THE GREAT GEOGRAPHICAL ATLAS

GEOGR

THE GREAT GRAPHICAL ATLAS

RAND McNALLY & COMPANY
CHICAGO, NEW YORK, SAN FRANCISCO
in association with
ISTITUTO GEOGRAFICO DE AGOSTINI, Novara
and MITCHELL BEAZLEY PUBLISHERS, London

Askja volcano, Iceland

Gerard Mercator (1512-1594), the cartographic genius of the world's great age of exploration, first coined the word atlas to describe a collection of maps (although Abraham Ortelius published the first modern atlas, at Antwerp in 1570). Mercator took the name of Atlas from the mythological figure, who symbolized for him the sum of terrestrial and celestial knowledge. When Mercator's *Atlas* was published in its fullest form, after his death, it consisted of the largest collection of maps yet assembled in book form, but it nevertheless fell short of the great cartographer's original and ambitious plan.

Mercator's intention had been to map the known world and to describe its creation and subsequent story. This is also the aim of *The Great Geographical Atlas*, which consists of an entirely new and complete collection of maps, a compendium of current geographical knowledge, and an account of the origin, development and present state of the Earth.

The major atlases of the world, from Mercator's time onward, have been published to satisfy a need for new information. As the rate of information gathering increased, so did the need for assimilating that information and making it available to the public. Current technology is at a point where man can survey the planet in the minutest detail. The resultant information explosion is in danger of overwhelming the ordinary atlas user. In *The Great Geographical Atlas*, this mass of information is organized and presented in the fullest, clearest and most elegant way.

To achieve this objective, three major international publishers of cartographic and Earth science material pooled their talents and resources: Istituto Geografico De Agostini, of Italy; Mitchell Beazley, of the United Kingdom; and Rand McNally, of the United States. The result is an atlas that reflects the ambition of Mercator, the original atlas-maker, by bringing together the conclusions of our current scientific and cartographic revolution. It marks the latest stage of internationality in map coverage and Earth science studies.

The spirit of the great atlases has always been international, although until very recently the Western countries were particularly emphasized. This internationality is implicit throughout the atlas, from the choices of projection to the coverage of Earth science subjects in the Encyclopedia Section. In one important way, however, the present atlas extends the international tradition, for it supplies to every country in which the atlas is published a special regional section of larger-scale maps, complete with local name forms and a separate index. This special map section offers a unique and satisfying solution to the needs of atlas users for definitive map coverage of the world, together with detailed maps of their own particular region. It honors and expands the spirit of internationality, and it serves the local requirements of individual users.

We believe that *The Great Geographical Atlas* is the definitive atlas to carry us forward into the 21st century, in terms of cartographic and encyclopedic excellence, and that it combines visual elegance with scientific authority and clarity in a fashion that has yet to be matched by any other work of a similar nature.

ANDREW MCNALLY IV
Rand McNally & Company

ACHILLE BOROLI
Istituto Geografico De Agostini

JAMES MITCHELL
Mitchell Beazley Publishers

PUBLISHING ADVISORY GROUP

Charles C. Bronson
Rand McNally & Company

Adolfo Boroli
Istituto Geografico De Agostini

Adrian Webster
Mitchell Beazley Publishers

RAND McNALLY & COMPANY

Product Director
Russell L. Voisin

Creative Director
Chris Arvetis

Managing Editor
Jon M. Leverenz

Geographic Research
V. Patrick Healy

Research Coordinator
Susan K. Eidsvoog

Cartographic Production
Ronald F. Peters

ISTITUTO GEOGRAFICO DE AGOSTINI

Product Director
Marco Drago

Cartographic/Geographic Director
Giuseppe Motta

Cartographic Editor
Vittorio Castelli

Geographic Research
Giovanni Baselli
Marta Colombo

Cartographic Production
Francesco Tosi

MITCHELL BEAZLEY PUBLISHERS

Editorial Director
Iain Parsons

Art Director
Ed Day

Senior Executive Art Editor
Michael McGuinness

Executive Editor
James Hughes

Sahara Desert, Souf, Algeria

THE GREAT GEOGRAPHICAL ATLAS essentially consists of three self-contained but interrelated parts. First, an Encyclopedia Section provides an authoritative survey of current scientific knowledge concerning Earth's structure, organization and life, from its origins to its present state. Next, the International Map Section contributes a newly created collection of maps, using the latest cartographical technology and presenting a detailed picture of the world, including its most recently mapped or modified areas. Finally, there is a special section of larger-scale maps specifically related to the country in which the edition is published. Thus the local and regional, as well as the international, requirements of the modern atlas user are met. The three sections have their own indexes and are supplemented by a digest of the latest geographical information.

INTERNATIONAL MAP SECTION

This full-scale production of a new set of maps of every part of the world is designed to satisfy a number of different needs. It provides new information on those areas of the world that have undergone political, demographic or infrastructural change. It makes use of the latest scientific and technological developments to give a more detailed picture of areas that have only recently been mapped. And it modifies the presentation of the maps in response to the new needs of atlas users. For such needs have greatly changed, both through the expansion of tourism and communications, and also through the influence of the media, so that today a new awareness of the world is emerging.

An international character is the hallmark of these maps, reflecting as it does the international context in which the mass of information presently available, geographical or otherwise, is increasingly collected and evaluated. For this reason, the planning, editing and production of the maps have all been undertaken to transcend the limitations of the traditional Western point of view. As a first step, every place-name or named geographical feature is given in its local form, using where necessary international systems of transcription and transliteration, or systems proposed by the countries concerned.

Secondly, the tendency to assign a major proportion of the maps to specific national areas has been discarded in favor of a more balanced coverage of every region in the world. Map scales have also been selected to reflect the importance—economic, cultural, historical and social—of all parts of the world. The international nature of the maps is further reinforced by the use of the metric system for such measurements as heights and depths. The sequential order of the maps gives a logical arrangement to each region, both in the internal relationship of its parts and in its global context.

Following a principle generally accepted in works of an international nature, *The Great Geographical Atlas* records the contemporary *de facto* disposition of states, boundaries and frontiers. It does not attempt to interpret *de jure* situations in contentious areas, or the territorial claims of contending parties. However, the application of this principle does not imply that the publishers necessarily accept or approve the political status recorded on the maps.

The reader's requirements have also been carefully considered, in conjunction with those that are consistent with a truly international approach. On continental and global maps, whether physical or political, all name forms relating to major geographical features—countries, oceans, seas, mountains, etc—appear in the English language; place-names for the most important towns and cities appear in English versions as well as in local forms. These same English-version names from the continental

THE MAKING OF THE ATLAS

maps recur on the larger-scale maps alongside the local forms. In addition, to satisfy the local and regional requirements of the reader, a special section of large-scale maps of the United States and Canada, complete with its own index, follows the International Map Section.

For ease of reference, continental maps giving separate coverage of physical and political features are juxtaposed. These are followed by larger-scale maps that combine both physical and political aspects, thus bringing together natural and man-made features. The larger-scale maps offer a wide range of physical detail, using hill shading and a graded range of color tints to indicate heights. They also provide political details such as settlements, administrative boundaries, and many other political and cultural features.

At each stage of production, the maps have been submitted to a rigorous process of research and updating to ensure that all data used are valid, accurate and fully up-to-date. Special care has been taken in the selection of the information shown, and map projections have been chosen to minimize distortion. A data bank was established to ensure consistency throughout the thousands of place-names used.

Projections chosen for the maps reflect the particular requirements of the various areas, and a computer and table plotter were used for their development, ensuring a degree of accuracy of 0.1 mm. For global maps, the projection chosen as best suited for representing the

whole Earth was the Hammer Azimuthal Equal-Area Projection with Wagner polar modification. However, the global map showing "Transportation and Time Zones" has been drawn on the grid of Mercator's cylindrical projection. Maps of continents and other extensive areas follow the Lambert Azimuthal Equal-Area Projection, since this is particularly suitable for representing continental areas with a minimum of shape and scale distortion. This projection enables the reader to compare the areas of different regions of the world, since the area scale is consistent throughout.

For the large-scale maps of such areas as the United States, European countries, etc, the Delisle Conic Equidistant Projection has been generally employed. Whenever possible, the same projection has been used for all maps relating to the same world area, so that they may be regarded as sections of a single map or as parts of a single whole. For example, all the maps of European countries that are scaled to 1:3,000,000 have been drawn on a single Delisle Conic Equidistant Projection which was developed on the latitudes 60° and 40° North, these being areas of minimum distortion. This technique allows distances to be calculated with extremely fine accuracy throughout the area.

Map scales have as far as possible been limited in number and employed according to the relevant needs—the more detail required, the larger the scale—and to enable comparisons to be made from area to area. For global maps the scales are 1:70,000,000 and 1:90,000,000; for continental maps 1:30,000,000, apart from Europe, which is scaled at 1:15,000,000; for the major geographical or political regions the scales are 1:12,000,000 and 1:9,000,000. Larger-scale maps giving details of more important areas are scaled at 1:6,000,000, 1:3,000,000 and 1:1,500,000. Numerical scales always follow the metric system; graphic scales are given both in metric and in statute mile systems.

The map coverage has been organized to show a physical or political unit in its entirety on a single spread. The relatively extensive areas of overlap between maps on adjacent pages is designed to maintain continuity and interrelation of locality from page to page.

Terrain is shown with the maximum detail and precision that the scale will allow. Relief and elevation have been depicted in a unique style, combining altimetric tinting and specially detailed shading techniques. The tints used show elevation and depth in a harmoniously graded range of colors. A refined hill-shading technique complements the tints, giving a three-dimensional appearance while showing the overall configuration of the area.

Hydrographic features such as rivers, lakes

and coasts have been clearly differentiated. Permanent rivers, for instance, are distinguished from intermittently flowing rivers; saltwater lakes are distinguished from freshwater lakes; defined shorelines are distinguished from undefined shorelines.

Place-name selection is of fundamental importance in any large atlas seeking to illustrate both the physical and the political–administrative aspects of the world. A suitable balance needs to be struck between names of natural and of man-made features if the continual interaction of the two is to be correctly recorded. The place-names are given in a wide variety of typefaces and typesizes to reflect the geographical, economic, demographic and historical importance of the subjects, and to give a unified and balanced picture of the human habitat and of man's relation to his territory.

Name forms have been standardized according to the principle, now internationally accepted and well established in reference atlases, of printing names and geographical terms in the language of the country concerned, and avoiding phonetic or traditional forms that may vary from country to country. The systems for transliteration and transcription are either those devised by internationally recognized geographical organizations or those that have been proposed by the countries concerned. For example, Russian, Bulgarian or Serb place-names originally in Cyrillic script have been transliterated according to the system established by the *Organisation Internationale de Normalisation*, and Chinese names have been transcribed according to the Pinyin system proposed by the Chinese government. Diacritical signs in each language or system of transliteration have been retained throughout.

Lettering and graphics have been designed to ensure quick and easy consultation. The more important features are represented in an integrated fashion appropriate to the varying needs of reference and research. To ensure that the large quantity of information on the maps is clearly legible, care has been taken in selecting typefaces that allow visual clarity. Eleven different typefaces have been used to indicate a broad range of physical and man-made features, with the size and weight of the characters reflecting the importance of the item. In accord with current cartographic practice, the typesizes for towns and cities are related to population densities and arranged in accordance with the map scales.

Geographical information of the most detailed kind has been assembled to accompany the international maps, together with a glossary of geographical terms used in the atlas. These appear in a separate section preceding the International Map Index. Documentation and data for these were drawn from original sources

Nepal, aerial view

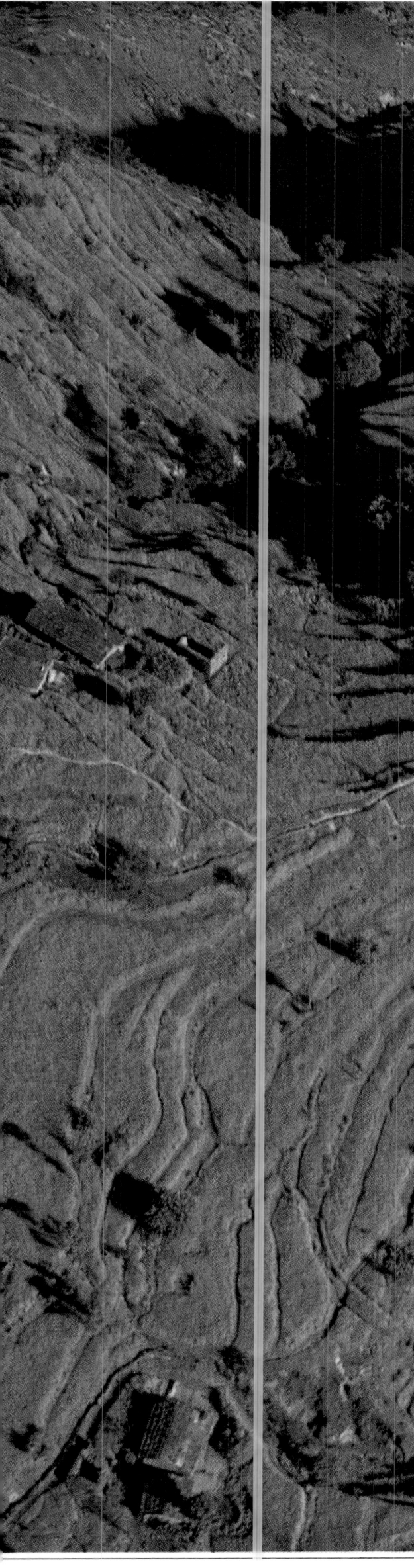

and from an extensive range of recent publications. In addition to cartographic sources, use was made of statistical surveys, census returns, geographical publications, special research projects in different parts of the world, analysis of satellite photographs, and many other information systems. All the information thus obtained has been evaluated, reviewed and compared in collaboration with the appropriate official bodies of the countries concerned.

The map indexes of *The Great Geographical Atlas* are twofold. One index relates to the larger-scale United States and Canada Map section, and is placed immediately after this section. The other, which comes at the end of the atlas, includes all names found in the International Map Section. This index carries an Introduction explaining its various unusual features, system of cross-references and graphic symbols, which are designed to provide the reader with maximum information regarding the nature and precise location of every entry.

ENCYCLOPEDIA SECTION

Recent decades have seen revolutionary changes in virtually all branches of the Earth sciences—those that relate to our planet and the life it supports. With this great increase in our knowledge has come an even greater demand on Earth's resources, as human populations soar and their needs multiply. The Encyclopedia Section of *The Great Geographical Atlas*, written by leading authorities in their fields and illustrated with original creative artwork, brings together the latest discoveries and conclusions of science regarding the Earth: its origins in the universe; its structural components and dynamics; its creation and evolution of life; its rich variety of habitats; its natural and physical resources; and its widespread and increasing modifications at the hands of man. The Section is divided into five parts, of which the first four are concerned directly with aspects of Earth science. The fifth part discusses the representation of the Earth's surface in graphic form—the art and science of mapping—and leads into the International Map Section with a precise explanation of how to make maximum use of the maps.

The Earth and the Universe, Part 1 of the Encyclopedia Section, places the Earth in its context within the cosmos. Recent advances in astronomy have led to an extraordinary increase in our knowledge of the heavens, including the discovery of background radiation that may mark the origin of the universe itself. This first part of the Section, compiled and authenticated by leading astronomers, interprets the discoveries of the space age.

Making and Shaping the Earth, Part 2 of the Encyclopedia Section, brings together the latest conclusions of geology to describe both the structure and the formation of our planet and also the forces that have provided the fine detailing of individual landscapes, with particular reference to the role played by man. Each of these subjects is discussed and illustrated with integrated artwork complementing the text—a unique feature that characterizes the treatment of all the subjects covered in the Encyclopedia Section.

The Emergence of Life, Part 3 of the Encyclopedia Section, is concerned with the origin, evolution and development of life on Earth. The sciences of biology and palaeontology have shared the information explosion affecting all the Earth sciences, and it is now possible to give a coherent account of the emergence, flourishing and disappearance of life forms throughout Earth's history. The section goes on to describe the zoogeographical regions of the world, with a full description of the various species as they have adapted to their ecological niches. Finally, there is an account of the origin, distribution and adaptation of the world's dominant species—man.

The Diversity of Life, Part 4 of the Encyclopedia Section, describes the range of habitats provided by Earth, from the polar regions to the equatorial forests. Each of these is seen both in terms of its natural life and with special reference to the needs and activities of man. Man's interaction with his habitat in terms of food, population, resources, communications, settlement patterns, urbanization and industrialization forms a key part of this section, and has been contributed by Professor Michael Wise, one of the world's leading authorities on these questions and the general consultant for the whole Encyclopedia Section. Illustrations and diagrams based on the most recent available statistics complement this authoritative text. The juxtaposition of natural and "man-made" habitats within each of the world's living communities, or biomes, reflects an awareness of the need to preserve the ecological balance while meeting the urgent demands of expanding populations and sophisticated social systems.

Understanding Maps is the title of the last part of the Encyclopedia Section, and it has been contributed by the Map Librarian of the British Library, Dr Helen Wallis. Pointing out that mapmaking appears to be an innate activity in human beings, the author provides an illuminating account of the development of mapmaking from the earliest times to the present day, with its advanced techniques of satellite photography and photogrammetrics. She then describes the language of mapping and its structure, the means whereby a three-dimensional world is translated into symbols on a two-dimensional surface. Finally, she explains how to read maps, with particular reference to the maps contained in *The Great Geographical Atlas*.

STRUCTURE OF THE ATLAS

The Great Geographical Atlas is arranged according to the following structure:

CONTENTS OF ENCYCLOPEDIA SECTION

Part 1

THE EARTH AND THE UNIVERSE

GRAPHICAL ATLAS

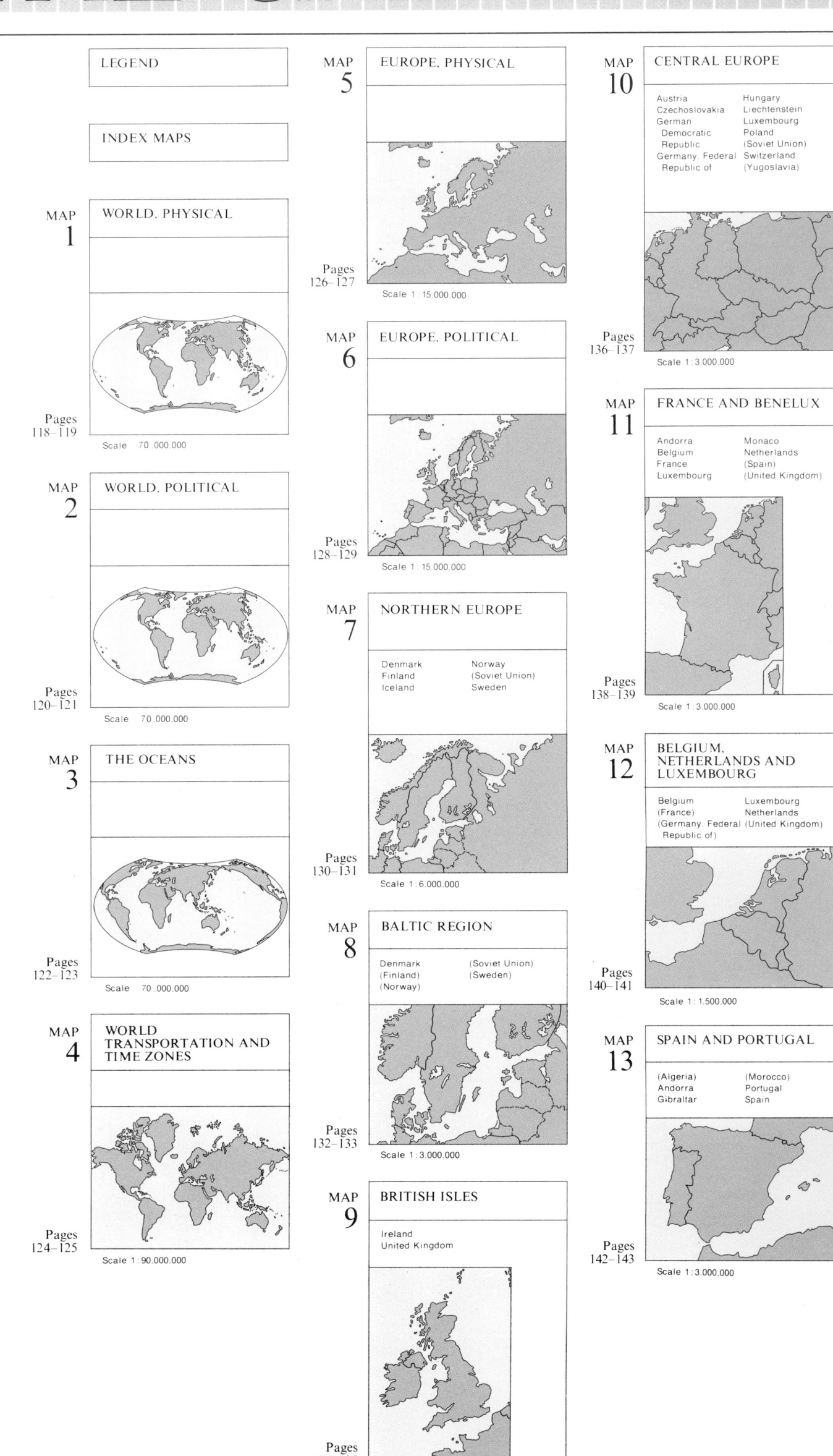

CONTENTS OF
INTERNATIONAL
MAP SECTION

An alphabetical list of major entities
appears on page XVI.

LEGEND

INDEX MAPS

MAP 1 — WORLD, PHYSICAL
Pages 118–119
Scale 70.000.000

MAP 2 — WORLD, POLITICAL
Pages 120–121
Scale 70.000.000

MAP 3 — THE OCEANS
Pages 122–123
Scale 70.000.000

MAP 4 — WORLD TRANSPORTATION AND TIME ZONES
Pages 124–125
Scale 1:90.000.000

MAP 5 — EUROPE, PHYSICAL
Pages 126–127
Scale 1:15.000.000

MAP 6 — EUROPE, POLITICAL
Pages 128–129
Scale 1:15.000.000

MAP 7 — NORTHERN EUROPE
Denmark
Finland
Iceland
Norway
(Soviet Union)
Sweden
Pages 130–131
Scale 1:6.000.000

MAP 8 — BALTIC REGION
Denmark
(Finland)
(Norway)
(Soviet Union)
(Sweden)
Pages 132–133
Scale 1:3.000.000

MAP 9 — BRITISH ISLES
Ireland
United Kingdom
Pages 134–135
Scale 1:3.000.000

MAP 10 — CENTRAL EUROPE
Austria
Czechoslovakia
German Democratic Republic
Germany, Federal Republic of
Hungary
Liechtenstein
Luxembourg
Poland
(Soviet Union)
Switzerland
(Yugoslavia)
Pages 136–137
Scale 1:3.000.000

MAP 11 — FRANCE AND BENELUX
Andorra
Belgium
France
Luxembourg
Monaco
Netherlands
(Spain)
(United Kingdom)
Pages 138–139
Scale 1:3.000.000

MAP 12 — BELGIUM, NETHERLANDS AND LUXEMBOURG
Belgium
(France)
(Germany, Federal Republic of)
Luxembourg
Netherlands
(United Kingdom)
Pages 140–141
Scale 1:1.500.000

MAP 13 — SPAIN AND PORTUGAL
(Algeria)
Andorra
Gibraltar
(Morocco)
Portugal
Spain
Pages 142–143
Scale 1:3.000.000

GRAPHICAL ATLAS

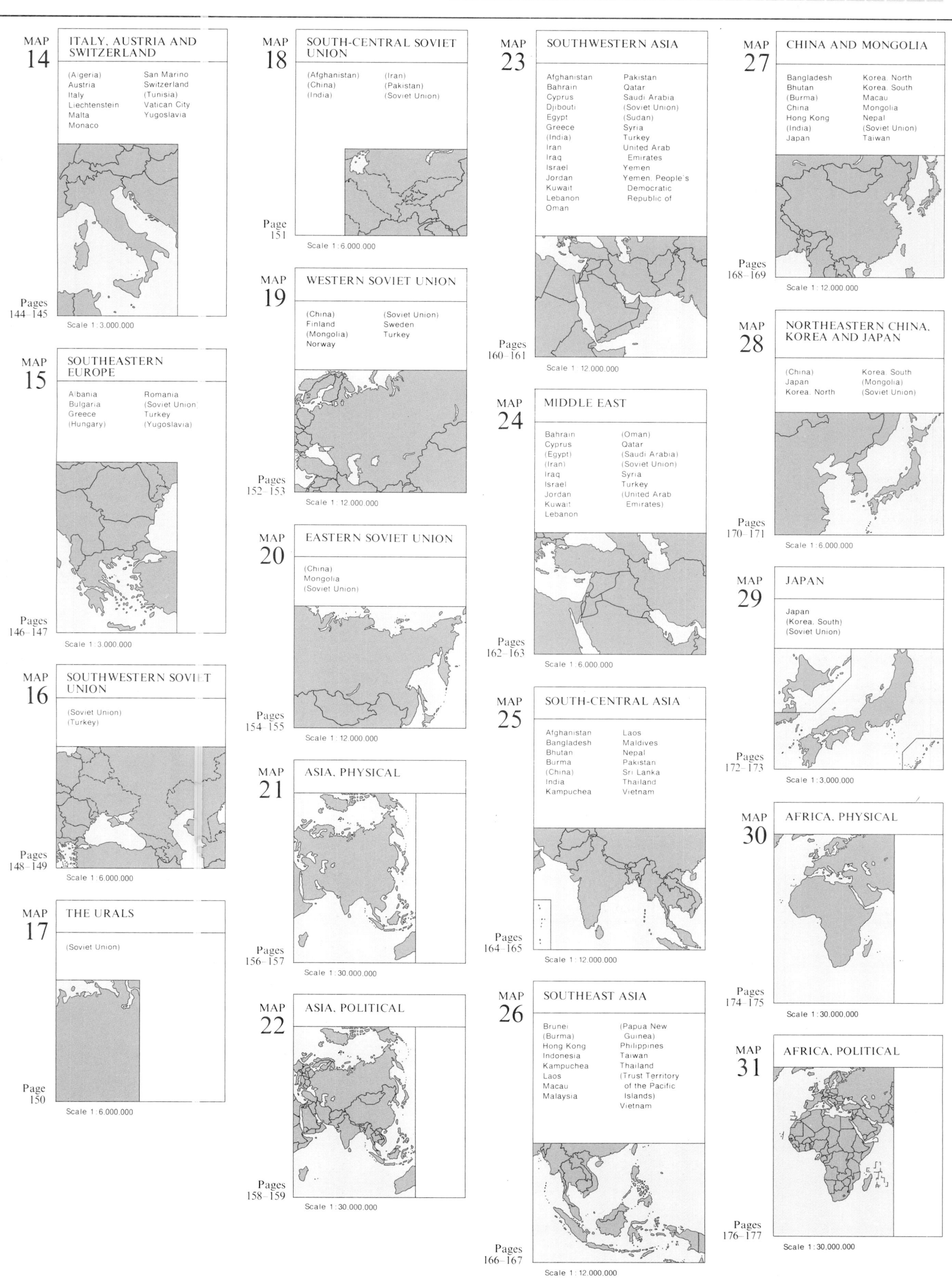

MAP 14 — ITALY, AUSTRIA AND SWITZERLAND

(Algeria)
Austria
Italy
Liechtenstein
Malta
Monaco
San Marino
Switzerland
(Tunisia)
Vatican City
Yugoslavia

Pages 144–145
Scale 1:3.000.000

MAP 15 — SOUTHEASTERN EUROPE

Albania
Bulgaria
Greece
(Hungary)
Romania
(Soviet Union)
Turkey
(Yugoslavia)

Pages 146–147
Scale 1:3.000.000

MAP 16 — SOUTHWESTERN SOVIET UNION

(Soviet Union)
(Turkey)

Pages 148–149
Scale 1:6.000.000

MAP 17 — THE URALS

(Soviet Union)

Page 150
Scale 1:6.000.000

MAP 18 — SOUTH-CENTRAL SOVIET UNION

(Afghanistan)
(China)
(India)
(Iran)
(Pakistan)
(Soviet Union)

Page 151
Scale 1:6.000.000

MAP 19 — WESTERN SOVIET UNION

(China)
Finland
(Mongolia)
Norway
(Soviet Union)
Sweden
Turkey

Pages 152–153
Scale 1:12.000.000

MAP 20 — EASTERN SOVIET UNION

(China)
Mongolia
(Soviet Union)

Pages 154–155
Scale 1:12.000.000

MAP 21 — ASIA, PHYSICAL

Pages 156–157
Scale 1:30.000.000

MAP 22 — ASIA, POLITICAL

Pages 158–159
Scale 1:30.000.000

MAP 23 — SOUTHWESTERN ASIA

Afghanistan
Bahrain
Cyprus
Djibouti
Egypt
Greece
(India)
Iran
Iraq
Israel
Jordan
Kuwait
Lebanon
Oman
Pakistan
Qatar
Saudi Arabia
(Soviet Union)
(Sudan)
Syria
Turkey
United Arab Emirates
Yemen
Yemen, People's Democratic Republic of

Pages 160–161
Scale 1:12.000.000

MAP 24 — MIDDLE EAST

Bahrain
Cyprus
(Egypt)
(Iran)
Iraq
Israel
Jordan
Kuwait
Lebanon
(Oman)
Qatar
(Saudi Arabia)
(Soviet Union)
Syria
Turkey
(United Arab Emirates)

Pages 162–163
Scale 1:6.000.000

MAP 25 — SOUTH-CENTRAL ASIA

Afghanistan
Bangladesh
Bhutan
Burma
(China)
India
Kampuchea
Laos
Maldives
Nepal
Pakistan
Sri Lanka
Thailand
Vietnam

Pages 164–165
Scale 1:12.000.000

MAP 26 — SOUTHEAST ASIA

Brunei
(Burma)
Hong Kong
Indonesia
Kampuchea
Laos
Macau
Malaysia
(Papua New Guinea)
Philippines
Taiwan
Thailand
(Trust Territory of the Pacific Islands)
Vietnam

Pages 166–167
Scale 1:12.000.000

MAP 27 — CHINA AND MONGOLIA

Bangladesh
Bhutan
(Burma)
China
Hong Kong
(India)
Japan
Korea, North
Korea, South
Macau
Mongolia
Nepal
(Soviet Union)
Taiwan

Pages 168–169
Scale 1:12.000.000

MAP 28 — NORTHEASTERN CHINA, KOREA AND JAPAN

(China)
Japan
Korea, North
Korea, South
(Mongolia)
(Soviet Union)

Pages 170–171
Scale 1:6.000.000

MAP 29 — JAPAN

Japan
(Korea, South)
(Soviet Union)

Pages 172–173
Scale 1:3.000.000

MAP 30 — AFRICA, PHYSICAL

Pages 174–175
Scale 1:30.000.000

MAP 31 — AFRICA, POLITICAL

Pages 176–177
Scale 1:30.000.000

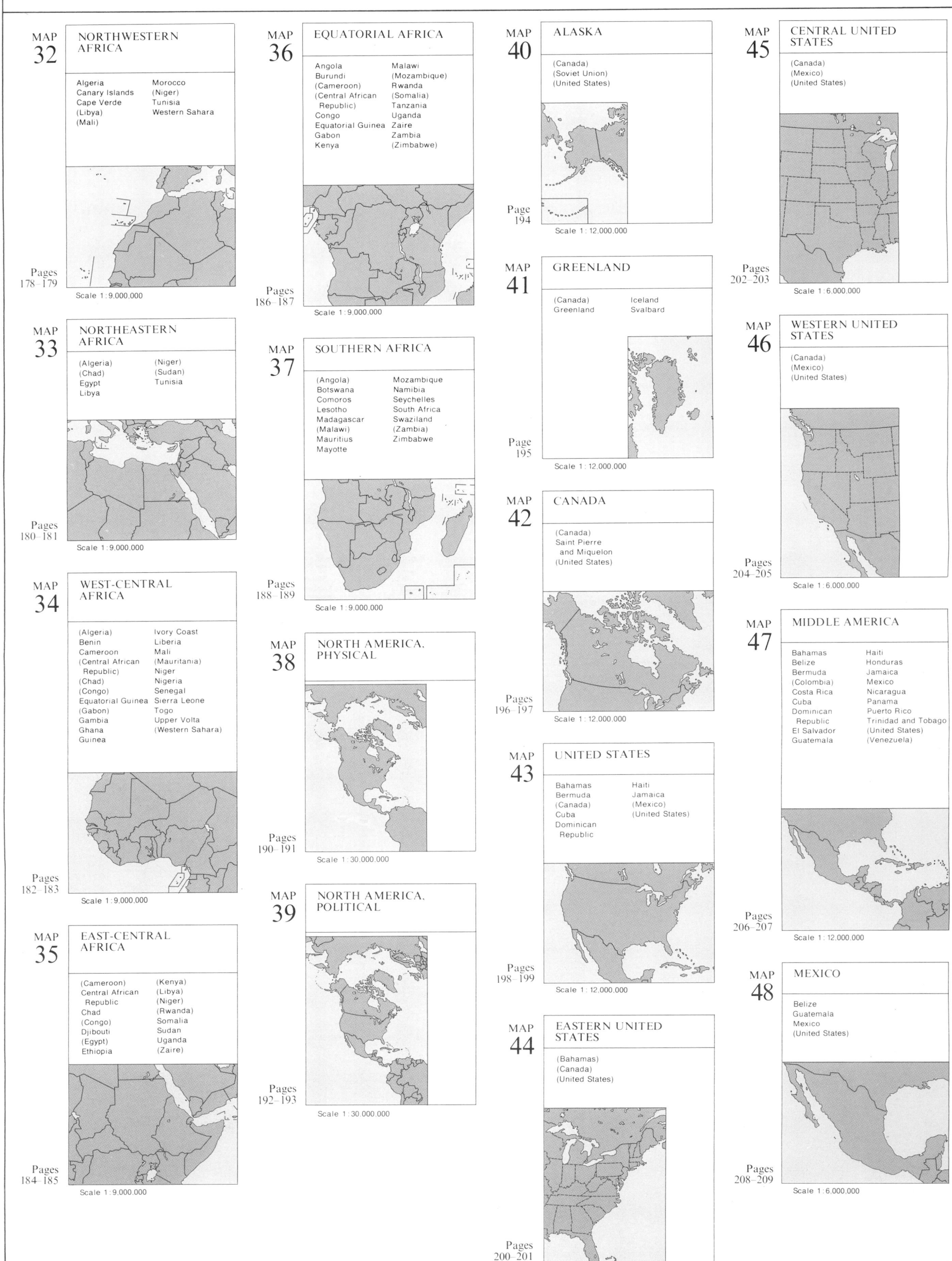

GRAPHICAL ATLAS

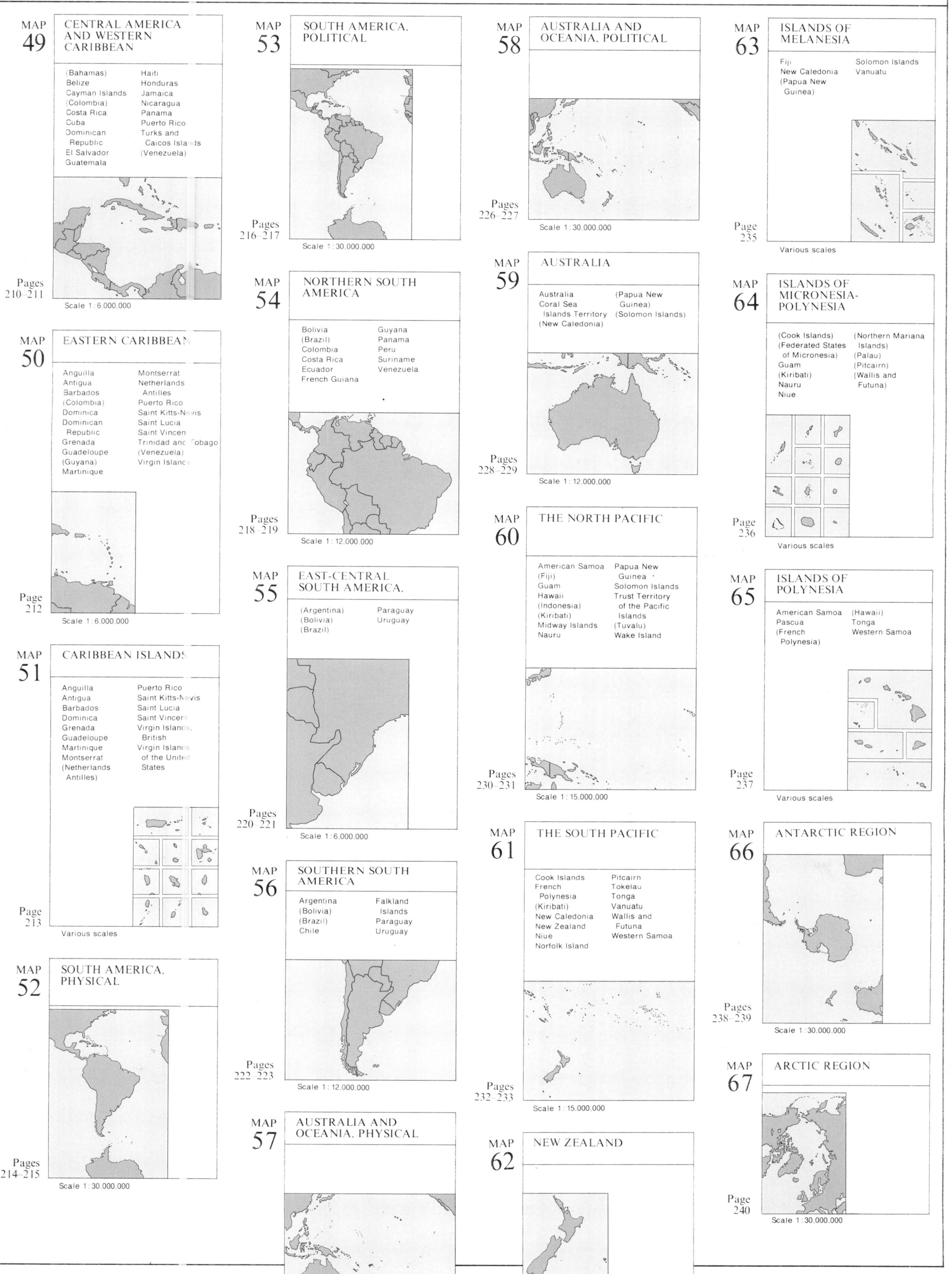

XV

THE GREAT GEOGRAPHICAL ATLAS

Alphabetical list of major entities in the International Map Section

CONTENTS OF
UNITED
STATES AND
CANADA
MAP SECTION

*Photographs pages IV, M. Cirani/Archivo IGDA,
Milano; VI, E. Pagani/Archivo IGDA, Milano;
VIII, M. Fantin/Archivo IGDA, Milano.*

ENCYCLOPEDIA SECTION

THE EARTH AND THE UNIVERSE

How the universe began · Earth's place in the Solar System
How the Earth became fit for life
Man looks at Earth from outer space

CREATION AND DESTRUCTION

Violent activity pervades our universe and has done so ever since the primordial fireball of creation. Evidence of violence comes from radio telescopes scanning the farthest reaches: entire galaxies may be exploding, torn apart by gravitational forces of unimaginable power. Some very large stars may burst apart in supernovas, spraying interstellar space with cosmic debris. From this violence new stars and new planets are constantly being formed throughout the universe.

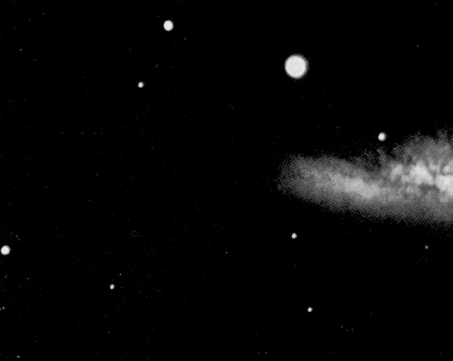

The Big Bang theory (left) of the origin of the universe envisages all matter originating from one point in time and space—a point of infinite density. In the intensely hot Big Bang all the material that goes to make up the planets, stars and galaxies that we see now began to expand outward in all directions. This expansion has been likened to someone blowing up a balloon on which spots have been painted. As the air fills and expands the balloon, the spots get farther away from each other. Likewise, clusters of galaxies that formed from the original superdense matter began, and continue, to move away from neighboring clusters. The Big Bang generated enormous temperatures and the remnants of the event still linger throughout space. A leftover, background radiation provides a uniform and measurable temperature of 3°C. It is generally believed that the universe will continue to expand into complete nothingness.

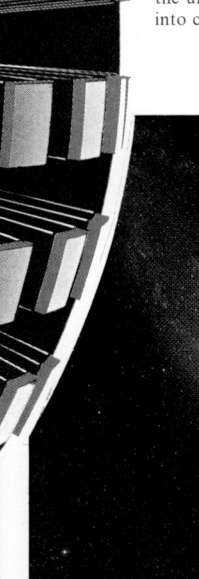

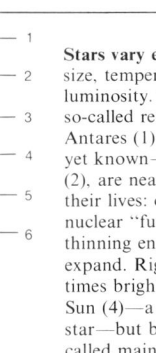

Stars vary enormously in size, temperature and luminosity. The largest, so-called red giants like Antares (1)—the biggest yet known—or Aldebaran (2), are nearing the end of their lives: diminishing nuclear "fuel" causes their thinning envelopes to expand. Rigel (3) is many times brighter than our Sun (4)—a middle-aged star—but both are so-called main-sequence stars. Epsilon Eridani (5) is rather like the Sun. Wolf 359 (6) is a red dwarf.

Our Solar System was formed from a collapsing cloud of gas and dust (A). Collapse made the center hotter and denser (B) until nuclear reactions started. Heat blew matter from the heart of the now flattened, spinning disc (C). Heavier materials condensed closest to the young Sun, now a hot star, eventually forming the inner ring of planets; the lighter ones accumulated farther out, making up the atmosphere and composition of the giant outer planets (D).

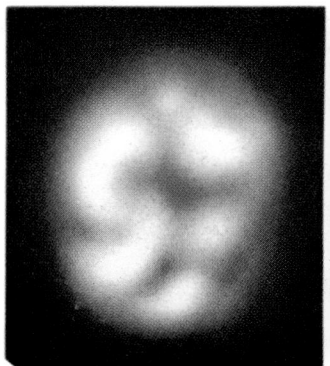

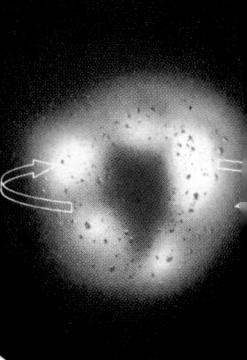

The Making of the Universe

Most astronomers believe that the universe began in a great explosion of matter and energy – the "Big Bang" – about 15,000 million years ago. This event was implied by Einstein's theory of general relativity, as well as by more recent astronomical observations and calculations. But the clinching evidence came in 1965, when two American radio astronomers discovered a faint, uniform, background radiation which permeated all space. This they identified as the remnants of the primordial Big Bang.

The generally accepted explanation for the so-called "cosmic microwave" background, detected by American astronomers Arno Penzias and Robert Wilson, is indeed that it is the echo of the Big Bang itself, the radio noise left over from the fireball of creation. In recognition of their discovery, Penzias and Wilson shared a Nobel Prize in 1978.

The Big Bang has also been identified by astronomers in other ways. All the evidence shows that the universe is expanding, and its constituent parts—clusters of galaxies, each containing thousands of millions of stars like our Sun—are moving away from each other at great speeds. From this and other evidence scientists deduce that long ago the galaxies must have been closer together, in a superdense phase, and that at some time in the remote past all the material in the universe must have started spreading out from a single point. But this "single point" includes not only all three-dimensional matter and space but also the dimension of time, as envisioned in Einstein's revolutionary concept of space-time. Einstein's theory of relativity describes the phenomenon, not in terms of galaxies moving through space in

then reused to form new stars and planets.

Thus, from the debris of such explosions new stars can form to repeat the creative cycle, and at each stage more of the heavy elements are produced. Today's heavenly bodies are very much the products of stellar violence in the universe, and indeed the universe itself is now seen to be an area of violent activity. During the past two decades the old idea of the universe as a place of quiet stability has been increasingly superseded by evidence of intense activity on all scales. Astronomers have identified what appear to be vast explosions involving whole galaxies, as well as those of individual stars.

Black holes
The evidence of just why these huge explosions occur is often hard to obtain, because the exploding galaxies may be so far away that light from them takes millions of years to reach telescopes on Earth. But it is becoming increasingly accepted by astronomers that such violent events may be associated with the presence of black holes at the centers of some galaxies.

These black holes are regions in which matter has become so concentrated that the force of gravity makes it impossible for anything—even light itself—to escape. As stars are pulled into super-massive black holes they are torn apart by gravitational forces, and their material forms into a swirling maelstrom from which huge explosions can occur. Collapse into black holes, accompanied by violent outbursts from the maelstrom, may be the ultimate fate of all matter in the universe. For our own Solar System, however, such a fate is far in the future: the Sun in its present form is believed to have enough "fuel" to keep it going for at least another 5,000 million years.

A star is born
The origins of the Earth and the Solar System are intimately connected with the structure of our own galaxy, the Milky Way. There are two main types of galaxies: flattened, disc-shaped spiral galaxies (like the Milky Way), and the more rounded elliptical galaxies, which range in form from near spheres to cigar shapes. The most important feature of a spiral galaxy is that it is rotating, a great mass of stars sweeping around a common center. In our galaxy the Sun, located some way out from the galaxy's center, takes about 225 million years to complete one circuit, called a cosmic year.

New stars are born out of the twisting arms of a spiral galaxy, with each arm marking a region of debris left over from previous stellar explosions. These arms are in fact clouds of dust and gas, including nitrogen and oxygen. As the spiral galaxy rotates over a period of millions of years, the twisting arms are squeezed by a high-density pressure wave as they pass through the cycle of the cosmic year. With two main spiral arms twining around a galaxy such as our own, large, diffuse clouds get squeezed twice during each orbit around the center of the galaxy.

Even if one orbit takes as long as hundreds of millions of years, a score or more squeezes have probably occurred since the Milky Way was first formed thousands of millions of years ago. At a critical point, such repeated squeezing increases the density of a gas cloud so much that it begins to collapse rapidly under the inward pull of its own gravity. A typical cloud of this kind contains enough material to make many stars. As it breaks up it collapses into smaller clouds—which are also collapsing—and these become stars in their own right.

Our own Solar System may have been formed in this way from such a collapsing gas cloud, which went on to evolve into the system of planets that we know today.

Billions of galaxies exist outside our own Milky Way, each thousands of light-years across and filled with millions of stars. Found in clusters, they are either elliptical or spiral in form. The clusters recede from each other following the space-time geometry, as established by Hubble in 1929, proving that the universe is expanding.

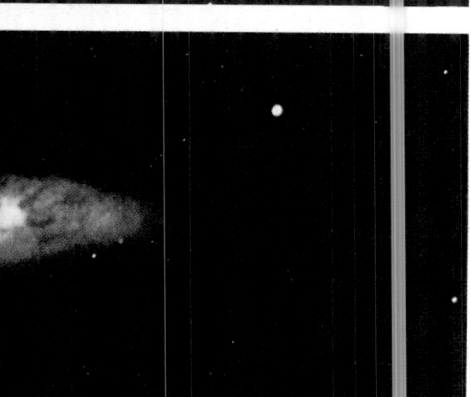

The "exploding" galaxy M82 may be an example of the violence of our universe. Clouds of hydrogen gas, equivalent in mass to 5,000,000 suns, have been ejected from the nucleus at 160 km (100 miles) per second. Black holes may cause the explosions, when gravity sucks in all matter, so that even light cannot escape.

Our own cluster of galaxies (below), the Local Group (A), consists of about 30 members, weakly linked by the force of gravity. Earth lies in the second-largest galaxy, the Milky Way (B)—here shown edge-on and at an angle—which is a spiral galaxy of about 100,000 million stars. Its rotating "arms" are great masses of clouds, dust and stars that sweep around a dense nucleus. In the course of this new stars are regularly created from dust and gas. Our Sun (S) lies 33,000 light-years from the nucleus and takes 225 million years to complete an orbit. The Andromeda Galaxy (C), known to astronomers as M31, is the largest of our Local Group. It too is a spiral, and lies about two million light-years away. Roughly 130,000 light-years in diameter, it appears as a flattened disc, and indicates how our galaxy would look if viewed from outside. Two smaller elliptical galaxies M32 and NGC 205, can also be seen.

Leo II
Leo I
Milky Way
LMC
SMC
Sculptor
Fornax
NGC 147
NGC 185
NGC 6822
M31
M33
M32
NGC 205
IC 1613
A
B
C

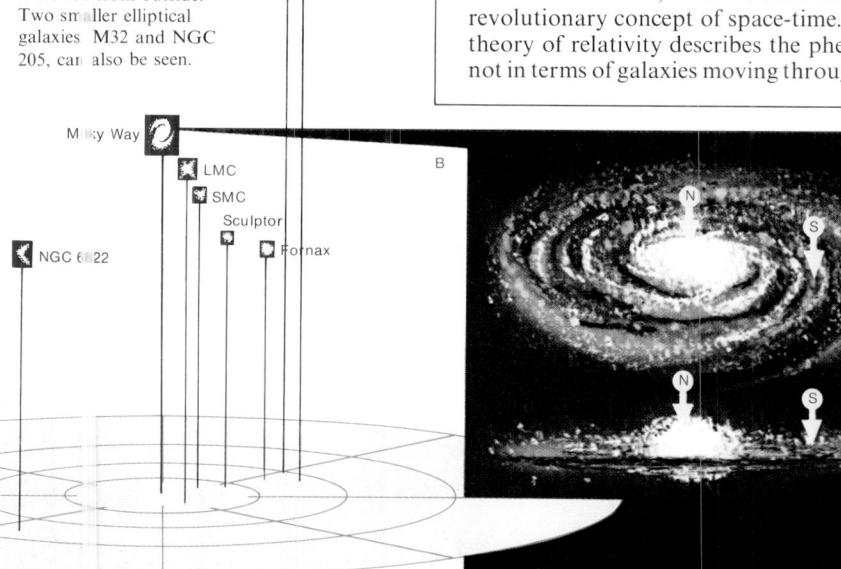

Nucleus (N)   Sun (S)

100,000 light-years

the expansion, but as being carried apart by the expansion of space-time itself. Space-time may be imagined as a rubber sheet speckled with paint blobs (galaxies), which move apart as the rubber sheet expands.

Galaxies consist of star systems, dust clouds and gases formed from the hot material exploding outward from the original cosmic fireball. Our own Milky Way system, the band of light that stretches across the night sky, is typical of many galaxies, containing millions of stars slowly rotating around a central nucleus.

Exploding space
The original material of the universe was hydrogen, the simplest of all elements. Nuclear reactions that occurred during the superdense phase of the Big Bang converted about 20 percent of the original hydrogen into helium, the next simplest element. So the first stars were formed from a mixture of about 80 percent hydrogen and 20 percent helium. All other matter in the universe, including the atoms of heavier elements such as carbon and oxygen—which help to make up the human body or the pages of this book—has been processed in further nuclear reactions. The explosion of a star—a relatively rare event called a supernova—scatters material across space, briefly radiating more energy than a trillion suns and ejecting matter into the cosmic reservoir of interstellar space. This is

Stars are being born (left) in the Great Nebula of Orion, visible from Earth. The brilliant light comes from a cluster of very hot young stars, the Trapezium, surrounded by a glowing aura of hydrogen gas. Behind the visible nebula there is known to be a dense cloud where radio astronomers have detected emissions from interstellar molecules, and have identified high-density globules. These probably indicate that stars are starting to form.

C
D

Earth in the Solar System

The Sun is an ordinary, medium-sized star located some two-thirds of the way from the center of our galaxy, the Milky Way. Yet it comprises more than 99 percent of the Solar System's total mass and provides all the light and heat that make life possible on Earth. This energy comes from nuclear reactions that take place in the Sun's hot, dense interior. The reactions convert hydrogen into helium, with the release of vast amounts of energy – the energy that keeps the Sun shining.

Nuclear reactions in the Sun's core maintain a temperature of some 15,000,000°C and this heat prevents the star from shrinking. The surface temperature is comparatively much lower —a mere 6,000°C. Thermonuclear energy-generating processes cause the Sun to "lose" mass from the center at the rate of four million tonnes of hydrogen every second. This mass is turned into energy (heat), and each gram of matter "burnt" produces the heat equivalent of 100 trillion electric fires. The Sun's total mass is so great, however, that it contains enough matter to continue radiating at its present rate for several thousand million years before it runs out of "fuel."

The Sun's retinue

The Solar System emerged from a collapsing gas cloud. In addition to the Sun there are at least nine planets, their satellites, thousands of minor planets (asteroids), comets and meteors. Most stars occur in pairs, triplets or in even more complicated systems, and the Sun is among a minority of stars in being alone except for its planetary companions. It does seem, however, that a single star with a planetary system offers the greatest potential for the development of life. When there are two or more stars in the same system, any planets are likely to have unstable orbits and to suffer from wide extremes of temperature.

The Solar System's structure is thought to be typical of a star that formed in isolation. As the hot young Sun threw material outward, inner planets (Mercury, Venus, Earth and Mars) were left as small rocky bodies, whereas outer planets (Jupiter, Saturn, Uranus and Neptune) kept their lighter gases and became huge "gas giants." Jupiter has two and a half times the mass of all the other planets put together. Pluto, a small object with a strange orbit, which sometimes carries it within the orbit of Neptune, is usually regarded as a ninth planet, but some astronomers consider it to be an escaped moon of Neptune or a large asteroid.

Planetary relations

Several planets are accompanied by smaller bodies called moons or satellites. Jupiter and Saturn have at least 17 and 22 respectively, whereas Earth has its solitary Moon. Sizes vary enormously, from Ganymede, one of Jupiter's large, so-called Galilean satellites, which has a diameter of 5,000 km (3,100 miles), to Mars' tiny Deimos, which is only 8 km (5 miles) across.

The Earth's Moon is at an average distance of 384,000 km (239,000 miles) and has a diameter of 3,476 km (2,160 miles). Its mass is $\frac{1}{81}$ of the Earth's. Although it is referred to as the Earth's satellite, the Moon is large for a secondary body. Some astronomers have suggested that the Earth/Moon system is a double planet. Certain theories of the origins of the Moon propose that it was formed from the solar nebula in the same way as the Earth was and very close to it. The Moon takes 27.3 days to orbit the Earth—exactly the same time that it takes to rotate once on its axis. As a result, it presents the same face to the Earth all the time.

Our planet's orbit around the Sun is not a perfect circle but an ellipse and so its distance from the Sun varies slightly. More importantly, the Earth is tilted, so that at different times of the year one pole or another "leans" toward the Sun. Without this tilt there would be no seasons. The angle of tilt is not constant: over tens of thousands of years the axis of the Earth "wobbles" like a slowly spinning top, so that the pattern of the seasons varies over the ages. These changes have been linked to recent ice ages, which seem to occur when the northern hemisphere has relatively cool summers.

Patterns of time

The Earth's movements on its axis and around the Sun give us our basic measurements of time—the day and the year—as well as setting the rhythm of the seasons and the ice ages. One rotation of the Earth on its axis—the time from one sunrise to the next—originally defined the day, and the time taken for one complete orbit around the Sun defined the year. Today, however, scientists define both the day and the year in terms of time units "counted" by precision instruments called atomic clocks.

A third basic rhythm is set not by the Sun but by the Moon, which runs through a cycle of phases $29\frac{1}{2}$ days long. This is the basis of the calendar month. But just as the modern calendar cannot cope with months $29\frac{1}{2}$ days long, so too it would have trouble with the precise year, which is, inconveniently, just less than $365\frac{1}{4}$ days long. This is the reason for leap years, by means of which an extra day is added to the month of February every fourth year.

Even this system does not keep the calendar exactly in step with the Sun. Accordingly, the leap year is left out in the years which complete centuries, such as 1900, but retained when they divide exactly by 400. The year 2000 will, therefore, be a leap year. With all these corrections, the average length of the calendar year is within 26 seconds of the year defined by the Earth's movements around the Sun. Thus the calendar will be one day out of step with the heavens in the year 4906.

Cosmic rubble

The other planets are too small and too far away to produce noticeable effects on the Earth, but the smallest members of the Sun's family, the asteroids, can affect us directly. Some of them have orbits that cross the orbit of the Earth around the Sun. From time to time they penetrate the Earth's atmosphere: small fragments burn up high in the atmosphere as meteors, whereas larger pieces may survive to strike the ground as meteorites. These in fact provide an echo of times gone by. All the planets, as the battered face of the Moon shows, suffered collisions from many smaller bodies in the course of their evolution from the collapsing pre-solar gas cloud.

Eclipses occur because the Moon, smaller than the Sun, is closer to Earth and looks just as big. This means that when all three are lined up the Moon can blot out the Sun, causing a solar eclipse. When the Earth passes through the main shadow cone, or umbra, the eclipse is total; in the area of partial shadow, or penumbra, a partial eclipse is seen. A similar effect is produced when Earth passes between the Moon and the Sun, causing a lunar eclipse. At most full moons, eclipses do not occur; the Moon passes either above or below the Earth's shadow, because the Moon's orbit is inclined at an angle of 5° to the orbit of the Earth.

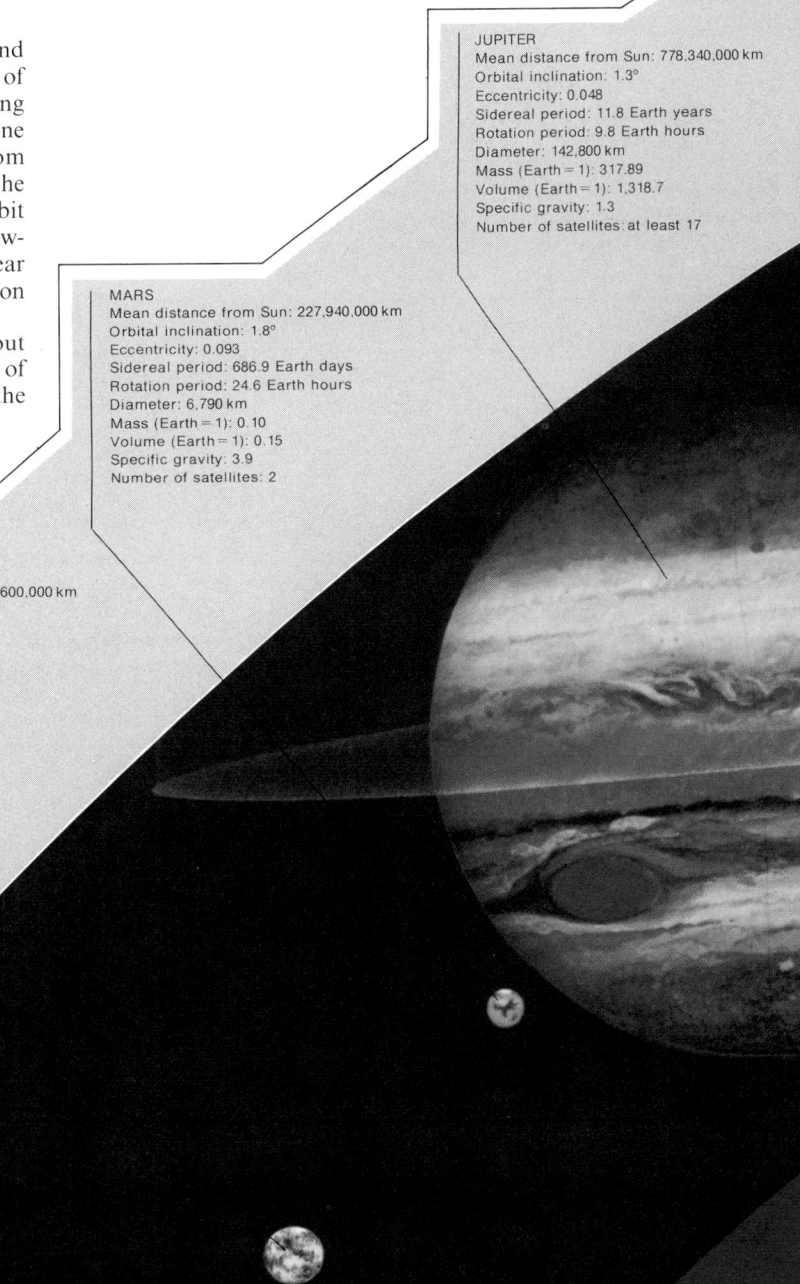

JUPITER
Mean distance from Sun: 778,340,000 km
Orbital inclination: 1.3°
Eccentricity: 0.048
Sidereal period: 11.8 Earth years
Rotation period: 9.8 Earth hours
Diameter: 142,800 km
Mass (Earth = 1): 317.89
Volume (Earth = 1): 1,318.7
Specific gravity: 1.3
Number of satellites: at least 17

MARS
Mean distance from Sun: 227,940,000 km
Orbital inclination: 1.8°
Eccentricity: 0.093
Sidereal period: 686.9 Earth days
Rotation period: 24.6 Earth hours
Diameter: 6,790 km
Mass (Earth = 1): 0.10
Volume (Earth = 1): 0.15
Specific gravity: 3.9
Number of satellites: 2

EARTH
Mean distance from Sun: 149,600,000 km
Orbital inclination: —
Eccentricity: 0.016
Sidereal period: 365.2 days
Rotation period: 23.9 hours
Diameter: 12,756 km
Mass: 1.00
Volume: 1.00
Specific gravity: 5.5
Number of satellites: 1

VENUS
Mean distance from Sun: 108,210,000 km
Orbital inclination: 3.3°
Eccentricity: 0.006
Sidereal period: 224.7 Earth days
Rotation period: 243 Earth days
Diameter: 12,100 km
Mass (Earth = 1): 0.81
Volume (Earth = 1): 0.85
Specific gravity: 5.2
Number of satellites: 0

MEMBERS OF THE SOLAR SYSTEM

The Sun has nine planetary attendants. They are best compared in terms of orbital data (distance from the Sun, inclination of orbit to the Earth's orbit, and eccentricity, which means the departure of a planet's orbit from circularity); planetary periods (the time for a planet to go around the Sun—sidereal periods, and the time it takes for one axial revolution—the rotation period); and physical data (equatorial diameter, mass, volume and density or specific gravity—the weight of a substance compared with the weight of an equal volume of water).

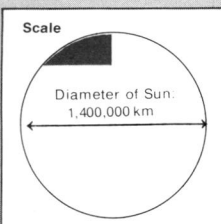

Scale

Diameter of Sun: 1,400,000 km

MERCURY
Mean distance from Sun: 57,910,000 km
Orbital inclination: 7°
Eccentricity: 0.205
Sidereal period: 87.9 Earth days
Rotation period: 58.7 Earth days
Diameter: 4,870 km
Mass (Earth = 1): 0.05
Volume (Earth = 1): 0.05
Specific gravity: 5.5
Number of satellites: 0

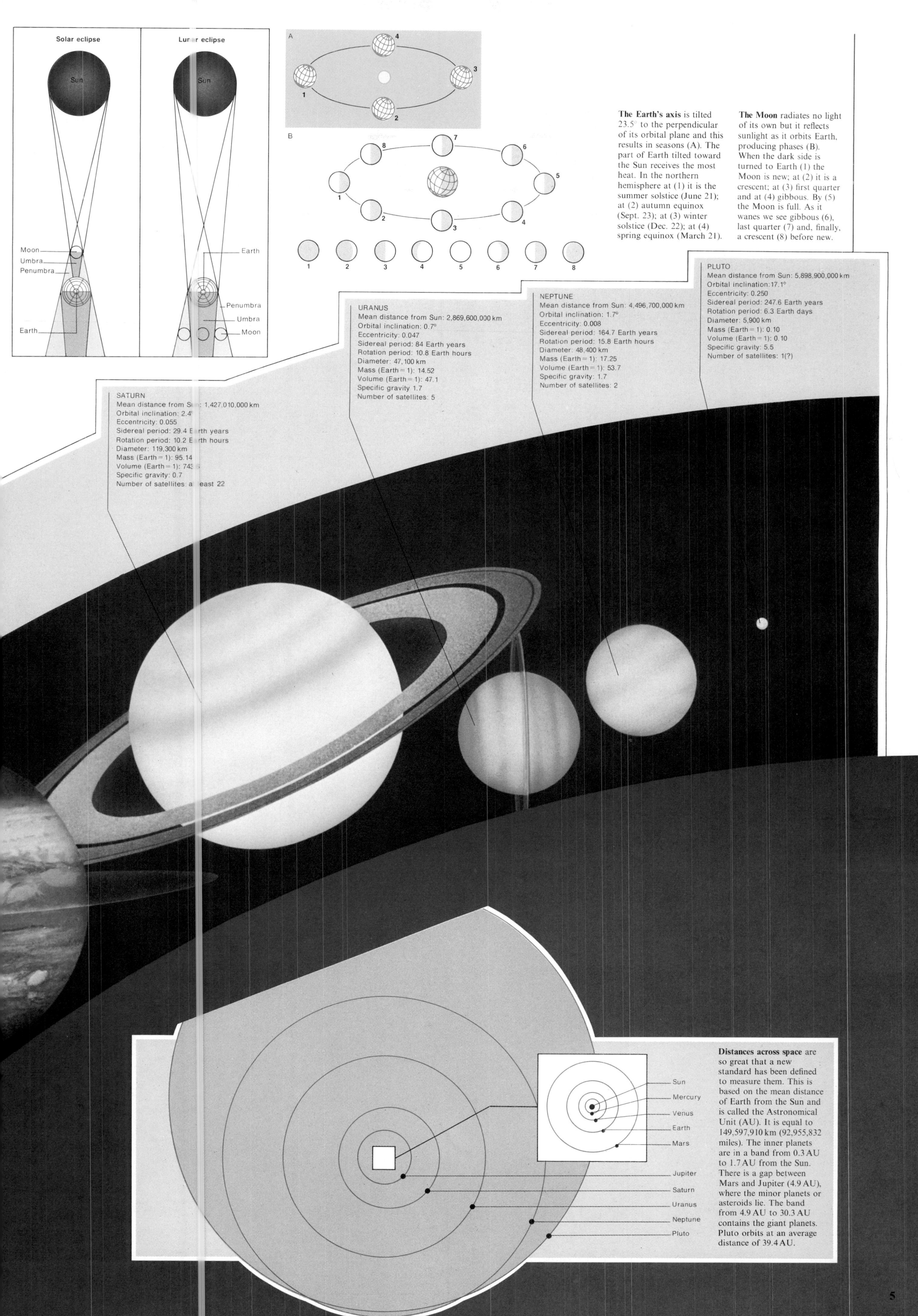

Solar eclipse Lunar eclipse

Sun   Sun

Moon
Umbra
Penumbra

Earth

Earth

Penumbra
Umbra
Moon

A

B

The Earth's axis is tilted 23.5° to the perpendicular of its orbital plane and this results in seasons (A). The part of Earth tilted toward the Sun receives the most heat. In the northern hemisphere at (1) it is the summer solstice (June 21); at (2) autumn equinox (Sept. 23); at (3) winter solstice (Dec. 22); at (4) spring equinox (March 21).

The Moon radiates no light of its own but it reflects sunlight as it orbits Earth, producing phases (B). When the dark side is turned to Earth (1) the Moon is new; at (2) it is a crescent; at (3) first quarter and at (4) gibbous. By (5) the Moon is full. As it wanes we see gibbous (6), last quarter (7) and, finally, a crescent (8) before new.

PLUTO
Mean distance from Sun: 5,898,900,000 km
Orbital inclination: 17.1°
Eccentricity: 0.250
Sidereal period: 247.6 Earth years
Rotation period: 6.3 Earth days
Diameter: 5,900 km
Mass (Earth = 1): 0.10
Volume (Earth = 1): 0.10
Specific gravity: 5.5
Number of satellites: 1(?)

NEPTUNE
Mean distance from Sun: 4,496,700,000 km
Orbital inclination: 1.7°
Eccentricity: 0.008
Sidereal period: 164.7 Earth years
Rotation period: 15.8 Earth hours
Diameter: 48,400 km
Mass (Earth = 1): 17.25
Volume (Earth = 1): 53.7
Specific gravity: 1.7
Number of satellites: 2

URANUS
Mean distance from Sun: 2,869,600,000 km
Orbital inclination: 0.7°
Eccentricity: 0.047
Sidereal period: 84 Earth years
Rotation period: 10.8 Earth hours
Diameter: 47,100 km
Mass (Earth = 1): 14.52
Volume (Earth = 1): 47.1
Specific gravity: 1.7
Number of satellites: 5

SATURN
Mean distance from Sun: 1,427,010,000 km
Orbital inclination: 2.4°
Eccentricity: 0.055
Sidereal period: 29.4 Earth years
Rotation period: 10.2 Earth hours
Diameter: 119,300 km
Mass (Earth = 1): 95.14
Volume (Earth = 1): 743.6
Specific gravity: 0.7
Number of satellites: at least 22

Sun
Mercury
Venus
Earth
Mars

Jupiter
Saturn
Uranus
Neptune
Pluto

Distances across space are so great that a new standard has been defined to measure them. This is based on the mean distance of Earth from the Sun and is called the Astronomical Unit (AU). It is equal to 149,597,910 km (92,955,832 miles). The inner planets are in a band from 0.3 AU to 1.7 AU from the Sun. There is a gap between Mars and Jupiter (4.9 AU), where the minor planets or asteroids lie. The band from 4.9 AU to 30.3 AU contains the giant planets. Pluto orbits at an average distance of 39.4 AU.

Earth as a Planet

Viewed from space, the Earth appears to be an ordinary member of the group of inner planets orbiting the Sun. But the Earth is unique in the Solar System because it has an atmosphere that contains oxygen. It is the nature of this surrounding blanket of air that has allowed higher life forms to evolve on Earth and provides their life-support system. At the same time the atmosphere acts as a shield to protect living things from the damaging effects of radiation from the Sun.

Any traces of gas that may have clung to the newly formed Earth were soon swept away into space by the heat of the Sun before it attained a stable state powered by nuclear fusion. Farther out in the Solar System, the Sun's heat was never strong enough to blow these gases away into space, so that even today the giant planets retain atmospheres composed of these primordial gases—mostly methane and ammonia.

The evolution of air

Until the Sun "settled down," Earth was a hot, airless ball of rock. The atmosphere and oceans—like the atmospheres of Venus and Mars—were produced by the "outgassing" of material from the hot interior of the planet as the crust cooled. Volcanoes erupted constantly and produced millions of tonnes of ash and lava. They also probably yielded, as they do today, great quantities of gas, chiefly carbon dioxide, and water vapor. A little nitrogen and various sulphur compounds were also released. Other things being equal, we would expect rocky planets, like the young Earth, to have atmospheres rich in carbon dioxide and water vapor. Venus and Mars do indeed have carbon dioxide atmospheres today, but the Earth now has a nitrogen/oxygen atmosphere. This results from the fact that life evolved on Earth, converting the carbon dioxide to oxygen and storing carbon in organic remains such as coal. Some carbon dioxide was also dissolved in the oceans. The Earth's oxygen atmosphere is a clear sign of life; the carbon dioxide atmospheres of Venus and Mars suggest the absence of life. Why did the Earth begin to evolve in a different way from the other inner planets?

When the Sun stabilized, Earth, Venus and Mars started off down the same evolutionary road, and carbon dioxide and water vapor were the chief constituents of the original atmospheres. On Venus the temperature was hot enough for the water to remain in a gaseous form, and both the water vapor and carbon dioxide in the Venusian atmosphere trapped heat by means of the so-called "greenhouse effect." In this process, radiant energy from the Sun passes through the atmospheric gases and warms the ground. The warmed ground re-radiates heat energy, but at infrared wavelengths, with the result that carbon dioxide and water molecules absorb it and stop it escaping from the planet. Instead of acting like a window, the atmosphere acts like a mirror for outgoing energy. As a result, the surface of Venus became hotter still. Today the surface temperature has stabilized at more than 500°C.

Mars, farther out from the Sun than Earth, was never hot enough for the greenhouse effect to dominate. The red planet once had a much thicker atmosphere than it does today, but, being smaller than the Earth, its gravity is too weak to retain a thick atmosphere. As a result, the planet cooled into a frozen desert as atmospheric gases escaped into space. Mars then, in fact, suffered a climatic change. At one time—hundreds of millions of years ago—there must have been running water because traces of old riverbeds still scar the Martian surface. Today, however, Mars has a thin atmosphere of carbon dioxide and surface temperatures below zero.

Earth—the ideal home

On Earth conditions were just right. Water stayed as a liquid and formed the oceans, while some carbon dioxide from outgassing went into the atmosphere, and some dissolved in the oceans. The resulting modest greenhouse effect

The thermosphere extends from 80 km (50 miles) up to 400 km (250 miles). Within this zone temperatures rise steadily with height to as much as 1,650°C (3,000°F), but the air is so thin that temperature is not a meaningful concept. At this height the air is mostly composed of nitrogen molecules to a height of 200 km (125 miles), when oxygen molecules become the dominant constituent.

The mesosphere is between 50 and 80 km (30 and 50 miles) above ground level. The stratopause is its lower limit and the mesopause its upper. This zone of the atmosphere is mainly distinguished by its ever decreasing temperatures and, unlike the stratosphere, it does not absorb solar energy.

The stratosphere is the level above the troposphere and extends as far as 50 km (30 miles). The chemical composition of the air up to this height is nearly constant and, in terms of volume, it is composed of nitrogen (78%) and oxygen (20%). The rest is mostly argon and other trace elements. The percentage of carbon dioxide (0.003) is small but crucial because this gas absorbs heat. There is virtually no water vapor or dust in this region of the atmosphere, but it does include the ozone layer, which is strongest between 20 km (12 miles) and 40 km (24 miles) high.

The troposphere extends from ground level to a height of between 10 and 15 km (6 and 9 miles). This height varies with latitude and season of the year: it is greater at the Equator than at the poles. Most weather phenomena occur in this zone. Mixed with the gases of the troposphere is water vapor and millions of tiny dust particles, around which vapor condenses to form clouds. The upper limit of this zone is called the tropopause.

EARTH'S OUTER SKIN

The Earth's atmosphere is wafer thin when compared with the size of the planet. Half of the atmosphere's mass lies in the 5.5 km (3½ miles) nearest the ground and more than 99 percent of it lies within 40 km (24 miles) of the Earth.

Scale

Atmosphere
Earth

Earth's radius: 6,378 km

Thermosphere

Mesosphere

Stratosphere

Troposphere

210 km

160

80

50

40

10

sea level   10   80

Stratosphere and Mesosphere

Troposphere

Earth reduced by 90% in proportion to this scale

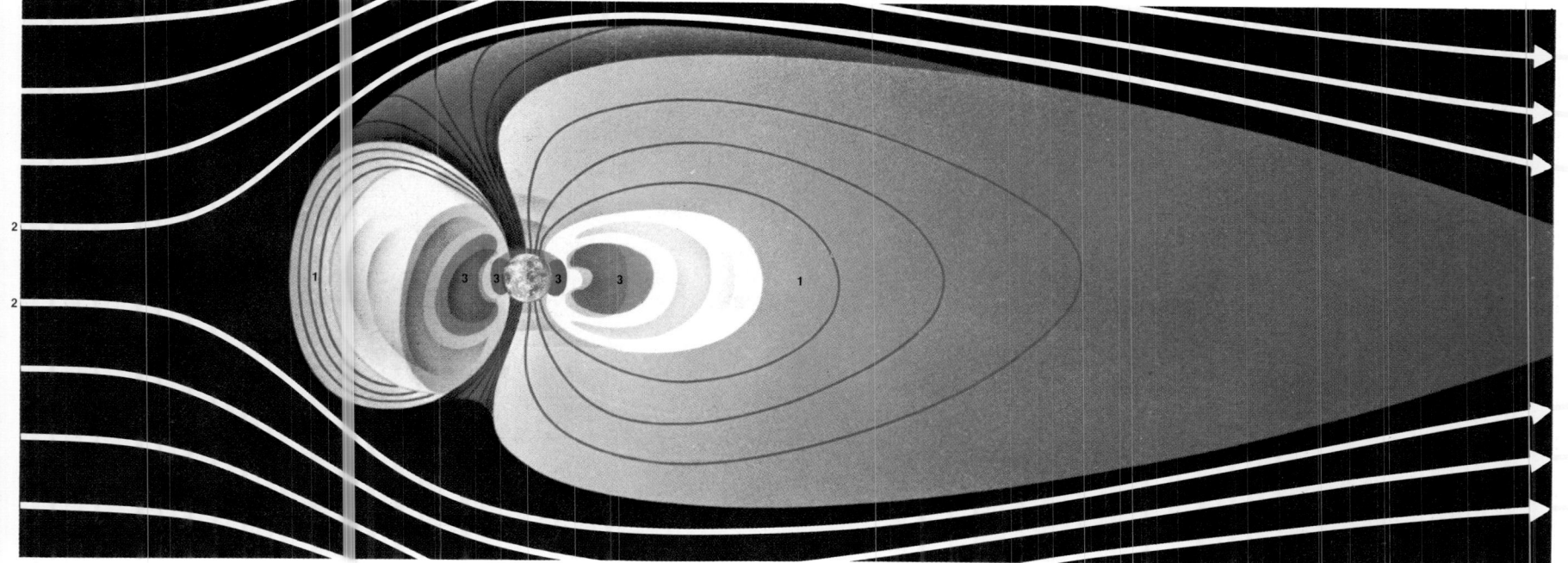

was compensated for by the formation of shiny white clouds of water droplets which reflected some of the Sun's radiation back into space. Our planet stabilized with an average temperature of 15°C. This proved ideal for the emergence of life, which evolved first in the seas and then moved onto land, converting carbon dioxide into oxygen as it did so.

In any view from space, planet Earth is dominated by water—in blue oceans and white clouds—and water is the key to life as we know it. Animal life—oxygen-breathing life—could only evolve after earlier forms of life had converted the atmosphere to an oxygen-rich state. The nature of the air today is a product of life as well as being vital to its existence.

An atmospheric layer cake

Starting at ground level, the first zone of the atmosphere is the troposphere, kept warm near the ground by the greenhouse effect but cooling to a chilly −60°C at an altitude of 15 km (9 miles). Above the troposphere is a warming layer, the stratosphere, in which energy from the Sun is absorbed and temperatures increase to reach 0°C at an altitude of 50 km (30 miles). The energy—in the form of ultraviolet radiation—is absorbed by molecules of ozone, a form of oxygen. Without the ozone layer in the atmosphere, ultraviolet rays would penetrate the

The Earth's magnetic field behaves as if there were a huge bar magnet placed inside the globe, with its magnetic axis tilted at a slight angle to the geographical north–south axis. The speed of rotation of the liquid core differs from that of the mantle, producing an effect like a dynamo (below). The region in which the magnetic field extends beyond the Earth is the magnetosphere (1). Streams of charged particles (2) from the Sun distort its shape into that of a teardrop. Zones of the magnetosphere include the Van Allen Belts (3), which are regions of intense radioactivity where magnetic particles are "trapped."

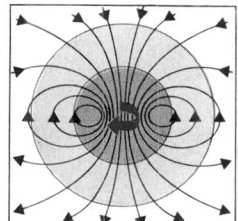

ground and sterilize the land surface: without life, there would be no oxygen from which an ozone layer could form.

Above the stratosphere, another cooling layer, the mesosphere, extends up to 80 km (50 miles), at which point the temperature has fallen to about −100°C. Above this level the gases of the atmosphere are so thin that the standard concept of temperature is no real guide to their behavior, and from the mesosphere outwards the atmosphere is best described in terms of its electrical properties.

In the outer layers of the atmosphere, the Sun's energy is absorbed by individual atoms in such a way that it strips electrons off them, leaving behind positively charged ions, which give the region its name—the ionosphere. A few hundred kilometers above the Earth's surface, gravity is so feeble that electromagnetic forces begin to determine the behavior of the charged particles, which are shepherded along the lines of force in the Earth's magnetic field. Above 500 km (300 miles), the magnetic field is so dominant that yet another region, the magnetosphere, is distinguished. This is the true boundary between Earth and interplanetary space.

The magnetosphere has been likened to the hull of "spaceship Earth." Charged particles (the solar wind) streaming out from the Sun are deflected around Earth by the magnetosphere

like water around a moving ship, while the region of the Earth's magnetic influence in space trails "downstream" away from the Sun like the wake of a ship. The Van Allen Belts, at altitudes of 3,000 and 15,000 km (1,850 and 9,300 miles) are regions of space high above the Equator where particles are trapped by the magnetic field. Particles spilling out of the belts spiral towards the polar regions of Earth, producing the spectacle of the auroras—the northern and southern lights. The Earth and Mercury are the only inner planets with magnetospheres such as this. The cause of the Earth's magnetism is almost certainly the planet's heavy molten core, which is composed of magnetic materials.

The Earth's atmosphere exhibits a great variety of characteristics on a vertical scale. As well as variations of temperature and the electrical properties of the air, there are differences in chemical composition—in the mixture of gases and water vapor—according to altitude. The Earth's gravitational pull means that air density and pressure decrease with altitude. Pressure of about 1,000 millibars at sea level falls to virtually nothing (10^{-42} millibars) by a height of 700 km (435 miles) above the Earth. All these factors, and their interrelationships, help to maintain the Earth's atmosphere as a protective outer covering or radiation shield and an essential life-support system.

The ionosphere is another name for the atmospheric layer beyond 80 km (50 miles). The region is best described in terms of the electrical properties of its constituents rather than by temperature. It is here that ionization occurs. Gamma and X-rays from the Sun are absorbed by atoms and molecules of nitrogen and oxygen and, as a result, each molecule or atom gives up one or more of its electrons, thus becoming a positively charged ion. These ions reflect radio waves and are used to bounce back radio waves transmitted from the surface of the Earth.

The exosphere is the layer above the thermosphere and it extends from 400 km (250 miles) up to about 700 km (435 miles), the point at which, it may be said, space begins. It is almost a complete vacuum because most of its atoms and molecules of oxygen escape the Earth's gravity.

The magnetosphere includes the exosphere, but it extends far beyond the atmosphere—to a distance of between 64,000 and 130,000 km (40,000 and 80,000 miles) above the Earth. It represents the Earth's external magnetic field and its outer limit is called the magnetopause.

The atmosphere protects the Earth from harmful solar radiation and also from bombardment by small particles from space. Most meteors (particles orbiting the Sun) burn up in the atmosphere, but meteorites (debris of minor planets) reach the ground. Of all incoming solar radiation, only visible light, radio waves and infrared rays reach the surface of Earth. X-rays are removed in the ionosphere, and ultraviolet and some infrared radiations are filtered out in the stratosphere. Studies of such radiations have, therefore, to be made from observatories in space.

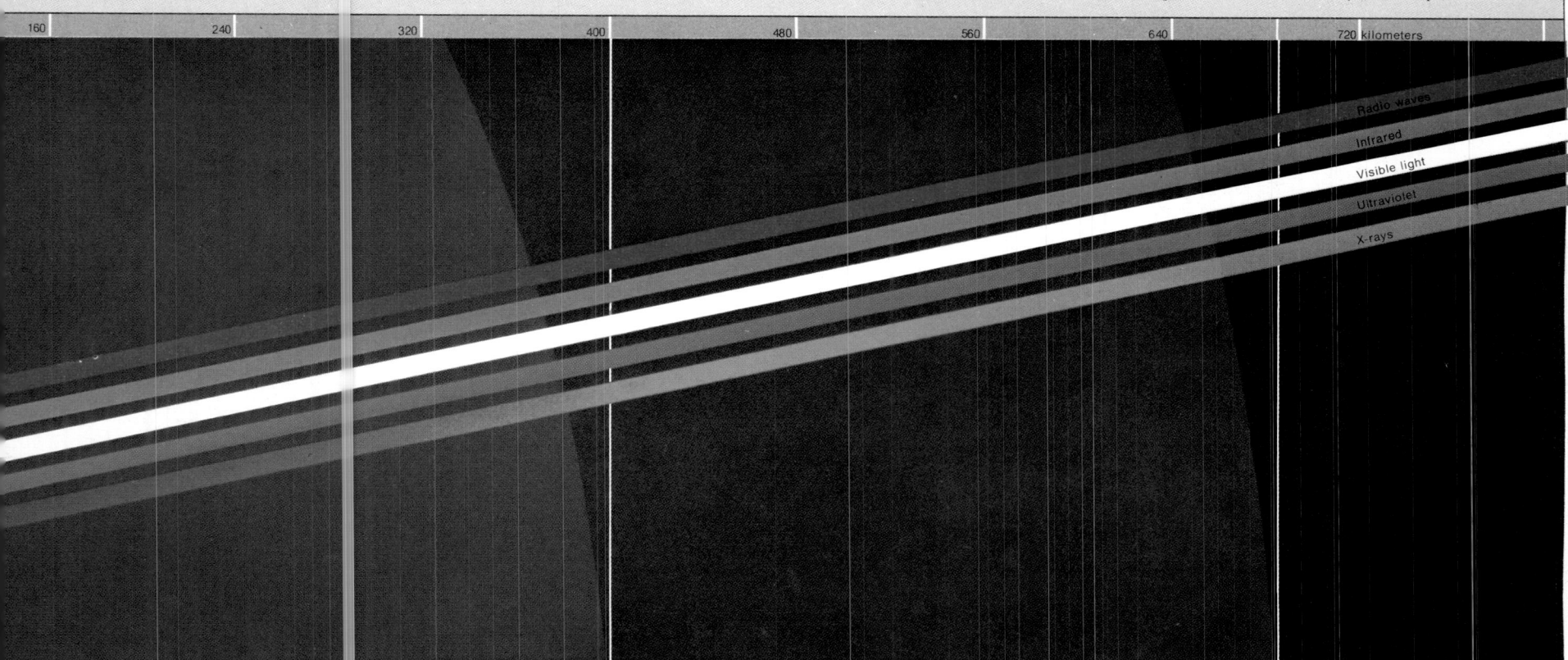

160 240 320 400 480 560 640 720 kilometers

Thermosphere/Ionosphere   Exosphere/Magnetosphere   Space

Man Looks at the Earth

Orbiting satellites keep a detailed watch on the Earth's land surface, oceans and atmosphere, feeding streams of data to meteorologists, geologists, oceanographers, farmers, fishermen and many others. Some information would be unobtainable by any other means. Surveys from orbit are quicker and less expensive than from aircraft, for example, because a satellite can scan a much larger area. And, surprisingly enough, certain features on the ground are easier to see from space.

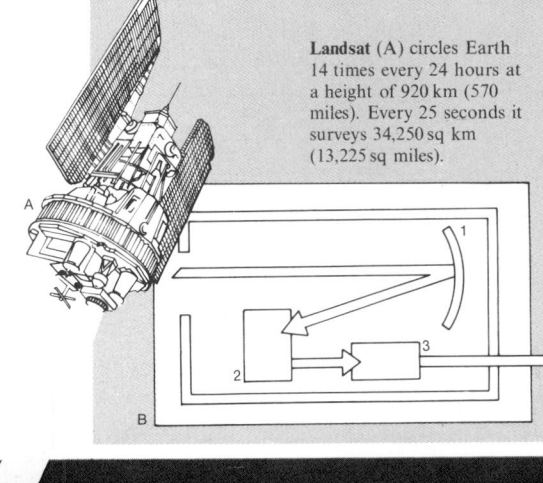

Landsat (A) circles Earth 14 times every 24 hours at a height of 920 km (570 miles). Every 25 seconds it surveys 34,250 sq km (13,225 sq miles).

MAPPING AND MEASURING

Man has been looking at Earth from satellites since the beginning of the 1960s, and has firmly established the value of surveys from space to those engaged in a variety of earthly pursuits. Chief of these activities are resource management, ranging from monitoring the spread of deserts and river silting to locating likely mineral deposits; environmental protection, which includes observing delicate ecosystems and natural disasters; and a whole range of mapping and land-use planning.

Satellites give us a greater overview of numerous aspects of life on Earth than any earthbound eye could see.

Of all the information gleaned from satellites, accurate weather forecasts are of particular social and economic value. The first weather satellite was Tiros 1 (Television and Infrared Observation Satellite), launched by the United States in 1960. By the time Tiros 10 ceased operations in 1967, the series had sent back more than half a million photographs, firmly establishing the value of satellite imagery.

Tiros was superseded by the ESSA (Environmental Science Services Administration) and the NOAA (National Oceanic and Atmospheric Administration) satellites. These orbited the Earth from pole to pole, and they covered the entire globe during the course of a day. Other weather satellites, such as the European Meteosat, are placed in geostationary orbit over the Equator, which means they stay in one place and continually monitor a single large region.

Watching the weather

In addition to photographing clouds, weather satellites monitor the extent of snow and ice cover, and they measure the temperature of the oceans and the composition of the atmosphere. Information about the overall heat balance of our planet gives clues to long-term climatic change, and includes the effects on climate of human activities such as the burning of fossil fuels and deforestation.

Infrared sensors allow pictures to be taken at night as well as during the day. The temperature of cloud tops, measured by infrared devices, is a guide to the height of the clouds. In a typical infrared image, high clouds appear white because they are the coldest, lower clouds and land areas appear gray, and oceans and lakes are black. Information on humidity in the atmosphere is provided by sensors tuned to wavelengths between 5.5 and 7 micrometers, at which water vapor strongly absorbs the radiation.

To "see" inside clouds, where infrared and visible light cannot penetrate, satellites use sensors tuned to short-wavelength radio waves (microwaves) around the 1.5 centimeter wavelength. These sensors can reveal whether or not clouds will give rise to heavy rainfall, snow or hail. Microwave sensors are also useful for locating ice floes in polar regions, making use of the different microwave reflections from land ice, sea ice and open water.

Satellites that send out such pictures are in relatively low orbits, at a height feeding about 1,000 km (620 miles), and they pass over each part of the Earth once every 12 hours. But to build up a global model of the Earth's weather and climate, meteorologists need continual information on wind speed and direction at various levels in the atmosphere, together with temperature and humidity profiles. This data is provided by geostationary satellites. Cloud photographs taken every half-hour give information on winds, and computers combine this with temperature and humidity soundings to give as complete a model as is possible of the Earth's atmosphere.

Increasing attention is also being paid to the Earth's surface, notably by means of a series of satellites called Landsat (originally ERTS or Earth Resource Technology Satellites), the first of which was launched by the United States in 1972. The third and current Landsat is in a similar pole-to-pole orbit as the weather satellites, but its cameras are more powerful and they make more detailed surveys of the Earth. Landsat rephotographs each part of the Earth's surface every 18 days.

How to map resources

The satellite has two sensor systems: a television camera, which takes pictures of the Earth using visible light; and a device called a multispectral scanner, which scans the Earth at several distinct wavelengths, including visible light and infrared. Data from the various channels of the multispectral scanner can be combined to produce so-called false-color images, in which each wavelength band is assigned a color (not necessarily its real one) to emphasize features of interest.

An important use of Landsat photographs is for making maps, particularly of large countries with remote areas that have never been adequately surveyed from the ground. Several countries, including Brazil, Canada and China, have set up ground stations to receive Landsat data directly. Features previously unknown or incorrectly mapped, including rivers, lakes and glaciers, show up readily on Landsat images. Urban mapping and hence planning are aided by satellite pictures that can distinguish areas of industry, housing and open parkland.

Landsat photographs have also proved invaluable for agricultural land-use planning.

They are used for estimates of soil types and for determining land-use patterns. Areas of crop disease or dying vegetation are detectable by their different colors. Yields of certain crops such as wheat can now be accurately predicted from satellite imagery, so that at last it is becoming possible to keep track of the worldwide production of vital food crops. Fresh water, too, is one of our most valuable resources, and knowing its sources and seasonal variation is vital to irrigation projects.

Finally, the geologist and mineral prospector have benefited from remote sensing. Features such as fault lines and different types of sediments and rocks show up clearly on Landsat pictures. This allows geologists to select promising areas in which the prospector can look for mineral deposits.

Another way to study the Earth is by bouncing radar beams off it. Radar sensing indicates the nature of soil or rock on land and movement of water at sea, for example. This was not done by Landsat, but by equipment aboard the United States' Skylab and by a short-lived American satellite called Seasat. The Soviet Union has included Earth surveying in its Salyut program, and resource mapping is also a feature of the spacelab aboard the American space shuttle. All these activities help man to manage the limited resources on our planet and to preserve the environment.

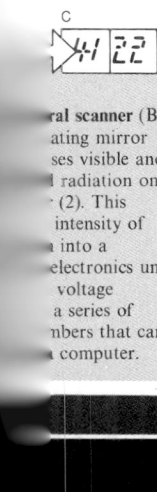

...ral scanner (B)
...ating mirror
...ses visible and
...d radiation on
...r (2). This
...intensity of
...into a
...electronics unit
...voltage
...a series of
...nbers that can
...a computer.

The numbers (C) are then
transmitted back to a
receiving station (D) as a
radio frequency at the rate
of 15 million units a
second. The numbers are
translated back into the
digital voltage pattern and
converted by computer (E)
into the equivalent binary
numbers, each of which
represents a color.

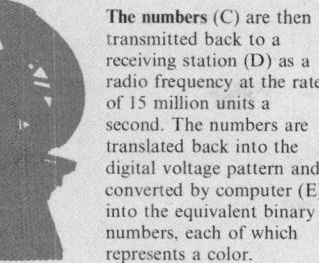

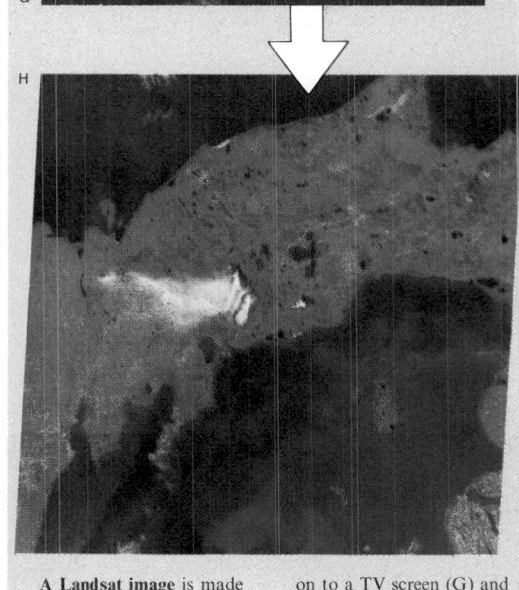

A Landsat image is made
up of very many points,
each of which is obtained
by means of the procedure
described above. Each
number in the image (F)
represents the radiation
from a small area of land,
or pixel, 0.44 hectares (1.1
acres) in size. A computer
then translates the numbers
into different colors, or
different shades of one
color, which are projected
on to a TV screen (G) and
the image is seen for the
first time. Finally,
photographs of this false-
color image are produced
(H). This picture, showing
a forest fire in the Upper
Peninsula, Michigan, is of
use to those engaged in
forest management. Other
satellite data of use in
forestry include types of
trees, patterns of growth
and the spread of disease.

**Observation of waterways
and coastal areas** (above)
shows pollution and
deposition of sediments.
This is of importance to
the fishing industry. Fish
congregate in areas where
upwelling brings nutrients
to the surface, for example.
The large yellow-orange
halo around Akimiski
Island in James Bay (A)—
a southern extension of
Hudson Bay in Canada—
is fine sediment resulting
from wave action on a silty
shore. Seeing the sediment
in this way helps to
determine current patterns
in the Bay. In a
predominantly desert area,
the Nile delta (B) stands
out dramatically. The red
is an intensively cultivated
area: cotton is the main
crop. The larger irrigation
canals can be seen on the
photograph. Thermal
imagery, or heat capacity
mapping, is used to
identify rocks, to study the
effects of urban "heat
islands," to estimate soil
moisture and snow melt,

and to map shallow
ground water. In this
photograph of the
northeast coast of North
America (C) purple
represents the coldest
temperatures—in Lakes
Erie and Ontario. The
coldest parts of the
Atlantic Ocean are deep
blue, whereas warmer
waters near the coast are
light blue. Green is the
warmer land, but also the
Gulf Stream in the lower
right part of the image.
Brown, yellow and orange
represent successively
warmer land surface areas.
Red is hot regions around
cities and coal-mining
regions found in eastern
Pennsylvania (to the upper
left of center in the
picture); and, finally, gray
and white are the very
hottest areas—the urban
heat islands of Baltimore,
Philadelphia and New
York City. Black areas in
the upper left are cold
clouds. The temperature
range of the image is
about 30°C (55°F).

The Earth seen from space
shows phases just like the
Moon, Mercury and Venus
do to us. These dramatic
photographs were taken
from a satellite moving at

35,885 km (22,300 miles)
above South America at
7.30 am (1), 10.30 am (2),
noon (3), 3.30 pm (4) and
at 10.30 pm (5), and clearly
show the Earth in phase.

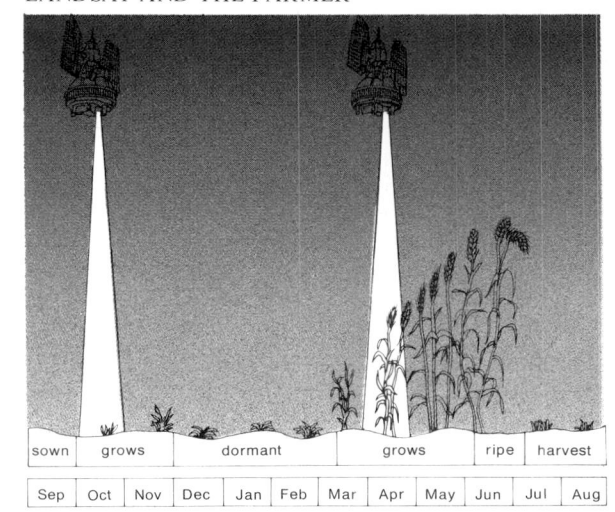

Weather satellite imagery
can save lives and property
by giving advance warning
of bad weather conditions,
as well as providing day-
to-day forecasts. This Tiros
image (left) shows a cold
front moving west of
Ireland with low-level wave
clouds over southern and
central England. There are
low-pressure systems over
northern France and to the
northwest of Ireland.

LANDSAT AND THE FARMER

sown	grows	dormant	grows	ripe	harvest

Sep	Oct	Nov	Dec	Jan	Feb	Mar	Apr	May	Jun	Jul	Aug

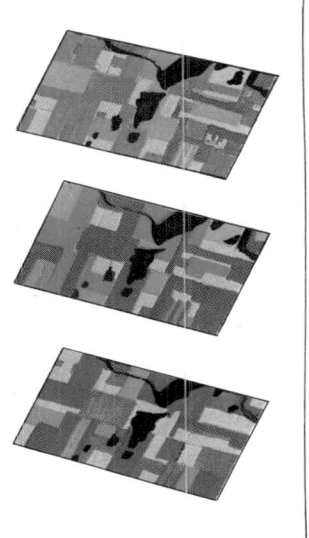

Agriculturists benefit from
"multitemporal analysis"
by satellites (left). This is
the comparison of data
from the same field
recorded on two or more
dates. It is also able to
differentiate crops, which
may have an identical
appearance, or signature,
on one day, but on another
occasion exhibit different
rates of growth. The
pattern of growth is
different for small grains
than most other crops. A
"biowindow" is the period
of time in which vegetation
is observed. These three
biowindows (right) show
the emergence and ripening
(light blue to red to dark
blue) of wheat in May,
July and August.

Part 2

MAKING AND SHAPING THE EARTH

The structure and substance of the Earth
Forces that move continents · Forces that fashion Earth's landscapes
How man has changed the face of the Earth

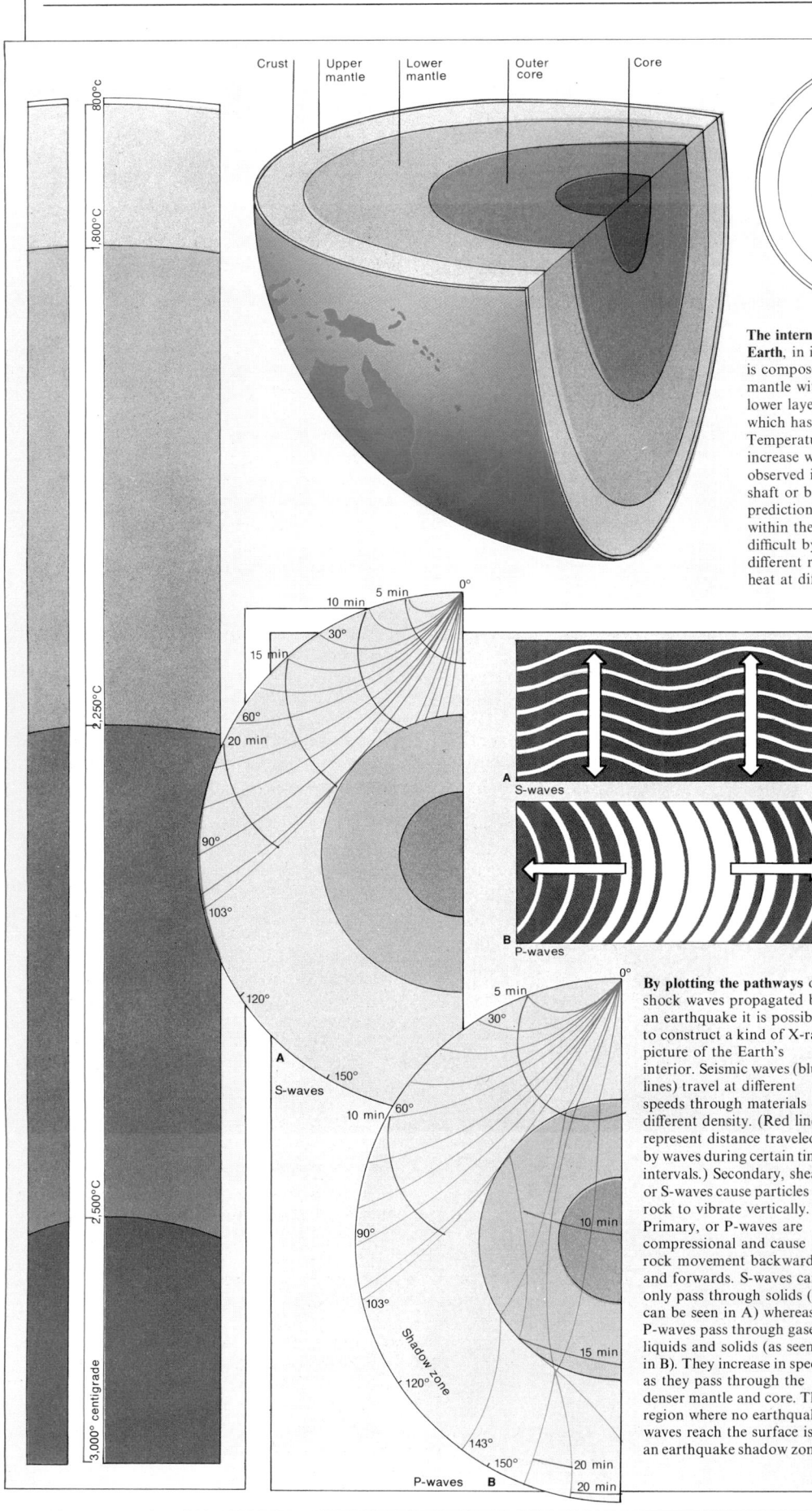

Crust | Upper mantle | Lower mantle | Outer core | Core

0–33 km
(0–19 miles)
33–700 km
(19–435 miles)
700–2,900 km
(435–1,800 miles)
2,900–5,165 km
(1,800–3,205 miles)
5,165–6,385 km
(3,205–3,965 miles)

The internal structure of the Earth, in its simplest form, is composed of a crust, a mantle with an upper and lower layer, and a core, which has an inner region. Temperatures in the Earth increase with depth, as is observed in a deep mine shaft or bore-hole, but the prediction of temperatures within the Earth is made difficult by the fact that different rocks conduct heat at different rates: rock salt, for example, has 10 times the heat conductivity of coal. Also, estimates have to take into account the abundance of heat-generating atoms in a rock. Radioactive atoms are concentrated toward the Earth's surface so the planet has, in effect, a thermal blanket to keep it warm. The temperature at the center of the Earth is believed to be approximately 3,000°C (5,400°F).

A NEW GEOLOGY

A revolution in geological thinking during the first half of this century transformed man's ideas about the structure of the planet Earth. The science of palaeomagnetism, which studies the magnetic properties of rocks and the history of the Earth's magnetic field, and later the new science of marine geology, contributed greatly to the refinement of theories such as continental drift. Man has even looked beyond the Earth for knowledge of this planet's innermost depths.

By plotting the pathways of shock waves propagated by an earthquake it is possible to construct a kind of X-ray picture of the Earth's interior. Seismic waves (blue lines) travel at different speeds through materials of different density. (Red lines represent distance traveled by waves during certain time intervals.) Secondary, shear or S-waves cause particles of rock to vibrate vertically. Primary, or P-waves are compressional and cause rock movement backwards and forwards. S-waves can only pass through solids (as can be seen in A) whereas P-waves pass through gases, liquids and solids (as seen in B). They increase in speed as they pass through the denser mantle and core. The region where no earthquake waves reach the surface is an earthquake shadow zone.

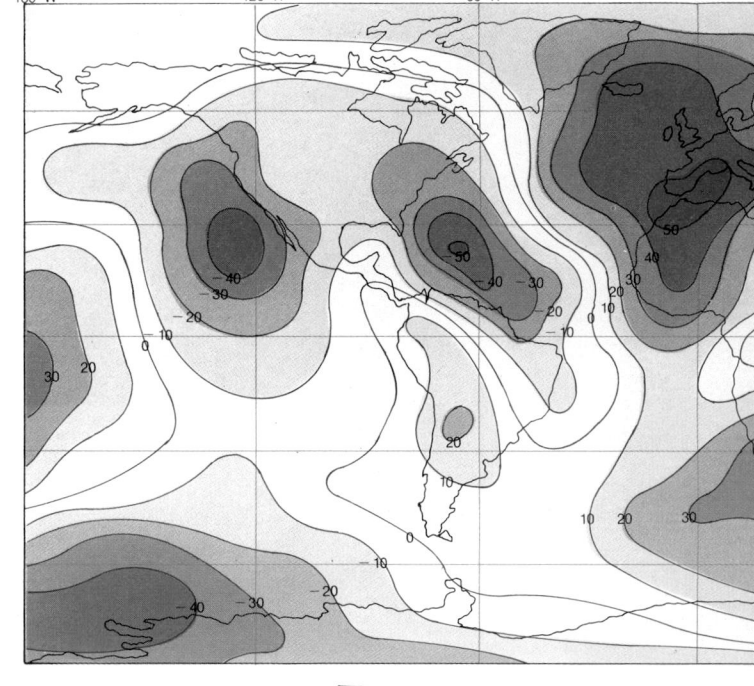

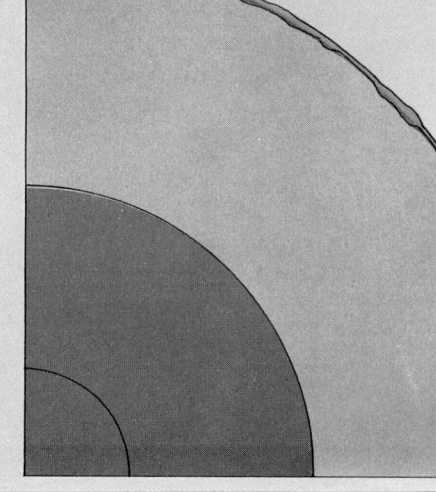

The chemical composition of the Earth varies from crust to core. The upper crust of continents (sial) is mainly granite, rich in aluminum and silicon, whereas oceanic crust (sima) is largely basalt, made of magnesium and silicon. The mantle is composed of rocks that are rich in magnesium and iron silicates, whereas the core, it is believed, is made of iron and nickel oxides.

A Silicon
B Aluminum
C Iron
D Calcium
E Magnesium
F Nickel
G Other

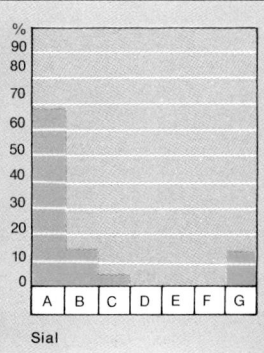
Sial

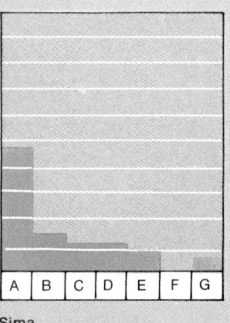
Sima

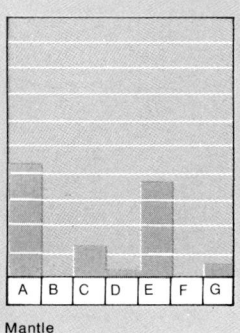
Mantle

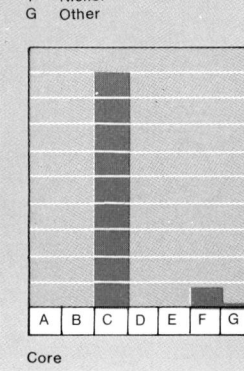
Core

Earth's Structure

The Earth is made up of concentric shells of different kinds of material. Immediately beneath us is the crust; below that is the mantle; and at the center of the globe is the core. Knowledge of the internal structure of Earth is the key to an understanding of the substances of Earth and an appreciation of the forces at work, not only deep in the center of the planet but also affecting the formation of surface features and large-scale landscapes. The workings of all these elements are inextricably linked.

A 17th-century diagram of the Earth shows an internal structure of fire and subterranean rivers.

Our knowledge of the Earth is largely restricted to the outer crust. The deepest hole that man has drilled reaches only 10 km (6 miles)—less than 1/600th of the planet's radius—and so our knowledge about the rest of the Earth has had to come via indirect means: by the study of earthquake waves, and a comparison between rocks on Earth and those that make up meteorites—small fragments of asteroids and other minor planetary bodies that originated from similar materials to the Earth.

The Earth's crust
The outermost layer of the Earth is called the crust. The crust beneath the oceans is different from the material that makes up continental crust. Ocean crust is formed at mid-ocean ridges where melted rocks (magma) from the mantle rise up in great quantities and solidify to form a layer a few kilometers thick over the mantle. As this ocean crust spreads out from the ridge it becomes covered with deep-ocean sediments. The ocean crust was initially called "sima," a word made up from the first two letters of the characteristic elements—silicon and magnesium. Sima has a density of 2.9 gm/cc (1 gm/cc is the density of water).

Continental crust was named "sial"—from silicon and aluminum, the most abundant elements. Sial is lighter than sima with a density of 2.7 gm/cc. The continental crust is like a series of giant rafts, 17 to 70 km (9–43 miles) thick. As a result of numerous collisions and breakages, these continental rafts have been bulldozed into their present shape, but they have been forming for at least 4,000 million years. The oldest known rocks, in Greenland, are 3,750 million years old, which is only about 800 million years younger than the Earth itself. The complex history of the continents' evolution over this vast time span makes construction of an ideal cross section difficult, but the rocks of the lower two-thirds of the crust appear to be denser (2.9 gm/cc) than the upper levels.

The Moho, or Mohorovičić discontinuity, discovered in 1909, marks the base of the crust and the beginning of the mantle rocks, where the density increases from 2.9 to 3.3 gm/cc. The Moho is at an average depth of 10 km (6 miles) under the sea and 35 km (20 miles) below land.

The mantle
Our knowledge of the mantle comes from mantle rocks that are sometimes brought to the surface. These are even more enriched in magnesium oxides than the sima, with lesser amounts of iron and calcium oxides. The uppermost mantle to a depth of between 60 and 100 km (40–60 miles), together with the overlying crust, forms the rigid lithosphere, which is divided into plates. Below this is a pasty layer, or asthenosphere, extending to a depth of 700 km (435 miles). The upper mantle is separated from the lower mantle by another discontinuity where the density of the rock increases from 3.3 to 4.3 gm/cc.

Scientists now believe that the mantle is the planetary motor force behind the movements of the continents. By studying in detail the chemistry of the volcanic rocks that have come directly from the mantle, they have gathered much information about this mantle motor. The rocks that come up along oceanic ridges and form new oceanic crust reveal by their chemical composition that they have formed from mantle that has undergone previous melting. By contrast, islands such as Hawaii and Iceland have formed from mantle material that, for the most part, has never been melted before. One explanation for these chemical observations is that, while the top 700 km (435 miles) of the mantle region is moving in accordance with movement of the plates, the mantle beneath it is moving independently and sending occasional rivers of unaltered material through the surface to form islands like volcanic Hawaii.

The core
Structurally, the most important boundary in the Earth lies at a depth of 2,900 km (1,800 miles) below the surface, where the rock density almost doubles from about 5.5 to 9.9 gm/cc. This is known as the Gutenberg discontinuity and was discovered in 1914. Below this level the material must have the properties of a liquid since certain earthquake waves cannot penetrate it. Scientists infer from the composition of meteorites, some of which are composed of iron and nickel, that this deep core material is composed largely of iron, with some nickel and perhaps lighter elements such as silicon. The processes involved in the formation of a planet have been compared to the separation of the metals (the core) from the slag (the mantle and crust) in a blast furnace.

The core has a radius of 3,485 km (2,165 miles) and makes up only one-sixth of the Earth's volume, yet it has one-third of its mass. In the middle of the liquid outer core there is an even denser ball with a radius of 1,220 km (760 miles)—two-thirds the size of the Moon—where, under intense pressure, the metals have solidified. The inner core is believed to be solid iron and nickel and is 20 percent denser (12–13 gm/cc) than the surrounding liquid.

Electric currents in the core are the only possible source of the Earth's magnetic field. This drifts and alters in a way which could arise only from some deeply buried fluid movement. At the top of the core, the pattern of the field moves about 100 m (330 ft) west each day. Every million years or so during the Earth's history, the north–south magnetic poles have switched so that compasses pointed south, not north.

The dynamo that generates magnetism and its strange variations is still not fully understood. Motion in the core may be powered by giant slabs of metal that crystallize out from the liquid and sink to join the inner core. Our knowledge of the Earth's structure has increased greatly over the last 50 years, but many intriguing questions remain to be answered.

The Earth is not a sphere but an ellipsoid (below) that is flattened at the poles, where the radius is 6,378 km (3,960 miles), and bulging at the Equator, where the radius is 6,536 km (4,060 miles). This results from the Earth's rapid rotation. But, rather than a perfect ellipsoid, the true shape is a "geoid"—the actual shape of sea level—which is lumpy, with variations away from ellipsoid of up to 80 m (260 ft) (left). This reflects major variations in density in Earth's outer layers.

The Earth as a Geoid

• Geomagnetic poles

Oersteds
0.20
0.25
0.30
0.35
0.40
0.45
0.50
0.55
0.60
0.65
0.70

The Earth's magnetic field is strongest at the poles and weakest in equatorial regions. If the field were simply like a bar magnet inside the globe, lines of intensity would mirror lines of latitude; but the field is inclined at an angle of 11° to the Earth's axis. The geomagnetic poles are similarly inclined and they do not coincide with the geographic poles. In reality, the field is much more complex than that of a bar magnet. In addition, over long periods of time, the magnetic poles and the north–south orientation of the field change slowly. The strength of the Earth's magnetic field is measured in units called oersteds.

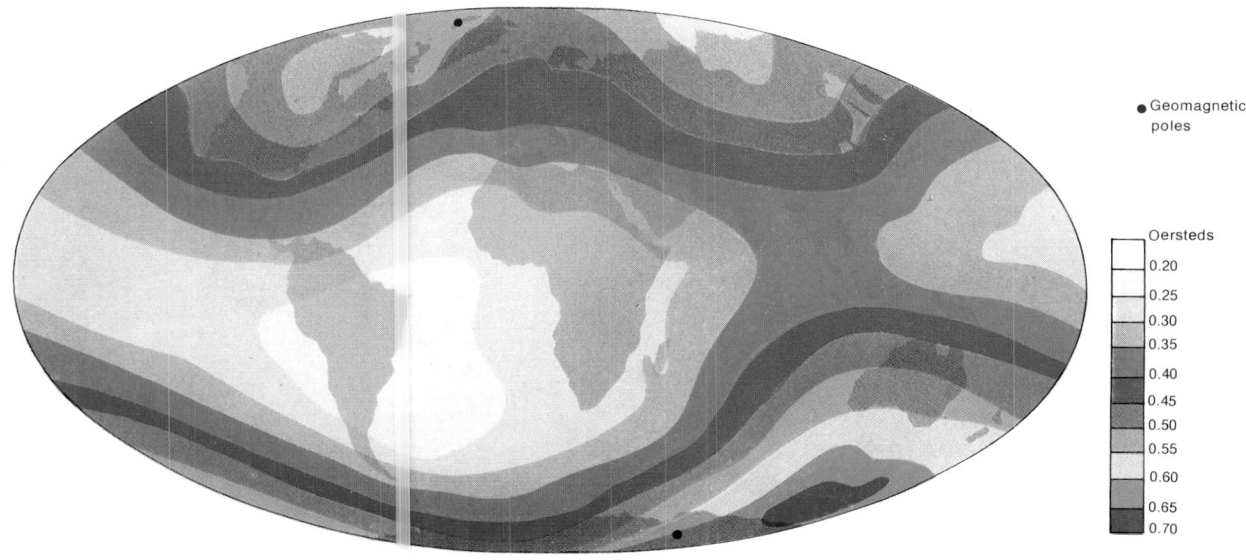

Earth's Moving Crust

The top layer of the Earth is known as the lithosphere and is composed of the crust and the uppermost mantle. It is divided into six major rigid plates and several smaller platelets that move relative to each other, driven by movements that lie deep in the Earth's liquid mantle. The plate boundaries correspond to the zones of earthquakes and the sites of active volcanoes. The concept of plate tectonics – that the Earth's crust is mobile despite being rigid – emerged in the 1960s and helped to confirm the early twentieth-century theory of continental drift proposed by Alfred Wegener.

THE DYNAMIC EARTH

As early as the 17th century, the English philosopher Francis Bacon noted that the coasts on either side of the Atlantic were similar and could be fitted together like pieces of a jigsaw puzzle. Three hundred years later Alfred Wegener proposed the theory of continental drift, but no one would believe the Earth's rigid crust could move. Today, geological evidence has provided the basis for the theory of plate tectonics, which demonstrates that the Earth's crust is slowly but continually moving.

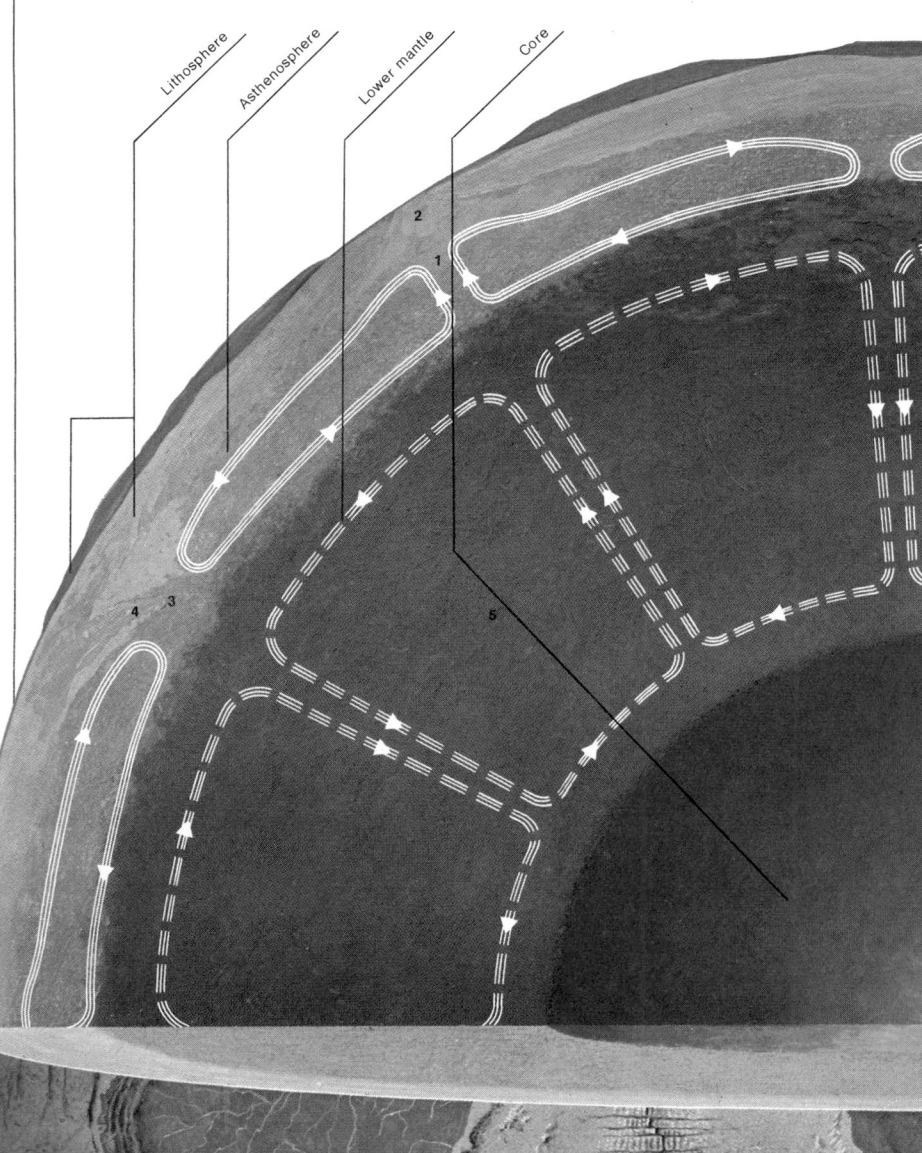

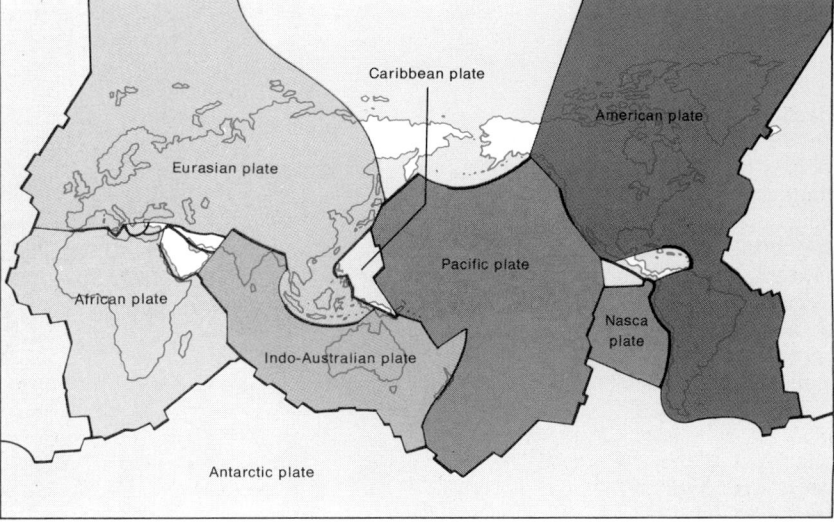

Earth's lithosphere—the rocky shell, or crust—is made up of six major plates and several smaller platelets, each separated from each other by ridges, subduction zones or transcurrent faults. The plates grow bigger by accretion along the mid-ocean ridges, are destroyed at subduction zones beneath the trenches, and slide beside each other along the transcurrent faults. The African and Antarctic plates have no trenches along their borders to destroy any of their crust, so they are growing bigger. This growth is compensated by the subduction zone that is developing to the north of the Tonga Islands and subduction zones in the Pacific. Conversely, the Pacific and Indo-Australian plates are shrinking. Along the plate boundaries magma wells up from the mantle to form volcanoes. Here, too, are the origins of earthquakes as the plates collide or slide slowly past each other.

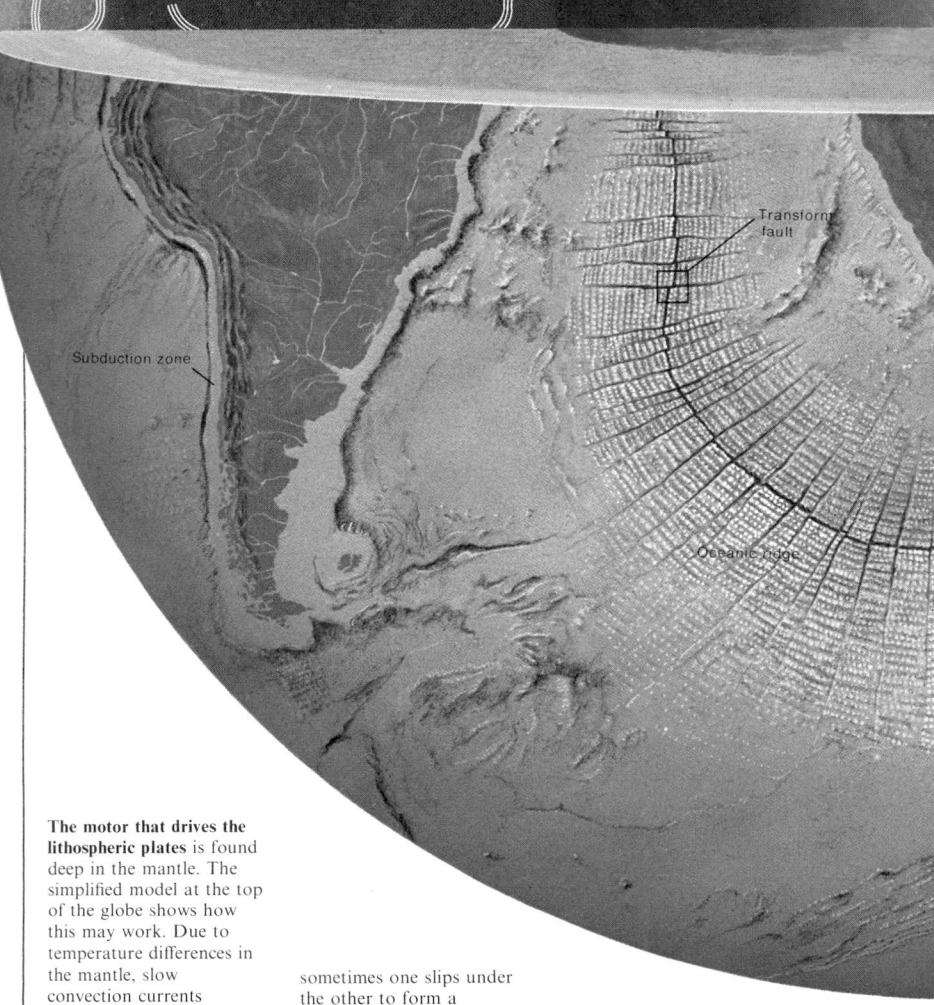

Subduction zones are the sites of destruction of the ocean crust. As one plate passes beneath another down into the mantle, the ocean floor is pulled downward and a deep ocean trench is formed. The movement taking place along the length of the subduction zone causes earthquakes, while melting of the rock at depth produces magma that rises to create the volcanoes that form island arcs.

An oceanic ridge is formed when two plates move away from each other. As they move, molten magma from the mantle forces its way to the surface. This magma cools and is in turn injected with new magma. Thus the oceanic ridge is gradually forming the newest part of Earth's crust.

The motor that drives the lithospheric plates is found deep in the mantle. The simplified model at the top of the globe shows how this may work. Due to temperature differences in the mantle, slow convection currents circulate. Where two current cycles move upwards together and separate (1), the plates bulge and move apart along mid-ocean ridges (2). Where there is a downward moving current (3), the plates move together and sometimes one slips under the other to form a subduction zone (4). Another model proposes that the convection currents are found deep in the mantle (5). Only time and more research, however, will reveal the true mechanism of plate movement.

Transform, or transcurrent, faults are found where two plates slide past each other. They may, for example, link two parts of a ridge (A, B). A study of the magnetic properties of the seabed may suggest a motion shown by the white arrows, but the true movements of the plates are shown by the red arrows. The transform fault is active only between points (2) and (3). Between points (1) and (2) and between (3) and (4) the scar of the fault is healed and the line of the fault is no longer a plate boundary.

The early evidence for continental drift was gathered by Alfred Wegener, a German meteorologist. He noticed that the coastlines on each side of the Atlantic Ocean could be made to fit together, and that much of the geological history of the flanking continents—shown by fossils, structures and past climates—also seemed to match. Wegener compared the two sides of the Atlantic with a sheet of torn newspaper and reasoned that if not just one line of print but 10 lines match then there is a good case for arguing that the two sides were once joined. Yet for 50 years continental drift was generally considered to be a fanciful dream.

Seafloor spreading
In the 1950s the first geological surveys of the oceans began, and a 60,000 km (37,300 mile) long chain of mountains was discovered running down the center of the Atlantic Ocean, all round the Antarctic, up to the Indian Ocean, into the Red Sea and up the Eastern Pacific Ocean into Alaska. Along the axis of this mid-ocean ridge system there was often a narrow, deep rift valley. In places this ridge was offset along sharp fractures in the ocean floor.

The breakthrough in developing the global plate tectonic theory came with the first large-scale survey of the ocean floor. Magnetometers, which were developed during World War II for tracking submarines, showed the ocean floor to be magnetically striped. The ocean floor reveals magnetic characteristics because the ocean crust basalts are full of tiny crystals of the magnetic mineral magnetite. As the basalt cooled, the magnetic field of these crystals aligned itself with the Earth's magnetic field. This would be insignificant if it were not for the fact that the magnetic pole of the Earth has switched from north to south at different times in the past. Half the magnetite compasses of the ocean floor point south rather than north.

In the middle 1960s, two Cambridge geophysicists, Drummond Matthews and Fred Vine, noticed that the pattern of stripes was symmetrical around the mid-ocean ridge. Such an extraordinary and unlikely symmetry could mean only one thing—any two matching stripes must originally have been formed together at the mid-ocean ridge and then moved away from each other as newer crust formed between them to create new stripes. It was soon calculated that the North Atlantic Ocean was growing wider by about 2 cm (¾ in) a year. At last, drifting continents was accepted.

Consumption of the seafloor
Seafloor spreading soon became included in an even more sensational model—plate tectonics. If the oceans are growing wider, then either the whole planet is expanding or the spreading ocean floor is consumed elsewhere. In the late 1950s a global network of seismic stations had been set up to monitor nuclear explosions and earthquakes. For the first time the positions of all earthquakes could be accurately defined.

It was found that the zones of earthquake activity were predominantly narrow, following the mid-ocean ridges and extending along the rim of the Pacific, beneath the island arcs of the

West Pacific and beneath the continental margins in the East Pacific as well as underlying the Alpine-Himalayan Mountain Belt. The seismic zones around the Pacific dipped away from the ocean and continued to depths as great as 700 km (430 miles). They intercepted the surface at the curious arc-shaped deep-ocean trenches. It had been known for 20 years that the pull of gravity over these trenches is strangely reduced, so to survive they must continually be dragged downwards. Here was the site of ocean-floor consumption—now known as a subduction zone. Subduction zones must be efficient at consuming ocean crust because no known ocean crust is older than 200 million years—less than five percent of Earth's lifetime.

The oceanic lithosphere (the Earth's rocky crust) is extraordinarily rigid. Even where the oceanic lithosphere becomes consumed within subduction zones it still maintains its rigidity. As it bends down into the Earth it tends to corrugate, forming very long folds. These corrugations give rise to the pattern of chains of deep-ocean trenches and chains of volcanic islands formed above the subduction zone.

As oceanic lithosphere grows older it cools, contracts and sinks. From the depth of the ocean floor it is possible to make an accurate estimate of the age of the crust beneath. Even the steepness of the subduction zone is a function of the age, and therefore the density, of the lithosphere. The oldest crust provides the strongest downward pull and hence the steepest angle of dip of the subduction zone.

As well as the spreading ridges (constructive margins) and the subduction zones (destructive margins) there is another kind of plate boundary (conservative margins), where the plates slip past one another along a major fault such as the San Andreas Fault of California.

The past positions of the continents
Continental drift is thus the result of the creation and destruction of oceanic lithosphere, but only the continents can record the oceanic plate motions taking place more than 200 million years ago. The discovery of ancient lines of subduction zone volcanoes can testify to the destruction of long-gone oceans. One particularly important technique for finding the positions of the continents is to study the magnetism of certain rocks, particularly lavas, that record the position of the north–south magnetic poles at the time when the rock cooled. If the rock "compass" points, for example, west, then the continent must have rotated by 90°. The vertical dip of the rock compass can reveal the approximate latitude of the rock at its formation (the dip increases from horizontal at the Equator to vertical at the magnetic poles).

As longitude is entirely arbitrary (defined on the position of Greenwich) one can only hope to gain the relative positions of the continents with regard to one another. The best additional information is provided by studies of fossils—if the remains of shallow-water marine organisms are very different they must have been separated by an ocean. The full impact of continental drift on the development of land animals and plants is only beginning to be realized.

THE DRIFTING CONTINENTS
It is now accepted that the continents have changed their positions during the past millions of years, and by studying the magnetism preserved in the rocks the configuration of the continents has been plotted for various geological times. The sequence of continental drifting, illustrated below, begins with one single landmass—the so-called supercontinent Pangaea—and the ancestral Pacific Ocean, called the Panthalassa Ocean. Pangaea first split into a northern landmass called Laurasia and a southern block called Gondwanaland, and subsequently into the continents we see today. The maps illustrate the positions of the continents in the past, where they are now and their predicted positions in 50 million years' time.

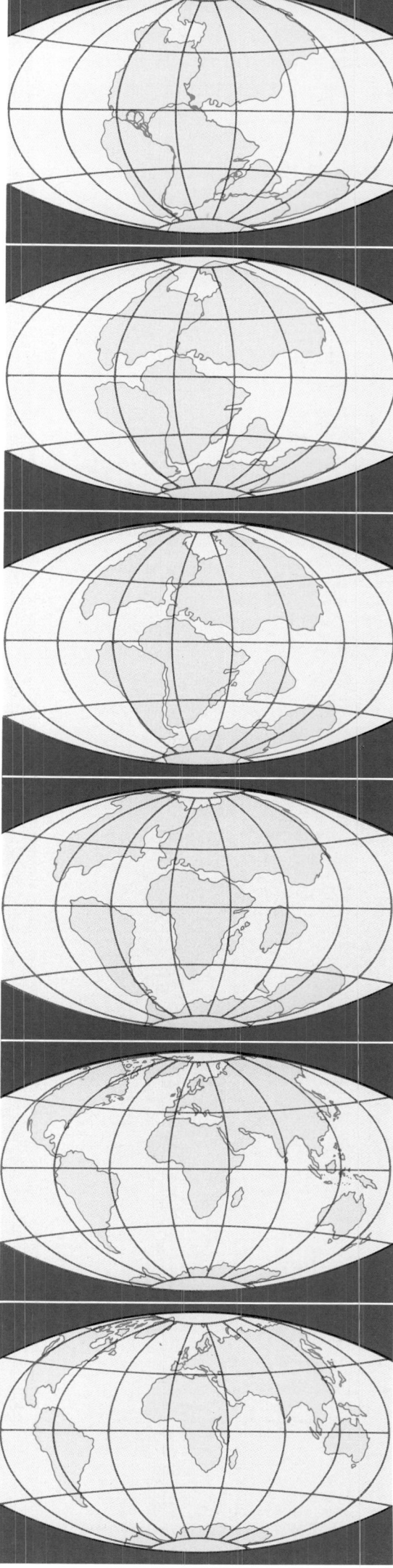

225 million years ago one large landmass, the supercontinent Pangaea, exists and Panthalassa forms the ancestral Pacific Ocean. The Tethys Sea separates Eurasia and Africa and forms an ancestor of the Mediterranean Sea.

180 million years ago Pangaea splits up, the northern block of continents, Laurasia, drifts northwards and the southern block, Gondwanaland, begins to break up. India separates and the South American–African block divides from Australia–Antarctica. New ocean floor is created between the continents.

135 million years ago the Indian plate continues its northward drift and Eurasia rotates to begin to close the eastern end of the Tethys Sea. The North Atlantic and the Indian Ocean have opened up and the South Atlantic is just beginning to form.

65 million years ago Madagascar has split from Africa and the Tethys Sea has closed, with the Mediterranean Sea opening behind it. The South Atlantic Ocean has opened up considerably, but Australia is still joined to the Antarctic and India is about to collide with Asia.

The present day: India has completed its northward migration and collided with Asia, Australia has set itself free from Antarctica, and North America has freed itself from Eurasia to leave Greenland between them. During the past 65 million years (a relatively short geological span of time) nearly half of the present-day ocean floor has been created.

50 million years in the future, Australia may continue its northward drift, part of East Africa will separate from the mainland, and California west of the San Andreas Fault will separate from North America and move northwards. The Pacific Ocean will become smaller, compensating for the increase in size of both the Atlantic and Indian oceans. The Mediterranean Sea will disappear as Africa moves to the north.

Magnetic surveys of the seabed helped build the plate tectonics theory. Research vessels equipped with magnetometers sailed back and forth over a mid-ocean ridge and recorded the varying magnetism of the seabed. The Earth's magnetic pole has switched from north to south at different times in the past, and this mapping revealed a striped magnetic pattern on the seabed. It was noticed that the stripes on either side of the ridge were symmetrical. The explanation was that the matching stripes must have formed together and moved apart as more crust was injected between them—a notion that was subsequently supported by dating of the seafloor.

3 2 1 0 1 3

Time in millions of years

Folds, Faults and Mountain Chains

The continents are great rafts of lighter rock that float in the mantle of the Earth. When drifting continents collide, great mountain chains are thrown up as the continental crust is forced to thicken to absorb the impact of the collision. The highest mountains are formed out of thick piles of sediment that are built up from the debris of erosion constantly washed off the land and deposited on the continental margins. Through the massive deformations of rock faults and folds these remains of old mountains become recycled, thus building new mountains from the remains of old ones.

For the formation of mountain ranges such as the Appalachians or the Himalayas, or the Caledonian mountain chain of Norway, Scotland and Newfoundland, the pattern of development is very much the same. First, a widening ocean with passive margins is located between two continents.

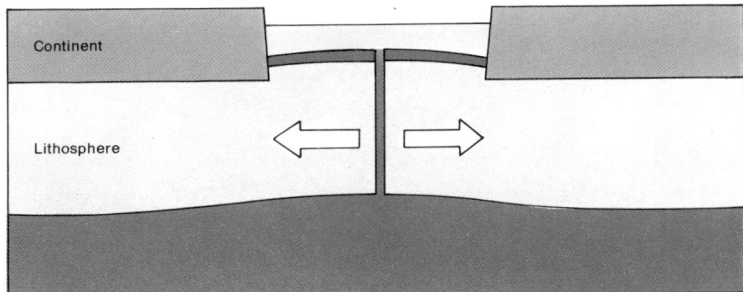

As more ocean floor is created the continents move farther apart, and at the edge of each continent sediment accumulates from the debris of erosion. These piles of thick sediment are known as sedimentary basins.

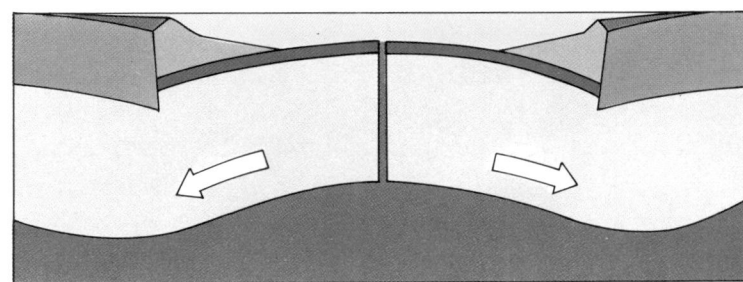

For the formation of the Appalachians, the ancestral Atlantic Ocean began to close, a subduction zone was formed at the ocean–continent boundary, and the oceanic lithosphere began to be absorbed into the mantle. Magma intruded to form granite "plutons" and volcanoes, and much of the sedimentary basin was metamorphosed.

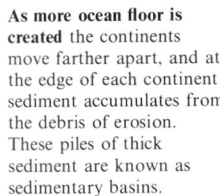

The ocean continued to close until North America and Africa were joined together, further compressing the sediments in the sedimentary basin at the passive ocean margin. The two continents were joined like this between 350 and 225 million years ago.

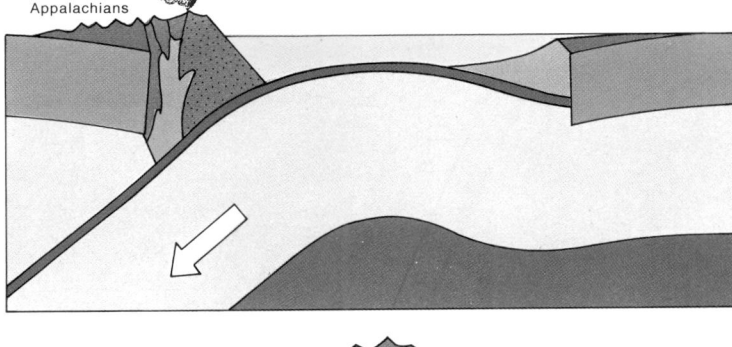

About 180 million years ago, after the original Appalachians had been worn down in size, the present Atlantic Ocean opened along a new break in the continental crust, offset from the line of the original mountains. As the continents split, so the crust became stretched along great curved faults.

Parts of the ancient Appalachian mountains have been eroded to sea level, leaving the Appalachians, that formed on the edge of the old continent, inland.

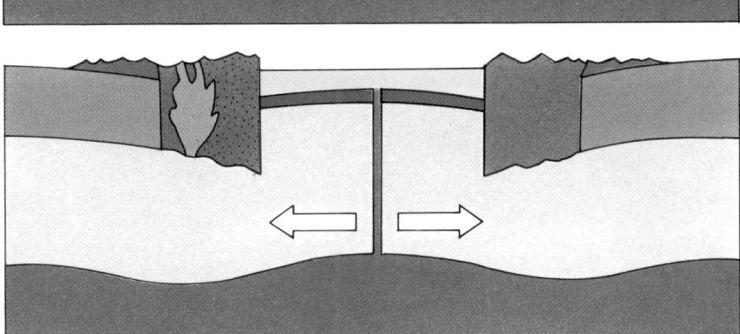
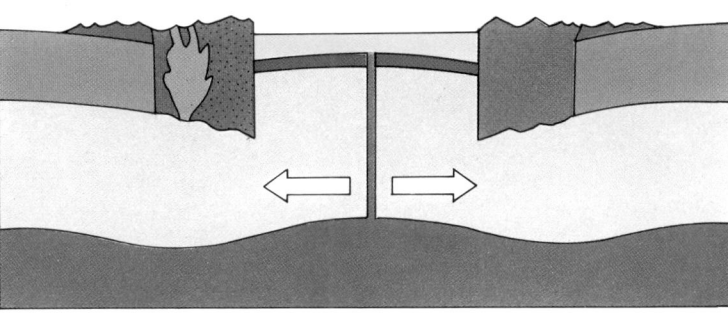

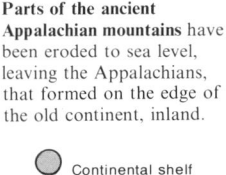
- ⬤ Continental shelf
- ⬤ Granite
- ⬤ Metamorphic rock
- ⬤ Sediment
- ⬤ Ocean crust

BIRTH AND DEATH OF A MOUNTAIN

Mountains are thrust upward by the pressure exerted by the moving plates of the Earth's crust, and are formed out of the sediments that have been eroded from the continental masses. Young mountains are lofty and much folded, but the agents of erosion and weathering soon begin to reduce their height, and over many millions of years the mountain range is eroded to sea level. This eroded material accumulates in the sea at the edge of the continents and becomes the building material for another phase of mountain building.

ISOSTASY

The continents float in the Earth's mantle, and because they are only slightly less dense (2.67 g/cc compared to 3.27 g/cc), 85% of their bulk lies below sea level. Thus the higher the mountain the deeper the mountain root. And as the crust can exist only to a maximum depth of about 70 km (43 miles) before it is liquefied in the mantle, mountains can never rise above a maximum of 10 km (6 miles) above sea level.

Folds are generally related to underlying faults. The commonest simple folds are monoclines, formed when a single fault exhibits underlying movement. With continued movement a simple symmetrical anticline (1) may fold unevenly to form an asymmetric anticline (2). More movement bends the strata further into a recumbent fold (3) and eventually the strata break to form an overthrust fold (4). Over a long period an overthrust fold may be pushed many kilometers from its original position to form a nappe (5). Faults are generally of three kinds: faults of tension known as normal faults, when one block drops down (6); faults of horizontal shear (7), known as strike-slip faults; and faults of compression (8), known as thrust faults.

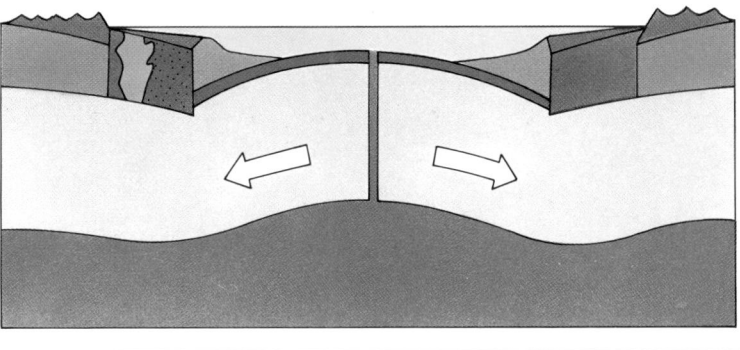

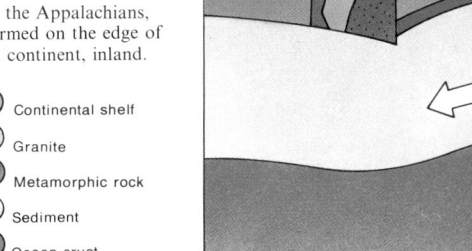

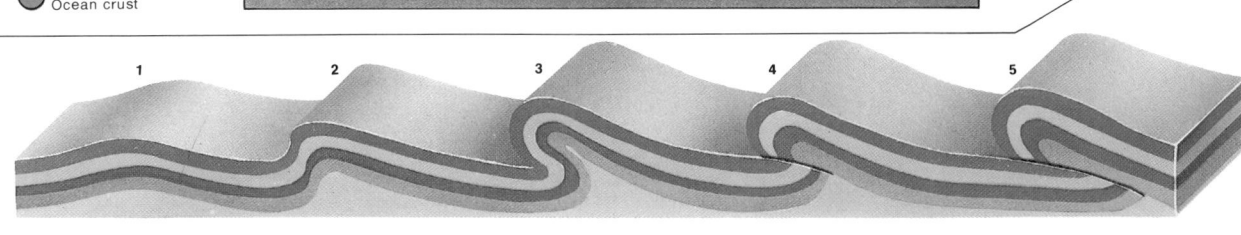

Continents float in the Earth's mantle like icebergs in the sea—more than four-fifths of their bulk lies beneath the surface. The continental crust is 28 km (17 miles) thick at sea level, and where mountains rise above this level there is a corresponding thickening in the crust beneath. The maximum thickness of crust is 70 km (43 miles), so mountains can only ever rise to a maximum height of approximately 10 km (6 miles) above sea level. This relation between upper and underlying crust is known as isostasy, or state of equal pressure.

As mountains become eroded, the process of isostatic rebound allows them to recover about 85 cm (34 in) for every 1 meter (40 in) removed. When, after about 100 million years, a major mountain range has been eroded down to sea level, the rocks exposed at the surface are those that were 15–25 km (9–15 miles) underground when the mountains were at their highest. Such rocks are coarsely crystalline, and make up the fabric of the old, tough continental crust.

Sedimentary basins
As early as the nineteenth century it was noticed that the biggest mountains formed where there had previously been the thickest pile of sediments. According to the principle of isostasy, a thick pile of sediments can form only where the Earth's crust is thin and sinking. The Aegean Sea in the eastern Mediterranean, for example, is at present being pulled apart, and therefore becoming thinner. Over the next few million years, as the Aegean crust sinks, a thick pile of sediments—a sedimentary basin—will accumulate. Most sedimentary basins are at present shallow seas, and form the continental shelves. The depth of water over these shelf seas has been determined by the erosion that accompanied the lowest sea levels of the past 100 million years— about 140 m (460 ft) below the present sea level.

Mountain building
When continents collide, it is the regions of stretched crust that are the first to absorb some of the impact. Such a former sedimentary basin is being turned into the Zagros Mountains of southwestern Iran as Arabia advances northeastward into Asia. The individual blocks of continental crust appear to be sliding back along curved faults, and the sediments that have built up over the thinned crust are now being forced into folds.

Early in the life of such a sedimentary basin sea water may become cut off from the ocean and evaporate to form extensive deposits of salt. Such salt deposits reduce friction and allow the folded pile of sediments overlying the continental blocks to become disconnected and to slide up to 100 km (62 miles) away from the collision zone. In the Zagros Mountains this process has only just begun, but in older mountain ranges, such as the Canadian Rockies or the European Alps, the formation of nappes— disconnected sediment piles forced ahead of the main compression zone—has been widespread.

As mountain ranges often form out of the sedimentary basins along the boundaries between a continent and the ocean, new mountains tend to add on to the fringes of the continents. In North America, for example, the oldest remnants of ranges that make up large tracts of the Canadian shield are found in the center of the continent, while the process of mountain building is continuing in the west.

Other continents show a more complex pattern of mountain ranges through subsequent phases of splitting and amalgamation, and the Himalayas and the Urals have formed where smaller continents have come together to make up the continent of Asia.

The boundary between the continent and the ocean along the western coast of the Atlantic Ocean is not a plate boundary and is therefore termed passive, in contrast to active boundaries such as the eastern coast of the Pacific Ocean, where the ocean plate is moving down into the mantle at a subduction zone beneath the Andean mountain chain. The highest Andean mountains are tall volcanoes of andesite (formed from magmas pouring off the underlying subduction zone). The bulk of the mountain range consists of enormous underground batholiths, in which the magma has solidified before being able to erupt, and compressed and uplifted sedimentary basins formed along the continental margin.

The crustal region immediately beyond the volcanoes that form above subduction zones, however, is very often in tension and in the process of being pulled apart. This appears to be caused by mantle material being dragged down with the oceanic lithosphere. Small ocean basins, such as the Sea of Japan, may open up under such conditions.

Folds and faults
When movement of the Earth's crust has taken place along a planar fracture through sedimentary rocks, it can be easily identified by the breaks in the layers, and such planes of movement are known as faults. Folds form where rock layers bend rather than break. Generally, faults form when rocks are brittle, and folds are found when rocks are plastic.

Sediments close to the surface are often so soft that they behave plastically, as do rocks at depths greater than 15–20 km (9–12 miles), where the continental crust is of sufficiently high temperature and pressure for slow rock flow to take place. Thus most continental faults are found between these levels. All major folds found in soft sediments apparently have a fault of some kind beneath them, and it is the failure of the fault to pass right through to the surface that creates the fold.

Folds are often extremely complicated and some geologists have tended to describe them in extraordinary detail, but in fact they are little more than brush strokes in the overall picture. Pre-existing faults beneath the folds tend to determine the folds' orientation. Once a continental fault has formed, it provides a plane of weakness wherever the continental crust is subject to stress. Many faults around the Mediterranean Sea came into existence during a period of tension, and these are now being reactivated and produce the large earthquakes associated with the continuing collision of Africa with Europe.

At the end of all the complications and intricacies of continental collision, the final phase of mountain building—that involving uplift—remains perhaps the least understood. In the last two million years, for example, while man has been increasingly active on Earth, 2,500,000 sq km (almost 1,000,000 sq miles) of Tibet has risen 4,000 m (2 miles). But the origin of such gigantic and rapid movement lies within the Earth's mantle.

The highest mountains are the product of continental collisions. As the rocks are squeezed, folded and faulted, the original continental crust becomes shortened and thickened. Although the overall extent and height of mountain chains is controlled by mountain building, the whole range can only be viewed from a spacecraft. For the earthbound mountain visitor the familiar shapes of peaks and valleys are those formed by mountain destruction (1). Snow at high altitudes consolidates to form ice that moves slowly downhill in the form of glaciers. To wear away a mountain range at an average of 5 km (3 miles) above sea level requires the removal of more than 20 km (12 miles) of rock, as the thick continental crust that floats in the underlying mantle rises to compensate for the loss of surface mass. Half-eroded mountains (2), such as the Appalachians, pictured above, may linger on for tens of millions of years until, like large regions of the Canadian interior, the mountains are all eroded away and only the hard crystalline surface rocks that were once buried 20 km (12 miles) underground remain (3).

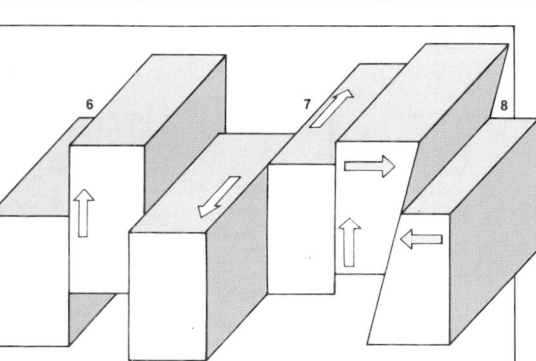

Earth's Minerals

Minerals are the basic ingredients of the Earth, from crust to core. They make up not only the ores on which man has based much of his technology, and the gemstones which he values for their beauty or rarity, but also the components of rocks, pebbles and sands. Two million years ago minerals – in the form of stones – provided early man with his first tools. Today, man's use of minerals, such as uranium for nuclear power or silicon for microcomputers, is revolutionizing our lives.

Minerals, and the metals derived from them, have always had an inherent fascination for man, as well as providing the basis for his technology. Gold in particular, which was worked in Egypt as early as 5000 BC, still retains its mysterious attraction. Because of its chemical inactivity it is imperishable, immutable and nontarnishing, and has served as the basis of world trade for almost 2,000 years. Copper has been smelted since the early part of the third millennium BC, to be replaced eventually by harder alloys. Arsenical bronze, for instance, bridged the gap between the Copper and Bronze ages (bronze is an alloy of copper and tin). More complex technology was needed for the working of iron, which began *c.*1100 BC, whereas brass (an alloy of copper and zinc) did not appear until Roman times.

Although the steel-making process had its roots in antiquity, it was not until the nineteenth century that new techniques changed man's attitude to minerals. Before the modern age of plastics, the capacity to produce steel was the hallmark of industrial development, and together with coal it formed the linchpin of western industrial progress. Today minerals have come to assume their greatest importance as exploitable—but nonrenewable—resources.

Components of the Earth
The terms "mineral," "rock" and "stone" are often used interchangeably, but in fact all rocks are made up of minerals, which are natural and usually inorganic substances with a particular chemical makeup and crystal structure.

Certain stones have properties that satisfy basic human needs for beauty and color. Some possess a flashing sparkle, others have special optical characteristics such as refraction and dispersion ("fire"), or contain inclusions that give rise to phenomena like the "asterism" found in opals and sapphires. About 100 such minerals are classified as gemstones and valued for their beauty, durability or rarity.

Most minerals occur as either pure (ore) deposits or mixed with other minerals in rocks—an economically important difference. Their exploitation has been vastly extended in recent decades through our greater understanding of the mineral-forming processes that take place in the Earth's crust. All mineral ores result from a separation process in which a mineral-rich solution separates into its various components according to the temperature, pressure and composition of the original mixture. Precipitation is the simplest kind of separation, as when calcium salts separate from circulating groundwater to yield stalactites and stalagmites in caves, in the form of calcite crystals.

Mineral formation
Most deposits of metallic ores originate in the intense physicochemical activity that takes place at the boundaries between the Earth's huge crustal plates. Very high concentrations of minerals occur in association with warm solutions coming from springs in the seabed, notably along the spreading zones in the southeastern Pacific Ocean, the Red Sea, the African Rift Valley and the Gulf of Aden. This process also occurs in shallow-water volcanic areas, as near the Mediterranean island of Thira and the submarine volcano of Bahu Wuhu, Indonesia. Cold seawater penetrates the crust and leaches out minerals from the basalts of these "hot spots," returning to the surface of the seabed as hot springs. The minerals then precipitate in the cold, oxygen-rich seawater.

Mineral separation may also occur when part of the deep-seated magma forces its way into the upper layers of the Earth's crust and begins to cool. The great plugs of magma that form the

rock kimberlite, in which diamonds are found, must have come from a depth of at least 100 km (62 miles). If the magma reaches the surface through fissures as extrusive rocks, the pattern of minerals in the surrounding rocks is also changed by a process called contact metamorphism, with various bands or zones of minerals occurring at various distances from the contact boundary.

As rocks become weathered, mineral concentrations that resist weathering may be left. Alternatively, all the weathered materials may be transported by running water, becoming concentrated as they are sorted out according to their different densities. Gold is the best-known example of this alluvial type of mineral deposit—known as a placer deposit. If the minerals are washed into the sea, they may be distributed over deltas or over the seafloor, but when this happens the concentrations of minerals are usually very low.

Mineral energy
Fossil fuels such as coal and petroleum are major mineral sources of energy. But with the twentieth-century discovery of nuclear fission, uranium also became an important energy resource. The richest deposits occur, as with other minerals, as veins deposited in fractures by hot-water movements. These deposits, consisting of a uranium oxide called pitchblende, were the first to be mined, for example at Joachimstal (Czechoslovakia), Great Bear Lake (Canada) and Katanga (Zaire). Weathered products of such rocks, redeposited as sandstones, also contain uranium, as in Wyoming (USA) and in the Niger basin. In many respects uranium is similar to silver: both occur with similar geological abundance, their ores are enriched about 2,000 times during processing, and the metals are recovered by using chemicals to dissolve the metal selectively and then by "stripping" the metal from the solution.

MINERALS FROM THE OCEAN
Ocean sediments that originally came from land contain organic matter that absorbs the oxygen in the sediments. As a result, solutions of minerals such as manganese and iron are released, seeping upwards through the debris. When they come in contact with the oxygen in seawater they are precipitated, condensing into so-called "manganese" nodules in amounts that may eventually prove to be a valuable source of mineral wealth. Metallic elements also accumulate very slowly from the seawater itself.

METAL-RICH BRINES
Scientists have recently discovered deep hollows on the floor of the Red Sea and other similar enclosed basins connected with rift valleys. These prevent normal circulation of water and form undersea pools of hot, high-density brines. The brines contain sulphur and other minerals in very high concentrations, and overlie sediments rich in metals such as zinc, copper, lead, silver and gold. Hot springs in fissures below the pools escape into them, carrying up solutions of the metallic minerals which combine with sulphur to create a concentrated broth rich in metals.

METALS FROM THE INTERIOR
Rift zones on the bed of the Pacific Ocean, where the Earth's crustal plates are slowly separating, provide sensational visual evidence of metallic ores in the actual process of creation. Seawater percolates through the fractured surface to the molten rock below, where it leaches out the soluble metallic components, erupting in superheated hydrothermal springs to form geysers of mineral-rich water. Oxygen in the cold water of the seafloor causes the minerals to condense out, precipitating in plumes of dark powder. Continental drift, collision and sedimentation over millions of years will eventually incorporate these deposits into the landmasses.

Uranium, chromium and many other minerals are widely distributed through the Earth's crust, but they are valuable as a resource only if the technology exists to extract them economically. In mineral development, the high-grade ores are worked out first, followed by the poorer deposits if demand remains or increases. With uranium, the low-grade deposits contain far more of the total quantity of the mineral, but these are worth exploiting because of uranium's importance and because the technology exists. Chromium, on the other hand, is currently extracted only from high-grade ores. Large deposits of low-grade ores do exist, but technology for exploiting them economically has not yet been developed.

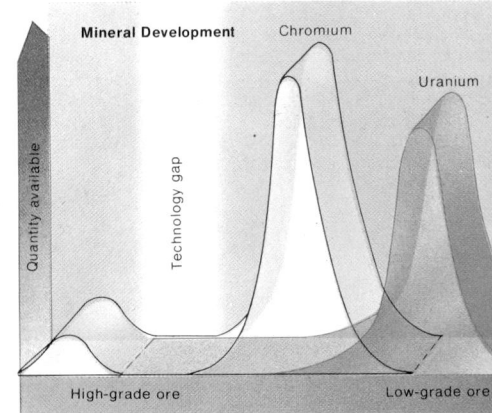

Mineral Development — Chromium — Uranium — Quantity available — Technology gap — High-grade ore — Low-grade ore

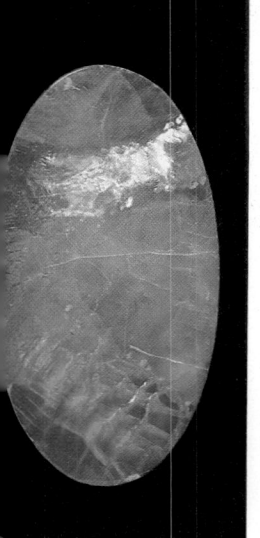

Opal (above), a silica

Sapphire gemstone (left), a form of the dull gray mineral carborundum (below), owes its color to inclusions of titanium and iron. If cut with a rounded top it gives a starry effect known as asterism.

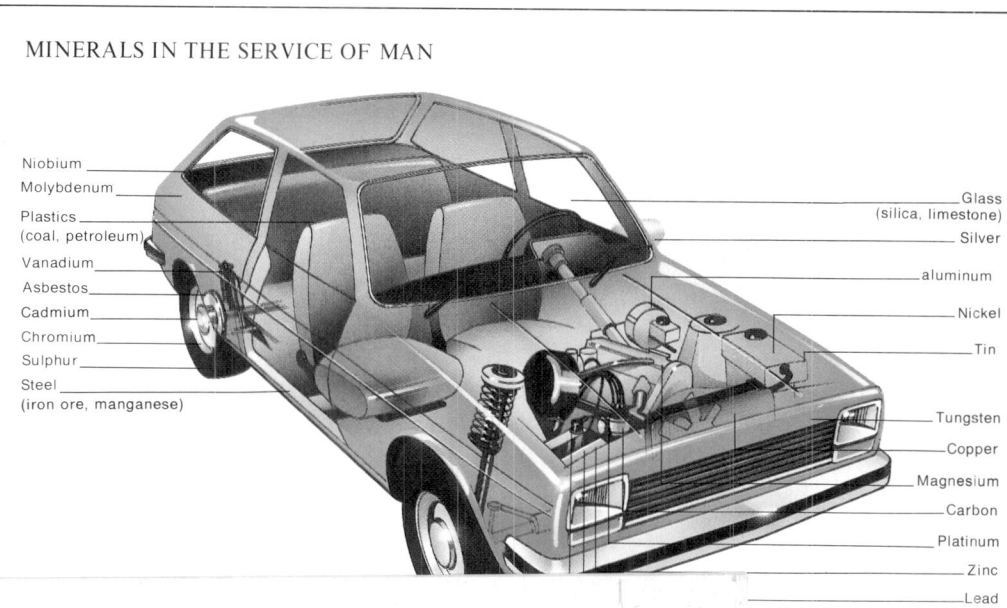

MINERALS IN THE SERVICE OF MAN

Niobium
Molybdenum
Plastics
(coal, petroleum)
Vanadium
Asbestos
Cadmium
Chromium
Sulphur
Steel
(iron ore, manganese)

Glass
(silica, limestone)
Silver
aluminum
Nickel
Tin
Tungsten
Copper
Magnesium
Carbon
Platinum
Zinc
Lead
Mica

mined and processed. A copper ore, for instance, only yields about 0.7 percent of metal, so to equip a single car's radiator with copper well over one and a half tonnes of rock will have to be excavated, of which 99.3 percent will simply be discarded.

Newsweek

The Gulf War Zone

A Series of Hammond Pull-out Maps

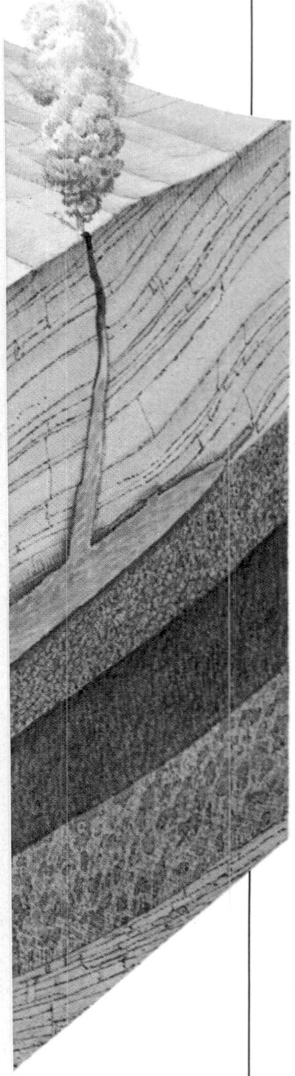

MINERALS
etrating the
m important
cooling, the
erals are the first
to the bottom.
o separate out
se heat affects
using mineral
changes in banded zones.

Earthquakes and Volcanoes

Earthquakes and volcanic eruptions challenge man's faith in the stability of the world, but these violent releases of energy testify to our planet's ever-dynamic activity. Earthquakes are caused when the rigid crust is driven past or over itself by underlying movements that extend deep into the Earth's mantle. Stress builds up until it exceeds the strength of the rocks, when there follows a sudden movement. Volcanoes occur where molten rock, or magma, from the mantle forces its way to the surface through lines of weakness in the crust, often at the lithospheric plate boundaries.

MODIFIED MERCALLI SCALE

I Earthquake not felt, except by a few.

II Felt on upper floors by few at rest. Swinging of suspended objects.

III Quite noticeable indoors, especially on upper floors. Standing cars may sway.

IV Felt indoors. Dishes and windows rattle, standing cars rock. Like a heavy truck hitting a building.

V Felt by nearly all, many wakened. Fragile objects broken, plaster cracked, trees and poles disturbed.

VI Felt by all, many run outdoors. Slight damage, heavy furniture moved, some fallen plaster.

VII People run outdoors. Average homes slightly damaged, substandard ones badly damaged. Noticed by car drivers.

VIII Well-built structures slightly damaged, others badly damaged. Chimneys and monuments collapse. Car drivers disturbed.

IX Well-designed buildings badly damaged, substantial ones greatly damaged, shifted off foundations. Conspicuous ground cracks open up.

X Well-built wood-structures destroyed, masonry structures destroyed. Rails bent, ground cracked, landslides. Rivers overflow.

XI Few masonry structures left standing. Bridges and underground pipes destroyed. Broad cracks in ground. Earth slumps.

XII Damage total. Ground waves seem like sea waves. Line of sight disturbed, objects thrown into the air.

The Earth's crust generally breaks along pre-existing planes of weakness, or faults. Such breakages give rise to an "explosive" release of stress that is familiar to surface dwellers as the vibrations of an earthquake.

Not all earthquakes, however, take place along pre-existing faults, otherwise no new faults would be generated. Many recent large earthquakes have been located immediately north of the Tonga Islands because a giant rent is developing through previously unbroken ocean crust. The crust to the south is being swallowed down into the mantle and that to the north continues at the surface to be subducted farther to the west. Once a fault has formed, however, it remains a plane of weakness even though the two sides tend to become partly resealed, so that when movement does occur there is a considerable release of energy.

Measuring earthquakes

Earthquakes are quantified in two ways. The actual energy release (magnitude) at the source of the earthquake (the focus) is measured on the Richter scale, a log scale where every unit of increase represents approximately 24 times the energy release. A magnitude 7 earthquake is roughly equivalent to the explosion of a one megaton nuclear bomb (one million tonnes of TNT). The strongest earthquake recorded this century was a magnitude 8.5 event in Alaska in 1964. Earthquakes as they are perceived are measured on the Modified Mercalli scale by their impact in terms of the amount of surface destruction. A medium-size earthquake under a town, such as that beneath Tangshan, China, in 1976 which killed more than a quarter of a million people, might record higher on the Mercalli scale than the Alaska event, which affected a large but sparsely populated region.

The magnitude of the earthquake depends on the frictional resistance that has to be overcome before movement can take place. This total frictional resistance, therefore, increases with the area of the fault plane. So the bigger the fault plane that moves, the bigger the earthquake. The largest earthquakes occur on wide fault planes that dip at a very shallow angle and can pass through a great deal of relatively shallow crust that will not deform plastically.

Earthquakes are unlikely to occur where rocks are plastic and can flow to accommodate the buildup of stress. Some faults, such as the San Andreas Fault in the western United States, pass from brittle rocks into a plastic zone at depths of only a few kilometers. Therefore, the next San Francisco earthquake cannot be as great as the 1964 Alaskan one, although this may be of little comfort to the potential victims. Along some sections of the San Andreas Fault the plastic zone comes directly to the surface, and motion occurs without large earthquakes.

Earthquake prediction is still in its infancy, although it is recognized that a number of phenomena may occur before a major earthquake—the ground may swell, the electrical conductivity of groundwater may change, and the water height of wells may rapidly alter.

How volcanoes are formed

Volcanoes, although spectacular, are safer than earthquakes. While an average of 20,000 people are killed each year in earthquakes, only about 400 are killed by volcanoes; and many of the victims die from starvation due to crop failure after heavy ash falls.

Volcanoes are formed when molten rock (magma) escapes through the Earth's crust to the Earth's surface. Most of this magma forms within the upper mantle between 30 and 100 km (20–60 miles) underground. The temperature increases with depth between 20° and 50°C per

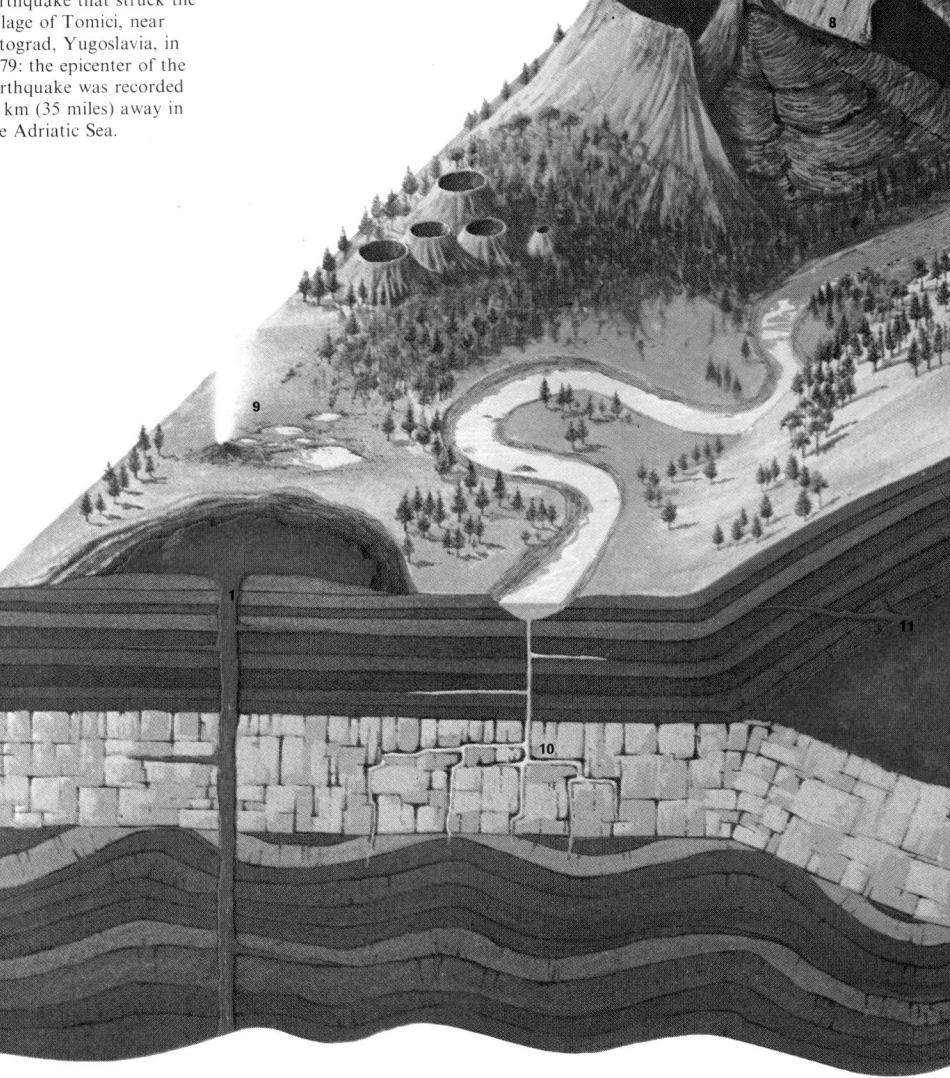

Earthquakes occur when slabs of the Earth's crust move in relation to each other. The focus of the earthquake is the point where movement occurs (1), and the epicenter is the point on the surface directly above it (2). Blue lines represent zones of surface damage as measured on the Modified Mercalli scale.

The aftermath of an earthquake that struck the village of Tomici, near Titograd, Yugoslavia, in 1979: the epicenter of the earthquake was recorded 55 km (35 miles) away in the Adriatic Sea.

km (35°–90°F per 3,250 ft) from the crust to the mantle, but even so the rocks are normally not hot enough to melt.

Basaltic magmas, found along mid-ocean spreading ridges and oceanic islands, are formed when hot, deep mantle rises and, on reduction of pressure, begins to melt. Such "basic" magmas generally have low silica and water content, a high temperature and flow easily—often, as in Hawaii, "quietly erupting" to form volcanoes with very gentle gradients known as shield volcanoes. Silica-rich magma forms under continental crust. Ocean crust sucks up water after it has formed at the oceanic spreading ridges and much of this water later becomes taken with the crust down a subduction zone, where it helps to lower the melting point of both mantle and ocean-crust rocks.

By the time these magmas reach the surface they are cooler and have a higher water content than basalts. These "intermediate" or andesite magmas are also more viscous (less willing to flow) because they contain more silica. The eruptions are more explosive as the water and other gases dissolve out of the magma as it approaches the surface, and the lava remains close to the volcanic vent, building up the archetypal steep-sided conical stratified volcano, such as Mount Fujiyama in Japan. Sometimes the conical form may be destroyed in catastrophic eruptions, as has happened at Mount St Helens in the United States.

The most violent of all eruptions are found where magmas from the mantle have penetrated and melted a great thickness of continental rocks, so as to create highly viscous silica- and water-rich "acid" magmas. As such magmas approach the surface they may turn into a red-hot froth that blasts out from fissures to cover enormous areas in a volcanic material known as ignimbrite. The most extensive eruption known to have occurred in the past 2,000 years was probably on Mount Taupo, on North Island, New Zealand. In AD 150 it discharged some

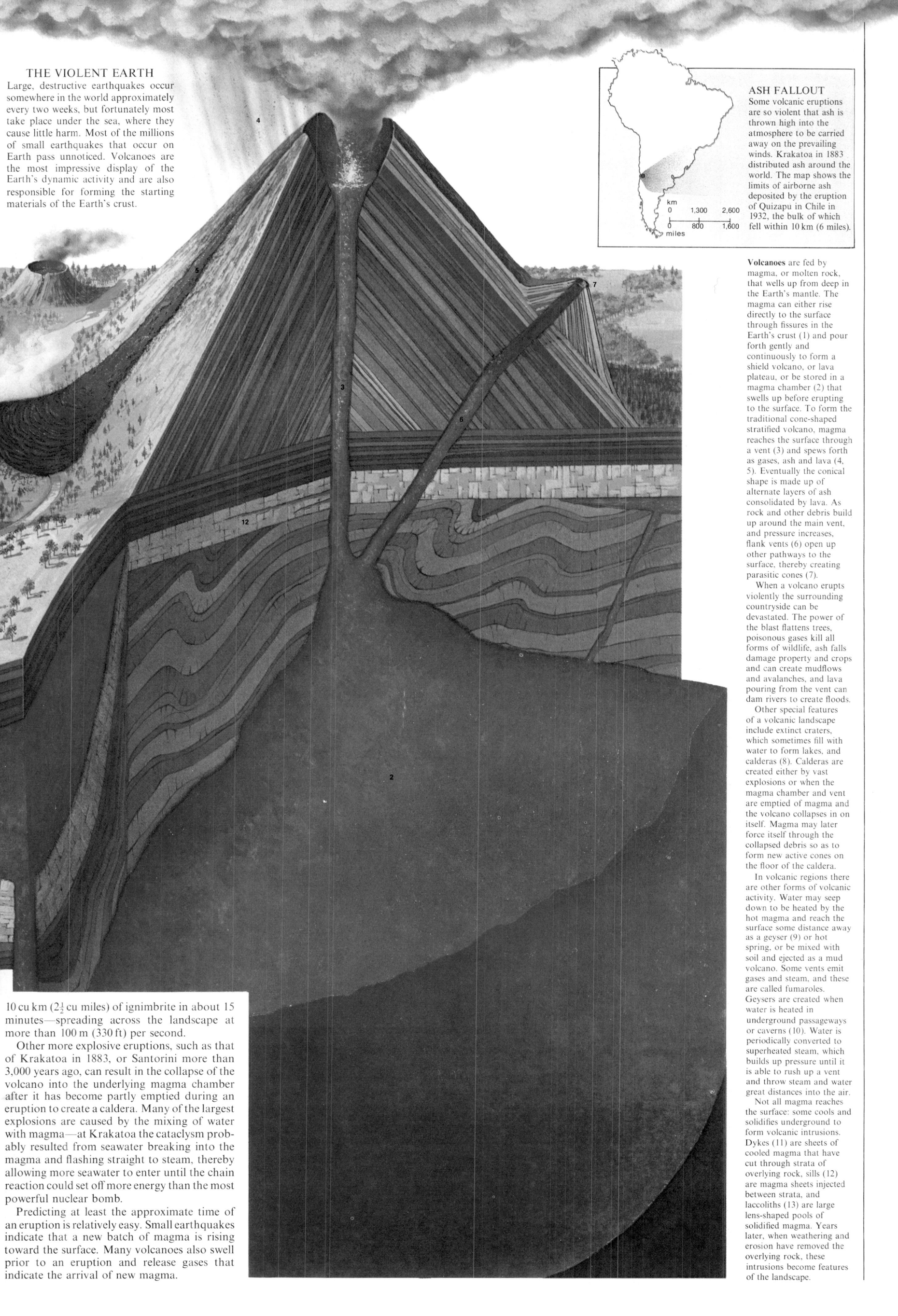

THE VIOLENT EARTH

Large, destructive earthquakes occur somewhere in the world approximately every two weeks, but fortunately most take place under the sea, where they cause little harm. Most of the millions of small earthquakes that occur on Earth pass unnoticed. Volcanoes are the most impressive display of the Earth's dynamic activity and are also responsible for forming the starting materials of the Earth's crust.

Volcanoes are fed by magma, or molten rock, that wells up from deep in the Earth's mantle. The magma can either rise directly to the surface through fissures in the Earth's crust (1) and pour forth gently and continuously to form a shield volcano, or lava plateau, or be stored in a magma chamber (2) that swells up before erupting to the surface. To form the traditional cone-shaped stratified volcano, magma reaches the surface through a vent (3) and spews forth as gases, ash and lava (4, 5). Eventually the conical shape is made up of alternate layers of ash consolidated by lava. As rock and other debris build up around the main vent, and pressure increases, flank vents (6) open up other pathways to the surface, thereby creating parasitic cones (7).

When a volcano erupts violently the surrounding countryside can be devastated. The power of the blast flattens trees, poisonous gases kill all forms of wildlife, ash falls damage property and crops and can create mudflows and avalanches, and lava pouring from the vent can dam rivers to create floods.

Other special features of a volcanic landscape include extinct craters, which sometimes fill with water to form lakes, and calderas (8). Calderas are created either by vast explosions or when the magma chamber and vent are emptied of magma and the volcano collapses in on itself. Magma may later force itself through the collapsed debris so as to form new active cones on the floor of the caldera.

In volcanic regions there are other forms of volcanic activity. Water may seep down to be heated by the hot magma and reach the surface some distance away as a geyser (9) or hot spring, or be mixed with soil and ejected as a mud volcano. Some vents emit gases and steam, and these are called fumaroles. Geysers are created when water is heated in underground passageways or caverns (10). Water is periodically converted to superheated steam, which builds up pressure until it is able to rush up a vent and throw steam and water great distances into the air.

Not all magma reaches the surface: some cools and solidifies underground to form volcanic intrusions. Dykes (11) are sheets of cooled magma that have cut through strata of overlying rock, sills (12) are magma sheets injected between strata, and laccoliths (13) are large lens-shaped pools of solidified magma. Years later, when weathering and erosion have removed the overlying rock, these intrusions become features of the landscape.

10 cu km (2½ cu miles) of ignimbrite in about 15 minutes—spreading across the landscape at more than 100 m (330 ft) per second.

Other more explosive eruptions, such as that of Krakatoa in 1883, or Santorini more than 3,000 years ago, can result in the collapse of the volcano into the underlying magma chamber after it has become partly emptied during an eruption to create a caldera. Many of the largest explosions are caused by the mixing of water with magma—at Krakatoa the cataclysm probably resulted from seawater breaking into the magma and flashing straight to steam, thereby allowing more seawater to enter until the chain reaction could set off more energy than the most powerful nuclear bomb.

Predicting at least the approximate time of an eruption is relatively easy. Small earthquakes indicate that a new batch of magma is rising toward the surface. Many volcanoes also swell prior to an eruption and release gases that indicate the arrival of new magma.

The Oceans

Earth is the water planet. Of all the planets of the solar system only the Earth has abundant liquid water, and 97 percent of this surface water is found in the seas and oceans. The water of the oceans appears to be passive and unchanging, whereas the rain and rivers seem active, but this is far from true. In reality the oceans are a turmoil of giant sluggish rivers – far larger than any of the land rivers – and of circulating surface currents that are driven by the prevailing winds.

No topographic map of the Earth can be drawn unless there is some kind of base line from which to measure depths and heights. This base line has always been taken as the level of the sea, yet the sea is perpetually changing level. One can choose some kind of average to call "sea level," but even today different countries have defined that base line in different ways. The currents found within the sea itself can also give the water surface a slope—the calm Sargasso Sea off the northern coast of South America is, for example, about 1.5 m (5 ft) higher than the water to the west adjacent to the Gulf Stream.

Waves

The changes in the level of the sea, at its surface, provide the most familiar image of motion within the waters. Various changes take place over many different time periods, but the most rapid are those that we call waves.

Waves are produced by the wind moving over the water and catching on the surface. They can move at between 15 and 100 km/hr (10–60 mph) and wave crests may be separated by up to 300 m (1,000 ft) in the open ocean. In general, the greater the wavelength, the faster the wave's speed and the farther the distance traveled by the wave. Waves that have traveled a long way from the winds that created them are known as swell. Without the wind continually pushing them they become symmetrical and smooth. Wind waves produce spilling breakers more like the rapids of a mountain torrent, whereas swell produces giant plunging breakers.

A combination of strong winds and low atmospheric pressure associated with storms can cause yet another kind of wave, known as a storm surge. A storm surge is formed by the water being driven ahead of the wind, and rising as the atmospheric pressure weighing down on the water decreases. Where storms drive water into funnel-shaped coasts, the water can rise more than 10 m (33 ft) above normal sea level, flooding large areas of low-lying land at the head of the bay. Venice, the Netherlands and Bangladesh have been particularly subject to destructive storm surges. Other catastrophic changes in sea level have their origins in the seabed. These are tsunamis (Japanese for "high-water in the harbor") and are generally triggered by underwater earthquakes that suddenly raise or lower large areas of the seafloor.

Tides

As the Earth orbits around the Sun the water in the oceans experiences a changing pull of gravity from both the Moon and the Sun. The Sun is overhead once a day, and because the Moon is itself orbiting the Earth, it is overhead once every 24 hours 50 minutes. The pull of gravity from the Sun is less than half that from the Moon, and so it is the Moon that sets the rhythm of the water movements we call tides. The variation in gravitational pull from the Moon is extremely small, however, and even if the whole of the Earth were covered with deep water a tide of only about 30 cm (12 in) would be produced, rushing around the world keeping pace with the circling Moon. Yet the tides in shallow coastal regions are often very much higher than this—for example, up to 18 m (60 ft) in the Bay of Fundy, Canada. The seas and bays with the highest tides are located where the whole mass of water is resonating—rebounding backwards and forwards like water in a bath, as the smaller tides in the outlying oceans push it twice each day.

The Bay of Fundy experiences a particularly high tidal range because it happens to have a resonant frequency—a range of movement—very close to the 12½-hour frequency between tides. Large enclosed seas such as the Mediterranean have very small tides because there is no outside push from an ocean to set them resonating. In contrast, where water movement associated with the tides passes through a narrow channel it can produce tidal currents of up to 30 km/hr (19 mph), such as the famous maelstrom of northern Norway.

After these relatively short-lived disturbances the sea returns to its normal, or at least to its average, level again. When the total volume of free water at the Earth's surface alters, or when the shapes of the ocean basins vary, the sea level itself may start to wander.

How does the volume of water vary? It can be buried in rocks—but the steam clouds above volcanoes return such water so it is normally recycled rather than lost. Some vapor can be broken down through radiation in the upper atmosphere and the hydrogen lost to outer space, but this is relatively insignificant. Or it can be frozen and stacked up on land in the form of ice—this is significant as we are still living in an ice age. The lowest ice-age sea levels produced beaches at about 130 m (430 ft) below present sea level, and the low-lying coastal regions of that period have now become flooded to form the continental shelves.

The salt content of the oceans

Average ocean water contains about 35 parts per 1,000 of salts which include 14 elements in concentrations greater than 1 part per million—the most abundant being sodium and chlorine. Where there is considerable surface evaporation, for example in enclosed seas such as the Dead Sea, the salt concentration builds up and the water becomes denser. Where the sea-surface is turning to ice the salt also becomes concentrated in the water.

The coldest, saltiest ocean water comes from the Antarctic. As it is also the densest it hugs the ocean bottom as it flows northwards, reaching as far as the latitudes of Spain. A similar current from the Arctic is slightly lighter and therefore rides above it—but traveling southwards, as far as the southern Atlantic. A second slightly lighter body of Antarctic water rides above the Arctic water—again traveling northwards. Where these water movements meet each other they rise up, bringing to the surface oxygenated water that can support a profusion of life in oceans that have been compared to a desert because of their lack of biological activity. Unlikely as it seems, it is the icy, stormy, polar waters that provide the lungs of the oceans.

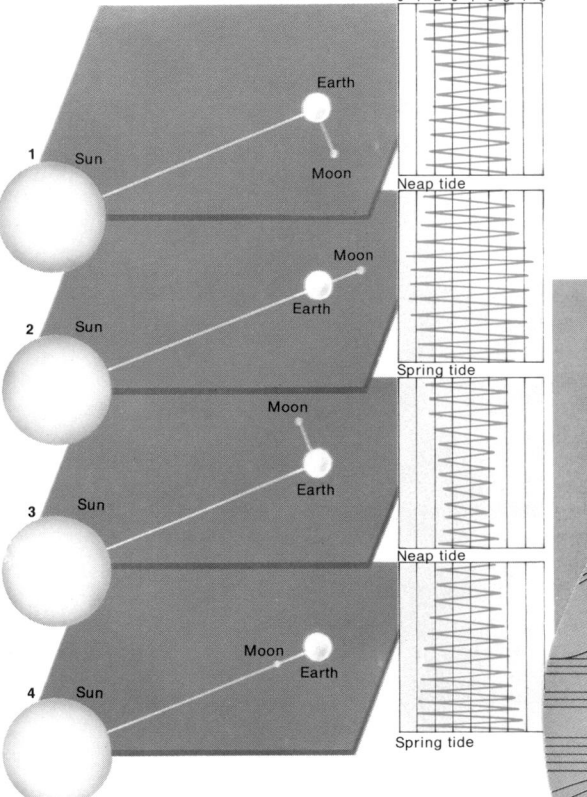

Both the Sun and the Moon exert gravitational pull on the water in the oceans, but the pull of the Sun is less than half that of the Moon. It is the Moon, therefore, that sets the rhythm of the tides. Because the Moon orbits the Earth every 24 hours and 50 minutes, the time of high or low tide advances approximately an hour each day. When the Moon is in its first and last quarters (1, 3) it forms a right angle with the Earth and the Sun and the gravitational fields are opposed, thus causing only a small difference between high and low tide. These are called neap tides. When the Sun, Moon and Earth lie in a straight line (2, 4), at the full and the new Moon, then the high tides become higher and the low tides lower. These are the spring tides. The graph illustrates tidal range over a period of a month.

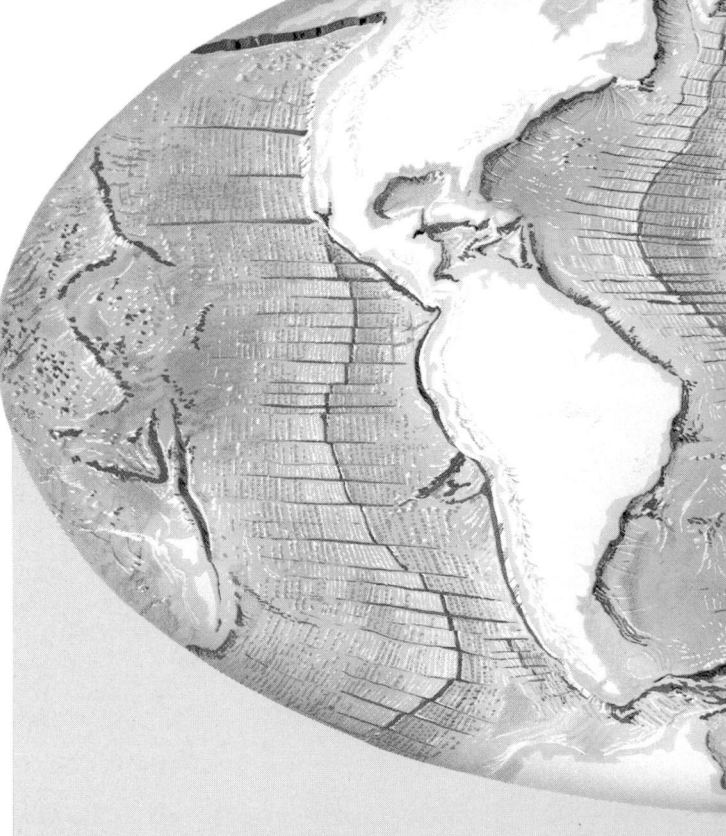

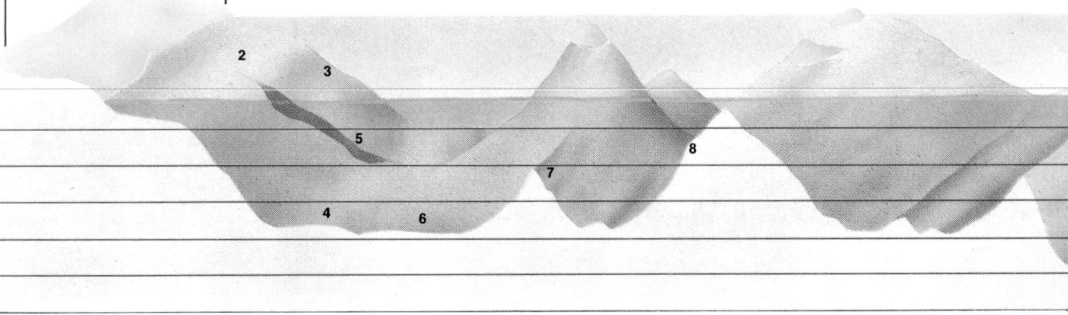

1 Continent
2 Continental shelf
3 Continental slope
4 Continental rise
5 Submarine canyon
6 Abyssal plain
7 Abyssal hills
8 Mid-ocean ridge
9 Oceanic trench
10 Island arc
11 Continental sea

THE CHANGING OCEANS

Nearly two-thirds of the Earth's surface is covered by the seas and oceans and this great expanse of water is continually in movement. The most familiar movements are waves formed by the wind and the rising and falling tides that respond to the position of the Moon. But even greater movements take place. Currents driven by prevailing winds form whirlpools an ocean in width, and below the surface flow great rivers of colder water. Sea level is also rising as ice melts from the polar caps.

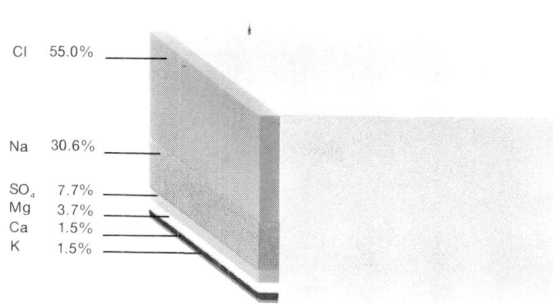

Cl	55.0%
Na	30.6%
SO₄	7.7%
Mg	3.7%
Ca	1.5%
K	1.5%

Seawater is about 96% pure water and the rest is made up of dissolved salts. Many elements are present in minute quantities, but only chlorine (Cl), sodium (Na), sulphate (SO₄), magnesium (Mg), calcium (Ca) and potassium (K) appear in concentrations of more than 1% of the total dissolved salts.

Polar easterlies · Southwesterlies · Northeast trades · Southeast trades · Northwesterlies · Polar easterlies

60° N · 30° N · 0° · 30° S · 60°S

B

A

The surface currents of the world's oceans (A) are driven by the prevailing winds (B). The winds and the spinning motion of the Earth drive the currents into gyres—massive whirlpools the width of an ocean. These gyres draw warm water away from the Equator and pull cold polar waters towards it. The centers of gyres are characterized by areas of high pressure, around which winds circulate. Because the Earth is spinning, gyres formed in the northern hemisphere rotate in a clockwise direction, whereas those of the southern hemisphere turn anticlockwise. In all, there are five major gyres, made up of the 38 major named currents. The formation of warm (red) and cold (blue) surface currents is not difficult to understand, given the regions from which they flow. However, even in temperate and subtropical regions, the warm waters of the oceans' surfaces have a permanent layer of cold water beneath them. This cold layer has been formed in the polar regions, where, as the ocean waters have been chilled, they have sunk and then spread out into all the other major ocean basins of the world. The warm subtropical and temperate waters float like an oil slick, from 10 m to 550 m (33–1,900 ft) thick, on top of this cold layer. There is very little mixing between the two layers because the warm water is lighter than the cold water.

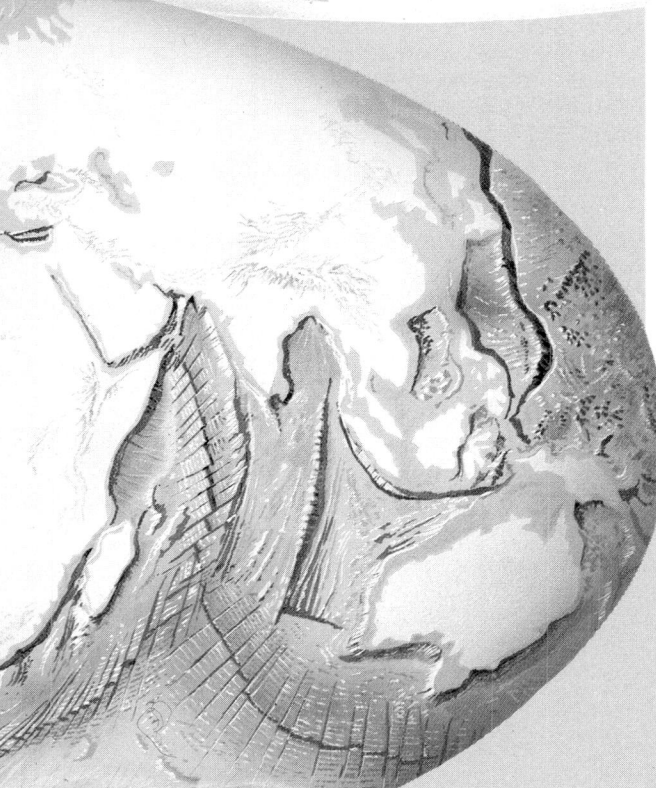

Much of the Earth's water is locked up as ice and stacked on the land. As the ice melts the sea level rises. Only 20,000 years ago the sea level was a full 100 m (330 ft) lower than it is today, and the continental shelves were dry land. About 10,000 years ago the sea level was rising as fast as 3 cm (1 in) each year. Today the melting ice is causing the sea level to rise about 1 mm (0.04 in) each year: only a small increment, but if all the ice melted, the sea level would rise by about 60 m (197 ft) and would flood many of the world's major cities.

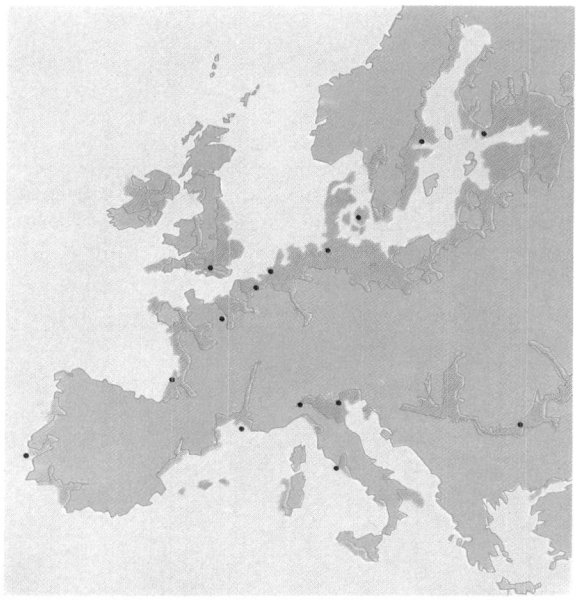

○ <60 m
○ >60 m
• Major cities

The seabed, more uniform than the land surface, also contains a landscape of underwater features that resemble the plains, valleys and mountains of the continents. Off the edge of continents lie the flat, shallow continental shelves, which are bounded by the steeper incline of the continental slope, which meets the true ocean floor at the continental rise.

Here deep submarine canyons may be found. These seem to be in a process of continual erosion from turbidity currents. River water pouring into major estuaries and carrying sediment can also scour out the slope—especially during periods of low sea level. The abyssal plain is rarely interrupted by volcanic hills and

mountains. The largest chains are at the mid-ocean ridge, where two crustal plates are moving apart and new ocean floor is being created. At some ocean margins deep trough-shaped valleys or trenches are the sites of ocean floor consumption at a subduction zone. The volcanic island arcs that form behind it sometimes isolate a continental sea.

TSUNAMIS

Tsunamis are generated by massive underwater earthquakes (A) and are common around the Pacific. They can travel at more than 700 km/hr (435 mph) and individual waves may occur at intervals of 15 minutes, or 200 km (125 miles). Low-lying atolls of the Pacific have extremely steep sides underwater, and are generally unharmed, but the gently shelving islands such as Hawaii slow down the tsunami and build it into a giant wave 30 m (100 ft) or more in height. This map plots the hourly position of a tsunami that originated south of Alaska.

A

Landscape-makers: Water

Of all the natural agents of erosion at work on the Earth's surface, water is probably the most powerful. Many of the finer details of the landscape, from the contouring of hills and valleys to the broad spread of plains, are the work of water. In recent years we have come to understand more fully the subtle factors at work in a river, for example, as it deepens mountain gorges or builds up sedimentary layers in its approach to the sea. The full force of a waterfall, the instability of a meandering stream, the multiple layering of river terraces – all are features of this most versatile landscape-maker.

Ninety-seven percent of the world's water is in the oceans, another two percent is locked up in the ice caps of Greenland and Antarctica, which leaves one percent only on the surface of Earth, under the ground and in the air. The importance of this one percent is, however, inestimable: most life forms could not exist without it, and yet at the same time many are threatened by it, in the form of flood and storm.

The Sun's energy "powers" the evaporation of water from the oceans. Water vapor then circulates in the atmosphere and is precipitated as rain or snow over land, from which it eventually drains back to the oceans. This is the vast, never-ending water cycle. Water in the air that falls as, for example, rain is replaced on average every 12 days. The total water supply remains constant and is believed to be exactly the same as it was 3,000 million years ago.

From raindrops to rivers

Rain falling on to the surface of the land has a great deal of energy: large drops may hit the ground with a terminal velocity of about 35 km/hr (20 mph). If the rain falls on bare soil, it splashes upwards, breaking off and transporting tiny fragments of soil, which come to rest downhill. Vegetation-covered soil breaks the impact and some of the rain may evaporate without ever reaching the ground.

Soil is rather like a sponge. If the holes or pores are very small, rain finds it difficult to penetrate and water runs over the surface of the soil. If the pores are large, rain infiltrates, filling up the pore spaces. Soils that are thin, have low infiltration rates, or already have a lot of water in them, are very susceptible to overland flow. The water may then concentrate into a channel called a gully, and this can have a dramatic effect upon the landscape. The creation of gullies, together with the splash effect, leads to soil erosion. The problem is particularly severe in semiarid regions, where rainfall is sporadic but intense, vegetation is sparse and over-grazing is common. In extreme cases, badlands are formed and by this time recuperation of the

land is impossible or is prohibitively expensive.

Where the infiltration rate is high, water percolates through the soil and eventually into the bedrock. There are two well-defined regions, the saturated and the unsaturated. The upper limit of the saturated zone is the water table. Beneath this, water moves at a rate of a few meters a day, but in rocks such as limestone it can move much more quickly along cracks and joints. In most rock types there are some soluble components which are removed as water continually flows through. In limestone regions, the dissolution of calcium salts results in spectacular cave formations.

Groundwater often provides a vital source for domestic consumption. In porous materials, especially chalk, water is stored in large quantities. Such strata are called aquifers and in some areas, notably North Africa, it is believed that water being pumped up now resulted from rainfall when the climate was wetter tens of thousands of years ago.

Water from a number of sources—from overland flow, soil seepage and springs draining aquifers—produces the flow in rivers. Groundwater appears days or even weeks after a heavy rainfall, but overland flow reaches the channel in hours, producing the sudden peak in flow that may cause flooding and occasionally great damage farther downstream. Flood waves usually rise quickly in mountain areas and the wave moves downstream as the river collects more and more water from its tributaries. Eventually, although the volume continues to increase downstream, the flood wave becomes broader and flatter, so it moves more slowly and causes less damage. The most serious floods occur after intense rainfall on already saturated soils where upland rivers issue on to plains.

Rivers at work

The work of a river from its source to its mouth involves three processes, the first of which is erosion. This includes corrasion, or abrasion— the grinding of rocks and stones against the river's banks and bed—which produces both

---

The hydrological cycle involves a vast transfer of water from sea to air to land, and back to sea again. Water evaporates from the world's oceans and is carried by maritime air masses towards land, where it condenses and is precipitated in the form of rain or snow. This water then evaporates from the ground surface; drains off the surface into lakes, rivers or seas; seeps as groundwater into rivers, lakes or seas; or is taken in by vegetation from the soil and then transpired.

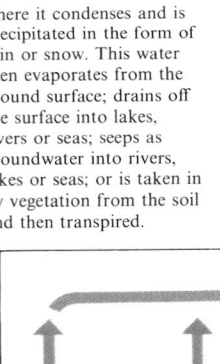

A RIVER SYSTEM

Rivers form by the accumulation of runoff water, groundwater and from springs and small streams. Few rivers reach the sea without gaining tributaries, thus forming a river system. Highland regions at source are called catchment areas and the total area drained by a river system is the drainage basin.

The course of a river from source to mouth includes distinctive stages and land forms. All rivers flow from high ground to lower ground. Many rise in an upland area where precipitation is heavy. The upper course is where vertical erosion is dominant and the resulting valley is narrow, deep and V-shaped. A gorge is formed if this downcutting is particularly rapid. If the river has a winding course, the valley walls project to produce interlocking spurs. In the middle course erosion is lateral rather than vertical and the valley takes a more open V-shape. The river may start to meander and bluffs are formed as interlocking spurs are eroded across an almost flat flood plain. In the lower course the river deposits much material as it meanders across an almost flat flood plain. The bed is sometimes higher than the plain and the river has raised banks, or levées, formed from material deposited when the river is in flood. Ox-bow lakes are common, as is a delta where the slow-flowing river enters the sea.

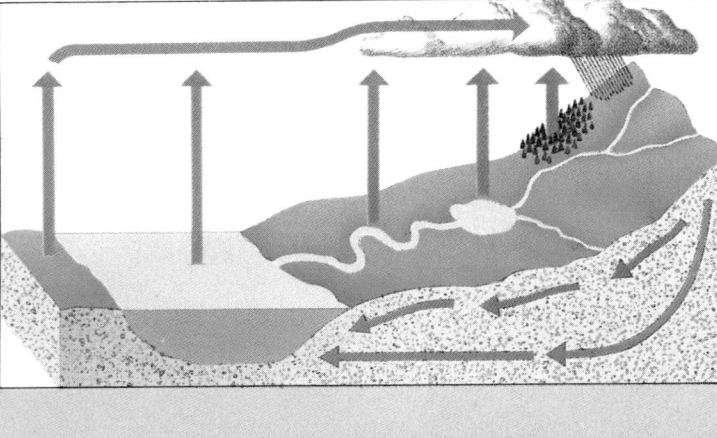

When a river reaches the sea, providing the coast is sheltered and the sea is shallow with no strong currents, its speed is checked and material is deposited (1). The river then forms distributaries (2) in order to continue its flow to the sea. A delta forms its characteristic fan shape (3) as it grows sideways and seawards. A river needs active erosion in its upper course in order to form a delta.

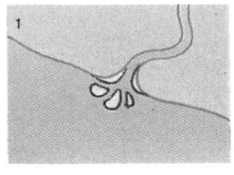
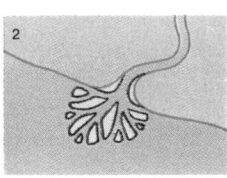
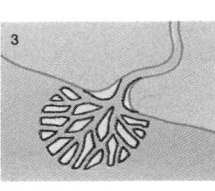

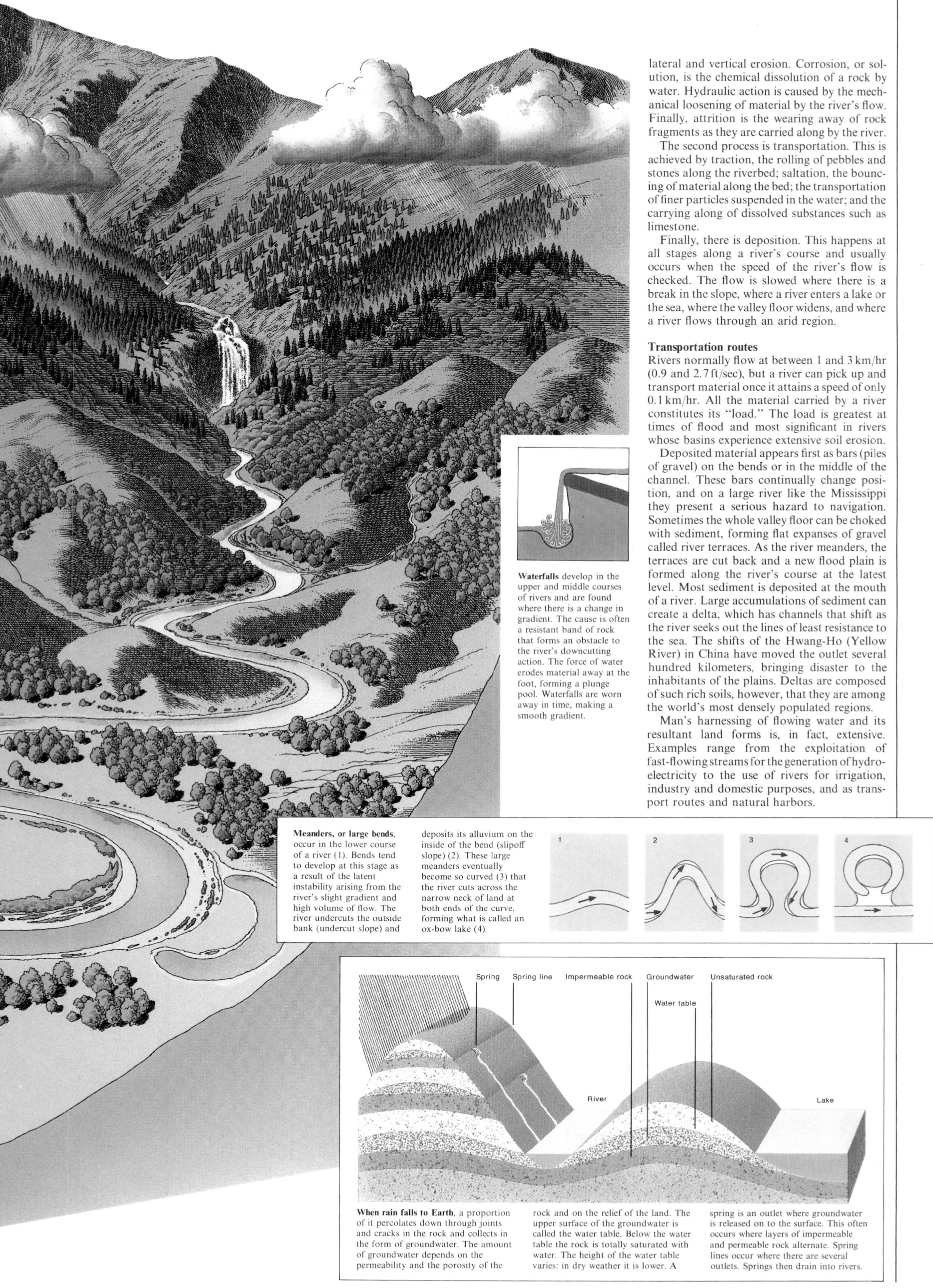

lateral and vertical erosion. Corrosion, or solution, is the chemical dissolution of a rock by water. Hydraulic action is caused by the mechanical loosening of material by the river's flow. Finally, attrition is the wearing away of rock fragments as they are carried along by the river.

The second process is transportation. This is achieved by traction, the rolling of pebbles and stones along the riverbed; saltation, the bouncing of material along the bed; the transportation of finer particles suspended in the water; and the carrying along of dissolved substances such as limestone.

Finally, there is deposition. This happens at all stages along a river's course and usually occurs when the speed of the river's flow is checked. The flow is slowed where there is a break in the slope, where a river enters a lake or the sea, where the valley floor widens, and where a river flows through an arid region.

Transportation routes

Rivers normally flow at between 1 and 3 km/hr (0.9 and 2.7 ft/sec), but a river can pick up and transport material once it attains a speed of only 0.1 km/hr. All the material carried by a river constitutes its "load." The load is greatest at times of flood and most significant in rivers whose basins experience extensive soil erosion.

Deposited material appears first as bars (piles of gravel) on the bends or in the middle of the channel. These bars continually change position, and on a large river like the Mississippi they present a serious hazard to navigation. Sometimes the whole valley floor can be choked with sediment, forming flat expanses of gravel called river terraces. As the river meanders, the terraces are cut back and a new flood plain is formed along the river's course at the latest level. Most sediment is deposited at the mouth of a river. Large accumulations of sediment can create a delta, which has channels that shift as the river seeks out the lines of least resistance to the sea. The shifts of the Hwang-Ho (Yellow River) in China have moved the outlet several hundred kilometers, bringing disaster to the inhabitants of the plains. Deltas are composed of such rich soils, however, that they are among the world's most densely populated regions.

Man's harnessing of flowing water and its resultant land forms is, in fact, extensive. Examples range from the exploitation of fast-flowing streams for the generation of hydro-electricity to the use of rivers for irrigation, industry and domestic purposes, and as transport routes and natural harbors.

Waterfalls develop in the upper and middle courses of rivers and are found where there is a change in gradient. The cause is often a resistant band of rock that forms an obstacle to the river's downcutting action. The force of water erodes material away at the foot, forming a plunge pool. Waterfalls are worn away in time, making a smooth gradient.

Meanders, or large bends, occur in the lower course of a river (1). Bends tend to develop at this stage as a result of the latent instability arising from the river's slight gradient and high volume of flow. The river undercuts the outside bank (undercut slope) and deposits its alluvium on the inside of the bend (slipoff slope) (2). These large meanders eventually become so curved (3) that the river cuts across the narrow neck of land at both ends of the curve, forming what is called an ox-bow lake (4).

When rain falls to Earth, a proportion of it percolates down through joints and cracks in the rock and collects in the form of groundwater. The amount of groundwater depends on the permeability and the porosity of the rock and on the relief of the land. The upper surface of the groundwater is called the water table. Below the water table the rock is totally saturated with water. The height of the water table varies: in dry weather it is lower. A spring is an outlet where groundwater is released on to the surface. This often occurs where layers of impermeable and permeable rock alternate. Spring lines occur where there are several outlets. Springs then drain into rivers.

Landscape-makers: Ice and Snow

A series of glacial periods has punctuated the Earth's history for the last two million years. During the last glacial, the ice covered an area nearly three times larger than that covered by ice sheets and glaciers today. Its remnants are still found in the ice caps of the world: most present-day glacial ice is in Antarctica and Greenland in two great ice sheets which together contain about 97 percent of all the Earth's ice. The rest is in glaciers in Iceland, the Alps and other high mountain chains.

During the Earth's major glacial periods, ice sheets almost as big as that of present-day Antarctica spread over the northern part of North America, reaching as far south as the Ohio River, and over northern Europe as far south as southern England, the Netherlands and southern Poland. Today glacial activity is more restricted, but the mechanisms by which it carves dramatic features of the Earth's landscape remain the same.

Types of glacier

There are six main types of ice mass: cirque glaciers, which occupy basin-shaped depressions in mountain areas; valley glaciers; piedmont glaciers, in which the ice spreads in a lobe over a lowland; floating ice tongues and ice shelves; mountain ice caps; and ice sheets. Climate and relief are responsible for these differences, but glaciers can also be classified according to their internal temperatures.

Cold glaciers are those in which the ice temperature is below freezing point and they are frozen to the rock beneath. This condition, which hinders the movement of glaciers, exists in many parts of Antarctica and Greenland, where air temperatures are low, as well as at high altitudes in some lower-latitude mountain regions. Temperate glaciers, on the other hand, show internal temperatures at or close to the melting point of ice. Unlike cold glaciers, they are not frozen to the rock beneath and can therefore slide over it. Ice melts on the surface of the glacier when the weather is warm, and underneath the glacier as it is warmed by geothermal heat from inside the Earth. Streams collecting meltwater may flow over, through or under the ice and emerge at the ice edge. In other glaciers, cold ice may overlie temperate ice.

Glaciers are formed from snow that, as it accumulates year after year, becomes compacted, turning first into "névé" or "firn" and eventually, after several years or even decades, into glacial ice. This process of accumulation is offset by ablation, through which ice is lost by melting, evaporation or, in glaciers that end in the sea or in lakes, by calving. If accumulation exceeds ablation, the glacier increases in size; conversely, if ablation is higher, the glacier shrinks and eventually disappears.

Glaciers move because of the force of gravity. The fastest-moving glaciers, for example those of coastal Greenland which descend steeply from areas of great accumulation, move at speeds of more than 20 m (65 ft) a day. A few meters a day is more common, however. Some glaciers move exceptionally quickly in surges, which usually last for a few weeks; rates of more than 100 m (330 ft) a day have been recorded. At the other extreme, some glaciers or parts of glaciers—the central zones of ice sheets and ice caps for example—are virtually motionless. When the ice in a glacier is subject to pressure or tension—as it flows down a valley, for example—it behaves rather like a plastic substance and changes its shape to fit the contours of the valley. Part or all of the movement of a glacier is accomplished by means of this internal deformation. In temperate glaciers, or glaciers whose lower layers are temperate, there is also basal sliding. Movement of a glacier produces cracks or crevasses in areas where stress exceeds the strength of the ice.

The work of glaciers

Glaciers and ice sheets can profoundly modify the landscape by both erosion and deposition. Measured rates of erosion of bedrock may be as much as several millimeters a year. Rock surfaces are scratched, or striated, and worn down by the constant grinding action (abrasion) of rock fragments embedded in the base of the ice. The extreme pressure of thick glacial ice on a basal boulder has been known to rupture solid bedrock beneath it.

The products of bedrock erosion range from fine clays and silts produced by abrasion, to large boulders picked up and transported by the ice. Some rocks have been carried hundreds of kilometers, from southern Scandinavia to

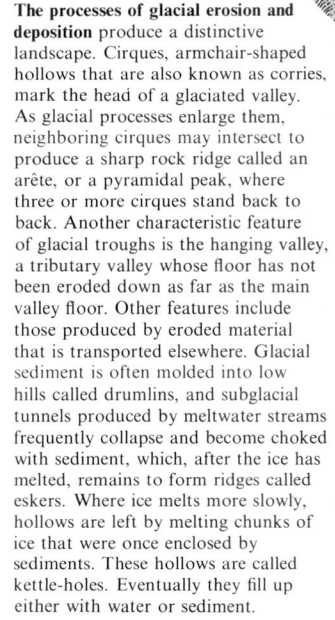

Pyramidal peak

Cirque

Arête

Névé

Medial moraine

Lateral moraine

Marginal crevasses

A U-shaped valley, such as Langdale (below) in the English Lake District, is a clear indication of a glaciated past. The floor is quite flat and the valley sides rise steeply from it.

A crevasse (below left) is created by stress within a glacier. Internally, the ice is rather like plastic but its surface is rigid and brittle. This causes tension and cracking on the surface.

This erratic (below right) is made of Silurian grit, yet it sits on a limestone perch. Ice left Yorkshire 20,000 years ago, since when the limestone surface has been lowered by solution.

1

2

3

Before the onset of glaciation a mountain region is often sculpted largely by the work of rivers and the processes of weathering. The hills are rounded and the valleys are V-shaped (1). During a period of glacial activity, valleys become filled with snow and eventually glaciers and, after thousands of years, the region shows a typically glaciated landscape (2). When the ice has finally disappeared there remains a glacial trough (3) with hanging valleys, truncated spurs, waterfalls and all the landforms associated with deposition of material.

The processes of glacial erosion and deposition produce a distinctive landscape. Cirques, armchair-shaped hollows that are also known as corries, mark the head of a glaciated valley. As glacial processes enlarge them, neighboring cirques may intersect to produce a sharp rock ridge called an arête, or a pyramidal peak, where three or more cirques stand back to back. Another characteristic feature of glacial troughs is the hanging valley, a tributary valley whose floor has not been eroded down as far as the main valley floor. Other features include those produced by eroded material that is transported elsewhere. Glacial sediment is often molded into low hills called drumlins, and subglacial tunnels produced by meltwater streams frequently collapse and become choked with sediment, which, after the ice has melted, remains to form ridges called eskers. Where ice melts more slowly, hollows are left by melting chunks of ice that were once enclosed by sediments. These hollows are called kettle-holes. Eventually they fill up either with water or sediment.

A glaciated valley exhibits a distinctive shape and profile. A cross section shows a U-shape, while longitudinally the valley floor is marked by a series of rocky steps and basins. The zone of accumulation is characterized by a cirque, in which snow collects to produce a firn field. A bergschrund is a type of crevasse that opens up near the top of the firn field where the head of the glacier is pulled away from the cirque walls. A rock step is where the gradient becomes much steeper. The speed of the ice flow is accelerated and consequent tension within the ice creates a number of deep crevasses called an ice fall. The zone of ablation has large accumulations of various kinds of rock debris.

Glacial erosion of rock surfaces is typified by a roche moutonnée, a resistant rock hummock that lies in the path of the ice. The upstream side is smooth as a result of abrasion by rock debris that is frozen into the base of the glacier. This debris scratches and scrapes rock, producing striations. The downstream side is rough as a result of ice plucking. Meltwater removes the small blocks of rock.

eastern England, for example, and such far-traveled rocks are termed erratics. The finer sediments, compacted at the base of the glacier by the weight of the overlying ice, form till or boulder clay.

The surface of a glacier is often strewn with rock debris, which either rests on the ice or is within the glacier and revealed as the ice melts. Lateral moraines consist of rock debris that has accumulated along the sides of the glacier as a result of rockfall from, and erosion of, the valley sides. Where two glaciers join, the inner lateral moraines merge to form a medial moraine. In the ablation zone, the surface of the glacier becomes increasingly laden with debris "melting out" so that the ice may become completely buried. At the end of the glacier all rock debris is dumped, forming a terminal moraine.

Meltwater streams pouring out from glaciers or flowing in tunnels beneath them can be powerful agents of erosion and can transport large quantities of sediment. Bedrock surfaces become potholed and carved by channels that are eroded with great speed. As the streams emerge from the edge of the ice, they carry with them and deposit vast quantities of sand and gravel which form flood plains (outwash plains). Alternatively, meltwater streams may deposit sediment between the edge of the glacier and valley side, leaving a "kame terrace" when the ice finally melts. Meltwater streams feeding glacial lakes that are dammed by a glacier or moraine, for example, construct deltas of sand and gravel and lay down finer sediments (varved clays) on the lake floor.

Snow processes

Snow plays a smaller part than glacial ice in landform sculpture. Its most important role is in avalanches, which, in mountain regions, regularly bring down thousands of tonnes of rock debris. The mixture of snow, rock and other debris forms avalanche boulder tongues on the flat ground where the avalanche comes to rest and the snow melts. Gullies (avalanche chutes) on mountain slopes are swept clean of loose debris several times a year and they are gradually enlarged. Snow patches that remain stationary on more gentle slopes or in hollows encourage rock weathering under and around them. Such a process, termed nivation, may lead to deepening and enlargement of hollows and further snow accumulation. This is one way in which new glaciers are formed.

A great variety of material arrives at the terminus or snout of a glacier—ranging from large blocks of rock and boulders to very finely ground rock "flour." All the material is dropped in a haphazard way as the ice melts. The mixture of clay and boulders is termed glacial till. If the ice margin remains stationary, till accumulates to form a terminal moraine. If the snout recedes continuously, no ridge forms.

Landscape-makers: The Seas

The coastline is both the birthplace and the graveyard of the land. Over tens of thousands of years, geological uplift of a continent, or a fall in sea level, may create an emerging fringe of new land, whereas a period of submergence drowns the coasts and floods the adjacent river valleys, destroying land but producing some of the most attractive coastal landscapes. More rapid are the changes brought about by the sea itself. Erosion of coastal rocks or beaches can cut back the coastline at a rate of several meters a year, whereas other coastlines are built up at a comparable rate from marine sediments.

Changing coastlines are apparent on a human time scale. In temperate latitudes, beaches tend to be combed down and narrowed by winter waves, only to be restored during the calmer weather of summer. They may be lost one week and replenished the next, demonstrating an invaluable ability to recover from the wounds of all but the most devastating storms. Cliffs are generally much less dynamic, particularly if composed of resistant rock, but any loss that they suffer is permanent because there is no process that is capable of rebuilding them.

Coasts vary greatly around the world. Tropical areas often have wide beaches made up of fine material which in many cases forms broad mangrove swamps that collect sediment and build up the coast. In more exposed tropical zones coral reefs are common, either fringing the shore or (particularly where the sea level is rising) separated from the shore by a lagoon to give a barrier reef. Continued submergence of a small island surrounded by such a reef may produce an atoll. In contrast, Arctic beaches are narrow and coarse, and may be icebound for up to 10 months each year. Recession of soft rock cliffs results more from melting of ice in the ground than from wave erosion.

Waves at work

Across great expanses of open ocean energy is transferred from the wind to the sea surface to produce waves, thus fueling the machine that ultimately creates the coast. Originating as waves with heights of up to 20 or even 30 m (65–100 ft), they lose part of their energy quite rapidly as they travel, and once they have been reduced in height to the lower but more widely spaced ocean swell, they continue to travel across enormous distances.

The coasts of western Europe receive waves produced almost 10,000 km (6,200 miles) away off Cape Horn, and swell reaching California has sometimes crossed more than 11,000 km

Cliffs are attacked by waves at the zone that lies between high tide (HT) and low tide (LT). The rate of erosion depends on the strength and jointing pattern of the rock and the angle at which the strata are presented to the sea. Erosion begins when water and rocks are hurled at the cliff and new fragments are broken off. The pressure of the water also compresses air in joints and cracks to shatter the rock face. As the base of the cliff is attacked, a notch (1) may be cut, and as this is made deeper the cliff above collapses. Eventually a wave-cut platform (2) is created, the top of which is exposed at low tide. The debris from the cliff is carried along the coast or deposited offshore (3). The shallow seabed now slows down incoming waves: they attack the cliff (4), but their energy is reduced. In calm water, for example at the head of a bay (5), wave energy is diffused and light material such as sand is deposited as beaches.

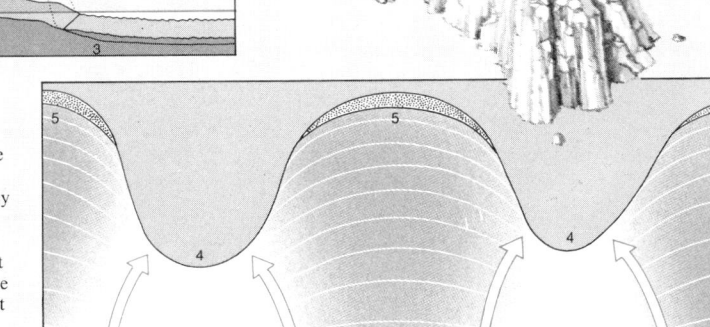

THE SEA COAST

The coastline is continually changing, whether day by day as the tides sift and sort the sand and shingle on the beaches, or over tens of thousands of years as the erosive power of waves carves out headlands and bays. And over millions of years the coastline is subjected to major changes of sea level, whether it is the land uplifting or sinking, or the sea itself rising or receding. Today, interference by man can damage the coast. Dam building and river-channel engineering drastically reduce the amount of sediment reaching the coast; and sea walls built to protect the coast and groynes constructed to retard sand removal both pose a long-term threat to adjacent coasts, which become starved of the sediment that previously supplied their beaches.

When a headland has been created (below), wave erosion continues on both sides and a cave (1) may be formed. After many years of wave action the cave will break through to the other side and an arch (2) may be created.

Light material such as mud, sand and shingle is carried by the sea. Waves tend to push the particles obliquely up a beach (right), but the backwash moves the material down again at right-angles to the shore. Thus the materials move in a zigzag fashion along the beach (1). This is known as longshore drift. When the load-carrying capacity of the waves is reduced for any reason, the material is deposited and forms a variety of features. The largest beaches (2) are found in the calmest waters such as in bays or at river mouths, with the finest grains sorted out nearest to the sea and larger pebbles stranded higher up. Spits (3) and bars (4) are sand ridges deposited across a bay or river mouth. When one end of the ridge is attached to the land it is called a spit. Spits are very often shaped like a hook as waves are refracted around the tip of land. Bars are formed where sand is deposited in shallow water offshore across the entrances to bays and run parallel to the coastline. Dunes, pictured above, are formed when sand on the beach is driven inland by onshore winds. Very often they isolate flooded land behind them to form coastal features such as salt marshes and mud flats.

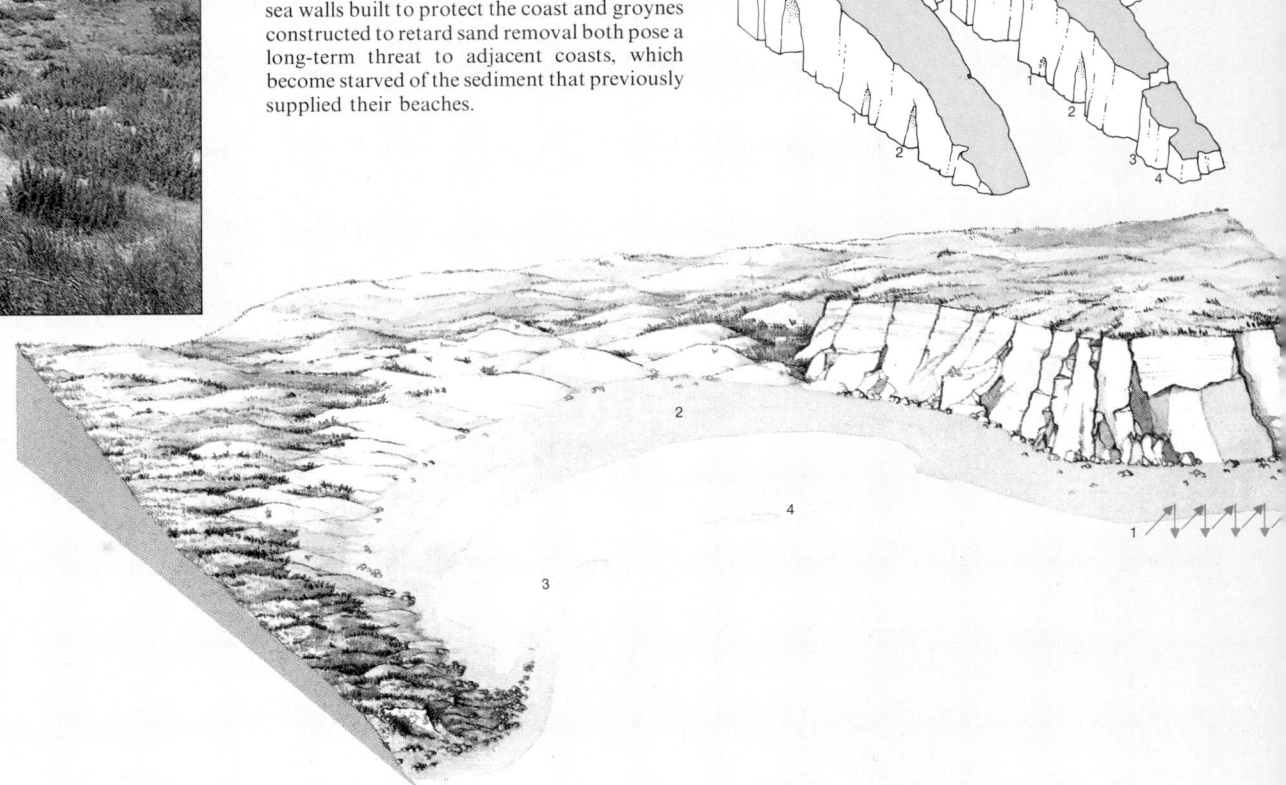

There are two major kinds of coastline—coastlines of submergence and coastlines of emergence. They are created by either a sinking or an uplift of the land, or by a change in sea level. A coastline with wave-cut cliffs and a river valley (A), for example, that experiences a rise in sea level will produce a new coastline (B) with a drowned estuary, coastal uplands isolated as islands, and a submerged coastal plain. The same coastline subjected to a drop in sea level (C) results in an extended river, abandoned cliffs far inland, and a raised beach that forms a new coastal plain.

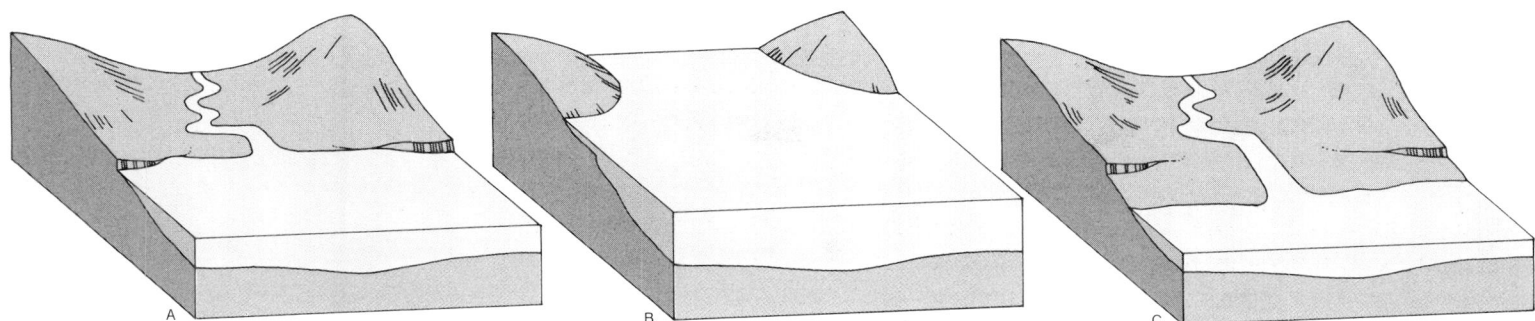

(6,800 miles) of the Pacific from the storm belt south of New Zealand. The waves thus act as a giant conveyor for the energy that is finally used up in a few seconds of intense activity. Few other natural systems gather their energy so widely and then concentrate it so effectively.

A ball floating on the sea surface shows that, although a passing wave form moves forward, the water (and ball) follow a near-circular path and end up almost where they started. Beneath the surface the water follows similar orbits, but the amount of movement becomes progressively less with depth, until it dies out altogether. The greater the wavelength (the distance between crests) the greater is the depth of disturbance.

Long-swell waves approaching a gentle shore start disturbing the seabed far from the coast and these waves slow up, pack closer together and increase in height until they become unstable, thus producing the spilling white surf that carries much sediment to build up wide sandy beaches. Shorter local storm waves disturb the water to less depth, and thus reach much closer inshore before they interact with the seabed. Such waves do not therefore break until they plunge directly down on to the beach, leading to severe erosion, which results in the production of steep pebble beaches.

Waves slow up in shallow water, and so an undulating seabed causes their crests to bend and change their direction of approach. As a result, waves converge toward headlands (where their erosional attack is concentrated), but they diverge as they enter bays, spreading out their energy and encouraging the deposition of the sediment they carry across the seabed close inshore. The high-energy waves at the headlands remove any rock fragments that become detached and transport them to the beaches that form at the bayheads.

Erosional coasts

Much of the local variability of coastal scenery results from differing rates of erosion on different types of rock. Bays are cut back rapidly into soft rocks such as clay, sand or gravel. Headlands are evidence that the sea takes longer to remove higher areas of harder rock such as granite or limestone. Despite the enormous power of storm waves, erosion of resistant rocks is slow and relies on any weakness that the sea can exploit.

Joints, faults and bedding planes are etched out by the water and by rock fragments hurled against them by breaking waves. Air compressed into such crevices by water pressure widens and deepens them into cracks and then into caves. In this way a solid cliff face can be eroded to form the great variety of features.

Resistant rocks can form steep, simple cliffs of great height—more than 600 m (2,000 ft) in some places—and the sea may have to undercut them to produce collapse and retreat. Cliffs of weaker rocks rarely reach 100 m (330 ft) in height and are more rapidly eroded by atmospheric processes, by running water and by landslips. There the role of the sea is largely confined to removing the rock debris from the foot of the cliff. Soft rock cliffs are gently sloping but complex in form.

Coasts of deposition

Although waves bend as they approach the shore, they rarely become completely parallel to the coastline. Wave crests drive sediment obliquely toward the beach, whereas the troughs carry it back directly offshore down the beach slope. In this way, sand and pebbles are transported in a zigzag motion, called longshore drift, away from the areas where they are produced. One such source of material is cliff erosion, but on average about 95 percent of the material moving on to beaches was originally carried to the coast by rivers.

Beaches are built up wherever longshore drift is impeded (for example, by a headland) or where wave and current energy is reduced (as at the head of a bay). An abundant supply of sediment may build a sandbar across the mouth of a bay or in shallow water offshore. Where the coast changes direction, longshore drift may continue in its original direction and build a spit out from the land. Depositional features may become strengthened by vegetation. Plants may take root and bind together newly deposited sediments, but they constitute relatively delicate coasts that are vulnerable to erosion if for any reason they are not continually supplied with fresh deposits of sediment.

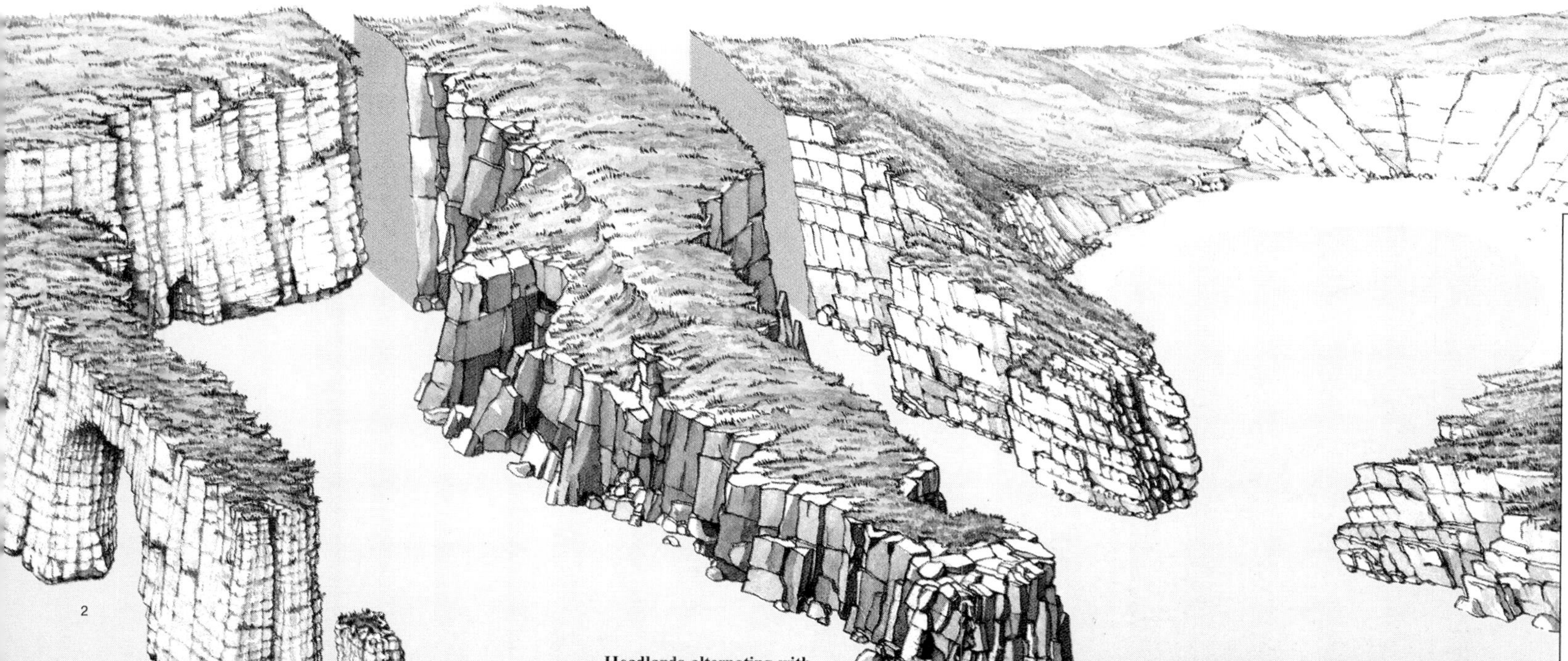

Further wave erosion (above) causes the roof of the arch to collapse, leaving an isolated column of rock called a stack (3). Another cave, and then an arch, may be formed behind the stack, which itself may be eroded to a short stump (4).

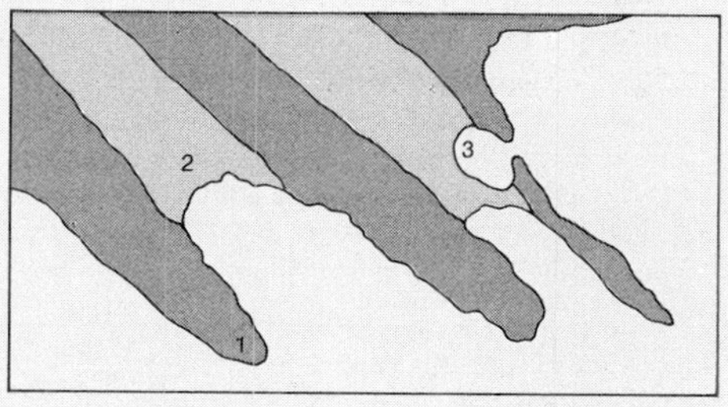

Headlands alternating with bays are found where bands of strong (1) and weak (2) rocks meet the coast at an angle and there is a varied resistance to erosion. The bays are first carved out of the softer rock, leaving the waves to attack the headlands of hard rock. If, in contrast, the strata lie parallel to the coast, then the hard rock has few irregular indentations except where the sea has broken through to the soft rock behind and has scoured out a cove (3).

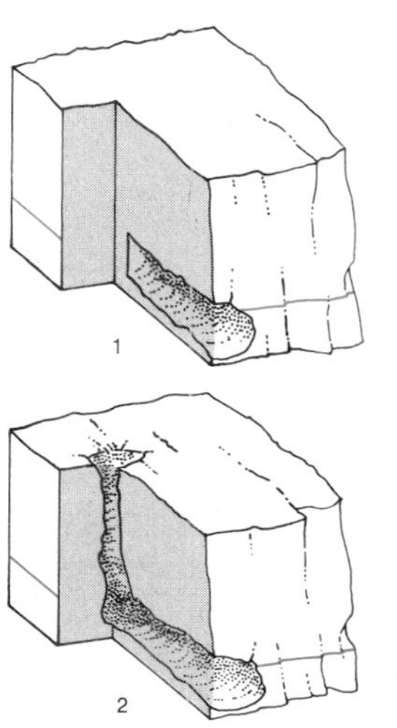

Gloups are formed when waves first erode a cave, then extend it backward as a long shaft running into the cliff (1). If the roof collapses at one point, a blowhole, or gloup (2), is formed. If the whole roof collapses, a deep cleft called a geo is created.

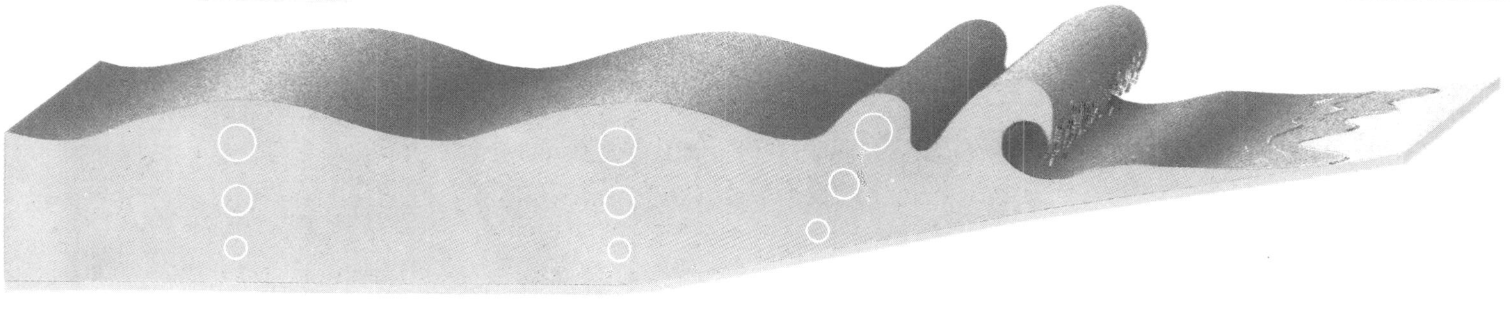

Waves are generated by wind on the surface of the sea. It is the shape of the wave that travels forward—the individual water particles move in near-circular orbits. Disturbance diminishes with depth to about half a wavelength. Waves break when they strike a sloping shore, and the wave height is about the same as the depth of the water.

Landscape-makers: Wind and Weathering

Winds are part of the global circulation of air and they can affect landforms wherever surface material is loose and unprotected by vegetation. The effects of a strong wind are a familiar sight—whether in the dust clouds that rise from a plowed field after a dry spell, or in the sand swept along the beach on a windy day. Weathering is the disintegration and decomposition of rocks through their exposure to the atmosphere. It includes the changes that destroy the original structure of rocks, and few on the Earth's surface have not been weathered at one time or another in the history of our evolving landscape.

Active and fixed dunes in Africa and western Asia

Sand dunes cover only 20 percent of the world's deserts, and tend to be concentrated in a small number of sand seas, or ergs, such as the Erg Bourharet in Algeria (above).

Longitudinal, or seif, dunes (below) are long, narrow ridges that lie parallel to the direction of prevailing winds. Surface heating and wind flow produce vertical spiraling motions of air.

Direction of wind

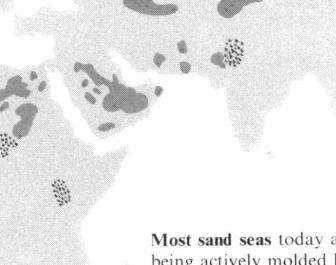

Most sand seas today are being actively molded by winds. The landscape has long been shaped by wind, and some dune fields produced in dry climates in the distant past may be "fossilized" now by soils and vegetation cover. Desertification often occurs where this vegetation is disturbed by man.

☐ Fixed sand dunes

▨ Active sand dunes

EROSION AND WEATHERING

Winds result from the differential heating of regions of the globe. They act indirectly as agents of erosion through water or waves, but they also directly affect the surface of the Earth, molding landforms either by erosion or deposition. The nature of weathering processes and the rate at which they operate depend upon climate, the properties of the rock and the conditions of the biosphere. Both wind erosion and the various weathering processes are significant landscape-makers.

Many rocks are formed deep in the Earth, where they are in equilibrium with the forces that created them. If they become exposed at the surface, they are in disequilibrium with atmospheric forces. This brings about the changes —adjustments to atmospheric and organic agents—that we call weathering. Products of weathering are moved by agents of erosion, one of which is the wind. Where the surface is protected, for example by vegetation, the wind has little effect, but where strong winds attack loose surface material that is unprotected, erosion, abrasion and deposition may occur, producing characteristic landforms.

How wind shapes the surface

Strong winds occur in many places, but nowhere are they more effective in forming the surface of the land than in deserts, where their work is largely unhindered by vegetation. There the wind can pick up material and then, charged with sand particles, blast away at the ground, carrying away the debris and depositing it. Many notorious desert winds are associated with sand movement and dust storms—the harmattan of West Africa and the sirocco of the Middle East, for example.

Wind erosion occurs where winds charged with sand attack soils or rock. Dry soils may be broken up and the resulting debris, which includes soil nutrients, is carried away as dust. This poses a serious problem, especially when arid and semiarid lands experience drought. Wind erosion involving the lifting and blowing away of loose material from the ground surface is called deflation.

Erosion by sand and rock fragments carried by winds is called abrasion. In this way winds erode individual surface pebbles into distinctive shapes known as ventifacts. They can also mold larger rock masses into aerodynamic shapes known as yardangs—features that often look rather like upturned rowing boats. Some of these features are so large that they have been identified only since satellite photographs have become available. Finally, winds erode by attrition, which involves the mutual wearing down of particles as they are carried along.

Winds can transport material in three different ways. They can lift loose, sand-sized particles into the air and carry them downwind along trajectories that resemble those of ballistic missiles: the particles rise steeply and descend along gentle flight paths. This produces a bouncing movement known as saltation in a layer extending approximately 1 m (3 ft) above the

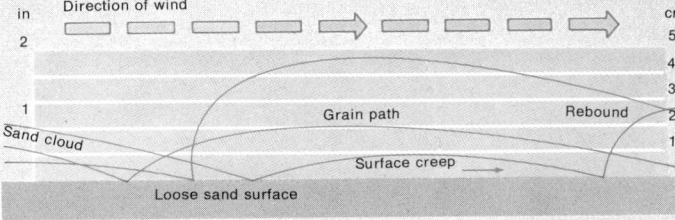

Direction of wind

Grain path — Rebound

Sand cloud

Surface creep

Loose sand surface

Sand particles move in a series of long jumps—a process called saltation. Particles describe a curved path (above), the height and length of which depends upon the mass of the grain, the wind velocity and the number of other particles moving around. Saltation only occurs in a layer extending up to approximately 1 m (3 ft) above the ground surface. Sand grains moving in this way are also responsible for the abraded base of features such as pedestal rocks (right). These landforms are weathered first—for example by the crystallization of salts—and are then eroded by the sand-laden winds.

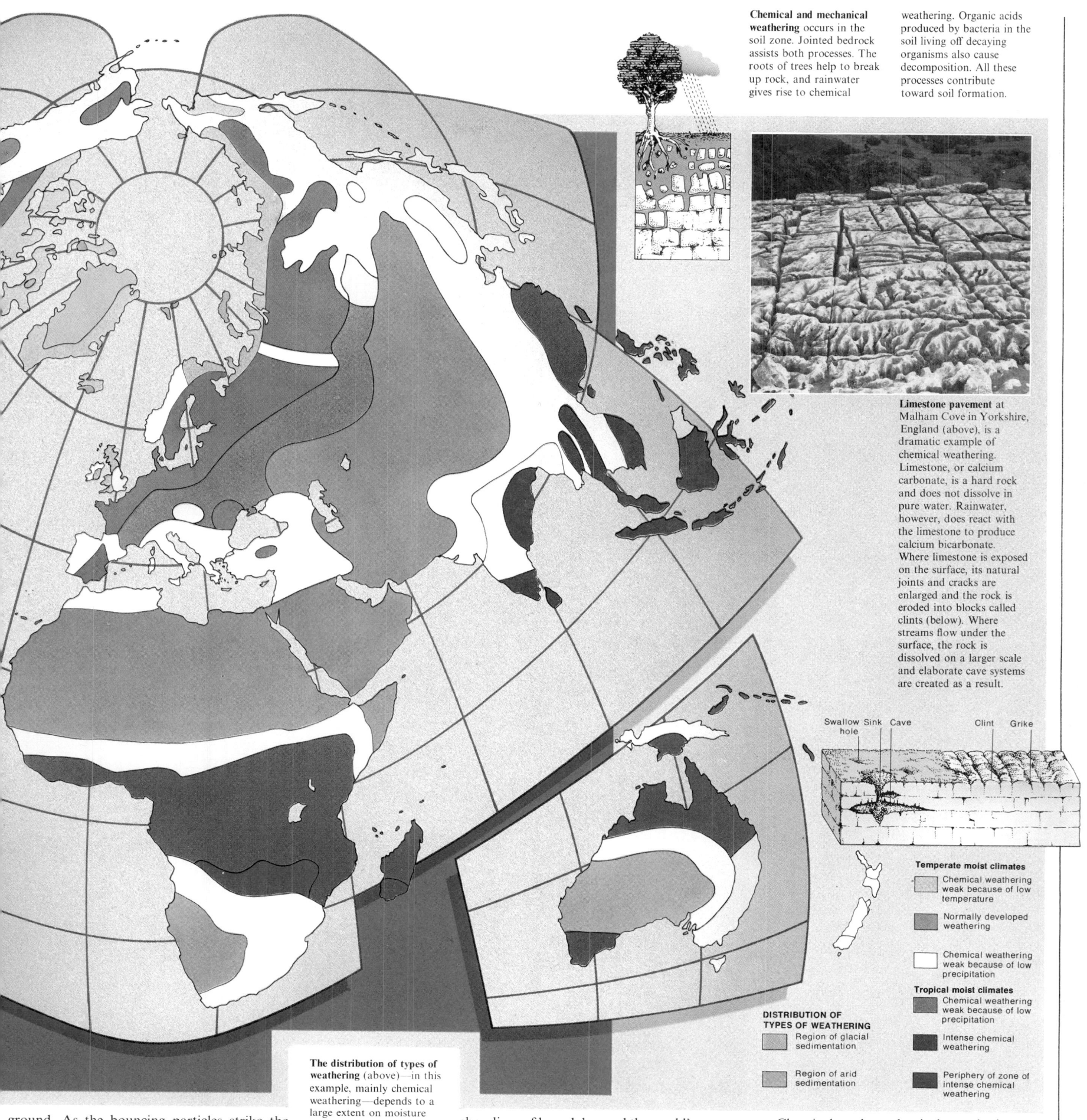

Chemical and mechanical weathering occurs in the soil zone. Jointed bedrock assists both processes. The roots of trees help to break up rock, and rainwater gives rise to chemical weathering. Organic acids produced by bacteria in the soil living off decaying organisms also cause decomposition. All these processes contribute toward soil formation.

Limestone pavement at Malham Cove in Yorkshire, England (above), is a dramatic example of chemical weathering. Limestone, or calcium carbonate, is a hard rock and does not dissolve in pure water. Rainwater, however, does react with the limestone to produce calcium bicarbonate. Where limestone is exposed on the surface, its natural joints and cracks are enlarged and the rock is eroded into blocks called clints (below). Where streams flow under the surface, the rock is dissolved on a larger scale and elaborate cave systems are created as a result.

Swallow Sink Cave   Clint Grike
hole

Temperate moist climates
☐ Chemical weathering weak because of low temperature
☐ Normally developed weathering
☐ Chemical weathering weak because of low precipitation

Tropical moist climates
☐ Chemical weathering weak because of low precipitation
☐ Intense chemical weathering
☐ Periphery of zone of intense chemical weathering

DISTRIBUTION OF TYPES OF WEATHERING
☐ Region of glacial sedimentation
☐ Region of arid sedimentation

The distribution of types of weathering (above)—in this example, mainly chemical weathering—depends to a large extent on moisture and temperature. When classifying regions with different rates of chemical weathering in terms of climatic zones, many areas of the world can be placed into one of two principal categories: tropical moist climates and temperate moist climates. The white areas on the map are mountain ranges or regions of tectonic activity where there is no appreciable weathering mantle.

ground. As the bouncing particles strike the surface, they push other particles along the ground (creep or drift). Fine particles that are disturbed by saltation rise up into the airflow and are carried away as dust (suspension).

The materials eroded and transported by winds must eventually come to rest in features of deposition, the most extensive of which are sand dunes. Sand seas at first sight appear to be random and complex, rather like a choppy ocean, but their features generally fall into three size groups: small ripples, which have a wavelength of up to 3 m (10 ft) and a height of 20 cm (8 in); dunes, with a wavelength of 20–300 m (65–1,000 ft) and a height of up to 30 m (68 ft); and sand mountains or "draa," which have a wavelength of 1–3 km (0.6–1.5 miles) and rise to a height of up to 200 m (650 ft). Within each size group various forms can be explained in terms of the nature of the sand and the kinds of winds that blow over it. Where winds blow consistently from one direction, long linear dunes form parallel or transverse to the wind direction. Where sand supply is limited, horned "barchan" dunes may form. If winds blow from several directions during a year, then star-shaped dunes and other complex patterns appear. Sand dunes are also common along the

shorelines of large lakes and the world's oceans, where onshore winds can pile quite extensive areas of loose drifting sand.

Agents of weathering

Weathering takes two forms: mechanical weathering breaks up rock without altering its mineral constituents, whereas chemical weathering changes in some way the nature of mineral crystals. One agent of mechanical weathering is temperature change. It used to be thought that rocks disintegrated as a result of a huge daily range of temperature (thermal weathering). Despite travelers' tales of rocks splitting in the desert night with cracks like pistol shots, there is little evidence to support this view. In the presence of water, however, alternate heating and cooling of rocks does result in fracture. Frost is also an effective rock breaker. The freezing of water and expansion of ice in the cracks and pores of rocks create disruptive pressures; alternate freezing and thawing eventually causes pieces of rock to break off in angular fragments. Finally, the roots of plants and trees grow into the joints of rock and widen them, thus loosening the structure of the rock. Animals burrowing through the soil can have a similar effect on rocks.

Chemical and mechanical weathering can work hand in hand. In arid regions, for example, the crystallization of salts results in the weathering of rock. As water evaporates from the rock surface, salt crystals grow (from minerals dissolved in the water) in small openings in the rock. In time these crystals bring to bear enough pressure to break off rock fragments from the parent block.

Chemical weathering is most effective in humid tropical climates, however, and it usually involves the decomposition of rocks as a result of their exposure to air and rainwater, which contains dissolved chemicals. Carbon dioxide from the air, for example, becomes dissolved in rainwater, making it into weak carbonic acid. This reacts with minerals such as calcite, which is found in many rocks. Similarly, rocks can be oxidized by oxygen in the air. This happens to rocks that contain iron, for example, if they are exposed on the surface: a reddish iron oxide is produced which causes the rocks to crumble.

Over many thousands, even millions, of years, the processes of mechanical and chemical weathering have affected many of the rocks on the Earth's surface. When rocks are weakened in such a way, they then fall prey to the agents of erosion—water, ice, winds and waves.

Landscape-makers: Man

Man has done much to reshape the face of the planet since his first appearance on Earth more than two million years ago. Early man did little to harm the environment but, with the rise of agriculture, the landscape began to change. An increasing population and the growth of urban settlements gradually created greater demands for agricultural land and living space. But industrialization during the last 200 years has had the biggest impact. Man's search for and exploitation of the Earth's resources has to a large extent transformed the natural landscape and at the same time created totally artificial man-made environments.

MAN THE GEOLOGICAL AGENT

In 1864 a conservationist named George Perkins Marsh introduced the thesis that "man in fact made the Earth" rather than the converse. The idea of man as a geological agent was further developed in the 1920s. Man modifies the landscape in many ways; sometimes he transforms the Earth completely—he even creates land where no land was before.

Man's major impact on the landscape has been through forest clearance. He made the first attack on natural forests about 8,000 years ago in Neolithic times in northern and western Europe, as revealed by the changing composition of tree pollen deposited in bogs. After Roman times, especially in the Mediterranean region, there was another spate of forest clearance, so that by the Middle Ages little original forest survived in the Old World. As population and emigration increased, it was the turn of trees in the New World and Africa to fall before the axe and plow. Man's present voracious appetite for timber and its products could, if unchecked, clear most of the Earth's great forests by the end of this century.

Forest clearance not only changes the appearance of the landscape but can alter the balance of nature within a region. The hydrological cycle may be affected, and soil erosion may be increased, which in turn chokes rivers with sediment and leads to the silting up of harbors and estuaries. The coastal area of Valencia in Spain, for example, has widened by nearly 4 km (2.5 miles) since Roman times, much of which can be accounted for by forest clearance, and subsequent soil erosion and the deposition of the material by rivers as they near the sea. Reafforestation of an area can reduce soil erosion and the threat of flooding. Landscape management can reduce wind speeds: for example, shelter belts in the Russian steppes have been planted over distances of more than 100 km (62 miles).

Water management

The second great impact of man has been on the waterways of the world. The most spectacular changes are caused by the construction of dams to make vast new lakes. Such projects have frequently had effects far beyond those originally anticipated. The Aswan High Dam on the River Nile was completed in 1970, creating Lake Nasser and making possible the irrigation of an additional 550,000 hectares (1,358,000 acres) in upper Egypt. But some would argue that the dam holds back silt from the rivers and stores it in the lake, a fact that has seriously reduced the rate of silting in the Nile delta. This has resulted in increased salinity and some loss of fertility of the soil, as well as changes to the delta's coastline. The storage of silt in Lake Nasser has caused increased erosion of the riverbed downstream and the undermining of the foundations of bridges and barrages.

Other man-made changes to rivers include straightening and canalization, usually for

Massive power plants (left) symbolize man's modifications to the landscape in modern, industrialized society. Demand for energy and mineral resources has led to the creation of huge holes in the ground like this borax mine (below left) in the Mojave desert in California. The open pit is 100 m (330 ft) deep, 1,460 m (4,800 ft) long and 915 m (3,000 ft) wide. In opening up resource areas in Brazil, the Trans-Amazonian highway has disturbed the forest (below).

Hong Kong's bustling waterfront (below) captures the true essence of urban man. If space is in short supply, he expands his world vertically and maximizes his use of every square meter. Central business districts in the world's major cities reflect this concern with space.

flood protection, but also to prevent the channel from shifting. As long ago as the third millennium BC, during the reign of Emperor Yao, a hydraulic engineer was apparently appointed to control the wandering course of the Hwang-Ho (Yellow River), and the system he devised survived for at least 1,500 years. Even so, over the centuries, the river has changed course radically, and today measures are still being taken to control the fine sediment that the river carries and the flooding caused by its deposition. The Missouri River in the United States is estimated to erode material from an area of about 3,680 hectares (9,000 acres) annually over a length of 1,220 km (758 miles). It is little wonder that engineers attempt to control rivers by means of realignment or try to "train" a river's flow by using concrete stays.

New land from old

The continuing pressure of population on food resources and the need to create new agricultural land illustrate still further the impact of man as a landscape shaper. As part of irrigation projects land is often leveled and new waterways are created in the form of canals. Pakistan has one of the most extensive man-made irrigation systems in the world. It controls almost completely the flow of the Indus, Sutlej and Punjab rivers through some 640 km (400 miles) of linking canals.

A huge demand for rice in many parts of southeastern Asia has led to farmers terracing steep slopes on many mountainous islands. In the Netherlands, about one-third of the entire cultivated area of the country is land that has been reclaimed from the sea. In the future more grandiose schemes are likely. Any large-scale expansion of agricultural land in the Soviet Union will be mainly dependent on water supply. There have been plans since the 1930s to divert northward-flowing rivers to irrigated areas in the south and west. This idea, and it is believed that it might become a reality by the turn of the century, could have serious implications for the waters of the Arctic Ocean. If the amount of fresh water flowing into the ocean is reduced, salinity will increase, thus affecting the melting of ice floes and, consequently, sea level.

Man has also made his mark along the coastlines, from small-scale measures, such as

the construction of groynes—wooden piles that reduce the amount of sand that is transported along the beach by wave action—to large-scale man-made harbors.

Modern man, the urban dweller of the machine age, has brought great changes to the face of the landscape. The need for materials for the construction of the urban fabric has led to the creation of huge quarries, in which building stone and road-building materials are extracted from the ground. Demand for energy and minerals leads to extensive modification of the landscape, especially where mineral deposits are near the surface and can be extracted by open-cast mining. The largest holes on Earth (excluding ocean basins) are those that result from the extraction of fuel (coal) and minerals.

The side effects of mining can be detrimental to the environment. Land may subside and despoilation of the landscape by slag heaps, for example, is considerable. Escaping coal dust can suffocate vegetation in a mining area, and gases given off during some mining operations can also damage plant and animal life.

Reclamation of spoiled areas is obligatory in many countries. Old open-cast workings are often filled with water to be used for recreational facilities, and slag heaps are treated and planted with vegetation: research has produced certain strains of plants that will grow even in the most acidic soils.

The true impact of man

During the last hundred years or so man has become much more aware of his role as an agent of landscape creation and destruction. The significance of man the landscape-maker, in comparison with slow, natural changes, is the speed with which he effects transformation, the sheer amount of energy which he can apply to a relatively small area, and the selectiveness and determination with which he applies that energy. Man's increased impact has not been a smooth and continuous process: it has occurred at different rates in different places and at different times. While it can be argued that some landscapes have been constructed which themselves conserve and often beautify the natural environment, man's active role has primarily been destructive: he has transformed the Earth's surface, perhaps irreversibly.

THE DUTCH POLDERS

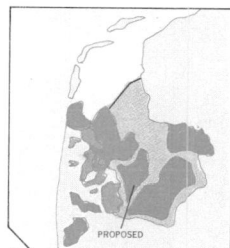

Reclamation of the Dutch polders from the North Sea is an example of man creating land. Many centuries ago a large part of what is now the western Netherlands was beneath the sea. From the 15th to the 17th centuries (A) dykes were constructed to enclose land and protect it against inundation from the sea, and enable it to be farmed. Later, windmills were used to drain away sea water. Further reclamation in the 19th and 20th centuries (B) has brought the total area to

165,000 hectares (408,000 acres). In 1932 a 40 km (25 mile) dam was completed, enclosing the Zuider Zee—which is now a freshwater lake that was renamed the IJsselmeer—and reducing Holland's vulnerable coastline by 320 km (200 miles). To create a polder, a dyke is built and the water pumped out. Reeds are grown to help dry out the soil. After a few years drains are put in to remove water remaining. Newly created polders (light blue) show up well on this satellite image (top).

Man-made environments have become increasingly complex and large scale. Highway construction—this vast interchange (left) is in Chicago—is typical of the extensive use of land for modern transport systems alone. The acreage of land use classified as urban continues to increase. Man's endeavors to make still more land available for his many purposes have extended to cultivating previously inhospitable desert lands (above). More than half the land in Israel is naturally unproductive because of its aridity. By means of elaborate water carriage and storage schemes and scientifically researched irrigation projects, the desert has been totally transformed from a barren wasteland into intensively cultivated fields. Output from agriculture can also be increased by terracing. In densely populated areas, or mountainous regions, as in Luzon in the Philippines (right), man's skillful landscaping has completely reshaped the topography.

Part 3

THE EMERGENCE OF LIFE

How life on Earth began and developed
How life has evolved and spread over the planet
How man came to inherit the Earth

THE STAGES OF LIFE

Simple organic molecules, the precursors of life, could certainly have evolved in Earth's primitive atmosphere. Energy from the Sun, volcanoes and electric storms had the power to combine the basic chemicals into the amino acids and other molecules that are the constituents of living matter, forming droplets of "pre-life" in pools and on shorelines. Concentrations of droplets collected around some minerals, coagulating in a "soup" of long-chain polymers—proteins and nucleic acids which together form the living cell. Thus far have scientists re-created life's origins, but the combining of proteins and nucleic acids into a living unit remains to be achieved.

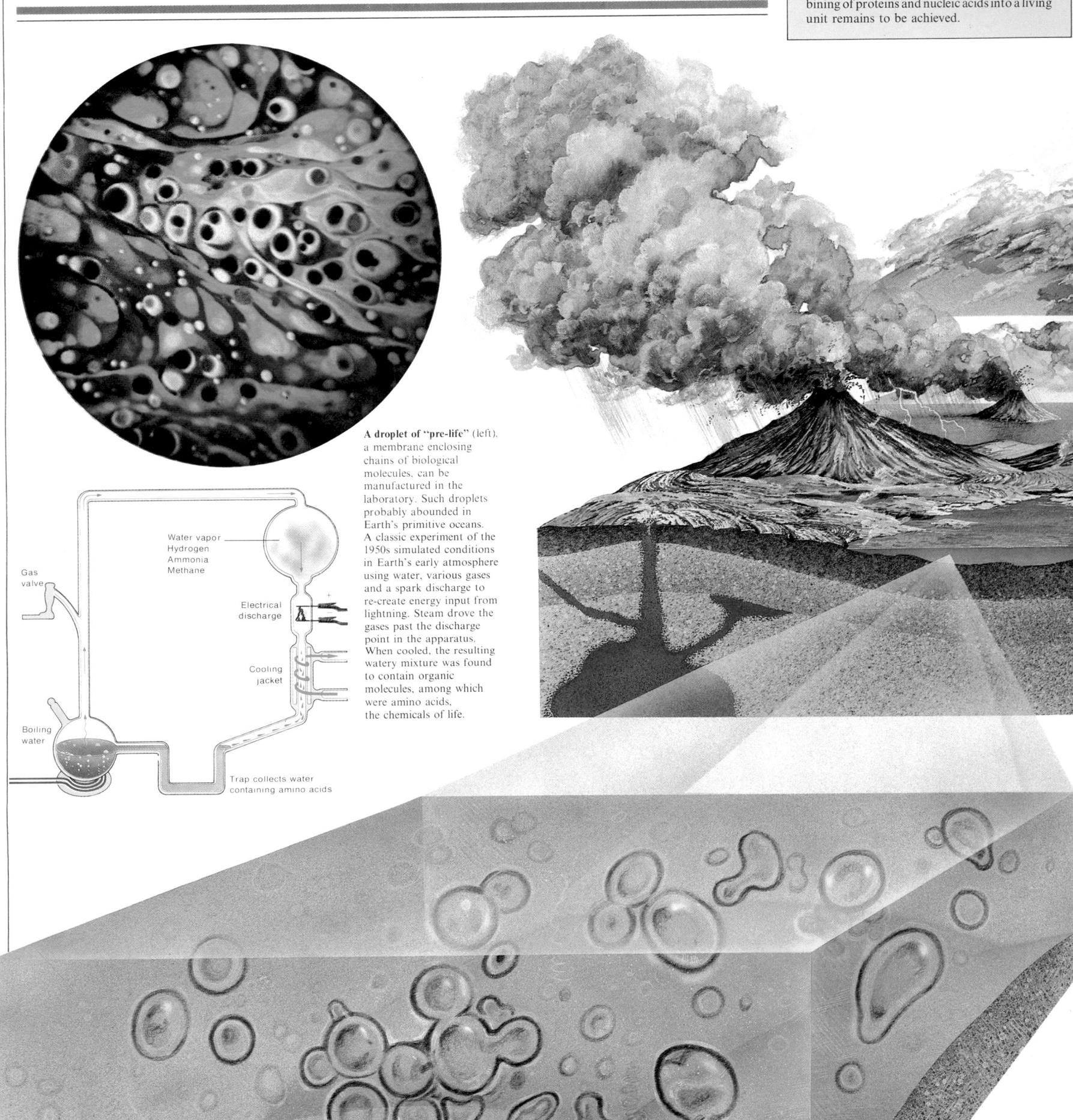

A droplet of "pre-life" (left), a membrane enclosing chains of biological molecules, can be manufactured in the laboratory. Such droplets probably abounded in Earth's primitive oceans. A classic experiment of the 1950s simulated conditions in Earth's early atmosphere using water, various gases and a spark discharge to re-create energy input from lightning. Steam drove the gases past the discharge point in the apparatus. When cooled, the resulting watery mixture was found to contain organic molecules, among which were amino acids, the chemicals of life.

Gas valve

Water vapor
Hydrogen
Ammonia
Methane

Electrical discharge

Cooling jacket

Boiling water

Trap collects water containing amino acids

LIFE BEGINS

A "primordial soup" of organic molecules, each separated from the water by a membrane, formed thick concentrations in Earth's shallow pools. From these evolved the long-chain polymers that form proteins and nucleic acids in every living cell.

The Source of Life

Life may have come to Earth from outer space – some meteorites contain life-like organic molecules – but the basic constituents of life, the biochemical structures called proteins and nucleic acids, could just as well have formed on Earth itself. By simulating possible primitive conditions on Earth, and applying a likely energy source, American scientists of the 1950s manufactured, from inorganic substances, the amino acids that form the subunits of all living things.

THE RADIANT SUN
A dense atmosphere of water vapor and various gases—but not oxygen—formed round the cooling planet Earth after its creation 4,600 million years ago. Oxygen in the atmosphere would have prevented the evolution of life from nonliving organic matter by blocking the Sun's ultraviolet radiation (which may have provided energy for the forming of organic compounds), and free oxygen would also have destroyed such compounds as they began to accumulate.

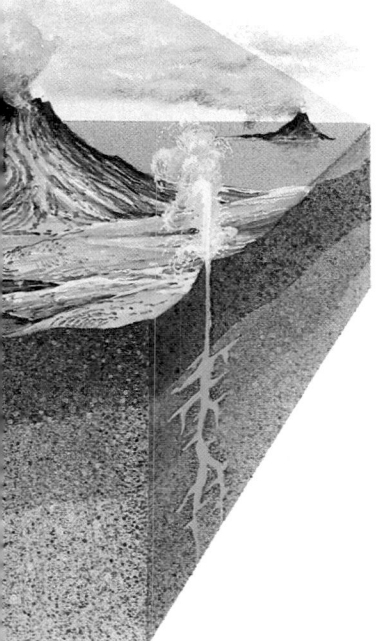

THE PRIMITIVE ATMOSPHERE
Volcanic eruptions drove water vapor and gases into the atmosphere of the young Earth; lightning and other discharges of atmospheric electricity accompanied the torrential rain; dissolved minerals collected in the pools. These were some of the preconditions for life on Earth, whereby mixtures of organic compounds in water may have combined to form more complex units essential for life.

Water played a key part in the creation of life on Earth. At first the temperature of the newly formed planet was far too high for water to exist in a liquid state. Instead, it formed a dense atmosphere of steam, which, as the Earth cooled, condensed into droplets of rain that poured down for perhaps thousands of years. This torrential, thundery rain eroded the land and dissolved the minerals, which collected in pools on the surface.

Earth's original atmosphere was also very different from today's. Most importantly, it contained no free oxygen, the gas which makes air-breathing life possible; the primitive atmosphere was composed of carbon monoxide, carbon dioxide, hydrogen and nitrogen. But the absence of oxygen created two conditions that are essential if life is to evolve. First, without oxygen the atmosphere could have no layer of ozone (an oxygen compound), which now acts as a barrier to most of the Sun's high-energy radiation (mainly ultraviolet light). Second, the absence of free oxygen meant that any complex chemicals that might be formed would not immediately break down again. Thus the molecules of life could form.

The chemistry of life

Life may be distinguished from nonlife in three ways: living organisms are able to increase the complexity of their parts through synthetic, self-building reactions; they obtain and use energy by breaking down chemical compounds; and they can make new copies of themselves.

It is the combined properties of the chemicals

THE MAKING OF AN AMINO ACID

The 20 amino acids found in the proteins of all living things are produced by combination, or synthesis, of basic molecules: the latter existed almost from the beginnings of Earth's history. Scientists have shown how molecules such as hydrogen, nitrogen and carbon monoxide can be combined to produce certain intermediate organic units. Further processing of these units involves the removal of water molecules to complete the amino acid.

Hydrogen
Methane
Carbon monoxide
Carbon dioxide
Ammonia
Nitrogen
Water

Water
Hydrogen cyanide
Aldehydes
Amino acid

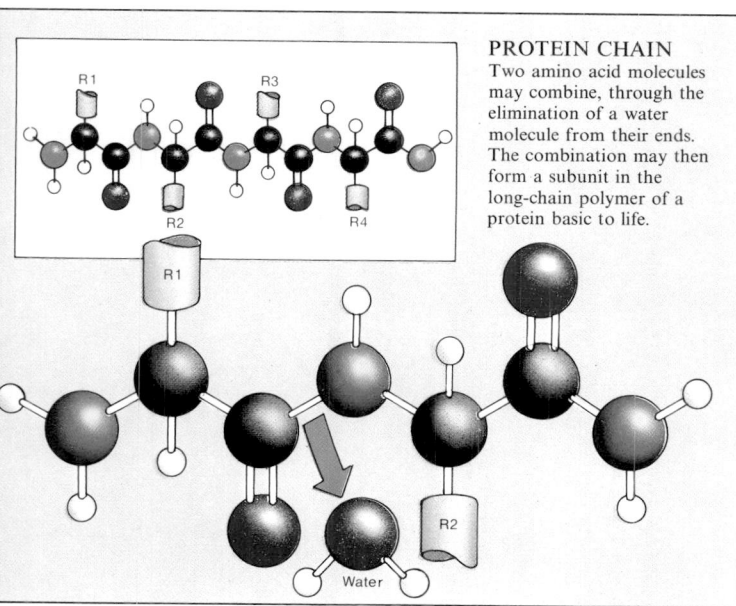

PROTEIN CHAIN
Two amino acid molecules may combine, through the elimination of a water molecule from their ends. The combination may then form a subunit in the long-chain polymer of a protein basic to life.

R1 R3
R2 R4
R1
R2
Water

of life that make them so special, not just the chemicals themselves. Experiments in the last few decades have given us a very good idea of how life could have arisen from the simple, non-living chemicals which compose it. In the early 1950s, Harold Urey and Stanley Miller simulated the atmosphere of a primitive world by filling a flask with water, ammonia, methane and hydrogen. They supplied it with energy in the form of heat and an electric spark—to simulate lightning—and the experiment was left to run for a week.

Analyzing the mixture formed, they found it contained many chemicals that are associated with living things, particularly nitrogen compounds called amino acids—the really important chemicals of life. Further experiments brought together other gas mixtures, including the one that is now thought to have covered the young Earth, and these gave similar results, as long as there was no free oxygen present. The resulting mixture of organic compounds in water came to be known as the "primordial

soup," and it is from this "soup" that life may have emerged.

Miller and Urey had shown that the basic substances of life can be derived from a primitive atmosphere. But there are still large gaps in our understanding of how these substances became more organized and self-regulating: in other words, how they became alive. More complex molecular structures somehow developed through the linking up of the basic units to form long, chain-like sequences of larger units, called polymers. But how this happened is still not fully understood.

The two most important classes of biological molecules are proteins and nucleic acids, both of which are polymers. Proteins are the building materials of living matter, the chief components of muscles, skin and hair. They also form enzymes—the chemicals that control biochemical reaction in living cells. Nucleic acids—DNA (deoxyribonucleic acid) and RNA (ribonucleic acid)—are so called because they are found in the central nuclei of cells. They are the cell's genetic material, the raw stuff of heredity. They act as the memories and the messengers of life, storing information in units called genes, and releasing that information to the cells when it is needed. Nucleic acids can reproduce themselves and, without this ability, life would not exist or continue.

The basic units that link together to form proteins are amino acids, and all proteins in living organisms are made up of just 20 different amino acids. In chemical terms, a protein molecule is a polymer consisting of a long chain of amino acid units joined together in a particular sequence, and the code to this sequence is held by DNA.

How living chemicals joined

Experiments with simulated primordial conditions have produced many amino acids other than the 20 commonly found in proteins. All amino acids (and other types of chemicals) tend to "stick" onto the surface of clay, but those 20 found in proteins stick particularly well to clays rich in the metal nickel. This suggests that the first proteins may have been formed in pools or on the fringes of seas, where the primordial soup was in contact with nickel-rich clays. There heat from the Sun or a volcano could have combined the amino acids to form a primitive protein.

The four classes of chemicals that form the basic components of nucleic acids have also, like the amino acids, been "cooked up" in a primordial soup, and they too will stick to clay to form long-chain polymers. And, just as nickel-rich clays are best at absorbing the amino acid constituents of protein, so clays rich in zinc absorb the building blocks of nucleic acids. This suggests that such clays could have been the birthplace of genes, which are the "messengers" of inheritance.

However, the coupling of proteins and nucleic acids, which together form the living cell, has yet to be explained, and it is improbable that proteins or nucleic acids alone could have provided the basis for life.

The Russian biochemist I. A. Oparin has shown that, in water, solutions of polymers (such as proteins) have a tendency to form droplets surrounded by an outer membrane very like that which encloses living cells. As these droplets grow by absorbing more polymers, some split in two when they become too large for stability. If such a droplet had protein enzymes to harness energy and make more polymers, and if it had nucleic acids with instructions for making those proteins, and if each new droplet received a complete copy of the nucleic acid instructions, the droplet would be alive—it would be a living cell.

The Structure of Life

All life forms stem from a single cell, and every cell contains in its nucleus instructions for the re-creation of the organism of which it forms a part. These are encoded in chromosomes, which contain the miraculous molecular substance of DNA, sectioned into units of heredity called genes. The genetic code determines in detail the physical characteristics of an individual creature, so that variations in DNA cause variations in the individual. Scientists believe that it is the interaction of the individual variation with the environment that ultimately leads to the evolution of the similar, interbreeding groups of creatures that are known as species.

THE HIDDEN SECRET
Dramatic discoveries in recent decades have revolutionized biology, the primary life science. Scientists can now trace parts of the genetic blueprint that lays down the pattern for every form of life, linking the large-scale unfolding of species that we know as evolution with the ultramicroscopic activity of the molecules within the nucleus of every cell. This may be the secret behind the rich diversity of life on Earth.

Deoxyribonucleic acid (DNA) consists of a "backbone" of alternating sugar and phosphate molecules, and to each sugar is attached one of four nitrogenous bases (adenine, guanine, thymine and cytostine, or A, G, T, C). A single gene might contain 2,000 of these bases, and in the body cell of a human being the 46 chromosomes (thread-like bodies of DNA and protein) run to 3,000 million bases. The sequence of these bases stores the information for making amino acids into proteins, just as the sequence of letters in this sentence stores the information for making a particular verbal structure. But the DNA alphabet has only four letters (A, G, T, C).

The thread of life

DNA is a double molecule, resembling a twisted ladder, its two main strands twining around each other to form the famous double helix. The strands are linked by pairs of bases—A and T, or G and C—whose shape is such that each pair fits together neatly, like pieces of a jigsaw, to form the rungs of the DNA ladder. As a result, the information on the strands can be duplicated by "unzipping" the double helix and making new strands by using the old ones as templates. DNA stores, duplicates and passes on the information that makes life alive.

Cells multiply by splitting in two, and each newly made cell thus gets instructions for its existence by the mechanism of heredity, the gene. But heredity is a word more often applied to the passing on of DNA from an organism to its offspring. In sexual reproduction the offspring gets some of the DNA (usually half) from one parent, and the rest from the other, ending up with a unique mix all of its own.

The laws of heredity

Man has long known that characteristics can be passed on from one generation to the next, for he has been selectively breeding crops and animals for thousands of years. However, it was not until the mid-nineteenth century that an obscure Austrian monk, Gregor Mendel (1822–84), discovered the laws that govern inheritance, and his work was ignored until the beginning of the twentieth century, when more powerful microscopes made possible the direct observation of the cell.

Mendel experimented with pea plants because they had easily recognizable traits, and because, although normally self-fertilizing, they could be cross-fertilized with pollen from a different plant. Mendel made many crosses between different pure-bred plants and found that in the offspring, or hybrids, some characters always prevailed over others: red flowers over white, tall plants over short, and so on. He called the prevailing characters dominant, and the nonprevailing characters recessive. He then let the first-generation hybrids self-fertilize, and found not only that the recessive traits reappeared in the hybrids' offspring, but also that they reappeared in a constant proportion of three dominant to one recessive; the second generation contained three times as many red-flowered peas as white-flowered peas.

To explain his results, Mendel proposed that each plant had two hereditary "factors"— today called alleles—for each character, and that the dominant factor suppressed the recessive factor. If a plant inherited both a dominant and a recessive factor, the dominant one would prevail. Only if both factors were recessive would the recessive character be apparent. Mendel found many other pairs of traits where one form was dominant and the other recessive. He established that permutations arising from the crossing of the two first-generation hybrids allows the dominant gene to be present in three out of four crosses in the second generation; but

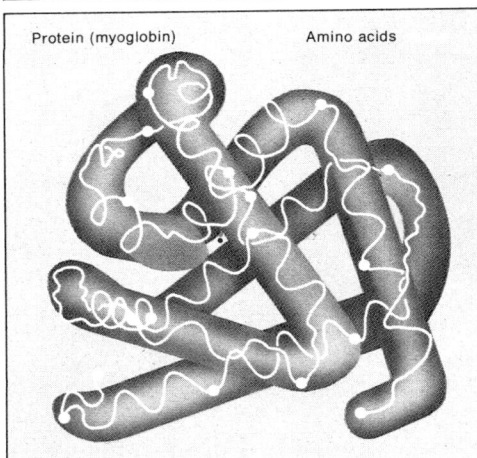

Genes

Protein (myoglobin)   Amino acids

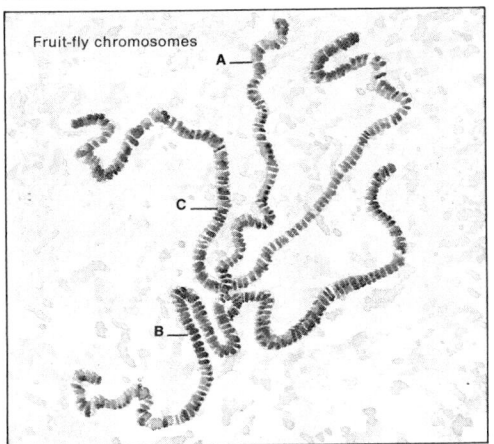

Fruit-fly chromosomes

Chromosomes

Cell

The cell is the basic unit of all life, and every cell contains in its nucleus the thread-like structures, called chromosomes, that control heredity. Each species has its own number of chromosomes, and the number is always the same for that species. Chromosomes are sectioned into genes, units of heredity made of DNA molecules. DNA acts like a code, specifying the order and number of amino acids that make up proteins— the organic compounds characteristic of all life.

Chromosomes (below left) of the fruit fly, much magnified, show bands of DNA arranged in sections that correspond exactly with specific genes, the chemical units of heredity. The proof of this correspondence came when the American geneticist Hermann Muller introduced the use of ionizing radiation to damage the fruit flies' chromosomes at ultra-microscopic points, causing precise point mutations in offspring of parents whose DNA had been damaged at the places indicated. Random mutations may occur in any organism, and not only as a result of radiation. A gradual accumulation of minor mutations may lead to evolutionary change.

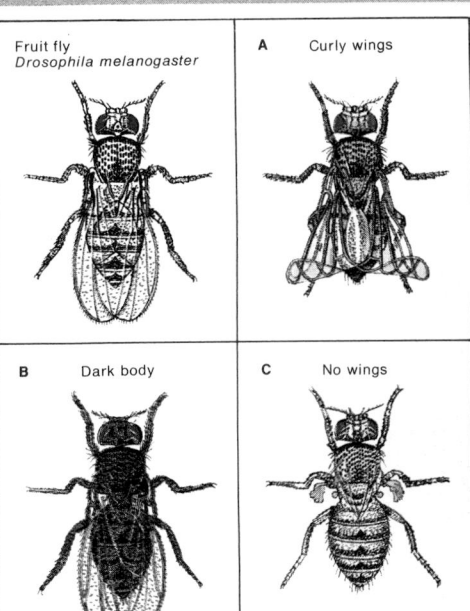

Fruit fly
Drosophila melanogaster

A   Curly wings

B   Dark body

C   No wings

in the fourth cross, only the two recessive alleles of the genes are present. So there is always a three-to-one ratio of dominant to recessive.

Theories of evolution

Mendel's work was of course unknown to his contemporaries, Charles Darwin and Alfred Russel Wallace, who even then were providing solutions to the major mystery of biology—the way that species evolve, change and develop over time. Evolution was not a new idea in Darwin's day. In 1809 the French naturalist Jean-Baptiste Lamarck had proposed a theory of the inheritance of acquired characteristics, suggesting that new habits learned by an organism in response to environmental change may become physically incorporated in the animal's descendants. For instance, the fact that the ancestral giraffe had to stretch its neck to reach food might give its offspring long necks to enable them to reach food more easily. Less satisfactory than the "natural selection" theory of Darwin and Wallace (who independently reached the same conclusion), Lamarckism founders on the fact that there is no genetic mechanism enabling acquired characters to pass on in this way.

Darwin's theory of natural selection has three key elements: all individuals vary, and some variations are passed on to the next generation; the gap between the potential and the actual number of offspring reproduced by organisms is very wide and implies that not all will survive; organisms best adapted to the environment will survive, their offspring will have been selected, and the favorable variation

will spread through the population, perhaps eventually changing it.

Genetic variation, the mainspring of natural selection, is reflected in variations of DNA, the material substance of heredity. Changes in the order of DNA's nitrogenous bases—called mutations—produce changes in the proteins which are usually, but not always, harmful. More important than these is the effect of genes recombining in sexually reproduced offspring.

Sexual reproduction provides the offspring with two sets of DNA, one from each parent. The processes that give rise to a half-set of chromosomes in a sperm or egg shuffle and recombine the genes on each chromosome to provide new combinations. Then, when sperm and egg fuse together at fertilization, the half-sets come together and even more combinations are produced. The world's enormous diversity of life can be explained in terms of a struggle that favors certain genetic combinations.

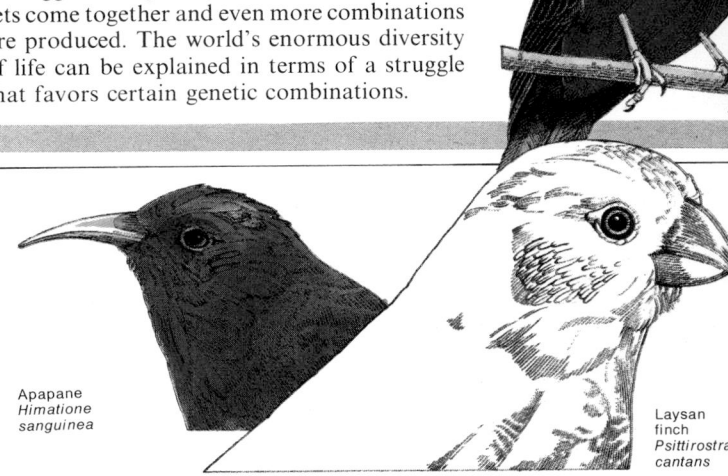

Iiwi
Vestiaria coccinea

Apapane
Himatione sanguinea

Laysan finch
Psittirostra cantans

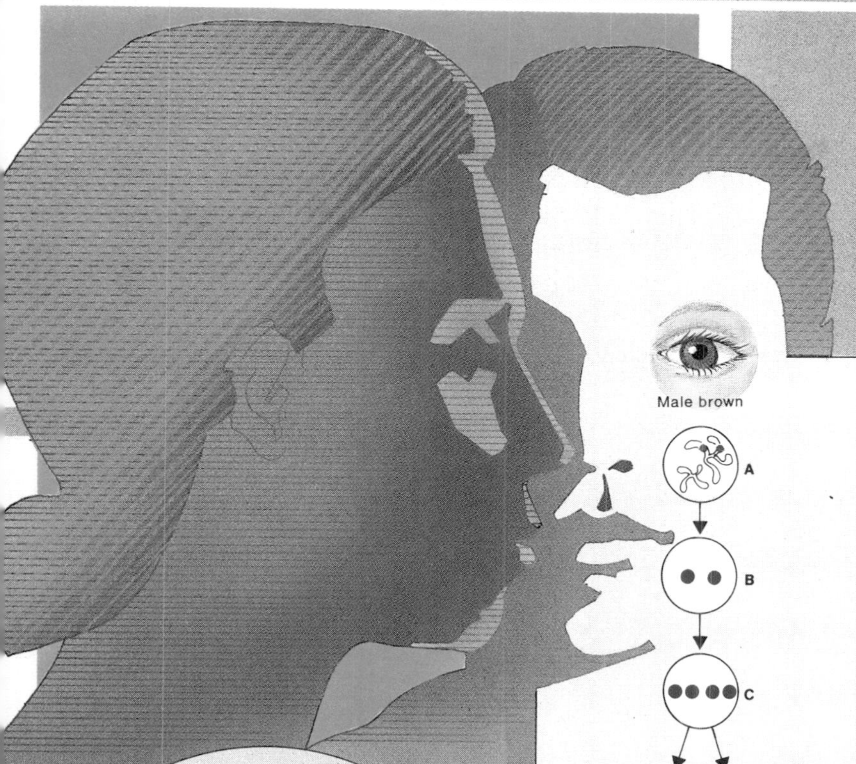

Some human traits, such as eye color, are inherited as single factors (below). In such cases one gene is dominant over the other, recessive, gene, and the gene giving a brown eye color is always dominant over that which gives a blue eye color. The chromosomes carrying eye-color genes (A) pair (B) and duplicate (C, D) before dividing twice (E, F) in the process known as meiosis, or reduction division. This ensures that the offspring gets half the chromosomes from the male and half from the female parent, so each new cell gets both genes when sperm and egg unite. But because brown-eye genes are dominant over blue, all offspring have brown eyes, with the blue-eye gene hidden. But if two brown-eyed parents carry recessive blue-eye genes, half the male sperm cells have blue-eye genes, and the female eggs carry a gene for either blue or brown eyes. So the two recessive genes have a one-in-four chance of being combined to produce a blue-eyed child, no brown-eye genes being present.

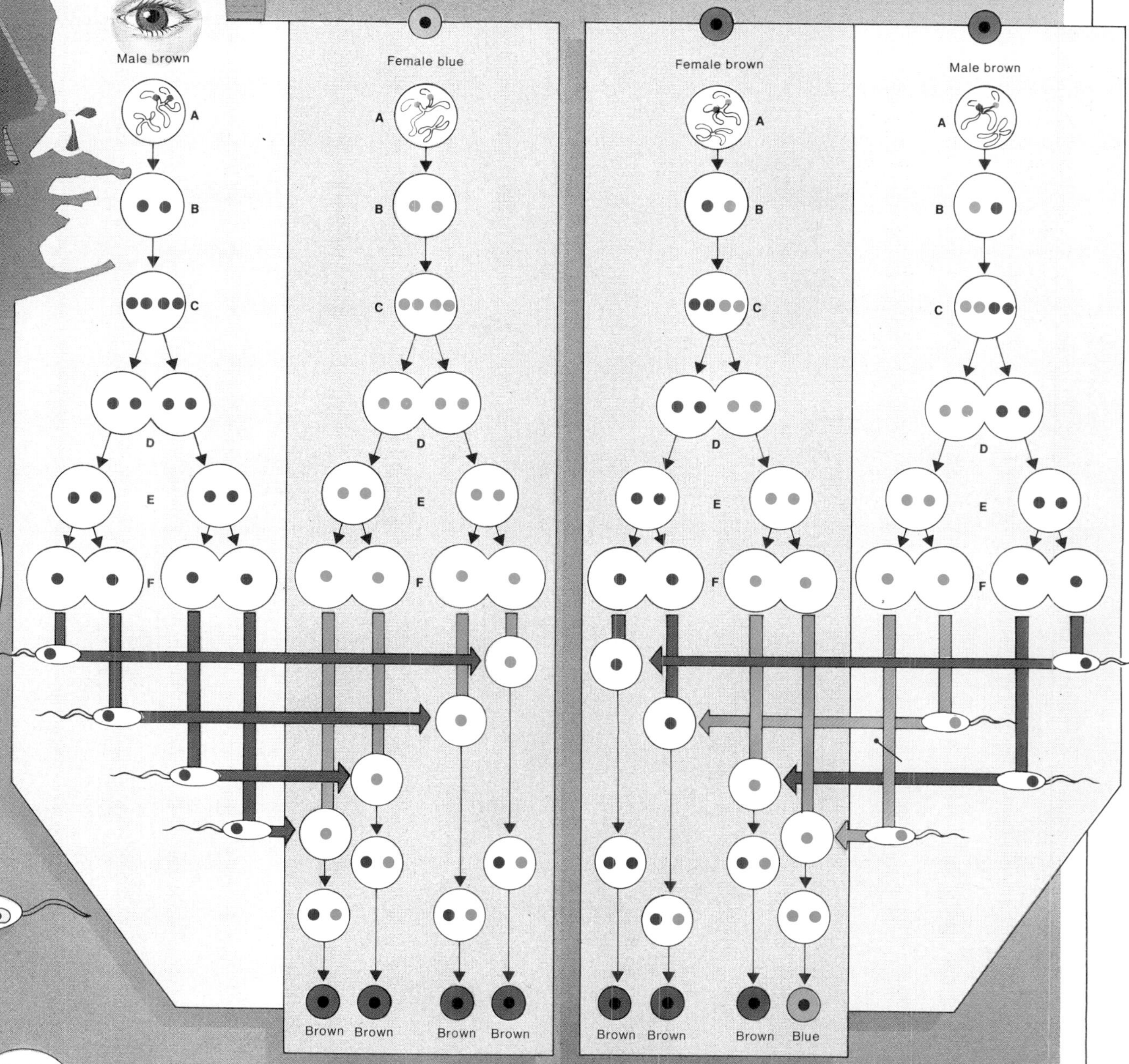

Male brown

Female blue

Female brown

Male brown

A

B

C

D

E

F

Brown Brown Brown Brown Brown Brown Brown Blue

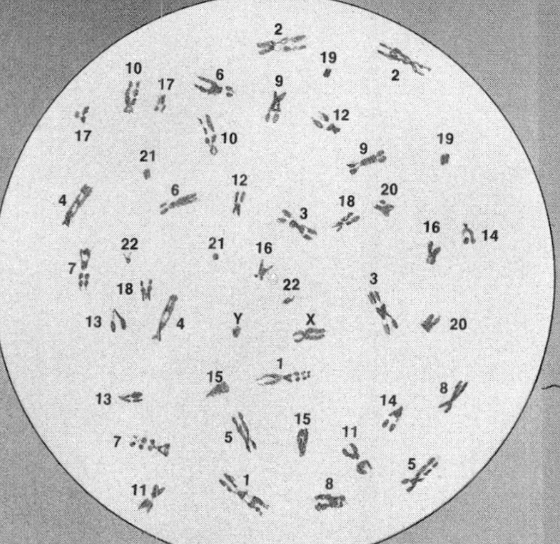

Egg

Sperm

Zygote

Replication

Meiosis

Recombination

Body cell division

First division

Second division

Second division

Sperm cells

A human body cell (above) contains 46 chromosomes—22 matching pairs and the chromosomes (X, Y) which determine sex. Males have X and Y, females X and X. In sexual reproduction (right) traits carried by the male sperm and the female egg combine in the zygote, the fertilized egg from which new life starts. All growth is the result of repeated cell division, or mitosis, where the nucleus forms paired chromosomes that duplicate themselves; the cell splits, and the chromosomes re-form in the nucleus of the new cells. Sex cells are produced by reduction division, or meiosis, with each cell taking only one from each pair of chromosomes, which exchange corresponding segments in the process called recombination. The genes are thus reshuffled at each generation, so that new combinations of gene traits are available for selection each time meiosis takes place. The result is genetic diversity, with many possibilities for the species to adapt to a changing environment.

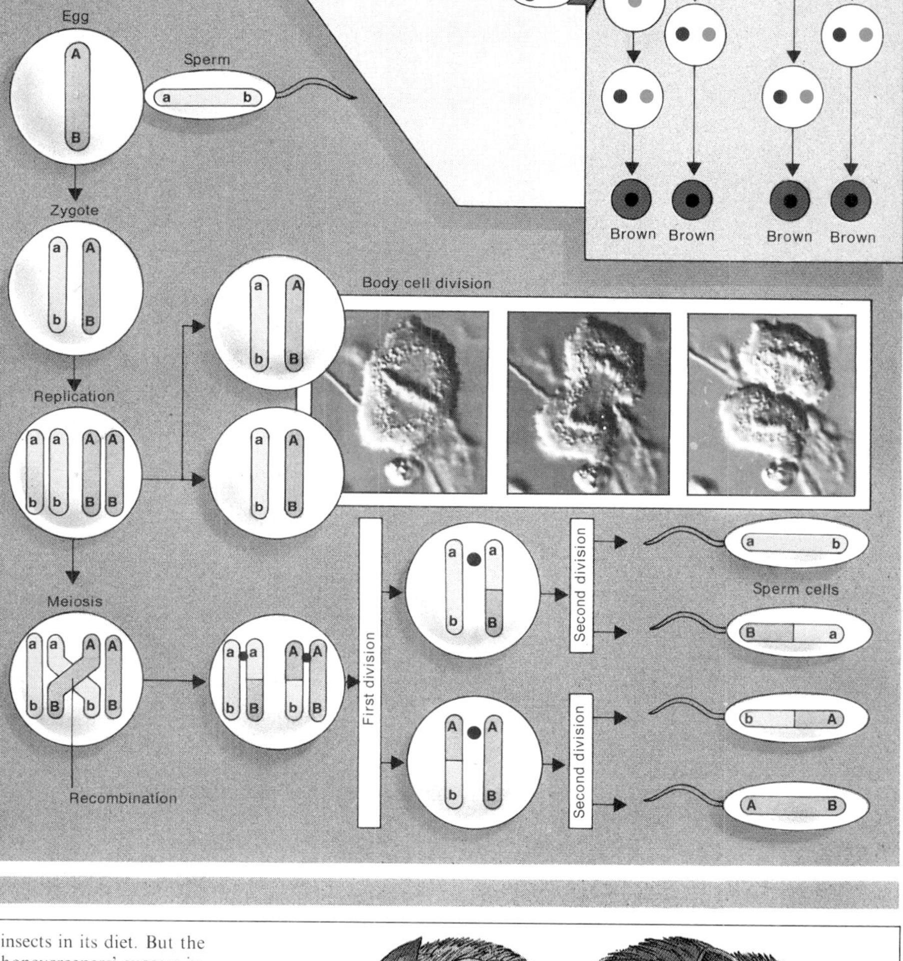

A diversity of forms (left) has stemmed from a single ancestor of the Hawaiian honeycreeper, which now numbers 14 species. These have adapted in their mid-Pacific isolation to fill niches usually taken by other birds, ranging from the nectar-feeding iiwi to the Laysan finch with its thick beak for cracking seeds, and the short-billed apapane, which includes insects in its diet. But the honeycreepers' success in divergence may have led to overspecialization, with at least eight species now extinct. The Australian marsupial mouse and the Indian spiny mouse (right) look very similar, due to the fact that they fill similar ecological niches, but they belong to groups evolving separately for almost 100 million years.

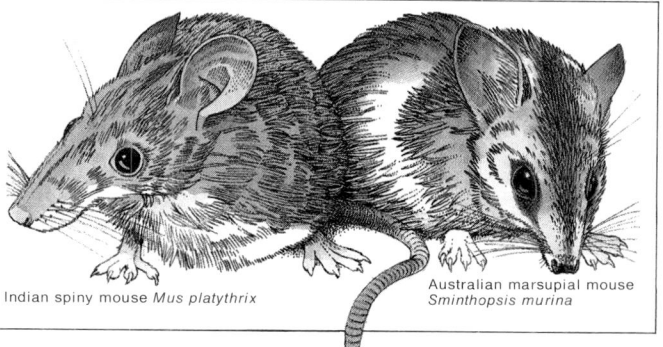

Indian spiny mouse *Mus platythrix*

Australian marsupial mouse *Sminthopsis murina*

VARIANT FORMS

Dark forms of many insects, such as the peppered moth *Biston betularia*, have developed widely in industrial areas of the world since the industrial age. The dark variant, resulting from a single genetic mutation, escapes the eye of predators against the black, lichen-free bark of soot-darkened trees (top), whereas the typical pale form is very conspicuous. In rural, unpolluted areas where tree trunks are light and lichen covered (bottom) the well-concealed pale form is much commoner. *Biston*'s rapid evolutionary response is remarkable: in 1849 only one dark example was recorded at Manchester, England, but by 1900 98% of the moths caught in the area were of the dark type. A similar change occurred in other industrial areas, during the period when the most coal was being burned and the population was most rapidly expanding. But with today's clean-air laws the number of pale moths in these areas is once again on the increase.

Earliest Life Forms

Earth's original atmosphere lacked oxygen, without which there could be no survival for air-breathing creatures. This vital gas was supplied by life itself, in the form of microscopic organisms that flourished in the atmosphere of the time and emitted oxygen as "waste." In this way a breathable atmosphere built up; increasingly complex life forms were able to develop in the seas; early plants and insects gained a foothold on the shores; and, finally, larger animals could survive on land.

A BREATHABLE ATMOSPHERE

Without oxygen, life as we know it could not exist; yet Earth's original atmosphere contained practically none. The oxygenation of the atmosphere was the work of the planet's first life—primeval bacteria and algae. Of these, some released oxygen as waste while consuming carbon dioxide or nitrogen in photosynthesis. Colonies of algae forming stromatolites ("stony carpets") generated even more oxygen, but this was first taken up by ocean rocks, visible today as "banded iron formations." Once all the ocean rocks were oxidized, an oxygen-rich atmosphere could develop, with an ozone layer to filter out harmful radiation from the Sun.

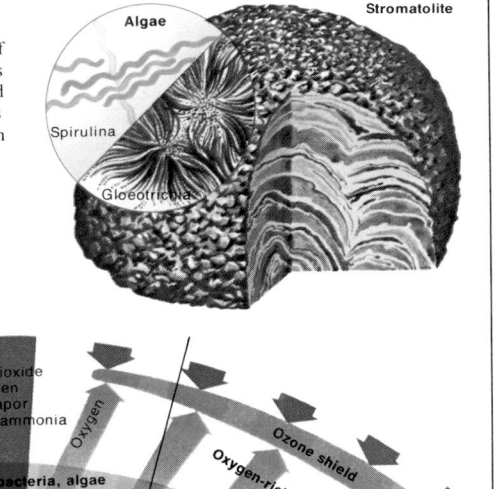

Algae
Spirulina
Gloeotrichia
Stromatolite

Sunlight
Ultraviolet rays
Ocean
Oxygen-free atmosphere
Carbon dioxide
Nitrogen
Water vapor
Primitive bacteria
Carbon dioxide
Nitrogen
Water vapor
Hydrogen in ammonia
Photosynthetic bacteria, algae
Stromatolites
Oxygen
Banded iron formation
Sediments
Oxygen
Oxygen-rich atmosphere
Ozone shield
Photosynthetic oxygen-using bacteria

Scientists have identified bacteria-like microfossils in the rocks that were formed more than 3,500 million years ago. Some of these organisms appear to have been capable of photosynthesis—the process of utilizing sunlight, water and carbon dioxide for "food," with release of oxygen as the vitally important by-product. As a result, surplus oxygen very gradually accumulated in the Earth's atmosphere, forming an upper-atmosphere shield of ozone (which kept out damaging ultraviolet radiation from the Sun) and providing an oxygen-rich atmosphere in which breathing life could develop.

At least five types of microfossil have been found in ancient sediments of Western Australia, aged about 3,560 million years, and these provide the earliest evidence of life so far discovered. Other early proof of life comes from the so-called "stromatolites," some of which may date back as far as 3,400 million years. These curious columns, growing in warm, shallow waters, are formed of blue-green algae which have entrapped chalky sediments, bacteria and other microfossils. Their study is made easier by the fact that similar structures have developed at later geological times, and some are even being formed at the present day.

Living below the surface of the water and not initially reliant on oxygen for life, such bacteria and algae were shielded from the Sun's ultraviolet rays as they imperceptibly altered the Earth's atmosphere. For hundreds of millions of years life of this kind persisted, with few obvious developments or changes.

Breathing life

About 1,800 million years ago, the effects of these microscopic photosynthesizers became dramatically apparent in the "rusting" of the ocean rocks, when the red color of the rocks being formed at that time indicates that there was enough free oxygen on Earth to bring about the process known as oxidation. Once the ocean rocks capable of absorbing oxygen had done so, forming the red "banded iron formations" known to geologists, oxygen could enter the atmosphere in ever greater quantities.

It has been estimated that a breathable atmosphere existed on Earth about 1,700 million years ago, and aerobic (oxygen-using) organisms first became abundant not very long afterwards. These organisms were single celled, and it may have been almost 1,000 million years before multicellular animals evolved. The fossilized remains of animals alive 800 million years ago have been found in many parts of the world, but it is not yet known whether multicellular animals had a long history before these earliest known forms, or whether they had developed and radiated rapidly from a creature capable of feeding as well as photosynthesizing.

One of the earliest collections of animals of this type was discovered in the Ediacara Sandstones of the Flinders Range in Australia, where some 650 million years ago the rocks once formed part of an ancient beach. Here a spectacular collection of soft-bodied animals, similar to today's coelenterates (such as jellyfish) and worms, was washed ashore and preserved in silt from the nearby shallow sea. Comparable, mainly floating forms have been found in other parts of the world in rocks dating from between 650 and 580 million years ago.

The first vertebrates

One of the most important changes in animal life seems to have occurred about 580 million years ago. At that date many creatures evolved hard, protective shells, which also acted as areas of muscle attachment and as support for their bodies—in other words, as external skeletons. Hard shells were more easily preserved as fossils than the soft bodies of earlier animals, so rich collections have been recovered from rocks of the Cambrian Period, beginning 580 million years ago, as well as from later strata.

The first fish-like animals—the earliest true vertebrates—are found in rocks of the Ordovician Period, from about 500 million years ago, and these were in many ways very similar to the lampreys and hagfishes of today. But unlike them, these ancient creatures were heavily armored with external bone. They must have been poor swimmers, living mainly on the seabed and filtering edible particles from the sediments, which they sucked into their jawless mouths. From them arose true fishes, with backbones, jaws and teeth, and they came to replace the less efficient earlier forms.

During the Devonian Period, about 400 million years ago, the fishes diversified greatly, adapting to fit all kinds of aquatic environments. Some grew to a huge size, such as *Dunkleosteus*, which achieved a length of up to 9 m (29 ft 7 in), although it belonged to a group of fishes that retained heavy armor. Some of these curious creatures probably used their stilt-like pectoral fins to hitch themselves across the beds of the pools in which they lived.

From water to land

The fishes that teemed in the seas and fresh waters of the Devonian world found their way into difficult environments such as swamps and oasis pools, where there was a danger of drying out in the warmer weather. Many of these fishes had rudimentary lungs, and one group developed powerful jointed fins.

Such marginal habitats were not ideal for fishes, but they were nevertheless rich in species, and it is from them that the first land vertebrates developed. When the water dried up they survived, for their strong fins held them up so that they did not flop over helplessly.

They found themselves in a new, dry world, but one which was already inhabited, at least round the water's edges, with plants related to modern liverworts, mosses and club mosses. There were also numerous invertebrate animals such as millipedes, spiders and wingless insects. These plants and animals provided shelter and food, so that the environment was not wholly hostile to larger animals.

The first steps on land probably took the form of strong flexions of the body—desperate swimming movements which swung the fins forward, pegging the animal's position in the drying mud. But in a very short time geologically, animals had evolved in which the rays of the lobe fins had vanished, leaving stubby legs with which the animals—no longer fishes but amphibians—could haul themselves over land. But they still had to return to water to breed and lay eggs.

THE FIRST SHELLED CREATURES

These evolved (right) in the seas when conditions allowed soft-bodied life to form protective casings. In the fossil record of 550 million years ago, soft and shelled forms are found. The trilobites (1, 2, 3)— a now extinct order of woodlouse-like animals— dominated the scene, but other early arthropods (4) included a possible insect ancestor (5), and there may even have been an ancestor to fish (6). Sponges (7), crinoids (8), early moluscs (9), bristleworms (10) and lamp-shells (11) were plentiful, but other creatures (12) are bewilderingly strange.

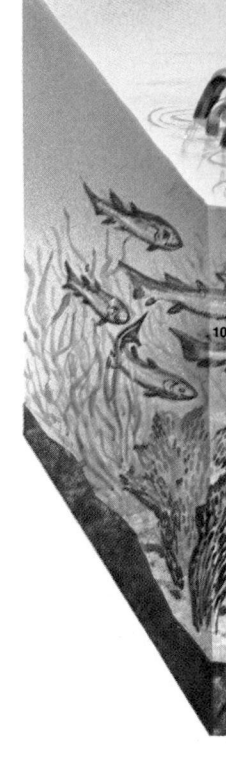

THE FIRST AMPHIBIANS

Amphibians (1) emerged some 345 million years ago (right), inhabiting swampy environments with luxuriant vegetation—club mosses and ferns (2, 3) that made up the early coal forests. Lungfish (4) were well adapted to life in oxygen-poor waters, but the move to land was probably made by related fish with a passage linking nostrils to throat—*Eusthenopteron* (5). Land offered food (6, 7, 8) and suitably damp conditions for a possibly stranded aquatic animal.

Palaeozoic | Mesozoic | Cenozoic

500 | 400 | 300 | 200 | 100 | 0

Millions of years ago

A timescale of life on Earth emerges from the record of fossils embedded in rock strata. Major breaks in faunas (animal assemblages) separate eras coinciding roughly with periods of intense mountain-building activity. These eras are broken down into geological periods, which are separated by lesser faunal breaks and which are generally named from the area where rocks of that age were first discovered. The geological eras and periods do not imply particular rock types.

600 | Shelled/skeletal animals | **CAMBRIAN** | 550 | First fishes | **ORDOVICIAN**

Soft-bodied animals

The Solar System forms
5,000 million years
Earth forms
4,000
Oldest micro-fossils
Oxygen-creating bacteria
Stromatolites, blue-green algae
3,000
Ozone shield forms
Oxygen in atmosphere
2,000
Breathable atmosphere
Many oxygen-using animals
Sexual reproduction
1,000
900
Multi-cellular life
800
700
Soft-bodied animals

THE AGE OF JELLYFISH

Jellyfish (left) and other soft-bodied animals flourished in the pre-Cambrian seas, more than 600 million years ago. The forms of one group, imprinted on sand, have been preserved as fossils in the Australian Ediacara Sandstones. They include varieties similar to modern jellyfish (1, 2); worm-like crawlers (3); sea pens (4) very like modern types; segmented worms (5); "three-legged" creatures like no known animal (6); and sand casts of burrowing worms (7).

LIFE ON SEA AND LAND

For more than half the Earth's existence, its atmosphere has been hostile to air-breathing life. Then, about 1,600 million years ago, the photosynthesizing action of minute organisms built up enough free oxygen in the atmosphere for more complex oxygen-dependent forms to develop. The first multicellular life led to the soft-bodied animals of the pre-Cambrian time—worms, jellyfish and sea pens. About 580 million years ago many animals developed hard parts, including shells. Over 1,200 new marine species date from this period, and the evolutionary explosion came to fill the Earth's seas with fishes. Some of these had powerful jointed fins and rudimentary lungs, and lived in swamps where primitive plants and insects had already made the move to land. As the pools dwindled the stranded animals could survive by breathing air.

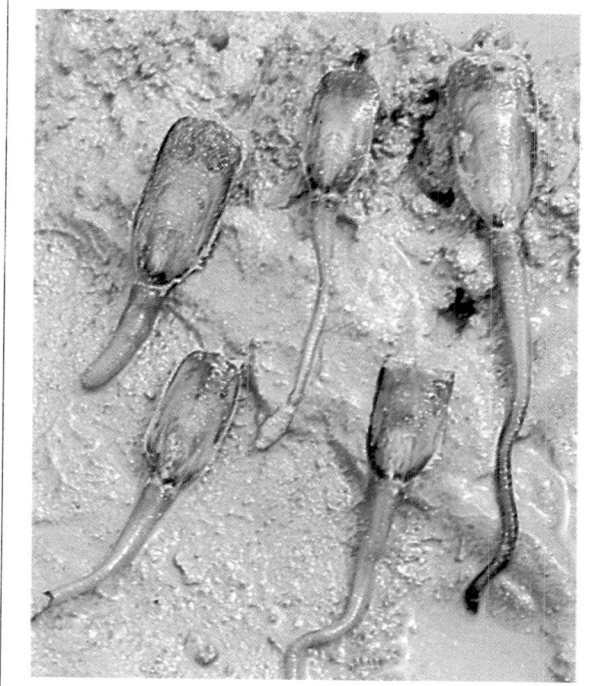

LIVING FOSSILS

Some life forms that emerged 570 million years ago have survived virtually unchanged to the present day. These "living fossils" include *Lingula* (left), today found in warm, brackish coastal waters, poor in oxygen and unsuited to most life, off the Pacific and Indian oceans. *Neopilina* (below), a primitive marine mollusc first found alive in 1952, has features unlike other molluscs but suggesting much closer affinities with the annelids (worms) and arthropods (insects, crabs, etc.).

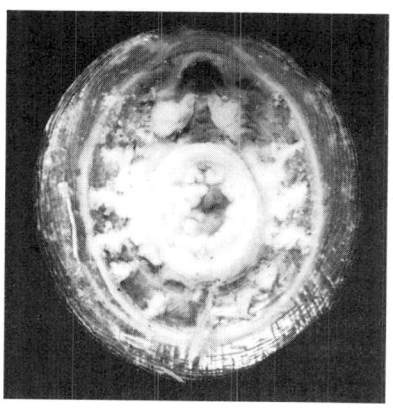

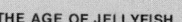

THE AGE OF JELLYFISH
1 Jellyfish (*Ediacaria*)
2 Jellyfish (*Medusina*)
3 Flatworm (*Dickinsonia costata*)
4 Sea pens (*Rangea, Charnia*)
5 Segmented worms (*Spriggina floundersi*)
6 Unknown animal (*Tribrachidium*)
7 Burrowing worm (fossil casts)
8 Sponges and algae (hypothetical)

THE FIRST SHELLED CREATURES
1 Trilobites (*Waptia*)
2 Trilobites (*Marella splendens*)
3 Trilobite (*Olenoides serratus*)
4 Primitive arthropod (*Perspicaris dictynna*)
5 Primitive arthropod (*Aysheaia pedunculata*)
6 Ancestral lancelet fish (*Branchiostoma*)
7 Sponge (*Vauxia*)
8 Crinoids (*Echmatocrinus*)
9 Mollusc (*Wiwaxia*)
10 Bristleworm (*Nereis*)
11 Brachiopod (*Lingulella*)
12 Unknown animal (*Hailucigenia sparsa*)

THE AGE OF FISHES
1 Primitive plant (*Nematophyton*)
2 Psilophite plant (*Asteroxylon*)
3 Psilophite plant (*Rhynia*)
4 Primitive insect (*Rhyniella*)
5 Placoderm fish (*Bothriolepis*)
6 Placoderm fish (*Phyllolepis*)
7 Placoderm fish (*Dunkleosteus*)
8 Early shark (*Cladoselache*)
9 Lungfish (*Dipterus*)
10 Lobe-fin fish (*Osteolepis*)
11 Crustacean (*Montecaris*)

THE FIRST AMPHIBIANS
1 Amphibian (*Ichthyostega*)
2 Club moss (*Cyclostigma*)
3 Fern (*Pseudosporochnus*)
4 Lungfish (*Scaumenacia*)
5 Rhipidistian fish (*Eusthenopteron*)
6 Millipede (*Acantherpestes ornatus*)
7 Early scorpion (*Palaeophonus*)
8 Spider-like creature (*Palaeocharinoides*)
9 Small plant (*Sciadophyton*)

THE AGE OF FISHES

Fishes (left) filled the brackish Devonian waters, about 350 million years ago, while primitive plants and insects had pioneered the land. Giant weeds (1) grew above muddy waters, and vascular plants (2, 3) colonized the shores, sheltering early insects (4). Primitive fishes (5, 6, 7) remained, but ray-finned types (8)—ancestors of modern fish—were dominant. However, it was from the lobe-finned fishes (9, 10) that the first land vertebrates emerged.

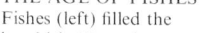

The Age of Reptiles

When the Carboniferous Period began, the world was already populated with animals and plants of many kinds. The oceans were full of fishes, invertebrates and aquatic plants. The land, meanwhile, was producing dramatic new species: giant mosses and ferns, spiders and insects and, most important of all, the rapidly evolving amphibians. These creatures were taking the first evolutionary steps on a path that would lead to some of the most remarkable creatures ever to live – the dinosaurs.

The broad, low-lying, swampy plains of the late Carboniferous provided ideal conditions for the world's early plants. They spread and diversified, and some of them grew to enormous size. Giant club mosses, huge horsetails and luxuriant tree ferns took on the proportions of modern-day trees and formed the world's first forests. These new forests were full of animal life: primitive spiders and scorpions hunting their prey, giant dragonflies hovering over the marshy waters and other insects scavenging or hunting on the mossy forest floor or in the branches of the "trees." In the huge coal-forest swamps, the most advanced of all animals, the amphibians, were rapidly evolving. Some of these would ultimately return to life in the water. But others were developing stronger legs and were becoming better able to cope with an existence on dry land.

It was from this second group that the reptiles evolved—the first animals to be equipped with waterproof skins. Unlike their amphibian ancestors, they could stay out of the water indefinitely without losing their body fluids through their skins. They were no longer tied to the water's edge and the pattern of life was revolutionized. The world was soon inhabited by the first wave of land vertebrates—reptiles, which then rapidly diversified.

Included among these first reptiles were creatures known as sailbacks. They had a row of long, bony spines that supported a great fin running down from the back of their heads to the base of their tails. This whole apparatus functioned as a heat-exchange organ: the fin absorbed heat from the atmosphere in the early, cooler parts of the day, when the animal was cold, and blushed off warmth later, when it became overheated. Unlike the cold-blooded reptiles, sailbacked reptiles could, to a certain extent, regulate their body temperatures.

Mammal-like reptiles

It was only about 50 million years later, however, that animals skeletally identical to mammals were found throughout the world. Almost certainly these creatures had a degree of warm-bloodedness. But they were all rather small—the biggest was no larger than a domestic cat—and this may account for their decline. They were destined to be overshadowed for many millions of years by the dinosaurs.

The late Triassic Period, about 200 million years ago, is marked by a sudden decline in the

THE RULING REPTILES

Seymouria and other advanced amphibians evolved to form the first reptiles, such as *Scutosaurus*. From these a multitude of adaptations evolved. Some herbivores, such as *Corythosaurus*, developed 2,000 or more teeth, to help them consume tough, fibrous food plants. Another herbivorous group attained enormous size—*Brachiosaurus* weighed as much as 80 tonnes—and this may have been an adaptation to regulate body temperature (large objects lose and gain heat more slowly than small objects). Another adaptation, but one that developed mainly in the carnivores, was that of offensive weaponry: *Deinonychus* had a huge sickle-shaped claw on each hind foot and the later *Tyrannosaurus* combined a massive body with a jagged mouthful of 60 teeth. Armor plating was a defensive adaptation, produced by herbivores such as *Triceratops*, whereas speed of movement was developed both by some herbivores and by small carnivores such as *Struthiomimus*.

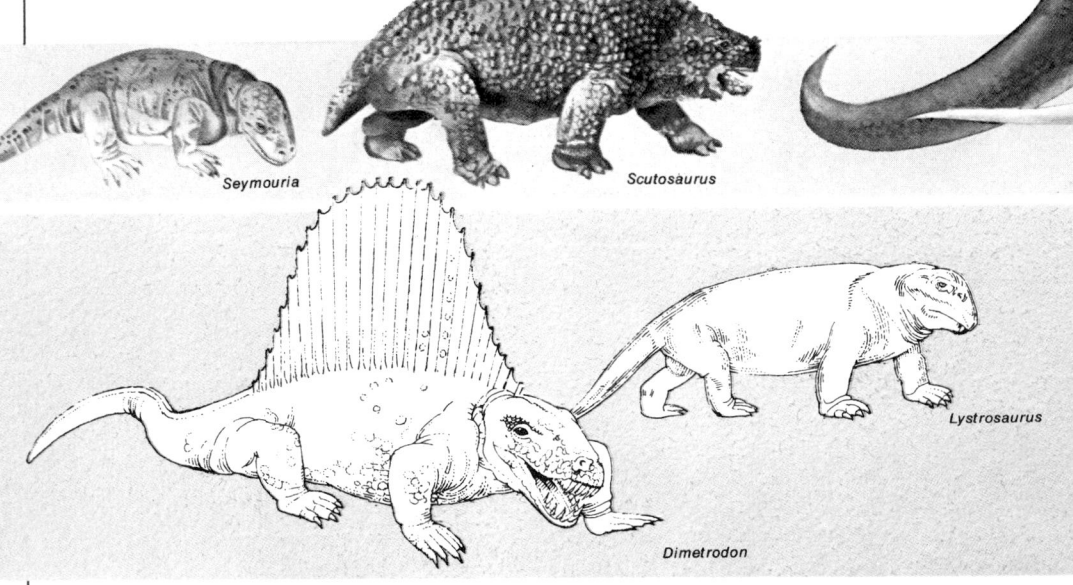

Corythosaurus

Seymouria

Scutosaurus

Deinonychus

Lystrosaurus

Dimetrodon

THE MAMMAL LINE

Sailbacks such as *Dimetrodon* mark the beginning of mammal history. These reptiles had developed the first method of regulating body temperature—each was equipped with a large fin on its back which acted as a heat-exchange organ, a living solar panel. From these strange creatures, para-mammals such as *Lystrosaurus* evolved, animals with many mammal-like features. Some of the later members of this group, such as *Thrinaxodon*, probably even had fur on their bodies. Then, about 200 million years ago, the first true warm-blooded mammals, such as *Morganucodon*, developed. But by this time the group as a whole was declining in response to reptilian competition. Mammals would have to wait 140 million years before becoming successful again.

Thrinaxodon

Morganucodon

COAL FORMATION

Coal consists of carbon from plant remains and most of it was formed in the swamp-forests from which reptiles emerged. First, peat formed from rotted vegetation. Sea levels rose, ocean covered the peat bogs and marine sediments were laid down. The resulting pressure converted peat to coal. The cycle recurred and the deepest coal seams were compressed and hardened.

Coal-forming forest swamp

Peat layer

Lignite seam

Bituminous seam

Anthracite seam

Palaeozoic			Mesozoic		Cenozoic	
500	400	300	200	100	0	

Millions of years ago

Three geological eras mark the evolution of life on Earth. It was the Mesozoic era, beginning 230 million years ago, that spanned the age of reptiles. Until then, throughout the Palaeozoic era, life had been slowly evolving from the primitive organisms that appeared 400 million years earlier.

By the Mesozoic, the earliest reptiles had developed. Among their descendants were dinosaurs and early representatives of the mammalian line. Mammals, however, would have to wait another 165 million years, until the Cenozoic, before they achieved dominance.

The plant communities underwent as many developments in the course of the Mesozoic era as did the reptiles. The end of the Palaeozoic saw changes in climate—the Permian Period was much drier than the Carboniferous. Giant horsetails, ferns and club mosses that had formed the world's first forests gave way to other types of plant: early conifers and their relatives

(the gymnosperms) came to the fore. These new species, such as the Cycadales, had evolved a new, improved method of reproduction—using seeds not spores. By Jurassic times, the climate had changed again and the moist conditions supported dense forests of ferns and of conifers. The final major Mesozoic development took place in Cretaceous times, when the flowering plants evolved.

Cycadale

Gingko biloba

CARBONIFEROUS | 300 | Earliest reptiles | PERMIAN | Early conifers | 250 | First radiation of reptiles | TRIASSIC | First mammals

40

EVOLUTION AND ADAPTATION

Once their amphibian ancestors had crawled from the swamps, reptiles rapidly evolved and developed a remarkable range of adaptations: they took to the air, invaded the seas and held dominion over the land. By early Jurassic times, they had firmly established their claim to the title Ruling Reptiles. Another group of early reptile descendants led to the mammals, and although these were long overshadowed by the dinosaurs, they were destined to rise to dominance.

mammal-like reptiles and by the extraordinary evolutionary radiation of the so-called Archosaurs ("ruling reptiles"). These began to fill every available ecological niche. They evolved into carnivores, herbivores and omnivores. They included the Crocodilians, which adapted to a life in the water; the flying pterosaurs, which were the first vertebrates to fly, and, most important of all, the dinosaurs, whose evolutionary reign over the land was to endure for the next 140 million years.

Dinosaurs adapted well to life on the land. They developed "fully erect" limbs (not unlike those of the later higher mammals) rather than the splayed legs found in most other reptiles. The new position of their limbs, which gave them the necessary mobility on dry land, was also accompanied by a general increase in size. But the dinosaurs were not the only land reptiles of the time; many other forms, including tortoises, snakes and lizards, were also carving their niches during the Mesozoic era.

Similarly, the pterosaurs did not remain the only creatures of the sky. By 170 million years ago, birds in the form of claw-winged *Archaeopteryx* had evolved, and these were to prove a serious challenge to the primitive winged reptiles which had poor flying abilities.

Aquatic reptiles

Just as the land and the air were rapidly inhabited by newly evolving forms, so the water produced many new developments. Several of the Mesozoic reptiles began to adapt to aquatic life in ways often parallel to present-day mammals: the long-necked, fish-eating plesiosaurs led a life much like that of seals; the larger

pliosaurs had a streamlined shape similar to that of certain whales; some mollusc-eating placodonts could be likened to the walrus; and the elegant icthyosaurs were in many ways like dolphins. Large invertebrates were also found in the seas. The most dramatic of these were the ammonites—shelled relatives of the octopus—some of which grew to more than 2 m (6 ft) in size. Among fishes a new type emerged, the Teleosts, and these were destined to become the dominant fishes of the modern world.

Wholesale extinction

At the end of the Cretaceous Period, the reptiles were flourishing. Then suddenly, 65 million years ago, a catastrophe occurred. Virtually every species, including all the large animals, were wiped out. Throughout the Mesozoic, a series of dinosaurs and other reptiles had been evolving and slowly becoming extinct, but they were always replaced by other species. This wholesale extinction was unprecedented.

The cause of the catastrophe is unknown, but since the nature of the Earth itself was unchanged, it seems likely that some outside phenomenon was responsible. One theory suggests that a large meteorite collided with the Earth, throwing enough dust into the atmosphere to blot out the sun for several years—long enough to kill almost all the green plants on land and in the sea. If this was the case, only small animals that fed on carrion, decaying vegetation, seeds or nuts could hope to survive. Whatever the cause, the reign of the reptiles was at an end, leaving the small, adaptable mammals and birds to recolonize the virtually empty planet during the Cenozoic era.

Brachiosaurus

Tyrannosaurus rex

Struthiomimus

Rhamphorhynchus

Triceratops

Archaeopteryx

Plesiosaurus

Ichthyornis

Plesiosaurs evolved at the same time as the dinosaurs and were as successful in their marine environment as were the dinosaurs on land. They were most common in Jurassic times.

Pterosaurs such as *Rhamphorhynchus* were the first vertebrates to take to the sky. They were not strong fliers and probably glided on air currents much of the time.

Birds are relatives of the reptiles. The first bird, *Archaeopteryx*, evolving in Jurassic times, had many reptilian features—a long, bony tail, toothed mouth and clawed wings. By Cretaceous times, birds such as *Ichthyornis* had a more familiar form.

Norfolk Island pine
Araucaria heterophylla

Williamsonia

Common oak
Quercus robur

Fig tree
Ficus sp

Plane tree
Platanus sp

tion of reptiles **JURASSIC** First birds   150   **CRETACEOUS** First flowering plants   100 First modern fishes   Extinction of dinosaurs

The Age of Mammals

After the time of the great dying, 65 million years ago, reptiles never regained the importance they had achieved during the Mesozoic era. A new era, the Cenozoic, had begun. On the continental landmasses, mammals and birds, newly released from 160 million years of reptilian domination, began to occupy their niches in the rich, empty habitats. They flourished and diversified, and the cold-blooded reptiles became second-class citizens in a world of warm-blooded animals.

While reptiles still dominated the world, during the late Mesozoic, a new group of mammals had arisen. These were the first creatures on Earth to give birth to fully formed, live young. Until this time, the most advanced of the mammals had been marsupials whose young were still virtually embryos at birth and had to develop in the mother's pouch, or marsupium. The new mammals had evolved a more sophisticated system—the mother retained the fetus safely inside her body until it was fully formed, nourishing it during this time through a special organ, the placenta, developed during pregnancy. These mammals, the placentals, were destined to become the major mammalian group.

Although all the Mesozoic placentals were small, they had already evolved into a number of different forms that existed alongside the dinosaurs. Besides the insectivores, which were the ancestral type, they included early representatives of the Primates (precursors of modern monkeys and apes), the Carnivores, and the now extinct Condylarthrans (primitive hoofed mammals). When suddenly, 65 million years ago, there was no longer competition from the large land reptiles, these early groups rapidly evolved and extravagant forms developed.

But just as the first reptiles had passed through an early evolution, largely to be replaced by a second evolutionary wave, so the first large mammals were, in many cases, superseded by other, more successful lines. In the earliest part of the Cenozoic era, the different groups of placentals, although not closely related, all tended to be heavy limbed and heavy tailed and to walk on the whole length of their feet (as do modern bears) or on thick, stubby toes. These ungainly, thickset mammals soon died out. Some became extinct because their descendants, more efficiently adapted to their environment, overtook and replaced them. Others, such as the powerful taeniodonts and the large rodent-like tillodonts, seem to have been evolutionary blind alleys.

Spectacular developments
It was the Oligocene Period, 36 million years ago, that saw the end of most of these early essays in mammalian gigantism, but, in many parts of the world, they were replaced by others just as spectacular. In South America, the giant sloths and glyptodonts (massive relatives of the armadillos) survived until comparatively recently. The ground sloths, at least, were contemporaries of the first men on the continent.

As each group of early mammals evolved, during the early and middle part of the Cenozoic era, many of their developments closely reflected changes taking place in their environment. The first horse-like creature, for example, was *Hyracotherium*, also called *Eohippus* or "dawn horse." It lived 54 million years ago and was a small, multi-toed creature, well adapted to its densely forested habitat. The teeth of its descendants gradually changed in size and complexity, but it was not until the Miocene Period, nearly 20 million years later, that any radical alterations took place. This was the time when grasses (the Gramineae), until then a rare family of plants, came to the fore. The world's plains suddenly became clothed in a food plant very suitable for the attention of grazing creatures such as the early horses.

Animals of the grasslands
Horses and many other animals moved from the forests to make use of this new and abundant food supply. Once on the plains, different adaptations for survival were required: high-crowned teeth to deal with tough grasses; limbs enabling the animal to run tirelessly without extra, unwanted weight from supporting side toes (which were lost); large eyes capable of seeing for long distances and placed far back on the head for detecting predators approaching from any direction (as a result of which, however, the ability to judge distances ahead had to be sacrificed). Thus, the modern horses are plains-dwelling animals, perfectly adapted to their present way of life.

Mammals reached the climax of diversity during the Pliocene Period, 10 million years ago. But in the following period, the Pleistocene, ice sheets swept down from the polar regions and from the high mountains of the north, bringing massive and sudden changes to the ecology of virtually every region in the world. This dramatic disturbance to the environment brought extinction to an enormous number of species.

The survivors consisted mainly of the smaller species. Unfortunately for many of them, however, they included *Homo sapiens*. Man rose to success at the end of the Pleistocene and has, in the last 10,000 years, taken dominion over virtually every part of the world. During this time, he has proved far more destructive to other animal species than any natural force has ever been. More than 5,000 years ago, the giant sloths may have been a dying species, but there is no doubt that early human hunters hurried on their extinction. Since then, the list of species eliminated by man has grown ever longer. Today the human race is causing the extinction of both animals and plants at a rate comparable to that of 65 million years ago, when some dramatic natural catastrophe swept the dinosaurs from the face of the world. Unless man, the super-efficient species, can curb his numbers and his destructive activities, a new age of dying may soon be upon the world.

By early Cenozoic times, many forms had evolved from the insectivorous mammals of the Mesozoic Period. *Miacis*, *Hyaenodon* and *Oxyaena* were flesh eaters. Plant-eating mammals, such as Taeniodonts, *Arsinoitherium* and *Phenacodus* (one of the first hoofed mammals), had also evolved, while other early forms, such as *Andrewsarchus*, were omnivorous. The early Primates, however, remained insect eaters for millions of years.

EARLY STAGES

Miacis

Andrewsarchus

Hyaenodon

Diatryma

Euryapteryx

CENOZOIC BIRDS
Giant flightless birds came to the fore more than once during the Cenozoic era. *Diatryma*, a massive, flesh-eating bird, ruled the North American grasslands in early Cenozoic times, while mammals were still small, fairly primitive and easily dominated. *Euryapteryx* and its relatives (the moas) evolved in New Zealand, where, because there were no mammals, they filled an empty ecological niche.

The Carnivores diversified into two major types—the cats and their kin (Aeluroidea), and the dogs and their relatives (Arctoidea). During the Oligocene Period, about 36 million years ago, Aeluroidea gave rise not only to early relatives of modern cats, such as sabre-toothed *Hoplophoneus*, but also to two other families, the civets and the hyenas. At the same time, Arctoidea also diversified and produced the dogs, weasels, bears and racoons. It was a complex group, with many forms that were later to become extinct—the massive bear-dogs, such as *Daphoenus*, for example, which lived during the Miocene Period. Cats and dogs evolved to exploit different habitats. The cats adapted to life in forests, and learned to hide and then stalk and ambush their prey. Dogs evolved as plains animals, and used pack-hunting techniques to catch fleet-footed, grassland animals.

Perissodactyls and Artiodactyls were two important groups that evolved from the primitive hoofed mammals; Perissodactyls had an odd number of toes on each foot, Artiodactyls had an even number. These two groups suffered very different fortunes. Artiodactyls are still at the height of their success; the early stock produced the modern pig, camel, deer, giraffe, hippopotamus, antelope, sheep, goat and cow. Perissodactyls, however, are in decline and the only survivors are the horse, rhinoceros and tapir. But they were once important and many, now-extinct, kinds such as *Moropus* and *Brontotherium* existed alongside more familiar types such as *Hyracotherium*. Few remained after the Pliocene Period, however. This was when the Artiodactyls came to the fore. They, too, had had casualties—the pig-like *Archaeotherium* was by then extinct—but many other Artiodactyls, such as the early giraffe, *Palaeotragus*, were evolving. Most important, however, was small *Archaeomeryx*, for it had developed the key to Artiodactyl success—it was a ruminant and this enabled it to make the best possible use of the world's new grasslands.

Palaeozoic | Mesozoic | Cenozoic
500 | 400 | 300 | 200 | 100 | 0
Millions of years ago

Three geological eras mark the slow evolution of life on Earth. The Palaeozoic era, 570 million years ago, saw the appearance of the first primitive life forms. By the end of the era, 340 million years later, the reptiles had evolved and the following Mesozoic era was the age of reptilian domination. This reign over the land ended 65 million years ago as the Cenozoic era began. Then mammals came to the fore and the age of mammalian dominance of the world had dawned.

EARLY GRASSES
Grasses first appeared in the densely forested lands of 60 million years ago. Probably similar to the sedges (right) found in wet woodland areas today, they offered an attractive meal to many mammals. But it was not until the Miocene Period, when a change in climate reduced forest cover, that grasses became widespread. Then many forest creatures migrated to grassland areas.

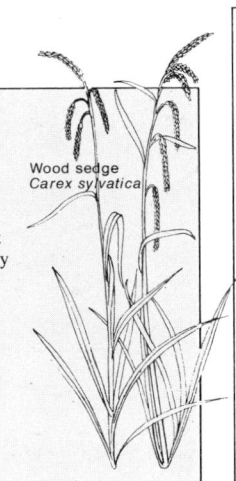

Wood sedge
Carex sylvatica

THE MARSUPIALS
Thylacosmilus and mouse-like *Argyrolagus* were two of the many forms of marsupial mammal that evolved in Cenozoic times in South America. Almost everywhere else, the marsupials, unable to compete with their more efficient placental cousins, met with an early extinction. But in two remote regions—South America (then separate from North America) and Australia—there was no competition from placentals, and there the marsupials flourished.

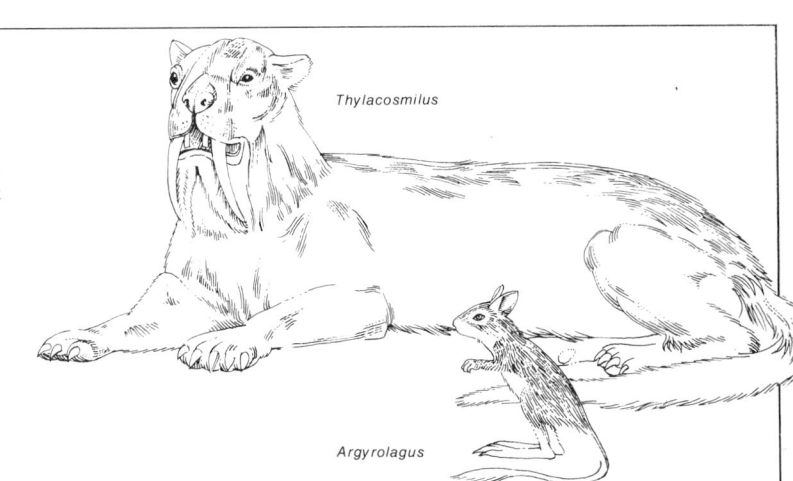

Thylacosmilus

Argyrolagus

TERTIARY | First radiation of mammals and birds | Forest horses | Second radiation of mammal
Palaeocene | 60 | Eocene | 50 | 40 | Oligocene

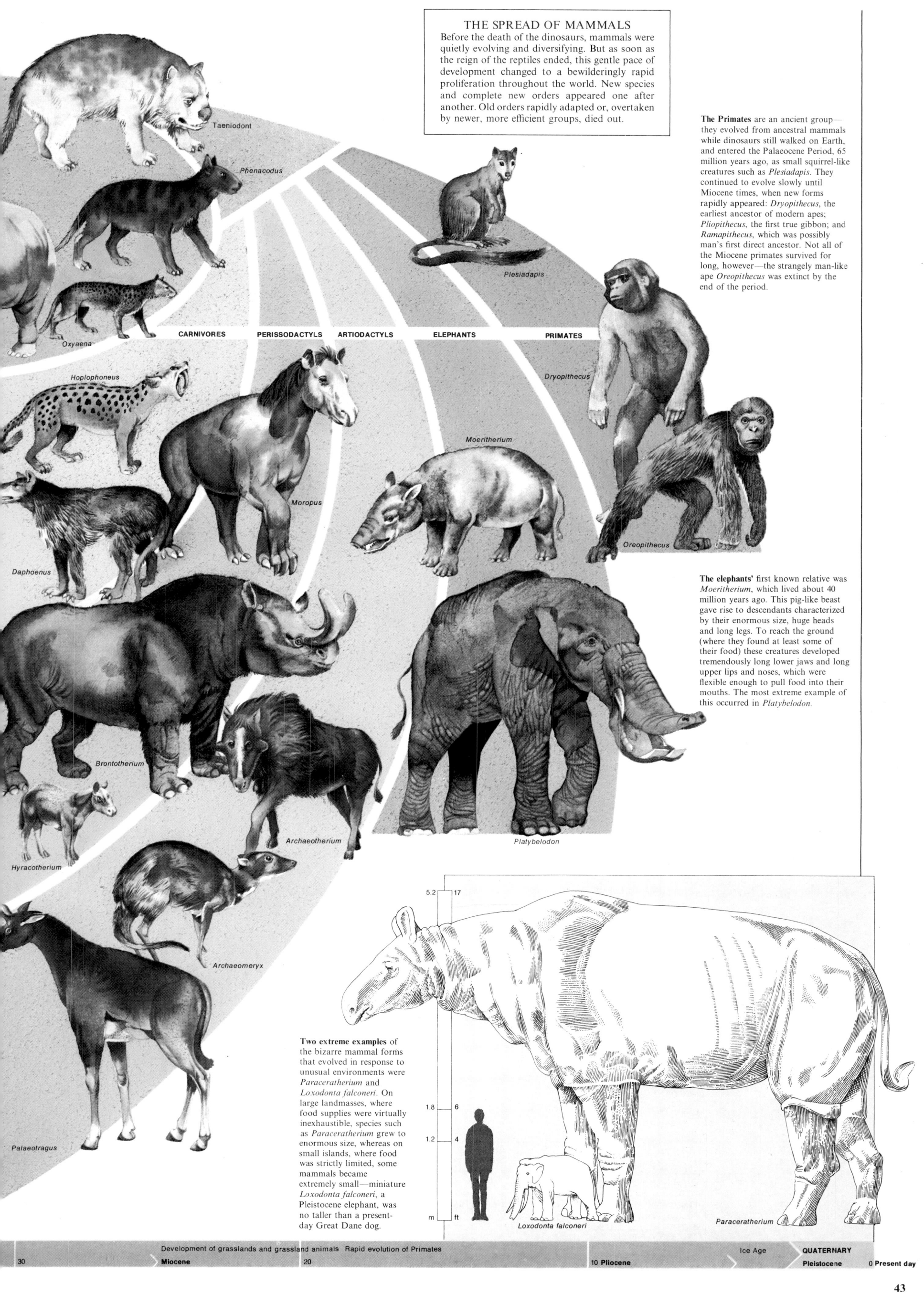

THE SPREAD OF MAMMALS

Before the death of the dinosaurs, mammals were quietly evolving and diversifying. But as soon as the reign of the reptiles ended, this gentle pace of development changed to a bewilderingly rapid proliferation throughout the world. New species and complete new orders appeared one after another. Old orders rapidly adapted or, overtaken by newer, more efficient groups, died out.

The Primates are an ancient group—they evolved from ancestral mammals while dinosaurs still walked on Earth, and entered the Palaeocene Period, 65 million years ago, as small squirrel-like creatures such as *Plesiadapis*. They continued to evolve slowly until Miocene times, when new forms rapidly appeared: *Dryopithecus*, the earliest ancestor of modern apes; *Pliopithecus*, the first true gibbon; and *Ramapithecus*, which was possibly man's first direct ancestor. Not all of the Miocene primates survived for long, however—the strangely man-like ape *Oreopithecus* was extinct by the end of the period.

The elephants' first known relative was *Moeritherium*, which lived about 40 million years ago. This pig-like beast gave rise to descendants characterized by their enormous size, huge heads and long legs. To reach the ground (where they found at least some of their food) these creatures developed tremendously long lower jaws and long upper lips and noses, which were flexible enough to pull food into their mouths. The most extreme example of this occurred in *Platybelodon*.

Two extreme examples of the bizarre mammal forms that evolved in response to unusual environments were *Paraceratherium* and *Loxodonta falconeri*. On large landmasses, where food supplies were virtually inexhaustible, species such as *Paraceratherium* grew to enormous size, whereas on small islands, where food was strictly limited, some mammals became extremely small—miniature *Loxodonta falconeri*, a Pleistocene elephant, was no taller than a present-day Great Dane dog.

Taeniodont

Phenacodus

Oxyaena

Plesiadapis

CARNIVORES   PERISSODACTYLS   ARTIODACTYLS   ELEPHANTS   PRIMATES

Hoplophoneus

Dryopithecus

Moeritherium

Moropus

Oreopithecus

Daphoenus

Brontotherium

Platybelodon

Hyracotherium

Archaeotherium

Archaeomeryx

Palaeotragus

Loxodonta falconeri

Paraceratherium

5.2 | 17

1.8 | 6

1.2 | 4

m | ft

Spread of Life

Different parts of the Earth have their own characteristic groups of animals, and this pattern of distribution caused nineteenth-century zoologists to divide the world into zoogeographical regions. Charles Darwin suggested how these assemblages of animals may have come about by the process of evolution. But we now know that movements of the Earth's land surfaces are also responsible for the present-day distribution of many of the world's animal species and groups.

The evolution of a major group of animals, such as the reptiles or the mammals, tends to follow a set pattern in five stages. First the original ancestral group spreads out, with each sub-group adapting to its environment. This process, called adaptive radiation, results in a variety of different kinds of animals, each suited to life in a particular niche or habitat—determined largely by food supply and environmental conditions. The different kinds then move into all of the areas they can reach in which the environment is right, producing the second stage of widespread distribution.

Competition for food or living space, or changes in climate may then cause some forms to decline and disappear from parts of the range, resulting in a third stage of discontinuous distribution. Any further reduction leads to isolated relict populations—the fourth stage—in which the animal exists only in one or two limited areas. The final stage is extinction.

In all distribution patterns, however, there is not only an ecological element but also a historical one, with past events determining where animals are and where they are not. There are thus two basic types of distribution: continuous, where the area is not interrupted by an insurmountable barrier (such as a mountain range), and discontinuous, where the area of distribution is subdivided and there is no way that members of one group can interchange with members of another.

One of these factors—the earliest and most important—is the (continuing) movement of the Earth's tectonic plates. This caused the supercontinent Pangaea to break up, probably in the Triassic Period (225–180 million years ago), and the continental masses to drift apart to their present positions. New oceans developed, separating the Americas from the Euro-African block and splitting both from Antarctica. Madagascar and Australia became islands, India moved north from Africa to join the Asian block, and mountain ranges such as the Alps, Andes, Rockies and Himalayas were thrown up. As a result, animal types that had already evolved on Pangaea or its fragments before they had significantly separated (i.e. all the major invertebrate groups and most of the earlier vertebrates) can be expected to exist on all the present-day continents.

Bridging the continents

Independently of these activities, ice ages occurred from time to time, resulting in the vast accumulations of ice at the poles and a consequent general lowering of the sea level by as much as 100 m (330 ft). This temporarily exposed the previously submerged continental shelves, providing additional land for colonization, and new corridors that linked existing areas, such as the land bridge that appeared between Alaska and Siberia.

Groups that had evolved after the breakup of Pangaea, e.g. the hare, squirrel and dog families, made use of land bridges as the climate allowed, and came to occupy more than one

continent. Flying animals—birds and bats—also made intercontinental crossings and established themselves on both sides of oceans, although a surprising number of these have remained very restricted in distribution. But most animals have to stay where they are because of special dietary or environmental requirements, or because they are "trapped" on islands, such as Madagascar and Australia, and cannot get off. These areas have the most distinctive faunas in the world.

Barriers and corridors

The extent to which an expanding group can spread from its original area depends on whether there are barriers, such as mountain ranges, deserts or seas, or corridors that link major areas in which the animals can live. Different animals have different environmental requirements, and so a topographical feature that is a barrier for one may be a corridor for another.

The dispersal of many animals is achieved by "hopping" from lake to lake across a continent, or from island to island across a sea. Some, such as insects, are good at this, whereas others, such as land mammals, are bad. Thus a considerable range of weevils (Curculionidae) are found on islands from New Caledonia to the Marquesas, some 6,500 km (4,000 miles) across the southern Pacific Ocean, whereas the marsupials of the region are concentrated in Australia, Papua New Guinea and a few adjacent islands, with only one genus reaching the Celebes and none crossing Wallace's Line into Borneo.

An example of colonization by "hopping" is seen on the volcanic island of Krakatoa near Java, which exploded in 1883 destroying all life. Within 25 years there were 263 species of animals on the island. Most were insects, but there were three species of land snails, two species of reptiles and 16 of birds. In another 22 years, 46 species of vertebrates had arrived, including two species of rats.

The effect of man

Animal distribution cannot be considered merely as a natural phenomenon, because it has been greatly and increasingly modified by man's impact on the environment. Agricultural practice has made large sections of the land area unsuitable for many of the animals that originally lived there, notably through the clearing of forests and the draining of marshes.

Man has also introduced animals, either deliberately or accidentally, to regions where they were not endemic. The rabbit in Australia and the deer in New Zealand were both deliberately introduced, but rats, cockroaches and many other animals have been accidentally transported throughout the world on ships and aircraft. The enormous growth in human population has driven many animals from their natural homes and into more remote environments, such as mountains. Indeed, in the past century human interference has altered the pattern of animal distribution more drastically than any topographic or climatic change.

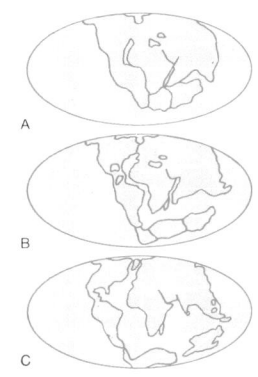

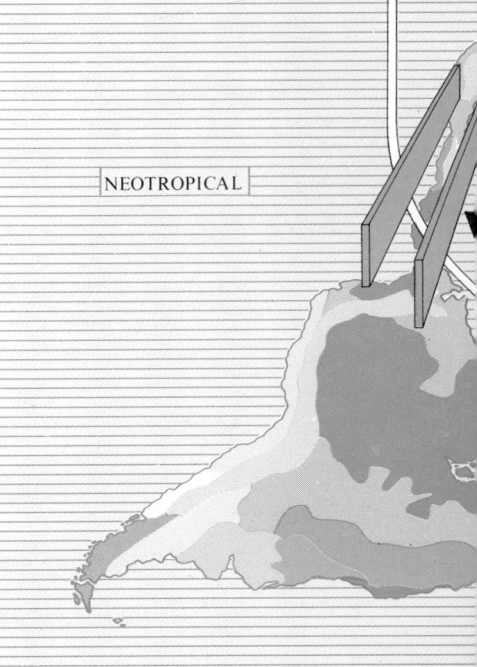

Earth's original single landmass, Pangaea (A), probably began to break up more than 200 million years ago. Species that had already evolved diversified on the Noah's Arks of the drifting supercontinents (B), called Laurasia and Gondwanaland. As the process continued (C), related animals flourished in the separated continents of the southern hemisphere.

PATTERNS OF ANIMALS

Over the ages the shape of the Earth has changed. Whole continents have moved; mountains and deserts have grown; land bridges between continents have opened and closed. These events, together with food supply, climate and other animals, account for the present natural pattern of life in the six zoogeographical regions, each containing a unique mix of animals. But man's activities have drastically affected this natural distribution in all parts of the world.

NEARCTIC	NEOTROPICAL
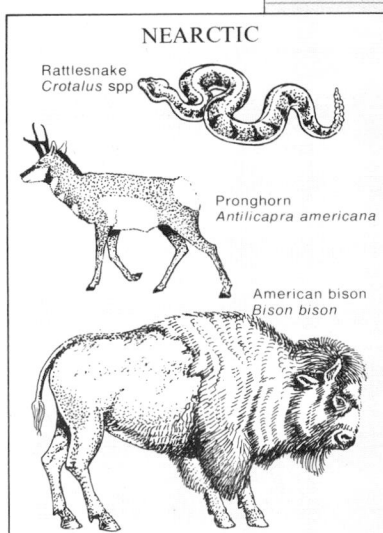	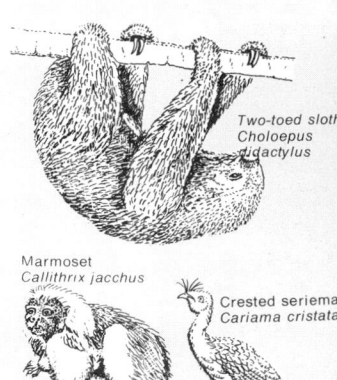

The Nearctic or "New North" region covers all of North America, from the highlands of Mexico in the south to Greenland and the Aleutian Islands in the north. Its climate and vegetation resemble that of the Palearctic region, and many of its mammals crossed over from the Palearctic via the Bering land bridge, which linked Siberia and Alaska when the sea level was lower. Animals unique to the Nearctic group include the pronghorn, an antelope-like mammal that inhabits the grasslands and plains of western and central America, and the bison, another large mammal that inhabits the prairies. Several species of rattlesnake also belong to the Nearctic group, although they are not exclusive to this region.

The Neotropical or "New Tropical" region consists of South America, the West Indies and most of Mexico. The climate and vegetation are mostly tropical—only the southern tip is in the temperate zone—and it is linked to the Nearctic by the Central American corridor. The Neotropical region has more distinctive families than any other. These include, among mammals, the sloth, which inhabits the tropical forests and has adapted to an upside-down existence. Among birds, the long-legged crested seriema is also unique to the region. Neotropical monkeys, such as the marmoset, have lateral-facing nostrils, which distinguish them from their downward-nosed relatives found in the Old World.

Land routes around the world have altered with the ages, sometimes allowing invaders to penetrate new lands, or closing to form natural sanctuaries for less efficient animals. The Central American isthmus (A) opened South America to placental mammals from the north. The Sahara desert closed most of Africa (B) to Eurasian species. Asia and Australia (C) share "island hoppers" in the transitional zones, but sea barriers have kept the regions separate.

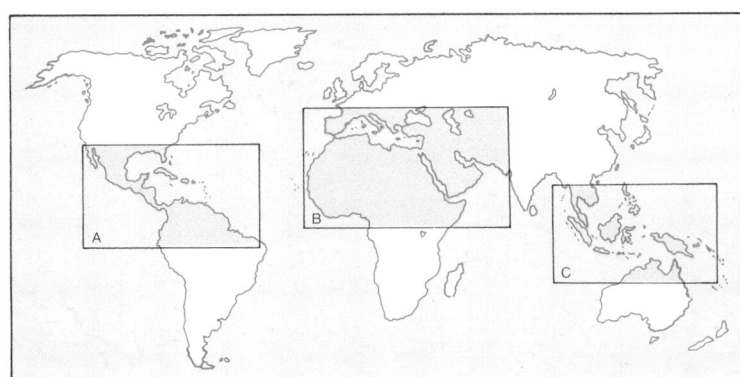

A land bridge between the Americas emerged about three million years ago, breaking the long isolation of the south. The primitive pouched mammals which had developed there were now threatened by more advanced mammals from the north, and many extinctions followed. Northern invaders included peccaries, raccoons and a llama-like camelid. But members of the armadillo and opossum families were successful in making their way to the northern region.

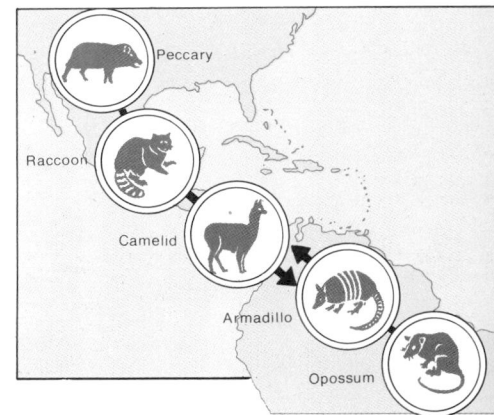

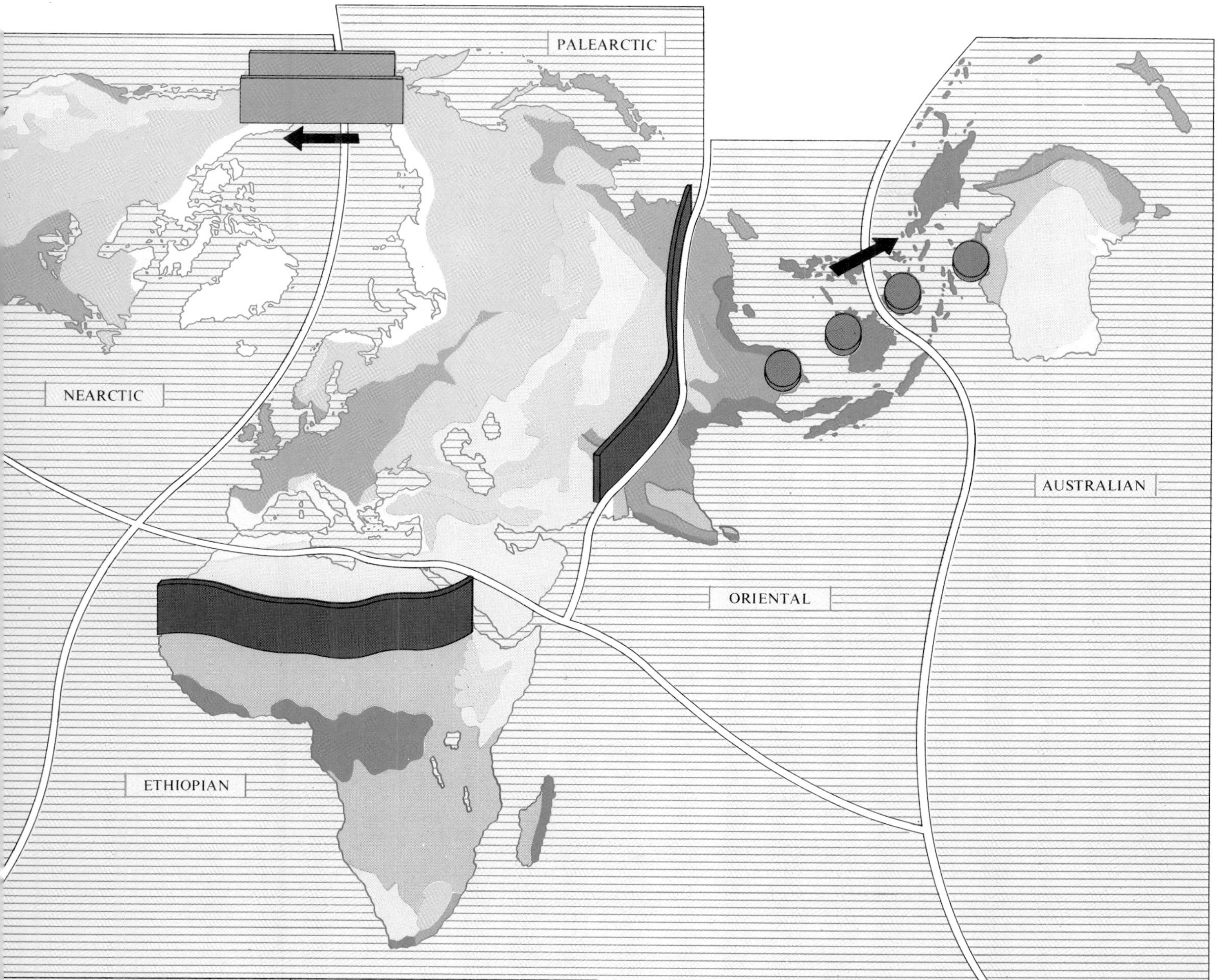

NEARCTIC

ETHIOPIAN

AUSTRALIAN

ORIENTAL

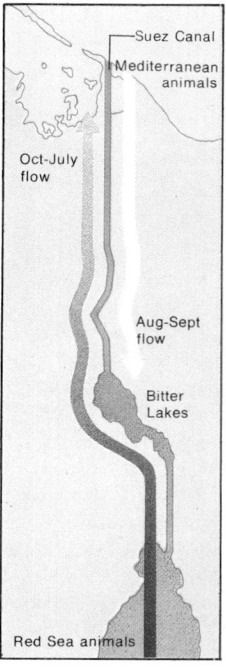

Suez Canal
Mediterranean animals
Oct-July flow
Aug-Sept flow
Bitter Lakes
Red Sea animals

The man-made filter of the Suez Canal, cut in 1869, is an animal corridor between the Mediterranean and Red Sea. But movement is mainly from the latter, for the channel passes through the hot, salty Bitter Lakes, favoring animals adapted to these conditions, and the current flows northwards for 10 months of the year. However, not all the 130 invading species are likely to survive Mediterranean conditions.

PALEARCTIC

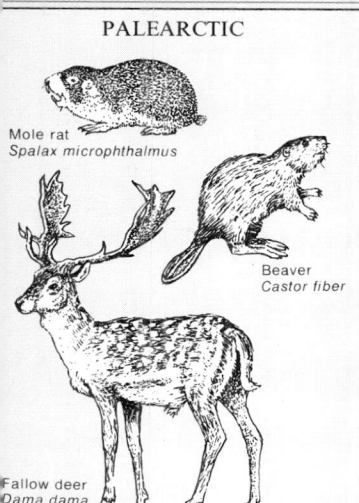

Mole rat
Spalax microphthalmus

Beaver
Castor fiber

Fallow deer
Dama dama

The Palearctic or "Old North" region covers the entire northerly part of the Old World, with seas to the north, east and west. To the south, the Sahara desert and the Himalaya mountains form barriers that separate the Palearctic from the Ethiopian and Oriental regions, although these regions are all part of the same landmass. One of the few species of mammals unique to the Palearctic is the Mediterranean mole rat, a thick-furred rodent. Another Palearctic rodent, the beaver, is shared with the Nearctic region. Fallow deer occur throughout Europe. They have been introduced by man into many other parts of the world, but their origin is almost certainly Mediterranean.

ETHIOPIAN

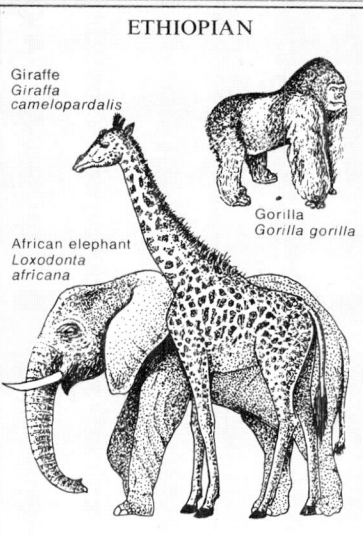

Giraffe
Giraffa camelopardalis

Gorilla
Gorilla gorilla

African elephant
Loxodonta africana

The Ethiopian region includes southern Arabia as well as all Africa south of the Sahara. It resembles in many ways the Neotropical region and is almost as rich in unique families. Its fauna also has much in common with the Oriental region. Unique mammals include the giraffe, at 5.5 m (18 ft) the tallest of living land animals, which inhabits the savanna. The region also supports two of the world's four great apes, the gorilla and the chimpanzee, which are found in the forests of western and central Africa. (The other great apes, the orangutan and the gibbon, are Oriental.) The African elephant is distinguished from its Indian relative by its greater size and by its huge ears and massive tusks.

Polar
Tundra
Taiga
Mountain
Temperate forest
Temperate grassland
Mediterranean
Savanna
Tropical rainforest
Monsoon
Desert
Barrier
Corridor
Stepping stone
Prevailing movement

ORIENTAL

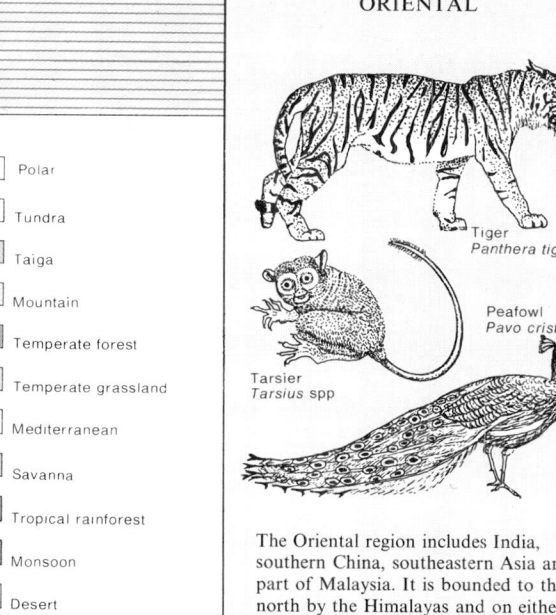

Tiger
Panthera tigris

Peafowl
Pavo cristatus

Tarsier
Tarsius spp

The Oriental region includes India, southern China, southeastern Asia and part of Malaysia. It is bounded to the north by the Himalayas and on either side by ocean, and is separated from the Australian region by a line known as Wallace's Line. It shares a quarter of its mammal families with Africa, but has more primates than any other region. The tarsier, a small relative of the monkey, is unique to southeastern Asia and represents an important early stage of primate evolution. The tiger was once widespread, but its natural habitats are steadily diminishing and the tiger itself is in danger of extinction by man. The peacock is one of the region's many brilliantly colored birds.

AUSTRALIAN

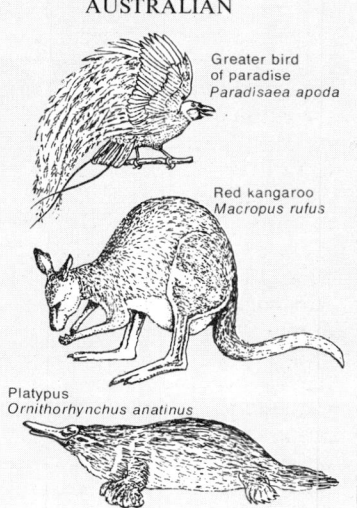

Greater bird of paradise
Paradisaea apoda

Red kangaroo
Macropus rufus

Platypus
Ornithorhynchus anatinus

The Australian region is unique in having no land connection with any other region. Its native fauna has developed in isolation from the rest of the world for at least 50 million years. Most of the mammals are marsupial—animals such as the kangaroo that carry their young in a pouch. Even more of a biological curiosity than the marsupials is the duckbilled platypus, a monotreme or egg-laying mammal. It lives along the banks of streams in Australia and Tasmania, and lays small, leathery eggs like those of snakes and turtles, but it is a true mammal and nurses its young with milk. Some 13 bird families are unique to the region, including the magnificent bird of paradise.

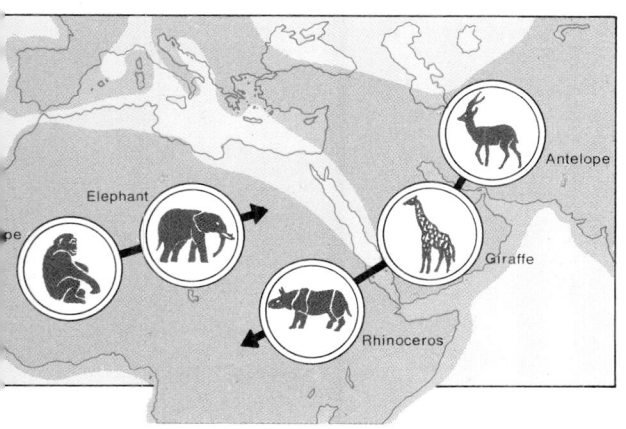

Elephant
Antelope
Giraffe
Rhinoceros

A desert barrier gradually began to form in northern Africa about nine million years ago, replacing the forest corridor between the Ethiopian and Palearctic regions. During the change, many animals typical of the African plains moved in from the north, including ancestors of today's antelopes, giraffes and rhinoceroses. But African animals also moved up north: early elephants and, much later, apes, which may have been precursors of modern man.

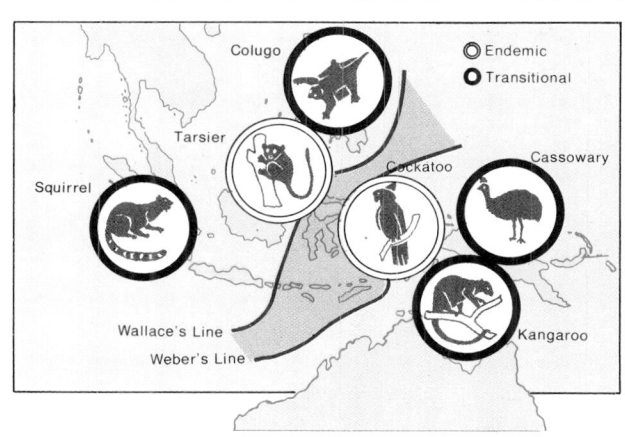

Colugo
Tarsier
Squirrel
Cockatoo
Cassowary
Kangaroo

Endemic
Transitional

Wallace's Line
Weber's Line

The transitional area of "Wallacea" contains animals from both the Oriental and Australian regions, bounded by Wallace's and Weber's Lines, but few have crossed to the other region. Some Oriental mammals, such as tarsiers, are found in Wallacea, but the gliding colugo and varieties of squirrel are not. The Australian cockatoo has reached the transition area, but the flightless cassowary and the tree kangaroo have not.

Spread of Man

Modern Man, *Homo sapiens sapiens*, has proved a highly successful animal since his emergence some 50,000 years ago: today more than 4,000 million members of this subspecies of the *Homo* (Man) group occupy the Earth, living in even the most inhospitable regions. But the fossil record shows that man's lineage goes back millions of years, with different stages of development leading to a greater control of the environment, and with climate itself helping man's ultimate domination of Earth.

Man's lineage may go back at least 14 million years to a small woodland creature known as *Ramapithecus* (Rama's ape). Since the first discoveries of *Ramapithecus* in the Indian sub-continent, its fossils have come to light in many parts of the world, including China, eastern Europe, Turkey and eastern Africa. Fossil remains show that it survived for several million years until, about eight million years ago, there is a tantalizing gap in the fossil record. Then, about four and a half million years later (according to recent discoveries in eastern Africa), we have solid evidence of an upright hominid—a member of man's zoological family. This is "Lucy," a fossil skeleton found in 1973 by Donald Johanson and Tom Gray, and subsequently classified with many other finds as *Australopithecus afarensis*.

This may be man's ancestral "rootstock," but a little later there existed two kinds of "ape-man" (*Australopithecus*), and our own direct ancestor Handy Man (*Homo habilis*). Datable volcanic ash found with the fossils provides a time scale and indicates that, about two million years ago, ape-man and "true" man lived side by side in the lush grassland that then covered the eastern African plains.

One and a half million years ago, according to the fossil evidence, there was again only one hominid species. The varieties of australopithecines had died out, and Handy Man (*Homo habilis*) had apparently evolved into Upright Man (*Homo erectus*). Remains of Upright Man have been found in many regions of the world, from various parts of Africa and Europe to China and Indonesia, although not in the Americas. But there is reason to believe that it was in Africa, well over one million years ago, that he evolved from his ancestor, and began a very gradual expansion out of the continent.

Upright Man had about one million years to spread across the Old World, adapting as he did so to local conditions, just as people of today are adapted in their various ways. He was a nomadic hunter gatherer, socially organized in groups. His skills included the use of fire and cooking, as well as the making of quite large structures out of wood. Recent discoveries suggest that, during the million years of his existence, *Homo erectus* gradually evolved into the next stage of man – *Homo sapiens*.

The next step is revealed most clearly in fossils from more than 100,000 to less than 50,000 years ago. Called Neanderthal Man in Europe, Solo Man in Indonesia, and Rhodesian Man in southern Africa, these types of human being were all descendants of *Homo erectus*.

Variable in brain size, but with prominent eyebrow ridges and receding jaws, they may have been dead ends on the evolutionary road; or some may have led to, or been incorporated in, Modern Man (*Homo sapiens sapiens*).

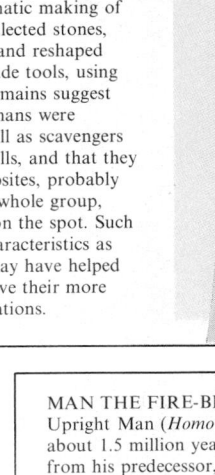

THE AFRICAN CRADLE

Handy Man (*Homo habilis*), who shared the East African grasslands two million years ago with a related "ape-man" species, was a slender and agile creature with a human way of walking and a capacity for conceptual thought, as evidenced in systematic making of tools. Handy Man collected stones, often from far away, and reshaped them into purpose-made tools, using other stones. Fossil remains suggest that these earliest humans were efficient hunters as well as scavengers of larger predators' kills, and that they brought food to campsites, probably sharing it among the whole group, rather than eating it on the spot. Such specifically human characteristics as the sharing of food may have helped our ancestors to survive their more primitive hominid relations.

MAN THE FIRE-BRINGER

Upright Man (*Homo erectus*) emerged about 1.5 million years ago, evolving from his predecessor, Handy Man. For one million years these people developed and adapted, spreading over most of the Old World and following a nomadic hunter-gatherer life-style, assisted by a more sophisticated tool technology. The cooler climates of northern Asia and Europe may have encouraged their most impressive innovation—the use of fire for warmth, cooking and hunting game—and also their ability to construct quite elaborate shelters. It seems likely that they possessed language; and traces of ocher lumps at a campsite perhaps 400,000 years old suggest the possibility of ritual adornment or some kind of body painting.

THE HUMANIZING OF MAN

Modern man's predecessor, although called Wise Man (*Homo sapiens*), was long regarded as more brutish than human. But widespread finds have now changed this image, as can be seen in an old and an updated reconstruction of the same Neanderthal skull (right). Many scientists believe that these people showed a human concern for each other, burying their dead with ceremonial reverence, and looking after disabled members of the group. In their Neanderthal form they inhabited Europe and the Middle East from about 100,000 to 40,000 years ago, and were perhaps adapted to ice-age conditions. *Homo sapiens* counterparts of Neanderthal Man also occur in Africa and southeastern Asia.

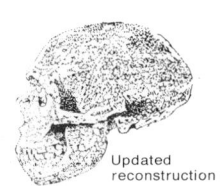

Updated reconstruction

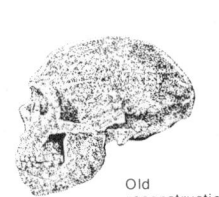

Old reconstruction

The burial of a Neanderthal man took place 60,000 years ago at Shanidar in the Iraq highlands. Fossil traces suggest that the body was laid on a bed of branches, and that flowers were brought to the grave and placed deliberately around the body. The flowers included many varieties still known locally for their medicinal properties. Ritual burials occur at many Neanderthal sites, from the Pyrenees to Soviet Asia, and indicate a sensitivity that contradicts Neanderthal Man's traditional image.

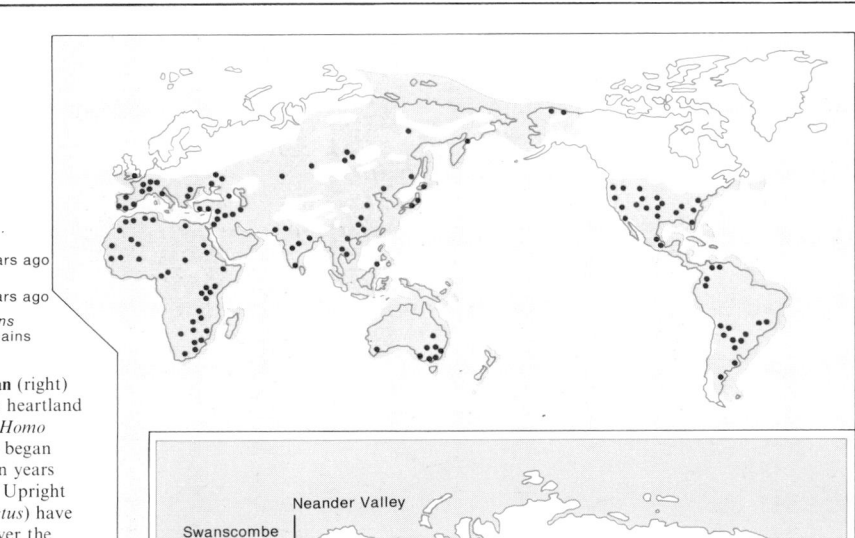

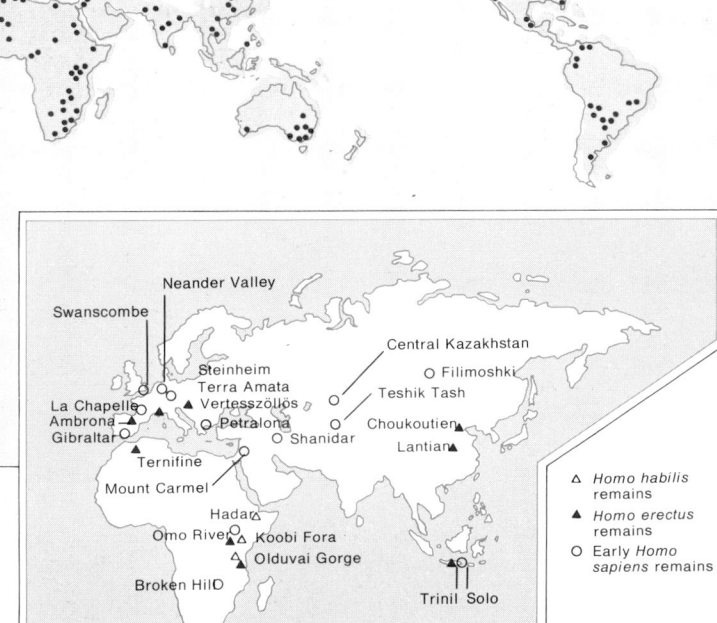

The spread of man (right) from the African heartland of Handy Man (*Homo habilis*) probably began about one million years ago. Remains of Upright Man (*Homo erectus*) have been found all over the Old World, and show a gradual physical and cultural evolution toward a later *Homo sapiens* ancestor, beginning about 350,000 years ago. Between 70,000 and 12,000 years ago, glacial periods locked up the sea water as ice (top), lowering sea levels and opening a land bridge to America that was used by later nomadic peoples. But they had to cross open sea to reach Australia.

Land areas c. 19,000 years ago
Ice sheets c. 19,000 years ago
• Homo sapiens sapiens remains

Neander Valley
Swanscombe
Steinheim
Terra Amata
La Chapelle
Ambrona
Gibraltar
Vertesszöllös
Petralona
Ternifine
Mount Carmel
Hadar
Omo River
Koobi Fora
Olduvai Gorge
Broken Hill
Central Kazakhstan
Filimoshki
Teshik Tash
Shanidar
Choukoutien
Lantian
Trinil Solo

△ Homo habilis remains
▲ Homo erectus remains
○ Early Homo sapiens remains

THE AGE OF ART

Toward the end of the last Ice Age, from about 35,000 years ago, truly modern humans began to depict their world in wonderfully vivid terms. The age of art may have reached its peak at Lascaux, France, some 15,000 years ago, but less well-preserved cave paintings from Africa show that the artistic impulse was equally present elsewhere. Called Cro-Magnon Man in Europe, these people spread to all parts of the world, crossing to the Americas by way of the Bering land bridge (when ice locked up the water of the straits), and even venturing over the seas to Australia. Physically these people were just like present-day humans. They led a nomadic, hunter-gathering life, living in large, organized groups, hunting such animals as mammoths, reindeer, bison and horses, and using a technology, as well as an artistry, far in advance of anything previously developed.

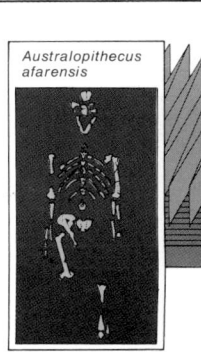

Fossils almost four million years old, found since 1973, may mark the ancestral "rootstock" of humanity, but the earliest form of true man is thought to be *Homo habilis*, who shared his African habitat with "ape-man" relatives some two million years ago. His successor, *Homo erectus*, spread over Asia and Europe, evolving gradually into modern man's predecessors, creatures whose large brow ridges belie many typically human characteristics. These were replaced by Modern Man.

Australopithecus afarensis

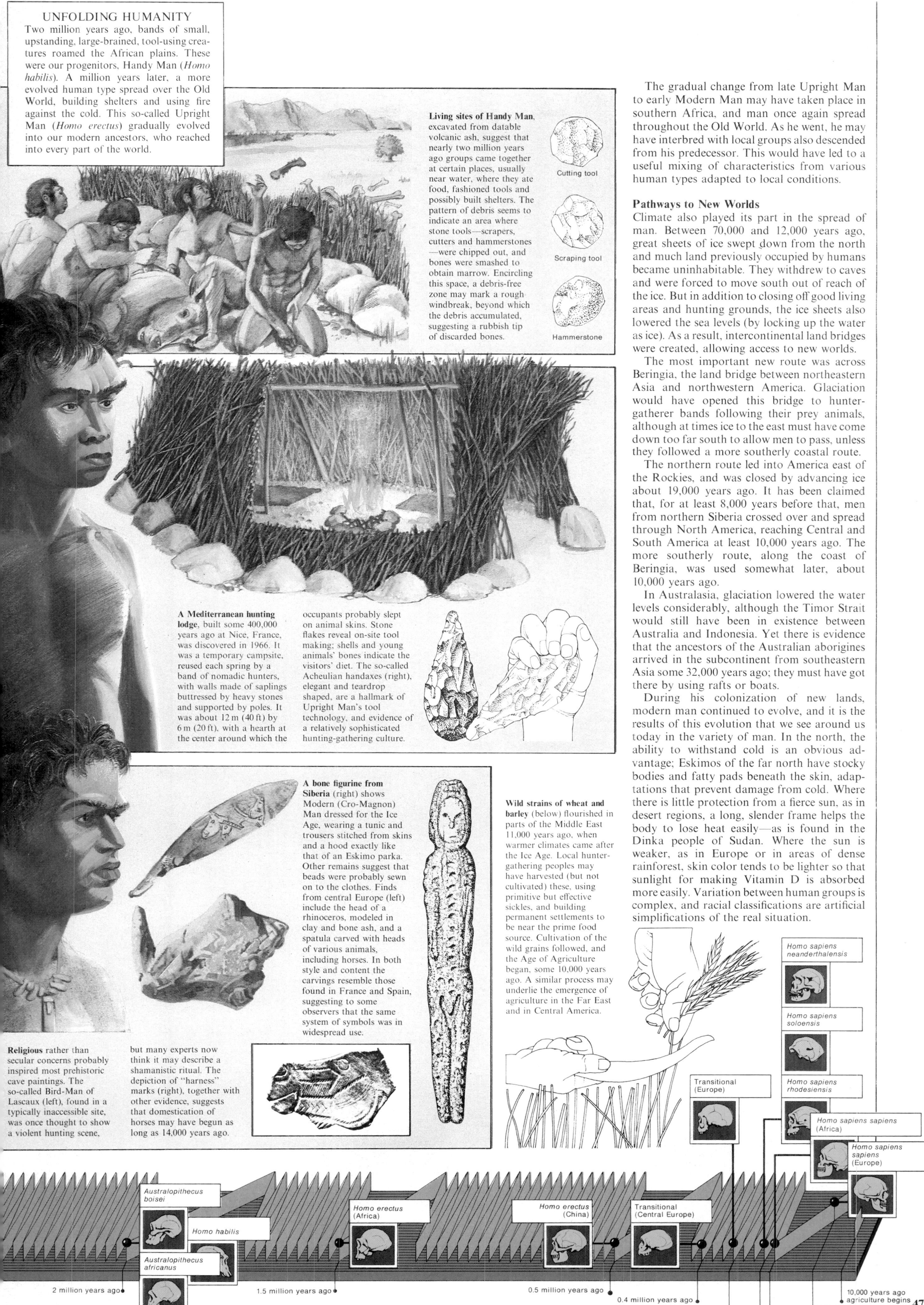

Two million years ago, bands of small, upstanding, large-brained, tool-using creatures roamed the African plains. These were our progenitors, Handy Man (*Homo habilis*). A million years later, a more evolved human type spread over the Old World, building shelters and using fire against the cold. This so-called Upright Man (*Homo erectus*) gradually evolved into our modern ancestors, who reached into every part of the world.

Living sites of Handy Man, excavated from datable volcanic ash, suggest that nearly two million years ago groups came together at certain places, usually near water, where they ate food, fashioned tools and possibly built shelters. The pattern of debris seems to indicate an area where stone tools—scrapers, cutters and hammerstones—were chipped out, and bones were smashed to obtain marrow. Encircling this space, a debris-free zone may mark a rough windbreak, beyond which the debris accumulated, suggesting a rubbish tip of discarded bones.

Cutting tool

Scraping tool

Hammerstone

The gradual change from late Upright Man to early Modern Man may have taken place in southern Africa, and man once again spread throughout the Old World. As he went, he may have interbred with local groups also descended from his predecessor. This would have led to a useful mixing of characteristics from various human types adapted to local conditions.

Pathways to New Worlds
Climate also played its part in the spread of man. Between 70,000 and 12,000 years ago, great sheets of ice swept down from the north and much land previously occupied by humans became uninhabitable. They withdrew to caves and were forced to move south out of reach of the ice. But in addition to closing off good living areas and hunting grounds, the ice sheets also lowered the sea levels (by locking up the water as ice). As a result, intercontinental land bridges were created, allowing access to new worlds.

The most important new route was across Beringia, the land bridge between northeastern Asia and northwestern America. Glaciation would have opened this bridge to hunter-gatherer bands following their prey animals, although at times ice to the east must have come down too far south to allow men to pass, unless they followed a more southerly coastal route.

The northern route led into America east of the Rockies, and was closed by advancing ice about 19,000 years ago. It has been claimed that, for at least 8,000 years before that, men from northern Siberia crossed over and spread through North America, reaching Central and South America at least 10,000 years ago. The more southerly route, along the coast of Beringia, was used somewhat later, about 10,000 years ago.

In Australasia, glaciation lowered the water levels considerably, although the Timor Strait would still have been in existence between Australia and Indonesia. Yet there is evidence that the ancestors of the Australian aborigines arrived in the subcontinent from southeastern Asia some 32,000 years ago; they must have got there by using rafts or boats.

During his colonization of new lands, modern man continued to evolve, and it is the results of this evolution that we see around us today in the variety of man. In the north, the ability to withstand cold is an obvious advantage; Eskimos of the far north have stocky bodies and fatty pads beneath the skin, adaptations that prevent damage from cold. Where there is little protection from a fierce sun, as in desert regions, a long, slender frame helps the body to lose heat easily—as is found in the Dinka people of Sudan. Where the sun is weaker, as in Europe or in areas of dense rainforest, skin color tends to be lighter so that sunlight for making Vitamin D is absorbed more easily. Variation between human groups is complex, and racial classifications are artificial simplifications of the real situation.

A Mediterranean hunting lodge, built some 400,000 years ago at Nice, France, was discovered in 1966. It was a temporary campsite, reused each spring by a band of nomadic hunters, with walls made of saplings buttressed by heavy stones and supported by poles. It was about 12 m (40 ft) by 6 m (20 ft), with a hearth at the center around which the occupants probably slept on animal skins. Stone flakes reveal on-site tool making; shells and young animals' bones indicate the visitors' diet. The so-called Acheulian handaxes (right), elegant and teardrop shaped, are a hallmark of Upright Man's tool technology, and evidence of a relatively sophisticated hunting-gathering culture.

A bone figurine from Siberia (right) shows Modern (Cro-Magnon) Man dressed for the Ice Age, wearing a tunic and trousers stitched from skins and a hood exactly like that of an Eskimo parka. Other remains suggest that beads were probably sewn on to the clothes. Finds from central Europe (left) include the head of a rhinoceros, modeled in clay and bone ash, and a spatula carved with heads of various animals, including horses. In both style and content the carvings resemble those found in France and Spain, suggesting to some observers that the same system of symbols was in widespread use.

Wild strains of wheat and barley (below) flourished in parts of the Middle East 11,000 years ago, when warmer climates came after the Ice Age. Local hunter-gathering peoples may have harvested (but not cultivated) these, using primitive but effective sickles, and building permanent settlements to be near the prime food source. Cultivation of the wild grains followed, and the Age of Agriculture began, some 10,000 years ago. A similar process may underlie the emergence of agriculture in the Far East and in Central America.

Religious rather than secular concerns probably inspired most prehistoric cave paintings. The so-called Bird-Man of Lascaux (left), found in a typically inaccessible site, was once thought to show a violent hunting scene, but many experts now think it may describe a shamanistic ritual. The depiction of "harness" marks (right), together with other evidence, suggests that domestication of horses may have begun as long as 14,000 years ago.

Homo sapiens neanderthalensis

Homo sapiens soloensis

Homo sapiens rhodesiensis

Transitional (Europe)

Homo sapiens sapiens (Africa)

Homo sapiens sapiens (Europe)

Australopithecus boisei

Homo habilis

Australopithecus africanus

Homo erectus (Africa)

Homo erectus (China)

Transitional (Central Europe)

2 million years ago   1.5 million years ago   0.5 million years ago   0.4 million years ago   250,000 years ago   100,000 years ago   50,000 years ago   35,000 years ago   10,000 years ago agriculture begins

Part 4

THE DIVERSITY OF LIFE

Earth's habitats from the Poles to the Equator
Plants and animals of the Earth's natural regions
Man the preserver and man the destroyer

WEATHER STATIONS
1 MASSAWA (Ethiopia)
°C TEMPERATURE °F
40 30 20 10 0
100 80 60 40
J F M A M J J A S O N D
cm RAINFALL in
20 10 0
8 4 0
Very hot and dry all year round, rain infrequent, nights cool
2 ALLAHABAD (India)
°C TEMPERATURE
40 30 20 10 0
J F M A M J J A S O N D
cm RAINFALL
20 10 0
Heavy summer rain, mild and dry winter, three seasons

180° 150° 120° 90° 60° 30° 0° 30° 60° 90° 120° 150°
Arctic Circle
60°
30°
Tropic of Cancer
Equator
Tropic of Capricorn
30°
60°
Antarctic Circle
1 2 3 4 5 6 7 8 9 10 11
The Natural Regions
Desert
Monsoon
Tropical rainforest
Savanna
Mediterranean
Temperate grassland
Temperate forest
Mountain
Taiga
Tundra
Polar
CLIMATE, RAINFALL AND THE BIOMES
Tundra
Taiga
Temperate forest
Temperate grassland
Mediterranean
Desert
Savanna
Monsoon
Tropical rainforest
10/26
0°C/32°F
10/37.5
20/68
0 cm/0 in
100/39
200/78
300/117

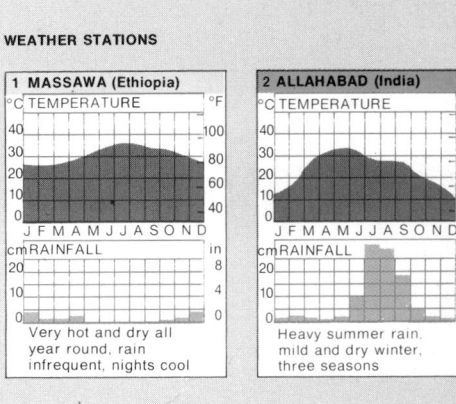

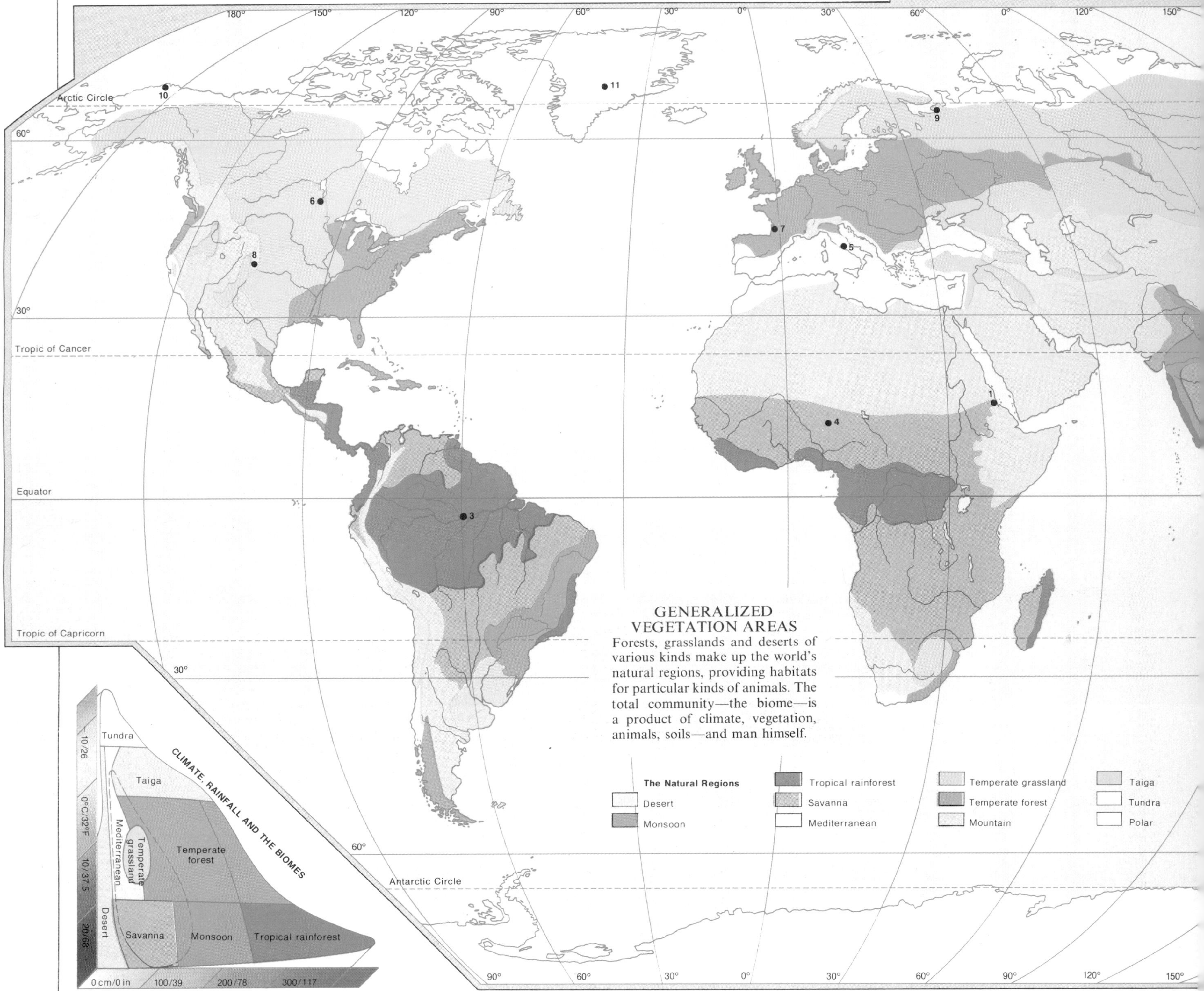

GENERALIZED VEGETATION AREAS

Forests, grasslands and deserts of various kinds make up the world's natural regions, providing habitats for particular kinds of animals. The total community—the biome—is a product of climate, vegetation, animals, soils—and man himself.

Temperature and rainfall (above) govern the world's zones of plant and animal life. Dryness prevents tree growth both in icy tundra and in hot deserts. Wetter conditions cause savannas and grasslands to yield to forest biomes, tropical or temperate (the dotted line indicates zones within which variations occur).

A broad correlation (below) between soil types, climate and vegetation areas shows the interconnections that define the biomes. The soil of the biome is related to climatic conditions and is also modified by plant and animal activity, but soil types are not necessarily confined to any one particular biome.

SOIL AND THE BIOMES

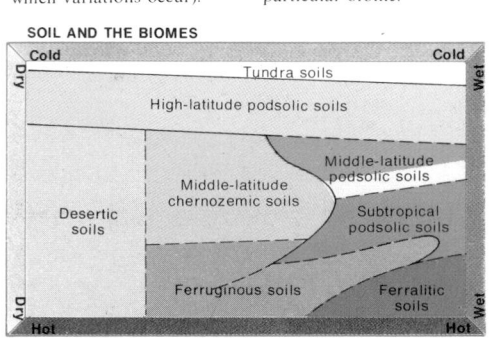

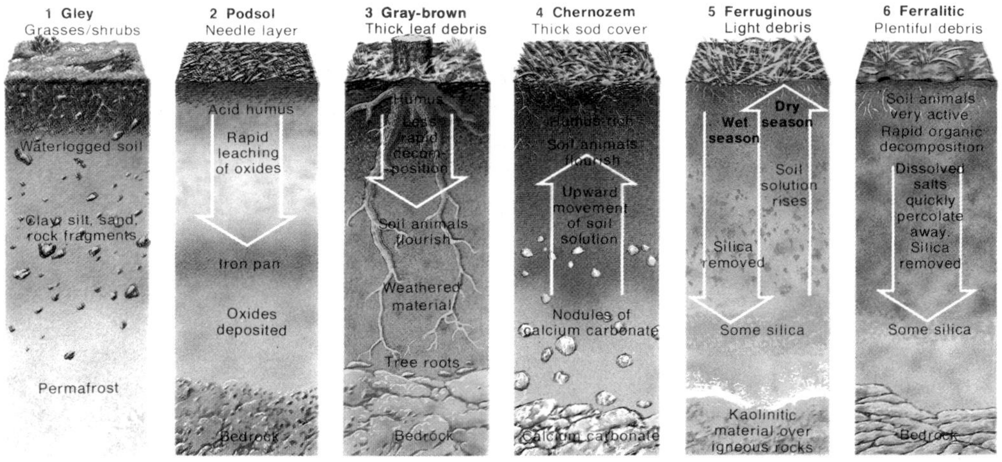

Cold
Cold
Dry
Wet
Tundra soils
High-latitude podsolic soils
Desertic soils
Middle-latitude chernozemic soils
Middle-latitude podsolic soils
Subtropical podsolic soils
Ferruginous soils
Ferralitic soils
Dry
Wet
Hot
Hot

1 Gley
Grasses/shrubs
Waterlogged soil
Clay, silt, sand, rock fragments
Permafrost
2 Podsol
Needle layer
Acid humus
Rapid leaching of oxides
Iron pan
Oxides deposited
Bedrock
3 Gray-brown
Thick leaf debris
Humus
Less rapid decom-position
Soil animals flourish
Weathered material
Tree roots
Bedrock
4 Chernozem
Thick sod cover
Humus-rich
Soil animals flourish
Upward movement of soil solution
Nodules of calcium carbonate
Calcium carbonate
5 Ferruginous
Light debris
Wet season
Dry season
Soil solution rises
Silica removed
Some silica
Kaolinitic material over igneous rocks
6 Ferralitic
Plentiful debris
Soil animals very active
Rapid organic decomposition
Dissolved salts quickly percolate away.
Silica removed
Some silica
Bedrock

Soil profiles (above) from surface to bedrock reflect the influence of climate and vegetation on the rock. Depths vary from 1 m in the tundra to 30–40 m at the Equator. Waterlogged gley (1) may form above tundra permafrost. Podsol (2) is typical of taiga forests, where spring snow-melt is heavily leached through a needle layer, sometimes forming an iron "pan." Gray-brown forest soil (3) has rich, organic humus, as has chernozem (4), the typical temperate grassland soil. Ferruginous soils (5) occur in dry-season tropical climates (monsoon, savanna), and ferralitic soils (6) where there is constant rainfall.

ECOSYSTEM DYNAMICS

An ecosystem consists o group of organisms and physical environment. A marshland ecosystem fro North America (right) shows the dynamic interactions between pla and animal communities and their habitats, whic include climate, soil and water. The energy and food in the system initia derive from the Sun—th main energy source for living things, notably plants. Plants are food for herbivores, on land and in water; herbivores are food for carnivores; decomposers (bacteria a fungi) nourish plants, breaking down dead boc into compounds.

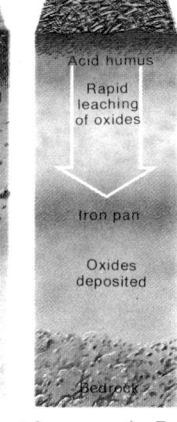

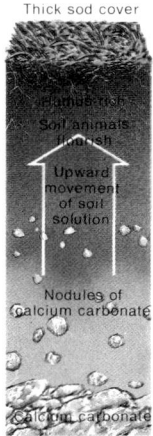

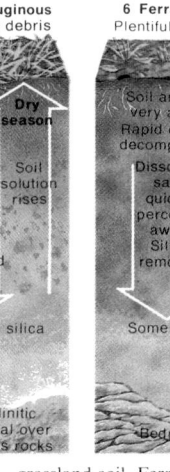

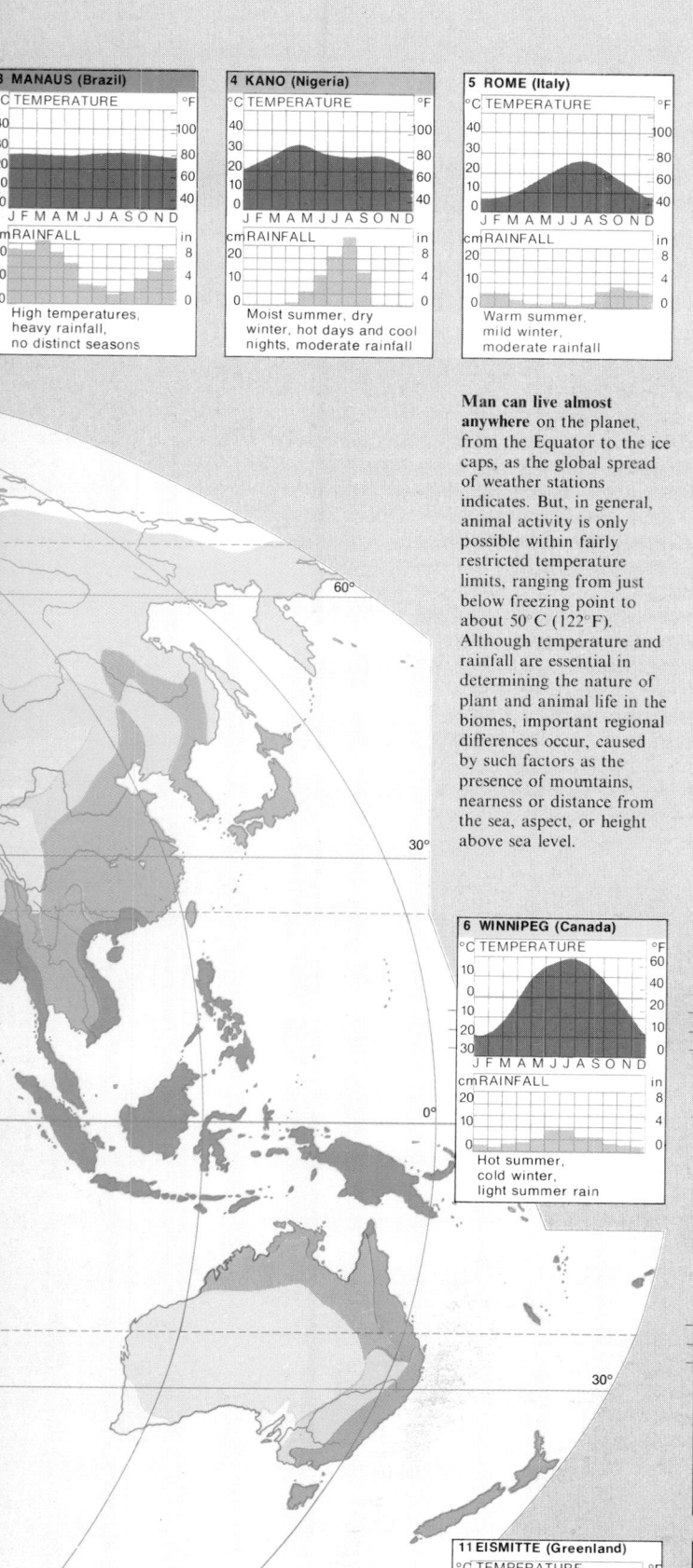

3 MANAUS (Brazil)
°C TEMPERATURE °F
High temperatures, heavy rainfall, no distinct seasons

4 KANO (Nigeria)
°C TEMPERATURE °F
Moist summer, dry winter, hot days and cool nights, moderate rainfall

5 ROME (Italy)
°C TEMPERATURE °F
Warm summer, mild winter, moderate rainfall

Man can live almost anywhere on the planet, from the Equator to the ice caps, as the global spread of weather stations indicates. But, in general, animal activity is only possible within fairly restricted temperature limits, ranging from just below freezing point to about 50 C (122°F). Although temperature and rainfall are essential in determining the nature of plant and animal life in the biomes, important regional differences occur, caused by such factors as the presence of mountains, nearness or distance from the sea, aspect, or height above sea level.

6 WINNIPEG (Canada)
°C TEMPERATURE °F
cmRAINFALL in
Hot summer, cold winter, light summer rain

7 BORDEAUX (France)
°C TEMPERATURE °F
cmRAINFALL in
Warm summer, mild winter, four distinct seasons

8 PIKE'S PEAK (USA)
°C TEMPERATURE °F
cmRAINFALL in
4,300 m (14,111ft)
Temperature decreases with increasing altitude

9 ARKHANGELSK (USSR)
°C TEMPERATURE °F
cmRAINFALL in
Short summer, long and cold winter, light summer rain

10 BARROW (Alaska)
°C TEMPERATURE °F
cmRAINFALL in
Brief summer, very long and cold winter, very light rainfall

11 EISMITTE (Greenland)
°C TEMPERATURE °F
RAINFALL
No data
Very light precipitation, annual temperature variation 15.3°C/27.5°F

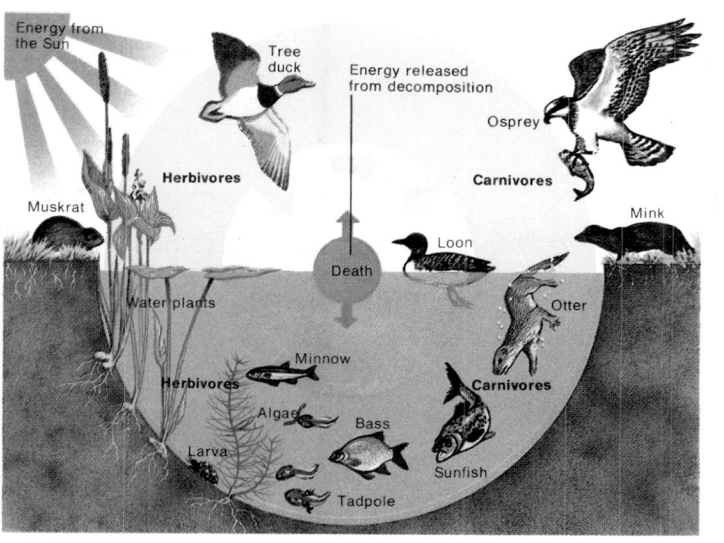

Energy from the Sun
Tree duck
Energy released from decomposition
Osprey
Herbivores
Carnivores
Muskrat
Mink
Death
Loon
Otter
Water plants
Minnow
Herbivores
Carnivores
Algae
Bass
Larva
Sunfish
Tadpole

Earth's Natural Regions

Geographers have long looked for ways of classifying conditions such as climate, soil and vegetation to describe the general similarities and differences from area to area throughout the world. By identifying distinctive patterns of climate and vegetation they have provided a convenient global division into natural regions or biomes. And recent developments in ecology – the study of plants and animals in relation to their environments – have given such divisions a greater depth.

Divisions according to climate were first suggested by the Greek philosopher Aristotle, and his ideas were still in use until about 100 years ago. Aristotle posited a number of climatic zones—called torrid, temperate and frigid —defined by latitude. But with time it became increasingly apparent that the complex distribution of atmospheric pressure, winds, rainfall and temperature could not be related to such a simple frame. Nineteenth-century scientists divided the world into 35 climatic provinces. Then in 1900 the German meteorologist Wladimir Köppen produced a more sophisticated climatic classification based on temperature and moisture conditions related to the needs of plants. At about the same time other scientists studied the distribution of vegetation types throughout the world. These studies together provided the basis for much of the later work on climatic regions.

An important step forward was made in 1904 by the British geographer A. J. Herbertson. He argued that subdivision of physical environments should take into account the distribution of the various phenomena as they related to each other. He conceived the idea of *natural regions*, each with "a certain unity of configuration (relief), climate and vegetation." His final classification contained four groups or regions: Polar Types, Cool Temperate Types, Warm Temperate Types and Tropical Hot Lands. Herbertson's scheme, controversial at first, was later much used for teaching geography.

Ecology

Meanwhile the study of environmental problems had been advanced by the idea of *ecology*, the relationship of living things between each other and their surroundings. The term was first used in 1868 by Ernst Haeckel, the German biologist, but it was not until the end of the nineteenth century that scientists really began to study life forms in relation to their habitat. In addition to the central ideas of interdependence between the members of plant and animal communities and between the community and the physical environment, there now came the suggestion that communities develop in a sequence that leads to a "climax"—a final step of equilibrium or balance. Their climax stage depends on conditions of climate or soil.

Later the British botanist A. G. Tansley, a leading exponent of ecological thinking, introduced the term *ecosystem* to describe a group of living organisms and its effective environment. Tansley's definition of 1935 referred to the whole system, including "not only the organism complex, but also the whole complex of physical factors forming what we call the environment of the biome." The idea became very influential and has been used in the social sciences as well as in the natural ones. But it is difficult to apply in practice, partly because of the highly complex and often diverse interactions that take place in different parts of the ecosystem.

Ecologists have developed special methods and have given particular attention to the ways in which energy is transferred within the system. The term *biome* refers to the whole complex of organisms, both animals and plants, that live together naturally as a society. By *environment* is meant all the external conditions that affect the life and development of an organism.

Biomes

The biomes shown on the map are broadly drawn generalizations. They should be regarded as idealized regions, within which many local variations may exist—for example, of climate or soil conditions. On a larger scale such features as mountain ranges may cause variations at a regional level. Scientists have tried to work out "hierarchies" that include many levels or orders of scale leading to the major climatic-vegetation realms or biomes. These realms give a broad picture that is useful at the world level of scale, and which forms a starting point for further analysis. Any map of the biomes has to have lines to indicate the boundaries of each region, but these too are generalizations. Although climate and vegetation do sometimes change abruptly from place to place, more often there are transitional zones, and the boundaries on the maps give the broad locations of these.

Herbertson's concept of natural regions attempted also to take account of the influence of man as an important factor in the environment. But he was not totally successful in including man in his analysis, no doubt because of the complexity of the problems involved and because of the immense influence that man has had upon the natural vegetation of the world. The cutting of forests, the drainage and reclamation of land, the introduction, use and spread of cultivated plants, the domestication of animals, the development of sophisticated systems of agriculture and many other actions all create, over large areas of the biomes, landscapes that are more man-made than natural.

Resource systems

An idea that clarifies the study of the interrelations of societies and environments, and the ways in which these change with the passage of time, is that of the *resource system*. This is a model of a population of human beings and their social and economic characteristics, including their technical skills and resources, together with those aspects of the natural environment that affect them and which they influence. The model includes the sequences by which natural materials are obtained, transformed and used. It tries to show how societies are organized according to their natural resources, the effects of that use, and the ways in which natural conditions limit or expand the life and work of the society. But it is easier to apply such a model to societies that have direct relations with natural conditions, through farming, fishing or forestry, than to great urban–industrial complexes.

The sections that follow present a picture of the diversity of habitats from ice caps to equatorial forests, the principal ways man has modified the environment and the problems of maintaining healthy resource systems.

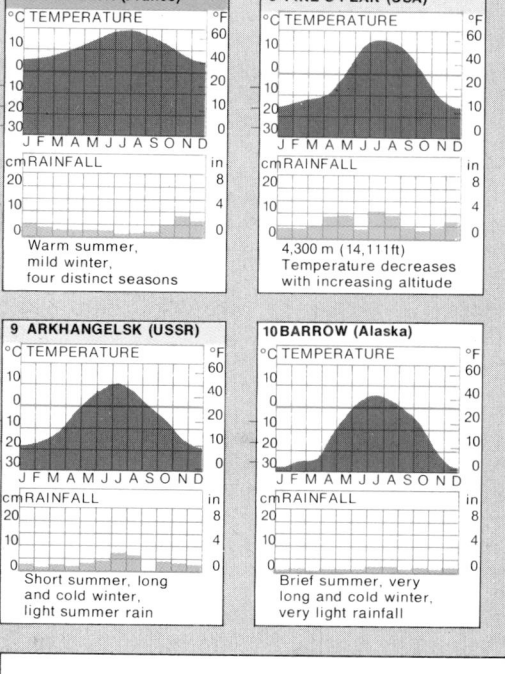

Climate and Weather

The pattern of world climates depends largely on great circulations of air in the atmosphere. These movements of air are driven by energy from the Sun, and they transfer surplus heat from the tropics to the polar regions. Over a long period of time – such as months, seasons or years – they create the climate. Over a short period – day by day, or week by week – they form the weather. Together, climate and weather are among the most significant natural components of the world's diverse environments.

The world's tropical zones receive more heat from the Sun than they re-emit into space, and so their land and sea surfaces become warm. The polar regions, on the other hand, emit more radiation than they receive, and so they become cold. Warm air is less dense than cold air, and this means that atmospheric pressure becomes low at the Equator and high at the poles. As a result, a circulation of air—both vertical and horizontal—is set up. But because of the Earth's rotation and the distribution of land and sea there is not a simple air circulation pattern in each hemisphere; winds are deflected to the right in the northern hemisphere and to the left in the southern hemisphere, a phenomenon known as the Coriolis effect.

A climatic patchwork
When warm air rises it expands and cools and the water vapor it is carrying condenses to form clouds. For this reason heavy, showery rain is frequent in the belt of rising air near the Equator. In the subtropical zones (where the air is sinking), clouds evaporate and the weather is fine. Air moves out of the subtropical high-pressure belts in the lower atmosphere. Some of it flows towards the poles and meets colder air, flowing out of the polar high-pressure region, in a narrow zone called the polar front. This convergence of air is concentrated around low-pressure systems known as depressions.

The pattern of climates does not remain constant throughout the year because of seasonal changes in the amount of radiation from the Sun—the "fuel" of the atmospheric engine. In June, when the northern hemisphere is tilted towards the Sun, the radiation is at a maximum at latitude 23°N and all the climatic belts shift northwards. In December it is summer in the southern hemisphere and all the belts move southwards.

Climate is also affected by the distribution of land and sea across the globe. The temperature of the land changes more quickly than that of

TYPES OF WEATHER
There is a constant flow of air between the world's polar and tropical regions, and this has a prime effect on the weather in other regions. In the high and middle latitudes cold and warm fronts succeed each other, and along coasts sea fogs often form. In temperate and tropical regions thunderstorms are frequent, and the tropics are characterized by the turbulent storms known as hurricanes in the Caribbean area and typhoons in the Pacific.

POLAR WEATHER
Weather in high latitudes is marked by consistently low temperatures—on the ice caps temperatures are nearly always below freezing. At the poles the sun never rises for six months of the year and for the remaining six months it never sets. Even in summer it stays low on the horizon and its rays are so slanted that they bring very little warmth. On the tundra the temperature rises above freezing for a few months in summer, but severe frosts are likely to occur at any time. As well as being bitterly cold, polar weather is predominantly dry. The lower the temperature the less moisture the air can contain. Clouds, when they form, are high, thin sheets of cirrostratus. Composed of ice crystals, they often produce a halo effect around the sun. Snow, when it falls, is usually dry and powdery.

DEPRESSIONS
Low-pressure weather systems, or depressions, form when polar and subtropical air masses converge. Cloud and rain usually occur at the boundary, or front, of the different air masses. Seen in cross section, a fully developed depression shows both warm (A) and cold (B) fronts. As the wave of warm air rises over the cold, its moisture condenses into the "layered" clouds that usually precede a warm front. Behind the warm front, cold air forces under the warm air, producing the wedge-shaped cold front.

FOG
Fogs form as a result of the condensation of water vapor in the air; they may occur when warm, moist air is cooled by its passage over a cold surface. Off the coast of California, for example, air near the surface of the sea is cooled by the cold California current and sea fog is frequent. The air at higher levels is still warm and acts like a lid over the fog, and mountains prevent the fog from dispersing in an easterly direction. Fumes and smoke are trapped by this temperature inversion, creating the notorious Los Angeles smog.

THUNDERSTORMS
These develop when air is unstable to a great height. Particularly violent storms occur when cold, dry air masses meet warm, moist air, causing the latter to rise rapidly. As the warm air surges upwards it cools and its moisture condenses into cumulonimbus, or thunder, clouds. Flat cloud tops mark the level where stable air occurs again. Quickly moving raindrops and hail in the clouds become electrically charged and cause lightning, and the explosion of heated air along the path of the flash creates the sound wave that is heard as thunder.

HURRICANES
These are tropical storms on a vast scale that build up over warm oceans. Their core is an area of low pressure around which large quantities of warm, moist air are carried to the high atmosphere at great speed. The Earth's rotation is responsible for the huge swirling movement: in the northern hemisphere the movement is anticlockwise, in the southern hemisphere it is clockwise. Towering bands of clouds produce torrential rain. The central region, or "eye," of a hurricane, however, has light winds, clear skies and no rainfall.

THE WORLD'S CLIMATIC REGIONS
Climate is the characteristic weather of a region over a long period of time. It is often described in terms of average monthly and yearly temperatures and rainfall. These in turn depend largely on latitude, which determines whether a region is basically hot or cold and whether it has pronounced seasonal changes. Climate is also influenced by prevailing winds, by ocean currents and by geographical features such as the distribution of land and water. Highland climates are influenced by altitude and are always cooler than those of nearby lowland regions. Tropical climates are always warm. Near the Equator rain falls for most of the year, but towards the subtropics the wet and dry seasons are more marked. Temperate climates reflect the conflict between warm and cold air masses. They range from the Mediterranean type with hot, dry summers and mild, moist winters to the cooler, wetter climates of higher latitudes. The subarctic is mainly cold and humid; polar climates are always cold and mainly dry.

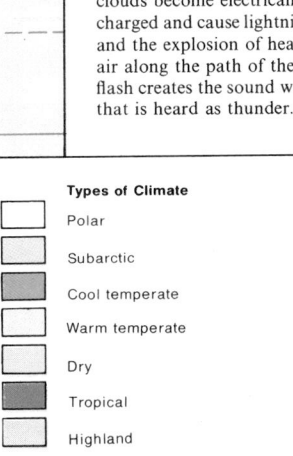

Types of Climate
- Polar
- Subarctic
- Cool temperate
- Warm temperate
- Dry
- Tropical
- Highland

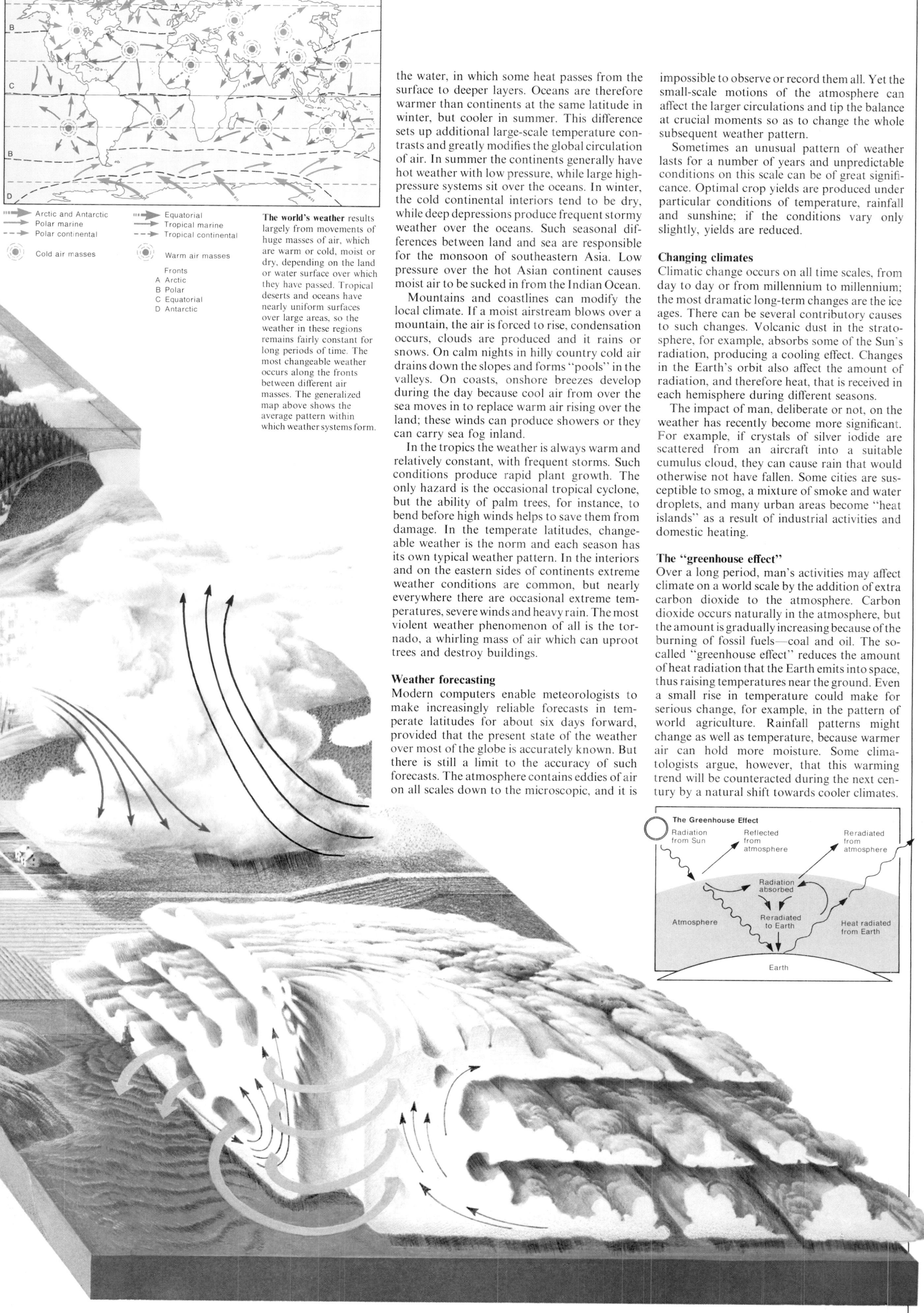

The world's weather results largely from movements of huge masses of air, which are warm or cold, moist or dry, depending on the land or water surface over which they have passed. Tropical deserts and oceans have nearly uniform surfaces over large areas, so the weather in these regions remains fairly constant for long periods of time. The most changeable weather occurs along the fronts between different air masses. The generalized map above shows the average pattern within which weather systems form.

the water, in which some heat passes from the surface to deeper layers. Oceans are therefore warmer than continents at the same latitude in winter, but cooler in summer. This difference sets up additional large-scale temperature contrasts and greatly modifies the global circulation of air. In summer the continents generally have hot weather with low pressure, while large high-pressure systems sit over the oceans. In winter, the cold continental interiors tend to be dry, while deep depressions produce frequent stormy weather over the oceans. Such seasonal differences between land and sea are responsible for the monsoon of southeastern Asia. Low pressure over the hot Asian continent causes moist air to be sucked in from the Indian Ocean.

Mountains and coastlines can modify the local climate. If a moist airstream blows over a mountain, the air is forced to rise, condensation occurs, clouds are produced and it rains or snows. On calm nights in hilly country cold air drains down the slopes and forms "pools" in the valleys. On coasts, onshore breezes develop during the day because cool air from over the sea moves in to replace warm air rising over the land; these winds can produce showers or they can carry sea fog inland.

In the tropics the weather is always warm and relatively constant, with frequent storms. Such conditions produce rapid plant growth. The only hazard is the occasional tropical cyclone, but the ability of palm trees, for instance, to bend before high winds helps to save them from damage. In the temperate latitudes, changeable weather is the norm and each season has its own typical weather pattern. In the interiors and on the eastern sides of continents extreme weather conditions are common, but nearly everywhere there are occasional extreme temperatures, severe winds and heavy rain. The most violent weather phenomenon of all is the tornado, a whirling mass of air which can uproot trees and destroy buildings.

Weather forecasting
Modern computers enable meteorologists to make increasingly reliable forecasts in temperate latitudes for about six days forward, provided that the present state of the weather over most of the globe is accurately known. But there is still a limit to the accuracy of such forecasts. The atmosphere contains eddies of air on all scales down to the microscopic, and it is

impossible to observe or record them all. Yet the small-scale motions of the atmosphere can affect the larger circulations and tip the balance at crucial moments so as to change the whole subsequent weather pattern.

Sometimes an unusual pattern of weather lasts for a number of years and unpredictable conditions on this scale can be of great significance. Optimal crop yields are produced under particular conditions of temperature, rainfall and sunshine; if the conditions vary only slightly, yields are reduced.

Changing climates
Climatic change occurs on all time scales, from day to day or from millennium to millennium; the most dramatic long-term changes are the ice ages. There can be several contributory causes to such changes. Volcanic dust in the stratosphere, for example, absorbs some of the Sun's radiation, producing a cooling effect. Changes in the Earth's orbit also affect the amount of radiation, and therefore heat, that is received in each hemisphere during different seasons.

The impact of man, deliberate or not, on the weather has recently become more significant. For example, if crystals of silver iodide are scattered from an aircraft into a suitable cumulus cloud, they can cause rain that would otherwise not have fallen. Some cities are susceptible to smog, a mixture of smoke and water droplets, and many urban areas become "heat islands" as a result of industrial activities and domestic heating.

The "greenhouse effect"
Over a long period, man's activities may affect climate on a world scale by the addition of extra carbon dioxide to the atmosphere. Carbon dioxide occurs naturally in the atmosphere, but the amount is gradually increasing because of the burning of fossil fuels—coal and oil. The so-called "greenhouse effect" reduces the amount of heat radiation that the Earth emits into space, thus raising temperatures near the ground. Even a small rise in temperature could make for serious change, for example, in the pattern of world agriculture. Rainfall patterns might change as well as temperature, because warmer air can hold more moisture. Some climatologists argue, however, that this warming trend will be counteracted during the next century by a natural shift towards cooler climates.

The Greenhouse Effect

Radiation from Sun
Reflected from atmosphere
Reradiated from atmosphere
Radiation absorbed
Atmosphere
Reradiated to Earth
Heat radiated from Earth
Earth

Resources and Energy

Resources, it has been said, comprise mankind's varying needs from generation to generation and are valued because of the uses societies can make of them. They represent human appraisals and are the products of man's ingenuity and experience. While natural resources remain vitally important in themselves, they must always be regarded as the rewards of human skill in locating, extracting and exploiting them. The development of resources depends on many factors, including the existence of a demand, adequate transport facilities, the availability of capital and the accessibility, quality and quantity of the resource itself.

The world's extraction of its resources highlights the inequality of their distribution. Each resource shown on the map is attributed to the three countries with the largest production percentages of that commodity. So, in 1976, the three leading bauxite producers were Australia (26.69%), Jamaica (14.19%) and Rep. of Guinea (13.9%). Usually, the larger and more wealthy a state the greater its monopoly of resources—although the tiny Pacific island of New Caledonia produces more than 14% of the world's nickel. China is reputed to mine 75% of the world's tungsten and to be increasing its oil supply rapidly. Energy consumption figures are for the year 1976, since when there have been some outstanding changes to patterns of availability, perhaps most noticeably in Britain's new-found oil and gas surplus. Bahrain and Tobago, too small to be shown on this map, also have surpluses of energy production.

A dictionary defines the term "resource" as "a means of aid or support," implying anything that lends support to life or activity. Man has always assessed nature with an eye to his own needs, and it is these varying needs that endow resources with their usefulness. Fossil fuels such as oil have lain long in the Earth, but it was not until about 1900 that the large-scale needs fostered by the rising demands of motor vehicles led to the development of new techniques for locating and extracting this raw material. Today oil has also become precious in the manufacture of a wide variety of industrial products, which themselves are resources that are much used by other industries.

The nature of resources

Resources can be most usefully classified in two groups: "renewable" and "nonrenewable." The latter is composed of materials found at or near the Earth's surface, which are sometimes known as "physical" resources. They include such essential minerals as uranium, iron, copper, nickel, bauxite, gold, silver, lead, mercury and tungsten. Oil, coal and natural gas are the principal nonrenewable fuel and energy resources, but after they have been used for producing heat or power their utility is lost and part of the geological capital of 325 million years of history is gone for ever. Some minerals such as iron and its product, steel, can be recycled and renewed, however. "Renewable" resources are basically biological, being the food and other vegetable matter which life needs to sustain human needs. Provided soil quality is maintained, their productivity may even be increased as better strains of plants and breeds of animals are developed.

Work has long been in progress to improve renewable resources, and has moved forward to manufacturing vegetable-flavored protein (VFP) from soybeans as a meat substitute and to viable experiments to extract protein from leaves. In Brazil, many cars have been converted to run successfully on alcohol extracted from sugar. One renewable resource—the tree—can be closely related to other resources: some conservationists are alarmed at the overuse of firewood as a source of fuel and energy in the semiarid areas of Africa. This may be an important factor in increasing the tendency for the deserts to spread in that continent, and in such a situation there is a new realization of the concept of closely managing resources such as soil, timber and fisheries. This is partly because we have a clearer understanding of the ecology of vegetation and the important interdependence of climate, soil, plants and animal life. Much, however, remains to be done.

The politics of nonrenewable resources

Today we are naturally troubled about the availability of natural resources. Oil is a prime cause for concern. Although many believe that production will grow until the mid-2020s and that new oil reserves will be discovered, oil's scarcity, based on a growing rate of demand and increasingly wasteful use, is now widely accepted. Because, like many resources, it is unevenly distributed, those countries with large and accessible supplies—such as the members of OPEC—have used their political power on a number of occasions to raise oil's price, with adverse effects on the economies of most importers. Ironically, these substantial price rises have had the effect of stimulating exploration and development in many new areas; there are already signs of increased production in China.

Other nonrenewable resources are also distributed unevenly, but have not been mined on any scale comparable with their availability; vast reserves of coal in the USSR and China have not been worked on any scale resembling their known extent.

New energy sources

As resources such as oil become less available and more expensive, the renewable resources of power such as water, wind, waves and solar energy, all of which are currently under study or development, will receive new injections of capital. Attention will also have to be paid to more widespread nuclear energy production. Energy has been called "the ultimate resource," and it is imperative that we make wise provisions for its future availability.

Future resources

It has been calculated that within four years of the launch of Sputnik I, more than 3,000 products resulting from space research were put into commercial production. These included new alloys, ceramics, plastics, fabrics and chemical compounds. Satellite developments have meant that land use can now be measured quickly and potential mineral sources closely identified. A satellite capable of converting solar power to electricity and contributing to the Earth's energy deficit has been widely discussed, while the Moon and planets have been mooted as future possible sources of minerals.

Conclusions

Resources are, in the main, the products of man's skill, ingenuity and expertise, and their widespread use, as in the case of timber and iron for shipbuilding, became apparent only as man's needs for them became clear. Our forebears were once concerned about the availability of flint, seaweed, charcoal and natural rubber; countries even went to war over supplies of spices. Today our requirements are slightly different—we no longer depend only on local sites for resources, and improved transport facilities and appropriate technologies have lowered the costs of obtaining materials for manufacture.

Nevertheless, the principles remain the same. A continual search for new resources capable of exploitation and wide application must be maintained, together with a close regard for the value of the renewable resources such as animal and vegetable products required to support man in his search for new resources. Perhaps the most vital consideration is the need for wise policies of conservation relating to the proven reserves of nonrenewable resources still in the ground, and the careful future use of such valuable deposits known or thought to exist.

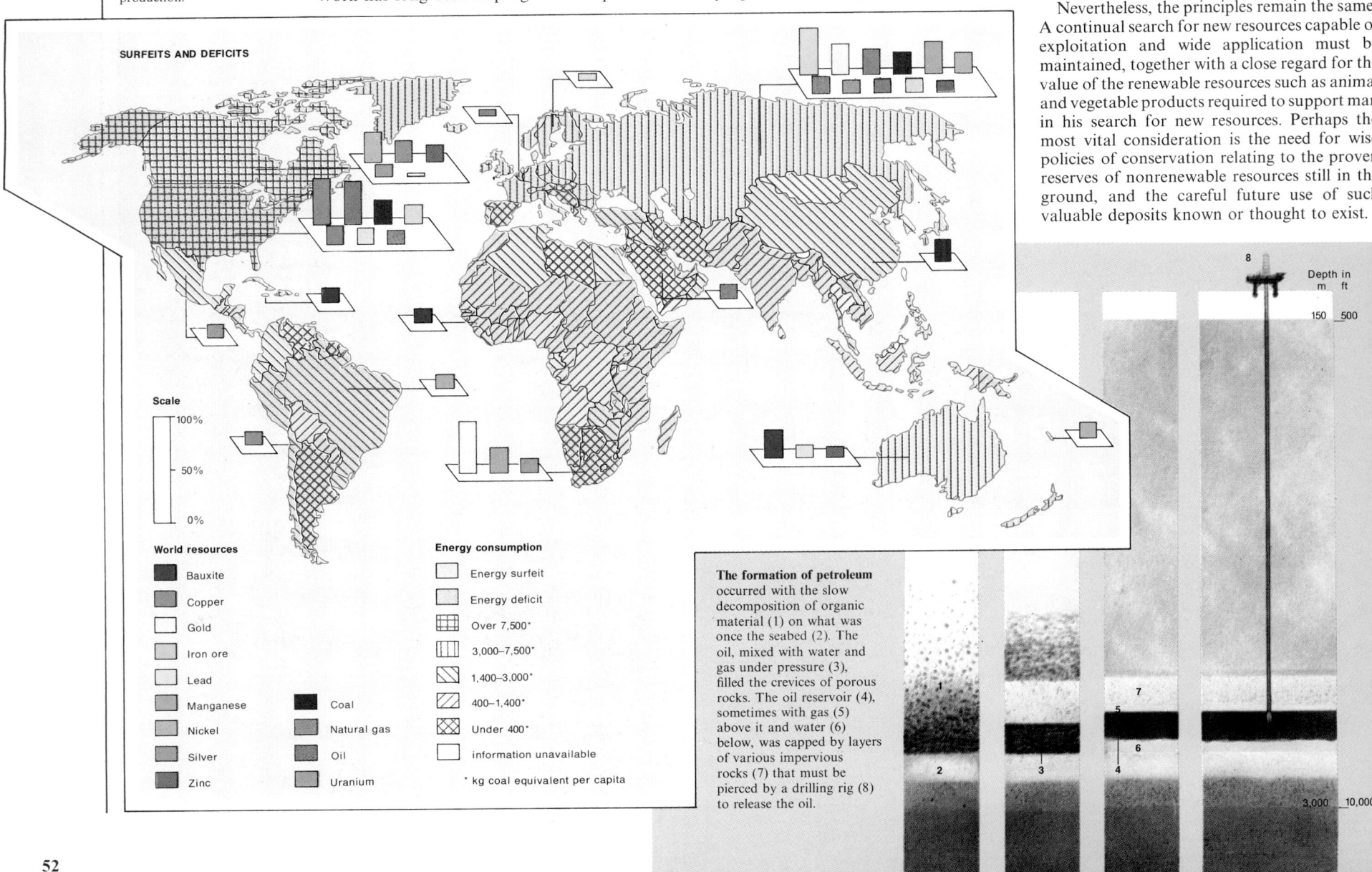

SURFEITS AND DEFICITS

Scale
100%
50%
0%

World resources
- Bauxite
- Copper
- Gold
- Iron ore
- Lead
- Manganese
- Nickel
- Silver
- Zinc
- Coal
- Natural gas
- Oil
- Uranium

Energy consumption
- Energy surfeit
- Energy deficit
- Over 7,500*
- 3,000–7,500*
- 1,400–3,000*
- 400–1,400*
- Under 400*
- information unavailable

* kg coal equivalent per capita

The formation of petroleum occurred with the slow decomposition of organic material (1) on what was once the seabed (2). The oil, mixed with water and gas under pressure (3), filled the crevices of porous rocks. The oil reservoir (4), sometimes with gas (5) above it and water (6) below, was capped by layers of various impervious rocks (7) that must be pierced by a drilling rig (8) to release the oil.

Depth in
m   ft
150 500
3,000 10,000

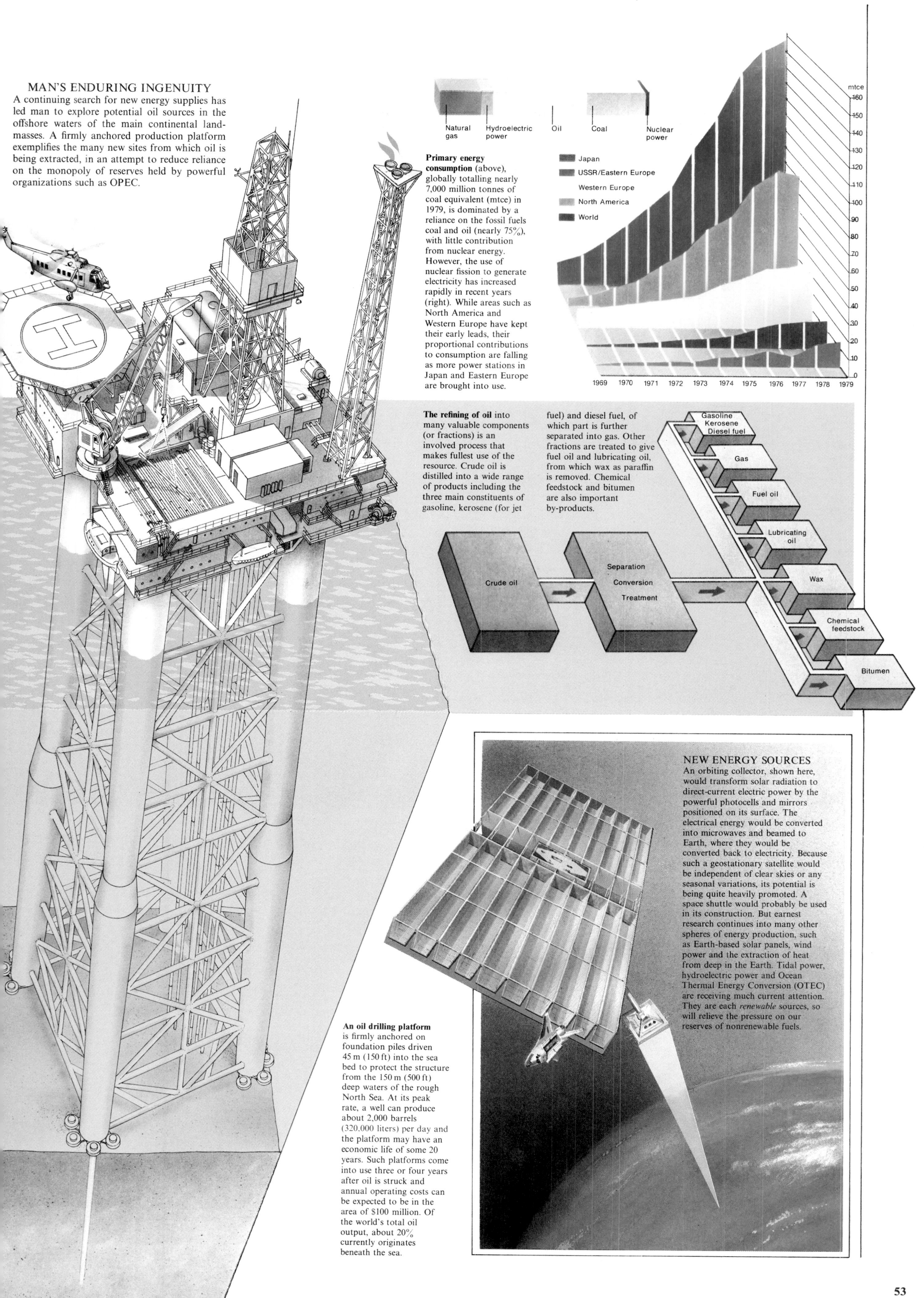

MAN'S ENDURING INGENUITY

A continuing search for new energy supplies has led man to explore potential oil sources in the offshore waters of the main continental landmasses. A firmly anchored production platform exemplifies the many new sites from which oil is being extracted, in an attempt to reduce reliance on the monopoly of reserves held by powerful organizations such as OPEC.

Natural gas   Hydroelectric power

Oil   Coal   Nuclear power

Japan
USSR/Eastern Europe
Western Europe
North America
World

mtce

Primary energy consumption (above), globally totalling nearly 7,000 million tonnes of coal equivalent (mtce) in 1979, is dominated by a reliance on the fossil fuels coal and oil (nearly 75%), with little contribution from nuclear energy. However, the use of nuclear fission to generate electricity has increased rapidly in recent years (right). While areas such as North America and Western Europe have kept their early leads, their proportional contributions to consumption are falling as more power stations in Japan and Eastern Europe are brought into use.

1969 1970 1971 1972 1973 1974 1975 1976 1977 1978 1979

The refining of oil into many valuable components (or fractions) is an involved process that makes fullest use of the resource. Crude oil is distilled into a wide range of products including the three main constituents of gasoline, kerosene (for jet fuel) and diesel fuel, of which part is further separated into gas. Other fractions are treated to give fuel oil and lubricating oil, from which wax as paraffin is removed. Chemical feedstock and bitumen are also important by-products.

Crude oil

Separation
Conversion
Treatment

Gasoline
Kerosene
Diesel fuel

Gas

Fuel oil

Lubricating oil

Wax

Chemical feedstock

Bitumen

NEW ENERGY SOURCES

An orbiting collector, shown here, would transform solar radiation to direct-current electric power by the powerful photocells and mirrors positioned on its surface. The electrical energy would be converted into microwaves and beamed to Earth, where they would be converted back to electricity. Because such a geostationary satellite would be independent of clear skies or any seasonal variations, its potential is being quite heavily promoted. A space shuttle would probably be used in its construction. But earnest research continues into many other spheres of energy production, such as Earth-based solar panels, wind power and the extraction of heat from deep in the Earth. Tidal power, hydroelectric power and Ocean Thermal Energy Conversion (OTEC) are receiving much current attention. They are each *renewable* sources, so will relieve the pressure on our reserves of nonrenewable fuels.

An oil drilling platform is firmly anchored on foundation piles driven 45 m (150 ft) into the sea bed to protect the structure from the 150 m (500 ft) deep waters of the rough North Sea. At its peak rate, a well can produce about 2,000 barrels (320,000 liters) per day and the platform may have an economic life of some 20 years. Such platforms come into use three or four years after oil is struck and annual operating costs can be expected to be in the area of $100 million. Of the world's total oil output, about 20% currently originates beneath the sea.

Population Growth

Every minute of every day, more than 250 children are born into the world. The Earth's population now stands at about 4,300 million and is continuing to grow extremely rapidly. The problems associated with such growth are enormous – already, about two-thirds of the world's people are underfed, according to United Nations' recommended standards of nutrition. And an even greater number live in very poor housing conditions, have inadequate access to medical facilities, receive little or no education and, at present, have no hope of improving their lot. As yet, there are no simple or immediate solutions.

World population (millions)

- ■ World population
- ▨ Projected world population

If the world's population continues to grow at its present rate, by the year 2000 there could be more than 6,400 million people on Earth (above). Such growth rates are only a recent phenomenon—for most of mankind's existence on Earth the numbers grew slowly (right). Then in the late 18th century, scientific and industrial developments and the discovery of new food sources (the prairies of the New World) raised living standards. Death rates declined and populations grew rapidly.

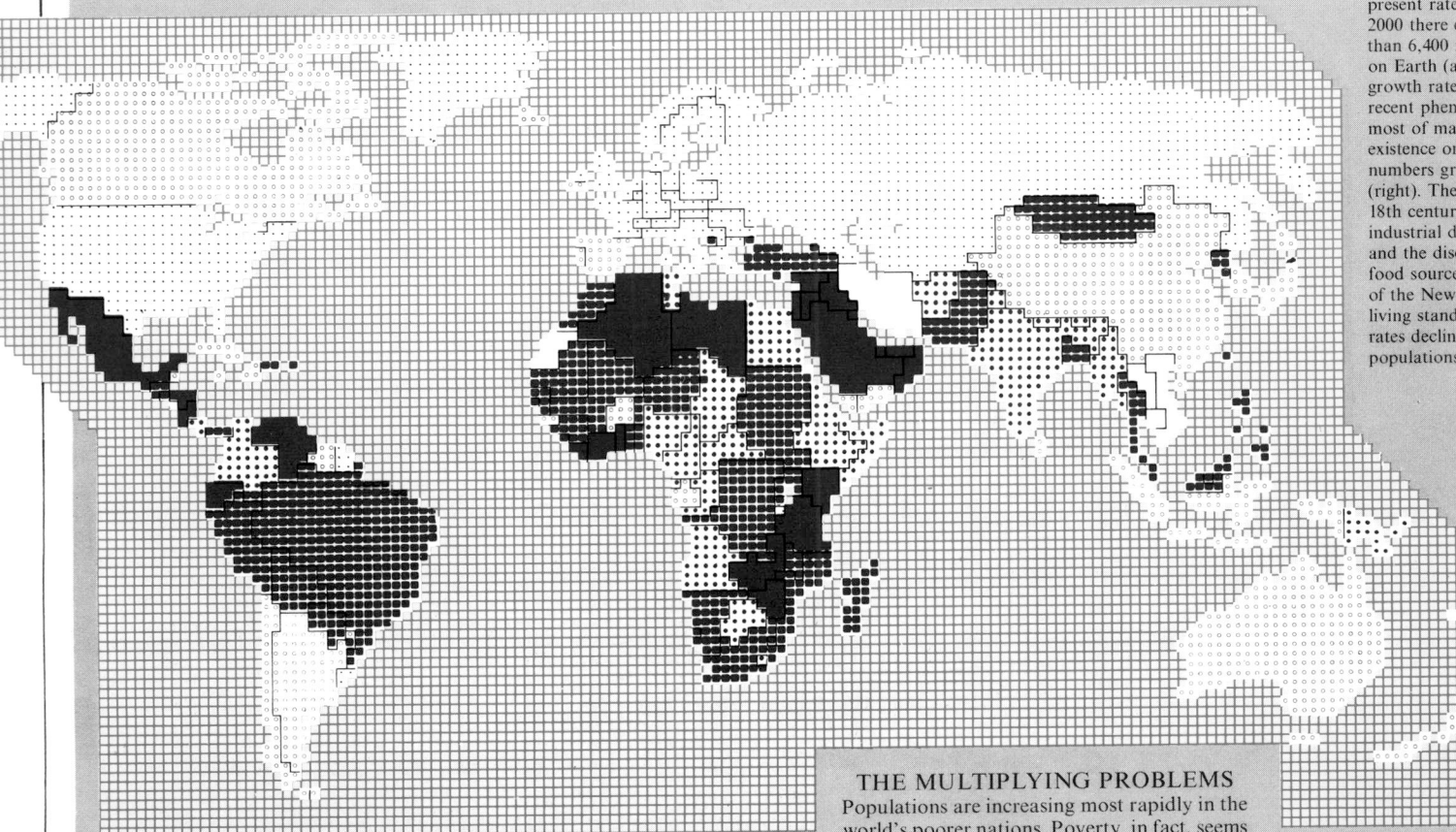

Average annual population growth rate 1970–1978

- ■ 3% and over
- ▦ 2.5% to less than 3%
- ▣ 2% to less than 2.5%
- ⬚ 1.0% to less than 2%
- ▢ Less than 1%
- □ Information unavailable

THE MULTIPLYING PROBLEMS

Populations are increasing most rapidly in the world's poorer nations. Poverty, in fact, seems to be at the heart of many of the complex interrelated problems created by rapid population growth. Poor countries, for example, are the least able to feed increasing numbers of people, while at the same time their lack of educational and medical facilities means that family planning is often inadequate and birth rates remain relatively high.

In 1830, there were only about 1,000 million people on Earth. By 1930, this figure had doubled. And by 1975, it had doubled again. If the present rate of increase continues, it will have doubled again by the year 2020.

This may not happen—it is extremely difficult to predict how world population will behave. What is certain is that it will continue to increase and, moreover, that this increase will not be evenly distributed. Since more than 50 percent of the human race lives in Asia, it is inevitable that the largest population increases will take place there. In fact, by the year 2000, the population of Asia may well have grown from about 2,000 million to more than 3,600 million. Substantial increases, of 400 million or more, will probably also occur in Africa, and Latin America is growing equally quickly.

In more prosperous North America and Europe, however, population growth seems to be stabilizing as women have fewer children and families become smaller—several countries, such as West Germany, now record a zero population growth rate. The poorer countries, the so-called Third World, are therefore gaining, and will probably continue to gain, an increasing share of the world's people. In 1930, about 64 percent of the human race lived in the poor countries of Asia, Africa and Latin America. By 1980, this proportion had increased to more than 75 percent. Population growth in these regions is creating enormous problems. It is estimated that there are now

more than 800 million people living in absolute poverty in the developing world, and these numbers can but increase as populations swell.

An obvious solution is to reduce birth rates, but this cannot be achieved quickly. In much of Africa and Asia, a very high proportion of the population is made up of young people who are, or soon will be, of childbearing age. Population increases are therefore inevitable. This will probably change as family planning becomes more widespread and women have fewer children, but such relief lies in the future and is likely to affect the poorest countries last. The most pressing problem for the growing numbers of impoverished people today is that of hunger.

Food – the fundamental problem

In theory, no food supply problem should exist—already enough food is produced in the world to feed a population of 5,500 million people. In fact, however, two-thirds of this food is consumed by the rich industrialized nations, and supplies are not reaching many of those in need. The developed nations dominate world food markets because developing nations, and people within those nations, are too poor to buy food, and are themselves unable to produce sufficient quantities to feed their growing populations. The answer to undernutrition and malnutrition lies largely in raising the incomes of poor peoples and improving distribution of supplies of food.

At a local level, food produced or imported

by developing countries must reach those in need at a price they can afford. One way of doing this is to encourage the rural poor to produce their own food. Small-scale, intensively farmed plots often prove to be the most efficient form of agriculture in areas where labor is plentiful. At present, many of the rural poor are either without land, or hold plots on extremely unfavorable terms of tenancy. By providing land, appropriate technology (small-scale, inexpensive farming equipment such as windpumps to draw water for irrigation), financial aid and information and education, small farmers could be helped to farm their land as effectively and efficiently as possible.

At a national level, too, developing countries must become more self-sufficient in food. This has already been achieved in some countries. India, although at one time heavily dependent upon imports of one of its staple foodstuffs—rice—has now increased production on such a scale that imports are no longer necessary. Unfortunately, for many developing countries this is not the case. Zaire, for example, was once an exporter of food. Today the country can no longer produce enough to keep pace with the demands of its own expanding population. At a world level, food production must be maintained as well, for unless production is kept high, prices are unstable and at times of bad harvests the poorer nations cannot afford to import essential supplies.

Food alone, however, is not enough to solve

FEEDING THE WORLD

How are the growing numbers of people on Earth to be fed when millions are already undernourished? In the short term, the food problem could be solved by improving distribution of supplies that are already available. But the world can also be made to produce more food. Fertilizers and pest control can make land more productive and genetic engineering could produce higher-yielding and more nutritious crops.

The world will have to produce more food than it does today (below) if future populations are to be fed. At present, large areas of the Earth's land surface cannot be farmed—they are either too cold, dry, marshy, mountainous or forested. Cultivatable areas could be extended, given the necessary investment.

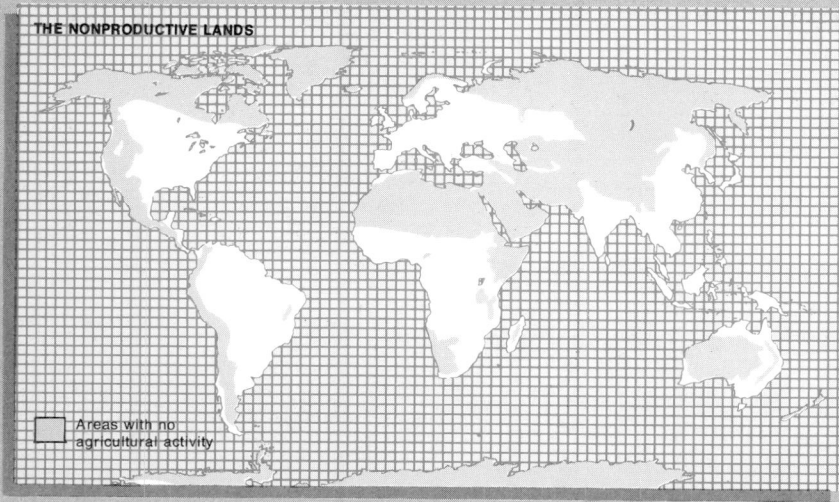

THE NONPRODUCTIVE LANDS

☐ Areas with no agricultural activity

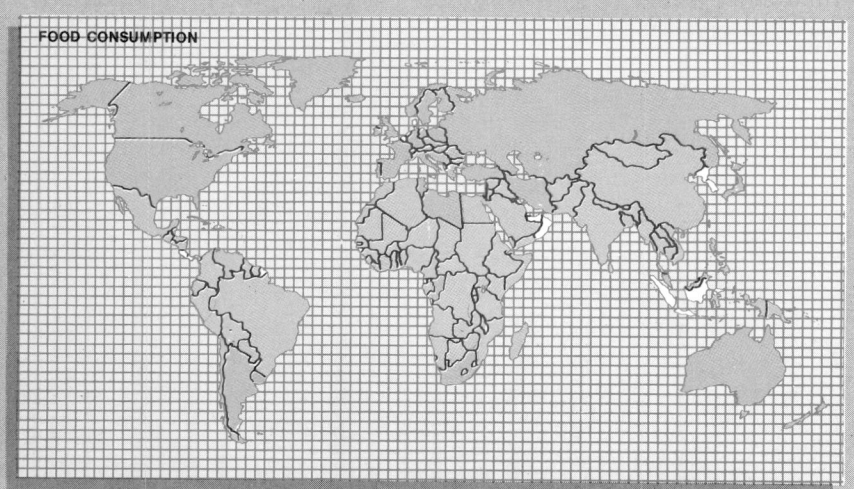

FOOD CONSUMPTION

Calories per capita
- Less than 95% of needs
- 95% to 115% of needs
- More than 115% of needs
- Information unavailable

Malnutrition is widespread throughout the developing nations of Africa, Asia and South America. The problem is made worse by the fact that populations in these countries are growing more rapidly than anywhere else in the world.

the problems created by population growth. Broadly based economic development, such as in manufacturing and industry, is essential if developing countries are to have the income and other resources to enable them to cope with their evergrowing numbers of people.

Economic growth

To achieve economic development, certain obstacles must be overcome. First, the Third World needs energy supplies at a price it can afford, for, with the exception of Nigeria and the now-rich Middle East, most developing regions are woefully short of the energy resources needed to fuel growth. Second, for sustained economic development a skilled labor force is required, as are educational facilities to provide the necessary skills from within the nations themselves. Third, investment is required to enable developing nations to exploit the resources they do have—minerals, for example. And this investment must be on terms that are as beneficial to the developing nations as they are to powerful multinational organizations that frequently fund such projects. Finally, and most important, more enlightened social and political outlooks are needed within many countries if their growing populations of impoverished people are to benefit from any economic development and consequent increase in national wealth.

It has been said that wealth is the best method of contraception and, judging by the history of population growth in the rich industrialized nations, this seems to be the case. If it is, economic development of the Third World may well alleviate many of the problems created by population growth.

THE HEALTH OF NATIONS

Many developing nations are severely short of medical and welfare facilities for their growing populations. Yet these are the very countries with high incidences of disease—mainly because of malnutrition, lack of clean water supplies, and inadequate and overcrowded housing. Furthermore, without health services family planning facilities are not widely available, and expanding populations continue to strain existing resources.

Birth and Death Rates
- High birth rate/High death rate
- High birth rate/Moderate or low death rate
- Low birth rate/Low death rate
- Information unavailable

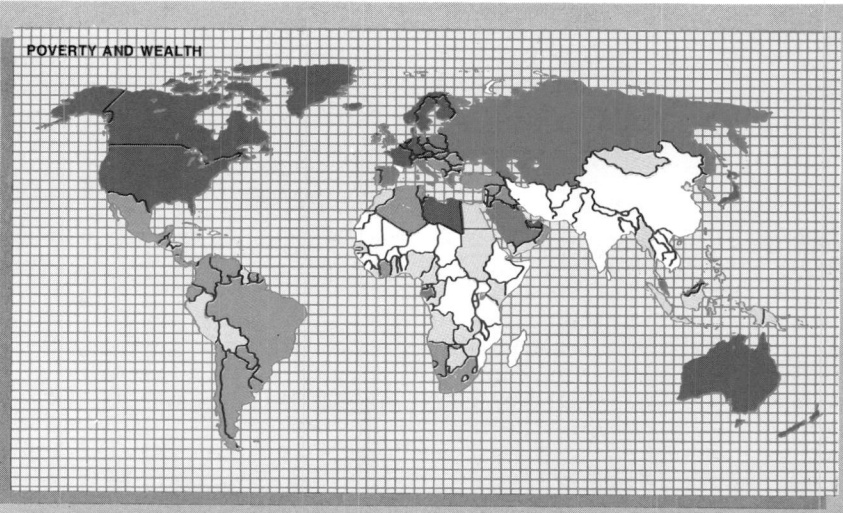

PATTERNS OF POPULATION GROWTH

As a country's health facilities improve, its mortality rates decline. Birth rates, however, do not immediately fall (above). Thus, ironically, an improvement in facilities at first exacerbates the problem of rapid growth in population. A country with a declining death rate and a high birth rate gains an increasing percentage of young people who are, or will be, of child-bearing age. Population pyramids (right) plot the percentage balance between age and youth in a nation.

[Population pyramid chart: Burundi and West Germany, by Age groups 0–4 through 80+, Male and Female, scale 10 8 6 4 2 0 2 4 6 8 10]

INCOME

When the income level of a population is raised sufficiently, it seems that birth rates ultimately decline. This has been the pattern that has emerged in the Western world. If this is the case, then economic development of the Third World countries could eventually help to stabilize world population growth, as well as provide nations with the means to cope. It could also help provide for their growing numbers.

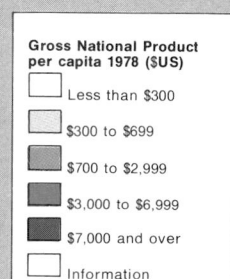

Gross National Product per capita 1978 ($US)
- Less than $300
- $300 to $699
- $700 to $2,999
- $3,000 to $6,999
- $7,000 and over
- Information unavailable

POVERTY AND WEALTH

A nation's Gross National Product (GNP), when divided by the number of its population, gives some indication of the relative wealth (or poverty) of its people. But because national wealth is not evenly distributed in many countries (particularly in South America), this figure can conceal the extreme poverty of very large numbers of a nation's people.

EDUCATIONAL RESOURCES

Education is essential if the people of the developing world are to be equipped to improve their lot. Basic education on health and hygiene could dramatically reduce the incidence of disease; education about birth control would help lower birth rates; agricultural advice could help the rural poor to produce more food. Finally, general schooling is required to provide skilled labor.

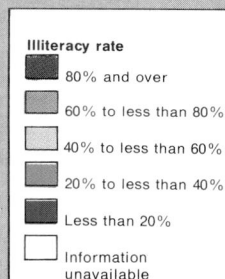

ILLITERACY

Illiteracy rate
- 80% and over
- 60% to less than 80%
- 40% to less than 60%
- 20% to less than 40%
- Less than 20%
- Information unavailable

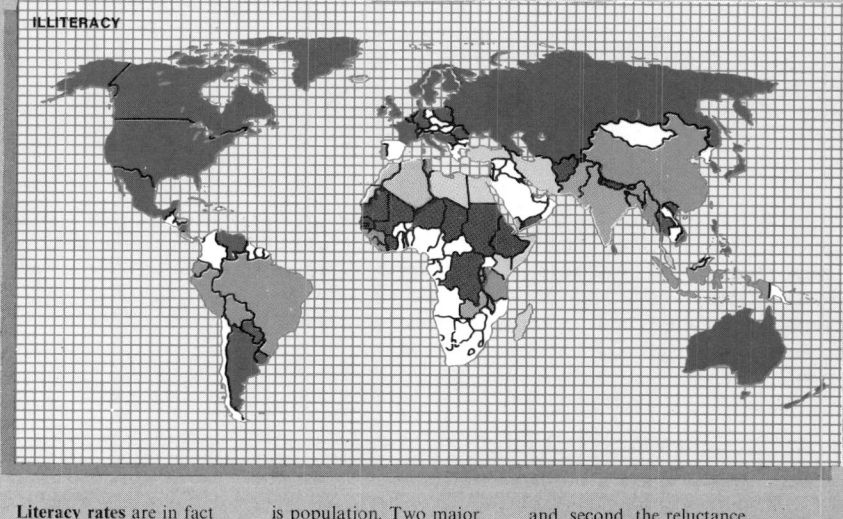

Literacy rates are in fact improving in developing countries and national expenditure on schools is growing more quickly than is population. Two major problems are, first, the social traditions that severely restrict the number of girls attending school and, second, the reluctance of many rural poor to send to school children who provide valuable manual labor on the land.

Human Settlement

Man is naturally a gregarious animal. As an agriculturist he first settled in small communities, but it was not long before the emergence of towns and cities. Now nearly half the world's people live in these larger settlements, and by the year 2000, for the first time in history, more people will live in cities than in the countryside. Cities have grown up for various reasons, and are unevenly distributed across the world; but it is in the developing countries that the most rapid rates of urban growth are today taking place.

City life has a long and varied history going back to the early population centers of the Tigris–Euphrates, Indus and Nile valleys. Administrative and political needs led to the development of capital cities. Some, like London and Paris, evolved on conveniently located river crossings; others, such as Canberra, Islamabad and Brasilia, have locations that were deliberately planned.

Types of towns and cities
Market towns were established to exchange produce and, as trade expanded, hierarchies of service centers became established. These ranged from small "central places" that supplied rural areas with simple goods and services from elsewhere, to large cities that provided highly specialized services. Through such centrally placed systems, rural areas became connected with major industrialized areas. Mining towns such as Johannesburg, South Africa, and Broken Hill, Australia, sprang up as man began to exploit the Earth's mineral resources, their locations determined by the presence of rich ore deposits. Fishing ports and settlements dependent on forestry fall into the same group.

Increasing specialization, exemplified by the Black Country, England, and the Ruhr, West Germany, was a feature of European industrial development in the eighteenth and nineteenth centuries, and was based on the availability of capital investment and the presence of sources of fuel and power, especially water and steam power. Such industrialized cities relied on newly developed forms of transport to bring in new materials and to carry away manufactured products. Chicago is a good example of the relationship between the development of rail and water routes and the growth of a city as a market, agricultural processing and manufacturing center. As transport developed, further specialized centers concentrated on locomotive, ship or aircraft construction.

Uneven settlement patterns
Across the world, density and distribution of population are uneven. The land surface of the Earth as a whole has a density of 28 people per sq km (73 per sq mile) although Manhattan, for example, has 26,000 per sq km (63,340 per sq mile) and Australia has only 1.5 per sq km (4 per sq mile). In Brazil, towns and cities are mostly sited in the rich southeast, in contrast to a sparseness of settlement in its interior. Contrasts also occur between Mediterranean North Africa and the deserted Sahara to the south; or Canada of the St. Lawrence and the Canadian Shield to the north. Here the causes are not hard to find: extremes of climate, terrain and vegetation form effective barriers to settlement. Geographers estimate that two-thirds of the world's population lives within 500 km (310 miles) of the sea.

Any true consideration of human settlements must, however, be placed within the context of the economic, political and social systems in which they have evolved. Physical considerations alone cannot fully explain the urban concentrations of Western Europe, Japan or the northeastern USA, or the comparative absence of cities elsewhere. Only 5 percent of Malawi's and 4.7 percent of New Guinea's populations live in towns; in Belgium the percentage is 87, in Australia 86, in the UK 78 and in the USA 73.5. The figure for Norway is only 42 percent. Urbanization is a varied phenomenon and cities grow for many reasons.

The attractions of the city
Cities have always acted as magnets to poor or unemployed rural populations, and migrations from the countryside have assisted high rates of

THE DISTRIBUTION OF POPULATION
Human settlement is highly uneven because it is related to many social and topographical factors. At first, man was tied to the sites of his crops and the grazing land of his cattle; life in nonrural centers only became a typical feature of population development as specialized services came into demand and towns and cities arose to support these needs. But during the 20th century there has been a vast increase in urban populations, particularly in Third World countries.

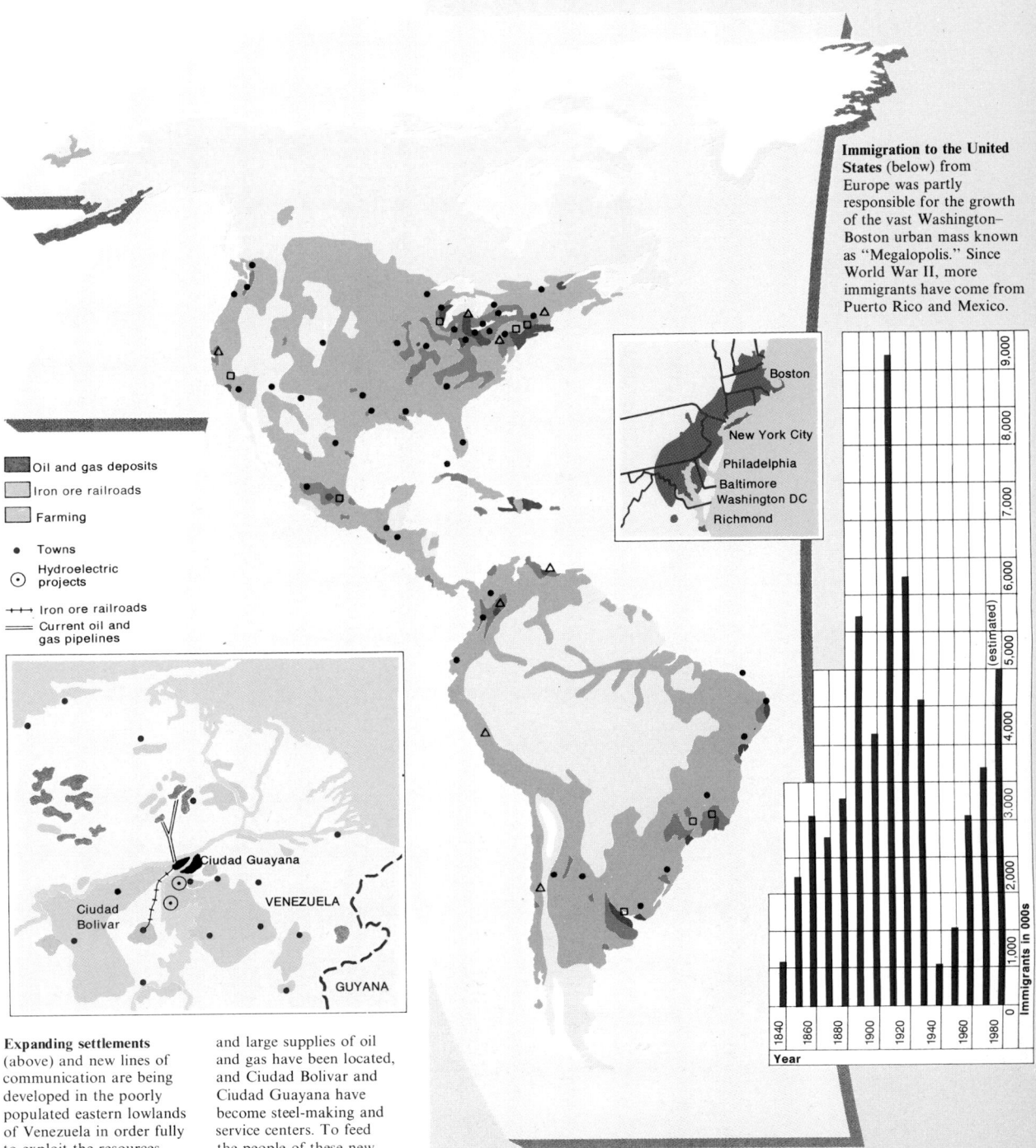

Oil and gas deposits
Iron ore railroads
Farming
• Towns
⊙ Hydroelectric projects
+++ Iron ore railroads
=== Current oil and gas pipelines

Boston
New York City
Philadelphia
Baltimore
Washington DC
Richmond

Ciudad Guayana
Ciudad Bolivar
VENEZUELA
GUYANA

Immigration to the United States (below) from Europe was partly responsible for the growth of the vast Washington–Boston urban mass known as "Megalopolis." Since World War II, more immigrants have come from Puerto Rico and Mexico.

9,000 / 8,000 / 7,000 / 6,000 / 5,000 (estimated) / 4,000 / 3,000 / 2,000 / 1,000 / 0
Immigrants in 000s
1840 / 1860 / 1880 / 1900 / 1920 / 1940 / 1960 / 1980
Year

Expanding settlements (above) and new lines of communication are being developed in the poorly populated eastern lowlands of Venezuela in order fully to exploit the resources being discovered there. Huge deposits of iron ore and large supplies of oil and gas have been located, and Ciudad Bolivar and Ciudad Guayana have become steel-making and service centers. To feed the people of these new settlements, agriculture has been greatly expanded.

city growth. Very large cities—Tokyo, New York and Los Angeles—are still found in the northern world, but many cities with far faster growth rates are sited in the Third World, especially in Asia. There the total number of inhabitants living in towns and cities is still much lower than in Europe, but centers such as Shanghai, Karachi, Bandung, New Delhi, Seoul, Jakarta and Manila are among the world's most rapidly expanding urban centers. Perhaps as many as a third of these city dwellers in Asia, Africa and Latin America put up with makeshift housing in shanty towns that present enormous problems of health, sanitation, education and unemployment: city growth in the developing world is a daunting prospect.

People on the move
In the past, one solution to population pressure on the land could be found in the migrations which occurred on a large scale from Asia into Europe, from Europe to the Americas and Australasia, and from China into southeastern Asia. But as claims are being made on almost every habitable area of the Earth, mass migrations have largely declined in importance. Many nations restrict movement to or from

their countries. Australia has strict immigration quotas; Vietnam and the USSR restrict emigration for largely ideological reasons. Large movements of labor still take place, however, from the poorer regions of the Mediterranean to the industrial cities of France and Germany. Migrant workers from neighboring countries in Africa also play an essential part in the mining economy of South Africa.

New trends in urbanization
In many industrialized countries, a strong process of decentralization is leading to reductions in the populations of cities and corresponding increases in those of the suburbs and beyond. In 1951 the geographer Jean Gottman showed how groups of city regions tend to form chains of functionally linked cities, to which he gave the term "megalopolis." His prime example was Megalopolis, USA, stretching from north of Boston to south of Washington DC. Similar settlements occur in the Tokyo–Yokohama–Osaka area of Japan and the Ruhr megalopolis of northwestern Europe. Ultimately, equally drastic and large-scale patterns are likely to emerge in the already overcrowded human settlements of the Third World.

Migrating refugees, the world total of which increases on average by 2,000–3,000 every day, can affect settlement patterns. The Ugandan children (below) fled to the northern province of Karamoja in the wake of the 1979 war with Tanzania and the resultant famine that occurred in much of Uganda.

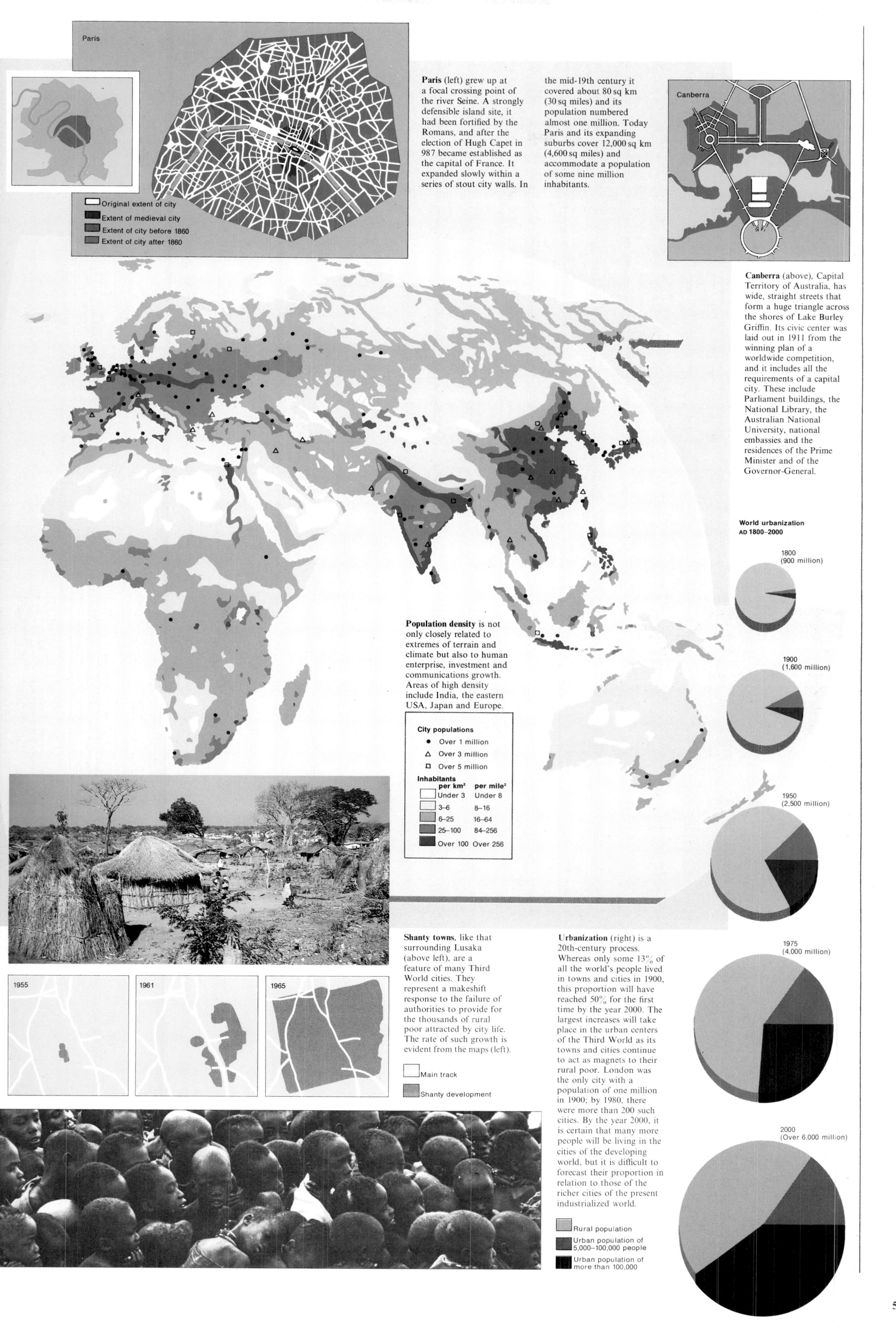

Paris

Paris (left) grew up at a focal crossing point of the river Seine. A strongly defensible island site, it had been fortified by the Romans, and after the election of Hugh Capet in 987 became established as the capital of France. It expanded slowly within a series of stout city walls. In the mid-19th century it covered about 80 sq km (30 sq miles) and its population numbered almost one million. Today Paris and its expanding suburbs cover 12,000 sq km (4,600 sq miles) and accommodate a population of some nine million inhabitants.

☐ Original extent of city
■ Extent of medieval city
■ Extent of city before 1860
■ Extent of city after 1860

Canberra

Canberra (above), Capital Territory of Australia, has wide, straight streets that form a huge triangle across the shores of Lake Burley Griffin. Its civic center was laid out in 1911 from the winning plan of a worldwide competition, and it includes all the requirements of a capital city. These include Parliament buildings, the National Library, the Australian National University, national embassies and the residences of the Prime Minister and of the Governor-General.

Population density is not only closely related to extremes of terrain and climate but also to human enterprise, investment and communications growth. Areas of high density include India, the eastern USA, Japan and Europe.

City populations
● Over 1 million
△ Over 3 million
☐ Over 5 million

Inhabitants

per km²	per mile²
Under 3	Under 8
3–6	8–16
6–25	16–64
25–100	84–256
Over 100	Over 256

Shanty towns, like that surrounding Lusaka (above left), are a feature of many Third World cities. They represent a makeshift response to the failure of authorities to provide for the thousands of rural poor attracted by city life. The rate of such growth is evident from the maps (left).

1955   1961   1965

☐ Main track
■ Shanty development

Urbanization (right) is a 20th-century process. Whereas only some 13% of all the world's people lived in towns and cities in 1900, this proportion will have reached 50% for the first time by the year 2000. The largest increases will take place in the urban centers of the Third World as its towns and cities continue to act as magnets to their rural poor. London was the only city with a population of one million in 1900; by 1980, there were more than 200 such cities. By the year 2000, it is certain that many more people will be living in the cities of the developing world, but it is difficult to forecast their proportion in relation to those of the richer cities of the present industrialized world.

☐ Rural population
■ Urban population of 5,000–100,000 people
■ Urban population of more than 100,000

World urbanization AD 1800–2000

1800 (900 million)

1900 (1,600 million)

1950 (2,500 million)

1975 (4,000 million)

2000 (Over 6,000 million)

Trade and Transport

It is a commonplace that we live in a "shrinking" world. During the last century the development of communications has been so rapid that man appears almost to have conquered the challenge of distance; but such a concept depends on the kind of area to be covered and the cost of transporting goods in relation to their value, bulk and perishability. People, goods and services become accessible by trade. Transport makes trade possible: trade's demands lead to improvements in transport.

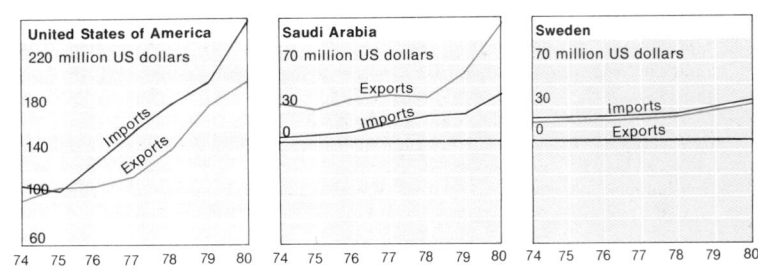

Exports in millions of US dollars (A)

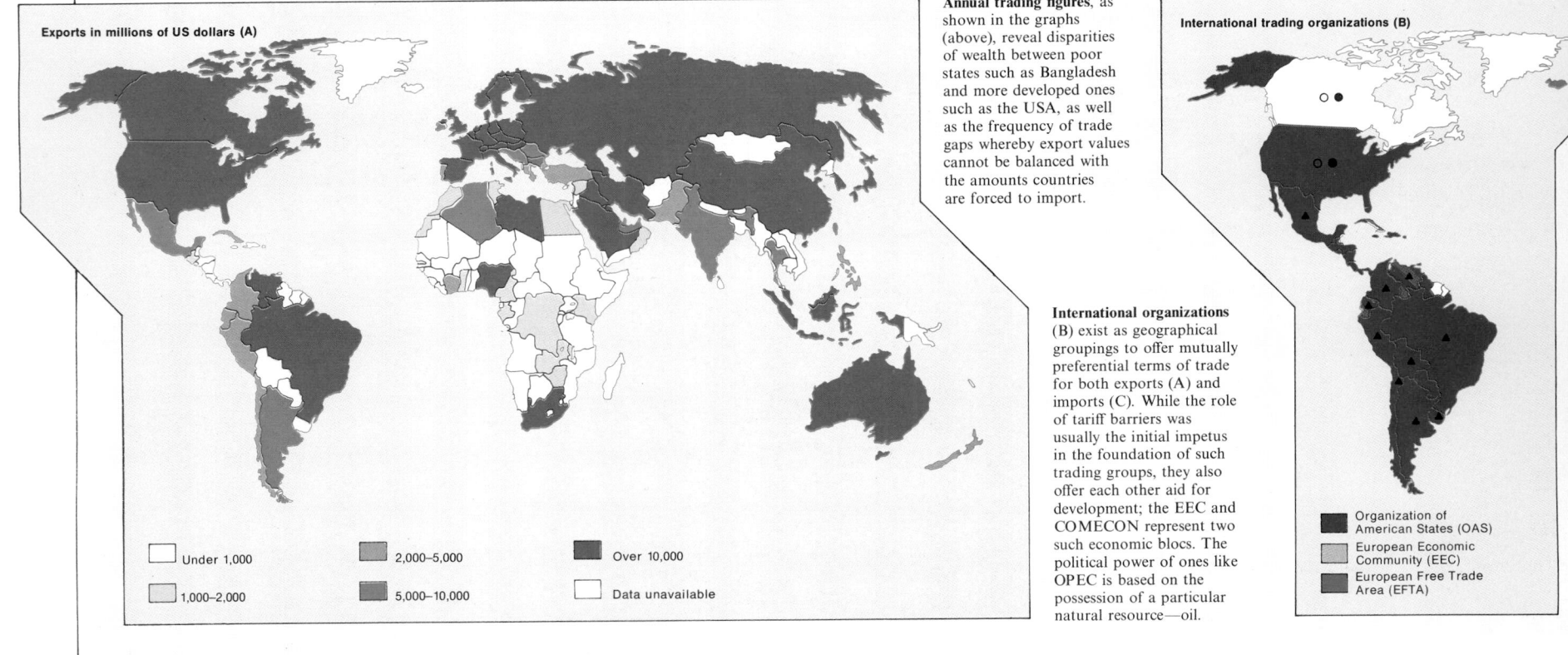

Annual trading figures, as shown in the graphs (above), reveal disparities of wealth between poor states such as Bangladesh and more developed ones such as the USA, as well as the frequency of trade gaps whereby export values cannot be balanced with the amounts countries are forced to import.

International trading organizations (B)

International organizations (B) exist as geographical groupings to offer mutually preferential terms of trade for both exports (A) and imports (C). While the role of tariff barriers was usually the initial impetus in the foundation of such trading groups, they also offer each other aid for development; the EEC and COMECON represent two such economic blocs. The political power of ones like OPEC is based on the possession of a particular natural resource—oil.

Legend (A):
- Under 1,000
- 1,000–2,000
- 2,000–5,000
- 5,000–10,000
- Over 10,000
- Data unavailable

Legend (B):
- Organization of American States (OAS)
- European Economic Community (EEC)
- European Free Trade Area (EFTA)

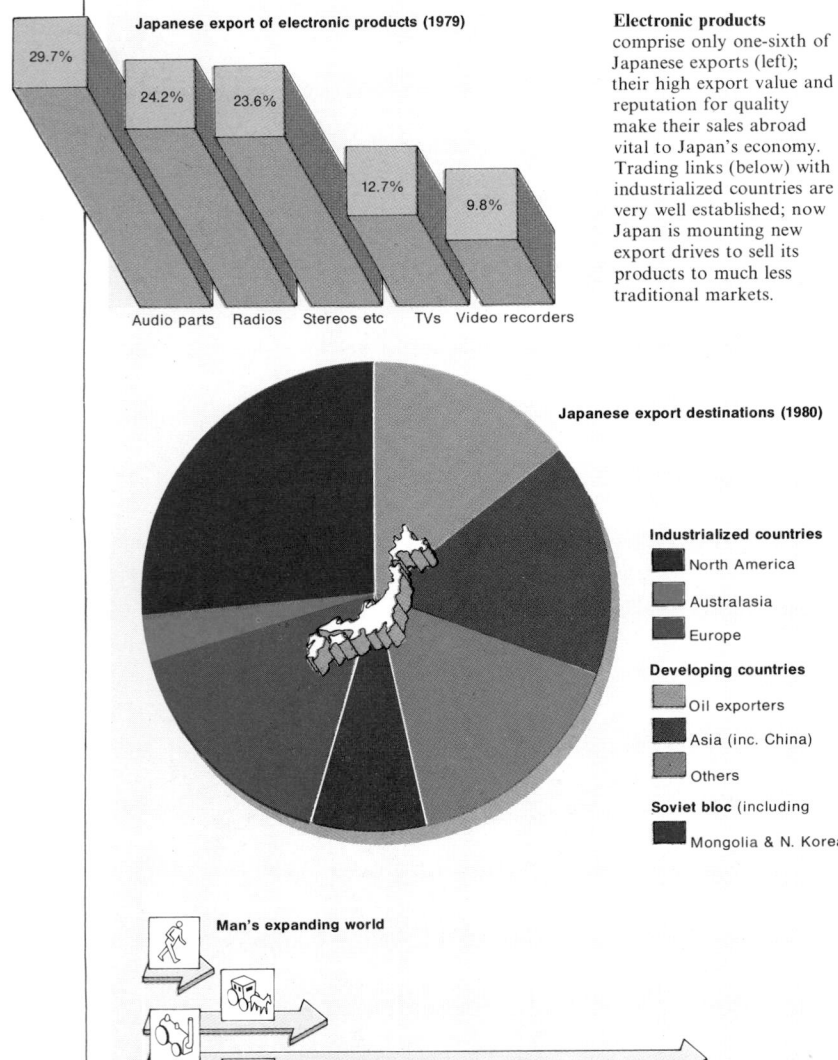

Japanese export of electronic products (1979)

29.7% Audio parts
24.2% Radios
23.6% Stereos etc
12.7% TVs
9.8% Video recorders

Electronic products comprise only one-sixth of Japanese exports (left); their high export value and reputation for quality make their sales abroad vital to Japan's economy. Trading links (below) with industrialized countries are very well established; now Japan is mounting new export drives to sell its products to much less traditional markets.

Japanese export destinations (1980)

Industrialized countries
- North America
- Australasia
- Europe

Developing countries
- Oil exporters
- Asia (inc. China)
- Others

Soviet bloc (including
- Mongolia & N. Korea)

Man's expanding world

It is only a little more than two centuries since navigators completed the mapping of the world's major landmasses and much less since the mapping of the continental interiors was completed—even today some gaps still remain. Canals like the Suez (1869) and Panama (1915) reduced the extent of long sea voyages—the Suez Canal shortened the distance from northwestern Europe to India by 15,000 km (9,300 miles)—so that in transport terms, the various parts of the world became more accessible, especially as steamships and motor vessels replaced sailing ships, and time distances were reduced still further by the airplane.

Locational advantages

Inland waterways, roads and railroads opened up new areas for mining or specialized agriculture, and created opportunities for the manufacture of goods and for the distribution of the finished products. The contrast, however, between locations such as London, Tokyo or Chicago (which are accessible to all forms of transport) and parts of South America where modern transport hardly penetrates, has become much more marked over the years. New transport developments tend to connect major centers first of all, and thus increase their already high locational status.

Such developments must nevertheless be seen in the light of the demand for communications and trade between different points, the nature of the goods being carried and the actual cost of transport. Transport improvements have allowed different parts of the world to share ideas and products; ironically, they have also made such places more dissimilar, since each area of the Earth has had the chance to specialize in the services it can provide most efficiently.

Specialization of area

Before the widespread development of canals and railroads, road transport was expensive and towns and villages tended to be more self-sufficient. Railroads played a vital role in reducing transport costs in relation to distance and in providing an opportunity for different areas to specialize. After the emergence of railroad networks in North America, specialized areas of agricultural production quickly developed because they were well adjusted to the climatic conditions needed for growing maize (corn), cotton, fruit and fresh vegetables for the new urban markets. In the southern hemisphere, steamships and the introduction of refrigeration enabled meat, butter and cheese to be kept fresh on their journeys to the north.

This concept of specialization of area is basic to world trading patterns, since regions tend to concentrate on commodities and services that they can exchange for other specialized goods and products from other regional or world markets. Countries and areas do best when they concentrate on products for which they have comparative cost advantages in terms of the presence of natural resources, the availability of the skills to develop them, and a demand for the products. Enterprise in adapting natural conditions for the production of goods at competitive price levels is also important. Settlers in New

Technological change in transport has resulted in important reductions in the cost of trade. A man trading on foot might travel half the area a draft horse could cover in a 12-hour day, but it was the acceptance of steam after *The Rocket* (1829) that made trade more reliable and greatly expanded the potential for international commerce. Modern jet airliners can easily fly thousands of kilometers in half a day, and while they are being used more and more for freight, most bulk freight is still carried by train or by specialized cargo vessel. The graph below plots changing transport technology.

0   120   240   360   480   600   720   840   960   1,080   1,200   1,320   1,440   1,560
Kilometers traveled in 12 hours

THE WEALTH OF NATIONS

Economists measure a country's richness in terms of Gross National Product (GNP), the value of the goods and services available for consumption and for adding to its wealth. The difference in value between its exported and imported goods is often an important aspect of a nation's economy, and effective systems to transport such goods must play a major role in overseas trade. The 1980 Brandt Report highlighted the huge gap between the income of the rich world and the poverty of many developing states, but solutions to such problems of inequality will be difficult to obtain.

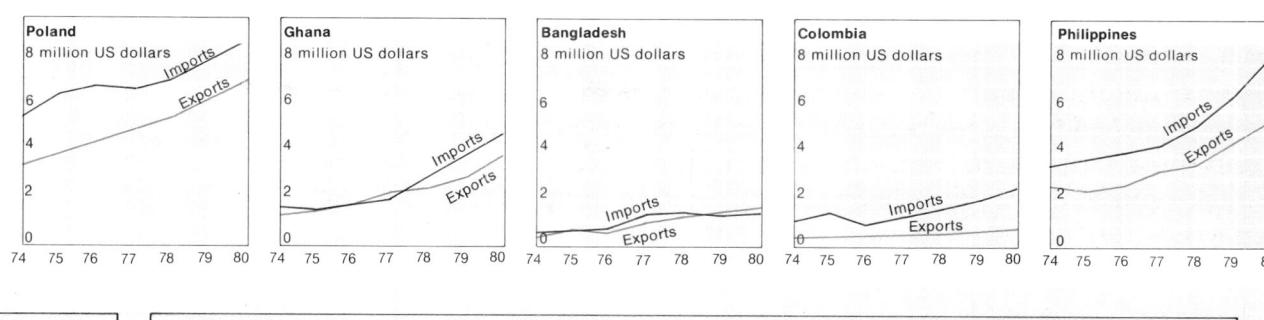

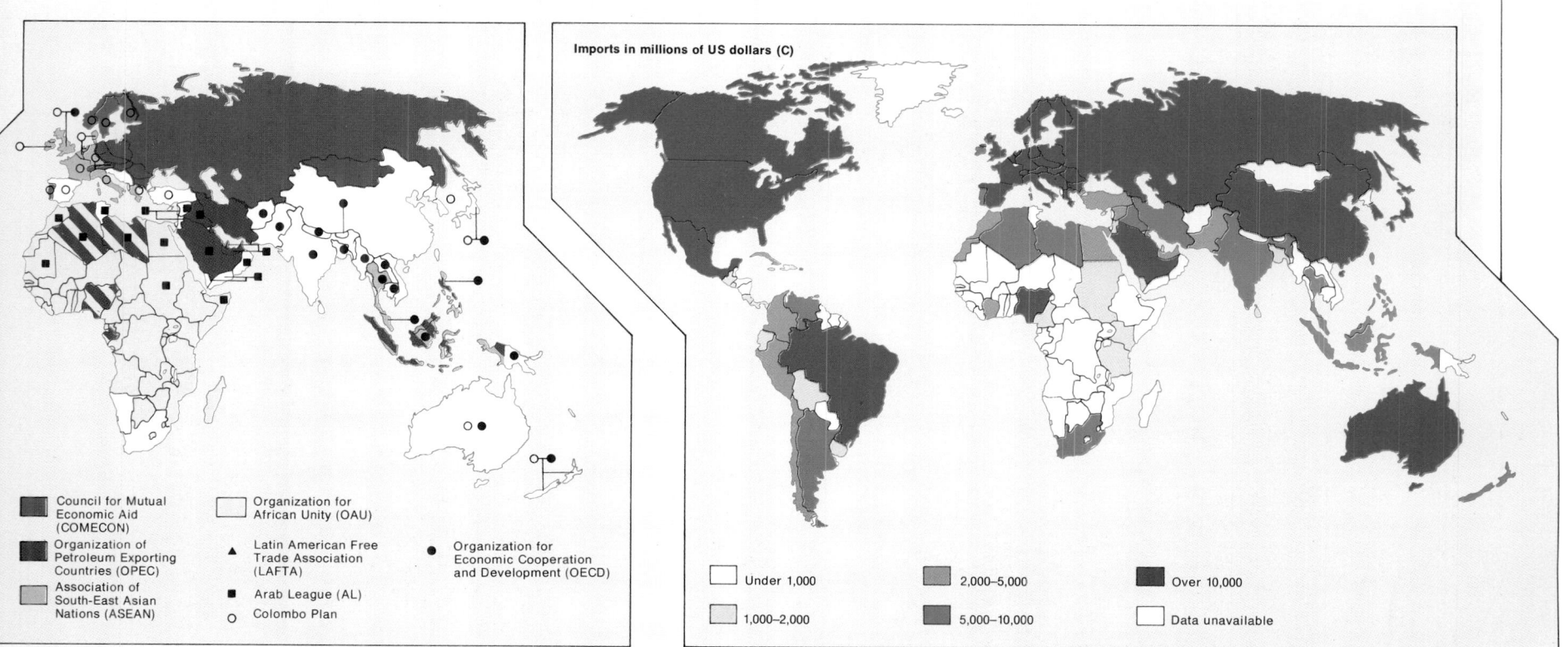

Imports in millions of US dollars (C)

Council for Mutual Economic Aid (COMECON)

Organization for African Unity (OAU)

Organization of Petroleum Exporting Countries (OPEC)

▲ Latin American Free Trade Association (LAFTA)

● Organization for Economic Cooperation and Development (OECD)

Association of South-East Asian Nations (ASEAN)

■ Arab League (AL)

○ Colombo Plan

Under 1,000 | 2,000–5,000 | Over 10,000
1,000–2,000 | 5,000–10,000 | Data unavailable

Zealand, for example, had little hesitation in clearing the prevailing tussock grass to create a new pastoral environment for their large-scale production of sheep and dairy products.

In the real world, however, there are many impediments to the operation of a free market system, and it is unwise for states like New Zealand to assume that they will always dominate Commonwealth dairy trade.

Impediments to free markets

Countries erect protectionist tariff barriers to assist their home industries and/or to obtain extra revenue. Import or export quotas may be imposed, and trade agreements with other countries give special preference to certain commodities. Problems arise from the exchange of currencies and their fluctuations in value. Tariff barriers may be erected for political, welfare or defense reasons. Sometimes special measures may be adopted to encourage the internal production of certain goods rather than obtaining them more cheaply from abroad, and such methods may be economically important to a country that has always relied on the export of raw materials for its income but now wishes domestically to manufacture previously imported goods.

Political ties are vital to the groupings of certain countries. For reasons of international politics, countries such as those of the Soviet bloc trade with each other rather than with the outside world; and historical links, as between the UK and the Commonwealth, France and her ex-colonies, and Spain and Portugal with

Latin America, are also influential. The European Economic Community (EEC) is composed of countries that have formed a strong bloc among the developed countries.

Rich man, poor man

The developed countries of "the North" have more than 80 percent of the world's manufacturing income but only a quarter of its population, whereas the poorer peoples of "the South" number 3,000 million and receive only a fifth of world income. Attempts have been made to obtain a better economic balance. The 1948 General Agreement on Tariffs and Trade (GATT) and the United Nations Conference on Trade and Development (UNCTAD) provided mechanisms for multinational trade negotiations, and the World Bank and the International Monetary Fund (IMF) together with the 1960 International Development Association (IDA) have all provided easier loans for less developed states.

The widening gap between rich and poor countries has led to understandable demands for a new international order calling for basic changes in the structure of world production, aid and trade, and the transfer of resources. The 1980 Independent Commission on International Development Issues (The Brandt Commission) advocated just such a transfer to the Third World. But during a major world recession there seems little sign of any international political will strong enough to take action on the scale needed to solve the problems that contrasts in wealth and poverty involve.

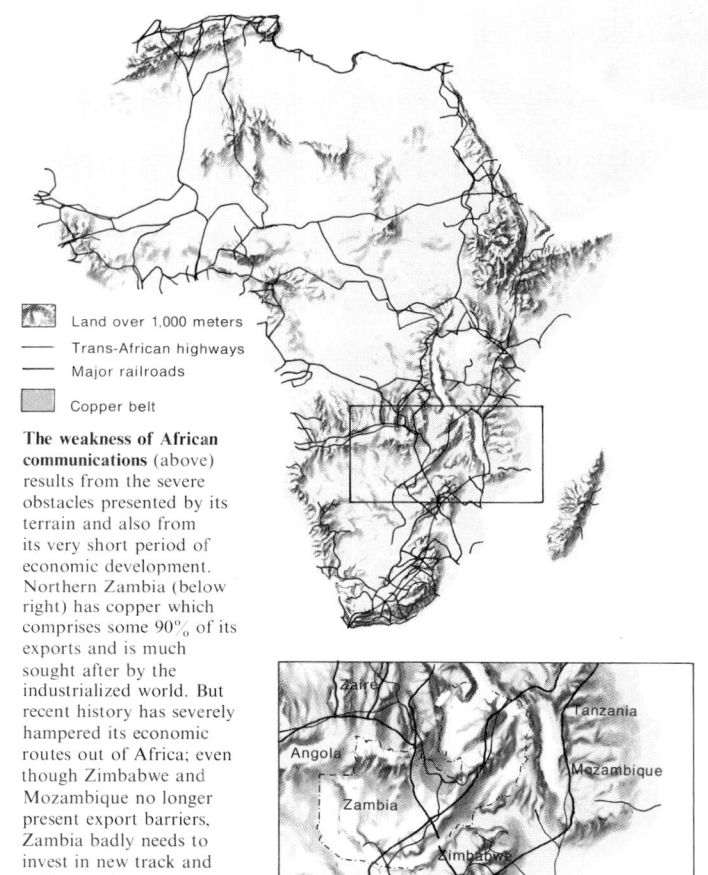

Land over 1,000 meters

— Trans-African highways

— Major railroads

Copper belt

The weakness of African communications (above) results from the severe obstacles presented by its terrain and also from its very short period of economic development. Northern Zambia (below right) has copper which comprises some 90% of its exports and is much sought after by the industrialized world. But recent history has severely hampered its economic routes out of Africa; even though Zimbabwe and Mozambique no longer present export barriers, Zambia badly needs to invest in new track and rolling stock.

1,800 | 1,920 | 2,040 | 2,160 | 2,280 | 2,400 | 2,520 | 2,640 | 2,760 | 2,880 | 3,000 | 3,120 | 3,240 | 3,360

Polar Regions

Sunless in winter, and capped with permanent land ice and shifting sea ice, the world's polar regions present an image of intense and everlasting cold. But permanent ice caps have been the exception rather than the rule in the 4,600 million years of Earth's history. The most recent intensification of the present ice age (which began at least two million years ago) reached its maximum about 20,000 years ago and still continues to fluctuate. Polar conditions preclude all but the toughest life forms on land, but the plankton-rich waters attract many animals, and man is beginning to exploit the polar regions' potential.

There have been about a dozen ice ages since the world began. During the intervening periods there was still a zonal pattern of world temperatures, with hot equatorial regions and cooler poles. But the ice caps, which are both chilling and self-sustaining, were absent altogether—the poles being cold temperate rather than icebound. The shiny ice surfaces of today's poles reflect more than 90 percent of the solar radiation which reaches them from the low-angled summer sun, while in winter the sun never rises at all. Thus the regions are now permanently ice capped.

Antarctica, the great southern polar continent, lies under an ice mantle 14 million sq km (5.4 million sq miles) in area, and sometimes more than 4,000 m (13,000 ft) thick. Many of its neighboring islands also carry permanent ice. In the Arctic, the three islands of Greenland lie under a pall of ice of subcontinental size, more than 1.8 million sq km (700,000 sq miles) in area and up to 3,000 m (9,800 ft) thick.

The ice cover of polar seas varies. The central core of the Arctic Ocean carries a mass of permanent pack ice, slowly circulating within the polar basin, which is added to each winter by a belt of ice forming over the open sea. Currents and winds break this up to form pack ice that also circulates, gradually melting in summer or drifting south. Antarctica too is surrounded by fast ice, which breaks up in spring to form a broad belt of persistent pack ice. Circulating slowly about the continent, the pack ice forms huge gyres spreading far to the north, dotted with tabular bergs that have broken away from the continental ice sheet.

The frozen land

In the present glacial phase, the ice caps reached their farthest spread about 20,000 years ago, and then began the retreat which brought them, some 10,000 to 12,000 years ago, to their current position and size. Since then the climate of the polar regions has been both warmer and colder than it is at the present time.

The coldness of the poles is caused by the tilt of the Earth's axis, which prevents sunlight from reaching them at all in the winter. Even in summer, little heat is received from the sun because of the low angle at which its rays reach the surface; much even of this is reflected away by the ice.

The fluctuating nature of the polar climates creates very difficult conditions for plants and animals. Very little will grow on the terrestrial ice caps, but water scarcity rather than cold is the most important factor inhibiting plant growth: the small patches of lichens, algae and mosses that occur on rock faces and nunataks (points of rock jutting above the land ice) are usually in the path of a snowmelt runnel. Vegetation patches sometimes contain tiny populations of insects and mites, which may be active for only a few days each year when the sun warms them from a state of dormancy.

However, these tiny scattered plant communities appear all over Antarctica wherever rock surfaces break through the ice cap, and have been seen less than 300 km (190 miles) from the South Pole, and on peaks 2,000 m (6,600 ft) above sea level. Insects and mites occur within 600 km (380 miles) of the Pole itself. In specially favored positions on the Antarctic Peninsula and the offshore islands, carpets of moss and grasses may be seen. Conditions around the northern terrestrial ice cap are similar, with aridity, strong winds and cold discouraging all but the hardiest plants and the smallest, toughest animal colonies.

The frozen seas

The marine ice caps, by contrast, are relatively lively places, especially during summer, when days are long and the sea ice is patchy. Water-lanes between floes are often rich in microscopic algae and the minute zooplanktonic animals that feed on them. These animals in turn attract fish, sea birds and seals in their thousands, as well as whales—including the largest baleen species. Some of the richest patches of sea are close to islands where strong currents stir the water and bring nutrients to the surface, and these attract semipermanent populations of seals and birds. The birds breed on the island cliffs and feed in the sheltered waters among the ice; the seals may breed on the ice itself, producing their pups on a floating nursery where food is close at hand.

Different species of seals are found on inshore and offshore ice environments. In the Arctic, bearded and ringed seals, which produce their young in spring as the inshore ice begins to break up, are often preyed upon by floe-riding polar bears; Eskimos too prize both species for their meat, blubber and skins. Farther out on the offshore pack ice live hooded and harp seals, where their pups are safe from all but the ship-borne commercial hunters. In the Antarctic, Weddell seals are the inshore species, whereas crabeater and Ross seals prefer the distant pack ice. Crabeaters, which feed largely on planktonic krill (once thought to be crab larvae), are probably the most numerous of all seal species, with a population estimated at 10 to 15 million.

Sea ice in the north provides a precarious platform on which coastal human populations of the Arctic, such as Eskimos, can extend their winter hunting range. When the land is snowbound and animals are scarce, the sea may still provide food for hunters skilled in fishing, and in stalking seals to their breathing holes.

Nonindigenous inhabitants of the ice caps have greatly increased in recent years, following the discovery and exploitation of oil in the north, as well as other valuable minerals in both the regions. Scientists and technicians today occupy bases and weather stations which in some cases, such as the Amundsen-Scott at the South Pole, are several decades old and have to be maintained by means of aircraft.

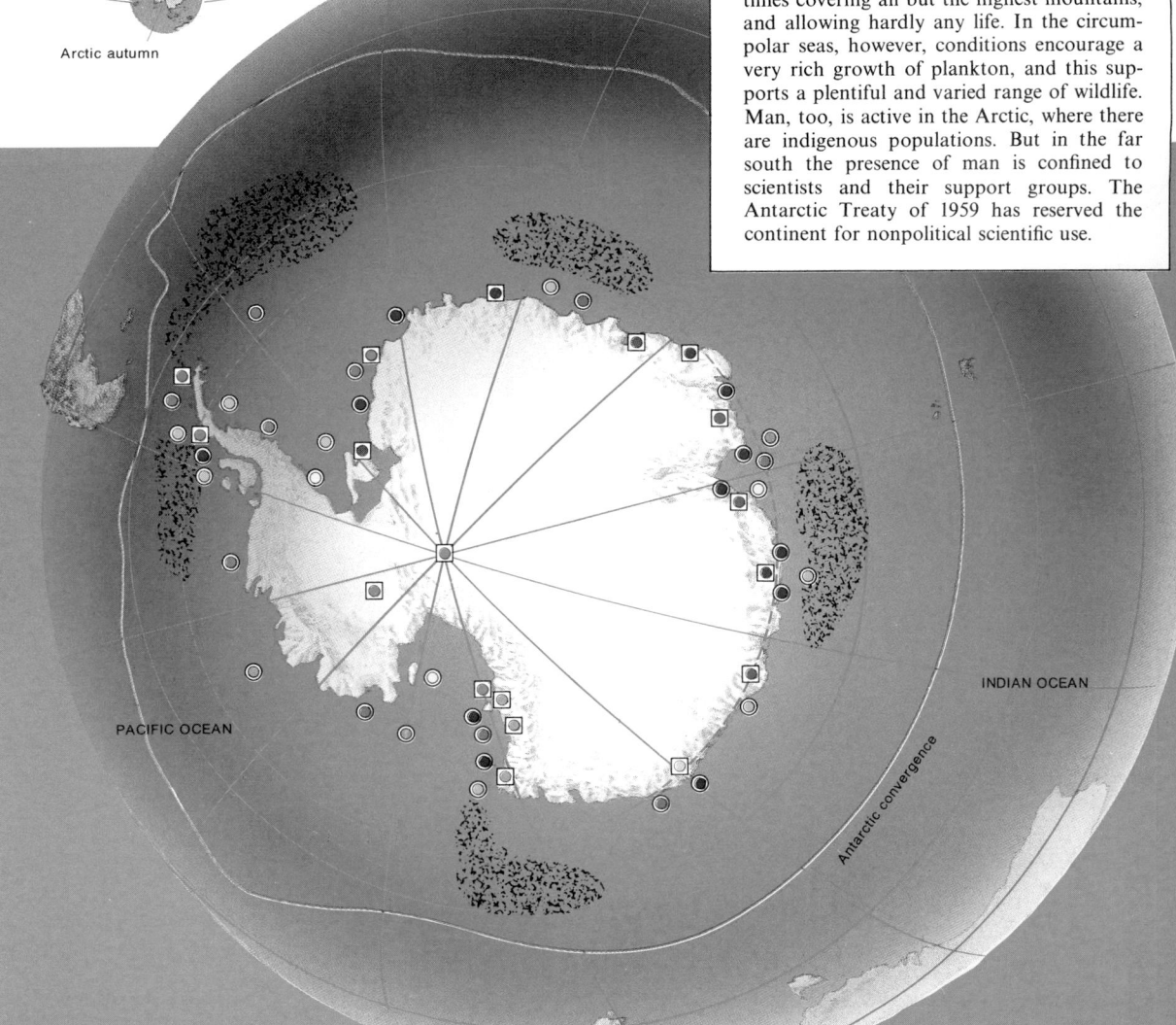

Arctic spring
Arctic winter
Arctic summer
Arctic autumn

ATLANTIC OCEAN
INDIAN OCEAN
PACIFIC OCEAN
Antarctic convergence

EARTH'S FROZEN LIMITS

The permanent ice around Earth's poles covers whole oceans, as well as landmasses of immense size. These ice sheets fluctuate, and on land may be thousands of meters thick, sometimes covering all but the highest mountains, and allowing hardly any life. In the circumpolar seas, however, conditions encourage a very rich growth of plankton, and this supports a plentiful and varied range of wildlife. Man, too, is active in the Arctic, where there are indigenous populations. But in the far south the presence of man is confined to scientists and their support groups. The Antarctic Treaty of 1959 has reserved the continent for nonpolitical scientific use.

THE FAR SOUTH

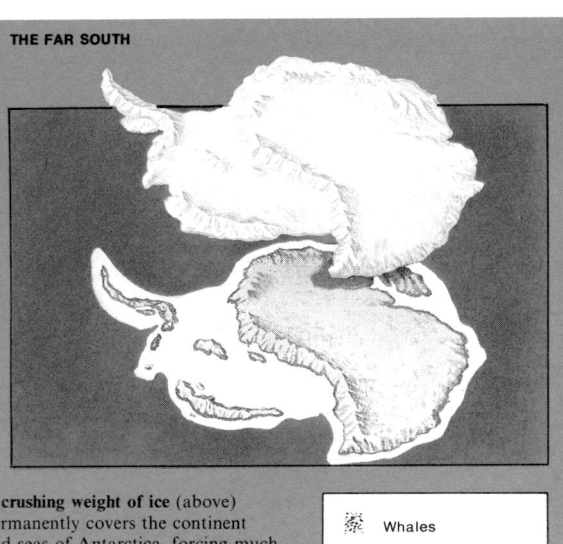

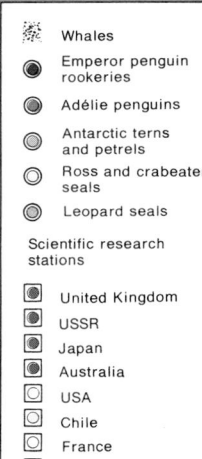

A crushing weight of ice (above) permanently covers the continent and seas of Antarctica, forcing much of the land below sea level. The Antarctic convergence (right), the line at which northern and southern water masses meet, marks a sharp change in temperature and marine life. Especially in areas of upwelling, nutrients make these waters rich in plankton. This feeds a multitude of shrimp-like krill that provide food for a huge number of other animals—fish, penguins, flying birds, seals and whales. The Antarctic landmass allows little natural life, but since the 1959 Antarctic Treaty it has proved to be an area of international scientific cooperation.

Whales
Emperor penguin rookeries
Adélie penguins
Antarctic terns and petrels
Ross and crabeater seals
Leopard seals

Scientific research stations

United Kingdom
USSR
Japan
Australia
USA
Chile
France
New Zealand
Argentina

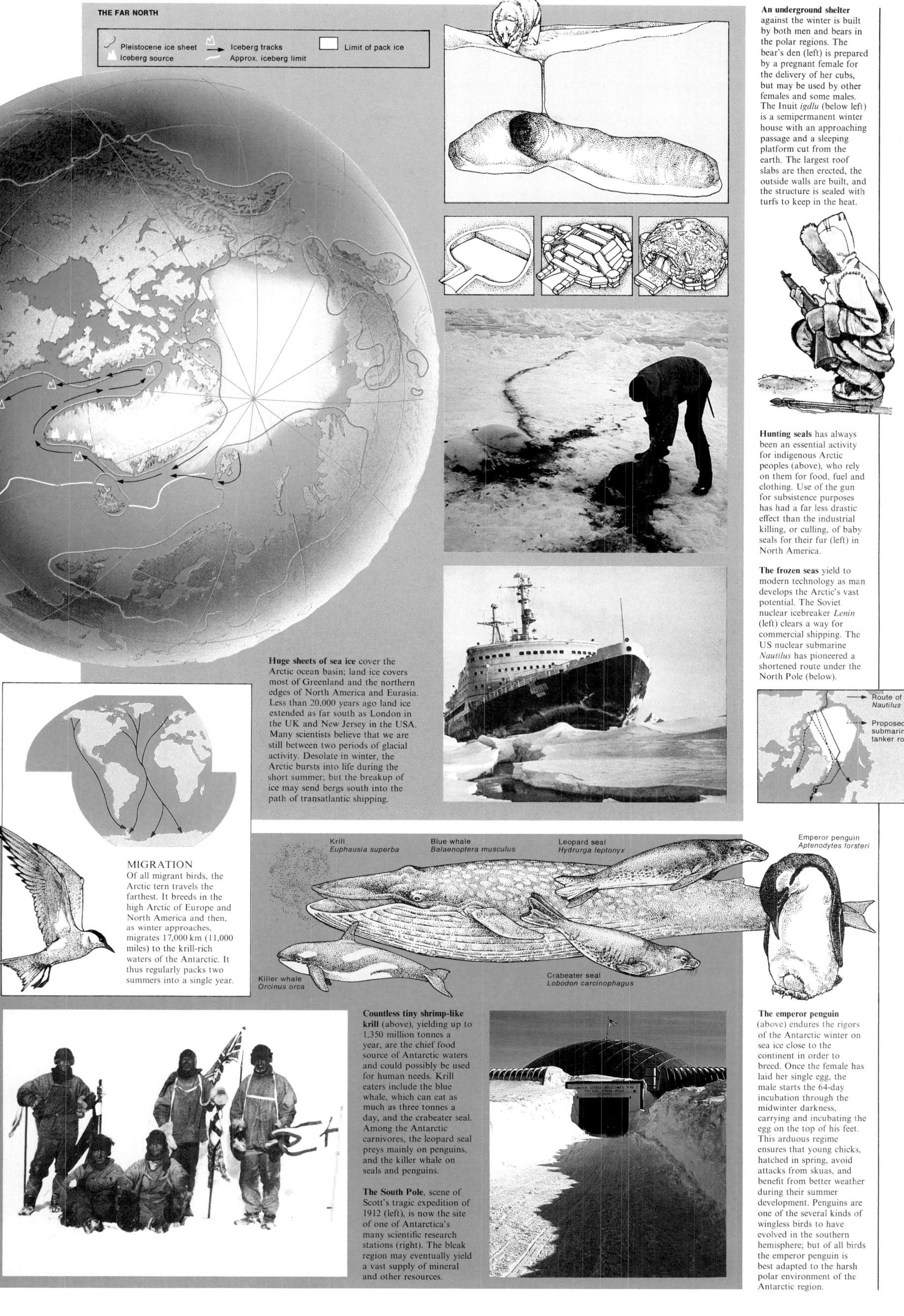

Pleistocene ice sheet | Iceberg tracks | Limit of pack ice
Iceberg source | Approx. iceberg limit

An underground shelter against the winter is built by both men and bears in the polar regions. The bear's den (left) is prepared by a pregnant female for the delivery of her cubs, but may be used by other females and some males. The Inuit *igdlu* (below left) is a semipermanent winter house with an approaching passage and a sleeping platform cut from the earth. The largest roof slabs are then erected, the outside walls are built, and the structure is sealed with turfs to keep in the heat.

Hunting seals has always been an essential activity for indigenous Arctic peoples (above), who rely on them for food, fuel and clothing. Use of the gun for subsistence purposes has had a far less drastic effect than the industrial killing, or culling, of baby seals for their fur (left) in North America.

The frozen seas yield to modern technology as man develops the Arctic's vast potential. The Soviet nuclear icebreaker *Lenin* (left) clears a way for commercial shipping. The US nuclear submarine *Nautilus* has pioneered a shortened route under the North Pole (below).

→ Route of *Nautilus* 1958
→ Proposed submarine tanker routes

Huge sheets of sea ice cover the Arctic ocean basin; land ice covers most of Greenland and the northern edges of North America and Eurasia. Less than 20,000 years ago land ice extended as far south as London in the UK and New Jersey in the USA. Many scientists believe that we are still between two periods of glacial activity. Desolate in winter, the Arctic bursts into life during the short summer; but the breakup of ice may send bergs south into the path of transatlantic shipping.

MIGRATION
Of all migrant birds, the Arctic tern travels the farthest. It breeds in the high Arctic of Europe and North America and then, as winter approaches, migrates 17,000 km (11,000 miles) to the krill-rich waters of the Antarctic. It thus regularly packs two summers into a single year.

Krill
Euphausia superba

Blue whale
Balaenoptera musculus

Leopard seal
Hydrurga leptonyx

Emperor penguin
Aptenodytes forsteri

Killer whale
Orcinus orca

Crabeater seal
Lobodon carcinophagus

Countless tiny shrimp-like krill (above), yielding up to 1,350 million tonnes a year, are the chief food source of Antarctic waters and could possibly be used for human needs. Krill eaters include the blue whale, which can eat as much as three tonnes a day, and the crabeater seal. Among the Antarctic carnivores, the leopard seal preys mainly on penguins, and the killer whale on seals and penguins.

The South Pole, scene of Scott's tragic expedition of 1912 (left), is now the site of one of Antarctica's many scientific research stations (right). The bleak region may eventually yield a vast supply of mineral and other resources.

The emperor penguin (above) endures the rigors of the Antarctic winter on sea ice close to the continent in order to breed. Once the female has laid her single egg, the male starts the 64-day incubation through the midwinter darkness, carrying and incubating the egg on the top of his feet. This arduous regime ensures that young chicks, hatched in spring, avoid attacks from skuas, and benefit from better weather during their summer development. Penguins are one of the several kinds of wingless birds to have evolved in the southern hemisphere; but of all birds the emperor penguin is best adapted to the harsh polar environment of the Antarctic region.

Tundra and Taiga

Tundra is land that has been exposed for only about 8,000 years, since the retreat of the ice caps, and only relatively recently occupied by plants. In consequence, few plants and animals have yet had time to adapt to the virtually soilless and treeless environment. The less rigorous conditions of neighboring taiga forest allow a longer growing season and a somewhat wider range of species. The delicately balanced ecology of both areas is being increasingly threatened, however, by the activities of man.

"Tundra," from a Lapp word meaning "rolling, treeless plain," defines the narrow band of open, low ground that surrounds the Arctic Ocean. It lies north of the line beyond which the temperature of the warmest month usually fails to reach 10°C (50°F). North of this trees do not generally grow well, so the line forms a natural frontier between tundra and the broad band of coniferous forest that circles the northern hemisphere to its south between about 60°N and 48°N. This forest, forming the world's largest and most uninterrupted area of vegetation, is usually referred to by its Russian name of "taiga."

Cheerless landscapes

The tundra presents a desolate and restrictive environment for most of the year: in winter there are several months of semidarkness. While there is considerable variation in the climates of places at the same latitude, temperatures average only −5°C (23°F) and are well below freezing for many months of the year. Frost-free days are restricted to a few weeks in midsummer and even then, although days are warmer, the sun is never high in the sky. Nearly all tundra has been free from ice for only a few thousand years. As a result, it either has no soil at all or has developed only a thin covering of

sandy, muddy or peaty soil, successfully colonized by only a few types of plants.

Trimmed by such grazing animals as hares, musk oxen and reindeer or caribou, and by strong winds carrying abrasive rock dust and ice particles, typical tundra vegetation forms a low, patchy mat a few centimeters deep. Much of it grows on permafrost — ground that thaws superficially in summer but remains perennially frozen beneath the surface. Here drainage is poor, shallow ponds are frequent and the scanty soils tend to be waterlogged and acidic. Nevertheless, a small number of grasses, sedges, mosses and marsh plants may grow well and the summer tundra in flower can be an impressive sight. Knee-high forests of dwarf birch, willow and alder grow in valleys sheltered from the strong and biting wind.

The taiga also is a dark and monotonous habitat. Again, while there is a good deal of variation in climatic conditions, on average the region has somewhat milder summers than the tundra with mean average temperatures of 2–6°C (34–42°F), less wind and a slightly longer growing season. The taiga is mostly older than the tundra, and its soils have had longer to mature. They support a small number of tree species, with coniferous spruce, pine, fir and

larch predominating. Short-season broadleaves such as willows, alders, birches and poplars tend to occur on the better soils of river valleys and the edges of forest lakes.

Animals of the far north

The number of animal species supported throughout the year by tundra and taiga is also comparatively small, with interdependent populations that may fluctuate wildly from season to season. In winter both tundra and taiga are silent, although far from deserted. Mice, voles and lemmings remain active, living in tunnels under the snow, which keeps them well insulated from the wind and subzero temperatures. Above the snow Arctic hares forage; they tend to gather in snow-free areas where food can still be found. Arctic foxes are mainly tundra animals and the musk oxen, too, winter on high, exposed tundra where their dense, shaggy coats protect them from the worst

The circumpolar north that surrounds the permanently frozen ice cap is dominated by tundra—open plain that remains snowfree for only several months in the summer—and taiga, the vast coniferous forest stretching right round the northern hemisphere. The Siberian taiga, for example, is one-third larger than the entire United States.

Tundra	Taiga

Producers

- USSR
- USA

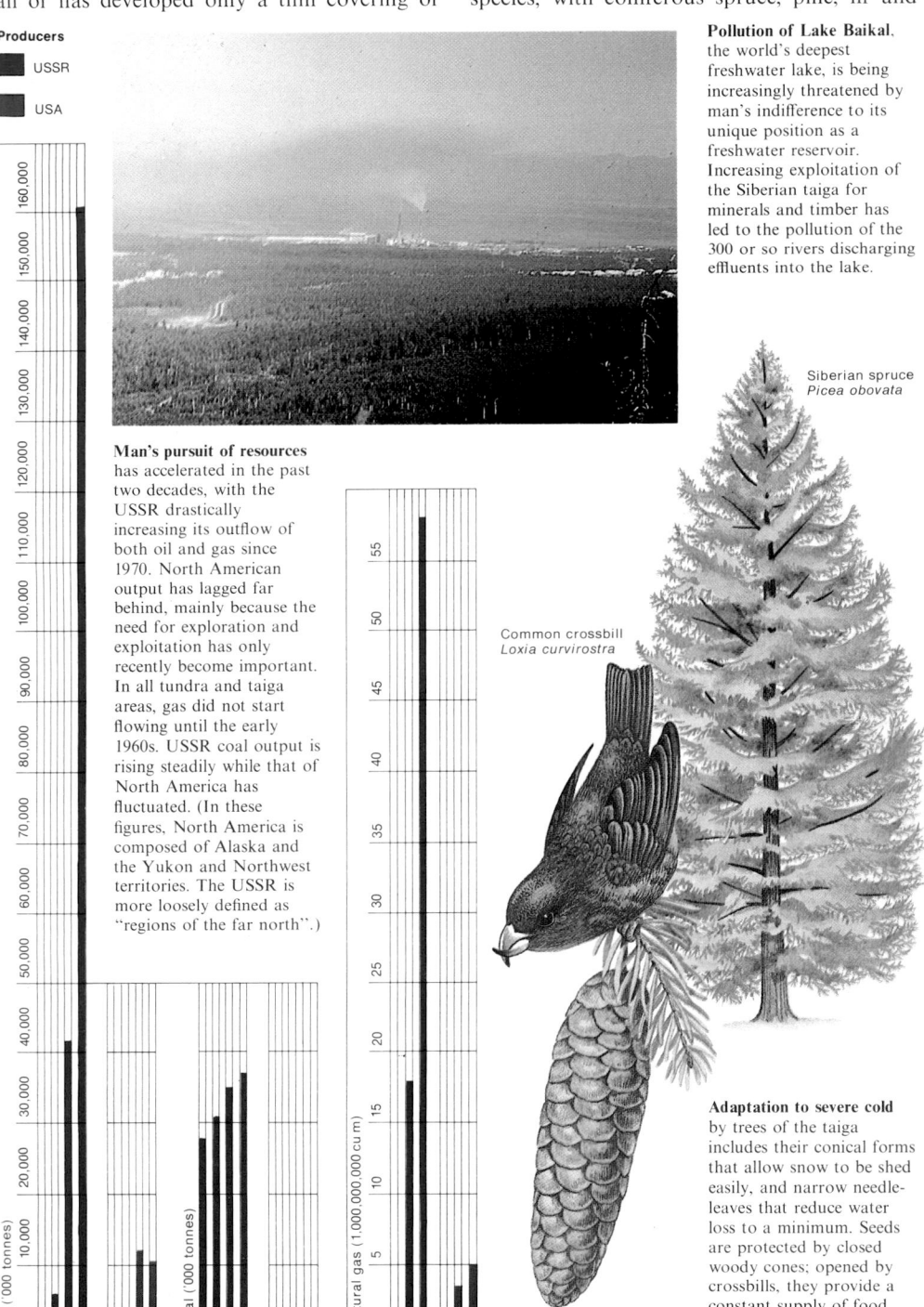

Man's pursuit of resources has accelerated in the past two decades, with the USSR drastically increasing its outflow of both oil and gas since 1970. North American output has lagged far behind, mainly because the need for exploration and exploitation has only recently become important. In all tundra and taiga areas, gas did not start flowing until the early 1960s. USSR coal output is rising steadily while that of North America has fluctuated. (In these figures, North America is composed of Alaska and the Yukon and Northwest territories. The USSR is more loosely defined as "regions of the far north".)

Oil ('000 tonnes)
Coal ('000 tonnes)
Natural gas (1,000,000,000 cu m)

Pollution of Lake Baikal, the world's deepest freshwater lake, is being increasingly threatened by man's indifference to its unique position as a freshwater reservoir. Increasing exploitation of the Siberian taiga for minerals and timber has led to the pollution of the 300 or so rivers discharging effluents into the lake.

Siberian spruce
Picea obovata

Common crossbill
Loxia curvirostra

Adaptation to severe cold by trees of the taiga includes their conical forms that allow snow to be shed easily, and narrow needle-leaves that reduce water loss to a minimum. Seeds are protected by closed woody cones; opened by crossbills, they provide a constant supply of food during winter.

Reindeer or caribou
Rangifer tarandus

Raven
Corvus corax

January
February
March
April
May
June

Arctic fox
Alopex lagopus

Capercaillie
Tetrao urogallus

Snowy owl
Nyctea scandiaca

Brown lemming
Lemmus lemmus

Arctic skua
Stercorarius parasiticus

Movement in these regions takes many directions. The capercaillie spends all winter in the taiga, where it thrives on the abundant conifer needles, buds and shoots. Some move southward into deciduous woods during the summer months. The Arctic skua breeds on the tundra but moves to the warmer oceans in winter, while the tundra movements of the all-scavenging raven and the snowy owl are governed by those of their

prey. The raven picks clean the carcasses left by other predators; the snowy owl feeds on small rodents such as mice and lemmings, as does the Arctic fox. Lemmings remain static and inconspicuous in normal years but some populations expand rapidly every third or fourth year, leading to mass local migration in every direction, possibly caused by an abundance of vegetation that encourages more frequent breeding.

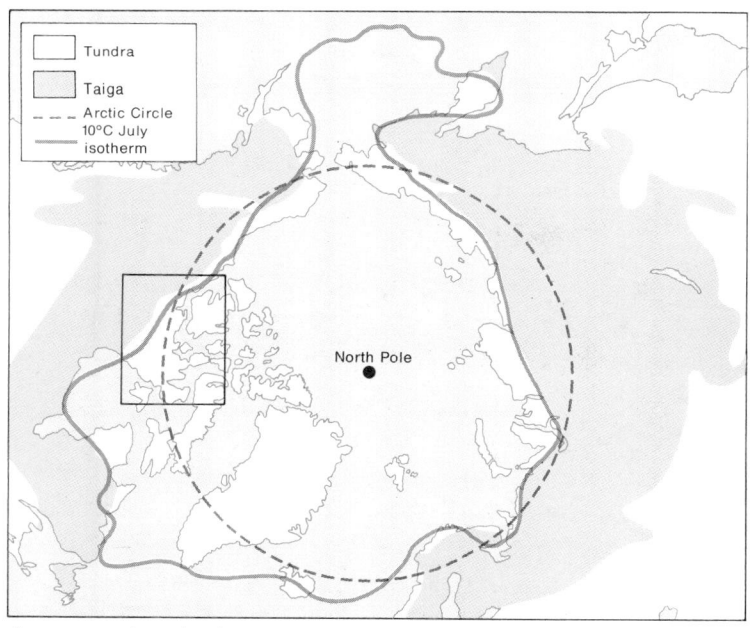

weather. Bears, badgers, beavers and squirrels are common taiga mammals. Elk and reindeer (in North America, moose and caribou) winter in the shelter of the taiga; wolves are mostly woodland animals in winter, following their prey to the open tundra in spring. Red foxes, coyotes, mink and wolverines also move to the tundra in summer.

Snow buntings, ptarmigans and snowy owls live on the tundra throughout the coldest months and are fully adapted to life there. Crossbills and capercaillies are among taiga residents, equipped to live on its abundant conifer buds, seeds and needles. Enormous populations of migrant birds, especially water birds and waders, fly north to both tundra and taiga with the spring thaw. Waxwings, bramblings, siskins and redpolls leave their temperate latitudes to feed on the lush and fast-growing vegetation and the profusion of insects that appear as soon as the snows begin to melt.

Man in the northlands

These circumpolar regions act as a strategic buffer between the USA and the USSR. Situated between the world's greatest centers of population, they are now crisscrossed with air routes. A total population of about nine million people currently inhabits the tundra and taiga. Numbers have been increased by the immigration of technicians and administrators during the last few decades; oil prospecting and mining, forest exploitation and other activities of these newcomers is altering the seminomadic lives of the million or so aboriginal peoples such as the Khanty (Ostyaks) and Nentsy (Samoyeds) of the USSR, the Samer (Lapps) of Scandinavia and the Soviet Union, and the Inuit (formerly Eskimos) of North America. New roads, exploitation of minerals and forests, and pipeline construction have disrupted the migration of their reindeer (caribou) and their land has been appropriated for hydroelectric schemes.

In the taiga, the Soviets are constructing railroads and towns and extracting huge amounts of timber; they have prospected widely and successfully for gold, nickel, iron, tin, mica, diamonds and tungsten, and have discovered vast reserves of oil and natural gas in western Siberia. Alaskan oil, discovered in 1968, now flows across the state at 54–62°C (130–145°F), and to protect the permafrost from this heat the pipeline has had to be elevated for half its 1,300 km (800 mile) length. The pipe's route to the ice-free port of Valdez has interfered with the migration of caribou; hunting and other pressures have led to a drop in their population from three million to some 200,000 in about 30 years. Only official protection has saved the musk ox from a similar fate. These bleak areas are so vast and inhospitable that living space there will never be threatened. However, if only on a local scale, their ecologies are under increasing pressure from man.

The summer tundra—seen here in Swedish Lapland—provides a wide cover of low plants including "reindeer mosses" and other lichens. Grazing reindeer return minerals to the soil. Shallow ponds form as the frozen ground above the permafrost thaws for a few months in summer. Mountains stay partly snow covered in the warmest weather and are a prominent physical feature of the tundra.

Many Norwegian Lapps (or Samer) derive their income from reindeer, which they domesticated many centuries ago to provide meat, milk and skins. Now they follow them through the seasons along well-worn and familiar routes. Such nomadic life styles are becoming rarer as Samer settle down.

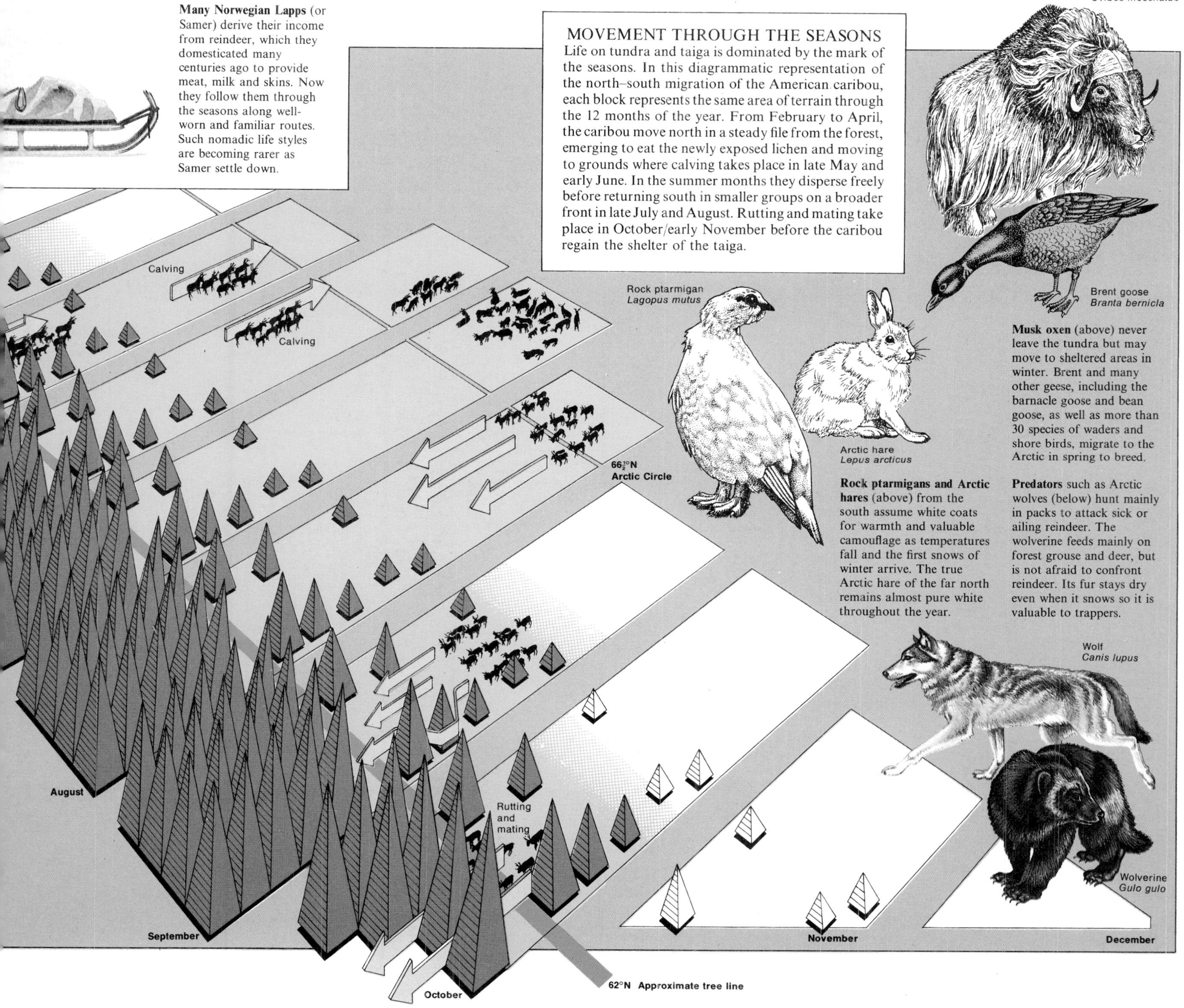

Musk ox
Ovibos moschatus

MOVEMENT THROUGH THE SEASONS

Life on tundra and taiga is dominated by the mark of the seasons. In this diagrammatic representation of the north–south migration of the American caribou, each block represents the same area of terrain through the 12 months of the year. From February to April, the caribou move north in a steady file from the forest, emerging to eat the newly exposed lichen and moving to grounds where calving takes place in late May and early June. In the summer months they disperse freely before returning south in smaller groups on a broader front in late July and August. Rutting and mating take place in October/early November before the caribou regain the shelter of the taiga.

Rock ptarmigan
Lagopus mutus

Arctic hare
Lepus arcticus

Brent goose
Branta bernicla

Musk oxen (above) never leave the tundra but may move to sheltered areas in winter. Brent and many other geese, including the barnacle goose and bean goose, as well as more than 30 species of waders and shore birds, migrate to the Arctic in spring to breed.

Rock ptarmigans and Arctic hares (above) from the south assume white coats for warmth and valuable camouflage as temperatures fall and the first snows of winter arrive. The true Arctic hare of the far north remains almost pure white throughout the year.

Predators such as Arctic wolves (below) hunt mainly in packs to attack sick or ailing reindeer. The wolverine feeds mainly on forest grouse and deer, but is not afraid to confront reindeer. Its fur stays dry even when it snows so it is valuable to trappers.

Wolf
Canis lupus

Wolverine
Gulo gulo

Calving
Calving
66½°N Arctic Circle
Rutting and mating
August
September
October
November
December
62°N Approximate tree line

Temperate Forests

At one time, dense, primeval forests blanketed large areas of North America, Europe and eastern Asia. Almost all of the trees that flourished in these temperate regions were deciduous – they shed their leaves in autumn, stood bare branched through winter and produced new foliage every spring. Little of this forest now exists. The few remaining pockets, however, still provide habitats for a large range of shade-loving plants: lichens and fungi, tree-hugging mosses, scrambling creepers and shrubs. And this vegetation in turn provides sanctuary for a surprisingly wide variety of forest creatures.

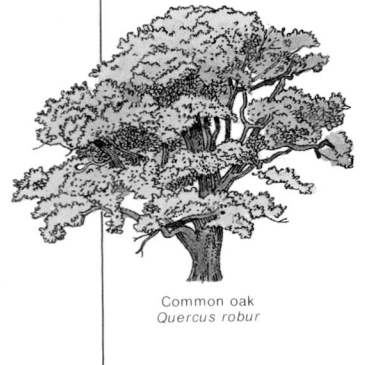

Common oak
Quercus robur

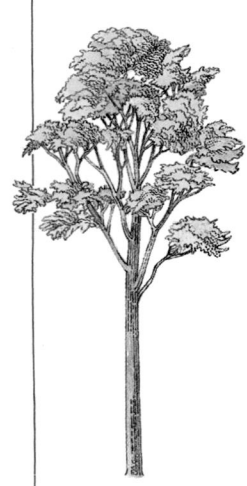

Silver beech
Nothofagus menziesii

Deciduous trees such as the oak (top) make up the temperate forests in cooler temperate regions. In milder, wetter climates, where the seasons are less distinct, evergreens such as southern beech (above) are typical temperate species.

The greater part of the temperate forest zone lies in the northern hemisphere, where winter soil temperatures reduce the ability of plants to absorb water. Hence the trees tend to shed their leaves, which use up moisture through evaporation. In the southern hemisphere, however, the temperate latitudes encourage a type of rainforest in such areas as southern Chile, Tasmania, New Zealand and parts of southeastern Australia. Here the climate is maritime, often with high rainfall and frequent fogs, and evergreen rather than deciduous types of trees grow. Temperate rainforests also occur in the northern hemisphere, in China and in northwestern and northeastern North America.

Deciduous forest consists of a mixture of trees, sometimes with one variety predominant. In central Europe, beech is the leading – and sometimes the only – tree species, whereas oaks mixed with other species made up the forest farther west and east. In North America, beech and maple were once extensive.

The climate in temperate forest zones varies sharply according to seasons – summers tend to be warm, winters moderately cold, and rainfall fairly regular. In fact, the seasonal rhythm is a central feature of temperate forests, and it affects the entire ecosystem – the whole community of plants and animals found there. Soils are generally of the fertile "brown earth" type: the leaf litter of deciduous forests in particular breaks down easily, and is quickly worked into the soil by burrowing animals such as earthworms. In wetter or rockier regions, the soil is more "podsolic" – bleached, sandy and less fertile than the true brown earths.

After the ice

Two million years ago, a series of ice sheets began to extend into the temperate latitudes. In Europe, species moving south before the advancing cold were cut off from the warmer climates by the east–west run of mountains. As a result, many varieties of plants and animals

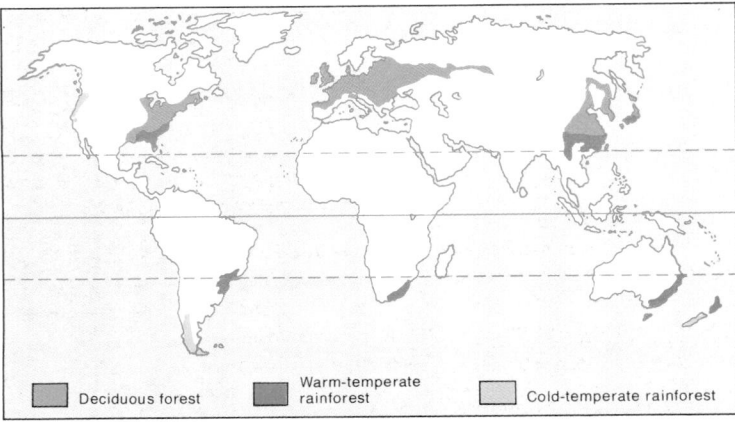

Natural distribution: in the northern hemisphere's temperate zone deciduous forests occur in the cooler areas – in eastern USA, northeastern China, Korea, the northern parts of Japan's Honshu island and western Europe. These forests only give way to evergreens in the warmer and wetter parts of the zone. In the southern hemisphere, the climate is generally rather milder throughout the temperate zone and so there are virtually no deciduous forests. Evergreen forests, however, can be found in southeastern South Africa, Chile, New Zealand, Australia and Tasmania.

| Deciduous forest | Warm-temperate rainforest | Cold-temperate rainforest |

were killed off. Species were reduced still further in islands such as Britain, where the newly formed barriers of the English Channel, Irish Sea and North Sea made recolonization even more difficult after the ice had retreated.

Eastern Asia was one of the few areas in the world that escaped the extreme climatic changes of the ice ages and therefore its temperate forests, unlike those of Europe, still contain an enormous variety of tree species. North America also fared better than Europe, for although glaciers at one time extended deep into the continent, the north–south direction of the mountain ranges allowed relatively easy migration of trees southwards as the climate worsened. Hence most species survived and were able to reoccupy their former territories when the ice retreated. As a result, some 40 species of deciduous trees occur in the North American forests, and contribute to the spectacular display of color during the autumn, notably in

the eastern USA. But a combination of climatic change and, more recently and importantly, of intense human activity, has meant that the remnants of temperate forest seen today differ greatly from the original forest in both composition and form. Only in remote regions such as the southern Appalachian Mountains do substantial areas of the original forest survive. Elsewhere, regrowth has occurred, but much of this is essentially scrub woodland.

The forest structure

Mature temperate deciduous forest is made up of distinct horizontal layers, particularly where the dominant tree is the oak, which allows enough light for a rich shrub layer to grow beneath it. The largest trees, such as oak, maple or ash, may be 25–50 m (80–160 ft) tall, and beneath them grows a prominent layer of smaller trees such as hazel, hornbeam or yew. Lower down again, a varied ground cover of perennial herbs, ferns, lichens and mosses flourishes in the comparative dampness of the forest floor. Because the trees are bare of leaves in winter, many of the plants growing on the forest floor take advantage of the warmth and light of spring to flower early in the year before the main trees come into full leaf and prevent the sun from reaching them. Various woody climbers, such as ivy and honeysuckle, are also present, growing over the trees and shrubs.

Much of the food supply in temperate forests is locked up in the trees themselves, but the annual fall of leaves in the deciduous forests produces a soil rich in nourishment. This supports a vast quantity of life, ranging in size from earthworms and insects to microscopic bacteria of the soil. The death of individual trees and branches also releases the food supply back to the earth. In shady, damp locations, insects, fungi, bacteria and other decomposing agents break down the leaves and other plant and animal debris more quickly, returning them to the soil as food for new plants.

Creatures of the forest

Temperate forests once contained many varieties of animal life, including several species of large animals. Herbivores such as wild oxen, wood bison, elk and moose ate grass and leaves; scavengers such as wild pigs rooted in the forest floor; predators such as wolves preyed on the other animals. Most of these have now been hunted to extinction by man or are extremely rare. Smaller animals still survive in comparatively large numbers, and include squirrels, chipmunks and raccoons, hedgehogs, wood mice, badgers and foxes.

The bird life of temperate forests is very diverse. Some species are insect eaters, exploring the bark and crevices for insects and grubs. Others, such as the wood pigeon, concentrate on seeds. Yet others, like the tawny owl, are predators. Complex interactions between predators and prey have developed at all levels of the forest, from the high canopy to the rotting ground litter, with each group evolving more efficient techniques of capture or escape in a kind of evolutionary race for survival.

The invertebrate insect life is also extremely varied and numerous, and forms a key component of the ecosystem. Oaks are particularly rich in insect life, and more than 100 species of moths feed on their leaves.

The plant and animal life of the temperate forest is remarkably rich and plentiful. And yet it is only a fraction of what once existed. Ever since man has occupied these regions he has found them so suited to his needs that he has long since cleared most of the original tree cover, replaced it with "civilization" and, in the process, destroyed innumerable species of forest wildlife.

THE SEASONAL CYCLE

It is the cycle of the four seasons that gives the temperate deciduous forest its distinctive character. All animals and plants have adapted their ways of life to cope with the seasonal changes in heat, light, moisture and food. The yearly shedding and regrowth of the forest's leaves is one of the most striking and important of adaptations to the seasonal cycle and one that affects all other life in the forest. In summer the leafy canopy of the trees blocks out the sunlight from the forest floor and creates unsuitable conditions for many other plants to flourish. When the leaves fall they form a layer over the soil and provide winter protection for the plant roots and hibernating animals beneath the ground. Finally, once the dead leaves have been broken down, they give fertility to the soil and provide food for future generations of plants.

SPRING

Between February and April, the low spring sun climbs steadily higher in the sky and, streaming through the still leafless branches of the trees, falls more directly on the forest floor, warming the soil and melting the last frosts. As soon as the days become warmer the sluggish sap in the trees begins to flow more quickly, carrying nutrients to the branches, where leaf buds start to form.

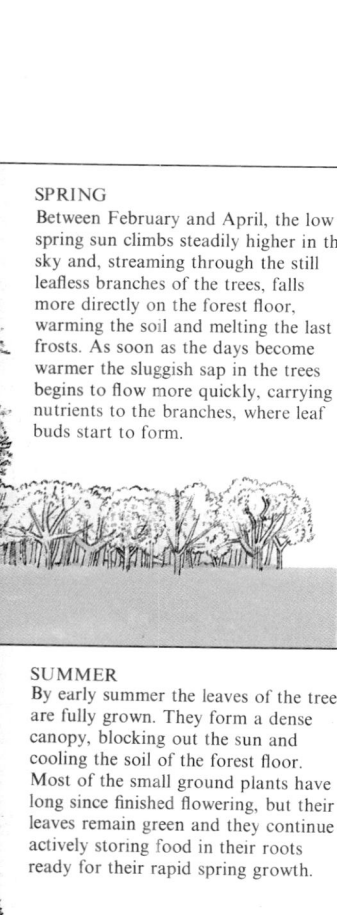

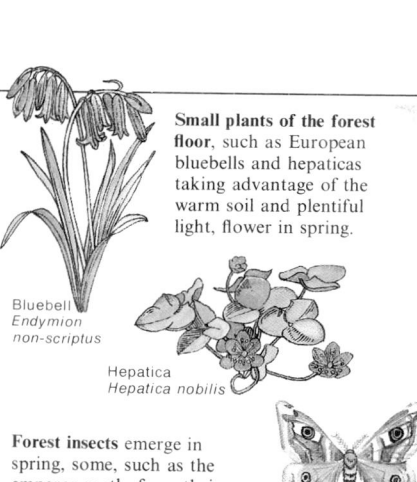

Bluebell
Endymion non-scriptus

Hepatica
Hepatica nobilis

Small plants of the forest floor, such as European bluebells and hepaticas taking advantage of the warm soil and plentiful light, flower in spring.

Forest insects emerge in spring, some, such as the emperor moth, from their winter cocoons, some from hibernation and some newly hatched from eggs.

Small emperor moth
Saturnia pavonia

European blackbird *Turdus merula*

Birds building nests in early spring make use of the forest's winter litter— broken twigs, dead leaves and dried grasses all serve as construction materials.

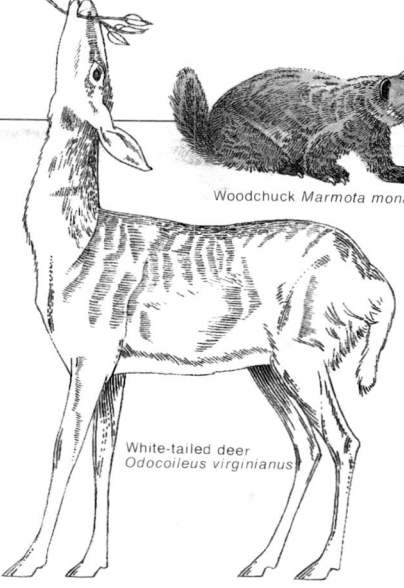

Woodchuck *Marmota monax*

Western European hedgehog *Erinaceus europaeus*

White-tailed deer *Odocoileus virginianus*

New plant growth and the increase in insects provide food for such animals as the North American woodchuck and the European hedgehog that wake thin and hungry from months of hibernation. Deer and other non-hibernating animals are also weak and thin— indeed many may have died during the harsh weather. The spring birth of young, however, soon restores their numbers.

SUMMER

By early summer the leaves of the trees are fully grown. They form a dense canopy, blocking out the sun and cooling the soil of the forest floor. Most of the small ground plants have long since finished flowering, but their leaves remain green and they continue actively storing food in their roots ready for their rapid spring growth.

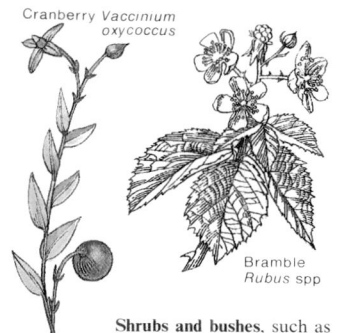

Cranberry *Vaccinium oxycoccus*

Bramble
Rubus spp

Shrubs and bushes, such as bramble and cranberry, form tangled flowering masses wherever sunlight manages to filter through the forest's gloomy canopy.

Hordes of insects inhabit the forest in summer, living off the vast supply of food plants. The European stag beetle feeds on the sap of chestnut and oak trees.

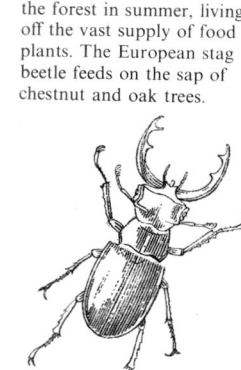

Stag beetle
Lucanus cervus

The North American pewee and the willow warbler are two of the forest's many summer visitors that feed on the insect population. Some seed-eating birds, finches for example, also take advantage of this summer food supply.

Willow warbler
Phylloscopus trochilus

Eastern wood pewee
Contopus virens

Hazel mouse
Muscardinus avellanarius

The hazel mouse protects its young by raising them in a summer nest, which it builds in a tree: almost every creature in the forest is viewed as a source of food by some other animal and the young litters are particularly at risk.

AUTUMN

As the autumn days grow shorter and cooler the forest foliage begins to turn color; the trees are responding to the drop in temperature and are cutting off the food supply to their leaves, which lose their green color and fall to the ground, forming a thick carpet on the forest's floor. Rain, frost, insects, earthworms and fungi then break down the leaves, making them part of the fertile forest soil.

Ripe fruits and seeds of the forest trees—acorns, beech nuts and hazel nuts—drop to the ground, where a few are buried in the layers of dead leaves and remain protected until they sprout in the early spring.

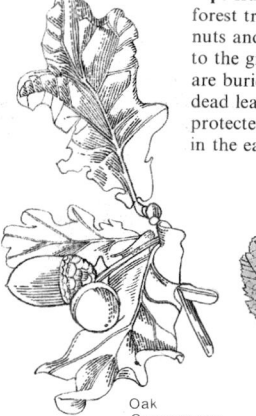

Common hazel
Corylus avellana

Oak
Quercus spp

Preparing for winter, the acorn woodpecker stores seeds in holes that it drills in tree trunks. Chipmunks hide supplies of nuts in their winter nests.

Acorn woodpecker
Melanerpes formicivorus

Eastern chipmunk
Tamias striatus

American black bear
Ursus americanus

The black bear of North America, like other winter hibernators, consumes vast quantities of food during autumn to build up its winter stores of food in the form of body fat.

WINTER

By winter, only evergreen shrubs and a few small hardy plants remain green. Many of the plants of the forest floor lose their green leaves during the first deep frost. The leaves of the trees still lie rotting on the bare ground, but within the soil, beneath the protective layers of leaf litter, plants are growing and spring flowers are developing buds.

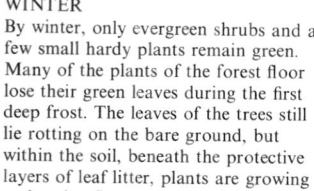

Late-fruiting plants, such as holly, mistletoe and dog rose, provide food for winter residents of the temperate forest such as the European hawfinch.

Holly
Ilex spp

Hawfinch
Coccothraustes coccothraustes

European woodcock
Scolopax rusticola

Woodcocks are insect-eaters. They can survive winter by prizing insects from the soil with their long beaks, providing that the ground is not too deeply frozen.

North American screech owl
Otus asio

Owls and foxes remain fairly active in winter, regularly leaving their nests or lairs to catch small animals or birds that are also in search of food.

Red fox
Vulpes vulpes

European badger
Meles meles

European badgers, like racoons, opossums, bears and skunks, are "shallow" hibernators. On mild winter days they wake and go to search for food.

THE EVERGREEN TEMPERATE RAINFORESTS

There are two main kinds of temperate rainforest, the warm temperate, such as can still be found on North Island, New Zealand (left), and the cold temperate, such as that of the Chilean coast. Both of these kinds of forest have one major feature in common: they have enough water for even the most moisture-greedy plants, such as mosses and ferns, to grow throughout the year. The animal life of the forest is also affected by the abundance of rain, so that snails, slugs, frogs and other water-loving creatures flourish. Most temperate rainforest is of the warm-temperate kind, normally found on the edges of subtropical regions, and the vegetation, with palms, lianas, bamboos, as well as ferns and mosses, is similar to, although less rich than, the tropical rainforest's vegetation. The cold-temperate rainforests grow in cooler regions but their coastal position means that the climate is milder and wetter than inland (where deciduous trees dominate). Their vegetation is less lush and less varied than the warm-temperate forests, but mosses and ferns grow in abundance. Broad-leaved evergreens, such as New Zealand's southern beech, are the most common trees of these forests, although on the northwestern coast of North America Douglas firs and other conifers outnumber the broad-leaved evergreen species.

Man and the Temperate Forests

Temperate forests have suffered enormously at the hands of man. For the great civilizations of China, Europe and, later, North America the forests not only yielded cropland for expanding populations but also contributed materials and fuel for early technologies. More recently the demands of industry have reduced the forests still further. But today, scientists believe that this depleted resource could again play an important role in providing energy, food and materials for future generations.

PERMANENT SETTLEMENT
The Bronze Age and, later, the Iron Age laid the foundations of Chinese and Western civilizations. The forest shrank as permanent settlements grew (3) and, with the use of metals and improved technology, agricultural land was extended (4). But the forest was recognized as an important resource and areas were protected. Management techniques were introduced that, especially in medieval Europe, changed dense forest to coppice woods (5).

EARLY INDUSTRIAL TIMES
Sources of cropland and timber had been discovered in the New World, but in the Far East and Europe forests were drastically reduced. Virtually no Chinese forest remained, and in Europe nations began importing timber to serve growing industrial needs (6). To help solve shortages, plantations were established on country estates (7), which were often landscaped into parkland and planted with introduced species of trees (8).

PREHISTORIC FORESTS
Hunter gatherers made clearings in the forest when they cut brushwood for building shelters and for fuel (1): human impact on the temperate forest was small. But 7,000 years ago in Europe, 6,000 years ago in eastern Asia and 1,000 years ago in eastern North America, the first farming communities of the temperate forest (2) began to clear larger pockets of forest to provide land for crops and timber for houses and tools.

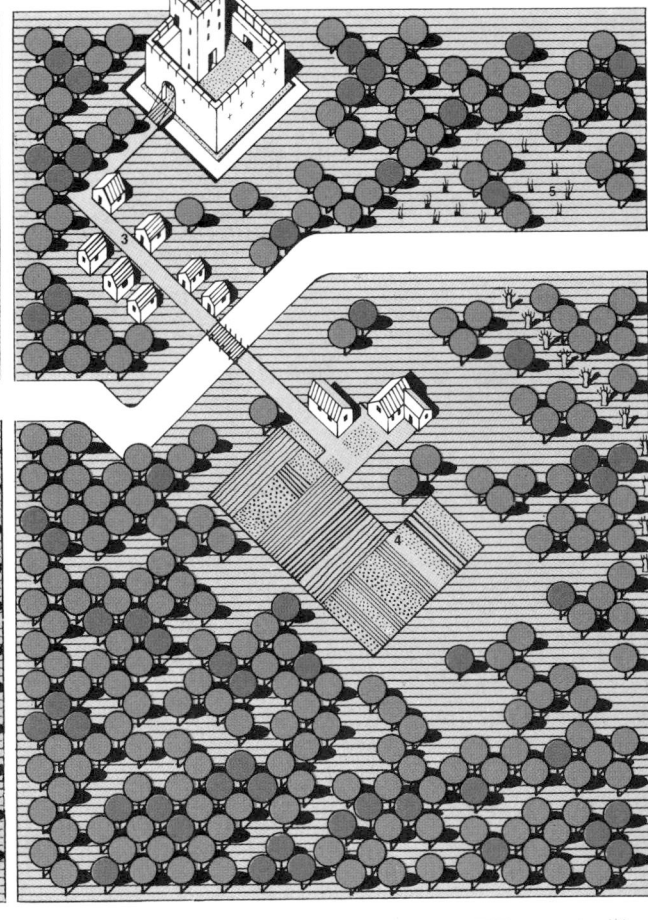
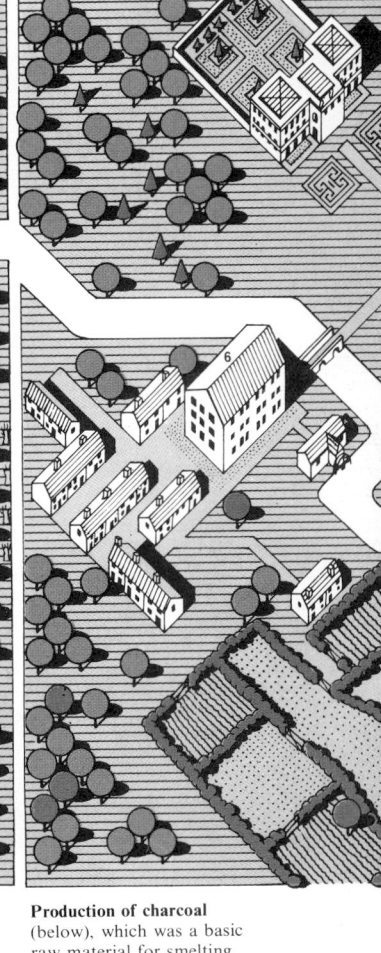

Production of charcoal (below), which was a basic raw material for smelting in early industrial times, was responsible for much deforestation of the land.

The aurochs, or wild ox, was one of the many forest animals that provided food for early hunter gatherers. Once man began to farm the land, he domesticated some of these animals—the wild boar, the aurochs and the wild turkey.

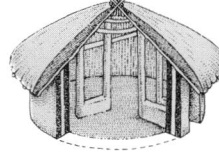

The dwellings of the late Neolithic Chinese were relatively sophisticated, reflecting an increasingly settled way of life that was soon to alter the landscape as forests were felled to provide building materials and land to plant crops.

The fortified villages and the farms of the Eastern Woodland Indians were set in semipermanent clearings cut in the North American forest. Before European settlement, however, human populations were small and deforestation was negligible.

Grain harvesting is depicted in a Chinese tomb image. By the 1st century AD, China contained nearly 60 million people, and agriculture, along with stock raising and metal mining, was drastically depleting the tree cover.

Coppicing and pollarding allowed continual cropping of forests. Branches were cut from trees, the bases of which were left to regrow shoots. This technique reduced the density of tree cover, encouraging a richer growth of ground plants.

Coppicing

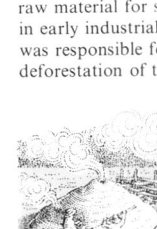

Pollarding

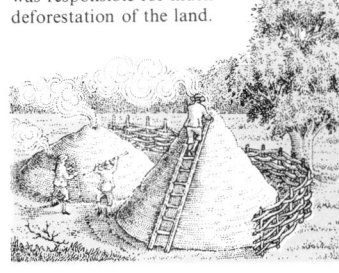

Human interference with the forests goes back deep into prehistory. There is evidence that fire was used to stampede hunted animals in southern Europe as long as 400,000 years ago. Human populations, while they remained small, had only a slight effect on the vast stretches of primeval forest. Even so, hunting practices and the use of fire to clear land reduced some of the forests of Europe and Asia even before the invention of agriculture. In the New World, too, Eastern Woodland Indians had already affected the North American forests, and early Maori hunters had burned much of the tree cover of New Zealand by the time Europeans arrived.

Nevertheless it was the development of agriculture in Neolithic (New Stone Age) times that had the first really destructive effect on the temperate forests. Clearings were made for crops and the felled trees provided fuel and building material for the new communities. Large forest animals suffered as well, some (such as deer) being hunted for food and others (such as wolves) because they threatened grazing animals. But it was the population increase resulting from the new, settled way of life that caused the extension of man-made cropland deep into former forests.

With man's development of metals, more forests were destroyed: wood and charcoal were used for smelting and the new iron tools made tree clearance easier and more thorough. Firing of forests was also a familiar military ploy, used by such warriors as the Romans.

Medieval woodlands
By medieval times, large tracts of forest had been cleared in Europe and in the Far East, although in the former area there remained extensive royal hunting forest reserves. Local woodlands were carefully managed to serve the needs of the community; the techniques used included pollarding and coppicing.

Pollarding involved the cropping of main branches at a certain height above ground. In coppicing, the "coppice with standards" method was used to harvest the smaller species, such as hazel and hornbeam, whereas the standards (such as oaks) were cut on a longer rotation of 100 years or so. Alternatively, the oak itself could be part of the coppice crop, its stems being cut near ground level so that shoots arose from the stump, to be cut 10 to 20 years later. For local communities, industries and cities, forests provided a variety of materials for building, tanning and fencing, as well as dyestuffs, charcoal and domestic fuel.

The growth of the iron and shipbuilding industries in the sixteenth century devastated so much woodland and forest that in many regions good timber became scarce and had to be imported from considerable distances. The pressure on woodland continued until the production of coke and cheap coal brought some relaxation, but by the early twentieth century the coppice system had broken down and management of Europe's woodlands had largely been abandoned. In Europe the poor state of the deciduous forests was further worsened by two world wars. Many countries have since set up organizations with the specific task of restoring reserves of timber. Economic pressures, however, have led to the planting mainly of quick-growing conifers, rather than typical trees of the temperate deciduous forest.

New World forests
The migrants who settled in the New World were the descendants of the people who had largely destroyed the forests of Europe. Confronted by the temperate deciduous forests of eastern North America, they virtually continued where they had left off. Tracts were cleared to create arable and range land and to provide the massive amounts of timber needed for the colonization, industrialization and urbanization of North America. With the opening of the prairie lands for agriculture, however,

Disturbance to the natural vegetation has occurred throughout the temperate forest zone. Exploitation of this biome's greatest resource, its agricultural potential, has been one of the major causes of deforestation. The only forests that have escaped major disturbance are in remote areas, too rocky or too steep for cultivation. Today, intensive farming is still a major economic activity of the temperate forest regions. But farmland is not the only important resource to have disturbed the forests. Mining for key minerals such as copper, iron and coal, all of which made possible the development of Western and Chinese civilization, has also contributed to destruction of the forest cover. For centuries the forests provided man with food, fuel and materials, but, ironically, it has been the removal of the forest that has enabled man to exploit the most important of these regions' resources.

THE CHANGING LANDSCAPE

Mankind has been occupying the temperate forest regions for many thousands of years, at first with little effect on the natural forest ecology. But during the last 2,000 years human activity has destroyed the original tree cover at an accelerating pace. As populations increased and economies developed—at different rates in the three major regions—forests disappeared to be replaced by farms, cities, industries and communications networks. Today, scarcely any of the original forest cover remains.

THE 19TH CENTURY
The Industrial Revolution developed in Europe and the New World, large towns and cities sprang up (9), pushing back the woodlands and forests still farther. This process was aided by the spreading network of railroads (10). Coke, iron and other minerals were replacing timber products as raw materials for growing industries (11), but demands were still made on the forests to provide, for example, railway sleepers and mine pit props.

FORESTS TODAY
The 20th century has seen an increasing trend towards urbanization in areas that were once temperate forest. Housing complexes (12) and new factory sites (13) cover large areas, while roadbuilding (14), industrial agriculture (15) and open-cast mining (16) destroy remaining woodland. Leisure areas (17) and nature reserves protect some woods, but plantations of exotic conifers (18) do not always provide suitable wildlife habitats.

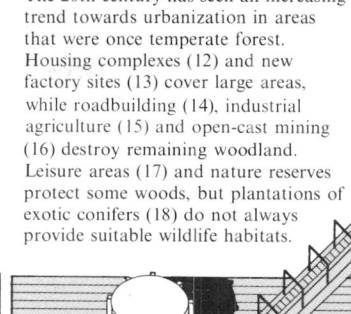

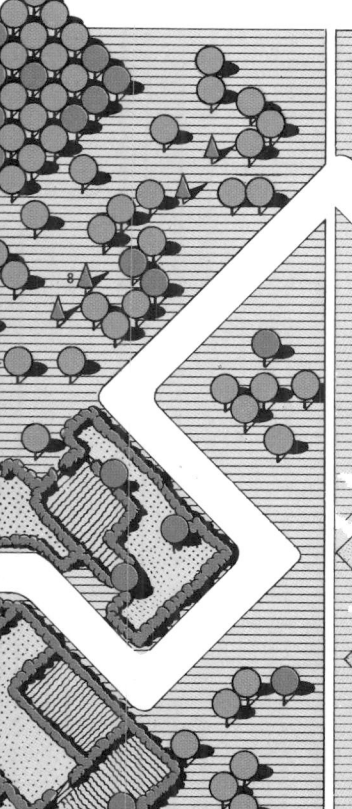

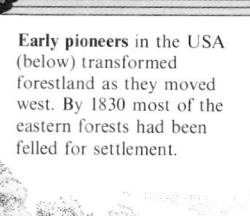

Early pioneers in the USA (below) transformed forestland as they moved west. By 1830 most of the eastern forests had been felled for settlement.

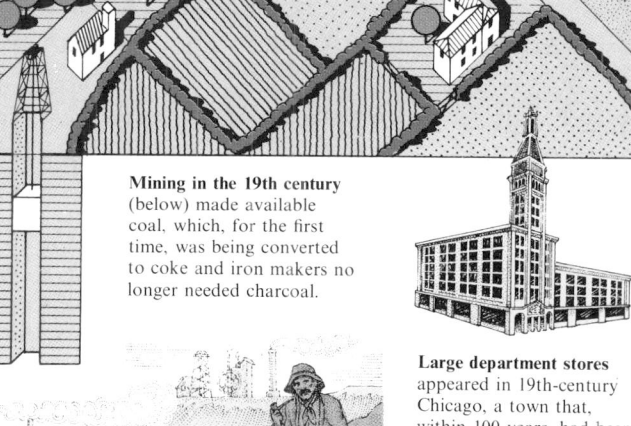

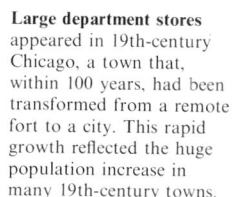

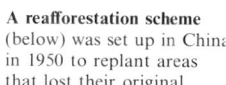

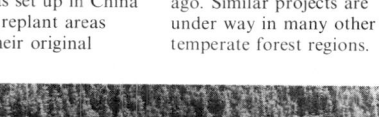

Mining in the 19th century (below) made available coal, which, for the first time, was being converted to coke and iron makers no longer needed charcoal.

Large department stores appeared in 19th-century Chicago, a town that, within 100 years, had been transformed from a remote fort to a city. This rapid growth reflected the huge population increase in many 19th-century towns.

A reafforestation scheme (below) was set up in China in 1950 to replant areas that lost their original forest cover many centuries ago. Similar projects are under way in many other temperate forest regions.

The European wood bison has escaped extinction because one herd of the animals has lived, for centuries, in a royal hunting reserve. Today, wildlife parks throughout temperate regions protect endangered forest species.

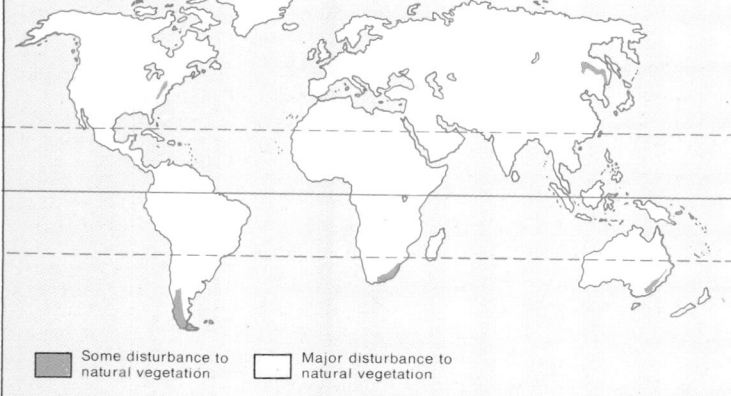

Some disturbance to natural vegetation

Major disturbance to natural vegetation

the pressures shifted, some of the east coast deciduous forest grew up again, and it is possible that parts of the eastern USA may have nearly as much forest cover now as when the settlers first arrived. Nevertheless, other areas of forestland have been destroyed in recent decades by strip mining and the creation of a vast road and rail network. In the southern hemisphere, especially in the last 200 years, the temperate rainforests of Australia and New Zealand have been subjected to much the same pattern of events, although on a smaller and somewhat less devastating scale.

Conservation
Today the general need to preserve and extend the woodlands is clearly recognized, but great uncertainty exists about their future. The demand for hardwoods for veneers, quality papermaking and furniture still exceeds supply. Oak is still the preferred material for some types of boat building and, especially in Europe, for joinery work. But one of the major difficulties with forestry as a land use is forecasting future trends within the industry, largely as a result of the long-term nature of the crop—hardwood trees planted today will not yield their timber until well into the next century. Government tax policies can be all important in deciding whether the majority of woodlands are, or will

continue to be, sound economic investments.

Temperate forests and woodlands still exist in sizeable quantities in central Europe and the USA, but many of today's plots, particularly in western Europe, are far too small for efficient conservation of plant and animal life, and are isolated from other woods. As a result, successful breeding and exchange of genetic material is very difficult, especially when modern agriculture is rapidly destroying the linking corridors of hedgerows. The use of woodlands for recreation is also presenting considerable problems. Controlling agencies have been formed to cope with leisure demands, and a start has been made in the multiple use of forests for recreation, conservation and timber felling, but progress still needs to be made in harmonizing these potentially conflicting interests. Meanwhile, natural expanses of woodland and forest are still being lost to agricultural and urban expansion and to plantations of nonnative conifers.

Temperate forests are a biologically efficient form of land use. In terms of biomass—the amount of living material (animal and plant) in any one area—they could still play an important role in the provision of food, materials and even renewable energy. Thus on scientific, economic and aesthetic grounds a strong case can be made for immediate conservation measures.

Mediterranean Regions

Forests of evergreen trees once covered much of the Mediterranean regions. They flourished in spite of the hot, rainless summer months – as the original plant life, they had evolved to survive such harsh conditions. Man, however, has proved to be a greater threat than the climate. He introduced domestic animals and cleared the land to grow crops; the natural vegetation was burned, browsed and plowed into nonexistence. Man's activities left behind tracts of impoverished soil which rapidly became scrubland. Today, scrub is the most typical vegetation in all the Mediterranean climate zones throughout the world.

CONVERGENCE
Isolated from each other by enormous areas of land and ocean, regions with a Mediterranean type of climate rarely have any plant species in common. But, by a process known as "convergent evolution," the plant communities in each of these areas have produced remarkably similar responses to their similar environments. This can be seen in the conifer communities, the broad-leaved evergreen trees, and in the various hardy shrubs and ground plants typical of each of the regions.

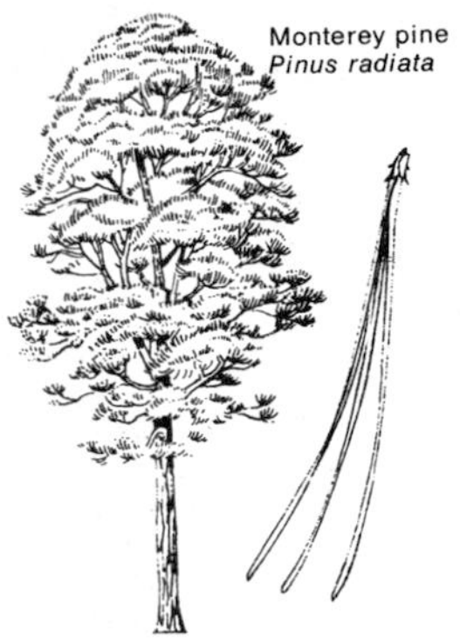
Monterey pine
Pinus radiata

California's Monterey pine and other Mediterranean conifers—South African podocarps and Chile pines, for example—have needle-shaped leaves that prevent rapid loss of water from such trees during drought.

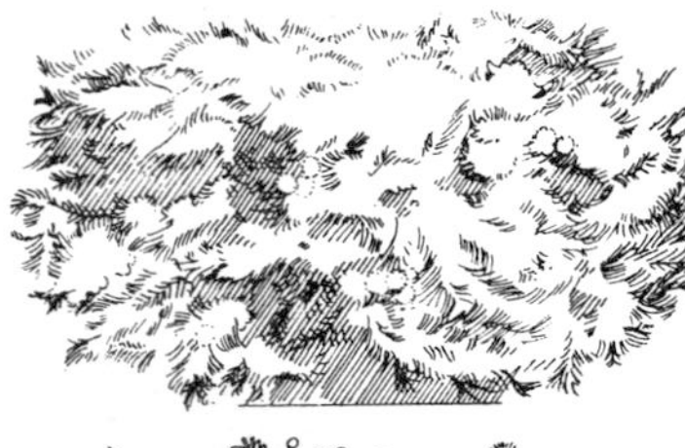

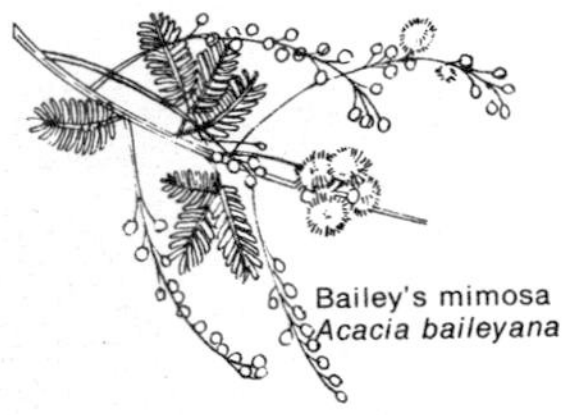
Bailey's mimosa
Acacia baileyana

Nonconiferous evergreens such as Australia's acacias and eucalypts, Chile's *quillajas* and California's evergreen oaks are typical Mediterranean trees. Their leathery leaves limit summer moisture loss.

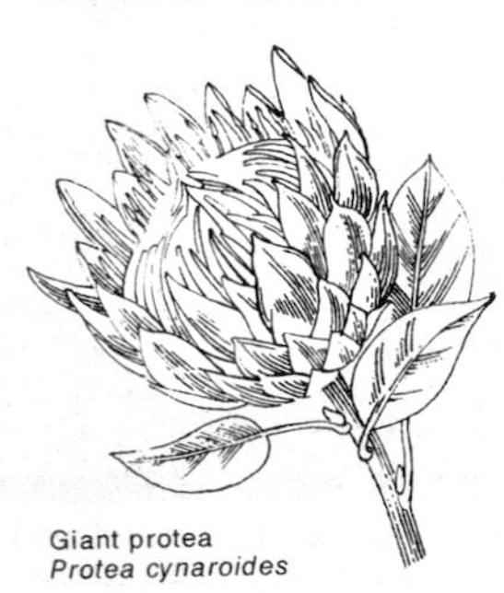
Giant protea
Protea cynaroides

Shrubs and ground plants show various adaptations to drought. South African proteas and Europe's laurel have thick evergreen leaves. Narrow leaves and water-storing roots are other common adaptations.

Long, hot, dry summers and warm, moist winters form the seasonal rhythm of the "Mediterranean" year. This climatic pattern can be found in small areas of nearly every continent in the world, typically on the western side of landmasses and in the mild, temperate latitudes. North America's "Mediterranean" is in California, South America's occurs in Chile and Africa's lies at the southern tip of Cape Province. Australia has two small "Mediterranean" areas, one on the southern coast and one on the western. Europe's Mediterranean region, which has given its name to this climate, covers much of the southern part of the continent and extends into northern Africa.

Wherever Mediterranean conditions prevail, the native plant life has adapted to survive the scanty annual rainfall and the long summer droughts. Some species have developed deep root systems that can tap low summer water tables, and many of the ground plants—such as bulbs and aromatic herbs—grow vigorously only in early summer while rain still moistens the soil. But it is the broad-leaved evergreens with their drought-resistant leaves that are the most typical of the Mediterranean areas.

This natural pattern of vegetation has been drastically altered by man. In southern Europe in particular, almost all the original evergreen forests have long since been destroyed and thickets of fast-growing, tough scrub plants have grown up in their place. This scrub, which once probably covered only small areas, is now so widespread that it is considered the most typically Mediterranean of all kinds of vegetation. It is the *maquis* of France, the *macchia* of Italy and the *mattoral* of Spain. A similar type of vegetation (although containing different species) can also be found in South Africa's fynbos, in California's chapparal, and in Australia's tracts of natural mallee scrub.

Classical land use

Southern Europe, with its long history of human settlement, farming and pastoralism, is the most altered of all the Mediterranean regions. Over the centuries vast tracts of original vegetation have been removed, either by farmers (for crop growing) or by grazing animals. And, particularly on the steep slopes and rocky outcrops, this has resulted in extensive deterioration and erosion of the soil. Agriculture generally has less serious effects upon the vegetation than has animal grazing. Mankind has learned, over many hundreds of years, which are the most suitable crops for the various soils, terrain and climatic conditions of the region. The Mediterranean "triad" of wheat on the lowlands and olives and vines on the hills has been a successful combination since Classical times.

Pastoral plundering of the land, however, has more serious consequences. The virtually omnivorous goat is particularly damaging and can strip a whole forest of its foliage, bark, shrubs, ground plants and grass. After such an assault the vegetation rarely returns to its former condition; normally, a scrubby growth of kermes oak and shrubs springs up to form a typical maquis-type vegetation.

The rise and fall of each great Mediterranean civilization has seen forests destroyed in one area after another. The Greek colonization of southern Italy was provoked by deforestation and soil erosion in Attica. The Romans extended clearance north to the Po valley and into eastern Tunisia. From the seventh century onwards, Muslims made great inroads into the forests of North Africa as well as southern and eastern Spain; and in the north of Spain and southern France, medieval monks cleared forested valleys. During the seventeenth and eighteenth centuries large areas of Provence and Italy were cleared to plant vines and this process continued in the 1800s, when the great wine-producing areas of Languedoc and Algeria were established. During this time the iron industries of Spain and northern Italy, with their growing need for charcoal, were adding to the destruction. Recent reafforestation efforts have been puny compared to past degradation.

Protected species

But throughout this history of forest removal some tree species have been protected. These have been the natural tree crops that have, at times, supported complete peasant economies. The chestnut forests of Corsica, for example, sustained a large rural population until this century; the chestnuts provided flour for bread and fodder for pigs. In Portugal and Sardinia the cork-oak forests are still important today.

It is the olive, however, symbol of peace and of New Testament landscapes, that is the Mediterranean's most characteristic tree crop. Of all the Mediterranean plants, it is the most perfectly adapted to its environment, with its deep roots to search out scarce water and its hard, shiny leaves to conserve what it finds. In fact, the summer drought is essential to olive growers for it encourages the build-up of oil in the fruit. Paradoxically, however, the olive—like the vine, the fig and many other "Mediterranean" crops—did not originate in the Mediterranean but was introduced from Asia Minor.

In spite of massive destruction of the natural landscape, mankind has learned many valuable lessons during his occupation of this region. Ideas that were to become important in laying the foundations of sound land management policy were developed in the Mediterranean area. Hillside terracing, irrigation, crop rotation and manuring were all, from necessity, practiced from early times. The flourishing agricultural industries of the world's other Mediterranean regions—the wine industry of California, the vast soft-fruit plantations of Australia and the citrus industry of South Africa—all owe a considerable debt to the generations of farmers who learned to exploit the red soils of the Mediterranean basin.

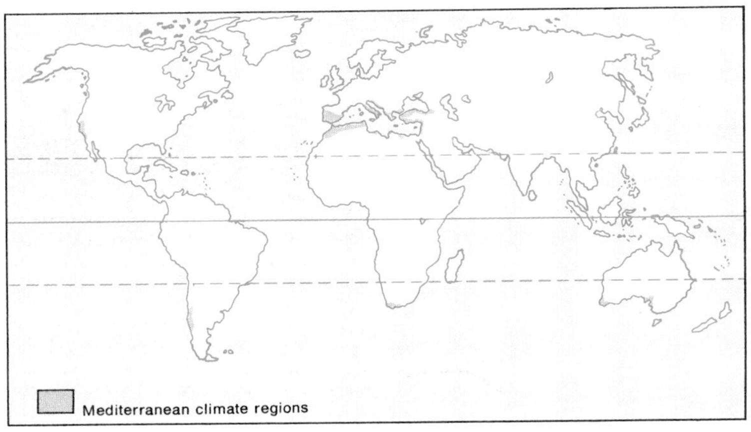
Mediterranean climate regions

The Mediterranean regions occur between the latitudes 30° and 40°, on the western and southwestern sides of the continents. These areas are affected in summer by the high-pressure systems of nearby desert regions, and in winter by wet, low-pressure systems brought in from the oceans and over the land by the prevailing Westerlies. This distinct seasonal shifting of major influences on the climate produces the hot, waterless summers and warm, moist, sometimes stormy winters typical of the Mediterranean climate.

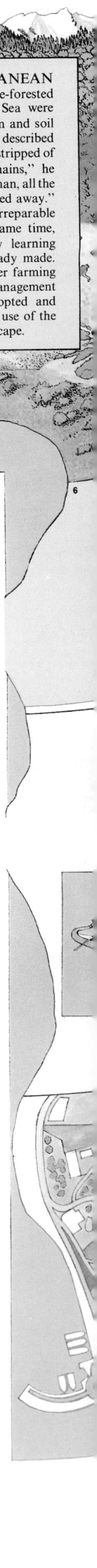
6

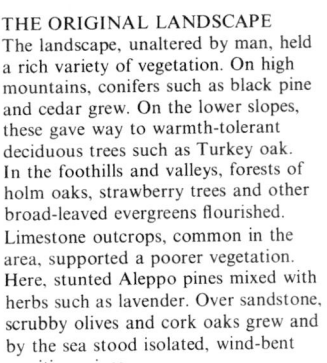

MAN AND THE MEDITERRANEAN
Even by Classical times, the once-forested lands fringing the Mediterranean Sea were suffering from massive deforestation and soil erosion. In the 5th century BC, Plato described the bare, dry hills of Attica, recently stripped of their woodlands. "What now remains," he wrote, "is like the skeleton of a sick man, all the fat and soft earth having been wasted away." By the end of the Classical period, irreparable damage had been done. At the same time, however, mankind was gradually learning through the mistakes he had already made. Suitable patterns of land use, better farming practices and improved land management techniques were slowly being adopted and were enabling man to make better use of the much-altered Mediterranean landscape.

THE ORIGINAL LANDSCAPE
The landscape, unaltered by man, held a rich variety of vegetation. On high mountains, conifers such as black pine and cedar grew. On the lower slopes, these gave way to warmth-tolerant deciduous trees such as Turkey oak. In the foothills and valleys, forests of holm oaks, strawberry trees and other broad-leaved evergreens flourished. Limestone outcrops, common in the area, supported a poorer vegetation. Here, stunted Aleppo pines mixed with herbs such as lavender. Over sandstone, scrubby olives and cork oaks grew and by the sea stood isolated, wind-bent maritime pines.

THE CLASSICAL AGE
Civilizations followed one after another, each taking its toll of the environment. In the mountains, forests were felled, the tall, straight conifers sought after by shipbuilders such as the Phoenicians, and deciduous hardwood timber in demand for charcoal to fuel growing industries. Some replanting did take place, especially as groves of crop trees such as chestnuts. Below in the foothills, agriculture and the grazing of animals had destroyed vast areas of natural forest. Terracing techniques, however, helped to stop soil erosion, and irrigation reached the height of its Classical art with Roman aqueducts and canals. Tree crops, such as olives, were found best suited to the thin hill soils. On the plains, especially where alluvial soils had been deposited, cereals were grown. Meanwhile, towns sprang up and the coastline became densely populated as ships and ports were built and sea trade grew. Exotic food plants, such as pomegranate trees, citron trees and vines, were brought into the region by merchant seamen.

THE MEDITERRANEAN TODAY
The region today bears the scars of many centuries of human activity. The once-forested mountains will never return to their former state, although some regrowth and some replanting (mostly with introduced tree species) has occurred. As in Classical times, hillsides are terraced and planted with vines and fruit trees. But with modern irrigation and fertilizing, land is less readily exhausted and abandoned now. On the plains, native shrubs, such as lavender, are commercially cultivated and grain is widely grown, particularly durum wheat used for making pasta. Cork oaks are planted, especially over dry sandstone areas, but indigenous vegetation has not suffered by this—scrubby woodland is more widespread than ever and can be found throughout the landscape. Perhaps the single most important part of the Mediterranean basin today is the coastline, for this has produced the region's major modern industry—tourism.

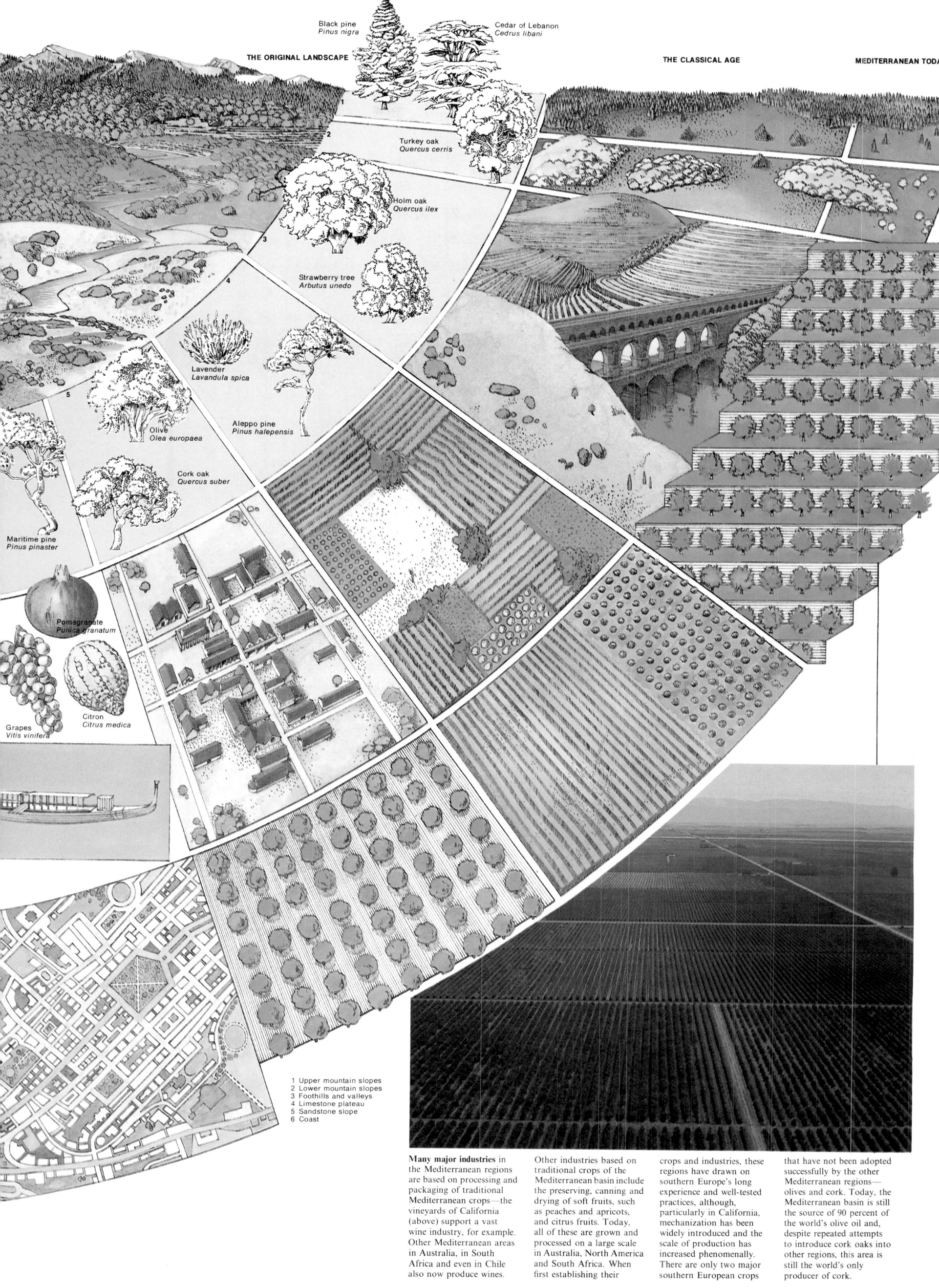

Black pine
Pinus nigra

Cedar of Lebanon
Cedrus libani

Turkey oak
Quercus cerris

Holm oak
Quercus ilex

Strawberry tree
Arbutus unedo

Lavender
Lavandula spica

Aleppo pine
Pinus halepensis

Olive
Olea europaea

Cork oak
Quercus suber

Maritime pine
Pinus pinaster

Pomagranate
Punica granatum

Grapes
Vitis vinifera

Citron
Citrus medica

1 Upper mountain slopes
2 Lower mountain slopes
3 Foothills and valleys
4 Limestone plateau
5 Sandstone slope
6 Coast

Many major industries in
the Mediterranean regions
are based on processing and
packaging of traditional
Mediterranean crops—the
vineyards of California
(above) support a vast
wine industry, for example.
Other Mediterranean areas
in Australia, in South
Africa and even in Chile
also now produce wines.

Other industries based on
traditional crops of the
Mediterranean basin include
the preserving, canning and
drying of soft fruits, such
as peaches and apricots,
and citrus fruits. Today,
all of these are grown and
processed on a large scale
in Australia, North America
and South Africa. When
first establishing their

crops and industries, these
regions have drawn on
southern Europe's long
experience and well-tested
practices, although,
particularly in California,
mechanization has been
widely introduced and the
scale of production has
increased phenomenally.
There are only two major
southern European crops

that have not been adopted
successfully by the other
Mediterranean regions—
olives and cork. Today, the
Mediterranean basin is still
the source of 90 percent of
the world's olive oil and,
despite repeated attempts
to introduce cork oaks into
other regions, this area is
still the world's only
producer of cork.

Temperate Grasslands

Compared with other flowering plants, grasses are newcomers to the Earth. They appeared only 60 million years ago, but since then they have proved to be an extremely successful family of plants. Today, the grasses dominate large areas of the world's natural vegetation and play a vital part in the intricate balance of plant and animal life in these regions. In spite of the inroads made by man, vast stretches of original grassland still cover the interiors of the North American and Eurasian landmasses.

The prairies of North America and the steppes of Eurasia extend far into the interiors of the northern continents. These are the best known and the most extensive of the world's temperate grasslands. The southern hemisphere, however, has examples in the veld of South Africa and the pampas of South America. Extensive grasslands also occur in southern Australia, although these are sometimes described as semiarid scrub because of the high average temperatures and the prolonged droughts in the region.

Temperate grasslands probably developed wherever the rainfall was too low to support forest and too high to result in semiarid regions, conditions found typically in the interiors of large continents. Continental interiors tend to be somewhat drier than coastal regions, but they are also characterized by extreme changes in temperature from one season to the next. In the North American grasslands, for example, winter temperatures may fall well below freezing whereas summer temperatures of 38°C (100°F) are not unusual. And these sharp fluctuations in seasonal temperature greatly influence how much of the rainfall is made available to plants. In summer particularly, when most of the rain falls, high temperatures, strong winds and lack of protective tree cover cause much of the moisture to evaporate before it can be absorbed into the soil.

Climatic conditions are not the only factor responsible for the distribution and form of the temperate grasslands. There are many pointers that indicate the importance of fire in determining their continuing existence and their extent. Natural fires, caused by lightning and fueled by the dry summer grasses, have always been a feature of these regions, but more recently, man-made fires have been crucial in fixing the boundary between forest and grassland.

Trees and shrubs frequently invade the margins of grasslands, but whenever there is a fire few of them survive. Grasses, however, have certain characteristics that enable them to withstand the potentially destructive impact of fire. The growing point of grasses is at the base of the leaves, close to the ground, and so destruction of the leaves above this point does not interrupt growth—in fact it may stimulate it. These same characteristics also serve to protect grasses from destruction by grazing animals. The large animals of these lands, such as the North American bison and the Eurasian horse, are able to crop the grasses without permanently damaging their food supply.

Grazers and predators

Large migrating herbivores with a strong herd instinct characterize one of the major types of temperate grassland animal. In the North American grasslands the bison (which may have numbered 60 million before being virtually exterminated by settlers) and the antelope-like pronghorn were the major examples of large herbivores. In Eurasia large herds of saiga antelopes, wild horses and asses at one time roamed the steppes, although they too have suffered from human activities, as has South America's largest grassland herd animal, the pampas deer. As these herds of grazing animals have been reduced, so have the carnivorous animals of the grasslands that preyed upon them. At one time, however, these predators played an important part in protecting the grasslands by continually keeping the numbers of grazing herd animals in check.

RUNNING AND LEAPING HERBIVORES

Saiga
Saiga tatarica

American bison
Bison bison

European hare
Lepus europaeus

Guanaco
Lama guanicoe

Springhaas
Pedetes cafer

RUNNING CARNIVORES

Plains wolf
Canis lupus nubilus

Coyote
Canis latrans

Maned wolf
Chrysocyon brachyurus

SMALL BURROWING ANIMALS

European souslik
Citellus citellus

Marsupial mole
Notoryctes typhlops

Prairie dog
Cynomys ludovicianus

Viscacha
Lagostomus maximus

SMALL CARNIVORES

Black-footed ferret
Mustela nigripes

Marbled polecat
Vormela peregusna

Pampas cat
Lynchailurus pajeros

Gopher snake
Pituophis melanoleucus

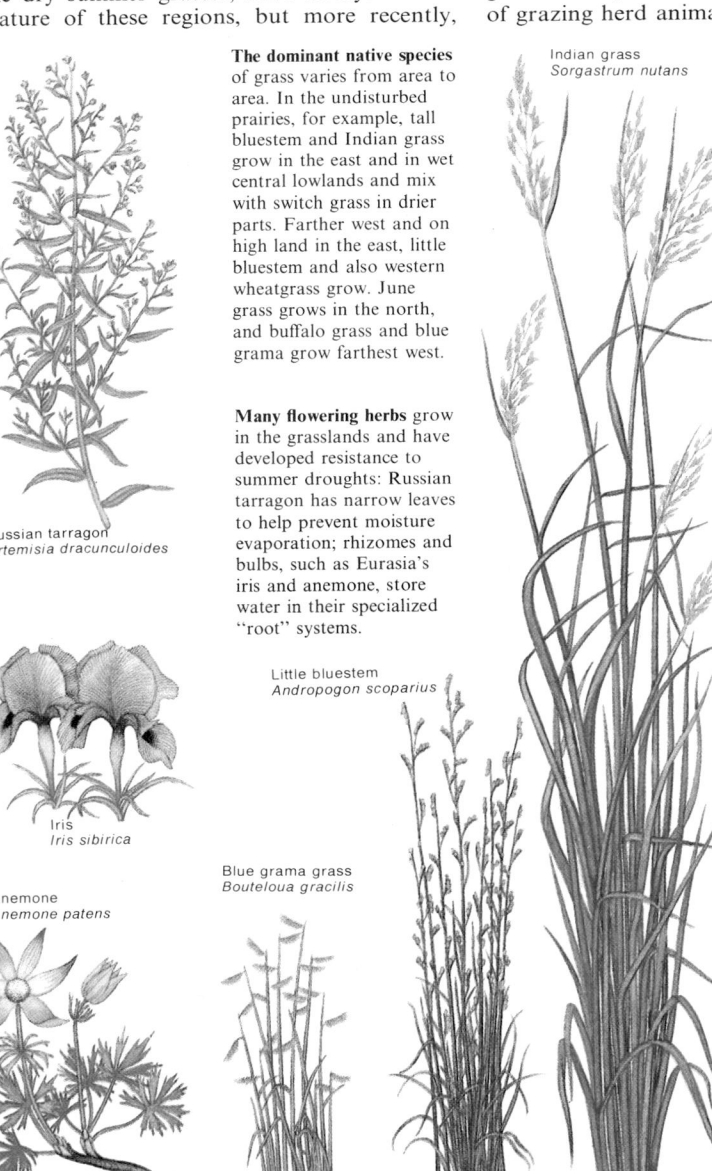

The dominant native species of grass varies from area to area. In the undisturbed prairies, for example, tall bluestem and Indian grass grow in the east and in wet central lowlands and mix with switch grass in drier parts. Farther west and on high land in the east, little bluestem and also western wheatgrass grow. June grass grows in the north, and buffalo grass and blue grama grow farthest west.

Many flowering herbs grow in the grasslands and have developed resistance to summer droughts: Russian tarragon has narrow leaves to help prevent moisture evaporation; rhizomes and bulbs, such as Eurasia's iris and anemone, store water in their specialized "root" systems.

Russian tarragon
Artemisia dracunculoides

Iris
Iris sibirica

Anemone
Anemone patens

Indian grass
Sorgastrum nutans

Little bluestem
Andropogon scoparius

Blue grama grass
Bouteloua gracilis

The natural distribution of the temperate grasslands is dictated mainly by rainfall: most occur in continental interiors where there is too little rain for forest but enough to prevent desert from forming. Between these limits the large range in rainfall allows three main types of grassland: tall grass in wetter areas, mid-grass, and short grass in drier parts. The largest grasslands exist in North America, Eurasia, South America, in Australia's Murray–Darling river basin and on the South African plateau.

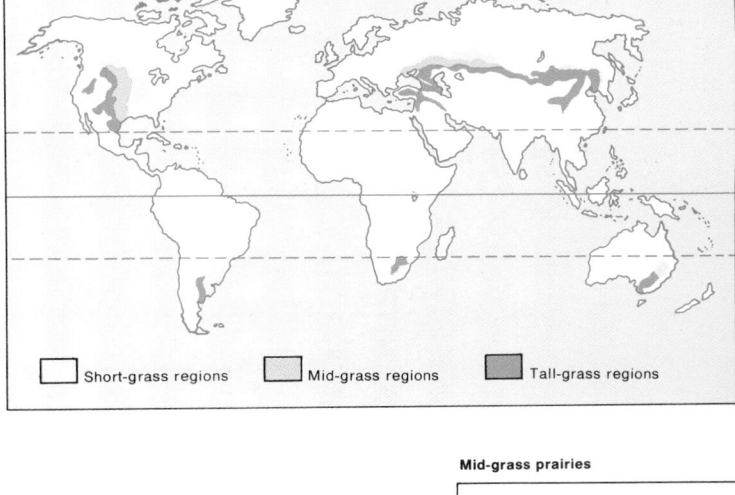

Short-grass regions   Mid-grass regions   Tall-grass regions

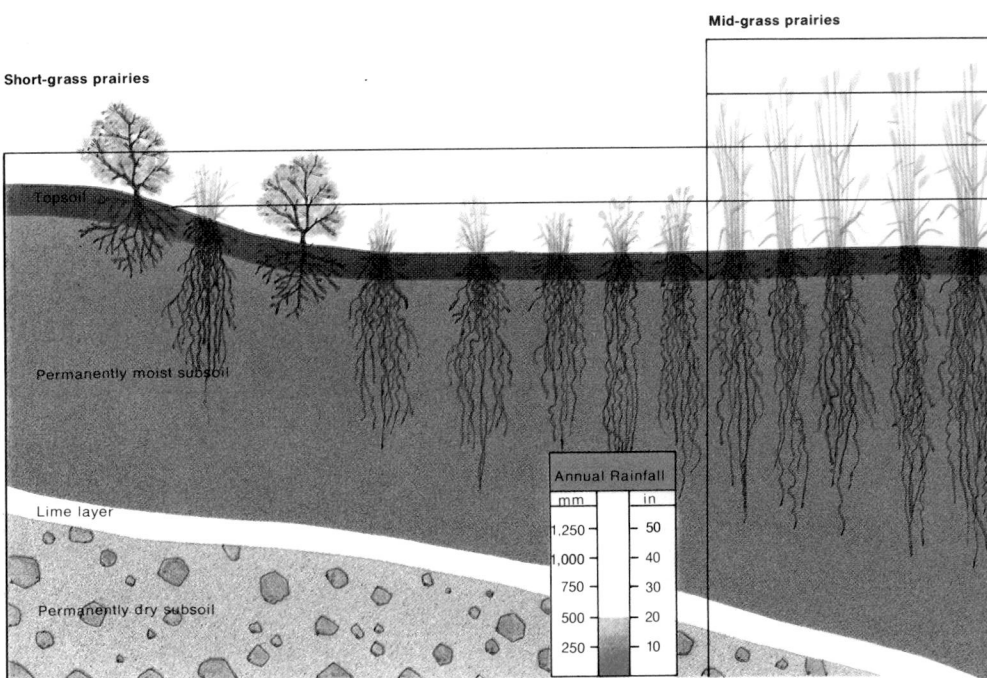

Short-grass prairies

Mid-grass prairies

Topsoil

Permanently moist subsoil

Lime layer

Permanently dry subsoil

Annual Rainfall

mm	in
1,250	50
1,000	40
750	30
500	20
250	10

GRASSLAND ADAPTATION

Animals of these regions have had to adapt to a difficult environment: vast, treeless expanses of grass offer little protection from harsh weather or predators. Different animals have found various answers to the problem and a clearly defined pattern of these adaptations can be traced throughout the grasslands.

Running and leaping herbivores survive because of their ability to move faster than a pursuer. The larger animals such as the Eurasian saiga, North America's bison and pronghorn and the guanaco of South America are runners. The leaping herbivores are usually smaller creatures that escape danger by bounding away to bolt-holes. They include the European hare and the African springhaas.

Running carnivores follow, and prey on, running and leaping herbivores. These animals, such as the coyote and the now extinct plains wolf of North America, and South America's maned wolf, also depend on speed—to enable them to catch their prey.

Small burrowing animals hide from predators by digging under the ground. Some, such as Australia's marsupial mole, spend most of their lives below ground. Others, such as the European souslik, South America's viscacha and North America's prairie dog, live and sleep under the ground but come to the surface to find food.

Small carnivores concentrate on the burrowers as their main source of food. They either, like the pampas cat, rely on surprise attack of their prey, or, like Eurasia's marbled polecat and the grasslands' many kinds of snake, depend on their long, lithe shape to follow creatures into their burrows.

Two distinctive types of grassland bird can be distinguished: the sky birds, which spend long periods of time on the wing, and the ground birds.

Birds of the sky include songbirds such as the skylark which, having no perch from which to proclaim its territory, sings in the sky, and birds of prey such as Eurasia's tawny eagle and North America's red-tailed hawk and prairie falcon, which ride the thermals scanning the ground for their prey.

Ground birds rarely take to the wing, although none has actually lost the ability to fly when necessary. They include birds such as the New World sage grouse and burrowing owl (which lives below ground in abandoned prairie dog burrows), the black grouse of Eurasia and songbirds such as North America's meadowlark.

Insects and other invertebrates have developed many different survival techniques. Some use camouflage: the praying mantis resembles a leaf bud and the tumble bug is the color of the dark grassland soil. Grasshoppers are miniature leaping herbivores and earthworms are small-scale versions of the grassland burrowers.

Skylark
Alauda arvensis

Red-tailed hawk
Buteo jamaicensis

Tawny eagle
Aquila rapax

Prairie falcon
Falco mexicanus

BIRDS OF THE SKY

Western meadowlark
Sturnella neglecta

Burrowing owl
Speotyto cunicularia

Sage grouse
Centrocercus urophasianus

Black grouse
Lyurus tetrix

GROUND BIRDS

Tumble bug
Canthonlaevis drury

Lubber grasshopper
Romalea microptera

INSECTS AND OTHER INVERTEBRATES

Common earthworm
Lumbricus terrestris

Praying mantis
Mantis religiosa

Another major type of animal found in the temperate grasslands, and one that is better adapted to survive man's activities, is the small, burrowing animal, for example the prairie dog and the gopher of North America, the viscacha of South America and the little ground squirrel known as the souslik in Eurasia.

Unlike the large herd animals, these creatures tend not to migrate. Many of them live together in complex, permanent, underground communities. The colonial "townships" of the prairie dog, for example, may house more than one million individuals, which each year excavate vast quantities of the grassland soil. This has considerable effect upon the structure of the soil. By bringing up earth from lower layers to the surface, these animals are responsible for changing the mineral content of certain areas of topsoil. This then encourages isolated pockets of different plant species to flourish.

A third group of grassland animals, consisting of insects and other invertebrates such as earthworms, has an even more important effect upon the soil. They live in or on the soil and play a vital role in maintaining grassland fertility. These creatures may be herbivores, carnivores or primary (first stage) decomposers (which break down such material as dead grass and animal remains). These three types of activity allow a complete range of organic matter to be processed and incorporated into the earth, where it is further broken down by the second-stage decomposers, the countless millions of soil bacteria. In this way nutrients continuously flow back to the earth and restore its fertility.

Fertile black earths

The topsoil of temperate grassland regions, therefore, contains large amounts of organic material, which is produced every year and is quickly incorporated into the soil. The low and intermittent rainfall and the protective cover of grasses mean that the topsoil undergoes little chemical leaching, a process in which minerals are removed and carried down to lower layers by rainfall percolating through the earth. The soils are thus dark in color, generally fertile and of the "black earth" type ("chernozem" in Russian) which is, at least at first, capable of producing high yields of crops.

The most suitable and most widely grown crops are, predictably, the cultivated grasses, and it is these grasses that provide more food for mankind (either directly as grain or indirectly as animal fodder) than any other source. The temperate grassland biome is therefore an important agricultural resource. Undisturbed natural grasslands, however, are also valuable resources. They need to be preserved both for the information that they can provide about how complex communities of wildlife function efficiently, and because, as a rich source of genetic material, they hold many of the answers to the major agricultural problems that probably lie ahead for the human race.

A typical cross section, based on the North American prairies, shows temperate grasslands in relation to rainfall. Annual rainfall determines the depth of the permanently moist subsoil, which in turn dictates the length to which grass roots can grow. Tall grasses have deep root systems and need a considerable depth of moist subsoil. As the rainfall decreases, they gradually give way to shorter grass species. Short grasses require less water and their shallower roots are well suited to drier regions. On dry margins, desert plants start to dominate, and on the wet margins, trees appear.

Tall-grass prairies

cm	ft
215	7
180	6
150	5
120	4
90	3
60	2
30	1
0	0

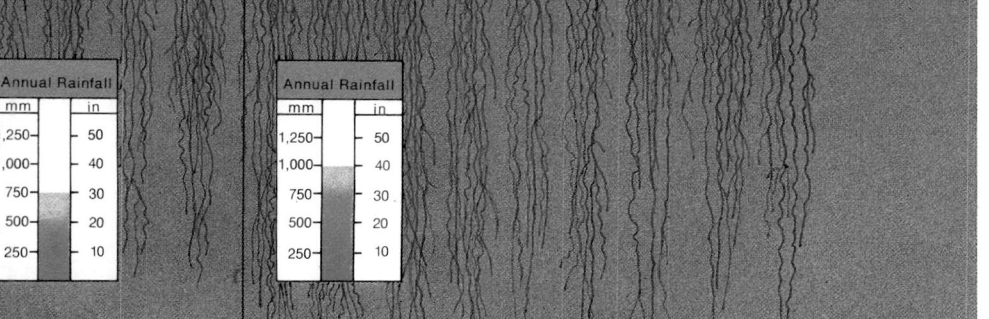

Annual Rainfall	
mm	in
1,250	50
1,000	40
750	30
500	20
250	10

Annual Rainfall	
mm	in
1,250	50
1,000	40
750	30
500	20
250	10

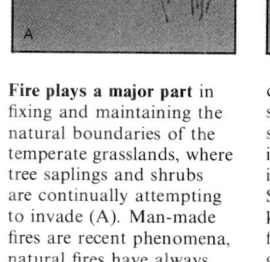

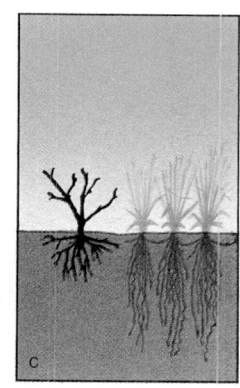

Fire plays a major part in fixing and maintaining the natural boundaries of the temperate grasslands, where tree saplings and shrubs are continually attempting to invade (A). Man-made fires are recent phenomena, natural fires have always occurred. In summer, low-pressure systems build up in continental interiors, causing violent electrical storms. The dry sward of summer grass is easily ignited by lightning and fire is quickly spread by wind. Shrubs and saplings are killed or badly damaged by fire, but grasses, with their growing points close to the soil, remain unharmed (B). They may even benefit from this "pruning" and grow more quickly. Some species grow new buds from their underground shoots. Removal of the main shoot may encourage growth of "tillers" (shoots growing out sideways), which then increase the spread of the grasses as they begin to invade the area left vacant by the dead, or slowly recuperating, shrubs (C).

Man and the Temperate Grasslands

The vast areas of temperate grassland lay virtually empty until the end of the eighteenth century. Over the next 125 years they were occupied by millions of people, most of them migrants from overcrowded Europe. By 1914, the grasslands had become the granaries and the stockyards of the world. Today, they are still the most important food-producing regions on Earth and their riches, properly distributed, are the world's first reserve against the possibility of a hungry future for the human race.

The great nineteenth-century migration to the grasslands proved of immense significance to the human race. It meant that, within a single century, the area of productive land available was suddenly enlarged by thousands of millions of hectares. In all of mankind's history, such a thing had never happened before.

But before the grasslands could be occupied a number of major problems had to be solved. First, in order to reach these regions it was almost always necessary to travel deep into the continental interiors, and there were few navigable rivers and no mechanized forms of transportation for early pioneers. Second, with virtually no indigenous population, newcomers had to learn by their mistakes how best to exploit the new and unfamiliar environment. Third, even if settlers succeeded in using the land, they still had to find markets for their produce.

A number of technological developments, however, that took place in the nineteenth century provided the right combination of circumstances for the opening up of the grasslands. The Industrial Revolution in Europe produced the steamship and the railway locomotive, which created both a means of travel to and from these distant parts and an internal transport system for moving produce to ports and markets. It also produced the kind of machinery needed to plow and farm the great new open spaces; it made it possible for one family to cultivate an area 50 times as large as that which most farmers had known in Europe. Industrialization also threw thousands of Europeans out of work, and therefore provided a large supply of eager migrants. And it crowded further thousands into cities, thus creating vast markets for the settlers' produce.

It was the coming together of these various circumstances that acted as the catalyst and converted, for example, the Russian penetration of the Eurasian steppes in the late eighteenth

THE CRADLE OF AGRICULTURE

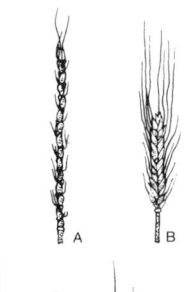
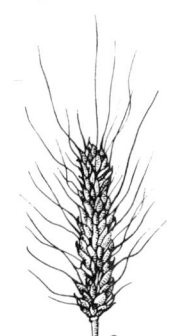

Stands of wild einkorn (A), emmer wheat (B) and wild barleys can be seen today in the grassy foothills that flank the Taurus and the Zagros mountains, and the uplands of northern Israel. It was in this region 10,000 years ago that the world's earliest farmers gathered seeds from these species and sowed the first crops. Wild einkorn is probably the oldest of all wheats and the parent of every modern variety—including the most important and most widely grown kind of grain in the world today, common bread wheat (C).

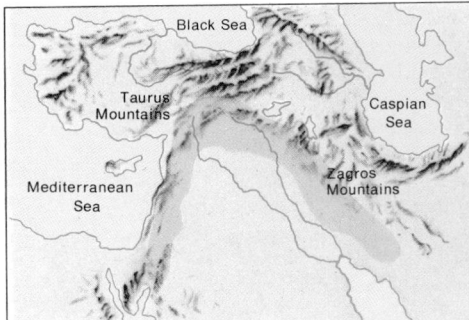

GRASSLAND EXPLOITATION

Today, temperate grasslands provide mankind with a superabundance of food. But the vast potential of these regions was not exploited until the mid-19th century, when mass migration by Europeans, combined with new technology, allowed full-scale development and settlement.

BEFORE EUROPEAN SETTLEMENT
The grasslands were sparsely populated. Most of the indigenous tribespeoples were nomadic hunters and gatherers. They wandered widely over the regions, making temporary camps (1) as they followed the movement of their quarry—the plentiful herds of grazing animals (2). These peoples made little impact on the natural grasslands.

GRASSLAND SETTLERS
Early pioneers relied on animal-drawn transport (3), primitive farm tools (4) and unpredictable free-range livestock grazing (5). During the 19th century, farming became more productive: better equipment cultivated larger areas (6); barbed wire made stock raising efficient (7); railways and the telegraph improved communication (8).

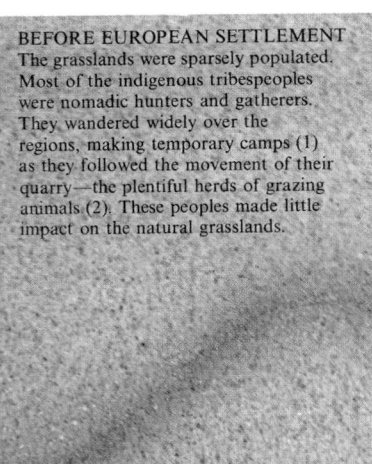

Tehuelche Indians (above) adopted horses for hunting from early Spanish settlers to the pampas. In South Africa and North America, too, the introduced horse became a valued asset for grassland hunters. For people of the Eurasian steppes, for example the Mongols (right), native horses have always been culturally important.

The **South African veld** was first settled by Europeans after 1836 (left). Dutch farmers (Boers), rejecting British rule of the Cape Colony, trekked north in search of new land. Moving into the Transvaal they discovered rich grassland, recently emptied of its original inhabitants, who had fled to escape the aggressive attentions of neighboring Zulus.

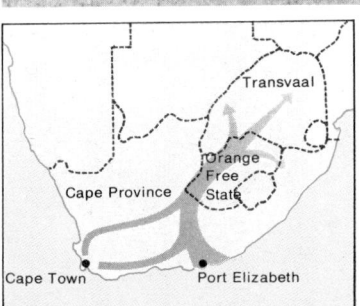

Cape Province / Transvaal / Orange Free State / Cape Town / Port Elizabeth

Vaqueros were the original cowboys (left). Tending herds of cattle for the missionaries in 18th-century California, they developed techniques and traditions that served hundreds of later cowboys working the prairie ranges. In other grassland regions, as free-range stock raising became important, similar "cowboy" professions evolved—the Australian stockman and the gaucho of South America.

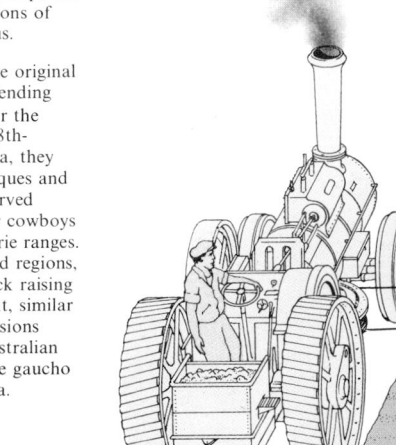

century into the explosive movement of hundreds of thousands of settlers a few years later. In the USA, too, by the year 1850, settlement had reached and then rapidly crossed the Mississippi. In the Argentine, genuine colonization of the pampas had begun, in South Africa, the Boers had reached the high veld, and in Australia pioneer settlers were moving outwards from the various areas of coastal settlement into the scrub grasslands of the interior.

Farmers or ranchers?

The fundamental question posed for these settlers was whether their newly found land should be used for crops or for livestock. Most grasslands have a dry edge and a wet edge, and it was therefore sensible to use the drier parts for stock raising and the wetter parts for cultivation. But the question was complicated by the fact that most of the newcomers were cultivators, and also that the line dividing dry from wet was vague—worse, it shifted from year to year.

Early attempts to define the dividing line tended to be ignored by the settlers themselves, and they pushed the limit of cultivation into areas where plowing the soil led to its destruction. Several generations of farmers had to learn this bitter lesson, and they learned only slowly: the worst disasters on the American grasslands occurred in the 1930s and created the infamous Dust Bowl region in the dry grasslands of the Midwest. Similarly, the Soviet Virgin Lands Program for growing cereal crops on the dry steppes was established in 1954 and is still experiencing difficulties.

Special methods are required both for farming and for ranching the grasslands successfully. Farming has to take account of the open, treeless surface, the scanty and variable rainfall and the comparatively shallow topsoil. To minimize the risk of soil erosion, farmers plant windbreaks, plow fields along the contour, and protect the soil with a covering of the previous year's stubble and by planting cover crops in rotation with cereals. Ranchers, too, have learned to live with variable rainfall. They build stock ponds, irrigate areas of fodder crops to be used as a reserve in dry years and avoid overstocking and consequent overgrazing, which destroys the quality of the grass.

Food for the world

Today, the world's principal trading supplies of cereals and meat flow from these lands, over the networks of railway which link the grasslands to mill towns, slaughter yards and ports of shipment such as Adelaide in Australia, Buenos Aires in Argentina and Montreal in Canada. Without these links to large towns, the grasslands would be of little value, for even today their populations are sparse and the local markets are relatively insignificant.

Throughout most of the world, however, the human population continues to soar and it remains to be seen whether the grasslands can continue to supply these growing numbers with food. Undoubtedly, the output of cereals and meat can be increased, although at considerable cost in fertilizers, new crop strains, more irrigation and more machines. On the other hand, the problem at present is not mainly one of production, nor will it be in the near future. The land can produce more, but there is no point in doing so unless the yields can be made available where they are most needed.

The world's hungry people live in other regions, many of them in countries that are unable to afford imported food supplies, particularly during those years when prices are high. The major importers of temperate grassland produce are the rich industrialized nations, such as those of western Europe. Furthermore, much of the grain imported by those countries is not consumed by humans but used to feed stalled, beef-producing cattle—a highly inefficient way of using these supplies. Consequently, unless producer nations and wealthy importing nations can create a system for produce to reach those in need of it, extra output from the grasslands will be irrelevant.

9

MODERN-DAY FARMING
Livestock feed on carefully selected grasses, which are sown and fertilized by aircraft (9). Fodder crops are grown as reserve animal feed (10), and stock ponds ensure against drought (11). Feedlots (12) fatten stock on grain (13). Cereal farms (14) are highly mechanized, and road and rail serve even the remotest regions (15).

The steam-driven plow (below) went through many developments to reduce its unwieldiness and heaviness. The version produced in 1858 used a traction engine and pulley wheel system. The plow was drawn back and forth between these by a power-driven cable. This design was, however, superseded by the steam tractor, which, although unsuited to small European fields, was ideal for drawing multifurrow plows across the grasslands.

Sand-smothered farms in the heart of the Dust Bowl were rapidly abandoned during the 1930s and 40s (above). This was one costly lesson that man had to learn in the process of developing the grasslands. Traditionally grazing land, the western part of the prairies was first plowed this century. Years of drought arrived, crops died and the desert encroached.

World cereal supplies flow from temperate grasslands (right). North America is the most important producing region, for although almost all nations produce grain, few can grow enough to feed their populations and even fewer have any surplus to export or hold in reserve against poor harvests. But North America, with its prairie cornfields and its small population, exports many millions of tonnes.

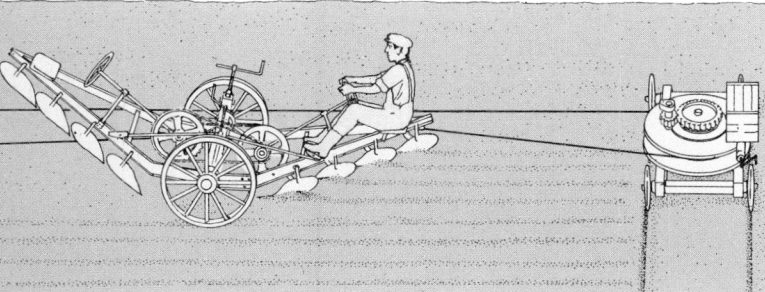

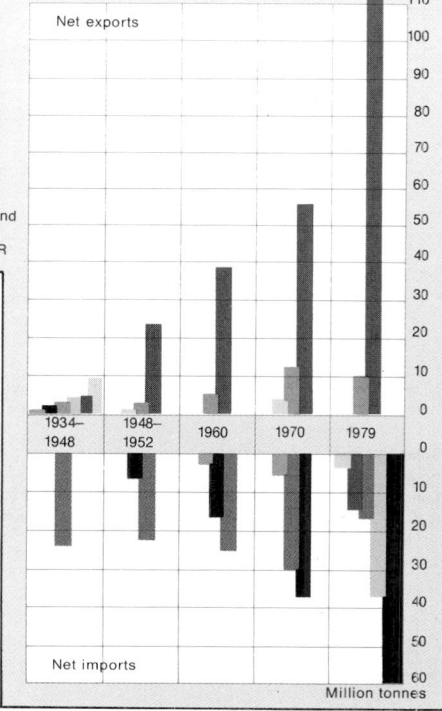

World grain-trading regions

- Africa
- North America
- South America
- Asia
- Western Europe
- Australia and New Zealand
- Eastern Europe and USSR

Net exports

1934– 1948–1952 1960 1970 1979
1948

Net imports

Million tonnes

Deserts

Much of the Earth's land surface is so short of water that it is defined as desert. Not all deserts are hot, sandy wastelands; some are cold, some are rocky, but all lack moisture for most of the year. Even so, a surprising variety of plants and animals have adapted to these hostile environments. Plants have developed ingenious ways of surviving long periods of drought, and many desert animals shelter during the intense heat of the day, emerging only at night to feed.

LIFE IN THE DESERT
The overriding need to obtain and conserve water dictates the pattern of desert life. Many plants close their pores during the day and most daytime creatures limit their activity to early morning and late afternoon. At night the temperature drops sharply and dew provides welcome moisture. Some plants bloom at night, and the desert is alive with insects, night-hunting birds, reptiles and small mammals.

DESERTS BY DAY

Many birds are at home in the desert. The lanner falcon of Africa and Asia gets all the moisture it needs from its diet of small birds and rodents. Sandgrouse live in the open deserts of Eurasia and North Africa; mainly seed eaters, they must make long flights each day to find water. Roadrunners, in American deserts, hunt insects, lizards and small rattlesnakes.

Lanner falcon
Falco biarmicus

Pallas's sandgrouse
Syrrhaptes paradoxus

Roadrunner
Geococcyx californianus

Large mammals are nomadic and obtain most of the moisture they need from plants. Camels can go for long periods without food or water because their humped back stores fat which can be drawn on when food is scarce, and water stored in their body tissues prevents dehydration. Addax antelopes survive entirely on plants. They roam remote parts of the Sahara, their broad hooves enabling them to travel easily over soft sand. Gazelles rely on speed. Small and fleet footed, they are able to disperse quickly over great distances to find food and water.

Arabian camel
Camelus dromedarius

Asian camel
Camelus bactrianus

Addax antelope
Addax nasomaculatus

Dorcas gazelle
Gazella dorcas

Insects and reptiles are well adapted to desert life. Desert locusts, when overpopulation threatens their food supply, change from a solitary to a swarming migratory form. Harvester ants store seeds against times of drought; desert tortoises withstand drought by becoming torpid. Lizards are cold blooded and need the sun to warm them, but must shelter from the intense heat of midday. The thorny devil, a small Australian ant-eating lizard, is protected from potential predators by its prickly scales.

Desert locust
Schistocerca gregaria

swarming adult

Harvester ants
Pogonomyrmex sp

Desert tortoise
Gopherus polyphemus

solitary hopper

Gridiron-tailed lizard
Callisaurus draconoides

Thorny devil
Moloch horridus

Desert plants have evolved various ways of coping successfully with drought. The ocotillo of southwestern America sheds its leaves, reducing its need for water. Euphorbias, and cacti such as the prickly pear, store water in their stems. Blue kleinia, a South African succulent, has a waxy coating that limits water loss. Agaves mature very slowly, building up reserves of food and water in their leaves before they flower. Esparto, a needlegrass, is typical of many desert grasses.

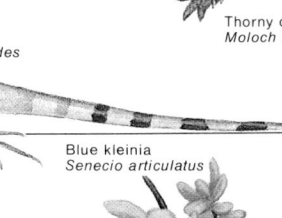

Blue kleinia
Senecio articulatus

Ocotillo
Fouquieria splendens

Euphorbia
Euphorbia obesa

Prickly pear
Opuntia ficus-indica

Agave
Agave americana

Deserts occur where rainfall is low and infrequent and where any moisture quickly evaporates or disappears instantly into the parched ground. In the driest deserts, rainfall rarely exceeds 100 mm (4 in) a year, and is so unreliable that some places may have no rain for 10 years or more. These are deserts in the truest sense of the word: harsh wildernesses that are almost totally without life. Regions with less than 255 mm (10 in) of rain a year are generally classified as arid and those with less than 380 mm (15 in) as semiarid.

Hot deserts have very high daytime temperatures in summer, although they drop sharply at night, and the winters are relatively mild. In the so-called cold deserts the summers are hot but the winters are so cold that temperatures may fall as low as −30°C (−22°F).

Desert climates and landscapes
In the subtropical latitudes, swept by hot, drying winds, high-pressure weather systems prevent rain clouds from forming. In these regions, rain comes only from local storms or follows low-pressure weather systems (often seasonal) when they move in across the desert. Large areas of central Asia have become desert because they are so far from the sea that clouds have shed all their rain before they reach them. Other deserts occur because mountains cut them

off from moisture-bearing winds. The Andes, for example, shelter the drylands of Argentina, and a high sierra stops rain from reaching the Mojave and Great Basin deserts of North America. Rain is also rare on the western sides of continents where cold ocean currents flow from the polar regions towards the Equator.

Desert climates vary not only from place to place but also with time. Over short periods rainfall is much less predictable than it is in temperate regions and droughts are frequent. Some droughts, such as those that occur along the southern fringe of the Sahara, are so severe that it may seem that the climate has changed permanently. But most droughts are short-lived and are followed by years of normal (although sparse) rainfall. Over longer periods of time, however, desert climates do change. Prehistoric cave drawings in the Saharan highlands, for example, show that elephants, rhinoceroses and even hippopotamuses—animals that are at home in wetter climates—lived in these now dry, barren uplands in a more moist period between 7,000 and 4,000 years ago.

Desert landscapes also vary enormously. They are as contrasted as the Colorado canyon country of the United States and the sandy wastes of the Middle East, but most include one or more of several basic features: steep, rocky mountain slopes, broad plains, basin floors

dominated by dry lake beds or sand seas, and canyon-like valleys. In low-lying areas, evaporation sometimes leaves a glistening residue of salt. Where there is soil, it is often sandy or consists of little more than fragmented rock, and because plant life is usually sparse there is little or no humus to enrich the ground.

Where water is life
Plant growth depends on water, and desert plants are usually widely spaced to reduce competition for what little moisture is available. Many plants rely on short, sharp rainstorms; others make use of dew and grow in locations, such as crevices in rocks, where water can accumulate. Some complete their life cycle in a single wet season, producing seeds that lie dormant during the following drought and germinate only when enough moisture is available for them to grow. These are the ephemerals that carpet the desert with a brief but brilliant display of flowers shortly after rain has fallen.

Most desert plants, however, are able to tolerate or resist drought. These are the xerophytes ("dry plants") and phreatophytes ("deep-water plants"). Xerophytic trees and shrubs have a wide-spreading network of shallow roots that take in water from a large area of ground. Many xerophytes also limit the amount of water

Esparto grass
Stipa tenacissima

Adaptations to desert life: kangaroo rats, jerboas and gerbils (A) make prodigious leaps with their long back legs to escape predators, and some desert lizards (B) run at high speed on their hind legs when pursued, using their tail for balance. Spadefoot toads have scoop-like hind feet with which they dig burrows to avoid the intense heat of day. Skinks use flattened toes fringed with scales to "swim" through the sand. Fan-toed geckos have toes that spread into fans at the tips, enabling them to walk easily on sand dunes, and the Namib palmate gecko has webbed feet that support it on loose sand.

The saguaro dominates the desert landscapes of Mexico and southern America. Immensely slow growing, it can take 200 years to reach its full height, and more than four-fifths of its weight may be water stored in its stem to be used in times of drought. To minimize water loss, it opens its pores only at night to absorb carbon dioxide and to help radiate heat accumulated by day.

Five great arid regions are bordered by semi-arid steppe and scrub. Cold deserts—the Gobi in central Asia, the Great Basin in North America and the Patagonian Desert in South America—lie in the higher latitudes. Cold ocean currents also affect climate, causing fogs to form over coastal deserts in southwest Africa, South America and Baja California, Mexico.

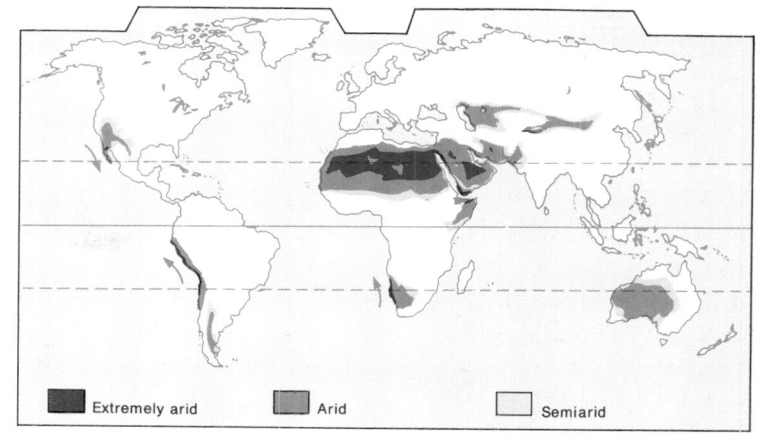

Extremely arid   Arid   Semiarid

White-throated poorwill
Phalaenoptilus nuttallii

Elf owl
Micrathene whitneyi

Great horned owl
Bubo virginianus

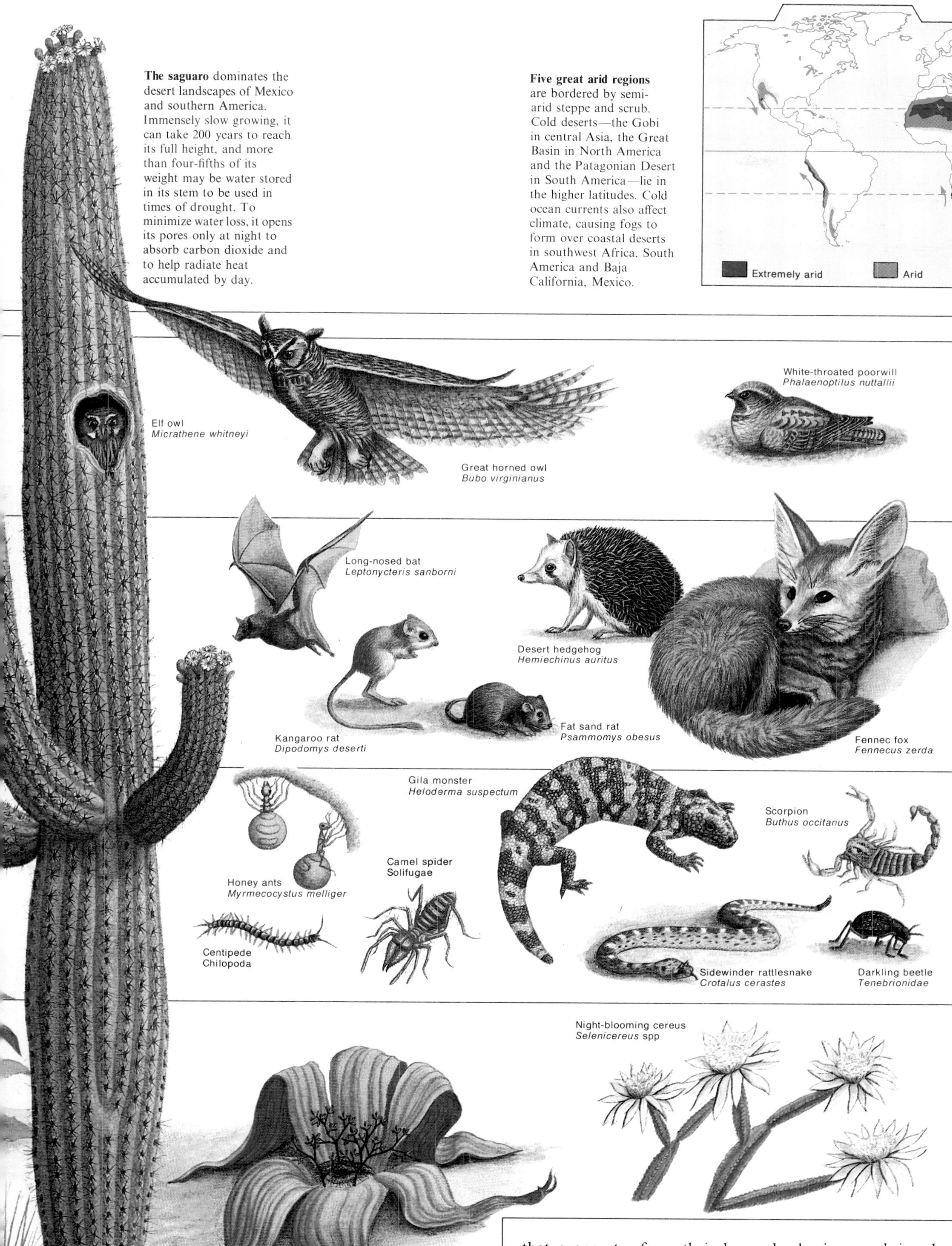

Owls and nightjars hunt under cover of darkness. Elf owls shelter by day, emerging at dusk to catch insects, and great horned owls often come into the desert at night to hunt. The poorwill, a small desert nightjar, is known to American Indians as "the sleeper." An insect eater, it sometimes survives the rigors of winter, when food is scarce, by hibernating.

Long-nosed bat
Leptonycteris sanborni

Desert hedgehog
Hemiechinus auritus

Kangaroo rat
Dipodomys deserti

Fat sand rat
Psammomys obesus

Fennec fox
Fennecus zerda

Most small animals are active at night. Nectar-eating bats visit plants that blossom at night, pollinating the flowers while they feed. American kangaroo rats obtain water from a dry diet of seeds and conserve moisture by producing very concentrated urine. The sand rat of North Africa feeds on salty succulents and excretes great quantities of extremely salty urine. Hedgehogs are mainly insect eaters; the long ears of desert species help to disperse body heat. The Saharan fennec, the smallest type of desert fox, hunts lizards, rodents and locusts.

Gila monster
Heloderma suspectum

Scorpion
Buthus occitanus

Honey ants
Myrmecocystus melliger

Camel spider
Solifugae

Centipede
Chilopoda

Sidewinder rattlesnake
Crotalus cerastes

Darkling beetle
Tenebrionidae

Among insects and other invertebrates the hunt for food intensifies at night. Honey ants gather nectar; centipedes and camel spiders hunt insects. The gila monster, a poisonous American lizard, eats centipedes, eggs and sometimes other lizards, and uses its tail to store fat. The sidewinder, a small rattlesnake, is active mainly at night, leaving its distinctive parallel tracks in the sand. Scorpions emerge from their burrows to stalk insects and spiders, and darkling beetles feed on dry, decomposing vegetation.

Night-blooming cereus
Selenicereus spp

Some desert plants are nocturnal, in the sense that they bloom only at night or make use of the dew that forms when the temperature falls. The welwitschia, unique to the Namib Desert in southwest Africa, has broad, sprawling leaves on which moisture condenses at night. The night-blooming cereus of the American deserts flowers for a single night in summer. Like other nocturnal plants, its flowers are luminously pale and strongly scented to attract pollinating night insects.

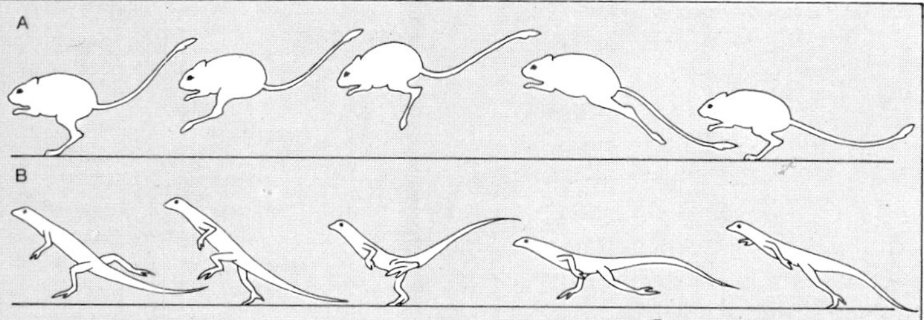

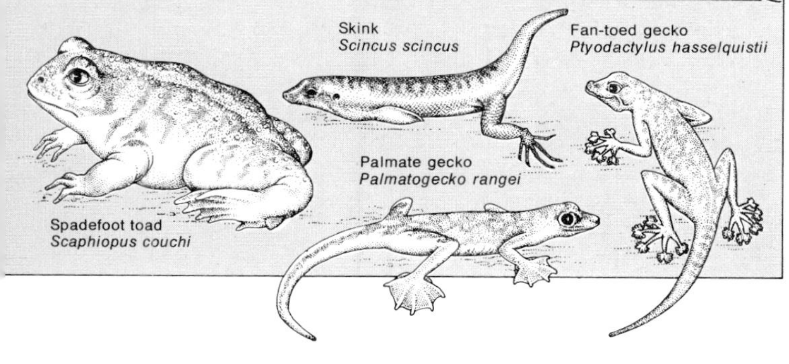

Welwitschia
Welwitschia mirabilis

Saguaro cactus
Cereus giganteus

A

B

Skink
Scincus scincus

Fan-toed gecko
Ptyodactylus hasselquistii

Palmate gecko
Palmatogecko rangei

Spadefoot toad
Scaphiopus couchi

that evaporates from their leaves by having small leaves, or by shedding them in the dry season. Some produce a protective covering of hairs or a coating of wax to prevent loss of moisture and to help to withstand heat.

Succulent plants, such as cacti and euphorbias, store water in their thick stems. Their leaves are usually reduced to spines, and their round or cylindrical shape also helps to reduce water loss. Spines have the added advantage in the desert of discouraging foraging animals.

The drought-resisting phreatophytes—date palms, mesquite and cottonwood trees, for example—have a similar variety of adaptations to dry conditions, but their most typical feature is a long tap root that draws water from great depths. Many plants can also tolerate the presence of salt in the soil. These are the halophytes ("salt plants") such as saltbush and other small shrubs that grow in and around salt pans.

The struggle to survive

Animals, too, need to obtain and conserve water at all costs and to be able to adjust to extremes of temperature. Most are small enough to shelter under stones or in burrows during the intense heat of day; others survive adverse conditions by becoming dormant or by migrating. For most desert creatures it is also an advantage to be inconspicuous, and many are

pale in color so that they are hard to see against their light background of sand or stones.

Many animals, especially those that are active by day, show adaptations that are strikingly similar to those of desert plants. Frogs and toads are activated by rain, emerging from dormancy to feed and mate in temporary pools and then quickly burying themselves until the next rain falls. Mammals have hairy coats that reduce water loss and also help to keep their body temperature at a tolerable level. Most desert insects have a waxy coating that serves much the same purpose.

Some geckos and other lizards store food, in the form of fat, in their tails, and camels store fat in their humped backs to sustain them when food is scarce. Honey ants force-feed nectar to some members of the colony, creating living "honey pots" for the rest of the community to feed from in times of drought. Many creatures are able to survive on the moisture contained in their food, and rarely need to drink. Most desert dwellers also have extremely efficient kidneys that produce very concentrated urine, so that little or no moisture is lost in the process.

Man enjoys no such advantages. Nevertheless, he still seeks to live in deserts, as he has for thousands of years, and the pressures he exerts on the environment may well have irrevocably changed much of the world's desert landscapes.

Man and the Deserts

Water is the key to man's survival in deserts: where water has been available, great civilizations have flourished, and man's dream of making the desert bloom has become a reality. More recently, discoveries of great mineral wealth have spurred the opening up of some of Earth's most inhospitable regions. But while man's ingenuity has made many deserts both habitable and productive, the human tendency to increase the extent of deserts has become a problem of international proportions.

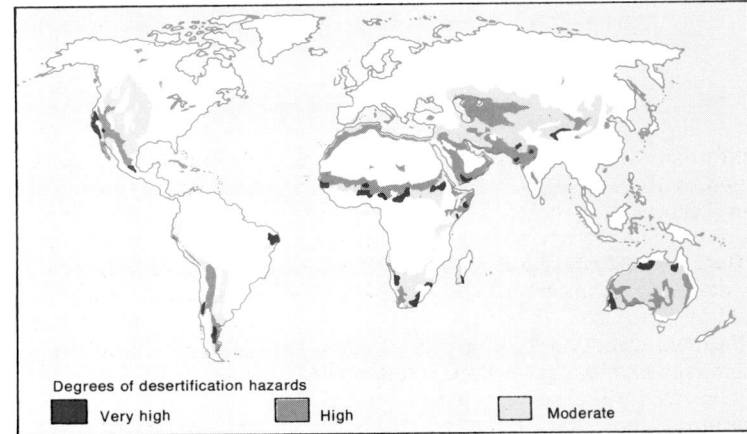

Degrees of desertification hazards

▮ Very high ▮ High ▯ Moderate

Given water, much is possible, and not surprisingly man has tended to settle where water is most readily available: along the courses of rivers (such as the Nile) that rise outside the desert, and around oases fed by springs or by wells that tap groundwater supplies. But desert rainfall is so unreliable that often runoff and spring flow are uncertain in quantity and timing. Much groundwater is either also unreliable or it is fossil water that has accumulated in the geological past and is not being replenished by today's rainfall. Thus in areas such as southern Libya and some of the oasis settlements of the Arabian Gulf, and in America's arid west, groundwater is a nonrenewable resource that is being rapidly depleted.

Making water go farther

Man has also used great ingenuity to secure water supplies and to transport them to where they are needed. Runoff from flash floods that follow rare desert storms may be collected in channels and distributed to crops in nearby fields, and terracing slopes to trap runoff is a traditional way of obtaining the maximum benefit from limited rainfall. Reservoirs, ranging from the small night tanks of the southern Atacama desert in Chile to the massive artificial lakes along the Colorado river in the United States, store seasonally or perennially unreliable runoff. Also, surface runoff may be increased by reducing the permeability of runoff surfaces, a

solution engineered by the Nabataeans in the Negev desert more than 2,000 years ago and being reemployed by the Israelis today.

The transport of water is a fundamental desert activity. Open canals are typical, usually carrying water to irrigated fields—a practice used throughout the fertile crescent of Mesopotamia more than 8,000 years ago and still widespread today. A striking alternative are the ancient qanats, which limit the evaporation of water while it is in transit. Qanats are still found in the Middle East, although today pipelines are increasingly used.

Ultimately the conversion of salt water to fresh water may ensure plentiful supplies for many desert regions. The process is expensive, but large-scale desalination has already become a reality in some affluent communities such as oil-rich Saudi Arabia and Kuwait. Increasing emphasis is also being placed on more efficient use of existing freshwater supplies: in Egypt and Israel, waste water from towns is being purified and recycled for use in agriculture.

Cultivating the desert

The successful control of water has enabled large areas of otherwise arid and semiarid land to be made productive. The Egyptian civilization along the Nile depended, and still depends, on the management of seasonal floodwaters. In North America, the large-scale, long-distance piping of water has made central

Desertification—the advance of desert areas across the Earth—now affects more than 30 million sq km (12 million sq miles) and deserts are continuing to expand at an alarming rate. In recent years, on the southern edge of the Sahara alone, as much as 650,000 sq km (250,900 sq miles) of land that was once productive have been lost, and in places there is little left to show where the Sahara ends and the Sahel–Sudan region begins. Intense and often inappropriate human pressures are major causes, frequently aggravated by drought: overcultivating vulnerable land, chopping down trees for fuelwood and grazing too many livestock, especially on the margins of arid lands.

THE SHIFTING SANDS

Recent decades have seen unprecedented changes in the world's deserts. Increasing pressure on the environment, especially from pastoralists and farmers, has caused extensive damage and a rapid expansion of barren land. In many desert regions, nomadism has long been the only way in which man could survive, except in oases. Today, even these traditional ways of life are changing as the exploitation of oil and other mineral resources, and the introduction of new agricultural techniques, are drawing many of the deserts into a spectacular new age of development.

The traditional pastoral response to limited water supplies and forage in desert regions is nomadic livestock herding, still practiced by the Tuareg of the northern Sahara (right) and by tribal groupings in Mongolia (left). The nomadic way of life has, however, become severely restricted in recent years. Long-distance migrations are often incompatible with the requirements of the modern state, and the poor rewards no longer match the incentives to settle in towns and cities.

Oases have provided welcome refuges in deserts since ancient times. Secure water supplies from wells or springs make settled life possible in the midst of the most arid landscapes. Many oases are intensively cultivated with three tiers of vegetation: tall date palms shade orchards of citrus fruits, apricots, peaches, pomegranates and figs, and both palms and orchard trees shade the ground crops of vegetables and cereals. Irrigation channels distribute water to the desert soils, which are frequently rich in plant foods although they lack humus. Windbreaks help to protect cultivated land from erosion and from migrating dunes, although many oases are losing the battle with encroaching sands and the oasis people are leaving to find work in the oil fields.

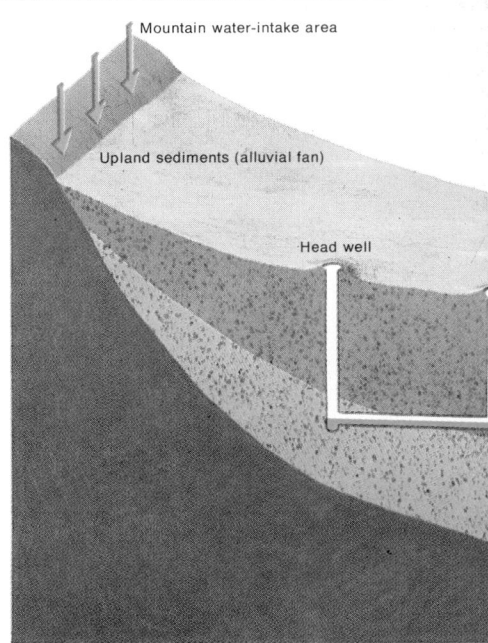

Mountain water-intake area

Upland sediments (alluvial fan)

Head well

California the most productive agricultural region in the world. But while irrigation can bring enormous benefits, it can also create problems. Too much water causes waterlogging of the land, and where water evaporates in the dry desert air, concentrations of dissolved salts build up in the soil.

Farming without irrigation is possible only where rainfall, although meager, is sufficient to sustain crops with a short growing season. Soil moisture is conserved by using dry surface mulches, by fallowing and crop rotation, by planting seeds sparsely and by controlling weeds. Geneticists are also producing new varieties of cereal crops that can survive for weeks without water. Dry farming, however, is precarious. Especially at times of drought it can cause serious problems of soil erosion, chiefly by the action of wind.

Man the desert maker
The extension of dry farming into unsuitable regions, and waterlogging and the accumulation of salts in irrigated areas, are major causes of desertification—the spread of deserts into formerly habitable land. Other major causes are the overgrazing of livestock on land with too little forage and the removal of trees and shrubs for firewood by communities that have no alternative fuel supply. A sequence of drier than normal years does the rest.

Many scientists believe that desertification can be reversed, provided the pressures on the land are reduced sufficiently to allow vegetation to recover. But desertification affects such huge areas, often crossing national frontiers, that broad-scale, international cooperation is needed to coordinate reductions in population and livestock pressures and to improve understanding of drought.

In some countries the battle against desertification has already begun. In China, extensive planting of drought-tolerant trees has created windbreaks to control sand movement and to protect farmland. In Algeria, a broad belt of trees has been planted to keep the Sahara at bay, and in Iran, advancing dunes have been halted by spraying them with petroleum residue: when the spray dries it forms a mulch that retains moisture and allows vegetation to grow, and much desert land has been reclaimed.

The deserts' riches
The exploitation of resources has also led to an "opening up" of many deserts. The rushes for precious metals in Arizona, Australia and South Africa started man's development of these regions in the nineteenth century. Some minerals, such as the evaporite deposits of Searles Basin in California and the nitrates of the Atacama desert in Chile, are actually products of the arid environment.

A resource that deserts also possess in abundance is solar power, and in many hot, dry regions the heat of the sun is used to evaporate mineral-rich solutions of salts, as well as being harnessed as a source of energy. Sunshine and the dry, clear air are also drawing ever-increasing numbers of tourists to the "sun cities" of the western United States and to Saharan oases, which were, until recently, only remote desert outposts.

No resource, however, has created as much attention or wealth as has oil. Oil has transformed the fortunes of several desert nations and provided an economic boom that has led to rapid industrialization and spectacular urban growth. The benefits of such growth in terms of affluence are substantial. The problems—the weakening of traditional desert societies, the submerging of traditional cities in the concrete labyrinths of modern complexes, and the precariousness of prosperity that is based on finite resources—are also clear.

Mineral wealth provides a powerful incentive for man's development of arid lands, and today the flow of oil rather than water is often a measure of a desert nation's prosperity. In some of the world's most desolate regions, flares signal the presence of modern "oases" where fossil fuels are being extracted—products, like the fossil waters that are sometimes trapped in the same sedimentary rocks, of the desert's geological past. Uranium, another mineral "fuel," also often lies beneath desert sands. Arid environments may also provide a rich harvest of other minerals: potash, phosphates and nitrates, valuable sources of commercial fertilizers; gypsum, manganese and salt; and borax, source of the element boron, used in nuclear reactors.

A "plastic" revolution has helped transform much of Israel's desert hinterland into productive farmland. Plastic cloches, plastic mulches and greenhouses trap moisture and reduce evaporation, and water trickled through thin plastic tubes irrigates the plants' roots with a minimum of wastage. Such innovative agricultural techniques enable Israel to produce most of its own food requirements, and fruit and vegetables grown in the relatively mild desert winters are also exported to Europe, where they command high prices.

One of the most ingenious ways man has devised of bringing water to desert regions is by the ancient underground system known as the qanat. Invented by the Persians in the first millennium BC, qanats tap groundwater in upland sediments and carry it by gravity to the surface on lower land. The head well is dug first, sometimes to a depth of 100 m (330 ft), until water is reached. A line of shafts is then sunk to provide ventilation and to give access to the channel being tunneled below. Work begins at the mouth end, and a typical channel is 10–20 km (6–12 miles) long when completed, depending on the depth of the head well and the slope of the land. Its slight gradient ensures that water flows freely but gently down to ground level. Surface canals then divert the water to where it is needed. Thousands of such qanats are still in use, their routes marked by mounds of excavated debris.

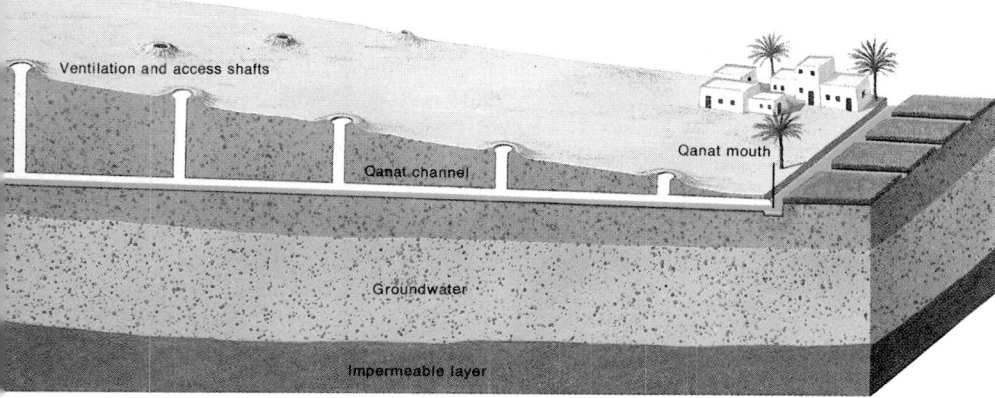

Ventilation and access shafts

Qanat mouth

Qanat channel

Groundwater

Impermeable layer

Guayule
Parthenium argentatum

Jojoba
Simmondsia californica

"Rubber" dandelion
Taraxacum kok-saghyz

Many desert plants have a bright future when they are grown on a commercial scale. Oil from the bean-like seeds of the jojoba plant, native to America's arid southwest, is remarkably similar to oil from sperm whales and has a multitude of uses, particularly as a high-grade industrial lubricant. Other promising plants are the latex-yielding guayule shrub of American and Mexican deserts, and a variety of dandelion from central Asia, both of which are being cultivated as a source of rubber.

Savannas

Between the tropical rainforest and desert regions lie large stretches of savanna, which are characterized by seasonal rainfall and long periods of drought. Those nearest to the forests usually take the form of open woodland, whereas those nearest to the deserts consist of widely scattered thorn scrub or tufts of grass. Unlike temperate grasslands, where the summers are hot but the winters are cold, savanna regions are always warm and in the wet season rain falls in heavy tropical downpours.

The most extensive areas of savanna are in Africa, north and south of the rainforest, and in South America, where the two main regions are the *llanos* of Venezuela, north of the Amazon rainforest, and the *campos* of Brazil in the south. Smaller areas of savanna also occur in Australia, India and southeastern Asia.

Savannas range from thickly wooded grasslands to almost treeless plains. Some are the result of man's destruction of the forest, and most are maintained in their present state by the high incidence of fire, both natural and man-made. The grasses tend to be taller and coarser than their temperate counterparts and they grow in tufts rather than as a uniform ground cover. In areas of high rainfall some grasses grow up to 4.5 m (15 ft) tall. Trees and bushes are usually widely spaced so that they do not compete with each other for water in the dry season. Humid, or moist, savannas experience 3 to 5 dry months a year, dry savannas 6 to 7 months, and thornbush savannas 8 to 10 months. Rainfall also varies widely, from more than 1,200 mm (47 in) a year in humid savannas to as little as 200 mm (8 in) where the savanna merges into desert.

Types of savannas

Humid woodland savanna presents an abrupt contrast to the rainforest. Trees tend to be scattered and some are so low growing that they are dwarfed by the tall grass that springs up during the summer rains. In the dry season the grass fuels fierce fires, which destroy all except thick-barked, large-leaved deciduous trees. Consequently, the proportion of fire-resistant trees and shrubs is large, and the grass quickly regenerates with the coming of the next rains.

In Africa this type of savanna is known as Guinea savanna north of the rainforest and as miombo savanna south of the rainforest. In South America it is known as *campo cerrado*, from the Portuguese words meaning field (*campo*) and dense. (*Campos sujos* are *campos* in which stretches of open grassland predominate and *campos limpos* are grasslands from which trees are entirely absent.) The *llanos*, or plains, of northern South America are grasslands interspersed with forests and swamps.

North of the Guinea savanna in Africa lies a belt known as Sudan savanna. The annual rainfall is in the range 500 to 1,000 mm (20–40 in) and the dry season lasts from October to April. This is typical dry savanna. Tall grasses between 1 and 1.5 m (3–5 ft) form an almost continuous ground cover and acacias and other thorny trees dot the landscape, together with branching dôm palms and massive water-storing baobab trees. Because of the interrupted tree cover the old name given to many savannas of this type was orchard steppe, and this description gives a good idea of the countryside. Like the humid woodland savannas it is maintained by regular burning of the grass in the dry season, and there is a delicate balance and interaction between climate, soil, vegetation, animals and fire. On the desert margins the grasses grow in short tufts and the scattered acacias are seldom more than 3 m (10 ft) tall. The scrub and grasses are too widely dispersed for fires to spread, and this type of savanna is modified not by fire but by aridity and blistering heat.

Thorn-scrub and thorn-forest savannas frequently form transitional zones between tropical forests and grasslands. The *caatinga*, or "light forest," of northeastern Brazil is a typical thorn-forest savanna. Long, hot, dry seasons alternate with erratic downpours of rain, and the rate of evaporation is high. Drought-resisting trees and thorny shrubs mix with bromeliads, cacti and palm trees.

Abundance of life

No other environment supports animals so spectacular in size and so immense in numbers as do the African savannas. In spite of the concentration of animal life, however, competition for food is not severe. Each species has its own preferences and feeds from different levels of the vegetation. Giraffes and elephants can easily reach the upper branches of trees, antelopes feed on bushes at different heights from the ground, zebras and impalas eat the grasses and warthogs root for the underground parts of plants. With the onset of the dry season, massed herds assemble for the great migrations that are a major part of savanna life, moving to areas where rain has recently fallen and new grass is plentiful.

Following the grazing animals are the large predators: the lions, leopards and cheetahs. Wild dogs hunt in packs, and the scavengers—jackals, hyenas and vultures—move in to dispose of the remains of the kill.

The savannas of South America and Australia are much poorer in animal species. The only mammal of any size on the South American savanna is the elusive, nocturnal maned wolf, which eats almost anything from small animals to wild fruit. On the Australian savanna the largest inhabitant is the kangaroo, and the prime predator—apart from man—is the dingo, or native dog.

Many of the resident savanna birds are ground-living species such as the ostrich in Africa and its counterparts, the rhea in South America and the emu in Australia. The warm African climate attracts large numbers of visiting birds, which migrate each year across the Sahara to escape from the severe winter of the northern hemisphere.

For many thousands of years man has lived in harmony with the savanna. Within the last century, however, and in recent decades in particular, the savanna has come under increasing pressure. Inevitably, there is competition between the needs of the environment and those of the human population, and the future of the savanna is very much in the balance.

On each side of the Equator are broad tracts of tropical grassland known as savannas. In these regions there are distinct wet and dry seasons and temperatures are high all the year round, seldom falling below 21°C (70°F). Rain falls mainly in the hottest months, whereas the cooler months are generally dry. Thorn-scrub and thorn-forest savannas occur where the rainfall is more erratic; they have relatively little grass cover, and trees and bushes can tolerate long periods of drought.

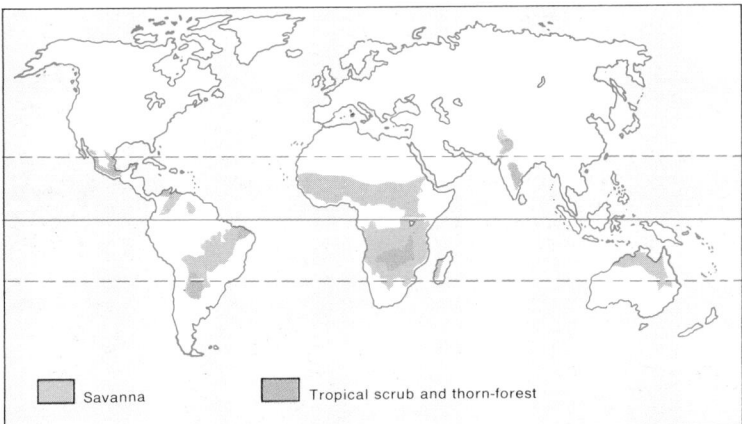

Savanna Tropical scrub and thorn-forest

THE AFRICAN SAVANNA

More than a third of Africa is savanna, the vast parklike plains and gently rolling foothills providing the setting for a supreme wildlife spectacle. Vegetation is the basis of the immense wealth of animal life. It supports the large herds of grazing animals, and they return nutrients to the grassland in their droppings. The plant eaters, in turn, provide food for the hunters and for the scavengers that play an indispensable role by keeping the savanna free from carrion. Most of the plant-eating animals are agile and swift-footed, which enables them to escape from their enemies, and live in herds, which also provides some protection in the open habitat. Many of the animals, both predators and prey, are camouflaged: stripes or spots, at a distance, help to break up their outline; dappled markings merge with the pattern of sunlight and shade in the undergrowth; and tawny colors make them difficult to see against a background of dry grass.

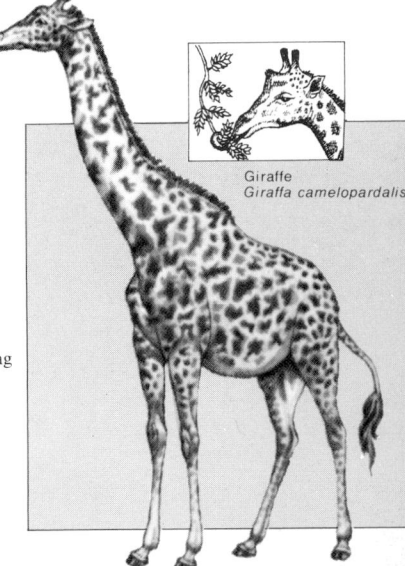

Giraffe
Giraffa camelopardalis

THE PLANT EATERS
Most plant eaters have adapted to feeding at a particular level of the vegetation. Giraffes browse on acacia tips that other animals cannot reach and elephants use their trunks to tear down succulent branches and leaves, although both feed on low-growing vegetation when it is easily available. Elephants will also uproot trees to gather leaves that are otherwise out of reach. The black rhinoceros plucks low-growing twigs and leaves by grasping them with its upper lip (the white rhinoceros has a broad, square mouth for grazing on grass). Eland often use their horns to collect twigs by twisting and breaking them. Zebra, wildebeest, topi and gazelle all graze on the same grasses, but at different stages of the plants' growth.

HUNTERS OF THE PLAINS
The plant eaters provide rich hunting for the carnivores. Lions kill the largest prey and hunt in family groups; the lioness usually makes the kill but the male is the first to eat. The leopard is a solitary hunter. It lies in ambush or stalks its prey, mainly at night, in brush country where it has ground cover. Cheetahs are the swiftest of all the hunters. They usually hunt in pairs in open grassland, stalking their prey and then charging in a lightning-fast sprint. Hunting dogs travel in well-organized packs. They exhaust their quarry by chasing it to a standstill and attacking as a team. Whereas lions, leopards and cheetahs usually kill by leaping for the neck or throat, packs of hunting dogs characteristically attack from the rear.

Lion
Panthera leo

Jackal
Canis aureus

THE SCAVENGERS
When the hunters have eaten, the scavengers move in. Jackals, small and quick, make darting runs to snatch titbits while packs of hyenas use their powerful bone-crushing jaws to demolish the bulk of the carcass. Hyenas are the most voracious of the carnivores, often driving the primary predator from its kill. Vultures are frequently the first to see a kill as they circle high in the sky, but must await their turn to feed on the skin and scraps because their descent attracts the more aggressive scavengers. Carrion beetles, carrion flies and the larvae of the horn-boring moth dispose of what is left. Most of the large scavengers, particularly the hyenas, also do their own hunting, singling out prey that is small, weak or sickly.

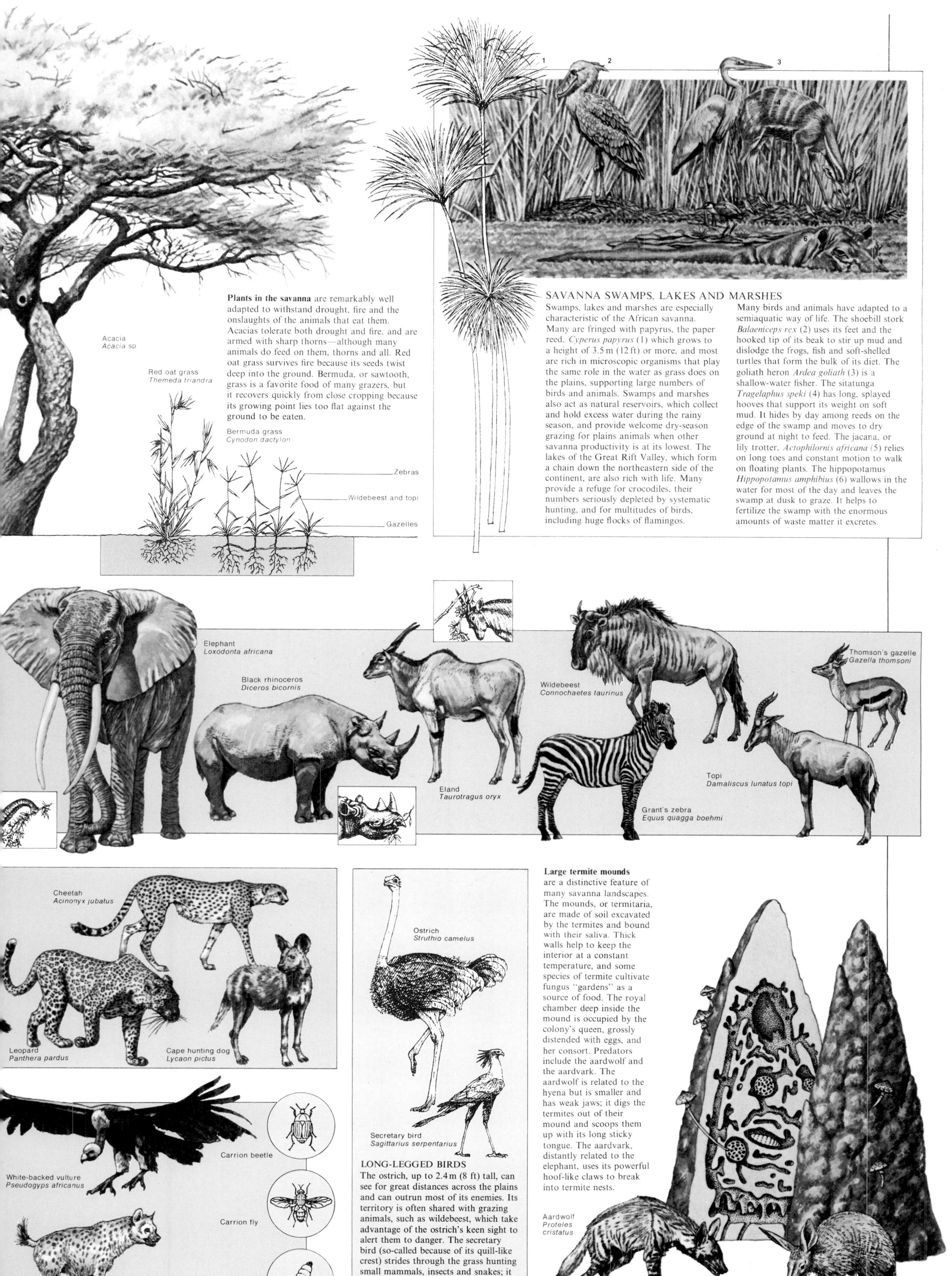

Plants in the savanna are remarkably well adapted to withstand drought, fire and the onslaughts of the animals that eat them. Acacias tolerate both drought and fire, and are armed with sharp thorns—although many animals do feed on them, thorns and all. Red oat grass survives fire because its seeds twist deep into the ground. Bermuda, or sawtooth, grass is a favorite food of many grazers, but it recovers quickly from close cropping because its growing point lies too flat against the ground to be eaten.

Acacia
Acacia sp

Red oat grass
Themeda triandra

Bermuda grass
Cynodon dactylon

Zebras

Wildebeest and topi

Gazelles

SAVANNA SWAMPS, LAKES AND MARSHES

Swamps, lakes and marshes are especially characteristic of the African savanna. Many are fringed with papyrus, the paper reed, *Cyperus papyrus* (1) which grows to a height of 3.5 m (12 ft) or more, and most are rich in microscopic organisms that play the same role in the water as grass does on the plains, supporting large numbers of birds and animals. Swamps and marshes also act as natural reservoirs, which collect and hold excess water during the rainy season, and provide welcome dry-season grazing for plains animals when other savanna productivity is at its lowest. The lakes of the Great Rift Valley, which form a chain down the northeastern side of the continent, are also rich with life. Many provide a refuge for crocodiles, their numbers seriously depleted by systematic hunting, and for multitudes of birds, including huge flocks of flamingos.

Many birds and animals have adapted to a semiaquatic way of life. The shoebill stork *Balaeniceps rex* (2) uses its feet and the hooked tip of its beak to stir up mud and dislodge the frogs, fish and soft-shelled turtles that form the bulk of its diet. The goliath heron *Ardea goliath* (3) is a shallow-water fisher. The sitatunga *Tragelaphus speki* (4) has long, splayed hooves that support its weight on soft mud. It hides by day among reeds on the edge of the swamp and moves to dry ground at night to feed. The jacana, or lily trotter, *Actophilornis africana* (5) relies on long toes and constant motion to walk on floating plants. The hippopotamus *Hippopotamus amphibius* (6) wallows in the water for most of the day and leaves the swamp at dusk to graze. It helps to fertilize the swamp with the enormous amounts of waste matter it excretes.

Elephant
Loxodonta africana

Black rhinoceros
Diceros bicornis

Eland
Taurotragus oryx

Wildebeest
Connochaetes taurinus

Grant's zebra
Equus quagga boehmi

Topi
Damaliscus lunatus topi

Thomson's gazelle
Gazella thomsoni

Cheetah
Acinonyx jubatus

Leopard
Panthera pardus

Cape hunting dog
Lycaon pictus

White-backed vulture
Pseudogyps africanus

Spotted hyena
Crocuta crocuta

Carrion beetle

Carrion fly

Horn-boring moth larva

Ostrich
Struthio camelus

Secretary bird
Sagittarius serpentarius

LONG-LEGGED BIRDS

The ostrich, up to 2.4 m (8 ft) tall, can see for great distances across the plains and can outrun most of its enemies. Its territory is often shared with grazing animals, such as wildebeest, which take advantage of the ostrich's keen sight to alert them to danger. The secretary bird (so-called because of its quill-like crest) strides through the grass hunting small mammals, insects and snakes; it kills snakes by battering them with its powerful, long-clawed feet.

Large termite mounds
are a distinctive feature of many savanna landscapes. The mounds, or termitaria, are made of soil excavated by the termites and bound with their saliva. Thick walls help to keep the interior at a constant temperature, and some species of termite cultivate fungus "gardens" as a source of food. The royal chamber deep inside the mound is occupied by the colony's queen, grossly distended with eggs, and her consort. Predators include the aardwolf and the aardvark. The aardwolf is related to the hyena but is smaller and has weak jaws; it digs the termites out of their mound and scoops them up with its long sticky tongue. The aardvark, distantly related to the elephant, uses its powerful hoof-like claws to break into termite nests.

Aardwolf
Proteles cristatus

Aardvark
Orycteropus afer

Man and the Savannas

In their natural state, savannas are among the most strikingly productive of all Earth's regions. Before the coming of man they supported a wealth of animal life that has seldom been surpassed. As yet they are relatively undeveloped, but many of them lie in areas where the pressures of population growth are becoming increasingly acute. Wisely used, they offer great hope for the future, both as cattle lands and for the cultivation of food crops. But without proper management savannas can rapidly turn into wasteland, and man will be the poorer for the loss of such a great natural resource.

Throughout much of the savannas the climate is semiarid and the soils tend to be poor: stripped of their plant cover, they bake hard and crack during the long months of hot sunshine, and during the wet season they often become water-logged or are washed away by the rains. Man's indiscriminate use of fire, unwise agricultural methods and the unrestricted grazing of domestic animals have already led to much soil loss, and erosion is widespread in tropical Africa, Asia, South America and Australia.

Systematic burning has long been practiced by the people of the savannas. Large areas are burned each year to clear land for agriculture or to remove dead grass and encourage a fresh growth to feed livestock. The resulting ash provides much-needed nutrients for crops, and the grasses rapidly produce new green shoots that provide a rich pasture for domestic herds. But although the short-term effects may be beneficial, repeated burning is harmful to the vegetation, the animals and the soil.

Trees are always more or less damaged by fire. Their trunks become twisted and gnarled, fresh shoots are killed and young trees are prevented from growing. Constant burning can destroy some species altogether, and when they disappear so too does the wildlife that depends on them for food and shelter.

Grasses, on the other hand, may be encouraged by burning, and the lush new growth that springs up when the first rains break the long dry season provides welcome nourishment for domestic herds and game animals alike. But whereas game animals move freely over the range, cropping grasses at various stages of growth, cattle tend to feed on grass only in the neighborhood of wells and other sources of drinking water. They may trample the soil and continue to graze the same area until the grass is completely suppressed.

The hazards of large projects
Cultivation in marginal areas that are unsuited to intensive agriculture also contributes to the impoverishment of the savanna. The Sahel and Sudan savannas on the fringes of the Sahara are particularly vulnerable to large-scale development projects that fail to take account of local climate and soil. Mechanized agriculture in fragile areas bordering the desert may well lead to soil erosion and dustbowl conditions, and large-scale irrigation schemes often result in waterlogging and an accumulation of salts in the soil. Cultivation in the savannas requires understanding and care. Many smaller schemes are safer—and usually more productive—than a few large ones, but not all planners yet realize that agricultural methods that are effective in temperate regions seldom come up to expectations in tropical climates.

Man first inhabited the savannas, as he did many other regions of the world, as a hunter and gatherer. He took from the land only what he needed from day to day, and although he used fire as a hunting tool, his impact was little more than that of any other savanna inhabitant. In East Africa, groups of nomadic Hadza (left) still hunt game and collect roots, fruit and the honey of wild bees, building grass huts as temporary shelters.

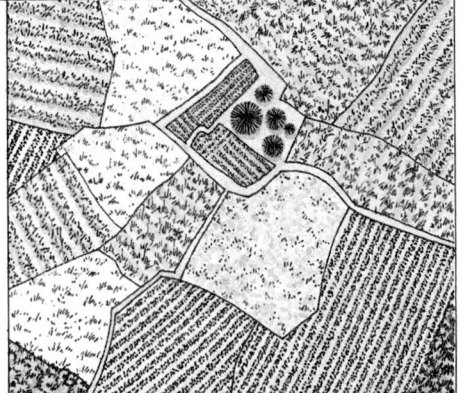

Small farms are scattered over much of the savannas. Plots close to houses are farmed continuously; beyond them lie the main fields, where periods of cultivation are usually followed by periods of fallow. Maize, millet and peanuts are the main food crops, and early and late crops are sometimes sown on the same plot to extend the growing season. Most of the work is done by hand, and any surplus to a family's needs is sold.

THE VULNERABLE WILDERNESS

Nowhere has man's impact on the tropical grasslands been felt more keenly than in Africa, although much of what is happening in Africa is happening also in savannas elsewhere. The majority of the people still live on the land, where the determining factor is the length and severity of the annual dry season. In the moister savannas the people are primarily cultivators, while in savannas that are too dry to sustain agriculture the main occupation is raising livestock. Most of the savannas are as yet sparsely settled, but competition is inevitably growing between man and wildlife, particularly in Africa, for the remaining tracts of relatively untouched wilderness.

The development of mineral resources and industries has led to an increasing movement of people—mainly young adults—from rural areas to towns and mining centers, attracted by opportunities for work—often at the expense of agriculture, since the heavy work of farming is left to the women, old people and children. Mining enterprises such as those in the Zambian Copper Belt (above), may recruit large labor forces from the surrounding countryside. Mining also dramatically alters the landscape, especially where the bedrock containing the ore reaches the surface and is quarried in huge terraces. The need for electricity to power mining and other industries leads, in turn, to the development of hydro-electric schemes, many of which entail resettling people whose villages are flooded by the creation of large artificial lakes.

Large areas of savanna have been set aside in East and Central Africa, and to a lesser extent in South America and Australia, as national parks and reserves where the landscape is kept intact and animals can be studied in their natural habitats. In Africa, observation platforms are frequently built close to waterholes where animals congregate to drink, and wardens use light aircraft to patrol the vast areas involved. Camel units are also used to patrol near-desert regions where much of the wildlife flourishes. Animals, such as elephants, whose numbers can grow out of control in the protected environment of the reserves are culled by licensed hunters to prevent the vegetation being destroyed. Culling maintains the health of the community as a whole and is also an economic source of meat in many countries where the people are short of protein foods.

Similarly, the introduction of European breeds of cattle into the savannas has not been an unqualified success. Not only are these breeds more susceptible to tropical pests and diseases than are the local varieties, but they are also adversely affected by the hot climate and their productivity is greatly reduced. In Africa and Brazil, native breeds are replacing more recent importations, and their productivity is being enhanced by selective breeding. In Australia, where most of the cattle are of British stock, tropical zebu, or humped cattle, are being introduced into the herds.

In the future, much more of the savanna may be developed as ranch lands, because the temperate grasslands will become less able to support enough animals to satisfy the world demand for meat. The *llanos* of Venezuela, the *campos* of Brazil and the tropical grasslands of Argentina and Australia already carry large herds of beef cattle. Throughout the savannas, however, ranching is still hampered by lack of water, poor natural pasture and remoteness from markets. In Africa, where herding is mainly nomadic, the sinking of wells by government organizations is changing the traditional ways of life, and cattle raising on a commercial

scale is likely to become increasingly important. In Africa, too, the conservation and controlled cropping of game animals could become one of the most productive—and constructive—forms of land use.

Game as a resource
The value of game animals as a source of food is considerable. Buffaloes, for example, and kangaroos in Australia, can thrive on natural grasses that will not even maintain the weight of domestic stock, and they show greater gains in weight than African and European cattle on most forms of vegetation, while several species of antelopes can survive on a water ration that is wholly inadequate for cattle.

In recent years attention has been directed toward the economics of controlled cropping of wild game, and of ranching animals such as eland, which can be kept as if they were domesticated stock and can convert poor pasture into excellent meat. Game animals are also more resistant than cattle to the tsetse fly, which infests large areas of Africa and transmits the disease trypanosomiasis (known as nagana in cattle and as sleeping sickness in man).

But for the most part game animals are still

considered to be a nuisance by man, and it is perhaps fortunate that by denying much of the savanna to domestic animals—and to man— the tsetse fly has preserved these regions from exploitation at the expense of the game. Many countries have also set aside large tracts of savanna as national parks and game reserves, where the natural environment is preserved and the wildlife can thrive.

Safeguarding the savanna
At a time when the pressure of the expanding human population calls for the development of areas hitherto uninhabited or only sparsely populated, it may seem paradoxical to maintain that the development of national parks and nature reserves is essential to the welfare of mankind. The aim of game conservation, however, is not simply to preserve rare or unusual animals for the enjoyment of posterity, or even for their scientific interest. It is to ensure that the land is put to its most economic and efficient use. The next few decades will show whether the savannas of the world will be developed into major sources of food and revenue for the countries that own them, or whether they will be misused and degraded into desert.

Commercial agriculture is important to the economies of many savanna countries. Cotton and coffee are major cash crops in Africa and Brazil, together with maize, tobacco, sisal and peanuts—crops that need a cycle of wet and dry seasons and year-round warmth. But large-scale cultivation of one crop tends to attract pests and diseases, and dependence on a single crop makes the economy vulnerable to fluctuating world prices.

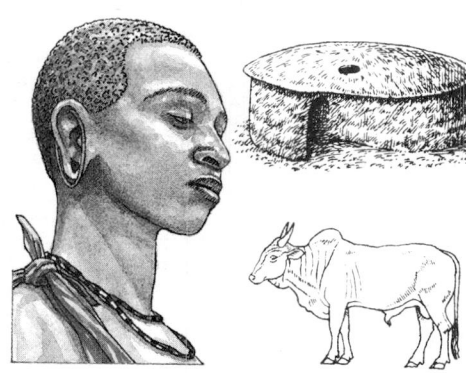

Cattle rearing takes the place of cultivation in areas that are too dry to be cropped successfully. In Africa, people such as the Masai are nomadic herders, moving their cattle long distances in search of pasture. Wealth is counted in terms of the numbers rather than the quality of the cattle they own, but improved management of their herds and better control of animal diseases are now making their cattle much more productive.

SAVANNA FIRES
Fires have been sweeping the savannas for thousands of years. Hunters set fires to flush game from cover, farmers use fire to clear land for crops, and cattle owners burn off parched, unpalatable grasses to make way for a fresh new growth for their stock. At the end of the dry season, when fires are particularly fierce, large areas of savanna lie under a thin haze of smoke.

Poaching, together with the takeover of wildlife ranges by farms and livestock, has led many animals to near-extinction in areas where they were once plentiful. Poisoned arrows are capable of killing even the biggest African game: sometimes they are set as traps and are triggered by the animal itself walking into a trip line. More sophisticated poachers use machine-guns and high-powered assault rifles, and airlift their illicit cargos of skins, ivory and rhinoceros horn. Illegal hunting for meat, which is dried and sold, has also become a large, highly organized and very profitable business in many areas.

Game animals also provide the spectacular displays that attract tourists and make tourism an important source of income for many developing nations. Today, most tourists pursue game with cameras instead of guns. The hunting that led to the wholesale slaughter of wildlife in previous years is banned, and so is the traffic in trophies, although even in the sanctuary provided by parks and reserves animals still fall prey to poachers.

Animals are frequently transferred from areas where they are at risk to safer areas such as game parks and reserves. In Kenya, helicopters came to the rescue of a herd of rare antelopes when their range was threatened by a proposed irrigation scheme and moved them to Tsavo National Park. Animals are also moved to introduce new blood to small, isolated herds or to restock areas from which they have been lost.

Tropical Rainforests

Tropical rainforests, extremely rich in both plant and animal life, consist of a series of layered or stratified habitats. These range from the dark and humid forest floor through a layer of shrubs to the emerging tops of the scattered giant trees towering above the dense main canopy of the forest. Each layer of vegetation is a miniature life zone containing a wide selection of animal species. These can be divided into a number of ecological groups according to their various ways of life, and many have evolved special adaptations to enable them to make maximum use of the plentiful food supply surrounding them.

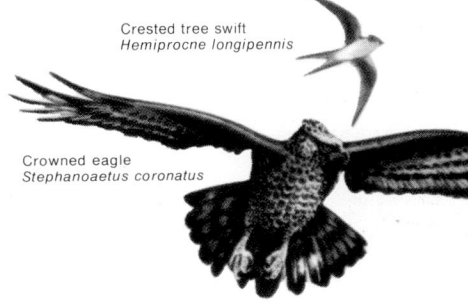

Crested tree swift
Hemiprocne longipennis

Crowned eagle
Stephanoaetus coronatus

Tropical rainforests occur only in the regions close to the Equator; they have a heavy rainfall and a uniformly hot and moist climate. There are slightly more of these forests in the northern half of the world than in the southern half and they occur at altitudes of up to 1,500 m (5,000 ft). Temperatures are normally between 24°C and 30°C (77°–86°F) and rarely fall below 21°C (70°F) or rise above 32°C (90°F). The skies are often cloudy and the rain falls more or less evenly throughout the year. Rainfall is usually more than 2,000 mm (78 in) a year and is never less than 1,500 mm (59 in). A distinctive feature of this tropical, humid climate is that the average daily temperature range is much greater than the range between the hottest and coolest months.

A stratified habitat

There are usually three to five overlapping layers in the mature tropical rainforest. The tallest trees (called "emergents") rise above a closed, dense canopy formed by the crowns of less tall trees, which nevertheless can reach more than 40 m (130 ft) tall. Below this canopy is a third or middle layer of trees—the understory; their crowns do not meet but they still form a dense layer of growth about 5–20 m (16–65 ft) tall. The fourth layer consists of woody shrubs of varying heights between 1–5 m (3–16 ft). The bottom layer comprises decomposers (fungi) that rarely reach 50 cm (20 in) in height.

Although the trees are so tall, few of them have really thick trunks. Nearly all are evergreens, shedding their dark, leathery leaves and growing new ones continuously. Many of the larger species grow buttresses—thin, triangular slabs of hardwood that spread out from the bases of their trunks. These support the trees, so removing the need for a heavy outlay of energy and resources on deep root systems. Hanging lianas (vines), thin and strong as rope, vanish like cables into the mass of foliage. They are especially abundant on riverbanks, where the canopy of trees is thinner; their leaves and flowers appear only among the treetops.

Epiphytes—plants that grow on other plants but do not take their nourishment from them—festoon the trunks and branches of trees, and up to 80 may grow on a single tree. They include many kinds of orchid and bromeliad. Their aerial roots make use of a humus substitute derived from the remains of other plants, often

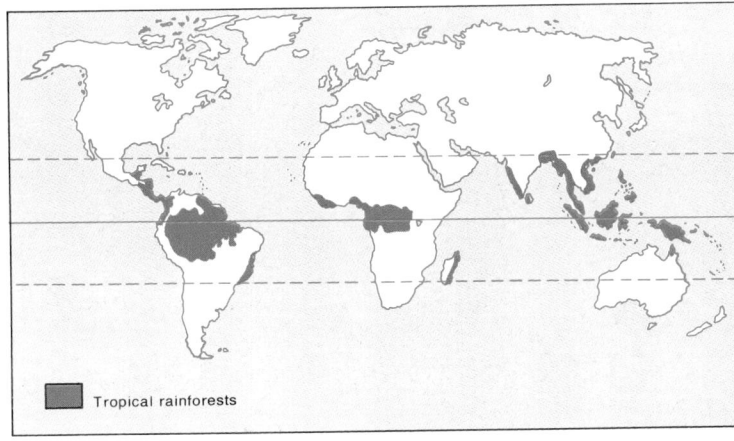

Tropical rainforests

Tropical rainforests are located in the hot and wet equatorial lands of Latin America, West Africa, Madagascar and Asia. These areas have consistently high temperatures throughout the year and receive high rainfall from the moist and unstable winds blowing in from the oceans.

The hummingbird numbers about 300 species, most of which are confined to the forests of South America. It is renowned for its ability to hover while gathering nectar, a feat achieved by the almost 180° rotations of its wings, which beat rapidly more than 80 times per second.

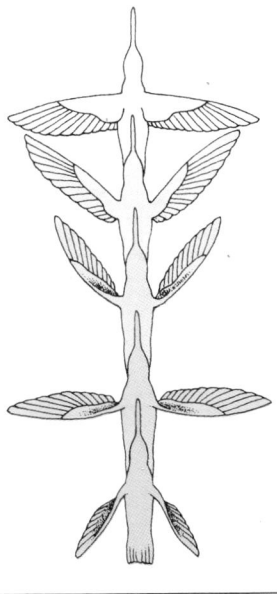

brought together by ants. The bases of their leaves may be broad and bowl shaped and collect and hold water; they also provide homes for a variety of insects and reptiles.

Rainforest soils are not as fertile as might be supposed by the luxuriance of their vegetation. On the contrary, the silicates and compounds necessary for plant growth are leached away by the rain to leave red or yellow soils of poor quality. This process, known as laterization, is widespread in the humid tropics. Humus is rapidly broken down by bacteria, fungi and termites, while earthworms, which in more temperate regions normally contribute to the mixing of humus with mineral particles, are usually absent.

In rainforests there are often up to 25 different tree species on a single hectare of land (60 species to the acre). Most temperate forests have only a fifth of this number, with nothing like the abundance of plants that grow in the tropics. This incredible variety supports—directly or indirectly—a corresponding variety of animal species which has an abundant food supply because the forest never ceases to be productive. This is why most mammals do not move far; they stay where their food grows.

Life in the canopy

The dense leaves and branches of the canopy provide the most food and so support the greatest number of species. Macaws and toucans (from the American tropics) and parrots and trogons (which live in forests throughout the tropics) eat the fruit growing in the

THE LAYERS OF THE FOREST

Stratification—the existence of distinct layers of forest vegetation—is especially pronounced in the tropics, where there are usually five main storys. These can overlap greatly and may vary in height from area to area. The large differences between the layers present many varied habitats and ecological niches for a very wide range of animals.

CANOPY LAYER

This dense story exerts a powerful influence on the levels below since its trees, which grow between 20 m (65 ft) and 40 m (130 ft) tall, form such a thick layer of vegetation that they cut off sunlight from the forest below. The canopy is noted for the diversity of its fauna. Many birds and animals are adapted to running along branches to get the flowers, fruits or nuts that form their diets. The pointed tips of canopy leaves encourage rapid drainage.

Sacred langur
Presbytis entellus

Tree shrew
Tupaia glis

MIDDLE LAYER

This understory comprises trees from 5 m (16 ft) to 20 m (65 ft) tall whose long, narrow crowns do not become quite so dense as those of the canopy. There is very often no clear distinction, however, between this level and the canopy. Middle-layer trees are strong enough to bear large animals such as leopards that spend part of their lives on the ground. Epiphytes are plentiful in this layer.

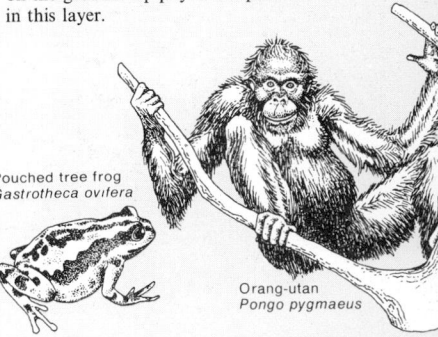

Leopard
Panthera pardus

Pouched tree frog
Gastrotheca ovifera

Orang-utan
Pongo pygmaeus

Moth orchid
Phalaenopsis sanderana

Flowering plants of the forest include epiphytes such as bromeliads and orchids like the species of *Phalaenopsis* illustrated here. Epiphytes grow on other plants such as trees where they can receive sunlight and are nourished by humus in the bark. Many epiphytic orchids have swellings in their roots or at the bases of their leaves where water can be stored. Seventy species of *Phalaenopsis* grow in southeast Asian forests and *P. sanderana*, one of the most beautiful, was first discovered in the Philippines in 1882.

SHRUB LAYER

The vegetation of this level is sparse in comparison with that above it and consists of treelets and woody shrubs that rarely reach 5 m (16 ft). These grow up in any available space between the abundant boles of large trees. Life in this story exists equally well at ground level.

Four-striped squirrel
Funisciurus lemniscatus

Tree pangolin
Manis tricuspis

Oriental civet
Viverra tangalunga

GROUND LAYER

Shade-tolerant herbs, ferns and tree seedlings represent the only flora at ground level; there is no grass there. Light is less than one percent of full daylight so that many mammals are well camouflaged in the gloom, whereas others have compact bodies to facilitate movement through the undergrowth. Ants and termites are well adapted to the high humidity and darkness of the forest floor. Fungi and a host of invertebrates quickly break down the litter of rotting leaves, fruit and fallen branches to provide vital nutrients for the fast-growing trees of the tropical rainforest.

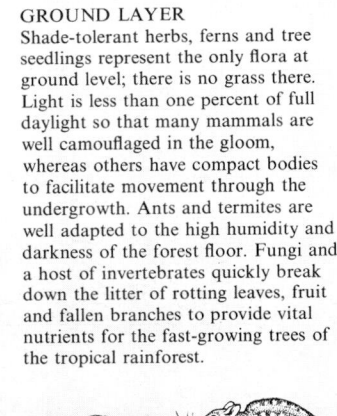

Okapi
Okapia johnstoni

Forest buffalo
Syncerus caffer nanus

Indian tiger
Panthera tigris tigris

Malayan tapir
Tapirus indicus

Congo forest mouse
Deomys ferrugineus

Short-eared elephant shrew
Macroscelides proboscideus

Orange-rumped agouti
Dasyprocta aguti

Mandrill
Mandrillus sphinx

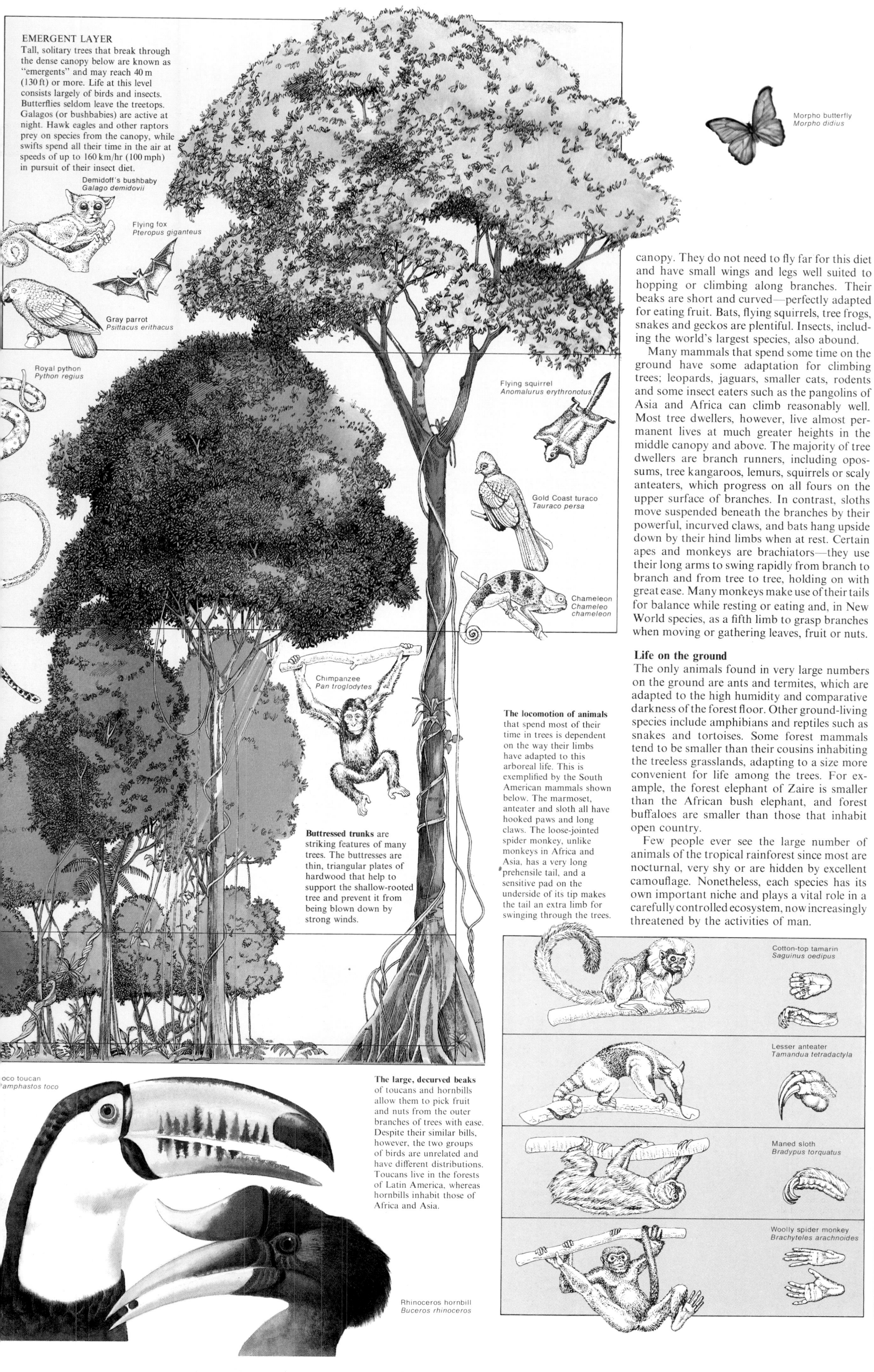

Tall, solitary trees that break through the dense canopy below are known as "emergents" and may reach 40 m (130 ft) or more. Life at this level consists largely of birds and insects. Butterflies seldom leave the treetops. Galagos (or bushbabies) are active at night. Hawk eagles and other raptors prey on species from the canopy, while swifts spend all their time in the air at speeds of up to 160 km/hr (100 mph) in pursuit of their insect diet.

Demidoff's bushbaby
Galago demidovii

Flying fox
Pteropus giganteus

Gray parrot
Psittacus erithacus

Royal python
Python regius

Morpho butterfly
Morpho didius

Flying squirrel
Anomalurus erythronotus

Gold Coast turaco
Tauraco persa

Chameleon
Chameleo chameleon

Chimpanzee
Pan troglodytes

Buttressed trunks are striking features of many trees. The buttresses are thin, triangular plates of hardwood that help to support the shallow-rooted tree and prevent it from being blown down by strong winds.

The locomotion of animals that spend most of their time in trees is dependent on the way their limbs have adapted to this arboreal life. This is exemplified by the South American mammals shown below. The marmoset, anteater and sloth all have hooked paws and long claws. The loose-jointed spider monkey, unlike monkeys in Africa and Asia, has a very long prehensile tail, and a sensitive pad on the underside of its tip makes the tail an extra limb for swinging through the trees.

oco toucan
amphastos toco

The large, decurved beaks of toucans and hornbills allow them to pick fruit and nuts from the outer branches of trees with ease. Despite their similar bills, however, the two groups of birds are unrelated and have different distributions. Toucans live in the forests of Latin America, whereas hornbills inhabit those of Africa and Asia.

Rhinoceros hornbill
Buceros rhinoceros

canopy. They do not need to fly far for this diet and have small wings and legs well suited to hopping or climbing along branches. Their beaks are short and curved—perfectly adapted for eating fruit. Bats, flying squirrels, tree frogs, snakes and geckos are plentiful. Insects, including the world's largest species, also abound.

Many mammals that spend some time on the ground have some adaptation for climbing trees; leopards, jaguars, smaller cats, rodents and some insect eaters such as the pangolins of Asia and Africa can climb reasonably well. Most tree dwellers, however, live almost permanent lives at much greater heights in the middle canopy and above. The majority of tree dwellers are branch runners, including opossums, tree kangaroos, lemurs, squirrels or scaly anteaters, which progress on all fours on the upper surface of branches. In contrast, sloths move suspended beneath the branches by their powerful, incurved claws, and bats hang upside down by their hind limbs when at rest. Certain apes and monkeys are brachiators—they use their long arms to swing rapidly from branch to branch and from tree to tree, holding on with great ease. Many monkeys make use of their tails for balance while resting or eating and, in New World species, as a fifth limb to grasp branches when moving or gathering leaves, fruit or nuts.

Life on the ground

The only animals found in very large numbers on the ground are ants and termites, which are adapted to the high humidity and comparative darkness of the forest floor. Other ground-living species include amphibians and reptiles such as snakes and tortoises. Some forest mammals tend to be smaller than their cousins inhabiting the treeless grasslands, adapting to a size more convenient for life among the trees. For example, the forest elephant of Zaire is smaller than the African bush elephant, and forest buffaloes are smaller than those that inhabit open country.

Few people ever see the large number of animals of the tropical rainforest since most are nocturnal, very shy or are hidden by excellent camouflage. Nonetheless, each species has its own important niche and plays a vital role in a carefully controlled ecosystem, now increasingly threatened by the activities of man.

Cotton-top tamarin
Saguinus oedipus

Lesser anteater
Tamandua tetradactyla

Maned sloth
Bradypus torquatus

Woolly spider monkey
Brachyteles arachnoides

Man and the Tropical Rainforests

Every three seconds a portion of original rainforest the size of a football field disappears as man fells the trees and extends his cultivation. Although tropical conditions allow rapid regrowth of secondary forest, the loss of primary forest is destroying thousands of plant and animal species that will never again be seen on Earth. Even by conservative estimates, it is likely that all the world's primary tropical forest will have disappeared within 85 years unless the trend is reversed.

The activities of man have only recently begun to threaten the tropical rainforest. Since prehistoric times, forests have offered shelter to people who, lacking any knowledge of agriculture, have existed as hunters and gatherers. They used only stone and wooden weapons such as bows and arrows to kill their animal prey, and collected berries, fruit and honey from their surroundings. Their influence on the forest environment was minimal and today a few races such as African pygmies and the Punans of Borneo still live in such a simple state of balance with nature. The Punans, for example, have no permanent homes, but use leaves and branches to construct temporary shelters that are used for only a few weeks before being abandoned. The pygmies build similar homes.

Shifting agriculture

Most forest dwellers, however, live in more permanent settlements and grow most of their food in forest clearings they have made. Such people are expert at chopping down trees in order to set fire to them, and this "slash-and-burn" farming results in small areas littered with charred logs and stumps whose ashes enrich the ground. Crops such as wild tapioca (cassava or manioc) are widely grown, but after a year or two the soil loses the little fertility it once had so that a new tract of forest has to be cleared and burned. Such shifting agriculture provides food for more than 200 million inhabitants of the Third World. As a farming system it has been used throughout the world for more than 2,000 years. When there were few farmers per kilometer the land was allowed to lie fallow for at least 10 years so that the soil could recover. Today, however, population pressures are so great that fallow periods have been drastically reduced and a swift repetition of slash-and-burn degrades and removes nutrients from the soil.

Effects on world climate

Tropical forest floors seldom have deep layers of humus so that, once trees are removed, the shallow topsoil is exposed and soon becomes eroded. In turn, this reduces the capacity of the ground to retain moisture, and without this sponge-like effect runoff can become very erratic and lead to floods, such as those that frequently occur in India and Bangladesh. Estuary sedimentation is often greatly increased

A DIMINISHING RESOURCE
This idealized tract of rainforest includes many of the activities of man that are daily endangering the survival of the forest. Shifting "slash-and-burn" cultivation and excessive logging present the greatest threats. Antidotes such as reafforestation have so far made very little headway.

Living in harmony with the forest are small groups of hunter gatherers who mainly live on a flesh diet, killing their prey with bows and arrows. Nuts and berries supplement this diet, and leaves gathered from the immediate jungle cover their temporary dome-shaped shelters. These are abandoned as an area becomes exhausted and the tribe moves on. Twenty or so pygmies need about 500 sq km (200 sq miles) to support themselves.

Selective logging by gangs of men seeking out the straightest and most valuable hardwood species has been the most common form of tree extraction, even though 75 percent of the canopy might have to be destroyed to remove just a few important trees. Today heavy axes are being replaced by power saws that have no difficulty in cutting down the large buttresses that were once left behind.

Plantation forestry has made increasing inroads into the forests over the decades. The commercial advantage of products that can be cropped several times during the hardwoods' maturation period is becoming increasingly apparent to farmers in the regions. Many rubber plantations in southeastern Asia consist of small holdings that have tended to encroach upon the forest, and intercropping now takes place between the long-established trees.

Shifting cultivation converts thousands of square kilometers of primary forest to substandard cultivation every year. Forest is cleared by slash-and-burn, the resulting fertile clearing is cropped with staples such as manioc, and then left to degrade to secondary forest once the ash-strewn ground has lost its poor fertility. Inevitably, the ground becomes permanently degraded. One encouraging antidote to the futility of such shifting agriculture is the recent strategy of agroforestry (as used by countries such as Nigeria and Thailand), which encourages the planting of fast-growing trees at the same time as the farmer's normal crops. Such intercropping offers considerable financial incentives to the small itinerant farmer.

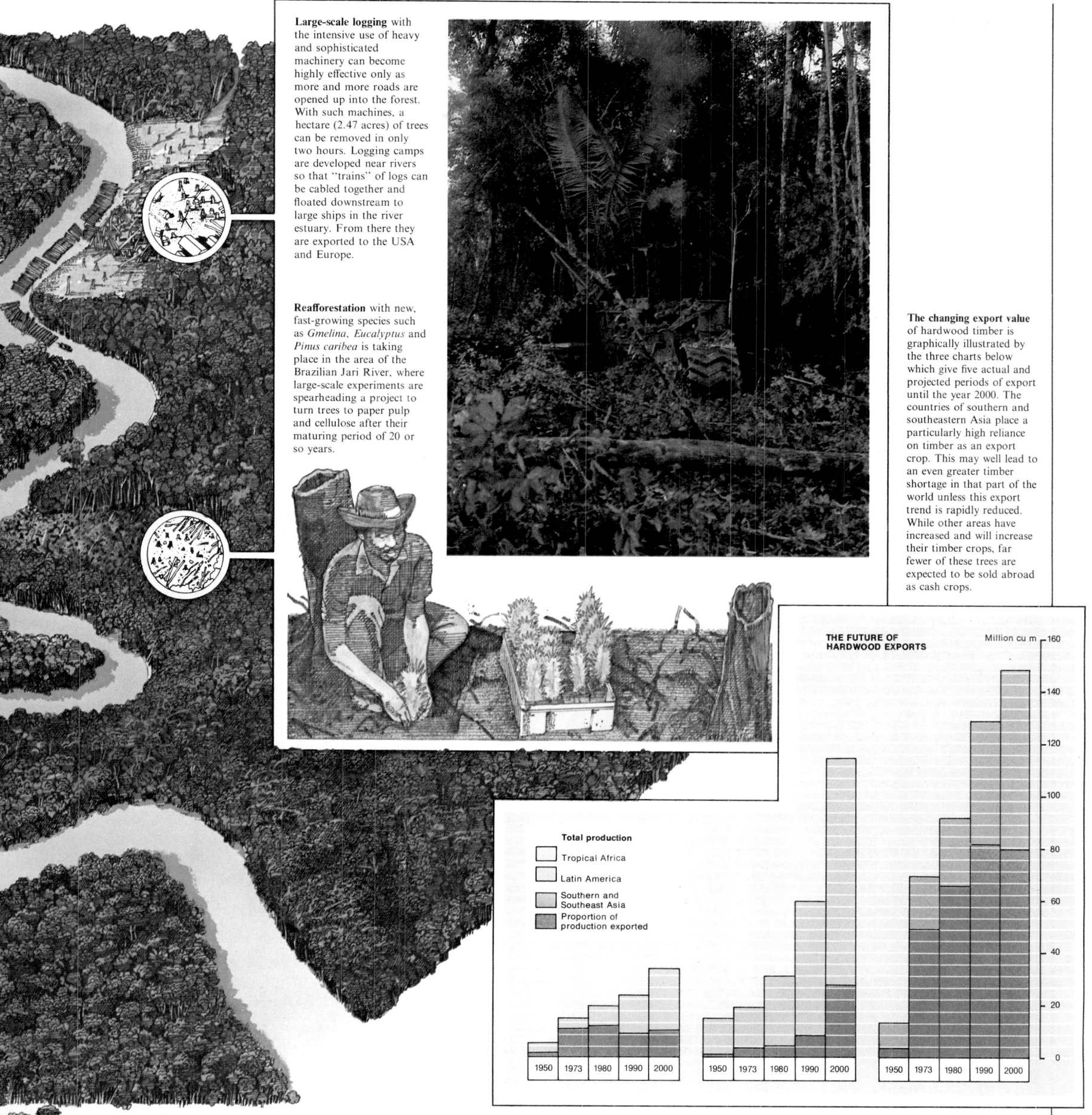

Large-scale logging with the intensive use of heavy and sophisticated machinery can become highly effective only as more and more roads are opened up into the forest. With such machines, a hectare (2.47 acres) of trees can be removed in only two hours. Logging camps are developed near rivers so that "trains" of logs can be cabled together and floated downstream to large ships in the river estuary. From there they are exported to the USA and Europe.

Reafforestation with new, fast-growing species such as *Gmelina*, *Eucalyptus* and *Pinus caribea* is taking place in the area of the Brazilian Jari River, where large-scale experiments are spearheading a project to turn trees to paper pulp and cellulose after their maturing period of 20 or so years.

The changing export value of hardwood timber is graphically illustrated by the three charts below which give five actual and projected periods of export until the year 2000. The countries of southern and southeastern Asia place a particularly high reliance on timber as an export crop. This may well lead to an even greater timber shortage in that part of the world unless this export trend is rapidly reduced. While other areas have increased and will increase their timber crops, far fewer of these trees are expected to be sold abroad as cash crops.

THE FUTURE OF HARDWOOD EXPORTS   Million cu m

Total production

- Tropical Africa
- Latin America
- Southern and Southeast Asia
- Proportion of production exported

1950 1973 1980 1990 2000

as the forest topsoil is simply washed away by torrential rain. In parts of Asia, deforestation has caused changes in water flow that have interfered with the production of new high-yield rice crops.

Tropical forests contain an enormous store of carbon, and some authorities believe that its release into the air (as carbon dioxide) when the forest is burned down may be as great in volume as that released by the rest of the world's fossil fuels. The higher proportion of carbon dioxide in the atmosphere may lead to an increase in global temperatures, especially at the poles. Trees also release oxygen into the air through photosynthesis, and some scientists have estimated that half of the world's oxygen is derived from this source. Others estimate that half of the rainfall of the Amazon basin is generated by the forest itself, so that any great reduction in tree cover would turn Amazonia into a much drier region.

Threats to Amazonia
Much attention has been paid to the situation of Amazonia, covering as it does some 6.5 million sq km (2½ million sq miles). In an attempt to give better access to timber and mineral reserves, the Brazilian government's

building of the TransAmazonian Highway (3,000 km or 1,860 miles long) has opened the way to deforestation, and settlers have been encouraged to make small holdings on the cleared forest beside the road. Between 1966 and 1978, the government calculated that farmers and big business interests had turned 80,000 sq km (31,000 sq miles) of forest into grazing land for 6 million cattle intended for hamburgers. However, like the wholesale extraction of timber, this has proved to be of doubtful economic value. Because costs rise steeply as less accessible areas are tapped, expenses tend to eliminate logging profits.

Threats in Africa
Even greater threats to tropical forest land have come from less cautious and realistic governments, such as that of Ivory Coast. There neither shifting agriculture nor excessive logging for valuable export sales appear to be under any sort of control. Accordingly, between 1966 and 1974, the area of forest declined from 156,000 sq km (60,000 sq miles) to 54,000 sq km (20,000 sq miles), much of the latter being secondary forest that can never be returned to its original status. Like many other developing countries, Ivory Coast has been more keen to

cut down and export its profitable timbers than to think about protecting its invaluable forest environment. Inevitably, forest farmers move into cleared areas and often establish plantation cash crops such as coffee, cocoa and rubber, while the establishment of national parks to curtail depletion has often had very little profitable effect. The Malaysian rainforest is also disappearing rapidly, through widescale logging and open-cast mining for bauxite (aluminum ore).

A large proportion of the world's rainforest occurs in tropical countries faced with severe problems of population control. It is therefore inevitable that the pressures on such forests will be great. Human interference does more than merely destroy the primary forest, to be replaced in time by secondary growth; more importantly, the wholesale removal of trees also drastically reduces the vast genetic reservoir contained in the number of plant and animal species the forests harbor. This in itself is a sound ecological argument for preserving forests and for reversing current trends towards monoculture in the tropics. All the warnings about forest depletion appear to be clear, yet there seems little hope that man will heed them until it is too late.

Monsoon Regions

The word monsoon often conjures up the image of torrential rain and steaming tropical jungles. Yet such a view is misleading, for very great contrasts occur in the regions of the tropical world with a monsoon climate. What distinguishes monsoon regions is not so much the amount of rainfall or the permanently high temperatures, but the dramatic contrast between seasons, with an extended dry season as an essential feature. And in fact the word monsoon derives from the Arabic word for season.

THE SEASON OF RAIN
Life in the monsoon regions balances on the expectation of seasonal heavy rain. In much of India, for instance, 85 percent of the annual rainfall occurs during the limited monsoon periods, and humans as well as plants and animals depend on it wholly. About half the world's people live in these regions, in communities whose rhythm of life necessarily reflects the rains' seasonal nature.

This contrast between wet and dry seasons reflects the reversals of winds over sea and land, which in the northern hemisphere blow from the northeast in the dry winter season, and from the southwest in the wet summer periods.

The monsoon regions occur most widely in southern, southeastern and eastern Asia to the south of latitude 25°N, and in western and central Africa north of the Equator, but there are also smaller regions with a characteristically monsoon climate in eastern Africa, northern Australia and central America. Despite the similar overall climatic pattern, however, the monsoon regions are otherwise very diverse.

Before human settlement the original vegetation of the monsoon regions reflected the dominance of an extended dry season followed by a period of violent rainfall. Typical forest cover was provided by the sal (*Shorea robusta*) deciduous forest, which adjusts to extended periods of moisture deficiency by shedding its leaves. However, within the monsoon region rainfall varies from 200 mm (8 in) a year to more than 20,000 mm (800 in), and the rainy periods may vary between three and nine months.

The range of vegetation found in the monsoon regions reflects this diversity. Where tropical rainforest alters into monsoon forest, as in eastern Java, there is a sharp fall in the total number of plant and animal species, and species adapted to endure seasonal drought begin to be seen. At the other extreme of rainfall the forest thins and shades into semidesert vegetation in India's northwest. But if there is a "type" of monsoon vegetation it is tropical deciduous forest, with sal as the dominant species.

As well as contrasts in climate, the monsoon regions also exhibit pronounced changes in temperature and vegetation as a result of variations in altitude. The Western Ghats of India and the foothills of the Himalayas in Assam both rise to more than 2,500 m (8,200 ft). Temperatures decrease sharply at such altitudes with corresponding changes in vegetation. In southern India on the Nilgiri Hills a wet temperate forest is characteristic, with an intermingling of temperate and tropical species. Magnolias, planes and elms all grow there.

Agriculture in monsoon regions

Despite its extensive area there is no part of the monsoon world that is untouched by man and by man's activities. In southern Asia, agricultural activity can be traced back at least 5,000 years, and there have been agricultural settlements throughout the monsoon regions for at least 1,500 years. Man's activity and the grazing of domesticated animals have interfered with, and progressively modified, the natural vegetation. The range of species indicates that, in the whole of the monsoon biome, there is now virtually no primary forest left. The pace of man's interference has speeded up considerably over the last 100 years. As a result, less than 10 percent of the land in southern Asia is now forested, and other parts of the monsoon

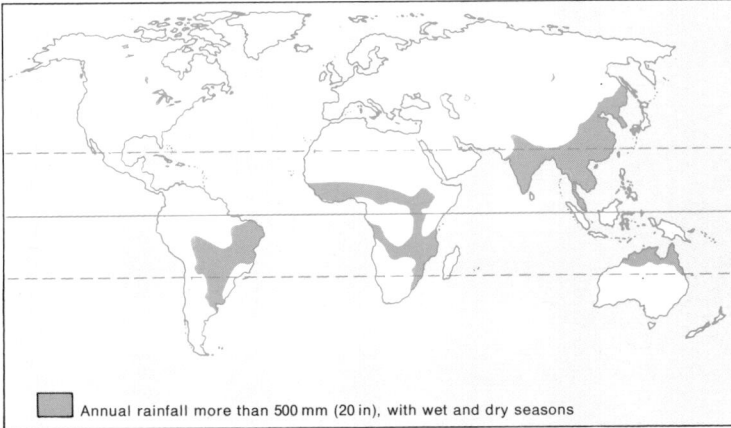

Many parts of the world experience "monsoon" winds, blowing from sea to land in summer, and from land to sea in winter; but typical monsoon vegetation is most clearly seen in the regions of southeastern Asia and the Indian subcontinent. In climatic terms, however, the monsoon circulation of seasonal wind reversals, with wetter summers and dry winters, also affects considerable areas of Africa, South America and northern Australia.

Annual rainfall more than 500 mm (20 in), with wet and dry seasons

regions are similarly losing their forest cover.

Many of today's farming methods incorporate traditional cultivation practices, but there have also been very significant changes in recent decades. Traditional agriculture in the monsoon regions has been developed to take into account the seasonal nature of its rainfall pattern and the total rainfall received. The fundamental role of water throughout the region and the absence of low temperatures have placed great importance on either cultivating crops that can tolerate the seasonal rainfall pattern, or on providing irrigation.

Through most of southern Asia, overwhelmingly the most populous of the monsoon regions, the most important single crop is rice, which covers about one-third of the total cultivated area. Rice needs a great deal of water and for this reason is grown mainly in areas of high irrigation, such as the delta lands of the southern and eastern coasts of India, and in areas where rainfall is more than 1,500 mm (59 in) a year. Its cultivation creates a very distinctive landscape as a result of the fact that rice must spend much of its growing period with a few centimeters of water over the soil.

Rice cultivation gives the monsoon regions their characteristic pattern of paddy fields, but other cereal crops such as wheat, the millets and sorghum are also very important. These can tolerate far drier conditions than can rice and occur in areas such as central India or upland Thailand, where uncertain and less abundant rainfall puts a premium on drought tolerance.

Even with traditional crops, man has often interfered extensively with the environment in order to increase yields and attempt to guarantee successful cropping. Traditional irrigation schemes range from diverting rivers at times of flood, in order to lead water to dry land, to digging wells and building small reservoirs. But recent technological developments have brought a new dimension to agricultural activity in the monsoon regions. Large-scale dam and irrigation canal schemes have become important in Africa as well as in monsoon Asia. The introduction and speed of electric or diesel "pumpsets" have transformed well irrigation in regions with extensive groundwater. The

Heat differences in the atmosphere cause the seasonal wind reversals (left) characteristic of monsoon circulation. In January the northern hemisphere is tilted away from the sun, and cold, dry winds blow from the central Asian landmass toward the Equator. Here they change direction (an effect of the Earth's rotation), converge with other winds, and drop their rain. In July the situation is reversed when the heated Asian landmass attracts a flow of cooler air from the equatorial oceans, which moves northward with the sun. The moist air condenses on reaching land, and the monsoon rains descend.

reliable water supply that irrigation can give has brought in its train the opportunity for farmers to adopt a wide range of new farming practices. Chemical fertilizers and new strains of seed have made possible great increases in the productivity of the land in many parts of the monsoon regions, but their use is generally restricted to areas of reliable water supply.

Subsistence cultivation over thousands of years has been by far the most important element in the transformation of the landscape and vegetation of the monsoon world, but the introduction of plantation cultivation during the last centuries has also had a major effect. Tea plantations, for instance, have led to the almost total replacement of natural vegetation in the hills of southern India and Sri Lanka.

Populations in all the countries of the monsoon regions are rapidly increasing, and demands for economic development are constantly growing, placing increasing pressures on the environment, pressures which to date have seemed almost irresistible.

DISAPPEARING ANIMALS
The dwindling wildlife of southeastern Asia includes species that may be regarded locally as pests—a fact that makes their protection difficult outside game reserves. Animals such as the tiger and the wild pig are doubly threatened as human cultivation spreads into the natural habitat: their hunting and foraging grounds are reduced, and their destruction of crops or livestock provides villagers with an obvious incentive for killing them in order to protect their own livelihoods.

Tiger
Panthera tigris

Wild pig
Sus scrofa

SELF-SUFFICIENCY IN CHINA
Local materials are turned into saleable products at a ratan factory in southern China. This factory is not owned by the state but by the village-sized brigade responsible for the manufacturing. The brigade functions as a smaller economic unit within the Ting Chow people's commune of 20 to 30 villages, but is encouraged to act independently, owning what it creates. The commune takes care of such matters as waterways—it contains 82 km (51 miles) of canals.

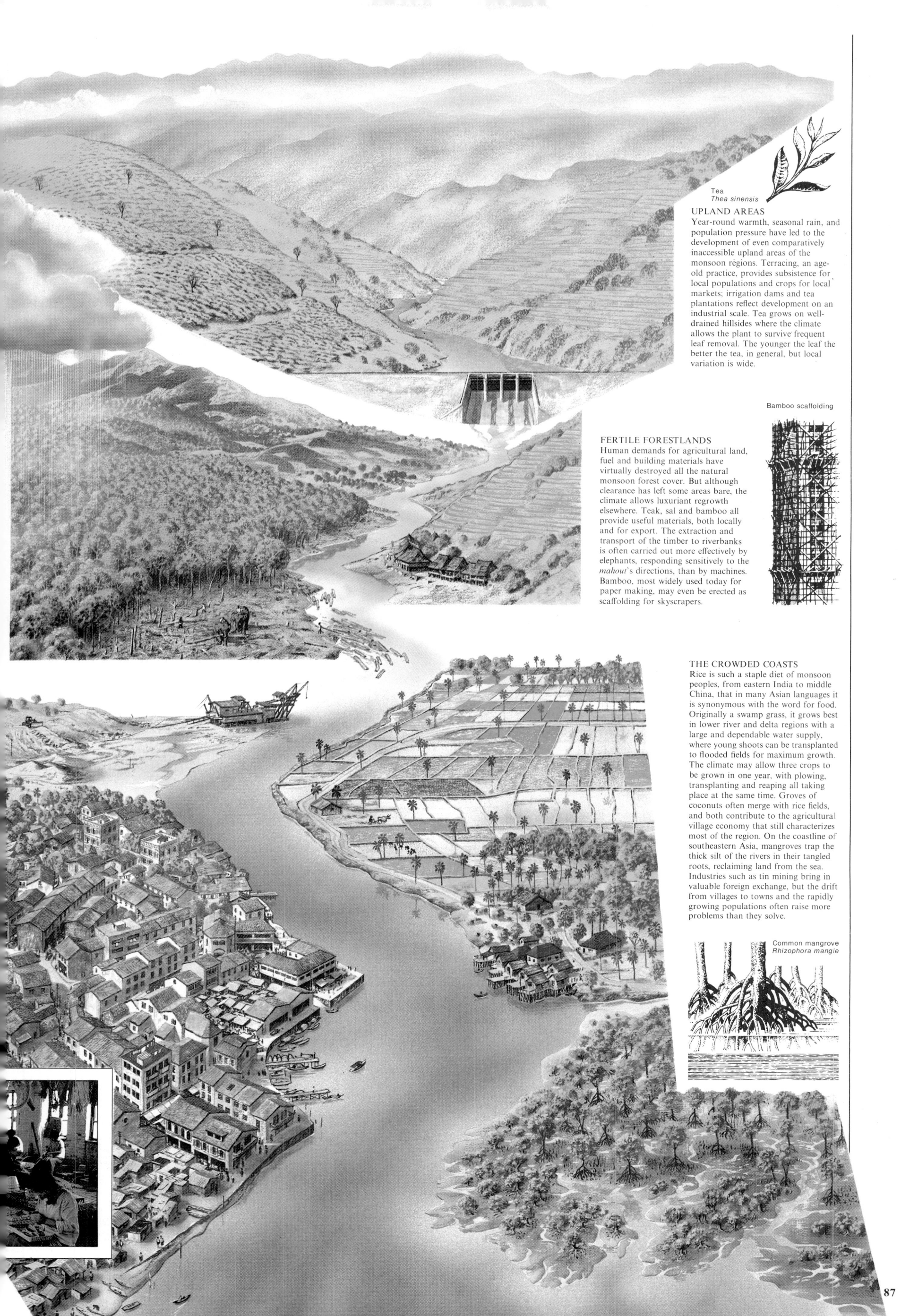

Tea
Thea sinensis

UPLAND AREAS

Year-round warmth, seasonal rain, and population pressure have led to the development of even comparatively inaccessible upland areas of the monsoon regions. Terracing, an age-old practice, provides subsistence for local populations and crops for local markets; irrigation dams and tea plantations reflect development on an industrial scale. Tea grows on well-drained hillsides where the climate allows the plant to survive frequent leaf removal. The younger the leaf the better the tea, in general, but local variation is wide.

Bamboo scaffolding

FERTILE FORESTLANDS

Human demands for agricultural land, fuel and building materials have virtually destroyed all the natural monsoon forest cover. But although clearance has left some areas bare, the climate allows luxuriant regrowth elsewhere. Teak, sal and bamboo all provide useful materials, both locally and for export. The extraction and transport of the timber to riverbanks is often carried out more effectively by elephants, responding sensitively to the *mahout*'s directions, than by machines. Bamboo, most widely used today for paper making, may even be erected as scaffolding for skyscrapers.

THE CROWDED COASTS

Rice is such a staple diet of monsoon peoples, from eastern India to middle China, that in many Asian languages it is synonymous with the word for food. Originally a swamp grass, it grows best in lower river and delta regions with a large and dependable water supply, where young shoots can be transplanted to flooded fields for maximum growth. The climate may allow three crops to be grown in one year, with plowing, transplanting and reaping all taking place at the same time. Groves of coconuts often merge with rice fields, and both contribute to the agricultural village economy that still characterizes most of the region. On the coastline of southeastern Asia, mangroves trap the thick silt of the rivers in their tangled roots, reclaiming land from the sea. Industries such as tin mining bring in valuable foreign exchange, but the drift from villages to towns and the rapidly growing populations often raise more problems than they solve.

Common mangrove
Rhizophora mangle

Mountain Regions

A quarter of Earth's land surface lies at heights of 1,000 m (3,300 ft) or more above sea level. But the highland regions are thinly populated by man, who is, generally speaking, a lowland dweller (most major population centers are less than 100 m (330 ft) above sea level). Some formerly lowland animals have fled from man to the harsh refuge of the mountains, joining with specially adapted plants and wildlife, but today man himself is finding the highland regions increasingly useful and desirable.

The world's highest mountain peaks rise to almost 9.6 km (6 miles) above sea level, but these heights are small compared to the total diameter of the Earth. The rough surface of an orange would have mountains higher than the Himalayas if scaled up to world size. But mountain environments, although they vary enormously from system to system, all tend to demand remarkable endurance and adaptability from the plants and animals that inhabit them.

Altitude rather than geological variation determines conditions of life on mountains. The temperature falls by 2°C with every 300 m (3.4°F every 1,000 ft)—hence the snowcapped beauty of the heights—and life forms must be adapted to increasingly harsh conditions as height increases. As a result, zones of different life occur at different levels, from tropical forests (at the base of low-latitude mountains) to arctic-type life in the zone of ice and snow at the summit. The latitude of the mountain affects the heights to which these zones extend: trees occur at 2,300 m (7,500 ft) in the southern Alps, whereas farther north, in central Sweden, trees cannot survive above 1,000 m (3,300 ft).

Life at the top

The specially adapted plant and animal life of the mountains occurs above the tree line, for here the variations in living conditions reach their greatest extremes. A plant that has found a foothold on a bare rock face may have to endure intense heat, even where the average temperature is low, when the summer sun blazing through the clear air warms the slabs to tropical temperatures. But when that part of the mountain falls into shadow, the temperature decreases very rapidly, often assisted by the high winds that blow almost constantly throughout the year in many mountain areas.

Soil necessary for plant life develops with the breakdown of the rock through the agency of water, frost and ice. Lichens, whose acids may aid in this destruction, can survive at very high levels, and as they die may add some humus to the newly forming soil. This may first accumulate in sheltered places where plants requiring high humidity, such as mosses and filmy ferns, are found. Flowering plants follow where a greater depth of soil has formed, although some grow in cracks between rocks.

Flowering plants of the mountains all tend to be small (to avoid harsh, drying winds), deep rooted (to anchor the plant firmly), and abundantly flowering (to benefit from the short growing season). Many unrelated species have independently developed a similar cushion form. This enables them to shed excess rainwater easily and to retain heat better in a tight tangle of stems and leaves, where the temperature may be more than 10°C (18°F) higher than that of the outside air. Insects sheltering there are well placed to perform the vital task of pollination. But pollinating insects are relatively rare at high altitudes, and some mountain plants are wind pollinated. The brilliant color of many others may be to increase their attractiveness for the insects. Nearly all upland plants are very slow-growing perennials, and many are evergreen, with leaves that exploit all available light.

Some large animals, such as the ibex or the Rocky Mountain goat, are adapted to spend their lives among the rocks and slopes. These stocky creatures, with hooves that act rather like suction cups, produce their summer young in the security of the heights, although in winter they descend to the shelter of the upper forests. Among smaller mammals, most of which are rodents, some dig burrows in which they hibernate through the winter. Others have very thick insulating coats, and may stay awake through the coldest weather in burrows under the snow.

Refugees from the lowlands

Some mountain animals, particularly carnivorous mammals and birds, have been driven by human persecution into remote mountain fastnesses. Many birds of prey, which could otherwise survive well in lowland areas, have their last strongholds among the mountains. They survive by feeding on small rodents, many of which are extremely wary. Some upland birds feed on insects or on seeds, but their number is comparatively small. The Alpine chough is one of the most interesting of mountain birds, for it has learned to find food among the scraps provided by climbers and skiers, whom it often follows to very high altitudes.

Insects and other small invertebrates, like their Arctic counterparts, may take several years to mature. Some are wingless, and many tend to fly low in order not to be blown away from their home range. Jumping spiders have been seen at heights of 6,700 m (22,000 ft) on the

slopes of Mount Everest, where they exist on small flies and springtails, but even above this level springtails and glacier "fleas" occur where there are no plants, apparently surviving on wind-blown insects and pollen grains.

Man and the mountains

The remote beauty of the mountains has led many peoples to identify them as the abode of the gods, but man himself prefers to live in the more convenient lowlands. The rarefied atmosphere of the heights makes physical work difficult, although some mountain-dwelling peoples have developed adaptations of the blood system to enable them to carry scarce oxygen more efficiently. The short growing season prevents cultivation of all but the hardiest cereal crops, and most uplanders rely on their livestock—cattle, sheep, llamas or yaks—for their existence. The animals are often driven to high pasture during the summer, descending to the valleys in the winter.

Modern, urbanized man finds the beauty and freshness of mountains increasingly attractive. Climbers have invaded most of the world's mountain regions, and in winter hosts of skiers flock to the resorts. Many important wildlife sanctuaries and national parks, particularly in the United States, are in mountain areas.

Lowland populations often rely on the pure mountain streams for both water and energy. Whole upland valleys are sometimes flooded to store water for distant conurbations. And the forceful flow of the water as it descends from the snow-fed heights is frequently harnessed to produce electricity for entire regions hundreds of kilometers away. The clear mountain air also offers the best conditions for astronomical observation, and most observatories today are built in dry, cloudless mountain areas.

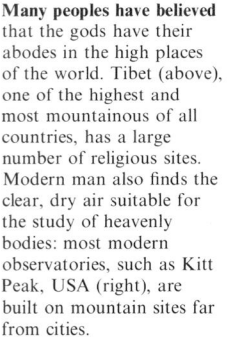

Many peoples have believed that the gods have their abodes in the high places of the world. Tibet (above), one of the highest and most mountainous of all countries, has a large number of religious sites. Modern man also finds the clear, dry air suitable for the study of heavenly bodies: most modern observatories, such as Kitt Peak, USA (right), are built on mountain sites far from cities.

Activity in Earth's crust has produced mountains in every continent (left). Some thrust up sharply, while older mountains have been eroded to rounded shapes. The Scottish Highlands were made by mountain-building forces 400 million years ago (170 million years before the Appalachians and the Urals). The Rockies are 70 million years old and the Alps 15 million years old.

Ancient mountains (Caledonian orogenesis)	Intermediate mountains (Hercynian orogenesis)	Recent mountains (Alpine orogenesis)

MOUNTAIN ADAPTATIONS

Saussurea
Saussurea tridactyla

Ingenious adaptations to harsh mountain conditions have been evolved by many plants, most of which have tiny cells with thick sap that does not freeze easily. Saussurea masks itself with white hair to reduce evaporation from the leaf surface. Alpine soldanellas are active even under snow, pushing up their flowers before the thaw.

Alpine soldanella
Soldanella alpina

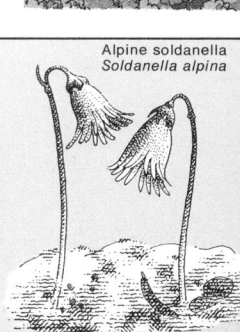

7,600 m / 25,000 ft

Jumping spider
Salticus scenicus

Alpine chough
Pyrrhocorax graculus

Cushion pink
Parrya lanuginosa

SNOWBOUND PEAKS

Perpetual snow, violent winds and atmospheric dryness impose harsh conditions on life in the high Himalayas. But wind-blown organic debris from the plains does support some life forms—springtails, flies and jumping spiders—where the air is too dry to allow even lichens to survive. Lower down, a cushion plant may take root in a rock-base niche, but there is little other vegetation. Among birds, the Alpine chough is a scavenger that has followed Everest expeditions to heights of 7,900 m (26,000 ft).

4,900 m / 16,000 ft

Fly
Diptera sp

Primula
Primula rosea

Blue sheep
Pseudois nayaur

Royle's pika
Ochotona roylei

Himalayan blue poppy
Meconopsis horridula

4,300 m / 14,000 ft

Domestic yak
Bos grunniens

3,700 m / 12,000 ft

Snow leopard
Panthera uncia

MOUNTAIN MEADOWS

Between the snow line and the zone of coniferous trees, the Himalayan slopes exhibit a glorious variety of flowering plants during summer. Small and slow growing, these often have bright flowers which attract pollinating insects such as fly-like *Diptera*. The pika and other small, thick-furred rodents are the most common animals, although larger creatures, such as blue (bharal) sheep and yaks, also find summer pasturage at these heights. Snow leopards tend to inhabit the coniferous forests, but they travel up to higher parts to prey on the grazing herds. Few people live within the zone, but some Sherpas take their yak herds as high as 4,600 m (15,000 ft) for summer grazing, and even grow crops of potatoes at this height. Their permanent villages, however, are on the lower alpine slopes.

3,000 m / 10,000 ft

FORESTED SLOPES

Isolated birches mark the tree line—the transition from meadow to coniferous and rhododendron forest. In the upper parts of the forest, trees are dwarfed by cold and lack of moisture, and are twisted and bent from the wind. These low and tangled masses provide shelter for animals such as the Asian black bear and the red panda. Below the conifers lies a zone of broad-leaved evergreens, and in the foothills these in turn give way to tropical monsoon forests of sal trees (*Shorea robusta*) and thickets of bamboo. The raucous flocks of hill mynahs represent just one of the many kinds of birds found in this zone, which has the widest range of wildlife of all the kinds of mountain vegetation. Unfortunately, many species are in danger of extinction, for here man has settled, cut down forests and terraced hillsides to grow crops.

2,400 m / 8,000 ft

Rhododendron
Rhododendron sp

1,800 m / 6,000 ft

Asiatic black bear
Selenarctos thibetanus

Red panda
Ailurus fulgens

Hill mynah bird
Gracula religiosa

1,200 m / 4,000 ft

◻ Permanent snow

▨ Coniferous forest

▨ Bamboo

◻ Alpine meadows

▨ Rhododendron groves

▨ Tropical monsoon forest

▨ Isolated birches

◻ Broadleaved evergreen forest

Rocky Mountain goat
Oreamnos americanus

Animals and humans adapt to mountain conditions in many ways. The Rocky Mountain goat (left) has evolved a fleecy undercoat and hooves with concave pads to grip on any surface. Comparison of the blood counts (right) of a lowlander (A) and an Andean (B) shows how the latter has a higher total content and more red cells.

A   B

12
6   10
5   8
4
3   6
2   4
1   2

liters pints

The golden eagle *Aquila chrysaetos* (left) epitomizes the grandeur of the heights. Although it lives and nests in remote regions, it could equally well find its food in the lowlands were it not for human competition. An eagle's territory may cover 130 sq km (50 sq miles): it preys on small mammals and even (it is believed) on young deer and lambs. It mates for life and returns each year to the same nest.

Freshwater Environments

Broad, muddy rivers, fast-running streams, miniature ponds and deep, ancient lakes all provide their own distinctive environments for populations of animals and colonies of aquatic plants. And in spite of the fact that these, the world's freshwater systems, contain only a minute proportion of the Earth's total supplies of water, the remarkable variety and richness of the wildlife they support make them among the most valuable and significant of all the world's natural habitats.

Fresh water is never really pure for, like sea water, and indeed like all other natural waters, it contains various dissolved minerals. Fresh water differs from seawater only in the relatively low concentrations of the minerals it contains. But these mineral traces are extremely important; they provide essential nutrients without which freshwater plants could not exist. And without plant life, there would be virtually no animal life either.

Not all parts of every freshwater system are rich in both plants and animals. Large, deep lakes are very similar to oceans—no light can penetrate their gloomy depths, and few plants can live in these conditions. The surface waters, on the other hand, where light is plentiful, teem with microscopic floating plants, mainly single-celled algae such as desmids and diatoms. The edges of lakes provide a different set of conditions again, for here the water is shallow and light can penetrate right through it. Plants can take root in the silt on the bottom, grow up through the water and thrust their leaves out into the light and air. Edges of lakes and, for the same reasons, the waters of small ponds are usually full of such plant life, which in turn supports many freshwater animals.

Running waters

Just as the still waters of lakes and ponds offer a variety of habitats, so the running waters of rivers support many different forms of life, each adapted to the particular conditions of its environment. In the upper reaches, where rivers are scarcely more than upland streams, water is fast flowing and clear of silt. Few plants, except close-clinging mosses, can gain a hold on the bare stony bottom and most of the fish are well muscled and strong bodied to enable them to withstand the constant tug of the current. As a river swells to form a mature lowland water course, however, it becomes slower moving and the water is warmer and richer in nutrients. Plants grow readily in these lower reaches and provide a supply of food for aquatic animals.

With such a wide range of conditions, freshwater environments support an enormous variety of animal life—insects, fishes, amphibians, reptiles, mammals and birds. In some ways insects are the most important of all these creatures: freshwater systems contain more insects and other invertebrates, representing a greater variety of species, than any other kind of animal. Furthermore, these, the smallest representatives of the freshwater animal world, provide one of the most important links in the complex freshwater food chain.

Insects may be the most numerous, but fishes are probably the most familiar of all freshwater creatures, and they certainly show some of the greatest varieties of adaptations to the many different habitats. Their sizes vary from the tiny, 14 mm ($\frac{1}{2}$ in) of the virtually transparent dwarf goby fish found in small streams and lakes in the Philippines to the 4 m (14 ft) of the arapaima found in deep rivers in tropical South America. Their feeding habits vary from those of the ferocious carnivorous piranha of South America to those of the North American paddle fish which, although more than three times the size of the largest piranha, feed solely on microscopic organisms which they filter from the water with their specially adapted throats.

The breeding habits of freshwater fish also vary widely, from the carefully maternal instincts of the African mouthbreeding cichlids—these retain the developing eggs safely in their mouths until the offspring hatch—to the rather more common ejection of eggs into the water, where their fertilization and survival is simply left to chance. Other adaptations include the ability to breathe air (as does the African lungfish), to leap waterfalls (a common practice among migrating salmon) and to emit an electric shock of up to 600 volts (an adaptation of the South American electric eel).

Creatures of the water's edge

Of all the other major groups of animals, amphibians (such as frogs and toads) are probably the most reliant on freshwater systems. Because their skins must not dry out and they have to lay their eggs in water, few amphibians can venture far from the water's edge. And because they cannot tolerate the salt in seawater (it causes them to lose their body fluids through their skins) they are totally dependent upon fresh water for their existence. Reptiles, rather less typical of freshwater environments, range in size from miniature North American terrapins to the giant crocodiles that live along the banks of the Nile. Freshwater mammals, on the other hand, with the considerable exception of the hippopotamus, all tend to be rather small creatures such as otters, beavers, coypus, aquatic moles and water shrews.

Birds are another important group of freshwater creatures. Although few birds are truly aquatic an enormous number of species live in or near freshwater systems and take advantage of the various food supplies: the plants and fish within the waters; the bankside vegetation and small animal life; and the many forms of freshwater insects. Marshes and swamps, for example, provide some of the richest bird habitats in the world.

Also numbered among the species dependent on Earth's freshwater systems is man. And although strictly a nonaquatic, land-living animal, man uses more fresh water than any other creature. His needs seem to be inexhaustible as he harnesses, channels, diverts and often pollutes freshwater systems throughout the world. Unfortunately, the vast requirements of the human race are not always compatible with the rather more humble needs of all other species that depend upon fresh water.

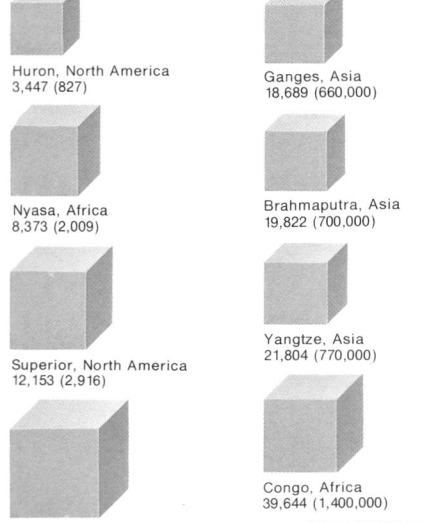

Volume of Lakes in cu km (cu miles)	Discharge of Rivers in cu m (cu ft) per second
Huron, North America 3,447 (827)	Ganges, Asia 18,689 (660,000)
Nyasa, Africa 8,373 (2,009)	Brahmaputra, Asia 19,822 (700,000)
Superior, North America 12,153 (2,916)	Yangtze, Asia 21,804 (770,000)
Tanganyika, Africa 19,418 (4,659)	Congo, Africa 39,644 (1,400,000)
Baikal, Asia 23,260 (5,581)	Amazon, South America 212,376 (7,500,000)

The five largest lakes in the world hold more than 53% of all fresh water that flows over the land. The rest of the world's lakes account for another 45%.

The world's largest river, the Amazon, discharges more than one-fifth of all fresh water that flows from the mouths of the world's rivers into the oceans.

THE UPPER REACHES
Here, water flows rapidly. Tumbling over bare rocks and stones, it is chilly, oxygen-rich and free of silt. Bird life attracted to these reaches includes the sure-footed dipper, which walks the stream bed hunting for caddis larvae. Slightly farther downstream, but where the river is still narrow and easily dammed, beavers are found. Few plants can live within the water, but river crowfoot has feathery underwater leaves that remain intact where most other plants would be shredded by the current. Many fish, such as trout, have streamlined bodies to offer the least resistance to the stream's pull, while others survive on the bottom by bracing against the rocks—the bullhead, for example. Insects have various means of anchoring themselves to the stream bed—blackfly larvae have hooks to fix themselves to pebbles.

Dipper
Cinclus cinclus

Beaver
Castor fiber

River crowfoot
Ranunculus fluitans

Brown trout
Salmo trutta

Blackfly larvae
Simulium spp

Bullhead
Cottus bairdi

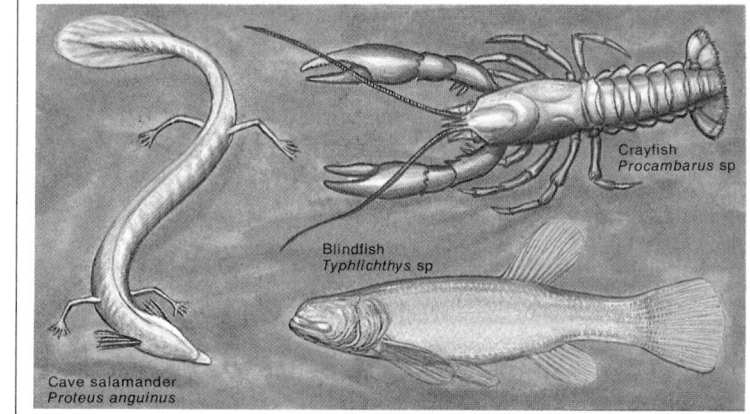

Cave salamander
Proteus anguinus

Blindfish
Typhlichthys sp

Crayfish
Procambarus sp

THE LIFE OF A RIVER

As a river makes its way from its upland source to the sea, it gradually changes its character. And at every stage in its progress, the animals and plants that inhabit the riverbanks and the waters reflect these changes by their adaptations to their environments. Most distinctive and dramatic are those adaptations produced in the wildlife of the upper and lower river reaches.

African spoonbill
Platalea alba

Southern painted turtle
Chrysemys picta dorsalis

THE LOWER REACHES

The slowly flowing river and its muddy banks are rich in animals and plants. Many birds live along the water's edge; spoonbills wade in the shallows, filtering food from the water with their beaks. The banks, fringed with reedmaces and other plants, provide habitats for many reptiles, such as the American painted turtle, and mammals, such as the platypus. Plants also grow on the water—they range from large waterlilies to tiny algae that are food for river fishes: Africa's upside-down-feeding catfish, for example. In these waters, mammals as well as fish are to be found—Amazonian manatees live entirely aquatic lives. The plentiful river plants, such as curled pondweed, provide food for water snails and other herbivores, and cover for predators such as pike. Crustacea and insects living in the silt of the riverbed are food for bottom-feeding fish such as the strange-looking North American paddle fish.

LAKES: CHANGE AND EVOLUTION

No two lakes are alike: each is virtually a self-contained world for its population of aquatic animals and plants. Furthermore, no individual lake remains the same for long: in every lake, slow, inexorable changes in conditions are gradually but constantly changing the balance of species inhabiting the lake bed, the bankside and the water.

Changing conditions may be caused by one of several processes. Accumulating sediments, one of the most common of these processes, may eliminate a lake altogether. The water becomes shallower as sediments thicken (1) and these sediments are then added to and consolidated by water plants taking root. Ultimately, land plants (2) invade the area.

Lakes develop their own peculiar species when the aquatic wildlife that evolves within them has no means of migrating to other freshwater systems to interbreed. The world's only existing species of freshwater seal, for example, is found in just one lake—isolated Lake Baikal in Asia.

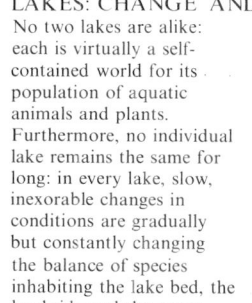

Baikal seal
Phoca sibirica

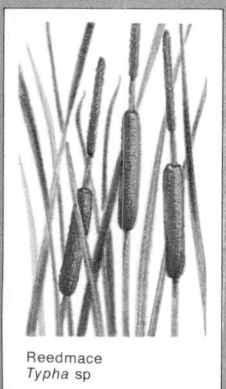

Reedmace
Typha sp

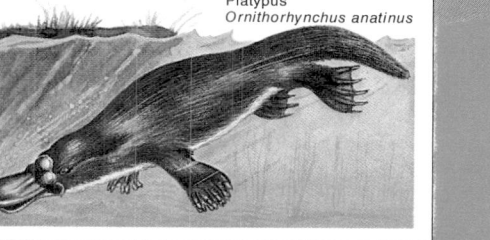

Platypus
Ornithorhynchus anatinus

Waterlily
Nymphaea sp

African catfish
Synodontis batensoda

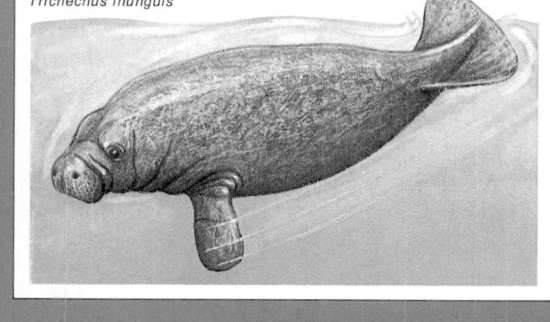

Amazonian manatee
Trichechus inunguis

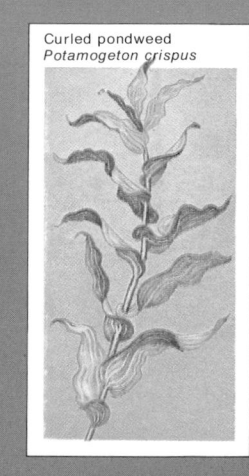

Curled pondweed
Potamogeton crispus

White ramshorn snail
Planorbis albus

Pike
Esox lucius

DARK WATERS

Underground rivers that flow through many of the world's cave systems support surprising numbers of creatures that have adapted to the permanent darkness. Many of these, such as the American cave crayfish, have lost the coloration of their surface-living kin. Some, such as Kentucky blind fishes, no longer possess eyes. Some salamanders are sighted and black when born, but become blind and colorless by adulthood.

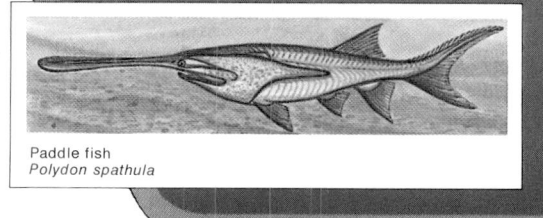

Paddle fish
Polydon spathula

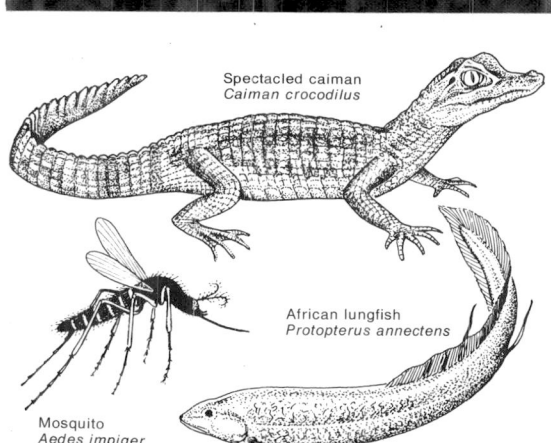

Spectacled caiman
Caiman crocodilus

African lungfish
Protopterus annectens

Mosquito
Aedes impiger

WETLANDS

Marshes and swamps are the richest of freshwater habitats. Wading birds, such as Asia's painted stork *Ibis leucocephalus* (above), are particularly common. Reptiles include caimans, which lay their eggs in swamps' warm, rotting vegetation. Of the many insects, mosquitoes are probably the most numerous, and of the many fishes, African lungfish are perhaps best adapted to life in wetlands. They survive drought, when marshes dry up, by their ability to breathe air.

Man and the Freshwater Environments

From earliest times, man has been finding new uses for and making new demands upon the world's freshwater resources. Today, the whole of modern society depends upon a vast supply to serve its agricultural, industrial, domestic and other needs. To meet the ever-growing demand for water, man has performed remarkable engineering feats: altering the courses of rivers, creating and destroying lakes, drowning valleys and tapping water sources that lie deep within the Earth.

THE VERSATILE RESOURCE

Every day, more than seven trillion liters (12 trillion pints) of water are removed from the world's freshwater systems. Almost all of this water is then directed to one of four destinations—some is destined for industry, a certain amount is piped to towns and cities for use in public services and in homes, some is fed to agricultural regions, and the rest is stored in reservoirs for future use.

INDUSTRY 19.5%

DOMESTIC 4.4%

AGRICULTURE 73.8%

RESERVOIRS 2.3%

Water is essential to human life. Simply to remain alive, an active adult living in a temperate climate needs a liquid intake of about two liters (3½ pints) every day. In warmer climates, the body's fluid requirements are even greater. Consequently, man has always been tied to reliable sources of drinking water—rivers, springs, lakes and ponds—and the availability of these, until very recently, has dictated the routes of all his wanderings and determined the sites of all his settlements.

From the time of the earliest human settlements, however, man has looked upon freshwater systems not simply as a source of drinking water but also as an increasingly useful resource for a multitude of other purposes. Today, water enters into virtually every aspect of modern life, and enormous quantities are used in agriculture, in industry, in the home, in the production of energy, for transport and for recreation.

The farmer's resource

Of all the major activities that rely on fresh water, agriculture is by far the world's largest consumer. In much of Europe and North America, rainfall is usually plentiful and lack of sufficient water for crops is rarely a problem. But in other parts of the world the climate simply does not produce enough rainfall and water shortages are a perennial problem. There, irrigation is not just a sophisticated technique to improve the yields and increase the varieties of crops grown; it is, and always has been, an essential element of agriculture.

Methods of irrigation range from small-scale devices—such as miniature windpumps—used in many developing countries simply to lift water from rivers for bankside crops, to vast dams, reservoirs and canal systems such as the Indus River project in Pakistan, which irrigates 10 million hectares (25 million acres) of land.

Traditional irrigation techniques usually involve using open channels or furrows for conducting water to fields. But one of the major problems with these, particularly in hot climates, is that much of the water evaporates and is lost before it can be used. Several new techniques, such as sprinklers and drip-feed systems, have recently been developed, however, to help make more efficient use of available supplies.

Although the most severe water deficiencies are experienced in the dry subtropical and tropical regions of the world, the temperate regions of North America and Europe, in spite of their relatively wet climates, do suffer shortages. Large towns and cities rarely have enough locally available rainfall or river flow to satisfy both domestic demand and the insatiable needs of industry. In the developed nations, industry consumes more water than any other activity.

Industrial demands

Fresh water is not only an integral part of almost every manufacturing process, it has other important industrial uses. As a source of power, it has been used since the early days of civilization—water wheels were one of man's first industrial inventions. Today, these simple devices are rarely seen in industrial societies, but water power is more important than ever before. Giant dams allow enormous volumes of water to be controlled and the power harnessed to drive turbines and generate electricity.

Freshwater systems have also, for centuries, provided industry with an important means of transporting its goods, and canal systems are still an essential part of industrial infrastructure in many countries of the world: the Europa Canal, when completed, will link three of Europe's major rivers, the Rhine, Main and Danube, and so form a continuous waterway running east–west across the breadth of Europe.

Man obtains fresh water by trapping it as it passes through one of the stages in the hydrological cycle—the never-ending circulation of Earth's waters from the ocean, to the atmosphere, to land. This cycle can be traced from the point at which water evaporates from the sea. The water vapor is blown across the land and falls as rain, hail or snow. Some then evaporates, but the rest completes the cycle by flowing over the land or through the soil or rocks back to the sea. It is at this point in its journey that man obtains his water supplies—from lakes (1), boreholes and wells (2) and dammed rivers (3). These supplies are then either used locally, or are transported by pipe or canal (4) to reservoirs (5) where they are stored ready for distribution.

➡ Movement of water in the hydrological cycle

▨ Water-bearing rock

Already, the finished sections of the canal are carrying oil, chemicals, fertilizers, coal, coke and building materials to and from some of Europe's major industrial regions.

Many of Europe's waterways date back to the great canal-building days of the Industrial Revolution. Although a few of these are still used for commerce, many are today considered too narrow to transport economical quantities of goods. Some, however, are now finding a role to play in one of the world's fastest-growing new industries—the leisure market. Today, canals provide a wide range of aquatic activities for holiday makers, tourists and sportsmen.

Recreation and sport

Freshwater systems throughout the world, in fact, are rapidly being recognized and developed as major recreational resources. Lakes and reservoirs are stocked with fish for anglers, silted waterways are dredged to provide sailing and swimming facilities, and old quarries and open-cast workings are landscaped and flooded to provide entirely new freshwater systems purely for leisure pursuits. The projects not only help to rejuvenate previously misused land, they also provide significant incomes to otherwise underdeveloped areas, especially highland regions that are too remote to attract other industries, and are unsuitable for farming.

Unfortunately, however, few of the world's freshwater systems can continue indefinitely to absorb the ever-growing demands that are being made upon them. Overuse of water resources is already a problem and has led to the pollution and destruction of many water systems—in some places overtapping has lowered water tables so drastically that rivers and lakes have been permanently destroyed. Although steps have been taken to protect certain waterways, legislation to guard against misuse and overuse is costly, time consuming and, inevitably, comes up against vested interests. Nevertheless, stringent conservation measures are becoming increasingly necessary if society is to maintain one of its most precious resources.

RESERVOIRS

About 70 trillion liters (15 trillion gallons) of fresh water are held in storage during any one year. Reservoirs ensure a continuous supply of water in spite of the inevitable seasonal fluctuations in demand and in the natural supply from rivers and rainfall. And where reservoirs are formed by damming rivers, there are additional benefits—the vast quantities of water held can be controlled and the power used to generate electricity. The Kariba Dam in Zimbabwe (right) has the potential for producing 8,500 million kilowatt hours of electrical power every year.

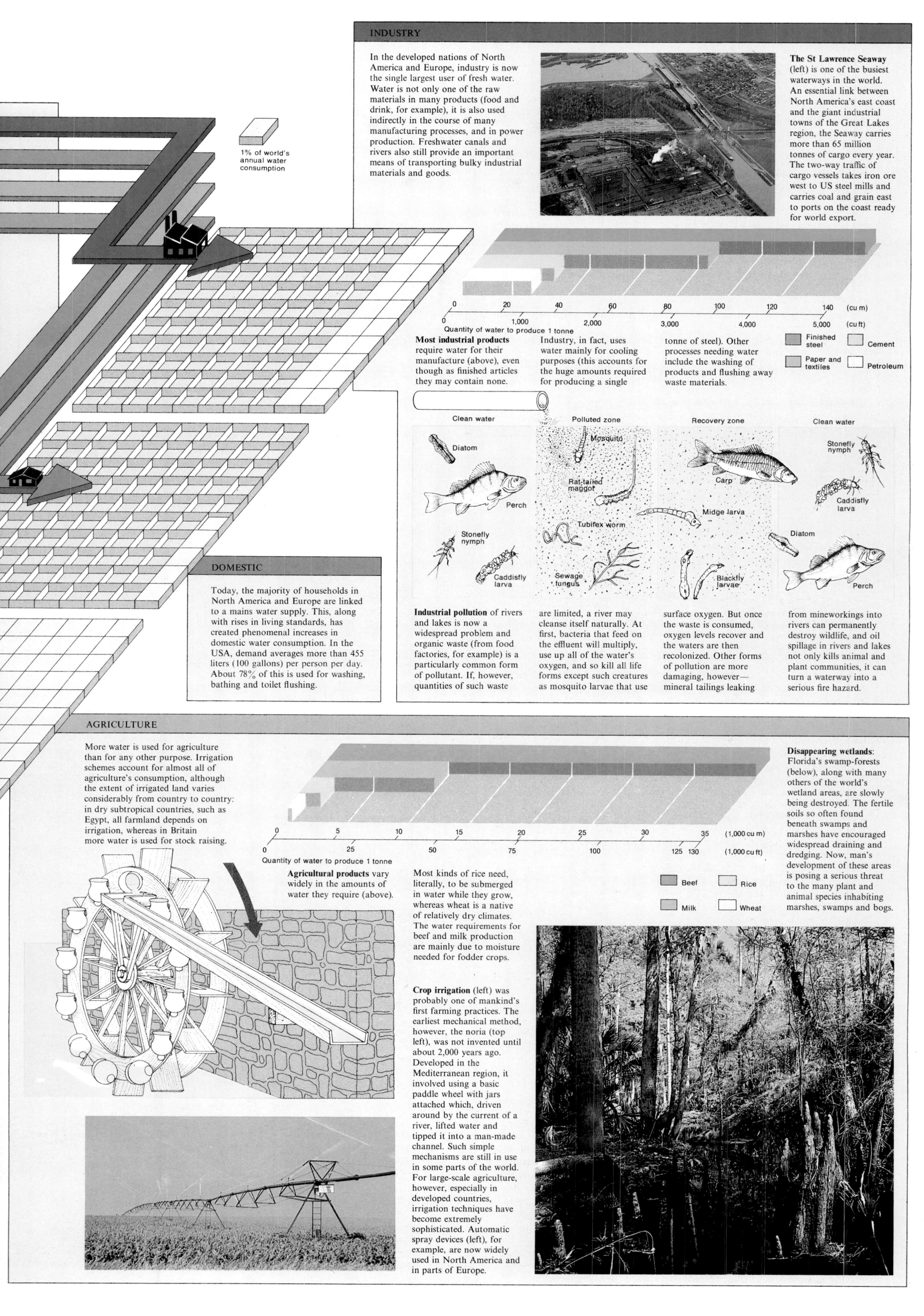

In the developed nations of North America and Europe, industry is now the single largest user of fresh water. Water is not only one of the raw materials in many products (food and drink, for example), it is also used indirectly in the course of many manufacturing processes, and in power production. Freshwater canals and rivers also still provide an important means of transporting bulky industrial materials and goods.

The St Lawrence Seaway (left) is one of the busiest waterways in the world. An essential link between North America's east coast and the giant industrial towns of the Great Lakes region, the Seaway carries more than 65 million tonnes of cargo every year. The two-way traffic of cargo vessels takes iron ore west to US steel mills and carries coal and grain east to ports on the coast ready for world export.

Quantity of water to produce 1 tonne

0 20 40 60 80 100 120 140 (cu m)
0 1,000 2,000 3,000 4,000 5,000 (cu ft)

Finished steel   Cement
Paper and textiles   Petroleum

Most industrial products require water for their manufacture (above), even though as finished articles they may contain none.

Industry, in fact, uses water mainly for cooling purposes (this accounts for the huge amounts required for producing a single tonne of steel). Other processes needing water include the washing of products and flushing away waste materials.

Clean water
Diatom
Perch
Stonefly nymph
Caddisfly larva

Polluted zone
Mosquito
Rat-tailed maggot
Tubifex worm
Sewage fungus

Recovery zone
Carp
Midge larva
Blackfly larvae

Clean water
Stonefly nymph
Caddisfly larva
Diatom
Perch

Industrial pollution of rivers and lakes is now a widespread problem and organic waste (from food factories, for example) is a particularly common form of pollutant. If, however, quantities of such waste are limited, a river may cleanse itself naturally. At first, bacteria that feed on the effluent will multiply, use up all of the water's oxygen, and so kill all life forms except such creatures as mosquito larvae that use surface oxygen. But once the waste is consumed, oxygen levels recover and the waters are then recolonized. Other forms of pollution are more damaging, however—mineral tailings leaking from mineworkings into rivers can permanently destroy wildlife, and oil spillage in rivers and lakes not only kills animal and plant communities, it can turn a waterway into a serious fire hazard.

1% of world's annual water consumption

Today, the majority of households in North America and Europe are linked to a mains water supply. This, along with rises in living standards, has created phenomenal increases in domestic water consumption. In the USA, demand averages more than 455 liters (100 gallons) per person per day. About 78% of this is used for washing, bathing and toilet flushing.

More water is used for agriculture than for any other purpose. Irrigation schemes account for almost all of agriculture's consumption, although the extent of irrigated land varies considerably from country to country: in dry subtropical countries, such as Egypt, all farmland depends on irrigation, whereas in Britain more water is used for stock raising.

Disappearing wetlands: Florida's swamp-forests (below), along with many others of the world's wetland areas, are slowly being destroyed. The fertile soils so often found beneath swamps and marshes have encouraged widespread draining and dredging. Now, man's development of these areas is posing a serious threat to the many plant and animal species inhabiting marshes, swamps and bogs.

0 5 10 15 20 25 30 35 (1,000 cu m)
0 25 50 75 100 125 130 (1,000 cu ft)

Quantity of water to produce 1 tonne

Agricultural products vary widely in the amounts of water they require (above).

Most kinds of rice need, literally, to be submerged in water while they grow, whereas wheat is a native of relatively dry climates. The water requirements for beef and milk production are mainly due to moisture needed for fodder crops.

Beef   Rice
Milk   Wheat

Crop irrigation (left) was probably one of mankind's first farming practices. The earliest mechanical method, however, the noria (top left), was not invented until about 2,000 years ago. Developed in the Mediterranean region, it involved using a basic paddle wheel with jars attached which, driven around by the current of a river, lifted water and tipped it into a man-made channel. Such simple mechanisms are still in use in some parts of the world. For large-scale agriculture, however, especially in developed countries, irrigation techniques have become extremely sophisticated. Automatic spray devices (left), for example, are now widely used in North America and in parts of Europe.

Seawater Environments

The oceans form by far the largest of the world's habitable environments, covering almost three-quarters of the Earth's surface at an average depth of more than 3,500 m (11,500 ft). Little more than a century ago, scientists believed that the deep sea's low temperatures, perpetual darkness and immense pressures made life in these regions completely untenable. But we now know that animals live at all depths in the ocean, even at the bottom of trenches more than 11,000 m (36,000 ft) deep.

THE PATTERN OF MARINE LIFE
The distribution of life in the seas is like an inverted pyramid whose broad base is formed by billions of minute single-celled plants—the phytoplankton. Plants need sunlight and nutrient salts, so phytoplankton occurs only in the upper, sunlit layers and where salts are present. Elsewhere, the distribution of marine life thins out rapidly.

Shore life belongs to both land and sea, and thus has to cope with a wide range of conditions. Seaweeds get all their food from the sea and are quite unlike land plants. Many animals take refuge below the surface: tellin shell molluscs sift food particles through special "lips"; lugworms swallow sand, digesting any organic matter; cockles take in food and eject waste through two siphons. Some birds have bills adapted for opening bivalve molluscs.

Oystercatcher *Haematopus* sp

Tellin shell *Tellina tenuis*

Lugworm *Arenicola marina*

Cockle *Cardium edile*

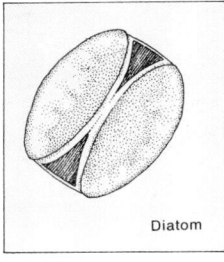
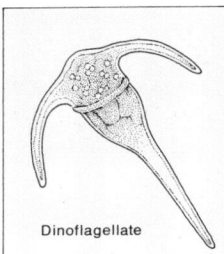
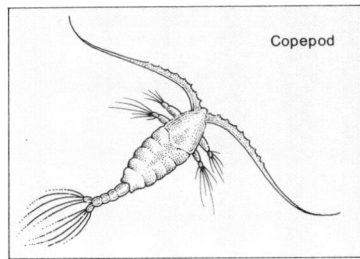

Marine plant life consists largely of diatoms—minute single-celled specks, each enclosed in a lidded box of silicon. Dinoflagellates, classed as plants but able to swim, dominate warmer waters. Both are food for copepods, the flea-sized grazers whose total weight, in the North Sea alone, is some seven million tonnes.

Diatom

Dinoflagellate

Copepod

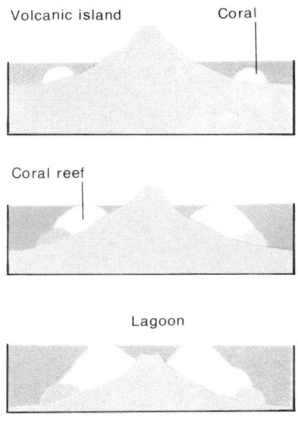

A coral atoll, forming in warm shallow water round an extinct volcano, makes up a living aquarium for thousands of tropical marine life forms. Countless billions of tiny polyps, each secreting a hard, calcareous skeleton, form the first layer of the reef, but die as the volcano gradually sinks. Their skeletons provide a base for further layers of corals, which enclose the sinking island to create a shallow, salt water lagoon. Different coral species in the same reef provide homes for a great variety of life.

Volcanic island   Coral

Coral reef

Lagoon

Life is by no means evenly distributed throughout the oceans, either vertically or horizontally. The great majority of marine creatures are concentrated in the upper few hundred meters, for the biological organization of life in the seas, as on land, depends on photosynthesis (the process by which plants use the Sun's energy to combine carbon dioxide and water to produce more complex compounds). This near-surface layer is the euphotic ("well-lighted") zone.

Some of the Sun's rays are reflected from the surface of the sea, and those that penetrate are scattered and absorbed as they pass through the water, so that even in the clearest oceanic water there is insufficient light to support photosynthesis at depths greater than about 100 m (330 ft). In turbid inshore regions, where the water is less clear, this near-surface layer may be reduced to a very few meters. So the large seaweeds that anchor themselves to the seabed are restricted to the small areas of the sea where the water is sufficiently shallow to allow them to photosynthesize. Of much greater importance over most of the oceans are the tiny floating plants of the phytoplankton, which live suspended in the sunlit surface layers.

Pastures of the sea
Phytoplankton, like all plant life, requires not only sunlight for survival but also adequate supplies of nutrient salts and chemical trace elements. River waters carry down considerable quantities of dissolved mineral salts and other

matter, so that high levels of phytoplankton production may occur locally around major estuaries. But a far more important source of nutrient supply to the euphotic zone is the recycling of salts that have sunk into the deeper layers, locked up in the bodies of plants and animals or in their fecal pellets.

In those areas of the oceans that overlie the continental shelves (about six percent of the total), the depth is nowhere more than about 200 m (650 ft), and the nutrient-rich bottom water is fairly readily brought back to the surface by currents and the stirring effect of storms. This stirring can reach much greater depths in near-polar latitudes, where the "water column" is not layered by temperature but remains more or less uniformly cold from top to bottom. In the Antarctic, cold (and therefore heavy) surface water sinks and is replaced by nutrient-rich water that may surface from depths of 1,000 m (3,300 ft).

In subtropical and tropical regions of the open ocean, where the warm surface layer is only a few tens of meters deep, the temperature falls rapidly with depth. There is little exchange between deep and shallow layers, and the euphotic zone receives an adequate supply of nutrient salts only in certain areas. These occur between westward-flowing and eastward-flowing currents in each of the major oceans. The Earth's rotation causes these currents to diverge so as to create an upwelling of nutrient-rich water along their common boundaries.

Finally, in restricted coastal regions of the tropics and subtropics the local climatic conditions cause an offshore movement of surface water, which is again replaced by upwelling nutrient-rich deep water. The central oceanic regions, including the deep blue subtropical waters, are in effect the deserts of the sea.

Sea grazers and carnivores
The abundance of animals in the oceans closely follows that of the plants. But very few of the larger marine animals can feed directly on the phytoplankton because the individual plants are so small—often only a fraction of a millimeter across. Instead, the phytoplankton supports an amazingly diverse community of planktonic animals, which also spend their lives in mid-water and are swept along by the ocean currents. This community, the zooplankton, includes many different protozoans (single-celled animals), crustaceans, worms and molluscs, and also the juvenile stages of fishes and of many invertebrate animals that live as adults on the seabed. Most members of the zooplankton are very small and many of them graze on the phytoplankton. But some planktonic animals, particularly among the jellyfish and salps, may be a meter or more across and are voracious carnivores feeding on their planktonic neighbors. In turn, the zooplankton provides food for many of the active swimmers such as the fishes and baleen whales, while at the top of the food chain are larger carnivores including

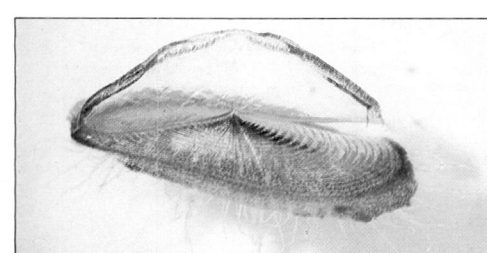

The by-the-wind sailor, *Velella*, is a so-called colonial animal, consisting of a whole collection of animals that function as a single individual. The gas-filled float of its body carries a vertical sail to catch the wind, and below dangle a group of modified polyps specialized for particular roles such as deterrence, reproduction, feeding and digesting.

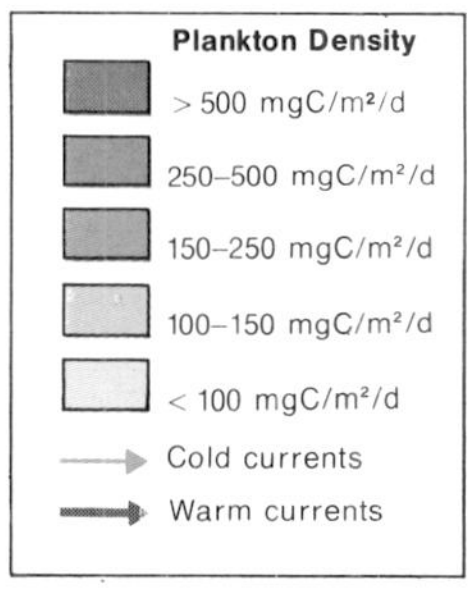

Plankton Density

> 500 mgC/m²/d
250–500 mgC/m²/d
150–250 mgC/m²/d
100–150 mgC/m²/d
< 100 mgC/m²/d
→ Cold currents
→ Warm currents

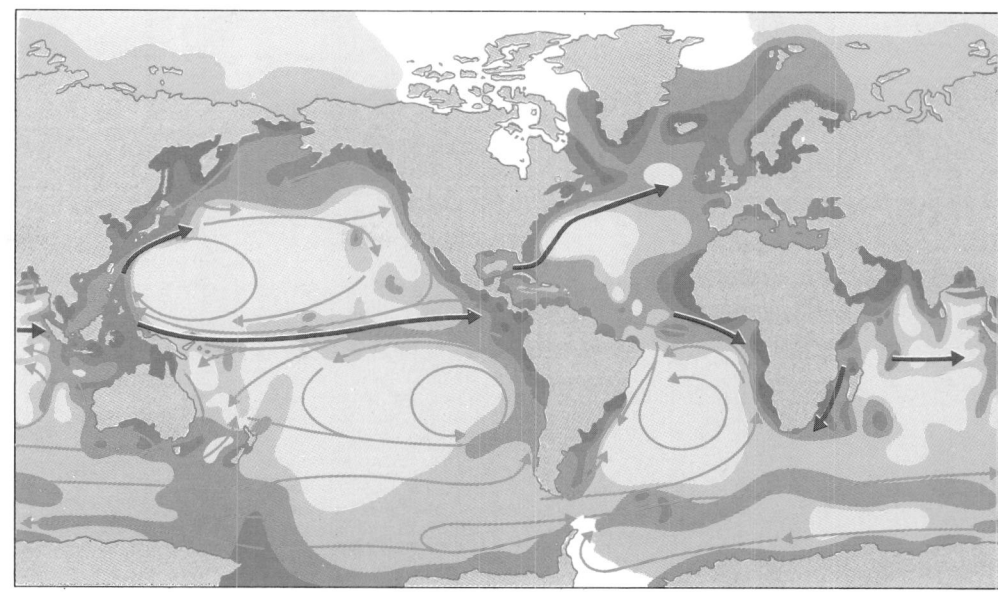

Phytoplanktonic cells need not only sunlight but also nutrient salts, and so they are restricted to areas where these are available: coastal regions, high latitudes (particularly the Antarctic), narrow tongues extending across the tropical regions of the main ocean basins, and a number of subtropical upwelling regions.

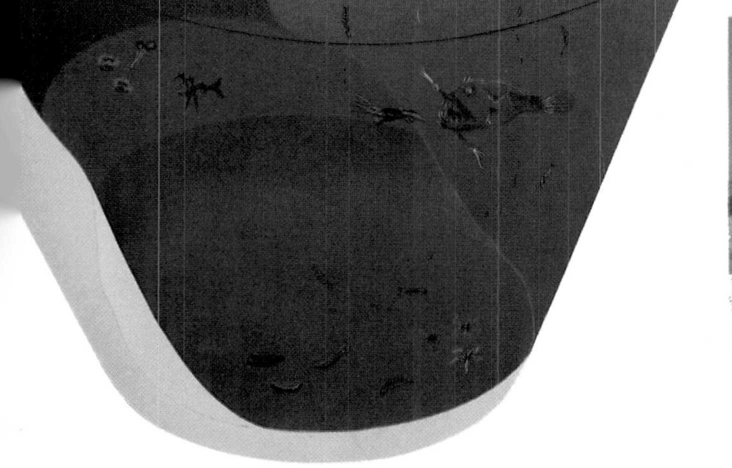

Zones of life (below) extend from the teeming euphotic ("well-lighted") layer to the sparsely populated bathypelagic ("deep-sea") depths, while benthic ("bottom") life occurs at all seabed levels. Phytoplankton (plant life) (1) dictates the pattern of the rest, flourishing where surface conditions allow nutrient salts to well up from lower depths. Herbivores such as minute zooplankton (2) provide food for a host of surface-layer life, which in turn feeds larger predators. Dead animals and fecal pellets fall to lower levels, where they sustain life, but in far smaller quantity.

1 Phytoplankton
2 Zooplankton
3 Blue whale *Balaenoptera musculus*
4 Herring *Clupea harengus*
5 Gray seal *Halichoerus grypus*
6 Bluefin tuna *Thunnus thynnus*
7 Bottlenosed dolphin *Tursiops truncatus*
8 Mackerel *Scomber scomber*
9 Common squid *Loligo* spp
10 White shark *Carcharadon carcharias*
11 Hatchet fish *Argyropelecus hemigymnus*
12 Giant squid *Architeuthis* spp
13 Sea anemone *Cerianthus orientalis*
14 Tripod fish *Benthosaurus grallator*
15 Scarlet shrimp *Notostomus longirostris*
16 Angler fish *Linophryne bicornis*
17 Brittle star *Ophiothrix fragilis*
18 Sea cucumber class Holothuroidea

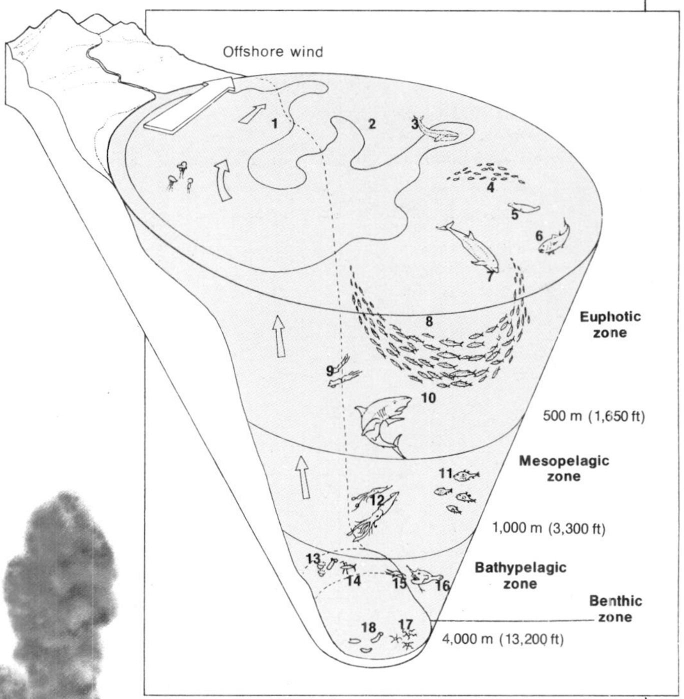

Offshore wind

Euphotic zone

500 m (1,650 ft)

Mesopelagic zone

1,000 m (3,300 ft)

Bathypelagic zone

Benthic zone

4,000 m (13,200 ft)

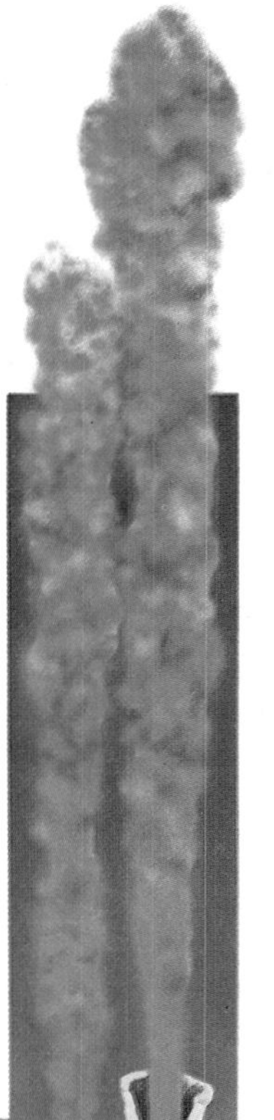

Bizarre life forms new to science live in the sunless depths, where plumes of hot mineral-rich water gush through deep-sea vents in the Earth's crust. These oases of life support huge, gutless tubeworms more than 1.5 m (5 ft) long, which appear to take food particles from the hot vents through blood-red tentacles. Other creatures include blind crabs and large white clams.

sharks, tuna-like fishes and toothed whales.

Beneath the euphotic zone, of course, there can be no herbivores at all, although some animals that spend the daylight hours in the deeper layers move upwards at night to feed in the plankton-rich surface waters. All of the permanent members of the deep-living communities are dependent for food upon material that sinks or is carried downwards from the euphotic zone. Many of them feed on dead animal remains and fecal material as it sinks through the water column or after it reaches the seabed. These detritus eaters in turn support the predatory carnivores that feed upon the detritivores or upon each other.

In shallow areas the food material that reaches the bottom supports complex communities, notably the rich and varied groups of invertebrates and fishes associated with coral reefs. In the deep sea, however, where the euphotic zone is separated from the seabed by several kilometers of water, much of the sinking material is recycled within the water column and relatively little reaches the bottom. Life on the deep-sea floor therefore becomes more and more sparse with increasing depth, but in recent years scientists have discovered that this community includes a surprising number of fishes, some many meters in length. So far man's knowledge of these deep-sea communities is relatively meager, but with our increasing use of the deep oceans we may need to know much more about the life in this environment.

Man and the Seawater Environments

For thousands of years man has used the oceans as a source of food and other materials, and as a repository for wastes. But only in the last 100 years have technological advances and fast-growing human populations had a significant effect, to a point where overfishing and pollution are becoming a cause for concern. Harvesting of krill and seaweeds may ease the pressure on traditional seafoods, but legal restrictions on dumping of wastes or on overfishing are notoriously hard to enforce.

Until about the middle of the nineteenth century the seas had always seemed to be a boundless source of food and of income for fishermen who were brave enough to face the elements with their relatively small sailing ships and primitive gear. But once fishing vessels began to be fitted with steam engines in the 1880s they became relatively independent of the weather, while improvements in the fishing gear itself, such as steam-powered winches in trawling and harpoon guns in whaling, made the whole business of fishing much more efficient.

At first these advances resulted in enormous increases in catches, but in many fisheries this was rapidly followed by a distressing fall in the catch per unit of effort—that is, it was becoming more and more difficult in successive years to catch the same amount of fish as before. In most fisheries the initial response to this situation was to increase the size and number of fishing vessels and to search for new fishing grounds. But as the fishing pressure on the stocks increased, with smaller fish being captured, often before they were able to reproduce, the catch per unit of effort frequently continued to fall.

In many cases attempts were made to counter the effects of overfishing by introducing regulations to control the mesh size of the nets, so allowing the small fish to escape; by establishing closed seasons or quotas of fish which might legitimately be taken from a particular fishing ground in any one year; or even, as in the case of the British herring fishery in the late 1970s, by imposing a complete ban on fishing. Moral questions also sometimes intervene, as in whaling operations, which, many conservationists believe, have driven some species close to extinction despite attempts to rationalize the fisheries.

Fisheries in decline

The North Sea trawl fishery, the first to be affected by the new technology in the nineteenth century, has been declining in terms of catch per unit of effort since the early decades of this century. Dramatic but short-lived improvements after the "closed seasons" of the two world wars proved that fishing pressure had a serious effect on stocks, but by the 1970s many North Sea fishing ports had become almost deserted. This decline put pressure on more distant fishing grounds used by European fishermen, and recent decades have been marked by a series of fishing disputes, with nations fighting for the continued existence of their fisheries despite clear evidence that there are not enough catchable fish to satisfy everyone.

A similar story of declining catches during the present century could be told of many of the old-established fisheries around the world, but at the same time the demand for fish in a protein-hungry world has increased. To satisfy this demand the total annual world catch increased by about seven percent from the end of World War II until the early 1970s, by this time reaching a figure of around 60–70 million tonnes. But this increase was achieved only by exploiting previously unfished stocks or new geographical areas. Such an increase cannot go on indefinitely, for we are rapidly running out of "new" areas and some of the new fisheries have already shown the same symptoms of overfishing as the older ones—and sometimes even more dramatically.

New foods from the sea

The indications are that the present total catch is close to the maximum that can be obtained from relatively conventional fisheries even with careful management, and that, to increase the total, or even to sustain it, we must look to completely new sources such as krill, the shrimp-like food of the whalebone whales.

Estimates of the sustainable annual catch of krill in the Antarctic range from about 50 to 500 million tonnes, that is up to about seven times as much as the current total from all other fisheries put together. Of course, the use of such an enormous quantity of small crustaceans would present considerable problems. Part of it might be converted into a protein-rich paste for human consumption, but much would be used indirectly as a feed for farm animals.

Many larger seaweeds are already cropped in several parts of the world, particularly in Japan, and are used not only for human food but also for animal food and in many industrial processes. About one million tonnes of seaweed are taken each year, but because seaweeds grow naturally only in relatively shallow areas of the oceans this figure could probably not be significantly increased using natural populations. However, seaweeds can be grown artificially on frames floating over deep water. Experiments suggest that, by enriching the surface layers through artificial upwelling of nutrient-rich deep water, each square kilometer of such a floating seaweed farm could produce enough food to feed 1,000–2,000 people, and enough energy and other products to satisfy the needs of a further 1,000. With an estimated 260 million sq km (100 million sq miles) of "arable" surface, the seas might thus support up to 10 times the present world population.

Polluted waters

Of course, the present century has seen an increase not only in what man takes out of the sea but also in the harmful substances that he throws into it. Not only oil but many other substances are dumped into the seas accidentally or intentionally, usually either in the discharged effluent from industrial plant or as a result of agricultural chemicals being leached into rivers and thence into the ocean. In many cases the amounts are very small compared with the amounts present in the oceans as a whole; the problem is that they are usually released, and accumulate, in restricted inshore areas near which we live and from which we obtain most of our sea-caught food.

Since the 1930s there have been both national and international attempts to control pollution by legislation, and since 1958 a series of United Nations conferences has sought agreement on many aspects of international maritime law, including pollution. Despite many prophecies of imminent doom, it does not seem that marine pollution yet poses any general threat to humanity. Nevertheless, with ever-increasing industrialization and the production of more and more toxic materials, including radioactive wastes, it is essential that we monitor the effects of man's activities on the ocean.

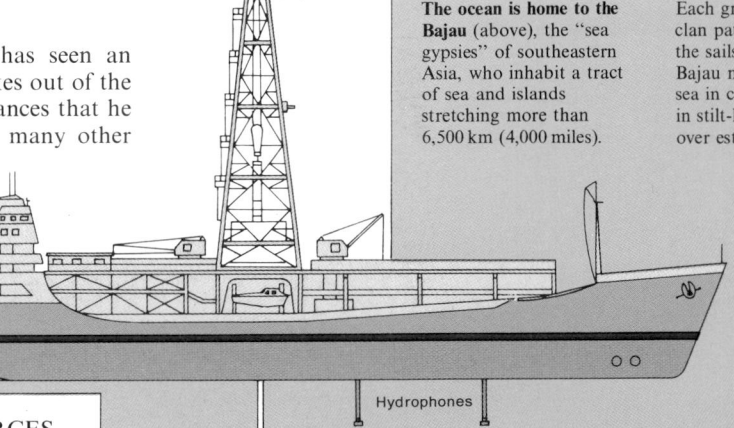

The ocean is home to the **Bajau** (above), the "sea gypsies" of southeastern Asia, who inhabit a tract of sea and islands stretching more than 6,500 km (4,000 miles).

Each group has its own clan pattern, blazoned on the sails of their *praus*. The Bajau may live on the open sea in clusters of boats, or in stilt-house villages built over estuaries.

THE MARINE RESOURCES

Modern technology has enabled man to expand his age-old exploitation of the seas to the limit in some areas, and a need for the careful management of our marine resource is imperative. But in some fields, such as energy and the extraction of fresh water, the seas may yield inexhaustible riches.

The deep-sea drilling ship *Glomar Challenger* (above) plays an important role in surveying and prospecting the oceans. It can drill in water depths of 7,000 m (23,000 ft) and obtain core samples 1,200 m (4,000 ft) below the ocean bed. The ship is positioned over the drill hole through signals from a sonar beacon to hydrophones in the hull.

Drilling derrick

Hydrophones

Sonar beacons

Core sample tube

Drilling head

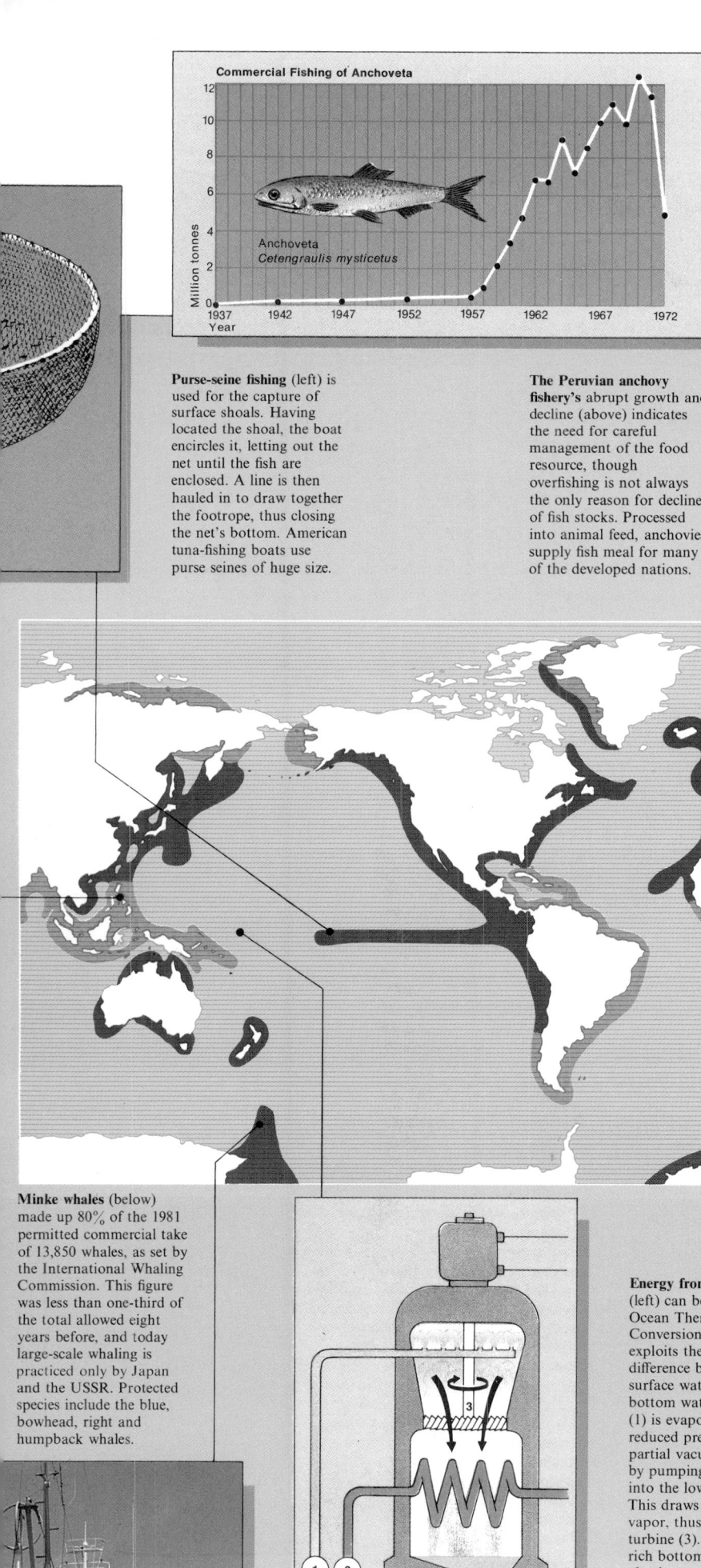

Commercial Fishing of Anchoveta

Anchoveta
Cetengraulis mysticetus

Million tonnes — Year (1937–1972)

Purse-seine fishing (left) is used for the capture of surface shoals. Having located the shoal, the boat encircles it, letting out the net until the fish are enclosed. A line is then hauled in to draw together the footrope, thus closing the net's bottom. American tuna-fishing boats use purse seines of huge size.

The Peruvian anchovy fishery's abrupt growth and decline (above) indicates the need for careful management of the food resource, though overfishing is not always the only reason for decline of fish stocks. Processed into animal feed, anchovies supply fish meal for many of the developed nations.

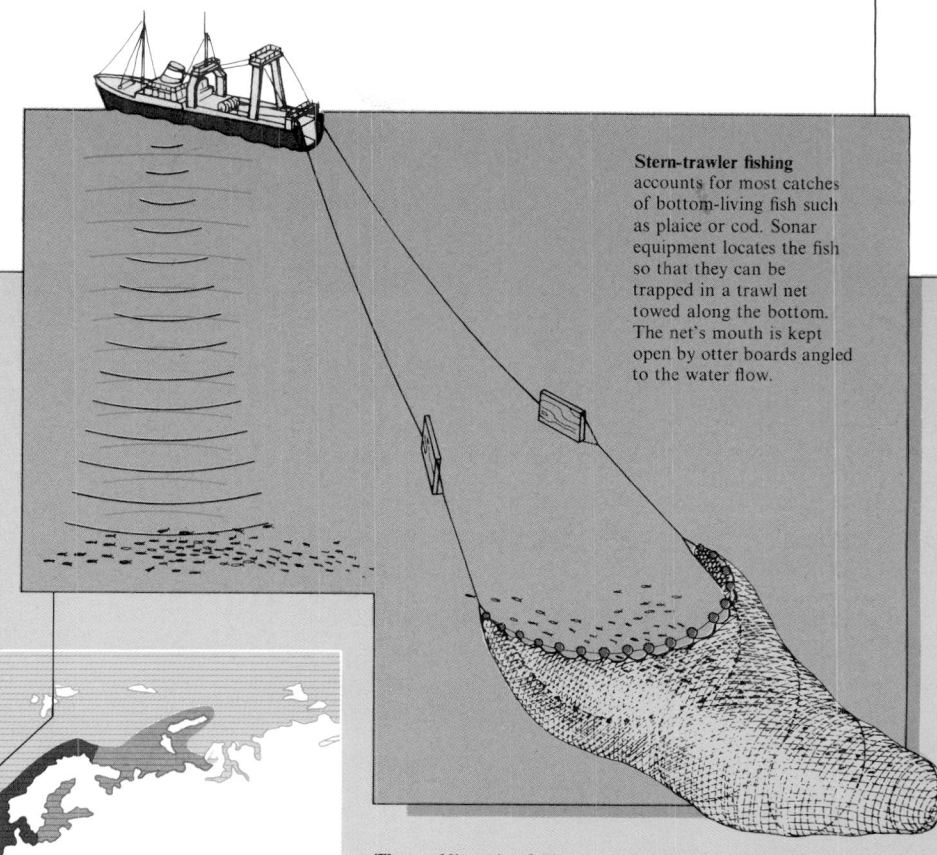

Stern-trawler fishing accounts for most catches of bottom-living fish such as plaice or cod. Sonar equipment locates the fish so that they can be trapped in a trawl net towed along the bottom. The net's mouth is kept open by otter boards angled to the water flow.

The world's major fishing grounds (left) tend to occur in regions of high plankton productivity, with the industrial fleets of the developed nations dominant in the northern hemisphere, and small-scale fishing by local populations commoner in the south.

Remote fishing grounds can be exploited by industrial fleets, as when whaling vessels operate in the Antarctic waters. But small-scale fishermen from underdeveloped nations in many parts of the world may also venture far from land, often in unpowered boats.

■ Industrial fishing

■ Small-scale fishing

Minke whales (below) made up 80% of the 1981 permitted commercial take of 13,850 whales, as set by the International Whaling Commission. This figure was less than one-third of the total allowed eight years before, and today large-scale whaling is practiced only by Japan and the USSR. Protected species include the blue, bowhead, right and humpback whales.

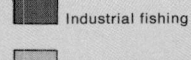

Energy from the oceans (left) can be obtained by Ocean Thermal Energy Conversion (OTEC), which exploits the temperature difference between warm surface water and cold bottom water. The former (1) is evaporated under reduced pressure when a partial vacuum is formed by pumping cold water (2) into the lower chamber. This draws down the vapor, thus turning the turbine (3). The nutrient-rich bottom water may also be a source of food for fish farms. The first commercial OTEC plant, Japanese made, has been constructed for the Pacific island of Nauru, where conditions for operation are ideal.

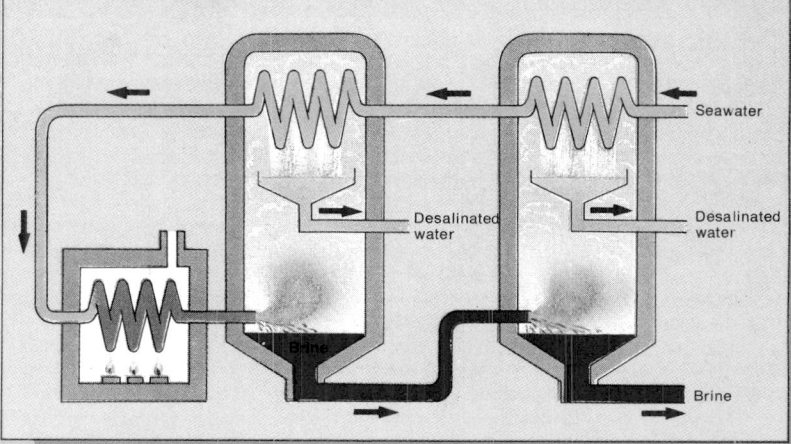

Seawater — Desalinated water — Brine

Fresh water is distilled from the sea (above) at many desalination plants in the Middle East. The cold seawater is heated and then discharged into a vessel at reduced pressure, where the cooling coils of seawater in the upper part condense the water vapor. The briny water that is left passes through several similar stages, at lower pressures, with more water vapor being evaporated and condensed at each stage. Such systems can operate by means of waste steam from electricity generating plants, as at Abu Dhabi.

ENERGY, INDUSTRY AND THE SEAS

The volume of oil carried annually along the world's major tanker routes (below) exceeds 1,400 million tonnes, of which some six million tonnes enter the seas through dumping or accidents. Coastlines of developed nations are worst affected by oil (right) and discharge of industrial wastes.

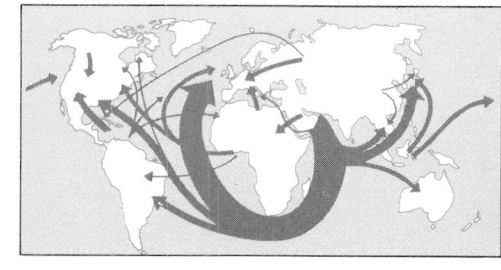

Part 5

UNDERSTANDING MAPS
What maps are and how they are made
New horizons and latest developments in maps and mapmaking
How to read the language of maps

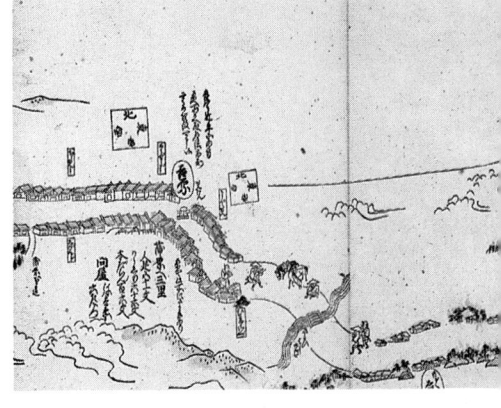

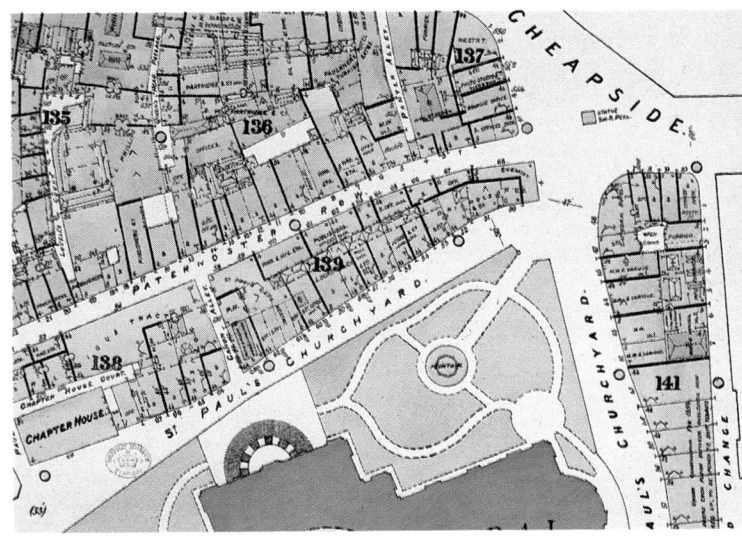

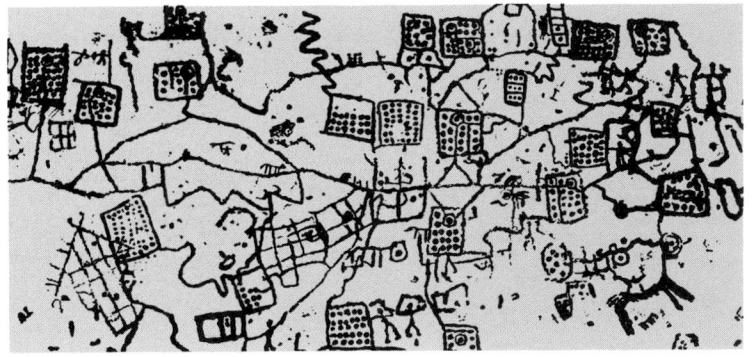

Elegant road maps with pictorial and geographical features have been produced by many different cultures. The woodcut map of the Tōkaidō (detail above), the great Japanese highway, 555 km (345 miles) long, between Edo (Tokyo) and Kyoto, was drawn as a panorama by the famous artist Moronobu in 1690. Its pictorial details do not prevent it being an accurate representation of the road's track. A Mexican map of the Tepetlaoztoc valley (right) drawn in 1583 marks roads with footprints between parallel lines, and hill ranges with wavy lines. Symbols in panels represent place-names.

Maps defining territory and ownership are almost as old as the human territorial instinct itself. The rock-carving maps of the Val Camonica, Italy (above), dating from the second and first millennia BC, show stippled square fields, paths, river lines, houses, and even humans and animals. It is uncertain whether their purpose was legal, but the need to establish ownership is a basic function of many maps, as seen in a detail from Goad's 19th-century insurance map of London (left), where every occupation is recorded.

America first appears as a separate continent (below) in an inset to Martin Waldseemüller's world map of 1507, with the two hemispheres facing each other. Presiding over the Old World is Claudius Ptolemy, the 2nd-century geographer whose remarkably scientific maps, copied and recopied over a thousand years, were revised and emended by Waldseemüller to show some of the results of Portuguese exploration. His New World counterpart is the Italian Amerigo Vespucci, one of the early explorers of the continent, after whom it was named. This is the first map to show the Pacific (not yet named) as an ocean between America and Asia. The west coast of South America, still to be explored by Europeans, seems to be inspired guesswork. The island between the landmasses is Cipango (Japan) known from Marco Polo.

1 2

The earliest surviving Chinese globe (above) was made in 1623 by two Jesuit missionaries, probably for the emperor of China. The long legend in Chinese expresses terms and ideas derived from early Chinese cosmology. It describes the Earth as "floating in the Heavens like the yolk of an egg . . . with all objects having mass tending toward its center"—one of the first known references to gravity.

High-altitude photography (left) allows accurate updating of topographic maps (right), while data gathering by satellites (above) expands the range. Landsat satellites carry electronic remote-sensing equipment that detects the energy emitted by surface materials and translates it into images. Healthy plants may show as bright red, sparse vegetation as pink, barren lands as light gray, and urban areas as green or dark gray. The folded shape of the Appalachians (1) is clearly seen; the Canada–US border (2) is revealed by land-use patterns; silt from the Mississippi (3) builds up the delta. Sudan irrigation (4) shows up as brilliant red.

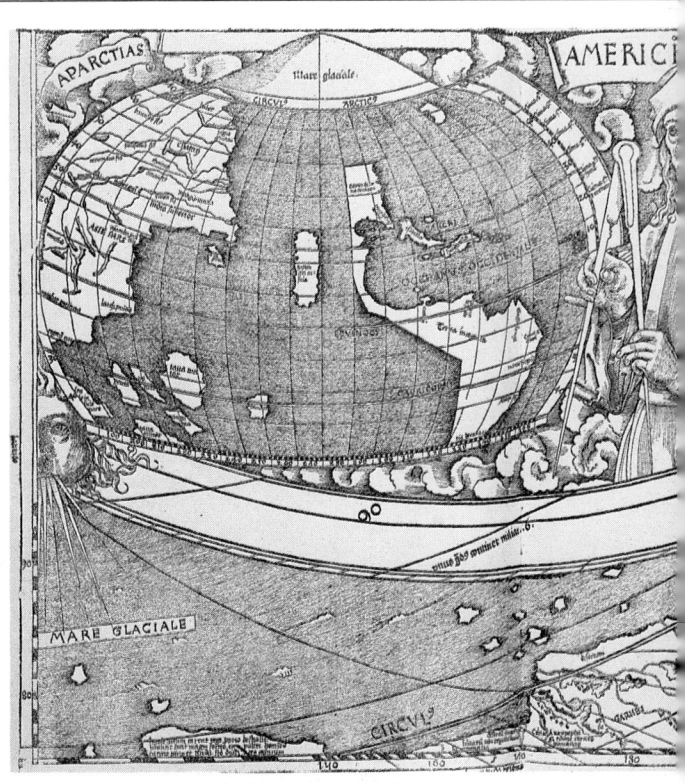

Mapping, Old and New

Mapmaking must have its origins in the earliest ages of human history, since people of preliterate as well as literate cultures possess an innate skill in map drawing. This innate capacity is further indicated by the ease with which almost anyone can sketch in the sand or on paper simple directions for showing the way. But maps may also define territory and express man's idea of the world in graphic representation. Today, modern technology has vastly extended the scope of cartography.

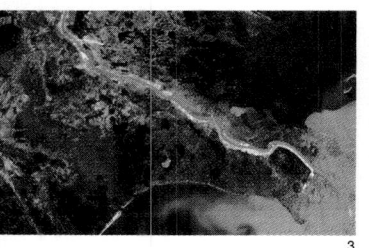
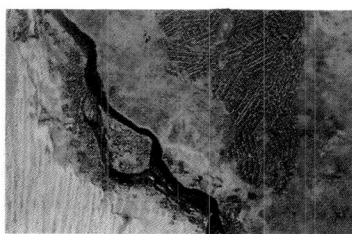

Many non-European cultures developed ingenious route-map techniques: the North American Indians, for example, made sketch maps of routes on birch bark. These were diagrammatic maps in which directions and distances were not accurate but relationships were true, as in New York Subway or London Underground maps. The people of the Marshall Islands in the western Pacific made route maps over the seas, depicting the direction of the main seasonal wave swells in relation to the islands.

Although maps of routes are the simplest type of map in concept, they developed complex forms as cartography progressed. A road map of the whole Roman Empire, drawn about AD 280, survives today in a thirteenth-century copy known as the Peutinger Table. Hernando Cortes, the Spanish conqueror, made his way across Mexico in the 1520s with the help of preconquest Mexican maps painted on cloth. These showed roads with double lines or colored bands marked with footprints. Another type of map is the strip map depicting a single road along its entire length. Pictorial maps of the Tōkaidō highway from Edo to Kyoto in Japan, made from a survey of 1651, were popular in the Edo period of Japanese history.

Nautical charts evolved as a special type of direction-finding map to meet the needs of seamen. Those of the late Middle Ages came to be known as "portolan" charts, from the word "portolani," or sailing directions. They showed the sea and adjacent coasts superimposed on a network of radiating compass lines.

Territorial maps

Another basic type of map derives from man's sense of territorial possession. The earliest example of a "cadastral" plan (a map showing land parcels and property boundaries) appears to be that preserved as rock carvings at Bedolina in Val Camonica in northern Italy. However, in the ancient civilizations of Mesopotamia and Egypt, land surveying had become an established profession by 2000 BC. An idea of what Egyptian surveyors' plans of 1000 BC were like can be seen from the "Fields of the Dead" representing the Egyptians' idea of life after death. These show plots of land surrounded by water and intersected by canals. The Romans used cadastral surveys to determine land ownership and assess tax liability.

Another form of map showing territorial demarcations is the map of administrative units. The Chinese in the thirteenth century AD were making official district maps to help in the organization of grain supplies and the collection of taxes. Many of their gazetteers (*fang chih*), written in the form of local geographies and

histories from the eleventh century onward, were illustrated with maps. Political maps showing the boundaries of states were increasingly significant in European cartography from the sixteenth century onward.

A third major class of map is the general or topographical map expressing man's perception of the world, its regions and its place in the universe. A Babylonian world map of the seventh century BC is drawn on a clay tablet and shows the Earth as a circular disc surrounded by the Earthly Ocean. With the ancient Greeks, geography developed on scientific principles. The treatise on mapmaking by Claudius Ptolemy (AD 87–150), later known as the *Geographia*, was the most famous cartographic text of the period. It influenced the Arabic geographers of the Middle Ages, notably Muhammad Ibn Muhammad, Al-Idrisi (1099–1164), and with the revival of Ptolemy in fifteenth-century Europe became one of the major works of the Renaissance. Published, with engraved maps, at Bologna in 1477, the *Geographia* ranks as the first printed atlas in the western world. The invention of techniques of engraving in wood and copper facilitated a wide diffusion of geographical knowledge through the map-publishing trade. The first atlas made up of modern maps to a uniform design was Abraham Ortelius's *Theatrum Orbis Terrarum* published at Antwerp in 1570. From 1492, when Martin Behaim made his "Erdapfel" at Nürnberg, globes also became popular, and globemakers vied with each other to make larger and more elaborate ones to keep pace with the growth of knowledge about the world.

Over the last two hundred years cartography has made rapid and remarkable advances. Observatories built in Paris in 1671 and at Greenwich in 1675 enabled the location of places to be established more exactly with the use of astronomical tables. Improvements in surveying instruments facilitated more accurate and rapid land survey. France was the pioneer in establishing (from 1679 onward) a national survey on a geometrical basis of triangulation. By the end of the eighteenth century national surveys on small and medium scales had been begun by most European countries. In the United States the Geological Survey was set up in 1879 to undertake the topographical and geological mapping of the country.

Mapping today

Since World War II cartographic techniques have undergone a revolution. The use of air survey and photogrammetry has made it possible to map most of the Earth's surface. Electronic distance measurement by laser or light beams in surveying, and digital computers in mapping, are among the most recent advances in methods. Mosaics or air photography are used to produce orthophoto maps which can supplement or substitute for the conventional topographic map. Artificial satellites and manned space craft make it possible to provide a world-wide framework of geodetic networks. Earth Resource Technology Satellites (ERTS) imagery has made it possible to map mountain ranges in Africa and features on the surface of Antarctica that were hitherto unknown. The imagery is made available by means of remote-sensing instruments, carried by the satellites, that are sensitive to invisible portions of the electromagnetic spectrum—longer and shorter wavelengths than can be sensed by the human eye. Remote-sensing instruments usually work in the infrared bands. They can also pick up the energy emitted by all types of surface material—rocks, soils, vegetation, water and man-made structures—and produce photographs or images from it.

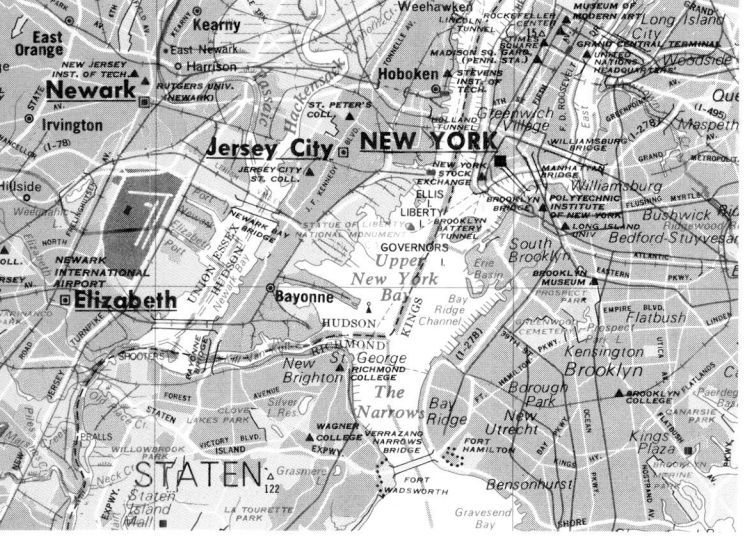

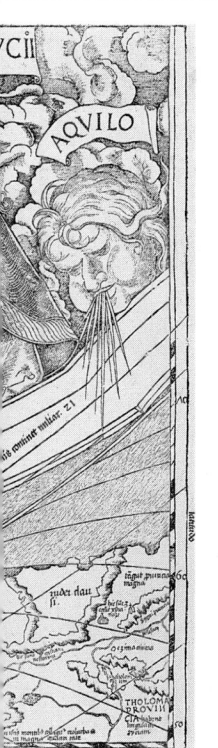

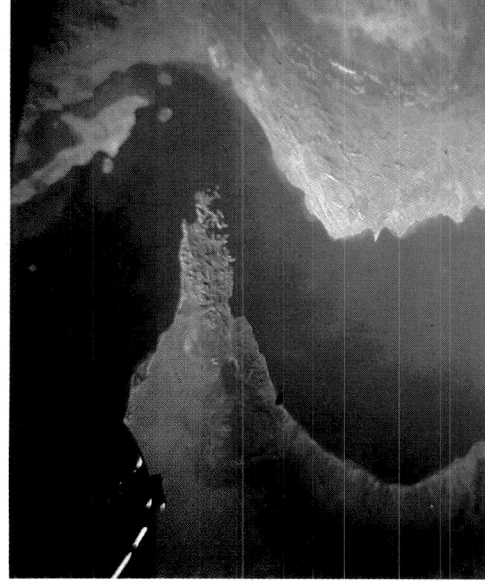

Space technology helps cartographers to map even interior details of the planet: its geology and mineral wealth. A photo (below) taken from Gemini 12 at an altitude of 272 km (168 miles) forms the basis of a geologic sketch map of

SW Asia (below right), showing the oil-rich area around the region between the Persian Gulf and the Gulf of Oman. The symbol S on the map indicates salt plugs; diamonds show fold trends; double-headed arrows anticlines.

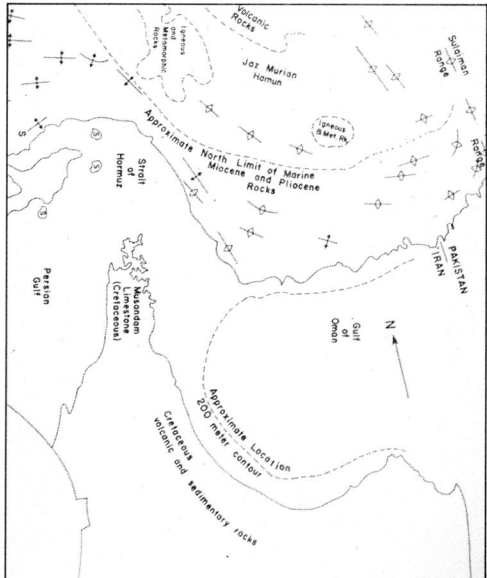

The Language of Maps

Mapmakers for more than 4,000 years have tried to find the best way to represent the shape and features of the three-dimensional Earth on two-dimensional paper, parchment and cloth. The measurement of distance and direction is a basic requirement for accurate surveys, but until about 1800 theoretical understanding of the method was well in advance of the technical equipment available. Today the use of lasers and light beams sometimes takes the place of direct measurement on the ground.

A reference system must be used to show distance and direction correctly in the construction of maps. The simplest type is the rectangular or square grid. The Chinese mapmaker Pei Xin made a map with a grid in about AD 270, and this system remained in continuous use in China until modern times. The Roman system of centuriation, a form of division of public lands on a square or rectangular basis, was also a "coordinate" system starting from a point of origin at the intersection of two perpendicular axes. Roman surveyors' maps, dating from the first century AD, are the earliest known European maps based on a grid system.

Latitude and longitude

Makers of small-scale regional maps and of world maps in early times also had to take account of the fact that the Earth is a sphere. The Greeks derived from the Babylonians the idea of dividing a circle into 360 degrees. In the second century BC the Greek geographer Eratosthenes (c. 276–194 BC) was the first to calculate the circumference of the globe and was reported to have made a world map based on the concept of the Earth's sphericity. From this the Greeks went on to develop the system of spherical coordinates which remains in use today. The poles at each end of the Earth's axis provide reference points for the Earth in its rotation in relation to the celestial sphere. Parallel circles around the Earth are degrees of latitude and express the idea of distance north or south of the Equator. Lines of longitude running north and south through the poles express east–west distances. One meridian is chosen as the meridian of origin, known as the prime meridian.

Whereas latitude from early times could be observed from the height of the Sun or (in the northern hemisphere) from the position of the Pole Star at night, accurate observations of longitude were not possible until the middle of the eighteenth century, when the chronometer was invented and more accurate astronomical tables were provided. In 1884 most countries agreed, at an international conference in Washington DC, to adopt the prime meridian through the Royal Greenwich Observatory in England and to calculate longitude to 180 degrees east and west of Greenwich.

Projection and distortion

The mathematical system by which the spherical surface of the Earth is transferred to the plane surface of a map is called a map projection. The Greek geographer Ptolemy gave instructions in his geographical treatise of AD 150 for the construction of two projections. When the *Geographia* was revised in Europe in the fifteenth century, and navigators began sailing across the oceans, mapmakers devised new projections more appropriate to the expanding geographical knowledge of the world. The Dutch geographer Gerard Mercator invented the projection named after him, applying it to his world chart of 1569. This cylindrical projection, in which all points are at true compass courses from each other, was of great benefit to navigators and is still one of the most commonly

used projections. Another advance was made when Johann Heinrich Lambert of Alsace (1728–1777) invented the azimuthal equal-area projection, in which the sizes of all areas are represented on the projection in correct proportion to one another, and the conformal projection, in which at any point on the map the scale is constant in all directions.

Since all projections involve deformation of the geometry of the globe, the cartographer has to choose the one that best suits the purpose of his map. "Conformal" or "orthomorphic" projections, in which angular relations (or shape) are preserved, are widely used for the construction of topographical maps. "Equivalent" or "equal-area" projections retain relative sizes and are particularly useful for general reference maps displaying economic, historical, political and other geographical phenomena.

Since the mid-fifteenth century, European mapmakers have generally arranged their maps with north at the top of the sheet. Earlier maps, however, were not standardized in this way. The circular world maps of the Middle Ages were orientated with east at the top, because this was where the terrestrial paradise was traditionally sited. Indeed, the word "orientation" originally meant the arrangement of something so as to face east.

Map scale

Scale is another basic property of a map. The scale of a map is the ratio of the distance on the map to the actual distance represented. Whereas the Babylonians, Egyptians, Greeks and Romans drew surveys to scale, in medieval Europe mapmakers used customary methods of estimating. The earliest known local map since Roman times which is drawn to scale (it displays a scale bar) is a plan of Vienna, 1422.

Projection, grid, orientation and scale form the framework of a map. The language of maps in concept and content is much more complex. To represent the surface of the Earth on a map, the cartographer must select and generalize from a vast quantity of material, using symbols and conventional signs as codes.

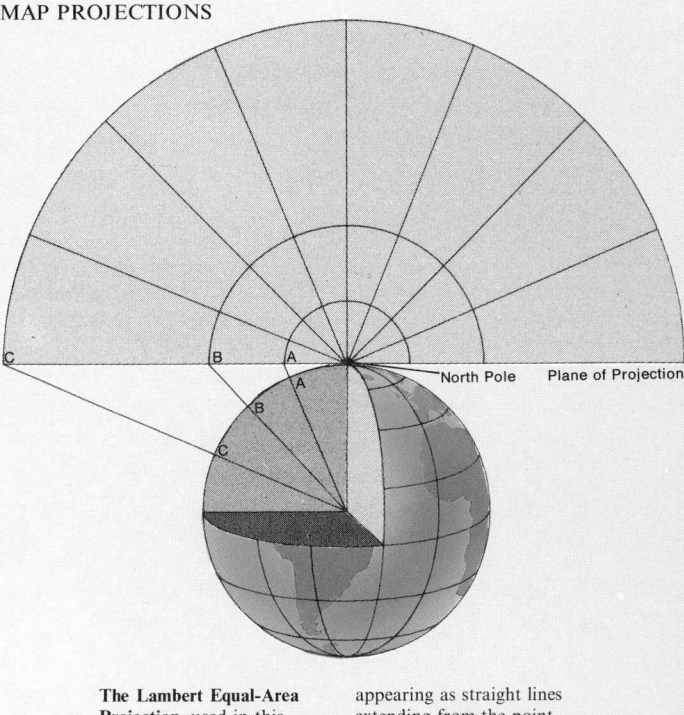

MAP PROJECTIONS

The Lambert Equal-Area Projection, used in this atlas, may be visualized as a flat plane placed at a tangent to the globe, with the lines of longitude appearing as straight lines extending from the point of tangency, the North Pole (above). Deformation increases away from this point (below).

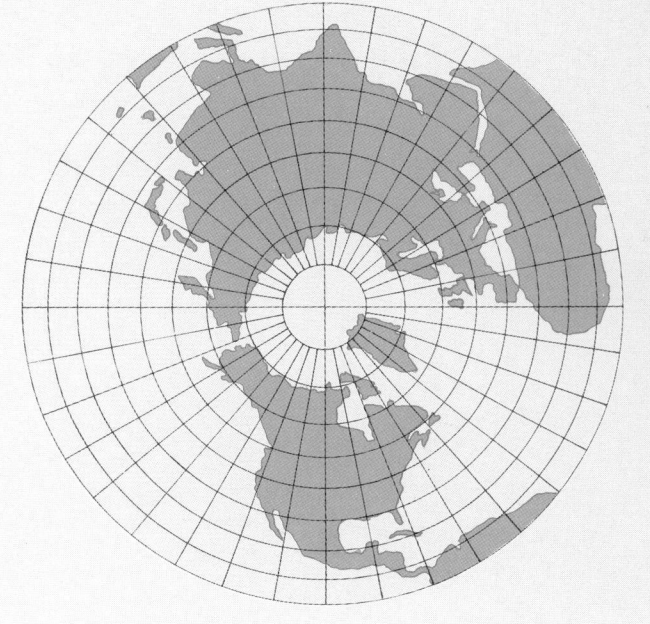

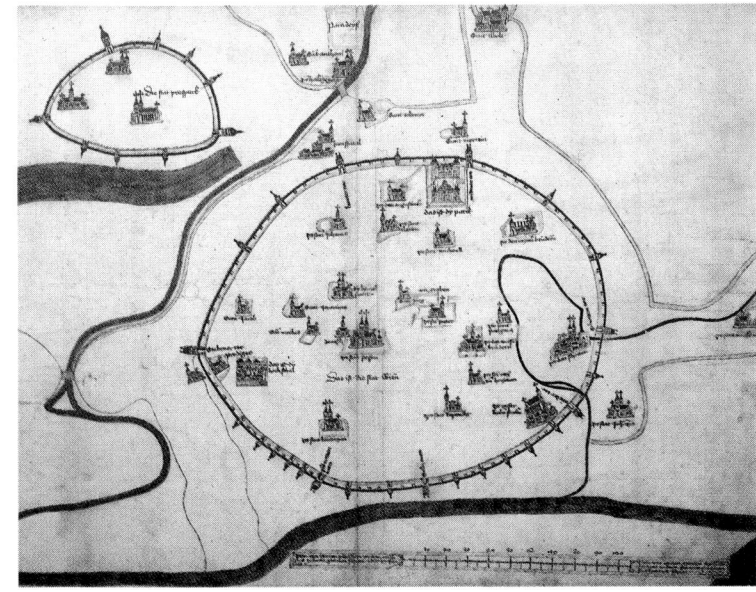

Map scales express the relationship between a distance measured on the map and the true distance on the ground. A plan of Vienna (left), originally made in 1422, is drawn in the bird's-eye-view style typical of early medieval town plans. But the scale bar at its foot shows that it has been explicitly drawn to scale, indicating that the concept of a uniform scale had been grasped in medieval Europe.

Direction and distance are concepts used in the relative location of two or more points (below). These concepts are organized according to a general frame of reference, with direction following the grid system of coordinates. Thus places shown in (A) can be precisely located in terms of longitude and of latitude (B), with the degrees further subdivided into one-sixtieths of minutes.

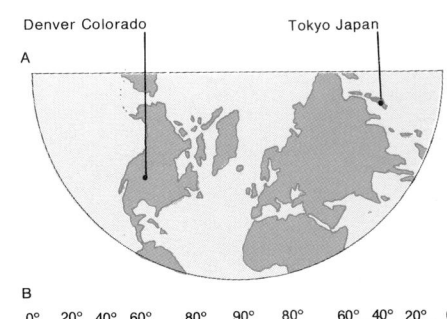

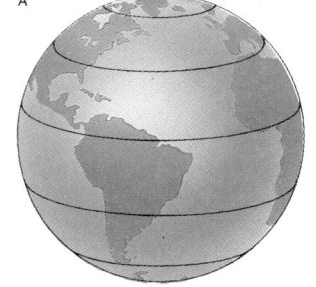 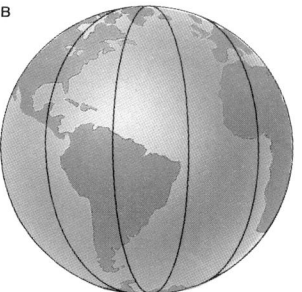 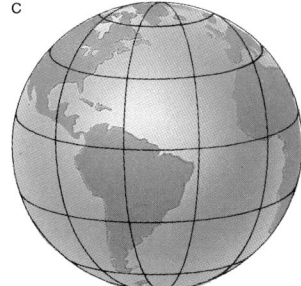

Superimposed on the globe (left), lines of latitude (A) and longitude (B) allow every place to be exactly located in terms of a coordinate system (C). The parallels of latitude measure distance from 0° to 90° north and south of the Equator. The meridians of longitude measure distance from 0° to 180° east and west of a "prime meridian" at Greenwich.

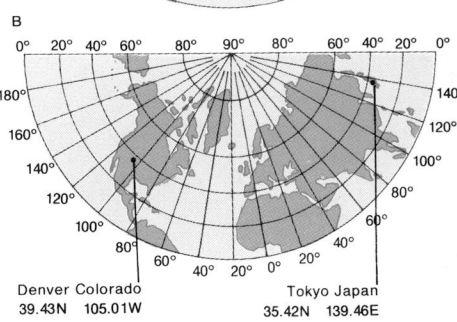

The Hammer Projection (far right), developed from the Lambert Projection of one hemisphere (right), is designed to show the whole world in a single view, and is used in this atlas in a version modified by Wagner and known as the Hammer-Wagner Projection. The Earth appears as an ellipse because the lines of longitude are plotted at twice their horizontal distance from the center line, and numbered at twice their previous values. The central meridian is half the length of the Equator.

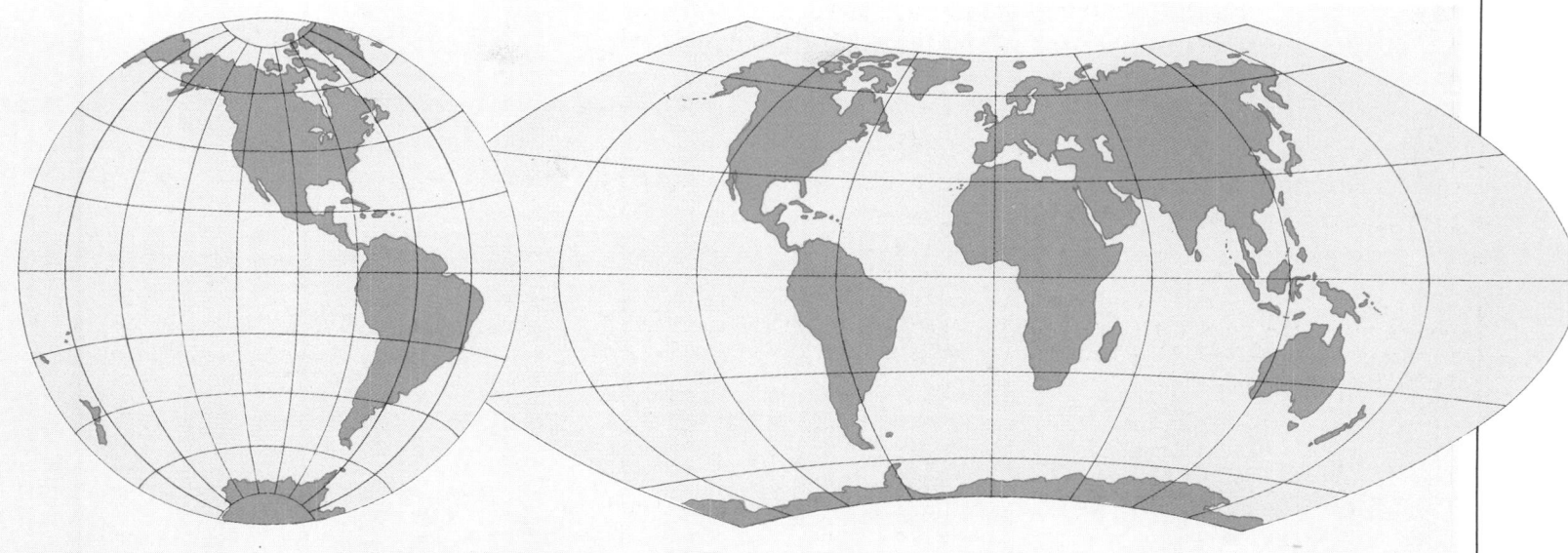

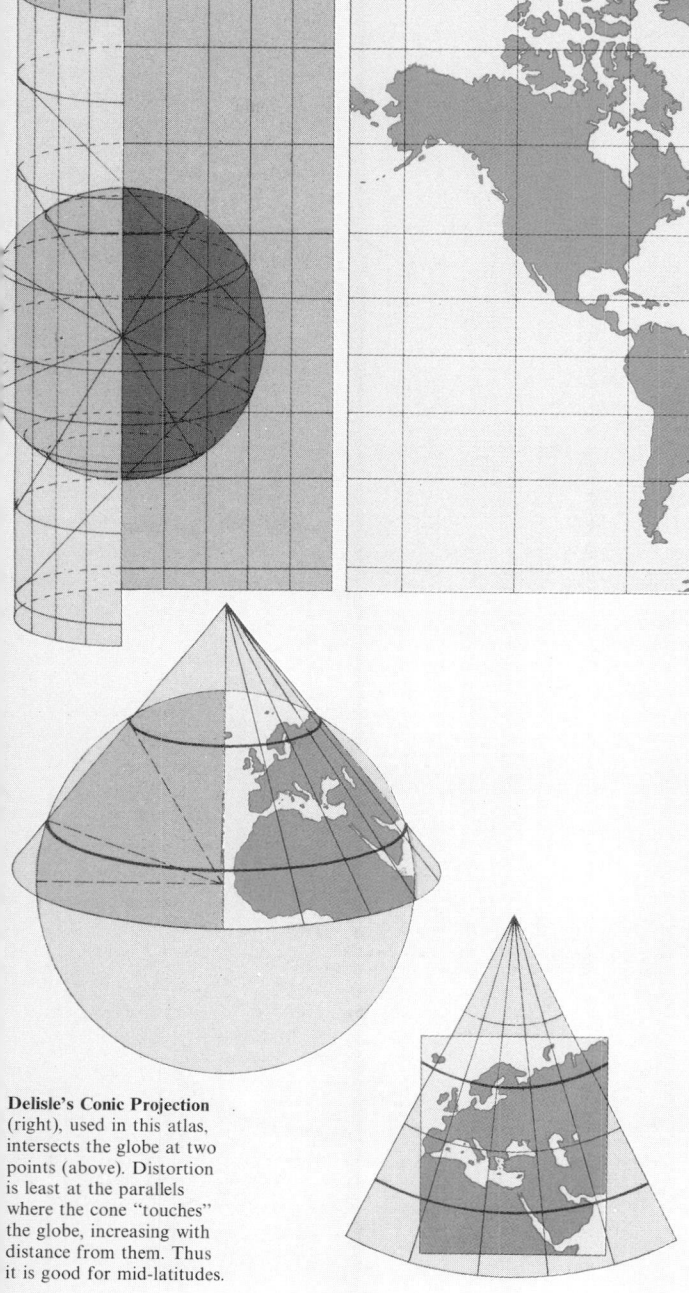

Delisle's Conic Projection (right), used in this atlas, intersects the globe at two points (above). Distortion is least at the parallels where the cone "touches" the globe, increasing with distance from them. Thus it is good for mid-latitudes.

In a cylindrical projection like Gall's (above left), the sphere is "unwrapped" on to a cylinder, making a complete transformation to a flat surface. Mercator's Projection (above), devised in 1569, is a cylindrical projection that aids navigation by showing all compass directions as straight lines. A projection (below), based on Peters', distorts shape to show land surface area ratios, emphasizing the Third World.

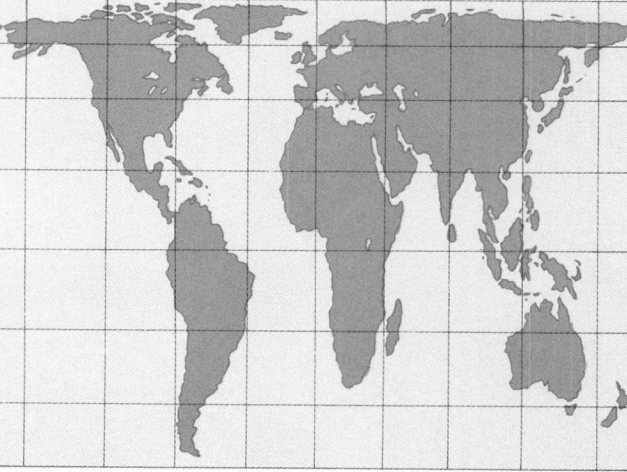

Photogrammetric plotting instruments (above) are now used in the preparation of large-scale accurate topographic maps. These are sophisticated machines that provide very precise measurements, plotting the map data in orthogonal projection.

The theodolite (above), a basic surveying instrument dating back to the 16th century, can measure angles and directions horizontally and vertically. A swivel telescope with cross-hairs inside it permits accurate alignment, and it may be used in the field.

EARTH MEASUREMENT THROUGH THE AGES

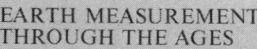

Surveying—the technique of making accurate measurements of the Earth's surface—is as old as civilization and has been an essential element in mankind's development of his environment. The need to establish land boundaries arose at least 3,500 years ago in the fertile valleys of the Nile, Tigris and Euphrates rivers. Man's urge to explore and to describe the world also led to the development of instruments determining position, distance and direction. The astrolabe, sometimes called the world's oldest scientific instrument, may date to the 3rd century BC. Today's techniques make increasing use of computers.

An Egyptian wall painting (left) from the middle of the second millennium BC shows what appears to be the measurement of a grain field by means of a rope with knots at regular intervals on its length.

The astrolabe (right), used in classical times to observe the positions of celestial bodies, became a navigational instrument in the Middle Ages, when it was developed to permit establishment of latitude.

How to Use Maps

Today maps play a role more important than ever before in increasing our knowledge of the Earth, its regions and peoples. How maps communicate knowledge is now a subject of scientific study. The process comprises the collection and mapping of the data and the reading of the map. In this final stage the map user is all important. Through him the map is transformed into an image in the mind, and the effectiveness of the map depends on the reader being able to understand it.

The cartographer's map has to convey an objective picture of reality. To compile the map the cartographer selects and generalizes information, taking into account the purpose of his map. If he is making a topographical reference map, he has to reduce the three-dimensional landforms of the Earth on to the flat surface of the map. He adds cultural detail such as towns, roads and railroads, and features not apparent to the eye, such as administrative boundaries. On the topographical base map he adds appropriate place-names, using typefaces which reflect their class and significance. All this requires the classification of phenomena, with emphasis to direct the reader's attention.

Themes and symbolization

The cartographer who seeks not merely to represent visible features but to convey geographical ideas about specific phenomena uses the techniques of thematic cartography, where the emphasis is on one or two elements, or themes. Maps today provide one of the most effective means of communicating many kinds of data and ideas relating to the world and its peoples. Their extensive use makes them an important force in education, planning, recreation and in many other human affairs.

The map is designed in code, with symbols to represent features, and a legend, or key, to explain them. There are three types of symbol: point, line and area. Point symbols usually denote places, which may be distinguished into classes by the shape, color and size of the symbol. Line symbols express connections, such as roads or traffic flow, and they may also define and distinguish areas. Area symbols in which variations of color are often combined with patterns of lines or dots are used to depict spatial phenomena, such as types of soil, vegetation and density of population.

How much detail can be shown on a map will depend on its scale, which controls the process of generalization. Scale expresses the relationship of the distance on the map to the distance on the Earth, with the distance on the map always given as the unit ·1. It is denoted in various ways: as a representative fraction such as 1:1,000,000; as a written statement; or by means of a graph or bar. Some map scales have become widely used and are generally familiar to map users. The scale 1:25,000 is ideal for walkers and relief can be shown in detail. That of 1:50,000 is a typical medium scale for national surveys. The publication of an international map of the world on a scale of one to

one million (1:1,000,000) has been in progress since 1909. On this scale 1 mm represents 1 km on the ground. The regional maps of countries in this atlas are drawn on scales of 1:6,000,000, 1:3,000,000 and 1:1,500,000; those of the continents are at 1:30,000,000 and 1:15,000,000. The Map Section index maps show the arrangement.

Terrain depiction

Since the early days of map making in ancient Chinese and classical Greek and Roman civilizations, map makers have been concerned to show the configuration of the land. For many centuries they symbolized mountains and hills by pictorial features often looking like caterpillars or sugar loaves. As topographical mapping developed in Europe from the seventeenth century onward, new techniques were devised to improve the visual impression of the features and to depict them accurately in terms of height and location. The system of hachuring (shading with fine parallel or crossed lines), first used in 1674, gives a good idea of relief but not of height. The use of contours, which became general from the nineteenth century onward, is more exact in representing actual elevation, but for many regions, especially those of irregular relief, the appearance of the land is lost.

The addition of hypsometric tints (tints between contours which show elevation) helps clarify the elevation. Applying shadows to the form of the land through the process called hill shading or relief shading creates a visual impression of the configuration of the land surface. Hypsometric tints combined with hill shading gives both elevation information and surface form of the area being depicted, leading to an almost three-dimensional effect.

Maps are classed (right) as either general (A) or thematic (B,C). The purpose of a general reference map is to provide locational information, showing how the positions of various geographical phenomena relate to each other. Thematic maps concentrate on a particular type of information, or theme, such as the distribution of people (B) or rainfall (C), and are generally based on statistical data.

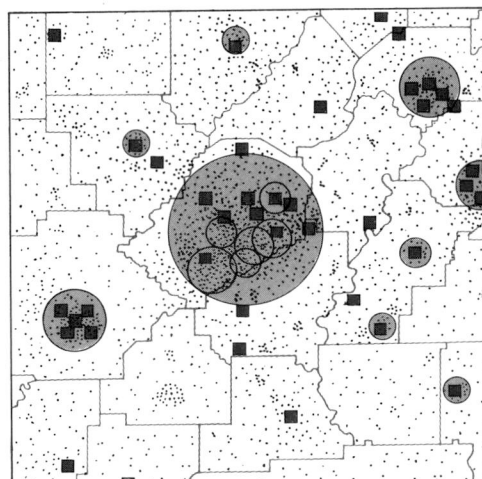

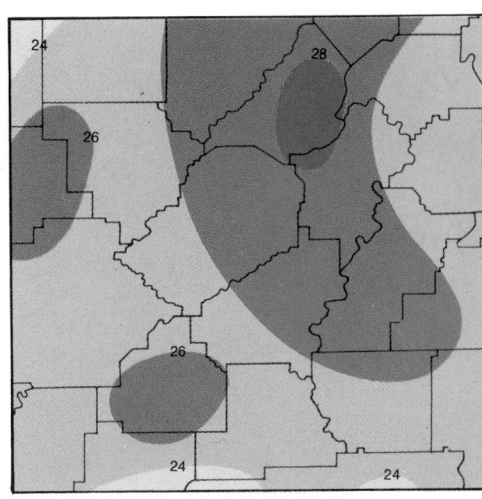

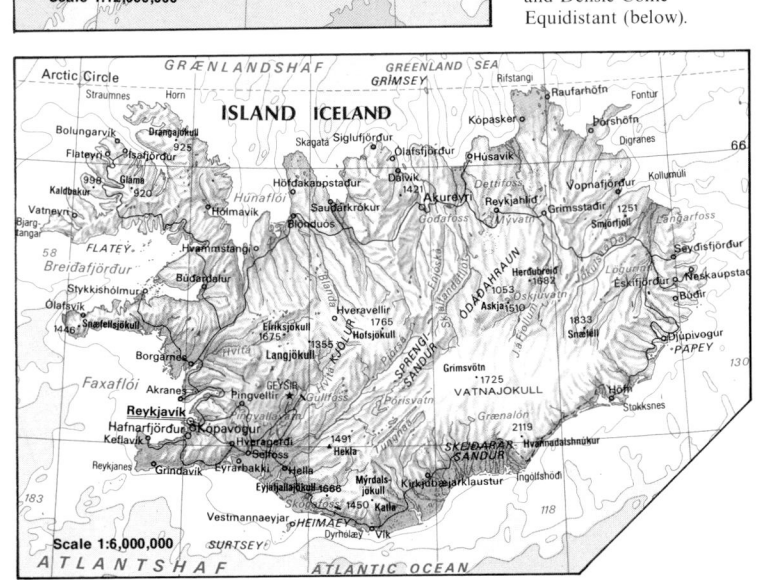

The ratio between a map's dimensions and those of the physical world is defined by the map scale (left and below), with the map distance always given as the unit 1. The larger the reduction, the smaller the scale, so that a scale of 1:6,000,000—1 mm (.04 in) to 6 km (3.74 miles)—is twice that of 1:12,000,000 (.04 in to 7.5 miles). The size of the scale reflects the amount of detail that needs to be shown. The projections are the Lambert Azimuthal Equal-Area (left) and Delisle Conic Equidistant (below).

Scale 1:12,000,000

Scale 1:6,000,000

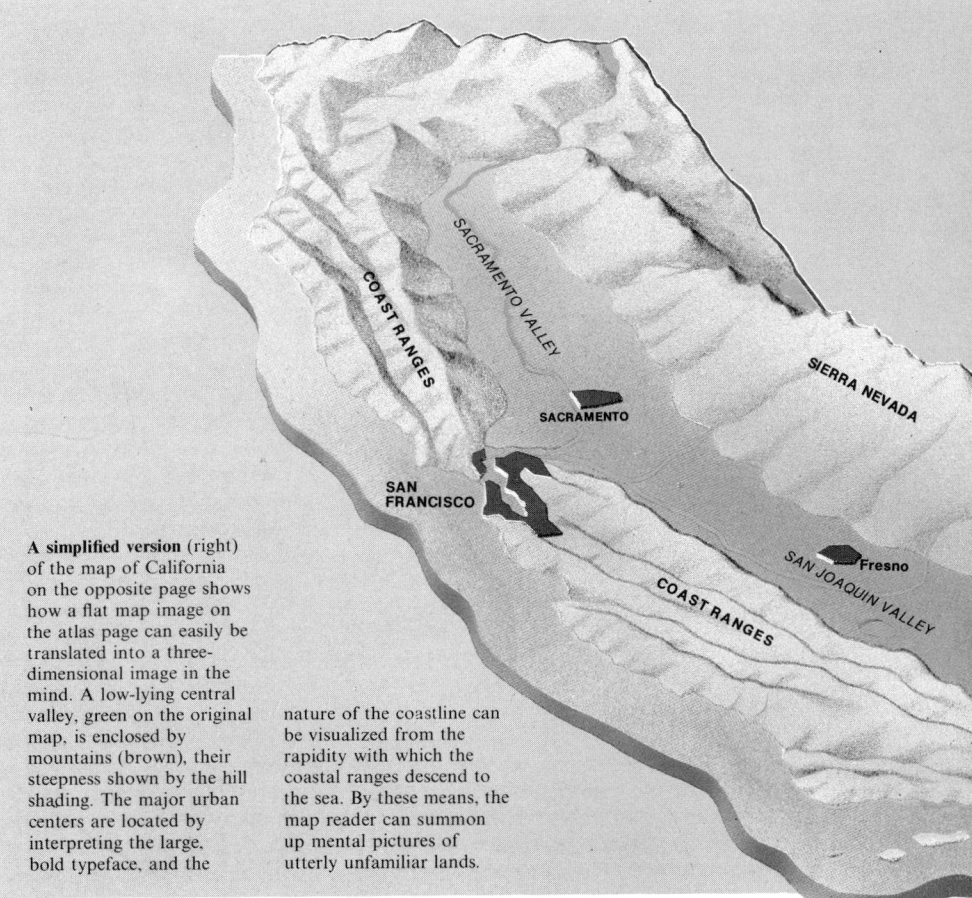

A simplified version (right) of the map of California on the opposite page shows how a flat map image on the atlas page can easily be translated into a three-dimensional image in the mind. A low-lying central valley, green on the original map, is enclosed by mountains (brown), their steepness shown by the hill shading. The major urban centers are located by interpreting the large, bold typeface, and the nature of the coastline can be visualized from the rapidity with which the coastal ranges descend to the sea. By these means, the map reader can summon up mental pictures of utterly unfamiliar lands.

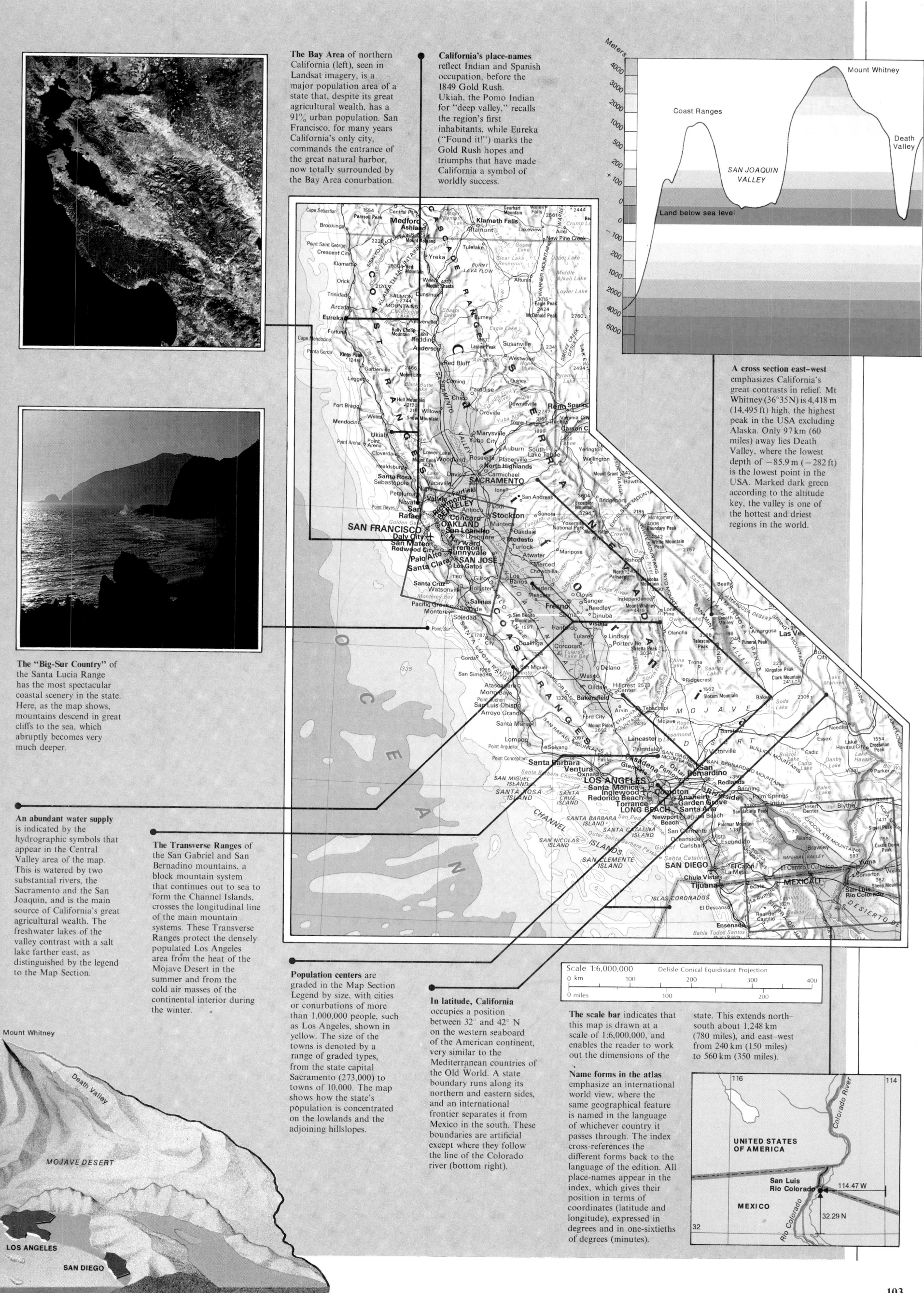

The Bay Area of northern California (left), seen in Landsat imagery, is a major population area of a state that, despite its great agricultural wealth, has a 91% urban population. San Francisco, for many years California's only city, commands the entrance of the great natural harbor, now totally surrounded by the Bay Area conurbation.

California's place-names reflect Indian and Spanish occupation, before the 1849 Gold Rush. Ukiah, the Pomo Indian for "deep valley," recalls the region's first inhabitants, while Eureka ("Found it!") marks the Gold Rush hopes and triumphs that have made California a symbol of worldly success.

A cross section east–west emphasizes California's great contrasts in relief. Mt Whitney (36°35N) is 4,418 m (14,495 ft) high, the highest peak in the USA excluding Alaska. Only 97 km (60 miles) away lies Death Valley, where the lowest depth of −85.9 m (−282 ft) is the lowest point in the USA. Marked dark green according to the altitude key, the valley is one of the hottest and driest regions in the world.

The "Big-Sur Country" of the Santa Lucia Range has the most spectacular coastal scenery in the state. Here, as the map shows, mountains descend in great cliffs to the sea, which abruptly becomes very much deeper.

An abundant water supply is indicated by the hydrographic symbols that appear in the Central Valley area of the map. This is watered by two substantial rivers, the Sacramento and the San Joaquin, and is the main source of California's great agricultural wealth. The freshwater lakes of the valley contrast with a salt lake farther east, as distinguished by the legend to the Map Section.

The Transverse Ranges of the San Gabriel and San Bernadino mountains, a block mountain system that continues out to sea to form the Channel Islands, crosses the longitudinal line of the main mountain systems. These Transverse Ranges protect the densely populated Los Angeles area from the heat of the Mojave Desert in the summer and from the cold air masses of the continental interior during the winter.

Population centers are graded in the Map Section Legend by size, with cities or conurbations of more than 1,000,000 people, such as Los Angeles, shown in yellow. The size of the towns is denoted by a range of graded types, from the state capital Sacramento (273,000) to towns of 10,000. The map shows how the state's population is concentrated on the lowlands and the adjoining hillslopes.

In latitude, California occupies a position between 32° and 42° N on the western seaboard of the American continent, very similar to the Mediterranean countries of the Old World. A state boundary runs along its northern and eastern sides, and an international frontier separates it from Mexico in the south. These boundaries are artificial except where they follow the line of the Colorado river (bottom right).

The scale bar indicates that this map is drawn at a scale of 1:6,000,000, and enables the reader to work out the dimensions of the state. This extends north–south about 1,248 km (780 miles), and east–west from 240 km (150 miles) to 560 km (350 miles).

Name forms in the atlas emphasize an international world view, where the same geographical feature is named in the language of whichever country it passes through. The index cross-references the different forms back to the language of the edition. All place-names appear in the index, which gives their position in terms of coordinates (latitude and longitude), expressed in degrees and in one-sixtieths of degrees (minutes).

Scale 1:6,000,000 Delisle Conical Equidistant Projection

Mount Whitney

Death Valley

MOJAVE DESERT

LOS ANGELES

SAN DIEGO

UNITED STATES OF AMERICA

MEXICO

Colorado River

San Luis Rio Colorado

Rio Colorado

114.47 W

32.29 N

116

114

32

INTERNATIONAL MAP SECTION CREDITS AND ACKNOWLEDGMENTS

Cartographic and Geographic Director
Giuseppe Motta

Geographic Research
G. Baselli
M. Colombo

Toponymy and Translation
C. Carpine
M. Colombo
H. R. Fischer
R. Nuñez de las Cuevas
Rand McNally
Cartographic Research Staff
I. Straube

Computerized Data Organization
C. Bardesono
E. Ciano
G. Comoglio
E. Di Costanzo

Index
S. Osnaghi
T. Tomasini

Cartographic Editor
V. Castelli

Cartographic Compilation
G. Albera
L. Cairo
C. Camera
G. Conti
G. Fizzotti
G. Gambaro
M. Mochetti
O. Passarelli
M. Peretti
G. Rassiga
A. Saino
F. Valsecchi

Terrain Illustration
S. Andenna
E. Ferrari

Cartographic Production
F. Tosi
G. Capitini
A. Carnero

Filmsetting
S. Fiorini
P. L. Gatta
E. Geranio
G. Ghezzi
L. Lorena
R. Martelli
E. Morchio
M. Morganti
C. Pezzana
P. Uglietti
D. Varalli

Photographic Processing
G. Fracassina
G. Klaus
L. Mella

Coordination
S. Binda
L. Pasquali
G. Zanetta

The editors wish to thank the many organizations, institutions and individuals who have given their valuable help and advice during the preparation of this International Map Section. Special thanks are extended to the following:

Agenzia Novosti, Rome, Italy
D. Arnold, Acting Chief of Documentation and Terminology Section, United Nations, New York, USA
Australian Bureau of Statistics, Brisbane, Australia
J. Breu, United Nations Group of Experts on Geographical Names, Vienna, Austria
Bureau Hydrographique International, Monaco, Principality of Monaco
Canada Map Office, Ottawa, Canada
Cartactual, Budapest, Hungary
Census and Statistical Department, Tripoli, Libya
Central Bureau of Statistics, Accra, Ghana
Central Bureau of Statistics, Jerusalem, Israel
Central Bureau of Statistics, Ministry of Economic Planning and Development, Nairobi, Kenya
Central Department of Statistics, Riyadh, Saudi Arabia
Central Statistical Board of the USSR, Moscow, USSR
Central Statistical Office, London, UK
Centro de Informaçao e Documentaçao Estadistica, Rio de Janeiro, Brazil
Committee for the Reform of Chinese Written Language, Peking, China
Danmark Statistik, Copenhagen, Denmark
Defense Mapping Agency, Distribution Office for Latin America, Miami, USA
Defense Mapping Agency, Washington DC, USA
Department of National Development and Energy, Division of National Mapping, Belconnen ACT, Australia
Department of State Coordinator for Maps and Publications, Washington DC, USA
Department of State Map Division, Sofia, Bulgaria
Department of Statistics, Wellington, New Zealand
Direcçao Nacional de Estadistica, Maputo, Mozambique
Dirección de Cartografia Naciónal, Caracas, Venezuela
Dirección de Estadistica y Censo de la Repubblica de Panamá, Panama
Dirección General de Estadistica, Mexico City, Mexico
Dirección General de Estadística y Censos, San Salvador, El Salvador
Direcția Centrala de Statistică, Bucharest, Romania
Directorate of National Mapping, Kuala Lumpur, Malaysia
Directorate of Overseas Surveys, London, UK
Elaborazione Dati e Disegno Automatico, Torino, Italy
Federal Office of Statistics, Lagos, Nigeria
Federal Office of Statistics, Prague, Czechoslovakia
Geographical Research Institute, Hungarian Academy of Sciences, Budapest, Hungary
Geological Map Service, New York, USA
G. Gomez de Silva, Chief Conference Services Section, United Nations Environment Programme, New York, USA
Government of the People's Republic of Bangladesh, Statistics Division, Ministry of Planning, Dacca, Bangladesh
High Commissioner for Trinidad and Tobago, London, UK
L. Iarotski, World Health Organization, Geneva, Switzerland
Information Division, Valletta, Malta
Institut für Angewandte Geodäsie, Frankfurt, West Germany
Institut Géographique, Abidjan, Ivory Coast
Institut Géographique du Zaïre, Kinshasa, Zaïre
Institut Géographique National, Brussels, Belgium
Institut Géographique National, Paris, France
Institut Haïtien de Statistique, Port-au-Prince, Haiti
Institut National de Géodésie et Cartographie, Antananarivo, Madagascar
Institut National de la Statistique, Tunis, Tunisia
Institute of Geography, Polish Academy of Sciences, Warsaw, Poland
Instituto Geográfico Militar, Buenos Aires, Argentina
Instituto Nacional de Estadistica, La Paz, Bolivia
Instituto Nacional de Estadistica, Madrid, Spain
Istituto Centrale di Statistica, Rome, Italy
Istituto Geografico Militare, Florence, Italy
Istituto Idrografico della Marina, Genoa, Italy
Landesverwaltung des Fürstentums, Vaduz, Liechtenstein
Ministère des Affaires Economiques, Brussels, Belgium
Ministère des Ressources Naturelles, des Mines et des Carrières, Kigali, Rwanda
Ministère des Travaux Publics, des Transports et de l'Urbanisme, Ouagadougou, Upper Volta
Ministry of Finance, Department of Statistics and Research, Nicosia, Cyprus

Ministry of Lands, Housing and Urban Development, Surveys and Mapping Division, Dar es Salaam, Tanzania
Ministry of the Interior, Jerusalem, Israel
National Census and Statistics Office, Manila, Philippines
National Central Bureau of Statistics, Stockholm, Sweden
National Geographic Society, Washington DC, USA
National Institute of Polar Research, Tokyo, Japan
National Ocean Survey, Riverdale, Maryland, USA
National Statistical Institute, Lisbon, Portugal
National Statistical Office, Zomba, Malawi
National Statistical Service of Greece, Athens, Greece
J. Novotny, Prague, Czechoslovakia
Office Nationale de la Recherche Scientifique et Technique, Yaoundé, Cameroon
Officina Comercial del Gobierno de Colombia, Rome, Italy
Ordnance Survey of Ireland, Dublin, Ireland
Österreichisches Statistisches Zentralamt, Vienna, Austria
Państwowe Przedsiebiorstwo Wydawnictw Kartograficznych, Warsaw, Poland
Scott Polar Research Institute, University of Cambridge, Cambridge, UK
Secrétariat d'Etat au Plan, Algiers, Algeria
Servicio Geografico Militar, Montevideo, Uruguay
Z. Shiying, Research Institute of Surveying and Mapping, Peking, China
Statistisches Bundesamt, Wiesbaden, West Germany
Statistisk Sentralbyrå, Oslo, Norway
Survey and National Mapping Department, Kuala Lumpur, Malaysia
Ufficio Turismo e Informazioni della Turchia, Rome, Italy
United States Board on Geographic Names, Washington DC, USA
M. C. Wu, Chinese Translation Service, United Nations, New York, USA
Z. Youguang, Committee for the Reform of Chinese Written Language, Peking, China

The editors are also grateful for the assistance provided by the following embassies, consulates and official state representatives:

Angolan Embassy, Rome
Australian Embassy, Rome
Austrian Embassy, Rome
Embassy of Bangladesh, Rome
Embassy of Botswana, Brussels
Brazilian Embassy, Rome
British Embassy, Rome
Burmese Embassy, Rome
Embassy of Cameroon, Rome
Embassy of Cape Verde, Lisbon
Consulate of Chad, Rome
Chilean Embassy, Rome
Embassy of the People's Republic of China in Italy, Rome
Danish Embassy, Rome
Embassy of El Salvador, Rome
Ethiopian Embassy, Rome
Finnish Embassy, Rome
Embassy of the German Democratic Republic, Rome
Greek Embassy, Rome
Honduras Republic Embassy, Rome
Hungarian Embassy, Rome
Consulate General of Iceland, Rome
Embassy of India, Rome
Embassy of the Republic of Indonesia, Rome
Embassy of the Islamic Republic of Iran, Rome

Irish Embassy, Rome
Embassy of Israel, Rome
Japanese Embassy, Rome
Korean Embassy, Rome
Luxembourg Embassy, Rome
Embassy of Malta, Rome
Mexican Embassy, Rome
Moroccan Embassy, Rome
Netherlands Embassy, Rome
Embassy of New Zealand, Rome
Embassy of Niger, Rome
Embassy of Pakistan, Rome
Peruvian Embassy, Rome
Philippine Embassy, Rome
Romanian Embassy, Rome
Somali Embassy, Rome
South African Embassy, Rome
Spanish Embassy, Rome
Consulate General of Switzerland, Milan
Royal Thai Embassy, Rome
Consulate of Upper Volta, Rome
Uruguay Embassy, Rome
Embassy of the Socialist Republic of Vietnam in Italy, Rome
Permanent Mission of Yemen to United Nations Educational, Scientific and Cultural Organization, Paris

INTERNATIONAL MAP SECTION

Hydrographic and Topographic Features
Symboles hydrographiques et morphologiques
Gewässer- und Geländeformen
Idrografia, Morfologia
Hidrografía y morfología

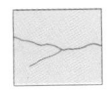

River, Stream
Cours d'eau permanent
Ständig wasserführender Fluß
Corso d'acqua perenne
Corriente de agua de régimen permanente

Intermittent Stream
Cours d'eau intermittent
Zeitweilig wasserführender Fluß
Corso d'acqua periodico
Corriente de agua intermitente

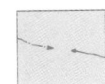

Disappearing Stream
Perte de cours d'eau
Versickernder Fluß
Corso d'acqua che si inabissa
Corriente de agua que desaparece

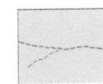

Undefined or Fluctuating River Course
Cours d'eau incertain
Fluß mit veränderlichem Lauf
Fiume dal corso incerto
Corriente de agua incerta

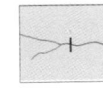

Waterfall, Rapids, Cataract
Chute, Rapide, Cataracte
Wasserfall, Stromschnelle, Katarakt
Cascata, Rapida, Cateratta
Cascada, Rapido, Catarata

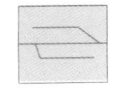

Canal
Canal
Kanal
Canale
Canal

Navigable Canal
Canal navigable
Schiffbarer Kanal
Canale navigabile
Canal navegable

Swamp
Marais
Sumpf
Palude d'acqua dolce
Pantano

Salt Marsh
Marais d'eau salée
Salzsumpf
Palude d'acqua salata
Pantano de agua salada

Salt Pan
Marais salant
Salzpfanne
Salina
Salina

Lake
Lac d'eau douce
Süßwassersee
Lago d'acqua dolce
Lago de agua dulce

Intermittent Lake
Lac d'eau douce temporaire
Zeitweiliger Süßwassersee
Lago d'acqua dolce periodico
Lago de agua dulce intermitente

Salt Lake
Lac d'eau salée
Salzsee
Lago d'acqua salata
Lago de agua salada

Intermittent Salt Lake
Lac d'eau salée temporaire
Zeitweiliger Salzsee
Lago d'acqua salata periodico
Lago de agua salada intermitente

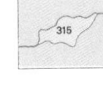

Dry Lake Bed
Lac asséché
Trockener Seeboden
Alveo di lago asciutto
Lecho de lago seco

Lake Surface Elevation
Cote du lac au-dessus du niveau de la mer
Höhe des Seespiegels
Altitudine del lago
Elevación de lago sobre el nivel del mar

Lake Depth
Profondeur du lac
Seetiefe
Profondità del lago
Profundidad del lago

Sand Area
Région de sable, Désert
Sandgebiet, Sandwüste
Area sabbiosa, Deserto
Zona arenosa, desierto

Sandbank, Sandbar
Banc de sable
Sandbank
Bassofondo sabbioso
Banco submarino de arena

Port Facilities
Installations portuaires
Hafenanlagen
Impianti portuali
Instalaciones portuarias

Rocks
Écueils, Roches
Klippen, Felsriffe
Scogli, Rocce
Escollos, Rocas

Reef, Atoll
Barrière, Atoll
Riff, Atoll
Barriera, Atollo
Barrera de arrecifes

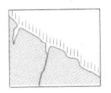

Mangrove
Mangrove
Mangrove
Mangrovie
Manglar

Continental Ice-cap
Glacier continental
Inlandeis, Gletscher
Ghiacciaio continentale
Glaciar continental

Glacial Tongue
Langue glaciaire
Gletscherzunge
Lingua di ghiaccio
Lengua de glaciar

Rocky Areas (Antarctica)
Région de roches (Antarctique)
Eisfreie Gebiete (Antarktika)
Aree rocciose (Antartide)
Area rocosa (Antártida)

Defined Shoreline
Trait de côte définie
Küsten- oder Uferlinie
Linea di costa definita
Línea de costa definida

Undefined or Fluctuating Shoreline
Trait de côte indéfinie
Unbestimmte oder veränderliche Uferlinie
Linea di costa indefinita
Línea de costa indefinida

Mountain Range
Chaîne de montagnes
Bergkette
Catena di monti
Cadena montañosa

Elevation
Cote, Altitude
Höhenzahl
Quota altimetrica
Cota altimétrica

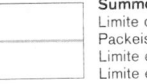

Summer Limit of Pack Ice
Limite du pack en été
Packeisgrenze im Sommer
Limite estivo del pack ghiacciato
Límite estival de banco de hielo

Winter Limit of Pack Ice
Limite du pack en hiver
Packeisgrenze im Winter
Limite invernale del pack ghiacciato
Límite invernal de banco de hielo

Limit of Icebergs
Limite des glaces flottantes
Treibeisgrenze
Limite dei ghiacci alla deriva
Límite de hielo a la deriva

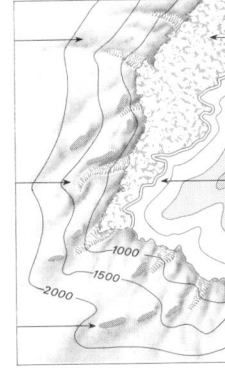

Ice Shelf
Banquise
Schelfeis oder Eisschelf
Banchisa polare (Ice-shelf)
Banquisa

Limit of Ice Shelf
Limite de la banquise
Schelfeisgrenze
Limite della banchisa
Límite de la banquisa

Contour Lines in Continental Ice
Courbes de niveau dans les régions glaciaires
Höhenlinien auf vergletschertem Gebiet
Curve altimetriche nelle aree ghiacciate
Curvas de nivel en áreas heladas

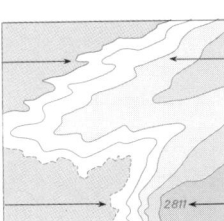

Bathymetric Contour
Courbe bathymétrique
Tiefenlinie
Curva batimetrica
Curva batimétrica

Depth of Water
Valeur de sonde
Tiefenzahl
Quota batimetrica
Cota batimétrica

Mountain
Mont
Berg, Bergmassiv
Monte
Monte

Mountain Pass, Gap
Passage, Col, Port
Paß, Joch, Sattel
Passo, Colle, Valico
Paso, Collado, Puerto de montaña

Key to Elevation and Depth Tints
Hypsométrie, Bathymétrie
Höhenstufen, Tiefenstufen
Altimetria, Batimetria
Altimetría, Batimetría

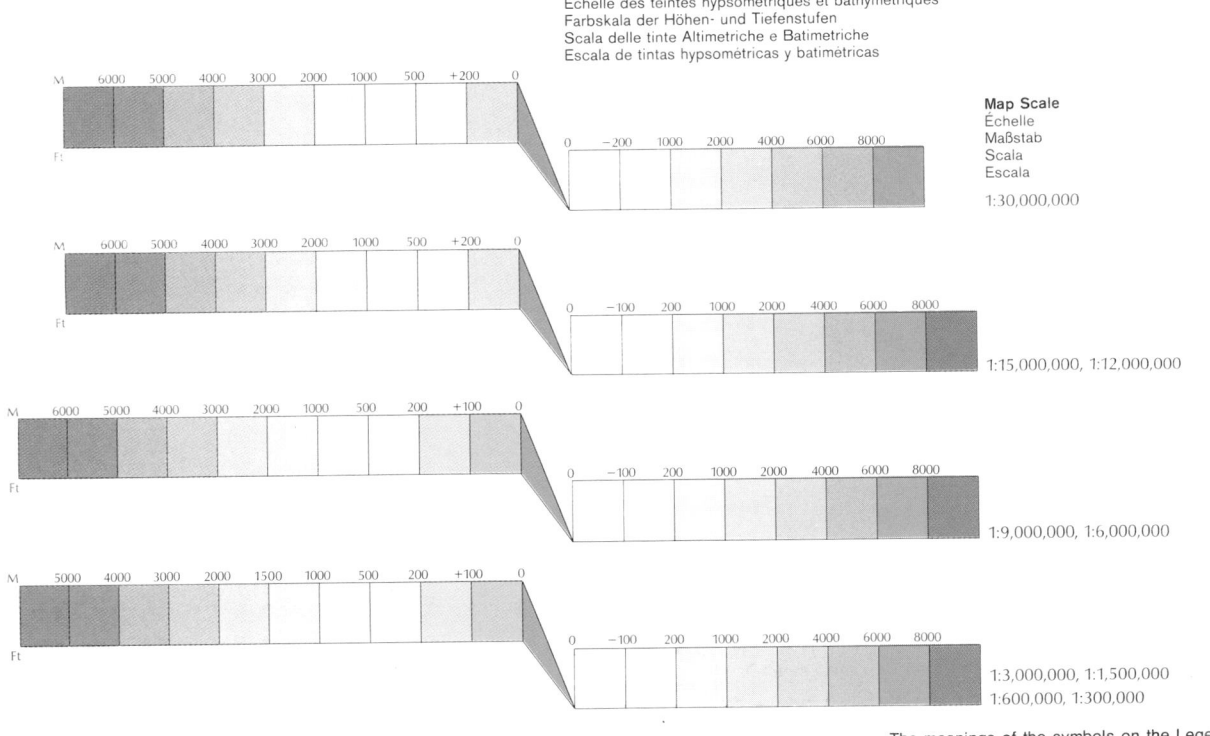

Scales in Metric and English Measures
Échelle des teintes hypsométriques et bathymétriques
Farbskala der Höhen- und Tiefenstufen
Scala delle tinte Altimetriche e Batimetriche
Escala de tintas hypsométricas y batimetricas

Land Elevation Below Sea Level
Dépression et cote au-dessous du niveau de la mer
Senke mit Tiefenzahl unter dem Meeresspiegel
Depressione e quota sotto il livello del mare
Depresión y elevación bajo el nivel del mar

Map Scale
Échelle
Maßstab
Scala
Escala

1:30,000,000

1:15,000,000, 1:12,000,000

1:9,000,000, 1:6,000,000

1:3,000,000, 1:1,500,000
1:600,000, 1:300,000

Map Projections
Projections cartographiques
Kartennetzentwürfe
Proiezioni cartografiche
Proyecciones cartográficas

The projections appearing in this atlas have been plotted by computer

Les réseaux des projections ont été obtenus par élaboration automatique à partir de formules mathématiques

Die Kartennetze aller im Atlas vorkommenden Abbildungen wurden mit Hilfe der Datenverarbeitung (EDV) völlig neu errechnet

I disegni delle proiezioni presenti in quest'opera sono stati realizzati interamente ex-novo con l'uso del computer e del plotter a partire dalle formule matematiche

El reticulado de las proyecciones (redes geográficas) incluidas en esta obra han sido obtenidas por proceso automático a partir de las formulas matemáticas

The meanings of the symbols on the Legend pages are in English, French, German, Italian, and Spanish languages to permit the interpretation of the maps by a broad readership.

Boundaries, Capitals
Frontières, Soulignements — Confini, Sottolineature
Grenzen, Unterstreichungen — Límites, Subrayados

Defined International Boundary
Frontière internationale définie
Staatsgrenze
Confine di Stato definito
Límite de Nación definido

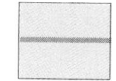

Second-order Political Boundary
Frontière d'État fédéré, Région
Bundesstaats-, Regionsgrenze
Confine di Stato federato, Regione
Límite de Estado federado, Región

International Boundary (Continent Maps)
Frontière internationale (Continents)
Staatsgrenze (Erdteilkarten)
Confine di Stato (Carte dei Continenti)
Límite de Nación (Continentes)

Third-order Political Boundary
Frontière de Province, Comté, Bezirk
Provinz-, Grafschafts-, Bezirksgrenze
Confine di Provincia, Contea, Bezirk
Límite de Provincia, Condado, Bezirk

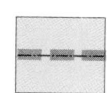

Undefined International Boundary
Frontière internationale indéfinie
Nicht genau festgelegte Staatsgrenze
Confine di Stato indefinito
Límite de Nación indefinido

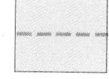

Administrative District Boundary (U.S.S.R.)
Frontière de Circonscription
Kreisgrenze
Confine di Circondario
Límite de Circunscripción administrativa

International Ocean Floor Boundary Defined by Treaty or Bilateral Agreement
Frontière d'état en mer définie par traités et conventions bilatéraux
Durch Verträge festgelegte Staatsgrenze im Meeresgebiet
Confine di Stato nel mare definito da trattati e convenzioni bilaterali
Límite de Nación en el Mar definido por los tratados bilaterales

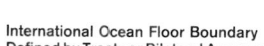

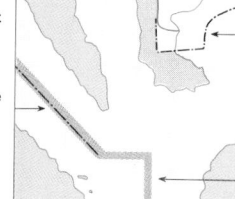

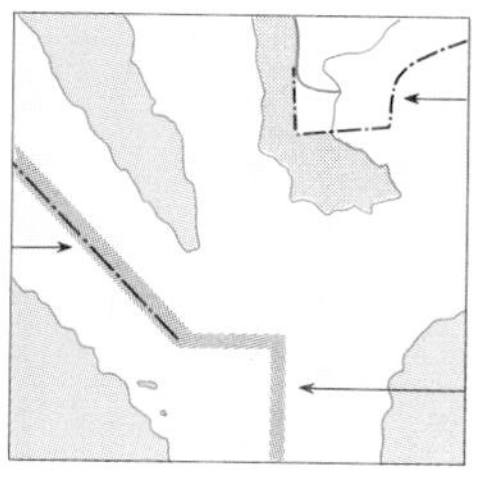

International Ocean Floor Boundary
Frontière d'état en mer
Staatsgrenze im Meeresgebiet
Confine di Stato nel mare
Límite de Nación en el mar

Undefined Ocean Floor Boundary
Frontière indéfinie d'état tracée en meer
Unbstimmte Staatsgrenze im Meeresgebiet
Confine di Stato indefinito nel mare
Límite indefinido de Nación en el mar

ROMA — **National Capital**
Capitale d'État
Hauptstadt eines unabhängigen Staates
Capitale di Stato
Capital de Nación

Kristiansand — **Third - order Capital**
Capitale de Province, Comté, Bezirk
Provinz-, Grafschafts-, Bezirkshauptstadt
Capoluogo di Provincia, Contea, Bezirk
Capital de Provincia, Condado, Bezirk

RIGA — **Dependency or Second-order Capital**
Capitale d'État fédéré, Région
Bundesstaats-, Regionshauptstadt
Capitale di Stato federato, Regione
Capital de Estado federado, Región

Anadyr — **Administrative District Capital (U.S.S R.)**
Capitale de Circonscription
Kreishauptstadt
Capoluogo di Circondario
Capital de Circunscripción administrativa

Other Symbols
Symboles divers — Simboli vari
Sonstige Zeichen — Signos varios

LUTON AIRPORT — **International Airport**
Aéroport international
Internationaler Flughafen
Aeroporto internazionale
Aeropuerto internacional

SANTAS CREUS — **Church, Monastery, Abbey**
Monastère, Église, Abbaye
Kloster, Kirche, Abtei
Monastero, Chiesa, Abbazia
Monasterio, Iglesia, Abadía

Lighthouse
Phare
Leuchtturm
Faro
Faro

DAMPIERRE — **Castle**
Château
Burg, Schloß
Castello
Castillo

BUI DAM — **Dam**
Barrage
Staudamm, Staumauer
Diga artificiale, Sbarramento
Presa

PAESTUM — **Ruin, Archeological Site**
Ruine, Centre archéologique
Ruine, Archäologisches Zentrum
Rovina, Zona archeologica
Ruina, Zona arqueológica

L.-GREENWICH, V.-IJmuiden — **Section of a City**
Faubourg
Stadt- oder Ortsteil
Sobborgo urbano
Suburbio

MOLENS VAN KINDERDIJK — **Monument, Historic Site, etc.**
Monument
Denkmal
Monumento
Monumento

Bidon V — **Uninhabited Locality, Hamlet**
Ville inhabitée, Ferme, Hameau
Unbewohnte Stadt, Gehöft, Weiler
Città disabitata, Fattoria, Nucleo di case
Ciudad despoblada, Granja, Casar

HADRIAN'S WALL — **Wall**
Muraille
Wall, Mauer
Vallo, Muraglia
Muralla

Bi'r Nāhid — **Periodically Inhabited Oasis**
Oasis habitées périodiquement
Zeitweilig bewohnte Oase
Oasi periodicamente abitate
Oasis periódicamente habitados

GIANT'S CAUSEWAY — **Point of Interest**
Curiosité
Sehenswürdigkeit
Curiosità
Curiosidad

Casey (Australia) — **Scientific Station**
Base géophysique
Geophysikalische Beobachtungsstation
Base geofisica
Base geofísica

CUEVAS DE ARTÁ — **Cave**
Grotte, Caverne
Höhle
Grotta, Caverna
Cueva, Gruta

Populated Places
Population — Popolazione
Bevölkerung — Población

Continent Maps
Cartes des Continents — Carte dei Continenti
Erdteilkarten — Mapas de Continentes
< 25 000
25 000-100 000
100 000-250 000
250 000-1 000 000
> 1 000 000

Regional Maps
Cartes à plus grande échelle — Carte di sviluppo
Karten größeren Maßstabs — Mapas a gran escala
< 10 000
10 000-25 000
25 000-100 000
100 000-250 000
250 000-1 000 000
> 1 000 000

Symbols represent population of inhabited localities
Les symboles représentent le nombre d'habitants des localités
Die Signaturen entsprechen der Einwohnerzahl des Ortes
I simboli sono relativi al valore demografico dei centri abitati
Los símbolos son proporcionales a la población del lugar

Town area symbol represents the shape of the urban area
Le petit plan de la ville reproduit la configuration de l'aire urbaine
Die Plansignatur stellt die Gestalt des Stadtgebietes dar
La piantina della città rappresenta la configurazione dell'area urbana
El pequeño plano de la ciudad representa la forma del area urbana

Transportation
Communications — Comunicazioni
Verkehrsnetz — Comunicaciones

Primary Railway
Chemin de fer principal
Hauptbahn
Ferrovia principale
Ferrocarril principal

Secondary Railway
Chemin de fer secondaire
Sonstige Bahn
Ferrovia secondaria
Ferrocarril secundario

Motorway, Expressway
Autoroute
Autobahn
Autostrada
Autopista

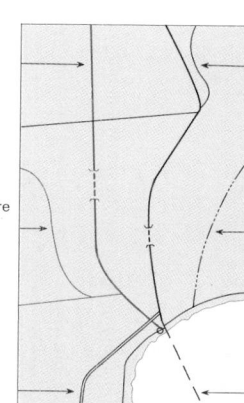

Road
Route de grande communication, Autres Routes
Fernverkehrsstraße, andere Straßen
Strada principale, Altre Strade
Carretera principal, Otras Carreteras

Trail, Caravan Route
Piste, Voie caravanière
Wüstenpiste, Karawanenweg
Pista nel deserto, Carovaniera
Pista en el desierto, Vía de Carabanas

Ferry, Shipping Lane
Bac, Ligne maritime
Fähre, Schiffahrtslinie
Traghetto, Linea di navigazione
Transbordador (Ferry), Línea de navegación

Type Styles
Caractères utilisés pour la toponymie — Caratteri usati per la toponomastica
Zur Namenschreibung verwendete Schriftarten — Caracteres utilizados para la toponimia

ITALY / Hessen RIBE — **Political Units**
Etat, Dépendance, Division administrative
Staat, abhängiges Gebiet, Verwaltungsgliederung
Stato, Dipendenza, Divisione amministrativa
Nación, Dependencia, División administrativa

Ankaratra, Monte Bianco, Tsiafajavona, Ngorongoro Crater, Nevado del Tolima, Kings Peak — **Small Mountain Range, Mountain, Peak**
Petit massif, Mont, Cime
Bergmassiv, Berg, Gipfel
Piccolo gruppo montuoso, Monte, Vetta
Macizo pequeño, Monte, Cima

LABRADOR SEA, Gulf of Alaska, Hudson Bay, Estrecho de Magallanes — **Sea, Gulf, Bay, Strait**
Mer, Golfe, Baie, Détroit
Meer, Golf, Bucht, Meeresstraße
Mare, Golfo, Baia, Stretto
Mar, Golfo, Bahía, Estrecho

SAXONY / THRACE SUSSEX — **Historical or Cultural Region**
Région historique ou culturelle
Historische oder Kulturlandschaft
Regione storico - culturale
Región histórica y cultural

Cabo de São Vicente, Land's End, Mizen Head, Point Conception, Col de la Perche, Passo della Cisa — **Cape, Point, Pass**
Cap, Pointe, Passe
Kap, Landspitze, Paß
Capo, Punta, Passo
Cabo, Punta, Paso

West Mariana Basin, Galapagos Fracture Zone, Mid-Atlantic Ridge — **Undersea Features**
Formes du relief sous-marin
Formen des Meeresbodens
Forme del rilievo sottomarino
Formas del relieve submarino

PATAGONIA / BASSIN DE RENNES / PENÍNSULA DE YUCATÁN — **Physical Region (plain, peninsula)**
Région physique (plaine, péninsule)
Landschaft (Ebene, Halbinsel)
Regione fisica (pianura, penisola)
Región natural (llanura, península)

MAHÉ, ALDABRA ISLANDS, CORSE, CHANNEL ISLANDS, SULU ARCHIPELAGO — **Island, Archipelago**
Ile, Archipel
Insel, Archipel
Isola, Arcipelago
Isla, Archipiélago

Tarfaya, Tombouctou, Agadir, Nouakchott, BRAZZAVILLE, CASABLANCA — **Size of type indicates relative importance of inhabited localities**
La dimension des caractères indique l'importance d'une localité
Die Schriftgröße entspricht der Gesamtbedeutung des Ortes
La grandezza del carattere è proporzionale all'importanza della località
La dimensión de los caracteres de imprenta indica la importancia de la localidad

PYRENEES / CUMBRIAN MOUNTAINS / SIERRA DE GÁDOR, LA SILA — **Mountain Range**
Chaîne de montagnes
Bergkette, Gebirge
Catena di monti
Cadena montañosa

Thames, Po, Victoria Falls, Lotagipi Swamp, Göta kanal, Lago Maggiore — **River, Waterfall, Cataract, Canal, Lake**
Fleuve, Chute d'eau, Cataracte, Canal, Lac
Fluß, Wasserfall, Katarakt, Kanal, See
Fiume, Cascata, Cateratta, Canale, Lago
Río, Cascada, Catarata, Canal, Lago

INDEX MAPS

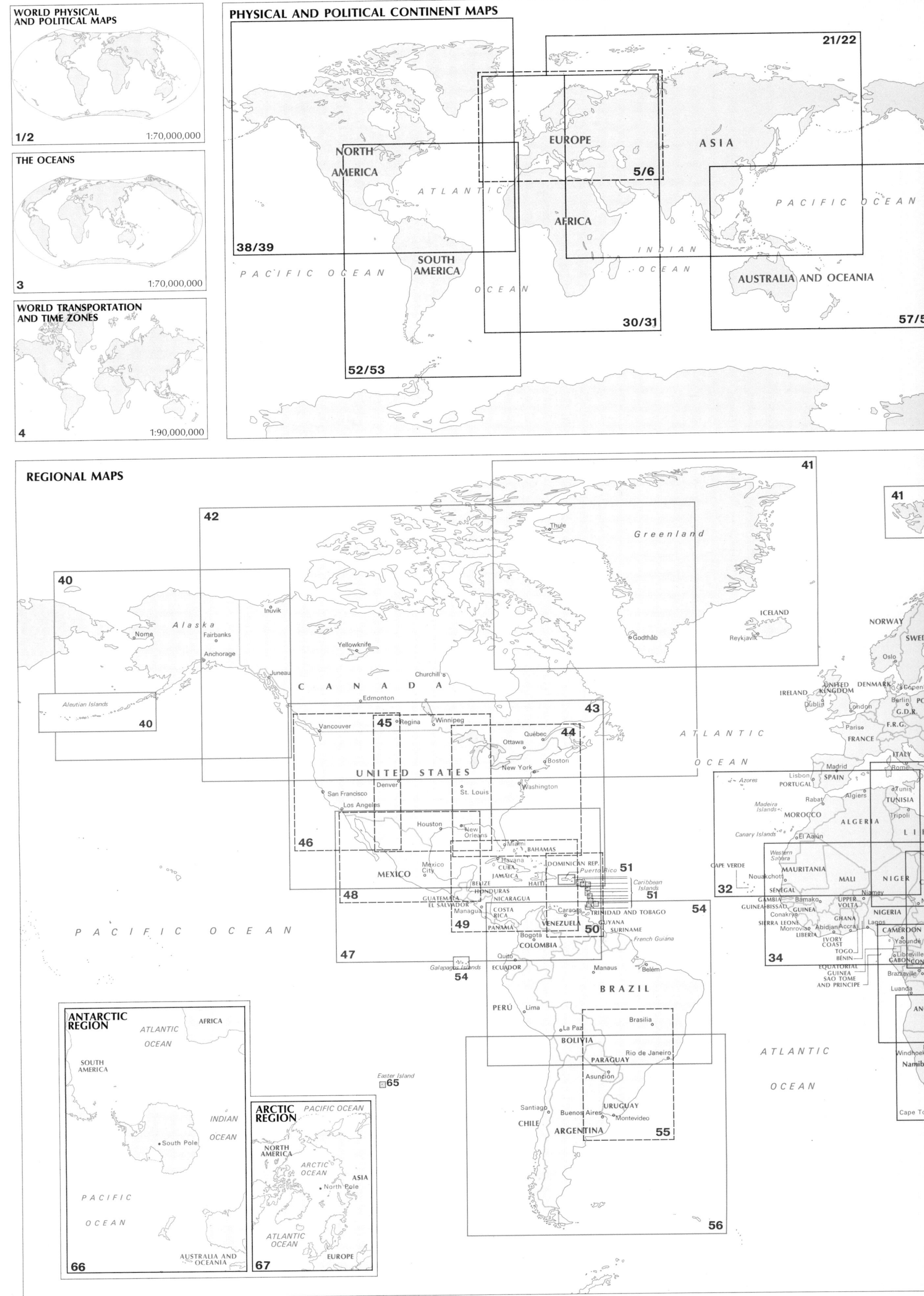

WORLD PHYSICAL AND POLITICAL MAPS

1/2   1:70,000,000

THE OCEANS

3   1:70,000,000

WORLD TRANSPORTATION AND TIME ZONES

4   1:90,000,000

PHYSICAL AND POLITICAL CONTINENT MAPS

21/22

NORTH AMERICA

EUROPE
5/6

ASIA

ATLANTIC

PACIFIC OCEAN

AFRICA

INDIAN OCEAN

38/39

SOUTH AMERICA

PACIFIC OCEAN

AUSTRALIA AND OCEANIA

OCEAN

30/31

57/5

52/53

REGIONAL MAPS

41

41

42

40

Alaska

Nome   Inuvik
Fairbanks
Anchorage
Yellowknife
Juneau   Churchill

Aleutian Islands

40

Thule   Greenland

ICELAND
Godthåb   Reykjavik

NORWAY   SWED

Oslo

IRELAND   UNITED   DENMARK
KINGDOM
Dublin   London   Berlin   POL
G.D.R.
FRANCE   F.R.G.

CANADA

Edmonton

43

45   Regina   Winnipeg   44
Vancouver   Ottawa   Québec
UNITED STATES   New York   Boston
Denver   Washington
San Francisco   St. Louis
Los Angeles

46   Houston   New
Orleans   Miami
BAHAMAS
Mexico   CUBA   Havana
City   DOMINICAN REP.
Puerto Rico
MEXICO   BELIZE   JAMAICA   51
48   HONDURAS   HAITI   Caribbean   51
GUATEMALA   NICARAGUA   Islands
EL SALVADOR   COSTA   Trinidad and tobago   54
49   Managua   RICA   Caracas
PANAMÁ   VENEZUELA   50   SURINAME
COLOMBIA   GUYANA
47   Bogotá   French Guiana
Quito   ECUADOR
Galapagos Islands   54
54   Manaus   Belém

BRAZIL

PERÚ   Lima

Brasilia
La Paz
BOLIVIA
PARAGUAY   Rio de Janeiro

Easter Island
65

Asunción

URUGUAY

Santiago   Buenos Aires
Montevideo
CHILE   ARGENTINA   55

56

PACIFIC   OCEAN

ATLANTIC   OCEAN

Madrid   Lisbon   Rome
Azores   PORTUGAL   SPAIN   ITALY
Algiers   Tunis
Rabat   TUNISIA
Madeira   MOROCCO
Islands   ALGERIA   Tripoli
Canary Islands   El Aaiún   LIB
Western
Sahara
CAPE VERDE   MAURITANIA
32   Nouakchott
MALI   NIGER   N
GAMBIA   Bamako   UPPER
SENEGAL   VOLTA   Niamey
GUINEA-BISSAU   GUINEA   NIGERIA
SIERRA LEONE   Conakry   GHANA
Monrovia   Abidjan   Accra   CAMEROON
LIBERIA   IVORY   Lagos
COAST   TOGO   Yaoundé
34   BÉNIN   Libreville   GONG
EQUATORIAL   GABON   K
GUINEA
SAO TOME   Brazzaville
AND PRINCIPE   Luanda
ANG

ATLANTIC

OCEAN

Windhoek   BO
Namibia

Cape Tow

ANTARCTIC REGION

AFRICA
ATLANTIC
OCEAN

SOUTH
AMERICA

INDIAN
OCEAN

South Pole

PACIFIC

OCEAN

66   AUSTRALIA AND
OCEANIA

ARCTIC REGION

PACIFIC OCEAN

NORTH
AMERICA
ARCTIC
OCEAN

North Pole   ASIA

ATLANTIC
OCEAN

67   EUROPE

REGIONAL MAPS OF EUROPE

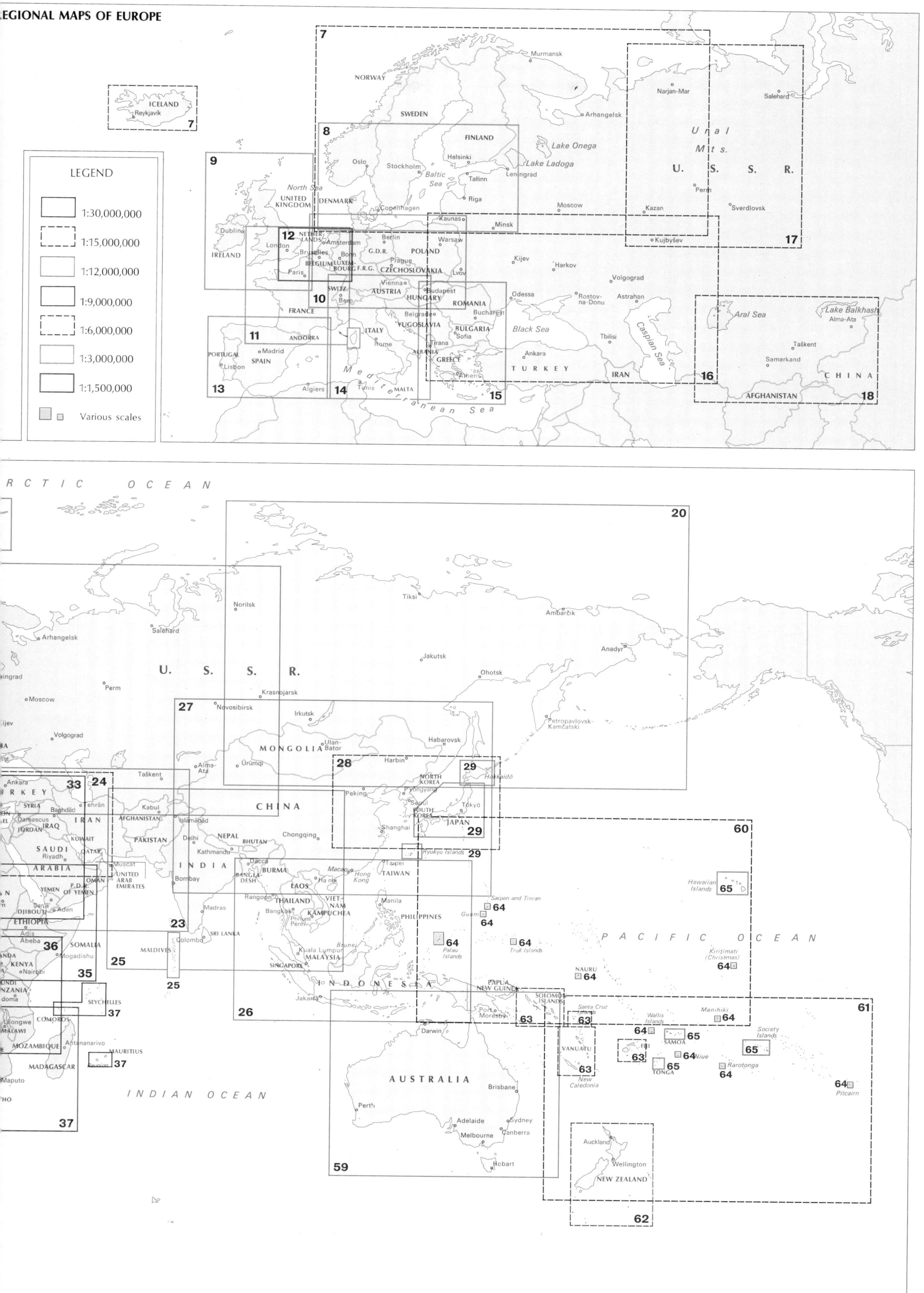

LEGEND

☐	1:30,000,000
☐	1:15,000,000
☐	1:12,000,000
☐	1:9,000,000
☐	1:6,000,000
☐	1:3,000,000
☐	1:1,500,000
☐	Various scales

Map 1 **WORLD, PHYSICAL**

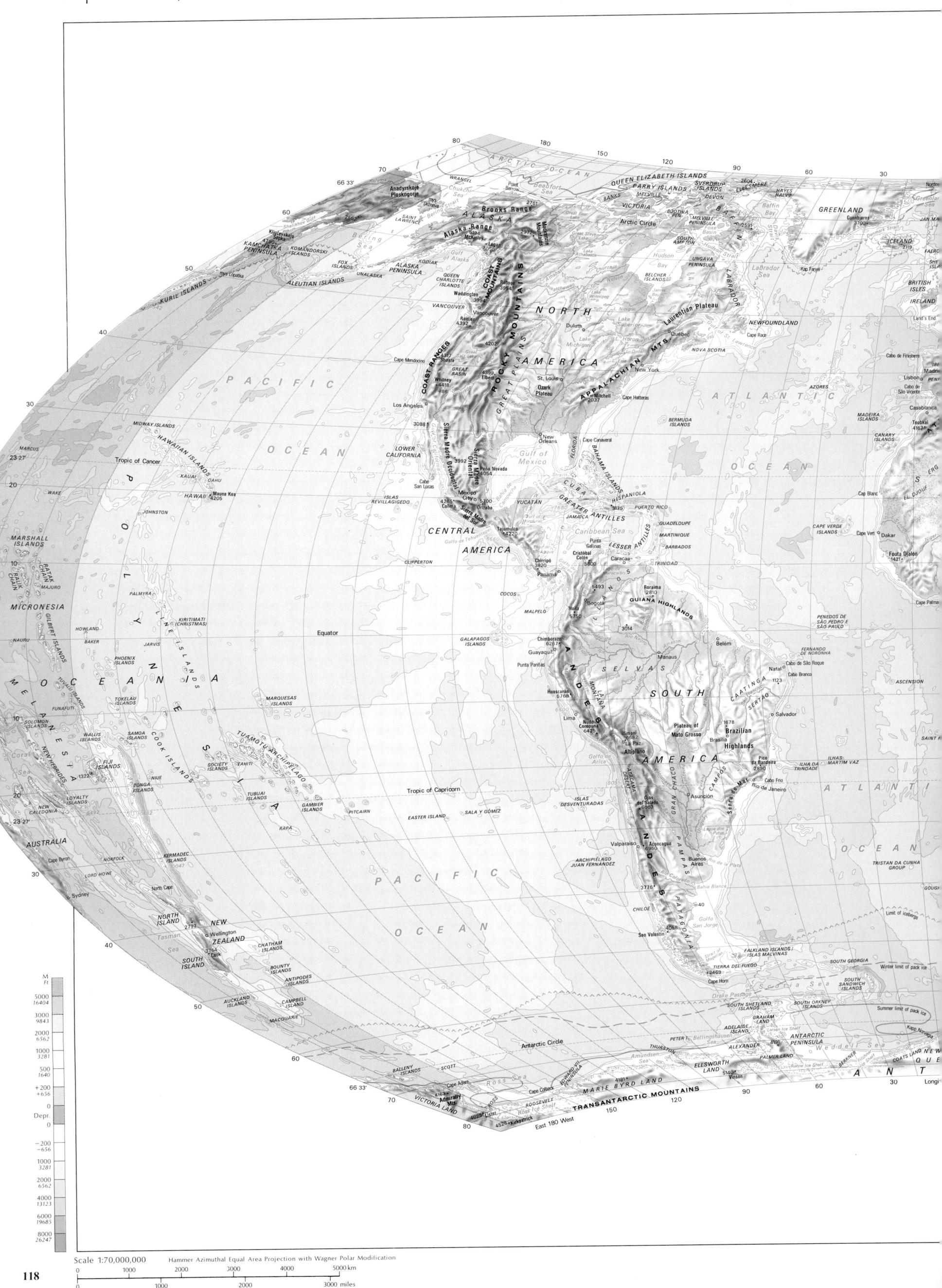

Scale 1:70,000,000   Hammer Azimuthal Equal Area Projection with Wagner Polar Modification

| 0 | 1000 | 2000 | 3000 | 4000 | 5000 km |
| 0 | | 1000 | 2000 | | 3000 miles |

Map 2 **WORLD, POLITICAL**

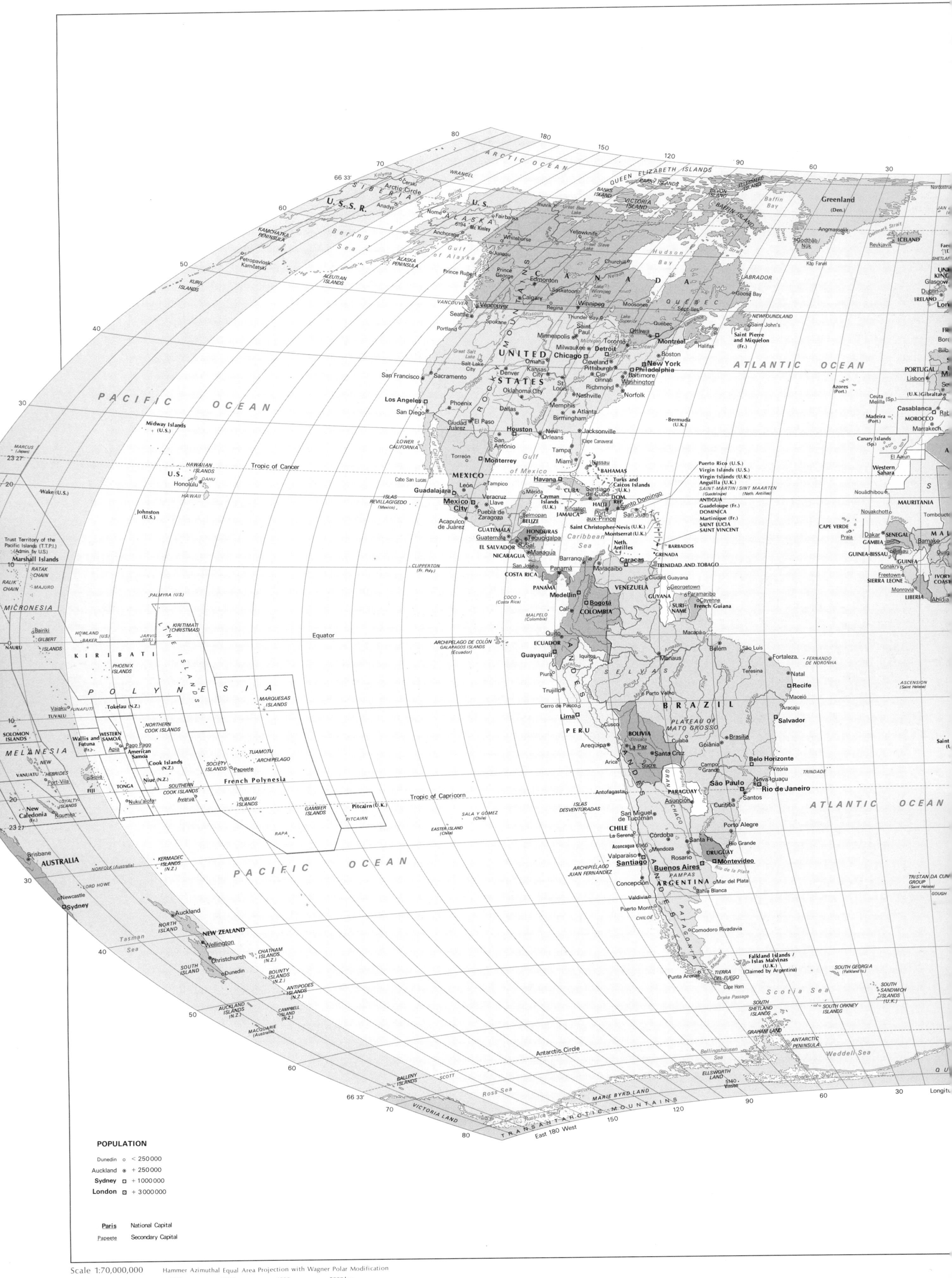

POPULATION

Dunedin ○ < 250 000
Auckland ⊛ + 250 000
Sydney □ + 1 000 000
London ◻ + 3 000 000

Paris National Capital
Papeete Secondary Capital

Scale 1:70,000,000   Hammer Azimuthal Equal Area Projection with Wagner Polar Modification

0   1000   2000   3000   4000   5000 km

0   1000   2000   3000 miles

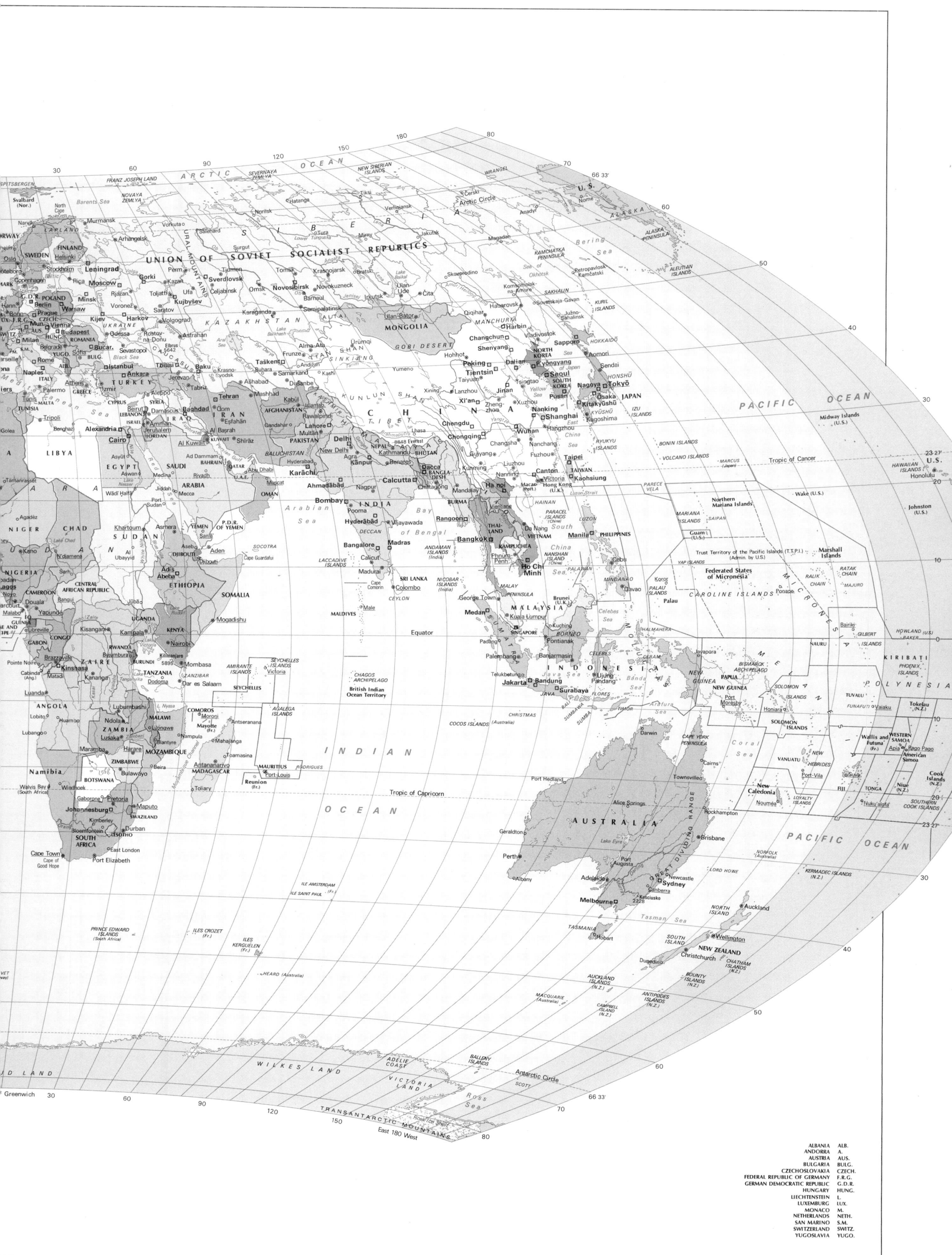

Map 3 **THE OCEANS**

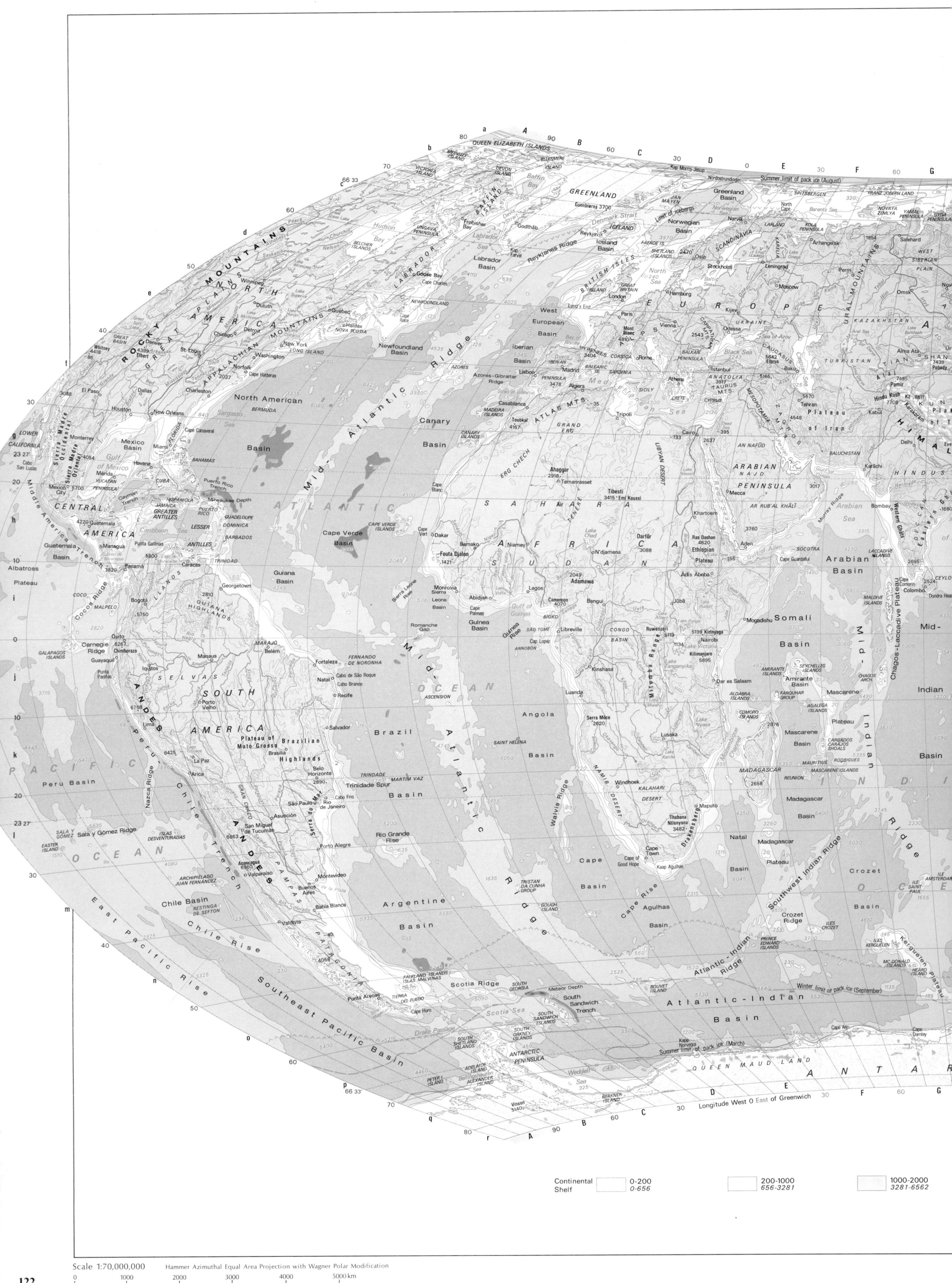

Continental Shelf
| | 0-200 | 200-1000 | 1000-2000 |
| | 0-656 | 656-3281 | 3281-6562 |

Scale 1:70,000,000   Hammer Azimuthal Equal Area Projection with Wagner Polar Modification

0   1000   2000   3000   4000   5000 km

0   1000   2000   3000 miles

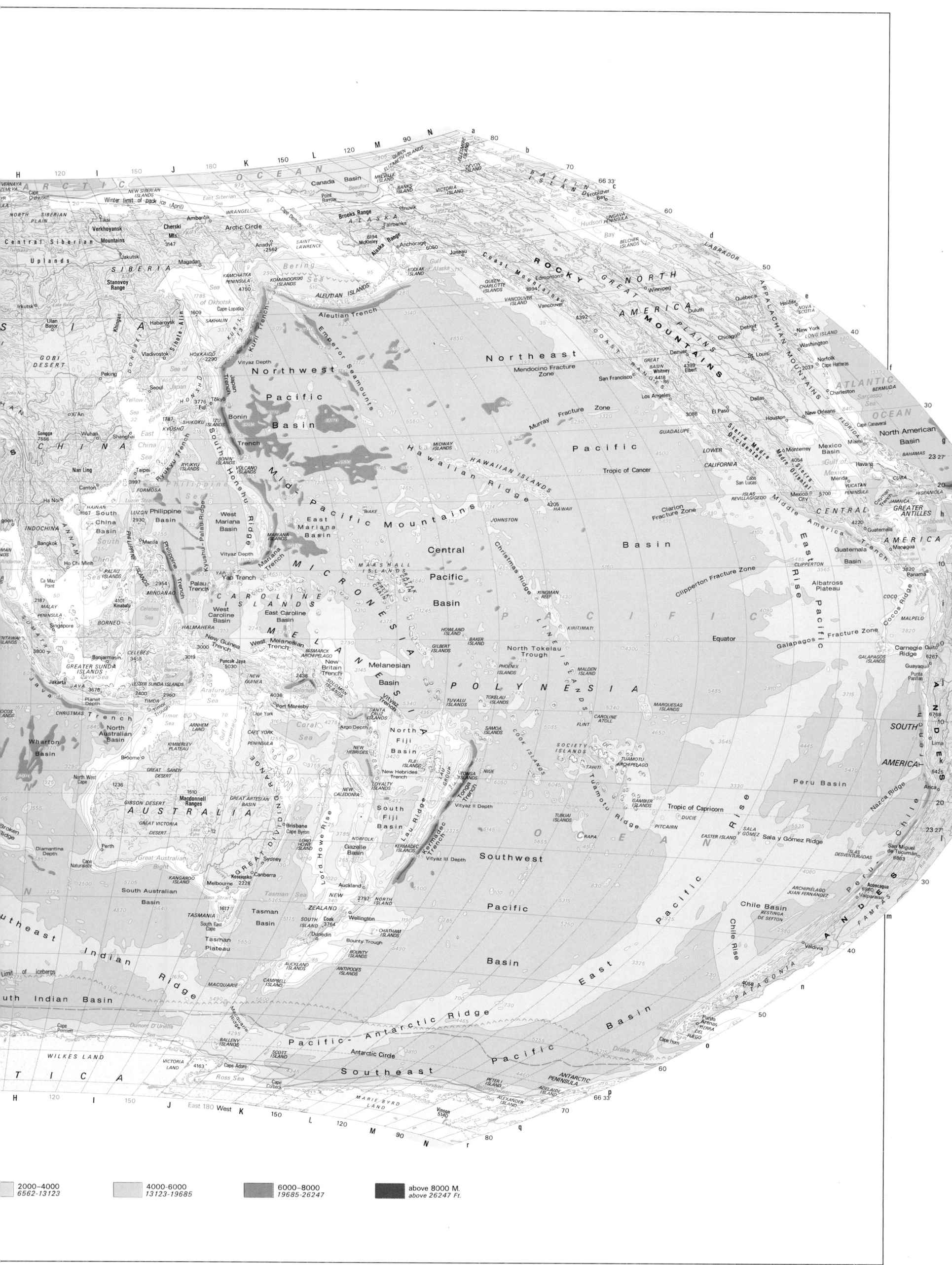

2000–4000
6562-13123

4000–6000
13123-19685

6000–8000
19685-26247

above 8000 M.
above 26247 Ft.

Map 4 **WORLD TRANSPORTATION AND TIME ZONES**

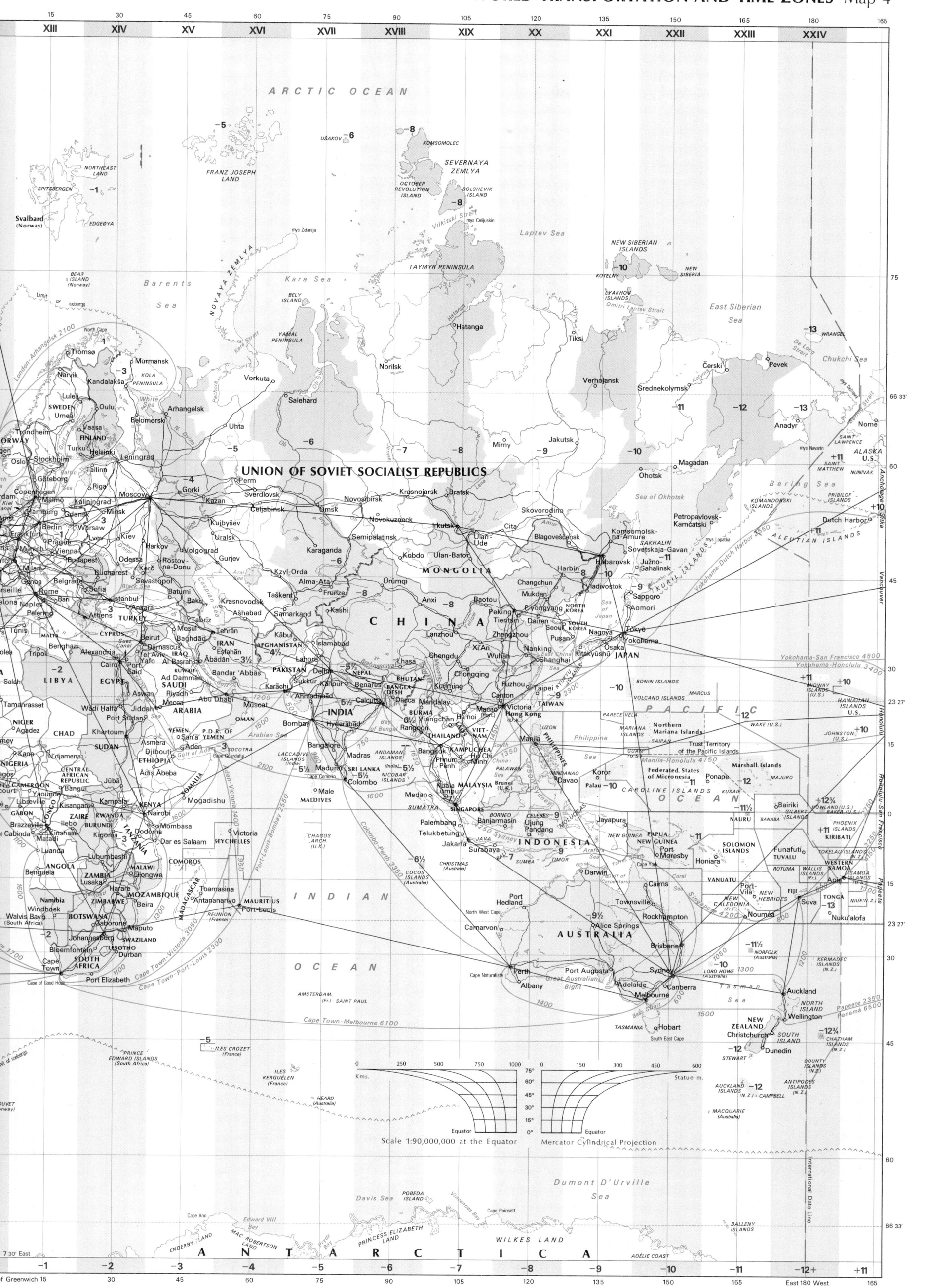

Map 5 **EUROPE, PHYSICAL**

GREENLAND

KING FREDERIK VI COAST

KING CHRISTIAN IX LAND

GREENLAND SEA

Denmark Strait

Mohns Ridge

Lofoten Basin

Limit of icebergs

ICELAND
VATNAJÖKULL

Arctic Circle

Reykjanes Ridge

Iceland Basin

Faroe-Iceland Ridge

FAEROE ISLANDS

Norwegian Basin

NORWEGIAN SEA

ATLANTIC OCEAN

Mid-Atlantic Ridge

West European Basin

Rockall Rise

Rockall

Ireland Trough

SHETLAND ISLANDS

ORKNEY ISLANDS

HEBRIDES

SCOTLAND

GRAMPIAN MTS.

NORTH SEA

NORWAY

SVEALAND

GÖTALAND

BRITISH ISLES

IRELAND

GREAT BRITAIN

PENNINES

WALES

JYLLAND

GERMAN PLAIN

POMERANIA

SILESIA

CELTIC SEA

ENGLISH CHANNEL

CORNWALL

ISLES OF SCILLY

NORMANDY

BRITTANY

PARIS BASIN

FRENCH PLAIN

ARDENNES

BOHEMIA

MORAVIAN Upland

BAVARIA

BAVARIAN PLATEAU

VOSGES

JURA

BLACK FOREST

Iberian Basin

AZORES

GRACIOSA
SÃO JORGE
PICO
TERCEIRA
SÃO MIGUEL
SANTA MARIA

Bay of Biscay

GALICIA

CANTABRIAN MTS.

AQUITAINE BASIN

PYRENEES

MASSIF CENTRAL

LANGUEDOC

PROVENCE

ALPS

SLOVENIA

APENNINES

ADRIATIC SEA

DALMATIA

BOSNIA

SUBMESETA NORTE

IBERIAN PENINSULA

SISTEMA CENTRAL

IBERIAN MOUNTAINS

ARAGON

CATALONIA

Gulf of Lion

LIGURIAN SEA

CORSICA

ITALY

TUSCAN ARCHIPELAGO

ALGARVE

SIERRA MORENA

ANDALUSIA

LA MANCHA

SUBMESETA SUR

BALEARIC ISLANDS

IBIZA
MAJORCA
MINORCA
FORMENTERA

SARDINIA

TYRRHENIAN SEA

Tyrrhenian Basin

SISTEMAS BÉTICOS

SIERRA NEVADA

Algerian Basin

LIPARI ISLANDS

EGADI ISLANDS

USTICA

PELAGIE ISLANDS

MALTA

CANARY ISLANDS

LA PALMA
GOMERA
HIERRO
TENERIFE
GRAN CANARIA
FUERTEVENTURA
LANZAROTE

MADEIRA ISLANDS

PORTO SANTO
ILHAS DESERTAS

RIF

TELL ATLAS

ATLAS MOUNTAINS

MIDDLE ATLAS

HIGH ATLAS

ANTI ATLAS

SAHARAN ATLAS

HAUTS PLATEAUX

MEDITERRANEAN

GRAND ERG OCCIDENTAL

GRAND ERG ORIENTAL

HAMADA DU DRAA

HAMADA DU GUIR

TRIPOLITANIA

JABAL NAFUSAH

AL HAMADAH AL HAMRA

Gulf of Sidra

Scale 1:15,000,000   Lambert Azimuthal Equal Area Projection

0 200 400 600 800 1000 km

0 250 500 miles

Longitude East 10 of Greenwich

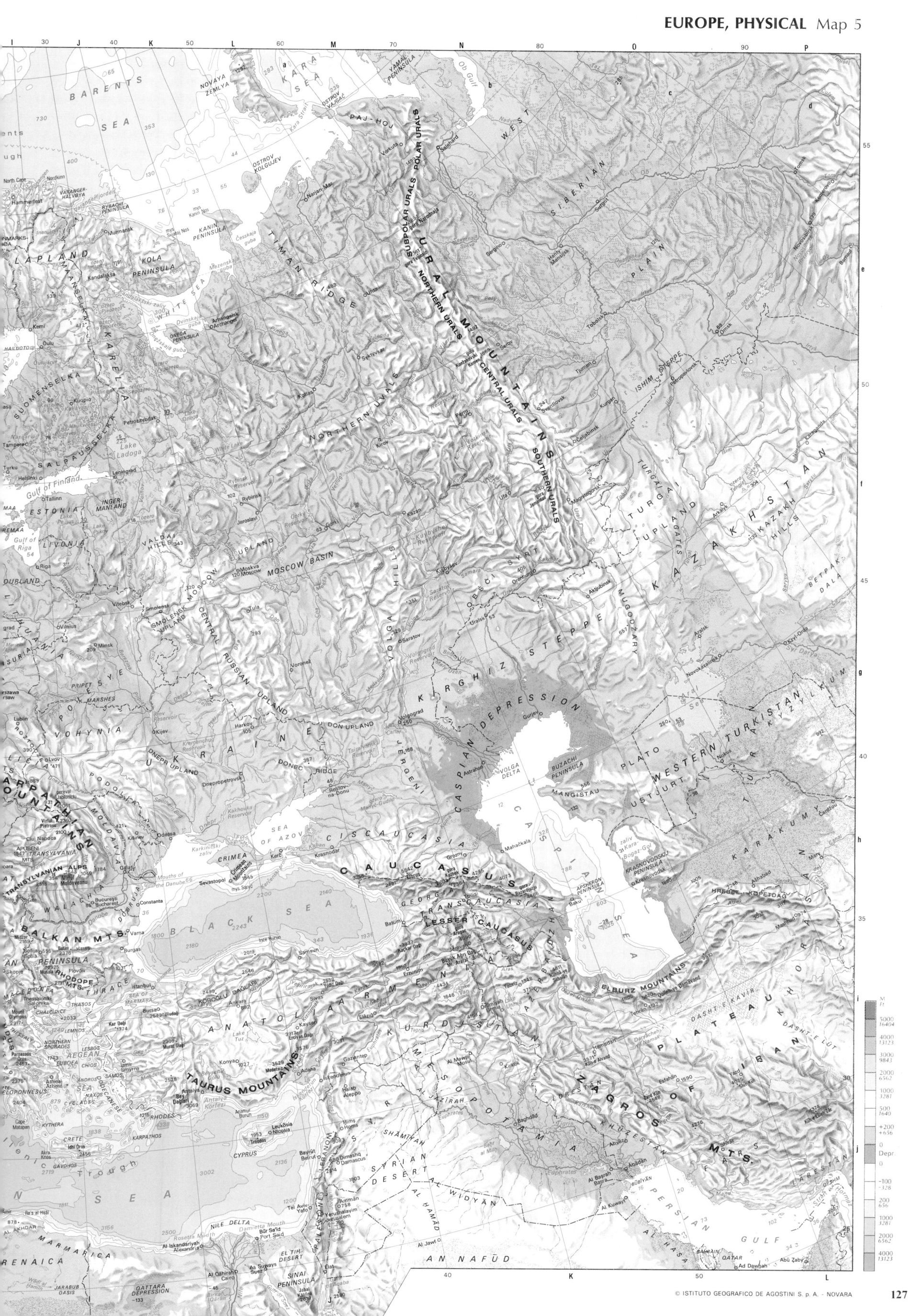

Map 6 **EUROPE, POLITICAL**

KING FREDERIK VI COAST
KING CHRISTIAN IX LAND
Greenland (Den.)
Greenland Sea
JAN MAYEN (Norway)
Denmark Strait
ICELAND
Reykjavik
Arctic Circle
Norwegian Sea

NORWAY
SWEDEN
Oslo
Bergen
Stavanger
Kristiansand
Trondheim
Ålesund

Faeroe Islands (Den.)
FØROYAR / FÆRØERNE
SHETLAND ISLANDS
ORKNEY ISLANDS
HEBRIDES

DENMARK
København Copenhagen
Malmö
Göteborg
Helsingør

North Sea
Skagerrak
Kattegat

Inverness
Aberdeen
Dundee
Edinburgh
Glasgow
Newcastle upon Tyne
IRELAND
Galway
Limerick
Cork
Waterford
Dublin
Belfast
UNITED KINGDOM
Manchester
Liverpool
Leeds
Sheffield
Nottingham
Birmingham
Leicester
Norwich
Kingston-upon-Hull
Teesside
Cardiff
Bristol
Swansea
London
Southampton
Plymouth
Brighton
Dover
LAND'S END
ISLES OF SCILLY
Celtic Sea
Irish Sea
English Channel

ATLANTIC OCEAN

NETHERLANDS
Amsterdam
Den Haag
Rotterdam
Groningen
Utrecht
s-Gravenhage
Antwerpen
BELGIUM
Bruxelles Brussel
Liège
LUXEMBOURG

GERMAN FED. REP. OF GERMANY
Hamburg
Bremen
Bremerhaven
Hannover
Berlin
Magdeburg
DEM. REP.
Leipzig
Dresden
Köln Cologne
Düsseldorf
Dortmund
Bonn
Frankfurt
Wiesbaden
Mannheim
Würzburg
Nürnberg
Stuttgart
München Munich
Karl-Marx-Stadt
Lübeck
Rostock
Kiel
Flensburg
Kristiansand

POLAND
Szczecin Stettin
Gdańsk Danzig
Gdynia
Poznań
Wrocław Breslau
Katowice
Wałbrzych
CZECHOSLOVAKIA
Praha Prague
Plzeň
Brno
Ostrava
Bratislava

FRANCE
Paris
Brest
Saint-Malo
Caen
Le Havre
Rouen
Amiens
Reims
Metz
Nancy
Strasbourg
Mulhouse
Rennes
Nantes
Angers
Tours
Orléans
Le Mans
Troyes
Dijon
Besançon
Bourges
Poitiers
La Rochelle
Limoges
Clermont-Ferrand
Saint-Étienne
Lyon
Bordeaux
Toulouse
Montpellier
Nîmes
Avignon
Marseille
Toulon
Nice
Grenoble
Perpignan

SWITZERLAND
Bern
Genève Geneva
Zürich
Lausanne
LIECHTENSTEIN
AUSTRIA
Wien Vienna
Salzburg
Innsbruck
Linz
Graz
Klagenfurt

ITALY
Milano Milan
Torino Turin
Genova Genoa
Venezia Venice
Verona
Bologna
Firenze Florence
Livorno Leghorn
Roma Rome
VATICAN CITY
Napoli Naples
Bari
Brindisi
Taranto
Cagliari
Palermo
Messina
Catania
Siracusa Syracuse
Reggio di Calabria
Trieste
Parma
Brescia
Ancona
Pescara
Foggia
Salerno
SAN MARINO
SARDINIA
SICILY
CORSICA (Fr.)
Ajaccio
Bastia
Mt. Etna
Ligurian Sea
Tyrrhenian Sea
Ionian Sea
ANDORRA la Vella
PYRENEES

YUGOSLAVIA
Ljubljana
Zagreb
Rijeka
Zadar
Split
Dubrovnik
Osijek
Pécs
Szombathely

PORTUGAL
Lisboa Lisbon
Porto
Coimbra
Braga
Setúbal
Évora
Faro

SPAIN
Madrid
Barcelona
Valencia
Sevilla
Zaragoza Saragossa
Málaga
Bilbao
Córdoba
Murcia
Granada
Valladolid
Oviedo
Gijón
Santander
San Sebastián
Pamplona
Burgos
León
Salamanca
Badajoz
Toledo
Cádiz
Huelva
Almería
Cartagena
Alicante
Albacete
Castellón de la Plana
Tarragona
Vigo
La Coruña
Gibraltar (U.K.)
Algeciras
BALEARIC ISLANDS
Palma
MAJORCA
MINORCA
IBIZA
Bay of Biscay

Azores (Portugal)
GRACIOSA
SÃO JORGE
TERCEIRA
PICO
FAIAL
SÃO MIGUEL
SANTA MARIA
Angra do Heroísmo
Ponta Delgada

MADEIRA ISLANDS
Madeira (Portugal)
Funchal
PORTO SANTO
ILHAS DESERTAS
ILHAS SELVAGENS

Canary Islands (Spain)
LA PALMA
TENERIFE
GOMERA
HIERRO
GRAN CANARIA
LANZAROTE
FUERTEVENTURA
Santa Cruz de Tenerife
Las Palmas de Gran Canaria

MOROCCO
Casablanca
Rabat
Marrakech
Fès
Meknès
Kenitra
Tanger Tangier
Tétouan
Ceuta (Spain)
Melilla (Spain)
Agadir
Essaouira
Safi
El Jadida
Oujda
ATLAS MOUNTAINS

ALGERIA
Alger Algiers
Oran
Constantine
Annaba
Bejaïa
Skikda
Sétif
Tizi Ouzou
Blida
Tiaret
Béchar
GRAND ERG OCCIDENTAL
GRAND ERG ORIENTAL

TUNISIA
Tunis
Bizerte
Sousse
Sfax
Gabès
Gafsa
Kairouan
MALTA
Valletta
PANTELLERIA (Italy)

LIBYA
Tarābulus Tripoli
Misrātah
TRIPOLITANIA

MEDITERRANEAN SEA
Gulf of Gabès
DJERBA

Scale 1:15,000,000 Lambert Azimuthal Equal-Area Projection
0 200 400 600 800 1000 km
0 250 500 miles
Longitude East 10 of Greenwich

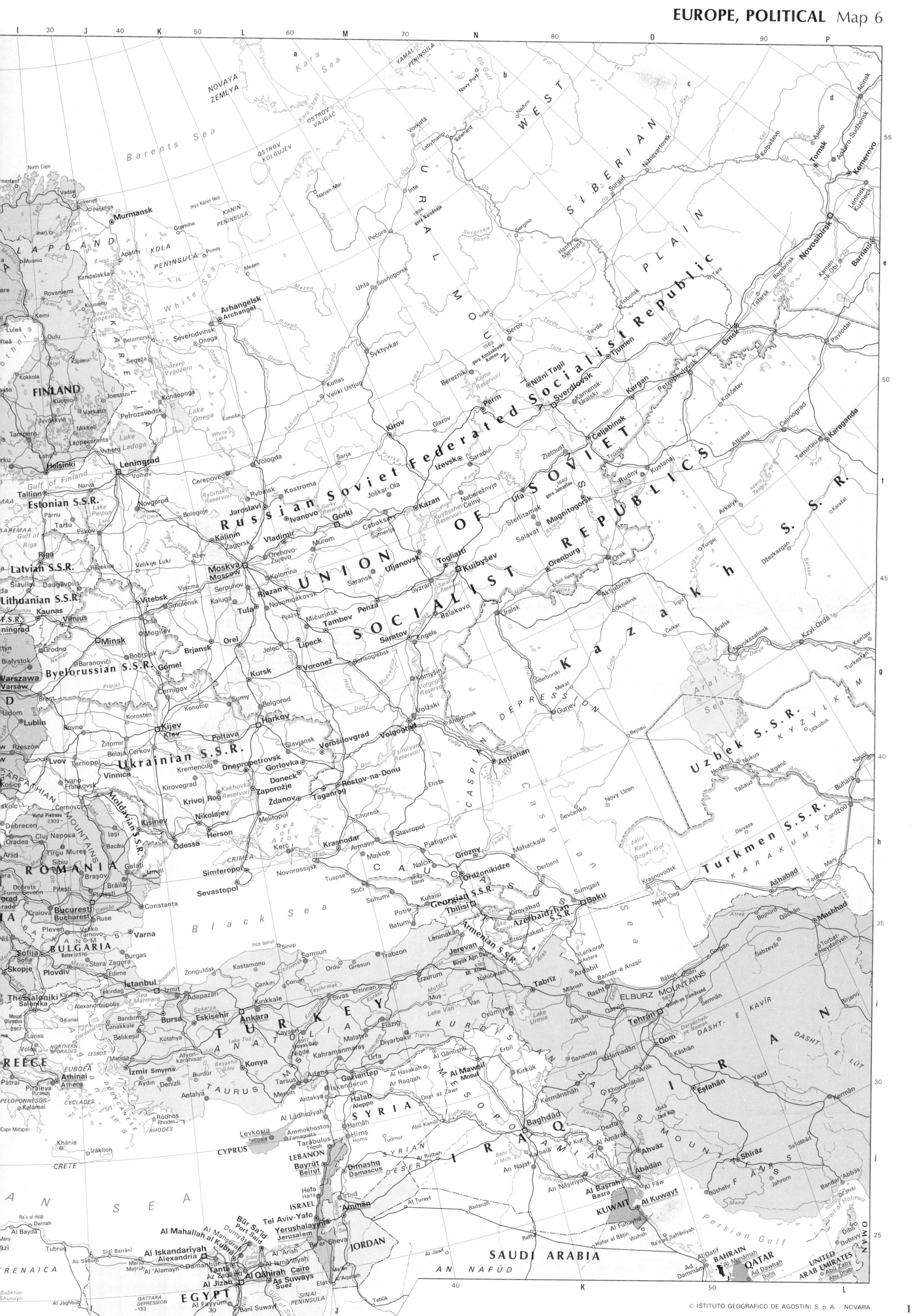

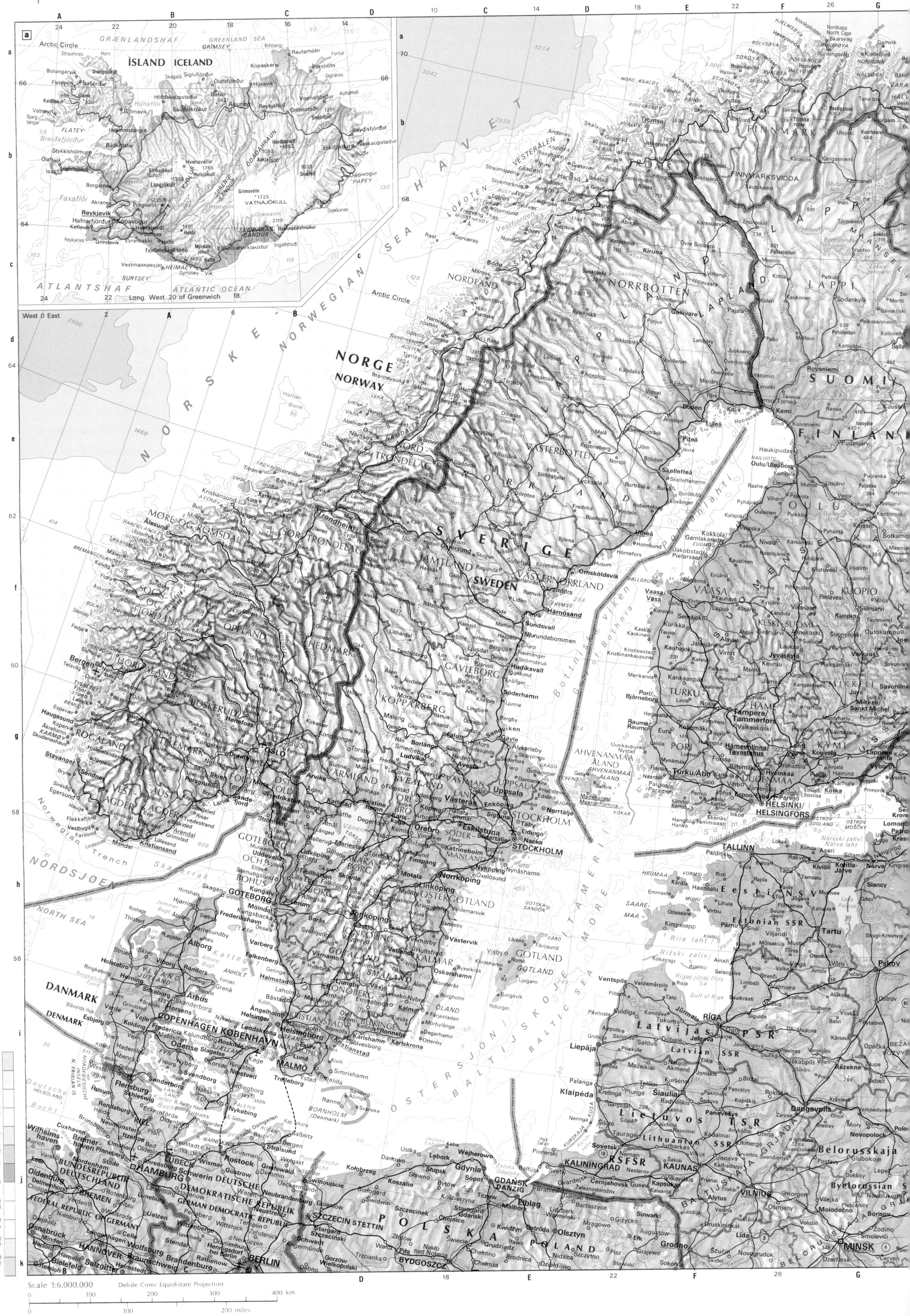

Map 7 NORTHERN EUROPE

ÍSLAND ICELAND

GRÆNLANDSHAF
GREENLAND SEA

Arctic Circle

Reykjavik

ATLANTSHAF   ATLANTIC OCEAN

Long. West 20 of Greenwich

West 0 East

NORSKE-HAVET
NORWEGIAN SEA

Arctic Circle

NORGE
NORWAY

FINNMARK

FINNMARKSVIDDA

LAPPLAND
LAPPI

LOFOTEN
VESTERÅLEN

NORRBOTTEN

Kiruna

NORDLAND

Bodø

VÄSTERBOTTEN

SUOMI
FINLAND

Oulu/Uleåborg

NORD-
TRØNDELAG

SØR-TRØNDELAG

Trondheim

JÄMTLAND

SVERIGE
SWEDEN

VÄSTERNORRLAND

Sundsvall

Härnösand

MØRE OG ROMSDÅL

Ålesund

VAASA
VASA

OPPLAND

HEDMARK

GÄVLEBORG

Hudiksvall

KUOPIO

Kuopio

SOGN OG FJORDANE

HORDALAND

Bergen

KOPPARBERG

Falun

VÄRMLAND

TAMPERE/
TAMMERFORS

TURKU
Björneborg

BUSKERUD

OSLO

VÄSTMANLAND

Västerås

UPPSALA

HÄMEENLINNA

TELEMARK

ROGALAND

Stavanger

SVEALAND

ÖREBRO

Örebro

STOCKHOLM

AHVENANMAA
ÅLAND

UUDENMAA

HELSINKI/
HELSINGFORS

Turku/Åbo

VEST-AGDER   AUST-AGDER

Kristiansand

GÖTEBORG
OCH BOHUS

ÄLVSBORG

Eskilstuna

Södertälje

NACKA

STOCKHOLM

TALLINN

NORDSJØEN
NORTH SEA

Skagerrak

GÖTEBORG

ÖSTERGÖTLAND

Linköping

Norrköping

EESTI NSV

Estonian SSR

Tartu

SKAGEN

DANMARK
DENMARK

JYLLAND
JUTLAND

Århus

SMÅLAND

KRONOBERG

Växjö

KALMAR

ÖLAND

GOTLAND

Visby

Latvijas
PSR

Latvian SSR

RĪGA

Gulf of Riga

KØBENHAVN
COPENHAGEN

MALMÖ

BLEKINGE

Karlskrona

BORNHOLM
(Danmark)

ØSTERSJÖN
BALTIC SEA
BALTIJSKOJE MORE

Liepāja

Lietuvos
TSR
Lithuanian SSR

Klaipeda

HAMBURG

BUNDESREPUBLIK
DEUTSCHLAND
FEDERAL REPUBLIC OF GERMANY

BERLIN

DEUTSCHE
DEMOKRATISCHE
REPUBLIK
GERMAN DEMOCRATIC REPUBLIC

SZCZECIN STETTIN

POLSKA
POLAND

GDANSK
DANZIG

KALININGRAD
RSFSR

KAUNAS

VILNIUS

MINSK

Byelorussian SSR
BELORUSSKAJA

BYDGOSZCZ

Scale 1:6,000,000   Delisle Conic Equidistant Projection
0   100   200   300   400 km
0   100   200 miles

M
Ft
2000
6562
1000
3281
500
1643
200
656
+100
+328
Depr.
−100
−328
200
656
1000
3281
2000
6562

SOJUZ SOVĚTSKICH SOCIALISTIČESKICH RESPUBLIK (SSSR)

UNION OF SOVIET SOCIALIST REPUBLICS (USSR)

Rossijskaja Sovětskaja Federativnaja Socialističeskaja Respublika (RSFSR)

Russian Soviet Federated Socialist Republic (RSFSR)

8 Arhangelskaja oblast
8A Nanecki nac. okrug
11 Brjanskaja oblast
14 Gorkovskaja oblast
15 Ivanovskaja oblast
17 Jaroslavskaja oblast
18 Kaliningradskaja oblast
19 Kalininskaja oblast
22 Kalužskaja oblast
23 Kirovskaja oblast
24 Kostromskaja oblast
25 Kujbyševskaja oblast
28 Leningradskaja oblast
29 Lipeckaja oblast
31 Moskovskaja oblast
32 Murmanskaja oblast
33 Novgorodskaja oblast
36 Orenburgskaja oblast
37 Orlovskaja oblast
38 Penzenskaja oblast
39 Permskaja oblast
39A Komi-Permjacki nac. okrug

40 Pskovskaja oblast
42 Rjazanskaja oblast
44 Saratovskaja oblast
45 Smolenskaja oblast
47 Tambovskaja oblast
48 Tjumenskaja oblast
48A Hanty-Mansijski nac. okrug
50 Tulskaja oblast
51 Uljanovskaja oblast
52 Vladimirskaja oblast
53 Vologodskaja oblast

Belorusskaja SSR

Byelorussian SSR

3 Grodnenskaja oblast
4 Minskaja oblast
5 Mogilevskaja oblast
6 Vitebskaja oblast

BARENCEVO MORE
BARENTS SEA
Pečorskoje more
Pechora Sea

MURMANSK
KOLSKI POLUOSTROV
KOLA PENINSULA
Kirovsk
Apatity
Kandalakša
Moncegorsk

OSTROV KOLGUJEV
Narjan-Mar

ARHANGELSK
Severodvinsk
Onega
Belomorsk
Kem
Segeža
Petrozavodsk
Kondopoga

Rossijskaja Sovětskaja Federativnaja Socialističeskaja Respublika
Russian SFSR

Syktyvkar
Veliki Ustjug
Kotlas

LENINGRAD
Volhov
Tihvin

Vologda
Čerepovec
Rybinsk
JAROSLAVL
Kostroma
IVANOVO
KIROV
Slobodskoj

IŽEVSK
UDMURTSKAJA ASSR
Solikamsk
Berezniki
PERM

Dzeržinsk
GORKI
Vladimir
Murom
Arzamas
KAZAN
TATARSKAJA ASSR
ČUVAŠSKAJA ASSR
Čeboksary
MARIJSKAJA ASSR
Joškar-Ola

MOSKVA
MOSCOW
Kalinin
Zagorsk
Noginsk
Elektrostal
Podolsk
Kolomna
Serpuhov
Kaluga
TULA
Novomoskovsk

RJAZAN
MORDOVSKAJA ASSR
Saransk
PENZA
ULJANOVSK
TOGLIATTI
KUJBYŠEV
SYZRAN
Novokujbyševsk

Smolensk
BSSR
SSR

Longitude East 32 of Greenwich

Map 8 **BALTIC REGION**

Scale 1:3,000,000   Delisle Conic Equidistant Projection

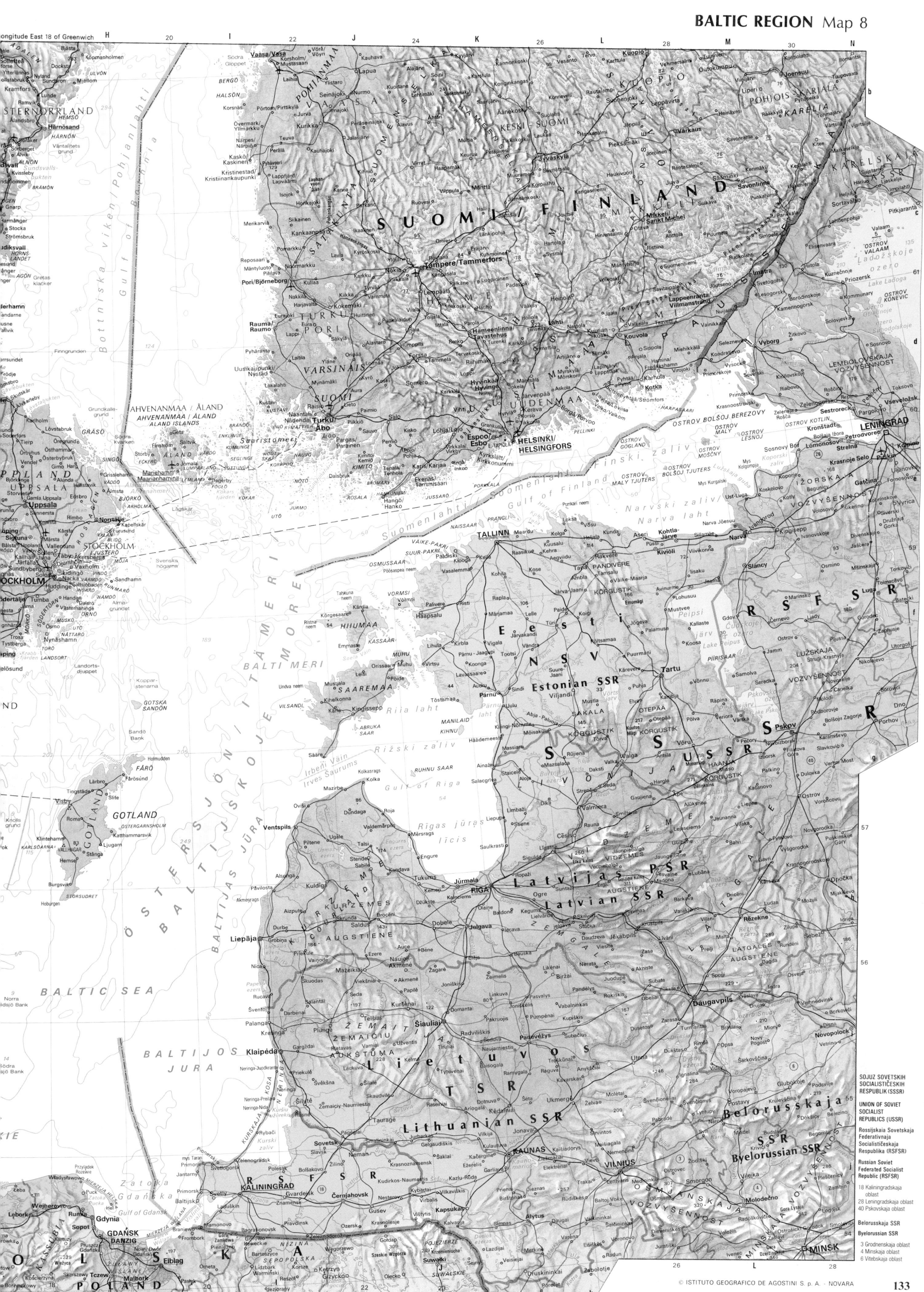

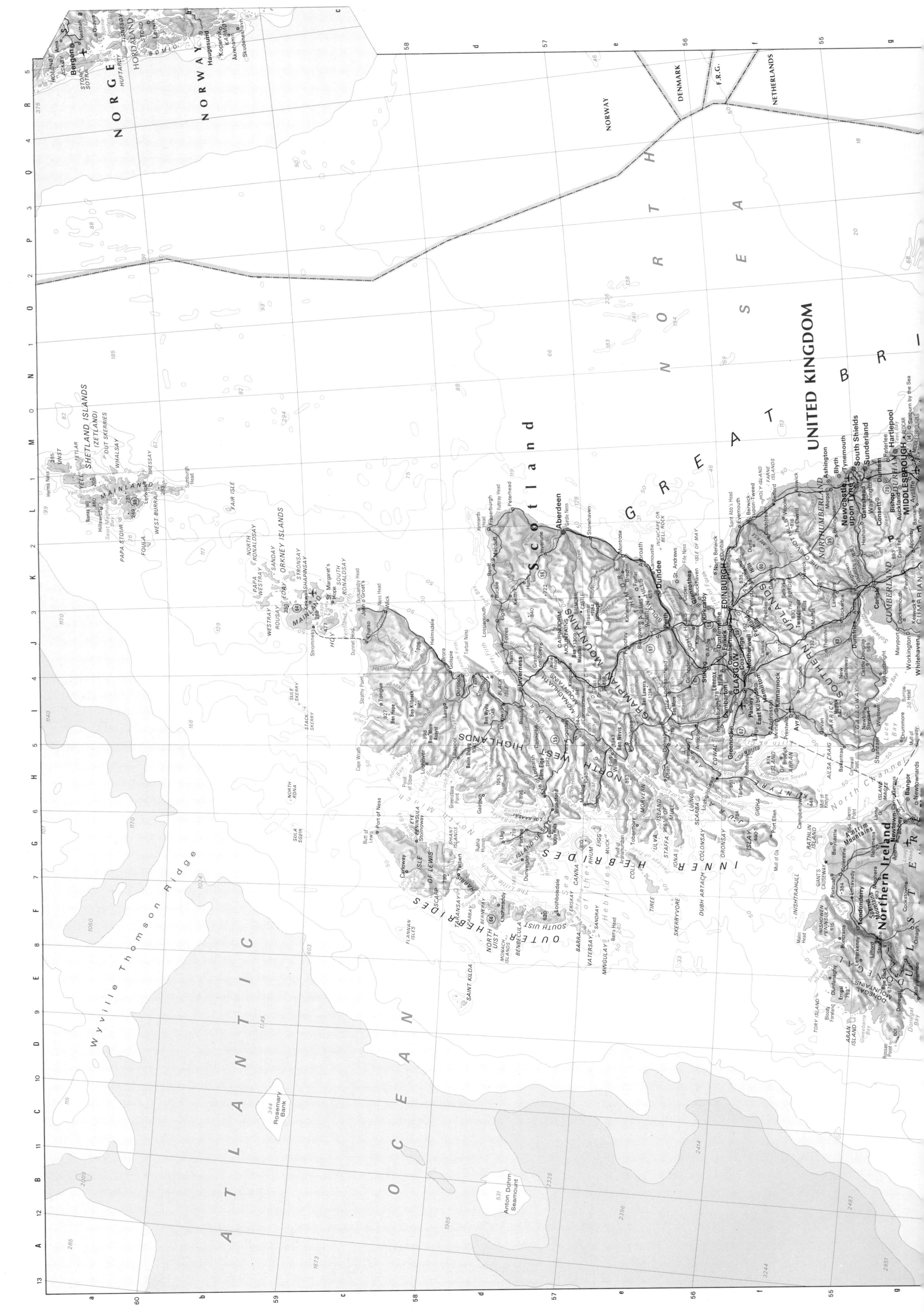

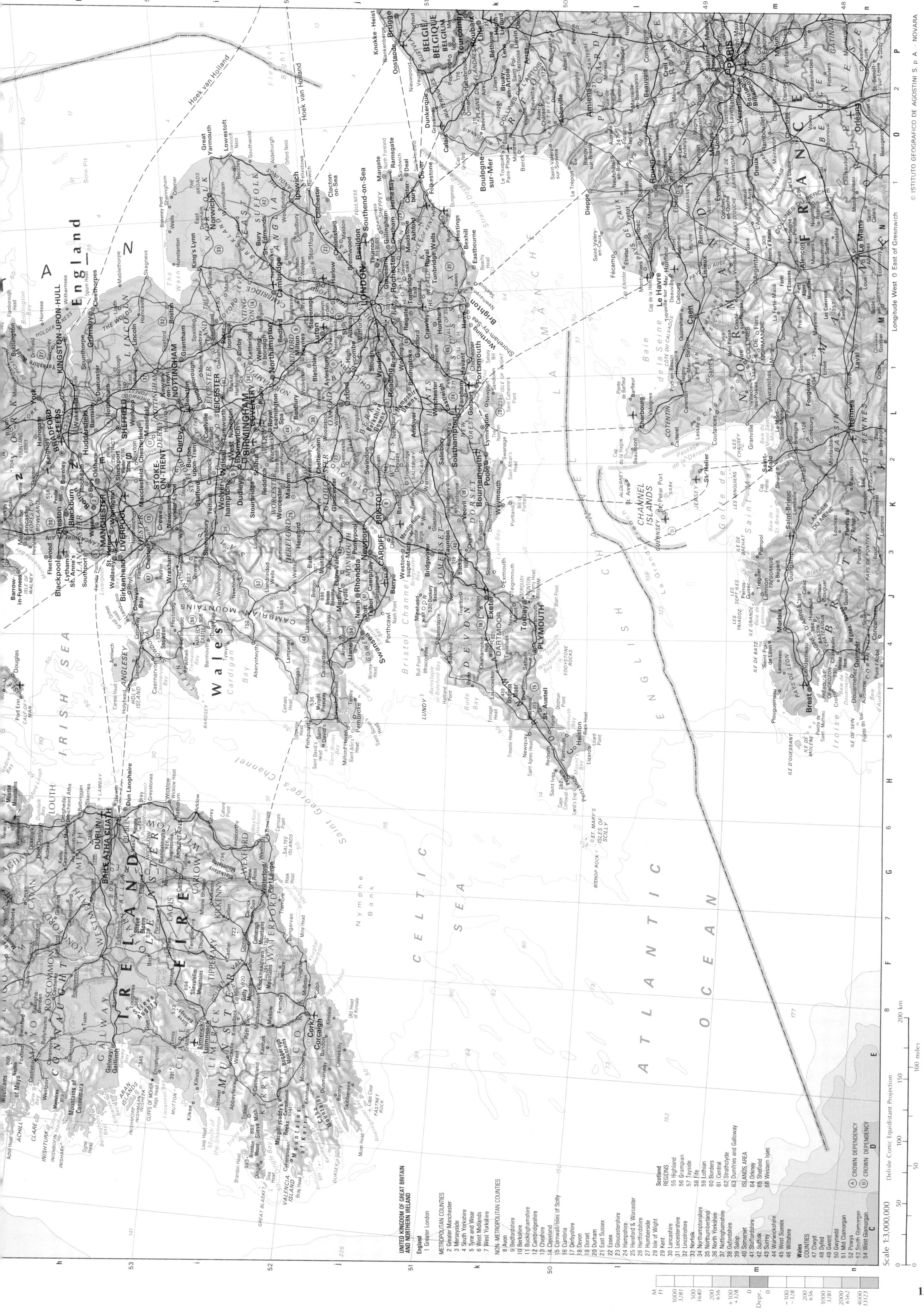

England

Wales

IRELAND / EIRE

FRANCE

BELGIQUE / BELGIË / BELGIEN

LONDON

CHANNEL ISLANDS

NORMANDIE

BRETAGNE

PICARDIE

ATLANTIC OCEAN

CELTIC SEA

IRISH SEA

Saint George's Channel

Bristol Channel

ENGLISH CHANNEL

LA MANCHE

Baie de la Seine

Golfe de Saint-Malo

Nymphe Bank

© ISTITUTO GEOGRAFICO DE AGOSTINI S p A - NOVARA

Longitude West 0 East of Greenwich

UNITED KINGDOM OF GREAT BRITAIN AND NORTHERN IRELAND

England
1 Greater London

METROPOLITAN COUNTIES
2 Greater Manchester
3 Merseyside
4 South Yorkshire
5 Tyne and Wear
6 West Midlands
7 West Yorkshire

NON-METROPOLITAN COUNTIES
8 Avon
9 Bedfordshire
10 Berkshire
11 Buckinghamshire
12 Cambridgeshire
13 Cheshire
14 Cleveland
15 Cornwall/Isles of Scilly
16 Cumbria
17 Derbyshire
18 Devon
19 Dorset
20 Durham
21 East Sussex
22 Essex
23 Gloucestershire
24 Hampshire
25 Hereford & Worcester
26 Hertfordshire
27 Humberside
28 Isle of Wight
29 Kent
30 Lancashire
31 Leicestershire
32 Lincolnshire
33 Norfolk
34 Northamptonshire
35 Northumberland
36 North Yorkshire
37 Nottinghamshire
38 Oxfordshire
39 Salop
40 Somerset
41 Staffordshire
42 Suffolk
43 Surrey
44 Warwickshire
45 West Sussex
46 Wiltshire

Wales
COUNTIES
47 Clwyd
48 Dyfed
49 Gwent
50 Gwynedd
51 Mid Glamorgan
52 Powys
53 South Glamorgan
54 West Glamorgan

Scotland
REGIONS
55 Highland
56 Grampian
57 Tayside
58 Fife
59 Lothian
60 Borders
61 Central
62 Strathclyde
63 Dumfries and Galloway

ISLANDS AREA
64 Orkney
65 Shetland
66 Western Isles

Ⓐ **CROWN DEPENDENCY**
Ⓑ **CROWN DEPENDENCY**

Delisle Conic Equidistant Projection

Scale 1:3,000,000

Map 10 **CENTRAL EUROPE**

DEUTSCHE
DEMOKRATISCHE
REPUBLIK

GERMAN
DEMOCRATIC
REPUBLIC

BEZIRKE

1 Berlin (Ost)
2 Cottbus
3 Dresden
4 Erfurt
5 Frankfurt
6 Gera
7 Halle
8 Karl-Marx-Stadt
9 Leipzig
10 Magdeburg
11 Neubrandenburg
12 Potsdam
13 Rostock
14 Schwerin
15 Suhl

Scale 1:3,000,000   Delisle Conic Equidistant Projection

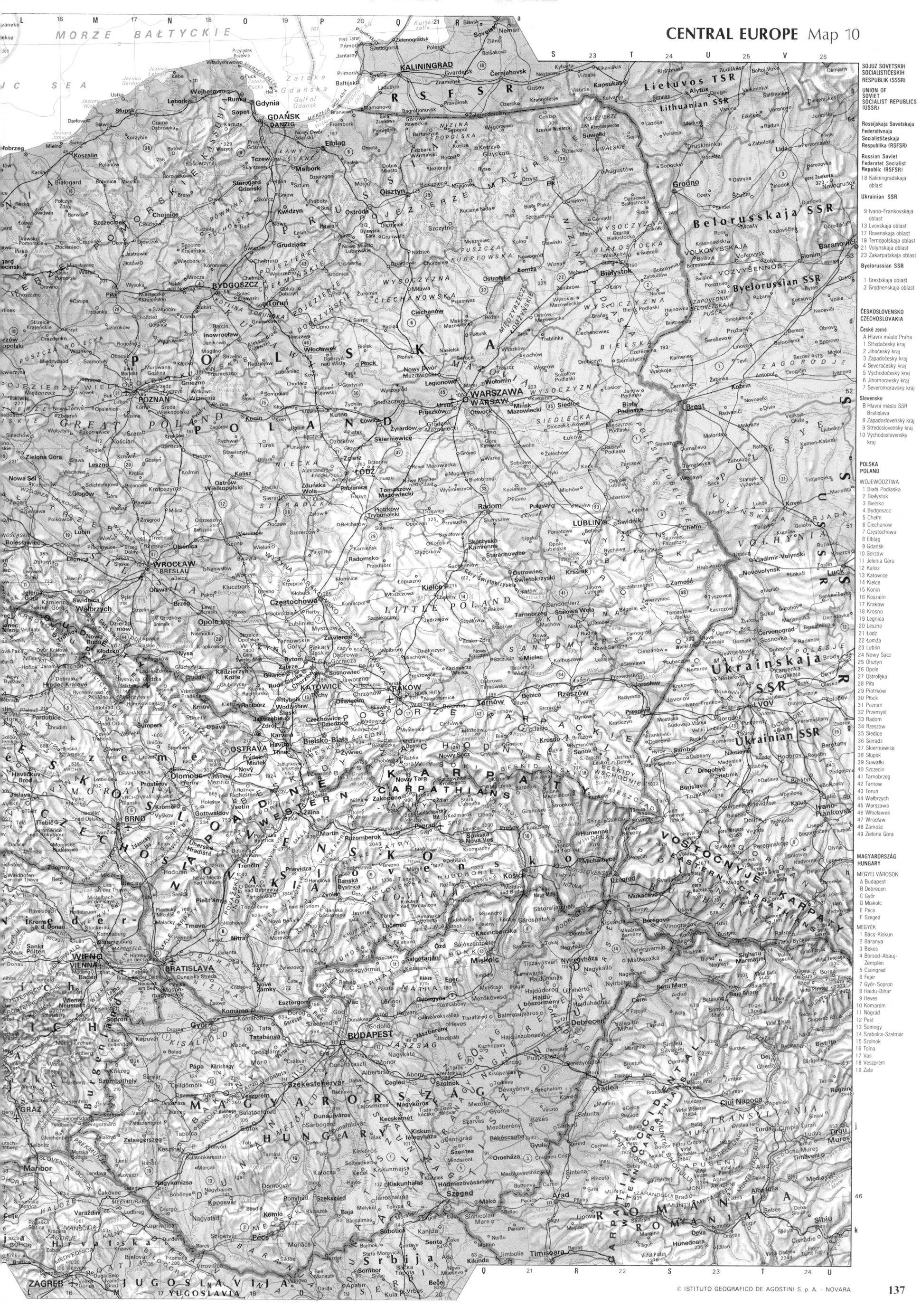

Map 11 **FRANCE AND BENELUX**

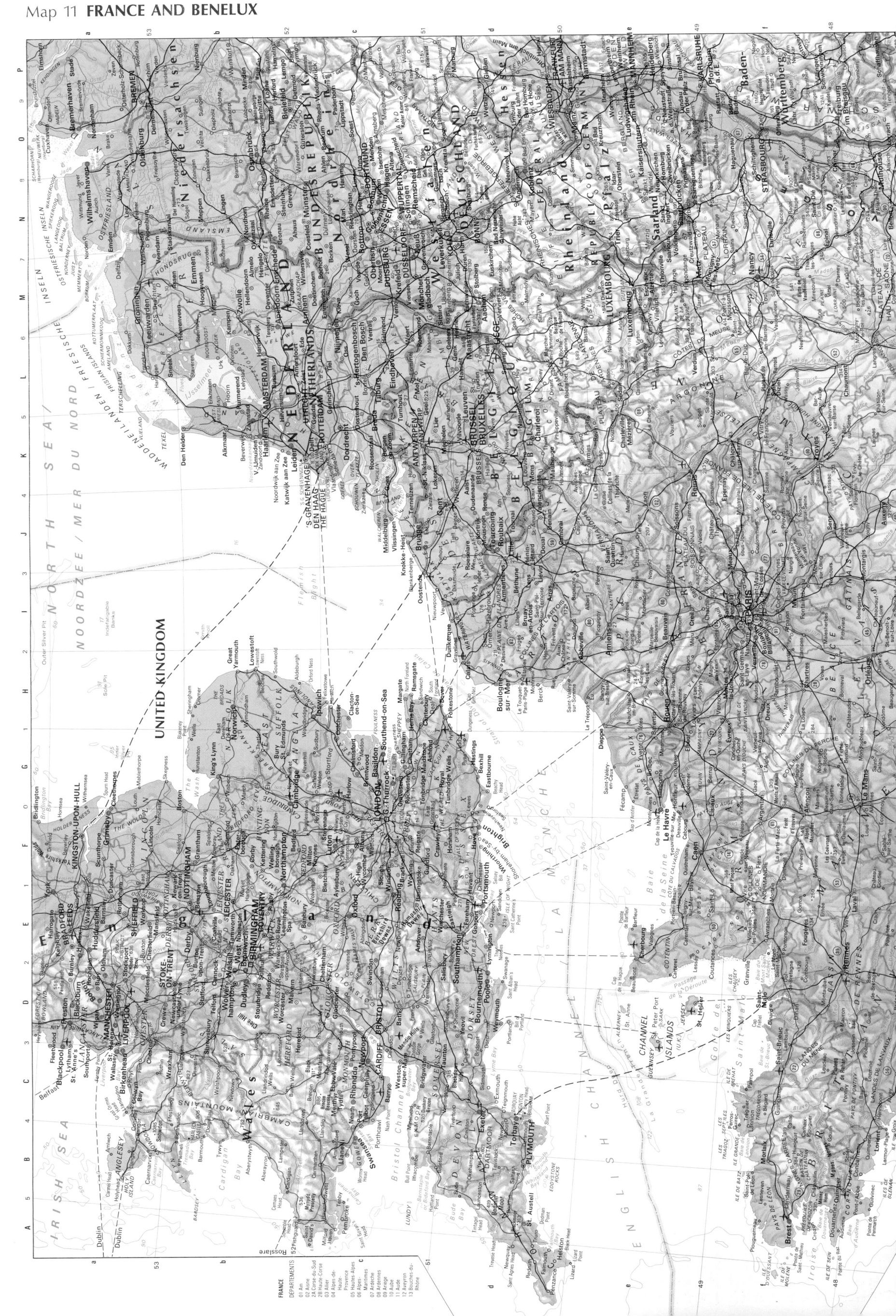

Scale 1:3,000,000

Delisle Conic Equidistant Projection

Map 12 **BELGIUM, NETHERLANDS AND LUXEMBOURG**

UNITED KINGDOM

England

NORTH SEA / NOORDZEE / MER DU NORD

Flemish Bight

ENGLISH CHANNEL / LA MANCHE

Strait of Dover / Pas de Calais

FRANCE

NORMANDIE

Baie de la Seine
Bay of the Seine

CÔTE DU CALVADOS

PAYS DE CAUX

SEINE-MARITIME

PICARDIE

SOMME

PAS-DE-CALAIS

NORD

VLAANDEREN

WEST-

GENT / GHENT

Brugge

Oostende

London

Paris

FRANCE

DEPARTEMENTOS
75 Ville de Paris
92 Hauts-de-Seine
93 Seine-Saint-Denis
94 Val-de-Marne

M ft
500 1640
200 656
100 328
0
Depr.

Scale 1:1,500,000   Delisle Conic Equidistant Projection

0   25   50   75   100 km

0   25   50 miles

Map 12

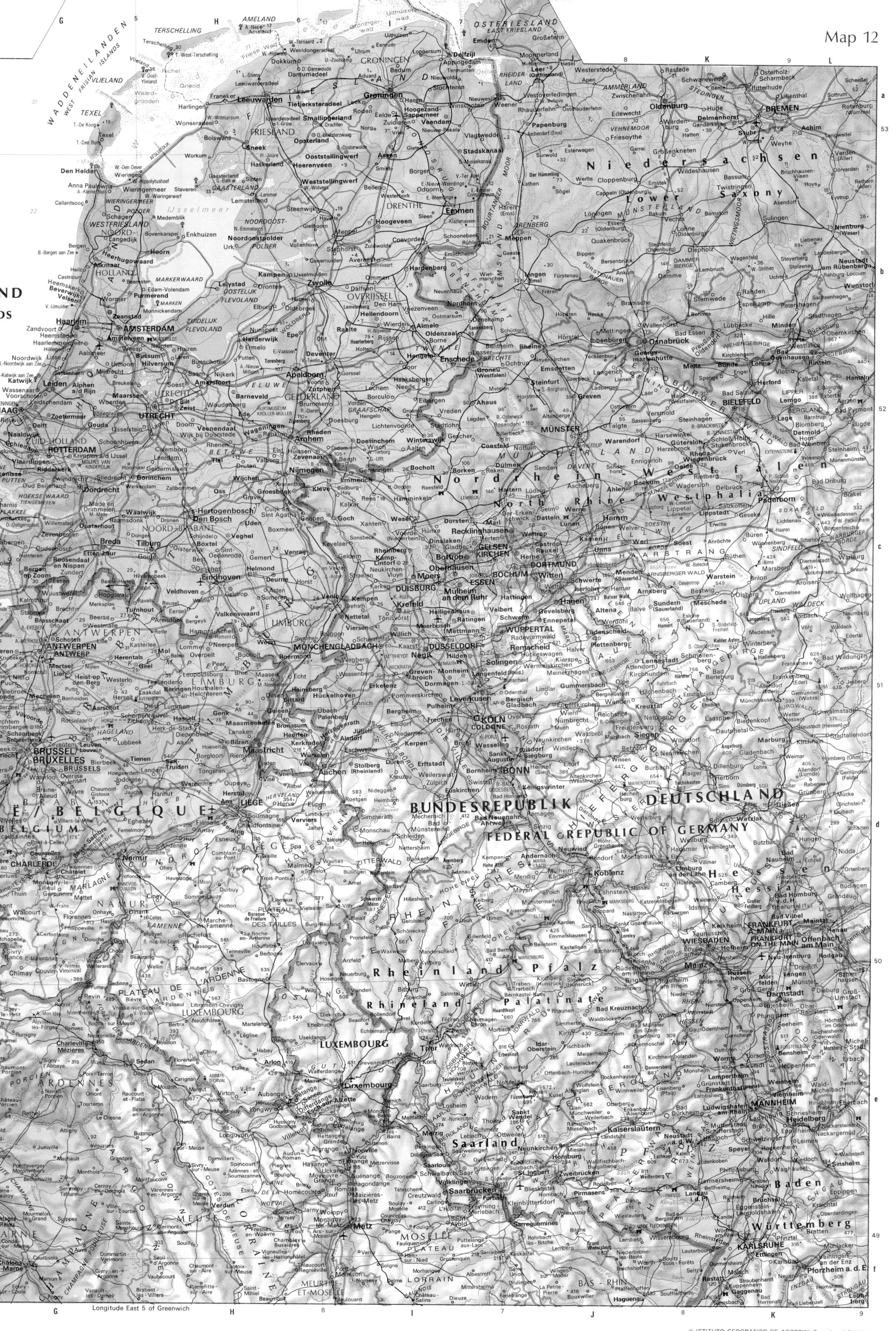

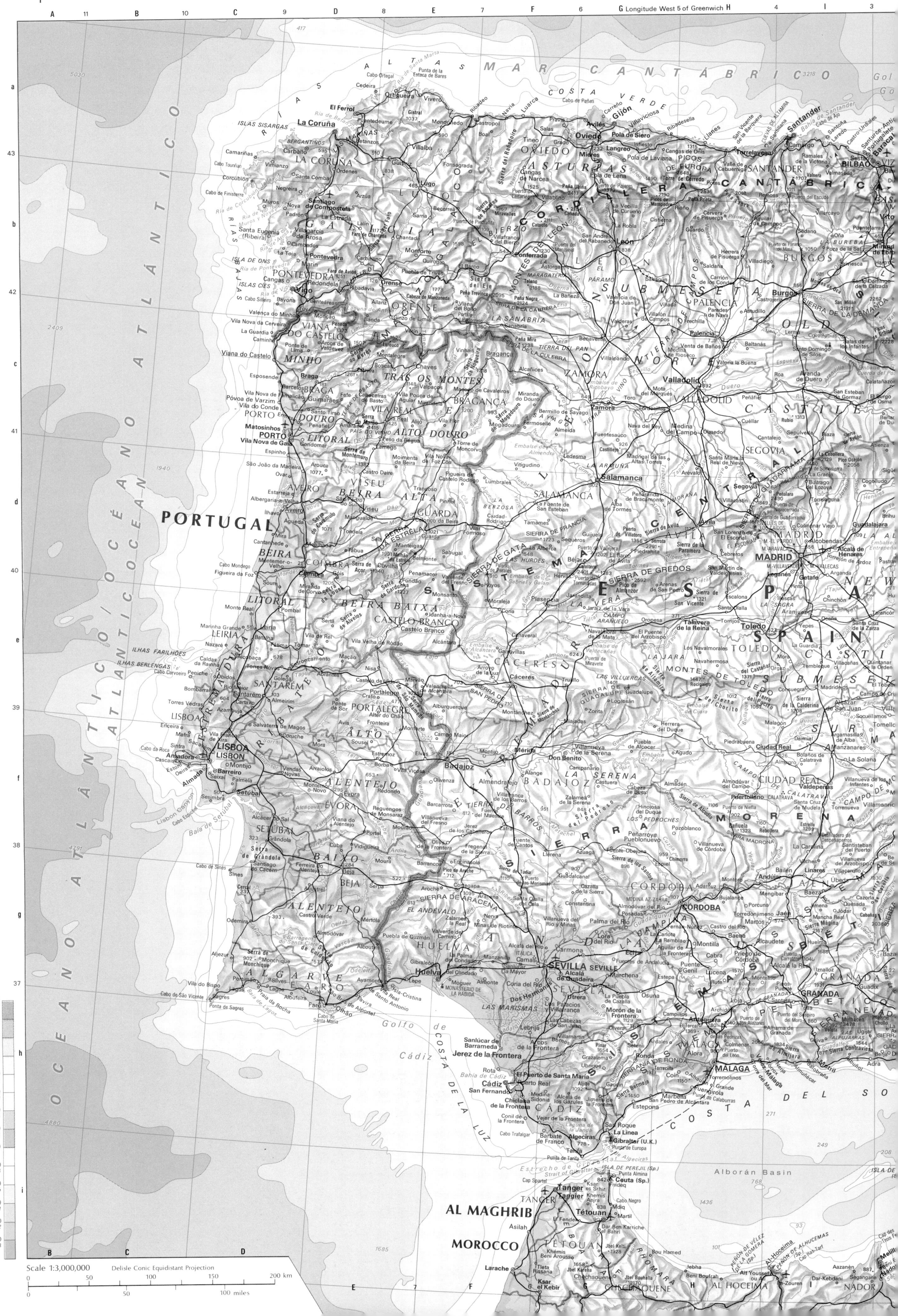

Map 13 **SPAIN AND PORTUGAL**

Longitude West 5 of Greenwich

MAR CANTÁBRICO

COSTA VERDE

OCÉANO ATLÂNTICO / ATLANTIC OCEAN

PORTUGAL

SPAIN

ESPAÑA

MADRID

LISBOA / LISBON

PORTO

AL MAGHRIB

MOROCCO

Scale 1:3,000,000   Delisle Conic Equidistant Projection

0   50   100   150   200 km

0   50   100 miles

Map 14 **ITALY, AUSTRIA AND SWITZERLAND**

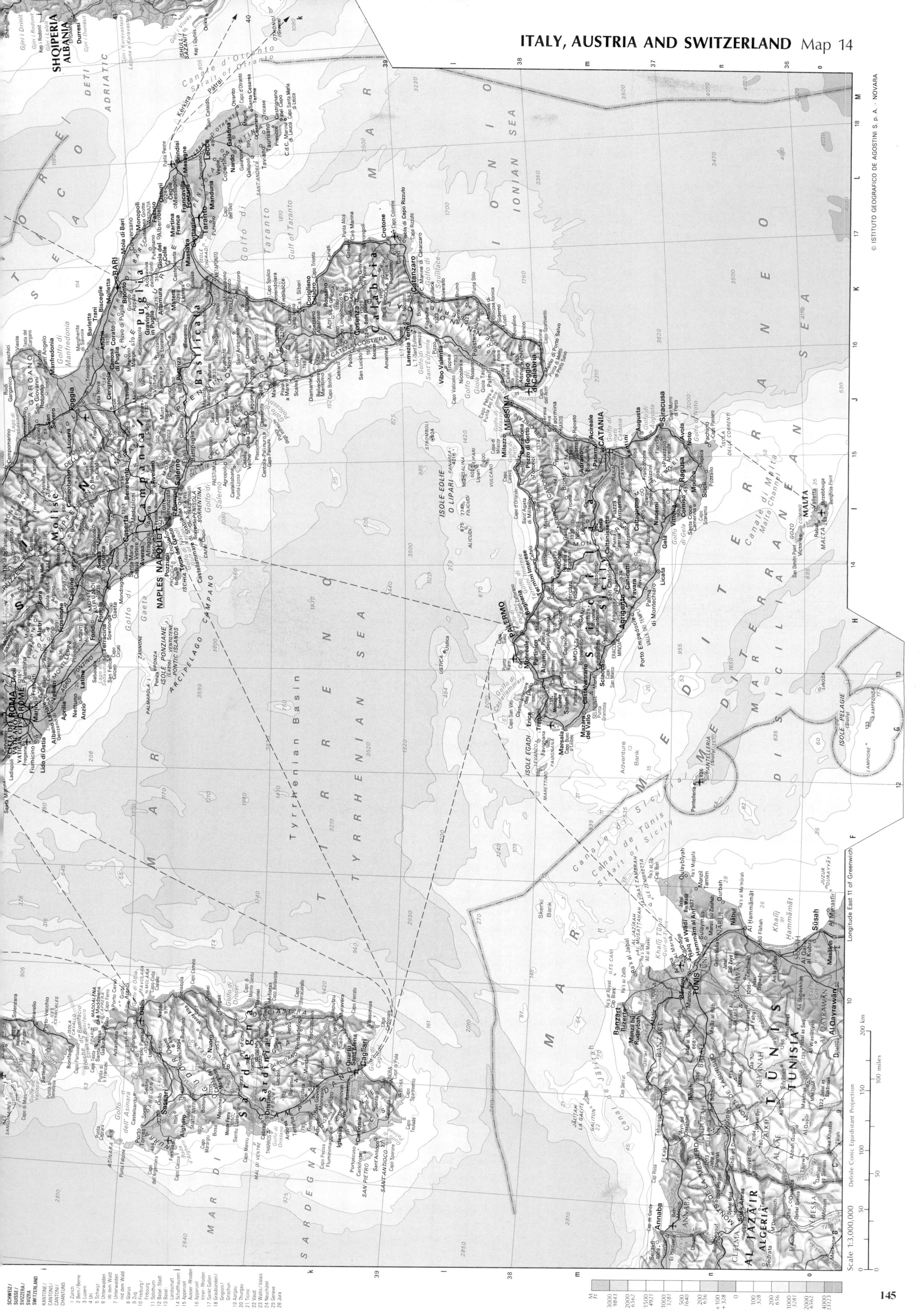

Map 15 **SOUTHEASTERN EUROPE**

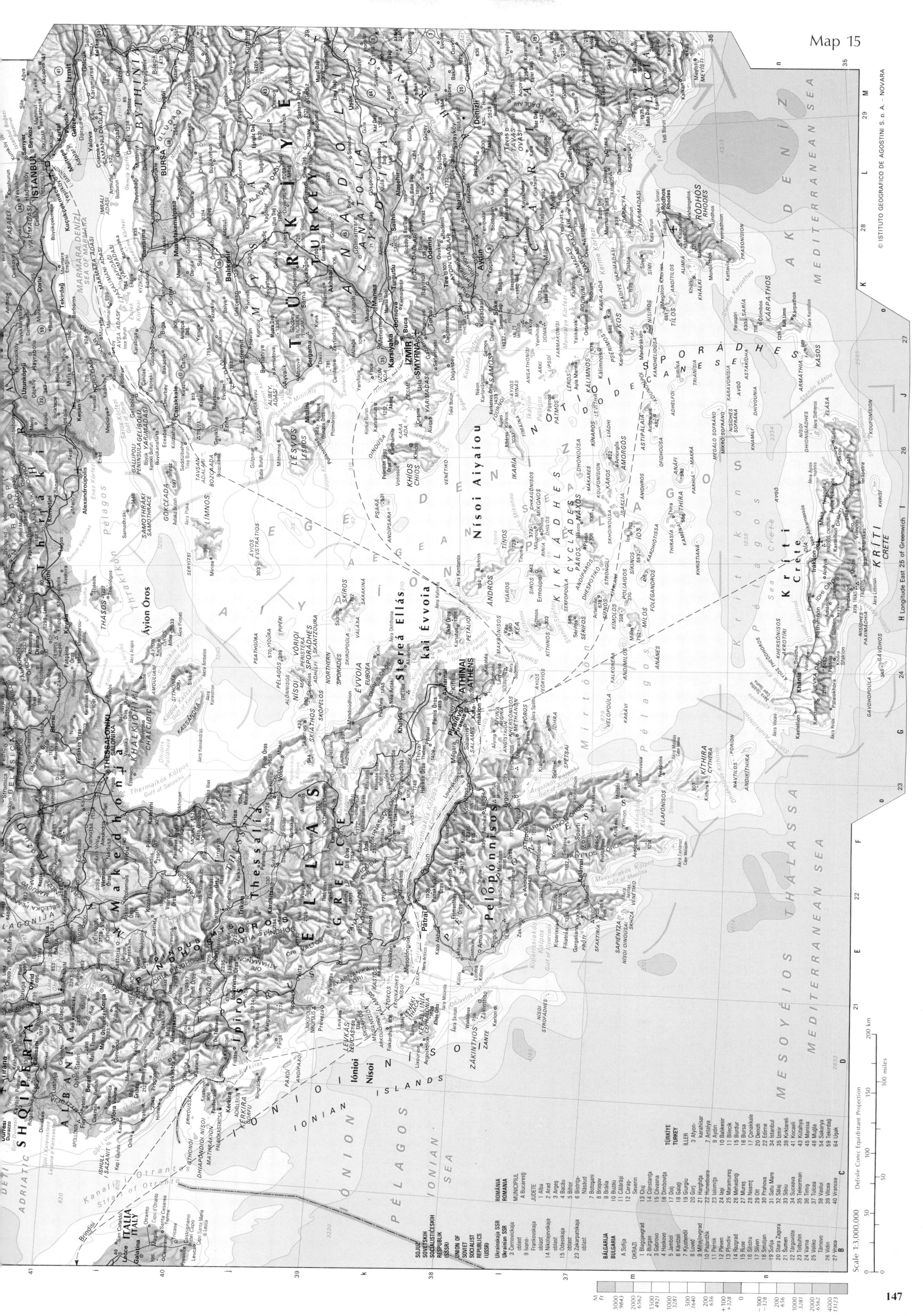

Map 15

Scale 1:3,000,000

Delisle Conic Equidistant Projection

Map 16 **SOUTHWESTERN SOVIET UNION**

Scale 1:6,000,000
Delisle Conic Equidistant Projection

SOJUZ SOVETSKIH
SOCIALISTIČESKIH
RESPUBLIK (SSSR)

UNION OF
SOVIET
SOCIALIST
REPUBLICS (USSR)

Rossijskaja Sovetskaja
Federativnaja
Socialističeskaja
Respublika (RSFSR)

Russian Soviet
Federated Socialist
Republic (RSFSR)

3 Krasnodarski kraj
3A Adygejskaja
  avtonomnaja oblast
6 Stavropolski kraj
6A Karačajevo-
  Čerkesskaja
10 Belgorodskaja oblast
11 Brjanskaja oblast
12 Čeljabinskaja oblast
14 Gorkovskaja oblast
15 Ivanovskaja oblast
17 Jaroslavskaja oblast
18 Kaliningradskaja
  oblast
19 Kalininskaja oblast
20 Kalužskaja oblast
23 Kirovskaja oblast
24 Kostromskaja oblast
25 Kujbyševskaja oblast
26 Kurganskaja oblast
27 Kurskaja oblast
29 Lipeckaja oblast
31 Moskovskaja oblast
33 Novgorodskaja oblast
36 Orenburgskaja oblast
37 Orlovskaja oblast
38 Penzenskaja oblast
40 Pskovskaja oblast
41 Rostovskaja oblast
42 Rjazanskaja oblast
44 Saratovskaja oblast
46 Smolenskaja oblast
47 Tambovskaja oblast
50 Tulskaja oblast
51 Uljanovskaja oblast
52 Vladimirskaja oblast
53 Volgogradskaja oblast
55 Voronežskaja oblast

Ukrainskaja SSR

Ukrainian SSR

1 Čerkasskaja oblast
2 Černigovskaja oblast
3 Černovickaja oblast
4 Dnepropetrovskaja
  oblast
5 Doneckaja oblast
6 Harkovskaja oblast
7 Hersonskaja oblast
8 Hmelnickaja oblast
9 Ivano-Frankovskaja
  oblast
10 Kijevskaja oblast
11 Kirovogradskaja oblast
12 Krymskaja oblast
13 Lvovskaja oblast
14 Nikolajevskaja oblast
15 Odesskaja oblast
16 Poltavskaja oblast
17 Rovenskaja oblast
18 Sumskaja oblast
19 Ternopolskaja oblast
20 Vinnickaja oblast
21 Volynskaja oblast
22 Vorošilovgradskaja
  oblast
23 Zakarpatskaja oblast
24 Zaporožskaja oblast
25 Žitomirskaja oblast

Belorusskaja SSR

Byelorussian SSR

1 Brestskaja oblast
2 Gomelskaja oblast
3 Grodnenskaja oblast
4 Minskaja oblast
5 Mogilevskaja oblast
6 Vitebskaja oblast

Kazahskaja SSR

Kazakh SSR

1 Aktjubinskaja oblast
7 Gurjevskaja oblast
9 Kzyl-Ordinskaja oblast
11 Kustanaiskaja oblast
17 Mangyšlakskaja
  oblast
18 Uralskaja oblast

Gruzinskaja SSR

Georgian SSR

1 Jugo-Osetinskaja
  avtonomnaja oblast

Azerbajdžanskaja SSR

Azerbaidzhan SSR

1 Nagorno-Karabahskaja
  avtonomnaja oblast

Turkmenskaja SSR

Turkmen SSR

1 Ašhabadskaja oblast
3 Krasnovodskaja oblast
5 Tašauzskaja oblast

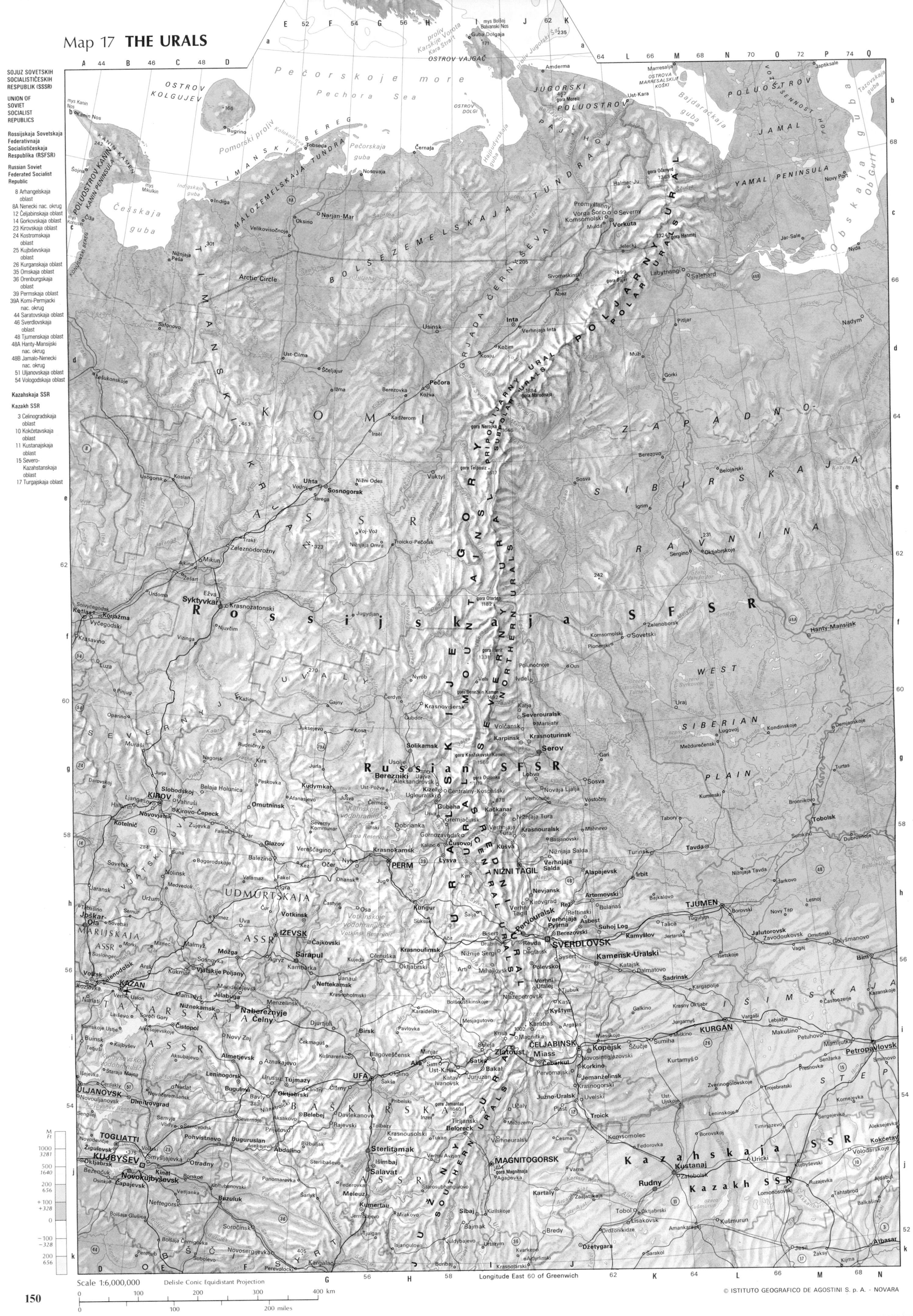

Map 17 THE URALS

Scale 1:6,000,000   Delisle Conic Equidistant Projection

Longitude East 60 of Greenwich

© ISTITUTO GEOGRAFICO DE AGOSTINI S. p. A. - NOVARA

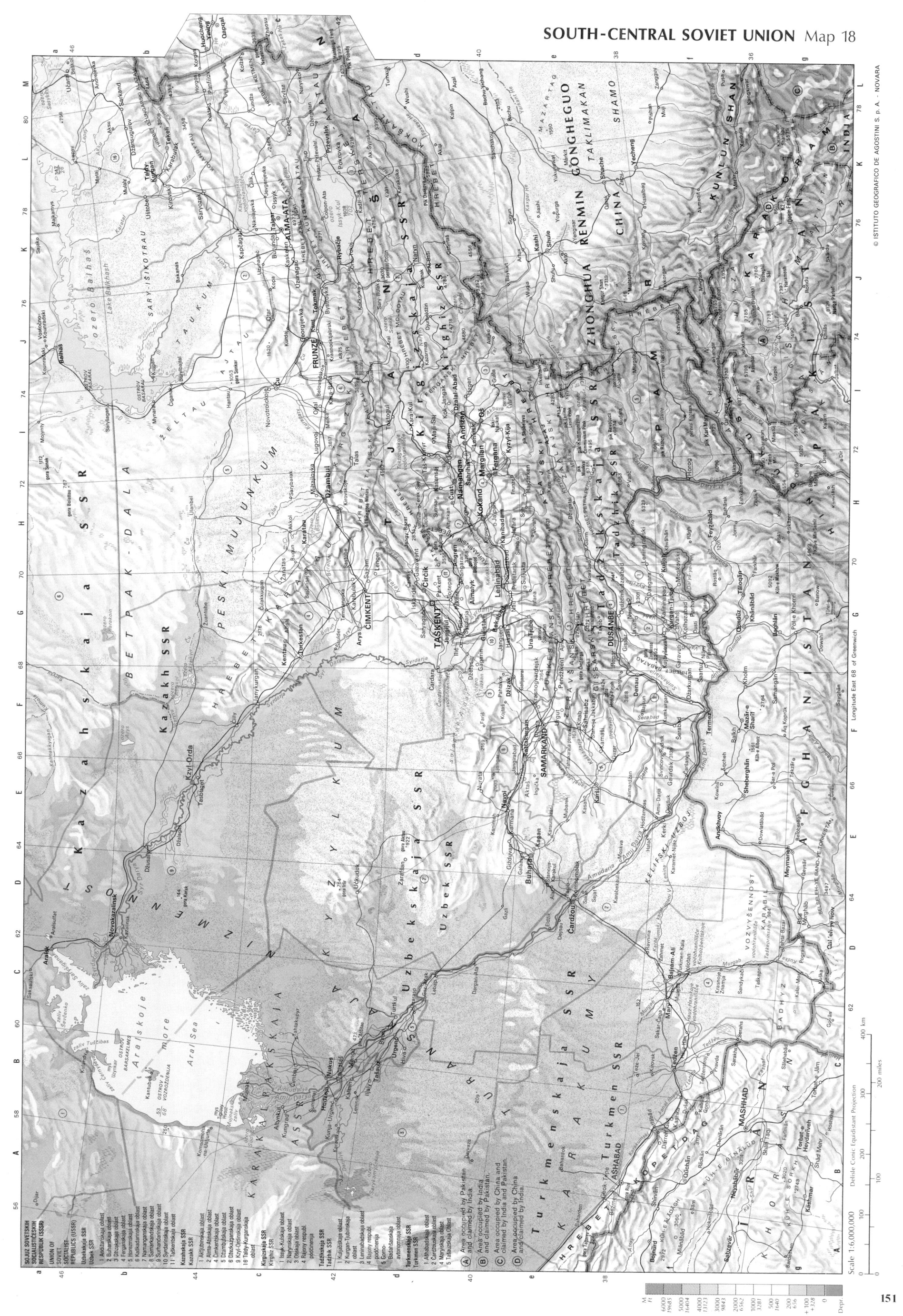

SOJUZ SOVETSKICH
SOCIALISTICESKICH
RESPUBLIK (SSSR)

UNION OF
SOVIET
SOCIALIST
REPUBLICS (USSR)

Uzbek SSR
1 Andizanskaja oblast
2 Buharskaja oblast
3 Dzizakskaja oblast
4 Ferganskaja oblast
5 Kaškadarinskaja oblast
6 Namanganskaja oblast
7 Samarkandskaja oblast
8 Surhandarinskaja oblast
9 Syrdarinskaja oblast
10 Syrdarinskaja oblast
11 Taškentskaja oblast

Kazakh SSR

Kirgiz SSR
1 Issyk-Kuľskaja oblast
2 Narynskaja oblast
3 Oškaja oblast
4 Rajony respubl
podčinenija

Tadžik SSR
1 Kuljabskaja oblast
2 Kurgan-Tjubinsk
3 Leninabadskaja oblast
4 Rajony respubl
podčinenija
5 Gorno-
avtonomnaja oblast

Turkmen SSR
1 Ašhabadskaja oblast
2 Čardžouskaja oblast
3 Maryjskaja oblast
4 Taškauzskaja oblast
5 Tašauzskaja oblast

(A) Area occupied by Pakistan
and claimed by India.
(B) Area occupied by India
and claimed by Pakistan.
(C) Area occupied by China and
claimed by India and Pakistan.
(D) Area occupied by China
and claimed by India.

Scale 1:6,000,000

Deisle Conic Equidistant Projection

151

Ukrainskaja SSR
Ukrainian SSR
11 Kirovogradskaja oblast
12 Krymskaja obl.
13 Lvovskaja obl.
14 Nikolajevskaja oblast
15 Odesskaja obl.
16 Poltavskaja obl.
17 Rovenskaja obl.
18 Sumskaja obl.
19 Ternopolskaja obl.
20 Vinnickaja obl.
21 Volynskaja obl.
22 Vorošilovgradskaja oblast
23 Zakarpatskaja obl.
24 Zaporožskaja obl.
25 Žitomirskaja obl.

Belorusskaja SSR
Byelorussian SSR
1 Brestskaja obl.
2 Gomelskaja obl.
3 Grodnenskaja obl.
4 Minskaja obl.
5 Mogilevskaja obl.
6 Vitebskaja obl.

Uzbekskaja SSR
Uzbek SSR
1 Andižanskaja obl.
2 Buharskaja obl.
3 Džizakskaja obl.
4 Ferganskaja obl.
5 Horezmskaja obl.
6 Kaškadarinskaja oblast
7 Namanganskaja oblast
8 Samarkandskaja oblast
9 Surhandarinskaja oblast
10 Syrdarinskaja obl.
11 Taškentskaja obl.

Kazahskaja SSR
Kazakh SSR
1 Aktjubinskaja obl.
2 Alma-Atinskaja oblast
3 Celinogradskaja oblast
4 Čimkentskaja obl.
5 Džambulskaja obl.
6 Džezkazganskaja oblast
7 Gurjevskaja obl.
8 Karagandinskaja oblast
9 Kzyl-Ordinskaja oblast
10 Kokčetavskaja oblast
11 Kustanajskaja obl.
12 Mangyšlakskaja oblast
13 Pavlodarskaja obl.
14 Semipalatinskaja oblast
15 Severo-Kazahstanskaja oblast
16 Taldy-Kurganskaja oblast
17 Turgajskaja obl.
18 Uralskaja obl.
19 Vostočno-Kazahstanskaja oblast

Gruzinskaja SSR
Georgian SSR
1 Jugo-Osetinskaja avt. oblast

Azerbajdžanskaja SSR
Azerbaidzhan SSR
1 Nagorno-Karabahskaja avt. oblast

Kirgizskaja SSR
Kirghiz SSR
1 Issyk-Kulskaja oblast
2 Narynskaja obl.
3 Ošskaja obl.
4 Rajony respubl. podčinenija

Tadžikskaja SSR
Tadzhik SSR
1 Kuljabskaja oblast
2 Kurgan-Tjubinskaja oblast
3 Leninabadskaja oblast
4 Rajony respubl. podčinenija
5 Gorno-Badahšanskaja avt. oblast

Turkmenskaja SSR
Turkmen SSR
1 Ašhabadskaja obl.
2 Čardžouskaja obl.
3 Krasnovodskaja oblast
4 Maryjskaja obl.
5 Tašauzskaja obl.

M	
Ft	
6000	19685
5000	16404
4000	13123
3000	9843
2000	6562
1000	3281
500	1640
+200	+656
0	
Depr.	
0	
−100	−328
200	656
1000	3281
2000	6562

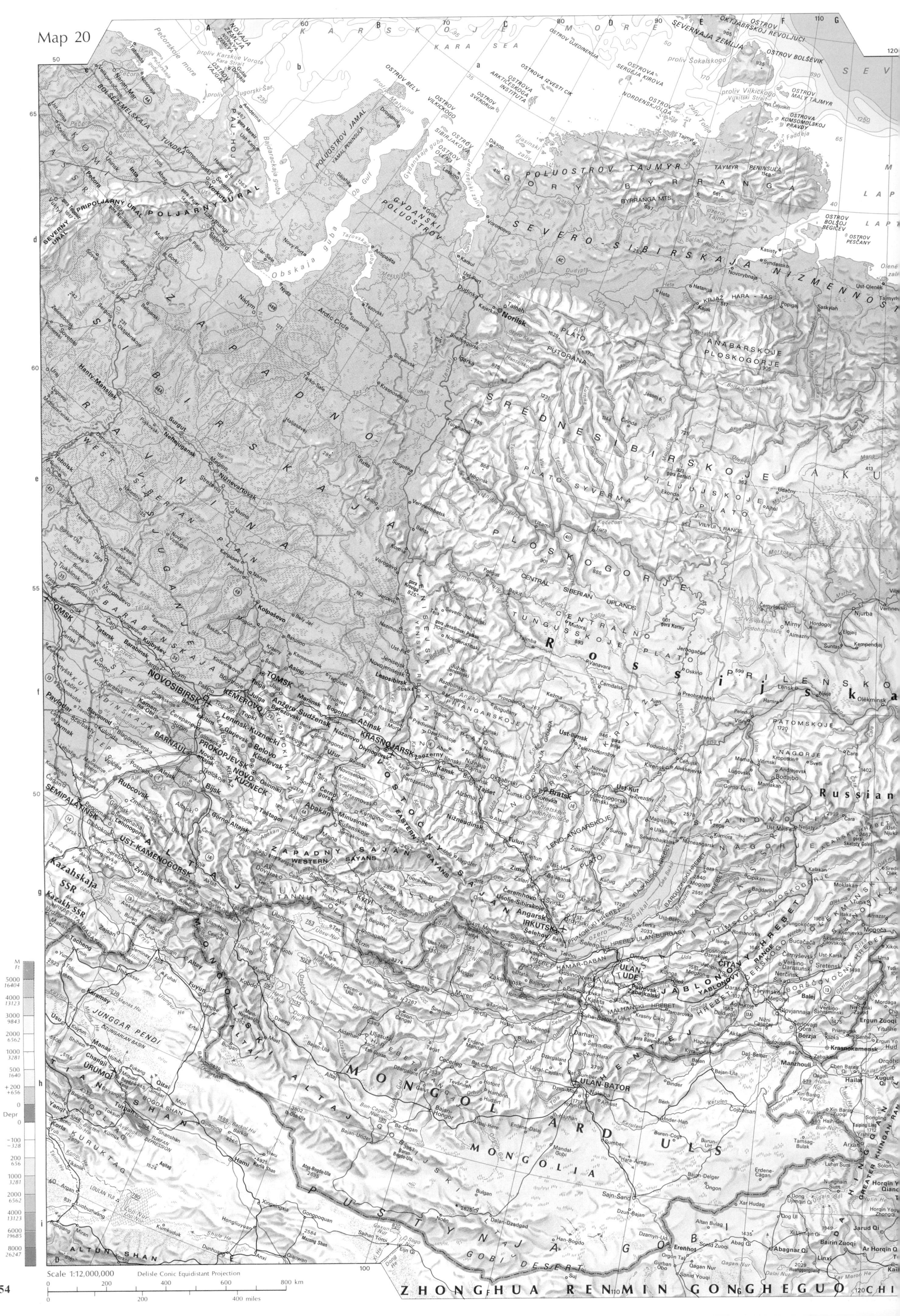

Map 20

154

Scale 1:12,000,000   Delisle Conic Equidistant Projection

0   200   400   600   800 km

0   200   400 miles

ZHONGHUA RENMIN GONGHEGUO

Sojuz Sovetskih Socialisticeskih Respublik (SSSR)
UNION OF SOVIET SOCIALIST REPUBLICS (USSR)

Rossijskaja Sovetskaja Federativnaja Socialisticeskaja Respublika (RSFSR)
Russian Soviet Federated Socialist Republic (RSFSR)

1 Altajski kraj
1A Gorno-Altajskaja avtonomnaja oblast
2 Habarovski kraj
2A Jevrejskaja avtonomnaja oblast
4 Krasnojarski kraj
4A Hakasskaja avtonomnaja oblast
4B Evenkijski nac. okrug
4C Tajmyrski (Dolgano-Neneckij) nac. okrug
5 Primorski kraj
7 Amurskaja oblast
8A Nenecki nac. okrug
13 Citinskaja oblast
13A Aginski Burjatski nac. okrug
16 Irkutskaja oblast
16A Ust-Ordynski Burjatski nac. okrug
21 Kamcatskaja oblast
21A Korjakski nac. okrug
22 Kemerovskaja oblast
30 Magadanskaja oblast
30A Cukotski nac. okrug
34 Novosibirskaja oblast
35 Omskaja oblast
43 Sahalinskaja oblast
48 Tjumenskaja oblast
48A Hanty-Mansijski nac. okrug
48B Jamalo-Nenecki nac. okrug
49 Tomskaja oblast

Kazahskaja SSR
Kazakh SSR

13 Pavlodarskaja oblast
14 Semipalatinskaja oblast
19 Vostocno-Kazahstanskaja oblast

Longitude East 150 of Greenwich

Map 21 **ASIA, PHYSICAL**

PACIFIC

Aleutian Trench
ALEUTIAN ISLANDS
Kuril Trench
FOX ISLANDS
Shishaldin Volcano
KODIAK
ANDREANOF ISLANDS
RAT ISLANDS
NEAR ISLANDS
KOMANDORSKI ISLANDS
KAMCHATKA PENINSULA
KURIL ISLANDS
HOKKAIDO
SAKHALIN
HONSHU

ALASKA PENINSULA
KENAI PENINSULA
ALASKA RANGE
Bering Sea
SEWARD PENINSULA
SAINT LAWRENCE
SAINT MATTHEW
NUNIVAK
PRIBILOF ISLANDS
Norton Sound
Cape Romanzof
Prince of Wales
Okhotsk Sea
SREDINNY HREBET
KORJAKSKOJE NAGORJE
SIHOTE - ALIN
Bureya Range

ALASKA
BROOKS RANGE
Chukchi Sea
CHUKCHI PENINSULA
Anadyr Gulf
KOLYMA RANGE
CHERSKI MOUNTAINS
VERKHOYANSK MOUNTAINS
SUNTAR HREBET
DZHUGDZHUR RANGE
STANOVOY RANGE
LESSER KHINGAN RANGE
GREATER KHINGAN RANGE
MANCHURIA
STANOVOY UPLAND
ALDAN PLATEAU
YABLONOVY RANGE
GOBI DESERT

Richardson Mountains
Point Hope
Point Barrow
WRANGEL
New Siberian Islands
EASTERN SIBERIA
NIZMENNOST
KOLYMSKAJA
LENA MOUNTAINS
Baikal Range
ALTAI
KHANGAI MTS.
MONGOLIAN ALTAI

VICTORIA
BANKS
MELVILLE ISLAND
PRINCE PATRICK
PARRY ISLANDS
McClure Strait
ARCTIC OCEAN
Canada Basin
Makarov Basin
Alpha Cordillera
North Pole
Lomonosov Ridge
Eurasia Basin
NEW SIBERIAN ISLANDS
ANJOU ISLANDS
LYAKHOV ISLANDS
KOTELNY ISLANDS
TAYMYR PENINSULA
BYRRANGA MOUNTAINS
NORTH SIBERIAN PLAIN
CENTRAL SIBERIAN UPLAND
WEST SIBERIAN PLAIN
VASJUGANJE
EASTERN SAYANS
WESTERN SAYANS
KUZNEČKI ALATAU
DZUNGARIAN BASIN
TIAN SHAN
TURFAN DEPRESSION

PRINCE OF WALES
SOMERSET ISLAND
BATHURST
CORNWALLIS
DEVON
AXEL HEIBERG ISLANDS
ELLESMERE
North Magnetic Pole
Cape Columbia
SEVERNAYA ZEMLYA
KOMSOMOLEC
BOLSHEVIK
OCTOBER REVOLUTION ISLAND
PIONER
VIZE
Arctic Circle
Yenisey
Ob'
TARIM BASIN
KAZAKH HILLS
KAZAKHSTAN
Dudinka

BAFFIN
Baffin Bay
Lancaster Sound
KNUD RASMUSSEN LAND
PEARY LAND
KING FREDERIK VIII LAND
Nansen Cordillera
Fram Basin
Nansen Basin
FRANZ JOSEPH LAND
ALEXANDRY
GEORGIJ
GREEM-BELL
BELY ISLAND
Winter limit of pack ice (April)
Summer limit of pack ice (August)
NOVAYA ZEMLYA
Kara Sea
GYDA PENINSULA
YAMAL PENINSULA
KAJGAC
Novosibirsk
Omsk
ISHIM STEPPE
URAL MOUNTAINS
KIRGHIZ STEPPE

GREENLAND
KING CHRISTIAN X LAND
KING FREDERIK VI COAST
Denmark Strait
Greenland Sea
Greenland Basin
SPITSBERGEN
BEAR ISLAND
Barents Sea
KOLGUJEV
KANIN PENINSULA
TIMAN RIDGE
NORTHERN UVALS
MOSCOW BASIN
VOLGA UPLAND
CASPIAN DEPRESSION
Caspian Sea

DISKO
JAN MAYEN
Mohns Ridge
Norwegian Sea
Norwegian Basin
SCANDINAVIA
KJØLEN
KARELIA
KOLA PENINSULA
White Sea
Murmansk
CENTRAL RUSSIAN UPLAND
VALDAI HILLS
CISCAUCASIA
CAUCASUS
TRANSCAUCASIA
ARMENIA

ICELAND
Reykjavik
Reykjanes Ridge
Mid-Atlantic Ridge
ATLANTIC OCEAN
FAEROE ISLANDS
SHETLAND ISLANDS
Gulf of Bothnia
Trondheim
VESTLAND
Stockholm
GOTLAND
ÖLAND
Baltic Sea
RIGA
LIVONIA
Leningrad
Moskva
UKRAINE
CRIMEA
MOLDAVIA
Black Sea
ANATOLIA
TAURUS MTS.
ZAGROS
MESOPOTAMIA

Rockall Rise
BRITISH ISLES
GREAT BRITAIN
ORKNEY ISLANDS
HEBRIDES
North Sea
SCOTLAND
Glasgow
Dublin
IRELAND
ENGLAND
London
Celtic Sea
Land's End
English Channel
BRITTANY
Paris
FLANDERS
Hamburg
Berlin
FRIESLAND
Amsterdam
BOHEMIA
BOHEMIAN FOREST
SILESIA
SUDETEN
POLAND
GALICIA
PODOLIA
POLESYE
CARPATHIAN MTS.
BALKAN MTS.
BALKAN PENINSULA
THRACE
MACEDONIA
CYPRUS
SYRIAN DESERT

Bordeaux
MASSIF CENTRAL
Mont Blanc
ALPS
APENNINES
PYRENEES
CORSICA
SARDINIA
Milano
Roma
Adriatic Sea
Ionian Sea
Tyrrhenian Sea
PINDUS MTS.
CRETE
PELOPONNESUS
RHODES
Mediterranean Sea
NILE DELTA
QATTARA

© ISTITUTO GEOGRAFICO DE AGOSTINI S. p. A. - NOVARA

Scale 1:30,000,000

Lambert Azimuthal Equal Area Projection

Longitude East 80 of Greenwich

2000 km

1000 miles

Map 22 **ASIA, POLITICAL**

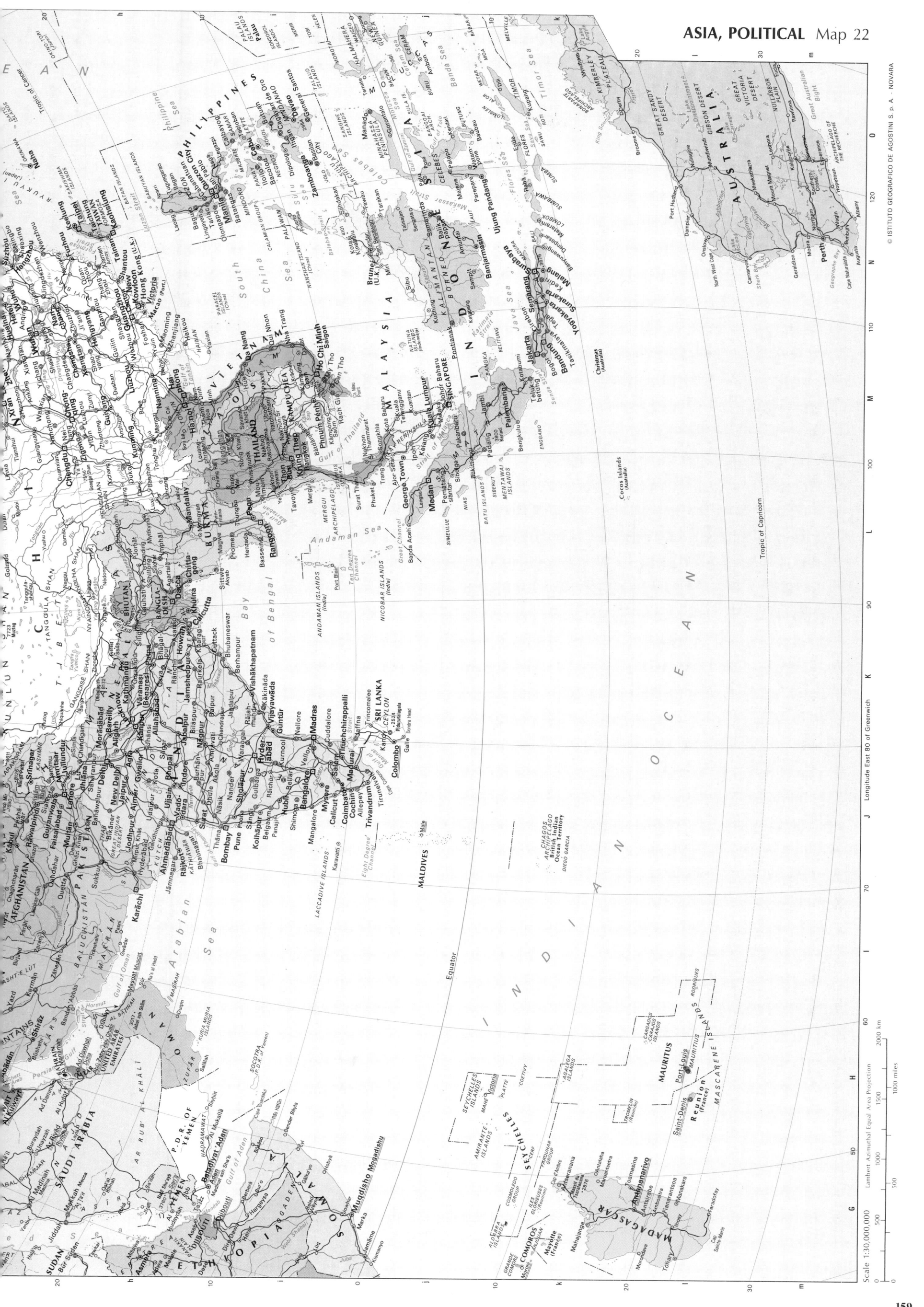

© ISTITUTO GEOGRAFICO DE AGOSTINI S. p. A. - NOVARA

Scale 1:30,000,000

Lambert Azimuthal Equal Area Projection

Longitude East 80 of Greenwich

Tropic of Capricorn

Equator

INDIAN OCEAN

AUSTRALIA

GREAT SANDY DESERT

GIBSON DESERT

GREAT VICTORIA DESERT

NULLARBOR PLAIN

KIMBERLEY PLATEAU

Perth

PHILIPPINES

Quezon City

Manila

Davao

South China Sea

VIETNAM

LAOS

THAILAND

KAMPUCHEA

BURMA

Ho Chi Minh

Saigon

Phnom Penh

Bangkok

Rangoon

Hanoi

MALAYSIA

INDONESIA

SUMATRA

BORNEO

KALIMANTAN

CELEBES

Kuala Lumpur

Singapore

Jakarta

Bandung

Surabaya

Brunei (U.K.)

Medan

Palembang

Banjarmasin

Ujung Pandang

Java Sea

Banda Sea

Timor Sea

Arafura Sea

NEW GUINEA

HALMAHERA

CERAM

MOLUCCAS

Cocos Islands (Australia)

Christmas (Australia)

INDIA

Bombay

Calcutta

Madras

New Delhi

Hyderabad

Bangalore

Ahmadabad

Kanpur

Nagpur

Pune

BANGLA-DESH

Dacca

Chittagong

NEPAL

Kathmandu

BHUTAN

SRI LANKA

CEYLON

Colombo

Bay of Bengal

Andaman Sea

ANDAMAN ISLANDS (India)

NICOBAR ISLANDS (India)

LACCADIVE ISLANDS

MALDIVES

Malé

Arabian Sea

PAKISTAN

Karāchi

AFGHANISTAN

Kabul

Lahore

CHINA

TIBET

KUNLUN SHAN

TANGGULA SHAN

HENGDUAN SHAN

Chengdu

Kunming

Guangzhou

Hong Kong (U.K.)

Macao (Port.)

TAIWAN

Taipei

Kaohsiung

Xi'an

Hangzhou

Suzhou

Nanning

Guilin

OMAN

Masqat (Muscat)

UNITED ARAB EMIRATES

QATAR

BAHRAIN

Persian Gulf

Gulf of Oman

Hormuz

SAUDI ARABIA

Mecca

Medina

AL KUWAIT

P.D.R. OF YEMEN

Aden

YEMEN

Ṣan'ā'

SUDAN

ETHIOPIA

Asmara

Addis Ababa

SOMALIA

Muqdisho Mogadishu

Djibouti

Gulf of Aden

SOCOTRA (P.D.R. of Yemen)

RUB' AL KHĀLĪ

MADAGASCAR

Antananarivo

COMOROS

Mayotte (France)

SEYCHELLES ISLANDS

Victoria

AMIRANTE ISLANDS

CHAGOS ARCHIPELAGO British Indian Ocean Territory

DIEGO GARCIA

MAURITIUS

Port-Louis

Réunion (France)

Saint-Denis

MASCARENE ISLANDS

RODRIGUES

CARGADOS CARAJOS ISLANDS

2000 km

1000 miles

159

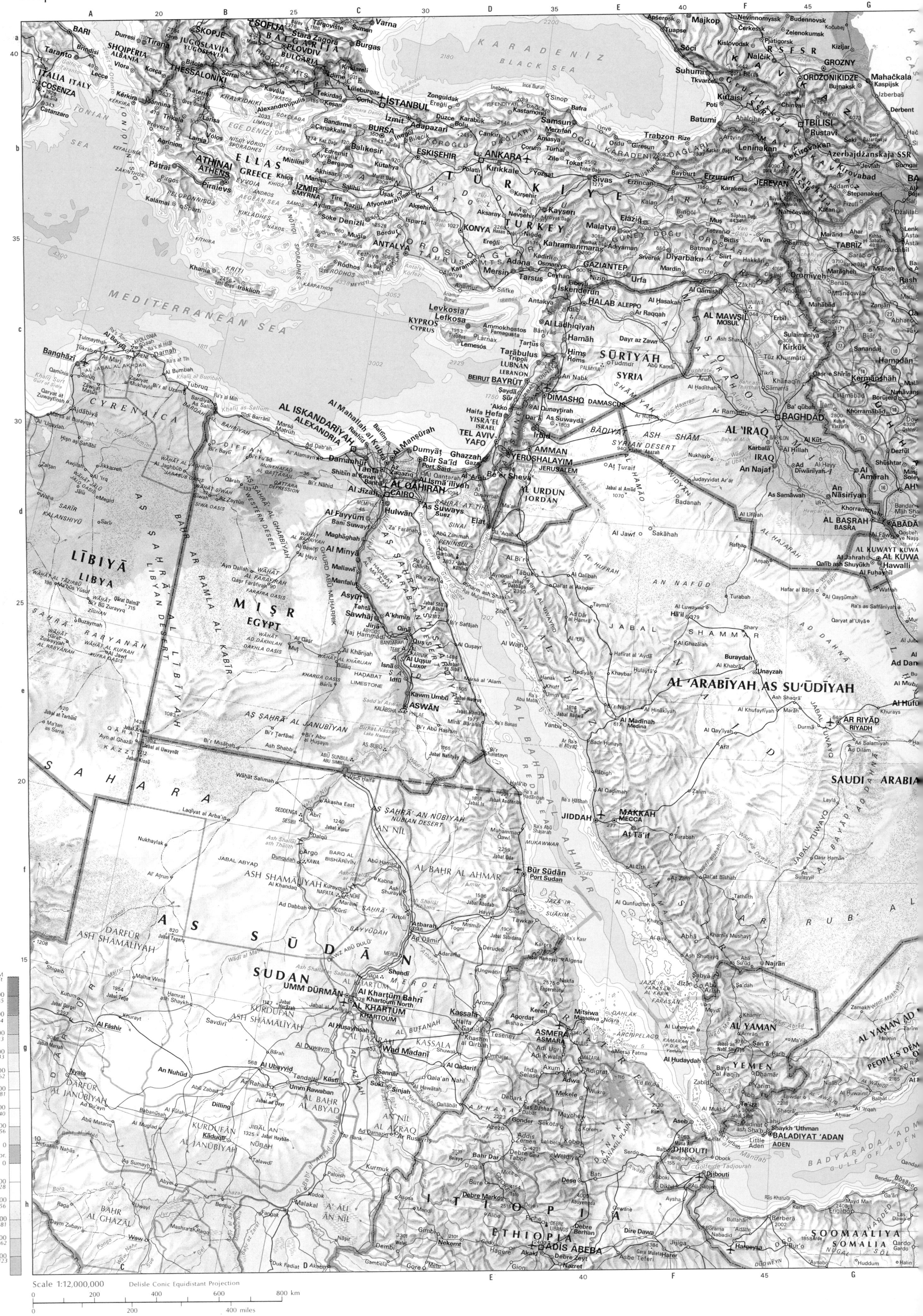

Map 23 **SOUTHWESTERN ASIA**

BLACK SEA
KARADENIZ

RSFSR

TBILISI
JEREVAN
GROZNY
ORDŽONIKIDZE

TÜRKİYE
TURKEY

ANKARA
İSTANBUL
İZMİR
BURSA
ESKİŞEHİR
KONYA
ANTALYA

ELLAS
GREECE
ATHÍNAI
ATHENS

ITALIA
ITALY

MEDITERRANEAN SEA

KYPROS
CYPRUS
Levkosia/
Lefkosa

HALAB ALEPPO
SÜRIYA
SYRIA
DIMASHQ DAMASCUS

LUBNÁN
LEBANON
BEIRUT BAYRÚT

YISRA'EL
ISRAEL
TEL AVIV-YAFO

AL ISKANDARĪYAH
ALEXANDRIA
AL QĀHIRAH
CAIRO

YERUSHALAYIM
JERUSALEM
AMMAN
AL URDUN
JORDAN

AL 'IRAQ
IRAQ
BAGHDĀD
AL BAŞRAH
BASRA

AL KUWAYT KUWA
AL KUWA

TABRIZ

MIŞR
EGYPT

LĪBIYĀ
LIBYA

CYRENAICA

SAHARA

AL 'ARABĪYAH AS SU'ŪDĪYAH
SAUDI ARABIA
AR RIYĀḌ
RIYADH

AN NAFŪD

JABAL SHAMMAR

AL MADĪNAH
Medina

MAKKAH
MECCA
JIDDAH

AL BAHR AL AHMAR
RED SEA

AS SŪDĀN
SUDAN

AL KHARTŪM
KHARTOUM
UMM DURMĀN

DARFŪR

Būr Sūdān
Port Sudan

AL YAMAN
YEMEN

YAMAN

SOOMAALIYA
SOMALIA
DJIBOUTI

ITIOPIA
ETHIOPIA
ADIS ABEBA
ADDIS ABABA

GULF OF ADEN
BALADIYAT 'ADAN
ADEN

Scale 1:12,000,000
Delisle Conic Equidistant Projection

0   200   400   600   800 km
0   200   400 miles

M Ft
6000 19685
5000 16404
4000 13123
3000 9843
2000 6562
1000 3281
500 1640
+200 +656
Depr.
0
−100 −328
200 656
1000 3281
4000 13123

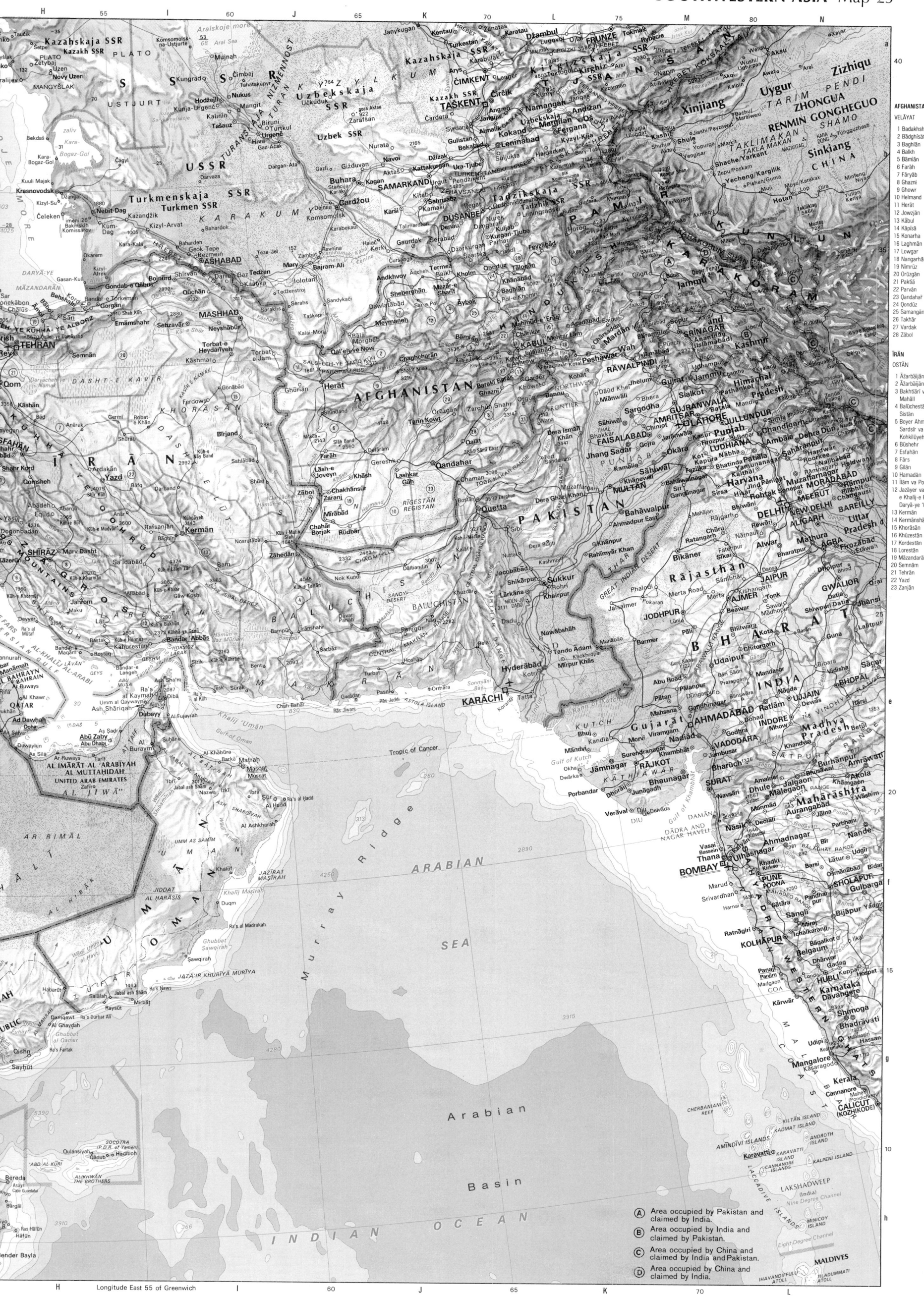

AFGHANISTAN

VELÄYAT

1 Badakhshan
2 Bädghīsāt
3 Baghlān
4 Balkh
5 Bāmiān
6 Farāh
7 Fāryāb
8 Ghazni
9 Ghowr
10 Helmand
11 Herāt
12 Jowzjān
13 Kābul
14 Kāpīsā
15 Konarha
16 Laghmān
17 Lowgar
18 Nangarhār
19 Nīmrūz
20 Orūzgān
21 Paktiā
22 Parvān
23 Qandahār
24 Qondūz
25 Samangān
26 Takhār
27 Vardak
28 Zābol

ĪRĀN

OSTĀN

1 Āzarbāījān-e Gharbī
2 Āzarbāījān-e Sharqī
3 Bakhtiārī va Chahār
  Mahāll
4 Balūchestān va
  Sīstān
5 Boyer Ahmadi-ye
  Sardsīr va
  Kühkīlūyeh
6 Büshehr
7 Esfahān
8 Fārs
9 Gīlān
10 Hamadān
11 Īlām va Poshtkūh
12 Jazāyer va Banāder-
   e Khalīj-e Fārs va
   Daryā-ye 'Omān
13 Kermān
14 Kermānshāhān
15 Khorāsān
16 Khüzestān
17 Kordestān
18 Lorestān
19 Māzandarān
20 Semnān
21 Tehrān
22 Yazd
23 Zanjān

Area occupied by Pakistan and claimed by India.

Area occupied by India and claimed by Pakistan.

Area occupied by China and claimed by India and Pakistan.

Area occupied by China and claimed by India.

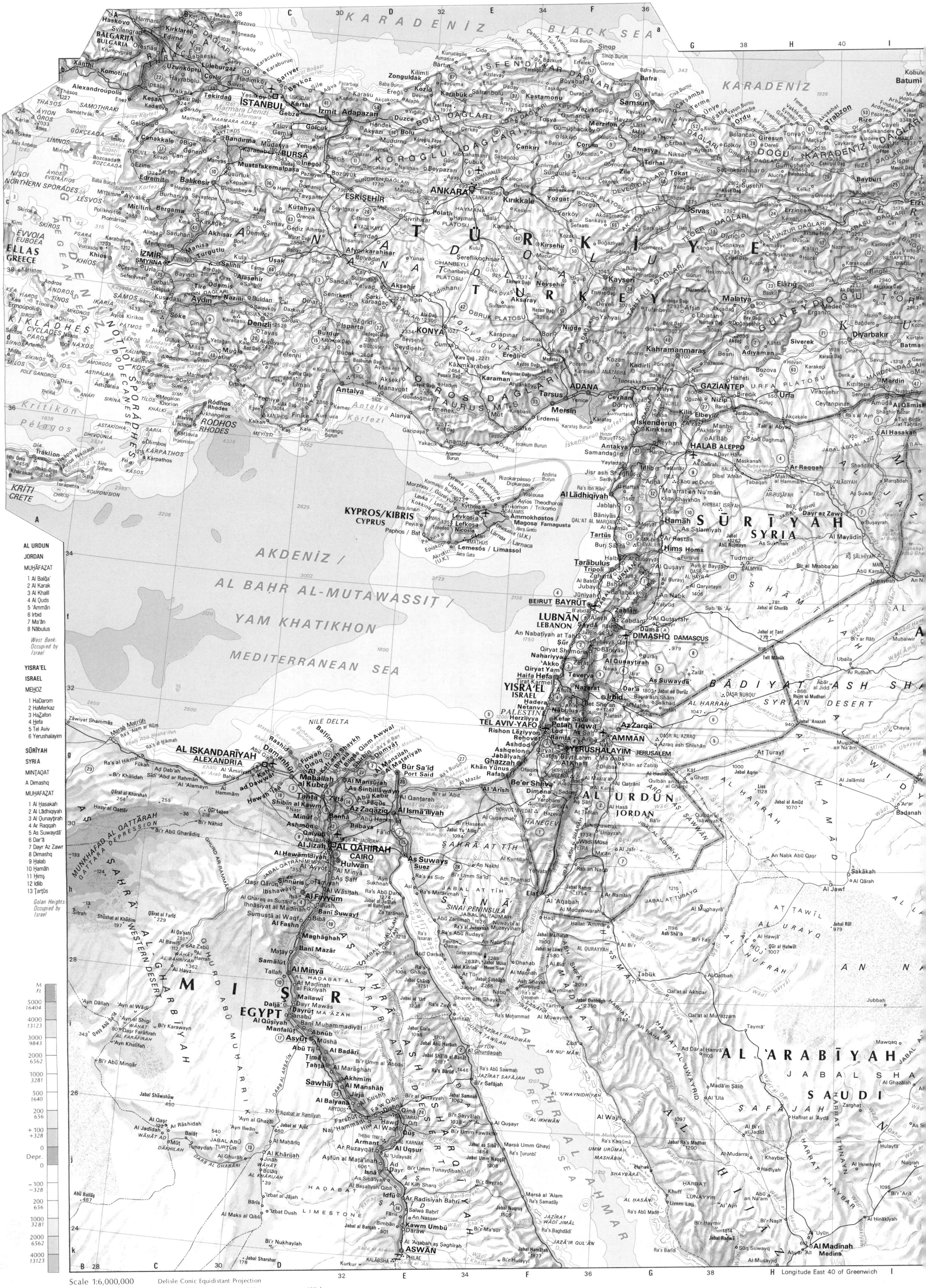

KARADENIZ — BLACK SEA — KARADENIZ

BÅLGARIJA / BULGARIA

TÜRKİYE / TURKEY

İSTANBUL
BURSA
ANKARA
ESKİŞEHİR
İZMİR / SMYRNA
KONYA
ADANA
GAZİANTEP
Malatya
Sivas
Trabzon
Samsun
Diyarbakır
Mardin

ELLAS / GREECE

KRITI / CRETE

KYPROS / KIBRIS
CYPRUS
Nicosia / Lefkosa

AKDENİZ / AL BAHR AL-MUTAWASSIT / YAM KHATIKHON / MEDITERRANEAN SEA

HALAB ALEPPO
Hamāh
Hims Homs
SŪRİYAH / SYRIA
Ar Raqqah

BEIRUT BAYRŪT
LUBNĀN / LEBANON
DIMASHQ DAMASCUS

YISRA'EL / ISRAEL
TEL AVIV-YAFO
YERUSHALAYIM / JERUSALEM

AL URDUN / JORDAN
'AMMĀN

BĀDIYAT ASH SHĀM / SYRIAN DESERT

AL ISKANDARİYAH / ALEXANDRIA
AL QĀHIRAH / CAIRO
NILE DELTA

MISR / EGYPT

SĪNĀ / SINAI PENINSULA

AL 'ARABİYAH SA'ŪDİ / SAUDI

AL BAHR AL AHMAR / RED SEA

AL MADĪNAH / Medina

ASWĀN

Scale 1:6,000,000 Delisle Conic Equidistant Projection

0   100   200   300   400 km
0   100   200 miles

Longitude East 40 of Greenwich

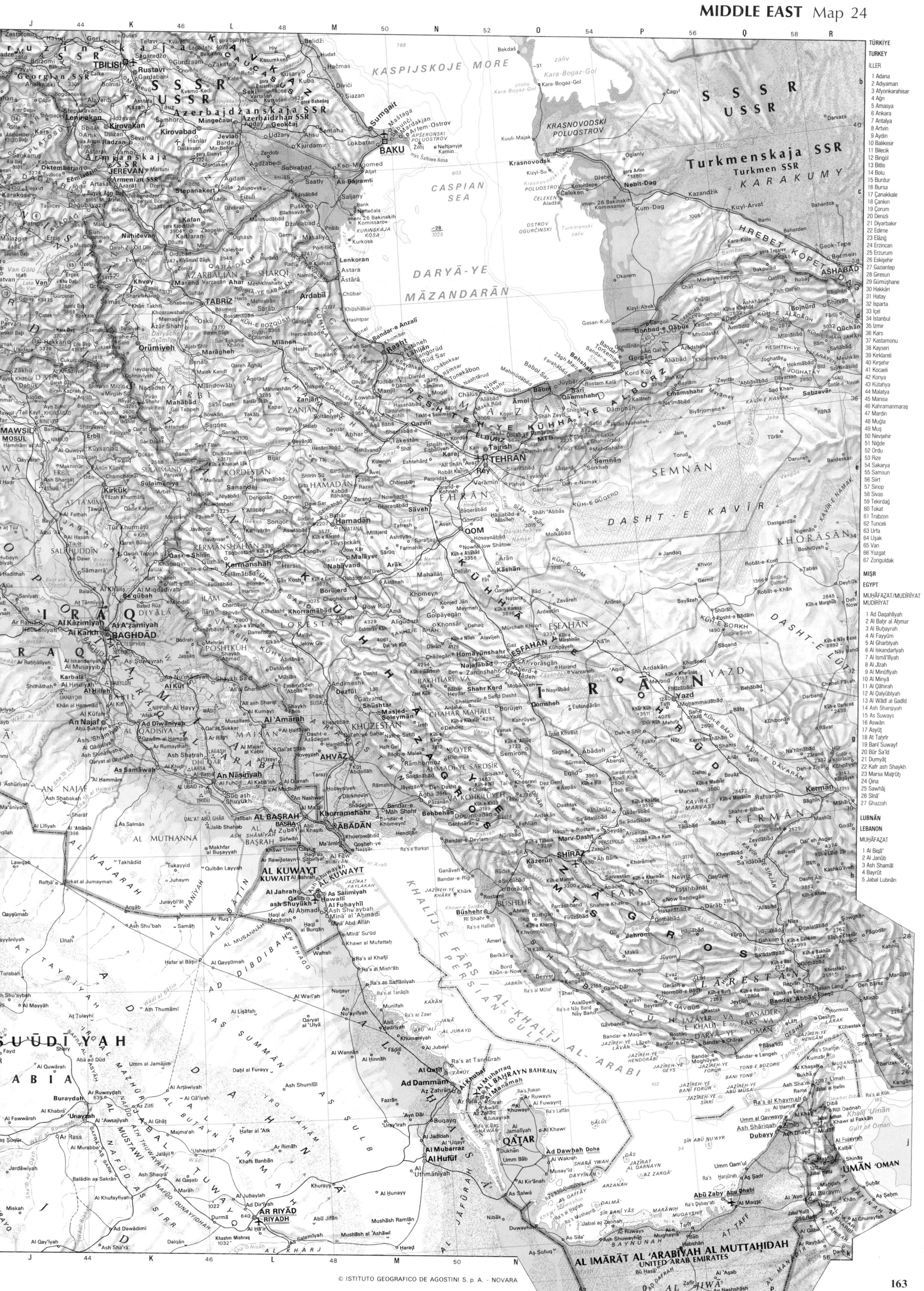

TÜRKIYE
TURKEY
ILLER
1 Adana
2 Adiyaman
3 Afyonkarahisar
4 Ağrı
5 Amasya
6 Ankara
7 Antalya
8 Artvin
9 Aydın
10 Balıkesir
11 Bilecik
12 Bingöl
13 Bitlis
14 Bolu
15 Burdur
16 Bursa
17 Çanakkale
18 Çankırı
19 Çorum
20 Denizli
21 Diyarbakır
22 Edirne
23 Elâzığ
24 Erzincan
25 Erzurum
26 Eskişehir
27 Gaziantep
28 Giresun
29 Gümüşhane
30 Hakkâri
31 Hatay
32 Isparta
33 İçel
34 İstanbul
35 İzmir
36 Kars
37 Kastamonu
38 Kayseri
39 Kırklareli
40 Kırşehir
41 Kocaeli
42 Konya
43 Kütahya
44 Malatya
45 Manisa
46 Kahramanmaraş
47 Mardin
48 Muğla
49 Muş
50 Nevşehir
51 Niğde
52 Ordu
53 Rize
54 Sakarya
55 Samsun
56 Siirt
57 Sinop
58 Sivas
59 Tekirdağ
60 Tokat
61 Trabzon
62 Tunceli
63 Urfa
64 Uşak
65 Van
66 Yozgat
67 Zonguldak

MISR
EGYPT
MUHĀFAZAT/MUDĪRĪYAT
MUDĪRĪYAT
1 Ad Daqahlīyah
2 Al Baḥr al Aḥmar
3 Al Buḥayrah
4 Al Fayyūm
5 Al Gharbīyah
6 Al Iskandarīyah
7 Al Ismā'īlīyah
8 Al Jīzah
9 Al Minūfīyah
10 Al Minyā
11 Al Qāhirah
12 Al Qalyūbīyah
13 Al Wādī al Gadīd
14 Ash Sharqīyah
15 As Suways
16 Aswān
17 Asyūṭ
18 At Taḥrīr
19 Banī Suwayf
20 Būr Sa'īd
21 Dumyāṭ
22 Kafr ash Shaykh
23 Marsa Maṭrūḥ
24 Qinā
25 Sawhāj
26 Sīnā'
27 Ghazzah

LUBNĀN
LEBANON
MUHĀFAZAT
1 Al Biqā'
2 Al Janūb
3 Ash Shamāl
4 Bayrūt
5 Jabal Lubnān

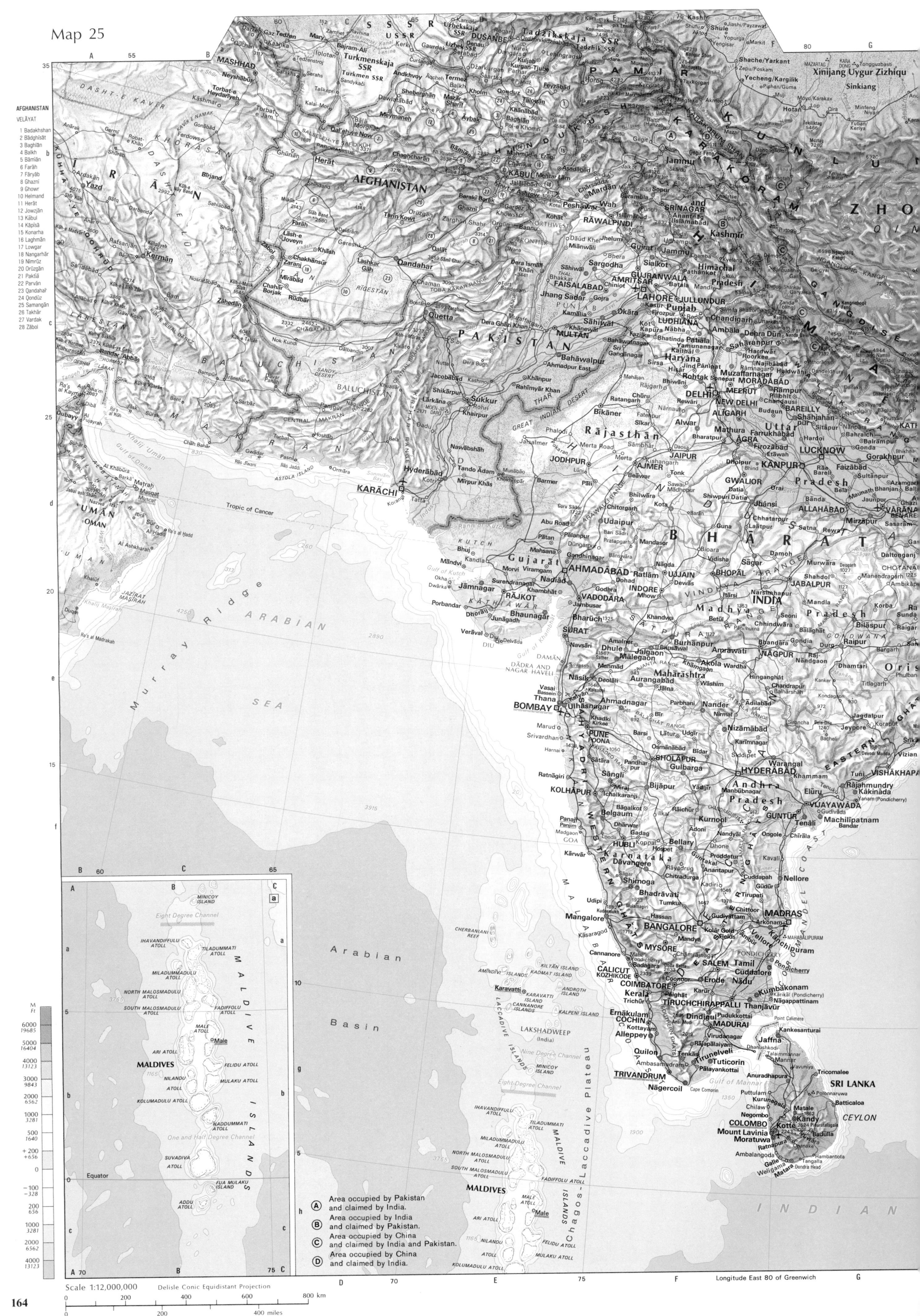

Map 25

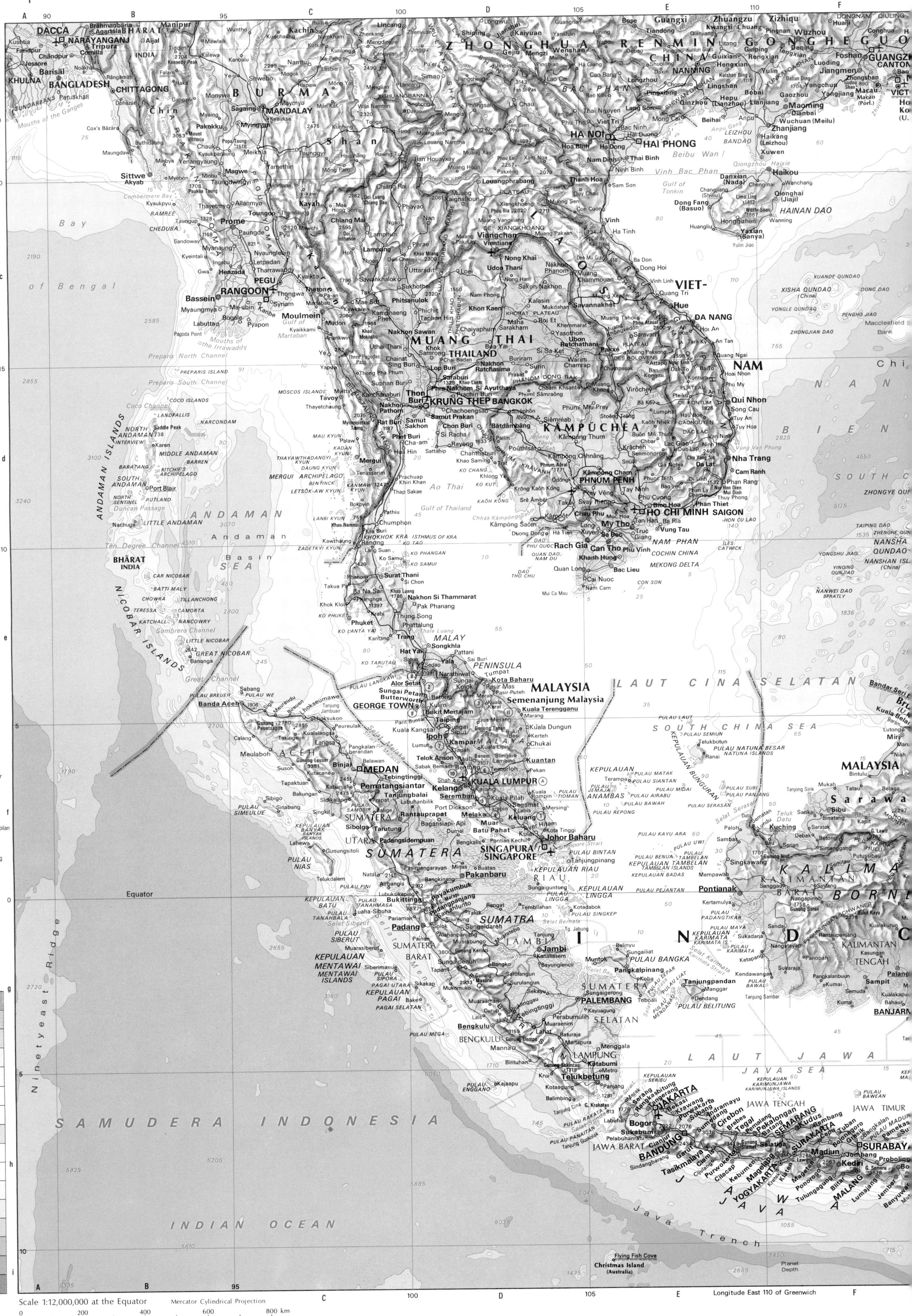

Map 26 **SOUTHEAST ASIA**

MALAYSIA
Semenanjung
Malaysia

WILAYAH
PERSEKUTUAN

A Kuala Lumpur

NEGERI

1 Johor
2 Kedah
3 Kelatan
4 Melaka
5 Negeri Sembilan
6 Pahang
7 Perak
8 Perlis
9 Pulau Pinang
10 Selangor
11 Terengganu

Scale 1:12,000,000 at the Equator   Mercator Cylindrical Projection

0   200   400   600   800 km
0   200   400 miles

Longitude East 110 of Greenwich

TAIWAN

NIPPON JAPAN

LUZON

PILIPINAS
PHILIPPINES

MANILA
QUEZON CITY

PHILIPPINE SEA

Philippine Basin

PACIFIC OCEAN

West Mariana Basin

Philippine Trench

MINDANAO

ZAMBOANGA

DAVAO

SULU SEA

Sulu Basin

SULU ARCHIPELAGO

CELEBES SEA

Celebes Basin

CAROLINE ISLANDS

Trust Territory of the Pacific Islands
(Administered by the United States)

PALAU ISLANDS

West Caroline Basin

YAP ISLANDS

HALMAHERA

MALUKU

MOLUCCA SEA

LAUT SERAM
SERAM CERAM

INDONESIA

SULAWESI
CELEBES

MAKASAR
UJUNG PANDANG

LAUT FLORES

BANDA SEA

IRIAN JAYA

NEW GUINEA
PAPUA
NEW GUINEA

PULAU IRIAN

KEPULAUAN TANIMBAR

ARAFURA SEA
LAUT ARAFURA

TIMOR SEA
LAUT TIMOR

NUSA TENGGARA
PULAU SUMBA

AUSTRALIA

DARWIN

MELVILLE ISLAND

Tropic of Cancer

Equator

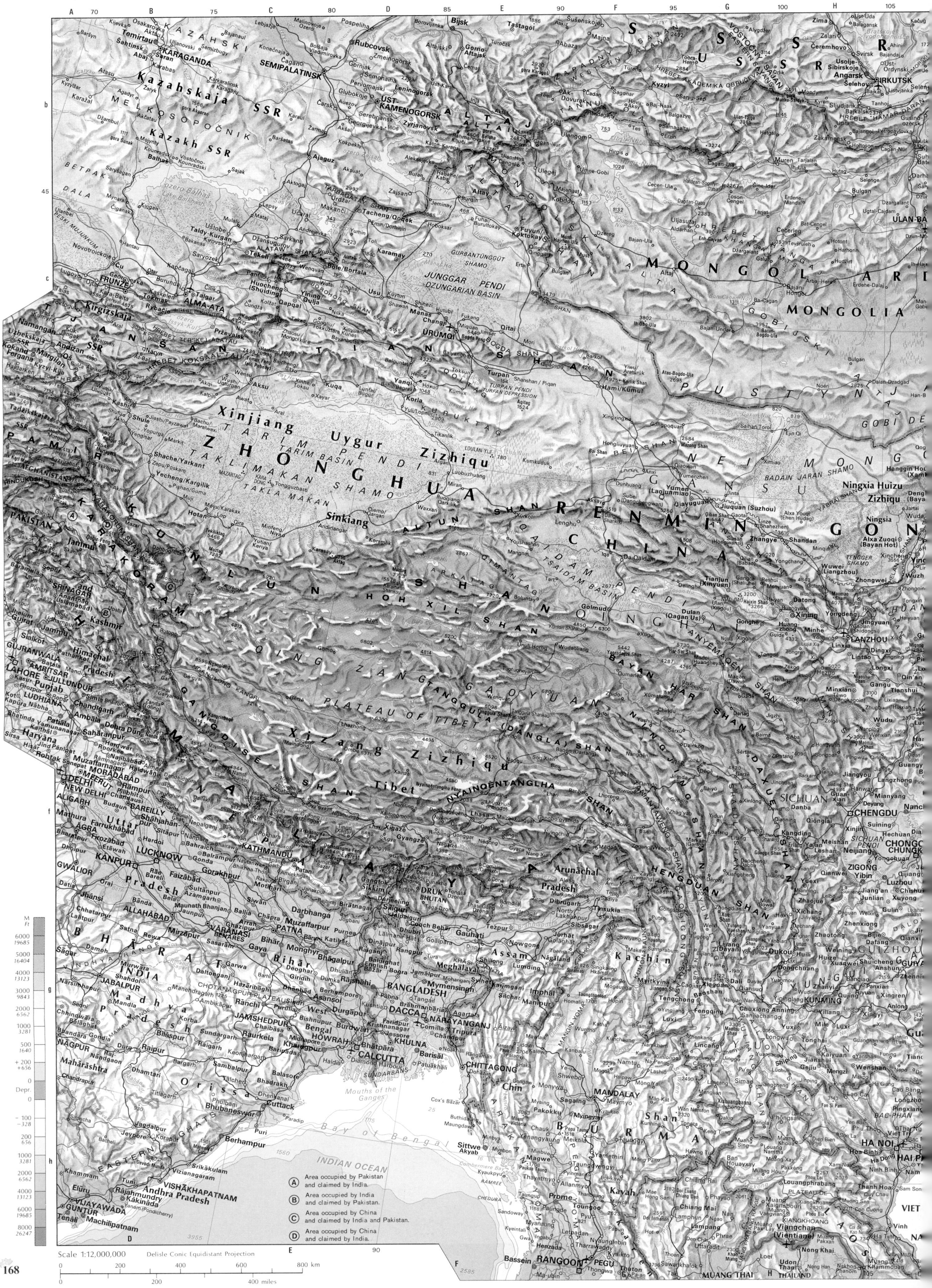

Map 27 **CHINA AND MONGOLIA**

M
Ft
6000 19685
5000 16404
4000 13123
3000 9843
2000 6562
1000 3281
500 1640
+ 200 +656
Depr.
0
- 100 -328
200 656
1000 3281
2000 6562
4000 13123
6000 19685
8000 26247

Ⓐ Area occupied by Pakistan and claimed by India.
Ⓑ Area occupied by India and claimed by Pakistan.
Ⓒ Area occupied by China and claimed by India and Pakistan.
Ⓓ Area occupied by China and claimed by India.

Scale 1:12,000,000   Delisle Conic Equidistant Projection

0   200   400   600   800 km
0   200   400 miles

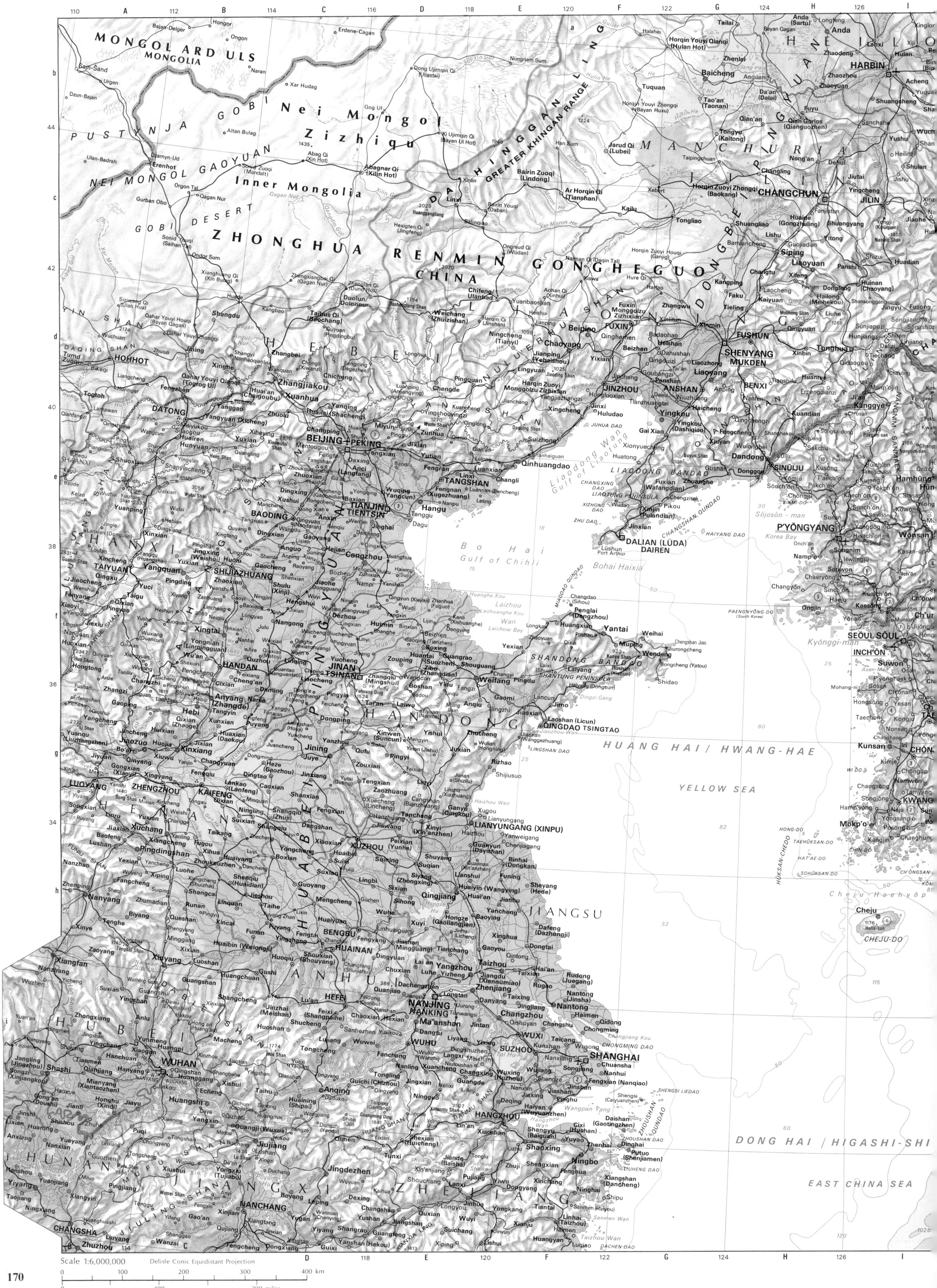

Map 28 **NORTHEASTERN CHINA, KOREA AND JAPAN**

MONGOL ARD ULS
MONGOLIA

PUSTYNJA GOBI Nei Mongol Zizhiqu

NEI MONGOL GAOYUAN Inner Mongolia

GOBI DESERT

ZHONGHUA RENMIN GONGHEGUO
CHINA

DA HINGGAN LING / GREATER KHINGAN RANGE

MANCHURIA

YIN SHAN

DAQING SHAN

HEBEI

SHANXI

BEIJING / PEKING

TIANJIN / TIENTSIN

TAIYUAN

SHIJIAZHUANG

HENAN

SHANDONG

SHANTUNG PENINSULA

LIAODONG BANDAO / LIAOTUNG PENINSULA

SHENYANG / MUKDEN

ANSHAN

BENXI

FUSHUN

JINZHOU

DALIAN (LÜDA) / DAIREN

Lüshun / Port Arthur

CHANGCHUN

JILIN

HARBIN

SIPING

LIAOYUAN

Bo Hai / Gulf of Chihli

Liaodong Wan / Gulf of Liaotung

Liaozhou / Laizhou Wan / Laichow Bay

HUANG HAI / HWANG-HAE

YELLOW SEA

SINŬIJU

DANDONG

PYŎNGYANG

SEOUL / SŎUL

INCH'ŎN

Korea Bay

Kyŏnggi-man

MADAO QUNDAO

CHANGSHAN-QUNDAO

Qingdao / Tsingtao

Yantai

Weihai

JIANGSU

NANJING / NANKING

SHANGHAI

HANGZHOU

WUXI

SUZHOU

WUHU

HEFEI

ANHUI

HUBEI

WUHAN

HUNAN

CHANGSHA

JIANGXI

NANCHANG

ZHEJIANG

NINGBO

Hangzhou Wan

DONG HAI / HIGASHI-SHI...

EAST CHINA SEA

Cheju / CHEJU-DO

Cheju-Haehyŏp

LUOYANG

ZHENGZHOU

KAIFENG

XUZHOU

LIANYUNGANG (XINPU)

BENGBU

HUAINAN

JINAN / TSINAN

HANDAN

ANYANG (Zhangde)

DATONG

HOHHOT

ZHANGJIAKOU

BAODING

TANGSHAN

QINHUANGDAO

YINGKOU

CHAOYANG

FUXIN

Scale 1:6,000,000   Delisle Conic Equidistant Projection

0 100 200 300 400 km
0 100 200 miles

NIPPON
JAPAN
1 Hokkaidō Ken
2 Aomori Ken
3 Iwate Ken
4 Miyagi Ken
5 Akita Ken
6 Yamagata Ken
7 Fukushima Ken
8 Ibaraki Ken
9 Tochigi Ken
10 Gunma Ken
11 Saitama Ken
12 Chiba Ken
13 Tōkyō To
14 Kanagawa Ken
15 Niigata Ken
16 Toyama Ken
17 Ishikawa Ken
18 Fukui Ken
19 Yamanashi Ken
20 Nagano Ken
21 Gifu Ken
22 Shizuoka Ken
23 Aichi Ken
24 Mie Ken
25 Shiga Ken
26 Kyōto Fu
27 Ōsaka Fu
28 Hyōgo Ken
29 Nara Ken
30 Wakayama Ken
31 Tottori Ken
32 Shimane Ken
33 Okayama Ken
34 Hiroshima Ken
35 Yamaguchi Ken
36 Tokushima Ken
37 Kagawa Ken
38 Ehime Ken
39 Kōchi Ken
40 Fukuoka Ken
41 Saga Ken
42 Nagasaki Ken
43 Kumamoto Ken
44 Ōita Ken
45 Miyazaki Ken
46 Kagoshima Ken

CHOSŎN M.I.K.
NORTH KOREA
1 Chagang-Do
2 Ch'ŏngjin Si
3 Hamgyŏng-Namdo
4 Hamgyong-Pukto
5 Hwanghae-Namdo
6 Hwanghae-Pukto
7 Kaesŏng Si
8 Kangwŏn-Do
9 P'yŏngan-Namdo
10 P'yŏngan-Pukto
11 P'yŏngyang Si
12 Yanggang-Do

TAEHAN-MIN'GUK
SOUTH KOREA
1 Cheju-Do
2 Chŏlla-Namdo
3 Chŏlla-Pukto
4 Ch'ungch'ŏng-Namdo
5 Ch'ungch'ŏng-Pukto
6 Kangwŏn-Do
7 Kyŏnggi-Do
8 Kyŏngsang-Namdo
9 Kyŏngsang-Pukto
10 Pusan Si
11 Sŏul Si

ZHONGHUA RENMIN GONGHEGUO
CHINA
1 Beijing Shi
2 Shanghai Shi
3 Tianjin Shi

Japan Basin
JAPONSKOJE MORE/
TONG-HAE/NIPPON-KAI
SEA OF JAPAN
Yamato Rise

NIPPON
JAPAN

HONSHŪ

CHOSŎN M.I.K.
NORTH KOREA

TAEHAN-MIN'GUK
SOUTH KOREA

HOKKAIDŌ
SAPPORO
HAKODATE
AOMORI
AKITA
SENDAI
NIIGATA
TŌKYŌ
YOKOHAMA
KAWASAKI
NAGOYA
KYŌTO
ŌSAKA
KŌBE
HIROSHIMA
KITAKYŪSHŪ
FUKUOKA
NAGASAKI
KUMAMOTO
KAGOSHIMA
SHIKOKU
KYŪSHŪ

PACIFIC OCEAN
TAIHEIYŌ

Nankai Trench
Shikoku Basin
Bonin Trench
Japan Trench

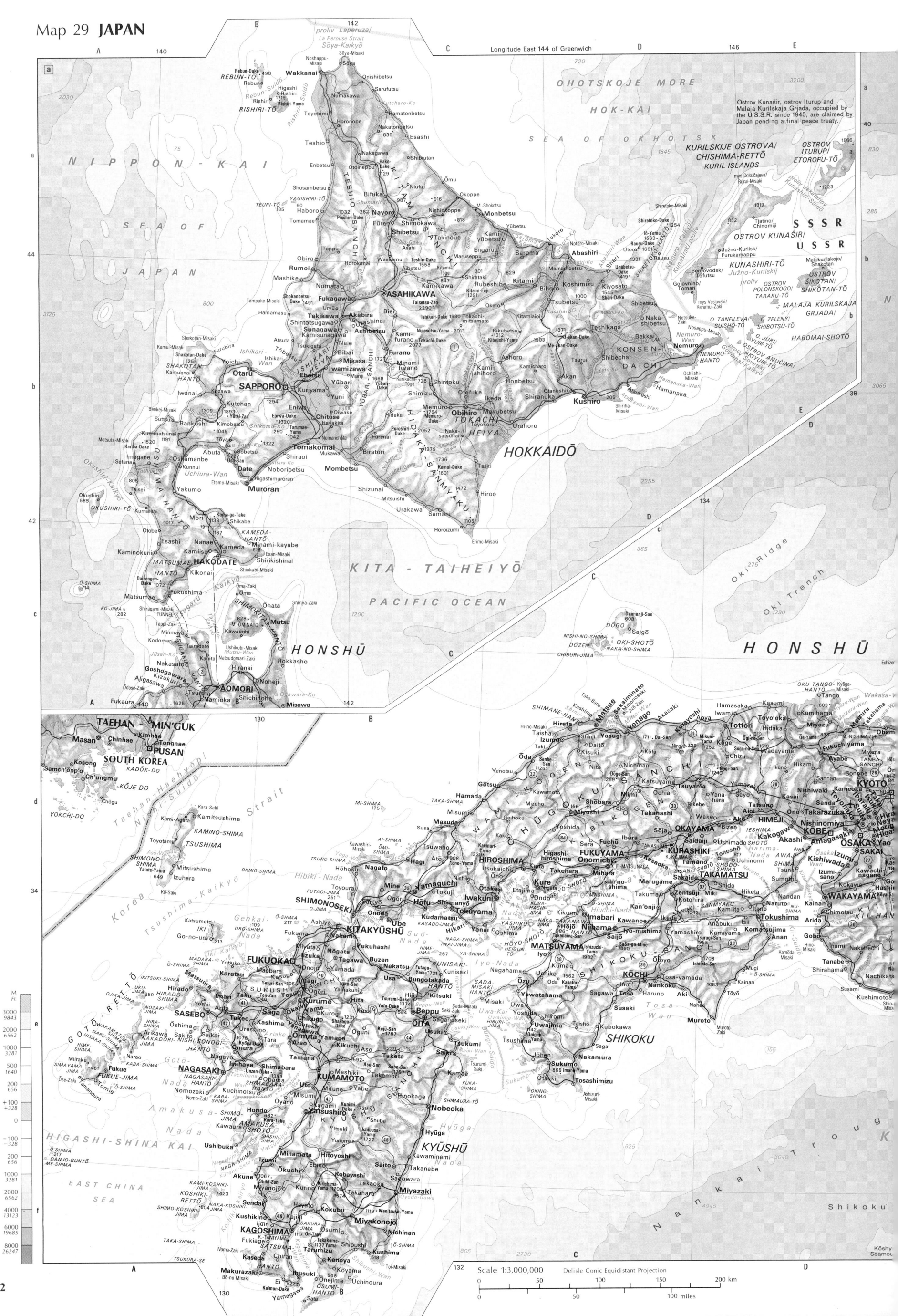

Map 29 **JAPAN**

Longitude East 144 of Greenwich

Ostrov Kunašir, ostrov Iturup and
Malaja Kurilskaja Grjada, occupied by
the U.S.S.R. since 1945, are claimed by
Japan pending a final peace treaty.

OHOTSKOJE MORE

HOK-KAI

SEA OF OKHOTSK

SSSR
USSR

OSTROV KUNAŠIR/
Južno-Kurilskij

KURILSKIJE OSTROVA/
CHISHIMA-RETTŌ
KURIL ISLANDS

OSTROV
ITURUP/
ETOROFU-TŌ

KUNASHIRI-TŌ

MALAJA KURILSKAJA
GRJADA

HABOMAI-SHOTŌ

NIPPON-KAI

SEA OF

JAPAN

WAKKANAI

ASAHIKAWA

SAPPORO

OTARU

CHITOSE

TOMAKOMAI

MURORAN

HAKODATE

HOKKAIDŌ

TOKACHI-
HEIYA

HIDAKA-SANMYAKU

KUSHIRO

OBIHIRO

NEMURO

KONSEN-
DAICHI

KITA - TAIHEIYŌ

PACIFIC OCEAN

HONSHŪ

HONSHŪ

Oki Ridge

Oki Trench

MUTSU

AOMORI

MISAWA

TAEHAN - MIN'GUK

PUSAN
MASAN

SOUTH KOREA

TSUSHIMA

Korea Strait

Tsushima-Kaikyō

MATSUE

TOTTORI

KYŌTO

HIROSHIMA

OKAYAMA

KURASHIKI

HIMEJI

KŌBE

ŌSAKA

SAKAI

WAKAYAMA

TAKAMATSU

FUKUYAMA

SHIMONOSEKI

YAMAGUCHI

KITAKYŪSHŪ

FUKUOKA

MATSUYAMA

KŌCHI

SHIKOKU

SHIKOKU-SANCHI

TOKUSHIMA

SASEBO

NAGASAKI

KUMAMOTO

ŌITA

BEPPU

KYŪSHŪ

MIYAZAKI

KAGOSHIMA

HIGASHI-SHINA KAI

EAST CHINA
SEA

Nankai Trough

M
Ft
3000 9843
2000 6562
1000 3281
500 1640
200 656
+ 100 +328
0
- 100 -328
200 656
1000 3281
2000 6562
4000 13123
6000 19685
8000 26247

Scale 1:3,000,000   Delisle Conic Equidistant Projection

0   50   100   150   200 km
0   50   100 miles

NIPPON
JAPAN
1 Hokkaidō Ken
2 Aomori Ken
3 Iwate Ken
4 Miyagi Ken
5 Akita Ken
6 Yamagata Ken
7 Fukushima Ken
8 Ibaraki Ken
9 Tochigi Ken
10 Gunma Ken
11 Saitama Ken
12 Chiba Ken
13 Tōkyō To
14 Kanagawa Ken
15 Niigata Ken
16 Toyama Ken
17 Ishikawa Ken
18 Fukui Ken
19 Yamanashi Ken
20 Nagano Ken
21 Gifu Ken
22 Shizuoka Ken
23 Aichi Ken
24 Mie Ken
25 Shiga Ken
26 Kyōto Fu
27 Ōsaka Fu
28 Hyōgo Ken
29 Nara Ken
30 Wakayama Ken
31 Tottori Ken
32 Shimane Ken
33 Okayama Ken
34 Hiroshima Ken
35 Yamaguchi Ken
36 Tokushima Ken
37 Kagawa Ken
38 Ehime Ken
39 Kōchi Ken
40 Fukuoka Ken
41 Saga Ken
42 Nagasaki Ken
43 Kumamoto Ken
44 Ōita Ken
45 Miyazaki Ken
46 Kagoshima Ken
47 Okinawa Ken

Map 30 **AFRICA, PHYSICAL**

Map 30

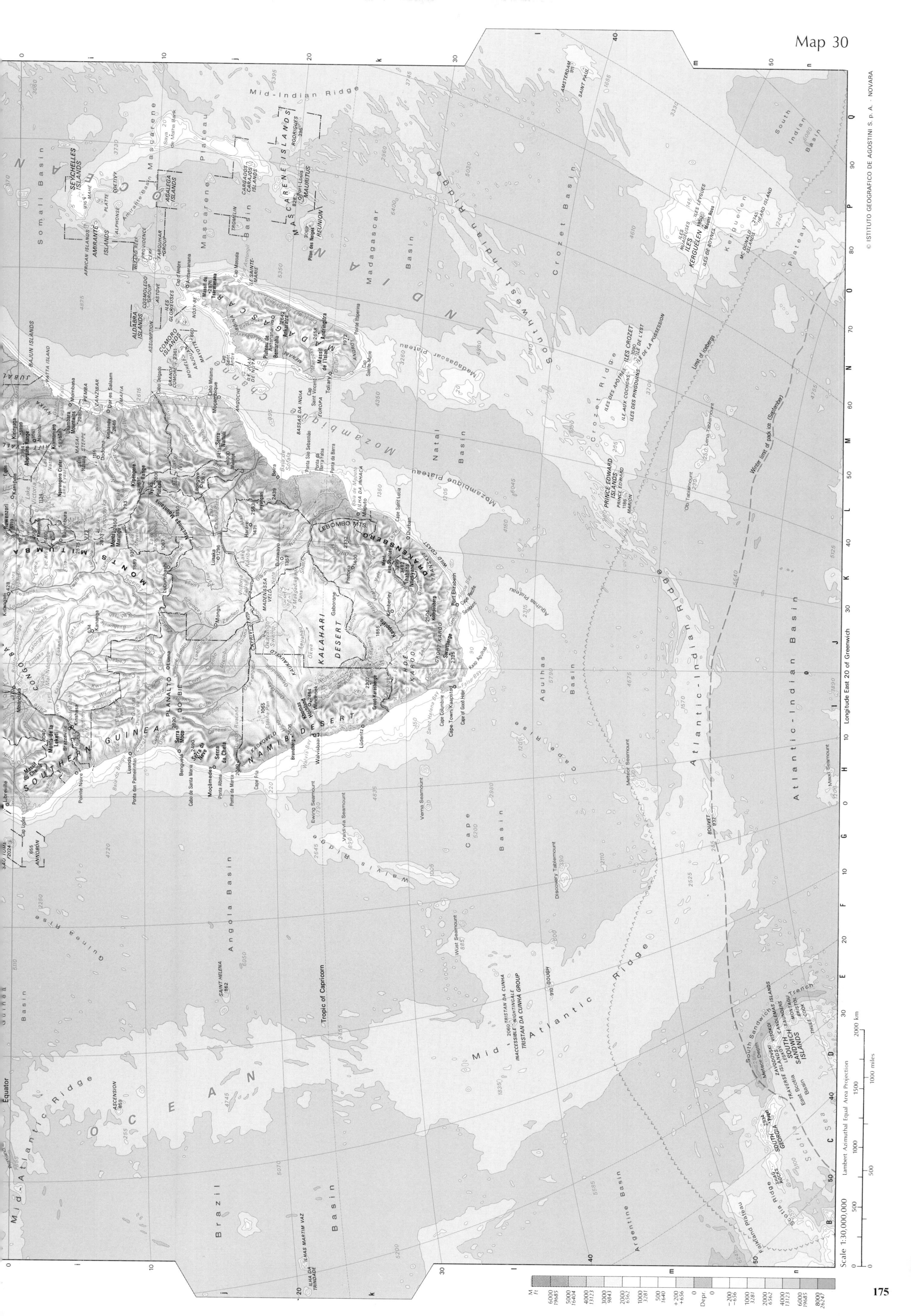

Map 31 **AFRICA, POLITICAL**

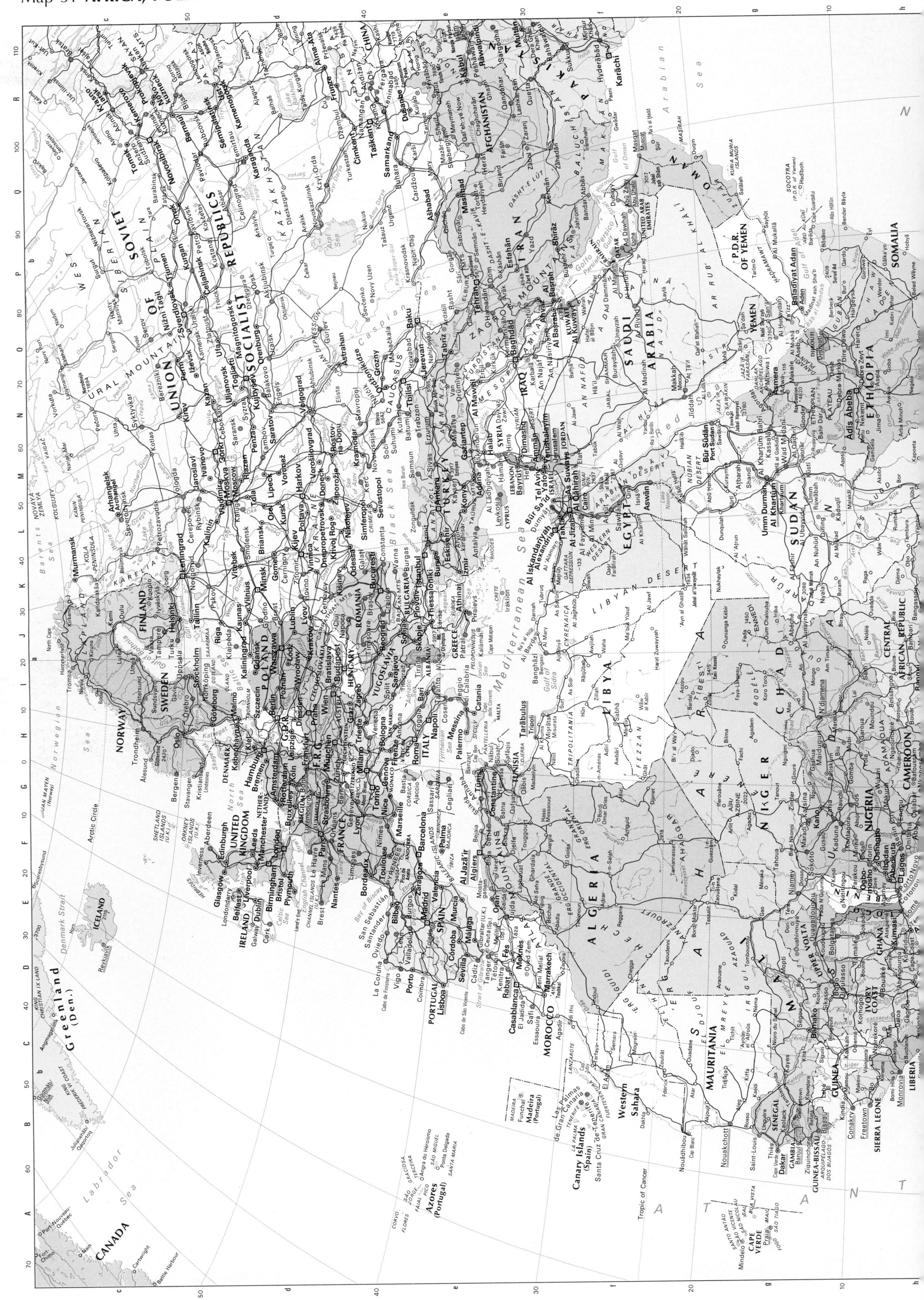

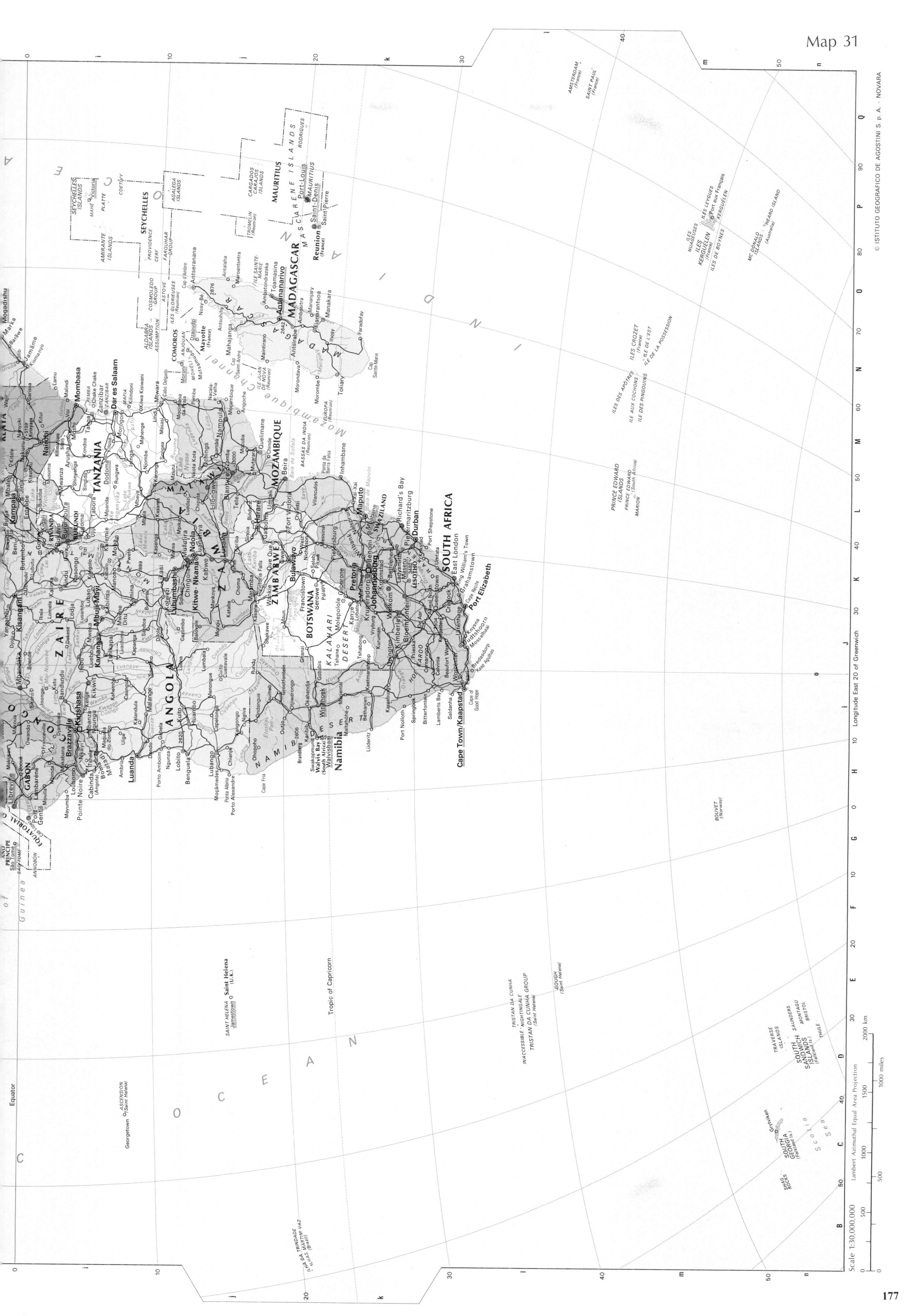

Map 31

© ISTITUTO GEOGRAFICO DE AGOSTINI S. p. A. - NOVARA

Scale 1:30,000,000   Lambert Azimuthal Equal Area Projection

177

Map 32

(A) Western Sahara is occupied by Morocco.

Scale 1:9,000,000   Lambert Azimuthal Equal Area Projection
0   200   400   600 km
0   200 miles

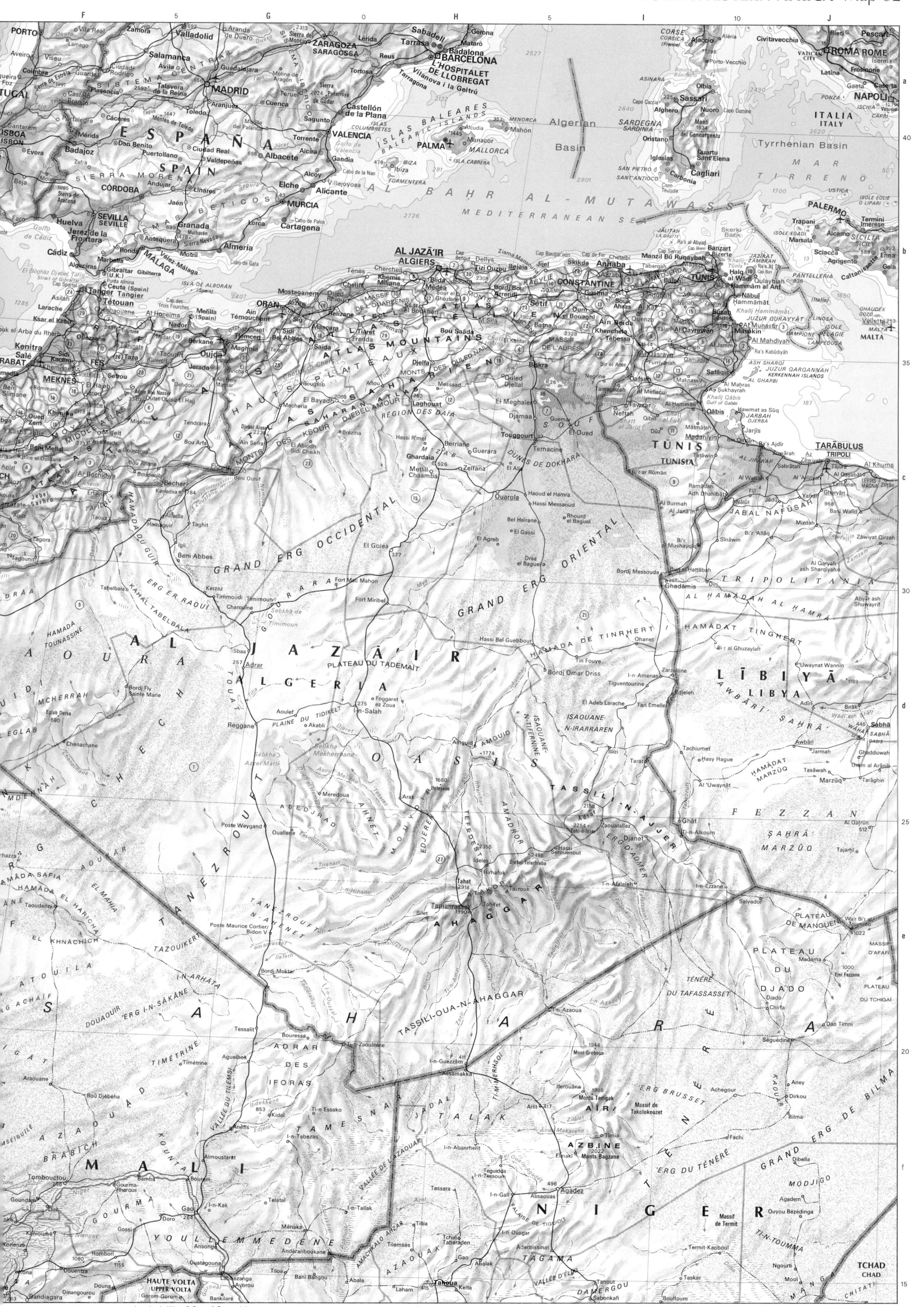

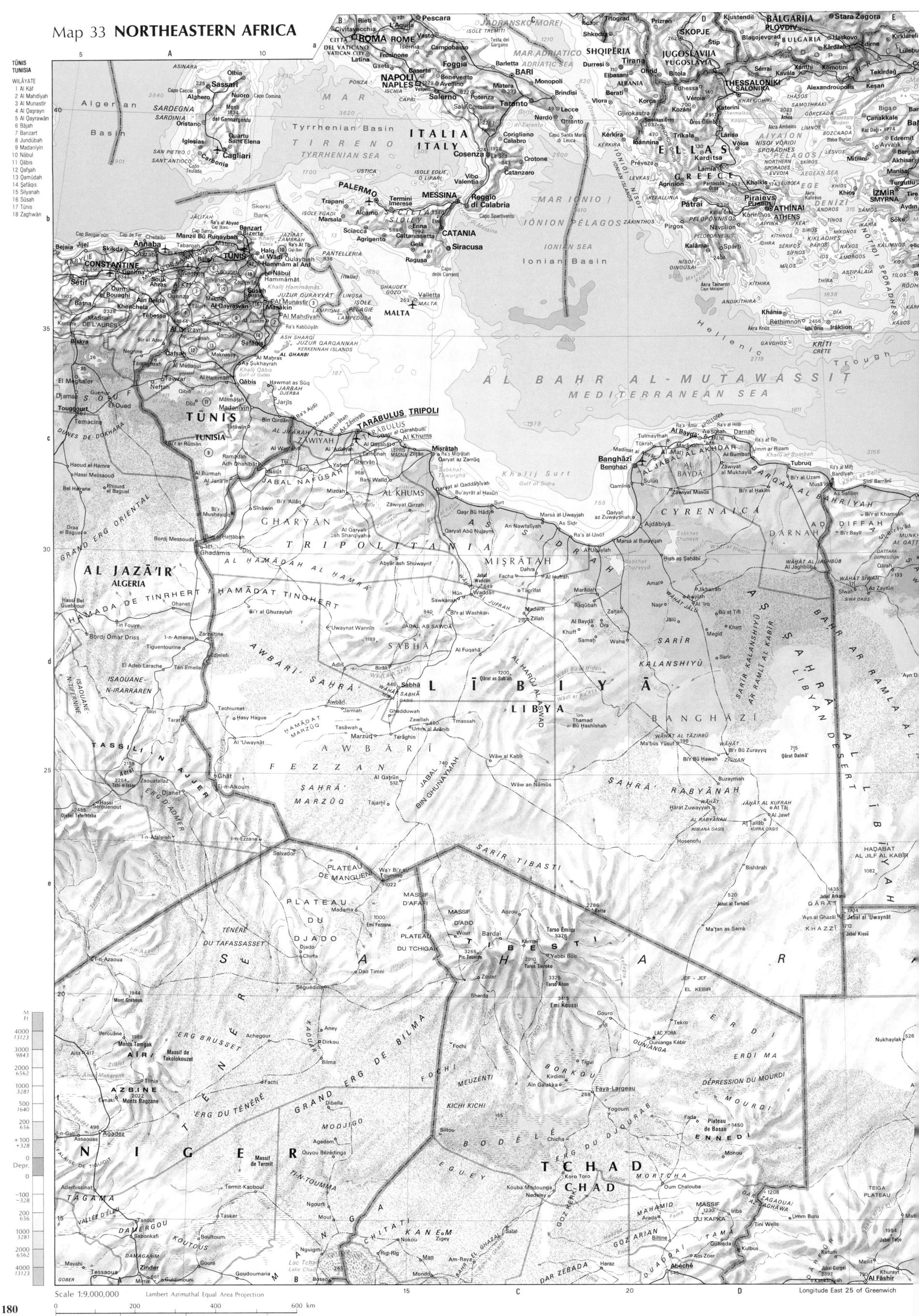

Map 33 **NORTHEASTERN AFRICA**

TÜNIS
TUNISIA
TUNISIE
WILÂYATE
1 Al Kâf
2 Al Mahdiyah
3 Al Munastir
4 Al Qaşrayn
5 Al Qayrawân
6 Bâjah
7 Banzart
8 Jundübah
9 Madanîyîn
10 Nâbul
11 Qâbis
12 Qafşah
13 Qamûdah
14 Şafâqis
15 Silyanah
16 Sûsah
17 Tûnis
18 Zaghwân

Scale 1:9,000,000   Lambert Azimuthal Equal Area Projection

0   200   400   600 km
0   200 miles

Longitude East 25 of Greenwich

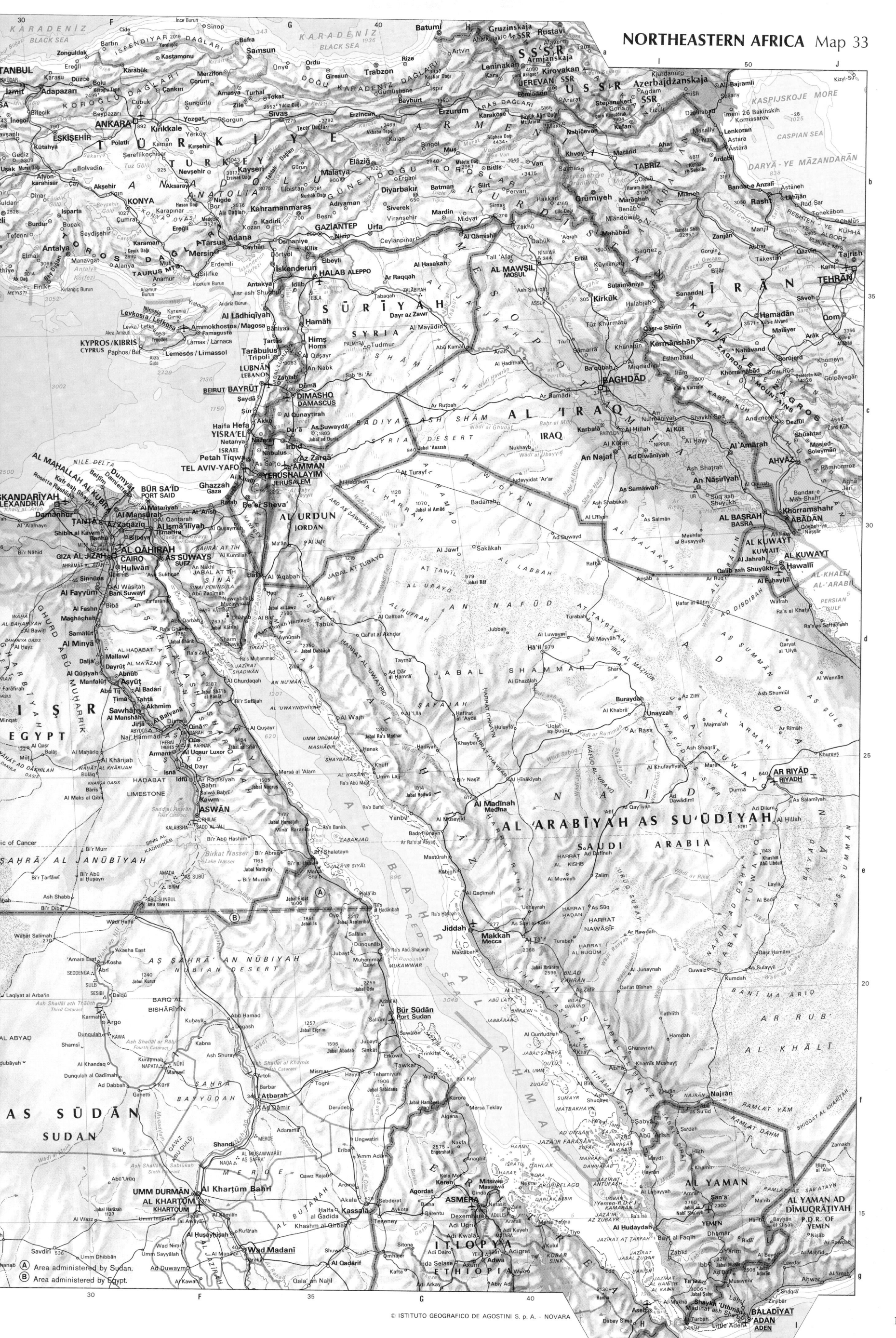

Ⓐ Area administered by Sudan.
Ⓑ Area administered by Egypt.

© ISTITUTO GEOGRAFICO DE AGOSTINI S. p. A. - NOVARA

181

Map 34 **WEST-CENTRAL AFRICA**

LIBERIA
COUNTIES
1 Bong
2 Cape Mount
3 Grand Bassa
4 Grand Gedeh
5 Lofa
6 Maryland
7 Montserrado
8 Nimba
9 Sinoe

**CÔTE D'IVOIRE
IVORY COAST**
DÉPARTEMENTS
1 Abengourou
2 Abidjan
3 Aboisso
4 Adzopé
5 Agboville
6 Biankouma
7 Bondoukou
8 Bongouanou
9 Bouaflé
10 Bouaké
11 Bouna
12 Boundiali
13 Dabakala
14 Daloa
15 Danané
16 Dimbokro
17 Divo
18 Ferkessédougou
19 Gagnoa
20 Guiglo
21 Issia
22 Katiola
23 Korhogo
24 Lakota
25 Man
26 Mankono
27 Odienné
28 Oumé
29 Sassandra
30 Seguela
31 Soubré
32 Tengréla
33 Touba
34 Zuenoula

**HAUTE-VOLTA
UPPER VOLTA**
DÉPARTEMENTS
1 Centre
2 Centre-Est
3 Centre-Nord
4 Centre-Ouest
5 Est
6 Hauts-Bassins
7 Komoé
8 Nord
9 Sahel
10 Sud-Ouest
11 Volta Noire

TOGO
RÉGIONS
1 Centre
2 Kara
3 Maritime
4 Plateaux
5 Savanes

BÉNIN
PROVINCES
1 Atakora
2 Atlantique
3 Borgou
4 Mono
5 Ouémé
6 Zou

Tropic of Cancer

Western Sahara

MŪRĪTĀNIYĀ
MAURITANIA

MALI

SÉNÉGAL

GAMBIA

GUINÉ-BISSAU
GUINEA-BISSAU

GUINÉE
GUINEA

SIERRA
LEONE

LIBERIA

CÔTE
D'IVOIRE
IVORY COAST

Cape Verde

Basin

ATLANTIC OCEAN
OCÉAN ATLANTIQUE

Sierra Leone

Basin

Guinea Basin

Mid-Atlantic Ridge

Equator

Ⓐ Abuja is the future federal capital of Nigeria.
Ⓑ The political subdivisions shown for Guinea represent statistical areas and are not recognized for administrative purposes.

Scale 1:9,000,000
Lambert Azimuthal Equal Area Projection
Longitude West 5 of Greenwich

0   200   400   600 km
0   200 miles

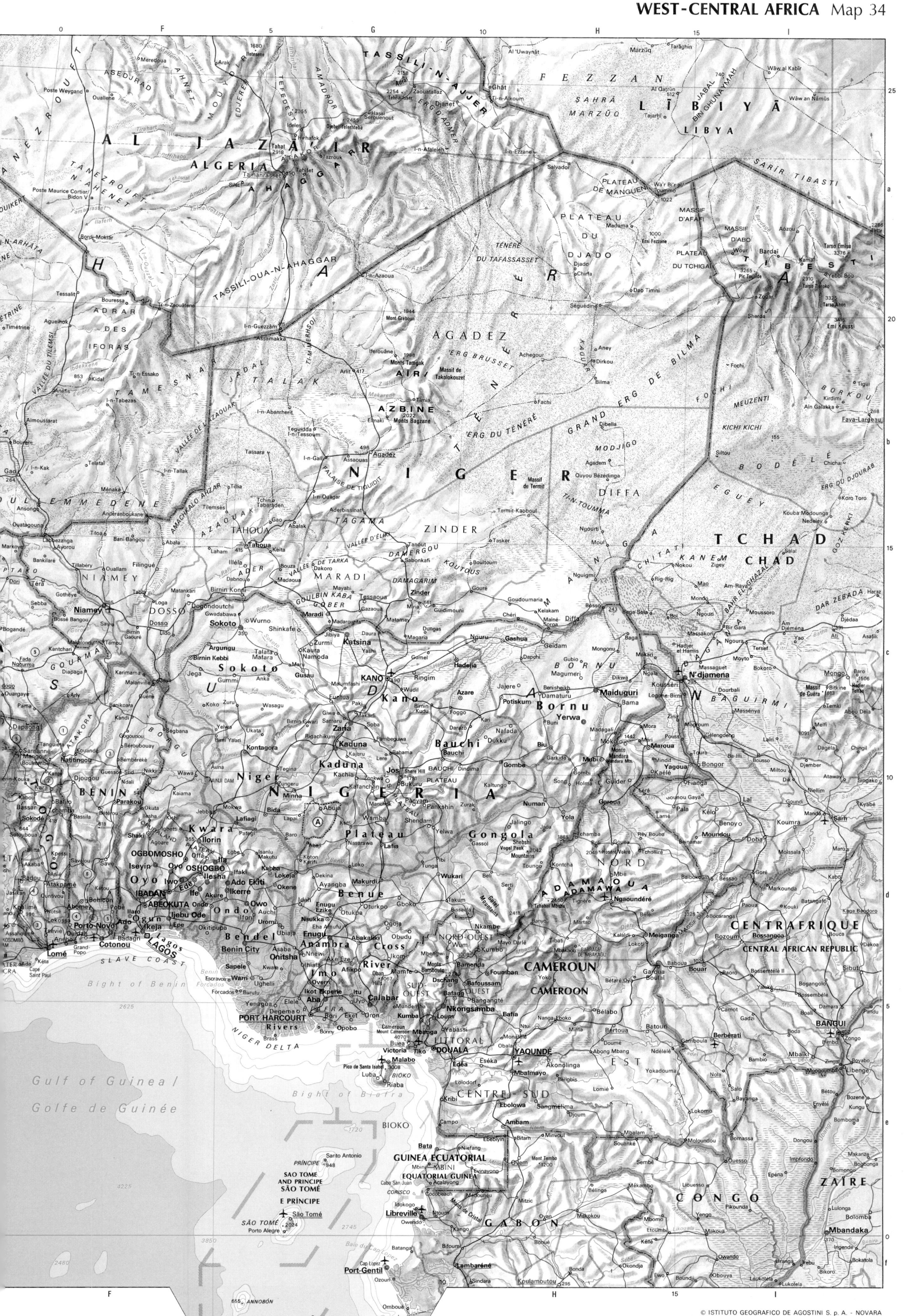

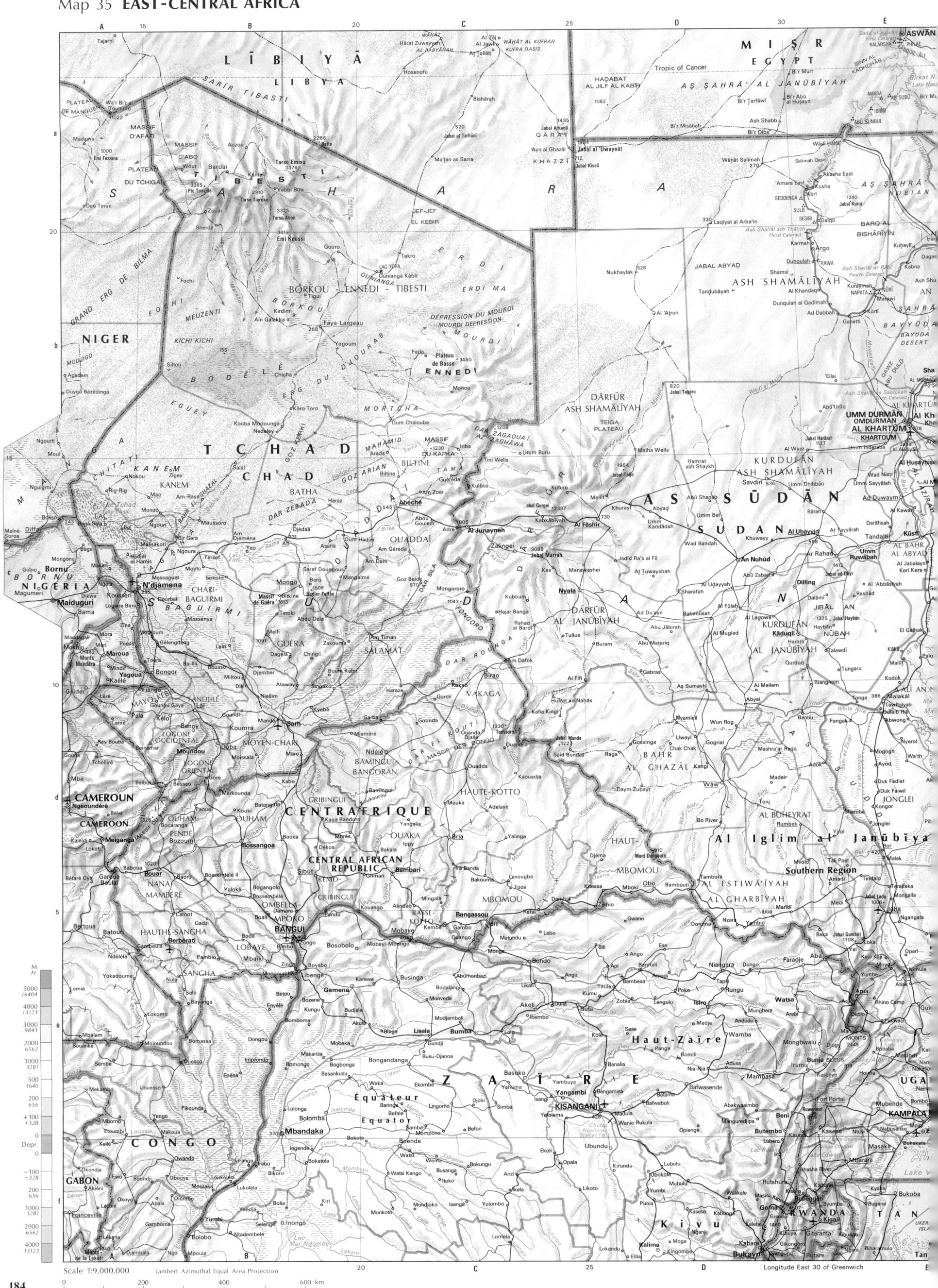

Map 35 **EAST-CENTRAL AFRICA**

Scale 1:9,000,000

Lambert Azimuthal Equal Area Projection

Longitude East 30 of Greenwich

Map 36 **EQUATORIAL AFRICA**

Scale 1:9,000,000   Lambert Azimuthal Equal Area Projection

0   200   400   600 km

0   200 miles

Map 37 **SOUTHERN AFRICA**

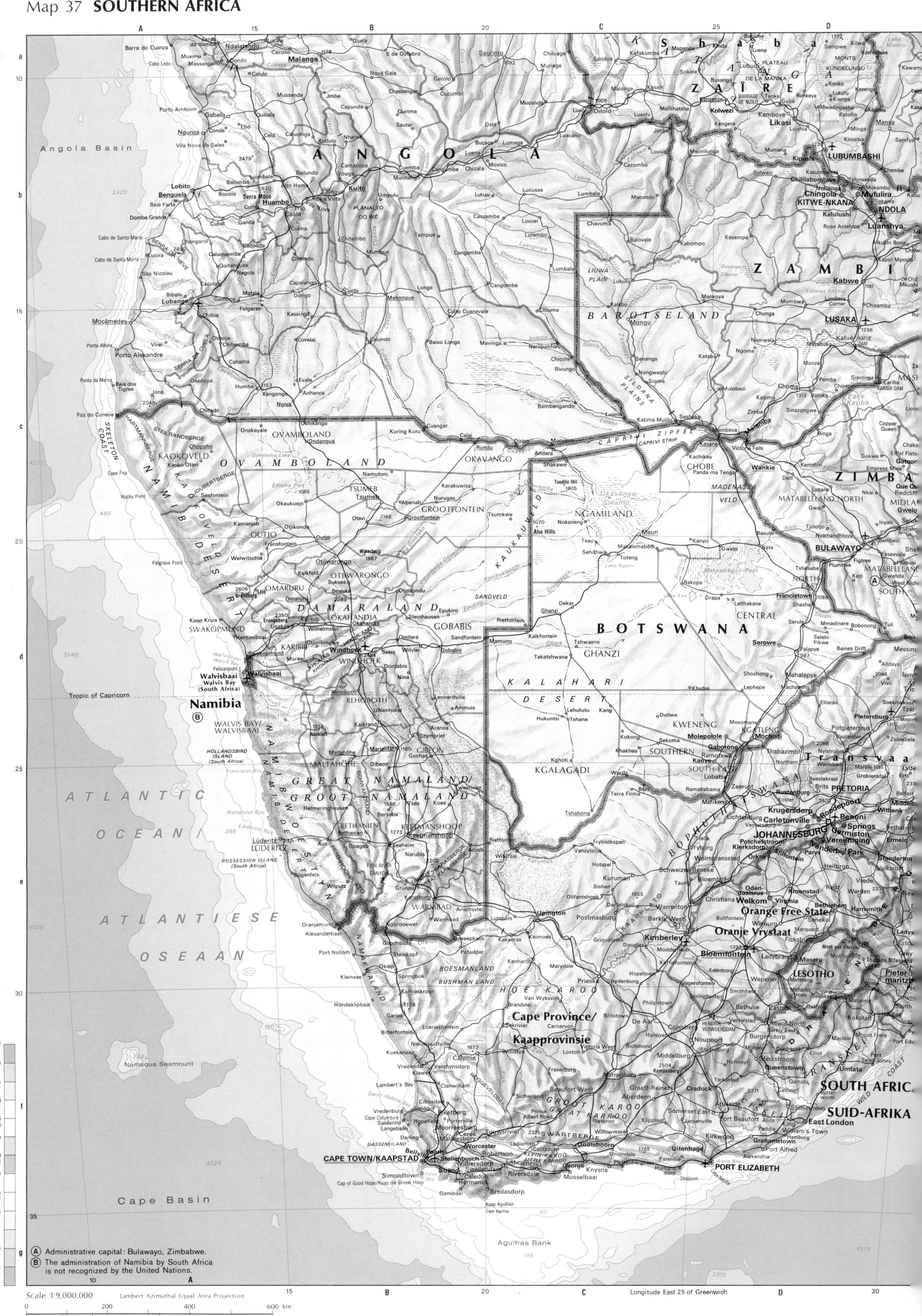

Map 38 **NORTH AMERICA, PHYSICAL**

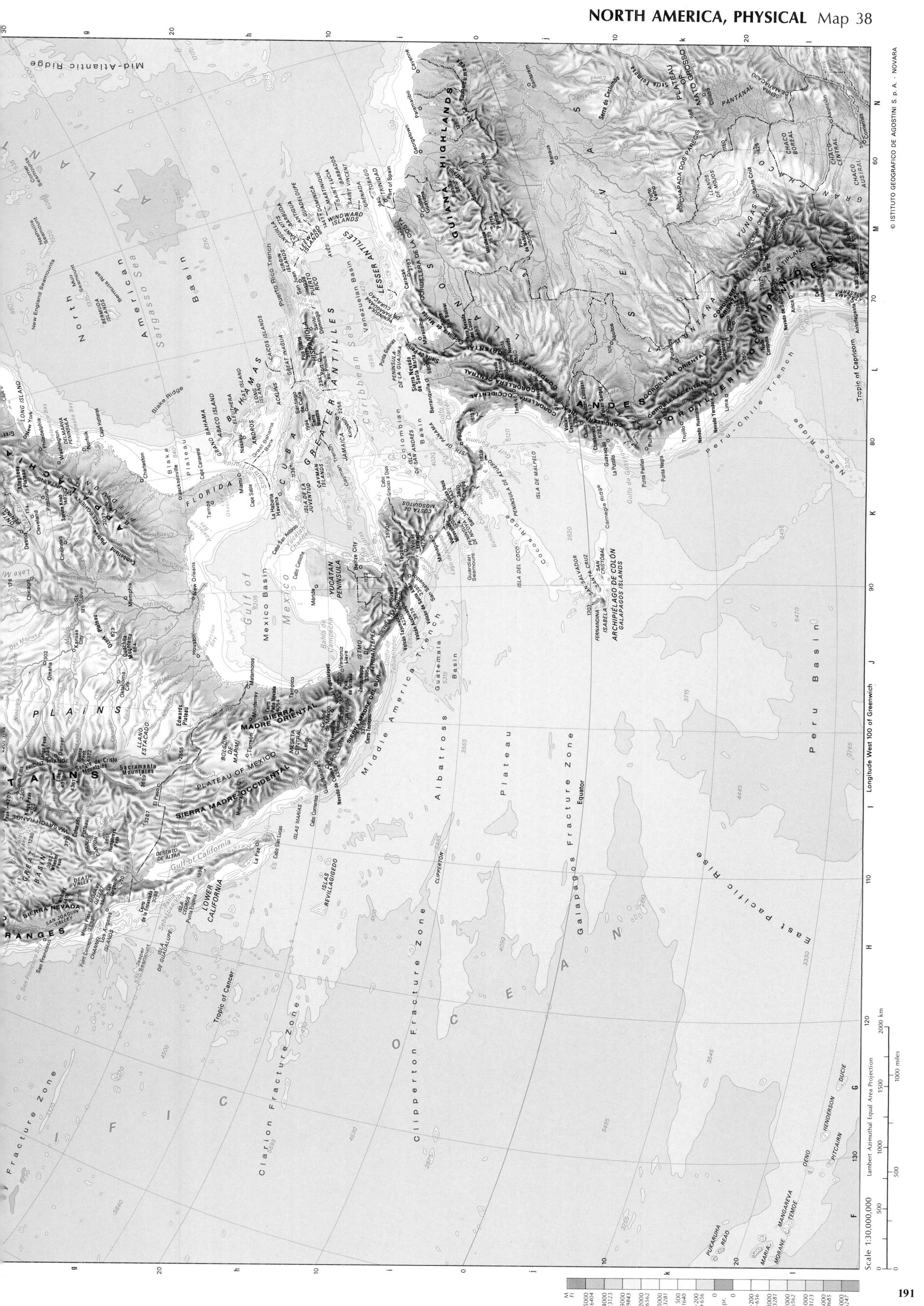

Scale 1:30,000,000   Lambert Azimuthal Equal Area Projection

Map 39 **NORTH AMERICA, POLITICAL**

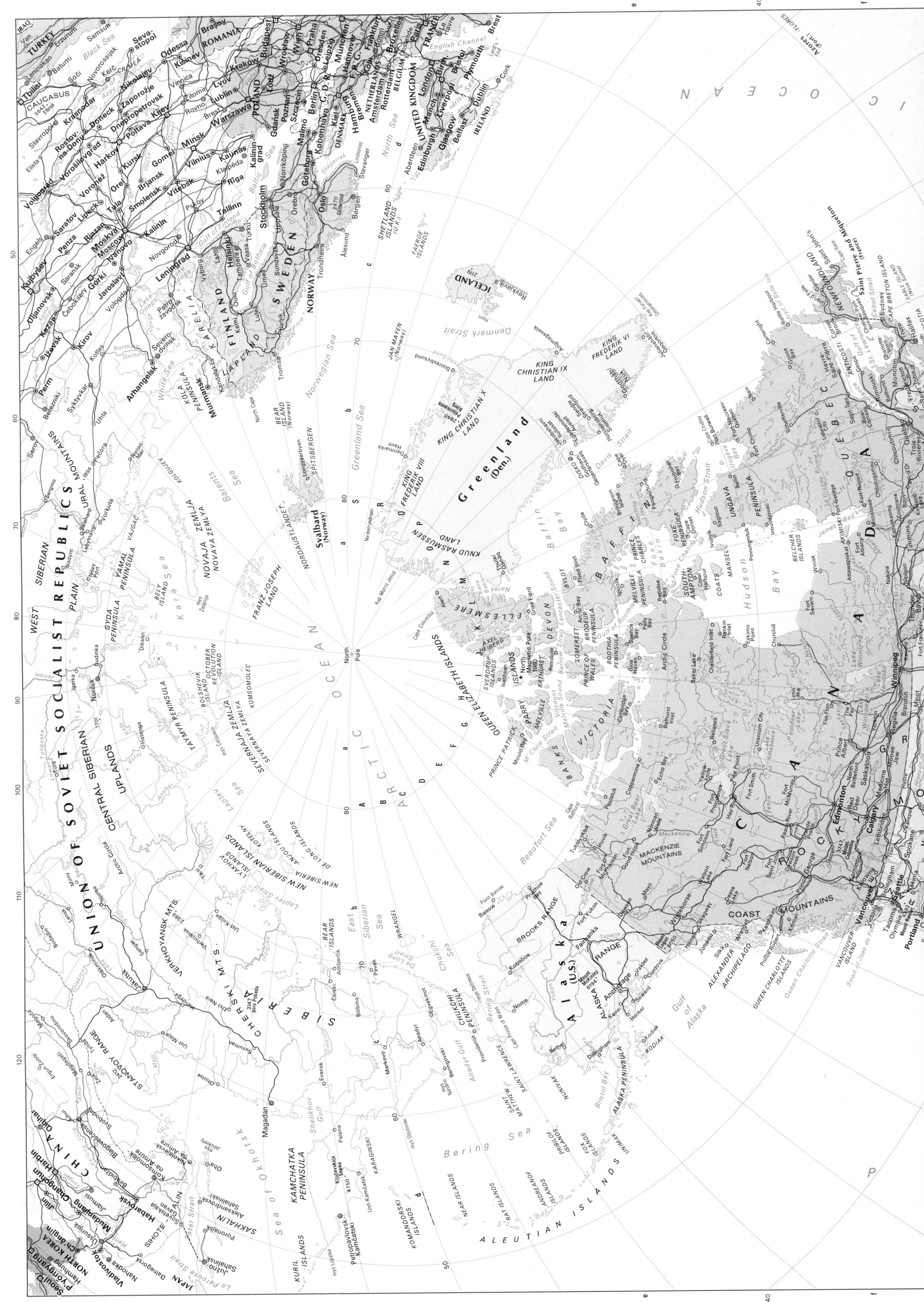

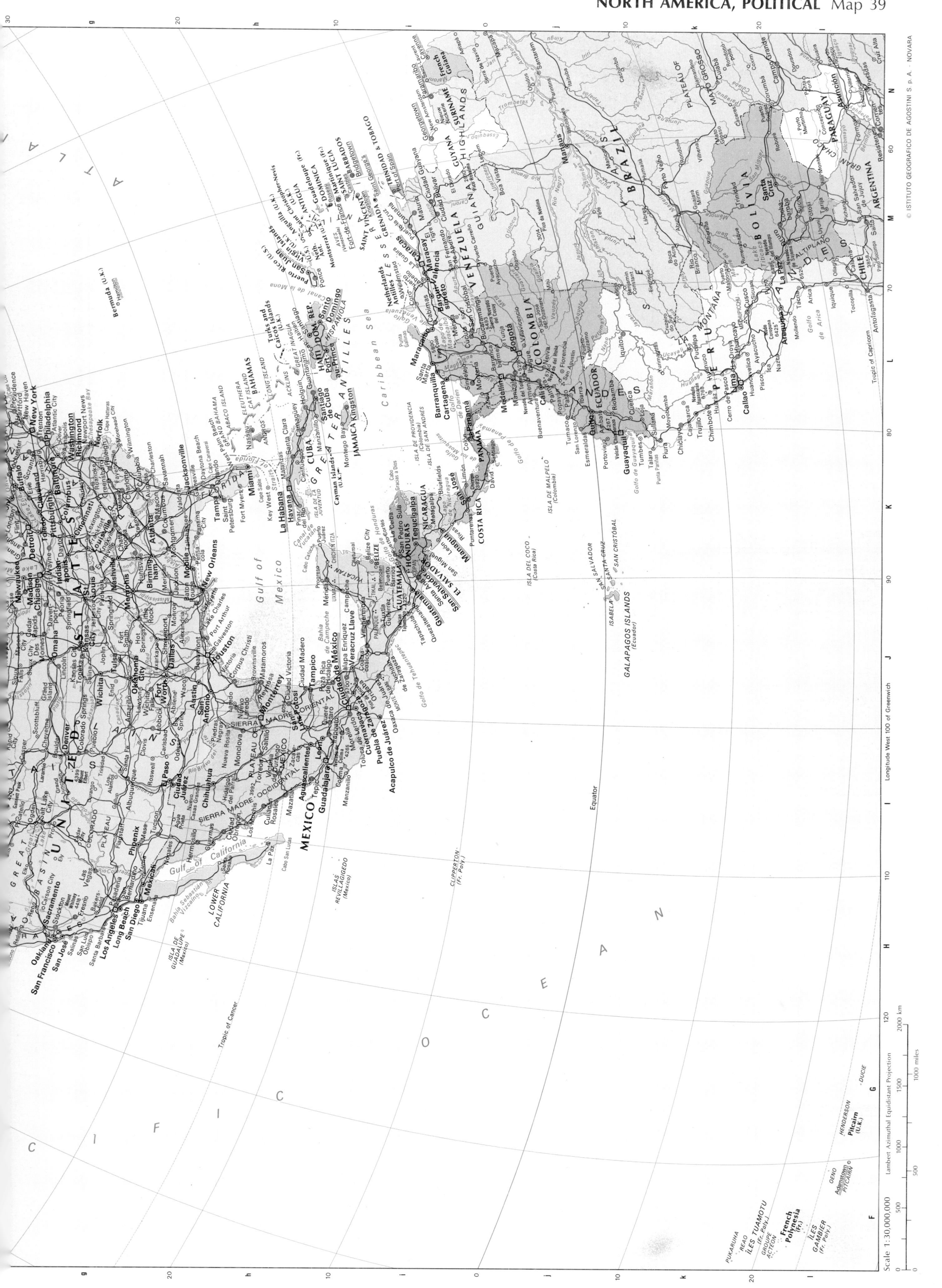

Map 40 ALASKA

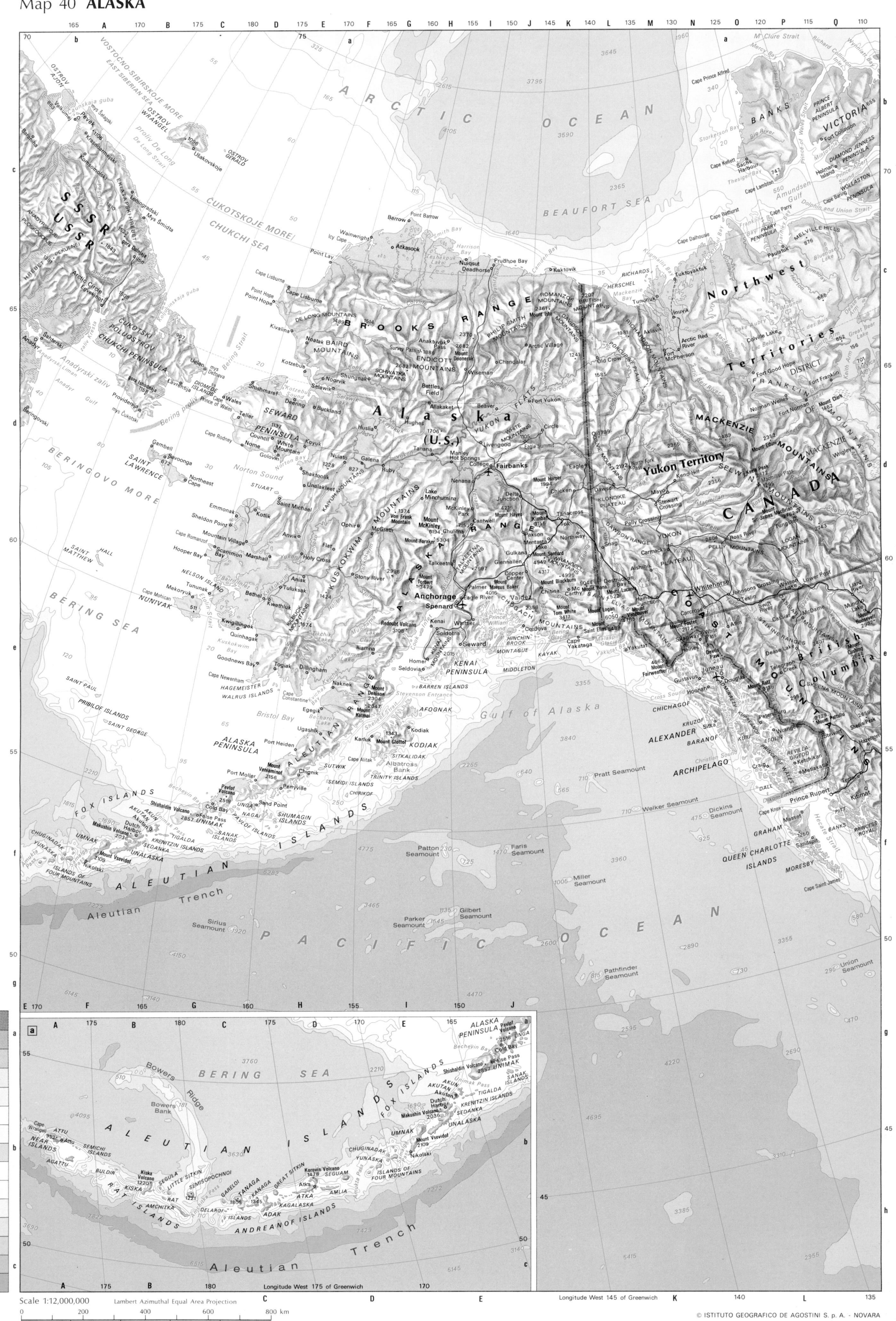

Scale 1:12,000,000   Lambert Azimuthal Equal Area Projection

© ISTITUTO GEOGRAFICO DE AGOSTINI S.p.A. - NOVARA

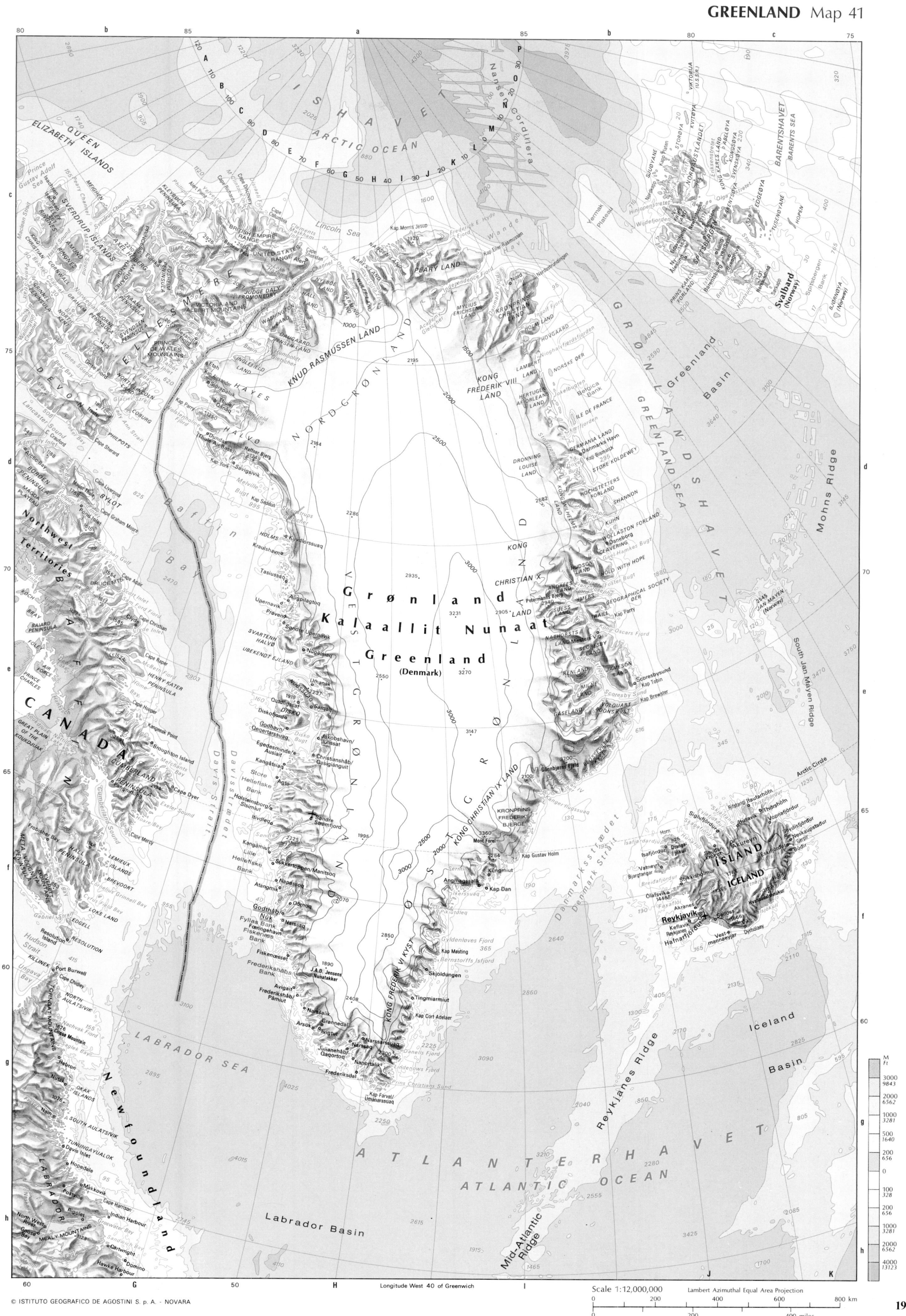

Scale 1:12,000,000
Lambert Azimuthal Equal Area Projection

Map 42 **CANADA**

Scale 1:12,000,000   Lambert Azimuthal Equal Area Projection

Longitude West 100 of Greenwich

0   200   400   600   800 km

0   200   400 miles

Map 43 **UNITED STATES**

Scale 1:12,000,000   Lambert Azimuthal Equidistant Projection

Longitude West 100 of Greenwich

Map 45

Map 46 WESTERN UNITED STATES

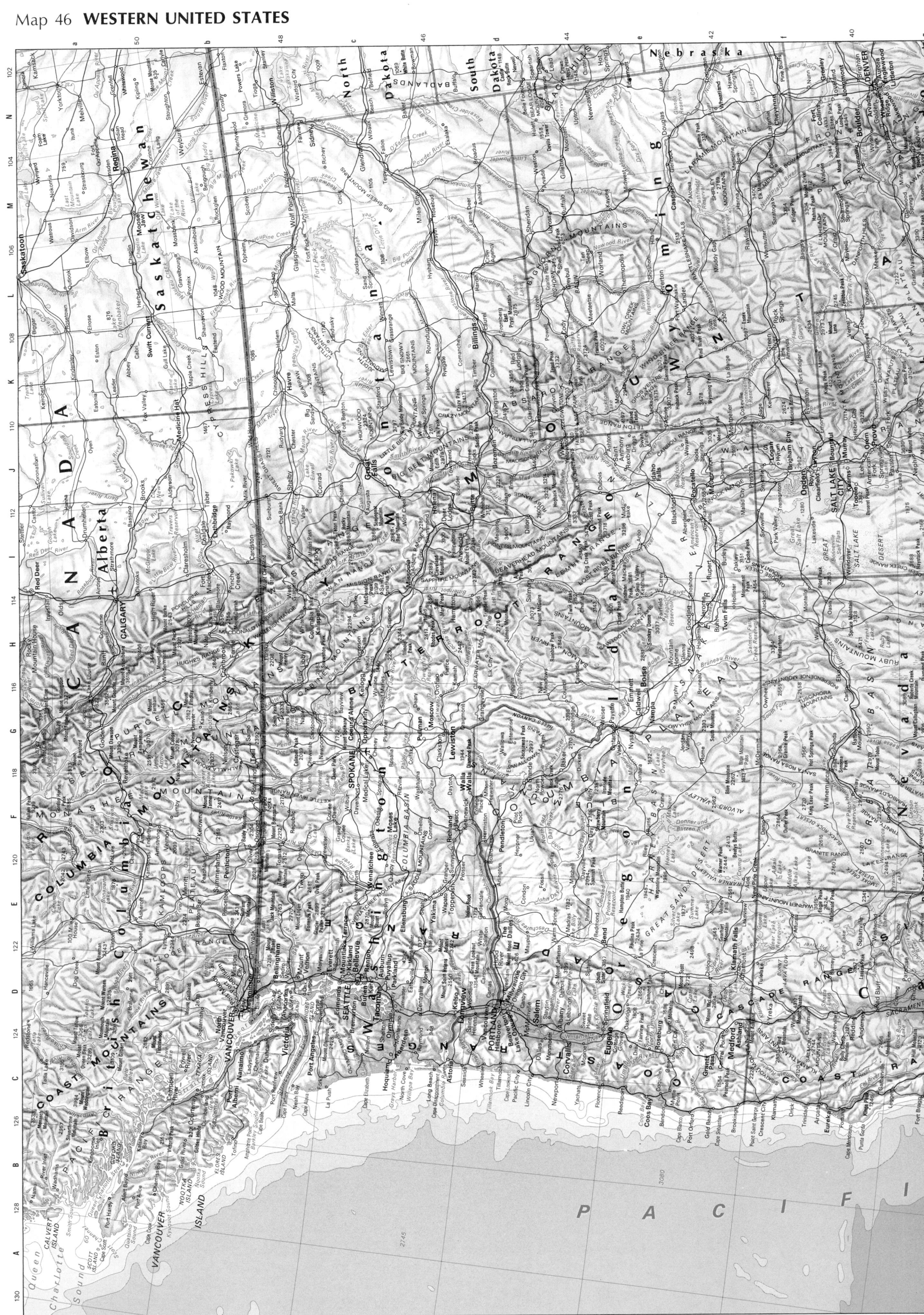

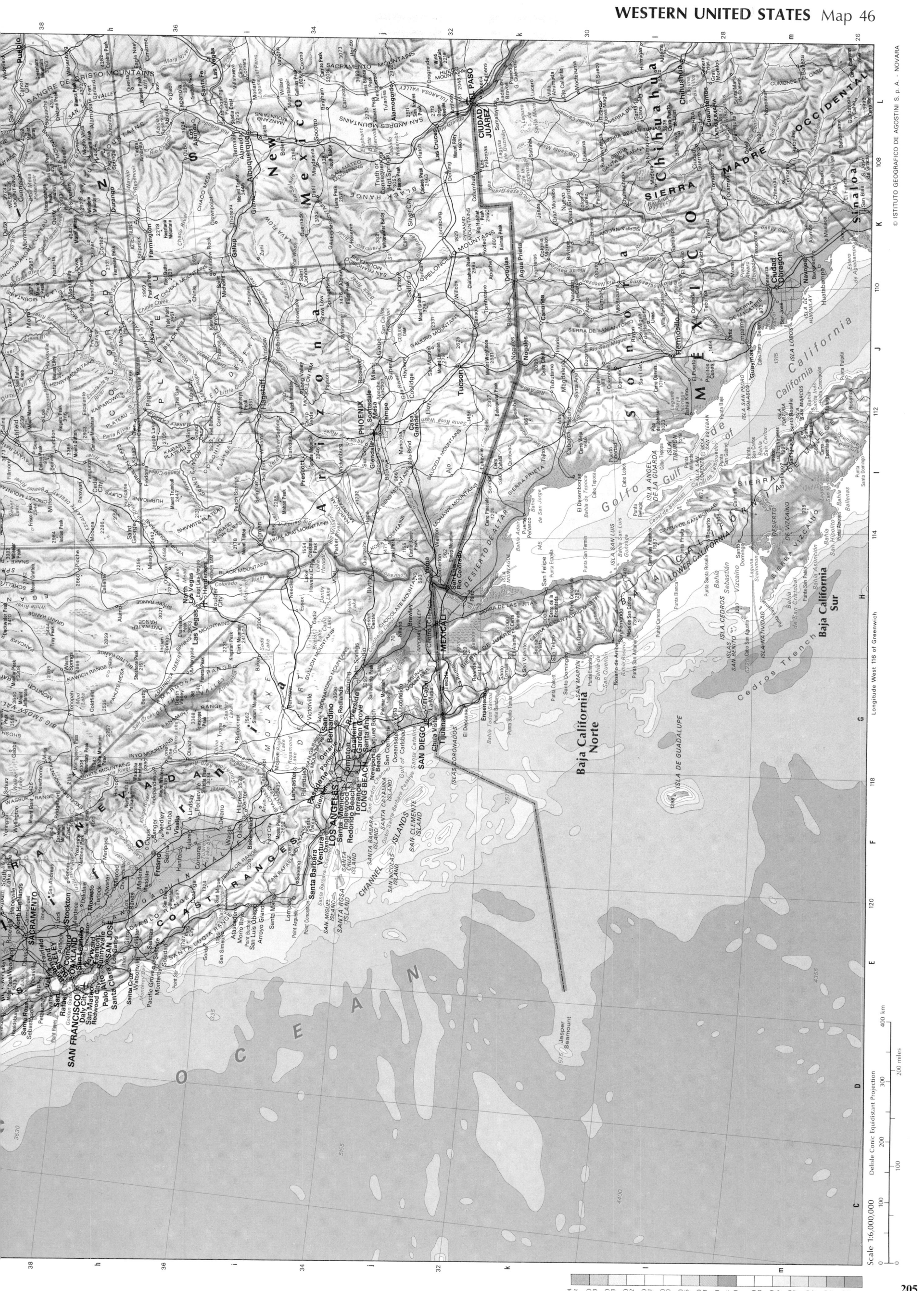

Scale 1:6,000,000

Delisle Conic Equidistant Projection

Longitude West 116 of Greenwich

Map 47 **MIDDLE AMERICA**

MÉXICO

ESTADOS

D.F. Distrito Federal
1 Aguascalientes
2 Baja California Norte
3 Baja California Sur
4 Campeche
5 Coahuila
6 Colima
7 Chiapas
8 Chihuahua
9 Durango
10 Guanajuato
11 Guerrero
12 Hidalgo
13 Jalisco
14 México
15 Michoacán
16 Morelos
17 Nayarit
18 Nuevo León
19 Oaxaca
20 Puebla
21 Querétaro
22 Quintana Roo
23 San Luis Potosí
24 Sinaloa
25 Sonora
26 Tabasco
27 Tamaulipas
28 Tlaxcala
29 Veracruz
30 Yucatán
31 Zacatecas

UNITED STATES

California · Arizona · New Mexico · Texas · Oklahoma · Kansas · Missouri · Arkansas · Louisiana · Mississippi

LOS ANGELES · San Diego · PHOENIX · Tucson · CIUDAD JUÁREZ · EL PASO · Albuquerque · DALLAS · FORT WORTH · SAN ANTONIO · HOUSTON · NEW ORLEANS · MEMPHIS · MOBILE

Gulf of Mexico/Golfo de México

Mexico Basin

Campeche Bank

BAJA CALIFORNIA · LOWER CALIFORNIA

MONTERREY · GUADALAJARA · CIUDAD DE MÉXICO · MÉXICO CITY · PUEBLA DE ZARAGOZA · VERACRUZ LLAVE · Acapulco de Juárez · Oaxaca de Juárez · MÉRIDA · PENÍNSULA DE YUCATÁN

GUATEMALA · SAN SALVADOR

OCÉANO PACÍFICO

PACIFIC OCEAN

Middle America Trench

Albatross Plateau

Guatemala Basin

ÎLE CLIPPERTON (Fr. Poly.)

ISLAS REVILLAGIGEDO (México)

ISLA DE GUADALUPE (México)

Equator

Scale 1:12,000,000   Lambert Azimuthal Equal Area Projection

Longitude West 90 of Greenwich

M Ft	
5000 16404	
4000 13123	
3000 9843	
2000 6562	
1000 3281	
500 1640	
+200 +656	
0 Depr.	
−100 −328	
1000 3281	
2000 6562	
4000 13123	
6000 19685	
8000 26247	

0   200   400   600   800 km
0   200   400 miles

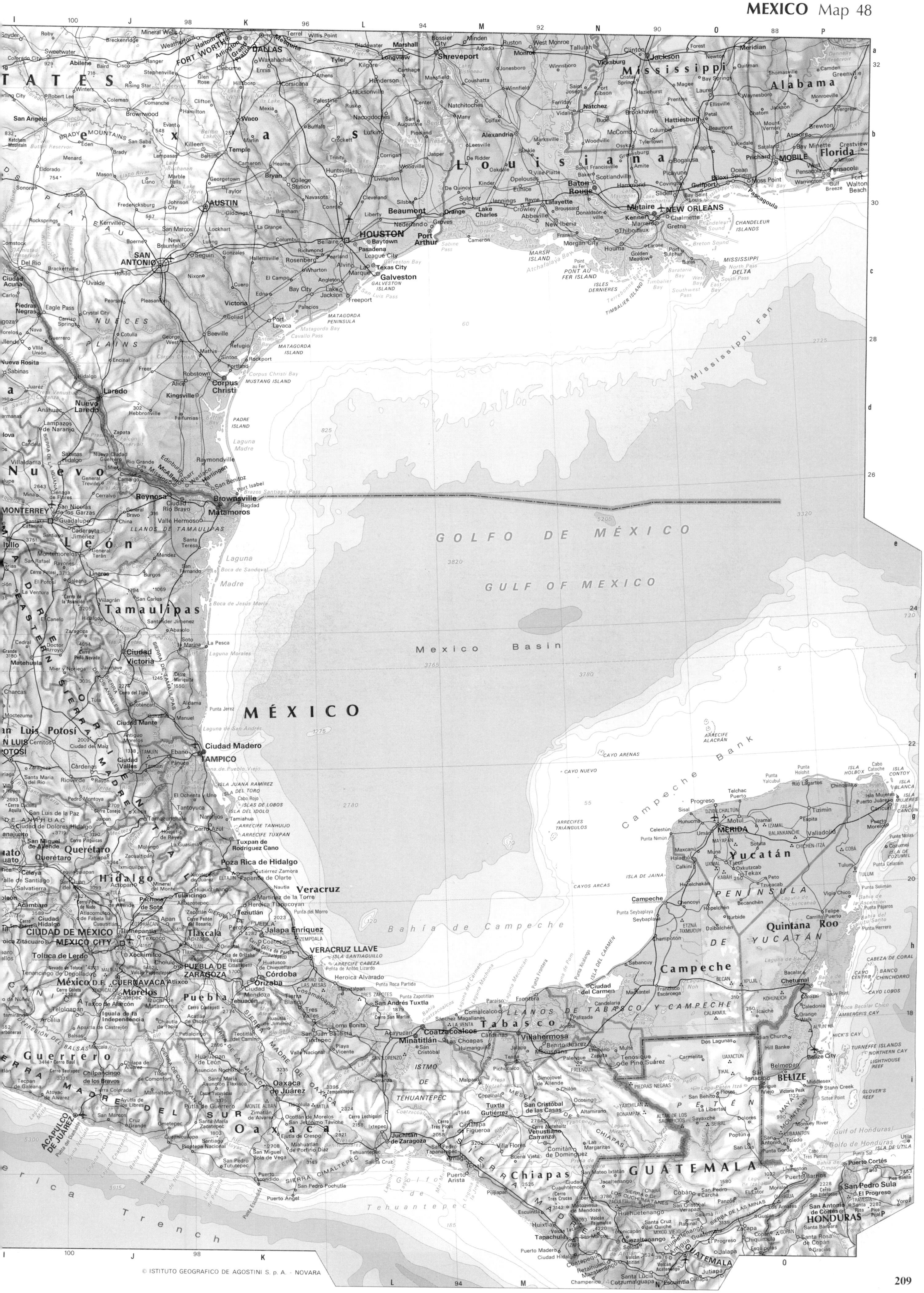

MISSISSIPPI
Alabama
Florida
Louisiana
TATES

GOLFO DE MÉXICO
GULF OF MEXICO
Mexico Basin

MÉXICO

Nuevo León
Tamaulipas

San Luis Potosí
Querétaro
Hidalgo
CIUDAD DE MÉXICO
MÉXICO CITY
Puebla
Morelos
Tlaxcala

Veracruz
Veracruz Llave

Guerrero
Oaxaca
Chiapas

Tabasco
Campeche
Yucatán
PENÍNSULA DE YUCATÁN
Quintana Roo
Mérida

Bahía de Campeche
Campeche Bank

GUATEMALA
HONDURAS
BELIZE

FORT WORTH
DALLAS
Shreveport
AUSTIN
SAN ANTONIO
HOUSTON
Galveston
Corpus Christi
Laredo
Nuevo Laredo
MONTERREY
Reynosa
Matamoros
Brownsville
NEW ORLEANS
MOBILE

TAMPICO
Ciudad Madero
Poza Rica de Hidalgo
Veracruz
ACAPULCO DE JUÁREZ
Oaxaca de Juárez
Tuxtla Gutiérrez
Coatzacoalcos
Villahermosa
Tapachula

ISTMO DE TEHUANTEPEC
Golfo de Tehuantepec

© ISTITUTO GEOGRAFICO DE AGOSTINI S.p.A. - NOVARA

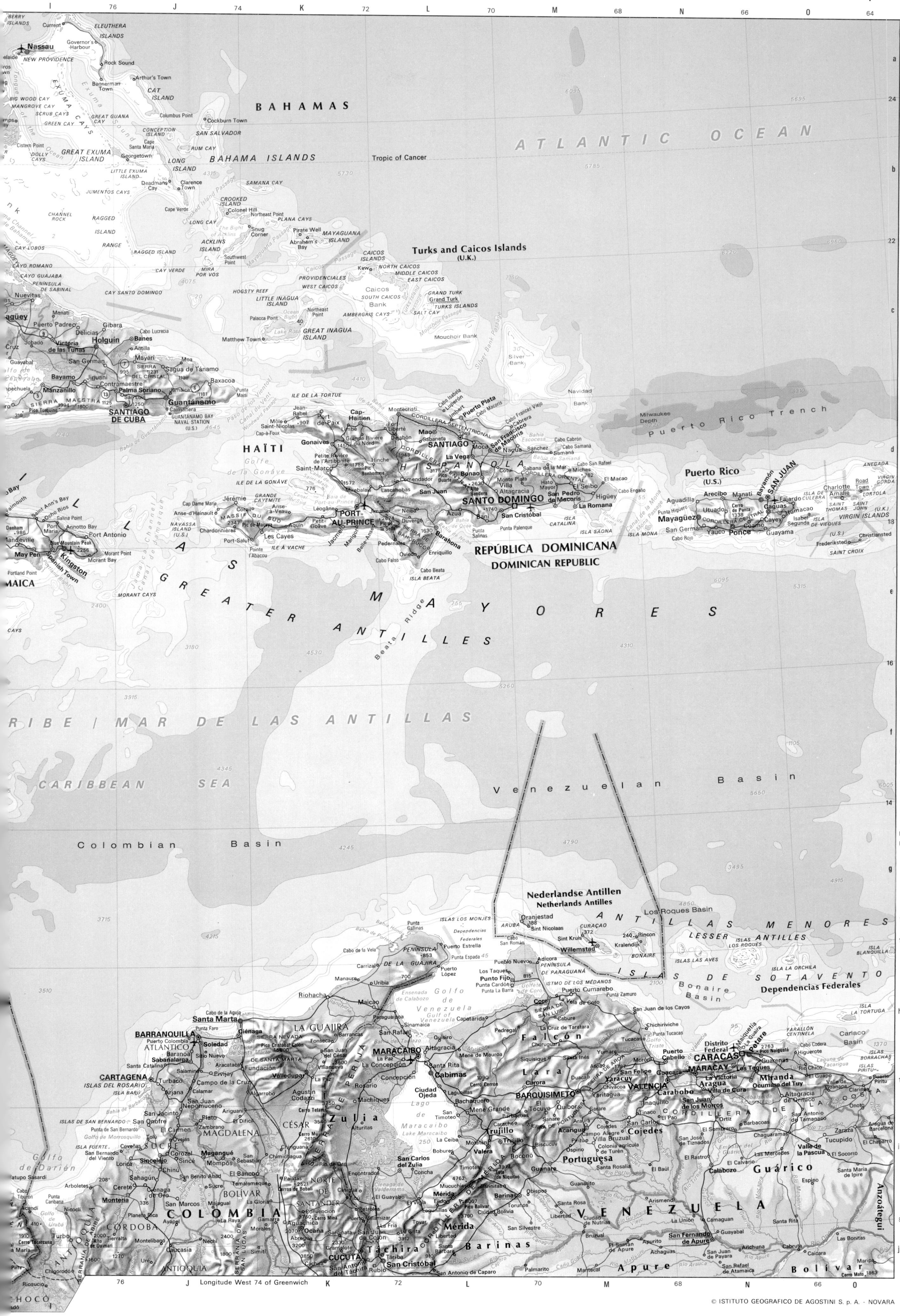

CUBA
PROVINCIAS
1 Camagüey
2 Ciego de Ávila
3 Cienfuegos
4 Ciudad de la Habana
5 Granma
6 Guantánamo
7 Holguín
8 La Habana
9 Las Tunas
10 Matanzas
11 Pinar del Río
12 Sancti Spíritus
13 Santiago de Cuba
14 Villaclara

BELIZE
DISTRICTS
1 Belize
2 Cayo
3 Corozal
4 Orange Walk
5 Stann Creek
6 Toledo

GUATEMALA
DEPARTAMENTOS
1 Alta Verapaz
2 Baja Verapaz
3 Chimaltenango
4 Chiquimula
5 El Progreso
6 Escuintla
7 Guatemala
8 Huehuetenango
9 Izabal
10 Jalapa
11 Jutiapa
12 Petén
13 Quezaltenango
14 Quiché
15 Retalhuleu
16 Sacatepéquez
17 San Marcos
18 Santa Rosa
19 Sololá
20 Suchitepéquez
21 Totonicapán
22 Zacapa

HONDURAS
DEPARTAMENTOS
1 Atlántida
2 Choluteca
3 Colón
4 Comayagua
5 Copán
6 Cortés
7 El Paraíso
8 Francisco Morazán
9 Gracias a Dios
10 Intibucá
11 Islas de la Bahía
12 La Paz
13 Lempira
14 Ocotepeque
15 Olancho
16 Santa Bárbara
17 Valle
18 Yoro

NICARAGUA
DEPARTAMENTOS
1 Boaco
2 Carazo
3 Chinandega
4 Chontales
5 Estelí
6 Granada
7 Jinotega
8 León
9 Madriz
10 Managua
11 Masaya
12 Matagalpa
13 Nueva Segovia
14 Río San Juan
15 Rivas
16 Zelaya

COSTA RICA
PROVINCIAS
1 Alajuela
2 Cartago
3 Guanacaste
4 Heredia
5 Limón
6 Puntarenas
7 San José

PANAMÁ
PROVINCIAS
1 Bocas del Toro
2 Chiriquí
3 Coclé
4 Colón
5 Darién
6 Herrera
7 Los Santos
8 Panamá
9 San Blas
10 Veraguas

BAHAMAS

BAHAMA ISLANDS

Tropic of Cancer

ATLANTIC OCEAN

Turks and Caicos Islands (U.K.)

HAÏTI

HISPANIOLA

SANTIAGO

PORT-AU-PRINCE

SANTO DOMINGO

REPÚBLICA DOMINICANA
DOMINICAN REPUBLIC

Puerto Rico (U.S.)

SAN JUAN

VIRGIN ISLANDS

SANTIAGO DE CUBA

Guantánamo

Holguín

Kingston

JAMAICA

GREATER ANTILLES / MAYORES

CARIBE / MAR DE LAS ANTILLAS

CARIBBEAN SEA

Colombian Basin

Venezuelan Basin

Nederlandse Antillen
Netherlands Antilles

ARUBA
CURAÇAO
BONAIRE

ANTILLAS MENORES
LESSER ANTILLES

ISLAS DE SOTAVENTO

Dependencias Federales

COLOMBIA

BARRANQUILLA
CARTAGENA
Santa Marta

MARACAIBO

MARACAY
CARACAS
VALENCIA
BARQUISIMETO

VENEZUELA

CÚCUTA
San Cristóbal
Mérida

Longitude West 74 of Greenwich

Map 50 **EASTERN CARIBBEAN**

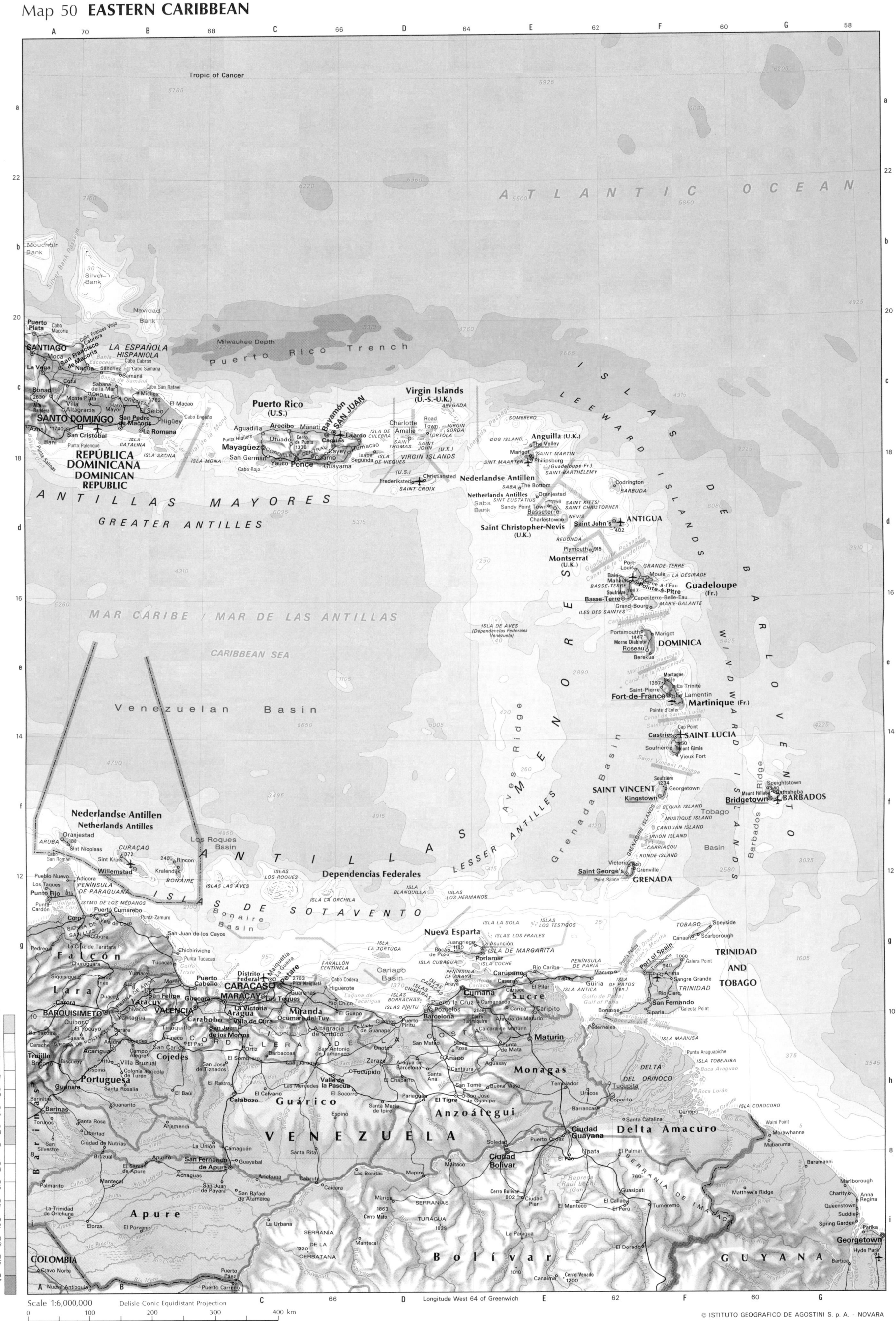

Scale 1:6,000,000

Delisle Conic Equidistant Projection

0   100   200   300   400 km

0   100   200 miles

Longitude West 64 of Greenwich

© ISTITUTO GEOGRAFICO DE AGOSTINI S.p.A. - NOVARA

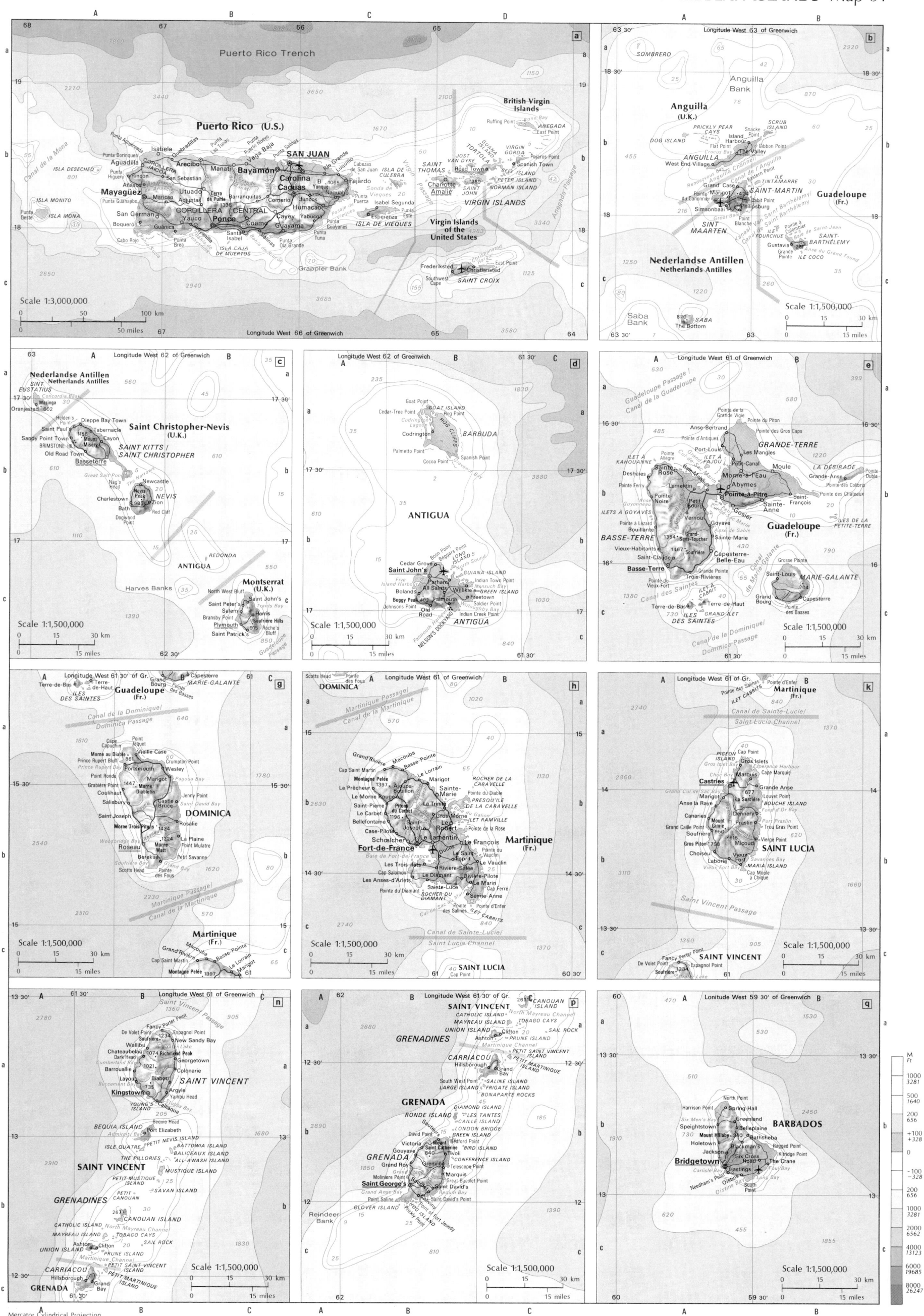

Scale 1:3,000,000

Puerto Rico Trench

Puerto Rico (U.S.)

SAN JUAN

Mayagüez
Ponce

British Virgin Islands
VIRGIN ISLANDS
Virgin Islands of the United States
SAINT CROIX

Scale 1:1,500,000

Anguilla (U.K.)
Guadeloupe (Fr.)
SAINT-MARTIN
SINT MAARTEN
SAINT-BARTHÉLEMY
Nederlandse Antillen / Netherlands Antilles
SABA
Saba Bank

Nederlandse Antillen / Netherlands Antilles
Saint Christopher-Nevis (U.K.)
SAINT KITTS / SAINT CHRISTOPHER
Basseterre
NEVIS
Charlestown
ANTIGUA
REDONDA
Montserrat (U.K.)
Plymouth
Scale 1:1,500,000

BARBUDA
Codrington
ANTIGUA
Saint John's
Scale 1:1,500,000

GRANDE-TERRE
Pointe-à-Pitre
BASSE-TERRE
Basse-Terre
Guadeloupe (Fr.)
MARIE-GALANTE
ILES DES SAINTES
Scale 1:1,500,000

Guadeloupe (Fr.)
ILES DES SAINTES
MARIE-GALANTE
DOMINICA
Roseau
Martinique (Fr.)
Montagne Pelée
Scale 1:1,500,000

DOMINICA
Martinique Passage / Canal de la Martinique
Montagne Pelée
Martinique (Fr.)
Fort-de-France
SAINT LUCIA
Scale 1:1,500,000

Martinique (Fr.)
Saint Lucia Channel / Canal de Sainte-Lucie
Castries
SAINT LUCIA
SAINT VINCENT
Scale 1:1,500,000

SAINT VINCENT
Richmond Peak
Kingstown
SAINT VINCENT
BEQUIA ISLAND
GRENADINES
CANOUAN ISLAND
MAYREAU ISLAND
UNION ISLAND
CARRIACOU
GRENADA
Grand Bay
Scale 1:1,500,000

SAINT VINCENT
GRENADINES
CANOUAN ISLAND
CARRIACOU
Hillsborough
GRENADA
Saint George's
Scale 1:1,500,000

BARBADOS
Speightstown
Mount Hillaby
Bridgetown
Scale 1:1,500,000

M	Ft
1000	3281
500	1640
200	656
+100	+328
0	0
−100	−328
200	656
1000	3281
2000	6562
4000	13123
6000	19685
8000	26247

Mercator Cylindrical Projection

Map 52   SOUTH AMERICA, PHYSICAL

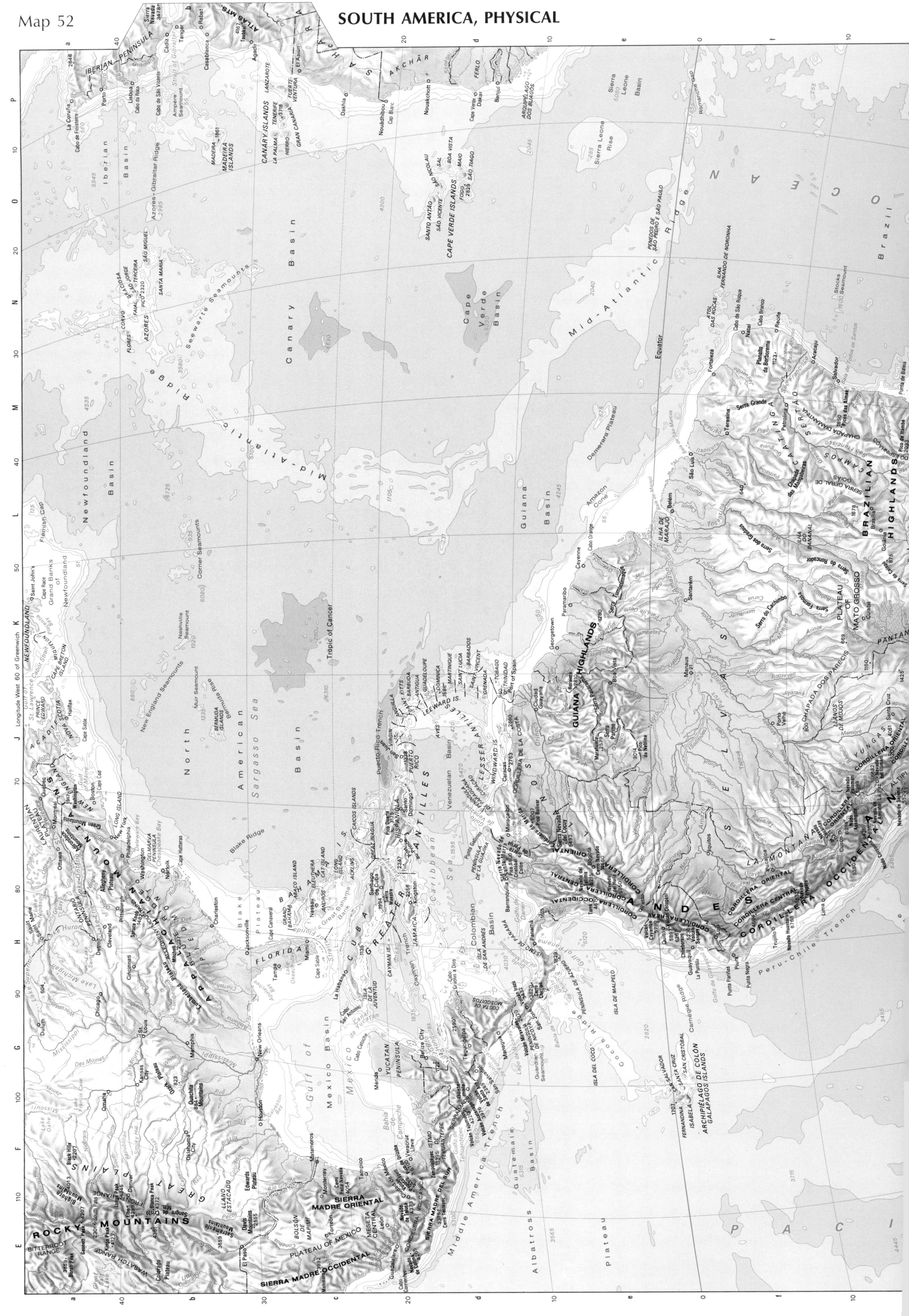

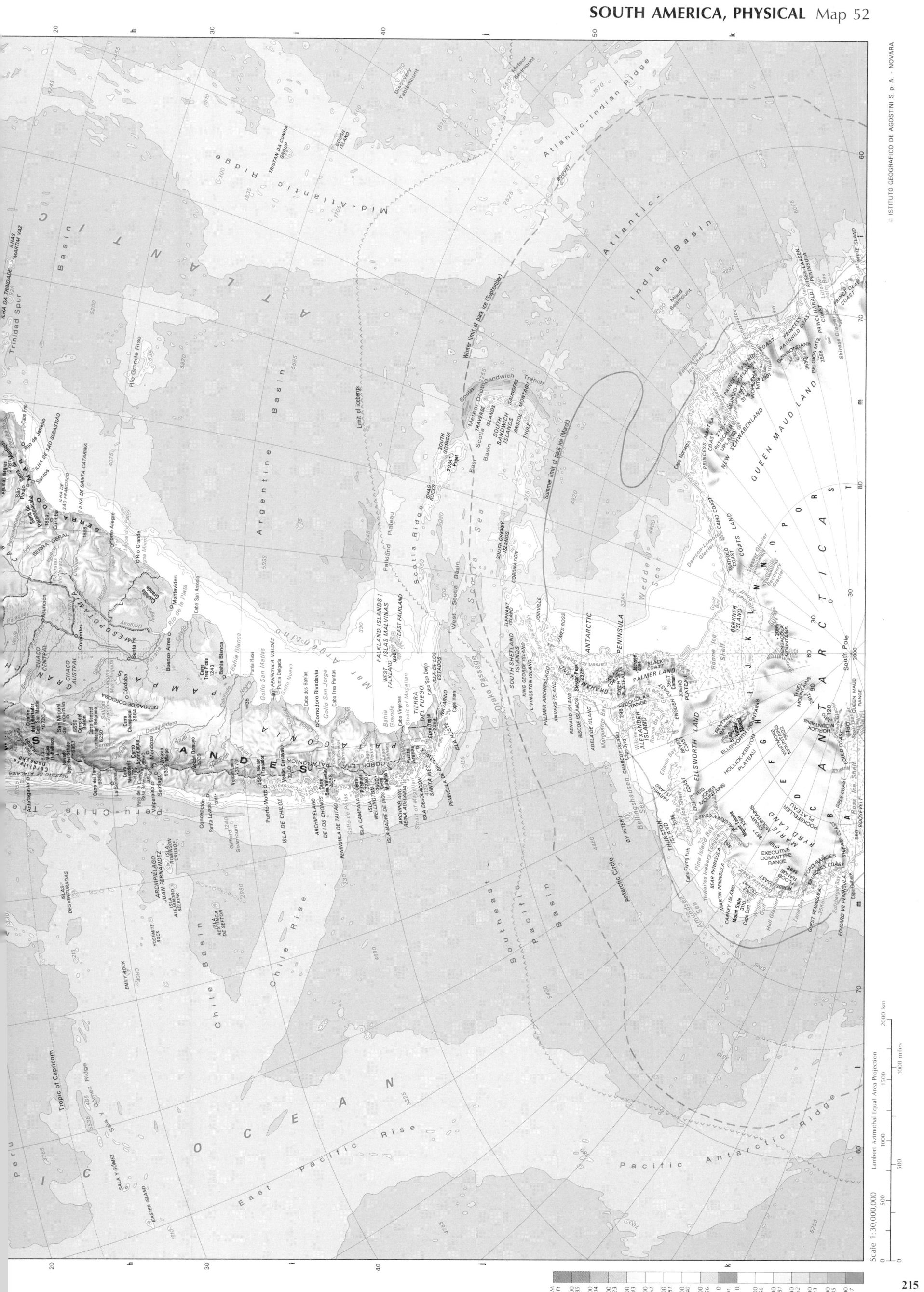

© ISTITUTO GEOGRAFICO DE AGOSTINI S. p. A. - NOVARA

Scale 1: 30,000,000 Lambert Azimuthal Equal Area Projection

2000 km

1000 miles

Map 53   SOUTH AMERICA, POLITICAL

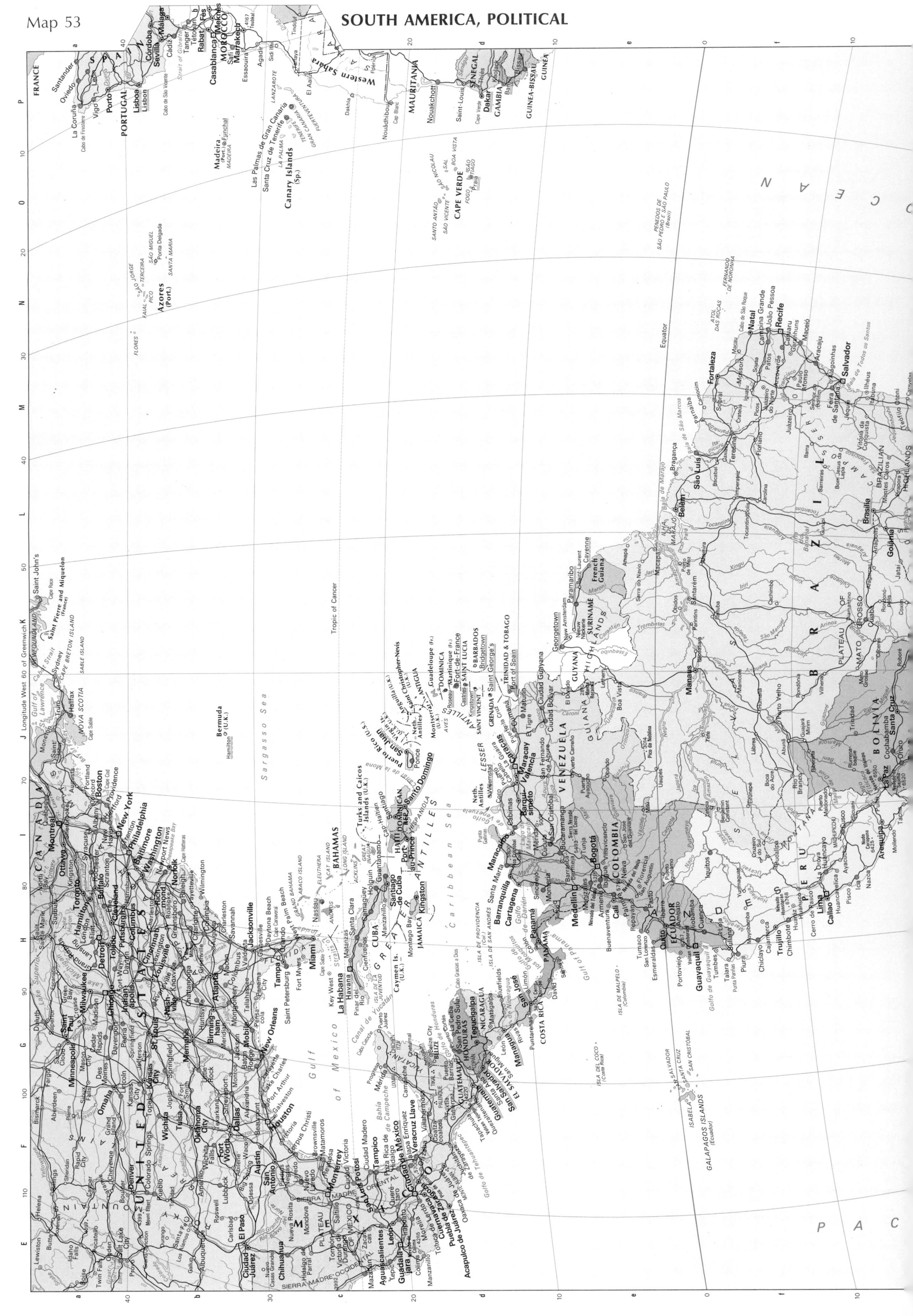

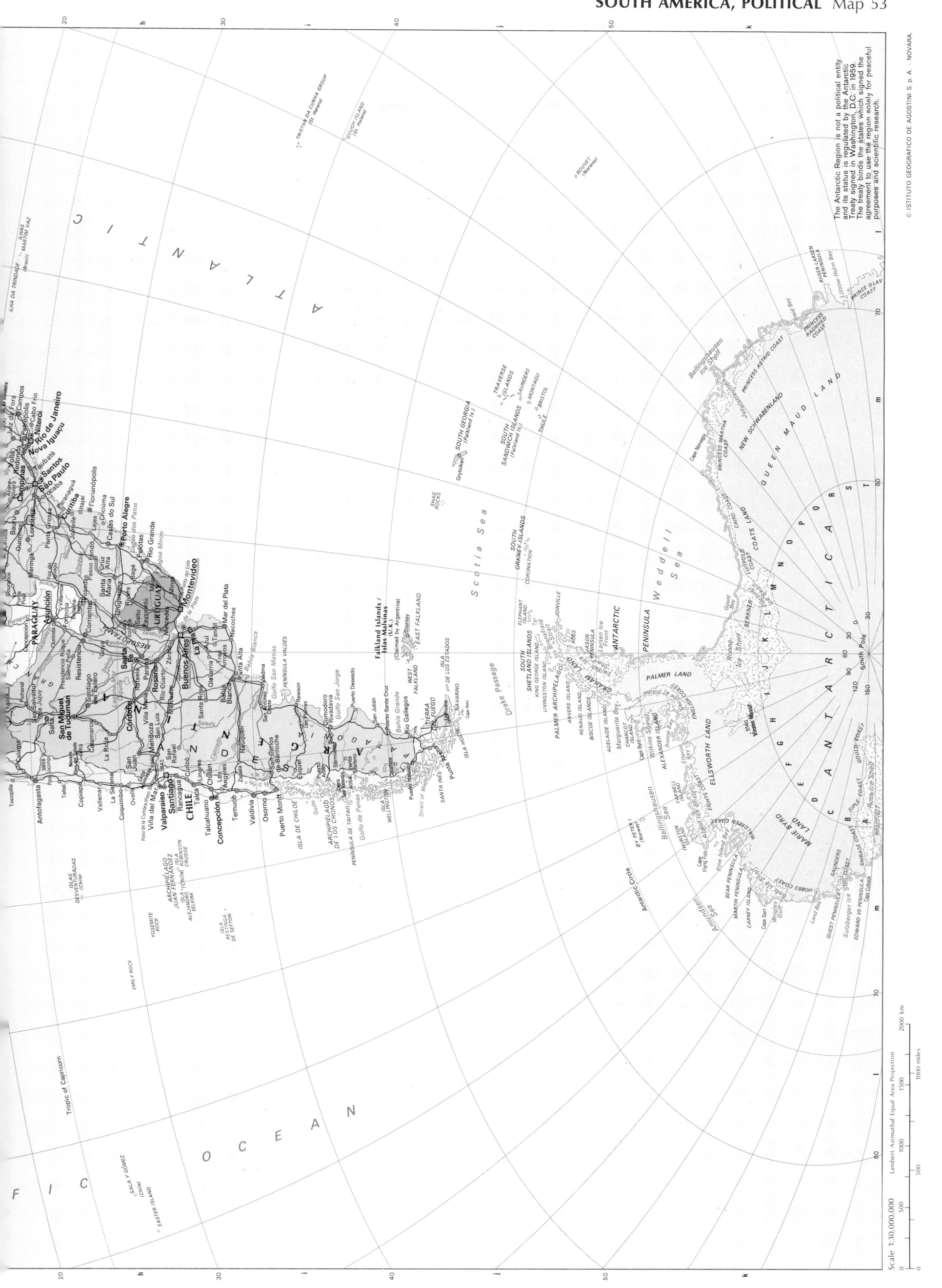

The Antarctic Region is not a political entity and its status is regulated by the Antarctic Treaty signed in Washington, D.C. in 1959. The treaty binds the states which signed the agreement to use the region solely for peaceful purposes and scientific research.

© ISTITUTO GEOGRAFICO DE AGOSTINI S. p. A. - NOVARA.

Scale 1:30,000,000

Lambert Azimuthal Equal Area Projection

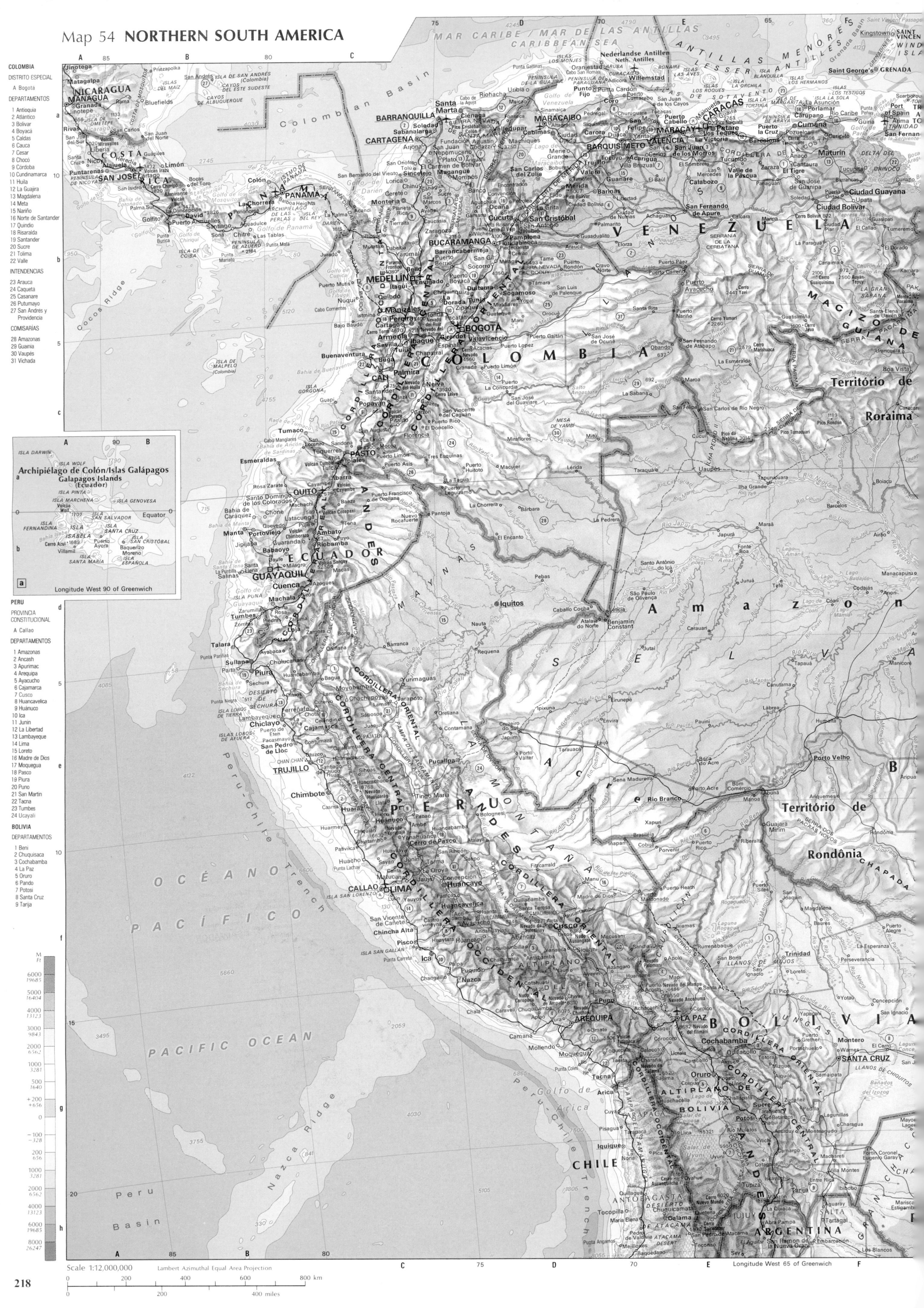

Map 54 **NORTHERN SOUTH AMERICA**

COLOMBIA
DISTRITO ESPECIAL
A Bogota
DEPARTAMENTOS
1 Antioquia
2 Atlántico
3 Bolívar
4 Boyacá
5 Caldas
6 Cauca
7 Cesar
8 Chocó
9 Córdoba
10 Cundinamarca
11 Huila
12 La Guajira
13 Magdalena
14 Meta
15 Nariño
16 Norte de Santander
17 Quindío
18 Risaralda
19 Santander
20 Sucre
21 Tolima
22 Valle
INTENDENCIAS
23 Arauca
24 Caquetá
25 Casanare
26 Putumayo
27 San Andres y
   Providencia
COMISARIAS
28 Amazonas
29 Guainía
30 Vaupés
31 Vichada

PERU
PROVINCIA
CONSTITUCIONAL
A Callao
DEPARTAMENTOS
1 Amazonas
2 Ancash
3 Apurimac
4 Arequipa
5 Ayacucho
6 Cajamarca
7 Cusco
8 Huancavelica
9 Huánuco
10 Ica
11 Junín
12 La Libertad
13 Lambayeque
14 Lima
15 Loreto
16 Madre de Dios
17 Moquegua
18 Pasco
19 Piura
20 Puno
21 San Martin
22 Tacna
23 Tumbes
24 Ucayali

BOLIVIA
DEPARTAMENTOS
1 Beni
2 Chuquisaca
3 Cochabamba
4 La Paz
5 Oruro
6 Pando
7 Potosí
8 Santa Cruz
9 Tarija

Archipiélago de Colón/Islas Galápagos
Galapagos Islands
(Ecuador)

Longitude West 90 of Greenwich

Scale 1:12,000,000   Lambert Azimuthal Equal Area Projection

Longitude West 65 of Greenwich

VENEZUELA
DISTRITO FEDERAL
A Caracas
ESTADOS
1 Anzoátegui
2 Apure
3 Aragua
4 Barinas
5 Bolívar
6 Carabobo
7 Cojedes
8 Falcón
9 Guárico
10 Lara
11 Mérida
12 Miranda
13 Nueva Esparta
14 Monagas
15 Portuguesa
16 Sucre
17 Táchira
18 Trujillo
19 Yaracuy
20 Zulia
TERRITORIOS
FEDERALES
21 Amazonas
22 Delta Amacuro
23 DEPENDENCIAS
FEDERALES
Islas Los Monjes
Isla La Tortuga
Islas Los Frailes
Isla La Sola
Islas Los Testigos
Islas Las Aves
Islas Los Roques
Isla La Orchila
Isla Blanquilla
Islas Los Hermanos
Isla de Patos
Isla de Aves

Map 55 **EAST-CENTRAL SOUTH AMERICA**

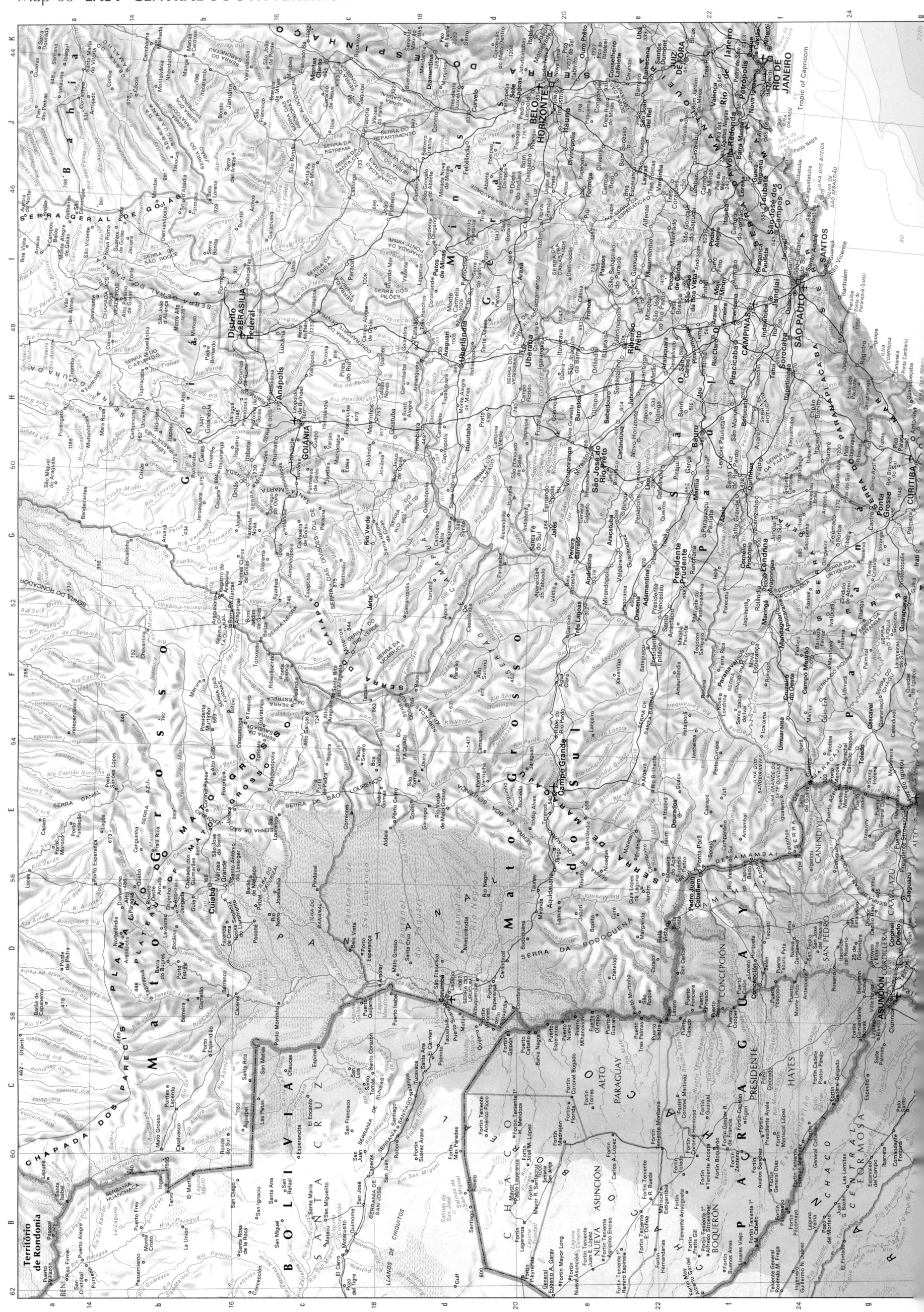

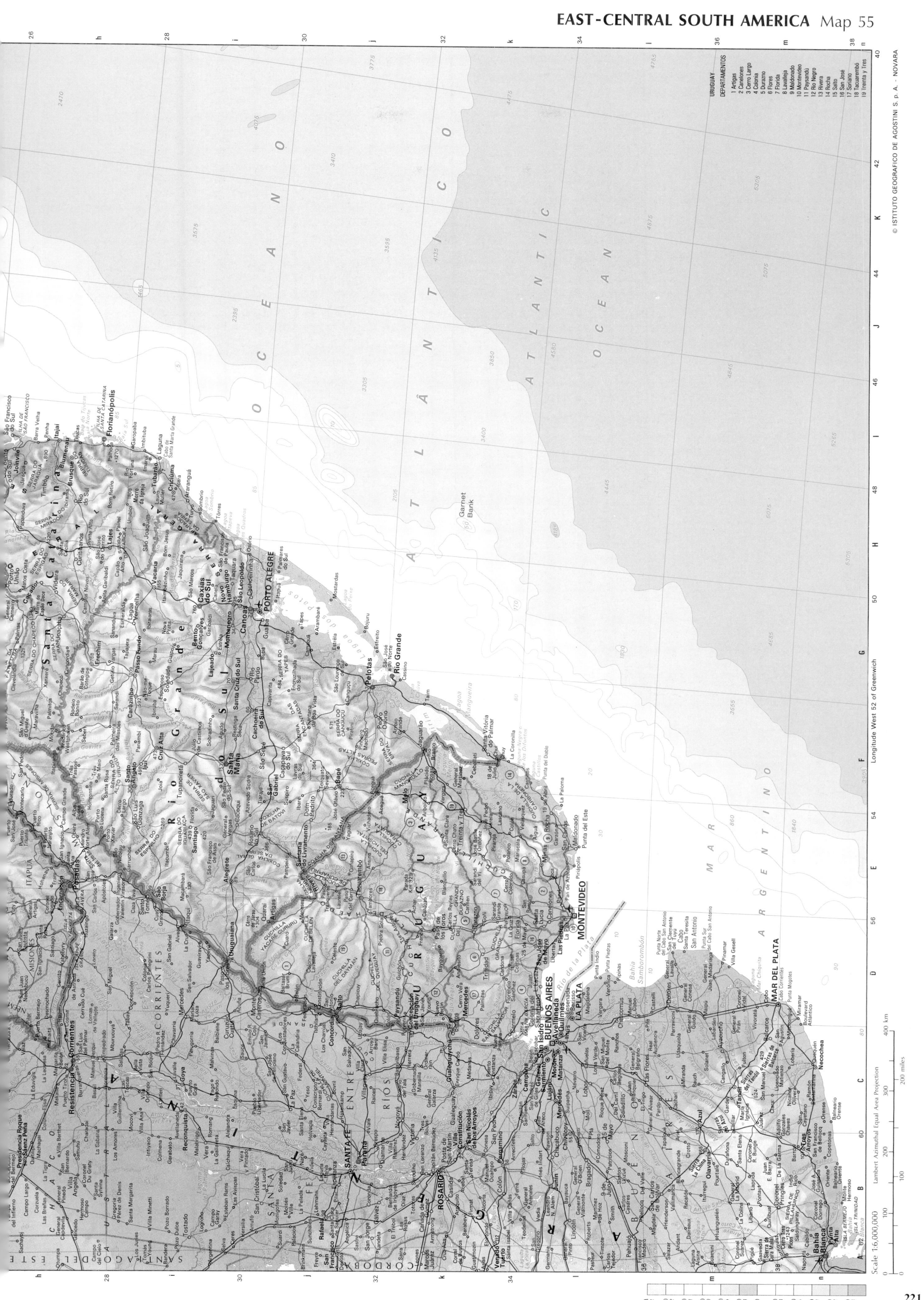

URUGUAY
DEPARTAMENTOS

1 Artigas
2 Canelones
3 Cerro Largo
4 Colonia
5 Durazno
6 Flores
7 Florida
8 Lavalleja
9 Maldonado
10 Montevideo
11 Paysandú
12 Río Negro
13 Rivera
14 Rocha
15 Salto
16 San José
17 Soriano
18 Tacuarembó
19 Treinta y Tres

Scale 1:6,000,000

Lambert Azimuthal Equal Area Projection

Longitude West 52 of Greenwich

Map 56 SOUTHERN SOUTH AMERICA

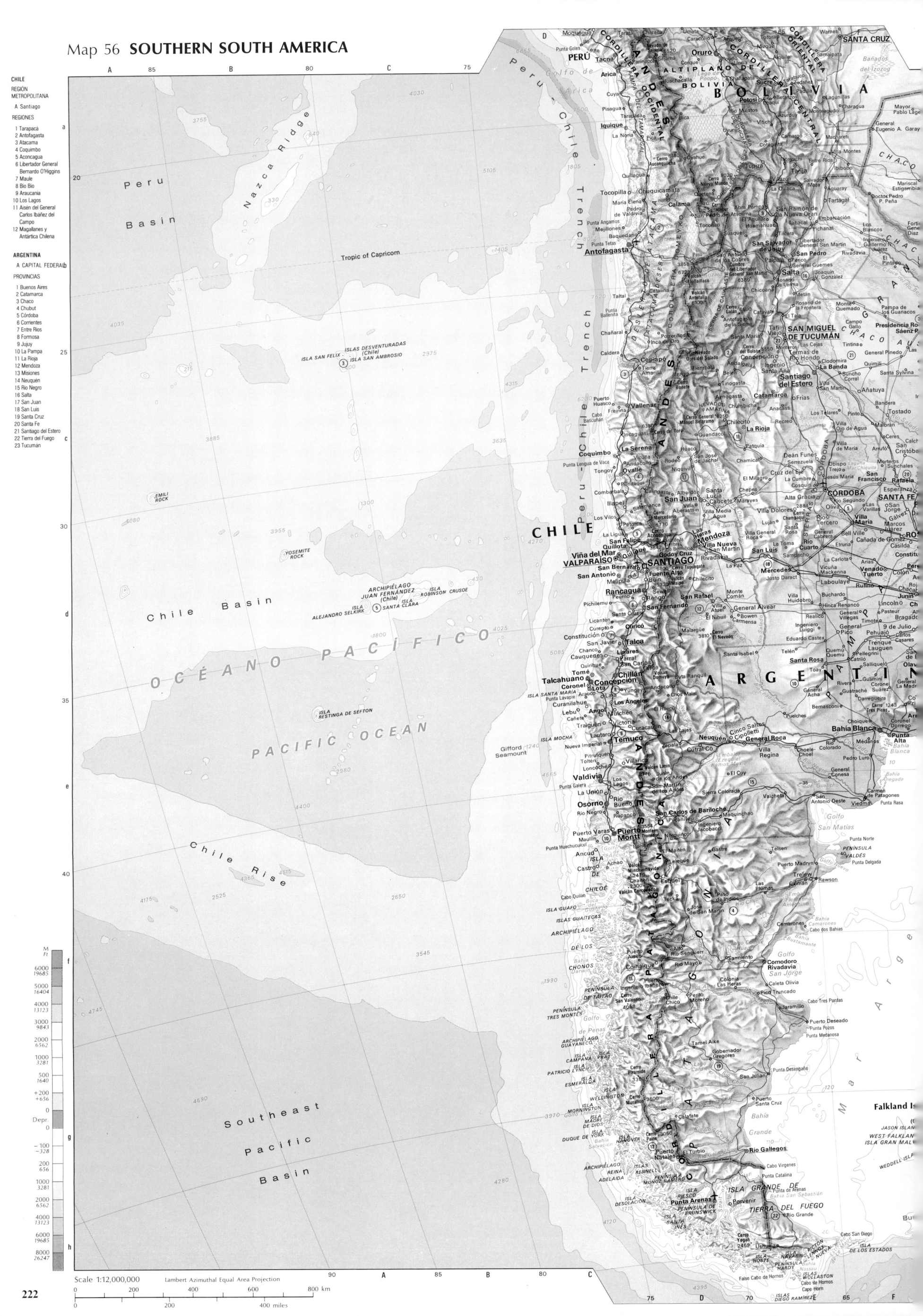

CHILE

REGIÓN
METROPOLITANA

A Santiago

REGIONES

1 Tarapacá
2 Antofagasta
3 Atacama
4 Coquimbo
5 Aconcagua
6 Libertador General
Bernardo O'Higgins
7 Maule
8 Bío Bío
9 Araucanía
10 Los Lagos
11 Aisén del General
Carlos Ibáñez del
Campo
12 Magallanes y
Antártica Chilena

ARGENTINA

A CAPITAL FEDERAL

PROVINCIAS

1 Buenos Aires
2 Catamarca
3 Chaco
4 Chubut
5 Córdoba
6 Corrientes
7 Entre Ríos
8 Formosa
9 Jujuy
10 La Pampa
11 La Rioja
12 Mendoza
13 Misiones
14 Neuquén
15 Río Negro
16 Salta
17 San Juan
18 San Luis
19 Santa Cruz
20 Santa Fe
21 Santiago del Estero
22 Tierra del Fuego
23 Tucumán

Scale 1:12,000,000   Lambert Azimuthal Equal Area Projection

0   200   400   600   800 km

0   200   400 miles

Map 57 **AUSTRALIA AND OCEANIA, PHYSICAL**

Scale 1:30,000,000   Lambert Azimuthal Equal Area Projection

0 500 1000 1500 2000 km

0 500 1000 miles

Map 58 **AUSTRALIA AND OCEANIA, POLITICAL**

CHINA
JAPAN
SOUTH KOREA

Chengdu · Zigong · Chongqing · Guiyang · Kunming · Nanning · Guangzhou · Canton · Hong Kong (U.K.) · Macao (Port.) · Nanjing · Nanking · Shanghai · Hangzhou · Wuhan · Changsha · Fuzhou · Xiamen · Amoy · Taipei · Kaohsiung

TAIWAN · FORMOSA

Tōkyō · Yokohama · Kyōto · Ōsaka · Kōbe · Nagoya · Fukuoka · Nagasaki · Kagoshima · Sendai · Sapporo · Niigata

KYŪSHŪ · SHIKOKU

THAILAND · VIET-NAM · KAMPUCHEA · Ho Chi Minh · Saigon · Hanoi · Haiphong · Da Nang · Qui Nhon

HAINAN · LUZON · Manila · Quezon City

PHILIPPINES

MINDORO · PANAY · NEGROS · CEBU · SAMAR · LEYTE · PALAWAN · MINDANAO · Zamboanga · Davao · General Santos

South China Sea · Philippine Sea · East China Sea · Sulu Sea · Celebes Sea

MALAYSIA · Brunei (U.K.) · Kuching · Pontianak · Balikpapan · Banjarmasin

KALIMANTAN · BORNEO · SUMATRA · CELEBES · HALMAHERA · CERAM

INDONESIA

Jakarta · Bandung · Semarang · Surabaya · Yogyakarta

Java Sea · Flores Sea · Banda Sea · Timor Sea · Arafura Sea

TIMOR · Kupang · Dili

Northern Mariana Islands · MARIANA ISLANDS · Guam (U.S.) · Agana · SAIPAN · TINIAN · ROTA

Trust Territory of the Pacific Islands (Admin. by U.S.)

Federated States of Micronesia

CAROLINE ISLANDS · Palau · Koror · YAP ISLANDS · TRUK ISLANDS · Ponape · KOSRAE (KUSAIE)

MICRONESIA

Marshall Islands · MARSHALL ISLANDS · BIKINI · KWAJALEIN · MAJURO · JALUIT · MILI

Wake (U.S.)

NAURU / NAOERO · BANABA

GILBERT ISLANDS · TARAWA · Bairiki · ABEMAMA

TUVALU

MELANESIA

NEW GUINEA · Jayapura · Wewak · Madang · Lae

PAPUA NEW GUINEA · Port Moresby

BISMARCK ARCHIPELAGO · NEW BRITAIN · NEW IRELAND · Rabaul · ADMIRALTY ISLANDS · MANUS

BOUGAINVILLE · CHOISEUL · SOLOMON ISLANDS · NEW GEORGIA · GUADALCANAL · Honiara · SAN CRISTOBAL · MALAITA

Gulf of Papua · Solomon Sea · Coral Sea

SANTA CRUZ ISLANDS

VANUATU · NEW HEBRIDES · Port-Vila · MALÉKOULA · ESPIRITU SANTO

New Caledonia (France) · Nouméa · LOYALTY ISLANDS

FIJI ISLANDS · VITI LEVU · VANUA LEVU

Norfolk (Australia) · Kingston

LORD HOWE · BALL'S PYRAMID

AUSTRALIA

GREAT SANDY DESERT · GIBSON DESERT · GREAT VICTORIA DESERT · SIMPSON DESERT · TANAMI DESERT · NULLARBOR PLAIN

ARNHEM LAND · KIMBERLEY · CAPE YORK PENINSULA

Darwin · Katherine · Wyndham · Derby · Broome · Port Hedland · Dampier · Carnarvon · Geraldton · Perth · Bunbury · Albany · Esperance · Kalgoorlie

Alice Springs · Tennant Creek · Mount Isa · Cloncurry · Townsville · Cairns · Cooktown · Normanton · Burketown

Rockhampton · Gladstone · Bundaberg · Maryborough · Gympie · Brisbane · Gold Coast · Toowoomba · Ipswich

Charleville · Roma · Dubbo · Tamworth · Armidale · Coffs Harbour · Lismore

Broken Hill · Port Augusta · Port Pirie · Adelaide · Whyalla · Port Lincoln

Mildura · Wagga Wagga · Canberra · Wollongong · Sydney · Newcastle · Maitland · Orange · Bathurst

Melbourne · Geelong · Ballarat · Bendigo · Warrnambool · Shepparton

Gulf of Carpentaria · Great Australian Bight

Spencer Gulf · KANGAROO ISLAND

Lake Eyre · Lake Torrens · Lake Gairdner · Lake Frome · Lake Carnegie · Lake Disappointment · Lake Mackay

BASS STRAIT

TASMANIA · Hobart · Launceston · Devonport · FURNEAUX GROUP · KING ISLAND

Tasman Sea

NEW ZEALAND

NORTH ISLAND · Auckland · Manukau · Hamilton · Whangarei · Wellington · New Plymouth

SOUTH ISLAND · Christchurch · Dunedin · Invercargill · Nelson · Blenheim · Hokitika · Timaru

STEWART ISLAND · AUCKLAND ISLANDS (New Zealand)

INDIAN OCEAN

Scale 1:30,000,000 · Lambert Azimuthal Equal Area Projection

0 500 1000 1500 2000 km
0 500 1000 miles

Longitude East 170 of Greenwich

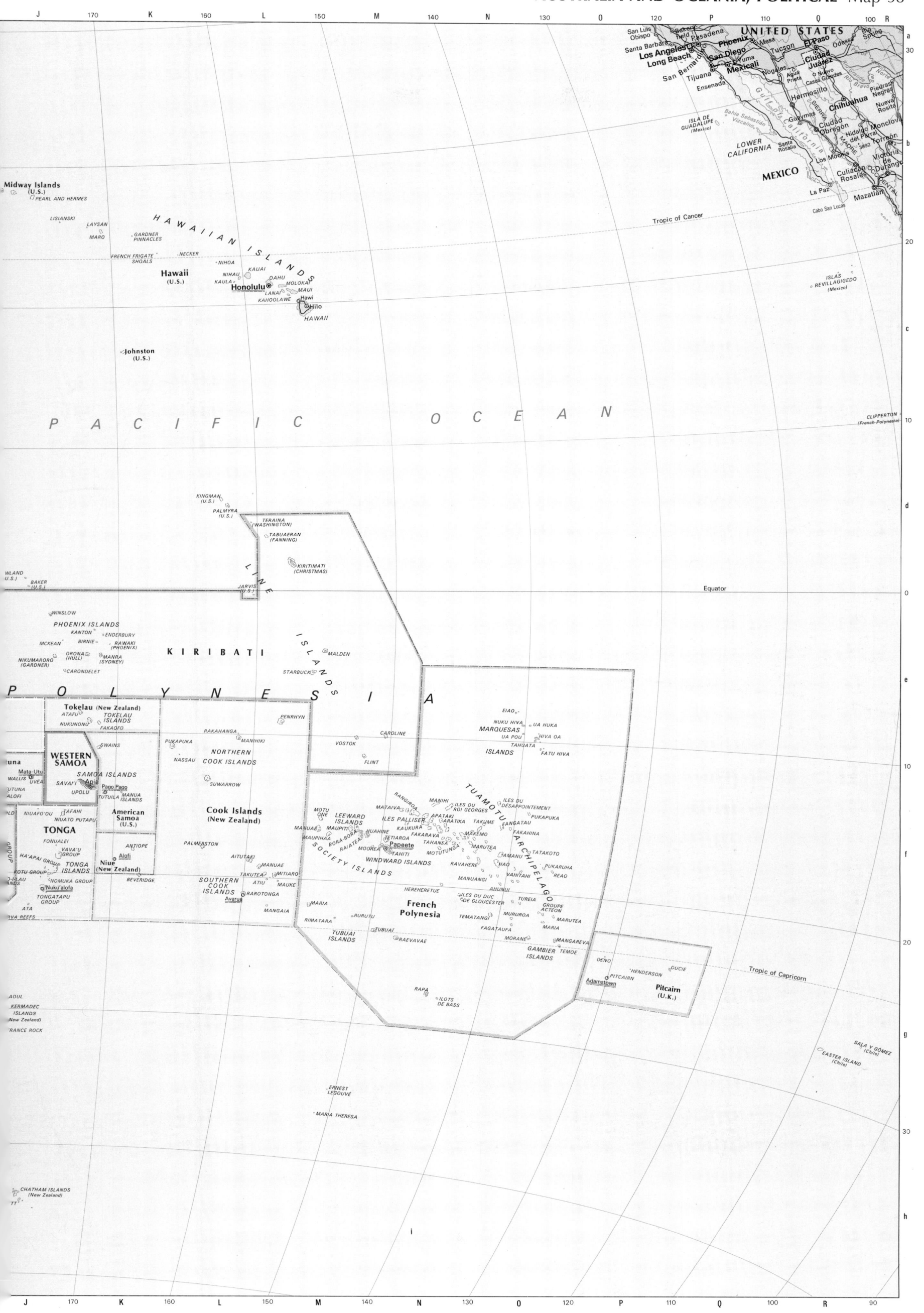

Map 59 **AUSTRALIA**

Map labels

INDONESIA

LAUT JAWA / Java Sea
LAUT FLORES / FLORES SEA
LAUT BALI
LAUT SAWU
SELAT SUMBA
TIMOR SEA
ARAFURA SEA

Kudus
SEMARANG
Magelang Madiun
SURAKARTA Kediri
YOGYA-KARTA
Tulungagung
MALANG
Banjuwangi
Surabaya
Gresik
Tuban
Rembang
Probolinggo
Bondowoso
JAWA / JAVA
NUSA PENIDA
PULAU LOMBOK
PULAU SUMBAWA
PULAU SUMBA
PULAU FLORES
PULAU LOMBLEN
PULAU ALOR
PULAU WETAR
PULAU ROMANG
PULAU TIMOR
PULAU ROTI
PULAU SAWU
Mataram
Singaraja
Denpasar
Waingapu
Waikabubak
Ende
Ruteng
Larantuka
Kupang
Baa
Atambua
Dili
Manatuto

KEPULAUAN TENGGARA
KEPULAUAN KANGEAN
KEPULAUAN BONE RATE
KEPULAUAN SOLOR
KEPULAUAN ALOR
KEPULAUAN BARAT DAYA
KEPULAUAN BABAR
KEPULAUAN LETI
KEPULAUAN SERMATA
KEPULAUAN TANIMBAR
KEPULAUAN KAI
Saumlaki
PULAU YAMDENA
PULAU SELARU
PULAU TRANGAN

INDIAN OCEAN

North Australian Basin
Java Trench
Planet Deep
Corona Bank
D'Artagnan Bank
Exmouth Plateau
Cuvier Basin
Tropic of Capricorn
Diamantina Deep
Diamantina Trench
South Australian Basin

TIMOR SEA
Timor Trough
ASHMORE ISLANDS
CARTIER ISLAND
HIBERNIA REEF
BROWSE ISLAND
SCOTT REEF
SERINGAPATAM REEF
Holothuria Banks
Cape Londonderry

Darwin
BATHURST ISLAND
MELVILLE ISLAND
Van Diemen Gulf
COBOURG PENINSULA
Cape Croker
COKER ISLAND
Maningrida Settlement
Milingimbi
ARNHEM LAND
Katherine
Mataranka
Larrimah
Birdum
Willeroo
Top Springs
Victoria River Downs
Wave Hill
Newcastle Waters
Elliot

KIMBERLEY
KIMBERLEY PLATEAU
KING LEOPOLD RANGES
Wyndham
Kununurra
Turkey Creek
Halls Creek
Fitzroy Crossing
Derby
Broome
DAMPIER LAND
KING SOUND
BUCCANEER ARCHIPELAGO
BONAPARTE ARCHIPELAGO
ADÈLE ISLAND
LACEPEDE ISLANDS
Cape Leveque
Mount Ord
Mount Wells
Mount Parker
Mount Napier
Christmas Creek

GREAT SANDY DESERT
CANNING BASIN
TANAMI DESERT
Tanami
The Granites
Barrow Creek
Tea Tree
NORTHERN TERRITORY

EIGHTY MILE BEACH
Port Hedland
Goldsworthy
Marble Bar
Nullagine
De Grey River
Roebourne
Dampier
DAMPIER ARCHIPELAGO
MONTE BELLO ISLANDS
BARROW ISLAND
MUIRON ISLANDS
North West Cape
Exmouth
Learmonth
Onslow
HAMERSLEY RANGE
CHICHESTER RANGE
PATERSON RANGE
ROBERTSON RANGE
Mount Bruce
Tom Price
Mount Meharry
OPHTHALMIA RANGE
Newman
Paraburdoo
Wittenoom
Roy Hill
Mundiwindi

WESTERN AUSTRALIA
GIBSON DESERT
GREAT VICTORIA DESERT
NULLARBOR PLAIN
AUSTRALIA

Lake Disappointment
Lake Mackay
Lake Macdonald
Lake Amadeus
Lake Neale
Lake Carnegie
Lake Wells
Lake Burnside
Lake Throssell
Lake Rason
MACDONNELL RANGES
MUSGRAVE RANGES
WARBURTON RANGE
RAWLINSON RANGE
TOMKINSON RANGES
PETERMANN RANGES
EVERARD RANGES
BIRKSGATE RANGE
Warburton Mission
Docker River
Giles Meteorological Station
Mount Olga
Erldunda
Kulgera
De Rose
Welbourn Hill
Mount Davies
Mount Woodroffe
Simpson Hill

BARLEE RANGE
ROBINSON RANGE
KENNEDY RANGE
CARNARVON RANGE
Carnarvon
Gascoyne Junction
Mount Augustus
Mount Egerton
Mount Vernon
Meekatharra
Wiluna
Lake Carnegie
Lake Way
Agnew
Leonora
Laverton
Lake Wells

BERNIER ISLAND
DORRE ISLAND
DIRK HARTOG ISLAND
Shark Bay
Denham
Cape Inscription
Hamelin
Useless Loop
NICHOLSON RANGE
WELD RANGE
Mount Murchison
Mount Hale
Mount Narryer
Cue
Mount Magnet
Sandstone
Mount Wyemandoo
Mount Singleton
Yalgoo
Mullewa
Morawa
Perenjori
Dalwallinu
Wongan Hills

Geraldton
HOUTMAN ABROLHOS
Northampton
Dongara
Mingenew
Three Springs
Carnamah
Moora
Watheroo
Jurien Bay
Lancelin
Gingin

PERTH
ROTTNET ISLAND
FREMANTLE
Rockingham
Mandurah
Pinjarra
Harvey
Waroona
Bunbury
Collie
Busselton
Margaret River
Augusta
Cape Naturaliste
Cape Leeuwin
Nannup
Bridgetown
Manjimup
Pemberton
Cape D'Entrecasteaux
Donnybrook
Boyup Brook
Kojonup
Katanning
Wagin
Narrogin
Nyabing
Gnowangerup
Cranbrook
Mount Barker
Denmark
Albany
King George Sound
STIRLING RANGE
Northam
York
Beverley
Brookton
Corrigin
Kondinin
Wickepin
Pingelly
Quairading
Cunderdin
Kellerberrin
Merredin
Bruce Rock
Southern Cross
Bullfinch
Koorda
Mukinbudin
Wyalkatchem
Goomalling
Kellerberrin
Lake Grace
Lake King
Ravensthorpe
Hopetoun
Esperance
Cape Arid
ARCHIPELAGO OF THE RECHERCHE
Hood Point
Cheyne Bay
Point Culver

Kalgoorlie
Coolgardie
Kambalda
Widgiemooltha
Norseman
Balladonia
Fraser Range
Zanthus
Rawlinna
Forrest
Cook
Ooldea
Nullarbor
Eucla
Eyre
Cape Culver
Twilight Cove

SOUTH AUSTRALIA
Maralinga
Ooldea
Penong
Fowlers Bay
Smoky Bay
Streaky Bay
Ceduna
Head of Bight
GREAT AUSTRALIAN BIGHT
Point Culver
INVESTIGATOR GROUP

INDIAN OCEAN

Elevation scale (metres / feet)

M / Ft	
4000 / 13123	
3000 / 9843	
2000 / 6562	
1000 / 3281	
500 / 1640	
+ 200 / +656	
0	
Depr.	
− 100 / −328	
200 / 656	
1000 / 3281	
2000 / 6562	
4000 / 13123	
6000 / 19685	
8000 / 26247	

228

Scale 1:12,000,000 Delisle Conic Equidistant Projection

0   200   400   600   800 km
0   200   400 miles

© ISTITUTO GEOGRAFICO DE AGOSTINI S. p. A. - NOVARA

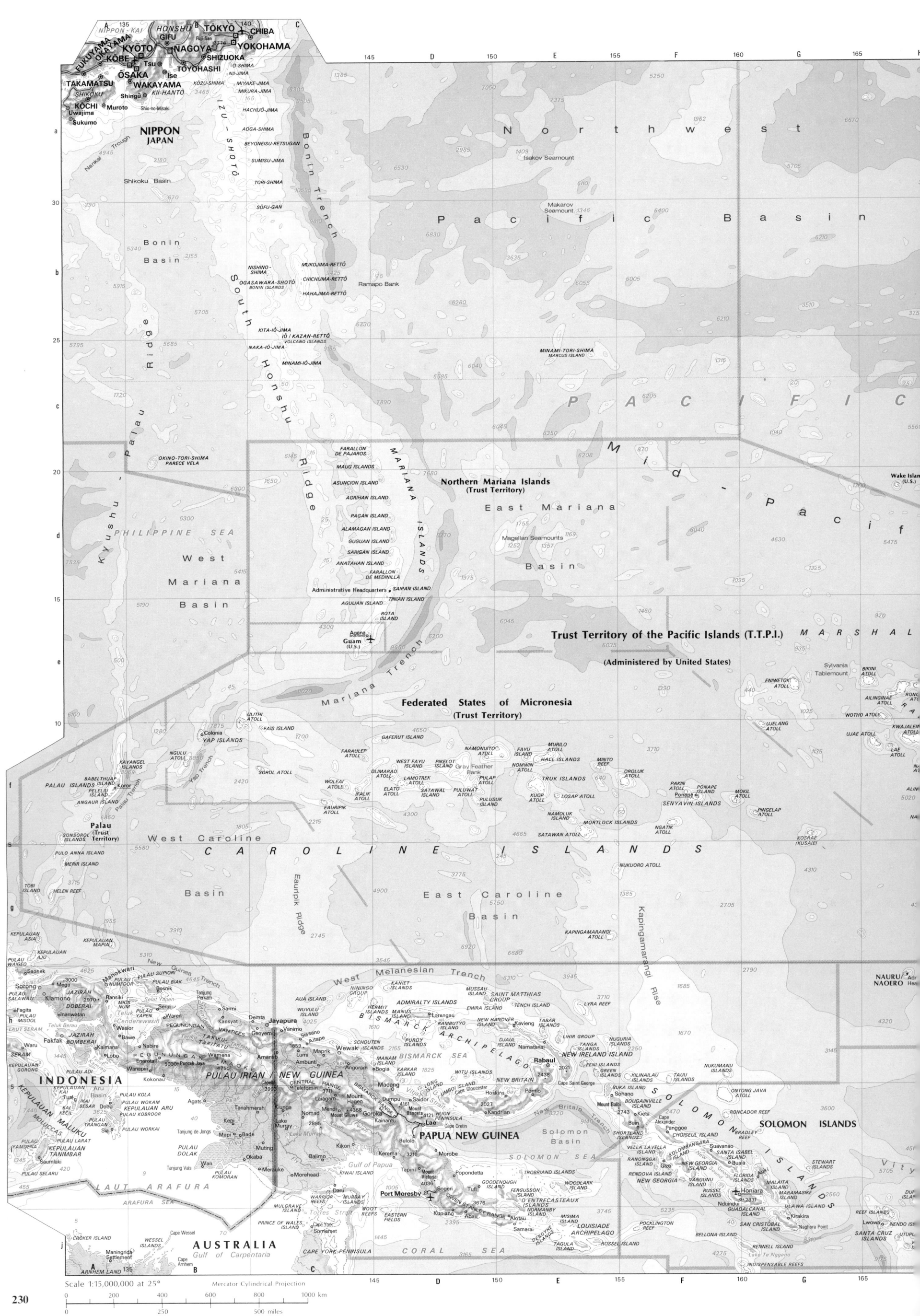

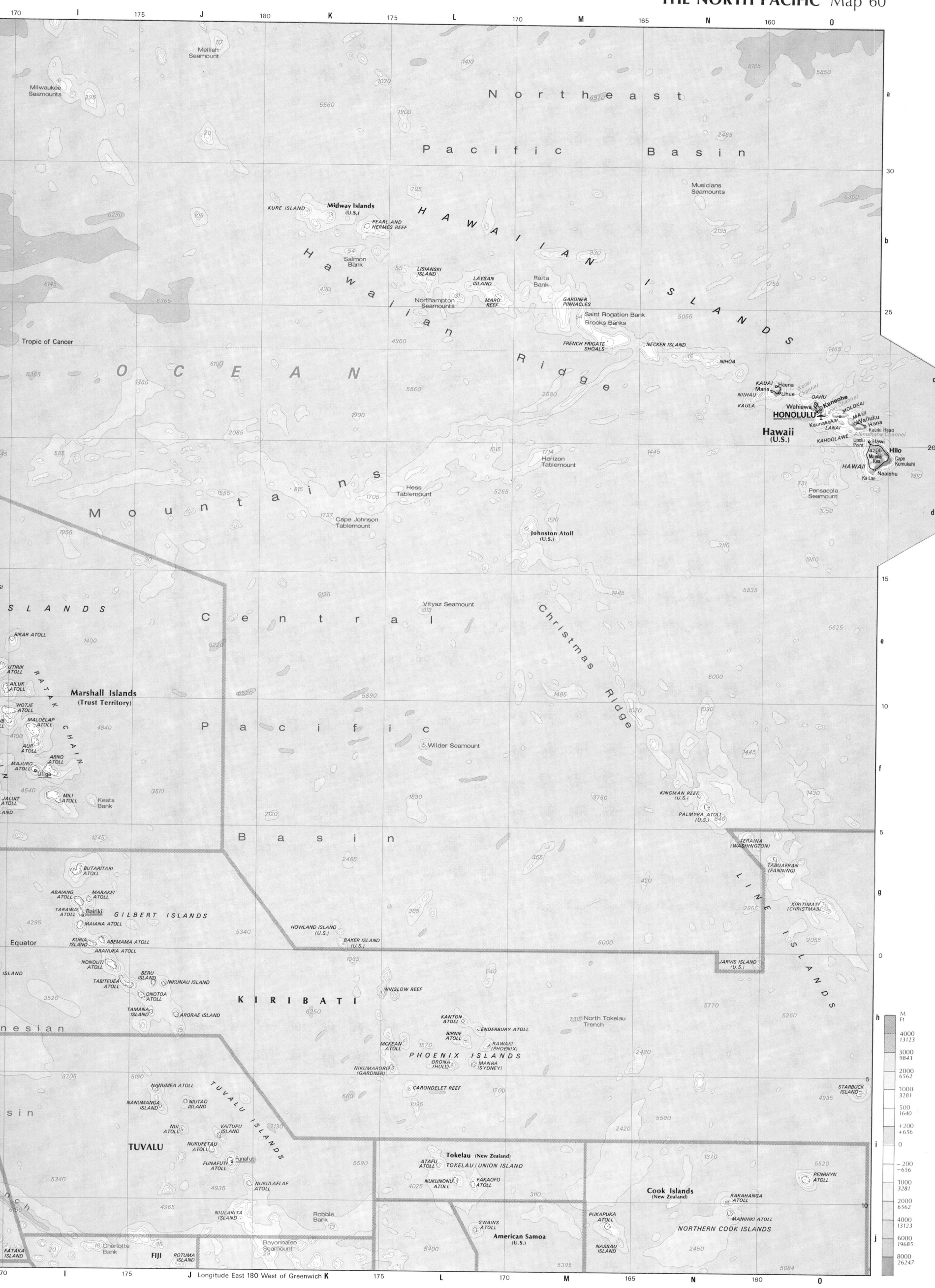

Map 61 THE SOUTH PACIFIC

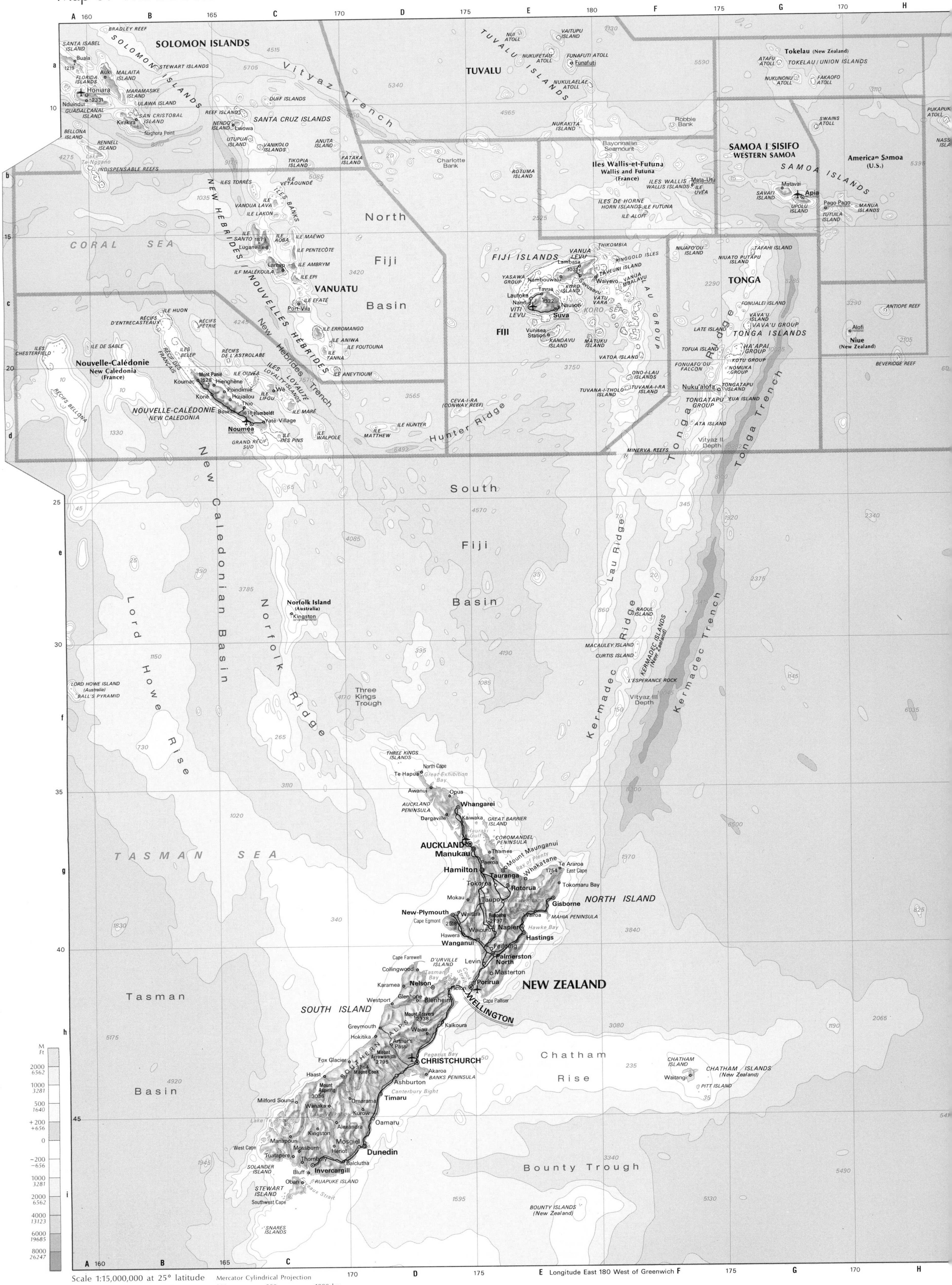

A 160 B 165 C 170 D 175 E 180 F 175 G 170 H

BRADLEY REEF

SOLOMON ISLANDS

SANTA ISABEL ISLAND

Buala

1219

Auki

MALAITA ISLAND

FLORIDA ISLANDS

Honiara 3331

MARAMASIKE ISLAND

ULAWA ISLAND

Nduindui

SAN CRISTOBAL ISLAND

Kirakira

GUADALCANAL ISLAND

4275

Nughota Point

BELLONA ISLAND

RENNELL ISLAND

Lake Te Nggano

3310

INDISPENSABLE REEFS

STEWART ISLANDS

Vityaz Trench

REEF ISLANDS

DUFF ISLANDS

5705

4515

SANTA CRUZ ISLANDS

NENDO ISLAND

Lwowa

UTUPUA ISLAND

VANIKOLO ISLANDS

ANUTA ISLAND

TIKOPIA ISLAND

FATAKA ISLAND

5085

1035

ÎLES TORRÈS

ÎLE VÉTAOUNDÉ

NEW HEBRIDES

ÎLES BANKS

VANUA LAVA

ÎLE MAÉWO

ÎLE LAKON

ÎLE SANTO 1879

ÎLE AOBA

Luganville

ÎLE PENTECÔTE

Lamap

ÎLF MALÉKOULA

ÎLE AMBRYM

ÎLE EPI

VANUATU

ÎLE ÉFATÉ

Port-Vila

ÎLE HUON

RÉCIFS D'ENTRECASTEAUX

RÉCIFS PÉTRIE

ÎLE DE SABLE

ÎLES CHESTERFIELD

RÉCIFS DE L'ASTROLABE

ÎLES BÉLEP

Nouvelle-Calédonie
New Caledonia
(France)

Koumac 61828

Henghène

Poindimié

Houailou

Koné

Thio

Bourail 618 Houdelot

NOUVELLE-CALÉDONIE
NEW CALEDONIA

Nouméa

GRAND RÉCIF SUD

ÎLE DES PINS

ÎLE WALPOLE

ÎLE MATTHEW

ÎLE HUNTER

New Hebrides Trench

ÎLES LOYAUTÉ

LOYALTY ISLANDS

ÎLE OUVÉA

ÎLE LIFOU

Wé

ÎLE MARÉ

Yaté-Village

Hienghène

NUI ATOLL

VAITUPU ISLAND

TUVALU ISLANDS

NUKUFETAU ATOLL

FUNAFUTI ATOLL

Funafuti

TUVALU

NUKULAELAE ATOLL

5340

5590

4965

NURAKITA ISLAND

ROTUMA ISLAND

Charlotte Bank

Bayonnaise Seamount

ÎLES WALLIS-ET-FUTUNA
Wallis and Futuna
(France)

ÎLES WALLIS
WALLIS ISLANDS
ÎLE UVÉA

Mata-Utu

ÎLES DE HORNE
HORN ISLANDS-ÎLE FUTUNA
ÎLE ALOFI

2525

North

Fiji

Basin

FIJI ISLANDS

THIKOMBIA

VANUA LEVU

Lambasa

NGGILDAD ISLES

Nambouwalu

TAVEUNI ISLAND

YASAWA GROUP

Lautoka

Tavua

Nandi 1322

Nausori

VITI LEVU

Suva

FIJI

Vunisea Station

KANDAVU ISLAND

KORO SEA

VATU VARA

MATUKU ISLAND

CEVA-I-RA
(CONWAY REEF)

ONO-I-LAU ISLANDS

TUVANA-I-THOLO ISLAND

TUVANA-I-RA ISLAND

VATOA ISLAND

3565

3750

5490

TOKELAU (New Zealand)

ATAFU ATOLL

NUKUNONU ATOLL

TOKELAU / UNION ISLANDS

FAKAOFO ATOLL

SWAINS ISLAND

PUKAPUKA ATOLL

NASSAU

SAMOA I SISIFO
WESTERN SAMOA

SAVAI'I ISLAND

Apia

UPOLU ISLAND

Matavai

Pago Pago

TUTUILA ISLAND

AMERICAN SAMOA
(U.S.)

MANUA ISLANDS

5395

SAMOA ISLANDS

NIUAFO'OU ISLAND

TAFAHI ISLAND

NIUATO PUTAPU ISLAND

Robbie Bank

FONUALEI ISLAND

VAVA'U ISLAND

VAVA'U GROUP

TONGA

LATE ISLAND

2290

HA'APAI GROUP

TOFUA ISLAND

KOTU GROUP

FONUAFO'OU FALCON

NOMUKA GROUP

Nuku'alofa

TONGATAPU GROUP

'EUA ISLAND

ATA ISLAND

TONGA ISLANDS

Tonga Trench

Lau Ridge

MINERVA REEFS

Vityaz II Depth

ANTIOPE REEF

Alofi

Niue
(New Zealand)

2105

BEVERIDGE REEF

3290

South

Fiji

Basin

4570

4085

3785

Norfolk Island
(Australia)

Kingston

4920

1085

Lord

Howe

Rise

LORD HOWE ISLAND
(Australia)
BALL'S PYRAMID

1150

New Caledonian Basin

Norfolk Ridge

Three Kings Trough

4120

Kermadec Ridge

RAOUL ISLAND

MACAULEY ISLAND

CURTIS ISLAND

L'ESPERANCE ROCK

Vityaz III Depth

KERMADEC ISLANDS
(New Zealand)

Kermadec Trench

4190

6025

8300

6500

TASMAN SEA

THREE KINGS ISLANDS

North Cape

Te Hapua Great Exhibition Bay

Awanui

Opua

AUCKLAND PENINSULA

Whangarei

Dargaville

Kaiwaka

GREAT BARRIER ISLAND

Hauraki Gulf

COROMANDEL PENINSULA

AUCKLAND

Manukau

Thames

Mount Maunganui

HAMILTON

Tauranga

Whakatane

Te Araroa

East Cape

Te Puke

Tokoroa

Rotorua

Tokomaru Bay

Mokau

Taupo

Gisborne

NORTH ISLAND

New-Plymouth

Waitara

MAHIA PENINSULA

Cape Egmont

Waiouru

Napier

Hawke Bay

Hawera

Hastings

Wanganui

Feilding

Palmerston North

D'URVILLE ISLAND

Levin

Cape Farewell

Collingwood

Masterton

NEW ZEALAND

Karamea

Porirua

Nelson

WELLINGTON

Westport

Blenheim

Cape Palliser

Greymouth

Glenhope

SOUTH ISLAND

Waiau

Kaikoura

Hokitika

Arthur's Pass

SOUTHERN ALPS

Mount Cook 3764

Pegasus Bay

Fox Glacier

CHRISTCHURCH

Akaroa

Haast

Ashburton

BANKS PENINSULA

Milford Sound

Mount Aspiring 3036

Omarama

Timaru

Canterbury Bight

Wanaka

Kurow

Oamaru

Manapouri

Alexandra

West Cape

Kingston

Heriot

Mossburn

Mosgiel

Dunedin

Thornbury

Balclutha

SOLANDER ISLAND

Bluff

Invercargill

Oban

STEWART ISLAND

Southwest Cape

SNARES ISLANDS

Chatham

Rise

CHATHAM ISLAND

CHATHAM ISLANDS
(New Zealand)

Waitangi

PITT ISLAND

Bounty Trough

BOUNTY ISLANDS
(New Zealand)

5130

5490

3340

1595

M Ft
2000 6562
1000 3281
500 1640
+200 +656
0 0
-200 -656
1000 3281
2000 6562
4000 13123
6000 19685
8000 26247

Scale 1:15,000,000 at 25° latitude   Mercator Cylindrical Projection

0   200   400   600   800   1000 km

0   250   500 miles

232

E Longitude East 180 West of Greenwich F

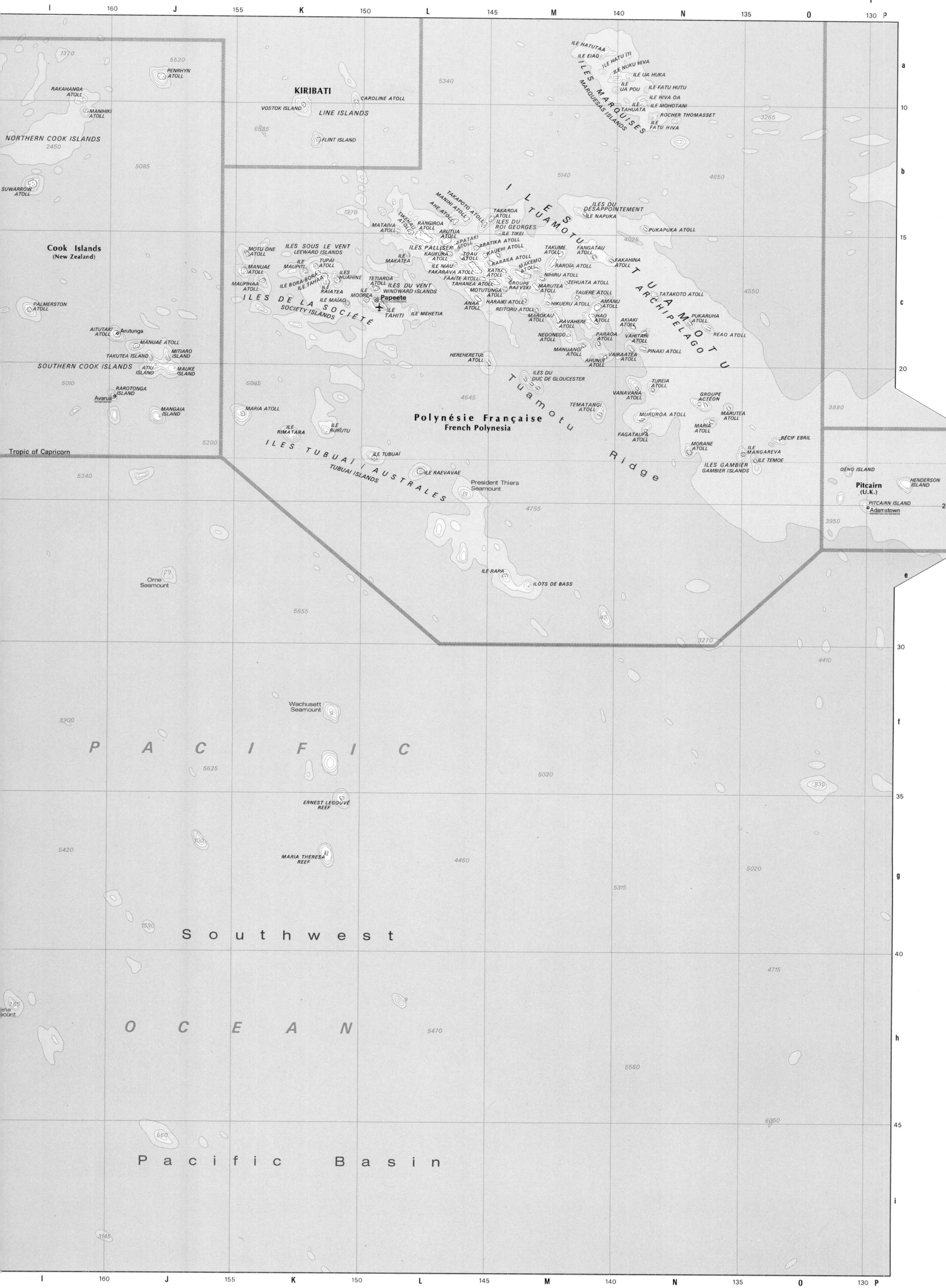

a

ILE HATUTAA
ILE EIAO
ILE HATU ITI
ILE NUKU HIVA
ILE UA HUKA
ILE UA POU
ILE FATU HUTU
ILE HIVA OA
ILE MOHOTANI
ILE TAHUATA
ROCHER THOMASSET
ILE FATU HIVA

1370
5520
RAKAHANGA ATOLL
PENRHYN ATOLL
MANIHIKI ATOLL

5340
KIRIBATI
CAROLINE ATOLL

ILES MARQUISES
MARQUESAS ISLANDS

10

VOSTOK ISLAND
LINE ISLANDS

NORTHERN COOK ISLANDS
2450

6685

FLINT ISLAND

5085

5140

4650

3265

b

SUWARROW ATOLL

I LES TUAMOTU
ILES DU DÉSAPPOINTEMENT
ILE NAPUKA
PUKAPUKA ATOLL

4025

1378
TAKAPOTO ATOLL
MANIHI ATOLL
AHE ATOLL
TAKAROA ATOLL
ILES DU ROI GEORGES
ILE TIKEI

T U A M O T U   A R C H I P E L A G O

Cook Islands
(New Zealand)

MOTU ONE ATOLL
ILES SOUS LE VENT
LEEWARD ISLANDS

RANGIROA ATOLL
MATAIVA ATOLL
ARUTUA ATOLL
ARATIKA ATOLL
KAUEHI ATOLL

TAKUME ATOLL
FANGATAU ATOLL
FAKAHINA ATOLL

MANUAE ATOLL

MAUPIHAA ATOLL
ILE BORA-BORA
ILE TAHAA
ILE MAUPITI
ILE TUPAI
ILE HUAHINE
APATAKI ATOLL
KAUKURA ATOLL
TOAU ATOLL
ILE NIAU
ILE MAKATEA

ARARAKA ATOLL
KATIU ATOLL
MAKEMO ATOLL
RAROIA ATOLL
NIHIRU ATOLL

TEHUATA ATOLL

TATAKOTO ATOLL

4550

PALMERSTON ATOLL
ILE RAIATEA
ILE MAIAO
TETIAROA ATOLL
FAKARAVA ATOLL
FAAITE ATOLL
TAHANEA ATOLL

GROUPE RAEVSKI
MARUTEA ATOLL
TAUERE ATOLL
AMANU ATOLL

PUKARUHA ATOLL
REAO ATOLL

c

AITUTAKI ATOLL
Arutunga
ILE MOOREA
Papeete
ILE TAHITI
ILES DU VENT
WINDWARD ISLANDS

MOTUTUNGA ATOLL
ANAA ATOLL
HIKUERU ATOLL
REITORU ATOLL

HARAIKI ATOLL
MAROKAU ATOLL
HAO ATOLL
AKIAKI ATOLL

VAHITAHI ATOLL

MANUAE ATOLL
MITIARO ISLAND
TAKUTEA ISLAND
ILES DE LA SOCIÉTÉ
SOCIETY ISLANDS
ILE MEHETIA

NEGONEGO ATOLL
RAVAHERE ATOLL
PARAOA ATOLL
PINAKI ATOLL

SOUTHERN COOK ISLANDS
ATIU ISLAND
MAUKE ISLAND

HEREHERETUE ATOLL

MANUANGI ATOLL
VAIRAATEA ATOLL

20

5010
RAROTONGA ISLAND
Avarua

6045

AHUNUI ATOLL

TUREIA ATOLL

PUKARUHA

3880

MANGAIA ISLAND

MARIA ATOLL

ILES DU DUC DE GLOUCESTER

VANAVANA ATOLL

GROUPE ACTÉON

5200

Tuamotu Ridge

TEMATANGI ATOLL

MURUROA ATOLL
MARUTEA ATOLL

RÉCIF EBRIL

d

Tropic of Capricorn

ILE RIMATARA
ILE RURUTU
Polynésie Française
French Polynesia

4645

FAGATAUFA ATOLL

MORANE ATOLL

MARIA ATOLL
ILE MANGAREVA
ILE TEMOE

OENO ISLAND

HENDERSON ISLAND

5340

ILES TUBUAI / AUSTRALES
TUBUAI ISLANDS
ILE TUBUAI

ILES GAMBIER
GAMBIER ISLANDS

Pitcairn
(U.K.)

ILE RAEVAVAE
President Thiers
Seamount

PITCAIRN ISLAND
Adamstown

25

4755

3950

ILE RAPA
ILOTS DE BASS

e

Orne Seamount

5655

48

3270

30

4410

Wachusett Seamount

P A C I F I C

3900

5625

5030

830

f

ERNEST LEGOUVÉ REEF

35

5420

MARIA THERESA REEF

4460

5315

5020

g

1530

S o u t h w e s t

40

4715

O C E A N

5470

h

5560

P a c i f i c   B a s i n

6050

45

3145

Map 62 **NEW ZEALAND**

NORTH ISLAND

SOUTH ISLAND

NEW ZEALAND

TASMAN SEA

PACIFIC OCEAN

Norfolk Ridge

New Caledonia Basin

Kermadec Trench

Chatham Rise

Bounty Trough

Campbell Plateau

Regions / Statistical areas:
Northland
Central Auckland
Auckland
South Auckland-Bay of Plenty
East Coast
Taranaki
Hawke's Bay
Wellington
Nelson
Marlborough
Westland
Canterbury
Otago
Southland

Cities and towns (selection):
Whangarei, Dargaville, Helensville, Waitemata, AUCKLAND, Manukau, Pukekohe, Thames, Hamilton, Cambridge, Morrinsville, Raglan, Tauranga, Rotorua, Tokoroa, Whakatane, Opotiki, Taupo, Gisborne, Wairoa, Napier, Hastings, Havelock North, New Plymouth, Stratford, Hawera, Wanganui, Palmerston North, Feilding, Masterton, Carterton, Levin, Upper Hutt, Lower Hutt, WELLINGTON, Picton, Blenheim, Nelson, Richmond, Motueka, Takaka, Collingwood, Westport, Greymouth, Hokitika, Ross, Reefton, Murchison, Kaikoura, CHRISTCHURCH, Lyttelton, Rangiora, Kaiapoi, Ashburton, Timaru, Oamaru, Dunedin, Mosgiel, Balclutha, Gore, Invercargill, Bluff, Queenstown, Wanaka, Alexandra, Cromwell

Physical features / other labels:
THREE KINGS ISLANDS, North Cape, Cape Reinga, Cape Maria van Diemen, NINETY MILE BEACH, Doubtless Bay, Great Exhibition Bay, CAVALLI ISLANDS, Bay of Islands, Cape Brett, POOR KNIGHTS ISLANDS, Hokianga Harbour, Kaipara Harbour, HEN AND CHICKENS ISLANDS, MOKOHINAU ISLANDS, LITTLE BARRIER ISLAND, GREAT BARRIER ISLAND, Hauraki Gulf, KAWAU ISLAND, Colville Channel, CUVIER ISLAND, COROMANDEL PENINSULA, MERCURY ISLANDS, MAYOR ISLAND, MOTITI ISLAND, WHITE ISLAND, MATAKANA ISLAND, Bay of Plenty, East Cape, Te Araroa, Tikitiki, Te Kaha, Tolaga Bay, MAHIA PENINSULA, PORTLAND ISLAND, Poverty Bay, Table Cape, Hawke Bay, Cape Kidnappers, Cape Egmont, Mount Egmont, North Taranaki Bight, South Taranaki Bight, KAPITI ISLAND, Cape Palliser, Cape Farewell, Farewell Spit, Golden Bay, D'URVILLE ISLAND, Tasman Bay, French Pass, Cape Stephens, Cape Jackson, Cape Campbell, Clarence, AUCKLAND ISLANDS (New Zealand), CAMPBELL ISLAND (New Zealand), SNARES ISLANDS, SOLANDER ISLAND, STEWART ISLAND, RUAPUKE ISLAND, CODFISH ISLAND, Foveaux Strait, Dusky Sound, Doubtful Sound, Milford Sound, George Sound, Caswell Sound, Thompson Sound, Breaksea Sound, RESOLUTION ISLAND, SECRETARY ISLAND, Jackson Bay, Cascade Point, Haast, Franz Josef Glacier, Fox Glacier, Mount Cook, Mount Tasman, Mount Aspiring, Lake Te Anau, Lake Manapouri, Lake Wakatipu, Lake Hawea, Lake Wanaka, Lake Pukaki, Lake Tekapo, BANKS PENINSULA, Pegasus Bay, Canterbury Bight, Lake Ellesmere, OTAGO PENINSULA, Green Island, CHATHAM ISLANDS (New Zealand), Cape Young, PITT ISLAND, Pitt Strait, BOUNTY ISLANDS (New Zealand), ANTIPODES ISLANDS (New Zealand)

Longitude East 174 of Greenwich

Scale 1:6,000,000

Delisle Conic Equidistant Projection

0   100   200   300 km
0   100 miles

M Ft
2000 6562
1000 3281
500 1640
+ 200 +656
0
− 100 −328
200 656
1000 3281
2000 6562
4000 13123
6000 19685
8000 26247

The political subdivisions shown for New Zealand represent statistical areas and are not recognized for administrative purposes.

234 ©ISTITUTO GEOGRAFICO DE AGOSTINI S. p. A. NOVARA

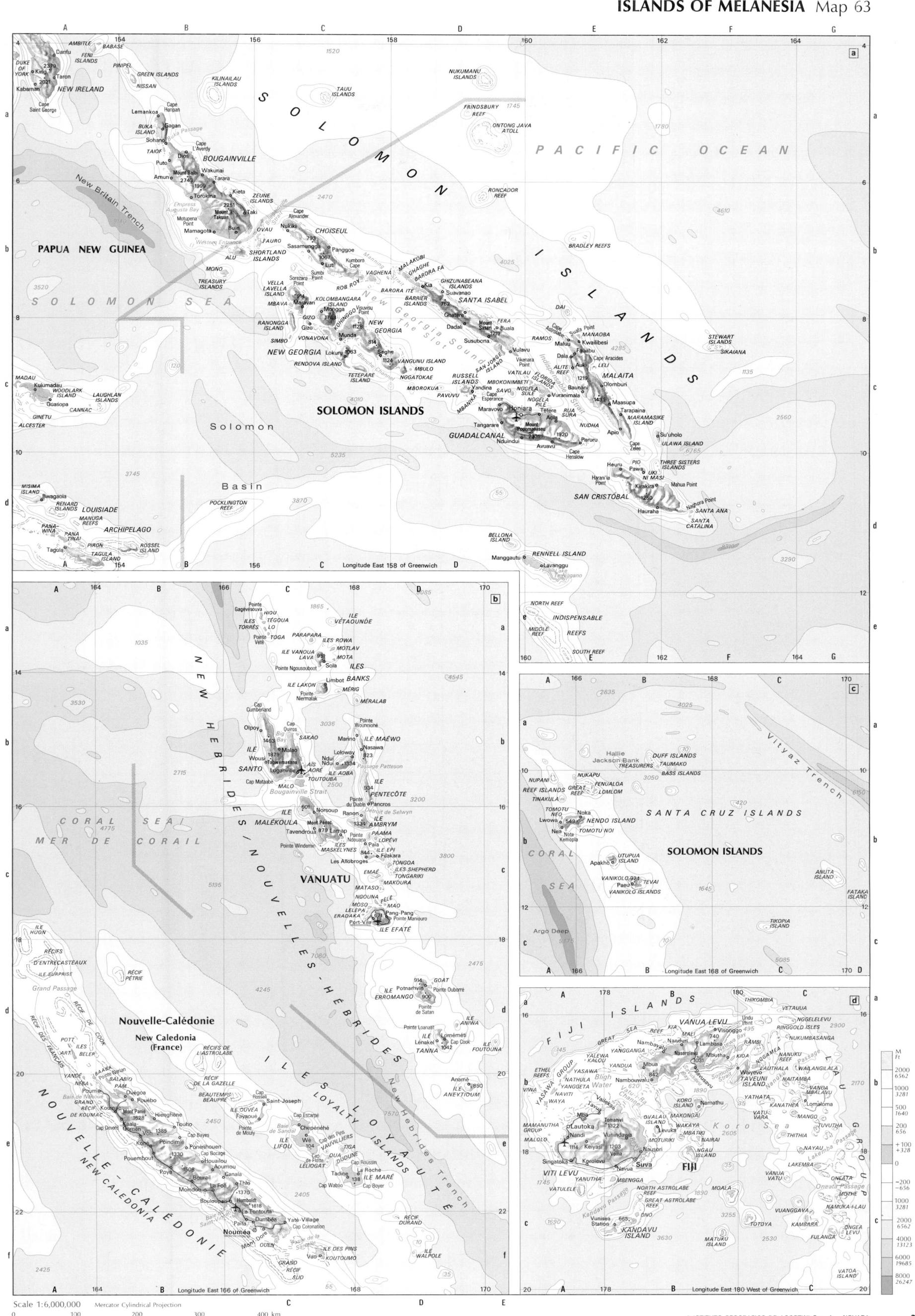

Map [a]

PACIFIC OCEAN

PAPUA NEW GUINEA

NEW IRELAND
DUKE OF YORK
Kabaman
Kiriu 2021
Taron
AMBITLE
Danfu 2379
FENI ISLANDS
BABASE
PINIPEL
GREEN ISLANDS
NISSAN
KILINAILAU ISLANDS
TAUU ISLANDS
NUKUMANU ISLANDS
FINDSBURY REEF 1745
ONTONG JAVA ATOLL
RONCADOR REEF
BRADLEY REEFS

Cape Saint George
Lemankos
Cape Harpan
BUKA ISLAND
Gagan
Sohano
Dios
Wakunai
Mount Balbi 2743
Puto
Amun
Torokina 1999
BOUGAINVILLE
Mount Takuan 2251
Motupena Point
Buin
Mamagota
Kieta
Taki
ZEUNE ISLANDS
OVAU
Nukiki
CHOISEUL
Cape Alexander

TAIOF
TARARA

SHORTLAND ISLANDS
ALU
MONO
TREASURY ISLANDS

SOLOMON   ISLANDS

Sasamungga
Panggoe
793
Kumboro Cape
Luti 1067
Sorezaru Point
Sumbi Point
ROB ROY
VAGHENA
MALAKOBI
GHAGHE
BARORA FA
Kia
BARORA ITE
Suavanao
GHZUNABEANA
BARRIER ISLANDS
752
Ghatere
SANTA ISABEL
Mount Sasari 762
Buala
DAI

VELLA LAVELLA ISLAND
Maravari 1768
Mbava 914
KOLOMBANGARA ISLAND
Mbogga
VISUVISU Point
RAMOS
MANAOBA
Suala Point
Dala
Cape Astrolabe
Fauabu
Kwaiilibesi
Cape Arackdes

RANONGGA ISLAND
Gizo 1128
Gizo
NEW GEORGIA
Dadaii
Susubona
SAN JORGE ISLAND
Vulavu
Vikenara Point
FERA
MALAITA
Malu'u
1219
Olomburi
STEWART ISLANDS
SIKAIANA

SIMBO
VONAVONA
Munda
814
Seghe
Lokuru 1053
VANGUNU ISLAND
MBULO
NGGATOKAE
MBOKONIMBETI
VATILAU
FLORIDA ISLANDS
Yandina
ALITE REEF
LELI
1431
Maasupa
Baunani
Vuranimala
Tarapaina
MARAMASIKE ISLAND

RENDOVA ISLAND
TETEPARE ISLAND
1124
MBULO
MBOROKUA
PAVUVU
RUSSELL ISLANDS
Cape Esperance
SAVO
NGGELA SULE
NGGELA PILE
Tetere
Apig
RUA SURA
NUDHA
Apio
ULAWA ISLAND
Su'uholo

MBANIKA
Maravovo
Honiara
Mount Popomanaseu 2447
Nduindui
Avuavu
1920
Paruru
Cape Zelee
THREE SISTERS ISLANDS

SOLOMON ISLANDS

GUADALCANAL
Tangarare

Solomon Basin
5235
3745
3870
4010

MADAU
Kulumadau
WOODLARK ISLAND
Guasiopa
CANNAC
LAUGHLAN ISLANDS
ALCESTER
GINETU

MISIMA ISLAND
Bwagaoia
RENARD ISLANDS
MANUGA REEFS
LOUISIADE ARCHIPELAGO
POCKLINGTON REEF

PANA WINA
PANA TINAI
PIRON
ROSSEL ISLAND
Tagula
TAGULA ISLAND

Heuru
Pawa
PIO
UKI NI MASI
Harani'a Point
Kirakira 1250
Mahua Point
Kira
SAN CRISTÓBAL
Hauraha
Nggura Point
SANTA ANA
SANTA CATALINA

BELLONA ISLAND
Manggautu
Lavanggu
RENNELL ISLAND
Lake Tegano

NORTH REEF
INDISPENSABLE REEFS
MIDDLE REEF
SOUTH REEF

Longitude East 158 of Greenwich

Map [b]

NEW   HEBRIDES / NOUVELLES-HÉBRIDES

VANUATU

Pointe Gagevesova
HIOU
TEGOUA
LO
TORRES
ILE VÉTAOUNDE
Pointe Vete
TOGA
PARAPARA
ILES ROWA
MOTLAV
MOTA
Pointe Ngousouboot
Sola
ILE VANOUA LAVA
MERA
ILES
BANKS
ILE LAKON
Limbot
MÉRIG
MÉRALAB
Pointe Niermalak

Cap Cumberland
Cap Quiros
Pointe Wounsono
Olpoy
Big Bay 1463
Cap Matabe
SANTO
ILE
1879
Malao
Wousi
Tasmasana
Luganville
AIS
AORÉ
MALO
Pointe du Diable
Pancros
Loloway
Nasawa
823
Ndui Ndui 1334
ILE AOBA
TOUTOUBA
2500
ILE MAÉWO
Marino
ILE PENTECÔTE
934
Norsoup
601
Ranon
Mount Petsei 1334
ILE AMBRYM
ILE
Lamap
Tavendrouä 879
MALÉKOULA
PAAMA
Pointe Windemie
Pointe Noduana
Paia
ILE LOPÉVI
ILES MASKELYNES
844
ILE EPI
Filakara
Les Allobroges
TONGOA
EMAE
ILES SHEPHERD
MATASO
TONGARIKI
MAKOURA
NGOUNA
PÉLE
MOSO
MAO
LELEPA
Pang-Pang
ERADAKA
Pointe Manuro
Port-Vila
ILE EFATÉ

Longitude East 166 of Greenwich

Map [c]

SOLOMON ISLANDS

SANTA CRUZ ISLANDS

Hallie Jackson Bank
DUFF ISLANDS
TREASURES
TAUMAKO
BASS ISLANDS
NUPANI
NUKAPU
REEF ISLANDS
FENUALOA
LOMLOM
TINAKULA
GREAT REEF
TOMOTU NEO
Noka
Lwowa 549
Nea
TOMOTU NOI
NENDO ISLAND
Note
Kemopla
UTUPUA ISLAND
Apakho
Paeu
TEVAI
VANIKOLO 924
VANIKOLO ISLANDS
ANUTA ISLAND
TIKOPIA ISLAND
FATAKA ISLAND

Argo Deep

CORAL   SEA

Longitude East 168 of Greenwich

Map [d]

FIJI   ISLANDS

FIJI

Udu Point
VETAUUA
THIKOMBIA
NGGELELEVU
RINGGOLD ISLES
NUKUMBASANGA
VANUA LEVU
KIA
MALI
NAIDI 740
RAMBI
Nambayanga
Naserelevu
Mbua
Mbutha
KIOA
NOGAMEA
NUKUNU
VANOA MBALAVU
WALANGILALA
NAITAMBA
ETHEL REEFS
YALEWA KALOU
YASAWA
YADUA
YANGGANGA
Wayevo
NATHULA
Lambasa 842
Namathu
TAVEUNI ISLAND
QUILALEVU
VANUA VATU
YASAWA GROUP
VIWA
YANGGETA
NAVITI
WAYA
Nambouwalu
KORO
KANANTHEA
Lomloma
MAMANUTHA GROUP
MALOLO
GROUP
NGGAMEA
MOTURIKI
VATU VARA
THITHIA
Nggrolevu
GVALALU ISLAND
MAKONGAI
WAKAYA
OVALAU
Levuka
OMBENG
Singatoka
Korolevu
Keiyasi 1203
Mbengga
NGAU ISLAND
NAIRAI
MBATIKI
LAKEMBA
VANUA VATU
ONEATA
MOALA
Nandi
Lautoka
VITI LEVU
Suva
Navua
MBENGGA
NORTH ASTROLABE REEF
GREAT ASTROLABE REEF
VUNIAVA Station 665
KANDAVU ISLAND
Kandavu Passage
TOTOYA
MATUKU ISLAND
NAMUKA-I-LAU
VUANGGAVA
KAMBARA
ONGEA LEVU
FULANGA
VATOA ISLAND

Longitude East 180 West of Greenwich

Scale 1:6,000,000   Mercator Cylindrical Projection

0   100   200   300   400 km

0   100   200 miles

© ISTITUTO GEOGRAFICO DE AGOSTINI S.p.A. - NOVARA

M Ft	
2000	6562
1000	3281
500	1640
200	656
+100	+328
0	
−200	−656
1000	3281
2000	6562
4000	13123
6000	19685
8000	26247

Map 64 **ISLANDS OF MICRONESIA-POLYNESIA**

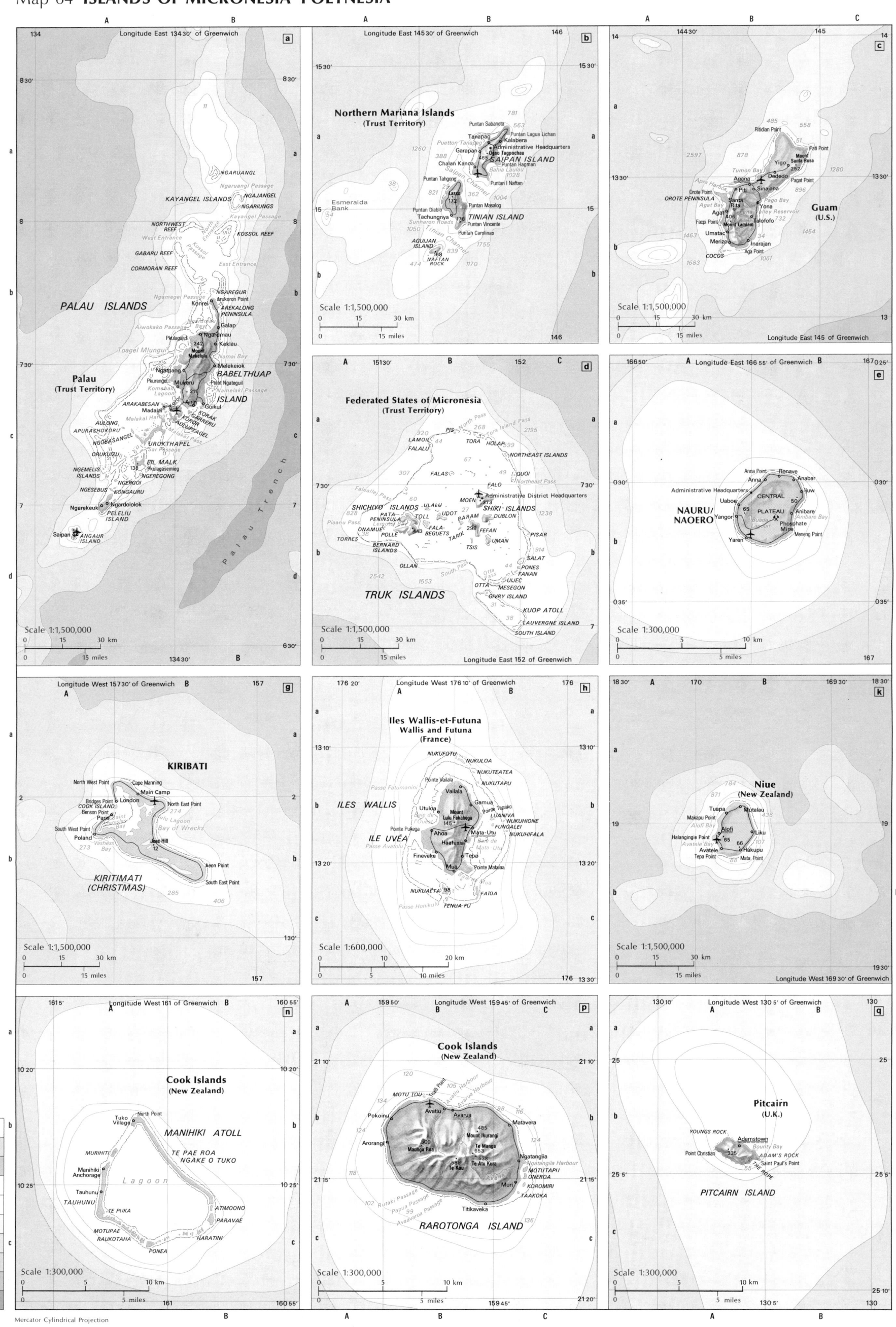

Scale 1:1,500,000 (Panel a — Palau)

Longitude East 134 30' of Greenwich

NGARUANGL
Ngaruangl Passage
KAYANGEL ISLANDS
NGAJANGEL
NGARJUNGS
NORTHWEST REEF
KOSSOL REEF
West Entrance
East Entrance
GABARU REEF
CORMORAN REEF
Kayangel Passage
NGAREGUR
Arakoron Point
Ngamegel Passage
AREKALONG PENINSULA
PALAU ISLANDS
Kokusai Bay
Kónrei
Galap
Ngaramau
Melekeiok
BABELTHUAP
Palau
(Trust Territory)
Ngatpang
Pkuragel
Truot Ngatagul
Muvera
Ngargemlengui
ISLAND
211
Namai Bay
Ngatmelai Passage
ARAKABESAN
Madalai
Airai
Gokul
KORÓR
GARRERU
Komabian
Lagoon
AULONG
KORÓR
NGARAPELENG
APURASHOKORU
NGOBASANGEL
URUKTHAPEL
ORUKUIZU
138
EIL MALK
NGEMELIS ISLANDS
Pkulagasemieg
NGEREGONG
NGESEBUS
KONGAURU
Ngardololok
Ngarekeukl
PELELIU ISLAND
Saipan
ANGAUR ISLAND
BERNARD ISLANDS
Palau Trench

Scale 1:1,500,000 (Panel b — Northern Mariana Islands)

Longitude East 145 30' of Greenwich

Northern Mariana Islands
(Trust Territory)
781
Puntan Sabaneta
563
Tanapag
Kalabera
Puntan Lagua Lichan
Puetton Tanapag
Administrative Headquarters
1260
388
Garapan
Osso Tagpochau
SAIPAN ISLAND
Chalan Kanoa
Puntan Hagman
1004
1028
Puntan Tahgong
Laolao
Puntan I Naftan
Puntan Masalog
Puntan Diablo
Tachungnya
176
172
TINIAN ISLAND
Sunharon Roads
Puntan Vincente
1050
Tinian Channel
Puntan Carolinas
1755
AGUIJAN ISLAND
835
168
474
NAFTAN ROCK
1170
Esmeralda Bank
54

Scale 1:1,500,000 (Panel c — Guam)

Longitude East 145 of Greenwich
14
144 30'
145
485
558
Ritidian Point
51
Pati Point
2597
878
1280
Yigo
Mount Santa Rosa
252
Tumon Bay
Dededo
Agaña
896
Pago Bay
Orote Point
Santa Rita
Sinajana
OROTE PENINSULA
Agat
Yona
Guam
(U.S.)
Agat Bay
732
Facpi Point
Mount Lamlam
Talofofo
1463
Umatac
34
Inarajan
Merizo
1454
Aga Point
COCOS
1683
1061

Scale 1:1,500,000 (Panel d — Truk)

Longitude East 152 of Greenwich
151 30'
152
Federated States of Micronesia
(Trust Territory)
PIS
North Pass
920
268
Tora Island Pass
2195
LAMOIL
TORA
NORTHEAST ISLANDS
FALALU
HOLAP
67
Northeast Pass
FALAS
49
QUOI
307
FALO
MOEN
Administrative District Headquarters
SHICHIYO ISLANDS
ULALU
SHIKI ISLANDS
828
PATA PENINSULA
UDOT
DUBLON
1238
ONAMUE
TOLL
PARAM
FALA-BEGUETS
TARIK
FEFAN
Piaanu Pass
POLLE
UMAN
PISAR
TORRES
TSIS
BERNARD ISLANDS
914
SALAT
OLLAN
PONES
FANAN
2542
1553
UUEC
MESEGON
OTTA
GIVRY ISLAND
KUOP ATOLL
TRUK ISLANDS
LAUVERGNE ISLAND
SOUTH ISLAND

Scale 1:300,000 (Panel e — Nauru)

Longitude East 166 55' of Greenwich
166 50'
167 025'
Anna Point
Ronave
Anna
Anabar
Uaboe
CENTRAL
50
PLATEAU
NAURU/NAOERO
65
Yangor
Anibare
Phosphate Mine
Anibare Bay
Yaren
Meneng Point

Scale 1:1,500,000 (Panel g — Kiribati)

Longitude West 157 30' of Greenwich
157
KIRIBATI
North West Point
Cape Manning
Main Camp
Bridges Point
London
COOK POINT
North East Point
Benson Point
274
Paris
South West Point
Poland
Joe's Hill
12
Vashess Bay
273
Aeon Point
South East Point
KIRITIMATI (CHRISTMAS)
285
406

Scale 1:600,000 (Panel h — Wallis and Futuna)

Longitude West 176 10' of Greenwich
176 20'
176
Iles Wallis-et-Futuna
Wallis and Futuna
(France)
NUKUFOTU
NUKULOA
13 10'
Pointe Vailala
NUKUTEATEA
NUKUTAPU
ILES WALLIS
Vailala
Gamua
Pointe Tepako
Utuloa
Mount Lulu Fakahega
145
NUKUHIONE
LUANIVA
FUNGALEI
Pointe Pukega
Ahoa
Mata-Utu
NUKUHIFALA
ILE UVÉA
Hsafusia
Passe Avatolu
Feveke
Tepa
Finenveke
Mua
Pointe Matalaa
NUKUAETA
98
FAIOA
FENUA-FU
Passe Honikulu
13 30'

Scale 1:1,500,000 (Panel k — Niue)

Longitude West 169 30' of Greenwich
18 30'
170
169 30'
784
871
Niue
(New Zealand)
LUANIU
436
Tuapa
Mutalau
Makapu Point
Alofi Bay
Alofi
Liku
Halangingie Point
65
66
107
Avatele Bay
Hakupu
Avatele
Tepa Point
Mata Point
19

Scale 1:300,000 (Panel n — Manihiki)

Longitude West 161 of Greenwich
161 15'
160 55'
Cook Islands
(New Zealand)
Tuko Village
North Point
MANIHIKI ATOLL
MURIHITI
TE PAE ROA
NGAKE O TUKO
Manihiki Anchorage
Lagoon
Tauhunu
10 25'
TAUHUNU
TE PUKA
ATIMOONO
MOTUPAE
PARAVAE
RAUKOTAHA
HARATINI
PONEA

Scale 1:300,000 (Panel p — Rarotonga)

Longitude West 159 45' of Greenwich
159 50'
Cook Islands
(New Zealand)
120
21 10'
Trap Point
MOTU TOU
Avatiu Harbour
Arorua Harbour
134
105
Avatiu
116
Pokoinu
Avarua
Matavera
Mount Ikurangi
485
Arorangi
Maunga Roa
Te Manga
653
Ngatangiia Harbour
124
MOTUTAPU
ONEROA
Te Kou
Te Atu Kura
KOROMIRI
118
Muri
TAAKOKA
Rutaki Passage
Titikaveka
136
Papua Passage
Avaavaroa Passage
RAROTONGA ISLAND

Scale 1:300,000 (Panel q — Pitcairn)

Longitude West 130 5' of Greenwich
130 10'
130
25
YOUNGS ROCK
Pitcairn
(U.K.)
Adamstown
Bounty Bay
Point Christian
335
ADAM'S ROCK
Saint Paul's Point
55
THE ROPE
PITCAIRN ISLAND
25 5'

Elevation legend:
M / Ft
200 / 656
+100 / +328
0
−100 / −328
200 / 656
1000 / 3281
2000 / 6562
4000 / 13123
6000 / 19685

Mercator Cylindrical Projection

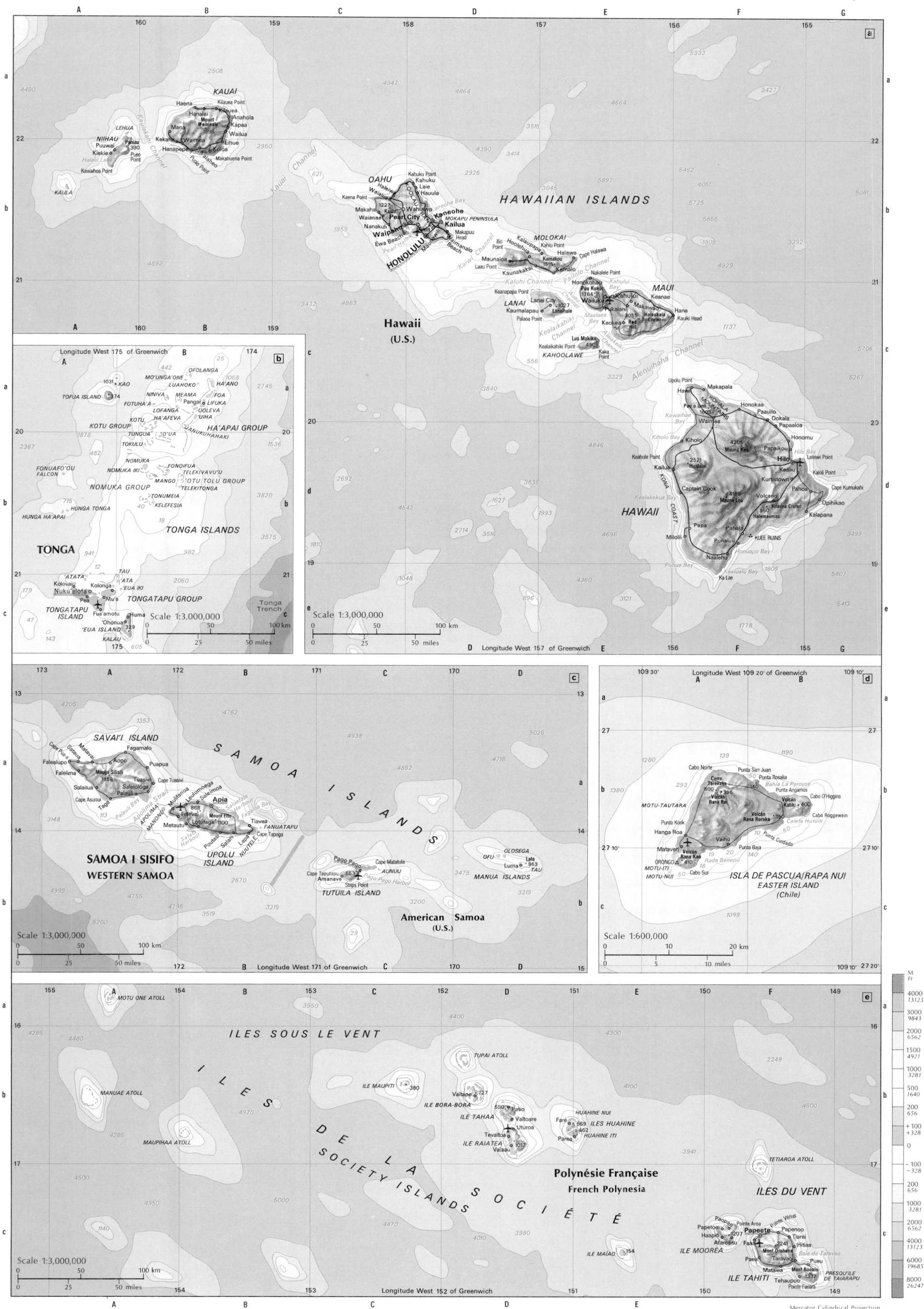

Mercator Cylindrical Projection

Map 66 **ANTARCTIC REGION**

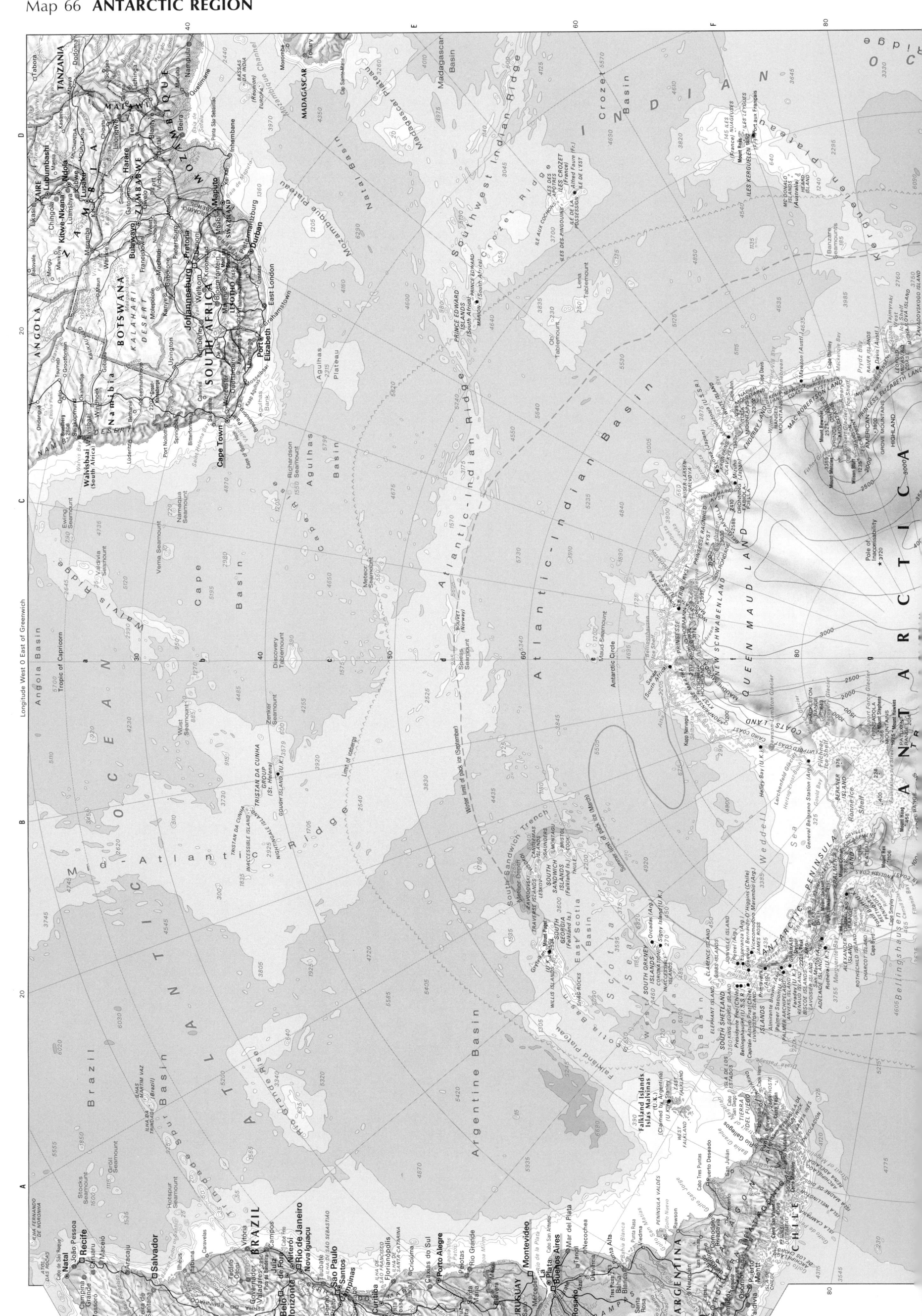

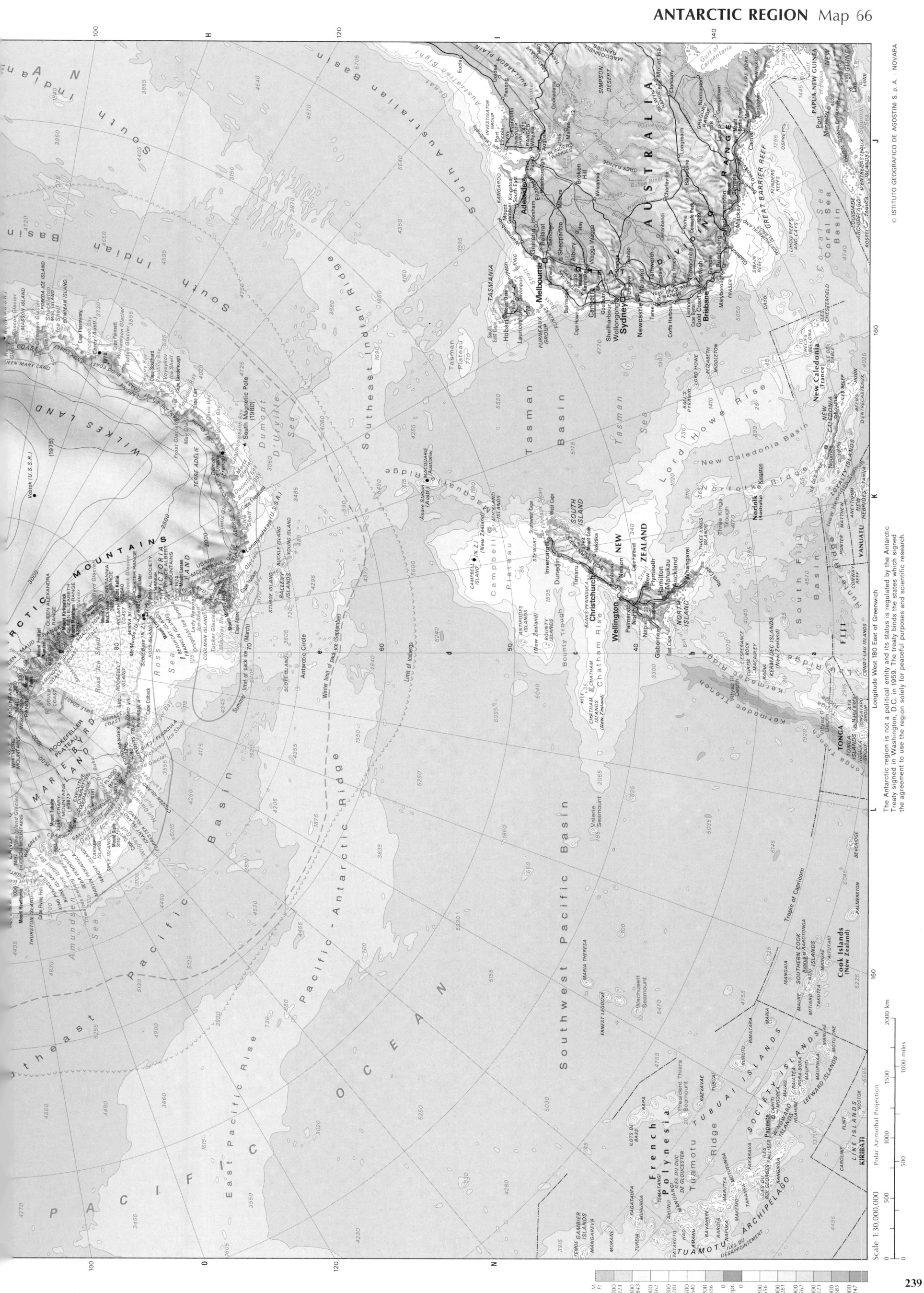

The Antarctic region is not a political entity and its status is regulated by the Antarctic Treaty signed in Washington, D.C. in 1959. The treaty binds the states which signed the agreement to use the region solely for peaceful purposes and scientific research.

Scale 1:30,000,000

Polar Azimuthal Projection

Longitude West 180 East of Greenwich

Map 67 **ARCTIC REGION**

Scale 1:30,000,000   Polar Azimuthal Projection

Longitude West 0 East of Greenwich

© ISTITUTO GEOGRAFICO DE AGOSTINI S.p.A. - NOVARA

UNITED STATES

AND CANADA

MAP SECTION

CONTENTS

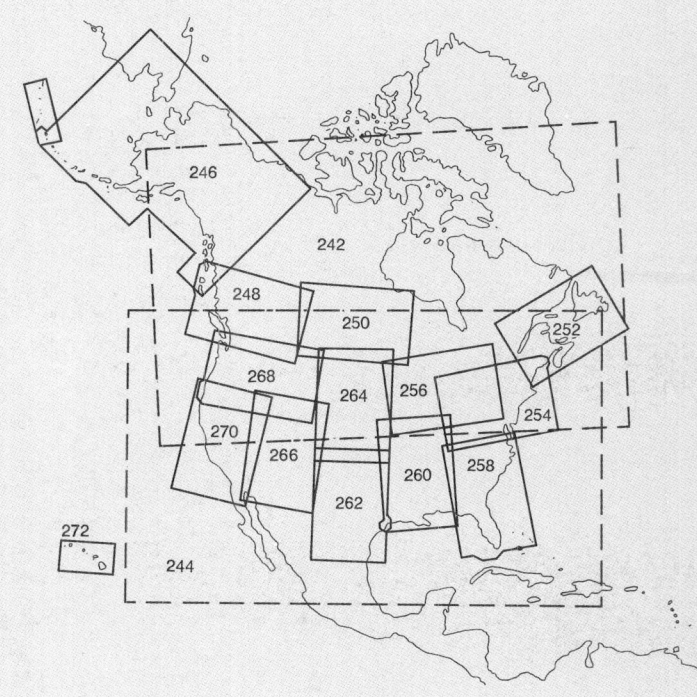

MAP LEGEND

Political Boundaries

▬ ▬ ▬ ▬	International (first-order political unit)
▬▬▬▬▬	State, Province, etc. (second-order political unit)

Capitals of Political Units

WASHINGTON	Independent Nation
Hamilton	Dependency
BERMUDA (U.K.)	Administering Country
Santa Fe	State, Province, etc.

Inhabited Localities

Map scale of 1:3,000,000, 1:6,000,000

.	0—10,000	⊡	100,000—250,000
o	10,000—25,000	▣	250,000—1,000,000
⊚	25,000—100,000	■	>1,000,000

Map scale of 1:12,000,000

.	0—50,000		
⊚	50,000—100,000	⊡	250,000—1,000,000
⊡	100,000—250,000	■	>1,000,000

The size of type indicates the relative economic and political importance of the locality

Gatlinburg	**Flaggstaff**	**Norfolk**
Gettysburg	**Ventura**	**NEW YORK**

Miscellaneous Cultural Features

GLACIER NATIONAL PARK ▲	National or State Park or Monument
FORT CLATSOP NAT. MEM. ▲	National or State Historic(al) Site, Memorial
SEMINOLE IND. RES.	Indian Reservation
FORT DIX	Military Installation
■ TANGLEWOOD ▲	Point of Interest (battlefield, historical site, etc.)
HOOVER DAM /	Dam

Transportation

Map scale of 1:3,000,000, 1:6,000,000 and 1:12,000,000

————	Primary Road
————	Secondary Road
----------	Minor Road, Trail
——+——+—	Primary Railway
—▭—	Bridge
—▭·—·—	Tunnel
—·—·—·—	Ferry
—·—·—·—	Intracoastal Waterway
DULLES INTERNATIONAL AIRPORT ✈	Airport

Hydrographic Features

Los Angeles Aqueduct	Aqueduct
SALTO ANGEL	Rapids, Falls
	Intermittent Stream
	Irrigation or Drainage Canal
The Everglades	Swamp
SEWARD GLACIER	Glacier
Lake Tahoe	Lake, Reservoir
	Salt Lake
	Dry Lake Bed
769 ▽	Depth of Water

Topographic Features

Mount McKinley ▲ 6194	Highest Elevation in Country
86 ▼	Lowest Elevation in Country
Targhee Pass 2156 —	Mountain Pass
(106)	Elevation of City
	Sand Area

	Salt Flat
	Lava

Elevation and depths are given in meters

Highest Elevation and Lowest Elevation of a continent are underlined

Elevation tints shown only on 1:3,000,000 and 1:6,000,000 scale maps

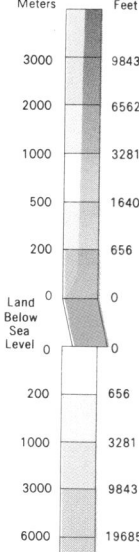

Meters	Feet
3000	9843
2000	6562
1000	3281
500	1640
200	656
Land Below Sea Level 0	0
0	0
200	656
1000	3281
3000	9843
6000	19685
9000	29520

Kilometers

Statute Miles

Scale 1:12,000,000

One centimeter represents 120 kilometers.
One inch represents approximately 190 miles.

Lambert Conformal Conic Projection

Copyright © by Rand McNally & Co.
Map prepared by Rand McNally & Co.
A-520200-264

UNITED STATES

PACIFIC OCEAN

Tropic of Cancer

CANADA
UNITED STATES

UNITED STATES
MEXICO

BRITISH COLUMBIA
ALBERTA
SASKATCHEWAN
MANITOBA

WASHINGTON
OREGON
IDAHO
MONTANA
NORTH DAKOTA
SOUTH DAKOTA
NEBRASKA
WYOMING
NEVADA
UTAH
COLORADO
KANSAS
CALIFORNIA
ARIZONA
NEW MEXICO
OKLAHOMA
TEXAS

GREAT BASIN

SIERRA MADRE OCCIDENTAL
SIERRA MADRE ORIENTAL
BAJA CALIFORNIA

Vancouver
Victoria
Seattle
Tacoma
Olympia
Portland
Salem
Eugene
Spokane
Yakima
Boise
Helena
Great Falls
Billings
Bozeman
Butte
Missoula
Calgary
Edmonton
Saskatoon
Regina
Winnipeg
Bismarck
Fargo
Rapid City
Sioux Falls
Pierre
San Francisco
Oakland
Sacramento
Stockton
Modesto
San Jose
Fresno
Bakersfield
Los Angeles
Long Beach
Santa Ana
Anaheim
Riverside
San Bernardino
Pasadena
San Diego
Oceanside
Escondido
Tijuana
Mexicali
Ensenada
Reno
Las Vegas
Salt Lake City
Provo
Ogden
Denver
Aurora
Colorado Springs
Pueblo
Phoenix
Mesa
Scottsdale
Tempe
Tucson
Yuma
Albuquerque
Santa Fe
El Paso
Ciudad Juárez
Amarillo
Lubbock
Wichita Falls
Fort Worth
Odessa
Midland
San Angelo
Abilene
Austin
San Antonio
Laredo
Nuevo Laredo
Reynosa
Monterrey
Saltillo
Torreón
Durango
Mazatlán
Culiacán
Ciudad Obregón
Hermosillo
Chihuahua
Guadalajara
Aguascalientes
Zacatecas
San Luis Potosí
Ciudad Victoria
Tampico
La Paz

Copyright © by Rand McNally & Co.
Map prepared by Rand McNally & Co.
A-520500-264

244

242-243

ONTARIO

QUÉBEC

Gulf of Saint Lawrence

CAPE BRETON ISLAND

PRINCE EDWARD ISLAND

NEW BRUNSWICK

NOVA SCOTIA

Halifax

Minneapolis
St. Paul

Duluth

Thunder Bay

Sault Ste. Marie

MONTRÉAL
Ottawa

TORONTO

MICHIGAN

Milwaukee

Lake Huron

DETROIT

CHICAGO

Cleveland

Buffalo

BOSTON

NEW YORK

PHILADELPHIA

Baltimore

WASHINGTON

Pittsburgh

Des Moines

St. Louis

Kansas City

Springfield

Cincinnati

Columbus

Indianapolis

Louisville

Nashville

Memphis

Little Rock

Richmond

Norfolk

Raleigh

Charlotte

Atlanta

Birmingham

Montgomery

Columbus

Jackson

Shreveport

Baton Rouge

New Orleans

Mobile

Pensacola

Tallahassee

Jacksonville

Daytona Beach

Orlando

Tampa
St. Petersburg

West Palm Beach

Fort Lauderdale

Miami

Key West

ATLANTIC

OCEAN

BERMUDA
(U.K.)

GULF OF

MEXICO

Nassau

Tropic of Cancer

B A H A M A

CARIBBEAN SEA

La Habana Havana

CUBA

WEST

INDIES

HISPANIOLA

HAITI

DOMINICAN REPUBLIC

Port-au-Prince

Santo Domingo

Santiago de Cuba

Mérida

YUCATAN PENINSULA

TURKS AND CAICOS ISLANDS
(U.K.)

Kilometers

Statute Miles

0   200   400   600   Km.

0   200   400   600   Mi.

Scale 1:12,000,000

One centimeter represents 120 kilometers.
One inch represents approximately 190 miles.

Albers Conical Equal-Area Projection

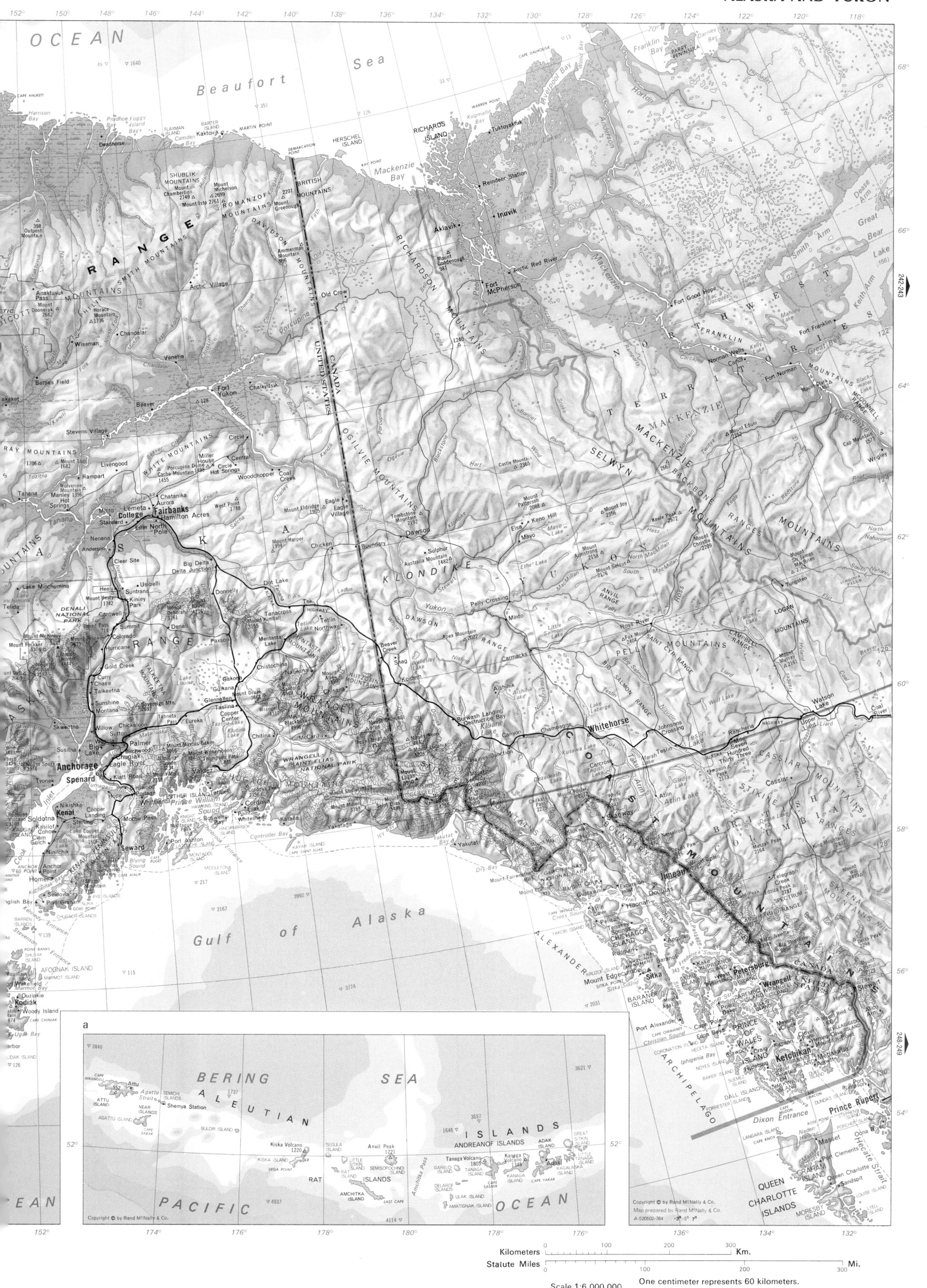

Kilometers
Statute Miles

Scale 1:6,000,000

One centimeter represents 60 kilometers.
One inch represents approximately 95 miles.
Lambert Conformal Conic Projection

PACIFIC

OCEAN

Kilometers 0 50 100 150 Km.

Statute Miles 0 50 100 150 Mi.

Scale 1:3,000,000
One centimeter represents 30 kilometers.
One inch represents approximately 47 miles.
Lambert Conformal Conic Projection

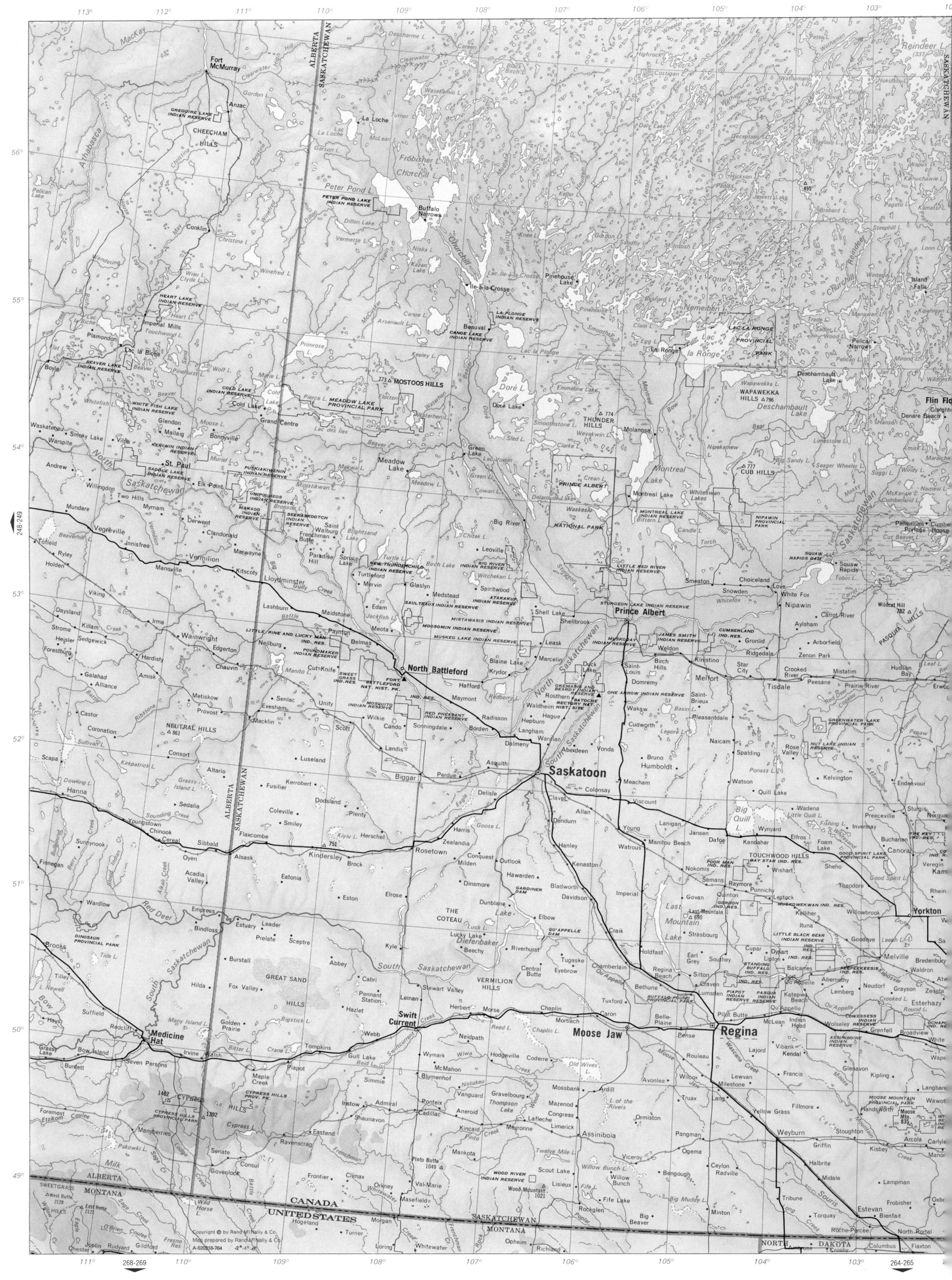

Kilometers

Statute Miles

Scale 1:3,000,000

One centimeter represents 30 kilometers.
One inch represents approximately 47 miles.
Lambert Conformal Conic Projection

LABRADOR
SEA

QUÉBEC
NEWF.

Red Bay
Cook's Harbour   CAPE BAULD
Pistolet Bay   QUIRPON ISLAND
West St. Modeste   Raleigh
Middle Bay   Forteau
Bradore   Blanc Sablon   St. Anthony
Old Port Bay   Salmon Bay
Port-St-Servan   Flower's Cove   Hare Bay
Shekatika Bay
St-Augustin-Saguenay   Brig Bay
ÎLE DES GÉNÉVRIERS   Saint Margaret Bay   GROAIS ISLAND
Baie des Hal Hal   Bartletts Harbour   Conche   GREY
La Tabatière   Roddickton   ISLANDS
Mutton Bay   SAINT JOHN ISLAND   BELL ISLAND
CAP DU GROS MÉCATINA   POINTE   Englee   Canada Bay
Tête-à-la-Baleine   RICHE   Port Riche
ÎLE DU PETIT MÉCATINA   Ingornachoix Bay   Hooping Harbour
Williamsport

LEWISPORTE
Passage Aylmer   River of Ponds   Harbour Deep

Pointe-à-Maurier   Daniel's Harbour   Blue Mountain   Little Harbour Deep   PARTRIDGE POINT   HORSE ISLANDS
649   Fleur-de-Lys   CAPE SAINT JOHN   FUNK ISLAND
Washicoutai   Pacquet   Confusion Bay
Kegaska   Gethsemani   Parson's Pond   Seal Cove   Baie Verte   La Scie   SOUTH   FOGO ISLAND
Wolf Bay   CAP WHITTLE   Cow Head   Shoe Cove   TWILLINGATE   Joe Batt's Arm
Saint Pauls Inlet   Nippers   Round Harbour   ISLAND   Fogo   CAPE FOGO
Jackson's Arm   Harbour   Durrell   Change Islands
GROS MORNE   Westport   Twillingate   WADHAM
NATIONAL PARK   Burlington   Green Bay   Little Bay Islands   Summerford   ISLANDS
Gros   Springdale   Beaumont   Fortune   Carmanville
Rocky Harbour   Morne   Hampden   Port Anson   Harbour   Doting Cove
806   Robert's Arm   Pilley's Island   Lumsden
Norris Point   Point Leamington   Birchy Bay   CAPE FREELS
Trout River   Bonne Bay   Campbellton   Newtown
(Woody Point)   Northern Arm   Gander Bay   Wesleyville
Mount Saint Gregory   Howley   Main Topsail   Botwood   Valleyfield
686   555   Hodges Hill   Glenwood   Greenspond
Old Man   Deer Lake   Bishop's   570   Norris
Mountain   Pasadena   Falls   Arm   Gander   Hare   Trinity
496   Cox's Cove   Millertown Junction   Badger   Windsor   Bay
Lark Harbour   Deer Lake   Grand Falls   Middle Brook   COTTEL ISLAND   290
CORNER BROOK   WILLIS ISLAND   St. Brendan's
814   Grand L.   Gambo   Salvage   Bonavista
Spruce Brook   Glover Island   Glovertown   Blackhead   CAPE BONAVISTA
LONG   Buchans   TERRA NOVA   Bay   Little Catalina
POINT   EXPLOITS DAM   Millertown   NATIONAL PARK   Eastport   Elliston
Port au Port   Lourdes   Red Indian   Keels   Catalina
PENINSULA   Piccadilly   Port Blandford   Port Union
Port au Port   Stephenville   NEWFOUNDLAND   Deer Pond   GRATES
Stephenville Crossing   Clarenville   Shoal Harbour   POINT
CAPE SAINT   St. George's   Island Pond   Crooked L.   BACCALIEU ISLAND
GEORGE   BARACHOIS POND   Hickman's Harbour   Bay de Verde
Flat Bay   PROVINCIAL PARK   Mount Sylvester   Old Perlican
Saint George's Bay   Mount Howley   376   Winterton   Hant's Harbour
Robinson   450   978   Great Burnt   Heart's   CAPE SAINT FRANCIS
St. David's   Pond   Content   Pouch Cove
Burnt   Come by Chance   Carbonear   Torbay
Codroy Pond   Pond   Head Bay   Sunnyside   Harbour Grace   St.   WABANA
635   d'Espoir   Terrenceville   Upper Island Cove   John's
South Branch   BLUE HILLS   St. Alban's   Davis   Spaniard's Bay   ST. JOHN'S
OF GOUTEAU   Rencontre   Bay Roberts   SIGNAL HILL
Codroy   Grand Bruit   East   Brigus   HISTORIC SITE
Tompkins   Doyles   Belleoram   Harbour Buffett   Whitbourne   Petty Harbour
Table Mountain   Burgeo   François   Hermitage   Bay Bulls
CAPE ANGUILLE   587   McCallum   English   Witless Bay
Rose-Blanche   Ramea   Cape la   Pass Island   Harbour West   Merasheen   Tors Cove
CAPE RAY   Burnt Island   RAMEA ISLANDS   Hune   Harbour Breton   Boxey   AVALON PENINSULA
Channel-Port   Isle-aux-Morts   Garnish   Fox Harbour   Dunville   Bay Bulls
aux-Basques   Bay   Grand   Marystown   Argentia   Colinet   Mount   Cape Broyle
L'Argent   Bank   Placentia   Carmel   Ferryland
NEWFOUNDLAND   Fortune   Burin   Creston   Renews
CANADA   Placentia Bay   Ship Cove
MIQUELON   240   BURIN   St. Bride's   Trepassey
SAINT PIERRE   Fortune   PENINSULA   Branch   St.   Portugal   Cove South
AND MIQUELON   Lawn   St. Lawrence   Vincent's   Cape Race
(France)   LANGLADE   Lamaline   CAPE SAINT MARY'S   St. Shotts   MISTAKEN POINT
Saint   228   CAPE FREELS   Trepassey
SAINT-PIERRE-   Pierre   Bay
ET-MIQUELON   SAINT-PIERRE

NEWFOUNDLAND
CANADA

Cabot   Strait

ST. PAUL ISLAND
(N.S.)

ÎLE DE LA MADELEINE
(Que.)   ÎLE DE L'EST
CAP COFFIN

Grand-Entrée   CAPE SAINT LAWRENCE   CAPE NORTH
ALRIGHT   Aspy Bay
Plaisance   Dingwall
D'ENTRÉE   CAPE BRETON   CAPE EGMONT
Hubert   HIGHLANDS   Ingonish
Pleasant Bay   NATIONAL PARK

Chéticamp   CAPE SMOKY
Grand-Étang
Margaree Harbour   Margaree   Saint Ann's Bay
Inverness   Indian Brook
Strathlorne   North Sydney   Sydney   New Waterford
Margaree   Mines   Dominion
Mabou   Baddeck   Sydney   Glace Bay
Whycocomagh   Bras   Iona   CAPE BRETON   Port Morien
d'Or   ISLAND   SCATARIE ISLAND
Judique   Mira Bay
West   St. George's   Louisbourg
Bay   FORTRESS OF LOUISBOURG
Port   L'Ardoise   NATIONAL HISTORIC PARK
grave   St. Peters   Gabarus
Hawkesbury   Arichat   Gabarus Bay   Fourchu
ISLE MADAME
MICHAUD POINT
Guysborough   CHEDABUCTO BAY
Queensport   Canso
Larrys River
dboro

ATLANTIC

OCEAN

SABLE ISLAND
(N.S.)

Kilometers
0   50   100   150
Km.
Statute Miles
0   50   100   150
Mi.

Scale 1:3,000,000

One centimeter represents 30 kilometers.
One inch represents approximately 47 miles.
Lambert Conformal Conic Projection

Copyright © by Rand McNally & Co.
Map prepared by Rand McNally & Co.
A-520219-764

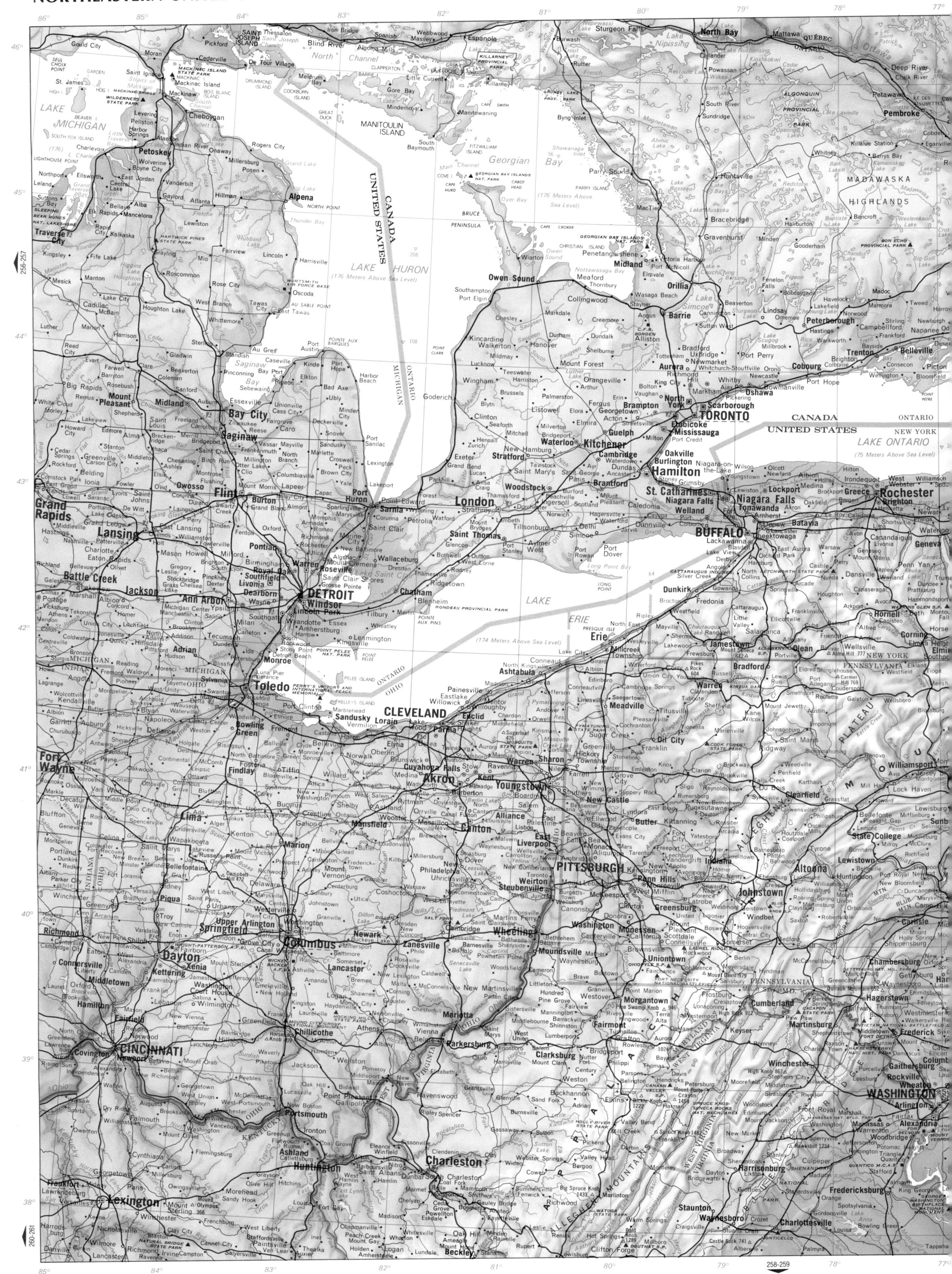

Kilometers 0 50 100 150 Km.

Statute Miles 0 50 100 150 Mi.

Scale 1:3,000,000

One centimeter represents 30 kilometers.
One inch represents approximately 47 miles.

Albers Conical Equal-Area Projection

Copyright © by Rand McNally & Co.
Map prepared by Rand McNally & Co.
A-920596-764

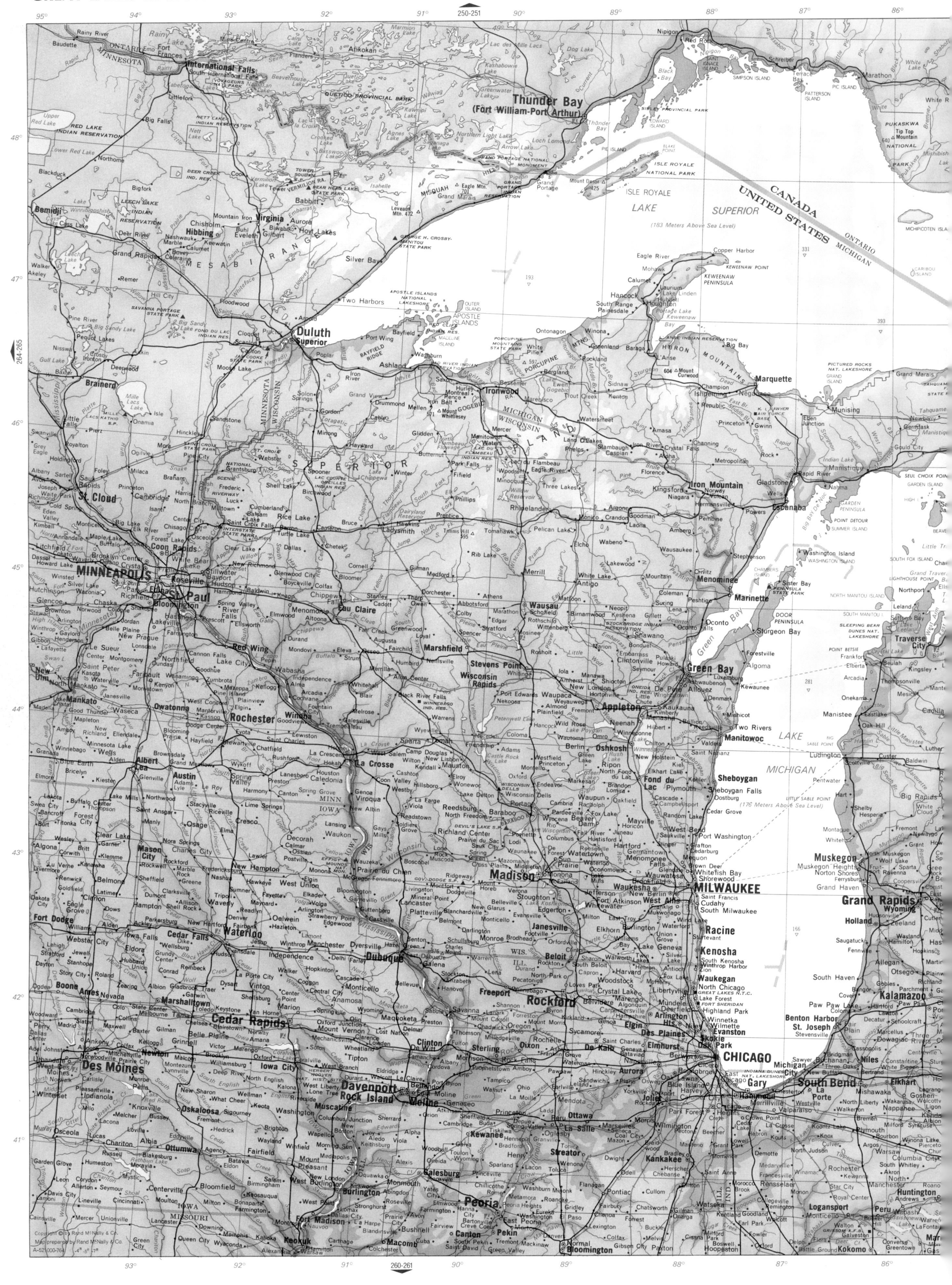

Kilometers
Statute Miles

Scale 1:3,000,000

One centimeter represents 30 kilometers.
One inch represents approximately 47 miles.

Albers Conical Equal-Area Projection

257

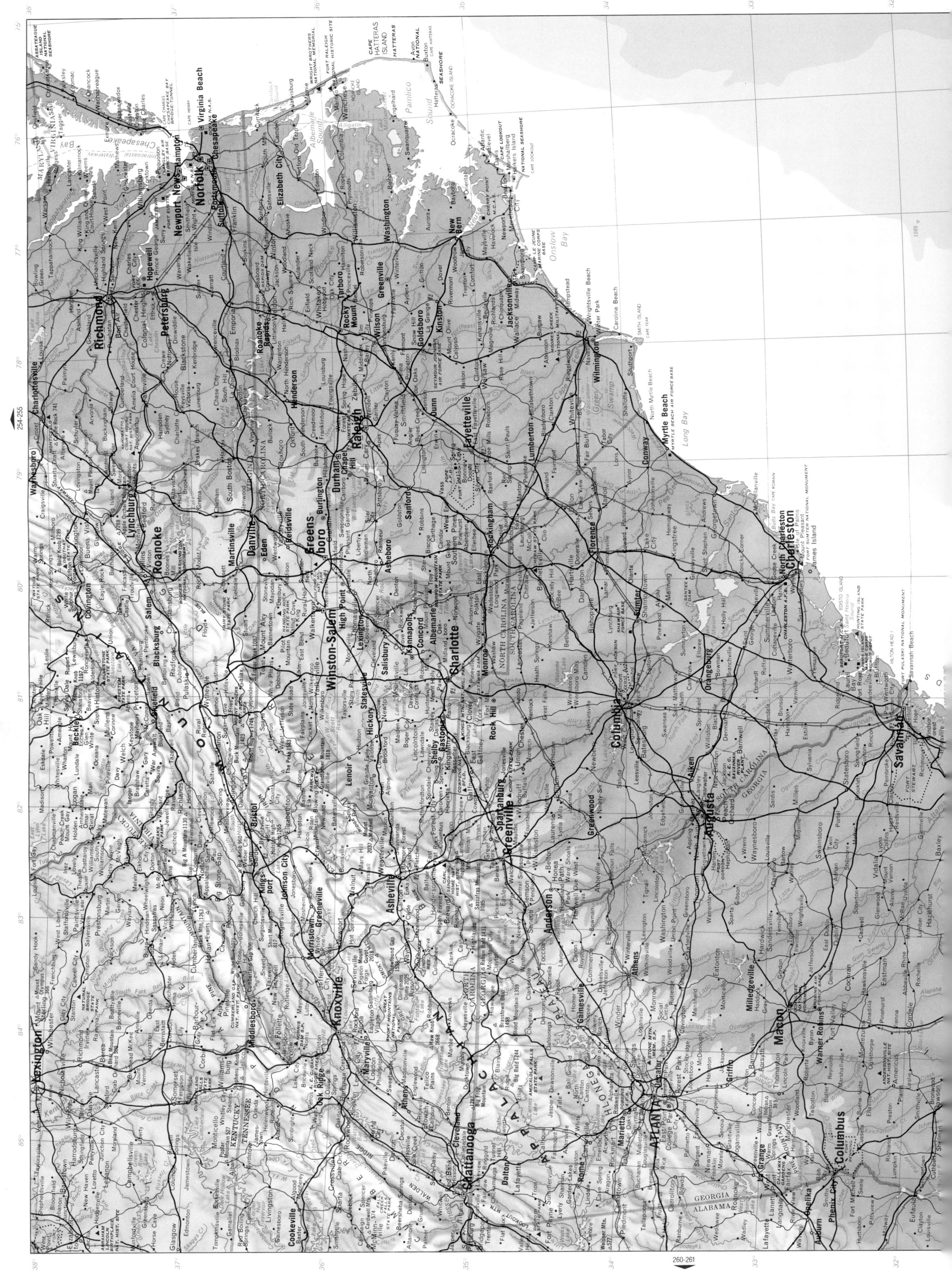

Scale 1:3,000,000

One centimeter represents 30 kilometers.
One inch represents approximately 47 miles.

Copyright © by Rand McNally & Co.
Map prepared by Rand McNally & Co.
A-831110-764

259

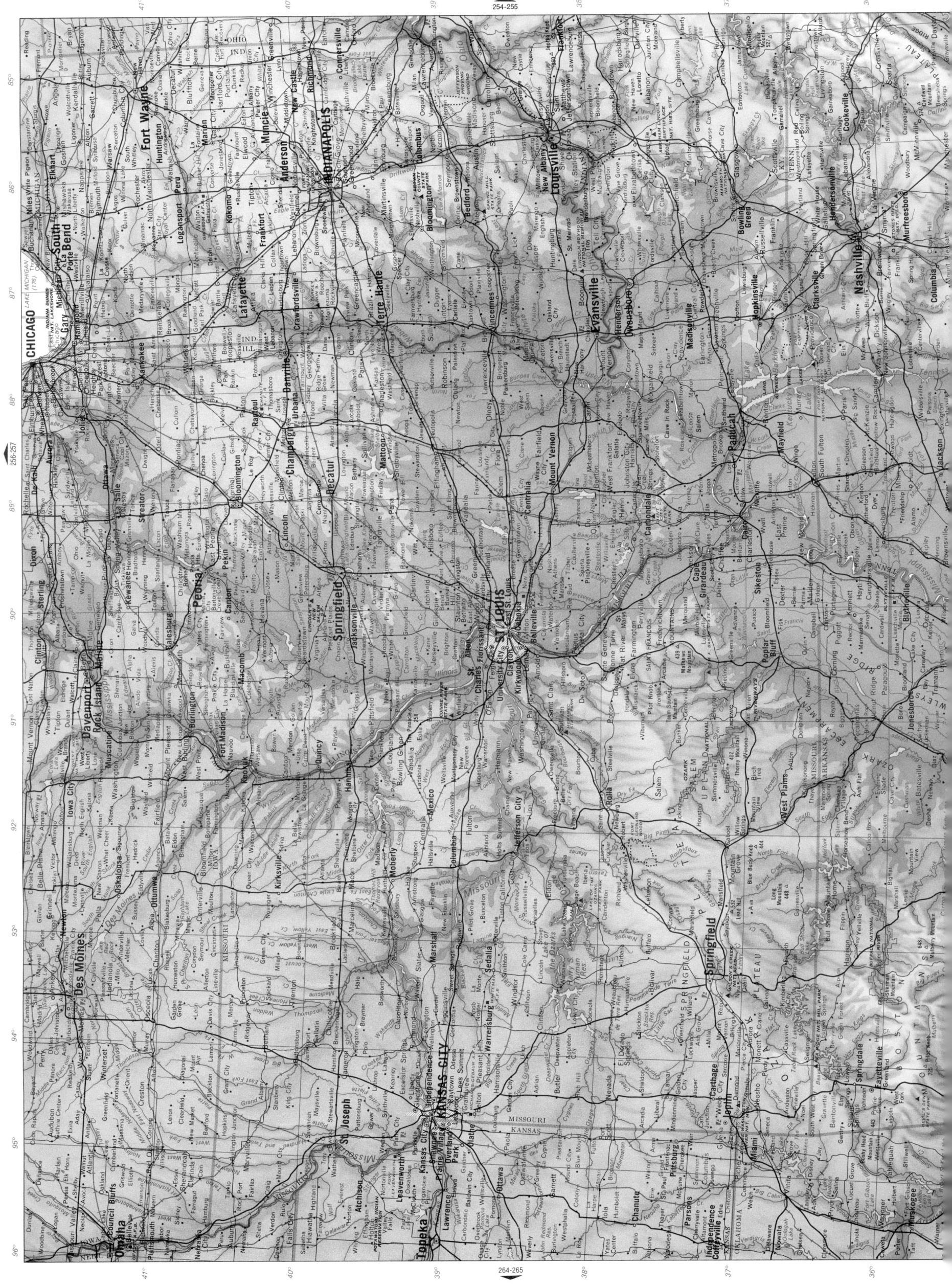

Scale 1:3,000,000

One centimeter represents 30 kilometers.
One inch represents approximately 47 miles.

Copyright © by Rand McNally & Co.
Map prepared by Rand McNally & Co.
A-58290-764

Kilometers
Statute Miles
Km.
Mi.

GULF OF MEXICO

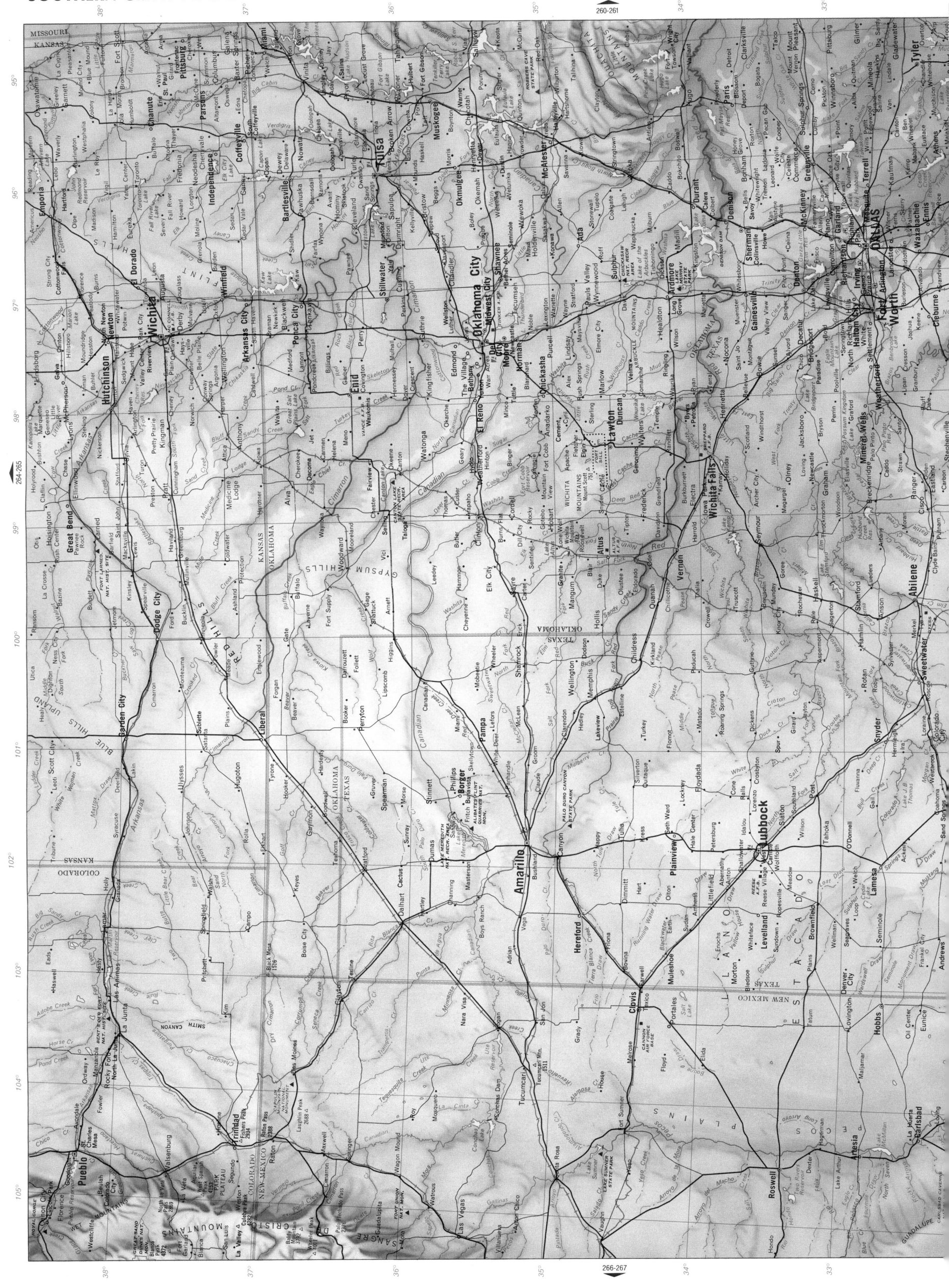

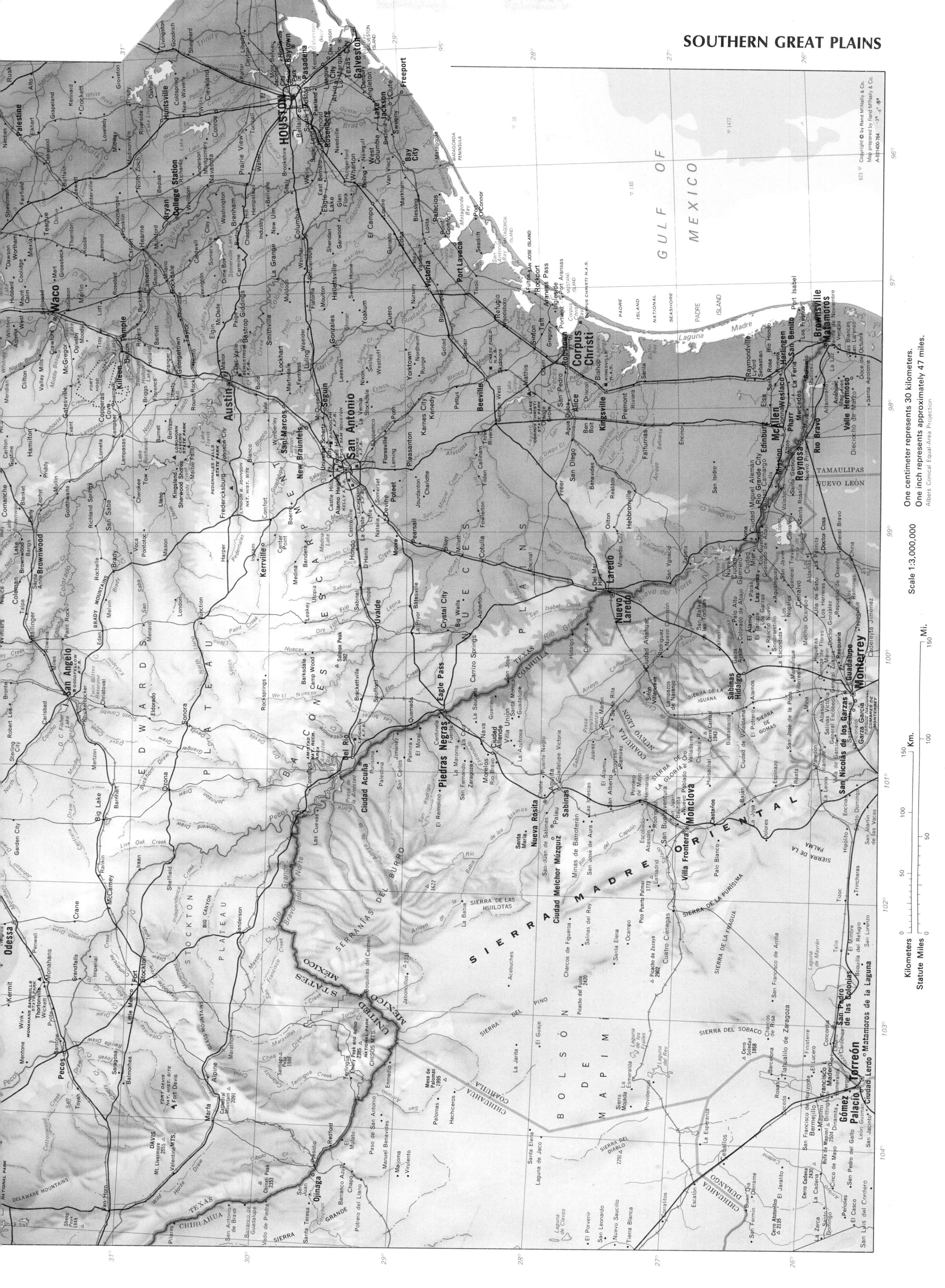

GULF OF MEXICO

One centimeter represents 30 kilometers.
One inch represents approximately 47 miles.
Albers Conical Equal-Area Projection

Scale 1:3,000,000

823 ▽ Copyright © by Rand McNally & Co.
Map prepared by Rand McNally & Co.
A-92400-764

Kilometers
Statute Miles
Km.
Mi.

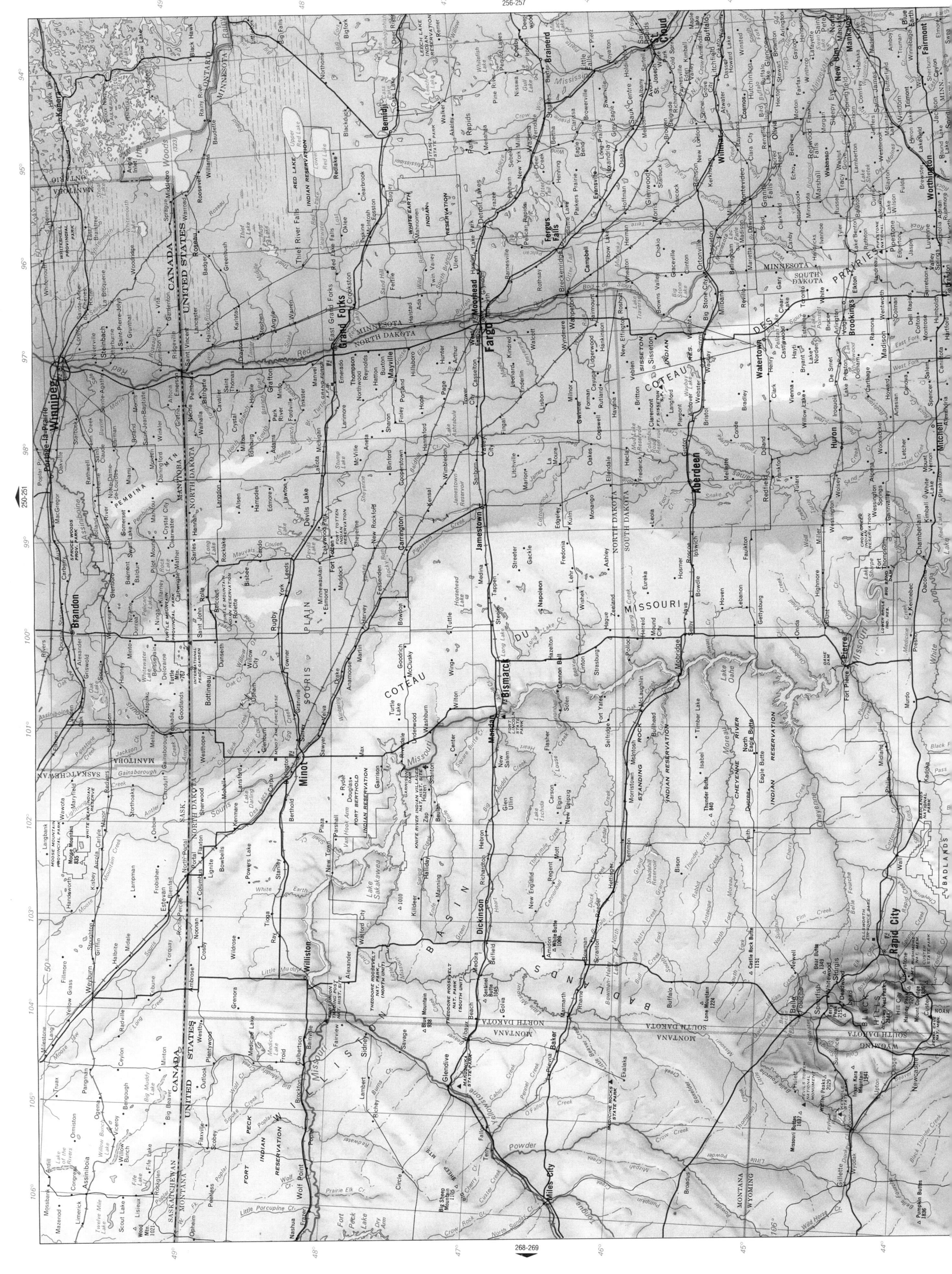

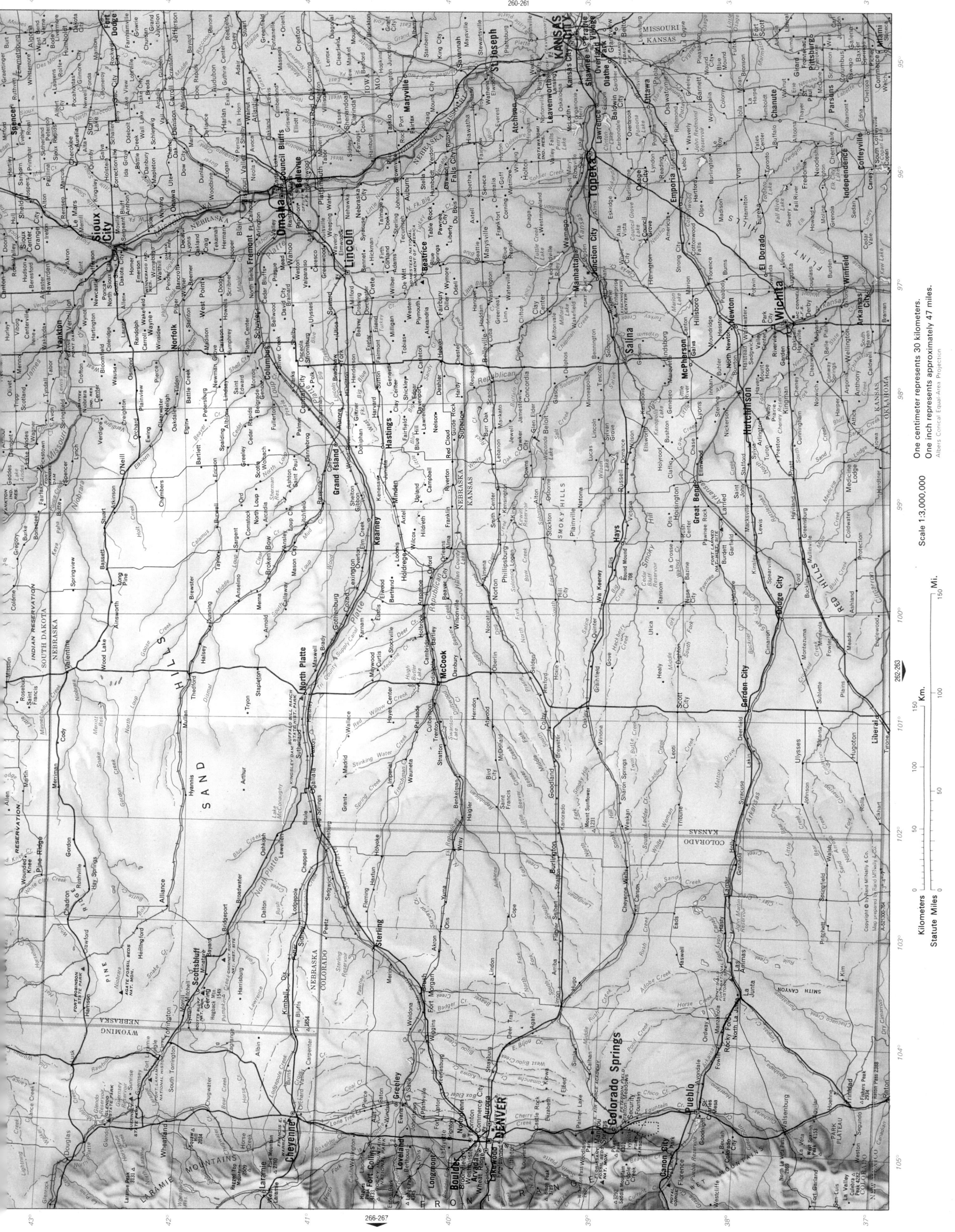

One centimeter represents 30 kilometers.
One inch represents approximately 47 miles.

Scale 1:3,000,000
Albers Conical Equal-Area Projection

262-263

Scale 1:3,000,000

One centimeter represents 30 kilometers.
One inch represents approximately 47 miles.
Albers Conical Equal-Area Projection

Kilometers

Statute Miles

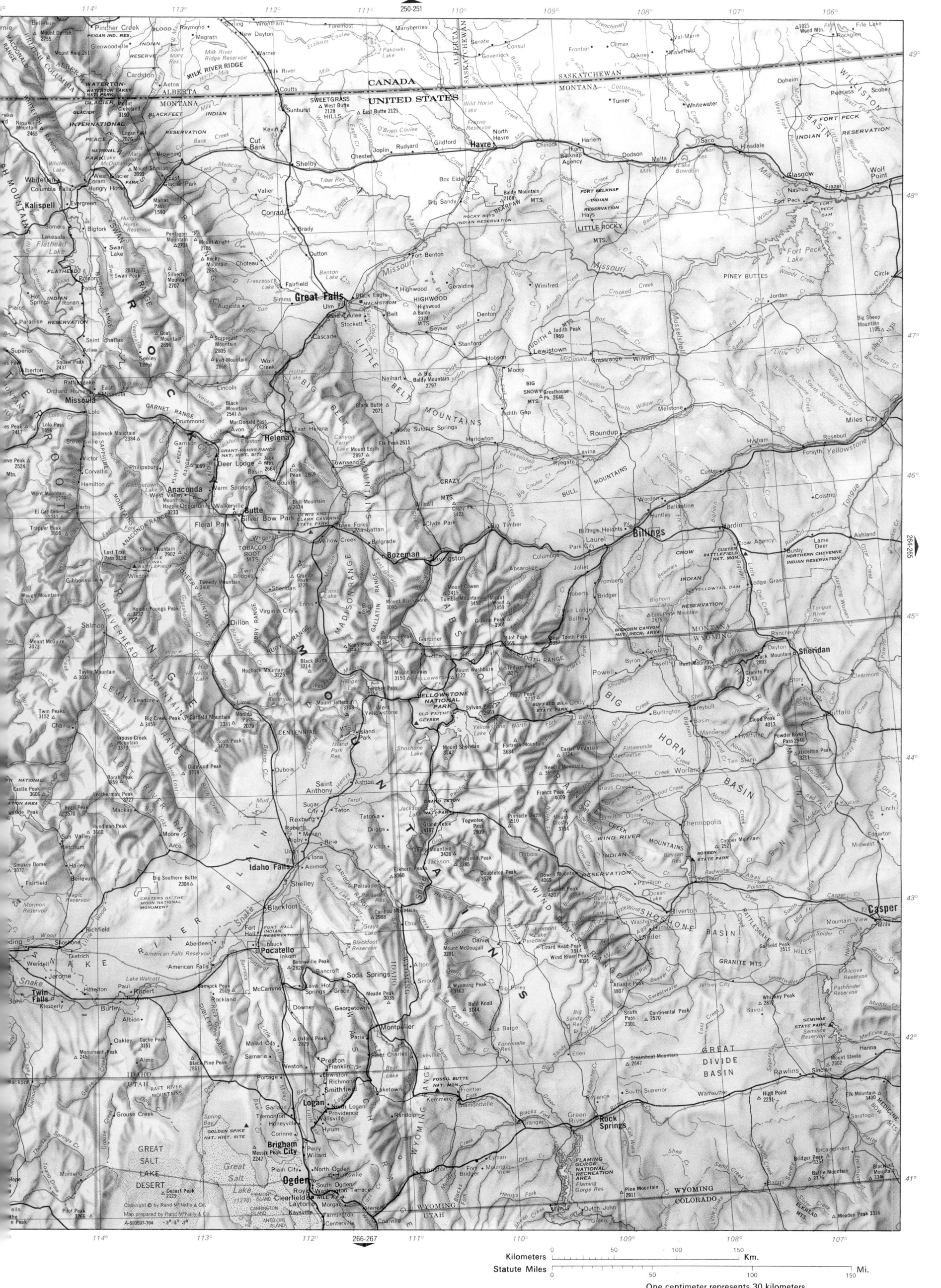

Kilometers

Statute Miles

Scale 1:3,000,000

One centimeter represents 30 kilometers.
One inch represents approximately 47 miles.

Albers Conical Equal-Area Projection

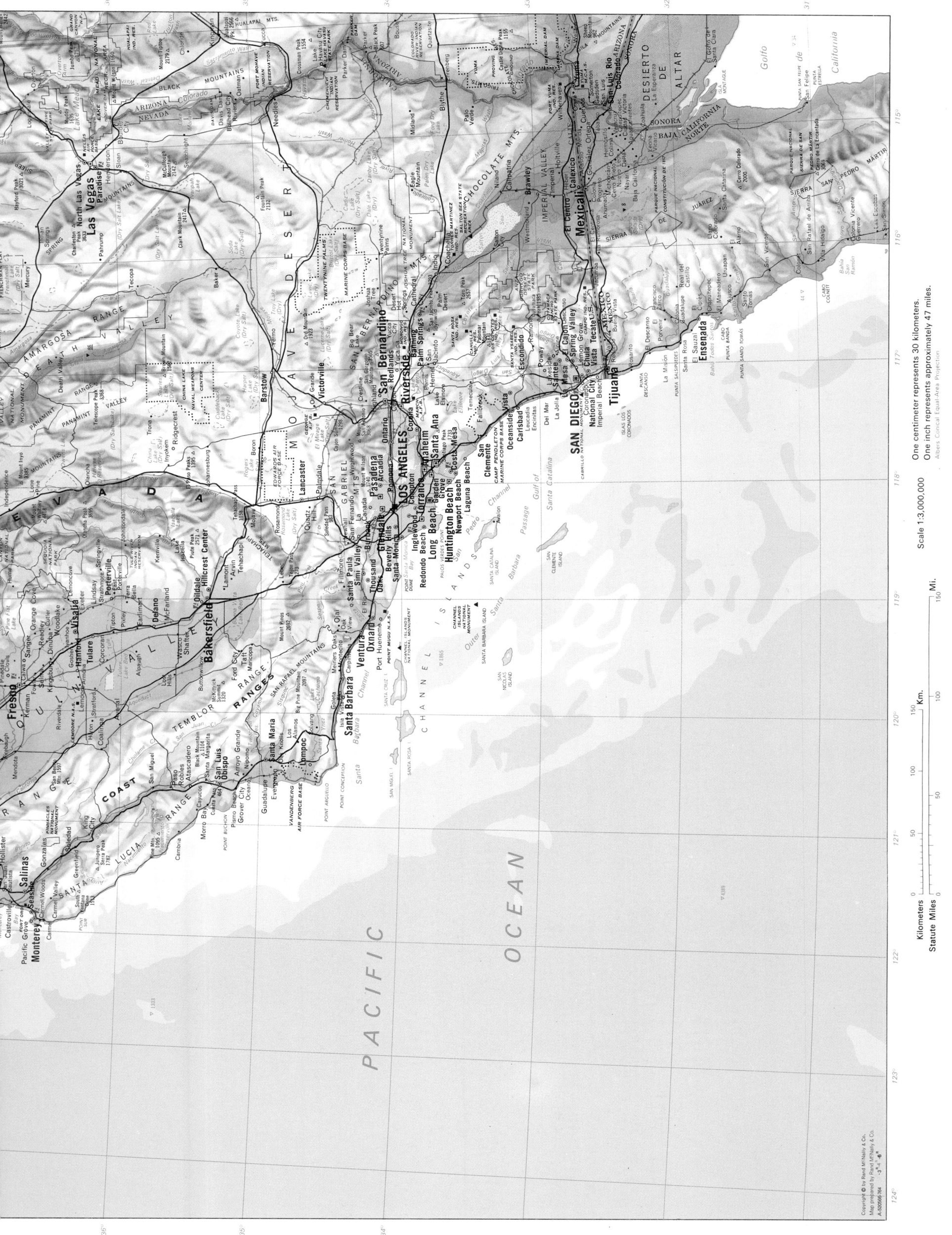

Scale 1:3,000,000

One centimeter represents 30 kilometers.
One inch represents approximately 47 miles.
Albers Conical Equal-Area Projection

Mi.

Km.

Kilometers

Statute Miles

HAWAII

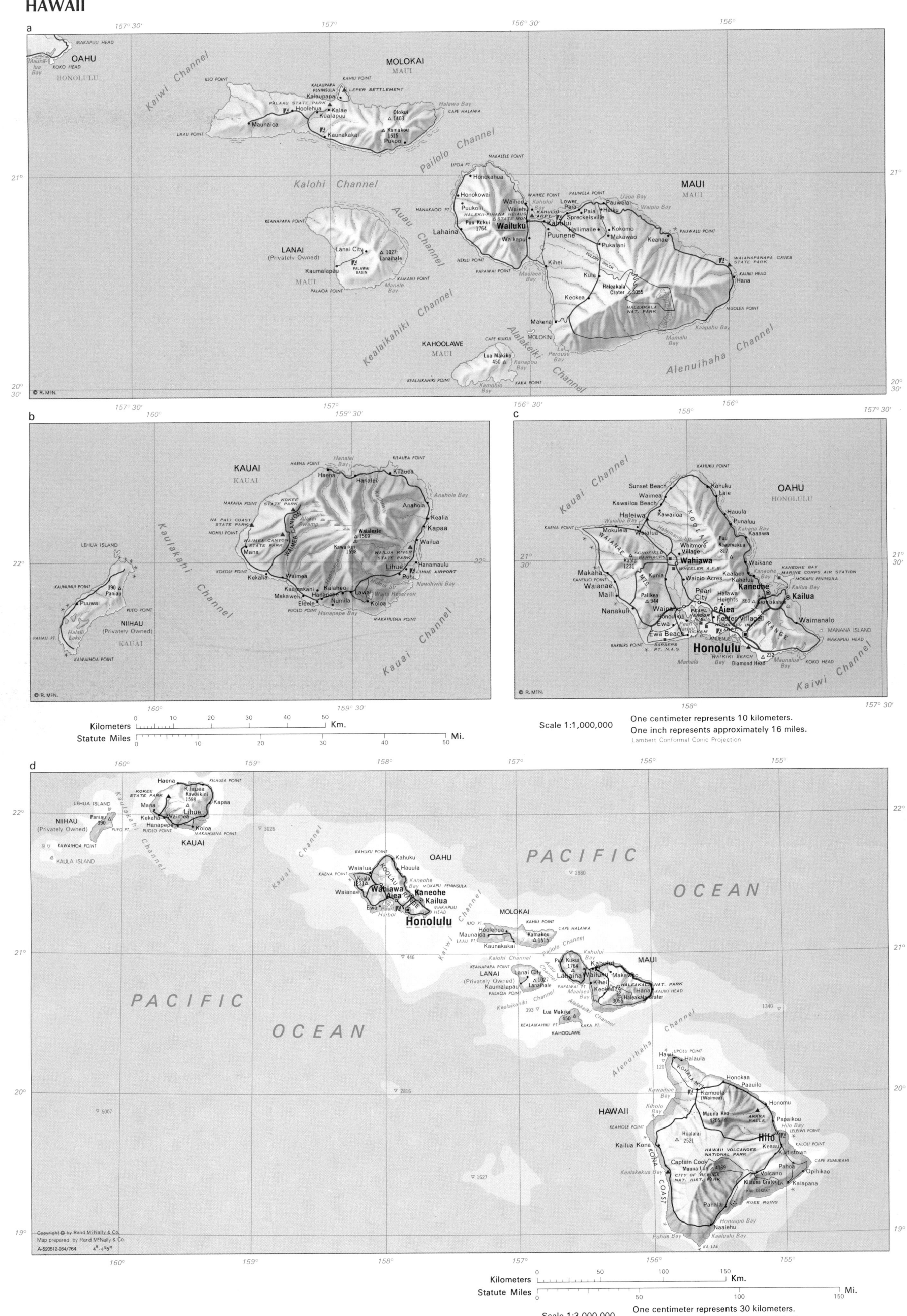

a

OAHU
MAKAPUU HEAD
Mauna-lua Bay   KOKO HEAD
HONOLULU

MOLOKAI
MAUI

KALAUPAPA PENINSULA
LEPER SETTLEMENT
PALAAU STATE PARK   Kamiu Point
Kalaupapa
Hoolehua Kalae
Kualapuu
Maunaloa   Olokui △1403
Kaunakakai   Kamakou △1515 Pukoo
LAAU POINT

NAKALELE POINT
UPOA PT.
Honokahua
Honokowai   WAIHEE POINT PAUWELA POINT
Kahului Ukoa Bay Waipio Bay
Puukolii Waihee Lower Pauwela Haiku
Waiehu Paia Paia
Puu Kukui Wailuku Spreckelsville
1764   Kahului
Lahaina   Kahului   PAUWALU POINT
Waikapu Haliimaile
Puunene Kokomo
Makawao
HEKILI POINT   Pukalani Keanae
WAIANAPANAPA
Kihei   STATE PARK CAVES
KAUIKI HEAD
Kula   Hana

LANAI   Keokea
(Privately Owned) Lanai City △1027
Lanaihale   Haleakala HUELO POINT
PALAWAI   Crater △3055
BASIN   HALEAKALA
Kaumalapau   NAT. PARK
Makena
KAMAIKI POINT
PALAOA POINT   Kaapahu Bay
Manele Bay   Makena
MOLOKINI

KAHOOLAWE   CAPE KUIKUI Mamalu Bay
MAUI   Alenuihaha Channel
Lua Makika △450 Kanapou Bay
KEALAIKAHIKI POINT Kamohio Bay EAKA POINT

b

KAUAI
KAUAI

Hanalei Bay KILAUEA POINT
HAENA POINT
Haena Hanalei Kilauea
MAKAHA POINT   KOKEE
STATE PARK
NA PALI COAST   Anahola Anahola Bay
STATE PARK   Kealia
NOHILI POINT   WAIMEA CANYON Waialeale Kapaa
STATE PARK △1569
Mana Kawaikini △1598
Lihue
KOOLE POINT   WAILUA RIVER LIHUE AIRPORT
Kekaha   STATE PARK
Waimea   Hanamaulu
Kaumakani Hanapepe   Nawiliwili Bay
Makaweli Wahiawa Lawai Wailua Reservoir
LEHUA ISLAND   Eleele Numila
PUOLO POINT Koloa
KAUNUNUI POINT 390   Hanapepe Bay
Puuwai △Paniau   MAKAHUENA POINT
PUEO POINT
NIIHAU
Halalii Lake (Privately Owned)
KAUAI
PAHAU PT.
KAWAIHOA POINT

c

KAHUKU POINT
OAHU
HONOLULU

Sunset Beach Kahuku
Waimea Laie
Kawailoa Beach Hauula
Haleiwa Kawailoa Punaluu
Mokuleia Waialua Kahana Bay
KAENA POINT Haleiwa   Kaaawa
Whitmore
Village Puu Kaaawa
Kaala   Kaleakala △812
Makaha △1231 Wahiawa
KANEILIO POINT   SCHOFIELD KANEOHE BAY
BARRACKS Kaneohe MARINE CORPS AIR STATION
Makaha   WHEELER A.F.B. Waikane MOKAPU PENINSULA
Waianae   Kunia Kaalaea
Maili   Waipio Acres Kahaluu Kaneohe
Palikea Kailua Kailua Bay
Nanakuli △944 Pearl Halawa
City   Heights △860 Kailua
Aiea
Honolulu Waimanalo
Ewa Pearl   Foster Village
Ewa Beach Harbor
BARBERS POINT   MANANA ISLAND
BARBERS   Honolulu MAKAPUU HEAD
PT. N.A.S.   △232
Honolulu Diamond Head
Mahala   WAIKIKI BEACH Maunalua KOKO HEAD
Bay   Bay
Kaiwi Channel

Scale 1:1,000,000   One centimeter represents 10 kilometers.
One inch represents approximately 16 miles.
Lambert Conformal Conic Projection

Kilometers 0 10 20 30 40 50 Km.
Statute Miles 0 10 20 30 40 50 Mi.

d

Haena KILAUEA POINT
KOKEE Kilauea
STATE PARK Kawaikini
△1598 Kapaa
Mana Lihue
NIIHAU Paniau Kekaha Waimea
(Privately Owned) △390 Hanapepe Koloa
PUEO PT. KAUAI
Puuwai
KAWAIHOA POINT
KAULA ISLAND
LEHUA ISLAND

PACIFIC
OCEAN

△3026
KAHUKU POINT
Waialua Kahuku OAHU
Kaala Haleiwa
KAENA POINT   Kaneohe
△1231 Wahiawa Mokapu Peninsula
Waianae Aiea Kaneohe
Ewa Kailua
Pearl MAKAPUU HEAD
Honolulu Harbor KOKO HEAD

△2580

PACIFIC
OCEAN

IUO PT. MOLOKAI
Hoolehua KAHIU POINT
Maunaloa Kamakou CAPE HALAWA
△1515
Kaunakakai

△446   KALOHI CHANNEL
KEANAPAPA POINT   Puu Kukui Kahului
LANAI 1764 Wailuku MAUI
(Privately Owned) Lanai City Lahaina Makawao
△1027 Kihei HALEAKALA NAT. PARK
Kaumalapau Lanaihale Hana KAUIKI HEAD
PALAOA POINT △393 Haleakala Crater
Lua Makika △3055
△450
KEALAIKAHIKI PT.   Alalakeiki Channel
KAHOOLAWE   LAKA PT.

△5007   Alenuihaha Channel

△2816   UPOLU POINT
Hawi KOHALA MT.
Halaula Honokaa Paauilo
HAWAII   △120
Kawaihae   Kamuela Honomu
Bay   (Waimea)
Kiholo Mauna Kea ANAIKA Papaikou
Bay △4205 FALLS Hilo Bay
Hualalai Hilo
△2521
Kailua Kona HAWAII VOLCANOES Keaau
△1627   NATIONAL PARK Kurtistown
Captain Cook Mauna Loa Volcano Pahoa
Kealakekua Bay △4169 Kilauea Crater Opihikao
KONA COAST   Kalapana
KA'U DESERT KUEE RUINS
Pahala
Honuapo Bay
Naalehu
KA LAE Kaaluulu Bay
Pohue Bay

Copyright © by Rand McNally & Co.
Map prepared by Rand McNally & Co.
A-520512-264/764

Kilometers 0 50 100 150 Km.
Statute Miles 0 50 100 150 Mi.

Scale 1:3,000,000   One centimeter represents 30 kilometers.
One inch represents approximately 47 miles.
Lambert Conformal Conic Projection

United States and Canada Map Index

The index includes in a single alphabetical list some 24,000 names appearing on the maps. Each name is followed by a page reference and by the location of the feature on the map. The map location is designated by latitude and longitude coordinates. If a page contains several maps, a lowercase letter identifies the inset map. The page reference for two-page maps is always to the left hand page.

Most map features are indexed to the largest-scale map on which they appear. Countries, mountain ranges, and other extensive features are generally indexed to the map that shows them in their entirety.

The features indexed are of three types: *point, areal,* and *linear*. For *point* features (for example, cities, mountain peaks, dams), latitude and longitude coordinates give the location of the point on the map. For *areal* features (countries, mountain ranges, etc.), the coordinates generally indicate the approximate center of the feature. For *linear* features (rivers, canals, aqueducts), the coordinates locate a terminating point—for example, the mouth of a river, or the point at which a feature reaches the map margin.

ALPHABETIZATION Names are alphabetized in the order of the letters of the English alphabet. Diacritical marks are disregarded in alphabetization.

The names of physical features may appear inverted, since they are always alphabetized under the proper, not the generic, part of the name, thus: "St. Lawrence, Gulf of c". Otherwise every entry, whether consisting of one word or more, is alphabetized as a single continuous entity. "Lakeland," for example, appears after "La Crosse" and before "La Salle." Names beginning with articles (La Pocatière) are not inverted. Names beginning "Mc" are alphabetized as though spelled "Mac," and names beginning "St." and "Sainte" as though spelled "Saint."

In the case of identical names, towns are listed first, then political divisions, then physical features. Entries that are completely identical (including symbols, discussed below) are distinguished by abbreviations of their state or province names. (See list of abbreviations below.)

ABBREVIATION AND CAPITALIZATION Abbreviation and styling have been standardized. Periods are used after all abbreviations except those for state and province names, which follow the postal style (e.g. Alaska AK, Alberta AB).

All names are written with an initial capital letter. Capitalization of noninitial words in a name generally follows local practice.

SYMBOL The symbols that appear in the index graphically represent the broad categories of the features named, for example, ∧ for mountain (McKinley, Mount ∧). Superior numbers following some symbols in the Index indicate finer distinctions, for example, ∧¹ for volcano (Lassen Peak ∧¹). A list of the symbols and those with superior numbers is given below. All cross references are indicated by the symbol →.

LIST OF ABBREVIATIONS

	Name			Name			Name			Name			Name			Name
AB	Alberta		DE	Delaware		MA	Massachusetts		NC	North Carolina		OH	Ohio		TN	Tennessee
AK	Alaska		FL	Florida		MB	Manitoba		ND	North Dakota		OK	Oklahoma		TX	Texas
AL	Alabama		GA	Georgia		MD	Maryland		NE	Nebraska		ON	Ontario		U.S.	United States
AR	Arkansas		HI	Hawaii		ME	Maine		NF	Newfoundland		OR	Oregon		UT	Utah
AZ	Arizona		IA	Iowa		MI	Michigan		NH	New Hampshire		PA	Pennsylvania		VA	Virginia
BC	British Columbia		ID	Idaho		MN	Minnesota		NJ	New Jersey		PE	Prince Edward Island		VT	Vermont
CA	California		IL	Illinois		MO	Missouri		NM	New Mexico		PQ	Quebec		WA	Washington
Can.	Canada		IN	Indiana		MS	Mississippi		NS	Nova Scotia		RI	Rhode Island		WI	Wisconsin
CO	Colorado		KS	Kansas		MT	Montana		NT	Northwest Territories		SC	South Carolina		WV	West Virginia
CT	Connecticut		KY	Kentucky		N.A.	North America		NV	Nevada		SD	South Dakota		WY	Wyoming
DC	District of Columbia		LA	Louisiana		NB	New Brunswick		NY	New York		SK	Saskatchewan		YK	Yukon Territory

KEY TO SYMBOLS

∧ Mountain
∧¹ Volcano
∧² Hill
∧ Mountains
∧¹ Plateau
∧² Hills
)(Pass
∨ Valley, Canyon
≃ Plain
≃¹ Basin
≃² Delta

⊁ Cape
⊁¹ Peninsula
⊁² Spit, Sand Bar
I Island
I¹ Atoll
I² Rock
II Islands
II¹ Rocks
≛ Other Topographic Features
•¹ Continent
•² Coast, Beach

•³ Isthmus
•⁴ Cliff
•⁵ Cave, Caves
•⁶ Crater
•⁷ Depression
•⁸ Dunes
•⁹ Lava Flow
≃ River
≃¹ River Channel
≊ Canal
≊¹ Aqueduct

ᴸ Waterfall, Rapids
ᴗ Strait
c Bay, Gulf
c¹ Estuary
c² Fjord
c³ Bight
⦿ Lake, Lakes
⦿¹ Reservoir
≋ Swamp
▣ Ice Features, Glacier

▼ Other Hydrographic Features
▼¹ Ocean
▼² Sea
▼³ Anchorage
▼⁴ Oasis, Well, Spring
⊹ Submarine Features
⊹¹ Depression
⊹² Reef, Shoal
⊹³ Mountain, Mountains
⊹⁴ Slope, Shelf

□ Political Unit
□¹ Independent Nation
□² Dependency
□³ State, Canton, Republic
□⁴ Province, Region, Oblast
□⁵ Department, District, Prefecture
□⁶ County
□⁷ City, Municipality
□⁸ Miscellaneous
□⁹ Historical

⌄ Cultural Institution
⌄¹ Religious Institution
⌄² Educational Institution
⌄³ Scientific, Industrial Facility
⌁ Historical Site
⌁ Recreational Site
⊠ Airport
▪ Military Installation

• Miscellaneous
•¹ Region
•² Desert
•³ Forest, Moor
•⁴ Reserve, Reservation
•⁵ Transportation
•⁶ Dam
•⁷ Mine, Quarry
•⁸ Neighborhood
•⁹ Shopping Center

Name	Page	Lat "	Long "
A			
Abajo Mountains ∧	266	37.50 N	109.25 W
Abajo Peak ∧	266	37.51 N	109.28 W
Abbeville, GA	258	31.59 N	83.18 W
Abbeville, LA	260	29.58 N	92.08 W
Abbeville, MS	260	34.25 N	89.37 W
Abbeville, SC	258	34.11 N	82.23 W
Abbey	250	50.43 N	108.45 W
Abbotsford, BC	268	49.03 N	122.17 W
Abbotsford, WI	256	44.57 N	90.19 W
Abbott Butte ∧	268	42.57 N	122.33 W
Abernathy	262	33.50 N	101.51 W
Abernethy	250	50.45 N	103.25 W
Abert, Lake ⦿	268	42.38 N	120.13 W
Abiaca Creek ≃	260	33.20 N	90.15 W
Abilene, KS	264	38.55 N	97.13 W
Abilene, TX	262	32.27 N	99.44 W
Abingdon, IL	256	40.48 N	90.24 W
Abingdon, VA	258	36.43 N	81.59 W
Abiquiu	266	36.12 N	106.19 W
Abiquiu Reservoir ⦿¹	266	36.18 N	106.32 W
Abita Springs	260	30.29 N	90.02 W
Abitau ≃	242	59.53 N	109.03 W
Abitibi ≃	242	51.03 N	80.55 W
Abitibi, Lake ⦿	256	48.42 N	79.45 W
Abraham Lincoln Birthplace National Historic Site ⌁	260	37.32 N	85.44 W
Absaroka Range ∧	244	44.45 N	109.50 W
Absarokee	268	45.31 N	109.27 W
Absecon	254	39.26 N	74.30 W
Acadia National Park ⌁	254	44.18 N	68.15 W
Acadia Valley	250	51.08 N	110.13 W
Accomac	258	37.43 N	75.40 W
Accoville	258	37.46 N	81.50 W
Ackerly	262	32.32 N	101.43 W
Ackerman	260	33.19 N	89.10 W
Ackley	256	42.33 N	93.03 W
Acme	248	51.30 N	113.30 W
Acoma Indian Reservation •⁴	266	34.52 N	107.40 W
Acomita	266	35.03 N	107.35 W
Acton	248	43.37 N	80.02 W
Acton Vale	254	45.39 N	72.34 W
Acworth	258	34.04 N	84.41 W
Ada, MN	264	47.18 N	96.31 W
Ada, OH	254	40.46 N	83.49 W
Ada, OK	262	34.46 N	96.41 W
Ada, Mount ∧	246	56.41 N	134.41 W
Adair, IA	264	41.30 N	94.39 W
Adair, OK	262	36.26 N	95.16 W
Adair, Cape ⊁	242	71.24 N	71.13 W
Adairsville	258	34.22 N	84.56 W
Adairville	260	36.40 N	86.51 W
Adak Island I	247a	51.45 N	176.40 W
Adams, MA	254	42.37 N	73.07 W
Adams, MN	256	43.34 N	92.43 W
Adams, ND	264	40.28 N	96.31 W
Adams, NE	264	48.25 N	98.05 W
Adams, NY	254	43.49 N	76.01 W
Adams, TN	260	36.35 N	87.04 W
Adams, WI	256	43.58 N	89.49 W
Adams ≃	248	50.52 N	119.35 W
Adams, Mount ∧	268	46.12 N	121.28 W
Adamsville	248	51.13 N	119.33 W
Addis	260	30.21 N	91.16 W
Addison	262	41.59 N	84.21 W
Adel, GA	258	31.08 N	83.25 W
Adel, IA	260	41.37 N	94.01 W
Adelaide Peninsula ⊁¹	242	68.09 N	97.45 W
Adin	270	41.12 N	120.57 W
Adirondack Mountains ∧	254	44.00 N	74.00 W
Adirondack Park ⌁	254	44.00 N	74.20 W
Admiral	250	49.43 N	108.01 W
Admiralty Bay c	246	70.53 N	155.45 W
Admiralty Inlet c	242	73.00 N	86.00 W
Admiralty Island I, AK	246	57.50 N	134.30 W
Admiralty Island I, NT	242	69.30 N	101.00 W
Adobe Creek ≃	264	38.05 N	103.18 W
Adrian, GA	258	32.32 N	82.35 W
Adrian, MI	254	41.54 N	84.02 W
Adrian, MN	264	43.38 N	95.56 W
Adrian, MO	260	38.24 N	94.21 W
Adrian, OR	268	43.44 N	117.04 W
Adrian, TX	262	35.16 N	102.40 W
Adrian, WV	258	38.54 N	80.17 W
Advance	260	37.06 N	89.55 W
Advocate Harbour	252	45.20 N	64.47 W
Aetna	248	49.08 N	113.15 W
Affton	260	38.33 N	90.20 W
Afognak Island I	246	58.15 N	152.30 W
Afton, IA	260	41.02 N	94.12 W
Afton, NY	254	42.14 N	75.32 W
Afton, OK	262	36.42 N	94.58 W
Afton, WY	268	42.44 N	110.56 W
Agassiz	248	49.14 N	121.46 W
Agate	264	39.25 N	103.58 W
Agate Beach	268	44.41 N	124.04 W
Agate Fossil Beds National Monument ⌁	264	42.25 N	103.43 W
Agattu Island I	247a	52.25 N	173.35 E
Agattu Strait ᴗ	247a	52.35 N	173.25 E
Agawa ≃	256	47.21 N	84.38 W
Agawa Bay c	256	47.20 N	84.42 W
Agawam	248	48.00 N	112.10 W
Agency	256	41.00 N	92.18 W
Agency Lake ⦿	268	42.32 N	121.58 W
Agnes Lake ⦿	256	48.13 N	91.21 W
Agua Dulce	262	27.47 N	97.54 W
Agua Fria ≃	266	33.23 N	112.21 W
Aguanish	252	50.13 N	62.05 W
Aguanus ≃	252	50.13 N	62.05 W
Aguasabon ≃	256	48.46 N	87.07 W
Agu Bay c	242	70.18 N	86.30 W
Aguenier, Lac ⦿	252	50.43 N	68.13 W
Aguila	266	33.56 N	113.11 W
Aguilar	264	37.24 N	104.46 W
Ahklun Mountains ∧	246	59.15 N	161.00 W
Ahmic Lake ⦿	256	45.37 N	79.42 W
Ahoskie	258	36.17 N	76.59 W
Ahtanum Creek ≃	268	46.32 N	120.31 W
Aialik, Cape ⊁	246	59.42 N	149.31 W
Aiea	272c	21.23 N	157.56 W
Aigle, Lac à l' ⦿	252	51.12 N	65.25 W
Aiguebelle, Réserve (Aiguebelle Reserve) ⌁	256	48.33 N	78.45 W
Aiken	258	33.34 N	81.43 W
Aikens Lake ⦿	250	51.12 N	95.20 W
Ailsa Craig	256	43.08 N	81.33 W
Ainslie Lake ⦿	252	46.08 N	61.12 W
Ainsworth	264	42.33 N	99.51 W
Airdrie	248	51.18 N	114.02 W
Air Force Island I	242	67.55 N	74.10 W
Aishihik	246	61.35 N	137.30 W
Aishihik Lake ⦿	246	61.25 N	137.06 W
Aitkin	256	46.32 N	93.43 W
Aix, Mount ∧	268	46.47 N	121.15 W
Aiyansh	248	55.17 N	129.03 W
Ajax	248	43.51 N	79.02 W
Ajo	266	32.22 N	112.52 W
Akaka Falls ᴸ	272	19.52 N	155.09 W
Ak-Chin Indian Reservation •⁴	266	33.02 N	112.05 W
Akeley	256	47.00 N	94.44 W
Akhiok	246	56.57 N	154.10 W
Akiachak	246	60.55 N	161.27 W
Akiak	246	60.55 N	161.12 W
Akimiski Island I	242	53.00 N	81.20 W
Aklavik	246	68.12 N	135.00 W
Akpatok Island I	242	60.25 N	68.00 W
Akron, CO	264	40.10 N	103.13 W
Akron, IN	260	41.02 N	86.01 W
Akron, IA	264	42.49 N	96.33 W
Akron, NY	254	43.01 N	78.30 W
Akron, OH	254	41.05 N	81.31 W
Akron, PA	254	40.09 N	76.12 W
Akun Island I	246	54.12 N	165.35 W
Akutan	246	54.08 N	165.46 W
Akutan Island I	246	54.10 N	165.55 W
Akutan Pass ᴗ	246	54.00 N	166.10 W
Alabama □³, U.S.	244		
Alabama ≃	260	32.50 N	87.00 W
Alabaster	260	33.15 N	86.49 W
Alachua	258	29.47 N	82.30 W
Alafia ≃	258	27.52 N	82.23 W
Alakai Swamp ≋	272b	22.08 N	159.35 W
Alakanuk	246	62.41 N	164.37 W
Alalakeiki Channel ᴗ	272a	20.35 N	156.30 W
Alameda, CA	270	37.46 N	122.16 W
Alameda, NM	266	35.11 N	106.37 W
Alamo, GA	258	32.09 N	82.47 W
Alamo, NV	270	37.22 N	115.10 W
Alamo, TN	260	35.47 N	89.07 W
Alamo ≃	270	33.14 N	115.39 W
Alamogordo	266	32.53 N	105.57 W
Alamogordo Creek ≃	262	34.40 N	104.23 W
Alamo Heights	262	29.28 N	98.28 W
Alamo Indian Reservation •⁴	266	34.30 N	107.30 W
Alamosa	266	37.28 N	105.52 W
Alamosa ≃, CO	266	37.22 N	105.46 W
Alamosa ≃, NM	266	33.20 N	107.21 W
Alanson	256	45.27 N	84.47 W
Alapaha	258	31.23 N	83.13 W
Alapaha ≃	258	30.26 N	83.06 W
Alaska □³	244		
Alaska, Gulf of c	246	58.00 N	146.00 W
Alaska Peninsula ⊁¹	246	57.00 N	158.00 W
Alaska Range ∧	246	62.30 N	150.00 W
Alatna ≃	246	66.34 N	152.34 W
Alava, Cape ⊁	268	48.10 N	124.43 W
Alba, MI	256	44.59 N	84.58 W
Alba, TX	262	32.48 N	95.38 W
Albanel, Lac ⦿	242	50.55 N	73.12 W
Albany, GA	258	31.35 N	84.10 W
Albany, IN	260	40.18 N	85.14 W
Albany, MN	264	45.38 N	94.34 W
Albany, MO	260	40.15 N	94.20 W
Albany, NY	254	42.39 N	73.45 W
Albany, OH	258	39.14 N	82.12 W
Albany, TX	262	32.44 N	99.18 W
Albany, WI	256	42.43 N	89.26 W
Albany ≃	242	52.17 N	81.31 W
Albemarle	258	35.21 N	80.12 W
Albemarle Sound ᴗ	258	36.03 N	76.12 W
Alberene	258	37.53 N	78.37 W
Alberni Inlet c	268	49.07 N	124.50 W
Alberta □⁴, Can.	242	32.14 N	87.25 W
Alberta, Mount ∧	248	52.18 N	117.28 W
Albert Canyon	248	51.08 N	117.52 W
Albert City	264	42.47 N	94.57 W
Albert Edward Bay c	242	69.32 N	103.00 W
Albert Lea	256	43.39 N	93.22 W
Alberton, PE	252	46.49 N	64.04 W
Alberton, MT	268	47.00 N	114.29 W
Albertville	260	34.16 N	86.12 W
Albia	256	41.02 N	92.48 W
Albin	264	41.25 N	104.06 W
Albion, CA	270	39.13 N	123.46 W
Albion, ID	268	42.25 N	113.35 W
Albion, IL	260	38.23 N	88.04 W
Albion, IN	260	41.24 N	85.25 W
Albion, IA	256	42.07 N	92.59 W
Albion, MI	254	42.15 N	84.45 W
Albion, NE	264	41.42 N	98.00 W
Albion, NY	254	43.15 N	78.12 W
Albion, PA	254	41.53 N	80.22 W
Albion, WA	268	46.48 N	117.15 W
Albreda	248	52.38 N	119.09 W
Albuquerque	266	35.05 N	106.40 W
Alburg	254	44.59 N	73.18 W
Alcalde	266	36.05 N	106.03 W
Alcester	264	43.01 N	96.38 W
Alcoa	258	35.48 N	83.59 W
Alcolu	258	33.45 N	80.13 W
Alcorn College	260	31.52 N	91.09 W
Alcova	266	42.32 N	106.45 W
Alcova Reservoir ⦿¹	266	42.32 N	106.45 W
Alcovy ≃	258	33.26 N	83.50 W
Alden, IA	264	42.31 N	93.23 W
Alden, MN	256	43.40 N	93.34 W
Alder Creek ≃	268	45.50 N	119.56 W
Alder Lake ⦿	268	46.45 N	122.15 W
Alderson	258	37.43 N	80.39 W
Aledo	260	41.12 N	90.45 W
Alegros Mountain ∧	266	34.09 N	108.11 W
Aleknagik	246	59.17 N	158.38 W
Aleknagik, Lake ⦿	246	59.20 N	158.45 W
Alenuihaha Channel ᴗ	272a	20.26 N	156.00 W
Alert Bay	248	50.35 N	126.55 W
Aleutian Islands II	246	52.00 N	176.00 W
Aleutian Range ∧	246	59.00 N	155.00 W
Alex	262	34.55 N	97.47 W
Alexander, MB	250	49.50 N	100.17 W
Alexander, ND	264	47.51 N	103.39 W
Alexander Archipelago II	246	56.30 N	134.00 W
Alexander City	260	32.56 N	85.57 W
Alexander Indian Reserve •⁴	248	53.09 N	113.58 W
Alexandra Falls ᴸ	242	60.29 N	116.18 W
Alexandria, BC	248	52.38 N	122.27 W
Alexandria, ON	254	45.19 N	74.38 W
Alexandria, IN	260	40.16 N	85.41 W
Alexandria, KY	254	38.58 N	84.23 W
Alexandria, LA	260	31.18 N	92.27 W
Alexandria, MN	264	45.53 N	95.22 W
Alexandria, MO	260	40.27 N	91.28 W
Alexandria, NE	264	40.15 N	97.23 W
Alexandria, SD	264	43.39 N	97.47 W
Alexandria, TN	260	36.05 N	86.02 W
Alexandria, VA	254	38.48 N	77.03 W
Alexandria Bay	254	44.20 N	75.55 W
Alexis, IL	260	41.04 N	90.33 W
Alexis Creek	248	52.05 N	123.17 W
Alexis Indian Reserve •⁴	248	53.46 N	114.30 W
Alfred, ON	254	45.34 N	74.53 W
Alfred, ME	254	43.29 N	70.43 W
Alger	254	40.42 N	83.51 W
Algodones	266	35.23 N	106.29 W
Algoma	256	44.36 N	87.27 W
Algoma Mills	256	46.10 N	82.50 W
Algona	256	43.04 N	94.14 W
Algona, WA	268	47.17 N	122.15 W
Algonac	254	42.37 N	82.32 W
Algonquin	256	42.10 N	88.18 W
Algonquin Provincial Park ⌁	256	45.27 N	78.26 W
Algood	260	36.12 N	85.27 W
Aliaksin, Cape ⊁	246	55.30 N	160.43 W
Alibates Flint Quarries National Monument ⌁	262	35.35 N	101.39 W
Alice	262	27.45 N	98.04 W
Alice Arm	248	55.29 N	129.29 W
Aliceville	260	33.08 N	88.09 W
Aliquippa	254	40.37 N	80.15 W
Alitak, Cape ⊁	246	56.51 N	154.21 W
Alitak Bay c	246	57.00 N	154.05 W
Alix	248	52.24 N	113.11 W
Alkali Creek ≃, AB	250	50.52 N	110.30 W
Alkali Creek ≃, WY	268	43.16 N	107.40 W
Alkali Lake ⦿	248	51.47 N	121.54 W
Alkali Lake ⦿, NV	270	41.42 N	119.50 W
Alkali Lake ⦿, OR	268	43.10 N	120.02 W
Allagash ≃	252	47.05 N	69.02 W
Allakaket	246	66.34 N	152.41 W
Allan	250	51.53 N	106.04 W
Allard, Lac ⦿	252	50.32 N	63.31 W
Allard, Lac ⦿, PQ	256	47.20 N	78.51 W
Allardt	258	36.23 N	84.53 W
Allatoona Lake ⦿	258	34.10 N	84.38 W
Allegan	256	42.32 N	85.51 W
Allegany State Park ⌁	254	42.04 N	78.44 W
Alleghany ≃	254	40.27 N	80.00 W
Allegheny Mountains ∧	258	38.30 N	80.00 W
Allegheny Plateau ∧¹	254	41.30 N	78.00 W

United States and Canada Map Index

Name	Page	Lat °′	Long °′
Allegheny Reservoir ⊜[1]	254	42.00 N	78.56 W
Allemands, Lac Des ≃	260	29.55 N	90.35 W
Allen, NE	264	42.25 N	96.51 W
Allen, OK	262	34.53 N	96.25 W
Allen, SD	264	43.17 N	101.55 W
Allen, TX	262	33.06 N	96.40 W
Allen, Mount ▲	246	62.14 N	142.13 W
Allendale, IL	260	38.32 N	87.43 W
Allendale, SC	258	33.06 N	81.18 W
Allentown	254	40.36 N	75.29 W
Allerton	256	40.42 N	93.22 W
Alliance, AB	250	52.26 N	111.47 W
Alliance, NE	264	42.06 N	102.52 W
Alliance, OH	254	40.55 N	81.06 W
Alligator ≃	258	35.58 N	75.58 W
Alligator Creek ≃	258	31.58 N	82.22 W
Allison	256	42.45 N	92.48 W
Allison Harbour	248	51.03 N	127.30 W
Alliston	256	44.09 N	79.52 W
Allouez	256	44.29 N	88.01 W
Allred Peak ▲	266	40.32 N	108.33 W
Allumette Lake ⊜	254	45.53 N	77.13 W
Allumettes, Île des ▮	254	45.50 N	77.05 W
Allyn	268	47.23 N	122.50 W
Alma, PQ	252	48.33 N	71.39 W
Alma, AR	260	35.29 N	94.13 W
Alma, GA	258	31.33 N	82.28 W
Alma, KS	264	39.01 N	96.17 W
Alma, MI	256	43.23 N	84.39 W
Alma, NE	264	40.06 N	99.22 W
Alma, WI	256	44.20 N	91.55 W
Alma Center	256	44.26 N	90.55 W
Alma Hill ▲[2]	254	42.03 N	78.01 W
Almanor, Lake ⊜	270	40.15 N	121.08 W
Almena	264	39.54 N	99.43 W
Almira	268	47.43 N	118.56 W
Almo	268	42.06 N	113.38 W
Almond	256	44.16 N	89.24 W
Almont	256	42.55 N	83.03 W
Almonte	256	45.14 N	76.12 W
Alpaugh	270	35.53 N	119.29 W
Alpena, AR	260	36.17 N	93.18 W
Alpena, MI	256	45.04 N	83.26 W
Alpena, SD	264	44.11 N	98.22 W
Alpha, IL	260	41.12 N	90.23 W
Alpha, MI	256	46.02 N	88.22 W
Alpharetta	258	34.04 N	84.18 W
Alpine, AZ	266	33.51 N	109.09 W
Alpine, CA	270	32.50 N	116.47 W
Alpine, TX	262	30.22 N	103.40 W
Alright, Île ▮	252	47.25 N	61.47 W
Alsask	250	51.23 N	109.59 W
Alsea	268	44.23 N	123.36 W
Alsea ≃	268	44.26 N	124.05 W
Alsek ≃	242	59.10 N	138.10 W
Alsen	264	48.38 N	98.42 W
Alstead ≃	250	55.50 N	107.26 W
Alta	264	42.40 N	95.18 W
Altamaha ≃	258	31.19 N	81.17 W
Altamont, IL	260	39.04 N	88.46 W
Altamont, KS	264	37.12 N	95.18 W
Altamont, OR	268	42.12 N	121.44 W
Altamont, TN	260	35.26 N	85.43 W
Altario	250	51.55 N	110.09 W
Altar Wash ∨	266	32.05 N	111.19 W
Alta Vista, KS	264	38.52 N	96.29 W
Altavista, VA	258	37.06 N	79.17 W
Altha	258	30.34 N	85.08 W
Altheimer	260	34.19 N	91.51 W
Alto	262	31.39 N	95.04 W
Alton, IL	260	38.54 N	90.10 W
Alton, IA	264	42.59 N	96.01 W
Alton, KS	264	39.28 N	98.57 W
Alton, MO	260	36.42 N	91.24 W
Alton, NH	254	43.27 N	71.13 W
Altona	250	49.06 N	97.33 W
Altoona, AL	260	34.02 N	86.20 W
Altoona, IA	256	41.39 N	93.28 W
Altoona, KS	264	37.32 N	95.40 W
Altoona, PA	254	40.30 N	78.24 W
Altoona, WI	256	44.48 N	91.26 W
Alturas	270	41.29 N	120.32 W
Altus, AR	260	35.27 N	93.46 W
Altus, OK	262	34.38 N	99.20 W
Altus, Lake ⊜[1]	262	34.56 N	99.18 W
Altus Air Force Base ■	262	34.40 N	99.16 W
Alum Rock	270	37.23 N	121.50 W
Alva	262	36.48 N	98.40 W
Alvarado	262	32.24 N	97.13 W
Alvin	262	29.25 N	95.15 W
Alvord	262	33.22 N	97.42 W
Alvord Desert →[2]	268	42.30 N	118.25 W
Alvord Lake ⊜	268	42.23 N	118.36 W
Amadjuak Lake ⊜	242	65.00 N	71.00 W
Amagansett	254	40.58 N	72.08 W
Amak Island ▮	246	55.25 N	163.07 W
Amana	256	41.48 N	91.52 W
Amanda	254	39.39 N	82.45 W
Amaranth	250	50.36 N	98.43 W
Amargosa ≃	270	36.13 N	116.48 W
Amargosa Range ⛰	270	36.30 N	116.45 W
Amarillo	262	35.13 N	101.49 W
Amasa	256	46.14 N	88.27 W
Amatignak Island ▮	247a	51.15 N	179.08 W
Amberg	256	45.30 N	88.00 W
Ambler	246	67.05 N	157.52 W
Amboy, IL	260	41.44 N	89.20 W
Amboy, MN	264	43.59 N	94.10 W
Ambridge	254	40.36 N	80.14 W
Ambrose	264	48.57 N	103.29 W
Ambrosia Lake	266	35.26 N	107.54 W
Amchitka Island ▮	247a	51.30 N	179.00 E
Amchitka Pass Ш	247a	51.30 N	179.30 W
Ameagle	258	37.57 N	81.25 W
Amelia Court House	258	37.21 N	77.59 W
Amelia Island ▮	258	30.37 N	81.27 W
American, North Fork ≃	270	38.43 N	121.09 W
American, South Fork ≃	270	38.43 N	121.09 W
American Falls	268	42.47 N	112.51 W
American Falls Reservoir ⊜[1]	268	43.00 N	113.00 W
American Fork	266	40.23 N	111.48 W
Americus, GA	258	32.04 N	84.14 W
Americus, KS	264	38.30 N	96.16 W
Amery, MB	250	56.34 N	94.03 W
Amery, WI	256	45.19 N	92.22 W
Ames	256	42.02 N	93.37 W
Amesbury	254	42.51 N	70.56 W
Amet Sound Ш	252	45.47 N	63.13 W
Amherst, NS	252	45.49 N	64.14 W
Amherst, MA	254	42.23 N	72.31 W
Amherst, NY	254	42.58 N	78.48 W
Amherst, OH	254	41.24 N	82.14 W
Amherst, TX	262	34.01 N	102.25 W
Amherst, VA	258	37.35 N	79.03 W
Amherst, WI	256	44.27 N	89.17 W
Amherst, Île ▮	252	47.13 N	62.57 W
Amherstburg	256	42.06 N	83.06 W
Amherstdale	258	37.47 N	81.49 W
Amherst Island ▮	256	44.08 N	76.45 W
Amherstview	256	44.13 N	76.38 W
Amicalola Falls State Park ♠	258	34.33 N	84.15 W
Amidon	264	46.29 N	103.19 W
Amisk	250	52.33 N	111.04 W
Amisk Lake ⊜	250	54.35 N	102.13 W
Amistad, Presa de la (Amistad Reservoir) ⊜[1]	262	29.34 N	101.15 W
Amistad National Recreation Area ♠	262	29.32 N	101.12 W
Amistad Reservoir ⊜[1]	244	29.34 N	101.15 W
Amite	260	30.44 N	90.30 W
Amite ≃	260	30.12 N	90.35 W
Amite, East Fork ≃	260	30.58 N	90.51 W
Amity, AR	260	34.16 N	93.28 W
Amity, OR	268	45.07 N	123.12 W
Amlia Island ▮	246	52.06 N	173.30 W
Ammerman Mountain ▲	246	68.21 N	141.03 W
Ammon	268	43.30 N	111.57 W
Ammonoosuc ≃	254	44.10 N	72.02 W
Amnicon ≃	256	46.41 N	91.52 W
Amory	260	33.59 N	88.29 W
Amos	242	48.35 N	78.07 W
Amqui	252	49.28 N	67.26 W
Amsterdam	254	42.57 N	74.11 W
Amukta Island ▮	246	52.29 N	171.15 W
Amukta Pass Ш	246	52.25 N	172.00 W
Amundsen Gulf ◖	242	71.00 N	124.00 W
Anacoco	260	31.15 N	93.20 W
Anacoco, Bayou ≃	260	30.52 N	93.34 W
Anaconda	268	46.08 N	112.57 W
Anaconda Range ⛰	268	45.55 N	113.30 W
Anacortes	268	48.30 N	122.37 W
Anadarko	262	35.04 N	98.15 W
Anaheim	270	33.51 N	117.57 W
Anahim Lake	248	52.28 N	125.18 W
Anahola	272b	22.09 N	159.19 W
Anahola Bay ◖	272b	22.09 N	159.18 W
Anahuac	260	29.46 N	94.41 W
Anaktuvuk ≃	246	69.32 N	151.30 W
Anaktuvuk Pass	246	68.10 N	151.50 W
Anama Bay	250	51.56 N	98.05 W
Anamoose	264	47.53 N	100.15 W
Anamosa	256	42.07 N	91.17 W
Anastasia Island ▮	258	29.48 N	81.16 W
Anawalt	258	37.15 N	81.26 W
Ancaster	256	43.12 N	80.00 W
Anchorage	246	61.13 N	149.53 W
Anchor Point	246	59.46 N	151.52 W
Anchor Point ≻	246	59.47 N	151.52 W
Andalusia	260	31.19 N	86.29 W
Anderson, AL	260	34.50 N	87.16 W
Anderson, AK	246	64.21 N	149.10 W
Anderson, CA	270	40.27 N	122.18 W
Anderson, IN	260	40.10 N	85.41 W
Anderson, MO	260	36.39 N	94.27 W
Anderson, SC	258	34.31 N	82.39 W
Anderson, TX	262	30.29 N	95.59 W
Anderson ≃	242	69.43 N	128.58 W
Anderson, Mount ▲	268	47.43 N	123.20 W
Anderson Creek ≃	260	33.18 N	94.26 W
Anderson Dam	268	43.30 N	115.30 W
Anderson Lake ⊜	248	50.41 N	122.07 W
Anderson Ranch Reservoir ⊜[1]	268	43.25 N	115.20 W
Andersonville National Historical Site ⊥	258	32.12 N	84.07 W
Andes, Lake ⊜	264	43.11 N	98.27 W
Andover, ME	254	44.38 N	70.45 W
Andover, MA	254	42.39 N	71.08 W
Andover, NY	254	42.09 N	77.48 W
Andover, OH	254	41.36 N	80.34 W
Andover, SD	264	45.25 N	97.54 W
Andreafsky ≃	246	52.02 N	163.16 W
Andreafsky, East Fork ≃	246	62.03 N	163.07 W
Andreanof Islands ▮▮	247a	52.00 N	176.00 W
Andrew	248	53.53 N	112.21 W
Andrew Gordon Bay ◖	242	64.23 N	75.30 W
Andrews, IN	260	40.52 N	85.36 W
Andrews, NC	258	35.12 N	83.49 W
Andrews, SC	258	33.27 N	79.34 W
Andrews, TX	262	32.19 N	102.33 W
Androscoggin ≃	254	43.55 N	69.55 W
Anegam	266	32.23 N	112.02 W
Aneroid	250	49.43 N	107.20 W
Aneta	264	47.41 N	97.59 W
Angelina ≃	260	30.53 N	94.12 W
Angels Camp	270	38.04 N	120.32 W
Angier	258	35.31 N	78.44 W
Angijak Island ▮	242	65.40 N	62.15 W
Angikuni Lake ⊜	242	62.13 N	99.50 W
Anglais, Baie des ◖	252	49.15 N	68.07 W
Angle Inlet	264	49.21 N	95.04 W
Angleton	262	29.10 N	95.26 W
Angling ≃	250	56.45 N	93.36 W
Angling Lake ⊜	250	53.55 N	93.52 W
Angola, IN	260	41.38 N	85.00 W
Angola, NY	254	42.38 N	79.02 W
Angoon	246	57.30 N	134.35 W
Angostura Reservoir ⊜[1]	264	43.18 N	103.27 W
Anguilla	260	32.58 N	90.50 W
Anguille, Cape ≻	252	47.55 N	59.25 W
Angus	256	44.19 N	79.53 W
Angusville	250	50.44 N	101.01 W
Angwin	270	38.34 N	122.26 W
Aniak	246	61.35 N	159.33 W
Aniak ≃	246	61.34 N	159.30 W
Aniakchak National Monument ♠	246	56.50 N	157.50 W
Animas	266	31.57 N	108.48 W
Animas ≃	266	36.43 N	108.13 W
Animas Peak ▲	266	31.35 N	108.47 W
Animas Valley ∨	266	32.05 N	108.50 W
Anita	264	41.27 N	94.46 W
Anjigami Lake ⊜	256	47.51 N	84.34 W
Ankeny	256	41.44 N	93.36 W
Anna, IL	260	37.28 N	89.15 W
Anna, TX	262	33.21 N	96.33 W
Anna, Lake ⊜[1]	254	38.04 N	77.45 W
Annandale, MN	264	45.16 N	94.08 W
Annandale, VA	254	38.49 N	77.09 W
Annapolis	254	38.59 N	76.30 W
Annapolis Basin ◖	252	44.39 N	65.42 W
Annapolis Royal	252	44.45 N	65.31 W
Ann Arbor	256	42.18 N	83.45 W
Annette	246	55.03 N	131.34 W
Annette Island ▮	246	55.10 N	131.28 W
Annieopsquotch Mountains ⛰	252	48.20 N	57.30 W
Anniston	260	33.40 N	85.50 W
Annville, KY	258	37.19 N	83.58 W
Annville, PA	254	40.19 N	76.31 W
Anoka	256	45.11 N	93.23 W
Anselmo	264	41.37 N	99.52 W
Ansley	264	41.18 N	99.23 W
Anson	262	32.45 N	99.54 W
Anson Lake ⊜	250	56.45 N	100.47 W
Ansonville	258	35.06 N	80.07 W
Ansted	254	38.08 N	81.06 W
Antelope Creek ≃, NV	270	40.00 N	117.24 W
Antelope Creek ≃, OR	268	42.28 N	117.13 W
Antelope Creek ≃, SD	264	45.19 N	102.27 W
Antelope Creek ≃, WY	264	43.29 N	105.23 W
Antelope Island ▮	266	40.57 N	112.12 W
Antelope Peak ▲	270	41.19 N	114.58 W
Antelope Reservoir ⊜[1]	268	42.54 N	117.13 W
Antelope Wash ∨	270	39.33 N	116.17 W
Antero Reservoir ⊜[1]	266	39.00 N	105.55 W
Anthon	264	42.23 N	95.52 W
Anthony, FL	258	29.18 N	82.07 W
Anthony, KS	264	37.09 N	98.02 W
Anthony, NM	266	32.00 N	106.36 W
Anthony Creek ≃	258	37.54 N	80.20 W
Anthony Peak ▲	270	39.51 N	122.58 W
Anticosti, Île d' ▮	252	49.30 N	63.00 W
Antietam National Battlefield Site ⊥	254	39.24 N	77.47 W
Antigo	256	45.09 N	89.09 W
Antigonish	252	45.35 N	61.55 W
Antimony	266	38.07 N	111.55 W
Antioch	256	42.29 N	88.06 W
Antler ≃	250	49.08 N	101.00 W
Antlers	262	34.14 N	95.37 W
Anton	262	33.49 N	102.10 W
Anton Chico	266	35.12 N	105.09 W
Antonito	266	37.05 N	106.00 W
Antwerp	254	41.11 N	84.45 W
Anuenue ▮	272c	21.18 N	157.53 W
Anvik	246	62.40 N	160.12 W
Anvik ≃	246	62.39 N	160.14 W
Anvil Peak ▲	247a	52.00 N	179.35 E
Anvil Range ⛰	246	62.30 N	133.50 W
Anza-Borrego Desert State Park ♠	270	33.00 N	116.26 W
Anzac	250	56.27 N	111.02 W
Apache	262	34.54 N	98.22 W
Apache Junction	266	33.25 N	111.33 W
Apache Lake ⊜[1]	266	33.36 N	111.16 W
Apache Peak ▲	266	31.49 N	110.25 W
Apalachee ≃	258	33.32 N	83.17 W
Apalachee Bay ◖	258	30.00 N	84.13 W
Apalachicola	258	29.44 N	84.59 W
Apalachicola ≃	258	29.44 N	84.59 W
Apalachicola Bay ◖	258	29.40 N	85.00 W
Apeganau Lake ⊜	250	55.35 N	99.35 W
Apex	258	35.44 N	78.51 W
Apex Mountain ▲	246	62.28 N	138.04 W
Apishapa ≃	264	38.08 N	103.57 W
Apollo	254	40.35 N	79.34 W
Apopka, Lake ⊜	258	28.37 N	81.38 W
Apostle Islands ▮▮	256	46.50 N	90.30 W
Apostle Islands National Lakeshore ♠	256	46.55 N	91.00 W
Appalachia	258	36.54 N	82.47 W
Appalachian Mountains ⛰, N.A.	242	44.00 N	73.00 W
Appalachian Mountains ⛰, N.A.	244	41.00 N	77.00 W
Apple ≃, U.S.	256	42.11 N	90.14 W
Apple ≃, WI	256	45.09 N	92.45 W
Apple Creek ≃, IL	260	39.22 N	90.37 W
Apple Creek ≃, MO	260	37.35 N	89.32 W
Apple Creek ≃, ND	264	46.40 N	100.46 W
Applegate ≃	268	42.26 N	123.27 W
Apple Orchard Mountain ▲	258	37.31 N	79.31 W
Appleton, MN	264	45.12 N	96.01 W
Appleton, WI	256	44.16 N	88.25 W
Appleton City	260	38.11 N	94.02 W
Appling	258	33.33 N	82.19 W
Appomattox	258	37.21 N	78.50 W
Appomattox ≃	258	37.18 N	77.18 W
Appomattox Court House National Historical Park ♠	258	37.23 N	78.48 W
Aquarius Plateau ⛰[1]	266	38.05 N	111.40 W
Aquilla	262	31.51 N	97.13 W
Aquilla Creek ≃	262	31.40 N	97.10 W
Arab	260	34.19 N	86.29 W
Arabi	260	29.57 N	90.02 W
Arago, Cape ≻	268	43.18 N	124.25 W
Aragon	258	34.03 N	85.03 W
Aransas ≃	262	28.04 N	97.14 W
Aransas Pass	262	27.54 N	97.09 W
Arapaho	262	35.34 N	98.57 W
Arapahoe	264	40.18 N	99.54 W
Aravaipa Creek ≃	266	32.50 N	110.43 W
Arborfield	250	53.06 N	103.39 W
Arborg	250	50.55 N	97.15 W
Arbuckle	270	39.01 N	122.03 W
Arbuckle, Lake ⊜	258	27.41 N	81.24 W
Arbuckle Mountains ⛰	262	34.25 N	97.20 W
Arbuckles, Lake of the ⊜[1]	262	34.25 N	97.00 W
Arc, Bayou des ≃	260	35.00 N	91.30 W
Arcade, CA	270	34.02 N	118.15 W
Arcade, NY	254	42.32 N	78.25 W
Arcadia, CA	270	34.08 N	118.01 W
Arcadia, FL	258	27.14 N	81.52 W
Arcadia, IN	260	40.11 N	86.01 W
Arcadia, IA	264	42.05 N	95.03 W
Arcadia, KS	264	37.38 N	94.37 W
Arcadia, LA	260	32.33 N	92.55 W
Arcadia, MI	256	44.30 N	86.14 W
Arcadia, MO	260	37.34 N	90.38 W
Arcadia, NE	264	41.25 N	99.07 W
Arcadia, PA	254	40.47 N	78.51 W
Arcadia, SC	258	34.57 N	82.00 W
Arcadia, WI	256	44.15 N	91.30 W
Arcanum	254	39.59 N	84.33 W
Arcata	270	40.52 N	124.05 W
Arc Dome ▲	270	38.51 N	117.22 W
Archbold	254	41.31 N	84.18 W
Archdale	258	35.56 N	79.57 W
Archer	258	29.32 N	82.31 W
Archer City	262	33.36 N	98.38 W
Arches National Park ♠	266	38.42 N	109.45 W
Arco	268	43.38 N	113.18 W
Arcola, SK	250	49.37 N	102.30 W
Arcola, IL	260	39.41 N	88.19 W
Arcola, MS	260	33.16 N	90.53 W
Arcosanti	266	34.21 N	112.06 W
Arctic Bay	242	73.02 N	85.11 W
Arctic Red ≃	242	67.27 N	133.46 W
Arctic Red River	246	67.27 N	133.46 W
Arctic Village	246	68.08 N	145.19 W
Arden, MB	250	50.17 N	99.14 W
Arden, CA	270	38.36 N	121.23 W
Ardill	250	49.53 N	105.49 W
Ardmore, AL	260	34.59 N	86.52 W
Ardmore, OK	262	34.10 N	97.08 W
Ardmore, PA	254	40.01 N	75.18 W
Arena, Point ≻	270	38.57 N	123.44 W
Arenosa Creek ≃	262	28.52 N	96.44 W
Argenta	260	39.59 N	88.49 W
Argentia	252	47.18 N	53.59 W
Argonia	264	37.16 N	97.46 W
Argonne	256	45.40 N	88.53 W
Argos	260	41.14 N	86.15 W
Arguello, Point ≻	270	34.35 N	120.39 W
Argyle	264	48.20 N	96.49 W
Arichat	252	45.31 N	61.01 W
Arikaree ≃	264	40.01 N	101.56 W
Arikaree, North Fork ≃	264	39.39 N	102.57 W
Arikaree, South Fork ≃	264	39.39 N	102.57 W
Aristazabal Island ▮	248	52.30 N	129.05 W
Ariton	260	31.36 N	85.43 W
Arizona □[3], U.S.	244		
	266	34.00 N	112.00 W
Arjay	258	36.48 N	83.41 W
Arkabutla Lake ⊜[1]	260	34.45 N	90.06 W
Arkadelphia	260	34.07 N	93.04 W
Arkansas □[3]	244	34.50 N	93.40 W
Arkansas ≃, U.S.	244		
	260	33.48 N	91.04 W
Arkansas, Salt Fork ≃	262	36.36 N	97.03 W
Arkansas City, AR	260	33.36 N	91.12 W
Arkansas City, KS	264	37.04 N	97.02 W
Arkansas Post National Memorial ⊥	260	33.55 N	91.26 W
Arkoma	260	35.21 N	94.26 W
Arkport	254	42.24 N	77.42 W
Arlee	268	47.10 N	114.05 W
Arlington, GA	258	31.27 N	84.44 W
Arlington, IA	256	42.45 N	91.40 W
Arlington, KS	264	37.54 N	98.11 W
Arlington, KY	260	36.47 N	89.01 W
Arlington, MN	264	44.36 N	94.05 W
Arlington, NE	264	41.27 N	96.21 W
Arlington, OH	254	40.54 N	83.39 W
Arlington, OR	268	45.16 N	120.13 W
Arlington, SD	264	44.22 N	97.08 W
Arlington, TN	260	35.18 N	89.40 W
Arlington, TX	262	32.44 N	97.07 W
Arlington, VT	254	43.05 N	73.09 W
Arlington, VA	254	38.52 N	77.05 W
Arlington, WA	268	48.12 N	122.08 W
Arlington Heights	256	42.05 N	87.59 W
Arm ≃	250	50.46 N	105.00 W
Arma	264	37.33 N	94.42 W
Armada	256	42.51 N	82.53 W
Armells Creek ≃	268	47.37 N	108.40 W
Armijo	266	35.03 N	106.41 W
Armit Lake ⊜	242	64.10 N	91.32 W
Armona	270	36.19 N	119.42 W
Armour	264	43.19 N	98.21 W
Armstrong, BC	248	50.27 N	119.12 W
Armstrong, IA	264	43.24 N	94.29 W
Armstrong, MO	260	39.16 N	92.42 W
Armstrong, Mount ▲	246	63.12 N	133.16 W
Armstrong Station	242	50.18 N	89.02 W
Arnaud ≃	242	59.59 N	69.46 W
Arnaudville	260	30.24 N	91.56 W
Arnett	262	36.08 N	99.46 W
Arnold, CA	270	38.15 N	120.21 W
Arnold, MN	256	46.53 N	92.05 W
Arnold, MO	260	38.26 N	90.23 W
Arnold, NE	264	41.26 N	100.12 W
Arnolds Park	264	43.22 N	95.08 W
Arnprior	256	45.26 N	76.21 W
Aroostook ≃	252	46.48 N	67.45 W
Aropuk Lake ⊜	246	61.12 N	163.50 W
Arp	262	32.13 N	95.04 W
Arrey	266	32.51 N	107.19 W
Arriba	264	39.17 N	103.17 W
Arrow Creek ≃	268	47.43 N	109.50 W
Arrow Dam →[6]	248	49.20 N	117.49 W
Arrow Lake ⊜	256	48.08 N	90.18 W
Arrowrock Reservoir ⊜[1]	268	43.36 N	115.51 W
Arrowsmith Bay ◖	242	68.00 N	95.15 W
Arrowwood	248	50.44 N	113.09 W
Arroyo Grande	270	35.07 N	120.34 W
Arroyo Hondo	266	36.32 N	105.40 W
Arsenault Lake ⊜	250	55.06 N	108.30 W
Artesia, MS	260	33.25 N	88.39 W
Artesia, NM	262	32.51 N	104.24 W
Artesian	264	44.00 N	97.55 W
Arthabaska	254	46.02 N	71.55 W
Arthur, ON	256	43.50 N	80.32 W
Arthur, IL	260	39.43 N	88.28 W
Arthur, NE	264	41.35 N	101.41 W
Arthur, ND	264	47.06 N	97.13 W
Arthur, TN	258	36.33 N	83.40 W
Arthur Fiord ◖[2]	242	76.33 N	93.11 W
Artillery Lake ⊜	242	63.09 N	107.52 W
Arvada	266	39.50 N	105.05 W
Arvida	252	48.25 N	71.11 W
Arvin	270	35.12 N	118.50 W
Arvonia	258	37.41 N	78.20 W
Asbestos	254	45.46 N	71.57 W
Asbury Park	254	40.13 N	74.01 W
Ashburn	258	31.43 N	83.39 W
Ash Creek ≃	270	41.05 N	121.08 W
Ashcroft	248	50.43 N	121.17 W
Ashdown	260	33.41 N	94.08 W
Asheboro	258	35.42 N	79.49 W
Ashern	250	51.11 N	98.21 W
Asherton	262	28.27 N	99.46 W
Asheville	258	35.34 N	82.33 W
Asheweig ≃	242	54.17 N	87.12 W
Ash Flat	260	36.14 N	91.37 W
Ashford	258	31.11 N	85.14 W
Ash Fork	266	35.13 N	112.29 W
Ash Grove	260	37.19 N	93.35 W
Ashland, AL	260	33.16 N	85.50 W
Ashland, IL	260	34.53 N	90.01 W
Ashland, KS	264	37.11 N	99.46 W
Ashland, KY	254	38.28 N	82.38 W
Ashland, ME	252	46.38 N	68.24 W
Ashland, MS	260	34.50 N	89.11 W
Ashland, MO	260	38.47 N	92.16 W
Ashland, MT	268	45.35 N	106.16 W
Ashland, NE	264	41.03 N	96.22 W
Ashland, NH	254	43.42 N	71.38 W
Ashland, OH	254	40.52 N	82.19 W
Ashland, OR	268	42.12 N	122.42 W
Ashland, PA	254	40.47 N	76.21 W
Ashland, VA	258	37.45 N	77.29 W
Ashland, WI	256	46.35 N	90.53 W
Ashland, Mount ▲	268	42.05 N	122.43 W
Ashland City	260	36.16 N	87.04 W
Ashley, IL	260	38.20 N	89.11 W
Ashley, MI	256	43.11 N	84.29 W
Ashley, ND	264	46.02 N	99.22 W
Ashley, OH	254	40.25 N	82.57 W
Ashley Creek ≃	266	40.21 N	109.22 W
Ashmore	260	39.32 N	88.01 W
Ashtabula	254	41.52 N	80.48 W
Ashtabula, Lake ⊜[1]	264	47.11 N	97.58 W
Ashton, ID	268	44.04 N	111.27 W
Ashton, IL	260	41.52 N	89.13 W
Ashton, IA	264	43.19 N	95.47 W
Ashton, NE	264	41.15 N	98.48 W
Ashuanipi Lake ⊜	242	52.35 N	66.10 W
Ashuelot ≃	254	42.46 N	72.29 W
Ashville, AL	260	33.50 N	86.15 W
Ashville, OH	254	39.43 N	82.57 W
Ashwaubenon	256	44.29 N	88.03 W
Asipoquobah Lake ⊜	250	53.40 N	91.15 W
Asotin	268	46.20 N	117.03 W
Aspen	266	39.11 N	106.49 W
Aspen Butte ▲	268	42.19 N	122.05 W
Aspen Lake ⊜	268	42.18 N	122.00 W
Aspermont	262	33.08 N	100.14 W
Aspid, Mount ▲	246	53.30 N	167.33 W
Aspy Bay ◖	252	46.55 N	60.25 W
Asquith	250	52.08 N	107.13 W
Assaikwatamo ≃	250	56.52 N	95.50 W
Assateague Island ▮	254	38.05 N	75.10 W
Assateague Island National Seashore ♠	254	38.18 N	75.19 W
Assean Lake ⊜	250	56.13 N	96.30 W
Assiniboia	250	49.38 N	105.59 W
Assiniboine ≃	250	49.53 N	97.08 W
Assiniboine, Mount ▲	242	50.52 N	115.39 W
Assiniboine Indian Reserve →[4]	250	50.21 N	103.28 W
Assinika ≃	250	52.37 N	96.10 W
Assumption	260	39.31 N	89.03 W
Astoria, IL	260	40.14 N	90.21 W
Astoria, OR	268	46.11 N	123.50 W
Atakakup Indian Reserve →[4]	250	53.24 N	106.55 W
Atascadero	270	35.29 N	120.40 W
Atascosa ≃	262	28.26 N	98.12 W
Atchafalaya ≃	260	29.53 N	91.28 W
Atchafalaya Bay ◖	260	29.25 N	91.20 W
Atchison	264	39.34 N	95.07 W
Athabasca	248	54.43 N	113.17 W
Athabasca ≃	242	58.40 N	110.50 W
Athabasca, Lake ⊜	242	59.07 N	110.00 W
Athalmer	248	50.32 N	116.02 W
Athapapuskow Lake ⊜	250	54.33 N	101.40 W
Athena	268	45.49 N	118.30 W
Athens, ON	254	44.38 N	75.57 W
Athens, AL	260	34.48 N	86.58 W
Athens, GA	258	33.57 N	83.23 W
Athens, IL	260	39.58 N	89.44 W
Athens, LA	260	32.39 N	93.01 W
Athens, ME	254	44.55 N	69.41 W
Athens, MI	256	42.05 N	85.14 W
Athens, NY	254	42.16 N	73.49 W
Athens, OH	254	39.20 N	82.06 W
Athens, PA	254	41.57 N	76.31 W
Athens, TN	258	35.27 N	84.36 W
Athens, TX	262	32.12 N	95.51 W
Athens, WV	258	37.25 N	81.01 W
Athens, WI	256	45.02 N	90.05 W
Athol	254	42.36 N	72.14 W
Aticonipi, Lac ⊜	252	51.52 N	59.22 W
Atikokan	256	48.45 N	91.37 W
Atikonak Lake ⊜	242	52.40 N	64.30 W
Atka	246	52.12 N	174.12 W
Atka Island ▮	246	52.15 N	174.30 W
Atkins	260	35.14 N	92.56 W
Atkinson, IL	260	41.25 N	90.01 W
Atkinson, NE	264	42.32 N	98.59 W
Atkinson, NC	258	34.28 N	78.06 W
Atkinson Lake ⊜	250	55.59 N	94.48 W
Atlanta, GA	258	33.45 N	84.23 W
Atlanta, IL	260	40.16 N	89.14 W
Atlanta, MI	256	45.00 N	84.09 W
Atlanta, MO	260	39.54 N	92.29 W
Atlanta, TX	260	33.07 N	94.10 W
Atlantic, IA	264	41.24 N	95.01 W
Atlantic, NC	258	34.54 N	76.20 W
Atlantic Beach	258	30.20 N	81.24 W
Atlantic City	254	39.22 N	74.26 W
Atlantic Ocean ≋[1]	244	50.00 N	15.00 W
Atlantic Peak ▲	268	42.37 N	109.00 W
Atlin	246	59.35 N	133.42 W
Atlin Lake ⊜	246	59.20 N	133.45 W
Atmore	260	31.02 N	87.29 W
Atna Peak ▲	248	53.57 N	128.03 W
Atna Range ⛰	248	55.25 N	127.00 W
Atnarko ≃	248	52.22 N	126.04 W
Atoka	262	34.23 N	96.08 W
Atomic Energy Commission Nevada Test Site ☢[3]	270	37.00 N	116.10 W
Atomic Energy Commission Savannah River Plant ☢[3]	258	33.15 N	81.40 W
Atrisco	266	34.59 N	106.41 W
Attalla	260	34.01 N	86.05 W
Attawapiskat	242	52.55 N	82.26 W
Attawapiskat ≃	242	52.57 N	82.18 W
Attawapiskat Lake ⊜	242	52.18 N	87.54 W
Attica, IN	260	40.17 N	87.15 W
Attica, KS	264	37.15 N	98.13 W
Attica, NY	254	42.52 N	78.17 W
Attica, OH	254	41.04 N	82.53 W
Attleboro	254	41.56 N	71.17 W
Attoyac Bayou ≃	260	31.29 N	94.18 W
Attu	247a	52.56 N	174.45 E
Attu Island ▮	247a	52.55 N	173.00 E
Atwater, SK	250	50.47 N	102.10 W
Atwater, CA	270	37.21 N	120.36 W
Atwater, MN	264	45.08 N	94.47 W
Atwood, IL	260	39.48 N	88.28 W
Atwood, KS	264	39.48 N	101.03 W
Atwood, TN	260	35.59 N	88.41 W
Auau Channel Ш	272a	20.51 N	156.45 W
Aubinadong ≃	256	46.51 N	83.22 W
Aubrey Cliffs •[4]	266	35.45 N	113.00 W
Aubry Lake ⊜	242	67.23 N	126.30 W
Auburn, AL	258	32.36 N	85.29 W
Auburn, CA	270	38.54 N	121.04 W
Auburn, IL	260	39.36 N	89.45 W
Auburn, IN	260	41.22 N	85.04 W
Auburn, KY	260	36.52 N	86.43 W
Auburn, ME	254	44.06 N	70.14 W
Auburn, MA	254	42.12 N	71.50 W
Auburn, MI	256	43.36 N	84.04 W
Auburn, NE	264	40.23 N	95.51 W
Auburn, NY	254	42.56 N	76.34 W
Auburn, WA	268	47.18 N	122.13 W
Aucilla ≃	258	30.05 N	83.59 W
Audubon	264	41.43 N	94.55 W
Auglaize ≃	254	41.17 N	84.21 W
Au Gres	256	44.03 N	83.42 W
Au Gres ≃	256	44.02 N	83.40 W
Au Gres, East Branch ≃	256	44.05 N	83.41 W
Augusta, AR	260	35.17 N	91.22 W
Augusta, GA	258	33.29 N	81.57 W
Augusta, IL	260	40.14 N	90.57 W
Augusta, KS	264	37.41 N	96.58 W
Augusta, KY	254	38.46 N	84.00 W
Augusta, ME	254	44.19 N	69.47 W
Augusta, MT	268	47.30 N	112.24 W
Augusta, WI	256	44.41 N	91.07 W
Augustine Island ▮	246	59.22 N	153.28 W
Augustines, Lac des ⊜	256	47.37 N	76.05 W
Aulander	258	36.14 N	77.06 W
Aulitivik Island ▮	242	69.32 N	67.50 W
Aulneau Peninsula ≻[1]	250	49.23 N	94.29 W
Ault	264	40.30 N	104.45 W
Aurelia	264	42.42 N	95.28 W
Aurora, ON	256	44.00 N	79.28 W
Aurora, AK	246	64.51 N	147.46 W
Aurora, CO	264	39.44 N	104.52 W
Aurora, IL	260	42.46 N	88.19 W
Aurora, IN	260	39.04 N	84.54 W
Aurora, ME	252	44.51 N	68.20 W
Aurora, MN	256	47.31 N	92.14 W
Aurora, MO	260	36.58 N	93.43 W
Aurora, NE	264	40.52 N	98.00 W
Aurora, NC	258	35.18 N	76.47 W
Aurora, NY	254	42.46 N	76.42 W
Aurora, OH	254	41.19 N	81.21 W
Aurora, UT	266	38.55 N	111.56 W
Aurora, WV	254	39.19 N	79.33 W
Ausable ≃, ON	256	43.19 N	81.46 W
Au Sable ≃, MI	256	44.25 N	83.20 W
Au Sable, North Branch ≃	256	44.40 N	84.23 W
Au Sable, South Branch ≃	256	44.40 N	84.23 W
Au Sable Forks	254	44.27 N	73.41 W
Au Sable Point ≻	256	44.20 N	83.20 W
Austin, MB	250	49.57 N	98.56 W
Austin, IN	260	38.45 N	85.48 W
Austin, MN	256	43.40 N	92.59 W
Austin, NV	270	39.30 N	117.04 W
Austin, PA	254	41.38 N	78.05 W
Austin, TX	262	30.16 N	97.45 W
Austin Channel Ш	242	75.35 N	103.25 W
Austinville	258	36.51 N	80.55 W
Australia Mountain ▲	246	63.36 N	138.08 W
Auteuil, Lac d' ⊜	252	50.38 N	61.17 W
Aux Barques, Pointe ≻	256	44.04 N	82.58 W
Auxier	258	37.44 N	82.46 W
Auxvasse	260	39.01 N	91.54 W
Auxvasse Creek ≃	260	38.41 N	91.49 W
Ava, IL	260	37.53 N	89.30 W
Ava, MO	260	36.57 N	92.40 W
Avalon	270	33.49 N	118.16 W
Avalon Peninsula ≻[1]	252	47.30 N	53.30 W
Avant	262	36.29 N	96.04 W
Avatanak Island ▮	246	54.03 N	165.19 W
Avenal	270	36.00 N	120.08 W
Avery, ID	268	47.15 N	115.49 W
Avery, TX	260	33.33 N	94.47 W
Avery Island	260	29.55 N	91.55 W
Avis	254	41.11 N	77.19 W
Avoca, IA	264	41.29 N	95.20 W
Avoca, NY	254	42.25 N	77.25 W
Avola	248	51.47 N	119.19 W
Avon, IL	256	40.40 N	90.26 W
Avon, MN	264	45.37 N	94.27 W
Avon, MT	268	46.36 N	112.36 W
Avon, NC	258	35.21 N	75.30 W
Avon, NY	254	42.55 N	77.45 W
Avon, SD	264	43.00 N	98.04 W
Avon ≃	252	45.10 N	64.15 W
Avondale, AZ	266	33.26 N	112.21 W
Avondale, CO	264	38.14 N	104.21 W
Avonlea	250	50.00 N	105.04 W
Avonmore	254	40.32 N	79.28 W
Avon Park	258	27.36 N	81.31 W
Awuna ≃	246	69.04 N	155.30 W
Axis	260	30.55 N	88.02 W
Axtell, KS	264	39.52 N	96.15 W
Axtell, NE	264	40.29 N	99.08 W
Ayden	258	35.25 N	77.20 W
Ayer	254	42.34 N	71.35 W
Aylmer, Mount ▲	248	51.19 N	115.26 W
Aylmer, Passage Ш	252	50.33 N	59.23 W
Aylmer East	254	45.24 N	75.51 W
Aylmer Lake ⊜	242	64.05 N	108.30 W
Aylmer West	256	42.46 N	80.59 W
Aylsham	250	53.11 N	103.49 W
Aynor	258	34.00 N	79.12 W
Ayr	256	43.17 N	80.27 W
Azalea Park	258	28.32 N	81.15 W
Aztec	266	36.49 N	107.59 W
Aztec Peak ▲	266	33.48 N	110.55 W
Aztec Ruins National Monument ♠	266	36.51 N	108.10 W
Azure Lake ⊜	248	52.23 N	120.00 W
B			
Babb	248	48.51 N	113.26 W
Babbitt, MN	256	47.43 N	91.57 W
Babbitt, NV	270	38.39 N	118.37 W
Babel, Mont de ▲	252	51.27 N	68.42 W
Babine	248	55.19 N	126.37 W
Babine ≃	248	55.42 N	127.40 W
Babine Lake ⊜	248	54.45 N	126.00 W
Babine Range ⛰	248	55.00 N	126.25 W
Baboquivari Mountains ⛰	266	31.45 N	111.35 W
Baboquivari Peak ▲	266	31.46 N	111.35 W
Baccalieu Island ▮	252	48.08 N	52.48 W
Back ≃	242	67.15 N	95.15 W
Backbone Ranges ⛰	246	63.30 N	129.00 W
Back Creek ≃	254	38.02 N	79.54 W
Baconton	258	31.23 N	84.10 W
Bad ≃, MI	256	43.18 N	84.06 W
Bad ≃, SD	264	44.22 N	100.22 W
Bad ≃, WI	256	46.38 N	90.40 W
Bad, South Fork ≃	264	44.02 N	101.40 W
Bad Axe	256	43.48 N	83.00 W
Baddeck	252	46.07 N	60.45 W
Badger, NF	252	48.59 N	56.02 W
Badger, MN	264	48.47 N	96.01 W
Badger Creek ≃, CO	264	40.17 N	103.42 W
Badger Creek ≃, CO	266	38.28 N	105.52 W
Badin Lake ⊜[1]	258	35.27 N	80.06 W
Badlands ⛰	264	46.45 N	103.30 W
Badlands ⛰[2]	264	43.30 N	102.20 W
Badlands National Park ♠	264	43.47 N	102.15 W
Bad River Indian Reservation →[4]	256	46.33 N	90.40 W
Badwater Creek ≃	268	43.17 N	108.08 W
Baezaeko ≃	248	53.09 N	123.48 W
Baffin Bay ◖, N.A.	242	73.00 N	66.00 W
Baffin Bay ◖, TX	262	27.15 N	97.33 W
Baffin Island ▮	242	68.00 N	70.00 W
Bagdad, AZ	266	34.34 N	113.11 W
Bagdad, FL	260	30.36 N	87.02 W
Baggs	268	41.02 N	107.39 W
Bagley	264	47.31 N	95.24 W
Bagnell Dam →[6]	260	38.11 N	92.39 W
Baie-Comeau	252	49.13 N	68.10 W

Symbols in the index entries are identified on page 273.

Name	Page	Lat ° ′	Long ° ′
Baie-Comeau-Hauterive, Parc de ♠	252	49.30 N	68.05 W
Baie-des-ha! Ha!	252	50.56 N	58.56 W
Baie-du-Renard	252	49.17 N	61.50 W
Baie-Johan-Beetz	252	50.17 N	62.48 W
Baies, Lac des ⊜	256	47.18 N	77.40 W
Baie-Saint-Claire	252	49.54 N	64.30 W
Baie-Saint-Paul	252	47.27 N	70.30 W
Baie-Trinité	252	49.25 N	67.18 W
Baie Verte	252	49.56 N	56.11 W
Bailey	258	35.47 N	78.07 W
Baillie ≃	242	65.10 N	104.24 W
Baillie-Hamilton Island ❙	242	75.53 N	94.35 W
Baillie Islands ❙❙	242	70.33 N	128.10 W
Bainbridge, GA	258	30.54 N	84.34 W
Bainbridge, NY	254	42.18 N	75.29 W
Bainbridge, OH	254	39.14 N	83.16 W
Bainville	264	48.08 N	104.13 W
Baird	262	32.24 N	99.24 W
Baird Inlet ⊂	246	60.45 N	164.00 W
Baird Mountains ⛰	246	67.35 N	161.30 W
Baird Peninsula ≻[1]	242	69.00 N	75.15 W
Bairoil	268	42.15 N	107.33 W
Baker, CA	270	35.16 N	116.04 W
Baker, FL	260	30.48 N	86.40 W
Baker, LA	260	30.35 N	91.10 W
Baker, MT	264	46.22 N	104.17 W
Baker, OR	268	44.47 N	117.50 W
Baker, Mount ∧	268	48.47 N	121.49 W
Baker Butte ∧	266	34.27 N	111.22 W
Baker Creek ≃	248	52.59 N	122.30 W
Baker Island ❙	246	55.20 N	133.36 W
Baker Lake	242	64.15 N	96.00 W
Baker Lake ⊜	242	64.10 N	95.30 W
Bakersfield	270	35.23 N	119.01 W
Bakersville	258	36.01 N	82.09 W
Balaton	264	44.14 N	95.52 W
Balcarres	250	50.48 N	103.33 W
Balcones Escarpment •[4]	262	29.30 N	99.15 W
Bald Eagle Creek ≃	254	41.08 N	77.24 W
Baldhill Creek ≃	264	47.09 N	98.03 W
Bald Knob	260	35.19 N	91.34 W
Bald Knob ∧	258	37.56 N	79.51 W
Bald Knoll ∧	268	42.24 N	110.29 W
Bald Mountain ∧, CT	254	41.59 N	72.25 W
Bald Mountain ∧, NJ	254	41.07 N	74.12 W
Bald Mountain ∧, OR	268	44.36 N	117.53 W
Bald Mountain ∧, OR	268	43.16 N	121.21 W
Baldock Lake ⊜	250	56.33 N	97.57 W
Baldur	250	49.23 N	99.15 W
Baldwin, FL	258	30.18 N	81.59 W
Baldwin, LA	260	29.51 N	91.33 W
Baldwin, MI	256	43.54 N	85.51 W
Baldwin, WI	256	44.58 N	92.22 W
Baldwin City	264	38.47 N	95.11 W
Baldwin Peninsula ≻[1]	246	66.44 N	162.15 W
Baldwinsville	254	43.09 N	76.20 W
Baldwinville	254	42.36 N	72.05 W
Baldwyn	260	34.31 N	88.38 W
Baldy Mountain ∧, BC	248	51.28 N	120.02 W
Baldy Mountain ∧, MB	250	51.28 N	100.44 W
Baldy Mountain ∧, MT	268	48.09 N	109.39 W
Baldy Mountain ∧, NM	266	36.38 N	105.13 W
Baldy Peak ∧	266	33.55 N	109.35 W
Baleine, Rivière à la ≃	242	58.15 N	67.40 W
Balfour	258	35.21 N	82.28 W
Ball	260	31.25 N	92.25 W
Ballantine	268	45.57 N	108.09 W
Ball Ground	258	34.21 N	84.23 W
Ballinger	262	31.44 N	99.57 W
Ballston Spa	254	43.00 N	73.51 W
Ballville	254	41.20 N	83.09 W
Balmertown	250	51.04 N	93.44 W
Balmorhea	262	30.59 N	103.45 W
Balsam Lake	256	45.27 N	92.27 W
Balsam Lake ⊜	256	44.35 N	78.50 W
Baltic Bay ⊂	256	48.22 N	83.43 W
Baltimore, MD	254	39.17 N	76.37 W
Baltimore, OH	254	39.51 N	82.36 W
Baluarte, Arroyo ∨	262	27.09 N	98.07 W
Balzac	248	51.10 N	114.01 W
Bamaji Lake ⊜	250	51.09 N	91.25 W
Bamberg	258	33.17 N	81.02 W
Bamfield	248	48.50 N	125.08 W
Banana River ⊂	258	28.25 N	80.38 W
Bancroft, ON	256	45.03 N	77.51 W
Bancroft, ID	268	42.43 N	111.53 W
Bancroft, IA	264	43.18 N	94.13 W
Bancroft, NE	264	42.00 N	96.34 W
Banded Peak ∧	266	37.06 N	106.38 W
Bandelier National Monument ♠	266	35.45 N	106.20 W
Bandera	262	29.44 N	99.04 W
Bandon	268	43.07 N	124.25 W
Banff	248	51.10 N	115.34 W
Banff National Park ♠	248	51.38 N	116.22 W
Bangor, ME	254	44.49 N	68.47 W
Bangor, MI	256	42.18 N	86.07 W
Bangor, PA	254	40.52 N	75.13 W
Bangs	262	31.43 N	99.08 W
Bangs, Mount ∧	266	36.48 N	113.51 W
Banister ≃	258	36.42 N	78.48 W
Banks	260	31.44 N	85.50 W
Banks, Point ≻	246	58.36 N	152.18 W
Banksian ≃	250	53.41 N	94.10 W
Banks Island ❙, BC	248	53.25 N	130.10 W
Banks Island ❙, NT	242	73.15 N	121.30 W
Banks Lake ⊜[1]	268	47.45 N	119.15 W
Banner Elk	258	36.12 N	81.54 W
Bannertown	258	36.29 N	80.34 W
Banning	270	33.56 N	116.52 W
Bannock Creek ≃	268	42.53 N	112.40 W
Bannock Peak ∧	268	42.36 N	112.42 W
Bapchule	266	33.12 N	111.50 W
Baptiste Lake ⊜	256	45.07 N	78.02 W
Baraboo	256	43.28 N	89.45 W
Baraboo Range ⛰[2]	256	43.25 N	89.40 W
Barachois Pond Provincial Park ♠	252	48.26 N	58.14 W
Baraga	256	46.47 N	88.30 W
Baranof	246	57.05 N	134.50 W
Baranof Island ❙	246	57.00 N	135.00 W
Barataria	260	29.44 N	90.08 W
Barataria Bay ⊂	260	29.22 N	89.57 W
Barbers Point ≻	272c	21.18 N	158.07 W
Barbers Point Naval Air Station ■	272c	21.19 N	158.04 W
Barberton	254	41.01 N	81.36 W
Barboursville	254	38.24 N	82.18 W
Barbourville	258	36.52 N	83.53 W
Bardoux, Lac ⊜	252	51.09 N	67.50 W
Bardstown	260	37.49 N	85.28 W
Bardswell Group ❙❙	248	52.10 N	128.20 W
Bardwell	260	36.52 N	89.01 W
Bardwell Lake ⊜[1]	262	32.16 N	96.39 W
Bar Harbor	254	44.23 N	68.13 W
Baring, Cape ≻	242	70.05 N	117.20 W
Baring Channel ⊔	242	73.48 N	98.50 W
Bark ≃	256	42.55 N	88.50 W
Barkerville	248	53.04 N	121.31 W
Barkerville Historical Park ⊥	248	53.04 N	121.30 W
Bark Lake ⊜, ON	256	46.54 N	82.28 W
Bark Lake ⊜, ON	256	45.27 N	77.51 W
Barkley, Lake ⊜[1]	260	36.40 N	87.55 W
Barkley Sound ⊔	248	48.53 N	125.20 W
Barksdale	262	29.44 N	100.02 W
Barling	260	34.20 N	94.17 W
Barlow	260	37.03 N	89.03 W
Barnegat	254	39.45 N	74.13 W
Barnegat Bay ⊂	254	39.52 N	74.07 W
Barnesboro	254	40.40 N	78.47 W
Barnes Lake ⊜	250	56.23 N	98.06 W
Barnesville, GA	258	33.04 N	84.09 W
Barnesville, MN	264	46.39 N	96.25 W
Barnesville, OH	254	39.59 N	81.11 W
Barnhart	262	31.08 N	101.10 W
Barnsdall	262	36.34 N	96.10 W
Barnstable	254	41.42 N	70.18 W
Barnwell, AB	248	49.46 N	112.15 W
Barnwell, SC	258	33.15 N	81.23 W
Barons	248	50.00 N	113.05 W
Barrackville	254	39.30 N	80.10 W
Barre, MA	254	42.26 N	72.06 W
Barre, VT	254	44.12 N	72.30 W
Barren ≃	260	37.11 N	86.37 W
Barren Islands ❙❙	246	58.55 N	152.15 W
Barren River Lake ⊜[1]	260	36.45 N	86.02 W
Barrhead	248	54.08 N	114.24 W
Barrie	256	44.24 N	79.40 W
Barrie Island ❙	256	45.55 N	82.40 W
Barrilla Draw ∨	262	31.21 N	103.23 W
Barrington	252	43.34 N	65.34 W
Barrington Lake ⊜	250	56.55 N	100.15 W
Barron	256	45.24 N	91.51 W
Barrow	246	71.17 N	156.47 W
Barrow, Point ≻	246	71.23 N	156.30 W
Barrows	250	52.49 N	101.27 W
Barrow Strait ⊔	242	74.21 N	94.10 W
Barry	260	39.42 N	91.02 W
Barrys Bay	256	45.29 N	77.41 W
Barryton	256	43.45 N	85.09 W
Barstow, CA	270	34.54 N	117.01 W
Barstow, TX	262	31.28 N	103.24 W
Barter Island ❙	246	70.08 N	143.35 W
Bartholomew, Bayou ≃	260	32.43 N	92.04 W
Bartlesville	262	36.45 N	95.59 W
Bartlett, NE	264	41.53 N	98.33 W
Bartlett, NH	254	44.05 N	71.17 W
Bartlett, TN	260	35.12 N	89.52 W
Bartlett, TX	262	30.48 N	97.26 W
Bartlett Cove	246	58.27 N	135.55 W
Bartlett Reservoir ⊜[1]	266	33.52 N	111.37 W
Bartletts Harbour	252	50.57 N	57.00 W
Bartley	264	40.15 N	100.18 W
Barton	254	44.45 N	72.11 W
Bartonville	256	40.39 N	89.39 W
Bartow, FL	258	27.54 N	81.50 W
Bartow, GA	258	32.53 N	82.29 W
Barview	268	43.21 N	124.18 W
Barwick	258	30.54 N	83.44 W
Bashaw	248	52.35 N	112.58 W
Basile	260	30.29 N	92.36 W
Basin, MT	268	46.16 N	112.16 W
Basin, WY	268	44.23 N	108.02 W
Basin Lake ⊜	250	52.38 N	105.18 W
Baskahegan Lake ⊜	254	45.30 N	67.48 W
Baskatong, Réservoir ⊜[1]	242	46.48 N	75.50 W
Basket Lake ⊜	250	49.43 N	92.00 W
Bassano	248	50.47 N	112.28 W
Bassett, NE	264	42.35 N	99.32 W
Bassett, VA	258	36.46 N	79.59 W
Bassett Creek ≃	260	31.25 N	87.56 W
Bassett Peak ∧	266	32.30 N	110.17 W
Bassetts Creek ≃	260	31.27 N	87.55 W
Bassfield	260	31.30 N	89.44 W
Bass Harbor	254	44.16 N	68.19 W
Bass River	252	45.25 N	63.47 W
Basswood Lake ⊜, ON	256	46.20 N	83.23 W
Basswood Lake ⊜, N.A.	244	48.06 N	91.40 W
Bastian	258	37.09 N	81.09 W
Bastrop, LA	260	32.47 N	91.55 W
Bastrop, TX	262	30.07 N	97.19 W
Batavia, IL	260	41.51 N	88.19 W
Batavia, IA	256	41.00 N	92.10 W
Batavia, NY	254	43.00 N	78.11 W
Batavia, OH	254	39.05 N	84.11 W
Batchawana ≃	256	46.55 N	84.32 W
Batchawana Mountain ∧	256	47.04 N	84.24 W
Batesburg	258	33.54 N	81.33 W
Bates Creek ≃	268	42.41 N	106.37 W
Batesville, AR	260	35.46 N	91.39 W
Batesville, IN	260	39.18 N	85.13 W
Batesville, MS	260	34.18 N	90.00 W
Batesville, TX	262	28.57 N	99.37 W
Bath, ME	254	43.55 N	69.49 W
Bath, NY	254	42.20 N	77.19 W
Bathgate	264	48.53 N	97.29 W
Bathurst	252	47.36 N	65.39 W
Bathurst, Cape ≻	242	70.35 N	128.00 W
Bathurst Inlet	242	66.50 N	108.01 W
Bathurst Inlet ⊂	242	68.10 N	108.50 W
Bathurst Island ❙	242	76.00 N	100.30 W
Batoche Rectory National Historic Site ⊥	250	52.41 N	106.02 W
Baton Rouge	260	30.23 N	91.11 W
Batson	260	30.15 N	94.37 W
Battle ≃	242	52.42 N	108.15 W
Battle Creek, IA	264	42.19 N	95.36 W
Battle Creek, MI	256	42.19 N	85.11 W
Battle Creek, NE	264	42.00 N	97.36 W
Battle Creek ≃, N.A.	268	48.36 N	109.11 W
Battle Creek ≃, CA	270	40.21 N	122.11 W
Battle Creek ≃, ID	268	42.14 N	116.32 W
Battle Creek ≃, TX	262	32.50 N	98.58 W
Battle Creek, North Fork ≃	270	40.26 N	122.00 W
Battle Creek, South Fork ≃	270	40.26 N	122.00 W
Battle Ground, IN	260	40.31 N	86.50 W
Battle Ground, WA	268	45.47 N	122.32 W
Battle Harbour	242	52.16 N	55.35 W
Battle Lake	264	46.17 N	95.43 W
Battlement Mesa ∧	266	39.20 N	108.00 W
Battle Mountain	270	40.38 N	116.56 W
Battle Mountain ∧	268	41.02 N	107.16 W
Baudette	264	48.43 N	94.36 W
Bauld, Cape ≻	252	51.38 N	55.25 W
Bauxite	260	34.33 N	92.30 W
Baxley	258	31.47 N	82.21 W
Baxter, IA	256	41.49 N	93.09 W
Baxter, MN	264	46.20 N	94.16 W
Baxter, TN	260	36.09 N	85.38 W
Baxter Springs	264	37.02 N	94.44 W
Baxter State Park ♠	254	46.00 N	68.58 W
Baxterville	260	31.06 N	89.36 W
Bay	260	35.45 N	90.34 W
Bayard, FL	258	30.09 N	81.31 W
Bayard, IA	264	41.51 N	94.33 W
Bayard, NE	264	41.45 N	103.20 W
Bayard, NM	266	32.46 N	108.08 W
Bayard, WV	254	39.16 N	79.22 W
Bayboro	258	35.09 N	76.46 W
Bay Bulls	252	47.19 N	52.49 W
Bay City, MI	256	43.36 N	83.53 W
Bay City, OR	268	45.31 N	123.53 W
Bay City, TX	262	28.59 N	95.58 W
Bay Creek ≃, IL	260	37.16 N	88.31 W
Bay Creek ≃, IL	260	39.20 N	90.46 W
Bay de Verde	252	48.05 N	52.54 W
Bay du Nord ≃	252	47.44 N	55.25 W
Bayfield, CO	266	37.14 N	107.36 W
Bayfield, WI	256	46.49 N	90.49 W
Bayfield, Île ❙	252	51.13 N	58.23 W
Bayfield Ridge ∧	256	46.45 N	91.25 W
Bay L'Argent	252	47.33 N	54.54 W
Bay Minette	260	30.53 N	87.47 W
Bayou Bodcau Reservoir ⊜[1]	260	32.45 N	93.30 W
Bayou D'Arbonne Lake ⊜[1]	260	32.45 N	92.25 W
Bayou La Batre	260	30.24 N	88.15 W
Bay Port, MI	256	43.51 N	83.23 W
Bayport, MN	256	45.01 N	92.47 W
Bay Roberts	252	47.36 N	53.16 W
Bays, Lake of ⊜	256	45.15 N	79.04 W
Bay Saint Louis	260	30.19 N	89.20 W
Bay Shore	254	40.44 N	73.15 W
Bayside	256	44.07 N	77.30 W
Bay Springs	260	31.53 N	89.17 W
Baytown	260	29.44 N	94.58 W
Bazine	264	38.27 N	99.42 W
Beach	264	46.55 N	103.52 W
Beach Haven	254	39.34 N	74.14 W
Beachville	256	43.05 N	80.49 W
Beacon	254	41.30 N	73.58 W
Beacon Hill	268	46.08 N	122.57 W
Beacon Rock State Park ♠	268	45.38 N	122.03 W
Beale, Cape ≻	248	48.44 N	125.20 W
Beale Air Force Base ■	270	39.08 N	121.20 W
Beals Creek ≃	262	32.10 N	100.51 W
Beanblossom Creek ≃	260	39.20 N	86.39 W
Bear ≃, SK	250	54.33 N	103.58 W
Bear ≃, U.S.	266	41.30 N	112.08 W
Bear ≃, CA	270	38.57 N	121.35 W
Bear, Mount ∧	246	61.17 N	141.09 W
Bear Bay ⊂	242	75.47 N	87.00 W
Bear Brook State Park ♠	254	43.05 N	71.26 W
Bear Butte ∧	264	44.28 N	103.26 W
Bear Creek ≃, U.S.	260	34.46 N	88.05 W
Bear Creek ≃, U.S.	262	37.45 N	101.23 W
Bear Creek ≃, AL	260	33.11 N	88.05 W
Bear Creek ≃, CO	264	39.40 N	105.00 W
Bear Creek ≃, ND	264	46.10 N	98.06 W
Bear Creek ≃, OR	268	44.06 N	120.46 W
Bear Creek ≃, OR	268	42.26 N	122.58 W
Bear Creek ≃, WY	264	41.41 N	104.13 W
Bearden	260	33.43 N	92.37 W
Beardmore	242	49.36 N	87.57 W
Beardstown	260	40.01 N	90.26 W
Bear Head Creek ≃	260	30.18 N	93.35 W
Bear Head Lake ⊜	250	55.33 N	96.10 W
Bear Head Lake State Park ♠	256	47.49 N	92.04 W
Bear-in-the-Lodge Creek ≃	264	43.41 N	101.50 W
Bear Lake	248	56.11 N	126.51 W
Bear Lake ⊜, AB	248	55.16 N	119.00 W
Bear Lake ⊜, BC	248	56.06 N	126.45 W
Bear Lake ⊜, MB	250	55.08 N	96.00 W
Bear Lake ⊜, U.S.	244	42.00 N	111.20 W
Bear Mountain ∧, KY	258	37.32 N	84.16 W
Bear Mountain ∧, OR	268	43.51 N	122.53 W
Bearpaw Mountains ⛰	268	48.15 N	109.30 W
Bear River	252	44.34 N	65.39 W
Bear Tooth Pass)(	268	44.58 N	109.28 W
Beartooth Range ⛰	268	45.00 N	109.30 W
Bear Town	260	31.14 N	90.28 W
Beaton	248	50.44 N	117.44 W
Beatrice, AL	260	31.38 N	87.19 W
Beatrice, NE	264	40.16 N	96.44 W
Beattie	264	39.52 N	96.25 W
Beatton ≃	242	56.10 N	120.25 W
Beatty	270	36.54 N	116.46 W
Beattyville	258	37.35 N	83.42 W
Beauceville-Est	254	46.12 N	70.46 W
Beauchêne, Lac ⊜	256	46.39 N	78.55 W
Beaucoup Creek ≃	260	37.47 N	89.17 W
Beaudry, Lac ⊜	256	47.44 N	78.55 W
Beaufort, NC	258	34.43 N	76.40 W
Beaufort, SC	258	32.26 N	80.40 W
Beaufort Marine Corps Air Station ■	258	32.30 N	80.44 W
Beaufort Sea ▾[2]	242	73.00 N	140.00 W
Beauharnois	254	45.19 N	73.52 W
Beaumont, NF	252	49.34 N	55.36 W
Beaumont, CA	270	33.56 N	116.58 W
Beaumont, MS	260	31.11 N	88.55 W
Beaumont, TX	260	30.05 N	94.06 W
Beaupré	252	47.03 N	70.54 W
Beauséjour	250	50.04 N	96.33 W
Beauvais Creek ≃	268	45.29 N	107.45 W
Beaver, AK	246	66.22 N	147.24 W
Beaver, OK	262	36.49 N	100.31 W
Beaver, PA	254	40.42 N	80.18 W
Beaver, UT	266	38.17 N	112.38 W
Beaver, WV	258	37.45 N	81.09 W
Beaver ≃, Can.	242	59.43 N	124.16 W
Beaver ≃, Can.	242	54.30 N	107.45 W
Beaver ≃, U.S.	262	36.35 N	99.30 W
Beaver ≃, NY	254	43.54 N	75.30 W
Beaver ≃, PA	254	40.40 N	80.18 W
Beaver ≃, UT	266	39.10 N	112.57 W
Beaver City	264	40.08 N	99.50 W
Beaver Creek	246	62.22 N	140.52 W
Beaver Creek ≃, U.S.	264	47.20 N	103.39 W
Beaver Creek ≃, U.S.	264	40.04 N	99.20 W
Beaver Creek ≃, U.S.	264	43.25 N	103.59 W
Beaver Creek ≃, AK	246	66.15 N	147.32 W
Beaver Creek ≃, CO	264	40.20 N	103.33 W
Beaver Creek ≃, ID	268	44.02 N	112.14 W
Beaver Creek ≃, IL	260	38.33 N	89.30 W
Beaver Creek ≃, MO	260	36.38 N	93.02 W
Beaver Creek ≃, MT	268	48.29 N	107.24 W
Beaver Creek ≃, NE	264	40.42 N	97.20 W
Beaver Creek ≃, NE	264	41.26 N	97.42 W
Beaver Creek ≃, ND	264	46.15 N	100.29 W
Beaver Creek ≃, TX	262	33.53 N	98.49 W
Beaver Creek ≃, WY	268	42.58 N	108.26 W
Beaver Crossing	264	40.47 N	97.17 W
Beaver Dam, KY	260	37.24 N	86.52 W
Beaver Dam, WI	256	43.28 N	88.50 W
Beaver Dam Wash ∨	266	36.54 N	114.55 W
Beaverdell	248	49.26 N	119.05 W
Beaver Falls	254	40.46 N	80.19 W
Beaverhead ≃	268	45.31 N	112.21 W
Beaverhead Mountains ⛰	268	45.00 N	113.20 W
Beaverhill Lake ⊜, AB	248	53.27 N	112.32 W
Beaver Hill Lake ⊜, MB	250	54.16 N	94.53 W
Beaverhouse Lake ⊜	256	48.32 N	92.05 W
Beaver Island ❙	256	45.40 N	85.31 W
Beaver Lake ⊜	250	54.43 N	111.50 W
Beaver Lake ⊜[1]	260	36.20 N	93.55 W
Beaver Lake Indian Reserve ➛[4]	250	54.39 N	111.54 W
Beaverlodge	248	55.13 N	119.26 W
Beaver Mountains ⛰	246	62.54 N	156.58 W
Beavers Bend State Park ♠	260	34.08 N	94.42 W
Beaverton, ON	256	44.26 N	79.09 W
Beaverton, MI	256	43.53 N	84.29 W
Beaverton, OR	268	45.29 N	122.48 W
Bécancour ≃	254	46.22 N	72.27 W
Beccero Creek ≃	262	28.05 N	98.55 W
Becharof Lake ⊜	246	58.00 N	156.30 W
Bechevin Bay ⊂	246	55.00 N	163.27 W
Beckley	258	37.46 N	81.13 W
Beckville	260	32.14 N	94.27 W
Becky Peak ∧	270	39.58 N	114.36 W
Bedeque Bay ⊂	252	46.22 N	63.53 W
Bedford, PQ	254	45.07 N	72.59 W
Bedford, IN	260	38.52 N	86.29 W
Bedford, IA	264	40.40 N	94.44 W
Bedford, KY	260	38.36 N	85.19 W
Bedford, PA	254	40.01 N	78.30 W
Bedford, VA	258	37.20 N	79.31 W
Bedias	262	30.46 N	95.57 W
Beebe	260	35.04 N	91.53 W
Beech ≃	260	35.37 N	88.10 W
Beech Creek	260	37.11 N	87.03 W
Beecher	260	41.21 N	87.38 W
Beech Fork ≃	260	37.46 N	85.41 W
Beech Grove	260	39.43 N	86.03 W
Beechy	250	50.51 N	107.25 W
Beemer	264	41.56 N	96.48 W
Bee Ridge	258	27.16 N	82.31 W
Beersheba Springs	260	35.28 N	85.39 W
Beetz, Lac ⊜	252	50.34 N	62.42 W
Beeville	262	28.24 N	97.45 W
Beggs	262	35.45 N	96.04 W
Behm Canal ⊔	246	55.41 N	131.35 W
Beiseker	248	51.23 N	113.32 W
Bel Air	254	39.32 N	76.21 W
Bélanger ≃	250	53.26 N	97.40 W
Belcher	260	32.45 N	93.50 W
Belcher Islands ❙❙	242	56.20 N	79.30 W
Belcourt	264	48.50 N	99.45 W
Belding	256	43.06 N	85.14 W
Belen	266	34.40 N	106.46 W
Belfast	254	44.27 N	69.01 W
Belfield	264	46.53 N	103.12 W
Belfry, KY	258	37.37 N	82.16 W
Belfry, MT	268	45.09 N	109.01 W
Belgrade, MN	264	45.27 N	95.00 W
Belgrade, MT	268	45.47 N	111.11 W
Belgrade, NE	264	41.28 N	98.04 W
Belhaven	258	35.33 N	76.37 W
Belington	254	39.01 N	79.56 W
Belize Inlet ⊂	248	51.08 N	127.15 W
Belknap Crater •[6]	268	44.17 N	121.50 W
Belkofski	246	55.05 N	162.02 W
Bell ≃, PQ	242	49.48 N	77.38 W
Bell ≃, YK	246	67.17 N	137.46 W
Bella Bella	248	52.09 N	128.07 W
Bella Coola	248	52.22 N	126.46 W
Bella Coola ≃	248	52.22 N	126.43 W
Bellair	258	30.10 N	81.45 W
Bellaire, MI	256	44.59 N	85.13 W
Bellaire, OH	254	40.02 N	80.45 W
Bellaire, TX	262	29.43 N	95.03 W
Bellamy	260	32.22 N	88.08 W
Belle, MO	260	38.17 N	91.43 W
Belle, WV	254	38.14 N	81.32 W
Belle ≃	256	42.43 N	82.30 W
Belle Bay ⊂	252	47.36 N	55.18 W
Bellefontaine	254	40.22 N	83.46 W
Bellefonte	254	40.55 N	77.46 W
Belle Fourche	264	44.40 N	103.51 W
Belle Fourche ≃	264	44.26 N	102.19 W
Belle Fourche Reservoir ⊜[1]	264	44.44 N	103.42 W
Belle Glade	258	26.41 N	80.40 W
Belle Isle ❙	242	51.55 N	55.20 W
Belle Isle, Strait of ⊔	242	51.35 N	56.30 W
Belleoram	252	47.31 N	55.25 W
Belle-Plaine, SK	250	50.24 N	105.09 W
Belle Plaine, IA	256	41.54 N	92.17 W
Belle Plaine, KS	264	37.24 N	97.17 W
Belle Plaine, MN	256	44.37 N	93.46 W
Belleview	258	29.04 N	82.03 W
Belleville, IL	260	38.31 N	90.00 W
Belleville, KS	264	39.49 N	97.38 W
Belleville, PA	254	40.36 N	77.43 W
Belleville, WI	256	42.52 N	89.32 W
Bellevue, AB	248	49.35 N	114.22 W
Bellevue, ID	268	43.28 N	114.16 W
Bellevue, IA	256	42.16 N	90.26 W
Bellevue, MI	256	42.12 N	83.29 W
Bellevue, NE	264	41.09 N	95.54 W
Bellevue, OH	254	41.17 N	82.50 W
Bellevue, TX	262	33.38 N	98.01 W
Bellevue, WA	268	47.37 N	122.12 W
Bellin	242	60.01 N	70.01 W
Bellingham, MN	264	45.08 N	96.17 W
Bellingham, WA	268	48.49 N	122.29 W
Bell Island ❙, NF	252	50.44 N	55.35 W
Bell Island ❙, NF	252	47.36 N	52.58 W
Bell Island Hot Springs	248	55.56 N	131.34 W
Bellmead	262	31.35 N	97.06 W
Bellot Strait ⊔	242	71.58 N	94.45 W
Bellows Falls	254	43.08 N	72.27 W
Bell Peninsula ≻[1]	242	63.50 N	82.00 W
Bells, TN	260	35.43 N	89.05 W
Bells, TX	262	33.37 N	96.25 W
Bells Corners	254	45.19 N	75.50 W
Bellville, OH	254	40.37 N	82.31 W
Bellville, TX	262	29.57 N	96.16 W
Bellwood, NE	264	41.21 N	97.14 W
Bellwood, PA	254	40.36 N	78.20 W
Belly ≃	248	49.46 N	113.02 W
Belmond	256	42.51 N	93.37 W
Belmont, MB	250	49.24 N	99.27 W
Belmont, MS	260	34.31 N	88.13 W
Belmont, NH	254	43.27 N	71.29 W
Belmont, NY	254	42.13 N	78.02 W
Belmont, SC	258	34.02 N	81.01 W
Belmont, WI	256	42.44 N	90.20 W
Beloit, KS	264	39.28 N	98.06 W
Beloit, WI	256	42.31 N	89.02 W
Belot, Lac ⊜	242	66.55 N	126.18 W
Belpre	254	39.17 N	81.34 W
Belspring	258	37.11 N	80.36 W
Belt	268	47.23 N	110.55 W
Belt Creek ≃	268	47.36 N	111.02 W
Belted Range ⛰	270	37.25 N	116.10 W
Belton, MO	260	38.49 N	94.32 W
Belton, SC	258	34.31 N	82.30 W
Belton, TX	262	31.04 N	97.28 W
Belton Lake ⊜[1]	262	31.08 N	97.23 W
Belvidere, IL	256	42.15 N	88.50 W
Belvidere, NJ	254	40.49 N	75.05 W
Belview	264	44.36 N	95.20 W
Belzoni	260	33.11 N	90.29 W
Bement	260	39.55 N	88.34 W
Bemidji	264	47.29 N	94.53 W
Bemis	260	35.35 N	88.49 W
Benavides	262	27.36 N	98.25 W
Ben Bolt	262	27.39 N	98.05 W
Benbrook Lake ⊜[1]	262	32.38 N	97.27 W
Bend	268	44.03 N	121.19 W
Bendeleben, Mount ∧	246	65.10 N	164.03 W
Bengough	250	49.24 N	105.08 W
Benham	258	36.58 N	82.57 W
Benito	250	51.55 N	101.31 W
Benjamin	262	33.35 N	99.48 W
Benkelman	264	40.03 N	101.32 W
Benld	260	39.06 N	89.48 W
Ben Lomond	270	37.05 N	122.05 W
Benndale	260	30.52 N	88.48 W
Bennet	264	40.41 N	96.30 W
Bennett Lake ⊜	250	53.28 N	96.05 W
Bennettsville	258	34.37 N	79.41 W
Bennington, KS	264	39.02 N	97.36 W
Bennington, VT	254	42.53 N	73.12 W
Benoit	260	33.39 N	91.01 W
Benson, AZ	266	31.58 N	110.18 W
Benson, MN	264	45.19 N	95.36 W
Benson, NC	258	35.23 N	78.33 W
Bentley	248	52.28 N	114.04 W
Benton, AR	260	34.34 N	92.35 W
Benton, IL	260	38.00 N	88.55 W
Benton, KY	260	36.52 N	88.21 W
Benton, LA	260	32.42 N	93.44 W
Benton, MS	260	32.50 N	90.15 W
Benton, MO	260	37.06 N	89.34 W
Benton, PA	254	41.12 N	76.23 W
Benton, TN	258	35.10 N	84.39 W
Benton, WI	256	42.34 N	90.23 W
Benton City	268	46.16 N	119.29 W
Benton Harbor	256	42.06 N	86.27 W
Bentonia	260	32.38 N	90.22 W
Benton Lake ⊜	268	47.40 N	111.20 W
Bentonville	260	36.22 N	94.13 W
Bent's Old Fort National Historic Site ⊥	264	38.05 N	103.28 W
Ben Wheeler	262	32.27 N	95.42 W
Beowawe	270	40.35 N	116.29 W
Berclair	262	28.32 N	97.36 W
Berea, KY	258	37.34 N	84.17 W
Berea, OH	254	41.22 N	81.52 W
Berea, SC	258	34.53 N	82.28 W
Berens ≃	242	52.21 N	97.02 W
Berens Island ❙	250	52.18 N	97.17 W
Berens River	250	52.22 N	97.02 W
Beresford, NB	252	47.42 N	65.42 W
Beresford, SD	264	43.05 N	96.47 W
Bergen	254	43.05 N	77.57 W
Bergland	256	46.35 N	89.34 W
Bergoo	254	38.29 N	80.18 W
Bergstrom Air Force Base ■	262	30.12 N	97.40 W
Bering Glacier ⊻	246	60.15 N	143.30 W
Berkeley	270	37.57 N	122.18 W
Berkeley Springs	254	39.38 N	78.14 W
Berkshire Hills ⛰[2]	254	42.20 N	73.10 W
Berland ≃	248	54.01 N	116.50 W
Berlin, MD	254	38.20 N	75.13 W
Berlin, NH	254	44.29 N	71.10 W
Berlin, NJ	254	39.48 N	74.57 W
Berlin, PA	254	39.55 N	78.57 W
Berlin, WI	256	43.58 N	88.55 W
Berlinguet Inlet ⊂	242	71.10 N	85.35 W
Berlin-ichthyosaur State Park ♠	270	38.51 N	117.35 W
Berlin Lake ⊜[1]	254	41.00 N	81.00 W
Bermen, Lac ⊜	242	53.35 N	68.55 W
Bernalillo	266	35.18 N	106.33 W
Berne	260	40.39 N	84.57 W
Bernice	260	32.49 N	92.39 W
Bernie	260	36.40 N	89.58 W
Bernier Bay ⊂	242	71.00 N	87.30 W
Berry	260	33.39 N	87.36 W
Berry Creek ≃	250	50.50 N	111.36 W
Berryessa, Lake ⊜[1]	270	38.35 N	122.14 W
Berryville, AR	260	36.22 N	93.34 W
Berryville, VA	254	39.09 N	77.59 W
Bersimis 2 Dam ➛[6]	252	49.22 N	69.47 W
Bersimis Indian Reserve ➛[4]	252	49.05 N	68.37 W
Berté, Lac ⊜	252	50.48 N	68.30 W
Bertha	264	46.16 N	95.04 W
Berthold	264	48.19 N	101.44 W
Berthoud	266	40.18 N	105.05 W
Berthoud Pass)(	266	39.45 N	105.45 W
Bertram	262	30.45 N	98.03 W
Bertrand, MI	256	41.46 N	86.16 W
Bertrand, NE	264	40.32 N	99.38 W
Berwick, NS	252	45.03 N	64.44 W
Berwick, LA	260	29.42 N	91.13 W
Berwick, ME	254	43.16 N	70.51 W
Berwick, PA	254	41.03 N	76.15 W
Berwyn	260	41.50 N	87.47 W
Besnard Lake ⊜	250	55.24 N	106.05 W
Bessemer, AL	260	33.25 N	86.57 W
Bessemer, MI	256	46.27 N	89.24 W
Bessemer, PA	254	40.59 N	80.30 W
Bessemer City	258	35.17 N	81.17 W
Bethalto	260	38.55 N	90.03 W
Bethany, IL	260	39.39 N	88.44 W
Bethany, MO	260	40.16 N	94.02 W
Bethany, OK	262	35.31 N	97.38 W
Bethel, AK	246	60.48 N	161.46 W
Bethel, CT	254	41.22 N	73.25 W
Bethel, ME	254	44.25 N	70.48 W
Bethel, NC	258	35.48 N	77.22 W
Bethel, OH	254	38.58 N	84.05 W
Bethel Acres	262	35.19 N	97.00 W
Bethel Springs	260	35.14 N	88.36 W
Bethesda, MD	254	38.59 N	77.06 W
Bethesda, OH	254	40.01 N	81.04 W
Bethlehem, PA	254	40.37 N	75.25 W
Bethlehem, WV	254	40.02 N	80.40 W
Bethune, SK	250	50.43 N	105.08 W
Bethune, SC	258	34.25 N	80.21 W
Betsiamites	252	48.56 N	68.38 W
Betsiamites ≃	252	48.56 N	68.38 W
Betsiamites, Pointe ≻	252	48.55 N	68.37 W
Betsie, Point ≻	256	44.42 N	86.16 W
Betsy Layne	258	37.33 N	82.38 W
Bettendorf	256	41.32 N	90.30 W
Bettles Field	246	66.55 N	151.30 W
Beulah, CO	264	38.05 N	104.59 W
Beulah, MI	256	44.38 N	86.06 W
Beulah, MS	260	33.42 N	90.59 W
Beulah, ND	264	47.16 N	101.47 W
Beulah Reservoir ⊜[1]	268	43.56 N	118.09 W
Beulaville	258	34.55 N	77.46 W
B. Everett Jordan Lake ⊜[1]	258	35.45 N	79.00 W
Beverly, MA	254	42.33 N	70.53 W
Beverly, OH	254	39.33 N	81.38 W
Beverly Hills	270	34.03 N	118.26 W
Beverly Lake ⊜	242	64.36 N	100.30 W
Bevier	260	39.45 N	92.34 W
Bexley	254	39.58 N	82.56 W
Bibb City	258	32.30 N	84.59 W
Bic	252	48.22 N	68.42 W
Biche, Lac la ⊜	248	54.50 N	112.03 W
Bickle Knob ∧	254	38.56 N	79.44 W
Bicknell, IN	260	38.47 N	87.19 W
Bicknell, UT	266	38.20 N	111.33 W
Biddeford	254	43.30 N	70.26 W
Bidwell	254	38.55 N	82.18 W
Bidwell, Mount ∧	270	41.58 N	120.10 W
Bieber	270	41.07 N	121.08 W
Bieler Lake ⊜	242	70.20 N	73.00 W
Bienfait	250	49.08 N	102.47 W
Bienville	260	32.21 N	92.59 W
Bienville, Lac ⊜	242	55.05 N	72.40 W
Big ≃, AK	246	63.00 N	154.56 W
Big ≃, MO	260	38.28 N	90.37 W
Big A Mountain ∧	258	37.03 N	82.02 W
Big Bald ∧	258	34.45 N	84.19 W
Big Bald Mountain ∧	252	47.12 N	66.25 W
Big Baldy ∧	268	44.47 N	115.13 W
Big Baldy Mountain ∧	268	46.58 N	110.37 W
Big Bar Creek	248	51.12 N	122.06 W
Big Basin Redwoods State Park ♠	270	37.09 N	122.17 W
Big Bay	256	46.49 N	87.44 W
Big Bay De Noc ⊂	256	45.46 N	86.43 W
Big Bear Lake	270	34.15 N	116.53 W
Big Beaver	250	49.08 N	105.10 W
Big Belt Mountains ⛰	268	46.40 N	111.25 W
Big Bend National Park ♠	262	29.12 N	103.12 W
Big Bend Reservoir ⊜[1]	248	52.57 N	115.37 W
Big Black ≃	260	32.00 N	91.05 W
Big Blue ≃	264	39.11 N	96.32 W
Big Blue, West Fork ≃	264	40.42 N	96.59 W
Big Bonito Creek ≃	266	33.34 N	109.56 W
Big Brady Creek ≃	262	31.07 N	98.59 W
Big Bureau Creek ≃	260	41.17 N	89.21 W
Big Cabin Creek ≃	262	36.26 N	95.08 W
Big Canoe Creek ≃	260	33.52 N	86.04 W
Big Canyon ∨	262	30.05 N	101.55 W
Big Chino Wash ∨	266	34.52 N	112.28 W
Big Clifty	260	37.33 N	86.09 W
Big Coulee Creek ≃	268	46.17 N	108.56 W
Big Cow Creek ≃	260	30.34 N	93.44 W
Big Creek, BC	248	51.44 N	123.03 W
Big Creek, CA	270	37.12 N	119.09 W
Big Creek ≃, BC	248	51.40 N	122.50 W
Big Creek ≃, ON	256	42.36 N	80.27 W
Big Creek ≃, U.S.	260	40.16 N	94.03 W
Big Creek ≃, AR	260	34.21 N	91.03 W
Big Creek ≃, ID	268	45.06 N	114.44 W
Big Creek ≃, KS	264	38.47 N	98.55 W
Big Creek ≃, LA	260	32.10 N	91.53 W
Big Creek ≃, MO	260	40.02 N	94.07 W
Big Creek ≃, TX	262	31.09 N	96.52 W
Big Creek, East Fork ≃	260	40.16 N	94.03 W
Big Creek Peak ∧	268	44.28 N	113.32 W
Big Cypress Creek ≃	260	33.00 N	94.51 W
Big Cypress Indian Reservation ➛[4]	258	26.14 N	80.49 W
Big Cypress Swamp ≡	258	26.10 N	81.38 W
Big Delta	246	64.09 N	145.50 W
Big Dry Creek ≃	268	47.30 N	106.19 W
Big Eau Pleine ≃	256	44.48 N	90.00 W
Big Elm Creek ≃	262	30.53 N	96.56 W
Bigelow Bight ⊂[3]	254	43.15 N	70.30 W
Big Escambia Creek ≃	260	30.58 N	87.14 W
Big Falls	256	48.12 N	93.48 W
Bigflat	260	36.00 N	92.24 W
Big Flat Creek ≃	260	31.33 N	87.31 W
Bigfork, MN	256	47.45 N	93.39 W
Bigfork, MT	268	48.04 N	114.04 W
Big Fork ≃	256	48.31 N	93.43 W

Symbols in the index entries are identified on page 273.

Bigf – Brea

United States and Canada Map Index

Name Page Lat° ' Long° '

Big Frog Mountain ∧ 258 35.00 N 84.32 W
Biggar 250 52.04 N 108.00 W
Biggers 260 36.20 N 90.48 W
Biggs 270 39.25 N 121.43 W
Big Gull Lake ⊜ 256 44.50 N 76.58 W
Big Gully Creek ≃ 250 53.13 N 109.03 W
Big Hole ≃ 268 45.34 N 112.20 W
Big Hole National Battlefield ⊥ 268 45.35 N 113.35 W
Bighorn ≃ 244 46.09 N 107.28 W
Big Horn Basin ≃¹ 268 44.15 N 108.10 W
Bighorn Canyon National Recreation Area ♦ 268 45.00 N 108.15 W
Big Horn Lake ⊜¹ 268 45.06 N 108.08 W
Bighorn Mountains ⩘ 244 44.00 N 107.30 W
Big Island 258 37.32 N 79.22 W
Big Island I, NT 242 62.43 N 70.43 W
Big Island I, ON 250 49.10 N 94.40 W
Big Knob ∧ 258 36.40 N 82.31 W
Big Koniuji Island I 246 55.06 N 159.33 W
Big Lake, AK 246 61.33 N 149.52 W
Big Lake, MN 256 45.20 N 93.45 W
Big Lake, TX 262 31.12 N 101.28 W
Big Lake ⊜ 254 45.10 N 67.40 W
Big Lookout Mountain ∧ 268 44.37 N 117.17 W
Big Lost ≃ 268 43.50 N 112.44 W
Big Monon Ditch ≅ 260 40.52 N 86.46 W
Big Mossy Point ≻ 250 53.42 N 98.03 W
Big Mountain ∧, BC 246 56.53 N 131.31 W
Big Mountain ∧, NV 270 41.17 N 119.04 W
Big Mountain Creek ≃ 248 55.04 N 118.39 W
Big Muddy ≃ 260 37.35 N 89.31 W
Big Muddy, Casey Fork ≃ 260 38.06 N 88.57 W
Big Muddy Creek ≃, MT 264 48.08 N 104.36 W
Big Muddy Creek ≃, ND 264 46.37 N 101.24 W
Big Muddy Lake ⊜ 250 49.08 N 104.54 W
Big Nasty Creek ≃ 264 45.41 N 102.51 W
Big Nemaha North Fork ≃ 264 40.04 N 95.43 W
Big Otter ≃ 258 37.07 N 79.23 W
Big Pine 270 37.10 N 118.17 W
Big Pine Creek ≃ 260 40.18 N 87.15 W
Big Pine Mountain ∧ 270 34.42 N 119.39 W
Big Piney 268 42.32 N 110.07 W
Big Piney ≃ 260 37.53 N 92.04 W
Big Piney Creek ≃ 260 35.20 N 93.20 W
Bigpoint 260 30.35 N 88.29 W
Big Porcupine Creek ≃ 268 46.16 N 106.43 W
Big Prairie Creek ≃ 260 32.35 N 87.45 W
Big Quill Lake ⊜ 250 51.55 N 104.22 W
Big Raccoon Creek ≃ 260 39.46 N 87.22 W
Big Rapids 256 43.42 N 85.29 W
Big Rib ≃ 256 44.56 N 89.41 W
Big Rideau Lake ⊜ 256 44.45 N 76.14 W
Big River 250 53.50 N 107.01 W
Big River Indian Reserve ◆⁴ 250 53.33 N 107.10 W
Big Sable ≃ 256 44.02 N 86.31 W
Big Sable Point ≻ 256 44.03 N 86.31 W
Big Salmon ≃ 246 61.52 N 134.56 W
Big Salmon Range ⩘ 246 60.20 N 132.40 W
Big Sand Lake ⊜ 242 57.45 N 99.42 W
Big Sandy, MT 268 48.11 N 110.07 W
Big Sandy, TN 260 36.15 N 88.05 W
Big Sandy, TX 262 32.35 N 95.07 W
Big Sandy ≃, U.S. 254 38.25 N 82.36 W
Big Sandy ≃, AZ 266 34.19 N 113.31 W
Big Sandy ≃, TN 260 36.15 N 88.06 W
Big Sandy ≃, WY 268 41.51 N 109.47 W
Big Sandy, Levisa Fork ≃ 254 37.24 N 82.26 W
Big Sandy, Tug Fork ≃ 254 38.06 N 82.36 W
Big Sandy Creek ≃, CO 264 38.06 N 102.29 W
Big Sandy Creek ≃, GA 258 32.42 N 82.57 W
Big Sandy Creek ≃, MT 268 48.34 N 109.48 W
Big Sandy Creek ≃, NE 264 40.13 N 97.18 W
Big Sandy Creek ≃, TX 262 33.11 N 97.40 W
Big Sandy Creek ≃, TX 262 32.33 N 95.05 W
Big Sandy Lake ⊜, SK 250 54.26 N 104.04 W
Big Sandy Lake ⊜, MN 256 46.45 N 93.17 W
Big Sandy Reservoir ⊜¹ 268 42.16 N 109.26 W
Big Satilla Creek ≃ 258 31.27 N 82.03 W
Bigsby Island I 250 49.04 N 94.35 W
Big Sheep Mountains ⩘ 264 47.10 N 105.30 W
Big Signal Peak ∧ 270 39.31 N 123.06 W
Big Sioux ≃ 264 42.30 N 96.25 W
Big Sky 268 45.17 N 111.17 W
Big Slough ≃ 258 30.56 N 84.33 W
Big Smoky Valley ∨ 270 38.30 N 117.15 W
Big Snowy Mountains ⩘ 268 46.50 N 109.30 W
Big Southern Butte ∧ 268 43.23 N 113.01 W
Big Spring 262 32.15 N 101.28 W
Big Springs 264 41.04 N 102.05 W
Big Spruce Knob ∧ 254 38.16 N 80.12 W
Big Squaw Mountain ∧ 254 45.30 N 69.45 W
Bigstick Lake ⊜ 250 50.16 N 109.20 W
Bigstone ≃ 250 55.55 N 94.36 W
Big Stone City 264 45.18 N 96.28 W
Big Stone Gap 258 36.52 N 82.47 W
Bigstone Lake ⊜, MB 250 53.42 N 95.44 W
Big Stone Lake ⊜, U.S. 264 45.25 N 96.40 W
Big Sunflower ≃ 260 32.40 N 90.40 W
Big Swamp Creek ≃ 260 32.19 N 86.49 W
Big Swan Creek ≃ 260 35.46 N 87.24 W
Big Thompson ≃ 264 40.21 N 104.45 W
Big Timber 268 45.50 N 109.57 W
Big Trout Lake ⊜ 242 53.45 N 90.00 W
Big Valley 248 52.02 N 112.46 W
Big Walnut Creek ≃ 260 39.30 N 86.57 W
Big Wells 262 28.34 N 99.34 W
Big White Mountain ∧ 248 49.42 N 118.58 W
Big Wills Creek ≃ 260 33.59 N 86.00 W
Big Wood ≃ 268 42.52 N 114.54 W
Bijou Creek ≃ 264 40.17 N 103.52 W
Billings, MO 260 37.04 N 93.33 W
Billings, MT 268 45.47 N 108.27 W
Billings, OK 262 36.32 N 97.27 W
Billings Heights 268 45.50 N 108.33 W
Bill Williams ≃ 266 34.17 N 114.03 W
Bill Williams Mountain ∧ 266 35.12 N 112.12 W
Billy Chinook, Lake ⊜¹ 268 44.33 N 121.20 W
Biloxi 260 30.24 N 88.53 W
Biloxi ≃ 260 30.26 N 89.00 W
Biltmore Forest 258 35.32 N 82.32 W
Bindloss 250 50.52 N 110.16 W
Binford 264 47.34 N 98.21 W
Binger 262 35.18 N 98.21 W
Bingham 254 45.03 N 69.53 W
Binghamton 254 42.08 N 75.54 W
Binscarth 250 50.37 N 101.16 W
Birch ≃, AB 242 58.30 N 112.15 W
Birch ≃, WV 254 38.35 N 80.53 W
Birch Creek ≃, AK 246 66.30 N 146.30 W
Birch Creek ≃, ID 268 43.51 N 112.43 W
Birch Creek ≃, MT 268 47.45 N 109.34 W
Birch Hills 250 52.59 N 105.25 W
Birch Island 248 51.36 N 119.55 W
Birch Island I 250 52.25 N 99.55 W
Birch Lake ⊜, ON 250 51.24 N 92.20 W
Birch Lake ⊜, SK 250 53.28 N 108.07 W
Birch Mountains ⩘² 242 57.30 N 112.30 W
Birch River 250 52.23 N 101.06 W
Birch Run 256 43.15 N 83.48 W
Birch Tree 260 37.00 N 91.30 W
Birchwood, AK 246 61.28 N 149.22 W
Birchwood, WI 256 45.40 N 91.33 W
Birchy Bay 252 49.21 N 54.44 W
Bird City 264 39.45 N 101.32 W
Bird Creek ≃ 262 36.13 N 95.44 W
Bird Island 264 44.46 N 94.54 W
Birdtail Creek ≃ 250 50.16 N 101.12 W
Birken 248 50.29 N 122.36 W
Birmingham, AL 260 33.31 N 86.49 W
Birmingham, IA 256 40.53 N 91.57 W
Birmingham, MI 256 42.33 N 83.15 W
Birnamwood 256 44.56 N 89.13 W
Birtle 250 50.25 N 101.03 W
Bisbee, AZ 266 31.27 N 109.55 W
Bisbee, ND 264 48.37 N 99.23 W
Biscayne Bay C 258 25.33 N 80.15 W
Biscayne National Monument ♦ 258 25.25 N 80.12 W
Biscoe, AR 260 34.49 N 91.24 W
Biscoe, NC 258 35.22 N 79.47 W
Biscotasi Lake ⊜ 256 47.19 N 82.07 W
Bishop, CA 270 37.22 N 118.24 W
Bishop, TX 262 27.35 N 97.48 W
Bishop's Falls 252 49.01 N 55.30 W
Bishopville 258 34.13 N 80.20 W
Bismarck, MO 260 37.46 N 90.38 W
Bismarck, ND 264 46.48 N 100.47 W
Bison 264 45.31 N 102.28 W
Bison Peak ∧ 266 39.14 N 105.30 W
Bissett 250 51.02 N 95.40 W
Bistcho Lake ⊜ 242 59.40 N 118.40 W
Bistineau, Lake ⊜¹ 260 32.25 N 93.22 W
Bitter Creek ≃, UT 266 39.58 N 109.25 W
Bitter Creek ≃, WY 268 41.31 N 109.27 W
Bitter Lake ⊜ 250 50.08 N 109.48 W
Bittern Lake ⊜ 250 53.55 N 105.50 W
Bitterroot ≃ 268 46.52 N 114.06 W
Bitterroot, East Fork ≃ 268 45.57 N 114.08 W
Bitterroot, West Fork ≃ 268 45.57 N 114.08 W
Bitterroot Range ⩘ 244 47.06 N 115.10 W
Bivins 260 33.01 N 94.12 W
Biwabik 256 47.32 N 92.23 W
Bixby 262 35.57 N 95.53 W
Black ≃, MB 250 50.49 N 96.20 W
Black ≃, ON 256 48.42 N 80.38 W
Black ≃, ON 256 44.32 N 77.22 W
Black ≃, ON 256 44.42 N 79.19 W
Black ≃, ON 256 48.36 N 86.16 W
Black ≃, U.S. 260 35.38 N 91.19 W
Black ≃, AK 246 66.39 N 144.50 W
Black ≃, AZ 266 33.44 N 110.13 W
Black ≃, LA 260 31.16 N 91.50 W
Black ≃, MI 256 46.40 N 90.03 W
Black ≃, MI 256 43.00 N 82.25 W
Black ≃, MI 256 45.39 N 84.29 W
Black ≃, NM 262 32.14 N 104.03 W
Black ≃, NC 258 34.35 N 78.16 W
Black ≃, NY 254 43.59 N 76.04 W
Black ≃, SC 258 33.24 N 79.15 W
Black ≃, VT 254 43.16 N 72.27 W
Black ≃, VT 254 44.55 N 72.13 W
Black ≃, WI 256 43.57 N 91.22 W
Black, East Fork ≃ 256 44.26 N 90.42 W
Black Bay C 256 48.40 N 88.30 W
Black Bear Creek ≃ 262 36.25 N 96.38 W
Black Birch Lake ⊜ 250 56.54 N 107.45 W
Blackburn, Mount ∧ 246 61.44 N 143.26 W
Black Butte ∧, MT 268 46.47 N 110.56 W
Black Butte ∧, MT 268 44.54 N 111.51 W
Black Butte Lake ⊜¹ 270 39.45 N 122.20 W
Black Canyon of the Gunnison National Monument ♦ 266 38.32 N 107.42 W
Black Creek 248 49.50 N 125.08 W
Black Creek ≃, AZ 266 35.16 N 109.14 W
Black Creek ≃, FL 258 30.03 N 81.42 W
Black Creek ≃, MS 260 33.01 N 90.21 W
Black Creek ≃, MS 260 30.39 N 88.39 W
Black Creek ≃, SC 258 34.18 N 79.37 W
Black Creek, North Fork ≃ 258 30.05 N 81.51 W
Black Creek, South Fork ≃ 258 30.05 N 81.51 W
Black Cypress Bayou ≃ 260 32.42 N 93.55 W
Black Diamond, AB 248 50.42 N 114.14 W
Black Diamond, WA 268 47.18 N 122.00 W
Blackduck 264 47.44 N 94.33 W
Black Duck ≃ 242 56.51 N 89.02 W
Black Eagle 268 47.31 N 111.17 W
Blackfalds 248 52.23 N 113.47 W
Blackfeet Indian Reservation ◆⁴ 268 48.40 N 113.00 W
Blackfoot 268 43.11 N 112.20 W
Blackfoot ≃, ID 268 43.08 N 112.30 W
Blackfoot ≃, MT 268 46.52 N 113.53 W
Blackfoot, North Fork ≃ 268 46.59 N 113.07 W
Blackfoot Indian Reserve ◆⁴ 248 50.45 N 113.00 W
Blackfoot Reservoir ⊜¹ 268 42.55 N 111.35 W
Blackhall Mountain ∧ 268 41.02 N 106.41 W
Black Hawk 250 48.48 N 93.59 W
Black Hawk Creek ≃ 256 42.30 N 92.21 W
Blackhead Bay C 252 48.34 N 53.15 W
Black Hills ⩘ 244 44.00 N 104.00 W
Black Island I 250 51.10 N 96.30 W
Black Lake 254 46.03 N 71.21 W
Black Lake ⊜, SK 242 59.10 N 105.20 W
Black Lake ⊜, MI 256 45.28 N 84.15 W
Black Lake ⊜, NY 254 44.31 N 75.35 W
Black Lake Bayou ≃ 260 32.01 N 93.09 W
Black Mesa ∧, AZ 266 36.35 N 110.20 W
Black Mesa ∧, OK 262 36.57 N 102.59 W
Blackmore, Mount ∧ 268 45.27 N 111.01 W
Black Mountain 258 35.37 N 82.19 W
Black Mountain ∧, CA 270 35.24 N 120.21 W
Black Mountain ∧, ID 268 46.53 N 115.33 W
Black Mountain ∧, KY 258 36.54 N 82.54 W
Black Mountain ∧, MT 268 46.44 N 112.31 W
Black Mountain ∧, OR 268 45.13 N 119.17 W
Black Mountain ∧, WY 268 44.45 N 107.22 W
Black Mountains ⩘ 266 35.30 N 114.30 W
Black Peak ∧ 266 34.08 N 114.13 W
Black Pine Peak ∧ 268 42.08 N 113.08 W
Black Pipe Creek ≃ 264 43.47 N 101.14 W
Black Point ≻ 246 57.00 N 153.18 W
Black Range ⩘ 266 33.20 N 107.50 W
Black River 254 44.01 N 75.48 W
Black River Falls 256 44.23 N 90.52 W
Black Rock 260 36.06 N 91.06 W
Black Rock Desert ◆² 270 41.10 N 119.00 W
Blacksburg, SC 258 35.07 N 81.31 W
Blacksburg, VA 258 37.14 N 80.25 W
Blacks Fork ≃ 266 41.24 N 109.38 W
Blacks Harbour 252 45.03 N 66.47 W
Blackshear 258 31.18 N 82.14 W
Blackshear, Lake ⊜¹ 258 31.56 N 83.56 W
Blackstone 258 37.04 N 78.00 W
Blackstone ≃, AB 248 52.50 N 116.07 W
Blackstone ≃, YK 246 65.51 N 137.12 W
Black Thunder Creek ≃ 264 43.33 N 104.41 W
Blackville 258 33.22 N 81.16 W
Black Warrior ≃ 260 32.32 N 87.51 W
Blackwater ≃, U.S. 260 30.36 N 87.02 W
Blackwater ≃, MO 260 38.56 N 92.51 W
Blackwater Draw ∨ 262 33.35 N 101.50 W
Blackwater Lake ⊜ 242 64.00 N 123.05 W
Blackwell, OK 262 36.48 N 97.17 W
Blackwell, TX 262 32.05 N 100.19 W
Bladenboro 258 34.33 N 78.48 W
Bladworth 250 51.18 N 106.09 W
Blaine, MN 256 45.11 N 93.14 W
Blaine, WA 268 48.59 N 122.44 W
Blaine Creek ≃ 254 38.11 N 82.37 W
Blaine Lake 250 52.50 N 106.54 W
Blair, NE 264 41.33 N 96.08 W
Blair, OK 262 34.47 N 99.20 W
Blair, WI 256 44.18 N 91.14 W
Blairmore 248 49.36 N 114.26 W
Blairstown 256 41.55 N 92.05 W
Blairsville, GA 258 34.53 N 83.58 W
Blairsville, PA 254 40.26 N 79.16 W
Blakely 258 31.23 N 84.56 W
Blake Point ≻ 256 48.11 N 88.25 W
Blakesburg 256 40.58 N 92.38 W
Blalock Island I 268 45.53 N 119.41 W
Blanca 266 37.27 N 105.31 W
Blanca, Sierra ⩘ 266 31.15 N 105.26 W
Blanca Peak ∧ 266 37.35 N 105.29 W
Blanchard 262 35.08 N 97.39 W
Blanchard ≃ 254 41.02 N 84.18 W
Blanchardville 256 42.49 N 89.52 W
Blanche ≃ 256 47.34 N 79.32 W
Blanchester 254 39.17 N 83.55 W
Blanco 262 30.06 N 98.25 W
Blanco ≃ 262 29.51 N 97.55 W
Blanco, Cañon ∨ 266 35.20 N 105.05 W
Blanco, Cape ≻ 268 42.50 N 124.32 W
Blanco, Rio ≃ 266 37.07 N 107.03 W
Blanco Creek ≃ 262 28.19 N 97.19 W
Blanc-Sablon 252 51.25 N 57.07 W
Bland, MO 260 38.18 N 91.38 W
Bland, VA 258 37.06 N 81.07 W
Blanding 266 37.37 N 109.29 W
Blandinsville 256 40.33 N 90.52 W
Blanket 262 31.49 N 98.47 W
Blasdell 254 42.47 N 78.49 W
Bledsoe 262 33.38 N 103.01 W
Blenheim 256 42.20 N 82.00 W
Blessing 262 28.52 N 96.13 W
Blewett Falls Lake ⊜¹ 258 35.03 N 79.54 W
Blind River 256 46.10 N 82.58 W
Blissfield 256 41.50 N 83.52 W
Block Island 254 41.10 N 71.34 W
Block Island I 254 41.11 N 71.35 W
Blockton 264 40.37 N 94.29 W
Bloedel 248 50.07 N 125.23 W
Blood Indian Creek ≃ 250 50.55 N 111.03 W
Blood Indian Reserve ◆⁴ 248 49.30 N 113.10 W
Blood Mountain ∧ 258 34.44 N 83.56 W
Bloodvein ≃ 250 51.45 N 96.44 W
Bloomer 256 45.07 N 91.29 W
Bloomfield, ON 256 43.59 N 77.14 W
Bloomfield, IN 260 39.01 N 86.56 W
Bloomfield, IA 256 40.45 N 92.25 W
Bloomfield, KY 260 37.55 N 85.19 W
Bloomfield, MO 260 36.53 N 89.56 W
Bloomfield, NE 264 42.36 N 97.39 W
Bloomfield, NM 266 36.43 N 107.59 W
Blooming Grove 262 32.06 N 96.43 W
Blooming Prairie 256 43.52 N 93.03 W
Bloomington, IL 256 40.29 N 89.00 W
Bloomington, IN 260 39.10 N 86.32 W
Bloomington, MN 256 44.50 N 93.17 W
Bloomington, TX 262 28.39 N 96.54 W
Bloomington, WI 256 42.53 N 90.55 W
Bloomsburg 254 41.00 N 76.27 W
Bloomville 254 41.03 N 83.01 W
Blossburg 254 41.41 N 77.04 W
Blossom 262 33.40 N 95.23 W
Blouin, Lac ⊜ 256 48.10 N 77.44 W
Blountstown 258 30.27 N 85.03 W
Blountsville 260 34.05 N 86.35 W
Blountville 258 36.32 N 82.19 W
Blowing Rock 258 36.08 N 81.41 W
Blue ≃, AZ 266 33.13 N 109.11 W
Blue ≃, CO 266 40.03 N 106.24 W
Blue ≃, IN 260 38.11 N 86.19 W
Blue ≃, OK 262 33.53 N 95.56 W
Blue Buck Knob ∧² 260 36.57 N 92.07 W
Blue Creek ≃, ID 268 42.02 N 116.08 W
Blue Creek ≃, NE 264 41.19 N 102.10 W
Blue Creek ≃, NM 262 32.50 N 105.00 W
Blue Creek ≃, UT 266 41.31 N 112.24 W
Blue Cypress Lake ⊜ 258 27.44 N 80.45 W
Blue Earth 264 43.38 N 94.06 W
Blue Earth ≃ 264 44.09 N 94.02 W
Bluefield, VA 258 37.15 N 81.17 W
Bluefield, WV 258 37.16 N 81.13 W
Blue Hill, ME 254 44.25 N 68.36 W
Blue Hill, NE 264 40.20 N 98.27 W
Blue Hill Bay C 254 44.15 N 68.30 W
Blue Hills of Couteau ⩘² 252 47.59 N 57.43 W
Blue Island 260 41.40 N 87.41 W
Bluejoint Lake ⊜ 268 42.35 N 119.40 W
Blue Knob State Park ♦ 254 40.16 N 78.35 W
Blue Mesa Reservoir ⊜¹ 266 38.27 N 107.10 W
Blue Mound, IL 260 39.42 N 89.07 W
Blue Mound, KS 264 38.05 N 95.00 W
Blue Mountain 260 34.40 N 89.02 W
Blue Mountain ∧, NB 252 47.49 N 66.19 W
Blue Mountain ∧, NF 252 50.24 N 57.10 W
Blue Mountain ∧, AR 260 34.41 N 94.03 W
Blue Mountain ∧, MT 264 47.16 N 104.10 W
Blue Mountain ∧, NH 254 44.47 N 71.28 W
Blue Mountain ∧, PA 254 40.15 N 77.30 W
Blue Mountain ∧² 256 48.15 N 80.07 W
Blue Mountains ⩘, U.S. 244 45.30 N 118.15 W
Blue Mountains ⩘, ME 254 44.50 N 70.35 W
Bluenose Lake ⊜ 242 68.30 N 119.35 W
Blue Rapids 264 39.41 N 96.39 W
Blue Ridge, AB 248 54.08 N 115.22 W
Blue Ridge, GA 258 34.52 N 84.20 W
Blue Ridge ⩘ 244 37.00 N 82.00 W
Blue River 248 52.05 N 119.17 W
Bluesky 248 56.04 N 118.14 W
Blue Springs 264 40.09 N 96.40 W
Bluestone ≃ 258 37.34 N 80.59 W
Bluestone Dam ◆⁶ 258 37.36 N 80.53 W
Bluestone Lake ⊜¹ 258 37.30 N 80.50 W
Bluestone State Park ♦ 258 37.37 N 80.56 W
Bluewater 266 35.15 N 107.59 W
Bluff 266 37.17 N 109.33 W
Bluff City 258 36.28 N 82.16 W
Bluff Creek ≃, U.S. 262 36.58 N 97.26 W
Bluff Creek ≃, KS 264 37.02 N 99.29 W
Bluff Dale 262 32.21 N 98.01 W
Bluff Park 260 33.27 N 86.47 W
Bluffs 260 39.45 N 90.32 W
Bluffton, IN 260 40.44 N 85.11 W
Bluffton, OH 254 40.54 N 83.54 W
Bluffton, SC 258 32.14 N 80.52 W
Bluffy Lake ⊜ 250 50.47 N 92.55 W
Blumenhof 250 50.01 N 107.41 W
Blunt 264 44.31 N 99.59 W
Bly 268 42.24 N 121.02 W
Blying Sound ɯ 246 59.50 N 149.15 W
Blyth 256 43.44 N 81.26 W
Blythe 270 33.37 N 114.36 W
Blytheville 260 35.56 N 89.55 W
Blytheville Air Force Base 260 35.57 N 89.57 W
Board Camp Mountain ∧ 270 40.42 N 123.43 W
Boardman 254 41.02 N 80.40 W
Boardman ≃ 256 44.46 N 85.38 W
Boat Basin 248 49.29 N 126.25 W
Boaz 260 34.12 N 86.10 W
Bobcaygeon 256 44.33 N 78.33 W
Bobs Lake ⊜ 256 44.40 N 76.35 W
Bobtown 254 39.46 N 79.59 W
Boca de Quadra ɯ 248 55.08 N 130.50 W
Boca Grande 258 26.45 N 82.16 W
Boca Raton 258 26.21 N 80.05 W
Bodcau Creek ≃ 260 33.01 N 93.31 W
Bode 264 42.52 N 94.17 W
Bodega Bay C 270 38.15 N 123.00 W
Bodine, Mount ∧ 248 55.37 N 125.49 W
Boerne 262 29.47 N 98.44 W
Boeuf ≃ 260 31.52 N 91.47 W
Bogachiel ≃ 268 47.55 N 124.28 W
Bogalusa 260 30.47 N 89.52 W
Bogata 262 33.28 N 95.13 W
Boger City 258 35.29 N 81.13 W
Bogue Chitto 260 31.28 N 90.26 W
Bogue Chitto ≃ 260 30.35 N 89.49 W
Bogue Chitto Creek ≃ 260 32.10 N 87.14 W
Bogue Phalia ≃ 260 33.15 N 90.44 W
Boiestown 252 46.27 N 66.25 W
Boiling Springs 258 35.16 N 81.40 W
Bois, Lac des ⊜ 242 66.40 N 125.15 W
Bois Blanc Island I 256 45.45 N 84.28 W
Bois Brule ≃ 256 46.45 N 91.37 W
Bois d'Arc Creek ≃ 262 33.50 N 95.50 W
Bois de Sioux ≃ 264 46.16 N 96.36 W
Boise 268 43.37 N 116.13 W
Boise ≃ 268 43.49 N 117.01 W
Boise, Middle Fork ≃ 268 43.42 N 115.38 W
Boise, North Fork ≃ 268 43.42 N 115.38 W
Boise, South Fork ≃ 268 43.36 N 115.51 W
Boise City 262 36.44 N 102.31 W
Boissevain 250 49.14 N 100.03 W
Boistfort Peak ∧ 268 46.29 N 123.12 W
Bokchito 262 34.01 N 96.09 W
Bokes Creek ≃ 254 40.19 N 83.10 W
Boles 262 34.47 N 94.03 W
Boley 262 35.29 N 96.29 W
Boligee 260 32.45 N 88.02 W
Boling 262 29.16 N 95.57 W
Bolingbrook 260 41.42 N 88.03 W
Bolivar, MO 260 37.37 N 93.25 W
Bolivar, NY 254 42.04 N 78.14 W
Bolivar, TN 260 35.16 N 88.59 W
Bolivar Peninsula ≻¹ 260 29.27 N 94.39 W
Bolton, ON 256 43.53 N 79.44 W
Bolton, MS 260 32.21 N 90.28 W
Bolton, NC 258 34.20 N 78.25 W
Bolton Lake ⊜ 250 54.16 N 95.47 W
Bon Air 258 37.32 N 77.34 W
Bonanza, OR 268 42.12 N 121.24 W
Bonanza, UT 266 40.01 N 109.11 W
Bonanza Peak ∧ 268 48.14 N 120.52 W
Bonaparte 256 40.42 N 91.48 W
Bonaparte ≃ 248 50.46 N 121.17 W
Bonaparte, Mount ∧ 268 48.45 N 119.08 W
Bonaparte Lake ⊜ 248 51.16 N 120.35 W
Bonasila Dome ∧ 246 62.19 N 160.30 W
Bonaventure 252 48.03 N 65.29 W
Bonaventure ≃ 252 48.02 N 65.28 W
Bonaventure, Île I 252 48.30 N 64.10 W
Bonavista 252 48.39 N 53.07 W
Bonavista, Cape ≻ 252 48.42 N 53.05 W
Bonavista Bay C 252 48.45 N 53.20 W
Bond 260 30.54 N 89.10 W
Bonduel 256 44.44 N 88.27 W
Bon Echo Provincial Park ♦ 256 44.52 N 77.15 W
Bonesteel 264 43.04 N 98.57 W
Bonham 262 33.35 N 96.11 W
Bonifay 260 30.48 N 85.41 W
Bonilla Island I 248 53.29 N 130.36 W
Bonita 260 32.55 N 91.40 W
Bonita Springs 258 26.21 N 81.47 W
Bonito, Rio ≃ 266 33.13 N 105.16 W
Bonne Bay (Woody Point) 252 49.30 N 57.56 W
Bonne Bay C 252 49.33 N 57.55 W
Bonnechere ≃ 256 45.31 N 76.33 W
Bonner 268 46.52 N 113.52 W
Bonners Ferry 268 48.41 N 116.18 W
Bonnet, Lac du ⊜ 250 50.22 N 95.55 W
Bonne Terre 260 37.55 N 90.33 W
Bonnet Plume ≃ 246 65.55 N 134.58 W
Bonneville Dam ◆⁶ 268 45.33 N 121.54 W
Bonneville Peak ∧ 268 42.46 N 112.08 W
Bonneville Salt Flats ≃ 266 40.45 N 113.52 W
Bonnie Doone 258 35.05 N 78.58 W
Bonnyville 250 54.16 N 110.44 W
Bono 260 35.55 N 90.50 W
Bonpas Creek ≃ 260 38.16 N 87.59 W
Bon Secour 260 30.19 N 87.44 W
Bonshaw 252 46.12 N 63.21 W
Bon Wier 260 30.44 N 93.39 W
Book Cliffs ◆⁴ 266 39.20 N 109.00 W
Booker 262 36.27 N 100.32 W
Booker T. Washington National Monument ♦ 258 37.01 N 79.45 W
Boomer 254 38.09 N 81.17 W
Boone, IA 256 42.04 N 93.53 W
Boone, NC 258 36.13 N 81.41 W
Boone ≃ 256 42.19 N 93.56 W
Boone Draw ∨ 262 33.51 N 103.42 W
Boone Lake ⊜¹ 258 36.25 N 82.25 W
Boones Mill 258 37.07 N 79.57 W
Booneville, AR 260 35.08 N 93.55 W
Booneville, KY 258 37.29 N 83.40 W
Booneville, MS 260 34.39 N 88.34 W
Boonsboro 254 39.30 N 77.39 W
Boonville, CA 270 39.00 N 123.22 W
Boonville, IN 260 38.03 N 87.16 W
Boonville, MO 260 38.58 N 92.44 W
Boonville, NY 254 43.29 N 75.20 W
Bootahnie Indian Reserve ◆⁴ 248 50.24 N 121.31 W
Booth 260 32.30 N 86.41 W
Booth, Lac ⊜ 256 46.45 N 78.34 W
Boothbay Harbor 254 43.51 N 69.38 W
Boothia, Gulf of C 242 71.00 N 91.00 W
Boothia Peninsula ≻¹ 242 70.30 N 95.00 W
Boothville 260 29.19 N 89.24 W
Borah Peak ∧ 268 44.08 N 113.48 W
Borden 250 52.25 N 107.13 W
Borden Lake ⊜ 256 47.50 N 83.18 W
Borden Peninsula ≻¹ 242 73.00 N 83.00 W
Borger 262 35.39 N 101.24 W
Borgne, Lake C 260 30.05 N 89.40 W
Boron 270 35.00 N 117.39 W
Boscobel 256 43.08 N 90.42 W
Bosque Farms 266 34.53 N 106.40 W
Bossier City 260 32.31 N 93.43 W
Boston, GA 258 30.47 N 83.47 W
Boston, MA 254 42.21 N 71.04 W
Boston Bar 248 49.52 N 121.26 W
Boston Mountains ⩘ 260 35.50 N 93.20 W
Boswell, IN 260 40.31 N 87.23 W
Boswell, OK 262 34.02 N 95.52 W
Boswell, PA 254 40.10 N 79.02 W
Boswell Bay 246 60.24 N 146.08 W
Bosworth 260 39.28 N 93.20 W
Bothwell 256 42.38 N 81.52 W
Botkins 254 40.28 N 84.11 W
Bottineau 264 48.50 N 100.27 W
Botwood 252 49.09 N 55.21 W
Boucher ≃ 252 49.10 N 69.06 W
Boucher, Lac ⊜ 252 51.07 N 59.35 W
Boularderie Island I 252 46.15 N 60.30 W
Boulder, CO 266 40.01 N 105.17 W
Boulder, MT 268 46.14 N 112.07 W
Boulder ≃ 268 45.52 N 111.57 W
Boulder City 270 35.59 N 114.50 W
Boulder Creek ≃, CO 266 40.09 N 105.01 W
Boulder Creek ≃, UT 266 37.47 N 111.22 W
Boundary 246 64.04 N 141.06 W
Boundary Peak ∧ 270 37.51 N 118.21 W
Bountiful 266 40.53 N 111.53 W
Bourbeuse ≃ 260 38.24 N 90.53 W
Bourbeuse, Dry Fork ≃ 260 38.16 N 91.26 W
Bourbon, IN 260 41.18 N 86.07 W
Bourbon, MO 260 38.09 N 91.15 W
Bourg 260 29.34 N 90.36 W
Bourget 254 45.26 N 75.09 W
Bouse 266 33.56 N 114.00 W
Bouse Wash ∨ 266 34.02 N 114.20 W
Bovey 264 47.17 N 93.25 W
Bovill 268 46.51 N 116.24 W
Bovina 262 34.31 N 102.53 W
Bow ≃, AB 250 49.56 N 111.42 W
Bow ≃, SK 250 54.56 N 105.13 W
Bowbells 264 48.48 N 102.15 W
Bow Creek ≃ 264 39.35 N 99.14 W
Bowden 248 51.55 N 114.02 W
Bowdle 264 45.27 N 99.39 W
Bowdoin, Lake ⊜ 268 48.24 N 108.41 W
Bowdon, GA 258 33.32 N 85.15 W
Bowdon, ND 264 47.28 N 99.43 W
Bowen 260 40.14 N 91.04 W
Bowie, AZ 266 32.19 N 109.29 W
Bowie, MD 254 39.00 N 76.47 W
Bowie, TX 262 33.34 N 97.51 W
Bow Island 250 49.52 N 111.22 W
Bowling Green, FL 258 27.38 N 81.50 W
Bowling Green, KY 260 37.00 N 86.27 W
Bowling Green, MO 260 39.20 N 91.12 W
Bowling Green, OH 254 41.22 N 83.39 W
Bowling Green, VA 254 38.03 N 77.21 W
Bowman, GA 258 34.12 N 83.02 W
Bowman, ND 264 46.11 N 103.24 W
Bowman, SC 258 33.21 N 80.41 W
Bowman, Mount ∧ 248 51.10 N 121.55 W
Bowman Bay C 242 65.30 N 73.40 W
Bowman-Haley Lake ⊜¹ 264 46.00 N 103.20 W
Bowmanville 256 43.55 N 78.41 W
Bowron ≃ 248 54.04 N 121.48 W
Bowron Lake Porvincial Park ♦ 248 53.10 N 121.06 W
Bowsman 250 52.14 N 101.14 W
Box Butte Creek ≃ 264 42.28 N 102.37 W
Box Elder 264 48.19 N 110.01 W
Boxelder Creek ≃, U.S. 264 45.59 N 103.57 W
Box Elder Creek ≃, CO 264 40.23 N 104.28 W
Boxelder Creek ≃, CO 264 40.33 N 105.00 W
Box Elder Creek ≃, MT 268 46.57 N 108.04 W
Boxelder Creek ≃, SD 264 44.01 N 102.27 W
Boxey 252 47.25 N 55.34 W
Boxey Point ≻ 252 47.24 N 55.35 W
Boyce 260 31.23 N 92.40 W
Boyceville 256 45.03 N 92.02 W
Boyd, MN 264 44.51 N 95.54 W
Boyd, TX 262 33.05 N 97.34 W
Boyd's Cove 252 49.27 N 54.39 W
Boydton 258 36.40 N 78.24 W
Boyer ≃ 264 41.28 N 95.55 W
Boyertown 254 40.20 N 75.38 W
Boykins 258 36.35 N 77.12 W
Boyle, AB 248 54.35 N 112.49 W
Boyle, MS 260 33.42 N 90.50 W
Boylston 260 32.26 N 86.17 W
Boyne ≃, MB 250 49.34 N 97.52 W
Boyne ≃, ON 256 44.10 N 79.49 W
Boyne City 256 45.13 N 85.01 W
Boynton 262 35.39 N 95.39 W
Boynton Beach 258 26.32 N 80.03 W
Boysen Reservoir ⊜¹ 268 43.19 N 108.11 W
Boysen State Park ♦ 268 43.23 N 108.07 W
Boys Ranch 262 35.32 N 102.15 W
Bozeman 268 45.41 N 111.02 W
Brabant Lake ⊜ 250 56.00 N 103.43 W
Bracebridge 256 45.02 N 79.19 W
Brackendale 248 49.46 N 123.09 W
Bracken Lake ⊜ 250 53.37 N 99.50 W
Brackettville 262 29.19 N 100.24 W
Bradenton 258 27.29 N 82.34 W
Bradford, ON 256 44.07 N 79.34 W
Bradford, AR 260 35.25 N 91.27 W
Bradford, IL 260 41.11 N 89.39 W
Bradford, OH 254 40.08 N 84.26 W
Bradford, PA 254 41.58 N 78.39 W
Bradford, TN 260 36.05 N 88.51 W
Bradford, VT 254 43.59 N 72.09 W
Bradley, AR 260 33.06 N 93.39 W
Bradley, FL 258 27.48 N 81.59 W
Bradley, IL 260 41.09 N 87.52 W
Bradley, SD 264 45.05 N 97.39 W
Bradore Bay 252 51.28 N 57.14 W
Bradshaw, NE 264 40.53 N 97.45 W
Bradshaw, WV 258 37.21 N 81.49 W
Brady, MT 268 48.02 N 111.51 W
Brady, NE 264 41.01 N 100.22 W
Brady, TX 262 31.08 N 99.20 W
Brady Mountains ⩘² 262 31.20 N 99.40 W
Braham 256 45.41 N 93.28 W
Braidwood 260 41.16 N 88.13 W
Brainard 264 41.11 N 97.00 W
Brainerd 264 46.21 N 94.12 W
Bralorne 248 50.47 N 122.49 W
Braman 262 36.55 N 97.20 W
Brampton 256 43.41 N 79.46 W
Branch 252 46.53 N 53.57 W
Branchville 258 33.15 N 80.49 W
Brandenburg 260 38.00 N 86.10 W
Brandon, MB 250 49.50 N 99.57 W
Brandon, FL 258 27.56 N 82.17 W
Brandon, MS 260 32.16 N 89.59 W
Brandon, SD 264 43.36 N 96.37 W
Brandon, VT 254 43.48 N 73.05 W
Brandon, WI 256 43.44 N 88.47 W
Brandy Peak ∧ 268 42.36 N 123.53 W
Branford 258 29.58 N 82.56 W
Branson 260 36.39 N 93.13 W
Brantford 256 43.08 N 80.16 W
Brant Lake 254 43.41 N 73.45 W
Brantley 260 31.35 N 86.22 W
Brantville 252 47.22 N 64.58 W
Bras d'Or Lake ⊜ 252 45.52 N 60.50 W
Brasstown Bald ∧ 258 34.52 N 83.48 W
Brattleboro 254 42.51 N 72.34 W
Brave 254 39.44 N 80.16 W
Bravo del Norte (Rio Grande) ≃ 244 25.55 N 97.09 W
Brawley 270 32.59 N 115.31 W
Brawley Peaks ∧ 270 38.15 N 118.55 W
Brawley Wash ∨ 266 32.34 N 111.26 W
Bray Island I 242 69.20 N 76.45 W
Braymer 260 39.35 N 93.48 W
Brazeau ≃ 248 52.55 N 115.15 W
Brazeau, Mount ∧ 248 52.33 N 117.21 W
Brazeau Dam ◆⁶ 248 52.45 N 115.30 W
Brazil 260 39.32 N 87.08 W
Brazoria 262 29.03 N 95.34 W
Brazos ≃ 262 28.53 N 95.23 W
Brazos, Clear Fork ≃ 262 33.01 N 98.40 W
Brazos, Double Mountain Fork ≃ 262 33.15 N 100.00 W
Brazos, Salt Fork ≃ 262 33.15 N 100.00 W
Brea 270 33.55 N 117.54 W
Breakenridge, Mount ∧ 248 49.43 N 121.56 W

Symbols in the index entries are identified on page 273.

Name Page Lat °' Long °'

Breaks Interstate Park ♦ 258 37.17 N 82.18 W
Breaux Bridge 260 30.16 N 91.54 W
Breckenridge, CO 266 39.29 N 106.03 W
Breckenridge, MI 256 43.24 N 84.29 W
Breckenridge, MN 264 46.16 N 96.35 W
Breckenridge, MO 260 39.44 N 93.49 W
Breckenridge, TX 262 32.45 N 98.54 W
Breda 264 42.11 N 94.59 W
Bredenbury 250 50.57 N 102.03 W
Breese 260 38.36 N 89.32 W
Bremen, GA 258 33.43 N 85.09 W
Bremen, IN 260 41.27 N 86.09 W
Bremen, OH 254 39.42 N 82.26 W
Bremerton 268 47.34 N 122.38 W
Bremner ≈ 256 48.41 N 85.31 W
Bremond 262 31.10 N 96.41 W
Brem River 248 50.26 N 124.39 W
Brenham 262 30.10 N 96.24 W
Brent, AL 260 32.56 N 87.10 W
Brent, FL 260 30.27 N 87.15 W
Brentwood, NY 254 40.47 N 73.14 W
Brentwood, TN 260 36.01 N 86.47 W
Breton 248 53.07 N 114.28 W
Breton Islands II 260 29.28 N 89.11 W
Breton Sound ⊔ 260 29.30 N 89.30 W
Brevard 258 35.09 N 82.44 W
Brevig Mission 246 65.20 N 166.29 W
Brevoort Island I 242 63.30 N 64.20 W
Brewer 254 44.48 N 68.46 W
Brewster, KS 264 39.22 N 101.23 W
Brewster, MN 264 43.42 N 95.28 W
Brewster, NE 264 41.56 N 99.52 W
Brewster, OH 254 40.43 N 81.36 W
Brewster, WA 268 48.06 N 119.47 W
Brewton 260 31.07 N 87.04 W
Brian Boru Peak ▲ 248 55.05 N 127.35 W
Brian Head ▲ 266 37.41 N 112.50 W
Bricelyn 256 43.34 N 93.49 W
Brices Cross Roads National Battlefield Site ⊥ 260 34.31 N 88.41 W
Briceville 258 36.11 N 84.11 W
Briçonnet, Lac ⊜ 252 51.27 N 60.11 W
Bridge ≈ 248 50.45 N 121.55 W
Bridge City 260 30.01 N 93.51 W
Bridge Lake 248 51.29 N 120.43 W
Bridgeport, ON 256 43.29 N 80.29 W
Bridgeport, AL 260 34.57 N 85.43 W
Bridgeport, CA 270 38.10 N 119.13 W
Bridgeport, CT 254 41.11 N 73.11 W
Bridgeport, IL 260 38.43 N 87.46 W
Bridgeport, MI 256 43.22 N 83.53 W
Bridgeport, NE 264 41.40 N 103.06 W
Bridgeport, TX 262 33.13 N 97.45 W
Bridgeport, WA 268 48.00 N 119.40 W
Bridgeport, WV 254 39.17 N 80.15 W
Bridgeport, Lake ⊜¹ 262 33.13 N 97.48 W
Bridger 268 45.18 N 108.55 W
Bridge River Indian Reserve ◆⁴ 248 50.45 N 122.00 W
Bridger Peak ▲ 268 41.12 N 107.02 W
Bridgeton 254 39.26 N 75.14 W
Bridgetown 252 44.51 N 65.18 W
Bridgeville 254 38.45 N 75.36 W
Bridgewater, NS 252 44.23 N 64.31 W
Bridgewater, ME 252 46.25 N 67.51 W
Bridgewater, MA 254 41.59 N 70.58 W
Bridgewater, SD 264 43.33 N 97.30 W
Bridgewater, VA 254 38.18 N 78.59 W
Bridgman 256 41.57 N 86.33 W
Brier Creek ≈ 258 32.47 N 81.26 W
Brig Bay 252 51.04 N 56.55 W
Briggs 262 30.53 N 97.56 W
Brigham City 266 41.31 N 112.01 W
Brighton, ON 256 44.02 N 77.44 W
Brighton, CO 266 39.59 N 104.49 W
Brighton, IL 260 39.02 N 90.08 W
Brighton, IA 256 41.10 N 91.49 W
Brighton, MI 256 42.32 N 83.47 W
Brighton, NY 254 43.08 N 77.34 W
Brighton Indian Reservation ◆⁴ 258 27.04 N 81.05 W
Brightsand Lake ⊜ 250 53.36 N 108.52 W
Brigus 252 47.32 N 53.13 W
Brilliant, BC 248 49.19 N 117.38 W
Brilliant, AL 260 34.01 N 87.46 W
Brillion 256 44.11 N 88.04 W
Brinkley 260 34.53 N 91.12 W
Brion, Île I 252 47.48 N 61.28 W
Bristol, CT 254 41.41 N 72.57 W
Bristol, FL 258 30.26 N 84.58 W
Bristol, NH 254 43.36 N 71.45 W
Bristol, PA 254 40.06 N 74.52 W
Bristol, RI 254 40.06 N 74.52 W
Bristol, SD 264 45.21 N 97.45 W
Bristol, TN 258 36.36 N 82.11 W
Bristol, VT 254 44.08 N 73.05 W
Bristol, VA 258 36.36 N 82.11 W
Bristol Bay C 246 58.00 N 159.00 W
Bristol Lake ⊜ 270 34.28 N 115.41 W
Bristow 262 35.50 N 96.23 W
Britannia Beach 248 49.38 N 123.12 W
British Columbia □⁴, Can. 242
248 54.00 N 125.00 W
British Mountains ⋀ 242 69.00 N 140.20 W
Britt 256 43.06 N 93.48 W
Britton 264 45.48 N 97.45 W
Broad ≈, U.S. 258 34.00 N 81.04 W
Broad ≈, GA 258 33.59 N 82.39 W
Broadalbin 254 43.03 N 74.12 W
Broadback ≈ 242 51.21 N 78.52 W
Broad Pass)(246 63.18 N 149.09 W
Broadus 264 45.27 N 105.25 W
Broadview 250 50.20 N 102.30 W
Broadwater 264 41.36 N 102.51 W
Broadway 254 38.38 N 78.46 W
Brochet 242 57.53 N 101.40 W
Brochet, Lac du ⊜ 252 49.40 N 69.37 W
Brock 250 51.27 N 108.42 W
Brockport 254 43.13 N 77.56 W
Brockton, MA 254 42.05 N 71.01 W
Brockton, MT 264 48.09 N 104.55 W
Brockville 256 44.35 N 75.41 W
Brockway 254 41.15 N 78.47 W
Brocton 254 42.23 N 79.27 W
Brodeur Peninsula ≻¹ 242 73.00 N 88.00 W
Brodhead, KY 258 37.24 N 84.25 W
Brodhead, WI 256 42.37 N 89.22 W
Brodnax 258 36.42 N 78.02 W
Brogan 268 44.15 N 117.31 W
Broken Arrow 262 36.03 N 95.48 W
Broken Bow, NE 264 41.24 N 99.38 W
Broken Bow, OK 260 34.02 N 94.44 W
Broken Bow Lake ⊜¹ 260 34.10 N 94.40 W
Brokenhead ≈ 250 50.25 N 96.40 W
Bromptonville 254 45.28 N 71.57 W
Bronlund Peak ▲ 242 57.26 N 126.38 W
Bronson, FL 258 29.27 N 82.38 W
Bronson, KS 264 37.54 N 95.04 W
Bronson, MI 256 41.52 N 85.12 W
Bronson, TX 260 31.21 N 94.01 W
Bronson Lake ⊜ 250 53.52 N 109.43 W
Bronte 262 31.53 N 100.18 W
Bronwood 258 31.50 N 84.22 W
Brooch, Lac ⊜ 252 50.44 N 67.58 W
Brook 260 40.52 N 87.22 W
Brookeland 260 31.09 N 94.00 W
Brooker 258 29.53 N 82.20 W
Brookfield, NS 252 45.15 N 63.17 W
Brookfield, MO 260 39.47 N 93.04 W
Brookfield, WI 256 43.04 N 88.09 W
Brookford 258 35.42 N 81.21 W
Brookhaven 260 31.35 N 90.26 W
Brookings, OR 268 42.03 N 124.17 W
Brookings, SD 264 44.19 N 96.48 W
Brookland 260 35.55 N 90.34 W
Brooklet 258 32.23 N 81.40 W
Brooklyn, NS 252 44.03 N 64.42 W
Brooklyn, IA 256 41.44 N 92.27 W
Brooklyn, MI 256 42.06 N 84.15 W
Brooklyn, MS 260 31.03 N 89.11 W
Brooklyn Center 256 45.05 N 93.20 W
Brookmere 248 49.49 N 120.53 W
Brookneal 258 37.03 N 78.57 W
Brookport 260 37.08 N 88.38 W
Brooks, AB 250 50.35 N 111.53 W
Brooks, ME 254 44.33 N 69.07 W
Brooks, Mount ▲ 246 63.11 N 150.40 W
Brooks Air Force Base ■ 262 29.21 N 98.25 W
Brooks Bay C 248 50.13 N 127.55 W
Brookshire 262 29.47 N 95.57 W
Brooks Mountain ▲ 246 65.33 N 167.09 W
Brooks Range ⋀ 246 68.00 N 154.00 W
Brooksville, FL 258 28.33 N 82.23 W
Brooksville, KY 258 38.41 N 84.04 W
Brooksville, MS 260 33.14 N 88.35 W
Brookville, IN 260 39.25 N 85.01 W
Brookville, PA 254 41.09 N 79.05 W
Brookville Lake ⊜¹ 260 39.30 N 85.00 W
Broomfield 266 39.56 N 105.04 W
Brooten 264 45.30 N 95.07 W
Broughton Island I 242 67.35 N 63.50 W
Browerville 264 46.05 N 94.52 W
Brown, Mount ▲ 250 48.52 N 111.09 W
Brown, Point ≻ 268 46.56 N 124.10 W
Brown City 256 43.13 N 82.59 W
Brown County State Park ♦ 260 39.09 N 86.14 W
Brown Deer 256 43.10 N 87.59 W
Browne Bay C 242 73.08 N 97.30 W
Brownfield 262 33.11 N 102.16 W
Browning, MO 260 40.02 N 93.10 W
Browning, MT 268 48.34 N 113.01 W
Browning Entrance C 248 53.41 N 130.30 W
Brown Lake ⊜ 242 65.55 N 91.15 W
Brownlee Reservoir ⊜¹ 268 44.40 N 117.05 W
Brown Mountain ▲ 270 35.41 N 117.01 W
Brownsburg, PQ 254 45.41 N 74.25 W
Brownsburg, IN 260 39.51 N 86.24 W
Brownsdale 256 43.44 N 92.52 W
Brownstown, IL 260 39.00 N 88.57 W
Brownstown, IN 260 38.53 N 86.03 W
Browns Valley 264 45.36 N 96.50 W
Brownsville, KY 260 37.12 N 86.16 W
Brownsville, LA 260 32.30 N 92.10 W
Brownsville, OR 268 44.24 N 122.59 W
Brownsville, PA 254 40.01 N 79.53 W
Brownsville, TN 260 35.36 N 89.15 W
Brownsville, TX 262 25.54 N 97.30 W
Brownton 264 44.44 N 94.21 W
Brownvale 248 56.08 N 117.53 W
Brownville, AL 260 33.24 N 87.52 W
Brownville, ME 254 45.18 N 69.02 W
Brownville, NE 264 40.24 N 95.42 W
Brownville Junction 254 45.21 N 69.03 W
Brownwood 262 31.43 N 98.59 W
Brownwood, Lake ⊜¹ 262 31.51 N 99.02 W
Broxton 258 31.38 N 82.53 W
Bruce, MS 260 33.59 N 89.21 W
Bruce, SD 264 44.26 N 96.54 W
Bruce, WI 256 45.28 N 91.20 W
Bruce Lake ⊜ 250 50.49 N 93.20 W
Bruce Mines 256 46.18 N 83.48 W
Bruce Peninsula ≻¹ 256 44.50 N 81.20 W
Bruderheim 248 53.47 N 112.56 W
Bruin Point ▲ 266 39.39 N 110.22 W
Brule 264 41.06 N 101.53 W
Brule ≈ 256 45.57 N 88.12 W
Brûlé, Lac ⊜ 242 52.17 N 63.52 W
Brundidge 260 31.43 N 85.49 W
Bruneau 268 42.53 N 115.48 W
Bruneau ≈ 268 42.57 N 115.58 W
Bruneau, East Fork ≈ 268 42.34 N 115.38 W
Brunette Island I 252 47.16 N 55.54 W
Bruno 250 52.15 N 105.30 W
Brunson 258 32.56 N 81.11 W
Brunswick, GA 258 31.10 N 81.29 W
Brunswick, ME 254 43.55 N 69.58 W
Brunswick, MD 254 39.19 N 77.37 W
Brunswick, MO 260 39.26 N 93.08 W
Brunswick, OH 254 41.14 N 81.50 W
Brunswick Lake ⊜ 256 49.00 N 83.23 W
Brunswick Naval Air Station ■ 254 43.54 N 69.56 W
Brush 264 40.15 N 103.37 W
Brush Creek ≈ 266 40.25 N 109.20 W
Brushy Creek ≈, OK 262 34.55 N 95.34 W
Brushy Creek ≈, TX 262 30.43 N 97.03 W
Brussels 256 43.44 N 81.15 W
Bryan, OH 254 41.28 N 84.33 W
Bryan, TX 262 30.40 N 96.22 W
Bryant, AR 260 34.36 N 92.30 W
Bryant, SD 264 44.35 N 97.28 W
Bryant Creek ≈ 260 36.36 N 92.17 W
Bryant Mountain ▲ 254 42.28 N 72.58 W
Bryce Canyon National Park ♦ 266 37.29 N 112.12 W
Bryson, PQ 254 45.41 N 76.37 W
Bryson, TX 262 33.10 N 98.23 W
Bryson City 258 35.26 N 83.27 W
Buchanan, SK 250 51.43 N 102.45 W
Buchanan, GA 258 33.48 N 85.11 W
Buchanan, MI 260 41.50 N 86.22 W
Buchanan, VA 258 37.32 N 79.41 W
Buchanan, Lake ⊜¹ 262 30.48 N 98.25 W
Buchan Gulf C 242 71.47 N 74.16 W
Buchans 252 48.49 N 56.52 W
Buchon, Point ≻ 270 35.15 N 120.54 W
Buckatunna 260 31.27 N 88.32 W
Buckatunna Creek ≈ 260 31.30 N 88.32 W
Buck Creek ≈, U.S. 262 34.35 N 99.58 W
Buck Creek ≈, KY 258 36.59 N 84.29 W
Buckeye 266 33.22 N 112.35 W
Buckeye Lake 254 39.56 N 82.29 W
Buckhannon 254 38.59 N 80.14 W
Buckholts 262 30.52 N 97.08 W
Buckhorn ≈ 246 66.13 N 161.10 W
Buckhorn Draw V 262 30.39 N 100.52 W
Buckingham, PQ 254 45.35 N 75.25 W
Buckingham, VA 258 37.32 N 78.37 W
Buck Lake ⊜ 248 53.00 N 114.45 W
Buckland 246 66.16 N 161.20 W
Buckley, IL 256 40.36 N 88.02 W
Buckley, WA 268 47.10 N 122.02 W
Bucklin, KS 264 37.33 N 99.38 W
Bucklin, MO 260 39.47 N 92.53 W
Buck Mountain ▲, VA 258 36.40 N 81.15 W
Buck Mountain ▲, WA 268 48.26 N 119.50 W
Buckner Creek ≈ 264 38.11 N 99.34 W
Bucksport 254 44.34 N 68.48 W
Buctouche 252 46.28 N 64.43 W
Bucyrus 254 40.48 N 82.58 W
Buda, IL 260 41.20 N 89.41 W
Buda, TX 262 30.05 N 97.51 W
Bude 260 31.28 N 90.51 W
Buena Vista, CO 266 38.50 N 106.08 W
Buena Vista, GA 258 32.19 N 84.31 W
Buena Vista, MS 260 33.47 N 88.56 W
Buena Vista, VA 258 37.44 N 79.21 W
Buena Vista Lake Bed ⊜ 270 35.11 N 119.17 W
Buffalo, IA 256 41.27 N 90.43 W
Buffalo, KS 264 37.42 N 95.42 W
Buffalo, MN 256 45.10 N 93.53 W
Buffalo, MO 260 37.39 N 93.06 W
Buffalo, NY 254 42.54 N 78.53 W
Buffalo, OH 254 39.55 N 81.31 W
Buffalo, OK 262 36.50 N 99.38 W
Buffalo, SC 258 34.43 N 81.41 W
Buffalo, SD 264 45.35 N 103.33 W
Buffalo, TX 262 31.28 N 96.04 W
Buffalo, WY 268 44.21 N 106.42 W
Buffalo ≈, Can. 242 60.55 N 115.00 W
Buffalo ≈, AR 260 36.10 N 92.26 W
Buffalo ≈, MN 264 47.06 N 96.49 W
Buffalo ≈, MS 260 31.04 N 91.34 W
Buffalo ≈, TN 260 36.00 N 87.50 W
Buffalo ≈, WI 256 44.22 N 91.55 W
Buffalo Bill Ranch State Historical Park ♦ 264 41.10 N 100.48 W
Buffalo Bill Reservoir ⊜¹ 268 44.29 N 109.13 W
Buffalo Bill State Park ♦ 268 44.30 N 109.14 W
Buffalo Center 256 43.23 N 93.57 W
Buffalo Creek ≈, U.S. 264 45.57 N 102.56 W
Buffalo Creek ≈, IA 256 42.06 N 91.18 W
Buffalo Creek ≈, KS 264 39.35 N 97.43 W
Buffalo Creek ≈, OK 262 36.47 N 99.15 W
Buffalo Lake 264 44.44 N 94.37 W
Buffalo Lake ⊜, AB 248 52.27 N 112.54 W
Buffalo Lake ⊜, NT 242 60.10 N 115.30 W
Buffalo Narrows 250 55.51 N 108.30 W
Buffalo National River ♦ 260 35.58 N 92.53 W
Buffalo Pound Provincial Park ♦ 250 50.36 N 105.30 W
Buford 258 34.07 N 84.00 W
Buford Dam ◆⁶ 258 34.11 N 84.03 W
Buhl, ID 268 42.36 N 114.46 W
Buhl, MN 256 47.30 N 92.47 W
Buhler 264 38.08 N 97.46 W
Buies Creek 258 35.24 N 78.45 W
Bulan 258 37.18 N 83.10 W
Buldir Island I 247a 52.21 N 175.54 E
Bulkley ≈ 248 55.13 N 127.40 W
Bulkley Ranges ⋀ 248 54.30 N 127.30 W
Bull ≈ 268 49.28 N 115.26 W
Bullard 262 32.08 N 95.19 W
Bull Creek ≈, NV 270 38.40 N 115.40 W
Bull Creek ≈, SD 264 45.40 N 103.18 W
Bull Creek ≈, SD 264 43.41 N 99.28 W
Bull Creek ≈, TX 262 32.36 N 101.10 W
Bullfrog Creek ≈ 266 37.19 N 110.44 W
Bull Harbour 248 50.54 N 127.55 W
Bullhead 264 45.46 N 101.05 W
Bullhead City 266 35.09 N 114.34 W
Bull Lake Creek ≈ 268 43.14 N 109.02 W
Bull Lake Reservoir ⊜¹ 268 43.11 N 109.07 W
Bull Mountain ▲ 266 46.05 N 112.04 W
Bull Mountains ⋀ 268 46.05 N 109.00 W
Bullock 258 36.30 N 78.33 W
Bullpound Creek ≈ 250 51.05 N 111.58 W
Bullrun Rock ▲ 268 44.21 N 118.17 W
Bulls Bay C 258 32.59 N 79.33 W
Bulls Gap 258 36.15 N 83.05 W
Bull Shoals 260 36.22 N 92.37 W
Bull Shoals Dam ◆⁶ 260 36.20 N 92.33 W
Bull Shoals Lake ⊜¹ 244 36.30 N 92.50 W
Bully Creek ≈ 268 43.58 N 117.15 W
Bumpus, Mount ▲² 242 69.33 N 112.40 W
Buna 260 30.26 N 93.58 W
Bunavista 262 35.39 N 101.28 W
Bunceton 260 38.47 N 92.48 W
Bundick Creek ≈ 260 30.36 N 92.57 W
Bunker 260 37.27 N 91.13 W
Bunker Hill, IL 260 39.03 N 89.57 W
Bunker Hill, IN 260 40.40 N 86.06 W
Bunker Hill, OR 268 43.21 N 124.12 W
Bunker Hill ▲ 270 39.15 N 117.08 W
Bunkie 260 30.57 N 92.11 W
Bunnell 258 29.28 N 81.15 W
Buras 260 29.21 N 89.32 W
Burbank, CA 270 34.12 N 118.18 W
Burbank, WA 268 46.12 N 119.01 W
Burden 264 37.19 N 96.45 W
Burdett, AB 250 49.50 N 111.32 W
Burdett, KS 264 38.11 N 99.31 W
Burford 256 43.06 N 80.26 W
Burgaw 258 34.33 N 77.56 W
Burgeo 252 47.37 N 57.37 W
Burgess 258 37.53 N 76.21 W
Burgettstown 254 40.23 N 80.23 W
Burgin 258 37.45 N 84.46 W
Burien 268 47.27 N 122.21 W
Burin 252 47.02 N 55.10 W
Burin Peninsula ≻¹ 252 47.00 N 55.40 W
Burkburnett 262 34.06 N 98.34 W
Burke 264 43.11 N 99.18 W
Burke Channel ⊔ 248 52.07 N 127.38 W
Burkesville 260 36.48 N 85.22 W
Burleson 262 32.33 N 97.19 W
Burley 268 42.32 N 113.48 W
Burlingame, CA 270 37.35 N 122.22 W
Burlingame, KS 264 38.45 N 95.50 W
Burlington, NF 252 49.45 N 56.02 W
Burlington, ON 256 43.19 N 79.47 W
Burlington, CO 264 39.18 N 102.16 W
Burlington, IA 256 40.49 N 91.14 W
Burlington, KS 264 38.12 N 95.45 W
Burlington, ME 254 45.12 N 68.26 W
Burlington, NJ 254 40.04 N 74.51 W
Burlington, NC 258 36.05 N 79.26 W
Burlington, ND 264 48.17 N 101.26 W
Burlington, VT 254 44.29 N 73.13 W
Burlington, WA 268 48.28 N 122.20 W
Burlington, WI 256 42.41 N 88.17 W
Burlington, WY 268 44.27 N 108.26 W
Burlington Junction 260 40.27 N 95.04 W
Burnaby 248 49.15 N 122.57 W
Burnaby Island I 248 52.24 N 131.20 W
Burnet 262 30.46 N 98.14 W
Burnett Bay C 242 73.53 N 124.00 W
Burney 270 40.53 N 121.40 W
Burnham 254 40.38 N 77.34 W
Burns, KS 264 38.05 N 96.53 W
Burns, OR 268 43.35 N 119.03 W
Burns, TN 260 36.03 N 87.19 W
Burns, WY 264 41.11 N 104.21 W
Burns Creek ≈ 264 47.22 N 104.25 W
Burns Flat 262 35.21 N 99.10 W
Burnside 258 36.59 N 84.36 W
Burnside ≈ 242 66.51 N 108.04 W
Burns Lake 248 54.14 N 125.46 W
Burnsville, AL 260 32.28 N 86.53 W
Burnsville, MS 260 34.51 N 88.19 W
Burnsville, NC 258 35.55 N 82.18 W
Burnsville, WV 254 38.51 N 80.40 W
Burnt ≈, ON 256 44.35 N 78.46 W
Burnt ≈, OR 268 44.22 N 117.14 W
Burnt Corn Creek ≈ 260 31.06 N 87.04 W
Burnt Island 252 47.36 N 58.53 W
Burntwood ≈ 250 56.08 N 96.30 W
Burntwood Lake ⊜ 250 55.29 N 100.07 W
Burr Oak 264 39.52 N 98.18 W
Burro Creek ≈ 266 34.32 N 113.35 W
Burro Peak ▲ 266 32.35 N 108.26 W
Burrton 264 38.02 N 97.41 W
Burrwood 260 28.58 N 89.22 W
Burstall 250 50.40 N 109.54 W
Burt 264 43.12 N 94.13 W
Burt Lake ⊜ 256 45.27 N 84.40 W
Burton, BC 248 49.59 N 117.54 W
Burton, MI 256 43.02 N 83.36 W
Burton, TX 262 30.11 N 96.36 W
Burton, Lake ⊜¹ 258 34.50 N 83.33 W
Burwash 256 46.19 N 80.48 W
Burwash Landing 246 61.21 N 139.00 W
Burwell 264 41.47 N 99.08 W
Busby 268 45.32 N 106.58 W
Bush ≈ 258 34.08 N 81.36 W
Bushland 262 35.11 N 102.04 W
Bushnell, FL 258 28.40 N 82.07 W
Bushnell, IL 260 40.33 N 90.30 W
Bushton 264 38.31 N 98.24 W
Bushy Head Mountain ▲ 260 36.02 N 94.35 W
Busseron Creek ≈ 260 38.55 N 87.31 W
Bussey 256 41.12 N 92.53 W
Bute Inlet C 248 50.37 N 124.53 W
Butler, AL 260 32.05 N 88.13 W
Butler, GA 258 32.34 N 84.14 W
Butler, IN 260 41.26 N 84.52 W
Butler, MO 260 38.16 N 94.20 W
Butler, OH 254 40.35 N 82.26 W
Butler, OK 262 35.38 N 99.11 W
Butler, PA 254 40.52 N 79.54 W
Butner 258 36.08 N 78.49 W
Butte, MT 268 46.00 N 112.32 W
Butte, NE 264 42.58 N 98.51 W
Butte Creek ≈, CA 270 39.12 N 121.59 W
Butte Creek ≈, OR 268 45.09 N 122.46 W
Butte Falls 268 42.33 N 122.34 W
Butte Mountains ⋀ 270 39.50 N 115.05 W
Butter Creek ≈ 268 45.52 N 119.19 W
Butterfield 264 43.58 N 94.48 W
Butternut 256 46.01 N 90.30 W
Buttle Lake ⊜ 248 49.46 N 125.36 W
Button Islands II 242 60.35 N 64.45 W
Buttonwillow 270 35.24 N 119.28 W
Buxton, NC 258 35.16 N 75.32 W
Buxton, ND 264 47.36 N 97.06 W
Buxton, Mount ▲ 248 51.35 N 127.55 W
Byam Channel ⊔ 242 75.20 N 105.20 W
Byam Martin Channel ⊔ 242 75.45 N 104.00 W
Byam Martin Island I 242 75.15 N 104.00 W
Byers 262 34.04 N 98.11 W
Byesville 254 39.58 N 81.32 W
Byhalia 260 34.52 N 89.41 W
Bylas 266 33.08 N 110.07 W
Bylot Island I 242 73.13 N 78.34 W
Byng Inlet 256 45.46 N 80.33 W
Bynum, MT 248 47.59 N 112.19 W
Bynum, NC 258 35.47 N 79.08 W
Byrd, Lac ⊜ 254 47.01 N 76.56 W
Byrdstown 260 36.34 N 85.08 W
Byron, GA 258 32.39 N 83.46 W
Byron, IL 256 42.08 N 89.15 W
Byron, WY 268 44.48 N 108.30 W

C

Caamaño Sound ⊔ 248 52.49 N 129.28 W
Caballo Reservoir ⊜¹ 266 32.58 N 107.18 W
Cabano 252 47.41 N 68.53 W
Cabin Creek ≈ 264 46.55 N 104.52 W
Cabinet Mountains ⋀ 268 48.08 N 115.46 W
Cable 256 46.13 N 91.17 W
Cabonga, Réservoir ⊜¹ 242 47.20 N 76.35 W
Cabool 260 37.07 N 92.06 W
Cabot 260 34.58 N 92.01 W
Cabot, Mount ▲ 254 44.31 N 71.24 W
Cabot Head ≻ 256 45.14 N 81.17 W
Cabot Strait ⊔ 242 47.20 N 59.30 W
Cabri 250 50.37 N 108.28 W
Cabrillo National Monument ♦ 270 32.41 N 117.15 W
Cacaoui, Lac ⊜ 252 50.53 N 66.58 W
Cacapon ≈ 254 39.37 N 78.16 W
Cacapon State Park ♦ 254 39.32 N 78.23 W
Cache 262 34.38 N 98.38 W
Cache ≈, AR 260 34.42 N 91.20 W
Cache ≈, IL 260 37.04 N 89.10 W
Cache Creek 248 50.48 N 121.19 W
Cache Creek ≈ 270 38.42 N 121.42 W
Cache la Poudre ≈ 264 40.25 N 104.36 W
Cache la Poudre, North Fork ≈ 266 40.54 N 105.22 W
Cache Mountain ▲ 246 65.31 N 147.20 W
Cache Peak ▲ 268 42.11 N 113.40 W
Cachuma, Lake ⊜¹ 270 34.35 N 119.55 W
Cactus 262 36.04 N 102.00 W
Cactus Flat ≚ 270 37.45 N 116.45 W
Cactus Peak ▲ 270 37.47 N 116.53 W
Caddo, OK 262 34.07 N 96.16 W
Caddo, TX 262 32.38 N 98.40 W
Caddo ≈ 260 33.10 N 93.05 W
Caddo Creek ≈ 262 34.14 N 96.59 W
Caddo Lake ⊜¹ 260 32.42 N 94.01 W
Caddo Mills 262 33.04 N 96.14 W
Cadillac, SK 250 49.44 N 107.43 W
Cadillac, MI 256 44.15 N 85.24 W
Cadiz, KY 260 36.52 N 87.50 W
Cadiz, OH 254 40.16 N 81.00 W
Cadiz Lake ⊜ 270 34.18 N 115.24 W
Cadomin 248 53.02 N 117.20 W
Cadott 256 44.57 N 91.09 W
Cadron Creek, North Fork ≈ 260 35.17 N 92.29 W
Cadwell 258 32.20 N 83.03 W
Cahaba ≈ 260 32.20 N 87.05 W
Cahokia 260 38.33 N 90.10 W
Cahto Peak ▲ 270 39.41 N 123.35 W
Cahuilla Indian Reservation ◆⁴ 270 33.30 N 116.43 W
Caillou Bay C 260 29.06 N 90.56 W
Cain Creek ≈ 264 44.17 N 98.10 W
Cains ≈ 252 46.40 N 65.47 W
Cainsville 260 40.26 N 93.47 W
Cairn Mountain ▲ 246 61.10 N 155.20 W
Cairns Lake ⊜ 250 51.42 N 94.30 W
Cairo, GA 258 30.53 N 84.12 W
Cairo, IL 260 37.00 N 89.11 W
Cairo, NE 264 41.00 N 98.36 W
Cairo, WV 254 39.13 N 81.09 W
Cajon Summit)(270 34.21 N 117.27 W
Calais 254 45.11 N 67.17 W
Calamity Creek ≈ 262 29.41 N 103.42 W
Calamus ≈ 264 41.48 N 99.09 W
Calapooia ≈ 268 44.38 N 123.08 W
Calapooya Mountains ⋀ 268 43.30 N 122.50 W
Calaveras ≈ 270 38.12 N 120.41 W
Calcasieu ≈ 260 30.05 N 93.20 W
Calcasieu Lake ⊜ 260 29.50 N 93.17 W
Caldwell, ID 268 43.40 N 116.41 W
Caldwell, KS 264 37.02 N 97.37 W
Caldwell, OH 254 39.45 N 81.31 W
Caldwell, TX 262 30.32 N 96.42 W
Caledonia, NS 252 44.22 N 65.02 W
Caledonia, ON 256 43.04 N 79.56 W
Caledonia, MN 256 43.38 N 91.29 W
Caledonia, MS 260 33.39 N 88.20 W
Caledonia, NY 254 42.58 N 77.51 W
Caledonia, OH 254 40.38 N 82.58 W
Calera, AL 260 33.06 N 86.45 W
Calera, OK 262 33.55 N 96.26 W
Calexico 270 32.40 N 115.30 W
Calfkiller ≈ 260 35.49 N 85.29 W
Calfpasture ≈ 254 37.58 N 79.28 W
Calgary 248 51.03 N 114.05 W
Calhan 264 39.02 N 104.18 W
Calhoun, AL 260 32.03 N 86.33 W
Calhoun, GA 258 34.30 N 84.57 W
Calhoun, KY 260 37.32 N 87.16 W
Calhoun, MO 260 38.28 N 93.37 W
Calhoun, TN 258 35.17 N 84.45 W
Calhoun City 260 33.51 N 89.19 W
Calhoun Falls 258 34.06 N 82.36 W
Calico Rock 260 36.07 N 92.09 W
Caliente 270 37.37 N 114.31 W
California, MO 260 38.38 N 92.34 W
California, PA 254 40.04 N 79.53 W
California □³, U.S. 244
270 37.30 N 119.30 W
California Aqueduct ≚¹ 270 33.52 N 117.12 W
California Creek ≈ 262 33.05 N 99.33 W
Calion 260 33.20 N 92.32 W
Calipatria 270 33.08 N 115.31 W
Calispell Peak ▲ 268 48.26 N 117.30 W
Calistoga 270 38.35 N 122.35 W
Callaghan, Mount ▲ 270 39.42 N 116.57 W
Callahan 258 30.34 N 81.49 W
Callahan, Mount ▲ 266 39.26 N 108.07 W
Callander 256 46.13 N 79.23 W
Callaway 264 41.17 N 99.56 W
Callaway Gardens ♦ 258 32.51 N 84.52 W
Calliham 262 28.29 N 98.21 W
Calling Lake 248 55.15 N 113.12 W
Calling Lake ⊜ 248 55.13 N 113.15 W
Calmar, AB 248 53.16 N 113.49 W
Calmar, IA 256 43.11 N 91.52 W
Calm Lake ⊜ 256 48.46 N 92.04 W
Caloosahatchee ≈ 258 26.31 N 82.01 W
Calumet, MI 256 47.14 N 88.27 W
Calumet, MN 256 47.19 N 93.17 W
Calumet City 260 41.37 N 87.31 W
Calvert, AL 260 31.09 N 88.01 W
Calvert, TX 262 30.59 N 96.40 W
Calvert City 260 37.02 N 88.21 W
Calvert Island I 248 51.35 N 128.00 W
Calvin 262 34.58 N 96.15 W
Calwa 270 36.42 N 119.46 W
Calypso 258 35.09 N 78.06 W
Camachigama, Lac ⊜ 256 47.50 N 76.19 W
Camanche 256 41.47 N 90.15 W
Camanche Reservoir ⊜¹ 270 38.13 N 120.58 W
Camas Creek ≈, ID 268 43.20 N 114.24 W
Camas Creek ≈, ID 268 44.53 N 114.44 W
Camas Creek ≈, ID 268 43.53 N 112.21 W
Camas Creek ≈, OR 268 45.01 N 118.59 W
Cambria, CA 270 35.34 N 121.05 W
Cambria, WI 256 43.33 N 89.06 W
Cambria Ice Field ⊠ 248 55.55 N 129.30 W
Cambridge, ON 256 43.22 N 80.19 W
Cambridge, ID 268 44.34 N 116.41 W
Cambridge, IL 260 41.18 N 90.12 W
Cambridge, IA 256 41.54 N 93.32 W
Cambridge, MD 254 38.34 N 76.04 W
Cambridge, MA 254 42.22 N 71.06 W
Cambridge, MN 256 45.31 N 93.14 W
Cambridge, NE 264 40.17 N 100.10 W
Cambridge, NY 254 43.02 N 73.23 W
Cambridge, OH 254 40.02 N 81.35 W
Cambridge Bay 242 69.03 N 105.05 W
Cambridge City 260 39.49 N 85.10 W
Cambridge Fiord C² 242 71.20 N 74.44 W
Cambridge Springs 254 41.48 N 80.04 W
Camden, AL 260 31.59 N 87.17 W
Camden, AR 260 33.35 N 92.50 W
Camden, DE 254 39.07 N 75.33 W
Camden, ME 254 44.12 N 69.04 W
Camden, MS 260 32.42 N 89.50 W
Camden, NJ 254 39.57 N 75.07 W
Camden, NC 258 36.20 N 76.10 W
Camden, NY 254 43.02 N 75.45 W
Camden, OH 254 39.38 N 84.39 W
Camden, SC 258 34.16 N 80.36 W
Camden, TN 260 36.04 N 88.06 W
Camden Bay C 246 70.00 N 145.00 W
Camden Hills State Park ♦ 254 44.17 N 69.05 W
Camdenton 260 38.00 N 92.45 W
Camelback Mountain ▲ 246 62.33 N 157.20 W
Camels Hump ▲ 254 44.19 N 72.53 W
Cameron, LA 260 29.48 N 93.19 W
Cameron, MO 260 39.44 N 94.14 W
Cameron, SC 258 33.33 N 80.43 W
Cameron, TX 262 30.51 N 96.59 W
Cameron, WV 254 39.50 N 80.34 W
Cameron, WI 256 45.25 N 91.44 W
Cameron Hills ⋀² 242 59.48 N 118.00 W
Camilla 258 31.14 N 84.12 W
Camino 270 38.44 N 120.41 W
Campaign 260 35.46 N 85.38 W
Campbell, CA 270 37.17 N 121.57 W
Campbell, MN 264 46.06 N 96.25 W
Campbell, MO 260 36.30 N 90.04 W
Campbell, NE 264 40.18 N 98.44 W
Campbellford 256 44.18 N 77.48 W
Campbell Hill ▲² 254 40.22 N 83.43 W
Campbell Island 248 52.10 N 128.09 W
Campbell Lake ⊜ 248 50.01 N 125.27 W
Campbell Range ⋀ 246 61.08 N 129.45 W
Campbell River 248 50.01 N 125.15 W
Campbells Bay 254 45.44 N 76.36 W
Campbellsport 256 43.36 N 88.17 W
Campbellsville 260 37.21 N 85.20 W
Campbellton, NB 252 48.00 N 66.40 W
Campbellton, NF 252 49.17 N 54.56 W
Campbellton, PE 252 46.47 N 64.18 W
Campbellton, FL 260 30.57 N 85.24 W
Camp Douglas 256 43.55 N 90.16 W
Camperville 250 51.59 N 100.09 W
Camp Hill, AL 260 32.43 N 85.39 W
Camp Hill, PA 254 40.14 N 76.55 W
Camp Howard Ridge ▲ 268 45.43 N 116.25 W
Camp Lejeune Marine Corps Base ■ 258 34.40 N 77.21 W
Campo 264 37.06 N 102.35 W
Campobello Island I 252 44.53 N 66.55 W
Campo Indian Reservation ◆⁴ 270 32.40 N 116.20 W
Camp Pendleton Marine Corps Base ■ 270 33.19 N 117.18 W
Camp Point 260 40.03 N 91.04 W
Campti 260 31.54 N 93.07 W
Campton 258 37.44 N 83.33 W
Camp Verde 266 34.34 N 111.51 W
Camp Wood 262 29.40 N 100.01 W
Camrose 248 53.01 N 112.50 W
Camsell ≈ 242 65.40 N 118.07 W
Canaan, CT 254 42.02 N 73.20 W
Canaan, VT 254 45.00 N 71.32 W
Canaan ≈ 252 45.55 N 65.45 W
Canaan Valley State Park ♦ 254 39.02 N 79.32 W
Canada □¹ 242 60.00 N 95.00 W
Canada Bay C 252 50.43 N 56.10 W
Canadian 262 35.55 N 100.23 W
Canadian ≈, U.S. 244 35.27 N 95.03 W
Canadian ≈, CO 266 40.53 N 106.20 W
Canadian, Deep Fork ≈ 262 35.28 N 95.50 W
Canadian Forces Base Borden ■ 256 44.17 N 79.55 W
Canajoharie 254 42.54 N 74.35 W
Canal Flats 248 50.09 N 115.48 W
Canal Fulton 254 40.54 N 81.36 W
Canal Point 258 26.52 N 80.38 W
Canal Winchester 254 39.51 N 82.48 W
Canandaigua 254 42.54 N 77.17 W
Canaseraga 254 42.28 N 77.47 W
Canastota 254 43.10 N 75.45 W
Canaveral, Cape ≻ 258 28.27 N 80.32 W
Canaveral National Seashore ♦ 258 28.45 N 80.45 W
Canby, CA 270 41.27 N 120.52 W
Canby, MN 264 44.43 N 96.16 W
Canby, OR 268 45.16 N 122.42 W
Candies Creek ≈ 258 35.18 N 84.51 W
Candle 246 65.55 N 161.56 W
Candle Lake ⊜ 250 53.50 N 105.18 W
Candlestick 260 32.15 N 90.20 W
Candlewood, Lake ⊜ 254 41.32 N 73.27 W
Cando, SK 250 52.23 N 108.14 W
Cando, ND 264 48.32 N 99.12 W
Candor, NC 258 35.18 N 79.45 W
Candor, NY 254 42.14 N 76.21 W
Cane ≈, LA 260 31.31 N 92.43 W
Cane ≈, NC 258 36.00 N 82.16 W
Cane Creek ≈ 260 36.29 N 90.28 W
Caney 264 37.01 N 95.56 W
Caney ≈ 262 36.20 N 95.42 W
Caney Creek ≈, AR 260 33.46 N 93.07 W
Caney Creek ≈, TX 262 30.07 N 95.10 W
Caney Creek ≈, TX 262 28.46 N 95.39 W
Caniapiscau 242 57.40 N 69.30 W
Caniapiscau, Lac ⊜ 242 54.10 N 69.55 W
Canim Lake 248 51.46 N 120.54 W
Canim Lake ⊜ 248 51.52 N 120.45 W
Canim Lake Indian Reserve ◆⁴ 248 51.47 N 121.00 W
Canisteo 254 42.16 N 77.36 W
Canisteo ≈ 254 42.07 N 77.08 W
Canistota 264 43.36 N 97.18 W
Canmore 248 51.05 N 115.21 W
Cannel City 258 37.47 N 83.17 W
Cannelton 260 37.55 N 86.45 W
Cannes, Bayou des ≈ 260 30.12 N 92.35 W
Canning 252 45.09 N 64.25 W
Canning ≈ 246 70.05 N 145.30 W
Cannington 256 44.21 N 79.02 W
Cannon ≈ 256 44.35 N 92.33 W
Cannon Air Force Base ■ 262 34.23 N 103.18 W
Cannonball 264 46.24 N 100.38 W
Cannonball ≈ 264 46.26 N 100.38 W
Cannon Beach 268 45.55 N 123.57 W
Cannon Falls 256 44.31 N 92.54 W
Canoe 248 50.45 N 119.13 W
Canoe ≈ 248 52.09 N 118.27 W
Canoe Creek Indian Reserve ◆⁴ 248 51.32 N 122.15 W
Canoe Lake ⊜ 250 55.11 N 108.15 W
Canoe Lake Indian Reserve ◆⁴ 250 55.08 N 108.12 W
Canol 246 65.14 N 126.56 W
Canon 258 34.21 N 83.07 W
Canon City 266 38.27 N 105.14 W
Canonsburg 254 40.15 N 80.11 W
Canoochee ≈ 258 31.59 N 81.18 W
Canora 250 51.37 N 102.26 W
Canova 264 43.53 N 97.30 W
Canova Beach 258 28.08 N 80.34 W
Canso 252 45.20 N 61.00 W
Canso, Strait of ⊔ 252 45.37 N 61.25 W
Canterbury 252 45.53 N 67.29 W
Cantin Lake ⊜ 250 53.27 N 95.10 W
Canton, GA 258 34.14 N 84.29 W
Canton, IL 256 40.33 N 90.02 W
Canton, KS 264 38.23 N 97.26 W
Canton, ME 254 44.28 N 70.19 W
Canton, MN 256 43.32 N 91.56 W

Symbols in the index entries are identified on page 273.

Name	Page	Lat °′	Long °′
Canton, MS	260	32.37 N	90.02 W
Canton, MO	260	40.08 N	91.32 W
Canton, NC	258	35.32 N	82.50 W
Canton, NY	254	44.36 N	75.10 W
Canton, OH	254	40.48 N	81.22 W
Canton, OK	262	36.03 N	98.35 W
Canton, PA	254	41.39 N	76.51 W
Canton, SD	264	43.18 N	96.35 W
Canton, TX	262	32.33 N	95.52 W
Canton Lake ◎[1]	262	36.08 N	98.36 W
Canton Lake State Recreational Area ♦	262	36.08 N	98.39 W
Cantonment	260	30.38 N	87.19 W
Cantwell	246	63.23 N	148.57 W
Canutillo	266	31.55 N	106.36 W
Canyon, YK	246	60.52 N	137.02 W
Canyon, TX	262	34.59 N	101.55 W
Canyon City	268	44.23 N	118.57 W
Canyon Creek	248	54.22 N	115.05 W
Canyon Creek ≈, AZ	266	33.49 N	110.40 W
Canyon Creek ≈, ID	268	42.59 N	115.59 W
Canyon de Chelly National Monument ♦	266	36.01 N	109.26 W
Canyon Ferry Lake ◎[1]	268	46.33 N	111.37 W
Canyon Lake ◎[1]	262	29.52 N	98.16 W
Canyonlands National Park ♦	266	38.10 N	110.00 W
Canyonville	268	42.56 N	123.17 W
Capac	256	43.01 N	82.56 W
Capaotigamau, Lac ◎	252	50.18 N	68.14 W
Cap aux Meules, Île du I	252	47.23 N	61.54 W
Cap-Chat	252	49.06 N	66.42 W
Cap-Chat, Parc de ♦	252	48.55 N	66.50 W
Cape Breton Highlands National Park ♦	252	46.45 N	60.45 W
Cape Breton Island I	252	46.00 N	60.30 W
Cape Broyle	252	47.06 N	52.57 W
Cape Canaveral	258	28.24 N	80.37 W
Cape Charles	258	37.16 N	76.01 W
Cape Cod Bay C	254	41.52 N	70.22 W
Cape Cod National Seashore ♦	254	41.56 N	70.06 W
Cape Coral	258	26.33 N	81.57 W
Cape Dorset	242	64.14 N	76.32 W
Cape Elizabeth	254	43.34 N	70.12 W
Cape Fear ≈	258	33.53 N	78.00 W
Cape Girardeau	260	37.19 N	89.32 W
Cape Hatteras National Seashore ♦	258	35.30 N	76.35 W
Cape la Hune	252	47.33 N	56.52 W
Cape Lisburne	246	68.52 N	166.05 W
Cape Lookout National Seashore ♦	258	34.40 N	76.23 W
Cape May	254	38.56 N	74.55 W
Cape May Court House	254	39.05 N	74.50 W
Cape Pole	246	55.58 N	133.48 W
Cape Porpoise	254	43.22 N	70.26 W
Cape Romanzof	246	61.49 N	165.56 W
Cape Sable Island I	252	43.25 N	65.37 W
Cape Tormentine	252	46.08 N	63.47 W
Cape Vincent	254	44.08 N	76.20 W
Cape Yakataga	246	60.04 N	142.26 W
Capitachouane ≈	256	47.36 N	76.54 W
Capitan	266	33.35 N	105.35 W
Capitan Peak ▲	266	33.36 N	105.16 W
Capitola	270	36.59 N	121.57 W
Capitol Peak ▲	270	41.50 N	117.18 W
Capitol Reef National Park ♦	266	38.11 N	111.20 W
Capitol View	258	33.57 N	80.56 W
Caplan	252	48.06 N	65.41 W
Cap Mountain ▲	246	63.25 N	123.29 W
Cap-Pelé	252	46.13 N	64.18 W
Capreol	256	46.43 N	80.56 W
Capron	256	42.24 N	88.44 W
Captain Cook	272	19.30 N	155.55 W
Captina Creek ≈	254	39.52 N	80.48 W
Capulin Mountain National Monument ♦	262	36.48 N	103.55 W
Caraquet	252	47.48 N	64.57 W
Caraway	260	35.46 N	90.19 W
Carberry	250	49.52 N	99.20 W
Carbon, AB	248	51.29 N	113.09 W
Carbon, TX	262	32.16 N	98.50 W
Carbon ≈	268	47.07 N	122.13 W
Carbondale, CO	266	39.24 N	107.13 W
Carbondale, IL	260	37.44 N	89.13 W
Carbondale, KS	264	38.49 N	95.41 W
Carbondale, PA	254	41.35 N	75.30 W
Carbonear	252	47.45 N	53.13 W
Carbon Hill	260	33.48 N	87.32 W
Carcajou ≈	242	65.37 N	128.43 W
Carcross	246	60.10 N	134.42 W
Cardigan	252	46.14 N	62.37 W
Cardigan Bay C	252	46.10 N	62.30 W
Cardigan State Park ♦	254	43.38 N	71.54 W
Cardinal	254	44.47 N	75.23 W
Cardinal Lake ◎	248	56.14 N	117.44 W
Cardington	254	40.30 N	82.53 W
Cardston	248	49.12 N	113.18 W
Cardwell	260	36.03 N	90.17 W
Cardwell Mountain ▲	260	35.41 N	85.41 W
Careen Lake ◎	250	57.00 N	108.10 W
Carencro	260	30.19 N	92.03 W
Caretta	258	37.20 N	81.41 W
Carey	254	40.57 N	83.23 W
Caribbean Sea ▼[2]	244	20.00 N	80.00 W
Cariboo ≈	248	52.40 N	121.40 W
Cariboo Mountains ⛰	248	53.00 N	121.00 W
Caribou	252	46.52 N	68.01 W
Caribou ≈	242	59.20 N	94.44 W
Caribou Island I	256	47.22 N	85.49 W
Caribou Mountain ▲, ID	268	43.06 N	111.18 W
Caribou Mountain ▲, ME	254	45.26 N	70.38 W
Caribou Mountains ⛰	242	59.12 N	115.40 W
Caribou Range ⛰	268	43.05 N	111.15 W
Carleton, MI	256	42.04 N	83.23 W
Carleton, NE	264	40.18 N	97.41 W
Carleton, Mount ▲	252	47.23 N	66.53 W
Carleton Place	256	45.08 N	76.09 W
Carlin	270	40.43 N	116.07 W
Carlinville	260	39.17 N	89.53 W
Carlisle, AR	260	34.47 N	91.45 W
Carlisle, IN	260	38.58 N	87.25 W
Carlisle, IA	256	41.30 N	93.29 W
Carlisle, KY	254	38.19 N	84.02 W
Carlisle, PA	254	40.12 N	77.12 W
Carlisle Island I	246	52.52 N	170.02 W
Carl Junction	260	37.11 N	94.34 W
Carl Sandburg Home National Historic Site ⊥	258	35.16 N	82.27 W
Carlsbad, CA	270	33.10 N	117.21 W
Carlsbad, NM	262	32.25 N	104.14 W
Carlsbad, TX	262	31.36 N	100.38 W
Carlsbad Caverns National Park ♦	262	32.08 N	104.35 W
Carlton, MN	256	46.40 N	92.25 W
Carlton, OR	268	45.18 N	123.11 W
Carlton, TX	262	31.55 N	98.10 W
Carlyle, SK	250	49.38 N	102.16 W
Carlyle, IL	260	38.37 N	89.22 W
Carlyle Lake ◎[1]	260	38.40 N	89.18 W
Carmacks	246	62.05 N	136.18 W
Carman	250	49.32 N	98.00 W
Carmangay	248	50.08 N	113.07 W
Carmanville	252	49.24 N	54.17 W
Carmel, CA	270	36.33 N	121.55 W
Carmel, IN	260	39.59 N	86.08 W
Carmel, NY	254	41.26 N	73.41 W
Carmel Valley	270	36.29 N	121.43 W
Carmel Woods	270	36.34 N	121.54 W
Carmen	262	36.35 N	98.28 W
Carmer Hill ▲[2]	254	41.54 N	77.58 W
Carmi	260	38.05 N	88.10 W
Carmichael	270	38.38 N	121.19 W
Carmine	262	30.09 N	96.41 W
Carnduff	250	49.10 N	101.50 W
Carnegie	262	35.06 N	98.36 W
Carnwath ≈	242	68.26 N	128.50 W
Caro	256	43.29 N	83.24 W
Carol City	258	25.56 N	80.16 W
Caroleen	258	35.17 N	81.48 W
Carolina Beach	258	34.02 N	77.54 W
Caron	250	50.28 N	105.52 W
Caron, Lac ◎	256	48.00 N	78.53 W
Carp	256	45.21 N	76.02 W
Carp ≈	256	46.02 N	84.42 W
Carpenter	264	41.03 N	104.22 W
Carpenter Lake ◎	248	51.00 N	122.55 W
Carpentersville	256	42.07 N	88.17 W
Carpinteria	270	34.24 N	119.31 W
Carpio	264	48.27 N	101.43 W
Carp Lake ◎	248	54.45 N	123.20 W
Carrabelle	258	29.51 N	84.40 W
Carrboro	258	35.54 N	79.04 W
Carrie, Mount ▲	268	47.53 N	123.39 W
Carriere	260	30.32 N	89.39 W
Carrière, Lac ◎	256	47.14 N	77.12 W
Carriers Mills	260	37.41 N	88.38 W
Carrington	264	47.27 N	99.08 W
Carrington Island I	266	41.00 N	112.37 W
Carrizo Creek ≈	262	36.05 N	102.36 W
Carrizo Mountain ▲	266	33.41 N	105.42 W
Carrizo Mountains ⛰	266	36.45 N	109.10 W
Carrizo Springs	262	28.31 N	99.52 W
Carrizo Wash ∨, U.S.	266	34.36 N	109.26 W
Carrizo Wash ∨, CA	270	33.05 N	115.56 W
Carrizozo	266	33.38 N	105.53 W
Carroll, IA	264	42.04 N	94.52 W
Carroll, NE	264	42.17 N	97.17 W
Carroll Lake ◎	250	51.07 N	95.05 W
Carrollton, AL	260	33.16 N	88.05 W
Carrollton, GA	258	33.35 N	85.05 W
Carrollton, IL	260	39.18 N	90.24 W
Carrollton, KY	260	38.41 N	85.11 W
Carrollton, MI	256	43.27 N	83.54 W
Carrollton, MS	260	33.30 N	89.55 W
Carrollton, MO	260	39.22 N	93.30 W
Carrollton, OH	254	40.34 N	81.05 W
Carrollton, TX	262	32.57 N	96.54 W
Carrolltown	254	40.36 N	78.43 W
Carrot ≈	242	53.50 N	101.17 W
Carrot River	250	53.17 N	103.35 W
Carrville	260	32.33 N	85.52 W
Carry Falls Reservoir ◎[1]	254	44.25 N	74.45 W
Carseland	248	50.51 N	113.28 W
Carson, ND	264	46.25 N	101.34 W
Carson, WA	268	45.44 N	121.49 W
Carson ≈	270	39.45 N	118.40 W
Carson, East Fork ≈	270	39.00 N	119.49 W
Carson City, MI	256	43.11 N	84.51 W
Carson City, NV	270	39.10 N	119.46 W
Carson Lake ◎	270	39.19 N	118.43 W
Carson Range ⛰	270	39.15 N	120.20 W
Carson Sink ◎	270	39.45 N	118.30 W
Carstairs	248	51.34 N	114.06 W
Carter	262	35.13 N	99.30 W
Carter Lake	264	41.18 N	95.54 W
Carter Mountain ▲	268	44.12 N	109.25 W
Carters Lake ◎[1]	258	34.35 N	84.35 W
Cartersville	258	34.10 N	84.48 W
Carterville	260	37.46 N	89.05 W
Carthage, AR	260	34.04 N	92.33 W
Carthage, IL	256	40.25 N	91.08 W
Carthage, IN	260	39.44 N	85.34 W
Carthage, MS	260	32.46 N	89.32 W
Carthage, MO	260	37.11 N	94.19 W
Carthage, NC	258	35.21 N	79.25 W
Carthage, NY	254	43.59 N	75.37 W
Carthage, SD	264	44.10 N	97.43 W
Carthage, TN	260	36.15 N	85.57 W
Carthage, TX	260	32.09 N	94.20 W
Cartwright, MB	250	49.06 N	99.20 W
Cartwright, NF	242	53.42 N	57.01 W
Caruthersville	260	36.11 N	89.39 W
Cary, MS	260	32.49 N	90.56 W
Cary, NC	258	35.47 N	78.46 W
Caryville, FL	260	30.46 N	85.49 W
Caryville, TN	258	36.18 N	84.14 W
Casa Grande	266	32.53 N	111.45 W
Casa Grande National Monument ♦	266	32.50 N	111.32 W
Casas Adobes	266	32.19 N	110.59 W
Cascade, BC	248	49.01 N	118.13 W
Cascade, ID	268	44.31 N	116.02 W
Cascade, IA	256	42.18 N	91.01 W
Cascade, MT	268	47.16 N	111.42 W
Cascade, WI	256	43.40 N	88.00 W
Cascade Locks	268	45.40 N	121.54 W
Cascade Range ⛰, N.A.	242, 244	49.00 N	120.00 W
Cascade Reservoir ◎[1]	268	44.35 N	116.06 W
Cascapédia ≈	252	48.11 N	65.54 W
Casco Bay C	254	43.40 N	70.00 W
Cascumpec Bay C	252	46.45 N	64.03 W
Caseville	256	43.56 N	83.16 W
Casey, IL	260	39.18 N	87.59 W
Casey, IA	264	41.31 N	94.32 W
Casey, Mount ▲	268	48.26 N	116.42 W
Cashie ≈	258	35.53 N	76.49 W
Cashiers	258	35.06 N	83.06 W
Cashmere	268	47.31 N	120.28 W
Cashton	256	43.43 N	90.47 W
Casper	268	42.51 N	106.19 W
Casper Creek, Middle Fork ≈	268	43.01 N	106.29 W
Caspian	256	46.03 N	88.38 W
Cass ≈	256	43.23 N	83.59 W
Cass City	256	43.36 N	83.10 W
Casselman	254	45.19 N	75.05 W
Casselton	264	46.54 N	97.13 W
Cassiar	246	59.16 N	129.40 W
Cassiar Mountains ⛰	242	59.00 N	129.00 W
Cass Lake	264	47.23 N	94.36 W
Cass Lake ◎	264	47.25 N	94.32 W
Cassopolis	256	41.55 N	86.01 W
Cassville, MO	260	36.41 N	93.52 W
Cassville, WI	256	42.43 N	90.59 W
Castalia	254	41.24 N	82.48 W
Castile	254	42.38 N	78.03 W
Castillo de San Marcos National Monument ♦	258	29.44 N	81.20 W
Castine	254	44.23 N	68.48 W
Castle Air Force Base ■	270	37.22 N	120.34 W
Castleberry	260	31.17 N	87.02 W
Castle Cape ›	246	56 15 N	158.06 W
Castle Crags State Park ♦	270	41.10 N	122.20 W
Castle Creek ≈	268	43.06 N	116.16 W
Castle Dale	266	39.13 N	111.01 W
Castle Dome Peak ▲	266	33.05 N	114.08 W
Castlegar	248	49.19 N	117.40 W
Castle Hills	262	29.32 N	98.31 W
Castle Mountain ▲	246	64.32 N	135.25 W
Castle Peak ▲, CO	266	39.01 N	106.52 W
Castle Peak ▲, ID	268	44.02 N	114.35 W
Castle Rock, CO	264	39.22 N	104.51 W
Castle Rock, WA	268	46.17 N	122.54 W
Castle Rock ▲, OR	268	44.02 N	118.11 W
Castle Rock ▲, VA	258	37.57 N	78.44 W
Castle Rock Butte ▲	264	45.00 N	103.27 W
Castle Rock Lake ◎[1]	256	43.56 N	89.58 W
Castleton	254	43.37 N	73.11 W
Castlewood, SD	264	44.43 N	97.02 W
Castlewood, VA	258	36.54 N	82.17 W
Castor	250	52.13 N	111.53 W
Castor ≈	260	36.51 N	89.44 W
Castor Creek ≈	260	31.47 N	92.22 W
Castroville, CA	270	36.46 N	121.45 W
Castroville, TX	262	29.21 N	98.53 W
Casummit Lake	250	51.28 N	92.24 W
Cat ≈	250	51.07 N	91.25 W
Catahoula Lake ◎	260	31.30 N	92.06 W
Catalina	252	48.31 N	53.05 W
Cataract Creek ≈	266	36.03 N	112.35 W
Catawba ≈	258	34.36 N	80.54 W
Catawba Dam ➝[6]	258	34.57 N	81.04 W
Catfish Creek ≈	262	31.47 N	95.56 W
Cathedral City	270	33.47 N	116.28 W
Cathedral Gorge State Park ♦	270	37.50 N	114.30 W
Cathedral Mountain ▲	262	30.10 N	103.40 W
Cathedral Provincial Park ♦	268	49.05 N	120.10 W
Cathlamet	268	46.12 N	123.23 W
Cat Island I	260	30.13 N	89.06 W
Cat Lake ◎	250	51.40 N	91.50 W
Catlettsburg	254	38.25 N	82.36 W
Catlin	260	40.04 N	87.42 W
Catnip Mountain ▲	270	41.52 N	119.23 W
Catonsville	254	39.16 N	76.44 W
Catoosa	262	36.11 N	95.45 W
Catskill	254	42.13 N	73.52 W
Catskill Creek ≈	254	42.12 N	73.51 W
Catskill Mountains ⛰	254	42.10 N	74.30 W
Catskill Park ♦	254	42.00 N	74.30 W
Catt, Mount ▲	248	54.21 N	128.47 W
Cattaraugus	254	42.20 N	78.52 W
Cattaraugus Creek ≈	254	42.35 N	79.10 W
Cattaraugus Indian Reservation ➝[4]	254	42.33 N	78.56 W
Cauchon Lake ◎	250	55.25 N	96.30 W
Causapscal	252	48.22 N	67.14 W
Causapscal, Parc de ♦	252	48.20 N	66.55 W
Caution, Cape ›	248	51.10 N	127.47 W
Cavalier	264	48.48 N	97.37 W
Cave City, AR	260	35.57 N	91.33 W
Cave City, KY	260	37.08 N	85.58 W
Cave Creek ≈	266	33.34 N	112.07 W
Cave In Rock	260	37.29 N	88.10 W
Cave Spring	258	34.07 N	85.20 W
Cawatose, Lac ◎	256	47.20 N	77.07 W
Cawker City	264	39.30 N	98.26 W
Cawood	258	36.47 N	83.14 W
Cawston	248	49.11 N	119.45 W
Cayce	258	33.59 N	81.04 W
Cayucos	270	35.27 N	120.54 W
Cayuga, ON	256	42.56 N	79.51 W
Cayuga, IN	260	39.57 N	87.28 W
Cayuga, ND	264	46.04 N	97.23 W
Cayuga, TX	262	31.57 N	95.57 W
Cayuga Heights	254	42.28 N	76.30 W
Cayuga Lake ◎	254	42.45 N	76.45 W
Cayuta Creek ≈	254	41.59 N	76.30 W
Cazenovia	254	42.56 N	75.51 W
Cebolla Creek ≈	266	38.29 N	107.13 W
Cebollita Peak ▲	266	34.43 N	107.51 W
Cecil	258	31.05 N	83.11 W
Cecil Field Naval Air Station ■	258	30.12 N	81.52 W
Cecilia	260	37.40 N	85.57 W
Cedar ≈, U.S.	256	41.17 N	91.21 W
Cedar ≈, MI	256	43.53 N	84.29 W
Cedar ≈, MI	256	45.25 N	87.21 W
Cedar ≈, NE	264	41.22 N	97.57 W
Cedar ≈, NY	254	43.51 N	74.11 W
Cedar, West Fork ≈	256	42.37 N	92.29 W
Cedar Bayou ≈	260	29.41 N	94.56 W
Cedar Bluff Reservoir ◎[1]	264	38.47 N	99.47 W
Cedar Bluffs	264	41.24 N	96.37 W
Cedar Breaks National Monument ♦	266	37.29 N	112.53 W
Cedarburg	256	43.17 N	87.59 W
Cedar City, MO	260	38.36 N	92.11 W
Cedar City, UT	266	37.41 N	113.04 W
Cedar Creek ≈, U.S.	256	41.17 N	91.21 W
Cedar Creek ≈, AL	260	32.13 N	87.06 W
Cedar Creek ≈, AZ	266	33.48 N	110.18 W
Cedar Creek ≈, GA	258	34.08 N	85.19 W
Cedar Creek ≈, ID	268	42.24 N	114.49 W
Cedar Creek ≈, IA	256	40.58 N	91.40 W
Cedar Creek ≈, IA	264	42.08 N	94.35 W
Cedar Creek ≈, IA	264	42.24 N	94.59 W
Cedar Creek ≈, MO	260	38.38 N	92.13 W
Cedar Creek ≈, ND	264	46.07 N	101.18 W
Cedar Creek ≈, TX	262	32.53 N	98.37 W
Cedar Creek ≈, TX	262	30.02 N	97.17 W
Cedar Creek Reservoir ◎[1]	262	32.20 N	96.10 W
Cedaredge	266	38.54 N	107.56 W
Cedar Falls	256	42.32 N	92.27 W
Cedar Grove, WV	254	38.13 N	81.26 W
Cedar Grove, WI	256	43.33 N	87.45 W
Cedar Hill	260	36.33 N	87.01 W
Cedar Hills	258	30.16 N	81.45 W
Cedar Key	258	29.08 N	83.02 W
Cedar Lake	260	41.22 N	87.26 W
Cedar Lake ◎, ON	256	46.02 N	78.30 W
Cedar Lake ◎, TX	262	32.49 N	102.17 W
Cedar Lake ◎[1]	250	53.15 N	100.10 W
Cedar Mountain ▲	270	41.36 N	120.16 W
Cedar Rapids, IA	256	41.59 N	91.40 W
Cedar Rapids, NE	264	41.34 N	98.09 W
Cedar Springs	256	43.13 N	85.33 W
Cedartown	258	34.01 N	85.15 W
Cedarvale, BC	248	55.01 N	128.20 W
Cedar Vale, KS	264	37.06 N	96.30 W
Cedarville, CA	270	41.32 N	120.10 W
Cedarville, MI	256	46.00 N	84.22 W
Cedarville, NJ	254	39.20 N	75.12 W
Cedar Wash ∨	266	35.53 N	111.25 W
Ceepeecee	248	49.52 N	126.43 W
Celeste	262	33.18 N	96.12 W
Celina, OH	254	40.33 N	84.34 W
Celina, TN	260	36.33 N	85.30 W
Celina, TX	262	33.19 N	96.47 W
Cement	262	34.57 N	98.09 W
Centennial Mountains ⛰	268	44.35 N	111.55 W
Centennial Wash ∨	266	33.14 N	112.46 W
Center, CO	266	37.45 N	106.06 W
Center, MO	260	39.30 N	91.32 W
Center, NE	264	42.37 N	97.53 W
Center, ND	264	47.07 N	101.18 W
Center, TX	260	31.48 N	94.11 W
Centerburg	254	40.18 N	82.42 W
Center City	256	45.24 N	92.49 W
Center Hill	258	28.38 N	82.03 W
Center Hill Lake ◎[1]	260	36.00 N	85.45 W
Center Moriches	254	40.48 N	72.48 W
Center Mountain ▲	268	45.06 N	115.13 W
Center Point, AL	260	33.38 N	86.41 W
Center Point, IA	256	42.11 N	91.46 W
Center Point, TX	262	29.57 N	99.02 W
Centerville, IN	260	39.49 N	85.00 W
Centerville, IA	256	40.43 N	92.52 W
Centerville, MO	260	37.26 N	90.58 W
Centerville, PA	254	41.44 N	79.46 W
Centerville, SD	264	43.07 N	96.58 W
Centerville, TN	260	35.47 N	87.28 W
Centerville, TX	262	31.16 N	95.59 W
Centerville, UT	266	40.55 N	111.52 W
Central, AK	246	65.34 N	144.48 W
Central, AZ	266	32.52 N	109.48 W
Central, NM	266	32.46 N	108.09 W
Central, SC	258	34.44 N	82.47 W
Central Butte	250	50.47 N	106.30 W
Central City, IL	260	41.14 N	88.16 W
Central City, IA	256	42.12 N	91.31 W
Central City, KY	260	37.18 N	87.07 W
Central City, NE	264	41.07 N	98.00 W
Central City, PA	254	40.06 N	78.48 W
Central Heights	266	32.25 N	110.48 W
Centralia, IL	260	38.31 N	89.08 W
Centralia, KS	264	39.44 N	96.08 W
Centralia, MO	260	39.13 N	92.08 W
Centralia, WA	268	46.43 N	122.58 W
Centralia Draw ∨	262	31.27 N	101.16 W
Central Lake	256	45.04 N	85.16 W
Central Point	268	42.23 N	122.57 W
Central Square	254	43.17 N	76.09 W
Central Utah Canal ≡	266	39.35 N	112.12 W
Central Valley	270	40.41 N	122.22 W
Centre	260	34.09 N	85.40 W
Centre Peak ▲	248	55.41 N	126.26 W
Centreville, AL	260	32.56 N	87.08 W
Centreville, MD	254	39.03 N	76.04 W
Centreville, MI	256	41.55 N	85.32 W
Centreville, MS	260	31.05 N	91.04 W
Century, FL	260	30.58 N	87.16 W
Century, WV	254	39.06 N	80.11 W
Cereal	250	51.25 N	110.48 W
Ceresco	264	41.03 N	96.39 W
Cerrillos	266	35.26 N	106.08 W
Cerro Gordo	260	39.53 N	88.44 W
Ceylon, SK	250	49.28 N	104.36 W
Ceylon, MN	264	43.32 N	94.38 W
Chaatl Island I	248	53.00 N	132.25 W
Chaco ≈	266	36.46 N	108.39 W
Chaco Canyon National Monument ♦	266	36.06 N	108.00 W
Chaco Mesa ▲	266	35.47 N	107.35 W
Chacon, Cape ›	246	54.42 N	132.00 W
Chacuaco Creek ≈	264	37.34 N	103.38 W
Chadbourn	258	34.19 N	78.50 W
Chadron	264	42.50 N	103.02 W
Chadwick	256	42.01 N	89.53 W
Chaffee	260	37.11 N	89.40 W
Chakachamna Lake ◎	246	61.13 N	152.35 W
Chaleur Bay C	252	48.00 N	65.45 W
Chalk Draw ∨	262	29.36 N	103.15 W
Chalk River	256	46.01 N	77.27 W
Chalkyitsik	246	66.39 N	143.43 W
Challis	268	44.30 N	114.14 W
Chalmette	260	29.56 N	89.58 W
Chama	266	36.54 N	106.35 W
Chama, Rio ≈	266	36.03 N	106.05 W
Chamberlain, SK	250	50.50 N	105.34 W
Chamberlain, SD	264	43.49 N	99.20 W
Chamberlain Lake ◎	252	46.17 N	69.20 W
Chamberlin, Mount ▲	246	69.16 N	144.55 W
Chambers, AZ	266	35.11 N	109.26 W
Chambers, NE	264	42.12 N	98.45 W
Chambersburg	254	39.56 N	77.39 W
Chambers Creek ≈	262	31.58 N	96.10 W
Chambers Island I	256	45.11 N	87.12 W
Chamblee	258	33.54 N	84.18 W
Chamois	260	38.41 N	91.46 W
Champagne	246	60.47 N	136.29 W
Champaign	260	40.07 N	88.14 W
Champdoré, Lac ◎	242	55.55 N	65.49 W
Champion, AB	248	50.14 N	113.09 W
Champion, MI	256	46.31 N	87.58 W
Champion, OH	254	41.17 N	80.51 W
Champlain	254	44.59 N	73.27 W
Champlain, Lake ◎, N.A.	242, 244	44.45 N	73.15 W
Chanchelulla Peak ▲	270	40.28 N	122.59 W
Chandalar	246	67.30 N	148.30 W
Chandalar ≈	246	66.36 N	145.48 W
Chandalar, East Fork ≈	246	67.05 N	147.16 W
Chandalar, Middle Fork ≈	246	67.10 N	148.19 W
Chandalar, North Fork ≈	246	67.10 N	148.19 W
Chandeleur Islands II	260	29.48 N	88.51 W
Chandeleur Sound ⊔	260	29.55 N	89.10 W
Chandler, PQ	252	48.21 N	64.41 W
Chandler, AZ	266	33.18 N	111.50 W
Chandler, IN	260	38.03 N	87.22 W
Chandler, OK	262	35.42 N	96.53 W
Chandler, TX	262	32.18 N	95.29 W
Chandler ≈	246	69.27 N	151.30 W
Chandler Lake ◎	246	68.15 N	152.43 W
Chandlerville	260	40.03 N	90.09 W
Chandos Lake ◎	256	44.49 N	78.00 W
Change Islands	252	49.40 N	54.25 W
Channel Islands II	270	34.00 N	120.00 W
Channel Islands National Monument ♦	270	34.00 N	119.26 W
Channel-Port-aux-Basques	252	47.34 N	59.09 W
Channelview	260	29.46 N	95.07 W
Channing, MI	256	46.09 N	88.05 W
Channing, TX	262	35.41 N	102.20 W
Chantrey Inlet C	242	67.48 N	96.20 W
Chanute	264	37.41 N	95.27 W
Chanute Air Force Base ■	260	40.18 N	88.09 W
Chapel Hill, NC	258	35.55 N	79.04 W
Chapel Hill, TN	260	35.38 N	86.41 W
Chapelle Creek ≈	264	44.16 N	99.55 W
Chapin	260	39.46 N	90.24 W
Chapleau	256	47.50 N	83.24 W
Chapleau ≈	256	48.29 N	82.57 W
Chaplin	250	50.28 N	106.40 W
Chaplin ≈	260	37.50 N	85.11 W
Chaplin Lake ◎	250	50.18 N	106.35 W
Chapman, KS	264	38.58 N	97.01 W
Chapman, NE	264	41.02 N	98.09 W
Chapman, Cape ›	242	69.12 N	88.59 W
Chapman, Mount ▲	248	51.50 N	118.20 W
Chapman Creek ≈	264	38.58 N	97.00 W
Chapman Lake ◎	250	56.58 N	98.12 W
Chapmanville	254	37.58 N	82.01 W
Chappell	264	41.06 N	102.28 W
Chappell Hill	262	30.09 N	96.16 W
Chardon	254	41.35 N	81.12 W
Chariton	256	41.01 N	93.19 W
Chariton ≈	260	39.19 N	92.57 W
Chariton, Mussel Fork ≈	260	39.24 N	92.55 W
Chariton, South Fork ≈	256	40.52 N	93.00 W
Charles, Cape ›	258	37.08 N	75.58 W
Charles City, IA	256	43.04 N	92.40 W
Charles City, VA	258	37.20 N	77.04 W
Charles Island I	242	62.40 N	74.15 W
Charles Mound ▲[2]	256	42.30 N	90.14 W
Charleston, AR	260	35.18 N	94.02 W
Charleston, IL	260	39.30 N	88.10 W
Charleston, MS	260	34.00 N	90.04 W
Charleston, MO	260	36.55 N	89.21 W
Charleston, SC	258	32.48 N	79.57 W
Charleston, WV	254	38.21 N	81.38 W
Charleston Air Force Base ■	258	32.55 N	80.03 W
Charleston Peak ▲	270	36.16 N	115.42 W
Charlestown, IN	260	38.27 N	85.40 W
Charlestown, NH	254	43.14 N	72.26 W
Charles Town, WV	254	39.17 N	77.52 W
Charlevoix	256	45.19 N	85.16 W
Charlevoix, Lake ◎	256	45.15 N	85.08 W
Charley ≈	246	65.20 N	142.49 W
Charlie Creek ≈	258	27.21 N	81.49 W
Charlie Lake	248	56.16 N	120.57 W
Charlotte, MI	256	42.36 N	84.50 W
Charlotte, NC	258	35.14 N	80.50 W
Charlotte, TN	260	36.11 N	87.24 W
Charlotte, TX	262	28.52 N	98.43 W
Charlotte Court House	258	37.03 N	78.39 W
Charlotte Harbor C	258	26.45 N	82.12 W
Charlotte Lake ◎	248	52.11 N	125.20 W
Charlottesville	254	38.02 N	78.29 W
Charlottetown	252	46.14 N	63.08 W
Charlton Island I	242	52.00 N	79.30 W
Charron Lake ◎	250	52.45 N	95.15 W
Charter Oak	264	42.04 N	95.35 W
Chase, BC	248	50.49 N	119.41 W
Chase, AK	246	62.27 N	150.07 W
Chase, KS	264	38.21 N	98.21 W
Chase, Mount ▲	252	46.07 N	68.29 W
Chase City	258	36.48 N	78.28 W
Chase Field Naval Air Station ■	262	28.21 N	97.40 W
Chaska	256	44.47 N	93.35 W
Chatanika	246	65.07 N	147.31 W
Chatanika ≈	246	65.04 N	149.18 W
Chateaugay	254	44.56 N	74.05 W
Château-Richer	252	46.58 N	71.01 W
Chatfield	256	43.51 N	92.11 W
Chatham, NB	252	47.02 N	65.28 W
Chatham, ON	256	42.24 N	82.11 W
Chatham, IL	260	39.40 N	89.42 W
Chatham, LA	260	32.19 N	92.27 W
Chatham, MA	254	41.41 N	69.58 W
Chatham, NY	254	42.22 N	73.36 W
Chatham, VA	258	36.50 N	79.24 W
Chatham Head	252	47.00 N	65.33 W
Chatham Sound ⊔	248	54.32 N	130.35 W
Chatham Strait ⊔	246	57.30 N	134.45 W
Chatom	260	31.28 N	88.16 W
Chatsquot Mountain ▲	248	53.08 N	127.30 W
Chatsworth, GA	258	34.46 N	84.46 W
Chatsworth, IL	256	40.45 N	88.18 W
Chattahoochee	258	30.42 N	84.51 W
Chattahoochee ≈	244	30.52 N	84.57 W
Chattanooga	260	35.03 N	85.19 W
Chattaroy	258	37.42 N	82.17 W
Chaudière ≈	252	46.45 N	71.17 W
Chauekuktuli, Lake ◎	246	60.03 N	158.45 W
Chauncey	254	39.24 N	82.08 W
Chautauqua Lake ◎	254	42.12 N	79.27 W
Chauvin, AB	250	52.42 N	110.07 W
Chauvin, LA	260	29.24 N	90.40 W
Chavannes, Lac ◎	256	46.51 N	77.10 W
Chazy	254	44.53 N	73.26 W
Cheaha Mountain ▲	260	33.30 N	85.47 W
Cheakamus Indian Reserve ➝[4]	248	49.48 N	123.11 W
Cheat, Shavers Fork ≈	254	39.06 N	79.33 W
Chebanse	256	41.00 N	87.54 W
Chebogue Point ›	252	43.45 N	66.07 W
Cheboygan	256	45.39 N	84.29 W
Checleset Bay C	248	50.03 N	127.40 W
Checotah	262	35.28 N	95.31 W
Chedabucto Bay C	252	45.23 N	61.10 W
Cheecham Hills ⛰[2]	250	56.20 N	111.10 W
Cheektowaga	254	42.55 N	78.46 W
Chefornak	246	60.13 N	164.12 W
Chehalis	268	46.40 N	122.58 W
Chehalis ≈	268	46.57 N	123.50 W
Chelan	268	47.51 N	120.01 W
Chelan, Lake ◎	268	48.05 N	120.30 W
Chelmsford	256	46.35 N	81.12 W
Chelsea, IA	256	41.55 N	92.24 W
Chelsea, MI	256	42.19 N	84.01 W
Chelsea, OK	262	36.32 N	95.26 W
Chelsea, VT	254	43.59 N	72.27 W
Chelyan	254	38.12 N	81.30 W
Chemainus	248	48.55 N	123.43 W
Chemehuevi Indian Reservation ➝[4]	270	34.30 N	114.23 W
Cheminis, Colline ▲[2]	256	48.08 N	79.31 W
Chemult	268	43.13 N	121.47 W
Chemung Lake ◎	256	44.25 N	78.22 W
Chena ≈	246	64.48 N	147.55 W
Chenango ≈	254	42.05 N	75.55 W
Chenango Bridge	254	42.10 N	75.52 W
Chénéville	254	45.53 N	75.03 W
Cheney, KS	264	37.38 N	97.47 W
Cheney, WA	268	47.29 N	117.34 W
Cheney Reservoir ◎[1]	264	37.45 N	97.50 W
Cheneyville	260	31.01 N	92.17 W
Chenil, Lac ◎	252	51.51 N	59.41 W
Chenoa	256	40.45 N	88.43 W
Cheraw	258	34.42 N	79.53 W
Cheraw State Park ♦	258	34.36 N	79.55 W
Cheriton	258	37.17 N	75.58 W
Chernofski	246	53.24 N	167.33 W
Cherokee, AL	260	34.46 N	87.58 W
Cherokee, IA	264	42.45 N	95.33 W
Cherokee, KS	264	37.21 N	94.49 W
Cherokee, OK	262	36.45 N	98.21 W
Cherokee, TX	262	30.59 N	98.43 W
Cherokee Indian Reservation ➝[4]	258	35.25 N	83.24 W
Cherokee Lake ◎[1]	258	36.16 N	83.20 W
Cherokees, Lake O' The ◎[1]	260	36.39 N	94.49 W
Cherokee Village	260	36.18 N	91.33 W
Cherry Creek ≈, AZ	266	33.41 N	110.49 W
Cherry Creek ≈, CO	266	39.45 N	105.01 W
Cherry Creek ≈, MT	264	46.48 N	105.15 W
Cherry Creek ≈, ND	264	47.41 N	103.02 W
Cherry Creek ≈, SD	264	44.36 N	101.30 W
Cherry Creek ≈, TX	262	31.13 N	103.34 W
Cherry Hill	254	39.55 N	75.01 W
Cherry Point Marine Corps Air Station ■	258	34.54 N	76.54 W
Cherryvale	264	37.16 N	95.33 W
Cherry Valley	260	35.24 N	90.45 W
Cherryville	258	35.23 N	81.23 W
Chesaning	256	43.11 N	84.07 W
Chesapeake	258	36.43 N	76.15 W
Chesapeake Bay C, U.S.	244, 254	38.40 N	76.25 W
Chesapeake Bay Bridge-Tunnel ➝[5]	258	37.00 N	76.02 W
Chesapeake Beach	254	38.41 N	76.32 W
Chesapeake City	254	39.32 N	75.49 W
Chesdin, Lake ◎[1]	258	37.15 N	77.33 W
Cheshire	254	42.34 N	73.10 W
Cheslatta Lake ◎	248	53.44 N	125.18 W
Chesley	256	44.17 N	81.05 W
Chesnee	258	35.09 N	81.52 W
Chest Creek ≈	254	40.53 N	78.44 W
Chester, CA	270	40.19 N	121.14 W
Chester, IL	260	37.55 N	89.49 W
Chester, MT	268	48.31 N	110.58 W
Chester, NE	264	40.01 N	97.37 W
Chester, OK	262	36.13 N	98.55 W
Chester, PA	254	39.51 N	75.21 W
Chester, SC	258	34.43 N	81.12 W
Chester, VT	254	43.16 N	72.36 W
Chester, VA	258	37.21 N	77.27 W
Chester Basin	252	44.34 N	64.19 W
Chesterfield, SC	258	34.44 N	80.05 W
Chesterfield, VA	258	37.23 N	77.31 W
Chesterfield Inlet	242	63.21 N	90.42 W
Chesterfield Inlet C	242	63.25 N	90.45 W
Chesterhill	254	39.29 N	81.52 W
Chesterton	260	41.37 N	87.04 W
Chestertown	254	39.13 N	76.04 W
Chesterville	254	45.06 N	75.14 W
Chesuncook Lake ◎	254	46.00 N	69.20 W
Chetco ≈	268	42.03 N	124.16 W
Chetek	256	45.19 N	91.39 W
Chéticamp	252	46.38 N	61.01 W
Chetopa	264	37.02 N	95.05 W
Chetwynd	248	55.42 N	121.40 W
Chevak	246	61.39 N	165.17 W
Chevelon Creek ≈	266	34.57 N	110.31 W
Cheviot	254	39.11 N	84.35 W
Chewaucan ≈	268	42.30 N	120.18 W
Chewelah	268	48.17 N	117.43 W
Cheyenne, OK	262	35.37 N	99.40 W
Cheyenne, WY	264	41.08 N	104.49 W
Cheyenne ≈	244	44.40 N	101.15 W
Cheyenne, Dry Fork ≈	264	43.25 N	105.23 W
Cheyenne River Indian Reservation ➝[4]	264	45.05 N	101.20 W
Cheyenne Wells	264	38.51 N	102.11 W
Chibougamau	242	49.55 N	74.22 W
Chicago	260	41.53 N	87.38 W
Chicago Heights	260	41.30 N	87.38 W

Symbols in the index entries are identified on page 273.

Name	Page	Lat ° ′	Long ° ′
Chic-Chocs, Monts ⛰	252	48.55 N	66.00 W
Chic-Chocs, Parc des ♣	252	49.05 N	65.42 W
Chichagof Island I	246	57.30 N	135.30 W
Chickahominy ≃	258	37.14 N	76.53 W
Chickaloon	246	61.48 N	148.28 W
Chickamauga	258	34.52 N	85.18 W
Chickamauga Lake ◎[1]	260	35.22 N	85.02 W
Chickamin ≃	248	55.47 N	130.58 W
Chickasaw	260	30.46 N	88.05 W
Chickasaw Bogue ≃	260	32.17 N	87.55 W
Chickasaw Creek ≃	260	30.44 N	88.03 W
Chickasawhatchie Creek ≃	258	31.19 N	84.29 W
Chickasawhay ≃	260	31.00 N	88.45 W
Chickasaw National Recreation Area ♣	262	34.25 N	96.59 W
Chickasha	262	35.02 N	97.58 W
Chicken	246	64.04 N	141.56 W
Chico, CA	270	39.44 N	121.50 W
Chico, TX	262	33.18 N	97.48 W
Chicobi, Lac ◎	256	48.53 N	78.30 W
Chico Creek ≃	264	38.15 N	104.20 W
Chicopee, GA	258	34.16 N	83.51 W
Chicopee, MA	254	42.10 N	72.36 W
Chicot State Park ♣	260	30.47 N	92.19 W
Chicoutimi	252	48.26 N	71.04 W
Chicoutimi ≃	252	48.26 N	71.05 W
Chicoutimi, Parc de ♣	252	48.30 N	70.15 W
Chidley, Cape ≻	242	60.23 N	64.26 W
Chiefland	258	29.29 N	82.52 W
Chien, Bayou de ≃	260	36.35 N	89.11 W
Chiginagak, Mount ∧	246	57.08 N	156.59 W
Chigmit Mountains ⛰	246	60.00 N	153.00 W
Chignecto, Cape ≻	252	45.20 N	64.57 W
Chignecto Bay C	252	45.35 N	64.45 W
Chignik	246	56.18 N	158.23 W
Chignik Bay C	246	56.22 N	158.15 W
Chignik Lagoon	246	56.14 N	158.44 W
Chignik Lake	246	56.20 N	158.29 W
Chikaskia ≃	262	36.37 N	97.15 W
Chikuminuk Lake ◎	246	60.14 N	159.00 W
Chilako ≃	248	53.54 N	122.59 W
Chilanko Forks	248	52.06 N	124.10 W
Chilco Lake Indian Reserve ➤[4]	248	51.25 N	124.07 W
Chilcotin ≃	248	51.45 N	122.24 W
Childersburg	260	33.16 N	86.21 W
Childress	262	34.25 N	100.13 W
Chilhowie	258	36.48 N	81.41 W
Chilkat Pass)(	246	59.43 N	136.35 W
Chilko ≃	248	52.08 N	123.30 W
Chilko Lake ◎	248	51.20 N	124.05 W
Chillicothe, IL	256	40.55 N	89.29 W
Chillicothe, MO	260	39.48 N	93.33 W
Chillicothe, OH	254	39.20 N	82.59 W
Chillicothe, TX	262	34.10 N	99.31 W
Chilliwack	248	49.10 N	121.57 W
Chiloquin	268	42.35 N	121.52 W
Chilton	256	44.02 N	88.10 W
Chimayo	266	36.00 N	105.56 W
Chimney Rock ∧	264	41.42 N	103.20 W
Chimney Rock National Historic Site ♣	264	41.39 N	103.20 W
China Grove	258	35.34 N	80.35 W
China Lake ◎	270	35.46 N	117.39 W
China Lake Naval Weapons Center ■	270	35.35 N	117.10 W
Chinati Peak ∧	262	29.57 N	104.29 W
Chinchaga ≃	242	58.50 N	118.20 W
Chincoteague	258	37.56 N	75.23 W
Chiniak, Cape ≻	246	57.36 N	152.08 W
Chinitna Point ≻	246	59.43 N	153.02 W
Chin Lakes ◎	248	49.37 N	112.13 W
Chinle	266	36.09 N	109.33 W
Chinle Creek ≃	266	37.12 N	109.43 W
Chinle Wash ∨	266	36.54 N	109.45 W
Chino	270	34.01 N	117.42 W
Chinook, AB	250	51.27 N	110.56 W
Chinook, MT	268	48.35 N	109.14 W
Chinook Cove	248	51.14 N	120.10 W
Chino Valley	266	34.45 N	112.27 W
Chinquapin	258	34.50 N	77.49 W
Chip Lake ◎	248	53.40 N	115.20 W
Chipley	260	30.47 N	85.32 W
Chipman	252	46.11 N	65.53 W
Chipola ≃	258	30.01 N	85.05 W
Chippewa ≃, MI	256	43.35 N	84.17 W
Chippewa ≃, MN	264	44.56 N	95.44 W
Chippewa ≃, WI	256	44.25 N	92.10 W
Chippewa, East Branch ≃	264	45.20 N	95.36 W
Chippewa, East Fork ≃	256	45.53 N	91.05 W
Chippewa, Lake ◎	256	45.56 N	91.13 W
Chippewa Falls	256	44.56 N	91.24 W
Chireno	260	31.30 N	94.21 W
Chiricahua Mountains ⛰	266	31.50 N	109.15 W
Chiricahua National Monument ♣	266	32.02 N	109.19 W
Chiricahua Peak ∧	266	31.52 N	109.20 W
Chirikof Island I	246	55.50 N	155.35 W
Chisago City	256	45.22 N	92.53 W
Chisana	246	62.09 N	142.10 W
Chisholm, AL	260	32.25 N	86.15 W
Chisholm, ME	254	44.29 N	70.12 W
Chisholm, MN	256	47.29 N	92.53 W
Chisholm Mills	248	54.55 N	114.08 W
Chisos Mountains ⛰	262	29.15 N	103.20 W
Chistochina	246	62.34 N	144.40 W
Chitek Lake ◎, MB	250	52.26 N	99.25 W
Chitek Lake ◎, SK	250	53.44 N	107.47 W
Chitina	246	61.31 N	144.27 W
Chitina ≃	246	61.30 N	144.28 W
Chiwawa ≃	268	47.47 N	120.40 W
Chloride	266	35.25 N	114.19 W
Choccolocco Creek ≃	260	33.33 N	86.11 W
Chocolate Mountains ⛰, AZ	266	33.10 N	114.25 W
Chocolate Mountains ⛰, CA	270	33.20 N	115.15 W
Choctawhatchee, East Fork ≃	260	31.21 N	85.33 W
Choctawhatchee, West Fork ≃	260	31.21 N	85.33 W
Choctawhatchee Bay C	260	30.25 N	86.21 W
Choctaw Indian Reservation ➤[4]	260	32.49 N	89.14 W
Choiceland	250	53.27 N	104.25 W
Chokio	264	45.34 N	96.10 W
Cholame Creek ≃	270	35.39 N	120.22 W
Chosen	258	26.42 N	80.41 W
Choteau	268	47.49 N	112.11 W
Choteau Creek ≃	264	42.51 N	98.09 W
Chouteau	262	36.11 N	95.21 W
Chowan ≃	258	36.00 N	76.40 W
Chowchilla	270	37.07 N	120.16 W
Chowchilla ≃	270	37.07 N	120.32 W
Chown, Mount ∧	248	53.24 N	119.22 W
Chrisman	260	39.48 N	87.41 W
Christian ≃	246	66.36 N	145.49 W
Christian, Cape ≻	242	70.31 N	68.18 W
Christian Island I	256	44.50 N	80.10 W
Christiansburg	258	37.08 N	80.24 W
Christian Sound ⋓	246	55.56 N	134.40 W
Christie, Mount ∧	246	63.02 N	129.40 W
Christie Bay C	242	62.32 N	111.10 W
Christie Lake ◎	250	56.54 N	96.56 W
Christina ≃	250	56.40 N	111.03 W
Christina Lake ◎, AB	250	55.38 N	110.55 W
Christina Lake ◎, BC	248	49.05 N	118.14 W
Christmas Lake ◎	268	43.18 N	120.36 W
Christmas Mountain ∧	246	64.34 N	160.34 W
Christopher	260	37.58 N	89.03 W
Christoval	262	31.12 N	100.30 W
Chuathbaluk	246	61.40 N	159.15 W
Chubbuck	268	42.55 N	112.28 W
Chuchi Lake ◎	248	55.10 N	124.33 W
Chu Chua	248	51.21 N	120.10 W
Chuchuwayha Indian Reserve ➤[4]	248	49.21 N	120.06 W
Chugach Islands II	246	59.06 N	151.42 W
Chugach Mountains ⛰	246	61.00 N	145.00 W
Chugiak	246	61.25 N	149.30 W
Chuginadak Island I	246	52.49 N	169.50 W
Chugwater	264	41.46 N	104.49 W
Chugwater Creek ≃	264	42.07 N	104.51 W
Chuius Mountain ∧	248	54.51 N	124.30 W
Chula Vista	270	32.39 N	117.05 W
Chunchula	260	30.55 N	88.12 W
Chupadera Arroyo ∨	266	33.47 N	106.37 W
Church Hill	258	36.31 N	82.47 W
Churchill	242	58.46 N	94.10 W
Churchill ≃, Can.	242	58.47 N	94.12 W
Churchill ≃, NF	242	53.30 N	60.10 W
Churchill, Cape ≻	242	58.46 N	93.12 W
Churchill, Mount ∧, BC	248	49.58 N	123.51 W
Churchill, Mount ∧, AK	246	61.25 N	141.43 W
Churchill Falls ʟ	242	53.35 N	64.27 W
Churchill Lake ◎	250	55.55 N	108.20 W
Church Point	260	30.24 N	92.13 W
Church Rock	266	35.46 N	108.35 W
Churdan	264	42.09 N	94.29 W
Churn Creek ≃	248	51.30 N	122.17 W
Churubusco	260	41.14 N	85.19 W
Chuska Mountains ⛰	266	36.15 N	108.50 W
Chuska Peak ∧	266	35.53 N	108.50 W
Cibecue	266	34.03 N	110.29 W
Cibolo Creek ≃, TX	262	28.57 N	97.53 W
Cibolo Creek ≃, TX	262	29.34 N	104.24 W
Cicero, IL	260	41.51 N	87.45 W
Cicero, IN	260	40.08 N	86.01 W
Cicero Creek ≃	260	40.01 N	86.01 W
Cimarron, KS	264	37.48 N	100.21 W
Cimarron, NM	262	36.31 N	104.55 W
Cimarron ≃, U.S.	244	36.10 N	96.17 W
Cimarron ≃, NM	262	36.20 N	104.31 W
Cimarron, North Fork ≃	262	37.25 N	101.13 W
Cincinnati, IA	256	40.38 N	92.56 W
Cincinnati, OH	254	39.06 N	84.31 W
Cinema	248	53.11 N	122.30 W
Circle, AK	246	65.50 N	144.04 W
Circle, MT	264	47.25 N	105.35 W
Circle Hot Springs	246	65.28 N	144.39 W
Circleville, OH	254	39.36 N	82.57 W
Circleville, UT	266	38.10 N	112.16 W
Circleville Mountain ∧	266	38.12 N	112.24 W
Cisco	262	32.23 N	98.59 W
Cisne	260	38.31 N	88.26 W
Cispus ≃	268	46.25 N	122.10 W
Cissna Park	256	40.34 N	87.54 W
Citra	258	29.25 N	82.06 W
Citronelle	260	31.06 N	88.14 W
Citrus Heights	270	38.42 N	121.17 W
City of Refuge National Historical Park ♣	272	19.25 N	155.54 W
City Point	258	28.24 N	80.45 W
C.J. Strike Reservoir ◎[1]	268	42.57 N	115.53 W
C K Creek ≃	268	47.36 N	108.29 W
Clackamas ≃	268	45.22 N	122.36 W
Claflin	264	38.31 N	98.32 W
Claiborne	260	31.32 N	87.31 W
Claire, Lake ◎	242	58.35 N	112.05 W
Clair Engle Lake ◎[1]	270	40.52 N	122.43 W
Clairmont	248	55.16 N	118.47 W
Clairton	254	40.18 N	79.53 W
Clam ≃, MI	256	44.05 N	85.00 W
Clam ≃, WI	256	45.57 N	92.33 W
Clam, North Fork ≃	256	45.46 N	92.18 W
Clam Gulch	246	60.15 N	151.22 W
Clam Lake ◎	250	55.19 N	105.43 W
Clan Alpine Mountains ⛰	270	39.40 N	117.55 W
Clandonald	250	53.34 N	110.44 W
Clanton	260	32.50 N	86.38 W
Clapperton Island I	256	46.02 N	82.13 W
Clara	260	31.35 N	88.42 W
Clara City	264	44.57 N	95.22 W
Clare	256	43.49 N	84.46 W
Claremont, CA	270	34.06 N	117.43 W
Claremont, NH	254	43.23 N	72.20 W
Claremont, SD	264	45.40 N	98.01 W
Claremont ∧	270	39.53 N	120.57 W
Claremore	262	36.19 N	95.36 W
Clarence, IA	256	41.53 N	91.04 W
Clarence, MO	260	39.44 N	92.16 W
Clarence, Port C	246	65.15 N	166.40 W
Clarence Cannon Lake ◎[1]	260	39.30 N	91.45 W
Clarence Strait ⋓	246	55.25 N	132.00 W
Clarendon, AR	260	34.42 N	91.18 W
Clarendon, PA	254	41.47 N	79.06 W
Clarendon, TX	262	34.56 N	100.53 W
Clarenville	252	48.10 N	53.58 W
Claresholm	248	50.02 N	113.35 W
Clarinda	264	40.44 N	95.02 W
Clarion, IA	256	42.44 N	93.44 W
Clarion, PA	254	41.13 N	79.24 W
Clarion ≃	254	41.07 N	79.41 W
Clarissa	264	46.08 N	94.57 W
Clark	264	44.53 N	97.44 W
Clark, Lake ◎	246	60.15 N	154.15 W
Clark, Mount ∧	246	64.25 N	124.12 W
Clark, Point ≻	256	44.04 N	81.45 W
Clark Creek ≃	264	39.05 N	96.42 W
Clarkdale	266	34.46 N	112.03 W
Clarke City	252	50.12 N	66.38 W
Clarke Lake ◎	250	54.25 N	106.51 W
Clarkesville	258	34.37 N	83.31 W
Clarkfield	264	44.48 N	95.48 W
Clark Fork	268	48.08 N	116.11 W
Clark Hill Lake ◎[1]	244	33.50 N	82.20 W
Clark Mountain ∧	270	35.32 N	115.35 W
Clarks, LA	260	32.02 N	92.08 W
Clarks, NE	264	41.13 N	97.50 W
Clarks ≃	260	37.03 N	88.33 W
Clarks, West Fork ≃	260	36.59 N	88.31 W
Clarksburg	254	39.17 N	80.21 W
Clarksdale	260	34.12 N	90.34 W
Clark's Harbour	252	43.26 N	65.38 W
Clarks Hill	260	40.15 N	86.43 W
Clarkson, KY	260	37.30 N	86.13 W
Clarkson, NE	264	41.43 N	97.13 W
Clarks Point	246	58.51 N	158.30 W
Clarks Summit	254	41.30 N	75.42 W
Clarkston	268	46.25 N	117.03 W
Clarksville, AR	260	35.28 N	93.28 W
Clarksville, IN	260	38.17 N	85.45 W
Clarksville, IA	256	42.47 N	92.40 W
Clarksville, TN	260	36.32 N	87.21 W
Clarksville, TX	262	33.37 N	95.03 W
Clarksville, VA	258	36.37 N	78.34 W
Clarkton, MO	260	36.27 N	89.58 W
Clarkton, NC	258	34.29 N	78.39 W
Clatskanie	268	46.06 N	123.12 W
Clatskanie ≃	268	46.08 N	123.14 W
Claude	262	35.07 N	101.22 W
Clavet	250	52.00 N	106.23 W
Claxton	258	32.10 N	81.55 W
Clay, KY	260	37.29 N	87.49 W
Clay, TX	262	30.23 N	96.21 W
Clay, WV	254	38.28 N	81.05 W
Claybank Creek ≃	260	31.10 N	85.44 W
Clay Center, KS	264	39.23 N	97.08 W
Clay Center, NE	264	40.32 N	98.03 W
Clay City, IL	260	38.41 N	88.21 W
Clay City, IN	260	39.17 N	87.07 W
Clay City, KY	258	37.52 N	83.55 W
Clay Creek ≃	264	38.06 N	102.31 W
Clayhole Wash ∨	266	36.59 N	113.17 W
Clayhurst	248	56.15 N	120.01 W
Claymont	254	39.48 N	75.28 W
Clayoquot Sound ⋓	248	49.11 N	126.08 W
Claypool	266	33.25 N	110.51 W
Claysburg	254	40.18 N	78.27 W
Clay Springs	266	34.22 N	110.18 W
Clayton, AL	258	31.53 N	85.27 W
Clayton, DE	254	39.17 N	75.38 W
Clayton, GA	258	34.53 N	83.23 W
Clayton, IL	260	40.02 N	90.57 W
Clayton, LA	260	31.44 N	91.33 W
Clayton, MO	260	38.39 N	90.20 W
Clayton, NM	262	36.27 N	103.11 W
Clayton, NC	258	35.39 N	78.28 W
Clayton, NY	254	44.14 N	76.05 W
Clayton, OK	262	34.35 N	95.21 W
Clear ≃	248	56.11 N	119.42 W
Clear, Cape ≻	246	59.48 N	147.54 W
Clear, Lake ◎	256	45.25 N	77.12 W
Clear Boggy Creek ≃	262	34.03 N	95.47 W
Clearbrook	264	47.42 N	95.26 W
Clear Creek ≃, AL	260	34.00 N	87.19 W
Clear Creek ≃, AZ	266	34.59 N	110.38 W
Clear Creek ≃, CA	270	40.31 N	122.22 W
Clear Creek ≃, MO	260	38.00 N	93.56 W
Clear Creek ≃, MT	268	48.46 N	109.25 W
Clear Creek ≃, NE	264	41.08 N	99.06 W
Clear Creek ≃, TN	258	36.05 N	84.42 W
Clear Creek ≃, TX	262	33.16 N	97.03 W
Clear Creek ≃, WY	268	44.53 N	106.04 W
Clearfield, IA	264	40.48 N	94.29 W
Clearfield, PA	254	41.02 N	78.27 W
Clearfield, UT	266	41.07 N	112.01 W
Clearfield Creek ≃	254	41.02 N	78.24 W
Clear Lake, IA	256	43.08 N	93.23 W
Clear Lake, SD	264	44.45 N	96.41 W
Clear Lake, WI	256	45.15 N	92.16 W
Clear Lake ◎	250	50.42 N	100.00 W
Clear Lake ◎[1], CA	270	39.02 N	122.50 W
Clear Lake ◎[1], LA	260	31.55 N	93.05 W
Clearlake Highlands	270	38.57 N	122.38 W
Clear Lake Reservoir ◎[1]	270	41.52 N	121.08 W
Clearmont	268	44.38 N	106.23 W
Clear Site	246	64.19 N	149.11 W
Clearwater, BC	248	51.38 N	120.02 W
Clearwater, MB	250	49.08 N	99.01 W
Clearwater, FL	258	27.58 N	82.48 W
Clearwater, KS	264	37.30 N	97.30 W
Clearwater, NE	264	42.10 N	98.11 W
Clearwater, SC	258	33.28 N	81.55 W
Clearwater ≃, Can.	242	56.44 N	111.25 W
Clearwater ≃, AB	248	52.23 N	114.50 W
Clearwater ≃, BC	248	51.42 N	120.00 W
Clearwater ≃, ID	268	46.25 N	117.02 W
Clearwater ≃, MN	264	47.54 N	96.16 W
Clearwater ≃, MT	268	46.58 N	113.23 W
Clearwater, Middle Fork ≃	268	46.09 N	115.59 W
Clearwater, North Fork ≃	268	46.30 N	116.19 W
Clearwater, South Fork ≃	268	46.09 N	115.59 W
Clearwater Lake ◎, BC	248	52.15 N	120.13 W
Clearwater Lake ◎, MB	250	54.05 N	101.00 W
Clearwater Mountains ⛰	268	46.00 N	115.30 W
Clearwater Provincial Park ♣	250	54.03 N	101.10 W
Clebit	260	34.21 N	94.52 W
Cleburne	262	32.21 N	97.23 W
Cle Elum	268	47.12 N	120.56 W
Cle Elum ≃	268	47.11 N	121.01 W
Cle Elum Lake ◎[1]	268	47.18 N	121.06 W
Clementsport	252	44.40 N	65.37 W
Clemson	258	34.41 N	82.50 W
Clendenin	254	38.29 N	81.21 W
Clermont, PQ	252	47.41 N	70.14 W
Clermont, FL	258	28.33 N	81.46 W
Cleveland, AL	260	33.59 N	86.35 W
Cleveland, GA	258	34.36 N	83.46 W
Cleveland, MS	260	33.45 N	90.50 W
Cleveland, NC	258	35.44 N	80.40 W
Cleveland, OH	254	41.30 N	81.41 W
Cleveland, OK	262	36.19 N	96.28 W
Cleveland, TN	258	35.10 N	84.53 W
Cleveland, TX	262	30.21 N	95.05 W
Cleveland, VA	258	36.57 N	82.09 W
Cleveland, Mount ∧	268	48.56 N	113.51 W
Cleveland Peninsula ≻[1]	248	55.45 N	132.00 W
Clewiston	258	26.45 N	80.56 W
Clifton, AZ	266	33.03 N	109.18 W
Clifton, IL	256	40.56 N	87.56 W
Clifton, KS	264	39.34 N	97.17 W
Clifton, TN	260	35.23 N	88.01 W
Clifton, TX	262	31.47 N	97.35 W
Clifton Forge	258	37.49 N	79.49 W
Climax, SK	250	49.13 N	108.23 W
Climax, CO	266	39.22 N	106.11 W
Climax, GA	258	30.53 N	84.26 W
Climax, MI	256	42.14 N	85.20 W
Clinch ≃	258	35.53 N	84.29 W
Clinchco	258	37.10 N	82.22 W
Clingmans Dome ∧	244	35.35 N	83.30 W
Clint	266	31.35 N	106.14 W
Clinton, BC	248	51.05 N	121.35 W
Clinton, ON	256	43.37 N	81.32 W
Clinton, AL	260	32.55 N	88.00 W
Clinton, AR	260	35.36 N	92.28 W
Clinton, CT	254	41.17 N	72.32 W
Clinton, IL	260	40.09 N	88.57 W
Clinton, IN	260	39.40 N	87.24 W
Clinton, IA	256	41.51 N	90.12 W
Clinton, KY	260	36.40 N	89.02 W
Clinton, LA	260	30.52 N	91.01 W
Clinton, ME	254	44.38 N	69.30 W
Clinton, MA	254	42.25 N	71.41 W
Clinton, MI	256	42.04 N	83.58 W
Clinton, MN	264	45.28 N	96.26 W
Clinton, MS	260	32.20 N	90.20 W
Clinton, MO	260	38.22 N	93.46 W
Clinton, NC	258	35.00 N	78.20 W
Clinton, OK	262	35.31 N	98.59 W
Clinton, SC	258	34.29 N	81.53 W
Clinton, TN	258	36.06 N	84.08 W
Clinton, WI	256	42.34 N	88.52 W
Clinton-Colden Lake ◎	242	63.58 N	107.27 W
Clinton Lake ◎[1]	264	38.55 N	95.25 W
Clintonville	256	44.37 N	88.46 W
Clintwood	258	37.09 N	82.27 W
Clio, AL	260	31.43 N	85.36 W
Clio, MI	256	43.11 N	83.44 W
Clio, SC	258	34.35 N	79.33 W
Clo-oose	248	48.40 N	124.49 W
Cloquet	256	46.43 N	92.28 W
Cloquet ≃	256	46.52 N	92.35 W
Cloudcroft	266	32.58 N	105.45 W
Cloud Peak ∧	268	44.25 N	107.10 W
Cloudy Mountain ∧	246	63.11 N	156.05 W
Clover	258	35.07 N	81.14 W
Clover Creek ≃	268	43.00 N	115.11 W
Cloverdale, AL	260	34.56 N	87.46 W
Cloverdale, CA	270	38.48 N	123.01 W
Cloverdale, IN	260	39.31 N	86.48 W
Clover Pass	246	55.28 N	131.47 W
Cloverport	260	37.50 N	86.38 W
Clovis, CA	270	36.49 N	119.42 W
Clovis, NM	262	34.24 N	103.12 W
Clute	262	29.01 N	95.24 W
Clyde, AB	248	54.09 N	113.39 W
Clyde, NT	242	70.25 N	68.30 W
Clyde, KS	264	39.36 N	97.24 W
Clyde, NC	258	35.32 N	82.55 W
Clyde, NY	254	43.05 N	76.52 W
Clyde, OH	254	41.18 N	82.59 W
Clyde, TX	262	32.24 N	99.30 W
Clyde ≃, NS	252	43.35 N	65.25 W
Clyde ≃, ON	256	44.58 N	76.22 W
Clyde ≃, VT	254	44.56 N	72.12 W
Clyde Lake ◎	250	55.18 N	111.28 W
Clyde Park	268	45.53 N	110.36 W
Clymer	254	40.40 N	79.01 W
Coachella	270	33.41 N	116.10 W
Coachella Canal ≅	270	33.34 N	116.00 W
Coahoma	262	32.18 N	101.18 W
Coal ≃	246	59.39 N	126.57 W
Coal City	260	41.17 N	88.17 W
Coal Creek	246	65.22 N	143.10 W
Coal Creek ≃, CO	264	40.30 N	104.26 W
Coal Creek ≃, IN	260	39.57 N	87.25 W
Coal Creek ≃, WA	268	47.19 N	118.36 W
Coaldale	248	49.43 N	112.37 W
Coal Fire Creek ≃	260	33.15 N	88.18 W
Coal Fork	254	38.19 N	81.32 W
Coalgate	262	34.32 N	96.13 W
Coal Grove	254	38.30 N	82.39 W
Coal Harbour	248	50.36 N	127.35 W
Coal Hill	260	35.26 N	93.40 W
Coalhurst	248	49.45 N	112.56 W
Coalinga	270	36.09 N	120.21 W
Coalmont	248	49.31 N	120.41 W
Coalport	254	40.45 N	78.32 W
Coal River	246	59.45 N	126.55 W
Coalspur	248	53.11 N	117.01 W
Coal Valley ∨	270	38.56 N	115.25 W
Coalville	266	40.55 N	111.24 W
Coast Mountains ⛰	242	55.00 N	129.00 W
Coast Ranges ⛰	244	41.00 N	123.30 W
Coatesville	254	39.59 N	75.49 W
Coaticook	254	45.08 N	71.48 W
Coats Island I	242	62.30 N	83.00 W
Cobalt	256	47.24 N	79.41 W
Cobb Creek ≃	262	35.05 N	98.25 W
Cobden, ON	256	45.38 N	76.53 W
Cobden, IL	260	37.32 N	89.15 W
Cobequid Bay C	252	45.21 N	63.45 W
Cobequid Mountains ⛰	252	45.30 N	63.30 W
Cobham ≃	242	53.15 N	93.58 W
Cobleskill	254	42.41 N	74.29 W
Cobourg	256	43.58 N	78.10 W
Coburg Island I	242	76.00 N	79.25 W
Coburn Mountain ∧	254	45.28 N	70.06 W
Cochetopa Creek ≃	266	38.31 N	106.47 W
Cochise Head ∧	266	32.03 N	109.18 W
Cochiti Indian Reservation ➤[4]	266	35.37 N	106.20 W
Cochran	258	32.23 N	83.21 W
Cochrane, AB	248	51.11 N	114.28 W
Cochrane, ON	242	49.04 N	81.01 W
Cochrane, WI	256	44.14 N	91.50 W
Cochrane ≃	242	57.52 N	101.38 W
Cochranton	254	41.31 N	80.03 W
Cockburn Island I	256	45.55 N	83.22 W
Cocoa	258	28.21 N	80.44 W
Cocoa Beach	258	28.19 N	80.36 W
Cocodrie Lake ◎[1]	260	30.58 N	92.25 W
Coconino Plateau ⛰[1]	266	35.50 N	112.30 W
Cod, Cape ≻	254	41.42 N	70.15 W
Coderre	250	50.10 N	106.23 W
Codesa	248	55.45 N	118.04 W
Cod Island I	242	57.45 N	61.50 W
Codroy	252	47.53 N	59.24 W
Codroy Pond	252	48.04 N	58.52 W
Cody, NE	264	42.56 N	101.15 W
Cody, WY	268	44.32 N	109.03 W
Coeburn	258	36.57 N	82.28 W
Coeur d'Alene	268	47.41 N	116.46 W
Coeur d'Alene ≃	268	47.28 N	116.48 W
Coeur d'Alene, South Fork ≃	268	47.33 N	116.15 W
Coeur d'Alene Indian Reservation ➤[4]	268	47.18 N	116.45 W
Coeur d'Alene Lake ◎[1]	268	47.32 N	116.48 W
Coeur d'Alene Mountains ⛰	268	47.50 N	116.05 W
Coffeen	260	39.05 N	89.24 W
Coffeeville	260	33.59 N	89.40 W
Coffeyville	264	37.02 N	95.37 W
Coffin, Ile I	252	47.33 N	61.30 W
Coggon	256	42.17 N	91.32 W
Cogswell	264	46.07 N	97.47 W
Cohocton ≃	254	42.09 N	77.05 W
Cohoe	246	60.23 N	151.18 W
Cohoes	254	42.46 N	73.42 W
Coils Creek ≃	270	39.32 N	116.16 W
Coin	264	40.40 N	95.14 W
Cokato	264	45.05 N	94.11 W
Cokeville	268	42.05 N	110.57 W
Colbert	262	33.51 N	96.30 W
Colborne	256	44.00 N	77.53 W
Colby, KS	264	39.24 N	101.03 W
Colby, WI	256	44.55 N	90.19 W
Colchester, CT	254	41.34 N	72.20 W
Colchester, IL	256	40.25 N	90.48 W
Cold Bay	246	55.11 N	162.30 W
Cold Bay C	246	55.13 N	162.33 W
Cold Lake	250	54.27 N	110.10 W
Cold Lake ◎	250	54.33 N	110.05 W
Cold Lake Indian Reserve ➤[4]	250	54.33 N	110.10 W
Cold Spring, MN	264	45.27 N	94.26 W
Coldspring, TX	262	30.36 N	95.08 W
Cold Springs Creek ≃	264	44.32 N	104.06 W
Coldwater, KS	264	37.16 N	99.19 W
Coldwater, MI	256	41.57 N	84.60 W
Coldwater, MS	260	34.41 N	89.59 W
Coldwater, OH	254	40.29 N	84.38 W
Coldwater ≃	260	34.11 N	90.13 W
Coldwater Creek ≃	262	36.40 N	101.08 W
Coldwater Indian Reserve ➤[4]	248	50.04 N	120.48 W
Colebrook	254	44.54 N	71.30 W
Cole Camp	260	38.28 N	93.12 W
Coleen ≃	246	67.05 N	142.31 W
Coleman, AB	248	49.38 N	114.30 W
Coleman, FL	258	28.48 N	82.04 W
Coleman, MI	256	43.46 N	84.35 W
Coleman, TX	262	31.50 N	99.26 W
Coleman, WI	256	45.04 N	88.02 W
Coleman, Lake ◎[1]	262	32.02 N	99.30 W
Colen Lakes ◎	250	54.33 N	95.25 W
Coleraine	256	47.17 N	93.27 W
Coleridge	264	42.30 N	97.13 W
Coles	260	31.17 N	91.03 W
Coleto Creek ≃	262	28.41 N	97.01 W
Coleville	250	51.43 N	109.16 W
Colfax, CA	270	39.06 N	120.57 W
Colfax, IL	256	40.34 N	88.37 W
Colfax, IN	260	40.12 N	86.40 W
Colfax, IA	256	41.41 N	93.14 W
Colfax, LA	260	31.31 N	92.42 W
Colfax, WA	268	46.53 N	117.22 W
Colfax, WI	256	45.00 N	91.44 W
Colinet	252	47.13 N	53.33 W
Colinton	248	54.37 N	113.15 W
Collbran	266	39.14 N	107.57 W
College	246	64.51 N	147.47 W
Collegedale	260	35.04 N	85.03 W
College Park	258	33.39 N	84.27 W
College Place	268	46.03 N	118.23 W
College Station	262	30.37 N	96.21 W
Collegeville	260	40.56 N	87.09 W
Colleymount	248	54.01 N	126.09 W
Colleyville	262	32.53 N	97.09 W
Collier-Seminole State Park ♣	258	25.59 N	81.36 W
Collierville	260	35.03 N	89.40 W
Collingwood	256	44.29 N	80.13 W
Collins, GA	258	32.11 N	82.07 W
Collins, IA	256	41.54 N	93.18 W
Collins, MS	260	31.39 N	89.33 W
Collins ≃	260	35.48 N	85.37 W
Collins, Mount ∧[2]	256	47.51 N	80.59 W
Collins Bay	256	44.15 N	76.36 W
Collinston	260	32.41 N	91.52 W
Collinsville, AL	260	34.16 N	85.52 W
Collinsville, MS	260	32.30 N	88.51 W
Collinsville, OK	262	36.22 N	95.51 W
Collinsville, TX	262	33.32 N	96.54 W
Collinwood	260	35.10 N	87.44 W
Collister	268	43.38 N	116.15 W
Colman	264	43.59 N	96.49 W
Colmesneil	260	30.54 N	94.25 W
Colo	256	42.01 N	93.19 W
Cologne	256	44.47 N	93.46 W
Coloma, MI	256	42.11 N	86.19 W
Coloma, WI	256	44.02 N	89.31 W
Colome	264	43.15 N	99.43 W
Colon	256	41.57 N	85.19 W
Colonial Heights	258	37.15 N	77.25 W
Colonsay	250	51.59 N	105.53 W
Colony	264	38.04 N	95.22 W
Colorado	246	63.09 N	149.26 W
Colorado □[3], U.S.	244	39.30 N	105.30 W
Colorado □[3], U.S.	266	39.00 N	105.30 W
Colorado ≃, N.A.	244	31.54 N	114.57 W
Colorado ≃, TX	262	28.36 N	95.58 W
Colorado, Arroyo ∨	266	34.58 N	107.13 W
Colorado, North Fork ≃	266	40.12 N	105.50 W
Colorado, Williams Fork ≃	266	40.03 N	106.11 W
Colorado City, AZ	266	36.58 N	112.58 W
Colorado City, CO	264	37.59 N	104.52 W
Colorado City, TX	262	32.24 N	100.52 W
Colorado National Monument ♣	266	39.04 N	108.25 W
Colorado Plateau ⛰[1]	244	36.30 N	108.00 W
Colorado River Aqueduct ≅[1]	270	33.50 N	117.23 W
Colorado River Indian Reservation ➤[4]	270	34.00 N	114.25 W
Colorado Springs	264	38.50 N	104.49 W
Colquitt	258	31.10 N	84.44 W
Colstrip	268	45.53 N	106.38 W
Colt	260	35.08 N	90.49 W
Colton, CA	270	34.04 N	117.20 W
Colton, SD	264	43.47 N	96.56 W
Columbia, AL	258	31.18 N	85.07 W
Columbia, CA	270	38.02 N	120.24 W
Columbia, IL	260	38.27 N	90.12 W
Columbia, KY	260	37.06 N	85.18 W
Columbia, LA	260	32.06 N	92.05 W
Columbia, MD	254	39.13 N	76.52 W
Columbia, MS	260	31.15 N	89.56 W
Columbia, MO	260	38.57 N	92.20 W
Columbia, NC	258	35.55 N	76.15 W
Columbia, PA	254	40.02 N	76.30 W
Columbia, SC	258	34.00 N	81.03 W
Columbia, TN	260	35.37 N	87.02 W
Columbia ≃, N.A.	242		
	244	46.15 N	124.05 W
Columbia, Mount ∧	242	52.09 N	117.25 W
Columbia Basin ≚[1]	268	46.45 N	119.05 W
Columbia City	260	41.10 N	85.29 W
Columbia Falls, ME	254	44.39 N	67.44 W
Columbia Falls, MT	268	48.23 N	114.11 W
Columbia Icefield ⊠	248	52.10 N	117.30 W
Columbia Lake ◎	248	50.15 N	115.57 W
Columbia Lake Indian Reserve ➤[4]	248	50.25 N	115.57 W
Columbia Mountains ⛰	248	51.30 N	118.30 W
Columbiana, AL	260	33.11 N	86.36 W
Columbiana, OH	254	40.53 N	80.42 W
Columbia Plateau ⛰[1]	270	44.00 N	117.30 W
Columbia Road Reservoir ◎[1]	264	45.45 N	98.15 W
Columbiaville	256	43.09 N	83.25 W
Columbus, GA	258	32.29 N	84.59 W
Columbus, IN	260	39.13 N	85.55 W
Columbus, KS	264	37.10 N	94.50 W
Columbus, MS	260	33.30 N	88.25 W
Columbus, MT	268	45.38 N	109.15 W
Columbus, NE	264	41.25 N	97.22 W
Columbus, NM	266	31.50 N	107.38 W
Columbus, NC	258	35.15 N	82.12 W
Columbus, ND	264	48.54 N	102.47 W
Columbus, OH	254	39.57 N	83.00 W
Columbus, TX	262	29.42 N	96.33 W
Columbus, WI	256	43.21 N	89.01 W
Columbus Air Force Base ■	260	33.38 N	88.26 W
Columbus Grove	254	40.55 N	84.04 W
Columbus Junction	256	41.17 N	91.22 W
Columbus Salt Marsh ≚	270	38.04 N	117.58 W
Colusa	270	39.13 N	122.01 W
Colville	268	48.33 N	117.54 W
Colville ≃, AK	246	70.25 N	150.30 W
Colville ≃, WA	268	48.37 N	118.05 W
Colville Indian Reservation ➤[4]	268	48.15 N	119.00 W
Colville Lake ◎	242	67.10 N	126.00 W
Comanche, OK	262	34.22 N	97.58 W
Comanche, TX	262	31.54 N	98.36 W
Comanche Creek ≃, CO	264	39.53 N	104.19 W
Comanche Creek ≃, TX	262	31.06 N	102.24 W
Combahee ≃	258	32.30 N	80.31 W
Comb Wash ∨	266	37.13 N	109.42 W
Come by Chance	252	47.51 N	53.58 W
Comer	258	34.04 N	83.08 W
Comfort, NC	258	35.00 N	77.30 W
Comfort, TX	262	29.58 N	98.49 W
Comfort, Cape ≻	242	65.08 N	83.21 W
Comfrey	264	44.07 N	94.54 W
Commerce, GA	258	34.12 N	83.28 W
Commerce, OK	260	36.56 N	94.53 W
Commerce, TX	262	33.15 N	95.54 W
Commerce City	264	39.49 N	104.55 W
Committee Bay C	242	68.30 N	86.30 W
Como, MS	260	34.31 N	90.03 W
Como, TX	262	33.03 N	95.28 W
Como Lake ◎	256	47.55 N	83.30 W
Comox	248	49.40 N	124.55 W
Compton	270	33.54 N	118.13 W
Comstock, NE	264	41.33 N	99.14 W
Comstock, TX	262	29.41 N	101.11 W
Comstock Park	256	43.02 N	85.40 W
Conasauga ≃	258	34.33 N	84.55 W
Conception, Point ≻	270	34.27 N	120.27 W
Conception Bay C	252	47.45 N	53.00 W
Conchas ≃	262	35.23 N	104.18 W
Conchas Dam	262	35.22 N	104.11 W
Conchas Lake ◎[1]	262	35.25 N	104.14 W
Conche	252	50.53 N	55.54 W
Concho	266	34.28 N	109.36 W
Concho ≃	262	31.34 N	99.43 W
Concord, CA	270	37.59 N	122.02 W
Concord, GA	258	33.05 N	84.26 W
Concord, MI	256	42.10 N	84.38 W
Concord, NH	254	43.12 N	71.32 W
Concord, NC	258	35.25 N	80.35 W
Concordia, KS	264	39.34 N	97.39 W
Concordia, MO	260	38.59 N	93.34 W
Concrete	268	48.32 N	121.45 W
Conde	264	45.09 N	98.06 W
Condon	268	45.14 N	120.11 W
Cone	262	33.48 N	101.23 W
Conecuh ≃	260	30.58 N	87.14 W
Conejos	266	37.05 N	106.01 W
Conejos ≃	266	37.18 N	105.44 W
Cone Mountain ∧	246	66.12 N	156.03 W
Confederation Lake ◎	250	51.05 N	92.44 W
Confluence	254	39.49 N	79.21 W
Confusion Bay C	252	49.58 N	55.47 W
Congaree ≃	258	33.45 N	80.37 W
Congress	250	49.46 N	106.00 W
Coniston	256	46.29 N	80.51 W
Conjuror Bay C	242	65.45 N	118.07 W
Conklin	250	55.38 N	111.05 W
Conklingville Dam ➤[6]	254	43.17 N	74.02 W
Conneaut	254	41.57 N	80.34 W
Conneautville	254	41.36 N	80.18 W
Connecticut □[3]	244	41.45 N	72.45 W
Connecticut ≃	244	41.17 N	72.21 W
Connell	268	46.40 N	118.52 W
Connell, Mount ∧	248	49.18 N	115.38 W
Connellsville	254	40.01 N	79.35 W
Connersville	260	39.39 N	85.08 W
Conn Lake ◎	242	70.34 N	73.30 W
Conover	258	35.42 N	81.12 W
Conquest	250	51.32 N	107.17 W

Symbols in the index entries are identified on page 273.

United States and Canada Map Index

Symbols in the index entries are identified on page 273.

Name Page Lat° ' Long° '

Dawson, YK 246 64.04 N 139.25 W
Dawson, GA 258 31.47 N 84.26 W
Dawson, MN 264 44.56 N 96.03 W
Dawson, NE 264 40.08 N 95.50 W
Dawson, TX 262 31.54 N 96.43 W
Dawson, Mount ∧ 248 51.09 N 117.25 W
Dawson Bay C 250 52.55 N 100.50 W
Dawson Creek 248 55.46 N 120.14 W
Dawson Inlet C 242 61.50 N 93.25 W
Dawson Range ∧∧ 246 62.40 N 139.00 W
Dawson Springs 260 37.10 N 87.41 W
Dawsonville 258 34.25 N 84.07 W
Daysland 248 52.52 N 112.15 W
Day Star Indian Reserve →[4] 250 51.43 N 104.14 W
Dayton, OH 254 39.45 N 84.15 W
Dayton, OR 268 45.13 N 123.05 W
Dayton, PA 254 40.53 N 79.15 W
Dayton, TN 258 35.30 N 85.00 W
Dayton, TX 260 30.03 N 94.54 W
Dayton, VA 254 38.25 N 78.56 W
Dayton, WA 268 46.19 N 117.59 W
Dayton, WY 268 44.53 N 107.16 W
Daytona Beach 258 29.12 N 81.00 W
Dayville 268 44.28 N 119.32 W
Dead ≃ 256 46.34 N 87.24 W
Deadhorse 246 70.11 N 148.27 W
Dead Horse Point State Park ♦ 266 38.28 N 109.44 W
Dead Lake @ 250 55.40 N 105.01 W
Deadman ≃ 248 50.45 N 120.55 W
Deadman's Creek Indian Reserve →[4] 248 50.49 N 121.00 W
Deadwood 264 44.23 N 103.44 W
Deadwood ≃ 268 44.05 N 115.40 W
Deadwood Reservoir @[1] 268 44.19 N 115.40 W
Deale 254 38.47 N 76.33 W
Deal Island 254 38.09 N 75.56 W
Dean ≃ 248 52.50 N 126.57 W
Dean Channel ⊔ 248 52.33 N 127.13 W
Deans Dundas Bay C 242 72.15 N 118.25 W
Dearborn 256 42.18 N 83.10 W
Dearborn ≃ 268 47.07 N 111.55 W
Dease ≃ 246 59.54 N 128.30 W
Dease Arm C 242 66.52 N 119.37 W
Dease Lake @ 246 58.35 N 130.02 W
Dease Strait ⊔ 242 68.40 N 108.00 W
Death Valley 270 36.18 N 116.25 W
Death Valley ∨ 270 36.30 N 117.00 W
Death Valley National Monument ♦ 270 36.30 N 117.00 W
Deatsville 260 32.37 N 86.24 W
De Bary 258 28.52 N 81.15 W
Debauch Mountain ∧ 246 64.31 N 159.52 W
De Beque 266 39.20 N 108.13 W
De Berry 260 32.18 N 94.10 W
Deborah, Mount ∧ 246 63.38 N 147.15 W
Decatur, AL 260 34.36 N 86.59 W
Decatur, GA 258 33.46 N 84.18 W
Decatur, IL 260 39.51 N 89.32 W
Decatur, IN 260 40.50 N 84.56 W
Decatur, MI 256 42.17 N 85.58 W
Decatur, MS 260 32.26 N 89.07 W
Decatur, NE 264 42.00 N 96.15 W
Decatur, TN 258 35.31 N 84.47 W
Decatur, TX 262 33.14 N 97.35 W
Decaturville 260 35.35 N 88.07 W
Decelles, Réservoir @[1] 256 47.42 N 78.08 W
Deception, Mount ∧ 268 47.49 N 123.14 W
Deception Lake @ 250 56.33 N 104.15 W
Dechêne, Lac @ 252 51.15 N 67.51 W
Decherd 260 35.13 N 86.05 W
Deckard Mountain ∧ 260 34.47 N 93.08 W
Decker Lake 248 54.17 N 125.50 W
Deckerville 256 43.32 N 82.44 W
Decorah 256 43.18 N 91.48 W
Deenwood 258 31.14 N 82.23 W
Deep ≃ 258 35.36 N 79.03 W
Deep Bay C 250 56.25 N 103.00 W
Deep Creek ≃, ID 268 42.15 N 116.40 W
Deep Creek ≃, TX 262 32.31 N 100.55 W
Deep Creek ≃, TX 262 32.45 N 99.10 W
Deep Creek ≃, UT 266 40.10 N 113.50 W
Deep Creek Indian Reserve →[4] 248 52.16 N 122.07 W
Deep Red Creek ≃ 262 34.17 N 98.39 W
Deep River, ON 256 46.06 N 77.30 W
Deep River, CT 254 41.23 N 72.26 W
Deep River, IA 256 41.35 N 92.22 W
Deepwater 260 38.16 N 93.47 W
Deepwater Creek ≃ 260 38.16 N 93.43 W
Deer ≃ 254 44.55 N 74.43 W
Deer Creek 264 46.24 N 95.19 W
Deer Creek ≃, U.S. 254 39.37 N 76.09 W
Deer Creek ≃, CA 270 39.56 N 122.04 W
Deer Creek ≃, IN 260 40.34 N 86.41 W
Deer Creek ≃, KS 264 39.40 N 99.06 W
Deer Creek ≃, MS 260 32.33 N 90.47 W
Deer Creek ≃, NE 264 40.28 N 100.00 W
Deer Creek ≃, OH 254 39.27 N 83.00 W
Deer Creek ≃, OK 262 35.38 N 98.28 W
Deer Creek ≃, WY 268 43.09 N 107.42 W
Deer Creek Indian Reservation →[4] 256 47.50 N 93.25 W
Deerfield, IL 256 42.10 N 87.51 W
Deerfield, KS 264 37.59 N 101.08 W
Deerfield Beach 258 26.19 N 80.06 W
Deering 246 66.05 N 162.43 W
Deer Island I, NB 252 45.00 N 66.57 W
Deer Island I, AK 246 54.53 N 162.25 W
Deer Isle 254 44.13 N 68.41 W
Deer Lake 252 49.10 N 57.26 W
Deer Lake @, NF 252 49.07 N 57.35 W
Deer Lake @, ON 250 52.40 N 94.30 W
Deer Lodge 268 46.24 N 112.44 W
Deer Mountain ∧ 254 45.01 N 70.56 W
Deer Park, AL 260 31.13 N 88.19 W
Deer Park, WA 268 47.57 N 117.28 W
Deerpass Bay C 242 65.56 N 122.25 W
Deer Pond @ 252 48.30 N 54.45 W
Deer River 256 47.20 N 93.48 W
Deer Trail 264 39.37 N 104.02 W
Deerwood 256 46.28 N 93.54 W
Defiance, IA 264 41.49 N 95.20 W
Defiance, OH 254 41.17 N 84.22 W
Defiance, Mount ∧ 268 45.38 N 121.43 W
Defiance Plateau ∧∧[1] 266 36.00 N 109.15 W
De Forest 256 43.15 N 89.20 W
De Funiak Springs 260 30.43 N 86.07 W
Dégelis (Saint-Rose-du-Dégelis) 252 47.33 N 68.39 W
De Graff 254 40.19 N 83.55 W
De Gray Lake @[1] 260 34.15 N 93.15 W
De Kalb, IL 260 41.59 N 88.41 W
De Kalb, MS 260 32.46 N 88.39 W
De Kalb, TX 260 33.31 N 94.37 W
De La Blache, Lac @ 252 50.05 N 69.29 W
De Land 258 29.02 N 81.18 W
Delano, CA 270 35.41 N 119.15 W
Delano, MN 256 45.02 N 93.47 W
Delano Peak ∧ 266 38.22 N 112.23 W
Delarof Islands II 247a 51.30 N 178.45 W
Delaronde Lake @ 250 54.05 N 107.05 W
Delavan 260 40.22 N 89.33 W
Delaware, OH 254 40.18 N 83.04 W
Delaware, OK 262 36.47 N 95.38 W
Delaware □[3], U.S. 244; 254 39.10 N 75.30 W
Delaware ≃ 264 39.03 N 95.24 W
Delaware, East Branch ≃ 254 41.55 N 75.17 W
Delaware, West Branch ≃ 254 41.56 N 75.17 W
Delaware Bay C 244 39.05 N 75.15 W
Delaware City 254 39.34 N 75.36 W
Delaware Mountains ∧∧ 262 31.35 N 104.40 W
Delburne 248 52.12 N 113.14 W
Delcambre 260 29.57 N 91.57 W
Del City 262 35.27 N 97.27 W
De Leon 262 32.07 N 98.32 W
De Leon Springs 258 29.07 N 81.21 W
Delhi, ON 256 42.51 N 80.30 W
Delhi, IA 256 42.26 N 91.20 W
Delhi, LA 260 32.27 N 91.30 W
Delhi, NY 254 42.17 N 74.55 W
Delia 248 51.38 N 112.23 W
Delight 260 34.02 N 93.30 W
Delisle 250 51.55 N 107.08 W
Dell City 266 31.56 N 105.12 W
Dellenbaugh, Mount ∧ 266 36.07 N 113.32 W
Dell Rapids 264 43.50 N 96.43 W
Del Mar, CA 270 32.58 N 117.16 W
Delmar, DE 254 38.27 N 75.34 W
Delmar, IA 256 42.00 N 90.37 W
Delmar, MD 254 38.27 N 75.34 W
Del Mar Hills 262 27.37 N 99.26 W
Delmas 250 52.55 N 108.36 W
Delmont 264 43.16 N 98.10 W
Del Norte 266 37.41 N 106.21 W
De Long Mountains ∧∧ 246 68.20 N 162.00 W
Deloraine 250 49.12 N 100.29 W
Delorme, Lac @ 242 54.31 N 69.52 W
Delphi 260 40.36 N 86.41 W
Delphos, KS 264 39.16 N 97.46 W
Delphos, OH 254 40.50 N 84.20 W
Delray Beach 258 26.28 N 80.04 W
Del Rio 262 29.22 N 100.54 W
Delta, CO 266 38.44 N 108.04 W
Delta, MO 260 37.12 N 89.44 W
Delta, OH 254 41.34 N 84.00 W
Delta, UT 266 39.21 N 112.35 W
Delta ≃ 246 64.09 N 146.18 W
Delta Beach 250 50.11 N 98.19 W
Delta City 260 33.04 N 90.48 W
Delta Junction 246 64.02 N 145.41 W
Delta Peak ∧ 246 56.39 N 129.34 W
Del Valle 262 30.12 N 97.40 W
Demarcation Point ≻ 246 69.40 N 141.15 W
Deming 266 32.16 N 107.45 W
Demmitt 248 55.26 N 119.54 W
De Montigny, Lac @ 256 48.08 N 77.54 W
Demopolis 260 32.31 N 87.50 W
Demorest 258 34.31 N 83.32 W
Demotte 260 41.12 N 87.12 W
Denali 246 63.11 N 147.28 W
Denali National Park ♦ 246 63.15 N 150.30 W
Denare Beach 250 54.40 N 102.05 W
Denbigh, Cape ≻ 246 64.23 N 161.31 W
Denham Springs 260 30.29 N 90.57 W
Denison, IA 264 42.01 N 95.21 W
Denison, TX 262 33.45 N 96.33 W
Denison, Mount ∧ 246 58.25 N 154.27 W
Denison Dam →[6] 262 33.50 N 96.34 W
Denmark, SC 258 33.19 N 81.09 W
Denmark, WI 256 44.21 N 87.50 W
Denmark Bay C 242 70.33 N 103.20 W
Dennison 254 40.24 N 81.19 W
Dennis Port 254 41.39 N 70.08 W
Denton, MD 254 38.53 N 75.50 W
Denton, MT 268 47.19 N 109.57 W
Denton, NC 258 35.38 N 80.06 W
Denton, TX 262 33.13 N 97.08 W
Denton Creek ≃ 262 32.58 N 96.57 W
Denver, CO 266 39.43 N 105.01 W
Denver, IA 256 42.40 N 92.20 W
Denver, PA 254 40.14 N 76.08 W
Denver City 262 32.58 N 102.50 W
De Pere 256 44.27 N 88.04 W
Depew, NY 254 42.54 N 78.42 W
Depew, OK 262 35.48 N 96.31 W
Depoe Bay 268 44.49 N 124.04 W
Deport 262 33.32 N 95.19 W
Deposit 254 42.04 N 75.25 W
Depue 260 41.19 N 89.19 W
De Queen 260 34.02 N 94.21 W
De Quincy 260 30.27 N 93.26 W
Derby, KS 264 37.33 N 97.16 W
Derby, ME 254 45.14 N 68.59 W
Derby, NY 254 42.41 N 78.58 W
Derby Line 254 45.00 N 72.06 W
De Ridder 260 30.51 N 93.17 W
Dermott 260 33.32 N 91.26 W
Dernieres, Isles II 260 29.02 N 90.47 W
Derry 254 42.53 N 71.19 W
Derwent 250 53.39 N 110.58 W
Des Allemands 260 29.50 N 90.28 W
Des Arc 260 34.58 N 91.30 W
Descanso 270 32.51 N 116.37 W
Deschambault Lake 250 54.55 N 103.22 W
Deschambault Lake @ 250 54.40 N 103.35 W
Descharme Lake @ 250 57.05 N 109.13 W
Deschênes 254 45.23 N 75.48 W
Deschutes ≃, OR 268 45.38 N 120.54 W
Deschutes ≃, WA 268 47.02 N 122.54 W
Deschutes-Umatilla Plateau ∧∧[1] 268 45.00 N 119.40 W
Deseret Peak ∧ 266 40.28 N 112.38 W
Deseronto 256 44.12 N 77.03 W
Désert ≃ 256 46.23 N 75.58 W
Désert, Lac @ 256 46.35 N 76.19 W
Desert Hot Springs 270 33.58 N 116.30 W
Desert Lake @ 270 37.58 N 115.15 W
Desert Peak ∧ 266 41.11 N 113.22 W
Desert Valley ∨ 270 41.15 N 118.20 W
Desha 260 35.44 N 91.42 W
Deshler, NE 264 40.08 N 97.44 W
Deshler, OH 254 41.12 N 83.54 W
Des Lacs ≃ 264 48.17 N 101.25 W
Desloge 260 37.53 N 90.33 W
Desmarais 248 55.56 N 113.49 W
De Smet 264 44.23 N 97.33 W
De Smet, Lake @[1] 268 44.29 N 106.45 W
Des Moines, IA 256 41.35 N 93.37 W
Des Moines, NM 262 36.46 N 103.50 W
Des Moines ≃ 244 40.22 N 91.26 W
Des Moines, East Fork ≃ 256 42.41 N 94.12 W
Desor, Mount ∧[2] 256 47.58 N 89.01 W
De Soto, IL 260 37.49 N 89.14 W
De Soto, MO 260 38.08 N 90.33 W
De Soto National Memorial ⊥ 258 27.31 N 82.40 W
De Soto State Park ♦ 258 34.28 N 85.36 W
Des Plaines 256 42.02 N 87.54 W
Destin 260 30.24 N 86.30 W
Destruction Bay 246 61.15 N 138.48 W
Detour, Point ≻ 256 45.36 N 86.37 W
De Tour Village 256 46.00 N 83.53 W
Detrital Wash ∨ 266 36.02 N 114.28 W
Detroit, MI 256 42.20 N 83.03 W
Detroit, OR 268 44.44 N 122.09 W
Detroit, TX 262 33.40 N 95.16 W
Detroit ≃ 256 42.06 N 83.08 W
Detroit Beach 256 41.55 N 83.20 W
Detroit Lake @[1] 268 44.42 N 122.10 W
Detroit Lakes 264 46.49 N 95.51 W
De Valls Bluff 260 34.47 N 91.28 W
De View, Bayou ≃ 260 34.48 N 91.18 W
Devils ≃ 262 29.39 N 100.58 W
Devil's Den State Park ♦ 260 35.46 N 94.16 W
Devils Lake 264 48.07 N 98.59 W
Devils Lake @ 264 48.01 N 98.52 W
Devil's Lake State Park ♦ 256 43.24 N 89.44 W
Devils Paw ∧ 246 58.44 N 133.50 W
Devils Postpile National Monument ♦ 270 37.37 N 119.05 W
Devils Tower National Monument ♦ 264 44.31 N 104.57 W
Devine, BC 248 50.32 N 122.30 W
Devine, TX 262 29.08 N 98.54 W
Devon 248 53.22 N 113.44 W
Devon Island I 242 75.00 N 87.00 W
Dewar 262 35.27 N 95.56 W
Dewdney 248 49.10 N 122.12 W
Dewey 262 36.48 N 95.56 W
Deweyville 260 30.18 N 93.45 W
De Witt, AR 260 34.18 N 91.20 W
De Witt, IA 256 41.49 N 90.33 W
De Witt, MI 256 42.51 N 84.34 W
De Witt, NE 264 40.24 N 96.55 W
De Witt, NY 254 43.02 N 76.04 W
Dexter, ME 254 45.01 N 69.18 W
Dexter, MI 256 42.20 N 83.53 W
Dexter, MO 260 36.48 N 89.57 W
Dexter, NM 262 33.12 N 104.22 W
Dexter, NY 254 44.01 N 76.03 W
Dexterity Fiord C[2] 242 71.11 N 73.03 W
Dezadeash Lake @ 246 60.28 N 136.58 W
D'hanis 262 29.20 N 99.17 W
Diablo, Canyon ∨ 266 35.18 N 110.59 W
Diablo, Mount ∧ 270 37.53 N 121.55 W
Diablo Plateau ∧∧[1] 266 31.30 N 105.30 W
Diablo Range ∧∧ 270 37.00 N 121.20 W
Diagonal 264 40.48 N 94.20 W
Diamond 260 37.00 N 94.19 W
Diamond Head •[6] 272c 21.16 N 157.49 W
Diamond Lake @ 268 43.10 N 122.09 W
Diamond Peak ∧, ID 268 44.09 N 113.05 W
Diamond Peak ∧, OR 268 43.33 N 122.09 W
Diamond Peak ∧, WA 268 46.07 N 117.32 W
Diamondville 268 41.47 N 110.32 W
Diana, Baie C 242 60.50 N 69.50 W
Diaz 260 35.40 N 91.18 W
D'Iberville 260 30.26 N 88.54 W
Diboll 260 31.11 N 94.47 W
Dickens 262 33.37 N 100.50 W
Dickinson, ND 264 46.53 N 102.47 W
Dickinson, TX 262 29.28 N 95.03 W
Dickson, OK 262 34.11 N 96.58 W
Dickson, TN 260 36.05 N 87.23 W
Didsbury 248 51.40 N 114.08 W
Diefenbaker, Lake @[1] 250 51.00 N 106.55 W
Dieppe 252 46.06 N 64.45 W
Dierks 260 34.07 N 94.01 W
Dietrich 268 42.55 N 114.16 W
Digby 252 44.37 N 65.46 W
Digby Neck ≻[1] 252 44.30 N 66.10 W
Digges Islands II 242 62.35 N 77.50 W
Dighton 264 38.29 N 100.28 W
Dike 256 42.28 N 92.38 W
Dill City 262 35.17 N 99.08 W
Diller 264 40.07 N 96.56 W
Dilley 262 28.40 N 99.10 W
Dillingham 246 59.02 N 158.29 W
Dillon, CO 266 39.37 N 106.04 W
Dillon, MT 268 45.13 N 112.38 W
Dillon, SC 258 34.25 N 79.22 W
Dillon ≃ 250 55.56 N 108.57 W
Dillon Lake @ 250 55.45 N 109.30 W
Dillon Lake @[1] 254 40.02 N 82.10 W
Dillon Mountain ∧ 266 33.51 N 108.48 W
Dillon Reservoir @[1] 266 39.35 N 106.02 W
Dillon State Park ♦ 254 40.03 N 82.08 W
Dillwyn 258 37.32 N 78.27 W
Dilworth 264 46.53 N 96.42 W
Dime Box 262 30.21 N 96.50 W
Dimmitt 262 34.33 N 102.19 W
Dingwall 252 46.54 N 60.28 W
Dinnebito Wash ∨ 266 35.29 N 111.14 W
Dinorwic 250 49.41 N 92.30 W
Dinorwic Lake @ 250 49.37 N 92.33 W
Dinosaur 266 40.15 N 109.01 W
Dinosaur National Monument ♦ 266 40.32 N 108.58 W
Dinosaur Provincial Park ♦ 250 50.45 N 111.30 W
Dinsmore, SK 250 51.20 N 107.26 W
Dinsmore, FL 258 30.26 N 81.46 W
Dinuba 270 36.32 N 119.23 W
Dinwiddie 258 37.05 N 77.35 W
Diomede 246 65.47 N 169.00 W
Dionne, Lac @ 252 49.26 N 67.55 W
Dirty Devil ≃ 266 37.53 N 110.24 W
Disappointment, Cape ≻ 268 46.18 N 124.03 W
Disappointment Creek ≃ 266 38.01 N 108.51 W
Discovery Passage ⊔ 248 50.00 N 125.15 W
Dishman 268 47.39 N 117.17 W
Dishna ≃ 246 63.37 N 157.18 W
Dismal ≃ 264 41.50 N 100.05 W
Dismal Lakes @ 242 67.26 N 117.07 W
Disney, OK 260; 262 36.29 N 95.01 W
Disraëli 254 45.54 N 71.21 W
Dissimieux, Lac @ 252 49.51 N 69.48 W
District of Columbia □[5] 244 38.54 N 77.01 W
Divernon 260 39.34 N 89.39 W
Dix 264 41.14 N 103.29 W
Dix ≃ 258 37.49 N 84.43 W
Dixfield 254 44.32 N 70.27 W
Dixie Valley ∨ 270 39.50 N 117.55 W
Dix-Milles, Lac @ 256 46.46 N 77.45 W
Dixon, CA 270 38.27 N 121.49 W
Dixon, IL 260 41.50 N 89.29 W
Dixon, KY 260 37.31 N 87.41 W
Dixon, MO 260 37.59 N 92.06 W
Dixon, NM 266 36.12 N 105.53 W
Dixon Entrance ⊔ 242 54.25 N 132.30 W
Dixons Mills 260 32.04 N 87.47 W
Doaktown 252 46.33 N 66.08 W
Dobbins Air Force Base ■ 258 33.54 N 84.31 W
Dobson 258 36.24 N 80.43 W
Dock Junction 258 31.11 N 81.31 W
Doddridge 260 33.06 N 93.54 W
Doddsville 260 33.39 N 90.31 W
Dodge 264 41.43 N 96.52 W
Dodge Center 256 44.02 N 92.51 W
Dodge City 264 37.45 N 100.01 W
Dodgeville 256 42.58 N 90.08 W
Dodsland 250 51.48 N 108.49 W
Dodson, LA 260 32.05 N 92.39 W
Dodson, MT 268 48.24 N 108.15 W
Dodson, TX 262 34.46 N 100.02 W
Doe River 248 56.00 N 120.05 W
Doerun 258 31.19 N 83.55 W
Dog ≃ 256 48.51 N 89.37 W
Dog Creek 248 51.35 N 122.15 W
Dog Creek ≃ 268 47.44 N 109.36 W
Dog Ear Creek ≃ 264 43.42 N 99.59 W
Dog Island I 258 29.48 N 84.35 W
Dog Lake @, MB 250 51.02 N 98.30 W
Dog Lake @, ON 256 48.18 N 84.10 W
Dog Lake @, ON 256 48.46 N 89.32 W
Dogpound Creek ≃ 248 51.50 N 114.24 W
Doland 264 44.54 N 98.06 W
Dolbeau 242 48.53 N 72.14 W
Dolgeville 254 43.06 N 74.46 W
Dolgoi Island I 246 55.10 N 161.45 W
Dolores 266 37.28 N 108.30 W
Dolores ≃ 266 38.49 N 109.17 W
Dolphin and Union Strait ⊔ 242 69.05 N 114.45 W
Dome Creek 248 53.44 N 121.01 W
Dominion 252 46.13 N 60.01 W
Dominion, Cape ≻ 242 66.13 N 74.28 W
Dominion City 250 49.08 N 97.09 W
Domremy 250 52.47 N 105.44 W
Dona Ana 266 32.23 N 106.49 W
Donalda 248 52.35 N 112.34 W
Donaldson 260 34.14 N 92.55 W
Donaldsonville 260 30.06 N 90.59 W
Donalsonville 258 31.03 N 84.53 W
Doneraile 258 34.19 N 79.53 W
Donie 262 31.29 N 96.13 W
Doniphan, MO 260 36.37 N 90.50 W
Doniphan, NE 264 40.46 N 98.22 W
Donjek ≃ 246 62.35 N 140.00 W
Donkey Creek ≃ 264 44.12 N 104.58 W
Donna 262 26.10 N 98.03 W
Donnelly, AB 248 55.44 N 117.06 W
Donnelly, AK 246 63.41 N 145.53 W
Donnelly, ID 268 44.44 N 116.05 W
Donner 260 29.42 N 90.58 W
Donner Pass)(270 39.19 N 120.20 W
Donner und Blitzen ≃ 268 43.17 N 118.49 W
Donora 254 40.11 N 79.52 W
Don Peninsula ≻[1] 248 52.30 N 128.10 W
Doon 264 43.17 N 96.14 W
Doonerak, Mount ∧ 246 67.56 N 150.37 W
Door Peninsula ≻[1] 256 44.55 N 87.20 W
Dora 260 33.44 N 87.05 W
Doraville 258 33.54 N 84.17 W
Dorcheat, Bayou ≃ 260 32.30 N 93.21 W
Dorchester, NB 252 45.54 N 64.31 W
Dorchester, ON 256 42.59 N 81.04 W
Dorchester, NE 264 40.39 N 97.07 W
Dorchester, WI 256 45.00 N 90.20 W
Dorchester, Cape ≻ 242 65.29 N 77.30 W
Dorchester Crossing 252 46.10 N 64.34 W
Doré ≃ 250 54.56 N 107.45 W
Doré Lake 250 54.31 N 107.06 W
Doré Lake @ 250 54.46 N 107.17 W
Dorena 268 43.47 N 122.55 W
Dorena Lake @[1] 268 43.46 N 122.55 W
Dorrance 264 38.51 N 98.35 W
Dorris 270 41.58 N 121.55 W
Dorset Peak ∧ 254 43.19 N 73.02 W
Dorton 258 37.17 N 82.35 W
Dos Palos 270 36.59 N 120.37 W
Dothan 258 31.13 N 85.24 W
Doting Cove 252 49.27 N 53.57 W
Double, Lac @ 252 50.46 N 70.23 W
Double Springs 260 34.09 N 87.24 W
Doubletop Peak ∧ 268 43.21 N 110.17 W
Douglas, AK 246 58.16 N 134.22 W
Douglas, AZ 266 31.21 N 109.33 W
Douglas, GA 258 31.31 N 82.51 W
Douglas, ND 264 47.51 N 101.30 W
Douglas, WY 264 42.45 N 105.24 W
Douglas, Cape ≻ 246 58.52 N 153.18 W
Douglas, Mount ∧ 246 58.52 N 153.31 W
Douglas Channel ⊔ 248 53.30 N 129.12 W
Douglas Creek ≃ 266 40.06 N 108.46 W
Douglas Lake 248 50.10 N 120.12 W
Douglas Lake @[1] 258 36.00 N 83.22 W
Douglas Lake Indian Reserve →[4] 248 50.10 N 120.49 W
Douglass 264 37.31 N 97.01 W
Douglas Station 250 49.53 N 99.46 W
Douglasville 258 33.45 N 84.45 W
Douthat State Park ♦ 258 37.55 N 79.50 W
Dove Creek 266 37.46 N 108.54 W
Dove Creek ≃, TX 262 31.20 N 100.36 W
Dove Creek ≃, UT 266 41.37 N 113.15 W
Dover, AR 260 35.24 N 93.07 W
Dover, DE 254 39.10 N 75.32 W
Dover, ID 268 48.15 N 116.36 W
Dover, NH 254 43.12 N 70.56 W
Dover, NJ 254 40.53 N 74.34 W
Dover, NC 258 35.13 N 77.26 W
Dover, OH 254 40.32 N 81.29 W
Dover, OK 262 35.59 N 97.55 W
Dover, TN 260 36.29 N 87.50 W
Dover Air Force Base ■ 254 39.08 N 75.28 W
Dover-Foxcroft 254 45.11 N 69.13 W
Dowagiac 256 41.59 N 86.06 W
Dowagiac ≃ 256 41.51 N 86.16 W
Dow City 264 41.56 N 95.30 W
Dowling Lake @ 248 51.44 N 112.00 W
Downey 268 42.26 N 112.07 W
Downieville 270 39.34 N 120.50 W
Downing 260 40.29 N 92.22 W
Downingtown 254 40.00 N 75.42 W
Downs 264 39.30 N 98.33 W
Downs Mountain ∧ 268 43.18 N 109.40 W
Downsville 254 42.05 N 75.00 W
Downton, Mount ∧ 248 52.42 N 124.51 W
Downton Lake @ 248 50.51 N 123.00 W
Dows 256 42.39 N 93.30 W
Doyle 270 40.02 N 120.06 W
Doyles 252 47.50 N 59.12 W
Doylestown, OH 254 40.58 N 81.42 W
Doylestown, PA 254 40.19 N 75.08 W
Doyline 260 32.32 N 93.25 W
Dozier 260 31.30 N 86.28 W
Dozois, Réservoir @[1] 256 47.30 N 77.05 W
Dracut 254 42.40 N 71.18 W
Drag Lake @ 256 45.05 N 78.24 W
Dragoon 266 32.02 N 110.02 W
Drain 268 43.40 N 123.19 W
Drake 264 47.55 N 100.23 W
Drake Peak ∧ 268 42.19 N 120.07 W
Drakesboro 260 37.13 N 87.03 W
Drakes Branch 258 37.00 N 78.36 W
Draper, NC 258 36.31 N 79.41 W
Draper, UT 266 40.32 N 111.52 W
Drayton, ND 264 48.38 N 97.11 W
Drayton, SC 258 34.58 N 81.54 W
Drayton Valley 248 53.13 N 114.59 W
Dresden, ON 256 42.35 N 82.11 W
Dresden, OH 254 40.07 N 82.01 W
Dresden, TN 260 36.18 N 88.42 W
Drew 260 33.49 N 90.32 W
Drews Reservoir @[1] 268 42.10 N 120.40 W
Driftpile ≃ 248 55.23 N 115.40 W
Drift Pile River Indian Reserve →[4] 248 55.18 N 115.45 W
Driftwood ≃, BC 248 55.43 N 126.15 W
Driftwood ≃, IN 260 39.12 N 85.56 W
Driftwood Creek ≃ 264 40.11 N 100.39 W
Driggs 268 43.44 N 111.14 W
Driscoll 262 27.40 N 97.45 W
Driskill Mountain ∧[2] 260 32.25 N 92.54 W
Drum, Mount ∧ 246 62.07 N 144.35 W
Drumheller 248 51.28 N 112.42 W
Drummond, MT 268 46.40 N 113.09 W
Drummond, WI 256 46.20 N 91.15 W
Drummond Island I 256 46.00 N 83.40 W
Drummondville 254 45.53 N 72.29 W
Drumright 262 35.59 N 96.36 W
Dry Arm C 268 47.45 N 106.20 W
Dry Bay C 246 59.08 N 138.25 W
Dryberry Lake @ 250 49.33 N 93.53 W
Dry Cimarron ≃ 264 36.54 N 102.59 W
Dry Creek ≃, CA 270 38.35 N 122.51 W
Dry Creek ≃, CA 270 38.14 N 121.24 W
Dry Creek ≃, OR 268 43.34 N 117.21 W
Dry Creek ≃, WY 268 43.13 N 108.54 W
Dry Creek ≃, WY 268 41.23 N 109.38 W
Dry Creek ≃, WY 268 44.30 N 108.03 W
Dry Creek Mountain ∧ 270 41.22 N 116.22 W
Dryden 250 49.47 N 92.50 W
Dry Devils ≃, TX 262 30.20 N 100.57 W
Dry Devils ≃, TX 262 29.47 N 100.59 W
Dry Frio ≃ 262 29.17 N 99.39 W
Dry Lake @ 264 48.15 N 98.58 W
Dry Prong 260 31.35 N 92.32 W
Dry Ridge 254 38.41 N 84.35 W
Dry Tortugas II 258 24.38 N 82.55 W
Dubach 260 32.42 N 92.39 W
Dubawnt ≃ 242 64.33 N 100.06 W
Dubawnt Lake @ 242 63.08 N 101.30 W
Dublin, GA 258 32.32 N 82.54 W
Dublin, TX 262 32.05 N 98.21 W
Dublin, VA 258 37.06 N 80.41 W
Dubois, ID 268 44.10 N 112.14 W
Dubois, IN 260 38.27 N 86.48 W
Du Bois, NE 264 40.02 N 96.04 W
Du Bois, PA 254 41.07 N 78.46 W
Dubois, WY 268 43.33 N 109.38 W
Dubuque 256 42.30 N 90.41 W
Duchesne 266 40.10 N 110.24 W
Duchesne ≃ 266 40.05 N 109.41 W
Duck ≃ 260 36.02 N 87.52 W
Duck Bay 250 52.10 N 100.09 W
Duck Creek ≃, NV 270 40.06 N 114.43 W
Duck Creek ≃, ND 264 46.03 N 102.14 W
Duck Creek ≃, TX 262 33.14 N 100.42 W
Duck Creek ≃, WI 256 44.33 N 88.02 W
Duck Hill 260 33.38 N 89.43 W
Duck Lake 250 52.47 N 106.13 W
Duck Lake @ 250 54.52 N 98.11 W
Duck Mountain ∧ 250 51.35 N 101.00 W
Duck Mountain Provincial Park ♦, MB 250 51.36 N 100.55 W
Duck Mountain Provincial Park ♦, SK 250 51.38 N 101.53 W
Ducktown 258 35.03 N 84.23 W
Duck Valley Indian Reservation →[4] 270 42.00 N 116.10 W
Dudleyville 266 32.58 N 110.47 W
Due West 258 34.20 N 82.23 W
Dufault, Lac @ 256 48.19 N 79.00 W
Duffer Peak ∧ 270 41.40 N 118.44 W
Dufur 268 45.27 N 121.08 W
Dugdemona ≃ 260 31.47 N 92.22 W
Dugger 260 39.04 N 87.16 W
Du Gué ≃ 242 57.21 N 70.45 W
Dugway Proving Ground ■ 266 40.10 N 113.15 W
Duke 262 34.40 N 99.34 W
Duke Island I 246 54.56 N 131.20 W
Duke of York Bay C 242 65.25 N 84.50 W
Dulce 266 36.56 N 107.00 W
Duluth, GA 258 34.00 N 84.09 W
Duluth, MN 256 46.47 N 92.06 W
Dumas, AR 260 33.53 N 91.29 W
Dumas, TX 262 35.52 N 101.58 W
Dume, Point ≻ 270 34.00 N 118.48 W
Dumoine ≃ 254 46.13 N 77.51 W
Dumoine, Lac @ 256 46.53 N 77.54 W
Dumont 256 42.45 N 92.58 W
Dumont, Lac @ 254 46.04 N 76.27 W
Dunbar 254 38.22 N 81.45 W
Dunblane 250 51.11 N 106.52 W
Duncan, BC 248 48.47 N 123.42 W
Duncan, AZ 266 32.43 N 109.06 W
Duncan, MS 260 34.03 N 90.45 W
Duncan, OK 262 34.30 N 97.57 W
Duncan ≃ 248 50.11 N 116.57 W
Duncan Dam →[6] 248 50.15 N 116.55 W
Duncan Lake @ 248 50.20 N 117.00 W
Duncannon 254 40.23 N 77.02 W
Dundalk, ON 256 44.10 N 80.24 W
Dundalk, MD 254 39.15 N 76.31 W
Dundas, ON 256 43.16 N 79.58 W
Dundas, MN 256 44.26 N 93.12 W
Dundas Island I 248 54.33 N 130.55 W
Dundas Peninsula ≻[1] 242 74.50 N 111.30 W
Dundee, FL 258 28.07 N 81.37 W
Dundee, MI 256 41.57 N 83.40 W
Dundee, MS 260 34.32 N 90.27 W
Dundee, NY 254 42.31 N 76.59 W
Dundurn 250 51.49 N 106.30 W
Dunedin 258 28.00 N 82.47 W
Dungannon 258 36.50 N 82.28 W
Dunkirk, IN 260 40.23 N 85.13 W
Dunkirk, NY 254 42.29 N 79.20 W
Dunkirk, OH 254 40.48 N 83.39 W
Dunlap, IA 264 41.51 N 95.36 W
Dunlap, TN 260 35.23 N 85.23 W
Dunmore 254 41.25 N 75.38 W
Dunn 258 35.19 N 78.37 W
Dunnellon 258 29.03 N 82.28 W
Dunning 264 41.50 N 100.06 W
Dunnville 256 42.54 N 79.36 W
Dunrea 250 49.25 N 99.44 W
Dunseith 264 48.50 N 100.02 W
Dunsmuir 270 41.13 N 122.16 W
Dunster 248 53.08 N 119.50 W
Dunville 252 47.16 N 53.54 W
Du Page ≃ 260 41.25 N 88.14 W
Duparquet, Lac @ 256 48.28 N 79.16 W
Dupree 264 45.03 N 101.36 W
Dupuyer 248 48.11 N 112.30 W
DuQuoin 260 38.01 N 89.14 W
Duran 266 34.28 N 105.24 W
Durand, IL 256 42.26 N 89.20 W
Durand, MI 256 42.55 N 83.59 W
Durand, WI 256 44.38 N 91.58 W
Durango 266 37.16 N 107.53 W
Durant, IA 256 41.36 N 90.54 W
Durant, MS 260 33.04 N 89.51 W
Durant, OK 262 34.00 N 96.23 W
Durbin 254 38.33 N 79.50 W
Durham, ON 256 44.10 N 80.49 W
Durham, CA 270 39.44 N 121.48 W
Durham, NH 254 43.08 N 70.56 W
Durham, NC 258 35.59 N 78.54 W
Durham Heights ∧ 242 71.08 N 122.56 W
Durrell 252 49.40 N 54.44 W
Dushore 254 41.31 N 76.24 W
Duson 260 30.12 N 92.11 W
Dustin 262 35.17 N 96.01 W
Dutch Creek ≃ 260 35.03 N 93.24 W
Dutch Harbor 246 53.53 N 166.32 W
Dutch John 266 40.55 N 109.24 W
Dutchman Draw ∨ 266 37.00 N 113.29 W
Dutton, ON 256 42.39 N 81.30 W
Dutton, MT 268 47.51 N 111.43 W
Dutton, Mount ∧, AK 246 55.10 N 162.15 W
Dutton, Mount ∧, UT 266 38.01 N 112.13 W
Duval, Lac @ 254 46.19 N 76.55 W
Dwight 260 41.05 N 88.26 W
Dyer 260 36.04 N 88.59 W
Dyer, Cape ≻ 242 66.37 N 61.18 W
Dyer Bay C 256 45.10 N 81.18 W
Dyersburg 260 36.03 N 89.23 W
Dyersville 256 42.29 N 91.08 W
Dyess Air Force Base ■ 262 32.25 N 99.51 W
Dyment 250 49.37 N 92.19 W
Dysart, SK 250 50.56 N 104.02 W
Dysart, IA 256 42.10 N 92.18 W

E

Eads 264 38.29 N 102.47 W
Eagar 266 34.06 N 109.11 W
Eagle, AK 246 64.46 N 141.16 W
Eagle, CO 266 39.39 N 106.50 W
Eagle ≃, NF 242 53.35 N 57.25 W
Eagle ≃, YK 246 67.20 N 137.10 W
Eagle ≃, CO 266 39.39 N 107.04 W
Eagle Bay 248 50.56 N 119.12 W
Eagle Butte 264 45.00 N 101.14 W
Eagle Chief Creek ≃ 262 36.22 N 98.27 W
Eagle Creek ≃, SK 250 52.22 N 107.24 W
Eagle Creek ≃, AZ 266 32.58 N 109.25 W
Eagle Creek ≃, IN 260 39.43 N 86.12 W
Eagle Creek ≃, KY 260 38.36 N 85.04 W
Eagle Creek ≃, MT 268 48.12 N 111.11 W
Eagle Creek ≃, NM 262 32.47 N 104.20 W
Eagle Creek ≃, OR 268 44.45 N 117.10 W
Eagle Grove 256 42.40 N 93.54 W
Eagle Lake, ME 252 47.02 N 68.36 W
Eagle Lake, TX 262 29.35 N 96.20 W
Eagle Lake @, BC 248 51.55 N 124.25 W
Eagle Lake @, ON 250 49.42 N 93.13 W
Eagle Lake @, ON 250 50.39 N 94.54 W
Eagle Lake @, CA 270 40.39 N 120.44 W
Eagle Lake @, ME 252 46.20 N 69.20 W
Eagle Mountain 270 33.49 N 115.27 W
Eagle Mountain ∧ 268 46.20 N 115.07 W
Eagle Mountain Lake @[1] 262 32.55 N 97.30 W
Eagle Nest Butte ∧ 264 43.27 N 101.39 W
Eagle Pass 262 28.43 N 100.30 W
Eagle Peak ∧ 270 41.17 N 120.12 W
Eagle River, AK 246 61.19 N 149.34 W
Eagle River, MI 256 47.24 N 88.18 W
Eagle River, WI 256 45.55 N 89.15 W
Eagle Rock 258 37.38 N 79.48 W
Eaglesham 248 55.47 N 117.53 W
Eagleton Village 258 35.46 N 83.56 W
Eagletown 260 34.01 N 94.35 W
Eagle Village 246 64.47 N 141.07 W
Eardley Lake @ 250 52.32 N 96.05 W
Ear Falls 250 50.38 N 93.13 W
Earle 260 35.16 N 90.28 W
Earl Grey 250 50.56 N 104.45 W
Earlham 260 41.30 N 94.07 W
Earlimart 270 35.53 N 119.16 W
Earlington 260 37.16 N 87.30 W
Earl Park 260 40.42 N 87.25 W
Earlville, IL 260 41.35 N 88.55 W
Earlville, NY 254 42.44 N 75.33 W
Early, IA 264 42.28 N 95.09 W
Early, TX 262 31.45 N 98.54 W
Earth 262 34.14 N 102.24 W
Easley 258 34.50 N 82.36 W
East ≃, ON 256 45.20 N 79.17 W

Symbols in the index entries are identified on page 273.

Name	Page	Lat	Long
East ≃, CO	266	38.40 N	106.51 W
East Alamosa	266	37.28 N	105.49 W
East Alton	260	38.53 N	90.06 W
East Angus	254	45.29 N	71.40 W
East Aurora	254	42.46 N	78.37 W
East Bay ⊂	266	29.30 N	94.35 W
East Bend	258	36.13 N	80.31 W
East Berlin	258	39.56 N	76.59 W
East Bernard	262	29.32 N	96.04 W
East Bernstadt	258	37.11 N	84.07 W
East Bijou Creek ≃	264	39.51 N	104.08 W
East Brady	254	40.59 N	79.37 W
East Braintree	250	49.37 N	95.38 W
East Brewton	258	31.05 N	87.04 W
East Butte ∧	268	48.52 N	111.09 W
East Cache Creek ≃	262	34.08 N	98.16 W
East Canada Creek ≃	254	43.00 N	74.45 W
East Cape ⃗, AK	247a	51.21 N	179.29 E
East Cape ⃗, FL	258	25.07 N	81.05 W
East Carbon	266	39.33 N	110.25 W
East Channel ≃[1]	246	69.20 N	134.00 W
East Chicago	256	41.38 N	87.27 W
East Corinth	254	45.00 N	69.01 W
East Cote Blanche Bay ⊂	260	29.35 N	91.40 W
East Coulee	248	51.20 N	112.19 W
East Dismal Swamp ≊	258	35.45 N	76.35 W
East Dublin	258	32.32 N	82.52 W
East Dubuque	260	42.30 N	90.39 W
East Ely	270	39.15 N	114.53 W
Eastend	250	49.31 N	108.48 W
East Fayetteville	258	35.05 N	78.51 W
East Flat Rock	258	35.17 N	82.32 W
East Gaffney	258	35.05 N	81.42 W
East Gallatin ≃	268	45.53 N	111.20 W
East Glacier Park	268	48.27 N	113.13 W
East Grand Forks	264	47.56 N	97.01 W
East Grand Rapids	256	42.56 N	85.35 W
East Greenwich	254	41.40 N	71.27 W
Easthampton	254	42.16 N	72.40 W
East Helena	268	46.35 N	111.56 W
East Jordan	256	45.10 N	85.07 W
East Kelowna	248	49.51 N	119.25 W
Eastlake, MI	256	44.15 N	86.18 W
Eastlake, OH	256	41.34 N	81.35 W
Eastland	262	32.24 N	98.49 W
East Lansing	256	42.44 N	84.29 W
East Laurinburg	258	34.46 N	79.27 W
East Liverpool	256	40.38 N	80.35 W
East Longmeadow	254	42.04 N	72.31 W
East Lynn Lake ⊞	258	38.05 N	82.20 W
East Machias	254	44.44 N	67.24 W
Eastmain	242	52.15 N	78.30 W
Eastmain ≃	242	52.15 N	78.35 W
Eastman	258	32.12 N	83.11 W
East Millinocket	254	45.37 N	68.35 W
East Missoula	268	46.52 N	113.58 W
East Moline	260	41.31 N	90.25 W
East Naples	258	26.08 N	81.46 W
East Nishnabotna ≃	264	40.39 N	95.37 W
East Nodaway ≃	264	40.38 N	95.01 W
East Olympia	268	46.58 N	122.50 W
Easton, MD	254	38.46 N	76.04 W
Easton, PA	254	40.42 N	75.12 W
Eastover	258	33.52 N	80.41 W
East Palatka	258	29.40 N	81.35 W
East Palestine	254	40.50 N	80.33 W
East Pecos	266	34.35 N	105.39 W
East Peoria	260	40.40 N	89.34 W
East Pine	248	55.43 N	121.13 W
Eastpoint, FL	258	29.45 N	84.52 W
East Point, GA	258	33.40 N	84.27 W
East Point ⃗	252	46.27 N	61.58 W
Eastport, NF	252	48.39 N	53.45 W
Eastport, ME	254	44.54 N	67.00 W
East Porterville	270	36.04 N	118.56 W
East Prairie	258	36.47 N	89.23 W
East Prairie ≃	264	46.25 N	105.20 W
East Pryor Mountain ∧	268	45.11 N	108.20 W
East Rockingham	258	34.57 N	79.45 W
East Rosebud Creek ≃	268	45.38 N	109.27 W
East Saint Louis	260	38.38 N	90.09 W
East Salt Creek ≃	266	39.13 N	108.54 W
East Shoal Lake ⊞	250	50.23 N	97.37 W
East Spencer	258	35.41 N	80.26 W
East Stroudsburg	254	41.00 N	75.11 W
East Sullivan	254	44.30 N	68.09 W
East Tawas	256	44.17 N	83.29 W
East Troy	256	42.47 N	88.24 W
East Twin ≃	256	44.08 N	87.34 W
Eastville	258	37.21 N	75.57 W
East Walker ≃	270	38.53 N	119.10 W
East Wenatchee	248	47.25 N	120.16 W
East Wilmington	258	34.13 N	77.53 W
East Yegua Creek ≃	262	30.19 N	96.45 W
East Yellow Creek ≃	256	39.38 N	93.04 W
Eaton, IN	260	40.21 N	85.21 W
Eaton, OH	260	39.45 N	84.38 W
Eatonia	250	51.13 N	109.23 W
Eaton Rapids	256	42.36 N	84.39 W
Eatonton	258	33.20 N	83.23 W
Eatonville	268	46.52 N	122.16 W
Eau Claire ≃, WI	254	44.49 N	91.31 W
Eau Claire ≊, WI	256	44.55 N	89.37 W
Eau Claire, WI	256	44.49 N	91.31 W
Eau-Claire, Lac à l' ⊞	242	56.10 N	74.25 W
Eau Claire, North Fork ≃	256	44.44 N	90.59 W
Eau Claire, South Fork ≃	256	44.44 N	90.59 W
Eau Galle ≃	256	44.37 N	92.00 W
Ebb and Flow Indian Reserve ◄[4]	250	51.05 N	99.05 W
Ebb and Flow Lake ⊞	250	51.05 N	98.56 W
Eben Junction	256	46.24 N	87.00 W
Ebensburg	254	40.29 N	78.44 W
Eccles	258	37.47 N	81.16 W
Echeconnee Creek ≃	258	32.39 N	83.36 W
Echimamish ≃	250	54.20 N	97.27 W
Echo	250	54.20 N	95.25 W
Echoing ≃	250	55.51 N	92.05 W
Echoing Lake ⊞	250	54.31 N	92.15 W
Eckville	248	52.21 N	114.22 W
Eclectic	258	32.38 N	86.02 W
Ecleto Creek ≃	262	28.52 N	97.45 W
Eclipse Sound ⹀	242	72.38 N	79.00 W
Econfina ≃	258	30.02 N	83.55 W
Ecorse	256	42.15 N	83.09 W
Ecru	266	34.21 N	89.01 W
Ecstall ≃	248	54.09 N	129.56 W
Ecum Secum	252	44.58 N	62.08 W
Edam	250	53.12 N	108.46 W
Eddyville, IA	260	41.09 N	92.38 W
Eddyville, KY	260	37.03 N	88.04 W
Edehon Lake ⊞	242	60.25 N	97.15 W
Eden, MS	260	32.59 N	90.20 W
Eden, TX	262	31.13 N	99.51 W
Eden, WY	268	42.03 N	109.26 W
Eden Hill ∧[2]	254	41.20 N	73.19 W
Eden Lake ⊞	256	56.38 N	100.15 W
Edenton	258	36.04 N	76.39 W
Eden Valley	264	45.19 N	94.33 W
Edgar, NE	264	40.22 N	97.58 W
Edgar, WI	264	44.55 N	90.00 W
Edgard	260	30.03 N	90.34 W
Edgartown	254	41.23 N	70.31 W
Edgefield	258	33.47 N	81.56 W
Edgeley	264	46.22 N	98.43 W
Edgemont	264	43.18 N	103.50 W
Edge Mountain ∧	246	58.12 N	152.06 W
Edgerton, AB	250	52.45 N	110.27 W
Edgerton, MN	264	43.52 N	96.08 W
Edgerton, OH	256	41.27 N	84.45 W
Edgerton, WI	256	42.50 N	89.04 W
Edgerton, WY	268	43.25 N	106.15 W
Edgewater, AL	258	33.32 N	86.57 W
Edgewater, FL	258	29.00 N	80.54 W
Edgewood, BC	248	49.47 N	118.08 W
Edgewood, IL	260	38.55 N	88.40 W
Edgewood, IA	260	42.39 N	91.24 W
Edgewood, MD	254	39.25 N	76.18 W
Edgewood, TX	262	32.42 N	95.53 W
Edina, MN	256	44.55 N	93.20 W
Edina, MO	260	40.10 N	92.11 W
Edinboro	254	41.52 N	80.08 W
Edinburg, IL	260	39.39 N	89.23 W
Edinburg, IN	260	39.21 N	85.58 W
Edinburg, MS	260	32.48 N	89.20 W
Edinburg, ND	264	48.30 N	97.52 W
Edinburg, TX	262	26.18 N	98.10 W
Edinburg, VA	258	38.49 N	78.34 W
Edison	258	31.33 N	84.44 W
Edisto ≃	258	32.39 N	80.24 W
Edisto, North Fork ≃	258	33.16 N	80.53 W
Edisto, South Fork ≃	258	33.16 N	80.53 W
Edisto Island	258	32.35 N	80.20 W
Edith, Mount ∧	268	46.26 N	111.11 W
Edmond	262	35.39 N	97.29 W
Edmonds	268	47.48 N	122.22 W
Edmonton, AB	248	53.33 N	113.28 W
Edmonton, KY	260	36.59 N	85.37 W
Edmore, MI	256	43.25 N	85.03 W
Edmore, ND	264	48.25 N	98.27 W
Edmund Lake ⊞	250	54.45 N	93.15 W
Edmundston	254	47.22 N	68.20 W
Edna, KS	264	37.04 N	95.22 W
Edna, TX	262	28.59 N	96.39 W
Edna Bay	246	55.57 N	133.40 W
Edson Butte ∧	268	42.52 N	124.20 W
Edson	248	53.35 N	116.26 W
Eduni, Mount ∧	246	64.15 N	128.04 W
Edward Island ⹀	256	48.24 N	88.36 W
Edwards, MS	260	32.20 N	90.36 W
Edwards, NY	254	44.20 N	75.15 W
Edwards ≃	262	41.09 N	90.59 W
Edwards Air Force Base ⊡	270	34.54 N	117.52 W
Edwards Butte ∧	268	45.23 N	123.41 W
Edwards Plateau ⋀[1]	262	31.20 N	101.00 W
Edwardsville	260	38.49 N	89.58 W
Edziza Peak ∧	246	57.40 N	130.36 W
Eek	246	60.12 N	162.15 W
Eek ≃	246	60.12 N	162.15 W
Eel ≃, CA	270	40.40 N	124.20 W
Eel ≃, IN	260	40.45 N	86.22 W
Eel, Middle Fork ≃	270	39.42 N	123.21 W
Eel, North Fork ≃	270	39.57 N	123.26 W
Eel, South Fork ≃	270	40.22 N	123.55 W
Effigy Mounds National Monument □	260	43.06 N	91.13 W
Effingham, IL	260	39.07 N	88.33 W
Effingham, KS	264	39.31 N	95.24 W
Egan Range ⋀	270	39.00 N	115.00 W
Eganville	256	45.32 N	77.06 W
Egegik	246	58.13 N	157.22 W
Egeria Mountain ∧	248	53.55 N	130.22 W
Egg Creek ≃	264	48.22 N	100.47 W
Egg Harbor City	254	39.32 N	74.39 W
Egg Lake ⊞, MB	250	54.21 N	101.26 W
Egg Lake ⊞, SK	250	55.05 N	105.30 W
Eglin Air Force Base ⊡	258	30.29 N	86.30 W
Egmont, Cape ⃗	252	46.51 N	60.18 W
Egmont Bay ⊂	252	46.51 N	64.15 W
Egremont	248	54.02 N	113.08 W
Egypt, Lake of ⊞[1]	260	37.35 N	88.55 W
Ehrenberg	266	33.36 N	114.31 W
Ehrhardt	258	33.06 N	81.01 W
Eisenhower, Mount ∧	248	51.18 N	115.55 W
Ekalaka	264	45.53 N	104.33 W
Ekuk	246	58.49 N	158.34 W
Ekwan ≃	242	53.14 N	82.13 W
Ekwok	246	59.22 N	157.30 W
Elaine	260	34.18 N	90.51 W
Elba	258	31.25 N	86.04 W
Elbert, Mount ∧	266	39.07 N	106.27 W
Elberta	258	44.37 N	86.14 W
Elberton	258	34.07 N	82.52 W
Elbow	250	51.08 N	106.35 W
Elbow ≃	264	51.03 N	114.02 W
Elbow Lake	264	45.59 N	95.58 W
Elbow Lake ⊞	264	54.50 N	100.53 W
El Cajon	270	32.48 N	116.58 W
El Campo	262	29.12 N	96.16 W
El Capitan ∧	268	46.01 N	114.23 W
El Centro	270	32.48 N	115.34 W
Elcho	256	45.26 N	89.11 W
Eldon, IA	260	40.55 N	92.13 W
Eldon, MO	260	38.21 N	92.35 W
Eldora	260	42.19 N	93.26 W
El Dorado, AR	260	33.13 N	92.40 W
Eldorado, IL	260	37.49 N	88.26 W
El Dorado, KS	264	37.49 N	96.52 W
Eldorado, OK	262	34.28 N	99.39 W
Eldorado, TX	262	30.52 N	100.36 W
Eldorado Peak ∧	248	48.32 N	121.08 W
El Dorado Springs	260	37.52 N	94.01 W
Eldred	254	41.57 N	78.23 W
Eldridge	260	41.39 N	90.35 W
Eldridge, Mount ∧	246	64.46 N	141.48 W
Eleanor	258	38.32 N	81.56 W
Electra	262	34.02 N	98.55 W
Electric City	248	47.56 N	119.12 W
Eleele	246	21.55 N	159.35 W
Elephant Butte Reservoir ⊞[1]	266	33.19 N	107.10 W
Elephant Butte State Park ⊐	266	33.11 N	107.14 W
Elephant Mountain ∧	254	44.46 N	70.46 W
Eleva	256	44.35 N	91.28 W
Eleven Point ≃	260	36.09 N	91.05 W
Elfin Cove	246	58.12 N	136.20 W
Elfrida, AZ	266	31.41 N	109.41 W
Elfros	250	51.43 N	103.52 W
Elgin, IL	256	42.02 N	88.17 W
Elgin, ON	256	42.57 N	91.38 W
Elgin, MN	264	44.08 N	92.15 W
Elgin, ND	264	46.24 N	101.51 W
Elgin, OK	262	34.48 N	98.18 W
Elgin, OR	268	45.34 N	117.55 W
Elgin, TX	262	30.21 N	97.22 W
Eliasville	262	32.57 N	98.46 W
Elida	262	33.57 N	103.39 W
Eliot	254	43.09 N	70.48 W
Elizabeth, CO	264	39.22 N	104.36 W
Elizabeth, IL	256	42.19 N	90.13 W
Elizabeth, LA	260	30.52 N	92.48 W
Elizabeth, NJ	254	40.40 N	74.11 W
Elizabeth City	258	36.18 N	76.14 W
Elizabethton	258	36.21 N	82.13 W
Elizabethtown, IL	260	37.27 N	88.18 W
Elizabethtown, KY	260	37.42 N	85.52 W
Elizabethtown, NC	258	34.38 N	78.37 W
Elizabethtown, NY	254	44.13 N	73.36 W
Elizabethtown, PA	254	40.09 N	76.36 W
El Jebel	266	39.22 N	107.02 W
Elk ≃, AB	248	52.55 N	115.40 W
Elk ≃, BC	248	49.10 N	115.14 W
Elk ≃, U.S.	258	34.46 N	87.16 W
Elk ≃, CO	266	40.29 N	106.58 W
Elk ≃, KS	264	37.15 N	95.41 W
Elk ≃, MN	256	45.18 N	93.34 W
Elk ≃, MO	258	36.38 N	94.38 W
Elk ≃, WV	258	38.21 N	81.38 W
Elk ≃, WI	256	45.42 N	90.37 W
Elkader	256	42.51 N	91.24 W
Elk City	262	35.25 N	99.25 W
Elk City Lake ⊞	264	37.25 N	95.55 W
Elk Creek	270	39.36 N	122.32 W
Elk Creek ≃, OK	262	34.48 N	99.09 W
Elk Creek ≃, OR	268	43.38 N	123.34 W
Elk Creek ≃, SD	264	44.15 N	102.22 W
Elk Grove	270	38.25 N	121.22 W
Elkhart, IN	256	41.41 N	85.58 W
Elkhart, KS	264	37.00 N	101.54 W
Elkhart, TX	262	31.38 N	95.35 W
Elkhart Lake	256	43.50 N	88.01 W
Elkhead Creek ≃	266	40.31 N	107.26 W
Elkhead Mountains ⋀	266	40.50 N	107.05 W
Elkhorn, MB	250	49.58 N	101.14 W
Elk Horn, IA	264	41.36 N	95.03 W
Elkhorn, WI	256	42.40 N	88.33 W
Elkhorn ≃	264	41.07 N	96.19 W
Elkhorn, North Fork ≃	264	42.00 N	97.51 W
Elkhorn City	258	37.18 N	82.21 W
Elkhorn Peaks ⋀	268	43.22 N	111.06 W
Elkin	258	36.16 N	80.51 W
Elkins	258	38.55 N	79.51 W
Elk Island ⹀	250	50.45 N	96.32 W
Elk Island National Park □	248	53.37 N	112.45 W
Elkland	254	41.59 N	77.21 W
Elk Mountain ∧	264	41.41 N	106.25 W
Elk Mountain ∧	268	41.38 N	106.32 W
Elko, BC	248	49.18 N	115.07 W
Elko, NV	270	40.50 N	115.46 W
Elk Peak ∧	268	46.50 N	110.46 W
Elk Point, AB	250	53.54 N	110.54 W
Elk Point, SD	264	42.41 N	96.41 W
Elk Rapids	256	44.54 N	85.25 W
Elk River, ID	268	46.47 N	116.11 W
Elk River, MN	256	45.18 N	93.35 W
Elkton, KY	260	36.49 N	87.09 W
Elkton, MI	256	43.49 N	83.11 W
Elkton, SD	264	44.14 N	96.29 W
Elkton, VA	258	38.25 N	78.38 W
Elkville	260	37.55 N	89.14 W
Ellard Lake ⊞	250	54.33 N	91.55 W
Ellaville	258	32.15 N	84.18 W
Ellen, Mount ∧	266	38.07 N	110.49 W
Ellendale, MN	264	43.52 N	93.18 W
Ellendale, ND	264	46.00 N	98.32 W
Ellensburg	268	47.00 N	120.32 W
Ellenton	258	31.11 N	83.35 W
Ellenville	254	41.43 N	74.28 W
Ellerbee	258	35.04 N	79.46 W
Ellettsville	260	39.14 N	86.37 W
Ellice ≃	242	68.00 N	103.26 W
Ellicott City	254	39.16 N	76.48 W
Ellicottville	254	42.17 N	78.40 W
Ellijay	258	34.42 N	84.28 W
Ellington	260	37.14 N	90.58 W
Ellinwood	264	38.21 N	98.35 W
Elliot Lake	256	46.23 N	82.39 W
Elliott, IA	264	41.09 N	95.10 W
Elliott, MS	260	33.40 N	89.44 W
Elliott Key ⹀	258	25.27 N	80.11 W
Ellis	264	38.56 N	99.34 W
Elliston, NF	252	48.38 N	53.03 W
Elliston, MT	268	46.33 N	112.26 W
Ellisville	266	31.36 N	89.12 W
Elloree	258	33.32 N	80.34 W
Ellsworth, KS	264	38.44 N	98.14 W
Ellsworth, ME	254	44.33 N	68.26 W
Ellsworth, MI	256	45.10 N	85.15 W
Ellsworth, WI	256	44.44 N	92.29 W
Ellsworth Air Force Base ⊡	264	44.08 N	103.05 W
Ellwood City	254	40.51 N	80.17 W
Elm ≃, U.S.	254	45.36 N	98.19 W
Elm ≃, IL	260	38.14 N	88.14 W
Elm ≃, ND	264	47.15 N	96.50 W
Elma, IA	264	43.15 N	92.26 W
Elma, WA	268	47.00 N	123.25 W
Elm City	258	35.48 N	77.52 W
Elm Creek, MB	250	49.41 N	98.00 W
Elm Creek, NE	264	40.43 N	99.22 W
Elm Creek ≃, MN	256	43.45 N	94.11 W
Elm Creek ≃, SD	264	44.21 N	100.42 W
Elm Creek ≃, TX	262	28.54 N	100.12 W
Elm Creek ≃, TX	262	33.12 N	98.50 W
Elmdale	262	32.40 N	99.41 W
Elmer	254	39.36 N	75.10 W
Elmhurst	256	41.53 N	87.56 W
Elmira, ON	256	43.36 N	80.33 W
Elmira, PE	252	46.27 N	62.04 W
Elmira, NY	254	42.06 N	76.48 W
El Mirage	266	33.36 N	112.19 W
El Mirage Lake ⊞	270	34.38 N	117.35 W
Elmira Heights	254	42.08 N	76.49 W
Elmo	268	46.01 N	114.23 W
Elmore City	262	34.37 N	97.24 W
El Morro National Monument □	266	35.05 N	108.22 W
Elmsdale	252	44.58 N	63.36 W
Elm Springs	260	36.12 N	94.17 W
Elmvale	256	44.35 N	79.52 W
Elmwood, IL	260	40.47 N	89.58 W
Elmwood, NE	264	40.50 N	96.18 W
Elmwood, WI	256	44.47 N	92.09 W
Elnora, AB	248	51.59 N	113.12 W
Elnora, IN	260	38.53 N	87.05 W
Eloise	258	28.00 N	81.44 W
Elora, ON	256	43.41 N	80.26 W
Elora, TN	260	35.01 N	86.21 W
Eloy	266	32.45 N	111.33 W
El Paso, IL	260	40.44 N	89.01 W
El Paso, TX	266	31.45 N	106.29 W
El Paso Peaks ⋀	270	35.28 N	117.43 W
Elphinstone	250	50.33 N	100.19 W
El Portal	270	37.41 N	119.47 W
El Reno	262	35.32 N	97.57 W
El Rio	270	34.14 N	119.10 W
El Rito	266	36.21 N	106.11 W
El Rito ≃	266	36.12 N	106.14 W
Elrose	250	51.13 N	108.01 W
Elroy	256	43.45 N	90.16 W
Elsa, YK	246	63.55 N	135.28 W
Elsa, TX	262	26.18 N	97.59 W
Elsberry	260	39.10 N	90.47 W
Elsie	258	43.05 N	84.23 W
Elsinore	266	38.41 N	112.09 W
Elsinore, Lake ⊞	270	33.39 N	117.21 W
Elsmere	264	39.44 N	75.36 W
Elton	260	30.29 N	92.42 W
Elvins	266	37.50 N	90.34 W
Elwood, IN	260	40.17 N	85.50 W
Elwood, KS	264	39.45 N	94.52 W
Elwood, NE	264	40.36 N	99.52 W
Ely, MN	256	47.54 N	91.51 W
Ely, NV	270	39.15 N	114.53 W
Elyria	256	41.22 N	82.06 W
Embarras ≃, AB	248	53.27 N	116.37 W
Embarras ≃, IL	260	38.39 N	87.37 W
Embarras, North Fork ≃	260	38.55 N	87.59 W
Embarrass	264	44.40 N	88.42 W
Embarrass ≃, MN	256	47.24 N	92.25 W
Embarrass ≃, WI	256	44.23 N	88.45 W
Embarrass, Middle Branch ≃	256	44.43 N	88.55 W
Embreeville	258	36.11 N	82.28 W
Embrun	256	45.16 N	75.17 W
Emden	260	40.18 N	89.29 W
Emelle	260	32.44 N	88.19 W
Emerado	264	47.55 N	97.22 W
Emerald, MB	250	49.00 N	97.12 W
Emerson, AR	260	33.06 N	93.11 W
Emerson, GA	258	34.08 N	84.45 W
Emerson, IA	264	41.01 N	95.24 W
Emerson, NE	264	42.17 N	96.44 W
Emery, SD	264	43.36 N	97.37 W
Emery, UT	266	38.55 N	111.15 W
Eminence, KY	260	38.22 N	85.11 W
Eminence, MO	260	37.09 N	91.22 W
Emlenton	254	41.11 N	79.43 W
Emmaus	254	40.32 N	75.30 W
Emmeline Lake ⊞	250	55.00 N	106.22 W
Emmet	250	33.44 N	93.28 W
Emmetsburg	264	43.07 N	94.41 W
Emmett	268	43.52 N	116.30 W
Emmitsburg	254	39.42 N	77.20 W
Emmonak	246	62.46 N	164.30 W
Emo	256	48.38 N	93.50 W
Emory	262	32.52 N	95.46 W
Emory Peak ∧	262	29.13 N	103.17 W
Empire, LA	260	29.24 N	89.37 W
Empire, NV	270	40.37 N	119.21 W
Empire, OR	268	43.23 N	124.17 W
Emporia, KS	264	38.24 N	96.11 W
Emporia, VA	258	36.41 N	77.32 W
Emporium	254	41.31 N	78.14 W
Empress	250	50.57 N	110.00 W
Encampment	268	41.12 N	106.47 W
Encampment ≃	268	41.18 N	106.43 W
Encinal	262	28.02 N	99.21 W
Encinitas	270	33.03 N	117.17 W
Encino, NM	266	34.39 N	105.28 W
Encino, TX	262	26.57 N	98.08 W
Endako ≃	248	54.05 N	124.55 W
Endeavor	256	43.43 N	89.29 W
Endeavour	250	52.10 N	102.40 W
Enderby	248	50.33 N	119.08 W
Enderlin	264	46.37 N	97.36 W
Endicott, NY	254	42.06 N	76.03 W
Endicott, WA	268	46.56 N	117.41 W
Endicott Mountains ⋀	246	67.50 N	152.00 W
Enfield, NH	254	43.34 N	71.57 W
Enfield, NC	258	36.11 N	77.47 W
Engelhard	258	35.31 N	76.02 W
England	260	34.33 N	91.58 W
England Air Force Base ⊡	260	31.20 N	92.33 W
Englee	252	50.44 N	56.06 W
Englefield, Cape ⃗	242	69.51 N	85.39 W
Englehart	242	47.49 N	79.52 W
Englewood, BC	248	50.33 N	126.53 W
Englewood, CO	264	39.39 N	104.59 W
Englewood, FL	258	26.58 N	82.21 W
Englewood, TN	258	35.26 N	84.29 W
English, IN	260	38.20 N	86.28 W
English ≃, ON	250	50.12 N	95.00 W
English ≃, IA	260	41.25 N	91.32 W
English Bay	246	59.21 N	151.55 W
English Harbour West	252	47.38 N	55.29 W
Enid	262	36.19 N	97.48 W
Enid Lake ⊞	260	34.10 N	89.50 W
Enilda	248	55.25 N	116.18 W
Enka	258	35.26 N	82.38 W
Ennadai Lake ⊞	242	60.53 N	101.15 W
Ennis, MT	268	45.21 N	111.44 W
Ennis, TX	262	32.20 N	96.38 W
Ennis Lake ⊞[1]	268	45.26 N	111.41 W
Enochs	262	33.52 N	102.46 W
Enoch	266	37.46 N	113.01 W
Enoree	258	34.26 N	81.58 W
Enoree ≃	258	34.26 N	81.25 W
Enosburg Falls	254	44.55 N	72.48 W
Enragé, Point ⃗	252	44.16 N	64.15 W
Enterprise, AL	258	31.19 N	85.51 W
Enterprise, CA	270	39.32 N	121.22 W
Enterprise, MS	260	32.10 N	88.49 W
Enterprise, OR	268	45.25 N	117.17 W
Enterprise, UT	266	37.34 N	113.43 W
Entiat	268	47.40 N	120.14 W
Entiat ≃	268	47.40 N	120.17 W
Entiat, Lake ⊞[1]	268	47.40 N	120.17 W
Entrée, Ile d' ⹀	252	47.17 N	61.42 W
Entwistle	248	53.36 N	115.00 W
Enumclaw	268	47.12 N	121.59 W
Eolia	260	39.14 N	91.01 W
Epes	260	32.42 N	88.07 W
Ephraim	266	39.22 N	111.35 W
Ephrata, PA	254	40.11 N	76.10 W
Ephrata, WA	268	47.19 N	119.33 W
Equality	260	37.44 N	88.20 W
Equinox Mountain ∧	254	43.10 N	73.06 W
Erath	260	29.58 N	92.02 W
Erichsen Lake ⊞	242	70.38 N	80.21 W
Erick	262	35.13 N	99.52 W
Erickson, BC	248	49.05 N	116.30 W
Erickson, MB	250	50.30 N	99.55 W
Ericson	264	41.47 N	98.41 W
Erie, CO	264	40.03 N	105.03 W
Erie, IL	260	41.39 N	90.04 W
Erie, KS	264	37.34 N	95.15 W
Erie, PA	254	42.08 N	80.04 W
Erie, N.A. ⊞	244	42.15 N	81.00 W
Erie Canal → New York State Barge Canal ⧗	254	43.05 N	78.43 W
Eriksdale	250	50.52 N	98.06 W
Erin, ON	256	43.45 N	80.07 W
Erin, TN	260	36.19 N	87.46 W
Erling, Lake ⊞	260	33.05 N	93.35 W
Ermineskin Indian Reserve ◄[4]	248	52.52 N	113.30 W
Ernest Sound ⹀	248	55.52 N	132.10 W
Errol Heights	258	45.29 N	122.33 W
Erskine	264	47.40 N	96.00 W
Erwin, NC	258	35.20 N	78.41 W
Erwin, TN	258	36.09 N	82.25 W
Erwood	250	52.50 N	102.10 W
Escalante	266	37.47 N	111.36 W
Escalante ≃	266	37.17 N	110.53 W
Escalante Desert ⬳[2]	266	37.50 N	113.30 W
Escalon	270	37.48 N	120.60 W
Escambia ≃	260	30.32 N	87.11 W
Escanaba	256	45.45 N	87.04 W
Escanaba ≃	256	45.47 N	87.04 W
Escanaba, East Branch ≃	256	46.16 N	87.27 W
Escanaba, Middle Branch ≃	256	46.16 N	87.27 W
Escondido	270	33.07 N	117.05 W
Escuminac, Point ⃗	252	47.04 N	64.46 W
Eskdale	254	48.05 N	81.27 W
Eskimo Lakes ⊞	246	69.15 N	132.17 W
Eskimo Point	242	61.07 N	94.03 W
Eskridge	264	38.52 N	96.06 W
Esmond	264	48.02 N	99.46 W
Esnagi Lake ⊞	256	48.38 N	84.32 W
Espanola, ON	256	46.15 N	81.46 W
Espanola, NM	266	36.06 N	106.02 W
Esperanza Inlet ⹀	246	49.48 N	127.10 W
Espoir, Bay d' ⹀	252	47.50 N	55.51 W
Esquatzel Coulee V	268	46.17 N	119.07 W
Essex, ON	256	42.10 N	82.49 W
Essex, IA	264	40.50 N	95.18 W
Essex, MD	254	39.18 N	76.29 W
Essex, MT	268	48.17 N	113.37 W
Essex Junction	254	44.29 N	73.07 W
Essexville	256	43.37 N	83.50 W
Est, Ile de l' ⹀	252	47.37 N	61.26 W
Est, Pointe de l' ⃗	252	49.08 N	61.41 W
Estacada	268	45.17 N	122.20 W
Estacado, Llano ⬳	266	33.30 N	102.40 W
Estancia	266	34.45 N	106.04 W
Estelline, SD	264	44.35 N	96.54 W
Estelline, TX	262	34.33 N	100.26 W
Ester	246	64.51 N	148.01 W
Esterhazy	250	50.40 N	102.08 W
Estes Park	264	40.23 N	105.31 W
Estevan	250	49.08 N	102.59 W
Estevan Group ⹀	248	53.05 N	129.40 W
Estevan Point	248	49.23 N	126.33 W
Esther Island ⹀	246	60.50 N	148.05 W
Estherville	264	43.24 N	94.50 W
Estill	258	32.45 N	81.14 W
Eston	250	51.10 N	108.46 W
Estuary	250	50.56 N	109.46 W
Etamamiou ≃	252	50.17 N	59.58 W
Etchemin ≃	254	46.46 N	71.14 W
Ethan	264	43.33 N	97.59 W
Ethel, Mount ∧	266	40.23 N	103.09 W
Ethel Lake ⊞	246	40.39 N	106.41 W
Ethelbert	250	51.31 N	100.22 W
Ethridge, MT	248	48.34 N	112.07 W
Ethridge, TN	260	35.19 N	87.18 W
Etna, CA	270	41.27 N	122.54 W
Etna, WY	268	43.02 N	111.00 W
Etolin Island ⹀	246	56.08 N	132.26 W
Etolin Strait ⹀	246	60.20 N	165.15 W
Etomami ≃	250	52.48 N	102.33 W
Etonia Creek ≃	258	29.42 N	81.39 W
Etowah	258	35.20 N	84.32 W
Etowah ≃	258	34.15 N	85.11 W
Ettrick	258	37.14 N	77.25 W
Etzikom Coulee ≃	250	49.51 N	111.10 W
Euchiniko ≃	248	53.20 N	123.50 W
Euclid	256	41.34 N	81.32 W
Eudistes, Lac des ⊞	254	50.30 N	63.15 W
Eudora, AR	260	33.07 N	91.16 W
Eudora, KS	264	38.57 N	95.06 W
Eufaula, AL	258	31.54 N	85.09 W
Eufaula, OK	262	35.17 N	95.35 W
Eugene	268	44.02 N	123.05 W
Eunice, LA	260	30.30 N	92.25 W
Eunice, NM	266	32.26 N	103.09 W
Eupora	260	33.32 N	89.16 W
Eureka, AK	246	65.11 N	160.13 W
Eureka, CA	270	40.47 N	124.09 W
Eureka, IL	260	40.43 N	89.16 W
Eureka, KS	264	37.49 N	96.17 W
Eureka, MT	268	48.53 N	115.03 W
Eureka, NV	270	39.31 N	115.58 W
Eureka, SD	264	45.46 N	99.37 W
Eureka, UT	266	39.57 N	112.07 W
Eureka Springs	260	36.24 N	93.44 W
Eustace	262	32.19 N	96.19 W
Eustis, FL	258	28.51 N	81.41 W
Eustis, Lake ⊞	258	28.50 N	81.44 W
Eutaw	260	32.50 N	87.53 W
Eutsuk Lake ⊞	248	53.20 N	126.44 W
Eva	260	34.20 N	86.46 W
Evadale	262	30.21 N	94.04 W
Evans, CO	264	40.23 N	104.41 W
Evans, Lac ⊞	242	50.50 N	77.00 W
Evans, Mount ∧	266	39.35 N	105.38 W
Evansburg	248	53.36 N	114.59 W
Evans City	254	40.46 N	80.04 W
Evans Creek	258	36.02 N	85.47 W
Evansdale	260	42.25 N	92.17 W
Evans Strait ⹀	242	63.15 N	82.00 W
Evanston, IL	256	42.03 N	87.41 W
Evanston, WY	268	41.16 N	110.58 W
Evansville, IN	260	37.58 N	87.35 W
Evansville, MN	264	46.00 N	95.41 W
Evansville, WI	256	42.47 N	89.18 W
Evant	262	31.29 N	98.09 W
Evart	256	43.54 N	85.09 W
Eveleth	264	47.28 N	92.32 W
Evening Shade	260	36.04 N	91.37 W
Everest	264	39.40 N	95.25 W
Everett, PA	254	40.01 N	78.22 W
Everett, WA	268	47.59 N	122.12 W
Everett, Mount ∧	254	42.06 N	73.25 W
Everett Mountains ⋀	242	62.45 N	67.12 W
Everglades City	258	25.52 N	81.23 W
Everglades National Park □	258	25.27 N	80.53 W
Evergreen, AL	258	31.26 N	86.57 W
Evergreen, CA	270	35.54 N	120.26 W
Evergreen, MT	268	48.13 N	114.18 W
Everly	264	43.10 N	95.20 W
Evesham	250	52.24 N	109.50 W
Ewa	272c	21.21 N	158.02 W
Ewa Beach	272c	21.20 N	158.04 W
Ewen	256	46.32 N	89.17 W
Ewing, NE	264	42.16 N	98.21 W
Ewing, VA	258	36.38 N	83.26 W
Excelsior Mountain ∧	270	38.02 N	119.18 W
Excelsior Springs	260	39.20 N	94.13 W
Excursion Inlet	246	58.25 N	135.27 W
Exeter, ON	256	43.21 N	81.29 W
Exeter, CA	270	36.18 N	119.09 W
Exeter, NE	264	40.39 N	97.27 W
Exeter, NH	254	42.59 N	70.57 W
Exeter ≃	254	43.02 N	70.55 W
Exeter Sound ⹀	242	66.14 N	62.00 W
Exira	264	41.35 N	94.52 W
Exmore	258	37.32 N	75.50 W
Experiment	258	33.16 N	84.17 W
Exploits ≃	252	49.05 N	55.20 W
Exploits, Bay of ⊂	252	49.24 N	55.00 W
Exploits Dam ⧗	252	48.45 N	56.30 W
Exshaw	248	51.03 N	115.09 W
Eyak	246	60.32 N	145.36 W
Eyebrow	250	50.47 N	106.09 W
Eylar Mountain ∧	270	37.28 N	121.33 W
Eyota	256	43.59 N	92.14 W

F

Name	Page	Lat	Long
Fabens	266	31.30 N	106.10 W
Faber Lake ⊞	242	63.56 N	117.15 W
Factoryville	254	41.34 N	75.47 W
Faillon, Lac ⊞	254	48.21 N	76.38 W
Fairbank	256	42.38 N	92.03 W
Fairbanks, AK	246	64.51 N	147.43 W
Fair Bluff	258	34.19 N	79.02 W
Fairburn	258	33.34 N	84.35 W
Fairbury, IL	256	40.45 N	88.31 W
Fairbury, NE	264	40.08 N	97.11 W
Fairchance	254	39.49 N	79.45 W
Fairchild	256	44.36 N	90.58 W
Fairchild Air Force Base ⊡	268	47.38 N	117.38 W
Fairfax, AL	258	32.48 N	85.11 W
Fairfax, MN	264	44.32 N	94.43 W
Fairfax, MO	264	40.22 N	95.24 W
Fairfax, OK	262	36.34 N	96.42 W
Fairfax, SC	258	33.01 N	81.18 W
Fairfax, SD	264	43.02 N	98.54 W
Fairfax, VT	254	44.40 N	73.01 W
Fairfax, VA	258	38.51 N	77.18 W
Fairfield, AL	258	33.29 N	86.55 W
Fairfield, CA	270	38.15 N	122.03 W
Fairfield, ID	268	43.21 N	114.48 W
Fairfield, IL	260	38.23 N	88.22 W
Fairfield, IA	260	40.56 N	91.57 W
Fairfield, ME	254	44.35 N	69.36 W
Fairfield, MT	268	47.37 N	111.59 W
Fairfield, NE	264	40.26 N	98.06 W
Fairfield, OH	254	39.20 N	84.33 W
Fairfield, TX	262	31.44 N	96.10 W
Fairgrove	256	43.31 N	83.33 W
Fairhaven, MA	254	41.39 N	70.54 W
Fair Haven, NY	256	43.19 N	76.42 W
Fair Haven, VT	254	43.36 N	73.16 W
Fairhope	260	30.31 N	87.54 W
Fairland, IN	260	39.35 N	85.52 W
Fairland, OK	262	36.45 N	94.51 W
Fairmont, NE	264	40.38 N	97.35 W
Fairmont, NC	258	34.30 N	79.07 W
Fairmont, WV	258	39.29 N	80.09 W
Fairmont Hot Springs	248	50.19 N	115.53 W
Fairmount, GA	258	34.26 N	84.42 W
Fairmount, IL	260	40.03 N	87.56 W
Fairmount, IN	260	40.25 N	85.39 W
Fairmount, ND	264	46.03 N	96.36 W
Fair Ness ⃗	242	63.24 N	72.05 W
Fair Oaks, CA	270	38.39 N	121.16 W
Fair Oaks, GA	258	33.55 N	84.32 W
Fair Plain	258	42.05 N	86.28 W
Fairplains	258	36.11 N	81.10 W
Fairplay	264	39.13 N	106.00 W
Fairport	256	43.06 N	77.27 W
Fairview, AB	248	56.04 N	118.23 W
Fairview, GA	258	34.58 N	85.16 W
Fairview, IL	260	40.38 N	90.10 W
Fairview, KS	264	39.50 N	95.44 W
Fairview, MI	256	44.44 N	84.03 W
Fairview, MT	264	47.51 N	104.03 W
Fairview, OK	262	36.16 N	98.29 W
Fairview, TN	260	35.59 N	87.07 W
Fairview, UT	266	39.38 N	111.26 W
Fairview, WV	258	39.36 N	80.15 W
Fairview Park	260	39.41 N	87.25 W
Fairview Peak ∧, NV	270	39.14 N	118.08 W
Fairview Peak ∧, OR	268	43.35 N	122.39 W
Fairweather, Mount ∧	242	58.54 N	137.32 W
Fairy Stone State Park ⊐	258	36.48 N	80.06 W
Faison	258	35.07 N	78.08 W
Faith	264	45.02 N	102.02 W
Falcon, Cape ⃗	268	45.46 N	123.59 W
Falcón, Presa (Falcon Reservoir) ⊞	262	26.37 N	99.11 W
Falconbridge	256	46.35 N	80.48 W
Falcon Heights	268	42.08 N	121.45 W
Falcon Reservoir ⊞[1]	262	26.37 N	99.11 W
Falfurrias	262	27.14 N	98.09 W
Falkland	248	50.30 N	119.33 W
Falkville	260	34.22 N	86.55 W
Fall ≃	264	36.23 N	96.56 W
Fallbrook	270	33.23 N	117.15 W
Fall Creek	256	44.47 N	91.17 W
Fall Creek ≃	260	39.47 N	86.11 W
Falling Water ≃	260	36.02 N	85.47 W
Fallon, MT	264	46.50 N	105.07 W
Fallon, NV	270	39.28 N	118.47 W
Fall River, KS	264	37.36 N	96.02 W
Fall River, MA	254	41.43 N	71.08 W
Fall River, WI	256	43.23 N	89.03 W
Fall River Mills	270	41.00 N	121.26 W
Falls City, NE	264	40.03 N	95.36 W
Falls City, OR	268	44.52 N	123.26 W
Falls Creek	254	41.09 N	78.48 W
Falmouth, KY	260	38.41 N	84.20 W
Falmouth, ME	254	43.44 N	70.15 W
Falmouth, MA	254	41.33 N	70.37 W
Falmouth, VA	258	38.19 N	77.28 W
False Pass	246	54.52 N	163.24 W
Family Creek ≃	250	51.54 N	95.30 W
Fancy Creek ≃	264	39.28 N	96.45 W

Symbols in the index entries are identified on page 273.

Symbols in the index entries are identified on page 273.

Fres – Gran

United States and Canada Map Index

Name	Page	Lat° '	Long° '
Freshfield, Mount ∧	248	51.44 N	116.57 W
Fresno	270	36.45 N	119.45 W
Fresno ≃	270	37.05 N	120.33 W
Fresno Reservoir @[1]	268	48.41 N	109.57 W
Frewsburg	254	42.03 N	79.10 W
Friant	270	36.59 N	119.43 W
Friars Point	260	34.22 N	90.38 W
Friday Harbor	268	48.32 N	123.01 W
Fridley	256	45.06 N	93.15 W
Friend	264	40.38 N	97.17 W
Friendship, NY	254	42.12 N	78.08 W
Friendship, TN	260	35.55 N	89.14 W
Friendship, WI	256	43.58 N	89.49 W
Fries	258	36.43 N	80.59 W
Frio ≃	262	28.30 N	98.10 W
Frio Draw V	262	34.50 N	102.19 W
Friona	262	34.38 N	102.43 W
Frisco	262	33.09 N	96.49 W
Frisco City	260	31.26 N	87.24 W
Frisco Creek ≃	262	36.34 N	101.23 W
Fritch	262	35.38 N	101.36 W
Frobisher	250	49.12 N	102.26 W
Frobisher Bay	242	63.44 N	68.28 W
Frobisher Bay C	242	62.30 N	66.00 W
Frobisher Lake @	250	56.25 N	108.20 W
Frog Lake @	250	53.55 N	110.18 W
Froid	264	48.20 N	104.30 W
Fromberg	268	45.23 N	108.54 W
Frontenac	264	37.29 N	94.44 W
Frontier, SK	250	49.12 N	108.34 W
Frontier, WY	268	41.49 N	110.32 W
Front Range ∧∧	266	39.45 N	105.45 W
Front Royal	254	38.55 N	78.11 W
Frost	262	32.05 N	96.48 W
Frostburg	254	39.39 N	78.56 W
Frostproof	258	27.44 N	81.32 W
Fruita	266	39.09 N	108.44 W
Fruitdale, AL	260	31.20 N	88.25 W
Fruitdale, OR	268	42.24 N	123.20 W
Fruithurst	258	33.44 N	85.25 W
Fruitland, ID	268	44.00 N	116.55 W
Fruitland, MD	254	38.19 N	75.37 W
Fruitport	256	43.07 N	86.09 W
Fruitvale, BC	248	49.07 N	117.33 W
Fruitvale, WA	268	46.37 N	120.33 W
Fruitville	258	27.20 N	82.30 W
Fryeburg	254	44.01 N	70.59 W
Fryingpan ≃	266	39.22 N	107.02 W
Fulda	264	43.52 N	95.36 W
Fullerton, CA	270	33.52 N	117.55 W
Fullerton, NE	264	41.22 N	97.58 W
Fulton, AL	260	31.47 N	87.43 W
Fulton, AR	260	33.37 N	93.49 W
Fulton, IL	260	41.52 N	90.11 W
Fulton, KS	264	38.01 N	94.43 W
Fulton, KY	260	36.30 N	88.53 W
Fulton, MS	260	34.16 N	88.31 W
Fulton, MO	260	38.52 N	91.57 W
Fulton, NY	254	43.19 N	76.25 W
Fulton, TX	262	28.04 N	97.02 W
Fulton ≃	248	54.48 N	126.07 W
Fultondale	260	33.36 N	86.48 W
Fundy, Bay of C	242	45.00 N	66.00 W
Fundy National Park ♠	252	45.38 N	65.00 W
Funk Island I	252	49.46 N	53.10 W
Fuquay-Varina	258	35.35 N	78.48 W
Fury and Hecla Strait U	242	69.56 N	84.00 W
Fusilier	250	51.51 N	109.46 W
G			
Gabarus	252	45.50 N	60.09 W
Gabarus Bay C	252	45.51 N	60.07 W
Gabbs	270	38.52 N	117.55 W
Gable Mountain ∧	248	54.30 N	121.40 W
Gabriel Strait U	242	61.45 N	65.30 W
Gackle	264	46.38 N	99.09 W
Gadsden, AL	260	34.02 N	86.02 W
Gadsden, AZ	266	32.33 N	108.47 W
Gaffney	258	35.05 N	81.39 W
Gage	262	36.19 N	99.45 W
Gagetown	252	45.47 N	66.09 W
Gagnon	242	51.53 N	68.10 W
Gagnon, Lac @	254	46.07 N	75.07 W
Gail	262	32.46 N	101.27 W
Gaillard, Lac @	252	50.06 N	68.47 W
Gainesboro	260	36.21 N	85.39 W
Gainesville, FL	258	29.40 N	82.20 W
Gainesville, GA	258	34.18 N	83.50 W
Gainesville, MO	260	36.36 N	92.26 W
Gainesville, TX	262	33.37 N	97.08 W
Gainsborough	250	49.10 N	101.26 W
Gainsborough Creek ≃	250	49.10 N	101.02 W
Gaithersburg	254	39.09 N	77.12 W
Gakona	246	62.18 N	145.18 W
Galahad	250	52.31 N	111.56 W
Galatia	260	37.51 N	88.37 W
Galax	258	36.40 N	80.56 W
Gale, Lac @	256	46.46 N	76.51 W
Galena, AK	246	64.44 N	156.57 W
Galena, IL	256	42.25 N	90.26 W
Galena, KS	264	37.04 N	94.38 W
Galena, MO	260	36.48 N	93.28 W
Galena Park	262	29.44 N	95.14 W
Galesburg, IL	256	40.57 N	90.22 W
Galesburg, MI	256	42.14 N	85.25 W
Galesville	256	44.05 N	91.21 W
Galeton	254	41.44 N	77.39 W
Galiano Island I	248	48.56 N	123.29 W
Galion	254	40.44 N	82.47 W
Galisteo Creek ≃	266	35.31 N	106.22 W
Galiuro Mountains ∧∧	266	32.40 N	110.20 W
Gallatin, MO	260	39.55 N	93.58 W
Gallatin, TN	260	36.24 N	86.27 W
Gallatin ≃	268	45.56 N	111.29 W
Gallatin Range ∧∧	268	45.15 N	111.05 W
Gallegos Canyon V	266	36.41 N	108.07 W
Galliano	260	29.26 N	90.20 W
Gallinas ≃	262	35.10 N	104.55 W
Gallinas Peak ∧	266	34.13 N	105.45 W
Gallipolis	254	38.49 N	82.12 W
Galloo Island I	254	43.54 N	76.25 W
Gallup	266	35.32 N	108.44 W
Galt	270	38.15 N	121.18 W
Galva, IL	260	41.10 N	90.03 W
Galva, IA	264	42.30 N	95.25 W
Galva, KS	264	38.25 N	97.32 W
Galveston, IN	260	40.35 N	86.11 W
Galveston, TX	260	29.18 N	94.48 W
Galveston Bay C	260	29.36 N	94.57 W
Galveston Island I	260	29.13 N	94.55 W
Gamaliel	260	36.38 N	85.48 W
Gambell	246	63.46 N	171.46 W
Gambier	254	40.23 N	82.24 W
Gambo	252	48.46 N	54.14 W
Gammon ≃	250	51.07 N	95.09 W
Ganado, AZ	266	35.43 N	109.33 W
Ganado, TX	262	29.02 N	96.31 W
Gananoque	256	44.20 N	76.10 W
Gander	252	48.57 N	54.37 W
Gander ≃	252	49.15 N	54.30 W
Gander Bay	252	49.18 N	54.29 W
Gander Bay C	252	49.25 N	54.28 W
Gander Lake @	252	48.55 N	54.40 W
Ganges	248	48.51 N	123.30 W
Gang Ranch	248	51.33 N	122.20 W
Gannett Peak ∧	268	43.11 N	109.39 W
Gannvalley	264	44.02 N	98.59 W
Gantt	260	31.25 N	86.29 W
Garber	262	36.26 N	97.35 W
Garberville	270	40.06 N	123.48 W
Garde, Lac la @	256	46.46 N	78.14 W
Garden ≃	256	46.32 N	84.09 W
Garden City, GA	258	32.06 N	81.09 W
Garden City, KS	264	37.58 N	100.53 W
Garden City, MO	260	38.34 N	94.12 W
Garden City, TX	262	31.52 N	101.29 W
Gardendale	260	33.39 N	86.49 W
Garden Grove, CA	270	33.46 N	117.57 W
Garden Grove, IA	256	40.50 N	93.36 W
Garden Island I	256	45.49 N	85.30 W
Garden Lakes	258	34.17 N	85.16 W
Garden Peninsula >[1]	256	45.45 N	86.35 W
Garden Plain	264	37.39 N	97.41 W
Gardenton	250	49.05 N	96.40 W
Gardiner, ME	254	44.14 N	69.46 W
Gardiner, MT	268	45.02 N	110.42 W
Gardiner, OR	268	43.44 N	124.07 W
Gardiner Dam →[6]	250	51.17 N	106.51 W
Gardiners Bay C	254	41.08 N	72.10 W
Gardner, KS	264	38.49 N	94.56 W
Gardner, MA	254	42.34 N	72.00 W
Gardner Canal C	248	53.28 N	128.15 W
Gardnerville	270	38.56 N	119.45 W
Gareloi Island I	247a	51.47 N	178.48 W
Garfield, KS	264	38.05 N	99.14 W
Garfield, NM	266	32.46 N	107.16 W
Garfield, WA	268	47.01 N	117.09 W
Garfield Mountain ∧	268	44.31 N	112.37 W
Garfield Peak ∧	268	42.47 N	107.18 W
Gargantua, Cape >	256	47.36 N	85.02 W
Garibaldi, BC	248	49.58 N	123.09 W
Garibaldi, OR	268	45.34 N	123.55 W
Garibaldi, Mount ∧	248	49.51 N	123.01 W
Garibaldi Provincial Park ♠	248	50.00 N	122.50 W
Garland, AL	260	31.33 N	86.49 W
Garland, TX	262	32.54 N	96.39 W
Garland, UT	266	41.45 N	112.10 W
Garnavillo	256	42.52 N	91.14 W
Garner, IA	256	43.06 N	93.36 W
Garner, NC	258	35.43 N	78.37 W
Garnet Bay C	242	65.17 N	75.15 W
Garnet Range ∧∧	268	46.45 N	113.15 W
Garnett	264	38.17 N	95.14 W
Garnish	252	47.14 N	55.22 W
Garretson	264	43.43 N	96.30 W
Garrett, IN	260	41.21 N	85.08 W
Garrett, KY	258	37.29 N	82.50 W
Garrett Lake @	250	53.39 N	90.59 W
Garrison, MT	268	46.31 N	112.57 W
Garrison, ND	264	47.40 N	101.25 W
Garrison, TX	260	31.49 N	94.29 W
Garrison Dam →[6]	264	47.22 N	101.25 W
Garry Bay C	242	68.55 N	85.05 W
Garry Lake @	242	66.00 N	100.00 W
Garson	256	46.34 N	80.52 W
Garson Lake @	250	56.19 N	110.02 W
Garwin	256	42.06 N	92.40 W
Garwood	262	29.27 N	96.24 W
Gary, IN	260	41.36 N	87.20 W
Gary, SD	264	44.48 N	96.27 W
Gary, TX	260	32.07 N	94.22 W
Gary, WV	258	37.21 N	81.38 W
Garza-Little Elm Reservoir @[1]	262	33.08 N	97.00 W
Gas City	260	40.29 N	85.37 W
Gasconade ≃	260	38.40 N	91.33 W
Gasconade, Osage Fork ≃	260	37.45 N	92.26 W
Gasparilla Island I	258	26.46 N	82.16 W
Gaspé	252	48.50 N	64.29 W
Gaspé, Baie de ≃	252	48.46 N	64.17 W
Gaspé, Cap de >	252	48.45 N	64.10 W
Gaspé, Péninsule de >[1]	252	48.30 N	65.00 W
Gaspereau Lake @	252	44.57 N	64.34 W
Gaspésie, Parc de la ♠	252	48.55 N	66.00 W
Gassaway	254	38.40 N	80.47 W
Gaston	258	36.30 N	77.38 W
Gaston, Lake @[1]	258	36.35 N	78.00 W
Gastonia	258	35.16 N	81.11 W
Gate	262	36.51 N	100.04 W
Gate City	258	36.38 N	82.35 W
Gateshead Island I	242	70.22 N	100.27 W
Gates of the Arctic National Park ♠	246	67.45 N	153.30 W
Gatesville, NC	258	36.19 N	76.45 W
Gatesville, TX	262	31.26 N	97.45 W
Gateway	266	38.41 N	108.59 W
Gatineau	254	45.29 N	75.38 W
Gatineau ≃	254	45.27 N	75.40 W
Gatineau, Parc ♠, PQ	254	45.30 N	76.05 W
Gatineau, Parc (Gatineau Park) ♠, PQ	256	45.30 N	75.52 W
Gatlinburg	258	35.43 N	83.31 W
Gauer Lake @	250	57.00 N	97.50 W
Gauley ≃	254	38.10 N	81.12 W
Gauley Bridge	254	38.10 N	81.11 W
Gause	262	30.47 N	96.43 W
Gavins Point Dam →[6]	264	42.48 N	97.40 W
Gaylord, MI	256	45.02 N	84.40 W
Gaylord, MN	264	44.33 N	94.13 W
Gays Mills	256	43.19 N	90.51 W
Gearhart Mountain ∧	268	42.30 N	120.53 W
Geary, NB	252	45.46 N	66.29 W
Geary, OK	262	35.38 N	98.19 W
Geddes	264	43.15 N	98.42 W
Geiger	260	32.52 N	88.18 W
Geikie ≃	242	57.45 N	103.52 W
Geistown	254	40.17 N	78.52 W
Genesee	268	46.33 N	116.56 W
Genesee ≃	256	43.16 N	77.36 W
Geneseo, IL	260	41.27 N	90.09 W
Geneseo, KS	264	38.31 N	98.09 W
Geneseo, NY	254	42.48 N	77.49 W
Geneva, AL	260	31.02 N	85.52 W
Geneva, IL	260	41.53 N	88.18 W
Geneva, IN	260	40.36 N	84.58 W
Geneva, NE	264	40.32 N	97.36 W
Geneva, NY	254	42.52 N	77.00 W
Geneva, OH	254	41.48 N	80.57 W
Genevia	260	34.43 N	92.13 W
Genévriers, Île des I	252	51.15 N	58.26 W
Genoa, IL	256	42.06 N	88.42 W
Genoa, NE	264	41.27 N	97.44 W
Genoa, OH	254	41.31 N	83.22 W
Genoa, WI	256	43.35 N	91.13 W
Gens de Terre ≃	256	46.53 N	76.00 W
Gentry	260	36.16 N	94.29 W
George	264	43.21 N	96.00 W
George ≃	242	58.49 N	66.10 W
George, Cape >	252	45.53 N	61.53 W
George, Lake @, N.A.	256	46.28 N	84.10 W
George, Lake @, FL	258	29.17 N	81.36 W
George, Lake @, NY	254	43.35 N	73.35 W
George Air Force Base ■	270	34.35 N	117.22 W
George H. Crosby-Manitou State Park ♠	256	47.29 N	91.10 W
Georgetown, ON	256	43.39 N	79.55 W
Georgetown, PE	252	46.11 N	62.32 W
Georgetown, CO	266	39.42 N	105.42 W
Georgetown, DE	254	38.42 N	75.23 W
Georgetown, FL	258	29.23 N	81.38 W
Georgetown, GA	258	31.53 N	85.06 W
Georgetown, ID	268	42.29 N	111.22 W
Georgetown, IL	260	39.59 N	87.38 W
Georgetown, KY	254	38.13 N	84.33 W
Georgetown, MS	260	31.52 N	90.10 W
Georgetown, OH	254	38.52 N	83.54 W
Georgetown, SC	258	33.23 N	79.17 W
Georgetown, TX	262	30.38 N	97.41 W
Georgetown Lake @	268	46.11 N	113.17 W
George Washington Carver National Monument ♠	260	37.00 N	94.19 W
George West	262	28.20 N	98.07 W
Georgia □[3], U.S.	244, 258	32.50 N	83.15 W
Georgia, Strait of U	242	49.00 N	123.20 W
Georgiana	260	31.33 N	86.44 W
Georgian Bay C	256	45.15 N	80.50 W
Georgian Bay Islands National Park ♠	256	44.54 N	79.52 W
Gerald	260	38.24 N	91.20 W
Geraldine	268	47.36 N	110.16 W
Geraldton	242	49.44 N	86.57 W
Gerber	270	40.03 N	122.09 W
Gerber Reservoir @[1]	268	42.12 N	121.06 W
Gerdine, Mount ∧	246	61.35 N	152.26 W
Gering	264	41.50 N	103.40 W
Germansen, Mount ∧	248	55.37 N	124.50 W
Germansen Lake @	248	55.41 N	124.53 W
Germansen Landing	248	55.47 N	124.43 W
Germantown, IL	260	38.33 N	89.32 W
Germantown, TN	260	35.05 N	89.49 W
Germantown, WI	256	43.14 N	88.06 W
Germfask	256	46.15 N	85.55 W
Geronimo	262	34.28 N	98.23 W
Gethsémani	252	50.13 N	60.40 W
Gettysburg, PA	254	39.50 N	77.14 W
Gettysburg, SD	264	45.01 N	99.57 W
Gettysburg National Military Park ♠	254	39.49 N	77.15 W
Geyser	268	47.16 N	110.30 W
Geyserville	270	38.42 N	122.54 W
Giant City State Park ♠	260	37.39 N	89.12 W
Giant Mountain ∧	254	44.10 N	73.44 W
Gibbon	264	40.45 N	98.51 W
Gibbons	248	53.50 N	113.20 W
Gibbonsville	268	45.33 N	113.55 W
Gibsland	260	32.33 N	93.03 W
Gibson	258	33.14 N	82.36 W
Gibsonburg	254	41.23 N	83.19 W
Gibson City	256	40.28 N	88.22 W
Gibsons	248	49.24 N	123.30 W
Giddings	262	30.11 N	96.56 W
Gideon	260	36.27 N	89.55 W
Gifford	258	27.41 N	80.25 W
Gifford ≃	242	70.21 N	83.05 W
Gifford Fjord C[2]	242	69.57 N	81.55 W
Gila ≃	244	32.43 N	114.33 W
Gila, Middle Fork ≃	266	33.14 N	108.14 W
Gila Bend	266	32.57 N	112.43 W
Gila Bend Indian Reservation →[4]	266	33.00 N	112.46 W
Gila Bend Mountains ∧∧	266	33.10 N	113.10 W
Gila Cliff Dwellings National Monument ♠	266	33.02 N	108.16 W
Gila Mountains ∧∧	266	33.05 N	109.50 W
Gila River Indian Reservation →[4]	266	33.12 N	112.00 W
Gilbert, LA	260	32.03 N	91.39 W
Gilbert, MN	256	47.29 N	92.28 W
Gilbert, Mount ∧	248	50.51 N	124.20 W
Gilbertown	260	31.53 N	88.19 W
Gilbert Peak ∧	268	46.30 N	121.25 W
Gilbert Plains	250	51.09 N	100.29 W
Gildford, MT	250, 268	48.34 N	110.18 W
Gilford Island I	248	50.45 N	126.25 W
Gil Island I	248	53.13 N	129.15 W
Gillam	250	56.21 N	94.43 W
Gillespie	260	39.07 N	89.49 W
Gillett, AR	260	34.07 N	91.22 W
Gillett, WI	256	44.54 N	88.18 W
Gillette	264	44.18 N	105.30 W
Gillian, Lake @	242	69.32 N	75.23 W
Gilman, IL	256	40.46 N	87.59 W
Gilman, IA	256	41.53 N	92.47 W
Gilman, MT	248	47.31 N	112.21 W
Gilman, WI	256	45.10 N	90.48 W
Gilmer	260	32.44 N	94.57 W
Gilmore City	264	42.44 N	94.27 W
Gilroy	270	37.00 N	121.43 W
Giltner	264	40.47 N	98.09 W
Gimli	250	50.38 N	96.59 W
Ginkgo State Park ♠	268	46.59 N	120.01 W
Girard, IL	260	39.27 N	89.47 W
Girard, KS	264	37.31 N	94.51 W
Girard, OH	254	41.10 N	80.42 W
Girard, PA	254	42.00 N	80.19 W
Girard, TX	262	33.22 N	100.40 W
Girdwood	246	60.57 N	149.10 W
Girouxville	248	55.45 N	117.20 W
Gisborne Lake @	252	47.48 N	54.50 W
Giscome	248	54.04 N	122.22 W
Gjoa Haven	242	68.38 N	95.57 W
Glace Bay	252	46.12 N	59.57 W
Glacier	248	51.16 N	117.31 W
Glacier Bay C	246	58.40 N	136.00 W
Glacier Bay National Park ♠	246	58.45 N	136.30 W
Glacier National Park ♠, BC	248	51.15 N	117.35 W
Glacier National Park ♠, MT	268	48.35 N	113.40 W
Glacier Peak ∧	268	48.07 N	121.07 W
Gladbrook	256	42.11 N	92.43 W
Glade Creek ≃	268	45.54 N	119.42 W
Glade Spring	258	36.47 N	81.47 W
Gladewater	260	32.33 N	94.56 W
Gladstone, MB	250	50.13 N	98.57 W
Gladstone, MI	256	45.50 N	87.03 W
Gladstone, MO	260	39.13 N	94.34 W
Gladwin	256	43.59 N	84.29 W
Gladys Lake @	246	59.55 N	132.55 W
Glasco	264	39.22 N	97.50 W
Glasgow, KY	260	37.00 N	85.55 W
Glasgow, MO	260	39.14 N	92.50 W
Glasgow, MT	268	48.12 N	106.38 W
Glasgow, VA	258	37.38 N	79.27 W
Glaslyn	250	53.21 N	108.22 W
Glassboro	254	39.42 N	99.15 W
Glass Mountains ∧∧	262	30.25 N	103.15 W
Gleason	260	36.13 N	88.37 W
Gleichen	248	50.52 N	113.03 W
Glen Alpine	258	35.44 N	81.47 W
Glenavon	250	50.10 N	103.10 W
Glenboro	250	49.32 N	99.15 W
Glenburn	264	48.31 N	101.13 W
Glen Burnie	254	39.10 N	76.37 W
Glen Canyon	266	37.05 N	111.41 W
Glen Canyon V	266	37.10 N	110.50 W
Glen Canyon Dam →[6]	266	36.48 N	111.13 W
Glen Canyon National Recreation Area ♠	266	37.00 N	111.20 W
Glencoe, ON	256	42.45 N	81.43 W
Glencoe, AL	260	33.57 N	85.56 W
Glencoe, IL	256	42.08 N	87.45 W
Glencoe, MN	264	44.46 N	94.09 W
Glen Cove	254	40.52 N	73.37 W
Glendale, AZ	266	33.32 N	112.11 W
Glendale, CA	270	34.10 N	118.17 W
Glendale, MS	260	31.22 N	89.19 W
Glendale, OR	268	42.44 N	123.26 W
Glendale, UT	266	37.19 N	112.36 W
Glendale, WI	256	43.07 N	87.57 W
Glendive	264	47.06 N	104.43 W
Glendive Creek ≃	264	47.08 N	104.41 W
Glendo	264	42.30 N	105.02 W
Glendon	250	54.15 N	111.10 W
Glendo Reservoir @[1]	264	42.31 N	104.58 W
Glendo State Park ♠	264	42.33 N	104.58 W
Gleneden Beach	268	44.53 N	124.02 W
Glen Elder	264	39.30 N	98.18 W
Glen Flora	262	29.21 N	96.12 W
Glen Lyon	254	41.10 N	76.05 W
Glenmora	260	30.59 N	92.35 W
Glennallen	246	62.07 N	145.33 W
Glenns Ferry	268	42.57 N	115.18 W
Glennville	258	31.56 N	81.56 W
Glenoma	268	46.31 N	122.09 W
Glen Robertson	254	45.21 N	74.30 W
Glen Rock, PA	254	39.48 N	76.44 W
Glenrock, WY	264	42.52 N	105.52 W
Glen Rose	262	32.14 N	97.45 W
Glens Falls	254	43.19 N	73.39 W
Glen Ullin	264	46.49 N	101.50 W
Glenville, MN	256	43.34 N	93.17 W
Glenville, WV	254	38.56 N	80.50 W
Glen White	258	37.44 N	81.17 W
Glenwood, NF	252	48.59 N	54.52 W
Glenwood, AL	260	31.40 N	86.10 W
Glenwood, AR	260	34.20 N	93.33 W
Glenwood, GA	258	32.11 N	82.40 W
Glenwood, IA	264	41.03 N	95.45 W
Glenwood, MN	264	45.39 N	95.23 W
Glenwood, NM	266	33.19 N	108.53 W
Glenwood, UT	266	38.46 N	111.59 W
Glenwood, VA	258	36.35 N	79.22 W
Glenwood City	256	45.04 N	92.10 W
Glenwood Springs	266	39.33 N	107.19 W
Glenwoodville	248	49.22 N	113.21 W
Glidden, IA	264	42.04 N	94.44 W
Glidden, WI	256	46.09 N	90.34 W
Glide	268	43.18 N	123.06 W
Globe	266	33.24 N	110.47 W
Glorieta	266	35.35 N	105.46 W
Gloster	260	31.12 N	91.01 W
Gloucester, MA	254	42.37 N	70.40 W
Gloucester, VA	258	37.25 N	76.32 W
Glouster	254	39.30 N	82.05 W
Glover Creek ≃	260	34.02 N	94.56 W
Glover Island I	252	48.44 N	57.45 W
Gloversville	254	43.03 N	74.20 W
Glovertown	252	48.41 N	54.02 W
Glyndon	264	46.52 N	96.35 W
Goat Mountain ∧	268	47.21 N	113.21 W
Gobles	256	42.21 N	85.53 W
Godbout	252	49.19 N	67.37 W
Goderich	256	43.45 N	81.43 W
Godfrey	260	38.57 N	90.11 W
Gods ≃	250	56.22 N	92.51 W
Gods Lake	250	54.40 N	94.09 W
Gods Lake @	250	54.40 N	94.20 W
Gods Mercy, Bay of C	242	63.30 N	86.10 W
Goéland, Lac au @	242	49.47 N	76.48 W
Goélands, Lac aux @	242	55.27 N	64.17 W
Goff	264	39.40 N	95.56 W
Goff Creek ≃	262	36.43 N	101.29 W
Goffstown	254	43.01 N	71.36 W
Gogama	256	47.40 N	81.43 W
Gogebic, Lake @	256	46.30 N	89.35 W
Gogebic Range ∧∧[2]	256	46.45 N	89.25 W
Golconda, IL	260	37.22 N	88.29 W
Golconda, NV	270	40.57 N	117.30 W
Gold Beach	268	42.25 N	124.25 W
Goldboro	252	45.11 N	61.39 W
Gold Bridge	248	50.51 N	122.50 W
Gold Creek	246	62.46 N	149.41 W
Gold Creek ≃	248	49.04 N	115.12 W
Golden, BC	248	51.18 N	116.58 W
Golden, CO	266	39.46 N	105.13 W
Golden, IL	260	40.07 N	91.01 W
Golden City	260	37.24 N	94.05 W
Goldendale	268	45.49 N	120.50 W
Golden Ears Provincial Park ♠	248	49.30 N	122.25 W
Golden Hinde ∧	248	49.40 N	125.45 W
Golden Lake @	256	45.35 N	77.20 W
Golden Meadow	260	29.23 N	90.16 W
Golden Prairie	250	50.14 N	109.38 W
Golden Spike National Historic Site ⊥	266	41.38 N	112.35 W
Goldfield, IA	256	42.44 N	93.55 W
Goldfield, NV	270	37.42 N	117.14 W
Gold Mountain ∧	270	37.15 N	117.18 W
Goldonna	260	32.01 N	92.54 W
Goldpan Peak ∧	246	61.12 N	153.22 W
Gold River	248	49.41 N	126.08 W
Gold Rock	250	49.27 N	92.43 W
Goldsand Lake @	250	57.02 N	101.08 W
Goldsboro	258	35.23 N	77.59 W
Goldsmith	262	31.59 N	102.40 W
Goldston	258	35.36 N	79.20 W
Goldthwaite	262	31.27 N	98.34 W
Goleta	270	34.27 N	119.50 W
Goliad	262	28.40 N	97.23 W
Golovin	246	64.33 N	163.02 W
Golva	264	46.44 N	103.51 W
Gonzales, CA	270	36.31 N	121.32 W
Gonzales, LA	260	30.14 N	90.55 W
Gonzales, TX	262	29.30 N	97.27 W
Goochland	258	37.41 N	77.53 W
Goode, Mount ∧	246	61.20 N	148.02 W
Goodenough, Mount ∧	246	67.56 N	135.31 W
Gooderham	256	44.54 N	78.23 W
Goodeve	250	51.04 N	103.10 W
Goodfellow Air Force Base ■	262	31.26 N	100.25 W
Goodhope Bay C	246	66.10 N	163.45 W
Good Hope Mountain ∧	248	51.09 N	124.10 W
Goodhue	256	44.24 N	92.37 W
Gooding	268	42.56 N	114.43 W
Goodland, FL	258	25.55 N	81.39 W
Goodland, IN	260	40.46 N	87.18 W
Goodland, KS	264	39.21 N	101.43 W
Goodlands	250	49.05 N	100.35 W
Goodman, MS	260	32.58 N	89.55 W
Goodman, WI	256	45.38 N	88.21 W
Goodnews Bay	246	59.07 N	161.35 W
Goodnight	264	37.14 N	104.43 W
Goodrich, ND	264	47.28 N	100.08 W
Goodrich, TX	260	30.36 N	94.57 W
Good Spirit Lake @	250	51.34 N	102.40 W
Good Spirit Lake Provincial Park ♠	250	51.36 N	102.45 W
Goodview	256	44.04 N	91.41 W
Goodwater	260	33.04 N	86.03 W
Goodwell	262	36.36 N	101.38 W
Goodyear	266	33.26 N	112.21 W
Goose ≃, AB	248	54.58 N	117.11 W
Goose ≃, ND	264	47.28 N	96.52 W
Goose Bay	242	53.20 N	60.25 W
Gooseberry Creek ≃	268	43.55 N	108.04 W
Goose Creek	258	33.00 N	80.01 W
Goose Creek ≃, U.S.	268	42.33 N	113.46 W
Goose Creek ≃, KY	258	37.16 N	83.38 W
Goose Creek ≃, NE	264	42.02 N	100.03 W
Goose Island I	248	51.55 N	128.25 W
Goose Lake @, MB	250	54.26 N	101.30 W
Goose Lake @, ON	250	51.46 N	93.00 W
Goose Lake @, SK	250	51.45 N	107.23 W
Goose Lake @, U.S.	244	41.57 N	120.25 W
Gordo	260	33.19 N	87.54 W
Gordon, GA	258	32.53 N	83.20 W
Gordon, NE	264	42.48 N	102.12 W
Gordon, WI	256	46.15 N	91.48 W
Gordon Creek ≃	264	42.49 N	100.40 W
Gordon Horne Peak ∧	248	51.46 N	118.50 W
Gordon Indian Reserve →[4]	250	51.16 N	104.16 W
Gordon Lake @, AB	250	56.30 N	110.25 W
Gordon Lake @, SK	250	55.50 N	106.26 W
Gordonsville	254	38.08 N	78.11 W
Gore	252	45.07 N	63.43 W
Gore Bay	256	45.55 N	82.28 W
Goree	262	33.28 N	99.31 W
Gore Mountain ∧	254	44.55 N	71.48 W
Gore Point >	246	59.12 N	151.00 W
Goreville	260	37.33 N	88.58 W
Gorham, ME	254	43.41 N	70.26 W
Gorham, NH	254	44.23 N	71.10 W
Gorman	262	32.12 N	98.41 W
Goshen, NS	252	45.23 N	61.59 W
Goshen, CA	270	36.21 N	119.25 W
Goshen, IN	260	41.35 N	85.50 W
Goshen, NY	254	41.24 N	74.20 W
Goshute Indian Reservation →[4]	270	39.53 N	114.08 W
Goshute Lake @	270	40.08 N	114.38 W
Goshute Valley V	270	40.40 N	114.30 W
Gosport	260	39.21 N	86.40 W
Gotebo	262	35.04 N	98.53 W
Gothenburg	264	40.56 N	100.09 W
Gough Lake @	248	52.02 N	112.28 W
Gouin, Réservoir @[1]	242	48.38 N	74.54 W
Goulais ≃	256	46.43 N	84.27 W
Gould	260	33.59 N	91.34 W
Gould City	256	46.06 N	85.42 W
Goulds	258	25.33 N	80.23 W
Goulet Lake @	250	55.23 N	96.18 W
Gourlay Lake @	256	48.52 N	84.54 W
Gouverneur	254	44.20 N	75.28 W
Govan	250	51.18 N	105.00 W
Gove	264	38.58 N	100.29 W
Govenlock	250	49.15 N	109.48 W
Governor Dodge State Park ♠	256	43.00 N	90.07 W
Gowan ≃	250	55.49 N	94.08 W
Gowanda	254	42.28 N	78.56 W
Gower	260	39.32 N	94.34 W
Gowrie	264	42.17 N	94.17 W
Goyelle, Lac @	252	50.47 N	60.45 W
Grace	268	42.35 N	111.44 W
Gracefield	254	46.06 N	76.03 W
Graceville, FL	260	30.58 N	85.31 W
Graceville, MN	264	45.34 N	96.26 W
Grady, AR	260	34.05 N	91.42 W
Grady, NM	262	34.49 N	103.19 W
Graettinger	264	43.14 N	94.45 W
Graford	262	32.56 N	98.14 W
Grafton, IL	260	38.58 N	90.26 W
Grafton, ND	264	48.25 N	97.25 W
Grafton, WV	254	39.20 N	80.01 W
Grafton, WI	256	43.19 N	87.56 W
Graham, NC	258	36.05 N	79.25 W
Graham, TX	262	33.06 N	98.35 W
Graham, Mount ∧	266	32.42 N	109.52 W
Graham Creek ≃	260	38.49 N	85.39 W
Graham Island I	248	53.40 N	132.30 W
Graham Lake @	254	44.40 N	68.25 W
Graham Moore, Cape >	242	72.52 N	76.04 W
Graham Moore Bay C	242	75.26 N	101.25 W
Grainfield	264	39.07 N	100.28 W
Grambling	260	32.32 N	92.43 W
Granada	264	38.04 N	102.19 W
Granbury	262	32.27 N	97.47 W
Granby, PQ	254	45.24 N	72.44 W
Granby, CO	266	40.05 N	105.56 W
Granby, MO	260	36.55 N	94.15 W
Granby ≃	248	49.03 N	118.25 W
Granby, Lake @[1]	266	40.09 N	105.50 W
Grand ≃, ON	256	42.51 N	79.34 W
Grand ≃, U.S.	260	39.23 N	93.06 W
Grand ≃, U.S.	264	40.05 N	94.25 W
Grand ≃, MI	256	42.40 N	84.40 W
Grand ≃, OH	254	41.46 N	81.17 W
Grand ≃, SD	264	45.40 N	100.32 W
Grand ≃, WI	256	43.45 N	89.16 W
Grand, East Fork ≃	260	40.12 N	94.21 W
Grand, Lac @	256	47.10 N	76.57 W
Grand, North Fork ≃	264	45.47 N	102.16 W
Grand, South Fork ≃	264	45.43 N	102.17 W
Grand Bank	252	47.06 N	55.46 W
Grand Bay, NB	252	45.18 N	66.12 W
Grand Bay, AL	260	30.29 N	88.21 W
Grand Beach	250	50.35 N	96.40 W
Grand Bend	256	43.15 N	81.45 W
Grand Blanc	256	42.56 N	83.38 W
Grand Bruit	252	47.41 N	58.13 W
Grand-Calumet, Île du I	254	45.44 N	76.41 W
Grand Cane	260	32.05 N	93.49 W
Grand Canyon	266	36.03 N	112.09 W
Grand Canyon V	266	36.10 N	112.45 W
Grand Canyon National Park ♠	266	36.15 N	112.58 W
Grand Centre	250	54.25 N	110.13 W
Grand Chenier	260	29.46 N	92.58 W
Grand Coulee	268	47.56 N	119.00 W
Grand Coulee V	268	47.45 N	119.15 W
Grand Coulee Dam →[6]	268	47.57 N	118.59 W
Grande ≃	252	48.24 N	64.30 W
Grande, Rio (Bravo del Norte) ≃	244	25.55 N	97.09 W
Grande-Anse	252	47.48 N	65.11 W
Grand-Entrée	252	47.33 N	61.34 W
Grande-Prairie	248	55.10 N	118.48 W
Grande-Rivière	252	48.24 N	64.30 W
Grande Rivière de la Baleine ≃	242	55.16 N	77.47 W
Grande Ronde ≃	268	46.05 N	116.59 W
Grand-Étang	252	46.33 N	61.02 W
Grand Falls, NB	232	47.03 N	67.44 W
Grand Falls, NF	252	48.56 N	55.40 W
Grandfalls, TX	262	31.20 N	102.51 W
Grandfather Mountain ∧	258	36.07 N	81.48 W
Grandfield	262	34.13 N	98.41 W
Grand Forks, BC	248	49.02 N	118.27 W
Grand Forks, ND	264	47.55 N	97.03 W
Grand Forks Air Force Base ■	264	47.57 N	97.25 W
Grand Haven	256	43.04 N	86.13 W
Grandin, Lac @	242	63.59 N	119.00 W
Grand Island	264	40.55 N	98.21 W
Grand Island I	256	46.30 N	86.40 W
Grand Isle	260	29.14 N	90.00 W
Grand Junction, CO	266	39.05 N	108.33 W
Grand Junction, IA	264	42.02 N	94.14 W
Grand Junction, TN	260	35.03 N	89.10 W
Grand Lac du Nord @	252	50.54 N	67.06 W
Grand lac Germain @	252	51.12 N	66.41 W
Grand lac Victoria @	256	47.31 N	77.30 W
Grand Lake	266	40.15 N	105.49 W
Grand Lake @, NB	252	45.42 N	66.05 W
Grand Lake @, NF	252	49.00 N	57.25 W
Grand Lake @, N.A.	252	45.43 N	67.50 W
Grand Lake @, LA	260	29.55 N	92.47 W
Grand Lake @, ME	254	45.15 N	67.50 W
Grand Lake @, MI	256	45.18 N	83.30 W
Grand Lake @, OH	254	40.30 N	84.32 W
Grand Ledge	256	42.45 N	84.45 W
Grand Manan Channel U	252	44.45 N	66.52 W
Grand Manan Island I	252	44.40 N	66.50 W
Grand Marais	256	46.40 N	85.59 W
Grand Meadow	256	43.42 N	92.34 W
Grand'Mère	242	46.37 N	72.41 W
Grand Mesa ∧	266	39.00 N	108.00 W
Grandmesnil, Lac @	252	51.19 N	67.33 W
Grand-Pabos, Rivière du ≃	252	48.21 N	64.43 W
Grand Prairie	262	32.45 N	96.59 W
Grand Pré National Historic Park ♠	252	45.08 N	64.18 W
Grand Rapids, MB	250	53.08 N	99.20 W
Grand Rapids, MI	256	42.58 N	85.40 W
Grand Rapids, MN	256	47.14 N	93.31 W
Grand Saline	262	32.41 N	95.43 W
Grand Teton ∧	268	43.44 N	110.48 W
Grand Tower	260	37.38 N	89.30 W
Grand Traverse Bay C	256	45.02 N	85.30 W
Grand Traverse Bay, East Arm C	256	44.52 N	85.28 W
Grand Traverse Bay, West Arm C	256	44.52 N	85.35 W
Grand Valley	266	39.27 N	108.03 W
Grandview, MB	250	51.10 N	100.45 W
Grandview, MO	260	38.53 N	94.32 W
Grandview, TX	262	32.16 N	97.11 W
Grandview, WA	268	46.15 N	119.54 W
Grand View, WI	256	46.22 N	91.06 W
Grand Wash Cliffs •[4]	266	35.40 N	113.50 W
Granger, TX	262	30.43 N	97.27 W
Granger, UT	266	40.42 N	111.57 W
Granger, WA	268	46.21 N	120.11 W
Granger, WY	268	41.35 N	109.58 W
Granger Draw V	262	30.20 N	100.57 W
Grangeville	268	45.56 N	116.07 W
Grangousier Hill ∧[2]	256	47.35 N	84.56 W
Granite	262	34.58 N	99.23 W
Granite City	260	38.42 N	90.09 W
Granite Dam →[6]	252	48.06 N	57.20 W
Granite Falls, MN	264	44.49 N	95.33 W
Granite Falls, NC	258	35.48 N	81.26 W
Granite Falls, WA	268	48.05 N	121.58 W
Granite Lake @[1]	252	48.08 N	57.05 W
Granite Mountain ∧, AK	246	65.26 N	161.14 W
Granite Mountain ∧, AK	248	55.30 N	132.35 W
Granite Mountains ∧∧	268	42.35 N	107.30 W
Granite Pass)(	268	44.38 N	107.30 W
Granite Peak ∧, MT	268	45.10 N	109.48 W
Granite Peak ∧, MT	268	45.34 N	112.02 W

Symbols in the index entries are identified on page 273.

Name	Page	Lat° '	Long° '
Granite Peak ∧, NV	270	41.40 N	117.35 W
Granite Peak ∧, NV	270	40.48 N	119.25 W
Granite Range ∧∧	270	41.00 N	119.35 W
Graniteville, SC	258	33.34 N	81.48 W
Graniteville, VT	254	44.08 N	72.29 W
Gran Quivira National Monument ♠	266	34.05 N	106.14 W
Grant, FL	258	27.56 N	80.32 W
Grant, MI	256	43.20 N	85.49 W
Grant, NE	264	40.50 N	101.56 W
Grant ≃	256	42.40 N	90.45 W
Grant, Mount ∧	270	38.34 N	118.48 W
Grant City	260	40.29 N	94.25 W
Grant-Kohrs Ranch National Historic Site ⊥	268	46.25 N	112.40 W
Grant Park	260	41.14 N	87.39 W
Grant Point >1	242	68.19 N	98.53 W
Grant Range ∧∧	270	38.25 N	115.30 W
Grants	266	35.09 N	107.52 W
Grantsburg	256	45.47 N	92.41 W
Grants Pass	268	42.26 N	123.19 W
Grant-Suttie Bay C	242	69.47 N	77.15 W
Grantsville, UT	266	40.36 N	112.28 W
Grantsville, WV	254	38.55 N	81.06 W
Grantville	258	33.14 N	84.50 W
Granum	248	49.52 N	113.30 W
Granville, IL	260	41.16 N	89.14 W
Granville, ND	264	48.16 N	100.47 W
Granville, NY	254	43.24 N	73.16 W
Granville, OH	254	40.04 N	82.31 W
Granville, WV	254	39.39 N	79.59 W
Granville Lake ⊜	250	56.18 N	100.30 W
Grape Creek ≃	266	38.26 N	105.16 W
Grapeland	262	31.29 N	95.29 W
Grapevine Lake ⊜1	262	32.59 N	97.06 W
Grapevine Peak ∧	270	36.57 N	117.09 W
Gras, Lac de ⊜	242	64.30 N	110.30 W
Grasonville	254	38.57 N	76.13 W
Grass ≃, MB	250	56.03 N	96.33 W
Grass ≃, NY	254	44.59 N	74.46 W
Grass, North Branch ≃	254	44.25 N	75.06 W
Grass, South Branch ≃	254	44.22 N	75.05 W
Grass Creek	268	43.56 N	108.39 W
Grassflat	254	41.00 N	78.07 W
Grasshopper Creek ≃	268	45.06 N	112.47 W
Grass Lake	256	49.49 N	111.43 W
Grassrange	268	47.01 N	108.48 W
Grass River Provincial Park ♠	250	54.40 N	100.50 W
Grass Valley, CA	270	39.13 N	121.04 W
Grass Valley, OR	268	45.22 N	120.47 W
Grassy ≃	256	48.42 N	81.27 W
Grassy Island Lake ⊜	250	51.50 N	110.20 W
Grassy Lake	250	49.49 N	111.43 W
Grassy Plains	248	53.57 N	125.54 W
Grates Point >	252	48.10 N	52.57 W
Gravelbourg	250	49.53 N	106.34 W
Gravel Creek ≃	268	42.39 N	123.35 W
Gravell Point >	242	67.10 N	76.43 W
Gravenhurst	256	44.55 N	79.22 W
Grave Peak ∧	268	46.24 N	114.44 W
Gravette	260	36.26 N	94.27 W
Gravina Island I	248	55.17 N	131.45 W
Gray, GA	258	33.01 N	83.32 W
Gray, KY	258	36.57 N	84.00 W
Gray, ME	254	43.53 N	70.20 W
Grayback Mountain ∧, AK	246	57.08 N	153.54 W
Grayback Mountain ∧, OR	268	42.07 N	123.18 W
Grayling, AK	246	62.57 N	160.03 W
Grayling, MI	256	44.40 N	84.43 W
Grays ≃	268	46.18 N	123.41 W
Grays Harbor C	268	46.56 N	124.05 W
Grays Lake ☷	268	43.04 N	111.26 W
Grays Lake Outlet ≃	268	43.22 N	111.46 W
Grayson, SK	250	50.44 N	102.40 W
Grayson, AL	260	34.15 N	87.24 W
Grayson, KY	254	38.20 N	82.57 W
Grayson, LA	260	32.03 N	92.06 W
Grays Peak ∧	266	39.37 N	105.45 W
Graysville	260	35.27 N	85.05 W
Grayville	260	38.16 N	87.59 W
Great Barrington	254	42.12 N	73.22 W
Great Basin ⌣1	244	40.00 N	117.00 W
Great Bear ≃	246	64.54 N	125.35 W
Great Bear Lake ⊜	242	66.00 N	120.00 W
Great Beaver Lake ⊜	248	54.25 N	123.45 W
Great Bend	264	38.22 N	98.46 W
Great Burnt Lake ⊜	252	48.20 N	56.13 W
Great Central Lake ⊜	248	49.27 N	125.12 W
Great Chazy ≃	254	44.56 N	73.23 W
Great Coharie Creek ≃	258	34.50 N	78.22 W
Great Dismal Swamp ☷	258	36.30 N	76.30 W
Great Divide Basin ⌣1	268	42.00 N	108.10 W
Great Duck Island I	256	45.40 N	82.58 W
Great Falls, MB	250	50.27 N	96.02 W
Great Falls, MT	268	47.30 N	111.17 W
Great Falls, SC	258	34.34 N	80.54 W
Greathouse Peak ∧	268	46.46 N	109.21 W
Great La Cloche Island I	256	46.01 N	81.52 W
Great Lakes Naval Training Center ■	256	42.18 N	90.23 W
Great Plain of the Koukdjuak ⌣	242	66.00 N	73.00 W
Great Point >	254	41.23 N	70.03 W
Great Pubnico Lake ⊜	252	43.42 N	65.43 W
Great Sacandaga Lake ⊜	254	43.08 N	74.10 W
Great Salt Lake ⊜	266	41.10 N	112.30 W
Great Salt Lake Desert ◆2	266	40.40 N	113.30 W
Great Salt Plains Lake ⊜1	262	36.44 N	98.12 W
Great Sand Dunes National Monument ♠	266	37.43 N	105.36 W
Great Sand Hills ∧∧2	250	50.35 N	109.05 W
Great Sandy Desert ◆2	268	43.35 N	120.15 W
Great Sitkin Island I	247a	52.03 N	176.07 W
Great Slave Lake ⊜	242	61.30 N	114.00 W
Great Smoky Mountains ∧∧	258	35.35 N	83.30 W
Great Smoky Mountains National Park ♠	258	35.39 N	83.30 W
Greece	254	43.14 N	77.38 W
Greeley, CO	264	40.25 N	104.42 W
Greeley, KS	264	38.22 N	95.08 W
Greeley, NE	264	41.33 N	98.32 W
Greeleyville	258	33.35 N	79.58 W
Green ≃, NB	252	47.18 N	68.09 W
Green ≃, U.S.	244	38.11 N	109.53 W
Green ≃, U.S.	268	40.45 N	108.55 W
Green ≃, IL	260	41.28 N	90.23 W
Green ≃, KY	258	37.15 N	85.58 W
Green ≃, KY	260	37.55 N	87.30 W
Green ≃, ND	264	46.52 N	102.35 W
Green ≃, WA	268	47.33 N	122.20 W
Green ≃, WA	268	46.20 N	122.34 W
Greenacres	268	47.39 N	117.06 W
Green Bay	256	44.30 N	88.01 W
Green Bay C, NF	252	49.43 N	55.58 W
Green Bay C, U.S.	244		
	256	45.00 N	87.30 W
Greenbrier, AR	260	35.14 N	92.23 W
Green Brier, TN	260	36.27 N	86.49 W
Greenbrier ≃	258	37.39 N	80.53 W
Greenburg	260	30.51 N	90.40 W
Greenbush	264	48.42 N	96.11 W
Greencastle, IN	260	39.38 N	86.52 W
Greencastle, PA	254	39.47 N	77.44 W
Green City	260	40.16 N	92.57 W
Green Cove Springs	258	30.00 N	81.41 W
Greendale	260	39.07 N	84.52 W
Greene, IA	256	42.54 N	92.48 W
Greene, ME	254	44.11 N	70.08 W
Greene, NY	254	42.20 N	75.46 W
Greeneville	258	36.10 N	82.50 W
Greenfield, CA	270	36.19 N	121.15 W
Greenfield, IL	260	39.21 N	90.12 W
Greenfield, IA	264	41.18 N	94.28 W
Greenfield, MA	254	42.36 N	72.36 W
Greenfield, MO	260	37.25 N	93.51 W
Greenfield, OH	254	39.21 N	83.23 W
Greenfield, TN	260	36.09 N	88.48 W
Green Forest	260	36.20 N	93.26 W
Greenhorn Creek ≃	264	38.08 N	104.38 W
Green Lake, SK	250	54.17 N	107.47 W
Green Lake, WI	256	43.51 N	88.57 W
Green Lake ⊜, BC	248	51.24 N	121.15 W
Green Lake ⊜, SK	250	54.10 N	107.43 W
Green Lake ⊜, WI	256	43.41 N	88.57 W
Greenland, AR	260	36.00 N	94.10 W
Greenland, MI	256	46.46 N	89.06 W
Greenleaf	264	39.44 N	96.59 W
Green Lookout Mountain ∧	268	45.52 N	122.08 W
Green Mountain Reservoir ⊜1	266	39.52 N	106.17 W
Green Mountains ∧∧	254	43.45 N	72.45 W
Greenough, Mount ∧	246	69.10 N	141.35 W
Green Peter Lake ⊜1	268	44.28 N	122.30 W
Green Pond	260	33.12 N	87.11 W
Greenport	254	41.06 N	72.22 W
Green River, UT	266	38.59 N	110.10 W
Green River, WY	268	41.32 N	109.28 W
Green River Lake ⊜1	260	37.15 N	85.15 W
Greensboro, AL	260	32.42 N	87.36 W
Greensboro, FL	258	30.34 N	84.45 W
Greensboro, GA	258	33.35 N	83.11 W
Greensboro, MD	254	38.59 N	75.48 W
Greensboro, NC	258	36.04 N	79.47 W
Greensburg, IN	260	39.20 N	85.29 W
Greensburg, KS	264	37.36 N	99.18 W
Greensburg, KY	260	37.16 N	85.30 W
Greensburg, PA	254	40.18 N	79.33 W
Greens Peak ∧	266	34.07 N	109.35 W
Greenspond	252	49.04 N	53.34 W
Green Springs	254	41.15 N	83.03 W
Green Swamp ☷	258	34.10 N	78.20 W
Greentown	260	40.29 N	85.58 W
Greenup, IL	260	39.15 N	88.10 W
Greenup, KY	254	38.34 N	82.50 W
Green Valley, AZ	266	31.50 N	111.00 W
Green Valley, IL	256	40.24 N	89.38 W
Greenview	260	40.05 N	89.44 W
Greenville, AL	260	31.50 N	86.38 W
Greenville, CA	270	40.08 N	120.57 W
Greenville, FL	258	30.28 N	83.38 W
Greenville, GA	258	33.02 N	84.43 W
Greenville, IL	260	38.53 N	89.25 W
Greenville, KY	260	37.12 N	87.11 W
Greenville, ME	254	45.28 N	69.35 W
Greenville, MI	256	43.11 N	85.15 W
Greenville, MS	260	33.25 N	91.05 W
Greenville, MO	260	37.08 N	90.27 W
Greenville, NH	254	42.46 N	71.49 W
Greenville, NC	258	35.37 N	77.23 W
Greenville, OH	254	40.06 N	84.38 W
Greenville, PA	254	41.24 N	80.23 W
Greenville, SC	258	34.51 N	82.23 W
Greenville, TX	262	33.08 N	96.07 W
Greenwater Lake ⊜	256	48.34 N	90.26 W
Greenwater Lake Provincial Park ♠	250	52.33 N	103.33 W
Greenwich, CT	254	41.01 N	73.38 W
Greenwich, NY	254	43.05 N	73.30 W
Greenwich, OH	254	41.02 N	82.31 W
Greenwood, BC	248	49.05 N	118.41 W
Greenwood, AR	260	35.13 N	94.15 W
Greenwood, IN	260	39.37 N	86.07 W
Greenwood, MS	260	33.31 N	90.11 W
Greenwood, NE	264	40.58 N	96.27 W
Greenwood, SC	258	34.12 N	82.10 W
Greenwood, WI	256	44.46 N	90.36 W
Greenwood, Lake ⊜1	258	34.15 N	82.02 W
Greer	258	34.56 N	82.14 W
Greers Ferry Lake ⊜1	260	35.30 N	92.10 W
Greeson, Lake ⊜1	260	34.10 N	93.45 W
Gregoire Lake Indian Reserve ◆4	250	56.28 N	111.10 W
Gregory, MI	256	42.28 N	84.05 W
Gregory, SD	264	43.14 N	99.26 W
Gregory, TX	262	27.55 N	97.17 W
Grenada	260	33.47 N	89.55 W
Grenada Lake ⊜1	260	33.50 N	89.40 W
Grenfell	250	50.25 N	102.56 W
Grenola	264	37.21 N	96.27 W
Grenora	264	48.37 N	103.56 W
Grenville Channel ⩌	248	53.40 N	129.40 W
Gresham	268	45.30 N	122.26 W
Gresham Park	258	33.42 N	84.19 W
Gretna, MB	250	49.02 N	97.35 W
Gretna, LA	260	29.55 N	90.03 W
Gretna, VA	258	36.57 N	79.22 W
Greville Bay C	252	45.22 N	64.38 W
Grey ≃	252	47.38 N	57.05 W
Greybull	268	44.30 N	108.03 W
Greybull ≃	268	44.28 N	108.03 W
Grey Eagle	264	45.50 N	94.45 W
Grey Islands II	252	50.50 N	55.37 W
Greylock, Mount ∧	254	42.38 N	73.10 W
Greys ≃	268	43.10 N	111.00 W
Gribbel Island I	248	53.25 N	129.00 W
Gridley, CA	270	39.22 N	121.42 W
Gridley, IL	256	40.45 N	88.53 W
Griffin, SK	250	49.40 N	103.26 W
Griffin, GA	258	33.15 N	84.16 W
Griffin, Lake ⊜	258	28.52 N	81.51 W
Griffiss Air Force Base ■	254	43.14 N	75.26 W
Griffith Island I	242	74.35 N	95.30 W
Grifton	258	35.23 N	77.26 W
Griggsville	260	39.42 N	90.43 W
Grimsby	256	43.12 N	79.34 W
Grimshaw	248	56.11 N	117.36 W
Grindstone Island (Cap-aux-Meules)	252	47.23 N	61.52 W
Grinnell	256	41.45 N	92.43 W
Grinnell Peninsula >1	242	76.40 N	95.00 W
Grissom Air Force Base ■	260	40.40 N	86.08 W
Griswold, MB	250	49.45 N	100.25 W
Griswold, IA	264	41.14 N	95.08 W
Grizzly Bear Mountain ∧	242	65.22 N	121.00 W
Grizzly Mountain ∧, ID	268	47.43 N	116.06 W
Grizzly Mountain ∧, OR	268	44.26 N	120.57 W
Grizzly Mountain ∧, WA	268	48.25 N	118.30 W
Groais Island I	252	50.57 N	55.35 W
Groesbeck	262	31.31 N	96.32 W
Gronlid	250	53.06 N	104.28 W
Groom	262	35.12 N	101.06 W
Groom Lake ⊜	270	37.15 N	115.48 W
Gros Mécatina, Cap du >	252	50.45 N	59.00 W
Gros Morne ∧	252	49.36 N	57.48 W
Gros Morne National Park ♠	252	49.40 N	57.45 W
Grosse Île I	252	47.37 N	61.31 W
Grosse Pointe	256	42.24 N	82.55 W
Grosvenor, Lake ⊜	246	58.40 N	155.15 W
Gros Ventre ≃	268	43.33 N	110.46 W
Groswater Bay C	242	54.20 N	57.30 W
Groton, CT	254	41.19 N	72.12 W
Groton, NY	254	42.35 N	76.22 W
Groton, SD	264	45.27 N	98.06 W
Grottoes	254	38.16 N	78.56 W
Grouard Mission	248	55.31 N	116.09 W
Groundbirch	248	55.47 N	120.55 W
Groundhog ≃	242	49.43 N	81.58 W
Grouse Creek ≃, KS	264	37.00 N	96.55 W
Grouse Creek ≃, UT	266	41.22 N	113.55 W
Grouse Creek Mountain ∧	268	44.22 N	113.54 W
Grove	260	36.36 N	94.46 W
Grove City, MN	264	45.09 N	94.41 W
Grove City, OH	254	39.53 N	83.06 W
Grove City, PA	254	41.10 N	80.05 W
Grove Hill	260	31.42 N	87.47 W
Groveland	258	28.34 N	81.51 W
Grover City	270	35.07 N	120.37 W
Groves	260	29.57 N	93.55 W
Groveton, NH	254	44.36 N	71.31 W
Groveton, TX	262	31.03 N	95.08 W
Grovetown	258	33.27 N	82.12 W
Growler Peak ∧	266	32.24 N	113.07 W
Growler Wash V	266	32.35 N	113.30 W
Gruetli	260	35.22 N	85.40 W
Grulla	262	26.16 N	98.39 W
Grundy	258	37.17 N	82.06 W
Grundy Center	256	42.22 N	92.47 W
Grundy Lake Provincial Park ♠	256	45.48 N	80.34 W
Grunthal	250	49.25 N	96.52 W
Gruver	262	36.16 N	101.24 W
Gu Achi	266	32.20 N	112.02 W
Guadalupe	270	34.58 N	120.34 W
Guadalupe ≃	262	28.30 N	96.53 W
Guadalupe Mountains ∧∧	262	32.20 N	105.00 W
Guadalupe Mountains National Park ♠	262	31.55 N	104.55 W
Guadalupe Peak ∧	262	31.50 N	104.52 W
Guadalupita	266	36.08 N	105.14 W
Gualala	270	38.46 N	123.32 W
Guano Creek ≃	268	42.12 N	119.31 W
Guéguen, Lac ⊜	256	48.06 N	77.13 W
Guelph	256	43.33 N	80.15 W
Guerneville	270	38.30 N	123.00 W
Guernsey	264	42.16 N	104.45 W
Guernsey Reservoir ⊜1	264	42.19 N	104.48 W
Guernsey State Park ♠	264	42.20 N	104.50 W
Gueydan	260	30.02 N	92.30 W
Guide Rock	264	40.04 N	98.20 W
Guildhall	254	44.34 N	71.34 W
Guilford	254	45.14 N	69.29 W
Guilford Courthouse National Military Park ♠	258	36.01 N	79.45 W
Guillaume-Delisle, Lac ⊜	242	56.15 N	76.17 W
Guin	260	33.58 N	87.55 W
Guinecourt, Lac ⊜	252	50.55 N	69.16 W
Gulf Hammock	258	29.15 N	82.43 W
Gulf Islands National Seashore ♠, U.S.	260	30.19 N	87.15 W
Gulf Islands National Seashore ♠, U.S.	260	30.14 N	88.42 W
Gulfport, FL	258	27.44 N	82.43 W
Gulfport, MS	260	30.22 N	89.06 W
Gulf Shores	260	30.17 N	87.41 W
Gulf State Park ♠	260	30.16 N	87.40 W
Gulkana	246	62.16 N	145.23 W
Gull Lake	250	50.08 N	108.27 W
Gull Lake ⊜, AB	248	52.35 N	114.00 W
Gull Lake ⊜, ON	250	51.18 N	91.58 W
Gull Lake ⊜, MN	264	46.25 N	94.20 W
Gullrock Lake ⊜	250	50.58 N	93.40 W
Gum Swamp Creek ≃	258	32.08 N	82.55 W
Gunisao ≃	250	53.54 N	97.58 W
Gunisao Lake ⊜	250	53.33 N	96.15 W
Gunnar	242	59.23 N	108.53 W
Gunnison, CO	266	38.33 N	106.56 W
Gunnison, UT	266	39.09 N	111.49 W
Gunnison ≃	266	39.03 N	108.35 W
Gunnison, Lake Fork ≃	266	38.28 N	107.19 W
Gunnison, North Fork ≃	266	38.47 N	107.50 W
Gunpowder State Park ♠	254	39.37 N	76.40 W
Guntersville	260	34.21 N	86.18 W
Guntersville Dam ◆6	260	34.13 N	86.23 W
Guntersville Lake ⊜1	260	34.45 N	86.03 W
Gu Oidak Wash V	266	31.57 N	112.21 W
Gurdon	260	33.55 N	93.09 W
Gustavus	246	58.25 N	135.44 W
Gustine, CA	270	37.16 N	120.60 W
Gustine, TX	262	31.51 N	98.24 W
Guthrie, KY	260	36.39 N	87.10 W
Guthrie, OK	262	35.53 N	97.25 W
Guthrie, TX	262	33.37 N	100.19 W
Guthrie Center	264	41.41 N	94.30 W
Guthrie Lake ⊜	250	55.17 N	100.38 W
Guttenberg	256	42.47 N	91.06 W
Guyandotte ≃	254	38.26 N	82.23 W
Guymon	262	36.41 N	101.29 W
Guyot, Mount ∧	258	35.42 N	83.15 W
Guysborough	252	45.23 N	61.30 W
Guyton	258	32.20 N	81.24 W
Gwinn	256	46.17 N	87.26 W
Gwinner	264	46.14 N	97.40 W
Gym Peak ∧	266	32.04 N	107.35 W
Gypsum, CO	266	39.39 N	106.57 W
Gypsum, KS	264	38.42 N	97.26 W
Gypsum Creek ≃, U.S.	266	37.09 N	109.52 W
Gypsum Creek ≃, KS	264	38.51 N	97.25 W
Gypsum Hills ∧∧2	262	36.25 N	99.20 W
Gypsum Point >	242	61.53 N	114.35 W
Gypsumville	250	51.45 N	98.35 W
H			
Hache, Lac la ⊜	248	51.50 N	121.30 W
Hackberry, AZ	266	35.22 N	113.44 W
Hackberry, LA	260	29.59 N	93.21 W
Hackberry Creek ≃	264	38.48 N	100.03 W
Hackensack	254	40.53 N	74.03 W
Hackett	260	35.11 N	94.25 W
Hackettstown	254	40.51 N	74.50 W
Hackleburg	260	34.17 N	87.50 W
Haddam	264	39.51 N	97.18 W
Haddock	258	33.02 N	83.26 W
Hadley Bay C	242	72.30 N	107.45 W
Hadlock	268	48.02 N	122.46 W
Haena	272b	22.14 N	159.34 W
Haena Point >	272b	22.14 N	159.34 W
Hafford	250	52.48 N	107.20 W
Hagan	258	32.09 N	81.56 W
Hagemeister Island I	246	58.40 N	161.00 W
Hagensborg	248	52.23 N	126.33 W
Hagerman, ID	268	42.49 N	114.54 W
Hagerman, NM	262	33.07 N	104.20 W
Hagerstown, IN	260	39.55 N	85.10 W
Hagerstown, MD	254	39.39 N	77.43 W
Hagersville	256	42.58 N	80.03 W
Haggin, Mount ∧	268	46.05 N	113.05 W
Hague, SK	250	52.30 N	106.25 W
Hague, ND	264	46.02 N	99.59 W
Hagues Peak ∧	266	40.29 N	105.38 W
Hahira	258	30.57 N	83.22 W
Haig, Mount ∧	248	49.17 N	114.29 W
Haigler	264	40.01 N	101.56 W
Haiku	272a	20.55 N	156.20 W
Hailey	268	43.31 N	114.19 W
Haileybury	256	47.27 N	79.38 W
Haileyville	262	34.52 N	95.36 W
Haines, AK	246	59.15 N	135.25 W
Haines, OR	268	44.55 N	117.56 W
Haines City	258	28.07 N	81.37 W
Haines Junction	246	60.45 N	137.30 W
Haiwee Reservoir ⊜1	270	36.10 N	117.57 W
Halalii Lake ⊜	272b	21.52 N	160.11 W
Halaula	272	20.14 N	155.46 W
Halawa, Cape >	272a	21.10 N	156.43 W
Halawa Bay C	272a	21.10 N	156.44 W
Halawa Heights	272c	21.23 N	157.55 W
Halbrite	250	49.20 N	103.32 W
Hale	260	39.36 N	93.20 W
Haleakala Crater ●6	272a	20.43 N	156.13 W
Haleakala National Park ♠	272a	20.44 N	156.13 W
Hale Center	262	34.04 N	101.51 W
Haleiwa	272c	21.35 N	158.07 W
Halekii-Pihana Heiaus State Monument ⊥	272a	20.54 N	156.29 W
Haleyville	260	34.14 N	87.37 W
Halfmoon Bay	248	49.31 N	123.54 W
Halfway, MD	254	39.37 N	77.46 W
Halfway, OR	268	44.53 N	117.07 W
Halfway ≃	242	56.10 N	121.35 W
Halfway Lake ⊜	250	55.03 N	98.24 W
Haliburton	256	45.03 N	78.03 W
Halifax, NS	252	44.39 N	63.36 W
Halifax, NC	258	36.20 N	77.35 W
Halifax, VA	258	36.46 N	78.56 W
Halifax Citadel National Historic Park ♠	252	44.40 N	63.36 W
Halifax Harbour C	252	44.35 N	63.31 W
Haliimaile	272a	20.52 N	156.20 W
Halkett, Cape >	246	70.49 N	152.12 W
Hallam Peak ∧	248	52.11 N	118.46 W
Hallandale	258	25.59 N	80.09 W
Hallettsville	262	29.27 N	96.56 W
Halliday	264	47.21 N	102.20 W
Hall Island I	246	60.40 N	173.05 W
Hall Lake ⊜	242	68.41 N	82.17 W
Hall Mountain ∧	268	48.49 N	117.15 W
Hallock	264	48.47 N	96.57 W
Hallowell	254	44.17 N	69.48 W
Hall Peninsula >1	242	63.30 N	66.00 W
Halls	260	35.53 N	89.24 W
Halls Creek ≃	266	37.18 N	110.45 W
Hallstead	254	41.58 N	75.45 W
Hallsville, MO	260	39.07 N	92.13 W
Hallsville, TX	260	32.30 N	94.34 W
Halsey, NE	264	41.54 N	100.16 W
Halsey, OR	268	44.23 N	123.07 W
Halstad	264	47.21 N	96.50 W
Halstead	264	38.00 N	97.30 W
Haltom City	262	32.48 N	97.16 W
Halvorson, Mount ∧	248	53.15 N	120.33 W
Hamber Provincial Park ♠	248	52.25 N	117.40 W
Hamburg, AR	260	33.14 N	91.48 W
Hamburg, IA	264	40.36 N	95.39 W
Hamburg, NJ	254	41.09 N	74.35 W
Hamburg, NY	254	42.43 N	78.50 W
Hamburg, PA	254	40.34 N	75.59 W
Hamden, CT	254	41.21 N	72.56 W
Hamden, OH	254	39.10 N	82.32 W
Hamilton, ON	256	43.15 N	79.51 W
Hamilton, AL	260	34.09 N	88.06 W
Hamilton, AK	246	62.54 N	163.53 W
Hamilton, GA	258	32.45 N	84.53 W
Hamilton, IL	256	40.24 N	91.21 W
Hamilton, KS	264	37.59 N	96.10 W
Hamilton, MI	256	42.41 N	86.00 W
Hamilton, MO	260	39.45 N	94.01 W
Hamilton, MT	268	46.15 N	114.09 W
Hamilton, NC	258	35.57 N	77.12 W
Hamilton, NY	254	42.50 N	75.33 W
Hamilton, OH	254	39.26 N	84.30 W
Hamilton, TX	262	31.42 N	98.07 W
Hamilton, Lake ⊜1	260	34.30 N	93.05 W
Hamilton, Mount ∧, AK	246	61.10 N	159.46 W
Hamilton, Mount ∧, CA	270	37.21 N	121.38 W
Hamilton, Mount ∧, NV	270	39.14 N	115.32 W
Hamilton Acres	246	64.51 N	147.40 W
Hamilton City	270	39.45 N	122.01 W
Hamilton Creek Indian Reserve ◆4	248	50.11 N	120.30 W
Hamilton Dome	268	43.46 N	108.34 W
Hamilton Inlet C	242	54.00 N	57.30 W
Hamilton Mountain ∧	254	43.25 N	74.22 W
Hamilton Sound ⩌	252	49.30 N	54.30 W
Hamiota	250	50.11 N	100.36 W
Hamlet	258	34.53 N	79.42 W
Hamlet, Mount ∧	246	68.47 N	165.57 W
Hamlin, TX	262	32.53 N	100.08 W
Hamlin, WV	254	38.17 N	82.06 W
Hamlin Lake ⊜	256	44.03 N	86.27 W
Hamlin Valley Wash V	266	38.53 N	114.01 W
Hammon	262	35.38 N	99.23 W
Hammond, IN	260	41.36 N	87.30 W
Hammond, LA	260	30.30 N	90.28 W
Hammond, WI	256	44.59 N	92.26 W
Hammondsport	254	42.25 N	77.13 W
Hammonton	254	39.38 N	74.48 W
Hampden, NF	252	49.33 N	56.51 W
Hampden, ME	254	44.45 N	68.50 W
Hampden, ND	264	48.32 N	98.40 W
Hampden Sydney	258	37.15 N	78.29 W
Hampshire	256	42.06 N	88.32 W
Hampstead	258	34.22 N	77.49 W
Hampton, NB	252	45.32 N	65.51 W
Hampton, AR	260	33.32 N	92.28 W
Hampton, FL	258	29.52 N	82.07 W
Hampton, GA	258	33.23 N	84.17 W
Hampton, IA	256	42.45 N	93.12 W
Hampton, NE	264	40.53 N	97.53 W
Hampton, NH	254	42.56 N	70.50 W
Hampton, NJ	254	40.42 N	74.58 W
Hampton, SC	258	32.52 N	81.07 W
Hampton, TN	258	36.17 N	82.12 W
Hampton, VA	258	37.01 N	76.22 W
Hampton Bays	254	40.53 N	72.31 W
Hampton Butte ∧	268	43.46 N	120.17 W
Hams Fork ≃	268	41.35 N	109.59 W
Hana	272a	20.45 N	155.59 W
Hanahan	258	32.55 N	80.00 W
Hanakaoo Point >	272a	20.55 N	156.42 W
Hanalei	272b	22.07 N	159.30 W
Hanalei Bay C	272b	22.13 N	159.31 W
Hanamaulu	272b	21.59 N	159.22 W
Hanapepe	272b	21.55 N	159.35 W
Hanapepe ≃	272b	21.54 N	159.36 W
Hanapepe Bay C	272b	21.54 N	159.35 W
Hanbury ≃	242	63.37 N	104.33 W
Hanceville, BC	248	51.55 N	123.03 W
Hanceville, AL	260	34.04 N	86.46 W
Hancock, MD	254	39.42 N	78.11 W
Hancock, MI	256	47.07 N	88.35 W
Hancock, MN	264	45.30 N	95.48 W
Hancock, NY	254	41.57 N	75.17 W
Hancock, WI	256	44.08 N	89.31 W
Hancock, Lake ⊜	258	27.58 N	81.50 W
Handsworth	250	49.48 N	103.00 W
Haney	248	49.13 N	122.36 W
Hanford	270	36.20 N	119.39 W
Hanging Rock State Park ♠	258	36.25 N	80.15 W
Hanging Woman Creek ≃	268	45.19 N	106.31 W
Hangman Creek ≃	268	47.38 N	117.27 W
Hankinson	264	46.04 N	96.54 W
Hanley	250	51.37 N	106.27 W
Hanmer	256	46.30 N	80.56 W
Hanna, AB	250	51.38 N	111.54 W
Hanna, OK	262	35.12 N	95.53 W
Hanna, WY	268	41.52 N	106.34 W
Hanna City	256	40.42 N	89.48 W
Hannaford	264	47.19 N	98.11 W
Hannah	264	48.58 N	98.42 W
Hannah Bay C	242	51.05 N	79.45 W
Hannibal	260	39.42 N	91.22 W
Hanover, ON	256	44.09 N	81.02 W
Hanover, IL	256	42.15 N	90.17 W
Hanover, IN	260	38.43 N	85.28 W
Hanover, KS	264	39.54 N	96.53 W
Hanover, NH	254	43.42 N	72.18 W
Hanover, NM	266	32.48 N	108.04 W
Hanover, PA	254	39.48 N	76.59 W
Hanover, VA	258	37.46 N	77.22 W
Hansard	248	54.05 N	121.52 W
Hanska	264	44.09 N	94.30 W
Hanson Lake ⊜	250	54.42 N	102.49 W
Hant's Harbour	252	48.01 N	53.16 W
Hantsport	252	45.04 N	64.11 W
Hantzsch ≃	242	67.32 N	72.25 W
Hapeville	258	33.40 N	84.24 W
Hap Hawkins Lake ⊜1	268	44.58 N	112.51 W
Happy	262	34.45 N	101.52 W
Happy Camp	270	41.48 N	123.22 W
Happy Jack	266	34.45 N	111.11 W
Harbor	268	42.03 N	124.15 W
Harbor Beach	256	43.51 N	82.39 W
Harbor Springs	256	45.26 N	85.00 W
Harbour Breton	252	47.29 N	55.48 W
Harbour Buffett	252	47.31 N	54.05 W
Harbour Deep	252	50.22 N	56.31 W
Harbour Grace	252	47.42 N	53.13 W
Harbourville	252	45.09 N	64.49 W
Harcuvar Mountains ∧∧	266	34.00 N	113.30 W
Hardeeville	258	32.17 N	81.05 W
Hardesty	262	36.37 N	101.12 W
Hardin, IL	260	39.09 N	90.37 W
Hardin, MT	268	45.44 N	107.37 W
Harding, Lake ⊜1	258	32.40 N	85.06 W
Harding Lake ⊜	250	56.13 N	98.23 W
Hardinsburg	260	37.47 N	86.28 W
Hardisty	250	52.40 N	111.18 W
Hardisty Lake ⊜	242	64.30 N	117.45 W
Hardscrabble Wash V	266	34.39 N	109.28 W
Hardtner	264	37.01 N	98.39 W
Hardwick, GA	258	33.09 N	83.13 W
Hardwick, VT	254	44.30 N	72.22 W
Hardwicke Island I	248	50.30 N	125.30 W
Hardwood	260	30.49 N	91.23 W
Hardwood Ridge ∧	254	41.15 N	75.23 W
Hardy, AR	260	36.19 N	91.29 W
Hardy, NE	264	40.01 N	97.56 W
Hardy Bay C	242	75.02 N	115.16 W
Hare Bay	252	48.51 N	54.01 W
Hare Bay C	252	51.18 N	55.50 W
Hare Indian ≃	242	66.18 N	128.38 W
Hargrave ≃	250	54.24 N	98.48 W
Hargrave Lake ⊜	250	54.29 N	99.40 W
Harkers Island	258	34.42 N	76.34 W
Harlan, IA	264	41.39 N	95.19 W
Harlan, KY	258	36.51 N	83.19 W
Harlan County Lake ⊜1	264	40.04 N	99.16 W
Harlem, FL	258	26.44 N	80.58 W
Harlem, GA	258	33.25 N	82.19 W
Harlem, MT	268	48.32 N	108.47 W
Harlingen	262	26.11 N	97.42 W
Harlowton	268	46.26 N	109.50 W
Harman	254	38.55 N	79.32 W
Harmony, IN	260	39.32 N	87.04 W
Harmony, ME	254	44.58 N	69.33 W
Harmony, MN	256	43.33 N	92.01 W
Harney, Lake ⊜	258	28.45 N	81.03 W
Harney Basin ⌣1	268	43.15 N	120.40 W
Harney Lake ⊜	268	43.14 N	119.07 W
Harney Peak ∧	264	44.00 N	103.30 W
Harper, KS	264	37.17 N	98.01 W
Harper, TX	262	30.18 N	99.15 W
Harper, Mount ∧	246	64.14 N	143.50 W
Harper Lake ⊜	270	35.02 N	117.17 W
Harpers Ferry National Historical Park ♠	254	39.13 N	77.45 W
Harquahala Mountain ∧	266	33.49 N	113.21 W
Harrell	260	33.31 N	92.24 W
Harricana ≃	242	51.15 N	79.45 W
Harriman	258	35.56 N	84.33 W
Harriman State Park ♠	254	41.14 N	74.09 W
Harrington, DE	254	38.56 N	75.35 W
Harrington, ME	254	44.37 N	67.49 W
Harrington, WA	268	47.29 N	118.15 W
Harris, SK	250	51.44 N	107.35 W
Harris, MN	256	45.35 N	92.59 W
Harris, Lake ⊜	258	28.46 N	81.49 W
Harrisburg, AR	260	35.34 N	90.43 W
Harrisburg, IL	260	37.44 N	88.33 W
Harrisburg, NE	264	41.33 N	103.44 W
Harrisburg, OR	268	44.16 N	123.10 W
Harrisburg, PA	254	40.16 N	76.52 W
Harrison, AR	260	36.14 N	93.07 W
Harrison, ID	268	47.27 N	116.47 W
Harrison, MI	256	44.01 N	84.48 W
Harrison, NE	264	42.41 N	103.53 W
Harrison, Cape >	242	54.55 N	57.55 W
Harrison Bay C	246	70.30 N	151.30 W
Harrisonburg	260	31.46 N	91.49 W
Harrison Islands II	242	69.13 N	90.30 W
Harrison Lake ⊜	248	49.30 N	121.50 W
Harrisonville	260	38.39 N	94.21 W
Harriston, ON	256	43.54 N	80.53 W
Harriston, MS	260	31.44 N	91.02 W
Harrisville, MI	256	44.39 N	83.17 W
Harrisville, NY	254	44.09 N	75.19 W
Harrisville, WV	254	39.13 N	81.03 W
Harrodsburg	258	37.46 N	84.51 W
Harrold	262	34.05 N	99.02 W
Harrop Lake ⊜	250	52.38 N	95.58 W
Harrow	256	42.02 N	82.55 W
Harrowsmith	256	44.24 N	76.40 W
Harry S Truman Reservoir ⊜1	260	38.10 N	93.45 W
Hart, MI	256	43.42 N	86.22 W
Hart, TX	262	34.23 N	102.07 W
Hart ≃	246	65.51 N	136.22 W
Hartford, AL	260	31.06 N	85.42 W
Hartford, AR	260	35.01 N	94.23 W
Hartford, CT	254	41.46 N	72.41 W
Hartford, KS	264	38.18 N	95.58 W
Hartford, KY	260	37.27 N	86.55 W
Hartford, MI	256	42.12 N	86.10 W
Hartford, SD	264	43.37 N	96.57 W
Hartford, WI	256	43.19 N	88.22 W
Hartford City	260	40.27 N	85.22 W
Hartington	264	42.37 N	97.16 W
Hart Lake ⊜	268	42.24 N	119.51 W
Hartland, NB	252	46.18 N	67.32 W
Hartland, ME	254	44.53 N	69.27 W
Hartley, IA	264	43.11 N	95.29 W
Hartley, TX	262	35.53 N	102.24 W
Hartley Bay	248	53.25 N	129.15 W
Hart Mountain ∧	250	52.29 N	101.25 W
Hartney	250	49.28 N	100.30 W
Hartselle	260	34.27 N	86.56 W
Hartshorne	262	34.51 N	95.34 W
Hartsville, SC	258	34.23 N	80.04 W
Hartsville, TN	260	36.24 N	86.10 W
Hartville	260	37.15 N	92.31 W
Hartwell	258	34.21 N	82.56 W
Hartwell Lake ⊜1	258	34.30 N	82.55 W
Hartwick Pines State Park ♠	256	44.47 N	84.41 W
Harvard, IL	256	42.25 N	88.37 W
Harvard, NE	264	40.37 N	98.06 W
Harvey, NB	252	45.43 N	64.43 W
Harvey, IL	260	41.37 N	87.39 W
Harvey, ND	264	47.47 N	99.56 W
Haskell, OK	262	35.50 N	95.40 W
Haskell, TX	262	33.10 N	99.44 W
Hasparos Canyon V	266	33.50 N	105.02 W
Hassayampa ≃	266	33.20 N	112.43 W
Hastings, ON	256	44.18 N	77.57 W
Hastings, FL	258	29.40 N	81.30 W
Hastings, MI	256	42.39 N	85.17 W
Hastings, MN	256	44.44 N	92.51 W
Hastings, NE	264	40.35 N	98.23 W
Hasty	264	38.07 N	102.58 W
Haswell	264	38.27 N	103.09 W
Hatch, NM	266	32.40 N	107.09 W
Hatch, UT	266	37.39 N	112.26 W
Hatchet Creek ≃	260	32.52 N	86.20 W
Hatchet Lake	252	44.35 N	63.40 W
Hatchie ≃	260	35.35 N	89.53 W
Hatch Wash V	266	38.32 N	109.36 W
Hat Creek ≃, U.S.	264	43.16 N	103.36 W
Hat Creek ≃, CA	270	40.59 N	121.33 W
Hatfield, AR	260	34.29 N	94.23 W
Hatfield, MA	254	42.22 N	72.36 W
Hatteras	258	35.13 N	75.42 W
Hatteras, Cape >	258	35.13 N	75.32 W
Hatteras Island I	258	35.25 N	75.30 W
Hattiesburg	260	31.19 N	89.16 W
Hatton, AL	260	32.06 N	86.35 W
Hatton, ND	264	47.38 N	97.27 W
Haubstadt	260	38.12 N	87.34 W
Haultain ≃	250	55.51 N	106.46 W
Haut, Isle au I	254	44.03 N	68.38 W
Hauterive	252	49.12 N	68.16 W
Hauula	272c	21.37 N	157.55 W
Havana, AR	260	35.07 N	93.32 W
Havana, FL	258	30.38 N	84.25 W
Havana, IL	260	40.18 N	90.04 W
Havana, ND	264	45.57 N	97.37 W
Havasu, Lake ⊜1	266	34.30 N	114.20 W
Havasu Creek ≃	266	36.19 N	112.46 W

Symbols in the index entries are identified on page 273.

Symbols in the index entries are identified on page 273.

Name	Page	Lat °′	Long °′
Huntsville, MO	260	39.26 N	92.33 W
Huntsville, TN	258	36.25 N	84.29 W
Huntsville, TX	262	30.43 N	95.33 W
Huntsville, UT	266	41.16 N	111.46 W
Hurd, Cape ➤	256	45.13 N	81.44 W
Hurley, MS	260	30.40 N	88.30 W
Hurley, NM	266	32.42 N	108.08 W
Hurley, SD	264	43.17 N	97.05 W
Hurley, WI	256	46.28 N	90.08 W
Hurlock	254	38.38 N	75.52 W
Huron, CA	270	36.12 N	120.06 W
Huron, OH	254	41.24 N	82.33 W
Huron, SD	264	44.22 N	98.13 W
Huron ≃	256	42.03 N	83.14 W
Huron, Lake ⊜, N.A.	244		
	256	44.30 N	82.15 W
Huron Mountains ⛰[2]	256	46.45 N	87.45 W
Hurricane, AK	246	62.59 N	149.38 W
Hurricane, UT	266	37.11 N	113.17 W
Hurricane, WV	254	38.26 N	82.01 W
Hurricane Cliffs •[4]	266	37.20 N	113.10 W
Hurricane Creek ≃, AR	260	34.05 N	92.23 W
Hurricane Creek ≃, GA	258	31.23 N	82.19 W
Hurricane Creek ≃, IL	260	38.53 N	89.13 W
Hurricane Wash ∨	266	37.00 N	113.23 W
Hurt	258	37.06 N	79.20 W
Hurtsboro	258	32.14 N	85.25 W
Huslia	246	65.42 N	156.25 W
Hussar	248	51.03 N	112.41 W
Hustisford	256	43.21 N	88.36 W
Hutchinson, KS	264	38.05 N	97.56 W
Hutchinson, MN	264	44.54 N	94.22 W
Hutchinson Island I	258	27.25 N	80.17 W
Hutch Mountain ∧	266	34.47 N	111.22 W
Hutsonville	260	39.07 N	87.39 W
Hutte Sauvage, Lac de la ⊜	242	56.15 N	64.45 W
Huttig	260	33.02 N	92.11 W
Hutto	262	30.33 N	97.33 W
Huxford	260	31.13 N	87.28 W
Huxley	248	51.56 N	113.14 W
Hyannis, MA	254	41.39 N	70.17 W
Hyannis, NE	264	41.59 N	101.44 W
Hyattville	268	44.15 N	107.36 W
Hyco ≃	258	36.40 N	78.45 W
Hyco Lake ⊜[1]	258	36.30 N	79.05 W
Hydaburg	246	55.12 N	132.49 W
Hyden	258	37.10 N	83.22 W
Hyde Park, NY	254	41.47 N	73.56 W
Hyde Park, VT	254	44.36 N	72.37 W
Hyder	246	55.55 N	130.01 W
Hydraulic	248	52.36 N	121.42 W
Hydro	262	35.33 N	98.35 W
Hyland ≃	242	59.50 N	128.10 W
Hymera	260	39.11 N	87.18 W
Hyndman	254	39.49 N	78.44 W
Hyndman Peak ∧	268	43.45 N	114.08 W
Hyrum	266	41.38 N	111.51 W
Hysham	268	46.18 N	107.14 W
Hythe	248	55.20 N	119.33 W

I

Iaeger	258	37.28 N	81.49 W
Iamonia, Lake ⊜	258	30.38 N	84.14 W
Iatt, Lake ⊜[1]	260	31.35 N	92.40 W
Ibapah Peak ∧	266	39.50 N	113.55 W
Iberia	260	38.05 N	92.18 W
Iberville	254	45.18 N	73.14 W
Iberville, Lac d' ⊜	242	55.55 N	73.15 W
Iberville, Mont d' ∧	242	58.53 N	63.43 W
Iceberg Pass)(	266	40.25 N	105.45 W
Ice Mountain ∧	248	54.25 N	121.08 W
Ichawaynochaway Creek ≃	258	31.10 N	84.28 W
Icicle Creek ≃	268	47.34 N	120.40 W
Icy Bay C	246	60.00 N	141.15 W
Icy Cape ➤	246	70.20 N	161.52 W
Icy Strait Ұ	246	58.18 N	135.30 W
Ida	256	41.55 N	83.34 W
Idabel	260	33.54 N	94.50 W
Ida Grove	264	42.21 N	95.28 W
Idaho □[3], U.S.	244		
	268	45.00 N	115.00 W
Idaho City	268	43.50 N	115.50 W
Idaho Falls	268	43.30 N	112.02 W
Idaho Springs	266	39.45 N	105.31 W
Idalou	262	33.40 N	101.41 W
Iditarod ≃	246	63.02 N	158.58 W
Idyllwild	270	33.45 N	116.43 W
Igiugig	246	59.20 N	155.55 W
Igloolik	242	69.24 N	81.49 W
Ignacio	266	37.07 N	107.38 W
Igvak, Cape ➤	246	57.26 N	156.00 W
Ikatan	246	54.45 N	163.19 W
Ikolik, Cape ➤	246	57.17 N	154.48 W
Ikpikpuk ≃	246	70.50 N	154.25 W
Ikti, Cape ➤	246	56.00 N	158.30 W
Ikuktlitlig Mountain ∧	246	59.16 N	161.27 W
Île-à-la-Crosse	250	55.27 N	107.53 W
Île-à-la-Crosse, Lac ⊜	250	55.40 N	107.45 W
Îles, Lac des ⊜	250	54.26 N	109.25 W
Ilford	250	56.04 N	95.35 W
Iliamna	246	59.45 N	154.54 W
Iliamna Lake ⊜	246	59.30 N	155.00 W
Iliff	264	40.45 N	103.04 W
Ilion	254	43.01 N	75.02 W
Ilio Point ➤	272a	21.13 N	157.15 W
Illinois □[3], U.S.	244		
	260	40.00 N	89.00 W
Illinois ≃, U.S.	260	35.30 N	95.06 W
Illinois ≃, CO	266	40.45 N	106.18 W
Illinois ≃, IL	256	38.58 N	90.27 W
Illinois ≃, OR	268	42.33 N	124.03 W
Illinois Peak ∧	268	47.02 N	115.04 W
Illiopolis	260	39.51 N	89.15 W
Imboden	260	36.12 N	91.10 W
Imlay	270	40.39 N	118.09 W
Imlay City	256	43.02 N	83.05 W
Immokalee	258	26.25 N	81.25 W
Imnaha ≃	268	45.49 N	116.46 W
Imperial, SK	250	51.22 N	105.27 W
Imperial, CA	270	32.51 N	115.34 W
Imperial, NE	264	40.31 N	101.39 W
Imperial, TX	262	31.16 N	102.41 W
Imperial Beach	270	32.35 N	117.08 W
Imperial Dam ⇀[6]	266	32.55 N	114.30 W
Imperial Mills	250	55.00 N	111.44 W
Imperial Valley ∨	270	32.50 N	115.30 W
Imuruk Basin ⊜	246	65.06 N	165.36 W
Imuruk Lake ⊜	246	65.36 N	163.10 W
Ina	260	38.09 N	88.54 W
Incline Village	270	39.16 N	119.56 W
Independence, CA	270	36.48 N	118.12 W
Independence, IA	256	42.28 N	91.54 W
Independence, KS	264	37.13 N	95.42 W
Independence, KY	254	38.57 N	84.32 W
Independence, LA	260	30.38 N	90.30 W
Independence, MO	260	39.05 N	94.24 W
Independence, OR	268	44.51 N	123.11 W
Independence, VA	258	36.37 N	81.09 W
Independence, WI	256	44.21 N	91.25 W
Independence ≃	254	43.45 N	75.20 W
Independence Creek ≃	262	30.27 N	101.44 W
Independence Mountains ⛰	270	41.15 N	116.00 W
Indialantic	258	28.05 N	80.34 W
Indian ≃, MI	256	45.59 N	86.15 W
Indian ≃, NY	254	43.58 N	75.17 W
Indiana	254	40.37 N	79.09 W
Indiana □[3], U.S.	244		
	260	40.00 N	86.15 W
Indiana Dunes National Lakeshore ♠	260	41.40 N	87.00 W
Indianapolis	260	39.46 N	86.09 W
Indian Bayou ≃	260	34.14 N	91.52 W
Indian Brook	252	46.23 N	60.32 W
Indian Creek ≃, IL	260	41.26 N	88.46 W
Indian Creek ≃, IN	260	38.07 N	86.16 W
Indian Creek ≃, MO	260	36.33 N	94.29 W
Indian Creek ≃, NM	266	36.11 N	108.23 W
Indian Creek ≃, SD	264	44.39 N	103.19 W
Indian Creek ≃, TN	260	35.13 N	88.08 W
Indian Grave Mountain ∧[2]	258	32.59 N	84.21 W
Indian Head	250	50.32 N	103.40 W
Indian Lake	254	43.47 N	74.16 W
Indian Lake ⊜, ON	256	47.08 N	82.08 W
Indian Lake ⊜, MI	256	45.59 N	86.20 W
Indianola, IA	256	41.22 N	93.34 W
Indianola, MS	260	33.27 N	90.39 W
Indianola, NE	264	40.14 N	100.25 W
Indian Peak ∧, UT	266	38.16 N	113.53 W
Indian Peak ∧, WY	268	44.47 N	109.51 W
Indian River	256	45.25 N	84.37 W
Indian River C	258	28.00 N	80.30 W
Indian Rock ∧	268	45.59 N	120.49 W
Indian Springs	270	36.34 N	115.40 W
Indiantown	258	27.01 N	80.28 W
Indio	270	33.43 N	116.13 W
Indus	250	48.37 N	93.50 W
Industry, IL	260	40.20 N	90.36 W
Industry, TX	262	29.58 N	96.30 W
Inez, KY	258	37.52 N	82.32 W
Inez, TX	262	28.54 N	96.47 W
Ingersoll	256	43.02 N	80.53 W
Ingleside	262	27.53 N	97.13 W
Inglewood	270	33.58 N	118.21 W
Inglis	250	50.57 N	101.15 W
Ingonish	252	46.42 N	60.22 W
Ingornachoix Bay C	252	50.38 N	57.20 W
Ingram	262	30.04 N	99.14 W
Inkom	268	42.48 N	112.15 W
Inkster	264	48.09 N	97.39 W
Inland Lake ⊜, MB	250	52.17 N	99.42 W
Inland Lake ⊜, AK	246	66.27 N	159.47 W
Inman, KS	264	38.14 N	97.47 W
Inman, SC	258	35.03 N	82.05 W
Inman Mills	258	35.02 N	82.06 W
Innisfail	248	52.02 N	113.57 W
Innisfree	250	53.22 N	111.32 W
Innoko ≃	246	62.14 N	159.45 W
Inola	262	36.09 N	95.31 W
Inoucdjouac	242	58.27 N	78.06 W
Inspiration	266	33.25 N	110.53 W
Instow	250	49.44 N	108.16 W
International Falls	256	48.36 N	93.25 W
International Peace Garden ♠, N.A.	250	49.00 N	100.07 W
International Peace Garden ♠, N.A.	264	49.00 N	100.04 W
Interstate Park ♠	256	45.23 N	92.40 W
Intracoastal Waterway ≚, U.S.	254	38.10 N	76.20 W
Intracoastal Waterway ≚, U.S.	258	33.40 N	79.00 W
Intracoastal Waterway ≚, U.S.	260	30.15 N	88.00 W
Intracoastal Waterway ≚, U.S.	262	28.45 N	95.40 W
Inuvik	242	68.25 N	133.30 W
Invermay	250	51.48 N	103.09 W
Invermere	248	50.30 N	116.02 W
Inverness, NS	252	46.14 N	61.18 W
Inverness, CA	270	38.06 N	122.51 W
Inverness, FL	258	28.51 N	82.20 W
Inverness, MS	260	33.21 N	90.35 W
Inwood, MB	250	50.34 N	97.32 W
Inwood, IA	264	43.18 N	96.26 W
Inyan Kara Mountain ∧	264	44.13 N	104.21 W
Inyo, Mount ∧	270	36.44 N	117.59 W
Inyokern	270	35.39 N	117.49 W
Inyo Mountains ⛰	270	36.40 N	118.10 W
Inzana Lake ⊜	248	54.58 N	124.40 W
Iola, KS	264	37.55 N	95.24 W
Iola, WI	256	44.36 N	89.08 W
Iona, NS	252	45.58 N	60.48 W
Iona, ID	268	43.32 N	111.56 W
Ione, CA	270	38.21 N	120.56 W
Ione, OR	268	45.30 N	119.50 W
Ione, WA	268	48.45 N	117.25 W
Ionia	256	42.59 N	85.04 W
Iosegun ≃	248	54.44 N	117.11 W
Iosegun Lake	248	54.29 N	116.50 W
Iota	260	30.20 N	92.29 W
Iowa	260	30.14 N	93.01 W
Iowa □[3], U.S.	244		
	256	42.15 N	93.15 W
Iowa ≃	256	41.10 N	91.02 W
Iowa, South Fork ≃	256	42.18 N	93.04 W
Iowa City	256	41.40 N	91.32 W
Iowa Falls	256	42.31 N	93.16 W
Iowa Park	262	33.57 N	98.40 W
Ipava	260	40.21 N	90.19 W
Iphigenia Bay C	246	55.40 N	133.55 W
Ipswich, MA	254	42.41 N	70.50 W
Ipswich, SD	264	45.27 N	99.02 W
Ira	262	32.35 N	101.00 W
Iraan	262	30.54 N	101.54 W
Irene	264	43.05 N	97.10 W
Ireton	264	42.58 N	96.19 W
Irish, Mount ∧	270	37.38 N	115.24 W
Irma	250	52.55 N	111.14 W
Iron Belt	256	46.25 N	90.19 W
Iron Bridge	256	46.17 N	83.14 W
Iron City	260	35.01 N	87.35 W
Iron Creek ≃	250	52.43 N	111.14 W
Irondale, AL	260	33.32 N	86.42 W
Irondale, MO	260	37.50 N	90.41 W
Irondequoit	254	43.12 N	77.36 W
Iron Mountain	256	45.49 N	88.04 W
Iron Mountain ∧	266	33.27 N	111.10 W
Iron Mountains ⛰	258	36.30 N	81.50 W
Iron River, MI	256	46.05 N	88.39 W
Iron River, WI	256	46.34 N	91.24 W
Ironton, MN	256	46.28 N	93.59 W
Ironton, MO	260	37.36 N	90.38 W
Ironton, OH	254	38.31 N	82.40 W
Ironwood	256	46.27 N	90.10 W
Iroquois, ON	254	44.51 N	75.19 W
Iroquois, SD	264	44.22 N	97.51 W
Iroquois ≃	256	41.05 N	87.49 W
Iroquois Falls	256	48.46 N	80.41 W
Irricana	248	51.19 N	113.37 W
Irrigon	268	45.54 N	119.30 W
Irvine, AB	250	49.57 N	110.16 W
Irvine, KY	258	37.42 N	83.58 W
Irvines Landing	248	49.38 N	124.03 W
Irving, IL	260	39.12 N	89.24 W
Irving, TX	262	32.49 N	96.56 W
Irvington	260	37.53 N	86.17 W
Irwinton	258	32.49 N	83.10 W
Isaac Lake ⊜	248	53.10 N	120.50 W
Isabel	264	45.24 N	101.26 W
Isabella Lake ⊜[1]	270	35.40 N	118.26 W
Isabelle ≃	256	47.50 N	91.41 W
Isanti	256	45.29 N	93.15 W
Ishpeming	256	46.30 N	87.40 W
Iskut ≃	246	56.42 N	131.45 W
Island	260	37.27 N	87.09 W
Island Falls, SK	250	55.32 N	102.21 W
Island Falls, ME	254	46.00 N	68.16 W
Island Lake	250	53.58 N	94.47 W
Island Lake ⊜	250	53.47 N	94.25 W
Island Park	268	44.24 N	111.19 W
Island Park Reservoir ⊜[1]	268	44.25 N	111.29 W
Island Pond	254	44.49 N	71.53 W
Island Pond ⊜	252	48.25 N	56.23 W
Islands, Bay of C	252	49.10 N	58.15 W
Isla Vista	270	34.25 N	119.53 W
Isle	256	46.08 N	93.29 W
Isle-aux-Morts	252	47.35 N	58.59 W
Isle of Hope	258	31.58 N	81.05 W
Isle of Palms	258	32.47 N	79.48 W
Isle of Wight	258	36.54 N	76.43 W
Isle Royale National Park ♠	256	48.00 N	89.00 W
Islesboro Island I	254	44.20 N	68.53 W
Isleta	266	34.55 N	106.42 W
Isleta Indian Reservation ⇀[4]	266	34.55 N	106.45 W
Isleton	270	38.10 N	121.37 W
Islets Caribou	252	49.30 N	67.14 W
Isola	260	33.16 N	90.36 W
Israel ≃	254	44.29 N	71.35 W
Isto, Mount ∧	246	69.12 N	143.48 W
Istokpoga, Lake ⊜	258	27.22 N	81.17 W
Italy	262	32.11 N	96.53 W
Itasca	262	32.10 N	97.09 W
Itasca State Park ♠	264	47.18 N	95.18 W
Itchen Lake ⊜	242	65.33 N	112.50 W
Ithaca, MI	256	43.18 N	84.36 W
Ithaca, NY	254	42.27 N	76.30 W
Itkillik ≃	246	70.08 N	150.57 W
Itomamo, Lac ⊜	252	49.11 N	70.28 W
Itta Bena	260	33.30 N	90.20 W
Ituna	250	51.10 N	103.30 W
Iuka	260	34.49 N	88.11 W
Iva	258	34.19 N	82.40 W
Ivanhoe, CA	270	36.23 N	119.13 W
Ivanhoe, MN	264	44.28 N	96.15 W
Ivanhoe, VA	258	36.50 N	80.58 W
Ivanhoe ≃	256	48.40 N	82.11 W
Ivanhoe Lake ⊜	256	48.05 N	82.38 W
Ivanof Bay	246	55.54 N	159.29 W
Ivanpah Lake ⊜	270	35.35 N	115.25 W
Ivujivik	242	62.24 N	77.55 W

J

Jaboncillos Creek ≃	262	27.23 N	97.45 W
Jacinto City	262	29.46 N	95.16 W
Jack Creek ≃	268	42.59 N	121.32 W
Jackfish Lake ⊜	250	53.05 N	108.25 W
Jackhead Harbour	250	51.52 N	97.16 W
Jackman	254	45.38 N	70.16 W
Jackman Station	254	45.37 N	70.15 W
Jack Mountain ∧, MT	268	46.21 N	112.18 W
Jack Mountain ∧, WA	268	48.47 N	120.57 W
Jackpot	270	41.59 N	114.40 W
Jacksboro, TN	258	36.20 N	84.11 W
Jacksboro, TX	262	33.13 N	98.10 W
Jackson, AL	260	31.31 N	87.53 W
Jackson, CA	270	38.21 N	120.46 W
Jackson, GA	258	33.18 N	83.58 W
Jackson, KY	258	37.33 N	83.23 W
Jackson, LA	260	30.50 N	91.13 W
Jackson, MI	256	42.15 N	84.24 W
Jackson, MN	264	43.37 N	95.01 W
Jackson, MS	260	32.18 N	90.12 W
Jackson, MO	260	37.23 N	89.40 W
Jackson, NC	258	36.23 N	77.25 W
Jackson, OH	254	39.03 N	82.39 W
Jackson, SC	258	33.20 N	81.47 W
Jackson, TN	260	35.37 N	88.49 W
Jackson, WY	268	43.29 N	110.38 W
Jackson ≃	258	37.47 N	79.46 W
Jackson, Lake ⊜	258	30.30 N	84.17 W
Jackson Center	254	40.27 N	84.02 W
Jackson Creek ≃	250	49.18 N	100.50 W
Jackson Lake ⊜[1], GA	258	33.22 N	83.52 W
Jackson Lake ⊜[1], WY	268	43.55 N	110.40 W
Jackson Mountain ∧	254	44.46 N	70.32 W
Jackson's Arm	252	49.52 N	56.47 W
Jacksonville, AL	260	33.49 N	85.46 W
Jacksonville, AR	260	34.52 N	92.07 W
Jacksonville, FL	258	30.20 N	81.40 W
Jacksonville, IL	260	39.44 N	90.14 W
Jacksonville, NC	258	34.45 N	77.26 W
Jacksonville, OR	268	42.19 N	122.57 W
Jacksonville, TX	262	31.58 N	95.17 W
Jacksonville Beach	258	30.18 N	81.24 W
Jacksonville Naval Air Station ■	258	30.14 N	81.41 W
Jacques, Lac à ⊜	246	66.10 N	127.25 W
Jacques-Cartier, Détroit de Ұ	252	50.00 N	63.30 W
Jacques-Cartier, Mont ∧	252	48.59 N	65.57 W
Jacquet River	252	47.55 N	66.00 W
Jacumba	270	32.37 N	116.11 W
Jadito Wash ∨	266	35.22 N	110.50 W
Jaffrey	254	42.50 N	72.04 W
Jagged Mountain ∧	246	58.38 N	162.02 W
Jake Creek Mountain ∧	270	41.13 N	116.54 W
Jal	262	32.07 N	103.12 W
James ≃, AB	248	51.55 N	114.34 W
James ≃, U.S.	244	42.52 N	97.18 W
James ≃, MO	260	36.45 N	93.30 W
James ≃, VA	258	36.57 N	76.26 W
James, Lake ⊜[1]	258	35.45 N	81.55 W
James Bay C	242	53.30 N	80.30 W
James City	258	35.05 N	77.02 W
James Island	258	32.42 N	79.58 W
Jamesport	260	39.58 N	93.48 W
James Ross, Cape ➤	242	74.40 N	114.25 W
James Ross Strait Ұ	242	69.40 N	95.30 W
James Smith Indian Reserve ⇀[4]	250	53.08 N	104.52 W
Jamestown, CA	270	37.57 N	120.25 W
Jamestown, KS	264	39.36 N	97.52 W
Jamestown, KY	260	36.59 N	85.04 W
Jamestown, NC	258	35.59 N	79.56 W
Jamestown, ND	264	46.54 N	98.42 W
Jamestown, NY	254	42.06 N	79.14 W
Jamestown, OH	254	39.39 N	83.44 W
Jamestown, TN	258	36.26 N	84.57 W
Jamestown ⊥	258	37.12 N	76.46 W
Jamestown Reservoir ⊜[1]	264	47.15 N	98.40 W
Janesville, CA	270	40.18 N	120.32 W
Janesville, MN	256	44.07 N	93.42 W
Janesville, WI	256	42.41 N	89.01 W
Jan Lake ⊜	250	54.55 N	102.55 W
Jansen	250	51.47 N	104.43 W
Jarales	266	34.37 N	106.46 W
Jarbidge ≃	270	42.19 N	115.39 W
Jarratt	258	36.48 N	77.28 W
Jarreau	260	30.39 N	91.29 W
Jarvie	248	54.27 N	113.59 W
Jarvis	256	42.53 N	80.06 W
Jarvisburg	258	36.09 N	75.52 W
Jasonville	260	39.10 N	87.12 W
Jasper, AB	248	52.53 N	118.05 W
Jasper, AL	260	33.50 N	87.17 W
Jasper, AR	260	36.00 N	93.11 W
Jasper, FL	258	30.31 N	82.57 W
Jasper, GA	258	34.28 N	84.26 W
Jasper, IN	260	38.24 N	86.56 W
Jasper, MN	264	43.51 N	96.24 W
Jasper, MO	260	37.20 N	94.18 W
Jasper, TN	260	35.04 N	85.38 W
Jasper, TX	260	30.55 N	94.01 W
Jasper Lake ⊜	248	53.07 N	118.00 W
Jasper National Park ♠	248	52.53 N	118.03 W
Java	264	45.30 N	99.53 W
Jay, FL	260	30.57 N	87.09 W
Jay, OK	260	36.25 N	94.48 W
Jay Cooke State Park ♠	256	46.41 N	92.23 W
Jaynes	266	32.16 N	111.01 W
Jay Peak ∧	254	44.55 N	72.32 W
Jayton	262	33.15 N	100.34 W
J B Thomas, Lake ⊜[1]	262	32.35 N	101.10 W
Jeanerette	260	29.55 N	91.40 W
Jeddore Lake ⊜[1]	252	48.03 N	55.55 W
Jeffers	264	44.03 N	95.12 W
Jefferson, GA	258	34.07 N	83.35 W
Jefferson, IA	264	42.01 N	94.23 W
Jefferson, NC	258	36.26 N	81.28 W
Jefferson, OH	254	41.44 N	80.46 W
Jefferson, OR	268	44.43 N	123.01 W
Jefferson, SC	258	34.39 N	80.23 W
Jefferson, SD	264	42.36 N	96.34 W
Jefferson, TX	260	32.46 N	94.21 W
Jefferson, WI	256	43.01 N	88.48 W
Jefferson ≃	268	45.56 N	111.30 W
Jefferson, Mount ∧, ID	268	44.34 N	111.30 W
Jefferson, Mount ∧, NV	270	38.46 N	116.55 W
Jefferson, Mount ∧, OR	268	44.40 N	121.47 W
Jefferson City, MO	260	38.34 N	92.10 W
Jefferson City, TN	258	36.07 N	83.30 W
Jefferson Proving Ground ■	260	38.50 N	85.25 W
Jeffersonton	254	38.38 N	77.55 W
Jeffersontown	260	38.12 N	85.35 W
Jeffersonville, GA	258	32.41 N	83.20 W
Jeffersonville, IN	260	38.17 N	85.44 W
Jeffersonville, OH	254	39.39 N	83.34 W
Jeffrey City	268	42.29 N	107.49 W
Jeffries Creek ≃	258	34.05 N	79.32 W
Jekyll Island I	258	31.04 N	81.25 W
Jekyll Island State Park ♠	258	31.02 N	81.25 W
Jellico	258	36.35 N	84.08 W
Jelm Mountain ∧	266	41.06 N	105.58 W
Jemez ≃	266	35.22 N	106.31 W
Jemez Indian Reservation ⇀[4]	266	35.35 N	106.45 W
Jemez Springs	266	35.46 N	106.42 W
Jena	260	31.41 N	92.08 W
Jenkins	258	37.10 N	82.38 W
Jenkinsville	258	34.16 N	81.17 W
Jenkintown	254	40.06 N	75.08 W
Jenks	262	36.01 N	95.58 W
Jennings, FL	258	30.36 N	83.06 W
Jennings, LA	260	30.13 N	92.39 W
Jensen	266	40.22 N	109.17 W
Jensen Beach	258	27.15 N	80.14 W
Jens Munk Island I	242	69.42 N	79.30 W
Jeptha Knob ∧[2]	260	38.11 N	85.07 W
Jerimoth Hill ∧[2]	254	41.52 N	71.47 W
Jerome, AZ	266	34.45 N	112.07 W
Jerome, ID	268	42.43 N	114.31 W
Jersey City	254	40.44 N	74.02 W
Jersey Mountain ∧	268	45.29 N	115.34 W
Jersey Shore	254	41.12 N	77.16 W
Jerseyville	260	39.07 N	90.20 W
Jervis Inlet C	248	49.46 N	124.10 W
Jessup	254	41.28 N	75.34 W
Jessup, Lake ⊜	258	28.43 N	81.14 W
Jesup, GA	258	31.36 N	81.53 W
Jesup, IA	256	42.29 N	92.04 W
Jet	262	36.40 N	98.11 W
Jetmore	264	38.03 N	99.54 W
Jeune Landing	248	50.27 N	127.30 W
Jewel Cave National Monument ♠	264	43.42 N	103.50 W
Jewell, IA	256	42.20 N	93.39 W
Jewell, KS	264	39.40 N	98.10 W
Jewell Ridge	258	37.11 N	81.48 W
Jewett, IL	260	39.13 N	88.15 W
Jewett, TX	262	31.22 N	96.09 W
Jewett City	254	41.36 N	71.59 W
Jewett Lake ⊜	250	56.09 N	104.40 W
Jicarilla Indian Reservation ⇀[4]	266	36.40 N	107.00 W
Jim Ned Creek ≃	262	31.50 N	99.07 W
Jim Thorpe	254	40.52 N	75.45 W
Joanna	258	34.25 N	81.49 W
Joaquin	260	31.58 N	94.03 W
Job Peak ∧	270	39.35 N	118.14 W
Jocko ≃	268	47.20 N	114.17 W
Joe Batt's Arm	252	49.44 N	54.10 W
Joffre, Mount ∧	248	50.32 N	115.13 W
Joggins	252	45.42 N	64.27 W
Johannesburg	270	35.22 N	117.38 W
John ≃	246	66.55 N	151.35 W
John Day	268	44.25 N	118.57 W
John Day ≃	268	45.44 N	120.39 W
John Day, Middle Fork ≃	268	44.55 N	119.18 W
John Day, North Fork ≃	268	44.45 N	119.38 W
John Day, South Fork ≃	268	44.28 N	119.31 W
John Day Fossil Beds National Monument ♠	268	44.34 N	119.39 W
Johney Creek ≃	262	28.27 N	98.54 W
John F. Kennedy Space Center ✦[3]	258	28.40 N	80.40 W
John H. Kerr Reservoir ⊜[1]	258	36.35 N	78.35 W
John Martin Reservoir ⊜[1]	264	38.05 N	103.02 W
John Redmond Reservoir ⊜[1]	264	38.18 N	95.55 W
Johns Creek ≃	258	37.30 N	80.06 W
Johnson, AR	260	36.06 N	94.10 W
Johnson, KS	264	37.34 N	101.45 W
Johnson, NE	264	40.24 N	96.01 W
Johnson, VT	254	44.38 N	72.41 W
Johnsonburg	254	41.29 N	78.41 W
Johnson City, NY	254	42.07 N	75.57 W
Johnson City, TN	258	36.19 N	82.21 W
Johnson City, TX	262	30.17 N	98.25 W
Johnson Creek ≃	268	44.58 N	115.30 W
Johnsondale	270	35.58 N	118.32 W
Johnson Draw ∨, TX	262	31.58 N	101.41 W
Johnson Draw ∨, TX	262	30.08 N	101.07 W
Johnsons Crossing	246	60.29 N	133.16 W
Johnsonville	258	33.49 N	79.27 W
Johnston, IA	256	41.40 N	93.42 W
Johnston, SC	258	33.50 N	81.48 W
Johnston City	260	37.49 N	88.56 W
Johnstone Strait Ұ	248	50.25 N	126.00 W
Johnstown, CO	264	40.20 N	104.54 W
Johnstown, NY	254	43.00 N	74.22 W
Johnstown, OH	254	40.09 N	82.41 W
Johnstown, PA	254	40.20 N	78.55 W
Joiner	260	35.31 N	90.09 W
Joliet, IL	260	41.32 N	88.05 W
Joliet, MT	268	45.29 N	108.58 W
Joliette	254	46.01 N	73.27 W
Jonathan Dickinson State Park ♠	258	27.01 N	80.08 W
Jones	262	35.34 N	97.17 W
Jonesboro, AR	260	35.50 N	90.42 W
Jonesboro, GA	258	33.32 N	84.21 W
Jonesboro, IL	260	37.27 N	89.16 W
Jonesboro, IN	260	40.29 N	85.38 W
Jonesboro, LA	260	32.15 N	92.43 W
Jonesboro, ME	254	44.40 N	67.35 W
Jonesboro, TN	258	36.18 N	82.28 W
Jonesburg	260	38.51 N	91.18 W
Jones Mill	260	34.27 N	92.50 W
Jonesport	254	44.32 N	67.36 W
Jones Sound Ұ	242	76.00 N	85.00 W
Jonestown	260	34.14 N	90.28 W
Jonesville, LA	260	31.38 N	91.49 W
Jonesville, MI	256	41.59 N	84.40 W
Jonesville, NC	258	36.15 N	80.51 W
Jonesville, SC	258	34.50 N	81.41 W
Jonesville, VA	258	36.41 N	83.07 W
Jonquière	252	48.24 N	71.15 W
Joplin, MO	260	37.06 N	94.31 W
Joplin, MT	268	48.34 N	110.46 W
Joppa	260	37.12 N	88.51 W
Jordan, MN	256	44.40 N	93.37 W
Jordan, MT	268	47.19 N	106.55 W
Jordan, NY	254	43.04 N	76.28 W
Jordan ≃	266	40.49 N	112.08 W
Jordan Bay C	252	43.45 N	65.12 W
Jordan Creek ≃	268	42.52 N	117.38 W
Jordan Valley	268	42.58 N	117.03 W
Jornado del Muerto ⇀[2]	266	33.20 N	106.50 W
Joseph	268	45.21 N	117.14 W
Joseph, Lac ⊜	242	52.45 N	65.15 W
Joseph, Lake ⊜	256	45.14 N	79.45 W
Joseph City	266	34.57 N	110.20 W
Joseph Creek ≃	268	46.03 N	117.01 W
Joshua	262	32.28 N	97.23 W
Joshua Tree	270	34.08 N	116.19 W
Joshua Tree National Monument ♠	270	33.55 N	116.00 W
Jourdanton	262	28.55 N	98.33 W
Joy	260	41.12 N	90.55 W
Joy, Mount ∧	246	63.46 N	132.55 W
Joyce	260	31.58 N	92.37 W
J. Percy Priest Lake ⊜[1]	260	36.05 N	86.30 W
Juan de Fuca, Strait of Ұ	244	48.18 N	124.00 W
Juan Perez Sound Ұ	248	52.30 N	131.18 W
Jubilee Lake ⊜	252	48.04 N	55.11 W
Jude Island I	252	47.15 N	54.59 W
Judique	252	45.52 N	61.30 W
Judith ≃	268	47.44 N	109.38 W
Judith Gap	268	46.41 N	109.45 W
Judith Mountains ⛰	268	47.12 N	109.15 W
Judith Peak ∧	268	47.13 N	109.13 W
Judson	258	34.50 N	82.27 W
Judsonia	260	35.16 N	91.38 W
Julesburg	264	40.59 N	102.16 W
Jumbo Peak ∧	270	36.12 N	114.11 W
Jump ≃	256	45.17 N	91.05 W
Jump, North Fork ≃	256	45.25 N	90.40 W
Jump, South Fork ≃	256	45.25 N	90.40 W
Junction, TX	262	30.29 N	99.46 W
Junction, UT	266	38.14 N	112.13 W
Junction City, AR	260	33.01 N	92.43 W
Junction City, KS	264	39.02 N	96.50 W
Junction City, KY	258	37.35 N	84.48 W
Junction City, OR	268	44.13 N	123.12 W
Juneau, AK	246	58.20 N	134.27 W
Juneau, WI	256	43.24 N	88.42 W
June Lake	270	37.47 N	119.04 W
Juniata	264	40.36 N	98.30 W
Juniata ≃	254	40.24 N	77.01 W
Junior	254	38.59 N	79.57 W
Juniper	252	46.33 N	67.13 W
Junipero Serra Peak ∧	270	36.08 N	121.25 W
Jupiter	258	26.56 N	80.06 W
Jupiter ≃	252	49.29 N	63.37 W
Juskatla	248	53.37 N	132.18 W

K

Kaaawa	272c	21.33 N	157.51 W
Kaala ∧	272c	21.31 N	158.09 W
Kaalaea	272c	21.28 N	157.51 W
Kaalualu Bay C	272	18.58 N	155.37 W
Kaapahu Bay C	272a	20.39 N	156.05 W
Kabenung Lake ⊜	256	48.16 N	85.00 W
Kabetogama Lake ⊜	256	48.28 N	92.59 W
Kabinakagami Lake ⊜	256	48.54 N	84.25 W
Kachemak Bay C	246	59.35 N	151.30 W
Kadoka	264	43.50 N	101.31 W
Kaegudeck Lake ⊜	252	48.07 N	55.11 W
Kaena Point ➤	272c	21.35 N	158.17 W
Kagalaska Island I	247a	51.47 N	176.23 W
Kagamil Island I	246	53.00 N	169.43 W
Kagawong Lake ⊜	256	45.49 N	82.18 W
Kahaluu	272c	21.28 N	157.50 W
Kahana Bay C	272c	21.34 N	157.52 W
Kahiu Point C	272a	21.13 N	156.58 W
Kahoka	260	40.25 N	91.43 W
Kahoolawe I	272a	20.33 N	156.37 W
Kahuku	272c	21.41 N	157.57 W
Kahuku Point ➤	272c	21.43 N	157.59 W
Kahului	272a	20.54 N	156.28 W
Kahului Airport ⊠	272a	20.54 N	156.26 W
Kahului Bay C	272a	20.54 N	156.28 W
Kaibab Gulch ∨	266	37.01 N	111.52 W
Kaibab Indian Reservation ⇀[4]	266	36.55 N	112.40 W
Kaibab Plateau ⛰[1]	266	36.30 N	112.15 W
Kaibito Plateau ⛰[1]	266	36.40 N	111.20 W
Kailua	272c	21.24 N	157.44 W
Kailua Bay C	272c	21.25 N	157.44 W
Kailua Kona	272	19.39 N	155.59 W
Kaiparowits Plateau ⛰[1]	266	37.20 N	111.15 W
Kaiwi Channel Ұ	272b	21.15 N	157.30 W
Kaiyuh Mountains ⛰	246	64.00 N	158.00 W
Kakagi Lake ⊜	250	49.13 N	93.52 W
Kaka Point ➤	272a	20.31 N	156.33 W
Kake	246	56.58 N	133.46 W
Kakhonak	246	59.26 N	154.51 W
Kakisa Lake ⊜	242	60.55 N	117.40 W
Kaktovik	246	70.08 N	143.37 W
Kakwa ≃	248	54.36 N	118.28 W
Kalae	272a	21.10 N	157.00 W
Ka Lae ➤	272	18.55 N	155.41 W
Kalaheo	272b	21.56 N	159.32 W
Kalama	268	46.01 N	122.51 W
Kalama ≃	268	46.02 N	122.52 W
Kalamalka Lake ⊜	248	50.09 N	119.22 W
Kalamazoo	256	42.17 N	85.32 W
Kalamazoo ≃	256	42.40 N	86.10 W
Kalapana	272	19.22 N	154.58 W
Kalaupapa	272a	21.11 N	156.59 W
Kalaupapa Peninsula ➤[1]	272a	21.13 N	156.58 W
Kaleden	248	49.23 N	119.35 W
Kalgin Island I	246	60.28 N	151.55 W
Kalihiwai ≃	272b	22.13 N	159.26 W
Kalispell	268	48.12 N	114.19 W
Kalkaska	256	44.44 N	85.11 W
Kalliecahoolie Lake ⊜	250	54.14 N	95.29 W
Kalohi Channel Ұ	272a	21.00 N	156.56 W
Kaloli Point ➤	272	19.38 N	154.57 W
Kalona	256	41.29 N	91.43 W
Kalone Peak ∧	248	52.38 N	126.37 W
Kalskag	246	61.30 N	160.23 W
Kaltag	246	64.20 N	158.44 W
Kamaiki Point ➤	272a	20.46 N	156.50 W
Kamakou ∧	272a	21.07 N	156.52 W
Kamaniskeg Lake ⊜	256	45.25 N	77.42 W
Kamas	266	40.38 N	111.17 W
Kamatsi Lake ⊜	250	56.10 N	102.15 W
Kamay	262	33.51 N	98.48 W
Kamiah	268	46.14 N	116.02 W
Kamiak Butte ∧	268	46.52 N	117.10 W
Kamilukuak Lake ⊜	242	62.22 N	101.40 W
Kaminak Lake ⊜	242	62.10 N	95.00 W
Kaminuriak Lake ⊜	242	63.00 N	95.40 W
Kamishak Bay C	246	59.15 N	153.45 W
Kamloops	248	50.40 N	120.20 W
Kamloops Indian Reserve ⇀[4]	248	50.42 N	120.20 W
Kamloops Lake ⊜	248	50.43 N	120.33 W
Kamohio Bay C	272a	20.31 N	156.36 W
Kampsville	260	39.18 N	90.37 W
Kamsack	250	51.34 N	101.54 W
Kamuchawie Lake ⊜	250	56.18 N	101.59 W
Kamuela (Waimea)	272	20.01 N	155.41 W
Kanaaupscow ≃	242	53.39 N	77.09 W
Kanab	266	37.03 N	112.32 W
Kanab Creek ≃	266	36.24 N	112.38 W
Kanab Plateau ⛰[1]	266	36.40 N	112.45 W
Kanaga Island I	247a	51.45 N	177.10 W
Kanaga Volcano ∧[1]	247a	51.50 N	177.09 W
Kanairiktok ≃	242	55.05 N	60.20 W
Kananaskis ≃	248	51.05 N	115.03 W
Kanapou Bay C	272a	20.33 N	156.33 W
Kanarraville	266	37.32 N	113.11 W
Kanawha	256	42.56 N	93.48 W
Kanawha ≃	254	38.50 N	82.08 W
Kandahar	250	51.46 N	104.21 W
Kandik ≃	246	65.24 N	142.34 W
Kane, IL	260	39.11 N	90.21 W
Kane, PA	254	41.40 N	78.49 W
Kaneilio Point ➤	272c	21.27 N	158.12 W
Kanektok ≃	246	59.45 N	161.55 W
Kaneohe	272c	21.25 N	157.48 W
Kaneohe Bay C	272c	21.28 N	157.49 W
Kaneohe Bay Marine Corps Air Station ■	272c	21.27 N	157.46 W
Kankakee	260	41.07 N	87.52 W
Kankakee ≃	256	41.23 N	88.16 W
Kannapolis	258	35.30 N	80.37 W
Kanopolis	264	38.43 N	98.09 W

Symbols in the index entries are identified on page 273.

Name	Page	Lat °′	Long °′
Kanopolis Lake ⊜[1]	264	38.38 N	98.00 W
Kanorado	264	39.20 N	102.02 W
Kanosh	266	38.48 N	112.26 W
Kansas	260	39.33 N	87.56 W
Kansas □[3], U.S.	244		
	264	38.45 N	98.15 W
Kansas ≃	264	39.07 N	94.36 W
Kansas City, KS	264	39.07 N	94.39 W
Kansas City, MO	260	39.05 N	94.35 W
Kantishna ≃	246	64.45 N	149.58 W
Kanuti ≃	246	66.26 N	153.02 W
Kapaa	272b	22.05 N	159.19 W
Kapikik Lake ⊜	250	51.32 N	91.57 W
Kapiskau ≃	242	52.47 N	81.55 W
Kaplan	260	30.00 N	92.17 W
Kaposvar Creek ≃	250	50.31 N	101.55 W
Kapuskasing	242	49.25 N	82.26 W
Kapuskasing ≃	242	49.49 N	82.00 W
Kapuskasing Lake ⊜	256	48.30 N	82.55 W
Karloske ≃	250	55.41 N	93.56 W
Karlstad	264	48.35 N	96.31 W
Karluk	246	57.34 N	154.28 W
Karnack	260	32.40 N	94.10 W
Karnak	260	37.18 N	88.58 W
Karnes City	262	28.53 N	97.54 W
Karsakuwigamak Lake ⊜	250	56.22 N	99.30 W
Karthaus	254	41.07 N	78.07 W
Kasaan	246	55.32 N	132.24 W
Kasba Lake ⊜	242	60.18 N	102.07 W
Kashabowie Lake ⊜	256	48.42 N	90.25 W
Kashegelok	246	60.50 N	157.50 W
Kashunuk ≃	246	61.18 N	165.36 W
Kasigluk	246	60.52 N	162.32 W
Kasilof	246	60.23 N	151.18 W
Kaskaskia ≃	260	37.59 N	89.56 W
Kaslo	248	49.55 N	116.55 W
Kasota	256	44.18 N	93.57 W
Kasson	256	44.03 N	92.45 W
Katahdin, Mount ▲	254	45.55 N	68.55 W
Katalla	246	60.12 N	144.31 W
Kateel ≃	246	65.28 N	157.35 W
Katepwa Beach	250	50.42 N	103.38 W
Kates Needle ▲	242	57.03 N	132.03 W
Katimik Lake ⊜	250	52.54 N	99.22 W
Katmai, Mount ▲	246	58.17 N	154.56 W
Katmai National Park ♠	246	58.30 N	155.00 W
Kauai □[6]	272b	21.59 N	159.22 W
Kauai ▮	272b	22.00 N	159.30 W
Kauai Channel ⊔	272b	21.45 N	158.50 W
Kau Desert ◆[2]	272	19.21 N	155.19 W
Kaufman	262	32.35 N	96.19 W
Kauiki Head ➤	272a	20.45 N	155.59 W
Kaukauna	256	44.17 N	88.17 W
Kaulakahi Channel ⊔	272b	22.00 N	159.53 W
Kaumakani	272b	21.06 N	157.02 W
Kaumalapau	272a	20.47 N	156.59 W
Kaunakakai	272a	21.06 N	157.01 W
Kaununui Point ➤	272b	21.56 N	160.10 W
Kaw	262	36.46 N	96.50 W
Kawagama Lake ⊜	256	45.18 N	78.45 W
Kawaihae Bay ⊂	272	20.02 N	155.50 W
Kawaihoa Point ➤	272b	21.47 N	160.12 W
Kawaikini ▲	272b	22.05 N	159.29 W
Kawailoa	272c	21.36 N	158.05 W
Kawailoa Beach	272c	21.37 N	158.05 W
Kawich Peak ▲	270	37.58 N	116.27 W
Kawich Range ⛰	270	37.40 N	116.30 W
Kawinaw Lake ⊜	250	52.52 N	99.30 W
Kaw Lake ⊜[1]	262	36.55 N	96.57 W
Kawnipi Lake ⊜	256	48.24 N	91.14 W
Kayak Island ▮	246	59.52 N	144.30 W
Kaycee	268	43.43 N	106.38 W
Kayenta	266	36.42 N	110.16 W
Kay Point ➤	246	69.18 N	138.22 W
Kaysville	266	41.02 N	111.56 W
Kazan ≃	242	64.02 N	95.30 W
Kazan Lake ⊜	250	55.33 N	108.21 W
Keaau	272	19.37 N	155.02 W
Keahole Point ➤	272	19.44 N	156.03 W
Kealaikahiki Channel ⊔	272a	20.37 N	156.50 W
Kealaikahiki Point ➤	272a	20.32 N	156.42 W
Kealakekua Bay ⊂	272	19.28 N	155.56 W
Kealia	272b	22.06 N	159.19 W
Keams Canyon	266	35.49 N	110.12 W
Keanae	272a	20.52 N	156.09 W
Keanapapa Point ➤	272a	20.54 N	157.04 W
Kearney, MO	260	39.22 N	94.22 W
Kearney, NE	264	40.42 N	99.05 W
Kearns	266	40.39 N	111.59 W
Kearny	266	33.03 N	110.55 W
Kechika ≃	246	59.36 N	127.05 W
Kedgwick	252	47.39 N	67.21 W
Keefers	248	50.02 N	121.33 W
Keele ≃	242	64.24 N	124.50 W
Keele Peak ▲	246	63.26 N	130.19 W
Keeley Lake ⊜	250	54.54 N	108.08 W
Keels	252	48.36 N	53.24 W
Keene, KY	258	37.57 N	84.38 W
Keene, NH	254	42.56 N	72.17 W
Keene, TX	262	32.24 N	97.20 W
Keeney Knob ▲	258	37.47 N	80.42 W
Keeseville	254	44.30 N	73.29 W
Keesler Air Force Base ■	260	30.26 N	88.55 W
Keewatin, ON	250	49.46 N	94.34 W
Keewatin, MN	256	47.24 N	93.05 W
Keewatin □[5]	242	65.00 N	95.00 W
Kégashka, Lac ⊜	252	50.20 N	61.25 W
Kegaska	252	50.12 N	61.17 W
Keglo, Baie ⊂	242	59.10 N	65.50 W
Keg River	242	57.48 N	117.52 W
Kehiwin Indian Reserve ◆[4]	250	54.07 N	110.48 W
Keiser	260	35.41 N	90.06 W
Keith Arm ⊂	242	65.20 N	122.15 W
Keithley Creek	248	52.45 N	121.24 W
Keithsburg	260	41.06 N	90.56 W
Keizer	268	44.57 N	123.01 W
Kejimkujik National Park ♠	252	44.21 N	65.18 W
Kekaha	272b	21.58 N	159.43 W
Kekek ≃	256	48.24 N	75.48 W
Kekertaluk Island ▮	242	68.10 N	66.30 W
Kekurnoi, Cape ➤	246	57.44 N	155.15 W
Keller Lake ⊜, NT	242	64.00 N	121.30 W
Keller Lake ⊜, SK	250	56.04 N	106.46 W
Kellett, Cape ➤	242	71.59 N	125.34 W
Kelleys Island ▮	254	41.36 N	82.42 W
Kelliher	250	51.15 N	103.44 W
Kellogg, ID	268	47.32 N	116.07 W
Kellogg, IA	256	41.43 N	92.54 W
Kellogg, MN	256	44.18 N	91.59 W
Kelly Air Force Base ■	262	29.24 N	98.35 W
Kelly Lake ⊜	246	65.30 N	126.10 W
Kellyville	262	35.57 N	96.13 W
Kelowna	248	49.53 N	119.29 W
Kelsey Bay	248	50.24 N	125.57 W
Kelsey Lake ⊜	250	53.37 N	101.02 W
Kelseyville	270	38.59 N	122.50 W
Kelso	268	46.09 N	122.54 W
Keltie Inlet ⊂	242	64.28 N	73.28 W
Kelvington	250	52.10 N	103.30 W
Kemah	262	29.32 N	95.01 W
Kemano	248	53.34 N	127.56 W
Kemmerer	268	41.48 N	110.32 W
Kemp	262	32.26 N	96.14 W
Kemp, Lake ⊜[1]	262	33.45 N	99.13 W
Kempner	262	31.05 N	98.00 W
Kempt, Lac ⊜	242	47.25 N	74.22 W
Kemptville	254	45.01 N	75.38 W
Kenai	246	60.33 N	151.15 W
Kenai Fjords National Park ♠	246	59.45 N	150.00 W
Kenai Mountains ⛰	246	60.00 N	150.00 W
Kenai Peninsula ➤[1]	246	60.10 N	150.00 W
Kenansville, FL	258	27.53 N	80.59 W
Kenansville, NC	258	34.58 N	77.58 W
Kenaston	250	51.30 N	106.18 W
Kenbridge	258	36.58 N	78.08 W
Kendal	250	50.15 N	103.37 W
Kendall, FL	258	25.41 N	80.19 W
Kendall, WI	256	43.48 N	90.21 W
Kendall, Cape ➤	242	63.36 N	87.09 W
Kendallville	260	41.27 N	85.16 W
Kendrick, FL	258	29.22 N	82.12 W
Kendrick, ID	268	46.37 N	116.39 W
Kenedy	262	28.49 N	97.51 W
Kenesaw	264	40.37 N	98.39 W
Kenilworth	266	39.42 N	110.47 W
Kenly	258	35.36 N	78.07 W
Kenmare	264	48.40 N	102.05 W
Kennard	262	31.22 N	95.11 W
Kennebec	264	43.54 N	99.52 W
Kennebec ≃	254	44.00 N	69.50 W
Kennebecasis Bay ⊂	252	45.25 N	66.00 W
Kennebunk	254	43.23 N	70.33 W
Kennedy	260	33.35 N	87.59 W
Kennedy, Cape → Canaveral, Cape ➤	258	28.27 N	80.32 W
Kennedy, Mount ▲, BC	248	50.49 N	125.33 W
Kennedy, Mount ▲, YK	246	60.30 N	139.00 W
Kennedy Entrance ⊔	246	59.00 N	152.00 W
Kennedy Lake ⊜	248	49.05 N	125.40 W
Kenner	260	29.59 N	90.15 W
Kennetcook	252	45.11 N	63.44 W
Kennett	260	36.14 N	90.03 W
Kennett Square	254	39.51 N	75.43 W
Kennewick	268	46.12 N	119.07 W
Kenney Dam ◆[6]	248	53.37 N	124.58 W
Kénogami	252	48.26 N	71.14 W
Kenogami ≃	242	51.06 N	84.28 W
Kenogamissi Lake ⊜	256	48.15 N	81.31 W
Keno Hill	246	63.55 N	135.18 W
Kenora	250	49.47 N	94.29 W
Kenosha	256	42.35 N	87.49 W
Kenova	254	38.24 N	82.35 W
Kensal	264	47.18 N	98.44 W
Kensett	260	35.12 N	91.41 W
Kensington, PE	252	46.26 N	63.38 W
Kensington, KS	264	39.46 N	99.02 W
Kensington Park	258	27.22 N	82.31 W
Kent, OH	254	41.09 N	81.22 W
Kent, WA	268	47.23 N	122.14 W
Kent Bay ⊂	242	69.59 N	96.02 W
Kentland	260	40.46 N	87.27 W
Kenton, MI	256	46.28 N	88.54 W
Kenton, OH	254	40.39 N	83.36 W
Kenton, TN	260	36.12 N	89.01 W
Kent Peninsula ➤[1]	242	68.30 N	107.00 W
Kentucky □[3], U.S.	244		
	260	37.30 N	85.15 W
Kentucky ≃	260	38.41 N	85.11 W
Kentucky, Middle Fork ≃	258	37.35 N	83.40 W
Kentucky, North Fork ≃	258	37.34 N	83.42 W
Kentucky, South Fork ≃	258	37.34 N	83.42 W
Kentucky Lake ⊜[1]	244	36.25 N	88.05 W
Kentville	252	45.05 N	64.30 W
Kentwood	260	30.56 N	90.31 W
Kenyon	256	44.16 N	92.59 W
Keokuk	256	40.24 N	91.24 W
Keosauqua	256	40.44 N	91.58 W
Keota, IA	256	41.21 N	91.57 W
Keota, OK	260	35.15 N	94.55 W
Keowee, Lake ⊜[1]	258	34.45 N	82.55 W
Kerby	268	42.12 N	123.39 W
Keremeos	248	49.12 N	119.50 W
Kerens	262	32.08 N	96.14 W
Kerkhoven	264	45.12 N	95.19 W
Kerman	270	36.43 N	120.04 W
Kermit	262	31.51 N	103.06 W
Kermode, Mount ▲	248	52.57 N	131.51 W
Kern ≃	270	35.13 N	119.17 W
Kern, South Fork ≃	270	35.40 N	118.27 W
Kernersville	258	36.07 N	80.04 W
Kernville	270	35.43 N	118.26 W
Kerrobert	250	51.55 N	109.08 W
Kerr Reservoir ⊜[1]	244	36.35 N	70.28 W
Kerrville	262	30.03 N	99.08 W
Kershaw	258	34.33 N	80.35 W
Kersley	248	52.49 N	122.25 W
Kesagami Lake ⊜	242	50.23 N	80.15 W
Keshena	256	44.52 N	88.38 W
Ketchikan	246	55.21 N	131.35 W
Ketchum	268	43.41 N	114.22 W
Kettering	254	39.41 N	84.10 W
Kettle ≃	248	48.42 N	118.07 W
Kettle Creek ≃	254	41.18 N	77.51 W
Kettle Falls	268	48.36 N	118.03 W
Kettle River Range ⛰	268	48.30 N	118.40 W
Keuka Lake ⊜	254	42.27 N	77.10 W
Kevin	268	48.45 N	111.58 W
Kewanee	260	41.14 N	89.56 W
Kewanna	260	41.01 N	86.25 W
Kewaunee	256	44.27 N	87.30 W
Keweenaw Bay ⊂	256	46.56 N	88.23 W
Keweenaw Peninsula ➤[1]	256	47.12 N	88.25 W
Keweenaw Point ➤	256	47.30 N	87.50 W
Keya Paha ≃	264	42.54 N	99.00 W
Keyes	262	36.49 N	102.15 W
Keyhole Reservoir ⊜[1]	264	44.21 N	104.51 W
Keyhole State Park ♠	264	44.19 N	104.48 W
Key Largo	258	25.04 N	80.28 W
Key Largo ▮	258	25.16 N	80.19 W
Keyser	254	39.26 N	78.59 W
Keystone, IA	256	42.00 N	92.12 W
Keystone, SD	264	43.54 N	103.25 W
Keystone, WV	258	37.25 N	81.27 W
Keystone Lake ⊜[1]	262	36.15 N	96.25 W
Keystone Peak ▲	266	31.53 N	111.13 W
Keysville	258	37.04 N	78.29 W
Keytesville	260	39.26 N	92.56 W
Key West	258	24.33 N	81.48 W
Key West Naval Air Station ■	258	24.34 N	81.41 W
Kgun Lake ⊜	246	61.32 N	163.45 W
Kiamichi ≃	262	33.57 N	95.14 W
Kiana	246	66.59 N	160.25 W
Kickapoo ≃	256	43.05 N	90.53 W
Kickapoo Creek ≃, IL	260	40.08 N	89.27 W
Kickapoo Creek ≃, TX	262	31.31 N	99.58 W
Kickapoo Creek ≃, TX	262	32.16 N	95.28 W
Kicking Horse Pass)(	248	51.27 N	116.18 W
Kiel	256	43.55 N	88.02 W
Kiester	256	43.32 N	93.42 W
Kigun, Cape ➤	246	52.00 N	175.21 W
Kihei	272a	20.47 N	156.28 W
Kiholo Bay ⊂	272	19.52 N	155.56 W
Kikerk Lake ⊜	242	67.20 N	113.20 W
Kilauea	272b	22.13 N	159.25 W
Kilauea Crater •[6]	272	19.25 N	155.17 W
Kilauea Point ➤	272b	22.14 N	159.24 W
Kilbuck Mountains ⛰	246	60.30 N	159.45 W
Kildare, Cape ➤	252	46.52 N	63.58 W
Kildonan	248	49.00 N	125.00 W
Kilgore	260	32.23 N	94.53 W
Kilian Island ▮	242	73.35 N	107.53 W
Killaloe Station	256	45.33 N	77.25 W
Killam	250	52.47 N	111.51 W
Killarney, MB	250	49.12 N	99.42 W
Killarney, ON	256	45.58 N	81.31 W
Killarney Provincial Park ♠	256	46.05 N	81.30 W
Killbuck	254	40.30 N	81.59 W
Killdeer	264	47.22 N	102.45 W
Killeen	262	31.08 N	97.44 W
Killen	260	34.52 N	87.32 W
Killik ≃	246	69.00 N	153.58 W
Killington Mountain ▲	254	43.36 N	72.49 W
Killpecker Creek ≃	268	41.35 N	109.14 W
Kilmarnock	258	37.43 N	76.23 W
Kilmichael	260	33.27 N	89.34 W
Kim	264	37.15 N	103.21 W
Kimball, MN	264	45.19 N	94.18 W
Kimball, NE	264	41.14 N	103.40 W
Kimball, SD	264	43.45 N	98.57 W
Kimball, Mount ▲	246	63.14 N	144.39 W
Kimberley	248	49.41 N	115.59 W
Kimberling City	260	36.38 N	93.28 W
Kimberly, ID	268	42.32 N	114.22 W
Kimberly, WI	256	44.17 N	88.20 W
Kimiwan Lake ⊜	248	55.45 N	116.54 W
Kim-me-ni-oli Wash ∨	266	36.07 N	108.11 W
Kimsquit	248	52.49 N	126.58 W
Kinbasket Lake ⊜	248	51.58 N	118.03 W
Kincaid, SK	250	49.39 N	107.00 W
Kincaid, IL	260	39.35 N	89.25 W
Kincaid, Lake ⊜[1]	260	39.35 N	89.30 W
Kincardine	256	44.11 N	81.38 W
Kinchafoonee Creek ≃	258	31.38 N	84.10 W
Kincheloe Air Force Base ■	256	46.15 N	84.28 W
Kincolith	248	55.00 N	129.57 W
Kinde	256	43.56 N	83.00 W
Kinder	260	30.29 N	92.51 W
Kindersley	250	51.27 N	109.10 W
Kindred	264	46.39 N	97.01 W
Kineo, Mount ▲	254	45.42 N	69.44 W
King	258	36.17 N	80.22 W
King and Queen Court House	258	37.40 N	76.53 W
King City, ON	256	43.56 N	79.32 W
King City, CA	270	36.13 N	121.08 W
King City, MO	260	40.03 N	94.31 W
Kingcome Inlet ⊂	248	50.50 N	126.10 W
King Cove	246	55.04 N	162.19 W
Kingfield	254	44.57 N	70.09 W
Kingfisher	262	35.52 N	97.56 W
King George	254	38.16 N	77.11 W
King George, Mount ▲	248	50.35 N	115.24 W
King George Islands ▮▮	242	57.20 N	78.25 W
King Hill	268	43.00 N	115.12 W
King Island ▮, BC	248	52.12 N	127.42 W
King Island ▮, AK	246	64.58 N	168.05 W
King Lear Peak ▲	270	41.12 N	118.34 W
Kingman, AZ	266	35.12 N	114.04 W
Kingman, KS	264	37.39 N	98.07 W
Kingman, ME	254	45.33 N	68.12 W
King Mountain ▲, BC	246	58.17 N	128.54 W
King Mountain ▲, OR	268	43.49 N	118.52 W
King Mountain ▲, OR	268	42.42 N	123.14 W
King Peak ▲	270	40.10 N	124.08 W
Kings	260	32.26 N	90.50 W
Kings ≃, AR	260	36.29 N	93.35 W
Kings ≃, CA	270	36.03 N	119.49 W
Kings ≃, NV	270	41.31 N	118.08 W
Kings, Middle Fork ≃	270	36.50 N	118.52 W
Kings, North Fork ≃	270	36.52 N	119.08 W
King Salmon	246	58.14 N	157.24 W
King Salmon ≃	246	58.15 N	157.30 W
Kings Beach	270	39.14 N	120.01 W
Kingsburg	270	36.31 N	119.33 W
Kings Canyon National Park ♠	270	36.48 N	118.30 W
Kingsford	256	45.48 N	88.04 W
Kingsgate	248	49.00 N	116.11 W
Kingsland, AR	260	33.52 N	92.18 W
Kingsland, GA	258	30.48 N	81.41 W
Kingsland, TX	262	30.40 N	98.26 W
Kingsley, IA	264	42.35 N	95.58 W
Kingsley, MI	256	44.35 N	85.32 W
Kingsley Dam ◆[6]	264	41.11 N	101.39 W
Kings Mountain	258	35.15 N	81.20 W
Kings Mountain National Military Park ♠	258	35.07 N	81.33 W
Kings Peak ▲	266	40.46 N	110.22 W
King's Point	252	49.35 N	56.11 W
Kingsport	258	36.32 N	82.33 W
Kingston, NS	252	44.59 N	64.57 W
Kingston, ON	256	44.18 N	76.34 W
Kingston, GA	258	34.15 N	84.57 W
Kingston, MA	254	41.59 N	70.43 W
Kingston, MO	260	39.39 N	94.02 W
Kingston, NY	254	41.56 N	74.00 W
Kingston, OH	254	39.28 N	82.55 W
Kingston, OK	262	34.00 N	96.43 W
Kingston, PA	254	41.16 N	75.54 W
Kingston, TN	258	35.52 N	84.31 W
Kingstree	258	33.40 N	79.50 W
Kingsville, ON	256	42.02 N	82.45 W
Kingsville, TX	262	27.31 N	97.52 W
Kingsville Naval Air Station ■	262	27.31 N	97.47 W
King William	258	37.41 N	77.01 W
King William Island ▮	242	69.00 N	97.30 W
Kingwood	254	39.28 N	79.41 W
Kinistino	250	52.57 N	105.00 W
Kinmundy	260	38.46 N	88.51 W
Kinnaird	248	49.17 N	117.39 W
Kinojévis ≃	256	48.23 N	78.21 W
Kinsley	264	37.55 N	99.25 W
Kinsman	254	41.27 N	80.36 W
Kinston, AL	260	31.13 N	86.11 W
Kinston, NC	258	35.16 N	77.35 W
Kinuseo Falls ⌞	248	54.47 N	121.12 W
Kinuso	248	55.20 N	115.25 W
Kinzua	268	44.59 N	120.03 W
Kinzua Creek ≃	254	41.47 N	78.50 W
Kinzua Dam ◆[6]	254	41.50 N	79.01 W
Kioshkokwi Lake ⊜	256	46.05 N	78.52 W
Kiowa, CO	264	39.21 N	104.28 W
Kiowa, KS	264	37.01 N	98.29 W
Kiowa, OK	262	34.43 N	95.54 W
Kiowa Creek ≃, U.S.	262	36.46 N	99.55 W
Kiowa Creek ≃, CO	264	40.20 N	104.05 W
Kipahigan Lake ⊜	250	55.20 N	101.55 W
Kipawa ≃	256	47.03 N	79.23 W
Kipawa, Lac ⊜	256	46.55 N	79.00 W
Kipawa, Parc de ♠	256	47.15 N	78.15 W
Kipling	250	50.10 N	102.38 W
Kipnuk	246	59.56 N	164.03 W
Kirbyville	260	30.40 N	93.54 W
Kirkland, IL	256	42.06 N	88.51 W
Kirkland, TX	262	34.23 N	100.04 W
Kirkland, WA	268	47.41 N	122.12 W
Kirkland Creek ≃	266	34.32 N	113.00 W
Kirkland Lake	256	48.09 N	80.02 W
Kirklin	260	40.12 N	86.22 W
Kirkness Lake ⊜	250	51.32 N	93.56 W
Kirkpatrick Lake ⊜	250	51.52 N	111.18 W
Kirksville	260	40.12 N	92.35 W
Kirkwood, IL	256	40.52 N	90.45 W
Kirkwood, MO	260	38.35 N	90.24 W
Kirtland	266	36.44 N	108.21 W
Kirtland Air Force Base ■	266	35.02 N	106.37 W
Kirwin	264	39.40 N	99.07 W
Kirwin Reservoir ⊜[1]	264	39.39 N	99.50 W
Kisaralik ≃	246	60.51 N	161.16 W
K.I. Sawyer Air Force Base ■	256	46.21 N	87.25 W
Kisbey	250	49.38 N	102.41 W
Kishikas ≃	250	52.45 N	91.43 W
Kishwaukee ≃	256	42.11 N	89.08 W
Kiska Island ▮	247a	52.00 N	177.30 E
Kiskatinaw ≃	248	56.06 N	120.08 W
Kiska Volcano ▲[1]	247a	52.07 N	177.36 E
Kiski Lake ⊜	250	54.46 N	98.55 W
Kiskittogisu Lake ⊜	250	54.13 N	98.20 W
Kiskitto Lake ⊜	250	54.16 N	98.34 W
Kispiox	248	55.21 N	127.41 W
Kispiox ≃	248	55.16 N	127.41 W
Kispiox Mountain ▲	248	55.25 N	127.57 W
Kisseynew Lake ⊜	250	54.58 N	101.35 W
Kissimmee	258	28.18 N	81.24 W
Kissimmee ≃	258	27.10 N	80.53 W
Kissimmee, Lake ⊜	258	27.55 N	81.16 W
Kississing	250	55.07 N	101.07 W
Kississing Lake ⊜	250	55.10 N	101.20 W
Kistigan Lake ⊜	250	54.38 N	92.37 W
Kit Carson	264	38.46 N	102.48 W
Kitchener	256	43.27 N	80.29 W
Kitimat	248	54.03 N	128.33 W
Kitimat ≃	248	54.06 N	128.38 W
Kitimat Ranges ⛰	248	53.30 N	128.50 W
Kitlope ≃	248	53.10 N	127.45 W
Kitlope Lake ⊜	248	53.07 N	127.47 W
Kitscoty	250	53.20 N	110.20 W
Kittanning	254	40.49 N	79.32 W
Kittery	254	43.05 N	70.45 W
Kittery Point	254	43.05 N	70.41 W
Kittitas	268	46.59 N	120.25 W
Kitt Peak National Observatory ✲[3]	266	31.58 N	111.36 W
Kitwanga	248	55.06 N	128.03 W
Kitwangar Indian Reserve ◆[4]	248	55.06 N	128.04 W
Kivalina	246	67.59 N	164.33 W
Kiwalik	246	66.02 N	161.50 W
Kiyiu Lake ⊜	250	51.38 N	108.55 W
Klahoose Indian Reserve ◆[4]	248	50.31 N	124.19 W
Klamath	270	41.32 N	124.02 W
Klamath ≃	244	41.33 N	124.04 W
Klamath Falls	268	42.13 N	121.46 W
Klamath Marsh ☰	268	42.54 N	121.44 W
Klamath Mountains ⛰	268	41.40 N	123.20 W
Klatt Road	246	61.05 N	149.48 W
Klawock	246	55.33 N	133.06 W
Kleena Kleene	248	51.58 N	124.59 W
Klemme	256	43.01 N	93.36 W
Klemtu	248	52.36 N	128.31 W
Klickitat	268	45.49 N	121.09 W
Klickitat ≃	268	45.42 N	121.17 W
Klinaklini ≃	248	51.05 N	125.36 W
Klondike □[9]	246	63.30 N	139.00 W
Klondike ≃	246	64.05 N	139.26 W
Klotz, Lac ⊜	242	60.32 N	73.40 W
Kluane Lake ⊜	246	61.15 N	138.40 W
Klukwan	246	59.24 N	135.54 W
Klutina Lake ⊜	246	61.37 N	146.55 W
Knapp	256	44.57 N	92.05 W
Kneehills Creek ≃	248	51.30 N	112.50 W
Knee Lake ⊜, MB	250	55.03 N	94.40 W
Knee Lake ⊜, SK	250	55.51 N	107.00 W
Knickerbocker	262	31.16 N	100.38 W
Knife ≃	264	47.20 N	101.23 W
Knife Lake ⊜	250	53.47 N	91.20 W
Knife River Indian Villages National Historical Site ⊥	264	47.21 N	101.23 W
Knight Inlet ⊂	248	50.41 N	125.40 W
Knight Island ▮	246	60.20 N	147.45 W
Knights Landing	270	38.48 N	121.43 W
Knightstown	260	39.48 N	85.32 W
Knik Arm ⊂	246	61.25 N	149.45 W
Knippa	262	29.18 N	99.38 W
Knob Noster	260	38.46 N	93.33 W
Knox, IN	260	41.18 N	86.37 W
Knox, PA	254	41.14 N	79.32 W
Knox, Cape ➤	248	54.11 N	133.04 W
Knox City	262	33.25 N	99.49 W
Knoxville, GA	258	32.44 N	84.01 W
Knoxville, IL	256	40.55 N	90.17 W
Knoxville, IA	256	41.19 N	93.06 W
Knoxville, TN	258	35.58 N	83.56 W
Kobuk	246	66.54 N	156.52 W
Kobuk ≃	246	66.45 N	161.00 W
Kobuk Valley National Park ♠	246	67.20 N	159.00 W
Koch Island ▮	242	69.38 N	78.15 W
Koch Peak ▲	268	45.02 N	111.28 W
Kodiak	246	57.48 N	152.23 W
Kodiak Island ▮	246	57.30 N	153.30 W
Kofa Mountains ⛰	266	33.20 N	114.00 W
Kogaluc ≃	242	59.40 N	77.35 W
Kogaluc, Baie ⊂	242	59.20 N	77.50 W
Kogaluk ≃	242	56.12 N	61.44 W
Kohala Mountains ⛰	272	20.05 N	155.45 W
Kohatk Wash ∨	266	32.38 N	111.55 W
Kohler	256	43.44 N	87.46 W
Koidern	246	61.58 N	140.25 W
Kokanee Glacier Provincial Park ♠	248	49.47 N	117.10 W
Kokee State Park ♠	272b	22.08 N	159.40 W
Koko Head ➤	272c	21.16 N	157.42 W
Kokole Point ➤	272b	21.59 N	159.46 W
Kokolik ≃	246	69.46 N	165.00 W
Kokomo, HI	272a	20.53 N	156.19 W
Kokomo, IN	260	40.29 N	86.08 W
Kokomo, MS	260	31.12 N	90.00 W
Kokrines	246	64.56 N	154.42 W
Kokrines Hills ⛰[2]	246	65.15 N	154.00 W
Koksoak ≃	242	58.32 N	68.10 W
Koliganek	246	59.48 N	157.25 W
Koloa	272b	21.55 N	159.28 W
Kona Coast •[2]	272	19.25 N	155.55 W
Konawa	262	34.58 N	96.45 W
Kondiaronk, Lac ⊜	256	46.56 N	76.45 W
Kongakut ≃	246	69.48 N	141.50 W
Kongiganak	246	59.58 N	162.45 W
Koocanusa, Lake ⊜[1]	248	49.00 N	115.10 W
Koolau Range ⛰	272c	21.35 N	158.00 W
Koontz Lake	260	41.25 N	86.29 W
Koosharem	266	38.31 N	111.53 W
Kooskia	268	46.09 N	115.59 W
Kootenai ≃	242	49.18 N	117.39 W
Kootenay (Kootenai) ≃	248	49.15 N	117.39 W
Kootenay Indian Reserve ◆[4]	248	49.37 N	115.45 W
Kootenay Lake ⊜	248	49.35 N	116.50 W
Kootenay National Park ♠	248	51.00 N	116.00 W
Korner	248	48.59 N	112.15 W
Korovin Island ▮	246	55.25 N	160.15 W
Korovin Volcano ▲[1]	246	52.22 N	174.10 W
Kosciusko	260	32.58 N	89.35 W
Koshkonong	260	36.36 N	91.39 W
Koshkonong, Lake ⊜	256	42.52 N	88.58 W
Koskaecodde Lake ⊜	252	48.00 N	55.20 W
Kosse	262	31.18 N	96.38 W
Kotcho Lake ⊜	242	59.05 N	121.10 W
Kotlik	246	63.02 N	163.33 W
Kotzebue	246	66.53 N	162.39 W
Kotzebue Sound ⊔	246	66.20 N	163.00 W
Kouchibouguac Bay ⊂	252	46.50 N	64.50 W
Kouchibouguac National Park ♠	252	46.50 N	65.00 W
Kougarok Mountain ▲	246	65.41 N	165.13 W
Koukdjuak ≃	242	66.45 N	73.09 W
Kountze	260	30.23 N	94.19 W
Kouts	260	41.19 N	87.02 W
Koyuk	246	64.56 N	161.08 W
Koyuk ≃	246	64.55 N	161.12 W
Koyukuk	246	64.53 N	157.43 W
Koyukuk ≃	246	64.56 N	157.30 W
Koyukuk, Middle Fork ≃	246	67.03 N	151.04 W
Koyukuk, North Fork ≃	246	67.03 N	151.04 W
Koyukuk, South Fork ≃	246	66.35 N	151.57 W
Krebs	262	34.56 N	95.43 W
Kremmling	266	40.03 N	106.24 W
Krenitzin Islands ▮▮	246	54.08 N	166.00 W
Kress	262	34.22 N	101.45 W
Krotz Springs	260	30.32 N	91.45 W
Krusenstern, Cape ➤	246	67.07 N	163.43 W
Krusenstern National Monument ♠	246	67.30 N	163.40 W
Kruzof Island ▮	246	57.10 N	135.40 W
Krydor	250	52.47 N	107.03 W
Kualapuu	272a	21.09 N	157.01 W
Kuee Ruins ⊥	272	19.21 N	155.23 W
Kugaluk ≃	246	69.10 N	131.00 W
Kugmallit Bay ⊂	246	69.33 N	133.25 W
Kuikui, Cape ➤	272a	20.36 N	156.35 W
Kuiu Island ▮	246	57.45 N	134.10 W
Kuk ≃	246	70.36 N	160.00 W
Kukaklek Lake ⊜	246	59.09 N	155.20 W
Kukpowruk ≃	246	69.35 N	163.00 W
Kukpuk ≃	246	68.23 N	166.20 W
Kula	272a	20.46 N	156.20 W
Kulik Lake ⊜	246	68.55 N	155.00 W
Kulm	264	46.24 N	98.57 W
Kumukahi, Cape ➤	272	19.31 N	154.49 W
Kuna	268	43.30 N	116.25 W
Kunghit Island ▮	248	52.06 N	131.04 W
Kunia	272c	21.29 N	158.07 W
Kuparuk ≃	246	70.25 N	148.55 W
Kupreanof Island ▮	246	56.50 N	133.30 W
Kupreanof Point ➤	246	55.34 N	159.35 W
Kurtistown	272	19.36 N	155.04 W
Kusawa Lake ⊜	246	60.20 N	136.15 W
Kuskokwim ≃	246	60.17 N	162.27 W
Kuskokwim, North Fork ≃	246	63.06 N	154.37 W
Kuskokwim, South Fork ≃	246	63.06 N	154.37 W
Kuskokwim Bay ⊂	246	59.45 N	162.25 W
Kuskokwim Mountains ⛰	246	62.30 N	156.00 W
Kutztown	254	40.31 N	75.47 W
Kuyuyukak, Cape ➤	246	56.54 N	156.50 W
Kuzitrin ≃	246	65.10 N	165.28 W
Kvichak Bay ⊂	246	58.48 N	157.30 W
Kwethluk	246	60.49 N	161.27 W
Kwethluk ≃	246	60.46 N	161.26 W
Kwigillingok	246	59.51 N	163.08 W
Kwiguk	246	62.45 N	164.28 W
Kyle, SK	250	50.50 N	108.02 W
Kyle, SD	264	43.26 N	102.10 W
Kyle, TX	262	29.59 N	97.53 W
Kyte ≃	260	42.00 N	89.19 W
Kyuquot	248	50.02 N	127.23 W
Kyuquot Sound ⊔	248	50.05 N	127.15 W
L			
Laau Point ➤	272a	21.06 N	157.19 W
Labadieville	260	29.50 N	90.57 W
La Baie	252	48.19 N	70.53 W
La Barge	268	42.16 N	110.12 W
La Barge Creek ≃	268	42.14 N	110.10 W
Labelle, PQ	254	46.16 N	74.44 W
La Belle, FL	258	26.46 N	81.26 W
La Belle, MO	260	40.07 N	91.55 W
Laberge, Lake ⊜	246	61.11 N	135.12 W
La Biche ≃	248	55.01 N	112.44 W
Labrador ◆[1]	242	54.00 N	62.00 W
Labrador Sea ▾[2]	242	57.00 N	53.00 W
Labrieville, Parc de ♠	252	49.20 N	69.40 W
La Broquerie	250	49.28 N	96.27 W
L'Acadie ≃	254	45.29 N	73.16 W
Lac Allard	252	50.38 N	63.28 W
La Canada	270	34.12 N	118.12 W
Lac Courte Oreilles Indian Reservation ◆[4]	256	45.55 N	91.19 W
Lac du Flambeau	256	45.58 N	89.53 W
Lac du Flambeau Indian Reservation ◆[4]	256	45.59 N	89.53 W
La Center	260	37.04 N	88.58 W
Lacey	268	47.07 N	122.49 W
Lachine	254	45.26 N	73.40 W
Lachkaltsap Indian Reserve ◆[4]	248	55.03 N	129.34 W
Lachute	254	45.38 N	74.20 W
La Cinta Creek ≃	262	35.24 N	104.06 W
Lackawanna	254	42.49 N	78.50 W
Lackawanna ≃	254	41.21 N	75.47 W
Lackland Air Force Base ■	262	29.27 N	98.37 W
Lacla Biche	250	54.46 N	111.58 W
Lac la Hache	248	51.49 N	121.28 W
Lac la Ronge Provincial Park ♠	250	55.14 N	104.45 W
Laclede, ID	248	49.58 N	116.45 W
Laclede, MO	260	39.47 N	93.10 W
Lac-Mégantic	254	45.36 N	70.53 W
Lacombe, AB	248	52.28 N	113.44 W
Lacombe, LA	260	30.19 N	89.58 W
Lacon	260	41.02 N	89.24 W
Lacona	256	41.12 N	93.23 W
Laconia	254	43.31 N	71.29 W
La Conner	268	48.23 N	122.30 W
Lacoochee	258	28.28 N	82.10 W
La Coste	262	29.19 N	98.49 W
Lac qui Parle ≃	264	45.01 N	95.53 W
Lac qui Parle, West Branch ≃	264	44.55 N	96.02 W
La Crescent	256	43.50 N	91.19 W
La Crosse, IN	260	41.19 N	86.53 W
La Crosse, KS	264	38.32 N	99.18 W
La Crosse, VA	258	36.42 N	78.06 W
Lacrosse, WA	268	46.49 N	117.53 W
La Crosse, WI	256	43.49 N	91.15 W
La Crosse ≃	256	43.49 N	91.16 W
Lac Seul	250	50.20 N	92.16 W
Lac Seul Indian Reserve ◆[4]	250	50.15 N	92.10 W
La Cygne	264	38.21 N	94.46 W
Ladd	260	41.23 N	89.13 W
Ladder Creek ≃	264	38.48 N	100.52 W
Laddonia	260	39.15 N	91.39 W
Ladner	248	49.05 N	123.05 W
Ladoga	260	39.55 N	86.48 W
Ladonia	262	33.25 N	95.57 W
Ladson	258	32.59 N	80.09 W
Ladue ≃	246	63.09 N	140.25 W
Lady Ann Strait ⊔	242	75.40 N	79.50 W
Lady Evelyn Lake ⊜	256	47.20 N	80.10 W
Ladysmith, BC	248	48.58 N	123.49 W
Ladysmith, WI	256	45.28 N	91.12 W
La Farge	256	43.35 N	90.38 W
Lafayette, AL	258	32.54 N	85.24 W
Lafayette, CA	270	37.54 N	122.07 W
Lafayette, CO	266	40.00 N	105.05 W
Lafayette, GA	258	34.42 N	85.17 W
Lafayette, IN	260	40.25 N	86.53 W
Lafayette, LA	260	30.14 N	92.01 W
Lafayette, MN	264	44.27 N	94.24 W
Lafayette, TN	260	36.32 N	86.01 W
Lafayette, Mount ▲	254	44.10 N	71.38 W
Lafayette Southwest	260	30.11 N	92.03 W
La Feria	262	26.09 N	97.50 W
Laflamme ≃	256	48.56 N	77.18 W
Laflèche	250	49.43 N	106.35 W
La Follette	258	36.23 N	84.07 W
La Fontaine	260	40.40 N	85.43 W
Lafourche, Bayou ≃	260	29.05 N	90.14 W
Lagarto Creek ≃	262	28.08 N	97.56 W
Lago, Mount ▲	268	48.51 N	120.32 W
La Grande	268	45.20 N	118.05 W
La Grande ≃	242	53.50 N	79.00 W
La Grange, GA	258	33.02 N	85.02 W
Lagrange, IN	260	41.39 N	85.25 W
La Grange, KY	260	38.24 N	85.23 W
La Grange, ME	254	45.10 N	68.51 W
La Grange, MO	260	40.03 N	91.35 W
La Grange, NC	258	35.19 N	77.47 W
La Grange, TX	262	29.54 N	96.52 W
Lagrange, WY	264	41.38 N	104.10 W
La Grue Bayou ≃	260	34.05 N	91.10 W
La Guadeloupe (Saint Évariste)	254	45.57 N	70.56 W
Laguna	266	35.02 N	107.23 W
Laguna Beach	270	33.33 N	117.51 W
Laguna Creek ≃	266	36.54 N	109.45 W
Laguna Dam ◆[6]	270	32.50 N	114.31 W
Laguna Indian Reservation ◆[4]	266	35.00 N	107.20 W
Lahaina	272a	20.52 N	156.41 W
La Harpe, IL	256	40.35 N	90.58 W
La Harpe, KS	264	37.55 N	95.18 W
La Have ≃	252	44.14 N	64.20 W
La Have Islands ▮▮	252	44.12 N	64.23 W
Lahontan Reservoir ⊜[1]	270	39.24 N	119.07 W
La Huerta	262	32.27 N	104.13 W
Laie	272c	21.39 N	157.56 W
L'Aigle Creek ≃	260	33.12 N	92.08 W

Symbols in the index entries are identified on page 273.

Name	Page	Lat ° ′	Long ° ′
Laingsburg	256	42.54 N	84.21 W
Laird Hill	260	32.21 N	94.54 W
La Jara	266	37.16 N	105.58 W
La Jara Canyon ∨	266	36.50 N	107.30 W
La Jara Creek ≃	266	37.22 N	105.46 W
Lajord	250	50.14 N	104.09 W
La Junta	264	37.59 N	103.33 W
Lake	260	32.21 N	89.20 W
Lake Alfred	258	28.05 N	81.44 W
Lake Andes	264	43.09 N	98.32 W
Lake Arthur, LA	260	30.05 N	92.41 W
Lake Arthur, NM	262	33.00 N	104.22 W
Lake Benton	264	44.16 N	96.17 W
Lake Brownwood	262	31.49 N	99.02 W
Lake Butler	258	30.01 N	82.20 W
Lake Carmel	254	41.27 N	73.40 W
Lake Charles	260	30.13 N	93.12 W
Lake Chelan National Recreation Area ♠	268	48.20 N	120.40 W
Lake City, AR	260	35.49 N	90.26 W
Lake City, CO	266	38.02 N	107.19 W
Lake City, FL	258	30.12 N	82.38 W
Lake City, IA	264	42.16 N	94.44 W
Lake City, MI	256	44.20 N	85.13 W
Lake City, MN	256	44.27 N	92.16 W
Lake City, PA	254	42.01 N	80.21 W
Lake City, SC	258	33.52 N	79.45 W
Lake City, TN	258	36.13 N	84.09 W
Lake Clark National Park ♠	246	60.30 N	153.15 W
Lake Corpus Christi State Park ♠	262	28.05 N	97.52 W
Lake Cowichan	248	48.50 N	124.03 W
Lake Creek ≃, OR	268	44.04 N	123.47 W
Lake Creek ≃, TX	262	30.16 N	95.29 W
Lake Crystal	264	44.06 N	94.13 W
Lake Dallas	262	33.07 N	97.02 W
Lake Delton	256	43.35 N	89.47 W
Lake Elsinore	270	33.40 N	117.20 W
Lakefield, ON	256	44.26 N	78.16 W
Lakefield, MN	264	43.41 N	95.10 W
Lake Forest, FL	258	30.24 N	81.41 W
Lake Forest, IL	256	42.15 N	87.50 W
Lake Fork ≃	266	40.13 N	110.07 W
Lake Fork Creek ≃	262	32.36 N	95.21 W
Lake Geneva	256	42.36 N	88.26 W
Lake George	254	43.26 N	73.43 W
Lake Harbor	258	26.42 N	80.48 W
Lake Harbour	242	62.51 N	69.53 W
Lake Hattie Reservoir ⊜[1]	266	41.15 N	105.55 W
Lake Havasu City	266	34.27 N	114.22 W
Lake Havasu State Park ♠	266	34.29 N	114.21 W
Lake Helen	258	28.59 N	81.14 W
Lakehurst	254	40.01 N	74.19 W
Lake Isabella	270	35.39 N	118.28 W
Lake Jackson	262	29.02 N	95.27 W
Lakeland, FL	258	28.03 N	81.57 W
Lakeland, GA	258	31.02 N	83.04 W
Lake Linden	256	47.11 N	88.26 W
Lake Louise	248	51.26 N	116.11 W
Lake Mead National Recreation Area ♠	270	36.00 N	114.30 W
Lake Meredith National Recreation Area ♠	262	35.40 N	101.40 W
Lake Mills, IA	256	43.25 N	93.32 W
Lake Mills, WI	256	43.05 N	88.55 W
Lake Minchumina	246	63.53 N	152.19 W
Lakemont	254	40.31 N	78.23 W
Lake Murray State Park ♠	262	34.01 N	97.00 W
Lake Norden	264	44.35 N	97.13 W
Lake Odessa	256	42.47 N	85.08 W
Lake of the Ozarks State Park ♠	260	38.08 N	92.40 W
Lake Oswego	268	45.26 N	122.39 W
Lake Ozark	260	38.12 N	92.38 W
Lake Park, FL	258	26.49 N	80.04 W
Lake Park, IA	264	43.27 N	95.19 W
Lake Park, MN	264	46.53 N	96.06 W
Lake Placid, FL	258	27.18 N	81.22 W
Lake Placid, NY	254	44.17 N	73.59 W
Lake Pleasant	254	43.28 N	74.25 W
Lakeport, CA	270	39.03 N	122.55 W
Lakeport, MI	256	43.07 N	82.30 W
Lake Preston	264	44.22 N	97.23 W
Lake Providence	260	32.48 N	91.11 W
Lake Shore, FL	258	30.17 N	81.43 W
Lakeshore, MS	260	30.15 N	89.28 W
Lakeside, NS	252	44.38 N	63.41 W
Lakeside, AZ	266	34.09 N	109.58 W
Lakeside, CA	270	32.52 N	116.55 W
Lakeside, MT	268	48.01 N	114.13 W
Lakeside, OR	268	43.34 N	124.11 W
Lake Stevens	268	48.01 N	122.04 W
Lake Sumner State Park ♠	262	34.38 N	104.24 W
Lake Superior Provincial Park ♠	256	47.32 N	84.50 W
Lake Tahoe-Nevada State Park ♠	270	39.13 N	119.55 W
Laketown	266	41.49 N	111.19 W
Lake View, AR	260	34.25 N	90.50 W
Lakeview, GA	258	34.59 N	85.16 W
Lake View, IA	264	42.18 N	95.03 W
Lakeview, MI	256	42.18 N	85.12 W
Lakeview, MI	256	43.27 N	85.17 W
Lake View, NY	254	42.43 N	78.56 W
Lakeview, OH	254	40.29 N	83.56 W
Lakeview, OR	268	42.11 N	120.21 W
Lake View, SC	258	34.21 N	79.10 W
Lakeview, TX	260	29.55 N	93.54 W
Lakeview, TX	262	34.40 N	100.42 W
Lakeview Mountain ∧	248	49.03 N	120.09 W
Lake Village	260	33.20 N	91.17 W
Lakeville	256	44.39 N	93.14 W
Lake Wales	258	27.54 N	81.35 W
Lake Wilson	264	43.59 N	95.57 W
Lakewood, CO	266	39.44 N	105.06 W
Lakewood, NJ	254	40.06 N	74.13 W
Lakewood, NY	254	42.06 N	79.20 W
Lakewood, OH	254	41.29 N	81.48 W
Lakewood, WI	256	45.18 N	88.31 W
Lakewood Center	268	47.10 N	122.31 W
Lakewood Park	264	48.04 N	98.56 W
Lake Worth	258	26.37 N	80.03 W
Lake Worth Village	262	32.49 N	97.27 W
Lakin	264	37.56 N	101.15 W
Lakota, IA	264	43.23 N	94.06 W
Lakota, ND	264	48.02 N	98.21 W
La Loche	250	56.29 N	109.27 W
La Loche, Lac ⊜	250	56.25 N	109.30 W
La Luz	266	32.59 N	105.54 W
La Malbaie	252	47.39 N	70.10 W
Lamaline	252	46.52 N	55.49 W
Lamar, CO	264	38.05 N	102.37 W
Lamar, MO	260	37.29 N	94.17 W
Lamar, SC	258	34.10 N	80.04 W
Lamar ≃	268	44.56 N	110.24 W
La Marque	260	29.22 N	94.58 W
Lambert, MS	260	34.12 N	90.24 W
Lambert, MT	264	47.41 N	104.37 W
Lamberton	264	44.14 N	95.16 W
Lambertville	254	40.22 N	74.57 W
Lambeth	256	42.54 N	81.18 W
Lambton, Cape ≻	242	71.05 N	123.10 W
Lame Deer	268	45.37 N	106.40 W
Lamèque	252	47.47 N	64.38 W
La Mesa, CA	270	32.46 N	117.01 W
La Mesa, NM	266	32.07 N	106.42 W
Lamesa, TX	262	32.44 N	101.57 W
Lamine ≃	260	38.59 N	92.51 W
Lamming Mills	248	53.22 N	120.18 W
La Moille, IL	260	41.32 N	89.17 W
Lamoille, NV	270	40.44 N	115.29 W
Lamoille ≃	254	44.35 N	73.10 W
La Moine ≃	260	39.59 N	90.31 W
La Moine, East Fork ≃	260	40.24 N	90.56 W
Lamoni	256	40.37 N	93.56 W
Lamont, AB	248	53.46 N	112.48 W
Lamont, CA	270	35.15 N	118.55 W
Lamont, IA	256	42.36 N	91.39 W
Lamont, OK	262	36.41 N	97.33 W
La Monte	260	38.46 N	93.25 W
La Mothe, Réservoir ⊜[1]	252	48.46 N	71.09 W
La Motte, Lac ⊜	256	48.24 N	78.03 W
La Moure	264	46.21 N	98.18 W
Lampasas	262	31.04 N	98.11 W
Lampasas ≃	262	30.59 N	97.24 W
Lampman	250	49.23 N	102.45 W
Lanai I	272a	20.50 N	156.55 W
Lanai City	272a	20.50 N	156.55 W
Lanaihale ∧	272a	20.49 N	156.52 W
Lanark, ON	256	45.01 N	76.22 W
Lanark, IL	256	42.06 N	89.50 W
Lancaster, ON	254	45.15 N	74.30 W
Lancaster, CA	270	34.42 N	118.08 W
Lancaster, KY	258	37.37 N	84.35 W
Lancaster, MN	264	48.52 N	96.48 W
Lancaster, MO	260	40.31 N	92.32 W
Lancaster, NH	254	44.29 N	71.34 W
Lancaster, NY	254	42.54 N	78.40 W
Lancaster, OH	254	39.43 N	82.36 W
Lancaster, PA	254	40.02 N	76.19 W
Lancaster, SC	258	34.43 N	80.46 W
Lancaster, TX	262	32.36 N	96.46 W
Lancaster, VA	258	37.46 N	76.28 W
Lancaster, WI	256	42.51 N	90.43 W
Lancaster Sound ⊔	242	74.13 N	84.00 W
Lance Creek	264	43.02 N	104.39 W
Lance Creek ≃	264	43.22 N	104.16 W
Land Between the Lakes ♠	260	36.55 N	88.05 W
Lander	268	42.50 N	108.44 W
Landing Lake ⊜	250	55.17 N	97.26 W
Landis, SK	250	52.12 N	108.28 W
Landis, NC	258	35.33 N	80.37 W
Lando	258	34.43 N	81.01 W
Land O'lakes	256	46.10 N	89.13 W
Landreth Draw ∨	262	31.14 N	102.29 W
Landrum	258	35.11 N	82.11 W
Landsman Creek ≃	264	39.35 N	102.19 W
Lanesboro	256	43.43 N	91.59 W
Lanett	258	32.57 N	85.12 W
Lanezi Lake ⊜	248	53.03 N	120.56 W
Lang	250	49.56 N	104.23 W
Langara Island I	248	54.14 N	133.00 W
Langbank	250	50.05 N	102.20 W
Lang Bay	248	49.47 N	124.21 W
Langdale	258	32.44 N	85.11 W
Langdon	264	48.46 N	98.22 W
Langenburg	250	50.50 N	101.43 W
Langford	264	45.36 N	97.50 W
Langham	250	52.22 N	106.57 W
Langley, BC	248	49.06 N	122.39 W
Langley, OK	262	36.30 N	95.04 W
Langley, SC	258	33.31 N	81.50 W
Langley Air Force Base ■	258	37.05 N	76.21 W
Langlois	268	42.56 N	124.27 W
Langruth	250	50.24 N	98.38 W
L'Anguille ≃	260	34.44 N	90.40 W
Lanigan	250	51.52 N	105.02 W
L'Annonciation	254	46.25 N	74.52 W
L'Anse	256	46.45 N	88.27 W
L'Anse Indian Reservation ◆[4]	256	46.48 N	88.22 W
Lansford	264	48.38 N	101.23 W
Lansing, IA	256	43.22 N	91.13 W
Lansing, KS	264	39.14 N	94.55 W
Lansing, MI	256	42.43 N	84.34 W
Lantana	258	26.35 N	80.03 W
Laona	256	45.34 N	88.40 W
Lapeer	256	43.03 N	83.19 W
La Perouse Bay C	272a	20.35 N	156.25 W
La Pine	268	43.40 N	121.30 W
La Plata, MD	254	38.32 N	76.59 W
La Plata, MO	260	40.02 N	92.29 W
La Plata ≃	266	36.54 N	108.15 W
La Plata Peak ∧	266	39.02 N	106.28 W
La Plonge Indian Reserve ◆[4]	250	55.15 N	107.36 W
La Pocatière	252	47.22 N	68.41 W
La Poile Bay C	252	47.38 N	58.20 W
Laporte, CO	266	40.38 N	105.08 W
La Porte, IN	260	41.36 N	86.43 W
Laporte, PA	254	41.25 N	76.30 W
La Porte City	256	42.19 N	92.12 W
La Potherie, Lac ⊜	242	58.50 N	74.24 W
La Prele Creek ≃	264	42.50 N	105.30 W
La Pryor	262	28.57 N	99.51 W
Lapwai	268	46.24 N	116.48 W
Laramie	264	41.19 N	105.35 W
Laramie ≃	264	42.12 N	104.32 W
Laramie Mountains ⋀	264	42.00 N	105.40 W
Laramie Peak ∧	264	42.17 N	105.27 W
Larb Creek ≃	268	48.25 N	107.16 W
Larchwood	264	43.27 N	96.26 W
Lardeau	248	50.09 N	116.57 W
Larder Lake ⊜	256	48.05 N	79.36 W
L'Ardoise	252	45.37 N	60.45 W
Laredo	262	27.31 N	99.30 W
Laredo Sound ⊔	248	52.32 N	128.53 W
Larga, Laguna ⊜	262	27.30 N	97.25 W
Largo	258	27.55 N	82.47 W
Largo, Cañon ∨	266	36.40 N	107.43 W
Largo Creek ≃	266	34.29 N	108.51 W
Larimore	264	47.54 N	97.38 W
Lark Harbour	252	49.06 N	58.23 W
Larned	264	38.11 N	99.06 W
La Ronge	250	55.06 N	105.17 W
Larose	260	29.35 N	90.23 W
Larrys River	252	45.13 N	61.23 W
Larsen Bay	246	57.33 N	154.04 W
La Rue	254	40.35 N	83.23 W
Larus Lake ⊜	250	51.17 N	94.40 W
La Sal	266	38.19 N	109.15 W
La Salle, CO	264	40.21 N	104.42 W
La Salle, IL	260	41.20 N	89.06 W
La Sal Mountains ⋀	266	38.30 N	109.10 W
Las Animas	264	38.04 N	103.13 W
La Sarre	256	48.48 N	79.12 W
La Sarre ≃	256	48.43 N	79.16 W
La Scie	252	49.57 N	55.36 W
Las Cruces	266	32.23 N	106.29 W
Lashburn	250	53.08 N	109.36 W
Las Moras Creek ≃	262	29.00 N	100.39 W
Lasqueti Island I	248	49.29 N	124.17 W
Las Raices Creek ≃	262	28.09 N	99.02 W
Lassen Peak ∧[1]	270	40.29 N	121.31 W
Lassen Volcanic National Park ♠	270	40.30 N	121.19 W
L'Assomption ≃	254	45.43 N	73.29 W
Last Mountain ∧	250	51.07 N	104.54 W
Last Mountain Lake ⊜	250	51.05 N	105.10 W
Las Vegas, NV	270	36.11 N	115.08 W
Las Vegas, NM	266	35.36 N	105.13 W
La Tabatière	252	50.50 N	58.58 W
Laterrière	252	48.18 N	71.06 W
Lathrop	260	39.33 N	94.20 W
Latimer	256	42.46 N	93.22 W
Latornell ≃	248	54.58 N	118.00 W
Latouche Island I	246	60.00 N	147.55 W
Latrobe	254	40.19 N	79.23 W
Latta	258	34.21 N	79.26 W
La Tuque	242	47.26 N	72.47 W
Lauderdale	260	32.31 N	88.31 W
Laughery Creek ≃	260	39.02 N	84.53 W
Laughlin Air Force Base ■	262	29.22 N	100.47 W
Laughlin Peak ∧	262	36.38 N	104.12 W
La Union	266	31.57 N	106.39 W
Laurel, DE	254	38.33 N	75.34 W
Laurel, FL	258	27.08 N	82.27 W
Laurel, IN	260	39.30 N	85.11 W
Laurel, MD	254	39.06 N	76.51 W
Laurel, MS	260	31.42 N	89.08 W
Laurel, MT	268	45.40 N	108.46 W
Laurel, NE	264	42.26 N	97.06 W
Laurel ≃	258	36.57 N	84.18 W
Laurel Bay	258	32.27 N	80.48 W
Laureldale	254	40.23 N	75.55 W
Laurel Hill	258	34.49 N	79.35 W
Laurel Ridge State Park ♠	254	39.58 N	79.23 W
Laurelville	254	39.28 N	82.44 W
Laurens, IA	264	42.51 N	94.51 W
Laurens, SC	258	34.30 N	82.01 W
Laurentides, Parc des ♠	252	47.40 N	71.30 W
Laurie Lake ⊜	250	56.34 N	101.54 W
Laurier	250	50.54 N	99.33 W
Laurinburg	258	34.47 N	79.27 W
Laurium	256	47.14 N	88.26 W
Lauzon	252	46.50 N	71.10 W
Lava Beds National Monument ♠	270	41.42 N	121.30 W
Lavaca ≃	262	28.50 N	96.36 W
Lavaca Bay C	262	28.35 N	96.35 W
Lava Hot Springs	268	42.37 N	112.01 W
Laval	254	45.33 N	73.44 W
La Valley	266	37.06 N	105.22 W
La Vérendrye, Parc de ♠	256	47.30 N	77.30 W
La Vergne	260	36.02 N	86.39 W
Laverne	262	36.43 N	99.54 W
La Vernia	262	29.21 N	98.07 W
La Veta	264	37.31 N	105.00 W
Lavic Lake ⊜	270	34.40 N	116.21 W
Lavieille, Lake ⊜	256	45.51 N	78.14 W
Lavillette	252	47.16 N	65.18 W
Lavina	268	46.18 N	108.56 W
La Vista	264	41.10 N	96.03 W
La Volla	270	32.51 N	117.16 W
Lavonia	258	34.26 N	83.06 W
Lawai	272b	21.55 N	159.31 W
Lawford Lake ⊜	250	54.30 N	96.43 W
Lawler	256	43.04 N	92.09 W
Lawn, NF	252	46.57 N	55.32 W
Lawn, TX	262	32.08 N	99.49 W
Lawn Bay C	252	46.53 N	55.35 W
Lawndale	258	35.25 N	81.34 W
Lawrence, IN	260	39.50 N	86.02 W
Lawrence, KS	264	38.58 N	95.14 W
Lawrence, MA	254	42.42 N	71.09 W
Lawrence, NE	264	40.17 N	98.16 W
Lawrenceburg, IN	260	39.06 N	84.51 W
Lawrenceburg, KY	254	38.02 N	84.54 W
Lawrenceburg, TN	260	35.15 N	87.20 W
Lawrence Fork ≃	264	41.36 N	103.14 W
Lawrenceville, IL	260	38.44 N	87.41 W
Lawrenceville, NJ	254	40.18 N	74.44 W
Lawrenceville, VA	258	36.45 N	77.51 W
Lawson	260	39.26 N	94.12 W
Lawtey	258	30.03 N	82.04 W
Lawton, MI	256	42.10 N	85.50 W
Lawton, ND	264	48.18 N	98.22 W
Lawton, OK	262	34.37 N	98.25 W
Lawyer Creek ≃	268	46.14 N	116.01 W
Layton	266	41.04 N	111.58 W
Laytonville	270	39.41 N	123.29 W
Leachville	260	35.56 N	90.15 W
Lead	264	44.21 N	103.46 W
Leadbetter Point ≻	268	46.38 N	124.03 W
Leader	250	50.53 N	109.31 W
Lead Hill ∧[2]	260	37.06 N	92.38 W
Leadore	268	44.41 N	113.21 W
Leadville	266	39.15 N	106.20 W
Leaf ≃, MN	264	46.29 N	94.53 W
Leaf ≃, MS	260	31.00 N	88.45 W
Leaf Lake ⊜	250	53.02 N	102.07 W
League City	262	29.31 N	95.05 W
Leakesville	260	31.09 N	88.33 W
Leakey	262	29.44 N	99.46 W
Leaksville	258	36.29 N	79.53 W
Lealman	258	27.50 N	82.41 W
Leamington	256	42.03 N	82.36 W
Leary	258	31.29 N	84.31 W
Leask	250	53.00 N	106.45 W
Leatherman Peak ∧	268	44.05 N	113.44 W
Leavenworth, KS	264	39.19 N	94.55 W
Leavenworth, WA	268	47.36 N	120.40 W
Leawood	260	37.03 N	94.31 W
Lebam	268	46.34 N	123.33 W
Lebanon, IN	260	40.03 N	86.28 W
Lebanon, KS	264	39.49 N	98.33 W
Lebanon, KY	260	37.34 N	85.15 W
Lebanon, MO	260	37.41 N	92.40 W
Lebanon, NH	254	43.38 N	72.15 W
Lebanon, OH	254	39.26 N	84.13 W
Lebanon, OR	268	44.32 N	122.54 W
Lebanon, PA	254	40.20 N	76.25 W
Lebanon, SD	264	45.04 N	99.46 W
Lebanon, TN	260	36.12 N	86.18 W
Lebanon, VA	258	36.54 N	82.05 W
Lebanon Junction	260	37.50 N	85.44 W
Lebec	270	34.50 N	118.52 W
Lebo	264	38.25 N	95.51 W
Le Center	256	44.24 N	93.44 W
Le Claire	256	41.36 N	90.21 W
Lecompte	260	31.05 N	92.24 W
Le Doré, Lac ⊜	252	51.17 N	61.23 W
Leduc	248	53.16 N	113.33 W
Lee	254	42.19 N	73.15 W
Leechburg	254	40.38 N	79.36 W
Leech Lake ⊜, SK	250	51.04 N	102.30 W
Leech Lake ⊜, MN	264	47.09 N	94.23 W
Leech Lake Indian Reservation ◆[4]	264	47.30 N	94.27 W
Leedey	262	35.52 N	99.21 W
Leeds, AL	260	33.33 N	86.33 W
Leeds, ND	264	48.17 N	99.27 W
Leelanau, Lake ⊜	256	44.55 N	85.43 W
Leesburg, FL	258	28.49 N	81.53 W
Leesburg, GA	258	31.44 N	84.10 W
Leesburg, VA	254	39.07 N	77.34 W
Lees Summit	260	38.55 N	94.23 W
Leesville, LA	260	31.08 N	93.16 W
Leesville, SC	258	33.56 N	81.31 W
Leesville, TX	262	29.24 N	97.45 W
Leesville Lake ⊜[1], OH	254	40.30 N	81.10 W
Leesville Lake ⊜[1], VA	258	37.05 N	79.25 W
Lee Vining	270	37.58 N	119.07 W
Lefors	262	35.26 N	100.48 W
Leftrook Lake ⊜	250	56.05 N	98.36 W
Legal	248	53.57 N	113.35 W
Leggett	270	39.52 N	123.43 W
Le Grand	270	37.14 N	120.15 W
Lehi	266	40.24 N	111.51 W
Lehigh	262	34.28 N	96.13 W
Lehigh Acres	258	26.36 N	81.39 W
Lehighton	254	40.49 N	75.45 W
Lehman Caves National Monument ♠	270	39.01 N	114.14 W
Lehr	264	46.17 N	99.21 W
Lehua Island I	272b	22.01 N	160.06 W
Leighton	260	34.42 N	87.32 W
Leinan	250	50.30 N	107.46 W
Leipsic	254	41.06 N	83.59 W
Leitchfield	260	37.29 N	86.18 W
Leland, IL	260	41.37 N	88.48 W
Leland, MI	256	45.01 N	85.45 W
Leland, MS	260	33.24 N	90.54 W
Leleiwi Point ≻	272	19.44 N	155.00 W
Le Mars	264	42.47 N	96.10 W
Lemay	260	38.32 N	90.17 W
Lemay, Lac ⊜	252	50.35 N	68.25 W
Lemberg	250	50.44 N	103.13 W
Lemeta	246	64.52 N	147.44 W
Lemhi ≃	268	45.12 N	113.53 W
Lemhi Pass)(	268	44.58 N	113.27 W
Lemhi Range ⋀	268	44.30 N	113.25 W
Lemieux Islands II	242	64.30 N	64.40 W
Leming	262	29.04 N	98.29 W
Lemitar	266	34.09 N	106.55 W
Lemmon	264	45.56 N	102.10 W
Lemmon, Mount ∧	266	32.26 N	110.47 W
Lemoine, Lac ⊜	256	48.00 N	78.00 W
Lemoncove	270	36.23 N	119.01 W
Lemon Grove	270	32.44 N	117.02 W
Lemont	254	40.49 N	77.49 W
Lemoore	270	36.18 N	119.47 W
Lemoore Naval Air Station ■	270	36.15 N	119.57 W
Lena, IL	256	42.23 N	89.50 W
Lena, WI	256	44.57 N	88.03 W
Lennox	264	43.21 N	96.53 W
Lennoxville	254	45.22 N	71.51 W
Lenoir	258	35.55 N	81.32 W
Lenoir City	258	35.48 N	84.16 W
Lenore Lake ⊜	250	52.30 N	105.00 W
Lenox, GA	258	31.16 N	83.28 W
Lenox, IA	264	40.53 N	94.34 W
Lenox, MA	254	42.22 N	73.17 W
Lenox, TN	260	36.05 N	89.30 W
Leola, AR	260	34.10 N	92.35 W
Leola, SD	264	45.43 N	98.56 W
Leominster	254	42.32 N	71.45 W
Leon, IA	256	40.44 N	93.45 W
Leon, KS	264	37.42 N	96.46 W
Leon ≃	262	30.59 N	97.24 W
Leona ≃	262	28.45 N	99.11 W
Leonard, ND	264	46.39 N	97.15 W
Leonard, TX	262	33.23 N	96.15 W
Leonardtown	254	38.17 N	76.38 W
Leonardville	264	39.22 N	96.51 W
Leon Creek ≃	262	31.11 N	102.45 W
Leonville	260	30.29 N	91.59 W
Leoti	264	38.29 N	101.21 W
Leoville	250	53.37 N	107.35 W
Lepanto	260	35.36 N	90.20 W
Leper Settlement ⊽	272a	21.12 N	156.58 W
L'Épiphanie	254	45.51 N	73.30 W
Lepreau, Point ≻	252	45.04 N	66.27 W
Leroux Wash ∨	266	34.54 N	110.12 W
Le Roy, IL	260	40.21 N	88.46 W
Le Roy, KS	264	38.05 N	95.38 W
Le Roy, MN	256	43.31 N	92.30 W
Le Roy, NY	254	42.59 N	77.59 W
Leslie, AR	260	35.50 N	92.34 W
Leslie, GA	258	31.57 N	84.05 W
Leslie, MI	256	42.27 N	84.26 W
Leslie, WV	254	38.03 N	80.43 W
Lesser Slave ≃	248	55.10 N	114.03 W
Lesser Slave Lake ⊜	248	55.25 N	115.30 W
Lestock	250	51.18 N	104.00 W
Le Sueur	256	44.27 N	93.54 W
Letcher	264	43.54 N	98.08 W
Letchworth State Park ♠	254	42.42 N	77.56 W
Lethbridge, AB	248	49.42 N	112.50 W
Lethbridge, NF	252	48.21 N	53.52 W
Leucadia	270	33.04 N	117.18 W
Levack	256	46.38 N	81.23 W
Levan	266	39.33 N	111.52 W
Levelland	262	33.35 N	102.23 W
Levelock	246	59.07 N	156.52 W
Levering	256	45.38 N	84.47 W
Lévis	252	46.48 N	71.11 W
Levisa Fork ≃	258	38.06 N	82.36 W
Levittown, NY	254	40.41 N	73.31 W
Levittown, PA	254	40.09 N	74.50 W
Lewellen	264	41.20 N	102.09 W
Lewes	254	38.47 N	75.08 W
Lewis, IA	264	41.18 N	95.05 W
Lewis, KS	264	37.56 N	99.15 W
Lewis ≃	268	45.51 N	122.48 W
Lewis, East Fork ≃	268	45.52 N	122.43 W
Lewis, Mount ∧	270	40.24 N	116.51 W
Lewis and Clark Caverns State Park ♠	268	45.49 N	111.13 W
Lewis and Clark Lake ⊜[1]	264	42.50 N	97.45 W
Lewisburg, KY	260	36.59 N	86.57 W
Lewisburg, PA	254	40.58 N	76.53 W
Lewisburg, TN	260	35.27 N	86.48 W
Lewisburg, WV	258	37.48 N	80.27 W
Lewis Hills ⋀[2]	252	48.48 N	58.30 W
Lewisport	260	37.56 N	86.54 W
Lewisporte	252	49.15 N	55.03 W
Lewis Range ⋀, N.A.	242, 244	48.30 N	113.15 W
Lewis Run	254	41.52 N	78.40 W
Lewis Smith Lake ⊜[1]	260	34.05 N	87.07 W
Lewiston, CA	270	40.43 N	122.48 W
Lewiston, ID	268	46.25 N	117.01 W
Lewiston, ME	254	44.06 N	70.13 W
Lewiston, MI	256	44.53 N	84.18 W
Lewiston, MN	256	44.00 N	91.49 W
Lewiston, NY	254	43.10 N	79.03 W
Lewiston, UT	266	41.58 N	111.51 W
Lewiston Orchards	268	46.23 N	116.59 W
Lewistown, IL	260	40.24 N	90.09 W
Lewistown, MO	260	40.05 N	91.49 W
Lewistown, MT	268	47.04 N	109.26 W
Lewistown, PA	254	40.36 N	77.31 W
Lewisville, NB	252	45.06 N	64.46 W
Lewisville, AR	260	33.22 N	93.35 W
Lewisville, TX	262	33.03 N	97.00 W
Lewvan	250	50.00 N	104.06 W
Lexa	260	34.36 N	90.45 W
Lexington, GA	258	33.52 N	83.07 W
Lexington, IL	256	40.39 N	88.47 W
Lexington, KY	254	38.03 N	84.30 W
Lexington, MA	254	42.27 N	71.14 W
Lexington, MI	256	43.16 N	82.32 W
Lexington, MS	260	33.07 N	90.03 W
Lexington, MO	260	39.11 N	93.52 W
Lexington, NE	264	40.47 N	99.45 W
Lexington, NC	258	35.49 N	80.15 W
Lexington, OK	262	35.01 N	97.20 W
Lexington, OR	268	45.27 N	119.41 W
Lexington, SC	258	34.00 N	81.14 W
Lexington, TN	260	35.39 N	88.24 W
Lexington, TX	262	30.25 N	97.01 W
Lexington, VA	258	37.47 N	79.27 W
Lexington Park	254	38.16 N	76.27 W
Leyond ≃	250	51.40 N	96.32 W
Liard ≃	242	61.52 N	121.18 W
Libby	268	48.23 N	115.33 W
Libby Dam ◆[6]	268	48.24 N	115.20 W
Liberal, KS	264	37.02 N	100.55 W
Liberal, MO	260	37.34 N	94.31 W
Liberty, IN	260	39.38 N	84.56 W
Liberty, KY	258	37.19 N	84.56 W
Liberty, MS	260	31.09 N	90.48 W
Liberty, MO	260	39.15 N	94.25 W
Liberty, NE	264	40.05 N	96.29 W
Liberty, NC	258	35.51 N	79.34 W
Liberty, NY	254	41.48 N	74.45 W
Liberty, SC	258	34.48 N	82.42 W
Liberty, TX	260	30.03 N	94.47 W
Liberty Center	254	41.27 N	84.07 W
Liberty Hill	262	30.40 N	97.55 W
Libertyville	256	42.17 N	87.57 W
Lick Creek ≃	258	36.11 N	83.10 W
Licking	260	37.30 N	91.51 W
Licking ≃, KY	254	39.06 N	84.30 W
Licking ≃, KY	258	38.05 N	83.35 W
Licking, North Fork ≃	254	38.35 N	84.13 W
Licking, South Fork ≃	254	38.41 N	84.20 W
Liddon Gulf C	242	75.03 N	113.00 W
Lidgerwood	264	46.05 N	97.09 W
Lièvre, Rivière du ≃	254	45.31 N	75.26 W
Lighthouse Point	258	26.17 N	80.07 W
Lighthouse Point ≻, FL	258	29.54 N	84.21 W
Lighthouse Point ≻, MI	256	45.13 N	85.32 W
Lightning Creek ≃, SK	250	49.12 N	101.43 W
Lightning Creek ≃, WY	264	43.11 N	104.44 W
Lignite	264	48.53 N	102.34 W
Ligonier, IN	260	41.28 N	85.35 W
Ligonier, PA	254	40.15 N	79.14 W
Lihue	272b	21.59 N	159.22 W
Lihue Airport ⊠	272b	21.59 N	159.21 W
Likely	248	52.37 N	121.34 W
Lilbourn	260	36.35 N	89.37 W
Lillington	258	35.24 N	78.49 W
Lillooet	248	50.42 N	121.56 W
Lillooet ≃	248	49.45 N	122.08 W
Lillooet Lake ⊜	248	50.13 N	122.29 W
Lily	258	37.02 N	84.17 W
Lima, MT	268	44.38 N	112.36 W
Lima, NY	254	42.54 N	77.37 W
Lima, OH	254	40.46 N	84.06 W
Lima Reservoir ⊜[1]	268	44.38 N	112.17 W
Limerick	250	49.40 N	106.15 W
Lime Springs	256	43.27 N	92.17 W
Limestone	252	46.55 N	67.50 W
Limestone Bay C	250	53.50 N	98.50 W
Limestone Lake ⊜, MB	250	56.35 N	96.00 W
Limestone Lake ⊜, SK	250	54.36 N	103.18 W
Limestone Point ≻[1]	250	53.50 N	98.50 W
Limestone Point Lake ⊜	250	55.07 N	100.32 W
Lime Village	246	61.21 N	155.28 W
Limon	264	39.16 N	103.41 W
Linch	268	43.37 N	106.12 W
Lincoln, AR	260	35.57 N	94.25 W
Lincoln, CA	270	38.54 N	121.17 W
Lincoln, IL	260	40.09 N	89.22 W
Lincoln, KS	264	39.02 N	98.09 W
Lincoln, ME	254	45.22 N	68.30 W
Lincoln, MI	256	44.41 N	83.25 W
Lincoln, MO	260	38.23 N	93.20 W
Lincoln, MT	268	46.58 N	112.41 W
Lincoln, NE	264	40.48 N	96.42 W
Lincoln, NH	254	44.03 N	71.40 W
Lincoln, Mount ∧	266	39.21 N	106.07 W
Lincoln Boyhood National Memorial ⊥	260	38.10 N	86.58 W
Lincoln City	268	44.59 N	123.59 W
Lincoln Creek ≃	264	40.54 N	97.06 W
Lincoln Park, CO	264	37.35 N	104.12 W
Lincoln Park, GA	258	32.52 N	84.19 W
Lincoln Park, MI	256	42.14 N	83.09 W
Lincoln's New Salem State Park ♠	260	39.58 N	89.52 W
Lincolnton, GA	258	33.48 N	82.28 W
Lincolnton, NC	258	35.29 N	81.14 W
Lincoln Village	270	38.01 N	121.19 W
Lind	268	46.58 N	118.37 W
Linda	270	39.08 N	121.34 W
Lindale, GA	258	34.11 N	85.11 W
Lindale, TX	262	32.31 N	95.25 W
Lind Coulee ∨	268	47.00 N	119.10 W
Linden, AL	260	32.18 N	87.47 W
Linden, IN	260	40.11 N	86.55 W
Linden, MI	256	42.49 N	83.47 W
Linden, TN	260	35.37 N	87.50 W
Linden, TX	260	33.01 N	94.22 W
Lindon	264	39.44 N	103.24 W
Lindsay, ON	256	44.21 N	78.44 W
Lindsay, CA	270	36.12 N	119.05 W
Lindsay, NE	264	41.42 N	97.42 W
Lindsay, OK	262	34.50 N	97.38 W
Lindsborg	264	38.35 N	97.40 W
Lindstrom	256	45.23 N	92.52 W
Line Creek ≃	260	33.34 N	88.42 W
Linesville	254	41.39 N	80.26 W
Lineville, AL	260	33.19 N	85.45 W
Lineville, IA	256	40.35 N	93.32 W
Lingle	264	42.08 N	104.21 W
Linn, KS	264	39.41 N	97.05 W
Linn, MO	260	38.29 N	91.51 W
Linton, IN	260	39.02 N	87.10 W
Linton, ND	264	46.16 N	100.14 W
Linville	258	36.04 N	81.52 W
Linwood	268	47.42 N	117.23 W
Lipan	262	32.31 N	98.03 W
Lipoa Point ≻	272a	21.02 N	156.38 W
Lipscomb	262	36.14 N	100.16 W
Lipton	250	50.54 N	103.50 W
Lisbon, ME	254	44.02 N	70.06 W
Lisbon, NH	254	44.13 N	71.55 W
Lisbon, ND	264	46.27 N	97.41 W
Lisbon, OH	254	40.47 N	80.46 W
Lisbon Falls	254	44.03 N	70.03 W
Lisburne, Cape ≻	246	68.52 N	166.14 W
Lisieux	250	49.17 N	105.59 W
Lisman	260	32.05 N	88.17 W
Lismore	252	45.42 N	62.16 W
Listowel	256	43.44 N	80.57 W
Litchfield, IL	260	39.11 N	89.39 W
Litchfield, MI	256	42.03 N	84.46 W
Litchfield, MN	264	45.08 N	94.31 W
Litchfield, NE	264	41.09 N	99.09 W
Litchfield Park	266	33.30 N	112.22 W
Litchville	264	46.39 N	98.11 W
Lithonia	258	33.43 N	84.06 W
Lititz	254	40.09 N	76.18 W
Little ≃, AL	258	34.16 N	85.40 W
Little ≃, AL	260	31.18 N	87.46 W
Little ≃, AL	260	34.16 N	85.40 W
Little ≃, GA	258	30.51 N	83.21 W
Little ≃, GA	258	33.39 N	82.32 W
Little ≃, GA	258	33.14 N	83.24 W
Little ≃, KY	260	36.51 N	87.58 W
Little ≃, LA	260	31.38 N	91.49 W
Little ≃, NC	258	35.15 N	78.42 W
Little ≃, NC	258	35.21 N	78.02 W
Little ≃, OK	262	35.00 N	96.25 W
Little ≃, SC	258	34.10 N	81.11 W
Little ≃, SC	258	33.56 N	82.25 W
Little ≃, SC	258	34.11 N	81.45 W
Little ≃, TN	258	35.51 N	83.57 W
Little ≃, TX	262	30.51 N	96.41 W
Little ≃, VA	258	37.05 N	80.32 W
Little, Mountain Fork ≃	260	33.57 N	94.34 W
Little Arkansas ≃	264	37.43 N	97.22 W
Little Bay Islands	252	49.39 N	55.47 W
Little Bear ≃	266	41.42 N	111.57 W
Little Bear Creek ≃	262	37.43 N	101.43 W
Little Beaver Creek ≃, U.S.	264	46.17 N	103.56 W
Little Beaver Creek ≃, U.S.	264	39.49 N	101.03 W
Little Belt Mountains ⋀	268	46.45 N	110.35 W
Little Bighorn ≃	268	45.44 N	107.34 W
Little Bitterroot ≃	268	47.30 N	114.19 W
Little Black ≃	260	36.25 N	90.45 W
Little Black Bear Indian Reserve ◆[4]	250	51.00 N	103.12 W
Little Blackfoot ≃	268	46.31 N	112.48 W
Little Blue ≃	264	39.41 N	96.40 W
Little Bow ≃	248	49.53 N	112.29 W
Little Bow Lake ⊜	248	50.12 N	112.41 W
Little Buffalo ≃	242	61.00 N	113.46 W
Little Bullhead	250	51.40 N	96.51 W
Little Catalina	252	48.33 N	53.02 W
Little Cedar ≃	256	42.57 N	92.31 W
Little Chariton, East Fork ≃	260	39.20 N	92.50 W
Little Chute	256	44.17 N	88.16 W
Little Colorado ≃	266	36.11 N	111.48 W
Little Cottonwood ≃	264	44.15 N	94.20 W
Little Creek ≃	258	33.13 N	83.24 W
Little Current	256	45.58 N	81.56 W
Little Current ≃	242	50.57 N	84.36 W
Little Cypress Bayou ≃	260	32.41 N	94.15 W
Little Deschutes ≃	268	43.51 N	121.27 W
Little Diomede Island I	246	65.45 N	168.57 W
Little Dry Creek ≃	268	47.21 N	106.22 W
Little Eau Pleine ≃	256	44.40 N	89.41 W
Little Falls, MN	264	45.59 N	94.21 W
Little Falls, NY	254	43.03 N	74.52 W
Littlefield	262	33.55 N	102.20 W
Littlefork	256	48.24 N	93.33 W
Little Fork ≃	256	48.31 N	93.35 W
Little Fort	248	51.25 N	120.12 W
Little Harbour Deep	252	50.15 N	56.33 W
Little Haw Creek ≃	258	29.23 N	81.24 W
Little Humboldt ≃	270	41.00 N	117.43 W
Little Humboldt, North Fork ≃	270	41.24 N	117.10 W
Little Humboldt, South Fork ≃	270	41.24 N	117.10 W
Little Hurricane Creek ≃	258	31.23 N	82.19 W
Little Juniata ≃	254	40.34 N	78.03 W
Little Kanawha ≃	254	39.16 N	81.34 W
Little Kanawha, West Fork ≃	254	38.57 N	81.16 W
Little Koniuji Island I	246	55.01 N	159.26 W
Little Lake ⊜	260	29.30 N	90.10 W
Little Laramie ≃	266	41.28 N	105.44 W
Little Limestone Lake ⊜	250	53.46 N	99.18 W
Little Lost ≃	268	43.46 N	112.58 W
Little Malad ≃	268	42.05 N	112.17 W
Little Manistee ≃	256	44.15 N	86.19 W
Little Mecatina ≃	252	50.28 N	59.35 W
Little Mexico	262	30.56 N	102.52 W
Little Missouri ≃, U.S.	244	47.30 N	102.25 W
Little Missouri ≃, AR	260	33.49 N	92.54 W
Little Muddy ≃, IL	260	37.50 N	89.11 W
Little Muddy ≃, ND	264	48.12 N	103.36 W
Little Mulberry Creek ≃	260	32.26 N	86.51 W
Little Nemaha ≃	264	40.19 N	95.40 W
Little Niangua ≃	260	38.04 N	92.54 W
Little Ohoopee ≃	258	32.27 N	82.24 W
Little Osage ≃	260	38.02 N	94.14 W
Little Owyhee ≃, U.S.	268	42.16 N	116.52 W
Little Owyhee ≃, U.S.	268	42.28 N	117.15 W
Little Pee Dee ≃	258	33.42 N	79.11 W
Little Pic ≃	256	48.48 N	86.37 W
Little Pine and Lucky Man Indian Reserve ◆[4]	250	52.56 N	109.05 W
Little Platte ≃	260	39.24 N	94.41 W
Little Popo Aggie ≃	268	42.54 N	108.35 W
Little Porcupine Creek ≃, MT	268	48.02 N	106.04 W
Little Porcupine Creek ≃, MT	268	46.18 N	106.34 W
Little Powder ≃	264	45.28 N	105.20 W
Little Quill Lake ⊜	250	51.55 N	104.05 W
Little Red ≃	260	35.11 N	91.27 W

Symbols in the index entries are identified on page 273.

Litt – Mala
United States and Canada Map Index

Name Page Lat° ′ Long° ′
Little Red, Middle Fork ≃ 260 35.37 N 92.11 W
Little Red Deer ≃ 248 52.04 N 114.09 W
Little Red River Indian Reserve ◆4 250 53.30 N 105.58 W
Little River 264 38.24 N 98.01 W
Little Rock, AR 260 34.44 N 92.15 W
Little Rock, IA 264 43.26 N 95.55 W
Little Rock ≃ 264 43.16 N 96.15 W
Little Rock Air Force Base ■ 260 34.55 N 92.10 W
Little Rocky Mountains ▲ 268 47.50 N 108.10 W
Little Sable Point > 256 43.38 N 86.32 W
Little Sac ≃ 260 37.39 N 93.46 W
Little Sachigo Lake ⊜ 250 54.09 N 92.11 W
Little Salkehatchie ≃ 258 32.37 N 80.53 W
Little Salmon ≃ 268 45.25 N 116.19 W
Little Salmon Lake ⊜ 246 62.12 N 134.45 W
Little Salt Lake ⊜ 266 37.55 N 112.53 W
Little Sandy ≃ 254 38.35 N 82.51 W
Little Sandy, East Fork ≃ 254 38.30 N 82.50 W
Little Sandy Creek ≃ 268 42.06 N 109.27 W
Little Sioux ≃ 264 41.49 N 96.04 W
Little Sioux, West Fork ≃ 264 42.04 N 96.00 W
Little Sitkin Island I 247a 51.55 N 178.30 E
Little Smoky ≃ 248 55.42 N 117.38 W
Little Snake ≃ 266 40.27 N 108.26 W
Little Southwest Miramichi ≃ 252 46.57 N 65.50 W
Littlestown 254 39.45 N 77.05 W
Little Tallapoosa ≃ 258 33.18 N 85.34 W
Little Tanaga Island I 247a 51.48 N 176.10 W
Little Tennessee ≃ 258 35.47 N 84.15 W
Littleton, CO 266 39.37 N 105.01 W
Littleton, NH 254 44.18 N 71.46 W
Littleton, NC 258 36.26 N 77.54 W
Littleton, WV 254 39.42 N 80.31 W
Little Traverse Bay C 256 45.24 N 85.03 W
Little Turtle ≃ 250 48.46 N 92.36 W
Little Valley 254 42.15 N 78.48 W
Little Vermillion Lake ⊜ 250 51.16 N 93.50 W
Little Wabash ≃ 260 37.54 N 88.05 W
Little Washita ≃ 262 34.58 N 97.51 W
Little White ≃ 264 43.44 N 100.40 W
Little Wichita ≃ 262 33.54 N 97.59 W
Little Wichita, East Fork ≃ 262 33.52 N 98.07 W
Little Wind ≃ 268 42.57 N 108.29 W
Little Wind, North Fork ≃ 268 43.01 N 108.53 W
Little Wind, South Fork ≃ 268 43.01 N 108.53 W
Little Wolf ≃ 256 44.23 N 88.48 W
Little Wood ≃ 268 42.57 N 114.21 W
Lively 256 46.26 N 81.09 W
Livengood 246 65.32 N 148.33 W
Live Oak, CA 270 39.17 N 121.40 W
Live Oak, FL 258 30.18 N 82.59 W
Live Oak Creek ≃ 262 30.39 N 101.42 W
Livermore, CA 270 37.41 N 121.46 W
Livermore, IA 264 42.52 N 94.11 W
Livermore, KY 260 37.29 N 87.08 W
Livermore Falls 254 44.28 N 70.11 W
Liverpool, NS 252 44.02 N 64.43 W
Liverpool, PA 254 40.34 N 77.00 W
Liverpool, Cape > 242 73.38 N 78.06 W
Liverpool Bay C, NT 246 69.45 N 130.00 W
Liverpool Bay C, NS 252 44.02 N 64.41 W
Livingston, AL 260 32.35 N 88.11 W
Livingston, CA 270 37.23 N 120.43 W
Livingston, IL 260 38.58 N 89.46 W
Livingston, KY 258 37.18 N 84.13 W
Livingston, LA 260 30.30 N 90.45 W
Livingston, MT 268 45.40 N 110.34 W
Livingston, TN 258 36.23 N 85.19 W
Livingston, TX 260 30.43 N 94.56 W
Livingston, WI 256 42.54 N 90.26 W
Livingstone, Lake ⊜1 262 30.50 N 95.30 W
Livingston Manor 254 41.54 N 74.50 W
Livonia, LA 260 30.33 N 91.33 W
Livonia, MI 256 42.25 N 83.23 W
Livonia, NY 254 42.49 N 77.40 W
Lizard Head Peak ▲ 268 42.47 N 109.11 W
Lizard Point Indian Reserve ◆4 250 50.40 N 100.57 W
Llano 262 30.45 N 98.41 W
Llano ≃ 262 30.35 N 98.25 W
Lloydminster 250 53.17 N 110.00 W
Lloyds ≃ 252 48.33 N 57.13 W
Loa 266 38.24 N 111.38 W
Loami 260 39.40 N 89.51 W
Lobelville 260 35.47 N 87.49 W
Lobstick Lake ⊜ 242 54.00 N 64.50 W
Lochsa ≃ 268 46.08 N 115.36 W
Lockeport 252 43.42 N 65.07 W
Lockesburg 260 33.58 N 94.10 W
Lockhart 262 29.53 N 97.41 W
Lock Haven 254 41.08 N 77.27 W
Lockney 262 34.07 N 101.27 W
Lockport, MB 250 50.05 N 96.56 W
Lockport, IL 260 41.36 N 88.03 W
Lockport, LA 260 29.39 N 90.32 W
Lockport, NY 254 43.10 N 78.42 W
Lockwood 260 37.23 N 93.57 W
Locust Creek ≃ 260 39.40 N 93.17 W
Locust Fork ≃ 260 33.33 N 87.11 W
Locust Grove 262 36.12 N 95.10 W
Lodge Creek ≃ 268 48.36 N 109.15 W
Lodge Grass 268 45.19 N 107.22 W
Lodgepole, AB 248 53.06 N 115.19 W
Lodgepole, NE 264 41.09 N 102.38 W
Lodgepole Creek ≃ 264 41.02 N 102.10 W
Lodi, CA 270 38.08 N 121.16 W
Lodi, OH 254 41.03 N 82.01 W
Lodi, WI 256 43.19 N 89.32 W
Logan, IA 264 41.39 N 95.47 W
Logan, KS 264 39.40 N 99.34 W
Logan, NM 262 35.22 N 103.25 W
Logan, OH 254 39.32 N 82.25 W
Logan, UT 266 41.44 N 111.50 W
Logan, WV 258 37.51 N 81.59 W
Logan ≃, AB 250 55.09 N 111.42 W
Logan ≃, UT 266 41.44 N 111.57 W
Logan, Mount ▲, YK 246 60.34 N 140.24 W
Logan, Mount ▲, WA 268 48.32 N 120.57 W
Logan Creek ≃, MO 260 37.11 N 90.49 W
Logan Creek ≃, NE 264 41.37 N 96.29 W
Logandale 270 36.36 N 114.29 W
Logan Martin Lake ⊜1 260 33.40 N 86.15 W
Logan Mountains ▲ 246 61.30 N 129.00 W
Logan Pass)(268 48.42 N 113.43 W
Logansport, IN 260 40.45 N 86.21 W
Logansport, LA 260 31.58 N 93.58 W
Loganville 258 33.50 N 83.54 W
Lohrville 264 42.17 N 94.33 W
Loïs, Lac ⊜ 256 48.34 N 78.44 W
Loks Land I 242 62.26 N 64.38 W
Lola, Mount ▲ 270 39.26 N 120.22 W
Loleta 270 40.38 N 124.13 W
Lolita 262 28.50 N 96.32 W
Lolo 268 46.45 N 114.05 W
Lolo Creek ≃, ID 268 46.26 N 116.10 W
Lolo Creek ≃, MT 268 46.45 N 114.03 W
Lolo Pass)(268 46.38 N 114.35 W
Lomax 256 40.41 N 91.04 W
Lometa 262 31.13 N 98.24 W
Lomira 256 43.35 N 88.27 W
Lomond 248 50.21 N 112.39 W
Lomond, Loch ⊜, NS 252 45.46 N 60.35 W
Lomond, Loch ⊜, ON 256 48.26 N 89.19 W
Lompoc 270 34.38 N 120.27 W
Lonaconing 254 39.34 N 78.59 W
London, ON 256 42.59 N 81.14 W
London, AR 260 35.20 N 93.15 W
London, KY 258 37.08 N 84.05 W
London, OH 254 39.53 N 83.27 W
London, TX 262 30.41 N 99.35 W
Londonderry 252 45.29 N 63.36 W
Lone Grove 262 34.11 N 97.16 W
Lonely Lake ⊜ 250 51.09 N 99.05 W
Lone Mountain ▲, NV 270 38.02 N 117.29 W
Lone Mountain ▲, SD 264 45.23 N 103.44 W
Lone Oak, KY 260 37.02 N 88.40 W
Lone Oak, TX 262 33.01 N 95.57 W
Lone Pine 270 36.36 N 118.04 W
Lone Rock 256 43.11 N 90.12 W
Lone Star 260 32.56 N 94.43 W
Lone Tree 256 41.29 N 91.26 W
Lone Tree Creek ≃ 264 40.25 N 104.35 W
Lone Wolf 262 34.59 N 99.15 W
Long Arroyo V 262 33.04 N 104.17 W
Long Bay C 258 33.35 N 78.45 W
Long Beach, CA 270 33.46 N 118.11 W
Long Beach, MS 260 30.22 N 89.07 W
Long Beach, NY 254 40.35 N 73.41 W
Long Beach, WA 268 46.21 N 124.03 W
Longboat Key 258 27.24 N 82.39 W
Long Branch 254 40.18 N 74.00 W
Long Branch ≃ 260 39.23 N 91.49 W
Long Cane Creek ≃ 258 33.57 N 82.24 W
Long Creek 268 44.43 N 119.06 W
Long Creek ≃ 250 49.07 N 103.00 W
Long Harbour 252 47.26 N 53.48 W
Long Harbour C 252 47.44 N 55.01 W
Longhorn Cavern State Park ♦ 262 30.20 N 98.30 W
Long Island I, NF 252 47.35 N 54.05 W
Long Island I, NT 242 54.50 N 79.20 W
Long Island I, NS 252 44.20 N 66.15 W
Long Island I, AK 248 54.54 N 132.45 W
Long Island I, NY 254 40.50 N 73.00 W
Long Island Sound ⊔ 244 41.05 N 72.58 W
Long Lake 254 43.58 N 74.25 W
Long Lake ⊜, MI 256 45.12 N 83.30 W
Long Lake ⊜, ND 264 48.50 N 99.10 W
Long Lake ⊜, ND 264 46.43 N 100.07 W
Long Lake ⊜, NY 254 44.04 N 74.20 W
Long Lake Creek ≃ 264 46.40 N 100.13 W
Longleaf 260 31.00 N 92.34 W
Long Leaf Park 258 34.12 N 77.56 W
Long-legged Lake ⊜ 250 50.46 N 94.08 W
Longmeadow 254 42.03 N 72.34 W
Longmont 266 40.10 N 105.06 W
Long Mountain ▲ 260 36.41 N 92.26 W
Long Pine 264 42.32 N 99.42 W
Long Point >, MB 250 53.02 N 98.40 W
Long Point >, NF 252 48.48 N 58.46 W
Long Point >1 256 42.34 N 80.15 W
Long Point Bay C 256 42.40 N 80.14 W
Long Prairie 264 45.59 N 94.52 W
Long Prairie ≃ 264 46.20 N 94.36 W
Long Range Mountains ▲ 252 49.20 N 57.30 W
Long Reach C 252 45.26 N 66.09 W
Long-Sault 254 45.02 N 74.53 W
Longs Peak ▲ 266 40.15 N 105.37 W
Long Tom ≃ 268 44.23 N 123.15 W
Longton 264 37.23 N 96.05 W
Longueuil 254 45.32 N 73.30 W
Long Valley Wash V 270 39.56 N 115.21 W
Longview, AB 248 50.32 N 114.14 W
Longview, NC 258 35.44 N 81.23 W
Longview, TX 260 32.30 N 94.44 W
Longview, WA 268 46.08 N 122.57 W
Longwood Park 258 34.55 N 79.42 W
Longworth 248 53.55 N 121.28 W
Lonoke 260 34.47 N 91.54 W
Lonsdale 264 44.29 N 93.25 W
Loogootee 260 38.41 N 86.55 W
Looking Glass ≃ 256 42.52 N 84.54 W
Lookout, Cape >, NC 258 34.35 N 76.32 W
Lookout, Cape >, OR 268 45.20 N 124.00 W
Lookout Mountain ▲, U.S. 258 34.25 N 85.40 W
Lookout Mountain ▲, OR 268 44.20 N 120.22 W
Lookout Pass)(268 47.27 N 115.42 W
Lookout Point Lake ⊜1 268 43.52 N 122.40 W
Lookout Ridge ▲ 246 69.07 N 158.36 W
Loomis 264 40.29 N 99.31 W
Loon ≃ 250 55.50 N 101.59 W
Loon Creek ≃ 268 44.49 N 114.49 W
Loon Lake ⊜ 250 55.51 N 102.00 W
Loop 262 32.55 N 102.25 W
Lorain 254 41.28 N 82.10 W
Loraine 262 32.25 N 100.43 W
Lord Mayor Bay C 242 69.44 N 92.00 W
Lordsburg 266 32.21 N 108.43 W
Loreauville 260 30.03 N 91.44 W
Lorenzo 262 33.40 N 101.32 W
Lorette 250 49.44 N 96.52 W
Loretto, KY 260 37.38 N 85.25 W
Loretto, TN 260 35.05 N 87.26 W
L'Orignal 254 45.37 N 74.42 W
Lorimor 260 41.07 N 94.03 W
Loring 268 48.47 N 107.52 W
Loring Air Force Base ■ 252 46.57 N 67.54 W
Loris 258 34.04 N 78.53 W
Lorman 260 31.49 N 91.03 W
Lorne 252 47.53 N 66.08 W
Los Alamos, CA 270 34.44 N 120.17 W
Los Alamos, NM 266 35.53 N 106.19 W
Los Angeles 270 34.03 N 118.15 W
Los Angeles Aqueduct ≃1 270 35.22 N 118.05 W
Los Banos 270 37.04 N 120.51 W
Los Coyotes Indian Reservation ◆4 270 33.20 N 116.35 W
Los Ebanos 262 26.14 N 98.34 W
Los Fresnos 262 26.04 N 97.29 W
Los Gatos 270 37.14 N 121.59 W
Los Lunas 266 34.48 N 106.44 W
Los Molinos 270 40.03 N 122.06 W
Los Olmos Creek ≃, TX 262 26.21 N 98.48 W
Los Olmos Creek ≃, TX 262 27.20 N 97.40 W
Los Padillas 266 34.58 N 106.43 W
Los Pinos ≃ 266 36.56 N 107.36 W
Lost ≃, U.S. 270 41.56 N 121.30 W
Lost ≃, IN 260 38.33 N 86.49 W
Lost ≃, MN 264 47.51 N 96.02 W
Lost ≃, WV 254 39.05 N 78.36 W
Lost Creek ≃, AL 260 33.38 N 87.14 W
Lost Creek ≃, AR 260 34.10 N 92.31 W
Lost Creek ≃, UT 266 41.04 N 111.32 W
Lost Creek ≃, WY 268 42.01 N 108.11 W
Lost Draw V 262 32.58 N 102.02 W
Lost Hills 270 35.37 N 119.41 W
Lostine ≃ 268 45.33 N 117.29 W
Lost Nation 256 41.58 N 90.49 W
Lost River Range ▲ 268 44.10 N 113.35 W
Lost Trail Pass)(268 45.41 N 113.57 W
Lothair 258 37.15 N 83.10 W
Lott 262 31.12 N 97.02 W
Lotts Creek ≃ 258 32.09 N 81.47 W
Loudon 258 35.44 N 84.20 W
Loudonville 254 40.38 N 82.14 W
Louin 260 31.59 N 89.16 W
Louisa, KY 258 38.07 N 82.36 W
Louisa, VA 258 38.01 N 78.01 W
Louisbourg 252 45.55 N 59.58 W
Louis Bull Indian Reserve ◆4 248 52.53 N 113.31 W
Louisburg, KS 264 38.37 N 94.41 W
Louisburg, NC 258 36.06 N 78.18 W
Louisdale 252 45.36 N 61.04 W
Louise, MS 260 32.59 N 90.35 W
Louise, TX 262 29.06 N 96.25 W
Louise, Lake ⊜ 246 62.20 N 146.30 W
Louise Island I 248 52.58 N 131.50 W
Louisiana 260 39.27 N 91.03 W
Louisiana □3, U.S. 244
260 31.15 N 92.15 W
Louisville, GA 258 33.00 N 82.24 W
Louisville, IL 260 38.46 N 88.30 W
Louisville, KY 260 38.16 N 85.45 W
Louisville, MS 260 33.07 N 89.03 W
Louisville, NE 264 41.00 N 96.10 W
Louisville, OH 254 40.50 N 81.16 W
Louis-XIV, Pointe > 242 54.37 N 79.45 W
Lount Lake ⊜ 250 50.10 N 94.20 W
Loup ≃ 264 41.24 N 97.19 W
Loup City 264 41.17 N 98.58 W
Lourdes 252 48.39 N 59.00 W
Louse Creek ≃ 264 46.22 N 100.57 W
Loutre ≃ 260 38.42 N 91.25 W
Loutre, Bayou de ≃ 260 32.41 N 92.08 W
Louviers 266 39.28 N 105.01 W
Love 250 53.29 N 104.09 W
Lovelady 262 31.08 N 95.27 W
Loveland 266 40.24 N 105.05 W
Lovell 268 44.50 N 108.24 W
Lovelock 270 40.11 N 118.28 W
Lovely 258 37.50 N 82.24 W
Loves Park 256 42.19 N 89.03 W
Lovilia 256 41.08 N 92.55 W
Loving, NM 262 32.17 N 104.06 W
Loving, TX 262 33.16 N 98.31 W
Lovingston 258 37.46 N 78.52 W
Lovington, IL 260 39.43 N 88.38 W
Lovington, NM 262 32.57 N 103.21 W
Low 254 45.48 N 75.57 W
Low, Cape > 242 63.07 N 85.18 W
Lowden 256 41.52 N 90.56 W
Lowell, AR 260 36.15 N 94.08 W
Lowell, IN 260 41.18 N 87.25 W
Lowell, MA 254 42.39 N 71.18 W
Lowell, MI 256 42.56 N 85.20 W
Lowell, OR 268 43.55 N 122.47 W
Lowell, Lake ⊜1 268 43.33 N 116.40 W
Lower Arrow Lake ⊜ 248 49.40 N 118.08 W
Lower Brule Indian Reservation ◆4 264 44.05 N 99.44 W
Lower Fort Garry National Historic Park ♦ 250 50.07 N 96.55 W
Lower Kalskag 246 61.31 N 160.22 W
Lower Keechi Creek ≃ 262 31.08 N 95.46 W
Lower Klamath Lake ⊜ 270 41.55 N 121.42 W
Lower Lake ⊜ 270 41.15 N 120.02 W
Lower Manitou Lake ⊜ 250 49.15 N 93.00 W
Lower Paia 272a 20.55 N 156.23 W
Lower Post 242 59.55 N 128.30 W
Lower Red Lake ⊜ 264 48.00 N 94.50 W
Lower Ugashik Lake ⊜ 246 57.30 N 156.56 W
Lower West Pubnico 252 43.38 N 65.48 W
Lower Wood's Harbour 252 43.31 N 65.44 W
Lowmoor 258 37.47 N 79.53 W
Lowry Air Force Base ■ 266 39.43 N 104.53 W
Lowry City 260 38.08 N 93.44 W
Lowville 254 43.47 N 75.29 W
Loxley 260 30.37 N 87.45 W
Loyal 256 44.44 N 90.30 W
Loyalsock Creek ≃ 254 41.14 N 76.56 W
Loyalton 270 39.41 N 120.14 W
Lua Makika ▲6 272a 20.34 N 156.34 W
Lubbock 262 33.35 N 101.51 W
Lubbub Creek ≃ 260 33.04 N 88.10 W
Lubec 254 44.52 N 66.59 W
Lucan 256 43.11 N 81.24 W
Lucania, Mount ▲ 246 61.01 N 140.28 W
Lucas, IA 256 41.02 N 93.28 W
Lucas, KS 264 39.04 N 98.32 W
Lucasville 254 38.53 N 83.00 W
Lucedale 260 30.55 N 88.35 W
Lucerne 270 39.06 N 122.48 W
Lucerne Lake ⊜ 270 34.31 N 57.00 W
Lucero, Lake ⊜ 266 32.42 N 106.25 W
Luck 256 45.34 N 92.28 W
Luckiamute ≃ 268 44.45 N 123.09 W
Luck Lake ⊜ 250 51.05 N 107.07 W
Lucknow 256 43.57 N 81.31 W
Lucky Lake 250 51.00 N 107.10 W
Lucky Peak Lake ⊜1 268 43.33 N 116.00 W
Ludington 256 43.57 N 86.27 W
Ludlow, CO 266 37.20 N 104.35 W
Ludlow, MA 254 42.10 N 72.29 W
Ludlow, VT 254 43.24 N 72.42 W
Ludowici 258 31.43 N 81.45 W
Lueders 262 32.48 N 99.37 W
Lufkin 260 31.20 N 94.44 W
Lukachukai Wash V 266 36.39 N 109.36 W
Luke Air Force Base ■ 266 33.32 N 112.22 W
Lukeville 266 31.53 N 112.49 W
Lula 260 34.27 N 90.29 W
Luling 262 29.41 N 97.39 W
Lulu Island I 248 55.28 N 133.30 W
Lumber ≃ 258 34.12 N 79.10 W
Lumber City 258 31.56 N 82.41 W
Lumberport 254 39.23 N 80.21 W
Lumberton, MS 260 31.00 N 89.27 W
Lumberton, NC 258 34.37 N 79.00 W
Lumberton, TX 260 30.16 N 94.10 W
Lumby 248 50.15 N 118.58 W
Lumpkin 258 32.03 N 84.48 W
Lumsden, NF 252 49.19 N 53.37 W
Lumsden, SK 250 50.34 N 104.53 W
Luna Pier 256 41.48 N 83.27 W
Lund, BC 248 49.58 N 124.44 W
Lund, NV 270 38.52 N 115.00 W
Lundale 258 37.48 N 81.45 W
Lundar 250 50.42 N 98.02 W
Lunenburg, NS 252 44.23 N 64.19 W
Lunenburg, VA 258 36.58 N 78.16 W
Luray 258 38.40 N 78.28 W
Luscar 248 53.04 N 117.24 W
Luseland 250 52.05 N 109.30 W
Lusk 264 42.46 N 104.27 W
Lutcher 260 30.02 N 90.42 W
Lutesville 260 37.18 N 89.59 W
Luther, MI 256 44.02 N 85.41 W
Luther, OK 262 35.40 N 97.12 W
Luther Lake ⊜ 256 43.55 N 80.26 W
Luttrell 258 36.12 N 83.44 W
Lutz 258 28.09 N 82.28 W
Luverne, AL 260 31.43 N 86.16 W
Lu Verne, IA 264 42.55 N 94.05 W
Luverne, MN 264 43.39 N 96.13 W
Luxana Bay C 248 52.03 N 131.00 W
Luxapallila Creek ≃ 260 33.28 N 88.26 W
Luxemburg 256 44.32 N 87.42 W
Luxora 260 35.45 N 89.56 W
Lycoming Creek ≃ 254 41.13 N 77.02 W
Lydia Mills 258 34.28 N 81.55 W
Lyell, Mount ▲ 248 51.57 N 117.06 W
Lyell Island I 248 52.40 N 131.30 W
Lyerly 258 34.20 N 85.27 W
Lyford 262 26.24 N 97.48 W
Lykens 254 40.34 N 76.43 W
Lyle 256 43.30 N 92.57 W
Lyles 260 35.55 N 87.21 W
Lyman, NE 264 41.55 N 104.02 W
Lyman, SC 258 34.56 N 82.09 W
Lyman, WY 268 41.20 N 110.18 W
Lynch, KY 258 36.58 N 82.55 W
Lynch, NE 264 42.50 N 98.28 W
Lynch, Lac ⊜ 254 46.25 N 77.05 W
Lynchburg, OH 254 39.14 N 83.48 W
Lynchburg, SC 258 34.04 N 80.04 W
Lynchburg, TN 260 35.17 N 86.22 W
Lynchburg, VA 258 37.24 N 79.10 W
Lynches ≃ 258 33.50 N 79.22 W
Lynden 268 48.57 N 122.27 W
Lyndon, KS 264 38.36 N 95.41 W
Lyndon, KY 260 38.16 N 85.34 W
Lyndon B. Johnson National Historical Site ⊥ 262 30.15 N 98.38 W
Lyndonville 254 44.32 N 72.01 W
Lyndora 254 40.51 N 79.55 W
Lynn, AL 260 34.03 N 87.33 W
Lynn, IN 260 40.03 N 84.56 W
Lynn, MA 254 42.28 N 70.57 W
Lynn Canal C 246 58.50 N 135.15 W
Lynndyl 266 39.31 N 112.22 W
Lynn Garden 258 36.35 N 82.34 W
Lynn Haven 260 30.15 N 85.39 W
Lynn Lake 250 56.51 N 101.03 W
Lynnville 256 41.35 N 92.47 W
Lynx Lake ⊜ 242 62.25 N 106.15 W
Lyon Inlet C 242 66.32 N 83.53 W
Lyon Mountain 254 44.43 N 73.55 W
Lyon Mountain ▲ 254 44.41 N 73.53 W
Lyons, CO 266 40.13 N 105.16 W
Lyons, GA 258 32.12 N 82.19 W
Lyons, IN 260 38.59 N 87.05 W
Lyons, KS 264 38.21 N 98.12 W
Lyons, MI 256 42.59 N 84.57 W
Lyons, NE 264 41.56 N 96.28 W
Lyons, NY 254 43.04 N 77.00 W
Lytle 262 29.14 N 98.48 W
Lytton 248 50.14 N 121.34 W

M

Maalaea Bay C 272a 20.47 N 156.29 W
Mabank 262 32.22 N 96.06 W
Mabel Lake ⊜ 248 50.35 N 118.44 W
Maben 260 33.33 N 89.05 W
Mableton 258 33.49 N 84.35 W
Mabou 252 46.05 N 61.22 W
Mabton 268 46.13 N 120.00 W
McAdam 252 45.36 N 67.20 W
McAdoo 254 40.54 N 76.01 W
McAlester 262 34.56 N 95.46 W
Macalister 248 52.27 N 122.24 W
McAllen 262 26.12 N 98.15 W
MacAlpine Lake ⊜ 242 66.40 N 103.15 W
Macamic, Lac ⊜ 256 48.48 N 78.59 W
McArthur 254 39.15 N 82.29 W
McAuley 250 50.16 N 101.23 W
McBain 256 44.12 N 85.13 W
McBee 258 34.28 N 80.15 W
McBeth Fjord C2 242 69.38 N 68.30 W
McBride 248 53.18 N 120.10 W
McCall 268 44.55 N 116.06 W
McCall Creek 260 31.31 N 90.42 W
McCallum 252 47.38 N 56.15 W
McCamey 262 31.08 N 102.13 W
McCammon 268 42.39 N 112.12 W
McCarteney Creek ≃ 268 47.13 N 120.05 W
McCarthy 246 61.26 N 142.55 W
McCauley Island I 248 53.40 N 130.15 W
McCaysville 258 34.59 N 84.23 W
McChord Air Force Base ■ 268 47.08 N 122.29 W
McClarty Lake ⊜ 250 54.28 N 100.20 W
McCleary 268 47.03 N 123.16 W
McClellan Creek ≃ 262 35.22 N 100.34 W
McClellanville 258 33.05 N 79.28 W
MacClenny 258 30.18 N 82.07 W
McCloud 270 41.15 N 122.08 W
McCloud ≃ 270 40.46 N 122.18 W
McClure, IL 260 37.19 N 89.26 W
McClure, PA 254 40.42 N 77.19 W
McClure, Lake ⊜1 270 37.37 N 120.16 W
McClusky 264 47.29 N 100.27 W
McColl 258 34.40 N 79.33 W
McComas 258 37.23 N 81.17 W
McComb, MS 260 31.14 N 90.27 W
McComb, OH 254 41.06 N 83.48 W
McConald, Lake ⊜ 248 48.35 N 113.55 W
McConaughy, Lake ⊜1 264 41.15 N 101.50 W
McConnell Air Force Base ■ 264 37.38 N 97.15 W
McConnell Range ▲ 246 64.00 N 123.50 W
McConnellsburg 254 39.56 N 77.59 W
McConnelsville 254 39.39 N 81.51 W
McCook 264 40.12 N 100.38 W
McCormick 258 33.55 N 82.17 W
McCoy Creek ≃ 268 43.02 N 118.50 W
McCoy Lake ⊜ 250 52.35 N 92.19 W
McCreary 250 50.46 N 99.30 W
McCrory 260 35.16 N 91.12 W
McCullough Mountain ▲ 270 35.36 N 115.11 W
McCune 264 37.21 N 95.01 W
McCurtain 260 35.09 N 94.58 W
McCusker ≃ 250 55.32 N 108.40 W
McDade 262 30.17 N 97.15 W
McDavid 260 30.52 N 87.19 W
McDermitt 270 41.59 N 117.36 W
McDermott 254 38.50 N 83.04 W
MacDill Air Force Base ■ 258 27.51 N 82.29 W
McDonald 264 39.47 N 101.22 W
McDonald, Lake ⊜ 268 48.35 N 113.55 W
McDonald Creek ≃ 268 47.01 N 108.09 W
MacDonald Pass)(268 46.34 N 112.18 W
Macdonald Range ▲ 248 49.12 N 114.46 W
McDonough 258 33.27 N 84.09 W
McDougall, Mount ▲ 268 42.54 N 110.36 W
MacDowell Lake ⊜ 250 52.15 N 92.45 W
McDowell Peak ▲ 266 33.40 N 111.50 W
McElmo Creek ≃ 266 37.13 N 109.12 W
McEwen 260 36.06 N 87.38 W
McFadden 268 41.39 N 106.08 W
McFarland, CA 270 35.41 N 119.14 W
McFarland, WI 256 43.01 N 89.17 W
MacFarlane ≃ 242 59.12 N 107.58 W
McGavock Lake ⊜ 250 56.32 N 101.25 W
McGehee 260 33.38 N 91.24 W
McGill 270 39.23 N 114.47 W
McGillivray, Lac ⊜ 254 46.04 N 77.06 W
McGrath 246 62.58 N 155.38 W
McGraw 254 42.36 N 76.06 W
MacGregor 250 49.57 N 98.49 W
McGregor, IA 256 43.01 N 91.11 W
McGregor, TX 262 31.26 N 97.24 W
McGregor ≃ 248 54.11 N 122.00 W
McGregor Lake ⊜ 248 50.31 N 112.53 W
McGuire, Mount ▲ 268 45.10 N 114.36 W
McHenry, IL 256 42.21 N 88.16 W
McHenry, MS 260 30.42 N 89.08 W
Machias 254 44.43 N 67.28 W
Machias ≃ 254 44.43 N 67.22 W
Machias Bay C 254 44.40 N 67.20 W
Machichi ≃ 250 57.03 N 92.06 W
Macho, Arroyo del V 262 33.36 N 104.28 W
McInnes Lake ⊜ 250 52.12 N 93.45 W
McIntosh, AL 260 31.16 N 88.02 W
McIntosh, MN 264 47.38 N 95.53 W
McIntosh, SD 264 45.55 N 101.21 W
McIntosh Lake ⊜ 250 55.45 N 105.08 W
McIntyre Bay C 248 54.05 N 131.55 W
Mackay 268 43.55 N 113.37 W
McKay Creek ≃ 268 45.40 N 118.50 W
MacKay Lake ⊜ 242 63.55 N 110.25 W
McKeand ≃ 242 65.26 N 68.10 W
McKee 258 37.25 N 84.01 W
McKee Creek ≃ 260 39.46 N 90.36 W
McKeesport 254 40.21 N 79.52 W
McKenzie, AL 260 31.33 N 86.43 W
McKenzie, TN 260 36.08 N 88.31 W
Mackenzie □5 242 65.00 N 115.00 W
Mackenzie ≃ 242 69.15 N 134.08 W
McKenzie ≃ 268 44.07 N 123.06 W
Mackenzie Bay C 242 69.00 N 136.30 W
McKenzie Bridge 268 44.05 N 123.04 W
McKenzie Island 250 51.05 N 93.48 W
McKenzie Lake ⊜ 250 54.12 N 102.30 W
Mackenzie Mountains ▲ 242 64.00 N 130.00 W
Mackinac, Straits of ⊔ 256 45.49 N 84.42 W
Mackinac Bridge ♦5 256 45.50 N 84.45 W
Mackinac Island 256 45.51 N 84.37 W
Mackinac Island I 256 45.51 N 84.38 W
Mackinac Island State Park ♦ 256 45.52 N 84.40 W
Mackinaw 256 40.32 N 89.21 W
Mackinaw ≃ 256 40.33 N 89.44 W
Mackinaw City 256 45.47 N 84.44 W
McKinley, Mount ▲ 246 63.30 N 151.00 W
McKinley Park 246 63.44 N 148.54 W
McKinleyville 270 40.57 N 124.06 W
McKinney 262 33.12 N 96.37 W
McKittrick Summit ▲ 270 35.18 N 119.46 W
Macklin 250 52.20 N 109.56 W
McKnight Lake ⊜ 250 56.03 N 101.08 W
Macksville 264 37.58 N 98.58 W
McLain 260 31.06 N 88.50 W
McLaughlin 264 45.49 N 100.49 W
McLaughlin ≃ 250 53.46 N 97.38 W
McLaurin 260 31.10 N 89.13 W
McLean, SK 250 50.30 N 104.04 W
McLean, IL 260 40.19 N 89.10 W
McLean, TX 262 35.14 N 100.36 W
McLean Lake ⊜ 250 56.27 N 109.15 W
McLean Mountain ▲ 252 47.07 N 68.50 W
McLeansboro 260 38.06 N 88.32 W
McLennan 248 55.42 N 116.54 W
McLeod ≃ 248 54.08 N 115.42 W
McLeod Bay C 242 62.53 N 110.00 W
McLeod Lake 248 54.59 N 123.02 W
McLoughlin, Mount ▲ 268 42.27 N 122.19 W
McLoughlin Bay C 242 67.50 N 99.00 W
McLouth 264 39.12 N 95.12 W
McLure 248 51.03 N 120.14 W
McMahon 250 50.05 N 107.32 W
MacMillan ≃ 246 62.52 N 135.55 W
McMillan, Lake ⊜1 262 32.40 N 104.20 W
McMinnville, OR 268 45.13 N 123.12 W
McMinnville, TN 260 35.41 N 85.46 W
McNary 266 34.04 N 109.51 W
McNeil 260 33.21 N 93.13 W
McNeil, Mount ▲ 248 54.35 N 130.14 W
McNeill 260 30.40 N 89.38 W
Macomb 256 40.27 N 90.40 W
Macon, GA 258 32.50 N 83.38 W
Macon, IL 260 39.43 N 89.00 W
Macon, MS 260 33.07 N 88.34 W
Macon, MO 260 39.44 N 92.28 W
Macon, Bayou ≃ 260 31.55 N 91.33 W
Macoun Lake ⊜ 250 56.32 N 103.50 W
Macoupin Creek ≃ 260 39.11 N 90.36 W
McPhail ≃ 250 52.44 N 96.31 W
McPherson 264 38.22 N 97.40 W
McQueeney 262 29.35 N 98.02 W
McRae, AR 260 35.07 N 91.49 W
McRae, GA 258 32.04 N 82.53 W
McRoberts 258 37.12 N 82.40 W
MacTier 256 45.08 N 79.47 W
McVeigh 258 37.32 N 82.15 W
McVille 264 47.46 N 98.11 W
McWilliams 260 31.50 N 87.06 W
Mad ≃, ON 256 44.25 N 79.54 W
Mad ≃, CA 270 40.57 N 124.07 W
Mad ≃, OH 254 39.46 N 84.11 W
Mad ≃, VT 254 44.18 N 72.41 W
Madame, Isle I 252 45.33 N 61.02 W
Madawaska 252 47.21 N 68.20 W
Madawaska ≃ 254 45.27 N 76.21 W
Madawaska Highlands ▲1 256 45.15 N 77.35 W
Maddock 264 47.58 N 99.32 W
Madeleine, Îles de la I 252 47.30 N 61.45 W
Madeleine-Centre 252 49.15 N 65.21 W
Madelia 264 44.03 N 94.25 W
Madeline Island I 256 46.50 N 90.40 W
Madera 270 36.57 N 120.03 W
Madill 262 34.06 N 96.46 W
Madison, AL 260 34.42 N 86.45 W
Madison, FL 258 30.28 N 83.25 W
Madison, GA 258 33.36 N 83.28 W
Madison, IN 260 38.44 N 85.23 W
Madison, KS 264 38.08 N 96.08 W
Madison, ME 254 44.48 N 69.53 W
Madison, MN 264 45.01 N 96.11 W
Madison, MO 260 39.28 N 92.13 W
Madison, NE 264 41.50 N 97.27 W
Madison, NC 258 36.23 N 79.58 W
Madison, OH 254 41.46 N 81.03 W
Madison, SD 264 44.00 N 97.07 W
Madison, VA 258 38.23 N 78.15 W
Madison, WV 254 38.04 N 81.49 W
Madison, WI 256 43.05 N 89.22 W
Madison ≃ 268 45.56 N 111.30 W
Madison, West Fork ≃ 268 44.55 N 111.35 W
Madison Heights 258 37.25 N 79.08 W
Madison Range ▲ 268 45.15 N 111.20 W
Madisonville, KY 260 37.20 N 87.30 W
Madisonville, LA 260 30.24 N 90.09 W
Madisonville, TN 258 35.31 N 84.22 W
Madisonville, TX 262 30.57 N 95.55 W
Madoc 256 44.30 N 77.28 W
Madras 268 44.38 N 121.08 W
Madre, Laguna C 262 27.00 N 97.35 W
Madrid, AL 258 31.01 N 85.24 W
Madrid, IA 256 41.53 N 93.49 W
Madrid, NE 264 40.51 N 101.33 W
Madsen 250 50.58 N 93.55 W
Maeser 266 40.28 N 109.32 W
Mafeking 250 52.41 N 101.06 W
Magaguadavic Lake ⊜ 252 45.43 N 67.12 W
Magazine Mountain ▲ 260 35.10 N 93.38 W
Magdalena 266 34.07 N 107.14 W
Magee 260 31.52 N 89.44 W
Maggie Creek ≃ 270 40.43 N 116.05 W
Magic Reservoir ⊜1 268 43.17 N 114.23 W
Magill Lake ⊜ 250 54.45 N 94.58 W
Magiss Lake ⊜ 250 52.59 N 91.40 W
Magna 266 40.42 N 112.06 W
Magnet 250 51.19 N 99.30 W
Magnetawan ≃ 256 45.46 N 80.37 W
Magnolia, AR 260 33.16 N 93.14 W
Magnolia, MN 264 43.39 N 96.05 W
Magnolia, MS 260 31.09 N 90.28 W
Magnolia, NC 258 34.54 N 78.03 W
Magog 254 45.16 N 72.09 W
Magpie 252 50.19 N 64.30 W
Magpie ≃, ON 256 47.56 N 84.50 W
Magpie ≃, PQ 252 50.19 N 64.27 W
Magpie, Lac ⊜ 252 51.00 N 64.41 W
Magpie-Ouest ≃ 252 51.02 N 64.42 W
Magrath 248 49.25 N 112.52 W
Magruder Mountain ▲ 270 37.25 N 117.33 W
Maguse Lake ⊜ 242 61.40 N 95.10 W
Mahanoy City 254 40.49 N 76.08 W
Mahnomen 264 47.19 N 96.01 W
Mahogany Mountain ▲ 268 43.14 N 117.16 W
Mahomet 260 40.12 N 88.24 W
Mahone Bay 252 44.27 N 64.23 W
Mahone Bay C 252 44.30 N 64.15 W
Mahony Lake ⊜ 246 65.30 N 125.20 W
Mahood Falls 248 51.50 N 120.39 W
Mahood Lake ⊜ 248 51.55 N 120.24 W
Mahtomedi 256 45.04 N 92.57 W
Maiden 258 35.35 N 81.13 W
Maidstone 250 53.06 N 109.18 W
Maili 272c 21.25 N 158.11 W
Main Channel ⊔ 256 45.22 N 81.50 W
Maine □3, U.S. 244
254 45.15 N 69.15 W
Main Topsail ▲ 252 49.08 N 56.33 W
Maitland 252 45.19 N 63.30 W
Maitland ≃ 256 43.45 N 81.43 W
Makaha 272c 21.28 N 158.13 W
Makaha Point > 272b 22.08 N 159.44 W
Makah Indian Reservation ◆4 268 48.20 N 124.41 W
Makahuena Point > 272b 21.52 N 159.27 W
Makaoo Indian Reserve ◆4 250 53.40 N 110.02 W
Makapuu Head > 272c 21.19 N 157.39 W
Makawao 272a 20.52 N 156.19 W
Makaweli 272b 21.55 N 159.38 W
Makena 272a 20.39 N 156.27 W
Makobe Lake ⊜ 256 47.27 N 80.25 W
Makoshika State Park ♦ 264 47.03 N 104.41 W
Makushin Volcano ▲1 246 53.53 N 166.50 W
Makwa Lake ⊜ 250 54.04 N 109.15 W
Malad ≃ 266 41.35 N 112.07 W
Malad City 268 42.12 N 112.15 W
Malaga 262 32.14 N 104.04 W
Malagash 252 45.46 N 63.23 W
Malakoff 262 32.10 N 96.01 W
Malartic 242 48.08 N 78.08 W
Malartic, Lac ⊜ 256 48.15 N 78.07 W

Symbols in the index entries are identified on page 273.

Name	Page	Lat ° ′	Long ° ′
Malaspina Glacier	246	59.50 N	140.30 W
Malaspina Strait	248	49.44 N	124.20 W
Malbaie ≃	252	47.39 N	70.09 W
Malbaie, Baie de	252	48.35 N	64.14 W
Malcom	256	41.43 N	92.33 W
Malden	260	36.34 N	89.57 W
Malheur ≃	268	44.03 N	116.59 W
Malheur, North Fork ≃	268	43.45 N	118.04 W
Malheur, South Fork ≃	268	43.33 N	118.10 W
Malheur Lake	268	43.20 N	118.45 W
Maligne ≃	248	52.56 N	118.02 W
Maligne Lake	248	52.40 N	117.31 W
Malin	268	42.01 N	121.24 W
Maljamar	262	32.51 N	103.46 W
Mallaig	250	54.13 N	111.22 W
Mallery Lake	242	63.55 N	98.25 W
Malmstrom Air Force Base	268	47.30 N	111.10 W
Malone, FL	258	30.57 N	85.10 W
Malone, NY	254	44.51 N	74.17 W
Malpeque Bay	252	46.30 N	63.47 W
Malta, MT	268	48.21 N	107.52 W
Malta, OH	254	39.39 N	81.52 W
Malvern, AR	260	34.22 N	92.49 W
Malvern, IA	264	41.00 N	95.35 W
Malvern, OH	254	40.41 N	81.11 W
Mamakwash Lake	250	51.38 N	92.56 W
Mamalu Bay	272a	20.37 N	156.09 W
Ma-Me-O Beach	248	52.58 N	113.59 W
Mamie	258	36.08 N	75.50 W
Mammoth, AZ	266	32.43 N	110.38 W
Mammoth, WV	254	38.16 N	81.22 W
Mammoth Cave National Park	260	37.08 N	86.13 W
Mammoth Lakes	270	37.38 N	118.58 W
Mammoth Spring	260	36.30 N	91.33 W
Mamou	260	30.38 N	92.25 W
Man	258	37.45 N	81.53 W
Mana	272b	22.02 N	159.46 W
Manana	272c	21.20 N	157.40 W
Manasquan	254	40.07 N	74.03 W
Manassa	266	37.11 N	105.56 W
Manassas	254	38.45 N	77.28 W
Manassas National Battlefield Park	254	38.50 N	77.32 W
Manatee ≃	258	27.32 N	82.38 W
Manawa	256	44.28 N	88.55 W
Manawan Lake	250	55.24 N	103.14 W
Mancelona	256	44.54 N	85.04 W
Manchester, CT	254	41.47 N	72.31 W
Manchester, GA	258	32.51 N	84.37 W
Manchester, IA	256	42.29 N	91.27 W
Manchester, KY	258	37.09 N	83.46 W
Manchester, MA	254	42.34 N	70.46 W
Manchester, MI	256	42.09 N	84.02 W
Manchester, NH	254	42.59 N	71.28 W
Manchester, OH	254	38.41 N	83.36 W
Manchester, TN	260	35.29 N	86.05 W
Manchester, VT	254	43.10 N	73.05 W
Mancos	266	37.21 N	108.18 W
Mancos ≃	266	36.59 N	108.59 W
Mandan	264	46.50 N	100.54 W
Manderson	268	44.16 N	107.58 W
Mandeville	260	30.22 N	90.04 W
Manele Bay	272a	20.45 N	156.53 W
Mangham	260	32.19 N	91.47 W
Mangum	262	34.53 N	99.30 W
Manhattan, KS	264	39.11 N	96.35 W
Manhattan, MT	268	45.52 N	111.20 W
Manicouagan ≃	252	49.11 N	68.13 W
Manicouagan 2 Dam [6]	252	49.20 N	68.24 W
Manicouagan, Réservoir [1]	252	51.30 N	68.19 W
Manigotagan	250	51.06 N	96.18 W
Manigotagan ≃	250	51.07 N	96.20 W
Manila, AR	260	35.53 N	90.10 W
Manila, UT	266	40.59 N	109.43 W
Manilla	264	41.53 N	95.14 W
Manistee	256	44.15 N	86.19 W
Manistee ≃	256	44.15 N	86.21 W
Manistique	256	45.57 N	86.15 W
Manistique ≃	256	45.57 N	86.15 W
Manistique, West Branch ≃	256	46.02 N	86.09 W
Manistique Lake	256	46.15 N	85.45 W
Manito	260	40.25 N	89.47 W
Manitoba [4], Can.	250		
	242	54.00 N	97.00 W
Manitoba, Lake	250	51.00 N	98.45 W
Manito Lake	250	52.45 N	109.45 W
Manitou	250	49.15 N	98.31 W
Manitou ≃	250	48.58 N	93.20 W
Manitou, Lac, PQ	252	50.54 N	65.18 W
Manitou, Lac, PQ	252	50.29 N	63.54 W
Manitou Beach	250	51.43 N	105.26 W
Manitou Lake	256	45.48 N	82.00 W
Manitoulin Island	256	45.45 N	82.30 W
Manitou Springs	264	38.52 N	104.55 W
Manitowaning	256	45.45 N	81.49 W
Manitowish Waters	256	46.09 N	89.53 W
Manitowoc	256	44.06 N	87.40 W
Manitowoc ≃	256	44.05 N	87.39 W
Maniwaki	254	46.23 N	75.58 W
Mankato, KS	264	39.47 N	98.12 W
Mankato, MN	264	44.10 N	94.01 W
Mankota	250	49.25 N	107.04 W
Manley Hot Springs	246	65.00 N	150.37 W
Manly	256	43.17 N	93.12 W
Mannford	262	36.09 N	96.21 W
Manning, IA	264	41.55 N	95.03 W
Manning, ND	264	47.14 N	102.47 W
Manning, SC	258	33.42 N	80.13 W
Manning Provincial Park	248	49.07 N	120.54 W
Mannington	254	39.32 N	80.20 W
Mannville	250	53.20 N	111.10 W
Manokotak	246	58.40 N	159.09 W
Manor, SK	250	49.36 N	102.05 W
Manor, TX	262	30.20 N	97.33 W
Manouane ≃	252	49.30 N	71.11 W
Manouane, Lac	252	50.41 N	70.45 W
Manouanis ≃	252	50.28 N	70.08 W
Manouanis, Lac	252	50.51 N	70.20 W
Mansel Island	242	62.00 N	79.50 W
Mansfield, AR	260	35.04 N	94.13 W
Mansfield, GA	258	33.31 N	83.44 W
Mansfield, IL	260	40.13 N	88.31 W
Mansfield, LA	260	32.02 N	93.43 W
Mansfield, MA	254	42.02 N	71.13 W
Mansfield, MO	260	37.06 N	92.35 W
Mansfield, OH	254	40.46 N	82.31 W
Mansfield, PA	254	41.48 N	77.05 W
Mansfield, TX	262	32.34 N	97.09 W
Mansfield, Mount	254	44.33 N	72.49 W
Manson	264	42.32 N	94.32 W
Manson ≃	248	55.42 N	123.47 W
Mansura	260	31.04 N	92.03 W
Mantagao ≃	250	51.50 N	97.48 W
Manteca	270	37.48 N	121.13 W
Manteno	260	41.14 N	87.50 W
Manteo	258	35.55 N	75.40 W
Manti	266	39.16 N	111.38 W
Manton	256	44.24 N	85.24 W
Mantorville	256	44.05 N	92.45 W
Mantua	254	41.17 N	81.14 W
Manvel	264	48.04 N	97.10 W
Many	260	31.34 N	93.29 W
Manyberries	250	49.24 N	110.42 W
Many Island Lake	250	50.08 N	110.03 W
Manzano	266	34.39 N	106.21 W
Manzanola	264	38.06 N	103.52 W
Manzano Peak	266	34.35 N	106.26 W
Maple ≃, U.S.	264	45.47 N	98.33 W
Maple ≃, IA	264	42.00 N	95.59 W
Maple ≃, MI	256	42.59 N	84.57 W
Maple ≃, MN	256	44.05 N	94.00 W
Maple ≃, ND	264	46.56 N	96.55 W
Maple Creek	250	49.55 N	109.27 W
Maple Creek ≃	264	41.33 N	96.27 W
Maple Lake	256	45.14 N	94.00 W
Maple Mount	260	37.42 N	87.26 W
Maplesville	260	32.47 N	86.52 W
Mapleton, IA	264	42.10 N	95.47 W
Mapleton, MN	256	43.56 N	93.57 W
Mapleton, OR	268	44.02 N	123.52 W
Mapleton, UT	266	40.08 N	111.36 W
Maquereau, Pointe au	252	48.12 N	64.47 W
Maquoketa	256	42.04 N	90.40 W
Maquoketa ≃	256	42.11 N	90.19 W
Maquoketa, North Fork ≃	256	42.05 N	90.40 W
Maraiche Lake	250	54.28 N	102.01 W
Marais des Cygnes ≃	260	38.02 N	94.14 W
Marana	266	32.27 N	111.13 W
Marathon, ON	256	48.40 N	86.25 W
Marathon, NY	254	42.26 N	76.02 W
Marathon, TX	262	30.12 N	103.15 W
Marathon, WI	256	44.56 N	89.50 W
Maravillas Creek ≃	262	29.34 N	102.47 W
Marble, MN	256	47.19 N	93.18 W
Marble, NC	258	35.10 N	83.55 W
Marble Canyon	266	36.30 N	111.50 W
Marble Falls	262	30.34 N	98.17 W
Marblehead	254	41.32 N	82.44 W
Marble Hill	260	37.18 N	89.58 W
Marble Rock	256	42.58 N	92.52 W
Marceau, Lac	252	51.25 N	66.41 W
Marcelin	250	52.55 N	106.47 W
Marceline	260	39.43 N	92.57 W
Marcellus	256	42.03 N	85.49 W
March Air Force Base	270	33.54 N	117.15 W
Marcola	268	44.10 N	122.52 W
Marcus	264	42.50 N	95.48 W
Marcus Baker, Mount	246	61.26 N	147.45 W
Marcy, Mount	254	44.07 N	73.56 W
Marengo, IL	256	42.15 N	88.37 W
Marengo, IN	260	38.22 N	86.21 W
Marengo, IA	256	41.48 N	92.04 W
Marenisco	256	46.23 N	90.30 W
Marfa	262	30.18 N	104.01 W
Margaree	252	46.24 N	61.05 W
Margaree Harbour	252	46.26 N	61.07 W
Margaret Bay	248	51.20 N	127.29 W
Margaretville	254	42.09 N	74.39 W
Margate	258	26.18 N	80.12 W
Margate City	254	39.20 N	74.31 W
Margot Lake	250	52.28 N	93.10 W
Marian Lake	242	63.00 N	116.10 W
Marianna, AR	260	34.46 N	90.46 W
Marianna, FL	258	30.47 N	85.14 W
Marias ≃, N.A.	248	48.25 N	111.45 W
Marias ≃, MT	268	47.56 N	110.30 W
Marias Pass	268	48.19 N	113.21 W
Maricopa, AZ	266	33.04 N	112.03 W
Maricopa, CA	270	35.03 N	119.24 W
Maricourt (Wakeham Bay)	242	61.36 N	71.58 W
Marie Lake	250	54.37 N	110.18 W
Marienville	254	41.28 N	79.07 W
Maries ≃	260	38.30 N	92.01 W
Marietta, FL	258	30.19 N	81.47 W
Marietta, GA	258	33.57 N	84.33 W
Marietta, MN	264	45.01 N	96.25 W
Marietta, OH	254	39.25 N	81.27 W
Marietta, OK	262	33.56 N	97.07 W
Marieville	254	45.26 N	73.10 W
Marine City	256	42.43 N	82.30 W
Marinette	256	45.06 N	87.38 W
Maringouin	260	30.29 N	91.31 W
Marion, AL	260	32.32 N	87.26 W
Marion, AR	260	35.13 N	90.12 W
Marion, IL	260	37.44 N	88.56 W
Marion, IN	260	40.33 N	85.40 W
Marion, IA	256	42.02 N	91.36 W
Marion, KS	264	38.21 N	97.01 W
Marion, KY	260	37.20 N	88.05 W
Marion, LA	260	32.54 N	92.15 W
Marion, MI	256	44.06 N	85.09 W
Marion, MS	260	32.25 N	88.39 W
Marion, NC	258	35.41 N	82.01 W
Marion, ND	264	46.37 N	98.20 W
Marion, OH	254	40.35 N	83.08 W
Marion, SC	258	34.11 N	79.24 W
Marion, SD	264	43.25 N	97.16 W
Marion, VA	258	36.50 N	81.31 W
Marion, WI	256	44.21 N	89.05 W
Marion, Lake	258	28.05 N	81.32 W
Marion, Lake [1]	258	33.30 N	80.25 W
Marion Junction	260	32.26 N	87.14 W
Marion Lake [1]	264	38.24 N	97.08 W
Marionville	260	37.00 N	93.38 W
Mariposa	270	37.29 N	119.58 W
Marissa	260	38.15 N	89.45 W
Markdale	256	44.19 N	80.39 W
Marked Tree	260	35.32 N	90.25 W
Markesan	256	43.42 N	88.59 W
Markham, ON	256	43.52 N	79.16 W
Markham, TX	262	28.57 N	96.04 W
Markham Bay	242	63.30 N	71.48 W
Markle	260	40.50 N	85.20 W
Markleeville	270	38.41 N	119.47 W
Marks	260	34.16 N	90.16 W
Marksville	260	31.08 N	92.04 W
Marlboro, AB	248	53.33 N	116.45 W
Marlboro, NY	254	41.36 N	73.58 W
Marlborough	254	42.21 N	71.33 W
Marlette	256	43.20 N	83.05 W
Marlin	262	31.18 N	96.53 W
Marlinton	254	38.13 N	80.06 W
Marlow	262	34.39 N	97.57 W
Marmaduke	260	36.11 N	90.23 W
Marmarth	264	46.18 N	103.54 W
Marmaton ≃	260	38.00 N	94.19 W
Marmet	254	38.15 N	81.04 W
Marmion Lake [1]	256	48.54 N	91.30 W
Marmora	256	44.29 N	77.41 W
Marmot Bay	246	58.00 N	152.20 W
Marmot Island	246	58.13 N	151.51 W
Marne	256	43.02 N	85.50 W
Maroa	260	40.02 N	88.57 W
Marquand	260	37.26 N	90.10 W
Marquesas Keys	258	24.34 N	82.08 W
Marquette, KS	264	38.33 N	97.50 W
Marquette, MI	256	46.33 N	87.24 W
Marrero	260	29.54 N	90.07 W
Mars	254	40.42 N	80.06 W
Marseilles	260	41.20 N	88.43 W
Marshall, AR	260	35.55 N	92.38 W
Marshall, IL	260	39.23 N	87.42 W
Marshall, MI	256	42.16 N	84.58 W
Marshall, MN	264	44.27 N	95.47 W
Marshall, MO	260	39.07 N	93.12 W
Marshall, NC	258	35.48 N	82.41 W
Marshall, TX	260	32.33 N	94.23 W
Marshall, VA	254	38.52 N	77.52 W
Marshallberg	258	34.44 N	76.31 W
Marshalltown	256	42.03 N	92.55 W
Marshallville	258	32.27 N	89.56 W
Marshfield, MO	260	37.15 N	92.54 W
Marshfield, WI	256	44.40 N	90.10 W
Mars Hill, ME	252	46.31 N	67.52 W
Mars Hill, NC	258	35.47 N	82.29 W
Marsh Island	260	29.35 N	91.53 W
Marsh Lake	246	60.25 N	134.18 W
Marsh Peak	266	40.43 N	109.50 W
Marshville	258	34.59 N	80.26 W
Marshyhope Creek ≃	254	38.32 N	75.45 W
Marsing	268	43.33 N	116.48 W
Mart	262	31.33 N	96.50 W
Marten Lake	256	46.42 N	79.41 W
Marten Mountain	248	55.28 N	114.43 W
Martha's Vineyard	254	41.25 N	70.40 W
Martin, KY	258	37.34 N	82.45 W
Martin, MI	256	42.37 N	85.39 W
Martin, ND	264	47.50 N	100.07 W
Martin, SD	264	43.10 N	101.44 W
Martin, TN	260	36.21 N	88.51 W
Martindale	262	29.50 N	97.51 W
Martinez, CA	270	37.55 N	121.55 W
Martinez, GA	258	33.31 N	82.05 W
Martin Lake [1]	260	32.50 N	85.55 W
Martin Point	246	70.08 N	143.16 W
Martinsburg, PA	254	40.19 N	78.20 W
Martinsburg, WV	254	39.27 N	77.58 W
Martins Ferry	254	40.06 N	80.44 W
Martinsville, IL	260	39.20 N	87.53 W
Martinsville, IN	260	39.26 N	86.25 W
Martinsville, VA	258	36.41 N	79.52 W
Martre, Lac la	242	63.15 N	116.55 W
Marvell	260	34.33 N	90.55 W
Marvine, Mount	266	38.40 N	111.39 W
Marwayne	250	53.32 N	110.20 W
Maryfield	250	49.48 N	101.32 W
Maryland [3], U.S.	244		
	254	39.00 N	76.45 W
Maryneal	262	32.14 N	100.27 W
Marys ≃, IL	260	37.53 N	89.47 W
Marys ≃, NV	270	41.04 N	115.16 W
Marys Creek ≃	268	42.18 N	115.48 W
Mary's Igloo	246	65.09 N	165.04 W
Marys Peak	268	44.30 N	123.33 W
Marystown	252	47.10 N	55.09 W
Marysvale	266	38.27 N	112.11 W
Marysville, BC	248	49.38 N	115.57 W
Marysville, NB	252	45.59 N	66.35 W
Marysville, CA	270	39.09 N	121.35 W
Marysville, KS	264	39.51 N	96.39 W
Marysville, MI	256	42.54 N	82.29 W
Marysville, OH	254	40.14 N	83.22 W
Marysville, PA	254	40.20 N	76.56 W
Marysville, WA	268	48.03 N	122.11 W
Maryville, MO	260	40.21 N	94.52 W
Maryville, TN	258	35.46 N	83.58 W
Mascot	258	36.04 N	83.44 W
Mascoutah	260	38.29 N	89.48 W
Masefield	250	49.09 N	107.48 W
Maskwa ≃	250	50.33 N	96.08 W
Mason, MI	256	42.35 N	84.26 W
Mason, OH	254	39.17 N	84.19 W
Mason, TN	260	35.25 N	89.33 W
Mason, TX	262	30.45 N	99.14 W
Mason, WV	254	39.01 N	82.01 W
Mason City, IL	260	40.12 N	89.42 W
Mason City, IA	256	43.09 N	93.12 W
Mason City, NE	264	41.13 N	99.18 W
Mason Creek	248	55.40 N	124.29 W
Masontown	254	39.51 N	79.54 W
Massachusetts [3], U.S.	244		
	254	42.15 N	71.50 W
Massachusetts Bay	254	42.20 N	70.50 W
Massacre Lake	270	41.39 N	119.35 W
Massena, IA	264	41.15 N	94.46 W
Massena, NY	254	44.56 N	74.54 W
Masset	248	54.02 N	132.09 W
Masset Inlet	248	53.42 N	132.20 W
Massey	256	46.12 N	82.05 W
Massillon	254	40.48 N	81.32 W
Massive, Mount	266	39.12 N	106.28 W
Masterson	262	35.38 N	101.58 W
Matachewan	256	47.56 N	80.39 W
Matador	262	34.01 N	100.49 W
Matagorda	262	28.41 N	95.58 W
Matagorda Bay	262	28.35 N	96.20 W
Matagorda Island	262	28.15 N	96.30 W
Matagorda Peninsula [1]	262	28.32 N	96.07 W
Matamoras	254	41.22 N	74.42 W
Matane	252	48.51 N	67.32 W
Matane, Parc de	252	48.45 N	67.00 W
Matanuska ≃	246	61.30 N	149.15 W
Matapédia	252	47.58 N	66.57 W
Matapédia, Lac	252	48.33 N	67.33 W
Matchi-Manitou, Lac	256	48.00 N	77.04 W
Matewan	258	37.37 N	82.10 W
Mather, MB	250	49.06 N	99.07 W
Mather, PA	254	39.56 N	80.05 W
Matheson	256	48.32 N	80.28 W
Matheson Island	250	51.44 N	96.56 W
Mathews	258	37.26 N	76.19 W
Mathis	262	28.06 N	97.50 W
Matinenda Lake	256	46.22 N	82.57 W
Matinicus Island	254	43.54 N	68.55 W
Matonipi ≃	252	51.21 N	69.45 W
Mattagami ≃	242	50.43 N	81.29 W
Mattagami Heights	256	48.29 N	81.22 W
Mattagami Lake	256	47.54 N	81.35 W
Mattamuskeet, Lake	258	35.30 N	76.11 W
Mattaponi ≃	258	37.31 N	76.47 W
Mattawa, ON	256	46.19 N	78.42 W
Mattawa, WA	268	46.44 N	119.54 W
Mattawa ≃	256	46.19 N	78.43 W
Mattawamkeag	254	45.31 N	68.21 W
Mattawamkeag ≃	254	45.30 N	68.24 W
Matterhorn	270	41.49 N	115.23 W
Matthews Mountain	260	37.29 N	90.21 W
Mattole ≃	270	40.18 N	124.21 W
Mattoon, IL	260	39.29 N	88.22 W
Mattoon, WI	256	45.01 N	89.02 W
Mattox Draw	264	38.03 N	101.11 W
Mattydale	254	43.06 N	76.09 W
Maud, OK	262	35.08 N	96.46 W
Maud, TX	260	33.20 N	94.21 W
Mauger, Île	252	51.05 N	58.45 W
Maui [6]	272a	20.53 N	156.30 W
Maui	272a	20.45 N	156.15 W
Mauldin	258	34.47 N	82.19 W
Maumee	254	41.34 N	83.39 W
Maumee ≃	254	41.42 N	83.28 W
Maumelle, Lake [1]	260	34.55 N	92.40 W
Mauna Kea [1]	272	19.50 N	155.28 W
Maunaloa	272a	21.08 N	157.13 W
Mauna Loa [1]	272	19.29 N	155.36 W
Maunalua Bay	272c	21.17 N	157.44 W
Maunoir, Lac	242	67.30 N	125.00 W
Maupin	268	45.11 N	121.05 W
Maurepas, Lake	260	30.15 N	90.30 W
Maury ≃	258	37.37 N	79.27 W
Maury Channel	242	75.44 N	94.40 W
Mauston	256	43.48 N	90.05 W
Mauvais Coulee	264	48.21 N	99.06 W
Mauvaise Terre Creek ≃	260	39.43 N	90.38 W
Maverick	266	33.43 N	109.32 W
Mawdesley Lake	250	54.01 N	100.39 W
Max	264	47.49 N	101.18 W
Maxon Creek ≃	262	29.53 N	102.24 W
Maxton	258	34.44 N	79.21 W
Maxville	254	45.17 N	74.51 W
Maxwell, CA	270	39.17 N	122.11 W
Maxwell, IA	256	41.53 N	93.24 W
Maxwell, NE	264	41.05 N	100.31 W
Maxwell, NM	262	36.32 N	104.33 W
Maxwell Air Force Base	260	32.23 N	86.21 W
Maxwell Bay	242	74.35 N	89.00 W
May	262	31.59 N	98.55 W
May ≃	250	55.43 N	111.22 W
May, Cape	254	38.58 N	74.55 W
May, Mount	248	54.02 N	119.58 W
Maybeury	258	37.22 N	81.22 W
Mayer	266	34.24 N	112.14 W
Mayersville	260	32.54 N	91.03 W
Mayerthorpe	248	53.57 N	115.08 W
Mayfield, KY	260	36.44 N	88.38 W
Mayfield, UT	266	39.07 N	111.42 W
Mayfield Creek ≃	260	36.57 N	89.05 W
Mayfield Lake [1]	268	46.30 N	122.30 W
Mayflower	260	34.58 N	92.26 W
May Inlet	242	76.15 N	100.45 W
Maymont	250	52.33 N	107.40 W
Maynard	256	42.46 N	91.53 W
Maynardville	258	36.15 N	83.48 W
Mayo, YK	246	63.35 N	135.54 W
Mayo, FL	258	30.03 N	83.10 W
Mayodan	258	36.25 N	79.58 W
Mayo Lake	246	63.46 N	135.10 W
Mayport Naval Station	258	30.22 N	81.24 W
Mays Landing	254	39.27 N	74.44 W
Maysville, KY	254	38.39 N	83.46 W
Maysville, MO	260	39.48 N	94.35 W
Maysville, NC	258	34.59 N	77.14 W
Maysville, OK	262	34.49 N	97.24 W
Mayville, MI	256	43.20 N	83.21 W
Mayville, ND	264	47.30 N	97.19 W
Mayville, NY	254	42.15 N	79.30 W
Mayville, WI	256	43.30 N	88.33 W
Maywood	264	40.39 N	100.37 W
Mazatzal Mountains	266	34.00 N	111.55 W
Mazatzal Peak	266	34.03 N	111.28 W
Mazenod	250	49.53 N	106.14 W
Mazeppa	256	44.17 N	92.32 W
Mazomanie	256	43.11 N	89.48 W
Mazon	260	41.14 N	88.25 W
M'Clintock Channel	242	71.00 N	101.00 W
M'Clure, Cape	242	74.35 N	121.08 W
M'Clure Strait	242	74.30 N	116.00 W
Meacham	250	52.08 N	105.45 W
Mead, Lake [1]	244	36.05 N	114.25 W
Meade, KS	264	37.17 N	100.20 W
Meade, NE	264	41.14 N	96.30 W
Meade ≃	246	70.50 N	156.25 W
Meaden Peak	266	40.46 N	107.03 W
Meade Peak	268	42.30 N	111.15 W
Meadow, TX	262	33.20 N	102.12 W
Meadow, UT	266	38.53 N	112.24 W
Meadow Creek ≃	268	46.03 N	115.18 W
Meadow Lake	250	54.08 N	108.26 W
Meadow Lake	250	54.07 N	108.20 W
Meadow Lake Provincial Park	250	54.28 N	109.10 W
Meadow Valley Wash	270	36.39 N	114.35 W
Meadowview	258	36.46 N	81.52 W
Meadville, MS	260	31.28 N	90.54 W
Meadville, MO	260	39.47 N	93.18 W
Meadville, PA	254	41.38 N	80.09 W
Meaford	256	44.36 N	80.35 W
Meaghers Grant	252	44.55 N	63.15 W
Meakerville	246	60.32 N	145.00 W
Meander River	242	59.02 N	117.42 W
Mebane	258	36.06 N	79.16 W
Mechanic Falls	254	44.07 N	70.24 W
Mechanicsburg	254	40.04 N	83.34 W
Mechanicsville, IA	256	41.54 N	91.15 W
Mechanicsville, VA	258	37.36 N	77.22 W
Mechanicville	254	42.54 N	73.42 W
Medaryville	260	41.05 N	86.55 W
Medford, OK	262	36.48 N	97.44 W
Medford, OR	268	42.19 N	122.52 W
Medford, WI	256	45.09 N	90.20 W
Medfra	246	63.06 N	154.44 W
Media	254	39.54 N	75.23 W
Mediapolis	256	41.00 N	91.10 W
Medical Lake	268	47.34 N	117.41 W
Medicine Bow	266	41.54 N	106.12 W
Medicine Bow ≃	268	42.00 N	106.40 W
Medicine Bow Mountains	268	41.30 N	106.30 W
Medicine Creek ≃, MO	260	39.43 N	93.24 W
Medicine Creek ≃, NE	264	40.17 N	100.10 W
Medicine Creek ≃, SD	264	44.06 N	99.42 W
Medicine Hat	250	50.03 N	110.40 W
Medicine Knoll Creek ≃	264	44.19 N	100.05 W
Medicine Lake	264	48.30 N	104.30 W
Medicine Lake	264	48.28 N	104.24 W
Medicine Lodge	264	37.17 N	98.35 W
Medicine Lodge ≃	262	36.49 N	98.20 W
Medicine Rocks State Park	264	45.09 N	104.35 W
Medina, ND	264	46.54 N	99.18 W
Medina, NY	254	43.13 N	78.23 W
Medina, OH	254	41.08 N	81.52 W
Medina, TX	262	29.48 N	99.15 W
Medina ≃	262	29.12 N	98.20 W
Medina Lake [1]	262	29.35 N	98.58 W
Medio Creek ≃	262	28.19 N	97.19 W
Medora, IN	260	38.49 N	86.10 W
Medora, ND	264	46.55 N	103.31 W
Medstead	250	53.19 N	108.02 W
Meductic	252	46.00 N	67.29 W
Medway	254	45.37 N	68.35 W
Medway ≃	252	44.08 N	64.36 W
Meeker	266	40.02 N	107.55 W
Meeks Bay	270	39.02 N	120.08 W
Meelpaeg Lake [1]	252	48.16 N	56.35 W
Meeteetse	268	44.09 N	108.52 W
Mégantic, Lac	254	45.32 N	70.53 W
Megargel	262	33.27 N	98.56 W
Mégiscane ≃	256	48.29 N	77.08 W
Mégiscane, Lac	256	48.35 N	75.55 W
Meherrin ≃	258	36.26 N	76.57 W
Meigs	258	31.04 N	83.06 W
Meiners Oaks	270	34.30 N	119.17 W
Meiss Lake	270	41.52 N	122.04 W
Mekoryuk	246	60.23 N	166.12 W
Melbourne, AR	260	36.04 N	91.54 W
Melbourne, FL	258	28.05 N	80.37 W
Melbourne, IA	256	41.57 N	93.06 W
Melbourne Island	242	68.30 N	104.45 W
Melcher	256	41.13 N	93.14 W
Meldrum Bay	256	45.56 N	83.07 W
Meldrum Creek	248	52.07 N	122.20 W
Mélèzes, Rivière aux ≃	242	57.40 N	69.29 W
Melfort	250	52.52 N	104.36 W
Melita	250	49.16 N	101.00 W
Mellen	256	46.20 N	90.40 W
Mellette	264	45.09 N	98.30 W
Melozitna ≃	246	64.46 N	155.29 W
Melrose, MN	264	45.40 N	94.49 W
Melrose, NM	262	34.26 N	103.38 W
Melrose, WI	256	44.08 N	91.01 W
Melstone	268	46.36 N	107.52 W
Melton Hill Lake [1]	258	36.00 N	84.15 W
Melvern	264	38.30 N	95.38 W
Melvern Lake [1]	264	38.30 N	95.50 W
Melville, SK	250	50.55 N	102.48 W
Melville, LA	260	30.42 N	91.45 W
Melville, Lake	242	53.45 N	59.30 W
Melville Hills [2]	242	69.20 N	122.00 W
Melville Island	242	75.15 N	110.00 W
Melville Peninsula [1]	242	68.00 N	84.00 W
Melville Sound	242	68.05 N	107.30 W
Melvin, IL	256	40.34 N	88.15 W
Melvin, KY	258	37.21 N	82.43 W
Melvin, TX	262	31.13 N	99.35 W
Melvin Lake	250	57.08 N	100.15 W
Memewin, Lac	256	46.29 N	78.42 W
Memphis, FL	258	27.32 N	82.34 W
Memphis, MI	256	42.54 N	82.46 W
Memphis, MO	260	40.28 N	92.10 W
Memphis, TN	260	35.08 N	90.03 W
Memphis, TX	262	34.44 N	100.32 W
Memphis Naval Air Station	260	35.21 N	89.52 W
Mena	260	34.35 N	94.15 W
Menahga	264	46.45 N	95.06 W
Menan	268	43.43 N	112.00 W
Menard	262	30.55 N	99.47 W
Menasha	256	44.13 N	88.26 W
Mendenhall	260	31.58 N	89.52 W
Mendenhall, Cape	246	59.51 N	166.15 W
Mendocino	270	39.19 N	123.48 W
Mendocino, Cape	270	40.25 N	124.25 W
Mendon, IL	260	40.05 N	91.17 W
Mendon, MI	256	42.00 N	85.27 W
Mendota, CA	270	36.45 N	120.23 W
Mendota, IL	260	41.33 N	89.07 W
Menihek Lakes	242	54.00 N	66.35 W
Menlo Park	270	37.28 N	122.13 W
Menno	264	43.14 N	97.34 W
Meno	262	36.24 N	98.11 W
Menominee	256	45.06 N	87.37 W
Menominee ≃	256	45.05 N	87.36 W
Menomonee Falls	256	43.11 N	88.07 W
Menomonie	256	44.53 N	91.55 W
Mentasta Lake	246	62.55 N	143.45 W
Mentasta Mountains	246	62.40 N	143.07 W
Mentone	262	31.42 N	103.36 W
Mentor	254	41.40 N	81.20 W
Meota	250	53.02 N	108.27 W
Meramec ≃	260	38.23 N	90.21 W
Meramec, Dry Fork ≃	260	37.58 N	91.31 W
Meramec State Park	260	38.14 N	91.05 W
Merasheen	252	47.25 N	54.21 W
Merasheen Island	252	47.30 N	54.15 W
Merced	270	37.18 N	120.29 W
Merced ≃	270	37.21 N	120.58 W
Merced, South Fork ≃	270	37.39 N	119.53 W
Mercedes	262	26.09 N	97.55 W
Mercer, MO	260	40.31 N	93.32 W
Mercer, PA	254	41.14 N	80.15 W
Mercer, WI	256	46.10 N	90.04 W
Mercersburg	254	39.50 N	77.54 W
Merchants Bay	242	67.10 N	62.50 W
Mercoal	248	53.10 N	117.05 W
Mercury	270	36.40 N	115.59 W
Mercy Bay	242	74.05 N	119.00 W
Meredith	254	43.39 N	71.30 W
Meredith, Lake [1]	262	35.36 N	101.42 W
Meredosia	260	39.50 N	90.34 W
Meriden	254	41.32 N	72.48 W
Meridian, GA	258	31.27 N	81.23 W
Meridian, ID	268	43.37 N	116.24 W
Meridian, MS	260	32.22 N	88.42 W
Meridian, TX	262	31.55 N	97.39 W
Meridian Naval Air Station	260	32.33 N	88.34 W
Meridianville	260	34.51 N	86.35 W
Merigold	260	33.50 N	90.50 W
Merino	264	40.29 N	103.21 W
Merkel	262	32.28 N	100.01 W
Merlin, ON	256	42.14 N	82.14 W
Merlin, OR	268	42.31 N	123.25 W
Merna	264	41.29 N	99.46 W
Merrickville	254	44.55 N	75.50 W
Merrill, IA	264	42.43 N	96.15 W
Merrill, MI	256	43.25 N	84.20 W
Merrill, OR	268	42.01 N	121.36 W
Merrill, WI	256	45.11 N	89.41 W
Merrillan	256	44.27 N	90.50 W
Merrillville	260	41.29 N	87.20 W
Merrimack ≃	254	42.49 N	70.49 W
Merriman	264	42.55 N	101.42 W
Merritt	248	50.07 N	120.47 W
Merritt Island	258	28.21 N	80.42 W
Merritt Reservoir [1]	264	42.35 N	100.55 W
Mer Rouge	260	32.47 N	91.48 W
Merryville	260	30.45 N	93.33 W
Mersey ≃	252	44.02 N	64.43 W
Mertzon	262	31.16 N	100.49 W
Mervin	250	53.20 N	108.53 W
Merwin, Lake [1]	268	45.59 N	122.26 W
Mesa	266	33.25 N	111.50 W
Mesabi Range [2]	256	47.30 N	92.50 W
Mesa Mountain	266	37.55 N	106.38 W
Mesa Verde National Park	266	37.13 N	108.30 W
Mescalero	266	33.09 N	105.46 W
Mescalero Indian Reservation [4]	266	33.12 N	105.40 W
Mesgouez, Lac	242	51.24 N	75.05 W
Mesick	256	44.24 N	85.43 W
Mesilinka ≃	248	56.09 N	124.28 W
Mesilla	266	32.16 N	106.48 W
Mesquite, NV	270	36.48 N	114.04 W
Mesquite, TX	262	32.46 N	96.36 W
Messix Peak	266	41.29 N	112.31 W
Meszah Peak	246	58.28 N	131.26 W
Metairie	260	29.59 N	90.09 W
Metaline Falls	268	48.52 N	117.22 W
Metamora	256	40.47 N	89.22 W
Meteghan	252	44.11 N	66.10 W
Meteor Crater [6]	266	35.02 N	111.02 W
Methow ≃	268	48.03 N	119.53 W
Metiskow	250	52.24 N	110.38 W
Metlakatla, BC	248	54.20 N	130.27 W
Metlakatla, AK	246	55.08 N	131.35 W
Meto, Bayou ≃	260	34.05 N	91.26 W
Metolius ≃	268	44.36 N	121.17 W
Metropolis	260	37.09 N	88.44 W
Metropolitan	256	46.00 N	87.53 W
Metter	258	32.24 N	82.03 W
Mexia	262	31.41 N	96.29 W
Mexican Hat	266	37.09 N	109.52 W
Mexico, ME	254	44.34 N	70.33 W
Mexico, MO	260	39.10 N	91.53 W
Mexico, NY	254	43.28 N	76.14 W
Mexico, Gulf of	244	25.00 N	90.00 W
Mexico Bay	254	43.31 N	76.17 W
Mexico Beach	260	29.58 N	85.24 W
Meyers Chuck	246	55.44 N	132.12 W
Meyersdale	254	39.45 N	79.05 W
Meyronne	250	49.39 N	106.50 W
Meziadin Lake	246	56.04 N	129.18 W
Miami, MB	250	49.21 N	98.11 W
Miami, AZ	266	33.24 N	110.52 W
Miami, FL	258	25.46 N	80.12 W
Miami, OK	260	36.53 N	94.53 W
Miami, TX	262	35.42 N	100.38 W
Miami Beach	258	25.47 N	80.08 W
Miami Canal	258	25.47 N	80.15 W
Miamisburg	254	39.38 N	84.17 W
Miami Springs	258	25.49 N	80.17 W
Mica Mountain	266	32.13 N	110.33 W
Micanopy	258	29.30 N	82.17 W
Michaud Point	252	45.34 N	60.40 W
Michel	248	49.43 N	114.49 W
Michel Peak	248	53.35 N	126.26 W
Michelson, Mount	246	69.19 N	144.17 W
Michigamee ≃	256	46.04 N	88.13 W
Michigan	264	48.07 N	98.07 W
Michigan [3], U.S.	244		
	256	44.00 N	85.00 W
Michigan ≃	266	40.52 N	106.20 W
Michigan, Lake	244	44.00 N	87.00 W
Michigan Center	256	42.14 N	84.20 W
Michigan City	260	41.43 N	86.54 W
Michikamau Lake	242	54.15 N	64.00 W
Michipicoten Bay	256	47.55 N	84.56 W
Michipicoten Island	256	47.45 N	85.45 W
Midale	250	49.22 N	103.27 W
Middle ≃, BC	248	54.50 N	125.08 W
Middle ≃, IA	256	41.29 N	93.24 W
Middle ≃, MN	264	48.22 N	97.04 W
Middle Alkali Lake	270	41.28 N	120.04 W
Middle Bay	252	51.28 N	57.30 W
Middleboro	254	41.49 N	70.55 W
Middle Bosque ≃	262	31.31 N	97.16 W
Middlebourne	254	39.30 N	80.54 W
Middlebro	250	49.01 N	95.21 W
Middle Brook	252	48.45 N	54.13 W
Middleburg, NY	254	42.36 N	74.20 W
Middleburg, PA	254	40.47 N	77.03 W
Middleburg, VA	254	38.58 N	77.44 W
Middlebury	254	44.01 N	73.10 W
Middle Channel ≃ [1]	246	69.05 N	136.00 W
Middle Concho ≃	262	31.27 N	100.25 W
Middle Fabius ≃	260	39.58 N	91.35 W
Middlefield	254	41.28 N	81.05 W
Middle Loup ≃	264	41.17 N	98.23 W
Middle Musquodoboit	252	45.03 N	63.09 W
Middle Nodaway ≃	264	40.54 N	95.00 W
Middle Pease ≃	262	34.15 N	100.07 W
Middle Point	254	40.51 N	84.27 W
Middle Popo Aggie ≃	268	42.51 N	108.42 W
Middleport	254	39.00 N	82.03 W
Middle Raccoon ≃	264	41.34 N	94.12 W
Middle Rush Creek ≃	264	38.52 N	103.29 W
Middlesboro	258	36.36 N	83.43 W
Middlesex	258	35.47 N	78.12 W
Middle Stewiacke	252	45.13 N	63.08 W
Middleton, NS	252	44.57 N	65.04 W
Middleton, MI	256	43.11 N	84.43 W
Middleton, TN	260	35.04 N	88.54 W
Middleton, WI	256	43.06 N	89.30 W
Middleton Island	246	59.25 N	146.25 W
Middletown, CA	270	38.45 N	122.37 W
Middletown, CT	254	41.33 N	72.39 W
Middletown, DE	254	39.25 N	75.47 W
Middletown, IL	260	40.11 N	89.35 W
Middletown, IN	260	40.03 N	85.32 W
Middletown, KY	260	38.15 N	85.32 W
Middletown, MD	254	39.27 N	77.33 W
Middletown, NY	254	41.27 N	74.25 W
Middletown, OH	254	39.29 N	84.25 W
Middletown, PA	254	40.12 N	76.44 W
Middletown, RI	254	41.32 N	71.17 W
Middletown, VA	254	39.02 N	78.17 W
Middleville	256	42.43 N	85.28 W
Middle Yegua Creek ≃	262	30.19 N	96.47 W
Middle Yuba ≃	270	39.22 N	121.12 W
Midgic	252	45.59 N	64.18 W
Midland, ON	256	44.45 N	79.53 W
Midland, CA	270	33.52 N	114.48 W
Midland, MI	256	43.37 N	84.14 W
Midland, NC	258	35.14 N	80.30 W
Midland, SD	264	44.04 N	101.10 W
Midland, TX	262	32.00 N	102.05 W
Midlothian	262	32.29 N	97.00 W
Midnapore	248	50.55 N	114.05 W
Midvale	268	44.28 N	116.44 W
Midville	258	32.49 N	88.14 W
Midway, AL	258	32.05 N	85.31 W
Midway, KY	254	38.09 N	84.41 W
Midway, TX	262	31.02 N	95.45 W
Midway, UT	266	40.31 N	111.28 W
Midway Park	258	34.43 N	77.21 W
Midwest	268	43.25 N	106.16 W
Midwest City	262	35.27 N	97.24 W
Mifflinburg	254	40.55 N	77.03 W
Mikkwa ≃	242	58.25 N	114.45 W
Milaca	256	45.45 N	93.39 W

Symbols in the index entries are identified on page 273.

Name	Page	Lat	Long
Milan, GA	258	32.01 N	83.04 W
Milan, IN	260	39.07 N	85.08 W
Milan, MI	256	42.05 N	83.40 W
Milan, MN	264	45.07 N	95.55 W
Milan, MO	260	40.12 N	93.07 W
Milan, NM	266	35.09 N	107.54 W
Milan, OH	256	41.18 N	82.36 W
Milan, TN	260	35.55 N	88.46 W
Milano	262	30.43 N	96.52 W
Milbank	264	45.13 N	96.38 W
Milbanke Sound ⊔	248	52.18 N	128.33 W
Milbridge	254	44.32 N	67.53 W
Milburn	262	34.14 N	96.33 W
Milden	250	51.30 N	107.31 W
Mildmay	256	44.03 N	81.07 W
Mildred	254	41.29 N	76.23 W
Miles	262	31.36 N	100.11 W
Miles City	264	46.25 N	105.51 W
Mile Seven Hundred Thirty Three	246	60.03 N	131.07 W
Milestone	250	50.00 N	104.30 W
Milford, CT	254	41.13 N	73.04 W
Milford, DE	254	38.55 N	75.25 W
Milford, IL	260	40.38 N	87.42 W
Milford, IN	260	41.25 N	85.51 W
Milford, IA	264	43.20 N	95.09 W
Milford, ME	254	44.57 N	68.39 W
Milford, MA	254	42.08 N	71.32 W
Milford, MI	256	42.35 N	83.36 W
Milford, NH	254	42.50 N	71.39 W
Milford, NJ	254	40.34 N	75.06 W
Milford, PA	254	41.19 N	74.48 W
Milford, UT	268	38.24 N	113.01 W
Milford Center	254	40.11 N	83.26 W
Milford Dam	264	39.02 N	96.54 W
Milford Lake	264	39.15 N	97.00 W
Milford Station	252	45.03 N	63.26 W
Milk ≈	248	48.05 N	106.15 W
Milk Creek ≈	266	40.24 N	107.45 W
Milk River	248	49.09 N	112.05 W
Milk River Ridge ⚲¹	248	49.15 N	112.30 W
Milk River Ridge Reservoir ⚲¹	248	49.15 N	112.17 W
Millard	264	41.13 N	96.07 W
Millboro	258	37.59 N	79.36 W
Millbrook, ON	256	44.09 N	78.27 W
Millbrook, NY	254	41.47 N	73.42 W
Millbury	254	42.11 N	71.46 W
Mill City	268	44.45 N	122.29 W
Millcreek, UT	268	40.43 N	111.51 W
Mill Creek, WV	258	38.44 N	79.58 W
Mill Creek ≈, IN	260	39.30 N	86.57 W
Mill Creek ≈, IA	264	42.47 N	95.31 W
Mill Creek ≈, KS	264	39.55 N	96.56 W
Millcreek Township	254	42.05 N	80.10 W
Milledgeville, GA	258	33.04 N	83.14 W
Milledgeville, IL	260	41.58 N	89.46 W
Mille Lacs, Lac des ⊕	256	48.50 N	90.30 W
Mille Lacs Kathio State Park ♦	256	46.08 N	93.43 W
Mille Lacs Lake ⊕	256	46.15 N	93.40 W
Millen	258	32.48 N	81.57 W
Miller, MO	260	37.13 N	93.50 W
Miller, SD	264	44.31 N	98.59 W
Miller, Mount ∧	246	60.25 N	142.23 W
Miller House	246	65.32 N	145.11 W
Miller Mountain ∧	270	38.03 N	118.12 W
Miller Peak ∧	266	31.23 N	110.17 W
Millersburg, KY	258	38.18 N	84.10 W
Millersburg, MI	256	45.20 N	84.04 W
Millersburg, OH	256	40.33 N	81.55 W
Millersburg, PA	254	40.33 N	76.58 W
Millers Creek	262	33.27 N	99.14 W
Millers Ferry	262	32.06 N	87.22 W
Millersport	254	39.54 N	82.32 W
Millersville	254	41.57 N	73.31 W
Millerton Lake ⚲	270	37.01 N	119.41 W
Millertown Junction	252	48.49 N	56.33 W
Millet	262	53.06 N	113.28 W
Millett	262	28.35 N	99.12 W
Mill Hall	254	41.06 N	77.29 W
Milligan, FL	260	30.45 N	86.38 W
Milligan, NE	264	40.30 N	97.23 W
Milligan Gulch ∨	266	33.37 N	107.02 W
Millington, MI	256	43.17 N	83.32 W
Millington, TN	260	35.21 N	89.54 W
Millinocket	254	45.39 N	68.43 W
Mill Island I	242	64.00 N	78.00 W
Millport	258	33.34 N	88.05 W
Millry	260	31.33 N	88.19 W
Mills Lake ⊕	242	61.30 N	118.10 W
Milltown, IN	260	38.21 N	86.17 W
Milltown, MT	268	46.53 N	113.52 W
Milltown, WI	256	45.32 N	92.30 W
Mill Valley	270	37.54 N	122.32 W
Millville	254	39.24 N	75.02 W
Millwood	254	39.04 N	78.02 W
Millwood Lake ⚲	260	33.45 N	94.00 W
Milnor	264	46.16 N	97.27 W
Milo, AB	248	50.34 N	112.53 W
Milo, IA	264	41.17 N	93.27 W
Milo, ME	254	45.15 N	68.59 W
Milpitas	270	37.26 N	121.54 W
Milpitas Wash ∨	270	33.18 N	114.44 W
Milroy, IN	260	39.30 N	85.28 W
Milroy, PA	254	40.43 N	77.35 W
Milton, ON	256	43.31 N	79.53 W
Milton, DE	254	38.47 N	75.19 W
Milton, FL	260	30.38 N	87.03 W
Milton, IA	264	40.41 N	92.10 W
Milton, ND	264	48.38 N	98.03 W
Milton, PA	254	41.01 N	76.51 W
Milton, VT	254	44.38 N	73.07 W
Milton, WV	258	38.26 N	82.08 W
Milton, WI	254	42.47 N	88.56 W
Milton-freewater	268	45.56 N	118.23 W
Miltonvale	264	39.21 N	97.27 W
Milverton	256	43.34 N	80.55 W
Milwaukee	256	43.02 N	87.55 W
Milwaukee ≈	256	43.02 N	87.54 W
Milwaukie	268	45.27 N	122.38 W
Mimbres ≈	266	32.25 N	107.45 W
Mimbres Mountains ∧	266	32.45 N	107.45 W
Mims	258	28.40 N	80.51 W
Mina	270	38.24 N	118.07 W
Minago ≈	250	54.34 N	98.08 W
Minam ≈	268	45.37 N	117.43 W
Minas Basin C	252	45.20 N	64.00 W
Minas Channel	252	45.15 N	64.45 W
Minatare	264	41.48 N	103.30 W
Minchumina, Lake ⊕	246	63.52 N	152.15 W
Minco	262	35.19 N	97.57 W
Mindemoya, ON	256	45.44 N	82.10 W
Minden, ON	256	44.55 N	78.43 W
Minden, IA	264	41.28 N	95.32 W
Minden, LA	260	32.37 N	93.17 W
Minden, NE	264	40.30 N	98.57 W
Minden, NV	270	38.57 N	119.45 W
Minden, WV	258	37.59 N	81.07 W
Minden City	256	43.40 N	82.47 W
Mindenmines	256	37.28 N	94.35 W
Mineola	262	32.40 N	95.29 W
Mineral	258	46.43 N	122.11 W
Mineral Point	256	42.52 N	90.11 W
Mineral Springs	260	33.53 N	93.55 W
Mineral Wells	262	32.48 N	98.07 W
Minersville, PA	254	40.41 N	76.16 W
Minersville, UT	268	38.13 N	112.55 W
Minerva	254	40.44 N	81.06 W
Mineville	254	44.05 N	73.31 W
Mingan	252	50.18 N	64.02 W
Mingan, Îles de ⊔¹	252	50.12 N	63.35 W
Mingo Junction	254	40.19 N	80.37 W
Mingo Lake ⊕	242	64.35 N	72.10 W
Minier	260	40.26 N	89.19 W
Miniota	250	50.08 N	101.00 W
Minisinakwa Lake ⊕	256	47.40 N	81.43 W
Ministikwan Lake ⊕	250	54.01 N	109.39 W
Minitonas	250	52.07 N	101.00 W
Minneapolis, KS	264	39.08 N	97.42 W
Minneapolis, MN	264	44.59 N	93.13 W
Minnechaduza Creek ≈	264	42.54 N	100.29 W
Minnedosa	250	50.14 N	99.51 W
Minnedosa ≈	250	49.53 N	100.08 W
Minnehaha	268	45.39 N	122.37 W
Minneola	254	37.26 N	100.01 W
Minnesa Creek ≈	262	35.31 N	102.48 W
Minnesota □³, U.S.	244		
Minnesota ≈	256	46.00 N	94.15 W
Minnesota Lake	256	43.51 N	93.50 W
Minnewanka, Lake ⊕	248	51.15 N	115.20 W
Minnewaukan	264	48.04 N	99.15 W
Minnitaki Lake ⊕	250	49.58 N	92.00 W
Minocqua	256	45.52 N	89.43 W
Minong	256	46.06 N	91.49 W
Minonk	256	40.54 N	89.02 W
Minot	264	48.14 N	101.18 W
Minot Air Force Base ∗	264	48.26 N	101.21 W
Minster	254	40.24 N	84.23 W
Minto, MB	250	49.25 N	100.01 W
Minto, NB	252	46.05 N	66.05 W
Minto, YK	246	62.34 N	136.51 W
Minto, AK	246	64.53 N	149.11 W
Minto, ND	264	48.17 N	97.15 W
Minto, Lac ⊕	242	51.00 N	73.37 W
Minto Inlet C	242	71.20 N	117.00 W
Minton	250	49.05 N	105.35 W
Minturn	266	39.35 N	106.26 W
Mio	256	44.39 N	84.08 W
Mira	254	46.03 N	60.00 W
Mira Bay C	252	46.02 N	59.56 W
Miramichi Bay C	252	47.08 N	65.08 W
Miranda	270	40.14 N	123.49 W
Mirando City	262	27.26 N	99.00 W
Mirond Lake ⊕	250	55.06 N	102.47 W
Mirror	248	52.28 N	113.07 W
Miscou Centre	252	47.57 N	64.34 W
Miscou Island I	252	47.57 N	64.33 W
Miscou Point ⊁	252	48.03 N	64.32 W
Misema ≈	256	47.54 N	79.53 W
Misenheimer	258	35.29 N	80.17 W
Mishawaka	260	41.40 N	86.11 W
Misheguk Mountain ∧	246	68.15 N	161.03 W
Mishibishu Lake ⊕	256	48.05 N	85.25 W
Mishicot	256	44.14 N	87.38 W
Misquamabein Lake ⊕	250	53.30 N	91.05 W
Missinaibi ≈	242	50.44 N	81.29 W
Missinaibi Lake ⊕	256	48.23 N	83.40 W
Mission, SD	264	43.18 N	100.40 W
Mission, TX	262	26.13 N	98.20 W
Mission City	248	49.08 N	122.18 W
Mission Mountain ∧	250	34.15 N	94.33 W
Mission Range ∧	248	47.30 N	113.55 W
Mississagi ≈	256	46.10 N	83.01 W
Mississagi Provincial Park ♦	256	46.35 N	82.30 W
Mississinewa ≈	260	40.46 N	86.02 W
Mississippi □³, U.S.	244		
Mississippi ≈, ON	256	45.26 N	76.16 W
Mississippi ≈, U.S.	244		
Mississippi Delta ⊵²	260	29.10 N	89.15 W
Mississippi Lake ⊕	256	45.05 N	76.12 W
Mississippi Sound ⊔	260	30.15 N	88.40 W
Missoula	268	46.52 N	114.01 W
Missouri □³	244		
Missouri ≈	260	38.30 N	90.30 W
Missouri, Coteau du ⚬⁶	264	46.00 N	99.30 W
Missouri Buttes ∧²	264	44.37 N	104.47 W
Missouri Valley	264	41.33 N	95.53 W
Mistaken Point ⊁	252	46.38 N	53.10 W
Mistanipisipou ≈	252	51.32 N	61.50 W
Mistassibi ≈	242	48.53 N	72.13 W
Mistassibi-Nord-Est ≈	252	49.50 N	71.56 W
Mistassini, Lac ⊕	242	51.00 N	73.37 W
Mistatim	250	52.52 N	103.22 W
Mistawasis Indian Reserve ⊷⁴	250	53.06 N	106.48 W
Mistikokan ≈	256	57.00 N	91.27 W
Mitchell, ON	256	43.28 N	81.12 W
Mitchell, IN	260	38.44 N	86.28 W
Mitchell, NE	264	41.57 N	103.48 W
Mitchell, OR	268	44.34 N	120.09 W
Mitchell, SD	264	43.43 N	98.01 W
Mitchell, Lake ⚲	258	32.50 N	86.30 W
Mitchell, Mount ∧	258	35.46 N	82.16 W
Mitchellville	264	41.46 N	93.22 W
Mitis, Lac ⊕	252	48.17 N	67.45 W
Mitsito ≈	250	54.50 N	98.58 W
Mitkof Island I	246	56.45 N	132.50 W
Mitrofania Island I	246	55.51 N	158.49 W
Mize	260	31.52 N	89.34 W
Mizpah Creek ≈	264	46.16 N	105.17 W
Moab	268	38.35 N	109.33 W
Moar Lake ⊕	250	52.00 N	95.09 W
Mobeetie	262	35.31 N	100.26 W
Moberly	260	39.25 N	92.26 W
Moberly ≈	250	56.12 N	120.55 W
Moberly Lake	250	55.48 N	121.45 W
Mobile, AL	260	30.42 N	88.05 W
Mobile, AZ	266	33.03 N	112.16 W
Mobile Bay C	260	30.25 N	88.00 W
Mobridge	264	45.32 N	100.26 W
Mocksville	258	35.54 N	80.34 W
Moclips	268	47.14 N	124.13 W
Modeste, Mount ∧	248	48.37 N	124.06 W
Modesto	270	37.39 N	121.00 W
Moenkopi	266	36.07 N	111.13 W
Moenkopi Wash ∨	266	36.54 N	111.26 W
Moffet Point ⊁	246	55.26 N	162.32 W
Moffit	264	46.41 N	100.18 W
Mogollon Mountains ∧	266	33.25 N	108.40 W
Mogollon Rim ∧⁷	266	32.30 N	111.00 W
Mohall	264	48.46 N	101.31 W
Mohave, Lake ⚲	270	35.25 N	114.38 W
Mohawk ≈	256	47.18 N	88.26 W
Mohawk ≈	254	42.47 N	73.42 W
Mohawk Mountain ∧	254	41.49 N	73.17 W
Mohican ≈	254	40.22 N	82.09 W
Mohican, Cape ⊁	246	60.12 N	167.28 W
Mohicanville Reservoir ⚲¹	254	40.45 N	82.00 W
Moira ≈	256	44.09 N	77.23 W
Moisie	252	50.11 N	66.05 W
Moisie ≈	252	50.12 N	66.04 W
Moisie, Baie C	252	50.16 N	65.56 W
Mojave	270	35.03 N	118.10 W
Mojave ≈	270	35.06 N	116.04 W
Mojave Desert ⊹²	270	35.00 N	117.00 W
Mokapu Peninsula ⊁¹	272c	21.27 N	157.45 W
Mokelumne ≈	270	38.13 N	121.28 W
Mokelumne, North Fork ≈	270	38.22 N	120.37 W
Mokuleia	272c	21.35 N	158.09 W
Molalla	268	45.09 N	122.35 W
Molalla ≈	268	45.18 N	122.43 W
Molanosa	250	54.30 N	105.33 W
Molega Lake ⊕	252	44.22 N	64.53 W
Moline, IL	260	41.30 N	90.31 W
Moline, KS	264	37.22 N	96.18 W
Molino	260	30.43 N	87.20 W
Moller, Port C	246	55.51 N	160.25 W
Molokai I	272a	21.07 N	157.00 W
Molokini I	272a	20.38 N	156.30 W
Molson Lake ⊕	250	54.12 N	96.45 W
Momence	260	41.10 N	87.40 W
Mona	266	39.49 N	111.51 W
Monaca	254	40.41 N	80.17 W
Monadnock, Mount ∧	254	42.52 N	72.07 W
Monahans	262	31.36 N	102.54 W
Monahans Draw ∨	262	31.55 N	101.46 W
Monahans Sandhills State Park ♦	262	31.38 N	102.50 W
Monango	264	46.10 N	98.43 W
Monarch	248	47.59 N	110.25 W
Monarch Mountain ∧	248	51.54 N	125.53 W
Monarch Pass)(	266	38.30 N	106.19 W
Monashee Mountains ∧	248	50.30 N	118.30 W
Monashee Provincial Park ♦	248	50.28 N	118.11 W
Moncks Corner	258	33.12 N	80.01 W
Moncton	252	46.06 N	64.47 W
Mondovi	256	44.34 N	91.40 W
Monero	266	36.54 N	106.52 W
Monessen	254	40.09 N	79.53 W
Monett	260	36.55 N	93.55 W
Monette	260	35.53 N	90.21 W
Mongaup ≈	254	41.25 N	74.45 W
Monico	256	45.35 N	89.09 W
Monida Pass)(	268	44.33 N	112.18 W
Monitor Range ∧	270	38.45 N	116.30 W
Monitor Valley ∨	270	39.00 N	116.40 W
Monmouth, IL	256	40.55 N	90.39 W
Monmouth, OR	268	44.51 N	123.14 W
Monmouth Mountain ∧	248	51.00 N	123.47 W
Monmouth Peak ∧	248	44.48 N	123.33 W
Mono Lake ⊕	270	38.00 N	119.00 W
Monon	260	40.52 N	86.53 W
Monona, IA	264	43.03 N	91.23 W
Monona, WI	256	43.03 N	89.20 W
Monongahela	254	40.11 N	79.56 W
Monongahela ≈	254	39.33 N	79.55 W
Monroe, GA	258	33.47 N	83.43 W
Monroe, IN	260	40.58 N	84.52 W
Monroe, LA	260	32.33 N	92.07 W
Monroe, MI	256	41.55 N	83.24 W
Monroe, NE	264	41.28 N	97.36 W
Monroe, NC	258	34.59 N	80.33 W
Monroe, NY	254	41.20 N	74.11 W
Monroe, OR	268	44.19 N	123.18 W
Monroe, UT	268	38.38 N	112.07 W
Monroe, VA	258	37.30 N	79.08 W
Monroe, WA	268	47.51 N	121.58 W
Monroe, WI	256	42.36 N	89.38 W
Monroe, Lake ⚲	258	28.52 N	81.16 W
Monroe City, IN	260	38.37 N	87.21 W
Monroe City, MO	260	39.39 N	91.44 W
Monroeville, AL	260	31.31 N	87.20 W
Monroeville, IN	260	40.58 N	84.52 W
Monroeville, OH	254	41.15 N	82.42 W
Monroeville, PA	254	40.26 N	79.47 W
Monson	254	45.17 N	69.30 W
Montague, PE	252	46.10 N	62.39 W
Montague, CA	270	41.44 N	122.32 W
Montague, MI	256	43.25 N	86.22 W
Montague, TX	262	33.40 N	97.43 W
Montague Island I	246	60.00 N	147.30 W
Montague Peak ∧	246	60.15 N	147.01 W
Montana □³, U.S.	244		
Montana Indian Reserve ⊷⁴	248	52.43 N	113.25 W
Montauk	254	41.03 N	71.57 W
Montauk Point ⊁	254	41.04 N	71.52 W
Mont Belvieu	262	29.51 N	94.54 W
Montcevelles, Lac de ⊕	252	51.07 N	60.38 W
Montclair, CA	270	34.06 N	117.41 W
Montclair, NJ	254	40.49 N	74.13 W
Monteagle	260	35.15 N	85.50 W
Montebello	270	34.01 N	118.07 W
Monte Creek	248	50.39 N	119.57 W
Montecito	270	34.26 N	119.39 W
Montegut	260	29.29 N	90.33 W
Montello, NV	270	41.16 N	114.12 W
Montello, WI	256	43.48 N	89.20 W
Monterey, CA	270	36.37 N	121.55 W
Monterey, TN	258	36.09 N	85.16 W
Monterey, VA	258	38.25 N	79.35 W
Monterey Bay C	270	36.48 N	121.55 W
Montesano	268	46.59 N	123.36 W
Montevallo	260	33.06 N	86.52 W
Montevideo	264	44.57 N	95.43 W
Monte Vista	266	37.35 N	106.09 W
Montezuma, GA	258	32.18 N	84.02 W
Montezuma, IN	260	39.48 N	87.22 W
Montezuma, IA	264	41.35 N	92.32 W
Montezuma, KS	264	37.36 N	100.27 W
Montezuma Castle National Monument ⌂	266	34.30 N	112.00 W
Montezuma Creek ≈	266	37.17 N	109.20 W
Montfort	256	42.58 N	90.26 W
Montgomery, AL	260	32.23 N	86.18 W
Montgomery, LA	260	31.40 N	92.53 W
Montgomery, MN	256	44.26 N	93.35 W
Montgomery, PA	254	41.10 N	76.52 W
Montgomery, TX	262	30.23 N	95.42 W
Montgomery, WV	258	38.11 N	81.19 W
Monticello, AR	260	33.38 N	91.47 W
Monticello, FL	260	30.33 N	83.52 W
Monticello, GA	258	33.18 N	83.40 W
Monticello, IL	260	40.01 N	88.34 W
Monticello, IN	260	40.45 N	86.46 W
Monticello, KY	258	36.50 N	84.51 W
Monticello, IA	264	42.15 N	91.12 W
Monticello, MN	256	45.18 N	93.48 W
Monticello, MS	260	31.33 N	90.07 W
Monticello, MO	260	40.07 N	91.43 W
Monticello, NY	254	41.39 N	74.42 W
Monticello, UT	268	37.52 N	109.21 W
Monticello, WI	256	42.45 N	89.35 W
Mont-Joli	252	48.35 N	68.11 W
Mont-Laurier	252	46.33 N	75.30 W
Montmagny	252	46.59 N	70.33 W
Montmorency ≈	252	46.59 N	71.09 W
Montmorency	252	46.53 N	71.07 W
Mont Orford, Parc ♦	252	45.22 N	72.05 W
Montour Falls	254	42.21 N	76.51 W
Montoursville	254	41.15 N	76.55 W
Montpelier, ID	268	42.19 N	111.18 W
Montpelier, IN	260	40.33 N	85.17 W
Montpelier, MS	258	33.43 N	88.57 W
Montpelier, OH	254	41.35 N	84.36 W
Montpelier, VT	254	44.16 N	72.35 W
Montreal, PQ	254	45.31 N	73.34 W
Montreal, WI	256	46.26 N	90.14 W
Montreal ≈, ON	256	47.08 N	79.27 W
Montreal ≈, ON	256	47.14 N	84.39 W
Montreal ≈, SK	250	55.06 N	105.19 W
Montreal, U.S.	256	46.44 N	90.25 W
Montreal Lake	250	54.03 N	105.46 W
Montreal Lake ⊕	250	54.20 N	105.40 W
Montreal Lake Indian Reserve ⊷⁴	250	54.00 N	105.45 W
Montrose, CO	266	38.29 N	107.53 W
Montrose, IA	264	40.31 N	91.25 W
Montrose, MI	256	43.11 N	83.54 W
Montrose, PA	254	41.50 N	75.53 W
Montrose, SD	264	43.42 N	97.11 W
Montross	258	38.06 N	76.50 W
Monts, Pointe des ⊁	252	49.20 N	67.23 W
Mont-Sainte-Anne, Parc du ♦	252	47.08 N	70.55 W
Montvale	258	37.23 N	79.43 W
Monument	266	38.30 N	104.19 W
Monument Draw ∨, U.S.	262	32.26 N	102.10 W
Monument Draw ∨, TX	262	30.51 N	102.33 W
Monument Peak ∧, CO	266	39.43 N	107.55 W
Monument Peak ∧, ID	268	42.07 N	114.14 W
Monument Valley ∨	266	37.05 N	110.20 W
Moodie Island I	242	64.37 N	65.30 W
Moody	262	31.19 N	97.21 W
Moody Air Force Base ∗	258	30.59 N	83.11 W
Moorcroft	268	44.16 N	104.57 W
Moore, ID	268	43.44 N	113.22 W
Moore, MT	248	46.59 N	109.42 W
Moore, OK	262	35.20 N	97.29 W
Moore, TX	262	29.03 N	99.01 W
Moorefield	258	39.04 N	78.58 W
Moore Haven	258	26.50 N	81.05 W
Mooreland	262	36.26 N	99.12 W
Moore Reservoir ⚲¹	254	44.25 N	71.50 W
Mooresville, IN	260	39.37 N	86.22 W
Mooresville, NC	258	35.35 N	80.48 W
Moorhead, MN	264	46.53 N	96.45 W
Moorhead, MS	260	33.27 N	90.30 W
Mooringsport	260	32.41 N	93.58 W
Moosehead Lake ⊕	254	45.40 N	69.40 W
Moose Heights	250	53.05 N	122.30 W
Moose Island I	250	51.42 N	97.10 W
Moose Jaw	250	50.23 N	105.32 W
Moose Jaw ≈	250	50.34 N	105.17 W
Moose Lake, MB	250	53.43 N	100.20 W
Moose Lake, MN	256	46.26 N	92.45 W
Moose Lake ⊕, AB	250	54.13 N	110.55 W
Moose Lake ⊕, MB	250	56.30 N	95.15 W
Mooselookmeguntic Lake ⊕	254	44.53 N	70.48 W
Moose Mountain ∧	268	49.45 N	122.37 W
Moose Mountain Creek ≈	250	49.12 N	102.10 W
Moose Mountain Provincial Park ♦	250	49.48 N	102.25 W
Moose Pass	246	60.29 N	149.22 W
Moosomin	250	50.07 N	101.40 W
Moosomin Indian Reserve ⊷⁴	250	53.06 N	108.14 W
Moosonee	252	51.17 N	80.39 W
Mora, MN	256	45.53 N	93.18 W
Mora, NM	266	35.58 N	105.20 W
Mora ≈	264	43.18 N	97.09 W
Mora, Arroyo de la ∨	262	34.05 N	104.18 W
Moran, MI	256	45.59 N	84.50 W
Moran, TX	262	32.33 N	99.10 W
Moran State Park ♦	248	48.41 N	122.52 W
Moravia, IA	264	40.53 N	92.49 W
Moravia, NY	254	42.43 N	76.25 W
Morden	250	49.11 N	98.05 W
Moreau ≈	264	45.18 N	100.43 W
Moreauville	260	31.02 N	91.58 W
Morehead	258	38.11 N	83.25 W
Morehead City	258	34.43 N	76.43 W
Morehouse	260	36.51 N	89.41 W
Moreland, GA	258	33.17 N	84.46 W
Moreland, KY	258	37.30 N	84.49 W
Morell	252	46.25 N	62.42 W
Morenci, AZ	266	33.05 N	109.22 W
Morenci, MI	256	41.43 N	84.13 W
Moresby Island I	248	52.50 N	131.55 W
Morey Peak ∧	270	38.37 N	116.17 W
Morgan, GA	258	31.32 N	84.36 W
Morgan, MN	264	44.25 N	94.56 W
Morgan, MT	248	49.00 N	107.50 W
Morgan, TX	262	32.01 N	97.37 W
Morgan, UT	268	41.02 N	111.41 W
Morgan City, AL	260	34.28 N	86.34 W
Morgan City, LA	260	29.42 N	91.12 W
Morgan Creek ≈	262	32.19 N	100.55 W
Morganfield	260	37.41 N	87.55 W
Morgan Hill	270	37.08 N	121.39 W
Morganton	258	35.45 N	81.41 W
Morgantown, IN	260	39.22 N	86.16 W
Morgantown, KY	260	37.14 N	86.41 W
Morgantown, MS	260	31.34 N	91.20 W
Morgantown, WV	254	39.38 N	79.57 W
Morganza	260	30.44 N	91.36 W
Moriah, Mount ∧	270	39.17 N	114.12 W
Moriarty	266	34.59 N	106.03 W
Morice ≈	248	54.24 N	126.45 W
Morice Lake ⊕	248	54.00 N	127.37 W
Morinville	248	53.48 N	113.39 W
Morkill ≈	248	53.23 N	120.30 W
Morley	256	43.29 N	85.27 W
Mormon Lake ⊕	266	34.57 N	111.27 W
Mormon Peak ∧	270	36.57 N	114.30 W
Mormon Reservoir ⚲¹	268	43.16 N	114.49 W
Morning Sun	264	41.05 N	91.15 W
Moro	268	45.29 N	120.44 W
Morocco	260	40.57 N	87.27 W
Moro Creek ≈	260	33.18 N	92.22 W
Morongo Indian Reservation ⊷⁴	270	33.59 N	116.50 W
Moroni	266	39.32 N	111.35 W
Morrill	264	41.58 N	103.56 W
Morrilton	260	35.09 N	92.45 W
Morrin	248	51.40 N	112.47 W
Morris, MB	250	49.21 N	97.22 W
Morris, IL	260	41.22 N	88.26 W
Morris, MN	264	45.35 N	95.55 W
Morris, OK	262	35.36 N	95.51 W
Morris ≈	254	39.21 N	77.22 W
Morrisburg	254	44.54 N	75.11 W
Morrison	260	41.49 N	89.58 W
Morrisonville	260	39.25 N	89.27 W
Morristown, AZ	266	33.51 N	112.37 W
Morristown, IN	260	39.40 N	85.42 W
Morristown, MN	256	44.13 N	93.26 W
Morristown, NJ	254	40.48 N	74.29 W
Morristown, SD	264	45.56 N	101.43 W
Morristown, TN	258	36.13 N	83.18 W
Morrisville, NY	254	42.54 N	75.39 W
Morrisville, PA	254	40.13 N	74.47 W
Morrisville, VT	254	44.34 N	72.44 W
Morro Bay	270	35.22 N	120.51 W
Morrow	260	30.50 N	92.05 W
Morrow Mountain State Park ♦	258	35.23 N	80.05 W
Morrow Point Reservoir ⚲¹	266	38.25 N	107.30 W
Morse, SK	250	50.25 N	107.03 W
Morse, LA	260	30.07 N	92.30 W
Morse, TX	262	36.04 N	101.29 W
Morson	250	49.03 N	94.18 W
Mortlach	250	50.28 N	106.03 W
Morton, IL	260	40.37 N	89.28 W
Morton, MN	264	44.33 N	94.59 W
Morton, MS	260	32.21 N	89.40 W
Morton, TX	262	33.44 N	102.46 W
Morton, WA	268	46.34 N	122.17 W
Mortons Gap	260	37.14 N	87.28 W
Morven, GA	258	30.56 N	83.30 W
Morven, NC	258	34.52 N	80.01 W
Morzhovoi	246	54.55 N	163.18 W
Moscow	268	46.44 N	117.00 W
Moselle	260	31.30 N	89.17 W
Mosers River	252	44.59 N	62.15 W
Moses Lake	268	47.08 N	119.17 W
Moses Point	246	64.42 N	162.03 W
Mosheim	258	36.11 N	82.57 W
Mosinee	256	44.47 N	89.43 W
Mosquero	262	35.47 N	103.58 W
Mosquito Creek Lake ⚲¹	254	41.22 N	80.45 W
Mosquito Indian Reserve ⊷⁴	250	52.30 N	108.15 W
Mosquito State Park ♦	254	41.25 N	80.45 W
Mossbank	250	49.55 N	105.59 W
Mossleigh	248	50.43 N	113.20 W
Moss Mountain ∧	258	38.04 N	83.56 W
Moss Point	260	30.25 N	88.32 W
Mossy ≈	250	54.05 N	103.00 W
Mostoos Hills ∧²	250	54.50 N	108.45 W
Mott	264	46.22 N	102.20 W
Moulton, AL	260	34.29 N	87.18 W
Moulton, IA	264	40.41 N	92.41 W
Moultrie	258	31.11 N	83.47 W
Moultrie, Lake ⚲¹	258	33.20 N	80.05 W
Mound Bayou	260	33.54 N	90.44 W
Mound City, IL	260	37.05 N	89.10 W
Mound City, KS	264	38.08 N	94.49 W
Mound City, MO	264	40.07 N	95.14 W
Mound City, SD	264	45.44 N	100.04 W
Mound City Group National Monument ⌂	254	39.23 N	83.00 W
Moundridge	264	38.12 N	97.31 W
Mounds, IL	260	37.07 N	89.12 W
Mounds, OK	262	35.53 N	96.04 W
Moundsville	260	39.55 N	80.44 W
Moundville	260	32.59 N	87.38 W
Mountain ≈	242	65.41 N	128.50 W
Mountain City, NV	270	41.50 N	115.58 W
Mountain City, TN	258	36.28 N	81.48 W
Mountain Creek ≈	258	32.43 N	86.29 W
Mountain Grove	260	37.08 N	92.16 W
Mountain Home, AR	260	36.20 N	92.23 W
Mountain Home, ID	268	43.08 N	115.41 W
Mountain Home Air Force Base ∗	268	43.03 N	115.52 W
Mountain Iron	256	47.32 N	92.37 W
Mountain Lake	256	43.56 N	94.55 W
Mountain Park	262	34.44 N	93.10 W
Mountain Pine	260	34.34 N	93.10 W
Mountain Point	246	55.18 N	131.32 W
Mountain View, AR	260	35.52 N	92.07 W
Mountain View, CA	270	37.23 N	122.04 W
Mountain View, MO	260	36.59 N	91.42 W
Mountain View, OK	262	35.06 N	98.45 W
Mountain View, WY	268	41.16 N	110.20 W
Mountain Village	246	62.05 N	163.44 W
Mount Airy, MD	254	39.23 N	77.09 W
Mount Airy, NC	258	36.31 N	80.37 W
Mount Angel	268	45.04 N	122.48 W
Mount Assiniboine Provincial Park ♦	248	50.54 N	115.40 W
Mount Ayr	264	40.43 N	94.14 W
Mount Brydges	256	42.54 N	81.29 W
Mount Calm	262	31.45 N	96.53 W
Mount Carmel, NF	252	47.09 N	53.29 W
Mount Carmel, IL	260	38.25 N	87.46 W
Mount Carmel, PA	254	40.48 N	76.25 W
Mount Carroll	256	42.06 N	89.58 W
Mount Clare	254	39.13 N	80.21 W
Mount Clemens	256	42.36 N	82.53 W
Mount Desert Island I	254	44.20 N	68.20 W
Mount Dora	258	28.48 N	81.38 W
Mount Edgecumbe	246	57.03 N	135.21 W
Mount Enterprise	260	31.55 N	94.41 W
Mount Forest	256	43.59 N	80.44 W
Mount Gay	258	37.51 N	82.00 W
Mount Gilead, NC	258	35.10 N	79.56 W
Mount Gilead, OH	254	40.33 N	82.50 W
Mount Holly	258	35.18 N	81.01 W
Mount Holly Springs	254	40.07 N	77.11 W
Mount Hope, KS	264	37.52 N	97.40 W
Mount Hope, WV	258	37.54 N	81.10 W
Mount Horeb	256	43.00 N	89.44 W
Mount Ida	260	34.34 N	93.38 W
Mount Jackson	258	38.45 N	78.39 W
Mount Jewett	254	41.44 N	78.38 W
Mount Juliet	258	36.12 N	86.31 W
Mount Kisco	254	41.12 N	73.44 W
Mount Lebanon	254	40.23 N	80.03 W
Mount Morris, IL	256	42.03 N	89.26 W
Mount Morris, MI	256	43.07 N	83.42 W
Mount Morris, NY	254	42.44 N	77.53 W
Mount Olive, IL	260	39.04 N	89.43 W
Mount Olive, MS	260	31.46 N	89.39 W
Mount Olive, NC	258	35.12 N	78.04 W
Mount Olivet	258	38.32 N	84.02 W
Mount Orab	254	39.02 N	83.56 W
Mount Pleasant, ON	256	43.05 N	80.19 W
Mount Pleasant, IA	264	40.58 N	91.33 W
Mount Pleasant, MI	256	43.35 N	84.47 W
Mount Pleasant, NC	258	35.24 N	80.26 W
Mount Pleasant, PA	254	40.09 N	79.33 W
Mount Pleasant, SC	258	32.47 N	79.52 W
Mount Pleasant, TN	260	35.32 N	87.13 W
Mount Pleasant, TX	260	33.09 N	94.58 W
Mount Pleasant, UT	266	39.33 N	111.27 W
Mount Pocono	254	41.08 N	75.22 W
Mount Pulaski	260	40.01 N	89.17 W
Mount Rainier National Park ♦	268	46.52 N	121.43 W
Mount Revelstoke National Park ♦	248	51.06 N	118.00 W
Mount Robson Provincial Park ♦	248	52.58 N	118.50 W
Mount Rogers National Recreation Area ♦	258	36.42 N	81.30 W
Mount Rushmore National Memorial ⊥	264	43.50 N	103.24 W
Mount Savage	254	39.42 N	78.53 W
Mount Seymour Provincial Park ♦	248	49.23 N	122.57 W
Mount Shasta	270	41.19 N	122.19 W
Mount Spokane State Park ♦	268	47.58 N	117.13 W
Mount Sterling, IL	260	39.59 N	90.45 W
Mount Sterling, KY	258	38.04 N	83.56 W
Mount Sterling, OH	254	39.43 N	83.16 W
Mount Stewart	252	46.22 N	62.52 W
Mount Uniacke	252	44.54 N	63.50 W
Mount Union	254	40.23 N	77.53 W
Mount Vernon, AL	260	31.05 N	88.01 W
Mount Vernon, GA	258	32.11 N	82.36 W
Mount Vernon, IL	260	38.19 N	88.55 W
Mount Vernon, IN	260	37.56 N	87.54 W
Mount Vernon, IA	264	41.55 N	91.23 W
Mount Vernon, KY	258	37.21 N	84.20 W
Mount Vernon, MO	260	37.06 N	93.49 W
Mount Vernon, OH	254	40.23 N	82.29 W
Mount Vernon, OR	268	44.25 N	119.07 W
Mount Vernon, SD	264	43.43 N	98.16 W
Mount Vernon, TX	260	33.11 N	95.13 W
Mount Vernon, WA	248	48.25 N	122.20 W
Mount Victory	254	40.32 N	83.31 W
Mouton Island I	252	43.54 N	64.46 W
Moville	264	42.29 N	96.04 W
Moweaqua	260	39.38 N	89.01 W
Moyie	248	49.17 N	115.50 W
Moyie Springs	268	48.43 N	116.11 W
Mozhabong Lake ⊕	256	46.57 N	82.05 W
Muckalee Creek ≈	258	31.38 N	84.09 W
Mud ≈, KY	258	37.13 N	86.54 W
Mud ≈, WV	258	38.25 N	82.17 W
Mud Creek ≈, NE	264	41.01 N	98.54 W
Mud Creek ≈, OK	262	33.55 N	97.28 W
Mud Creek ≈, SD	264	45.11 N	98.24 W
Mud Creek ≈, TX	262	31.48 N	94.58 W
Muddy ≈	270	36.27 N	114.22 W
Muddy Boggy Creek ≈	262	34.03 N	95.47 W
Muddy Creek ≈, MO	260	38.51 N	93.48 W
Muddy Creek ≈, WY	268	42.52 N	106.25 W
Muddy Creek ≈, WY	268	41.16 N	110.20 W
Muddy Creek ≈, UT	268	38.24 N	110.42 W
Muddy Creek ≈, WY	266	41.59 N	106.08 W

Symbols in the index entries are identified on page 273.

Name	Page	Lat ° ′	Long ° ′
Muddy Creek ≃, WY	268	43.17 N	108.14 W
Muddy Creek ≃, WY	268	41.32 N	110.13 W
Muddy Creek ≃, WY	268	41.01 N	107.42 W
Muddy Peak ∧	270	36.18 N	114.42 W
Mudjatik ≃	250	56.02 N	107.36 W
Mud Lake ⊜, ID	268	43.53 N	112.24 W
Mud Lake ⊜, MN	264	48.20 N	95.58 W
Mud Lake ⊜, NV	270	37.52 N	117.04 W
Mud Lake Reservoir ⊜[1]	264	45.50 N	98.10 W
Muenster	262	33.39 N	97.23 W
Muir, Mount ∧	246	61.06 N	148.24 W
Mukilteo	268	47.57 N	122.18 W
Mukutawa ≃	250	53.10 N	97.28 W
Mukwonago	256	42.52 N	88.20 W
Mulberry, AR	260	35.30 N	94.03 W
Mulberry, FL	258	27.54 N	81.59 W
Mulberry, IN	260	40.21 N	86.40 W
Mulberry ≃	260	35.28 N	94.03 W
Mulberry Creek ≃, AL	260	32.27 N	86.52 W
Mulberry Creek ≃, TX	262	34.37 N	100.55 W
Mulberry Fork ≃	260	33.33 N	87.11 W
Mulberry Mountain ∧	260	35.42 N	92.56 W
Mulchatna ≃	246	59.39 N	157.08 W
Muldoon	262	29.49 N	97.04 W
Muldraugh	260	37.56 N	85.59 W
Muldrow	260	35.24 N	94.36 W
Mule Creek ≃	264	37.05 N	99.00 W
Muleshoe	262	34.13 N	102.43 W
Mulgrave	252	45.37 N	61.23 W
Mulgrave Hills ⩘[2]	246	67.42 N	163.24 W
Mulhall	262	36.04 N	97.24 W
Mullan	268	47.28 N	115.48 W
Mullen	264	42.03 N	101.01 W
Mullens	258	37.35 N	81.23 W
Mullett Lake ⊜	256	45.30 N	84.30 W
Mullica ≃	254	39.33 N	74.25 W
Mullin	262	31.33 N	98.40 W
Mullins	258	34.12 N	79.15 W
Mullinville	264	37.35 N	99.29 W
Mulvane	264	37.29 N	97.14 W
Mumford	262	30.44 N	96.34 W
Muncie	260	40.11 N	85.23 W
Muncy	254	41.12 N	76.47 W
Mundare	248	53.36 N	112.20 W
Munday	262	33.27 N	99.38 W
Mundelein	256	42.16 N	88.00 W
Munford	260	35.27 N	89.47 W
Munfordville	260	37.16 N	85.54 W
Munising	256	46.25 N	86.40 W
Munro Lake ⊜	250	54.38 N	95.16 W
Munson	248	51.34 N	112.45 W
Munsons Corners	254	42.35 N	76.13 W
Munuscong Lake ⊜	256	46.10 N	84.08 W
Muolea Point ›	272a	20.41 N	156.01 W
Murchison	262	32.17 N	95.45 W
Murder Creek ≃	260	31.04 N	87.06 W
Murdo	264	43.53 N	100.43 W
Murfreesboro, AR	260	34.04 N	93.41 W
Murfreesboro, NC	258	36.27 N	77.06 W
Murfreesboro, TN	260	35.51 N	86.23 W
Muriel Lake ⊜	250	54.10 N	110.40 W
Murphy, ID	268	43.13 N	116.33 W
Murphy, NC	258	35.05 N	84.01 W
Murphy Lake ⊜	248	52.00 N	121.00 W
Murphys	270	38.08 N	120.28 W
Murphysboro	260	37.46 N	89.20 W
Murray, IA	256	41.03 N	93.57 W
Murray, KY	260	36.37 N	88.19 W
Murray, UT	266	40.40 N	111.53 W
Murray ≃	248	55.40 N	121.10 W
Murray, Lake ⊜[1]	258	34.04 N	81.23 W
Murray, Mount ∧	246	60.54 N	128.49 W
Murray Bay → La Malbaie	252	47.39 N	70.10 W
Murray City	254	39.31 N	82.10 W
Murray Harbour	252	46.00 N	62.31 W
Murray Head ›	252	46.00 N	62.28 W
Murray Maxwell Bay C	242	70.00 N	80.00 W
Murray River	252	46.01 N	62.37 W
Murrayville	260	39.35 N	90.15 W
Murtle Lake ⊜	248	52.08 N	119.38 W
Murvaul Creek ≃	260	32.05 N	94.12 W
Muscatatuck ≃	260	38.46 N	86.10 W
Muscatine	256	41.25 N	91.03 W
Muscle Shoals	260	34.45 N	87.40 W
Musclow, Mount ∧	248	53.17 N	127.09 W
Musclow Lake ⊜	250	51.25 N	94.56 W
Muscoda	256	43.11 N	90.27 W
Muscongus Bay C	254	43.55 N	69.20 W
Musgravetown	252	48.24 N	53.53 W
Muskeg ≃	248	54.01 N	119.03 W
Muskeg Lake Indian Reserve ◆[4]	250	52.58 N	106.57 W
Muskegon	256	43.14 N	86.16 W
Muskegon ≃	256	43.14 N	86.20 W
Muskegon Heights	256	43.12 N	86.12 W
Muskingum ≃	254	39.27 N	81.30 W
Muskoday Indian Reserve ◆[4]	250	53.06 N	105.30 W
Muskogee	262	35.45 N	95.22 W
Muskoka, Lake ⊜	256	45.00 N	79.25 W
Muskowekwan Indian Reserve ◆[4]	250	51.19 N	104.06 W
Muskrat Creek ≃	268	43.09 N	108.11 W
Muskratdam Lake ⊜	250	53.25 N	91.40 W
Muskrat Lake ⊜	256	45.40 N	76.55 W
Muskwa ≃	242	58.45 N	122.35 W
Muskwa Lake ⊜	248	56.09 N	114.38 W
Musquanousse, Lac ⊜	252	50.22 N	61.05 W
Musquaro, Lac ⊜	252	50.38 N	61.05 W
Musquodoboit Harbour	252	44.47 N	63.09 W
Musselshell ≃	268	47.21 N	107.58 W
Mustang Draw V	262	32.12 N	101.36 W
Mustang Island I	262	28.00 N	96.55 W
Mustinka ≃	264	45.45 N	96.38 W
Mutton Bay	252	50.47 N	59.02 W
Muzon, Cape ›	246	54.41 N	132.44 W
Myakka ≃	258	26.56 N	82.11 W
Myakka River State Park ♠	258	27.15 N	82.17 W
Myerstown	254	40.22 N	76.19 W
Myrnam	250	53.40 N	111.14 W
Myrtle Beach	258	33.42 N	78.52 W
Myrtle Beach Air Force Base ■	258	33.41 N	78.56 W
Myrtle Beach State Park ♠	258	33.37 N	78.58 W
Myrtle Creek	268	43.01 N	123.17 W
Myrtle Grove	260	30.25 N	87.18 W
Myrtle Point	268	43.04 N	124.08 W
Myrtletowne	270	40.47 N	124.04 W
Mystic, CT	254	41.21 N	71.58 W
Mystic, IA	256	40.47 N	92.57 W
Myton	266	40.12 N	110.04 W
N			
Naalehu	272	19.04 N	155.35 W
Nabesna	246	62.22 N	143.00 W
Nabesna ≃	246	63.03 N	141.52 W
Nabisipi ≃	252	50.14 N	62.13 W
Naches ≃	268	46.38 N	120.31 W
Nachvak Fiord C[2]	242	59.03 N	63.45 W
Nacimiento ≃	270	35.49 N	120.45 W
Nacimiento Reservoir ⊜[1]	270	35.45 N	121.00 W
Naco	266	31.20 N	109.57 W
Nacogdoches	260	31.36 N	94.39 W
Naden Harbour C	248	54.00 N	132.35 W
Nagai Island I	246	55.11 N	159.55 W
Nagasin Lake ⊜	256	47.44 N	83.37 W
Nahma	256	45.50 N	86.40 W
Nahunta	258	31.12 N	81.59 W
Naicam	250	52.25 N	104.30 W
Nain	242	56.32 N	61.41 W
Nairn	260	29.27 N	89.38 W
Nakalele Point ›	272a	21.02 N	156.35 W
Nakina	242	50.10 N	86.42 W
Naknek	246	58.44 N	157.02 W
Naknek Lake ⊜	246	58.40 N	156.15 W
Nakusp	248	50.15 N	117.48 W
Namakan Lake ⊜	256	48.27 N	92.35 W
Nambe Indian Reservation ◆[4]	266	35.52 N	105.57 W
Nameigos Lake ⊜	256	48.46 N	84.43 W
Namekagon ≃	256	46.05 N	92.06 W
Namew Lake ⊜	250	54.13 N	101.56 W
Nampa, AB	248	56.02 N	117.08 W
Nampa, ID	268	43.34 N	116.34 W
Namu	248	51.49 N	127.52 W
Nanaimo	248	49.10 N	123.56 W
Nanakuli	272c	21.23 N	158.09 W
Nanawan ≃	250	53.13 N	97.13 W
Nanika Lake ⊜	248	53.45 N	127.40 W
Nantais, Lac ⊜	242	60.59 N	74.00 W
Nanticoke	254	41.12 N	76.00 W
Nanticoke ≃	254	38.16 N	75.56 W
Nanton	248	50.21 N	113.46 W
Nantucket	254	41.17 N	70.06 W
Nantucket Island I	254	41.16 N	70.03 W
Nantucket Sound ʊ	254	41.30 N	70.15 W
Nanty Glo	254	40.28 N	78.50 W
Nanushuk ≃	246	69.18 N	151.00 W
Naococane, Lac ⊜	242	52.52 N	70.40 W
Naosap Lake ⊜	250	54.51 N	101.24 W
Napa	270	38.18 N	122.17 W
Napa ≃	270	38.07 N	122.18 W
Napakiak	246	60.42 N	161.57 W
Na Pali Coast State Park ♠	272b	22.05 N	159.45 W
Napamute	246	61.33 N	158.42 W
Napanee	256	44.15 N	76.57 W
Napaskiak	246	60.42 N	161.54 W
Naperville	260	41.47 N	88.09 W
Napetipi ≃	252	51.21 N	58.08 W
Napinka	250	49.17 N	100.50 W
Naples, FL	258	26.08 N	81.48 W
Naples, ID	268	48.34 N	116.24 W
Naples, NY	254	42.37 N	77.25 W
Naples, TX	260	33.12 N	94.41 W
Napoleon, ND	264	46.30 N	99.46 W
Napoleon, OH	254	41.23 N	84.08 W
Napoleonville	260	29.57 N	91.01 W
Nappanee	260	41.27 N	86.00 W
Naramata	248	49.36 N	119.35 W
Nara Visa	262	35.37 N	103.06 W
Narraway ≃	248	54.48 N	119.56 W
Narrows	258	37.20 N	80.48 W
Nash	260	33.27 N	94.08 W
Nashua, IA	256	42.57 N	92.32 W
Nashua, MT	268	48.08 N	106.22 W
Nashua, NH	254	42.46 N	71.27 W
Nashville, AR	260	33.57 N	93.51 W
Nashville, GA	258	31.12 N	83.15 W
Nashville, IL	260	38.21 N	89.23 W
Nashville, IN	260	39.12 N	86.15 W
Nashville, MI	256	42.36 N	85.05 W
Nashville, NC	258	35.58 N	77.58 W
Nashville, TN	260	36.09 N	86.48 W
Nashwaak ≃	252	45.57 N	66.37 W
Nashwaaksis	252	45.59 N	66.39 W
Nashwauk	256	47.23 N	93.10 W
Naskaupi ≃	242	53.45 N	60.50 W
Nass ≃	248	55.00 N	129.50 W
Nassau	254	42.31 N	73.37 W
Nassawadox	258	37.28 N	75.51 W
Nastapoca ≃	242	56.55 N	76.33 W
Nastapoka Islands II	242	57.00 N	76.50 W
Nasukoin Mountain ∧	268	48.48 N	114.35 W
Nat ≃	256	48.48 N	82.07 W
Natal	248	49.44 N	114.50 W
Natalia	262	29.11 N	98.52 W
Natalkuz Lake ⊜	248	53.26 N	125.20 W
Natanes Plateau ⩘[1]	266	33.35 N	110.15 W
Natashquan	252	50.12 N	61.49 W
Natashquan ≃	242	50.06 N	61.49 W
Natashquan, Pointe de ›	252	50.06 N	61.44 W
Natashquan-Est ≃	252	51.20 N	61.40 W
Natchez	260	31.34 N	91.23 W
Natchez Trace Parkway ♠	260	36.08 N	86.49 W
Natchitoches	260	31.46 N	93.05 W
Natick	254	42.17 N	71.21 W
Nation ≃	248	55.28 N	125.35 W
National City	270	32.40 N	117.06 W
Nation Lakes ⊜	248	55.10 N	125.00 W
Natipi, Lac ⊜	252	51.27 N	71.23 W
Native Bay C	242	63.52 N	82.30 W
Natoma	264	39.11 N	99.01 W
Natural Bridges National Monument ♠	266	37.30 N	110.08 W
Natural Bridge State Park ♠	258	37.47 N	83.42 W
Naturita	266	38.14 N	108.34 W
Naturita Creek ≃	266	38.13 N	108.32 W
Naugatuck	254	41.30 N	73.04 W
Naughton	256	46.24 N	81.12 W
Nauvoo	256	40.33 N	91.23 W
Navajo ≃	266	37.01 N	107.10 W
Navajo Creek ≃	266	36.59 N	111.24 W
Navajo-Hopi Indian Reservation ◆[4]	266	36.15 N	110.30 W
Navajo Mountain ∧	266	37.02 N	110.52 W
Navajo National Monument ♠	266	36.40 N	110.33 W
Navajo Reservoir ⊜[1]	266	36.55 N	107.30 W
Navarre	254	40.43 N	81.32 W
Navarro ≃	270	39.11 N	123.45 W
Navarro Mills Lake ⊜[1]	262	31.56 N	96.45 W
Navasota	262	30.23 N	96.05 W
Navasota ≃	262	30.20 N	96.09 W
Navassa	258	34.16 N	77.58 W
Navidad ≃	262	28.41 N	96.35 W
Nawiliwili Bay C	272b	21.57 N	159.21 W
Naylor	260	36.34 N	90.36 W
Nazareth	254	40.44 N	75.19 W
Nazko ≃	248	53.07 N	123.34 W
Neah Bay	268	48.22 N	124.37 W
Near Islands II	247a	52.40 N	173.30 E
Nebo	260	39.27 N	90.47 W
Nebo, Mount ∧	266	39.49 N	111.46 W
Nebraska □[3], U.S.	244		
	264	41.30 N	100.00 W
Nebraska City	264	40.41 N	95.52 W
Necedah	256	44.02 N	90.05 W
Nechako ≃	248	53.56 N	122.42 W
Nechako Plateau ⩘[1]	248	54.00 N	124.30 W
Nechako Range ⩘	248	53.20 N	124.30 W
Nechako Reservoir ⊜[1]	248	53.25 N	125.10 W
Neche	264	48.59 N	97.33 W
Neches	262	31.52 N	95.30 W
Neches ≃	260	29.55 N	93.52 W
Nederland	260	29.58 N	93.60 W
Neebish Island I	256	46.16 N	84.09 W
Needle Mountain ∧	268	44.05 N	109.37 W
Needles	270	34.51 N	114.37 W
Needville	262	29.24 N	95.51 W
Neenah	256	44.11 N	88.28 W
Neepawa	250	50.13 N	99.29 W
Negaunee	256	46.30 N	87.36 W
Neguac	252	47.15 N	65.05 W
Nehalem ≃	268	45.40 N	123.56 W
Nehawka	264	40.50 N	95.59 W
Neidpath	250	50.08 N	107.15 W
Neihart	268	46.56 N	110.44 W
Neilburg	250	52.50 N	109.38 W
Neillsville	256	44.34 N	90.36 W
Nekoosa	256	44.19 N	89.54 W
Neligh	264	42.08 N	98.02 W
Nellis Air Force Base ■	270	36.14 N	115.02 W
Nelson, BC	248	49.29 N	117.17 W
Nelson, NE	264	40.12 N	98.04 W
Nelson ≃	250	57.04 N	92.30 W
Nelson Creek ≃	270	40.36 N	114.28 W
Nelson House	250	55.47 N	98.51 W
Nelson Island I	246	60.35 N	164.45 W
Nelson Lake ⊜	250	55.44 N	100.00 W
Nelson Reservoir ⊜[1]	268	48.30 N	107.34 W
Nelsonville	254	39.27 N	82.14 W
Nemacolin	254	39.52 N	79.56 W
Nemadji ≃	256	46.41 N	92.02 W
Nemaha	264	40.20 N	95.40 W
Nemegosenda ≃	256	48.31 N	82.53 W
Nemeiben Lake ⊜	250	55.20 N	105.20 W
Nenana	246	64.34 N	149.07 W
Nenana ≃	246	64.30 N	149.00 W
Neodesha	264	37.25 N	95.41 W
Neoga	260	39.19 N	88.27 W
Neola, IA	264	41.27 N	95.37 W
Neola, UT	266	40.26 N	110.02 W
Neon	258	37.12 N	82.43 W
Neopit	256	44.59 N	88.50 W
Neosho	260	36.52 N	94.22 W
Neosho ≃	260	35.48 N	95.18 W
Nepewassi Lake ⊜	256	46.20 N	80.40 W
Nephi	266	39.43 N	111.50 W
Nepisiguit ≃	252	47.37 N	65.38 W
Nepisiguit Bay C	252	47.46 N	65.32 W
Neptune	254	40.12 N	74.02 W
Neptune Beach	258	30.19 N	81.24 W
Nerka, Lake ⊜	246	59.30 N	158.45 W
Ness City	264	38.27 N	99.54 W
Nesselrode, Mount ∧	242	58.58 N	134.18 W
Nestucca ≃	268	45.12 N	123.57 W
Nettilling Fiord C[2]	242	66.02 N	68.12 W
Nettilling Lake ⊜	242	66.30 N	70.40 W
Nett Lake ⊜	256	48.10 N	93.10 W
Nett Lake Indian Reservation ◆[4]	256	48.06 N	93.10 W
Nettleton	260	34.05 N	88.44 W
Neudorf	250	50.44 N	102.59 W
Neuse ≃	258	35.06 N	76.30 W
Neutral Hills ⩘[2]	250	52.10 N	110.50 W
Nevada, IA	256	42.01 N	93.27 W
Nevada, MO	260	37.51 N	94.22 W
Nevada, OH	254	40.49 N	83.08 W
Nevada □[3], U.S.	244		
	270	39.00 N	117.00 W
Nevada, Sierra ⩘	270	38.00 N	119.15 W
Nevada City	270	36.16 N	121.01 W
Nevada Creek ≃	268	46.54 N	113.02 W
New ≃, N.A.	270	33.08 N	115.44 W
New ≃, U.S.	258	38.10 N	81.12 W
New ≃, AZ	266	33.31 N	112.18 W
New ≃, FL	258	29.50 N	84.40 W
New ≃, FL	258	29.55 N	82.25 W
New ≃, NC	258	34.32 N	77.20 W
New ≃, SC	258	32.09 N	80.50 W
New ≃, TN	258	36.25 N	84.38 W
New, North Fork ≃	258	36.33 N	81.21 W
New Albany, IN	260	38.18 N	85.49 W
New Albany, MS	260	34.29 N	89.00 W
New Albin	256	43.30 N	91.17 W
Newark, AR	260	35.42 N	91.27 W
Newark, DE	254	39.41 N	75.45 W
Newark, NJ	254	40.44 N	74.10 W
Newark, NY	254	43.03 N	77.06 W
Newark, OH	254	40.04 N	82.24 W
Newark Lake ⊜	270	39.41 N	115.44 W
Newark Valley	254	42.14 N	76.11 W
New Athens	260	38.19 N	89.53 W
New Augusta	260	31.12 N	89.02 W
Newaygo	256	43.25 N	85.48 W
New Baden	260	38.32 N	89.42 W
New Baltimore	256	42.41 N	82.44 W
New Bedford	254	41.38 N	70.56 W
Newberg	268	45.18 N	122.58 W
New Berlin, IL	260	39.44 N	89.55 W
New Berlin, NY	254	42.38 N	75.20 W
New Berlin, WI	256	42.58 N	88.07 W
Newbern, AL	260	32.36 N	87.38 W
New Bern, NC	258	35.07 N	77.03 W
Newbern, TN	260	36.07 N	89.16 W
Newberry, FL	258	29.39 N	82.37 W
Newberry, MI	256	46.21 N	85.30 W
Newberry, SC	258	34.17 N	81.37 W
New Bethlehem	254	41.00 N	79.20 W
New Bloomfield	254	40.25 N	77.11 W
New Boston, IL	260	41.10 N	91.00 W
New Boston, OH	254	38.45 N	82.56 W
New Boston, TX	260	33.28 N	94.25 W
New Braunfels	262	29.42 N	98.08 W
New Bremen	254	40.26 N	84.23 W
New Britain	254	41.40 N	72.47 W
New Brockton	260	31.23 N	85.57 W
Newbrook	248	54.19 N	112.57 W
New Brunswick	254	40.29 N	74.27 W
New Brunswick □[4], Can.	242		
	252	46.30 N	66.15 W
New Buffalo	256	41.47 N	86.45 W
Newburg	260	37.55 N	91.54 W
Newburgh, ON	256	44.19 N	76.52 W
Newburgh, IN	260	37.57 N	87.24 W
Newburgh, NY	254	41.30 N	74.01 W
Newburyport	254	42.49 N	70.53 W
New Carlisle, PQ	252	48.01 N	65.20 W
New Carlisle, OH	254	39.56 N	84.02 W
Newcastle, NB	252	47.00 N	65.34 W
Newcastle, ON	256	43.55 N	78.35 W
Newcastle, CA	270	38.53 N	121.08 W
New Castle, CO	266	39.34 N	107.32 W
New Castle, DE	254	39.40 N	75.34 W
New Castle, IN	260	39.55 N	85.22 W
New Castle, KY	260	38.26 N	85.10 W
Newcastle, ME	254	44.02 N	69.33 W
Newcastle, NE	264	42.39 N	96.53 W
Newcastle, OK	262	35.20 N	97.36 W
New Castle, PA	254	41.00 N	80.20 W
Newcastle, TX	262	33.12 N	98.44 W
New Castle, VA	258	37.30 N	80.07 W
Newcastle, WY	264	43.50 N	104.11 W
Newcastle Mine	248	51.28 N	112.46 W
New City	254	41.09 N	73.59 W
Newcomerstown	254	40.16 N	81.36 W
New Concord	254	40.00 N	81.44 W
New Cumberland	254	40.30 N	80.36 W
New Dayton	248	49.25 N	112.23 W
New Denver	248	49.59 N	117.22 W
New Don Pedro Reservoir ⊜[1]	270	37.43 N	120.23 W
New Edinburg	260	33.46 N	92.14 W
New Effington	264	45.51 N	96.55 W
New Egypt	254	40.04 N	74.32 W
Newell, IA	264	42.36 N	95.00 W
Newell, SD	264	44.43 N	103.25 W
Newell, WV	254	40.37 N	80.36 W
Newell, Lake ⊜	250	50.25 N	111.56 W
New Ellenton	258	33.24 N	81.42 W
Newellton	260	32.10 N	91.14 W
New England	264	46.32 N	102.52 W
Newenham, Cape ›	246	58.37 N	162.12 W
Newfane, NY	254	43.17 N	78.43 W
Newfane, VT	254	42.59 N	72.39 W
New Florence, MO	260	38.54 N	91.27 W
New Florence, PA	254	40.23 N	79.05 W
New Fork ≃	268	42.33 N	109.58 W
Newfound Gap)(	258	35.37 N	83.25 W
Newfoundland □[4]	242	52.00 N	56.00 W
Newfoundland I	252	48.30 N	56.00 W
New Franklin	260	39.01 N	92.44 W
New Freedom	254	39.44 N	76.42 W
Newgate	248	49.00 N	115.10 W
New Germany	252	44.33 N	64.43 W
New Glarus	256	42.49 N	89.38 W
New Glasgow	252	45.35 N	62.39 W
Newgulf	262	29.16 N	95.54 W
Newhalem	268	48.41 N	121.16 W
Newhalen	246	59.43 N	154.54 W
Newhall	270	34.23 N	118.31 W
New Hamburg	256	43.23 N	80.42 W
New Hampshire □[3], U.S.	244		
	254	43.35 N	71.40 W
New Hampton	256	43.03 N	92.19 W
New Harmony	260	38.08 N	87.56 W
New Hartford, CT	254	41.53 N	72.59 W
New Hartford, IA	256	42.34 N	92.37 W
New Haven, CT	254	41.18 N	72.56 W
New Haven, IL	260	37.55 N	88.08 W
New Haven, IN	260	41.04 N	85.01 W
New Haven, KY	260	37.39 N	85.36 W
New Haven, MO	260	38.37 N	91.13 W
New Haven, WV	254	38.59 N	81.58 W
New Hazelton	248	55.15 N	127.35 W
Newhebron	260	31.44 N	83.58 W
New Hogan Lake ⊜[1]	270	38.07 N	120.50 W
New Holland, OH	254	39.33 N	83.15 W
New Holland, PA	254	40.06 N	76.05 W
New Holstein	256	43.57 N	88.05 W
New Hope	260	34.32 N	86.24 W
New Hope Lake ⊜[1]	258	35.45 N	79.00 W
New Iberia	260	30.00 N	91.49 W
New Jersey □[3], U.S.	244		
	254	40.15 N	74.30 W
New Johnsonville	260	36.01 N	87.58 W
New Kensington	254	40.34 N	79.46 W
New Kent	258	37.31 N	76.59 W
Newkirk	262	36.53 N	97.03 W
New Lake ⊜	258	35.38 N	76.20 W
Newland	258	36.05 N	81.56 W
New Leipzig	264	46.22 N	101.57 W
New Lexington	254	39.43 N	82.13 W
New Lisbon	256	43.53 N	90.10 W
New Liskeard	256	47.30 N	79.40 W
Newllano	260	31.06 N	93.17 W
New London, CT	254	41.21 N	72.07 W
New London, IA	256	40.55 N	91.24 W
New London, MN	264	45.18 N	94.56 W
New London, MO	260	39.35 N	91.24 W
New London, NH	254	43.25 N	71.59 W
New London, OH	254	41.05 N	82.24 W
New London, TX	260	32.15 N	94.56 W
New London, WI	256	44.23 N	88.45 W
New Madrid	260	36.36 N	89.32 W
Newman, CA	270	37.19 N	121.01 W
Newman, IL	260	39.48 N	87.59 W
Newman Grove	264	41.45 N	97.47 W
Newmarket, ON	256	44.03 N	79.28 W
New Market, AL	260	34.55 N	86.26 W
New Market, IA	264	40.44 N	94.54 W
Newmarket, NH	254	43.05 N	70.56 W
New Market, VA	254	38.39 N	78.40 W
New Martinsville	254	39.39 N	80.52 W
New Meadows	268	44.58 N	116.32 W
New Mexico □[3], U.S.	244		
	266	34.30 N	106.00 W
New Milford, CT	254	41.35 N	73.25 W
New Milford, PA	254	41.52 N	75.44 W
Newnan	258	33.23 N	84.48 W
Newnans Lake ⊜	258	29.39 N	82.13 W
New Norway	248	52.53 N	112.58 W
New Orleans	260	29.58 N	90.07 W
New Orleans Naval Air Station ■	260	29.51 N	90.01 W
New Oxford	254	39.52 N	77.04 W
New Paltz	254	41.45 N	74.05 W
New Paris	254	39.51 N	84.48 W
New Philadelphia	254	40.30 N	81.27 W
New Pine Creek	268	42.01 N	120.18 W
New Plymouth	268	43.58 N	116.49 W
Newport, PQ	252	48.16 N	64.45 W
Newport, AR	260	35.37 N	91.17 W
Newport, IN	260	39.53 N	87.24 W
Newport, KY	254	39.06 N	84.29 W
Newport, ME	254	44.50 N	69.17 W
Newport, NH	254	43.21 N	72.09 W
Newport, NC	258	34.48 N	76.51 W
Newport, OR	268	44.38 N	124.03 W
Newport, PA	254	40.29 N	77.08 W
Newport, RI	254	41.13 N	71.18 W
Newport, TN	258	35.58 N	83.11 W
Newport, VT	254	44.57 N	72.12 W
Newport, WA	268	48.11 N	117.03 W
Newport Beach	270	33.37 N	117.56 W
Newport News	258	37.04 N	76.28 W
New Port Richey	258	28.16 N	82.43 W
New Prague	256	44.32 N	93.34 W
New Providence	260	36.32 N	87.23 W
New Richland	256	43.54 N	93.30 W
New Richmond, PQ	252	48.10 N	65.52 W
New Richmond, OH	254	38.57 N	84.17 W
New Richmond, WI	256	45.07 N	92.32 W
New Road	252	44.45 N	63.28 W
New Roads	260	30.42 N	91.26 W
New Rochelle	254	40.55 N	73.47 W
New Rockford	264	47.41 N	99.15 W
New Ross	252	44.44 N	64.27 W
Newry	258	34.43 N	82.55 W
New Salem	264	46.51 N	101.25 W
New Sharon	256	41.28 N	92.39 W
New Smyrna Beach	258	29.02 N	80.56 W
New Stuyahok	246	59.29 N	157.20 W
New Tazewell	258	36.27 N	83.33 W
New Thunderchild Indian Reserve ◆[4]	250	53.30 N	108.50 W
Newtok	246	60.56 N	164.38 W
Newton, GA	258	31.19 N	84.20 W
Newton, IL	260	38.59 N	88.10 W
Newton, IA	256	41.42 N	93.03 W
Newton, KS	264	38.03 N	97.21 W
Newton, MA	254	42.21 N	71.11 W
Newton, MS	260	32.19 N	89.10 W
Newton, NJ	254	41.03 N	74.45 W
Newton, NC	258	35.40 N	81.13 W
Newton, TX	260	30.51 N	93.46 W
Newton Falls	254	44.13 N	74.59 W
Newtown, NF	252	49.12 N	53.31 W
New Town, ND	264	47.59 N	102.30 W
New Ulm, MN	264	44.19 N	94.28 W
New Ulm, TX	262	29.53 N	96.29 W
New Vienna	254	39.19 N	83.42 W
Newville	254	40.10 N	77.24 W
New Vineyard	254	44.48 N	70.07 W
New Washington	254	40.58 N	82.51 W
New Waterford	252	46.15 N	60.05 W
New Waverly	262	30.32 N	95.29 W
New Westminster	248	49.12 N	122.55 W
New Whiteland	260	39.33 N	86.05 W
New Wilmington	254	41.07 N	80.20 W
New World Island I	252	49.35 N	54.40 W
New York	254	40.43 N	74.01 W
New York □[3], U.S.	244		
	254	43.00 N	75.00 W
New York Mills	264	46.31 N	95.22 W
New York State Barge Canal ≍	254	43.05 N	78.43 W
Ney Lake ⊜	250	54.38 N	92.25 W
Nezperce	268	46.14 N	116.14 W
Nez Perce Indian Reservation ◆[4]	268	46.20 N	116.30 W
Nez Perce National Historical Park ♠	268	45.50 N	116.15 W
Nezpique, Bayou ≃	260	30.12 N	92.35 W
Niagara	256	45.46 N	88.02 W
Niagara Falls, ON	256	43.06 N	79.04 W
Niagara Falls, NY	254	43.06 N	79.02 W
Niagara-on-the-Lake	256	43.15 N	79.04 W
Niangua ≃	260	37.58 N	92.48 W
Niantic	260	39.51 N	89.10 W
Niceville	260	30.31 N	86.29 W
Nicholasville	258	37.53 N	84.34 W
Nicholls	258	31.31 N	82.38 W
Nicholson, MS	260	30.29 N	89.42 W
Nicholson, PA	254	41.38 N	75.47 W
Nickerson	264	38.08 N	98.05 W
Nicola	248	50.10 N	120.40 W
Nicola ≃	248	50.25 N	121.18 W
Nicola Lake ⊜	248	50.10 N	120.25 W
Nicola Mameet Indian Reserve ◆[4]	248	50.11 N	120.49 W
Nicolet	254	46.13 N	72.37 W
Nicolet-Sud-Ouest ≃	254	46.13 N	72.36 W
Nicollet	264	44.17 N	94.11 W
Night Hawk Lake ⊜	256	48.28 N	81.00 W
Nightmute	246	60.29 N	164.00 W
Niihau I	272b	21.55 N	160.10 W
Nikip Lake ⊜	250	52.53 N	91.53 W
Nikishka	246	60.44 N	151.19 W
Nikolai	246	62.58 N	154.09 W
Nikolski	246	53.15 N	168.22 W
Niland	270	33.14 N	115.31 W
Niles, IL	256	42.01 N	87.49 W
Niles, MI	256	41.50 N	86.15 W
Niles, OH	254	41.11 N	80.45 W
Nilgaut, Lac ⊜	256	46.36 N	77.15 W
Nimpkish Lake ⊜	248	50.25 N	126.59 W
Nimrod Lake ⊜[1]	260	34.55 N	93.20 W
Nina Bang Lake ⊜	242	70.51 N	79.07 W
Nine Mile Creek ≃	266	39.50 N	109.53 W
Ninette	250	49.22 N	99.43 W
Ninety Six	258	34.11 N	82.01 W
Ninga	250	49.13 N	99.51 W
Ninilchik	246	60.03 N	151.41 W
Ninnescah ≃	264	37.20 N	97.10 W
Ninnescah, North Fork ≃	264	37.34 N	97.42 W
Ninnescah, South Fork ≃	264	37.34 N	97.42 W
Niobrara	264	42.45 N	98.02 W
Niobrara ≃	244	42.45 N	98.00 W
Niordenskiold ≃	246	62.05 N	136.18 W
Niota	258	35.31 N	84.33 W
Nipawin	250	53.22 N	104.00 W
Nipawin Provincial Park ♠	250	54.00 N	104.40 W
Nipekamew Lake ⊜	250	54.24 N	104.58 W
Nipigon	256	49.01 N	88.16 W
Nipigon, Lake ⊜	242	49.50 N	88.30 W
Nipigon Bay C	256	48.53 N	87.50 W
Nipin ≃	250	55.45 N	109.02 W
Nipisi Lake ⊜	248	55.47 N	114.57 W
Nipissing, Lake ⊜	256	46.17 N	80.00 W
Nipissis, Lac ⊜	252	51.02 N	66.10 W
Nipisso, Lac ⊜	252	50.52 N	65.50 W
Nipomo	270	35.03 N	120.29 W
Nippers Harbour	252	49.48 N	55.52 W
Niska Lake ⊜	250	55.35 N	108.38 W
Nisling ≃	246	62.27 N	139.30 W
Nisqually ≃	268	47.06 N	122.42 W
Nisswa	264	46.31 N	94.17 W
Nisutlin ≃	246	60.10 N	132.30 W
Nith ≃	256	43.12 N	80.22 W
Nithi River	248	54.01 N	125.01 W
Nitinat Lake ⊜	248	48.45 N	124.45 W
Nitro	254	38.25 N	81.50 W
Niverville	250	49.37 N	97.01 W
Nixa	260	37.03 N	93.18 W
Nixon, NV	270	39.50 N	119.21 W
Nixon, TX	262	29.16 N	97.46 W
Noatak	246	67.34 N	162.59 W
Noatak ≃	246	67.00 N	162.30 W
Noble, IL	260	38.42 N	88.13 W
Noble, OK	262	35.08 N	97.24 W
Noblesville	260	40.03 N	86.01 W
Nocatee	258	27.09 N	81.53 W
Nocona	262	33.47 N	97.44 W
Nodaway ≃	260	39.54 N	94.58 W
Nodier, Lac ⊜	256	47.38 N	78.26 W
Noel	260	36.33 N	94.29 W
Nogales	266	31.20 N	110.56 W
Nohili Point ›	272b	22.04 N	159.47 W
Noire ≃	254	45.54 N	76.57 W
Nokomis, SK	250	51.30 N	105.00 W
Nokomis, FL	258	27.07 N	82.27 W
Nokomis, IL	260	39.18 N	89.18 W
Nokomis Lake ⊜	250	56.58 N	103.02 W
Nolan ≃	262	32.07 N	97.26 W
Nolichucky ≃	258	36.07 N	83.14 W
Nolin ≃	260	37.13 N	86.15 W
Nolin Lake ⊜[1]	260	37.20 N	86.10 W
Nome	246	64.30 N	165.24 W
Nominingue	254	46.24 N	75.02 W
Nonacho Lake ⊜	242	61.42 N	109.40 W
Nondalton	246	60.00 N	154.49 W
Nonvianuk Lake ⊜	246	59.00 N	155.15 W
Nooksack ≃	268	48.46 N	122.35 W
Noonan	264	48.54 N	103.01 W
Noorvik	246	66.50 N	161.12 W
Nootka Island I	248	49.32 N	126.42 W
Nootka Sound ʊ	248	49.33 N	126.38 W
Noralee	248	53.59 N	126.26 W
Noranda	256	48.15 N	79.02 W
Nora Springs	256	43.09 N	93.01 W
Norborne	260	39.18 N	93.40 W
Norcatur	264	39.50 N	100.11 W
Norcross	258	33.57 N	84.13 W
Nordegg	248	52.28 N	116.04 W
Nordegg ≃	248	52.53 N	115.18 W
Nordheim	262	28.55 N	97.36 W
Nordman	248	48.38 N	116.57 W
Norfolk, NE	264	42.02 N	97.25 W
Norfolk, VA	258	36.40 N	76.14 W
Norfolk Naval Base ■	258	36.57 N	76.18 W
Norfork Lake ⊜[1]	260	36.25 N	92.10 W
Norlina	258	36.27 N	78.12 W
Normal, AL	260	34.47 N	86.34 W
Normal, IL	256	40.31 N	88.59 W
Norman, AR	260	34.27 N	93.41 W
Norman, OK	262	35.13 N	97.26 W
Norman, Lake ⊜[1]	258	35.35 N	80.55 W
Normangee	262	31.02 N	96.07 W
Norman Park	258	31.16 N	83.38 W
Norman Wells	242	65.17 N	126.51 W
Norphlet	260	33.19 N	92.40 W
Norquay	250	51.53 N	102.05 W
Norridgewock	254	44.43 N	69.48 W
Norris	258	36.12 N	84.04 W
Norris Arm	252	49.05 N	55.15 W
Norris City	260	37.59 N	88.20 W
Norris Dam State Park ♠	258	36.14 N	84.07 W
Norris Lake ⊜[1]	258	36.20 N	83.55 W
Norris Point	252	49.31 N	57.53 W
Norristown	254	40.07 N	75.21 W
North	258	33.37 N	81.06 W
North ≃, NF	242	57.30 N	62.05 W
North ≃, AL	260	33.15 N	87.30 W
North ≃, IA	256	41.31 N	93.27 W
North ≃, MO	260	39.52 N	91.27 W
North ≃, WA	268	46.45 N	123.53 W
North, Cape •[2]	252	47.02 N	60.25 W
North Adams, MA	254	42.42 N	73.07 W
North Adams, MI	256	41.58 N	84.32 W
North Albany	268	44.39 N	123.06 W
Northampton, MA	254	42.19 N	72.38 W
Northampton, PA	254	40.41 N	75.30 W
North Anna ≃	258	37.48 N	77.25 W
North Anson	254	44.52 N	69.54 W
North Asheboro	258	35.44 N	79.49 W
North Atlanta	258	33.51 N	84.21 W
North Augusta	258	33.30 N	81.58 W
North Aulatsivik Island I	242	59.50 N	64.00 W
North Baltimore	254	41.11 N	83.41 W
North Battleford	250	52.47 N	108.17 W
North Bay	256	46.19 N	79.28 W
North Bend, BC	248	49.53 N	121.27 W
North Bend, NE	264	41.28 N	96.47 W
North Bend, OR	268	43.24 N	124.14 W
North Bennington	254	42.56 N	73.15 W
North Berwick	254	43.17 N	70.45 W
North Boggy Creek ≃	262	34.23 N	96.04 W
North Bosque ≃	262	31.40 N	97.24 W
North Branch, MI	256	43.14 N	83.12 W
North Branch, MN	256	45.31 N	92.58 W
North Canadian ≃	262	35.17 N	95.31 W
North Canton, GA	258	34.15 N	84.29 W
North Canton, OH	254	40.53 N	81.24 W
North Caribou Lake ⊜	242	52.50 N	90.40 W
North Carolina □[3], U.S.	244		
	258	35.30 N	80.00 W
North Cascades National Park ♠	268	48.30 N	121.00 W
North Channel ʊ	256	46.02 N	82.50 W
North Charleston	258	32.53 N	80.00 W
North Chicago	256	42.20 N	87.51 W
North College Hill	254	39.12 N	84.32 W
North Collins	254	42.36 N	78.56 W
North Concho ≃	262	31.27 N	100.25 W
North Conway	254	44.03 N	71.08 W
North Creek	254	43.42 N	73.59 W
North Crossett	260	33.11 N	91.57 W
North Croton Creek ≃	262	33.24 N	100.00 W
North Dakota □[3], U.S.	244		
	264	47.30 N	100.15 W
North Eagle Butte	264	45.02 N	101.15 W
North East, MD	254	39.36 N	75.56 W
North East, PA	254	42.13 N	79.50 W
Northeast Cape	246	63.18 N	168.42 W
Northeast Cape ›	246	63.17 N	168.45 W
Northeast Cape Fear ≃	258	34.11 N	77.57 W
Northeast Harbor	254	44.18 N	68.17 W

Symbols in the index entries are identified on page 273.

Symbols in the index entries are identified on page 273.

Name	Page	Lat ° ′	Long ° ′
Outer Santa Barbara Passage	270	33.10 N	118.30 W
Outlook, SK	250	51.30 N	107.03 W
Outlook, MT	264	48.53 N	104.47 W
Outpost Mountain	246	69.08 N	151.12 W
Ouzinkie	246	57.55 N	152.30 W
Overbrook	264	38.47 N	95.33 W
Overflowing	250	53.10 N	101.05 W
Overland Park	264	38.59 N	94.40 W
Overton, NE	264	40.44 N	99.32 W
Overton, NV	270	36.33 N	114.27 W
Overton, TX	260	32.16 N	94.59 W
Overton Arm	270	36.20 N	114.25 W
Ovett	260	31.29 N	89.02 W
Ovid, MI	256	43.01 N	84.22 W
Ovid, NY	254	42.41 N	76.49 W
Owasso	262	36.16 N	95.51 W
Owatonna	256	44.05 N	93.14 W
Owego	254	42.06 N	76.16 W
Owen	256	44.57 N	90.33 W
Owens	270	36.31 N	117.57 W
Owensboro	260	37.46 N	87.07 W
Owens Lake	270	36.25 N	117.56 W
Owen Sound	256	44.34 N	80.56 W
Owen Sound	256	44.40 N	80.55 W
Owensville, IN	260	38.16 N	87.41 W
Owensville, MO	260	38.21 N	91.29 W
Owenton	254	38.32 N	84.50 W
Owikeno Lake	248	51.41 N	127.00 W
Owingsville	254	38.09 N	83.46 W
Owl, AB	250	54.54 N	111.57 W
Owl, MB	242	57.51 N	92.44 W
Owl Creek, U.S.	264	44.41 N	103.29 W
Owl Creek, MT	268	45.18 N	107.21 W
Owl Creek, WY	268	43.41 N	108.11 W
Owl Creek, South Fork	268	43.43 N	108.32 W
Owl Creek Mountains	268	43.30 N	108.35 W
Owosso	256	43.00 N	84.10 W
Owyhee	270	41.57 N	116.06 W
Owyhee	268	43.46 N	117.02 W
Owyhee, Lake	268	43.28 N	117.20 W
Owyhee, South Fork	268	42.26 N	116.53 W
Oxbow	250	49.14 N	102.11 W
Ox Creek	264	48.37 N	100.17 W
Oxford, NS	252	45.44 N	63.52 W
Oxford, AL	260	33.37 N	85.50 W
Oxford, IN	260	40.31 N	87.15 W
Oxford, IA	256	41.43 N	91.47 W
Oxford, KS	264	37.16 N	97.10 W
Oxford, ME	254	44.08 N	70.30 W
Oxford, MD	254	38.42 N	76.10 W
Oxford, MI	256	42.49 N	83.16 W
Oxford, MS	260	34.22 N	89.32 W
Oxford, NE	264	40.15 N	99.38 W
Oxford, NC	258	36.19 N	78.35 W
Oxford, NY	254	42.27 N	75.36 W
Oxford, OH	254	39.30 N	84.44 W
Oxford, PA	254	39.47 N	75.59 W
Oxford, WI	256	43.47 N	89.34 W
Oxford House	250	54.56 N	95.16 W
Oxford House Indian Reserve	250	54.54 N	95.15 W
Oxford Junction	256	41.59 N	90.57 W
Oxford Lake	250	54.51 N	95.37 W
Oxford Peak	268	42.16 N	112.06 W
Oxnard	270	34.12 N	119.11 W
Oyama	248	50.07 N	119.22 W
Oyen	250	51.22 N	110.28 W
Oyster Creek	262	28.59 N	95.18 W
Ozark, AR	260	35.29 N	93.50 W
Ozark, MO	260	37.01 N	93.12 W
Ozark Escarpment	260	36.15 N	91.15 W
Ozark National Scenic Riverways	260	37.10 N	91.10 W
Ozark Plateau	244	37.00 N	93.00 W
Ozark Reservoir	260	35.35 N	94.00 W
Ozarks, Lake of the	260	38.10 N	92.50 W
Ozette Lake	268	48.06 N	124.38 W
Ozona	262	30.43 N	101.12 W
P			
Paauilo	272	20.02 N	155.22 W
Pablo	268	47.36 N	114.07 W
Pace, FL	260	30.36 N	87.09 W
Pace, MS	260	33.42 N	90.52 W
Pacific, BC	248	54.46 N	128.17 W
Pacific, MO	260	38.29 N	90.45 W
Pacifica	270	37.38 N	122.29 W
Pacific Creek	268	42.08 N	109.24 W
Pacific Grove	270	36.38 N	121.56 W
Pacific Ocean	244	30.00 N	120.00 W
Pacific Ranges	248	50.45 N	125.30 W
Pacific Rim National Park	268	48.35 N	124.40 W
Packard Mountain	254	42.28 N	72.21 W
Pacolet	258	34.50 N	81.27 W
Pacolet Mills	258	34.55 N	81.45 W
Pacquet	252	49.59 N	55.53 W
Paddle	248	54.05 N	114.15 W
Paddle Prairie	242	57.57 N	117.29 W
Paden City	254	39.36 N	80.56 W
Padloping Island	242	67.07 N	62.35 W
Padre Island	262	27.00 N	97.15 W
Paducah, KY	260	37.05 N	88.36 W
Paducah, TX	262	34.01 N	100.18 W
Pagato	250	55.49 N	102.05 W
Pagato Lake	250	56.08 N	102.30 W
Page, AZ	266	36.57 N	111.27 W
Page, ND	264	47.09 N	97.34 W
Pageland	258	34.46 N	80.24 W
Pagoda Peak	266	40.10 N	107.20 W
Pagosa Springs	266	37.16 N	107.01 W
Paguate	266	35.08 N	107.23 W
Pahala	272	19.12 N	155.29 W
Pahau Point	272b	21.49 N	160.15 W
Pahoa	272	19.28 N	154.51 W
Pahokee	258	26.49 N	80.40 W
Pahrump	270	36.12 N	115.59 W
Pahsimeroi	268	44.41 N	114.03 W
Paia	272a	20.54 N	156.22 W
Paige	262	30.13 N	97.07 W
Pailolo Channel	272a	21.05 N	156.42 W
Painesdale	256	47.02 N	88.41 W
Painesville	254	41.43 N	81.15 W
Paint	256	45.58 N	88.15 W
Paint Creek	262	30.18 N	99.54 W
Painted Desert	266	36.00 N	111.20 W
Painted Rock Reservoir	266	33.00 N	112.50 W
Paint Lake	250	55.28 N	97.57 W
Paint Rock	262	31.30 N	99.55 W
Paint Rock	260	34.28 N	86.28 W
Paintsville	258	37.49 N	82.48 W
Paisley	268	42.42 N	120.32 W
Pakowki Lake	250	49.22 N	110.57 W
Pakwash Lake	250	50.45 N	93.30 W
Palaau State Park	272a	21.11 N	157.00 W
Palacios	262	28.42 N	96.13 W
Palaoa Point	272a	20.44 N	156.58 W
Palatka	258	29.39 N	81.38 W
Palawai Basin	272a	20.47 N	156.55 W
Palen Dry Lake	270	33.46 N	115.12 W
Palestine, AR	260	34.59 N	90.56 W
Palestine, IL	260	39.00 N	87.37 W
Palestine, TX	262	31.46 N	95.38 W
Palestine, Lake	262	32.06 N	95.27 W
Palikea	272c	21.26 N	158.06 W
Palisade, CO	266	39.07 N	108.21 W
Palisade, NE	264	40.21 N	101.07 W
Palisades	268	43.21 N	111.13 W
Palisades Reservoir	268	43.15 N	111.05 W
Palling	248	54.21 N	125.55 W
Palm Bay	258	28.02 N	80.35 W
Palm Beach	258	26.42 N	80.02 W
Palmdale	270	34.35 N	118.07 W
Palm Desert	270	33.43 N	116.22 W
Palmer, AK	246	61.36 N	149.07 W
Palmer, MA	254	42.09 N	72.20 W
Palmer, MI	256	46.27 N	87.35 W
Palmer, NE	264	41.13 N	98.15 W
Palmer, TN	260	35.21 N	85.34 W
Palmer, TX	262	32.26 N	96.40 W
Palmer Lake	264	39.07 N	104.55 W
Palmers Crossing	260	31.16 N	89.15 W
Palmerston	256	43.50 N	80.51 W
Palmerton	254	40.48 N	75.37 W
Palmetto, FL	258	27.31 N	82.35 W
Palmetto, GA	258	33.31 N	84.40 W
Palmetto, LA	260	30.43 N	91.55 W
Palm Springs	270	33.50 N	116.33 W
Palmyra, IL	260	39.26 N	90.00 W
Palmyra, MO	260	39.48 N	91.31 W
Palmyra, NY	254	43.04 N	77.14 W
Palmyra, PA	254	40.18 N	76.36 W
Palmyra, VA	258	37.51 N	78.16 W
Palo Alto	270	37.27 N	122.09 W
Palo Blanco Creek	262	27.10 N	97.52 W
Palo Duro Canyon State Park	262	34.55 N	101.42 W
Palo Duro Creek, U.S.	262	36.39 N	100.58 W
Palo Duro Creek, TX	262	35.00 N	101.55 W
Palo Flechado Pass	266	36.25 N	105.20 W
Palomar Mountain	270	33.22 N	116.50 W
Palomas Creek	266	33.03 N	107.16 W
Palo Pinto	262	32.46 N	98.18 W
Palo Pinto Reservoir	262	32.38 N	98.18 W
Palos Verdes Point	270	33.47 N	118.26 W
Palouse	268	46.55 N	117.04 W
Palouse	268	46.35 N	118.13 W
Palouse, South Fork	268	46.53 N	117.22 W
Palo Verde	270	33.26 N	114.44 W
Paluxy	262	32.15 N	97.43 W
Pamlico	258	35.20 N	76.30 W
Pamlico Sound	258	35.20 N	75.55 W
Pampa	262	35.32 N	100.58 W
Pamplico	258	34.00 N	79.34 W
Pamunkey	258	37.32 N	76.48 W
Pana	260	39.23 N	89.05 W
Panaca	270	37.47 N	114.23 W
Panacea	258	30.02 N	84.23 W
Panache, Lake	256	46.15 N	81.20 W
Panama, IL	260	39.02 N	89.32 W
Panama, OK	260	35.10 N	94.40 W
Panama City	260	30.10 N	85.41 W
Panamint Range	270	36.30 N	117.20 W
Panamint Valley	270	36.15 N	117.20 W
Pangburn	260	35.15 N	91.51 W
Pangman	250	49.39 N	104.38 W
Pangnirtung	242	66.08 N	65.44 W
Pangnirtung Fiord	242	66.06 N	65.58 W
Panguitch	266	37.49 N	112.26 W
Panhandle	262	35.21 N	101.23 W
Paniau	272b	21.57 N	160.05 W
Pankof, Cape	246	54.40 N	163.04 W
Panola	260	32.57 N	88.16 W
Panora	264	41.42 N	94.22 W
Panther Creek, ID	268	45.19 N	114.24 W
Panther Creek, KY	260	37.45 N	87.19 W
Panther Creek, South Fork	260	37.42 N	87.05 W
Paola	264	38.35 N	94.53 W
Paoli	260	38.33 N	86.28 W
Paonia	266	38.52 N	107.36 W
Papago Indian Reservation	266	32.20 N	112.00 W
Papaikou	272	19.47 N	155.06 W
Papawai Point	272a	20.47 N	156.33 W
Papillion	264	41.09 N	96.03 W
Papineau, Lac	254	45.48 N	74.46 W
Papineau, Parc de	254	45.55 N	75.20 W
Paradise, CA	270	39.46 N	121.37 W
Paradise, MT	268	47.23 N	114.48 W
Paradise, NV	270	36.09 N	115.10 W
Paradise, TX	262	33.09 N	97.41 W
Paradise Hill, SK	250	53.32 N	109.28 W
Paradise Hill, AK	246	62.25 N	160.03 W
Paradise Valley, AZ	266	33.32 N	111.57 W
Paradise Valley, NV	270	41.30 N	117.32 W
Paragonah	266	37.53 N	112.46 W
Paragould	260	36.03 N	90.29 W
Paramus	254	40.57 N	74.04 W
Parchment	256	42.19 N	85.33 W
Pardeeville	256	43.32 N	89.18 W
Parent	242	47.55 N	74.37 W
Parent, Lac	256	48.38 N	77.03 W
Paria	266	36.52 N	111.36 W
Pariette Draw	266	40.02 N	109.45 W
Paris, ON	256	43.12 N	80.23 W
Paris, AR	260	35.18 N	93.44 W
Paris, ID	268	42.14 N	111.24 W
Paris, IL	260	39.36 N	87.42 W
Paris, KY	254	38.13 N	84.14 W
Paris, ME	254	44.16 N	70.30 W
Paris, MO	260	39.29 N	92.00 W
Paris, TN	260	36.19 N	88.20 W
Paris, TX	262	33.40 N	95.33 W
Park	264	48.28 N	97.09 W
Park, North Branch	264	48.26 N	97.27 W
Park, South Branch	264	48.26 N	97.27 W
Park City, KS	264	37.46 N	97.19 W
Park City, MT	268	45.38 N	108.55 W
Park City, UT	266	40.39 N	111.30 W
Parkdale, PE	252	46.15 N	63.07 W
Parkdale, OR	268	45.31 N	121.36 W
Parker, AZ	266	34.09 N	114.17 W
Parker, FL	260	30.08 N	85.36 W
Parker, SD	264	43.24 N	97.08 W
Parker, Cape	242	75.04 N	79.40 W
Parker City	260	40.11 N	85.12 W
Parker Dam	270	34.17 N	114.09 W
Parker Dam	270	34.18 N	114.07 W
Parker Peak	264	43.24 N	103.41 W
Parkersburg, IL	260	38.36 N	88.03 W
Parkersburg, IA	256	42.35 N	92.47 W
Parkersburg, WV	254	39.17 N	81.32 W
Parkers Prairie	264	46.09 N	95.20 W
Park Falls	256	45.56 N	90.32 W
Park Forest	260	41.28 N	87.38 W
Parkhill	256	43.09 N	81.41 W
Parkin	260	35.16 N	90.34 W
Parkland	268	47.09 N	122.26 W
Park Plateau	264	37.15 N	104.45 W
Park Range	266	40.00 N	106.30 W
Park Rapids	264	46.55 N	95.04 W
Park River	264	48.24 N	97.45 W
Parkrose	268	45.34 N	122.33 W
Parksley	258	37.47 N	75.39 W
Parkston	264	43.24 N	97.59 W
Parksville	248	49.19 N	124.19 W
Parkville, MD	254	39.23 N	76.32 W
Parkville, MO	260	39.11 N	94.41 W
Parkwater	268	47.40 N	117.18 W
Parle, Lac qui	264	45.07 N	96.00 W
Parma, ID	268	43.47 N	116.57 W
Parma, MI	256	42.15 N	84.36 W
Parma, MO	260	36.37 N	89.48 W
Parma, OH	254	41.22 N	81.43 W
Parowan	266	37.51 N	112.57 W
Parrish, AL	260	33.44 N	87.17 W
Parrish, FL	258	27.35 N	82.25 W
Parris Island Marine Corps Recruit Depot	258	32.21 N	80.41 W
Parrsboro	252	45.24 N	64.20 W
Parry, Cape	242	70.08 N	124.24 W
Parry, Mount	248	52.53 N	128.45 W
Parry Bay	242	68.07 N	82.00 W
Parry Island	256	45.18 N	80.10 W
Parry Peninsula	246	69.45 N	124.30 W
Parry Sound	256	45.21 N	80.02 W
Parshall	264	47.57 N	102.08 W
Parsnip	248	55.10 N	123.00 W
Parsons, KS	264	37.20 N	95.16 W
Parsons, TN	260	35.39 N	88.07 W
Parsons, WV	254	39.06 N	79.41 W
Parson's Pond	252	50.02 N	57.43 W
Parsons Pond	252	50.00 N	57.35 W
Partridge Crop Lake	250	55.38 N	97.27 W
Partridge Point	252	50.09 N	56.10 W
Pasadena, NF	252	49.01 N	57.36 W
Pasadena, CA	270	34.09 N	118.09 W
Pasadena, TX	262	29.42 N	95.13 W
Pascagama, Lac	256	48.34 N	75.36 W
Pascagoula	260	30.23 N	88.31 W
Pascagoula	260	30.21 N	88.34 W
Pascalis, Lac	256	48.16 N	77.24 W
Pasco	268	46.14 N	119.06 W
Pascoag	254	41.57 N	71.42 W
Pasley Bay	242	70.40 N	96.27 W
Paso Robles	270	35.38 N	120.41 W
Pasqua Indian Reserve	250	50.45 N	104.02 W
Pasquia Hills	250	53.13 N	102.37 W
Pasquia Lake	250	53.37 N	101.20 W
Pasquotank	258	36.10 N	76.03 W
Passadumkeag	254	45.11 N	68.37 W
Passadumkeag Mountain	254	45.10 N	68.20 W
Passaic	254	40.51 N	74.08 W
Passamaquoddy Bay	252	45.06 N	66.59 W
Pass Creek	264	43.45 N	101.28 W
Pass Island	252	47.29 N	56.11 W
Pastecho	248	56.07 N	114.15 W
Pasteur, Lac	252	50.13 N	66.58 W
Pastol Bay	246	63.07 N	163.15 W
Pastora Peak	266	36.47 N	109.10 W
Patagonia	266	31.33 N	110.45 W
Pataha Creek	268	46.31 N	117.59 W
Pataula Creek	258	31.46 N	85.02 W
Patchogue	254	40.46 N	73.00 W
Pateros	268	48.03 N	119.54 W
Paterson	254	40.55 N	74.10 W
Pathfinder Reservoir	268	42.30 N	106.50 W
Pat Mayse Reservoir	262	33.40 N	95.35 W
Patoka	260	38.45 N	89.06 W
Patoka	260	38.25 N	87.44 W
Patrick Air Force Base	258	28.15 N	80.36 W
Patsaliga Creek	260	31.22 N	86.31 W
Patten	252	46.01 N	68.27 W
Patterson, CA	270	37.28 N	121.07 W
Patterson, GA	258	31.23 N	82.08 W
Patterson, LA	260	29.42 N	91.18 W
Patterson, Mount	246	64.04 N	134.39 W
Patterson Creek	254	39.34 N	78.23 W
Patterson Island	256	48.39 N	87.00 W
Pattison	260	31.53 N	90.53 W
Patton	254	40.38 N	78.39 W
Pattonsburg	260	40.03 N	94.08 W
Pattullo, Mount	246	56.14 N	129.39 W
Patuxent	254	38.18 N	76.25 W
Paul	268	42.40 N	113.36 W
Paul, Lac à	252	49.52 N	70.46 W
Paulding, MS	260	32.02 N	89.02 W
Paulding, OH	254	41.08 N	84.35 W
Paulina Peak	268	43.41 N	121.15 W
Pauline, Mount	248	53.33 N	119.54 W
Paullina	264	42.59 N	95.41 W
Paull Lake	250	56.08 N	104.50 W
Pauloff Harbor (Pavlof Harbor)	246	54.27 N	162.42 W
Pauls Valley	262	34.44 N	97.13 W
Pauwalu Point	272a	20.52 N	156.08 W
Pauwela	272a	20.56 N	156.19 W
Pauwela Point	272a	20.57 N	156.19 W
Pavant Range	266	38.45 N	112.15 W
Pavilion	248	50.52 N	121.50 W
Pavillion	268	43.15 N	108.42 W
Pavlof Bay	246	55.30 N	161.32 W
Pavlof Volcano	246	55.24 N	161.52 W
Pavo	258	30.57 N	83.45 W
Paw Creek	258	35.17 N	80.56 W
Pawhuska	262	36.40 N	96.20 W
Pawnee, IL	260	39.35 N	89.35 W
Pawnee, OK	262	36.20 N	96.48 W
Pawnee	264	38.10 N	99.06 W
Pawnee City	264	40.07 N	96.09 W
Pawnee Creek	264	40.34 N	103.14 W
Pawnee Rock	264	38.16 N	99.01 W
Pawpaw, IL	260	41.41 N	88.59 W
Paw Paw, MI	256	42.13 N	85.53 W
Paw Paw, WV	254	39.32 N	78.27 W
Paw Paw Lake	256	42.12 N	86.15 W
Pawtucket	254	41.53 N	71.23 W
Paxson	246	63.02 N	145.30 W
Paxton, IL	256	40.27 N	88.06 W
Paxton, NE	264	41.07 N	101.21 W
Payette	268	44.05 N	116.56 W
Payette	268	44.05 N	116.57 W
Payette, Middle Fork	268	44.05 N	116.07 W
Payette, North Fork	268	44.05 N	116.07 W
Payette, South Fork	268	44.06 N	116.00 W
Payette Lake	268	44.57 N	116.05 W
Payne	254	41.05 N	84.44 W
Payne, Bassin	242	60.00 N	70.00 W
Payne, Lac	242	59.25 N	74.00 W
Paynes Creek	270	40.16 N	122.11 W
Paynesville	264	45.23 N	94.43 W
Paynton	250	53.01 N	108.56 W
Payson, AZ	266	34.14 N	111.20 W
Payson, IL	260	39.49 N	73.14 W
Payson, UT	266	40.03 N	111.44 W
Pea	260	31.01 N	85.51 W
Peabody, KS	264	38.10 N	97.07 W
Peabody, MA	254	42.32 N	70.55 W
Peace, Can.	242	59.00 N	111.25 W
Peace, FL	258	26.55 N	82.05 W
Peace River	248	56.14 N	117.17 W
Peach Creek	258	37.53 N	81.59 W
Peach Creek, TX	262	29.24 N	97.19 W
Peach Creek, TX	262	30.07 N	95.10 W
Peachland	248	49.46 N	119.44 W
Peach Orchard	258	33.22 N	82.03 W
Peach Springs	266	35.32 N	113.25 W
Peacock Hills	242	66.05 N	110.45 W
Peaked Mountain	252	46.34 N	68.49 W
Peale, Mount	266	38.26 N	109.14 W
Pearce	266	31.54 N	109.49 W
Peard Bay	246	70.51 N	159.10 W
Pea Ridge National Military Park	260	36.29 N	94.06 W
Pearisburg	258	37.20 N	80.44 W
Pearl, IL	260	39.28 N	90.38 W
Pearl, MS	260	32.18 N	90.12 W
Pearl	244	30.11 N	89.32 W
Pearland	262	29.34 N	95.17 W
Pearl City	272c	21.24 N	157.59 W
Pearl Creek	264	44.15 N	98.08 W
Pearl Harbor	272c	21.22 N	157.58 W
Pearl Harbor Naval Base	272c	21.21 N	157.57 W
Pearl Peak	270	40.14 N	115.32 W
Pearl River, LA	260	30.23 N	89.45 W
Pearl River, NY	254	41.04 N	74.02 W
Pearsall	262	28.53 N	99.06 W
Pearse Island	248	54.51 N	130.21 W
Pearsoll Peak	268	42.18 N	123.50 W
Pearson	258	31.18 N	82.51 W
Pearson Lake	250	56.15 N	97.15 W
Pease	262	34.12 N	99.07 W
Pease Air Force Base	254	43.06 N	70.49 W
Pecan Bayou	262	31.28 N	98.43 W
Pecan Gap	262	33.26 N	95.51 W
Pecatonica	256	42.19 N	89.22 W
Pecatonica	256	42.27 N	89.05 W
Peck	256	43.16 N	82.49 W
Pecos, NM	266	35.29 N	105.41 W
Pecos, TX	262	31.25 N	103.30 W
Pecos	244	29.42 N	101.22 W
Pecos National Monument	266	35.26 N	105.56 W
Pecos Plains	262	33.20 N	104.30 W
Pedernales	262	30.26 N	98.04 W
Pedernales Falls State Park	262	30.20 N	98.14 W
Pedro Bay	246	59.47 N	154.07 W
Peebles	254	38.57 N	83.24 W
Pee Dee	244	33.21 N	79.16 W
Peekaboo Mountain	254	45.45 N	67.53 W
Peekskill	254	41.17 N	73.55 W
Peel	246	67.37 N	134.40 W
Peel Channel	246	68.13 N	135.00 W
Pe Ell	268	46.34 N	123.18 W
Peel Point	242	73.22 N	114.35 W
Peel Sound	242	73.15 N	96.30 W
Peepeekeesis Indian Reserve	250	50.52 N	103.24 W
Peerless	264	48.47 N	105.50 W
Peers	248	53.40 N	116.00 W
Peesane	250	52.52 N	103.36 W
Peetz	264	40.58 N	103.07 W
Peguis Indian Reserve	250	51.20 N	97.35 W
Peigan Indian Reserve	248	49.35 N	113.40 W
Peirce, Cape	246	58.35 N	161.47 W
Pekin, IL	256	40.35 N	89.40 W
Pekin, IN	260	38.30 N	86.00 W
Pelahatchie	260	32.19 N	89.48 W
Pelee, Point	256	41.54 N	82.30 W
Pelham, AL	260	33.17 N	86.49 W
Pelham, GA	258	31.08 N	84.09 W
Pelican	246	57.57 N	136.14 W
Pelican	264	46.17 N	96.08 W
Pelican Bay	250	52.45 N	100.20 W
Pelican Lake	256	45.30 N	89.10 W
Pelican Lake, AB	248	55.47 N	113.15 W
Pelican Lake, MB	250	49.20 N	99.35 W
Pelican Lake, MB	250	53.50 N	96.08 W
Pelican Lake, MB	250	52.30 N	100.20 W
Pelican Lake, SK	250	55.08 N	103.00 W
Pelican Lake, SD	264	44.52 N	97.11 W
Pelican Mountain	248	55.35 N	113.40 W
Pelican Narrows	250	55.10 N	102.56 W
Pelican Rapids, MB	250	52.45 N	100.42 W
Pelican Rapids, MN	264	46.34 N	96.05 W
Pella	256	41.25 N	92.55 W
Pell City	260	33.35 N	86.17 W
Pelletier Lake	250	56.30 N	97.00 W
Pellston	256	45.33 N	84.47 W
Pelly	250	51.52 N	101.55 W
Pelly	246	62.47 N	137.19 W
Pelly Bay	242	68.53 N	89.51 W
Pelly Crossing	246	62.50 N	136.35 W
Pelly Lake	242	65.59 N	101.12 W
Pelly Mountains	246	62.00 N	133.00 W
Peloncillo Mountains	266	32.15 N	109.00 W
Pemadumcook Lake	254	45.40 N	68.55 W
Pemberton	248	50.20 N	122.48 W
Pemberton Indian Reserve	248	50.19 N	122.42 W
Pembina	264	48.58 N	97.15 W
Pembina, AB	248	54.45 N	114.15 W
Pembina, N.A.	250	48.56 N	97.15 W
Pembina Mountains	264	49.00 N	98.05 W
Pembine	256	45.38 N	87.59 W
Pembroke, ON	256	45.49 N	77.07 W
Pembroke, GA	258	32.08 N	81.37 W
Pembroke, KY	260	36.47 N	87.21 W
Pembroke, ME	254	44.57 N	67.10 W
Pembroke, NC	258	34.41 N	79.12 W
Pembroke, VA	258	37.19 N	80.38 W
Pembroke, Cape	242	62.56 N	81.55 W
Pemichigamau Lake	250	56.16 N	99.33 W
Pemigewasset	254	43.26 N	71.40 W
Pemmican Portage	250	53.56 N	102.17 W
Pemynoos Indian Reserve	248	50.29 N	121.15 W
Pen Argyl	254	40.52 N	75.16 W
Penasco	266	36.10 N	105.41 W
Peñasco, Rio	262	32.45 N	104.19 W
Pence	256	46.25 N	90.16 W
Pender	264	42.07 N	96.43 W
Pendleton, IN	260	40.01 N	85.45 W
Pendleton, OR	268	45.40 N	118.47 W
Pendleton, SC	258	34.39 N	82.47 W
Pend Oreille	248	49.04 N	117.37 W
Pend Oreille, Lake	268	48.10 N	116.11 W
Pend Oreille, Mount	268	48.25 N	116.10 W
Penetanguishene	256	44.47 N	79.55 W
Penfield	254	41.13 N	78.34 W
Penhold	248	52.08 N	113.52 W
Peninsula State Park	256	45.09 N	87.14 W
Penitas	262	26.17 N	98.27 W
Pennant Point	252	44.26 N	63.39 W
Pennant Station	250	50.33 N	108.12 W
Pennask Lake	248	50.00 N	120.05 W
Pennask Mountain	248	49.53 N	120.07 W
Pennel Creek	264	46.34 N	104.52 W
Penn Hills	254	40.28 N	79.53 W
Pennington Gap	258	36.41 N	83.02 W
Pennsauken	254	39.58 N	75.04 W
Pennsboro	254	39.17 N	80.58 W
Penns Creek	254	40.48 N	76.51 W
Penns Grove	254	39.43 N	75.28 W
Pennsylvania, U.S.	244		
	254	40.45 N	77.30 W
Penny	248	53.50 N	121.17 W
Penn Yan	254	42.40 N	77.03 W
Pennycutaway	250	56.43 N	92.44 W
Penny Strait	242	76.30 N	97.00 W
Penobscot	254	44.30 N	68.50 W
Penobscot, East Branch	254	45.35 N	68.32 W
Penobscot, West Branch	254	45.35 N	68.32 W
Penobscot Bay	254	44.15 N	68.52 W
Pensacola	260	30.25 N	87.13 W
Pensacola Bay	260	30.25 N	87.06 W
Pensacola Naval Air Station	260	30.21 N	87.19 W
Pensaukee	256	44.49 N	87.55 W
Pense	250	50.25 N	105.00 W
Pentagon Mountain	268	47.56 N	113.07 W
Pentecôte, Lac	252	49.53 N	67.20 W
Penticton	248	49.30 N	119.35 W
Penticton Indian Reserve	248	49.30 N	119.40 W
Pentwater	256	43.47 N	86.26 W
Penwell	262	31.44 N	102.35 W
Peoples Creek	268	48.24 N	108.19 W
Peoria, AZ	266	33.35 N	112.14 W
Peoria, IL	256	40.42 N	89.36 W
Peoria Heights	256	40.45 N	89.34 W
Peotone	260	41.20 N	87.47 W
Pepaw	250	52.40 N	102.23 W
Pepin	256	44.27 N	92.09 W
Pepin, Lake	256	44.30 N	92.15 W
Pequop Mountains	270	40.45 N	114.40 W
Pequot Lakes	264	46.36 N	94.19 W
Peralta	266	34.50 N	106.41 W
Percé	252	48.31 N	64.13 W
Perche Creek	260	38.49 N	92.24 W
Perdido	260	31.00 N	87.37 W
Perdido	260	30.29 N	87.26 W
Perdido Bay	260	30.21 N	87.27 W
Perdu, Lac	252	50.44 N	70.14 W
Perdue	250	52.04 N	107.32 W
Pere Marquette	256	43.57 N	86.27 W
Pere Marquette, Big South Branch	256	43.56 N	86.10 W
Perham	264	46.36 N	95.34 W
Péribonca	252	48.45 N	72.05 W
Péribonca, Lac	252	50.04 N	71.15 W
Peridot	266	33.18 N	110.28 W
Perkasie	254	40.22 N	75.18 W
Perkins	262	35.58 N	97.02 W
Perkinston	260	30.47 N	89.08 W
Perkiomen Creek	254	40.07 N	75.28 W
Perkiomen Creek, East Branch	254	40.15 N	75.27 W
Perow	248	54.31 N	126.26 W
Perrault Falls	250	50.19 N	93.11 W
Perrin	262	33.02 N	98.04 W
Perrine	258	25.36 N	80.21 W
Perris	270	33.47 N	117.14 W
Perris, Lake	270	33.50 N	117.10 W
Perro, Laguna del	266	34.40 N	105.57 W
Perry, FL	258	30.07 N	83.35 W
Perry, GA	258	32.27 N	83.44 W
Perry, IA	260	41.50 N	94.06 W
Perry, KS	264	39.05 N	95.24 W
Perry, MI	256	42.50 N	84.13 W
Perry, MO	260	39.26 N	91.40 W
Perry, NY	254	42.43 N	78.00 W
Perry, OK	262	36.17 N	97.17 W
Perry, UT	266	35.18 N	105.22 W
Perry Lake	264	39.20 N	95.30 W
Perrysburg	254	41.33 N	83.38 W
Perry's Victory and International Peace Memorial	254	41.33 N	82.50 W
Perrysville	254	40.40 N	82.19 W
Perryton	262	36.24 N	100.48 W
Perryville, AK	246	55.54 N	159.10 W
Perryville, AR	260	35.00 N	92.48 W
Perryville, KY	258	37.39 N	84.58 W
Perryville, MO	260	37.43 N	89.52 W
Persia	264	41.34 N	95.35 W
Persimmon Creek	260	31.31 N	86.50 W
Perth	256	44.54 N	76.15 W
Perth Amboy	254	40.31 N	74.16 W
Perth-Andover	252	46.45 N	67.42 W
Peru, IL	260	41.20 N	89.08 W
Peru, IN	260	40.45 N	86.04 W
Peru, NE	264	40.29 N	95.44 W
Peru, NY	254	44.35 N	73.32 W
Peshtigo	256	45.03 N	87.45 W
Peshtigo	256	44.58 N	87.40 W
Petal	260	31.21 N	89.17 W
Petaluma	270	38.14 N	122.39 W
Petawawa	256	45.54 N	77.17 W
Petawawa	256	45.55 N	77.15 W
Petenwell Dam	256	44.01 N	90.02 W
Petenwell Lake	256	44.10 N	89.57 W
Peterborough, ON	256	44.18 N	78.19 W
Peterborough, NH	254	42.53 N	71.57 W
Peter Lake	242	63.08 N	92.48 W
Peterman	260	31.36 N	87.18 W
Peter Pond Lake	250	55.55 N	108.44 W
Peter Pond Lake Indian Reserve	250	55.55 N	109.00 W
Petersburg, AK	246	56.50 N	132.59 W
Petersburg, IL	260	40.01 N	89.51 W
Petersburg, IN	260	38.30 N	87.17 W
Petersburg, MI	256	41.54 N	83.43 W
Petersburg, NE	264	41.51 N	98.05 W
Petersburg, TN	260	35.19 N	86.38 W
Petersburg, TX	262	33.52 N	101.36 W
Petersburg, VA	258	37.13 N	77.24 W
Petersburg, WV	254	39.00 N	79.07 W
Peterson	264	42.55 N	95.21 W
Peterson Field	264	38.49 N	104.42 W
Petit Bois Island	260	30.12 N	88.26 W
Petitcodiac	252	45.56 N	65.10 W
Petitcodiac	252	45.50 N	64.33 W
Petite-Cascapedia, Parc de la	252	48.30 N	65.50 W
Petite Rivière de La Baleine	242	56.00 N	76.45 W
Petit Jean	260	35.10 N	92.56 W
Petit Jean State Park	260	35.06 N	92.57 W
Petit Lac du Nord	252	50.50 N	67.10 W
Petit Mécatina, Île du	252	50.33 N	59.20 W
Petit-Mecatina, Rivière du	242	50.28 N	59.35 W
Petitot	242	60.14 N	123.29 W
Petitsikapau Lake	242	54.45 N	66.25 W
Petoskey	256	45.22 N	84.57 W
Petownikip Lake	250	52.56 N	92.02 W
Petre, Point	256	43.50 N	77.09 W
Petrified Forest National Park	266	34.55 N	109.49 W
Petrolia, ON	256	42.52 N	82.09 W
Petrolia, TX	262	34.01 N	98.14 W
Petronila Creek	262	27.32 N	97.32 W
Petros	258	36.06 N	84.26 W
Pettus	262	28.37 N	97.48 W
Petty Harbour	252	47.28 N	52.43 W
Pharr	262	26.12 N	98.11 W
Pheasant Creek	250	50.35 N	103.28 W
Pheba	260	33.35 N	88.57 W
Phelps, NY	254	42.57 N	77.03 W
Phelps, WI	256	46.04 N	89.05 W
Phelps Lake	258	35.46 N	76.27 W
Phenix City	258	32.29 N	85.01 W
Philadelphia, MS	260	32.46 N	89.07 W
Philadelphia, NY	254	44.09 N	75.43 W
Philadelphia, PA	254	39.57 N	75.07 W
Philadelphia, TN	258	35.41 N	84.24 W
Phil Campbell	260	34.21 N	87.42 W
Philip	264	44.02 N	101.40 W
Philipp	260	33.45 N	90.12 W
Philippi	254	39.09 N	80.02 W
Philipsburg, MT	268	46.20 N	113.18 W
Philipsburg, PA	254	40.53 N	78.05 W
Philip Smith Mountains	246	68.30 N	148.00 W
Phillips, ME	254	44.49 N	70.21 W
Phillips, TX	262	35.42 N	101.22 W
Phillips, WI	256	45.41 N	90.24 W
Phillipsburg, GA	258	31.34 N	83.31 W
Phillipsburg, KS	264	39.45 N	99.19 W
Phillipsburg, NJ	254	40.42 N	75.12 W
Philmont	254	42.15 N	73.39 W
Philo, IL	260	40.01 N	88.09 W
Philo, OH	254	39.52 N	81.55 W
Philomath	268	44.32 N	123.22 W
Philpots Island	242	74.48 N	80.00 W
Phoenix, AZ	266	33.27 N	112.05 W
Phoenix, NY	254	43.14 N	76.18 W
Phoenixville	254	40.08 N	75.31 W
Piacouadie, Lac	252	51.16 N	70.54 W
Pian, Lac	256	47.50 N	79.08 W
Piapot	250	50.00 N	109.11 W
Piapot Indian Reserve	250	50.45 N	104.26 W
Piashti, Lac	252	50.29 N	62.52 W
Pibroch	248	54.16 N	113.52 W
Pic	256	48.36 N	86.18 W
Picacho	266	32.43 N	111.30 W
Picanoc	254	46.05 N	76.03 W
Picayune	260	30.26 N	89.41 W
Piccadilly	252	48.34 N	58.55 W
Piceance Creek	266	40.05 N	108.14 W
Picher	260	36.59 N	94.50 W
Pic Island	256	48.43 N	86.38 W
Pickardville	248	54.03 N	113.53 W
Pickens, MS	260	32.53 N	89.58 W
Pickens, SC	258	34.53 N	82.42 W
Pickens, WV	254	38.39 N	80.13 W
Pickensville	260	33.14 N	88.16 W
Pickerel	256	45.55 N	80.50 W
Pickerel Lake	250	52.36 N	99.30 W
Pickering	256	43.52 N	79.02 W
Pickford	256	46.10 N	84.22 W
Pickle Crow	242	51.30 N	90.04 W
Pickstown	264	43.04 N	98.32 W
Pickton	262	33.02 N	95.24 W
Pickwick Lake	260	34.55 N	88.10 W
Pickwick Landing Dam	260	35.00 N	88.21 W
Picton	256	44.00 N	77.08 W
Pictou	252	45.41 N	62.43 W
Pictou Island	252	45.50 N	62.34 W
Picture Butte	248	49.53 N	112.47 W
Pictured Rocks National Lakeshore	256	46.35 N	86.20 W
Picuris Indian Reservation	266	36.12 N	105.42 W
Piedmont, AL	258	33.55 N	85.37 W
Piedmont, MO	260	37.09 N	90.42 W
Piedmont, SC	258	34.42 N	82.28 W
Piedmont Lake	254	40.08 N	81.11 W
Piedra	266	37.01 N	107.24 W
Pie Island	256	48.15 N	89.05 W

Symbols in the index entries are identified on page 273.

United States and Canada Map Index

Symbols in the index entries are identified on page 273.

Name	Page	Lat ° '	Long ° '

Name	Page	Lat °′	Long °′
Roslyn	268	47.13 N	120.59 W
Rosman	258	35.03 N	82.49 W
Ross	246	61.59 N	132.26 W
Ross Barnett Reservoir	260	32.30 N	90.00 W
Rossburn	250	50.40 N	100.52 W
Rosseau, Lake	256	45.10 N	79.35 W
Rossford	254	41.37 N	83.33 W
Ross Fork Creek	268	47.05 N	109.43 W
Rossignol, Lake	252	44.10 N	65.10 W
Ross Island	250	54.14 N	97.45 W
Rossiter	254	40.53 N	78.56 W
Ross Lake	248	48.53 N	121.04 W
Ross Lake National Recreation Area	268	48.45 N	121.00 W
Rossland	248	49.05 N	117.48 W
Ross River	246	61.59 N	132.27 W
Rossville, GA	258	34.59 N	85.16 W
Rossville, IL	260	40.23 N	87.40 W
Rossville, IN	260	40.25 N	86.36 W
Rossville, KS	264	39.08 N	95.57 W
Rosthern	250	52.40 N	106.17 W
Roswell, GA	258	34.01 N	84.22 W
Roswell, NM	262	33.24 N	104.32 W
Rotan	262	32.51 N	100.28 W
Rothesay	252	45.23 N	66.00 W
Rothsay	264	46.28 N	96.17 W
Rothschild	256	44.54 N	89.50 W
Rothwell	252	46.04 N	66.04 W
Rotterdam	254	42.48 N	74.01 W
Roubideau Creek	266	38.44 N	108.10 W
Roubidoux Creek	260	37.51 N	92.13 W
Rouge	254	45.39 N	74.42 W
Rough	260	37.29 N	87.08 W
Rough River Lake	260	37.40 N	86.25 W
Rouleau	250	50.11 N	104.55 W
Roulette	254	41.47 N	78.09 W
Round Harbour	252	47.37 N	56.00 W
Round Lake	264	43.32 N	95.28 W
Round Lake, NF	252	51.08 N	56.33 W
Round Lake, ON	256	45.38 N	77.32 W
Round Lake, SK	250	50.33 N	102.23 W
Round Mound	264	38.55 N	99.39 W
Round Mountain	270	38.43 N	117.04 W
Round Pond	252	48.10 N	56.00 W
Round Rock	262	30.31 N	97.41 W
Roundup	268	46.27 N	108.33 W
Round Valley Indian Reservation	270	39.50 N	123.20 W
Rouses Point	254	45.00 N	73.22 W
Routhierville	252	48.11 N	67.09 W
Rouvray, Lac	252	49.18 N	70.49 W
Rouyn	256	48.15 N	79.01 W
Rowan Lake	250	49.18 N	93.32 W
Rowena	262	31.39 N	100.03 W
Rowland	258	34.32 N	79.18 W
Rowlesburg	254	39.21 N	79.40 W
Rowley	242	70.16 N	77.45 W
Rowley Island	242	69.08 N	78.50 W
Roxboro	258	36.24 N	78.59 W
Roxie	260	31.30 N	91.04 W
Roxton	262	33.33 N	95.44 W
Roy, NM	262	35.57 N	104.12 W
Roy, UT	266	41.10 N	112.02 W
Roy, WA	268	47.00 N	122.33 W
Royal	264	43.04 N	95.17 W
Royal Center	260	40.52 N	86.30 W
Royal City	268	46.54 N	119.38 W
Royale, Isle	256	48.00 N	89.00 W
Royal Gorge	266	38.17 N	105.45 W
Royal Oak	256	42.30 N	83.08 W
Royalton	264	45.50 N	94.18 W
Royse City	262	32.59 N	96.20 W
Royston	258	34.17 N	83.06 W
Rozhnof, Cape	246	55.58 N	160.58 W
Rubicon	270	39.00 N	120.44 W
Ruby	246	64.44 N	155.30 W
Ruby	268	45.34 N	112.21 W
Ruby Dome	270	40.37 N	115.28 W
Ruby Lake	270	40.10 N	115.30 W
Ruby Mountains	270	40.25 N	115.35 W
Ruby Range	268	45.15 N	112.15 W
Ruby Valley	270	40.30 N	115.15 W
Rudyard, MI	256	46.14 N	84.36 W
Rudyard, MT	268	48.34 N	110.33 W
Rudyerd Bay	248	55.35 N	130.44 W
Ruffin	258	33.00 N	80.49 W
Rufus	268	45.42 N	120.44 W
Rugby	264	48.22 N	100.00 W
Rugged Mountain	248	50.02 N	126.41 W
Ruidoso	266	33.20 N	105.40 W
Ruidoso, Rio	266	33.23 N	105.16 W
Ruidoso Downs	266	33.21 N	105.34 W
Rule	262	33.11 N	99.54 W
Rule Creek	264	38.02 N	103.02 W
Ruleville	260	33.44 N	90.33 W
Rulo	264	40.03 N	95.26 W
Rum	256	45.11 N	93.23 W
Rumford	254	44.33 N	70.33 W
Rump Mountain	254	45.12 N	71.04 W
Runge	262	28.54 N	97.43 W
Running Water Draw	262	33.58 N	101.30 W
Rupert, ID	268	42.37 N	113.41 W
Rupert, WV	258	37.58 N	80.41 W
Rupert, Rivière de	242	51.29 N	78.45 W
Rupert House	242	51.30 N	78.45 W
Rural Hall	258	36.15 N	80.18 W
Rural Retreat	258	36.54 N	81.17 W
Rush, ND	264	47.00 N	96.54 W
Rush, WI	256	44.34 N	92.19 W
Rush Center	264	38.28 N	99.19 W
Rush City	256	45.41 N	92.58 W
Rush Creek, CO	264	38.22 N	102.32 W
Rush Creek, NE	264	41.27 N	102.32 W
Rush Creek, OH	254	39.38 N	82.33 W
Rush Creek, OK	262	34.42 N	97.10 W
Rushford	256	43.49 N	91.46 W
Rush Lake, ON	256	47.48 N	82.12 W
Rush Lake, WI	256	43.49 N	89.00 W
Rushmore	264	43.37 N	95.48 W
Rush Springs	262	34.47 N	97.58 W
Rushville, IL	260	40.07 N	90.34 W
Rushville, IN	260	39.37 N	85.27 W
Rushville, NE	264	42.43 N	102.28 W
Rusk	262	31.48 N	95.09 W
Ruskin	258	27.43 N	82.26 W
Russell, MB	250	50.47 N	101.15 W
Russell, ON	254	45.17 N	75.17 W
Russell, IA	256	40.59 N	93.12 W
Russell, KS	264	38.54 N	98.52 W
Russell, KY	254	38.32 N	82.42 W
Russell, MN	264	44.19 N	95.57 W
Russell, PA	254	41.56 N	79.08 W
Russell, Cape	242	75.15 N	117.35 W
Russell, Mount	246	62.48 N	151.52 W
Russell Cave National Monument	260	34.54 N	85.48 W
Russell Creek	260	37.14 N	85.30 W
Russell Island	242	73.55 N	98.25 W
Russell Lake	250	56.15 N	101.30 W
Russell Point	242	73.30 N	115.00 W
Russells Point	254	40.28 N	83.54 W
Russell Springs	260	37.03 N	85.05 W
Russellville, AL	260	34.30 N	87.44 W
Russellville, AR	260	35.17 N	93.08 W
Russellville, KY	260	36.51 N	86.53 W
Russellville, MO	260	38.31 N	92.26 W
Russian	270	38.27 N	123.08 W
Russian Mission	246	61.34 N	159.34 W
Russiaville	260	40.25 N	86.16 W
Rustburg	258	37.17 N	79.06 W
Ruston	260	32.32 N	92.38 W
Ruth, MS	260	31.23 N	90.19 W
Ruth, NV	270	39.17 N	114.59 W
Rutherford	260	36.08 N	88.59 W
Rutherfordton	258	35.22 N	81.57 W
Ruthton	264	44.11 N	96.06 W
Ruthven	264	43.08 N	94.54 W
Rutland, BC	248	49.53 N	119.24 W
Rutland, ND	264	46.03 N	97.30 W
Rutland, VT	254	43.36 N	72.59 W
Rutledge, GA	258	33.38 N	83.37 W
Rutledge, TN	258	36.17 N	83.31 W
Rutter	256	46.06 N	80.40 W
Ryan	262	34.01 N	97.57 W
Ryan	248	50.25 N	122.43 W
Ryan Peak	268	43.54 N	114.25 W
Rycroft	248	55.45 N	118.43 W
Ryder	264	47.55 N	101.40 W
Ryderwood	268	46.23 N	123.03 W
Ryegate	268	46.18 N	109.15 W
Rye Patch Reservoir	270	40.38 N	118.18 W
Rykerts	248	49.00 N	116.35 W
Ryley	248	53.17 N	112.26 W
S			
Sabak, Cape	247a	52.20 N	173.45 E
Sabana	262	32.03 N	98.34 W
Sabetha	264	39.54 N	95.48 W
Sabina	254	39.29 N	83.38 W
Sabinal	262	29.19 N	99.28 W
Sabinal	262	29.06 N	99.27 W
Sabine	244	30.00 N	93.45 W
Sabine Bay	242	75.35 N	109.30 W
Sabine Lake	260	29.50 N	93.50 W
Sabine Pass	260	29.44 N	93.52 W
Sabine Peninsula	242	76.20 N	109.30 W
Sable, Cape, NS	252	43.25 N	65.35 W
Sable, Cape, FL	258	25.12 N	81.05 W
Sable, Rivière du	242	55.30 N	68.21 W
Sable Island	252	43.55 N	59.50 W
Sables, River aux	256	46.13 N	82.04 W
Sabourin, Lac	256	47.58 N	77.41 W
Sabula	256	42.04 N	90.10 W
Sac	260	38.01 N	93.43 W
Sacajawea Peak	268	45.15 N	117.17 W
Sacaton	266	33.05 N	111.44 W
Sac City	264	42.25 N	95.00 W
Sachigo	242	55.06 N	88.58 W
Sachigo Lake	250	53.49 N	92.08 W
Sachs Harbour	242	72.00 N	125.00 W
Sackets Harbor	254	43.57 N	76.07 W
Sackville	252	45.54 N	64.22 W
Saco, ME	254	43.29 N	70.28 W
Saco, MT	268	48.28 N	107.21 W
Saco	252	43.27 N	70.22 W
Saco Bay	254	43.30 N	70.15 W
Sacramento	270	38.03 N	121.56 W
Sacramento, CA	270	38.03 N	121.56 W
Sacramento, NM	266	32.16 N	105.31 W
Sacramento Mountains	266	33.10 N	105.50 W
Sacramento Valley	270	39.15 N	122.00 W
Sacramento Wash	266	34.43 N	114.28 W
Sacred Heart	264	44.47 N	95.21 W
Saddle Lake Indian Reserve	250	54.00 N	111.40 W
Saddle Mountain, CO	266	38.50 N	105.28 W
Saddle Mountain, OR	268	45.58 N	123.41 W
Saddle Mountains	268	46.50 N	119.55 W
Sadler Lake	250	55.17 N	103.45 W
Saegertown	254	41.43 N	80.09 W
Safford	266	32.50 N	109.43 W
Sagak, Cape	246	52.48 N	169.08 W
Saganaga Lake	244	48.14 N	90.52 W
Saganash Lake	256	49.04 N	82.35 W
Sagavanirktok	246	70.20 N	148.00 W
Sage Creek, N.A.	268	48.58 N	110.06 W
Sage Creek, U.S.	268	44.50 N	108.26 W
Sage Creek, MT	268	48.20 N	110.03 W
Sage Creek, MT	268	47.16 N	109.43 W
Sagerton	262	33.05 N	99.58 W
Saginaw	256	43.25 N	83.58 W
Saginaw	256	43.39 N	83.51 W
Saginaw Bay	256	43.50 N	83.40 W
Saglek Bay	242	58.35 N	63.00 W
Saglouc	242	62.14 N	75.38 W
Saguache	266	38.05 N	106.08 W
Saguache Creek	266	37.52 N	105.51 W
Saguaro National Monument	266	32.12 N	110.38 W
Saguenay	252	48.08 N	69.44 W
Sahuarita	266	31.57 N	110.58 W
Sailor Creek	268	42.56 N	115.29 W
Sainte-Agathe	250	49.34 N	97.10 W
Sainte-Agathe-des-Monts	254	46.03 N	74.17 W
Saint Alban's, NF	252	47.52 N	55.51 W
Saint Albans, VT	254	44.49 N	73.05 W
Saint Albans, WV	254	38.23 N	81.49 W
Saint Albert	248	53.38 N	113.38 W
Saint-Alexandre-de-Kamouraska	252	47.41 N	69.38 W
Sainte-Amélie	250	50.59 N	99.21 W
Saint-André-Avellin	254	45.43 N	75.03 W
Saint Andrews	258	32.47 N	80.00 W
Saint Andrew's Channel	252	46.03 N	60.38 W
Saint Anne	260	41.01 N	87.43 W
Sainte-Anne, Lac, AB	248	53.43 N	114.27 W
Sainte-Anne, Lac, PQ	252	50.05 N	67.50 W
Sainte-Anne-de-Beaupré	252	47.02 N	70.56 W
Sainte-Anne-de-Madawaska	252	47.15 N	68.02 W
Sainte-Anne-des-Chênes	250	49.40 N	96.40 W
Sainte-Anne-des-Monts	252	49.08 N	66.30 W
Saint Ann's Bay	252	46.20 N	60.30 W
Saint-Anselme	252	46.37 N	70.58 W
Saint Ansgar	256	43.23 N	92.55 W
Saint Anthony, NF	252	51.22 N	55.35 W
Saint Anthony, ID	268	43.58 N	111.41 W
St.-Antoine	252	46.22 N	64.45 W
Saint-Augustin	252	51.14 N	58.41 W
Saint Augustine	258	29.54 N	81.19 W
Saint-Augustin-Nord-Ouest	252	51.16 N	58.42 W
Saint-Augustin-Saguenay	252	51.14 N	58.39 W
Saint-Basile	252	47.21 N	68.14 W
Saint Boniface	250	49.55 N	97.06 W
Saint Brendan's	252	48.52 N	53.40 W
Saint Bride, Mount	248	51.30 N	115.57 W
Saint Bride's	252	46.55 N	54.10 W
Saint-Brieux	250	52.38 N	104.52 W
Saint Catharines	256	43.10 N	79.15 W
Saint Catherines Island	258	31.38 N	81.10 W
Saint Charles, AR	260	34.22 N	91.08 W
Saint Charles, ID	268	42.07 N	111.23 W
Saint Charles, IL	260	41.54 N	88.19 W
Saint Charles, MI	256	43.18 N	84.09 W
Saint Charles, MN	256	43.58 N	92.04 W
Saint Charles, MO	260	38.47 N	90.29 W
Saint Charles Mesa	264	38.15 N	104.32 W
Saint Clair, MI	256	42.49 N	82.30 W
Saint Clair, MO	260	38.20 N	90.59 W
Saint Clair	256	42.37 N	82.31 W
Saint Clair, Lake	256	42.25 N	82.41 W
Saint Clair Shores	256	42.30 N	82.54 W
Saint Clairsville	254	40.05 N	80.54 W
Saint-Claude	250	49.40 N	98.22 W
Saint Cloud, FL	258	28.15 N	81.17 W
Saint Cloud, MN	264	45.33 N	94.10 W
Saint Croix, N.A.	252	45.10 N	67.10 W
Saint Croix, U.S.	256	44.45 N	92.49 W
Saint Croix Falls	256	45.24 N	92.38 W
Saint Croix Island National Monument	254	45.08 N	67.08 W
Saint Croix State Park	256	46.00 N	92.40 W
Saint Cyr Range	246	61.10 N	131.10 W
Saint David, AZ	266	31.54 N	110.13 W
Saint David, IL	256	40.30 N	90.03 W
Saint David's	252	48.12 N	58.52 W
Saint Edward	264	41.34 N	97.52 W
Saint Eleanor's	252	46.25 N	63.49 W
Saint-Éleuthère	252	47.29 N	69.17 W
Saint Elias, Cape	246	59.52 N	144.30 W
Saint Elias, Mount	242	60.18 N	140.55 W
Saint Elias Mountains	246	60.30 N	139.30 W
Saint Elmo	260	39.02 N	88.51 W
Saint-Éloi	252	48.02 N	69.14 W
Saint-Eustache	254	45.34 N	73.53 W
Saint-Fabien	252	48.18 N	68.52 W
Saint-Félicien	242	48.39 N	72.26 W
Sainte-Félicité	252	48.54 N	67.20 W
Saint-Félix-de-Valois	254	46.11 N	73.26 W
Sainte-Foy	252	46.47 N	71.17 W
Saint Francis, KS	264	39.46 N	101.48 W
Saint Francis, SD	264	43.09 N	100.54 W
Saint Francis, WI	256	42.58 N	87.52 W
Saint Francis, N.A.	252	47.10 N	68.57 W
Saint Francis, U.S.	260	34.38 N	90.35 W
Saint Francis, Cape	252	47.50 N	52.47 W
Saint Francisville	260	30.47 N	91.23 W
Saint-François	254	46.07 N	72.55 W
Saint-François, Lac	254	45.55 N	71.10 W
Saint Francois Mountains	260	37.30 N	90.35 W
Saint-Gabriel	254	46.17 N	73.23 W
Saint Gabriel-deGaspé	252	48.31 N	64.32 W
Saint-Gabriel-de-Rimouski	252	48.25 N	68.10 W
Saint-Gaudens National Historic Site	254	43.29 N	72.19 W
Sainte Genevieve	260	37.59 N	90.03 W
Saint George, NB	252	45.08 N	66.49 W
Saint George, ON	256	43.15 N	80.15 W
Saint George, AK	246	56.36 N	169.32 W
Saint George, SC	258	33.11 N	80.35 W
Saint George, UT	266	37.06 N	113.35 W
Saint George, Cape, NF	252	48.27 N	59.15 W
Saint George, Cape, FL	258	29.35 N	85.04 W
Saint George, Point	270	41.47 N	124.15 W
Saint George Island, AK	246	56.35 N	169.35 W
Saint George Island, FL	258	29.39 N	84.55 W
Saint George's	252	48.26 N	58.29 W
Saint George's Bay, NF	252	48.20 N	59.00 W
Saint Georges Bay, NS	252	45.50 N	61.45 W
Saint George Sound	258	29.47 N	84.42 W
Saint Gregory, Mount	252	49.19 N	58.13 W
Saint Helena	270	38.30 N	122.28 W
Saint Helena Sound	258	32.27 N	80.25 W
Saint Helens	268	45.52 N	122.48 W
Saint Helens, Mount	268	46.12 N	122.11 W
Saint-Hyacinthe	254	45.38 N	72.57 W
Saint-Ignace, NB	252	46.42 N	65.05 W
Saint Ignace, MI	256	45.52 N	84.43 W
Saint Ignace Island	256	48.48 N	87.55 W
Saint Ignatius	268	47.19 N	114.06 W
Saint-Isidore	252	47.33 N	65.03 W
Saint James, MI	256	45.45 N	85.31 W
Saint James, MN	264	43.59 N	94.38 W
Saint James, MO	260	38.00 N	91.37 W
Saint James, NY	254	40.53 N	73.09 W
Saint James, Cape	248	51.56 N	131.01 W
Saint-Jean	254	45.19 N	73.16 W
Saint-Jean, PQ	252	48.46 N	64.26 W
Saint-Jean, PQ	252	50.17 N	64.20 W
Saint-Jean, Lac	242	48.35 N	72.05 W
Saint-Jean-Baptiste	250	49.16 N	97.21 W
Saint-Jean-Port-Joli	252	47.13 N	70.16 W
Saint-Jérôme	254	45.46 N	74.00 W
Saint Jo	262	33.42 N	97.31 W
Saint Joe	268	47.21 N	116.42 W
Saint John, NB	252	45.16 N	66.03 W
Saint John, KS	264	38.00 N	98.46 W
Saint John, ND	264	48.57 N	99.43 W
Saint John, WA	268	47.05 N	117.35 W
Saint John	242	45.15 N	66.04 W
Saint John, Cape	252	50.00 N	55.32 W
Saint John, Lake	252	48.23 N	54.41 W
Saint John Bay	252	50.54 N	57.08 W
Saint John Island	252	50.49 N	57.14 W
Saint John's, NF	252	47.34 N	52.43 W
Saint Johns, AZ	266	34.30 N	109.22 W
Saint Johns, MI	256	43.00 N	84.33 W
Saint Johns	258	30.24 N	81.24 W
Saint Johnsbury	254	44.25 N	72.01 W
Saint Joseph, NB	252	45.59 N	64.34 W
Saint Joseph, IL	260	40.07 N	88.02 W
Saint Joseph, LA	260	31.55 N	91.14 W
Saint Joseph, MI	256	42.06 N	86.29 W
Saint Joseph, MN	264	45.34 N	94.19 W
Saint Joseph, MO	260	39.46 N	94.51 W
Saint Joseph, TN	260	35.02 N	87.31 W
Saint Joseph, U.S.	256	41.05 N	85.08 W
Saint Joseph, U.S.	256	42.07 N	86.29 W
Saint Joseph, Lake	242	51.05 N	90.35 W
Saint Joseph Bay	260	29.47 N	85.21 W
Saint Joseph Channel	256	46.16 N	83.51 W
Saint Joseph d'Alma → Alma	252	48.33 N	71.39 W
Saint-Joseph-de-Beauce	252	46.18 N	70.53 W
Saint Joseph Island	256	46.13 N	83.57 W
Saint-Jovite	254	46.07 N	74.36 W
Sainte-Julienne	254	45.58 N	73.43 W
Saint-Lambert	254	45.30 N	73.30 W
Saint Landry	260	30.51 N	92.15 W
Saint-Laurent	250	50.24 N	97.56 W
Saint Lawrence	252	46.55 N	55.24 W
Saint Lawrence, N.A.	242 244	49.30 N	67.00 W
Saint Lawrence, Cape	252	47.03 N	60.37 W
Saint Lawrence, Gulf of	242	48.00 N	62.00 W
Saint Lawrence Island	246	63.30 N	170.30 W
Saint-Lazare	250	50.26 N	101.16 W
Saint-Léandre	252	48.44 N	67.36 W
Saint-Léonard	252	47.10 N	67.56 W
Saint-Léonard-d'Aston	254	46.06 N	72.22 W
Saint-Louis, SK	250	52.56 N	105.49 W
Saint Louis, MI	256	43.25 N	84.36 W
Saint Louis, MO	260	38.38 N	90.11 W
Saint Louis	256	46.45 N	92.06 W
Saint-Louis-de-Kent	252	46.44 N	64.58 W
Saint Louis Park	256	44.56 N	93.22 W
Saint Lucie Canal	258	27.10 N	80.15 W
Saint Lucie Inlet	258	27.10 N	80.10 W
Saint Margaret Bay	252	51.01 N	56.58 W
Saint Margaret's Bay	252	44.35 N	64.00 W
Sainte-Marguerite	252	50.09 N	66.36 W
Sainte-Marguerite, Baie	252	50.06 N	66.36 W
Saint Maries	268	47.19 N	116.35 W
Saint Maries	268	47.19 N	116.33 W
Saint Marks	258	30.09 N	84.12 W
Saint Marks	258	30.08 N	84.12 W
Sainte-Marthe-de-Gaspé	252	49.12 N	66.10 W
Saint Martin, Lake	250	51.37 N	98.29 W
Saint Martins	252	45.21 N	65.32 W
Saint Martinville	260	30.07 N	91.50 W
Saint Mary, BC	248	49.37 N	115.38 W
Saint Mary, N.A.	248	49.37 N	112.52 W
Saint Mary, Cape	252	44.05 N	66.13 W
Saint Mary Lake	268	48.40 N	113.30 W
Saint Mary Reservoir	248	49.19 N	113.12 W
Saint Mary's, NF	252	46.55 N	53.34 W
Saint Mary's, ON	256	43.16 N	81.08 W
Saint Marys, AK	246	62.04 N	163.10 W
Saint Marys, GA	258	30.44 N	81.33 W
Saint Marys, KS	264	39.12 N	96.04 W
Saint Marys, MO	260	37.52 N	89.58 W
Saint Marys, OH	254	40.33 N	84.23 W
Saint Marys, PA	254	41.26 N	78.34 W
Saint Marys, WV	254	39.23 N	81.12 W
Saint Mary's, NS	252	45.02 N	61.54 W
Saint Marys, U.S.	254	41.05 N	85.08 W
Saint Marys, U.S.	258	30.43 N	81.27 W
Saint Mary's, Cape	252	46.49 N	54.12 W
Saint Marys, North Prong	258	30.22 N	82.06 W
Saint Marys, South Prong	258	30.22 N	82.06 W
Saint Mary's Bay, NF	252	46.50 N	53.47 W
Saint Mary's Bay, NS	252	44.25 N	66.10 W
Saint Matthew Island	246	60.30 N	172.45 W
Saint Matthews, KY	260	38.15 N	85.39 W
Saint Matthews, SC	258	33.40 N	80.46 W
Saint-Maurice	242	46.21 N	72.31 W
Saint Meinrad	260	38.10 N	86.49 W
Saint Michael	246	63.29 N	162.02 W
Saint Michaels	254	38.47 N	76.14 W
Saint Nazianz	256	44.00 N	87.55 W
Saint-Pacôme	252	47.24 N	69.57 W
Saint-Pamphile	252	46.58 N	69.47 W
Saint Paris	254	40.07 N	83.58 W
Saint-Pascal	252	47.32 N	69.49 W
Saint-Patrick, Lac	254	46.22 N	77.21 W
Saint Paul, AB	250	53.59 N	111.17 W
Saint Paul, IN	260	39.26 N	85.38 W
Saint Paul, KS	264	37.32 N	95.11 W
Saint Paul, MN	256	44.58 N	93.07 W
Saint Paul, NE	264	41.13 N	98.27 W
Saint Paul, VA	258	36.54 N	82.19 W
Saint-Paul	252	51.26 N	57.40 W
Saint Paul Island	246	57.07 N	170.17 W
Saint Paul Island, NS	252	47.15 N	60.10 W
Saint Paul Island, AK	246	57.10 N	170.15 W
Saint Pauls	258	34.48 N	78.58 W
Saint Pauls Inlet	252	49.50 N	57.45 W
Saint Peter	256	44.17 N	93.57 W
Saint Peters	252	45.40 N	60.52 W
Saint Peters Bay	252	46.25 N	62.35 W
Saint Petersburg	258	27.46 N	82.38 W
Saint-Pierre, Lac, PQ	252	50.08 N	68.26 W
Saint-Pierre, Lac, PQ	254	46.12 N	72.52 W
Saint Pierre and Miquelon	242	46.55 N	56.10 W
Saint-Pierre-Jolys	250	49.26 N	96.59 W
Saint-Prosper-de-Dorchester	254	46.13 N	70.29 W
Saint-Quentin	252	47.30 N	67.23 W
Saint Regis	268	47.18 N	115.06 W
Saint Regis	268	47.18 N	115.05 W
Saint Regis, East Branch	254	44.39 N	74.28 W
Saint Regis, West Branch	254	44.47 N	74.46 W
Saint Regis Falls	254	44.40 N	74.33 W
Saint Regis Indian Reservation	254	44.59 N	74.39 W
Saint-Rémi-d'Amherst	254	46.01 N	74.47 W
Saint Robert	260	37.50 N	92.09 W
Saint-Romuald-d'Etchemin	252	46.45 N	71.14 W
Sainte-Rose-du-Lac	250	51.03 N	99.32 W
Saint Shotts	252	46.38 N	53.35 W
Saint Simons Island	258	31.08 N	81.24 W
Saint Simons Island	258	31.14 N	81.21 W
Saint Stephen, NB	252	45.12 N	67.17 W
Saint Stephen, SC	258	33.24 N	79.55 W
Sainte-Thérèse-de-Blainville	254	45.39 N	73.49 W
Saint Thomas, ON	256	42.47 N	81.12 W
Saint Thomas, ND	264	48.37 N	97.27 W
Saint-Tite-des-Caps	252	47.08 N	70.47 W
Saint-Urbain-de-Charlevoix	252	47.33 N	70.32 W
Saint Vincent	264	48.58 N	97.14 W
Saint Vincent's	252	46.48 N	53.38 W
Saint Walburg	250	53.39 N	109.12 W
Saint-Yvon	252	49.10 N	64.48 W
Sakakawea, Lake	264	47.50 N	102.20 W
Sakami	242	53.40 N	76.40 W
Sakami, Lac	242	53.15 N	76.45 W
Saks	260	33.42 N	85.52 W
Sakwaso Lake	250	53.01 N	91.55 W
Salado, Rio	266	34.16 N	106.52 W
Salado Creek, NM	262	34.35 N	104.25 W
Salado Creek, TX	262	29.14 N	98.25 W
Salamanca	254	42.09 N	78.43 W
Salamonie	260	40.50 N	85.43 W
Salamonie Lake	256	40.46 N	85.37 W
Salcha	246	64.29 N	147.00 W
Sale	250	49.45 N	97.08 W
Sale Creek	260	35.23 N	85.07 W
Salem, AR	260	36.22 N	91.49 W
Salem, IL	260	38.38 N	88.57 W
Salem, IN	260	38.36 N	86.06 W
Salem, IA	256	40.51 N	91.38 W
Salem, KY	260	37.16 N	88.16 W
Salem, MA	254	42.31 N	70.55 W
Salem, MO	260	37.39 N	91.32 W
Salem, NH	254	42.47 N	71.12 W
Salem, NJ	254	39.34 N	75.28 W
Salem, NY	254	43.10 N	73.20 W
Salem, OH	254	40.54 N	80.52 W
Salem, OR	268	44.57 N	123.01 W
Salem, SD	264	43.44 N	97.23 W
Salem, UT	266	40.03 N	111.40 W
Salem, VA	258	37.17 N	80.03 W
Salem, WV	254	39.17 N	80.34 W
Salem Upland	260	37.25 N	91.30 W
Salida	266	38.32 N	106.00 W
Salina, KS	264	38.50 N	97.37 W
Salina, OK	262	36.20 N	95.05 W
Salina, UT	266	38.58 N	111.51 W
Salinas	270	36.40 N	121.39 W
Salinas	270	36.45 N	121.48 W
Saline, LA	260	32.10 N	92.58 W
Saline, MI	256	42.10 N	83.47 W
Saline, AR	260	33.44 N	93.58 W
Saline, AR	260	33.10 N	92.08 W
Saline, IL	260	37.35 N	88.08 W
Saline, KS	264	38.51 N	97.30 W
Saline, North Fork	260	37.44 N	88.19 W
Saline Bayou	260	31.45 N	92.58 W
Saline Lake	260	31.55 N	92.55 W
Salisbury, MD	254	38.22 N	75.36 W
Salisbury, MO	260	39.25 N	92.48 W
Salisbury, NC	258	35.40 N	80.29 W
Salisbury, PA	254	39.45 N	79.05 W
Salisbury Island	242	63.30 N	77.00 W
Salish Mountains	268	48.15 N	114.45 W
Salitpa	260	31.37 N	88.01 W
Salkehatchie	258	32.37 N	80.53 W
Sallisaw	260	35.28 N	94.47 W
Sallisaw Creek	260	35.23 N	94.52 W
Salmo	248	49.12 N	117.17 W
Salmon	268	45.11 N	113.54 W
Salmon, BC	248	54.05 N	122.34 W
Salmon, NB	252	46.06 N	65.56 W
Salmon, N.A.	254	45.02 N	74.31 W
Salmon, CA	270	41.23 N	123.29 W
Salmon, ID	268	45.51 N	116.46 W
Salmon, NY	254	43.35 N	76.12 W
Salmon, OR	268	45.22 N	122.02 W
Salmon, East Fork	268	44.16 N	114.19 W
Salmon, Middle Fork	268	45.18 N	114.36 W
Salmon, North Fork	270	41.16 N	123.18 W
Salmon, South Fork, CA	270	41.16 N	123.18 W
Salmon, South Fork, ID	268	45.23 N	115.31 W
Salmon Arm	248	50.42 N	119.16 W
Salmon-Bay	252	51.26 N	57.36 W
Salmon Falls Creek	270	42.43 N	114.51 W
Salmon Mountain	254	45.14 N	71.08 W
Salmon Mountains	270	41.00 N	123.00 W
Salmon Peak	262	29.28 N	100.10 W
Salmon River Mountains	268	44.45 N	115.30 W
Salmon Valley	248	54.05 N	122.41 W
Salo	254	43.27 N	70.22 W
Salome	266	33.47 N	113.37 W
Salt, U.S.	268	43.08 N	111.02 W
Salt, AZ	266	33.23 N	112.18 W
Salt, KY	260	38.00 N	85.57 W
Salt, MO	260	39.28 N	91.04 W
Salt, Elk Fork	260	39.28 N	91.53 W
Salt, Middle Fork	260	39.28 N	91.49 W
Salt, North Fork	260	39.30 N	91.47 W
Salt, South Fork	260	39.28 N	91.49 W
Salt Basin	262	31.50 N	105.00 W
Saltcoats	250	51.03 N	102.12 W
Salt Creek, CA	270	36.15 N	116.49 W
Salt Creek, IL	260	40.08 N	89.50 W
Salt Creek, KS	264	39.06 N	97.44 W
Salt Creek, NM	262	33.35 N	104.23 W
Salt Creek, OK	262	36.32 N	96.43 W
Salt Creek, OR	268	43.43 N	122.26 W
Salt Creek, WY	268	43.41 N	106.20 W
Salt Draw	262	31.19 N	103.28 W
Salt Fork State Park	254	40.08 N	81.33 W
Saltillo, MS	260	34.23 N	88.41 W
Saltillo, TN	260	35.23 N	88.13 W
Salt Lake	262	34.05 N	103.05 W
Salt Lake City	266	40.46 N	111.53 W
Salton City	270	33.19 N	115.59 W
Salton Sea	270	33.19 N	115.50 W
Salton Sea State Recreation Area	270	33.29 N	115.53 W
Salt River Indian Reservation	266	33.31 N	111.48 W
Saltspring Island	248	48.47 N	123.30 W
Saltville	258	36.53 N	81.46 W
Salt Wells Creek	268	41.39 N	108.59 W
Saluda, SC	258	34.00 N	81.46 W
Saluda, VA	258	37.36 N	76.36 W
Saluda	258	34.00 N	81.04 W
Salvador, Lake	260	29.45 N	90.15 W
Salvage	252	48.41 N	53.38 W
Salyer	270	40.54 N	123.35 W
Salyersville	258	37.45 N	83.04 W
Sam A. Baker State Park	260	37.16 N	90.34 W
Samalga Pass	246	52.48 N	169.25 W
Samaria	268	42.07 N	112.20 W
Samoset	258	27.28 N	82.33 W
Sam Rayburn Reservoir	260	31.27 N	94.37 W
Samson	260	31.07 N	86.09 W
Samson Indian Reserve	248	52.48 N	113.10 W
Samtown	260	31.20 N	92.26 W
San Agustin, Plains of	266	33.50 N	108.00 W
Sanak Islands	246	54.25 N	162.35 W
San Andreas	270	38.12 N	120.41 W
San Andres Mountains	266	32.55 N	106.45 W
San Angelo	262	31.28 N	100.26 W
San Anselmo	270	37.59 N	122.34 W
San Antonio, NM	266	33.55 N	106.52 W
San Antonio, TX	262	29.28 N	98.31 W
San Antonio	262	28.30 N	96.50 W
San Antonio, Mount	270	34.17 N	117.39 W
San Antonio, Rio	266	37.11 N	105.55 W
San Antonio Bay	262	28.20 N	96.45 W
San Antonio Mountain	266	36.52 N	106.02 W
Sanatorium	260	31.55 N	89.47 W
San Augustine	260	31.32 N	94.07 W
San Augustin Pass	266	32.26 N	106.34 W
San Benito	262	26.08 N	97.38 W
San Benito	270	36.53 N	121.34 W
San Benito Mountain	270	36.22 N	120.38 W
San Bernard	262	28.52 N	95.27 W
San Bernardino	270	34.06 N	117.17 W
San Bernardino Mountains	270	34.10 N	117.00 W
San Blas, Cape	260	29.40 N	85.22 W
Sanborn, IA	264	43.11 N	95.39 W
Sanborn, MN	264	44.13 N	95.08 W
Sanborn, ND	264	46.57 N	98.13 W
San Bruno	270	37.37 N	122.25 W
San Carlos, AZ	266	33.21 N	110.27 W
San Carlos, CA	270	37.31 N	122.16 W
San Carlos	266	33.16 N	110.27 W
San Carlos Indian Reservation	266	33.23 N	110.09 W
San Carlos Reservoir	266	33.13 N	110.24 W
San Clemente	270	33.26 N	117.37 W
San Clemente Island	270	32.54 N	118.29 W
San Cristobal Wash	266	32.47 N	113.44 W
Sand	250	54.22 N	111.05 W
Sand Arroyo Creek	264	37.29 N	101.29 W
Sand Coulee	268	47.24 N	111.10 W
Sand Coulee Creek	268	47.27 N	111.18 W
Sand Creek, AZ	266	35.46 N	112.27 W
Sand Creek, IN	260	39.03 N	85.51 W
Sand Creek, KS	264	37.26 N	98.12 W
Sand Creek, MN	256	45.56 N	92.39 W
Sand Creek, MT	268	47.18 N	106.45 W
Sand Creek, SD	264	44.02 N	98.05 W
Sand Creek, WY	264	43.27 N	105.26 W
Sand Creek, WY	268	41.02 N	107.52 W
Sand Creek, WY	268	44.16 N	107.55 W
Sanders	266	35.13 N	109.20 W
Sanderson	262	30.09 N	102.24 W
Sandersville, GA	258	32.59 N	82.48 W
Sandersville, MS	260	31.47 N	89.02 W
Sandfly Lake	250	55.45 N	106.05 W
Sand Fork	254	38.55 N	80.45 W
Sand Hill	264	47.36 N	96.52 W
Sand Hills	264	42.00 N	101.00 W
Sandia Crest	266	35.13 N	106.27 W
Sandia Indian Reservation	266	35.15 N	106.30 W
San Diego, CA	270	32.43 N	117.09 W
San Diego, TX	262	27.46 N	98.14 W
San Diego	270	32.46 N	117.13 W
San Diego Aqueduct	270	32.55 N	116.55 W
San Diego Creek	262	27.47 N	98.03 W
Sandies Creek	262	29.06 N	97.20 W
Sand Key	258	27.53 N	82.51 W
Sand Lake	250	50.05 N	94.39 W
Sandoval	260	38.37 N	89.07 W
Sand Point, AK	246	55.20 N	160.30 W
Sandpoint, ID	268	48.16 N	116.33 W
Sandspit	248	53.14 N	131.50 W
Sand Springs, OK	262	36.09 N	96.07 W
Sand Springs, TX	262	32.15 N	101.22 W
Sandston	258	37.31 N	77.19 W
Sandstone	256	46.08 N	92.52 W
Sandusky, MI	256	43.25 N	82.50 W
Sandusky, OH	254	41.27 N	82.42 W
Sandusky	254	41.27 N	83.00 W
Sandwich, IL	260	41.39 N	88.37 W
Sandwich, MA	254	41.46 N	70.30 W
Sandwich Bay	242	53.35 N	57.15 W
Sandwick	248	49.42 N	124.59 W
Sandy, OR	268	45.24 N	122.16 W
Sandy, UT	266	40.36 N	111.52 W
Sandy, ME	254	44.45 N	69.52 W
Sandy, OR	268	45.34 N	122.24 W
Sandy, VA	258	36.35 N	79.25 W
Sandy Bay Indian Reserve	250	50.33 N	98.40 W
Sandy Bay Mountain	254	45.47 N	70.25 W
Sandy Creek, U.S.	262	34.25 N	99.35 W
Sandy Creek, U.S.	262	36.50 N	98.10 W
Sandy Creek, NC	258	36.08 N	78.02 W
Sandy Creek, NY	254	43.44 N	76.15 W
Sandy Creek, OH	254	40.38 N	81.26 W
Sandy Creek, TX	262	30.34 N	98.26 W
Sandy Creek, TX	262	29.02 N	96.33 W
Sandy Hook, KY	258	38.05 N	83.08 W
Sandy Hook, MS	260	31.02 N	89.48 W
Sandy Hook	254	40.27 N	74.00 W
Sandy Lake, NF	252	49.16 N	57.00 W
Sandy Lake, ON	250	53.00 N	93.07 W
Sandy Springs	258	33.55 N	84.23 W
San Elizario	266	31.35 N	106.16 W
San Felipe Creek	270	33.09 N	115.46 W
San Felipe Indian Reservation	266	35.26 N	106.26 W
San Felipe Pueblo	266	35.27 N	106.28 W
San Fernando	270	34.17 N	118.26 W
San Fernando Creek	262	27.28 N	97.46 W
Sanford, CO	266	37.16 N	105.54 W
Sanford, FL	258	28.48 N	81.16 W
Sanford, ME	254	43.26 N	70.46 W
Sanford, MI	256	43.40 N	84.23 W
Sanford, NC	258	35.29 N	79.10 W
Sanford, TX	262	35.42 N	101.32 W
Sanford, Mount	246	62.13 N	144.09 W
San Francisco	270	37.48 N	122.24 W
San Francisco	266	32.59 N	109.22 W
San Francisco Bay	270	37.43 N	122.17 W
San Francisco Creek	262	29.53 N	102.19 W

Symbols in the index entries are identified on page 273.

Name	Page	Lat° ′	Long° ′
San Francisco Mountains	266	33.45 N	109.00 W
San Gabriel	262	30.46 N	97.01 W
San Gabriel, North Fork	262	30.38 N	97.41 W
San Gabriel, South Fork	262	30.38 N	97.41 W
San Gabriel Mountains	270	34.20 N	118.00 W
Sangamon	260	40.07 N	90.20 W
Sanger, CA	270	36.42 N	119.27 W
Sanger, TX	262	33.22 N	97.10 W
Sangerville	254	45.10 N	69.21 W
San Gorgonio Mountain	270	34.06 N	116.50 W
Sangre de Cristo Mountains	266	37.30 N	105.15 W
Sangsues, Lac aux	256	46.29 N	77.57 W
Sangudo	248	53.53 N	114.54 W
Sanibel Island	258	26.27 N	82.06 W
San Ildefonso Indian Reservation	266	35.53 N	106.08 W
San Isabel Creek	262	27.39 N	99.38 W
San Isidro	262	26.43 N	98.27 W
San Jacinto	270	33.47 N	116.57 W
San Jacinto, East Fork	262	30.05 N	95.09 W
San Jacinto, West Fork	262	30.02 N	95.15 W
San Jacinto Peak	270	33.49 N	116.41 W
San Joaquin	270	38.03 N	121.50 W
San Joaquin Valley	270	36.50 N	120.10 W
San Jon	262	35.06 N	103.20 W
San Jose, CA	270	37.20 N	121.53 W
San Jose, FL	258	30.15 N	81.36 W
San Jose, IL	260	40.18 N	89.36 W
San Jose, NM	266	35.24 N	105.29 W
San Jose	248	52.14 N	122.15 W
San Jose, Rio	266	34.52 N	107.01 W
San Jose Island	262	28.10 N	96.45 W
San Juan	244	37.11 N	110.54 W
San Juan Basin	266	36.15 N	108.20 W
San Juan Bautista	270	36.51 N	121.32 W
San Juan Creek	270	35.40 N	120.22 W
San Juan Indian Reservation	266	36.03 N	106.04 W
San Juan Island National Historical Park	268	48.28 N	123.00 W
San Juan Islands	268	48.36 N	122.50 W
San Juan Mountains	266	37.35 N	107.10 W
San Leandro	270	37.43 N	122.09 W
San Luis, AZ	266	32.29 N	114.47 W
San Luis, CO	266	37.12 N	105.25 W
San Luis Creek	266	37.42 N	105.44 W
San Luis Obispo	270	35.17 N	120.40 W
San Luis Peak	266	37.59 N	106.56 W
San Luis Reservoir	270	37.07 N	121.05 W
San Luis Rey	270	33.12 N	117.24 W
San Luis Valley	266	37.25 N	106.00 W
San Manuel	266	32.36 N	110.38 W
San Marcos	262	29.53 N	97.57 W
San Marcos	262	29.29 N	97.28 W
San Mateo, CA	270	37.35 N	122.19 W
San Mateo, FL	258	29.36 N	81.35 W
San Mateo, NM	266	35.20 N	107.39 W
San Miguel	270	35.45 N	120.42 W
San Miguel	266	38.23 N	108.48 W
San Miguel Creek	262	28.30 N	98.25 W
San Miguel Island	270	34.02 N	120.22 W
San Nicolas Island	270	33.15 N	119.31 W
San Pablo Bay	270	38.06 N	122.22 W
San Pedro	262	27.48 N	97.41 W
San Pedro, N.A.	266	32.59 N	110.47 W
San Pedro, AZ	266	32.59 N	110.47 W
San Pedro Channel	270	33.35 N	118.25 W
San Pedro Peaks	266	36.07 N	106.49 W
San Pitch	266	39.03 N	111.51 W
Sanpoil	268	47.53 N	118.41 W
San Rafael, CA	270	37.59 N	122.31 W
San Rafael, NM	266	35.06 N	107.53 W
San Rafael	266	38.47 N	110.07 W
San Rafael Desert	266	38.40 N	110.30 W
San Rafael Mountains	270	34.45 N	119.50 W
San Rafael Swell	266	38.40 N	110.45 W
San Saba	262	31.12 N	98.43 W
San Saba	262	31.15 N	98.35 W
Sans Bois Creek	260	35.20 N	94.50 W
San Simon	266	32.16 N	109.14 W
San Simon	266	32.50 N	109.39 W
San Simon Wash	266	31.45 N	112.25 W
Santa Ana	270	33.43 N	117.54 W
Santa Ana Indian Reservation	266	35.28 N	106.37 W
Santa Anna	262	31.45 N	99.19 W
Santa Barbara	270	34.25 N	119.42 W
Santa Barbara Channel	270	34.15 N	119.55 W
Santa Barbara Island	270	33.28 N	119.02 W
Santa Catalina, Gulf of	270	33.20 N	117.45 W
Santa Catalina Island	270	33.23 N	118.26 W
Santa Clara, CA	270	37.21 N	121.57 W
Santa Clara, UT	266	37.08 N	113.39 W
Santa Clara, CA	270	34.14 N	119.16 W
Santa Clara, UT	266	37.05 N	113.36 W
Santa Clara Indian Reservation	266	35.59 N	106.10 W
Santa Cruz	270	36.58 N	122.01 W
Santa Cruz	266	33.19 N	112.14 W
Santa Cruz Island	270	34.01 N	119.45 W
Santa Fe	266	35.42 N	106.57 W
Santa Fe, FL	258	29.53 N	82.53 W
Santa Fe, NM	266	35.36 N	106.20 W
Santa Fe Baldy	266	35.50 N	105.46 W
Santa Lucia Range	270	36.00 N	121.20 W
Santa Margarita	270	35.23 N	120.37 W
Santa Maria	270	34.57 N	120.26 W
Santa Maria	266	34.19 N	34.31 W
Santa Monica	270	34.01 N	118.30 W
Santa Monica Bay	270	33.54 N	118.25 W
Santa Paula	270	34.21 N	119.04 W
Santaquin	266	39.59 N	111.47 W
Santa Rita	248	48.42 N	112.19 W
Santa Rosa, CA	270	38.26 N	122.43 W
Santa Rosa, NM	262	34.57 N	104.41 W
Santa Rosa, TX	262	26.15 N	97.50 W
Santa Rosa Beach	260	30.23 N	86.14 W
Santa Rosa Indian Reservation	270	33.35 N	116.35 W
Santa Rosa Island, CA	270	33.58 N	120.06 W
Santa Rosa Island, FL	260	30.22 N	86.55 W
Santa Rosa Range	270	41.35 N	117.40 W
Santa Rosa Wash	266	33.00 N	112.00 W
Santa Ynez	270	35.41 N	120.36 W
Santa Ysabel Indian Reservation	270	33.11 N	116.41 W
Santee	270	32.50 N	116.58 W
Santee	258	33.14 N	79.28 W
Santee Dam	258	33.24 N	80.12 W
Santee Indian Reservation	264	42.45 N	97.50 W
Santiago Peak, CA	270	33.43 N	117.32 W
Santiago Peak, TX	262	29.47 N	103.25 W
Santiam Pass	268	44.25 N	121.51 W
Santo	262	32.36 N	98.13 W
Santo Domingo Indian Reservation	266	35.30 N	106.25 W
Santo Domingo Pueblo	266	35.31 N	106.22 W
San Xavier Indian Reservation	266	32.05 N	111.08 W
San Ygnacio	262	27.03 N	99.27 W
Saorre, Mount	242	64.27 N	84.30 W
Sapello	262	35.47 N	104.59 W
Sapelo Island	258	31.28 N	81.15 W
Sappa Creek	264	40.07 N	99.38 W
Sappa Creek, Middle Fork	264	39.40 N	100.53 W
Sappa Creek, South Fork	264	39.47 N	100.35 W
Sapphire Mountains	268	46.20 N	113.45 W
Sapulpa	262	36.00 N	96.06 W
Saragosa	262	31.01 N	103.39 W
Saraland	260	30.49 N	88.04 W
Saranac	256	42.56 N	85.13 W
Saranac	254	44.42 N	73.27 W
Saranac Lake	254	44.20 N	74.08 W
Sarasota	258	27.20 N	82.34 W
Saratoga, CA	270	37.16 N	122.02 W
Saratoga, TX	260	30.17 N	94.31 W
Saratoga, WY	268	41.27 N	106.48 W
Saratoga National Historical Park	254	43.00 N	73.38 W
Saratoga Springs	254	43.05 N	73.47 W
Sarcee Indian Reserve	248	50.58 N	114.06 W
Sarcoxie	260	37.03 N	94.07 W
Sardis, AL	260	32.17 N	86.59 W
Sardis, GA	258	32.58 N	81.46 W
Sardis, MS	260	34.26 N	89.55 W
Sardis, TN	260	35.27 N	88.18 W
Sardis Lake	260	34.27 N	89.43 W
Sarepta	260	32.54 N	93.27 W
Sargent, GA	258	33.31 N	84.51 W
Sargent, NE	264	41.38 N	99.22 W
Sarles	264	48.57 N	99.00 W
Sarnia	256	42.58 N	82.23 W
Sarpy Creek	268	46.15 N	107.09 W
Sartell	264	45.37 N	94.12 W
Sasaginnigak Lake	250	51.36 N	95.40 W
Sasakwa	262	34.57 N	96.31 W
Saseginaga, Lac	256	47.06 N	78.35 W
Saskatchewan	242	54.00 N	105.00 W
Saskatchewan	250	53.12 N	99.16 W
Saskatoon	250	52.07 N	106.38 W
Sasmik, Cape	247a	51.36 N	177.55 W
Saspamco	262	29.14 N	98.18 W
Sassafras	258	37.14 N	83.06 W
Sassafras Mountain	258	35.03 N	82.48 W
Satah Mountain	248	52.29 N	124.41 W
Satanta	264	37.26 N	100.59 W
Satellite Beach	258	28.11 N	80.35 W
Satilla	258	30.59 N	81.28 W
Satilpa Creek	260	31.39 N	88.05 W
Satsuma	260	30.51 N	88.03 W
Satus Creek	268	46.16 N	120.07 W
Saucier	260	30.38 N	89.08 W
Saugatuck	256	42.40 N	86.12 W
Saugeen	256	44.30 N	81.22 W
Saugerties	254	42.05 N	73.57 W
Saugstad, Mount	248	52.15 N	126.31 W
Sauk, MN	264	45.36 N	94.10 W
Sauk, WA	268	48.30 N	121.37 W
Sauk Centre	264	45.44 N	94.57 W
Sauk City	256	43.17 N	89.43 W
Sauk Rapids	264	45.34 N	94.09 W
Saukville	256	43.23 N	87.55 W
Sault-au-Mouton	252	48.33 N	69.15 W
Sault aux Cochons, Rivière du	252	48.44 N	69.04 W
Saulteaux	248	55.16 N	114.25 W
Saulteaux Indian Reserve	250	53.08 N	108.18 W
Sault Sainte Marie, ON	256	46.31 N	84.20 W
Sault Sainte Marie, MI	256	46.30 N	84.21 W
Saumon, Rivière au	254	45.41 N	71.27 W
Saumons, Riviere aux	252	49.25 N	62.15 W
Sauquoit	254	43.00 N	75.16 W
Sausalito	270	37.51 N	122.29 W
Savage, MD	254	39.08 N	76.49 W
Savage, MT	264	47.27 N	104.21 W
Savane	252	51.08 N	71.26 W
Savanna, IL	256	42.05 N	90.08 W
Savanna, OK	262	34.50 N	95.51 W
Savannah, GA	258	32.04 N	81.05 W
Savannah, MO	260	39.56 N	94.50 W
Savannah, TN	260	35.14 N	88.14 W
Savannah	244	32.02 N	80.53 W
Savannah Beach	258	32.01 N	80.51 W
Savanna Portage State Park	256	46.51 N	93.10 W
Savery Creek	268	41.01 N	107.27 W
Savona	248	50.45 N	120.50 W
Savoonga	246	63.42 N	170.27 W
Savoy	262	33.34 N	96.21 W
Sawatch Range	266	39.10 N	106.25 W
Saw Log Creek	264	38.07 N	99.42 W
Sawtooth National Recreation Area	268	44.00 N	114.55 W
Sawyer, MI	256	41.53 N	86.35 W
Sawyer, ND	264	48.05 N	101.03 W
Sawyers Hill	252	47.11 N	53.52 W
Saxis	258	37.55 N	75.43 W
Saxon	256	46.29 N	90.25 W
Saxton	254	40.13 N	78.15 W
Saybrook	260	40.26 N	88.32 W
Saylorville Lake	256	41.48 N	93.46 W
Sayre, OK	262	35.18 N	99.38 W
Sayre, PA	254	41.59 N	76.32 W
Sayreville	254	40.28 N	74.21 W
Sayward	248	50.22 N	125.55 W
Scammon	264	37.17 N	94.49 W
Scammon Bay	246	61.53 N	165.38 W
Scammon Bay	246	61.53 N	165.54 W
Scandia	264	39.48 N	97.47 W
Scanlon	256	46.42 N	92.23 W
Scapa	250	51.52 N	111.59 W
Scapegoat Mountain	268	47.19 N	112.50 W
Scappoose	268	45.45 N	122.53 W
Scatarie Island	252	46.00 N	59.44 W
Sceptre	250	50.51 N	109.15 W
Schaller	264	42.30 N	95.18 W
Schefferville	242	54.48 N	66.50 W
Schell Creek Range	270	39.10 N	114.40 W
Schenectady	254	42.47 N	73.53 W
Schenevus Creek	254	42.29 N	74.59 W
Schertz	262	29.33 N	98.16 W
Schlater	260	33.38 N	90.21 W
Schleswig	264	42.10 N	95.26 W
Schofield	256	44.54 N	89.36 W
Schofield Barracks	272c	21.30 N	158.04 W
Schoharie	254	42.40 N	74.19 W
Schoharie Creek	254	42.57 N	74.18 W
Schoodic Lake	254	45.21 N	68.54 W
Schoolcraft	256	42.07 N	85.38 W
Schreiber	256	48.48 N	87.15 W
Schriever	260	29.45 N	90.49 W
Schroon	254	43.29 N	73.49 W
Schroon Lake	254	43.47 N	73.46 W
Schulenburg	262	29.41 N	96.54 W
Schultz Lake	242	64.45 N	97.30 W
Schumacher	256	48.28 N	81.18 W
Schuyler, NE	264	41.27 N	97.04 W
Schuyler, VA	258	37.47 N	78.42 W
Schuylkill	254	39.53 N	75.12 W
Schuylkill Haven	254	40.38 N	76.10 W
Schwatka Mountains	246	67.25 N	157.00 W
Scio, OH	254	40.24 N	81.05 W
Scio, OR	268	44.42 N	122.51 W
Scioto	254	38.44 N	83.01 W
Scipio	266	39.15 N	112.06 W
Scobey	264	48.47 N	105.25 W
Scofield Reservoir	266	39.47 N	111.09 W
Scooba	260	32.50 N	88.29 W
Scotia, NE	264	41.28 N	98.42 W
Scotia, NY	254	44.54 N	73.33 W
Scotia Lake	256	47.05 N	81.23 W
Scotland, ON	256	43.01 N	80.22 W
Scotland, SD	264	43.09 N	97.43 W
Scotland, TX	262	33.40 N	98.28 W
Scotland Neck	258	36.02 N	77.32 W
Scotlandville	260	30.31 N	91.11 W
Scotsburn	252	45.39 N	62.51 W
Scott, SK	250	52.23 N	108.50 W
Scott, MS	260	33.36 N	91.04 W
Scott	270	41.48 N	123.02 W
Scott, Cape	248	50.47 N	128.26 W
Scott, Mount, OK	262	34.44 N	98.32 W
Scott, Mount, OR	268	42.56 N	122.01 W
Scott Air Force Base	260	38.32 N	89.52 W
Scott City, KS	264	38.29 N	100.54 W
Scott City, MO	260	37.12 N	89.32 W
Scottdale	254	40.06 N	79.35 W
Scott Islands	248	50.48 N	128.40 W
Scott Mountain	268	44.11 N	115.47 W
Scott Peak	268	44.21 N	112.50 W
Scottsbluff	264	41.52 N	103.40 W
Scotts Bluff National Monument	264	41.49 N	103.41 W
Scottsboro	260	34.40 N	86.02 W
Scottsburg	260	38.41 N	85.46 W
Scottsdale	266	33.30 N	111.56 W
Scotts Hill	260	35.32 N	88.16 W
Scott State Park	264	38.40 N	100.54 W
Scottsville	260	36.45 N	86.11 W
Scottville	256	43.57 N	86.17 W
Scout Lake	250	49.22 N	106.00 W
Scranton, IA	264	42.01 N	94.33 W
Scranton, ND	264	46.09 N	103.09 W
Scranton, PA	254	41.24 N	75.40 W
Screven	258	31.29 N	82.01 W
Scribner	264	41.40 N	96.40 W
Scugog, Lake	256	44.10 N	78.51 W
Scurry	262	32.31 N	96.23 W
Seabird Island Indian Reserve	248	49.17 N	121.42 W
Seaboard	258	36.24 N	77.26 W
Seadrift	262	28.30 N	96.47 W
Seaford	254	38.39 N	75.37 W
Seaforth	256	43.33 N	81.24 W
Seager Wheeler Lake	250	54.27 N	103.30 W
Seagraves	262	32.57 N	102.34 W
Seahorse Point	242	63.47 N	80.09 W
Sea Islands	244	31.20 N	81.20 W
Sea Isle City	254	39.09 N	74.42 W
Seal	242	59.04 N	94.48 W
Seal Cove, NB	252	44.39 N	66.51 W
Seal Cove, NF	252	47.28 N	53.05 W
Seale	258	32.18 N	85.10 W
Sealevel	258	34.52 N	76.23 W
Seal Harbor	254	44.18 N	68.14 W
Seal Lake	242	54.18 N	61.40 W
Sealy	262	29.47 N	96.09 W
Searchlight	270	35.28 N	114.55 W
Searcy	260	35.15 N	91.44 W
Searles Lake	270	35.43 N	117.20 W
Searsport	254	44.28 N	68.56 W
Seaside, CA	270	36.37 N	121.50 W
Seaside, OR	268	46.02 N	123.55 W
Seaside Park	254	39.55 N	74.05 W
Seattle	268	47.36 N	122.20 W
Sebago Lake	254	43.50 N	70.35 W
Sebastian	262	26.20 N	97.47 W
Sebastian, Cape	268	42.19 N	124.26 W
Sebastopol, CA	270	38.24 N	122.49 W
Sebastopol, MS	260	32.34 N	89.27 W
Sebec Lake	254	45.18 N	69.18 W
Sebeka	264	46.38 N	95.05 W
Sebewaing	256	43.44 N	83.27 W
Sebree	260	37.36 N	87.32 W
Sebring	258	27.30 N	81.26 W
Secesh	268	45.02 N	115.43 W
Sechelt	248	49.28 N	123.45 W
Seco, Arroyo	270	36.25 N	121.20 W
Seco Creek, NM	266	32.59 N	107.18 W
Seco Creek, TX	262	29.02 N	99.08 W
Section	260	34.35 N	85.59 W
Security	264	38.45 N	104.44 W
Sedalia, AB	250	51.41 N	110.40 W
Sedalia, MO	260	38.42 N	93.14 W
Sedan	264	37.08 N	96.11 W
Sedanka, Cape	246	53.49 N	166.06 W
Sedanka Island	246	53.50 N	166.10 W
Sedgefield	258	35.10 N	80.51 W
Sedgewick	250	52.46 N	111.41 W
Sedgewick, Mount	266	35.11 N	108.06 W
Sedgwick, CO	264	40.56 N	102.31 W
Sedgwick, KS	264	37.55 N	97.25 W
Sedgwick, ME	254	44.18 N	68.37 W
Sedona	266	34.52 N	111.46 W
Sedro Woolley	268	48.30 N	122.14 W
Seeber Lake	250	53.52 N	93.03 W
Seekaskootch Indian Reserve	250	53.43 N	109.55 W
Seeley Lake	268	47.11 N	113.29 W
Seelyville	260	39.30 N	87.16 W
Seemalik Butte	246	60.09 N	167.08 W
Seguam Island	246	52.17 N	172.30 W
Seguam Pass	246	52.08 N	172.45 W
Seguin	262	29.34 N	97.58 W
Segula Island	247a	52.01 N	178.07 E
Segundo	264	37.07 N	104.45 W
Seibert	264	39.18 N	102.52 W
Seiling	262	36.09 N	98.56 W
Seine, MB	250	49.54 N	97.07 W
Seine, ON	256	48.40 N	92.49 W
Selah	268	46.39 N	120.32 W
Selawik	246	66.37 N	160.03 W
Selawik	246	66.36 N	160.20 W
Selawik Lake	246	66.30 N	160.40 W
Selby	264	45.31 N	100.02 W
Selbyville	254	38.28 N	75.13 W
Selden	264	39.33 N	100.34 W
Seldovia	246	59.27 N	151.43 W
Selfridge	264	46.02 N	100.56 W
Seligman, AZ	266	35.20 N	112.53 W
Seligman, MO	260	36.31 N	93.56 W
Selinsgrove	254	40.48 N	76.52 W
Selkirk	250	50.09 N	96.52 W
Selkirk Mountains	242	51.00 N	117.40 W
Seller Lake	250	55.00 N	94.32 W
Sellers	258	34.17 N	79.28 W
Sellersburg	260	38.24 N	85.45 W
Sells	266	31.55 N	111.53 W
Selma, AL	260	32.25 N	87.01 W
Selma, CA	270	36.34 N	119.37 W
Selma, NC	258	35.32 N	78.17 W
Selmer	260	35.11 N	88.36 W
Selmont	260	32.23 N	87.01 W
Selous, Mount	246	62.57 N	132.31 W
Selway	268	46.08 N	115.36 W
Selwyn, Mount	248	55.59 N	123.36 W
Selwyn Lake	242	59.55 N	104.35 W
Selwyn Mountains	246	63.10 N	130.20 W
Semans	250	51.25 N	104.44 W
Semichi Islands	247a	52.42 N	174.00 E
Semidi Islands	246	56.07 N	156.44 W
Seminary	260	31.34 N	89.30 W
Seminoe Reservoir	268	42.00 N	106.50 W
Seminoe State Park	268	42.05 N	106.55 W
Seminole, OK	262	35.14 N	96.41 W
Seminole, TX	262	32.43 N	102.39 W
Seminole, Lake	244	30.46 N	84.50 W
Seminole Draw	262	32.26 N	102.10 W
Semisopochnoi Island	247a	52.00 N	179.35 E
Semmens Lake	250	55.03 N	94.11 W
Semple Lake	250	55.02 N	95.38 W
Senate	250	49.18 N	109.41 W
Senath	260	36.08 N	90.10 W
Senatobia	260	34.39 N	89.58 W
Seneca, IL	260	41.19 N	88.36 W
Seneca, KS	264	39.50 N	96.04 W
Seneca, MO	260	36.51 N	94.37 W
Seneca, OR	268	44.08 N	118.58 W
Seneca, SC	258	34.41 N	82.57 W
Seneca, Mount	254	42.01 N	78.49 W
Seneca Creek	262	36.36 N	102.52 W
Seneca Falls	254	42.55 N	76.48 W
Seneca Lake	254	42.40 N	76.57 W
Senecaville Lake	254	39.55 N	81.25 W
Senlac	250	52.29 N	109.41 W
Senneterre	242	48.23 N	77.15 W
Senoia	258	33.18 N	84.33 W
Sentinel	262	35.09 N	99.10 W
Sentinel Butte	264	46.53 N	103.50 W
Sentinel Peak	248	54.54 N	121.57 W
Sentinel Plain	266	32.45 N	113.15 W
Separation Creek	268	41.59 N	107.28 W
Sept-Iles (Seven Islands)	252	50.12 N	66.23 W
Sepulga	260	31.11 N	86.46 W
Sequatchie	260	35.02 N	85.38 W
Sequim	268	48.05 N	123.06 W
Sequoia National Park	270	36.30 N	118.30 W
Sergeant Bluff	264	42.24 N	96.22 W
Serigny	242	56.47 N	66.00 W
Serpent, Lac du	252	49.50 N	71.37 W
Serpent, Rivière au	252	49.33 N	71.14 W
Sespe Creek	270	34.23 N	118.57 W
Seth Ward	262	34.13 N	101.42 W
Seton Lake	248	50.45 N	122.05 W
Seton Portage	248	50.43 N	122.18 W
Settee Lake	250	57.03 N	96.55 W
Setting Lake	250	55.00 N	98.38 W
Seul, Lac	250	50.20 N	92.30 W
Seul Choix Point	256	45.56 N	85.52 W
Seven Islands → Sept-Iles	252	50.12 N	66.23 W
Sevenmile Creek	254	39.28 N	84.33 W
Seven Persons	250	49.52 N	110.54 W
Seven Sisters Peaks	248	54.58 N	128.10 W
Seventy (70) Mile House	248	51.18 N	121.24 W
Severn	242	56.02 N	87.36 W
Severna Park	254	39.04 N	76.33 W
Severy	264	37.37 N	96.14 W
Sevier	266	39.04 N	113.06 W
Sevier, East Fork	266	38.14 N	112.12 W
Sevier Bridge Reservoir	266	39.21 N	111.57 W
Sevier Desert	266	39.25 N	112.50 W
Sevier Lake	266	38.55 N	113.09 W
Sevierville	258	35.52 N	83.34 W
Seville, FL	258	29.19 N	81.30 W
Seville, OH	254	41.01 N	81.52 W
Sewanee	260	35.12 N	85.55 W
Seward, AK	246	60.06 N	149.26 W
Seward, NE	264	40.55 N	97.06 W
Seward, PA	254	40.25 N	79.01 W
Seward Glacier	246	60.22 N	140.15 W
Seward Peninsula	246	65.00 N	164.00 W
Sexsmith	248	55.21 N	118.47 W
Seymour, CT	254	41.24 N	73.04 W
Seymour, IN	260	38.58 N	85.53 W
Seymour, IA	256	40.44 N	93.07 W
Seymour, MO	260	37.09 N	92.46 W
Seymour, TX	262	33.35 N	99.16 W
Seymour, WI	256	44.31 N	88.20 W
Seymour	248	51.05 N	126.50 W
Seymour Inlet	248	51.03 N	127.10 W
Seymour Johnson Air Force Base	258	35.21 N	77.58 W
Seymourville	260	30.16 N	91.13 W
Shabotik	256	48.50 N	85.34 W
Shackan Indian Reserve	248	50.17 N	112.10 W
Shadehill Reservoir	264	45.45 N	102.15 W
Shades Creek	260	33.11 N	87.02 W
Shadow Mountain National Recreation Area	266	40.07 N	105.48 W
Shady Cove	268	42.37 N	122.49 W
Shady Grove	258	30.17 N	83.38 W
Shadyside	254	39.58 N	80.45 W
Shafer Butte	268	43.47 N	116.05 W
Shafter	270	35.30 N	119.16 W
Shageluk	246	62.36 N	159.32 W
Shaker Heights	254	41.29 N	81.36 W
Shakopee	256	44.48 N	93.32 W
Shaktoolik	246	64.20 N	161.09 W
Shalalth	248	50.44 N	122.13 W
Shaler Mountains	242	72.35 N	110.45 W
Shallotte	258	33.58 N	78.23 W
Shallowater	262	33.41 N	101.59 W
Shamattawa	250	55.52 N	92.05 W
Shamokin	254	40.47 N	76.34 W
Shamrock, FL	258	29.39 N	83.08 W
Shamrock, TX	262	35.13 N	100.15 W
Shannon, GA	258	34.20 N	85.04 W
Shannon, IL	256	42.09 N	89.44 W
Shannon, MS	260	34.07 N	88.43 W
Shannontown	258	33.53 N	80.21 W
Sharatin Mountain	246	57.49 N	152.41 W
Sharbot Lake	256	44.46 N	76.41 W
Sharktooth Mountain	242	58.35 N	127.57 W
Sharon, ND	264	47.36 N	97.54 W
Sharon, PA	254	41.14 N	80.31 W
Sharon, TN	260	36.14 N	88.50 W
Sharon, WI	256	42.30 N	88.44 W
Sharon Springs	264	38.54 N	101.45 W
Sharpe, Lake	264	44.05 N	99.55 W
Sharpe Lake	250	54.24 N	93.30 W
Shasta	270	40.36 N	122.29 W
Shasta	270	41.50 N	122.35 W
Shasta, Mount	270	41.20 N	122.20 W
Shasta Lake	270	40.50 N	122.25 W
Shattuck	262	36.16 N	99.53 W
Shaunavon	250	49.40 N	108.25 W
Shaw	260	33.36 N	90.46 W
Shaw Air Force Base	258	33.58 N	80.29 W
Shawanaga Inlet	256	45.32 N	80.24 W
Shawano	256	44.47 N	88.36 W
Shaw Creek	258	33.34 N	81.30 W
Shawinigan	242	46.33 N	72.45 W
Shawinigan Falls → Shawinigan	242	46.33 N	72.45 W
Shawmere	256	48.40 N	82.29 W
Shawnee, KS	264	39.01 N	94.43 W
Shawnee, OH	254	39.36 N	82.13 W
Shawnee, OK	262	35.20 N	96.55 W
Shawneetown	260	37.42 N	88.08 W
Shawville	254	45.36 N	76.30 W
Sheboygan	256	43.46 N	87.36 W
Sheboygan	256	43.45 N	87.42 W
Sheboygan Falls	256	43.44 N	87.49 W
Shediac	252	46.13 N	64.32 W
Shedin Peak	248	55.55 N	127.32 W
Sheenjek	246	66.45 N	144.33 W
Sheep	248	50.44 N	113.51 W
Sheep Creek, AB	248	54.04 N	119.00 W
Sheep Creek, U.S.	270	42.27 N	115.36 W
Sheep Creek, UT	266	40.55 N	109.39 W
Sheep Mountain, AZ	266	32.32 N	114.14 W
Sheep Mountain, WY	268	43.33 N	110.32 W
Sheep Peak	262	31.14 N	104.59 W
Sheep Range	270	36.45 N	115.05 W
Sheepscot	254	44.00 N	69.50 W
Sheet Harbour	252	44.55 N	62.32 W
Sheffield, AL	260	34.46 N	87.40 W
Sheffield, IL	260	41.21 N	89.44 W
Sheffield, IA	256	42.54 N	93.13 W
Sheffield, PA	254	41.42 N	79.02 W
Sheffield, TX	262	30.41 N	101.49 W
Sheffield Lake	252	49.20 N	56.35 W
Sheho	250	51.38 N	103.12 W
Shekatika Bay	252	51.17 N	58.20 W
Shelagyote Peak	248	55.58 N	127.12 W
Shelbina	260	39.47 N	92.02 W
Shelburn	260	39.11 N	87.24 W
Shelburne, NS	252	43.46 N	65.19 W
Shelburne, ON	256	44.04 N	80.12 W
Shelburne Falls	254	42.36 N	72.44 W
Shelby, IA	264	41.31 N	95.27 W
Shelby, MI	256	43.37 N	86.22 W
Shelby, MS	260	33.57 N	90.46 W
Shelby, MT	268	48.30 N	111.51 W
Shelby, NE	264	41.12 N	97.26 W
Shelby, NC	258	35.17 N	81.32 W
Shelby, OH	254	40.53 N	82.40 W
Shelbyville, IL	260	39.24 N	88.48 W
Shelbyville, IN	260	39.31 N	85.47 W
Shelbyville, KY	260	38.13 N	85.14 W
Shelbyville, MO	260	39.48 N	92.02 W
Shelbyville, TN	260	35.29 N	86.27 W
Shelbyville, Lake	260	39.30 N	88.40 W
Sheldon, IA	264	43.11 N	95.51 W
Sheldon, MO	260	37.40 N	94.18 W
Sheldon Point	246	62.32 N	164.52 W
Shelikof Strait	246	57.30 N	155.00 W
Shell	250	50.58 N	101.24 W
Shellbrook	250	53.13 N	106.24 W
Shell Creek, U.S.	266	40.56 N	108.37 W
Shell Creek, NE	264	41.27 N	96.58 W
Shell Creek, ND	264	47.59 N	102.17 W
Shell Creek, WY	268	44.31 N	108.03 W
Shelley, BC	248	54.00 N	122.37 W
Shelley, ID	268	43.23 N	112.07 W
Shell Lake, SK	250	53.18 N	107.07 W
Shell Lake, WI	256	45.45 N	91.55 W
Shellman	258	31.46 N	84.37 W
Shell Rock	256	42.43 N	92.35 W
Shell Rock	256	42.38 N	92.30 W
Shellsburg	256	42.06 N	91.52 W
Shelton, CT	254	41.19 N	73.05 W
Shelton, NE	264	40.47 N	98.44 W
Shelton, WA	268	47.13 N	123.06 W
Shemogue	252	46.09 N	64.11 W
Shenandoah, IA	264	40.46 N	95.22 W
Shenandoah, PA	254	40.49 N	76.12 W
Shenandoah, VA	254	38.29 N	78.37 W
Shenandoah, North Fork	254	38.57 N	78.12 W
Shenandoah, South Fork	254	38.57 N	78.12 W
Shenandoah National Park	254	38.48 N	78.12 W
Shepard	248	50.57 N	113.55 W
Shepherd, MI	256	43.32 N	84.41 W
Shepherd, TX	262	30.30 N	95.01 W
Shepherd Bay	242	68.56 N	93.40 W
Shepherdstown	254	39.26 N	77.48 W
Shepherdsville	260	37.59 N	85.43 W
Sheppard Air Force Base	262	33.58 N	98.30 W
Sheppard Peak	246	57.41 N	132.37 W
Sherard, Cape	242	74.36 N	80.25 W
Sherbrooke, NS	252	45.08 N	61.59 W
Sherbrooke, PQ	254	45.25 N	71.54 W
Sherbrooke Lake	252	44.40 N	64.35 W
Sherburn	264	43.39 N	94.43 W
Sherburne	254	42.41 N	75.30 W
Sheridan, AR	260	34.19 N	92.24 W
Sheridan, IN	260	40.08 N	86.13 W
Sheridan, MT	268	45.27 N	112.12 W
Sheridan, OR	268	45.06 N	123.24 W
Sheridan, TX	262	29.29 N	96.40 W
Sheridan, WY	268	44.48 N	106.58 W
Sheridan, Mount	268	44.16 N	110.32 W
Sherman, MS	260	34.22 N	88.57 W
Sherman, NY	254	42.10 N	79.36 W
Sherman, TX	262	33.38 N	96.36 W
Sherman Creek	254	40.23 N	77.02 W
Sherman Mills	254	45.52 N	68.23 W
Sherman Mountain	260	36.01 N	93.17 W
Sherman Reservoir	264	41.20 N	98.55 W
Sherman Station	254	45.54 N	68.26 W
Sherrard	260	41.19 N	90.31 W
Sherridon	250	55.07 N	101.05 W
Sherrill	254	43.04 N	75.35 W
Sherwood, PE	252	46.17 N	63.08 W
Sherwood, AR	260	34.49 N	92.14 W
Sherwood, ND	264	48.58 N	101.38 W
Sherwood, OH	254	41.17 N	84.33 W
Sherwood, TN	260	35.05 N	85.56 W
Sherwood Park	248	53.31 N	113.19 W
Sherwood Shores	262	30.36 N	98.22 W
Shetek, Lake	264	44.08 N	95.42 W
Sheyenne	264	47.39 N	99.07 W
Sheyenne	264	47.05 N	96.50 W
Shickley	264	40.25 N	97.43 W
Shickshinny	254	41.09 N	76.09 W
Shidler	262	36.47 N	96.40 W
Shields	268	45.43 N	110.28 W
Shillington	254	40.18 N	75.58 W
Shiloh	254	39.49 N	84.15 W
Shiloh National Military Park	260	35.06 N	88.21 W
Shiner	262	29.26 N	97.10 W
Shinglehouse	254	41.58 N	78.12 W
Shinnston	254	39.24 N	80.18 W
Shiocton	256	44.27 N	88.35 W
Ship Cove	252	47.06 N	54.05 W
Ship Island	260	30.13 N	88.55 W
Shipman	258	37.43 N	78.51 W
Shippegan	252	47.45 N	64.42 W
Shippegan Island	252	47.48 N	64.36 W
Shippensburg	254	40.03 N	77.31 W
Shiprock	266	36.47 N	108.41 W
Ship Rock	266	36.42 N	108.50 W
Shirley	260	39.53 N	85.35 W
Shishaldin Volcano	246	54.45 N	163.57 W
Shishmaref	246	66.14 N	166.09 W
Shishmaref Inlet	246	66.07 N	165.50 W
Shively	260	38.11 N	85.49 W
Shivwits Plateau	266	36.15 N	113.40 W
Shoal	260	30.41 N	86.39 W
Shoal Creek, U.S.	260	40.28 N	92.42 W
Shoal Creek, U.S.	260	34.50 N	87.33 W
Shoal Creek, U.S.	260	37.05 N	94.42 W
Shoal Creek, IL	260	38.28 N	89.35 W
Shoal Creek, MO	260	39.44 N	93.32 W
Shoal Harbour	252	48.11 N	53.59 W
Shoal Lake	250	50.26 N	100.34 W
Shoal Lake	250	49.32 N	95.00 W
Shoals	260	38.40 N	86.47 W
Shoe Cove	252	47.45 N	52.44 W
Shoreacres	248	49.26 N	117.32 W
Shorewood	256	43.05 N	87.53 W
Short Mountain	258	36.23 N	83.10 W
Shortsville	254	42.57 N	77.14 W
Shoshone	268	42.56 N	114.24 W
Shoshone	268	44.52 N	108.11 W
Shoshone, North Fork	268	44.29 N	109.18 W
Shoshone, South Fork	268	44.27 N	109.14 W
Shoshone Basin	268	43.05 N	108.05 W
Shoshone Lake	268	44.22 N	110.43 W
Shoshone Mountains	270	39.25 N	117.15 W
Shoshone Peak	270	36.56 N	116.16 W
Shoshone Range	270	40.20 N	116.50 W
Shoshoni	268	43.14 N	108.07 W
Show Low	266	34.15 N	110.02 W
Shreve	254	40.41 N	82.01 W
Shreveport	260	32.30 N	93.45 W
Shrewsbury	254	42.18 N	71.43 W
Shubenacadie	252	45.20 N	63.30 W
Shubenacadie Lake	252	44.55 N	63.36 W
Shublik Mountains	246	69.31 N	145.40 W
Shubuta	260	31.52 N	88.42 W
Shuksan, Mount	268	48.50 N	121.36 W
Shulaps Peak	248	50.57 N	122.31 W
Shullsburg	256	42.34 N	90.14 W
Shumagin Islands	246	55.07 N	159.45 W
Shungnak	246	66.53 N	157.02 W
Shuqualak	260	32.59 N	88.34 W
Shuswap	248	50.50 N	119.00 W
Shuswap Lake	248	50.57 N	119.15 W
Shuyak Island	246	58.35 N	152.30 W
Siasconset	254	41.16 N	69.58 W
Sibbald	250	51.23 N	110.09 W
Sibley, IA	264	43.24 N	95.45 W
Sibley, LA	260	32.33 N	93.18 W
Sibley, MS	260	31.23 N	91.24 W
Sibley Provincial Park	256	48.30 N	88.30 W
Sicamous	248	50.50 N	119.00 W
Sicily Island	260	31.51 N	91.40 W
Sidnaw	256	46.30 N	88.43 W
Sidney, BC	248	48.39 N	123.24 W
Sidney, IL	260	40.01 N	88.04 W
Sidney, IA	264	40.45 N	95.39 W
Sidney, MT	264	47.43 N	104.09 W
Sidney, NE	264	41.09 N	102.59 W
Sidney, NY	254	42.19 N	75.24 W
Sidney, OH	254	40.17 N	84.09 W
Sidney Lanier, Lake	258	34.15 N	83.57 W
Sidon	260	33.25 N	90.12 W
Sierra Blanca	266	31.11 N	105.21 W
Sierra Blanca Peak	266	33.23 N	105.48 W
Sierra Vista	266	31.33 N	110.18 W
Siesta Key	258	27.19 N	82.34 W
Sifton	250	51.21 N	100.07 W
Signal Hill National Historic Park	252	47.30 N	52.42 W
Signal Mountain	260	35.07 N	85.21 W
Signal Mountain	254	44.12 N	72.20 W
Signal Peak	266	37.19 N	113.29 W
Sigourney	256	41.20 N	92.12 W
Sigurd	266	38.50 N	111.58 W
Sikanni Chief	242	58.20 N	121.50 W
Sikeston	260	36.53 N	89.35 W
Silas	260	31.46 N	88.20 W
Siler City	258	35.44 N	79.28 W
Siletz	268	44.43 N	123.55 W
Siletz	268	44.54 N	124.00 W
Sillem Island	242	70.55 N	71.30 W
Siloam Springs	260	36.11 N	94.32 W
Silsbee	260	30.21 N	94.11 W
Silsby Lake	250	55.29 N	95.46 W
Silton	250	50.48 N	104.55 W
Silver	262	32.04 N	100.40 W
Silver Bay	256	47.17 N	91.16 W
Silver Bell	266	32.23 N	111.30 W
Silver Bow Park	268	46.01 N	112.28 W
Silver City, NM	266	32.46 N	108.17 W
Silver City, NC	258	35.00 N	79.12 W
Silver Creek, MS	260	31.36 N	89.59 W
Silver Creek, NE	264	41.19 N	97.40 W
Silver Creek, NY	254	42.33 N	79.10 W
Silver Creek, AZ	266	34.44 N	110.02 W
Silver Creek, IL	260	38.20 N	89.52 W
Silver Creek, KY	258	37.48 N	84.30 W
Silver Creek, OR	268	43.16 N	119.13 W
Silverdale	268	47.39 N	122.42 W
Silver Falls State Park	268	44.48 N	122.50 W
Silver Lake, KS	264	39.06 N	95.52 W
Silver Lake, OR	268	43.08 N	120.56 W
Silver Lake, WI	256	42.33 N	88.07 W
Silver Lake, OR	268	43.22 N	119.24 W
Silver Lake, OR	268	43.06 N	120.53 W
Silver Spring	254	39.02 N	77.03 W

Symbols in the index entries are identified on page 273.

Silv – Ston

United States and Canada Map Index

Name	Page	Lat ° ′	Long ° ′
Silver Star Mountain	268	48.33 N	120.35 W
Silver Star Provincial Park	248	50.22 N	119.05 W
Silverthrone Mountain	248	51.31 N	126.06 W
Silvertip Mountain	268	47.47 N	113.15 W
Silverton, BC	248	49.57 N	117.21 W
Silverton, CO	266	37.49 N	107.40 W
Silverton, OR	268	45.01 N	122.47 W
Silverton, TX	262	34.28 N	101.19 W
Silvies	268	43.22 N	118.48 W
Simcoe	256	42.50 N	80.18 W
Simcoe, Lake	256	44.20 N	79.20 W
Similkameen	248	48.56 N	119.26 W
Simi Valley	270	34.16 N	118.47 W
Simla	264	39.09 N	104.05 W
Simmesport	260	30.59 N	91.49 W
Simmie	250	49.57 N	108.06 W
Simms	268	47.30 N	111.55 W
Simon, Lac	254	45.58 N	75.05 W
Simonette	248	55.07 N	118.00 W
Simonhouse Lake	250	54.30 N	101.10 W
Simoom Sound	248	50.45 N	126.45 W
Simpson	260	31.16 N	93.00 W
Simpson Island	256	48.48 N	87.40 W
Simpson Lake, NT	242	68.39 N	91.19 W
Simpson Lake, NT	246	68.10 N	126.35 W
Simpson Peak	246	59.44 N	131.27 W
Simpson Peninsula	242	68.34 N	88.45 W
Simpson Strait	242	68.27 N	97.45 W
Simpsonville	258	34.44 N	82.15 W
Simsbury	254	41.52 N	72.48 W
Sinclair	268	41.47 N	107.07 W
Sinclair, Lake	258	33.11 N	83.16 W
Sinclair Mills	248	54.02 N	121.41 W
Singer	260	30.39 N	93.25 W
Sinking Creek	260	37.55 N	86.31 W
Sinnamahoning	254	41.19 N	78.06 W
Sinton	262	29.41 N	95.58 W
Sioux Center	264	43.05 N	96.10 W
Sioux City	264	42.30 N	96.23 W
Sioux Falls	264	43.32 N	96.44 W
Sioux Lookout	250	50.06 N	91.55 W
Sioux Narrows	250	49.25 N	94.06 W
Sioux Rapids	264	42.53 N	95.09 W
Sipiwesk	250	55.27 N	97.24 W
Sipiwesk Lake	250	55.05 N	97.35 W
Sipsey	260	33.00 N	88.10 W
Sipsey Creek	260	33.53 N	88.17 W
Sir Alexander, Mount	248	53.56 N	120.23 W
Sirdar	248	49.15 N	116.37 W
Sir Douglas, Mount	248	50.44 N	115.20 W
Sir James MacBrien, Mount	242	62.07 N	127.41 W
Sir Sandford, Mount	248	51.40 N	117.52 W
Sir Wilfrid Laurier, Mount	248	52.47 N	119.45 W
Sisib Lake	250	52.35 N	99.22 W
Sisipuk Lake	250	55.45 N	101.50 W
Siskiyou Mountains	270	41.55 N	123.15 W
Siskiyou Pass	268	42.03 N	122.36 W
Sisquoc	270	34.54 N	120.18 W
Sisseton	264	45.40 N	97.03 W
Sisseton Indian Reservation	264	45.40 N	97.02 W
Sisson Branch Reservoir	252	47.16 N	67.20 W
Sissonville	254	38.32 N	81.38 W
Sister Bay	256	45.11 N	87.07 W
Sisters	268	44.17 N	121.33 W
Sistersville	254	39.34 N	81.00 W
Sitidgi Lake	242	68.32 N	132.42 W
Sitka	246	57.03 N	135.14 W
Sitkalidak Island	246	57.10 N	153.14 W
Sitka National Monument	246	57.05 N	135.15 W
Sitka Point	246	57.00 N	135.49 W
Sitka Sound	246	57.00 N	135.30 W
Sitkinak Island	246	56.35 N	154.12 W
Sitkinak Strait	246	56.39 N	154.06 W
Siuslaw	268	44.01 N	124.08 W
Sixshooter Draw	262	30.51 N	102.33 W
Sixteenmile Creek	268	46.06 N	111.23 W
Skaggs Creek	260	36.54 N	86.04 W
Skagit	268	48.20 N	122.25 W
Skagway	246	59.28 N	135.19 W
Skeena	248	54.09 N	130.02 W
Skeena Crossing	248	55.06 N	127.49 W
Skeena Mountains, BC	246, 248	57.00 N	128.30 W
Skeleton Creek	262	35.58 N	97.25 W
Skellytown	262	35.34 N	101.11 W
Skiatook	262	36.22 N	96.01 W
Skidegate	248	53.15 N	132.00 W
Skidegate Inlet	248	53.14 N	132.00 W
Skidmore	262	28.15 N	97.41 W
Skihist Mountain	248	50.11 N	121.54 W
Skilak Lake	246	60.25 N	150.25 W
Skillet Fork	260	38.08 N	88.07 W
Skokie	256	42.02 N	87.46 W
Skowhegan	254	44.46 N	69.43 W
Skownan	250	51.57 N	99.36 W
Skull Valley	266	34.30 N	112.41 W
Skull Valley Indian Reservation	266	40.24 N	112.45 W
Skuna	260	33.54 N	89.41 W
Skunk	256	40.42 N	91.07 W
Skwentna	246	61.58 N	151.11 W
Skwentna	246	62.00 N	151.08 W
Skykomish	268	47.50 N	122.03 W
Skykomish, North Fork	268	47.47 N	121.33 W
Skykomish, South Fork	268	47.47 N	121.33 W
Skyland	258	35.29 N	82.31 W
Slate Creek	264	37.08 N	97.09 W
Slater, IA	256	41.53 N	93.41 W
Slater, MO	260	39.13 N	93.04 W
Slater Creek	266	40.59 N	107.23 W
Slaton	262	33.26 N	101.39 W
Slaughter	260	30.48 N	91.08 W
Slave	242	61.18 N	113.39 W
Slave Lake	248	55.17 N	114.46 W
Slayton	264	43.59 N	95.45 W
Sledge	260	34.26 N	90.13 W
Sledge Island	246	64.29 N	166.13 W
Sled Lake	250	54.27 N	107.25 W
Sleeping Bear Dunes National Lakeshore	256	44.50 N	86.08 W
Sleepy Eye	264	44.18 N	94.43 W
Sleetmute	246	61.42 N	157.11 W
Slidell	260	30.17 N	89.47 W
Slide Mountain	254	42.00 N	74.23 W
Sliderock Mountain	268	46.35 N	113.33 W
Sligo	254	41.07 N	79.29 W
Slinger	256	43.20 N	88.17 W
Slippery Rock	254	41.04 N	80.03 W
Sloan, IA	264	42.14 N	96.14 W
Sloan, NV	270	35.57 N	115.13 W
Slocan	248	49.46 N	117.28 W
Slocan Lake	248	49.56 N	117.22 W
Slosh Indian Reserve	248	50.44 N	122.13 W
Smackover	260	33.22 N	92.44 W
Smackover Creek	260	33.22 N	92.24 W
Smeaton	250	53.30 N	104.49 W
Smeaton Bay	248	55.20 N	130.50 W
Smethport	254	41.49 N	78.27 W
Smiley, SK	250	51.37 N	109.29 W
Smiley, TX	262	29.16 N	97.38 W
Smith	248	55.10 N	114.02 W
Smith, U.S.	258	36.29 N	79.45 W
Smith, CA	270	41.56 N	124.12 W
Smith, MT	268	47.25 N	111.29 W
Smith, OR	268	43.43 N	124.05 W
Smith, Cape	256	45.48 N	81.35 W
Smith Arm	242	66.15 N	124.00 W
Smith Bay	246	70.51 N	154.25 W
Smith Canyon	264	37.46 N	103.26 W
Smith Center	264	39.47 N	98.47 W
Smith Creek	264	43.58 N	99.20 W
Smithers, BC	248	54.47 N	127.10 W
Smithers, WV	254	38.11 N	81.18 W
Smithfield, NC	258	35.30 N	78.21 W
Smithfield, UT	266	41.50 N	111.50 W
Smithfield, VA	258	36.59 N	76.38 W
Smith Island	258	33.52 N	77.59 W
Smithland	260	37.09 N	88.24 W
Smith Mountain Lake	258	37.10 N	79.40 W
Smith Peak	268	48.50 N	116.39 W
Smith Point	252	45.51 N	63.25 W
Smith River	270	41.56 N	124.09 W
Smiths	258	32.32 N	85.06 W
Smiths Falls	256	44.54 N	76.01 W
Smiths Grove	260	37.03 N	86.12 W
Smith Sound	248	51.18 N	127.48 W
Smithton	260	38.41 N	93.05 W
Smithville, GA	258	31.54 N	84.15 W
Smithville, MS	260	33.59 N	88.23 W
Smithville, MO	260	39.23 N	94.35 W
Smithville, TN	260	35.58 N	85.49 W
Smithville, TX	262	30.00 N	97.09 W
Smoke Creek	264	48.18 N	104.41 W
Smoke Creek Desert	270	40.30 N	119.40 W
Smokey Dome	268	43.29 N	114.56 W
Smoky	248	56.10 N	117.21 W
Smoky, Cape	252	46.38 N	60.21 W
Smoky Hill	264	39.03 N	96.48 W
Smoky Hill, North Fork	264	39.28 N	98.26 W
Smoky Hills	264	39.15 N	99.00 W
Smoky Lake	248	54.07 N	112.28 W
Smoot	268	42.37 N	110.55 W
Smoothstone	250	55.20 N	106.39 W
Smoothstone Lake	250	54.40 N	106.50 W
Smyrna, DE	254	39.18 N	75.36 W
Smyrna, GA	258	33.53 N	84.31 W
Smyrna, TN	260	35.59 N	86.31 W
Smythe, Mount	242	57.54 N	124.53 W
Snag	246	62.24 N	140.22 W
Snake, YK	246	65.58 N	134.10 W
Snake, U.S.	244	46.12 N	119.02 W
Snake, MN	256	45.49 N	92.46 W
Snake, MN	264	48.26 N	97.07 W
Snake, NE	264	42.47 N	100.48 W
Snake Creek, MT	268	48.32 N	108.53 W
Snake Creek, NE	264	42.01 N	102.45 W
Snake Creek, SD	264	44.58 N	98.29 W
Snake Indian	248	53.11 N	118.00 W
Snake Range	270	39.00 N	114.15 W
Snake River Plain	268	43.00 N	113.00 W
Snake Valley	270	39.20 N	113.55 W
Sneads	258	30.42 N	84.56 W
Sneedville	258	36.32 N	83.13 W
Snelling	270	37.31 N	120.26 W
Snipe Lake	248	55.07 N	116.46 W
Snohomish	268	47.55 N	122.06 W
Snoqualmie	268	47.32 N	121.50 W
Snoqualmie Pass	268	47.25 N	121.25 W
Snover	256	43.28 N	82.58 W
Snowbird Lake	242	60.41 N	103.00 W
Snow Canyon State Park	266	37.11 N	113.42 W
Snowden	250	53.30 N	104.41 W
Snowdoun	260	32.15 N	86.18 W
Snowdrift	242	62.23 N	110.47 W
Snowflake	266	34.30 N	110.05 W
Snow Hill, MD	254	38.11 N	75.24 W
Snow Hill, NC	258	35.27 N	77.40 W
Snow Lake	250	54.53 N	100.02 W
Snowmass Mountain	266	39.07 N	107.04 W
Snow Mountain	270	39.23 N	122.45 W
Snow Peak	268	48.35 N	118.29 W
Snowshoe Peak	268	48.13 N	115.41 W
Snow Water Lake	270	41.07 N	115.00 W
Snowy Mountain	254	43.42 N	74.23 W
Snowyside Peak	268	43.57 N	114.58 W
Snyder, OK	262	34.40 N	98.57 W
Snyder, TX	262	32.44 N	100.55 W
Soap Creek	256	40.55 N	92.14 W
Soap Lake	268	47.23 N	119.29 W
Social Circle	258	33.39 N	83.43 W
Society Hill	258	34.31 N	79.51 W
Socorro, NM	266	34.04 N	106.54 W
Socorro, TX	266	31.39 N	106.18 W
Soda Creek	248	52.21 N	122.18 W
Soda Lake	270	35.08 N	116.04 W
Soda Springs	268	42.39 N	111.36 W
Soddy-Daisy	260	35.17 N	85.10 W
Sodus	254	43.14 N	77.04 W
Sointula	248	50.38 N	127.01 W
Solana	258	26.57 N	82.01 W
Soldier Creek	264	39.04 N	95.39 W
Soldier Pond	252	47.09 N	68.35 W
Soldiers Grove	256	43.24 N	90.47 W
Soldotna	246	60.29 N	151.04 W
Soledad	270	36.26 N	121.19 W
Soledad Pass	270	34.30 N	118.07 W
Soleduck	268	47.55 N	124.35 W
Solen	264	46.23 N	100.48 W
Solomon, AZ	266	32.49 N	109.38 W
Solomon, KS	264	38.55 N	97.22 W
Solomon	264	38.54 N	97.22 W
Solomon, North Fork	264	39.29 N	98.26 W
Solomon, South Fork	264	39.29 N	98.26 W
Solon, IA	256	41.48 N	91.30 W
Solon, ME	254	44.57 N	69.52 W
Solon Springs	256	46.22 N	91.48 W
Solvang	270	34.36 N	120.08 W
Solvay	254	43.04 N	76.12 W
Somers	268	48.05 N	114.13 W
Somerset, MB	250	49.24 N	98.39 W
Somerset, CO	266	38.56 N	107.16 W
Somerset, KY	258	37.05 N	84.36 W
Somerset, MA	254	41.45 N	71.09 W
Somerset, OH	254	39.48 N	82.18 W
Somerset, PA	254	40.01 N	79.05 W
Somerset, TX	262	29.13 N	98.40 W
Somerset, WI	256	45.08 N	92.40 W
Somerset Island	242	73.15 N	93.30 W
Somers Point	254	39.20 N	74.36 W
Somersworth	254	43.16 N	70.52 W
Somerton	266	32.36 N	114.43 W
Somerville, NJ	254	40.34 N	74.37 W
Somerville, TN	260	35.15 N	89.21 W
Somerville, TX	262	30.21 N	96.32 W
Somerville Lake	262	30.18 N	96.40 W
Somo	256	45.29 N	89.48 W
Sonningdale	250	52.24 N	107.40 W
Sonoita Creek	266	31.30 N	110.58 W
Sonoma	270	38.17 N	122.28 W
Sonoma Peak	270	40.52 N	117.36 W
Sonora, CA	270	37.59 N	120.23 W
Sonora, TX	262	30.34 N	100.39 W
Sonora Desert	266	33.00 N	114.00 W
Sontag	260	31.39 N	90.12 W
Soo → Sault Sainte Marie	256	46.30 N	84.21 W
Sooke	248	48.23 N	123.43 W
Sopchoppy	258	30.04 N	84.29 W
Soperton	258	32.23 N	82.35 W
Sophia	258	37.43 N	81.15 W
Sorel	254	46.02 N	73.07 W
Sorrento	260	30.11 N	90.51 W
Soso	260	31.45 N	89.16 W
Soudan	256	47.49 N	92.10 W
Souderton	254	40.19 N	75.19 W
Soufflot, Lac	256	47.24 N	78.31 W
Sougahatchee Creek	260	32.38 N	85.50 W
Souhegan	254	42.51 N	71.29 W
Sounding Creek	250	52.06 N	110.28 W
Souris, MB	250	49.38 N	100.15 W
Souris, PE	252	46.21 N	62.15 W
Souris	242	49.39 N	99.34 W
Souris Plain	264	48.15 N	100.15 W
Sourlake	260	30.09 N	94.25 W
Sourland Mountain	254	40.29 N	74.43 W
South, IA	256	41.29 N	93.20 W
South, NC	258	34.20 N	78.03 W
South, VA	258	37.46 N	79.23 W
Southampton, NS	252	45.35 N	64.15 W
Southampton, ON	256	44.29 N	81.23 W
Southampton, NY	254	40.53 N	72.24 W
Southampton, Cape	242	62.09 N	83.40 W
Southampton Island	242	64.20 N	84.40 W
South Anna	258	37.48 N	77.25 W
South Aulatsivik Island	242	56.45 N	61.30 W
Southaven	260	34.59 N	90.03 W
South Bald Mountain	266	40.45 N	105.41 W
South Baldy	266	33.59 N	107.11 W
Southbank	248	54.02 N	125.46 W
South Bay	258	26.40 N	80.43 W
South Bay, MB	250	56.43 N	99.00 W
South Bay, NT	242	63.58 N	83.30 W
South Bay, ON	256	45.38 N	81.50 W
South Baymouth	256	45.33 N	82.01 W
South Beloit	256	42.29 N	89.02 W
South Bend, IN	260	41.41 N	86.15 W
South Bend, WA	268	46.40 N	123.48 W
South Bentinck Arm	248	52.15 N	126.15 W
South Boston	258	36.42 N	78.54 W
South Branch	252	47.55 N	59.02 W
Southbridge	254	42.05 N	72.02 W
South Brookfield	252	44.23 N	64.58 W
South Burlington	254	44.28 N	73.13 W
South Carolina, U.S.	244, 258	34.00 N	81.00 W
South Channel	256	45.38 N	84.32 W
South Charleston	254	38.22 N	81.44 W
South Coffeyville	262	36.59 N	95.38 W
South Concho	262	31.21 N	100.28 W
South Dakota, U.S.	244, 264	44.15 N	100.00 W
South Deerfield	254	42.29 N	72.37 W
Southeast Cape	246	62.55 N	169.42 W
South English	256	41.30 N	91.56 W
Southern Indian Lake	250	57.10 N	98.40 W
Southern Pines	258	35.11 N	79.24 W
Southern Ute Indian Reservation	266	37.05 N	107.45 W
Southey	250	50.56 N	104.30 W
South Fabius	260	39.54 N	91.30 W
South Fallsburg	254	41.43 N	74.38 W
Southfield	256	42.29 N	83.17 W
South Fork	266	37.40 N	106.37 W
South Fort George	248	53.54 N	122.45 W
South Fox Island	256	45.25 N	85.50 W
South Fulton	260	36.30 N	88.53 W
Southgate	256	42.12 N	83.13 W
South Grand	260	38.18 N	93.28 W
South Hadley Falls	254	42.14 N	72.36 W
South Haven, KS	264	37.03 N	97.24 W
South Haven, MI	256	42.24 N	86.16 W
South Heart	248	55.34 N	116.11 W
South Henderson	258	36.17 N	78.25 W
South Henik Lake	242	61.30 N	97.30 W
South Hero	254	44.39 N	73.19 W
South Hill	258	36.44 N	78.08 W
South Holston Lake	258	36.35 N	82.00 W
South Houston	262	29.40 N	95.14 W
South Indian Lake	250	56.46 N	98.57 W
Southington	254	41.36 N	72.53 W
South International Falls	256	48.35 N	93.24 W
South Kenosha	256	42.33 N	87.51 W
South Ladder Creek	264	38.41 N	101.34 W
South Lake Tahoe	270	38.57 N	119.57 W
Southland	262	33.22 N	101.33 W
Southlawn	260	39.45 N	89.37 W
South Llano	262	30.30 N	99.46 W
South Loup	264	41.04 N	98.40 W
South Lyon	256	42.28 N	83.39 W
South MacMillan	246	63.03 N	133.18 W
South Manitou Island	256	45.01 N	86.07 W
South Medford	268	42.18 N	122.50 W
South Miami	258	25.42 N	80.17 W
South Mills	258	36.27 N	76.20 W
South Milwaukee	256	42.55 N	87.52 W
South Moose Lake	250	53.46 N	100.08 W
South Mountain	268	42.44 N	116.54 W
South Nahanni	242	61.03 N	123.20 W
South Naknek	246	58.43 N	157.05 W
South Nation	254	45.35 N	75.06 W
South Ogden	266	41.12 N	111.59 W
South Palo Duro Creek	262	36.06 N	101.29 W
South Paris	254	44.13 N	70.31 W
South Pass	268	42.22 N	108.55 W
South Pekin	256	40.30 N	89.39 W
South Pittsburg	260	35.01 N	85.42 W
South Platte	244	41.07 N	100.42 W
South Platte, North Fork	266	39.25 N	105.10 W
South Porcupine	256	48.28 N	81.13 W
Southport, FL	260	30.17 N	85.39 W
Southport, IN	260	39.40 N	86.09 W
Southport, NC	258	33.55 N	78.01 W
Southport, NY	254	42.03 N	76.49 W
South Portland	254	43.38 N	70.15 W
South Range	256	47.04 N	88.39 W
South Revelstoke	248	50.48 N	118.11 W
South River	256	45.45 N	79.25 W
South Rockwood	256	42.04 N	83.16 W
South Salt Lake	266	40.43 N	111.53 W
South San Francisco	270	37.39 N	122.24 W
South Santiam	268	44.41 N	123.00 W
South Saskatchewan	250	53.15 N	105.05 W
South Saugeen	256	44.08 N	81.02 W
South Sioux City	264	42.28 N	96.24 W
South Skunk	256	41.15 N	92.02 W
South Slocan	248	49.28 N	117.32 W
South Spicer Island	242	68.06 N	79.13 W
South Sulphur	262	33.23 N	95.18 W
South Superior	268	41.46 N	108.58 W
South Thompson	248	50.41 N	120.21 W
South Torrington	264	42.03 N	104.11 W
South Tucson	266	32.12 N	110.58 W
South Twillingate Island	252	49.37 N	54.47 W
South Umpqua	268	43.20 N	123.25 W
South Ventana Cone	270	36.17 N	121.38 W
South Wabasca Lake	248	55.54 N	113.45 W
Southwest Cape	246	63.18 N	171.27 W
South West City	260	36.31 N	94.37 W
Southwest Harbor	254	44.17 N	68.20 W
Southwest Miramichi	252	46.58 N	65.35 W
South Weymouth Naval Air Station	254	42.09 N	70.57 W
South Whitley	260	41.05 N	85.38 W
South Wichita	262	33.43 N	99.29 W
South Williamson	258	37.40 N	82.16 W
South Windham	254	43.44 N	70.26 W
South Yadkin	258	35.45 N	80.27 W
South Yamhill	268	45.13 N	123.08 W
Sovereign Mountain	246	62.08 N	148.36 W
Spalding, SK	250	52.20 N	104.30 W
Spalding, NE	264	41.41 N	98.22 W
Spaniard's Bay	252	47.37 N	53.17 W
Spanish	256	46.12 N	82.21 W
Spanish	256	46.11 N	82.19 W
Spanish Fork	266	40.07 N	111.39 W
Spanish Peak	268	44.24 N	119.46 W
Sparkman	260	33.55 N	92.51 W
Sparks, GA	258	31.11 N	83.26 W
Sparks, NV	270	39.32 N	119.45 W
Sparland	260	41.02 N	89.26 W
Sparlingville	256	42.58 N	82.30 W
Sparrows Point	254	39.13 N	76.29 W
Sparta, GA	258	33.17 N	82.58 W
Sparta, IL	260	38.07 N	89.42 W
Sparta, KY	254	38.41 N	84.55 W
Sparta, MI	256	43.10 N	85.42 W
Sparta, NJ	254	41.01 N	74.39 W
Sparta, NC	258	36.30 N	81.07 W
Sparta, TN	260	35.56 N	85.29 W
Sparta, WI	256	43.57 N	90.47 W
Spartanburg	258	34.57 N	81.55 W
Spear, Cape	252	47.32 N	52.32 W
Spearfish	264	44.30 N	103.52 W
Spearman	262	36.12 N	101.12 W
Spearville	264	37.51 N	99.45 W
Spectrum Range	246	57.30 N	130.40 W
Spednic Lake	252	45.36 N	67.35 W
Speedway	260	39.47 N	86.15 W
Spenard	246	61.11 N	149.55 W
Spence Bay	242	69.32 N	93.31 W
Spencer, IN	260	39.17 N	86.46 W
Spencer, IA	264	43.09 N	95.09 W
Spencer, MA	254	42.15 N	71.60 W
Spencer, NE	264	42.53 N	98.42 W
Spencer, NC	258	35.37 N	80.26 W
Spencer, SD	264	43.44 N	97.36 W
Spencer, TN	260	35.45 N	85.28 W
Spencer, WV	254	38.48 N	81.21 W
Spencer, WI	256	44.46 N	90.18 W
Spencer, Cape, NB	252	45.12 N	65.55 W
Spencer, Cape, AK	246	58.14 N	136.40 W
Spencer, Point	246	65.18 N	166.50 W
Spencer Creek	260	39.33 N	91.20 W
Spencerville	254	40.42 N	84.21 W
Spences Bridge	248	50.25 N	121.21 W
Sperryville	254	38.39 N	78.14 W
Spicer	264	45.14 N	94.56 W
Spickard	260	40.14 N	93.35 W
Spillimacheen	248	50.55 N	116.20 W
Spindale	258	35.22 N	81.55 W
Spirit Lake, ID	268	47.58 N	116.52 W
Spirit Lake, IA	264	43.26 N	95.06 W
Spirit River	248	55.47 N	118.50 W
Spiritwood	250	53.22 N	107.31 W
Spiro	260	35.16 N	94.37 W
Split, Cape	252	45.20 N	64.30 W
Split Lake	250	56.08 N	96.15 W
Split Rock Creek	264	43.34 N	96.35 W
Spofford	262	29.11 N	100.25 W
Spokane	268	47.40 N	117.23 W
Spokane	268	47.44 N	118.20 W
Spokane, Mount	268	47.55 N	117.07 W
Spokane Indian Reservation	268	47.55 N	118.00 W
Spoon	256	40.18 N	90.04 W
Spooner	256	45.50 N	91.53 W
Spotsylvania	254	38.12 N	77.35 W
Sprague, MB	250	49.02 N	95.38 W
Sprague, WA	268	47.18 N	117.59 W
Sprague	268	42.34 N	121.51 W
Sprague, North Fork	268	42.26 N	121.07 W
Sprague, South Fork	268	42.26 N	121.07 W
Spray	268	44.50 N	119.48 W
Spray Lakes Reservoir	248	50.55 N	115.20 W
Spreckelsville	272a	20.54 N	156.25 W
Spring, U.S.	260	36.52 N	94.44 W
Spring, AR	260	36.08 N	91.05 W
Spring, North Fork	260	37.18 N	94.21 W
Spring, South Fork	260	36.19 N	91.30 W
Spring Bay	266	41.40 N	112.50 W
Spring City, TN	258	35.42 N	84.52 W
Spring City, UT	266	39.29 N	111.30 W
Spring Coulee	264	48.31 N	100.54 W
Spring Creek, U.S.	264	40.30 N	101.21 W
Spring Creek, GA	258	30.54 N	84.45 W
Spring Creek, NV	270	39.55 N	117.50 W
Spring Creek, ND	264	47.15 N	101.48 W
Spring Creek, SD	264	43.52 N	113.00 W
Spring Creek, SD	264	45.54 N	100.18 W
Spring Creek, TX	262	30.02 N	95.16 W
Springdale, NF	252	49.30 N	56.04 W
Springdale, AR	260	36.11 N	94.08 W
Springdale, SC	258	33.57 N	81.06 W
Springdale, UT	266	37.11 N	113.00 W
Springdale, WA	268	48.04 N	117.45 W
Spring Dale, WV	258	37.53 N	80.48 W
Springer	262	36.22 N	104.36 W
Springerville	266	34.08 N	109.17 W
Springfield, NB	252	46.01 N	67.03 W
Springfield, CO	264	37.24 N	102.37 W
Springfield, FL	260	30.09 N	85.37 W
Springfield, GA	258	32.22 N	81.18 W
Springfield, IL	260	39.47 N	89.40 W
Springfield, KY	260	37.41 N	85.13 W
Springfield, MA	254	42.07 N	72.36 W
Springfield, MN	264	44.14 N	94.59 W
Springfield, MO	260	37.14 N	93.17 W
Springfield, OH	254	39.56 N	83.49 W
Springfield, OR	268	44.03 N	123.01 W
Springfield, SC	258	33.30 N	81.17 W
Springfield, SD	264	42.49 N	97.54 W
Springfield, TN	260	36.31 N	86.52 W
Springfield, VT	254	43.18 N	72.29 W
Springfield, Lake	260	39.40 N	89.35 W
Springfield Plateau	260	37.10 N	93.30 W
Spring Glen, FL	258	30.18 N	81.36 W
Spring Glen, UT	266	39.38 N	110.52 W
Spring Green	256	43.11 N	90.04 W
Spring Grove, MN	256	43.33 N	91.38 W
Spring Grove, PA	254	39.52 N	76.52 W
Springhill, NS	252	45.39 N	64.03 W
Springhill, LA	260	33.00 N	93.28 W
Spring Hill, TN	260	35.45 N	86.56 W
Spring Hope	258	35.57 N	78.06 W
Springhouse	248	51.55 N	122.07 W
Spring Lake	258	35.10 N	78.58 W
Spring Mill State Park	260	38.43 N	86.25 W
Spring Mountains	270	36.10 N	115.40 W
Springtown	262	32.58 N	97.41 W
Springvale	254	43.28 N	70.48 W
Spring Valley, CA	270	37.40 N	121.14 W
Spring Valley, IL	260	41.20 N	89.12 W
Spring Valley, MN	256	43.41 N	92.23 W
Spring Valley, NY	254	41.07 N	74.03 W
Spring Valley, WI	256	44.51 N	92.14 W
Spring Valley	270	39.15 N	114.25 W
Spring Valley Creek	270	39.20 N	114.25 W
Springview	264	42.49 N	99.45 W
Springville, AL	260	33.46 N	86.30 W
Springville, CA	270	36.08 N	118.49 W
Springville, IA	256	42.03 N	91.27 W
Springville, NY	254	42.31 N	78.40 W
Springville, UT	266	40.10 N	111.37 W
Sproat Lake	248	49.16 N	125.03 W
Spruce Brook	252	48.45 N	58.11 W
Spruce Grove	248	53.32 N	113.55 W
Spruce Knob	254	38.42 N	79.32 W
Spruce Knob-Seneca Rocks National Recreation Area	254	38.50 N	79.20 W
Spruce Lake	250	53.32 N	109.14 W
Spruce Mountain, AZ	266	34.28 N	112.24 W
Spruce Mountain, NV	270	40.33 N	114.49 W
Spruce Pine, AL	260	34.23 N	87.45 W
Spruce Pine, NC	258	35.55 N	82.04 W
Spruce Woods Provincial Park	250	49.42 N	99.05 W
Spur	262	33.28 N	100.52 W
Spurfield	248	55.13 N	114.16 W
Spurger	260	30.42 N	94.11 W
Spurr, Mount	246	61.18 N	152.15 W
Spuzzum	248	49.41 N	121.25 W
Spy Hill	250	50.36 N	101.41 W
Squally Channel	248	53.10 N	129.15 W
Squamish	248	49.42 N	123.09 W
Squamish	248	49.45 N	123.09 W
Squam Lake	254	43.45 N	71.32 W
Square Butte Creek	264	46.55 N	100.55 W
Square Lake	252	47.03 N	68.20 W
Squatteck	252	47.53 N	68.43 W
Squaw Cap Mountain	252	47.53 N	66.53 W
Squaw Creek, ID	268	43.51 N	116.22 W
Squaw Creek, OR	268	44.27 N	121.20 W
Squaw Harbor	246	55.11 N	160.30 W
Squaw Hill	264	41.48 N	105.02 W
Squaw Peak	268	47.10 N	114.21 W
Squaw Rapids	250	53.41 N	103.20 W
Squaw Rapids Dam	250	53.40 N	103.25 W
Squilax	248	50.52 N	119.35 W
Squire	258	37.14 N	81.36 W
Squirrel	246	66.57 N	160.27 W
Stacyville	256	43.26 N	92.47 W
Stafford, KS	264	37.58 N	98.36 W
Stafford, VA	254	38.25 N	77.24 W
Stafford Springs	254	41.57 N	72.18 W
Staffordsville	258	37.50 N	82.50 W
Staked Plain → Estacado, Llano	244	33.30 N	102.40 W
Stambaugh	256	46.04 N	88.38 W
Stamford, CT	254	41.03 N	73.32 W
Stamford, NY	254	42.25 N	74.37 W
Stamford, TX	262	32.57 N	99.48 W
Stamford, Lake	262	33.05 N	99.35 W
Stamps	260	33.22 N	93.30 W
Stanaford	258	37.49 N	81.10 W
Stanardsville	254	38.18 N	78.26 W
Stanberry	260	40.13 N	94.35 W
Standard, AB	248	51.07 N	112.59 W
Standard, AK	246	64.47 N	148.32 W
Standing Buffalo Indian Reserve	250	50.53 N	103.54 W
Standing Rock Indian Reservation	264	45.50 N	101.10 W
Standish	256	43.59 N	83.57 W
Stanfield, AZ	266	32.53 N	111.58 W
Stanfield, OR	268	45.47 N	119.13 W
Stanford, KY	258	37.32 N	84.40 W
Stanford, MT	268	47.09 N	110.13 W
Stanhope	256	42.17 N	93.48 W
Stanislaus	270	37.40 N	121.14 W
Stanislaus, Middle Fork	270	38.09 N	120.21 W
Stanislaus, North Fork	270	38.09 N	120.21 W
Stanley, NB	252	46.17 N	66.44 W
Stanley, NC	258	35.21 N	81.06 W
Stanley, ND	264	48.19 N	102.23 W
Stanley, VA	254	38.34 N	78.31 W
Stanley, WI	256	44.58 N	90.56 W
Stanton, IA	264	40.59 N	95.06 W
Stanton, KY	258	37.54 N	83.52 W
Stanton, MI	256	43.18 N	85.05 W
Stanton, NE	264	41.57 N	97.14 W
Stanton, ND	264	47.19 N	101.23 W
Stanton, TN	260	35.28 N	89.24 W
Stanton, TX	262	32.08 N	101.48 W
Stantonsburg	258	35.37 N	77.49 W
Stanwood	268	48.15 N	122.23 W
Staples	264	46.21 N	94.48 W
Stapleton, AL	260	30.45 N	87.48 W
Stapleton, NE	264	41.29 N	100.31 W
Star, MS	260	32.06 N	90.03 W
Star, NC	258	35.24 N	79.47 W
Starbuck, MB	250	49.46 N	97.36 W
Starbuck, MN	264	45.37 N	95.32 W
Starbuck, WA	268	47.31 N	118.08 W
Star City, SK	250	52.53 N	104.21 W
Star City, AR	260	33.56 N	91.51 W
Star City, IN	260	40.58 N	86.33 W
Stargo	266	33.04 N	109.21 W
Starke	258	29.57 N	82.07 W
Starkville	260	33.28 N	88.48 W
Star Peak	270	40.32 N	118.10 W
Starvation Reservoir	266	40.15 N	110.30 W
State Center	256	42.01 N	93.10 W
State College, MS	260	33.26 N	88.47 W
State College, PA	254	40.48 N	77.52 W
State Line, MS	260	31.26 N	88.28 W
Stateline, NV	270	38.57 N	119.57 W
Statenville	258	30.42 N	83.02 W
State Road	258	36.19 N	80.52 W
Statesboro	258	32.27 N	81.47 W
Statesville	258	35.47 N	80.53 W
Staunton, IL	260	39.01 N	89.47 W
Staunton, VA	254	38.09 N	79.04 W
Staunton → Roanoke	244	35.56 N	76.43 W
Stave Lake	248	49.15 N	122.21 W
Stavely	248	50.10 N	113.38 W
Stayner	256	44.25 N	80.05 W
Stayton	268	44.48 N	122.48 W
Steamboat Mountain	268	41.58 N	108.58 W
Steamboat Springs	266	40.29 N	106.50 W
Stearns	258	36.42 N	84.28 W
Stebbins	246	63.32 N	162.18 W
Steel	256	48.46 N	86.54 W
Steele, MO	260	36.05 N	89.50 W
Steele, ND	264	46.51 N	99.55 W
Steele, Mount	268	41.50 N	107.00 W
Steeleville	260	38.00 N	89.40 W
Steelville	260	37.58 N	91.22 W
Steens Mountain	268	42.35 N	118.40 W
Steephill Lake	250	55.58 N	103.08 W
Steep Rock	250	51.26 N	98.48 W
Stefansson Island	242	73.17 N	106.45 W
Steinbach	250	49.32 N	96.41 W
Steinhatchie	258	29.40 N	83.24 W
Stella	264	40.14 N	95.46 W
Stellaquo Indian Reserve	248	54.03 N	124.55 W
Stellarton	252	45.34 N	62.40 W
Steller, Mount	246	60.30 N	143.02 W
Stephen	264	48.27 N	96.53 W
Stephens	260	33.25 N	93.04 W
Stephens City	254	39.05 N	78.13 W
Stephens Island	248	54.10 N	130.45 W
Stephens Knob	258	36.37 N	84.20 W
Stephenson	256	45.20 N	87.38 W
Stephens Passage	246	57.50 N	133.50 W
Stephenville, NF	252	48.33 N	58.35 W
Stephenville, TX	262	32.13 N	98.12 W
Stephenville Crossing	252	48.30 N	58.26 W
Steptoe Valley	270	39.25 N	114.45 W
Sterling, AK	246	60.28 N	150.08 W
Sterling, CO	264	40.37 N	103.13 W
Sterling, IL	260	41.48 N	89.42 W
Sterling, KS	264	38.13 N	98.12 W
Sterling, MI	256	44.02 N	84.02 W
Sterling, NE	264	40.28 N	96.23 W
Sterling, OK	262	34.45 N	98.10 W
Sterling City	262	31.50 N	100.59 W
Sterling Reservoir	264	40.47 N	103.17 W
Sterlington	260	32.42 N	92.05 W
Stettler	248	52.19 N	112.43 W
Steubenville	254	40.22 N	80.37 W
Stevens Creek	258	33.34 N	82.03 W
Stevenson, AL	260	34.52 N	85.50 W
Stevenson, WA	268	45.42 N	121.53 W
Stevenson Entrance	246	57.45 N	152.20 W
Stevenson Lake	250	53.56 N	96.09 W
Stevens Pass	268	47.45 N	121.04 W
Stevens Peak	268	47.27 N	115.46 W
Stevens Point	256	44.31 N	89.34 W
Stevens Village	246	66.00 N	155.05 W
Stevensville, MI	256	42.01 N	86.31 W
Stevensville, MT	268	46.30 N	114.05 W
Stewardson	260	39.16 N	88.38 W
Stewart, BC	248	55.56 N	129.59 W
Stewart, MN	264	44.43 N	94.29 W
Stewart	246	63.18 N	139.25 W
Stewartstown	254	39.45 N	76.35 W
Stewartsville	260	39.45 N	94.30 W
Stewart Valley	250	50.36 N	107.50 W
Stewartville	256	43.51 N	92.29 W
Stewiacke	252	45.08 N	63.21 W
Stickney	264	43.35 N	98.26 W
Stigler	262	35.15 N	95.08 W
Stikine	242	56.40 N	132.30 W
Stikine Ranges	246	58.45 N	130.00 W
Stillhouse Hollow Lake	262	31.00 N	97.35 W
Stillmore	258	32.27 N	82.13 W
Stillwater, BC	248	49.46 N	124.18 W
Stillwater, MN	256	45.04 N	92.49 W
Stillwater, OK	262	36.07 N	97.04 W
Stillwater	268	45.38 N	109.17 W
Stillwater Range	270	39.50 N	118.15 W
Stillwell	260	35.49 N	94.38 W
Stimson, Mount	268	48.31 N	113.36 W
Stine Mountain	268	45.44 N	113.07 W
Stinking Water Creek	264	40.22 N	101.07 W
Stinnett	262	35.50 N	101.27 W
Stirling, AB	248	49.30 N	112.31 W
Stirling, ON	256	44.18 N	77.33 W
Stirling City	270	39.54 N	121.32 W
Stirrat	258	37.44 N	82.00 W
Stittsville	254	45.15 N	75.55 W
Stockbridge, GA	258	33.33 N	84.14 W
Stockbridge, MI	256	42.27 N	84.11 W
Stockbridge Indian Reservation	256	44.52 N	88.53 W
Stockdale	262	29.14 N	97.58 W
Stockett	268	47.21 N	111.10 W
Stockholm	252	47.03 N	68.08 W
Stockton, AL	260	31.00 N	87.52 W
Stockton, CA	270	37.57 N	121.17 W
Stockton, IL	256	42.21 N	90.01 W
Stockton, KS	264	39.26 N	99.16 W
Stockton, MO	260	37.42 N	93.48 W
Stockton, UT	266	40.27 N	112.22 W
Stockton Plateau	262	30.30 N	102.30 W
Stockton Reservoir	260	37.40 N	93.45 W
Stockton Springs	254	44.29 N	68.52 W
Stockville	264	40.32 N	100.23 W
Stoneboro	254	41.20 N	80.07 W
Stonefort	260	37.37 N	88.42 W
Stone Harbor	254	39.03 N	74.45 W
Stone Indian Reserve	248	51.54 N	123.12 W
Stone Mountain	258	33.49 N	84.10 W
Stone Mountain	254	44.34 N	71.40 W
Stone Mountain Memorial State Park	258	33.49 N	84.06 W
Stoner	248	53.36 N	122.40 W
Stones, East Fork	260	35.59 N	86.27 W
Stones, West Fork	260	35.59 N	86.27 W
Stones River National Battlefield	260	35.52 N	86.26 W
Stoneville	258	36.28 N	79.54 W
Stonewall, MB	250	50.09 N	97.21 W
Stonewall, LA	260	32.16 N	93.50 W
Stonewall, MS	260	32.08 N	88.47 W
Stonewall, OK	262	34.39 N	96.31 W
Stoney Creek	256	43.13 N	79.46 W
Stonington, IL	260	39.44 N	89.12 W
Stonington, ME	254	44.09 N	68.40 W
Stony, AK	246	61.45 N	156.35 W
Stony, MN	256	47.44 N	91.47 W

Symbols in the index entries are identified on page 273.

Name	Page	Lat °′	Long °′
Toba Inlet	248	50.20 N	124.50 W
Tobias	264	40.25 N	97.20 W
Tobin, Mount	270	40.22 N	117.32 W
Tobin Lake	250	53.40 N	103.35 W
Tobique	252	46.46 N	67.42 W
Tobyhanna	254	41.11 N	75.25 W
Toccoa	258	34.35 N	83.19 W
Toccoa	258	34.59 N	84.23 W
Tochcha Lake	248	54.56 N	125.54 W
Tofield	248	53.22 N	112.40 W
Tofino	248	49.09 N	125.54 W
Togiak	246	59.04 N	160.24 W
Togiak Bay	246	59.00 N	160.30 W
Togiak Lake	246	59.38 N	159.35 W
Togwotee Pass	268	43.45 N	110.04 W
Tohakum Peak	270	40.11 N	119.27 W
Tohopekaliga, Lake	258	28.12 N	81.23 W
Toiyabe Range	270	39.10 N	117.10 W
Tok	246	63.20 N	142.59 W
Toklat	246	64.27 N	150.17 W
Toksook Bay	246	60.32 N	165.06 W
Toledo, IL	260	39.16 N	88.15 W
Toledo, IA	256	42.00 N	92.35 W
Toledo, OH	254	41.39 N	83.32 W
Toledo, OR	268	44.37 N	123.56 W
Toledo Bend Reservoir	244	31.30 N	93.45 W
Tolleson	266	33.27 N	112.16 W
Tolono	260	39.59 N	88.16 W
Tolovana	246	64.51 N	149.45 W
Toluca	256	41.00 N	89.08 W
Tomah	256	43.59 N	90.30 W
Tomahawk	256	45.28 N	89.44 W
Tomasina	256	46.40 N	76.16 W
Tomball	262	30.06 N	95.37 W
Tombigbee	244	31.04 N	87.58 W
Tombstone	266	31.43 N	110.04 W
Tombstone Mountain	246	64.25 N	138.30 W
Tomichi Creek	266	38.31 N	106.58 W
Tomiko Lake	256	46.32 N	79.49 W
Tompkins, NF	252	47.48 N	59.13 W
Tompkins, SK	250	50.04 N	108.47 W
Tompkinsville	260	36.42 N	85.41 W
Toms	254	39.57 N	74.07 W
Toms River	254	39.58 N	74.12 W
Tonasket	268	48.42 N	119.26 W
Tonawanda	254	43.01 N	78.53 W
Tonganoxie	264	39.07 N	95.05 W
Tongue, U.S.	268	46.24 N	105.52 W
Tongue, ND	264	48.56 N	97.18 W
Tongue, TX	262	34.07 N	100.25 W
Tongue River Reservoir	268	45.06 N	106.47 W
Tonica	260	41.13 N	89.04 W
Tonkawa	262	36.41 N	97.18 W
Tonopah	270	38.04 N	117.14 W
Tonto Creek	266	33.46 N	111.15 W
Tonto National Monument	266	33.34 N	111.02 W
Tooele	266	40.32 N	112.18 W
Toolik	246	69.55 N	149.30 W
Toomsboro	258	32.50 N	83.05 W
Toosey Indian Reserve	248	51.56 N	122.29 W
Topawa	266	31.48 N	111.51 W
Topeka	264	39.03 N	95.41 W
Topley	248	54.49 N	126.18 W
Toppenish	268	46.23 N	120.19 W
Toppenish Creek	268	46.20 N	120.11 W
Topsham	254	43.56 N	69.58 W
Toquima Range	270	39.00 N	117.00 W
Toquop Wash	270	36.45 N	114.11 W
Torbay	252	47.40 N	52.44 W
Torbert, Mount	246	61.25 N	152.24 W
Torbrook	252	44.55 N	64.59 W
Torch	250	53.50 N	103.05 W
Torch Lake	256	45.00 N	85.19 W
Tornado Mountain	248	49.58 N	114.39 W
Torngat Mountains	242	59.00 N	64.00 W
Tornillo	266	31.27 N	106.05 W
Tornillo Creek	262	29.11 N	103.00 W
Toronto, ON	256	43.39 N	79.23 W
Toronto, KS	264	37.48 N	95.57 W
Toronto, OH	254	40.28 N	80.36 W
Toronto, SD	264	44.34 N	96.39 W
Toronto Lake	264	37.46 N	95.57 W
Toro Peak	270	33.32 N	116.25 W
Torquay	250	49.08 N	103.31 W
Torrance	270	33.50 N	118.19 W
Torrance Lake	250	57.04 N	98.12 W
Torres Martinez Indian Reservation	270	33.35 N	116.02 W
Torrington, CT	254	41.48 N	73.08 W
Torrington, WY	264	42.04 N	104.11 W
Tors Cove	252	47.13 N	52.51 W
Totagatic	256	46.05 N	92.11 W
Totson Mountain	246	64.26 N	157.15 W
Tottenham	256	44.01 N	79.49 W
Touchet	268	46.02 N	118.41 W
Touchwood Hills	250	51.35 N	104.17 W
Touchwood Lake, AB	250	54.50 N	111.23 W
Touchwood Lake, MB	250	54.29 N	95.00 W
Tougaloo	260	32.24 N	90.09 W
Toulnustouc	252	49.35 N	68.24 W
Toulnustouc-Nord-Est	252	50.56 N	67.44 W
Toulon	260	41.06 N	89.52 W
Toulon Lake	270	40.01 N	118.40 W
Touraine	254	45.34 N	75.47 W
Toutle	268	46.17 N	122.55 W
Toutle, South Fork	268	46.20 N	122.44 W
Tow	262	30.53 N	98.28 W
Towanda, KS	264	37.48 N	97.02 W
Towanda, PA	254	41.46 N	76.26 W
Towanda Creek	254	41.45 N	76.26 W
Tower	256	47.48 N	92.17 W
Tower City, ND	264	46.55 N	97.40 W
Tower City, PA	254	40.35 N	76.33 W
Tower Hill	260	39.23 N	88.58 W
Tower Soudan State Park	256	47.50 N	92.15 W
Town Creek	260	34.24 N	86.11 W
Towner	264	48.21 N	100.25 W
Townsend	268	46.19 N	111.31 W
Towson	254	39.24 N	76.36 W
Toyah	262	31.19 N	103.47 W
Toyah Creek	262	31.18 N	103.27 W
Tozi, Mount	246	65.41 N	150.58 W
Tozitna	246	65.08 N	152.23 W
Tracadie	252	47.31 N	64.54 W
Tracy, PQ	254	46.01 N	73.09 W
Tracy, CA	270	37.44 N	121.25 W
Tracy, MN	264	44.14 N	95.37 W
Tracy City	260	35.16 N	85.44 W
Trade Lake	250	55.22 N	103.44 W
Tradewater	260	37.31 N	88.03 W
Traer	256	42.12 N	92.28 W
Trail	248	49.06 N	117.42 W
Trail Ridge	258	30.35 N	82.05 W
Trammel	258	37.01 N	82.18 W
Trammel Creek	260	36.52 N	86.23 W
Tramperos Creek (Punta de Agua Creek), U.S.	262	35.32 N	102.27 W
Tramperos Creek, NM	262	36.05 N	103.15 W
Tranters Creek	258	35.33 N	77.05 W
Trapper Peak	268	45.54 N	114.18 W
Traverse, Lake	264	45.43 N	96.40 W
Traverse Bay	250	50.40 N	96.25 W
Traverse City	256	44.46 N	85.37 W
Traverse Peak	246	65.10 N	159.12 W
Travers Reservoir	248	50.14 N	112.51 W
Travis, Lake	262	30.27 N	98.00 W
Travis Air Force Base	270	38.16 N	121.55 W
Treble Mountain	248	55.50 N	129.51 W
Treherne	250	49.38 N	98.41 W
Tremblant, Mont	254	46.16 N	74.35 W
Trembleur Lake	248	54.51 N	125.07 W
Tremont, IL	256	40.28 N	89.29 W
Tremont, PA	254	40.38 N	76.23 W
Tremonton	266	41.43 N	112.10 W
Trempealeau	256	44.00 N	91.26 W
Trempealeau	256	44.02 N	91.32 W
Trent, ON	256	44.06 N	77.34 W
Trent, NC	258	35.05 N	77.02 W
Trente-et-un-Milles, Lac des	254	46.12 N	75.49 W
Trenton, NS	252	45.37 N	62.38 W
Trenton, ON	256	44.06 N	77.35 W
Trenton, FL	258	29.37 N	82.49 W
Trenton, GA	258	34.52 N	85.31 W
Trenton, KY	260	36.43 N	87.16 W
Trenton, MO	260	40.05 N	93.37 W
Trenton, NE	264	40.11 N	101.01 W
Trenton, NJ	254	40.13 N	74.45 W
Trenton, NC	258	35.04 N	77.21 W
Trenton, TN	260	35.59 N	88.56 W
Trenton, TX	262	33.26 N	96.20 W
Trentwood	268	47.42 N	117.13 W
Trepassey	252	46.44 N	53.22 W
Trepassey Bay	252	46.40 N	52.20 W
Tres Montosas	266	34.06 N	107.28 W
Tres Palacio	262	28.45 N	96.09 W
Trevorton	254	40.47 N	76.41 W
Trevose	254	40.09 N	74.59 W
Trezevant	260	36.01 N	88.37 W
Triangle	254	38.33 N	77.20 W
Tribune, SK	250	49.15 N	103.50 W
Tribune, KS	264	38.28 N	101.45 W
Tribune Channel	248	50.50 N	126.16 W
Tri County Supply Canal	264	40.49 N	100.06 W
Trident Peak	270	41.54 N	118.25 W
Trigo Mountains	266	33.15 N	114.35 W
Trilby	258	28.28 N	82.12 W
Trimont	264	43.45 N	94.45 W
Trinchera Creek	266	37.19 N	105.45 W
Trinidad, CO	264	37.10 N	104.31 W
Trinidad, TX	262	32.09 N	96.06 W
Trinity, NF	252	48.59 N	53.55 W
Trinity, TX	262	30.57 N	95.22 W
Trinity, CA	270	41.11 N	123.42 W
Trinity, TX	260	29.47 N	94.42 W
Trinity, Clear Fork	262	32.46 N	97.21 W
Trinity, Elm Fork	262	32.47 N	96.54 W
Trinity, South Fork	270	40.54 N	123.35 W
Trinity, West Fork	262	32.48 N	96.51 W
Trinity Bay, NF	252	48.00 N	53.40 W
Trinity Bay, TX	260	29.40 N	94.45 W
Trinity Islands	246	56.33 N	154.25 W
Trinity Mountain	268	43.36 N	115.26 W
Trinity Mountains	270	41.00 N	122.30 W
Trinity Peak	270	40.14 N	118.45 W
Trion	258	34.33 N	85.19 W
Tripoli	256	42.48 N	92.16 W
Tripp	264	43.13 N	97.58 W
Triumph	260	29.20 N	89.30 W
Trochu	248	51.50 N	113.13 W
Trois-Rivières	254	46.21 N	72.33 W
Trona	270	35.45 N	117.23 W
Trophy Mountain	248	51.47 N	119.48 W
Tropic	266	37.37 N	112.05 W
Trotwood	254	39.48 N	84.18 W
Troublesome Creek	258	37.29 N	83.21 W
Troup	262	32.09 N	95.07 W
Trout	260	31.42 N	92.11 W
Trout	242	61.19 N	119.51 W
Trout Creek, MI	256	46.28 N	89.01 W
Trout Creek, MT	248	47.50 N	115.36 W
Trout Creek, AZ	266	34.56 N	113.36 W
Trout Creek, OR	268	44.48 N	121.03 W
Trout Creek, OR	268	42.23 N	118.36 W
Trout Creek Pass	266	38.54 N	105.58 W
Trout Lake, BC	248	50.35 N	117.26 W
Trout Lake, NT	242	60.35 N	121.10 W
Trout Lake, ON	250	51.13 N	93.20 W
Trout Lake, ON	256	46.18 N	79.20 W
Trout Lake, ON	256	46.13 N	80.35 W
Trout Peak	268	44.36 N	109.32 W
Trout River	252	49.29 N	58.08 W
Troutville	258	37.25 N	79.53 W
Troy, AL	260	31.48 N	85.58 W
Troy, ID	268	46.44 N	116.46 W
Troy, IN	260	38.00 N	86.49 W
Troy, KS	264	39.47 N	95.05 W
Troy, MO	260	38.59 N	90.59 W
Troy, MT	268	48.28 N	115.53 W
Troy, NH	254	42.50 N	72.11 W
Troy, NC	258	35.22 N	79.53 W
Troy, NY	254	42.43 N	73.40 W
Troy, OH	254	40.02 N	84.13 W
Troy, PA	254	41.47 N	76.47 W
Troy, TN	260	36.20 N	89.10 W
Troy, TX	262	31.12 N	97.18 W
Troy Lake	270	34.49 N	116.33 W
Troy Peak	270	38.19 N	115.30 W
Truax	250	49.55 N	104.58 W
Truchas	266	36.03 N	105.49 W
Truchas Peak	266	35.58 N	105.39 W
Truckee	270	39.20 N	120.11 W
Truckee	270	39.51 N	119.24 W
Truite, Lac à la	256	47.16 N	78.17 W
Trujillo Creek	262	35.28 N	102.52 W
Truman	264	43.50 N	94.26 W
Trumann	260	35.41 N	90.31 W
Trumansburg	254	42.33 N	76.40 W
Trumbull	254	41.15 N	73.12 W
Trumbull, Mount	266	36.25 N	113.10 W
Truro	252	45.22 N	63.16 W
Truscott	262	33.45 N	99.49 W
Truth or Consequences (Hot Springs)	266	33.08 N	107.15 W
Truxton Wash	266	35.38 N	114.04 W
Tryon, NE	264	41.33 N	100.57 W
Tryon, NC	258	35.13 N	82.14 W
Tsacha Lake	248	53.05 N	124.40 W
Tsala Apopka Lake	258	28.52 N	82.20 W
Tsaydaychuz Peak	248	53.02 N	126.35 W
Tschida, Lake	264	46.36 N	101.54 W
Tsimpsean Indian Reserve	248	54.30 N	130.22 W
Tsitsutl Peak	248	52.44 N	125.47 W
Tualatin	268	45.20 N	122.39 W
Tubac	266	31.37 N	111.03 W
Tuba City	266	36.08 N	111.14 W
Tucannon	268	46.33 N	118.11 W
Tuckerman	260	35.44 N	91.12 W
Tuckerton	254	39.36 N	74.20 W
Tucson	266	32.13 N	110.58 W
Tucumcari	262	35.10 N	103.44 W
Tucumcari Mountain	262	35.08 N	103.42 W
Tugaske	250	50.53 N	106.16 W
Tug Fork	258	38.06 N	82.36 W
Tugidak Island	246	56.30 N	154.36 W
Tuktoyaktuk	242	69.27 N	133.02 W
Tulare, CA	270	36.13 N	119.21 W
Tulare, SD	264	44.44 N	98.31 W
Tulare Lake Bed	270	36.03 N	119.49 W
Tularosa	266	33.04 N	106.01 W
Tularosa	266	33.41 N	108.46 W
Tularosa Valley	266	32.45 N	106.10 W
Tule	270	36.03 N	119.50 W
Tule Creek	262	34.40 N	101.14 W
Tulelake	270	41.57 N	121.29 W
Tule Lake Sump	270	41.54 N	121.32 W
Tule River Indian Reservation	270	36.02 N	118.42 W
Tule Valley	266	39.20 N	113.25 W
Tulia	262	34.32 N	101.46 W
Tulik Volcano	246	53.22 N	168.03 W
Tullahoma	260	35.22 N	86.11 W
Tullock Creek	268	46.08 N	107.27 W
Tullos	260	31.49 N	92.19 W
Tulsa	262	36.09 N	95.58 W
Tulsequah	242	58.35 N	133.35 W
Tuluksak	246	61.06 N	160.58 W
Tumacacori National Monument	266	31.25 N	111.01 W
Tumble Mountain	268	45.19 N	110.02 W
Tumwater	268	47.01 N	122.54 W
Tunago Lake	246	66.18 N	125.50 W
Tunas Creek	262	31.01 N	102.11 W
Tungsten	246	62.00 N	127.40 W
Tunica	260	34.41 N	90.23 W
Tunkhannock	254	41.32 N	75.57 W
Tunnel Hill	258	34.51 N	85.03 W
Tunnelton	254	39.24 N	79.45 W
Tuntutuliak	246	60.22 N	162.38 W
Tununak	246	60.35 N	165.16 W
Tunungayualok Island	242	56.05 N	61.05 W
Tuolumne	270	37.58 N	120.14 W
Tuolumne	270	37.36 N	121.10 W
Tupelo, MS	260	34.16 N	88.43 W
Tupelo, OK	262	34.37 N	96.26 W
Tupelo National Battlefield	260	34.13 N	88.44 W
Tupper	248	55.31 N	120.02 W
Tupper Lake	254	44.13 N	74.29 W
Turin	248	49.58 N	112.31 W
Turkey	262	34.23 N	100.54 W
Turkey	256	42.43 N	91.01 W
Turkey Creek, U.S.	264	39.58 N	96.02 W
Turkey Creek, IA	264	41.20 N	95.05 W
Turkey Creek, KS	264	38.53 N	97.11 W
Turkey Creek, NE	264	40.23 N	96.53 W
Turkey Creek, OK	262	35.58 N	97.56 W
Turkey Creek, TX	262	28.42 N	99.58 W
Turkey Run State Park	260	39.54 N	87.13 W
Turley	262	36.14 N	95.58 W
Turlock	270	37.30 N	120.51 W
Turnagain	246	59.06 N	127.35 W
Turnagain Arm	246	61.00 N	150.00 W
Turnbull, Mount	266	33.04 N	110.16 W
Turnbull Dry Lake	268	43.10 N	118.00 W
Turner, MT	268	48.51 N	108.24 W
Turner, OR	268	44.51 N	122.57 W
Turners Falls	254	42.36 N	72.33 W
Turner Valley	248	50.40 N	114.17 W
Turnor Lake	250	56.32 N	108.38 W
Turon	264	37.48 N	98.26 W
Turrell	260	35.23 N	90.15 W
Turret Peak	266	34.15 N	111.53 W
Turtle, MB	250	51.07 N	99.39 W
Turtle, ON	250	48.51 N	92.45 W
Turtle, ND	264	48.20 N	97.08 W
Turtle, North Branch	264	47.57 N	97.35 W
Turtle Creek	252	45.58 N	64.53 W
Turtle Creek, SD	264	44.55 N	98.29 W
Turtle Creek, WI	256	42.29 N	89.03 W
Turtle Flambeau Flowage	256	46.05 N	90.11 W
Turtleford	250	53.23 N	108.56 W
Turtle Lake, ND	264	47.31 N	100.53 W
Turtle Lake, WI	256	45.24 N	92.08 W
Turtle Lake	250	53.35 N	108.40 W
Turtle Mountain Indian Reservation	264	48.51 N	99.45 W
Turtle Mountain Provincial Park	250	49.03 N	100.15 W
Tusas, Rio	266	36.23 N	106.03 W
Tuscaloosa	260	33.13 N	87.33 W
Tuscarora Mountain	254	40.10 N	77.45 W
Tuscarora Mountains	270	41.00 N	116.20 W
Tuscola, IL	260	39.48 N	88.17 W
Tuscola, TX	262	32.12 N	99.48 W
Tuscumbia, AL	260	34.44 N	87.42 W
Tuscumbia, MO	260	38.14 N	92.28 W
Tuskegee	260	32.26 N	85.42 W
Tustumena Lake	246	60.12 N	150.50 W
Tuttle, ND	264	47.09 N	100.00 W
Tuttle, OK	262	35.17 N	97.49 W
Tuttle Creek Lake	264	39.22 N	96.40 W
Tututalak Mountain	246	67.46 N	161.10 W
Tutwiler	260	34.01 N	90.26 W
Tuxford	250	50.35 N	105.35 W
Tuya	242	58.05 N	130.50 W
Tuzigoot National Monument	266	34.40 N	111.52 W
Tweed	256	44.29 N	77.19 W
Tweedsmuir Provincial Park	248	52.55 N	126.05 W
Tweedy Mountain	268	45.29 N	112.58 W
Twelve Mile Lake	250	49.29 N	106.14 W
Twentyfive Mile Wash	266	37.33 N	111.07 W
Twentynine Palms	270	34.08 N	116.03 W
Twentynine Palms Marine Corps Base	270	34.25 N	116.10 W
Twillingate	252	49.39 N	54.46 W
Twin Bridges	268	45.33 N	112.20 W
Twin Butte Creek	264	38.46 N	100.56 W
Twin Buttes	268	44.20 N	122.15 W
Twin Buttes Reservoir	262	31.20 N	100.35 W
Twin City	258	32.35 N	82.10 W
Twin Creek	254	39.33 N	84.21 W
Twin Falls	268	42.34 N	114.28 W
Twin Hills	246	59.23 N	159.58 W
Twin Lakes, GA	258	30.42 N	83.12 W
Twin Lakes, WI	256	42.32 N	88.15 W
Twin Peaks	268	44.35 N	114.29 W
Twinsburg	254	41.19 N	81.27 W
Twin Valley	264	47.16 N	96.16 W
Twisp	268	48.22 N	120.07 W
Twitchell Reservoir	270	35.00 N	120.19 W
Twitya	242	64.10 N	128.12 W
Two Butte Creek	264	38.02 N	102.08 W
Two Harbors	256	47.01 N	91.40 W
Two Hills	250	53.43 N	111.45 W
Two Medicine	268	48.29 N	112.14 W
Two River Lake	250	53.52 N	91.27 W
Two Rivers	256	44.09 N	87.34 W
Two Rivers	264	48.49 N	97.09 W
Two Rivers Reservoir	262	33.17 N	104.45 W
Tye	262	32.27 N	99.52 W
Tyende Creek	266	36.50 N	109.43 W
Tygarts Creek	254	38.43 N	82.57 W
Tygh Valley	268	45.15 N	121.10 W
Tyler, MN	264	44.17 N	96.08 W
Tyler, TX	262	32.21 N	95.18 W
Tylertown	260	31.07 N	90.09 W
Tyndall	264	42.59 N	97.52 W
Tyndall Air Force Base	260	30.04 N	85.35 W
Tyonek	246	61.02 N	151.17 W
Tyrone, OK	262	36.57 N	101.04 W
Tyrone, PA	254	40.40 N	78.14 W
Ty Ty	258	31.28 N	83.39 W
U			
Uaoa Bay	272a	20.56 N	156.16 W
Ubly	256	43.43 N	82.56 W
Uchi Lake	250	51.05 N	92.35 W
Ucluelet	248	48.57 N	125.33 W
Ucon	268	43.36 N	111.58 W
Udall	264	37.23 N	97.07 W
Ugak Bay	246	57.25 N	152.45 W
Uganik Island	246	57.53 N	153.28 W
Ugashik	246	57.32 N	157.25 W
Ugashik Bay	246	57.34 N	157.38 W
Ugyak, Cape	246	58.17 N	154.04 W
Uhlman Lake	250	56.40 N	98.23 W
Uhrichsville	254	40.24 N	81.20 W
Uinta	266	40.14 N	109.51 W
Uintah and Ouray Indian Reservation	266	40.20 N	110.20 W
Uinta Mountains	266	40.45 N	110.05 W
Ukiah, CA	270	39.09 N	123.13 W
Ukiah, OR	268	45.08 N	118.56 W
Ukolnoi Island	246	55.14 N	161.34 W
Ulak Island	247a	51.22 N	179.00 W
Ulen	264	47.05 N	96.16 W
Ullin	260	37.17 N	89.11 W
Ulm	268	47.26 N	111.30 W
Ulysses, KS	264	37.35 N	101.22 W
Ulysses, NE	264	41.04 N	97.12 W
Umatilla, FL	258	28.55 N	81.40 W
Umatilla, OR	268	45.55 N	119.21 W
Umatilla	268	45.55 N	119.20 W
Umatilla, Lake	268	45.44 N	120.35 W
Umatilla Indian Reservation	268	45.41 N	118.31 W
Umfreville Lake	250	50.18 N	94.45 W
Umnak Island	246	53.25 N	168.10 W
Umnak Pass	246	53.20 N	167.45 W
Umpqua	268	43.42 N	124.03 W
Umstead State Park	258	35.52 N	78.47 W
Unadilla, GA	258	32.16 N	83.44 W
Unadilla, NY	254	42.20 N	75.19 W
Unadilla	254	42.20 N	75.25 W
Unalakleet	246	63.53 N	160.47 W
Unalaska	246	53.52 N	166.32 W
Unalaska Island	246	53.45 N	166.45 W
Uncompahgre	266	38.45 N	108.06 W
Uncompahgre Peak	266	38.04 N	107.28 W
Uncompahgre Plateau	266	38.30 N	108.25 W
Underwood	264	47.27 N	101.08 W
Unga Island	246	55.15 N	160.45 W
Ungava, Peninsule d'	242	60.00 N	74.00 W
Ungava Bay	242	59.30 N	67.30 W
Unicoi	258	36.12 N	82.21 W
Unimak Island	246	54.50 N	164.00 W
Unimak Pass	246	54.35 N	164.43 W
Union, IA	256	42.15 N	93.04 W
Union, LA	260	30.06 N	90.54 W
Union, ME	254	44.13 N	69.17 W
Union, MS	260	32.34 N	89.14 W
Union, MO	260	38.27 N	91.00 W
Union, NJ	254	40.42 N	74.16 W
Union, OR	268	45.13 N	117.52 W
Union, SC	258	34.43 N	81.37 W
Union, WA	268	47.21 N	123.06 W
Union, WV	258	37.36 N	80.33 W
Union Bay	248	49.35 N	124.53 W
Union City, GA	258	33.35 N	84.33 W
Union City, IN	260	40.12 N	84.49 W
Union City, MI	256	42.04 N	85.08 W
Union City, OH	254	40.10 N	84.48 W
Union City, PA	254	41.54 N	79.51 W
Union City, TN	260	36.26 N	89.03 W
Union Gap	268	46.34 N	120.34 W
Union Grove	256	42.41 N	88.03 W
Union Park	258	28.30 N	81.15 W
Union Point	258	33.37 N	83.04 W
Union Springs, AL	260	32.09 N	85.49 W
Union Springs, NY	254	42.50 N	76.42 W
Uniontown, AL	260	32.22 N	87.31 W
Uniontown, KY	260	37.46 N	87.56 W
Uniontown, PA	254	39.54 N	79.44 W
Unionville, MI	256	43.39 N	83.28 W
Unionville, MO	260	40.29 N	93.01 W
Unipouheos Indian Reserve	250	53.52 N	110.21 W
United	254	40.13 N	79.31 W
United States	244	38.00 N	97.00 W
United States Air Force Academy	264	39.00 N	104.55 W
United States Military Academy	254	41.23 N	73.28 W
United States Naval Academy	254	38.59 N	76.30 W
Unity, SK	250	52.27 N	109.10 W
Unity, ME	254	44.40 N	69.14 W
Universal City	262	29.33 N	98.17 W
University	260	34.21 N	89.32 W
University City	260	38.39 N	90.19 W
University Park, NM	266	32.17 N	106.45 W
University Park, TX	262	32.52 N	96.47 W
Upatoi Creek	258	32.22 N	84.58 W
Upham	264	48.35 N	100.44 W
Upland	264	40.19 N	98.54 W
Upnuk Lake	246	60.21 N	158.58 W
Upolu Point	272	20.16 N	155.51 W
Upper Arlington	254	40.00 N	83.03 W
Upper Arrow Lake	248	50.30 N	117.55 W
Upper Blackville	252	46.39 N	65.52 W
Upper Darby	254	39.58 N	75.16 W
Upper Fraser	248	54.07 N	121.56 W
Upper Goose Lake	250	51.44 N	92.44 W
Upper Hat Creek	248	50.38 N	121.35 W
Upper Humber	252	49.10 N	57.28 W
Upper Iowa	256	43.29 N	91.14 W
Upper Island Cove	252	47.39 N	53.12 W
Upper Keechi Creek	262	31.23 N	95.42 W
Upper Klamath Lake	268	42.23 N	122.55 W
Upper Lake	270	39.10 N	122.54 W
Upper Lake	270	41.44 N	120.08 W
Upper Liard	246	60.02 N	128.55 W
Upper Manitou Lake	250	49.24 N	92.48 W
Upper Musquodoboit	252	45.08 N	62.57 W
Upper Red Lake	264	48.10 N	94.40 W
Upper Sandusky	254	40.50 N	83.17 W
Upper Sheila	252	47.28 N	64.56 W
Upper Ugashik Lake	246	57.40 N	156.43 W
Upper Windigo Lake	250	52.30 N	91.35 W
Upright, Cape	246	60.17 N	172.15 W
Upton, KY	260	37.27 N	85.53 W
Upton, WY	264	44.06 N	104.38 W
Urania	260	31.52 N	92.18 W
Uranium City	242	59.34 N	108.36 W
Uravan	266	38.22 N	108.44 W
Urbana, AR	260	33.11 N	92.25 W
Urbana, IL	260	40.07 N	88.12 W
Urbana, MO	260	37.51 N	93.10 W
Urbana, OH	254	40.07 N	83.45 W
Urbandale	256	41.38 N	93.48 W
Uriah	260	31.18 N	87.30 W
Urich	260	38.28 N	94.02 W
Ursa	260	40.04 N	91.22 W
Usibelli	246	63.51 N	148.47 W
Usk, BC	248	54.38 N	128.25 W
Usk, WA	268	48.19 N	117.17 W
Utah, U.S.	244		
	266	39.30 N	111.30 W
Utah Lake	266	40.13 N	111.49 W
Ute	264	42.03 N	95.42 W
Ute Creek	262	35.21 N	103.50 W
Ute Mountain Indian Reservation	266	37.10 N	108.35 W
Ute Reservoir	262	36.21 N	103.31 W
Utica, KS	264	38.39 N	100.10 W
Utica, MI	256	42.38 N	83.02 W
Utica, MS	260	32.07 N	90.37 W
Utica, NE	264	40.54 N	97.21 W
Utica, NY	254	43.05 N	75.14 W
Utica, OH	254	40.14 N	82.27 W
Utik Lake	250	55.16 N	96.00 W
Utikoomak Indian Reserve	248	55.57 N	115.30 W
Utikuma Lake	248	55.50 N	115.25 W
Utopia	262	29.37 N	99.32 W
Utukok	246	70.04 N	162.18 W
Uvalda	258	32.02 N	82.31 W
Uvalde	262	29.13 N	99.47 W
Uxbridge	256	44.06 N	79.07 W
Uyak	246	57.38 N	154.00 W
Uyak Bay	246	57.36 N	153.57 W
V			
Vacaville	270	38.21 N	121.59 W
Vaiden	260	33.20 N	89.45 W
Vail, CO	266	39.38 N	106.21 W
Vail, IA	264	42.04 N	95.12 W
Valatie	254	42.25 N	73.41 W
Valders	256	44.09 N	87.53 W
Val-des-Bois	254	45.54 N	75.35 W
Valdese	258	35.44 N	81.34 W
Valdez	246	61.07 N	146.16 W
Val-d'Or	242	48.07 N	77.47 W
Valdosta	258	30.50 N	83.17 W
Vale	268	43.59 N	117.15 W
Valemount	248	52.50 N	119.15 W
Valentine, NE	264	42.52 N	100.33 W
Valentine, TX	262	30.34 N	104.29 W
Valets, Lac	256	48.32 N	76.30 W
Valier, IL	260	38.01 N	89.03 W
Valier, MT	268	48.18 N	112.15 W
Vallecitos	266	36.30 N	106.01 W
Vallejo	270	38.07 N	122.14 W
Valles Caldera	266	35.52 N	106.33 W
Valley	264	41.19 N	96.21 W
Valley Bend	254	38.46 N	79.56 W
Valley Center	264	37.50 N	97.22 W
Valley City	264	46.55 N	97.59 W
Valley Creek	262	31.43 N	100.02 W
Valley Falls	264	39.21 N	95.28 W
Valley Farms	266	32.59 N	111.27 W
Valleyfield, NF	252	49.08 N	53.37 W
Valleyfield, PQ	254	45.15 N	74.08 W
Valley Forge National Historical Park	254	40.06 N	75.27 W
Valley Head, AL	258	34.34 N	85.37 W
Valley Head, WV	254	38.33 N	80.02 W
Valley Mills	262	31.39 N	97.28 W
Valley of Fire State Park	270	36.26 N	114.30 W
Valley Springs	264	43.35 N	96.28 W
Valley Station	260	38.06 N	85.52 W
Valleyview, AB	248	55.04 N	117.17 W
Valley View, TX	262	33.29 N	97.10 W
Valliant	262	34.00 N	95.02 W
Val-Marie	250	49.14 N	107.44 W
Valmeyer	260	38.18 N	90.19 W
Valparaiso, FL	260	30.29 N	86.30 W
Valparaiso, IN	260	41.28 N	87.03 W
Valparaiso, NE	264	41.05 N	96.50 W
Valsetz	268	44.50 N	123.39 W
Van	262	32.31 N	95.38 W
Van Alstyne	262	33.25 N	96.35 W
Vananda	248	49.45 N	124.33 W
Van Buren, AR	260	35.26 N	94.21 W
Van Buren, ME	252	47.09 N	67.56 W
Van Buren, MO	260	37.00 N	91.01 W
Vance Air Force Base	262	36.21 N	97.55 W
Vanceboro	254	45.34 N	67.26 W
Vanceburg	254	38.36 N	83.19 W
Vancleave	260	30.32 N	88.46 W
Vancouver, BC	248	49.16 N	123.07 W
Vancouver, WA	268	45.39 N	122.40 W
Vancouver, Cape	246	60.33 N	165.27 W
Vancouver, Mount	246	60.20 N	139.40 W
Vancouver Island	248	49.45 N	126.00 W
Vancouver Island Ranges	248	49.25 N	125.25 W
Vandalia, IL	260	38.58 N	89.06 W
Vandalia, MO	260	39.19 N	91.29 W
Vandalia, OH	254	39.53 N	84.12 W
Vandekerckhove Lake	250	57.02 N	101.25 W
Vandenberg Air Force Base	270	34.43 N	120.33 W
Vanderbilt, MI	256	45.09 N	84.40 W
Vanderbilt, TX	262	28.49 N	96.37 W
Vandergrift	254	40.36 N	79.34 W
Vanderhoof	248	54.01 N	124.01 W
Vandervoort	260	34.23 N	94.22 W
Van Duzen	270	40.33 N	124.08 W
Vanguard	250	49.55 N	107.20 W
Van Hook Arm	264	47.50 N	102.25 W
Van Horn	262	31.03 N	104.50 W
Van Horne	256	42.01 N	92.05 W
Vanier	254	45.26 N	75.40 W
Vankleek Hill	254	45.31 N	74.39 W
Van Lear	258	37.46 N	82.46 W
Vanndale	260	35.19 N	90.46 W
Vansant	258	37.14 N	82.06 W
Vansittart Island	242	65.50 N	84.00 W
Van Vleck	262	29.01 N	95.53 W
Van Wert	254	40.52 N	84.35 W
Van Winkle	260	32.17 N	90.15 W
Vardaman	260	33.47 N	89.10 W
Varnville	258	32.51 N	81.05 W
Vashon Island	268	47.24 N	122.27 W
Vass	258	35.15 N	79.17 W
Vassar	256	43.22 N	83.35 W
Vaughan	256	43.47 N	79.36 W
Vaughn	266	34.36 N	105.13 W
Vauxhall	248	50.04 N	112.07 W
Veazie	254	44.51 N	68.42 W
Veblen	264	45.52 N	97.17 W
Veedersburg	260	40.07 N	87.16 W
Vega	262	35.15 N	102.26 W
Vega Point	247a	51.49 N	177.16 E
Vegreville	248	53.30 N	112.03 W
Veguita	266	34.31 N	106.46 W
Velma	262	34.28 N	97.40 W
Velva	264	48.04 N	100.56 W
Venetie	246	66.30 N	147.26 W
Veniaminof, Mount	246	56.13 N	159.18 W
Venice, FL	258	27.06 N	82.27 W
Venice, LA	260	29.17 N	89.21 W
Ventura	270	34.17 N	119.18 W
Venus	258	27.04 N	81.21 W
Verde	266	33.33 N	111.40 W
Verden	262	35.05 N	98.05 W
Verdi	270	39.31 N	119.59 W
Verdigre	264	42.36 N	98.02 W
Verdigre Creek	264	42.42 N	98.03 W
Verdigris	260	35.48 N	95.19 W
Verdon	264	40.08 N	95.48 W
Verdun	254	45.27 N	73.34 W
Vergennes	254	44.10 N	73.15 W
Verigin	250	51.35 N	102.08 W
Vermejo	262	36.30 N	104.33 W
Vermette Lake	250	55.40 N	109.05 W
Vermilion, AB	250	53.22 N	110.51 W
Vermilion, OH	254	41.25 N	82.22 W
Vermilion, AB	250	53.44 N	110.18 W
Vermilion, ON	256	46.16 N	81.41 W
Vermilion, IL	260	41.19 N	89.04 W
Vermilion, LA	260	29.46 N	92.09 W
Vermilion, MN	256	48.16 N	92.30 W
Vermilion Bay	250	49.51 N	93.24 W
Vermilion Bay	260	29.40 N	92.00 W
Vermilion Hills	250	50.43 N	106.50 W
Vermilion Lake, ON	250	50.03 N	92.13 W
Vermilion Lake, MN	256	47.53 N	92.25 W
Vermilion Range	256	47.50 N	92.00 W
Vermillion	264	42.47 N	96.56 W
Vermillion, MN	256	44.45 N	92.51 W
Vermillion, SD	264	42.44 N	96.53 W
Vermillion, East Fork	264	43.44 N	97.03 W
Vermillion, West Fork	264	43.44 N	97.03 W
Vermillion Bluffs	266	40.50 N	108.30 W
Vermillion Creek, U.S.	268	40.45 N	108.45 W
Vermillion Creek, KS	264	39.12 N	96.13 W
Vermont	260	40.18 N	90.26 W
Vermont, U.S.	244		
	254	43.50 N	72.45 W
Vernal	266	40.27 N	109.32 W
Verndale	264	46.24 N	95.01 W
Verner	256	46.25 N	80.07 W
Vernon, BC	248	50.16 N	119.16 W
Vernon, AL	260	33.45 N	88.07 W
Vernon, CT	254	41.52 N	72.27 W
Vernon, FL	260	30.37 N	85.43 W
Vernon, IN	260	38.59 N	85.36 W
Vernon, TX	262	34.09 N	99.17 W
Vernon, UT	266	40.06 N	112.26 W
Vernonia	268	45.52 N	123.11 W
Vernon Lake	260	31.15 N	93.25 W
Vernon River	252	46.12 N	62.50 W
Vero Beach	258	27.38 N	80.24 W
Verona, ON	256	44.29 N	76.42 W
Verona, MS	260	34.12 N	88.43 W
Verona, WI	256	42.59 N	89.32 W
Versailles, IL	260	39.53 N	90.39 W
Versailles, IN	260	39.04 N	85.15 W
Versailles, KY	254	38.03 N	84.44 W
Versailles, MO	260	38.26 N	92.51 W
Versailles, OH	254	40.13 N	84.29 W
Vestavia Hills	260	33.27 N	86.47 W
Vevay	260	38.45 N	85.04 W
Vian	260	35.30 N	94.58 W
Vibank	250	50.20 N	103.55 W
Viborg	264	43.10 N	97.05 W
Viburnum	260	37.43 N	91.08 W
Vicco	258	37.13 N	83.04 W
Viceroy	250	49.27 N	105.22 W
Vici	262	36.09 N	99.18 W
Vicksburg, MI	256	42.06 N	85.32 W
Vicksburg, MS	260	32.14 N	90.56 W
Vicksburg National Military Park	260	32.24 N	90.52 W
Victor, ID	268	43.36 N	111.07 W
Victor, IA	256	41.44 N	92.18 W
Victor, MT	268	46.25 N	114.09 W
Victor, Lac	252	50.35 N	61.50 W
Victoria, BC	248	48.25 N	123.22 W
Victoria, PE	252	46.13 N	63.29 W
Victoria, KS	264	38.52 N	99.09 W
Victoria, TX	262	28.48 N	97.00 W
Victoria, VA	258	36.59 N	78.14 W
Victoria	252	48.45 N	56.40 W
Victoria Beach	250	50.43 N	96.33 W
Victoria Harbour	256	44.45 N	79.46 W
Victoria Island	242	71.00 N	114.00 W
Victoria Lake	252	48.18 N	57.30 W
Victoria Peak	248	50.03 N	126.06 W
Victoria Strait	242	69.15 N	100.30 W
Victoriaville	254	46.03 N	71.57 W
Victorville	270	34.32 N	117.18 W
Vidalia, GA	258	32.13 N	82.25 W
Vidalia, LA	260	31.34 N	91.26 W
Vidor	260	30.07 N	94.01 W
Vieillard, Lac du	256	47.23 N	78.02 W
Vienna, GA	258	32.06 N	83.47 W
Vienna, IL	260	37.25 N	88.54 W
Vienna, MD	254	38.29 N	75.49 W
Vienna, MO	260	38.11 N	91.57 W
Vienna, SD	264	44.42 N	97.30 W
Vienna, WV	254	39.20 N	81.26 W
Viking	250	53.06 N	111.46 W
Village Creek	260	35.28 N	91.19 W
Villa Grove	260	39.52 N	88.10 W
Villanueva	266	35.17 N	105.23 W
Villa Rica	258	33.44 N	84.55 W
Villas	254	39.02 N	74.56 W
Villebon, Lac	256	47.58 N	77.17 W
Ville-Marie	256	47.19 N	79.26 W
Ville Platte	260	30.42 N	92.16 W
Ville-Saint-Georges	254	46.07 N	70.40 W
Villisca	264	40.56 N	94.59 W
Vilna	250	54.07 N	111.55 W
Vina	270	39.56 N	122.03 W
Vinalhaven	254	44.03 N	68.50 W
Vinalhaven Island	254	44.05 N	68.52 W
Vincennes	260	38.41 N	87.32 W
Vincent	260	33.23 N	86.25 W
Vinegar Hill	268	44.43 N	118.34 W
Vine Grove	260	37.49 N	85.59 W
Vineland	254	39.29 N	75.02 W
Vinemont	260	34.10 N	86.52 W
Vineyard Haven	254	41.27 N	70.36 W
Vineyard Sound	254	41.25 N	70.46 W
Vinita	262	36.39 N	95.09 W
Vinton, IA	256	42.10 N	92.01 W
Vinton, LA	260	30.11 N	93.35 W
Vinton, VA	258	37.17 N	80.01 W
Viola, IL	260	41.12 N	90.35 W
Viola, WI	256	43.31 N	90.40 W
Virago Sound	248	54.00 N	132.36 W
Virden, MB	250	49.51 N	100.55 W
Virden, IL	260	39.30 N	89.46 W
Virden, NM	266	32.42 N	109.00 W
Virgil	264	37.59 N	96.01 W
Virgin	270	36.35 N	114.19 W
Virgin, North Fork	266	37.10 N	113.01 W
Virginia, IL	260	39.57 N	90.13 W
Virginia, MN	256	47.31 N	92.32 W
Virginia, U.S.	244		
	258	37.30 N	78.45 W
Virginia Beach	258	36.51 N	75.58 W

Symbols in the index entries are identified on page 273.

Name	Page	Lat °′	Long °′
Virginia City, MT	268	45.18 N	111.56 W
Virginia City, NV	270	39.19 N	119.39 W
Virginia Falls ↳	242	61.38 N	125.42 W
Virginia Peak ▲	270	39.45 N	119.28 W
Virginiatown	256	48.08 N	79.35 W
Viroqua	256	43.34 N	90.53 W
Visalia	270	36.20 N	119.18 W
Viscount	250	51.57 N	105.39 W
Viscount Melville Sound ⊔	242	74.10 N	113.00 W
Vista	270	33.12 N	117.15 W
Vita	250	49.08 N	96.34 W
Vivian	260	32.53 N	93.59 W
Voca	262	31.01 N	99.11 W
Voisin, Lac ◎	250	54.13 N	107.15 W
Volcano	272	19.26 N	155.14 W
Volga, IA	256	42.48 N	91.33 W
Volga, SD	264	44.19 N	96.56 W
Volga ≈	256	42.45 N	91.17 W
Vonda	250	52.19 N	106.06 W
Von Frank Mountain ▲	246	63.33 N	154.20 W
Voyageurs National Park ♠	256	48.30 N	93.00 W
Vredenburgh	260	31.49 N	87.19 W
Vsevidof, Mount ▲	246	53.07 N	168.43 W
Vulcan, AB	248	50.24 N	113.15 W
Vulcan, MI	256	45.47 N	87.53 W
W			
Wabamun	248	53.33 N	114.28 W
Wabamun Indian Reserve ➝[4]	248	53.30 N	114.30 W
Wabamun Lake ◎	248	53.33 N	114.35 W
Wabana	252	47.38 N	52.57 W
Wabasca	248	56.00 N	113.53 W
Wabasca ≈	242	58.22 N	115.20 W
Wabasca Indian Reserve ➝[4]	248	55.53 N	113.32 W
Wabash	260	40.48 N	85.49 W
Wabash ≈	244	37.46 N	88.02 W
Wabasha	256	44.23 N	92.02 W
Wabasso, FL	258	27.45 N	80.26 W
Wabasso, MN	264	44.24 N	95.15 W
Wabatongushi Lake ◎	256	48.26 N	84.15 W
Wabeno	256	45.26 N	88.39 W
Wabigoon Lake ◎	250	49.44 N	92.44 W
Wabowden	250	54.55 N	98.38 W
W.A.C. Bennett Dam ➝[6]	242	56.01 N	122.10 W
Waccamaw ≈	258	33.21 N	79.16 W
Waccamaw, Lake ◎	258	34.17 N	78.30 W
Waccasassa Bay ⊂	258	29.06 N	82.52 W
Wachapreague	258	37.36 N	75.41 W
Wachusett Mountain ▲	254	42.29 N	71.53 W
Wacissa	258	30.21 N	83.59 W
Waco	262	31.55 N	97.08 W
Waco Lake ◎[1]	262	31.34 N	97.13 W
Waconda Lake ◎[1]	264	39.30 N	98.35 W
Waconia	256	44.51 N	93.47 W
Wacouno ≈	252	50.54 N	65.57 W
Waddington	254	44.52 N	75.12 W
Waddington, Mount ▲	248	51.23 N	125.15 W
Wadena, SK	250	51.57 N	103.47 W
Wadena, MN	264	46.26 N	95.08 W
Wadesboro	258	34.58 N	80.04 W
Wadham Islands ▮▮	252	49.34 N	53.50 W
Wadhams	248	51.30 N	127.31 W
Wadley, AL	258	33.07 N	85.34 W
Wadley, GA	258	32.52 N	82.24 W
Wadsworth, NV	270	39.38 N	119.17 W
Wadsworth, OH	254	41.02 N	81.44 W
Waelder	262	29.42 N	97.18 W
Wager Bay ⊂	242	65.26 N	88.40 W
Wagner	264	43.05 N	98.18 W
Wagoner	262	35.58 N	95.22 W
Wagon Mound	262	36.01 N	104.42 W
Wagontire Mountain ▲	268	43.21 N	119.53 W
Wahiawa	272c	21.30 N	158.01 W
Wahoo	264	41.13 N	96.37 W
Wahpeton	264	46.16 N	96.36 W
Wahweap Creek ≈	266	36.57 N	111.29 W
Waialeale ▲	272b	22.04 N	159.30 W
Waialua	272c	21.34 N	158.08 W
Waialua Bay ⊂	272c	21.36 N	158.07 W
Waianae	272c	21.27 N	158.11 W
Waianae Mountains ⛰	272c	21.30 N	158.10 W
Waianapanapa Caves State Park ♠	272a	20.47 N	156.01 W
Waiehu	272a	20.55 N	156.30 W
Waihee	272a	20.56 N	156.31 W
Waihee Point ➤	272a	20.57 N	156.31 W
Waikane	272c	21.30 N	157.51 W
Waikapu	272a	20.51 N	156.30 W
Waikiki Beach ♠	272c	21.17 N	157.50 W
Wailua	272b	22.03 N	159.19 W
Wailua River State Park ♠	272b	22.02 N	159.21 W
Wailuku	272a	20.53 N	156.30 W
Waimanalo	272c	21.21 N	157.42 W
Waimea, HI	272b	21.58 N	159.42 W
Waimea, HI	272c	21.39 N	158.04 W
Waimea Canyon ∨	272b	22.04 N	159.39 W
Waimea Canyon State Park ♠	272b	22.04 N	159.40 W
Wainwright, AB	250	52.49 N	110.52 W
Wainwright, AK	246	70.38 N	160.01 W
Waipahu	272c	21.23 N	158.01 W
Waipio Acres	272c	21.28 N	158.01 W
Waipio Bay ⊂	272a	20.55 N	156.13 W
Waita Reservoir ◎[1]	272b	21.55 N	159.27 W
Waite Park	264	45.33 N	94.14 W
Waitsburg	268	46.16 N	118.09 W
Waka	262	36.17 N	101.03 W
Wakami ≈	256	47.43 N	82.22 W
Wakami Lake ◎	256	47.29 N	82.51 W
Wakarusa	260	41.32 N	86.01 W
Wakarusa ≈	264	38.57 N	95.05 W
Wakaw	250	52.39 N	105.44 W
Wa Keeney	264	39.01 N	99.53 W
Wakefield, KS	264	39.13 N	97.01 W
Wakefield, NE	264	42.16 N	96.52 W
Wakefield, RI	254	41.26 N	71.30 W
Wakefield, VA	258	36.58 N	76.59 W
Wake Forest	258	35.59 N	78.30 W
Wakeman ≈	248	51.00 N	126.30 W
Wakenda Creek ≈	260	39.19 N	93.16 W
Wake Village	260	33.26 N	94.07 W
Wakita	262	36.53 N	97.55 W
Wakomata Lake ◎	256	46.34 N	83.22 W
Wakonassin ≈	256	46.28 N	81.51 W
Wakonda	264	43.00 N	97.06 W
Walcott, BC	248	54.31 N	126.51 W
Walcott, IA	256	41.35 N	90.47 W
Walcott, ND	264	46.33 N	90.56 W
Walcott, Lake ◎[1]	268	42.40 N	113.23 W
Walden, CO	266	40.44 N	106.17 W
Walden, NY	254	41.34 N	74.11 W
Walden Ridge ▲	260	35.30 N	85.15 W
Waldheim	250	52.37 N	106.38 W
Waldo, BC	248	49.13 N	115.13 W
Waldo, AR	260	33.21 N	93.18 W
Waldoboro	254	44.06 N	69.23 W
Waldorf	254	38.37 N	76.54 W
Waldport	268	44.26 N	124.04 W
Waldron, SK	250	50.51 N	102.30 W
Waldron, AR	260	34.54 N	94.05 W
Waldron, IN	260	39.27 N	85.40 W
Waldron, MI	256	41.44 N	84.25 W
Wales	246	65.36 N	168.05 W
Wales Island ▮, NT	242	68.00 N	86.43 W
Wales Island ▮, NT	242	61.50 N	72.05 W
Walhalla, ND	264	48.55 N	97.55 W
Walhalla, SC	258	34.46 N	83.04 W
Walker, IA	256	42.17 N	91.47 W
Walker, MN	264	47.06 N	94.35 W
Walker ≈	270	38.54 N	118.47 W
Walker, Lac ◎	252	50.16 N	67.09 W
Walker Creek ≈, AZ	266	36.58 N	109.42 W
Walker Creek ≈, WY	264	43.09 N	104.52 W
Walker Lake ◎, MB	250	54.42 N	96.57 W
Walker Lake ◎, AK	246	67.10 N	154.26 W
Walker Lake ◎, NV	270	38.44 N	118.43 W
Walker River Indian Reservation ➝[4]	270	39.00 N	118.40 W
Walkersville	254	39.29 N	77.21 W
Walkerton, ON	256	44.07 N	81.09 W
Walkerton, IN	260	41.28 N	86.29 W
Walkertown	258	36.10 N	80.10 W
Walkerville	268	46.01 N	112.30 W
Wall	264	43.59 N	102.14 W
Wallace, ID	268	47.28 N	115.56 W
Wallace, NE	264	40.50 N	101.10 W
Wallace, NC	258	34.44 N	77.59 W
Wallaceburg	256	42.36 N	82.23 W
Walla Walla	268	46.08 N	118.20 W
Walla Walla Plateau ⛰[1]	268	46.20 N	117.45 W
Waller	262	30.04 N	95.56 W
Wallingford, CT	254	41.27 N	72.50 W
Wallingford, VT	254	43.28 N	72.59 W
Wallis	262	29.38 N	96.04 W
Wall Lake	264	42.16 N	95.05 W
Wallowa	268	45.34 N	117.32 W
Wallowa ≈	268	45.43 N	117.47 W
Wallowa Mountains ⛰	268	45.10 N	117.30 W
Walls	260	34.58 N	90.16 W
Walnut, IL	260	41.33 N	89.36 W
Walnut, IA	264	41.28 N	95.16 W
Walnut, KS	264	37.36 N	95.05 W
Walnut, MS	260	34.57 N	88.54 W
Walnut, NC	258	35.51 N	82.44 W
Walnut Canyon National Monument ♠	266	34.59 N	111.10 W
Walnut Cove	258	36.18 N	80.09 W
Walnut Creek ≈, KS	264	38.21 N	98.41 W
Walnut Creek ≈, OH	254	39.41 N	82.59 W
Walnut Creek, Middle Fork ≈	264	38.32 N	100.08 W
Walnut Creek, South Fork ≈	264	38.25 N	99.53 W
Walnut Grove, MN	264	44.13 N	95.28 W
Walnut Grove, MS	260	32.36 N	89.28 W
Walnut Ridge	260	36.04 N	90.57 W
Walnut Springs	262	32.03 N	97.45 W
Walpole	254	43.05 N	72.26 W
Walsenburg	264	37.37 N	104.47 W
Walsh, AB	250	49.57 N	110.03 W
Walsh, CO	264	37.23 N	102.17 W
Walterboro	258	32.55 N	80.39 W
Walter F. George Lake ◎[1]	258	31.49 N	85.08 W
Walters	262	34.22 N	98.19 W
Waltersville	260	32.22 N	90.52 W
Walthall	260	33.31 N	89.16 W
Waltham	254	42.23 N	71.14 W
Walthill	264	42.09 N	96.30 W
Walton, NS	252	45.14 N	64.00 W
Walton, IN	260	40.40 N	86.15 W
Walton, KY	254	38.52 N	84.37 W
Walton, NY	254	42.10 N	75.08 W
Walworth	256	42.32 N	88.36 W
Wamego	264	39.12 N	96.18 W
Wampsville	254	43.05 N	75.42 W
Wampum	254	40.54 N	80.21 W
Wamsutter	268	41.40 N	107.58 W
Wanamingo	256	44.18 N	92.47 W
Wanapitei ≈	256	46.02 N	80.51 W
Wanapitei Lake ◎	256	46.45 N	80.45 W
Wanapum Lake ◎[1]	268	47.00 N	120.00 W
Wanblee	264	43.34 N	101.40 W
Wanchese	258	35.51 N	75.38 W
Wandering ≈	248	55.05 N	112.30 W
Wanette	262	34.58 N	97.02 W
Wanham	248	55.44 N	118.24 W
Wanipigow ≈	250	51.11 N	96.18 W
Wapakoneta	254	40.34 N	84.12 W
Wapanucka	262	34.22 N	96.25 W
Wapato	268	46.27 N	120.25 W
Wapawekka Hills ⛰[2]	250	54.45 N	104.20 W
Wapawekka Lake ◎	250	54.55 N	104.40 W
Wapella	250	50.15 N	102.00 W
Wapello	256	41.11 N	91.11 W
Wapesi Lake ◎	250	50.34 N	92.21 W
Wapisu Lake ◎	250	55.47 N	99.11 W
Wapiti ≈	248	55.08 N	118.18 W
Wappapello, Lake ◎[1]	260	36.58 N	90.20 W
Wappingers Falls	254	41.36 N	73.55 W
Wapsipinicon ≈	256	41.44 N	90.20 W
Wapus ≈	256	47.11 N	76.06 W
Wapus Lake ◎	250	56.27 N	102.12 W
War	258	37.18 N	81.41 W
Warburton Bay ⊂	242	63.50 N	111.30 W
Ward Cove	248	55.24 N	131.43 W
Warden	268	46.58 N	119.02 W
Wardlow	250	50.54 N	111.33 W
Ward Mountain ▲	268	46.10 N	114.17 W
Wardner	248	49.25 N	115.26 W
Wardswell Draw ∨	262	32.39 N	102.35 W
Ware	254	42.16 N	72.15 W
Ware ≈	254	42.11 N	72.22 W
War Eagle Creek ≈	260	36.14 N	94.00 W
Wareham	254	41.46 N	70.43 W
Ware Shoals	258	34.24 N	82.15 W
Waring Mountains ⛰	246	66.50 N	159.00 W
Warkworth	256	44.12 N	77.53 W
Warland	248	48.30 N	115.17 W
Warman	250	52.20 N	106.34 W
Warminster	254	40.12 N	75.06 W
Warm Springs, GA	258	32.54 N	84.41 W
Warm Springs, MT	268	46.11 N	112.48 W
Warm Springs, OR	268	44.46 N	121.16 W
Warm Springs, VA	254	38.03 N	79.47 W
Warm Springs ≈	268	44.52 N	121.04 W
Warm Springs Indian Reservation ➝[4]	268	45.00 N	121.25 W
Warm Springs Reservoir ◎[1]	268	43.37 N	118.14 W
Warner, AB	248	49.17 N	112.12 W
Warner, NH	254	43.17 N	71.49 W
Warner, OK	262	35.31 N	95.18 W
Warner Lakes ◎	268	42.25 N	119.50 W
Warner Mountains ⛰	270	41.40 N	120.20 W
Warner Peak ▲	268	42.27 N	119.44 W
Warner Robins	258	32.37 N	83.36 W
Warpath ≈	250	52.21 N	98.26 W
Warr Acres	262	35.31 N	97.37 W
Warren, AR	260	33.37 N	92.04 W
Warren, IN	256	40.41 N	85.26 W
Warren, MI	256	42.31 N	83.01 W
Warren, MN	264	48.12 N	96.46 W
Warren, OH	254	41.14 N	80.52 W
Warren, PA	254	41.51 N	79.08 W
Warren Peaks ⛰	264	44.29 N	104.28 W
Warren Point ➤	246	69.44 N	132.30 W
Warrens	256	44.08 N	90.30 W
Warrensburg, MO	260	38.46 N	93.44 W
Warrensburg, NY	254	43.30 N	73.46 W
Warrenton, GA	258	33.24 N	82.40 W
Warrenton, MO	260	38.49 N	91.08 W
Warrenton, NC	258	36.24 N	78.09 W
Warrenton, OR	268	46.10 N	123.56 W
Warrenton, VA	254	38.43 N	77.48 W
Warrington	260	30.23 N	87.16 W
Warrior	260	33.49 N	86.49 W
Warrior Creek ≈	258	31.15 N	83.34 W
Warroad	264	48.54 N	95.19 W
Warsaw, IL	256	40.22 N	91.26 W
Warsaw, IN	260	41.14 N	85.51 W
Warsaw, KY	254	38.47 N	84.54 W
Warsaw, MO	260	38.15 N	93.23 W
Warsaw, NC	258	35.00 N	78.05 W
Warsaw, NY	254	42.44 N	78.08 W
Warsaw, OH	254	40.20 N	82.00 W
Warsaw, VA	258	37.57 N	76.46 W
Warspite	248	54.06 N	112.37 W
Wartburg	258	36.06 N	84.36 W
Wartrace	260	35.32 N	86.19 W
Warwick, PQ	254	45.56 N	71.59 W
Warwick, RI	254	41.43 N	71.28 W
Wasaga Beach	256	44.31 N	80.01 W
Wasatch Mountain State Park ♠	266	40.33 N	111.31 W
Wasatch Plateau ⛰[1]	266	39.20 N	111.30 W
Wasatch Range ⛰	266	41.15 N	111.30 W
Wascana Creek ≈	250	50.20 N	104.25 W
Wasco, CA	270	35.36 N	119.20 W
Wasco, OR	268	45.35 N	120.42 W
Waseca	256	44.05 N	93.30 W
Wasekamio Lake ◎	250	56.45 N	108.45 W
Washademoak Lake ◎	252	45.48 N	65.58 W
Washburn, IL	256	40.55 N	89.17 W
Washburn, ME	252	46.47 N	68.09 W
Washburn, ND	264	47.17 N	101.02 W
Washburn, WI	256	46.41 N	90.52 W
Washburn, Mount ▲	268	44.48 N	110.25 W
Washburn Lake ◎	242	70.03 N	106.50 W
Washicoutai	252	50.17 N	60.42 W
Washington, DC	254	38.54 N	77.01 W
Washington, GA	258	33.44 N	82.44 W
Washington, IL	256	40.42 N	89.24 W
Washington, IN	260	38.40 N	87.10 W
Washington, IA	256	41.18 N	91.42 W
Washington, KS	264	39.49 N	97.03 W
Washington, KY	254	38.37 N	83.49 W
Washington, LA	260	30.37 N	92.03 W
Washington, MO	260	38.33 N	91.01 W
Washington, NC	258	35.33 N	77.03 W
Washington, PA	254	40.10 N	80.15 W
Washington, TX	262	30.20 N	96.10 W
Washington, UT	266	37.08 N	113.30 W
Washington, VA	254	38.43 N	78.10 W
Washington □[3], U.S.	244		
	268	47.30 N	120.30 W
Washington, Mount ▲	254	44.15 N	71.15 W
Washington Court House	254	39.32 N	83.26 W
Washington Island	256	45.23 N	86.55 W
Washington Island ▮	256	45.23 N	86.55 W
Washington Terrace	266	41.12 N	111.59 W
Washita ≈	262	34.12 N	96.50 W
Washoe Lake ◎	270	39.15 N	119.47 W
Washow Bay ⊂	250	51.22 N	96.47 W
Washtucna	268	46.45 N	118.19 W
Wasilla	246	61.35 N	149.26 W
Waskada	250	49.06 N	100.46 W
Waskahigan ≈	248	54.45 N	117.12 W
Waskaiowaka Lake ◎	250	56.30 N	96.20 W
Waskatenau	248	54.07 N	112.47 W
Waskesiu Lake ◎	250	53.56 N	106.10 W
Waskom	260	32.29 N	94.04 W
Wass Lake ◎	250	53.40 N	95.25 W
Watabeag Lake ◎	256	48.14 N	80.32 W
Watatic, Mount ▲	254	42.42 N	71.53 W
Waterbury, CT	254	41.33 N	73.02 W
Waterbury, VT	254	44.20 N	72.46 W
Waterdown	256	43.20 N	79.53 W
Wateree ≈	258	33.45 N	80.37 W
Wateree Lake ◎[1]	258	34.25 N	80.50 W
Waterford, ON	256	42.56 N	80.17 W
Waterford, CA	270	37.38 N	120.46 W
Waterford, PA	254	41.57 N	79.59 W
Waterford, WI	256	42.46 N	88.13 W
Waterhen ≈	250	54.38 N	107.47 W
Waterhen Lake ◎, MB	250	52.06 N	99.34 W
Waterhen Lake ◎, SK	250	54.28 N	108.25 W
Waterloo, ON	256	43.28 N	80.31 W
Waterloo, PQ	254	45.21 N	72.31 W
Waterloo, AL	260	34.55 N	88.04 W
Waterloo, IL	260	38.20 N	90.09 W
Waterloo, IA	256	42.30 N	92.20 W
Waterloo, NY	254	42.54 N	76.52 W
Waterloo, WI	256	43.11 N	88.59 W
Waterman	260	41.46 N	88.46 W
Waterman Wash ∨	266	33.21 N	112.31 W
Waterproof	260	31.48 N	91.23 W
Watersmeet	256	46.13 N	89.11 W
Waterton-Glacier International Peace Park ♠	268	48.47 N	113.45 W
Waterton Lakes National Park ♠	248	49.05 N	113.50 W
Watertown, NY	254	43.59 N	75.55 W
Watertown, SD	264	44.54 N	97.07 W
Watertown, WI	256	43.12 N	88.43 W
Water Valley	260	34.09 N	89.38 W
Waterville, NS	252	45.03 N	64.41 W
Waterville, KS	264	39.42 N	96.45 W
Waterville, ME	254	44.33 N	69.38 W
Waterville, MN	256	44.13 N	93.34 W
Waterville, OH	254	41.30 N	83.43 W
Waterville, WA	268	47.39 N	120.04 W
Watervliet	254	42.44 N	73.42 W
Watford	256	42.57 N	81.53 W
Watford City	264	47.48 N	103.17 W
Wathaman ≈	242	57.16 N	102.52 W
Wathaman Lake ◎	250	56.55 N	103.43 W
Wathena	264	39.46 N	94.58 W
Watino	248	55.43 N	117.37 W
Watkins Glen	254	42.23 N	76.52 W
Watkins Glen State Park ♠	254	42.22 N	76.55 W
Watkinsville	258	33.52 N	83.25 W
Watoga State Park ♠	254	38.07 N	80.05 W
Watonga	262	35.51 N	98.25 W
Watonwan ≈	264	44.04 N	94.07 W
Watrous, SK	250	51.40 N	105.28 W
Watrous, NM	262	35.48 N	104.59 W
Watseka	256	40.47 N	87.44 W
Watson	250	52.07 N	104.31 W
Watson Lake	246	60.07 N	128.48 W
Watsontown	254	41.05 N	76.52 W
Watsonville	270	36.55 N	121.45 W
Watts Bar Lake ◎[1]	258	35.48 N	84.39 W
Wattsville	258	34.31 N	82.02 W
Waubay	264	45.20 N	97.18 W
Waubay Lake ◎	264	45.25 N	97.25 W
Wauchula	258	27.33 N	81.49 W
Waugh	250	49.40 N	95.13 W
Waugh Mountain ▲	268	45.29 N	114.47 W
Waukegan	256	42.22 N	87.50 W
Waukesha	256	43.01 N	88.14 W
Waukomis	262	36.15 N	97.53 W
Waukon	256	43.16 N	91.29 W
Waunakee	256	43.11 N	89.27 W
Wauneta	264	40.25 N	101.23 W
Waupaca	256	44.21 N	89.05 W
Waupun	256	43.38 N	88.44 W
Waurika	262	34.10 N	98.00 W
Waurika Lake ◎[1]	262	34.15 N	98.05 W
Wausa	264	42.30 N	97.32 W
Wausau	256	44.59 N	89.39 W
Wausaukee	256	45.23 N	87.57 W
Wauseon	254	41.33 N	84.09 W
Wautoma	256	44.04 N	89.17 W
Wauwatosa	256	43.03 N	88.00 W
Wauzeka	256	43.05 N	90.52 W
Waveland	260	30.16 N	89.29 W
Waverly, AL	258	32.44 N	85.35 W
Waverly, IL	260	39.36 N	89.57 W
Waverly, IA	256	42.44 N	92.29 W
Waverly, KS	264	38.23 N	95.36 W
Waverly, MN	256	45.04 N	93.57 W
Waverly, MO	260	39.12 N	93.31 W
Waverly, NE	264	40.55 N	96.32 W
Waverly, NY	254	42.00 N	76.32 W
Waverly, OH	254	39.07 N	82.59 W
Waverly, TN	260	36.05 N	87.48 W
Waverly, VA	258	37.02 N	77.06 W
Waverly Hall	258	32.41 N	84.44 W
Wawa	256	47.59 N	84.47 W
Wawanesa	250	49.36 N	99.41 W
Wawiag ≈	256	48.25 N	91.07 W
Wawota	250	49.55 N	102.00 W
Waxahachie	262	32.24 N	96.51 W
Waxhaw	258	34.55 N	80.45 W
Waycross	258	31.13 N	82.21 W
Wayland, IA	256	41.08 N	91.40 W
Wayland, KY	258	37.27 N	82.48 W
Wayland, MI	256	42.40 N	85.39 W
Wayland, NY	254	42.34 N	77.35 W
Waylyn	258	32.51 N	80.00 W
Wayne, AB	248	51.23 N	112.39 W
Wayne, MI	256	42.17 N	83.23 W
Wayne, NE	264	42.14 N	97.01 W
Wayne, NJ	254	40.55 N	74.17 W
Wayne, OK	262	34.55 N	97.19 W
Wayne, WV	254	38.13 N	82.27 W
Wayne City	260	38.21 N	88.38 W
Waynesboro, GA	258	33.06 N	82.01 W
Waynesboro, MS	260	31.40 N	88.39 W
Waynesboro, PA	254	39.45 N	77.35 W
Waynesboro, TN	260	35.19 N	87.45 W
Waynesboro, VA	254	38.04 N	78.53 W
Waynesburg, OH	254	40.40 N	81.16 W
Waynesburg, PA	254	39.54 N	80.11 W
Waynesville, IL	260	40.15 N	89.08 W
Waynesville, MO	260	37.50 N	92.12 W
Waynesville, NC	258	35.29 N	83.00 W
Waynoka	262	36.35 N	98.53 W
Weagamow Lake ◎	250	52.53 N	91.22 W
Weatherford, OK	262	35.32 N	98.42 W
Weatherford, TX	262	32.46 N	97.48 W
Weatherly	254	40.57 N	75.50 W
Weaubleau	260	37.54 N	93.32 W
Weaver	260	33.45 N	85.49 W
Weaver Lake ◎	250	52.45 N	96.35 W
Weaverville, CA	270	40.44 N	122.56 W
Weaverville, NC	258	35.42 N	82.34 W
Webb, SK	250	50.11 N	108.12 W
Webb, MS	260	33.57 N	90.21 W
Webb Air Force Base ■	262	32.14 N	101.31 W
Webb City	260	37.09 N	94.28 W
Webber Lake ◎	250	54.28 N	94.00 W
Weber ≈	266	41.13 N	112.16 W
Weber, Mount ▲	248	55.32 N	128.31 W
Weber City	258	36.37 N	82.34 W
Webster, AB	248	55.26 N	118.42 W
Webster, FL	258	28.37 N	82.03 W
Webster, MA	254	42.03 N	71.53 W
Webster, SD	264	45.20 N	97.31 W
Webster, WI	256	45.53 N	92.22 W
Webster City	256	42.28 N	93.49 W
Webster Springs	254	38.29 N	80.25 W
Wedge Mountain ▲	248	50.10 N	122.50 W
Wedgeport	252	43.44 N	65.59 W
Wedowee	258	33.19 N	85.29 W
Weed	270	41.25 N	122.23 W
Weedsport	254	43.03 N	76.34 W
Weedville	254	41.17 N	78.30 W
Weems	258	37.39 N	76.27 W
Weeping Water	264	40.52 N	96.08 W
Weimar	262	29.42 N	96.47 W
Weiner	260	35.37 N	90.54 W
Weippe	268	46.23 N	115.56 W
Weir, KS	264	37.19 N	94.46 W
Weir, MS	260	33.16 N	89.17 W
Weir ≈	250	56.54 N	93.21 W
Weir, Lake ◎	258	29.00 N	81.57 W
Weir River	250	56.49 N	94.04 W
Weirsdale	258	28.59 N	81.55 W
Weirton	254	40.25 N	80.35 W
Weiser	268	44.15 N	116.58 W
Weiser ≈	268	44.15 N	116.59 W
Weisner Mountain ▲	260	34.02 N	85.40 W
Weiss Lake ◎[1]	258	34.15 N	85.35 W
Wekusko Lake ◎	250	54.45 N	99.50 W
Welaka	258	29.29 N	81.40 W
Welch, OK	262	36.52 N	95.06 W
Welch, TX	262	32.56 N	102.08 W
Welch, WV	258	37.25 N	81.31 W
Welcome, MN	264	43.40 N	94.37 W
Welcome, SC	258	34.49 N	82.26 W
Weldon, SK	250	53.00 N	105.08 W
Weldon, IL	260	40.07 N	88.45 W
Weldon, NC	258	36.25 N	77.36 W
Weldon ≈	260	40.06 N	93.38 W
Weldona	264	40.21 N	103.58 W
Weleetka	262	35.20 N	96.08 W
Welland	256	42.59 N	79.15 W
Welland ≈	256	43.04 N	79.03 W
Welland Canal ≋	256	43.14 N	79.13 W
Wellborn, FL	258	30.14 N	82.49 W
Wellborn, TX	262	30.32 N	96.18 W
Wellesley Lake ◎	246	62.30 N	139.50 W
Wellfleet	254	41.56 N	70.02 W
Wellington, ON	256	43.57 N	77.21 W
Wellington, CO	264	40.42 N	105.00 W
Wellington, KS	264	37.16 N	97.24 W
Wellington, MO	260	39.08 N	93.59 W
Wellington, OH	254	41.10 N	82.13 W
Wellington, TX	262	34.51 N	100.13 W
Wellington, UT	266	39.32 N	110.44 W
Wellington Bay ⊂	242	69.30 N	106.30 W
Wellington Channel ⊔	242	75.00 N	93.00 W
Wellington Station	252	46.27 N	64.00 W
Wellman, IA	256	41.28 N	91.50 W
Wellman, TX	262	33.03 N	102.26 W
Wells, BC	248	53.06 N	121.34 W
Wells, MI	256	45.47 N	87.04 W
Wells, MN	256	43.44 N	93.44 W
Wells, NV	270	41.07 N	114.58 W
Wells, NY	254	43.24 N	74.17 W
Wells, TX	260	31.29 N	94.56 W
Wellsboro	254	41.45 N	77.18 W
Wellsburg, IA	256	42.26 N	92.56 W
Wellsburg, WV	254	40.16 N	80.37 W
Wells Gray Provincial Park ♠	248	52.20 N	120.00 W
Wellston, OH	254	39.07 N	82.32 W
Wellston, OK	262	35.41 N	97.06 W
Wellsville, KS	264	38.43 N	95.05 W
Wellsville, MO	260	39.04 N	91.34 W
Wellsville, NY	254	42.07 N	77.57 W
Wellsville, OH	254	40.36 N	80.39 W
Wellsville, UT	266	41.38 N	111.56 W
Wellton	266	32.40 N	114.08 W
Welsford	252	45.27 N	66.20 W
Welsh	260	30.14 N	92.49 W
Wembley	248	55.09 N	119.08 W
Wenatchee	268	47.25 N	120.19 W
Wenatchee ≈	268	47.27 N	120.19 W
Wenatchee Mountains ⛰	268	47.20 N	120.45 W
Wendell, ID	268	42.46 N	114.42 W
Wendell, NC	258	35.47 N	78.22 W
Wenden	266	33.49 N	113.32 W
Wendover	266	40.44 N	114.02 W
Wenebegon ≈	256	46.53 N	83.12 W
Wenebegon Lake ◎	256	47.24 N	83.08 W
Wenona	260	41.03 N	89.03 W
Wentworth, NC	258	36.24 N	79.53 W
Wentworth, SD	264	44.00 N	96.58 W
Wesconnett	258	30.14 N	81.44 W
Weskan	264	38.41 N	101.57 W
Weslaco	262	26.09 N	97.59 W
Weslemkoon Lake ◎	256	45.02 N	77.25 W
Wesley	256	43.05 N	93.59 W
Wesleyville, NF	252	49.09 N	53.34 W
Wesleyville, PA	254	42.08 N	80.01 W
Wessington	264	44.27 N	98.42 W
Wessington Springs	264	44.05 N	98.34 W
Wesson	260	31.42 N	90.23 W
West, MS	260	33.12 N	89.47 W
West, TX	262	31.48 N	97.06 W
West ≈	254	42.52 N	72.33 W
West Alexandria	254	39.45 N	84.32 W
West Allis	256	43.01 N	88.00 W
Westbank	248	49.50 N	119.38 W
West Bay, NS	252	45.43 N	61.10 W
Westbay, FL	260	30.17 N	85.52 W
West Bay ⊂, FL	260	30.16 N	85.47 W
West Bay ⊂, TX	260	29.15 N	94.57 W
West Bend, IA	264	42.57 N	94.27 W
West Bend, WI	256	43.25 N	88.11 W
West Bijou Creek ≈	264	39.51 N	104.08 W
West Blocton	260	33.07 N	87.07 W
Westbourne	250	50.09 N	98.35 W
West Bow Creek ≈	264	42.46 N	97.08 W
West Branch, IA	256	41.40 N	91.20 W
West Branch, MI	256	44.17 N	84.14 W
Westbridge	248	49.10 N	118.59 W
Westbrook, ME	254	43.41 N	70.21 W
Westbrook, MN	264	44.03 N	95.26 W
Westbrook, TX	262	32.21 N	101.01 W
West Burlington	256	40.49 N	91.09 W
West Butte ▲	268	48.57 N	111.32 W
Westby, MT	264	48.52 N	104.03 W
Westby, WI	256	43.39 N	90.51 W
West Cache Creek ≈	262	34.13 N	98.23 W
West Canada Creek ≈	254	43.01 N	74.58 W
West Carlisle	262	33.35 N	101.56 W
West Channel ≈[1]	246	68.51 N	136.10 W
West Chester	254	39.58 N	75.36 W
West Clear Creek ≈	266	34.34 N	111.51 W
Westcliffe	266	38.08 N	105.28 W
West Columbia, SC	258	34.00 N	81.04 W
West Columbia, TX	262	29.09 N	95.39 W
West Concord	256	44.09 N	92.54 W
West Cote Blanche Bay ⊂	260	29.40 N	91.45 W
West Des Moines	256	41.35 N	93.43 W
West Dolores ≈	266	37.35 N	108.21 W
West Elk Mountains ⛰	266	38.40 N	107.15 W
West Elk Peak ▲	266	38.43 N	107.13 W
West End, AR	260	34.13 N	92.03 W
West End, NC	258	35.15 N	79.33 W
Westerly	254	41.22 N	71.50 W
Western	264	40.24 N	97.12 W
Westernport	254	39.29 N	79.03 W
Western Shore	252	44.32 N	64.19 W
Westerville	254	40.08 N	82.56 W
West Fargo	264	46.53 N	96.54 W
West Farmington	254	44.40 N	70.10 W
Westfield, IL	260	39.27 N	88.01 W
Westfield, IN	260	40.02 N	86.08 W
Westfield, MA	254	42.08 N	72.45 W
Westfield, NJ	254	40.39 N	74.21 W
Westfield, NY	254	42.19 N	79.35 W
Westfield, PA	254	41.55 N	77.32 W
Westfield, WI	256	43.53 N	89.30 W
West Fiord ⊂[2]	242	76.02 N	90.00 W
West Fork	260	35.56 N	94.11 W
West Frankfort	260	37.54 N	88.55 W
Westgate	258	26.47 N	80.06 W
West Glacier	268	48.30 N	113.59 W
West Hamlin	254	38.17 N	82.12 W
West Hartford	254	41.46 N	72.45 W
Westhaven, CA	270	41.03 N	124.06 W
West Haven, CT	254	41.16 N	72.57 W
West Helena	260	34.33 N	90.39 W
Westhoff	262	29.12 N	97.28 W
Westhope	264	48.55 N	101.01 W
West Jefferson, NC	258	36.24 N	81.30 W
West Jefferson, OH	254	39.57 N	83.16 W
West Jordan	266	40.36 N	111.58 W
West Kettle ≈	248	49.07 N	119.00 W
West Kildonan	250	49.56 N	97.07 W
West Kingston	254	41.29 N	71.34 W
West Lafayette, IN	260	40.27 N	86.55 W
West Lafayette, OH	254	40.17 N	81.45 W
Westlake	260	30.15 N	93.15 W
West Laramie	264	41.17 N	105.40 W
West Lebanon	260	40.16 N	87.23 W
West Liberty, IA	256	41.34 N	91.16 W
West Liberty, KY	258	37.55 N	83.16 W
West Liberty, OH	254	40.15 N	83.46 W
West Little Owyhee ≈	268	42.28 N	117.15 W
Westlock	248	54.09 N	113.52 W
West Lorne	256	42.36 N	81.36 W
West Lubec	254	44.49 N	67.05 W
West Melbourne	258	28.04 N	80.38 W
West Memphis	260	35.08 N	90.11 W
West Mifflin	254	40.22 N	79.52 W
Westminster, CO	266	39.50 N	105.02 W
Westminster, MD	254	39.35 N	77.00 W
Westminster, SC	258	34.40 N	83.06 W
West Monroe	260	32.31 N	92.09 W
Westmont	254	40.19 N	78.57 W
West Montreal ≈	256	47.56 N	80.39 W
Westmoreland, KS	264	39.24 N	96.25 W
Westmoreland, TN	260	36.34 N	86.15 W
Westmorland	270	33.02 N	115.37 W
West Mountain ▲	254	43.51 N	74.43 W
West Nishnabotna ≈	264	40.39 N	95.37 W
West Nodaway ≈	264	40.38 N	95.01 W
West Nueces ≈	262	29.16 N	99.56 W
Weston, CO	264	37.08 N	104.48 W
Weston, ID	268	42.02 N	111.59 W
Weston, MO	260	39.25 N	94.54 W
Weston, NE	264	41.12 N	96.45 W
Weston, OH	254	41.21 N	83.48 W
Weston, OR	268	45.49 N	118.26 W
Weston, WV	254	39.02 N	80.28 W
West Orange	260	30.05 N	93.46 W
Westover, TN	260	35.36 N	88.55 W
Westover, WV	254	39.38 N	79.58 W
Westover Air Force Base ■	254	42.12 N	72.33 W
West Palm Beach	258	26.43 N	80.04 W
West Palm Beach Canal ≋	258	26.38 N	80.03 W
West Paris	254	44.20 N	70.35 W
West Pembroke	254	44.57 N	67.11 W
West Pensacola	260	30.27 N	87.15 W
West Petersburg	246	56.49 N	132.57 W
Westphalia	264	38.11 N	95.29 W
West Plains	260	36.44 N	91.51 W
West Point, CA	270	38.24 N	120.32 W
West Point, GA	258	32.52 N	85.10 W
West Point, IA	256	40.43 N	91.27 W
West Point, KY	260	37.59 N	85.57 W
West Point, MS	260	33.36 N	88.39 W
West Point, NE	264	41.51 N	96.43 W
West Point, NY	254	41.23 N	73.57 W
West Point, VA	258	37.32 N	77.06 W
West Point ▲	246	64.57 N	144.40 W
West Point ➤	252	46.37 N	64.25 W
West Point Lake ◎[1]	258	33.00 N	85.10 W
Westport, NF	252	49.47 N	56.38 W
Westport, NS	252	44.16 N	66.21 W
Westport, ON	256	44.41 N	76.26 W
Westport, CT	254	41.09 N	73.22 W
Westport, IN	260	39.11 N	85.34 W
Westport, OR	268	46.10 N	123.23 W
Westport, WA	268	46.53 N	124.06 W
West Portsmouth	254	38.46 N	83.02 W
West Prairie ≈	248	55.30 N	116.31 W
West Richland	268	46.18 N	119.20 W
West Road ≈	248	53.19 N	122.52 W
West Rosebud Creek ≈	268	45.29 N	109.27 W
West Rutland	254	43.36 N	73.03 W
West Sacramento	270	38.34 N	121.32 W
West Saint Mary's ≈	252	45.15 N	62.04 W
West Saint Modeste	252	51.36 N	56.42 W
West Salem, IL	260	38.31 N	88.01 W
West Salem, OH	254	40.58 N	82.06 W
West Salem, WI	256	43.54 N	91.05 W
West Salt Creek ≈	266	39.13 N	108.54 W
West Shoal Lake ◎	250	50.20 N	97.41 W
West Slope	268	45.31 N	122.46 W
West Spanish Peak ▲	264	37.23 N	104.59 W
West Terre Haute	260	39.28 N	87.27 W
West Twin ≈	256	44.08 N	87.34 W
West Union, IA	256	42.57 N	91.49 W
West Union, OH	254	38.48 N	83.32 W
West Union, WV	254	39.18 N	80.47 W
West Unity	254	41.35 N	84.26 W
West Valley	268	46.08 N	113.01 W
West Vancouver	248	49.22 N	123.12 W
Westville, NS	252	45.34 N	62.43 W
Westville, IN	260	41.33 N	86.54 W
Westville, OK	260	35.59 N	94.34 W
West Virginia □[3], U.S.	244		
	254	38.45 N	80.30 W
West Walker ≈	270	38.53 N	119.10 W
West Warwick	254	41.42 N	71.32 W
West Webster	254	43.12 N	77.30 W
Westwego	260	29.55 N	90.09 W
Westwold	248	50.28 N	119.45 W
Westwood	270	40.18 N	121.00 W
Westwood Lakes	258	25.44 N	80.22 W
West Yellow Creek ≈	260	39.38 N	93.04 W
West Yellowstone	268	44.30 N	111.05 W
Wetaskiwin	248	52.58 N	113.22 W
Wethersfield	254	41.43 N	72.40 W
Wetiko Hills ⛰[2]	250	54.30 N	92.20 W
Wetmore	264	39.38 N	95.49 W
Wet Mountains ⛰	266	38.00 N	105.10 W
Wetumka	262	35.14 N	96.15 W
Wetumpka	260	32.27 N	86.13 W
Wewahitchka	258	30.07 N	85.12 W
Wewoka	262	35.09 N	96.30 W
Weyakwin Lake ◎	250	54.30 N	106.00 W
Weyauwega	256	44.19 N	88.56 W
Weyburn	250	49.41 N	103.52 W
Weymouth, NS	252	44.25 N	66.00 W
Weymouth, MA	254	42.13 N	70.58 W
Wharton, TX	262	29.19 N	96.06 W
Wharton, WV	258	37.55 N	81.40 W
Wharton Lake ◎	242	64.00 N	99.55 W
What Cheer	256	41.24 N	92.21 W
Whatley	260	31.39 N	87.42 W
Whatshan Lake ◎	248	50.00 N	118.03 W
Wheatland, CA	270	39.01 N	121.25 W
Wheatland, IA	256	41.50 N	90.51 W
Wheatland, WY	264	42.03 N	104.57 W
Wheatland Reservoir ◎[1]	264	41.52 N	105.36 W
Wheatley, ON	256	42.06 N	82.27 W
Wheatley, AR	260	34.56 N	91.08 W
Wheaton, IL	260	41.52 N	88.06 W
Wheaton, MD	254	39.03 N	77.03 W
Wheaton, MN	264	45.48 N	96.30 W
Wheat Ridge	266	39.46 N	105.07 W
Wheelbarrow Peak ▲	270	37.27 N	116.05 W
Wheeler, MS	260	34.34 N	88.36 W
Wheeler, TX	262	35.27 N	100.16 W
Wheeler ≈	242	57.02 N	67.13 W
Wheeler Air Force Base ■	272c	21.29 N	158.03 W
Wheeler Lake ◎[1]	260	34.40 N	87.05 W
Wheeler Peak ▲, CA	270	38.25 N	119.17 W
Wheeler Peak ▲, NV	270	38.59 N	114.19 W
Wheeler Peak ▲, NM	266	36.34 N	105.25 W
Wheeling	254	40.05 N	80.42 W
Wheelwright	258	37.20 N	82.43 W
Whidbey Island ▮	268	48.15 N	122.40 W
Whidbey Island Naval Air Station ■	268	48.17 N	122.37 W
Whigham	258	30.53 N	84.19 W
Whiskey Peak ▲	268	42.18 N	107.35 W
Whiskeytown-Shasta-Trinity National Recreation Area ♠	270	40.45 N	122.15 W
Whisky Chitto Creek ≈	260	30.31 N	92.55 W
Whitakers	258	36.06 N	77.43 W
Whitbourne	252	47.25 N	53.32 W
Whitby	256	43.52 N	78.56 W
Whitchurch-Stouffville	256	43.58 N	79.15 W
White, GA	258	34.17 N	84.45 W
White, SD	264	44.26 N	96.39 W
White ≈, BC	248	50.23 N	115.35 W
White ≈, ON	256	48.33 N	86.16 W
White ≈, N.A.	242	63.10 N	139.36 W
White ≈, U.S.	244	33.53 N	91.03 W
White ≈, U.S.	244		
	264	43.45 N	99.30 W
White ≈, U.S.	266	40.04 N	109.41 W
White ≈, AZ	266	33.44 N	110.13 W
White ≈, IN	260	38.25 N	87.44 W
White ≈, NV	270	37.42 N	115.10 W
White ≈, OR	268	45.14 N	121.04 W
White ≈, TX	262	33.14 N	100.56 W
White ≈, VT	254	43.37 N	72.20 W
White ≈, WA	268	47.12 N	122.15 W
White ≈, WI	256	46.36 N	90.42 W
White, East Fork ≈, AZ	266	33.47 N	110.00 W
White, East Fork ≈, IN	260	38.33 N	87.14 W
White, North Fork ≈, AZ	266	33.47 N	110.00 W
White, North Fork ≈, CO	266	39.58 N	107.38 W
White, South Fork ≈	266	39.58 N	107.38 W
White Bay ⊂	252	50.00 N	56.30 W
White Bear Indian Reserve ➝[4]	250	49.15 N	102.15 W
White Bear Lake	256	45.05 N	93.01 W
White Bluff	260	36.06 N	87.13 W
White Breast Creek ≈	256	41.24 N	93.02 W
White Butte ▲	264	46.23 N	103.19 W
Whitecap Lake ◎	250	56.54 N	95.14 W
White Cap Mountain ▲	254	45.35 N	69.13 W
White Castle	260	30.10 N	91.09 W
White City	264	38.48 N	96.44 W
White Clay Creek ≈	264	43.12 N	102.48 W
White Cloud	256	43.33 N	85.46 W
Whitecourt	248	54.09 N	115.41 W
White Deer	262	35.26 N	101.10 W
White Earth ≈	264	48.09 N	102.42 W
White Earth Indian Reservation ➝[4]	264	47.18 N	95.50 W
Whiteface	262	33.36 N	102.37 W
Whiteface ≈	256	46.58 N	92.48 W
Whiteface Mountain ▲	254	44.22 N	73.54 W
Whitefield, ME	254	44.10 N	69.38 W
Whitefield, NH	254	44.22 N	71.36 W
Whitefish	268	48.25 N	114.20 W
Whitefish ≈	256	45.55 N	86.57 W

Symbols in the index entries are identified on page 273.

Symbols in the index entries are identified on page 273.

GEOGRAPHICAL INFORMATION AND INTERNATIONAL MAP INDEX

World Nations

This table gives the area, population, population density, form of government, capital and location of every country in the world.

Area figures include inland water.

The populations are estimates made by Rand McNally and Company on the basis of official data, United Nations estimates and other available information.

Besides specifying the form of government for all political areas, the table classifies them into five groups according to their political status. Units labeled A are independent sovereign nations. (Several of these are designated as members of the British Commonwealth of Nations.) Units labeled B are independent as regards internal affairs, but for purposes of foreign affairs they are under the protection of another country. Units labeled C are colonies, overseas territories, dependencies, etc. of other countries. Units labeled D are states, provinces or other major administrative subdivisions of important countries. Units in the table with no letter designation are regions, islands or other areas that do not constitute separate political units by themselves.

Map Plate numbers refer to the International Map section of the Atlas.

Country, Division, or Region English (Conventional)	Local Name	Area km²	Area sq mi	Population 1/1/82	Population Density per km²	Population Density per sq mi	Form of Government and Political Status		Capital	Continent and Map Plate	
Afars and Issas, see Djibouti	...									...	...
†AFGHANISTAN	Afghanistan	647,497	250,000	13,220,000	20	53	Socialist Republic	A	Kābul	Asia	23
AFRICA		30,323,000	11,708,000	490,300,000	16	42				Africa	30–31
Alabama, U.S.	Alabama	133,667	51,609	3,975,000	30	77	State (U.S.)	D	Montgomery	N. Amer.	44
Alaska, U.S.	Alaska	1,527,470	589,759	415,000	0.3	0.7	State (U.S.)	D	Juneau	N. Amer.	40
†ALBANIA	Shqiperia	28,748	11,100	2,820,000	98	254	Socialist Republic	A	Tirana	Europe	15
Alberta, Can.	Alberta	661,185	255,285	2,190,000	3.3	8.6	Province (Canada)	D	Edmonton	N. Amer.	42
†ALGERIA	Al Jazā'ir	2,381,741	919,595	19,270,000	8.1	21	Socialist Republic	A	Algiers (Al Jazā'ir)	Africa	32
American Samoa (U.S.)	American Samoa	197	76	34,000	173	447	Unincorporated Territory (U.S.)	C	Pago Pago	Oceania	65
Andaman and Nicobar Islands, India	Andaman and Nicobar	8,293	3,202	195,000	24	61	Territory of India	D	Port Blair	Asia	25
ANDORRA	Andorra	453	175	40,000	88	229	Co-Principality (Spanish and French protection)	B	Andorra la Vella	Europe	13
†ANGOLA	Angola	1,246,700	481,353	7,335,000	5.9	15	Socialist Republic	A	Luanda	Africa	36
ANGUILLA	Anguilla	90	34	7,900	90	232	Associated State (U.K.)	B	The Valley	N. Amer.	51
Anhwei, China	Anhui	139,859	54,000	49,055,000	351	908	Province (China)	D	Hefei	Asia	28
ANTARCTICA	...	14,000,000	5,405,000	...(1)	...	...				Ant.	66
†ANTIGUA (incl. Barbuda)	Antigua	440	170	77,000	175	453	Parliamentary State (Comm. of Nations)	A	Saint John's	N. Amer.	51
Arabian Peninsula	...	3,003,200	1,159,500	21,050,000	7.0	18				Asia	23
†ARGENTINA	Argentina	2,776,889	1,068,301	28,420,000	10	27	Federal Republic	A	Buenos Aires	S. Amer.	56
Arizona, U.S.	Arizona	295,024	113,909	2,795,000	9.5	25	State (U.S.)	D	Phoenix	N. Amer.	46
Arkansas, U.S.	Arkansas	137,539	53,104	2,335,000	17	44	State (U.S.)	D	Little Rock	N. Amer.	45
Armenian S.S.R., U.S.S.R.	Armjanskaja S.S.R.	29,800	11,506	3,115,000	105	271	Soviet Socialist Republic (U.S.S.R.)	D	Jerevan	Asia	16
Aruba (Neth. Ant.)	Aruba	193	75	67,000	347	893	Division of Netherlands Antilles		Oranjestad	N. Amer.	49
Ascension (U.K.)	Ascension	88	34	1,000	11	29	Dependency of St. Helena (U.K.)	C	Georgetown	Africa	30–31
ASIA	...	44,798,000	17,297,000	2,724,900,000	61	158				Asia	21–22
†AUSTRALIA	Australia	7,686,850	2,967,909	14,910,000	1.9	5.0	Parliamentary State (Federal) (Comm. of Nations)	A	Canberra	Oceania	59
Australian Capital Territory, Austl.	Australian Capital Territory	2,432	939	235,000	97	250	Territory (Australia)	D	Canberra	Oceania	59
†AUSTRIA	Österreich	83,850	32,375	7,510,000	90	232	Federal Republic	A	Vienna (Wien)	Europe	14
Azerbaidzhan S.S.R., U.S.S.R.	Azerbajdžanskaja S.S.R.	86,600	33,436	6,210,000	72	186	Soviet Socialist Republic (U.S.S.R.)	D	Baku	Asia	16
Azores (Port.)	Açores	2,335	902	235,000	101	261	Part of Portugal (3 districts)			Africa	32
†BAHAMAS	Bahamas	13,939	5,382	235,000	17	44	Parliamentary State (Comm. of Nations)	A	Nassau	N. Amer.	47
†BAHRAIN	Al Baḥrayn	662	256	400,000	604	1,563	Constitutional Monarchy	A	Al Manāmah	Asia	24
Balearic Islands, Spain	Islas Baleares	5,014	1,936	730,000	146	377	Province of Spain (Baleares)	D	Palma	Europe	13
Baltic Republics (U.S.S.R.)	...	174,000	67,182	7,555,000	43	112	Part of U.S.S.R. (3 republics)			Europe	8
†BANGLADESH	Bangladesh	143,998	55,598	91,860,000	638	1,652	Republic (Comm. of Nations)	A	Dacca	Asia	25
†BARBADOS	Barbados	430	166	260,000	605	1,566	Parliamentary State (Comm. of Nations)	A	Bridgetown	N. Amer.	51
†BELGIUM	Belgique (French) België (Flemish)	30,513	11,781	9,880,000	324	839	Constitutional Monarchy	A	Brussels (Bruxelles)	Europe	12
†BELIZE	Belize	22,963	8,866	160,000	7.0	18	Parliamentary State (Comm. of Nations)	A	Belmopan	N. Amer.	49
Benelux	...	74,259	28,672	24,535,000	330	856	Economic Union			Europe	12
†BENIN	Bénin	112,622	43,484	3,715,000	33	85	Socialist Republic	A	Porto-Novo	Africa	34
Bermuda (U.K.)	Bermuda	53	21	69,000	1,302	3,286	Colony (U.K.)	C	Hamilton	N. Amer.	47
†BHUTAN	Druk	47,000	18,147	1,345,000	29	74	Monarchy (Indian protection)	B	Thimphu	Asia	25
Bioko, Equat. Gui.	Bioko	2,034	785	94,000	46	120	Province of Equatorial Guinea	D	Malabo	Africa	34
†BOLIVIA	Bolivia	1,098,581	424,164	5,845,000	5.3	14	Republic	A	Sucre and La Paz	S. Amer.	54
Borneo, Indonesian	Kalimantan	539,460	208,287	6,815,000	13	33	Part of Indonesia (4 provinces)			Asia	26
†BOTSWANA	Botswana	600,372	231,805	875,000	1.5	3.8	Republic (Comm. of Nations)	A	Gaborone	Africa	37
†BRAZIL	Brasil	8,511,965	3,286,487	124,760,000	15	38	Federal Republic	A	Brasília	S. Amer.	54–56
British Columbia, Can.	British Columbia	948,596	366,255	2,725,000	2.9	7.4	Province (Canada)	D	Victoria	N. Amer.	42
British Honduras, see Belize	...	...	...	...	...	...					
British Indian Ocean Territory (U.K.)	British Indian Ocean Territory	60	23	...(1)	...	...	Colony (U.K.)	C	...	Africa	22
British Solomon Islands, see Solomon Islands	...	...	...	...	...	...					
BRUNEI	Brunei	5,765	2,226	245,000	42	110	Constitutional Monarchy (U.K. protection)	B	Bandar Seri Begawan	Asia	26
†BULGARIA	Balgarija	110,912	42,823	8,915,000	80	208	Socialist Republic	A	Sofia (Sofija)	Europe	15
†BURMA	Burma	676,577	261,228	35,710,000	53	137	Socialist Republic	A	Rangoon	Asia	25
†BURUNDI	Burundi	27,834	10,747	4,705,000	169	438	Republic	A	Bujumbura	Africa	36
†Byelorussian S.S.R., U.S.S.R.	Belorusskaja S.S.R.	207,600	80,155	9,755,000	47	122	Soviet Socialist Republic (U.S.S.R.)	D	Minsk	Europe	16
California, U.S.	California	411,015	158,694	24,155,000	59	152	State (U.S.)	D	Sacramento	N. Amer.	46
Cambodia, see Kampuchea	...	...	...	...	...	...					
†CAMEROON	Cameroun	475,442	183,569	8,860,000	19	48	Republic	A	Yaoundé	Africa	34
†CANADA	Canada	9,922,330	3,831,033	24,335,000	2.5	6.4	Parliamentary State (Federal) (Comm. of Nations)	A	Ottawa	N. Amer.	42
Canary Islands (Sp.)	...	7,273	2,808	1,685,000	232	600	Part of Spain (2 provinces)			Africa	32
†CAPE VERDE	Cabo Verde	4,033	1,557	330,000	82	212	Republic	A	Praia	Africa	32
Cayman Islands (U.K.)	Cayman Islands	259	100	18,000	69	180	Colony (U.K.)	C	Georgetown	N. Amer.	49
Celebes (Indonesia)	Sulawesi	189,216	73,057	10,755,000	57	147	Part of Indonesia (4 provinces)			Asia	26
†CENTRAL AFRICAN REPUBLIC	Centrafrique	622,984	240,535	2,300,000	3.7	9.6	Republic	A	Bangui	Africa	35
Central America	...	523,000	202,000	23,970,000	46	119				N. Amer.	49
Central Asia, Soviet (U.S.S.R.)	...	1,277,100	493,090	26,495,000	21	54	Part of U.S.S.R. (4 republics)			Asia	19
Ceylon, see Sri Lanka	...	...	...	...	...	...					

Country, Division, or Region English (Conventional)	Local Name	Area km²	Area sq mi	Population 1/1/82	Population Density per km²	Population Density per sq mi	Form of Government and Political Status		Capital	Continent and Map Plate	
†CHAD	Tchad	1,284,000	495,755	4,675,000	3.6	9.4	Republic	A	N'djamena	Africa . . .	35
Channel Islands (U.K.)	Channel Islands	195	75	133,000	682	1,773	. . . .		. . . . .	Europe . .	9
Chekiang, China	Zhejiang	101,787	39,300	38,115,000	374	970	Province (China)	D	Hangzhou	Asia	27
†CHILE	Chile	756,626	292,135	11,375,000	15	39	Republic	A	Santiago	S. Amer. .	56
†CHINA (excl. Taiwan)	Zhonghua Renmin Gongheguo	9,560,939	3,691,500	995,000,000	104	270	Socialist Republic	A	Peking (Beijing)	Asia	27
China (Nationalist), see Taiwan	. . .	. . .	. . .	. . .	. . .	. . .					
Christmas Island (Austl.)	Christmas Island	140	54	3,200	23	60	External Territory (Australia)	C	Flying Fish Cove	Oceania. .	26
Cocos (Keeling) Islands (Austl.)	Cocos (Keeling) Islands	14	5.4	400	29	74	External Territory (Australia)	C		Oceania. .	22
†COLOMBIA	Colombia	1,138,914	439,737	28,185,000	25	64	Republic	A	Bogotá	S. Amer. .	54
Colorado, U.S.	Colorado	270,000	104,248	2,960,000	11	28	State (U.S.)	D	Denver	N. Amer. .	45
Commonwealth of Nations	. . .	27,629,000	10,667,000	1,106,308,000	40	104	Political Union		. . . . . .	. . . .	. . .
†COMOROS	Comores	2,171	838	380,000	175	453	Republic	A	Moroni	Africa . . .	37
†CONGO	Congo	342,000	132,047	1,595,000	4.7	12	Socialist Republic	A	Brazzaville	Africa . . .	36
Connecticut, U.S.	Connecticut	12,973	5,009	3,165,000	244	632	State (U.S.)	D	Hartford	N. Amer. .	44
†COOK ISLANDS	Cook Islands	236	91	18,000	76	198	Self-governing Territory (New Zealand protection)	B	Avarua	Oceania. .	61
Corsica (Fr.)	Corse	8,681	3,352	184,000	21	55	Part of France (2 departments)		. . . . .	Europe . .	11
†COSTA RICA	Costa Rica	51,100	19,730	2,340,000	46	119	Republic	A	San José	N. Amer. .	49
†CUBA	Cuba	114,524	44,218	9,805,000	86	222	Socialist Republic	A	Havana (La Habana)	N. Amer. .	49
Curaçao (Neth. Ant.)	Curaçao	444	171	170,000	383	994	Division of Netherlands Antilles	. . .	Willemstad	N. Amer. .	49
†CYPRUS	Kypros (Greek) Kıbrıs (Turkish)	9,251	3,572	650,000	70	182	Republic (Comm. of Nations)	A	Nicosia (Levkosia)	Asia	24
†CZECHOSLOVAKIA	Československo	127,877	49,374	15,345,000	120	311	Socialist Republic	A	Prague (Praha)	Europe . .	10
Dahomey, see Benin	. . .	. . .	. . .	. . .	. . .	. . .					
Delaware, U.S.	Delaware	5,328	2,057	600,000	113	292	State (U.S.)	D	Dover	N. Amer. .	44
†DENMARK	Danmark	43,080	16,633	5,150,000	120	310	Constitutional Monarchy	A	Copenhagen (København)	Europe . .	8
Denmark and Possessions	. . .	2,220,079	857,177	5,246,000	2.4	6.1	. . . .	. . .	Copenhagen (København)	. . . .	. . .
District of Columbia, U.S.	District of Columbia	174	67	640,000	3,678	9,552	District (U.S.)	D	Washington	N. Amer. .	44
†DJIBOUTI	Djibouti	23,000	8,880	124,000	5.4	14	Republic	A	Djibouti	Africa . . .	35
†DOMINICA	Dominica	752	290	75,000	100	259	Republic (Comm. of Nations)	A	Roseau	N. Amer. .	51
†DOMINICAN REPUBLIC	República Dominicana	48,442	18,704	5,660,000	117	303	Republic	A	Santo Domingo	N. Amer. .	49
†ECUADOR	Ecuador	283,561	109,483	8,725,000	31	80	Republic	A	Quito	S. Amer. .	54
†EGYPT	Mişr	1,001,400	386,643	43,565,000	44	113	Socialist Republic	A	Cairo (Al Qāhirah)	Africa . . .	33
Ellice Islands, see Tuvalu	. . .	. . .	. . .	. . .	. . .	. . .					
†EL SALVADOR	El Salvador	21,041	8,124	5,270,000	250	649	Republic	A	San Salvador	N. Amer. .	49
England, U.K.	England	130,439	50,362	46,575,000	357	925	Administrative division of U.K.	D	London	Europe . .	9
†EQUATORIAL GUINEA	Guinea Ecuatorial	28,051	10,831	375,000	13	35	Republic	A	Malabo	Africa . . .	36
Estonian S.S.R., U.S.S.R.	Eest: N.S.V.	45,100	17,413	1,505,000	33	86	Soviet Socialist Republic (U.S.S.R.)	D	Tallinn	Europe . .	8
†ETHIOPIA	Itiopya	1,223,600	472,434	30,370,000	25	64	Monarchy.	A	Ādīs Ābeba	Africa . . .	35
Eurasia	. . .	54,730,000	21,132,000	3,291,300,000	60	156	. . . .		. . . . .	. . . .	. . .
EUROPE	. . .	9,932,000	3,835,000	666,400,000	67	174				Europe . .	5–6
FAEROE ISLANDS	Føroyar (Faeroese) Færøerne (Danish)	1,399	540	45,000	32	83	Part of Danish Realm	B	Tórshavn	Europe . .	6
Falkland Islands (Islas Malvinas) (excl. Dependencies) (U.K.)(3)	Falkland Islands	12,173	4,700	1,900	0.2	0.4	Colony (U.K.)	C	Stanley	S. Amer. .	56
†FIJI	Fiji	18,272	7,055	645,000	35	91	Parliamentary State (Comm. of Nations)	A	Suva	Oceania. .	63
†FINLAND	Suomi (Finnish) Finland (Swedish)	337,032	130,129	4,805,000	14	37	Republic	A	Helsinki (Helsingfors)	Europe . .	7
Florida, U.S.	Florida	151,670	58,560	10,215,000	67	174	State (U.S.)	D	Tallahassee	N. Amer. .	44
†FRANCE	France	547,026	211,208	54,045,000	99	256	Republic	A	Paris	Europe . .	11
France and Possessions	. . .	675,114	260,661	55,618,000	82	213	. . . .	. . .	Paris	. . . .	. . .
Franklin (Can.)	Franklin	1,422,559	549,253	8,000	0.01	0.01	District of Northwest Territories (Canada)			N. Amer. .	42
French Guiana (Fr.)	Guyane Française	91,000	35,135	66,000	0.7	1.9	Overseas Department (France)	D	Cayenne	S. Amer. .	54
French Polynesia (Fr.)	Polynésie Française	4,000	1,544	150,000	38	97	Overseas Territory (France)	C	Papeete	Oceania. .	61
French West Indies	. . .	2,879	1,112	620,000	215	558	. . . .		. . . . .	N. Amer. .	50
Fukien, China	Fujian	123,024	47,500	22,490,000	183	474	Province (China)	D	Fuzhou	Asia	27
†GABON	Gabon	267,667	103,347	560,000	2.1	5.4	Republic	A	Libreville	Africa . . .	36
Galapagos Islands, Ecuador	Archipiélago de Colón	7,964	3,075	6,100	0.8	2.0	Province of Ecuador (Galápagos)	D	Baquerizo Moreno	S. Amer. .	54
†GAMBIA	Gambia	11,295	4,361	625,000	55	143	Republic (Comm. of Nations)	A	Banjul	Africa . . .	34
Georgia, U.S.	Georgia	152,489	58,876	5,570,000	37	95	State (U.S.)	D	Atlanta	N. Amer. .	44
Georgian S.S.R., U.S.S.R.	Gruzinskaja S.S.R.	69,700	26,911	5,135,000	74	191	Soviet Socialist Republic (U.S.S.R.)	D	Tbilisi	Asia	16
†GERMAN DEMOCRATIC REPUBLIC	Deutsche Demokratische Republik	108,179	41,768	16,750,000	155	401	Socialist Republic	A	East Berlin (Ost-Berlin)	Europe . .	10
†GERMANY, FEDERAL REPUBLIC OF (incl. West Berlin)	Bundesrepublik Deutschland	248,650	96,004	61,680,000	248	642	Federal Republic	A	Bonn	Europe . .	10
Germany (Entire)	Deutschland	356,829	137,772	78,430,000	220	569				Europe . .	10
†GHANA	Ghana	238,537	92,100	11,730,000	49	127	Republic (Comm. of Nations)	A	Accra	Africa . . .	34
Gibraltar (U.K.)	Gibraltar	6.0	2.3	30,000	5,000	13,043	Colony (U.K.)	C	Gibraltar	Europe . .	13
Gilbert Islands, see Kiribati	. . .	. . .	. . .	. . .	. . .	. . .					
Great Britain, see United Kingdom	. . .	. . .	. . .	. . .	. . .	. . .	. . . .			. . . .	. . .
†GREECE	Ellas	131,944	50,944	9,840,000	75	193	Republic	A	Athens (Athínai)	Europe . .	15
GREENLAND	Grønland (Danish) Kalaallit Nunaat (Eskimo)	2,175,600	840,003	51,000	0.02	0.06	Part of Danish Realm	B	Godthåb	N. Amer. .	41
†GRENADA	Grenada	344	133	112,000	326	842	Parliamentary State (Comm. of Nations)	A	Saint George's	N. Amer. .	51
Guadeloupe (incl. Dependencies) (Fr.)	Guadeloupe	1,779	687	320,000	180	466	Overseas Department (France)	D	Basse-Terre	N. Amer. .	51
Guam (U.S.)	Guam	549	212	110,000	200	519	Unincorporated Territory (U.S.)	C	Agana	Oceania. .	64
†GUATEMALA	Guatemala	108,889	42,042	7,375,000	68	175	Republic	A	Guatemala	N. Amer. .	49
Guernsey (incl. Dependencies) (U.K.)	Guernsey	77	30	55,000	714	1,833	Bailiwick (U.K.)	C	St. Peter Port	Europe . .	9
†GUINEA	Guinée	245,857	94,926	5,200,000	21	55	Republic	A	Conakry	Africa . . .	34
†GUINEA-BISSAU	Guiné-Bissau	36,125	13,948	820,000	23	59	Republic	A	Bissau	Africa . . .	34
†GUYANA	Guyana	214,969	83,000	925,000	4.3	11	Republic (Comm. of Nations)	A	Georgetown	S. Amer. .	54
†HAITI	Haïti	27,750	10,714	5,145,000	185	480	Republic	A	Port-au-Prince	N. Amer. .	49
Hawaii, U.S.	Hawaii	16,706	6,450	995,000	60	154	State (U.S.)	D	Honolulu	N. Amer. .	60
Heilungkiang, China	Heilongjiang	705,254	272,300	31,340,000	44	115	Province (China)	D	Harbin	Asia	27
Hispaniola	La Española	76,192	29,418	10,805,000	142	367	. . . .		. . . . .	N. Amer. .	49
Holland, see Netherlands	. . .	. . .	. . .	. . .	. . .	. . .					

Country, Division, or Region English (Conventional)	Local Name	Area km²	Area sq mi	Population 1/1/82	Population Density per km²	Population Density per sq mi	Form of Government and Political Status	Capital	Continent and Map Plate
Honan, China	Henan	166,795	*64,400*	71,840,000	431	*1,116*	Province (China)	*D* Chengchow (Zhengzhou)	Asia 27
†HONDURAS	Honduras	112,088	*43,277*	3,880,000	35	*90*	Republic	*A* Tegucigalpa	N. Amer. 49
Hong Kong (U.K.)	Hong Kong	1,061	*410*	5,375,000	5,066	*13,110*	Colony (U.K.)	*C* Victoria	Asia 27
Hopeh, China	Hebei	192,954	*74,500*	59,925,000	311	*804*	Province (China)	*D* Shijiazhuang	Asia 28
Hunan, China	Hunan	210,566	*81,300*	52,435,000	249	*645*	Province (China)	*D* Changsha	Asia 27
†HUNGARY	Magyarország	93,036	*35,921*	10,715,000	115	*298*	Socialist Republic	*A* Budapest	Europe 10
Hupeh, China	Hubei	187,515	*72,400*	46,665,000	249	*645*	Province (China)	*D* Wuhan	Asia 27
†ICELAND	Ísland	103,000	*39,769*	230,000	2.2	*5.8*	Republic	*A* Reykjavík	Europe 7
Idaho, U.S.	Idaho	216,413	*83,557*	975,000	4.5	*12*	State (U.S.)	*D* Boise	N. Amer. 46
Illinois, U.S.	Illinois	150,028	*57,926*	11,650,000	78	*201*	State (U.S.)	*D* Springfield	N. Amer. 45
†INDIA (incl. part of Jammu and Kashmir)	Bhārat	3,203,975	*1,237,061*	695,230,000	217	*562*	Federal Socialist Republic (Comm. of Nations)	*A* New Delhi	Asia 25
Indiana, U.S.	Indiana	94,585	*36,519*	5,595,000	59	*153*	State (U.S.)	*D* Indianapolis	N. Amer. 44
†INDONESIA	Indonesia	1,919,270	*741,034*	151,500,000	79	*204*	Republic	*A* Jakarta	Asia 26
Inner Mongolia, China	Nei Mongol	424,499	*163,900*	8,555,000	20	*52*	Autonomous Region (China)	*D* Hohhot	Asia 27
Iowa, U.S.	Iowa	145,791	*56,290*	2,980,000	20	*53*	State (U.S.)	*D* Des Moines	N. Amer 45
†IRAN	Īrān	1,648,000	*636,296*	38,565,000	23	*61*	Republic	*A* Tehrān	Asia 23
†IRAQ	Al 'Irāq	434,924	*167,925*	13,465,000	31	*80*	Socialist Republic	*A* Baghdād	Asia 24
†IRELAND	Eire	70,283	*27,136*	3,495,000	50	*129*	Republic	*A* Dublin (Baile Átha Cliath)	Europe 9
ISLE OF MAN	Isle of Man	588	*227*	66,000	112	*291*	Self-governing Territory (U.K. protection)	*B* Douglas	Europe 9
†ISRAEL	Yisra'el	20,325	*7,848*	3,980,000	196	*507*	Republic	*A* Jerusalem (Yerushalayim)	Asia 24
Israeli Occupied Areas	...	7,000	*2,703*	1,235,000	176	*457*	...	...	Asia 24
†ITALY	Italia	301,262	*116,318*	57,270,000	190	*492*	Republic	*A* Rome (Roma)	Europe 14
†IVORY COAST	Côte d'Ivoire	320,763	*123,847*	8,145,000	25	*66*	Republic	*A* Abidjan	Africa 34
†JAMAICA	Jamaica	10,991	*4,244*	2,235,000	203	*527*	Parliamentary State (Comm. of Nations)	*A* Kingston	N. Amer. 49
†JAPAN	Nippon	372,313	*143,751*	118,650,000	319	*825*	Constitutional Monarchy	*A* Tōkyō	Asia 29
Java (incl. Madura) (Indon.)	Jawa	132,187	*51,038*	93,780,000	709	*1,837*	Part of Indonesia (5 provinces)	...	Asia 26
Jersey (U.K.)	Jersey	117	*45*	78,000	667	*1,733*	Bailiwick (U.K.)	*C* St. Helier	Europe 9
†JORDAN	Al Urdun	91,000	*35,135*	2,300,000	25	*65*	Constitutional Monarchy	*A* 'Ammān	Asia 24
†KAMPUCHEA	Kampuchea Prâcheathipâtéyy	181,035	*69,898*	6,965,000	38	*100*	Socialist Republic	*A* Phnum Pénh	Asia 26
Kansas, U.S.	Kansas	213,064	*82,264*	2,405,000	11	*29*	State (U.S.)	*D* Topeka	N. Amer. 45
Kansu, China	Gansu	720,276	*278,100*	20,895,000	29	*75*	Province (China)	*D* Lanzhou	Asia 27
Kashmir, Jammu and	Jammu and Kashmīr	222,802	*86,024*	9,920,000	45	*115*	In dispute (India and Pakistan)	... Srīnagar and Jammu	Asia 25
Kazakh S.S.R., U.S.S.R.	Kazahskaja S.S.R.	2,717,300	*1,049,155*	15,105,000	5.6	*14*	Soviet Socialist Republic (U.S.S.R.)	*D* Alma-Ata	Asia 19
Keewatin (Can.)	Keewatin	590,932	*228,160*	5,000	0.01	*0.02*	District of Northwest Territories (Canada)	...	N. Amer. 42
Kentucky, U.S.	Kentucky	104,623	*40,395*	3,745,000	36	*93*	State (U.S.)	*D* Frankfort	N. Amer. 44
†KENYA	Kenya	582,646	*224,961*	17,790,000	31	*79*	Republic (Comm. of Nations)	*A* Nairobi	Africa 36
Kerguelen Islands (Fr.)	Iles Kerguèlen	6,993	*2,700*	90	0.01	*0.03*	Part of French Southern and Antarctic Territory (France)	*C* ...	S. Amer. 30–31
Kiangsi, China	Jiangxi	164,723	*63,600*	28,260,000	172	*444*	Province (China)	*D* Nanchang	Asia 27
Kiangsu, China	Jiangsu	92,981	*35,900*	67,105,000	722	*1,869*	Province (China)	*D* Nanjing	Asia 28
Kirghiz S.S.R., U.S.S.R.	Kirgizskaja S.S.R.	198,500	*76,641*	3,655,000	18	*48*	Soviet Socialist Republic (U.S.S.R.)	*D* Frunze	Asia 18
KIRIBATI	Kiribati	754	*291*	59,000	78	*203*	Republic (Comm. of Nations)	*A* Bairiki	Oceania 60
Kirin, China	Jilin	271,690	*104,900*	22,385,000	82	*213*	Province (China)	*D* Changchun	Asia 27
KOREA, NORTH	Chosŏn Minjujuŭi In'min Konghwaguk	120,538(4)	*46,540(4)*	18,540,000	154	*398*	Socialist Republic	*A* P'yŏngyang	Asia 28
KOREA, SOUTH	Taehan-Min'guk	98,484(4)	*38,025(4)*	40,755,000	414	*1,072*	Republic	*A* Seoul (Sŏul)	Asia 28
Korea (Entire)	Chosŏn	220,284	*85,052*	59,295,000	269	*697*	...	...	Asia 28
†KUWAIT	Al Kuwayt	17,818	*6,880*	1,480,000	83	*215*	Constitutional Monarchy	*A* Al Kuwayt	Asia 24
Kwangsi, China	Guangxi	240,092	*92,700*	32,040,000	133	*346*	Province (China)	*D* Nanning	Asia 27
Kwangtung, China	Guangdong	211,602	*81,700*	54,725,000	259	*670*	Province (China)	*D* Canton (Guangzhou)	Asia 27
Kweichow, China	Guizhou	174,047	*67,200*	26,565,000	153	*395*	Province (China)	*D* Guiyang	Asia 27
Labrador (Can.)	Labrador	292,218	*112,826*	35,000	0.1	*0.3*	Part of Newfoundland Province (Canada)	...	N. Amer. 42
†LAOS	Laos	236,800	*91,429*	3,850,000	16	*42*	Socialist Republic	*A* Viangchan	Asia 26
Latin America	...	20,561,900	*7,938,600*	571,655,000	18	*47*	...	...	N.A., S.A. 52–53
Latvian S.S.R., U.S.S.R.	Latvijas P.S.R.	63,700	*24,595*	2,580,000	41	*105*	Soviet Socialist Republic (U.S.S.R.)	*D* Rīga	Europe 8
†LEBANON	Lubnān	10,400	*4,015*	3,275,000	315	*816*	Republic	*A* Beirut (Bayrūt)	Asia 24
†LESOTHO	Lesotho	30,355	*11,720*	1,385,000	46	*118*	Monarchy (Comm. of Nations)	*A* Maseru	Africa 37
Liaoning, China	Liaoning	229,473	*88,600*	45,970,000	200	*519*	Province (China)	*D* Mukden (Shenyang)	Asia 28
†LIBERIA	Liberia	111,369	*43,000*	1,975,000	18	*46*	Republic	*A* Monrovia	Africa 34
†LIBYA	Lībiyā	1,759,540	*679,362*	3,155,000	1.8	*4.6*	Socialist Republic	*A* Tripoli (Tarābulus)	Africa 33
LIECHTENSTEIN	Liechtenstein	169	*62*	27,000	169	*435*	Constitutional Monarchy	*A* Vaduz	Europe 14
Lithuanian S.S.R., U.S.S.R.	Lietuvos T.S.R.	65,200	*25,174*	3,470,000	53	*138*	Soviet Socialist Republic (U.S.S.R.)	*D* Vilnius	Europe 8
Louisiana, U.S.	Louisiana	125,675	*48,523*	4,300,000	34	*89*	State (U.S.)	*D* Baton Rouge	N. Amer. 45
†LUXEMBOURG	Luxembourg	2,586	*999*	355,000	137	*355*	Constitutional Monarchy	*A* Luxembourg	Europe 12
Macao (Port.)	Macau	16	*6.0*	275,000	17,188	*45,833*	Overseas Province (Portugal)	*D* Macau	Asia 27
Macias Nguema Biyogo, *see* Bioko	...	...	...	...	...	...	...	...	...
†Mackenzie (Can.)	Mackenzie	1,366,193	*527,490*	36,000	0.03	*0.07*	District of Northwest Territories (Canada)	...	N. Amer. 42
†MADAGASCAR	Madagasikara	587,041	*226,658*	9,085,000	15	*40*	Republic	*A* Antananarivo	Africa 37
Madeira Islands, Port.	Arquipélago da Madeira	796	*307*	265,000	333	*863*	District of Portugal (Madeira)	*D* Funchal	Africa 32
Maine, U.S.	Maine	86,027	*33,215*	1,115,000	13	*34*	State (U.S.)	*D* Augusta	N. Amer. 44
Malagasy Republic, see Madagascar	...	...	...	...	...	...	...	...	...
†MALAWI	Malawi	118,484	*45,747*	6,200,000	52	*136*	Republic (Comm. of Nations)	*A* Lilongwe	Africa 36
Malaya	Malaya	131,312	*50,700*	12,235,000	93	*241*	Part of Malaysia (11 States)	...	Asia 26
†MALAYSIA	Malaysia	332,632	*128,430*	14,495,000	44	*113*	Constitutional Monarchy (Comm. of Nations)	*A* Kuala Lumpur	Asia 26
†MALDIVES	Maldives	298	*115*	155,000	520	*1,348*	Republic	*A* Male	Asia 25
†MALI	Mali	1,240,000	*478,766*	7,175,000	5.8	*15*	Republic	*A* Bamako	Africa 34
†MALTA	Malta	316	*122*	360,000	1,139	*2,951*	Republic (Comm. of Nations)	*A* Valletta	Europe 14
Manitoba, Can.	Manitoba	650,087	*251,000*	1,045,000	1.6	*4.2*	Province (Canada)	*D* Winnipeg	N. Amer 42
Maritime Provinces (excl. Newfoundland) (Can.)	Maritime Provinces	134,584	*51,963*	1,677,000	12	*32*	Part of Canada (3 provinces)	...	N. Amer. 42
Marshall Islands (T.T.P.I.)	Marshall Islands	181	*70*	31,000	171	*443*	Part of Trust Territory of the Pacific Islands (U.S. administration)	*C* Uliga	Oceania 60

Country, Division, or Region English (Conventional)	Local Name	Area km²	sq mi	Population 1/1/82	Population Density per km²	sq mi	Form of Government and Political Status		Capital	Continent and Map Plate	
Martinique (Fr.)	Martinique	1,100	425	300,000	273	706	Overseas Department (France)	D	Fort-de-France	N. Amer. .	51
Maryland, U.S.	Maryland	27,394	10,577	4,300,000	157	407	State (U.S.)	D	Annapolis	N. Amer. .	44
Massachusetts, U.S.	Massachusetts	21,386	8,257	5,800,000	271	702	State (U.S.)	D	Boston	N. Amer. .	44
†MAURITANIA	Mūrītāniyā	1,030,700	397,955	1,730,000	1.7	4.3	Republic	A	Nouakchott	Africa . . .	32
†MAURITIUS (incl. Dependencies)	Mauritius	2,045	790	985,000	482	1,247	Parliamentary State (Comm. of Nations)	A	Port-Louis	Africa . . .	37
Mayotte (Fr.)	Mayotte	374	144	54,000	144	375	Overseas Department (France)	D	Dzaoudzi	Africa . . .	37
†MEXICO	México	1,972,547	761,604	70,515,000	36	93	Federal Republic	A	Mexico (Ciudad de México)	N. Amer .	48
Michigan, U.S.	Michigan	250,687	96,791	9,455,000	38	98	State (U.S.)	D	Lansing	N. Amer. .	44
Micronesia, Federated States of (T.T.P.I.)	Federated States of Micronesia	694	268	71,000			Part of Trust Territory of the Pacific Islands (U.S. administration)	C	Ponape	Oceania. .	60
Middle America	. . .	2,703,900	1,055,600	123,855,000	46	117				N. Amer. .	47
Midway Islands (U.S.)	Midway Islands	5.2	2.0	1,500	288	750	Unincorporated Territory (U.S.)	C	. . .	Oceania. .	60
Minnesota, U.S.	Minnesota	223,465	86,280	4,160,000	19	48	State (U.S.)	D	St. Paul	N. Amer. .	45
Mississippi, U.S.	Mississippi	123,584	47,716	2,565,000	21	54	State (U.S.)	D	Jackson	N. Amer. .	45
Missouri, U.S.	Missouri	180,487	69,686	5,015,000	28	72	State (U.S.)	D	Jefferson City	N. Amer. .	45
Moldavian S.S.R., U.S.S.R.	Moldavskaja S.S.R.	33,700	13,012	4,030,000	120	310	Soviet Socialist Republic (U.S.S.R.)	D	Kišinev	Europe . .	16
MONACO	Monaco	1.5	0.6	27,000	18,000	45,000	Constitutional Monarchy	A	Monaco	Europe . .	11
†MONGOLIA	Mongol Ard Uls	1,565,000	604,250	1,750,000	1.1	2.9	Socialist Republic	A	Ulan-Bator	Asia	27
Montana, U.S.	Montana	381,087	147,138	810,000	2.1	5.5	State (U.S.)	D	Helena	N. Amer. .	46
Montserrat (U.K.)	Montserrat	103	40	12,000	117	300	Colony (U.K.)	C	Plymouth	N. Amer. .	51
†MOROCCO (excl. Western Sahara)	Al Maghrib	446,550	172,414	21,795,000	49	126	Constitutional Monarchy	A	Rabat	Africa . . .	32
†MOZAMBIQUE	Moçambique	783,030	302,329	12,385,000	16	41	Socialist Republic	A	Maputo	Africa . . .	37
Muscat and Oman, see Oman	. . .	. . .	. . .	. . .	. . .					. . . .	. . .
Namibia (excl. Walvis Bay) (S. Afr.)(5)	Namibia	824,292	318,261	1,070,000	1.3	3.4	Under South African Administration	C	Windhoek	Africa . . .	37
NAURU	Nauru (English) Naoero (Nauruan)	21	8.2	7,900	376	963	Republic (Comm. of Nations)	A	Domaneab	Oceania. .	64
Nebraska, U.S.	Nebraska	200,018	77,227	1,595,000	8.0	21	State (U.S.)	D	Lincoln	N. Amer. .	45
†NEPAL	Nepal	140,797	54,362	15,520,000	110	285	Constitutional Monarchy	A	Kathmandu	Asia	25
†NETHERLANDS	Nederland	41,160	15,892	14,300,000	347	900	Constitutional Monarchy	A	Amsterdam	Europe . .	12
Netherlands Guiana, see Suriname	. . .	. . .	. . .	. . .	. . .					. . . .	. . .
NETHERLANDS ANTILLES	Nederlandse Antillen	993	383	260,000	262	679	Self-governing Territory (Netherlands protection)	B	Willemstad	N. Amer. .	50
Nevada, U.S.	Nevada	286,299	110,541	855,000	3.0	7.7	State (U.S.)	D	Carson City	N. Amer. .	46
New Brunswick, Can.	New Brunswick	73,436	28,354	705,000	9.6	25	Province (Canada)	D	Fredericton	N. Amer. .	42
New Caledonia (incl. Dependencies) (Fr.)	Nouvelle-Calédonie	19,058	7,358	140,000	7.3	19	Overseas Territory (France)	C	Nouméa	Oceania. .	63
New England (U.S.)	New England	172,514	66,608	12,550,000	73	188	Part of U.S. (6 states)			N. Amer. .	43
Newfoundland, Can.	Newfoundland	404,517	156,185	585,000	1.4	3.7	Province (Canada)	D	St. John's	N. Amer. .	42
Newfoundland (excl. Labrador) (Can.)	Newfoundland	112,299	43,359	550,000	4.9	13	Part of Newfoundland Province, Canada .			N. Amer. .	42
New Hampshire, U.S.	New Hampshire	24,097	9,304	950,000	39	102	State (U.S.)	D	Concord	N. Amer. .	44
New Hebrides, see Vanuatu	. . .	. . .	. . .	. . .	. . .					. . . .	. . .
New Jersey, U.S.	New Jersey	20,295	7,836	7,515,000	370	959	State (U.S.)	D	Trenton	N. Amer. .	44
New Mexico, U.S.	New Mexico	315,115	121,667	1,350,000	4.3	11	State (U.S.)	D	Santa Fe	N. Amer. .	45
New South Wales, Austl.	New South Wales	801,428	309,433	5,245,000	6.5	17	State (Australia)	D	Sydney	Oceania. .	59
New York, U.S.	New York	137,795	53,203	17,680,000	128	332	State (U.S.)	D	Albany	N. Amer. .	44
†NEW ZEALAND	New Zealand	269,057	103,883	3,195,000	12	31	Parliamentary State (Comm. of Nations)	A	Wellington	Oceania. .	62
†NICARAGUA	Nicaragua	130,000	50,193	3,035,000	23	60	Republic	A	Managua	N. Amer. .	49
†NIGER	Niger	1,267,000	489,191	5,538,000	4.4	11	Republic	A	Niamey	Africa . . .	34
†NIGERIA	Nigeria	923,768	356,669	80,765,000	87	226	Federal Republic (Comm. of Nations)	A	Lagos	Africa . . .	34
Ningsia, China	Ningxia	66,304	25,600	2,985,000	45	117	Autonomous Region (China)	D	Yinchuan	Asia	27
NIUE	Niue	263	102	3,000	11	29	Self-governing Territory (New Zealand)	B	Alofi	Oceania. .	64
Norfolk Island (Austl.)	Norfolk Island	36	14	2,300	64	164	External Territory (Australia)	C	Kingston	Oceania. .	61
NORTH AMERICA	. . .	24,360,000	9,406,000	379,400,000	16	40				N. Amer. .	38–39
North Borneo, see Sabah	. . .	. . .	. . .	. . .	. . .					. . . .	. . .
North Carolina, U.S.	North Carolina	136,198	52,586	5,985,000	44	114	State (U.S.)	D	Raleigh	N. Amer. .	44
North Dakota, U.S.	North Dakota	183,022	70,665	670,000	3.7	9.5	State (U.S.)	D	Bismarck	N. Amer. .	45
Northern Ireland, U.K.	Northern Ireland	14,120	5,452	1,545,000	109	283	Administrative division of United Kingdom	D	Belfast	Europe . .	9
Northern Mariana Islands (T.T.P.I.)	Northern Mariana Islands	474	183	18,000	38	98	Part of Trust Territory of the Pacific Islands (U.S. administration)	C	Saipan (island)	Oceania. .	60
Northern Territory, Austl.	Northern Territory	1,375,519	520,280	125,000	0.09	0.2	Territory (Australia)	D	Darwin	Oceania. .	59
Northwest Territories, Can.	Northwest Territories	3,379,684	1,304,903	49,000	0.01	0.04	Territory (Canada)	D	Yellowknife	N. Amer. .	42
†NORWAY (incl. Svalbard and Jan Mayen)	Norge	386,317	149,158	4,115,000	13	33	Constitutional Monarchy	A	Oslo	Europe . .	7
Nova Scotia, Can.	Nova Scotia	55,491	21,425	850,000	15	40	Province (Canada)	D	Halifax	N. Amer. .	42
OCEANIA (incl. Australia)	. . .	8,513,000	3,287,000	23,200,000	2.7	7.1				Oceania. .	57–58
Ohio, U.S.	Ohio	115,791	44,679	11,025,000	95	247	State (U.S.)	D	Columbus	N. Amer. .	44
Oklahoma, U.S.	Oklahoma	181,090	69,919	3,100,000	17	44	State (U.S.)	D	Oklahoma City	N. Amer. .	45
†OMAN	'Umān	212,457	82,030	930,000	4.4	11	Monarchy	A	Muscat (Masqat)	Asia	23
Ontario, Can.	Ontario	1,068,582	412,582	8,665,000	8.1	21	Province (Canada)	D	Toronto	N. Amer. .	42
Oregon, U.S.	Oregon	251,181	96,981	2,680,000	11	28	State (U.S.)	D	Salem	N. Amer. .	46
Orkney Islands (U.K.)	Orkney Islands	974	376	19,000	20	51	Part of Scotland, U.K. (Orkney Island Area)		Kirkwall	Europe . .	9
†PAKISTAN (incl. part of Jammu and Kashmir)	Pākistān	828,453	319,867	92,070,000	111	288	Federal Republic	A	Islāmābād	Asia	25
Palau (T.T.P.I.)	Palau	461	178	14,000	. . .	. . .	Part of Trust Territory of the Pacific Islands (U.S. administration) . .	C	Koror	Oceania. .	60
†PANAMA	Panamá	77,082	29,762	1,910,000	25	64	Republic	A	Panamá	N. Amer. .	49
†PAPUA NEW GUINEA	Papua New Guinea	462,840	178,703	3,115,000	6.7	17	Parliamentary State (Comm. of Nations)	A	Port Moresby	Oceania. .	60
†PARAGUAY	Paraguay	406,752	157,048	3,205,000	7.9	20	Republic	A	Asunción	S. Amer. .	56
Peking, China	Beijing	17,094	6,600	8,000,000	468	1,212	Autonomous City (China)	D	Beijing	Asia	28
Pennsylvania, U.S.	Pennsylvania	119,316	46,068	11,995,000	101	260	State (U.S.)	D	Harrisburg	N. Amer. .	44

Country, Division, or Region English (Conventional)	Local Name	Area km²	sq mi	Population 1/1/82	Population Density per km²	sq mi	Form of Government and Political Status		Capital	Continent and Map Plate
Persia, *see* Iran	. . .	. . .	. . .							. . .
†PERU	Peru	1,285,216	496,224	18,510,000	14	37	Republic	A	Lima	S. Amer. . 54
†PHILIPPINES	Pilipinas	300,000	115,831	50,960,000	170	440	Republic	A	Manila	Asia 26
Pitcairn (excl. Dependencies) (U.K.)	Pitcairn	4.7	1.8	65	14	36	Colony (U.K.)	C	Adamstown	Oceania. . 61
†POLAND	Polska	312,683	120,728	36,035,000	115	298	Socialist Republic	A	Warsaw (Warszawa)	Europe . . 10
†PORTUGAL	Portugal	88,940	34,340	10,050,000	113	293	Republic	A	Lisbon (Lisboa)	Europe . . 13
Portuguese Guinea, *see* Guinea-Bissau	. . .									. . .
Prairie Provinces (Can.)	Prairie Provinces	1,963,172	757,985	4,235,000	2.2	5.6	Part of Canada (3 provinces)			N. Amer. . 42
Prince Edward Island, Can.	Prince Edward Island	5,657	2,184	122,000	22	56	Province (Canada)	D	Charlottetown	N. Amer. . 42
PUERTO RICO	Puerto Rico	8,897	3,435	3,270,000	368	952	Commonwealth (U.S. protection)	B	San Juan	N. Amer. . 51
†QATAR	Qaṭar	11,000	4,247	235,000	21	55	Monarchy.	A	Ad Dawḩah (Doha)	Asia 24
Quebec, Can.	Québec	1,540,680	594,860	6,375,000	4.1	11	Province (Canada)	D	Québec	N. Amer. . 42
Queensland, Austl.	Queensland	1,727,522	667,000	2,310,000	1.3	3.5	State (Australia).	D	Brisbane	Oceania. . 59
Reunion (Fr.)	Réunion	2,510	969	525,000	209	542	Overseas Department (France)	D	Saint-Denis	Africa . . . 37
Rhode Island, U.S.	Rhode Island	3,144	1,214	950,000	302	783	State (U.S.)	D	Providence	N. Amer. . 44
Rhodesia, *see* Zimbabwe	. . .	. . .	. . .							
Rodrigues (Maur.)	Rodrigues	109	42	32,000	294	762	Part of Mauritius.		. . .	Africa . . . 30–31
†ROMANIA	România	237,500	91,699	22,445,000	95	245	Socialist Republic	A	Bucharest (Bucureşti)	Europe . . 15
Russian Soviet Federated Socialist Republic, U.S.S.R.	Rossijskaja S.F.S.R.	17,075,400	6,592,846	140,580,000	8.2	21	Soviet Federated Socialist Republic (U.S.S.R.).	D	Moscow (Moskva)	Eur./Asia . 19–20
†RWANDA	Rwanda	26,338	10,169	5,175,000	196	509	Republic	A	Kigali	Africa . . . 36
Sabah, Malaysia	Sabah	76,115	29,388	915,000	12	31	State of Malaysia.	D	Kota Kinabalu	Asia 26
St. Christopher-Nevis	St. Christopher-Nevis	269	104	41,000	152	394	Associated State (U.K.)	B	Basseterre	N. Amer. . 51
St. Helena (incl. Dependencies) (U.K.)	St. Helena	419	162	6,600	16	41	Colony (U.K.)	C	Jamestown	Africa . . . 31
†SAINT LUCIA	Saint Lucia	616	238	124,000	201	521	Parliamentary State (Comm. of Nations).	A	Castries	N. Amer. . 51
St. Pierre and Miquelon (Fr.)	St.-Pierre et Miquelon	242	93	6,700	28	72	Overseas Department (France)	D	Saint-Pierre	N. Amer. . 42
†ST. VINCENT	St. Vincent	389	150	128,000	329	853	Parliamentary State (Comm. of Nations).	A	Kingstown	N. Amer. . 50
Samoa (entire)	Samoa Islands	3,039	1,173	189,000	62	161				Oceania. . 65
SAN MARINO	San Marino	61	24	24,000	393	1,000	Republic	A	San Marino	Europe . . 14
†SAO TOME AND PRINCIPE	São Tomé e Príncipe	964	372	89,000	92	239	Republic	A	São Tomé	Africa . . . 34
Sarawak, Malaysia	Sarawak	125,205	48,342	1,345,000	11	28	State of Malaysia.	D	Kuching	Asia 26
Sardinia	Sardegna	24,090	9,301	1,605,000	67	173	Part of Italy (Sardegna Autonomous Region).	D	Cagliari	Europe . . 14
Saskatchewan, Can.	Saskatchewan	651,900	251,700	1,000,000	1.5	4.0	Province (Canada)	D	Regina	N. Amer. . 42
†SAUDI ARABIA	Al 'Arabīyah as Sa'ūdīyah	2,149,690	830,000	8,755,000	4.1	11	Monarchy.	A	Riyadh (Ar Riyāḍ)	Asia 23
Scandinavia (incl. Finland and Iceland)	. . .	1,320,900	510,000	22,680,000	17	44				Europe . . 7
Scotland, U.K.	Scotland	78,775	30,416	5,135,000	65	169	Administrative division of U.K.	D	Edinburgh	Europe . . 9
†SENEGAL	Sénégal	196,722	75,955	5,880,000	30	77	Republic	A	Dakar	Africa . . . 34
Senegambia	Senegambia	208,067	80,316	6,505,000	31	81	Economic Union			Africa . . . 34
†SEYCHELLES	Seychelles	443	171	68,000	153	398	Republic (Comm. of Nations)	A	Victoria	Africa . . . 37
Shanghai, China	Shanghai	5,698	2,200	11,300,000	1,893	5,136	Autonomous City (China)	D	Shanghai	Asia 28
Shansi, China	Shanxi	157,212	60,700	24,575,000	156	405	Province (China)	D	Taiyuan	Asia 27
Shantung, China	Shandong	153,586	59,300	83,380,000	543	1,406	Province (China)	D	Jinan	Asia 28
Shensi, China	Shaanxi	195,803	75,600	29,650,000	151	392	Province (China)	D	Xi'an	Asia 27
Shetland Islands (U.K.)	Shetland Islands	1,427	551	24,000	17	44	Part of Scotland, U.K. (Shetland Island Area).	. . .	Lerwick	Europe . . 9
Siam, *see* Thailand	. . .									. . . .
Sicily	Sicilia	25,708	9,926	5,040,000	196	508	Part of Italy (Sicilia Autonomous Region).	D	Palermo	Europe . . 14
†SIERRA LEONE	Sierra Leone	72,325	27,925	3,615,000	50	129	Republic (Comm. of Nations)	A	Freetown	Africa . . . 34
†SINGAPORE	Singapore (English) Singapura (Malay)	581	224	2,860,000	4,923	12,768	Republic (Comm. of Nations)	A	Singapore	Asia 26
Sinkiang, China	Xinjiang	1,646,714	635,800	9,550,000	5.8	15	Autonomous Region (China).	D	Ürümqi	Asia 27
†SOLOMON ISLANDS	Solomon Islands	29,800	11,500	235,000	7.9	20	Parliamentary State (Comm. of Nations).	A	Honiara	Oceania. . 63
†SOMALIA	Soomaaliya	637,657	246,200	5,100,000	8.0	21	Socialist Republic	A	Mogadishu (Muqdisho)	Africa . . . 35
†SOUTH AFRICA (incl. Walvis Bay)	South Africa (English) Suid-Afrika (Afrikaans)	1,221,042	471,447	30,495,000	25	65	Republic	A	Pretoria and Cape Town	Africa . . . 37
SOUTH AMERICA	. . .	17,828,000	6,883,000	247,800,000	14	36				S. Amer. . 52–53
South Australia, Austl.	South Australia	984,377	380,070	1,315,000	1.3	3.5	State (Australia).	D	Adelaide	Oceania. . 59
South Carolina, U.S.	South Carolina	80,432	31,055	3,190,000	40	103	State (U.S.)	D	Columbia	N. Amer. . 44
South Dakota, U.S.	South Dakota	199,552	77,047	695,000	3.5	9.0	State (U.S.)	D	Pierre	N. Amer. . 45
Southern Yemen, *see* Yemen, People's Democratic Republic of	. . .	. . .	. . .	. . .						
South Georgia (incl. Dependencies) (U.K.)[3]	South Georgia	4,092	1,580	20	.005	0.01	Dependency of Falkland Islands (U.K.).	C	. . .	S. Amer. . 56
South West Africa, *see* Namibia	. . .	. . .	. . .							
Soviet Union, *see* Union of Soviet Socialist Republics	. . .	. . .	. . .							
†SPAIN	España	504,741	194,882	37,865,000	75	194	Constitutional Monarchy	A	Madrid	Europe . . 13
Spanish North Africa (Sp.)[2]	Plazas de Soberanía en el Norte de África	32	12	127,000	3,969	10,583	Five Possessions (No Central Government).	C		Africa . . . 13
Spanish Sahara, *see* Western Sahara	. . .	. . .	. . .	. . .						. . . .
†SRI LANKA	Sri Lanka	65,000	25,097	15,605,000	240	622	Socialist Republic (Comm. of Nations).	A	Colombo	Asia 25
†SUDAN	As Sūdān	2,505,813	967,500	20,180,000	8.1	21	Republic	A	Khartoum (Al Kharṭūm)	Africa . . . 35
Sumatra	Sumatera	473,606	182,860	23,785,000	50	130	Part of Indonesia (7 provinces).			Asia 26
†SURINAME	Suriname	163,265	63,037	365,000	2.2	5.8	Republic	A	Paramaribo	S. Amer. . 54
†SWAZILAND	Swaziland	17,364	6,704	580,000	33	87	Monarchy (Comm. of Nations)	A	Mbabane	Africa . . . 37
†SWEDEN	Sverige	450,089	173,780	8,335,000	19	48	Constitutional Monarchy	A	Stockholm	Europe . . 7
SWITZERLAND	Schweiz (German) Suisse (French) Svizzera (Italian)	41,293	15,943	6,315,000	153	396	Federal Republic	A	Bern (Berne)	Europe . . 14
†SYRIA	Sūrīyah	185,180	71,498	9,475,000	51	133	Socialist Republic	A	Damascus (Dimashq)	Asia 24
Szechwan, China	Sichuan	569,020	219,700	106,765,000	188	486	Province (China)	D	Chengdu	Asia 27
Tadzhik S.S.R., U.S.S.R.	Tadžikskaja S.S.R.	143,100	55,251	3,950,000	28	71	Soviet Socialist Republic (U.S.S.R.)	D	Dušanbe	Asia 18

Country, Division, or Region English (Conventional)	Local Name	Area km²	Area sq mi	Population 1/1/82	Population Density per km²	Population Density per sq mi	Form of Government and Political Status		Capital	Continent and Map Plate	
TAIWAN	Taiwan	35,989	13,895	18,365,000	510	1,322	Republic	A	Taipei	Asia	27
†TANZANIA	Tanzania	945,087	364,900	19,115,000	20	52	Republic (Comm. of Nations)	A	Dodoma	Africa	36
Tasmania, Austl.	Tasmania	68,332	26,383	430,000	6.3	16	State (Australia)	D	Hobart	Oceania	59
Tennessee, U.S.	Tennessee	109,412	42,244	4,690,000	43	111	State (U.S.)	D	Nashville	N. Amer.	44
Texas, U.S.	Texas	692,405	267,339	14,520,000	21	54	State (U.S.)	D	Austin	N. Amer.	45
†THAILAND	Muang Thai	513,113	198,114	48,860,000	95	247	Constitutional Monarchy	A	Bangkok (Krung Thep)	Asia	26
Tibet, China	Xizang	1,221,697	471,700	1,690,000	1.4	3.6	Autonomous Region (China)	D	Lhasa	Asia	27
Tientsin, China	Tianjin	4,144	1,600	7,000,000	1,689	4,375	Autonomous City (China)	D	Tianjin	Asia	28
†TOGO	Togo	56,785	21,925	2,730,000	48	125	Republic	A	Lomé	Africa	34
Tokelau (N.Z.)	Tokelau	10	3.9	1,600	160	410	Island Territory (New Zealand)	C		Oceania	61
TONGA	Tonga	699	270	101,000	144	374	Constitutional Monarchy (Comm. of Nations)	A	Nuku'alofa	Oceania	61
Transcaucasia (U.S.S.R.)	. . .	186,100	71,853	14,460,000	78	201	Part of U.S.S.R. (3 republics)			Asia	16
†TRINIDAD AND TOBAGO	Trinidad and Tobago	5,128	1,980	1,165,000	227	588	Republic (Comm. of Nations)	A	Port of Spain	N. Amer.	50
Tristan da Cunha (U.K.)	Tristan da Cunha	104	40	300	2.9	7.5	Dependency of St. Helena (U.K.)	C	Edinburgh	Africa	30–31
Trucial States, see United Arab Emirates	. . .	. . .	. . .	. . .	. . .					. . . . . .	. . .
Trust Territory of the Pacific Islands	Trust Territory of the Pacific Islands	1,810	699	140,000	77	200	U.N. Trusteeship administered by U.S.	C	Saipan (island)	Oceania	60
Tsinghai, China	Qinghai	721,053	278,400	3,880,000	5.4	14	Province (China)	D	Xining	Asia	27
†TUNISIA	Tūnis	163,610	63,170	6,585,000	40	104	Republic	A	Tūnis	Africa	32
†TURKEY	Türkiye	779,452	300,948	46,435,000	60	154	Republic	A	Ankara	Eur./As.	24
Turkey in Europe		23,764	9,175	4,005,000	169	437	Part of Turkey			Europe	24
Turkmen S.S.R., U.S.S.R.	Turkmenskaja S.S.R.	488,100	188,456	2,875,000	5.9	15	Soviet Socialist Republic (U.S.S.R.)	D	Ašhabad	Asia	19
Turks and Caicos Islands (U.K.)	Turks and Caicos Islands	430	166	7,700	18	46	Colony (U.K.)	C	Grand Turk	N. Amer.	49
TUVALU	Tuvalu	26	10	8,100	312	810	Parliamentary State (Comm. of Nations)	A	Funafuti	Oceania	60
†UGANDA	Uganda	236,036	91,134	13,440,000	57	147	Republic (Comm. of Nations)	A	Kampala	Africa	36
†Ukrainian S.S.R., U.S.S.R.	Ukrainskaja S.S.R.	603,700	233,090	50,760,000	84	218	Soviet Socialist Republic (U.S.S.R)	D	Kiev (Kijev)	Europe	16
†UNION OF SOVIET SOCIALIST REPUBLICS	Sojuz Sovetskih Socialističeskih Respublik	22,274,900	8,600,383	268,740,000	12	31	Federal Socialist Republic	A	Moscow (Moskva)	Eur./Asia	19–20
U.S.S.R. in Europe	. . .	4,974,818	1,920,789	174,790,000	35	91	Part of U.S.S.R.			Europe	19
†UNITED ARAB EMIRATES	Al Imārāt al 'Arabīyah al Muttaḥidah	83,600	32,278	1,050,000	13	33	Federation of Monarchs	A	Abū Ẓaby	Asia	23
United Arab Republic, see Egypt	. . .	. . .	. . .	. . .	. . .					. . . . . .	. . .
†UNITED KINGDOM	United Kingdom	244,102	94,249	56,035,000	230	595	Constitutional Monarchy (Comm. of Nations)	A	London	Europe	9
United Kingdom and Possessions	. . .	294,415	113,676	62,049,000	211	546		. . .	London	. . . . . .	. . .
†UNITED STATES	United States	9,528,318	3,678,896	231,160,000	24	63	Federal Republic	A	Washington, D.C.	N. Amer.	43
United States and Possessions	. . .	9,540,129	3,683,456	234,817,000	25	64		. . .	Washington	. . . . . .	. . .
†UPPER VOLTA	Haute-Volta	274,200	105,869	7,180,000	26	68	Republic	A	Ouagadougou	Africa	34
†URUGUAY	Uruguay	176,215	68,037	2,930,000	17	43	Republic	A	Montevideo	S. Amer.	55
Utah, U.S.	Utah	219,932	84,916	1,510,000	6.9	18	State (U.S.)	D	Salt Lake City	N. Amer.	46
Uzbek S.S.R., U.S.S.R.	Uzbekskaja S.S.R.	447,400	172,742	16,015,000	36	93	Soviet Socialist Republic (U.S.S.R.)	D	Taškent	Asia	19
†VANUATU	Vanuatu	14,800	5,714	120,000	8.1	21	Parliamentary State (Comm. of Nations)	A	Port-Vila	Oceania	63
VATICAN CITY	Città del Vaticano	0.4	0.2	1,000	2,500	5,000	Ecclesiastical State	A	Vatican City (Città del Vaticano)	Europe	14
†VENEZUELA	Venezuela	912,050	352,144	14,515,000	16	41	Federal Republic	A	Caracas	S. Amer.	54
Vermont, U.S.	Vermont	24,887	9,609	530,000	21	55	State (U.S.)	D	Montpelier	N. Amer.	44
Victoria, Austl.	Victoria	227,619	87,884	3,955,000	17	45	State (Australia)	D	Melbourne	Oceania	59
†VIETNAM	Viet-nam Dan-chu Cong-hoa	329,556	127,242	55,455,000	168	436	Socialist Republic	A	Hanoi	Asia	26
Virginia, U.S.	Virginia	105,716	40,817	5,455,000	52	134	State (U.S.)	D	Richmond	N. Amer.	44
Virgin Islands (U.S.)	Virgin Islands	344	133	101,000	294	759	Unincorporated Territory (U.S.)	C	Charlotte Amalie	N. Amer.	51
Virgin Islands, British (U.K.)	British Virgin Islands	153	59	11,000	72	186	Colony (U.K.)	C	Road Town	N. Amer.	51
Wake Island (U.S.)	Wake Island	7.8	3.0	200	26	67	Unincorporated Territory (U.S.)	C	. . .	Oceania	60
Wales, U.K.	Wales	20,768	8,019	2,780,000	134	347	Administrative division of U.K.	D	Cardiff	Europe	9
Wallis and Futuna (Fr.)	Iles Wallis-et-Futuna	255	98	11,000	43	112	Overseas Territory (France)	C	Mata-Utu	Oceania	61
Washington, U.S.	Washington	176,617	68,192	4,205,000	24	62	State (U.S.)	D	Olympia	N. Amer.	46
Western Australia, Austl.	Western Australia	2,527,621	975,920	1,295,000	0.5	1.3	State (Australia)	D	Perth	Oceania	59
Western Sahara	. . .	266,000	102,703	120,000	0.5	1.2	Occupied by Morocco	C	El Aaiún	Africa	32
†WESTERN SAMOA	Samoa i Sisifo	2,842	1,097	155,000	55	141	Constitutional Monarchy (Comm. of Nations)	A	Apia	Oceania	65
West Indies	West Indies (English) Indias Occidentales (Spanish)	238,200	92,000	29,370,000	123	319				N. Amer.	47
West Virginia, U.S.	West Virginia	62,629	24,181	1,990,000	32	82	State (U.S.)	D	Charleston	N. Amer.	44
White Russia, see Byelorussian S.S.R.	. . .	. . .	. . .	. . .	. . .					. . . . . .	. . .
Wisconsin, U.S.	Wisconsin	171,499	66,216	4,810,000	28	73	State (U.S.)	D	Madison	N. Amer.	45
Wyoming, U.S.	Wyoming	253,597	97,914	485,000	1.9	5.0	State (U.S.)	D	Cheyenne	N. Amer.	46
†YEMEN	Al Yaman	195,000	75,290	6,140,000	31	82	Republic	A	Şan'ā'	Asia	23
†YEMEN, PEOPLE'S DEMOCRATIC REPUBLIC OF	Al Yaman ad Dīmuqrāṭīyah	332,968	128,560	2,060,000	6.2	16	Socialist Republic	A	Aden (Baladiyat 'Adan)	Asia	23
†YUGOSLAVIA	Jugoslavija	255,804	98,766	22,635,000	88	229	Federal Socialist Republic	A	Belgrade (Beograd)	Europe	14–15
Yukon Territory, Can.	Yukon Territory	482,515	186,300	24,000	0.05	0.1	Territory (Canada)	D	Whitehorse	N. Amer.	42
Yunnan, China	Yunnan	436,154	168,400	27,860,000	64	165	Province (China)	D	Kunming	Asia	27
†ZAIRE	Zaïre	2,345,409	905,567	29,060,000	12	32	Republic	A	Kinshasa (Léopoldville)	Africa	36
†ZAMBIA	Zambia	752,614	290,586	5,905,000	7.8	20	Republic (Comm. of Nations)	A	Lusaka	Africa	36
Zanzibar	Zanzibar	2,461	950	520,000	211	547	Part of Tanzania	D	Zanzibar	Africa	36
†ZIMBABWE	Zimbabwe	390,580	150,804	7,700,000	20	51	Republic (Comm. of Nations)	A	Harare	Africa	37
WORLD	. . .	149,754,000	57,821,000	4,532,000,000	30	78				. . . . . .	1–2

† Member of the United Nations (1981).
. . . None, or not applicable.
(1) No permanent population.
(2) Comprises Ceuta, Melilla, and several small islands.
(3) Claimed by Argentina.
(4) The 1,262 km² or 487 sq mi of the demilitarized zone are not included in either North or South Korea.
(5) In October 1966 the United Nations terminated the South African mandate over Namibia, a decision which South Africa did not accept.

World Geographical Tables

The Earth: Land and Water

	Total Area km²	sq mi	Area of Land km²	sq mi	%	Area of Oceans and Seas km²	sq mi	%
Earth	510,100,000	197,000,000	149,400,000	57,700,000	29.3	360,700,000	139,300,000	70.7
N. Hemisphere	255,050,000	98,500,000	106,045,650	40,950,000	41.6	149,004,350	57,550,000	58.4
S. Hemisphere	255,050,000	98,500,000	43,354,350	16,750,000	17.0	211,695,650	81,750,000	83.0

The Continents

Continent	Area km² sq mi	Population Estimate (1/1/82)	Population per km² sq mi	Mean Elevation m ft *	Highest Elevation m/ft	Lowest Elevation m/ft (below sea level)	Highest Recorded Temperature °C/°F	Lowest Recorded Temperature °C/°F
Europe	9,932,000 3,835,000	666,400,000	67 174	340 1,000	Mt. Elbrus, U.S.S.R. 5,642/18,510	Caspian Sea, U.S.S.R.-Iran −28/−92	Sevilla, Spain 50°/122°	Ust-Ščugor, U.S.S.R. −55°/−67°
Asia	44,798,000 17,297,000	2,724,900,000	61 158	960 3,150	Mt. Everest, China-Nepal 8,848/29,029	Dead Sea, Israel-Jordan −395/−1,296	Tirat Zevi, Israel 54°/129°	Ojmjakon, U.S.S.R.; Verkhoyansk U.S.S.R. −68°/−90°
Africa	30,323,000 11,708,000	490,300,000	16 42	750 2,450	Kilimanjaro, Tanzania 5,895/19,341	Lac Assal, Djibouti −155/−509	Al ʻAzīzīyah, Libya 58°/136°	Ifrane, Morocco −24°/−11°
North America	24,360,000 9,406,000	379,400,000	16 40	720 2,350	Mt. McKinley, United States 6,194/20,320	Death Valley, United States −86/−282	Death Valley, United States 57°/134°	Northice, Greenland −66°/−87°
South America	17,828,000 6,883,000	247,800,000	14 36	590 1,940	Aconcagua, Argentina 6,960/22,835	Salinas Chicas, Argentina −42/−138	Rivadavia, Argentina 49°/120°	Sarmiento, Argentina −33°/−27°
Oceania, incl. Australia	8,513,000 3,287,000	23,200,000	3 7	. . . .	Mt. Wilhelm, Papua N. Gui. 4,509/14,793	Lake Eyre, Australia −12/−39	Cloncurry, Australia 53°/128°	Charlotte Pass, Australia −22°/−8°
Australia	7,686,850 2,967,909	14,910,000	2 5	340 1,100	Mt. Kosciusko, Australia 2,228/7,310	Lake Eyre, Australia −12/−39	Cloncurry, Australia 53°/128°	Charlotte Pass, Australia −22°/−8°
Antarctica	14,000,000 5,405,000	. . . .	. . . .	2,600 8,550	Vinson Massif 5,140/16,864	unknown	Esperanza 14°/58°	Vostok −90°/−127°
World	149,754,000 57,821,000	4,532,000,000	30 78	840 2,750	Mt. Everest, China-Nepal 8,848/29,029	Dead Sea, Israel-Jordan −395/−1,296	Al ʻAzīzīyah, Libya 58°/136°	Vostok −90°/−127°

All temperatures are rounded to the nearest degree.   * Elevations in feet are converted from metric equivalents and rounded.

Principal Mountains

Mountain	Country	Height M	Ft
Europe			
Elbrus, Mount	U.S.S.R.	5,642	18,510
Dyhtau	U.S.S.R.	5,203	17,070
Blanc, Mont	△France-△Italy	4,810	15,781
Rosa, Monte	Italy-△Switzerland	4,633	15,200
Matterhorn	Italy-Switzerland	4,478	14,692
Jungfrau	Switzerland	4,158	13,642
Grossglockner	△Austria	3,797	12,457
Teide, Pico de	△Spain (Canary Is.)	3,718	12,198
Mulhacén	Spain	3,478	11,411
Aneto, Pico de	Spain	3,404	11,168
Etna, Mount	Italy	3,340	10,958
Corno Grande	Italy	2,914	9,560
Gerlachovský štít	△Czechoslovakia	2,655	8,711
Glittertind	△Norway	2,470	8,104
Narodnaja, gora	U.S.S.R.	1,894	6,214
Nevis, Ben	△United Kingdom	1,343	4,406
Snowdon	United Kingdom	1,085	3,560
Asia			
Everest, Mount	△China-△Nepal	8,848	29,029
K2 (Godwin Austen)	China-△Pakistan	8,611	28,251
Kånchenjunga	△India-Nepal	8,598	28,207
Dhaulagiri	Nepal	8,172	26,811
Annapurna	Nepal	8,078	26,503
Muztag	China	7,723	25,338
Tirich Mīr	Pakistan	7,690	25,230
Communism Peak (pik Kommunizma)	△U.S.S.R.	7,495	24,590
Pobeda Peak (pik Pobedy)	China-U.S.S.R.	7,439	24,406
Demavend, Mount (Qolleh-ye Damāvand)	△Iran	5,670	18,602
Ararat, Mount (Büyük Ağrı Dağı)	△Turkey	5,165	16,946
Jaya, Puncak	△Indonesia	5,030	16,503
Klyuchevskaya Sopka (vulkan Ključevskaja Sopka)	U.S.S.R.	4,750	15,584
Kinabalu, Gunong	△Malaysia	4,101	13,455
Yu Shan	△Taiwan	3,997	13,114
Kerinci, Gunong	Indonesia	3,800	12,467
Fuji-San	△Japan	3,776	12,388
Nabī Shuʻayb, Jabal an	△Yemen	3,760	12,336
Sauda, Qurnet es	△Lebanon	3,083	10,115
Shām, Jabal ash	△Oman	3,017	9,898
Apo, Mount	△Philippines	2,954	9,692
Hermon, Mount	Lebanon-△Syria	2,814	9,232
Mayon, Mount	Philippines	2,462	8,077

Mountain	Country	Height M	Ft
Africa			
Kilimanjaro	△Tanzania	5,895	19,341
Kirinyaga (Mount Kenya)	△Kenya	5,199	17,057
Margherita Peak (Ruwenzori Range)	△Uganda-△Zaire	5,119	16,795
Ras Dashen	△Ethiopia	4,620	15,157
Toubkal, Jebel	△Morocco	4,167	13,671
Cameroun, Mont	△Cameroon	4,070	13,353
North America			
McKinley, Mount	△U.S.	6,194	20,320
Logan, Mount	△Canada	6,050	19,849
Orizaba, Pico de (Volcán Citlaltépetl)	△Mexico	5,700	18,701
Popocatépetl, Volcán	Mexico	5,452	17,887
Whitney, Mount	U.S.	4,418	14,494
Elbert, Mount	U.S.	4,399	14,433
Rainier, Mount	U.S.	4,392	14,410
Shasta, Mount	U.S.	4,317	14,162
Pikes Peak	U.S.	4,301	14,410
Tajumulco, Volcán	△Guatemala	4,220	13,845
Kea, Mauna	U.S.	4,205	13,796
Grand Teton	U.S.	4,197	13,770
Waddington, Mount	Canada	3,994	13,104
Chirripó, Cerro	△Costa Rica	3,820	12,533
Hood, Mount	U.S.	3,426	11,239
Duarte, Pico	△Dominican Republic	3,175	10,417
Mitchell, Mount	U.S.	2,037	6,684
Clingmans Dome	U.S.	2,025	6,643
Washington, Mount	U.S.	1,917	6,288
South America			
Aconcagua, Cerro	△Argentina	6,960	22,835
Ojos del Salado, Nevado	Argentina-△Chile	6,863	22,516
Huascarán, Nevado	△Peru	6,768	22,205
Chimborazo, Volcán	△Ecuador	6,267	20,561
Cristóbal Colón, Pico	△Colombia	5,800	19,029
Bolívar, Pico	△Venezuela	5,007	16,427
Neblina, Pico da	△Brazil	3,014	9,888
Oceania			
Wilhelm, Mount	△Papua New Guinea	4,509	14,793
Cook, Mount	△New Zealand	3,764	12,349
Kosciusko, Mount	△Australia	2,228	7,310
Antarctica			
Vinson Massif	△Antarctica	5,140	16,864
Jackson, Mount	Antarctica	4,191	13,750

△Highest mountain in country.

Oceans, Seas, and Gulfs

Name	Area km²	Area sq mi	Greatest Depth m	Greatest Depth ft
Pacific Ocean	165,200,000	63,800,000	11,022	36,161
Atlantic Ocean	82,400,000	31,800,000	9,220	30,249
Indian Ocean	74,900,000	28,900,000	7,450	24,442
Arctic Ocean	14,000,000	5,400,000	5,450	17,881
Arabian Sea	3,863,000	1,492,000	5,800	19,029
South China Sea	3,447,000	1,331,000	5,560	18,241
Caribbean Sea	2,754,000	1,063,000	7,680	25,197
Mediterranean Sea	2,505,000	967,000	5,020	16,470
Bering Sea	2,270,000	876,000	4,191	13,750
Bengal, Bay of	2,172,000	839,000	5,258	17,251
Okhotsk, Sea of	1,580,000	610,000	3,372	11,063
Norwegian Sea	1,547,000	597,000	4,020	13,189
Mexico, Gulf of	1,544,000	596,000	4,380	14,370
Hudson Bay	1,230,000	475,000	259	850
Greenland Sea	1,205,000	465,000	4,846	15,899

Waterfalls

Waterfall	Country	River	Height m	Height ft
Angel	Venezuela	Churún	972	3,189
Tugela	South Africa	Tugela	948	3,110
Yosemite	United States	Yosemite Creek	739	2,425
Sutherland	New Zealand	Arthur	579	1,900
Gavarnie	France	Gave de Pau	421	1,381
Lofoi	Zaire	Lofoi	384	1,260
Krimml	Austria	Krimml	381	1,250
Takakkaw	Canada	Yoho	380	1,248
Staubbach	Switzerland	Staubbach	305	1,001
Mardalsfoss	Norway	. . .	297	974
Gersoppa	India	Sharavati	253	830
Kaieteur	Guyana	Potaro	247	810

Principal Rivers

River	Location	Length km	Length mi
Nile-Kagera	Africa	6,671	4,145
Yangtze (Chang Jiang)	China	6,300	3,915
Amazon-Ucayali	Brazil-Peru	6,280	3,902
Mississippi-Missouri-Red Rock	U.S.	6,019	3,741
Yellow (Huang He)	China	5,464	3,395
Ob-Irtysh	China-U.S.S.R.	5,410	3,362
Río de la Plata-Paraná	South America	4,700	2,920
Mekong	Asia	4,500	2,796
Paraná	South America	4,500	2,796
Amur	China-U.S.S.R.	4,416	2,744
Lena	U.S.S.R.	4,400	2,734
Mackenzie	Canada	4,241	2,635
Congo (Zaire)	Africa	4,200	2,610
Niger	Africa	4,160	2,585
Yenisey (Jenisej)	U.S.S.R.	4,092	2,543
Mississippi	U.S.	3,778	2,348
Missouri	U.S.	3,725	2,315
Ob	U.S.S.R.	3,680	2,287
Volga	U.S.S.R.	3,531	2,194
Murray-Darling	Australia	3,490	2,169
Madeira-Mamoré	Bolivia-Brazil	3,200	1,988
Purus	Brazil-Peru	3,200	1,988
Yukon	Canada-U.S.	3,185	1,979
Indus	Asia	3,180	1,976
Rio Grande	Mexico-U.S.	3,033	1,885
Syr Darya (Syrdarja)	U.S.S.R.	2,991	1,859
Brahmaputra	Asia	2,900	1,802
São Francisco	Brazil	2,900	1,802
Danube	Europe	2,860	1,777
Salween	Asia	2,849	1,770
Euphrates	Asia	2,760	1,715
Orinoco	Colombia-Venezuela	2,736	1,700
Darling	Australia	2,720	1,690
Ganges	Bangladesh-India	2,700	1,678
Saskatchewan	Canada	2,672	1,660
Zambezi	Africa	2,660	1,653
Tocantins	Brazil	2,640	1,640
Amu Darya (Amudarja)	Afghanistan-U.S.S.R.	2,600	1,616
Murray	Australia	2,589	1,609
Kolyma	U.S.S.R.	2,575	1,600
Paraguay	South America	2,549	1,584
Ural	U.S.S.R.	2,428	1,509
Arkansas	U.S.	2,333	1,450
Colorado	Mexico-U.S.	2,333	1,450
Irrawaddy	Burma	2,293	1,425
Dnepr	U.S.S.R.	2,201	1,368
Araguaia	Brazil	2,199	1,367
Kasai	Angola-Zaire	2,153	1,338
Tarim	China	2,137	1,328
Brazos	U.S.	2,106	1,309

Principal Islands

Island	Area km²	Area sq mi	Name	Highest Point m	Highest Point ft
Greenland (Grønland)	2,175,600	840,004	Gunnbjørns Fjeld	3,700	12,139
New Guinea	785,000	303,090	Puncak Jaya	5,030	16,503
Borneo	746,545	288,243	Gunong Kinabalu	4,101	13,455
Madagascar	587,041	226,658	Maromokotro	2,876	9,436
Baffin	476,065	183,810	unnamed	2,147	7,045
Sumatra (Sumatera)	473,606	182,860	Kerinci	3,800	12,467
Great Britain	227,581	87,870	Ben Nevis	1,343	4,406
Honshū	227,414	87,805	Fuji	3,776	12,388
Ellesmere	212,687	82,119	Barbeau Peak	2,604	8,543
Victoria	212,198	81,930	unnamed	655	2,150
Celebes (Sulawesi)	189,216	73,057	Rantekombola	3,455	11,335
South Island	150,461	58,093	Cook	3,764	12,349
Java (Jawa)	132,187	51,038	Semeru	3,676	12,060
North Island	114,728	44,297	Ruapehu	2,797	9,177
Cuba	114,524	44,218	Pico Turquino	1,994	6,542
Newfoundland	112,299	43,359	Lewis Hills	814	2,671
Luzon	104,687	40,420	Pulog	2,930	9,613
Iceland (Ísland)	103,000	39,769	Hvannadalshnúkur	2,119	6,952
Mindanao	94,630	36,537	Apo	2,954	9,692
Ireland	84,403	32,588	Carrantuohill	1,041	3,415
Hokkaidō	78,073	30,144	Daisetsu-Zan	2,290	7,513
Sakhalin (Sahalin)	76,400	29,498	Lopatina	1,609	5,279
Hispaniola	76,192	29,418	Pico Duarte	3,175	10,417
Banks	70,028	27,038	Durham	747	2,450
Tasmania	68,332	26,383	Ossa	1,617	5,305
Sri Lanka (Ceylon)	65,000	25,097	Pidurutalagala	2,524	8,281
Devon	55,247	21,331	Treuter	1,887	6,191
Novaya Zemlya (N. part)	48,904	18,882	unnamed	1,547	5,075
Tierra del Fuego	48,174	18,600	Yogan	2,469	8,100
Kyūshū	41,997	16,215	Kuju-San	1,787	5,863

Major Lakes

Lake	Country	Area km²	Area sq mi	Depth m	Depth ft
Caspian Sea	Iran-U.S.S.R	371,000	143,200	1,025	3,363
Superior	Canada-U.S.	82,414	31,820	406	1,333
Victoria	Africa	68,100	26,293	80	262
Aral Sea (Aral'skoje more)	U.S.S.R.	66,500	25,676	68	223
Huron	Canada-U.S.	59,596	23,010	229	750
Michigan	U.S.	58,016	22,400	281	923
Tanganyika	Africa	32,893	12,700	1,436	4,711
Baikal (ozero Bajkal)	U.S.S.R.	31,500	12,162	1,620	5,315
Great Bear	Canada	31,328	12,096	413	1,356
Nyasa	Africa	30,800	11,892	678	2,224
Great Slave	Canada	28,570	11,031	559	1,834
Erie	Canada-U.S.	25,745	9,940	64	210
Winnipeg	Canada	24,390	9,417	18	60
Ontario	Canada-U.S.	19,529	7,540	244	802
Ladoga (Ladožskoje ozero)	U.S.S.R.	18,400	7,104	225	738
Balkhash (ozero Balhaš)	U.S.S.R.	18,200	7,027	26	85
Chad (Lac Tchad)	Africa	16,300	6,293	4	13
Onega (Onežskoje ozero)	U.S.S.R.	9,610	3,710	120	393
Eyre	Australia	9,583	3,700	1	4
Rudolf	Ethiopia-Kenya	8,600	3,320	61	200
Nicaragua	Nicaragua	8,430	3,255	43	141
Titicaca	Bolivia-Peru	8,300	3,205	272	892
Athabasca	Canada	7,936	3,064	124	407
Gairdner	Australia	7,700	2,973	☆	☆
Reindeer	Canada	6,651	2,568	219	720
Issyk-Kul	U.S.S.R.	6,280	2,425	702	2,303
Urmia (Daryācheh-ye Orūmīyeh)	Iran	5,800	2,239	15	49
Torrens	Australia	5,776	2,230	☆	☆
Vänern	Sweden	5,585	2,156	100	328
Winnipegosis	Canada	5,374	2,075	12	38

☆Intermittently dry lake

Drainage Basins

Name	Continent	Area km²	Area sq mi
Amazon-Ucayali	South America	7,050,000	2,722,000
Congo (Zaire)	Africa	3,690,000	1,425,000
Mississippi-Missouri	North America	3,221,000	1,243,700
Río de la Plata-Paraná	South America	3,140,000	1,212,000
Ob	Asia	2,975,000	1,149,000
Nile	Africa	2,867,000	1,107,000
Yenisey (Jenisej)	Asia	2,580,000	996,000
Lena	Asia	2,490,000	961,000
Niger	Africa	2,092,000	808,000
Amur	Asia	1,855,000	716,000
Yangtze (Chang Jiang)	Asia	1,807,000	698,000
Mackenzie	North America	1,760,000	680,000
Saint Lawrence-Great Lakes	North America	1,463,000	565,000
Volga	Europe	1,360,000	525,000

World Geographical Tables

Historical Population of the World

AREA	1650	1750	1800	1850	1900	1914	1920	1939	1950	1982*
Europe	100,000,000	140,000,000	190,000,000	265,000,000	400,000,000	470,000,000	453,000,000	526,000,000	530,000,000	666,400,000
Asia	335,000,000	476,000,000	593,000,000	754,000,000	932,000,000	1,006,000,000	1,000,000,000	1,247,000,000	1,418,000,000	2,724,900,000
Africa	100,000,000	95,000,000	90,000,000	95,000,000	118,000,000	130,000,000	140,000,000	170,000,000	199,000,000	490,300,000
North America	5,000,000	5,000,000	13,000,000	39,000,000	106,000,000	141,000,000	147,000,000	186,000,000	219,000,000	379,400,000
South America	8,000,000	7,000,000	12,000,000	20,000,000	38,000,000	55,000,000	61,000,000	90,000,000	111,000,000	247,800,000
Oceania, incl. Australia	2,000,000	2,000,000	2,000,000	2,000,000	6,000,000	8,000,000	9,000,000	11,000,000	13,000,000	23,200,000
Australia					4,000,000	5,000,000	6,000,000	7,000,000	8,000,000	14,910,000
World	550,000,000	725,000,000	900,000,000	1,175,000,000	1,600,000,000	1,810,000,000	1,810,000,000	2,230,000,000	2,490,000,000	4,532,000,000

* Figures prior to 1982 are rounded to the nearest million.   Figures in italics represent very rough estimates.

Largest Countries: Population

	Country	Population 1/1/82
1.	China	995,000,000
2.	India	695,230,000
3.	U.S.S.R	268,740,000
4.	United States	231,160,000
5.	Indonesia	151,500,000
6.	Brazil	124,760,000
7.	Japan	118,650,000
8.	Pakistan	92,070,000
9.	Bangladesh	91,860,000
10.	Nigeria	80,765,000
11.	Mexico	70,515,000
12.	Germany, Fed. Rep.	61,680,000
13.	Italy	57,270,000
14.	United Kingdom	56,035,000
15.	Vietnam	55,455,000
16.	France	54,045,000
17.	Philippines	50,960,000
18.	Thailand	48,860,000
19.	Turkey	46,435,000
20.	Egypt	43,565,000
21.	Korea, South	40,755,000
22.	Iran	38,565,000
23.	Spain	37,865,000
24.	Poland	36,035,000
25.	Burma	35,710,000
26.	South Africa	30,495,000
27.	Ethiopia	30,370,000
28.	Zaire	29,060,000
29.	Argentina	28,420,000
30.	Colombia	28,185,000
31.	Canada	24,335,000
32.	Yugoslavia	22,635,000
33.	Romania	22,445,000
34.	Morocco	21,795,000
35.	Sudan	20,180,000
36.	Algeria	19,270,000
37.	Tanzania	19,115,000
38.	Korea, North	18,540,000
39.	Peru	18,510,000
40.	Taiwan	18,365,000
41.	Kenya	17,790,000
42.	German Dem. Rep.	16,750,000
43.	Sri Lanka	15,605,000
44.	Nepal	15,520,000
45.	Czechoslovakia	15,345,000

Largest Countries: Area

	Country	Area km²	sq mi
1.	U.S.S.R	22,274,900	8,600,383
2.	Canada	9,922,330	3,831,033
3.	China	9,560,939	3,691,500
4.	United States	9,528,318	3,678,896
5.	Brazil	8,511,965	3,286,487
6.	Australia	7,686,850	2,967,909
7.	India	3,203,975	1,237,061
8.	Argentina	2,766,889	1,068,301
9.	Sudan	2,505,813	967,500
10.	Algeria	2,381,741	919,595
11.	Zaire	2,345,409	905,567
12.	Greenland	2,175,600	840,004
13.	Saudi Arabia	2,149,690	830,000
14.	Mexico	1,972,547	761,604
15.	Indonesia	1,919,270	741,034
16.	Libya	1,759,540	679,362
17.	Iran	1,648,000	636,296
18.	Mongolia	1,565,000	604,250
19.	Peru	1,285,216	496,224
20.	Chad	1,284,000	495,755
21.	Niger	1,267,000	489,191
22.	Angola	1,246,700	481,353
23.	Mali	1,240,000	478,766
24.	Ethiopia	1,223,600	472,434
25.	South Africa	1,221,042	471,447
26.	Colombia	1,138,914	439,737
27.	Bolivia	1,098,581	424,164
28.	Mauritania	1,030,700	397,955
29.	Egypt	1,001,400	386,643
30.	Tanzania	945,087	364,900
31.	Nigeria	923,768	356,669
32.	Venezuela	912,050	352,144
33.	Pakistan	828,453	319,867
34.	Mozambique	783,030	302,329
35.	Turkey	779,452	300,948
36.	Chile	756,626	292,135
37.	Zambia	752,614	290,586
38.	Burma	676,577	261,228
39.	Afghanistan	647,497	250,000
40.	Somalia	637,657	246,200
41.	Central African Republic	622,984	240,535
42.	Botswana	600,372	231,805
43.	Madagascar	587,041	226,658
44.	Kenya	582,646	224,961
45.	France	547,026	211,208

Smallest Countries: Population

	Country	Population 1/1/82
1.	Vatican City	1,000
2.	Niue	3,000
3.	Anguilla	7,900
	Nauru	7,900
4.	Tuvalu	8,100
5.	Cook Islands	18,000
6.	San Marino	24,000
7.	Liechtenstein	27,000
	Monaco	27,000
8.	Andorra	40,000
9.	St. Kitts-Nevis	41,000
10.	Faeroe Islands	45,000
11.	Greenland	51,000
12.	Kiribati	59,000
13.	Isle of Man	66,000
14.	Seychelles	68,000
15.	Dominica	75,000
16.	Antigua	77,000
17.	Sao Tome and Principe	89,000
18.	Tonga	101,000
19.	Grenada	112,000
20.	Vanuatu	120,000
21.	Djibouti	124,000
	Saint Lucia	124,000
22.	St. Vincent	128,000
23.	Maldives	155,000
	Western Samoa	155,000
24.	Belize	160,000
25.	Iceland	230,000
26.	Bahamas	235,000
	Qatar	235,000
	Solomon Is.	235,000
27.	Brunei	245,000
28.	Barbados	260,000
	Netherlands Antilles	260,000
29.	Cape Verde	330,000
30.	Luxembourg	355,000
31.	Malta	360,000
32.	Suriname	365,000
33.	Equatorial Guinea	375,000
34.	Comoros	380,000
35.	Bahrain	400,000
36.	Gabon	560,000
37.	Swaziland	580,000
38.	Gambia	625,000

Smallest Countries: Area

	Country	Area km²	sq mi
1.	Vatican City	0.4	0.2
2.	Monaco	1.5	0.6
3.	Nauru	21	8.2
4.	Tuvalu	26	10
5.	San Marino	61	24
6.	Anguilla	88	34
7.	Liechtenstein	160	62
8.	Cook Islands	236	91
9.	Niue	263	102
10.	St. Kitts-Nevis	269	104
11.	Maldives	298	115
12.	Malta	316	122
13.	Grenada	344	133
14.	St. Vincent	389	150
15.	Barbados	430	166
16.	Antigua	440	170
17.	Seychelles	443	171
18.	Andorra	453	175
19.	Singapore	581	224
20.	Isle of Man	588	227
21.	Saint Lucia	616	238
22.	Bahrain	662	256
23.	Tonga	699	270
24.	Dominica	752	290
25.	Kiribati	754	291
26.	Sao Tome and Principe	964	372
27.	Netherlands Antilles	993	383
28.	Faeroe Islands	1,399	540
29.	Mauritius	2,045	790
30.	Comoros	2,171	838
31.	Luxembourg	2,586	999
32.	Western Samoa	2,842	1,097
33.	Cape Verde	4,033	1,557
34.	Trinidad and Tobago	5,128	1,980
35.	Brunei	5,765	2,226
36.	Puerto Rico	8,897	3,435
37.	Cyprus	9,251	3,572
38.	Lebanon	10,400	4,015
39.	Jamaica	10,991	4,244
40.	Qatar	11,000	4,247
41.	Gambia	11,295	4,361
42.	Bahamas	13,939	5,382
43.	Vanuatu	14,800	5,714
44.	Swaziland	17,364	6,704
45.	Kuwait	17,818	6,880

Highest Population Densities

	Country	Density per km²	sq mi		Country	Density per km²	sq mi
1.	Monaco	18,000	45,000	16.	St. Vincent	329	853
2.	Singapore	4,923	12,768	17.	Grenada	326	842
3.	Vatican City	2,500	5,000	18.	Belgium	324	839
4.	Malta	1,139	2,951	19.	Japan	319	825
5.	Bangladesh	638	1,652	20.	Lebanon	315	816
6.	Barbados	605	1,566	21.	Tuvalu	312	810
7.	Bahrain	604	1,563	22.	Netherlands Antilles	262	679
8.	Maldives	520	1,348	23.	El Salvador	250	649
9.	Taiwan	510	1,322	24.	Germany, Fed. Rep. of	248	642
10.	Mauritius	482	1,247	25.	Sri Lanka	240	622
11.	Korea, South	414	1,072	26.	United Kingdom	230	595
12.	San Marino	393	1,000	27.	Trinidad and Tobago	227	588
13.	Nauru	376	963	28.	India	217	562
14.	Puerto Rico	368	952	29.	Jamaica	203	527
15.	Netherlands	347	900	30.	Saint Lucia	201	521

Lowest Population Densities

	Country	Density per km²	sq mi		Country	Density per km²	sq mi
1.	Greenland	0.02	0.06		Oman	4.4	11
2.	Mongolia	1.1	2.9	15.	Congo	4.7	12
3.	Botswana	1.5	3.8	16.	Bolivia	5.3	14
4.	Mauritania	1.7	4.3	17.	Djibouti	5.4	14
5.	Libya	1.8	4.6	18.	Mali	5.8	15
6.	Australia	1.9	5.0	19.	Angola	5.9	15
7.	Gabon	2.1	5.4	20.	Yemen, P.D.R. of	6.2	16
8.	Iceland	2.2	5.8	21.	Papua New Guinea	6.7	17
	Suriname	2.2	5.8	22.	Belize	7.0	18
9.	Canada	2.5	6.4	23.	Zambia	7.8	20
10.	Chad	3.6	9.4	24.	Paraguay	7.9	20
11.	Central African Republic	3.7	9.6		Solomon Islands	7.9	20
12.	Saudi Arabia	4.1	11	25.	Somalia	8.0	21
13.	Guyana	4.3	11	26.	Algeria	8.1	21
14.	Niger	4.4	11		Vanuatu	8.1	21

Major Metropolitan Areas of the World

This table lists the major metropolitan areas of the world according to their estimated population on January 1, 1982. For convenience in reference, the areas are grouped by major region, and the number of areas in each region and size group is given.

There are 29 areas with more than 5,000,000 population each; these are listed in rank order of estimated population, with the world rank given in parentheses following the name. For example, New York's 1982 rank is second. Below the 5,000,000 level, the metropolitan areas are listed alphabetically within region, not in order of size.

For ease of comparison, each metropolitan area has been defined by Rand McNally & Company according to consistent rules. A metropolitan area includes a central city, surrounding communities linked to it by continuous built-up areas and more distant communities if the bulk of their population is supported by commuters to the central city. Some metropolitan areas have more than one central city, for example Tōkyō–Yokohama or San Francisco–Oakland–San Jose.

POPULATION CLASSIFICATION	UNITED STATES and CANADA	LATIN AMERICA	EUROPE (excl. U.S.S.R.)	U.S.S.R	ASIA	AFRICA-OCEANIA
Over 15,000,000 (4)	New York, U.S. (2)	Mexico City, Mex. (3)			Tōkyō-Yokohama, Jap. (1) Ōsaka-Kōbe-Kyōto, Jap. (4)	
10,000,000–15,000,000 (8)	Los Angeles, U.S. (12)	São Paulo, Braz. (5) Buenos Aires, Arg. (9)	London, U.K. (10)	Moscow (6)	Seoul, Kor. (7) Calcutta, India (8) Bombay, India (11)	
5,000,000–10,000,000 (17)	Chicago, U.S. (16) Philadelphia–Trenton– Wilmington, U.S. (26)	Rio de Janeiro, Braz. (15)	Paris, Fr. (13) Essen–Dortmund– Duisburg (The Ruhr), Ger., Fed. Rep. of (27) İstanbul, Tur. (29)	Leningrad (23)	Shanghai, China, (17) Delhi–New Delhi, India (18) Manila, Phil. (19) Jakarta, Indon. (20) Peking (Beijing), China (21), Tehrān, Iran (22) Bangkok, Thai. (24) Karāchi, Pak. (25) Tientsin (Tianjin), China (28)	Cairo, Eg. (14)
3,000,000–5,000,000 (32)	Boston, U.S. Detroit, U.S.– Windsor, Can. Montréal, Can. San Francisco– Oakland– San Jose, U.S. Toronto, Can. Washington, U.S.	Bogotá, Col. Caracas, Ven. Lima, Peru Santiago, Chile	Athens, Greece Barcelona, Sp. Berlin, Ger. Madrid, Sp. Milan, It. Rome, It.		Baghdād, Iraq Bangalore, India Chungking (Chongqing), China Dacca, Bngl. Lahore, Pak. Madras, India Mukden (Shenyang), China Nagoya, Jap. Pusan, Kor. Rangoon, Bur. Taipei, Taiwan Victoria, Hong Kong Wuhan, China	Alexandria, Eg. Johannesburg, S. Afr. Sydney, Austl.
2,000,000–3,000,000 (46)	Atlanta, U.S. Cleveland, U.S. Dallas– Fort Worth, U.S. Houston, U.S. Miami–Fort Lauderdale, U.S. Minneapolis–St. Paul, U.S. Pittsburgh, U.S. St. Louis, U.S. San Diego, U.S.– Tijuana, Mex. Seattle– Tacoma, U.S.	Belo Horizonte, Braz. Guadalajara, Mex. Havana, Cuba Medellín, Col. Monterrey, Mex. Porto Alegre, Braz. Recife, Braz.	Birmingham, U.K. Brussels, Bel. Bucharest, Rom. Budapest, Hung. Hamburg, Ger., Fed. Rep. of Katowice–Bytom– Gliwice, Pol. Lisbon, Port. Manchester, U.K. Naples, It. Warsaw, Pol.	Donetsk–Makeyevka Kiev Tashkent	Ahmadābād, India Ankara, Tur. Canton (Guangzhou), China Chengtu (Chendu), China Hanoi, Viet. Harbin, China Ho Chi Minh City (Saigon), Viet. Hyderābād, India Sian (Xi'an) China Singapore, Singapore Surabaya, Indon.	Algiers, Alg. Casablanca, Mor. Kinshasa, Zaire Lagos, Nig. Melbourne, Austl.
1,500,000–2,000,000 (37)	Baltimore, U.S. Phoenix, U.S.	Fortaleza, Braz. Salvador, Braz. San Juan, P.R.	Amsterdam, Neth. Cologne, Ger., Fed. Rep. of Copenhagen, Den. Frankfurt am Main, Ger., Fed. Rep. of Glasgow, U.K. Leeds–Bradford, U.K. Liverpool, U.K. Munich, Ger., Fed. Rep. of Stuttgart, Ger., Fed. Rep. of Turin, It. Vienna, Aus.	Baku Dnepropetrovsk Gorki Kharkov Novosibirsk	Bandung, Indon. Chittagong, Bngl. Colombo, Sri Lanka Damascus, Syria Fukuoka, Jap. Hiroshima–Kure, Jap. Kānpur, India Kaohsiung, Taiwan Kitakyūshū– Shimonoseki, Jap. Medan, Indon. Nanking (Nanjing), China Pune, India Sapporo, Jap. Taegu, Kor.	Cape Town, S. Afr. Durban, S. Afr.
1,000,000–1,500,000 (90)	Buffalo–Niagara Falls, U.S.–St. Catharines– Niagara Falls, Can. Cincinnati, U.S. Denver, U.S. El Paso, U.S.–Ciudad Juárez, Mex. Hartford–New Britain, U.S. Indianapolis, U.S. Kansas City, U.S. Milwaukee, U.S. New Orleans, U.S. Portland, U.S. San Antonio, U.S. Vancouver, Can.	Barranquilla, Col. Belém, Braz. Brasília, Braz. Cali, Col. Córdoba, Arg. Curitiba, Braz. Guatemala, Guat. Guayaquil, Ec. Montevideo, Ur. Rosario, Arg. Santo Domingo, Dom. Rep.	Antwerp, Bel. Belgrade, Yugo. Bilbao, Sp. Dublin, Ire. Düsseldorf, Ger., Fed. Rep. of Hannover, Ger., Fed. Rep. of Lille, Fr. Łódź, Pol. Lyon, Fr. Mannheim, Ger., Fed. Rep. of Marseille, Fr. Newcastle– Sunderland, U.K. Nürnberg, Ger., Fed. Rep. of Porto, Port. Prague, Czech. Rotterdam, Neth. Sofia, Bul. Stockholm, Swe. Valencia, Sp.	Alma–Ata Chelyabinsk Kazan Kuybyshev Minsk Odessa Omsk Perm Rostov-na-Donu Saratov Sverdlovsk Tbilisi Ufa Volgograd Yerevan	Anshan, China Asansol, India Beirut, Leb. Changchun, China Chengchow (Zhengzhou), China Faisalabad (Lyallpur), Pak. Fushun, China İzmir, Tur. Jaipur, India Kābul, Afg. Kuala Lumpur, Mala. Kunming, China Kuwait, Kuw. Lanchou (Lanzhou), China Lucknow, India Lüta (Dairen), China Nāgpur, India Patna, India P'yŏngyang, Kor. Rāwalpindi– Islāmābād, Pak. Riyadh, Sau. Ar. Semarang, Indon. Shihchiachuang (Shijiazhuang), China Surat, India Taiyuan, China Tel Aviv–Yafo, Isr. Tsinan (Jinan), China Tsingtao (Qingdao), China	Abidjan, I.C. Addis Ababa, Eth. Brisbane, Austl. Khartoum, Sud. Tunis, Tun.
Total by Region (234)	34	29	50	25	80	16

Populations of Major Cities

The largest and most important of the world's major cities are listed in the following table. Also included are some smaller cities because of their regional significance.

Local official name forms have been used throughout the table. When a commonly used "conventional" name form exists, it has been featured, with the official name following, within parentheses. Former names are identified by italics. Each city name is followed by the English name of its country. Whenever two well-known cities of the same name are in the same country, the state or province name has been added for identification.

Many cities have population figures within parentheses following the country name. These are metropolitan populations, comprising the central city and its suburbs. When a city is within the metropolitan area of another city the name of the metropolitan central city is specified in parentheses preceded by an (*). The symbol (†) identifies a political district population which includes some rural population. For these cities the estimated city population has been based upon the district figure.

The population of each city has been dated for ease of comparison. The date is followed by a letter designating: Census (C); Official Estimate (E); and in a few instances Unofficial Estimates (UE).

City and Country	Population	Date
Aachen, Fed. Rep. of Ger. (540,000)	242,971	79E
Abidjan, Ivory Coast	1,100,000	78E
Acapulco [de Juárez], Mexico	421,000	78E
Accra, Ghana (738,498)	633,880	70C
Adelaide, Australia (933,000)	13,400	79E
Aden (Baladīyat 'Adan), People's Dem. Rep. of Yemen	271,600	77E
Addis Ababa (Ādīs Ābeba), Ethiopia	1,125,340	78E
Āgra, India (770,352)	723,676	81C
Ahmadābād, India (2,400,000)	2,024,917	81C
Aleppo (Halab), Syria	878,000	78E
Alexandria (Al Iskandarīyah); Egypt (2,850,000)	2,409,000	78E
Algiers (Al Jazā'ir), Algeria (1,800,000)	1,503,720	74E
Allahābād, India (642,420)	609,232	81C
Alma-Ata, U.S.S.R. (970,000)	928,000	80E
'Ammān, Jordan	648,587	79E
Amritsar, India	589,227	81C
Amsterdam, Netherlands (1,810,000)	716,919	80E
Ankara, Turkey (2,290,000)	2,203,729	80C
Anshan, China	1,050,000	75UE
Antananarivo, Madagascar	484,000	77E
Antwerp, (Antwerpen, Anvers), Belgium (1,105,000)	194,073	80E
Asansol, India (1,050,000)	187,039	81C
Asunción, Paraguay (655,000)	463,700	78E
Athens (Athinai), Greece (2,540,241)	867,023	71C
Atlanta, U.S. (1,950,600)	425,022	80C
Auckland, New Zealand (775,000)	147,600	79E
Augsburg, Fed. Rep. of Ger. (390,000)	245,940	79E
Austin, U.S. (422,700)	345,496	80C
Baghdād, Iraq (2,183,800)	1,300,000	70E
Baku, U.S.S.R. (1,800,000)	1,030,000	80E
Baltimore, U.S. (1,883,100)	786,775	80C
Bamako, Mali	404,022	76C
Bandung, Indonesia (1,525,000)	1,462,637	80C
Bangalore, India (2,950,000)	2,482,507	81C
Bangkok (Krung Thep), Thailand (3,375,000)	3,133,834	72E
Barcelona, Spain (3,975,000)	1,902,713	78E
Barranquilla, Colombia (950,000)	859,000	73C
Basel, Switzerland (580,000)	182,143	80C
Basra (Al Başrah), Iraq	370,900	70E
Beirut (Bayrūt), Lebanon (1,010,000)	474,870	70E
Belém, Brazil (660,000)	565,097	70C
Belfast, U.K. (710,000)	354,400	78E
Belgrade (Beograd), Yugoslavia (1,150,000)	770,140	71C
Belo Horizonte, Brazil (2,450,000)	1,814,990	80C
Berlin, East (Ost), Ger. Dem. Rep. (*Berlin)	1,128,983	78E
Berlin, West, Fed. Rep. of Ger. (3,775,000)	1,902,250	79E
Bern, Switzerland (286,903)	145,254	80C
Bhopāl, India	672,329	81C
Bielefeld, Fed. Rep. of Ger. (525,000)	312,357	79E
Bilbao, Spain (995,000)	452,921	78E
Birmingham, U.K. (2,660,000)	1,033,900	79E
Birmingham, U.S. (697,900)	284,413	80C
Bogotá, Colombia (4,150,000)	4,067,000	79E
Bologna, Italy (550,000)	471,554	79E
Bombay, India (9,950,000)	8,227,332	81C
Bonn, Fed. Rep. of Ger. (555,000)	286,184	79E
Bordeaux, France (612,456)	223,131	75C
Boston, U.S. (3,738,800)	562,994	80C
Brasília, Brazil	1,202,683	80C
Brazzaville, Congo	175,000	70C
Bremen, Fed. Rep. of Ger. (800,000)	556,128	79E
Bremerhaven, Fed. Rep. of Ger. (190,000)	138,987	79E
Brisbane, Australia (1,014,700)	702,000	79E
Bristol, U.K. (635,000)	408,000	79E

City and Country	Population	Date
Brussels (Bruxelles, Brussel), Belgium (2,400,000)	143,957	80E
Bucharest (Bucureşti), Romania (2,050,000)	1,858,418	78E
Budapest, Hungary (2,600,000)	2,060,000	80C
Buenos Aires, Argentina (10,700,000)	2,908,001	80C
Buffalo, U.S. (1,154,600)	357,870	80C
Bursa, Turkey	466,178	80C
Cairo (Al Qāhirah), Egypt (8,500,000)	5,278,000	78E
Calcutta, India (11,100,000)	3,291,655	81C
Cali, Colombia (1,340,000)	1,293,000	79E
Canberra, Australia (241,500)	221,000	79E
Canton (Guangzhou), China	2,500,000	75UE
Cape Town (Kaapstad), South Africa (1,125,000)	697,514	70C
Caracas, Venezuela (2,475,000)	1,658,500	71C
Cardiff, U.K. (625,000)	282,000	79E
Casablanca (Dar-el-Beida), Morocco (1,575,000)	1,506,373	71C
Catania, Italy (515,000)	398,426	79E
Cebu, Philippines (500,000)	413,025	75C
Changchun, China	1,300,000	75UE
Changsha, China	840,000	75UE
Charleroi, Belgium (495,000)	221,911	80E
Chelyabinsk (Čeljabinsk), U.S.S.R. (1,215,000)	1,042,000	80E
Chengchou (Zhengzhou), China	1,100,000	75UE
Chengtu, (Chendu), China	1,800,000	75UE
Chicago, U.S. (7,803,800)	3,005,072	80C
Chittagong, Bangladesh (1,388,476)	980,000	81C
Chungking (Chongqing), China	2,900,000	75UE
Cincinnati, U.S. (1,476,600)	385,457	80C
Ciudad Juárez, Mexico (*El Paso, U.S.)	597,100	78E
Cleveland, U.S. (2,218,300)	573,822	80C
Cochin, India (552,408)	513,081	81C
Coimbatore, India (965,000)	700,923	81C
Cologne, (Köln), Fed. Rep. of Ger. (1,815,000)	976,136	79E
Colombo, Sri Lanka (1,540,000)	616,000	77E
Columbus, Ohio, U.S. (943,300)	564,871	80C
Copenhagen, (København), Denmark (1,470,000)	498,850	80E
Córdoba, Argentina (1,070,000)	1,052,147	80C
Coventry, U.K. (655,000)	339,300	79E
Curitiba, Brazil (1,300,000)	1,052,147	80C
Dacca, Bangladesh (3,458,602)	1,850,000	81C
Dakar, Senegal	798,792	76C
Dallas, U.S. (2,811,800)	904,078	80C
Damascus (Dimashq), Syria (1,550,000)	1,156,000	79E
Dar es Salaam, Tanzania	870,000	78C
Dayton, U.S. (898,000)	203,588	80C
Delhi, India (7,200,000)	4,865,077	81C
Denver, U.S. (1,414,200)	491,396	80C
Detroit, U.S. (4,399,000)	1,203,339	80C
Dnepropetrovsk, U.S.S.R. (1,460,000)	1,083,000	80E
Donetsk (Doneck), U.S.S.R. (2,075,000)	1,032,000	80E
Dortmund, Fed. Rep. of Ger. (*Essen)	609,954	79E
Douala, Cameroon	458,246	76C
Dresden, Ger. Dem. Rep. (640,000)	514,508	78E
Dublin (Baile Atha Cliath), Ireland (1,110,000)	544,586	79C
Duisburg, Fed. Rep. of Ger. (*Essen)	559,066	79E
Durban, South Africa (1,040,000)	736,852	70C
Düsseldorf, Fed. Rep. of Ger. (1,225,000)	594,770	79E
Edinburgh, U.K. (635,000)	455,126	79E
Edmonton, Canada (554,228)	461,361	76C
El Paso, U.S. (1,122,300)	425,259	80C
Essen, Fed. Rep. of Ger. (5,125,000)	652,501	79E

City and Country	Population	Date
Faisalabad, (Lyallpur), Pakistan	823,343	72C
Florence (Firenze), Italy (660,000)	462,690	79E
Fortaleza, Brazil (1,490,000)	1,338,733	80C
Frankfurt am Main, Fed. Rep. of Ger. (1,880,000)	628,203	79E
Freetown, Sierra Leone (335,000)	274,000	74C
Frunze, U.S.S.R.	543,000	80E
Fukuoka, Japan (1,575,000)	1,088,617	80C
Fushun, China	1,150,000	75UE
Gdańsk (Danzig), Poland (820,000)	449,200	79E
Geneva (Genève), Switzerland (435,000)	156,505	80C
Genoa (Genova), Italy (855,000)	782,476	79E
Gent, Belgium (470,000)	241,695	80E
Giza (Al Jizah), Egypt (*Cairo)	1,246,713	76C
Glasgow, U.K. (1,830,000)	794,316	79E
Gorki, U.S.S.R. (1,900,000)	1,358,000	80E
Göteborg, Sweden (665,000)	434,699	79E
Graz, Austria (275,000)	250,900	76E
Guadalajara, Mexico (2,350,000)	1,813,100	78E
Guatemala, Guatemala (945,000)	717,322	73C
Guayaquil, Ecuador	1,022,010	78E
Haifa (Hefa), Israel (415,000)	229,300	79E
Hamburg, Fed. Rep. of Ger. (2,260,000)	1,653,043	79E
Hangchou (Hangzhou), China	900,000	75UE
Hannover, Fed. Rep. of Ger. (1,005,000)	535,854	79E
Hanoi, Vietnam	1,600,000	71E
Harare (Salisbury), Zimbabwe (633,000)	118,500	79E
Harbin, China	2,400,000	75UE
Hartford, U.S. (1,055,700)	136,392	80C
Havana (La Habana), Cuba (2,000,000)	1,961,674	76E
Helsinki, Finland (885,000)	484,879	78E
Hiroshima, Japan (1,525,000)	899,394	80C
Ho Chi Minh City (Saigon), Vietnam (2,750,000)	1,804,900	71E
Honolulu, U.S. (762,900)	324,871	80C
Houston, U.S. (2,689,200)	1,594,086	80C
Hyderābād, India (2,750,000)	2,142,087	81C
Hyderābād, Pakistan (660,000)	600,796	72C
Ibadan, Nigeria	847,000	75E
Inch'ŏn, South Korea (*Seoul)	1,084,730	80C
Indianapolis, U.S. (1,104,200)	700,807	80C
Innsbruck, Austria (150,000)	120,400	76E
İstanbul, Turkey (4,765,000)	2,853,539	80C
İzmir, Turkey (1,190,000)	753,749	80C
Jacksonville, Florida, U.S. (615,300)	540,898	80C
Jaipur, India (1,025,000)	966,677	81C
Jakarta, Indonesia (6,700,000)	6,503,449	80C
Jerusalem (Yerushalayim), Israel (420,000)	398,200	79E
Jiddah, Saudi Arabia	561,104	74C
Johannesburg, South Africa (2,550,000)	654,232	70C
Kābul, Afghanistan	749,000	75E
Kananga, Zaire	601,000	74E
Kano, Nigeria	399,000	75E
Kānpur, India (1,875,000)	1,531,345	81C
Kansas City, Missouri, U.S. (1,254,600)	448,159	80C
Kaohsiung, Taiwan (1,480,000)	1,172,977	77E
Karāchi, Pakistan (4,500,000)	2,800,000	75E
Karaganda, U.S.S.R.	577,000	80E
Kathmandu, Nepal (215,000)	150,402	71C
Katowice, Poland (2,550,000)	351,300	79E
Kawasaki, Japan (*Tōkyō)	1,040,698	80C
Kazan', U.S.S.R. (1,050,000)	1,002,000	80E
Khabarovsk (Habarovsk), U.S.S.R.	538,000	80E
Khar'kov (Harkov), U.S.S.R. (1,750,000)	1,464,000	80E

City and Country	Population	Date
Khartoum (Al Kharṭūm), Sudan (790,000)	333,921	73C
Kiel, Fed. Rep. of Ger. (335,000)	250,750	79E
Kiev, (Kijev), U.S.S.R. (2,430,000)	2,192,000	80E
Kingston, Jamaica	665,050	78E
Kinshasa, Zaire	2,202,000	75E
Kishinev (Kišinev), U.S.S.R.	519,000	80E
Kitakyūshū, Japan (1,515,000)	1,065,084	80C
Kōbe, Japan (*Ōsaka)	1,367,392	80C
Kowloon, Hong Kong (*Victoria)	749,600	76C
Kraków, Poland (708,000)	706,100	79E
Krasnoyarsk (Krasnojarsk), U.S.S.R.	807,000	80E
Kuala Lumpur, Malaysia (750,000)	451,728	70C
Kueiyang (Guiyang), China	800,000	75UE
Kunming, China	1,225,000	75UE
Kuwait (Al Kuwayt), Kuwait (780,000)	78,116	75C
Kuybyshev (Kujbyšev), U.S.S.R. (1,440,000)	1,226,000	80E
Kwangju, South Korea	727,627	80C
Kyōto, Japan (*Ōsaka)	1,472,993	80C
Lagos, Nigeria (1,450,000)	1,060,800	75E
Lahore, Pakistan (2,200,000)	2,022,577	72C
Lanchou (Lanzhou), China	950,000	75UE
La Paz, Bolivia	654,713	76C
Leeds, U.K. (1,540,000)	724,300	79E
Leipzig, Ger. Dem. Rep. (710,000)	563,980	78E
Leningrad, U.S.S.R. (5,360,000)	4,119,000	80E
León, Mexico	590,000	78E
Liège, Belgium (765,000)	220,183	80E
Lille, France (1,015,000)	172,280	75C
Lima, Peru (3,350,000)	340,339	72C
Linz, Austria (290,000)	208,000)	76E
Lisbon, (Lisboa), Portugal (1,950,000)	829,900	75E
Liverpool, U.K. (1,535,000)	520,200	79E
Łódź, Poland (1,025,000)	830,800	79E
Lomas de Zamora, Argentina (*Buenos Aires)	508,620	80C
London, U.K. (11,050,000)	6,877,100	79E
Los Angeles, U.S. (9,840,200)	2,966,763	80C
Louisville, U.S. (881,100)	298,451	80C
Luanda, Angola	475,328	70C
Lubumbashi, Zaire	404,000	74E
Lucknow, India (1,060,000)	895,947	81C
Ludhiāna, India	606,250	81C
Lusaka, Zambia	641,000	80E
Lüta *(Dairen)*, China (1,700,000†)	1,100,000	75UE
Lvov, U.S.S.R.	676,000	80E
Lyon, France (1,170,660)	456,716	75C
Madras, India (4,475,000)	3,266,034	81C
Madrid, Spain (4,415,000)	3,367,438	78E
Madurai, India (960,000)	817,562	80C
Managua, Nicaragua	552,900	78E
Manchester, U.K. (2,800,000)	479,100	79E
Mandalay, Burma	458,000	77E
Manila, Philippines (5,500,000)	1,479,116	75C
Mannheim, Fed. Rep. of Ger. (1,395,000)	303,247	79E
Maputo *(Lourenço Marques)*, Mozambique	341,922	70C
Maracaibo, Venezuela	651,574	71C
Marseille, France (1,070,912)	908,600	75C
Mecca (Makkah), Saudi Arabia	366,801	74C
Medan, Indonesia (1,450,000)	1,378,955	80C
Medellín, Colombia (2,025,000)	1,477,000	79E
Melbourne, Australia (2,739,700)	65,800	79E
Memphis, U.S. (843,200)	646,356	80C
Mexico City (Ciudad de México), Mexico (14,400,000)	8,988,200	78E
Miami, U.S. (2,689,100)	346,931	80C
Milan (Milano), Italy (3,800,000)	1,677,109	79E
Milwaukee, U.S. (1,358,600)	636,212	80C
Minneapolis, U.S. (1,978,000)	370,951	80C
Minsk, U.S.S.R. (1,330,000)	1,295,000	80E
Mombasa, Kenya	342,000	79C
Monrovia, Liberia	204,210	74C
Monterrey, Mexico (1,925,000)	1,054,000	78E
Montevideo, Uruguay (1,350,000)	1,229,748	75C
Montréal, Canada (2,802,485)	1,080,546	76C
Morón, Argentina (*Buenos Aires)	596,769	80C
Moscow (Moskva), U.S.S.R. (11,950,000)	7,915,000	80E
Mukden (Shenyang), China	3,300,000	75UE
Multān, Pakistan (538,000)	504,365	72C
Munich (München), Fed. Rep. of Ger. (1,940,000)	1,299,693	79E
Mysore, India (476,446)	439,185	80C
Nagoya, Japan (3,700,000)	2,087,884	80C
Nāgpur, India (1,325,000)	1,215,425	81C
Nairobi, Kenya	835,000	79C
Nanking (Nanjing), China	1,800,000	75UE
Nantes, France (453,500)	256,693	75C
Naples (Napoli), Italy (2,740,000)	1,223,228	79E
Nashville, U.S. (608,400)	455,651	80C
Newcastle upon Tyne, U.K. (1,295,000)	287,300	79E
New Delhi, India (*Delhi)	271,990	81C
New Kowloon, Hong Kong (*Victoria)	1,628,880	76C
New Orleans, U.S. (1,175,800)	557,482	80C
New York, U.S. (16,573,600)	7,071,030	80C
Niamey, Niger	225,300	77E
Norfolk, U.S. (795,600)	219,214	80C
Nottingham, U.K. (645,000)	278,600	79E
Novokuznetsk (Novokuzneck), U.S.S.R.	545,000	80E
Novosibirsk, U.S.S.R. (1,460,000)	1,328,000	80E
Nürnberg, Fed. Rep. of Ger. (1,025,000)	484,184	79E
Odessa, U.S.S.R. (1,120,000)	1,057,000	80E
Okayama, Japan	545,737	80C
Oklahoma City, U.S. (742,000)	403,213	80C
Omaha, U.S. (548,400)	311,681	80C
Omsk, U.S.S.R. (1,040,000)	1,028,000	80E
Orlando, U.S. (568,300)	128,394	80C
Ōsaka, Japan (15,200,000)	2,648,158	80C
Oslo, Norway (725,000)	454,819	80E
Ostrava, Czechoslovakia (745,000)	325,473	79E
Ottawa, Canada (693,288)	304,462	76C
Palermo, Italy	693,949	79E
Panamá, Panama (645,000)	439,800	78E
Paris, France (9,450,000)	2,050,500	80E
Patna, India (1,025,000)	773,720	81C
Peking (Beijing), China (8,500,000†)	5,700,000	78E
Perm, U.S.S.R. (1,075,000)	1,008,000	80E
Perth, Australia (883,600)	88,850	79E
Philadelphia, U.S. (5,153,400)	1,688,210	80C
Phnom Penh (Phnum Pénh), Kampuchea	393,995	62C
Phoenix, U.S. (1,483,500)	764,911	80C
Pittsburgh, U.S. (2,165,100)	423,938	80C
Port-au-Prince, Haiti (800,000)	745,700	78E
Portland, Oregon, U.S. (1,220,000)	366,383	80C
Porto, Portugal (1,150,000)	335,700	75E
Porto Alegre, Brazil (2,225,000)	1,158,709	80C
Portsmouth, U.K. (490,000)	191,000	79E
Poznan', Poland (610,000)	545,600	79E
Prague (Praha), Czechoslovakia (1,275,000)	1,193,345	79E
Pretoria, South Africa (575,000)	545,450	70C
Providence, U.S. (897,000)	156,804	80C
Puebla [de Zaragoza], Mexico	678,000	78E
Pune, India (1,775,000)	1,202,848	81C
Pusan, South Korea	3,160,276	80C
P'yŏngyang, North Korea	840,000	67E
Québec, Canada (542,158)	177,082	76C
Quezon City, Philippines (*Manila)	956,864	75C
Quito, Ecuador	742,858	78E
Rabat, Morocco (540,000)	367,620	71C
Rangoon, Burma (3,000,000)	2,276,000	77E
Rāwalpindi, Pakistan (725,000)	372,919	72C
Recife *(Pernambuco)*, Brazil (2,300,000)	1,240,897	80C
Richmond, Virginia, U.S. (548,100)	219,214	80C
Rīga, U.S.S.R. (920,000)	843,000	80E
Rio de Janerio, Brazil (8,975,000)	5,184,292	80C
Riyadh (Ar Riyāḍ), Saudi Arabia	666,840	74C
Rochester, New York, U.S. (809,500)	241,741	80C
Rome (Roma), Italy (3,195,000)	2,911,671	79E
Rosario, Argentina (1,045,000)	935,471	80C
Rostov-na-Donu, U.S.S.R. (1,075,000)	946,000	80E
Rotterdam, Netherlands (1,085,000)	579,194	80E
Saarbrücken, Fed. Rep. of Ger. (390,000)	194,452	79E
Sacramento, U.S. (848,800)	275,741	80C
St. Louis, U.S. (2,216,100)	453,085	80C
St. Paul, U.S. (*Minneapolis)	270,230	80C
St. Petersburg, U.S. (699,800)	236,893	80C
Sakai, Japan (*Ōsaka)	810,120	80C
Salt Lake City, U.S. (686,200)	163,033	80C
Salvador, Brazil (1,725,000)	1,525,831	80C
Samarkand, U.S.S.R.	481,000	80E
San Antonio, U.S. (1,012,300)	785,410	80C
San Bernardino, U.S. (715,300)	118,057	80C
San Diego, U.S. (1,597,000)	875,504	80C
San Francisco, U.S. (4,665,500)	678,974	80C
San José, Costa Rica (519,400)	239,800	78E
San Juan, Puerto Rico (1,535,000)	422,701	80C
San Justo, Argentina (*Buenos Aires)	946,715	80C
San Salvador, El Salvador (720,000)	397,100	77E
Santiago, Chile (2,925,000)	517,473	70C
Santo Domingo, Dominican Rep.	979,608	76E
Santos, Brazil (610,000)	341,317	70C
São Paulo, Brazil (12,525,000)	8,584,896	80C
Sapporo, Japan (1,450,000)	1,401,758	80C
Saragossa (Zaragoza), Spain	563,375	78E
Saratov, U.S.S.R. (1,090,000)	864,000	80E
Seattle, U.S. (2,077,100)	493,846	80C
Semarang, Indonesia (1,050,000)	1,026,671	80C
Sendai, Japan (925,000)	664,799	80C
Seoul (Sŏul), South Korea (11,200,000)	8,366,756	80C
Sevilla, Spain (740,000)	630,329	78E
Shanghai, China (10,980,000†)	8,100,000	78E
Sheffield, U.K. (705,000)	544,200	79E
Shihchiachuang (Shijiazhuang), China	940,000	75UE
Sian (Xi'an), China	1,900,000	75UE
Singapore (Singapura), Singapore (2,600,000)	2,390,800	80E
Sofia (Sofija), Bulgaria (1,133,733)	1,047,920	79E
Southampton, U.K. (410,000)	207,800	79E
Stockholm, Sweden (1,384,310)	649,384	79E
Stuttgart, Fed. Rep. of Ger. (1,935,000)	581,989	79E
Suchow (Xuzhou), China	800,000	75UE
Suez (As Suways), Egypt	204,000	78E
Surabaya, Indonesia (2,150,000)	2,027,913	80C
Surat, India (960,000)	775,711	81C
Sverdlovsk, U.S.S.R. (1,450,000)	1,225,000	80E
Sydney, Australia (3,193,300)	49,750	79E
Taegu, South Korea	1,607,458	80C
Taichung, Taiwan	585,205	77E
Tainan, Taiwan	572,590	77E
Taipei, Taiwan (3,825,000)	2,196,237	77E
Taiyuan, China	1,350,000	75UE
Tallinn, U.S.S.R.	436,000	80E
Tampa, U.S. (573,100)	271,523	80C
Tashkent (Taškent), U.S.S.R. (2,015,000)	1,816,000	80E
Tbilisi, U.S.S.R. (1,240,000)	1,080,000	80E
Tegucigalpa, Honduras	316,800	77E
Tehrān, Iran (4,700,000)	4,496,159	76C
Tel Aviv-Yafo, Israel (1,350,000)	336,300	79E
The Hague ('s-Gravenhage), Netherlands (775,000)	456,886	80E
Thessaloníki *(Salonika)*, Greece (557,360)	345,799	71C
Tientsin (Tianjin), China (7,210,000†)	4,650,000	78E
Tirana, Albania	192,300	76E
Tōkyō, Japan (25,800,000)	8,349,209	80C
Toledo, U.S. (571,200)	354,635	80C
Toronto, Canada (2,803,101)	633,318	76C
Tripoli (Tarābulus), Libya	264,000	70E
Tsinan (Jinan), China	1,125,000	75UE
Tsingtao (Qingdao), China	1,200,000	75UE
Tsitsihar (Qiqihar), China	850,000	75UE
Tucson, U.S. (495,200)	330,537	80C
Tula, U.S.S.R. (615,000)	518,000	80E
Tulsa, U.S. (569,100)	360,919	80C
Tūnis, Tunisia (915,000)	550,404	75C
Turin (Torino), Italy (1,670,000)	1,160,686	79E
Ufa, U.S.S.R. (1,000,000)	986,000	80E
Ujung Pandang *(Makasar)*, Indonesia	709,038	80C
Ulan-Bator, Mongolia	287,000	70E
Vadodara, India (744,043)	733,656	81C
Valencia, Spain (1,140,000)	750,994	78E
Valparaiso, Chile (530,000)	250,358	70C
Vancouver, Canada (1,166,348)	410,188	76C
Vārānasi *(Benares)*, India (925,000)	704,772	81C
Venice (Venezia), Italy (445,000)	355,865	79E
Victoria, Hong Kong (3,975,000)	1,026,870	76C
Vienna (Wien), Austria (1,925,000)	1,572,300	79E
Vladivostok, U.S.S.R.	558,000	80E
Volgograd *(Stalingrad)*, U.S.S.R. (1,230,000)	939,000	80E
Voronezh (Voronež), U.S.S.R.	796,000	80E
Warsaw (Warszawa), Poland (2,080,000)	1,576,600	79E
Washington, U.S. (3,220,700)	637,651	80C
Wellington, New Zealand (349,900)	137,600	79E
Wiesbaden, Fed. Rep. of Ger. (795,000)	273,267	79E
Winnipeg, Canada (578,217)	560,874	76C
Wrocław *(Breslau)*, Poland	609,100	79E
Wuhan, China	3,000,000	75UE
Wuppertal, Fed. Rep. of Ger. (870,000)	394,605	79E
Yaoundé, Cameroon	313,706	76C
Yerevan, (Jerevan), U.S.S.R. (1,155,000)	1,036,000	80E
Yokohama, Japan (*Tōkyō)	2,773,322	80C
Zagreb, Yugoslavia	566,084	71C
Zaporozhye (Zaporožje), U.S.S.R.	799,000	80E
Zhdanov (Ždanov), U.S.S.R.	507,000	80E
Zürich, Switzerland (780,000)	369,522	80C

Metropolitan area populations are shown in parentheses.
* City is located within the metropolitan area of another city; for example, Kyōto, Japan (*Ōsaka).
† Population of entire municipality or district, including rural area.

C Census
E Official Estimate
UE Unofficial Estimate

Sources

The maps in the Atlas have been compiled from diverse source materials, which are cited in the following lists. The citations are organized by continent and region or country. Within each regional or country group, atlases are listed alphabetically by title and then followed by maps, which are listed according to scale, from the smallest to the largest. Other sources, listed alphabetically by title, follow the map listings.

GENERAL SOURCES

Atlante dei confini sottomarini, *A. Giuffrè Editore, Milano 1979*
Atlante Internazionale del Touring Club Italiano, *TCI, Milano 1977*
Atlas Mira, *G.U.G.K. Moskva 1967*
Atlas Okeanov-Atlantičeski i Indijski Okeany, *Ministerstvo Oborony SSSR-Vojenno-Morskoj Flot, Moskva 1977*
Atlas Okeanov-Tihi Okean, *Ministerstvo Oborony SSSR-Vojenno-Morskoj Flot, Moska 1974*
Atlas of the World, *National Geographic Society (N.G.S.), Washington 1981*
Atlas zur Ozeanographie, *Bibliographisches Institut, Mannheim 1971*
Bertelsmann Atlas International, *C. Bertelsmann Verlag GmbH, München 1963*
Grande Atlante degli Oceani, *Instituto Geografico De Agostini (I.G.D.A.), Novara 1978*
Meyers Neuer Geographischer Handatlas, *Bibliographisches Institut, Mannheim 1966*
The New International Atlas, *Rand McNally & Company, Chicago 1980*
The Odyssey World Atlas, *Western Publishing Company Inc., New York 1966*
The Times Atlas of the World, *John Bartholomew & Son Ltd, Edinburgh 1980*
The World Book Atlas, *World Book Encyclopedia Inc, 1979*
The World Shipping Scene, *Weststadt-Verlag, München 1963*
Weltatlas Erdöl und Erdgas, *George Westermann Verlag, Braunschweig 1976*
Pacific Ocean Floor 1:36,432,000, *N.G.S., Washington 1969*
Atlantic Ocean Floor 1:30,580,000, *N.G.S., Washington 1973*
Indian Ocean 1:25,720,000, *N.G.S. Washington 1967*
Deutsche Meereskarte 1:25,000,000, *Kartographisches Institut Meyer*
Carte générale du Monde 1:10,000,000, *Institut Géographique National (I.G.N.), Paris*
Artic Ocean Floor 1:9,757,000, *N.G.S., Washington 1971*
Carte du Monde 1:5,000,000, *I.G.N., Paris*
Karta Mira 1:2,500,000, *G.U.G.K., Moskva*
Carte Internationale du Monde 1:1,000,000, *Geographical Survey Institute*
Carte Aéronautique du Monde 1:1,000,000, *I.G.N., Paris*
Calendario Atlante, *I.G.D.A., Novara 1982*
Cartactual, *Cartographia, Budapest*
Demographic Yearbook, *United Nations, New York, 1978*
Duden Wörterbuch Geographischer Namen, *Bibliographisches Institut, Mannheim 1966*
Gazetteers (Various), *U.S. Board on Geographical Names, Washington*
Meyers Enzyklopädisches Lexikon, *Bibliographisches Institut, Mannheim 1972–81*
Schtag nach!-Die Staaten der Erde, *Bibliographisches Institut, Mannheim 1977*
Statistical Yearbook, *United Nations, New York, 1978*
Statistik des Auslandes-Länderkurzberichte, *Statistisches Bundesamt, Wiesbaden*
The Columbia Lippincott Gazetteer of the World, *Columbia University Press, New York 1961*
The Europa Year Book 1981, *Europa Publication Ltd., London*
The Statesman's Yearbook 1981–82, *The Macmillan Press Ltd., London*
Webster's New Geographical Dictionary, *G & C Merriam Co, Springfield 1972*

EUROPE

ALBANIA
Shqiperia-Hartë Fizike 1:500,000, *MMS "Hamid Shijaku", Tirana 1970*
Shqiperia Politiko Administrative 1:500,000, *MMS "Hamid Shijaku", Tirana 1969*
Gjeografia e Shqiperise per shkollat e mesme, *Shtëpia Botuese e Librit Shkollor, Tirana 1970*

AUSTRIA
Neuer Schulatlas, *Freytag-Berndt und Artaria KG, Wien 1971*
Generalkarte Österreich 1:200,000, *Mairs Geographischer Verlag, Stuttgart 1974*
Gemeindeverzeichnis von Österreich, *Österreichischen Statistischen Zentralamt, Wien 1970*
Geographisches Namenbuch Österreichs, *Verlag der Österreichischen Akademie der Wissenschaften, Wien 1975*
Statistisches Handbuch für die Republik Österreich, *Österreichischen Statistischen Zentralamt, Wien 1978*

BELGIUM
Atlas de Belgique-Atlas van België, *Comité National de Géographie, Bruxelles 1974*
België, Luxemburg, Belgien 1:350,000, *Pneu. Michelin, Bruxelles 1976*
Belgique, Grand-Duché de Luxembourg, *Pneu. Michelin, Paris 1978*
Lista Alphabetique des Communes-fusion de 1963 à 1977, *Institut National de Statistique, Bruxelles*
Statistique Demographiques 1980, *Institut National de Statistique, Bruxelles*

BULGARIA
Atlas Narodna Republika Bulgarija, *Glavno Upravlenie po Geodezija i Kartografija, Sofija 1973*
Bulgaria 1:1,000,000, *PPWK, Warszawa 1977*
Statističeski Godišnik na Narodna Republika Bălgarija 1973, *Ministerstvo na Informacijata i Săobšenijata, Sofija*

CZECHOSLOVAKIA
Atlas ČSSR, *Kartografie, Praha 1972*
Školní Zeměpisný Atlas Čescoslovenské Socialistické Republiky, *Kartografické* Nakladatelství, Praha 1970
Auto Atlas Č.S.S.R., *Kartografie, Praha 1971*
Č.S.S.R.-Fyzická Mapa 1:500,000, *Ústřední Správa Geodezie a Kartografie, Praha 1963*
Statistická Ročenka Č.S.S.R., *Federální Statistický Úřad, Praha 1980*

DENMARK
Haases Atlas, *P. Haase & Søns Forlag, København 1972*
Opgivne og Tilplantede Landbrugsarealer i Jylland, *Det Kongelige Danske Geografiske Selskab, København 1976*
Danmark 1:300,000, *Geodætisk Institut, København 1972*
Statistisk Årbog Danmark 1980, *Danmarks Statistik, København*

FINLAND
Oppikoulun Kartasto, *Werner Söderström Osakeyhtiö, Porvoo 1972*
Suomi-Finland 1:1,000,000, *Naanmittaushallituksen Kivipaino, Helsinki 1972*
Finland-Suomi 1:1,000,000, *Kümmerly & Frey, Bern 1981*
Suomen Tilastollinen Vuosikirja 1975, *Tilastokeskus, Helsinki*

FRANCE
Atlas Général Larousse, *Librairie Larousse, Paris 1976*
Atlas Général Bordas, *Bordas, Paris 1972*
Atlas Géographique Alpha, *I.G.D.A., Novara 1972*
Atlas Moderne Larousse, *Librairie Larousse-I.G.D.A., Paris 1976*
Carte Administrative de la France 1:1,400,000, *I.G.N., Paris 1977*
Carte de la France 1:1,000,000, *I.G.N., Paris 1971*
France: Routes-Autoroutes 1:1,000,000, *I.G.N., Paris 1978*
Carte Touristique 1:250,000, *I.G.N., Paris 1978*
France 1:200,000, *Pneu. Michelin, Paris*
Carte Touristique 1:100,000, *I.G.N., Paris*
Michelin 1977-France, *Pneu. Michelin, Paris*
Population de la France-Recensement 1975, *Institut National de la Statistique et des Études Économiques, Paris*

GERMAN DEMOCRATIC REPUBLIC
Haack Weltatlas, *V.E.B. Hermann Haack Geographisch-Kartographische Anstalt, Gotha-Leipzig 1972*
Weltatlas-Die Staaten der Erde und ihre Wirtschaft, *V.E.B. Hermann Haack Geographisch-Kartographische Anstalt, Gotha-Leipzig 1972*
Autokarte der D.D.R. 1:600,000, *V.E.B. Landkartenverlag, Berlin 1972*
Statistisches Jahrbuch der Deutschen Demokratischen Republik 1981, *Staatsverlag der D.D.R., Berlin*

GERMANY, FEDERAL REPUBLIC OF
Diercke Weltatlas, *Westermann Verlag, Braunschweig 1977*
Der Grosse Shell Atlas, *Mairs Geographischer Verlag, Stuttgart 1981–82*
Der Neue Weltatlas, *I.G.D.A., Novara 1977*
Deutschland-Strassenkarte 1:1,000,000, *Kümmerly & Frey, Bern 1981*
Bundesrepublik Deutschland-Übersichtskarte 1:500,000, *Institut für Angewandte Geodäsie, Frankfurt 1978*
Topographische Übersichtskarte 1:200,000, *Institut für Angewandte Geodäsie, Frankfurt*
Bevölkerung der Gemeinden, *Statistisches Bundesamt, Wiesbaden 1979*
Statistisches Jahrbuch für die B.R.D. 1980, *Statistisches Bundesamt, Wiesbaden*

GREECE
Greece-Autokarte 1:1,000,000, *Kümmerly & Frey, Bern*
Greece-Autokarte 1:650,000, *Freytag & Berndt, Wien*
Genikos Chartis tis Hellados 1:400,000, *Geografiki Hypiresia Stratoy, Athínai*
Etniki Statistiki Hypiresia tis Hellados 1:200,000, *E.S.Y.E., Athínai*
Statistiki Epetiris tis Hellados 1979, *E.S.Y.E., Athínai*

HUNGARY
Földrajzi Atlas a Középiskolák Számára, *Kartográfiai Vallalat, Budapest 1980*
A Magyar Népköztársaság 1:400,000, *Kartográfiai Vallalat, Budapest 1974*
Magyarorszag Domborzata és Vizei 1:350,000, *Kartogràfiai Vallalat, Budapest 1961*
Megye Terképe, *Cartographia, Budapest 1979–80*
A Magyar Népköztársaság Helységnévtára 1973, *Statisztikai Kiadó Vállalat, Budapest*
Statistical Pocket Book of Hungary 1980, *Statistical Publishing House, Budapest*

ICELAND
Landabréfabok, *Ríkisutgáfa Námsbóka, Reykjavik 1970*
Iceland-Road Guide, *Örn & Örlygur H.F., Reykjavik 1975*

IRELAND
Irish Student's Atlas, *Educational Company of Ireland, Dublin-Cork 1971*
Ireland 1:575,000, *Ordnance Survey Office, Dublin 1979*
Ireland 1:250,000, *Ordnance Survey Office, Dublin 1962*
Census of Population of Ireland 1979, *The Stationery Office, Dublin*

ITALY
Atlante Metodico, *I.G.D.A., Novara 1981*
Atlante Stradale d'Italia 1:200,000, *Touring Club Italiano, Milano*
Carta d'Italia 1:1,250,000, *Instituto Geografico Militare, Firenze 1972*
Carte batimetriche, *Istituto Idrografico della Marina, Genova*
Carta Generale d'Italia 1:500,000, *Touring Club Italiano, Milano 1979*
Carta Generale d'Italia 1:200,000, *I.G.M., Firenze*
Enciclopedia Italiana, *Istituto della Enciclopedia Italiana G. Treccani, Roma*
Il Mare, *I.G.D.A., Novara*
La Montagna, *I.G.D.A., Novara*
XI Censimento Generale della Popolazione 24 ottobre 1971, *Istituto Centrale di Statistica, Roma*
XII Censimento Generale della Popolazione 25 ottobre 1981, *Istituto Centrale di Statistica, Roma*

LUXEMBOURG
Grand-Duché de Luxembourg 1:100,000, *I.G.N., Paris 1970*
Annuaire Statistique-Luxembourg 1981–82, *Service Central de la Statistique et des Études Économiques, Paris*

NETHERLANDS
Atlas van Nederland, *Staatsdrukkerij-en Uitgeverijbedrijf,'s-Gravenhage*
De Grote Vara Gezinsatlas, *Vara Omroepvereniging, Hilversum 1975*
Der Kleine Bosatlas, *Wolter-Noordhoff, Groningen 1974*
Pays-Bas/Nederland 1:400,000, *Pneu. Michelin, Paris 1981*
Gegevens per Gemeente Betreffende de Loop der Bevolking in het Jaar 1980, *Centraal Bureau voor der Statistik, Amsterdam*

NORWAY
Atlas-Større Utgave for Gymnaset, *J. W. Cappelens Forlag A.S., Oslo 1969*
Bilkart Bok Road Atlas, *J. W. Cappelens Forlag A.S., Oslo 1967*
Norge-Bit-Og Turistkart 1:400,000, *J. W. Cappelens Forlag A.S., Oslo 1965*
Folketallet i Kommunene 1972–73, *Statistik Sentralbyraå, Oslo*
Statistisk Årbok 1981, *Statistik Sentralbyrå, Oslo*

POLAND
Atlas Geograficzny, *PPWK, Warszawa 1979*
Narodowy Atlas Polski, *Polska Akademia Nauk, Warszawa 1978*
Polska Kontynenty Świat, *P.P.W.K., Warszawa 1977*
Powszechny Atlas Świat, *P.P.W.K. Warszawa 1981*
Polska Rzeczpospolito. Ludowa-Mapa Administracyjna 1:500,000, *P.P.W.K., Warszawa 1980*
Rocznik Statystyczny 1978, *Glówny Urzad Statystyczny, Warszawa*

PORTUGAL
Portugal 1:1,500,000, *Pneu. Michelin, Paris 1981*
Mapa do Estado das Estradas de Portugal 1:550,000, *Automovel Club de Portugal, Lisboa 1979*
Carto. Corográfica de Portugal 1:400,000, *Instituto Geografico e Cadastral, Lisboa 1968*
Anuário Estatístico-Portugal 1974, *Instituto Nacional de Estatística, Lisboa*

ROMANIA
Atlas Geografic General, *Editura Didactica si Pedagogica, Bucureşti 1974*
Atlasul Republicii Socialiste România, *Institutul de Geologie si Geofizica, Bucureşti*
Rumanien-Bulgarien 1:1,000,000, *Freytag-Berndt und Artaria K.G., Wien*
Anuarul Statistic al Republicii Socialiste România 1980, *Direcţia Centrala de Statistică, Bucureşti*

SPAIN
Atlas Bachillerato Universal y de España, *Aguilar, Madrid 1968*
Atlas Básico Universal, *I.G.D.A. Teide, Novara 1969*
Gran Atlas Aguilar, *Aguilar, Madrid 1969*
Peninsula Iberica, Baleares y Canarias 1:1,000,000, *Instituto Geografico y Catastral, Madrid 1966*
Mapa Militar de España 1:800,000, *Servicio Geografico del Ejercito, Madrid 1971*
España 1:500,000, *Firestone Hispania, Madrid*
España-Mapa Oficial de Carreteras 1:400,000 *Ministerio de Obras Publica, Madrid*
España-Anuario Estadistico 1979, *Instituto Nacional de Estadistica, Madrid*

SWEDEN
Atlas Över Välden, *Generalstabens Litografiska Anstalt, Stockholm 1972*
Atlas Över Välden, *Natur Miljö Befolkning, Stockholm 1974*
Kak Bil Atlas, *Generalstabens Litografiska Anstalt, Stockholm 1973*
Sverige-Bilkarta 1:625,000, *A.B. Kartlitografen, Stockholm 1972*
Statistisk Årsbok 1980, *Statistiska Centralbyrån, Stockholm*

SWITZERLAND
Atlas der Schweiz, *Verlag des Bundesamtes fur Landestopographie, Wabern-Bern*
Schweizerischer Mittelschulatlas, *Konferenz der Kantonalen Erziehungsdirektoren, Zürich 1976*
Switzerland 1:300,000, *Kümmerly & Frey, Bern 1979*
Carte Nazionale de la Suisse 1:200,000, *Service Topographique Federale, Wabern-Bern*

U.S.S.R.
Atlas Avtomobilnyh Dorog, *G.U.G.K., Moskva 1976*
Atlas Obrazovanie i Razvitie Sojuza S.S.R., *G.U.G.K., Moskva 1972*
Malyi Atlas S.S.S.R., *G.U.G.K., Moskva 1973*
SSSR 1:8,000,000, *G.U.G.K., Moskva 1980*
SSSR 1:4,000,000, *G.U.G.K., Moskva 1972*
Latvijskaja SSR 1:600,000, *G.U.G.K., Moskva 1967*
Litovskaja SSR 1:600,000, *G.U.G.K., Moskva 1969*
S.S.S.R. Administrativno-Territorialnoje Delenie Sojuznyh Respublik, *Prezidium Verhovnogo Soveta Sojuza Sovetskih Socialističeskih Respublik Moskva 1971*

UNITED KINGDOM
Philips' Modern School Economic Atlas, *George Philip & Son Ltd, London 1981*
Roads Atlas of Great Britain and Ireland, *George Philip & Son Ltd, London 1971*
The Atlas of Britain and Northern Ireland, *Clarendon Press, Oxford 1963*
Route Planning Map 1:625,000, *Ordnance Survey, Southampton 1973*
Cartes 1:400,000, *Michelin Tyre Co. Ltd., London 1981*

YUGOSLAVIA
Atlas, *Izrađenou u Oour Kartografiji Tlos "Učila", Zagreb 1980*
Jugoslavija-Auto Atlas, *Jugoslavenski Leksikografski Zavod, Zagreb 1972*
Školki Atlas, *Izrađenou u Oour Kartografiji Tlos "Učila", Zagreb 1975*
Jugoslavija 1:1,000,000, *Grafički Zavod Hrvatske, Zagreb 1980*
Statistički Godišnjak Jugoslavije 1975, *Savezni Zavod za Statistiku, Beograd*

ASIA

ARABIAN PENINSULA
The Oxford Map of Saudi Arabia 1:2,600,000, *GEO-projects, Beirut 1981*
Arabian Peninsula 1:2,000,000, *United States Geological Survey, Washington 1963*
Arabische Republik Jemen 1:1,000,000, *Deutsch-Jemenitische Gesellschaft e V, Schwaig 1976*
The United Arab Emirates 1:750,000, *GEO-projects, Beirut 1981*

MIDDLE EAST
Atlas of Iran, *"Sahab" Geographic & Drafting Institute, Tehrán 1971*
Modern Büyük Atlas, *Arkin Kitabevi-I.G.D.A., Istanbul 1981*
The New Israel Atlas-Zev Vilnay, *Israel Universities Press, Yerushalaym 1968*
Iran 1:2,500,000, *Imperial Government of Iran, Tehrān 1968*
Guide Map of Iran 1:2,250,000, *Gita Shenassi Co. Ltd, Tehrān*
Guide Map of Iraq 1:2,000,000, *"Sahab" Geographic & Drafting Institute, Tehrān 1971*
Türkiye 1:2,000,000, *Ravenstein Verlag GmbH, Frankfurt 1975*
Iran 1:1,500,000, *Imperial Government of Iran, Tehrān 1968*
Iraq Tourist Map 1:1,500,000, *Summer Resorts and Tourism Service, Baghdād 1967*
The Oxford Map of Syria 1:1,000,000, *GEO-projects, Beirut 1980*
Turkey-Road Map 1:1,000,000, *Kümmerly & Frey, Bern 1980*
Türkei und Naher Osten 1:800,000, *Reis und Verkehrsverlag, Berlin-Stuttgart 1977*
Israel und Angrenzende Länder-Strassenkarte 1:750,000, *Kümmerly & Frey, Bern 1981*
The Oxford Map of Jordan 1:730,000, *GEO-projects, Beirut 1979*
Map of Israel 1:500,000, *Survey of Israel, Yerushalaym 1979*
The Oxford Map of Kuwait 1:500,000, *GEO-projects, Beirut 1980*
The Oxford Map of Qatar 1:270,000, *GEO-projects, Beirut 1980*
Israel Map of the Cease-Fire Lines 1:250,000, *Survey of Israel, Yerushalaym 1973*
Qatar-Visitor's Map 1:250,000, *Ministry of Information, Doha 1979*
Carte Générale du Liban 1:200,000, *Ministère de la Défense Nationale, Beirut 1967*
Qatar 1:200,000, *Hunting Surveys Ltd., Borchamwood 1975*
Bahrain Islands 1:63,360, *Public Works Department, Al Manāmah 1968*
The Oxford Map of Bahrain 1:57,750, *GEO-projects, Beirut 1980*
Bahrain—A Map for Visitors 1:50,000, *Ministry of Information, Al Manāmah 1976*
Annual Abstract of Statistics 1978, *Central Statistical Organization, Baghdād*
Genel Nüfus Sayımı 12 ekim 1980, *Başbakanlik Devlet İstatistik Enstitüsü, Ankara*
Kuwait—Annual Statistical Abstract, *Central Statistical Office-Ministry of Planning, Al Kuwayt 1976*
List of Localities—Geographical Information and Population 1948–1961–1972–1975, *Central Bureau of Statistics, Yerushalaym*
Recueil de Statistiques Libanaises No. 8-1972, *Direction Centrale de la Statistique, Bayrūt*
Republic of Cyprus—Statistical Abstract 1973, *The Statistics and Research Department, Levkosia*
Statistical Abstract—Syrian Arab Republic 1973, *Central Bureau of Statistics, Dimashq*
Statistical Abstract of Israel 1979, *Central Bureau of Statistics, Yerushalaym*
The Hashemite Kingdom of Jordan, Statistical Yearbook 1976, *Department of Statistics, Ammān*
Türkiye İstatistik Yıllığı 1975, *Başbakanlik Devlet İstatistik Enstitüsü, Ankara*

SOUTH ASIA
National Atlas of India, *National Atlas & Thematic Mapping Organization, Calcutta*
Oxford School Atlas for Pakistan, *Oxford University Press—Pakistan Branch, Karachi 1973*
Tourist Atlas of India, *National Atlas Organization, Calcutta*
Physical Map of India 1:4,500,000, *Survey of India, Calcutta 1974*
Political Map of India 1:4,500,000, *Survey of India, Calcutta 1972*
Railway Map of India 1:3,500,000, *Government of India, Calcutta 1971*
Pākistān 1:3,168,000, *Survey of Pākistān, Rāwalpindi 1966*
Bangladesh 1:2,800,000, *Survey of Bangladesh, Dacca 1979*
Burma 1:2,000,000, *Army Map Service, Washington 1963*
Physical and Political Map of Afghanistan 1:1,500,000, *Afghan Cartographic Institute, Kabul 1968*
Ceylon Physical 1:1,000,000, *Survey Department, Colombo 1973*
New Map of Afghanistan 1:1,000,000, *"Sahab" Geographic & Drafting Institute, Tehrān*
Pākistān 1:1,000,000, *Survey of Pākistān, Rāwalpindi 1968*
Motor Map of Ceylon 1:506,880, *Survey Department, Colombo 1973*
Nepal 1:506,880, *Ministry of Defence, London 1967*
Nepal 1:408,000, *Kümmerly & Frey, Bern 1980*
Bangladesh Population Census Report 1974, *Statistics Division-Ministry of Planning, Dacca*
Geomedical Monograph Series—Afghanistan, *Springer-Verlag, Berlin 1968*
Pakistan Statistical Yearbook 1978, *Statistics Division, Karachi*
Statistical Pocket Book of the Democratic Socialist Republic of Sri Lanka 1979, *Department of Census and Statistics, Colombo*

SOUTHEAST ASIA
Atlas Indonesia, *Yayasan Dwidjendra, Denpasar-Jakarta 1977*
Atlas of Thailand, *Royal Thai Survey Department, Bangkok 1974*
Secondary Atlas for Malaysia and Singapore, *Niugini Press Pty. Ltd., Port Moresby 1975*
Secondary School Atlas for Malaysia, *McGraw-Hill Far Eastern Publishers Ltd., Singapore 1970*
Hành Chính Viet Nam 1:2,500,000, *Hô Chí Minh 1976*
Maluku dan Irian Jaya 1:2,250,000, *Pembina, Jakarta 1975–76*
Bàu-dô Viet Nam 1:2,000,000, *Saigon 1972*
Laos Administratif 1:2,000,000, *Service Géographique National du Laos, Vientiane 1968*
Malaysia 1:2,000,000, *Jabatanarah Pemetaan Negara, 1976*
Map of Thailand and Bangkok 1:2,000,000, *The Shell Company of Thailand Ltd., Bangkok*
Vietnam 1:2,000,000, *G.U.G.K., Moskva 1972*
Kalimantan 1:1,500,000, *Pembina, Jakarta 1975–76*
Philippines 1:1,500,000, *Philippine Coast and Geodetic Survey, Manila 1968*
Cambodia & South Vietnam—Southeast Asia 1:1,250,000, *Army Map Service, Washington 1966*
Carte Générale du Laos, *Service Géographique National du Laos, Vientiane 1968*
Sumatera 1:790,000, *Pembina, Jakarta 1975–76*
Malaysia Barat—West Malaysia 1:760,000, *Jabatanarah Pemetaan Negara, 1968*
Jawa Barat & D.K.I. Jakarta 1:500,000, *Pembina, Jakarta 1974–75*
Jawa Tengah & D.I. Yogyakarta 1:500,000, *Pembina, Jakarta 1974–75*
Jawa Timur 1:500,000, *Pembina, Jakarta 1974–75*

Sabah 1:500,000, *Jabatanarah Pemetaan Negara, 1976*
Nusa Tenggara Barat & Nusa Tenggara Timur 1:330,000, *Pembina, Jakarta 1975*
Jawa Madura 1:225,000, *Pembina, Jakarta 1975–76*
Sulawesi 1:220,000, *Pembina, Jakarta 1975–76*
Gulongan Masharakat-Banchi Pendudok dan Perumahan Malaysia 1970, *Jabatan Perangkaan, Kuala Lumpur*
Sensus Penduluk 1971, *Biro Pusat Statistik, Jakarta*
Statistical Summary of Thailand 1978, *Statistical Reports Division, Bangkok*
Statistik Indonesia 1974–75, *Biro Pusat Statistik, Jakarta*

CHINA, MONGOLIA
Zhonghua Renmin Gongheguo Fen Sheng Dituji, *Ditu Chubanshe, Beijing 1977*
Zhonghua Renmin Gongheguo Ditu 1:6,000,000, *Ditu Chubanshe, Beijing 1980*
China 1:5,500,000, *Cartographia, Budapest 1967*
Zhonghua Renmin Gongheguo Ditu 1:4,000,000, *Ditu Chubanshe, Beijing 1980*
Mongolskaja Narodnaja Respublika 1:3,000,000, *G.U.G.K., Moskva 1972*
Taiwan/Formosa 1:500,000, *Army Map Service, Washington 1964*
China's Changing Map, *Methuen & Co., London 1972*

JAPAN, KOREA
Japan—The Pocket Atlas, *Heibonsha Ltd., Tōkyō 1970*
The National Atlas of Japan, *Geographical Survey Institute, Tōkyō 1977*
Teikoku's Complete Atlas of Japan, *Teikoku Shoin Company Ltd., Tōkyō 1977*
Tourist Map of Japan 1:5,300,000, *Japan National Tourist Organisation, Tōkyō 1974*
Republic of Korea 1:1,000,000, *Chungang Map & Chart Service, Sŏul 1973*
Northern Korea—Road Map of Korea, *Republic of Korea Army Map Service, Sŏul 1971*
Southern Korea 1:700,000, *Republic of Korea Army Map Service, Sŏul 1977*

AFRICA

The Atlas of Africa, *Editions Jeune Afrique, Paris 1973*
Africa 1:14,000,000, *N.G.S., Washington 1980*
Africa 1:9,000,000, *V.E.B. Hermann Haack, Gotha-Leipzig 1977*
Afrique/Africa 1:4,000,000, *Pneu. Michelin, Paris-London*
Africa 1:2,000,000, *Army Map Service, Washington*

NORTH WEST AFRICA
Atlas International de l'Ouest Africain 1:2,500,000, *Organisation de l'Unité Africaine, Dakar 1971*
Mauritanie 1:2,500,000, *I.G.N., Paris 1978*
Algérie-Tunisie 1:1,000,000, *Pneu. Michelin, Paris 1975*
Maroc 1:1,000,000, *Pneu. Michelin, Paris 1975*
Generalkarte Gran Canaria-Tenerife 1:150,000, *Mairs Geographischer Verlag, Stuttgart 1979*
Annuaire Statistique du Maroc, *Direction de la Statistique, Rabat 1976*
Code Géographique National—Code des Communes, *Secretariat d'État au Plan, Alger 1975*
Recensement Général de la Population et des Logements 1975, *Institut National de la Statistique, Tūnis*

NORTH EAST AFRICA
Egypte 1:750,000, *Kummerly & Frey, Bern 1977*
Population Census 1973, *Census and Statistical Department, Tarābulus*

WEST AFRICA
Atlas de Côte d'Ivoire, *Institut de Géographie Tropicale-Université d'Abidjan, Abidjan 1971*
Atlas de Haute-Volta, *Centre Voltaïque de la Recherche Scientifique, Ouagadougou 1969*
Atlas du Cameroun, *Institut de Recherches Scientifiques du Cameroun, Yaoundé*
Atlas for the United Republic of Cameroon, *Collins-Longman, Glasgow 1977*
Ghana Junior Atlas, *E. A. Boateng-Thomas Nelson and Sons Ltd., London 1965*
Liberia in Maps, *Stefan von Gnielinski, Hamburg 1972*
Oxford Atlas for Nigeria, *Oxford University Press, London-Ibadan 1971*
School Atlas for Sierra Leone, *Collins-Longman, Glasgow 1975*
République du Mali 1:2,500,000, *I.G.N., Paris 1971*
Ghana-Administrative 1:2,000,000, *Survey of Ghana, Accra 1968*
Road Map of Nigeria 1:585,000, *Federal Surveys, Lagos 1969*
République Unie du Cameroun 1:1,000,000, *I.G.N., Paris 1972*
République de Haute-Volta-Carte Routière 1:1,000,000, *I.G.N., Paris 1968*
Philips' School Room Map of Ghana 1:1,000,000, *George Philip & Son Ltd., London 1963*
Sénégal 1:1,000,000, *I.G.N., Paris 1974*
Sénégal-Carte Administrative 1:1,000,000, *I.G.N., Paris 1966*
Physical Map of Nigeria 1:1,000,000, *Federal Surveys, Lagos 1965*
République du Côte d'Ivoire 1:1,000,000, *I.G.N., Paris 1970*
Côte d'Ivoire 1:800,000, *Pneu. Michelin, Paris 1978*
Mapa da Guiné 1:650,000, *J. R. Silva, Lisboa 1969*
République du Dahomey-Carte Routière et Touristique 1:500,000, *I.G.N., Paris 1968*
Road Map of Ghana 1:500,000, *Survey of Ghana, Accra 1970*
The Gambia Road Map 1:500,000, *Survey Department The Gambia, Banjul 1973*
Nigeria-Digest of Statistics 1973, *Federal Office of Statistics, Lagos*

EAST AND CENTRAL AFRICA
Atlas Pratique du Tchad, *Institut Tchadien pour les Sciences Humaines, Paris 1972*
Sudan Roads 1:4,000,000, *Sudan Survey Department, Khartoum 1976*
Äthiopie/Ethiopia 1:4,000,000, *Medizinische Länderkunde/Geomedical Monograph Series, Berlin 1972*
Carte de l'Afrique Centrale 1:2,500,000, *I.G.N., Paris 1968*
Highway Map of Ethiopia 1:2,000,000, *Imperial Ethiopian Government, Addis Ababa 1961*
République du Tchad-Carte Routière 1:1,500,000, *I.G.N., Paris 1968*
République Centrafricaine-Carte Routière 1:1,500,000, *I.G.N., Paris 1969*
Territoire Française des Afars et des Issas 1:400,000, *Office Developpement du Tourisme, Djibouti 1970*
Ethiopia-Statistical Abstract 1976, *Central Statistical Office, Addis Ababa*

EQUATORIAL AFRICA
Atlas du Congo, *Office de la Recherche Scientifique et Techique Outre-Mer, Brazzaville 1969*
Atlas for Malawi, *Collins-Longman, Glasgow 1969*
Atlas of Uganda, *Department of Lands and Surveys, Kampala 1967*
Malawi in Maps, *University of London Press Ltd., London 1972*
Tanzania in Maps, *University of London Press, Ltd., London 1975*
The First Kenya Atlas, *George Philip & Son Ltd., London 1973*
Carte de l'Afrique Centrale 1:2,500,000, *I.G.N., Paris 1968*
Carta Rodoviária de Angola 1:2,000,000, *Lello S.A.R.L., Luanda 1974*
Republic of Zambia 1:1,500,000, *Surveyor General, Ministry of Lands and Natural Resources, Lusaka 1972*
Tanzania 1:1,250,000, *Shell & B.P. Tanzania Ltd., Dar es Salaam 1973*
Malawi 1:1,000,000, *Malawi Government, Blantyre 1971*
Road Map of Kenya 1:1,000,000, *George Philip & Son Ltd., London 1972*
République Populaire du Congo 1:1,000,000, *I.G.N., Paris 1973*
Gabon 1:1,000,000, *I.G.N., Paris 1975*
Statistical Abstract 1979, *Central Bureau of Statistics, Nairobi*

SOUTHERN AFRICA
Large Print Atlas for Southern Africa, *George Philip & Son Ltd., London 1976*
Atlas de Madagascar, *Association des Géographes de Madagascar, Antananarivo 1971*
Atlas for Mauritius, *Macmillan Education Ltd., London 1971*
Ontwikkelingsatlas-Development Atlas, *Republic of South Africa-Department of Planning, Pretoria 1966*
Botswana Road Map and Climate Chart 1:6,000,000, *Department of Surveys and Lands, Gaborone 1980*
Madagascar et Comores 1:4,000,000, *I.G.N., Paris 1970*
Suidelike Afrika/Southern Africa 1:2,500,000, *The Government Printer, Pretoria 1973*
Roads of Zimbabwe 1:2,100,000, *Shell Zimbabwe Ltd., Salisbury, 1980*
Carta de Moçambique 1:2,000,000, *Ministerio do Ultramar, Lisboa 1971*
Mapa Rodoviário de Moçambique 1:2,000,000, *J.A.E.M. 1972*
The Black Homelands of South Africa 1:1,900,000, *Perskor Boeke Tekenkantoor, Johannesburg*
Road Map of Zimbabwe 1:1,800,000, *A.A. of Zimbabwe, Salisbury 1980*
Zimbabwe-Mobil 1:1,470,000, *M.O. Collins Ltd., Salisbury 1976*
Rhodesia Relief 1:1,000,000, *Surveyor General, Salisbury 1973*
Lafatshe La Botswana/Republic of Botswana 1:1,000,000, *Department of Surveys and Lands, Gaborone 1970*
Suid Afrika/South Africa 1:500,000, *The Government Printer, Pretoria*
Lesotho, 1:250,000, *Government Overseas Surveys, Maseru 1969*
Île Maurice-Carte Touristique 1:100,000, *I.G.N., Paris 1978*
La Réunion-Carte Touristique 1:100,000, *I.G.N., Paris 1978*
Annual Statistical Bulletin 1973, *The Bureau of Statistics, Maseru*
Bi-Annual Digest of Statistics 1976, *Central Statistical Office, Port Louis*
Population Census 1970, *Department of Statistics, Pretoria*
Population de Madagascar au Ier Janvier 1972, *Direction Général du Gouvernement, Antananarivo*
South Africa 1980–81-Official Yearbook, *Chris van Rensburg Publications Ltd., Johannesburg*

NORTH AMERICA

CANADA
Atlas Larousse Canadien, *Les Editions Françaises Inc., Québec - Montréal 1971*
Oxford Regional Economic Atlas - United States & Canada, *Clarendon Press, Oxford 1967*
Road Atlas United States - Canada - Mexico, *Rand McNally & Co., Chicago 1981*
The National Atlas of Canada, *Department of Energy, Mines and Resources, Ottawa 1972*
Northwest Territories - Yukon Territory 1:4,000,000, *Department of Energy, Mines and Resources, Ottawa 1974*
Quebec and Newfoundland 1:3,700,000, *N.G.S., Washington 1980*
British Columbia, Alberta and the Yukon Territory 1:3,500,000, *N.G.S., Washington 1978*
Ontario 1:3,000,000, *N.G.S., Washington 1980*
Saskatchewan and Manitoba 1:2,600,000, *N.G.S., Washington 1979*
Canada Year Book 1978-79, *Minister of Industry, Trade and Commerce, Ottawa*

UNITED STATES
Oxford Regional Economic Atlas - United States & Canada, *Clarendon Press, Oxford 1967*
Road Atlas United States - Canada - Mexico, *Rand McNally & Co., Chicago 1981*
Transportation Map of the United States, *U.S. Department of Transportation, Washington 1976*
National Energy Transportation System 7,500,000, *U.S. Geological Survey, Reston, Virginia 1977*
Close-up: Alaska 1:3,295,000, *N.G.S., Washington 1975*
Close-up: The Southwest 1:2,124,000, *N.G.S., Washington 1977*
Close-up: The Northwest 1:2,000,000, *N.G.S., Washington 1973*
Close-up: The Southeast 1:1,780,000, *N.G.S., Washington 1975*
Close-up: California and Nevada 1:1,700,000, *N.G.S., Washington 1978*
Close-up: Florida 1:1,331,000, *N.G.S., Washington 1973*
Close-up: Illinois, Indiana, Ohio and Kentucky 1:1,267,000, *N.G.S., Washington 1977*
Close-up: The Northeast 1:1,215,000, *N.G.S., Washington 1978*
Close-up: The Mid-Atlantic States 1:886,000, *N.G.S., Washington 1973*
Topographic Maps 1:500,000, *U.S. Geological Survey, Washington*
Topographic Maps 1:250,000, *U.S. Geological Survey, Washington*
Togographic Maps 1:24,000, *U.S. Geological Survey, Washington*
Census of Population and Housing 1980, *Bureau of the Census, Washington*

MEXICO
Atlas of Mexico, *Bureau of Business Research, University of Texas, Austin 1975*
Road Atlas United States - Canada - Mexico, *Rand McNally & Co., Chicago 1981*
Mapas de los Estados-Serie Patria, *Libreria Patria S.A., México*
Carta Geografica de México 1:2,500,000, *Asociación Nacional Automovilística, Ciudad de México 1976*
Archeological Map of Middle America 1:2,250,000, *N.G.S., Washington 1968*

CENTRAL AMERICA AND THE CARIBBEAN
Atlas for Barbados, Windwards and Leewards, *Macmillan Education Ltd., London 1974*
Atlas for Guyana & Trinidad & Tobago, *Macmillan Education Ltd, London 1973*
Atlas for the Eastern Caribbean, *Collins-Longman, London 1977*
Atlas Nacional de Cuba, *Academia de Ciencias de Cuba, La Habana 1970*
Atlas of the Commonwealth of the Bahamas, *Kingston Publishers Ltd.-Ministry of Education, Kingston-Nassau 1976*
Jamaica in Maps, *University of London Press Ltd., London 1974*
West Indies and Central Amerika 1:4,500,000, *N.G.S., Washington 1981*
Mapa General-República de Honduras 1:1,000,000, *Instituto Geográfico Nacional, Tegucigalpa 1980*
Mapa Oficial de la República de Panamá 1:1,000,000, *Instituto Geográfico Nacional, Panamá 1979*
Mapa Preliminar de la República de Guatemala 1:1,000,000, *Instituto Geográfico Nacional, Guatemala 1976*
República de Nicaragua 1:1,000,000, *Instituto Geográfico Nacional, Managua 1975*
Belize 1:800,000, *Directorate of Overseas Surveys, London 1974*
Mapa de la República Dominicana 1:600,000, *Instituto Geográfico Universitario, Santo Domingo 1979*
Costa Rica - Mapa Fisico-Politico 1:500,000, *Instituto Geográfico de Costa Rica, San José 1974*
El Salvador 1:500,000, *Ministerio de Obras Públicas, San Salvador 1978*
Mapa Hipsométrico de la República de Guatemala 1:500,000, *Instituto Geográfico Nacional, Guatemala 1979*
Jamaica 1:280,000, *Fairey Surveys Ltd., Maidenhead 1974*
Mapa de Carreteras Estatales de Puerto Rico 1:250,000, *Autoridad de Carreteras Estatales, San Juan 1972*
Nicaragua-Costa Rica 1:250,000, *Instituto Geográfico Nacional, Managua 1972*
Puerto Rico e Islas Limitrofes 1:240,000, *U.S. Geological Survey, Washington 1970*
Turks & Caicos Islands 1:200,000, *Directorate of Overseas Surveys, London 1971*
Cayman Islands 1:150,000, *Directorate of Overseas Surveys, London 1972*
Trinidad 1:150,000, *Director of Surveys-Ministry of Defense, London 1970*
Guadeloupe-Carte Touristique 1:100,000, *I.G.N., Paris 1978*
Martinique-Carte Touristique 1:100,000, *I.G.N., Paris 1977*
Lesser Antilles-Antigua 1:50,000, *Directorate of Overseas Surveys, London 1973*
Tourist Map of Tobago 1:50,000, *Lands & Surveys Department, Port of Spain 1969*
Dominica 1:25,000, *Directorate of Overseas Surveys, London 1978*
Lesser Antilles-Barbuda 1:25,000, *Directorate of Overseas Surveys, London 1970*
Annuario Estadístico de Costa Rica 1977, *Direción General de Estadística, San José*
Annuario Estadístico de Cuba 1973, *Direción Central de Estadística, La Habana*
Caribbean Year Book 1978-80, *Caribook Ltd., Toronto*
Fact Sheets on the Commonwealth-Antigua, *British Information Services, London 1974*
Fact Sheets on the Commonwealth-Belize, *British Information Services, London 1976*
Guatemala-III Censo de Habitación 26 de marzo de 1973, *Direción General de Estadística, Guatemala*
Honduras-Annuario Estadístico 1978, *Direción General de Estadística, Censos, Tegucigalpa*
Nicaragua-Annuario Estadístico 1975, *Oficina Ejecutiva de Encuestas y Censos, Managua*
Statistical Yearbook for Latin America, *United Nations, New York 1976*
Zentralamerika-Karten zur Bevölkerungs und Wirtschaftsstruktur 1975, *H. Nuhn, P. Krieg & W. Schlick, Hamburg*

SOUTH AMERICA

NORTHERN SOUTH AMERICA
Atlas Basico de Colombia, *Instituto Geográfico Agustin Codazzi, Bogotá 1970*
Atlas de Colombia, *Instituto Geográfico Agustin Codazzi, Bogotá 1979*
Atlas de Venezuela, *Ministerio de Obras Públicas, Caracas 1970*
Atlas for Guyana, Trinidad & Tobago, *Macmillan Education Ltd., London 1973*
Atlas Histórico Geográfico y de Paisajes Peruanos, *Instituto Nacional de Planificación, Lima 1970*
Atlas Nacional do Brasil, *Instituto Brasileiro de Geografia*
Atlas Universal y del Perú, *Thomas Nelson & Sons Ltd., Sunbury on Thames 1968*
Brasil-Didáctico, Rodoviário, Turístico 1:5,000,000, *Gr. Editôra e Publicidade Ltda., Rio de Janeiro*
Mapa de la República de Bolivia 1:4,000,000, *Instituto Geográfico Militar, La Paz 1974*
Mapa Politico del Perú 1:2,400,000, *Editorial "Navarrete", Lima 1975*
Mapa de Carreteras del Perú 1:2,200,000, *Instituto Geográfico Militar, Lima 1979*
Mapa Fisico-Politico 1:2,000,000, *Instituto Geográfico Militar, Lima 1970*
Mapa Fisico de la República de Venezuela 1:2,000,000, *Ministerio de Obras Públicas, Bogotá 1975*
Brasil-Mapa Rodoviário 1:2,000,000, *Ministério dos Transportes, 1971*
Carte de la Guyane Française 1:1,500,000, *I.G.N., Paris 1973*
República de Colombia 1:1,500,000, *Ministerio de Hacienda y Credito Público, Bogotá 1979*
Ecuador 1:1,000,000, *Instituto Geográfico Militar, Quito 1971*
Kaart van Suriname 1:1,000,000, *C. Kersten & Co. N.V., Paramaribo*
Mapa de Bolivia 1:1,000,000, *Instituto Geográfico Militar, La Paz 1973*
Mapa Vial 1:1,000,000, *Ministerio de Obras Públicas, Caracas 1970*
República del Perú-Mapa Fisico-Politico, 1:1,000,000, *Instituto Geográfico Militar, Lima 1978*
Carte de la Guyane Française 1:500,000, *I.G.N., Paris 1976*
Suriname 1:500,000, *Uitgave Centraal Bureau Luchtkartering, 1969*
Guyana 1:500,000, *Ordnance Survey, Georgetown 1972*
Annuário Estatístico do Brasil 1978, *Fundacão Instituto Brasileiro de Geografia e Estatística, Rio de Janeiro*
Boletín Mensual de Estadística-agosto 1977, *D.A.N.E., Bogotá*
Dicionário Geográfico Brasileiro, *Editora Globo, Pôrto Alegre 1972*
Discover Bolivia, *Los Amigos del Libro, La Paz 1972*
Venezuela-Annuário Estadístico 1976, *Oficina Central de Estadística e Informatica, Caracas*

SOUTHERN SOUTH AMERICA
Atlas de la República Argentina, *Instituto Geográfico Militar, Buenos Aires 1972*
Atlas de la República Argentina, *Instituto Geográfico Militar, Santiago 1976*
Atlas de la República de Chile, *Instituto Geográfico Militar, Santiago 1970*
Atlas Escolar de Chile, *Instituto Geográfico Militar, Santiago 1978*
Atlas Universal y de la República Argentina, *Aguilar Argentina S.A. de Ediciones, Buenos Aires 1972*
Mapa de la República Argentina 1:5,000,000, *Instituto Geográfico Militar, Buenos Aires 1973*
Paraguay 1:1,000,000, *Instituto Geográfico Militar, Asuncíon 1974*
República Oriental del Uruguay 1:500,000, *Servicio Geográfico Militar, Montevideo 1961*
Uruguay-Moyennes et Petites Villes 1972, *Institut des Hautes Etudes de l'Amerique Latine, Paris*

AUSTRALIA AND OCEANIA

Atlas of Australian Resources, *Division of National Mapping, Canberra 1980*
New Zealand-Mobil Travel Map, *Mobil Oil New Zealand Ltd., Wellington 1973*
New Zealand Atlas, *A.R. Shearer Government Printer, Wellington 1976*
The Jacaranda Atlas, *Jacaranda Press Pty. Ltd., 1971*
The Jacaranda Atlas For New Zealand, *Jacaranda Press Pty. Ltd., 1971*
Australia-Geographic Map 1:2,500,000, *Minister for National Development, Canberra 1967*
Territory of Papua and New Guinea 1:2,500,000, *Division of National Mapping, Canberra 1970*
Carte de l'Oceanie Française 1:2,000,000, *I.G.N., Paris 1971*
Îles Tuamotu-Îles Marquises 1:2,000,000, *I.G.N., Paris 1969*
New Zealand-Map Guide 1:1,900,000, *New Zealand Tourist and Publicity Department, Wellington 1978*
Mobil New Zealand Road Map, *Mobil Oil New Zealand Ltd., Wellington 1973*
Fiji Islands-World Aeronautical Chart 1:1,000,000, *Ordnance Survey, Southampton 1970*
Close-up: Hawaii 1:675,000, *N.G.S., Washington 1978*
Archipel des Nouvelles-Hébrides 1:500,000, *I.G.N., Paris 1976*
New Zealand 1:500,000, *Department of Lands and Survey, Wellington 1976*
Nouvelle Calédonie 1:500,000, *I.G.N., Paris 1978*
Palau Islands 1:165,000, *Defense Mapping Agency Hydrographic Center, Washington 1973*
General Map of Tokelau Islands 1:100,000, *Department of Lands & Survey, Wellington 1969*
Tahiti-Carte Touristique 1:100,000, *I.G.N., Paris 1977*
Christmas Islands - Gilbert and Ellice Islands Colony 1:50,000, *Directorate of Overseas Survey, London 1970*
Tuvalu, *Government of Tuvalu 1979*
Annual Statistical Abstract-Fiji 1970-71, *Bureau of Statistics, Suva*
Australia - Population and Dwellings in Local Government Areas and Urban Centres 1976, *Australian Bureau of Statistics, Canberra*
Fact Sheet - Pitcairn Islands Group, *British Information Services, London 1974*
Fact Sheet - The Gilbert Islands, *British Information Services, London 1977*
Fact Sheet - The New Hebrides, *British Information Services, London 1976*
Fact Sheet - The Solomon Islands, *British Information Services, London 1976*
Fact Sheet - Tuvalu, *British Information Services, London 1977*
New Zealand Pocket Digest of Statistics 1979, *Department of Statistics, Wellington*
New Zealand Official Yearbook 1978, *Department of Statistics, Wellington*

POLAR REGIONS

Antarctica 1:11,250,000, *U.S. Naval Oceanographic Office, Washington 1965*
Antarctica 1:10,000,000, *American Geographical Society, New York 1970*
Antarctica 1:10,000,000, *Division of National Mapping, Canberra 1979*
Antarctica 1:5,000,000, *American Geographical Society, New York 1970*
Map of the Artic Region 1:5,000,000, *American Geographical Society, New York 1975*

Transliteration Systems

Toponymy: Criteria Used for the Writing of Names on the Maps

The language of geography is a language which defines geographic features in universally recognized terms. In creating this language, toponymy experts and cartographers have confronted complex problems in finding terms which are universally acceptable. So that the reader can fully understand the maps in this atlas, here is a brief explanation of how the toponyms (place-names for geographic features) have been written, particularly those relating to regions or countries where the Roman alphabet is not used. Among these are the Slavic-speaking nations such as the Soviet Union, Yugoslavia and Bulgaria; and China and Japan, which use ideographic characters. Of the European countries, Greece has its own alphabet, which is totally different from the Roman alphabet. Many of the Islamic countries use Arabic, with variations derived from local dialects.

There are two basic systems for Romanizing writing. The first is by phonetic transcription, using combinations of different alphabetical signs for each language when the phonetic sound in other languages should be maintained. For example, the Italian sound "sc" (which must be followed by an "e" or "i" to remain soft) in French is "ch," in English is "sh," and in German is "sch."

The second system is transliteration, in which the words, letters or characters of one language are represented or spelled in the letters or characters of another language.

Chinese, Japanese and Arabic Languages

Various Asian and African countries use non-Roman forms in their writing. For example, the Chinese and Japanese languages use ideographic characters instead of an alphabet, and these ideographic characters are transformed into the Roman alphabet through phonetic transcription. Until recently, one of the methods used for transforming Chinese was the Wade-Giles system, named for its English authors. Used in this atlas is the Pinyin system, which was approved by the Chinese government in 1958 and has been incorporated into the official maps of the People's Republic of China. The Pinyin system also has been adopted by the United States Board on Geographic Names and is used in official United Nations documents. The Pinyin names, however, often are accompanied by the Wade-Giles form, as the latter was widely known.

In Japan, ideographic characters are used, although the Roman alphabet is used in many Japanese scientific works. Japan uses two principal systems for standardizing names. They are the Kunreisiki, used by the government in official publications, and the Hepburn method. Adopted for this atlas is the Hepburn method, the system used in international English-language publications and by the United States Board on Geographic Names.

Romanization of the Arabic alphabet, which is used in many Islamic countries, is by transliteration. Since English and French are still used as an international language in many Arab countries, the name forms proposed by the major English and French sources have been taken into consideration. Generally, the systems proposed by the United States Board on Geographic Names and the Permanent Committee on Geographical Names have been used for most Asian countries and Arab-speaking countries.

Greek, Russian and Other Slavic Languages

Practically all written languages in Europe use the Roman alphabet. The differences in phonetics and grammar are shown by the use of diacritical marks and by groupings of consonants, vocals and syllables which give meaning to the various tones in the language. According to a centuries-old tradition, each written language maintains its formal characters, using the translated form rather than the phonetic transcription when a geographical term must be given in another language. This system, therefore, makes it more a translation than a transliteration.

In the Aegean area, Greek and the Greek alphabet are particularly significant because of historical links to the beginning of European civilization. The 1962 United States Board on Geographic Names and the Permanent Committee on Geographical Names systems, based on modern Greek pronunciation, have been used in transcribing toponyms from official sources for these maps. (The table that follows has an example indicating essential norms for Romanizing the modern Greek alphabet.)

A different situation arises in countries using the Cyrillic alphabet. Six principal Slavic languages using this alphabet are Russian, Byelorussian, Ukrainian, Bulgarian, Serbian, and Macedonian. The Cyrillic alphabet also is used by the non-Slavic people of the central Soviet Union. The nomenclature of these regions has been transliterated in accordance with the system proposed by the International Organization for Standardization, taking into consideration sounds and letters and uses of the diacritical marks normal in Slavic languages. The International Organization for Standardization method is accepted and used in bibliographical works and international documents. (The table which follows gives the relationship between the letters of the Cyrillic and Roman alphabets for the above six languages.) An exception to this transliteration is made by the Soviet Balkan republics of Estonia, Latvia and Lithuania. Here the name forms deriving from the national languages have been adopted, using the Roman alphabet.

Special Cases: Conventional Forms and Multilinguals

Cartographic nomenclature generally derives from the official nomenclature of the sovereign and nonsovereign countries, although a number of cases need an explanation.

In numerous situations, English conventional forms are used along with the local or conventional name in referring to a geographical entity outside the official language area. For example, Vienna, Prague, Copenhagen and Moscow are English forms for Wien, Praha, København and Moskva, respectively. There have been cases, however, where the conventional or historical form commonly used in English cartography has been applied with the same meaning. Thus, Peking and Nanking are the English conventional forms for Beijing and Nanjing, while Tsinan, Tientsin and Mukden are the former conventional spellings or names for Jinan, Tianjin and Shenyang, respectively. Other examples are Saigon, the former name for Ho Chi Minh, Vietnam; and Bangkok, the name for Krung Thep, which is used in Thailand.

The lack of reliable data for countries, especially ex-colonies without a firm national cartographic tradition, has made it necessary to utilize mapping skills of former colonist nations such as France, the United Kingdom and Belgium. A lack of data has led to the adoption of French and British forms in many areas, as these two languages are widely used for official purposes.

Another special case is that of the multilingual areas. Many countries and areas officially recognize two or more written and spoken languages; therefore, all of the principal written forms appear on the maps. This is true, for example, of Belgium where the official languages are French and Dutch (e.g. Bruxelles/Brussel) and of Italian regions such as Valle d'Aosta and Alto Adige, where French, German and Italian are used (e.g. Aosta/Aoste) (Bolzano/Bozen).

In preparing this atlas, each of these special cases has been taken into full consideration within the limits of the scale, space and readability of the maps.

Transliteration of the Cyrillic Alphabet
(International System—ISO)

Cyrillic Letter	Roman Letter		Cyrillic Letter	Roman Letter	
А а	a		О о	o	
Б б	b		П п	p	
В в	v		Р р	r	
Г г	g		С с	s	
Д д	d		Т т	t	
Е е	e	initially, after a vowel or after the mute sign "Ъ", becomes "je"	У у	u	
Ё ё	ë		Ф ф	f	
			Х х	h	
Ж ж	ž		Ц ц	c	
З з	z		Ч ч	č	
И и	i		Ш ш	š	
Й й	j	not written if preceded by "И" or "Ы"	Щ щ	šč	
			Ъ ъ	—	not written
К к	k		Ы ы	y	
Л л	l		Ь ь	—	not written
М м	m		Э э	e	
Н н	n		Ю ю	ju	
			Я я	ja	

Transcription of Modern Greek
(U. S. B. G. N. / P.C.G.N.)

Greek Letter (or combination)	Roman Letter (or combination)		Greek Letter (or combination)	Roman Letter (or combination)	
Α α	a		μπ	b	beginning a word
αι	ai			mb	within a word
αυ	av		Ν ν	n	
Β β	v		ντ	d	beginning a word
Γ γ	g			nd	within a word
γγ	ng		Ξ ξ	x	
γκ	g	beginning a word	Ο ο	o	
			οι	oi	
	ng	within a word	ου	ou	
Δ δ	d		Π π	p	
Ε ε	e		Ρ ρ	r	
ει	i		Σ σ	s	
ευ	ev		ς	s	ending a word
Ζ ζ	z		Τ τ	t	
Η η	i		τζ	tz	
ην	iv		Υ υ	i	
Θ θ	th		υι	i	
Ι ι	i		Φ φ	f	
Κ κ	k		Χ χ	kh	
Λ λ	l		Ψ ψ	ps	
Μ μ	m		Ω ω	o	

The "Geographical Glossary" lists the principal geographical terms used on the maps. All of these terms, including abbreviations, prefixes and suffixes, appear in the cartographic table as they appear on the maps. Terms are listed in accordance with the English alphabet, without consideration of diacritical marks on letters or of particular groups of letters.

Prefixes and suffixes relating to principal names or forming part of geographical toponyms are followed or preceded by a dash and the language to which they refer: e.g. Chi-/Dan. (Chi, a Danish prefix, means large); -bor/Slvn. (-bor, a Slovakian suffix, means city). Suffixes can also appear as words in themselves. In this case, the suffix and primary word are coupled together: e.g. Berg, -berg (Berg, which means mountain, can be used alone or as part of another word, such as Hapsberg).

Certain terms are followed or preceded by their abbreviation used on the maps. Both instances are listed: e.g. Fjord, Fj. and Fj., Fjord.

All geographical terms are identified by the language or languages to which each belongs. The language or languages in italics follows the term: e.g. Abbey/*Eng.*; -bad/*Nor., Dut., Swed., Germ.* Each term is translated into a corresponding English term or terms.

Below is a table identifying the abbreviations of various language names used on the maps. Note that certain abbreviations represent a group of languages, instead of one language: e.g. Ural. is the abbreviation for Uralic, a group word for Udmurt, Komi, and Nenets.

Alt. = Altaic (Turkmen, Tatar, Bashkir, Kazakh, Karalpak, Nogai, Kirghiz, Uzbek, Uigur, Altaic, Yakut, Khakass)

Ban. = Bantu (KiSwahili, ChiLuba, Lingala, KiKongo)

Cauc. = Caucasian (Chechen, Ingush, Kalmuck, Georgian)

Iran. = Iranian (Baluchi, Tagus)

Mel. = Melanesian (Fijian, New Caledonian, Micronesian, Nauruan)

Mong. = Mongolian (Buryat, Khalka Mongol)

Poly. = Polynesian (Maori, Samoan, Tongan, Tahitian, Hawaiian)

Sah. = Saharan (Kanuri, Tubu)

Som. = Somalian (Somali, Galla)

Sud. = Sudanese (Peul, Ehoué, Mossi, Yoruba, Ibo)

Ural. = Uralic (Udmurt, Komi, Nenets)

Because of their technical application to geography, some geographical terms may not fully correspond with the meaning given for them in some dictionaries.

Abbreviations of Language Names

Abbreviations in English	English	Abbreviations in English	English	Abbreviations in English	English
Afr.	Afrikaans	Bulg.	Bulgarian	Fr.	French
A.I.	American Indian	Burm.	Burmese	Gae.	Gaelic
Alb.	Albanian	Cat.	Catalan	Georg.	Georgian
Alt.	Altaic	Cauc.	Caucasian	Germ.	German
Amh.	Amharic	Chin.	Chinese	Gr.	Greek
Ar.	Arabic	Cz.	Czech	Hebr.	Hebrew
Arm.	Armenian	Dan.	Danish	Hin.	Hindi
Az.	Azerbaidzhani	Dut.	Dutch	Hung.	Hungarian
Ban.	Bantu	Eng.	English	Icel.	Icelandic
Bas.	Basque	Esk.	Eskimo	Indon.	Indonesian
Beng.	Bengali	Est.	Estonian	Ir.	Irish
Ber.	Berber	Far.	Faroese	Iran.	Iranian
Br.	Breton	Finn.	Finnish	It.	Italian
		Fle.	Flemish	Jap.	Japanese

Abbreviations in English	English	Abbreviations in English	English	Abbreviations in English	English
Khm.	Khmer	Pers.	Persian	Som.	Somalian
Kor.	Korean	Pol.	Polish	Sp.	Spanish
K.S.	Khoi-San	Poly.	Polynesian	Sud.	Sudanese
Laot.	Laotian	Port.	Portuguese	Swa.	Swahili
Lapp.	Lappish	Prov.	Provençal	Swed.	Swedish
Latv.	Latvian	Rmsh.	Romansh	Tam.	Tamil
Lith.	Lithuanian	Rom.	Romanian	Thai	Thai
Mal.	Malay	Rus.	Russian	Tib.	Tibetan
Malag.	Malagasy	Sah.	Saharan	Tur.	Turkish
Mel.	Melanesian	S.C.	Serbo-Croatian	Ural.	Uralic
Mong.	Mongolian	Sin.	Sinhalese	Urdu	Urdu
Nep.	Nepalese	Slvk.	Slovak	Viet.	Vietnamese
Nor.	Norwegian	Slvn.	Slovene	Wall.	Walloon
Pash.	Pashto			Wel.	Welsh

Glossary of Geographical Terms

A

Local Form	English
A- / *Ban.*	people
A' / *Icel.*	river
Å / *Dan.; Nor.; Swed.*	stream
a., an / *Germ.*	on
Aa / *Germ.*	stream
Aache / *Germ.*	stream
Aaiún / *Ar.*	springs
Aan / *Dut.; Fle.*	on
Āb / *Pers.*	stream
Ābād / *Pers.*	city, town
Abad, -abad / *Pers.*	city, town
Ābār / *Ar.*	spring
Abbadia / *It.*	abbey
Abbaye / *Fr.*	abbey
Abbazia / *It.*	abbey
Abbi / *Amh.*	great
Abd / *Ar.*	servant
Abeba / *Amh.*	flower
Aber / *Br.; Wel.*	estuary
Abhang / *Germ.*	slope
Abū / *Ar.*	father, master
Abyad / *Ar.*	white
Abyaḍ / *Ar.*	white
Abyār / *Ar.*	well
Abyss / *Eng.*	ocean depth, deep
Ach / *Germ.*	stream
Achaïf / *Ar.*	dunes
Ache / *Germ.*	stream
Achter / *Afr.; Dut.; Fle.*	back
Acqua / *It.*	water
Açu / *A.I.*	great
Açude / *Port.*	reservoir, dam
Ada / *Tur.*	island
Adalar / *Tur.*	archipelago
Adasr / *Tur.*	island
Addis / *Amh.*	new
Adi / *Amh.*	village
Adrar / *Ber.*	mount, mountains
Aéroport / *Fr.*	airport
Aeroporto / *It.; Port.*	airport
Aeropuerto / *Sp.*	airport
Af / *Som.*	mouth, gorge
Afsluitdijk / *Dut.*	dam
Agadir / *Ber.*	castle
Aḡïz / *Tur.*	mouth
Agro / *Sp.; It.*	plain
Agua / *Sp.*	water
Aguja / *Sp.*	needle
Agulha / *Port.*	needle, promontory
Ahal / *Georg.*	new
Aḥmar / *Ar.*	red
Ahrāmāt / *Ar.*	pyramids
Ahzar / *Ber.*	wadi
Aigialós / *Gr.*	coast
Aigue / *Prov.*	water
Aiguille / *Fr.*	needle
Ain / *Ar.*	spring

Local Form	English
Ait / *Ar.; Ber.*	sons
Aivi, -aivi / *Lapp.*	mountain
Ak / *Tur.*	white
'Aklé / *Ar.*	dunes
Akmeṇs / *Latv.*	stone
Ákra / *Gr.*	point
Akti / *Gr.*	coast
Ala / *Malag.*	forest
Ala / *Finn.*	low, lower
Alan / *Tur.*	field
Alb / *Rom.*	white
Albo / *Sp.*	white
Albufera / *Sp.*	lagoon
Alcalá / *Sp.*	castle
Alcázar / *Sp.*	castle
Aldea / *Sp.*	village
Alföld / *Hung.*	lowland
Ali / *Amh.*	mountain
Alia / *Poly.*	stream
Alin / *Mong.*	range
Alm / *Germ.*	mountain, pasture
Alor / *Mal.*	river
Alp / *Germ.*	mountain, pasture
Alpe / *Germ.; Fr.; It.*	mountain, pasture
Alps / *Eng.*	mountains
Alsó / *Hung.*	low, lower
Alt / *Germ.*	old
Altin / *Tur.*	lower
Altiplano / *Sp.*	plateau
Alto / *Sp.; It.; Port.*	high
Altopiano / *It.*	plateau
Älv / *Swed.*	river
Am / *Kor.*	mountain, peak
Amane / *Ber.*	water
Amba / *Amh.*	mountain
Ambato / *Malag.*	rock
An / *Gae.*	of
An, a. / *Germ.*	on
Ana / *Poly.*	grotto
Anatolikós / *Gr.*	eastern
Äng / *Swed.*	meadow
Angra / *Port.*	bay, anchorage
Ani- / *Malag.*	center
Áno / *Gr.*	upper
Ānou / *Ber.*	well
Anse / *Fr.*	inlet
Ant- / *Malag.*	center
Ao / *Chin.; Khm.; Thai*	gulf
'Āouâna / *Ar.*	well
Apã / *Rom.*	water
'Aqabat / *Ar.*	pass
Aqueduc / *Fr.*	aqueduct
Ar / *Mong.*	north
Ar / *Sin.; Tam.*	river
'Arâguîb / *Ar.*	hills
Arba / *Ar.*	mount
Arbore / *Rom.*	tree
Archipiélago / *Sp.*	archipelago
Arcipelago / *It.*	archipelago
Arḍ / *Ar.*	region

Local Form	English
Ard- / *Gae.*	high
Areg / *Ar.*	dune
Areia / *Port.*	beach
Arena / *Sp.*	beach
Argent / *Fr.*	silver
Arhipelag / *Rus.*	archipelago
Arkhaios / *Gr.*	old, antique
Arm / *Eng.; Germ.*	branch
Arquipélago / *Port.*	archipelago
Arr., Arroyo / *Sp.*	stream
Arrecife / *Sp.*	reef
Arroio / *Port.*	stream
Art / *Tur.*	pass, watershed
Aru / *Sin.; Tam.*	river
Ås / *Dan.; Nor.; Swed.*	hills
Asfar / *Ar.*	yellow
Asif / *Ber.*	river
Asky / *Alt.*	lower
Áspros / *Gr.*	white
Assa / *Ar.*	wadi
Atalaya / *Sp.*	frontier
Áth / *Gae.*	ford
Átha / *Gae.*	ford
Atol / *Port.*	atoll
Au / *Germ.*	meadow
Aue / *Germ.*	irrigated field
Aust / *Nor.*	east
Austur / *Icel.*	east
Ava / *Poly.*	canal
Aven / *Fr.*	doline, sink
Awa / *Poly.*	bay
Áyios / *Gr.*	saint
'Ayn / *Ar.*	spring, well
'Ayoún / *Ar.*	springs, wells
'Ayoûn / *Ar.*	spring
Aza / *Ber.*	wadi
Azraq / *Ar.*	light blue
Azul / *Port.; Sp.*	light blue
Azur / *Fr.*	light blue

B

Local Form	English
B., Bay / *Eng.*	bay
b., bei / *Germ.*	by
B., Bucht / *Germ.*	bay
Ba / *Sud.*	river
Ba- / *Ban.*	people
Ba / *Mel.*	hill, mountain
Baai / *Afr.*	bay
Bab / *Ar.*	gate
Bac / *Viet.*	north
Bach / *Germ.*	brook, torrent
Bacino / *It.*	reservoir
Back / *Eng.*	ridge
Back / *Swed.*	brook
Bäck / *Swed.*	brook
Backe / *Swed.*	hill
Bad, -bad / *Dan.; Germ.; Nor.; Swed.*	thermal springs
Baden, -baden / *Germ.*	thermal springs
Bādiyat / *Ar.*	desert

Local Form	English
Badwêynta / *Som.*	ocean
Badyarada / *Som.*	gulf
Baeg / *Kor.*	white
Bæk / *Dan.*	brook
Bælt / *Dan.*	strait
Bagni / *It.*	thermal springs
Baharu / *Mal.*	new
Bahía / *Port.*	bay
Bahia / *Sp.*	bay
Bahir / *Ar.*	river, lake, sea
Bahnhof / *Germ.*	railway station
Bahr / *Ar.*	wadi
Baḩr / *Ar.*	river, lake, sea
Baḩrat / *Ar.*	lake
Bahri / *Ar.*	north, northern
Baḩri / *Ar.*	north
Bahrīyah / *Ar.*	northern
Bai / *Chin.*	white
Băi / *Rom.*	thermal springs
Baia / *Port.*	bay
Baie / *Fr.*	bay
Baigne / *Fr.*	seaside resort
Baile / *Gae.*	city, town
Bain / *Fr.*	thermal springs
Bains / *Fr.*	thermal springs
Baixo / *Port.*	low, lower
Bajan / *Mong.*	rich
Bajo / *Sp.*	low
Bajrak / *Alb.*	tribe
Bakhtīyārī / *Pers.*	western
Bakki / *Icel.*	hill
Bālā / *Pers.*	high
Bald / *Eng.*	peak
Balka / *Rus.*	gorge
Balkan / *Bulg.; Tur.*	mountain range
Ballin / *Gae.*	mouth
Ballon / *Fr.*	dome
Bally / *Gae.*	city, town
Balta / *Rom.*	marsh
Báltos / *Gr.*	marsh
Ban / *Laot.*	village
Bana / *Jap.*	promontory
Baña / *Slvk.*	mine
Bañados / *Sp.*	marsh
Banc / *Fr.*	bank
Banco / *It.; Sp.*	bank
Band / *Pers.*	dam, mountain range
Bandao / *Chin.*	peninsula
Bandar / *Ar.; Mal.; Pers.*	port, market
Bang / *Indon.; Mal.*	stream
Bangou / *Sah.*	well
Banhado / *Port.*	marsh
Bani / *Ar.*	sons
Banja / *Bulg.; S.C.; Slvn.*	thermal springs
Banjaran / *Mal.*	mountain range
Banka / *Rus.*	sandbank
Banke / *Dan.*	bank
Baño / *Sp.*	thermal springs
Banský / *Cz.*	upper
Bánya / *Hung.*	mine
Bar / *Gae.*	peak
Bar / *Eng.*	sandbar

Geographical Glossary

Local Form	English	Local Form	English	Local Form	English	Local Form	English
Bar / Hin.	great	Bôca / Port.	gap, mouth	Büyük / Tur.	great	Ch'ŏn / Kor.	river
Bāra / Hin.	great	Bocage / Fr.	forest	By / Eng.	near	Chōsuji / Kor.	reservoir
Bara / S.C.	pond	Bocca / It.	gap, pass	By, -by / Dan.; Nor.;	city, town	Chott / Ar.	salt marsh
Barā / Urdu	great	Bocchetta / It.	gap, pass	Swed.		Chu / Chin.; Viet.	mountain, hill
Baraji / Tur.	dam	Bodden / Germ.	bay, lagoon	Bystrica / Cz.; Slvk.	stream	Chuŏr phnum / Khm.	mountain range
Barat / Indon.; Mal.	west, western	Boden / Germ.	soil	Bystrzyca / Pol.	stream	Chute / Fr.	waterfall
Barkas / Lith.	castle, city,	Běng / Khm.	lake, marsh			Chutes / Fr.	waterfalls
	town	Bog / Eng.	marsh			Cidade / Port.	city, town
Barlovento / Sp.	windward	Bogaz / Alt.; Az.; Tur.	strait	**C**		Ciems / Latv.	village
Barq / Ar.	hill	Bogăzi / Tur.	strait			Čierny / Slvk.	black
Barra / Port.; Sp.	bar, bank	Bogdo / Mong.	high	C., Cap / Cat.; Fr.; Rom.	cape	Cime / It.	peak
Barrage / Fr.	dam	Bogen / Nor.	bay	C., Cape / Eng.	cape	Cîmp / Rom.	field
Barragem / Port.	reservoir	Bois / Fr.	forest	C., Colle / It.	pass	Cimpie / Rom.	plain
Barranca / Sp.	gorge	Boka / S.C.	channel	Caatinga / A.I.	forest	Cinco / Sp.; Port.	five
Barranco / Port.; Sp.	gorge	Boloto / Rus.	marsh	Cabeça / Port.	peak	Citeli / Georg.	red
Barre / Fr.	bar	Bolšoj / Rus.	great	Cabeço / Port.	peak	Città / It.	city, town
Barun / Mong.	western	Bolsón / Sp.	basin	Cabeza / Sp.	peak	Ciudad / Sp.	city, town
Bas / Fr.	low	Bom / Port.	good	Cabezo / Sp.	peak, mountain	Ckali / Georg.	water
-bas / Rus.	reservoir	Bong / Kor.	peak	Cabo / Port.; Sp.	cape	Ckaro / Georg.	spring
Bassa / Port.	flat	Bongo / Malag.	upland	Cachoeira / Port.	waterfall, rapids	Co / Chin.	lake
Bassejn / Rus.	reservoir	Bor / Cz.; Rus.	coniferous forest	Cachopo / Port.	reef	Col / Cat.; Fr.	pass
Bassin / Fr.	basin	Bór / Pol.	forest	Cadena / Sp.	range	Colina / Port.; Sp.	hill
Bassure / Fr.	flat	-bor / Slvn.	city, town	Caer / Wel.	castle	Coll / Cat.	hill
Bassurelle / Fr.	flat	Bóras / Gr.	north	Cagan / Cauc.; Mong.	white	Collado / Sp.	pass
Bašta / S.C.	garden	Börde / Germ.	fertile plain	Cairn / Gae.	hill	Colle, C. / It.	pass
Bataille / Fr.	battle	Bordj / Ar.	fort	Čaj / Az.; Tur.	river	Collina / It.	hill
Batalha / Port.	battle	Bóreios / Gr.	northern	Cajdam / Mong.	salt marsh	Colline / Fr.	hill
Batang / Indon.; Mal.	river	Borg, -borg / Dan.; Nor.;	castle	Caka / Chin.	lake	Colonia / Sp.; It.	colony
Batha / Sah.	stream	Swed.		Cala / Sp.; It.	inlet	Coma / Sp.	hill country
Bațin / Ar.	depression	Borgo / It.	village	Calar / Sp.	plateau	Comb / Eng.	basin
Bāțlāq / Pers.	marsh	Born / Germ.	spring	Caldas / Sp.; Port.	thermal springs	Comba / Sp.	basin
Batu / Mal.	rock	Bory / Pol.	forest	Caleta / Sp.	inlet	Combe / Fr.	basin
Bayan / Mong.	rich	Bosch / Dut.; Fle.	forest	Camp / Cat.; Fr.; Eng.	field	Comté / Fr.	county, shire
Bayir / Tur.	mountain, slope	Bosco / It.	wood	Campagna / It.	plain	Con / Viet.	island
Bayou / Fr.	branch, stream	Bosque / Sp.	forest	Campagne / Fr.	plain	Conca / It.	depression
Bayt / Ar.	house	Bosse / Fr.	hill	Campo / Sp.; It.; Port.	field	Condado / Sp.	county, shire
Bazar / Pers.	market	Botn / Nor.	bay	Cañada / Sp.	gorge, ravine	Cone / Eng.	volcanic cone
Be / Malag.	great	Bou / Ar.	father, master	Canale / It.	canal, channel	Cône / Fr.	volcanic cone
Beau / Fr.	beautiful	Bouche / Fr.	mouth	Caño / Sp.	branch	Contraforte / Port.	front range
Becken / Germ.	basin	Boula / Sud.	well	Cañón / Sp.	gorge	Cordal / Sp.	crest
Bed / Eng.	river bed	Bourg / Fr.	city, town	Canyon / Eng.	gorge	Cordilheira / Port.	mountain range
Beek / Dut.	creek	Bourne, - bourne / Eng.	frontier	Cao / Viet.	mountain	Cordillera / Sp.	mountain range
Be'er / Hebr.	spring	Boven / Afr.	upper	Cap, C. / Cat.; Fr.; Rom.	cape	Coring / Chin.	lake
Bei / Chin.	north	Boz / Tur.	grey	Car / Gae.	castle	Corixa / A.I.	stream
Bei, b. / Germ.	by	Bozorg / Pers.	great	Càrn / Gae.	peak	Corno / It.	peak
Beida / Ar.	white	Brána / Cz.	gate	Carrera / Sp.	road	Cornone / It.	peak
Beinn / Gae.	mount	Braña / Sp.	mountain	Carrick / Gae.	rock	Corrente / It.; Port.	stream
Bel / Ar.	son		pasture	Casale / It.	hamlet	Corriente / Sp.	stream
Bel / Bulg.	white	Branche / Fr.	branch	Cascada / Sp.	waterfall	Costa / Sp.; It.; Port.	coast
Bel / Tur.	pass	Branco / Port.	white	Cascata / It.	waterfall	Côte / Fr.	coast
Beled / Ar.	village	Brațul / Rom.	branch	Castel / It.	castle	Coteau / Fr.	height, slope
Belen / Tur.	mount	Bravo / Sp.	wild	Castell / Cat.	castle	Coxilha / Port.	ridge
Belet / Ar.	village	Brazo / Sp.	branch	Castello / It.	castle	Craig / Gae.	rock
Beli / S.C.; Slvn.	white	Brdo / Cz.; S.C.	hill	Castelo / Port.	castle	Cratère / Fr.	crater
Beli / Tur.	pass	Bre / Nor.	glacier	Castillo / Sp.	castle	Cresta / Sp.; It.	crest
Bellah / Sah.	well	Bredning / Dan.	bay	Castro / Sp.; It.	village	Crêt / Fr.	crest
Belogorje / Rus.	mountains	Breg / Alb.; Bulg.; S.C.	hill, coast	Catarata / Sp.	cataract	Crête / Fr.	crest
Belt / Dan.; Germ.	strait	Brjag / Bulg.	bank	Catena / It.	mountain range	Crkva / S.C.	church
Bely / Rus.	white	Bro / Dan.; Nor.; Swed.	bridge	Catinga / Port.	degraded forest	Crni / S.C.; Slvn.	black
Bělý / Cz.	white	Brod / Bulg.; Cz.; Rus.;	ford	Cauce / Sp.	river bed	Crven / S.C.	red
Ben / Ar.	son	S.C.; Slvk.; Slvn.		Causse / Fr.	highland	Csatorna / Hung.	canal
Ben / Gae.	mount	Bród / Pol.	ford	Cava / It.	stone quarry	Cuchilla / Sp.	ridge
Bender / Pers.	port, market	Bron / Afr.	spring	Çay / Tur.	river	Cuenca / Sp.	basin
Bendi / Tur.	dam	Bronn / Germ.	spring	Cay / Eng.	islet, island	Cuesta / Sp.	escarpment
Beni / Ar.	son	Bru / Nor.	bridge	Caye / Fr.	island	Cueva / Sp.	cave
Beo / S.C.	white	Bruch / Germ.	peat-bog	Cayo / Sp.	islet, island	Čuka / Bulg.; S.C.	peak
Bereg / Rus.	bank	Bruchzone / Germ.	fracture zone	Ceann / Gae.	promontory	Çukur / Tur.	well
Berg, -berg / Afr.; Dut.;	mount	Bruck, -bruck / Germ.	bridge	Centralny / Rus.	middle	Cu Lao / Viet.	island
Fle.; Germ.; Nor.; Swed.		Brücke / Germ.	bridge	Ceren / Alb.	black	Cumbre / Sp.	peak
Berge / Afr.	mountain	Brug / Dut.; Fle.	bridge	Černi / Bulg.	black	Cun / Chin.	village
Bergen / Dut.; Fle.	dunes	Brugge / Dut.; Fle.	bridge	Černý / Cz.	black	Cura / A.I.	stone
Bergland / Germ.	upland	Bruk / Nor.	factory	Čërny / Rus.	black	Curr / Alb.	rock
Bermejo / Sp.	red	Brunn / Swed.	spring	Cerrillo / Sp.	hill	Cy., City / Eng.	city, town
Besar / Mal.	great	-brunn / Germ.	spring	Cerrito / Sp.	hill	Czarny / Pol.	black
Betsu / Jap.	river	Brunnen / Germ.	spring	Cerro / Sp.; Port.	hill, mountain		
Betta / Tam.	mountain	Brygg / Swed.	bridge	Cêrro / Port.	hill, mountain		
Bhani / Hin.	community	Brzeg / Pol.	coast	Červen / Bulg.	red	**D**	
Bharu / Mal.	new	Bü / Ar.	father, master	Červony / Rus.	red		
Bheag / Gae.	little	Bucht, B. / Germ.	bay	Cetate / Rom.	city, town	Da / Chin.	great
Bīābān / Pers.	desert	Bugt / Dan.	bay	Chaco / Sp.	scrubland	Da / Viet.	mountain, peak
Biały / Pol.	white	Buḥayrat / Ar.	lake, lagoon	Chãh / Pers.	well	Daal / Dut.; Fle.	valley
Bianco / It.	white	Bühel / Germ.	hill	Chaïf / Ar.	dunes	Daba / Mong.	pass
Bien / Viet.	lake	Bühl / Germ.	hill	Chaîne / Fr.	mountain range	Daba / Som.	pass
Bight / Eng.	bay	Buhta / Rus.	bay	Champ / Fr.	field	Daban / Chin.; Mong.	pass
Bijeli / S.C.	white	Bukit / Mal.	mountain, peak	Chang / Chin.	highland	Dae / Kor.	great
Bill / Eng.	promontory	Bukt / Nor.; Swed.	bay	Chapada / Port.	highland	Dağ / Tur.	mountain
Bilo / S.C.	range	Buku / Indon.	hill, mountain	Chapadão / Port.	highland	Dağ., Daği / Tur.	mountain
Bilý / Cz.	white	Bulag / Mong.; Tur.	spring	Château / Fr.	castle	Dăgh / Pers.; Tur.	mountain
Binnen / Dut.; Fle.; Germ.	inner	Bulak / Mong.; Tur.	spring	Châtel / Fr.	castle	Daği, Dağ. / Tur.	mountain
Biqā' / Ar.	valley	Bülāq / Tur.	spring	Chãy / Tur.	river	Dağlari / Tur.	mountain range
Bir / Ar.	well	Bult / Afr.	hill	Chedo / Kor.	archipelago	Dahar / Ar.	hill
Bi'r / Ar.	well	Bulu / Indon.	mountain	Chenal / Fr.	canal	Dahr / Ar.	plateau,
Birkat / Ar.	pond	Bur / Som.	mount	Cheng / Chin.	city, town, wall		escarpment
Bistrica / Bulg.; S.C.;	stream	Bür / Ar.	port	Cheon / Kor.	city, river	Dai / Chin.; Jap.	great
Slvn.		Burg, - burg / Afr.; Ar.;	castle	Chergui / Ar.	eastern	Daiet / Ar.	marsh
Bjarg / Icel.	rock	Dut.; Eng.; Germ.		Cherry, -cherry / Hin.;	city, town	Dak / Viet.	stream
Bjerg / Dan.	mount	Burgh / Eng.	city, town	Tam.		Dake / Jap.	mountain
Bjeshkët / Alb.	mountain	Burgo / Sp.	village	Chew / Amh.	salt mine, salt	Dakhla / Ar.	depression
	pasture	Burha / Hin.	old	Chhâk / Khm.	bay	Dakhlet / Ar.	depression, bay
Blaauw / Afr.	blue	Buri / Thai	city, town	Chhotla / Hin.	little	Dal, -dal / Afr.; Dan.;	valley
Blanc / Fr.	white	Burj / Ar.	village	Chi- / Ban.	great	Dut.; Fle.; Nor.; Swed.	
Blanco / Sp.	white	Burn / Eng.	stream	Chi / Chin.	marsh, lake	Dala / Alt.	steppe, plain
Blau / Germ.	blue	Burnu / Tur.	promontory	Chi / Kor.	lake, pond	Dalaj / Mong.	lake, sea
Bleu / Fr.	blue	Burqat / Ar.	mount, marsh	Chi- / Swa.	land	Dalan / Mong.	wall
Bluff / Eng.	cliff	Burun / Tur.	cape	Chiang / Thai	city, town	Dallol / Sud.	valley, torrent
Bo- / Ban.	people	Busen / Germ.	bay	Chico / Sp.	little	Dalur / Icel.	valley
Bo / Chin.	white	Busu / Ban.	land	Chine / Eng.	ridge	Damm / Germ.	dam
Bo / Swed.	habitation	Būtat / Ar.	lake, pond	Ch'on / Kor.	station	Dan / Kor.	point
Boca / Sp.	gap, mouth	Butte / Eng.; Fr.	flat-topped hill				

Local Form	English
Danau / Indon.	lake
Danda / Nep.	mountains
Dao / Chin.	island, peninsula
Dao / Viet.	island
Dar / Ar.	house, region
Dar / Swa.	port
Dara / Tur.	torrent, valley
Darb / Ar.	track
Darja / Alt.	river, sea
Darya, Daryā / Pers.	river, sea
Daryācheh / Pers.	lake, sea
Daš / Alt.; Az.	rock
Dasht / Pers.	desert, plain
Dawḥat / Ar.	bay
Dayr / Ar.	convent
De / Sp.; Fr.	of
Deal / Rom.	hill
Dearg / Gae.	red
Debre / Amh.	hill, monastery
Dega / Som.	stone
Deh / Pers.	village
Deḥ / Som.	stream
Deich / Germ.	dike
Dél / Hung.	south
Delft / Dut.; Fle.	deep
Delger / Mong.	wide, market
-den / Eng.	city, town
Deniz / Tur.	sea
Denizi / Tur.	sea
Dent / Fr.	peak
Deo / Laot.; Viet.	pass
Dépression / Fr.	depression
Depressione / It.	depression
Der / Som.	high
Dera / Hin.; Urdu	temple
Derbent / Tur.	gorge, pass
Dere / Tur.	river, valley
Désert / Fr.	desert
Desfiladero / Sp.	pass
Desh / Hin.	land, country
Desierto / Sp.	desert
Det / Alb.	sea
Détroit / Fr.	strait
Deux / Fr.	two
Dezh / Pers.	castle
Dhar / Ar.	heights, hills
Dhār / Hin.; Urdu	mountain
Dhitikós / Gr.	western
Dien / Khm.; Viet.	rice-field
Diep / Dut.; Fle.	deep, strait
Dijk, -dijk / Dut.; Fle.	dam
Ding / Chin.	mountain, peak
Dique / Sp.	dam
Di Sopra / It.	upper
Di Sotto / It.	lower
Distrito / Sp.; Port.	district
Diu / Hin.	island
Diz / Pers.	castle
Djebel / Ar.	mountain
Dji / Ban.	water
Djup / Swed.	deep
Do / Kor.	Island
Do / S.C.	valley
Dō / Jap.	island, administrative division
Dōho / Som.	valley
Doi / Thai	mountain, peak
Dol / Bulg.; Cz.; Rus.; S.C.	valley
Dol / Pol.	valley
Dolen / Bulg.	low
Dolgi / Rus.	long
Dolina / Bulg.; Cz.; Pol.; Rus.; S.C.; Slvn.	valley
Dolni / Bulg.	low
Dolni / Pol.	lower
Dolny / Pol.	lower
Domb / Hung.	hill
Dôme / Fr.	dome
Dong / Chin.; Viet.	east
Dong / Kor.	city, town
Dong / Thai	mountain
Dong / Viet.	marsh, plain
Donji / S.C.	low, lower
Dorf, -dorf / Germ.	village
Doroga / Rus.	road
Dorp, -dorp / Afr.; Dut.; Fle.	village
Dos / Rom.	ridge
Dos / Sp.	two
Douarn / Br.	land
Dougou / Sud.	settlement
Doukou / Sud.	settlement
Down / Eng.	hill
Drâa / Ar.	dunes, hills
Dracht / Germ.	sandbank
Draw / Eng.	ravine, valley
Drif / Afr.	ford
Drift / Afr.	ford
Droichead / Gae.	bridge
Droûs / Ar.	crest
Dry / Pash.	river
Dubh / Gae.	black
Dugi / S.C.	long
Dugu / Sud.	settlement
Dun / Gae.	castle
Duna / Sp.; It.	dune
Düne / Germ.	dune
Dungar / Hin.	mountain
Düngar / Hin.	mountain
Duong / Viet.	stream
Durchbruch / Germ.	gorge
Durg / Hin.	castle
-durga / Hin.	castle
Duży / Pol.	great
Dvor / Cz.	court
Dvorec / Rus.	castle
Dvůr / Cz.	castle
Dwór / Pol.	court
Džebel / Bulg.	mountain
Dzong / Tib.	fort, monastery

E

Local Form	English
Ea / Thai	river
Eau / Fr.	water
Ebe / Ban.	forest
Ebene / Germ.	plain
Eck / Germ.	point
Eclusa / Sp.	lock
Écluse / Fr.	lock
Écueil / Fr.	cliff
Edeien / Ber.	sand desert
Edjérir / Ber.	wadi
Egg / Germ.; Nor.	crest, point
Eglab / Ar.	hills
Ehi / Sah.	mountain
Eid / Nor.	isthmus
Eiland / Afr.	island
Eisen / Germ.	iron
Eisenerz / Germ.	iron ore
El / Amh.	well
Elv, -elv / Nor.	river
Embalse / Sp.	reservoir
Embouchure / Fr.	mouth
Emi / Sah.	mountain
En / Fr.	in
Ende / Germ.	end
Enneri / Sah.	stream
Ennis / Gae.	island
Enseada / Port.	Bay, inlet
Ensenada / Sp.	bay, inlet
Ér / Hung.	stream
Erdö / Hung.	forest
Erg / Ar.	sand desert
Erz / Germ.	ore
Espigão / Port.	plateau
Éstän / Pers.	land
Este / Sp.	east
Estero / Sp.	estuary, marsh
Estrecho / Sp.	strait
Estreito / Port.	strait
Estuaire / Fr.	estuary
Estuário / Port.	estuary
Estuario / Sp.; It.	estuary
Észak / Hung.	north
Étang / Fr.	pond
Ewaso / Ban.	river
Ey / Icel.	island
Eyja / Icel.	island
Eyjar / Icel.	islands
Eylandt / Dut.	island
Eżeras / Lith.	lake
Ezers / Latv.	lake

F

Local Form	English
Fa / Mel.	stream
Falaise / Fr.	cliff
Fall, -fall / Germ.; Eng.; Swed.	waterfall
Falls / Eng.	waterfall
Falu / Hung.	village
-falva / Hung.	village
Fan / Sah.	village
Faraglione / It.	cliff
Farallón / Sp.	cliff
Faro / Sp.; It.	lighthouse
Farvand / Dan.	strait
Fehér / Hung.	white
Fehn / Germ.	peat fen, peat-bog
Fekete / Hung.	black
Feld / Dan.; Germ.	field
Fell / Eng.	upland moor
Fell / Icel.	mountain
Fels / Germ.	rock
Fen / Eng.	marsh, peat-bog
Feng / Chin.	mountain, peak
Feste / Germ.	fort
Festung / Germ.	fort
Fier / Rom.	iron
Firn / Germ.	snow-field
Firth / Eng.	estuary, fjord
Fiume / It.	river
Fjäll / Swed.	mountain
Fjärd / Swed.	fjord
Fjell / Nor.	mountain
Fjöll / Icel.	mountain
Fjord, Fj. / Dan.; Nor.; Swed.	fjord
Fjörður / Icel.	fjord, bay
Fleuve / Fr.	river
Fließ / Germ.	torrent
Fljót / Icel.	river
Flój / Icel.	bay, gulf
Floresta / Sp.; Port.	forest
Flow / Eng.	strait
Flughafen / Germ.	airport
Fluß / Germ.	river
Fo / Mel.	stream
Foa / Mel.	stream
Foa / Poly.	cove
Foce / It.	mouth
Föld / Hung.	plain
Fonn / Nor.	glacier
Fontaine / Fr.	fountain
Fonte / It.; Port.	spring
Fontein / Afr.; Dut.	spring
Foort / Afr.; Dut.	ford
Forca / It.	pass
Forcella / It.	defile
Ford / Rus.	fjord
Förde / Germ.	fjord, gulf
Foreland / Eng.	promontory
Foresta / It.	forest
Forêt / Fr.	forest
Fors / Swed.	rapids, waterfall
Forst / Germ.; Dut.	forest
Forte / It.; Port.	fort
Fortin / Sp.	fort
Fosa / Sp.	trench
Foss / Icel.; Nor.	rapids, waterfall
Fossé / Fr.	trench
Foum / Ar.	pass
Fourche / Fr.	pass
Foz / Sp.; Port.	mouth
Frei / Germ.	free
Fronteira / Port.	frontier
Frontera / Sp.	frontier
Frontón / Sp.	promontory
Fuente / Sp.	spring
Fuerte / Sp.	fort
Fuji / Jap.	mountain
Fülat / Ar.	marsh
Furt / Germ.	ford
Fushë / Alb.	plain

G

Local Form	English
G., Gora / Bulg.; Rus.; S.C.	mountain, hill
G., Gunung / Indon.	mountain
Ga / Jap.	bay
Ga / Mel.	mountain, peak
Gabel / Germ.	pass
Gaissa / Lapp.	mountain
Gala / Sin.; Tam.	mountain
Gam / Hin.; Urdu	village
Gamle / Nor.; Swed.	old
Gana / Sud.	little
Gang / Germ.	passage
Gang / Chin.	port, bay
Gang / Kor.	stream, bay
Gang / Tib.	glacier
Ganga / Hin.	river
Ganj / Hin.; Urdu	market
-gaon / Hin.	city, town
Gaoyuan / Chin.	plateau
Gap / Kor.	point
Gar / Hin.	house
Gara / Bulg.	station
Gara / Ar.	hills, range
Garä / Rom.	station
Garaet / Ar.	marsh, intermittent lake
Garam / Beng.; Hin.; Urdu	village
-gard / Pol.	city, town
Gård, -gård / Dan.; Nor.; Swed.	farmhouse
Gardaneh / Pers.	pass
Gare / Fr.	railway station
Garet / Ar.	hill
Garh, -garh / Hin.; Urdu	castle
Garhi / Hin.; Nep.; Urdu	fort
Garten / Germ.	garden
Gat / Dan.; Fle.; Dut.	strait
Gata / Jap.	bay, lake
Gau, -gau / Germ.	district
Gäu, -gäu / Germ.	district
Gavan / Rus.	port
Gave / Bas.	torrent
Gawa / Jap.	river
Geb., Gebirge / Germ.	mountain range
Gebergte / Afr.; Dut.	mountain range
Gebirge, Geb. / Germ.	mountain range
Geç., Geçit / Tur.	pass
Geçidi / Tur.	pass
Geçit, Geç. / Tur.	pass
Geysir / Icel.	geyser
Ghar / Hin.; Urdu	house
Ghar / Pash.	mountain, mountain range
Gharbīyah / Ar.	western
Ghat / Hin.; Nep.; Urdu	pass
Ghubbat / Ar.	bay
Ghurd / Ar.	dune
Gi / Kor.	peninsula
Giang / Viet.	stream
Giri / Hin.; Urdu	mountain, hill
Girlo / Rus.	branch
Gjebel / Ar.	mountain
Gji / Alb.	bay
Glace / Fr.	ice
Glaciar / Sp.	glacier
Glacier / Eng.; Fr.	glacier
Glen / Gae.	valley
Gletscher / Germ.	glacier
Gobi / Mong.	desert
Godär / Pers.	ford
Gok / Kor.	river
Gök / Tur.	blue
Gol / Cauc.; Mong.	river
Göl / Tur.	lake
Gola / It.	gorge
Gold / Germ.; Eng.	gold
Golet / S.C.	mountain
Golf / Germ.	gulf
Golfe / Fr.	gulf
Golfete / Sp.	inlet
Golfo / Sp.; It.; Port.	gulf
Goljam / Bulg.	great
Gölü / Tur.	lake
Gong / Tib.	high
Gonggar / Tib.	mountain
Gongo / Ban.	mountain
Góra / Pol.	mountain
Gora, G. / Bulg.; Rus.; S.C.	mountain, hill
Gorica / S.C.; Slvn.	hill
Gorje / S.C.	mountain range
Gorlo / Rus.	gorge
Gorm / Gae.	blue
Gorni / Bulg.; S.C.; Slvn.	upper
Gornji / S.C.; Slvn.	upper
Górny / Pol.	high
Gorod / Rus.	city, town
Gorodok / Rus.	village
Gorski / Bulg.	upper
Gory / Rus.	mountains
-gou / Chin.	river
Goulbi / Sud.	river, lake
Goulbin / Sud.	wadi
Goulet / Fr.	gap
Gour / Ar.	hills, range
Gourou / Sud.	wadi
Goz / Sah.	dune
Graafschap / Dut.	county, shire
Graben / Germ.	ditch, canal
Gracht / Dut.	canal
Grad, -grad / Bulg.; Rus.; S.C.; Slvn.	city, town, castle
Gradac / S.C.	castle
Gradec / Bulg.	village
Gradec / Slvn.	castle
Græn / Icel.	green
Gran / Sp.; It.	great
Grande / Sp.; It.; Port.	great
Grao / Cat.; Sp.	gap
Grat / Germ.	crest
Grève / Fr.	beach
Grind / Germ.	peak
Grjada / Rus.	range
Gród, -gród / Pol.	castle, city, town
Grön / Icel.	green
Grond / Afr.	soil
Gronden / Dut.; Fle.	flat
Groot / Afr.; Dut.; Fle.	great
Groß / Germ.	great
Grotta / It.	grotto
Grotte / Fr.; Germ.	grotto
Grube / Germ.	mine
Grün / Germ.	green
Grunn / Nor.	ground
Gruppe / Germ.	mountain system
Gruppo / It.	mountain system
Gua / Mal.	cave
Guaçu / A.I.	great
Guan / Chin.	pass
Guazú / A.I.	great
Guba / Rus.	bay
Guchi / Jap.	strait
Guelb / Ar.	hill, mountain
Guelta / Ar.	well
Guic / Br.	village
Güney / Tur.	south, southern
Gunong / Mal.	mountain
Guntō / Jap.	archipelago
Gunung, G. / Indon.	mountain
Guo / Chin.	state, land
Gur / Rom.	mountain
Guri / Jap.	cliff
Gurud / Ar.	hills, dunes
Gyár / Hung.	factory

H

Local Form	English
Haag / Dut.; Fle.	hedge
-håb / Dan.	port
Haḍabat / Ar.	highland
Hadd / Ar.	point
Hadjer / Ar.	hill, mountain
Hae / Kor.	bay, sea
Haehyeop / Kor.	strait

Geographical Glossary

Local Form	English
Haf / Icel.	sea
Ḥafar / Ar.	well
Hafen / Germ.	port
Haff / Germ.	lagoon
Hafir / Ar.	spring, ditch
Hafnar / Icel.	port
Häfün / Som.	bay
Hage / Dan.	point
Hage / Dut.; Fle.	hedge
Hågna / Swed.	peak
Hai / Chin.	sea, lake, bay
Hain / Germ.	forest
Haixia / Chin.	strait
Ḥajar / Ar.	hill, mountain
Hajar / Ar.	hill country
Halbinsel / Germ.	peninsula
Halma / Hung.	hill
Halom / Hung.	hill
Halq / Ar.	gap
Hals / Nor.	peninsula
Halve / Dan.	peninsula
Halvøy / Nor.	peninsula
Hama / Jap.	beach
Hamāda / Ar.	rocky desert
Ḥamādah / Ar.	plateau
Ḥamādat / Ar.	plateau
Hammam / Ar.	thermal springs
Ḥammām / Ar.	well
Hamn / Nor.; Swed.	port
Hamrā' / Ar.	red
Hāmūn / Jap.	salt lake
Hana / Jap.	cape
Hana / Poly.	bay
Hane / Tur.	house
Hang / Kor.	port
Hank / Ar.	escarpment, plateau
Hantō / Jap.	peninsula
Har / Hebr.	mountain
Hara / Mong.	black
Harar / Swa.	well
Ḥarrah / Ar.	lava field
Ḥarrat / Ar.	lava field
Hasi / Ar.	well
Ḥasi / Ar.	well
Hassi / Ar.	well
Ḥasy / Ar.	well
Haug / Nor.	hill
Haupt- / Germ.	principal
Haure / Lapp.	lake
Haus / Germ.	house
Hausen / Germ.	village
Haut / Fr.	high
Hauteur / Fr.	hill
Hauts Plateaux / Fr.	highlands
Hauz / Pers.	reservoir
Hav / Dan.; Nor.; Swed.	sea, gulf
Haven / Eng.; Fle.; Dut.	port
Havn / Dan.; Nor.	port
Havre / Fr.	port
Hawr / Ar.	lake, marsh
Ház / Hung.	house
-háza / Hung.	house
Hazm / Ar.	height, mountain range
He / Chin.	river
Head / Eng.	headland
Hed / Dan.; Swed.	heath
Hegy / Hung.	mountain
Hegység / Hung.	mountain
Hei / Nor.	heath
Heide / Germ.	heath
Heijde / Dut.; Fle.	heath
Heilig / Germ.	saint
Heim, -heim / Germ.; Nor.	house
Heiya / Jap.	plain
-hely / Hung.	locality
Hem / Swed.	home
Hen / Br.	old
Higashi / Jap.	east, eastern
Hima / Hin.	ice
Himal / Nep.	peak
Hisar / Tur.	castle
Ho / Chin.	reservoir, river
Ho / Kor.	river, reservoir
Hō / Jap.	mountain
Hoch / Germ.	high, upper
Hochland / Germ.	highland
Hochplato / Afr.	highland
Hodna / Ar.	highland
Hoek / Dut.; Fle.	cape
Hof / Dut.; Germ.	court
Höfn / Icel.	port
Høg / Nor.	peak
Hög / Swed.	mountain
Hogna / Nor.	peak
Höhe / Germ.	peak
Høj / Dan.	hill
Hoj / Ural.	mountain range
Hok / Jap.	north
Hoku / Jap.	north, northern
Holm / Dan.; Nor.; Swed.	island
Holz / Germ.	forest
Hon / Viet.	island, point
Hong / Chin.; Viet.	red
Hono / Poly.	bay, anchorage
Hoog / Afr.; Dut.; Fle.	high
Hook / Eng.	point
Hoorn / Afr.; Dut.; Fle.	cape, point
Hora / Cz.; Slvk.	point
Horn / Eng.; Germ.; Icel.; Nor.; Swed.	point
Horni / Cz.	high
Horný / Slvk.	upper
Horst / Germ.	mountain
Horvot / Hebr.	ruins
Hory / Cz.; Slvk.	mountain range
Hout / Dut.; Fle.	forest
Hovd, -hovd / Dan.; Nor.	cape
Howz / Pers.	basin
Hrad / Cz.; Slvk.	castle, city, town
Hradiště / Cz.	citadel
Hřeben / Cz.	crest
Hrebet / Rus.	mountain range
Hu / Rmsh.	lake
Huang / Chin.	yellow
Hude / Germ.	pasture
Huerta / Sp.	market garden
Hügel / Germ.	hill
Hügelland / Germ.	hill country
Huis, -huis / Afr.; Dut.; Fle.	house
Huisie / Afr.	house
Huizen, -huizen / Dut.	houses
Huk / Afr.; Dan.; Swed.	cape
Hum / S.C.	hill
Hurst / Eng.	grove
Hus / Dut.; Nor.; Swed.	house
Huta / Pol.; Slvk.	hut
Hütte / Germ.	hut
Hver / Icel.	crater
Hvit / Icel.	white
Hvost / Rus.	spit

I

Local Form	English
I., Island / Eng.	island
Ierós / Gr.	holy
Igarapé / A.I.	river
Ighazer / Ber.	torrent
Ighil / Ber.	hill
Iguidi / Ber.	dunes
Ih / Mong.	great
Ike / Jap.	pond
Ile / Fr.	island
Ilha / Port.	island
Iller / Tur.	administrative division
Ilot / Fr.	islet
Imi / Ar.	spring
I-n / Ber.	well
Inch / Gae.	island
Inder / Dan.; Nor.	inner
Indre / Nor.	inner
Inferiore / It.	lower
Inish / Gae.	island
Insel / Germ.	island
Insulă / Rom.	island
Inver / Gae.	mouth
Irhazér / Ber.	wadi
Irmak / Tur.	river
'Irq / Ar.	dunes
Is / Nor.	glacier
Ís / Icel.	ice
Isblink / Dan.	glacier
Ishi / Jap.	rock
Iske / Alt.	old
Isla / Sp.	island
Iso / Finn.	great
Iso / Jap.	cliff
Isola / It.	island
Isthmós / Gr.	isthmus
Istmo / Sp.; It.	isthmus
Ita / A.I.	stone
Itä / Finn.	east
Itivdleq / Esk.	isthmus
Iwa / Jap.	rock, cliff
Iztočni / Bulg.	eastern
Izvor / Bulg.; Rom.; S.C.; Slvn.	spring

J

Local Form	English
J., Jazīrat / Ar.	island
J., Jiang / Chin.	river
Jabal / Ar.	mountain
Jaha / Ural.	river
Jam / Ural.	lake, river
Jama / Rus.	cave
Jan / Alt.	great
Janga / Tur.	north
Jangi / Alt.; Iran.	new
Janūbīyah / Ar.	southern
Jar / Rus.	bank
Järv / Est.	lake
Järve / Finn.	lake
Järvi / Finn.	lake
Jasirēd / Som.	island
Jaun / Latv.	new
Jaur / Lapp.	lake
Jaure / Lapp.	lake
Javr / Lapp.	lake
Javrre / Lapp.	lake
Jazā'ir / Ar.	islands
Jazīrat, J. / Ar.	island
Jazovir / Bulg.	reservoir
Jbel / Ar.	mountain
Jebel / Ar.	mountain
Jedid / Ar.	new
Jedo / Kor.	archipelago
Jezero / S.C.; Slvn.	lake
Jezioro / Pol.	lake
Jhil / Hin.; Urdu	lake
Jian / Chin.	mountain
Jiang, J. / Chin.	river
Jiao / Chin.	cape, cliff
Jibāl / Ar.	mountain
Jih / Cz.	south
Jima / Jap.	island
Jin / Kor.	cove
Jing / Chin.	spring
Jisr / Ar.	bridge
Joch / Germ.	pass
Jōgi / Est.	river
Jøkel / Nor.	glacier
Joki / Finn.	river
Jokka / Lapp.	river
Jökull / Icel.	glacier
Jord, -jord / Nor.	earth
Ju / Ural.	river
Judeţ / Rom.	district
Jugan / Ural.	river
Jura / Lith.	sea
Jūra / Latv.	sea
Jūras Līcis / Latv.	bay
Jūrmala / Latv.	beach
Jurt / Cauc.	village
Južni / Bulg.; S.C.; Slvn.	southern
Južny / Rus.	southern
Juzur / Ar.	islands

K

Local Form	English
Ka / Poly.	lake
Kaap / Afr.	cape
Kabīr / Ar.	great
Kae / Kor.	inlet
Kāf / Ar.	peak, mountain
Kafr / Ar.	village
Kaga / Ban.	hills, mountain range
Kahal / Ar.	plateau, escarpment
Kai / Jap.	sea
Kaikyō / Jap.	strait
Kaise / Lapp.	mountain
Kal / Pers.	stream
Kala / Az.; Kor.	fort
Kala / Finn.	river
Kala / Hin.	black
Kala / Tur.	castle
Kalaa / Ar.	castle
Kalaki / Georg.	city, town
Kale / Tur.	castle
Kali / Hin.	black
Kali / Indon.; Mal.	bay, river
Kallio / Finn.	rock
Kaln / Latv.	mountain
Kalós / Gr.	beautiful, good
Kamen / Bulg.; Rus.; S.C.; Slvn.	mountain, peak
Kámen / Cz.	rock
Kameň / Slvk.	rock
Kami / Jap.	upper
Kamień / Pol.	rock
Kamm / Germ.	crest
Kamp / Germ.	field
Kâmpóng / Khm.	village
Kámpos / Gr.	field
Kampung / Indon.; Mal.	village
Kan., Kanal / Alb.; Dan.; Germ.; Nor.; Rus.; S.C.; Slvn.; Swed.; Tur.	canal, channel
Kanaal / Dut.; Fle.	canal
Kanał / Pol.	canal
Kanal, Kan. / Alb.; Dan.; Germ.; Nor.; Rus.; S.C.; Slvn.; Swed.; Tur.	canal, channel
Kand, -kand / Pers.; Tur.	city, town
Kang / Chin.; Kor.	bay, river
Kangas / Fle.	heath
Kange / Esk.	east
Kangri / Tib.	snow-capped mountain
Kantara / Ar.	bridge
Kaôh / Khm.	island
Kap / Dan.; Germ.	cape
Kapija / S.C.	gate, gorge
Kapp / Nor.	cape
Kar / Tib.	white
Kar / Ural.	city, town
Kara / Tur.	black
Karang / Indon.; Mal.	sandbank, cliff
Kari / Finn.	cliff
Kariba / Ban.	gorge
Kariet / Ar.	village
Karki / Finn.	peninsula
Kastel / Germ.	castle
Kástron / Gr.	fort, city, town
Káto / Gr.	lower
Kaupstadur / Icel.	city, town
Kaupunki / Finn.	city, town
Kavīr / Pers.	salt desert
Kawa / Jap.	river
Kawm / Ar.	hill
Kebir / Ar.	great
Kedi / Georg.	mountain range
Kédia / Ar.	mountain, plateau
Kedim / Ar.	old
Kef / Ar.	mountain
Kefála / Gr.	mountain, peak
Kefar / Hebr.	village
Kei / Jap.	river
Kelet / Hung.	east
Ken / Gae.	cape
Kent / Alt.; Iran.; Tur.	city, town
Kenya / Swa.	fog
Kep / Alb.	cape
Kep., Kepulauan / Mal.	archipelago
Kepulauan, Kep. / Mal.	archipelago
Kereszt / Hung.	cross
Kerk / Dut.; Fle.	church
Keski / Finn.	middle
Kette / Germ.	mountain range
Keur / Sud.	village
Key / Eng.	coral island
Kha / Tib.	valley
Khal / Hin.	canal
Khalīj / Ar.	gulf
Khand / Hin.	district
Khao / Thai	hill, mountain
Kharābeh / Pers.	ruins
Khashm / Ar.	promontory
Khatt / Ar.	wadi
Khawr / Ar.	mouth, bay
Khazzān / Ar.	dam
Khemis / Ar.	fifth
Khersónisos / Gr.	peninsula
Khirbat / Ar.	ruins
Khlong / Thai	stream, mouth
Khokhok / Thai	isthmus
Khor / Ar.	mouth, bay
Khóra / Gr.	land
Khorion / Gr.	village
Khowr / Pers.	bay
Khrisós / Gr.	gold
Ki- / Ban.	little
Kibali / Sud.	river
Kil / Gae.	church
Kilde / Dan.	spring
Kilima / Swa.	mountain
Kill / Gae.	strait
Kilwa / Ban.	lake
Kin / Gae.	cape
Kinn / Nor.	cape, point
Kirche / Germ.	church
Kirk / Eng.	church
Kis / Hung.	little
Kisiwa / Swa.	island
Kita / Jap.	north, northern
Kızıl / Tur.	red
Klein / Afr.; Dut.; Germ.	little
Kliff / Germ.	cliff
Klint / Dan.	reef
Klip / Afr.; Dut.	rock, cliff
Klit / Dan.	dune
Kloof / Afr.; Dut.	gorge
Kloster / Dan.; Germ.; Nor.; Swed.	convent
Knob / Eng.	mountain
Knock / Gae.	mountain, hill
Ko / Jap.	bay, lake, little
Ko / Sud.	stream
Ko / Thai	island, point
Kebing / Dan.	town
Kogel / Germ.	dome
Kögen / Jap.	plateau
Koh / Hin.; Pers.	mountain, mountain range
Kol / Alt.	river, valley
Kol / Alt.; Tur.	lake
Koll / Nor.	peak
Kólpos / Gr.	gulf
Kong / Dan.; Nor.; Swed.	king
Kong / Indon.; Mal.	mountain
Kong / Viet.	mountain, hill
Konge / Ban.	river
König / Germ.	king
Koog / Afr.	polder
Kop / Afr.	hill
Kopec / Cz.; Slvk.	hill
Kopf / Germ.	peak
Köping / Swed.	town
Köprü / Tur.	bridge
Körfezi / Tur.	gulf
Korfi / Gr.	rock
Koro / Mel.	mountain, island
Koro / Sud.	old
Koru / Tur.	forest
Kosa / Rus.	spit
Koška / Rus.	cliff
Koski / Finn.	rapids
Kosui / Jap.	lake
Kot / Urdu	castle
Kota / Mal.	city, town
Kotal / Pash.; Pers.	pass
Kotar / S.C.	cultivated area
Kotlina / Pol.	basin

Local Form	English
Kotlovina / Rus.	basin, plain
Kou / Chin.	mouth, pass
Kourou / Sud.	well
Kowr / Pers.	river
Kowtal / Pers.	pass
Koy / Tur.	bay
Köy / Tur.	village
Kraal / Afr.	village
Kraina / Pol.	land
Kraj / Rus.; S.C.	land
Kraj / Rus.	administrative division
Krajina / S.C.	land
Krak / Ar.	hill, castle
Krans / Afr.	mountain
Kras / S.C.; Slvn.	karst landscape
Krasny / Rus.	red
Kreb / Ar.	hills, mountain range
Kriaž / Ar.	mountain range
Krš / S.C.	karst area, limestone area
Krung / Thai	city, town
Ksar / Ar.	castle
Ksour / Ar.	fortified village
Ku- / Ban.	river branch
Kuala / Mal.	river, mouth
Kubra / Ar.	bridge
Küçük / Tur.	little
Kuduk / Tur.	spring
Küh / Pers.	mountain
Kühhā / Pers.	mountain range
Kul / Alt.; Iran.; Tur.	lake
Kulam, -kulam / Hin.; Tam.	pond
Kulle / Swed.	hill
Kulm / Germ.	peak
Kultuk / Rus.	bay
Kum / Tur.	dunes, sand desert
Kuppe / Germ.	dome, seamount
Kurayb / Ar.	hill
Kurgan / Alt.	hill
Kurgan / Tur.	fort
Kuro / Jap.	black
Kurort / Bulg.; Germ.; Rus.	spa
Kust / Dut.; Fle.	coast
Kust- / Swed.	coast
Küste / Germ.	coast
Kút / Hung.	spring
Kuyu / Tur.	spring
Kvemo / Georg.	low, lower
Kwa / Ban.	village
Kylä / Finn.	village
Kyle / Gae.	strait, channel
Kyō / Jap.	strait
Kyrka / Swed.	church
Kyst / Dan.; Nor.	coast
Kyun / Burm.	island
Kyūryō / Jap.	hills, mountains
Kyzyl / Tur.	red
Kzyl / Tur.	red

L

Local Form	English
L., Lake, Lago / Eng.; It.; Port.; Sp.	lake
La / Tib.	pass
Laagte / Afr.	stream, valley
Labuan / Indon.; Mal.	bay, port
Lac / Fr.	lake
Lach / Som.	stream, wadi
Lacul / Rom.	lake
Lae / Poly.	cape, point
Laem / Thai	bay, port
Låg / Nor.; Swed.	low, lower
Lag / Swed.	stream, wadi
Läge / Swed.	beach
Lagh / Som.	stream, wadi
Lago, L. / It.; Port.; Sp.	lake
Lagoa / Port.	lagoon
Laguna / Alb.; It.; Rus.; Sp.	lagoon, lake
Lagune / Fr.	lagoon
Laht / Est.	bay
Lahti / Finn.	bay, gulf
Laks / Finn.	bay
Lalla / Ar.	saint
Lampi / Finn.	pond
Lande / Fr.	heath
Lang / Afr.; Dut.; Germ.	long
Lang / Viet.	village
Lao / Chin.	old
Lapa / Poly.	mountain range, peak
Largo / Port.; Sp.	basin
Las / Pol.	forest
Las, Läs / Som.	well
Laut / Mal.	sea
Law / Gae.	hill, mountain
Lázně / Cz.	thermal springs
Lednik / Rus.	glacier
Leite / Germ.	coast
Lekh / Nep.	mountain range

Local Form	English
Les / Bulg.; Cz.; Rus.; Slvk.	forest
Leso / Rus.	forested
Levante / It.; Sp.	eastern
Levkós / Gr.	white
Levy / Rus.	left
Lha / Tib.	temple
Lhari / Hin.; Nep.	mountain
Lho / Tib.	south
Lido / It.	sandbar
Liedao / Chin.	archipelago
Liehtao / Chin.	archipelago
Liels / Latv.	great
Lilla / Swed.	little
Lille / Dan.; Nor.	little
Liman / Alb.; Rus.; Tur.	lagoon, bay
Liman / Tur.	bay, port
Limin / Gr.	port
Limni / Gr.	lake
Ling / Chin.	mountain range, peak
Linna / Finn.	castle
Liqen / Alb.	lake
Lithos / Gr.	stone
Litoral / Port.; Sp.	littoral
Litorale / It.	littoral
Llan / Wel.	church
Llano / Sp.	plain
Llanura / Sp.	plain
Lo- / Ban.	river
Loch / Gae.	lake, inlet
Loch / Germ.	grotto
Loka / Slvn.	forest
Loma / Sp.	hill
Long / Indon.	stream
Loo / Dut.; Fle.	clearing
Lough / Gae.	lake
Loutrá / Gr.	thermal springs
Ložbina / Rus.	depression
Lu- / Ban.	river
Lua / Ban.	river
Lua / Mel.	island, reef
Lua / Poly.	crater
Luang / Thai	yellow
Luch / Germ.	peat-bog
Lücke / Germ.	pass
Lug / Rus.	meadow
Luka / S.C.; Slvn.	port
Lule / Lapp.	east, eastern
Lum / Alb.	river
Lund / Dan.; Swed.	forest
Lung / Rom.	long
Lung / Tib.	valley
Luoto / Finn.	shoal
Lurg / Pers.	salt flat
Lut / Pers.	desert

M

Local Form	English
M., Monte / It.; Port.; Sp.	mountain
Ma / Ar.	water
Ma- / Ban.	people
Maa / Est.; Finn.	island, land
Ma'arrat / Ar.	height
Machi / Jap.	district
Macizo / Sp.	massif
Madhya / Hin.	central
Madīnah / Ar.	city, town
Madīq / Ar.	strait
Mado / Swa.	well
Madu / Tam.	pond
Mae / Thai	stream
Mae nam / Thai	stream, mouth
Magh / Gae.	plain
Mägi / Est.	mountain
Măgura / Rom.	height
Mahā / Hin.	great
Mahal / Hin.; Urdu	palace
Mai / Amh.; Ban.	stream
Majdan / S.C.	quarry
Mäki / Finn.	mountain, hill
Makrós / Gr.	long
Mala / Hin.; Tam.	mountain
Malai / Hin.; Tam.	mountain
Malal / A.I.	fence
Malhão / Port.	dome
Mali / Alb.	mountain
Mali / S.C.; Slvn.	little
Malki / Bulg.	little
Malla / Tam.	mountain
Maly / Rus.	little
Malý / Cz.; Slvk.	little
Mały / Pol.	little
Man / Kor.	bay
Manastir / Bulg.; S.C.	monastery
Manche / Fr.	channel
Mar / It.; Port.; Sp.	sea
Mar / Tib.	red
Mar / Ural.	city, town
Marais / Fr.	marsh
Marché / Fr.	market
Mare / Fr.	pond
Mare / It.; Rom.	sea
Mare / Rom.	great
Marea / Rom.	sea
Marécage / Fr.	marsh
Marios / Lith.	reservoir

Local Form	English
Marisma / Sp.	marsh
Mark / Dan.; Nor.; Swed.	land
Markt / Germ.	market
Marsa / Ar.	anchorage, bay
Marsch / Germ.	marsh
Maru / Jap.	mountain
Mas / Prov.	farmhouse
Maşabb / Ar.	mouth
Mashra' / Ar.	landing, pier
Masivul / Rom.	massif
Massiv / Germ.; Rus.	massif
Mata / Poly.	point
Mata / Port.; Sp.	forest
Mata / Som.	waterfall
Mato / Port.; Sp.	forest
Matsu / Jap.	point
Mauna / Poly.	mountain
Mávros / Gr.	black
Mayo / Sud.	river
Maza / Lith.	little
Mazar / Pers.; Tur.	sanctuary
Mazs / Latv.	little
Me / Khm.	river
Me / Mel.	hill, mountain
Me / Thai	great
Medina / Ar.	city, town
Medjez / Ar.	ford
Meer / Dut.; Fle.	lake
Meer / Germ.	lake, sea
Megálos / Gr.	great
Mégas / Gr.	great
Megye / Hung.	district
Mélas / Gr.	black
Melkosopočnik / Rus.	hill country
Mellan / Swed.	central
Men / Chin.	gate, channel
Ménez / Br.	mountain
Menzel / Ar.	bivouac
Meos / Indon.	island
Mer / Fr.	sea
Mercato / It.	market
Merdja / Ar.	lagoon, marsh
Meri / Est.; Finn.	sea
Meridional / Rom.; Sp.	southern
Merín / A.I.	little
Merja / Ar.	lagoon, marsh
Mers / Ar.	port
Mersa / Ar.	port
Mesa / Sp.	mesa, tableland
Meseta / Sp.	plateau
Mésos / Gr.	central
Mesto / Bulg.; S.C.; Slvk.; Slvn.	city, town
Město / Cz.	city, town
Mestre / Port.	principal
Meydan / Tur.	square
Mezad / Hebr.	castle
Mezö / Hung.	field
Mgne., Montagne / Fr.	mountain
Mgnes., Montagnes / Fr.	mountains
Miao / Chin.	temple
Miasto / Pol.	city, town
Mic / Rom.	little
Middel / Afr.; Dut.; Fle.	middle
Midi / Fr.	noon, south
Między / Pol.	central
Miedzyrzecze / Pol.	interfluve
Mierzeja / Pol.	sand spit
Mifraz / Hebr.	bay, gulf
Miftah / Ar.	gorge
Mikrós / Gr.	little
Mina / Port.; Sp.	mine
Mīnā' / Ar.	port
Minami / Jap.	south, southern
Minamoto / Jap.	spring
Minato / Jap.	port
Mine / Jap.	peak
Mirim / A.I.	little
Misaki / Jap.	cape
Mittel- / Germ.	middle
Mo / Chin.	sand desert
Mo / Nor.; Swed.	heath
Moana / Poly.	lake
Mogila / Bulg.; Rus.	hill
Moku / Poly.	island
Mølle / Dan.	mill
Monasterio / Sp.	monastery
Mond / Afr.; Dut.; Fle.	mouth
Mong / Burm.; Thai; Viet.	city, town
Moni / Gr.	monastery
Mont / Cat.; Fr.	mountain
Montagna / It.	mountain
Montagne, Mgne. / Fr.	mountain
Montagnes, Mgnes. / Fr.	mountains
Montaña / Sp.	mountain
Monte, M. / It.; Port.; Sp.	mountain
Monts, Mts. / Fr.	mountains
Moos / Germ.	moor
Mór / Gae.	great
More / Bulg.; Rus.; S.C.	sea
More / Gae.	great
Mori / Jap.	mountain, forest
Morne / Fr.	mountain
Moron / Mong.	river
Morro / Port.; Germ.	hill, peak
Morrón / Sp.	mountain
Morze / Pol.	sea

Local Form	English
Most / Bulg.; Cz.; Pol.; Rus.; S.C.; Slvn.	bridge
Moto / Jap.	spring
Motte / Fr.	hill
Motu / Mel.; Poly.	island, rock
Moutier / Fr.	monastery
Movilă / Rom.	hill
Moyen / Fr.	central
Mta / Georg.	mountain
Mts., Monts, Mountains / Eng.; Fr.	mountains
Muang / Laot.; Thai	city, town, land
Muara / Indon.; Mal.	mouth
Muela / Sp.	mountain
Mühle / Germ.	mill
Mui / Mel.	point
Mui / Viet.	point, cape
Muiden / Dut.; Fle.	mouth
Muir / Gae.	sea
Mukh / Hin.	mouth
Mull / Gae.	promontory
Münde / Germ.	mouth
Mündung / Germ.	mouth
Municipiul / Rom.	commune
Munkhafad / Ar.	depression
Münster / Germ.	monastery
Munte / Rom.	mountain
Muntelé / Rom.	mountain
Munţii / Rom.	mountain range
Muren / Mong.	river
Mushāsh / Ar.	spring
Muz / Tur.	ice
Muztagh / Tur.	snow-capped mountain
Mwambo / Ban.	rock, cliff
Myit / Burm.	stream
Mynydd / Wel.	mountain
Myo / Burm.	city, town
Mýri / Icel.	marsh
Mys / Rus.	cape

N

Local Form	English
Na / Cz.; Pol.; Rus.; S.C.; Slvn.	on
Nab / Ar.	spring
Nad / Cz.; Pol.; Rus.	on
Nada / Jap.	bay, sea
Nadi, -nadi / Hin.; Urdu	river
Næs / Dan.	point
Nafūd / Ar.	dunes
Nag / Tib.	black
Nagar, -nagar / Hin.; Tib.	city, town
Nagaram / Hin.; Tam.	city, town
Nagorje / Rus.	plateau, mountains
Nagy / Hung.	great
Nahr / Ar.	river
Naikai / Jap.	sea
Naka / Jap.	central
Nakhon / Thai	city, town
Nam / Burm.; Laot.; Thai	river
Nam / Kor.	south
Namakzar / Pers.	salt desert
Nan / Chin.	south
Narrows / Eng.	strait
Narssaq / Esk.	plain, valley
Näs / Swed.	cape
Nationalpark / Swed.; Germ.	national park
Nau / Lith.	new
Nauja / Lith.	new
Navolok / Rus.	cape, promontory
Ne / Jap.	cliff
Neder / Fle.; Dut.	low
Neem / Est.	cape
Negro / Port.; Sp.	black
Negru / Rom.	black
Nehir / Tur.	river
Nei / Chin.	inner
Nene, -nene / Ban.	great
Néos / Gr.	new
Nero / It.	black
Nes / Icel.; Nor.	cape
Ness / Gae.	promontory
Neu / Germ.	new
Neuf / Fr.	new
Nevado / Sp.	snow-capped mountain
Nez / Fr.	cape
Ngok / Viet.	mountain, peak
Ngolo / Ber.	great
Ni / Kor.	village
Niecka / Pol.	basin
Niemi / Finn.	peninsula
Nieuw / Fle.; Dut.	new
Nij / Dut.	new
Nil / Hin.	blue
Nishi / Jap.	west
Niski / Pol.	lower
Nisko / S.C.	low
Nisoi / Gr.	islands
Nisos / Gr.	island
Nizina / Pol.	lowland
Nížina / Cz.	depression
Nízký / Cz.	low, lower

Geographical Glossary

Local Form	English
Nizmennost / Rus.	lowland, depression
Nižni / Rus.	low, lower
Nižný / Slvk.	low, lower
Nó / Mel.	stream
Nock / Gae.	ridge
Noir / Fr.	black
Non / Thai	hill
Nong / Thai	lake, marsh
Noord / Afr.; Fle.; Dut.	north
Noordoost / Afr.; Fle.; Dut.	northeast
Nor / Arm.	new
Nord / Fr.; It.; Germ.	north
Nördlich / Germ.	northern
Nørdre / Dan.; Nor.	northern
Norra / Swed.	northern
Nørre / Dan.	northern
Norte / Sp.	north
Nos / Bulg.; Rus.; S.C.; Slvn.	cape
Nosy / Malag.	island
Nótios / Gr.	southern
Nou / Rom.	new
Novi / Bulg.; S.C.; Slvn.	new
Novo / Port.	new
Novy / Rus.	new
Nový / Cz.; Slvk.	new
Now / Pers.	new
Nowy / Pol.	new
Nudo / Sp.	mountain
Nuevo / Sp.	new
Nui / Viet.	mountain
Numa / Jap.	marsh, lake
Nummi / Finn.	heath
Nunatak / Esk.	peak
Nuovo / It.	new
Nur / Chin.	lake
Nusa / Mal.	island
Nut, -nut / Nor.	peak
Nuwara / Sin.; Tam.	city, town
Nuwe / Afr.	new
Nyanza / Ban.	water, river, lake
Nyasa / Ban.	lake
Nyeong / Kor.	pass
Nyika / Ban.	upland
Nyöng / Kor.	mount, pass
Nyugat / Hung.	west

O

Local Form	English
Ō / Jap.	great
Ó / Hung.	old
Ö / Swed.	island
Ø, -ø / Dan.; Nor.	island
Öar / Swed.	islands
Ober / Germ.	upper
Oblast / Rus.	province
Obo / Mong.	mountain, hill
Occidental / Fr.; Rom.; Sp.	western
Océan / Fr.	ocean
Océano / Sp.	ocean
Oceano / It.; Port.	ocean
Ocnă / Rom.	salt mine
Odde / Dan.; Nor.	promontory
Oeste / Port.; Sp.	west
Oever / Fle.; Dut.	bank
Oewer / Afr.	bank
Oie / Germ.	islet
Ojos / Sp.	spring
Oka / Jap.	coast
Oke / Sud.	height
Okean / Rus.	ocean
Oki / Jap.	bay
Okrug / Rus.	district
Ola / Alt.	city, town
Omuramba / K.S.	stream
Onder / Afr.	under
Oni / Malag.	river
Oos / Afr.	east
Oost / Fle.; Dut.	east
Oostelijk / Dut.	eastern
Opatija / Slvn.	abbey
Or / Fr.	gold
Oraş / Rom.	city, town
Óri / Gr.	mountains
Oriental / Fr.; Port.; Rom.; Sp.	eastern
Orientale / It.	eastern
Orilla / Sp.	bank
Órmos / Gr.	bay
Óros / Gr.	mountain
Ország / Hung.	land
Ort / Germ.	cape
Orta / Tur.	central
Orto / Alt.	central
Oseaan / Afr.	ocean
Ōshima / Jap.	large island
Ost / Dan.; Germ.	east
Öst / Swed.	east
Ostän, -ostän / Pers.	province
Øster / Dan.; Nor.	east, eastern
Öster / Swed.	east, eastern
Östlich / Germ.	eastern
Ostrog / Rus.	castle
Ostrov / Rus.	island
Ostrovul / Rom.	island
Ostrów / Pol.	island
Ostrvo / S.C.	island
Otok / S.C.; Slvn.	island
Otrog / Rus.	front range (mountains)
Oua / Mel.	stream
Ouar / Ar.	rocky desert
Oud / Fle.; Dut.	old
Oued / Ar.	wadi
Ouest / Fr.	west
Ouled / Ar.	son
Oum / Ar.	mother
Ouro / Port.	gold
Outu / Poly.	cape
Ova / Ban.	people
Ova / Tur.	plain
Ovasi / Tur.	plain
Øver / Nor.	over
Över / Swed.	over
Övre / Swed.	over
Øy / Dan.; Nor.	island
oz., Ozero / Rus.	lake
Ozek / Alt.	hollow
Ozera / Rus.	lakes
Ozero, oz. / Rus.	lake

P

Local Form	English
P., Pulau / Mal.; Indon.	island
Pää / Finn.	principal
Pad / Rus.	valley
Padang / Indon.	plain
Padiş / Rom.	upland
Padół / Pol.	valley
Pădure / Rom.	forest
Pahorek / Cz.	hill
Pahorkatina / Cz.	plateau, hills
Pais / Port.; Sp.	land, country
Pak / Thai	mouth
Pala / It.	peak
Palaiós / Gr.	old
Palanka / S.C.	village
Pali / Poly.	cliff
-palli / Hin.	village
Pampa / Sp.	plain, prairie
Panda / Swa.	junction
Panev / Cz.	basin
Pantanal / Sp.	swamp
Pantano / Sp.	swamp, lake
Pao / Mel.	hill
Pará / A.I.	river
Paramera / Sp.	desert highland
Páramo / Sp.	moor
Paraná / A.I.	river
Parbat / Hin.; Urdu	mountain
Parc / Fr.	park
Parco / It.	park
Parco Nazionale / It.	national park
Pardo / Port.	grey
Parque / Sp.	park
Parque Nacional / Sp.; Port.	national park
Pas / Fr.; Rom.	pass, strait
Pasaje / Sp.	passage
Pasir / Mal.	sand, beach
Paso / Sp.	pass
Passágem / Port.	passage
Passe / Fr.	pass
Passo / It.; Port.	pass
Pasul / Rom.	pass
Patak / Hung.	stream
Patam, -patam / Hin.	city, town
Patnã / Hin.	city, town
Patnam, -patnam / Hin.	city, town
Pattinam, -pattinam / Hin.	city, town
Pays / Fr.	land, country
Pazar / Tur.	market
Pea / Est.	cape
Pech / Cat.	hill
Pedhiás / Gr.	plain
Pedra / Port.	rock, mountain
Peg., Pegunungan / Mal.; Indon.	mountain range
Pegunungan, Peg. / Mal.; Indon.	mountain range
Pélagos / Gr.	sea
Pele / Poly.	peak, hill
Pen / Br.	principal
Pen / Br.; Gae.	cape, mountain
Peña / Sp.	peak
Pendi / Chin.	basin
Pendiente / Sp.	slope
Penha / Port.	peak
Peninsula / Port.; Sp.	peninsula
Péninsule / Fr.	peninsula
Penisola / It.	peninsula
Peñon / Sp.	rock, island
Pente / Fr.	slope
Perekóp / Rus.	channel
Pereval / Rus.	pass
Perevoz / Rus.	ford
Pertuis / Fr.	strait
Peščara / S.C.	sandy soil
Peski / Rus.	sand desert
Petit / Fr.	little
Pétra / Gr.	rock
Phanom / Thai; Khm.	mountain range, mountain
Phau / Laot.	mountain
Phnum / Khm.	hill, mountain
Phu / Viet.	mountain, hill
Phum / Thai	forest
Phumĭ / Khm.	village
Pì / Chin.	cape
Piana, Pianura / It.	plain
Piano / It.	plain
Piatră / Rom.	stone
Pic / Cat.; Fr.	peak
Picacho / Sp.	peak
Piccolo / It.	little
Pico / Port.; Sp.	peak
Piedra / Sp.	rock, cliff
Pietra / It.	stone
Pieve / It.	parish
Pik / Rus.	peak
Pils / Latv.	city, town
Pinar / Sp.	pine forest
Pingyuan / Chin.	plain
Pioda / It.	crest
Pirgos / Gr.	tower, peak
Pish / Pers.	anterior, before
Pitkä / Finn.	great
Piton / Fr.	mountain, peak
Piz / Rmsh.	peak
Pizzo / It.	peak
Pjasăci / Bulg.	beach
Plaat / Fle.; Dut.	sandbank
Plage / Fr.	beach
Plaine / Fr.	plain
Plan / Fr.	plain
Planalto / Port.	plateau
Planina / Bulg.	mountain
Plano / Sp.	plain
Plas / Dut.; Fle.	lake, marsh
Plato / Bulg.; Rus.	plateau
Platosu / Tur.	plateau
Platte / Germ.	plain, plateau
Plav / S.C.	blue
Plavnja / Rus.	marsh
Playa / Sp.	beach
Ploskogorje / Rus.	plateau
Plou / Br.	church
Po / Kor.	port
Po / Chin.	lake, white
P'o / Kor.	bay, lake
Poa / Mel.	hill
Poarta / Rom.	pass
Poartă / Rom.	gate
Pobla / Cat.	village
Pobrzeże / Pol.	littoral, coast
Poço / Port.	well
Poço / Port.	point
Pod / Cz.; Pol.; Rus.; S.C.; Slvn.	bridge
Podkamenny / Rus.	stony
Poggio / It.	hill
Pohja / Finn.	north, northern
Pohjois- / Finn.	north
Pojezierze / Pol.	lake region
Pol / Pers.	bridge
Pol, -pol / Rus.	city, town
Pola / Port.; Sp.	village
Polder / Fle.; Dut.	reclaimed land
Pole / Pol.	field
Pólis / Gr.	city, town
Poljana / Bulg.; Rus.; S.C.; Slvn.	field, terrace
Poljarny / Rus.	polar
Polje / S.C.; Slvn.	valley, field, basin
Poluostrov / Rus.	peninsula
Pomorije / Bulg.	littoral
Pomorze / Pol.	littoral
Ponente / It.	western
Pont / Cat.; Fr.	bridge
Ponta / Port.	point
Ponte / It.; Port.	bridge
Póntos / Gr.	sea
Poort / Afr.; Fle.; Dut.	pass
Pore, -pore / Hin.; Urdu	city, town
Porog / Rus.	rapids
Porte / Fr.	gate
Portile / Rom.	gorge
Portillo / Sp.	pass
Portiţa / Rom.	small gate
Porto / It.	port
Pôrto / Port.	port
Posht / Pers.	back, posterior
Potjo / Indon.	peak
Potok / Bulg.; Cz.; Pol.; Rus.; S.C.; Slvn.	stream
Póvoa / Port.	village
Pozo / Sp.	well
Pozzo / It.	well
Pradesh / Hin.	region, state
Prado / Sp.	meadow
Praia / Port.	beach
Prato / It.	meadow
Prè / Fr.	meadow
Prealpi / It.	prealps
Presa / Sp.	reservoir
Presqu'île / Fr.	peninsula
Prêto / Port.	black
Priehradni nádrž / Cz.	reservoir
Pripoljarny / Rus.	subpolar
Pristan / Rus.	port
Prohod / Bulg.	pass
Proliv / Rus.	strait
Promontoire / Fr.	promontory
Průchod / Cz.	pass
Przedgorze / Pol.	front range (mountains)
Przełęcz / Pol.	pass
Przemysł / Pol.	industry
Przylądek / Pol.	cape
Pua / Mel.	hill
Puebla / Sp.	village
Puente / Sp.	bridge
Puerto / Sp.	port, pass
Puig / Cat.	peak
Puits / Fr.	well
Pul / Pash.	bridge
Pulau, P. / Mal.; Indon.	island
Pulau Pulau / Mal.	islands
Pulo / Mal.; Indon.	island
Puna / A.I.	upland
Puncak / Indon.	mountain
Punjung / Mal.; Indon.	mountain
Punt / Afr.	point
Punta / It.; Sp.	point
Pur, -pur / Hin.; Urdu	city, town
-pura / Hin.; Urdu	city, town
Pura / Indon.	city, town, temple
Puri, -puri / Hin.; Urdu	city, town
Pus / Alb.	spring
Pušča / Rus.	forest
Pustynja / Rus.	desert
Puszcza / Pol.	heath
Puszta / Hung.	lowland
Put / Afr.	well
Put / Rus.; S.C.	road
Putra, -putra / Hin.	son
Puu / Poly.	mountain, volcano
Puy / Fr.	peak
Pwell / Wel.	pond
Pyeong / Kor.	plain
Pyhä / Finn.	saint

Q

Local Form	English
Qagan / Mong.	white
Qala / Pash.	fortified town
Qal'at / Ar.	castle
Qalb / Ar.	hill
Qalīb / Ar.	spring
Qalíq / Ar.	spring
Qanāt / Ar.	canal
Qantara / Ar.	bridge
Qaqortoq / Esk.	white
Qar / Som.	mountain
Qara / Pers.	black
Qarah / Tur.	black
Qārat / Ar.	height, mountain
Qāret / Ar.	village, hill
Qaryah / Ar.	village
Qaryat / Ar.	village
Qaşr / Ar.	castle
Qawz / Ar.	dunes
Qeqertarssuaq / Esk.	peninsula
Qezel / Tur.	red
Qi / Chin.	river
Qing / Chin.	blue, green
Qiryat / Hebr.	city, town
Qolleh / Pers.	mountain, peak
Qu / Chin.	river, canal
Quan dao / Viet.	islands
Quebracho / Sp.	stream
Quebrada / Sp.	gorge, stream
Quedas / Port.	waterfalls
Qulbān / Ar.	well
Qundao / Chin.	archipelago
Qūr / Ar.	height, hill
Qytet / Alb.	city, town
Qyteti / Alb.	city, town

R

Local Form	English
R., Rio, River / Eng.; Sp.	river
Rada / It.; Sp.	anchorage
Rade / Fr.	anchorage
Rags / Latv.	cape
Rahad / Ar.	lake, pond
Rajon / Rus.	district
Rak / Fle.; Dut.	strait
Rakai / Poly.	reef
Ramla / Ar.	sand
Rancho / Port.; Sp.	farm, ranch
Rand / Afr.; Germ.	escarpment
Range / Eng.	mountain range
Rann / Hin.	marsh
Rano / Malag.	water
Ranta / Finn.	bank, beach
Rapide / Fr.	rapids
Ras / Amh.	peak
Rās / Ar.	point, cape

Local Form	English
Ras, Rås / Ar.	promontory, peak
Råsiga / Som.	promontory
Rass / Ar.	promontory, peak
Rassa / Lapp.	mountain
Råth / Gae.	castle
Raunina / Bulg.; Rus.	plain
Raz / Fr.	strait
Razliv / Rus.	flood plain
Récif / Fr.	reef
Recife / Port.	reef
Reede / Germ.; Dut.; Slvn.	anchorage
Reek / Afr.; Gae.	mountain range
Reg / Pash.	dunes
Région / Fr.	region
Rei / Port.	king
Reka / Bulg.; Rus.; S.C.; Slvn.	river
Řeka / Cz.	river
Réma / Gr.	torrent
Renne / Dan.; Nor.	deep
Represa / Port.	dam, reservoir
Represa / Sp.	dam, reservoir
República / Port.; Sp.	republic
République / Fr.	republic
Rés., Réservoir / Fr.	reservoir
Res., Reservoir / Eng.	reservoir
Réservoir, Rés. / Fr.	reservoir
Reshteh / Pers.	mountain range
Respublika / Rus.	republic
Restinga / Port.	cliff, sandbank
Retsugan / Jap.	reef
Rettō / Jap.	archipelago
Rev / Dan.; Nor.; Swed.	reef
Rey / Sp.	king
Ri / Tib.	mountain
Ría / Sp.	estuary
Riacho / Port.	stream
Rialto / It.	plateau
Rialto / It.	rise
Riba / Port.	bank
Ribeira / Port.	river
Ribeirão / Port.	stream
Ribeiro / Port.	stream
Ribera / Sp.	coast
Ribnik / Slvn.	pond
Rid / Bulg.	mountain range
Rif / Icel.	cliff
Riff / Germ.	reef
Rīg / Pash.	dunes
Rijeka / S.C.	river
Rimāl / Ar.	sand desert
Rincón / Sp.	peninsula between two rivers
Ring / Tib.	long
Rinne / Germ.	trench
Rio / Port.	river
Rio, R. / Sp.	river
Riu / Rom.	river
Riva / It.	bank
Rive / Fr.	bank
Rivera / Sp.	brook, stream
Rivier, -rivier / Afr.; Dut.; Fle.	river
Riviera / It.	coast
Rivière / Fr.	river
Roads / Eng.	anchorage
Roc / Fr.	rock
Roca / Port.; Sp.	rock
Rocca / It.	castle
Roche / Fr.	rock
Rocher / Fr.	rock
Rock / Eng.	rock
Rød / Pash.	river
Rode / Germ.	tilled soil
Rodnik / Rus.	spring
Rog / Rus.; S.C.; Slvn.	peak
Roi / Fr.	king
Rojo / Sp.	red
Roque / Sp.	rock
Rot / Germ.	red
Roto / Poly.	lake
Rouge / Fr.	red
Równina / Pol.	plain
Rt / S.C.; Slvn.	cape
Ru / Tib.	mountain
Ruck / Germ.	ridge
Rücken / Germ.	ridge
Rud / Pers.	river
Ruda / Cz.; Slvk.	mine
Ruda / Pol.	ore
Rūdbār / Pers.	river
Rudha / Gae.	point
Rudnik / Rus.; S.C.; Slvn.	mine
Rug / Fle.; Dut.	ridge
Ruggen / Afr.	ridge
Ruina / Sp.	ruins
Ruine / Fr.; Dut.; Germ.	ruins
Rujm / Ar.	hill
Run / Eng.	stream

S

Local Form	English
S., See / Germ.	lake, sea
Saar / Est.	island
Saari / Finn.	island
Sabbia / It.	sand
Sabkhat / Ar.	salt flat, salt marsh
Sable / Fr.; Eng.	beach
Sacca / It.	anchorage
Saco / Port.	bay
Sad / Cz.; Slvk.	park
Sad / Pers.	wall
Sadd / Ar.; Pers.	cataract, dam
Safid / Pash.; Urdu; Hin.	white
Şafrā' / Ar.	desert
Sāgar / Hin.	reservoir
Saguia / Ar.	irrigation canal
Sahara / Ar.	desert
Sahel / Ar.	plain, coast
Sahr / Iran.	city, town
Şaḥrā' / Ar.	desert
Said / Ar.	sweet
Saj / Alt.	stream, valley
Saki / Jap.	point
Sala / Latv.; Lith.	island
Saladillo / Sp.	salt desert
Salar / Sp.	salt lake
Sale / Ural.	village
Salina / It.; Sp.	salt flat, salt marsh
Saline / Dut.; Fr.; Germ.	salt flat, salt marsh
Salmi / Finn.	strait
Salseleh-ye Kūh / Pers.	mountain range
Salto / Port.; Sp.	waterfall, rapids
Salz / Germ.	salt
Samudera / Indon.	ocean
Samudra / Hin.	lake
Samut / Thai	sea
San / Jap.; Kor.	mountain
San / It.; Sp.	saint
Sanchi / Jap.	mountain range
Sand / Dan.; Eng.; Nor.; Swed.; Germ.	beach
Šand / Mong.	spring
Sandur / Icel.	sand
Sank / Pers.	rock
Sankt, St. / Germ.; Swed.	saint
Sanmaeg / Kor.	mountain range
Sanmyaku / Jap.	mountain range
Sansanné / Sud.	campsite
Santo / It.; Port.; Sp.	saint
Santuario / It.	sanctuary
São / Port.	saint
Sar / Pers.	cape; peak
Šar / Rus.; Tur.	strait
Saraf / Ar.	well
Sari / Finn.	island
Sari / Tur.	yellow
Sarīr / Ar.	rocky desert
Sary / Tur.	yellow
Sasso / It.	stone
Sat / Rom.	village
Sattel / Germ.	pass
Saurum / Latv.	strait
Schleuse / Germ.	lock
Schloß / Germ.	castle
Schlucht / Germ.	gorge
Schnee / Germ.	snow
Schwarz / Germ.	black
Scoglio / It.	cliff
Se / Jap.	bank, shoal
Sebkha / Ar.	salt flat
Sebkhet / Ar.	salt flat
Sed / Ar.	dam
Seda / Ural.	mountain
See, S. / Germ.	lake, sea
Sefra / Ar.	yellow
Segara / Indon.	lagoon
Şehir / Tur.	city, town
Seki / Jap.	dam
Selat / Mal.; Indon.	strait
Selatan / Indon.	southern
Selkä / Finn.	ridge, lake
Sella / It.	pass
Selo / Bulg.; Rus.; S.C.; Slvn.	village
Selsela Kohe / Pers.	mountain range
Selva / It.; Sp.	forest
Semenanjung / Mal.	peninsula
Sen / Jap.	mountain
Seong / Kor.	castle
Sep / Alt.	canal
Serir / Ar.	rocky desert
Serra / Cat.; Port.	mountain range
Serra / It.	mountain
Serrania / Sp.	mountain range
Sertão / Port.	steppe
Seto / Jap.	strait
Sett., Settentrionale / It.	northern
Settentrionale, Sett. / It.	northern
Seuil / Fr.	sill
Sev / Arm.	black
Sever / Rus.	north
Severny / Rus.	northern
Sfint / Rom.	saint
Sfintu / Rom.	saint
Sgeir / Gae.	cliff
Sha'b / Ar.	cliff
Shahr / Pers.; Hin.	city, town
Sha'ib / Ar.	stream
Shallāl / Ar.	cataract
Shām / Ar.	north; northern
Shamo / Chin.	sand desert
Shan / Chin.	mountain, mountain range
Shan / Gae.	old
Shand / Mong.	spring
Shankou / Chin.	pass
Shaqq / Ar.	wadi
Sharm / Ar.	bay
Sharqi / Ar.	east, eastern
Sharqīyah / Ar.	eastern
Shatt / Ar.	river, salt lake
Shatt / Ar.	stream
Shën / Alb.	saint
Sheng / Chin.	province
Shi / Chin.	city, town
Shibīn / Ar.	village
Shih / Chin.	rock
Shima / Jap.	island
Shimo / Jap.	lower
Shin / Jap.	new
Shō / Jap.	island
Shotō / Jap.	archipelago
Shū / Jap.	administrative division
Shui / Chin.	river
Shuiku / Chin.	reservoir
Shur / Pers.	salt
Sidhiros / Gr.	iron
Sidi / Ar.	master
Sieben / Germ.	seven
Sierra / Sp.	mountain range
Sikt / Ural.	village
Sillon / Fr.	furrow
Šine / Mong.	new
Sink / Eng.	depression
Sinn / Ar.	point
Sint / Dut.; Fle.	saint
Sirt / Tur.	mountain range
Sirtlar / Tur.	mountain range
Sistema / It.; Sp.	mountain system
Sīyāh / Pers.	black
Sjø / Nor.	lake
Sjö / Swed.	lake, sea
Skag / Icel.	peninsula
Skala / Bulg.; Rus.	rock
Skála / Slvk.	rock
Skar / Nor.	pass
Skär / Swed.	cliff
Skeir / Gae.	cliff
Skerry / Gae.	cliff
Skog / Nor.; Swed.	forest
Skóg / Icel.	forest
Skov / Dan.; Nor.	forest
Slatina / S.C.; Slvn.	mineral water
Slätt / Swed.	plain
Slieve / Gae.	mountain
Slot / Dut.; Fle.	castle
Slott / Nor.; Swed.	castle
Slough / Eng.	creek, pond, marsh
Sluis / Dut.; Fle.	sluice
Små / Swed.	little
Sne / Nor.	snow
Sneeuw / Afr.; Dut.	snow
Snežny / Rus.	snowy
Sne / Nor.	snow
So / Kor.	little
Sø / Dan.; Nor.	lake; sea
So / Ural.	passage
Söder / Swed.	south
Södra / Swed.	southern
Solončak / Rus.	salt flat
Sommet / Fr.	peak
Son / Viet.	mountain
Sønder / Dan.; Nor.	southern
Søndre / Dan.	southern
Sone / Jap.	bank
Song / Viet.	river
Sopka / Rus.	volcano
Sopočnik / Rus.	mountain system
Soprana / It.	upper
Šor, Sor / Alt.	salt marsh
Sos / Sp.	upon
Sotavento / Sp.	leeward
Sotoviento / Sp.	leeward
Sottana / It.	lower
Souk / Ar.	market
Souq / Ar.	market
Sour / Ar.	rampart
Source / Eng.; Fr.	spring
Souto / Port.	forest
Spitze / Germ.	peak
Spruit / Afr.	current
Sreden / Bulg.	central
Sredni / Rus.	central
Średni / Pol.	central
Srednji / S.C.; Slvn.	central
St., Saint, Sankt / Eng.; Fr.; Germ.; Swed.	saint
Stadhur / Icel.	city, town
Stadt, -stadt / Germ.	city, town
Stag / Eng.	city, town
Stagno / It.	pond
-stan / Hin.; Pers.; Urdu	land
Star / Bulg.	old
Stari / S.C.; Slvn.	old
Stary / Pol.; Rus.	old
Starý / Cz.; Slvk.	old
Stat / Afr.; Dan.; Fle.; Nor.; Dut.; Swed.	city, town
Stathmós / Gr.	railway station
Stausee / Germ.	reservoir
Stavrós / Gr.	cross
Sted / Dan.; Nor.	place
Stedt / Germ.	place
Stein, -stein / Nor.; Germ.	stone
Sten / Nor.; Swed.	stone
Stena / S.C.; Slvn.	rock
Stěna / Cz.	mountain range
Stenón / Gr.	strait, pass
Step / Rus.	steppe
-sthān / Hin.; Pers.; Urdu	land
Stift / Germ.	foundation
Štít / Cz.; Slvk.	peak
Stock / Germ.	massif
Stok / Pol.	slope
Stor / Dan.; Nor.; Swed.	great
Store / Dan.	great
Stræde / Dan.	strait
Strana / Rus.	land
Strand / Germ.; Nor.; Swed.; Afr.; Dan.	beach
Straße / Germ.	street, road
Strath / Gae.	valley
Straum / Nor.; Swed.	stream
Středni / Cz.	central
Stredný / Slvk.	central
Strelka / Rus.	spit
Stret / Nor.	strait
Stretto / It.	strait
Strom / Germ.	stream
Strøm / Nor.	stream
Ström / Swed.	stream
Stroom / Dut.	stream
Su / Jap.	sandbank
Su / Tur.	river
Suando / Finn.	pond
Suid / Afr.	south
Suidō / Jap.	strait
Sul / Port.	south
Sund / Dan.; Nor.; Swed.; Germ.	strait
Sungai / Mal.	river
Sunn / Nor.	south
Sūq / Ar.	market
Sur / Fr.	on
Sur / Sp.	south
Surkh / Pers.	red
Suu / Finn.	mouth, river mouth
Suur / Cat.	great
Svart / Nor.; Swed.	black
Sveti / S.C.; Slvn.	saint
Swa / Ban.	great
Swart / Afr.	black
Świety / Pol.	saint
Syrt / Alt.	ridge
Szállás / Hung.	village
Szczyt / Pol.	peak
Szeg / Hung.	bend
Székes / Hung.	residence
Szent / Hung.	saint
Sziget / Hung.	river island

T

Local Form	English
Tadi / Ban.	rock, cliff
Tae / Kor.	great
Tafua / Poly.	mountain
Tag / Alt.; Tur.	mountain
Tahta / Ar.	lower
Tahti / Ar.	lower
Tai / Chin.; Jap.	great
Taipale / Finn.	isthmus
Tajga / Rus.	forest
Take / Jap.	mountain
Tal / Germ.	valley
Tala / Mong.	plain, steppe
Tala / Ber.	spring
Tall / Ar.	hill
Talsperre / Germ.	dam
Tam / Viet.	stream
Tamgout / Ber.	peak
Tan / Chin.; Kor.	sandbank
Tana / Malag.	city, town
Tanana / Malag.	city, town
Tandjung / Mal.	cape, point
Tanezrouft / Ber.	desert
Tang / Tib.	upland
Tangeh / Pers.	strait
Tanjong / Mal.	cape, point
Tanjung, Tg. / Indon.	cape, point
Tanout / Ber.	well
Tao / Chin.	island
Taourirt / Ber.	peak
Targ / Pol.	market
Tărg / Bulg.	market
Tarn / Eng.	glacial lake
Tarso / Sah.	crater
Taš / Alt.	stone

Geographical Glossary

Local Form	English
Tassili / Ber.	upland
Tau / Tur.	mountain
Taung / Burm.	mountain
Ţawîl / Ar.	hill
Tégi / Sah.	hill
Teguidda / Ber.	well
Tehi / Ber.	pass, mountain
Teich / Germ.	pond
Tell / Tur.	hill
Telok / Mal.	bay, port
Teluk / Mal.	bay, port
Tempio / It.	temple
Ténéré / Ber.	rocky desert
Tengah / Indon.; Mal.	central
Tepe / Tur.	hill
Tepesi / Tur.	hill
Termas / Sp.	thermal springs
Terme / It.	thermal springs
Terra / It.; Dut.	land, earth
Terrazzo / It.	guyot, tablemount
Terre / Fr.	land, earth
Teso / Cat.	hill
Téssa / Ber.	wadi, depression
Testa / It.	point
Tête / Fr.	peak
Tetri / Georg.	white
Teu / Poly.	reef
Teze / Alt.	new
Tg., Tanjung / Indon.	cape, point
Thaba / Ban.	mountain
Thabana / Ban.	mountain
Thal / Germ.	valley
Thálassa / Gr.	sea
Thale / Thai	lagoon
Thamad / Ar.	well
Theós / Gr.	god
Thermes / Fr.	thermal springs
Thog / Tib.	high, upper
Tian / Chin.	field
Tiefe / Germ.	deep
Tierra / Sp.	land, earth
Timur / Indon.; Mal.	eastern
Tind / Nor.	mountain
Tinto / Sp.	black
Tirg / Rom.	market
Tis / Amh.	new
Tizgui / Ber.	forest
Tizi / Ber.	pass
Tjåkko / Lapp.	mountain
Tjärn / Swed.	tarn, glacial lake
Tji / Mal.	stream
To / Kor.	island
To / Mel.	stream
Tô / Jap.	island
Tó / Hung.	lake
To / Ural.	lake
Tobe / Tur.	hill
Tofua / Poly.	mountain
Tog / Som.	valley
Tōge / Jap.	pass
Tokoj / Alt.	forest
Tônle / Khm.	stream, lake
Tope / Dut.	peak
Toplice / S.C.; Slvn.	thermal springs
Topp / Nor.	peak
Tor / Gae.	rock
Tor / Germ.	gate
Torbat / Pers.	tomb
Törl / Germ.	pass
Torp / Swed.	hut
Torre / Cat.; It.; Sp.; Port.	tower
Torrente / It.; Sp.	torrent, stream
Tossa / Cat.	mountain, peak
Tota / Sin.	port
Tour / Fr.	tower
Traforo / It.	tunnel
Träsk / Swed.	lake
Trg / S.C.	market
Trog / Germ.	trough, trench
Trois / Fr.	three
Trung / Viet.	central
Tse / Tib.	peak, point
Tsi / Chin.	pond
Tskali / Georg.	river
Tsu / Jap.	bay
Tulûl / Ar.	hills
Tünel / Pers.	tunnel
Tunturi / Lapp.	mountain, tundra
Tur'ah / Ar.	irrigation canal
Turm / Germ.	tower
Turn / Rom.	tower
Turó / Cat.	dome
Tuz / Tur.	salt
Týn / Cz.	fortress

U

Local Form	English
U., Unter-, Upon / Eng.; Germ.	under, lower
Uaimh / Gae.	cave
Uchi / Jap.	bay
Udde / Swed.	cape
Údolní nádrž / Cz.	reservoir

Local Form	English
Uebi / Som.	river
Új- / Hung.	new
Ujście / Pol.	mouth
Ujung / Indon.	point, cape
Ul / Chin.; Mong.	mountain, mountain range
Ula / Mong.	mountain range
Ulan / Mong.	red
Uls / Mong.	state
Umi / Jap.	bay
Umm / Ar.	mother, spring
Umne / Mong.	south
Under / Mong.	mountain, peak
Ungur / Alt.	cave
Unter-, U. / Germ.	under, lower
Upar / Hin.	river
'Uqlat / Ar.	well
Ûr / Tam.	city, town
Ura / Jap.	bay, coast
Ura / Alt.	depression
Urd / Mong.	south
Uru / Tam.	city, town
Ušće / S.C.	mouth
Uske / Alt.	upper
Ust / Rus.	mouth
Ústí / Cz.	mouth
Ustup / Rus.	terrace
Utan / Indon.; Mal.	forest
Utara / Indon.	north, northern
Uusi / Finn.	new
Uval / Rus.	height
Úval / Cz.	mountain
'Uwaynät / Ar.	well
Uzboj / Alt.	river bed
Uzun / Tur.	long
Užürekis / Lith.	gulf

V

Local Form	English
Va / Alb.	ford
Va / Ural.	water, river
Vaara / Finn.	mountain
Väärti / Finn.	bay
Vad / Rom.	ford
Vær / Nor.	port
Våg / Nor.	bay
Vähä / Finn.	little
Väike / Est.	little
Väin / Est.	strait
Val / Fr.; It.	valley
Val / Rom.; Rus.	wall
Valico / It.	pass
Vall / Cat.	valley
Vall / Swed.	pasture
Valle / It.; Sp.	valley
Vallée / Fr.	valley
Vallei / Afr.	valley
Vallo / It.	wall
Valta / Finn.	cape
Váltos / Gr.	marsh
Valul / Rom.	wall
Vann / Dan.; Nor.	water, lake
Vanua / Mel.	land
Vár / Hung.	fort
Vara / Finn.	mountain
Varoš / S.C.	city, town
Város / Hung.	city, town
Varre / Lapp.	mountain
Vary / Cz.	spring
Vas / S.C.; Slvn.	village
Vásár / Hung.	market
Väst / Swed.	west
Väster / Swed.	western
Vatn / Icel.; Nor.	lake
Vatten / Swed.	water, lake
Vatu / Mel.; Poly.	island, reef
Vdhr., Vodohranilišče / Rus.	reservoir
Vechiu / Rom.	old
Vecs / Latv.	old
Veen / Dut.; Fle.	moor
Vega / Sp.	irrigated crops
Veld / Afr.; Dut.; Fle.	field
Veli / S.C.; Slvn.	great
Velik / Bulg.	great
Veliki / Rus.; S.C.; Slvn.	great
Veliký / Cz.	great
Velký / Cz.	great
Vel'ky / Slvk.	great
Vella / Cat.	old
Ver / Ural.	forest
Verde / It.; Sp.	green
Verh / Rus.	peak
Verhni / Rus.	upper
Verk / Swed.	factory
Vermelho / Port.	red
Vert / Fr.	green
Ves / Cz.	village
Vesi / Finn.	water, lake
Vest / Dan.; Nor.	west
Vester / Dan.; Nor.	western
Vestur / Icel.	west
Vetta / It.	summit
Viaduc / Fr.	viaduct

Local Form	English
Vidda / Nor.	upland
Vidde / Nor.	upland
Viejo / Sp.	old
Vier / Germ.	four
Viertel / Germ.	quarter
Vieux / Fr.	old
Vig / Dan.	bay
Vik / Icel.; Nor.; Swed.	gulf, bay
Vila / Port.	city, town
Villa / Sp.	city, town
Ville, -ville / Eng.; Fr.	city, town
Vinh / Viet.	bay
Virful / Rom.	peak, mountain
Virta / Finn.	river
Višni / Rus.	high
Visok / S.C.	high
Viz / Hung.	water
Víztároló / Hung.	reservoir
Vlakte / Dut.; Fle.	plain
Vlei / Afr.	pond
Vliet / Dut.; Fle.	river
Vloer / Afr.	depression
Voda / Bulg.; Cz.; Rus.; S.C.; Slvn.	water
Vodny put / Rus.	stream, canal
Vodohranilišče, vdhr. / Rus.	reservoir
Vodopad / Rus.	waterfall
Volcan / Fr.	volcano
Volcán / Sp.	volcano
Voll / Nor.	meadow
Vórios / Gr.	northern
Vorota / Rus.	gate
Vorrás / Gr.	north
Vostočny / Rus.	eastern
Vostok / Rus.	east
Vötn / Icel.	lake, water
Vož / Ural.	mouth
Vozvyšennost / Rus.	upland
Vpadina / Rus.	depression
Vrah / Bulg.	peak
Vrata / Bulg.; S.C.; Slvn.	pass
Vrch / Cz.; Slvk.	mountain
Vrch / S.C.; Slvn.	peak
Vrchni / Cz.	upper
Vrchovina / Cz.	upland
Vulcan / Rom.; Rus.	volcano
Vulcano / It.	volcano
Vulkan / Germ.; Rus.	volcano
Vuopio / Lapp.	bend
Vuori / Finn.	rock
Východný / Cz.	eastern
Vyšný / Slvk.	upper
Vysoki / Rus.	high
Vysoky / Cz.; Slvk.	high
Vyšši / Cz.	high

W

Local Form	English
W., Wâdî / Ar.	wadi
Wa / Ban.	people
Wabe / Amh.	stream
Wad / Ar.	wadi
Wad / Dut.	tidal flat
Wâdî, W. / Ar.	wadi
Wâḩät / Ar.	oasis
Wai / Mel.; Poly.	stream
Wal / Afr.	wall
Wala / Hin.	mountain range
Wald / Germ.	forest
Wan / Burm.	village
Wan / Chin.; Jap.	bay
Wand / Germ.	bluff
War / Som.	pond
Wär / Ar.	desert
-waram / Hin.; Tam.	village
Wasser / Germ.	water
Wat / Pol.	wall
Wat / Thai	church
Waterval / Afr.; Dut.	waterfall
Watt / Germ.	tidal flat
Wäw / Ar.	oasis
Weald / Eng.	wooded country
Webi / Som.	stream
Weg / Germ.	way, road
Wei / Chin.	cape, point
Weide / Germ.	pasture
Weiler / Germ.	village
Weiß / Germ.	white
Weon / Kor.	field
Wer / Som.	pond
Werder / Germ.	river island
Werk / Germ.	factory
Wes / Afr.	west
Westlich / Germ.	western
Westr- / Sca.	western
Wēyn / Som.	great
Wēyne / Som.	great
Wick / Eng.	village
Wiek / Germ.	bay
Wielki / Pol.	great
Wieś / Pol.	village
Wijk / Dut.; Fle.	quarter, district
-willer / Germ.	village

Local Form	English
Woda / Pol.	water
Woestyn / Afr.	desert
Wold / Dut.; Fle.; Eng.	forest
Wörth / Germ.	river island
Woud / Dut.; Fle.	forest
Wschodni / Pol.	eastern
Wysoczyzna / Pol.	upland
Wysoki / Pol.	upper
Wyspa / Pol.	island
Wyżyna / Pol.	highland
Wzgórze / Pol.	hill

X

Local Form	English
Xi / Chin.	west
Xia / Chin.	gorge, strait
Xian / Chin.	county, shire
Xiang / Chin.	village
Xiao / Chin.	little
Xin / Chin.	new
Xu / Chin.	island

Y

Local Form	English
Yam / Hebr.	lake, sea
Yama / Jap.	mountain
Yan / Chin.	mountain
Yang / Chin.	strait, ocean
Yani / Tur.	new
Yar / Tur.	gorge
Yarimada / Tur.	peninsula
Yazi / Tur.	plain
Yegge / Sah.	well
Yeni / Tur.	new
Yeon / Kor.	sea
Yeong / Kor.	mountain
Yeşil / Tur.	green
Ylä / Finn.	upper
Yli- / Finn.	upper
Yô / Jap.	ocean
Yobe / Sud.	great
Yöm / Kor.	island
Yoma / Burm.	mountain range
Yön / Kor.	lake, pond
Yŏng / Kor.	mountain, peak
Ytter / Nor.; Swed.	outer
Yttre / Swed.	outer
Yu / Chin.	old
Yu / Chin.	island
Yu / Jap.	thermal spring
Yüan / Chin.	spring, river
Yunhe / Chin.	canal

Z

Local Form	English
Zâb / Ar.	river
Zachodni / Pol.	western
Zaki / Jap.	cape
Zalew / Pol.	gulf
Zaliv / Bulg.; Rus.; S.C.; Slvn.	gulf
Zaljev / Slvn.	bay
Zámek / Cz.	castle
Zan / Jap.	mountain
Zand / Dut.; Fle.	sand
Zandt / Dut.; Fle.	sand
Zangbo / Chin.	river
Zapad / Rus.	west
Zapaden / Bulg.	western
Zapadni / S.C.; Slvn.	western
Západní / Cz.	western
Zapadny / Rus.	western
Zapovednik / Rus.	reserve
Zatoka / Pol.	gulf
Zavod / Rus.	roadstead
Zãwiyat / Ar.	monastery
Zdrój / Pol.	thermal springs
Ze / Dut.; Fle.	islet
Zee / Dut.; Fle.	sea
Zelëny / Rus.	green
Žem / Lith.	land, country
Zemé / Cz.; Slvk.	land, country
Zemlja / Rus.	land
Zen / Jap.	mountain
Zhan / Chin.	mountain
Zhen / Chin.	market
Zhong / Chin.	central
Zhou / Chin.	quarter, district
Zhuang / Chin.	village
Ziemia / Pol.	land
Zigos / Gr.	pass
Zipfel / Germ.	tip, point
Ziwa / Swa.	marsh
Zizhiqu / Chin.	autonomous region
Zlato / Bulg.	gold
Zuid / Dut.; Fle.	south
Zuidelijk / Dut.	southern
Žuława / Pol.	marsh
Zun / Mong.	east
Zwart / Dut.	black
Zwei / Germ.	two

International Map Index

All of the toponyms (place-names) which appear on the maps are listed in the International Map Index. Each entry includes the following: Place-name and, where applicable, other forms by which it is written or known; a symbol, where applicable, indicating what kind of feature it is; the number of the map on which it appears; and the map-reference letters and geographical coordinates indicating its location on the map.

Toponyms

Each toponym, or place-name, is written in full, with accents and diacritical marks. Since many countries have more than one official language, many of these forms are included on the maps. For example, many Belgian place-names are listed as follows: Bruxelles/Brussel; Antwerpen/Anvers, and vice versa, Brussel/Bruxelles; Anvers/Antwerpen. In Italy, certain regions have a special status—they are largely autonomous and officially bilingual. As a result, Index listings appear as follows: Aosta/Aoste; Alto Adige/Sud Tirol, and vice versa. One name, however, may be the only name on the map.

In China, the written forms of commonly used regional languages have been taken into account. These forms are enclosed in parenthesis following the official name: e.g. Xiangshan (Dancheng). However, when the regional is listed first, it is linked to the official name with an→: e.g. Dancheng→Xiangshan. The same style is used for former or historical name forms: e.g. Rhodesia→Zimbabwe and Zimbabwe (Rhodesia).

Place-names for major features (countries, major cities, and large physical features), where applicable, include the English conventional form identified by (EN) and linked to the local name or names with an = sign: e.g. Italia=Italy (EN), and vice versa, Italy (EN)=Italia. Former English names are linked in the Index to the conventional form by an→.

Symbols

The last component with the place-name is a symbol, where applicable, specifying the broad category of the feature named. A table preceding the Index lists all of the symbols used and their meanings; this information also appears as a footnote on each page of the Index. Place-names without symbols are cities and towns.

Alphabetization

Place-names are listed in English alphabetical order—26 letters, from A to Z—because of its international usage. Names including two or more words are listed alphabetically according to the first letter of the word: e.g. De Ruyter is listed under D; Le Havre is listed under L. Names with the prefix Mc are listed as if spelled Mac. The generic portion of a name (lake, sierra, mountain, etc.) is placed after the name: e.g. Lake Erie is listed as Erie, Lake; Sierra Morena is listed as Morena, Sierra. In Spanish, "ch" and "ll" groups and the letter "ñ" are included respectively under C, L, and N, without any distinction.

The same place-name sometimes is listed in the Index several times. It may because of the various translations of a name, or it may be that several places have the same name.

Various translations of a name appear as follows:

Danube (EN)=Dunav	Danube (EN)=Donau
Danube (EN)=Dunărea	Danube (EN)=Dunaj

Several places with the same name appear as follows; however, only in these cases is the location—abbreviated and enclosed in brackets—included. A table of these abbreviations precedes the Index.

Abbeville [U.S.]	Aberdeen [Scot.-U.K.]
Abbeville [Fr.]	Aberdeen [N.C.-U.S.]
Aberdeen [S. Afr.]	

Map Number

Each map in the atlas is identified by a number. Where multiple maps are on one page, each map is additionally identified by a boxed letter in the upper-right-hand corner of the map. In the Index listing following the place-name and its variations in language and spelling, where applicable, is the number of the map on which it appears. If the map is one of several on a page, the Index listing includes the map number and letter.

Although a place-name may appear on one or more maps, it is indexed to only one map. Most places are indexed to the regional maps. However, if a place-name appears on either the physical or political continental maps, it is indexed to one of the two types of map. For example, a river or mountain would be indexed to a physical continental map; a city or state would be indexed to a political continental map.

Map-Reference Letters and Geographical Coordinates

The next elements in the Index listing are the map-reference letters and the geographical coordinates, respectively, locating the place on the map.

Map-reference letters consist of a capital and a lowercase letter. Capital letters are across the top and bottom of the maps; lowercase letters are down the sides. The map-reference letters assigned to each place-name refer to the location of the name within the area formed by grid lines connecting the geographical coordinates on either sides of the letters.

Geographical coordinates are the latitude (N for North, S for South) and longitude (E for East, W for West) expressed in degrees and minutes and based on the prime meridian, Greenwich.

Map-reference letters and coordinates for extensive geographical features, such as mountain ranges and countries, are given for the approximate central point of the area. Those for waterways, such as canals and rivers, are given for the mouth of the river, the point where it enters another river or where the feature reaches the map margin. On this page are sample maps showing points to which features are indexed according to map-reference letters and coordinates.

On most maps there is not enough space to place all of the names of administrative subdivisions. In these cases the location of the place is shown on the map by a circled letter or number and the place-name and circled letter or number are listed in the map margin. The map-reference numbers and coordinates for these places refer to the location of the circled letter or number on the map.

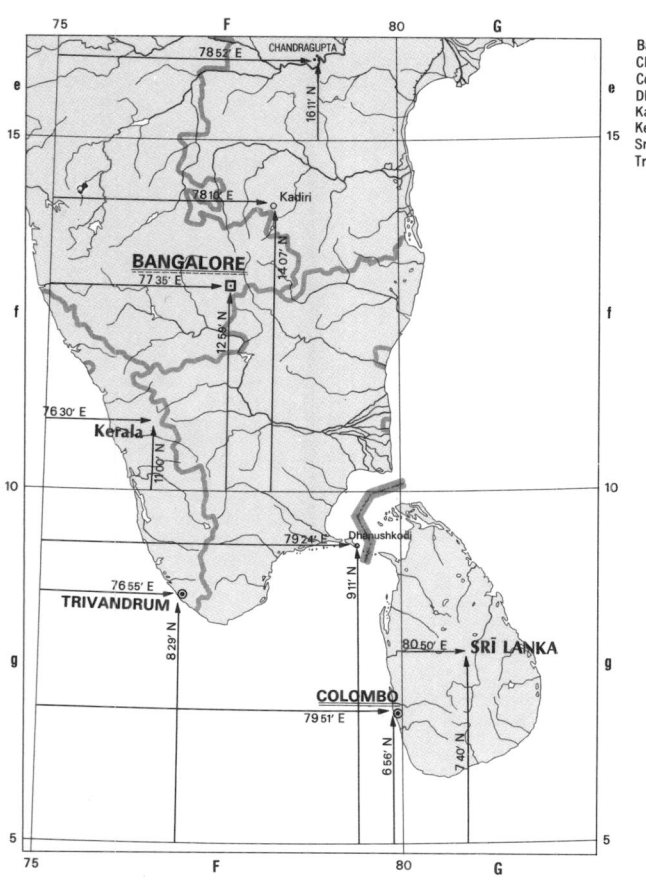

Bangalore	25 Ff	12°59'N	77°35'E
Chandragupta △	35 Fe	16°11'N	78°52'E
Colombo	25 Fg	6°56'N	79°51'E
Dhanushkodi	25 Fg	9°11'N	79°24'E
Kadiri	25 Ff	14°07'N	78°10'E
Kerala ▣	25 Ff	11°00'N	76°30'E
Sri Lanka ◻	25 Gg	7°40'N	80°50'E
Trivandrum	25 Fg	8°29'N	76°55'E

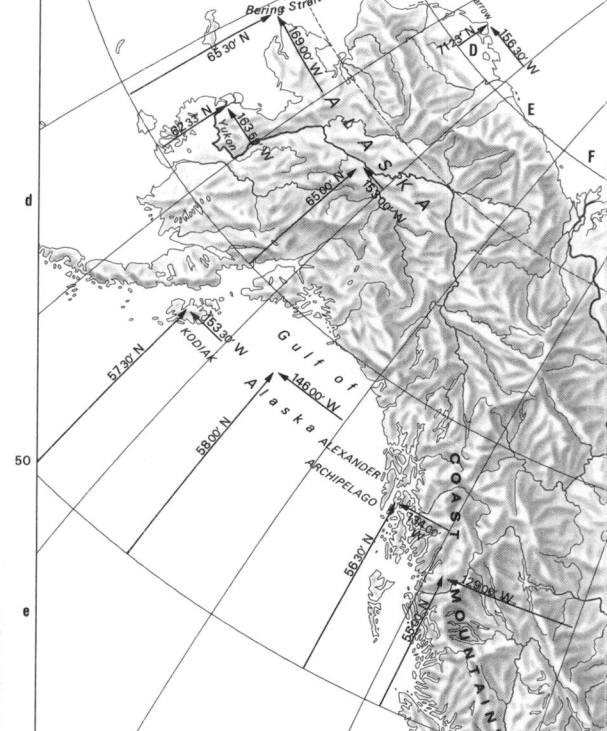

Alaska ▣	38 Dc	65°00'N	153°00'W
Alaska, Gulf of- ◖	38 Ed	58°00'N	146°00'W
Alexander Archipelago ▦	38 Fd	56°30'N	134°00'W
Barrow, Point- ▸	38 Db	71°23'N	156°30'W
Bering Strait ◻	38 Cc	65°30'N	169°00'W
Coast Mountains ▲	38 Gd	55°00'N	129°00'W
Kodiak ◈	38 Dd	57°30'N	153°30'W
Yukon ◺	38 Cc	62°33'N	163°59'W

List of Abbreviations

Abz.-U.S.S.R. Azerbaidzhan S.S.R., U.S.S.R.
Afg. Afghanistan
Afr. Africa
Agl. Anguilla
Ak.-U.S. Alaska, U.S.
Al.-U.S. Alabama, U.S.
Alb. Albania
Alg. Algeria
Alta.-Can. Alberta, Canada
Am. Sam. American Samoa
And. Andorra
Ang. Angola
Ant. Antarctica
Ar.-U.S. Arkansas, U.S.
Arg. Argentina
Arm.-U.S.S.R. Armenian S.S.R., U.S.S.R.
Asia Asia
Atg. Antigua
Aus. Austria
Austl. Australia
Az.-U.S. Arizona, U.S.
Azr. Azores
Bah. Bahamas
Bar. Barbados
B.A.T. British Antarctic Territory
B.C.-Can. British Columbia, Canada
Bel. Belgium
Ben. Benin
Ber. Bermuda
Bhr. Bahrain
Bhu. Bhutan
Blz. Belize
Bnd. Burundi
Bngl. Bangladesh
Bol. Bolivia
Bots. Botswana
Braz. Brazil
Bru. Brunei
Bul. Bulgaria
Bur. Burma
B.V.I. British Virgin Islands
Bye.-U.S.S.R. Byelorussian S.S.R., U.S.S.R.
Ca.-U.S. California, U.S.
Cam. Cameroon
C. Amer. Central America
Can. Canada
Can. Is. Canary Islands
C.A.R. Central African Republic
Cay. Is. Cayman Islands
Chad Chad
Chan. Is. Channel Islands
Chile Chile
China China
Cocos Is. Cocos Islands
Col. Colombia
Con. Congo
Cook Cook Islands
Cor. Sea Is. Coral Sea Islands
C.R. Costa Rica
Ct.-U.S. Connecticut, U.S.
Cuba Cuba
C.V. Cape Verde
Cyp. Cyprus

Czech. Czechoslovakia
D.C.-U.S. District of Columbia, U.S.
De.-U.S. Delaware, U.S.
Den. Denmark
Dji. Djibouti
Dom. Dominica
Dom. Rep. Dominican Republic
Ec. Ecuador
Eg. Egypt
El Sal. El Salvador
Eng.-U.K. England, U.K.
Eq. Gui. Equatorial Guinea
Est.-U.S.S.R. Estonian S.S.R., U.S.S.R.
Eth. Ethiopia
Eur. Europe
Falk. Is. Falkland Islands
Far. Is. Faeroe Islands
Fiji Fiji
Fin. Finland
Fl.-U.S. Florida, U.S.
Fr. France
F.R.G. Federal Republic of Germany
Fr. Gui. French Guiana
Fr. Poly. French Polynesia
F.S.M. Federated States of Micronesia
Ga.-U.S. Georgia, U.S.
Gabon Gabon
Gam. Gambia
G.D.R. German Democratic Republic
Geo.-U.S.S.R. Georgian S.S.R., U.S.S.R.
Ghana Ghana
Gib. Gibraltar
Grc. Greece
Gren. Grenada
Grld. Greenland
Guad. Guadeloupe
Guam Guam
Guat. Guatemala
Gui. Guinea
Gui. Bis. Guinea Bissau
Guy. Guyana
Haiti Haiti
Hi.-U.S. Hawaii, U.S.
H.K. Hong Kong
Hond. Honduras
Hun. Hungary
Ia.-U.S. Iowa, U.S.
Id.-U.S. Idaho, U.S.
Il.-U.S. Illinois, U.S.
In.-U.S. Indiana, U.S.
India India
Indon. Indonesia
I. of M. Isle of Man
Iran Iran
Iraq Iraq
Ire. Ireland
Isr. Israel
It. Italy
Jam. Jamaica
Jap. Japan
Jor. Jordan
Kam. Kampuchea

Kaz.-U.S.S.R. Kazakh S.S.R., U.S.S.R.
Kenya Kenya
Ker. Is. Kermandec Islands
Kir. Kiribati
Kirg.-U.S.S.R. Kirghiz S.S.R., U.S.S.R.
Ks.-U.S. Kansas, U.S.
Kuw. Kuwait
Ky.-U.S. Kentucky, U.S.
La.-U.S. Louisiana, U.S.
Laos Laos
Lat.-U.S.S.R. Latvian S.S.R., U.S.S.R.
Lbr. Liberia
Leb. Lebanon
Les. Lesotho
Lib. Libya
Liech. Liechtenstein
Lith.-U.S.S.R. Lithuanian S.S.R., U.S.S.R.
Lux. Luxembourg
Ma.-U.S. Massachusetts, U.S.
Mac. Macao
Mad. Madagascar
Mala. Malaysia
Mald. Maldives
Mali Mali
Malta Malta
Man.-Can. Manitoba, Canada
Mar. Is. Marshall Islands
Mart. Martinique
Maur. Mauritius
May. Mayotte
Mco. Monaco
Md.-U.S. Maryland, U.S.
Me.-U.S. Maine, U.S.
Mex. Mexico
Mi.-U.S. Michigan, U.S.
Mid. Is. Midway Islands
Mn.-U.S. Minnesota, U.S.
Mo.-U.S. Missouri, U.S.
Mold.-U.S.S.R. Moldavian S.S.R., U.S.S.R.
Mong. Mongolia
Mont. Montserrat
Mor. Morocco
Moz. Mozambique
Ms.-U.S. Mississippi, U.S.
Mt.-U.S. Montana, U.S.
Mtna. Mauritania
Mwi. Malawi
Nam. Namibia
N. Amer. North America
Nauru Nauru
N.B.-Can. New Brunswick, Canada
Nb.-U.S. Nebraska, U.S.
N.C.-U.S. North Carolina, U.S.
N. Cal. New Caledonia
N.D.-U.S. North Dakota, U.S.
Nep. Nepal
Neth. Netherlands
Neth. Ant. Netherlands Antilles
Newf.-Can. Newfoundland, Canada
N.H.-U.S. New Hampshire, U.S.

Nic. Nicaragua
Nig. Nigeria
Niger Niger
N. Ire.-U.K. Northern Ireland, U.K.
N.J.-U.S. New Jersey, U.S.
N. Kor. North Korea
N.M.-U.S. New Mexico, U.S.
N.M. Is. Northern Mariana Islands
Nor. Norway
Nor. I. Norfolk Island
N.S.-Can. Nova Scotia, Canada
Nv.-U.S. Nevada, U.S.
N.W.T.-Can. Northwest Territories, Canada
N.Y.-U.S. New York, U.S.
N.Z. New Zealand
Ocn. Oceania
Oh.-U.S. Ohio, U.S.
Ok.-U.S. Oklahoma, U.S.
Oman Oman
Ont.-Can. Ontario, Canada
Or.-U.S. Oregon, U.S.
Pa.-U.S. Pennsylvania, U.S.
Pak. Pakistan
Pal. Palau
Pan. Panama
Pap. N. Gui. Papua New Guinea
Par. Paraguay
Pas. Pascua
P.D.R.Y. People's Democratic Republic of Yemen
P.E.I.-Can. Prince Edward Island, Canada
Peru Peru
Phil. Philippines
Pit. Pitcairn
Pol. Poland
Port. Portugal
P.R. Puerto Rico
Qatar Qatar
Que.-Can. Quebec, Canada
Reu. Reunion
R.I.-U.S. Rhode Island, U.S.
Rom. Romania
R.S.F.S.R.- Russian U.S.S.R. Soviet Federated Socialist Republic, U.S.S.R.
Rwn. Rwanda
S. Afr. South Africa
S. Amer. South America
Sao T.P. Sao Tome and Principe
Sask.-Can. Saskatchewan, Canada
Sau. Ar. Saudi Arabia
S.C.-U.S. South Carolina, U.S.
Scot.-U.K. Scotland, U.K.
S.D.-U.S. South Dakota, U.S.
Sen. Senegal
Sey. Seychelles
Sing. Singapore
S. Kor. South Korea
S.L. Sierra Leone
S. Lan. Sri Lanka
S.M. San Marino
S.N.A. Spanish North Africa

Sol. Is. Solomon Islands
Som. Somalia
Sp. Spain
St. C.N. Saint Christopher-Nevis
St. Hel. Saint Helena
St. Luc. Saint Lucia
St. P.M. Saint Pierre and Miquelon
St. Vin. Saint Vincent
Sud. Sudan
Sur. Suriname
Sval. Svalbard
Swe. Sweden
Switz. Switzerland
Syr. Syria
Tad.-U.S.S.R. Tadzhik S.S.R., U.S.S.R.
Tai. Taiwan
Tan. Tanzania
T.C. Is. Turks and Caicos Islands
Thai. Thailand
Tn.-U.S. Tennessee, U.S.
Togo Togo
Ton. Tonga
Trin. Trinidad and Tobago
T.T.P.I. Trust Territory of the Pacific Islands
Tun. Tunisia
Tur. Turkey
Tur.-U.S.S.R. Turkman S.S.R., U.S.S.R.
Tuv. Tuvalu
Tx.-U.S. Texas, U.S.
U.A.E. United Arab Emirates
Ug. Uganda
U.K. United Kingdom
Ukr.-U.S.S.R. Ukrainian S.S.R., U.S.S.R.
Ur. Uruguay
U.S. United States
U.S.S.R. Union of Soviet Socialist Republics
Ut.-U.S. Utah, U.S.
U.V. Upper Volta
Uzb.-U.S.S.R. Uzbek S.S.R., U.S.S.R.
Va.-U.S. Virginia, U.S.
Van. Vanuatu
V.C. Vatican City
Ven. Venezuela
Viet. Vietnam
V.I.U.S. Virgin Islands of the U.S.
Vt.-U.S. Vermont, U.S.
Wa.-U.S. Washington, U.S.
Wake Wake Island
Wales-U.K. Wales, U.K.
W.F. Wallis and Futuna
Wi.-U.S. Wisconsin, U.S.
W. Sah. Western Sahara
W. Sam. Western Samoa
W.V.-U.S. West Virginia, U.S.
Wy.-U.S. Wyoming, U.S.
Yem. Yemen
Yugo. Yugoslavia
Yuk.-Can. Yukon, Canada
Zaire Zaire
Zam. Zambia
Zimb. Zimbabwe

List of Symbols

Plains and Associated Features
Plain, Basin, Lowland
Delta
Salt Flat

Valleys and Depressions
Valley, Gorge, Ravine, Canyon
Cave, Crater, Quarry
Karst Features
Depression
Polder, Reclaimed Marsh

Vegetational Features
Desert, Dunes
Forest, Woods
Heath, Steppe, Tundra, Moor
Oasis

Political/Administrative Units
Independent Nation
State, Canton, Region
Province, Department, County, Territory, District
Municipality
Colony, Dependency, Administered Territory

Geographical Regions
Continent
Physical Region
Historical or Cultural Region

Mountain Features
Mount, Mountain, Peak
Volcano
Hill
Mountains, Mountain Range
Hills, Escarpment
Plateau, Highland, Upland
Pass, Gap

Coastal Features
Cape, Point
Coast, Beach
Cliff
Peninsula, Promontory
Isthmus
Sandbank, Tombolo, Sandbar

Islands Rocks, Reefs
Island
Atoll
Rock, Reef
Islands, Archipelago
Rocks, Reefs
Coral Reef

Hydrographic Features
Well, Spring
Geyser, Fumarole
River, Stream, Brook
Waterfall, Rapids, Cataract
River Mouth, Estuary
Lake
Salt Lake
Intermittent Lake, Dry Lake Bed
Reservoir, Artificial Lake
Swamp, Marsh, Pond
Irrigation Canal, Navigable Canal, Ditch, Aqueduct

Ice Features
Glacier, Snowfield
Ice Shelf, Pack Ice

Marine Features
Ocean
Sea
Gulf, Bay
Strait, Fjord, Sea Channel
Lagoon, Anchorage

Submarine Features
Bank, Shoal
Seamount
Rise, Plateau, Tablemount
Seamount Chain, Ridge
Platform, Shelf
Basin, Depression
Escarpment, Slope, Sea Scarp
Fracture
Trench, Abyss, Valley, Canyon

Other Features
National Park, Nature Reserve
Scenic Area, Point of Interest
Recreation Site, Sports Arena
Cave, Cavern
Historic Site, Memorial, Mausoleum, Museum
Ruins
Wall, Walls, Tower, Castle, Fortress
Church, Abbey, Cathedral, Sanctuary
Temple, Synagogue, Mosque
Research or Scientific Station
Airport, Heliport
Port, Dock
Lighthouse
Mine
Tunnel
Dam, Bridge

A

Å	7	Cc	67.53N	12.59 E
Aa [Eur.]	12	Ic	51.50N	6.25 E
Aa [Fr.]	11	Ic	51.01N	2.06 E
Aa [Fr.]	12	Dd	50.44N	2.18 E
Aa [F.R.G.]	12	Kb	52.07N	8.41 E
Aa [F.R.G.]	12	Jb	52.15N	7.18 E
Aachen	10	Cf	50.46N	6.06 E
Aalen	10	Gh	48.50N	10.06 E
A'ālī an Nīl	35	Ed	9.15N	33.00 E
Aalsmeer	12	Gb	52.15N	4.45 E
Aalst/Alost	11	Kd	50.56N	4.02 E
Aalten	12	Ic	51.55N	6.35 E
Aalter	12	Fc	51.05N	3.27 E
Äänekoski	7	Fe	62.36N	25.44 E
Aa of Weerijs	12	Gc	51.35N	4.46 E
Aar	12	Kd	50.23N	8.00 E
Aarau	14	Cc	47.25N	8.02 E
Aarbergen	12	Kd	50.13N	8.03 E
Aare	14	Cc	47.37N	8.13 E
Aargau	14	Cc	47.30N	8.10 E
Aarlen/Arlon	11	Le	49.41N	5.49 E
Aarschot	11	Kd	50.59N	4.50 E
Aat/Ath	11	Jd	50.38N	3.47 E
Aazanèn	13	Ii	35.06N	3.02W
Āb	24	Md	36.00N	48.05 E
Aba [Nig.]	31	Hh	5.07N	7.22 E
Aba [Zaire]	31	Hk	3.52N	30.14 E
Aba/Ngawa	27	He	32.55N	101.45 E
Abā ad Dūd	24	Ki	27.02N	44.04 E
Abā as Su'ūd	23	Ff	17.28N	44.06 E
Abacaxis, Rio-	54	Gd	3.54S	58.50W
Abaco Island	38	Lg	26.25N	77.10W
Abacou, Pointe l'-	49	Kd	18.03N	73.47W
Abadab. Jabal-	35	Fb	18.53N	35.59 E
Ābādān	22	Gf	30.10N	48.50 E
Ābādeh [Iran]	23	Hc	31.10N	52.37 E
Ābādeh [Iran]	24	Oh	29.08N	52.52 E
Abadiânia	55	Hc	16.06S	48.48W
Abadla	31	Ge	31.01N	2.43W
Abaeté	55	Jd	19.09S	45.27W
Abaeté, Rio-	55	Jd	18.02S	45.12W
Abaetetuba	54	Id	1.42S	48.54W
Abagnar Qi (Xilin Hot)	22	Ne	43.58N	116.08 E
Abag Qi (Xin Hot)	27	Jc	44.01N	114.59 E
Abai	55	Eh	26.01S	55.57W
Abaiang Atoll	57	Id	1.51N	172.58 E
Abaj	19	Hf	49.38N	72.50 E
Abaji	34	Gd	8.28N	6.57 E
Abajo Mountains	46	Kh	37.50N	109.25W
Abakaliki	34	Gd	6.20N	8.03 E
Abakan	20	Ef	53.43N	91.30 E
Abakan	22	Ld	53.43N	91.26 E
Abakwasimbo	36	Eb	0.36N	28.43 E
Abala [Con.]	36	Cc	1.21S	15.30 E
Abala [Niger]	34	Fc	14.56N	3.26 E
Abalak	34	Gb	15.27N	6.17 E
Aban	20	Ee	56.40N	96.10 E
Abancay	54	Df	13.35S	72.55W
Abancourt	12	De	49.42N	1.46 E
Abanga	36	Bb	0.13N	10.28 E
Abano Terme	14	Fe	45.21N	11.47 E
Ābār al Jidd	24	Hf	32.50N	39.50 E
Abarqū	23	Hc	31.08N	53.17 E
Abarqu, Kavīr-e-	24	Og	31.00N	53.50 E
Abashiri	27	Pc	44.01N	144.17 E
Abashiri-Gawa	29a	Db	43.56N	144.09 E
Abashiri-Ko	29a	Da	44.00N	144.10 E
Abashiri-Wan	29a	Da	44.00N	144.35 E
Abasolo	48	Je	24.04N	98.22W
Abatski	19	Hd	56.18N	70.28 E
Abau	60	Dj	10.11S	148.42 E
Abava	7	Eh	57.06N	21.54 E
Abay=Blue Nile (EN)	30	Kg	15.38N	32.31 E
Abaya, Lake-	30	Kh	6.20N	37.55 E
Abaza	20	Ef	52.39N	90.06 E
Abbadia San Salvatore	14	Fh	42.53N	11.41 E
Abbah Quşūr	14	Co	35.57N	8.50 E
Āb Bārīk	24	Oh	29.45N	52.37 E
'Abbāsābād	24	Qd	36.20N	56.25 E
Abbekås	8	Ei	55.24N	13.36 E
Abberton Reservoir	12	Cc	51.50N	0.55 E
Abbeville [Fr.]	11	Hd	50.06N	1.50 E
Abbeville [La.-U.S.]	45	Jl	29.58N	92.08W
Abbeville [S.C.-U.S.]	44	Fh	34.10N	82.23W
Abbey	46	Ka	50.43N	108.45W
Abbeyfeale/Mainistir na Féile	9	Di	52.24N	9.18W
Abbiategrasso	14	Ce	45.24N	8.54 E
Abbot, Mount-	59	Jd	20.03S	147.45 E
Abbot Ice Shelf	66	Pf	72.45S	96.00W
'Abd Al 'Azīz, Jabal-	24	Id	36.25N	40.20 E
'Abd al Kurī	21	Hh	12.12N	52.13 E
Ābdānān	24	Lf	32.57N	47.26 E
Abdul Ghadir	35	Gc	10.42N	42.59 E
Abdulino	19	Fe	53.42N	53.38 E
Abe, Lake-	35	Gc	11.10N	41.45 E
Abéché	31	Jg	13.49N	20.49 E
Abeek	12	Hc	51.15N	6.00 E
Abe-Gawa	29	Fd	34.55N	138.22 E
Abeløya	41	Pc	79.00N	30.15 E
Abelvær	7	Cd	64.44N	11.11 E
Abemama Atoll	57	Id	0.21N	173.51 E
Abenab	37	Bc	19.12S	18.06 E
Abengourou	34	Ed	6.35N	3.25W
Abengourou	31	Gh	6.44N	3.29W
Åbenrå	7	Bi	55.02N	9.26 E
Åbenrå Fjord	8	Ci	55.05N	9.35 E
Abeokuta	31	Hh	7.09N	3.21 E
Āb-e-Pany	23	If	37.06N	68.20 E
Aberayron	9	Ii	52.15N	4.15W
Aberdare Range	30	Ki	0.25S	36.38 E
Aberdeen [Id.-U.S.]	46	Ie	42.57N	112.50W
Aberdeen [Md.-U.S.]	44	If	39.30N	76.14W
Aberdeen [Ms.-U.S.]	45	Lj	33.49N	88.33W
Aberdeen [N.C.-U.S.]	44	Hh	35.08N	79.26W
Aberdeen [S.Afr.]	37	Cf	32.29S	24.03 E
Aberdeen [Scot.-U.K.]	6	Fd	57.10N	2.04W
Aberdeen [S.D.-U.S.]	39	Je	45.28N	98.29W
Aberdeen [Wa.-U.S.]	43	Cb	46.59N	123.50W
Aberdeen Lake	42	Hd	64.28N	99.00W
Abergavenny	9	Kj	51.50N	3.00W
Aberystwyth	9	Ii	52.25N	4.05W
Abetone	14	Ef	44.08N	10.40 E
Abez	19	Gb	66.32N	61.46 E
Abhā	22	Gh	18.13N	42.30 E
Abhainn an Chláir/Clare	9	Dh	53.20N	9.03W
Abhainn an Lagáin/Lagan	9	Hg	54.37N	5.53W
Abhainn na Bandan/Bandon	9	Ej	51.40N	8.30W
Abhainn na Deirge/Derg	9	Fg	54.40N	7.25W
Abhar	24	Md	36.02N	49.45 E
Abhar	23	Gb	36.09N	49.13 E
Abhazskaja ASSR	19	Eg	43.00N	41.10 E
Abibe, Serrania de-	54	Cb	8.00N	76.30W
Abidjan	31	Gh	5.19N	4.02W
Abidjan	34	Ed	5.30N	4.30W
Abilene [Ks.-U.S.]	45	Hg	38.55N	97.13W
Abilene [Tx.-U.S.]	39	Jf	32.27N	99.44W
Abingdon	9	Lj	51.41N	1.17W
Abinsk	16	Kg	44.52N	38.10 E
Abiquiu	45	Ch	36.12N	106.19W
Abiquiu Reservoir	45	Ch	36.18N	106.32W
Abisko	7	Eb	68.20N	18.51 E
Abitibi	42	Jf	51.04N	80.55W
Abitibi, Lake-	38	Le	48.42N	79.45W
Abiy Adi	35	Fc	13.37N	39.01 E
Abiyata, Lake-	35	Fd	7.38N	38.36 E
Abja-Paluoja	8	Kf	58.02N	25.14 E
Abnūb	33	Fd	27.16N	31.09 E
Åbo/Turku	6	Ic	60.27N	22.17 E
Abo, Massif d'-	35	Ba	21.41N	16.08 E
Abóboras, Serra das-	55	Jc	16.12S	44.35W
Abodo	35	Ed	7.50N	34.25 E
Aboisso	34	Ed	5.28N	3.02W
Aboisso	34	Ed	5.28N	3.12W
Abomey	31	Hh	7.11N	1.59 E
Abong Mbang	34	He	3.59N	13.11 E
Abony	10	Pi	47.11N	20.00 E
Aborigen, Pik-	20	Jd	62.05N	149.10 E
Aborlar	26	Ge	9.26N	118.33 E
Aborrebierg	8	Ej	54.59N	12.32 E
Abou Deïa	35	Bc	11.27N	19.17 E
Abou Goulem	35	Cc	13.37N	21.38 E
Abovjan	16	Ni	40.14N	44.37 E
Abrād, Wādī-	23	Gf	15.51N	46.05 E
Abraham's Bay	49	Kb	22.21N	72.55W
Abramovski Bereg	7	Kc	66.25N	43.05 E
Abrántes	13	De	39.28N	8.12W
Abra Pampa	56	Gb	22.43S	65.42W
Abrego	49	Ki	8.04N	73.14W
Abreojos, Punta-	47	Bc	26.42N	113.35W
'Abrī	35	Ea	20.48N	30.20 E
Abrolhos, Arquipélago dos-	54	Kg	18.00S	38.40W
Abrud	15	Gc	46.16N	23.04 E
Abruka, Ostrov-/Abruka Saar	8	Jf	58.08N	22.25 E
Abruka Saar/Abruka, Ostrov-	8	Jf	58.08N	22.25 E
Abruzzi	14	Hh	42.20N	13.45 E
Absaroka Range	43	Fc	44.45N	109.50W
Abtenau	14	Hc	47.33N	13.21 E
Abū, Ḩād, Wādī-	24	Ei	27.46N	33.30 E
Abū ad Duhūr	24	Ge	35.44N	37.02 E
Abū 'Alī	24	Mi	27.20N	49.33 E
Abū al Khaşīb	24	Lg	30.27N	47.59 E
Abū an Na'am	24	Hj	25.14N	38.49 E
Abū 'Arīsh	23	Ff	16.58N	42.50 E
Abū Ballaş	33	Ee	24.26N	27.39 E
Abū Daghmah	24	Hd	36.25N	38.15 E
Abū Darbah	33	Fd	28.29N	33.20 E
Abu Dhabi (EN)=Abū Ẓaby	22	Hg	24.28N	54.22 E
Abū Ḩadrīyah	24	Mi	27.20N	48.58 E
Abū Ḩamad	31	Kg	19.32N	33.19 E
Abū Ḩammād	24	Dg	30.32N	31.40 E
Abū Ḩarbah, Jabal-	24	Ei	27.17N	33.13 E
Abū Ḩashā'ifah, Khalīj-	24	Bg	31.16N	27.25 E
Abuja	31	Hh	9.10N	7.11 E
Abu Jābirah	35	Dc	11.04N	26.51 E
Abū Jifān	24	Lj	24.31N	47.43 E
Abū Kabīr	24	Dg	30.44N	31.40 E
Abū Kamāl	23	Fc	34.27N	40.55 E
Abukuma-Gawa	29	Gb	38.06N	140.52 E
Abukuma-Sanchi	29	Gc	37.20N	140.45 E
Abū Latt	33	Hf	19.58N	40.08 E
Abū Libdah, Khashm-	33	Ie	22.58N	46.13 E
Abū Maţāriq	35	Dc	10.58N	26.17 E
Abu Mendi	35	Fc	11.47N	35.42 E
Abumonbazi	36	Db	3.42N	22.10 E
Abū Muḩarrik, Ghurd-	33	Ed	27.00N	30.00 E
Abū Musā, Jazīreh-ye-	23	Id	25.52N	55.03 E
Abunā	53	Jf	9.42S	65.23W
Abuná, Rio-	52	Jf	9.41S	65.23W
Abune Yosef	35	Fc	12.09N	39.12 E
Abū Qīr	24	Dg	31.19N	30.04 E
Abū Qīr, Khalīj-	24	Dg	31.20N	30.15 E
Abū Qumayyis, Ra's-	24	Nj	24.34N	51.30 E
Abu Road	25	Ed	24.29N	72.47 E
Abū Sawmah, Ra's-	24	Ei	26.51N	33.59 E
Abū Shanab	35	Dc	13.57N	27.47 E
Abu Simbel (EN)=Abū Sumbul	33	Fe	22.22N	31.38 E
Abū Şukhayr	24	Kg	31.52N	44.27 E
Abū Sumbul=Abu Simbel (EN)	33	Fe	22.22N	31.38 E
Abuta	28	Pc	42.31N	140.46 E
Abut Head	62	De	43.06S	170.15 E
Abū Tij	33	Fd	27.02N	31.19 E
Abū Ţurţūr, Jabal-	24	Cj	25.20N	30.00 E
Abū'Urūq	35	Eb	15.54N	30.27 E
Abuyemeda	35	Fc	10.38N	39.43 E
Abū Zabad	35	Dc	12.21N	29.15 E
Abū Ẓaby=Abu Dhabi (EN)	22	Hg	24.28N	54.22 E
Abū Zanīmah	33	Fd	29.03N	33.06 E
Abwong	35	Ed	9.07N	32.12 E
Åby	8	Gf	58.40N	16.11 E
Abyaḑ	35	Dc	13.46N	26.28 E
Abyaḑ, Al Baḩr al-=White Nile (EN)	30	Kg	15.38N	32.31 E
Abyaḑ, Al Baḩr al-=White Nile (EN)	35	Ec	12.40N	32.30 E
Abyaḑ, Ar Ra's al-	23	Ee	23.32N	38.32 E
Abyaḑ, Jabal-	35	Db	18.55N	28.40 E
Abyaḑ, Ra's al-=Blanc, Cape- (EN)	30	He	37.20N	9.50 E
Abyār Alī	24	Hj	24.25N	39.33 E
Abyār ash Shuwayrif	33	Bd	29.59N	14.16 E
Åbybro	7	Bh	57.09N	9.45 E
Abydos	33	Fd	26.11N	31.55 E
Abyei	35	Dd	9.36N	28.26 E
Ābyek	24	Nd	36.02N	50.31 E
Abymes	51e	Ab	16.16N	61.31W
Acacías	54	Dc	3.59N	73.47W
Academy Gletscher	41	Ib	81.45N	33.35W
Acadie	38	Me	46.00N	65.00W
Acaill/Achill	9	Dh	54.00N	10.00W
Acajutla	49	Cg	13.36N	89.50W
Acalayong	34	Ge	1.05N	9.40 E
Acámbaro	47	Dd	20.02N	100.44W
Acandí	54	Cb	8.31N	77.17W
Acaponeta	47	Cd	22.30N	105.22W
Acaponeta, Río-	48	Gf	22.20N	105.37W
Acapulco de Juárez	39	Jh	16.51N	99.55W
Acará	54	Id	1.57S	48.11W
Acarai, Serra-	54	Gc	1.50N	57.40W
Acaraú	54	Jd	2.53S	40.07W
Acaray, Río-	55	Eg	25.29S	54.42W
Acari, Rio- [Braz.]	54	Ge	5.18S	59.42W
Acari, Rio- [Braz.]	55	Jb	16.00S	45.03W
Acarigua	54	Eb	9.33N	69.12W
Acatenango, Volcán-	38	Jh	14.30N	91.40W
Acatlán de Osorio	48	Jh	18.12N	98.03W
Acayucan	47	Fe	17.57N	94.55W
Accéglio	14	Af	44.28N	7.00 E
Aččitau, Gora-	18	Cc	42.07N	60.31 E
Accomac	44	Jg	37.43N	75.40W
Accra	31	Gh	5.33N	0.13W
Acebal	55	Bk	33.14S	60.50W
Acebuches	48	Hc	28.15N	102.43W
Aceguá [Braz.]	55	Ej	31.52S	54.09W
Aceguá [Ur.]	55	Ej	31.52S	54.12W
Aceh	26	Cf	4.10N	96.50 E
Acerenza	14	Jj	40.48N	15.56 E
Acerra	14	Ij	40.57N	14.22 E
Achacachi	54	Eg	16.03S	68.43W
Achaguas	54	Eb	7.46N	68.14W
Achaïf, 'Erg-	34	Ea	20.49N	4.34W
Achao	56	Ff	42.28S	73.30W
Achegour	34	Hb	19.03N	11.53 E
Acheng	27	Mb	45.32N	126.56 E
Acheux-en-Amiénois	12	Ed	50.04N	2.32 E
Achiet-le-Grand	12	Ed	50.08N	2.47 E
Achill/Acaill	9	Dh	54.00N	10.00W
Achílleion	15	Cj	39.34N	19.55 E
Achill Head/Ceann Acla	9	Ch	53.59N	10.13W
Achim	10	Fc	53.02N	9.01 E
Achim	35	Bb	15.53N	19.31 E
Achterwasser	10	Jb	54.00N	13.57 E
Acı Gölü	24	Cd	37.50N	29.54 E
Ačinsk	22	Ld	56.17N	90.30 E
Acıpayam	24	Cd	37.25N	29.22 E
Acireale	14	Jm	37.37N	15.10 E
Acîş	15	Fb	47.32N	22.47 E
Ačisaj	18	Gc	43.33N	68.53 E
Ačit	17	Hh	56.48N	57.54 E
Ačit-Nur	27	Fb	49.30N	90.30 E
Acklins	38	Lg	22.25N	74.00W
Acklins, The Bight of-	49	Jb	22.30N	74.15W
Acle	12	Db	52.38N	1.33 E
Acobamba	54	Df	12.48S	74.34W
Acolin	11	Jh	46.49N	3.23 E
Aconcagua	56	Fd	32.15S	70.50W
Aconcagua, Cerro-	52	Ji	32.39S	70.00W
Açor, Serra de-	13	Ed	40.13N	7.48W
Açores=Azores (EN)	31	Ee	38.30N	28.00W
Açores, Arquipélago dos-=Azores (EN)	30	Ee	38.30N	28.00W
Acorizal	55	Db	15.12S	56.22W
Acoyapa	49	Eh	11.58N	85.10W
Acquapendente	14	Fh	42.44N	11.52 E
Acquasanta Terme	14	Hh	42.46N	13.24 E
Acquasparta	14	Gh	42.41N	12.33 E
Acquaviva delle Fonti	14	Kj	40.54N	16.50 E
Acqui Terme	14	Cf	44.41N	8.28 E
Acraman, Lake-	59	Hf	32.05S	135.25 E
Acre	54	Ee	9.00S	70.00W
Acre, Rio-	52	Jf	8.45S	67.22W
Acri	14	Kk	39.29N	16.23 E
Actéon, Groupe-	57	Ng	21.20S	136.30W
Actopan	48	Jg	20.16N	98.56W
Açu	54	Ke	5.34S	36.54W
Acuña	55	Di	29.55S	57.58W
Ada [Ghana]	34	Fd	5.47N	0.38 E
Ada [Ok.-U.S.]	43	He	34.46N	96.41W
Ada [Yugo.]	15	Dd	45.48N	20.08 E
Adaba	35	Fd	7.03N	39.31 E
'Adād	35	Hb	8.23N	46.48 E
'Adādle	35	Gd	9.45N	44.41 E
Adair, Bahía-	48	Cb	31.30N	113.50W
Adair, Cape -	42	Kb	71.31N	71.24W
Adaja	13	Hc	41.32N	4.52W
Adak	40a	Cb	51.45N	176.40W
Adalar	15	Mi	40.52N	29.07 E
'Adale	35	He	2.46N	46.20 E
Ådalen	8	Ga	63.20N	17.30 E
Adalselv	8	Dd	60.04N	10.11 E
Adam, Mount-	56	Hh	51.34S	60.04W
Adamantina	55	Ge	21.42S	51.04W
Adamaoua=Adamawa (EN)	30	Ih	7.00N	15.00 E
Adamawa (EN)=Adamaoua	30	Ih	7.00N	15.00 E
Adamello	14	Ed	46.09N	10.30 E
Adamovka	16	Ud	51.32N	59.59 E
Adams	45	Le	43.58N	89.49W
Adams, Mount-	43	Cb	46.12N	121.28W
Adams Lake	46	Fa	51.13N	119.33W
Adams River	42	Ff	50.54N	119.33W
Adam's Rock	64q	Ab	25.04S	130.05W
Adamstown	58	Ng	25.04S	130.05W
Adamuz	13	Hf	38.02N	4.31W
Adana	22	Ff	37.01N	35.18 E
Adapazarı	24	Db	40.46N	30.24 E
Adarama	35	Eb	17.05N	34.54 E
Adarān, Jabal-	33	Ig	13.46N	45.08 E
Adare, Cape-	66	Kf	71.17S	170.14 E
Adavale	59	Ie	25.55S	144.36 E
Adda [It.]	5	Gf	45.08N	9.53 E
Adda [Sud.]	35	Cd	9.51N	24.50 E
Aḑ Ḑab'ah	33	Ec	31.02N	28.26 E
Ad Dabbah	35	Eb	18.03N	30.57 E
Ad Dafinah	33	He	23.18N	41.58 E
Aḑ Ḑafrah	24	Ok	23.25N	53.25 E
Ad Dahnā'	21	Gg	24.30N	48.10 E
Addala-Šuhgelmeer, Gora-	16	Oh	42.20N	46.15 E
Aḑ Ḑālī'	33	Hg	13.42N	44.44 E
Ad Damazin	35	Ec	11.49N	34.23 E
Ad 'Dāmir	35	Eb	17.35N	33.58 E
Ad Dammām	22	Hg	26.26N	50.07 E
Ad Dār al Ḩamrā'	23	Ed	27.19N	37.44 E
Ad Dawādimī	23	Fe	24.28N	44.18 E
Ad Dawḩah=Doha (EN)	22	Hg	25.17N	51.32 E
Ad Dawr	24	Je	34.27N	43.47 E
Ad Dayr	33	Fd	25.20N	32.35 E
Ad Dibdibah	24	Lh	28.00N	46.30 E
Aḑ Ḑiffah	33	Ec	30.30N	25.30 E
Ad Dikākah	35	Ib	19.25N	51.30 E
Ad Dılam	23	Ge	23.59N	47.10 E
Ad Dindar	35	Ec	13.20N	34.05 E
Ad Dir'īyah	24	Lj	24.48N	46.32 E
Ad Dissān	33	Hf	16.56N	41.41 E
Addis Zemen	35	Fc	12.05N	37.44 E
Ad Dīwānīya	23	Fc	31.59N	44.56 E
Addu Atoll	21	Jj	0.25S	73.10 E
Ad Du'ayn	35	Dc	11.26N	26.09 E
Ad Duwayd	24	Jg	30.13N	42.18 E
Ad Duwaym	35	Ec	14.00N	32.19 E
Adel [Ga.-U.S.]	44	Fj	31.18N	83.25W
Adel [Or.-U.S.]	46	Fe	42.11N	119.54W
Adelaide [Austl.]	58	Eh	34.56S	138.36 E
Adelaide [Bah.]	44	Im	25.00N	77.31W
Adelaide [S.Afr.]	37	Df	32.42S	26.20 E
Adelaide Island	66	Qe	67.15S	68.30W
Adelaide Peninsula	42	Hc	68.05N	97.50W
Adelaide River	58	Ef	13.15S	131.06 E
Adelaye	35	Cd	7.07N	22.49 E
Adelboden	14	Bd	46.30N	7.33 E
Adèle Island	59	Ec	15.30S	123.10 E
Adélie, Terre-	66	Ie	67.00S	139.00 E
Ademuz	13	Kd	40.04N	1.17W
Aden (EN)=Baladiyat 'Adan	22	Gh	12.46N	45.01 E
Aden, Gulf of-	30	Lg	12.00N	48.00 E
Aden, Gulf of- (EN)='Admēd, Badyarada-	30	Lg	12.00N	48.00 E
Adenau	12	Id	50.23N	6.56 E
Ader	30	Hg	14.10N	5.05 E
Aderbissinat	34	Gb	15.37N	7.52 E
Adhan, Jabal-	24	Qj	25.27N	56.13 E
Adh Dhahībāt	32	Jc	32.01N	10.42 E
Adh Dhayd	24	Pj	25.17N	55.53 E
Adhélfi	15	Gj	39.08N	23.59 E
Adhelfoí	15	Jm	36.25N	26.37 E
'Adhırīyāt, Jıbāl- al-	24	Gg	30.25N	36.48 E
Adi, Pulau-	26	Jg	4.18S	133.26 E
Adiaké	34	Ed	5.16N	3.17W
Adi Arkay	35	Fc	13.31N	38.00 E
Adícora	54	Ea	11.57N	69.48W
Adi Dairo	35	Fc	14.21N	38.12 E
Adigala	35	Gc	10.24N	42.18 E
Adige/Etsch	5	Hf	45.10N	12.20 E
Adigrat	35	Fc	14.16N	39.28 E
Adi Keyeh	35	Fc	14.48N	39.23 E
Adi Kwala	35	Fc	14.37N	38.51 E
Ādilābād	25	Fe	19.40N	78.32 E
Adīrī	31	If	27.30N	13.16 E
Adirondack Mountains	38	Le	44.00N	74.00W
Adis Abeba	31	Kh	9.01N	38.46 E
Adis Alem	35	Fd	9.03N	38.24 E
Adi Ugri	35	Fc	14.53N	38.49 E
Adiyaman	23	Eb	37.46N	38.17 E
Adjud	15	Kc	46.06N	27.10 E
Adjuntas	51a	Bb	18.09N	66.43W
'Admēd, Badyarada-=Aden, Gulf of- (EN)	30	Lg	12.00N	48.00 E
Admer, Erg d'-	32	Ie	24.12N	9.10 E
Admiralty	40	Me	57.50N	134.30W
Admiralty Bay	51n	Ba	13.00N	61.16W
Admiralty Gulf	59	Fb	14.20S	125.50 E
Admiralty Inlet	42	Ib	72.30N	86.00W
Admiralty Islands	57	Fe	2.10S	147.00 E
Admiralty Mountains	66	Kf	71.45S	168.30 E
Admont	14	Ic	47.34N	14.27 E
Ado	34	Fd	6.36N	2.56 E
Ado Ekiti	34	Gd	7.38N	5.13 E
Adok	35	Ed	8.11N	30.19 E
Adolfo Gonzales Chaves	55	Bn	38.02S	60.06W
Adolfo López Mateos, Presa-	48	Fe	25.05N	107.20W
Adonara, Pulau-	26	Hh	8.20S	123.10 E
Ādoni	25	Fe	15.38N	77.17 E
Adra	13	Ih	36.44N	3.01W
Adrano	14	Im	37.40N	14.50 E
Adrar	30	Ff	20.30N	13.30W
Adrar	31	Gf	27.54N	0.17W
Adrar	30	Hf	25.12N	8.10 E
Adrar [Alg.]	32	Gd	27.00N	1.00W
Adrar [Mtna.]	32	Ee	21.00N	11.00W
Adré	35	Cc	13.28N	22.12 E
Adria	14	Ge	45.03N	12.03 E
Adrian	44	Ee	41.54N	84.02W
Adrianópolis	55	Hg	24.41S	48.50W
Adriatic, Deti-=Adriatic Sea (EN)	5	Hg	43.00N	16.00 E
Adriatico, Mar-=Adriatic Sea (EN)	5	Hg	43.00N	16.00 E
Adriatic Sea (EN)=Adriatic, Deti-	5	Hg	43.00N	16.00 E
Adriatic Sea (EN)=Adriatico, Mar-	5	Hg	43.00N	16.00 E
Adriatic Sea (EN)=Jadransko More	5	Hg	43.00N	16.00 E
Aduard	12	Ia	53.15N	6.25 E
Adula	14	Dd	46.30N	9.05 E
Adulis	35	Fb	15.15N	39.37 E
Adur	12	Bd	50.49N	0.16W
Adusa	36	Eb	1.23N	28.01 E
Adventure Bank (EN)	14	Gm	37.20N	12.10 E
Adwa	31	Kg	14.10N	38.55 E
Adyča	21	Pc	68.13N	135.03 E
Adygalah	20	Jd	62.57N	146.25 E
Adygejskaja Avt. Oblast	19	Eg	44.30N	40.05 E
Adžarskaja ASSR	19	Eg	41.40N	42.10 E
Adzopé	34	Ed	6.15N	3.45W
Adzopé	34	Ed	6.06N	3.52W
Adzva	17	Ic	66.36N	59.28 E
Aegean Sea (EN)=Aiyaíon Pélagos	5	Ih	39.00N	25.00 E
Aegean Sea (EN)=Ege Denizi	5	Ih	39.00N	25.00 E
Aegina (EN) = Aiyina	15	Gl	37.40N	23.30 E
Aegviidu	8	Ke	59.17N	25.37 E
Aeon Point	64g	Bb	1.46N	157.11W
Aerfort na Sionainne/Shannon	9	Ei	52.42N	8.57W
Ærø	8	Dj	54.55N	10.20 E
Ærøskøbing	8	Dj	54.53N	10.25 E
Aerzen	12	Lb	52.02N	9.16 E
Afafi, Massif d'-	34	Ha	22.15N	15.00 E
'Afak	24	Kf	32.04N	45.15 E
Afanasjevo	7	Mg	58.54N	53.16 E
Afareaitu	65e	Fc	17.33S	149.47W
Afars and Issas→Djibouti	31	Lg	11.30N	43.00 E
Aff	11	Dg	47.43N	2.?7W
Affollé	30	Fg	16.55N	10.25W
Affrica, Scoglio d'-	14	Eh	42.20N	10.05 E
Afghanistan	22	If	33.00N	65.00 E
Afgōye	35	He	2.09N	45.07 E
'Afīf	23	Fe	23.55N	42.56 E
Afikpo	34	Gd	5.53N	7.55 E
Afipski	16	Kg	44.52N	38.50 E
Aflou	32	Hc	34.07N	2.06 E
Afmadōw	35	Ge	0.29N	42.06 E
Afognak	40	Ie	58.15N	152.30W
Afonso Cláudio	54	Jh	20.05S	41.08W
Afon Teifi	9	Ii	52.06N	4.43W
Afon Tywi	9	Ij	51.40N	4.15W
Afragola	14	Ij	40.55N	14.18 E
Afrērā, Lake-	35	Gc	13.20N	41.03 E
Africa	30	Jh	10.00N	22.00 E
African Islands	30	Mi	4.53S	43.24 E
Afşin	24	Gc	38.36N	36.55 E
Afsluitdijk	11	La	53.00N	5.15 E
Afton	46	Je	42.44N	110.56W
Afuá	54	Hd	0.10S	50.23W
'Afula	24	Ff	32.36N	35.17 E
Afyonkarahisar	22	Ff	38.45N	30.40 E
Agadem	31	Ig	16.50N	13.17 E
Agadez	31	Hg	16.58N	7.59 E
Agadez	34	Hb	19.45N	10.15 E
Agadir	31	Ge	30.25N	9.37W
Agadir	32	Fc	30.00N	9.00W
Agadyr	19	Hf	48.17N	72.53 E
Agalega Islands	30	Mj	10.24S	56.30 E
Agalta, Sierra de-	47	Ge	15.00N	85.53W
Agan	19	Hc	61.23N	74.35 E
Agana	58	Fc	13.28N	144.45 E
Agano-Gawa	28	Of	37.57N	139.07 E
Aga Point	64c	Bb	13.14N	144.43 E
Agapovka	17	Ij	53.18N	59.10 E
Agaro	35	Fd	7.53N	36.36 E
Agartala	22	Lg	23.49N	91.16 E
Agassiz Pool	45	Ib	48.20N	95.58W
Agat	64c	Bb	13.23N	144.39 E
Agat Bay	64c	Bb	13.24N	144.39 E
Agats	58	Ee	5.33S	138.08 E
Agattu	40a	Ab	52.25N	173.35 E
Agawa Bay	44	Eb	47.22N	84.33W
Agawa Bay	44	Eb	47.20N	84.42W
Agboville	34	Ed	5.56N	4.13W
Agboville	34	Ed	6.00N	4.15W
Agdam	19	Eh	39.58N	46.57 E
Agdaš	16	Oi	40.38N	47.29 E
Agde	11	Jk	43.19N	3.28 E
Agde, Cap d'-	11	Jk	43.16N	3.30 E
Agder	8	Cf	58.25N	8.15 E
Agdz	32	Fc	30.27N	7.56W
Agdžabedi	16	Oi	40.03N	47.28 E
Agematsu	29	Ed	35.47N	137.41 E
Agen	11	Gj	44.12N	0.38 E
Ageo	29	Fd	35.58N	139.35 E
Agepsta, Gora-	16	Lh	43.32N	40.30 E
Ager	14	Hb	48.05N	13.51 E
Agere Mariam	35	Fd	5.39N	38.15 E
Agersø	8	Di	55.10N	11.10 E
Agger	12	Jd	50.48N	7.11 E
Āghā Jārī	23	Gc	30.42N	49.50 E
Aghireşu	15	Gc	46.53N	23.15 E
Agiabampo, Estero de-	48	Ed	26.15N	109.15W
Ağın	24	Hc	38.57N	38.43 E

Index Symbols

Independent Nation	Historical or Cultural Region	Pass, Gap	Depression	Coast, Beach	Rock, Reef	Waterfall Rapids	Canal	Lagoon	Escarpment, Sea Scarp	Historic Site	Port
State, Region	Mount, Mountain	Plain, Lowland	Polder	Cliff	Islands, Archipelago	River Mouth, Estuary	Glacier	Bank	Fracture	Ruins	Lighthouse
District, County	Volcano	Delta	Desert, Dunes	Peninsula	Rocks, Reefs	Lake	Ice Shelf, Pack Ice	Seamount	Trench, Abyss	Wall, Walls	Mine
Municipality	Hill	Salt Flat	Forest, Woods	Isthmus	Coral Reef	Salt Lake	Ocean	Tablemount	National Park, Reserve	Church, Abbey	Tunnel
Colony, Dependency	Mountains, Mountain Range	Valley, Canyon	Heath, Steppe	Sandbank	Well, Spring	Intermittent Lake	Sea	Ridge	Point of Interest	Temple	Dam, Bridge
Continent	Hills, Escarpment	Crater, Cave	Oasis	Island	Geyser	Reservoir	Gulf, Bay	Shelf	Recreation Site	Scientific Station	
Physical Region	Plateau, Upland	Karst Features	Cape, Point	Atoll	River, Stream	Swamp, Pond	Strait, Fjord	Basin	Cave, Cavern	Airport	

Index Symbols

- [▫] Independent Nation
- [▫] State, Region
- [▫] District, County
- [▫] Municipality
- [▫] Colony, Dependency
- [▫] Continent
- [▫] Physical Region
- [▫] Historical or Cultural Region
- [▲] Mount, Mountain
- [▲] Volcano
- [▲] Hill
- [▲] Mountains, Mountain Range
- [▲] Hills, Escarpment
- [▲] Plateau, Upland
- [▭] Pass, Gap
- [▭] Plain, Lowland
- [▭] Delta
- [▭] Salt Flat
- [▭] Valley, Canyon
- [▭] Crater, Cave
- [▭] Karst Features
- [▭] Depression
- [▭] Polder
- [▭] Desert, Dunes
- [▭] Forest, Woods
- [▭] Heath, Steppe
- [▭] Oasis
- [▲] Cape, Point
- [▭] Coast, Beach
- [▭] Cliff
- [▭] Peninsula
- [▭] Isthmus
- [▭] Sandbank
- [+] Island
- [◎] Atoll
- [S] River, Stream
- [▭] Rock, Reef
- [+] Islands, Archipelago
- [▭] River Mouth, Estuary
- [▭] Lake
- [▭] Salt Lake
- [▭] Well, Spring
- [▭] Intermittent Lake
- [▭] Reservoir
- [▭] Swamp, Pond
- [▭] Waterfall Rapids
- [▭] Glacier
- [▭] Ice Shelf, Pack Ice
- [▭] Ocean
- [▭] Sea
- [▭] Ridge
- [▭] Shelf
- [▭] Basin
- [▭] Canal
- [▭] Lagoon
- [▭] Bank
- [▭] Fracture
- [▭] Trench, Abyss
- [▭] Tablemount
- [▭] Seamount
- [◀] Gulf, Bay
- [▭] Strait, Fjord
- [▭] Cave, Cavern
- [▭] Escarpment, Sea Scarp
- [▭] Ruins
- [▭] Wall, Walls
- [▭] National Park, Reserve
- [▭] Point of Interest
- [▭] Recreation Site
- [▭] Church, Abbey
- [▭] Temple
- [▭] Scientific Station
- [▭] Airport
- [▭] Historic Site
- [▭] Port
- [▭] Lighthouse
- [▭] Mine
- [▭] Tunnel
- [▭] Dam, Bridge

Al Baḩrayn=Bahrain (EN) [1] 22 Hg 26.00N 50.29 E
Albaida 13 Lf 38.51N 0.31W
Alba Iulia 15 Gc 46.04N 23.35 E
Albalate del Arzobispo 13 Lc 41.07N 0.31W
Al Balyanā 33 Fd 26.14N 32.00 E
Alban 11 Ik 43.54N 2.28 E
Albanel, Lac- 42 Kf 51.05N 73.05W
Albani, Colli- 14 Gi 41.45N 12.45 E
Albania (EN)=Shqiperia [1] 6 Hg 41.00N 20.00 E
Albano, Lago- 14 Gi 41.45N 12.40 E
Albano Laziale 14 Gi 41.44N 12.39 E
Albany 38 Kd 52.17N 81.31W
Albany [Austl.] 58 Ch 35.02S 117.53 E
Albany [Ga.-U.S.] 43 Ke 31.35N 84.10W
Albany [Ky.-U.S.] 44 Eg 36.42N 85.08W
Albany [N.Y.-U.S.] 39 Le 42.39N 73.45W
Albany [Or.-U.S.] 43 Cc 44.38N 123.06W
Alba Posse 55 Eh 27.33S 54.42W
Albarche 13 He 39.58N 4.46W
Albardón 56 Gd 31.26S 68.32W
Albarracín 13 Kd 40.25N 1.26W
Albarracín, Sierra de- 13 Kd 40.30N 1.30W
Al Başalīyah Qiblī 24 Ej 25.06N 32.47 E
Al Başrah [3] 24 Lg 30.30N 47.27 E
Al Başrah=Basra (EN) 22 Gf 30.30N 47.47 E
Al Baṭḩā' 24 Kg 31.07N 45.54 E
Al Bāṭın 24 Lh 29.00N 46.35 E
Al Bāṭinah 21 Hg 23.45N 57.20 E
Albatross Bank (EN) 40 Ie 56.10N 152.20W
Albatross Bay 59 Ib 12.45S 141.43 E
Albatross Plateau (EN) 3 Mi 10.00N 103.00W
Albatross Point 62 Fc 38.07S 174.40 E
Al Batrūn 24 Fe 34.15N 35.39 E
Al Bawīṭī 33 Ed 28.21N 28.52 E
Al Bayāḑ 21 Gg 22.00N 47.00 E
Al Bayḑā' [3] 33 Dc 32.00N 21.30 E
Al Bayḑā' 33 Cd 28.21N 18.58 E
Al Bayḑā' 31 Je 32.46N 21.43 E
Al Bayḑā' 33 Ig 13.58N 45.35 E
Albegna 14 Fh 42.30N 11.11 E
Albemarle 44 Gh 35.21N 80.12W
Albemarle Sound 43 Ld 36.03N 76.12W
Albenga 14 Cf 44.03N 8.13 E
Alberdi 56 Ic 26.10S 58.09W
Albères, Chaîne des- 11 Il 42.28N 2.56 E
Albères, Montes-/Les Alberes 11 Il 42.28N 2.56 E
Albergaria-a-Velha 13 Dd 40.42N 8.29W
Alberique 13 Le 39.07N 0.31W
Alberobello 14 Lj 40.47N 17.16 E
Albert 11 Id 50.00N 2.39 E
Albert, Canal-/Albert Kanaal =Albert Canal (EN) 11 Ld 50.39N 5.37 E
Albert, Lake- [Afr.] 30 Kh 1.40N 31.00 E
Albert, Lake- [Or.-U.S.] 46 Ee 42.38N 120.13W
Albert, Lake- (EN)=Mobuto Sese Seko, Lac- 30 Kh 1.40N 31.00 E
Alberta [3] 42 Gf 55.00N 115.00W
Albert Canal (EN)=Albert, Canal-/Albert Kanaal 11 Ld 50.39N 5.37 E
Albert Canal (EN)=Albert Kanaal/Albert, Canal- 11 Ld 50.39N 5.37 E
Albert Edward, Mount- 59 Ja 8.23S 147.27 E
Albert Edward Bay 42 Hc 69.35N 103.10W
Alberti 56 He 35.02S 60.16W
Albertirsa 10 Pi 47.15N 19.37 E
Albert Kanaal/Albert, Canal- =Albert Canal (EN) 11 Ld 50.39N 5.37 E
Albert Lea 43 Ic 43.39N 93.22W
Albert Nile 30 Kh 3.36N 32.02 E
Albertville [Al.-U.S.] 44 Dh 34.16N 86.12W
Albertville [Fr.] 11 Mi 45.41N 6.23 E
Albestroff 12 If 48.56N 6.51 E
Albi 11 Ik 43.56N 2.09 E
Albia 45 Jf 41.02N 92.48W
Al Bid' 24 Fh 28.28N 35.01 E
Albina 54 Hb 5.30N 54.03W
Albina, Ponta- 30 Ij 15.51S 11.44 E
Albino 14 De 45.46N 9.47 E
Albion [Mi.-U.S.] 44 Ed 42.15N 84.45W
Albion [Nb.-U.S.] 45 Hf 41.42N 98.00W
Albion [N.Y.-U.S.] 44 Hd 43.15N 78.12W
Al Biqa' 24 Ge 34.10N 36.10 E
Al Bi'r 23 Ed 28.51N 36.15 E
Al Bi'r al Jadīd 23 Ed 26.01N 38.29 E
Al Birk 23 Ff 18.13N 41.33 E
Albis 14 Cc 47.20N 8.30 E
Albo, Monte- 14 Dj 40.32N 9.35 E
Albocácer/Albocasser 13 Md 40.21N 0.02 E
Albocasser/Albocácer 13 Md 40.21N 0.02 E
Alborán, Isla de- 5 Fh 35.58N 3.02W
Alboran Basin (EN) 13 Ii 36.00N 4.00W
Ålborg 6 Gd 57.03N 9.56 E
Ålborg Bugt 7 Ch 56.45N 10.30 E
Alborz, Reshteh-ye Kūhhā-ye-=Elburz Mountains (EN) 21 Hf 36.00N 53.00 E
Albox 13 Jg 37.23N 2.08W
Albret, Pays d'- 11 Fj 44.10N 0.20W
Ālbū 'Alī 24 Je 34.49N 43.35 E
Albufeira 13 Dg 37.05N 8.15W
Albū Gharz, Sabkhat- 24 Ie 34.45N 41.15 E
Al Buheyrat [3] 35 Dd 7.00N 29.30 E
Al Bumbah 33 Dc 32.13N 23.00 E
Albuñol 13 Ih 36.47N 3.12W
Albuquerque [Braz.] 55 Dd 19.23S 57.26W
Albuquerque [N.M.-U.S.] 39 If 35.05N 106.40W
Albuquerque, Cayos de- 47 Hf 12.10N 81.50W
Al Burayj 24 Ge 34.15N 36.46 E
Al Buraymī 23 Ie 24.15N 55.45 E
Al Burmah 32 Ic 31.45N 9.02 E
Alburquerque 13 Fe 39.13N 7.00W
Albury [Austl.] 58 Fh 36.05S 146.55 E
Albury [N.Z.] 62 Df 44.14S 170.53 E
Al Buṭanah 30 Kg 15.00N 35.00 E
Al Buṭayn 24 Kj 25.52N 45.50 E
Alby 8 Fb 62.30N 15.28 E
Alcácer do Sal 13 Df 38.22N 8.30W
Alcáçovar 13 Df 38.25N 8.13W
Alcalá de Chivert 13 Md 40.18N 0.14 E
Alcalá de Guadaira 13 Gg 37.20N 5.50W
Alcalá de Henares 13 Id 40.29N 3.22W
Alcalá del Júcar 13 Ke 39.12N 1.26W
Alcalá de los Gazules 13 Gh 36.28N 5.44W
Alcalá del Río 13 Gg 37.31N 5.59W
Alcalá la Real 13 Ig 37.28N 3.56W
Alcamo 14 Gm 37.59N 12.58 E
Alcanandre 13 Mc 41.37N 0.12 E
Alcañices 13 Fc 41.42N 6.21W
Alcañiz 13 Lc 41.03N 0.08W
Alcántara 13 Fe 39.43N 6.53W
Alcântara 54 Jd 2.24S 44.24W
Alcantara 14 Jm 37.49N 15.16 E
Alcántara, Embalse de- 13 Fe 39.45N 6.48W
Alcantarilla 13 Kg 37.58N 1.13W
Alcaraz 13 Jf 38.40N 2.29W
Alcaraz, Sierra de- 13 Jf 38.35N 2.25W
Alcaudete 13 Hg 37.36N 4.05W
Alcázar de San Juan 13 Ie 39.24N 3.12W
Alcester 63a Ac 9.33S 152.25 E
Alcira/Alzira 13 Le 39.09N 0.26W
Alcobaça [Braz.] 54 Kg 17.30S 39.13W
Alcobaça [Port.] 13 De 39.33N 8.59W
Alcobendas 13 Id 40.32N 3.38W
Alcoi/Alcoy 13 Lf 38.42N 0.28W
Alcolea del Pinar 13 Jc 41.02N 2.28W
Alcorta 55 Bk 33.32S 61.07W
Alcoutim 13 Eg 37.28N 7.28W
Alcova 46 Le 42.37N 106.36W
Alcoy/Alcoi 13 Lf 38.42N 0.28W
Alcubierre, Sierra de- 13 Lc 41.44N 0.29W
Alcudia 13 Pe 39.52N 3.07 E
Alcúdia, Badia d'-/Alcudia, Bahía de- 13 Pe 39.48N 3.13 E
Alcudia, Bahía de-/Alcúdia, Badia d'- 13 Pe 39.48N 3.13 E
Alcudia, Sierra de- 13 Hf 38.35N 4.35W
Aldabra Group 37b Ab 9.25S 46.22 E
Aldabra Islands 30 Li 9.25S 46.22 E
Aldama [Mex.] 48 Jf 22.55N 98.04W
Aldama [Mex.] 47 Cc 28.51N 105.54W
Aldan 22 Od 58.37N 125.24 E
Aldan [R.S.F.S.R.] 20 Hd 63.20N 129.25 E
Aldan [U.S.S.R.] 21 Oc 63.28N 129.35 E
Aldan Plateau (EN)= Aldanskoje Nagorje 21 Od 57.30N 127.30 E
Aldanskoje Nagorje=Aldan Plateau (EN) 21 Od 57.30N 127.30 E
Aldarhan 27 Gb 47.42N 96.36 E
Alde 12 Db 52.10N 1.32 E
Aldeburgh 9 Oi 52.09N 1.35 E
Aldeia 55 Ed 18.12S 55.10W
Aldeia, Serra da- 55 Ic 17.00S 46.50W
Alderney 9 Kl 49.43N 2.12W
Aldershot 12 Bc 51.15N 0.46W
Alderson 46 Ja 50.18N 111.26W
Aledo 45 Kf 41.12N 90.45W
Aleg 31 Fg 17.03N 13.53W
Alegranza 32 Ed 29.23N 13.30W
Alegre 54 Jh 20.46S 41.32W
Alegre, Rio- 55 Cb 15.14S 59.58W
Alegrete 56 Ic 29.46S 55.46W
Alej 20 Df 52.50N 83.35 E
Alejandra 55 Ci 29.54S 59.50W
Alejandro Selkirk, Isla- 52 Hi 33.45S 80.46W
Alejsk 20 Df 52.28N 82.45 E
Aleksandrija 16 He 48.40N 33.07 E
Aleksandrov 19 Dd 56.25N 38.42 E
Aleksandrov Gaj 19 Ee 50.08N 48.32 E
Aleksandrovka 16 He 48.59N 32.13 E
Aleksandrovsk 17 Hg 59.10N 57.35 E
Aleksandrovskoje 16 Mg 44.39N 43.00 E
Aleksandrovsk-Sahalinsk 22 Qd 50.54N 142.10 E
Aleksandrów Kujawski 10 Od 52.52N 18.42 E
Aleksandrów Łódzki 10 Pe 51.49N 19.19 E
Aleksandry, Zemlja- 21 Ga 80.45N 46.00 E
Aleksejevka [Kaz.-U.S.S.R.] 19 If 48.26N 85.40 E
Aleksejevka [Kaz.-U.S.S.R.] 19 He 51.58N 70.59 E
Aleksejevka [Kaz.-U.S.S.R.] 17 Nj 53.31N 69.28 E
Aleksejevka [R.S.F.S.R.] 19 De 50.39N 38.42 E
Aleksejevsk 20 Fe 57.50N 108.23 E
Aleksejevskoje 7 Mi 55.19N 50.03 E
Aleksin 16 Jb 54.31N 37.07 E
Aleksinac 15 Ef 43.32N 21.43 E
Alem 56 Ic 27.31S 55.15W
Ålem 7 Dh 56.57N 16.23 E
Alem Maya 35 Gd 9.27N 41.58 E
Ålen 8 Db 62.51N 11.17 E
Alençon 11 Gf 48.26N 0.05 E
Alenquer 54 Hd 1.56S 54.46W
Alenuihaha Channel 60 Oc 20.26N 156.00W
Alépé 34 Ed 5.30N 3.39W
Aleppo (EN)=Ḩalab 22 Ff 36.12N 37.10 E
Aléria 11a Ba 42.06N 9.31 E
Aléria, Plaine d'- 11a Ba 42.05N 9.30 E
Alert 39 Ma 82.30N 62.00W
Alert Bay 46 Ba 50.35N 126.55W
Alès 11 Kj 44.08N 4.05 E
Aleşd 15 Fb 47.04N 22.25 E
Alessandria 14 Cf 44.54N 8.37 E
Ålestrup 8 Ch 56.42N 9.30 E
Ålesund 6 Gc 62.28N 6.09 E
Aleutian Basin (EN) 38 Ad 57.00N 177.00 E
Aleutian Islands 38 Bd 52.00N 176.00W
Aleutian Range 38 Dd 59.00N 155.00W
Aleutian Trench (EN) 3 Je 51.00N 179.00 E
Alexander, Cape- 60 Fi 6.35S 156.30 E
Alexander, Kap- 41 Ec 78.10N 72.45W
Alexander Archipelago 38 Fd 56.30N 134.00W
Alexanderbaai 37 Be 28.40S 16.30 E
Alexander City 43 Je 32.56N 85.57W
Alexander Island 66 Qe 71.00S 70.00W
Alexandra 61 Ci 45.15S 169.24 E
Alexandra Fiord 42 Ka 79.17N 75.00W
Alexandretta (EN)= İskenderun 22 Ff 36.37N 36.07 E
Alexandretta, Gulf of- (EN) =İskenderun Körfezi 23 Eb 36.30N 35.40 E
Alexándria 15 Fi 40.38N 22.27 E
Alexandria [Austl.] 59 Hc 19.05S 136.40 E
Alexandria [La.-U.S.] 39 Jf 31.18N 92.27W
Alexandria [Mn.-U.S.] 43 Hb 45.53N 95.22W
Alexandria [Rom.] 15 If 43.59N 25.20 E
Alexandria [S.Afr.] 37 Df 33.39S 26.24 E
Alexandria [Va.-U.S.] 44 If 38.49N 77.06W
Alexandria (EN)=Al Iskandarīyah [Eg.] 31 Je 31.12N 29.54 E
Alexandria Bay 44 Jc 44.20N 75.55W
Alexandrina, Lake- 59 Hg 35.25S 139.10 E
Alexandrita 54 Hg 19.42S 50.27W
Alexandroúpolis 6 Ig 40.51N 25.52 E
'Aleyak, Godār-e- 24 Qd 36.30N 57.45 E
Alf 10 Df 50.03N 7.07 E
Alfabia, Sierra de- 13 Oe 39.45N 2.48 E
Alfambra 13 Kd 40.21N 1.07W
Al Fardah 35 Hc 14.51N 48.26 E
Alfaro 13 Kb 42.11N 1.45W
Al Fāshir 31 Jg 13.38N 25.21 E
Al Fashn 33 Fd 28.49N 30.54 E
Alfatar 15 Kf 43.57N 27.17 E
Al Fathah 24 Je 35.04N 43.34 E
Al Fāw 23 Gd 29.58N 48.29 E
Al Fawwārah 24 Ji 26.03N 43.05 E
Al Fayyūm 31 Kf 29.19N 30.58 E
Alfbach 12 Jd 50.03N 7.08 E
Alfeld 10 Fe 51.59N 9.50 E
Alfenas 54 Ih 21.26S 45.57W
Al Fifi 35 Dc 10.03N 25.01 E
Alfiós 15 El 37.37N 21.27 E
Alföld 5 If 47.15N 20.25 E
Alfonsine 14 Gf 44.30N 12.03 E
Alford 12 Ca 53.15N 0.11 E
Ålfotbreen 8 Ac 61.45N 5.40 E
Alfreton 12 Aa 53.06N 1.23W
Alfta 7 Df 61.21N 16.05 E
Al Fuḩayḩīl 23 Gd 29.05N 48.08 E
Al Fuhūd 24 Lg 30.58N 46.43 E
Al Fujayrah 23 Id 25.06N 56.21 E
Al Fūlah 35 Dc 11.48N 28.24 E
Al Fuqahā' 33 Cd 27.50N 16.21 E
Al Furāt=Euphrates (EN) 21 Gf 31.00N 47.25 E
Al Fuwayriṭ 24 Ni 26.02N 51.22 E
Alga 19 Ff 49.55N 57.20 E
Algador 13 Ie 39.55N 3.53W
Al Gārah 24 Ih 29.52N 40.15 E
Algarås 8 Ff 58.48N 14.14 E
Ålgård 8 Af 58.46N 5.51 E
Algarrobo 49 Jh 10.12N 74.04W
Algarve 13 Dg 37.10N 8.15W
Algarve 5 Fh 37.10N 8.15W
Algeciras 6 Fh 36.08N 5.30W
Algeciras, Bahía de- 13 Gh 36.09N 5.25W
Algena 35 Fb 17.20N 38.34 E
Algeria (EN)=Al Jazā'ir [1] 31 Hf 28.00N 3.00 E
Algerian Basin (EN) 5 Gh 39.00N 5.00 E
Al Gharaq as Sulṭānī 24 Dh 29.08N 30.42 E
Al Gharbi 32 Jc 34.40N 11.13 E
Al Ghāṭ 24 Ki 26.00N 45.03 E
Al Ghaydah 23 Hf 16.12N 52.15 E
Alghero 14 Cj 40.33N 8.19 E
Alghero, Rada d'- 14 Cj 40.35N 8.20 E
Älghult 8 Fg 57.01N 15.34 E
Al Ghurāb 24 Dj 25.20N 30.20 E
Al Ghurayfah 24 Qk 23.59N 56.29 E
Al Ghurdaqah 33 Fd 27.14N 33.50 E
Algiers (EN)=Al Jazā'ir 31 He 36.47N 3.03 E
Algiers (EN)=Al Jazā'ir [3] 32 Hb 36.35N 3.00 E
Algoa Bay 30 Jl 33.50S 25.50 E
Algodoeiro, Serra do- 55 Jc 16.30S 44.45W
Algoma 45 Md 44.36N 87.27W
Algoma Uplands 44 Fb 47.00N 83.35W
Algona 45 Ie 43.04N 94.14W
Algonquin Park 44 Hc 45.27N 78.26W
Algrange 12 Ie 49.21N 6.03 E
Al Ḩabakah 24 Jh 29.51N 42.16 E
Al Ḩadd 23 Ie 22.29N 59.58 E
Al Ḩadīdah 35 Ia 21.31N 50.28 E
Al Ḩadīthah 23 Fc 34.07N 42.23 E
Al Ḩadithah 24 Gg 31.28N 37.08 E
Al Ḩaḑr 24 Je 35.35N 42.44 E
Al Haffah 24 Ge 35.35N 36.02 E
Al Ḩahjarah 23 Fc 30.25N 44.30 E
Al Ḩā'ır 24 Lj 24.23N 46.50 E
Al Ḩajar 35 Hb 16.08N 47.50 E
Al Hajar 23 Ie 23.15N 57.30 E
Al Halfāyah 24 Lg 31.49N 47.26 E
Alhama 13 Kb 42.11N 1.45W
Al Ḩamād 21 Ff 32.00N 39.30 E
Alhama de Granada 13 Ih 37.00N 3.59W
Alhama de Murcia 13 Kg 37.51N 1.25W
Alhamilla, Sierra- 13 Jh 36.58N 2.20W
Al Ḩammāh 32 Ic 33.54N 9.48 E
Al Ḩammām [Eg.] 24 Cg 30.50N 29.23 E
Al Ḩammām [Iraq] 24 Kg 31.08N 44.04 E
Al Ḩamrā 24 Pj 25.42N 55.47 E
Al Hanīyah 24 Kh 29.10N 45.50 E
Al Ḩarrah 24 Ch 28.20N 29.07 E
Al Ḩarrah 24 Hg 31.00N 38.40 E
Al Harūj al Aswad 30 If 27.00N 17.10 E
Al Ḩasā 24 Fg 30.49N 35.59 E
Al Hasā' 21 Gg 26.35N 48.10 E
Al Ḩasakah 23 Fb 36.29N 40.45 E
Al Ḩasan 24 Je 34.39N 43.43 E
Al Ḩasānī 24 Gj 24.58N 37.05 E
Alhaurín el Grande 13 Hh 36.38N 4.41W
Al Ḩawāmidīyah 24 Dh 29.54N 31.15 E
Al Ḩawātah 35 Ec 13.25N 34.38 E
Al Ḩawjā' 24 Hh 28.59N 38.34 E
Al Ḩawrah 35 Hc 13.49N 47.35 E
Al Hayy 23 Gc 32.10N 46.03 E
Al Ḩayz 33 Ed 28.02N 28.39 E
Al Hibāk 23 He 20.20N 53.10 E
Al Ḩijāz 21 Fg 24.30N 38.30 E
Al Hillah 33 Ie 23.50N 46.51 E
Al Ḩillah 23 Fc 32.29N 44.25 E
Al Ḩinākīyah 23 Fe 24.51N 40.31 E
Al Hindiyah 24 Kf 32.32N 44.13 E
Al Ḩınnāh 24 Mi 26.56N 48.45 E
Al Hirmil 24 Ge 34.23N 36.23 E
Al Hoceima 32 Gb 35.15N 3.55W
Al Hoceima [3] 32 Gb 35.00N 4.15W
Alhucemas, Peñón de- 13 Ii 35.13N 3.53W
Al Ḩudaydah 22 Gh 14.48N 42.57 E
Al Ḩufrah 33 Cd 29.30N 17.55 E
Al Hufrah 23 Ed 28.49N 38.15 E
Al Hufūf 22 Gg 25.22N 49.34 E
Al Hūj 24 Hh 29.00N 38.25 E
Al Ḩunayy 24 Mj 24.48N 48.45 E
Al Ḩuşayḩişah 35 Ec 14.44N 33.18 E
Al Ḩuwaimī 23 Fg 13.58N 47.40 E
Al Ḩuwayyiṭ 24 Ij 25.36N 40.23 E
Al Ḩyyānīyah 24 Jh 28.42N 42.18 E
'Alīābād [Iran] 23 Id 28.37N 55.51 E
'Alīābād [Iran] 24 Le 35.04N 46.58 E
'Alīābād [Iran] 24 Nd 36.37N 51.33 E
Aliābād 24 Pd 36.56N 54.50 E
Alīābād, Kūh-e- 23 Hc 34.13N 50.46 E
Aliaga 13 Ld 40.40N 0.42W
Aliağa 24 Bc 38.48N 26.59 E
Aliákmon 15 Fi 40.30N 22.40 E
'Alī al Gharbī 24 Lf 32.27N 46.41 E
'Alī ash Sharqī 24 Lf 32.07N 46.44 E
Ali-Bajramly 19 Eh 39.55N 48.57 E
Alibej, Ozero- 15 Nd 45.50N 30.00 E
Alibey Adasi 15 Jj 39.20N 26.38 E
Alibo 35 Fd 9.53N 37.05 E
Alibori 34 Fc 11.56N 3.17 E
Alibunar 15 Dd 45.04N 20.58 E
Alicante 6 Fh 38.21N 0.29W
Alicante [3] 13 Lf 38.30N 0.30W
Alicante, Golfo de- 13 Lf 38.20N 0.15W
Alice [S.Afr.] 37 Df 32.47S 26.50 E
Alice [Tx.-U.S.] 43 Hf 27.45N 98.04W
Alice, Punta- 14 Lk 39.12N 17.09 E
Alice Springs 58 Eg 23.42S 133.53 E
Aliceville 44 Ci 33.08N 88.09W
Alicudi 14 Il 38.30N 14.20 E
Alīgarh 22 Jg 28.02N 78.17 E
Alīgūdarz 24 Mf 33.24N 49.41 E
Alihe → Oroqen Zizhiqi 27 La 50.35N 123.42 E
Alijó 13 Ec 41.16N 7.28W
Alijos, Rocas- 47 Ad 24.57N 115.44W
'Al Ijūq, Kūh-e- 24 Ng 31.30N 51.45 E
Al Ikhwan 21 Hh 12.08N 53.10 E
Al Ikhwān 24 Fi 26.19N 34.52 E
Alima 30 Ii 1.36S 16.36 E
Al Imārāt al 'Arabīyah al Muttaḩidah=United Arab Emirates (EN) [1] 22 Hg 24.00N 54.00 E
Alimiá 15 Km 36.16N 27.43 E
Alindao 35 Cd 5.02N 21.13 E
Alinglapalap Atoll 57 Hd 7.08N 168.16 E
Alingsås 7 Ch 57.56N 12.31 E
Aliquippa 44 Ge 40.38N 80.16W
Al 'Irāq=Iraq (EN) [1] 22 Gf 33.00N 44.00 E
Al'Irq 33 Dd 29.01N 21.31 E
Al 'Irqah 23 Gg 13.40N 47.18 E
Ali-Sabjeh 35 Gc 11.08N 42.43 E
'Alī Shāh 'Avaz 24 Ne 35.39N 51.04 E
Al Iskandarīyah [Eg.] = Alexandria (EN) 31 Je 31.12N 29.54 E
Al Iskandarīyah [Iraq] 24 Kf 32.53N 44.21 E
Aliskerovo 20 Lc 67.52N 167.40 E
Al Ismā'īlīyah=Ismailia (EN) 33 Fc 30.35N 32.16 E
Al Istiwā'īyah al Gharbīyah [3] 35 Dd 5.20N 28.30 E
Al Istiwā'īyah al Sharkīyah [3] 35 Ed 5.20N 33.50 E
Alistráti 15 Gh 41.04N 23.58 E
Alitak, Cape- 40 Ie 56.51N 154.21W
Alite Reef 63a Ec 8.53S 160.38 E
Alitus/Alytus 19 Ce 54.25N 24.08 E
Alivérion 15 Hk 38.25N 24.02 E
Aliwal North 31 Jl 30.44S 26.40 E
Al Jabalayn 35 Ec 12.36N 32.48 E
Al Jadīdah [Eg.] 24 Cj 25.34N 28.51 E
Al Jadīdah [Sau.Ar.] 24 Mj 25.39N 49.32 E
Al Jafr 24 Gg 30.18N 36.13 E
Al Jāfūrah 35 Ia 23.25N 50.17 E
Al Jāfūrah 24 Nj 25.00N 50.15 E
Al Jaghbūb 31 Jf 29.45N 24.31 E
Al Jahrah 23 Gc 29.20N 47.40 E
Al Jalāmīd 24 Ig 31.17N 40.06 E
Al Jamalīyah 24 Nj 25.37N 51.05 E
Al Jamm 32 Jb 35.18N 10.43 E
Al Janā'in 32 Jc 31.44N 10.09 E
Aljat 16 Pj 39.58N 49.27 E
Al Jawf [Lib.] 31 Jf 24.12N 23.18 E
Al Jawf [Sau.Ar.] 22 Fg 29.50N 39.52 E
Al Jazā'ir=Algeria (EN) [1] 31 Hf 28.00N 3.00 E
Al Jazā'ir=Algiers (EN) [3] 32 Hb 36.35N 3.00 E
Al Jazā'ir=Algiers (EN) 31 He 36.47N 3.03 E
Al Jazā'ir-El Harrach 13 Ph 36.43N 3.08 E
Al Jazīrah [3] 35 Ec 14.40N 33.30 E
Al Jazīrah [Asia] 21 Gf 35.10N 42.00 E
Al Jazīrah [Sud.] 30 Kg 14.25N 33.00 E
Aljezur 13 Dg 37.19N 8.48W
Aljibe 13 Gh 36.31N 5.37W
Al Jifārah 30 Ie 32.30N 11.45 E
Al Jiwā' 23 He 23.00N 54.00 E
Al Jīzah=Giza (EN) 31 Ke 30.01N 31.13 E
Al Jubayl 23 Gd 27.01N 49.40 E
Al Jubaylah 24 Lj 24.54N 46.27 E
Al Junaynah [Sau.Ar.] 33 He 20.17N 42.48 E
Al Junaynah [Sud.] 31 Jg 13.27N 22.27 E
Al Juraid 24 Mi 27.11N 49.52 E
Aljustrel 13 Dg 37.52N 8.10W
Alka 40a Db 52.15N 174.30W
Al Kaba'ish 24 Lg 30.58N 47.00 E
Al Kāf [3] 32 Ib 36.00N 9.00 E
Al Kāf 32 Ib 36.11N 8.43 E
Alkali Lake 46 Ff 41.42N 119.50W
Al Kamāsin 23 Fe 20.25N 44.48 E
Al Kāmilīn 35 Eb 15.05N 33.11 E
Al Karak 24 Fg 31.11N 35.42 E
Al Karkh 24 Kf 33.20N 44.20 E
Al Karnak 33 Fd 25.43N 32.39 E
Al Kawah 35 Ec 13.44N 32.30 E
Al Kāẓimīyah 24 Kf 33.22N 44.20 E
Alken 12 Hd 50.52N 5.18 E
Al Khabrā' 23 Fd 26.04N 43.33 E
Al Khābūra 23 Ie 23.50N 57.18 E
Al-Khalīj al- 'Arabi=Persian Gulf (EN) 21 Hg 27.00N 51.00 E
Al Khalīl 24 Fg 31.32N 35.06 E
Al Khālis 24 Kf 33.51N 44.32 E
Al Khandaq 35 Eb 18.36N 30.34 E
Al Khārijah 31 Kf 25.26N 30.33 E
Al Kharj 24 Lj 24.10N 47.30 E
Al Kharṭūm=Khartoum (EN) [3] 35 Eb 15.50N 33.00 E
Al Kharṭūm=Khartoum (EN) 31 Kg 15.36N 32.32 E
Al Kharṭūm Baḩrī= Khartoum North (EN) 31 Kg 15.38N 32.33 E
Al Khaşab 24 Qi 26.12N 56.15 E
Al Khaṭṭ 24 Qk 25.37N 56.01 E
Al Khawr 23 Hd 25.40N 51.30 E
Al Khidr 24 Kg 31.12N 45.33 E
Al Khubar 23 Hd 26.17N 50.12 E
Al Khufayfīyah 23 Fe 24.55N 44.42 E
Al Khums [3] 33 Bc 31.20N 14.10 E
Al Khums 31 Ie 32.39N 14.16 E
Al Khunn 35 Ha 23.18N 49.15 E
Al Khuwayr 24 Ni 26.04N 51.05 E
Al Kidn 35 Ia 22.30N 54.00 E
Al Kilḩ Sharq 24 Ej 25.03N 32.52 E
Alkionídhon, Kólpos- 15 Fk 38.05N 23.00 E
Al Kır'ānah 24 Nj 25.00N 51.03 E
Alkmaar 11 Kb 52.37N 4.44 E
Al Kūfah 24 Kf 32.02N 44.24 E
Al Kumayt 24 Lf 32.02N 46.52 E
Al Kuntillah 33 Fc 30.00N 34.41 E
Al Kushḩ 24 Ei 26.14N 32.05 E
Al Kut 23 Gc 32.30N 45.49 E
Al Kuwayt=Kuwait (EN) [1] 22 Gg 29.30N 47.45 E
Al Kuwayt=Kuwait (EN) 22 Gg 29.20N 47.59 E
Al Labbah 24 Ih 29.20N 41.30 E
Al Lādhiqīyah=Latakia (EN) 22 Ff 35.31N 35.07 E
Allagash River 44 Mb 47.05N 69.20W
Al Lagowa 35 Dc 11.24N 29.08 E
Allahābād 22 Kg 25.27N 81.51 E
Allah-Jun 20 Id 60.27N 134.57 E
Allah-Jun 20 Id 61.08N 137.59 E
Allahüekber DaGı 24 Jb 40.35N 42.32 E
Allakaket 40 Ic 66.34N 152.41W
Allanmyo 25 Je 19.22N 95.13 E
Allariz 13 Eb 42.11N 7.48W
All-Awash Island 51n Bb 12.55N 61.10W
Alldays 37 Dd 22.41S 29.06 E
Ålleberg 8 Ef 58.08N 13.36 E
Allegan 44 Ed 42.32N 85.51W
Allegheny Mountains 38 Lf 38.30N 80.00W
Allegheny Plateau 38 Le 41.30N 78.00W
Allegheny Reservoir 44 He 42.00N 78.56W
Allegheny River 43 Lc 40.27N 80.00W
Allègre, Pointe- 51e Ab 16.22N 61.45W
Allen 26 Hd 12.30N 124.17 E
Allen, Bog of- 9 Gh 53.20N 7.00W
Allen, Lough-/Loch Aillionn 9 Eg 54.08N 8.08W
Allendale 44 Gi 33.01N 81.19W
Allende 47 Dc 28.20N 100.51W
Allendorf (Eder) 12 Kc 51.02N 8.40 E
Allendorf (Lumda) 12 Kd 50.41N 8.50 E
Allentown 43 Lc 40.37N 75.30W
Alleppey 22 Ji 9.29N 76.19 E
Aller 10 Fd 52.57N 9.11 E
Allevard 11 Mi 45.24N 6.04 E
Allgäuer Alpen 10 Gi 47.20N 10.25 E
Alliance [Nb.-U.S.] 43 Gc 42.06N 102.52W
Alliance [Oh.-U.S.] 44 Ge 40.56N 81.06W
Allier [3] 11 Ih 46.30N 3.00 E
Allier 5 Gf 46.57N 3.05 E
Al Līfīyah 23 Fc 30.35N 43.09 E
Al Lişāfah 24 Li 27.37N 46.52 E
Alliston 44 Hc 44.09N 79.52W
Al Līth 23 Fe 20.09N 40.16 E
Alloa 9 Je 56.07N 3.49W
Allonnes 11 Gg 47.58N 0.09 E
Allos 11 Mj 44.14N 6.38 E
All Saints 51d Bb 17.03N 61.48W
Al Luḩayyah 23 Ff 15.43N 42.42 E
Al Luwaymī 23 Fd 27.54N 42.22 E
Alm 14 Hb 48.05N 13.55 E
Alma [Ga.-U.S.] 44 Fj 31.33N 82.28W
Alma [Mi.-U.S.] 44 Ed 43.23N 84.39W
Alma [Nb.-U.S.] 45 Gf 40.06N 99.22W
Alma [Que.-Can.] 42 Kg 48.32N 71.40W
Alma-Ata 22 Je 43.15N 76.57 E
Alma-Atinskaja Oblast [3] 19 Hg 44.00N 77.00 E
Almada 13 Cf 38.41N 9.09W
Almadén 13 Hf 38.46N 4.50W
Al Madīnah [Iraq] 24 Lg 30.57N 47.16 E
Al Madīnah [Sau.Ar.] = Medina (EN) 22 Fg 24.28N 39.36 E
Al Madīnah al Fikrīyah 24 Di 27.56N 30.49 E
'Al Madōw 35 Hc 10.59N 48.42 E
Al Mafraq 24 Gf 32.21N 36.12 E
Al Maghrib=Morocco (EN) [1] 31 Ge 32.00N 5.50W
Almagro 13 If 38.53N 3.43W
Almagrundet 8 He 59.06N 19.00 E

Index Symbols

[1] Independent Nation
[2] State, Region
[3] District, County
[4] Municipality
[5] Colony, Dependency
Continent
Physical Region
Historical or Cultural Region
Mount, Mountain
Volcano
Hill
Mountains, Mountain Range
Hills, Escarpment
Plateau, Upland
Pass, Gap
Plain, Lowland
Delta
Salt Flat
Valley, Canyon
Crater, Cave
Karst Features
Depression
Polder
Desert, Dunes
Forest, Woods
Heath, Steppe
Oasis
Cape, Point
Coast, Beach
Cliff
Peninsula
Isthmus
Sandbank
Island
Atoll
Rock, Reef
Islands, Archipelago
Rocks, Reefs
Coral Reef
Well, Spring
Geyser
River, Stream
Waterfall Rapids
River Mouth, Estuary
Lake
Salt Lake
Intermittent Lake
Reservoir
Swamp, Pond
Canal
Glacier
Ice Shelf, Pack Ice
Ocean
Sea
Gulf, Bay
Strait, Fjord
Lagoon
Bank
Seamount
Tablemount
Ridge
Shelf
Basin
Escarpment, Sea Scarp
Fracture
Trench, Abyss
National Park, Reserve
Point of Interest
Recreation Site
Cave, Cavern
Historic Site
Ruins
Wall, Walls
Church, Abbey
Temple
Scientific Station
Airport
Port
Lighthouse
Mine
Tunnel
Dam, Bridge

International Map Index

'Amm Adām 35 Fb 16.22N 36.09 E
'Ammān 22 Ff 31.57N 35.56 E
Ammanford 9 Jj 51.48N 3.59W
Ammarnäs 7 Dd 65.58N 16.12 E
Åmmeberg 8 Ff 58.52N 15.00 E
Ammer 10 Hi 47.57N 11.08 E
Ammerån 8 Ga 63.09N 16.13 E
Ammerland 10 Dc 53.15N 8.00 E
Ammersee 10 Hi 48.00N 11.08 E
Ammi-Moussa 13 Ni 35.52N 1.07 E
Ammóchōstos=Famagusta (EN) 23 Dc 35.07N 33.57 E
Amnja 17 Me 63.45N 67.07 E
Amnok-kang 27 Ld 39.55N 124.20 E
Āmol 23 Hb 36.23N 52.20 E
Amolar 55 Dd 18.01 S 57.30W
Amorgós 15 Im 36.50N 25.53 E
Amorgós 15 Im 36.50N 25.59 E
Amorinópolis 55 Gc 16.36 S 51.08W
Amory 45 Lj 33.59N 88.29W
Amos 42 Jg 48.34N 78.07W
Åmot [Nor.] 8 Be 59.35N 8.00 E
Åmot [Nor.] 7 Bg 59.54N 9.54 E
Åmotfors 8 Ee 59.46N 12.22 E
Amoucha 13 Rh 36.23N 5.25 E
Amouliani 15 Gi 40.20N 23.55 E
Amour, Djebel- 32 Hc 33.45N 1.45 E
Amourj 32 Ff 16.10N 7.35W
Ampanihy 37 Gd 24.40 S 44.45 E
Amparafaravola 37 Hc 17.36 S 48.12 E
Amparo 55 If 22.42 S 46.47W
Amper 10 Hh 48.10N 11.50 E
Ampère Seamount (EN) 5 Eh 35.05N 12.13W
Amphitrite Point 46 Cb 48.56N 125.35W
Amposta 13 Md 40.43N 0.35 E
Ampthill 12 Bb 52.02N 0.29W
Ampurdán/L'Empordà 13 Ob 42.12N 2.45 E
Ampurias 13 Pb 42.10N 3.05 E
Amqui 44 Na 48.28N 67.26W
'Amrān 23 Ff 15.41N 43.55 E
Amrāvati 22 Jg 20.56N 77.45 E
Am-Raya 35 Bc 14.05N 16.30 E
Amritsar 22 Jf 31.35N 74.53 E
Amrum 8 Cj 54.40N 8.20 E
Amsaga 32 Ee 20.07N 14.10W
Amsittene, Jebel- 32 Fc 31.11N 9.40W
Amstel 12 Gb 52.22N 4.56 E
Amstelveen 12 Gb 52.18N 4.53 E
Amsterdam 30 Ol 37.57 S 77.40 E
Amsterdam [Neth.] 6 Ge 52.22N 4.54 E
Amsterdam [N.Y.-U.S.] 44 Jd 42.56N 74.12W
Amsterdam-Rijnkanaal 12 Hc 51.57N 5.25 E
Amstetten 14 Ib 48.07N 14.52 E
Am Timan 31 Jg 11.02N 20.17 E
Amūd, Jabal al- 23 Ec 30.59N 39.20 E
Āmūdā 24 Id 37.05N 40.54 E
Amu-Darja 18 Ef 37.57N 65.15 E
Amudarja=Amu Darya (EN) 21 He 43.40N 59.01 E
Āmū Daryā=Amu Darya (EN) 21 He 43.40N 59.01 E
Amu Darya (EN)=Amudarja 21 He 43.40N 59.01 E
Amu Darya (EN)=Āmū Daryā 21 He 43.40N 59.01 E
Amudat 36 Fb 1.58N 34.56 E
Amukta Pass 40a Db 52.25N 172.00W
Amun 63a Ba 5.57 S 154.45 E
Amund Ringnes 42 Ha 78.15N 97.00W
Amundsen Bay 66 Ee 66.55 S 50.00 E
Amundsen Coast 66 Mg 85.30 S 159.00W
Amundsen Glacier 66 Mg 85.35 S 159.00W
Amundsen Gulf 38 Gb 71.00N 124.00W
Amundsen-Scott Station 66 Bg 90.00 S 0.00
Amundsen Sea (EN) 66 Of 72.30 S 112.00W
Amungen 8 Fc 61.10N 15.40 E
Amuntai 22 Nj 2.26 S 115.15 E
Amur 21 Qd 52.56N 141.10 E
'Amūr, Wādī 35 Eb 18.56N 33.34 E
Amurang 26 Hf 1.11N 124.35 E
Amursk 20 If 50.16N 136.55 E
Amurskaja Oblast 20 Hf 54.00N 128.00 E
Amurzet 20 Ig 47.41N 131.07 E
Amvrakia, Gulf of- (EN) = Amvrakikós Kólpos 15 Dk 39.00N 21.00 E
Amvrakikós Kólpos = Amvrakia, Gulf of- (EN) 15 Dk 39.00N 21.00 E
Amvrosijevka 16 Kf 47.44N 38.31 E
Am Zoer 35 Cc 14.13N 21.23 E
Anaa Atoll 61 Lc 17.25 S 145.30W
Anabar 64e Ba 0.29 S 166.57 E
Anabar 21 Nb 73.08N 113.36 E
Anabarskoje Ploskogorje 21 Mc 70.00N 108.00 E
An Abhainn Dubh/Blackwater 9 Gh 53.39N 6.43W
An Abhainn Mhór/Blackwater [Ire.] 9 Fj 51.51N 7.50W
An Abhainn Mhór/Blackwater [N.Ire.-U.K.] 9 Gg 54.30N 6.35W
Anabuki 29 Dd 34.02N 134.11 E
Anacasti 56 Gc 28.49 S 65.30W
Anaco 54 Fb 9.27N 64.28W
Anaconda 43 Eb 46.08N 112.57W
Anacortes 46 Db 48.30N 122.37W
Anadarko 45 Gi 35.04N 98.15W
Anadolu=Anatolia (EN) 21 Ff 39.00N 35.00 E
Anadyr 21 Tc 64.55N 176.05 E
Anadyr 22 Tc 64.45N 177.29 E
Anadyr Gulf (EN)=Anadyrski Zaliv 21 Uc 64.00N 179.00W
Anadyr Range (EN)=Anadyrskoje Ploskogorje 21 Tc 67.00N 174.00 E
Anadyrski Liman 20 Md 64.30N 178.00 E
Anadyrski Zaliv=Anadyr Gulf (EN) 21 Uc 64.00N 179.00W
Anadyrskoje Ploskogorje=Anadyr Range (EN) 21 Tc 67.00N 174.00 E
Anáfi 15 Im 36.22N 25.47 E
Anaghit 35 Fb 16.20N 38.39 E
Anagni 14 Hi 41.44N 13.09 E
'Ānah 23 Fc 34.28N 41.56 E
Anaheim 46 Gj 33.51N 117.57W
Anahola 65a Ba 22.09N 159.19W
Anáhuac 48 Id 27.14N 100.09W
Anahuac, Meseta de- 47 Dd 21.30N 101.00W
An Aird/Ards Peninsula 9 Hg 54.30N 5.30W
Anaj Mudi 21 Jh 10.10N 77.04 E
Anaktuvuk Pass 40 Ic 68.10N 151.50W
Analalava 37 Hb 14.38 S 47.45 E
Analavelona 37 Gd 22.37 S 44.10 E
Ana María, Golfo de- 49 Hc 21.25N 78.40W
Anambas, Kepulauan-=Anambas Islands (EN) 21 Mi 3.00N 106.00 E
Anambas Islands (EN)=Anambas, Kepulauan- 21 Mi 3.00N 106.00 E
Anambra 34 Gd 6.30N 7.30 E
Anamé 63b De 20.08 S 169.49 E
Anamizu 28 Nf 37.14N 136.54 E
Anamur 23 Db 36.06N 32.50 E
Anamur Burun 23 Db 36.03N 32.48 E
Anan [Jap.] 28 Mh 33.55N 134.39 E
Anan [Jap.] 29 Ed 35.19N 137.48 E
Anane, Djebel- 13 Mi 35.12N 0.47 E
Anánes 15 Hm 36.31N 24.08 E
Ananjev 16 Ff 47.43N 29.59 E
Anankwin 25 Je 15.41N 97.59 E
Anantapur 25 Ff 14.41N 77.36 E
Anantnāg (Islāmābād) 25 Fb 33.44N 75.09 E
Anapa 19 Dg 44.53N 37.19 E
Anapo 14 Jm 37.03N 15.16 E
Anápolis 53 Lg 16.20 S 48.58W
Anapu, Rio- 54 Hd 2.15 S 51.30W
Anār 23 Ic 30.53N 55.18 E
Anārak 23 Hc 33.20N 53.42 E
Anare Station 66 Jd 54.30 S 158.55 E
Anaro, Río- 49 Lj 7.48N 70.12W
Añasco 51a Ab 18.17N 67.10W
Anatahan Island 57 Fc 16.22N 145.40 E
Anatolia (EN)=Anadolu 21 Ff 39.00N 35.00 E
Anatoliki Rodhópi 15 Ih 41.44N 25.31 E
Añatuya 56 Hc 28.28 S 62.50W
Anauá, Rio- 54 Fc 0.58N 61.21W
Anazarba 24 Fd 37.15N 35.45 E
An Baile Meánach/Ballymena 9 Gg 54.52N 6.17W
An Bhanna/Bann 9 Gf 55.10N 6.46W
An Bhearú/Barrow 9 Gi 52.10N 7.00W
An Bhinn Bhui/Benwee Head 9 Dg 54.21N 9.48W
An Bhograch/Boggeragh Mountains 9 Ei 52.05N 9.00W
An Bhóinn/Boyne 9 Gh 53.43N 6.15W
An Bhrosnach/Brosna 9 Fh 53.13N 7.58W
An Blascaod Mór/Great Blasket 9 Ci 52.05N 10.32W
Anbyŏn 28 Ie 39.02N 127.32 E
An Cabhán/Cavan 9 Fh 53.55N 7.30W
An Cabhán/Cavan 9 Fg 54.00N 7.21W
An Caisleán Nua/Newcastle 9 Hg 54.12N 5.54W
An Caisleán Nua/Newcastle West 9 Di 52.27N 9.03W
An Caisleán Riabhach/Castlerea 9 Eh 53.46N 8.29W
An Caoláire Rua/Killary Harbour 9 Dh 53.38N 9.55W
Ancares, Sierra de- 13 Fb 42.46N 6.54W
Ancash 54 Ce 9.30 S 77.45W
Ancenis 11 Eg 47.22N 1.10W
An Chathair/Caher 9 Fi 52.22N 7.55W
An Cheacha/Caha Mountains 9 Dj 51.45N 9.45W
Anchorage 39 Ec 61.13N 149.53W
An Chorr Chríochach/Cookstown 9 Gg 54.39N 6.45W
Anci (Langfang) 27 Kd 39.29N 116.40 E
An Clár/Clare 9 Ei 52.50N 9.00W
An Cóbh/Cóbh 9 Ej 51.51N 8.17W
Ancohuma, Nevado- 54 Eg 15.51 S 68.36W
Ancona 6 Hg 43.38N 13.30 E
Ancón de Sardinas, Bahía de- 54 Cc 1.30N 79.50W
Ancre 11 Ie 49.54N 2.28 E
Ancuabe 37 Fb 12.58 S 39.51 E
Ancud 56 Ff 41.52 S 73.50W
Ancud, Golfo de- 56 Ff 42.05 S 73.00W
Anda 27 Mb 46.24N 125.20 E
Anda (Sartu) 28 Ha 46.35N 125.00 E
Andacollo [Arg.] 56 Fe 37.11 S 70.41W
Andacollo [Chile] 56 Fd 30.14 S 71.06W
Andahuaylas 54 Df 13.39 S 73.23W
An Daingean/Dingle 9 Ci 52.08N 10.15W
Andalgalá 56 Gc 27.36 S 66.19W
Åndalsnes 7 Be 62.34N 7.42 E
Andalucía=Andalusia (EN) 13 Hg 37.30N 4.30W
Andalucía=Andalusia (EN) 5 Fh 37.30N 4.30W
Andalusia 43 Je 31.19N 86.29W
Andalusia (EN)=Andalucía 13 Hg 37.30N 4.30W
Andalusia (EN)=Andalucía 5 Fh 37.30N 4.30W
Andaman and Nicobar 25 If 12.30N 92.45 E
Andaman Basin (EN) 21 Lh 10.00N 94.00 E
Andaman Islands 21 Lh 12.30N 92.43 E
Andaman Sea (EN) 21 Lh 10.00N 95.00 E
Andamooka 59 Hf 30.27 S 137.12 E
'Andān, Wādī- 23 Ie 21.05N 58.23 E
Andant 55 Am 36.34 S 62.07W
Andapa 37 Hb 14.38 S 49.33 E
Andara 37 Cc 18.03 S 21.27 E
Andelle 12 De 49.19N 1.14 E
Andenes 7 Db 69.19N 16.08 E
Andenne 12 Hd 50.29N 5.06 E
Andenne-Namêche 12 Hd 50.28N 5.00 E
Andéranboukane 34 Fb 15.26N 3.02 E
Anderlecht 12 Gd 50.50N 4.18 E
Anderlues 12 Gd 50.24N 4.16 E
Andermatt 14 Cd 46.38N 8.37 E
Andernach 10 Df 50.26N 7.24 E
Andernos-les-Bains 11 Ej 44.44N 1.06W
Anderson 42 Ec 69.42N 129.01W
Anderson [Ca.-U.S.] 46 Df 40.27N 122.18W
Anderson [In.-U.S.] 43 Jc 40.10N 85.41W
Anderson [S.C.-U.S.] 43 Ke 34.30N 82.39W
Anderstorp 8 Eg 57.17N 13.38 E
Andes (EN) = Andes, Cordillera de los- 52 Jh 20.00 S 67.00W
Andes, Cordillera de los- = Andes (EN) 52 Jh 20.00 S 67.00W
Andevoranto 37 Hc 18.48 S 49.02 E
Andfjorden 7 Db 69.10N 16.20 E
Andhra Pradesh 25 Fe 16.00N 79.00 E
Andía, Sierra de- 13 Kb 42.45N 2.00W
Andikhásia Ōri 15 Ej 39.47N 21.55 E
Andikira 15 Fk 38.23N 22.38 E
Andikithira = Andikithira (EN) 15 Gn 35.52N 23.18 E
Andikithira (EN) = Andikithira 15 Gn 35.52N 23.18 E
Andikithíron, Stenón- 15 Gn 35.45N 23.25 E
Andilamena 37 Hc 17.01 S 48.32 E
Andilanatoby 37 Hc 17.56 S 48.14 E
Andīmeshk 24 Mf 32.27N 48.21 E
Andímilos 15 Hm 36.47N 24.14 E
Andíparos 15 Il 37.00N 25.03 E
Andípaxoi 15 Dj 39.08N 20.14 E
Andípsara 15 Ik 38.33N 25.24 E
Andir He 27 Dd 38.00N 83.36 E
Andiria Burun 24 Fe 35.42N 34.35 E
Andırın 24 Gd 37.34N 36.20 E
Andirlangar 27 Dd 37.36N 83.50 E
Andírrion 15 Ek 38.20N 21.46 E
Andítilos 15 Km 36.22N 27.28 E
Andižan 22 Je 40.45N 72.22 E
Andižanskaja Oblast 19 Hg 40.45N 72.20 E
Andkhvoy 23 Kb 36.56N 65.08 E
Andŏng 27 Md 36.36N 128.44 E
Andorra (Valls d'Andorra) 6 Gg 42.30N 1.30 E
Andorra la Vella 6 Gg 42.31N 1.31 E
Andover 9 Lj 51.13N 1.28W
Andøya 7 Db 69.08N 15.54 E
Andradas 55 If 22.05 S 46.35W
Andradina 56 Jb 20.54 S 51.23W
Andraitx 13 Oe 39.35N 2.25 E
Andreanof Islands 38 Bd 52.00N 176.00W
Andreapol 7 Hh 56.39N 32.16 E
Andrées Land 41 Jd 73.20N 26.30W
Andrejevka [Kaz.-U.S.S.R.] 19 If 45.47N 80.35 E
Andrejevka [Ukr.-U.S.S.R.] 16 Je 49.32N 36.40 E
Andrejevo-Ivanovka 15 Nb 47.31N 30.21 E
Andrejevsk 20 Ge 58.10N 114.15 E
Andrelândia 55 Je 21.44 S 44.18W
Andresito 55 Dk 33.08 S 57.09W
Andrespol 10 Pe 51.43N 19.40 E
Andrews 45 Ej 32.19N 102.33W
Andria 14 Ki 41.13N 16.17 E
Andriamena 37 Hc 17.28 S 47.29 E
Andriba 37 Hc 17.36 S 46.53 E
Andrijevica 15 Cg 42.44N 19.48 E
Andringitra 30 Lk 22.20 S 46.55 E
Andrítsaina 15 El 37.29N 21.54 E
Androka 37 Gd 24.59 S 44.04 E
Androna, Plateau de l'- 37 Hc 15.30 S 48.20 E
Ándros 5 Ih 37.50N 24.50 E
Andros 38 Lg 24.25N 78.00W
Ándros 15 Hl 37.50N 24.56 E
Androscoggin River 44 Md 43.55N 69.55W
Androssan 9 If 55.40N 4.55W
Andros Town 47 Id 24.43N 77.47W
Androth Island 25 Ef 10.50N 73.41 E
Androy 30 Lk 25.00 S 45.40 E
Andruševka 16 Fe 49.59N 29.01 E
Andrychów 10 Pg 49.52N 19.21 E
Andselv 7 Eb 69.04N 18.30 E
Andudu 36 Eb 2.29N 28.41 E
Andújar 13 Hf 38.03N 4.04W
Andulo 36 Ce 11.28 S 16.43 E
Andu Tan 26 Fe 7.35N 114.15 E
Anduze 11 Jj 44.03N 3.59 E
An Ea agail/Errigal 9 Ef 55.02N 8.07W
Aneby 8 Fg 57.50N 14.48 E
Anéfis 34 Fb 18.03N 0.36 E
Anegada 47 Le 18.45N 64.20W
Anegada, Bahía- 56 Hf 40.15 S 62.15W
Anegada Passage 47 Le 18.30N 63.40W
Anécho 34 Fd 6.14N 1.36 E
An Éirne/Erne 9 Eg 54.30N 8.15W
An Eithne/Inny 9 Fh 53.35N 7.50W
An Eoghanach/Annalee 9 Fg 54.02N 7.25W
Anet 12 Df 48.51N 1.26 E
Aneto, Pico de- 5 Gg 42.38N 0.40 E
Aney 34 Hb 19.24N 12.56 E
Aneytioum, Ile- 57 Hg 20.12 S 169.49 E
An Feabhal 9 Ff 55.04N 7.15W
An Fhéil/Feale 9 Di 52.28N 9.40W
An Fheoir/Nore 9 Gi 52.25N 6.58W
Angamos, Punta- [Chile] 56 Fb 23.01 S 70.32W
Angamos, Punta- [Pas.] 65d Bb 27.04 S 109.17W
Angara 21 Ld 58.06N 93.00 E
Angarsk 22 Md 52.34N 103.54 E
Angarski, Pereval- 16 Ig 44.47N 34.25 E
Angarski Krjaž 20 Fe 57.30N 103.00 E
Angathonisi 15 Jl 37.28N 27.00 E
Angaur Island 57 Ed 6.54N 134.09 E
Ånge 7 De 62.31N 15.37 E
Änge 8 Fa 63.27N 14.03 E
An Gearran/Garron Point 9 Hf 55.05N 5.58W
Ángel, Cerro- 48 Hf 22.49N 102.34W
Ángel, Salto-=Angel Falls (EN) 52 Je 5.57N 62.30W
Angelburg 12 Kd 50.47N 8.25 E
Angel de la Guarda, Isla- 47 Bc 29.20N 113.25W
Angeles 26 Hc 15.09N 120.35 E
Angeles, Sierra de los- 48 Jf 23.10N 99.20W
Angel Falls (EN)=Ángel, Salto- 52 Je 5.57N 62.30W
Angel Falls (EN)=Churún Merú 52 Je 5.57N 62.30W
Ängelholm 7 Ch 56.15N 12.51 E
Angélica 55 Bj 31.33 S 61.33W
Angeln 10 Fb 54.40N 9.45 E
Ängelsberg 8 Ge 59.58N 16.02 E
Anger 35 Fd 9.40N 36.06 E
Angereb 35 Fc 13.44N 36.28 E
Ångermanälven 5 Hc 62.48N 17.56 E
Angermünde 10 Jc 53.02N 14.00 E
Angers 6 Ff 47.28N 0.33W
Angkor 25 Kf 13.26N 103.52 E
Angikuni Lake 42 Hd 62.10N 99.55W
Angístrion 15 Gl 37.40N 23.20 E
Anglem, Mount- 62 Bg 46.44 S 167.54 E
Anglés 13 Oc 41.57N 2.39 E
Anglesey 5 Fe 53.18N 4.20W
Anglet 11 Ek 43.29N 1.32W
Angleton 45 Il 29.10N 95.26W
Anglin 11 Gh 46.42N 0.52 E
Anglona 14 Cj 40.45N 8.45 E
Angmagssalik 67 Mc 65.45N 37.30W
Ango 36 Eb 4.02N 25.52 E
Angoche 31 Kj 16.12 S 39.54 E
Angoche, Ilha- 30 Kj 16.20 S 39.51 E
Angol 56 Fe 37.48 S 72.43W
Angola 31 Ij 12.30 S 18.30 E
Angola 44 Ee 41.38N 85.00W
Angola Basin (EN) 3 Ek 15.00 S 3.00 E
Angoram 60 Ch 4.04 S 144.04 E
Angostura 48 Ee 25.22N 108.11W
Angostura, Presa de la- 48 Mi 16.30N 92.30W
Angostura, Salto- 54 Dc 2.43N 70.57W
Angostura Reservoir 45 Ee 43.18N 103.27W
Angoulême 11 Gi 45.39N 0.09 E
Angoumois 11 Fi 45.30N 0.10W
Angra do Heroismo 32 Bb 38.42N 27.15W
Angra do Héroismo 31 Ee 38.39N 27.13W
Angra dos Reis 55 Jf 23.00 S 44.18W
Angren 19 Hg 41.03N 70.10 E
Angu 36 Db 3.33N 24.28 E
Anguang 28 Gb 45.36N 123.48 E
Anguilla 39 Mh 18.15N 63.05W
Anguilla 38 Mh 18.15N 63.05W
Anguilla, Canal de l'-=Anguilla Channel (EN) 51b Ab 18.09N 63.04W
Anguilla Bank (EN) 51b Ab 18.30N 63.03W
Anguilla Cays 49 Hb 23.31N 78.33W
Anguilla Channel (EN)=Anguilla, Canal de l'- 51b Ab 18.09N 63.04W
Anguli Nur 28 Cd 41.23N 114.30 E
Anguo 28 Ce 38.25N 115.20 E
Anhanca 36 Cf 16.47 S 15.33 E
Anhanguera 55 Hd 18.21 S 48.17W
An Hoa 25 Le 15.46N 108.03 E
Anholt 7 Ch 56.40N 11.35 E
Anhua (Dongping) 27 Jf 28.27N 111.15 E
Anhui Sheng (An-hui Sheng)=Anhwei (EN) 27 Ke 32.00N 117.00 E
An-hui Sheng→Anhui Sheng=Anhwei (EN) 27 Ke 32.00N 117.00 E
Anhwei (EN)=Anhui Sheng (An-hui Sheng) 27 Ke 32.00N 117.00 E
Anhwei (EN)=An-hui Sheng→Anhui Sheng 27 Ke 32.00N 117.00 E
Ani 29 Gb 39.59N 140.25 E
Aniak 40 Hd 61.34N 159.30W
An Iarmhí/Westmeath 9 Fh 53.30N 7.30W
Anibare 64e Bb 0.32 S 166.57 E
Anibare Bay 64e Bb 0.32 S 166.57 E
Aniche 12 Fd 50.20N 3.15 E
Ánidros 15 Im 36.37N 25.41 E
Anié 34 Fd 7.45N 1.12 E
Anie, Pic d'- 11 Fl 42.57N 0.43W
Aniene 14 Gi 41.56N 12.30 E
Anijangying → Luanping 28 Dd 40.55N 117.19 E
Anikščjaj/Anykščiai 7 Fi 55.31N 25.08 E
Animas Peak 45 Bk 31.35N 108.47W
Anina 15 Ed 45.05N 21.51 E
Anita Garibaldi 55 Gh 27.37 S 51.05W
Anittepe 15 Kh 41.21N 27.42 E
Aniva 20 Jg 46.41N 142.35 E
Aniva, Zaliv- 20 Jg 46.20N 142.40 E
Anivorano Nord 37 Hb 12.43 S 49.12 E
Aniwa, Ile- 57 Hf 19.16 S 169.35 E
Anizy-le-Château 12 Fe 49.30N 3.27 E
Anjala 7 Gf 60.41N 26.50 E
Anji 28 Ei 30.39N 119.41 E
Anjiang → Qianyang 27 Jf 27.19N 110.13 E
Anjō 29 Ed 34.57N 137.05 E
Anjou 11 Fg 47.20N 0.30W
Anjou, Ostrova-=Anjou Islands (EN) 21 Qb 75.30N 143.00 E
Anjouan/Nzwali 30 Lj 12.15 S 44.25 E
Anjou Islands (EN)=Anjou, Ostrova- 21 Qb 75.30N 143.00 E
Anjozorobe 37 Hc 18.24 S 47.52 E
Anju 27 Md 39.37N 125.40 E
Anjuj 20 Ig 49.20N 136.20 E
Anjujski Hrebet 20 Lc 67.20N 166.00 E
Anjuou, Val d'- 11 Fg 47.25N 0.15W
Anka 34 Gc 12.07N 5.55 E
Ankang (Xing'an) 22 Mf 32.37N 109.03 E
Ankara 22 Ff 39.56N 32.52 E
Ankaratra 30 Lj 19.25 S 47.12 E
Ankarsrum 7 Dh 57.42N 16.19 E
Ankavandra 37 Hc 18.45 S 45.18 E
Ankazoabo 37 Gd 22.16 S 44.30 E
Ankazobe 37 Hc 18.17 S 47.05 E
Ankeny 45 Jf 41.44N 93.36W
'Ankhor 35 Hc 10.47N 46.18 E
Anklam 10 Jc 53.52N 13.42 E
Ankober 35 Fd 9.40N 39.44 E
Ankoro 36 Ed 6.45 S 26.57 E
Ankum 12 Jb 52.33N 7.53 E
An Laoi/Lee 9 Ej 51.55N 8.30W
Anlong 27 If 25.02N 105.30 E
An Longfort/Longford 9 Fh 53.40N 7.40W
An Longfort/Longfort 9 Fh 53.44N 7.47W
An Lorgain/Lurgan 9 Gg 54.28N 6.20W
Anlu 27 Je 31.12N 113.46 E
An Mhí/Meath 9 Gh 53.35N 6.40W
An Mhuaidh/Moy 9 Dg 54.12N 9.08W
An Mhuir Cheilteach=Celtic Sea (EN) 5 Fe 51.00N 7.00W
An Muileann gCearr/Mullingar 9 Fh 53.32N 7.20W
An Muirthead/Mullet Peninsula 9 Cg 54.15N 10.04W
Ånn 7 Ce 63.15N 12.35 E
Ånn 8 Ea 63.19N 12.33 E
Ann, Cape- [Ant.] 66 Ee 66.10 S 51.22 E
Ann, Cape- [Ma.-U.S.] 44 Ld 42.39N 70.38W
Anna [Il.-U.S.] 45 Lh 37.28N 89.15W
Anna [Nauru] 64e Ba 0.29 S 166.56 E
Anna [R.S.F.S.R.] 19 Ee 51.29N 40.26 E
Annaba 31 He 36.54N 7.46 E
Annaba 32 Ib 35.35N 8.00 E
An Nabaṭiyah at Taḥtā 24 Gf 33.23N 35.29 E
Annaberg-Buchholz 10 If 50.34N 13.00 E
An Nabī Şāliḥ 24 Eh 28.38N 33.59 E
An Nabk 23 Ec 34.01N 36.44 E
An Nabk Abū Qaşr 24 Hg 30.21N 38.34 E
An Nafīḍah 14 En 36.08N 10.23 E
An Nafūd 21 Gg 28.30N 41.00 E
An Najaf 22 Gf 31.59N 44.20 E
An Najaf 24 Kg 31.20N 44.07 E
An Nakhl 33 Fd 29.55N 33.45 E
Annalee/An Eoghanach 9 Fg 54.02N 7.25W
Annam (EN)=Trung Phan 21 Me 15.00N 108.00 E
Annamitique, Chaîne- 25 Le 17.00N 106.00 E
Annan 9 Jg 54.59N 3.16W
Annan 9 Jg 55.00N 3.16W
Anna Paulowna 12 Gb 52.52N 4.52 E
Anna Paulowna-Kleine Sluis 12 Gb 52.52N 4.52 E
Anna Point 64e Ba 0.29 S 166.56 E
Annapolis 39 Lf 38.59N 76.30W
Annapolis Royal 44 Oc 44.45N 65.31W
Annapurna 21 Kg 28.34N 83.50 E
Ann Arbor 43 Kc 42.18N 83.45W
Anna Regina 50 Gi 7.16N 58.30W
An Nás/Naas 9 Gh 53.13N 6.39W
An Nashshāsh 24 Pk 23.05N 54.02 E
An Nashwah 24 Lg 30.49N 47.36 E
An Nāşirīyah 23 Gc 31.02N 46.16 E
An Nasser 24 Ej 24.36N 32.58 E
An Nawfalīyah 33 Cc 30.47N 17.50 E
Annecy 11 Mi 45.54N 6.07 E
Annecy, Lac d'- 11 Mi 45.51N 6.11 E
Annemasse 11 Mh 46.12N 6.15 E
Annevoie-Rouillon 12 Gd 50.21N 4.50 E
An Nīl 35 Ea 20.10N 33.00 E
An Nīl al Azraq 35 Ed 12.20N 34.15 E
Anning 27 Hg 24.58N 102.29 E
Anniston 43 Je 33.40N 85.50W
Annobón 30 Hi 1.32 S 5.38 E
Annonay 11 Ki 45.14N 4.40 E
Annotto Bay 49 Id 18.16N 76.46W
An Nu'ayrīyah 24 Mi 27.28N 48.27 E
An Nuhūd 31 Jg 12.42N 28.26 E
An Nu' Mān 24 Fi 27.06N 35.46 E
An Nu'mānīyah 24 Kf 32.32N 45.25 E
Annweiler am Trifels 12 Je 49.12N 7.58 E
Anoia/Noya 13 Nc 41.28N 1.56 E
Anoka 45 Jd 45.11N 93.23W
An Ómaigh/Omagh 9 Fg 54.36N 7.18W
Anori 54 Fd 3.47 S 61.38W
Anosyennes, Chaînes- 37 Hd 24.20 S 47.00 E
Ânou Makarene 34 Gb 18.07N 7.35 E
Áno Viánnos 15 In 35.03N 25.25 E
Anóyia 15 Hn 35.15N 24.54 E
Anping [China] 28 Ce 38.13N 115.32 E
Anping [China] 28 Gd 41.10N 123.25 E
An Pointe/Warrenpoint 9 Gg 54.06N 6.15W
Anpu 27 Ig 21.30N 110.00 E
Anpu Gang 27 Ig 21.25N 109.40 E
Anqing 22 Nf 30.32N 116.59 E
Anqiu 28 Ef 36.25N 119.12 E
An Ráth/Ráth Luirc 9 Ei 52.21N 8.41W
An Ribhéar/Kenmare River 9 Dj 51.50N 9.50W
Anröchte 12 Kc 51.34N 8.20 E
Ans 12 Hd 50.39N 5.32 E
Anşāb 23 Fd 29.11N 44.43 E
Ansauvillers 12 Ee 49.34N 2.24 E
Ansbach 10 Gg 49.18N 10.35 E
An Sciobairín/Skibbereen 9 Dj 51.33N 9.15W
An Seancheann/Kinsale, Old Head of- 9 Ej 51.36N 8.32W
Anse-à-Veau 49 Kd 18.30N 73.19W
Anse-Bertrand 51e Ab 16.29N 61.31W
Anse-d'Hainault 49 Jd 18.30N 74.27W
Anse la Raye 51k Ab 13.57N 61.03W
Anshan 22 Oe 41.08N 122.59 E
Anshun 22 Mg 26.15N 105.58 E
Ansina 56 Id 31.54 S 55.28W
Ansley 45 Gf 41.18N 99.23W
Anson Bay 59 Gb 13.20 S 130.05 E
Ansongo 34 Fb 15.40N 0.31 E
An Srath Bán/Strabane 9 Fg 54.49N 7.27W
Anta 54 Df 13.29 S 72.09W

Index Symbols

1 Independent Nation
2 State, Region
3 District, County
5 Municipality
Colony, Dependency
Continent
Physical Region
Historical or Cultural Region
Mount, Mountain
Volcano
Hill
Mountains, Mountain Range
Hills, Escarpment
Plateau, Upland
Pass, Gap
Plain, Lowland
Delta
Salt Flat
Valley, Canyon
Crater, Cave
Karst Features
Depression
Polder
Desert, Dunes
Forest, Woods
Heath, Steppe
Oasis
Cape, Point
Coast, Beach
Cliff
Peninsula
Isthmus
Sandbank
Island
Atoll
Rock, Reef
Islands, Archipelago
Rocks, Reefs
Coral Reef
Well, Spring
Geyser
River, Stream
Waterfall Rapids
River Mouth, Estuary
Lake
Salt Lake
Intermittent Lake
Reservoir
Swamp, Pond
Canal
Glacier
Ice Shelf, Pack Ice
Ocean
Sea
Gulf, Bay
Strait, Fjord
Lagoon
Bank
Seamount
Tablemount
Ridge
Shelf
Basin
Escarpment, Sea Scarp
Fracture
Trench, Abyss
National Park, Reserve
Point of Interest
Recreation Site
Cave, Cavern
Historic Site
Ruins
Wall, Walls
Church, Abbey
Temple
Scientific Station
Airport
Port
Lighthouse
Mine
Tunnel
Dam, Bridge

Antabamba 54 Df 14.19S 72.55W
Antakya=Antioch (EN) 23 Eb 36.14N 36.07 E
Antalaha 31 Mj 14.55S 50.15 E
Antalya 22 Ff 36.53N 30.42 E
Antalya, Gulf of- (EN)=Antalya Körfezi 23 Db 36.30N 31.00 E
Antalya Körfezi=Antalya, Gulf of- (EN) 23 Db 36.30N 31.00 E
An Tan 25 Le 15.26N 108.39 E
Antananarivo 31 Lj 18.55S 47.30 E
Antananarivo [3] 37 Hc 19.00S 46.40 E
Antanimora 37 Hd 24.48S 45.39 E
An tAonach/Nenagh 9 Ei 52.52N 8.12W
Antarctica (EN) 66 Bg 90.00S 0.00
Antarctic Peninsula (EN) 66 Qe 69.30S 65.00W
Antas, Cachoeira das- 55 Ha 13.06S 48.09W
Antas, Rio das- 55 Gi 29.04S 51.21W
An Teampall Mór/Templemore 9 Fi 52.48N 7.50W
Antela, Laguna de- 13 Eb 42.07N 7.41W
Antelao 14 Gd 46.27N 12.16 E
Antelope Creek 46 Me 43.29N 105.23W
Anten 8 Ef 58.03N 12.30 E
Antequera [Par.] 55 Dg 24.08S 57.07W
Antequera [Sp.] 13 Hg 37.01N 4.33W
Anthony 45 Cj 32.00N 106.34W
Anti-Atlas 30 Ge 30.00N 8.30W
Antibes 11 Nk 43.55N 7.07 E
Antibes, Cap d'- 11 Nk 43.32N 7.07 E
Antica, Isla- 50 Eg 10.24N 62.43W
Anticosti, Ile d'- 38 Me 49.30N 63.00W
Antigo 45 Ld 45.09N 89.09W
Antigonish 42 Lg 45.37N 61.58W
Antigua 38 Mh 17.03N 61.48W
Antigua [1] 39 Mh 17.03N 61.48W
Antigua Guatemala 47 Ff 14.34N 90.44W
Antiguo Cauce del Rio Bermejo 56 Hc 25.39S 60.11W
Antiguo Morelos 48 Jf 22.30N 99.05W
Antilla 49 Jc 20.50N 75.45W
Antillas, Mar de las-/Caribe, Mar-=Caribbean Sea (EN) 38 Lh 15.00N 73.00W
Antillas Mayores=Greater Antilles (EN) 38 Lh 20.00N 74.00W
Antillas Menores=Lesser Antilles (EN) 38 Mh 15.00N 61.00W
Antilles, Mer des-/Caraïbe, Mer-=Caribbean Sea (EN) 38 Lh 15.00N 73.00W
An tInbhear Mór/Arklow 9 Gi 52.48N 6.09W
Antioch 46 Eg 38.00N 121.49W
Antioch (EN)=Antakya 23 Eb 36.14N 36.07 E
Antioche, Pertuis d'- 11 Eh 46.05N 1.20W
Antiope Reef 57 Kf 18.18S 168.40W
Antioquia [2] 54 Cb 7.00N 75.30W
Antipajëta 20 Cc 69.09N 77.00 E
Antipodes Islands 57 Ii 49.40S 178.50 E
Antiques, Pointe d'- 51e Ab 16.26N 61.33W
An t-Iúr/Newry 9 Gg 54.11N 6.20W
Antler River 45 Fb 49.08N 101.00W
Antlers 45 Ii 34.14N 95.37W
Antofagasta [2] 56 Gb 23.30S 69.00W
Antofagasta 53 Ih 23.39S 70.24W
Antofagasta de la Sierra 56 Gc 26.04S 67.25W
Antofalla, Salar de- 56 Gc 25.44S 67.45W
Antofalla, Volcán- 56 Gc 25.34S 67.55W
Antoing 12 Fd 50.34N 3.27 E
Antón 49 Gi 8.24N 80.16W
Anton Dohrn Seamount (EN) 9 Cd 57.30N 11.00W
Antongil, Baie d'- 30 Lj 15.45S 49.50 E
Antonina 56 Kc 25.27S 48.43W
Antônio João 55 Ef 23.15S 55.31W
Antonito 45 Dh 37.05N 106.00W
Antón Lizardo, Punta de- 48 Lh 19.03N 95.58W
Antony 12 Ef 48.45N 2.18 E
Antopol 10 Ud 52.12N 24.53 E
Antracit 16 Ke 48.06N 39.06 E
Antreff 12 Ld 50.52N 9.15 E
Antrim/Aontroim 9 Gg 54.43N 6.13W
Antrim Mountains 9 Gf 55.00N 6.10W
Antrodoco 14 Hh 42.25N 13.05 E
Antsakabary 37 Hc 15.03S 48.56 E
Antsalova 37 Gc 18.42S 44.33 E
Antseranana [3] 37 Hb 13.40S 49.15 E
Antseranana 31 Lj 12.17S 49.17 E
An tSionainn/Shannon 5 Fe 52.36N 9.41W
Antsirabe 31 Lj 19.51S 47.01 E
An tSiúir/Suir 9 Gi 52.15N 7.00W
Antsla 7 Gh 57.52N 26.33 E
An tSláine/Slaney 9 Gi 52.21N 6.30W
Antsohihy 31 Lj 14.52S 47.58 E
An tSuca/Suck 9 Eh 53.16N 8.03W
Anttola 8 Lc 61.35N 27.39 E
Antu (Songjiang) 28 Jc 42.33N 128.20 E
An Tuc 25 Lf 13.57N 108.39 E
Antufash, Jazīrat- 33 Hf 15.42N 42.25 E
An Tulach/Tullow 9 Gi 52.48N 6.44W
An Tulach Mhór/Tullamore 9 Fh 53.16N 7.30W
Antwerp (EN)=Antwerpen/Anvers 6 Ge 50.38N 5.34 E
Antwerp (EN)=Anvers/Antwerpen 6 Ge 50.38N 5.34 E
Antwerpen [3] 12 Gc 51.10N 4.30 E
Antwerpen/Anvers=Antwerp (EN) 6 Ge 50.38N 5.34 E
Antwerpen-Ekeren 11 Kc 51.17N 4.25 E
Antwerpen-Hoboken 12 Gc 51.10N 4.21 E
Antwerpen-Merksem 12 Gc 51.15N 4.27 E
Antykan 20 If 54.55N 135.13 E
An Uaimh/Navan 9 Gh 53.39N 6.41W
Anuradhapura 25 Gg 8.21N 80.23 E
Anuta Island 57 Hf 11.38S 169.50 E
Anvers/Antwerpen=Antwerp (EN) 6 Ge 50.38N 5.34 E
Anvers Island 66 Qe 64.33S 63.35W
Anvik 40 Gd 62.40N 160.12W
Anxi 22 Le 40.30N 96.00 E
Anxiang 27 Jf 29.26N 112.11 E
Anxin 28 Ce 38.55N 115.56 E
Anxious Bay 59 Gf 33.25S 134.35 E
Anyang (Zhangde) 22 Nf 36.01N 114.25 E
A'nyêmaqen Shan 21 Lf 34.30N 100.00 E
Anyi 28 Cj 28.50N 115.31 E
Anykščiai/Anikščjaj 7 Fi 55.31N 25.08 E
Anyva, Mys- 20 Jg 46.00N 143.25 E
Anza 14 Ce 46.00N 8.17 E
Anze 28 Bf 36.09N 112.14 E
Anzegem 12 Fd 50.50N 3.28 E
Anžero-Sudžensk 22 Kd 56.07N 86.00 E
Anzi 36 Dc 0.52S 23.24 E
Anzio 14 Gi 41.27N 12.37 E
Anzoátegui [2] 54 Fb 9.00N 64.30W
Anzob, Pereval- 18 Ge 39.07N 68.53 E
Aoba, Ile- 61 Cc 15.25S 167.50 E
Ao Ban Don 25 Jg 9.20N 99.25 E
Aoga-Shima 27 Oe 32.30N 139.50 E
Aohan Qi (Xinhui) 28 Ec 42.18N 119.53 E
Aoiz 13 Kb 42.47N 1.22W
Aoji 28 Kc 42.31N 130.24 E
Aola 63a Ec 9.32S 160.29 E
Aomen/Macau=Macao (EN) [5] 22 Ng 22.10N 113.33 E
Aomen/Macau=Macao (EN) 27 Jg 22.12N 113.33 E
Aomori 22 Qe 40.49N 140.45 E
Aomori Ken [2] 28 Pd 40.40N 140.40 E
Aono-Yama 29 Bd 34.27N 131.48 E
Aontroim/Antrim 9 Gg 54.43N 6.13W
Aopo 65c Aa 13.29S 172.30W
Aôral, Phnum- 25 Kf 12.02N 104.10 E
Aoré 63b Cb 15.35S 167.10 E
Aosta / Aoste 14 Be 45.44N 7.20 E
Aosta, Val d'- 14 Be 45.45N 7.20 E
Aoste / Aosta 14 Be 45.44N 7.20 E
Aouk, Bahr- 30 Ih 8.51N 18.53 E
Aoukalé 35 Cd 9.10N 20.30 E
Aoukâr [Afr.] 32 Ge 24.00N 2.30W
Aoukâr [Mtna.] 30 Gg 17.30N 9.30W
Aoulef 32 Hd 26.58N 1.05 E
Aoumou 63b Be 21.24S 165.49 E
Aourou 34 Cc 14.28N 11.34W
Aoya 29 Cd 35.32N 133.59 E
Aozou 31 If 21.49N 17.25 E
Apa, Rio- 56 Ib 22.06S 58.00W
Apača 20 Kf 52.50N 157.10 E
Apache 46 Kk 31.44N 109.07W
Apache Junction 46 Jj 33.26N 111.32W
Apahida 15 Gc 46.49N 23.45 E
Apakho 63c Bb 11.25S 166.32 E
Apalachee Bay 38 Kg 29.30N 84.00W
Apalachicola 44 Ek 29.44N 84.59W
Apalachicola River 44 Ek 29.44N 84.59W
Apan 48 Jh 19.43N 98.25W
Apaporis, Río- 52 Jf 1.23S 69.25W
Aparecida do Taboado 54 Hg 20.05S 51.05W
Aparri 22 Oh 18.22N 121.39 E
Apataki Atoll 57 Mf 15.26S 146.20W
Apatin 15 Bd 45.40N 18.59 E
Apatity 6 Jb 67.34N 33.18 E
Apatzingán de la Constitucion 47 De 19.05N 102.21W
Apaxtla de Castrejón 48 Jh 18.09N 99.52W
Ape 7 Gh 57.32N 26.42 E
Apeldoorn 11 Lb 52.13N 5.58 E
Apeldoorn-Nieuw Milligen 12 Hb 52.14N 5.45 E
Apen 12 Ja 53.13N 7.48 E
Apennines (EN) = Appennini 5 Hg 43.00N 13.00 E
Apere, Río- 54 Ef 13.44S 65.18W
Aphrodisias 24 Cd 37.45N 28.40 E
Api 21 Kf 30.00N 80.57 E
Api 36 Eb 3.40N 25.26 E
Apia 58 Jf 13.50S 171.44W
Apiacás, Serra dos- 54 Gf 10.15S 57.15W
Apio 63a Ec 9.39S 161.23 E
Apipé Grande, Isla- 55 Di 27.30S 56.54W
Apizaco 48 Jh 19.25N 98.09W
Aplao 54 Dc 16.05S 72.31W
Apo, Mount- 21 Oi 6.59N 125.16 E
Apodi 54 Ke 5.39S 37.48W
Apolda 10 He 51.01N 11.30 E
Apolima 65c Aa 13.49S 172.07W
Apolima Strait 65c Aa 13.50S 172.10W
Apollo Bay 59 Ig 38.45S 143.40 E
Apollonia [Alb.] 15 Ci 40.43N 19.27 E
Apollonia [Lib.] 33 Dc 32.54N 21.58 E
Apolo 54 Ef 14.43S 68.31W
Apón, Río- 49 Kh 10.06N 72.23W
Apopka, Lake- 44 Gk 28.37N 81.38W
Aporé 55 Fd 18.58S 52.01W
Aporé, Rio- 52 Kg 19.27S 50.57W
Apostle Islands 43 Ib 46.50N 90.30W
Apostoles 56 Ic 27.55S 55.46W
Apostolovo 16 Hf 47.39N 33.43 E
Apoteri 54 Gc 4.02N 58.34W
Apôtres, Iles des- 30 Mm 45.40S 50.20 E
Appalachia 44 Fg 36.54N 82.48W
Appalachian Mountains 38 Lc 41.00N 77.00W
Äppelbo 8 Ed 60.30N 14.00 E
Appennini = Apennines (EN) 5 Hg 43.00N 13.00 E
Appennino Abruzzese 14 Hh 42.00N 13.55 E
Appennino Calabro 14 Kl 39.00N 16.30 E
Appennino Campano 14 Ii 40.50N 14.45 E
Appennino Ligure 14 Cf 44.30N 9.00 E
Appennino Lucano 14 Jj 40.30N 16.00 E
Appennino Tosco-Emiliano 14 Fg 44.00N 11.30 E
Appennino Umbro-Marchigiano 14 Gg 43.20N 12.55 E
Appenzell 14 Dc 47.20N 9.25 E
Appenzell Ausser-Rhoden [2] 14 Dc 47.20N 9.20 E
Appenzell Inner-Rhoden [2] 14 Dc 47.15N 9.25 E
Appingedam 12 Ia 53.19N 6.52 E
Appleby 9 Kg 54.36N 2.29W
Appleton 43 Jc 44.16N 88.25W
Appomattox 44 Hg 37.21N 78.51W
Apra Harbor 64c Bb 13.27N 144.38 E
Apricena 14 Ji 41.47N 15.27 E
Aprilia 14 Gi 41.36N 12.39 E
Apšeronsk 19 Dg 44.27N 39.44 E
Apšeronski Poluostrov=Apsheron Peninsula (EN) 5 Lg 41.00N 50.50 E
Apsheron Peninsula (EN)=Apšeronski Poluostrov 5 Lg 41.00N 50.50 E
Apt 11 Lk 43.53N 5.24 E
Apucarana 56 Jb 23.33S 51.29W
Apucarana, Serra da- 55 Gf 23.50S 51.20W
Apuka 20 Ld 60.23N 169.45 E
Apuka 20 Ld 60.25N 169.35 E
Apulia (EN) = Puglia [2] 14 Ki 41.15N 16.15 E
Apurashokoru 64a Ac 7.17N 134.18 E
Apure [2] 54 Eb 7.10N 68.50W
Apure, Río- 52 Je 7.37N 66.25W
Apurímac [2] 54 Df 14.00S 73.00W
Apurímac, Río- 52 Ig 12.17S 73.56W
Apurito 50 Bi 7.56N 68.27W
Apuseni, Munţii-=Apuseni Mountains (EN) 5 If 46.30N 22.30 E
Apuseni Mountains (EN)=Apuseni, Munţii- 5 If 46.30N 22.30 E
Āq 24 Kc 38.59N 45.27 E
Āqā 24 Me 35.00N 47.00 E
Aqaba (EN)=Al 'Aqabah 23 Dd 29.31N 35.00 E
Aqaba, Gulf of- (EN)='Aqabah, Khalīj al- 30 Kf 29.00N 34.40 E
Āqā Bāba 24 Md 36.20N 49.46 E
'Aqabah, Khalīj al-=Aqaba, Gulf of- (EN) 30 Kf 29.00N 34.40 E
Āqcheh 23 Kb 36.56N 66.11 E
'Aqdā 24 Of 32.26N 53.37 E
'Aqīq 35 Fb 18.14N 38.12 E
Aqitag 27 Fc 41.49N 90.38 E
Āqotāq 24 Ld 37.10N 47.05 E
Āq Qal'eh 24 Pd 37.01N 54.30 E
Aqqikkol Hu 27 Ed 37.00N 88.20 E
'Aqrah 24 Jd 36.45N 43.54 E
Aqrin, Jabal- 24 Hg 31.32N 38.18 E
Āq Şū 24 Ke 34.35N 44.31 E
Aquidabã, Rio- 55 De 20.58S 57.50W
Aquidabán, Río- 55 Df 23.11S 57.32W
Aquidauana 54 Gh 20.28S 55.48W
Aquidauana, Rio- 54 Gg 19.44S 56.50W
Aquidauna, Serra de- 55 Ee 20.50S 55.30W
Aquiles Serdán 48 Gc 28.36N 105.53W
Aquin 49 Kd 18.16N 73.24W
Aquitaine, Bassin d'-=Aquitane Basin (EN) 5 Fg 44.00N 0.10W
Aquitane Basin (EN)=Aquitaine, Bassin d'- 5 Fg 44.00N 0.10W
Ara 13 Mb 42.25N 0.09 E
'Arab, Baḩr al- 30 Jh 9.02N 29.28 E
'Arab, Khalīj al- 33 Ec 30.55N 29.05 E
'Arab, Shaţţ al- 21 Gf 30.28N 47.59 E
'Arabah, Wādī- 24 Eh 29.07N 32.39 E
'Arabah, Wādī al- 24 Fg 30.58N 32.24 E
Arabatskaja Strelka, Kosa- 16 Ig 45.40N 35.05 E
'Arabestān 24 Mg 30.30N 50.00 E
Arabian Basin (EN) 3 Gh 11.30N 65.00 E
Arabian Desert (EN)=Sharqīyah, Aş Şaḩrā' ash- 30 Kf 28.00N 32.00 E
Arabian Peninsula (EN) 21 Gg 25.00N 45.00 E
Arabian Sea (EN) 21 Ih 15.00N 65.00 E
Araç 24 Eb 41.15N 33.21 E
Aracá, Rio- 54 Fd 0.25S 62.55W
Aracaju 53 Mg 10.55S 37.04W
Aracataca 49 Jh 10.35N 74.13W
Aracati 54 Kd 4.34S 37.46W
Araçatuba 53 Kh 21.12S 50.25W
Aracena 13 Fg 37.53N 6.33W
Aracena, Sierra de- 13 Fg 37.56N 6.50W
Aracides, Cape- 63a Ec 8.39S 161.01 E
Aracruz 54 Jg 19.49S 40.16W
Araçuaí 54 Jg 16.52S 42.04W
Arad 6 If 46.11N 21.19 E
'Arad 24 Fg 31.15N 35.13 E
Arad [2] 15 Ec 46.11N 21.25 E
Arada 35 Cb 15.01N 20.40 E
'Arādah 35 Ia 22.59N 53.26 E
Arafali 35 Fb 15.04N 39.45 E
Ara Fana 35 Gd 6.01N 41.11 E
Arafune-Yama 29 Fc 36.12N 138.38 E
Arafura, Laut-=Arafura Sea (EN) 57 Ee 9.00S 133.00 E
Arafura, Sea (EN)=Arafura, Laut- 57 Ee 9.00S 133.00 E
Aragac, Gora- 5 Kg 40.31N 44.10 E
Aragarças 53 Kg 15.55S 52.15W
Aragón 13 Kb 42.13N 1.44W
Aragón 5 Fg 41.00N 1.00W
Aragón 13 Lc 41.00N 1.00W
Aragona 14 Hm 37.24N 13.37 E
Aragua [2] 54 Eb 10.00N 67.10W
Araguacema 54 Ie 8.50S 49.34W
Aragua de Barcelona 50 Dh 9.28N 64.49W
Aragua de Maturín 50 Eh 9.58N 63.29W
Araguaia, Rio- 52 Lf 5.21S 48.41W
Araguaiana 55 Gb 16.49S 53.05W
Araguaina 54 Ie 7.12S 48.12W
Araguao, Boca- 54 Fb 9.17N 60.48W
Araguao, Caño- 50 Fh 9.15N 60.50W
Araguapiche, Punta- 50 Fh 9.29N 60.56W
Araguari 54 Ig 18.38S 48.11W
Araguari, Rio- [Braz.] 52 Le 1.15N 49.55W
Araguari, Rio- [Braz.] 55 Hd 18.21S 48.40W
Araguatins 54 Ie 5.38S 48.07W
'Arâguîb 32 Ff 18.50N 7.45W
Aragvi 16 Ni 41.50N 44.43 E
Arai 28 Of 37.09N 138.06 E
Árainn/Inishmore 9 Dh 53.07N 9.45W
Árainn Mhór/Aran Island 9 Ef 55.00N 8.30W
Araioses 54 Jd 2.53S 41.55W
Arāk 22 Gf 34.05N 49.41 E
Arak 32 Hd 25.18N 3.45 E
Arakabesan 64a Ac 7.21N 134.27 E
Arakan [2] 25 Ie 19.00N 94.15 E
Arakan Yoma 21 Lh 19.00N 94.40 E
Arakawa 29 Fb 38.09N 139.25 E
Ara-Kawa [Jap.] 29 Fb 38.09N 139.23 E
Ara-Kawa [Jap.] 29 Fc 37.11N 138.15 E
Árakhthos 15 Ej 39.01N 21.03 E
Araks 21 Gf 39.56N 48.20 E
Aral [China] 27 Dc 40.38N 81.24 E
Aral [Kirg.-U.S.S.R.] 19 Hg 41.48N 74.25 E
Aral Sea (EN)=Aralskoje More 21 He 45.00N 60.00 E
Aralsk 22 Ie 46.48N 61.40 E
Aralskoje More=Aral Sea (EN) 21 He 45.00N 60.00 E
Aralsor, Ozero- 16 Pe 49.05N 48.15 E
Aralsulfat 19 Gf 46.50N 61.59 E
Aramac 59 Jd 22.59S 145.14 E
Arambaré 55 Gj 30.55S 51.29W
Ārān 24 Ne 34.03N 51.30 E
Aranda de Duero 13 Ic 41.41N 3.41W
Arandelovac 15 De 44.18N 20.35 E
Arandilla 13 Ic 41.40N 3.41W
Aran Island/Árainn Mhór 9 Dh 53.07N 9.43W
Aran Islands 9 Ef 55.00N 8.30W
Aranjunez 13 Id 40.02N 3.36W
Aranos 37 Bd 24.09S 19.09 E
Arañuelo, Campo- 13 Ge 39.55N 5.30W
Aranuka Atoll 57 Id 0.11N 173.36 E
Arao 29 Be 32.59N 130.27 E
Araouane 31 Gg 18.53N 3.35W
Arapahoe 45 Gf 40.18N 99.54W
Arapey Grande, Rio- 55 Dj 30.55S 57.49W
Arapiraca 54 Ke 9.45S 36.39W
Arápis, Ákra- 15 Gi 40.27N 24.00 E
Arapkir 24 Hc 39.03N 38.30 E
Arapoim, Rio- 55 Kb 15.45S 43.39W
Arapongas 56 Jb 23.23S 51.27W
Arapoti 55 Hg 24.08S 49.50W
'Ar'ar 24 Ig 30.59N 41.02 E
'Ar'ar, Wādī 24 Jg 31.23N 42.26 E
Araranguá 56 Kc 28.56S 49.29W
Araraquara 53 Lh 21.47S 48.10W
Araras 55 If 22.22S 47.23W
Araras, Açude- 54 Jd 4.20S 40.30W
Araras, Serra das- 55 Fd 18.45S 53.30W
Ararat [Arm.-U.S.S.R.] 19 Eh 39.50N 44.43 E
Ararat [Austl.] 59 Ig 37.17S 142.56 E
Ararat, Mount- (EN)=Büyük Ağri Daği 21 Gf 39.40N 44.24 E
Arari 54 Jd 3.28S 44.47W
Arari, Lago- 54 Id 0.37S 49.07W
Aras 21 Gf 39.56N 48.20 E
Aras Dağlari 24 Jc 40.00N 43.00 E
Aratika Atoll 57 Mf 15.32S 145.32W
Aratürük/Yiwu 27 Fc 43.15N 94.35 E
Arauca [2] 54 Db 6.30N 71.00W
Arauca 54 Db 7.03N 70.47W
Arauca, Río- 52 Je 7.24N 66.35W
Araucania [2] 56 Fe 37.50S 73.15W
Arauco 56 Fe 37.15S 73.19W
Araure 50 Bh 9.38N 69.15W
Aravaca, Madrid- 13 Id 40.27N 3.47W
Aravis 11 Mi 45.53N 6.28 E
Arawalli Range 21 Jg 25.00N 73.30 E
Araxá 54 Ig 19.35S 46.55W
Áraxos, Ákra- 15 Ek 38.10N 21.23 E
Araya 50 Dg 10.34N 64.15W
Araya, Peninsula de- 54 Fa 10.35N 64.00W
Arba 13 Kc 41.52N 1.18W
Arba'āt 35 Fb 19.50N 37.03 E
Arba'īn, Darb al- 24 Di 26.40N 30.50 E
Arbaj-Here 27 Hb 46.15N 102.48 E
Arba Minch 31 Kh 5.59N 37.38 E
'Arbat 24 Ke 35.25N 45.35 E
Arbatax 14 Dk 39.56N 9.42 E
Arboga 7 Dg 59.24N 15.50 E
Arbogaån 8 Ge 59.26N 16.04 E
Arbois 11 Lh 46.54N 5.46 E
Arboletes 49 Ii 8.52N 76.25W
Arbolito 55 Ek 32.39S 54.15W
Arbon 14 Dc 47.30N 9.25 E
Arbore 15 Ib 47.44N 25.56 E
Arborea 14 Ck 39.46N 8.35 E
Arborea 14 Ck 39.50N 8.50 E
Arborg 45 Ha 50.55N 97.15W
Arbrå 7 Dc 61.29N 16.23 E
Arbroath 9 Ke 56.34N 2.35W
Arbus 14 Ck 39.32N 8.36 E
Arc [Fr.] 11 Mi 45.34N 6.12 E
Arc [Fr.] 11 Lk 43.31N 5.07 E
Arcachon 11 Ej 44.39N 1.10W
Arcachon, Bassin d'- 11 Ej 44.42N 1.09W
Arcadia [Fl.-U.S.] 44 Gl 27.14N 81.52W
Arcadia [La.-U.S.] 45 Jj 32.33N 92.55W
Arcagly-Ajat 17 Jj 53.00N 61.50 E
Arcas, Cayos- 47 Fd 20.12N 91.58W
Arcata 46 Cf 40.52N 124.05W
Arcelia 48 Ih 18.17N 100.16W
Arcen, Areen en Velden- 12 Ic 51.28N 6.11 E
Arcevia 14 Gg 43.30N 12.56 E
Archangel (EN)=Arhangelsk 6 Kc 64.34N 40.32 E
Archaringa Creek 59 He 28.15S 135.15 E
Archer River 59 Ib 13.28S 141.41 E
Archer's Post 36 Gb 0.39N 37.41 E
Archidona 13 Hg 37.05N 4.23W
Arcidosso 14 Fh 42.52N 11.33 E
Arcipelago Campano 5 Hg 40.30N 13.20 E
Arcipelago Toscano=Tuscan Archipelago (EN) 5 Hg 42.45N 10.20 E
Arcis-sur-Aube 11 Kf 48.32N 4.08 E
Arciz 16 Fg 45.59N 29.27 E
Arco [Id.-U.S.] 46 Ie 43.38N 113.18W
Arco [It.] 14 Ee 45.55N 10.53 E
Arconce 11 Jh 46.27N 4.00 E
Arcos 55 Je 20.17S 45.32W
Arcos de Jalón 13 Jc 41.13N 2.16W
Arcos de la Frontera 13 Gh 36.45N 5.48W
Arcos de Valdevez 13 Dc 41.51N 8.25W
Arcoverde 53 Mf 8.25S 37.04W
Arctic Bay 39 Kb 73.02N 85.11W
Arctic Ocean 67 Be 85.00N 170.00 E
Arctic Ocean (EN)=Ishavet 67 Be 85.00N 170.00 E
Arctic Ocean (EN)=Severny Ledovity Okean 67 Be 85.00N 170.00 E
Arctic Red River 42 Ec 67.27N 133.45W
Arctic Red River 42 Ec 67.22N 133.30W
Arctic Village 40 Jc 68.08N 145.19W
Arda [Eur.] 15 Jh 41.39N 26.29 E
Arda [It.] 14 Ee 45.02N 10.02 E
Ardabīl [Iran] 22 Gf 38.15N 48.18 E
Ardabīl [Iraq] 24 Ie 34.24N 40.59 E
Ardahan 24 Jb 41.07N 42.41 E
Ardakāh 23 Hc 32.19N 53.59 E
Ardakān 24 Og 30.16N 52.01 E
Ardal 24 Ng 31.59N 50.39 E
Ardales 13 Hh 36.52N 4.51W
Ardalsfjorden 8 Bc 61.15N 7.30 E
Årdalstangen 7 Bf 61.14N 7.43 E
Ardanuç 24 Jb 41.08N 42.03 E
Ardatov [R.S.F.S.R.] 7 Ki 55.17N 43.12 E
Ardatov [R.S.F.S.R.] 7 Li 54.53N 46.13 E
'Arde 35 Hd 9.58N 46.04 E
Ardèche 11 Kj 44.16N 4.39 E
Ardèche [3] 11 Kj 44.40N 4.20 E
Ardee/Béal Átha Fhirdhia 9 Gh 53.52N 6.33W
Ardencaple Fjord 41 Jd 75.15N 20.10W
Ardenne, Plateau de l'-/Ardennen, Plateau van der-=Ardennes (EN) 5 Ge 50.10N 5.45 E
Ardennen, Plateau van der-/Ardenne, Plateau de l'-=Ardennes (EN) 5 Ge 50.10N 5.45 E
Ardennes [3] 11 Ke 49.40N 4.40 E
Ardennes (EN)=Ardenne, Plateau de l'-/Ardennen, Plateau van der- 5 Ge 50.10N 5.45 E
Ardennes (EN)=Ardennen, Plateau van der-/Ardenne, Plateau de l'- 5 Ge 50.10N 5.45 E
Ardennes, Canal des- 11 Ke 49.26N 4.02 E
Ardennes, Forêt des- 12 Ge 49.48N 4.50 E
Ardentes 11 Hh 46.45N 1.50 E
Ardeşen 24 Ib 41.12N 41.00 E
Ardestān 24 Of 33.22N 52.23 E
Árdhas 15 Jh 41.39N 26.29 E
Ardila 13 Ef 38.12N 7.28W
Ard Mhacha/Armagh 9 Gg 54.21N 6.39W
Ardmore 43 He 34.10N 97.08W
Ardnamurchan, Point of- 9 Ge 56.45N 6.30W
Ardon 16 Nh 43.07N 44.13 E
Ardooie 12 Fd 50.59N 3.12 E
Ardre 12 Fe 49.18N 3.40 E
Ardres 12 Dd 50.51N 1.59 E
Ards Peninsula/An Aird 9 Hg 54.30N 5.30W
Ar Dub'al Khālī 21 Hg 21.00N 51.00 E
Ardud 15 Fb 47.38N 22.53 E
Arebi 36 Eb 2.50N 29.38 E
Arecibo 47 Ke 18.28N 66.43W
Areen en Valden 12 Ic 51.28N 6.11 E
Areen en Velden-Arcen 12 Ic 51.28N 6.11 E
Arëgala/Ariogala 8 Ji 55.13N 23.30 E
Areia, Ribeirão da- 55 Jc 16.07S 45.52W
Areia Branca 54 Kd 4.57S 37.08W
Arekalong Peninsula 64a Bb 7.40N 134.38 E
Aremberg 12 Id 50.25N 6.49 E
Arena 26 He 9.14N 120.46 E
Arena, Point- 43 Cd 38.57N 123.44W
Arena, Punta- 47 Cd 23.30N 109.30W
Arena de la Ventana, Punta- 47 Cd 24.04N 109.52W
Arenápolis 54 Gf 14.26S 56.49W
Arenas, Cayo- 47 Fd 22.08N 91.24W
Arenas, Punta de- 56 Gh 53.09S 68.13W
Arenas de San Pedro 13 Gd 40.12N 5.05W
Arenberg 12 Jb 52.42N 7.20 E
Arendal 7 Bg 58.27N 8.48 E
Arendonk 12 Hc 51.19N 5.05 E
Arénys de Mar/Arenys de Mar 13 Oc 41.35N 2.33 E
Arenys de Mar/Arénys de Mar 13 Oc 41.35N 2.33 E
Areópolis 15 Fm 36.40N 22.23 E
Areq, Sebkha bou- 13 Ji 35.10N 2.45W
Arequipa 53 Ig 16.24S 71.33W
Arequipa [2] 54 Dg 16.00S 72.30W
Arequito 55 Bk 33.09S 61.28W
Arero 35 Fe 4.44N 38.50 E
Ares, Muela de- 13 Ld 40.28N 0.07W
Åreskutan 8 Ea 63.26N 13.06 E
Åreskutan 7 Ce 63.24N 13.06 E
Arévalo 13 Hc 41.04N 4.43W
Arezzo 14 Fg 43.25N 11.53 E
Arga 13 Kb 42.18N 1.47W
Argajas 17 Ji 55.31N 60.55 E
Argamasilla de Alba 13 Ie 39.07N 3.06W
Argan 27 Ec 40.09N 88.22 E
Arganda 13 Id 40.18N 3.26W
Arga-Sala 20 Gc 68.37N 112.05 E
Argelès-Gazost 11 Fk 43.01N 0.06W
Argelès-sur-Mer 11 Jl 42.33N 3.01 E
Argens 11 Mk 43.24N 6.44 E

Index Symbols

[1] Independent Nation
[2] State, Region
[3] District, County
[4] Municipality
[5] Colony, Dependency
Continent
Physical Region
Historical or Cultural Region
Mount, Mountain
Volcano
Hill
Mountains, Mountain Range
Hills, Escarpment
Plateau, Upland
Pass, Gap
Plain, Lowland
Delta
Salt Flat
Valley, Canyon
Crater, Cave
Karst Features
Depression
Polder
Desert, Dunes
Forest, Woods
Heath, Steppe
Oasis
Cape, Point
Coast, Beach
Cliff
Peninsula
Isthmus
Sandbank
Island
Atoll
Rock, Reef
Islands, Archipelago
Rocks, Reefs
Coral Reef
Well, Spring
Geyser
River, Stream
Waterfall Rapids
River Mouth, Estuary
Lake
Salt Lake
Intermittent Lake
Reservoir
Swamp, Pond
Canal
Glacier
Ice Shelf, Pack Ice
Ocean
Sea
Gulf, Bay
Strait, Fjord
Lagoon
Bank
Seamount
Tablemount
Ridge
Shelf
Basin
Escarpment, Sea Scarp
Fracture
Trench, Abyss
National Park, Reserve
Point of Interest
Recreation Site
Cave, Cavern
Historic Site
Ruins
Wall, Walls
Church, Abbey
Temple
Scientific Station
Airport
Port
Lighthouse
Mine
Tunnel
Dam, Bridge

Argent, Côte d'- 11 Ej 44.00N 1.30W
Argenta 14 Ff 44.37N 11.50 E
Argentan 11 Ff 48.45N 0.01W
Argentario, Monte- 14 Fh 42.24N 11.09 E
Argentat 11 Hi 45.06N 1.56 E
Argentera 14 Bf 44.10N 7.18 E
Argenteuil 11 If 48.57N 2.15 E
Argentiera, Capo dell'- 14 Cj 40.44N 8.08 E
Argentina 55 Ai 29.33S 62.17W
Argentina [1] 53 Ji 34.00S 64.00W
Argentine Basin (EN) 3 Cn 45.00S 45.00W
Argentino, Lago- 52 Ik 50.13S 72.25W
Argentino, Mar- 52 Kj 46.00S 59.40W
Argenton 11 Fg 47.05N 0.13W
Argenton-Château 11 Fh 46.59N 0.27W
Argenton-sur-Creuse 11 Hh 46.35N 1.31 E
Arges 15 Jd 44.04N 26.37 E
Arges [2] 15 Hd 45.00N 24.50 E
Arghandāb 23 Jc 31.27N 64.23 E
Argo 35 Eb 19.31N 30.25 E
Argo Depth (EN) 3 Jk 12.10S 165.40W
Argolikós Kólpos = Argolis, Gulf of- (EN) 15 Fl 37.20N 22.55 E
Argolis, Gulf of- (EN) = Argolikós Kólpos 15 Fl 37.20N 22.55 E
Argonne 12 He 49.30N 5.00 E
Argonne 11 Ke 49.30N 5.00 E
Árgos 15 Fl 37.38N 22.44 E
Árgos Orestikón 15 Ei 40.30N 21.16 E
Argostólion 15 Dk 38.11N 20.29 E
Arguedas 13 Kb 42.10N 1.36W
Argueil-Fry 12 De 49.37N 1.31 E
Arguello, Point- 46 Ei 34.35N 120.39W
Arguenon 11 Df 48.35N 2.13W
Argun 16 Nh 43.16N 45.52 E
Argun 21 Od 53.20N 121.28 E
Argungu 34 Fc 12.45N 4.31 E
Argyle 51n Ba 13.10N 61.10W
Argyle, Lake- 57 Df 16.15S 128.40 E
Argyll 9 Ie 56.20N 5.00W
Arhangelsk = Archangel (EN) 6 Kc 64.34N 40.32 E
Arhangelskaja Oblast [3] 19 Ec 63.30N 43.00 E
Arhara 20 Ig 49.30N 130.09 E
Arhavi 24 Ib 41.22N 41.16 E
Arholma 8 He 59.50N 19.05 E
Ar Horqin Qi (Tianshan) 27 Lc 43.55N 120.05 E
Århus [2] 8 Dh 56.10N 10.15 E
Århus 6 Hd 56.09N 10.13 E
Århus Bugt 8 Dh 56.10N 10.20 E
Arhust 27 Ib 47.42N 107.50 E
Ariadnoje 20 Ig 45.08N 134.25 E
Ariake-Kai 28 Kh 32.55N 130.27 E
Ariamsvlei 37 Be 28.08S 19.50 E
Ariano Irpino 14 Ji 41.09N 15.05 E
Ariari, Rio- 54 Dc 2.35N 72.47W
Arias 56 Hd 33.38S 62.25W
Ari Atoll 25a Bb 3.30N 72.45 E
Aribinda 34 Ec 14.14N 0.52W
Arica 53 Ig 18.29S 70.20W
Arica, Golfo de- 52 Ig 18.30S 70.30W
Arichuna 50 Ci 7.42N 67.08W
Arid, Cape- 59 Ef 34.00S 123.09 E
Arida 28 Mg 34.05N 135.07 E
Arida-Gawa 29 Dd 34.05N 135.06 E
Aridhaia 15 Fi 40.59N 22.04 E
Ariège 11 Hk 43.31N 1.25 E
Ariège [3] 11 Hk 43.00N 1.30 E
Ariel 55 Cm 36.32S 59.54W
Aries 15 Gc 46.26N 23.59 E
Ariguani 54 Db 9.50N 74.01W
Ariguani, Rio- 49 Ki 9.35N 73.46W
Arīḥā [Jor.] 24 Fg 31.52N 35.27 E
Arīḥā [Syr.] 24 Ge 35.48N 36.36 E
Arikaree River 45 Ff 40.01N 101.56W
Arikawa 29 Ae 32.59N 129.07 E
Arilje 15 Df 43.45N 20.06 E
Arima 54 Fa 10.38N 61.17W
Arinos 55 Ib 15.55S 46.04W
Arinos, Rio- 52 Kg 10.25S 58.20W
Arinos Novo, Rio- 55 Db 14.14S 56.01W
Ariogala/Arégala 8 Ji 55.13N 23.30 E
Aripuanã 54 Fe 9.10S 60.38W
Aripuanã, Rio- 52 Jf 5.07S 60.24W
Ariquemes 54 Fe 9.56S 63.04W
Arisa 35 Gc 11.11N 41.38 E
'Arish, Wādī al- 24 Eg 31.09N 33.49 E
Arismendi 49 Mi 8.29N 68.22W
Arita 29 Ae 33.11N 129.52 E
Aritzo 14 Dk 39.57N 9.12 E
Arixang/Wenquan 27 Dc 44.59N 81.04 E
Ariza 13 Jc 41.19N 2.03W
Arizaro, Salar de- 56 Gb 24.42S 67.45W
Arize, Massif de l'- 11 Hl 42.50N 1.30 E
Arizona [2] 43 Ee 34.00N 112.00W
Arizpe 48 Db 30.20N 110.10W
Årjäng 7 Cg 59.23N 12.08 E
Arjeplog 7 Dc 66.03N 17.54 E
Arjo 35 Fd 8.45N 36.30 E
Arjona 54 Ca 10.15N 75.21W
Arkadak 19 Ee 51.58N 43.28 E
Arkadelphia 43 Ie 34.07N 93.04W
Arkalyk 22 Id 50.13N 66.50 E
Arkansas 38 Jf 33.48N 91.04W
Arkansas [2] 43 Id 34.50N 93.40W
Arkansas City 43 Hd 37.04N 97.02W
Arkanū, Jabal- 33 De 22.15N 24.45 E
Arkatag 21 Kf 36.45N 89.10 E
Arkhángelos 15 Lm 36.12N 28.08 E
Árki 15 Jl 37.22N 26.45 E
Arklow/An tInbhear Mór 9 Gi 52.48N 6.09W
Arkona, Kap- 10 Jb 54.41N 13.26 E
Arkonam 25 Ff 13.06N 79.40 E
Arkösund 8 Gf 58.30N 16.56 E
Arkoúdhion 15 Dk 38.33N 20.43 E
Arktičeskoga Instituta, Ostrova- = Arkticheski Institut Islands (EN) 20 Da 75.20N 81.50 E
Arkticheski Institut Islands (EN) = Arktičeskoga Instituta, Ostrova- 20 Da 75.20N 81.50 E
Arlan, Gora- 16 Sj 39.43N 54.40 E
Arlanza 13 Hb 42.06N 4.09W
Arlanzón 13 Hb 42.03N 4.17W
Arlberg 14 Ec 47.08N 10.12 E
Arles 11 Kk 43.40N 4.38 E
Arlington [Or.-U.S.] 46 Ed 45.46N 120.13W
Arlington [Tx.-U.S.] 45 Hj 32.44N 97.07W
Arlington [Va.-U.S.] 43 Ld 38.52N 77.05W
Arlington Heights 45 Me 42.05N 87.59W
Arlit 31 Hg 19.00N 7.38 E
Arlon/Aarlen 11 Le 49.41N 5.49 E
Arlöv 8 Ei 55.39N 13.05 E
Arly 34 Fc 11.35N 1.28 E
Armagh/Ard Mhacha 9 Gg 54.21N 6.39W
Armagnac 11 Gk 43.45N 0.10 E
Armagnac, Collines de l'- 11 Gk 43.30N 0.30 E
Armah, Wādī- 23 Hf 18.12N 51.02 E
Arman 20 Ke 59.43N 150.12 E
Armançon 11 Jg 47.57N 3.30 E
Armandale, Perth- 59 Df 32.09S 116.00 E
Armant 33 Fd 25.37N 32.32 E
Armáthia 15 Jn 35.26N 26.52 E
Armavir 6 Kf 45.00N 41.08 E
Armenia 53 Ie 4.31N 75.41W
Armenia (EN) = Ermenistan 23 Fb 39.10N 43.00 E
Armenia (EN) = Ermenistan 21 Gf 39.10N 43.00 E
Armenian SSR (EN) = Armjanskaja SSR [2] 19 Eg 40.00N 45.00 E
Armentières 11 Id 50.41N 2.53 E
Armeria 48 Gh 18.56N 103.58W
Armi, Capo dell'- 14 Jm 37.57N 15.41 E
Armidale 58 Gh 30.31S 151.39 E
Armisvesi 8 Lb 62.30N 26.35 E
Armjansk 16 Hf 46.05N 33.41 E
Armjanskaja Sovetskaja Socialističeskaja Respublika [2] 19 Eg 40.00N 45.00 E
Armjanskaja SSR/Haikakan Sovetakan Socialistakan Respublika [2] 19 Eg 40.00N 45.00 E
Armjanskaja SSR = Armenian SSR (EN) [2] 19 Eg 40.00N 45.00 E
Armoricain, Massif- = Armorican Massif (EN) 5 Ff 48.00N 3.00W
Armorican Massif (EN) = Armoricain, Massif- 5 Ff 48.00N 3.00W
Armour 45 Ge 43.19N 98.21W
Arm River 46 Ma 50.46N 105.00W
Armstrong [Arg.] 55 Bk 32.47S 61.36W
Armstrong [B.C.-Can.] 46 Fa 50.27N 119.12W
Armstrong [Ont.-Can.] 42 If 50.18N 89.02W
Ārmūdū 24 Qd 37.15N 56.05 E
Armutçuk Dağ 15 Ki 40.05N 27.23 E
Armutlu 15 Li 40.31N 28.50 E
Armutova 15 Jj 39.23N 26.50 E
Arnaia 15 Gi 40.29N 23.36 E
Arnaud 42 Kd 60.00N 69.55W
Arnautis, Akrotérion- 24 Ee 35.06N 32.17 E
Arnay-le-Duc 11 Kg 47.08N 4.29 E
Arnedo 13 Jb 42.13N 2.06W
Årnes 7 Cf 60.09N 11.28 E
Arnhem 11 Lc 51.59N 5.55 E
Arnhem, Cape- 57 Ef 12.21S 136.21 E
Arnhem Bay 59 Hb 12.20S 136.10 E
Arnhem Land 57 Ef 13.10S 134.30 E
Arno 5 Hg 43.41N 10.17 E
Arno Atoll 57 Id 7.05N 171.41 E
Arnold 12 Aa 53.00N 1.08W
Arnon 11 Ig 47.13N 2.01 E
Arnøy 7 Ea 70.08N 20.36 E
Arnprior 44 Ic 45.26N 76.21W
Arnsberg 10 Ee 51.23N 8.05 E
Arnsberger Wald 12 Kc 51.26N 8.10 E
Arnsberg-Oeventrop 12 Kc 51.24N 8.08 E
Arnsburg 12 Kd 50.29N 8.48 E
Arnstadt 10 Gf 50.50N 10.57 E
Aro, Rio- 50 Di 8.01N 64.11W
Aroa 50 Bg 10.26N 68.54W
Aroa, Pointe- 65e Fc 17.28S 149.46W
Aroa, Rio- 50 Bg 10.41N 68.18W
Aroa, Sierra de- 50 Bg 10.15N 68.55W
Aroab 37 Be 26.47S 19.40 E
Aroánia Óri 15 Fl 37.57N 22.13 E
Aroche 13 Fg 37.57N 6.57W
Aroche, Pico de- 13 Ff 38.01N 6.56W
Aroeira 55 Ee 21.41S 54.25W
Arolsen 10 Ff 51.22N 9.01 E
Aroma 35 Fb 15.49N 36.08 E
Aron 11 Jh 46.50N 3.27 E
Arona 14 Ce 45.46N 8.34 E
Aroostook River 44 Nb 46.48N 67.45W
Arorae Island 57 Ie 2.38S 176.49 E
Arorangi 64p Bb 21.13S 159.49W
Aros, Rio- 48 Ec 29.30N 109.15W
Arosa 14 Dd 46.47N 9.40 E
Arosa, Ría de- 13 Db 42.28N 8.57W
Aros Papigochic, Rio- 48 Ec 29.09N 108.35W
Årøsund 8 Ci 55.15N 9.43 E
Arouca 13 Dd 40.56N 8.15W
Arpaçay 24 Jb 40.45N 43.25 E
Arpajon 11 If 48.35N 2.15 E
Arpino 14 Hi 41.39N 13.36 E
Arquata Scrivia 14 Cf 44.41N 8.53 E
Arque 54 Eg 17.48S 66.23W
Arques-la-Bataille 12 De 49.53N 1.08 E
Ar Rachidiya 32 Gc 31.55N 4.40W
Ar Rachidiya [3] 32 Gc 31.00N 4.00W
Ar Radisīyah Baḥrī 33 Fe 24.57N 32.53 E
Arrah 25 Gc 25.34N 84.40 E
Ar Rahad 35 Ec 12.43N 30.39 E
Ar Rahad 30 Kg 14.28N 33.31 E
Arraias 54 If 12.56S 46.57W
Arraias, Rio- [Braz.] 54 Hf 11.10S 53.35W
Arraias, Rio- [Braz.] 55 Ia 12.28S 47.18W
Arraiolos 13 Ef 38.43N 7.59W
Ar Ramādī 23 Fc 33.25N 43.17 E
Ar Ramlah 24 Fh 29.32N 35.57 E
Ar Ramlī al Kabīr 33 Dd 26.30N 22.10 E
Arran, Island of- 9 Hf 55.35N 5.15W
Ar Rank 35 Ec 11.45N 32.48 E
Ar Raqqah 23 Eb 35.56N 39.01 E
Arras 11 Id 50.17N 2.47 E
Ar Rāshidah 24 Cj 25.35N 28.56 E
Ar Rass 24 Jj 25.52N 43.28 E
Ar Rastān 24 Ge 34.55N 36.44 E
Arrats 11 Gj 44.06N 0.52 E
Ar Rawḍah [Sau.Ar.] 33 He 21.16N 42.50 E
Ar Rawḍah [Alg.] 13 Ki 35.23N 1.05W
Ar Rawḍah [P.D.R.Y.] 33 Ig 14.28N 47.17 E
Ar Rawḍatayn 24 Lh 29.53N 47.44 E
Ar Rayḥānī 24 Pk 23.37N 55.58 E
Arrecife 32 Ed 28.57N 13.32W
Arrecife Alacrán 47 Gd 22.24N 89.42W
Arrecifes 56 Hd 34.03S 60.07W
Arrecifes, Río- 55 Ck 33.46S 59.31W
Arrée, Montagnes d'- 11 Cf 48.26N 3.55W
Arresø 8 Ei 55.55N 12.05 E
Arriaga 48 Mi 16.14N 93.54W
Ar Rifā'ī 24 Lg 31.43N 46.07 E
Ar Rihāb 24 Kg 30.52N 45.30 E
Ar Rimāh 24 Lj 25.34N 47.09 E
Ar Rimāl 21 Hg 22.00N 52.50 E
Ar Riyāḍ = Riyadh (EN) 22 Gg 24.38N 46.43 E
Arrochar 9 Ie 56.12N 4.45W
Arroio Grande 55 Fk 32.14S 53.05W
Arrojado 55 Ja 13.29S 44.37W
Arrojado, Rio- 55 Ja 13.24S 44.20W
Arromanches-les-Bains 12 Be 49.20N 0.37W
Arros 11 Gk 43.40N 0.02 E
Arroscia 14 Cg 44.03N 8.11 E
Arroux 11 Jh 46.29N 3.58 E
Arrow, Lough-/Loch Arabhach 9 Eg 54.05N 8.20W
Arrowsmith, Mount- 61 Dh 43.21S 170.59 E
Arrowtown 62 Cf 44.56S 168.50 E
Arroyo Barú 55 Cj 31.52S 58.26W
Arroyo de la Luz 13 Fe 39.29N 6.35W
Arroyo Grande 46 Ei 35.07N 120.34W
Arroyos y Esteros 55 Dg 25.04S 57.06W
Arruda 55 Db 15.02S 56.07W
Arrufó 56 Hd 30.15S 61.45W
Ar Rumaythah 24 Kg 31.32N 45.12 E
Ar Ruq'ī 24 Lh 29.01N 46.33 E
Ar Rusāfah 24 He 35.02N 36.17 E
Ar Ruşayriş 31 Kg 11.51N 34.23 E
Ar Ruţbah 23 Fc 33.02N 40.17 E
Ar Ruwayḍah 24 Ki 26.23N 44.14 E
Ar Ruways [Qatar] 23 Hd 26.08N 51.13 E
Ar Ruways [U.A.E.] 23 He 24.08N 52.45 E
Ar Ruzayqāt 24 Ej 25.35N 32.28 E
Års 8 Ch 56.48N 9.32 E
Arsenjān 24 Oh 29.56N 53.18 E
Arsenjev 20 Ih 44.12N 133.20 E
Arsi [3] 35 Fd 7.10N 40.00 E
Arsk 7 Lh 56.07N 49.52 E
Årskogen 8 Gb 62.05N 17.20 E
Arslanköy 24 Fd 37.01N 34.17 E
Ars-sur-Moselle 12 Ie 49.05N 6.04 E
Arsuk 41 Hf 61.11N 48.30W
Årsunda 8 Gd 60.32N 16.44 E
Art 63b Ad 19.43S 163.39 E
Artá 13 Pe 39.42N 3.21 E
Arta 35 Gc 11.31N 42.50 E
Árta 15 Dj 39.09N 20.59 E
Artá, Cuevas de- 13 Pe 39.40N 3.24 E
Artašat 16 Nj 39.59N 44.33 E
Arteaga 48 Hh 18.28N 102.25W
Artem 20 Ih 43.23N 132.10 E
Artemisa 47 Hd 22.49N 82.46W
Artemón 15 Hm 36.57N 24.43 E
Artem-Ostrov 19 Fg 40.28N 50.18 E
Artemovsk [R.S.F.S.R.] 20 Ef 54.23N 93.30 E
Artemovsk [Ukr.-U.S.S.R.] 16 Ke 48.33N 38.03 E
Artemovski 17 Jh 57.25N 61.58 E
Artesa de Segre 13 Nc 41.54N 1.03 E
Artesia 43 Ge 32.51N 104.24W
Arthur 45 Ff 41.35N 101.31W
Arthur Creek 59 Hd 23.00S 136.58 E
Arthur River 59 Ih 41.00S 144.55 E
Arthur's Pass 61 Dh 42.57S 171.34 E
Arthur's Pass 62 De 42.54S 171.34 E
Arthur's Town 49 Ja 24.38N 75.32W
Arti 17 Ih 56.26N 58.32 E
Artibonite, Rivière de l'- 49 Kd 19.15N 72.47W
Artigas 56 Id 30.42S 56.28W
Artigas [2] 55 Dj 30.35S 57.00W
Artijarvi/Artsjö 8 Ld 60.45N 26.05 E
Artik 16 Mi 40.36N 43.58 E
Artillery Lake 42 Gd 63.08N 107.45W
Artois 11 Id 50.10N 2.30 E
Artois, Collines de l'- 11 Id 50.30N 2.15 E
Artoli 35 Eb 18.19N 33.54 E
Artsjö/Artijarvi 8 Ld 60.45N 26.05 E
Artux 27 Cd 39.40N 76.10 E
Artvin 23 Fa 41.11N 41.49 E
Artyk 20 Jd 64.12N 145.15 E
Aru 36 Fb 2.52N 30.51 E
Aru, Kepulauan- = Aru Islands (EN) 57 Ee 6.00S 134.30 E
Arua 31 Kh 3.01N 30.55 E
Aruanã 55 Gb 14.54S 51.05W
Aruba 54 Ea 12.30N 70.00W
Aru Bassin (EN) 26 Jg 5.00S 134.00 E
Aru Islands (EN) = Aru, Kepulauan- 57 Ee 6.00S 134.30 E
Arukoron Point 64a Bb 7.43N 134.38 E
Arun 9 Mk 50.48N 0.33W
Arunāchal Pradesh [3] 25 Ic 27.50N 94.50 E
Arundel 12 Bd 50.51N 0.33W
Arun He 27 Lb 47.36N 124.06 E
Arun Qi 27 Lb 48.09N 123.29 E
Arus, Tanjung- 26 Hf 1.24N 125.06 E
Arusha [3] 36 Gc 3.30S 36.00 E
Arusha 31 Ki 3.22S 36.41 E
Arutua Atoll 61 Lc 15.18S 146.44W
Arutunga 61 Jc 18.52S 159.46W
Aruwimi 30 Jh 1.13N 23.36 E
Arvada [Co.-U.S.] 45 Dg 39.50N 105.05W
Arvada [Wy.-U.S.] 46 Ld 44.40N 106.03W
Arve 11 Mh 46.12N 6.08 E
Arvert, Presqu'île d'- 11 Ei 45.45N 1.05W
Arvida 42 Kg 48.26N 71.11W
Arvidsjaur 7 Ed 65.35N 19.10 E
Arvika 7 Cg 59.39N 12.36 E
Årviksand 7 Ea 70.12N 20.32 E
Arvin 46 Fi 35.12N 118.50W
Aryānah 14 En 36.52N 10.11 E
Arys 18 Gc 42.48N 68.15 E
Arys 19 Gg 42.26N 68.48 E
Arys, Ozero- 18 Fb 45.50N 66.20 E
Arz 11 Dg 47.39N 2.06W
Arzachena 14 Di 41.05N 9.23 E
Arzamas 19 Ed 55.23N 43.50 E
Arzanah 24 Oj 24.47N 52.34 E
Aržano 14 Kg 43.35N 16.59 E
Arzew 32 Gb 35.51N 0.19W
Arzew, Golfe d'- 13 Li 35.50N 0.10W
Arzew, Salines d'- 13 Li 35.42N 0.18W
Arzfeld 12 Id 50.05N 6.16 E
Arzgir 19 Ef 45.22N 44.13 E
Arzúa 13 Db 42.56N 8.09W
As 12 Hc 51.01N 5.35 E
Ås 8 De 59.40N 10.48 E
Aš 10 If 50.13N 12.12 E
Aša 19 Fd 55.02N 57.18 E
Aså 8 Dg 57.09N 10.25 E
Asab 37 Be 25.29S 17.59 E
Asaba 34 Gd 6.11N 6.45 E
Asad, Buḩayrat al- 24 He 35.57N 38.10 E
Asadābād [Afg.] 23 Lc 34.52N 71.09 E
Asadābād [Iran] 24 Me 34.47N 48.07 E
Asafik 35 Bc 13.10N 19.26 E
Asahi [Jap.] 29 Fb 38.15N 139.30 E
Asahi [Jap.] 29a Ca 44.08N 142.35 E
Asahi [Jap.] 29 Gd 35.43N 140.35 E
Asahi [Jap.] 29 Ec 36.57N 137.34 E
Asahi-Dake 29 Fb 38.16N 139.55 E
Asahi-Gawa 29 Cd 34.36N 133.58 E
Asahikawa 22 Qe 43.46N 142.22 E
Asaka-Drainage 29 Gc 37.30N 140.15 E
Asale, Lake- 35 Gc 14.00N 40.20 E
'Asalūyeh 24 Oi 27.28N 52.37 E
Asama-Yama 28 Of 36.27N 138.30 E
Asan-Man 28 If 36.56N 126.51 E
Asansol 22 Kg 23.41N 86.59 E
Asarna 7 De 62.39N 14.21 E
Asarum 8 Fh 56.12N 14.50 E
'Asäyr = Guardafui, Cape- (EN) 30 Mg 11.49N 51.15 E
Asayta 35 Gc 11.33N 41.27 E
Asbest 17 Jh 57.01N 61.31 E
Asbestos 44 Lc 45.46N 71.57W
Asbe Teferi 35 Gd 9.05N 40.51 E
Asbury Park 44 Je 40.14N 74.01W
Ascension 30 Fi 7.57S 14.22W
Ascensión, Bahía de la- 47 Ge 19.40N 87.30W
Ascensión, Bahía de la- 48 Ph 19.40N 87.30W
Ascensión, Laguna de la- 48 Fb 31.05N 107.55W
Aschaffenburg 10 Fg 49.59N 9.09 E
Ascheberg 12 Jc 51.47N 7.37 E
Aschendorf (Ems), Papenburg- 12 Ja 53.04N 7.22 E
Aschersleben 10 He 51.45N 11.28 E
Aščikol, Ozero- 18 Fb 45.05N 67.20 E
Aščiozek 16 Pe 49.12N 48.06 E
Ascoli Piceno 14 Hh 42.51N 13.34 E
Ascoli Satriano 14 Ji 41.12N 15.34 E
Ascot 12 Bc 51.24N 0.40W
Aseb 31 Lg 13.00N 42.44 E
Åseda 7 Dh 57.10N 15.20 E
Asedjrad 30 Hf 24.42N 1.40 E
Asekejevo 16 Rc 53.36N 52.51 E
Asela 31 Kh 7.58N 39.08 E
As Ela 35 Gc 11.06N 42.06 E
Åsele 7 Dd 64.10N 17.20 E
Åsen [Nor.] 7 Ce 63.36N 11.03 E
Åsen [Swe.] 7 Cf 61.17N 13.50 E
Asendabo 35 Fd 9.47N 37.36 E
Asendorf 12 Kb 52.46N 9.00 E
Asenovgrad 15 Hg 42.01N 24.52 E
Åsensbruk 8 Ef 58.48N 12.25 E
Åseral 8 Bf 58.37N 7.25 E
Aseri/Azeri 7 Gg 59.29N 26.51 E
Asfeld 12 Ge 49.28N 4.07 E
Aşfūn al Maţā'inah 24 Ej 25.23N 32.32 E
Åsgårdstrand 8 De 59.21N 10.28 E
Ašhabad 22 Hf 37.57N 58.23 E
Ašhabadskaja Oblast [3] 19 Fh 38.30N 59.00 E
Ashanti [3] 34 Ed 6.45N 1.30W
Ashburn 44 Fj 31.43N 83.39W
Ashburton 61 Dh 43.54S 171.45 E
Ashburton River 57 Cg 21.40S 114.56 E
Ashdod 24 Fg 31.49N 34.39 E
Ashdown 45 Ij 33.41N 94.08W
Asheboro 44 Hh 35.42N 79.49W
Asheroft 46 Ea 50.43N 121.17W
Asheville 43 Kd 35.34N 82.33W
Ashford 9 Nj 51.09N 0.53 E
Ashford Airport 12 Cc 51.10N 0.59 E
Ash Fork 46 Ii 35.13N 112.29W
Ashibetsu 28 Qc 43.31N 142.11 E
Ashikaga 29 Fc 36.21N 139.27 E
Ashington 9 Lf 55.11N 1.34W
Ashiro 29 Ga 40.06N 141.01 E
Ashiya 29 Be 33.53N 130.40 E
Ashizuri-Misaki 28 Lh 32.44N 133.01 E
Ashkal, Qar'at al- 14 Dm 37.10N 9.40 E
Āshkhāneh 24 Qd 37.28N 57.00 E
Ashland [Ks.-U.S.] 45 Gh 37.11N 99.46W
Ashland [Ky.-U.S.] 43 Kd 38.28N 82.38W
Ashland [Mt.-U.S.] 46 Ld 45.35N 106.16W
Ashland [Oh.-U.S.] 44 Fe 40.52N 82.19W
Ashland [Or.-U.S.] 43 Cc 42.12N 122.42W
Ashland [Wi.-U.S.] 43 Ib 46.35N 90.53W
Ashland, Mount- 46 De 42.05N 122.43W
Ashley 45 Gc 46.02N 99.22W
Ashmore Islands 57 Df 12.15S 123.05 E
Ashmūn 24 Dg 30.18N 30.58 E
Ashoro 29a Cb 43.14N 143.31 E
Ashqelon 24 Fg 31.40N 34.35 E
Ash Shabakah 24 Jg 30.49N 43.39 E
Ash Shabb 33 Ee 22.19N 29.46 E
Ash Shā'ib 24 Gh 28.59N 37.07 E
Ash Sha'm 23 Id 26.02N 56.05 E
Ash Shamālīyah [3] 35 Db 18.40N 30.00 E
Ash 'Shāmīyah 24 Kg 31.57N 44.36 E
Ash Shāmīyah 24 Lg 30.15N 46.55 E
Ash Shaqq 24 Lh 28.20N 47.30 E
Ash Shaqrā' 23 Gd 25.15N 45.15 E
Ash Sha'rā' 24 Kj 24.16N 44.11 E
Ash Sharīqah 23 Id 25.22N 55.23 E
Ash Sharqāţ 23 Fb 35.27N 43.16 E
Ash Sharqī 32 Jc 34.45N 11.15 E
Ash Sharqī 24 Ge 34.00N 36.30 E
Ash Sharqīyah 23 Ie 22.15N 58.30 E
Ash Shatrah 24 Lg 31.25N 46.10 E
Ash Shawbak 24 Fg 30.32N 35.34 E
Ash Shaykh Ḩumayd 24 Fh 28.07N 34.34 E
Ash Shifā 24 Fh 28.30N 35.30 E
Ash Shiḩr 23 Gg 14.44N 49.35 E
Ash Shināfīyah 24 Kg 31.35N 44.39 E
Ash Shu'aybah [Kuw.] 24 Mh 29.03N 48.08 E
Ash Shu'aybah [Sau.Ar.] 24 Ji 27.53N 42.43 E
Ash Shu'bah 24 Kh 28.54N 44.44 E
Ash Shumlūl 24 Li 26.31N 47.20 E
Ash Shuqayq 23 Ff 17.44N 42.01 E
Ash Shurayk 35 Eb 18.48N 33.34 E
Ash Shuwayhāt 24 Oj 24.05N 52.28 E
Ash Shuwaykh 24 Lh 29.21N 47.55 E
Ashtabula 43 Kc 41.53N 80.47W
Ashtabula, Lake- 45 Hc 47.11N 97.58W
Ashtīyān 24 Me 34.30N 49.55 E
Ashton [Id.-U.S.] 46 Jd 44.04N 111.27W
Ashton [St.Vin.] 51n Bb 12.36N 61.27W
Ashuanipi 42 Kf 52.55N 66.00W
Ashuanipi Lake 42 Kf 52.45N 66.10W
Asia 21 Ke 40.00N 85.00 E
Asia, Kepulauan- 26 Jf 1.03N 131.18 E
Asiago 14 Fe 45.52N 11.30 E
Asiago, Altopiano di- 14 Fe 45.54N 11.30 E
Asilah 32 Fb 35.28N 6.02W
Asinara 5 Gg 41.04N 8.15 E
Asinara, Golfo dell'- 14 Cj 41.00N 8.35 E
Asino 20 De 56.58N 86.09 E
'Asīr 23 Ff 19.00N 42.00 E
Aškadar 17 Hi 53.37N 56.01 E
Aşkale 24 Ic 39.55N 40.42 E
Askanija-Nova 16 Hf 46.27N 33.52 E
Asker 8 De 59.50N 10.26 E
Askersund 7 Dg 58.53N 14.54 E
Askī Al Mawşil 24 Jd 36.34N 42.42 E
Askim [Nor.] 8 De 59.35N 11.10 E
Askim [Swe.] 8 Dg 57.38N 11.56 E
Áskion Óros 15 Ei 40.22N 21.34 E
Askiz 20 Ef 53.08N 90.32 E
Askja 5 Eb 65.03N 16.48W
Askola 8 Kd 60.32N 25.36 E
Äsköping 8 Ge 59.09N 16.04 E
Askøy 8 Ad 60.30N 5.05 E
Askøy 8 Ad 60.24N 5.11 E
Askrova 8 Ac 61.30N 4.55 E
Askvoll 7 Af 61.21N 5.04 E
Asl 24 Eh 29.30N 32.43 E
Aslanapa 15 Mj 39.13N 29.52 E
Asmara (EN) = Asmera 31 Kg 15.19N 38.57 E
Asmera = Asmara (EN) 31 Kg 15.19N 38.57 E
Åsnen 8 Fh 56.40N 14.40 E
Asni 32 Fc 31.15N 7.59W
Asnières-sur-Seine 12 Ef 48.55N 2.17 E
Aso 14 Hg 43.06N 13.51 E
Aso 29 Be 32.58N 131.02 E
Asola 14 Ee 45.13N 10.24 E
Asosa 31 Kg 10.02N 34.32 E
Aso-San 29 Be 32.53N 131.06 E
Asoteriba, Jabal- 35 Fa 21.51N 36.30 E
Asouf Mellene 32 Hd 25.40N 2.08 E
Asō-Wan 29 Ad 34.20N 129.15 E
Āspās 24 Og 30.40N 52.24 E
Aspe 13 Lf 38.21N 0.46W
Aspen 43 Fd 39.11N 106.49W
Aspermont 45 Fj 33.08N 100.14W
Aspiring, Mount- 61 Ch 44.23S 168.44 E
Aspromonte 14 Jl 38.10N 16.00 E
Assa 32 Fd 28.37N 9.25W
Aş Şadr 23 He 24.40N 54.41 E
Aş Şaff 24 Dh 29.34N 31.17 E
Aş Şāfī 24 Fg 31.02N 35.28 E
As Safīrah 24 Gd 36.04N 37.22 E
Aş Şaḩm 24 Qj 24.10N 56.53 E
Assahoun 34 Fd 6.27N 0.55 E
Aş Şa'īd 30 Kf 26.00N 32.00 E
Assal, Lac- 35 Gc 11.40N 42.22 E
As Salamīyah [Sau.Ar.] 23 Ge 24.12N 47.23 E
As Salamīyah [Syr.] 24 Ge 35.01N 37.03 E
Aş Şāliḩīyah 24 Ie 34.44N 40.45 E
As Sallūm 31 Je 31.34N 25.09 E
As Salmān 24 Kg 30.26N 44.30 E
As Salt 24 Ff 32.03N 35.44 E
As Salwá 23 He 24.45N 50.49 E

Index Symbols

[1] Independent Nation
[2] State, Region
[3] District, County
[4] Municipality
[5] Colony, Dependency
Continent
Physical Region
Historical or Cultural Region
Mount, Mountain
Volcano
Hill
Mountains, Mountain Range
Hills, Escarpment
Plateau, Upland
Pass, Gap
Plain, Lowland
Delta
Salt Flat
Valley, Canyon
Crater, Cave
Karst Features
Depression
Polder
Desert, Dunes
Forest, Woods
Heath, Steppe
Oasis
Cape, Point
Coast, Beach
Cliff
Peninsula
Isthmus
Sandbank
Island
Atoll
Rock, Reef
Islands, Archipelago
Rocks, Reefs
Coral Reef
Well, Spring
Geyser
River, Stream
Waterfall Rapids
River Mouth, Estuary
Lake
Salt Lake
Intermittent Lake
Reservoir
Swamp, Pond
Canal
Glacier
Ice Shelf, Pack Ice
Ocean
Sea
Gulf, Bay
Strait, Fjord
Lagoon
Bank
Seamount
Tablemount
Ridge
Shelf
Basin
Escarpment, Sea Scarp
Fracture
Trench, Abyss
National Park, Reserve
Point of Interest
Recreation Site
Cave, Cavern
Historic Site
Ruins
Wall, Walls
Church, Abbey
Temple
Scientific Station
Airport
Port
Lighthouse
Mine
Tunnel
Dam, Bridge

Index Symbols

[1] Independent Nation
[2] State, Region
[3] District, County
[4] Municipality
[5] Colony, Dependency
■ Continent
■ Physical Region

Historical or Cultural Region
Mount, Mountain
Volcano
Hill
Mountains, Mountain Range
Hills, Escarpment
Plateau, Upland

Pass, Gap
Plain, Lowland
Delta
Salt Flat
Valley, Canyon
Crater, Cave
Karst Features

Depression
Polder
Desert, Dunes
Forest, Woods
Heath, Steppe
Oasis
Cape, Point

Coast, Beach
Cliff
Peninsula
Rocks, Reefs
Coral Reef
Island
Atoll

Rock, Reef
Islands, Archipelago
Sandbank
Well, Spring
Geyser
River, Stream

Waterfall Rapids
River Mouth, Estuary
Lake
Salt Lake
Intermittent Lake
Sea
Gulf, Bay
Swamp, Pond

Canal
Glacier
Ice Shelf, Pack Ice
Ocean
Strait, Fjord

Lagoon
Bank
Seamount
Tablemount
Ridge
Shelf
Basin

Escarpment, Sea Scarp
Fracture
Trench, Abyss
National Park, Reserve
Point of Interest
Recreation Site
Cave, Cavern

Historic Site
Ruins
Wall, Walls
Church, Abbey
Temple
Scientific Station
Airport

Port
Lighthouse
Mine
Tunnel
Dam, Bridge

Index Symbols

[1] Independent Nation — Historical or Cultural Region — Pass, Gap — Depression — Coast, Beach — Rock, Reef — Waterfall Rapids — Canal — Lagoon — Escarpment, Sea Scarp — Historic Site — Port
[2] State, Region — Mount, Mountain — Plain, Lowland — Polder — Cliff — Islands, Archipelago — River Mouth, Estuary — Glacier — Bank — Fracture — Ruins — Lighthouse
[3] District, County — Volcano — Delta — Desert, Dunes — Peninsula — Rocks, Reefs — Lake — Ice Shelf, Pack Ice — Seamount — Trench, Abyss — Wall, Walls — Mine
[4] Colony, Dependency — Hill — Salt Flat — Forest, Woods — Isthmus — Coral Reef — Salt Lake — Ocean — Tableland — National Park, Reserve — Church, Abbey — Tunnel
[5] Continent — Mountains, Mountain Range — Valley, Canyon — Heath, Steppe — Sandbank — Well, Spring — Intermittent Lake — Sea — Ridge — Point of Interest — Temple — Dam, Bridge
[6] Physical Region — Hills, Escarpment — Crater, Cave — Oasis — Island — Geyser — Reservoir — Gulf, Bay — Shelf — Recreation Site — Scientific Station
Plateau, Upland — Karst Features — Cape, Point — Atoll — River, Stream — Swamp, Pond — Strait, Fjord — Basin — Cave, Cavern — Airport

International Map Index

Index Symbols

[1] Independent Nation	▨ Pass, Gap	▨ Rock, Reef	▨ Lagoon
[2] State, Region	▨ Plain, Lowland	▨ Rocks, Reefs	▨ Bank
[3] District, County	▨ Delta	▨ Coral Reef	▨ Seamount
[4] Municipality	▨ Salt Flat	▨ Well, Spring	▨ Tablemount
[5] Colony, Dependency	▨ Valley, Canyon	▨ Geyser	▨ Ridge
■ Continent	▨ Crater, Cave	🖾 River, Stream	▨ Shelf
▨ Physical Region	⊠ Karst Features		▨ Basin

Index Symbols (labels, full list):
[1] Independent Nation; [2] State, Region; [3] District, County; [4] Municipality; [5] Colony, Dependency; ■ Continent; ▨ Physical Region; ▨ Historical or Cultural Region; ▲ Mount, Mountain; ▲ Volcano; ▨ Hill; ▨ Mountains, Mountain Range; ▨ Hills, Escarpment; ▨ Plateau, Upland; Pass, Gap; Plain, Lowland; Delta; Salt Flat; Valley, Canyon; Crater, Cave; Karst Features; Depression; Polder; Desert, Dunes; Forest, Woods; Heath, Steppe; Oasis; Cape, Point; Coast, Beach; Cliff; Peninsula; Isthmus; Sandbank; Island; Islands, Archipelago; Atoll; Rock, Reef; Rocks, Reefs; Coral Reef; Well, Spring; Geyser; River, Stream; Waterfall Rapids; River Mouth, Estuary; Lake; Salt Lake; Intermittent Lake; Reservoir; Swamp, Pond; Canal; Glacier; Ice Shelf, Pack Ice; Ocean; Sea; Gulf, Bay; Strait, Fjord; Lagoon; Bank; Seamount; Tablemount; Ridge; Shelf; Basin; Escarpment, Sea Scarp; Fracture; Trench, Abyss; National Park, Reserve; Point of Interest; Recreation Site; Cave, Cavern; Historic Site; Ruins; Wall, Walls; Church, Abbey; Temple; Scientific Station; Airport; Port; Lighthouse; Mine; Tunnel; Dam, Bridge

Name	Page	Grid	Lat.	Long.
Baranoviči	6	Ie	53.08N	26.02 E
Baranovka	16	Ed	50.18N	27.41 E
Baranya [2]	10	Oj	46.05N	18.15 E
Barão de Capanema	55	Da	13.19S	57.52W
Barão de Cotegipe	55	Fh	27.37S	52.23W
Barão de Grajaú	54	Je	6.45S	43.01W
Barão de Melgaço	54	Gg	16.13S	55.58W
Baraque de Fraiture	11	Ld	50.15N	5.45 E
Baratang	25	If	12.13N	92.45 E
Barataria Bay	45	Ll	29.22N	89.57W
Barat Daja, Kepulauan-	21	Oj	7.25S	128.00 E
Barāwe	31	Lh	1.09N	44.03 E
Barbacena	53	Lh	21.14S	43.46W
Barbacoas [Ven.]	49	Li	9.49N	70.03W
Barbacoas [Ven.]	50	Ch	9.29N	66.58W
Barbacoas, Bahia de-	49	Jh	10.10N	75.35W
Barbado, Rio-	55	Cb	15.12S	58.58W
Barbados [1]	39	Nh	13.10N	59.32W
Barbados	38	Nh	13.10N	59.32W
Barbados Ridge (EN)	50	Gf	12.45N	59.35W
Barbagia	14	Dj	40.10N	9.10 E
Barbar	35	Eb	18.01N	33.59 E
Bárbara	54	Dd	0.52S	72.30W
Barbaros	15	Ki	40.54N	27.27 E
Barbas, Cabo-	32	De	22.18N	16.41W
Barbastro	13	Mb	42.02N	0.08 E
Barbate de Franco	13	Gh	36.12N	5.55W
Barbeau Peak	38	La	81.54N	75.01W
Barbeton	37	Ee	25.48S	31.03 E
Barbezieux	11	Fi	45.28N	0.09W
Barbourville	44	Fg	36.52N	83.53W
Barboza Ferraz	55	Fg	24.04S	52.03W
Barbuda	38	Mh	17.38N	61.48W
Barcaldine	58	Fg	23.33S	145.17 E
Barcarrota	13	Ff	38.31N	6.51W
Barcău	15	Ec	46.59N	21.07 E
Barcellona Pozzo di Gotto	14	Jl	38.09N	15.13 E
Barcelona [3]	13	Nc	41.40N	2.00 E
Barcelona [Sp.]	6	Gg	41.23N	2.11 E
Barcelona [Ven.]	54	Fa	10.08N	64.42W
Barcelonnette	11	Mj	44.23N	6.39 E
Barcelos [Braz.]	54	Fd	0.58S	62.57W
Barcelos [Port.]	13	Dc	41.32N	8.37W
Barcin	10	Nd	52.52N	17.57 E
Barcoo River	59	Ie	25.30S	142.50 E
Barcs	10	Nk	45.58N	17.28 E
Barda	16	Oi	40.25N	47.05 E
Bardagé	35	Ba	22.06N	16.28 E
Bardaï	31	If	21.21N	16.59 E
Bardār Shāh	24	Ld	36.45N	47.15 E
Bārdaw	14	En	36.49N	10.08 E
Bardawīl, Sabkhat al-	24	Eg	31.10N	33.10 E
Bardejov	10	Rg	49.18N	21.16 E
Bārḍēre	31	Lh	2.20N	42.20 E
Bardeskan	24	Qe	35.12N	57.58 E
Bardīyah	33	Ed	31.46N	25.06 E
Bardonecchia	14	Ae	45.05N	6.42 E
Bardsey	9	Ii	52.45N	4.45W
Bardstown	44	Eg	37.49N	85.28W
Barēda	31	Mg	11.52N	51.03 E
Bareilly	22	Jg	28.25N	79.23 E
Barencevo More=Barents Sea (EN)	67	Jd	74.00N	36.00 E
Barentin	11	Ge	49.33N	0.57 E
Barentsburg	67	Kd	78.04N	14.14 E
Barentshav=Barents Sea (EN)	67	Jd	74.00N	36.00 E
Barentsøya	41	Oc	78.27N	21.15 E
Barents Sea (EN)=Barencevo More	67	Jd	74.00N	36.00 E
Barents Sea (EN)=Barentshav	67	Jd	74.00N	36.00 E
Barents Trough (EN)	5	Ia	73.00N	29.00 E
Barentu	35	Fb	15.06N	37.36 E
Barfleur	11	Ee	49.40N	1.15W
Barfleur, Pointe de-	11	Ee	49.42N	1.16W
Barga	22	Kf	30.48N	81.17 E
Bārgāl	35	Ic	11.18N	51.07 E
Bargarh	25	Gd	21.20N	83.37 E
Barguelonne	11	Gj	44.07N	0.50 E
Barguzin	20	Ff	53.27N	108.58 E
Barguzinski Hrebet	20	Ff	54.30N	110.00 E
Bar Harbor	44	Mc	44.23N	68.13W
Barhi	25	Hd	24.18N	85.25 E
Bari [3]	35	Hd	10.00N	50.00 E
Bari	6	Hg	41.08N	16.51 E
Bari, Terra di-	14	Kj	41.05N	16.50 E
Ba Ria	25	Lf	10.30N	107.10 E
Barīdī, Ra's-	24	Gj	24.17N	37.31 E
Barika	13	Ri	35.22N	5.05 E
Barīm	33	Hg	12.39N	43.25 E
Barima, Río-	50	Fh	8.35N	60.25W
Barima River	50	Fh	8.35N	60.25W
Barinas	54	Db	8.38N	70.12W
Barinas [2]	54	Eb	8.10N	70.00W
Baring, Cape-	42	Fb	70.01N	117.28W
Baringa	36	Db	0.45N	20.52 E
Barinitas	49	Li	8.45N	70.25W
Baripāda	25	Hd	21.56N	86.43 E
Bariri	55	Hf	22.04S	48.44W
Bariri, Reprêsa-	55	Hf	22.21S	48.39W
Bārīs	33	Fe	24.40N	30.36 E
Bari Sādri	25	Ed	24.25N	74.28 E
Barisāl	25	Id	22.42N	90.22 E
Barisan, Pegunungan-=Barisan Mountains (EN)	21	Mj	3.00S	102.15 E
Barisan Mountains (EN)=Barisan, Pegunungan-	21	Mj	3.00S	102.15 E
Barito	21	Nj	3.32S	114.29 E
Barjols	11	Lk	43.33N	6.00 E
Barkā'	23	Ie	23.35N	57.55 E
Barkam	27	He	31.45N	102.32 E
Barkan, Ra's-e-	24	Mg	30.01N	49.35 E
Barkava	8	Lh	56.40N	26.45 E
Barkley, Lake-	43	Jd	36.40N	87.55W
Barkley Sound	46	Cb	48.53N	125.20W
Barkly East	37	Df	30.58S	27.33 E
Barkly Tableland	57	Ef	19.00S	138.00 E
Barkly West	37	Ce	28.05S	24.31 E
Barkol	27	Fc	43.35N	92.51 E
Barkol Hu	27	Fc	43.40N	92.39 E
Barlavento [3]	32	Cf	16.10N	24.40W
Bar-le-Duc	11	Lf	48.47N	5.10 E
Barlee, Lake-	57	Cg	29.10S	119.30 E
Barlee Range	59	Dd	23.35S	116.00 E
Barletta	14	Ki	41.19N	16.17 E
Barlinek	10	Lc	53.00N	15.12 E
Barlovento, Islas de-=Windward Islands (EN)	38	Mh	15.00N	61.00W
Barma	26	Jg	1.54S	133.00 E
Barmer	25	Ec	25.45N	71.23 E
Barmera	59	If	34.15S	140.28 E
Barmouth	9	Ii	52.43N	4.03W
Barnard Castle	9	Lg	54.33N	1.55W
Barnaul	22	Kd	53.22N	83.45 E
Barnes Ice Cap	42	Kc	70.00N	73.30W
Barnesville [Ga.-U.S.]	44	Ei	33.04N	84.09W
Barnesville [Mn.-U.S.]	45	Hc	46.39N	96.25W
Barnet, London-	12	Bc	51.39N	0.12W
Barneveld	12	Hb	52.08N	5.34 E
Barnim	10	Jd	52.40N	13.45 E
Barnsley	9	Lh	53.34N	1.28W
Barnstaple	9	Ij	51.05N	4.04W
Barnstaple (Bideford Bay)	9	Ij	51.05N	4.20W
Barnstorf	12	Kb	52.43N	8.30 E
Barntrup	12	Lc	51.59N	9.07 E
Barnwell	44	Gi	33.14N	81.21W
Baro	30	Kh	8.26N	33.14 E
Baro [Chad]	35	Bc	12.12N	18.58 E
Baro [Nig.]	34	Gd	8.36N	6.25 E
Baronnies	11	Lj	44.15N	5.30 E
Barora Fa	63a	Db	7.30S	158.20 E
Barora Ite	63a	Db	7.36S	158.24 E
Barotseland	36	Df	15.05S	24.00 E
Barqah=Cyrenaica (EN)	33	Dc	31.00N	22.30 E
Barqah=Cyrenaica (EN)	30	Je	31.00N	23.00 E
Barqah, Jabal al-	24	Ej	24.24N	32.34 E
Barqah al Bahrīyah=Marmarica (EN)	30	Je	31.40N	24.30 E
Barqū, Jabal-	14	Dn	36.04N	9.37 E
Barques, Pointe aux-	44	Fc	44.04N	82.58W
Barquisimeto	53	Jd	10.04N	69.19W
Barr	11	Nf	48.24N	7.27 E
Barr, Ra's al-	24	Nj	25.47N	50.34 E
Barra	53	Lg	11.05S	43.10W
Barra	9	Fd	57.00N	7.30W
Barra, Ponta da-	30	Kk	23.47S	35.32 E
Barra, Sound of-	9	Fd	57.10N	7.20W
Barraba	59	Kf	30.22S	150.36 E
Barra Bonita, Reprêsa-	55	Hf	22.38S	48.20W
Barra de Navidad	47	De	19.12N	104.41W
Barra do Bugres	54	Gg	15.05S	57.11W
Barra do Corda	54	Ie	5.30S	45.15W
Barra do Cuanza	36	Bd	9.18S	13.09 E
Barra do Dande	36	Bd	8.28S	13.22 E
Barra do Garças	54	Hg	15.53S	52.15W
Barra Falsa, Ponta da-	30	Kk	22.55S	35.37 E
Barra Head	9	Fe	56.46N	7.36W
Barra Mansa	54	Jh	22.32S	44.11W
Barrāmīyah, Wādī al-	24	Ej	25.00N	33.23 E
Barranca	54	Cd	4.50S	76.42W
Barrancabermeja	53	Ie	7.03N	73.52W
Barrancas [Col.]	49	Kh	10.57N	72.50W
Barrancas [Ven.]	54	Fb	8.42N	62.11W
Barrancas, Arroyo-	55	Cj	30.19S	59.25W
Barranco	55	Db	15.56S	57.41W
Barrancos	13	Ff	38.08N	6.59W
Barranqueras	56	Ic	27.29S	58.56W
Barranquilla	53	Id	10.59N	74.48W
Barranquitas	51a	Bb	18.12N	66.23W
Barra Patuca	49	Ef	15.50N	84.17W
Barras	54	Jd	4.15S	42.18W
Barra Velha	55	Hh	26.39S	48.43W
Barre	44	Kc	44.12N	72.30W
Barreira	55	Db	15.24S	57.52W
Barreiras	53	Lg	12.08S	45.00W
Barreirinha	54	Gd	2.47S	57.03W
Barreirinhas	54	Jd	2.45S	42.50W
Barreiro	13	Cf	38.40N	9.04W
Barreiro, Rio-	55	Fb	15.43S	52.45W
Barreiro Grande	55	Jd	18.12S	45.10W
Barreiros	54	Ke	8.49S	35.12W
Barren	25	If	12.16N	93.51 E
Barren, Iles-	37	Gc	18.25S	43.40 E
Barren Islands	40	Ie	58.55N	152.15W
Barretos	56	Kb	20.33S	48.33W
Barrie	42	Jh	44.24N	79.40W
Barrier Bay	66	Ge	67.45S	81.10 E
Barrier Islands	63a	Db	7.44S	158.32 E
Barrington Tops	59	Kf	32.00S	151.28 E
Barro Alto	55	Hb	15.04S	48.58W
Barrois, Plateau du-	11	Kf	48.45N	5.00 E
Barros, Lagoa dos-	55	Gi	29.56S	50.23W
Barros, Tierra de-	13	Ff	38.40N	6.25W
Barroso	55	Ke	21.11S	43.58W
Barrouallie	51n	Ba	13.14N	61.17W
Barrow [Ak.-U.S.]	39	Db	71.17N	156.47W
Barrow [Arg.]	55	Bn	38.18S	60.14W
Barrow/An Bhearú	9	Gi	52.10N	7.00W
Barrow, Point-	38	Db	71.23N	156.30W
Barrow Creek	58	Eg	21.33S	133.53 E
Barrow-in-Furness	9	Jg	54.07N	3.14W
Barrow Island	57	Cg	20.50S	115.25 E
Barrow Range	59	Fe	26.05S	127.30 E
Barrow Strait	38	Jb	74.21N	94.10W
Barru	26	Gg	4.25S	119.37 E
Barry	9	Jj	51.24N	3.18W
Barrytown	62	De	42.14S	171.20 E
Barsakelmes, Ostrov-	18	Bb	45.40N	59.55 E
Barsalogo	34	Ec	13.25N	1.03W
Barsatas	19	Hf	48.13N	78.33 E
Baršć/Forst	10	Ke	51.44N	14.38 E
Bārsi	25	Fe	18.14N	75.42 E
Barsinghausen	10	Fd	52.18N	9.27 E
Barstow	43	De	34.54N	117.01W
Bar-sur-Aube	11	Kf	48.14N	4.43 E
Bar-sur-Seine	11	Kf	48.07N	4.22 E
Baršyn	19	Gf	49.45N	69.36 E
Bārta/Barta	8	Ih	56.57N	20.57 E
Barta/Bārta	8	Ih	56.57N	20.57 E
Barṭallah	24	Jd	36.23N	43.25 E
Bartang	18	Hf	37.55N	71.33 E
Barth	10	Ib	54.22N	12.44 E
Bartholomew, Bayou-	45	Jj	32.43N	92.04W
Bartica	54	Gb	6.24N	58.37W
Bartın	24	Eb	41.38N	32.21 E
Bartle Frere, Mount-	57	Ff	17.23S	145.49 E
Bartlesville	43	Hd	36.45N	95.59W
Bartlett	45	Gf	41.53N	98.33W
Bartoszyce	10	Qb	54.16N	20.49 E
Bartow	44	Gl	27.54N	81.50W
Barú, Isla-	49	Jh	10.26N	75.35W
Barú, Volcán	47	Hg	8.48N	82.33W
Bārūd, Ra's-	24	Ei	26.47N	33.39 E
Barumini	14	Dk	39.42N	9.01 E
Barun-Bogdo-Ula	27	Hb	45.00N	100.20 E
Bāruni	25	Hc	25.29N	85.59 E
Barun-Šabartuj, Gora-	20	Fg	49.43N	109.58 E
Barun-Urt	27	Jb	46.40N	113.12 E
Barwice	10	Mc	53.45N	16.22 E
Barwon River	57	Fg	30.00S	148.05 E
Barycz	10	Me	51.42N	16.15 E
Baryš	7	Lj	53.40N	47.08 E
Baryš	7	Li	54.35N	46.47 E
Bāsa'īdū	24	Pi	26.39N	55.17 E
Basail	55	Ch	27.52S	59.18W
Basankusu	36	Cb	1.14N	19.48 E
Basaral, Ostrov-	18	Ib	45.25N	73.45 E
Basauri	13	Ja	43.13N	2.53W
Basavilbaso	55	Ck	32.22S	58.53W
Bas Champs	12	Dd	50.20N	1.41 E
Basco	26	Hb	20.27N	121.58 E
Bascuñán, Cabo-	56	Fc	28.51S	71.30W
Base	11	Gj	44.17N	0.18 E
Basel [2]	14	Bc	47.35N	7.40 E
Basel/Bâle	6	Gf	47.30N	7.30 E
Baselland [2]	14	Bc	47.30N	7.45 E
Basentello	14	Kj	40.40N	16.23 E
Basento	14	Kj	40.20N	16.49 E
Başeu	15	Kb	47.44N	27.15 E
Basey	26	Id	11.17N	125.04 E
Bashi Channel (EN)=Bashi Haixia	27	Lg	22.00N	121.00 E
Bashi Haixia=Bashi Channel (EN)	27	Lg	22.00N	121.00 E
Bāsht	24	Ng	30.21N	51.09 E
Ba Shui	28	Ci	30.25N	115.02 E
Basilan	21	Oi	6.34N	122.03 E
Basilan City (Isabela)	22	Oi	6.42N	121.58 E
Basilan Strait	26	He	6.49N	122.05 E
Basildon	9	Nj	51.34N	0.25 E
Basilicata [2]	14	Kj	40.30N	16.30 E
Basingstoke	9	Lj	51.16N	1.05W
Basjanovski	17	Jg	58.19N	60.44 E
Başkale	24	Jc	38.02N	44.00 E
Baskatong, Réservoir-	42	Jg	46.47N	75.50W
Baškaus	20	Df	51.09N	87.43 E
Baskil	24	Hc	38.35N	38.40 E
Baškirskaja ASSR [3]	19	Fe	55.00N	56.00 E
Baskunčak, Uzero-	16	Oe	48.10N	46.55 E
Bašmakovo	16	Mc	53.12N	43.03 E
Bāsmenj	24	Ld	37.59N	46.29 E
Basoko	36	Db	1.14N	23.36 E
Basongo	36	Dc	4.20S	20.24 E
Basque Provinces (EN)=Euzkadi/Vascongadas	13	Ja	43.00N	2.30W
Basque Provinces (EN)=Vascongadas/Euzkadi	13	Ja	43.00N	2.30W
Basra (EN)=Al Başrah	22	Gf	30.30N	47.47 E
Bas Rhin [3]	11	Nf	48.35N	7.40 E
Bass, Ilots de-	57	Mg	27.55S	143.26W
Bassano	46	Ia	50.47N	112.28W
Bassano del Grappa	14	Fe	45.46N	11.44 E
Bassar	34	Fd	9.15N	0.47 E
Bassas da India	30	Lk	21.25S	39.42 E
Bassein	22	Lh	16.47N	94.44 E
Bassein → Vasai	25	Ee	19.21N	72.48 E
Basse-Kotto [3]	35	Ce	5.00N	21.30 E
Basse-Pointe	51h	Ab	14.52N	61.07W
Basses, Pointe des-	51e	Bc	15.52N	61.17W
Basse-Sambre	12	Gd	50.27N	4.37 E
Basse Santa Su	34	Cc	13.19N	14.13W
Basse-Terre	50	Fd	16.10N	61.40W
Basse-Terre	47	Le	16.00N	61.44W
Basseterre	47	Le	17.18N	62.43W
Bassett	45	Ge	42.35N	99.32W
Bassigny	11	Lf	48.00N	5.30 E
Bassikounou	32	Ff	15.52N	5.58W
Bassila	34	Fd	9.01N	1.40 E
Bass Islands	63c	Ba	9.58S	167.17 E
Basso, Plateau de-	30	Jg	17.20N	22.40 E
Bass Strait	57	Fh	39.20S	145.30 E
Bassum	12	Kb	52.51N	8.44 E
Basswood Lake	45	Kb	48.05N	91.35W
Båstad	7	Ch	56.26N	12.51 E
Bastak	24	Pi	27.14N	54.22 E
Bastām	24	Pd	36.29N	55.04 E
Bastenaken/Bastogne	11	Le	50.00N	5.43 E
Bastia [Fr.]	6	Gg	42.42N	9.27 E
Bastia [It.]	14	Gg	43.04N	12.33 E
Bastogne/Bastenaken	11	Le	50.00N	5.43 E
Bastrop	45	Kj	32.47N	91.55W
Basudan Ula	27	Fe	33.05N	91.00 E
Basuo → Dongfang	27	Ih	19.14N	108.39 E
Basuto	37	Dc	19.52S	26.32 E
Bas-Zaïre [2]	36	Bd	5.30S	14.30 E
Bata	31	Hh	1.51N	9.45 E
Batabanó, Golfo de-	47	Hd	22.15N	82.30W
Batagaj	20	Ic	67.38N	134.38 E
Batagaj-Alyta	20	Ic	67.53N	130.31 E
Bataguaçu	54	Hh	21.42S	52.22W
Bataiporã	55	Ff	22.20S	53.17W
Batajnica	15	De	44.54N	20.17 E
Batajsk	19	Df	47.05N	39.46 E
Batak	15	Hh	41.57N	24.13 E
Bataklık Gölü	24	Ed	37.42N	33.07 E
Batala	25	Fb	31.48N	75.12 E
Batalha	13	De	39.39N	8.50W
Batama	36	Eb	0.56N	26.39 E
Batamaj	20	Hd	63.30N	129.25 E
Batamšinski	19	Fe	50.36N	58.17 E
Batan	26	Hb	20.30N	121.50 E
Batang	27	Ge	30.02N	99.10 E
Batanga	36	Ac	0.21S	9.18 E
Batangafo	35	Bd	7.18N	18.18 E
Batangas	22	Oh	13.45N	121.03 E
Batanghari	26	Mj	1.00S	104.00 E
Batan Islands	21	Og	20.30N	121.50 E
Batanta, Pulau-	26	Jg	0.50S	130.40 E
Bátaszék	10	Oj	46.11N	18.44 E
Batatais	55	Ie	20.53S	47.37W
Batavia	44	Hd	43.00N	78.11W
Bat-Cengel	27	Hb	47.47N	101.58 E
Batchawana	44	Eb	46.58N	84.34W
Batchelor	59	Gb	13.04S	131.01 E
Bătdâmbâng	22	Mh	13.06N	103.12 E
Batéké, Plateaux-	36	Cc	3.30S	15.45 E
Batel, Esteros del-	55	Ci	28.30S	58.20W
Batemans Bay	59	Kg	35.43S	150.11 E
Batesburg	44	Gi	33.56N	81.33W
Batesville [Ar.-U.S.]	45	Ki	35.46N	91.39W
Batesville [Ms.-U.S.]	45	Li	34.18N	90.00W
Bath [Eng.-U.K.]	9	Kj	51.23N	2.22W
Bath [Me.-U.S.]	44	Md	43.55N	69.49W
Bath [N.B.-Can.]	44	Nb	46.32N	67.33W
Bath [St.C.N.]	51c	Ab	17.08N	62.37W
Batha	30	Ig	12.47N	17.34 E
Batha [3]	35	Bc	14.00N	19.00 E
Bá Thrá Lí/Tralee Bay	9	Di	52.15N	9.59W
Bathsheba	50	Gf	13.13N	59.31W
Bá Thuath Reanna/Liscannor Bay	9	Di	52.55N	9.25W
Bathurst	38	Ib	76.00N	100.30W
Bathurst [Austl.]	59	Jf	33.25S	149.35 E
Bathurst [N.B.-Can.]	39	Me	47.36N	65.39W
Bathurst, Cape-	38	Gb	70.35N	128.00W
Bathurst Inlet	38	Ic	68.10N	108.50W
Bathurst Inlet	39	Ic	66.50N	108.01W
Bathurst Island	57	Ef	11.35S	130.25 E
Bati	35	Gc	11.13N	40.01 E
Batié	34	Ed	9.53N	2.55W
Bāţin, Wādī al-	23	Gc	30.25N	47.35 E
Batman	23	Fb	37.52N	41.07 E
Batman	24	Id	37.45N	41.00 E
Batna [3]	32	Ib	35.10N	6.00 E
Batna	31	He	35.34N	6.11 E
Ba To	25	Lf	14.46N	108.44 E
Bato Bato	26	Ge	5.06N	119.50 E
Batoka	36	Ef	16.47S	27.15 E
Baton Rouge	39	Jf	30.23N	91.11W
Batopilas	48	Fd	27.01N	107.44W
Batouri	34	He	4.26N	14.22 E
Batovi	55	Fb	15.53S	53.24W
Batovi, Coxilha de-	55	Ej	30.33S	54.27W
Båtsfjord	7	Ga	70.38N	29.44 E
Bat-Sumber	27	Ib	48.25N	106.42 E
Batticaloa	25	Gg	7.43N	81.42 E
Batti Maly	25	Ig	8.50N	92.51 E
Battipaglia	14	Ij	40.37N	14.58 E
Battle	12	Cd	50.55N	0.30 E
Battle	42	Gf	52.42N	108.15W
Battle Creek	46	Kb	48.36N	109.11W
Battle Creek	43	Jc	42.19N	85.11W
Battle Harbour	39	Nd	52.17N	55.35W
Battle Mountain	43	Dc	40.38N	116.56W
Battonya	10	Rj	46.17N	21.01 E
Battowia Island	51n	Bb	12.58N	61.09W
Batu	35	Fd	6.59N	39.37 E
Batu, Kepulauan-=Batu Islands (EN)	21	Lj	0.18S	98.28 E
Batuasa	26	Jg	3.32S	130.08 E
Batuata, Pulau-	26	Hh	6.12S	122.42 E
Batudaka, Pulau-	26	Hg	0.28S	121.48 E
Batui	26	Hg	1.17S	122.33 E
Batu Islands (EN)=Batu, Kepulauan-	21	Lj	0.18S	98.28 E
Batumi	6	Kg	41.38N	41.38 E
Batu Pahat	26	Df	1.51N	102.56 E
Baturaja	26	Dg	4.08S	104.10 E
Baturino	20	De	57.45N	85.12 E
Baturité	54	Kd	4.20S	38.53W
Batz, Ile de-	11	Bf	48.45N	4.01W
Bau	26	Ff	1.25N	110.09 E
Baubau	22	Oj	5.28S	122.38 E
Baucau	26	Ih	8.27S	126.27 E
Bauchi	31	Hg	10.19N	9.50 E
Bauchi [2]	34	Hc	10.40N	10.00 E
Bauchi Plateau	34	Gc	10.00N	9.30 E
Baud	11	Cg	47.52N	3.01W
Baudette	45	Ib	48.43N	94.36W
Baudo, Serrania de-	54	Cb	6.00N	77.05W
Baudour, Saint-Ghislain-	12	Fd	50.29N	3.49 E
Baugé	11	Fg	47.33N	0.06W
Bauges	11	Mi	45.38N	6.10 E
Baúl, Cerro-	48	Ii	17.38N	100.19W
Baula	26	Hg	4.09S	121.41 E
Bauld, Cape-	38	Nd	51.38N	55.25W
Bauman Fiord	42	Ia	77.45N	86.00W
Baume-les-Dames	11	Mg	47.21N	6.22 E
Baunach	10	Gg	49.59N	10.51 E
Baunani	63a	Ec	9.08S	160.51 E
Baunei	14	Dj	40.02N	9.40 E
Baures	54	Ff	13.35S	63.35W
Bauru	53	Lh	22.19S	49.04W
Baús	55	Fd	18.19S	53.10W
Baús, Serra dos-	55	Fd	18.20S	53.25W
Bauska	7	Fh	56.24N	24.13 E
Bautzen/Budyšin	10	Ke	51.11N	14.26 E
Bavaria (EN)=Bayern [2]	10	Hg	49.00N	11.30 E
Bavaria (EN)=Bayern	5	Hf	49.00N	11.30 E
Bavarian Forest (EN)=Bayerischer Wald	10	Ig	49.00N	12.55 E
Bavay	12	Fd	50.18N	3.47 E
Båven	8	Ge	59.00N	16.55 E
Bavispe	48	Eb	30.24N	108.50W
Bavispe, Río de-	48	Ec	29.15N	109.11W
Bavly	7	Mi	54.26N	53.18 E
Bawah, Pulau-	26	Ef	2.31N	106.03 E
Bawal, Pulau-	26	Fg	2.44S	110.06 E
Bawe	58	Ee	2.59S	134.43 E
Bawean, Pulau-	26	Fh	5.46S	112.40 E
Bawku	34	Ec	11.03N	0.15W
Baxian	27	Kd	39.03N	116.24 E
Baxol	27	Ge	30.07N	96.56 E
Bay [3]	35	Ge	2.50N	43.30 E
Bay/Baicheng	27	Dc	41.46N	81.52 E
Bayamo	47	Id	20.23N	76.39W
Bayamón	49	Nd	18.24N	66.09W
Bayan	28	Ia	46.05N	127.24 E
Bayanbulak	27	Dc	43.05N	84.05 E
Bayanga	35	Be	2.53N	16.19 E
Bayan Gol	27	Gd	37.18N	96.50 E
Bayan Gol → Dengkou	22	Me	40.25N	106.59 E
Bayan Har Shan	21	Lf	34.20N	97.00 E
Bayan Har Shankou	27	Ge	34.06N	97.38 E
Bayan Hot → Alxa Zuoqi	27	Id	38.50N	105.32 E
Bayan Hure → Chen Barag Qi	27	Kb	49.21N	119.25 E
Bayan Huxu → Horqin Youyi Zhongqi	27	Lb	45.04N	121.27 E
Bayano, Lago de-	49	Hi	9.00N	78.30W
Bayan Obo	27	Ic	41.50N	109.58 E
Bayan Qagan	28	Ga	46.11N	123.59 E
Bayan Qagan → Qahar Youyi Houqi	28	Bd	41.28N	113.10 E
Bayan Ul Hot → Xi Ujimqin Qi	27	Kc	44.31N	117.33 E
Bayas	48	Gf	23.32N	104.50W
Bayat	24	Fb	40.39N	34.15 E
Bayauca	55	Bl	34.51S	61.18W
Bayawan	26	He	9.20N	123.00 E
Bayāẕ	24	Pg	30.42N	55.28 E
Bayāzeh	24	Pf	30.42N	55.28 E
Baybay	26	Hd	10.41N	124.48 E
Bayburt	23	Fa	40.16N	40.15 E
Bay City [Mi.-U.S.]	43	Kc	43.36N	83.53W
Bay City [Tx.-U.S.]	43	Hf	29.09N	95.39W
Bayerische Alpen	10	Hi	47.30N	11.30 E
Bayerischer Wald=Bavarian Forest (EN)	10	Ig	49.00N	12.55 E
Bayern=Bavaria (EN)	5	Hf	49.00N	11.30 E
Bayern=Bavaria (EN) [2]	10	Hg	49.00N	11.30 E
Bayes, Cap-	63b	Be	20.57S	165.25 E
Bayeux	11	Fe	49.16N	0.42W
Bayfield	45	Kc	46.49N	90.49W
Bay Fiord	42	Ja	79.00N	84.00W
Baygorria	55	Dk	32.52S	56.44W
Baygorria, Lago Artificial de-	55	Dk	33.05S	57.00W
Bayḩān al Qişāb	33	Ig	14.48N	45.44 E
Bayındır	24	Bc	38.13N	27.40 E
Bayjī	24	Je	34.56N	43.29 E
Bay Minette	44	Dj	30.53N	87.47W
Baynūnah	24	Ok	23.50N	52.50 E
Bayombong	26	Hc	16.29N	121.09 E
Bayona	13	Db	42.07N	8.51W
Bayonnaise Seamount (EN)	57	Jf	12.00S	179.30W
Bayonne	6	Fg	43.29N	1.29W
Bayou Bodcau Lake	45	Jj	32.58N	93.30W
Bayou D'Arbonne Lake	45	Jj	32.45N	92.27W
Bayramiç	15	Jj	39.48N	26.37 E
Bayreuth	10	Hg	49.57N	11.35 E
Bayrūt=Beirut (EN)	22	Ff	33.53N	35.30 E
Bay Saint Louis	45	Lk	30.19N	89.20W
Bay Springs	45	Lk	31.59N	89.17W
Bayt al Faqīh	23	Fg	14.31N	43.17 E
Baytik Shan	27	Fb	45.15N	90.50 E
Bayt Laḩm=Bethlehem (EN)	24	Fg	31.43N	35.12 E
Baytown	43	If	29.44N	94.58W
Bayuda Desert (EN)=Bayyūḑah, Şaḩrā'-	30	Kg	18.00N	33.00 E
Bayunglencir	26	Dg	2.03S	103.41 E
Bayview	46	Gc	48.00N	116.30W
Bay View	62	Gc	39.26S	176.52 E
Bayy al Kabīr	33	Cc	31.11N	15.53 E
Bayyūḑah, Şaḩrā'-=Bayuda Desert (EN)	30	Kg	18.00N	33.00 E
Baza	13	Jg	37.29N	2.46W
Baza, Sierra de-	13	Jg	37.15N	2.45W
Bazardjuzju, Gora-	5	Kg	41.13N	47.51 E
Bazaruto, Ilha do-	37	Fd	21.40S	35.25 E
Bazas	11	Fj	44.26N	0.13W
Bazhong	27	Ie	31.54N	106.42 E
Bazoches-sur-Vesle	12	Fe	49.19N	3.37 E
Baztán	13	Ka	43.09N	1.31W
Beach	43	Gb	46.55N	103.52W
Beachy Head	9	Nk	50.44N	0.16 E
Beacon	44	Ke	41.31N	73.59W
Beaconsfield [Austl.]	59	Jh	41.12S	146.48 E
Beaconsfield [Eng.-U.K.]	12	Bc	51.36N	0.38W
Beagle, Canal-	56	Gh	54.53S	68.10W
Beagle Gulf	59	Gb	12.00S	130.20 E
Bealach an Doirín/Ballaghaderreen	9	Eh	53.55N	8.35W
Béalanana	37	Hb	14.33S	48.44 E
Béal an Átha/Ballina	9	Dg	54.07N	9.09W
Béal an Bheara/Gweebarra Bay	9	Eg	54.52N	8.20W
Béal Átha Fhirdhia/Ardee	9	Gh	53.52N	6.33W
Béal Átha hAmhnais/Ballyhaunis	9	Eh	53.46N	8.46W

Index Symbols

[1] Independent Nation
[2] State, Region
[3] District, County
[4] Municipality
[5] Colony, Dependency
Continent
Physical Region
Historical or Cultural Region
Mount, Mountain
Volcano
Hill
Mountains, Mountain Range
Hills, Escarpment
Plateau, Upland
Pass, Gap
Plain, Lowland
Delta
Salt Flat
Valley, Canyon
Crater, Cave
Karst Features
Depression
Polder
Desert, Dunes
Forest, Woods
Heath, Steppe
Oasis
Cape, Point
Coast, Beach
Cliff
Peninsula
Isthmus
Sandbank
Island
Atoll
Rock, Reef
Islands, Archipelago
Rocks, Reefs
Coral Reef
Well, Spring
Geyser
River, Stream
Waterfall Rapids
River Mouth, Estuary
Lake
Salt Lake
Intermittent Lake
Reservoir
Swamp, Pond
Canal
Glacier
Ice Shelf, Pack Ice
Ocean
Sea
Gulf, Bay
Strait, Fjord
Lagoon
Bank
Seamount
Tablemount
Ridge
Shelf
Basin
Escarpment, Sea Scarp
Fracture
Trench, Abyss
National Park, Reserve
Point of Interest
Recreation Site
Cave, Cavern
Historic Site
Ruins
Wall, Walls
Church, Abbey
Temple
Scientific Station
Airport
Port
Lighthouse
Mine
Tunnel
Dam, Bridge

Béal Átha na Muice/Swinford 9 Eh 53.57N 8.57W
Béal Átha na Sluaighe/Ballinasloe 9 Eh 53.20N 8.13W
Béal Átha Seanaidh/Ballyshannon 9 Eg 54.30N 8.11W
Beale, Cape- 46 Cb 48.44N 125.20W
Béal Easa/Foxford 9 Dh 53.59N 9.07W
Béal Feirste/Belfast 6 Fe 54.35N 5.55W
Beal Range 59 Ie 25.30S 141.30 E
Béal Tairbirt/Belturbet 9 Fg 54.06N 7.26W
Beanna Boirche/Mourne Mountains 9 Gg 54.10N 6.04W
Beannchar/Bangor 9 Hg 54.40N 5.40W
Beanntraí/Bantry 9 Dj 51.41N 9.27W
Bear Bay 42 Ia 75.45N 86.30W
Beardmore 45 Mb 49.36N 87.57W
Beardstown 45 Kg 39.59N 90.26W
Bear Island (EN)= Bjørnøya 5 Ha 74.30N 19.00 E
Bear Islands (EN)=Medveži, Ostrova- 21 Sb 70.52N 161.26 E
Bear Lake 43 Ec 42.00N 111.20W
Bear Lodge Mountains 45 Dd 44.35N 104.15W
Béarn 11 Fk 43.20N 0.45W
Bearpaw Mountains 46 Kb 48.15N 109.30W
Bear Peninsula 66 Of 74.35S 110.50W
Bear River 46 If 41.30N 112.08W
Bearskin Lake 42 If 53.57N 90.59W
Beās 25 Eb 31.10N 74.59 E
Beas de Segura 13 Jf 38.15N 2.53W
Beata, Cabo- 47 Je 17.36N 71.25W
Beata, Isla- 49 Le 17.35N 71.31W
Beata Ridge (EN) 47 Je 16.00N 72.30W
Beatrice 43 Hc 40.16N 96.44W
Beatrice, Cape- 59 Hb 14.15S 137.00 E
Beatton 42 Fe 56.06N 120.22W
Beatton River 42 Fe 56.10N 120.25W
Beatty 43 Dd 36.54N 116.46W
Beattyville 44 Ia 48.52N 77.10W
Beatys Butte 46 Fe 42.23N 119.20W
Beau-Bassin 37a Bb 20.13S 57.27 E
Beaucaire 11 Kk 43.48N 4.38 E
Beaucamps-le-Vieux 12 De 49.50N 1.47 E
Beaucanton 44 Ha 49.05N 79.15W
Beauce 11 Hf 48.22N 1.50 E
Beaudesert 59 Ke 27.59S 153.00 E
Beaufort [Mala.] 26 Ge 5.20N 115.45 E
Beaufort [S.C.-U.S.] 44 Gi 32.26N 80.40W
Beaufort/Befort 12 Ie 49.50N 6.18 E
Beaufort, Massif de- 11 Mi 45.50N 6.40 E
Beaufort Island 66 Kf 76.57S 166.56 E
Beaufort Sea 67 Eb 73.00N 140.00W
Beaufort West 31 Jl 32.20S 22.33 E
Beaugency 11 Hg 47.47N 1.38 E
Beaujolais, Monts du- 11 Kh 46.00N 4.22 E
Beauly 9 Id 57.29N 4.29W
Beaumesnil 12 Ce 49.01N 0.43 E
Beaumetz-lès-Loges 12 Ed 50.14N 2.39 E
Beaumont [Bel.] 12 Gd 50.14N 4.14 E
Beaumont [Fr.] 11 Gj 44.46N 0.46 E
Beaumont [Fr.] 11 Ee 49.40N 1.51W
Beaumont [Fr.] 12 Hf 48.51N 5.47 E
Beaumont [Ms.-U.S.] 45 Lk 31.11N 88.55W
Beaumont [N.Z.] 62 Cf 45.49S 169.32 E
Beaumont [Tx.-U.S.] 39 Jf 30.05N 94.06W
Beaumont-de-Lomagne 11 Gk 43.53N 0.59 E
Beaumont-en-Argonne 12 He 49.32N 5.03 E
Beaumont-le-Roger 12 Ce 49.05N 0.47 E
Beaumont-sur-Oise 12 Ee 49.08N 2.17 E
Beaumont-sur-Sarthe 11 Gf 48.13N 0.08 E
Beaune 11 Kg 47.02N 4.50 E
Beaupré 44 Lb 47.03N 70.53W
Beauraing 12 Gd 50.07N 4.48 E
Beaurepaire 11 Li 45.20N 5.03 E
Beausejour 42 Hf 50.04N 96.33W
Beautemps Beaupré 63b Ce 20.25S 166.08 E
Beauvais 11 Ie 49.26N 2.05 E
Beauval 12 Ed 50.06N 2.20 E
Beauvoir-sur-Mer 11 Dh 46.55N 2.03W
Beaver [Ak.-U.S.] 40 Jc 66.22N 147.24W
Beaver [Ok.-U.S.] 45 Fh 36.48N 100.30W
Beaver [Ut.-U.S.] 43 Ed 38.17N 112.38W
Beaver Creek [Co.-U.S.] 45 Ef 40.20N 103.33W
Beaver Creek [U.S.] 45 Ec 47.20N 103.39W
Beaver Creek [U.S.] 45 Gf 40.04N 99.20W
Beaver Creek [U.S.] 45 Ee 43.25N 103.59W
Beaver Dam 45 Le 43.28N 88.50W
Beaver Falls 44 Ge 40.45N 80.21W
Beaverhead Mountains 46 Id 45.00N 113.20W
Beaver Island 44 Ec 45.40N 85.31W
Beaver Lake 45 Jh 36.20N 93.55W
Beaver River [U.S.] 45 Gh 36.10N 98.45W
Beaver River [Ut.-U.S.] 46 Ig 39.10N 112.57W
Beaverton 46 Dd 45.29N 122.48W
Beāwar 25 Ec 26.06N 74.19 E
Bebedouro 56 Kb 20.56S 48.28W
Becan 48 Oh 18.37N 89.35W
Becanchén 48 Oh 19.50N 89.22W
Beccles 9 Oi 52.28N 1.34 E
Bečej 15 Dd 45.37N 20.03 E
Beceni 15 Jd 45.23N 26.47 E
Becerreá 13 Eb 42.51N 7.10W
Becerro, Cayos- 49 Ff 15.57N 83.17W
Béchar 31 Ge 31.37N 2.13W
Béchar [3] 32 Gd 30.00N 2.00W
Becharof Lake 40 He 58.00N 156.30W
Bechet 15 Gf 43.46N 23.57 E
Bechevin Bay 40 Ge 55.00N 163.27W
Bechyně 10 Kg 49.18N 14.28 E
Beckingen 12 Ie 49.24N 6.42 E
Beckley 43 Kd 37.46N 81.12W
Beckum 10 Ee 51.45N 8.02 E
Beckumer Berge 12 Kc 51.43N 8.10 E
Beclean 15 Hb 47.11N 24.11 E
Bédarieux 11 Jk 43.37N 3.09 E
Bedburg-Hau 12 Ic 51.46N 6.11 E
Bedele 35 Fd 8.27N 36.22 E
Bedesa 35 Gd 8.53N 40.46 E
Bedford 9 Mi 52.10N 0.50W
Bedford [Eng.-U.K.] 9 Mi 52.08N 0.29W
Bedford [In.-U.S.] 44 Df 38.52N 86.29W
Bedford [Pa.-U.S.] 44 He 40.00N 78.31W
Bedford [Va.-U.S.] 44 Hg 37.20N 79.31W
Bedford Level 9 Ni 52.30N 0.05 E
Bedford Point 51p Bb 12.13N 61.36W
Bedfordshire [3] 9 Mi 52.05N 0.20W
Bednja 14 Kd 46.18N 16.45 E
Bednodemjanovsk 16 Mc 53.55N 43.12 E
Bedourie 59 Hd 24.21S 139.28 E
Bedum 12 Ia 53.18N 6.39 E
Beech Grove 44 Df 39.43N 86.03W
Beecroft Head 59 Kg 35.01S 150.50 E
Beef Island 51a Db 18.27N 64.31W
Beelitz 10 Id 52.14N 12.58 E
Beemster 12 Gb 52.34N 4.56 E
Beerfelden 12 Ke 49.34N 8.59 E
Beernem 12 Fc 51.09N 3.20 E
Beerse 12 Gc 51.19N 4.52 E
Beersel 12 Gd 50.46N 4.18 E
Beersheba (EN)=Be'er Shevà 23 Dc 31.14N 34.47 E
Be'er Shevà=Beersheba (EN) 23 Dc 31.14N 34.47 E
Beerze 12 Hc 51.36N 5.19 E
Beeskow 10 Kd 52.10N 14.14 E
Beestekraal 37 De 25.23S 27.38 E
Beeston 9 Li 52.56N 1.12W
Beethoven Peninsula 66 Qf 71.40S 73.45W
Beetsterzwaag, Opsterland- 12 Ia 53.03N 6.04 E
Beeville 43 Hf 28.24N 97.45W
Befale 36 Db 0.28N 20.58 E
Befandriana Nord 37 Hc 15.15S 48.32 E
Befandriana Sud 37 Gd 22.06S 43.54 E
Befori 36 Db 0.06N 22.17 E
Befort/Beaufort 12 Ie 49.50N 6.18 E
Bega 15 Dd 45.13N 20.19 E
Bega 58 Fh 36.40S 149.50 E
Bégard 11 Cf 48.38N 3.18W
Begejski kanal 15 Dd 45.27N 20.27 E
Beggars Point 51d Bb 17.10N 61.48W
Bègle 11 Fj 44.48N 0.32W
Begna 7 Bf 60.35N 10.00 E
Begoml 8 Mj 54.46N 28.14 E
Begunicy 8 Me 59.35N 29.30 E
Behābād 24 Pg 31.52N 55.57 E
Behbehān 23 Hc 30.35N 50.14 E
Behring Point 49 Ia 24.27N 77.43W
Behshahr 23 Hb 36.43N 53.34 E
Bei'an 22 Oe 48.16N 126.29 E
Beibu Wan=Tonkin, Gulf of- (EN) 21 Mh 20.00N 108.00 E
Beida He 27 Gc 40.18N 99.01 E
Beihai 22 Mg 21.31N 109.07 E
Bei Hulsan Hu 27 Gd 36.55N 95.55 E
Bei Jiang 27 Jg 23.02N 112.58 E
Beijing=Peking (EN) 22 Nf 39.55N 116.23 E
Beijing Shi (Pei-ching Shih) [4] 27 Kc 40.15N 116.30 E
Beila 32 Df 18.10N 15.53W
Beilen 12 Ib 52.52N 6.32 E
Beiliutang He 28 Eg 34.12N 119.33 E
Beilrstroom 12 Ib 52.41N 6.12 E
Beilsteim 12 Jd 50.07N 7.15 E
Beilu He 27 Fe 34.34N 94.00 E
Beinamar 35 Bd 8.40N 15.23 E
Beine-Nauroy 12 Ge 49.15N 4.13 E
Beipiao 27 Lc 41.49N 120.45 E
Beira 31 Kj 19.50S 34.52 E
Beira Alta 13 Ed 40.40N 7.35W
Beira Baixa 13 Ee 39.55N 7.30W
Beira Litoral 13 Dd 40.15N 8.25W
Beiru He 28 Bh 33.40N 113.35 E
Beirut (EN)=Bayrūt 22 Ff 33.53N 35.30 E
Bei Shan 21 Le 41.30N 96.00 E
Beitstad 7 Cd 64.05N 11.22 E
Beiuş 15 Fc 46.40N 22.21 E
Beiwei Tan 27 Kg 21.10N 116.10 E
Beizhen [China] 27 Kd 37.24N 117.59 E
Beizhen [China] 28 Fd 41.36N 121.47 E
Beja 13 Ef 38.01N 7.52W
Beja [2] 13 Eg 37.58N 7.50W
Bejaia [3] 32 Ib 36.40N 5.10 E
Bejaia 31 He 36.45N 5.05 E
Bejaia, Golfe de- 13 Rh 36.45N 5.20 E
Béjar 13 Gd 40.23N 5.46W
Beji 25 Dc 29.47N 67.58 E
Bejneu 19 Ff 45.15N 55.05 E
Bejsug 16 Kf 46.02N 38.35 E
Bejsugski Liman 16 Kf 46.05N 38.25 E
Bekabad 19 Gg 40.13N 69.14 E
Bekasi 26 Eh 6.14S 106.59 E
Bekdaš 19 Fg 41.31N 52.40 E
Békés 10 Rj 46.46N 21.08 E
Békés [2] 10 Qj 46.45N 21.00 E
Békéscsaba 10 Rj 46.41N 21.06 E
Bekilli 15 Mk 38.14N 29.26 E
Bekily 37 Hd 24.12S 45.18 E
Bekkai 29a Db 43.25N 145.07 E
Bekoji 35 Fd 7.32N 39.15 E
Bekopaka 37 Gc 19.08S 44.45 E
Bekovo 16 Mc 52.29N 43.45 E
Bela [India] 25 Gc 25.56N 81.59 E
Bela [Pak.] 25 Dc 26.14N 66.19 E
Bélabo 34 He 4.52N 13.10 E
Bela Crkva 15 Ee 44.54N 21.26 E
Bela Dila 25 Ge 18.40N 80.55 E
Bela Floresta 55 Ge 20.36S 51.16W
Belaga 26 Ff 2.42N 113.47 E
Belaja [R.S.F.S.R.] 20 Mc 65.30N 173.15 E
Belaja [R.S.F.S.R.] 5 Ld 56.00N 54.32 E
Belaja [R.S.F.S.R.] 16 Kg 45.03N 39.25 E
Belaja Cerkov 6 Jf 49.49N 30.07 E
Belaja Gora 20 Jc 68.30N 146.15 E
Belaja Holunica 19 Fd 58.53N 50.50 E
Belaja Kalitva 19 Ef 48.09N 40.49 E
Bela Krajina 14 Je 45.35N 15.15 E
Bela Lorena 55 Ib 15.13S 46.01W
Belang 26 Hf 0.57N 124.47 E
Bela Palanka 15 Ff 43.13N 22.19 E
Belarbi 13 Li 35.09N 0.27W
Belaruskaja Sovetskaja Socialistyčnaja Respublika /Belorusskaja SSR [2] 19 Ce 53.50N 28.00 E
Belasica 15 Fh 41.21N 22.50 E
Bela Vista [Ang.] 36 Ce 12.33S 16.14 E
Bela Vista [Braz.] 54 Gh 22.06S 56.31W
Bela Vista [Braz.] 55 Dc 17.37S 57.01W
Bela Vista [Moz.] 37 Ee 26.20S 32.40 E
Belawan 26 Cf 3.47N 98.41 E
Běla Woda/Weißwasser 10 Ke 51.31N 14.38 E
Belayan 26 Gg 0.14S 116.36 E
Belbo 14 Cf 44.54N 8.31 E
Bełchatow 10 Pe 51.22N 19.21 E
Belcher Channel 42 Ia 77.20N 94.30W
Belcher Islands 38 Ld 56.20N 79.30W
Belchite 13 Lc 41.18N 0.45W
Belcy 19 Cf 47.46N 27.55 E
Bełczyna 10 Ne 51.25N 17.50 E
Belebej 19 Fe 54.10N 54.07 E
Belecke, Warstein- 12 Kc 51.29N 8.20 E
Beled 10 Ni 47.28N 17.06 E
Beled Wēyne 31 Lh 4.47N 45.12 E
Bélel 34 Hd 7.03N 14.26 E
Belém [Moz.] 37 Fb 14.08S 35.58 E
Belém [Braz.] 53 Lf 1.27S 48.29W
Belem [Mex.] 48 Dd 27.45N 110.28W
Belém de São Francisco 54 Ke 8.46S 38.58W
Belen 43 Fe 34.40N 106.46W
Belén [Arg.] 56 Gc 27.39S 67.02W
Belén [Nic.] 49 Eh 11.30N 85.53W
Belén [Par.] 55 Df 23.30S 57.06W
Belén [Ur.] 55 Dj 30.47S 57.47W
Belén, Cuchilla de- 55 Dj 30.55S 56.30W
Belén de Escobar 55 Cl 34.21S 58.47W
Belene 15 If 43.39N 25.07 E
Bélep, Iles- 57 Hf 19.45S 163.40 E
Beles 35 Fc 10.55N 35.10 E
Belev 16 Jc 53.50N 36.10 E
Beleye 35 Fc 11.24N 36.10 E
Belfast [Me.-U.S.] 44 Mc 44.27N 69.01W
Belfast [S.Afr.] 37 Ee 25.43S 30.03 E
Belfast/Béal Feirste 6 Fe 54.35N 5.55W
Belfast Lough/Loch Lao 9 Hg 54.40N 5.50W
Belfield 45 Ec 46.53N 103.12W
Belford 9 Lf 55.36N 1.49W
Belfort 11 Mg 47.45N 7.00 E
Belgaum 22 Jh 15.52N 74.30 E
Belgica Bank (EN) 67 Ld 78.28N 15.00W
Belgicafjella 66 Df 72.35S 31.10 E
België/Belgique=Belgium (EN) [1] 6 Ge 50.30N 4.30 E
Belgique/België=Belgium (EN) [1] 6 Ge 50.30N 4.30 E
Belgium (EN)=België/Belgique [1] 6 Ge 50.30N 4.30 E
Belgium (EN)=Belgique/België [1] 6 Ge 50.30N 4.30 E
Belgorod 6 Je 50.36N 36.35 E
Belgorod-Dnestrovski 19 Df 46.12N 30.17 E
Belgorodskaja Oblast [3] 19 De 50.45N 37.30 E
Belgrade (EN) = Beograd 6 Ig 44.50N 20.30 E
Bel Hairane 32 Ic 31.17N 6.20 E
Beli 34 Hd 7.52N 10.58 E
Belice 14 Gm 37.35N 12.52 E
Beli Drim 15 Dg 42.05N 20.20 E
Belidži 16 Pi 41.53N 48.20 E
Beli Lom 15 If 43.41N 26.00 E
Beli Manastir 14 Me 45.46N 18.37 E
Belimbegovo 15 Eh 42.00N 21.35 E
Belin 11 Fj 44.30N 0.47W
Belinga 36 Bb 1.04N 13.12 E
Belinski 16 Mc 52.58N 43.29 E
Belinyu 26 Eg 1.38S 105.46 E
Beliş 15 Gc 46.39N 23.02 E
Beli Timok 15 Ff 43.55N 22.18 E
Belize 39 Kh 17.15N 88.45W
Belize (British Honduras) 49 Ce 17.35N 88.35W
Belize City 39 Kh 17.30N 88.12W
Belize River 49 Ce 17.32N 88.14W
Beljajevka 16 Gf 46.29N 30.14 E
Beljanica 15 Ee 44.07N 21.43 E
Belka 8 Mg 57.40N 29.47 E
Belkovski, Ostrov- 20 Ia 75.30N 136.00 E
Bellac 11 Hh 46.07N 1.03 E
Bella Coola 42 Ef 52.22N 126.46W
Bellagio 14 De 45.59N 9.15 E
Bellaire [Oh.-U.S.] 44 Ge 40.02N 80.46W
Bellaire [Tx.-U.S.] 45 Il 29.43N 95.28W
Bellaria-Igea Marina 14 Gf 44.09N 12.28 E
Bellary 22 Jh 15.09N 76.56 E
Bella Unión 55 Dj 30.15S 57.35W
Bella Vista [Arg.] 56 Ic 28.30S 59.03W
Bella Vista [Par.] 55 Df 22.08S 56.31W
Bellavista, Capo- 14 Dk 39.56N 9.43 E
Bell Bay 42 Jb 71.10N 84.55W
Belle-Anse 49 Kd 18.14N 72.04W
Belledonne 11 Mi 45.18N 6.08 E
Bellefontaine [Mart.] 51h Ab 14.40N 61.10W
Bellefontaine [Oh.-U.S.] 44 Fe 40.22N 83.45W
Belle Fourche 43 Gc 44.40N 103.51W
Belle Fourche River 45 Ed 44.26N 102.19W
Bellegarde 11 If 47.59N 2.26 E
Bellegarde-sur-Valserine 11 Lh 46.06N 5.49 E
Belle Glade 44 Gl 26.41N 80.40W
Belle Ile 5 Ff 47.19N 3.11W
Belle Isle 42 Lf 51.55N 55.20W
Belle Isle, Strait of- 38 Nd 51.35N 56.30W
Bellencombre 12 De 49.42N 1.14 E
Belleplaine 51q Ab 13.15N 59.34W
Belleville [Fr.] 11 Kh 46.06N 4.45 E
Belleville [Il.-U.S.] 45 Lg 38.31N 90.00W
Belleville [Ks.-U.S.] 45 Hg 39.49N 97.38W
Belleville [Ont.-Can.] 42 Jh 44.10N 77.23W
Bellevue [Nb.-U.S.] 45 If 41.09N 95.54W
Bellevue [Wa.-U.S.] 46 Dc 47.37N 122.12W
Belley 11 Li 45.46N 5.41 E
Bellheim 12 Ke 49.12N 8.17 E
Bellin 39 Lc 60.00N 70.01W
Bellingham [Eng.-U.K.] 9 Kf 55.09N 2.16W
Bellingham [Wa.-U.S.] 39 Ge 48.46N 122.29W
Bellingsfors 8 Ef 58.59N 12.15 E
Bellingshausen 66 Re 62.12S 58.56W
Bellingshausen Ice Shelf 66 Ce 71.00S 89.00W
Bellingshausen Sea (EN) 66 Pf 71.00S 85.00W
Bellinzona 14 Dd 46.11N 9.02 E
Bello 54 Cb 6.19N 75.34W
Bellocq 55 Bl 35.55S 61.32W
Bellona, Récifs- 57 Gg 21.00S 159.00 E
Bellona Island 60 Fj 11.17S 159.47 E
Bellot Strait 42 Ib 72.00N 94.30W
Bellow Falls 44 Kd 43.08N 72.28W
Bell Peninsula 42 Jd 63.45N 81.30W
Bell River 42 Jg 49.49N 77.39W
Bell Rock→Inchcape 9 Ke 56.26N 2.24W
Bellsund 41 Nc 77.39N 14.15 E
Belluno 14 Gd 46.09N 12.13 E
Bell Ville 56 Hd 32.37S 62.42W
Bellville 37 Bf 33.53S 18.36 E
Belmond 45 Je 42.51N 93.37W
Belmont 44 Hd 42.14N 78.02W
Belmonte [Braz.] 54 Kg 15.51S 38.54W
Belmonte [Port.] 13 Ed 40.21N 7.21W
Belmonte [Sp.] 13 Je 39.34N 2.42W
Belmopan 39 Kh 17.15N 88.46W
Beloeil 12 Fd 50.35N 3.43 E
Belogorsk [R.S.F.S.R.] 22 Od 50.57N 128.25 E
Belogorsk [Ukr.-U.S.S.R.] 16 Ig 45.01N 34.33 E
Belogradčik 15 Ff 43.38N 22.41 E
Belogradčiški 15 Ff 43.38N 22.28 E
Belo Horizonte 53 Lg 19.55S 43.56W
Beloit [Ks.-U.S.] 45 Gg 39.28N 98.06W
Beloit [Wi.-U.S.] 43 Jc 42.31N 89.02W
Belojarovo 20 Hf 51.35N 128.55 E
Belojarski 19 Gc 63.40N 66.45 E
Beloje More=White Sea (EN) 5 Kb 66.00N 44.00 E
Beloje Ozero=White Lake (EN) 5 Jc 60.11N 37.35 E
Belokany 16 Oi 41.43N 46.28 E
Belomorsk 6 Jc 64.29N 34.43 E
Belomorsko-Baltijski Kanal =White Sea-Baltic Canal (EN) 5 Jc 63.30N 34.48 E
Belomorsko-Kulojskoje Plato 7 Jd 65.20N 41.50 E
Beloozersk 16 Dc 52.28N 25.13 E
Belopolje 19 De 51.09N 34.18 E
Belorečensk 16 Kg 44.43N 39.52 E
Beloreck 19 Fe 53.58N 58.24 E
Belorusskaja Grjada 16 Ec 53.50N 27.00 E
Belorusskaja Sovetskaja Socialističeskaja Respublika [2] 19 Ce 53.50N 28.00 E
Belorusskaja SSR/Belaruskaja Sovetskaja Socialistyčnaja Respublika [2] 19 Ce 53.50N 28.00 E
Belorusskaja SSR=Byelorussian SSR (EN) [2] 19 Ce 53.50N 28.00 E
Belo-sur-Mer 37 Gd 20.44S 44.00 E
Belo-sur-Tsiribihina 37 Gc 19.39S 44.32 E
Belot, Lac- 42 Ec 66.50N 126.20W
Belovo 20 Df 54.25N 86.18 E
Belovodsk 16 Ke 49.10N 39.33 E
Belovodskoe 18 Jc 42.47N 74.13 E
Belozersk 19 Dd 60.03N 37.48 E
Belper 12 Aa 53.02N 1.28W
Belted Range 46 Gh 37.25N 116.10W
Belton [Mo.-U.S.] 45 Ig 38.49N 94.32W
Belton [Tx.-U.S.] 45 Hk 31.04N 97.28W
Belton Lake 45 Hk 31.08N 97.32W
Belturbet/Béal Tairbirt 9 Fg 54.06N 7.26W
Beluha 21 Ke 49.48N 86.35 E
Belvedere Marittimo 14 Jk 39.37N 15.52 E
Belvidere 45 Le 42.15N 88.50W
Bely 7 Hi 55.50N 32.58 E
Bely, Ostrov-=Bely Island (EN) 21 Jb 73.10N 70.45 E
Belyando River 59 Jd 21.38S 146.50 E
Bely Čeremoš 15 Ia 48.06N 25.04 E
Bely Island (EN)=Bely, Ostrov- 21 Jb 73.10N 70.45 E
Bely Jar 20 De 58.26N 85.03 E
Belyje Berega 16 Ic 53.12N 34.42 E
Belz 16 Dd 50.23N 24.03 E
Bełżec 10 Tf 50.24N 23.26 E
Belzoni 45 Kj 33.11N 90.29W
Bełżyce 10 Se 51.11N 22.18 E
Bemaraha, Plateau de- 30 Lj 19.00S 45.15 E
Bembe 36 Bd 7.02S 14.18 E
Bembéréké 34 Fc 10.13N 2.40 E
Bembézar 13 Gg 37.45N 5.13W
Bembridge 12 Ad 50.41N 1.05W
Bemidji 43 Ib 47.29N 94.53W
Ben 24 Nf 32.32N 50.45 E
Benāb 23 Gb 37.18N 46.05 E
Benabarre/Benavarn 13 Mb 42.07N 0.29 E
Bena Dibele 36 Dc 4.07S 22.50 E
Bénaize 11 Hh 46.34N 1.04 E
Benalla 59 Jg 36.33S 145.59 E
Benares→Vārānasi 22 Kg 25.20N 83.00 E
Benasc/Benasque 13 Mb 42.36N 0.32 E
Benasque/Benasc 13 Mb 42.36N 0.32 E
Benavarn/Benabarre 13 Mb 42.07N 0.29 E
Benavente 13 Gc 42.00N 5.41W
Benbecula 9 Fd 57.27N 7.20W
Bencheng→Luannan 28 Ee 39.30N 118.42 E
Ben-Chicao, Col de- 13 Oh 36.12N 2.51 E
Bend 43 Cc 44.03N 121.19W
Bendaja 34 Cd 7.10N 11.15W
Bendel [2] 34 Gd 6.00N 5.50 E
Bendela 36 Cc 3.18S 17.36 E
Bender Bäyla 31 Mh 9.30N 50.30 E
Bendersiyada 35 Hc 11.14N 48.57 E
Bendery 19 Cf 46.48N 29.22 E
Bendigo 58 Fh 36.46S 144.17 E
Bendorf 12 Jd 50.26N 7.34 E
Bêne/Bene 8 Jh 56.28N 23.01 E
Bene/Bêne 8 Jh 56.28N 23.01 E
Bénéna 34 Ec 13.06N 4.22W
Benepú, Rada- 65d Ac 27.10S 109.25W
Benešov 10 Kg 49.47N 14.40 E
Benevento 14 Ii 41.08N 14.45 E
Bengal 21 Kg 24.00N 90.00 E
Bengal, Bay of- (EN) 21 Kh 15.00N 90.00 E
Bengamisa 36 Eb 0.57N 25.10 E
Bengbis 34 He 3.27N 12.27 E
Bengbu 22 Nf 32.47N 117.23 E
Benghazi (EN)=Banghāzī 31 Je 32.07N 20.04 E
Benghazi (EN)=Banghāzī [3] 33 Dd 27.00N 20.30 E
Benghisa Point 14 Io 35.50N 14.35 E
Bengkalis 26 Df 1.28N 102.08 E
Bengkulu [3] 26 Dg 3.48S 102.16 E
Bengkulu 22 Mj 3.48S 102.16 E
Bengo, Baía do- 36 Bd 8.43S 13.21 E
Bengo He 28 Eg 35.04N 118.22 E
Bengough 46 Mb 49.24N 105.08W
Bengtsfors 7 Cg 59.02N 12.13 E
Benguela 31 Ij 12.35S 13.26 E
Benguela [3] 36 Be 12.00S 15.00 E
Benguerir 32 Fc 32.14N 7.57W
Benguérua, Ilha- 37 Fd 21.53S 35.26 E
Bengue Viejo 49 Ce 17.05N 89.08W
Benguet, Cap- 32 Hb 36.55N 3.54 E
Beni 31 Jh 0.30N 29.28 E
Beni [2] 54 Ef 14.00S 65.30W
Beni, Rio- 52 Jg 10.23S 65.24W
Beni Abbes 32 Gc 30.08N 2.10W
Beni Baufrah 13 Hi 35.05N 4.18W
Benicarló 13 Md 40.25N 0.26 E
Benicasim 13 Md 40.03N 0.04 E
Beni Chougran, Monts des- 13 Mi 35.30N 0.15 E
Benidorm 13 Lf 38.32N 0.08W
Beni Enzar 13 Ji 35.14N 2.57W
Beni Haoua 13 Nh 36.32N 1.34 E
Beni Mellal 31 Ge 32.20N 6.21W
Beni Mellal [3] 32 Fc 32.30N 6.30W
Benin 34 Gd 5.45N 5.04 E
Bénin=Benin (EN) [1] 31 Hh 9.30N 2.15 E
Bénin (Dahomey) [1] 31 Hh 9.30N 2.15 E
Benin (EN)=Bénin [1] 31 Hh 9.30N 2.15 E
Benin, Bight of- 30 Hh 5.30N 4.00 E
Benin City 31 Hh 6.20N 5.38 E
Beni Ounif 32 Gc 32.03N 1.15W
Benisa 13 Mf 38.43N 0.03 E
Beni Saf 13 Ki 35.19N 1.23W
Benisheikh 34 Hc 11.48N 12.29 E
Benito Juárez 48 Mi 17.50N 92.32W
Benito Juárez, Presa- 48 Li 16.27N 95.30W
Benjamen Island 37b Bb 5.27S 53.21 E
Benjamin 45 Gj 33.35N 99.48W
Benjamin Aceval 55 Dg 24.58S 57.34W
Benjamin Constant 53 If 4.22S 70.02W
Benjamin Hill 48 Db 30.10N 111.10W
Benkei-Misaki 29a Bb 42.50N 140.11 E
Benkelman 45 Ff 40.03N 101.32W
Benkovac 14 Jf 44.02N 15.37 E
Ben Mehidi 14 Bn 36.46N 7.54 E
Bennett, Lake- 59 Gd 23.50S 131.00 E
Bennett, Ostrov- 20 Ja 76.45N 149.00 E
Benneydale 62 Fc 38.31S 175.21 E
Bennichab 32 Df 19.26N 15.21W
Bennington 44 Kd 42.53N 73.12W
Benom 26 Df 3.50N 102.06 E
Benoni 31 Jk 26.19S 28.27 E
Bénoué=Benue (EN) 30 Hh 7.48N 6.46 E
Benoy 35 Bd 8.59N 16.19 E
Benrath 12 Ic 51.10N 6.52 E
Bensekrane 13 Ki 35.04N 1.13W
Bensheim 10 Eg 49.41N 8.37 E
Ben Slimane 32 Fc 33.37N 7.07W
Benson [Az.-U.S.] 46 Jk 31.58N 110.18W
Benson [Mn.-U.S.] 45 Id 45.19N 95.36W
Benson Point 64g Ab 1.56N 157.30W
Bent 23 Id 26.17N 59.31 E
Benteng [Indon.] 26 Hg 0.24S 121.59 E
Benteng [Indon.] 26 Hh 6.08N 120.27 E
Bentheim 10 Dd 52.19N 7.10 E
Bentiaba 36 Be 14.29S 12.50 E
Bentinck 25 Jf 11.45N 98.03 E
Bentinck Island 59 Hc 17.05S 139.30 E
Bentiu 35 Dd 9.14N 29.50 E
Bento Conçalves 56 Jc 29.10S 51.31W
Bento Gomes, Rio- 55 Dc 16.40S 57.12W
Benton [Ar.-U.S.] 45 Ji 34.34N 92.35W
Benton [Il.-U.S.] 45 Lg 38.01N 88.55W
Bentong 26 Df 3.32N 101.55 E
Benton Harbor 44 Dd 42.07N 86.27W
Bentonville 45 Ih 36.22N 94.13W
Benua, Pulau- 26 Ef 0.56N 107.27 E
Benue [2] 34 Gd 7.15N 8.20 E
Benue 30 Hh 7.48N 6.46 E
Benue (EN)=Bénoué 30 Hh 7.48N 6.46 E
Benwee Head/An Bhinn Bhuí 9 Dg 54.21N 9.48W
Benxi 22 Oe 41.16N 123.48 E
Beo 26 If 4.15N 126.48 E
Beograd = Belgrade (EN) 6 Ig 44.50N 20.30 E
Beograd-Krnjača 15 De 44.52N 20.28 E
Beograd-Zemun 15 De 44.53N 20.25 E
Béoumi 34 Dd 7.40N 5.34W

Index Symbols

[1] Independent Nation
[2] State, Region
[3] District, County
[4] Municipality
[5] Colony, Dependency
Continent
Physical Region
Historical or Cultural Region
Mount, Mountain
Volcano
Hill
Mountains, Mountain Range
Hills, Escarpment
Plateau, Upland
Pass, Gap
Plain, Lowland
Delta
Salt Flat
Valley, Canyon
Crater, Cave
Karst Features
Depression
Polder
Desert, Dunes
Forest, Woods
Heath, Steppe
Oasis
Cape, Point
Coast, Beach
Cliff
Peninsula
Isthmus
Sandbank
Island
Atoll
Rock, Reef
Islands, Archipelago
Rocks, Reefs
Coral Reef
Well, Spring
Geyser
River, Stream
Waterfall Rapids
River Mouth, Estuary
Lake
Salt Lake
Intermittent Lake
Reservoir
Swamp, Pond
Canal
Glacier
Ice Shelf, Pack Ice
Ocean
Sea
Gulf, Bay
Strait, Fjord
Lagoon
Bank
Seamount
Tablemount
Ridge
Shelf
Basin
Escarpment, Sea Scarp
Fracture
Trench, Abyss
National Park, Reserve
Point of Interest
Recreation Site
Cave, Cavern
Historic Site
Ruins
Wall, Walls
Church, Abbey
Temple
Scientific Station
Airport
Port
Lighthouse
Mine
Tunnel
Dam, Bridge

Beppu	27	Ne	33.17N	131.30 E
Beppu-Wan	29	Be	33.20N	131.35 E
Bequia Head	51n	Ba	13.03N	61.12W
Bequia Island	50	Ff	13.01N	61.13W
Beraketa	37	Hd	24.11S	45.42 E
Berati	15	Ci	40.42N	19.57 E
Beratus, Gunung-	26	Gg	1.02S	116.20 E
Berau, Teluk-=McCluer Gulf (EN)	26	Jg	2.30S	132.30 E
Berberä	31	Lg	10.25N	45.02 E
Berbérati	31	Ih	4.16N	15.47 E
Berberia, Cabo-	13	Nf	38.38N	1.23 E
Berbice River	54	Gb	6.17N	57.32W
Berca	15	Jd	45.17N	26.41 E
Berchères-sur-Vesgre	12	Df	48.51N	1.33 E
Berchtesgaden	10	Ii	47.38N	13.00 E
Berck [Fr.]	12	Dd	50.24N	1.36 E
Berck [Fr.]	11	Hd	50.24N	1.34 E
Berck-Berck Plage	12	Dd	50.24N	1.34 E
Berck-Plage, Berck-	12	Dd	50.24N	1.34 E
Berda	16	Jf	46.47N	36.52 E
Berdâle	35	Hd	7.04N	47.51 E
Berdičev	19	Cf	49.53N	28.36 E
Berdigestjah	20	Hd	62.03N	126.50 E
Berdjansk	19	Df	46.43N	36.48 E
Berdsk	20	Df	54.47N	83.05 E
Beregomet	15	Ia	48.10N	25.24 E
Beregovo	19	Cf	48.13N	22.41 E
Bereku	36	Gc	4.27S	35.44 E
Berekua	50	Fe	15.14N	61.19W
Berekum	34	Ed	7.27N	2.35W
Berens	42	Hf	52.21N	97.01W
Berens River	42	Hf	52.22N	97.02W
Beresford	45	He	43.05N	96.47W
Berestečko	10	Vf	50.16N	25.14 E
Bereşti	15	Kc	46.06N	27.53 E
Berettyó	15	Ec	46.59N	21.07 E
Berettyóújfalu	10	Ri	47.13N	21.33 E
Bereza	19	Ce	52.33N	24.58 E
Berezan	16	Gd	50.19N	31.31 E
Berežany	16	De	49.29N	25.00 E
Berezina [Bye.-U.S.S.R.]	16	Dc	53.48N	25.59 E
Berezina [U.S.S.R.]	5	Je	52.33N	30.14 E
Berezino [Bye.-U.S.S.R.]	16	Fc	53.51N	29.00 E
Berezino [Bye.-U.S.S.R.]	8	Mj	54.55N	28.16 E
Berezino [Ukr.-U.S.S.R.]	15	Mc	46.16N	29.11 E
Bereznegovatoje	16	Hf	47.20N	32.49 E
Bereznik	19	Ec	62.53N	42.42 E
Berezniki	6	Ld	59.24N	56.46 E
Berezno	16	Ed	51.01N	26.45 E
Berezovka [Bye.-U.S.S.R.]	10	Vc	53.40N	25.37 E
Berezovka [R.S.F.S.R.]	17	Hd	64.59N	56.29 E
Berezovka [Ukr.-U.S.S.R.]	19	Df	47.12N	30.56 E
Berezovka Višerka	17	Hf	60.55N	56.50 E
Berezovo	19	Gc	63.58N	65.00 E
Berezovski [R.S.F.S.R.]	17	Jh	56.55N	60.50 E
Berezovski [R.S.F.S.R.]	20	De	55.39N	86.16 E
Berezovy	20	If	51.41N	135.52 E
Berga [Sp.]	13	Nb	42.06N	1.51 E
Berga [Swe.]	8	Gg	57.13N	16.02 E
Bergama	23	Cb	39.07N	27.10 E
Bergamo	14	De	45.41N	9.43 E
Bergantiños	13	Da	43.20N	8.45W
Bergby	7	Df	60.56N	17.02 E
Bergen [G.D.R.]	10	Jb	54.25N	13.26 E
Bergen [Neth.]	12	Gb	52.40N	4.42 E
Bergen [Nor.]	6	Gc	60.23N	5.20 E
Bergen/Mons	11	Jd	50.27N	3.56 E
Bergen aan Zee, Bergen-	12	Gb	52.40N	4.38 E
Bergen-Bergen aan Zee	12	Gb	52.40N	4.38 E
Bergen op Zoom	11	Kc	51.30N	4.17 E
Bergerac	11	Gj	44.51N	0.29 E
Bergeyk	12	Hc	51.19N	5.22 E
Bergh	12	Ic	51.53N	6.16 E
Bergheim	10	Cf	50.58N	6.39 E
Bergh-s'Heerenberg	12	Ic	51.53N	6.16 E
Bergisches Land	10	De	51.07N	7.10 E
Bergisch Gladbach	10	Df	50.59N	7.08 E
Bergkvara	8	Gh	56.23N	16.05 E
Bergneustadt	12	Jc	51.02N	7.39 E
Bergö	8	Ib	62.55N	21.10 E
Bergsjö	7	Df	61.59N	17.04 E
Bergslagen	8	Fd	60.05N	14.30 E
Bergstraße	12	Ke	49.40N	8.40 E
Bergues	12	Ed	50.58N	2.26 E
Bergum, Tietjerksteradeel-	12	Ha	53.12N	6.00 E
Bergviken	8	Gc	61.10N	16.45 E
Bergville	37	De	28.52S	29.18 E
Berh	27	Jb	47.45N	111.07 E
Berhala, Selat-	26	Dg	0.48S	104.25 E
Berhampore	25	Hd	24.06N	88.15 E
Berhampur	22	Kh	19.19N	84.47 E
Berici, Monti-	14	Fe	45.26N	11.31 E
Berīkān	24	Nh	28.17N	51.14 E
Berikulski	20	De	55.32N	88.08 E
Beringa, Ostrov-=Bering Island (EN)	20	Lf	55.00N	166.10 E
Beringen	12	Hc	51.03N	5.13 E
Bering Glacier	40	Kd	60.15N	143.30W
Bering Island (EN)= Beringa, Ostrov-	20	Lf	55.00N	166.10 E
Beringovo More=Bering Sea (EN)	38	Bd	60.00N	175.00W
Beringovski	22	Tc	63.07N	179.19 E
Bering Proliv=Bering Strait (EN)	38	Cc	65.30N	169.00W
Bering Sea	38	Bd	60.00N	175.00W
Bering Sea (EN)=Beringovo More	38	Bd	60.00N	175.00W
Bering Strait	38	Cc	65.30N	169.00W
Bering Strait (EN)=Bering Proliv	38	Cc	65.30N	169.00W
Berislav	16	Hf	46.51N	33.29 E
Berisso	55	Dl	34.52S	57.53W
Berit Daği	24	Gc	38.01N	36.52 E
Berïzak	24	Qi	26.06N	57.15 E
Berja	13	Jh	36.51N	2.57W
Berkåk	7	Be	62.50N	10.00 E
Berkane	32	Gc	34.56N	2.20W
Berkel	10	Cd	52.09N	6.12 E
Berkeley	43	Cd	37.57N	122.18W
Berkhamsted	12	Bc	51.45N	0.33W
Berkner Island	66	Rf	79.30S	49.30W
Berkovica	15	Gf	43.14N	23.07 E
Berks	9	Lj	51.15N	1.20W
Berkshire	9	Lj	51.30N	1.10W
Berkshire Downs	9	Lj	51.35N	1.25W
Berkshire Hills	44	Kd	42.20N	73.10W
Berlaimont	12	Fd	50.12N	3.49 E
Berlanga de Duero	13	Jc	41.28N	2.51W
Berlengas, Ilhas-	13	Ce	39.25N	9.30W
Berlevåg	7	Ga	70.51N	29.06 E
Berlin	43	Mc	44.29N	71.10W
Berlin (Ost)=East Berlin (EN)	10	Jd	52.30N	13.25 E
Berlin (Ost)=East Berlin (EN)	6	He	52.31N	13.24 E
Berlin (West)=West Berlin (EN)	6	He	52.31N	13.24 E
Berlin-Pankow	10	Jd	52.34N	13.24 E
Bermeja, Sierra-	13	Gh	36.30N	5.15W
Bermejillo	47	Dc	25.53N	103.37W
Bermejito, Rio-	55	Bg	25.39S	60.11W
Bermejo, Isla-	55	An	39.01S	62.01W
Bermejo, Paso-/Cumbre, Paso de la-	52	Ii	32.50S	70.05W
Bermejo, Rio- [Arg.]	52	Ji	31.52S	67.22W
Bermejo, Rio- [S.Amer.]	52	Kh	26.52S	58.23W
Bermen, lac-	42	Kf	53.35N	68.55W
Bermeo	13	Ja	43.26N	2.43W
Bermillo de Sayago	13	Fc	41.22N	6.06W
Bermuda	39	Mf	32.20N	64.45W
Bermuda Islands	39	Mf	32.20N	64.45W
Bermuda Rise (EN)	38	Mf	32.30N	65.00W
Bern	14	Bd	46.55N	7.40 E
Bern/Berne	6	Gf	46.55N	7.30 E
Bernalda	14	Kj	40.24N	16.41 E
Bernalillo	45	Ci	35.18N	106.33W
Bernard Islands	64d	Bb	7.18N	151.32 E
Bernardo de Irigoyen	55	Bk	32.10S	61.09W
Bernardo do Irigoyen	56	Jc	26.15S	53.39W
Bernasconi	56	He	37.54S	63.43W
Bernau bei Berlin	10	Jd	52.40N	13.35 E
Bernaville	12	Ed	50.08N	2.10 E
Bernay	11	Ge	49.06N	0.36 E
Bernburg	10	He	51.48N	11.44 E
Berndorf	14	Kc	47.57N	16.06 E
Berne [F.R.G.]	12	Ka	53.11N	8.29 E
Berne [In.-U.S.]	44	Ee	40.39N	84.57W
Berne/Bern	6	Gf	46.55N	7.30 E
Berner Alpen/Alpes Bernoises=Bernese Alps (EN)	14	Bd	46.25N	7.30 E
Berneray	9	Fd	57.43N	7.15W
Bernese Alps (EN)=Alpes Bernoises/Berner Alpen	14	Bd	46.25N	7.30 E
Bernese Alps (EN)=Berner Alpen/Alpes Bernoises	14	Bd	46.25N	7.30 E
Bernesga	13	Gb	42.28N	5.31W
Bernesq	12	Be	49.16N	0.56W
Bernier Bay	42	Ib	71.08N	88.00W
Bernier Island	59	Cd	24.50S	113.10 E
Bernina	14	Ed	46.25N	10.01 E
Bernina	5	Gf	46.22N	9.50 E
Berninapaß	14	Ed	46.25N	10.01 E
Bernissart	12	Fd	50.28N	3.38 E
Bernkastel-Kues	10	Dg	49.55N	7.04 E
Bernstorffs Isfjord	41	Hf	63.10N	40.45W
Berón de Astrada	55	Dh	27.33S	57.32W
Beroroha	37	Hd	21.39S	45.10 E
Béroubouay	34	Fc	10.32N	2.44 E
Beroun	10	Kg	49.58N	14.04 E
Berounka	10	Kg	50.00N	14.24 E
Berovo	15	Fh	41.43N	22.51 E
Berre, Étang de-	11	Lk	43.27N	5.08 E
Berriane	32	Hc	32.50N	3.46 E
Berrouaghia	13	Oh	36.08N	2.55 E
Berry	11	Hh	47.00N	2.00 E
Berry-au-Bac	12	Fe	49.24N	3.54 E
Berryessa, Lake-	46	Dg	38.37N	122.16W
Berry Head	9	Jk	50.24N	3.29W
Berry Islands	47	Ic	25.34N	77.45W
Berry River	46	Ja	50.50N	111.36W
Beršad	19	Cf	48.23N	29.33 E
Berseba	37	Be	26.01S	17.41 E
Bersenbrück	12	Jb	52.33N	7.56 E
Berthierville	44	Kb	46.05N	73.11W
Bertincourt	12	Ed	50.05N	2.59 E
Bertogne	12	Hd	50.05N	5.40 E
Bertolinia	54	Je	7.38S	43.57W
Bertoua	31	Ih	4.35N	13.41 E
Bertraghboy Bay	9	Dh	53.23N	9.50W
Bertrix	12	He	49.51N	5.15 E
Beru Island	57	Ie	1.20S	176.00 E
Berwick-upon-Tweed	9	Lf	55.46N	2.00W
Berwyn	9	Ji	52.53N	3.24W
Besalampy	37	Gc	16.44S	44.24 E
Besançon	6	Gf	47.15N	6.02 E
Besar, Gunung-	26	Gg	1.25S	115.39 E
Besbre	11	Jh	46.33N	3.44 E
Besed	16	Gc	52.38N	31.11 E
Besikama	26	Hh	9.36S	124.57 E
Beskid Mountains (EN)	5	Hf	49.40N	20.00 E
Beskid Niski	10	Rg	49.20N	21.30 E
Beskid Średni	10	Pg	49.45N	19.20 E
Beskid Wysoki	10	Pg	49.32N	20.00 E
Beskidy Wschodnie	10	Sg	49.20N	22.30 E
Beskidy Zachodnie	10	Pg	49.30N	19.30 E
Beskol	18	Ma	46.06N	81.01 E
Beslan	19	Eg	43.10N	44.35 E
Besna Kobila	15	Fg	42.32N	22.14 E
Besni	24	Gd	37.41N	37.52 E
Besparmak Dağ	15	Kl	37.30N	27.35 E
Bessao	35	Bd	7.53N	15.59 E
Bessarabia (EN)= Bessarabija	15	Lb	47.00N	28.30 E
Bessarabija=Bessarabia (EN)	15	Lb	47.00N	28.30 E
Bessarabka	16	Ff	46.20N	28.59 E
Bességes	11	Kj	44.17N	4.06 E
Bessemer	43	Je	33.25N	86.57W
Bessin	11	Fe	49.10N	1.00W
Bessines-sur-Gartempe	11	Hh	46.06N	1.22 E
Besšoki, Gora-	16	Rh	43.57N	52.30 E
Best	12	Hc	51.30N	5.24 E
Bestjah [R.S.F.S.R.]	20	Hc	66.00N	123.35 E
Bestjah [R.S.F.S.R.]	20	Hd	61.17N	128.50 E
Bestobe	19	He	52.30N	73.05 E
Bestwig	12	Kc	51.22N	8.24 E
Betafo	37	Hc	19.49S	46.50 E
Betanzos [Bol.]	54	Eg	19.34S	65.27W
Betanzos [Sp.]	13	Da	43.17N	8.12W
Betanzos, Ria de-	13	Da	43.23N	8.15W
Bétaré Oya	34	Hd	5.36N	14.05 E
Bétérou	34	Fd	9.12N	2.16 E
Beteta	13	Jd	40.34N	2.04W
Bethal	37	De	26.27S	29.28 E
Bethanien	37	Be	26.30S	17.00 E
Bethanien	31	Ik	26.32S	17.11 E
Bethany [Mo.-U.S.]	45	If	40.16N	94.02W
Bethany [Ok.-U.S.]	45	Hi	35.31N	97.38W
Bethel	39	Cc	60.48N	161.46W
Béthenivile	12	Ge	49.18N	4.22 E
Bethlehem [Pa.-U.S.]	44	Je	40.36N	75.22W
Bethlehem [S.Afr.]	31	Jk	28.15S	28.15 E
Bethlehem (EN)=Bayt Laḥm	24	Fg	31.43N	35.12 E
Bethulie	37	Df	30.32S	25.59 E
Béthune	11	Id	50.32N	2.38 E
Béthune	11	He	49.53N	1.09 E
Betioky	37	Gd	23.42S	44.22 E
Betong	25	Kg	5.45N	101.05 E
Betor	35	Fc	11.37N	39.00 E
Bétou	36	Cb	3.03N	18.31 E
Betpak-Dala	19	Gf	46.00N	70.00 E
Betroka	37	Hd	23.15S	46.05 E
Bet She'an	24	Ff	32.30N	35.30 E
Betsiamites, Rivière-	42	Kg	48.56N	68.38W
Betsiboka	30	Lj	16.03S	46.36 E
Bette	30	If	22.00N	19.12 E
Bettembourg/Bettemburg	12	Ie	49.31N	6.06 E
Bettemburg/Bettembourg	12	Ie	49.31N	6.06 E
Bettendorf	45	Kf	41.32N	90.30W
Bettles Field	40	Ic	66.53N	151.51W
Bettna	8	Gf	58.55N	16.38 E
Bettola	14	Df	44.47N	9.36 E
Betül	25	Fd	21.55N	77.54 E
Betuwe	11	Lc	51.55N	5.30 E
Betwa	25	Hc	25.55N	80.12 E
Betz	12	Ee	49.09N	2.57 E
Betzdorf	10	Df	50.47N	7.53 E
Beulah	44	Dc	44.38N	86.06W
Beult	12	Cc	51.13N	0.26 E
Beuvron	11	Hg	47.29N	1.15 E
Beuzeville	12	Ce	49.20N	0.21 E
Beveland	11	Jc	51.30N	3.40 E
Beveren	12	Gc	51.13N	4.15 E
Beveridge Reef	57	Kg	20.00S	168.00W
Beverley [Austl.]	59	Df	32.06S	116.56 E
Beverley [Eng.-U.K.]	9	Mh	53.51N	0.26W
Beverwijk	11	Kb	52.28N	4.40 E
Bewsher, Mount-	66	Ff	70.54S	65.28 E
Bexhill	9	Nk	50.50N	0.29 E
Bexley, London-	12	Cc	51.26N	0.09 E
Beyağaç	15	Ll	37.13N	28.57 E
Beyānlū	24	Ld	36.02N	47.53 E
Bey Daği	24	Hc	38.15N	38.22 E
Bey Dağlari	23	Db	36.40N	30.15 E
Beykoz	24	Cb	41.08N	29.05 E
Beyla	34	Dd	8.41N	8.38W
Beyoğlu, İstanbul	15	Lh	41.02N	28.59 E
Beyoneisu-Retsugan	27	Oe	31.55N	139.55 E
Beypazari	24	Db	40.10N	31.55 E
Beyra	35	Hd	6.57N	47.19 E
Beyram	24	Oi	27.26N	53.31 E
Beyşehir	24	Dd	37.41N	31.43 E
Beyşehir Gölü	23	Db	37.40N	31.30 E
Bezaha	37	Gd	23.29S	44.30 E
Bežanickaja Vozvyšennost	7	Gh	56.45N	29.30 E
Bežanicy	7	Gh	56.58N	29.57 E
Bezdan	15	Bd	45.51N	18.56 E
Bezděz	10	Kf	50.32N	14.43 E
Bezdež	10	Vd	52.18N	26.30 E
Bežeck	19	Dd	57.50N	36.41 E
Bezenčuk	7	Lj	53.01N	49.24 E
Bezerra, Rio-	55	Ia	13.16S	47.31W
Bezerros	54	Ke	8.14S	35.45W
Béziers	11	Jk	43.21N	3.15 E
Bezmein	19	Fh	38.05N	58.12 E
Bežta	19	Eg	42.08N	46.08 E
Bhadrakh	25	Hd	21.04N	86.30 E
Bhadrāvati	25	Ff	13.52N	75.43 E
Bhāgalpur	22	Kg	25.15N	87.00 E
Bhairawa	25	Gc	27.31N	83.24 E
Bhaironghati	25	Fb	31.01N	78.53 E
Bhakkar	25	Eb	31.38N	71.04 E
Bhamo	25	Jd	24.16N	97.14 E
Bhandāra	25	Fd	21.10N	79.39 E
Bhanjan	25	Gc	25.47N	83.36 E
Bhārat Juktarashtra=India (EN)	22	Jh	20.00N	77.00 E
Bharatpur	25	Fc	27.13N	77.29 E
Bharūch	25	Ed	21.46N	72.54 E
Bhatinda	25	Eb	30.12N	74.57 E
Bhātpāra	25	Hd	22.52N	88.24 E
Bhaunagar	22	Jg	21.46N	72.09 E
Bhera	25	Eb	32.29N	72.55 E
Bheri	25	Gc	28.44N	81.16 E
Bhīlwāra	25	Ec	25.21N	74.38 E
Bhīma	21	Jh	16.25N	77.17 E
Bhind	25	Fc	26.34N	78.48 E
Bhiwāni	25	Fc	28.47N	76.08 E
Bhopāl	22	Jg	23.16N	77.24 E
Bhubaneswar	22	Kg	20.14N	85.50 E
Bhuj	25	Dd	23.16N	69.40 E
Bhusāwal	25	Fd	21.03N	75.46 E
Bhutan (Druk-Yul)	22	Lg	27.30N	90.30 E
Bia	34	Ed	5.21N	3.11W
Bia, Phou-	21	Mh	18.36N	103.01 E
Biá, Rio-	54	Ed	3.28S	67.23W
Biābān, Kūh-e-	24	Qi	26.30N	57.25 E
Biabou	51n	Ba	13.12N	61.09W
Biafra	30	Hh	5.00N	7.30 E
Biafra, Bight of-	30	Hh	3.20N	9.20 E
Biak	26	Kg	1.10S	136.06 E
Biak, Pulau-	57	Ee	1.00S	136.00 E
Biała Piska	10	Sc	53.37N	22.04 E
Biała Podlaska	10	Td	52.00N	23.05 E
Biała Podlaska	10	Td	52.02N	23.06 E
Białobrzegi	10	Qe	51.40N	20.57 E
Białogard	10	Lb	54.01N	16.00 E
Białostocka, Wysoczyzna-	10	Tc	53.23N	23.10 E
Białowieża	10	Td	52.41N	23.50 E
Białystok	6	Ie	53.09N	23.09 E
Białystok	10	Tc	53.10N	23.10 E
Biancavilla	14	Im	37.38N	14.52 E
Bianco	14	Kl	38.05N	16.09 E
Bianco, Monte-	5	Gf	45.50N	6.52 E
Biankouma	34	Dd	7.44N	7.37W
Biankouma	34	Dd	7.43N	7.40W
Bianzhuang → Cangshan	28	Eg	34.51N	118.03 E
Biaro, Pulau-	26	If	2.05N	125.20 E
Biarritz	11	Ek	43.29N	1.34W
Biasca	14	Cd	46.22N	8.57 E
Bibā	33	Fd	28.55N	30.59 E
Bibai	27	Pc	43.19N	141.52 E
Bibala	36	Be	14.50S	13.30 E
Biban, Chaine des-	13	Qh	36.12N	4.25 E
Bibbiena	14	Fg	43.42N	11.49 E
Biberach an der Riß	10	Fh	48.06N	9.48 E
Bibiani	34	Ed	6.28N	2.20W
Bic	44	Ma	48.22N	68.42W
Bicaj	15	Dh	41.59N	20.25 E
Bicas	55	Ke	21.43S	43.04W
Bicaz	15	Jc	46.55N	26.04 E
Bicaz, Pasul-	15	Ic	46.49N	25.52 E
Bičenekski, Pereval-	16	Nj	39.33N	45.48 E
Bicester	9	Lj	51.54N	1.09W
Bichena	35	Fc	10.21N	38.14 E
Bickerton Island	59	Hb	13.45S	136.10 E
Bicske	10	Oi	47.29N	18.38 E
Bičura	20	Ff	50.36N	107.35 E
Bīd	24	Qd	36.33N	57.35 E
Bida	31	Hh	9.05N	6.01 E
Bīdar	25	Fe	17.54N	77.33 E
Bidasoa	13	Ka	43.22N	1.47W
Biddeford	43	Mc	43.30N	70.26W
Bideford	9	Ij	51.01N	4.13W
Bideford Bay → Barnstaple Bay	9	Ij	51.05N	4.20W
Bidon V/Poste Maurice Cortier	32	He	22.18N	1.05 E
Bié	36	Ce	13.00S	17.30 E
Bié, Planalto do-	30	Ij	13.30S	17.02 E
Biebrza	10	Sc	53.13N	22.28 E
Biecz	10	Rg	49.44N	21.14 E
Biedenkopf	10	Ef	50.55N	8.32 E
Biei	29a	Cb	43.35N	142.28 E
Biel/Bienne	14	Bc	47.10N	7.15 E
Bielefeld	10	Ed	52.02N	8.32 E
Bielefeld-Brackwede	12	Kc	51.59N	8.31 E
Bielefeld-Sennestadt	12	Kc	51.57N	8.35 E
Biella	14	Ce	45.34N	8.03 E
Bielsk	10	Pd	52.40N	19.49 E
Bielska, Wysoczyzna-	10	Sd	52.35N	23.00 E
Bielsko	10	Og	49.50N	19.00 E
Bielsko-Biała	10	Pg	49.49N	19.02 E
Bielsk Podlaski	10	Td	52.47N	23.12 E
Bien Dong=South China Sea (EN)	21	Ni	10.00N	113.00 E
Bien Hoa	25	Lf	10.57N	106.49 E
Bienne	11	Lh	46.20N	5.38 E
Bienne/Biel	14	Bc	47.10N	7.15 E
Bienvenida	13	Jd	40.30N	2.30W
Bienville, Lac-	42	Ke	55.20N	72.40W
Bierbeek	12	Gd	50.50N	4.46 E
Bieszczady	10	Sg	49.10N	22.35 E
Bièvre	12	He	49.56N	5.01 E
Biferno	14	Ji	41.59N	15.02 E
Bifoum	36	Bc	0.20S	10.23 E
Bifuka	28	Qb	44.29N	142.21 E
Biga	24	Bb	40.13N	27.14 E
Bigadiç	24	Cc	39.23N	28.08 E
Big Bald Mountain	44	Nb	47.37N	66.38W
Big Baldy Mountain	46	Jc	46.58N	110.37W
Big Bay [Mi.-U.S.]	44	Db	46.49N	87.44W
Big Bay [Van.]	63b	Cb	15.05S	166.54 E
Big Beaver House	42	If	52.58N	89.57W
Big Belt Mountains	46	Jc	46.40N	111.25W
Big Black River	45	Kj	32.00N	91.05W
Big Blue River	43	Hd	39.11N	96.32W
Big Creek Peak	46	Id	44.28N	113.32W
Big Dry Creek	46	Lc	47.30N	106.19W
Big Falls	45	Jb	48.11N	93.46W
Biggar	42	Gf	52.04N	108.00W
Biggenden	59	Ke	25.30S	152.00 E
Biggleswade	9	Mi	52.05N	0.17W
Big Hatchet Peak	45	Bk	31.37N	108.22W
Big Hole River	46	Id	45.34N	112.20W
Bighorn Basin	43	Fc	44.15N	108.10W
Bighorn Lake	46	Kd	45.08N	108.10W
Bighorn Mountains	38	Ie	44.00N	107.30W
Bighorn River	43	Fb	46.09N	107.28W
Bight, Head of-	59	Gf	31.30S	131.10 E
Big Island	42	Kd	62.43N	70.40W
Big Lake	44	Nc	45.10N	67.40W
Big Lake	45	Fk	31.12N	101.28W
Big Lost River	46	Ie	43.50N	112.44W
Big Muddy Creek	46	Mb	48.08N	104.36W
Big Muddy Lake	46	Mb	49.10N	104.54W
Bignona	34	Bc	12.49N	16.14W
Bigorre	11	Gk	43.06N	0.05 E
Big Porcupine Creek	46	Lc	46.17N	106.47W
Big Quill Lake	42	Hf	51.51N	104.18W
Big Rapids	44	Ed	43.42N	85.29W
Big River	42	Gf	53.50N	107.01W
Big River	42	Fb	72.50N	125.00W
Big Sand Lake	42	He	57.45N	99.45W
Big Sandy	46	Jb	48.11N	110.07W
Big Sandy Creek	45	Eg	38.06N	102.29W
Big Sandy River [Az.-U.S.]	46	Ii	34.19N	113.31W
Big Sandy River [Wy.-U.S.]	46	Kf	41.50N	109.48W
Big Sheep Mountains	46	Mc	47.03N	105.43W
Big Sioux River	43	Hc	42.30N	96.25W
Big Smoky Valley	43	Dd	38.30N	117.15W
Big Snowy Mountains	46	Kc	46.50N	109.30W
Big Spring	39	If	32.15N	101.28W
Big Spruce Knob	44	Gf	38.16N	80.12W
Big Stone Lake	45	Hd	45.25N	96.40W
Big Timber	46	Kd	45.50N	109.57W
Big Trout Lake	42	If	53.45N	90.00W
Biguglia, Étang de-	11a	Ba	42.36N	9.29 E
Big Wood Cay	49	Ia	24.21N	77.44W
Big Wood River	46	He	42.52N	114.55W
Bihać	14	Jf	44.49N	15.52 E
Bihār	25	Hd	25.00N	86.00 E
Bihār	25	Hc	25.11N	85.31 E
Biharamulo	36	Fc	2.38S	31.20 E
Bihor	15	Ec	47.00N	22.00 E
Bihoro	27	Pc	43.49N	144.07 E
Bihorului, Munții-	15	Fc	46.40N	22.45 E
Bija	21	Kd	52.25N	85.05 E
Bijagós, Arquipélago dos-=Bijagos Islands (EN)	30	Fg	11.15N	16.05W
Bijagós Islands (EN)=Bijagós, Arquipélago dos-	30	Fg	11.15N	16.05W
Bijapur	25	Fe	16.50N	75.42 E
Bijār	23	Gb	35.52N	47.36 E
Bijeljina	14	Nf	44.45N	19.13 E
Bijelo Polje	15	Cf	43.02N	19.45 E
Bijiang (Zhiziluo)	27	Gf	26.39N	99.00 E
Bijie	27	If	27.15N	105.16 E
Bijlikol, Ozero-	18	Hc	43.05N	70.40 E
Bijou Creek	45	Ef	40.17N	103.52W
Bijoutier Island	37b	Bb	7.04S	52.45 E
Bijsk	22	Kd	52.34N	85.15 E
Bikāner	22	Jg	28.01N	73.18 E
Bikar Atoll	57	Ic	12.15N	170.06 E
Bikeqi	28	Ad	40.45N	111.17 E
Bikin	20	Ig	46.43N	134.02 E
Bikin	20	Ig	46.51N	134.02 E
Bikini Atoll	57	Hc	11.35N	165.23 E
Bikoro	31	Ii	0.45S	18.07 E
Bilād Ghāmid	33	Hf	19.58N	41.38 E
Bilād Zahrān	33	He	20.15N	41.15 E
Bilāspur	22	Kg	22.03N	82.10 E
Bilate	35	Fd	6.34N	38.01 E
Bilauktaung Range	21	Lh	13.00N	99.00 E
Bilbao	6	Fg	43.15N	2.58W
Bilbays	33	Fc	30.25N	31.34 E
Bileća	14	Mh	42.53N	18.26 E
Bilecik	23	Ca	40.09N	29.59 E
Bilehsavār	24	Mc	39.28N	48.20 E
Bilé Karpaty=White Carpathians (EN)	10	Nh	48.55N	17.50 E
Bilesha Plain	36	Hb	0.35N	40.45 E
Biłgoraj	10	Sf	50.34N	22.43 E
Bili	36	Db	4.50N	22.29 E
Bili	36	Eb	4.09N	25.10 E
Bilibino	22	Sc	68.03N	166.20 E
Biliran	26	Hd	11.35N	124.28 E
Bilishti	15	Di	40.37N	20.59 E
Biliu He	28	Ge	39.30N	122.36 E
Bill Baileys Bank (EN)	9	Ca	60.40N	10.20W
Billerbeck	12	Jc	51.58N	7.18 E
Billericay	12	Cc	51.37N	0.35 E
Billingen	8	Ef	58.24N	13.45 E
Billings	39	Jf	37.04N	93.33W
Billings, Représa-	55	If	23.45S	46.40W
Billingshurst	12	Bc	51.01N	0.27W
Bill Williams River	46	Hi	34.17N	114.03W
Billy Chinook, Lake-	46	Ed	44.33N	121.20W
Bilma	31	Ig	18.41N	12.56 E
Biloela	59	Kd	24.24S	150.30 E
Bilo Gora	14	Le	45.50N	17.10 E
Biloku	54	Gc	1.46N	58.33W
Biloxi	43	Je	30.24N	88.53W
Bilqās Qism Awwal	24	Dg	31.13N	31.21 E
Bilteni	15	Ge	44.52N	23.17 E
Biltine	35	Cc	14.32N	20.55 E
Biltine	35	Cc	15.00N	21.00 E
Bilzen	12	Hd	50.51N	5.31 E
Bima	36	Eb	3.23N	25.09 E
Bimbān	24	Ej	24.26N	32.53 E
Bimberi Peak	59	Jg	35.40S	148.47 E
Bimbila	34	Fd	8.51N	0.04 E
Bimbo	35	Be	4.18N	18.33 E
Bimini Islands	47	Ic	25.44N	79.15W
Bināb	24	Md	36.35N	48.41 E
Binačka Morava	15	Eg	42.27N	21.47 E
Binaiya, Gunung-	26	Ig	3.11S	129.26 E
Binatang	26	Ff	2.10N	111.38 E
Binboga Daği	24	Gc	38.21N	36.32 E
Binche	12	Gd	50.24N	4.10 E
Binder	27	Jb	48.35N	110.36 E
Bindura	31	Kj	17.17S	31.20 E
Bine el Ouidane	32	Fc	32.08N	6.28W
Binéfar	13	Mc	41.51N	0.18 E
Binem	35	Bb	18.43N	19.40 E
Binga [Zaire]	36	Db	2.23N	20.30 E
Binga [Zimb.]	37	Dc	17.37S	27.20 E

Index Symbols

- Independent Nation
- State, Region
- District, County
- Municipality
- Colony, Dependency
- Continent
- Physical Region
- Historical or Cultural Region
- Mount, Mountain
- Volcano
- Hill
- Mountains, Mountain Range
- Hills, Escarpment
- Plateau, Upland
- Pass, Gap
- Plain, Lowland
- Delta
- Salt Flat
- Valley, Canyon
- Crater, Cave
- Karst Features
- Depression
- Polder
- Desert, Dunes
- Forest, Woods
- Heath, Steppe
- Oasis
- Cape, Point
- Coast, Beach
- Cliff
- Peninsula
- Isthmus
- Sandbank
- Island
- Atoll
- Rock, Reef
- Islands, Archipelago
- Rocks, Reefs
- Coral Reef
- Well, Spring
- Geyser
- River, Stream
- Waterfall Rapids
- River Mouth, Estuary
- Lake
- Salt Lake
- Intermittent Lake
- Reservoir
- Swamp, Pond
- Canal
- Glacier
- Ice Shelf, Pack Ice
- Ocean
- Sea
- Gulf, Bay
- Strait, Fjord
- Lagoon
- Bank
- Seamount
- Tablemount
- Ridge
- Shelf
- Basin
- Escarpment, Sea Scarp
- Fracture
- Trench, Abyss
- National Park, Reserve
- Point of Interest
- Recreation Site
- Cave, Cavern
- Historic Site
- Ruins
- Wall, Walls
- Church, Abbey
- Temple
- Scientific Station
- Airport
- Port
- Lighthouse
- Mine
- Tunnel
- Dam, Bridge

Index Symbols

[1] Independent Nation
[2] State, Region
[3] District, County
[4] Municipality
[5] Colony, Dependency
Continent
Physical Region

Historical or Cultural Region
Mount, Mountain
Volcano
Hill
Mountains, Mountain Range
Hills, Escarpment
Plateau, Upland

Pass, Gap
Plain, Lowland
Delta
Salt Flat
Valley, Canyon
Crater, Cave
Karst Features

Depression
Cliff
Desert, Dunes
Forest, Woods
Heath, Steppe
Oasis
Cape, Point

Coast, Beach
Polder
Peninsula
Isthmus
Sandbank
Island
Atoll

Rock, Reef
Islands, Archipelago
Rocks, Reefs
Coral Reef
Well, Spring
Geyser
River, Stream

Waterfall Rapids
River Mouth, Estuary
Lake
Salt Lake
Intermittent Lake
Reservoir
Swamp, Pond

Canal
Bank
Seamount
Ocean
Tablemount
Ridge
Shelf

Lagoon
Glacier
Ice Shelf, Pack Ice
Sea
Gulf, Bay
Strait, Fjord
Basin

Escarpment, Sea Scarp
Fracture
Trench, Abyss
National Park, Reserve
Point of Interest
Recreation Site
Scientific Station

Historic Site
Ruins
Wall, Walls
Church, Abbey
Temple
Scientific Station
Airport

Port
Lighthouse
Mine
Tunnel
Dam, Bridge

Bogcang Zangbo	27	Ee	31.56N	87.24 E
Bogda Feng	27	Ec	43.45N	88.32 E
Bogdan	15	Hg	42.37N	24.28 E
Bogdanovka	16	Mi	41.15N	43.36 E
Bogda Shan	21	Ke	43.35N	90.00 E
Bogen	7	Db	68.32N	17.00 E
Bogenfels	37	Be	27.23S	15.22 E
Bogense	8	Di	55.34N	10.06 E
Boggeragh Mountains/An Bhograch	9	Ei	52.05N	9.00W
Boggy Peak	51d	Bb	17.03N	61.51W
Boghar	13	Oi	35.55N	2.43 E
Boghni	13	Ph	36.32N	3.57 E
Bogia	60	Ch	4.16S	144.58 E
Bognor Regis	12	Bd	50.47N	0.39W
Bogny-sur-Meuse	12	Ge	49.54N	4.43 E
Bogoduhov	16	Id	50.12N	35.31 E
Bogomila	15	Eh	41.36N	21.28 E
Bogor	22	Mj	6.35S	106.47 E
Bogoridick	19	De	53.50N	38.08 E
Bogorodčany	10	Uh	48.45N	24.40 E
Bogorodsk	7	Kh	56.09N	43.32 E
Bogorodskoje [R.S.F.S.R.]	7	Mh	57.51N	50.48 E
Bogorodskoje [R.S.F.S.R.]	20	Jf	52.22N	140.30 E
Bogotá	53	Ie	4.36N	74.05W
Bogotol	20	De	56.17N	89.43 E
Bogøy	7	Dc	67.54N	15.11 E
Bogra	25	Hd	24.51N	89.22 E
Bogučany	20	Ee	58.23N	97.39 E
Bogučar	16	Le	49.57N	40.33 E
Bogué	32	Ef	16.36N	14.15W
Boguševsk	7	Hi	54.50N	30.13 E
Boguslav	19	Df	49.33N	30.54 E
Bo Hai=Chihli, Gulf of- (EN)	21	Nf	38.30N	120.00 E
Bohai Haixia	27	Ld	38.00N	121.30 E
Bohain-en-Vermandois	12	Fe	49.59N	3.27 E
Bohemia (EN)=Čechy	5	Hf	50.00N	14.30 E
Bohemia (EN)=Čechy	10	Kf	50.00N	14.30 E
Bohemian Forest (EN)= Böhmerwald	5	Hf	49.00N	13.30 E
Bohemian Forest (EN)= Český Les	10	Ig	49.50N	12.30 E
Bohemian Forest (EN)= Oberpfälzer Wald	10	Ig	49.50N	12.30 E
Bohemian Forest (EN)= Šumava	5	Hf	49.00N	13.30 E
Bohicon	34	Fd	7.12N	2.04 E
Böhmerwald=Bohemian Forest (EN)	5	Hf	49.00N	13.30 E
Bohmte	12	Kb	52.22N	8.19 E
Bohodoyou	34	Dd	9.46N	9.04W
Bohol	21	Oi	9.50N	124.10 E
Böhönye	10	Nj	46.24N	17.24 E
Bohor	14	Jd	46.04N	15.26 E
Bohu/Bagrax	27	Ec	41.58N	86.29 E
Bohus	8	Eg	57.51N	12.01 E
Bohuslän	8	Df	58.15N	11.50 E
Boiaçu	54	Fd	0.27S	61.46W
Boiano	14	Ii	41.29N	14.29 E
Boina	30	Lj	16.00S	46.30 E
Bois, Lac des -	42	Ec	66.50N	125.15W
Bois, Rio dos- [Braz.]	55	Gd	18.35S	50.02W
Bois, Rio dos- [Braz.]	55	Ha	13.55S	49.51W
Bois Blanc Island	44	Ec	45.45N	84.28W
Boischaut	11	Hb	46.40N	1.45 E
Boise	39	He	43.37N	116.13W
Boise City	45	Eh	36.44N	102.31W
Boise River	46	Ge	43.49N	117.01W
Boissay	12	De	49.31N	1.21 E
Boissevain	42	Hg	49.14N	100.03W
Boizenburg	10	Gc	53.23N	10.43 E
Bojador, Cabo-	30	Ff	26.08N	14.30W
Bojana	15	Ch	41.52N	19.22 E
Bojanowo	10	Me	51.42N	16.44 E
Bojarka	19	De	50.19N	30.20 E
Bojčinovci	15	Gf	43.28N	23.20 E
Bojnūrd	23	Ib	37.28N	57.19 E
Bojonegoro	26	Fh	7.09S	111.52 E
Bojuru	55	Gj	31.38S	51.26W
Bokatola	36	Cc	0.38S	18.46 E
Boké	34	Cc	10.56N	14.13W
Bokhara River	59	Je	29.55S	146.42 E
Bokn	8	Ae	59.15N	5.25 E
Boknafjorden	5	Gd	59.10N	5.35 E
Boko	36	Bc	4.47S	14.38 E
Bokol Mayo	35	Ge	4.31N	41.32 E
Bokoro	35	Bc	12.23N	17.03 E
Bokote	36	Dc	0.05S	20.08 E
Bokpyin	25	Jf	11.16N	98.46 E
Boksitogorsk	19	Dd	59.29N	33.52 E
Bokungu	36	Dc	0.41S	22.19 E
Bol [Chad]	35	Ac	13.30N	14.41 E
Bol [Yugo.]	14	Kg	43.16N	16.40 E
Bola, Bahr-	35	Bd	9.50N	18.59 E
Bolama	34	Bc	11.35N	15.28W
Bolands	51d	Bb	17.02N	61.53W
Bolaños, Río-	48	Gg	21.14N	104.08W
Bolattau, Gora-	18	Ha	46.44N	71.54 E
Bolayir	15	Ji	40.31N	26.45 E
Bolbec	11	Ge	49.34N	0.29 E
Bolda	16	Pg	45.58N	48.35 E
Bole [Eth.]	35	Fd	6.37N	37.22 E
Bole [Ghana]	34	Ed	9.02N	2.29W
Bole/Bortala	27	Dc	44.59N	81.57 E
Bolehov	16	Ce	49.03N	23.50 E
Bolesławiec	10	Le	51.16N	15.34 E
Bolgatanga	31	Gg	10.47N	0.51W
Bolgrad	16	Fg	45.40N	28.38 E
Bolhov	19	De	53.30N	36.01 E
Boli	27	Nb	45.46N	130.31 E
Bolia	36	Cc	1.36S	18.23 E
Boliden	7	Ed	64.52N	20.23 E
Bolinao, Cape-	26	Gc	16.22N	119.50 E
Bolintin Vale	15	Ie	44.27N	25.46 E
Bolívar [Col.] [2]	54	Db	9.00N	74.40W
Bolivar [Mo.-U.S.]	45	Jh	37.37N	93.25W
Bolivar [Tn.-U.S.]	44	Ch	35.15N	88.59W
Bolívar [Ven.] [2]	54	Fb	6.20N	63.30W
Bolívar, Cerro-	54	Fb	7.28N	63.25W
Bolívar, Pico-	52	Ie	8.30N	71.02W
Bolivia [1]	53	Jg	17.00S	65.00W
Bolivia, Altiplano de-	52	Jg	18.00S	68.00W
Boljevac	15	Ef	43.50N	21.58 E
Bollendorf	12	Ie	49.51N	6.22 E
Bollène	11	Kj	44.17N	4.45 E
Bollnäs	7	Df	61.21N	16.25 E
Bollon	59	Je	28.02S	147.28 E
Bollstabruk	8	Ga	63.00N	17.41 E
Bollullos par del Condado	13	Fg	37.20N	6.32W
Bolmen	7	Ch	56.55N	13.40 E
Bolnisi	16	Ni	41.28N	44.31 E
Bolobo	36	Cc	2.10S	16.14 E
Bolodek	20	If	53.43N	133.09 E
Bologna	6	Hg	44.29N	11.20 E
Bolognesi	54	Df	10.01S	74.05W
Bologoje	6	Jd	57.54N	34.02 E
Bolohovo	16	Jb	54.05N	37.52 E
Bolomba	36	Cb	0.29N	19.12 E
Bolombo	36	Dc	3.59S	21.22 E
Bolon	20	Ig	49.58N	136.04 E
Bolotnoje	20	De	55.41N	84.33 E
Bolovens, Plateau des-	25	Le	15.20N	106.20 E
Bolšaja Balahnja	20	Fb	73.37N	107.05 E
Bolšaja Berestovica	10	Uc	53.09N	24.02 E
Bolšaja Černigovka	7	Mj	52.08N	50.48 E
Bolšaja Glušica	7	Mj	52.24N	50.29 E
Bolšaja Ižora	8	Me	59.55N	29.40 E
Bolšaja Kinel	7	Mj	53.14N	50.32 E
Bolšaja Koksaga	7	Lh	56.07N	47.48 E
Bolšaja Kuonamka	20	Gc	70.50N	113.20 E
Bolšaja Oju	17	Jb	69.42N	60.42 E
Bolšaja Rogovaja	17	Jc	66.30N	60.40 E
Bolšaja Synja	17	Id	65.58N	58.01 E
Bolšaja Tap	17	Lg	59.55N	65.42 E
Bolšaja Ussurka	20	Ig	46.00N	133.30 E
Bolšaja Vladimirovka	19	He	50.53N	79.30 E
Bolšakovo	8	Ij	54.50N	21.36 E
Bolsena	14	Fh	42.39N	11.59 E
Bolsena, Lago di-	14	Fh	42.35N	11.55 E
Bolšerečje	19	Hd	56.06N	74.38 E
Bolšereck	20	Kf	52.22N	156.24 E
Bolšeustikinskoje	17	Ii	55.57N	58.20 E
Bolševik	20	Jd	62.40N	147.30 E
Bolševik, Ostrov-=Bolshevik Island (EN)	21	Mb	78.40N	102.30 E
Bolšezemelskaja Tundra	19	Fb	67.30N	58.30 E
Bolshevik Island (EN)= Bolševik, Ostrov-	21	Mb	78.40N	102.30 E
Bolšije Uki	19	Hd	56.57N	72.37 E
Bolšoj Anjuj	20	Lc	68.30N	160.50 E
Bolšoj Begičev, Ostrov-	20	Gb	74.20N	112.30 E
Bolšoj Berezovy, Ostrov-	8	Md	60.15N	28.35 E
Bolšoj Boktybaj, Gora- [Kaz.-U.S.S.R.]	19	Ff	48.30N	58.20 E
Bolšoj Boktybaj, Gora- [U.S.S.R.]	16	Ue	48.30N	58.25 E
Bolšoj Bolvanski Nos, Mys-	17	Ia	70.27N	59.05 E
Bolšoj Čeremšan	7	Li	54.12N	49.40 E
Bolšoje Muraškino	7	Ki	55.47N	44.46 E
Bolšoje Vlasjevo	20	Jf	53.25N	140.55 E
Bolšoje Zagorje	8	Mg	57.47N	28.58 E
Bolšoj Gašun	16	Mf	47.22N	42.42 E
Bolšoj Ik	17	Hj	51.47N	56.20 E
Bolšoj Irgiz	19	Ee	52.01N	47.24 E
Bolšoj Jenisej	20	Ef	51.40N	94.26 E
Bolšoj Jugan	19	Hc	60.55N	73.40 E
Bolšoj Kamen	20	Ih	43.08N	132.28 E
Bolšoj Klimecki, Ostrov-	7	Ie	62.00N	35.15 E
Bolšoj Kujalnik	16	Gf	46.46N	30.38 E
Bolšoj Kumak	16	Ud	51.22N	58.55 E
Bolšoj Ljahovski, Ostrov-	20	Jb	73.35N	142.00 E
Bolšoj Murta	20	Ee	56.55N	93.10 E
Bolšoj Nimnyr	20	He	58.08N	125.45 E
Bolšoj Pit	20	Ee	59.02N	91.40 E
Bolšoj Tjuters, Ostrov-	8	Le	59.50N	27.10 E
Bolšoj Uluj	20	Ee	56.45N	90.46 E
Bolšoj Uvat, Ozero-	17	Oh	57.35N	70.30 E
Bolšoj Uzen	5	Kf	48.50N	49.40 E
Bolsón, Cerro del-	52	Jh	27.13S	66.06W
Bolšovcy	10	Ug	49.08N	24.47 E
Bolsward	12	Ha	53.04N	5.30 E
Boltaña	13	Mb	42.27N	0.04 E
Bolton	9	Kh	53.35N	2.26W
Bolu	23	Da	40.44N	31.37 E
Bolu Dağları	24	Eb	41.05N	32.05 E
Bolungarvík	7a	Aa	66.09N	23.15W
Boluntay	27	Fd	36.29N	92.18 E
Bolva	16	Ic	53.17N	34.20 E
Bolvadin	24	Dc	38.42N	31.04 E
Bolzano/Bozen	6	Hf	46.31N	11.22 E
Bom, Rio-	55	Gf	23.56S	51.44W
Boma	31	Ii	5.51S	13.03 E
Bomassa	36	Cb	2.12N	16.12 E
Bombala	59	Jg	36.54S	149.14 E
Bombarral	13	Ce	39.16N	9.09W
Bombay	22	Jh	18.58N	72.50 E
Bomberai, Jazirah-	26	Jg	3.00S	133.00 E
Bombo	36	Fb	0.35N	32.32 E
Bomboma	36	Cb	2.26N	18.57 E
Bom Comércio	54	Ee	9.45S	65.54W
Bom Conselho	54	Ke	9.10S	36.41W
Bom Despacho	54	Ig	19.43S	45.15W
Bomdila	25	Ic	27.16N	92.23 E
Bomi/Bowo	27	Ge	30.02N	95.39 E
Bomi Hills	31	Fh	6.52N	10.45W
Bomili	36	Eb	1.40N	27.01 E
Bom Jardim de Goiás	55	Fc	16.17S	52.07W
Bom Jardim de Minas	55	Je	21.57S	44.11W
Bom Jesus	55	Gi	28.42S	50.24W
Bom Jesus da Lapa	53	Lg	13.15S	43.25W
Bom Jesus de Goiás	55	Hd	18.12S	49.37W
Bømlafjorden	8	Ae	59.40N	5.20 E
Bømlo	7	Ag	59.45N	5.10 E
Bomokandi	36	Eb	3.30N	26.08 E
Bomongo	36	Cb	1.22N	18.21 E
Bom Retiro	55	Hh	27.48S	49.31W
Bom Sucesso	55	Je	21.02S	44.46W
Bomu	30	Jh	4.08N	22.26 E
Bomu (EN)=Mbomou	30	Jh	4.08N	22.26 E
Bomu (EN)=Mbomou [3]	35	Cd	5.30N	23.30 E
Bon, Cape- (EN)=Ţīb, Ra's Aţ-	30	Ie	37.05N	11.03 E
Bona, Mount-	40	Kd	61.20N	141.50W
Bonaire	54	Ea	12.10N	68.15W
Bonaire Basin (EN)	50	Cg	11.25N	67.30W
Bonampak	48	Ni	16.43N	91.05W
Bonanza	49	Ef	14.01N	84.35W
Bonanza Peak	46	Eb	48.14N	120.52W
Bonao	49	Ld	18.56N	70.25W
Bonaparte, Mount-	46	Fb	48.45N	119.08W
Bonaparte Archipelago	57	Df	14.20S	125.20 E
Bonaparte Lake	46	Ea	51.16N	120.35W
Bonaparte Rocks	51p	Cb	12.24N	61.30W
Bonasse	50	Fg	10.05N	61.52W
Bonavista	42	Mg	48.39N	53.07W
Bonavista Bay	42	Mg	49.00N	53.20W
Bon-Cagan-Nur	27	Gb	45.35N	99.15 E
Bondeno	14	Ff	44.53N	11.25 E
Bondo	31	Jh	3.49N	23.40 E
Bondoukou	34	Ed	8.02N	2.48W
Bondoukou [3]	34	Ed	8.20N	2.55W
Bondowoso	26	Fh	7.55S	113.49 E
Bone, Gulf of- (EN)=Bone, Teluk-	21	Oj	4.00S	120.40 E
Bone, Teluk-=Bone, Gulf of- (EN)	21	Oj	4.00S	120.40 E
Bone Bay	51a	Db	18.45N	64.22W
Bonelohe	26	Hh	5.48S	120.27 E
Bönen	12	Jc	51.36N	7.46 E
Bone Rate, Kepulauan-	26	Hh	7.00S	121.00 E
Bone Rate, Pulau-	26	Hh	7.22S	121.08 E
Bonete, Cerro-	56	Gc	27.51S	68.47W
Bong	34	Cd	6.49N	10.19W
Bong [3]	34	Dd	7.00N	9.40W
Bonga	35	Fd	7.16N	36.14 E
Bongabong	26	Hd	12.45N	121.29 E
Bongandanga	36	Db	1.30N	21.03 E
Bongo, Massif des-	30	Jh	8.40N	22.25 E
Bongolava	37	Hc	18.35S	45.20 E
Bongor	31	Ig	10.17N	15.22 E
Bongouanou [3]	34	Ed	6.43N	4.12W
Bongouanou	34	Ed	6.39N	4.12W
Bonham	45	Hj	33.35N	96.11W
Bonheiden	12	Gc	51.02N	4.32 E
Bonhomme, Col du-	11	Nf	48.10N	7.06 E
Bonhomme, Pic-	49	Kd	19.05N	72.15W
Bonifacio	11a	Bb	41.23N	9.09 E
Bonifacio, Bocche di-= Bonifacio, Strait of- (EN)	5	Gg	41.18N	9.15 E
Bonifacio, Strait of- (EN)= Bonifacio, Bocche di-	5	Gg	41.18N	9.15 E
Bonifati, Capo-	14	Jk	39.33N	15.52 E
Bonin Basin (EN)	60	Bb	29.00N	137.00 E
Bonin Islands (EN)= Ogasawara-Shotō	21	Qg	27.00N	142.10 E
Bonin Trench (EN)	3	If	30.00N	145.00 E
Bonita Springs	44	Gl	26.21N	81.47W
Bonito [Braz.]	55	Jb	15.20S	44.46W
Bonito [Braz.]	55	De	21.08S	56.28W
Bonito, Pico-	47	Ge	15.38N	86.55W
Bonito, Rio- [Braz.]	55	Hb	15.18S	49.36W
Bonito, Rio- [Braz.]	55	Gc	16.31S	51.23W
Bonn	6	Ge	50.44N	7.06 E
Bonn-Bad Godesberg	10	Df	50.41N	7.09 E
Bonnebosq	12	Ce	49.12N	0.05 E
Bonnechère River	44	Ic	45.31N	76.33W
Bonners Ferry	46	Gb	48.41N	116.18W
Bonnet, Lac du-	45	Ia	50.22N	95.55W
Bonnétable	11	Gf	48.11N	0.26 E
Bonnet Plume	42	Ec	65.53N	134.58W
Bonneval	11	Hf	48.11N	1.24 E
Bonneville	11	Mh	46.05N	6.25 E
Bonneville Salt Flats	46	If	40.45N	113.50W
Bonnières-sur-Seine	12	De	49.02N	1.35 E
Bonningues-lès-Ardres	12	Ed	50.47N	2.01 E
Bonny	34	Ge	4.25N	7.10 E
Bono	14	Dj	40.25N	9.02 E
Bō-no-Misaki	29	Bf	31.15N	130.13 E
Bonorva	14	Cj	40.25N	8.46 E
Bontang	26	Gf	0.08N	117.30 E
Bonthain	26	Gh	5.32S	119.56 E
Bonthe	34	Cd	7.32N	12.30W
Bontoc	26	Hc	17.05N	120.58 E
Bonyhád	10	Oj	46.18N	18.32 E
Boo, Kepulauan-	26	Ig	1.12S	129.24 E
Boola	34	Dd	8.22N	8.43W
Booligal	59	If	33.52S	144.53 E
Boone [Ia.-U.S.]	45	Je	42.04N	93.53W
Boone [N.C.-U.S.]	44	Gg	36.13N	81.41W
Booneville [Ar.-U.S.]	45	Ji	35.08N	93.55W
Booneville [Ms.-U.S.]	45	Li	34.39N	88.34W
Boon Point	51d	Bb	17.10N	61.50W
Boonville [In.-U.S.]	44	Df	38.03N	87.16W
Boonville [Mo.-U.S.]	45	Jg	38.58N	92.44W
Boos	12	De	49.23N	1.12 E
Boothia, Gulf of-	38	Jb	71.00N	91.00W
Boothia Peninsula	38	Jb	70.30N	95.00W
Boot Reefs	60	Cj	10.00S	144.35 E
Booué	31	Ii	0.06S	11.56 E
Bophuthatswana	37	De	26.00S	25.30 E
Bopolu	34	Cd	7.04N	10.29W
Boppard	12	Jd	50.14N	7.36 E
Boquerón [3]	55	Bf	23.00S	61.00W
Boquerón	51a	Ab	18.03N	67.09W
Boquilla, Presa de la-	48	Gd	27.30N	105.30W
Boquillas del Carmen	48	Hc	29.17N	102.53W
Bor [Czech.]	10	Ig	49.43N	12.47 E
Bor [R.S.F.S.R.]	19	Ed	56.23N	44.07 E
Bor [Sud.]	31	Kh	6.12N	31.33 E
Bor [Swe.]	8	Fg	57.07N	14.10 E
Bor [Tur.]	24	Fd	37.54N	34.34 E
Bor [Yugo.]	15	Fe	44.06N	22.06 E
Bora-Bora, Ile-	57	Lf	16.30S	151.45W
Borah Peak	38	He	44.08N	113.14W
Boraldaj	18	Gc	42.30N	69.05 E
Bora Marina	14	Jm	37.56N	15.55 E
Bōramo	35	Gd	9.58N	43.07 E
Borås	7	Ch	57.43N	12.55 E
Borāzjān	24	Nh	29.16N	51.12 E
Borba [Braz.]	54	Gd	4.24S	59.35W
Borba [Port.]	13	Ef	38.48N	7.27W
Borborema, Planalto da-	52	Mf	7.00S	37.00W
Borca	15	Ib	47.11N	25.46 E
Borcea	15	Ke	44.20N	27.45 E
Borcea, Braţul-	15	Ke	44.40N	27.53 E
Borchgrevink Coast	66	Kf	73.00S	171.00 E
Borçka	24	Ib	41.22N	41.40 E
Borculo	12	Ib	52.07N	6.31 E
Borda da Mata, Serra-	55	Ie	21.18S	47.06W
Bordeaux	6	Fg	44.50N	0.34W
Borden	42	Ga	78.30N	110.30W
Borden Peninsula	38	Kb	73.00N	83.00W
Borders [3]	9	Kf	55.35N	3.00W
Bordertown	58	Fh	36.19S	140.47 E
Bordighera	14	Bg	43.46N	7.39 E
Bordj Bou Arreridj	32	Hb	36.04N	4.46 E
Bordj el Emir Abdelkader	13	Oi	35.52N	2.16 E
Bordj Fly Sainte Marie	32	Gd	27.18N	2.59W
Bordj-Menaïel	13	Ph	36.44N	3.43 E
Bordj Messouda	32	Ic	30.12N	9.25 E
Bordj Moktar	31	Hf	21.20N	0.56 E
Bordj Omar Driss	31	Hf	28.09N	6.49 E
Bord Khūn-e Now	24	Nh	28.03N	51.28 E
Bordon Camp	12	Bc	51.07N	0.51W
Boreal, Chaco-	52	Kh	23.00S	60.00W
Boren	8	Ff	58.35N	15.10 E
Borensberg	8	Ff	58.34N	15.17 E
Borgå/Porvoo	7	Ff	60.24N	25.40 E
Borgarnes	7a	Bb	64.32N	21.55W
Børgefjell	7	Cd	65.23N	13.50 E
Borgentreich	12	Lc	51.34N	9.15 E
Borger [Neth.]	12	Ib	52.55N	6.48 E
Borger [Tx.-U.S.]	43	Gd	35.39N	101.24W
Borgholm	7	Dh	56.53N	16.39 E
Borghorst, Steinfurt-	12	Jb	52.08N	7.25 E
Borgia	14	Kl	38.49N	16.30 E
Borgloon	12	Hd	50.48N	5.20 E
Borgomanero	14	Ce	45.42N	8.28 E
Borgorose	14	Hh	42.11N	13.15 E
Borgo San Dalmazzo	14	Bf	44.20N	7.30 E
Borgo San Lorenzo	14	Fg	43.57N	11.23 E
Borgosesia	14	Ce	45.43N	8.16 E
Borgou [3]	34	Fc	10.30N	2.50 E
Borgo Val di Taro	14	Df	44.29N	9.46 E
Borgo Valsugana	14	Fd	46.03N	11.27 E
Borgu	30	Hg	10.35N	3.40 E
Borgworm/Waremme	11	Ld	50.42N	5.15 E
Bori	34	Ge	4.42N	7.21 E
Borinquen, Punta-	51a	Ab	18.30N	67.10W
Borislav	19	Cf	49.18N	23.27 E
Borisoglebsk	6	Ke	51.23N	42.06 E
Borisov	19	Ce	54.15N	28.30 E
Borisovka	16	Jd	50.36N	36.06 E
Borispol	19	De	50.23N	30.59 E
Bo River	35	Dd	6.48N	27.55 E
Borja	14	Lf	44.31N	17.44 E
Borja [Peru]	54	Cd	4.26S	77.33W
Borja [Sp.]	13	Kc	41.50N	1.32W
Borjas Blancas/Les Borges Blanques	13	Mc	41.31N	0.52 E
Borken	10	Ce	51.51N	6.52 E
Borkou	30	Ig	18.15N	18.50 E
Borkou-Ennedi-Tibesti [3]	35	Bb	18.00N	19.00 E
Borkoviči	8	Mi	55.38N	28.23 E
Borkum	10	Cc	53.35N	6.41 E
Borlänge	7	Df	60.29N	15.25 E
Borlu	24	Cc	38.44N	28.27 E
Bormida	14	Cf	44.56N	8.40 E
Bormio	14	Ed	46.28N	10.22 E
Born	11	Fj	44.30N	1.00W
Borna	10	Ie	51.07N	12.30 E
Borndiep	12	Ha	53.25N	5.35 E
Borne	12	Ib	52.18N	6.45 E
Borneo/Kalimantan	21	Ni	1.00N	114.00 E
Bornheim	12	Id	50.46N	7.00 E
Bornholm	5	Hd	55.10N	15.00 E
Bornholm [2]	8	Fi	55.10N	15.00 E
Bornos	13	Gh	36.48N	5.44W
Bornova, İzmir-	24	Bc	38.27N	27.14 E
Bornu [2]	34	Hc	12.00N	12.40 E
Bornu	30	Ig	12.30N	13.00 E
Boro	30	Jh	8.52N	26.11 E
Borodino [R.S.F.S.R.]	7	Ii	55.32N	35.49 E
Borodino [R.S.F.S.R.]	20	Ee	55.57N	95.03 E
Borodinskoje	8	Md	61.00N	29.29 E
Borogoncy	20	Id	62.39N	131.08 E
Borohoro Shan	21	Ke	42.00N	85.00 E
Boromo	34	Ec	11.45N	2.56W
Borongan	26	Id	11.37N	125.26 E
Borotou	34	Dd	8.44N	7.30W
Borovan	15	Gf	43.26N	23.45 E
Borovec	15	Gg	42.16N	23.35 E
Boroviči	19	Dd	58.24N	33.56 E
Borovici	8	Mg	57.58N	29.47 E
Borovljanka	20	Df	52.38N	84.35 E
Borovo	14	Me	45.24N	18.59 E
Borovski	19	Gd	57.03N	65.44 E
Borovskoj	19	Ge	53.48N	64.17 E
Borrachas, Islas-	50	Dg	10.18N	64.44W
Borrān	35	Hc	10.11N	48.53 E
Borrby	8	Fi	55.27N	14.10 E
Borroloola	58	Ef	16.04S	136.17 E
Borş	15	Eb	47.07N	21.49 E
Borşa	15	Hb	47.39N	24.40 E
Borščovočny Hrebet= Borshchovochny Range (EN)	20	Gf	52.00N	118.30 E
Borsec	15	Ic	46.57N	25.34 E
Borshchovochny Range (EN) =Borščovočny Hrebet	20	Gf	52.00N	118.30 E
Borsod-Abaúj-Zemplén [2]	10	Qh	48.15N	21.00 E
Bortala/Bole	27	Dc	44.59N	81.57 E
Bortala He	27	Dc	44.53N	82.45 E
Bort-les-Orgues	11	Ii	45.24N	2.30 E
Borūjen	24	Ng	31.59N	51.18 E
Borūjerd	23	Gc	33.54N	48.46 E
Borzja	22	Nd	50.24N	116.31 E
Borzna	16	Hd	51.15N	32.29 E
Boržomi	16	Mi	41.50N	43.25 E
Borzsöny	10	Oi	47.55N	19.00 E
Borzyszkowy	10	Nb	54.03N	17.22 E
Bosa	14	Cj	40.18N	8.30 E
Bosanska Dubica	14	Ke	45.11N	16.48 E
Bosanska Gradiška	14	Le	45.09N	17.15 E
Bosanska Krupa	14	Kf	44.53N	16.10 E
Bosanski Brod	14	Me	45.08N	18.01 E
Bosanski Novi	14	Ke	45.03N	16.22 E
Bosanski Petrovac	14	Kf	44.34N	16.21 E
Bosanski Šamac	14	Me	45.04N	18.28 E
Bosansko Grahovo	23	Ff	44.11N	16.22 E
Bōsāso	31	Lg	11.13N	49.08 E
Bosavi, Mount-	59	Ia	6.35S	142.50 E
Bosbeek	12	Hc	51.06N	5.48 E
Bose	22	Mg	24.01N	106.32 E
Boshan	27	Kd	36.30N	117.50 E
Boshrūyeh	24	Qf	33.53N	57.26 E
Bosilegrad	15	Fg	42.30N	22.28 E
Bosingfeld, Extertal-	12	Lb	52.04N	9.07 E
Bosna	14	Me	45.04N	18.28 E
Bosna	15	Kg	42.11N	27.27 E
Bosna=Bosnia (EN)	5	Hg	44.00N	18.00 E
Bosna = Bosnia (EN)	14	Lf	44.00N	18.00 E
Bosna i Hercegovina = Bosnia-Hercegovina (EN) [2]	14	Lf	44.15N	17.50 E
Bosnia (EN) = Bosna	14	Lf	44.00N	18.00 E
Bosnia (EN)=Bosna	5	Hg	44.00N	18.00 E
Bosnia-Hercegovina (EN) = Bosna i Hercegovina [2]	14	Lf	44.15N	17.50 E
Bosnik	26	Kg	1.10S	136.14 E
Bošnjakovo	20	Jg	49.41N	142.10 E
Bosobolo	36	Cb	4.11N	19.54 E
Bōsō-Hantō	28	Pg	35.20N	140.10 E
Bosporus (EN)=İstanbul Boğazi	5	Ig	41.00N	29.00 E
Bosque Bonito	48	Gb	30.42N	105.06W
Bossangoa	31	Ih	6.29N	17.27 E
Bossé Bangou	34	Fc	13.21N	1.18 E
Bossembélé	35	Bd	5.16N	17.39 E
Bossemtélé II	35	Bd	5.41N	16.38 E
Bossier City	43	Ie	32.31N	93.43W
Bosso	34	Hc	13.42N	13.19 E
Bosso, Dallol-	30	Hg	12.25N	2.50 E
Bossut, Cape-	59	Ec	18.43S	121.38 E
Bostān	25	Db	30.26N	67.02 E
Bostānābād	24	Ld	37.50N	46.50 E
Bosten/Bagrax Hu	21	Ke	42.00N	87.00 E
Boston [Eng.-U.K.]	9	Mi	52.59N	0.01W
Boston [Ma.-U.S.]	39	Le	42.21N	71.04W
Boston Bar	46	Eb	49.52N	121.26W
Boston Deeps	12	Ca	53.00N	0.15 E
Boston Mountains	43	Id	35.50N	93.20W
Botan	24	Id	37.44N	41.48 E
Botas, Ribeirão das-	55	Fe	20.26S	53.43W
Botesdale	12	Db	52.20N	1.01 E
Botev	5	Ig	42.43N	24.55 E
Botevgrad	15	Gg	42.54N	23.47 E
Bothnia, Gulf of- (EN)= Bottniska viken	5	Hc	63.00N	20.00 E
Bothnia, Gulf of- (EN)= Pohjanlahti	5	Hc	63.00N	20.00 E
Boticas	13	Ec	41.41N	7.40W
Botletle	37	Cd	21.07S	24.42 E
Botlih	16	Oh	42.41N	46.13 E
Botna	15	Mc	46.48N	29.30 E
Botoşani [2]	15	Jb	47.40N	26.43 E
Botoşani	15	Jb	47.45N	26.40 E
Botrange	11	Md	50.30N	6.08 E
Botswana [1]	31	Jk	22.00S	24.00 E
Botte Donato	14	Kk	39.17N	16.27 E
Bottineau	43	Gb	48.50N	100.27W
Bottniska viken=Bothnia, Gulf of- (EN)	5	Hc	63.00N	20.00 E
Bottrop	10	Ce	51.31N	6.55 E
Botucatu	56	Kb	22.52S	48.26W
Botucatu, Serra de-	55	Hf	23.00S	48.20W
Botwood	42	Lg	49.08N	55.21W
Bouaflé	34	Dd	6.59N	5.45W
Bouaflé [3]	34	Dd	7.03N	5.48W
Bouaké	31	Gh	7.41N	5.02W
Bouaké [3]	34	Dd	7.45N	5.02W
Bou Anane	32	Gc	32.02N	3.03W
Bouar	31	Ih	5.57N	15.36 E
Bou Arfa	32	Gc	32.32N	1.57W
Boubín	10	Jh	48.58N	13.50 E
Bouca	31	Ih	6.30N	18.17 E
Bouchain	12	Fd	50.17N	3.19 E
Bouchegouf	14	Bn	36.28N	7.44 E
Bouche Island	51k	Bb	13.57N	60.53W
Bouches-du-Rhône [3]	11	Kk	43.30N	5.00 E
Boudenib	32	Gc	31.57N	3.36W
Boudeuse Cay	37b	Bb	6.05S	52.51 E
Boû Djébéha	34	Eb	18.33N	2.45W
Bouenza [3]	36	Bc	3.00S	13.00 E
Boufarik	13	Oh	36.34N	2.55 E
Bougaa	13	Rh	36.20N	5.05 E
Bougainville Island	57	Ge	6.00S	155.00 E
Bougainville Reef	59	Jc	15.30S	147.05 E
Bougainville Strait [Ocn.]	63a	Cb	6.40S	156.10 E
Bougainville Strait [Van.]	63b	Cb	15.50S	167.10 E
Bougouni	31	Gg	11.25N	7.28W

Index Symbols

- [1] Independent Nation
- [2] State, Region
- [3] District, County
- [4] Municipality
- Colony, Dependency
- Continent
- Physical Region
- Historical or Cultural Region
- Mount, Mountain
- Volcano
- Hill
- Mountains, Mountain Range
- Hills, Escarpment
- Plateau, Upland
- Pass, Gap
- Plain, Lowland
- Delta
- Salt Flat
- Valley, Canyon
- Crater, Cave
- Karst Features
- Depression
- Polder
- Desert, Dunes
- Forest, Woods
- Heath, Steppe
- Oasis
- Cape, Point
- Coast, Beach
- Cliff
- Peninsula
- Isthmus
- Sandbank
- Island
- Atoll
- Rock, Reef
- Islands, Archipelago
- Rocks, Reefs
- Coral Reef
- Well, Spring
- Geyser
- River, Stream
- Waterfall Rapids
- River Mouth, Estuary
- Lake
- Salt Lake
- Intermittent Lake
- Reservoir
- Swamp, Pond
- Canal
- Glacier
- Ice Shelf, Pack Ice
- Ocean
- Sea
- Gulf, Bay
- Strait, Fjord
- Lagoon
- Bank
- Seamount
- Tablemount
- Ridge
- Shelf
- Basin
- Escarpment, Sea Scarp
- Fracture
- Trench, Abyss
- National Park, Reserve
- Point of Interest
- Recreation Site
- Cave, Cavern
- Historic Site
- Ruins
- Wall, Walls
- Church, Abbey
- Temple
- Scientific Station
- Airport
- Port
- Lighthouse
- Mine
- Tunnel
- Dam, Bridge

International Map Index

Index Symbols

[1] Independent Nation	[)(] Pass, Gap	[▽] Depression	[▨] Coast, Beach
[2] State, Region	[▨] Plain, Lowland	[▨] Polder	[▨] Cliff
[3] District, County	[▽] Delta	[▨] Desert, Dunes	[▨] Peninsula
[4] Municipality	[▨] Salt Flat	[▨] Forest, Woods	[▨] Isthmus
[5] Colony, Dependency	[▷] Valley, Canyon	[▨] Heath, Steppe	[◻] Island
[■] Continent	[▨] Crater, Cave	[▨] Oasis	[◻] Islands, Archipelago
[■] Physical Region	[◫] Karst Features	[▶] Cape, Point	[◻] Atoll

[▨] Rock, Reef	[▨] Waterfall Rapids	[▨] Canal	[▨] Lagoon
[▨] Islands, Archipelago	[▨] River Mouth, Estuary	[▨] Ice Shelf, Pack Ice	[▨] Bank
[▨] Rocks, Reefs	[▨] Lake	[▨] Ocean	[▨] Seamount
[▨] Coral Reef	[▨] Salt Lake	[▨] Sea	[▨] Tablemount
[▨] Well, Spring	[▨] Intermittent Lake	[▨] Gulf, Bay	[▨] Ridge
[▨] Geyser	[▨] Sea	[▨] Strait, Fjord	[▨] Shelf
[S] River, Stream	[▨] Gulf, Bay	[▨] Swamp, Pond	[▨] Basin

[▨] Escarpment, Sea Scarp	[▨] Historic Site	[▨] Port
[▨] Fracture	[▨] Ruins	[▨] Lighthouse
[▨] Trench, Abyss	[▨] Wall, Walls	[▨] Mine
[▨] National Park, Reserve	[▨] Church, Abbey	[▨] Tunnel
[▨] Point of Interest	[▨] Temple	[▨] Dam, Bridge
[▨] Recreation Site	[▨] Scientific Station	
[▨] Cave, Cavern	[▨] Airport	

Bruchhausen Vilsen 12 Lb 52.50N 9.01 E
Bruchmühlbach Miesau 12 Je 49.23N 7.28 E
Bruchsal 10 Eg 49.08N 8.36 E
Bruck an der Leitha 14 Kb 48.01N 16.46 E
Bruck an der Mur 14 Jc 47.25N 15.17 E
Brue 9 Kj 51.13N 3.00W
Bruges/Brugge 11 Jc 51.13N 3.14 E
Brugg 14 Cc 47.29N 8.12 E
Brugge/Bruges 11 Jc 51.13N 3.14 E
Brugge-Assebroek 12 Fc 51.12N 3.16 E
Brüggen 12 Ic 51.15N 6.11 E
Brugge-Sint-Andries 12 Fc 51.12N 3.10 E
Brühl [F.R.G.] 12 Id 50.50N 6.54 E
Brühl [F.R.G.] 12 Ke 49.24N 8.32 E
Bruine Bank=Brown Bank (EN) 12 Fb 52.35N 3.20 E
Bruin Point 43 Ed 39.39N 110.22W
Brule River 44 Cc 45.57N 88.12W
Brumado 54 Jf 14.13S 41.40W
Brummen 12 Ib 52.06N 6.10 E
Brummo 8 Ef 58.50N 13.40 E
Brumunddal 7 Cf 60.53N 10.56 E
Bruna 14 Eh 42.45N 10.53 E
Brune 12 Fe 49.45N 3.47 E
Bruneau 46 He 42.53N 115.48W
Bruneau River 46 He 42.57N 115.58W
Bruneck / Brunico 14 Fd 46.48N 11.56 E
Brunehamel 12 Ge 49.46N 4.11 E
Brunei 22 Ni 4.30N 114.40 E
Brunei, Teluk- 21 Ni 5.05N 115.18 E
Brunette Downs 59 Hc 18.38S 135.57 E
Brunflo 8 Fa 63.05N 14.49 E
Brunico / Bruneck 14 Fd 46.48N 11.56 E
Brunna 8 Ge 59.52N 17.25 E
Brunner 62 De 42.26S 171.19 E
Brunner, Lake- 62 De 42.35S 171.25 E
Brunnsberg 8 Ec 61.17N 13.55 E
Brunsbüttel 10 Fc 53.54N 9.07 E
Brunssum 12 Hd 50.57N 5.57 E
Brunswick [Ga.-U.S.] 43 Ke 31.10N 81.29W
Brunswick [Me.-U.S.] 43 Nc 43.55N 69.58W
Brunswick, Peninsula de- 52 Ik 53.30S 71.25W
Brunswick Lake 44 Fa 49.00N 83.23W
Bruntál 10 Ng 49.59N 17.28 E
Bruny Island 59 Jh 43.30S 147.05 E
Brus 15 Ef 43.23N 21.02 E
Brus, Laguna de- 49 Ef 15.50N 84.35W
Brush 43 Gc 40.15N 103.37W
Brus Laguna 49 Ef 15.47N 84.35W
Brusque 56 Kc 27.06S 48.56W
Brussel/Bruxelles=Brussels (EN) 6 Ge 50.50N 4.20 E
Brussels (EN)=Brussel/Bruxelles 6 Ge 50.50N 4.20 E
Brussels (EN)=Bruxelles/Brussel 6 Ge 50.50N 4.20 E
Brusset, 'Erg- 34 Hb 18.55N 10.30 E
Brusturi 15 Fb 47.09N 22.15 E
Brusy 10 Nc 53.53N 17.45 E
Bruxelles/Brussel=Brussels (EN) 6 Ge 50.50N 4.20 E
Bruzual 50 Bh 8.03N 69.19W
Bryan [Oh.-U.S.] 44 Ee 41.30N 84.34W
Bryan [Tx.-U.S.] 43 He 30.40N 96.22W
Bryan Coast 66 Pf 73.35S 84.00W
Bryne 7 Ag 58.44N 5.39 E
Brza Palanka 15 Fe 44.28N 22.27 E
Brzava kanal 15 Dd 45.16N 20.49 E
Brzeg 10 Nf 50.52N 17.27 E
Brzeg Dolny 10 Me 51.15N 16.40 E
Brzeziny 10 Pe 51.48N 19.46 E
Brzozów 10 Sg 49.42N 22.02 E
Bsharri 24 Ge 34.15N 36.01 E
Bû 12 Df 48.48N 1.30 E
Bua 8 Eg 57.14N 12.07 E
Buada Lagoon 64e Ab 0.32S 166.54 E
Buala 58 Ge 8.10S 159.35 E
Bū al Ḩidān, Wādī- 33 Cd 27.25N 19.22 E
Buapinang 26 Hg 4.46S 121.34 E
Buatan 26 Df 0.44N 101.51 E
Bū aţ Tifl 33 Dd 28.54N 22.30 E
Bua Yai 25 Ke 15.34N 102.24 E
Bu'ayrāt al Ḩasūn 33 Cc 31.24N 15.44 E
Bubanza 36 Ec 3.06S 29.23 E
Bubaque 34 Bc 11.17N 15.50W
Būbīyan 24 Mh 29.45N 48.15 E
Bubu 36 Gd 6.03S 35.19 E
Bubye 37 Ed 22.20S 31.07 E
Buca 15 Kk 38.22N 27.11 E
Bučač 16 De 49.04N 25.23 E
Bucaćaća 20 Gf 52.59N 116.55 E
Buçaco 36 De 11.27S 20.12 E
Bucak 24 Dd 37.28N 30.36 E
Bucaramanga 53 Ie 7.08N 73.09W
Bucas Grande 26 Ie 9.40N 125.58 E
Buccament Bay 51n Ba 13.12N 61.17W
Buccaneer Archipelago 59 Ec 16.17S 123.20 E
Bucecea 15 Jb 47.46N 26.26 E
Buchanan 31 Fh 5.53N 10.03W
Buchanan, Lake- [Austl.] 59 Jd 21.30S 145.50 E
Buchanan, Lake- [Tx.-U.S.] 45 Gk 30.48N 98.25W
Buchanan Bay 42 Ka 78.55N 75.00W
Buchan Gulf 42 Kb 71.48N 74.06W
Buchardo 56 Hd 34.43S 63.31W
Bucharest (EN)=Bucureşti 6 Ig 44.26N 26.06 E
Buchen 10 Fg 49.31N 9.20 E
Buchholz in der Nordheide 10 Fc 53.20N 9.52 E
Buchon, Point- 46 Ei 35.15N 120.54W
Buchs 14 Dc 47.10N 9.30 E
Buchy 12 De 49.35N 1.22 E
Bückeburg 12 Lb 52.16N 9.03 E
Buckeye 46 Ij 33.22N 112.35W
Buckhaven 9 Je 56.11N 3.03W
Buckie 9 Kd 57.40N 2.58W
Buckingham [Eng.-U.K.] 12 Bb 52.00N 0.59W
Buckingham [Que.-Can.] 44 Jc 45.35N 75.25W
Buckingham Bay 59 Hb 12.10S 135.46 E
Buckinghamshire 9 Mj 51.50N 0.55W
Buckland 40 Gc 66.16N 161.20W
Buckle Island 66 Ke 66.47S 163.14 E
Buckley Bay 66 Je 68.16S 148.12 E
Bucks 9 Mj 51.50N 0.55W
Bucksport 44 Mc 44.34N 68.48W
Buco Zau 36 Bc 4.50S 12.33 E
Bu Craa 32 Ed 26.17N 12.46W
Bucureşti 15 Je 44.30N 26.05 E
Bucureşti=Bucharest (EN) 6 Ig 44.26N 26.06 E
Bucy-lès-Pierrepont 12 Fe 49.39N 3.54 E
Bucyrus 44 Fe 40.47N 82.57W
Bud 7 Be 62.55N 6.55 E
Budacu, Vîrful- 15 Ib 47.07N 25.41 E
Buda-Koševo 16 Gc 52.43N 30.39 E
Budapest 10 Pi 47.30N 19.05 E
Budapest 6 Hf 47.30N 19.05 E
Búdardalur 7a Bb 65.07N 21.46W
Budaun 25 Fc 28.03N 79.07 E
Budbud 35 He 4.13N 46.31 E
Budd Coast 66 He 66.30S 113.00 E
Buddusò 14 Dj 40.35N 9.15 E
Bude [Eng.-U.K.] 9 Ik 50.50N 4.33W
Bude [Ms.-U.S.] 45 Kk 31.28N 90.51W
Bude Bay 9 Ik 50.50N 4.37W
Budel 12 Hc 51.16N 5.30 E
Budennovsk 19 Eg 44.45N 44.08 E
Budeşti 15 Je 44.14N 26.27 E
Budia 13 Jd 40.38N 2.45W
Büdingen 10 Ff 50.18N 9.07 E
Búdir 7a Cb 64.56N 14.01W
Budjala 36 Cb 2.39N 19.42 E
Budkowiczanka 10 Nf 50.52N 17.33 E
Budogošč 7 Hg 59.19N 32.29 E
Budrio 14 Ff 44.32N 11.32 E
Budslav 8 Lj 54.49N 27.32 E
Budva 15 Bg 42.17N 18.51 E
Budyšin/Bautzen 10 Ke 51.11N 14.26 E
Budžjak 15 Lc 46.15N 28.45 E
Buea 34 Ge 4.09N 9.14 E
Buech 11 Lj 44.12N 5.57 E
Buenaventura [Col.] 53 Ie 3.53N 77.04W
Buenaventura [Mex.] 47 Cc 29.51N 107.29W
Buenaventura, Bahía de- 54 Cc 3.45N 77.15W
Buenavista 48 Ef 23.39N 109.42W
Buena Vista [Co.-U.S.] 45 Cg 38.50N 106.08W
Buena Vista [Mex.] 48 Mi 16.05N 93.00W
Buena Vista [Mex.] 48 Bb 31.10N 115.40W
Buena Vista [Ven.] 50 Eh 9.02N 63.49W
Buenavista, Bahía de- 49 Hb 22.30N 79.08W
Buendia, Embalse de- 13 Jd 40.25N 2.43W
Buenópolis 55 Jc 17.54S 44.11W
Buenos Aires 56 Ie 36.00S 60.00W
Buenos Aires [Arg.] 53 Ki 34.36S 58.27W
Buenos Aires [C.R.] 49 Fi 10.04N 84.26W
Buenos Aires, Lago- 52 Ij 46.30S 72.00W
Buffalo 42 Fe 60.52N 115.03W
Buffalo [N.Y.-U.S.] 39 Le 42.54N 78.53W
Buffalo [Ok.-U.S.] 45 Gh 36.50N 99.38W
Buffalo [S.D.-U.S.] 43 Gb 45.35N 103.33W
Buffalo [Tx.-U.S.] 45 Hk 31.28N 96.04W
Buffalo [Wy.-U.S.] 43 Fc 44.21N 106.42W
Buffalo Bill Reservoir 46 Kd 44.29N 109.13W
Buffalo Lake 42 Fd 60.12N 115.25W
Buffalo Narrows 42 Ge 55.51N 108.30W
Buffalo Pound Lake 46 Ma 50.38N 105.20W
Buffels 37 Be 29.41S 17.04 E
Bū Fīshah 14 En 36.18N 10.28 E
Buford 44 Fh 34.07N 84.00W
Buftea 15 Ie 44.34N 25.57 E
Bug 5 Ie 52.31N 21.05 E
Buga 54 Cc 3.55N 76.18W
Bugarach, Pech de- 11 Il 42.52N 2.23 E
Bugeat 11 Hi 45.36N 1.56 E
Bugene 36 Fc 1.35S 31.08 E
Bugey 11 Li 45.48N 5.30 E
Bugojno 23 Ff 44.03N 17.27 E
Bugøynes 7 Gb 69.58N 29.39 E
Bugrino 17 Db 68.48N 49.09 E
Bugsuk 26 Ge 8.15N 117.18 E
Bugt 27 Lb 48.47N 121.55 E
Bugulma 19 Fe 54.33N 52.48 E
Bugun 18 Hc 43.22N 70.10 E
Bugun 18 Gc 42.56N 68.36 E
Bügür/Luntai 27 Dc 41.46N 84.10 E
Buguruslan 19 Fe 53.39N 52.30 E
Buhara 22 If 39.49N 64.25 E
Buharskaja Oblast 19 Gg 41.20N 64.20 E
Bū Ḩaşā' 24 Ok 23.20N 53.20 E
Buhera 37 Ec 19.18S 31.29 E
Buh He 27 Gd 36.58N 99.48 E
Buhl 46 He 42.36N 114.46W
Bühl 10 Eh 48.42N 8.09 E
Bühödle 35 Hd 8.15N 46.20 E
Buhtarminskoje Vodohranilišče 19 If 49.10N 84.00 E
Bui Dam 34 Ed 8.22N 2.10W
Builth Wells 9 Ji 52.09N 3.24W
Buin [Chile] 56 Fd 33.44S 70.44W
Buin [Pap.N.Gui.] 60 Fi 6.50S 155.44 E
Buinsk 19 Ee 54.59N 48.17 E
Buir Nur 27 Kb 47.48N 117.42 E
Buitrago del Lozoya 13 Id 41.00N 3.38W
Buj 17 Gh 56.15N 54.12 E
Buj 19 Ed 58.29N 41.31 E
Bujalance 13 Hg 37.54N 4.22W
Bujanovac 15 Eg 42.28N 21.47 E
Bujaraloz 13 Lc 41.30N 0.09W
Buje 14 He 45.24N 13.40 E
Bujnaksk 19 Eg 42.49N 47.07 E
Bujukly 20 Jg 49.33N 142.55 E
Bujumbura 31 Ji 3.23S 29.22 E
Bujunda 20 Kd 62.00N 153.30 E
Buk 10 Md 52.22N 16.31 E
Bük 10 Mi 47.23N 16.45 E
Buk 10 Hb 54.10N 11.42 E
Buka Island 57 Ge 5.15S 154.35 E
Bukakata 36 Fc 0.18S 32.02 E
Bukama 31 Ji 9.12S 25.51 E
Buka Passage 63a Ba 5.25S 154.41 E
Bukavu 31 Ji 2.30S 28.52 E
Bukene 36 Fc 4.14S 32.53 E
Bukhā 24 Qi 26.10N 56.09 E
Bukit Besi 26 Df 4.46N 103.12 E
Bukit Mertajam 26 De 5.22N 100.28 E
Bukittinggi 22 Mj 0.19S 100.22 E
Bükk 10 Qh 48.05N 20.30 E
Bukoba 31 Ki 1.20S 31.49 E
Bukovina 15 Ia 48.00N 25.30 E
Bukowiec 10 Ld 52.23N 15.20 E
Bukuru 34 Gd 9.48N 8.52 E
Būl, Kūh-e- 23 Hc 30.48N 52.45 E
Bulajevo 19 He 54.53N 70.26 E
Bulan 26 Hd 12.40N 123.52 E
Bulanaš 17 Kh 57.16N 62.02 E
Bulancak 24 Hb 40.57N 38.14 E
Bulanık 24 Jc 39.05N 42.15 E
Būlāq 33 Fd 25.12N 30.32 E
Bulawayo 31 Jk 20.09S 28.34 E
Buldan 24 Cc 38.03N 28.51 E
Buldir 40a Bb 52.21N 175.54 E
Bulgan [Mong.] 27 Hc 44.05N 103.32 E
Bulgan [Mong.] 27 Hb 48.45N 103.34 E
Bulgan [Mong.] 27 Fb 46.05N 91.34 E
Bulgaria (EN)=Bălgarija 6 Ig 43.00N 25.00 E
Buli 26 If 0.53N 128.18 E
Buli, Teluk- 26 If 0.45N 128.30 E
Buliluyan, Cape- 26 Ge 8.20N 117.11 E
Bulki 35 Fd 6.01N 36.36 E
Bullahār 35 Gc 10.23N 44.27 E
Bullange/Büllingen 12 Id 50.25N 6.16 E
Bullaque 13 Hf 38.59N 4.17W
Bulla Regia 14 Cn 36.33N 8.45 E
Bullas 13 Kf 38.03N 1.40W
Bulle 14 Bd 46.37N 7.04 E
Buller 62 Dd 41.44S 171.35 E
Bullfinch 59 Df 30.59S 119.06 E
Büllingen/Bullange 12 Id 50.25N 6.16 E
Bullion Mountains 46 Hi 34.25N 116.00W
Bulloo River 57 Fg 28.43S 142.30 E
Bull Point [Eng.-U.K.] 9 Ij 51.12N 4.10W
Bull Point [Falk.Is.] 56 Ih 52.19S 59.18W
Bulls 62 Fd 40.10S 175.23 E
Bulls Bay 44 Hi 32.59N 79.33W
Bull Shoals Lake 45 Jh 36.30N 92.50W
Bully Choop Mountain 46 Df 40.35N 122.45W
Bully-les-Mines 12 Ed 50.26N 2.43 E
Bulo Berde 35 He 3.52N 45.40 E
Bulolo 60 Di 7.12S 146.39 E
Bulqiza 15 Dh 41.30N 20.21 E
Bulter 45 Ig 38.16N 94.20W
Bultfontein 37 De 28.20S 26.05 E
Bulukumba 26 Hh 5.33S 120.11 E
Bulungu [Zaire] 36 Cc 4.33S 18.36 E
Bulungu [Zaire] 36 Dd 6.04S 21.54 E
Bumba 31 Jh 2.11N 22.28 E
Bumbah, Khalīj al- 33 Dc 32.25N 23.06 E
Buna 15 Ch 41.52N 19.22 E
Buna 36 Gb 2.47N 39.31 E
Bunbury 58 Ch 33.19S 115.38 E
Buncrana/Bun Cranncha 9 Ff 55.08N 7.27W
Bun Cranncha/Buncrana 9 Ff 55.08N 7.27W
Bunda 36 Fc 2.03S 33.52 E
Bundaberg 58 Gg 24.52S 152.21 E
Bünde 10 Ed 52.12N 8.35 E
Bundesrepublik Deutschland =Germany, Federal Republic of- (EN) 6 Ge 51.00N 9.00 E
Bun Dobhráin/Bundoran 9 Eg 54.28N 8.17W
Bundoran/Bun Dobhráin 9 Eg 54.28N 8.17W
Bungay 12 Db 52.27N 1.27 E
Bungku 26 Hg 2.33S 121.58 E
Bungo 36 Cd 7.26S 15.24 E
Bungo Strait (EN)=Bungo-Suidō 28 Lh 32.40N 132.18 E
Bungo-Suidō=Bungo Strait (EN) 28 Lh 32.40N 132.18 E
Bungotakada 29 Be 33.33N 131.27 E
Bungsberg 10 Gb 54.12N 10.43 E
Bunguran, Kepulauan-=Natuna Islands (EN) 21 Mi 2.45N 109.00 E
Buni 34 Hc 11.12N 12.02 E
Bunja 31 Kh 1.34N 30.15 E
Bunji 25 Ea 35.40N 74.36 E
Bunker 45 Kh 37.27N 91.13W
Bunker Group 59 Kd 23.50S 152.20 E
Bunkeya 36 Ee 10.24S 26.58 E
Bunkie 45 Jk 30.57N 92.11W
Bunnerfjällen 8 Ea 63.10N 12.34 E
Buñol 13 Le 39.25N 0.47W
Bunschoten 12 Hb 52.14N 5.24 E
Buntingford 12 Bc 51.57N 0.01W
Buntok 26 Fg 1.42S 114.48 E
Bünyan 24 Fc 38.51N 35.52 E
Bunyu, Pulau- 26 Gf 3.30N 117.50 E
Buor-Haja, Guba- 20 Ib 71.00N 131.00 E
Buotama 20 Hd 61.17N 128.55 E
Buqayaq 23 Gd 25.56N 49.40 E
Buqda Kōsār 35 Ge 4.31N 44.49 E
Bur 20 Hb 71.40N 123.40 E
Bura 36 Gc 1.06S 39.57 E
Buram 35 Dc 10.49N 25.10 E
Buran 19 If 48.04N 85.15 E
Burang 27 De 30.18N 81.08 E
Burāq 24 Gf 33.10N 36.29 E
Buras 45 Ll 29.21N 89.32W
Buraydah 22 Gg 26.20N 43.59 E
Burbach 12 Kd 50.43N 8.03 E
Būrdab 35 Hd 9.05N 46.30 E
Burdekin River 59 Jc 19.39S 147.30 E
Burdêre 35 He 3.30N 45.37 E
Burdur 23 Db 37.43N 30.17 E
Burdur Gölü 24 Dd 37.44N 30.12 E
Burdwān 25 Ad 23.15N 87.51 E
Burdwood Bank (EN) 56 Ih 54.15S 59.00W
Bure 12 Db 52.38N 1.45 E
Bure [Eth.] 35 Fd 8.20N 35.08 E
Bure [Eth.] 35 Fc 10.43N 37.03 E
Bureå 7 Ed 64.37N 21.12 E
Bureinski Hrebet=Bureya Range (EN) 21 Pd 50.40N 134.00 E
Bureja 20 Hg 49.43N 129.51 E
Bureja 21 Oe 49.25N 129.35 E
Büren 10 Ee 51.33N 8.34 E
Buren-Cogt 27 Jb 46.45N 111.30 E
Bureya Range (EN)=Bureinski Hrebet 21 Pd 50.40N 134.00 E
Burfjord 7 Fb 69.56N 22.03 E
Būr Gābo 35 Gf 1.10S 41.50 E
Burgas 6 Ig 42.30N 27.28 E
Burgas 15 Kg 42.30N 27.20 E
Burgas, Gulf of- (EN)=Burgaski Zaliv 15 Kg 42.30N 27.33 E
Burgaski Zaliv=Burgas, Gulf of- (EN) 15 Kg 42.30N 27.33 E
Burg auf Fehmarn 10 Hb 54.26N 11.12 E
Burg auf Fehmarn-Puttgarden 10 Hb 54.30N 11.13 E
Burgaw 44 Ih 34.33N 77.56W
Burgaz Daği 15 Mk 38.25N 29.46 E
Burg bei Magdeburg 10 Hd 52.16N 11.51 E
Burgdorf [F.R.G.] 10 Gd 52.27N 10.01 E
Burgdorf [Switz.] 14 Bc 47.04N 7.37 E
Burgenland 14 Kc 47.30N 16.25 E
Burgersdorp 37 Df 31.00S 26.20 E
Burgess Hill 12 Bd 50.58N 0.08W
Burgfjället 7 Dd 64.56N 15.03 E
Burghausen 10 Ih 48.10N 12.50 E
Burghūth, Sabkhat al- 24 Ie 34.58N 41.06 E
Burglengenfeld 10 Ig 49.12N 12.02 E
Burgos 13 Ib 42.20N 3.40W
Burgos [Mex.] 48 Je 24.57N 98.57W
Burgos [Sp.] 6 Fg 42.21N 3.42W
Burg-Reuland 12 Id 50.12N 6.09 E
Burgsvik 7 Eh 57.03N 18.16 E
Burgundy (EN)=Bourgogne 5 Gf 47.00N 4.30 E
Burgundy (EN)=Bourgogne 11 Kg 47.00N 4.30 E
Burgwald 12 Kd 50.57N 8.48 E
Būr Hakkaba 35 Ge 2.43N 44.10 E
Burhaniye 24 Bc 39.30N 26.58 E
Burhānpur 22 Jg 21.18N 76.14 E
Burias 26 Hd 12.57N 123.08 E
Buribaj 17 Ij 51.57N 58.11 E
Burica, Punta- 47 Hg 8.03N 82.53W
Burien 46 Dc 47.27N 122.21W
Burin Peninsula 42 Lg 47.00N 55.40W
Buriram 25 Kf 14.59N 103.08 E
Buriti, Rio- 55 Ca 12.50S 58.28W
Buriti Alegre 55 Hd 18.09S 49.03W
Buriti Bravo 54 Je 5.50S 43.50W
Buriti dos Lopes 54 Jd 3.10S 41.52W
Buritis 55 Ib 15.37S 46.26W
Burj al Ḩattābah 32 Ic 30.20N 9.30 E
Burjasot 13 Le 39.31N 0.25W
Burjatskaja ASSR 20 Ff 53.00N 110.00 E
Burj Şāfitā 24 Ge 34.49N 36.07 E
Burkandja 20 Jd 63.27N 147.27 E
Burkburnett 45 Gi 34.06N 98.34W
Burke 45 Ge 43.11N 99.18W
Burke, Mount- 46 Ha 50.18N 114.30W
Burke Island 66 Of 73.08S 105.06W
Burke River 59 Hd 23.12S 139.33 E
Burkesville 44 Eg 36.48N 85.22W
Burketown 58 Ef 17.44S 139.22 E
Burley 43 Ec 42.32N 113.48W
Burli 16 Rd 51.28N 52.44 E
Burlingame 45 Ig 38.45N 95.50W
Burlington [Co.-U.S.] 43 Gd 39.18N 102.16W
Burlington [Ia.-U.S.] 43 Ic 40.49N 91.07W
Burlington [Ks.-U.S.] 45 Ig 38.12N 95.45W
Burlington [N.C.-U.S.] 44 Hg 36.06N 79.26W
Burlington [Ont.-Can.] 44 Hd 43.19N 79.43W
Burlington [Vt.-U.S.] 43 Mc 44.28N 73.14W
Burlington [Wi.-U.S.] 45 Le 42.41N 88.17W
Burma 22 Lg 22.00N 98.00 E
Burma (Myanma-Nainggan-Daw) 22 Lg 22.00N 98.00 E
Burnazului, Cîmpia- 15 Ie 44.10N 25.50 E
Burnett River 59 Kd 24.46S 152.25 E
Burney 46 Ef 40.53N 121.40W
Burnham Market 12 Cb 52.57N 0.44 E
Burnham-on-Crouch 12 Cc 51.37N 0.50 E
Burnie 59 Jh 41.04S 145.54 E
Burnley 9 Kh 53.48N 2.14W
Burns 43 Dc 43.35N 119.03W
Burnside 42 Gc 66.51N 108.04W
Burnside, Lake- 59 Ee 25.20S 123.10 E
Burns Lake 42 Ef 54.14N 125.46W
Burnsville 44 Fh 35.55N 82.18W
Burnt Lava Flow 46 Ef 41.35N 121.35W
Burnt River 44 Hc 44.35N 78.46W
Burntwood 42 He 56.08N 96.33W
Bur'o 31 Lh 9.30N 45.34 E
Burqin 27 Eb 47.43N 86.53 E
Burqin He 27 Eb 47.42N 86.50 E
Burqūm, Ḩarrat al- 33 He 20.54N 42.00 E
Burra 59 Hf 33.40S 138.56 E
Burragorang Lake 59 Kf 34.00S 150.25 E
Burreli 15 Ch 41.37N 20.00 E
Burrendong Reservoir 59 Jf 32.40S 149.10 E
Burriana 13 Le 39.53N 0.05W
Burro, Serranías del 48 Ic 28.50N 101.35W
Burrow Head 9 Ig 54.41N 4.24W
Bursa 22 Ee 40.11N 29.04 E
Būr Sa'īd=Port Said (EN) 31 Ke 31.16N 32.18 E
Burscheid 12 Jc 51.06N 7.07 E
Bürstadt 12 Ke 49.38N 8.27 E
Burštyn 16 De 49.16N 24.37 E
Būr Sūdān=Port Sudan (EN) 31 Kg 19.37N 37.14 E
Burt Lake 44 Ec 45.27N 84.40W
Burtnieku, Ozero- 8 Kg 57.35N 25.10 E
Burtnieku, Ozero-/Burtnieku Ezers 8 Kg 57.35N 25.10 E
Burtnieku Ezers 8 Kg 57.35N 25.10 E
Burtnieku Ezers/Burtnieku, Ozero- 8 Kg 57.35N 25.10 E
Burton 44 Fd 43.02N 83.36W
Burton Latimer 12 Bb 52.21N 0.40W
Burton-upon-Trent 9 Li 52.49N 1.36W
Burträsk 7 Ed 64.31N 20.39 E
Buru, Pulau- 57 De 3.24S 126.40 E
Burullus, Buḩayrat al- 24 Dg 31.30N 30.50 E
Burultokay/Fuhai 27 Eb 47.06N 87.23 E
Burum Gana 34 Hc 13.00N 11.57 E
Burūn, Ra's- 24 Eg 31.14N 33.04 E
Burundaj 19 Hg 43.20N 76.49 E
Burundi 31 Ki 3.15S 30.00 E
Bururi 36 Ec 3.57S 29.37 E
Burutu 34 Gd 5.21N 5.31 E
Bury 9 Kh 53.36N 2.17W
Burylbajtal 18 Ib 44.56N 73.59 E
Buryn 16 Hd 51.13N 33.48 E
Bury Saint Edmunds 9 Ni 52.15N 0.43 E
Burzil Pass 25 Ff 34.54N 75.06 E
Busalla 14 Cf 44.34N 8.57 E
Busanga [Zaire] 36 Ee 10.12S 25.23 E
Busanga [Zaire] 36 Dc 0.51S 22.04 E
Busanga Swamp 36 Ee 14.10S 25.50 E
Buşayrah 24 Ie 35.09N 40.26 E
Būsh 24 Dh 29.09N 31.08 E
Būshehr 23 Hd 28.00N 52.00 E
Būshehr 22 Hg 28.59N 50.50 E
Būshgān 24 Nh 28.48N 51.42 E
Bushimaie 29 Ji 6.02S 23.45 E
Bushmanland (EN) = Boesmanland 37 Be 29.30S 19.00 E
Busia 36 Fb 0.28N 34.06 E
Busigny 12 Fd 50.02N 3.28 E
Businga 36 Db 3.20N 20.53 E
Busira 30 Ii 0.15S 18.59 E
Busk 16 Dd 50.01N 24.37 E
Buskerud 7 Bf 60.30N 9.10 E
Busko-Zdrój 10 Qf 50.28N 20.44 E
Busoga 36 Fb 0.45N 33.30 E
Buşrá ash Shām 24 Gf 32.31N 36.29 E
Busselton 59 Df 33.39S 115.20 E
Bussum 11 Lb 52.16N 5.10 E
Bustamante, Bahía- 56 Gg 45.07S 66.27W
Buşteni 15 Id 45.24N 25.32 E
Busto Arsizio 14 Ce 45.37N 8.51 E
Buštyna 10 Th 48.03N 23.28 E
Busuanga 26 Hd 12.05N 120.05 E
Busu-Djanoa 36 Db 1.43N 21.23 E
Büsum 10 Eb 54.08N 8.51 E
Buta 31 Jh 2.48N 24.44 E
Butajira 35 Fd 8.08N 38.27 E
Buta Ranquil 56 Ge 37.03S 69.50W
Butare 36 Ec 2.36S 29.44 E
Butaritari Atoll 57 Id 3.03N 172.49 E
Bute, Island of- 9 Hf 55.50N 5.05W
Bute Inlet 46 Ca 50.37N 124.53W
Butembo 31 Jh 0.09N 29.17 E
Butera 14 Im 37.11N 14.11 E
Butere 36 Fb 0.13N 34.30 E
Butha Qi (Zalantum) 27 Lb 48.02N 122.42 E
Buthidaung 25 Id 20.52N 92.32 E
Butiá 56 Jd 30.07S 51.58W
Butiaba 36 Fb 1.49N 31.19 E
Butler 44 He 40.51N 79.55W
Butser Hill 12 Bd 50.57N 0.59W
Butte 39 He 46.00N 112.32W
Butterworth [Mala.] 26 Df 5.25N 100.24 E
Butterworth [S.Afr.] 37 Df 32.23S 28.04 E
Button Bay 42 Ie 58.45N 94.25W
Butuan 22 Oi 8.57N 125.33 E
Butung, Palau- 21 Oj 5.00S 122.55 E
Buturlinovka 16 Ld 50.48N 40.45 E
Butzbach 12 Kd 50.26N 8.41 E
Bützow 10 Hc 53.50N 11.59 E
Buxtehude 10 Fc 53.27N 9.42 E
Buxton [Eng.-U.K.] 9 Lh 53.15N 1.55W
Buxton [N.C.-U.S.] 44 Jh 35.16N 75.32W
Buyo 34 Dd 6.16N 7.03W
Büyük Ağri Dağı=Ararat, Mount- (EN) 21 Gf 39.40N 44.24 E
Büyükanafarta 15 Ji 40.17N 26.22 E
Büyükçekmece 15 Lh 41.01N 28.34 E
Büyükkarıştiran 15 Kh 41.18N 27.32 E
Büyük Kemikli Burun 15 Ji 40.18N 26.14 E
Büyük Mahya 15 Kh 41.47N 27.36 E
Büyük Menderes 23 Cb 37.57N 28.58 E
Büyükorhan 15 Lj 39.45N 28.55 E
Buyun Shan 27 Lc 40.06N 122.42 E
Buzači, Poluostrov- 16 Ff 45.00N 52.00 E
Buzan 16 Pf 46.18N 49.06 E
Buzançais 11 Hh 46.53N 1.25 E
Buzancy 12 Ge 49.25N 4.57 E
Buzău 15 Jd 45.09N 26.50 E
Buzău 15 Jd 45.09N 26.50 E
Buzău 15 Kd 45.26N 27.44 E
Buzaymah 33 De 24.55N 22.02 E
Buzen 29 Be 33.37N 131.08 E
Buzet 14 He 45.24N 13.59 E
Būzhān 24 Le 34.09N 47.05 E
Búzi 37 Ec 19.51S 34.30 E
Búzi 37 Ec 19.52S 34.46 E
Buziaş 15 Ed 45.39N 21.36 E
Búzios, Ilha dos- 55 Jf 23.48S 45.08W
Bužora, Gora- 10 Th 48.24N 23.15 E
Buzuluk 19 Fe 52.46N 52.17 E
Buzuluk [R.S.F.S.R.] 16 Md 50.13N 42.12 E
Buzuluk [R.S.F.S.R.] 16 Rc 52.47N 52.16 E
Buzzards Bay 44 Le 41.33N 70.47W

Index Symbols

- 1 Independent Nation
- 2 State, Region
- 3 District, County
- 4 Municipality
- 5 Colony, Dependency
- Continent
- Physical Region
- Historical or Cultural Region
- Mount, Mountain
- Volcano
- Hill
- Mountains, Mountain Range
- Hills, Escarpment
- Plateau, Upland
- Pass, Gap
- Plain, Lowland
- Delta
- Salt Flat
- Valley, Canyon
- Crater, Cave
- Karst Features
- Depression
- Polder
- Desert, Dunes
- Forest, Woods
- Heath, Steppe
- Oasis
- Cape, Point
- Coast, Beach
- Cliff
- Peninsula
- Isthmus
- Sandbank
- Island
- Atoll
- Rock, Reef
- Islands, Archipelago
- Rocks, Reefs
- Coral Reef
- Well, Spring
- Geyser
- River, Stream
- Waterfall Rapids
- River Mouth, Estuary
- Lake
- Salt Lake
- Intermittent Lake
- Reservoir
- Swamp, Pond
- Canal
- Glacier
- Ice Shelf, Pack Ice
- Ocean
- Sea
- Gulf, Bay
- Strait, Fjord
- Lagoon
- Bank
- Seamount
- Tablemount
- Ridge
- Shelf
- Basin
- Escarpment, Sea Scarp
- Fracture
- Trench, Abyss
- National Park, Reserve
- Point of Interest
- Recreation Site
- Cave, Cavern
- Historic Site
- Ruins
- Wall, Walls
- Church, Abbey
- Temple
- Scientific Station
- Airport
- Port
- Lighthouse
- Mine
- Tunnel
- Dam, Bridge

Çanakkale Boğazi = Dardanelles (EN) 5 Ig 40.15N 26.25 E
Canala 63b Be 21.32S 165.57 E
Canandaigua 44 Id 42.53N 77.19W
Cananea 47 Bb 30.57N 110.18W
Cananéia 55 Ig 25.01S 47.57W
Canapolis 55 Hd 18.44S 49.13W
Canarias, Islas-=Canary Islands (EN) [5] 31 Ff 28.00N 15.30W
Canarias, Islas-=Canary Islands (EN) 30 Ff 28.00N 15.30W
Canaries 51k Ab 13.55N 61.04W
Canaronero, Laguna- 48 Ff 23.00N 106.15W
Canarreos, Archipiélago de los- 47 Hd 21.50N 82.30W
Canary Basin (EN) 3 Dg 30.00N 25.00W
Canary Islands (EN)= Canarias, Islas- 30 Ff 28.00N 15.30W
Canary Islands (EN)= Canarias, Islas- [5] 31 Ff 28.00N 15.30W
Cañas [C.R.] 49 Eh 10.25N 85.07W
Cañas [Pan.] 49 Gj 7.27N 80.16W
Canastra, Serra da- 55 Ie 20.00S 46.20W
Canatlán 48 Ge 24.31N 104.47W
Cañaveral 13 Fe 39.47N 6.23W
Canaveral, Cape- 38 Kg 28.30N 80.35W
Canavese 14 Be 45.20N 7.40 E
Canavieiras 54 Kg 15.39S 38.57W
Canazei 14 Fd 46.28N 11.46 E
Canberra 58 Fh 35.17S 149.08 E
Canby [Mn.-U.S.] 45 Hd 44.43N 96.16W
Canby [Or.-U.S.] 46 Dd 45.16N 122.42W
Cance 11 Ki 45.12N 4.48 E
Canche 11 Hd 50.31N 1.39 E
Cancon 11 Gj 44.32N 0.37 E
Cancún 47 Gd 21.05N 86.46W
Cancún, Isla- 48 Pg 21.05N 86.46W
Çandarli 15 Jk 38.56N 26.56 E
Çandarli Körfezi 15 Jk 38.52N 26.55 E
Candé 11 Eg 47.34N 1.02W
Candela 48 Id 26.50N 100.40W
Candelaria 48 Nh 18.18N 91.21W
Candelaria, Cerro- 48 Hf 23.25N 103.43W
Candelaria, Rio- [Bol.] 55 Cc 17.17S 58.39W
Candelaria, Rio- [Mex.] 48 Nh 18.38N 91.15W
Candelaro 14 Ji 41.34N 15.53 E
Cândido de Abreu 55 Gg 24.35S 51.20W
Cândido Mendes 54 Id 1.27S 45.43W
Candlemas Island 66 Ad 57.03S 26.40W
Candói 55 Fg 25.43S 52.11W
Čandyr 16 Jj 38.13N 55.44 E
Canela 56 Jc 29.22S 50.50W
Canelli 14 Cf 44.43N 8.17 E
Canelones [2] 55 El 34.35S 56.00W
Canelones 55 Dl 34.32S 56.17W
Canendiyu [3] 55 Eg 24.20S 55.00W
Cañete [Chile] 56 Fe 37.48S 73.24W
Cañete [Sp.] 13 Kd 40.03N 1.39W
Cangallo 55 Cm 37.13S 58.42W
Cangamba 36 Ce 13.44S 19.53 E
Cangas 13 Db 42.16N 8.47W
Cangas de Narcea 13 Fa 43.11N 6.33W
Cangas de Onis 13 Ga 43.21N 5.07W
Cangola 36 Cd 7.58S 15.53 E
Cangombe 36 Ce 14.24S 19.59 E
Cangshan (Bianzhuang) 28 Eg 34.51N 118.03 E
Canguçu 55 Fj 31.24S 52.41W
Canguçu, Serra do- 55 Fj 31.20S 52.40W
Canguinha 55 Eb 14.42S 55.40W
Cangumbe 36 Ce 12.00S 19.09 E
Cangyuan 27 Gg 23.10N 99.15 E
Cangzhou 27 Kd 38.14N 116.58 E
Cani, Iles- 14 Em 37.21N 10.07 E
Caniapiscau 38 Md 57.40N 69.30W
Caniapiscau, Lac- 42 Kf 54.00N 70.10W
Canicatti 14 Hm 37.21N 13.51 E
Canigou, Pic du- 11 Il 42.31N 2.27 E
Canik Dağlari 24 Gb 40.50N 37.10 E
Canim Lake 46 Ea 51.52N 120.45W
Canindé 54 Kd 4.22S 39.19W
Canindé, Rio- 54 Je 6.15S 42.52W
Cañitas de Felipe Pescador 48 Hf 23.36N 102.43W
Çankaya 24 Ec 39.56N 32.52 E
Çankırı 23 Da 40.36N 33.37 E
Canna 9 Gd 57.03N 6.33W
Cannac 63a Ac 9.15S 153.29 E
Çannakale 23 Ca 40.09N 26.24 E
Cannanore 25 Ff 11.51N 75.22 E
Cannanore Islands 25 Ef 10.05N 72.10 E
Cannes 11 Nk 43.33N 7.01 E
Cannich 9 Id 57.20N 4.45W
Canning Basin 59 Ed 20.10S 123.00 E
Cannobio 14 Cd 46.04N 8.42 E
Cannock 9 Ki 52.42N 2.01W
Cannonball River 45 Fc 46.26N 100.38W
Cann River 59 Jg 37.34S 149.10 E
Caño, Isla del- 49 Fi 8.44N 83.53W
Canoas 56 Jc 29.56S 51.11W
Canoas, Punta- 48 Bc 29.25N 115.10W
Canoas, Rio- 56 Jc 27.36S 51.25W
Canoeiros 54 Ig 18.02S 45.31W
Canoinhas 55 Gh 26.10S 50.24W
Canoinhas, Rio- 55 Gh 26.07S 50.22W
Cañoles 13 Le 39.02N 0.29W
Canon City 43 Fd 38.27N 105.14W
Canon Fiord 42 Ja 80.15N 83.00W
Canonnier, Pointe du- 51b Ab 18.04N 63.10W
Canora 42 Hf 51.37N 102.26W
Canosa di Puglia 14 Ki 41.13N 16.04 E
Canouan Island 50 Ff 12.43N 61.20W
Canourgue 11 Jj 44.25N 3.13 E
Canso, Strait of- 42 Lg 45.35N 61.23W
Canta 54 Cf 11.25S 76.38W
Cantabrian Mountains (EN) =Cantábrica, Cordillera- 5 Fg 43.00N 5.00W
Cantábrica, Cordillera-= Cantabrian Mountains (EN) 5 Fg 43.00N 5.00W
Cantal 5 Gf 45.10N 2.50 E
Cantal [3] 11 Ii 45.05N 2.40 E
Cantalejo 13 Ic 41.15N 3.55W
Cantanhede 13 Dd 40.21N 8.36W
Cantaura 54 Fb 9.19N 64.21W
Cantavieja 13 Ld 40.32N 0.24W
Cantavir 15 Cd 45.55N 19.46 E
Canterbury [2] 62 De 43.30S 171.50 E
Canterbury 9 Oj 51.17N 1.05 E
Canterbury Bight 57 Ii 44.10S 172.00 E
Can Tho 22 Mi 10.02N 105.47 E
Cantiles, Cayo- 49 Fc 21.36N 82.02W
Canto do Buriti 54 Je 8.07S 42.58W
Canton [Il.-U.S.] 45 Kf 40.33N 90.02W
Canton [Mo.-U.S.] 45 Kf 40.08N 91.32W
Canton [Ms.-U.S.] 45 Kj 32.37N 90.02W
Canton [N.Y.-U.S.] 44 Jc 44.37N 75.11W
Canton [Oh.-U.S.] 43 Kc 40.48N 81.23W
Canton [S.D.-U.S.] 45 He 43.18N 96.35W
Canton (EN)=Guangzhou 22 Ng 23.07N 113.18 E
Cantù 14 De 45.44N 9.08 E
Cantwell 40 Jd 63.23N 148.57W
Cañuelas 55 Cl 35.03S 58.44W
Canumã, Rio- 52 Kf 3.55S 59.10W
Canutama 54 Fe 6.32S 64.20W
Canvey 12 Cc 51.31N 0.36 E
Čany 20 Ce 55.19N 76.56 E
Čany, Ozero- 21 Jd 54.50N 77.30 E
Cany-Barville 12 Ce 49.47N 0.38 E
Canyon [Mn.-U.S.] 45 Jc 47.02N 92.29W
Canyon [Tx.-U.S.] 43 Ge 34.59N 101.55W
Canyon [Wy.-U.S.] 46 Jd 44.44N 110.30W
Canyon Lake 45 Gl 29.52N 98.16W
Canzar 36 Dd 7.36S 21.33 E
Cao Bang 25 Ld 22.40N 106.15 E
Caojiahe → Qichun 28 Ci 30.15N 115.26 E
Caojian 27 Gf 25.38N 99.07 E
Caombo 36 Cd 8.42S 16.33 E
Caorle 14 Ge 45.36N 12.53 E
Caoxian 28 Cg 34.49N 115.33 E
Caozhou → Heze 27 Kd 35.14N 115.28 E
Capaccio 14 Jj 40.25N 15.05 E
Čapajev 19 Fe 50.14N 51.08 E
Čapajevsk 19 Ee 53.01N 49.36 E
Capanaparo, Rio- 54 Eb 7.01N 67.07W
Capanema [Braz.] 54 Id 1.12S 47.11W
Capanema [Braz.] 55 Fg 25.40S 53.48W
Capanema, Serra do- 55 Fh 26.05S 53.16W
Capão Alto 55 Gh 27.56S 50.30W
Capão Bonito 55 Hf 24.01S 48.20W
Capão Doce, Morro do- 55 Gh 26.43S 51.25W
Caparo, Rio- 49 Lj 7.46N 70.23W
Capatárida 49 Lh 11.11N 70.37W
Capbreton 11 Ek 43.38N 1.26W
Cap Breton Canyon (EN) 11 Ek 43.40N 1.50W
Capčama, Pereval- 18 Hd 41.34N 70.50 E
Cap-Chat 44 Na 49.06N 66.42W
Capcir 11 Il 42.45N 2.10 E
Cap-de-la-Madeleine 42 Kg 46.22N 72.32W
Capdenac-Gare 11 Ij 44.34N 2.05 E
Cape Barren Island 59 Jh 40.25S 148.10 E
Cape Basin (EN) 3 Em 37.00S 7.00 E
Cape Breton Island 38 Me 46.00N 60.30W
Cape Charles 44 Jg 37.17N 76.00W
Cape Coast 31 Gh 5.06N 1.15W
Cape Cod Bay 44 Le 41.52N 70.22W
Cape Coral 44 Gl 26.33N 81.58W
Cape Dorset 39 Lc 64.14N 76.32W
Cape Dyer 39 Mc 66.30N 61.18W
Cape Fear River 44 Ii 33.53N 78.00W
Cape Girardeau 43 Jd 37.19N 89.32W
Cape Johnson Tablemount (EN) 57 Jc 17.08N 177.15W
Capel 12 Bc 51.08N 0.19W
Cape Lisburne 40 Fc 68.52N 166.05W
Capelka 8 Mf 58.02N 29.07 E
Capelongo 31 Ij 14.29S 16.18 E
Capem 55 Ea 13.14S 55.14W
Cape May 44 Jf 38.56N 74.54W
Cape Mount [3] 34 Cd 7.05N 10.50W
Cape Province/ Kaapprovinsie [2] 37 Cf 32.00S 22.00 E
Cape Rise (EN) 3 En 42.00S 15.00 E
Cape Smith 42 Jd 60.44N 78.29W
Capesterre 51e Bc 15.54N 61.13W
Capesterre-Belle-Eau 50 Fd 16.03N 61.34W
Cape Town / Kaapstad 31 Il 33.55S 18.22 E
Cape Verde (EN)=Cabo Verde [1] 31 Eg 16.00N 24.00W
Cape Verde (EN)=Cap Vert [3] 34 Bc 14.45N 17.20W
Cape Verde Basin (EN) 3 Ch 15.00N 30.00W
Cape Verde Islands (EN)= Cabo Verde, Ilhas do- 30 Eg 16.00N 24.10W
Cape Yakataga 40 Kd 60.04N 142.26W
Cape York Peninsula 57 Ff 14.00S 142.30 E
Cap-Haïtien 39 Lh 19.45N 72.15W
Capiibary, Arroyo- 55 Dg 24.06S 56.26W
Capiibary, Rio- 55 Eg 25.30S 55.33W
Capim, Rio- 52 Lf 1.40S 47.47W
Capinópolis 55 Hd 18.41S 49.35W
Capira 49 Hi 8.45N 79.53W
Capital Federal [2] 55 Cl 34.36S 58.27W
Capitán Arturo Prat 66 Re 62.29S 59.39W
Capitán Bado 56 Ib 23.16S 55.32W
Capitán Bermúdez 55 Bk 32.49S 60.43W
Capitán Sarmiento 55 Cl 34.10S 59.48W
Capitão Noronha, Rio- 55 Ea 13.19S 54.36W
Capivara, Represa da- 55 Gf 22.40S 50.57W
Capivari, Rio- 55 Dd 19.16S 57.10W
Capivarita 55 Fj 30.18S 52.19W
Cap Lopez, Baie du- 36 Ac 0.40S 9.00 E
Čaplygin 16 Kc 53.17N 39.59 E
Cappeln (Oldenburg) 12 Kb 52.49N 8.07 E
Cap Point 50 Fe 14.07N 60.57W
Capraia 14 Dg 43.05N 9.50 E
Caprara, Punta- 14 Ci 41.07N 8.19 E
Capreol 44 Gb 46.43N 80.56W
Caprera 14 Di 41.10N 9.30 E
Capri 14 Ij 40.35N 14.15 E
Capri 14 Ij 40.33N 14.14 E
Capricorn, Cape- 59 Kd 23.30S 151.15 E
Capricorn Channel 59 Kd 22.15S 151.30 E
Capricorn Group 57 Gg 23.30S 152.00 E
Caprivi Strip (EN)=Caprivi Zipfel 30 Jj 18.00S 23.00 E
Caprivi Zipfel=Caprivi Strip (EN) 30 Jj 18.00S 23.00 E
Captain Cook 65a Fd 19.30N 155.55W
Captains Flat 59 Jg 35.35S 149.27 E
Captieux 11 Fj 44.17N 0.15W
Capua 14 Ii 41.06N 14.12 E
Capuchin, Cape- 51g Ba 15.38N 61.28W
Capunda 36 Ce 10.41S 17.23 E
Cap Vert=Cape Verde (EN) [3] 34 Bc 14.45N 17.20W
Caquetá [2] 54 Dc 1.00N 74.00W
Čara 21 Oc 60.17N 120.40 E
Čara [R.S.F.S.R.] 20 Ge 56.58N 118.17 E
Čara [R.S.F.S.R.] 20 Ge 58.54N 118.12 E
Carabobo [2] 54 Ea 10.10N 68.05W
Caracal 15 He 44.07N 24.21 E
Caracarai 54 Fc 1.50N 61.08W
Caracas 53 Jd 10.30N 66.56W
Carache 49 Li 9.38N 70.14W
Caracol 55 De 21.59S 57.02W
Caracol, Rio- 55 Df 22.13S 57.03W
Caracollo 54 Eg 17.39S 67.10W
Cara Droma Rúisc/Carrick-on-Shannon 9 Eh 53.57N 8.05W
Caraguatá, Cuchilla- 55 Ek 32.05S 54.54W
Caraguatatuba 55 Jf 23.37S 45.25W
Caraïbe, Mer-/Antilles, Mer des-=Caribbean Sea (EN) 38 Lh 15.00N 73.00W
Carajas, Serra dos- 54 He 6.00S 51.20W
Caramoan Peninsula 26 Hd 13.48N 123.40 E
Caramulo, Serra do- 13 Dd 40.34N 8.11W
Caraná, Rio- 55 Ca 13.20S 59.17W
Carandai 55 Ke 20.57S 43.48W
Carandazal 55 Dd 19.50S 57.09W
Caransebeș 15 Fd 45.25N 22.13 E
Carapá, Rio- 55 Eg 24.30S 54.20W
Carapelle 14 Ji 41.30N 15.55 E
Caraș 15 Ee 44.49N 21.20 E
Caraș Severin [2] 15 Ed 45.20N 22.00 E
Caratasca, Cayo- 49 Fe 16.02N 83.20W
Caratasca, Laguna de- 47 He 15.20N 83.50W
Caratinga 54 Jg 19.47S 42.08W
Carauari 54 Ed 4.52S 66.54W
Caraúbas 54 Ke 5.47S 37.34W
Caravaca 13 Kf 38.06N 1.51W
Caravelas 53 Mg 17.45S 39.15W
Caraveli 54 Dg 15.46S 73.22W
Caravelle, Presqu'île de la- 51h Bb 14.45N 60.55W
Caravelle, Rocher de la- 51h Bb 14.48N 60.53W
Caràzinho 56 Jc 28.18S 52.48W
Carazo [3] 49 Dh 11.45N 86.15W
Carballino 13 Db 42.26N 8.04W
Carballo 13 Da 43.13N 8.41W
Carberry 45 Gb 49.52N 99.20W
Carbet, Pitons du- 51h Ab 14.42N 61.07W
Carbon, Cap- [Alg.] 13 Rh 36.47N 5.06 E
Carbon, Cap- [Alg.] 13 Li 35.54N 0.20W
Carbonara, Capo- 14 Dk 39.06N 9.31 E
Carbondale [Il.-U.S.] 43 Jd 37.44N 89.13W
Carbondale [Pa.-U.S.] 44 Je 41.35N 75.31W
Carbonera, Cuchilla de la- 55 El 34.10S 54.00W
Carboneras 13 Kh 36.59N 1.54W
Carboneras, Cerro- 48 Ih 18.10N 101.10W
Carbones 13 Gg 37.36N 5.39W
Carbonia 14 Ck 39.10N 8.31 E
Carcans, Étang de- 11 Ei 45.06N 1.07W
Carcar 26 Hd 10.06N 123.38 E
Carcarañá, Rio- 55 Bk 32.27S 60.48W
Carcassonne 11 Ik 43.13N 2.21 E
Carcross 42 Ed 60.10N 134.42W
Çardak [Tur.] 15 Ji 40.22N 26.43 E
Çardak [Tur.] 24 Cd 37.48N 29.40 E
Čardara 19 Gg 41.15N 68.01 E
Čardarinskoje Vodohranilišče 18 Gd 41.05N 68.15 E
Cárdenas [Cuba] 47 Hd 23.02N 81.12W
Cárdenas [Mex.] 47 Ed 22.00N 99.40W
Cárdenas [Mex.] 48 Mi 17.59N 93.22W
Cárdenas, Bahía de- 49 Gb 23.05N 81.10W
Cardener/Cardoner 13 Nc 41.41N 1.51 E
Cardiel, Lago- 56 Fg 48.55S 71.15W
Cardiff 6 Fe 51.30N 3.13W
Cardigan 9 Ii 52.06N 4.40W
Cardigan Bay 5 Fe 52.30N 4.20W
Cardona [Sp.] 13 Nc 41.55N 1.41 E
Cardona [Ur.] 55 Dk 33.54S 57.22W
Cardoner/Cardener 13 Nc 41.41N 1.51 E
Cardozo 55 Dk 32.38S 56.21W
Cardston 42 Gg 49.12N 113.18W
Čardžou 22 If 39.06N 63.34 E
Čardžouskaja Oblast [3] 19 Gh 39.00N 63.00 E
Carei 15 Fb 47.41N 22.28 E
Careiro 54 Gd 3.12S 59.45W
Carentan 11 Ee 49.18N 1.14W
Carey 46 Ie 43.20N 113.58W
Carey, Lake- 57 Dg 29.05S 122.15 E
Cargados Carajos Islands 30 Mj 16.35S 59.40 E
Cargese 11a Aa 42.08N 8.35 E
Carhaix-Plouguer 11 Cf 48.17N 3.35W
Cari 14 Hi 41.23N 13.50 E
Caria 15 Ll 37.30N 29.00 E
Cariacica 54 Jh 20.16S 40.25W
Cariaco 50 Eg 10.29N 63.33W
Cariaco, Golfo de- 50 Eg 10.30N 64.00W
Cariaco Basin (EN) 50 Dg 10.37N 65.10W
Cariati 14 Kk 39.30N 16.57 E
Caribana, Punta- 49 Ii 8.37N 76.52W
Caribbean Sea 38 Lh 15.00N 73.00W
Caribbean Sea (EN)= Antillas, Mar de las-/ Caribe, Mar- 38 Lh 15.00N 73.00W
Caribbean Sea (EN)= Antilles, Mer des-/Caraïbe, Mer- 38 Lh 15.00N 73.00W
Caribbean Sea (EN)= Caribe, Mar-/Antillas, Mar de las- 38 Lh 15.00N 73.00W
Caribe, Mar-/Antillas, Mar de las-=Caribbean Sea (EN) 38 Lh 15.00N 73.00W
Cariboo Mountains 42 Ff 53.00N 121.00W
Caribou 42 Ie 59.20N 94.45W
Caribou 44 Mb 46.52N 68.01W
Caribou Island 44 Eb 47.27N 85.52W
Caribou Lake 45 La 50.25N 89.00W
Caribou Mountains 38 Hd 59.12N 115.40W
Caribou Range 46 Je 43.05N 111.15W
Caričin Grad 15 Eg 42.57N 21.45 E
Carignan 11 Le 49.38N 5.10 E
Carignano 14 Bf 44.55N 7.40 E
Cariñena 13 Kc 41.20N 1.13W
Carinhanha 54 Jf 14.08S 43.47W
Carinhanha, Rio- 55 Kb 14.20S 43.47W
Carini 14 Hl 38.08N 13.11 E
Carinola 14 Hi 41.11N 13.58 E
Carinthia (EN) = Kärnten [2] 14 Hd 46.45N 14.00 E
Carinthia (EN) = Kärnten 14 Hd 46.45N 14.00 E
Caripe 50 Eg 10.21N 63.29W
Caripito 54 Fa 10.08N 63.06W
Caris, Rio- 50 Eh 8.09N 63.46W
Carlet 13 Le 39.14N 0.31W
Carleton Place 44 Ic 45.07N 76.08W
Carletonville 37 De 26.23S 27.22 E
Carlin 46 Gf 40.43N 116.07W
Carling 12 Ie 49.10N 6.43 E
Carlingford Lough/Loch Cairlinn 9 Gg 54.05N 6.14W
Carlinville 45 Lg 39.17N 89.53W
Carlisle [Eng.-U.K.] 6 Fe 54.54N 2.55W
Carlisle [Pa.-U.S.] 44 Ie 40.12N 77.12W
Carlisle Bay 51q Ab 13.05N 59.37W
Carloforte 14 Ck 39.08N 8.18 E
Carlos Beguerie 55 Cl 35.29S 59.06W
Carlos Casares 56 He 35.38S 61.21W
Carlos Chagas 54 Jg 17.43S 40.45W
Carlos Reyles 55 Dk 33.03S 56.29W
Carlos Tejedor 55 Al 35.23S 62.25W
Carlow/Ceatharlach 9 Gi 52.50N 6.55W
Carlow/Ceatharlach [2] 9 Gi 52.50N 7.00W
Carloway 9 Gc 58.17N 6.47W
Carlsbad [Ca.-U.S.] 46 Gj 33.10N 117.21W
Carlsbad [N.M.-U.S.] 39 If 32.25N 104.14W
Carlyle 42 Hg 49.38N 102.16W
Carlyle Lake 45 Lg 38.40N 89.18W
Carmacks 42 Dd 62.05N 136.18W
Carmagnola 14 Bf 44.51N 7.43 E
Carmarthen 9 Ij 51.52N 4.19W
Carmarthen Bay 9 Ij 51.40N 4.30W
Carmaux 11 Ij 44.03N 2.09 E
Carmel Head 9 Ih 53.24N 4.34W
Carmelita 49 Be 17.21N 90.10W
Carmelo 56 Id 34.00S 58.17W
Carmen 55 Dk 33.15S 56.01W
Carmen, Isla- 47 Bc 25.57N 111.12W
Carmen, Isla del- 48 Nh 18.42N 91.40W
Carmen, Laguna del- 48 Mh 18.15N 93.50W
Carmen, Rio del- 48 Fb 30.42N 106.29W
Carmen, Sierra del- 48 Hc 29.00N 102.30W
Carmen de Patagones 56 Hf 40.48S 62.59W
Carmensa 56 Ge 35.08S 67.38W
Carmi 45 Lg 38.07N 88.10W
Carmichael 46 Eg 38.38N 121.19W
Carmo de Minas 55 Jf 22.07S 45.08W
Carmo do Paranaiba 55 Id 18.59S 46.21W
Carmona 13 Gg 37.28N 5.38W
Carnac 11 Cg 47.35N 3.05W
Carnamah 59 De 29.42S 115.53 E
Carnarvon [Austl.] 58 Cg 24.53S 113.40 E
Carnarvon [S.Afr.] 31 Jl 30.56S 22.08 E
Carnarvon Range 59 Ee 25.10S 121.00 E
Carnatic (EN) 21 Jh 10.30N 79.00 E
Carnegie, Lake- 57 Dg 26.10S 122.30 E
Carnegie Ridge (EN) 3 Nj 1.00S 85.00W
Carn Eige 9 Hd 57.30N 5.05W
Carney Island 66 Nf 73.57S 121.00W
Carnia 14 Gd 46.25N 13.00 E
Car Nicobar 25 Ig 9.10N 92.47 E
Carnot 35 Be 4.48N 16.03 E
Carnoustie 9 Ke 56.30N 2.44W
Carnsore Point/Ceann an Chairn 9 Gi 52.10N 6.22W
Carn Ui Néid/Mizen Head 5 Fe 51.27N 9.49W
Caro 44 Fd 43.29N 83.24W
Carol City 44 Gm 25.56N 80.16W
Carolina [Braz.] 53 Lf 7.20S 47.28W
Carolina [P.R.] 51a Cb 18.24N 65.57W
Carolina [S.Afr.] 37 Ee 26.05S 30.06 E
Carolina Beach 44 Ih 34.02N 77.54W
Carolinas, Puntan- 64b Bb 14.54N 145.38 E
Caroline Atoll 57 Le 9.58S 150.13W
Caroline Islands 57 Fd 8.00N 147.00 E
Carondelet Reef 57 Je 5.34S 173.51W
Caroní, Rio- 52 Je 8.21N 62.43W
Caronie → Nebrodi 14 Im 37.55N 14.35 E
Carora 54 Da 10.11N 70.05W
Carpathian Mountains (EN) 5 If 48.00N 24.00 E
Carpathian Mountains (EN) = Carpații Occidentali 15 Fc 46.30N 22.10 E
Carpathian Mountains (EN) = Carpații Orientali 15 Ib 47.30N 25.30 E
Carpații Meridionali= Transylvanian Alps (EN) 5 If 45.30N 22.10 E
Carpații Occidentali = Carpathian Mountains (EN) 15 Fc 46.30N 22.10 E
Carpații Orientali= Carpathian Mountains (EN) 15 Ib 47.30N 25.30 E
Carpen 15 Ge 44.20N 23.15 E
Carpentaria, Gulf of- 57 Ef 14.00S 139.00 E
Carpentras 11 Lj 44.03N 5.03 E
Carpi 14 Ef 44.47N 10.53 E
Carpina 54 Ke 7.51S 35.15W
Carr, Cape- 66 Ie 66.07S 130.51 E
Carraig Fhearghais/ Carrickfergus 9 Hg 54.43N 5.44W
Carraig na Siúire/Carrick-on-Suir 9 Fi 52.21N 7.25W
Carrantuohill 5 Fe 52.00N 9.45W
Carrara 14 Ef 44.05N 10.06 E
Carreiro, Rio- 55 Gi 29.07S 51.43W
Carreño 13 Ga 43.35N 5.46W
Carreta, Punta- 54 Cf 14.13S 76.18W
Carretero, Puerto- 13 Ig 37.28N 3.40W
Carriacou 50 Ff 12.30N 61.27W
Carrick 9 If 55.15N 4.40W
Carrickfergus/Carraig Fhearghais 9 Hg 54.43N 5.44W
Carrick-on-Shannon/cara Droma Rúisc 9 Eh 53.57N 8.05W
Carrick-on-Suir/Carraig na Siúire 9 Fi 52.21N 7.25W
Carrington 43 Hb 47.27N 99.08W
Carrión 13 Hc 41.53N 4.32W
Carrión de los Condes 13 Hb 42.20N 4.36W
Carrizal 49 Kh 11.58N 72.12W
Carrizo Peak 45 Dj 33.20N 105.38W
Carrizos 48 Gc 29.58N 105.16W
Carrizo Springs 45 Gl 28.31N 99.52W
Carrizo Wash 46 Ki 34.36N 109.26W
Carrizozo 45 Dj 33.38N 105.53W
Carroll 45 Ie 42.04N 94.52W
Carroll Inlet 66 Qf 73.18S 78.30W
Carrollton [Ga.-U.S.] 44 Ei 33.35N 85.05W
Carrollton [Il.-U.S.] 45 Kg 39.18N 90.24W
Carrollton [Ky.-U.S.] 44 Ef 38.41N 85.11W
Carrollton [Mo.-U.S.] 45 Jg 39.22N 93.30W
Carron, Loch- 9 Hd 57.30N 5.40W
Carrot 42 Hf 53.50N 101.18W
Carrowmore Lough 9 Dg 54.12N 9.47W
Çarşamba 24 Gb 41.12N 36.44 E
Çarşamba 24 Ed 37.53N 32.37 E
Čaršanga 19 Gh 37.31N 66.03 E
Čarsk 19 If 49.35N 81.05 E
Carson 46 Ed 45.44N 121.49W
Carson City 39 Hf 39.10N 119.46W
Carson Lake 46 Fg 39.19N 118.43W
Carson Sink 46 Fg 39.45N 118.30W
Cartagena [Col.] 53 Id 10.25N 75.32W
Cartagena [Sp.] 6 Fh 37.36N 0.59W
Cartago [3] 49 Fi 9.50N 83.45W
Cartago [Col.] 54 Cc 4.46N 75.56W
Cartago [C.R.] 47 Hg 9.52N 83.55W
Cartaxo 13 De 39.09N 8.47W
Carter, Mount- 59 Ib 13.05S 143.15 E
Carteret 12 Ee 49.23N 1.47W
Cartersville 44 Eh 34.10N 85.05W
Carterton 62 Fd 41.01S 175.31 E
Carthage [Mo.-U.S.] 45 Ih 37.11N 94.19W
Carthage [Tx.-U.S.] 45 Ij 32.09N 94.20W
Cartier 44 Gb 46.42N 81.32W
Cartier Island 57 Df 12.30S 123.30 E
Caruaru 53 Mf 8.17S 35.58W
Carúpano 54 Fa 10.40N 63.14W
Carutapera 54 Id 1.13S 46.01W
Čarvak 18 Gd 41.38N 69.56 E
Carvin 12 Ed 50.29N 2.58 E
Carvoeiro, Cabo- 13 Ce 39.21N 9.24W
Čaryn 18 Lc 43.50N 79.12 E
Čaryš 20 Df 52.22N 83.45 E
Casablanca [2] 32 Fc 33.37N 7.35W
Casablanca 31 Ge 33.36N 7.37W
Casa Branca 55 Ie 21.46S 47.05W
Casa Grande 43 Ee 32.53N 111.45W
Casalbordino 14 Ih 42.09N 14.35 E
Casale Monferrato 14 Ce 45.08N 8.27 E
Casalmaggiore 14 Ef 44.59N 10.26 E
Casalvasco 55 Cb 15.19S 59.59W
Casal Velino 14 Jj 40.11N 15.06 E
Casamance 34 Bc 12.33N 16.46W
Casamance [3] 34 Bc 12.50N 15.00W
Casanare [2] 54 Db 5.20N 72.00W
Casanare, Rio- 54 Eb 6.02N 69.51W
Casanay 50 Eg 10.30N 63.25W
Casa Nova 54 Je 9.25S 41.08W
Casarano 14 Mj 40.00N 18.10 E
Casas Grandes, Rio- 48 Eb 30.22N 107.31W
Casas-Ibáñez 13 Ke 39.17N 1.28W
Casca, Rio da- 55 Eb 14.52S 55.52W
Cascade 46 Hd 44.31N 115.59W
Cascade Point 62 Cf 44.01S 168.22 E
Cascade Range 38 Ge 45.00N 121.30W
Cascais 13 Cf 38.42N 9.25W
Cascavel 56 Jb 24.57S 53.28W
Cascia 14 Hh 42.43N 13.01 E
Casciana Terme 14 Eg 43.32N 10.38 E
Cascina 14 Eg 43.41N 10.33 E
Casentino 14 Fg 43.40N 11.50 E

Index Symbols

[1] Independent Nation
[2] State, Region
[3] District, County
[5] Municipality
Colony, Dependency
Continent
Physical Region
Historical or Cultural Region
Mount, Mountain
Volcano
Hill
Mountains, Mountain Range
Hills, Escarpment
Plateau, Upland
Pass, Gap
Plain, Lowland
Delta
Salt Flat
Valley, Canyon
Crater, Cave
Karst Features
Depression
Polder
Desert, Dunes
Forest, Woods
Heath, Steppe
Oasis
Cape, Point
Coast, Beach
Cliff
Peninsula
Isthmus
Sandbank
Island
Atoll
Rock, Reef
Islands, Archipelago
Rocks, Reefs
Coral Reef
Well, Spring
Geyser
River, Stream
Waterfall Rapids
River Mouth, Estuary
Lake
Salt Lake
Intermittent Lake
Reservoir
Swamp, Pond
Canal
Glacier
Ice Shelf, Pack Ice
Ocean
Sea
Gulf, Bay
Strait, Fjord
Lagoon
Bank
Seamount
Tablemount
Ridge
Shelf
Basin
Escarpment, Sea Scarp
Fracture
Trench, Abyss
National Park, Reserve
Point of Interest
Recreation Site
Cave, Cavern
Historic Site
Ruins
Wall, Walls
Church, Abbey
Temple
Scientific Station
Airport
Port
Lighthouse
Mine
Tunnel
Dam, Bridge

Case-Pilote	51h	Ab	14.38N	61.08W
Caserta	14	Ii	41.04N	14.20 E
Casey	66	He	66.17S	110.32 E
Casey Bay	66	Ee	67.00S	48.00 E
Cashel/Caiseal	9	Fi	52.31N	7.53W
Casigua	49	Ki	8.46N	72.30W
Casilda	56	Hd	33.03S	61.10W
Casimcea	15	Le	44.24N	28.33 E
Casino	59	Ke	28.52S	153.03 E
Casiquiare, Brazo-	54	Ec	2.01N	67.07W
Čáslav	10	Lg	49.55N	15.25 E
Casma	54	Ce	9.28S	78.19W
Časnačorr, Gora-	7	Hc	67.45N	33.29 E
Čašniki	7	Gi	54.52N	29.08 E
Casoli	14	Ih	42.07N	14.18 E
Casoria	14	Ij	40.54N	14.17 E
Caspe	13	Lc	41.14N	0.02W
Casper	39	Ie	42.51N	106.19W
Caspian Depression (EN)= Prikaspijskaja Nizmennost	5	Lf	48.00N	52.00 E
Caspian Sea (EN)= Kaspijskoje More	5	Lg	42.00N	50.30 E
Caspian Sea (EN)= Māzandarān, Daryā-ye-	5	Lg	42.00N	50.30 E
Cassai	30	Ii	3.02S	16.57 E
Cassamba	36	De	13.04S	20.25 E
Cassange, Rio-	55	Dc	17.06S	57.23W
Cassano allo Ionio	14	Kk	39.47N	16.19 E
Cass City	44	Fd	43.36N	83.10W
Cassel	12	Ed	50.47N	2.29 E
Casselton	45	Hc	46.54N	97.13W
Cássia	55	Ie	20.36S	46.56W
Cassiar	42	Ee	59.16N	129.40W
Cassiar Mountains	38	Gd	59.00N	129.00W
Cassilândia	54	Hg	19.09S	51.45W
Cassino [Braz.]	55	Fk	32.11S	52.10W
Cassino [It.]	14	Hi	41.30N	13.49 E
Cassis	11	Lk	43.13N	5.32 E
Cass Lake	45	Ic	47.23N	94.36W
Cass River	44	Fd	43.23N	83.59W
Cassununga	55	Fc	16.03S	53.38W
Castagneto Carducci	14	Eg	43.10N	10.36 E
Castagniccia	11a	Ba	42.25N	9.30 E
Castañar, Sierra del-	13	He	39.35N	4.10W
Castanhal	54	Id	1.18S	47.55W
Castaños	48	Id	26.47N	101.25W
Castelbuono	14	Im	37.56N	14.05 E
Castel di Sangro	14	Ii	41.47N	14.06 E
Castelfidardo	14	Hg	43.28N	13.33 E
Castelfranco Veneto	14	Fe	45.40N	11.55 E
Casteljaloux	11	Gj	44.19N	0.06 E
Castellabate	14	Ij	40.17N	14.57 E
Castellammare, Golfo di-	14	Gl	38.10N	12.55 E
Castellammare del Golfo	14	Gl	38.01N	12.53 E
Castellammare di Stabia	14	Ij	40.42N	14.29 E
Castellana Grotte	14	Lj	40.53N	17.10 E
Castellane	11	Mk	43.51N	6.31 E
Castellaneta	14	Kj	40.38N	16.56 E
Castelldefels	13	Nc	41.17N	1.58 E
Castelli [Arg.]	56	Hc	25.57S	60.37W
Castelli [Arg.]	55	Dm	36.06S	57.47W
Castelló de la Plana/ Castellón de la Plana	6	Fh	39.59N	0.02W
Castellón	13	Ld	40.10N	0.10W
Castellón de la Plana/ Castelló de la Plana	6	Fh	39.59N	0.02W
Castellón de la Plana-El Grao	13	Me	39.58N	0.01 E
Castellote	13	Ld	40.48N	0.19W
Castelnaudary	11	Hk	43.19N	1.57 E
Castelnau-de-Médoc	11	Fi	45.02N	0.48W
Castelnovo ne' Monti	14	Ef	44.26N	10.24 E
Castelo Branco	13	Ee	40.00N	7.30W
Castelo Branco	13	Ee	39.49N	7.30W
Castelo de Vide	13	Ee	39.25N	7.27W
Castelo do Piauí	54	Je	5.20S	41.33W
Castel San Giovanni	14	De	45.04N	9.26 E
Castelsardo	14	Cj	40.55N	8.43 E
Castelsarrasin	11	Hj	44.02N	1.06 E
Casteltermini	14	Hm	37.32N	13.39 E
Castelvetrano	14	Gm	37.41N	12.47 E
Castets	11	Ek	43.53N	1.09W
Castiglione del Lago	14	Gg	43.07N	12.03 E
Castiglione della Pescaia	14	Eh	42.46N	10.53 E
Castiglion Fiorentino	14	Fg	43.20N	11.55 E
Castilla la Nueva=New Castile (EN)	13	Id	40.00N	3.45W
Castilla la Vieja=Old Castile (EN)	13	Ic	41.30N	4.00W
Castillejo	13	Gc	41.14N	5.30W
Castillon-la-Bataille	11	Fj	44.51N	0.02W
Castillonnès	11	Gj	44.39N	0.36 E
Castillos	56	Jd	34.12S	53.50W
Castillos, Laguna de-	55	Fl	34.20S	53.54W
Castlebar/Caisleán an Bharraigh	9	Dh	53.52N	9.17W
Castle Bruce	51g	Bb	15.26N	61.16W
Castle Dome Peak	46	Hj	33.05N	114.08W
Castle Douglas	9	Jg	54.57N	3.56W
Castlegar	42	Fg	49.19N	117.40W
Castleisland/Oiléan Ciarraí	9	Di	52.14N	9.27W
Castlemaine	59	Ig	37.04S	144.13 E
Castle Peak	46	Hd	44.03N	114.32W
Castlepoint	62	Gd	40.55S	176.13 E
Castlepollard	9	Fh	53.41N	7.17W
Castlerea/An Caisleán Riabhach	9	Eh	53.46N	8.29W
Castlereagh Bay	59	Hb	12.10S	135.10 E
Castle Rock Butte	45	Ed	45.00N	103.27W
Castle Rock Lake	45	Le	43.56N	89.58W
Častoozerje	17	Mi	55.34N	67.53 E
Castor	46	Ja	52.13N	111.53W
Castres	11	Ik	43.36N	2.15 E
Castricum	12	Gb	52.33N	4.42 E
Castries	39	Mh	14.01N	61.00W
Castrignano del Capo	14	Mk	39.50N	18.20 E
Castro [Braz.]	56	Jb	24.47S	50.03W
Castro [Chile]	56	Ff	42.29S	73.46W
Castro Alves	54	Kf	12.45S	39.26W
Castrocaro Terme e Terra del Sole	14	Ff	44.10N	11.57 E
Castro Daire	13	Ed	40.54N	7.56W
Castro del Río	13	Hg	37.41N	4.28W
Castrojeriz	13	Hb	42.17N	4.08W
Castropol	13	Ea	43.32N	7.02W
Castrop-Rauxel	12	Jc	51.33N	7.19 E
Castro Urdiales	13	Ia	43.23N	3.13W
Castro Verde	13	Dg	37.42N	8.05W
Castrovillari	14	Kk	39.49N	16.12 E
Castrovirreyna	54	Cf	13.16S	75.19W
Castuera	13	Gf	38.43N	5.33W
Častyje	17	Gh	57.19N	54.59 E
Casupá	55	El	34.09S	55.38W
Caswell Sound	62	Bf	45.00S	167.10 E
Çat	24	Ic	39.40N	41.02 E
Čata	10	Oi	47.58N	18.40 E
Catacamas	49	Ef	14.54N	85.56W
Catahoula Lake	45	Jk	31.30N	92.06W
Çatak	24	Jc	38.01N	43.07 E
Çatak	24	Jd	37.53N	42.39 E
Catalan Coastal Range (EN) =Cadena Costero Catalana /Serralada Litoral Catalana	5	Gg	41.35N	1.40 E
Catalan Coastal Range (EN) =Serralada Litoral Catalana/Cadena Costero Catalana	5	Gg	41.35N	1.40 E
Catalão	54	Ig	18.10S	47.57W
Čatal Balkan	15	Jg	42.46N	27.00 E
Çatalca	15	Lh	41.09N	28.27 E
Çatal Dağ	15	Lj	39.51N	28.20 E
Catalina	56	Gc	25.13S	69.43W
Catalina, Isla-	49	Md	18.21N	69.00W
Catalina, Punta-	56	Gh	52.32S	68.47W
Catalonia (EN)=Cataluña/ Catalunya	5	Gg	42.00N	2.00 E
Catalonia (EN)=Cataluña/ Catalunya	13	Nc	42.00N	2.00 E
Catalonia (EN)=Catalunya/ Cataluña	5	Gg	42.00N	2.00 E
Catalonia (EN)=Catalunya/ Cataluña	13	Nc	42.00N	2.00 E
Cataluña/Catalunya= Catalonia (EN)	5	Gg	42.00N	2.00 E
Cataluña/Catalunya= Catalonia (EN)	13	Nc	42.00N	2.00 E
Catalunya/Cataluña= Catalonia (EN)	13	Nc	42.00N	2.00 E
Catalunya/Cataluña= Catalonia (EN)	5	Gg	42.00N	2.00 E
Çatalzeytin	24	Fb	41.57N	34.13 E
Catamarca	53	Jh	28.30S	65.45W
Catamarca	56	Gc	27.00S	67.00W
Catanduanes	21	Oh	13.45N	124.15 E
Catanduva	56	Kb	21.08S	48.58W
Catanduvas	55	Fg	25.12S	53.08W
Catania	6	Hh	37.30N	15.06 E
Catania, Golfo di-	14	Jm	37.25N	15.10 E
Catania, Piana di-	14	Im	37.25N	14.50 E
Catanzaro	6	Hh	38.54N	16.35 E
Catarman	26	Hd	12.30N	124.38 E
Catastrophe, Cape-	57	Eh	35.00S	136.00 E
Catatumbo, Río-	49	Li	9.21N	71.45W
Catbalogan	26	Hd	11.46N	124.53 E
Catemaco, Lago-	48	Lh	18.25N	95.05W
Catete	36	Bd	9.07S	13.41 E
Cathair na Mart/Westport	9	Dh	53.48N	9.32W
Cathair Saidhbhín/ Cahersiveen	9	Cj	51.57N	10.13W
Cathcart	37	Df	32.18S	27.09 E
Catherine, Mount-	46	Ig	39.05N	112.04W
Catholic Island	51n	Bb	12.40N	61.24W
Catio	34	Bc	11.17N	15.15W
Cat Island	38	Lg	24.30N	75.30W
Čatkal	18	Hd	41.36N	70.05 E
Čatkalski Hrebet	19	Hg	41.30N	70.50 E
Cat Lake	42	If	51.40N	91.52W
Catoche, Cabo-	38	Kg	21.36N	87.07W
Cato Island	57	Gg	23.15S	155.35 E
Catolé do Rocha	54	Ke	6.21S	37.45W
Catoute	13	Fb	42.45N	6.20W
Catria	14	Gg	43.28N	12.42 E
Catriló	56	He	36.26S	63.24W
Catrimani, Rio-	54	Fc	0.28N	61.44W
Catskill Mountains	44	Jd	42.10N	74.30W
Cattenom	12	Ie	49.25N	6.15 E
Cattolica	14	Gg	43.58N	12.44 E
Catu	54	Kf	12.21S	38.23W
Catuane	37	Ee	26.48S	32.14 E
Catumbela	36	Be	12.27S	13.29 E
Catur	37	Fb	13.45S	35.37 E
Catwick, Iles-	25	Lg	10.00N	109.00 E
Catwright	39	Nd	53.50N	56.45W
Catyrkël, Ozero-	18	Jd	40.35N	75.20 E
Catyrtaš	18	Kd	40.52N	76.23 E
Cauca	54	Cc	2.30N	77.00W
Cauca, Río-	52	Ie	8.54N	74.28W
Caucasia	54	Cb	7.59N	75.13W
Caucasus (EN)=Kavkaz, Bolšoj-	5	Kg	42.30N	45.00 E
Caucete	56	Gd	31.38S	68.16W
Caudebec-en-Caux	12	Ce	49.32N	0.44 E
Caudete	13	Lf	38.42N	0.59W
Caudry	11	Jd	50.08N	3.25 E
Caulonia	14	Kl	38.23N	16.24 E
Caumont-l'Eventé	12	Be	49.05N	0.48W
Caungula	31	Ii	8.26S	18.37 E
Čaunskaja Guba	20	Lc	69.30N	170.00 E
Caupolican	54	Ef	13.30S	68.30W
Cauquenes	56	Fe	35.58S	72.21W
Caura, Río-	52	Je	7.38N	64.53W
Causapscal	44	Na	48.22N	67.14W
Caussade	11	Hj	44.10N	1.32 E
Čausy	16	Gc	53.50N	30.59 E
Cauterets	11	Fl	42.53N	0.07W
Cauto, Río-	49	Ic	20.33N	77.15W
Cauvery	21	Jh	11.09N	78.52 E
Caux, Pays de-	11	Ge	49.40N	0.40 E
Cávado	13	Dc	41.32N	8.48W
Cavaillon	11	Lk	43.50N	5.02 E
Cavalcante	55	Ia	13.48S	47.30W
Cavalese	14	Fd	46.17N	11.27 E
Cavalli Islands	62	Ea	35.00S	173.55 E
Cavallo, Isola-	11a	Bb	41.22N	9.16 E
Cavallo Pass	45	Hl	28.25N	96.26W
Cavally	30	Gh	4.22N	7.32W
Cavan/An Cabhán	9	Fg	54.00N	7.21W
Cavan/An Cabhán	9	Fh	53.55N	7.30W
Cavarzere	14	Ge	45.08N	12.05 E
Çavdarhisar	15	Mj	39.12N	29.37 E
Çavdir	15	Ml	37.09N	29.42 E
Caviana, Ilha-	54	Hc	0.10N	50.05W
Cavili	26	He	9.17N	120.50 E
Cavour, Canale-	14	Be	45.11N	7.54 E
Cavtat	14	Mh	42.35N	18.13 E
Caxambu	55	Je	21.59S	44.56W
Caxias	53	Lf	4.50S	43.21W
Caxias do Sul	53	Kh	29.10S	51.11W
Caxito	36	Bd	8.34S	13.40 E
Çay	24	Dc	38.35N	31.02 E
Cayambe	54	Cc	0.05N	78.08W
Cayambe, Volcán-	52	Ie	0.02N	77.59W
Cayastá	55	Bj	31.12S	60.10W
Cayce	44	Gi	33.59N	81.04W
Çaycuma	24	Eb	41.25N	32.05 E
Çayeli	24	Ib	41.05N	40.44 E
Cayenne	53	Ke	4.56N	52.20W
Cayeux-Sur-Mer	12	Dd	50.11N	1.29 E
Cayey	49	Nd	18.07N	66.10W
Çayırlı	24	Ic	39.48N	40.01 E
Çaykara	24	Ib	40.45N	40.19 E
Caylus	11	Hj	44.14N	1.47 E
Cayman Brac	47	Ie	19.43N	79.49W
Cayman Islands	39	Kh	19.30N	80.30W
Cayman Islands	38	Kh	19.30N	80.30W
Cayman Ridge (EN)	47	He	19.30N	80.30W
Cayman Trench (EN)	3	Bh	19.00N	80.00W
Cayo	49	Ce	17.10N	88.50W
Cayon	51c	Ab	17.21N	62.43W
Cayones, Cayos-	49	Fe	16.05N	83.12W
Cay Sal Bank	47	Hd	23.45N	80.00W
Cayuga Lake	44	Id	42.45N	76.45W
Cazalla de la Sierra	13	Gg	37.56N	5.45W
Caza Pava	55	Di	28.17S	56.07W
Cazaux, Étang de-	11	Ej	44.29N	1.10W
Cazombo	31	Jj	11.54S	22.53 E
Cazorla	13	Jg	37.55N	3.00W
Cazorla, Sierra de-	13	Jf	37.55N	2.55W
Cea	13	Gb	42.00N	5.36W
Ceahlău	15	Ib	47.03N	25.58 E
Ceanannas Mór/Kells	9	Gh	53.44N	6.53W
Ceanna Caillighe/Hags Head	9	Di	52.57N	9.28W
Ceann Acla/Achill Head	9	Ch	53.59N	10.13W
Ceann an Chairn/Carnsore Point	9	Gi	52.10N	6.22W
Ceann Chill Mhantáin/ Wicklow Head	9	Hi	52.58N	6.00W
Ceann Gólaim/Slyne Head	9	Ch	53.24N	10.13W
Ceann Iorrais/Erris Head	5	Fe	54.19N	10.00W
Ceann Léime/Loop Head	9	Di	52.34N	9.56W
Ceann Ros Eoghain/Rossan Point	9	Eg	54.42N	8.48W
Ceann Sléibhe/Slea Head	9	Ci	52.06N	10.27W
Ceann Toirc/Kanturk	9	Ei	52.10N	8.55W
Ceará	54	Kd	5.00S	39.30W
Ceará-Mirim	54	Ke	5.38S	35.26W
Ceatharlach/Carlow	9	Gi	52.50N	7.00W
Ceatharlach/Carlow	9	Gi	52.50N	6.55W
Cébaco, Isla-	49	Gj	7.32N	81.09W
Ceballos	48	Gd	26.32N	104.09W
Čebarkul	17	Ji	54.58N	60.25 E
Čeboksary	6	Kd	56.09N	47.15 E
Cebollati	55	Fk	33.16S	53.47W
Cebollati, Río-	55	Fk	33.09S	53.38W
Cebollera, Sierra-	13	Jc	42.00N	2.40W
Ceboruco, Volcán-	48	Gg	21.09N	104.30W
Cebreros	13	Hd	40.27N	4.28W
Cebrikovo	15	Nb	47.09N	30.02 E
Cebu	21	Oh	10.20N	123.45 E
Cebu	22	Oh	10.18N	123.54 E
Cece	10	Oj	46.46N	18.39 E
Čečen, Ostrov-	16	Og	44.00N	47.45 E
Čečeno-Ingušskaja ASSR	19	Eg	43.15N	45.30 E
Cecen-Ula	27	Gb	48.45N	95.55 E
Cecerleg	22	Me	47.30N	101.27 E
Čečersk	16	Gc	52.56N	30.58 E
Čechy=Bohemia (EN)	5	Hf	50.00N	14.30 E
Čechy=Bohemia (EN)	10	Kf	50.00N	14.30 E
Cecina	14	Eg	43.18N	10.29 E
Cecina	14	Eg	43.10N	10.31 E
Čečuisk	20	Fe	58.07N	108.32 E
Cedar City	39	Hf	37.41N	113.04W
Cedar Creek	45	Fc	46.07N	101.18W
Cedar Creek Reservoir	45	Hj	32.20N	96.10W
Cedar Falls	43	Ic	42.32N	92.27W
Cedar Grove	51d	Bb	17.10N	61.49W
Cedar Lake	42	Hf	53.25N	100.00W
Cedar Rapids	39	Je	41.59N	91.40W
Cedar River [Nb.-U.S.]	45	Hf	41.22N	97.57W
Cedar River [U.S.]	43	Ic	41.17N	91.20W
Cedartown	44	Eh	34.01N	85.15W
Cedar-Tree Point	51d	Ba	17.42N	61.53W
Cedeira	13	Da	43.39N	8.03W
Cedral	48	If	23.48N	100.44W
Cedrino	14	Dj	40.23N	9.44 E
Cedro	54	Ke	6.36S	39.03W
Cedrón	13	Ie	39.48N	3.33W
Cedros, Isla- [Mex.]	47	Ac	28.12N	115.15W
Cedros, Isla [Mex.] =Cedros Island (EN)	38	Hg	28.10N	115.15W
Cedros Island (EN)=Cedros, Isla [Mex.]	38	Hg	28.10N	115.15W
Cedros Trench (EN)	47	Ac	27.45N	115.45W
Ceduna	59	Gf	32.07S	133.40 E
Cedynia	10	Kd	52.50N	14.14 E
Cefalù	14	Il	38.02N	14.01 E
Cega	13	Hc	41.33N	4.46W
Čegdomyn	22	Pd	51.07N	133.05 E
Čegem	16	Mh	43.36N	43.48 E
Cegléd	10	Pi	47.10N	19.48 E
Ceglie Messapico	14	Lj	40.39N	17.31 E
Cehegín	13	Kf	38.06N	1.48W
Cehotina	15	Bf	43.31N	18.45 E
Čehov [R.S.F.S.R.]	7	Ii	55.11N	37.29 E
Čehov [R.S.F.S.R.]	20	Jg	47.24N	142.05 E
Ceica	15	Fc	46.51N	22.11 E
Çekerek	24	Fb	40.34N	35.46 E
Çekerek	24	Fb	40.04N	35.31 E
Čekmaguš	17	Gi	55.10N	54.40 E
Cela	36	Ce	11.25S	15.07 E
Celano	14	Hh	42.05N	13.33 E
Celaya	47	Dd	20.31N	100.37W
Čelbas	16	Kf	46.06N	38.59 E
Célè	11	Hj	44.28N	1.38 E
Celebes/Sulawesi	21	Oj	2.00S	121.10 E
Celebes Basin (EN)	26	Hf	4.00N	122.00 E
Celebes Sea (EN)= Sulawesi, Laut-	21	Oj	3.00N	122.00 E
Čeleken	19	Fh	39.27N	53.10 E
Čeleken, Poluostrov-	16	Rj	39.25N	53.35 E
Celendín	54	Ce	6.52S	78.09W
Celerain, Punta-	48	Pg	20.16N	86.59W
Celeste	55	Dj	31.18S	57.04W
Celestún	48	Ng	20.52N	90.24W
Celinograd	22	Jd	51.10N	71.30 E
Celinogradskaja Oblast	19	Gh	51.00N	70.00 E
Čeljabinsk	22	Id	55.10N	61.24 E
Čeljabinskaja Oblast	19	Ge	54.00N	61.00 E
Celje	14	Jd	46.14N	15.16 E
Celjuskin, Mys-	21	Mb	77.45N	104.20 E
Čelkar	19	Ff	47.50N	59.29 E
Celldömölk	10	Ni	47.15N	17.09 E
Celle	10	Gd	52.37N	10.05 E
Celles	12	Fd	50.43N	3.27 E
Celles, Houyet-	12	Hd	50.19N	5.01 E
Cellina	14	Ge	46.02N	12.47 E
Celone	14	Ji	41.36N	15.41 E
Celorico da Beira	13	Ed	40.38N	7.23W
Celtic Sea	5	Fe	51.00N	7.00W
Celtic Sea (EN)=An Mhuir Cheilteach	5	Fe	51.00N	7.00W
Cemaes Head	9	Ii	52.07N	4.44W
Čemal	20	Df	51.25N	86.05 E
Čemdalsk	20	Fe	59.45N	103.18 E
Cemernica	14	Lf	44.30N	17.15 E
Čemerno	15	Df	43.36N	20.26 E
Çemişkezek	24	Hc	39.04N	38.55 E
Cenajo, Embalse de-	13	Kf	38.20N	1.55W
Cenderawasih, Teluk-	26	Kg	2.25S	135.10 E
Cengel	27	Eb	48.56N	89.10 E
Çengel Geçidi	24	Kc	39.45N	44.02 E
Ceno	14	Ef	44.41N	10.05 E
Centenary	37	Ec	16.44S	31.07 E
Centennial	46	Lf	41.51N	106.07W
Centennial Lake	44	Ic	45.15N	77.00W
Centennial Mountains	46	Jd	44.35N	111.55W
Center	45	Ik	31.48N	94.11W
Center Hill Lake	44	Eg	36.00N	85.45W
Centerville	45	Jf	40.43N	92.52W
Centinela, Farallón-	50	Cg	10.49N	66.05W
Centinela, Picacho del-	47	Dc	29.07N	102.27W
Cento	14	Ff	44.43N	11.17 E
Centrafrique=Central African Republic (EN)	31	Jh	7.00N	21.00 E
Central [Bots.]	37	Dd	21.30S	26.00 E
Central [Ghana]	34	Ed	5.30N	1.00W
Central [Kenya]	36	Gc	0.45S	37.00 E
Central [Mwi.]	36	Fe	13.30S	34.00 E
Central [Par.]	55	Dg	25.30S	57.30W
Central [Scot.-U.K.]	9	Ie	56.15N	4.10W
Central [Ug.]	36	Fb	0.10N	32.05 E
Central [Zam.]	36	Ee	15.00S	29.00 E
Central, Chaco-	52	Kh	25.00S	59.45W
Central, Cordillera- [Dom.Rep.]	47	Je	18.45N	70.30W
Central, Cordillera- [P.R.]	49	Nd	18.10N	66.35W
Central, Massif-	5	Gf	45.00N	3.10 E
Central, Meseta-	38	Ig	23.00N	103.00W
Central African Republic (EN)=Centrafrique	31	Jh	7.00N	21.00 E
Central Auckland	62	Fb	36.45S	174.40 E
Central Brāhui Range	25	Dc	29.20N	66.55 E
Central City	45	Hf	41.07N	98.00W
Centralia [Il.-U.S.]	45	Lg	38.31N	89.08W
Centralia [Wa.-U.S.]	43	Cb	46.43N	122.58W
Central Lowland	38	Ke	40.20N	90.00W
Central Makrān Range	21	Ig	26.40N	64.30 E
Centralno Tungusskoje Plato	20	Fd	61.15N	102.00 E
Centralny-Kospašski	17	Hg	59.03N	57.50 E
Central Pacific Basin (EN)	3	Ki	5.00N	175.00W
Central Plateau	64e	Bb	0.32S	166.56 E
Central Point	46	De	42.23N	122.57W
Central Range	57	Fe	5.00S	142.30 E
Central Russian Uplands (EN)=Srednerusskaja Vozvyšennost	5	Je	52.00N	38.00 E
Central Siberian Uplands (EN)=Srednesibirskoje Ploskogorje	21	Mc	65.00N	105.00 E
Central Urals (EN)=Sredni Ural	5	Ld	58.00N	59.00 E
Centre [Togo]	34	Fd	9.15N	1.00 E
Centre [U.V.]	34	Ec	12.00N	1.00W
Centre, Canal du-	11	Jh	46.28N	3.59 E
Centre-Est	34	Ec	11.30N	0.20W
Centre-Nord	34	Ec	13.20N	0.55W
Centre-Ouest	34	Ec	12.00N	2.20W
Centre-Sud	34	He	3.30N	11.50 E
Centro, Cayo-	48	Ph	18.35N	87.20W
Centuripe	14	Im	37.37N	14.44 E
Čepca	19	Fd	58.35N	50.05 E
Čepelare	15	Hh	41.44N	24.41 E
Cephalonia (EN)= Kefallinia	5	Ih	38.15N	20.35 E
Čepin	14	Me	45.32N	18.34 E
Ceplenița	15	Jb	47.23N	26.58 E
Cepu	26	Fh	7.09S	111.35 E
Cer	15	Ce	44.37N	19.28 E
Ceram Sea (EN)=Seram, Laut-	57	De	2.30S	128.00 E
Cerbatana, Serranía de la-	54	Eb	6.50N	66.15W
Cerbicales, Iles-	11a	Bb	41.33N	9.22 E
Cercal	13	Dg	37.47N	8.42W
Čerchov	10	Rg	49.10N	21.05 E
Čerdakly	7	Li	54.23N	48.51 E
Čerdyn	17	Hf	60.25N	56.29 E
Cère	11	Hj	44.55N	1.49 E
Čereha	7	Gh	57.47N	28.22 E
Čeremhovo	22	Md	53.09N	103.05 E
Čerepanovo	20	Df	54.13N	83.32 E
Čerepovec	6	Jd	59.08N	37.54 E
Ceres [Arg.]	56	Hc	29.53S	61.57W
Ceres [Braz.]	54	Ig	15.17S	49.35W
Ceres [S.Afr.]	37	Bf	33.21S	19.18 E
Céret	11	Il	42.29N	2.45 E
Cereté	54	Cb	8.53N	75.47W
Cerf Island	30	Mi	9.31S	51.01 E
Cerfontaine	12	Gd	50.10N	4.25 E
Cergy	12	Ee	49.02N	2.04 E
Cerignola	14	Ji	41.16N	15.54 E
Čerikov	16	Gc	53.35N	31.25 E
Cérilly	11	Ih	46.37N	2.50 E
Čerkasskaja Oblast	19	Df	49.15N	31.15 E
Čerkassy	19	Df	49.26N	32.04 E
Çerkeş	24	Eb	40.50N	32.54 E
Čerkessk	19	Eg	44.14N	42.04 E
Çerkezköy	15	Kh	41.17N	28.00 E
Čerlak	19	He	54.09N	74.58 E
Čerlakski	19	He	53.47N	74.31 E
Čermasàn	17	Gi	55.10N	55.20 E
Cermei	15	Ec	46.33N	21.51 E
Çermenika	15	Dh	41.03N	20.20 E
Čermoz	17	Hg	58.47N	56.10 E
Cerna [Rom.]	15	Ge	44.37N	23.57 E
Cerna [Rom.]	15	Fd	44.42N	22.25 E
Cerna [Rom.]	15	Fe	45.53N	22.58 E
Černaja	17	Hb	68.35N	56.31 E
Černaja [R.S.F.S.R.]	17	Hb	68.35N	56.30 E
Černaja [Ukr.-U.S.S.R.]	15	Mb	47.39N	29.11 E
Černa Skala, Prohod-	15	Fg	42.02N	22.47 E
Černatica	15	Hh	41.53N	24.33 E
Černavčicy	10	Td	52.11N	23.47 E
Cernavoda	15	Le	44.22N	28.01 E
Cernay	11	Ng	47.49N	7.10 E
Cernay-en-Dormois	12	Ge	49.13N	4.46 E
Černevo	8	Mf	58.35N	28.23 E
Černigov	6	Je	51.30N	31.18 E
Černigovskaja Oblast	19	De	51.20N	32.00 E
Černi Lom	15	If	43.33N	25.57 E
Černi vrăh	15	Gg	42.35N	23.15 E
Černjahovsk	19	Ce	54.38N	21.48 E
Černjanka	16	Jd	50.55N	37.49 E
Černobyl	19	De	51.17N	30.13 E
Černogorsk	20	Ef	53.45N	91.18 E
Černoje More=Black Sea (EN)	5	Jg	43.00N	35.00 E
Černo More=Black Sea (EN)	5	Jg	43.00N	35.00 E
Černomorskoje	16	Hg	45.31N	32.42 E
Černovcy	6	If	48.18N	25.56 E
Černovickaja Oblast	19	Cf	48.20N	26.10 E
Černuška	19	Fd	56.31N	56.03 E
Černy Jar	16	Oe	48.03N	46.05 E
Černyje Zemli	16	Nf	45.55N	46.00 E
Černyšëva, Grjada-	17	Ic	66.20N	59.45 E
Černyševa, Zaliv-	18	Bb	45.50N	59.10 E
Černyševsk	20	Gf	52.35N	117.02 E
Černyševski	20	Gd	62.58N	112.15 E
Černyškovski	16	Me	48.27N	42.14 E
Cérou	11	Hj	44.08N	1.52 E
Cerralvo	48	Jd	26.06N	99.37W
Cerralvo, Isla-	47	Cd	24.15N	109.55W
Cerredo, Torre de-	13	Ha	43.13N	4.50W
Cerriku	15	Ch	41.02N	19.57 E
Cerrito [Col.]	54	Db	6.51N	72.42W
Cerrito [Par.]	55	Dh	27.19S	57.40W
Cerritos	47	Dd	22.26N	100.17W
Cerro Azul	48	Kg	21.12N	97.44W
Cêrro Azul	56	Kb	24.50S	49.15W
Cerro Chato	55	Ek	33.06S	55.08W
Cerro Colorado	55	Ek	33.52S	55.33W
Cerro de las Mesas	48	Kh	18.47N	96.05W
Cerro de Pasco	53	Ig	10.41S	76.16W
Cêrro Grande	55	Gj	30.36S	51.45W
Cerro Largo	56	Jc	28.09S	54.45W
Cerro Largo	55	Ek	32.20S	54.20W
Cerron, Cerro-	49	Lh	10.19N	70.39W
Cerro San Valentín	52	Ij	46.36S	73.20W
Cerros Colorados, Embalse-	56	Ge	38.35S	68.40W
Cerro Vera	55	Dk	33.11S	57.28W
Cerrudo Cué	55	Dh	27.34S	57.57W
Čerski	22	Sc	68.45N	161.45 E
Čerskogo, Hrebet- [R.S.F.S.R.]	20	Gf	52.00N	114.00 E
Čerskogo, Hrebet- [R.S.F.S.R.] =Cherski Mountains (EN)	21	Qc	65.00N	145.00 E

Index Symbols

- Independent Nation
- State, Region
- District, County
- Municipality
- Colony, Dependency
- Continent
- Physical Region
- Historical or Cultural Region
- Mount, Mountain
- Volcano
- Hill
- Mountains, Mountain Range
- Hills, Escarpment
- Plateau, Upland
- Pass, Gap
- Plain, Lowland
- Delta
- Salt Flat
- Valley, Canyon
- Crater, Cave
- Karst Features
- Depression
- Polder
- Desert, Dunes
- Forest, Woods
- Heath, Steppe
- Oasis
- Cape, Point
- Coast, Beach
- Cliff
- Peninsula
- Isthmus
- Sandbank
- Island
- Atoll
- Rock, Reef
- Islands, Archipelago
- Rocks, Reefs
- Coral Reef
- Well, Spring
- Geyser
- River, Stream
- Waterfall Rapids
- River Mouth, Estuary
- Lake
- Salt Lake
- Intermittent Lake
- Reservoir
- Swamp, Pond
- Canal
- Glacier
- Ice Shelf, Pack Ice
- Ocean
- Sea
- Gulf, Bay
- Strait, Fjord
- Lagoon
- Bank
- Seamount
- Tablemount
- Ridge
- Shelf
- Basin
- Escarpment, Sea Scarp
- Fracture
- Trench, Abyss
- National Park, Reserve
- Point of Interest
- Recreation Site
- Cave, Cavern
- Historic Site
- Ruins
- Wall, Walls
- Church, Abbey
- Temple
- Scientific Station
- Airport
- Port
- Lighthouse
- Mine
- Tunnel
- Dam, Bridge

Certaldo 14 Fg 43.33N 11.02 E
Čertkovo 16 Le 49.20N 40.12 E
Cervaro 14 Ji 41.30N 15.52 E
Cervati 14 Jj 40.17N 15.29 E
Červeh 15 Jf 43.37N 26.02 E
Červen 16 Fc 53.43N 28.29 E
Červen brjag 15 Hf 43.16N 24.06 E
Cervera 13 Nc 41.40N 1.17 E
Cervera del Río Alhama 13 Kb 42.01N 1.57W
Cervera de Pisuerga 13 Hb 42.52N 4.30W
Cerveteri 14 Gh 42.00N 12.06 E
Cervia 14 Gf 44.15N 12.22 E
Cervin/Cervino 14 Be 45.58N 7.39 E
Cervino/Cervin 14 Be 45.58N 7.39 E
Cervione 11a Ba 42.20N 9.29 E
Červonoarmejsk 10 Vf 50.03N 25.18 E
Červonoarmejskoje 15 Ld 45.50N 28.38 E
Červonograd 19 Ce 50.24N 24.12 E
Cesano 14 Hg 43.45N 13.10 E
Cesar [2] 54 Db 9.50N 73.30W
César, Río- 49 Ki 9.00N 73.58W
Cesena 14 Gf 44.08N 12.15 E
Cesenatico 14 Gf 44.12N 12.24 E
Cēsis/Cesis 19 Cd 57.18N 25.18 E
Cesis/Cēsis 19 Cd 57.18N 25.18 E
Česká Lípa 10 Kf 50.42N 14.32 E
Česká Třebová 10 Mg 49.54N 16.27 E
České Budějovice 10 Kh 48.58N 14.29 E
České středohoří 10 Jf 50.35N 14.00 E
České země [2] 10 Kg 49.45N 15.00 E
Českomoravská Vrchovina=Moravian Upland (EN) 5 Hf 49.20N 15.30 E
Československá Socialistická Republika (ČSSR) [1] 6 Hf 49.30N 17.00 E
Československo=Czechoslovakia (EN) [1] 6 Hf 49.30N 17.00 E
Český Krumlov 10 Kh 48.49N 14.19 E
Český Les=Bohemian Forest (EN) 10 Ig 49.50N 12.30 E
Cesma 14 Kf 45.35N 16.29 E
Česma 17 Jj 53.50N 60.40 E
Çeşme 24 Bc 38.18N 26.19 E
Çeşme Yarimadasi 15 Jk 38.30N 26.30 E
Češskaja Guba=Chesha Bay (EN) 5 Kb 67.20N 46.30 E
Cessnock 59 Kf 32.50S 151.21 E
Cestos 30 Gh 5.27N 9.35W
Cesvaine/Cesvajne 8 Lh 56.55N 26.20 E
Cesvajne/Cesvaine 8 Lh 56.55N 26.20 E
Cetate 15 Ge 44.06N 23.03 E
Cetina 14 Kg 43.27N 16.42 E
Cetinje 15 Bg 42.24N 18.55 E
Çetinkaya 24 Gc 39.15N 37.38 E
Cetraro 14 Jk 39.31N 15.56 E
Cetynia 10 Sd 52.33N 22.26 E
Ceuta [5] 31 Ge 35.53N 5.19W
Ceva-i-Ra (Conway Reef) 57 Ig 21.45S 174.35 E
Cevedale/Zufallspitze 14 Ed 46.27N 10.37 E
Cévennes 5 Gg 44.40N 4.00 E
Ceyhan 23 Eb 36.45N 35.42 E
Ceyhan 23 Eb 37.04N 35.47 E
Ceylanpınar 24 Id 36.51N 40.02 E
Ceylon 21 Ki 7.30N 80.30 E
Ceylon→Srī Lanka [1] 22 Ki 7.40N 80.50 E
Cézallier 11 Ii 45.20N 3.00 E
Cèze 11 Kj 44.06N 4.42 E
Chaalis, Abbaye de- 12 Ee 49.10N 2.40 E
Cha-am 25 Jf 12.48N 99.58 E
Chabanais 11 Gi 45.52N 0.43 E
Chabjuwardoo Bay 59 Cd 22.55S 113.50 E
Chablais 11 Mh 46.20N 6.30 E
Chāboksar 24 Nd 36.58N 50.34 E
Chabówka 10 Pg 49.34N 19.58 E
Chacabuco 56 Hd 34.38S 60.29W
Chachan, Nevado- 54 Dg 16.12S 71.33W
Chachapoyas 54 Ce 6.13S 77.51W
Chachoengsao 25 Kf 13.41N 101.03 E
Chaco [2] 56 Hc 26.00S 60.30W
Chaco [3] 55 Bd 20.00S 60.30W
Chaco, Gran- 52 Jh 23.00S 60.00W
Chaco Mesa 45 Ci 35.50N 107.35W
Chaco River 45 Bh 36.46N 108.39W
Chad (EN)=Tchad [1] 31 Ig 15.00N 19.00 E
Chad, Lake- (EN)=Tchad, Lac- 30 Ig 13.20N 14.00 E
Chādegān 24 Nf 32.46N 50.38 E
Chadileuvú, Río- 56 Ee 38.49S 64.57W
Chadiza 36 Fe 14.04S 32.26 E
Chadron 43 Gc 42.50N 103.02W
Chaeryŏng 28 He 38.24N 125.37 E
Chafarinas, Islas- 13 Ji 35.11N 2.26W
Chāgai Hills 21 Ig 29.30N 64.15 E
Chagang-Do [2] 28 Ie 40.50N 126.30 E
Chaghcharān 22 If 34.31N 65.15 E
Chagny 11 Kh 46.55N 4.45 E
Chagos Archipelago 21 Jj 6.00S 72.00 E
Chagos-Laccadive Plateau (EN) 3 Gi 3.00N 73.00 E
Chagu, Serra do- 55 Fg 25.10S 52.40W
Chaguaramas 50 Ch 9.20N 66.16W
Chahār Borjak 23 Jc 30.17N 62.03 E
Chāh Bahār 23 Jd 25.18N 60.37 E
Chahbounia 13 Oi 35.33N 2.36 E
Ch'aho 28 Jd 40.12N 128.38 E
Chai Badan 25 Ke 15.05N 101.04 E
Chaibāsa 25 Hd 22.34N 85.49 E
Chaigoubu → Huai'an 28 Cd 40.40N 114.25 E
Chai He 28 Gc 42.20N 123.51 E
Chaillu, Massif du- 30 Ii 2.32S 11.10 E
Chainat 25 Ke 15.10N 100.10 E
Chaitén 56 Ff 42.55S 72.43W
Chaiyaphum 25 Ke 16.09N 102.02 E
Chajul 49 Bf 15.30N 91.02W
Chakari 37 Dc 18.09S 29.52 E
Chak Chak 35 Dd 8.40N 26.54 E
Chake Chake 31 Ki 5.15S 39.46 E
Chakhānsūr 23 Jc 31.10N 62.04 E
Chala 54 Dg 15.52S 74.16W
Chalais 11 Gi 45.17N 0.02 E
Chalaltenango 49 Cf 14.03N 88.56W
Chalan Kanoa 64b Ba 15.08N 145.43 E
Chālūs 22 Gf 37.16N 49.36 E
Chalbi Desert 30 Kh 3.00N 37.20 E
Chalchuapa 49 Cg 13.59N 89.41W
Chalcidice (EN)=Khalkidhikí 5 Ig 40.25N 23.25 E
Chālesbān 24 Ne 35.18N 50.03 E
Chaleur Bay 42 Kg 47.50N 65.30W
Chalhuanca 54 Df 14.17S 73.15W
Chaling 27 Jf 26.47N 113.32 E
Chalky Inlet 62 Bg 46.05S 166.30 E
Challans 11 Eh 46.51N 1.53W
Challapata 54 Eg 18.54S 66.47W
Challis 46 Hd 44.30N 114.14W
Chalmette 45 Ll 29.56N 89.58W
Châlons-sur-Marne 11 Kf 48.57N 4.22 E
Châlon-sur-Saône 11 Kh 46.47N 4.51 E
Chaltubo 16 Mh 42.19N 42.34 E
Chālūs 23 Hb 36.38N 51.26 E
Châlus 11 Gi 45.39N 0.59 E
Cham 10 Ig 49.13N 12.40 E
Chama 36 Fe 11.12S 33.10 E
Chama, Rio- 45 Ch 36.03N 106.05W
Chama, Río- 49 Li 9.03N 71.37W
Chaman 25 Db 30.55N 66.27 E
Chaman Bīd 24 Qd 37.25N 56.38 E
Chamba [India] 25 Fb 32.34N 76.08 E
Chamba [Tan.] 36 Ge 11.35S 36.58 E
Chambal 21 Jg 26.29N 79.15 E
Chambaran, Plateau de- 11 Li 45.10N 5.20 E
Chambas 49 Hb 22.12N 78.55W
Chamberlain 45 Ge 43.49N 99.20W
Chamberlain Lake 44 Mb 46.17N 69.20W
Chamberlain River 59 Fc 15.35S 127.51 E
Chambersburg 44 If 39.57N 77.40W
Chambéry 11 Li 45.34N 5.56 E
Chambeshi 30 Jj 11.53S 29.48 E
Chambley-Bussières 12 He 49.03N 5.54 E
Chambly 12 Ee 49.10N 2.15 E
Chambois 12 Cf 48.48N 0.07 E
Chambon, Lac de- 11 Ih 45.35N 2.55 E
Chambord 11 Hg 47.37N 1.31 E
Chamchamal 24 Ke 35.32N 44.50 E
Chame, Punta- 49 Hi 8.39N 79.42W
Chamela 48 Gh 19.32N 105.05W
Chamela, Bahía- 48 Gh 19.30N 105.10W
Chamelecón, Río- 49 Df 15.51N 87.49W
Chamical 56 Gd 30.21S 66.19W
Chamiss Bay 46 Ba 50.07N 127.22W
Chamoli 25 Fb 30.24N 79.21 E
Chamonix-Mont-Blanc 11 Mi 45.55N 6.52 E
Chamouchouane, Rivière- 44 Ka 48.40N 72.20W
Champagne 5 Gf 49.00N 4.30 E
Champagne 11 Kf 49.00N 4.30 E
Champagne Berrichonne 11 Hh 47.00N 2.00 E
Champagne Humide 11 Kf 48.20N 4.30 E
Champagne Pouilleuse 11 Kf 48.40N 4.20 E
Champagnole 11 Lh 46.45N 5.55 E
Champaign 43 Jc 40.07N 88.14W
Champaquí, Cerro- 52 Ji 31.59S 64.56W
Champasak 25 Lf 14.53N 105.52 E
Champaubert 12 Ff 48.53N 3.47 E
Champdoré, Lac- 42 Ke 55.55N 65.45W
Champeigne 11 Gg 47.15N 0.50 E
Champerico 49 Bf 14.18N 91.55W
Champlain, Lake- 43 Mc 44.45N 73.15W
Champlitte-et-le-Prélot 11 Lg 47.37N 5.31 E
Champotón 47 Fe 19.21N 90.43W
Champsaur 11 Mj 44.45N 6.10 E
Chāmrājnagar 25 Ff 11.55N 76.57 E
Chañaral 56 Fc 26.21S 70.37W
Chança 13 Eg 37.33N 7.31W
Chan Chan 54 Ce 8.07S 79.02W
Chanco 56 Fe 35.44S 72.32W
Chandalar 40 Jc 66.36N 145.48W
Chandalar 40 Jc 67.30N 148.30W
Chandausi 25 Fc 28.27N 78.46 E
Chandeleur Islands 43 Jf 29.48N 88.51W
Chandeleur Sound 45 Ll 29.55N 89.10W
Chandīgarh 22 Jf 30.44N 76.55 E
Chandler 42 Lg 48.21N 64.41W
Chandless, Rio 54 Ee 9.08S 69.51W
Chāndpur 25 Id 23.13N 90.39 E
Chandragupta 25 Fe 16.11N 78.52 E
Chandrapur 22 Jh 19.57N 79.18 E
Chang, Ko- 25 Kf 12.00N 102.23 E
Changajn Nuruu → Hangaj, Hrebet-=Khangai Mountains (EN) 21 Le 47.30N 100.00 E
Chang'an → Rong'an 27 If 25.16N 109.23 E
Changane 30 Kk 24.43S 33.32 E
Changbai 28 Jd 41.25N 128.11 E
Changbai Shan 21 Oe 42.00N 128.00 E
Changchun 22 Oe 43.51N 125.20 E
Changdao(Sihou) 28 Ff 37.56N 120.42 E
Changde 22 Ng 29.04N 111.42 E
Ch'angdo 28 Ie 38.30N 127.45 E
Changfeng (Shuijiahu) 28 Dh 32.29N 117.10 E
Changge 28 Bg 34.12N 113.45 E
Changhang 28 If 36.01N 126.42 E
Chang He 28 Ei 31.21N 118.21 E
Changhowŏn 28 If 37.07N 127.38 E
Changhua 27 Lg 24.05N 120.32 E
Changhŭng 28 Ig 34.40N 126.54 E
Changji 27 Ec 44.01N 87.16 E
Chang Jiang 28 Dj 28.59N 116.42 E
Changjiang (Shiliu) 27 Ih 19.20N 109.03 E
Chang Jiang (Yangtze Kiang) 21 Of 31.48N 121.10 E
Changjiang Kou 27 Le 31.24N 121.59 E
Changjin-gang 28 Id 40.30N 127.12 E
Changjin-ho 28 Id 40.30N 127.12 E
Changjin-ŭp 27 Mc 40.23N 127.15 E
Changli 28 Ee 39.43N 119.10 E
Changling 27 Lc 44.15N 123.58 E
Changlung 25 Fb 34.56N 77.29 E
Changping 28 Dd 40.14N 116.13 E
Changsha 22 Ng 28.12N 113.02 E
Changshan 28 Ej 28.55N 118.31 E
Changshan Qundao 28 Ge 39.10N 122.34 E
Changshu 28 Fi 31.38N 120.44 E
Changsŏng 28 Ig 35.19N 126.48 E
Changting 28 Jb 44.27N 128.50 E
Changtu 28 Hc 42.47N 124.08 E
Changuillo 54 Cf 14.40S 75.12W
Changuinola 49 Fi 9.26N 82.31W
Changwu 27 Id 35.17N 107.52 E
Changxing 28 Ei 31.01N 119.55 E
Changxing Dao 28 Fe 39.35N 121.42 E
Changyi 28 Ef 36.52N 119.25 E
Changyŏn 27 Md 38.15N 125.05 E
Changyuan 28 Cg 35.12N 114.40 E
Changzhi 27 Jd 36.07N 113.10 E
Changzhou 28 Ei 31.46N 119.56 E
Channel Islands [5] 9 Kl 49.20N 2.20W
Channel Islands [Chan.Is.] 5 Ff 49.20N 2.20W
Channel Islands [U.S.] 38 Hf 34.00N 120.00W
Channel Port-aux-Basques 39 Ne 47.35N 59.11W
Channel Rock 49 Ib 23.00N 77.55W
Channing 45 Ei 35.41N 102.20W
Chantada 13 Eb 42.37N 7.46W
Chantengo, Laguna- 48 Ji 16.35N 99.10W
Chanthaburi 25 Kf 12.35N 102.06 E
Chantilly 11 Ie 49.12N 2.28 E
Chantonnay 11 Eh 46.41N 1.03W
Chantrey Inlet 38 Jc 67.48N 96.20W
Chanute 45 Ih 37.41N 95.27W
Chanza 13 Eg 37.33N 7.31W
Chao'an (Chaozhou) 27 Kg 23.41N 116.37 E
Chaobai Xinhe 28 De 39.07N 117.41 E
Chao He 28 Dd 40.36N 117.08 E
Chao Hu 28 Di 31.31N 117.33 E
Chao Phraya 21 Mh 13.32N 100.36 E
Chaor He 27 Lb 46.49N 123.45 E
Chaoxian 27 Ke 31.37N 117.49 E
Chaoyang [China] 22 Oe 41.35N 120.26 E
Chaoyang [China] 27 Kg 23.17N 116.37 E
Chaoyang → Huinan 28 Ic 42.41N 126.03 E
Chaoyang → Jiayin 27 Nb 48.52N 130.21 E
Chaoyangchuan 28 Jc 42.53N 129.23 E
Chaoyangcun 27 La 50.01N 124.22 E
Chaozhong 27 La 50.53N 121.23 E
Chaozhou → Chao'an 27 Kg 23.41N 116.37 E
Chapada dos Guimarães 54 Gg 15.26S 55.45W
Chapadinha 54 Jd 3.44S 43.21W
Chapais 44 Ja 49.47N 74.56W
Chapala 48 Hg 20.18N 103.12W
Chapala, Lago de- 38 Ig 20.15N 103.00W
Chaparral 54 Cc 3.43N 75.28W
Chapecó 56 Jc 27.06S 52.36W
Chapecó, Rio- 55 Fh 27.06S 53.01W
Chapecó, Serra do- 55 Gh 26.44S 51.54W
Chapel Hill 44 Hh 35.55N 79.04W
Chapicuy 55 Dj 31.40S 57.55W
Chapleau 42 Jg 47.50N 83.24W
Chaplin 46 La 50.28N 106.40W
Chaplin Lake 46 La 50.18N 106.35W
Chapman, Cape - 42 Ic 69.15N 89.27W
Chappell 45 Ef 41.06N 102.28W
Chāpra 25 Gc 25.46N 84.45 E
Chapultepec 48 Hf 23.27N 103.04W
Chaqui 54 Eg 19.36S 65.32W
Char 32 Ee 21.31N 12.51W
Charadai 55 Ch 27.38S 59.54W
Charagua 54 Fg 19.48S 63.13W
Charām 24 Ng 30.45N 50.44 E
Charaña 54 Eg 17.36S 69.28W
Charcas 48 If 23.08N 101.07W
Charco de la Aguja 48 Gc 28.25N 104.01W
Charcot Island 66 Qe 69.45S 75.15W
Chard [Alta.-Can.] 42 Ge 55.48N 111.10W
Chard [Eng.-U.K.] 9 Kk 50.53N 2.58W
Chardāvol 24 Lf 33.45N 46.38 E
Chardonnières 49 Jd 18.16N 74.10W
Charente [3] 11 Gi 45.40N 0.05 E
Charente 11 Ei 45.57N 1.05W
Charente-Maritime [3] 11 Fi 45.30N 0.45W
Charentonne 12 Ce 49.07N 0.44 E
Chari 30 Ig 12.58N 14.31 E
Chari-Baguirmi [3] 35 Bc 12.00N 17.00 E
Chārīkār 23 Kb 35.01N 69.11 E
Charing 12 Cc 51.12N 0.48 E
Chariton 45 Jf 41.00N 93.19W
Chariton River 45 Jg 39.19N 92.57W
Charity 54 Gb 7.24N 58.36W
Charleroi 11 Kd 50.25N 4.26 E
Charleroi-Jumet 11 Kd 50.27N 4.26 E
Charleroi-Marcinelle 12 Gd 50.25N 4.28 E
Charles 42 Kd 62.38N 74.15W
Charles, Cape- [Can.] 38 Nd 52.13N 55.40W
Charles, Cape- [Va.-U.S.] 43 Ld 37.08N 75.58W
Charles, Peak- 59 Ef 32.52S 121.11 E
Charlesbourg 44 Lb 46.52N 71.16W
Charles City 43 Ic 43.04N 92.40W
Charles de Gaulle, Aéroport-=Charles de Gaulle Airport (EN) 12 Ee 49.02N 2.35 E
Charles de Gaulle Airport (EN)=Charles de Gaulle, Aéroport- 12 Ee 49.02N 2.35 E
Charleston [Il.-U.S.] 45 Lg 39.30N 88.10W
Charleston [Mo.-U.S.] 45 Lh 36.55N 89.21W
Charleston [Ms.-U.S.] 45 Ki 34.01N 90.04W
Charleston [N.Z.] 62 Dd 41.54S 171.27 E
Charleston [S.C.-U.S.] 39 Lf 32.48N 79.57W
Charleston [W.V.-U.S.] 39 Kf 38.21N 81.38W
Charleston Peak 43 Dd 36.16N 115.42W
Charles Town 44 If 39.18N 77.52W
Charlestown 50 Ed 17.12N 62.35W
Charleval 12 De 49.22N 1.23 E
Charleville 58 Fg 26.24S 146.15 E
Charleville-Mézières 11 Ke 49.46N 4.43 E
Charleville Mézières-Mohon 12 Ge 49.46N 4.43 E
Charlevoix 44 Ec 45.19N 85.16W
Charlieu 11 Kh 46.09N 4.11 E
Charlotte [Mi.-U.S.] 44 Ed 42.36N 84.50W
Charlotte [N.C.-U.S.] 39 Kf 35.14N 80.50W
Charlotte Amalie 47 Le 18.21N 64.56W
Charlotte Bank (EN) 57 If 11.47S 173.13 E
Charlotte Harbor 44 Fl 26.45N 82.12W
Charlottenberg 8 Ee 59.53N 12.17 E
Charlottesville 43 Ld 38.02N 78.29W
Charlottetown 39 Me 46.14N 63.08W
Charlton 59 Ig 36.16S 143.21 E
Charlton 42 Jf 52.00N 79.26W
Charly 12 Ff 48.58N 3.17 E
Charmes 11 Mf 48.22N 6.17 E
Charnley River 59 Ec 16.20S 124.53 E
Charny-sur-Meuse 12 He 49.12N 5.22 E
Charollais 11 Kh 46.26N 4.16 E
Charouïne 32 Gd 29.01N 0.16W
Charroux 11 Gh 46.09N 0.24 E
Chārsadda 25 Eb 34.09N 71.44 E
Charters Towers 58 Fg 20.05S 146.16 E
Chartres 11 Hf 48.27N 1.30 E
Charzykowskie, Jezioro- 10 Nc 53.47N 17.30 E
Chascomus 56 Ie 35.34S 58.01W
Chase 46 Fa 50.49N 119.41W
Chasŏng 28 Id 41.25N 126.35 E
Chassengue 36 Ce 10.26S 18.32 E
Chassezac 11 Kj 44.26N 4.19 E
Chassiron, Pointe de- 11 Eh 46.03N 1.24W
Chat 24 Pd 37.59N 55.16 E
Châtaigneraie 11 Ij 44.45N 2.20 E
Chātāl 24 Pd 37.40N 55.45 E
Château-Arnoux 11 Lj 44.06N 6.00 E
Chateaubelair 51n Ba 13.17N 61.15W
Châteaubriant 11 Eg 47.43N 1.23W
Château-Chinon 11 Jg 47.04N 3.56 E
Château-du-Loir 11 Gg 47.42N 0.25 E
Châteaudun 11 Hf 48.05N 1.20 E
Château-Gontier 11 Fg 47.50N 0.42W
Châteaulin 11 Bf 48.12N 4.05W
Châteaulin, Bassin de- 11 Cf 48.18N 3.50W
Châteaumeillant 11 Ih 46.34N 2.12 E
Châteauneuf-de-Randon 11 Jj 44.39N 3.04 E
Châteauneuf-sur-Cher 11 Ih 46.51N 2.19 E
Châteauneuf-sur-Loire 11 Ig 47.52N 2.14 E
Château-Porcien 12 Ge 49.32N 4.15 E
Châteaurenard 11 Kk 43.53N 4.51 E
Château-Renault 11 Gg 47.35N 0.54 E
Châteauroux 11 Hh 46.49N 1.42 E
Château-Salins 11 Mf 48.49N 6.30 E
Château-Thierry 11 Je 49.03N 3.24 E
Châteaux, Pointe des- 51e Bb 16.15N 61.11W
Châtelaillon-Plage 11 Eh 46.04N 1.05W
Châtelet 12 Gd 50.24N 4.31 E
Châtelguyon 11 Ji 45.55N 3.04 E
Châtellerault 11 Gh 46.48N 0.32 E
Chatelodo 55 De 21.19S 57.28W
Chatham [Eng.-U.K.] 9 Nj 51.23N 0.32 E
Chatham [N.B.-Can.] 42 Kg 47.02N 65.26W
Chatham [Ont.-Can.] 42 Jh 42.24N 82.11W
Chatham [Va.-U.S.] 44 Hg 36.49N 79.26W
Chatham Island 57 Ji 44.00S 176.30W
Chatham Islands 57 Ji 44.00S 176.30W
Chatham Rise (EN) 57 Ii 43.30S 180.00
Chatham Strait 40 Me 57.30N 134.45W
Châtillon-en-Bazois 11 Jg 47.03N 3.40 E
Châtillon-sur-Indre 11 Hh 46.59N 1.10 E
Châtillon-sur-Marne 12 Fe 49.06N 3.45 E
Châtillon-sur-Seine 11 Kg 47.51N 4.33 E
Chatom 44 Cj 31.28N 88.16W
Chatsworth 37 Ec 19.38S 30.50 E
Chattahoochee 44 Ej 30.42N 84.51W
Chattahoochee 38 Kf 30.52N 84.57W
Chattanooga 39 Kf 35.03N 85.19W
Chatteris 12 Cb 52.27N 0.03 E
Chaucas 55 Cc 16.46S 58.44W
Chaudfontaine 12 Hd 50.35N 5.38 E
Chaudière, Rivière- 44 Lb 46.43N 71.17W
Chauk 25 Id 20.53N 94.49 E
Chaulnes 12 Ee 49.49N 2.48 E
Chaumont 11 Lf 48.07N 5.08 E
Chaumont-en-Vexin 12 De 49.16N 1.53 E
Chaumont-Gistoux 12 Gd 50.41N 4.44 E
Chaumont-Porcien 12 Ge 49.39N 4.15 E
Chaumont-sur-Aire 12 Hf 48.56N 5.15 E
Chaumont-sur-Loire 11 Hg 47.29N 1.11 E
Chauny 11 Je 49.37N 3.13 E
Chau Phu 25 Lf 10.42N 105.07 E
Chausey, Iles- 11 Ef 48.53N 1.50W
Chauvigny 11 Gh 46.34N 0.39 E
Chavantina 54 Hf 14.40S 52.21W
Chavarría 55 Ci 28.57S 58.35W
Chaves [Braz.] 54 Id 0.10S 49.55W
Chaves [Port.] 13 Ec 41.44N 7.28W
Chavigny, Lac - 42 Je 58.00N 75.05W
Chavuma 36 De 13.05S 22.42 E
Chazelles-sur-Lyon 11 Ki 45.38N 4.23 E
Chbar 25 Lf 12.46N 107.10 E
Cheaha Mountain 44 Ei 33.30N 85.47W
Cheat River 44 Hf 39.45N 79.55W
Cheb 10 If 50.04N 12.23 E
Cheboygan 43 Kb 45.39N 84.29W
Chech, 'Erg- 30 Gf 25.00N 3.00W
Chechaouene [3] 32 Fb 35.00N 5.00W
Chechaouene 32 Fb 35.10N 5.16W
Checheng 27 Lg 22.05N 120.42 E
Che-Chiang Sheng → Zhejiang Sheng [2] 27 Kf 29.00N 120.00 E
Chech'ŏn 28 Jf 37.08N 128.12 E
Chęciny 10 Qf 50.48N 20.28 E
Cheddar Gorge 9 Kj 51.13N 2.47W
Cheduba 25 Ie 18.48N 93.38 E
Chée 12 Gf 48.45N 4.39 E
Cheektowaga 44 Hd 42.57N 78.38W
Chefu 37 Ed 22.27S 32.45 E
Chegga 31 Gf 25.22N 5.49W
Cheghelvandī 24 Mf 33.42N 48.25 E
Chehel Pāyeh 24 Qg 31.54N 57.14 E
Cheju 27 Me 33.31N 126.32 E
Cheju-Do 21 Of 33.25N 126.30 E
Cheju-Do [2] 28 Ih 33.25N 126.30 E
Cheju-Haehyŏp 28 Ih 33.40N 126.28 E
Chela, Serra da- 30 Ij 16.00S 13.10 E
Chelan 46 Ec 47.51N 120.01W
Chelan, Lake- 46 Eb 48.05N 120.30W
Chelforó, Arroyo- 55 Cm 36.55S 58.12W
Cheliff [3] 32 Hb 36.10N 1.45 E
Cheliff 30 He 36.02N 0.08 E
Cheliff 32 Hb 36.10N 1.20 E
Cheliff, Plaine du- 13 Mi 35.57N 0.45 E
Chellalat el Adhaouara 13 Pi 35.56N 3.25 E
Chelleh Khāneh, Kūh-e- 24 Md 36.52N 48.36 E
Chełm [2] 10 Te 51.10N 23.30 E
Chełm 10 Te 51.10N 23.28 E
Chelmer 12 Cc 51.44N 0.42 E
Chełmińskie, Pojezierze- 10 Oc 53.20N 19.00 E
Chełmno 10 Oc 53.22N 18.26 E
Chelmsford 9 Nj 51.44N 0.28 E
Chełmża 10 Oc 53.12N 18.37 E
Cheltenham 9 Kj 51.54N 2.04W
Chelva 13 Le 39.45N 0.59W
Chemainus 46 Db 48.55N 123.43W
Chemâma 32 Ef 16.50N 14.00 E
Chemba 37 Ec 17.09S 34.53 E
Chembe 36 Ee 11.58S 28.45 E
Chemillé 11 Fg 47.13N 0.43W
Chemult 46 Ee 43.13N 121.47W
Chenāb 21 Jg 29.13N 70.49 E
Chenachane 32 Gd 26.00N 4.15W
Chenachane 32 Gd 25.17N 3.10W
Chenārbāshi 24 Lf 33.20N 46.20 E
Chen Barag Qi (Bayan Hure) 27 Kb 49.21N 119.25 E
Chencha 35 Fd 6.17N 37.40 E
Chencoyí 48 Nh 19.48N 90.14W
Cheney 46 Gc 47.29N 117.34W
Cheney Reservoir 45 Hh 37.45N 97.50W
Cheng'an 28 Cf 36.27N 114.41 E
Chengde 27 Kc 41.00N 117.57 E
Chengdu 22 Mf 30.45N 104.04 E
Chengkou 27 Ie 31.54N 108.37 E
Chengmai 27 Ih 19.50N 109.59 E
Chengshan Jiao 27 Ld 37.24N 122.42 E
Chengxi Hu 28 Dh 32.22N 116.12 E
Chengzitan 27 Ld 39.31N 122.28 E
Chenisckali 16 Mh 42.06N 42.16 E
Chenjiagang 28 Eg 34.22N 119.48 E
Chenonceaux 11 Hg 47.20N 1.04 E
Chenxi 27 Jf 28.02N 110.15 E
Chenxian 27 Jf 25.49N 113.05 E
Chenying → Wannian 28 Dj 28.42N 117.04 E
Chépénéhé 63b Ce 20.47S 167.09 E
Chepes 56 Gd 31.21S 66.36W
Chepo 49 Hi 9.10N 79.06W
Cher [3] 11 Ig 47.00N 2.30 E
Cher 5 Gf 47.21N 0.29 E
Cheradi, Isole- 14 Lj 40.25N 17.10 E
Cherangany Hills 36 Gb 1.15N 35.27 E
Cheraw 44 Hh 34.42N 79.53W
Cherbaniani Reef 25 Ef 12.18N 71.53 E
Cherbourg 6 Ff 49.39N 1.39W
Cherchell 32 Hb 36.36N 2.12 E
Chère 11 Eg 47.42N 1.50W
Chergui, Chott Ech- 30 He 34.21N 0.30 E
Chéri 34 Hc 13.26N 11.21 E
Cherlen → Kerulen 21 Ne 48.48N 117.00 E
Cherokee 45 Ie 42.45N 95.33W
Cherokees, Lake O' the- 45 Ih 36.39N 94.49W
Cherski Mountains (EN)=Čerskogo, Hrebet- [R.S.F.S.R.] 21 Qc 65.00N 145.00 E
Chersterfield Inlet 39 Jc 63.21N 90.42W
Chertsey 12 Bc 51.23N 0.30W
Cherwell 9 Lj 51.44N 1.15W
Chesapeake 44 Ig 36.45N 76.15W
Chesapeake Bay 38 Lf 38.40N 76.25W
Chesapeake Bay Bridge-Tunnel 44 Ig 37.00N 76.02W
Chesha Bay (EN)=Češskaja Guba 5 Kb 67.20N 46.30 E
Chesham 12 Bc 51.42N 0.36W
Cheshire [3] 9 Kh 53.15N 2.30W
Cheshire Plain 9 Kh 53.20N 2.40W
Cheshunt 12 Bc 51.42N 0.02W
Chester 9 Kh 53.10N 2.55W
Chester [Eng.-U.K.] 9 Kh 53.12N 2.54W
Chester [Il.-U.S.] 45 Lh 37.55N 89.49W
Chester [Mt.-U.S.] 46 Jb 48.31N 110.58W
Chester [Pa.-U.S.] 44 Jf 39.50N 75.23W
Chester [S.C.-U.S.] 44 Gh 34.40N 81.12W
Chesterfield 9 Lh 53.15N 1.25W
Chesterfield, Ile- 37 Gc 16.20S 43.58 E
Chesterfield, Récifs et Iles-=Chesterfield Reefs and Islands (EN) 57 Gf 20.00S 159.00 E
Chesterfield Inlet 38 Jc 63.25N 90.45W
Chesterfield Reefs and Islands (EN)=Chesterfield, Récifs et Iles- 57 Gf 20.00S 159.00 E
Chesterton Range 59 Je 25.30S 147.30 E
Chestnut Ridge 44 He 40.10N 79.25W
Chesuncook Lake 44 Mb 46.00N 69.20W
Chetaibi 32 Ib 37.04N 7.23 E
Chetumal 39 Kh 18.35N 88.07W
Chetumal, Bahía de 47 Ge 18.20N 88.05W
Cheviot 62 Ee 42.49S 173.16 E
Chew Bahir=Stefanie, Lake- (EN) 30 Kh 4.38N 36.50 E
Chewelah 46 Gb 48.17N 117.43W
Cheyenne [Ok.-U.S.] 45 Gi 35.37N 99.40W

Index Symbols

[1] Independent Nation
[2] State, Region
[3] District, County
[4] Municipality
[5] Colony, Dependency
Continent
Physical Region
Historical or Cultural Region
Mount, Mountain
Volcano
Hill
Mountains, Mountain Range
Hills, Escarpment
Plateau, Upland
Pass, Gap
Plain, Lowland
Delta
Salt Flat
Valley, Canyon
Crater, Cave
Karst Features
Depression
Polder
Desert, Dunes
Forest, Woods
Heath, Steppe
Oasis
Cape, Point
Coast, Beach
Cliff
Peninsula
Isthmus
Sandbank
Island
Atoll
Rock, Reef
Islands, Archipelago
Rocks, Reefs
Coral Reef
Well, Spring
Geyser
River, Stream
Waterfall Rapids
River Mouth, Estuary
Lake
Salt Lake
Intermittent Lake
Reservoir
Swamp, Pond
Canal
Glacier
Ice Shelf, Pack Ice
Ocean
Sea
Gulf, Bay
Strait, Fjord
Lagoon
Bank
Seamount
Tablemount
Ridge
Shelf
Basin
Escarpment, Sea Scarp
Fracture
Trench, Abyss
National Park, Reserve
Point of Interest
Recreation Site
Cave, Cavern
Historic Site
Ruins
Wall, Walls
Church, Abbey
Temple
Scientific Station
Airport
Port
Lighthouse
Mine
Tunnel
Dam, Bridge

Cheyenne [Wy.-U.S.] 39 Ie 41.08N 104.49W
Cheyenne River 43 Gc 44.40N 101.15W
Cheyenne Wells 45 Eg 38.51N 102.11W
Cheyne Bay 59 Df 34.35S 118.50 E
Chhatarpur 25 Fd 24.54N 79.36 E
Chhindwāra 25 Fd 22.04N 78.56 E
Chi 25 Ke 15.11N 104.43 E
Chiamboni, Rās- 35 Gf 1.38S 41.36 E
Chiana, Val di- 14 Fg 43.15N 11.50 E
Chianciano Terme 14 Fg 43.02N 11.49 E
Chiang-hsi Sheng→Jangxi Sheng=Kiangsi (EN) [2] 27 Kf 28.00N 116.00 E
Chiang Mai 22 Lh 18.46N 98.58 E
Chiang Rai 22 Lh 19.54N 99.50 E
Chiang-su Sheng→Jiangsu Sheng=Kiangsu (EN) [2] 27 Ke 33.00N 120.00 E
Chiani 14 Gh 42.44N 12.07 E
Chianje 31 Ij 15.45S 13.54 E
Chianti 14 Fg 43.30N 11.25 E
Chiapa, Rio- 48 Mj 16.30N 93.10W
Chiapas [2] 47 Fe 16.30N 92.30W
Chiapas, Meseta de- 47 Fe 16.30N 92.00W
Chiaramonte Gulfi 14 Im 37.02N 14.42 E
Chiaravalle 14 Hg 43.36N 13.19 E
Chiaromonte 14 Kj 40.07N 16.13 E
Chiautla de Tapia 48 Jh 18.17N 98.36W
Chiavari 14 Df 44.19N 9.19 E
Chiavenna 14 Dd 46.19N 9.24 E
Chiayi 27 Lg 23.29N 120.27 E
Chiba 27 Pd 35.36N 140.07 E
Chiba Ken [2] 28 Pg 35.40N 140.20 E
Chibemba 36 Bf 15.45S 14.06 E
Chibia 36 Bf 15.11S 13.41 E
Chibougamau 39 Le 49.53N 74.21W
Chibougamau, Lac- 44 Ja 49.50N 74.15W
Chibougamau, Rivière- 44 Ja 49.50N 74.25W
Chiburi-Jima 28 Lf 36.00N 133.02 E
Chibuto 37 Ed 24.42S 33.33 E
Chicago 39 Ke 41.53N 87.38W
Chicago Heights 45 Mf 41.30N 87.38W
Chicala 36 Ce 11.59S 19.30 E
Chicapa 30 Ji 6.25S 20.48 E
Chic-Chocs, Monts- 44 Na 48.55N 66.45W
Chicha 35 Bb 16.52N 18.33 E
Chichagof 40 Le 57.30N 135.30W
Chichancanab, Laguna de- 48 Oh 19.54N 88.46W
Chichaoua 32 Fc 31.32N 8.46W
Chichas, Cordillera de- 54 Eh 20.30S 66.30W
Chicheng 27 Kc 40.55N 115.47 E
Chichén Itzá 49 Kg 20.40N 88.35W
Chichester 9 Mk 50.50N 0.48W
Chichester Range 59 Dd 22.20S 119.20 E
Chichibu 28 Og 35.59N 139.05 E
Chichigalpa 49 Dg 12.34N 87.02W
Chichijma-Rettō 60 Cb 27.06N 142.12 E
Chichilla de Monte-Aragón 13 Kf 38.55N 1.43W
Chichiriviche 49 Mh 10.56N 68.16W
Chickasawhay River 45 Lk 31.00N 88.45W
Chickasha 43 Hd 35.02N 97.58W
Chicken 40 Kd 64.04N 141.56W
Chiclana de la Frontera 13 Fh 36.25N 6.08W
Chiclayo 53 If 6.46S 79.50W
Chico 43 Cd 39.44N 121.50W
Chico, Rio- [Arg.] 52 Jj 43.48S 66.25W
Chico, Rio- [Arg.] 52 Jj 49.56S 68.32W
Chicoana 56 Gc 25.06S 65.33W
Chicomo 37 Ed 24.31S 34.17 E
Chiconono 37 Fb 12.57S 35.45 E
Chicopee 44 Kd 42.10N 72.36W
Chicote 36 Df 16.01S 21.48 E
Chicoutimi 39 Le 48.26N 71.04W
Chicoutimi Nord 44 La 48.29N 71.02W
Chicualacuala 37 Ed 22.05S 31.42 E
Chidenguele 37 Ed 24.55S 34.10 E
Chidley, Cape- 38 Mc 60.25N 64.30W
Chiemsee 10 Ii 47.54N 12.29 E
Chiengi 36 Ed 8.39S 29.10 E
Chienti 14 Hg 43.18N 13.45 E
Chieri 14 Be 45.01N 7.49 E
Chiers 12 He 49.39N 5.00 E
Chiese 14 Ee 45.08N 10.25 E
Chieti 14 Ih 42.21N 14.10 E
Chièvres 12 Fd 50.35N 3.48 E
Chifeng/Ulanhad 27 Kc 42.16N 118.57 E
Chifumage 36 De 12.10S 22.30 E
Chifwefwe 36 Fe 13.35S 29.35 E
Chigasaki 29 Fd 35.19N 139.24 E
Chignik 40 He 56.18N 158.23W
Chigombe 37 Ed 23.26S 33.19 E
Chigorodó 49 Ij 7.41N 76.41W
Chigubo 37 Ed 22.50S 33.31 E
Chigu Co 27 Ff 28.40N 91.50 E
Chi He 28 Dh 32.51N 117.59 E
Chihli, Gulf of- (EN)=Bo Hai 21 Nf 38.30N 120.00 E
Chihuahua [2] 47 Cc 28.30N 106.00W
Chihuahua 39 Ig 28.38N 106.05W
Chii-san 28 Ig 35.20N 127.44 E
Chikaskia River 45 Hh 36.37N 97.15W
Chikugo 29 Be 33.13N 130.30 E
Chikugo-Gawa 29 Be 33.10N 130.21 E
Chikuma-Gawa 29 Fc 37.00N 138.35 E
Chikwana 36 Ff 16.03S 34.48 E
Chilapa de Alvarez 48 Ji 17.36N 99.10W
Chilās 25 Ea 35.26N 74.05 E
Chilaw 25 Fg 7.34N 79.47 E
Chilcotin 42 Ff 51.46N 122.22W
Childers 59 Ke 25.14S 152.17 E
Childress 43 Ge 34.25N 100.13W
Chile [1] 53 Ii 30.00S 71.00W
Chile Basin (EN) 3 Mm 33.00S 90.00W
Chile Chico 56 Fg 46.33S 71.44W
Chilecito [Arg.] 56 Gd 33.53S 69.03W
Chilecito [Arg.] 56 Gc 29.10S 67.30W
Chile Rise (EN) 3 Mm 40.00S 90.00W
Chili 35 Cb 16.44N 20.53 E
Chilia, Braţul- 15 Md 45.13N 29.43 E
Chililabombwe 36 Ee 12.22S 27.50 E
Chi-lin Sheng→Jilin Sheng=Kirin (EN) [2] 27 Mc 43.00N 126.00 E
Chilko Lake 46 Ca 51.20N 124.05W
Chilko River 46 Da 52.00N 123.40W
Chillán 53 Ii 36.36S 72.07W
Chillar 56 Ie 37.18S 59.59W
Chillicothe [Il.-U.S.] 45 Lf 40.55N 89.29W
Chillicothe [Mo.-U.S.] 45 Jg 39.48N 93.33W
Chillicothe [Oh.-U.S.] 43 Kd 38.20N 82.59W
Chilliwack 46 Eb 49.10N 121.57W
Chiloé, Isla de- 52 Ij 42.30S 73.55W
Chilón 48 Mi 17.14N 92.25W
Chiloquin 46 Ee 42.35N 121.52W
Chilpancingo de los Bravos 47 Ee 17.33N 99.30W
Chiltern Hills 9 Mj 51.42N 0.48W
Chilton 45 Ld 44.02N 88.10W
Chiluage 36 Dd 9.31S 21.46 E
Chilumba 36 Fe 10.27S 34.16 E
Chilwa, Lake- 36 Fc 15.12S 35.50 E
Chimala 36 Fd 8.51S 34.01 E
Chimaltenango 49 Bf 14.39N 90.49W
Chimaltenango [3] 49 Bf 14.40N 90.55W
Chimán 49 Hi 8.42N 78.37W
Chimanas, Islas- 50 Dg 10.17N 64.38W
Chimay 12 Gd 50.03N 4.19 E
Chimborazo, Volcán- 52 If 1.28S 78.48W
Chimbote 53 If 9.05S 78.36W
Chimichagua 49 Ki 9.16N 73.49W
Chimoio 37 Ec 19.00S 33.23 E
Chimorra 13 Hf 38.18N 4.53W
Chin [2] 25 Id 22.00N 93.30 E
China [Jap.] 29b Bb 27.20N 128.36 E
China [Mex.] 48 Je 25.42N 99.14W
China (EN)=Zhonghua Renmin Gongheguo [1] 22 Mf 35.00N 105.00 E
Chinacates 48 Ge 25.00N 105.13W
China Lake 46 Gi 35.46N 117.39W
Chinandega 47 Gf 12.37N 87.09W
Chinandega [3] 49 Dg 12.45N 87.05W
Chinati Peak 45 Dl 29.57N 104.29W
Chincha Alta 54 Cf 13.27S 76.08W
Chinchaga 42 Fe 58.52N 118.19W
Chinchilla 59 Ke 26.45S 150.38 E
Chinchón 13 Id 40.08N 3.25W
Chinchorro, Banco- 47 Ge 18.35N 87.20W
Chincoteague 44 Jg 37.55N 75.23W
Chinde 31 Kj 18.34S 36.27 E
Chin-Do 28 Ig 34.25N 126.15 E
Chindu 27 Ge 33.30N 96.31 E
Chindwin 21 Lg 21.26N 95.15 E
Ch'ing-hai Sheng→Qinghai Sheng=Tsinghai (EN) [2] 27 Gd 36.00N 96.00 E
Chingil 35 Bc 10.33N 18.57 E
Chingola 31 Jj 12.32S 27.52 E
Chinguar 36 Ce 12.33S 16.22 E
Chinguetti 32 Ee 20.27N 12.21W
Chinguetti, Dahr de- 32 Ee 20.43N 12.20W
Chinhae 28 Jg 35.08N 128.40 E
Chiniot 25 Eb 31.43N 72.59 E
Chinipas 48 Ed 27.23N 108.32W
Chinju 27 Md 35.11N 128.05 E
Chinko 30 Jh 4.50N 23.53 E
Chinle 46 Kh 36.09N 109.33W
Chinle Creek 46 Kh 37.12N 109.43W
Chinmen 27 Kg 24.25N 118.25 E
Chino 29 Fd 36.00N 138.09 E
Chinon 11 Gg 47.10N 0.15 E
Chinook 46 Kb 48.35N 109.14W
Chinquila 48 Pg 21.30N 87.25W
Chinsali 36 Fe 10.33S 32.04 E
Chinteche 36 Fe 11.50S 34.10 E
Chinú 54 Cb 9.06N 75.24W
Chinvali 19 Eg 42.13N 43.57 E
Chiny 12 He 49.44N 5.20 E
Chinyŏng 28 Jg 35.18N 128.44 E
Chioco 37 Ec 16.25S 32.50 E
Chioggia 14 Ge 45.13N 12.17 E
Chios (EN)=Khios 5 Ih 38.22N 26.00 E
Chipata 31 Kj 13.39S 32.40 E
Chipepo 36 Ef 16.49S 27.50 E
Chipindo 36 Ce 13.48S 15.48 E
Chiping 28 Df 36.35N 116.16 E
Chipinga 37 Ed 20.12S 32.38 E
Chipman 44 Ob 46.11N 65.53W
Chippenham 9 Kj 51.28N 2.07W
Chippewa, Lake- 45 Kd 45.56N 91.13W
Chippewa Falls 43 Ic 44.56N 91.24W
Chippewa River [Wi.-U.S.] 45 Id 44.56N 95.44W
Chippewa River [U.S.] 45 Jd 44.25N 92.10W
Chipping Ongar 12 Cc 51.42N 0.15 E
Chiputneticook Lakes 44 Mc 45.45N 68.45W
Chiquián 54 Cf 10.09S 77.11W
Chiquimula [3] 49 Cf 14.40N 89.25W
Chiquimula 49 Cf 14.48N 89.33W
Chiquimulilla 49 Bf 14.05N 90.23W
Chiquinquirá 54 Db 5.37N 73.50W
Chiquitos, Llanos de- 54 Fg 18.00S 61.30W
Chirāla 25 Ge 15.49N 80.21 E
Chiran 29 Bf 31.22N 130.27 E
Chiredzi 31 Kk 21.03S 31.45 E
Chirfa 34 Ha 20.57N 12.21 E
Chirgua, Rio- 50 Bh 8.30N 68.01W
Chiricahua Peak 43 Fe 31.52N 109.20W
Chiriguaná 49 Ki 9.22N 73.37W
Chirikof 40 He 55.50N 155.35W
Chiriqui [3] 49 Fi 8.30N 82.00W
Chiriquí, Golfo de- 38 Ki 8.00N 82.20W
Chiriquí, Laguna de- 47 Hg 9.03N 82.00W
Chiriquí Grande 49 Fi 8.57N 82.07W
Chirnogi 15 Je 44.07N 26.34 E
Chiromo 36 Gf 16.33S 35.08 E
Chirripó, Cerro- 38 Ki 9.29N 83.29W
Chirripó, Rio- [C.R.] 49 Fh 10.03N 83.16W
Chirripó, Rio- [C.R.] 49 Fh 10.41N 83.41W
Chirundu 37 Dc 15.59S 28.54 E
Chisamba 36 Ee 14.59S 28.23 E
Chisāpāni Garhi 25 Hc 27.34N 85.08 E
Chisenga 36 Fd 9.56S 33.26 E
Chishui 27 If 28.30N 105.44 E
Chişineu Criş 15 Ec 46.32N 21.31 E
Chisone 14 Bf 44.49N 7.25 E
Chitado 36 Bf 17.18S 13.54 E
Chita-Hantō 29 Ed 34.50N 136.50 E
Chitati 35 Ac 14.40N 14.30 E
Chita-Wan 29 Ed 34.50N 136.55 E
Chitembo 36 Ce 13.31S 16.45 E
Chitina 40 Kd 61.31N 144.27W
Chitina 40 Kd 61.30N 144.28W
Chitipa 36 Fd 9.43S 33.16 E
Chitorgarh 25 Ed 24.53N 74.38 E
Chitose 28 Pc 42.49N 141.39 E
Chitradurga 25 Ff 14.14N 76.24 E
Chitrāl 25 Ea 35.51N 71.47 E
Chitré 47 Hg 7.58N 80.26W
Chittagong 22 Lg 22.20N 91.50 E
Chittoor 25 Ff 13.12N 79.07 E
Chiumbe 30 Ji 6.59S 21.12 E
Chiume 36 Df 15.08S 21.12 E
Chiusi 14 Fg 43.01N 11.57 E
Chiusi, Lago di- 14 Fg 43.05N 12.00 E
Chiva 13 Le 39.28N 0.43W
Chivacoa 50 Bg 10.10N 68.54W
Chivapuri, Rio- 50 Ci 6.25N 66.23W
Chivasso 14 Be 45.11N 7.53 E
Chivay 54 Dg 15.38S 71.36W
Chivilcoy 56 Hd 34.53S 60.01W
Chixoy o Negro, Rio- 49 Be 16.28N 90.33W
Chizou → Guichi 27 Ke 30.38N 117.30 E
Chizu 29 Dd 35.15N 134.14 E
Chōām Khsant 25 Kf 14.13N 104.56 E
Choapa, Rio- 56 Fd 31.38S 71.34W
Chobe 30 Jj 17.47S 25.10 E
Chobe [3] 37 Cc 18.30S 25.00 E
Choc Bay 51k Ba 14.03N 60.59W
Choch'iwŏn 28 If 36.36N 127.18 E
Chocó [2] 54 Cb 6.00N 77.00W
Chocolate Mountains 46 Hj 33.25N 114.10W
Chodecz 10 Pd 52.24N 19.01 E
Chodov 10 If 50.15N 12.45 E
Chodzież 10 Md 52.59N 16.56 E
Choele-Choel 56 Ge 39.16S 65.41W
Choique 56 He 38.28S 62.43W
Choiseul 51k Ab 13.47N 61.03W
Choiseul Island 57 Ge 7.00S 157.00 E
Choix 48 Ed 26.43N 108.17W
Chojna 10 Kd 52.58N 14.28 E
Chojnice 10 Nc 53.42N 17.34 E
Chojnów 10 Le 51.17N 15.56 E
Chōkai-San 21 Qf 39.10N 140.02 E
Choke 30 Kg 10.45N 37.35 E
Chókué 37 Ed 24.27S 32.55 E
Cho La 27 Ge 31.52N 98.51 E
Cholet 11 Fg 47.04N 0.53W
Chŏlla-Namdo [2] 28 Ig 34.45N 127.00 E
Chŏlla-Pukto [2] 28 Ig 35.45N 127.15 E
Cholo 36 Gf 16.04S 35.08 E
Cholula 48 Jh 19.04N 98.18W
Choluteca 47 Gf 13.18N 87.12W
Choluteca [3] 49 Dg 13.20N 87.10W
Choluteca, Rio- 49 Dg 13.07N 87.19W
Choma 31 Jj 16.49S 26.59 E
Chomo/Yadong 27 Ef 27.38N 89.03 E
Chomo Lhari 27 Ef 27.50N 89.16 E
Chomutov 10 Jf 50.28N 13.25 E
Ch'ŏnan 27 Md 36.48N 127.09 E
Chon Buri 25 Kf 13.22N 100.59 E
Chone 54 Bd 0.42S 80.07W
Ch'ŏngch'ŏn-gang 28 He 39.35N 125.28 E
Ch'ŏngjin 22 Oe 41.46N 129.49 E
Ch'ŏngjin Si [2] 28 Jd 41.45N 129.45 E
Chŏngju 27 Md 39.51N 125.15 E
Ch'ŏngju 27 Md 36.38N 127.30 E
Chongli (Xiwanzi) 28 Cd 40.57N 115.12 E
Chongming 28 Fi 31.38N 121.24 E
Chongming Dao 28 Fi 31.36N 121.33 E
Chongoroi 36 Be 13.34S 13.55 E
Chongqing (Yuzhou)=Chungking (EN) 22 Mg 29.34N 106.27 E
Chongqing→Yuzhou=Chungking (EN) 22 Mg 29.34N 106.27 E
Ch'ŏngsan-Do 28 Ig 34.11N 126.54 E
Chŏngŭp 28 Ig 35.34N 126.51 E
Chongyang 28 Cj 29.32N 114.02 E
Chongzuo 27 Ig 22.29N 107.22 E
Chŏnju 27 Md 35.49N 127.09 E
Chonos, Archipiélago de los- 52 Ij 45.00S 74.00W
Chontaleña, Cordillera- 49 Eh 11.50N 85.00W
Chontales [3] 49 Eg 12.05N 85.10W
Chopim, Rio- 55 Fg 25.35S 53.05W
Chopinzinho 55 Fg 25.51S 52.30W
Chorito, Sierra del- 13 He 39.25N 4.25W
Choroszcz 10 Sc 53.09N 22.59 E
Chorreras, Cerro- 48 Fd 26.02N 106.21W
Ch'ŏrwŏn 27 Md 38.15N 127.13 E
Chorzele 10 Qc 53.16N 20.55 E
Chorzów 10 Of 50.19N 18.57 E
Ch'osan 28 Hd 40.45N 125.50 E
Chośebuz/Cottbus 10 Ke 51.46N 14.20 E
Chōshi 28 Pg 35.44N 140.50 E
Chos Malal 56 Fe 37.23S 70.16W
Chosŏn M.I.K.=North Korea (EN) [1] 22 Oe 40.00N 127.30 E
Chosŏn Minjuju-Inmin-Konghwaguk=Chosŏn M.I.K. [1] 22 Oe 40.00N 127.30 E
Choszczno 10 Lc 53.10N 15.26 E
Chota 54 Ce 6.33S 78.39W
Chotanagpur Plateau 21 Kg 22.00N 86.00 E
Choteau 46 Ic 47.49N 112.11W
Chotla, Cerro de- 48 Ii 17.55N 101.31W
Choukchot, Djebel- 13 Qh 36.01N 4.11 E
Choum 32 Ee 21.18N 12.59W
Chovd→Kobdo 27 Fb 48.06N 92.11 E
Chövsgöl nuur→Hubsugul Nur 21 Md 51.00N 100.30 E
Chowchilla 46 Eh 37.07N 120.16W
Chowra 25 Ig 8.27N 93.02 E
Chréa 13 Oh 36.25N 2.53 E
Chřiby 10 Ng 49.10N 17.20 E
Christchurch 58 Ii 43.32S 172.37 E
Christian, Cape- 42 Kb 70.32N 68.18W
Christian, Point- 64q Ab 25.04S 130.07W
Christiana 37 De 27.52S 25.08 E
Christian IV Gletscher 41 Ie 68.40N 30.20W
Christiansburg 44 Gg 37.07N 80.26W
Christiansfeld 8 Ci 55.21N 9.29 E
Christianshåb/Qasigiánguit 41 Ge 68.45N 51.30W
Christiansø 8 Fi 55.20N 15.10 E
Christian Sound 40 Me 55.56N 134.40W
Christiansted 50 Dd 17.45N 64.40W
Christiansted Harbor 51a Dc 17.46N 64.42W
Christie Bay 42 Gd 62.45N 110.15W
Christmas→Kiritimati Atoll [5] 57 Ld 1.52N 157.20W
Christmas Creek 59 Fc 18.29S 125.23 E
Christmas Creek 59 Fc 18.53S 125.55 E
Christmas Island [5] 22 Mk 10.30S 105.40 E
Christmas Ridge (EN) 3 Ki 10.00N 165.00W
Chrudim 10 Lg 49.57N 15.47 E
Chrzanów 10 Pf 50.09N 19.24 E
Chrząstowa 10 Mc 53.35N 16.58 E
Chuansha 28 Fi 31.11N 121.42 E
Chübar 24 Mc 38.11N 48.51 E
Chubut [2] 56 Gf 44.00S 69.00W
Chubut, Rio- 52 Jj 43.20S 65.03W
Chucunague, Rio- 49 Ii 8.09N 77.44W
Chugach Mountains 40 Jd 61.00N 145.00W
Chuginadak 40 Ef 52.49N 169.50W
Chugoku-Sanchi 21 Pf 35.15N 133.20 E
Chu He 28 Eh 32.15N 119.03 E
Chuhuichupa 48 Ec 29.38N 108.22W
Chuí 55 Fk 33.41S 53.27W
Chuka 36 Gc 0.20S 37.39 E
Chukai 26 Df 4.15N 103.25 E
Chukchi Peninsula (EN)=Čukotski Poluostrov 21 Uc 66.00N 175.00W
Chukchi Plateau (EN) 67 Bd 78.00N 165.00W
Chukchi Sea 67 Bd 69.00N 171.00W
Chukchi Sea (EN)=Čukotskoje More 67 Bd 69.00N 171.00W
Chula Vista 46 Gj 32.39N 117.05W
Chulitna 40 Jd 62.55N 149.39W
Chullo 13 Jg 37.10N 2.57W
Chulucanas 54 Be 5.06S 80.10W
Chumbicha 56 Gc 28.52S 66.14W
Chumphon 25 Jf 10.32N 99.13 E
Chumunjin 28 Jf 37.53N 128.49 E
Ch'unch'ŏn 27 Md 37.52N 127.44 E
Chunga 36 Ef 15.03S 26.00 E
Ch'ungch'ŏng-Namdo [2] 28 If 36.30N 127.00 E
Ch'ungch'ŏng-Pukto [2] 28 Jf 36.45N 128.00 E
Ch'ungju 27 Md 36.58N 127.56 E
Chungking (EN)=Chongqing (Yuzhou) 22 Mg 29.34N 106.27 E
Chungking (EN)=Yuzhou→Chongqing 22 Mg 29.34N 106.27 E
Ch'ungmu 28 Jg 34.51N 128.26 E
Chunya 36 Fd 8.32S 33.25 E
Chuquibamba 54 Dg 15.50S 72.39W
Chuquibambilla 54 Df 14.07S 72.43W
Chuquicamata 56 Gb 22.19S 68.56W
Chuquisaca [2] 54 Fg 20.00S 64.20W
Chur/Cuera 14 Dd 46.50N 9.35 E
Churchill 39 Jd 58.46N 94.10W
Churchill [Can.] 38 Md 53.30N 60.10W
Churchill [Can.] 38 Jd 58.47N 94.12W
Churchill, Cape- 42 Ie 58.46N 93.12W
Churchill Falls 42 Lf 53.30N 64.10W
Churchill Lake 42 Ge 56.05N 108.15W
Churchill Peak 42 Ee 58.20N 125.02W
Churchill Range 66 Jg 81.30S 158.30 E
Chūru 25 Ec 28.18N 74.57 E
Churuguara 54 Ea 10.49N 69.32W
Churún Merú=Angel Falls (EN) 52 Je 5.57N 62.30W
Chuska Mountains 46 Kh 36.15N 108.50W
Chute-des Passes 42 Kg 49.50N 71.00W
Chuxian 27 Ke 32.16N 118.15 E
Chuxiong 27 Hf 25.02N 101.32 E
Chuy 55 Fk 33.41S 53.27W
Ciamis 26 Eh 7.20S 108.21 E
Cianjur 26 Eh 6.49S 107.08 E
Ciarraí/Kerry [2] 9 Di 52.10N 9.30W
Ciatura 16 Mh 42.17N 43.15 E
Cibuta, Cerro- 48 Db 31.02N 110.58W
Ćićarija 14 He 45.28N 13.54 E
Ćićevac 15 Ef 43.43N 21.27 E
Cicicleja 15 Nb 47.23N 30.50 E
Cicolano 14 Hh 42.15N 13.10 E
Cidacos 13 Kb 42.19N 1.55W
Cide 24 Eb 41.54N 33.00 E
Cidlina 10 Lf 50.09N 15.12 E
Ciechanów 10 Qd 52.53N 20.38 E
Ciechanów [2] 10 Qd 52.55N 20.40 E
Ciechanowiec 10 Sd 52.42N 22.31 E
Ciechanowska, Wysoczyzna- 10 Qc 53.10N 20.30 E
Ciego de Ávila 47 Id 21.51N 78.46W
Ciego de Ávila [3] 49 Hb 22.00N 78.40W
Ciénaga 54 Da 11.00N 74.14W
Ciénaga de Flores 48 Ie 25.57N 100.11W
Ciénaga de Oro 49 Ji 8.53N 75.38W
Cieneguita 48 Fd 27.57N 106.59W
Cienfuegos [3] 49 Gb 22.15N 80.30W
Cienfuegos 39 Kg 22.09N 80.27W
Cies, Islas de- 13 Db 42.13N 8.54W
Cieszanów 10 Tf 50.16N 23.08 E
Cieza 13 Kf 38.14N 1.25W
Çifteler 24 Dc 39.22N 31.03 E
Cifuentes 13 Jd 40.47N 2.37W
Čiganak 19 Hf 45.05N 73.58 E
Čigirin 16 He 49.03N 32.42 E
Cigüela 13 Ie 39.08N 3.44W
Cihanbeyli 24 Ec 38.40N 32.56 E
Cihanbeyli Platosu 24 Ec 38.40N 32.45 E
Čiharesi 16 Mh 42.47N 43.02 E
Cihuatlán 48 Gh 19.14N 104.35W
Čiily 19 Gg 44.13N 66.46 E
Cijara, Embalse de- 13 He 39.18N 4.52W
Cijulang 36 Eh 7.44S 108.27 E
Čik 15 Dd 45.42N 20.04 E
Čikoj 20 Ff 51.02N 106.39 E
Čikuraĉki, Vulkan- 20 Kf 50.15N 155.29 E
Cilacap 26 Eh 7.44S 109.00 E
Çıldır 24 Jb 41.08N 43.07 E
Çıldır Gölü 24 Jb 41.04N 43.15 E
Cilento 14 Jj 40.20N 15.20 E
Čilik 18 Lc 43.42N 78.14 E
Čilik 19 Hg 43.35N 78.12 E
Cill Airne/Killarney 9 Di 52.03N 9.30W
Cill Chainnigh/Kilkenny 9 Fi 52.39N 7.15W
Cill Chainnigh/Kilkenny [2] 9 Fi 52.40N 7.20W
Cill Chaoi/Kilkee 9 Di 52.41N 9.38W
Cill Dara/Kildare [2] 9 Gh 53.15N 6.45W
Cill Dara/Kildare 9 Gh 53.10N 6.55W
Cill Mhantáin/Wicklow 9 Gi 52.59N 6.03W
Cill Mhantáin/Wicklow [2] 9 Gi 53.00N 6.30W
Cill Mocheallóg/Kilmallock 9 Ei 52.25N 8.35W
Cill Rois/Kilrush 9 Di 52.39N 9.29W
Cilma 17 Fd 65.25N 52.05 E
Cilo Dağı 24 Kd 37.30N 44.00 E
Cimaltepec, Sierra- 47 Ee 16.00N 96.40W
Cimarron 38 Jf 36.10N 96.17W
Cimarron 45 Dh 36.31N 104.55W
Čimbaj 19 Fg 42.59N 59.47 E
Cimini, Monti- 14 Gh 42.24N 12.12 E
Cimišlija 16 Ff 46.32N 28.46 E
Čimkent 22 Ie 42.18N 69.36 E
Čimkentskaja Oblast [3] 19 Gg 43.00N 68.40 E
Cimljansk 19 Ef 47.37N 42.04 E
Cimljanskoje Vodohranilišče=Tsimlyansk Reservoir (EN) 5 Kf 48.00N 43.00 E
Cimone 5 Hg 44.12N 10.40 E
Cîmpeni 15 Gc 46.22N 23.03 E
Cîmpia Turzii 15 Gc 46.33N 23.53 E
Cîmpina 15 Id 45.08N 25.44 E
Cîmpulung 15 Id 45.16N 25.03 E
Cîmpulung Moldovenesc 15 Ib 47.32N 25.34 E
Čimtarga, Gora- 18 Ge 39.14N 68.12 E
Cina, Tanjung- 26 Dh 5.55S 104.35 E
Çinar 24 Id 37.39N 40.06 E
Çinarcik 15 Mi 40.39N 29.06 E
Cinaruco, Rio- 50 Ci 6.41N 67.07W
Cina Selatan, Laut-=South China Sea (EN) 21 Ni 10.00N 113.00 E
Cinaz 18 Gd 40.56N 68.45 E
Cinca 13 Mc 41.26N 0.21 E
Cincar 14 Lg 43.54N 17.04 E
Cincinnati 39 Kf 39.06N 84.31W
Cinco de Otubro 36 Cd 9.34S 17.50 E
Cinco Irmãos, Serra dos- 55 Ff 22.55S 52.50W
Cinco Saltos 56 Ge 38.49S 68.04W
Cindrelu, Virful- 15 Gd 45.35N 23.48 E
Çine 24 Cd 37.36N 28.04 E
Çine 15 Kl 37.46N 27.49 E
Ciney 11 Ld 50.18N 5.06 E
Čingirlau 19 Fe 51.07N 54.05 E
Cingoli 14 Hg 43.22N 13.13 E
Cintalapa de Figueroa 48 Mi 16.44N 93.43W
Cinto, Monte- 5 Gg 42.23N 8.56 E
Cintra, Golfo de- 32 De 23.00N 16.15W
Cinzas, Rio das- 55 Gf 22.56S 50.32W
Ciociaria 14 Hi 41.45N 13.15 E
Cionn Mhálanna/Malin Head 5 Fd 55.23N 7.24W
Cionn tSáile/Kinsale 9 Ej 51.42N 8.32W
Ciorani 15 Je 44.49N 26.25 E
Čiovo 14 Kg 43.30N 16.18 E
Cipa 20 Ge 55.20N 115.55 E
Cipikan 20 Gf 54.58N 113.21 E
Cipó 54 Kf 11.06S 38.31W
Cipolletti 56 Ge 38.56S 67.59W
Čiprovci 15 Ff 43.23N 22.53 E
Čir 16 Me 48.35N 42.55 E
Circeo, Capo- 14 Hi 41.14N 13.03 E
Čirčik 19 Gg 41.28N 69.35 E
Circle [Ak.-U.S.] 40 Kc 65.50N 144.04W
Circle [Mt.-U.S.] 46 Mc 47.25N 105.35W
Circleville 44 Ff 39.36N 82.57W
Cirebon 22 Mj 6.44S 108.34 E
Cirencester 9 Lj 51.44N 1.59W
Cirié 14 Be 45.14N 7.36 E
Čirinda 20 Fc 67.30N 100.35 E
Čirip, Vulkan- 20 Jg 45.20N 147.58 E
Čirka-Kem 7 Hd 64.45N 32.10 E
Cirò 14 Lk 39.23N 17.04 E
Cirò Marina 14 Lk 39.22N 17.08 E
Ciron 11 Fj 44.36N 0.18W
Čirpan 15 Ig 42.12N 25.20 E
Cirque Mountain 42 Le 58.55N 63.33W
Cisa, Passo della- 14 Df 44.28N 9.55 E
Ciscaucasia (EN) 5 Kf 45.00N 43.00 E
Cisco 45 Gj 32.23N 98.59W
Ciskei 37 Df 31.30S 26.40 E
Čišmy 19 Fe 54.35N 55.25 E
Cisnădie 15 Hd 45.43N 24.09 E
Cisne, Islas del- 47 He 17.22N 83.51W
Cistern Point 49 Ib 24.40N 77.45W
Cistierna 13 Gb 42.48N 5.07W
Čistoozernoje 20 Cf 54.43N 76.43 E
Čistopol 19 Fd 55.23N 50.39 E
Čita 22 Nd 52.03N 113.30 E
Çitak 15 Mk 38.08N 29.39 E

Index Symbols

- [1] Independent Nation
- [2] State, Region
- [3] District, County
- [4] Municipality
- [5] Colony, Dependency
- Continent
- Physical Region
- Historical or Cultural Region
- Mount, Mountain
- Volcano
- Hill
- Mountains, Mountain Range
- Hills, Escarpment
- Plateau, Upland
- Pass, Gap
- Plain, Lowland
- Delta
- Salt Flat
- Valley, Canyon
- Crater, Cave
- Karst Features
- Depression
- Polder
- Desert, Dunes
- Forest, Woods
- Heath, Steppe
- Oasis
- Cape, Point
- Coast, Beach
- Cliff
- Peninsula
- Isthmus
- Sandbank
- Island
- Atoll
- Rock, Reef
- Islands, Archipelago
- Rocks, Reefs
- Coral Reef
- Well, Spring
- Geyser
- River, Stream
- Waterfall Rapids
- River Mouth, Estuary
- Lake
- Salt Lake
- Intermittent Lake
- Reservoir
- Swamp, Pond
- Canal
- Glacier
- Ice Shelf, Pack Ice
- Ocean
- Sea
- Gulf, Bay
- Strait, Fjord
- Lagoon
- Bank
- Seamount
- Tablemount
- Ridge
- Shelf
- Basin
- Escarpment, Sea Scarp
- Fracture
- Trench, Abyss
- National Park, Reserve
- Point of Interest
- Recreation Site
- Cave, Cavern
- Historic Site
- Ruins
- Wall, Walls
- Church, Abbey
- Temple
- Scientific Station
- Airport
- Port
- Lighthouse
- Mine
- Tunnel
- Dam, Bridge

Citeli-Ckaro 16 Oi 41.28N 46.06 E
Čitinskaja Oblast [3] 20 Gf 52.30N 117.30 E
Citlaltépetl, Volcán-
→ Orizaba, Pico de- 38 Jh 19.01N 97.16W
Citrusdale 37 Bf 32.36 S 19.00 E
Città del Vaticano =
Vatican City (EN) [1] 6 Hg 41.54N 12.27 E
Città di Castello 14 Gg 43.27N 12.14 E
Cittanova 14 Kl 38.21N 16.05 E
Ciucaşu, Vîrful- 15 Id 45.31N 25.55 E
Ciucea 15 Fd 46.57N 22.49 E
Ciudad 48 Gf 23.44N 105.44W
Ciudad Acuña 47 Dc 29.18N 100.55W
Ciudad Altamirano 48 Ih 18.20N 100.40W
Ciudad Bolívar 53 Je 8.08N 63.33W
Ciudad Bolivia 54 Db 8.21N 70.34W
Ciudad Camargo [Mex.] 47 Ec 26.19N 98.50W
Ciudad Camargo [Mex.] 47 Cc 27.40N 105.10W
Ciudad Cuauhtémoc 48 Mj 15.37N 92.00W
Ciudad Darío 49 Dg 12.43N 86.08W
Ciudad de Areco 55 Cl 34.18S 59.46W
Ciudad de Dolores Hidalgo 48 Ig 21.10N 100.56W
Ciudad de la Habana [3] 49 Fb 23.10N 82.10W
Ciudad del Carmen 47 Fe 18.38N 91.50W
Ciudad del Maíz 48 Jf 22.24N 99.36W
Ciudad de México = Mexico
City (EN) 39 Jh 19.24N 99.09W
Ciudad de Nutrias 54 Eb 8.07N 69.19W
Ciudad de Río Grande 47 Dd 23.50N 103.02W
Ciudadela/Ciutadella 13 Pd 40.02N 3.50 E
Ciudad Guayana 53 Je 8.22N 62.40W
Ciudad Guerrero 47 Cc 28.33N 107.30W
Ciudad Guzmán 47 De 19.41N 103.29W
Ciudad Hidalgo [Mex.] 48 Mj 14.41N 92.09W
Ciudad Hidalgo [Mex.] 48 Ih 19.41N 100.34W
Ciudad Juárez 39 If 31.44N 106.29W
Ciudad Lerdo 47 Dc 25.32N 103.32W
Ciudad Madero 39 Jg 22.16N 97.50W
Ciudad Mante 47 Ed 22.44N 98.57W
Ciudad Mendoza 48 Kh 18.48N 97.11W
Ciudad Obregón 39 Ig 27.59N 109.56W
Ciudad Ojeda 54 Da 10.12N 71.19W
Ciudad Piar 54 Fb 7.27N 63.19W
Ciudad Real 13 If 38.59N 3.56W
Ciudad Real [3] 13 If 39.00N 4.00W
Ciudad Río Bravo 47 Ec 25.59N 98.06W
Ciudad-Rodrigo 13 Fd 40.36N 6.32W
Ciudad Valles 47 Ed 21.59N 99.01W
Ciudad Victoria 39 Jg 23.44N 99.08W
Ciutadella/Ciudadela 13 Pd 40.02N 3.50 E
Civa Burnu 24 Gb 41.22N 36.35 E
Cividale del Friuli 14 Hd 46.06N 13.25 E
Civilsk 7 Li 55.53N 47.29 E
Civita Castellana 14 Gh 42.17N 12.25 E
Civitanova Marche 14 Hg 43.18N 13.44 E
Civitavecchia 14 Fh 42.06N 11.48 E
Civitella del Tronto 14 Hh 42.46N 13.40 E
Çivril 24 Cc 38.56N 35.29 E
Cixerri 14 Ck 39.17N 8.59 E
Cixi (Hushan) 28 Fi 30.10N 121.14 E
Cixian 28 Cf 36.22N 114.22 E
Čiža 19 Eb 67.06N 44.19 E
Cizre 23 Fb 37.20N 42.12 E
Cjurupinsk 16 Hf 46.37N 32.43 E
Čkalovsk 7 Kh 56.47N 43.17 E
Clacton-on-Sea 9 Oj 51.48N 1.09 E
Clain 11 Gh 46.47N 0.33 E
Claire, Côte- 66 Ie 66.30 S 133.00 E
Claire, Lake - 42 Ge 58.30N 112.00W
Clair Engle Lake 46 Df 40.52N 122.43W
Claise 11 Gh 46.56N 0.42 E
Clamecy 11 Jg 47.27N 3.31 E
Clan Alpine Mountains 46 Gg 39.40N 117.55W
Clanton 44 Di 32.50N 86.38W
Clanwilliam 37 Bf 32.11 S 18.54 E
Claraz 55 Cm 37.54 S 59.17W
Clár Chlainne Mhuiris/
Claremorris 9 Eh 53.44N 9.00W
Clare [Austl.] 59 Hf 33.50 S 138.36 E
Clare [Mi.-U.S.] 44 Ed 43.49N 84.46W
Clare/Abhainn an Chláir 9 Dh 53.20N 9.03W
Clare/An Clár [2] 9 Ei 52.50N 9.00W
Clare/Cliara 9 Dh 53.49N 10.00W
Claremont 44 Kd 43.23N 72.21W
Claremore 45 Ih 36.19N 95.36W
Claremorris/Clár Chlainne
Mhuiris 9 Eh 53.44N 9.00W
Clarence 62 Ee 42.10 S 173.57 E
Clarence 62 Ee 42.10 S 173.56 E
Clarence, Cape - 42 Ib 73.55N 90.12W
Clarence Cannon
Reservoir 45 Kg 39.31N 91.45W
Clarence Island 66 Re 61.12 S 54.05W
Clarence River 59 Ke 29.25 S 153.22 E
Clarence Strait [Ak.-U.S.] 40 Me 55.25N 132.00W
Clarence Strait [Austl.] 59 Gb 12.00 S 131.00 E
Clarence Town 49 Jb 23.06N 74.59W
Clarendon 45 Fi 34.56N 100.53W
Clarenville 42 Mg 48.09N 53.58W
Claresholm 42 Gf 50.02N 113.35W
Clarinda 45 If 40.44N 95.02W
Clarines 50 Dh 9.56N 65.10W
Clarion, Isla- 47 Be 18.22N 114.44W
Clarion Fracture Zone (EN)
3 Lh 18.00N 130.00W
Clarion River 44 He 41.07N 79.41W
Clark 45 Hd 44.53N 97.44W
Clark, Lake- 40 Id 60.15N 154.15W
Clark, Mount - 42 Fd 64.25N 124.14W
Clarkdale 46 Ii 34.46N 112.03W
Clarke Range 59 Jd 20.50 S 148.35 E
Clark Fork 38 He 48.09N 116.15W
Clark Hill Lake 44 Fi 33.50N 82.20W
Clark Mountain 46 Hi 35.32N 115.35W
Clarksburg 43 Kd 39.17N 80.21W
Clarksdale 43 Ie 34.12N 90.34W
Clarks Fork 46 Kd 45.39N 108.43W
Clark's Harbour 44 Od 43.26N 65.38W
Clarkston 46 Gc 46.30N 117.03W
Clarksville [Ar.-U.S.] 45 Ji 35.28N 93.28W
Clarksville [Tn.-U.S.] 43 Jd 36.32N 87.21W
Clarksville [Tx.-U.S.] 45 Ij 33.37N 95.03W
Claro, Rio- [Braz.] 54 Hg 19.08 S 50.40W
Claro, Rio- [Braz.] 54 Hg 15.28 S 51.45W
Clary 12 Fd 50.00N 3.24 E
Claude 45 Fi 35.07N 101.22W
Claustra/Klosters 14 Dd 46.52N 9.52 E
Clavering 41 Jd 74.20N 21.10W
Claxton 44 Gi 32.10N 81.55W
Clay Belt 38 Kd 51.50N 82.00W
Clay Center 45 Hg 39.23N 96.08W
Clay Cross 12 Aa 53.09N 1.25W
Claye Souilly 12 Ef 48.57N 2.42 E
Clayton 43 Gd 36.27N 103.11W
Clear, Cape- 9 Dj 51.26N 9.31W
Clear Boggy Creek 45 Ii 34.03N 95.47W
Clear Creek [Az.-U.S.] 46 Ji 34.59N 110.38W
Clear Creek [U.S.] 46 Ld 44.53N 106.04W
Clearfield [Pa.-U.S.] 44 He 41.02N 78.27W
Clearfield [Ut.-U.S.] 46 If 41.07N 112.01W
Clear Fork Brazos 45 Gj 33.01N 98.40W
Clear Lake 43 Cd 39.02N 122.50W
Clear Lake [Ia.-U.S.] 45 Je 43.08N 93.23W
Clear Lake [S.D.-U.S.] 45 Hd 44.45N 96.41W
Clear Lake Reservoir 46 Ef 41.52N 121.08W
Clearwater 42 Ge 56.45N 111.22W
Clearwater 43 Kf 27.58N 82.48W
Clearwater Mountains 43 Db 46.00N 115.30W
Clearwater River [Alta.-Can.]
46 Ha 52.23N 114.50W
Clearwater River [U.S.] 46 Gc 46.25N 117.02W
Cleburne 43 He 32.21N 97.23W
Clécy 12 Bf 48.55N 0.29W
Clee Hills 9 Ki 52.25N 2.35W
Cleethorpes 9 Mh 53.34N 0.02W
Clères 12 De 49.36N 1.07 E
Clerf/Clervaux 12 Id 50.03N 6.02 E
Clermont [Austl.] 59 Jd 22.49 S 147.39 E
Clermont [Fr.] 11 Ie 49.23N 2.24 E
Clermont-en-Argonne 12 He 49.06N 5.04 E
Clermont-Ferrand 6 Gf 45.47N 3.05 E
Clermont-l'Hérault 11 Jk 43.37N 3.26 E
Clervaux/Clerf 12 Id 50.03N 6.02 E
Clervé 12 Ie 49.57N 6.01 E
Cles 14 Fd 46.22N 11.02 E
Clevedon 9 Kj 51.27N 2.51W
Cleveland 9 Lg 54.25N 1.05W
Cleveland [3] 9 Mg 54.40N 1.00W
Cleveland [Ms.-U.S.] 45 Kj 33.45N 90.50W
Cleveland [Oh.-U.S.] 39 Ke 41.30N 81.41W
Cleveland [Tn.-U.S.] 43 Kd 35.10N 84.53W
Cleveland [Tx.-U.S.] 45 Ik 30.21N 95.05W
Cleveland, Mount- 43 Eb 48.56N 113.51W
Cleveland Heights 44 Ge 41.30N 81.34W
Clevelândia 55 Fh 26.24 S 52.21W
Cleveland Mountain 46 Ic 46.37N 113.47W
Clew Bay/Cuan Mó 9 Dh 53.50N 9.50W
Cliara/Clare 9 Dh 53.49N 10.00W
Cliff 45 Bj 32.59N 108.36W
Clifton [Az.-U.S.] 43 Fe 33.03N 109.18W
Clifton [St.Vin.] 51n Bb 12.36N 61.26W
Clifton [Tx.-U.S.] 45 Hk 31.47N 97.35W
Clinch River 44 Eh 35.53N 84.29W
Cline, Mount- 46 Ga 52.10N 116.40W
Clines Corners 45 Di 35.01N 105.34W
Clingmans Dome 44 Fh 35.35N 83.30W
Clinton [Ar.-U.S.] 45 Ji 35.36N 92.28W
Clinton [B.C.-Can.] 42 Ff 51.05N 121.35W
Clinton [Ia.-U.S.] 43 Ic 41.51N 90.12W
Clinton [Il.-U.S.] 45 Lf 40.09N 88.57W
Clinton [Mo.-U.S.] 45 Jg 38.22N 93.46W
Clinton [Ms.-U.S.] 45 Kj 32.20N 90.20W
Clinton [N.C.-U.S.] 44 Hh 34.59N 78.20W
Clinton [N.Z.] 62 Cg 46.13 S 169.23 E
Clinton [Ok.-U.S.] 43 Hd 35.31N 98.59W
Clinton-Colden Lake 42 Gd 63.55N 107.30W
Clintonville 45 Ld 44.37N 88.46W
Clipperton 38 Ih 10.17N 109.13W
Clipperton, Fracture Zone
(EN) 3 Mi 10.00N 115.00W
Clisson 11 Eg 47.05N 1.17W
Cloates, Point- 59 Cd 22.45 S 113.40 E
Clochán an Aifir/
Giant's Causeway 9 Gf 55.15N 6.35W
9 Gf 55.15N 6.35W
Clodomira 56 Hc 27.35 S 64.08W
Cloich na Coillte/Clonakilty 9 Ej 51.37N 8.54W
Clonakilty/Cloich na Coillte 9 Ej 51.37N 8.54W
Cloncurry 58 Fg 20.42 S 140.30 E
Clones/Cluan Eois 9 Fg 54.11N 7.14W
Clonmel/Cluain Meala 9 Fi 52.21N 7.42W
Cloppenburg 10 Ed 52.51N 8.02 E
Cloquet 43 Ib 46.43N 92.28W
Clorinda 53 Kh 25.20 S 57.40W
Cloud Peak 43 Fc 44.25N 107.10W
Clouère 11 Gh 46.26N 0.17 E
Cloverdale 46 Dg 38.48N 123.01W
Clovis [Ca.-U.S.] 46 Fh 36.49N 119.42W
Clovis [N.M.-U.S.] 39 If 34.24N 103.12W
Cluain Meala/Clonmel 9 Fi 52.21N 7.42W
Cluan Eois/Clones 9 Fg 54.11N 7.14W
Cluj [2] 15 Gc 46.49N 23.35 E
Cluj Napoca 6 If 46.46N 23.36 E
Cluny 11 Kh 46.26N 4.39 E
Cluses 11 Mh 46.04N 6.36 E
Clusone 14 De 45.53N 9.57 E
Clutha 62 Cg 46.21 S 169.48 E
Clwyd 9 Jh 53.20N 3.30W
Clwyd [3] 9 Jh 53.10N 3.15W
Clyde 9 If 55.56N 4.29W
Clyde [N.W.T.-Can.] 39 Mb 70.25N 68.30W
Clyde [N.Z.] 62 Cf 45.11 S 169.19 E
Clyde, Firth of- 9 If 55.42N 5.00W
Clyde Inlet 42 Kb 70.20N 68.20W
Cna 5 Ke 54.32N 42.05 E
Cnoc Bréanainn/Brandon
Mount 9 Ci 52.14N 10.15W
Cnoc Fola/Bloody
Foreland 9 Ef 55.09N 8.17W
Cnoc Mhaoldonn/
Knockmealdown
Mountains 9 Fi 52.15N 8.00W
Cnori 16 Ni 41.35N 45.59 E
Cnossus (EN) = Knosós 15 In 35.18N 25.10 E
Côa 13 Ec 41.05N 7.06W
Coachella Canal 46 Hj 33.34N 116.00W
Coahuayana 48 Hh 18.44N 103.41W
Coahuila [2] 47 Dc 27.20N 102.00W
Coalcomán, Sierra de- 47 De 18.30N 102.55W
Coalcomán de Matamoros 48 Hh 18.47N 103.09W
Coaldale 46 Ib 49.43N 112.37W
Coalgate 45 Hi 34.32N 96.13W
Coalinga 46 Eh 36.09N 120.21W
Coalville 9 Li 52.44N 1.20W
Coamo 49 Nd 18.05N 66.22W
Coari 54 Fd 4.05 S 63.08W
Coari, Lago de- 54 Fd 4.15 S 63.25W
Coari, Rio- 52 Jf 4.30 S 63.33W
Coast [3] 36 Gc 3.00 S 39.30 E
Coast Mountains 38 Gd 55.00N 129.00W
Coast Plain (EN) =
Kustvlakte 11 Ic 51.00N 2.30 E
Coast Ranges 38 Ge 41.00N 123.30W
Coatbridge 9 If 55.52N 4.01W
Coatepec 48 Kh 19.27N 96.58W
Coatepel, Cerro- 48 Kh 18.25N 97.35W
Coatepeque 49 Bf 14.42N 91.52W
Coats 38 Kc 62.30N 83.00W
Coats Land (EN) 66 Af 77.00 S 28.00W
Coatzacoalcos 39 Jh 18.09N 94.25W
Coatzacoalcos, Bahía- 48 Lh 18.10N 94.27W
Coatzacoalcos, Río- 48 Lh 18.09N 94.24W
Coba 47 Gd 20.36N 87.35W
Cobadin 15 Le 44.05N 28.13 E
Cobalt 42 Jg 47.24N 79.41W
Cobán 47 Fe 15.29N 90.19W
Cobar 59 Jf 31.30 S 145.49 E
Cobb, Mount- 46 Dg 38.45N 122.40W
Cobb Seamount (EN) 38 Fe 46.46N 130.43W
Cóbh/An Cóbh 9 Ej 51.51N 8.17W
Cobija 54 Ef 11.02 S 68.44W
Cobo 55 Dm 37.48 S 57.38W
Cobourg 42 Jh 43.58N 78.10W
Cobourg Peninsula 59 Gb 11.20 S 132.15 E
Cóbuè 37 Eb 12.07 S 34.52 E
Coburg 42 Ja 75.57N 79.00W
Coburn Mountain 44 Lc 45.28N 70.06W
Coca, Pizzo di- 14 Ed 46.04N 10.01 E
Cocalinho 55 Gb 14.22 S 51.00W
Cocentaina 13 Lf 38.45N 0.26W
Cochabamba [2] 54 Eg 17.30 S 65.40W
Cochabamba 53 Jg 17.24 S 66.09W
Coche, Isla- 50 Eg 10.47N 63.56W
Cochem 10 Df 50.08N 7.09 E
Cochin 22 Ji 9.58N 76.14 E
Cochin China (EN) = Nam
Phan 21 Mg 11.00N 107.00 E
Cochinos, Bahía de- = Pigs,
Bay of- (EN) 49 Gb 22.07N 81.10W
Cochons, Ile aux- 30 Mm 46.05 S 50.08 E
Cochran 44 Fi 32.23N 83.21W
Cochrane 42 He 57.55N 101.32W
Cochrane [Alta.-Can.] 46 Ha 51.11N 114.28W
Cochrane [Ont.-Can.] 39 Ke 49.04N 81.01W
Cockburn, Canal- 56 Fh 54.20 S 71.30W
Cockburn, Mount- 59 Gd 22.46 S 130.36 E
Cockburn Bank 9 El 49.40N 8.50W
Cockburn Island 44 Fc 45.55N 83.22W
Cockburn Town 49 Ja 24.02N 74.31W
Cockermouth 9 Jg 54.40N 3.21W
Coclé [3] 49 Gi 8.30N 80.15W
Coco, Cayo- 49 Hb 22.30N 78.28W
Coco, Ile- 51b Bc 17.52N 62.49W
Coco, Isla del- 38 Ki 5.32N 87.04W
Coco, Río-o Segovia, Río- 38 Kh 15.00N 83.08W
Cocoa 43 Kf 28.21N 80.44W
Cocoa Beach 44 Gk 28.19N 80.36W
Cocoa Point 51d Ba 17.33N 61.46W
Cocobeach 36 Ab 0.59N 9.36 E
Coco Channel 25 If 14.00N 93.00 E
Coco Islands 25 If 14.05N 93.18 E
Coconino Plateau 46 Ii 35.50N 112.30W
Cocorocuma, Cayos- 49 Ff 15.45N 83.00W
Cocos 64c Bb 13.14N 144.39 E
Côcos 55 Jb 14.10 S 44.33W
Cocos Islands (Keeling
Islands) 21 Lk 12.10 S 96.55 E
Cocos Islands (Keeling
Islands) [5] 22 Lk 12.10 S 96.55 E
Cocos Ridge (EN) 3 Ni 5.30N 86.00W
Cocula 48 Hg 20.23N 103.50W
Cocuzzo 14 Kk 39.13N 16.08 E
Cod, Cape- 44 Me 41.50N 70.00W
Cod, Cape- 38 Le 41.42N 70.15W
Coda Cavallo, Capo- 14 Dj 40.51N 9.43 E
Codaeştî 15 Kc 46.52N 27.45 E
Codajás 54 Fd 3.50 S 62.05W
Codera, Cabo- 50 Cg 10.35N 66.04W
Codfish Island 62 Bg 46.45 S 167.40 E
Codigoro 14 Gf 44.49N 12.08 E
Codlea 15 Id 45.42N 25.27 E
Codó 54 Jd 4.29 S 43.53W
Codogno 14 De 45.09N 9.42 E
Codrington 50 Fd 17.38N 61.50W
Codrington Lagoon 51d Ba 17.39N 61.51W
Codrului, Munţii- 15 Fc 46.35N 22.10 E
Cody 43 Fc 44.32N 109.05W
Coen 58 Ff 13.56 S 143.12 E
Coesfeld 10 De 51.56N 7.09 E
Coetivy Island 30 Mi 7.08 S 56.16 E
Coeur d'Alene 43 Db 47.41N 116.46W
Coevorden 11 Mb 52.40N 6.45 E
Coffeyville 45 Ih 37.02N 95.37W
Coffs Harbour 58 Gh 30.18 S 153.08 E
Cofre de Perote, Cerro-
(Nauhcampatépetl) 48 Kh 19.29N 97.08W
Cofrentes 13 Ke 39.14N 1.04W
Coggeshall 12 Cc 51.52N 0.41 E
Coghinas 14 Cj 40.56N 8.48 E
Coghinas, Lago del- 14 Dj 40.45N 9.05 E
Coglians 14 Gd 46.37N 12.53 E
Cognac 11 Fi 45.42N 0.20W
Cogne 14 Be 45.37N 7.21 E
Cogolludo 13 Id 40.57N 3.05W
Čograjskoje
Vodohranilišče 16 Ng 45.30N 44.30 E
Coiba, Isla de- 47 Hg 7.27N 81.45W
Coig, Río- (Coyle) 56 Gh 50.58 S 69.11W
Coihaique 56 Fg 45.34 S 72.04W
Coimbatore 22 Jh 11.00N 76.58 E
Coimbra [2] 13 Dd 40.12N 8.25W
Coimbra [Braz.] 55 Dd 19.55 S 57.47W
Coimbra [Port.] 6 Fg 40.12N 8.25W
Coín 13 Hh 36.40N 4.45W
Coipasa, Salar de- 54 Eg 19.30 S 68.10W
Čojbalsan 22 Ne 48.04N 114.30 E
Cojedes 50 Bh 9.37N 68.55W
Cojedes [2] 54 Eb 9.20N 68.20W
Cojedes, Río- 50 Bh 8.44N 68.15W
Cojutepeque 49 Cg 13.43N 88.56W
Čoka 15 Dd 45.56N 20.09 E
Cokeville 46 Je 42.05N 110.55W
Cokover River 59 Ed 20.40 S 120.45 E
Čokurdah 20 Jb 70.38N 147.55 E
Colac [Austl.] 59 Ig 38.20 S 143.35 E
Colac [N.Z.] 62 Bg 46.22 S 167.53 E
Colatina 53 Lg 19.32 S 40.37W
Colbeck, Cape- 66 Mf 77.06 S 157.48W
Colbitz-Letzlinger Heide 10 Hd 52.27N 11.35 E
Colby 45 Fg 39.24N 101.03W
Colchester 9 Nj 51.54N 0.54 E
Cold Bay 40 Ge 55.11N 162.30W
Cold Lake 42 Gf 54.27N 110.10W
Coldstream 9 Kf 55.39N 2.15W
Coldwater [Ks.-U.S.] 45 Gh 37.16N 99.19W
Coldwater [Mi.-U.S.] 44 Ee 41.57N 85.00W
Colebrook 44 Lc 44.53N 71.30W
Coleman 45 Gk 31.50N 99.26W
Coleman River 59 Ic 15.06 S 141.38 E
Coleraine/Cúil Raithin 9 Gf 55.08N 6.40W
Coleridge, Lake- 62 De 43.20 S 171.30 E
Coles, Punta- 54 Dg 17.42 S 71.23W
Colesberg 37 Df 30.45 S 25.05 E
Colfax [La.-U.S.] 45 Jk 31.31N 92.42W
Colfax [Wa.-U.S.] 46 Gc 46.53N 117.22W
Colfontaine 12 Fd 50.25N 3.50 E
Colhué Huapí, Lago- 56 Gg 45.30 S 68.48W
Colibaşi 15 He 44.56N 24.54 E
Colibris, Pointe des- 51e Bb 16.17N 61.06W
Colima [2] 47 De 19.10N 104.00W
Colima 39 Ih 19.14N 103.43W
Colima, Nevado de- 38 Ih 19.33N 103.38W
Colinas 55 Hb 14.12S 48.03W
Coll 9 Ge 56.40N 6.35W
Collado Bajo 13 Kd 40.14N 1.50W
Collarada 13 Lb 42.43N 0.29W
Colle di Val d'Elsa 14 Fg 43.25N 11.07 E
Colleferro 14 Gi 41.44N 12.59 E
College 40 Jd 64.51N 147.47W
College Place 46 Fc 46.03N 118.23W
College Station 45 Hk 30.37N 96.21W
Collegno 14 Be 45.05N 7.34 E
Collie 59 Df 33.21 S 116.09 E
Collier Bay 59 Ec 16.10 S 124.15 E
Collierville 44 Ch 35.03N 89.40W
Collingwood [N.Z.] 61 Dh 40.41 S 172.41 E
Collingwood [Ont.-Can.] 44 Gc 44.29N 80.13W
Collinson Peninsula 42 Hb 70.00N 101.10W
Collinsville 59 Jd 20.34 S 147.51 E
Collmberg 10 Je 51.15N 13.02 E
Colmar 11 Nf 48.05N 7.22 E
Colmena 55 Bi 28.45 S 60.06W
Colmenar 13 Hh 36.54N 4.20W
Colmenar Viejo 13 Id 40.40N 3.46W
Colne 12 Cc 51.51N 0.59 E
Colne Point 12 Dc 51.46N 1.03 E
Colnett, Punta- 48 Ab 31.00N 116.20W
Cologne (EN) = Köln 6 Ge 50.56N 6.57 E
Colombia [2] 53 Ie 4.00N 72.00W
Colombia 55 He 20.10 S 48.40W
Colombian Basin (EN) 38 Lh 13.00N 76.00W
Colombier, Pointe à- 51b Bc 17.55N 62.53W
Colombo 22 Ji 6.56N 79.51 E
Colón [Arg.] 56 Hd 33.53 S 61.07W
Colón [Arg.] 56 Id 32.13 S 58.08W
Colón [Cuba] 47 Hd 22.43N 80.54W
Colón [Hond.] [3] 49 Ef 15.20N 84.30W
Colón [Pan.] [3] 49 Hi 9.30N 79.15W
Colón [Pan.] 39 Li 9.22N 79.54W
Colón [Ur.] 55 Ek 33.53 S 54.43W
Colon, Archipiélago de-/
Galápagos, Islas- =
Galapagos Islands (EN) 52 Gf 0.30 S 90.30W
Colón, Montañas de- 49 Ef 14.55N 84.45W
Colona 59 Gf 31.38 S 132.05 E
Colonarie 51n Ba 13.14N 61.08W
Colonarie 51n Ba 13.14N 61.08W
Colonel Hill 49 Jb 22.52N 74.15W
Colonia [2] 55 Dl 34.10 S 57.30W
Colonia 60 Bf 9.31N 138.08 E
Colonia agrícola de Turén 50 Bh 9.15N 69.05W
Colonia Carlos Pellegrini 55 Di 28.32 S 57.10W
Colonia del Sacramento 56 Id 34.28 S 57.51W
Colonia Elisa 55 Ch 26.56 S 59.32W
Colonia Juaréz 48 Eb 30.19N 108.05W
Colonia Las Heras 56 Gg 46.33 S 68.57W
Colonia Lavalleja 56 Id 31.06 S 57.01W
Colonial Heights 44 Ig 37.15N 77.25W
Colonia Morelos 48 Eb 30.50N 109.10W
Colonne, Capo- 14 Lk 39.02N 17.12 E
Colonsay 9 Ge 56.05N 6.10W
Colorado 49 Fh 10.46N 83.35W
Colorado [2] 43 Fd 39.30N 105.30W
Colorado, Cerro- 48 Bb 31.31N 115.31W
Colorado, Río- [Arg.] 52 Ji 39.50 S 62.08W
Colorado, Río- [N.Amer.] 38 Hf 31.45N 114.40W
Colorado City 45 Fj 32.24N 100.52W
Colorado Plateau 38 Hf 36.30N 118.00W
Colorado River [N.Amer.] 38 Hf 31.45N 114.40W
Colorado River [U.S.] 38 Jg 28.36N 95.58W
Colorados, Archipiélago de
los- 49 Eb 22.36N 84.20W
Colorado Springs 39 If 38.50N 104.49W
Colotlán 48 Hf 22.03N 103.16W
Colpon-Ata 18 Kc 42.39N 77.06 E
Coltishall 12 Db 52.44N 1.22 E
Colui 36 Cf 15.10 S 16.40 E
Columbia 38 Ge 46.15N 124.05W
Columbia [Ky.-U.S.] 44 Eg 37.06N 85.18W
Columbia [Mo.-U.S.] 43 Id 38.57N 92.20W
Columbia [Ms.-U.S.] 45 Lk 31.15N 89.56W
Columbia [Pa.-U.S.] 44 Ie 40.02N 76.30W
Columbia [S.C.-U.S.] 39 Kf 34.00N 81.03W
Columbia [Tn.-U.S.] 44 Dh 35.37N 87.02W
Columbia, Cape- 38 La 83.08N 70.35W
Columbia, Mount- 38 Hd 57.00N 117.00W
Columbia Basin 43 Db 46.45N 119.05W
Columbia Falls 46 Hb 48.23N 114.11W
Columbia Mountains 38 Hd 52.00N 119.00W
Columbia Plateau 38 He 44.00N 117.30W
Columbia Seamount (EN) 54 Lh 20.40 S 31.30W
Columbine, Cape- 30 Il 32.49 S 17.51 E
Columbretes, Islas-/
Columbrets, Els- 13 Me 39.52N 0.40 E
Columbrets, Els-/
Columbretes, Islas- 13 Me 39.52N 0.40 E
Columbus [Ga.-U.S.] 39 Kf 32.29N 84.59W
Columbus [In.-U.S.] 43 Jd 39.13N 85.55W
Columbus [Ks.-U.S.] 45 Ih 37.10N 94.50W
Columbus [Ms.-U.S.] 43 Je 33.30N 88.25W
Columbus [Mt.-U.S.] 46 Kd 45.38N 109.15W
Columbus [Nb.-U.S.] 43 Hc 41.25N 97.22W
Columbus [N.M.-U.S.] 45 Ck 31.50N 107.38W
Columbus [Oh.-U.S.] 39 Kf 39.57N 83.00W
Columbus [Tx.-U.S.] 45 Hl 29.42N 96.33W
Columbus Point 49 Ja 24.08N 75.16W
Colville 38 Dc 70.25N 150.30W
Colville, Cape- 62 Fb 36.28 S 175.21 E
Colville Channel 62 Fb 36.25 S 175.30 E
Colville Lake 42 Ec 67.10N 126.00W
Colville Lake 42 Ec 67.06N 126.00W
Col Visentin 14 Gd 46.05N 12.20 E
Colwyn Bay 9 Jh 53.18N 3.43W
Coma 35 Fd 8.27N 36.55 E
Comacchio 14 Gf 44.42N 12.11 E
Comacchio, Valli di- 14 Gf 44.40N 12.05 E
Comai (Damxoi) 27 Ff 28.26N 91.32 E
Comala 48 Hh 19.19N 103.45W
Comalcalco 47 Fe 18.16N 93.13W
Coman, Mount- 66 Qf 73.49 S 64.18W
Comanche [Mt.-U.S.] 46 Kc 46.02N 108.54W
Comanche [Tx.-U.S.] 45 Gk 31.54N 98.36W
Comandante Fontana 55 Cg 25.20 S 59.41W
Comandău 15 Jd 45.46N 26.16 E
Comăneşti 15 Jc 46.25N 26.26 E
Comayagua 47 Gf 14.25N 87.37W
Comayagua [3] 49 Df 14.30N 87.40W
Combarbala 56 Fd 31.11 S 71.02W
Combeaufontaine 11 Lg 47.43N 5.53 E
Combermere Bay 25 Ie 19.37N 93.34 E
Comblain-au-Pont 12 Hd 50.28N 5.35 E
Combles 12 Ed 50.01N 2.52 E
Combourg 11 Ef 48.25N 1.45W
Combraille 11 Jh 46.30N 3.10 E
Combrailles 11 Ih 46.15N 2.10 E
Comedero 48 Fe 24.37N 106.46W
Comendador 49 Ld 18.53N 71.42W
Comeragh Mountains/Na
Comaraigh 9 Fi 52.13N 7.35W
Comerío 51a Bb 18.13N 66.16W
Comilla 25 Id 23.27N 91.12 E
Comines 12 Fd 50.46N 3.01 E
Comines/Komen 12 Ed 50.46N 2.59 E
Comino 14 In 36.00N 14.20 E
Comino, Capo- 14 Dj 40.32N 9.49 E
Comiso 14 In 36.56N 14.36 E
Comitán de Dominguez 47 Fe 16.15N 92.08W
Commentry 11 Ih 46.17N 2.45 E
Commerce 45 Ij 33.15N 95.54W
Commercy 11 Lf 48.45N 5.35 E
Commiges 11 Gk 43.15N 0.45 E
Committee Bay 38 Kc 68.30N 86.30W
Commonwealth Bay 66 Je 66.54 S 142.40 E
Communism Peak (EN) =
Kommunizma, Pik- 21 Jf 38.57N 72.08 E
Como [China] 27 Ee 33.26N 85.21 E
Como [It.] 14 De 45.47N 9.05 E
Como, Lago di- 14 Dd 46.00N 9.15 E
Comodoro 55 Bl 35.19 S 60.31W
Comodoro Ravadavia 53 Jj 45.50 S 67.30W
Comondú 47 Bc 26.03N 111.46W
Comores/Comoros [1] 31 Lj 12.10 S 44.10 E
Comores, Archipel des- =
Comoro Islands (EN) 30 Lj 12.10 S 44.15 E
Comorin, Cape- 21 Ji 8.04N 77.34 E
Comoro Islands (EN) =
Comores, Archipel des- 30 Lj 12.10 S 44.15 E
Comoros/Comores [1] 31 Lj 12.10 S 44.10 E
Comox 46 Cb 49.40N 124.55W
Compiègne 11 Ie 49.25N 2.50 E
Compostela 47 Dd 21.14N 104.55W
Comprida, Ilha- 55 Ig 24.50 S 47.42W
Compton 46 Fj 33.54N 118.13W
Comstock 45 Fl 29.41N 101.11W
Comtal, Causse du- 11 Ij 44.26N 2.38 E

Index Symbols

[1] Independent Nation
[2] State, Region
[3] District, County
[4] Municipality
[5] Colony, Dependency
Continent
Physical Region
Historical or Cultural Region
Mount, Mountain
Volcano
Hill
Mountains, Mountain Range
Hills, Escarpment
Plateau, Upland
Pass, Gap
Plain, Lowland
Delta
Salt Flat
Valley, Canyon
Crater, Cave
Karst Features
Depression
Polder
Desert, Dunes
Forest, Woods
Heath, Steppe
Oasis
Cape, Point
Coast, Beach
Cliff
Peninsula
Isthmus
Sandbank
Island
Atoll
Rock, Reef
Islands, Archipelago
Rocks, Reefs
Coral Reef
Well, Spring
Geyser
River, Stream
Waterfall Rapids
River Mouth, Estuary
Lake
Salt Lake
Intermittent Lake
Reservoir
Swamp, Pond
Canal
Glacier
Ice Shelf, Pack Ice
Ocean
Sea
Gulf, Bay
Strait, Fjord
Lagoon
Bank
Seamount
Tablemount
Ridge
Shelf
Basin
Escarpment, Sea Scarp
Fracture
Trench, Abyss
National Park, Reserve
Point of Interest
Recreation Site
Cave, Cavern
Historic Site
Ruins
Wall, Walls
Church, Abbey
Temple
Scientific Station
Airport
Port
Lighthouse
Mine
Tunnel
Dam, Bridge

Crest	11	Lj	44.44N	5.02 E
Crested Butte	45	Cg	38.52N	106.59W
Creston [B.C.-Can.]	46	Gb	49.06N	116.31W
Creston [Ia.-U.S.]	43	Ic	41.04N	94.22W
Crestone Peak	45	Dh	37.58N	105.36W
Crestview	43	Je	30.46N	86.34W
Creswell	44	Ih	35.52N	76.23W
Creswell Bay	42	Ib	72.40N	93.30W
Creswell Creek	59	Hc	18.10S	135.11 E
Crete	45	Hf	40.38N	96.58W
Crete (EN) = Kriti	5	Ih	35.15N	24.45 E
Crete (EN) = Kriti [2]	15	Hn	35.35N	25.00 E
Crete, Sea of- (EN) = Kritikón Pélagos	15	Hn	36.00N	25.00 E
Créteil	11	If	48.47N	2.28 E
Cretin, Cape-	60	Di	6.40S	147.52 E
Creus, Cabo de-/Creus, Cap de-	5	Gg	42.19N	3.19 E
Creus, Cap de-/Creus, Cabo de-	5	Gg	42.19N	3.19 E
Creuse [3]	11	Hh	46.05N	2.00 E
Creuse	11	Gg	47.00N	0.34 E
Creutzwald	11	Me	49.12N	6.41 E
Crevecoeur-en-Auge	12	Ce	49.07N	0.01 E
Crèvecoeur-le-Grand	12	Ee	49.36N	2.05 E
Crevillente	13	Lf	38.15N	0.48W
Crewe	9	Kh	53.05N	2.27W
Crézancy	12	Fe	49.03N	3.30 E
Criciúma	53	Lh	28.40S	49.23W
Cricket Mountains	46	Ig	38.50N	113.00W
Crieff	9	Je	56.23N	3.52W
Criel-sur-Mer	12	Dd	50.01N	1.19 E
Criel sur Mer-Mesnil Val	12	Dd	50.03N	1.20 E
Crikvenica	14	Ie	45.11N	14.42 E
Crillon	12	De	49.31N	1.56 E
Crimea (EN) = Krymski Poluostrov	5	Jf	45.00N	34.00 E
Crimean Mountains (EN) = Krymskije Gory	5	Jg	44.45N	34.30 E
Crimmitschau	10	If	50.49N	12.23 E
Criquetot-l'Esneval	12	Ce	49.39N	0.16 E
Crissolo	14	Bf	44.42N	7.09 E
Cristal, Monts de-	36	Bb	0.30N	10.30 E
Cristal, Sierra del-	49	Jc	20.33N	75.31W
Cristalândia	54	If	10.36S	49.11W
Cristalina	54	Ig	16.45S	47.36W
Cristalino, Rio-	54	Hf	12.40S	50.40W
Cristallo	14	Gd	46.34N	12.12 E
Cristóbal Colón, Pico	52	Id	10.50N	73.45W
Cristuru Secuiesc	15	Ic	46.35N	25.47 E
Crişu Alb	15	Ec	46.42N	21.16 E
Crişu Negru	15	Ec	46.42N	21.16 E
Crişu Repede	15	Dc	46.55N	20.59 E
Crixás	55	Hb	14.27S	49.58W
Crixás-Açu, Rio-	54	Hf	13.19S	50.36W
Crixás Mirim, Rio-	55	Ga	13.28S	50.36W
Crkvena Planina	15	Fg	42.48N	22.22 E
Crna Gora	15	Eg	42.16N	21.35 E
Crna Gora	15	Ce	44.05N	19.50 E
Crna Gora = Montenegro (EN) [2]	15	Cg	42.30N	19.18 E
Crna Gora = Montenegro (EN)	15	Cg	42.30N	19.18 E
Crna Reka	15	Ef	43.50N	21.55 E
Crna reka	15	Eh	41.33N	21.59 E
Crni Drim	15	Dg	42.05N	20.23 E
Crni Timok	15	Ff	43.55N	22.18 E
Črni Vrh	14	Jd	46.29N	15.14 E
Crni vrh	14	Kf	44.36N	16.30 E
Črnomelj	14	Je	45.34N	15.12 E
Croatia (EN) = Hrvatska [2]	14	Jf	45.00N	15.30 E
Croatia (EN) = Hrvatska	5	Hf	45.00N	15.30 E
Croatia (EN) = Hrvatska	14	Je	45.00N	15.30 E
Crocker, Banjaran-	26	Ge	5.40N	116.20 E
Crockett	45	Ik	31.19N	95.28W
Crocq	11	Ii	45.52N	2.22 E
Crocus Bay	51b	Ab	18.13N	63.05W
Croisette, Cap-	11	Lk	43.13N	5.20 E
Croisic, Pointe du-	11	Dg	47.17N	2.33W
Croisilles	12	Ed	50.12N	2.53 E
Croissy-sur-Celle	12	Ee	49.42N	2.11 E
Croix, Lac la-	45	Jb	48.21N	92.05W
Croix-Haute, Col de la-	11	Lj	44.43N	5.40 E
Croker, Cape-	59	Gb	10.58S	132.35 E
Croker Bay	42	Jb	74.38N	83.15W
Croker Island	59	Gb	11.10S	132.30 E
Cromarty	9	Id	57.40N	4.02W
Cromer	9	Oi	52.56N	1.18 E
Cromwell	62	Cf	45.03S	169.14 E
Crooked Island	47	Jd	22.45N	74.13W
Crooked Island Passage	47	Jd	22.55N	74.35W
Crooked River	46	Ed	44.34N	121.16W
Crookston	43	Hb	47.47N	96.37W
Crosby [Mn.-U.S.]	45	Jc	46.28N	93.57W
Crosby [N.D.-U.S.]	45	Eb	48.55N	103.18W
Cross	34	Ge	4.55N	8.15 E
Cross City	44	Fk	29.32N	83.07W
Crossett	45	Kj	33.08N	91.58W
Cross Fell	9	Kg	54.42N	2.29W
Cross Lake	42	Hf	54.47N	97.22W
Crossman Peak	46	Hi	34.32N	114.07W
Cross River [2]	34	Gd	5.40N	8.10 E
Cross Sound	40	Le	58.10N	136.30W
Crotone	14	Lk	39.05N	17.08 E
Crotto	55	Bm	36.35S	60.10W
Crouch	12	Cc	51.37N	0.53 E
Crow Agency	46	Ld	45.36N	107.27W
Crowborough	12	Cc	51.03N	0.09 E
Crow Creek	45	Df	40.23N	104.29W
Crowell	45	Gj	33.59N	99.43W
Crow Lake	45	Jb	49.12N	93.57W
Crowley	45	Jk	30.13N	92.22W
Crowley, Lake-	46	Fh	37.37N	118.44W
Crowley Ridge	45	Ki	35.45N	90.45W
Crownpoint	45	Bi	35.42N	108.07W
Crown Prince Frederik	42	Ic	70.05N	86.40W
Crowsnest Pass	42	Gg	49.00N	114.30W
Crows Nest Peak	45	Ed	44.03N	103.58W
Croydon	59	Ic	18.12S	142.14 E
Croydon, London-	9	Mj	51.23N	0.07W
Crozet, Iles-	30	Mm	46.30S	51.00 E
Crozet Basin (EN)	3	Gm	39.00S	60.00 E
Crozet Ridge (EN)	3	Fn	45.00S	45.00 E
Crozon	11	Bf	48.15N	4.29W
Crozon, Presqu'île de-	11	Bf	48.15N	4.25W
Crucero, Cerro-	48	Gg	21.41N	104.25W
Cruces	49	Gb	22.21N	80.16W
Crump Lake	46	Fe	42.17N	119.50W
Crumpton Point	51g	Ba	15.35N	61.19W
Cruz, Cabo-	47	Ie	19.51N	77.44W
Cruz Alta [Arg.]	55	Bk	33.01S	61.49W
Cruz Alta [Braz.]	53	Kh	28.39S	53.36W
Cruz del Eje	56	Hd	30.44S	64.48W
Cruzeiro do Oeste	56	Jb	23.46S	53.04W
Cruzeiro do Sul	53	If	7.38S	72.36W
Cruzen Island	66	Mf	74.47S	140.42W
Cruz Grande	48	Ji	16.44N	99.08W
Crvanj	14	Mg	43.25N	18.11 E
Crvenka	15	Cd	45.39N	19.28 E
Crystal Brook	59	Hf	33.21S	138.13 E
Crystal City [Man.-Can.]	45	Gb	49.08N	98.57W
Crystal City [Tx.-U.S.]	45	Gl	28.41N	99.50W
Crystal Falls	44	Cb	46.06N	88.20W
Crystal Springs	45	Kk	31.59N	90.21W
Csákvár	10	Oi	47.24N	18.27 E
Cserhat	10	Pi	47.55N	19.30 E
Csongrád [2]	10	Qj	46.25N	20.15 E
Csongrad	10	Qj	46.42N	20.09 E
Csorna	10	Ni	47.37N	17.15 E
ČSSR → Československá Socialistická Republika [1]	6	Hf	49.30N	17.00 E
Csurgó	10	Nj	46.16N	17.06 E
Ctesiphon	24	Kf	33.05N	44.35 E
Ču	21	Ie	45.00N	67.44 E
Ču	22	Je	43.33N	73.45 E
Cuajinicuilapa	48	Ji	16.28N	98.25W
Cuale	36	Cd	7.40S	17.01 E
Cuamba	31	Kj	14.49S	36.33 E
Cuan an Fhóid Duibh/Blacksod Bay	9	Dg	54.08N	10.00W
Cuanavale	36	Cf	15.07S	19.14 E
Cuan Bhaile Átha Cliath/Dublin Bay	9	Gh	53.20N	6.06W
Cuan Chill Ala/Killala Bay	9	Dg	54.15N	9.10W
Cuan Dhun Dealgan/Dundalk Bay	9	Gh	53.57N	6.17W
Cuan Dhún Droma/Dundrum Bay	9	Hg	54.13N	5.45W
Cuando	30	Jj	18.27S	23.32 E
Cuando-Cubango [3]	36	Df	16.00S	20.30 E
Cuan Eochaille/Youghal Harbour	9	Fj	51.52N	7.50W
Cuangar	36	Cf	17.36S	18.37 E
Cuango	30	Ii	3.14S	17.22 E
Cuango [Ang.]	36	Cd	9.07S	18.05 E
Cuango [Ang.]	36	Cd	6.17S	16.41 E
Cuan Loch Garman/Wexford Harbour	9	Gi	52.20N	6.25W
Cuan Mó/Clew Bay	9	Dh	53.50N	9.50W
Cuan na Gaillimhe/Galway Bay	5	Fe	53.10N	9.15W
Cuan na gCaorach/Sheep Haven	9	Ff	55.10N	7.52W
Cuan Phort Láirge/Waterford Harbour	9	Gi	52.10N	6.57W
Cuan Shligigh/Sligo Bay	9	Eg	54.20N	8.40W
Cuanza	30	Ii	9.19S	13.08 E
Cuanza Norte [3]	36	Bd	8.50S	14.30 E
Cuanza Sul [3]	36	Be	10.50S	14.50 E
Cuareim, Arroyo-	55	Dj	30.12S	57.36W
Cuaró	55	Dj	30.37S	56.54W
Cuaró Grande, Arroyo-	55	Dj	30.18S	57.12W
Cuarto, Río-	56	Hd	33.25S	63.02W
Cuatir	36	Cf	17.01S	18.09 E
Cuatro Ciénegas de Carranza	48	Hd	26.59N	102.05W
Cuauhtémoc	47	Cc	28.25N	106.52W
Cuautitlán	48	Jh	19.40N	99.11W
Cuay Grande	55	Di	28.40S	56.17W
Cuba	38	Lg	21.30N	80.00W
Cuba [1]	39	Lg	21.30N	80.00W
Cuba [Mo.-U.S.]	45	Kg	38.04N	91.24W
Cuba [N.M.-U.S.]	45	Ch	36.01N	107.04W
Cuba [Port.]	13	Ef	38.10N	7.53W
Cubabi, Cerro-	48	Cb	31.42N	112.46W
Cubagua, Isla-	50	Dg	10.49N	64.11W
Cubal	36	Be	13.03S	14.15 E
Cubal [Ang.]	36	Be	11.29S	13.48 E
Cubal [Ang.]	36	Bf	15.22S	12.39 E
Cubango	30	Jj	18.53N	22.24 E
Çubuk	24	Eb	40.59N	32.05 E
Čubukulah, Gora-	20	Kc	66.23N	153.59 E
Cucalón, Sierra de-	13	Kd	40.59N	1.10W
Cuchi	36	Ce	14.40S	16.52 E
Cuchi	30	Ij	15.28S	17.21 E
Cuchibi	36	De	15.00S	20.45 E
Cuchilla Áquila, Cerro-	48	Ig	21.27N	101.03W
Cuchivero, Río-	50	Di	7.40N	65.57W
Cuchumatanes, Sierra de los-	49	Bf	15.35N	91.25W
Cuckfield	12	Bc	51.01N	0.08W
Cuckmere	12	Cd	50.45N	0.09 E
Cucuí	54	Ec	1.12N	66.50W
Cucumbi	36	Ce	10.17S	19.03 E
Cucurpe	48	Db	30.20N	110.43W
Cúcuta	53	Ie	7.54N	72.31W
Cudahy	45	Me	42.57N	87.52W
Cudalbi	15	Kd	45.47N	27.42 E
Cuddalore	22	Jh	11.45N	79.45 E
Cuddapah	25	Ff	14.28N	78.49 E
Čudovo	19	Dd	59.08N	31.41 E
Čudskoje Ozero = Peipus, Lake- (EN)	5	Id	58.45N	27.30 E
Cue	59	De	27.25S	117.54 E
Cuebe	36	Cf	15.48S	17.30 E
Cuelei	36	Cf	15.33S	17.21 E
Cuéllar	13	Hc	41.29N	4.19W
Cuemba	36	Ce	12.09S	18.07 E
Cuenca [3]	13	Ke	40.00N	2.00W
Cuenca [Ec.]	53	If	2.53S	78.59W
Cuenca [Sp.]	13	Jd	40.04N	2.08W
Cuenca, Serranía de-	5	Fg	40.10N	1.55W
Cuencamé de Ceniceros	48	He	24.53N	103.42W
Cuera/Chur	14	Dd	46.50N	9.35 E
Cuerda del Pozo, Embalse de la-	13	Jc	41.51N	2.44W
Cuernavaca	39	Jh	18.55N	99.15W
Cuero	45	Hl	29.06N	97.18W
Cuevas del Almanzora	13	Kg	37.18N	1.53W
Cugir	15	Gd	45.50N	23.22 E
Cugo	36	Cd	7.22S	17.06 E
Čugujev	16	Je	49.50N	36.41 E
Čugujevka	28	Mb	44.08N	133.53 E
Čuhloma	19	Ed	58.47N	42.41 E
Cuiabá	53	Kg	15.35S	56.05W
Cuiabá, Rio-	52	Kg	17.05S	56.36W
Cuiabá Mirim, Rio-	55	Ec	16.20S	55.55W
Cuidado, Punta-	65d	Bb	27.08S	109.19W
Cuijk, Cuijk en Sint Agatha-	12	Hc	51.44N	5.52 E
Cuijk en Sint Agatha-Cuijk	12	Hc	51.44N	5.52 E
Cuilapa	49	Bf	14.17N	90.18W
Cuillin Hills	9	Gd	57.14N	6.15W
Cuilo	30	Ii	3.22S	17.22 E
Cúil Raithin/Coleraine	9	Gf	55.08N	6.40W
Cuiluan	27	Mb	47.39N	128.34 E
Cuima	36	Ce	13.14S	15.38 E
Cuíto	30	Jj	18.01S	20.48 E
Cuito Cuanavale	31	Ij	15.13S	19.08 E
Cuitzeo, Lago de-	48	Ih	19.55N	101.05W
Cuiuni, Rio-	54	Fd	0.45S	63.07W
Cujmir	15	Fe	44.13N	22.56 E
Čukata	15	Ih	41.50N	25.15 E
Čukotski Nacionalny okrug [3]	20	Mc	66.00N	172.30 E
Čukotski Poluostrov = Chukchi Peninsula (EN)	21	Uc	66.00N	175.00W
Čukotskoje More = Chukchi Sea (EN)	67	Bd	69.00N	171.00W
Çukurca	24	Jd	37.15N	43.37 E
Çukurdaği	15	Ll	37.58N	28.44 E
Čulakkurgan	19	Gg	43.48N	69.12 E
Culan	11	Ih	46.33N	2.21 E
Cu Lao, Hon-	25	Lf	10.30N	109.13 E
Culasi	26	Hd	11.26N	122.03 E
Culbertson	46	Mb	48.09N	104.31W
Culebra, Isla de-	49	Od	18.19N	65.17W
Culebra, Sierra de la-	13	Fc	41.55N	6.20W
Culebra Peak	45	Dh	37.06N	105.10W
Culemborg	12	Hc	51.57N	5.14 E
Culiacán, Río de-	48	Fe	24.31N	107.41W
Culiacán Rosales	39	Ig	24.48N	107.24W
Culion	26	Gd	11.50N	119.55 E
Culion	26	Hd	11.53N	120.01 E
Culiseu, Rio-	54	Hf	12.14S	53.17W
Cullera	13	Le	39.10N	0.15W
Cullman	43	Je	34.11N	86.51W
Čulman	22	Od	56.52N	124.52 E
Culpeper	44	Hf	38.28N	78.01W
Culuene, Rio-	52	Kg	12.56S	52.51W
Culukidze	16	Mh	42.18N	42.25 E
Culver, Point-	59	Ef	32.54S	124.43 E
Culverden	62	Ee	42.46S	172.51 E
Čulym	20	De	55.06N	80.58 E
Čulym	21	Kd	57.40N	83.50 E
Čulyšman	20	Df	51.20N	87.45 E
Cuma	36	Ce	12.52S	15.04 E
Cumaná	53	Jd	10.28N	64.10W
Cumanacoa	50	Eg	10.15N	63.55W
Cumaovası	15	Kk	38.15N	27.09 E
Cumbal, Volcán-	54	Cc	0.57N	77.52W
Cumberland	9	Kg	54.40N	2.50W
Cumberland	38	Kf	37.09N	88.25W
Cumberland [B.C.-Can.]	46	Cb	49.37N	125.01W
Cumberland [Md.-U.S.]	43	Ld	39.39N	78.46W
Cumberland [Va.-U.S.]	44	Hg	37.31N	78.16W
Cumberland, Cap-	63b	Cb	14.39S	166.37 E
Cumberland, Lake-	44	Eg	36.57N	84.55W
Cumberland Bay	51n	Ba	13.16N	61.17W
Cumberland Island	44	Gj	30.51N	81.27W
Cumberland Islands	59	Jd	20.40S	149.10 E
Cumberland Lake	42	Hf	54.00N	102.20W
Cumberland Peninsula	38	Mc	66.50N	64.00W
Cumberland Plateau	38	Kf	36.00N	85.00W
Cumberland Sound	38	Mc	65.10N	65.30W
Cumbernauld	9	Jf	55.58N	3.59W
Cumbre, Paso de la-/Bermejo, Paso-	52	Ii	32.50S	70.05W
Cumbria [3]	9	Kg	54.35N	2.45W
Cumbrian Mountains	9	Jg	54.30N	3.05W
Čumerna	15	Ig	42.47N	25.58 E
Čumikan	20	If	54.42N	135.19 E
Cummins	59	Hf	34.16S	135.44 E
Cumnock	9	If	55.27N	4.16W
Cumpas	48	Eb	30.02N	109.48W
Çumra	24	Ed	37.34N	32.48 E
Čumyš	20	Df	53.30N	83.10 E
Čuna	21	Ld	57.42N	95.35 E
Cunagua	49	Hb	22.05N	78.20W
Cuñapirú	55	Ej	31.32S	55.35W
Cuñapirú, Arroyo-	55	Ej	31.12S	55.31W
Cuñapirú, Cuchilla de-	55	Ej	31.12S	55.36W
Cunaviche, Río-	50	Ci	7.19N	67.11W
Cunderdin	59	Df	31.39S	117.15 E
Cundinamarca [2]	54	Db	5.00N	74.00W
Čundža	19	Hg	43.32N	79.28 E
Cunene [3]	36	Cf	16.30S	15.00 E
Cunene = Kunene (EN)	30	Ij	17.20S	11.50 E
Cuneo	14	Bf	44.23N	7.32 E
Čunja	21	Lc	61.30N	96.20 E
Cunnamulla	58	Fg	28.04S	145.41 E
Čunski [R.S.F.S.R.]	20	Ee	56.03N	99.48 E
Čunski [R.S.F.S.R.]	20	Ee	57.23N	97.40 E
Cuorgné	14	Be	45.23N	7.39 E
Čupa	19	Db	66.17N	33.01 E
Cupar	9	Je	56.19N	3.01W
Cupica, Golfo de-	54	Cb	6.35N	77.30W
Ćuprija	15	Ef	43.56N	21.22 E
Cupula, Pico-	48	De	24.47N	110.50W
Čur	7	Mh	57.11N	53.01 E
Curaçá	54	Ke	8.59S	39.54W
Curacao	52	Jd	12.11N	69.00W
Curacautín	56	Fe	38.26S	71.53W
Cura Malal, Sierra de-	55	Am	37.44S	62.16W
Curanilahue	56	Fe	37.28S	73.21W
Čurapča	20	Id	61.56N	132.18 E
Curaray, Río-	54	Dd	2.20S	74.05W
Curcúbata, Vîrful-	15	Fc	46.25N	22.35 E
Curdimurka	58	Eg	29.30S	137.10 E
Curé	55	De	21.25S	56.25W
Cure	11	Jg	47.40N	3.41 E
Curepipe	37a	Bb	20.19S	57.31 E
Curepto	56	Fe	35.05S	72.01W
Curiapo	54	Fb	8.33N	61.00W
Curicó	53	Ii	34.59S	71.14W
Curicuriari, Rio-	54	Ed	0.14S	66.48W
Curitabanos	56	Jc	27.18S	50.36W
Curitiba	53	Lh	25.25S	49.15W
Curoca	36	Bf	15.43S	11.55 E
Currais Novos	54	Ke	6.15S	36.31W
Curralinho	54	Id	1.48S	49.47W
Curral-Velho	32	Cf	15.59N	22.48W
Current River	45	Kh	36.15N	90.57W
Currie	59	Ig	39.56S	143.52 E
Curtea de Argeş	15	Hd	45.08N	24.41 E
Curtici	15	Ec	46.21N	21.18 E
Curtis	45	Ff	40.38N	100.31W
Curtis Channel	59	Kd	23.55S	152.05 E
Curtis Island	57	Jh	30.35S	178.36W
Curtis Island [Austl.]	59	Kd	23.40S	151.10 E
Curuá, Rio- [Braz.]	55	Ga	13.26S	51.24W
Curuá, Rio- [Braz.]	54	Gd	1.55S	55.07W
Curuá, Rio- [Braz.]	52	Kf	5.23S	54.22W
Curuçá	54	Id	0.43S	47.50W
Curuçá, Rio-	54	Dd	4.27S	71.23W
Curuguaty	56	Ib	24.31S	55.42W
Curuguaty, Arroyo-	55	Dg	24.06S	56.02W
Curup	26	Dg	3.28S	102.32 E
Curupira, Sierra de-	54	Fc	1.25N	64.30W
Cururupu	54	Jd	1.50S	44.52W
Curuzú Cuatiá	56	Ic	29.47S	58.03W
Curvelo	54	Jg	18.45S	44.25W
Cusco	53	Ig	13.31S	71.59W
Cushing	45	Hi	35.59N	96.46W
Cushing, Mount -	42	Ee	57.36N	126.51W
Čusovaja	5	Ld	58.13N	56.30 E
Čusovoj	19	Fd	58.17N	57.50 E
Cusset	11	Jh	46.08N	3.28 E
Cusseta	44	Ei	32.18N	84.47W
Čust	18	Hd	41.00N	71.15 E
Custer	45	Ee	43.46N	103.36W
Cutato	36	Ce	10.33S	16.48 E
Cut Bank	43	Eb	48.38N	112.20W
Cutervo	54	Ce	6.22S	78.51W
Cuthbert	44	Ej	31.46N	84.48W
Cutral Có	56	Ge	38.56S	69.14W
Cutro	14	Kk	39.02N	16.59 E
Cuttack	22	Kg	20.30N	85.50 E
Čuvašskaja ASSR [3]	19	Ed	55.30N	47.10 E
Cuvelai	36	Cf	15.40S	15.47 E
Cuvette [3]	36	Cc	0.10S	15.30 E
Cuvier Basin (EN)	59	Cd	22.00S	111.00 E
Cuvier Island	62	Fb	36.25S	175.45 E
Cuvo ou Queve	30	Ij	10.50S	13.47 E
Cuxhaven	10	Ec	53.53N	8.42 E
Cuya	56	Fa	19.07S	70.08W
Cuyahoga Falls	44	Ge	41.08N	81.55W
Cuyo Islands	26	Hd	11.04N	120.57 E
Cuyubini, Río-	50	Fh	8.20N	60.20W
Cuyuni, Río-	52	Kf	6.23N	58.41W
Cuyuni River	52	Kf	6.23N	58.41W
Cuyutlán, Laguna-	48	Gh	19.00N	104.10W
Cuzco [2]	54	Df	12.30S	72.30W
Cuzna	13	Hf	38.04N	4.41W
Cvikov	10	Kf	50.48N	14.40 E
Čvrsnica	14	Lg	43.35N	17.35 E
Cyangugu	36	Ec	2.29S	28.54 E
Cybinka	10	Kd	52.12N	14.48 E
Cyclades (EN) = Kikládhes	5	Ih	37.00N	25.10 E
Čyjyrčyk, Pereval-	18	Id	40.15N	73.20 E
Cypress Hills	38	Ie	49.40N	109.30W
Cypress Lake	46	Kb	49.28N	109.29W
Cyprus (EN) = Kıbrıs/Kypros [1]	22	Ff	35.00N	33.00 E
Cyprus (EN) = Kıbrıs/Kypros	21	Ff	35.00N	33.00 E
Cyprus (EN) = Kypros/Kıbrıs [1]	22	Ff	35.00N	33.00 E
Cyprus (EN) = Kypros/Kıbrıs	21	Ff	35.00N	33.00 E
Cyrenaica (EN) = Barqah	33	Dc	31.00N	22.30 E
Cyrenaica (EN) = Barqah	30	Je	31.00N	23.00 E
Cyrene	33	Dc	32.48N	21.59 E
Cyrus Field Bay	42	Ld	62.50N	65.00W
Cysoing	12	Fd	50.34N	3.13 E
Cythera (EN) = Kíthira	15	Fm	36.09N	23.00 E
Czaplinek	10	Mc	53.34N	16.14 E
Czarna [Pol.]	10	Pe	51.12N	19.53 E
Czarna [Pol.]	10	Rf	50.30N	21.15 E
Czarna Białostocka	10	Tc	53.18N	23.19 E
Czarna Dąbrówka	10	Nb	54.20N	17.32 E
Czarna Hańcza	10	Tc	53.50N	23.47 E
Czarnków	10	Md	52.55N	16.34 E
Czchów	10	Qg	49.50N	20.39 E
Czechoslovakia (EN) = Československo [1]	6	Hf	49.30N	17.00 E
Czechowice-Dziedzice	10	Og	49.54N	19.00 E
Czeremcha	10	Td	52.32N	23.15 E
Czersk	10	Nc	53.48N	18.00 E
Częstochowa	6	He	50.49N	19.06 E
Częstochowa [2]	10	Pf	50.50N	19.05 E
Człopa	10	Mc	53.06N	16.08 E
Człuchów	10	Nc	53.41N	17.21 E

D

Da, Sông- = Black River (EN)	21	Mg	20.17N	106.34 E
Da'an (Dalai)	27	Lb	45.35N	124.16 E
Dabaga	36	Gd	8.07S	35.55 E
Dabakala	34	Ed	8.22N	4.26W
Dabakala [3]	34	Ed	8.27N	4.28W
Daban → Bairin Youqi	27	Kc	43.30N	118.37 E
Dabas	10	Pi	47.11N	19.19 E
Daba Shan	21	Mf	32.15N	109.00 E
Dabat	35	Fc	12.58N	37.45 E
Dabay Sima	35	Gc	12.43N	42.17 E
Dabba/Daocheng	27	Hf	29.01N	100.26 E
Dabbāgh, Jabal-	23	Ed	27.52N	35.45 E
Dabeiba	54	Cb	7.02N	76.16W
Dąbie	10	Od	52.06N	18.49 E
Dabie, Jezioro-	10	Kc	53.29N	14.40 E
Dabie Shan	21	Nf	31.15N	115.00 E
Dabl, Wādī- [Sau.Ar.]	24	Gh	28.35N	39.04 E
Dabl, Wādī- [Sau.Ar.]	24	Gh	29.05N	36.14 E
Dabnou	34	Gc	14.09N	5.22 E
Dabola	34	Cc	10.45N	11.07W
Daborow	35	Hd	6.11N	48.22 E
Dabou	34	Ed	5.19N	4.23W
Dabqig → Uxin Qi	27	Id	38.27N	109.08 E
Dabraš	15	Gh	41.40N	23.50 E
Dabrowa Białostocka	10	Tc	53.40N	23.20 E
Dąbrowa Górnicza	10	Pf	50.20N	19.11 E
Dąbrowa Tarnowska	10	Qf	50.11N	21.00 E
Dabsan Hu	27	Fd	36.58N	95.00 E
Dăbuleni	15	Hf	43.48N	24.05 E
Dabus	35	Fc	10.38N	35.10 E
Dacata	35	Gd	7.16N	42.15 E
Dacca	22	Lg	23.43N	90.25 E
Dachangzhen	28	Eh	32.13N	118.44 E
Dachau	10	Hh	48.16N	11.26 E
Dachen Dao	28	Fj	28.29N	121.53 E
Dachstein	14	Hc	47.30N	13.36 E
Dacia Seamount (EN)	5	Ei	31.10N	13.42W
Dačice	10	Lg	49.05N	15.26 E
Dac Lac, Caonguyen-	25	Lf	12.50N	108.05 E
Đacovica	15	Dg	42.23N	20.26 E
Dadali	63a	Dc	8.07S	159.06 E
Dadanawa	54	Gc	2.50N	59.30W
Daday	24	Eb	41.28N	33.28 E
Dade City	44	Fk	28.22N	82.12W
Dadou	11	Hk	43.44N	1.49 E
Dādra and Nagar Haveli [3]	25	Ed	20.20N	72.50 E
Dadu	25	Dc	26.44N	67.47 E
Dadu He	21	Mg	29.32N	103.44 E
Dadukou	28	Di	30.30N	117.03 E
Dăeni	15	Le	44.50N	28.07 E
Daet	26	Hd	14.05N	122.55 E
Dafang	27	If	27.06N	105.32 E
Dafeng (Dazhongji)	28	Fh	33.11N	120.27 E
Dagana	34	Bb	16.31N	15.30W
Dagana	35	Bc	13.05N	16.00 E
Daga Post	35	Ed	9.13N	33.58 E
Dağardi	15	Lj	39.26N	29.00 E
Dagash	35	Eb	19.22N	33.24 E
Dagda	8	Lh	56.04N	27.36 E
Dagdan-Daba	27	Gb	48.20N	96.50 E
Dagéla	35	Bc	10.40N	18.26 E
Dagestanskaja [3]	19	Eg	43.00N	47.00 E
Dagestanskije Ogni	19	Eg	42.06N	48.12 E
Dagezhen → Fengning	28	Dd	41.12N	116.39 E
Dagu	28	De	38.58N	117.40 E
Daguan	27	Hf	27.48N	103.54 E
Dagu He	28	Ff	37.34N	121.17 E
Daguokui Shan	28	Jb	45.19N	129.50 E
Dagupan	26	Hc	16.03N	120.20 E
Dagxoi → Yidun	27	Ge	30.25N	99.28 E
Dagzê	27	Ff	29.41N	91.24 E
Dagzê Co	27	Ee	31.54N	87.29 E
Daheiding Shan	27	Mb	47.58N	129.10 E
Dahei He	28	Ad	40.34N	111.05 E
Da Hinggan Ling = Greater Khingan Range (EN)	21	Oe	49.00N	122.00 E
Dahlak Archipelago	30	Lg	15.40N	40.30 E
Dahlak Kebir	35	Gb	15.38N	40.11 E
Daḥl al Furayy	24	Li	26.45N	47.03 E
Dahlem	12	Id	50.23N	6.33 E
Dahlonega Plateau	44	Fh	34.30N	83.45W
Dahm, Ramlat-	33	If	16.25N	45.45 E
Dahme	10	Je	51.52N	13.26 E
Dahmouni	13	Ni	35.25N	1.29 E
Dahn	12	Je	49.09N	7.47 E
Dahomey → Bénin [1]	31	Hh	9.30N	2.15 E
Dahongliutan	27	Cd	36.00N	79.12 E
Dahra	13	Mh	36.18N	0.55 E
Dahra [Lib.]	33	Cd	29.40N	17.40 E
Dahra [Sen.]	34	Bb	15.21N	15.29W
Dahra, Massif de-	13	Oh	36.30N	2.05 E
Dahūk [3]	24	Jd	36.57N	43.00 E
Dahūk	24	Jd	36.52N	43.00 E
Dahushan	28	Gd	41.37N	122.09 E
Daḥy, Nafūd ad-	33	Ie	22.00N	45.25 E
Dai	63a	Eb	7.53S	160.37 E
Daia	15	If	44.00N	25.59 E
Daïa, Région des-	32	Hc	33.30N	3.25 E
Daicheng	28	De	38.42N	116.37 E
Daigo	28	Pf	36.46N	140.21 E
Dai Hai	28	Bd	40.31N	112.43 E
Dailekh	25	Gc	28.50N	81.44 E
Daimanji-San	29	Cc	36.15N	133.19 E
Daimiel	13	Ie	39.04N	3.37W

Index Symbols

[1] Independent Nation
[2] State, Region
[3] District, County
[4] Municipality
[5] Colony, Dependency
Continent
Physical Region
Historical or Cultural Region
Mount, Mountain
Volcano
Hill
Mountains, Mountain Range
Hills, Escarpment
Plateau, Upland
Pass, Gap
Plain, Lowland
Delta
Salt Flat
Valley, Canyon
Crater, Cave
Karst Features
Depression
Polder
Desert, Dunes
Forest, Woods
Heath, Steppe
Oasis
Cape, Point
Coast, Beach
Cliff
Peninsula
Isthmus
Sandbank
Island
Atoll
Rock, Reef
Islands, Archipelago
Rocks, Reefs
Coral Reef
Well, Spring
Geyser
River, Stream
Waterfall Rapids
River Mouth, Estuary
Lake
Salt Lake
Intermittent Lake
Reservoir
Swamp, Pond
Canal
Glacier
Ice Shelf, Pack Ice
Ocean
Sea
Gulf, Bay
Strait, Fjord
Lagoon
Bank
Seamount
Tablemount
Ridge
Shelf
Basin
Escarpment, Sea Scarp
Fracture
Trench, Abyss
National Park, Reserve
Point of Interest
Recreation Site
Cave, Cavern
Historic Site
Ruins
Wall, Walls
Church, Abbey
Temple
Scientific Station
Airport
Port
Lighthouse
Mine
Tunnel
Dam, Bridge

Index Symbols

- ⬚① Independent Nation
- ⬚② State, Region
- ⬚③ District, County
- ⬚④ Municipality
- ⬚⑤ Colony, Dependency
- Continent
- Physical Region

- Historical or Cultural Region
- Mount, Mountain
- Volcano
- Hill
- Mountains, Mountain Range
- Hills, Escarpment
- Plateau, Upland

- Pass, Gap
- Plain, Lowland
- Delta
- Salt Flat
- Valley, Canyon
- Crater, Cave
- Karst Features

- Depression
- Polder
- Desert, Dunes
- Forest, Woods
- Heath, Steppe
- Oasis
- Cape, Point

- Coast, Beach
- Cliff
- Peninsula
- Rocks, Reefs
- Coral Reef
- Sandbank
- Island

- Rock, Reef
- Islands, Archipelago
- River Mouth, Estuary
- Lake
- Salt Lake
- Intermittent Lake
- Sea
- Gulf, Bay
- Strait, Fjord
- Basin

- Waterfall Rapids
- River Mouth, Estuary
- Canal
- Glacier
- Ice Shelf, Pack Ice
- Ocean
- Ridge
- Shelf
- Swamp, Pond

- Lagoon
- Bank
- Seamount
- Tablemount
- Trench, Abyss
- Fracture
- Point of Interest
- Recreation Site
- Cave, Cavern

- Escarpment, Sea Scarp
- National Park, Reserve
- Temple
- Scientific Station
- Airport

- Historic Site
- Ruins
- Wall, Walls
- Church, Abbey

- Port
- Lighthouse
- Mine
- Tunnel
- Dam, Bridge

Index Symbols

International Map Index

Index Symbols

[1] Independent Nation	Historical or Cultural Region	Pass, Gap	Depression
[2] State, Region	Mount, Mountain	Plain, Lowland	Polder
[3] District, County	Volcano	Delta	Desert, Dunes
[4] Municipality	Hill	Salt Flat	Forest, Woods
[5] Colony, Dependency	Mountains, Mountain Range	Valley, Canyon	Heath, Steppe
Continent	Hills, Escarpment	Crater, Cave	Oasis
Physical Region	Plateau, Upland	Karst Features	Cape, Point

Coast, Beach	Rock, Reef	Waterfall Rapids	Canal
Cliff	Islands, Archipelago	River Mouth, Estuary	Glacier
Peninsula	Rocks, Reefs	Lake	Ice Shelf, Pack Ice
Isthmus	Coral Reef	Salt Lake	Ocean
Sandbank	Island	Intermittent Lake	Tablemount
Island	Atoll	Sea	Ridge
Cape, Point	River, Stream	Gulf, Bay	Shelf
Swamp, Pond		Strait, Fjord	Basin

Lagoon	Escarpment, Sea Scarp	Historic Site	Port
Bank	Fracture	Ruins	Lighthouse
Seamount	Trench, Abyss	Wall, Walls	Mine
Tablemount	National Park, Reserve	Church, Abbey	Tunnel
Ridge	Point of Interest	Temple	Dam, Bridge
Shelf	Recreation Site	Scientific Station	
Basin	Cave, Cavern	Airport	
	Well, Spring		
	Geyser		
	Reservoir		

Dragon's Mouths/Dragón, Bocas del- 54 Fa 10.45N 61.46W
Dragør 8 Ei 55.36N 12.41 E
Draguignan 11 Mk 43.32N 6.28 E
Drahanska vrchovina 10 Mg 49.30N 16.45 E
Drain 46 De 43.40N 123.19W
Drake 45 Fc 47.55N 100.23W
Drake, Estrecho de-=Drake Passage (EN) 52 Jk 58.00S 70.00W
Drakensberg 30 Jk 29.00S 29.00 E
Drake Passage (EN)=Drake, Estrecho de- 52 Jk 58.00S 70.00W
Dráma 15 Hh 41.09N 24.09 E
Drammen 6 Hd 59.44N 10.15 E
Dramselva 8 De 59.44N 10.14 E
Drangajokull 7a Aa 66.09N 22.15W
Dranse 11 Mh 46.24N 6.30 E
Drau=Drava (EN) 5 Hf 45.33N 18.55 E
Dráva=Drava (EN) 5 Hf 45.33N 18.55 E
Drava (EN)=Drau 5 Hf 45.33N 18.55 E
Drava (EN)=Dráva 5 Hf 45.33N 18.55 E
Dravograd 14 Jd 46.35N 15.01 E
Drawa 10 Ld 52.52N 15.59 E
Drawno 10 Lc 53.13N 15.45 E
Drawsko, Jezioro- 10 Mc 53.33N 16.10 E
Drawsko Pomorskie 10 Lc 53.32N 15.48 E
Drayton Valley 42 Gf 53.13N 115.00W
Drean 14 Bn 36.41N 7.45 E
Dreieich 12 Ke 50.01N 8.43 E
Drenovci 14 Mf 44.55N 18.55 E
Drenthe [3] 12 Ib 52.45N 6.30 E
Dresden [2] 10 Je 51.10N 14.00 E
Dresden 6 He 51.03N 13.45 E
Dreux 11 Hf 48.44N 1.22 E
Drevsjø 7 Cf 61.54N 12.02 E
Drezdenko 10 Ld 52.51N 15.50 E
Dričeni/Driceni 8 Lh 56.39N 27.11 E
Driceni/Dričeni 8 Lh 56.39N 27.11 E
Driffield 9 Mg 54.01N 0.26W
Driggs 46 Je 43.44N 111.14W
Drina 5 Hg 44.53N 19.21 E
Drincea 15 Fe 44.07N 22.59 E
Drin Gulf (EN)=Drinit, Gjiri i- 15 Ch 41.45N 19.28 E
Drini 5 Hg 41.45N 19.34 E
Drini i Zi 15 Dg 42.05N 20.23 E
Drinit, Gjiri i-=Drin Gulf (EN) 15 Ch 41.45N 19.28 E
Drinjača 14 Nf 44.17N 19.10 E
Drinosi 15 Di 40.17N 20.02 E
Drissa 7 Gi 55.47N 27.57 E
Drisvjaty, Ozero-/Drūkšiu Ežeras 8 Lj 55.37N 26.45 E
Driva 8 Cb 62.40N 8.34 E
Drjanovo 15 Ig 42.58N 25.28 E
Drniš 14 Kg 43.52N 16.09 E
Drøbak 7 Cg 59.39N 10.39 E
Drocea, Vîrful- 15 Fc 46.12N 22.14 E
Drogheda/Droichead Átha 9 Gh 53.43N 6.21W
Drogičin 16 Dc 52.13N 25.10 E
Drogobyč 16 Ce 49.22N 23.33 E
Drohiczyn 10 Sd 52.24N 22.41 E
Droichead Átha/Drogheda 9 Gh 53.43N 6.21W
Droichead na Bandan/Bandon 9 Ej 51.45N 8.45W
Droichead na Banna/Banbridge 9 Gg 54.21N 6.16W
Drokija 16 Ee 48.01N 27.53 E
Drôme 12 Be 49.19N 0.45W
Drôme [3] 11 Lj 44.35N 5.10 E
Drömling 10 Hd 52.29N 11.04 E
Dronero 14 Bf 44.28N 7.22 E
Dronne 11 Fi 45.02N 0.09W
Dronning Fabiola-Fjella 66 Df 71.30S 35.40 E
Dronning Louise Land 41 Jc 76.45N 24.00W
Dronten 11 Lb 52.31N 5.42 E
Dropt 11 Fj 44.35N 0.06W
Drovjanoj 20 Cb 72.25N 72.45 E
Drowning River 45 Na 50.55N 84.35W
Druja 7 Gi 55.47N 27.29 E
Drūkšiu Ežeras/Drisvjaty, Ozero- 8 Lj 55.37N 26.45 E
Druk-Yul→Bhutan [1] 22 Lg 27.30N 90.30 E
Drulingen 12 Jf 48.52N 7.11 E
Drumheller 42 Gf 51.28N 112.42W
Drummond [Mt.-U.S.] 46 Ic 46.40N 113.09W
Drummond [Wi.-U.S.] 45 Kc 46.20N 91.15W
Drummond Island 44 Fb 46.00N 83.40W
Drummond Range 59 Jd 23.30S 147.15 E
Drummondville 42 Kg 45.50N 72.20W
Drummore 9 Ig 54.42N 4.54W
Drumochter, Pass of- 9 Ie 56.50N 4.12W
Drunen 12 Hc 51.41N 5.10 E
Druskininkai/Druskininkaj 7 Fi 54.04N 24.06 E
Druskininkaj/Druskininkai 7 Fi 54.04N 24.06 E
Drut 16 Gc 53.04N 30.35 E
Druten 12 Hc 51.54N 5.38 E
Družba 16 Hc 52.02N 33.59 E
Druzba 19 If 45.18N 82.29 E
Družkovka 16 Je 48.36N 37.33 E
Družnaja Gorka 8 Ne 59.11N 30.10 E
Družnino 17 Ih 56.48N 59.29 E
Družno, Jezioro- 10 Pb 54.08N 19.30 E
Drvar 14 Kf 44.22N 16.23 E
Drvenik 14 Lg 43.09N 17.15 E
Drwęca 10 Oc 53.00N 18.42 E
Dryden 42 Ig 49.47N 92.50W
Dry Fork 46 Me 43.30N 105.24W
Drygalski Ice Tongue 66 Kf 75.24S 163.30 E
Drygalski Island 66 Ge 65.45S 92.30 E
Drysdale River 59 Fb 13.59S 126.51 E
Dry Tortugas 43 Kg 24.38N 82.55W
Drzewica 10 Qe 51.27N 20.28 E
Drzewiczka 10 Qe 51.33N 20.35 E
Dschang 34 Hd 5.27N 10.04 E
Dua 36 Db 3.20N 20.53 E
Duaca 54 Ea 10.18N 69.10W
Duancun→Wuxiang 28 Bf 36.50N 112.51 E
Duarte, Pico- 38 Lh 19.00N 71.00W
Duartina 55 Hf 22.24S 49.25W
Dubawnt 42 Hd 64.30N 100.06W
Dubawnt Lake 38 Ic 63.08N 101.30W
Ḑubay'ah, Ra's- 24 Pj 24.20N 54.09 E
Dubayy 22 Hg 25.18N 55.18 E
Dubbo 58 Fh 32.15S 148.36 E
Dübener Heide 10 Ie 51.40N 12.40 E
Dubenski 16 Td 51.29N 56.38 E
Dubh Artach 9 Ge 56.08N 6.39W
Dubica 14 Ke 45.13N 16.48 E
Dublin 43 Ke 32.32N 82.54W
Dublin/Baile Átha Cliath [2] 9 Gh 53.20N 6.15W
Dublin/Baile Átha Cliath 6 Fe 53.20N 6.15W
Dublin Bay/Cuan Bhaile Átha Cliath 9 Gh 53.20N 6.06W
Dubljany 10 Tg 49.26N 23.16 E
Dublon 64d Bb 7.23N 151.53 E
Dubna 8 Lh 56.20N 26.31 E
Dubna 19 Dd 56.47N 37.10 E
Dubnica nad Váhom 10 Oh 48.58N 18.10 E
Dubno 19 Ce 50.29N 25.46 E
Du Bois 44 He 41.06N 78.46W
Dubois [Id.-U.S.] 46 Id 44.10N 112.14W
Dubois [Wy.-U.S.] 46 Ke 43.33N 109.38W
Dubossary 16 Ff 47.17N 29.10 E
Dubovka 19 Ef 49.03N 44.50 E
Dubovoje 10 Ih 48.08N 23.59 E
Dubreka 34 Cd 9.48N 13.31W
Dubrovica 16 Ed 51.34N 26.34 E
Dubrovnik 6 Hg 42.39N 18.07 E
Dubrovno 7 Hi 54.33N 30.41 E
Dubrovnoje 19 Gd 57.58N 69.25 E
Dubuque 43 Ic 42.30N 90.41W
Dubysa 8 Ji 55.02N 23.27 E
Duc de Gloucester, Iles du-=Duke of Gloucester Islands (En) 57 Mg 20.38S 143.20W
Duchang 28 Dj 29.16N 116.11 E
Duchesne 46 Jf 40.10N 110.24W
Duchess 59 Hd 21.22S 139.52 E
Ducie Atoll 57 Og 24.40S 124.47W
Duck River 44 Dg 36.02N 87.52W
Duckwater Peak 46 Hg 38.58N 115.26W
Duclair 12 Ce 49.29N 0.53 E
Duc Lap 25 Lf 12.27N 107.38 E
Ducos 51h Bb 14.34N 60.58W
Dudelange/Düdelingen 12 Ie 49.28N 6.06 E
Duderstadt 10 Ge 51.31N 10.16 E
Dudinka 22 Kc 69.25N 86.15 E
Dudley 9 Ki 52.30N 2.05W
Ḑūdo 35 Id 9.20N 50.14 E
Dudub 35 Hd 6.55N 46.42 E
Dudune 63b Ce 21.21S 167.44 E
Dudváh 10 Ni 47.58N 17.50 E
Dudweiler, Saarbrücken- 12 Je 49.17N 7.02 E
Düdwēyn 35 Gd 9.19N 44.53 E
Dudypta 20 Db 70.55N 89.50 E
Duékoué 34 Dd 6.45N 7.21W
Dueodde 8 Fj 54.59N 15.05 E
Duerna 13 Gb 42.19N 5.54W
Duero 5 Fg 41.08N 8.40W
Dufek Coast 66 Lg 84.30S 179.00W
Duffer Peak 46 Ff 41.40N 118.44W
Duff Islands 57 He 9.50S 167.10 E
Dugi Otok 14 Ii 44.00N 15.00 E
Dugo Selo 14 Ke 45.48N 16.15 E
Du Gué, Rivière- 42 Ke 57.20N 70.46W
Duhovnickoje 16 Pc 52.29N 48.15 E
Duijan Yan 27 He 31.01N 103.28 E
Duiru→Wuchuan 27 If 28.28N 107.57 E
Duisburg 10 Ce 51.26N 6.45 E
Duitama 54 Db 5.50N 73.02W
Dujūma 36 Ge 1.14N 42.34 E
Dukagjini 15 Cg 42.18N 19.45 E
Dūkān 26 Ke 35.56N 44.58 E
Dukan, Sad ad- 24 Kd 36.10N 44.56 E
Dukat 15 Fg 42.26N 22.21 E
Duke of Gloucester Islands (EN)=Duc de Gloucester, Iles du- 57 Mg 20.38S 143.20W
Duke of York 63a Aa 4.10S 152.28 E
Duke of York Bay 42 Jc 65.25N 84.50W
Duk Fadiat 35 Ed 7.45N 31.25 E
Duk Faiwil 35 Ed 7.30N 31.29 E
Dukhān 23 Hd 25.25N 50.48 E
Dukielska, Przełecz- 10 Rg 49.25N 21.42 E
Dukku 34 Hc 10.49N 10.46 E
Dukla 10 Rg 49.34N 21.41 E
Dukou 22 Mg 26.31N 101.44 E
Dūkštas/Dukštas 8 Li 55.32N 26.28 E
Dukštas/Dūkštas 8 Li 55.32N 26.28 E
Dulan (Qagan Us) 22 Lf 36.29N 98.29 E
Dulce, Bahia- 48 Ji 16.30N 98.50W
Dulce, Golfo- 47 Hg 8.36N 83.15W
Dulce, Rio- 52 Ji 30.31S 62.32W
Dulce Nombre de Culmi 49 Ef 15.09N 85.37W
Duldurga 20 Gf 50.38N 113.35 E
Dulgalah 21 Pc 67.30N 133.20 E
Dulia 36 Db 2.57N 24.08 E
Dülmen 10 De 51.50N 7.18 E
Dulovka 8 Mg 57.27N 28.29 E
Dulovo 15 Kf 43.49N 27.09 E
Duluth 39 Je 46.47N 92.06W
Dūmā 24 Gf 33.35N 36.24 E
Dumaguete 26 He 9.18N 123.18 E
Dumai 26 Df 1.41N 101.27 E
Dumaran 26 Gd 10.33N 119.51 E
Dumaresq River 59 Ke 28.40S 150.28 E
Dumas [Ar.-U.S.] 45 Kj 33.53N 91.29W
Dumas [Tx.-U.S.] 45 Fi 35.52N 101.58W
Dumayr 24 Gf 33.38N 36.40 E
Dumbarton 9 If 55.57N 4.35W
Dumbéa 63b Cf 22.09S 166.27 E
Dumbrăveni [Rom.] 15 Jb 47.39N 26.25 E
Dumbrăveni [Rom.] 15 Hc 46.14N 24.34 E
Dumfries 9 Jf 55.04N 3.37W
Dumfries and Galloway [3] 9 Jf 55.10N 3.35W
Dumka 25 Hd 24.16N 87.15 E
Dumlupinar 15 Mk 38.52N 30.00 E
Dümmer 10 Ed 52.31N 8.19 E
Dumoine, Lac- 44 Ib 46.52N 77.52W
Dumoine, Rivière- 44 Ib 46.13N 77.50W
Dumont d'Urville 66 Je 66.40S 140.01 E
Dumont D'Urville Sea (EN) 66 Je 63.00S 140.00 E
Dumpu 58 Fe 5.52S 145.46 E
Dümrek 15 Lk 38.40N 28.24 E
Dumuhe 28 La 46.21N 133.33 E
Dumyāṭ=Damietta (EN) 31 Ke 31.25N 31.48 E
Dumyāṭ, Maṣabb- 24 Dg 31.27N 31.51 E
Duna=Danube (EN) 5 If 45.20N 29.40 E
Dunaföldvár 10 Oi 46.48N 18.56 E
Dunaharaszti 10 Pi 47.21N 19.05 E
Dunaj 20 Ih 42.57N 132.20 E
Dunaj=Danube (EN) 5 If 45.20N 29.40 E
Dunajec 10 Qf 50.15N 20.44 E
Dunajevcy 16 Ee 48.51N 26.44 E
Dunajská Streda 10 Ni 47.01N 17.38 E
Dunakeszi 10 Pi 47.38N 19.08 E
Dunántúl 10 Nj 47.00N 18.00 E
Dunărea=Danube (EN) 5 If 45.20N 29.40 E
Dunărea Veche 15 Ld 45.17N 28.02 E
Dunării, Delta-=Danube, Mouths of the- (EN) 5 If 45.30N 29.45 E
Duna-Tisza Köze 10 Pj 46.45N 19.30 E
Dunaújváros 10 Oj 46.58N 18.56 E
Dunav=Danube (EN) 5 If 45.20N 29.40 E
Dunavăţu de Jos 15 Me 44.59N 29.13 E
Dunav-Tisa-Dunav kanal 15 Dd 45.10N 20.50 E
Dunback 62 Df 45.23S 170.38 E
Dunbar 9 Kf 56.00N 2.31W
Duncan [Az.-U.S.] 46 Kj 32.43N 109.06W
Duncan [B.C.-Can.] 46 Db 48.47N 123.42W
Duncan [Ok.-U.S.] 43 He 34.30N 97.57W
Duncan Passage 25 If 11.00N 92.00 E
Duncansby Head 5 Fd 58.39N 3.01W
Dundaga 8 Jg 57.31N 22.14 E
Dundalk 44 If 39.15N 76.31W
Dundalk/Dún Dealgan 9 Gg 54.01N 6.25W
Dundalk Bay/Cuan Dhun Dealgan 9 Gh 53.57N 6.17W
Dundas [Grld.] 41 Fc 76.30N 69.00W
Dundas [Ont.-Can.] 44 Hd 43.16N 79.58W
Dundas, Lake- 59 Ef 32.35S 121.50 E
Dundas Peninsula 42 Gb 74.40N 113.00W
Dundas Strait 59 Gb 11.20S 131.35 E
Dún Dealgan/Dundalk 9 Gg 54.01N 6.25W
Dundee [S.Afr.] 37 Ee 28.12S 30.16 E
Dundee [Scot.-U.K.] 6 Fd 56.28N 3.00W
Dund Hot→Zhenglan Qi 28 Cc 42.14N 115.59 E
Dundrum Bay/Cuan Dhún Droma 9 Hg 54.13N 5.45W
Dunedin [Fl.-U.S.] 44 Fk 28.02N 82.47W
Dunedin [N.Z.] 58 Ii 45.53S 170.31 E
Dunfanaghy 9 Ff 55.11N 7.59W
Dunfermline 9 Je 56.04N 3.29W
Dungannon/Dún Geanainn 9 Gg 54.31N 6.46W
Dún Garbhán/Dungarvan 9 Fi 52.05N 7.37W
Düngarpur 25 Ed 23.50N 73.43 E
Dungarvan/Dún Garbhán 9 Fi 52.05N 7.37W
Dungas 34 Gc 13.04N 9.20 E
Dungau 10 Ih 48.45N 12.30 E
Dún Geanainn/Dungannon 9 Gg 54.31N 6.46W
Dungeness 9 Nk 50.55N 0.58 E
Dungu 36 Eb 3.42N 28.40 E
Dungu 36 Eb 3.37N 28.34 E
Dunhua 27 Mc 43.22N 128.12 E
Dunhuang 27 Fc 40.10N 94.50 E
Dunkerque 11 Ic 51.03N 2.22 E
Dunkery Beacon 9 Jj 51.11N 3.35W
Dunkirk 43 Lc 42.29N 79.21W
Dunkwa 34 Ed 5.58N 1.47W
Dún Laoghaire 9 Gh 53.17N 6.08W
Dún Mánmhai/Dunmanway 9 Dj 51.43N 9.07W
Dunmanway/Dún Mánmhai 9 Dj 51.43N 9.07W
Dunn 44 Hh 35.19N 78.37W
Dún na nGall/Donegal [2] 9 Fg 54.50N 8.00W
Dún na nGall/Donegal 9 Eg 54.39N 8.06W
Dunnellon 44 Fk 29.03N 82.28W
Dunnet Head 9 Jc 58.39N 3.23W
Dunning 45 Ff 41.50N 100.06W
Dún Pádraig/Downpatrick 9 Hg 54.20N 5.43W
Dunqulah=Dongola (EN) 31 Kg 19.10N 30.29 E
Dunqulah al Qadīmah 35 Eb 18.13N 30.45 E
Dunqunāb 35 Fa 21.06N 37.05 E
Dunqunāb, Khalīj- 35 Fa 21.05N 37.08 E
Dunrankin 44 Fa 48.39N 83.04W
Duns 9 Kf 55.47N 2.20W
Dünsberg 12 Kd 50.39N 8.35 E
Dunsmuir 46 Df 41.13N 122.16W
Dunstable 12 Bc 51.53N 0.31W
Dunstan Mountains 62 Cf 44.55S 169.30 E
Dun-sur-Auron 11 Ih 46.53N 2.34 E
Dun-sur-Meuse 12 He 49.23N 5.11 E
Duntroon 62 Df 44.51S 170.41 E
Dunvegan 9 Gd 57.26N 6.35W
Duobukur 27 La 50.19N 124.57 E
Duolun/Dolonnur 27 Kc 42.10N 116.30 E
Duong Dong 25 Kf 10.13N 103.58 E
Dupree 45 Fd 45.03N 101.36W
Duqm 22 Hh 19.41N 57.32 E
Duque de Bragança, Quedas- 30 Ii 9.05S 16.10 E
Duque de Caxias 54 Jh 22.47S 43.18W
Duque de York, Isla- 56 Eh 50.40S 75.20W
Du Quoin 45 Lg 38.01N 89.14W
Durack Range 59 Fc 17.00S 128.00 E
Durack River 59 Fc 15.33S 127.52 E
Durağan 24 Fb 41.25N 35.04 E
Durance 5 Gg 43.55N 4.44 E
Durand 45 Kd 44.38N 91.58W
Durand, Récif- 63b Df 22.02S 168.39 E
Durango [2] 47 Dd 24.50N 104.50W
Durango [Co.-U.S.] 39 If 37.16N 107.53W
Durango [Sp.] 13 Ja 43.10N 2.37W
Durañona 55 Bm 37.15S 60.31W
Durant 43 He 33.59N 96.23W
Duras 11 Gj 44.40N 0.11 E
Duratón 13 Hc 41.37N 4.07W
Durazno 56 Id 33.22S 56.31W
Durazno [2] 55 Dk 33.05S 56.05W
Durazno, Cuchilla Grande del- 55 Dk 33.15S 56.15W
Durazzo (EN)=Durresi 15 Ch 41.19N 19.26 E
Durban 31 Kk 29.55S 30.56 E
Durbe 8 Ih 56.39N 21.14 E
Durbet-Daba, Pereval- 27 Eb 49.37N 89.25 E
Ḑurbo 35 Ic 11.30N 50.18 E
Durbuy 12 Hd 50.21N 5.28 E
Đurđevac 14 Ld 46.02N 17.04 E
Düren 10 Cf 50.48N 6.29 E
Durg 25 Gd 21.11N 81.17 E
Durgapūr 25 Hd 23.30N 87.15 E
Durgen-Nur 27 Fb 47.40N 93.30 E
Durham 9 Lg 54.45N 1.45W
Durham [3] 9 Lg 54.45N 1.40W
Durham [Eng.-U.K.] 9 Lg 54.47N 1.34W
Durham [N.C.-U.S.] 43 Ld 35.59N 78.54W
Durkee 46 Gd 44.36N 117.28W
Durlas/Thurles 9 Fi 52.41N 7.49W
Ḑurmā 23 Ge 24.37N 46.08 E
Durmersheim 12 Kf 48.56N 8.16 E
Durmitor 5 Hg 43.09N 19.02 E
Durnford, Punta- 32 De 23.37N 16.00W
Durresi=Durazzo (EN) 15 Ch 41.19N 19.26 E
Durrësit, Gjiri- 15 Ch 41.16N 19.28 E
Dursey/Oiléan Baoi 9 Cj 51.36N 10.12W
Dursunbey 24 Cc 39.35N 28.38 E
Durtal 11 Fg 47.40N 0.15W
Duru→Wuchuan 27 If 28.28N 107.57 E
Duruksi 35 Hd 8.29N 45.38 E
Durusu Gölü 15 Lh 41.20N 28.38 E
Durūz, Jabal ad- 24 Gf 32.40N 36.44 E
D'Urville Island 61 Dh 40.50S 173.50 E
Dušak 18 Cf 37.15N 60.01 E
Dusa Mareb 35 Hd 5.31N 46.24 E
Dušanbe 22 If 38.35N 68.48 E
Dušeti 16 Nh 42.05N 44.42 E
Dusetos 8 Li 55.42N 26.02 E
Dushan 22 Mg 25.55N 107.36 E
Dushan Hu 28 Dg 35.06N 116.48 E
Dusios Ežeras/Dusja, Ozero- 8 Jj 54.15N 23.45 E
Dusja, Ozero-/Dusios Ežeras 8 Jj 54.15N 23.45 E
Dusky Sound 62 Bf 45.45S 166.30 E
Düsseldorf 6 Ge 51.13N 6.46 E
Dusti 18 Gf 37.22N 68.43 E
Dutch Harbor 40a Eb 53.53N 166.32W
Dutlwe 37 Cd 23.58S 23.54 E
Dutton, Mount- 46 Ig 38.01N 112.13W
Duved 8 Ea 63.24N 12.52 E
Duvergé 49 Ld 18.22N 71.31W
Düvertepe 15 Lj 39.14N 28.27 E
Duvno 14 Lg 43.43N 17.14 E
Duwayhin 23 He 24.16N 51.20 E
Duwayhin, Khawr- 24 Nj 24.20N 51.25 E
Duyfken Point 59 Ib 12.35S 141.40 E
Duyun 27 If 26.20N 107.28 E
Düz 32 Ic 33.28N 9.01 E
Düzce 23 Da 40.50N 31.10 E
Dve Mogili 15 If 43.36N 25.52 E
Dvina (EN)=Daugava 19 Cd 57.04N 24.03 E
Dvina Gulf (EN)=Dvinskaja Guba 5 Jb 65.00N 39.45 E
Dvinskaja Guba=Dvina Gulf (EN) 5 Jb 65.00N 39.45 E
Dvor 14 Ke 45.04N 16.23 E
Dvuh Cirkov, Gora- 20 Lc 67.30N 168.20 E
Dvůr Králové nad Labem 10 Lf 50.26N 15.48 E
Dwārka 25 Dd 22.14N 68.58 E
Dworshak Reservoir 46 Hc 46.45N 116.00W
Dyer, Cape- 38 Mc 66.37N 61.18W
Dyero 34 Dc 12.50N 6.30W
Dyer Plateau 66 Qf 70.45S 65.30W
Dyersburg 43 Jd 36.03N 89.23W
Dyfed [3] 9 Ji 52.05N 4.00W
Dyhtau, Gora- 16 Mh 43.05N 43.12 E
Dyje 10 Mh 48.37N 16.56 E
Dyjsko-Svratecký úval 10 Mh 48.56N 16.25 E
Dyle 12 Gd 50.57N 4.40 E
Dylewska Góra 10 Pc 53.34N 19.57 E
Dynów 10 Sg 49.49N 22.14 E
Dyr, Djebel- 14 Cn 36.13N 8.46 E
Dyrhólaey 5 Ec 63.24N 19.08W
Dysnų Ežeras/Disnaj, Ozero- 7 Gi 55.35N 26.32 E
Dytike Rodhópi 15 Hh 41.45N 24.05 E
Dzabhan 21 Le 48.54N 93.23 E
Džagdy, Hrebet- 20 If 53.40N 131.00 E
Džalagaš 19 Gf 45.05N 64.40 E
Džalal-Abad 18 Id 40.56N 73.05 E
Džalilabad 19 Eh 39.12N 48.31 E
Džalinda 20 Hf 53.31N 123.59 E
Džambejty 16 Rd 50.14N 52.38 E
Džambul [Kaz.-U.S.S.R.] 22 Je 42.54N 71.22 E
Džambul [Kaz.-U.S.S.R.] 19 Hf 47.17N 71.42 E
Džambulskaja Oblast [3] 19 Hg 44.30N 72.30 E
Dzamyn-Ud 27 Jb 43.50N 111.45 E
Džanak 16 Si 40.30N 55.35 E
Džanga 19 Fg 40.01N 53.10 E
Džankoj 19 Df 45.42N 34.22 E
Džansugurov 19 Hf 45.23N 79.29 E
Džanybek 19 Ef 49.24N 46.50 E
Dzaoudzi 31 Lj 12.47S 45.17 E
Džardžan 20 Hc 68.55N 124.05 E
Džargalant 27 Gb 47.20N 99.35 E
Dzargalant 27 Ib 48.35N 105.50 E
Džarkurgan 19 Gh 37.29N 67.25 E
Džava 16 Mh 42.24N 43.53 E
Džebariki-Haja 20 Id 62.23N 135.50 E
Džebel [Bul.] 15 Ih 41.30N 25.18 E
Džebel [Tur.-U.S.S.R.] 16 Sj 39.37N 54.18 E
Džebrail 16 Oj 39.23N 47.01 E
Dzereg 27 Fb 47.08N 92.50 E
Džergalan 18 Lc 42.33N 79.02 E
Dzermuk 16 Nj 39.48N 45.39 E
Dzeržinsk [Bye.-U.S.S.R.] 16 Ec 53.44N 27.08 E
Dzeržinsk [R.S.F.S.R.] 19 Ed 56.16N 43.32 E
Dzeržinsk [Ukr.-U.S.S.R.] 16 Je 48.22N 37.50 E
Dzeržinskaja, Gora- 8 Lk 53.53N 27.10 E
Dzeržinskoje 20 Ee 56.49N 95.18 E
Džetygara 22 Id 52.11N 61.12 E
Džetysaj 18 Gd 40.49N 68.20 E
Džezkazgan [Kaz.-U.S.S.R.] 19 Gf 47.53N 67.27 E
Džezkazgan [Kaz.-U.S.S.R.] 22 Ie 47.47N 67.46 E
Džezkazganskaja Oblast [3] 19 Gf 47.30N 70.00 E
Dzhugdzhur Range (EN)=Džugdžur, Hrebet- 21 Pd 58.00N 136.00 E
Działdówka 10 Qd 52.58N 20.05 E
Działdowo 10 Qc 53.15N 20.10 E
Działoszyce 10 Qf 50.22N 20.21 E
Dzibalchén 48 Oh 19.31N 89.45W
Dzibilchaltún 48 Og 21.05N 89.36W
Dzierzgoń 10 Pc 53.56N 19.21 E
Dzierżoniów 10 Mf 50.44N 16.39 E
Džirgatal 18 He 39.13N 71.12 E
Džizak 19 Gg 40.07N 67.52 E
Džizakskaja Oblast [3] 19 Gg 40.20N 67.40 E
Džugdžur, Hrebet-=Dzhugdzhur Range (EN) 21 Pd 58.00N 136.00 E
Džūkste/Džukste 8 Jh 56.45N 23.10 E
Džukste/Džūkste 8 Jh 56.45N 23.10 E
Džulfa 16 Nj 38.59N 45.35 E
Džuma 18 Fe 39.44N 66.39 E
Dzun-Bajan 27 Jc 44.26N 110.03 E
Dzungarian Basin (EN)=Junggar Pendi 21 Ke 45.00N 88.00 E
Dzungarian Gate (EN)=Alataw Shankou 21 Ke 45.25N 82.25 E
Dzungarian Gate (EN)=Džungarskije Vorota 21 Ke 45.25N 82.25 E
Džungarski Alatau, Hrebet- 21 Ke 45.00N 81.00 E
Džungarskije Vorota=Dzungarian Gate (EN) 21 Ke 45.25N 82.25 E
Dzun-Hara 27 Ib 48.40N 106.40 E
Dzun-Mod 27 Ib 47.50N 106.57 E
Džurak-Sal 16 Mf 47.18N 43.36 E
Džusaly 19 Gf 45.29N 64.05 E
Džvari 16 Mh 42.42N 42.02 E

E

Éadan Doire/Edenderry 9 Fh 53.21N 7.03W
Eads 45 Eg 38.29N 102.47W
Eagle 40 Kd 64.46N 141.16W
Eagle 42 Lf 53.35N 57.25W
Eagle Creek 46 La 52.22N 107.24W
Eagle Lake 44 Mb 47.02N 68.36W
Eagle Lake [Ca.-U.S.] 46 Ef 40.39N 120.44W
Eagle Lake [Me.-U.S.] 44 Mb 46.20N 69.20W
Eagle Lake [Ont.-Can.] 45 Jb 49.42N 93.13W
Eagle Mountain 45 Kc 47.54N 90.33W
Eagle Nest 45 Dh 36.35N 105.14W
Eagle Pass 43 Gf 28.43N 100.30W
Eagle Peak [Ca.-U.S.] 43 Cc 41.17N 120.12W
Eagle Peak [Tx.-U.S.] 45 Dk 30.56N 105.01W
Eagle River [Ak.-U.S.] 40 Jd 61.19N 149.34W
Eagle River [Wi.-U.S.] 45 Ld 45.55N 89.15W
Eagle Summit 40 Jc 65.30N 145.38W
Ealing, London- 12 Bc 51.30N 0.19W
Ear Falls 45 Ja 50.38N 93.13W
Earn 9 Je 56.25N 3.30W
Earn, Loch- 9 Ie 56.23N 4.10W
Earnslaw, Mount- 62 Cf 44.37S 168.25 E
Easley 44 Fh 34.50N 82.36W
East Alligator River 59 Gb 12.08S 132.42 E
East Anglia 9 Ni 52.25N 1.00 E
East Angus 44 Lc 45.29N 71.40W
East Bay [Can.] 42 Jd 64.05N 81.30W
East Bay [U.S.] 45 Ll 29.05N 89.15W
East Berlin (EN)=Berlin (Ost) [2] 10 Jd 52.30N 13.25 E
East Berlin (EN)=Berlin (Ost) 6 He 52.31N 13.24 E
Eastbourne [Eng.-U.K.] 9 Nk 50.46N 0.17 E
Eastbourne [N.Z.] 62 Fd 41.17S 174.54 E
East Caicos 49 Lc 21.41N 71.30W
East Cape [Fl.-U.S.] 44 Gm 25.07N 81.05W
East Cape [N.Z.] 57 Ih 37.41S 178.33 E
East Caroline Basin (EN) 3 Ii 4.00N 146.45 E
East Chicago 44 De 41.38N 87.27W
East China Sea (EN)=Dong Hai 21 Og 29.00N 125.00 E
East China Sea (EN)=Higashi-Shina-Kai 21 Og 29.00N 125.00 E
East Coast [2] 62 Gc 38.20S 177.50 E
East Dereham 9 Ni 52.41N 0.56 E
Eastend 46 Kb 49.31N 108.48W
East Entrance 64a Bb 7.50N 134.40 E
Easter Island (EN)=Pascua, Isla de-/Rapa Nui 57 Qg 27.07S 109.22W
Easter Island (EN)=Rapa Nui/Pascua, Isla de- 57 Qg 27.07S 109.22W
Eastern [Ghana] [3] 34 Ed 6.30N 0.30W
Eastern [Kenya] [3] 36 Gb 0.05N 38.00 E
Eastern [S.L.] [3] 34 Cd 8.15N 11.00W
Eastern [Ug.] [3] 36 Fb 1.30N 33.50 E
Eastern [Zam.] [3] 36 Fe 13.00S 32.15 E
Eastern Fields 60 Dj 10.03S 145.22 E

Index Symbols

[1] Independent Nation
[2] State, Region
[3] District, County
[4] Municipality
[5] Colony, Dependency
Continent
Physical Region
Historical or Cultural Region
Mount, Mountain
Volcano
Hill
Mountains, Mountain Range
Hills, Escarpment
Plateau, Upland
Pass, Gap
Plain, Lowland
Delta
Salt Flat
Valley, Canyon
Crater, Cave
Karst Features
Depression
Polder
Desert, Dunes
Forest, Woods
Heath, Steppe
Oasis
Cape, Point
Coast, Beach
Cliff
Peninsula
Isthmus
Sandbank
Island
Atoll
Rock, Reef
Islands, Archipelago
Rocks, Reefs
Coral Reef
Well, Spring
Geyser
River, Stream
Waterfall Rapids
River Mouth, Estuary
Lake
Salt Lake
Intermittent Lake
Reservoir
Swamp, Pond
Canal
Glacier
Ice Shelf, Pack Ice
Ocean
Sea
Gulf, Bay
Strait, Fjord
Lagoon
Bank
Seamount
Tablemount
Ridge
Shelf
Basin
Escarpment, Sea Scarp
Fracture
Trench, Abyss
National Park, Reserve
Point of Interest
Recreation Site
Cave, Cavern
Historic Site
Ruins
Wall, Walls
Church, Abbey
Temple
Scientific Station
Airport
Port
Lighthouse
Mine
Tunnel
Dam, Bridge

International Map Index

Name	Grid	Lat	Long
Eastern Ghats ⊠	21 Jh	14.00N	78.50 E
Eastern Point ►	51b Ab	18.07N	63.01W
Eastern Sayans (EN) = Vostočny Sajan ⊠	21 Ld	53.00N	97.00 E
Eastern Siberia (EN) ⊠	21 Rc	65.00N	155.00 E
Eastern Sierra Madre (EN) = Madre Oriental, Sierra- ⊠	38 Jg	22.00N	99.30W
Eastern Turkistan (EN) ⊠	21 Jf	40.00N	80.00 E
East Falkland/Soledad, Isla- ◙	52 Kk	51.45S	58.50W
East Fork ◙	45 Ie	42.41N	94.12W
East Friesland (EN) = Ostfriesland ⊠	10 Dc	53.20N	7.40 E
East Frisian Islands (EN) = Ostfriesische Inseln ◙	10 Dc	53.45N	7.25 E
East Grand Forks	45 Hc	47.56N	97.01W
East Grand Rapids	44 Ed	42.56N	85.35W
East Greenland (EN) = Østgrenland ⊠	41 Id	72.00N	35.00W
East Grinstead	9 Mj	51.08N	0.01W
East Ilsley	12 Ac	51.32N	1.17W
East Kilbride	9 If	55.46N	4.10W
East Lansing	44 Ed	42.44N	84.29W
East Las Vegas	46 Hh	36.07N	115.01W
East Leigh	9 Lk	50.58N	1.22W
East London	31 Jl	33.00S	27.55 E
East Lynn Lake ◙	44 Ff	38.05N	82.20W
Eastmain	42 Jf	52.15N	78.34W
Eastmain ◙	42 Jf	52.14N	78.31W
Eastman	44 Fi	32.12N	83.11W
East Mariana Basin (EN) ⊠	3 Jh	12.00N	153.00 E
East Midlands Airport ◙	8 Ab	52.50N	1.20W
East Novaya Zemlya Trough (EN) ◙	67 Hd	73.30N	61.00 E
Easton	44 Je	40.41N	75.13W
East Pacific Rise (EN) ⊠	3 Ml	20.00S	110.00W
East Point	44 Ei	33.40N	84.27W
East Point [B.V.I.] ►	51a Db	18.43N	64.16W
East Point [V.I.U.S.] ►	51a Dc	17.46N	64.33W
Eastport	44 Nc	44.54N	67.00W
East Pryor Mountain ▲	46 Kd	45.14N	108.30W
East Retford	9 Mh	53.19N	0.56W
East Road ◙	12 Cd	51.00N	1.02 E
East Schelde (EN) = Oosterschelde ◙	11 Jc	51.30N	4.00 E
East Scotia Basin (EN) ◙	52 Mk	57.00S	35.00W
East Siberian Sea (EN) = Vostočno Sibirskoje More ◙	67 Cd	74.00N	166.00 E
East St. Louis	43 Id	38.38N	90.05W
East Sussex ◙	9 Nk	50.55N	0.15 E
East Tavaputs Plateau ◙	46 Kg	39.45N	109.30W
East Wear Bay ◙	12 Dc	51.08N	1.18 E
Eaton	44 Ef	39.44N	84.37W
Eatonia	46 Ka	51.13N	109.23W
Eatonton	44 Fi	33.20N	83.23W
Eatonville	46 Dc	46.51N	122.17W
Eau Claire	43 Ic	44.49N	91.31W
Eau-Claire, Lac à l' - ◙	42 Ke	56.20N	74.00W
Eauripik Atoll ◙	57 Fd	6.42N	143.03 E
Eauripik Ridge (EN) ◙	60 Cg	3.00N	142.00 E
Eauze	11 Gk	43.52N	0.06 E
Ebano	48 Jf	22.13N	98.24W
Ebbegebirge ⊠	10 Dc	51.10N	7.45 E
Ebbw Vale	9 Jj	51.47N	3.12W
Ebebiyin	34 He	2.09N	11.20 E
Ebeltoft	8 Dh	56.10N	10.41 E
Ebensburg	44 He	40.28N	78.44W
Ebensee	14 Hc	47.48N	13.46 E
Eberbach	10 Eg	49.28N	8.59 E
Eber Gölü ◙	24 Dc	38.38N	31.12 E
Ebersbach	51b Kc	51.01N	14.35 E
Eberswalde	10 Jd	52.50N	13.50 E
Ebetsu	28 Pc	43.07N	141.34 E
Ebino	28 Kh	32.02N	130.47 E
Ebinur Hu ◙	21 Ke	44.55N	82.55 E
Ebla ◙	23 Eb	35.42N	36.50 E
Ebo	36 Ce	11.02S	14.40 E
Ebola ◙	36 Db	3.20N	20.57 E
Eboli	14 Jj	40.36N	15.04 E
Ebolowa	31 Ih	2.54N	11.09 E
Ebombo	36 Ed	5.42S	26.07 E
Ebon Atoll ◙	57 Hd	4.38N	168.43 E
Ebre/Ebro ◙	5 Gg	40.43N	0.54 E
Ebre, Delta de l' - /Ebro, Delta del- ◙	13 Md	40.43N	0.54 E
Ebril, Récif- ◙	61 Od	22.40S	133.30W
Ebro/Ebre ◙	5 Gg	40.43N	0.54 E
Ebro, Delta del- /Ebre, Delta de l' - ◙	13 Md	40.43N	0.54 E
Ebro, Embalse del- ◙	13 Ia	43.00N	3.58W
Ebschlob ◙	10 Ef	50.58N	8.15 E
Ecaussines	12 Gd	50.34N	4.10 E
Ecbatana ◙	24 Me	34.48N	48.30 E
Eceabat	15 Ji	40.11N	26.21 E
Echdeiría	32 Ed	27.14N	10.27W
Echegarate, Puerto de- ◙	13 Jb	42.57N	2.14W
Echeng [China]	28 Ci	30.24N	114.52 E
Echeng [China]	27 Kd	36.10N	116.03 E
Echez ◙	13 Gk	43.28N	0.02 E
Echigo-Sanmyaku ⊠	29 Fc	37.30N	139.15 E
Echizen-Misaki ►	29 Dd	35.59N	135.57 E
Echo Bay	39 Hc	66.04N	118.00W
Echo Seamount (EN) ◙	32 Dc	25.23N	19.25W
Echt	12 Ie	51.06N	5.52 E
Echternach	12 Ie	49.49N	6.25 E
Echuca	59 Jg	36.10S	144.45 E
Echzell	12 Kd	50.23N	8.52 E
Ecija	13 Gg	37.32N	5.05W
Eckernförde	10 Fb	54.28N	9.50 E
Eckerö	7 Ef	60.15N	19.35 E
Eclipse Sound ◙	42 Jb	72.40N	79.00W
Eémiadzin	19 Kg	40.09N	44.18 E
Ecommoy	11 Gg	47.50N	0.16 E
Ecos	11 Gf	49.10N	1.39 E
Ecouis	12 De	49.19N	1.26 E
Écouves, Forêt d' - ⊠	11 Gf	48.32N	0.04 E
Écrin, Barre des- ▲	11 Mj	44.55N	6.22 E
Ecuador ◙	53 If	2.00S	77.30W
Ecury-sur-Coole	12 Gf	48.54N	4.20 E
Ed	7 Cf	58.54N	11.56 E
Edam-Volendam	12 Hb	52.30N	5.03 E
Edane	8 Ee	59.38N	12.49 E
Eday ◙	9 Kb	59.11N	2.47W
Edchera	32 Ed	27.02N	13.04W
Eddrachillis Bay ◙	9 Hc	58.19N	5.15W
Eddystone Point ►	59 Jh	41.00S	148.20 E
Eddystone Rocks ◙	9 Ik	50.15N	4.10W
Eddyville	44 Cg	37.03N	88.04W
Ede [Neth.]	11 Lb	52.03N	5.40 E
Ede [Nig.]	34 Fd	7.44N	4.26 E
Edéa	31 Ih	3.48N	10.08 E
Edelény	35 Gc	13.56N	41.40 E
Edefors	7 Ec	66.13N	20.54 E
Edéia	55 Hc	17.18S	49.55W
Edeleny	10 Qh	48.18N	20.44 E
Eden ◙	5 Jg	54.57N	3.01W
Eden [Austl.]	59 Jg	37.04S	149.54 E
Eden [Tx.-U.S.]	45 Gk	31.13N	99.51W
Edenburg	37 De	29.45S	25.56 E
Edenderry/Éadan Doire	9 Fh	53.21N	7.03W
Edenkoben	12 Ke	49.17N	8.09 E
Edenton	44 Ig	36.04N	76.39W
Eder	10 Fe	51.13N	9.27 E
Edersee ◙	12 Lc	51.11N	9.03 E
Edertal	12 Lc	51.09N	9.09 E
Edewecht	12 Ja	53.08N	7.59 E
Edgar Ranges ⊠	59 Ec	18.43S	123.25 E
Edgartown	44 Le	41.23N	70.31W
Edgecumbe	62 Gb	37.58S	176.50 E
Edgeley	45 Gc	46.22N	98.43W
Edgell ◙	42 Ld	61.50N	65.00W
Edgemont	45 Ee	43.18N	103.50W
Edgeya ►	67 Jd	77.45N	22.30 E
Édhessa	15 Fi	40.48N	22.03 E
Edina	45 Jd	44.55N	93.20W
Edinburg	43 Hf	26.18N	98.10W
Edinburgh	6 Fd	55.57N	3.13W
Edinburgh, Arrecife- ◙	49 Ff	14.50N	82.39W
Edincik	24 Bb	40.20N	27.51 E
Edingen/Enghien	12 Gd	50.42N	4.02 E
Edirne	24 Bb	41.40N	26.34 E
Edisto Island ◙	44 Gi	32.35N	80.10W
Edisto River ◙	44 Gi	32.39N	80.24W
Edith, Mount- ▲	46 Jc	46.26N	111.11W
Edith Ronne Land (EN) ◙	66 Qf	78.30S	61.00W
Edjeleh	32 Id	27.42N	9.53 E
Edjereh ⊠	32 He	24.35N	4.30 E
Edjérir ◙	34 Fb	18.06N	0.50 E
Edmond	45 Hi	35.39N	97.29W
Edmonds	46 Dc	47.48N	122.22W
Edmonton	39 Hd	53.33N	113.28W
Edmundston	42 Kg	47.22N	68.20W
Edna	45 Hl	28.42N	96.39W
Edremit	23 Cb	39.35N	27.01 E
Edremit, Gulf of- (EN) = Edremit Körfezi ◙	24 Bc	39.30N	26.45 E
Edremit Körfezi = Edremit, Gulf of- (EN) ◙	24 Bc	39.30N	26.45 E
Edsbro	7 Eg	59.54N	18.29 E
Edsbruk	8 Gf	58.02N	16.28 E
Edsbyn	8 Fc	61.23N	15.49 E
Edson	42 Hf	53.35N	116.26W
Edsvalla	8 Ee	59.26N	13.13 E
Eduardo Castex	56 He	35.54S	64.18W
Eduni, Mount- ▲	42 Ed	64.08N	128.10W
Edward, Lake- ◙	30 Ji	0.25 S	29.30 E
Edward, Lake- (EN) = Rutanzige, Lac- ◙	30 Ji	0.25 S	29.30 E
Edwards Creek	59 He	28.21S	135.51 E
Edwards Plateau ◙	38 If	31.20N	101.00W
Edward VIII Bay ◙	66 Ee	66.50S	57.00 E
Edward VII Peninsula ◙	66 Mf	77.40S	155.00W
Edzo	42 Fd	62.47N	116.08W
Eeklo	11 Jc	51.11N	3.34 E
Eelde	12 Ia	53.08N	6.33 E
Eel River ◙	43 Cc	40.40N	124.20W
Eems ◙	12 Hb	52.16N	5.20 E
Eems ◙	11 Na	53.19N	7.03 E
Eemskanaal ◙	12 Ia	53.19N	6.57 E
Eenrum	12 Ia	53.23N	6.25 E
Eersel	12 Hc	51.22N	5.19 E
Eggenstein Leopoldshafen	12 Ke	49.05N	8.23 E
Eggum	7 Cb	68.19N	13.42 E
Eghezée	12 Gd	50.36N	4.56 E
Egijn-Gol ◙	27 Ha	49.24N	103.36 E
Egletons	11 Ii	45.24N	2.03 E
Eglinton ◙	42 Fa	75.45N	118.50W
Egmont, Cape- ►	61 Dg	39.17S	173.45 E
Egmont, Mount- ▲	62 Fc	39.18S	174.04 E
Egnazia	14 Lj	40.50N	17.25 E
Eğridir	24 Dd	37.52N	30.51 E
Eğridir Gölü ◙	23 Db	38.02N	30.53 E
Eğrigöz Dağ ▲	15 Mj	39.21N	29.07 E
Egtved	8 Ci	55.37N	9.18 E
Éguas ou Correntina, Rio das- ◙	55 Ja	13.26S	44.14W
Eguey ◙	30 Ig	16.10N	16.10 E
Egvekinot	22 Tc	66.19N	179.10 E
Egypt (EN) = Misr ◙	27 Jf	27.00N	30.00 E
Eha Amufu	34 Gd	6.40N	7.46 E
Ehen Hudag → Alxa Youqi	27 Hd	39.12N	101.40 E
Ehime Ken ◙	28 Lh	33.35N	132.40 E
Ehingen	10 Fh	48.17N	9.44 E
Ehrang, Trier-	12 Ie	49.49N	6.41 E
Ehrwald	14 Ec	47.24N	10.55 E
Ei	29 Bf	31.13N	130.30 E
Eiao, Île- ◙	57 Me	8.00 S	140.40W
Eibar	13 Ja	43.11N	2.28W
Eibergen	12 Ib	52.07N	6.40 E
Eichsfeld ◙	10 Ge	51.25N	10.20 E
Eichstätt	10 Hh	48.53N	11.11 E
Eickelborn, Lippetal-	12 Kc	51.39N	8.13 E
Eide	8 Eb	62.55N	7.26 E
Eider ◙	10 Eb	54.19N	8.58 E
Eiderstedt ►	10 Eb	54.22N	8.50 E
Eidet	7 Cd	64.27N	13.37 E
Eidfjord	7 Bf	60.28N	7.05 E
Eidfjorden ◙	8 Bd	60.25N	6.45 E
Eidslandet	8 Ad	60.44N	5.45 E
Eidsvåg	7 Be	62.47N	8.03 E
Eidsvoll	7 Cf	60.19N	11.14 E
Eidsvollfjellet ▲	41 Nc	79.00N	13.00 E
Eierlandse Gat ◙	12 Ga	53.12N	4.52 E
Eifel ◙	10 Cf	50.15N	6.45 E
Eiffel Flats	37 Dc	18.15S	29.59 E
Eigenbrakel/Braine-l'Alleud	12 Gd	50.41N	4.22 E
Eigeraya ►	8 Af	58.25N	5.55 E
Eigg ◙	9 Ge	56.54N	6.10W
Eight Degree Channel ◙	21 Ji	8.00N	73.00 E
Eights Coast ◙	66 Pf	73.30S	96.00W
Eighty Mile Beach ◙	59 Dc	19.45S	121.00 E
Eigrim, Jabal- ▲	35 Fb	19.22N	35.18 E
Eijsden	12 Hd	50.46N	5.42 E
Eikeren ◙	8 Ce	59.40N	10.00 E
Eikesdalsvatnet ◙	8 Bc	62.35N	8.10 E
'Eilai	35 Eb	16.33N	30.54 E
Eildon, Lake- ◙	59 Jg	37.10S	145.50 E
Eiler Rasmussen, Kap- ►	41 Kb	82.40N	20.00W
Eil Malk ◙	64a Ac	7.09N	134.22 E
Eina	8 Dd	60.38N	10.36 E
Einasleigh	59 Ic	18.31S	144.05 E
Einasleigh River ◙	59 Ic	17.30S	142.17 E
Einbeck	10 Fe	51.49N	9.52 E
Eindhoven	11 Lc	51.26N	5.28 E
Einsiedeln	14 Cc	47.08N	8.45 E
Éire/Ireland ◙	6 Fe	53.00N	8.00W
Eiríksjökull ▲	7a Bb	64.46N	20.24W
Eirunepé	53 Jf	6.40S	69.52W
Eisack/Isarco ◙	14 Fd	46.27N	11.18 E
Eisacktal/Isarco, Valle- ◙	14 Fd	46.45N	11.35 E
Eisacktal/Valle Isarco ◙	14 Fd	46.45N	11.35 E
Eisenach	10 Gf	50.59N	10.19 E
Eisenberg	10 Hf	50.58N	11.54 E
Eisenberg (Pfalz)	12 Ke	51.15N	8.50 E
Eisenberg (Pfalz)	12 Ke	49.33N	8.06 E
Eisenerz	14 Ic	47.32N	14.53 E
Eisenerzer Alpen ⊠	14 Ic	47.30N	14.40 E
Eisenhüttenstadt	10 Kd	52.10N	14.42 E
Eisenstadt	14 Kc	47.51N	16.31 E
Eisenwurzen ⊠	14 Ic	47.56N	15.02 E
Eišiškės/Ejšiškes	7 Fi	54.14N	25.02 E
Eisleben	10 He	51.32N	11.33 E
Eitorf	12 Jd	50.46N	7.27 E
Eivissa/Ibiza = Iviza (EN) ◙	5 Gg	39.00N	1.25 E
Eje, Sierra del- ⊠	13 Fb	42.20N	6.55W
Ejea de los Caballeros	13 Kb	42.08N	1.08W
Ejeda	37 Gd	24.19S	44.21 E
Ejido	54 Db	8.33N	71.14W
Ejido Insurgentes	48 De	25.12N	111.45W
Ejin Horo Qi (Altan Xiret)	27 Jd	39.31N	109.45 E
Ejin Qi	22 Me	41.50N	100.50 E
Ejšiškes/Eišiškės	7 Fi	54.14N	25.02 E
Ejura	34 Fd	7.23N	1.22W
Ejutla de Crespo	47 Ge	16.34N	96.44W
Ekalaka	46 Md	45.53N	104.33W
Ekecek Dağı ▲	24 Fc	38.39N	34.03 E
Ekenäs/Tammisaari	7 Fg	59.58N	23.26 E
Ekeren, Antwerpen-	11 Kc	51.17N	4.25 E
Eket	34 Ge	4.39N	7.56 E
Eketahuna	62 Fd	40.39S	175.44 E
Ekhinádhes Nisoi ◙	15 Ek	38.25N	21.02 E
Ekiatapski Hrebet ⊠	20 Mc	68.40N	177.50 E
Ekibastuz	19 If	51.42N	75.22 E
Ekimčan	20 If	53.07N	133.02 E
Ekoli	36 Dc	0.23S	24.16 E
Ekoln ◙	8 Fe	59.45N	17.35 E
Ekombe	34 Ge	5.55N	5.25 E
Ekonda	20 Hc	65.47N	105.17 E
Eksjö	7 Dh	57.40N	14.57 E
Ekwan ◙	42 Jf	53.12N	82.15W
Ekwan ◙	42 Je	53.12N	82.15W
El Aaiún	32 Dd	27.10N	13.12W
El Aargub	32 De	20.48N	17.04W
El Aatf ◙	34 Fa	26.45N	0.45 E
El Abadia	13 Mi	36.13N	1.40 E
El-Abd ◙	32 Hc	30.45N	5.00 E
El Abiodh Sidi Cheikh	32 Hc	32.53N	0.34 E
El 'Açaba ◙	32 Ef	16.30N	12.00W
El 'Açaba ◙	30 Fg	16.49N	12.05W
El Adeb Larache	32 Id	27.22N	8.52 E
El Affroun	13 Oh	36.28N	2.37 E
Elafónisi Channel (EN) = Elafónisos, Stenón- ◙	15 Fm	36.25N	23.00 E
Elafónisos, Stenón- = Elafónisi Channel (EN) ◙	15 Fm	36.29N	22.58 E
El Agreb	32 Ic	30.48N	5.30 E
El Aguilar	56 Gb	32.12S	65.42W
El Alamo	48 Ab	31.34N	116.02W
El Alia	32 Ic	32.42N	5.26 E
El-Amria	13 Ki	35.32N	1.01W
Elan ◙	15 Lc	46.06N	28.04 E
El Andévalo ◙	13 Fg	37.40N	7.00W
El Aouinet	14 Bo	35.52N	7.54 E
El Arahal	13 Gg	37.16N	5.33W
El Aricha	32 Gc	34.13N	1.16W
Elása ◙	15 Jn	35.17N	26.20 E
Elassón	15 Fj	39.54N	22.11 E
Elat	24 Eg	29.33N	34.57 E
Eláti ◙	15 Dk	38.43N	20.39 E
Elato Atoll ◙	57 Fd	7.28N	146.10 E
El Attaf	13 Nh	36.13N	1.40 E
Eláziğ	23 Gb	38.41N	39.14 E
El Azúcar, Presa de- ◙	48 Je	26.15N	99.00W
Elba ◙	44 Dj	31.25N	86.04W
Elba ◙	5 Gg	42.45N	10.15 E
Elban	20 If	50.05N	136.30 E
El Banco	54 Db	9.01N	73.58W
El Barco de Ávila	13 Gd	40.21N	5.31W
El Barco de Valdeorras	13 Fb	42.25N	6.59W
Elbasani	15 Dh	41.06N	20.05 E
El Baúl	54 Eb	8.57N	68.17W
El Bayadh	32 Hc	33.41N	1.01 E
Elbe ◙	5 Ge	53.50N	9.00 E
Elbe (EN) = Labe ◙	5 Ge	53.50N	9.00 E
Elbe-Lübeck-Kanal ◙	10 Gc	53.50N	10.36 E
Elbert, Mount- ▲	38 If	39.07N	106.27W
Elbe-Seitenkanal ◙	10 Gd	52.22N	10.34 E
Elbeuf	11 Gf	49.17N	1.00 E
El Bierzo ◙	13 Fb	42.40N	6.50W
Elbistan	24 Gc	38.13N	37.12 E
Elbląg ◙	10 Pb	54.10N	19.25 E
Elbląski, Kanał- ◙	10 Pc	53.43N	19.53 E
El Bolsón	56 Ff	41.58S	71.31W
El Bonillo	13 Jf	38.57N	2.32W
Elbow	46 La	51.07N	106.35W
Elbow Cays ◙	49 Gb	23.57N	80.29W
Elbow Lake	45 Id	46.00N	95.58W
Elbrus ◙	5 Kg	43.21N	42.26 E
Elbsandsteingebirge ⊠	10 Kf	50.50N	14.12 E
'Élbúr	35 Je	4.40N	46.40 E
Elburg	11 Lb	52.26N	5.50 E
El Burgo de Osma	13 Ic	41.35N	3.04W
Elburgon	36 Gc	0.18S	35.49 E
El Burro	48 Ic	29.16N	101.55W
Elburz Mountains (EN) = Alborz, Reshteh-ye Kühhā-ye- ⊠	21 Hf	36.00N	53.00 E
El Callao	54 Fb	7.21N	61.49W
El Calvario	50 Ch	8.59N	67.00W
El Campo	45 Hl	29.12N	96.16W
El Canelo	48 Ie	24.19N	100.23W
El Cârmen	55 Cd	18.49S	58.33W
El Carmen de Bolívar	54 Cb	9.43N	75.07W
El Casco	48 Ge	25.34N	104.35W
El Castillo	49 Eh	11.01N	84.24W
El Centro	43 De	32.48N	115.34W
El Cerro	54 Fg	17.31S	61.34W
El Chaparro	50 Dh	9.10N	65.01W
Elche	13 Lf	38.15N	0.42W
Elcho Island ◙	59 Hb	11.55S	135.45 E
El Cury	56 Ge	39.56S	68.20W
Elda	13 Lf	38.29N	0.47W
Éldab	35 Hd	8.48N	46.56 E
Elde ◙	10 Ic	53.17N	12.40 E
'Él Dére	35 Jd	3.55N	47.10 E
El Dere	35 Gd	5.07N	43.12 E
El Descanso	48 Aa	32.12N	116.55W
El Desemboque	47 Bb	30.30N	112.59W
El Diamante	48 Jg	9.51N	74.14W
Eldikan	20 Id	60.38N	135.17 E
El Djouf ◙	30 Gf	21.25N	6.40W
El Dorado [Ar.-U.S.]	45 Cc	1.43N	75.17W
El Dorado [Ks.-U.S.]	45 Hh	30.52N	100.36 E
El Dorado [Mex.]	47 Jc	26.24S	54.38W
El Dorado [Ar.-U.S.]	43 Ie	33.13N	92.40W
El Dorado [Ks.-U.S.]	43 Hd	37.49N	96.52W
El Dorado [Mex.]	47 Cd	24.17N	107.31W
El Dorado [Ven.]	53 Le	6.44N	61.38W
El Dorado Paulista	55 Hg	24.32S	48.06W
El Dorado Springs	45 Jh	37.52N	94.01W
El Doncello	54 Cc	1.43N	75.17W
Eldoret	36 Gb	0.31N	35.17 E
Eldsberga	8 Eh	56.36N	12.59 E
El Dubbo	35 Gb	3.52N	44.45 E
Eldzik	18 Qe	39.25N	63.01 E
Elefantes, Rio dos- ◙	37 Dd	24.03S	32.40 E
El Eglab ◙	30 Gf	26.30N	5.00W
Eléja/Eleja	7 Fh	56.28N	23.41 E
Eléja/Eleja	7 Fh	56.28N	23.41 E
Elektrénai/Elektrenai	7 Gi	54.46N	24.47 E
Elektrenai/Elektrénai	8 Kj	54.46N	24.47 E
Elektrostal	19 Dd	55.48N	38.29 E
Elele	34 Gd	5.06N	6.49 E
Elena	15 Jg	42.56N	25.53 E
El Encanto [Bol.]	54 Cc	16.57S	59.24W
El Encanto [Col.]	54 Dd	1.37S	73.13W
Elephant Butte Reservoir ◙	45 Cj	33.19N	107.10W
Elephant Island ◙	66 Rl	61.10S	55.14W
Elephant Mountain ▲	45 Ek	30.02N	103.30W
Elesbão Veloso	54 Je	6.13S	42.08W
El Escorial ◙	13 Hd	40.35N	4.10W
Eleşkirt	24 Jc	39.49N	42.40 E
El Estor	49 Cf	15.32N	89.21W
Eleuthera ◙	38 Lg	25.15N	76.20W
Elevtheroúpolis	15 Gk	38.02N	23.32 E
Elevtheroúpolis	15 Hi	40.55N	24.15 E
El Fendek	13 Gi	35.34N	5.35W
El Ferrol del Caudillo	13 Da	43.29N	8.14W
El Fud	35 Gd	7.15N	42.51 E
El Fuerte [Mex.]	48 Hf	23.50N	103.06W
El Fuerte [Mex.]	47 Cc	26.25N	108.39W
'Él Gál	8 Eb	62.09N	12.04 E
El Gassi	35 Lc	11.23N	50.23 E
El Galhak	35 Ec	11.03N	32.42 E
El Gassi	32 Ic	30.55N	5.50 E
Elgepiggen ▲	20 Kd	62.45N	150.40 E
El Ghomri	7 Ce	62.10N	11.22 E
Elgin [Il.-U.S.]	13 Mi	35.41N	0.12 E
Elgin [N.D.-U.S.]	43 Jc	42.02N	88.17W
Elgin [Or.-U.S.]	45 Fc	46.24N	101.51W
Elgin [Scot.-U.K.]	46 Gd	45.34N	117.55W
Elginski	9 Jd	57.39N	3.20W
Elgjaj	20 Gd	64.48N	141.50 E
El Goléa	20 Gd	62.28N	117.37 E
Elgon, Mont- ▲	31 Ne	30.34N	2.53 E
El Grao, Castellón de la Plana-	30 Kh	1.08N	34.33 E
El Grao, Valencia-	35 Gd	5.04N	44.22 E
El Guapo	13 Me	39.58N	0.01 E
El Guayabo	13 Le	39.27N	0.20W
El Hadjar	50 Dg	10.09N	65.58W
El Hajeb	49 Ki	6.37N	72.20W
El-Ham-	14 Bo	36.48N	7.45 E
El Hammam	32 Fc	33.42N	5.22W
El Hank ◙	13 Li	35.50N	0.15W
El Harrach, Al Jazā'ir-	35 Hf	7.11N	48.55 E
Elhotovo	13 Ph	36.43N	3.08 E
Elhovo	16 Nh	43.20N	44.13 E
Élida	15 Jg	42.10N	26.34 E
Éliki, Vallée d' - ◙	45 Ej	33.57N	103.39W
Elila	34 Gc	14.45N	7.15 E
Elila ◙	36 Ec	2.43S	25.53 E
Elimäki	30 Ji	2.45S	25.53 E
Elin Pelin	15 Lg	42.40N	26.28 E
Elisejna	15 Gg	42.40N	23.36 E
Elisenvaara	15 Gf	43.05N	23.29 E
Elista	8 Mc	61.19N	29.47 E
Elizabeth [Austl.]	6 Kf	46.16N	44.14 E
Elizabeth [N.J.-U.S.]	58 Eh	34.45S	138.39 E
Elizabeth, Cape- ►	44 Je	40.40N	74.13W
Elizabeth City	43 Ld	36.18N	76.14W
Elizabeth Reef ◙	57 Gg	29.55S	159.05 E
Elizabethton	44 Fg	36.21N	82.13W
Elizabethtown [Ky.-U.S.]	44 Eg	37.42N	85.52W
Elizabethtown [N.C.-U.S.]	44 Hh	34.38N	78.37W
El Jadida ◙	32 Fc	32.54N	8.30W
El Jadida	31 Ga	33.15N	8.30W
El Jicaro	49 Dg	13.43N	86.08W
'Él Jilib	35 He	3.48N	47.07 E
Elk	10 Sc	53.50N	22.22 E
Elk ◙	10 Sc	53.32N	22.47 E
El Kala	32 Jb	36.54N	8.27 E
El Kantara	32 Ib	35.13N	5.43 E
El-Karimia	13 Nh	36.01N	1.33 E
Elk City [Id.-U.S.]	46 Gd	45.51N	115.29W
Elk City [Ok.-U.S.]	45 Gi	35.25N	99.25W
El Kelaa des Srarhna ◙	32 Fc	32.03N	7.30W
El Kelaa des Srarhna	32 Fc	32.03N	7.24W
El Kere	35 Gd	5.51N	42.06 E
Elkhart [In.-U.S.]	43 Jc	41.41N	85.58W
Elkhart [Ks.-U.S.]	45 Ff	37.00N	101.54W
El Khatt ◙	32 Ef	19.00N	12.25W
Elkhead Mountains ⊠	45 Cf	40.50N	107.05W
El Khnâchich ◙	34 Ea	21.20N	3.30W
Elkhorn River ◙	45 Hf	41.07N	96.19W
Elkins	44 Gf	38.56N	79.53W
Elk Lake	44 Gb	47.42N	80.11W
El Kseur	13 Oh	36.41N	4.50 E
Elk Mountain ▲	45 Cf	41.38N	106.32W
Elk Mountains ⊠	45 Cg	38.55N	106.50W
Elko	43 Ec	40.50N	115.46W
Elk Peak ▲	46 Jc	46.27N	110.46W
Elk River	45 Jd	45.18N	93.35W
Elk River ◙	44 Eg	38.21N	81.38W
Elku Kalns ▲	8 Kg	57.04N	25.23 E
Ellás = Greece (EN) ◙	5 Ih	39.00N	22.00 E
Ellé ◙	11 Cg	47.52N	3.32W
Eller Ringnes ◙	38 Ib	30.00N	104.00W
Ellen, Mount- ▲	38 Gd	38.07N	110.49W
Ellendale	45 Gc	46.00N	98.32W
Ellensburg	43 Cb	46.40N	120.32W
Ellenville	44 Je	41.43N	74.23W
Ellesmere, Lake- ◙	38 Kb	79.00N	82.00W
Ellesmere Island ◙	62 Ef	43.45S	172.30 E
Ellesmere Port	9 Kh	53.17N	2.54W
Ellice Islands → Tuvalu ◙	57 Ie	8.00S	178.00 E
Elliot [Austl.]	59 Hc	17.33S	133.35 E
Elliot [S.Afr.]	37 Df	31.18S	27.50 E
Elliot, Mount- ▲	59 Jc	19.29S	146.58 E
Elliot Lake	44 Gb	46.23N	82.39W
Elliras	37 Qd	23.40S	27.46 E
Ellisville	45 Lk	31.36N	89.12W
Ellös	7 Cg	58.11N	11.27 E
Ellsworth [Ks.-U.S.]	45 Gg	38.44N	98.14W
Ellsworth [Me.-U.S.]	44 Mc	44.33N	68.25W
Ellsworth [Nb.-U.S.]	45 Ef	42.04N	102.15W
Ellsworth Land (EN) ◙	66 Pf	75.30S	80.00W
Ellsworth Mountains ⊠	66 Pf	78.30S	85.00W
Ellwangen	10 Gh	48.57N	10.08 E

Elm 10 Gd 52.09N 10.53 E
El Macao 49 Md 18.46N 68.33W
Elmadağ 24 Ec 39.55N 33.15 E
Elma Daği 15 Mk 38.46N 29.32 E
El Maestrat/El Maestrazgo 13 Ld 40.30N 0.10W
El Maestrazgo/El Maestrat 13 Ld 40.30N 0.10W
El Mahia 34 Ea 22.30N 2.30W
El Maitén 56 Ff 42.03S 71.10W
Elmaki 34 Gb 17.55N 8.20 E
El Malah 13 Ph 36.18N 3.14 E
Elmalı 24 Ic 39.25N 40.35 E
Elmali 24 Cd 36.44N 29.56 E
El Manteco 50 Ei 7.27N 62.32W
El Marfil 55 Bb 15.35S 60.19W
El Marsa 13 Mh 36.24N 0.55 E
El Medo 35 Gd 5.41N 41.46 E
El Meghaïer 32 Ic 33.57N 5.56 E
Elmhurst 45 Mf 41.53N 87.56W
El Milagro 56 Gd 31.01S 65.59W
Elmira 43 Lc 42.06N 76.50W
El Mrâyer 32 Fe 21.30N 8.10W
El Mreïti 32 Fe 23.29N 7.52W
El Mreyyé 30 Gg 19.30N 7.00W
Elmshorn 10 Fc 53.45N 9.39 E
Elmstein 12 Je 49.22N 7.56 E
Elne 11 Il 42.36N 2.58 E
El Nevado, Cerro- 56 Ge 35.35S 68.30W
El Niabo 35 Fe 4.33N 39.59 E
El Nihuil 56 Gd 34.58S 68.40W
El Novillo 48 Ec 28.40N 109.30W
El Novillo, Presa- 48 Ec 29.05N 109.45W
El Ochenta y Uno 48 Kg 21.35N 97.57W
Elorn 11 Bf 48.27N 4.16W
Elortondo 55 Bk 33.42S 61.37W
Elorza 54 Eb 7.03N 69.31W
Elota, Rio- 48 Ff 23.52N 106.56W
El Oued 32 Ic 33.20N 6.53 E
Eloy 46 Jj 32.45N 111.33W
El Palmar 50 Fh 8.01N 61.53W
El Palmito 48 Ge 25.40N 104.59W
El Panadés/El Penedès 13 Nc 41.25N 1.30 E
El Pao [Ven.] 50 Eh 8.06N 62.33W
El Pao [Ven.] 50 Bh 9.38N 68.08W
El Paraíso [3] 49 Df 14.10N 86.30W
El Paraíso 49 Dg 13.51N 86.34W
El Páramo 13 Gb 42.25N 5.45W
El Pardo, Madrid- 13 Id 40.32N 3.46W
El Paso [Il.-U.S.] 45 Lf 40.44N 89.01W
El Paso [Tx.-U.S.] 39 If 31.45N 106.29W
El Penedès/El Panadés 13 Nc 41.25N 1.30 E
El Perú 50 Fi 7.19N 61.49W
El Pico 54 Fg 15.57S 64.42W
El Pilar 50 Eg 10.32N 63.09W
El Pintado 56 Hb 24.38S 61.27W
El Porvenir [Hond.] 49 Df 14.41N 87.11W
El Porvenir [Pan.] 49 Hi 9.12N 80.08W
El Porvenir [Ven.] 50 Bi 6.55N 68.42W
El Potosí 48 Ie 24.51N 100.19W
El Prat de Llobregat/Prat de Llobregat 13 Oc 41.20N 2.06 E
El Priorat/El Priorato 13 Mc 41.10N 1.00 E
El Priorato/El Priorat 13 Mc 41.10N 1.00 E
El Progreso [3] 49 Cf 14.50N 90.00W
El Progreso [Guat.] 49 Bf 14.51N 90.04W
El Progreso [Hond.] 47 Ge 15.21N 87.49W
El Puente del Arzobispo 13 Ge 39.48N 5.10W
El Puerto 48 Dc 28.45N 111.20W
El Puerto de Santa María 13 Fh 36.36N 6.13W
El Rastro 50 Ch 9.03N 67.27W
El Real de Santa María 49 Ii 8.08N 77.43W
El Reno 43 Hd 35.32N 97.57W
El Ribeiro 13 Db 42.25N 8.10W
Elrose 46 Ka 51.13N 108.01W
El Saler 13 Le 39.23N 0.20W
El Salto 47 Cd 23.47N 105.23W
El Salvador [1] 39 Kh 13.50N 88.55W
El Samán de Apure 50 Bi 7.55N 68.44W
El Sauce [Mex.] 48 De 24.34N 111.29W
El Sauce [Nic.] 49 Dg 12.53N 86.32W
El Sáuz 48 Fc 29.03N 106.15W
Elsberry 45 Kg 39.10N 90.47W
Elsdorf 12 Id 50.56N 6.34 E
Else 12 Kb 52.12N 8.40 E
El Seibo 49 Md 18.46N 68.52W
Elsen, Paderborn- 12 Kc 51.44N 8.41 E
Elsen Nur 27 Fd 35.08N 92.20 E
'Él Shâma 35 Ge 2.46N 41.03 E
El Socorro 50 Dh 8.59N 65.44W
El Sombrero 54 Eb 9.23N 67.03W
Elst 12 Hc 51.55N 5.52 E
Elsterwerda 10 Je 51.27N 13.32 E
El Sueco 47 Cc 29.54N 106.24W
El-Taht 13 Mi 35.27N 0.46 E
El Tajín 47 Ed 20.27N 97.23W
El Tala 56 Gc 26.07S 65.17W
Eltanin Bay 66 Pf 73.40S 82.00W
Eltham 62 Fc 39.26S 174.18 E
El Tigre 53 Je 8.55N 64.15W
El Tigre, Isla- 49 Dg 13.16N 87.38W
El Toboso 13 Je 39.31N 3.00W
El Tocuyo 54 Eb 9.47N 69.48W
Elton 16 Oe 49.08N 46.50 E
Elton, Ozero- 19 Ef 49.10N 46.40 E
El Torcal 13 Hh 36.55N 4.35W
El Trébol 55 Bk 32.12S 61.42W
El Trigo 55 Cl 35.52S 59.24W
El Triunfo [Hond.] 49 Dg 13.06N 87.00W
El Triunfo [Mex.] 48 Df 23.47N 110.08W
El Tuito 48 Gg 20.19N 105.22W
El Turbio 56 Fh 51.41S 72.05W
Eltville am Rhein 12 Kd 50.02N 8.07 E
Eltz 12 Jd 50.12N 7.18 E
Elūru 25 Ge 17.05N 82.15 E
Elva 7 Gg 58.13N 26.25 E
El Valle 49 Gi 8.31N 80.08W
El Valles/Valles 13 Oc 41.35N 2.15 E
Elvas 13 Ef 38.53N 7.10W
El Vejo, Cerro- 54 Db 7.30N 73.05W
El Venado, Isla- 49 Fh 11.57N 83.44W
El Vendrell/Vendrell 13 Nc 41.13N 1.32 E
Elverum 7 Cf 60.53N 11.34 E
El Viejo 49 Dg 12.40N 87.10W
El Viejo, Volcán 38 Kh 12.38N 87.11W
El Vigía 49 Li 8.38N 71.39W
El Vigía, Cerro- 48 Gg 21.25N 104.00W
El Wak 36 Hb 2.49N 40.56 E
Elwell, Lake- 46 Jb 48.22N 111.17W
Elwood 44 Ee 40.17N 85.50W
Ely [Eng.-U.K.] 9 Ni 52.24N 0.16 E
Ely [Mn.-U.S.] 43 Ib 47.54N 91.51W
Ely [Nv.-U.S.] 39 Hf 39.15N 114.53W
Elyria 44 Fe 41.22N 82.06W
El Yunque 51a Cb 18.18N 65.47W
Elz 12 Kd 50.25N 8.02 E
Elzbach 12 Jd 50.12N 7.22 E
Emaé 63b Dc 17.04S 168.22 E
Ema Jõgi/Emajygi 8 Lf 58.20N 27.15 E
Emajygi/Ema Jõgi 8 Lf 58.20N 27.15 E
Emali 36 Gc 2.05S 37.28 E
Emāmshahr [Iran] 23 Ib 36.25N 55.01 E
Emāmshahr [Iran] 22 Hf 36.50N 54.29 E
Emāmzādeh 'Abbās 24 Lf 32.25N 47.55 E
Emån 7 Dh 57.08N 16.30 E
Emba 19 Ff 48.50N 58.10 E
Emba 5 Lf 46.38N 53.04 E
Embaracai, Rio- 55 Ff 23.27S 53.58W
Embarcación 56 Hb 23.13S 64.06W
Embarras Portage 42 Ge 58.25N 111.27W
Embarras River 45 Mg 38.39N 87.37W
Embira, Rio- 54 De 7.19S 70.15W
Embrun 11 Mj 44.34N 6.30 E
Embu 36 Gc 0.32S 37.27 E
Emden 10 Dc 53.22N 7.13 E
Emeldžak 20 He 58.27N 126.57 E
Emerald 58 Fg 23.32S 148.10 E
Emerald 42 Ga 76.50N 114.00W
Emerson 45 Hb 49.00N 97.12W
Emet 24 Cc 39.20N 29.15 E
Emiliano Zapata 48 Ni 17.45N 91.46W
Emilia-Romagna [2] 14 Ef 44.45N 11.00 E
Emilio R. Coni 55 Cj 30.04S 58.16W
Emili Rock 52 Hh 29.40S 87.25W
Emin/Dorbiljin 27 Db 46.32N 83.39 E
Emine, Nos- 15 Kg 42.42N 27.54 E
Emira Island 60 Dh 1.40S 150.00 E
Emirdağ 24 Dc 39.01N 31.10 E
Emisu, Tarso- 30 If 21.13N 18.32 E
Emlichheim 10 Cd 52.37N 6.51 E
Emmaboda 7 Dh 56.38N 15.32 E
Emmaste 7 Fg 58.43N 22.36 E
Emme 14 Bd 47.10N 7.35 E
Emmeloord, Noordoostpolder- 12 Hb 52.42N 5.44 E
Emmelshausen 12 Jd 50.09N 7.34 E
Emmen 11 Mb 52.47N 6.55 E
Emmendingen 10 Dh 48.08N 7.51 E
Emmen-Emmer-Compascuum 12 Jb 52.49N 7.03 E
Emmen-Klazienaveen 12 Jb 52.44N 7.01 E
Emmen-Nieuw Weerdinge 12 Jb 52.52N 7.01 E
Emmental 14 Bd 46.55N 7.45 E
Emmen-Weerdinge 12 Ib 52.49N 6.57 E
Emmer 12 Lb 52.03N 9.23 E
Emmer-Compascuum, Emmen- 12 Jb 52.49N 7.03 E
Emmerich 10 Ce 51.50N 6.15 E
Emmet 59 Id 24.40S 144.28 E
Emmetsburg 45 Ie 43.07N 94.41W
Emmett 46 Ge 43.52N 116.30W
Emmonak 40 Gd 62.46N 164.30W
Emőd 10 Qi 47.56N 20.49 E
Emory 46 Jf 41.05N 111.16W
Emory Peak 43 Gf 29.13N 103.17W
Empalme 47 Bc 27.58N 110.51W
Empangeni 37 Ee 28.50S 31.48 E
Empedrado 56 Ic 27.57S 58.48W
Emperor Seamounts (EN) 3 Je 40.00N 171.00 E
Empoli 14 Eg 43.43N 10.57 E
Emporia [Ks.-U.S.] 43 Hd 38.24N 96.11W
Emporia [Va.-U.S.] 44 Ig 36.42N 77.33W
Emporium 44 He 41.31N 78.14W
Empress Augusta Bay 63a Bb 6.25S 155.05 E
Empress Mine 37 Dc 18.27S 29.27 E
Ems 11 Na 53.19N 7.03 E
Emsbach 12 Kd 50.24N 8.06 E
Emsdetten 10 Dd 52.11N 7.32 E
Ems-Jade-Kanal 10 Dc 53.19N 7.10 E
Emsland 10 Dd 52.50N 7.20 E
Emstek 12 Kb 52.50N 8.09 E
Emumägi/Emumjagi 8 Lf 58.54N 26.23 E
Emumjagi/Emumägi 8 Lf 58.54N 26.23 E
Ena 29 Ed 35.27N 137.24 E
Enånger 7 Df 61.32N 17.00 E
Enaratoli 26 Kg 3.55S 136.21 E
Enard Bay 9 Hc 58.06N 5.20W
Ena-San 29 Ed 35.26N 137.36 E
Enbetsu 28 Pb 44.44N 141.47 E
Encantada, Cerro de la- 38 Hf 31.00N 115.23W
Encantada, Sierra de la- 48 Hc 28.30N 102.20W
Encantadas, Serra das 55 Fj 30.40S 53.00W
Encantado, Cerro- 47 Bc 27.03N 112.30W
Encarnación 53 Kh 27.20S 55.54W
Encarnación de Diaz 48 Hg 21.31N 102.14W
Enchi 34 Ed 5.49N 2.49W
Encinal 45 Gl 28.02N 99.21W
Encinasola 13 Ff 38.08N 6.52W
Encontrados 54 Db 8.46N 72.30W
Encounter Bay 59 Hg 35.35S 138.45 E
Encrucijada 49 Hb 22.37N 79.52W
Encruzilhada do Sul 55 Fj 30.32S 52.31W
Encs 10 Rh 48.20N 21.08 E
Ende 22 Oj 8.50S 121.39 E
Endeavour Strait 59 Ib 10.50S 142.15 E
Endelave 8 Di 55.45N 10.15 E
Enderbury Atoll 57 Je 3.08S 171.05W
Enderby 46 Fa 50.33N 119.08W
Enderby Land 66 Ee 67.30S 53.00 E
Endicott Mountains 40 Ic 67.50N 152.00W
Ené, Río- 54 Df 11.09S 74.19W
Energetik 19 Fe 51.44N 58.48 E
Enez 24 Bb 40.44N 26.04 E
Enez Körfezi 15 Ii 40.45N 26.00 E
Enfer, Portes d'- 36 Ed 5.05S 27.30 E
Enfield 44 Ig 36.11N 77.47W
Enfield, London- 12 Bc 51.40N 0.04W
Engadin/Engiadin'ota/Engiadina 14 Dd 46.35N 10.00 E
Engadina/Engadin/Engiadin'ota 14 Dd 46.35N 10.00 E
Engaño, Cabo- 47 Ke 18.37N 68.20W
Engaru 28 Qb 44.03N 143.31 E
Engelberg 14 Cd 46.50N 8.24 E
Engelhard 44 Jh 35.31N 76.00W
Engels 6 Ke 51.30N 46.07 E
Engelskirchen 12 Jd 50.59N 7.24 E
Engenho 55 Db 15.10S 56.25W
Enger 12 Kb 52.08N 8.34 E
Engeren 8 Ec 61.35N 12.05 E
Engershatu 35 Fb 16.34N 38.15 E
Enggano, Pulau- 21 Mj 5.24S 102.16 E
Enghien/Edingen 12 Gd 50.42N 4.02 E
Engiadin'ota/Engadina/Engadin 14 Dd 46.35N 10.00 E
England 5 Fe 52.30N 1.30W
England [2] 9 Li 52.30N 1.30W
Englehart 42 Jg 47.49N 79.52W
Englewood 45 Dg 39.39N 104.59W
English 44 Df 38.20N 86.28W
English Bāzār 25 Hc 25.00N 88.09 E
English Channel 5 Fe 50.20N 1.00W
English Coast 66 Qf 73.30S 73.00W
English River 45 Ia 50.12N 95.00W
English River 45 Kb 49.13N 90.58W
Engozero, Ozero- 7 Hd 65.45N 33.30 E
Enguera 13 Lf 38.59N 0.41W
Engure/Engures 8 Jg 57.09N 23.06 E
Engures/Engure 8 Jg 57.09N 23.06 E
Engures, Ozero-/Engures Ezers 8 Jg 57.15N 23.10 E
Engures Ezers/Engures, Ozero- 8 Jg 57.15N 23.10 E
Enh-Gajvan 27 Gb 48.05N 97.35 E
Enid 39 Jf 36.19N 97.48W
Enid Lake 45 Li 34.10N 89.50W
Eniwa 28 Pc 42.53N 141.14 E
Eniwa-Dake 29a Bb 42.47N 141.17 E
Eniwetok Atoll 57 Hc 11.30N 162.15 E
Enkeldoorn 37 Ec 19.01S 30.53 E
Enkenbach Alsenborn 12 Je 49.29N 7.53 E
Enkhuizen 11 Lb 52.42N 5.17 E
Enklinge 8 Id 60.20N 20.45 E
Enköping 7 Dg 59.38N 17.04 E
Enna 14 Im 37.34N 14.16 E
Ennadai 42 Hd 61.10N 101.00W
Ennadei Lake 42 Hd 60.55N 101.20W
Enné 35 Bc 14.24N 18.45 E
Ennedi 30 Jg 17.15N 22.00 E
Ennell, Lough-/Loch Ainninn 9 Fh 53.28N 7.24W
Ennepetal 12 Jc 51.18N 7.21 E
Ennigerloh 12 Kc 51.50N 8.01 E
Enning 45 Ed 44.37N 102.31W
Ennis [Mt.-U.S.] 46 Jd 45.21N 111.44W
Ennis [Tx.-U.S.] 45 Hj 32.20N 96.38W
Ennis/Inis 9 Ei 52.50N 8.59W
Enniscorthy/Inis Córthaidh 9 Gi 52.30N 6.34W
Enniskillen/Inis Ceithleann 9 Fg 54.21N 7.38W
Ennistymon/Inis Díomáin 9 Di 52.57N 9.13W
Enns 14 Ib 48.12N 14.28 E
Enns 5 Hf 48.14N 14.30 E
Ennstaler Alpen 14 Ic 47.37N 14.35 E
Eno 7 He 62.48N 30.09 E
Enontekiö 7 Fb 68.23N 23.38 E
Enonvesi [Fin.] 8 Mb 62.10N 28.55 E
Enonvesi [Fin.] 8 Lc 61.20N 26.30 E
Enozero, Ozero- 7 Ib 68.10N 38.00 E
Enrekang 26 Gg 3.34S 119.47 E
Enrique Carbó 55 Ck 33.08S 59.14W
Enriquillo 49 Le 17.54N 71.14W
Enriquillo, Lago- 47 Je 18.27N 71.39W
Enschede 11 Mb 52.12N 6.53 E
Ensenada [Arg.] 55 Dl 34.51S 57.55W
Ensenada [Mex.] 39 Hf 31.52N 116.37W
Enshi 27 Ie 30.16N 109.26 E
Enshū-Nada 29 Ed 34.30N 138.00 E
Entebbe 31 Kh 0.04N 32.28 E
Entenbühl 10 Ig 49.46N 12.24 E
Enterprise [Al.-U.S.] 44 Ej 31.19N 85.51W
Enterprise [N.W.T.-Can.] 42 Fd 60.39N 116.08W
Enterprise [Or.-U.S.] 46 Gd 45.25N 117.17W
Entinas, Punta- 13 Jh 36.41N 2.46W
Entrada, Punta- 47 Ab 30.22N 115.59W
Entraygues-sur-Truyère 11 Ij 44.39N 2.34 E
Entrecasteaux, Récifs d'- 57 Hf 18.20S 163.00 E
Entrepeñas, Embalse de- 13 Jd 40.34N 2.42W
Entre Rios [2] 56 Id 32.00S 59.00W
Entre Rios 54 Fh 21.32S 64.12W
Entre Rios de Minas 55 Je 20.41S 44.04W
Entrevaux 11 Mk 43.57N 6.49 E
Entroncamento 13 De 39.28N 8.28W
Enugu 31 Hh 6.26N 7.29 E
Enugu Ezike 34 Gd 6.59N 7.27 E
Envermeu 12 De 49.54N 1.16 E
Envigado 54 Cb 6.08N 75.39W
Envira 54 De 7.18S 70.13W
Enyamba 36 Dc 3.40S 24.58 E
Enyélé 36 Cb 2.49N 18.06 E
Enz 10 Fh 49.00N 9.10 E
Enza 14 Ef 44.54N 10.31 E
Enzan 28 Og 34.52N 138.44 E
Enzgau 12 Kf 48.48N 8.37 E
Eo 13 Ea 43.28N 7.03W
Eochaill/Youghal 9 Fj 51.57N 7.50W
Eolie o Lipari, Isole-=Lipari Islands (EN) 5 Hh 38.35N 14.55 E
Epanomi 15 Fi 40.26N 22.56 E
Epazote, Cerro- 47 Cd 24.35N 105.07W
Epe [Neth.] 12 Hb 52.21N 5.59 E
Epe [Nig.] 34 Fd 6.35N 3.59 E
Epéna 36 Cb 1.22N 17.29 E
Épernay 11 Je 49.03N 3.57 E
Epe-Vaassen 12 Hb 52.17N 5.58 E
Ephesus (EN)=Efes 15 Kl 37.55N 27.20 E
Ephraim 46 Jg 39.22N 111.35W
Ephrata 46 Fc 47.19N 119.33W
Epi, Ile- 57 Hf 16.43S 168.15 E
Epidamnus 15 Ch 41.19N 19.26 E
Epidaurus (EN) = Epidhavros 15 Gl 37.38N 23.09 E
Epidhavros = Epidaurus (EN) 15 Gl 37.38N 23.09 E
Epila 13 Kc 41.36N 1.17W
Épinal 11 Mf 48.11N 6.27 E
Epirus (EN)=Ipiros 5 Ih 39.30N 20.40 E
Epirus (EN)=Ipiros 15 Dj 39.30N 20.40 E
Episkopi 24 Ee 34.40N 32.54 E
Epping 12 Cc 51.42N 0.07 E
Eppingen 12 Ke 49.08N 8.54 E
Epsom 9 Mj 51.20N 0.16W
Epte 11 He 49.04N 1.31 E
Epukiro 37 Bd 21.41S 19.08 E
Epukiro 37 Bd 21.28S 19.59 E
Epulu 36 Eb 1.15N 28.21 E
Eqlīd 23 Hc 30.55N 52.39 E
Équateur=Equator (EN) [2] 36 Eb 1.00N 20.00 E
Equator (EN)=Équateur [2] 36 Eb 1.00N 20.00 E
Equatorial Guinea (EN)=Guinea Ecuatorial [1] 1 Hh 2.00N 9.00 E
Equinox Mountain 44 Kd 43.15N 73.10W
Era [It.] 14 Eg 43.40N 10.38 E
Era [Sud.] 35 Dd 5.30N 29.50 E
Eraclea 14 Kj 40.15N 16.40 E
Eraclea Minoa 14 Hm 37.25N 13.18 E
Eradaka 63b Dc 17.39S 168.08 E
Eräjärvi 8 Kc 61.35N 24.34 E
Eratini 15 Fk 38.22N 22.14 E
Erbaa 24 Gb 40.42N 36.36 E
Erbach 10 Eg 49.39N 9.00 E
Erbeskopf 10 Dg 49.44N 7.05 E
Erbil [3] 24 Je 36.10N 44.00 E
Erbil 22 Gf 36.11N 44.01 E
Ercek 24 Jc 38.39N 43.36 E
Erçek Gölü 24 Jc 38.39N 43.32 E
Erciş 24 Jc 39.00N 43.19 E
Erciyas Daği 21 Ff 38.32N 35.28 E
Ercolano 14 Ij 40.48N 14.21 E
Ercsi 10 Oi 47.15N 18.54 E
Érd 10 Oi 47.22N 18.56 E
Erdaobaihe 27 Mc 42.28N 128.05 E
Erdao Jiang 28 Ic 42.35N 127.10 E
Erdek 24 Bb 40.24N 27.48 E
Erdek Körfezi 24 Bb 40.25N 27.45 E
Erdemli 24 Fd 36.37N 34.18 E
Erdene-Cagan 27 Kb 45.55N 115.30 E
Erdene-Dalaj 27 Hb 46.02N 104.55 E
Erdene-Mandal 27 Hb 48.30N 101.21 E
Erdi 30 Jg 19.05N 22.40 E
Erdi Ma 35 Cb 18.35N 23.30 E
Erding 10 Hh 48.18N 11.56 E
Erdinger Moos 10 Hh 48.20N 11.50 E
Erdre 11 Eg 47.13N 1.32W
Erebus, Mount- 66 Kf 77.32S 167.09 E
Erechim 56 Jc 27.38S 52.17W
Ereğli [Tur.] 23 Db 37.31N 34.04 E
Ereğli [Tur.] 23 Da 41.17N 31.25 E
Erei, Monti- 14 Im 37.35N 14.20 E
Ereke 26 Hg 4.45S 123.10 E
Eren 24 Dd 37.25N 30.05 E
Erenhot 22 Ne 43.35N 112.00 E
Erepecu, Lago do- 54 Gd 1.20S 56.35W
Eresma 13 Hc 41.26N 4.45W
Erétria 15 Gk 38.25N 23.48 E
Erfelek 24 Fb 41.55N 34.57 E
Erfengshan 28 Ag 35.50N 111.47 E
Erfoud 32 Gc 31.26N 4.14W
Erft 10 Ce 51.11N 6.44 E
Erftstadt 12 Id 50.48N 6.49 E
Erfurt 6 He 50.59N 11.02 E
Erfurt [2] 10 Gf 51.00N 11.00 E
Ergani 24 Hc 38.17N 39.46 E
Ergene 24 Bb 41.01N 26.22 E
Erges 13 Ee 39.40N 7.01W
Ergig, Bahr- 35 Bc 11.22N 15.24 E
Ērgļi/Ergli 7 Fh 56.55N 25.41 E
Ergli/Ērgļi 7 Fh 56.55N 25.41 E
Ergun He 21 Od 53.20N 121.28 E
Ergun Youqi (Labudalin) 27 La 50.16N 120.09 E
Ergun Zuoqi (Genhe) 22 Od 50.47N 121.32 E
Er Hai 27 Hf 25.45N 100.10 E
Eria 13 Gb 42.03N 5.44W
Eriba 35 Fb 16.37N 36.04 E
Eriboll, Loch- 9 Ic 58.30N 4.40W
Eric 42 Kf 51.52N 65.45W
Erice 14 Gl 38.02N 12.35 E
Ericeira 13 Cf 38.59N 9.25W
Erichsen Lake 42 Jb 70.38N 80.20W
Ericht, Loch- 9 Ie 56.50N 4.25W
Erick 45 Gi 35.13N 99.52W
Eridu [3] 24 Lg 36.00N 44.00 E
Erie 39 Ke 42.08N 80.04W
Erie, Lake- 38 Ke 42.15N 81.00W
'Erigābo 35 Hc 10.37N 47.24 E
Erigât 30 Gg 19.40N 4.50W
Erikoússa 15 Cj 39.53N 19.35 E
Eriksdale 45 Ga 50.52N 98.06W
Eriksenstretet 41 Oc 79.00N 26.00 E
Erikub Atoll 57 Id 9.08N 170.02 E
Erimanthos Óros 15 El 37.58N 21.48 E
Erimo-Misaki 27 Pc 41.55N 143.15 E
Eriskay 9 Fd 57.04N 7.13W
Eritrea 30 Kg 15.00N 40.00 E
Eritrea [3] 35 Fb 15.00N 39.00 E
Eritrea 35 Fb 15.00N 40.00 E
Erjas 13 Ee 39.40N 7.01W
Erkelenz 12 Ic 51.05N 6.19 E
Erken 8 He 59.50N 18.35 E
Erkowit 35 Fb 18.46N 37.07 E
Erlangdian→Dawu 28 Ci 31.33N 114.07 E
Erlangen 10 Hg 49.36N 11.01 E
Erlang Shan 27 Hf 29.58N 102.20 E
Erlauf 14 Jb 48.12N 15.11 E
Erldunda 59 Ge 25.14S 133.12 E
Erlenbach 12 Ke 49.07N 8.11 E
Erlong Shan 27 Mc 43.30N 128.44 E
Ermelo [Neth.] 12 Hb 52.19N 5.37 E
Ermelo [S.Afr.] 37 De 26.34S 29.58 E
Ermenek 24 Ed 36.38N 32.54 E
Ermenistan=Armenia (EN) 23 Fb 39.10N 43.00 E
Ermenistan=Armenia (EN) 21 Gf 39.10N 43.00 E
Ermenonville 12 Ee 49.08N 2.42 E
Ermesinde 13 Dc 41.13N 8.33W
Ermoúpolis 15 Hl 37.27N 24.56 E
Ernākulam 25 Fg 9.59N 76.17 E
Erndtebrück 12 Kd 50.59N 8.16 E
Erne/An Éirne 9 Eg 54.30N 8.15W
Ernée 11 Ff 48.18N 0.56W
Ernest Legouvé Reef 57 Lh 35.12S 150.35W
Ernici, Monti- 14 Hi 41.50N 13.20 E
Erode 25 Ff 11.21N 77.44 E
Eromanga 59 Ie 26.40S 143.16 E
Erongoberg 37 Bd 21.40S 15.40 E
Erpengdianzi 28 Hd 41.12N 125.29 E
Errego 37 Fc 16.02S 37.10 E
Errigal/An Ea agail 9 Ef 55.02N 8.07W
Erris Head/Ceann Iorrais 5 Fe 54.19N 10.00W
Erromango, Ile- 57 Hf 18.48S 169.05 E
Erseka 15 Di 40.20N 20.41 E
Erstein 11 Nf 48.26N 7.40 E
Ertai 27 Fb 46.02N 90.10 E
Ertil 19 Ee 51.50N 40.51 E
Ertix He 21 Ke 47.52N 84.16 E
Erts 37 De 25.08S 29.55 E
Ertvågøy 8 Ca 63.15N 8.25 E
Eruh 24 Jd 37.46N 42.15 E
Ervânia 55 Ee 21.43S 55.32W
Erve 11 Fg 47.50N 0.20W
Ervy-le-Châtel 11 Jf 48.02N 3.55 E
Erwin 44 Fg 36.09N 82.25W
Erwitte 12 Kc 51.37N 8.21 E
Eryuan 27 Gf 26.09N 99.56 E
Erzeni 15 Ch 41.26N 19.27 E
Erzgebirge=Ore Mountains (EN) 5 He 50.30N 13.15 E
Erzin 20 Ef 50.17N 95.10 E
Erzincan 23 Eb 39.44N 39.29 E
Erzurum 22 Gf 39.55N 41.17 E
Esan-Misaki 28 Pd 41.48N 141.12 E
Esashi [Jap.] 28 Pd 41.52N 140.07 E
Esashi [Jap.] 28 Qb 44.56N 142.35 E
Esashi [Jap.] 28 Pe 39.12N 141.09 E
Esbjerg 6 Gd 55.28N 8.27 E
Esbo/Espoo 7 Ff 60.13N 24.40 E
Escalante 46 Jh 37.47N 111.36W
Escalante Desert 46 Ih 37.50N 113.30W
Escalante River 46 Jh 37.17N 110.53W
Escalaplano 14 Dk 39.37N 9.21 E
Escalón 47 Dc 26.45N 104.20W
Escalona 13 Hd 40.10N 4.24W
Escanaba 39 Ke 45.45N 87.04W
Escanaba River 44 Dc 45.47N 87.04W
Escandón, Puerto de- 13 Ld 40.17N 1.00W
Escandorgue 11 Jk 43.46N 3.14 E
Escarpada Point 21 Oh 18.31N 122.13 E
Escarpé, Cap- 63b 20.41S 167.13 E
Escatrón 13 Lc 41.17N 0.19W
Escaut=Schelde (EN) 11 Kc 51.22N 4.15 E
Esch an der Alzette/Esch-sur-Alzette 11 Le 49.30N 5.59 E
Eschkopf 12 Je 49.19N 7.51 E
Esch-sur-Alzette/Esch an der Alzette 11 Le 49.30N 5.59 E
Eschwege 10 Ge 51.11N 10.04 E
Eschweiler 10 Cf 50.49N 6.17 E
Escocesa, Bahia- 49 Md 19.25N 69.45W
Escondida, Punta- 48 Kj 15.49N 97.03W
Escondido 46 Gj 33.07N 117.05W
Escondido, Río- 49 Fg 12.04N 83.45W
Escravos 34 Gd 5.36N 5.11 E
Escudo, Puerto del- 13 Ia 43.05N 3.50W
Escudo de Veraguas, Isla- 49 Gi 9.06N 81.33W
Escuintla [3] 49 Bf 14.10N 91.00W
Escuintla [Guat.] 47 Ff 14.18N 90.47W
Escuintla [Mex.] 48 Mj 15.20N 92.38W
Escuro, Rio- [Braz.] 55 Ic 17.31S 46.39W
Escuro, Rio- [Braz.] 55 Ha 12.50S 49.28W
Ese 36 Eb 4.04N 26.40 E
Ese-Hajja 20 Ic 67.35N 134.55 E
Eséka 34 He 3.39N 10.46 E
Eşen 24 Cd 36.27N 29.16 E
Esendere 24 Kd 37.46N 44.40 E
Esera 13 Mb 42.06N 0.15 E
Esfahān [3] 23 Hc 32.50N 51.50 E
Eşfahān=Isfahan (EN) 22 Hf 32.40N 51.38 E
Esfandārān 24 Og 31.52N 52.32 E
Esfarāyen, Reshteh-ye- 24 Qd 36.46N 57.10 E
Esgueva 13 Hc 41.40N 4.43W

Index Symbols

[1] Independent Nation
[2] State, Region
[3] District, County
[4] Municipality
[5] Colony, Dependency
Continent
Physical Region
Historical or Cultural Region
Mount, Mountain
Volcano
Hill
Mountains, Mountain Range
Hills, Escarpment
Plateau, Upland
Pass, Gap
Plain, Lowland
Delta
Salt Flat
Valley, Canyon
Crater, Cave
Karst Features
Depression
Polder
Desert, Dunes
Forest, Woods
Heath, Steppe
Oasis
Cape, Point
Coast, Beach
Cliff
Peninsula
Isthmus
Sandbank
Island
Atoll
Rock, Reef
Islands, Archipelago
Rocks, Reefs
Coral Reef
Well, Spring
Geyser
River, Stream
Waterfall Rapids
River Mouth, Estuary
Lake
Salt Lake
Intermittent Lake
Reservoir
Swamp, Pond
Canal
Glacier
Ice Shelf, Pack Ice
Ocean
Sea
Gulf, Bay
Strait, Fjord
Lagoon
Bank
Seamount
Tablemount
Ridge
Shelf
Basin
Escarpment, Sea Scarp
Fracture
Trench, Abyss
National Park, Reserve
Point of Interest
Recreation Site
Cave, Cavern
Historic Site
Ruins
Wall, Walls
Church, Abbey
Temple
Scientific Station
Airport
Port
Lighthouse
Mine
Tunnel
Dam, Bridge

Index Symbols

- ◻ Independent Nation
- ◻ State, Region
- ◻ District, County
- ◻ Municipality
- ◻ Colony, Dependency
- ◻ Continent
- ◻ Physical Region
- ◻ Historical or Cultural Region
- ◻ Mount, Mountain
- ◻ Volcano
- ◻ Hill
- ◻ Mountains, Mountain Range
- ◻ Hills, Escarpment
- ◻ Plateau, Upland
- ◻ Pass, Gap
- ◻ Plain, Lowland
- ◻ Delta
- ◻ Salt Flat
- ◻ Valley, Canyon
- ◻ Crater, Cave
- ◻ Karst Features
- ◻ Depression
- ◻ Polder
- ◻ Desert, Dunes
- ◻ Forest, Woods
- ◻ Heath, Steppe
- ◻ Oasis
- ◻ Cape, Point
- ◻ Coast, Beach
- ◻ Cliff
- ◻ Peninsula
- ◻ Isthmus
- ◻ Sandbank
- ◻ Island
- ◻ Atoll
- ◻ Rock, Reef
- ◻ Islands, Archipelago
- ◻ Rocks, Reefs
- ◻ Coral Reef
- ◻ Well, Spring
- ◻ Geyser
- ◻ River, Stream
- ◻ Waterfall Rapids
- ◻ River Mouth, Estuary
- ◻ Lake
- ◻ Salt Lake
- ◻ Intermittent Lake
- ◻ Reservoir
- ◻ Swamp, Pond
- ◻ Canal
- ◻ Glacier
- ◻ Ice Shelf, Pack Ice
- ◻ Ocean
- ◻ Sea
- ◻ Gulf, Bay
- ◻ Strait, Fjord
- ◻ Lagoon
- ◻ Bank
- ◻ Seamount
- ◻ Ridge
- ◻ Shelf
- ◻ Basin
- ◻ Escarpment, Sea Scarp
- ◻ Fracture
- ◻ Trench, Abyss
- ◻ National Park, Reserve
- ◻ Point of Interest
- ◻ Recreation Site
- ◻ Scientific Station
- ◻ Historic Site
- ◻ Ruins
- ◻ Wall, Walls
- ◻ Church, Abbey
- ◻ Temple
- ◻ Airport
- ◻ Port
- ◻ Lighthouse
- ◻ Mine
- ◻ Tunnel
- ◻ Dam, Bridge

Index Symbols

[1] Independent Nation	Pass, Gap	Rock, Reef
[2] State, Region	Plain, Lowland	River Mouth, Estuary
[3] District, County	Delta	Lake
[4] Municipality	Salt Flat	Salt Lake
[5] Colony, Dependency	Valley, Canyon	Intermittent Lake
Continent	Crater, Cave	Reservoir
Physical Region	Karst Features	Swamp, Pond
Historical or Cultural Region	Depression	Waterfall Rapids
Mount, Mountain	Polder	River, Stream
Volcano	Desert, Dunes	Coast, Beach
Hill	Forest, Woods	Cliff
Mountains, Mountain Range	Heath, Steppe	Islands, Archipelago
Hills, Escarpment	Oasis	Rocks, Reefs
Plateau, Upland	Cape, Point	Coral Reef
		Well, Spring
		Atoll

Canal	Lagoon	Escarpment, Sea Scarp	Historic Site	Port
Glacier	Bank	Fracture	Ruins	Lighthouse
Ice Shelf, Pack Ice	Seamount	Trench, Abyss	Wall, Walls	Mine
Ocean	Tablemount	National Park, Reserve	Church, Abbey	Tunnel
Sea	Gulf, Bay	Point of Interest	Temple	Dam, Bridge
Ridge	Basin	Recreation Site	Scientific Station	
Shelf		Cave, Cavern	Airport	
Strait, Fjord				

Friesoythe	10	Dc	53.01N	7.51 E
Frigate Island	51p	Cb	12.25N	61.29W
Friggesund	8	Gc	61.54N	16.32 E
Frignano	14	Ef	44.20N	10.50 E
Frindsbury Reef	63a	Da	5.00S	159.07 E
Frinnaryd	8	Fg	57.56N	14.49 E
Frinton-on-Sea	12	Dc	51.50N	1.15 E
Frio, Cabo-	52	Lh	22.53S	42.00W
Frio, Río-	49	Eh	11.08N	84.46W
Frio Draw	45	Ei	34.50N	102.08W
Friona	45	Ei	34.38N	102.43W
Frio River	45	Gl	28.30N	98.10W
Frisco Peak	46	Ig	38.31N	113.14W
Frisian Islands (EN)	5	Ge	54.00N	7.00 E
Fristad	8	Eg	57.50N	13.01 E
Fritsla	8	Eg	57.33N	12.47 E
Fritzlar	10	Fe	51.08N	9.17 E
Friuli	14	Ge	46.00N	13.00 E
Friuli-Venezia Giulia [2]	14	Gd	46.00N	13.00 E
Frobisher Bay	39	Mc	63.44N	68.28W
Frobisher Bay	38	Mc	62.30N	66.00W
Frobisher Lake	42	Ge	56.20N	108.20W
Froidchapelle	12	Gd	50.09N	4.20 E
Froissy	12	Ee	49.34N	2.13 E
Frolovo	19	Ef	49.45N	43.39 E
Fromberg	46	Kd	45.23N	108.54W
Frombork	10	Pb	54.22N	19.41 E
Frome	9	Kj	51.14N	2.20W
Frome, Lake-	57	Eh	30.50S	139.50 E
Frondenberg	12	Jc	51.28N	7.46 E
Fronteira	13	Ee	39.03N	7.39W
Fronteiras	54	Je	7.05S	40.37W
Frontera	48	Mh	18.32N	92.38W
Frontera, Punta-	48	Mh	19.36N	92.42W
Fronteras	48	Eb	30.56N	109.31W
Frontignan	11	Jk	43.27N	3.45 E
Frontino, Paramo-	54	Cb	6.28N	76.04W
Front Range	38	If	39.45N	105.45W
Front Royal	44	Hf	38.56N	78.13W
Frosinone	14	Hi	41.38N	13.19 E
Frösö	8	Fa	63.11N	14.32 E
Frostburg	44	Hf	39.39N	78.56W
Frost Glacier	66	Ie	67.05S	129.00 E
Frövi	8	Fe	59.28N	15.22 E
Frøya	7	Be	63.43N	8.42 E
Frøysjøen	8	Ac	61.50N	5.05 E
Frozen Strait	42	Jc	65.50N	84.30W
Fruges	11	Id	50.31N	2.08 E
Frunze [Kirg.-U.S.S.R.]	18	Hd	40.06N	71.45 E
Frunze [Kirg.-U.S.S.R.]	22	Je	42.54N	74.36 E
Frunzovka	15	Mb	47.20N	29.37 E
Fruška Gora	15	Cd	45.10N	19.35 E
Frutal	54	Ih	20.02S	48.55W
Frutigen	14	Bd	46.35N	7.40 E
Fry Canyon	46	Jh	37.38N	110.08W
Frýdek Místek	10	Og	49.41N	18.22 E
Frylinckspan	37	Ce	26.46S	22.28 E
Ftéri	15	Ej	39.09N	21.33 E
Fua'amotu	65b	Ac	21.15S	175.08W
Fua Mulaku Island	25a	Bc	0.15S	73.30 E
Fu'an	27	Kf	27.10N	119.44 E
Fu-chien Sheng → Fujian Sheng = Fukien (EN) [2]	27	Kf	26.00N	118.00 E
Fuchskauten	10	Ef	50.40N	8.05 E
Fuchū [Jap.]	29	Cd	34.34N	133.14 E
Fuchū [Jap.]	29	Fd	35.41N	139.28 E
Fuchun-Jiang	28	Fi	30.15N	120.15 E
Fuchunjiang-Shuiku	28	Ej	29.29N	119.31 E
Fucino, Conca del-	14	Hj	42.01N	13.31 E
Fudai	29	Ga	40.01N	141.52 E
Fuding	27	Lf	27.19N	120.08 E
Fuengirola	13	Hh	36.32N	4.37W
Fuente Alto	56	Fd	33.37S	70.35W
Fuente del Maestre	13	Ff	38.32N	6.27W
Fuente-Obejuna	13	Gf	38.16N	5.25W
Fuentesaúco	13	Gc	41.14N	5.30W
Fuentes de Andalucía	13	Gg	37.28N	5.21W
Fuentes de Cantos	13	Ff	38.15N	6.18W
Fuerte	47	Cc	25.54N	109.22W
Fuerte, Isla-	49	Ii	9.23N	76.11W
Fuerte, Sierra del-	48	Hd	27.30N	102.45W
Fuerte Olimpo	56	Ib	21.02S	57.54W
Fuerteventura	30	Ff	28.20N	14.00W
Fuga	26	Hc	18.52N	121.22 E
Fugong	27	Gf	27.03N	98.57 E
Fugou	28	Cg	34.04N	114.23 E
Fugu	27	Jd	39.02N	111.03 E
Fuguo → Zhanhua	28	Ef	37.42N	118.08 E
Fuhai/Burultokay	27	Eb	47.06N	87.23 E
Fuhayrī, Wādī-	23	Hf	16.04N	52.11 E
Fu He	28	Dj	28.36N	116.04 E
Fuji	28	Og	35.09N	138.38 E
Fujian Sheng (Fu-chien Sheng) = Fukien (EN) [2]	27	Kf	26.00N	118.00 E
Fujieda	29	Fd	34.51N	138.15 E
Fuji-Gawa	29	Fd	35.07N	138.38 E
Fujin	27	Nb	47.15N	132.01 E
Fujinomiya	29	Fd	35.12N	138.38 E
Fujioka	29	Fc	36.15N	139.03 E
Fuji-San	21	Pf	35.26N	138.43 E
Fujisawa	29	Fd	35.21N	139.27 E
Fuji-yoshida	29	Fd	35.29N	138.47 E
Fukagawa	27	Pc	43.43N	142.03 E
Fūkah	24	Bg	31.04N	27.55 E
Fukang	27	Ec	44.10N	87.59 E
Fuka-Shima	29	Be	32.43N	131.56 E
Fukiage	29	Bf	31.30N	130.20 E
Fukien (EN) = Fu-chien Sheng → Fujian Sheng [2]	27	Kf	26.00N	118.00 E
Fukien (EN) = Fujian Sheng (Fu-chien Sheng) [2]	27	Kf	26.00N	118.00 E
Fukuchiyama	28	Mg	35.18N	135.07 E
Fukue	28	Jh	32.41N	128.50 E
Fukueichiao	27	Lf	25.19N	121.34 E
Fukue-Jima	28	Jh	32.41N	128.48 E
Fukui	27	Od	36.04N	136.13 E
Fukui Ken [2]	28	Ng	36.00N	136.20 E

Fukuma	29	Be	33.47N	130.28 E
Fukuoka	22	Pf	33.35N	130.24 E
Fukuoka Ken [2]	28	Kh	33.28N	130.45 E
Fukuroi	29	Ed	34.45N	137.54 E
Fukushima [Jap.]	27	Pd	37.45N	140.28 E
Fukushima [Jap.]	27	Pc	41.29N	140.15 E
Fukushima Ken [2]	28	Pf	37.25N	140.10 E
Fukuyama	27	Ne	34.29N	133.22 E
Fūlādī, Kūh-e-	23	Kc	34.38N	67.32 E
Fūlād Mahalleh	24	Od	36.02N	53.44 E
Fulanga	63d	Cc	19.08S	178.34W
Fulda	5	Ge	51.25N	9.39 E
Fulda	10	Ff	50.33N	9.40 E
Fuliji	28	Dh	33.47N	116.59 E
Fulin → Hanyuan	27	Hf	29.25N	102.12 E
Fuling	27	If	29.40N	107.21 E
Fullerton	45	Hf	41.22N	97.58W
Fulton [Arg.]	55	Cm	37.25S	58.48W
Fulton [Il.-U.S.]	45	Kf	41.52N	90.11W
Fulton [Ky.-U.S.]	44	Cg	36.30N	88.53W
Fulton [Mo.-U.S.]	45	Kg	38.52N	91.57W
Fulton [N.Y.-U.S.]	44	Id	43.20N	76.26W
Fulufjället	8	Ec	61.33N	12.43 E
Fumaiolo	14	Gg	43.47N	12.04 E
Fumay	11	Kd	50.00N	4.42 E
Fumel	11	Gj	44.30N	0.58 E
Funabasi	28	Og	35.42N	139.59 E
Funabiki	29	Gc	37.26N	140.35 E
Funafuti	58	Ie	8.01S	178.00 E
Funafuti Atoll	57	Ie	8.31S	179.08 E
Funagata	29	Gb	38.42N	140.18 E
Funagata-Yama	29	Gb	38.27N	140.37 E
Funakoshi-Wan	29	Hb	39.25N	142.00 E
Funan	28	Ch	32.38N	115.35 E
Funäsdalen	7	Ce	62.32N	12.33 E
Funchal	31	Fe	32.38N	16.54W
Fundación	54	Da	10.29N	74.12W
Fundão	13	Ed	40.08N	7.30W
Fundy, Bay of-	38	Me	45.00N	66.00W
Funeral Peak	46	Gh	36.08N	116.37W
Fungalei	64h	Bb	13.17S	176.07W
Funhalouro	37	Ed	23.05S	34.24 E
Funing [China]	27	Ig	23.39N	105.33 E
Funing [China]	28	Eh	33.48N	119.47 E
Funing [China]	28	Ee	39.56N	119.15 E
Funiu Shan	27	Je	33.40N	112.10 E
Funtua	34	Gc	11.32N	7.19 E
Fuping	28	Ce	38.49N	114.15 E
Fuqing	27	Kf	25.47N	119.24 E
Furancungo	37	Eb	14.54S	33.37 E
Furano	28	Qc	43.21N	142.23 E
Füren	29a	Ca	44.17N	142.25 E
Furenai	29a	Cb	42.43N	142.15 E
Füren-Ko	29a	Db	43.20N	145.20 E
Fürg	24	Ph	28.18N	55.13 E
Fur Jiang	28	Hc	42.37N	125.33 E
Furmanov	7	Jh	57.16N	41.07 E
Furnas, Represa de-	54	Ih	21.20S	45.50W
Furnas, Serra das-	55	Fb	15.45S	53.20W
Furneaux Group	57	Fi	40.10S	148.05 E
Furnes/Veurne	11	Ic	51.04N	2.40 E
Furqlus	24	Ge	34.36N	37.05 E
Furrīyānah	32	Ic	34.57N	8.34 E
Fürstenau	12	Jb	52.31N	7.43 E
Furstenauer Berge	12	Jb	52.35N	7.45 E
Fürstenfeld	14	Kc	47.03N	16.05 E
Fürstenfeldbruck	10	Hh	48.11N	11.15 E
Furstenlager	12	Ke	49.42N	8.38 E
Fürstenwalde	10	Kd	52.22N	14.04 E
Fürth [F.R.G.]	10	Gg	49.28N	11.00 E
Fürth [F.R.G.]	12	Ke	49.39N	8.47 E
Furth im Wald	10	Ig	49.18N	12.51 E
Furubira	29a	Bb	43.16N	140.39 E
Furudal	7	Df	61.10N	15.08 E
Furukawa	27	Pd	38.34N	140.58 E
Furusund	8	He	59.40N	18.55 E
Fury and Hecla Strait	42	Jc	69.55N	84.00W
Fushan [China]	28	Ff	37.30N	121.15 E
Fushan [China]	28	Ag	35.58N	111.51 E
Fushë-Arëzi	15	Dg	42.04N	20.02 E
Fushë-Lura	15	Dh	41.48N	20.13 E
Fu Shui	28	Cj	29.52N	115.26 E
Fushun	22	Oe	41.46N	123.56 E
Fusong	27	Mc	42.20N	127.17 E
Füsselberg	12	Je	49.32N	7.14 E
Füssen	10	Gi	47.34N	10.42 E
Futa, Passo della-	14	Ff	44.05N	11.17 E
Futago-Yama	29	Be	33.35N	131.38 E
Futaoi-Jima	29	Bd	34.06N	130.47 E
Futog	15	Cd	45.15N	19.42 E
Futuna, Ile-	57	Jf	14.17S	178.09W
Fuwah	24	Dg	31.12N	30.33 E
Fuxian (Wafangdian)	27	Ld	39.38N	121.59 E
Fuxian Hu	27	Hg	24.30N	102.55 E
Fuxin	22	Oe	41.59N	121.38 E
Fuxin Monggolzu Zizhixian	28	Fc	42.06N	121.46 E
Fuyang	27	Ke	32.47N	115.46 E
Fuyang He	28	Dg	38.14N	116.05 E
Fuyang Zhan	28	Ch	32.56N	115.53 E
Fuyu [China]	27	Lb	45.10N	124.52 E
Fuyu [China]	27	Lb	47.48N	124.26 E
Fuyuan [China]	27	Lc	42.44N	124.57 E
Fuyuan [China]	27	Nb	48.21N	134.18 E
Fuyuan [China]	27	Hf	25.43N	104.20 E
Fuyun/Koktokay	22	Ke	47.13N	89.39 E
Füzesabony	10	Qi	47.45N	20.25 E
Fuzhou [China]	22	Ng	26.10N	119.20 E
Fuzhou [China]	27	Kf	27.58N	116.20 E
Fuzhou He	28	Fe	39.36N	121.35 E
Fyllas Bank (EN)	41	Gf	64.00N	53.00W
Fyn	5	Hd	55.20N	10.30 E
Fyn [2]	8	Di	55.20N	10.30 E
Fyne, Loch-	9	He	56.10N	5.20W
Fyresdal	7	Bg	59.11N	8.06 E
Fyresvatn	8	Ce	59.05N	8.10 E
Fzâra, Gara'et-	14	Bn	36.47N	7.30 E

G

Gaasbeek	12	Gd	50.48N	4.10 E
Gaasterland	12	Hb	52.54N	5.36 E
Gaasterland	12	Hb	52.53N	5.35 E
Gaasterland-Balk	12	Hb	52.54N	5.36 E
Gabaru Reef	64a	Bb	7.53N	134.31 E
Gabas	11	Fk	43.46N	0.42W
Gabba'	35	Id	8.02N	50.08 E
Gabbs	46	Gg	38.52N	117.55W
Gabela	31	Ij	10.52S	14.23 E
Gabès, Gulf of-(EN) = Qābis, Khalīj-	30	Ie	34.00N	10.25 E
Gabon	36	Ab	0.25N	9.20 E
Gabon [1]	31	Ii	1.00S	11.45 E
Gaborone	31	Jk	24.40S	25.55 E
Gabras	35	Dc	10.16N	26.14 E
Gabriel Strait	42	Kd	61.50N	65.40W
Gabriel y Galán, Embalse de-	13	Fd	40.15N	6.15W
Gabrovo	15	Ig	42.52N	25.19 E
Gabrovo [2]	15	Ig	42.52N	25.19 E
Gacé	11	Gf	48.48N	0.18 E
Gachsārān	24	Ng	30.12N	50.47 E
Gackle	45	Gc	46.38N	99.09W
Gacko	14	Mg	43.10N	18.32 E
Gadag	25	Fe	15.25N	75.37 E
Gäddede	7	Dd	64.30N	14.09 E
Gadê	27	Ge	34.13N	99.29 E
Gadjač	16	Id	50.22N	34.01 E
Gádor, Sierra de-	13	Jh	36.55N	2.45W
Gadsden	43	Je	34.02N	86.02W
Gadūk, Gardaneh-ye-	24	Oe	35.55N	52.55 E
Gadzi	35	Be	4.47N	16.42 E
Gael Hamkes Bugt	41	Jd	74.00N	22.00W
Găeşti	15	Ie	44.43N	25.19 E
Gaeta	14	Hi	41.12N	13.35 E
Gaeta, Golfo di-	14	Hi	41.05N	13.30 E
Gaferut Island	57	Fd	9.14N	145.23 E
Gaffney	44	Gh	35.05N	81.39W
Gagan	63a	Ba	5.14S	154.37 E
Gagarin [R.S.F.S.R.]	19	Dd	55.35N	35.01 E
Gagarin [Uzb.-U.S.S.R.]	18	Gd	40.40N	68.05 E
Gagévésouva, Pointe-	63b	Ca	13.04S	166.32 E
Gaggenau	12	Kf	48.48N	8.20 E
Gagnef	7	Df	60.35N	15.04 E
Gagnoa	31	Gh	6.08N	5.56W
Gagnoa [3]	34	Dd	6.03N	6.00W
Gagnon	42	Kf	51.55N	68.10W
Gagra	19	Eg	43.17N	40.15 E
Gahkom	24	Ph	28.12N	55.50 E
Gahkom, Kūh-e-	24	Ph	28.10N	55.57 E
Gaíba, Laguna-	55	Dc	17.45S	57.43W
Gail	14	Hd	46.36N	13.53 E
Gaillac	11	Hk	43.54N	1.55 E
Gaillefontaine	12	De	49.39N	1.37 E
Gaillimh/Galway	6	Fe	53.16N	9.03W
Gaillimh/Galway [2]	9	Eh	53.20N	9.00W
Gaillon	12	De	49.10N	1.20 E
Gailtaler Alpen	14	Gd	46.40N	13.00 E
Gaiman	56	Gf	43.17S	65.29W
Găineşti	15	Ib	47.25N	25.55 E
Gainesville [Fl.-U.S.]	39	Kg	29.40N	82.20W
Gainesville [Ga.-U.S.]	43	Ke	34.18N	83.50W
Gainesville [Mo.-U.S.]	45	Jh	36.36N	92.26W
Gainesville [Tx.-U.S.]	43	He	33.37N	97.08W
Gainsborough	9	Mh	53.24N	0.46W
Gairdner, Lake-	57	Eh	31.35S	136.00 E
Gairloch	9	Hd	57.43N	5.40W
Gaizina Kalns/Gajzinkalns	8	Kh	56.50N	25.59 E
Gaj	19	Fe	51.31N	58.30 E
Gajny	19	Fc	60.20N	54.15 E
Gajsin	19	Cf	48.50N	29.27 E
Gajvoron	16	Fe	48.22N	29.52 E
Gajzinkalns/Gaizina Kalns	8	Kh	56.50N	25.59 E
Galaasija	18	Ee	39.52N	64.27 E
Gălăbovo	15	Ig	42.08N	25.51 E
Gala Gölü	15	Ji	40.45N	26.12 E
Galaico, Macizo-	13	Eb	42.30N	7.20W
Galán, Cerro-	56	Gc	25.55S	66.52W
Galana	30	Li	3.09S	40.08 E
Galanta	10	Nh	48.12N	17.44 E
Galap	64a	Bb	7.38N	134.39 E
Galápagos, Islas-/Colón, Archipiélago de- = Galapagos Islands (EN)	52	Gf	0.30S	90.30W
Galapagos Fracture Zone (EN)	3	Mi	0.00	100.00W
Galapagos Islands (EN) = Colon, Archipiélago de-/Galápagos, Islas-	52	Gf	0.30S	90.30W
Galapagos Islands (EN) = Galápagos, Islas-/Colón, Archipiélago de-	52	Gf	0.30S	90.30W
Galarza	55	Di	28.06S	56.41W
Galashiels	9	Kf	55.37N	2.49W
Galaţi [2]	15	Kd	45.33N	27.56 E
Galaţi	6	If	45.27N	28.03 E
Galatina	14	Mj	40.10N	18.10 E
Galatone	14	Mj	40.09N	18.04 E
Galatzó	13	Oe	39.38N	2.29 E
Galdar	32	Dd	28.09N	15.39W
Galdhøpiggen	7	Bf	61.37N	8.17 E
Galeana [Mex.]	48	Fb	30.07N	107.38W
Galeana [Mex.]	48	Ie	24.50N	100.04W
Galeh Dār	24	Oi	27.38N	52.42 E
Galela	58	Dd	1.50N	127.50 E
Galena [Ak.-U.S.]	40	Hd	64.44N	156.57W
Galena [Il.-U.S.]	45	Ke	42.25N	90.26W
Galeota Point	50	Fg	10.08N	60.59W
Galera, Punta-	56	Fe	39.59S	73.43W
Galera, Rio-	55	Bb	14.25S	60.07W
Galera Point	50	Fg	10.49N	60.55W
Galesburg	43	Ic	40.57N	90.22W

Galga	10	Pi	47.33N	19.43 E
Gal Gaduud [3]	35	Hd	5.00N	47.00 E
Galheirão, Rio-	55	Ja	12.23S	45.05W
Galheiros	55	Ia	13.18S	46.25W
Gali	16	Lh	42.36N	41.42 E
Galič [R.S.F.S.R.]	19	Ed	58.23N	42.21 E
Galič [Ukr.-U.S.S.R.]	16	De	49.06N	24.43 E
Galicea Mare	15	Ge	44.06N	23.18 E
Galicia	5	Fg	43.00N	8.00W
Galicia	13	Eb	43.00N	8.00W
Galicia (EN) = Galicija	5	If	49.50N	21.00 E
Galicia (EN) = Galicija [Eur.]	10	Qg	49.50N	21.00 E
Galicia (EN) = Galicja	10	Qg	49.50N	21.00 E
Galicia (EN) = Galicja	5	If	49.50N	21.00 E
Galicija [Eur.] = Galicia (EN)	10	Qg	49.50N	21.00 E
Galicija [Ukr.-U.S.S.R.]	10	Jg	49.00N	24.00 E
Galicija = Galicia (EN)	5	If	49.50N	21.00 E
Galicja = Galicia (EN)	5	If	49.50N	21.00 E
Galicja = Galicia (EN)	10	Qg	49.50N	21.00 E
Galilee, Lake-	59	Jd	22.20S	145.55 E
Galimy	20	Kd	62.19N	156.00 E
Galina Point	49	Id	18.24N	76.53W
Galion	44	Fe	40.44N	82.46W
Galion, Baie du-	51h	Bb	14.44N	60.57W
Galiton	14	Cm	37.30N	8.52 E
Galiuro Mountains	46	Jj	32.40N	110.20W
Gālka'yo	31	Lh	6.49N	47.23 E
Galkino	17	Ki	55.40N	62.55 E
Gallarate	14	Ce	45.40N	8.47 E
Gallatin	44	Dg	36.24N	86.27W
Gallatin Range	46	Jd	45.15N	111.05W
Gallatin River	46	Jd	45.56N	111.29W
Galle	22	Ki	6.02N	80.13 E
Gállego	13	Lc	41.39N	0.51W
Gallegos, Río-	52	Jk	51.36S	68.59W
Gallinas, Punta-	52	Id	12.25N	71.40W
Gallinas Peak	45	Di	34.15N	105.45W
Gallipoli	14	Lj	40.03N	17.58 E
Gallipoli Peninsula (EN) = Gelibolu Yarimadası	15	Ji	40.20N	26.30 E
Gallipolis	44	Ff	38.49N	82.14W
Gällivare	6	Ib	67.08N	20.42 E
Galljaaral	18	Fd	40.02N	67.35 E
Gallo	13	Jd	40.48N	2.09W
Gällö	7	De	62.55N	15.14 E
Gallo, Capo-	14	Hl	38.15N	13.19 E
Gallo Mountains	45	Bi	34.00N	108.15W
Galloway	9	If	55.00N	4.25W
Galloway, Mull of-	9	Ig	54.38N	4.50W
Gallup	39	If	35.32N	108.44W
Gallur	13	Kc	41.52N	1.19W
Gallura	14	Dj	41.00N	9.15 E
Galmaarden/Gammerages	12	Fd	50.45N	3.58 E
Galole	36	Hc	1.30S	40.02 E
Galt	44	Gd	43.22N	80.19W
Gal Tardo	35	He	3.37N	45.58 E
Galtasen	8	Eg	57.48N	13.30 E
Galty Mountains/Na Gaibhlte	9	Ei	52.23N	8.11W
Galut	27	Hb	46.43N	100.08 E
Galveston	39	Jg	29.18N	94.48W
Galveston Bay	38	Jg	29.36N	94.57W
Galveston Island	45	Il	29.13N	94.55W
Gálvez	56	Hd	32.02S	61.13W
Galway/Gaillimh [2]	9	Eh	53.20N	9.00W
Galway/Gaillimh	6	Fe	53.16N	9.03W
Galway Bay/Cuan na Gaillimhe	5	Fe	53.10N	9.15W
Gamaches	12	De	49.59N	1.33 E
Gamagōri	29	Ed	34.49N	137.13 E
Gamarra	54	Db	8.19N	73.44W
Gamba [China]	27	Ef	28.17N	88.31 E
Gamba [Gabon]	36	Ac	2.37S	10.00 E
Gambaga	34	Ec	10.32N	0.26W
Gambela	31	Kh	8.15N	34.36 E
Gambell	40	Ed	63.46N	171.46W
Gambia	30	Fg	13.28N	16.34W
Gambia [1]	31	Fg	13.25N	16.00W
Gambie	34	Bc	13.28N	16.34W
Gambier, Iles- = Gambier Islands (EN)	57	Ng	23.09S	134.58W
Gambier Islands (EN) = Gambier, Iles-	57	Ng	23.09S	134.58W
Gambo	35	Ce	4.39N	22.16 E
Gamboma	36	Cc	1.53S	15.51 E
Gambos	36	Be	14.45S	14.05 E
Gamboula	35	Be	4.08N	15.09 E
Gamda → Zamtang	27	He	32.23N	101.05 E
Gamelão	55	Db	15.29S	57.50W
Gamkonora, Gunung-	26	If	1.21N	127.31 E
Gamlakarleby/Kokkola	6	Ic	63.50N	23.07 E
Gamla Uppsala	8	Ge	59.54N	17.38 E
Gamleby	7	Dh	57.54N	16.24 E
Gamo Gofa [3]	35	Fd	5.45N	37.20 E
Gamua	64h	Bb	13.15S	176.08W
Gamud	35	Fe	4.05N	38.06 E
Gamvik	7	Ga	71.03N	28.14 E
Ganāne, Webi- = Juba (EN)	30	Lh	0.15S	42.38 E
Gananoque	44	Ic	44.20N	76.10W
Ganāveh	24	Nh	29.32N	50.31 E
Gancedo	55	Bh	27.30S	61.42W
Gancevići	16	Ec	52.45N	26.29 E
Gand/Gent = Ghent (EN)	11	Jc	51.03N	3.43 E
Ganda	36	Be	12.59S	14.40 E
Gandadiwata, Bulu-	26	Gg	2.42S	119.27 E
Gandajika	36	Dd	6.45S	23.57 E
Gandak	25	Hc	25.39N	85.13 E
Gander	39	Ne	48.57N	54.34W
Ganderkesee	12	Ka	53.04N	8.33 E
Gandesa	13	Mc	41.03N	0.26 E
Gandhinagar	22	Jg	23.21N	72.40 E
Gāndhi Sāgar	25	Fd	24.30N	75.30 E
Gandía	13	Lf	38.58N	0.11W
Gandía-Grao de Gandía	13	Lf	38.59N	0.09W

Gandisê Shan	21	Kf	31.00N	83.00 E
Gandu	54	Kf	13.45S	39.30W
Ganetti	35	Eb	17.58N	31.13 E
Ganga = Ganges (EN)	21	Lg	23.20N	90.30 E
Gangaw	25	Id	22.10N	94.08 E
Gangca (Shaliuhe)	27	Hd	37.30N	100.14 E
Ganges	11	Jk	43.56N	3.42 E
Ganges (EN) = Ganga	21	Lg	23.20N	90.30 E
Ganges, Mouths of the- (EN)	21	Lg	23.20N	90.30 E
Gangi	14	Im	37.48N	14.12 E
Gango	36	Cd	9.48S	15.40 E
Gangtok	22	Kg	27.20N	88.37 E
Gangu	27	Ie	34.45N	105.12 E
Gangziyao	28	Cf	36.17N	114.06 E
Gan He	27	Mb	49.12N	125.14 E
Ganhe	27	La	50.43N	123.00 E
Gani	26	Ig	0.47S	128.13 E
Ganjgah	24	Md	37.42N	48.16 E
Gan Jiang	21	Ng	29.12N	116.00 E
Ganjig → Horqin Zuoyi Houqi	27	Lc	42.57N	122.14 E
Gannan	27	Lb	47.53N	123.26 E
Gannat	11	Jh	46.06N	3.12 E
Gannett Peak	38	Ie	43.10N	109.40W
Gansbaai	37	Bf	34.35S	19.22 E
Gansu Sheng (Kan-su Sheng) = Kansu (EN) [2]	27	Hd	38.00N	102.00 E
Ganta	34	Dd	7.14N	8.59W
Gantang → Taiping	28	Ei	30.18N	118.07 E
Ganyu (Qingkou)	28	Eg	34.50N	119.07 E
Ganzhou	22	Ng	25.49N	114.56 E
Gao [3]	34	Eb	18.15N	1.00W
Gao [Mali]	31	Hg	16.15N	0.01 E
Gao [Niger]	34	Gb	15.25N	5.45 E
Gao'an	27	Kf	28.27N	115.24 E
Gaobeidian → Xincheng	28	Ce	39.20N	115.50 E
Gaocheng	28	Ce	38.02N	114.50 E
Gaolan (Shidongsi)	27	Hd	36.23N	103.55 E
Gaoliangjian → Hongze	27	Ke	33.10N	119.58 E
Gaoligong Shan	27	Gf	25.45N	98.45 E
Gaolou Ling	27	Ig	24.47N	106.48 E
Gaomi	28	Ef	36.23N	119.45 E
Gaoping	27	Jd	35.46N	112.55 E
Gaoqing (Tianzhen)	28	Df	37.10N	117.50 E
Gaotai	27	Gd	39.20N	99.58 E
Gaotingzhen → Daishan	28	Gi	30.15N	122.13 E
Gaoua	34	Ec	10.20N	3.11W
Gaoual	34	Cc	11.45N	13.12W
Gaoyang	28	Ce	38.42N	115.47 E
Gaoyi	28	Cf	37.37N	114.37 E
Gaoyou	28	Eh	32.46N	119.27 E
Gaoyou Hu	27	Ke	32.50N	119.15 E
Gaozhou	27	Jg	21.56N	110.47 E
Gap	11	Mj	44.34N	6.05 E
Gar	27	Ce	32.12N	79.57 E
Gara, Lough-/Loch Uí Ghadra	9	Eh	53.55N	8.30W
Gara'ad	35	Hd	6.54N	49.20 E
Garabato	55	Bi	28.56S	60.09W
Garachiné	49	Hi	8.04N	78.22W
Garachiné, Punta-	49	Hi	8.06N	78.25W
Gara Dragoman	15	Fg	42.55N	22.56 E
Ga'raet el Oubeïra	14	Cn	36.50N	8.23 E
Gara Kostenec	15	Gg	42.18N	23.52 E
Garalo	34	Dc	11.00N	7.26W
Gara Muleta	35	Gd	9.05N	41.43 E
Garanhuns	53	Mf	8.54S	36.29W
Garapan	64b	Ba	15.12N	145.43 E
Garapuava	55	Ic	16.06S	46.33W
Garavuti	18	Gf	37.36N	68.29 E
Garba	35	Cd	9.12N	20.30 E
Garbahārrey	35	Ge	3.20N	42.17 E
Garberville	46	Df	40.06N	123.48W
Gārbosh, Kūh-e-	24	Nf	32.36N	50.04 E
Garça	55	Hf	22.14S	49.37W
Garças, Rio das-	55	Fb	15.54S	52.16W
Garcias	55	Fe	20.34S	52.13W
Gard [3]	11	Jj	44.00N	4.00 E
Gard	11	Kk	43.51N	4.37 E
Garda	14	Ee	45.34N	10.42 E
Garda, Lago di- = Garda, Lake- (EN)	5	Hf	45.35N	10.35 E
Garda, Lake- (EN) = Garda, Lago di-	5	Hf	45.35N	10.35 E
Gardabani	16	Ni	41.29N	45.05 E
Garde, Cap de-	14	Bn	36.58N	7.47 E
Gardelegen	10	Hd	52.32N	11.22 E
Garden City [Ga.-U.S.]	44	Gi	32.06N	81.09W
Garden City [Ks.-U.S.]	43	Gd	37.58N	100.53W
Garden Grove	46	Gj	33.46N	117.57W
Garden Peninsula	44	Dc	45.40N	86.35W
Gardermoen	8	Dd	60.13N	11.06 E
Gardey	55	Cm	37.17S	59.21W
Gardēz	23	Kc	33.37N	69.07 E
Gardiner	46	Jd	45.02N	110.42W
Gardiner Range	59	Fc	19.15S	128.50 E
Gardner → Nikumaroro Atoll	57	Je	4.40S	174.32W
Gardner Pinnacles	57	Kb	25.00N	167.55W
Gardno, Jezioro-	10	Nb	54.43N	17.05 E
Gardone Riviera	14	Ee	45.37N	10.34 E
Gardždai/Gargždaj	7	Ei	55.43N	21.24 E
Gareloi	40a	Cb	51.47N	178.48W
Garessio	14	Cf	44.12N	8.02 E
Garfagnana	14	Ef	44.05N	10.30 E
Gargaliánoi	15	El	37.04N	21.38 E
Gargano	5	Hg	41.50N	16.00 E
Gargano, Testa del-	14	Ki	41.35N	16.12 E
Gargantua, Cape-	44	Eb	47.36N	85.02W
Gargždaj/Gargždai	7	Ei	55.43N	21.24 E
Gari	19	Gd	59.28N	62.25 E
Garibaldi	55	Gi	29.15S	51.32W
Garibaldi, Mount-	46	Db	49.51N	123.01W
Garies	37	Bf	30.30S	18.00 E
Garigliano	14	Hi	41.13N	13.45 E
Garimpo	55	Ed	18.41S	54.50W
Garissa	31	Ki	0.28S	39.38 E

Index Symbols

- [1] Independent Nation
- [2] State, Region
- [3] District, County
- [4] Municipality
- [5] Colony, Dependency
- Continent
- Physical Region
- Historical or Cultural Region
- Mount, Mountain
- Volcano
- Hill
- Mountains, Mountain Range
- Hills, Escarpment
- Plateau, Upland
- Pass, Gap
- Plain, Lowland
- Delta
- Salt Flat
- Valley, Canyon
- Crater, Cave
- Karst Features
- Depression
- Polder
- Desert, Dunes
- Forest, Woods
- Heath, Steppe
- Oasis
- Cape, Point
- Coast, Beach
- Cliff
- Peninsula
- Isthmus
- Sandbank
- Island
- Atoll
- Rock, Reef
- Islands, Archipelago
- Rocks, Reefs
- Coral Reef
- Well, Spring
- Geyser
- River, Stream
- Waterfall Rapids
- River Mouth, Estuary
- Lake
- Salt Lake
- Intermittent Lake
- Reservoir
- Swamp, Pond
- Canal
- Glacier
- Ice Shelf, Pack Ice
- Ocean
- Sea
- Gulf, Bay
- Strait, Fjord
- Lagoon
- Bank
- Seamount
- Tablemount
- Ridge
- Shelf
- Basin
- Escarpment, Sea Scarp
- Fracture
- Trench, Abyss
- National Park, Reserve
- Point of Interest
- Recreation Site
- Cave, Cavern
- Historic Site
- Ruins
- Wall, Walls
- Church, Abbey
- Temple
- Scientific Station
- Airport
- Port
- Lighthouse
- Mine
- Tunnel
- Dam, Bridge

Garkida 34 Hc 10.25N 12.34 E
Garland 45 Hj 32.54N 96.39W
Garlasco 14 Ce 45.12N 8.55 E
Garliava/Garljava 8 Jj 54.46N 23.55 E
Garljava/Garliava 8 Jj 54.46N 23.55 E
Garm 18 He 39.02N 70.18 E
Garmisch-Partenkirchen 10 Hi 47.30N 11.06 E
Garmsar 24 Oe 35.20N 52.13 E
Garnet Bank (EN) 55 Hk 33.05S 49.25W
Garnet Range 46 Ic 46.45N 113.15W
Garnett 45 Ig 38.17N 95.14W
Garonne 5 Ff 45.02N 0.36W
Garonne, Canal latéral à la- 11 Fj 44.34N 0.09W
Garopaba 55 Hi 28.04S 48.40W
Garoua 31 Ih 9.18N 13.24 E
Garoua Boulaï 35 Ad 5.53N 14.33 E
Garoubi 34 Fc 13.07N 2.18 E
Garöwe 31 Lh 8.25N 48.33 E
Garpenberg 8 Gd 60.19N 16.12 E
Garphyttan 8 Fe 59.19N 14.56 E
Garrel 12 Kb 52.57N 8.01 E
Garreru 64a Bc 7.20N 134.33 E
Garri, Kūh-e- 24 Mf 33.59N 48.25 E
Garrigues 11 Kj 44.10N 4.30 E
Garrison 45 Fc 47.40N 101.25W
Garron Point/An Gearran 9 Hf 55.05N 5.58W
Garrovillas 13 Fe 39.43N 6.33W
Garruchos 55 Ei 28.11S 55.39W
Garry 9 Je 56.45N 3.45W
Garry Bay 42 Ic 69.00N 85.10W
Garry Lake 38 Jc 66.00N 100.00W
Garsen 36 Hc 2.16S 40.07 E
Gartar/Qianning 27 He 30.27N 101.29 E
Gartempe 11 Gh 46.47N 0.50 E
Gartog → Markam 27 Gf 29.32N 98.33 E
Garut 26 Eh 7.13S 107.54 E
Garuva 55 Hh 26.01S 48.51W
Garvie Mountains 62 Cf 45.30S 168.50 E
Garwa 25 Gd 24.11N 83.49 E
Garwolin 10 Re 51.54N 21.37 E
Gary 43 Jc 41.36N 87.20W
Garyarsa 27 De 31.40N 80.26 E
Garzê 27 Ge 31.42N 99.58 E
Garzón [Col.] 54 Cc 2.13N 75.38W
Garzón [Ur.] 56 Jd 34.36S 54.33W
Gasan-Kuli 19 Fh 37.29N 53.59 E
Gascogne = Gascony (EN) 11 Gk 43.30N 0.10 E
Gasconade River 45 Kg 38.40N 91.33W
Gascony (EN) = Gascogne 11 Gk 43.30N 0.10 E
Gascoyne Junction 59 De 25.03S 115.12 E
Gascoyne River 57 Cg 24.52S 113.37 E
Gasefjord 41 Je 70.00N 27.30W
Gaseland 41 Jd 70.20N 29.00W
Gash 30 Kg 16.48N 35.51 E
Gas Hu 27 Fd 38.08N 90.45 E
Gashua 31 Ig 12.52N 11.03 E
Gaspar Strait (EN)=Kelasa, Selat- 26 Eg 2.40S 107.15 E
Gaspé 39 Me 48.50N 64.29W
Gaspé, Cap de - 42 Lg 48.45N 64.10W
Gaspé, Péninsule de-= Gaspe Peninsula (EN) 38 Me 48.30N 65.00W
Gaspe Peninsula (EN)= Gaspé, Péninsule de- 38 Me 48.30N 65.00W
Gassan 29 Gb 38.34N 140.01 E
Gassol 34 Hd 8.32N 10.28 E
Gaston, Lake- 44 Ig 36.35N 78.00W
Gastonia 43 Kd 35.16N 81.11W
Gastoúni 15 El 37.51N 21.15 E
Gastre 56 Gf 42.17S 69.14W
Gästrikland 8 Gd 60.30N 16.30 E
Gata, Akrōtérion- 24 Ee 34.34N 33.02 E
Gata, Cabo de- 5 Fh 36.43N 2.12W
Gata, Sierra de- 13 Fd 40.15N 6.45W
Gătaia 15 Ed 45.26N 21.26 E
Gatčina 19 Dd 59.34N 30.09 E
Gate 45 Fh 36.51N 100.01W
Gate City 44 Fg 36.38N 82.37W
Gateshead 9 Lg 54.58N 1.37W
Gateshead 42 Hb 70.35N 100.15W
Gathemo 12 Bf 48.46N 0.58W
Gâtinais 11 If 48.00N 2.20 E
Gâtine, Hauteurs de- 11 Fh 46.38N 0.38W
Gatineau, Rivière- 42 Jg 45.27N 75.42W
Gatlinburg 44 Fh 35.43N 83.31W
Gato, Cumbres del- 48 Fd 27.00N 106.35W
Gatooma 31 Jj 18.21S 29.55 E
Gattinara 14 Ce 45.37N 8.22 E
Gatún 49 Hi 9.16N 79.55W
Gatún, Lago-=Gatun Lake (EN) 47 Ig 9.12N 79.55W
Gatun Lake (EN)=Gatún, Lago- 47 Ig 9.12N 79.55W
Gatvand 24 Mf 32.15N 48.50 E
Gatwick Airport 12 Bc 51.08N 0.12W
Gaucín 13 Gh 36.31N 5.19W
Gauhati 22 Lg 26.11N 91.44 E
Gauiena/Gaujiena 8 Lg 57.25N 26.28 E
Gauja 7 Fh 57.10N 24.16 E
Gaujiena/Gauiena 8 Lg 57.25N 26.28 E
Gaula [Nor.] 8 Da 63.21N 10.14 E
Gaula [Nor.] 8 Ac 61.22N 5.41 E
Gauldalen 8 Db 63.00N 11.00 E
Gauley River 44 Gf 38.10N 81.12W
Gau-Odernheim 12 Ke 49.46N 8.12 E
Gaurdak 19 Gh 37.49N 66.01 E
Gausdal 8 Cc 61.20N 9.55 E
Gausta 7 Bg 59.50N 8.39 E
Gāvbandī 24 Oi 27.12N 53.04 E
Gāvbūs, Kūh-e- 24 Oi 27.10N 54.00 E
Gavdhopoúla 15 Go 34.56N 24.00 E
Gávdhos 5 Ii 34.50N 24.05 E
Gāveh 24 Le 35.00N 46.58 E
Gavere 12 Fd 50.56N 3.40 E
Gavkhūnī, Bāţlāq-e- 24 Of 32.06N 52.52 E
Gāv Kosh 24 Le 34.00N 48.00 E
Gävle 6 Hc 60.40N 17.10 E
Gävleborg [2] 7 Df 61.30N 16.15 E
Gävlebukten 8 Gd 60.40N 17.20 E
Gavorrano 14 Eh 42.55N 10.54 E
Gavri 8 Lh 56.49N 27.58 E
Gavrilov-Jam 7 Jh 57.19N 39.51 E
Gāw Koshi 23 Id 28.38N 57.12 E
Gawler 59 Hf 34.37S 138.44 E
Gawler Ranges 57 Eh 32.30S 136.00 E
Gaxun Nur 21 Me 42.25N 101.00 E
Gaya [India] 22 Kg 24.47N 85.00 E
Gaya [Niger] 34 Fc 11.53N 3.27 E
Gaya He 28 Jc 42.58N 129.52 E
Gaylord 44 Ec 45.02N 84.40W
Gayndah 59 Ke 25.37S 151.36 E
Gaz 24 Nf 32.48N 51.37 E
Gaza [3] 37 Ed 23.30S 33.00 E
Gaz-Ačak 19 Gg 41.11N 61.27 E
Gazalkent 18 Gd 41.33N 69.46 E
Gazaoua 34 Gc 13.32N 7.55 E
Gazelle, Récif de la- 63b Be 20.11S 165.27 E
Gaziantep 22 Ff 37.05N 37.22 E
Gaziemir 15 Kk 38.19N 27.10 E
Gazimur 20 Hf 52.57N 120.22 E
Gazipaşa 24 Ed 36.17N 32.20 E
Gazli 19 Gg 40.09N 63.23 E
Gbarnga 31 Gh 7.00N 9.29W
Gboko 34 Gd 7.21N 8.58 E
Gbon 34 Dd 9.50N 6.27W
Gdańsk [2] 10 Ob 54.25N 18.40 E
Gdańsk=Danzig (EN) 6 He 54.23N 18.40 E
Gdansk, Gulf of- (EN)= Gdanska, Zatoka- 5 He 54.40N 19.15 E
Gdánska, Zatoka-=Gdansk, Gulf of- (EN) 5 He 54.40N 19.15 E
Gdov 7 Gg 58.47N 27.54 E
Gdynia 6 He 54.32N 18.33 E
Gearhart Mountain 46 Ee 42.30N 120.53W
Gêba 34 Bc 11.58N 15.00W
Gebe, Pulau- 26 Ig 0.05S 129.20 E
Gebze 24 Cb 40.48N 29.25 E
Gecha 35 Fd 7.29N 35.25 E
Gedi 36 Hc 3.18S 40.01 E
Gedinne 12 Ge 49.59N 4.56 E
Gediz 24 Cc 39.02N 29.25 E
Gedo 35 Ge 2.20N 41.20 E
Gedo [3] 35 Ge 3.00N 42.00 E
Gedo 35 Fd 9.00N 37.29 E
Gedser, Sydfalster- 7 Ci 54.35N 11.57 E
Gedser Odde 8 Dj 54.34N 11.59 E
Geel 11 Kc 51.10N 5.00 E
Geelong 58 Fh 38.08S 144.21 E
Geelvink Channel 59 Ce 28.30S 114.10 E
Geer 12 Hd 50.51N 5.42 E
Geeste 12 Jb 52.36N 7.16 E
Geesthacht 10 Gc 53.26N 10.22 E
Gē'gyai 27 De 32.29N 80.52 E
Ge Hu 28 Ei 31.36N 119.51 E
Geidam 34 Hc 12.53N 11.56 E
Geigar 35 Ec 11.59N 32.46 E
Geihoku 29 Cd 34.44N 132.17 E
Geikie 42 He 57.48N 103.46W
Geilo 7 Bf 60.31N 8.12 E
Geiranger 8 Bb 62.06N 7.12 E
Geisenheim 12 Je 49.59N 7.58 E
Geislingen an der Steige 10 Fh 48.37N 9.51 E
Geita 36 Fc 2.52S 32.10 E
Geithus 7 Bg 59.57N 9.59 E
Geiyo-Shotō 29 Cd 34.15N 132.45 E
Gejiu 22 Mg 23.22N 103.14 E
Gel [Sud.] 30 Jh 7.46N 29.36 E
Gel [Sud.] 35 Ed 6.08N 31.17 E
Gela 14 Im 37.04N 14.15 E
Gela, Golfo di- 14 Im 37.05N 14.10 E
Geladi 35 Hd 6.57N 46.25 E
Geldenaken/Jodoigne 12 Gd 50.43N 4.52 E
Gelderland [3] 12 Hb 52.10N 5.50 E
Geldermalsen 12 Hc 51.53N 5.19 E
Geldern 10 Ce 51.31N 6.20 E
Geldrop 12 Hc 51.25N 5.33 E
Geleen 11 Ld 50.58N 5.52 E
Gelembé 15 Kj 39.10N 27.50 E
Gelemso 35 Gd 8.48N 40.32 E
Gelendžik 19 Dg 44.33N 38.06 E
Gélengdeng 35 Bc 10.56N 15.32 E
Gelgaudiškis 8 Ji 55.02N 22.58 E
Gelibolu 24 Bb 40.24N 26.40 E
Gelibolu Yarimadası = Gallipoli Peninsula (EN) 15 Ji 40.20N 26.30 E
Gélise 11 Gj 44.11N 0.17 E
Gellinsör 35 Hd 6.24N 46.46 E
Gelnhausen 10 Ff 50.12N 9.11 E
Gelsenkirchen 10 De 51.31N 7.06 E
Gemena 31 Ih 3.15N 19.46 E
Gemerek 24 Gc 39.11N 36.05 E
Gemert 12 Hc 51.33N 5.41 E
Gemi, Jabal- 35 Ed 9.01N 34.09 E
Gemlik 24 Cb 40.26N 29.09 E
Gemlik Körfezi 24 Cb 40.25N 28.55 E
Gemona del Friuli 14 Hd 46.16N 13.09 E
Gemünden (Felda) 12 Ld 50.42N 9.03 E
Gemünden (Wohra) 12 Kd 50.58N 8.58 E
Gemünden am Main 10 Ff 50.03N 9.42 E
Genale 30 Lh 0.15S 42.38 E
Genç 24 Ic 38.46N 40.35 E
Gendringen 12 Ic 51.52N 6.23 E
Gendringen-Ulft 12 Ic 51.54N 6.24 E
Genemuiden 12 Ib 52.37N 6.02 E
General Acha 56 He 37.23S 64.36W
General Alvear [Arg.] 56 Gd 34.58S 67.42W
General Alvear [Arg.] 56 He 36.03S 60.01W
General Arenales 55 Bl 34.18S 61.18W
General Artigas 55 Dh 26.53S 56.17W
General Belgrano 56 Ie 35.46S 58.30W
General Belgrano Station 66 Af 77.50S 38.00W
General Bernardo O'Higgins 66 Re 63.19S 57.54W
General Bravo 48 Je 25.48N 99.10W
General Cabrera 56 Hd 32.48S 63.52W
General Capdevila 55 Bh 27.26S 61.28W
General Carneiro 55 Gh 26.28S 51.25W
General Carrera, Lago- 52 Ij 46.30S 72.00W
General Cepeda 48 Ie 25.23N 101.27W
General Conesa [Arg.] 55 Dm 36.30S 57.20W
General Conesa [Arg.] 56 Hf 40.06S 64.26W
General Enrique Martínez 55 Fk 33.12S 53.50W
General Galarza 55 Ck 32.43S 59.24W
General Güemes 56 Hb 24.40S 65.00W
General Guido 56 Ie 36.40S 57.46W
General José de San Martín 55 Ch 26.33S 59.21W
General Juan Madariaga 56 Ie 37.00S 57.09W
General La Madrid 56 He 37.16S 61.17W
General Lavalle 56 Ie 36.24S 56.58W
General Manuel Belgrano, Cerro- 52 Jh 29.01S 67.49W
General O'Brien 55 Bl 34.54S 60.45W
General Pico 56 He 35.40S 63.44W
General Pinedo 56 Hc 27.19S 61.17W
General Pinto 55 Bl 34.46S 61.53W
General Pirán 55 Dm 37.16S 57.45W
General Roca 56 Ge 39.02S 67.35W
General Salgado 55 Ge 20.39S 50.22W
General Santos 22 Oi 6.05N 125.10 E
General Sarmiento 55 Cl 34.33S 58.43W
General Terán 48 Je 25.16N 99.41W
General-Toševo 15 Lf 43.42N 28.02 E
General Treviño 48 Jd 26.14N 99.29W
General Trías 48 Fc 28.21N 106.22W
General Vargas 55 Ei 29.42S 54.40W
General Viamonte 55 Bl 35.01S 61.01W
General Villegas 56 He 35.02S 63.01W
Genesee River 44 Id 43.16N 77.36W
Geneseo 44 Id 42.46N 77.49W
Geneva [Al.-U.S.] 44 Ej 31.02N 85.52W
Geneva [Nb.-U.S.] 45 Hf 40.32N 97.36W
Geneva [N.Y.-U.S.] 44 Id 42.53N 76.59W
Geneva (EN) = Genève 6 Gf 46.10N 6.10 E
Geneva, Lake- (EN) = Léman, Lac- 5 Gf 46.25N 6.30 E
Genève [2] 14 Ad 46.10N 6.15 E
Genève = Geneva (EN) 6 Gf 46.10N 6.10 E
Genevois 11 Mh 46.00N 6.10 E
Genhe → Ergun Zuoqi 22 Od 50.47N 121.32 E
Geni 35 Ed 8.31N 33.10 E
Geničesk 19 Df 46.12N 34.48 E
Genil 13 Gg 37.42N 5.19W
Genk 11 Ld 50.58N 5.30 E
Genkai-Nada 29 Ae 33.45N 130.00 E
Gennargentu 5 Gg 40.00N 9.20 E
Gennep 12 Hc 51.42N 5.59 E
Genoa (EN) = Genova 6 Gg 44.25N 8.57 E
Genoa, Gulf of- (EN) = Genova, Golfo di- 5 Gg 44.10N 8.55 E
Genova = Genoa (EN) 6 Gg 44.25N 8.57 E
Genova, Golfo di- = Genoa, Gulf of- (EN) 5 Gg 44.10N 8.55 E
Genova-Nervi 14 Df 44.23N 9.02 E
Genova-Voltri 14 Cf 44.26N 8.45 E
Genovesa, Isla- 54a Ba 0.20N 89.58W
Gent/Gand=Ghent (EN) 11 Jc 51.03N 3.43 E
Gentbrugge, Gent- 12 Fc 51.03N 3.45 E
Gent-Gentbrugge 12 Fc 51.03N 3.45 E
Genthin 10 Id 52.24N 12.10 E
Gent-Sint-Amandsberg 12 Fc 51.04N 3.45 E
Genū, Kūhhā-ye- 23 Id 27.25N 56.09 E
Genyem 26 Lg 2.46S 140.12 E
Genzano di Lucania 14 Kj 40.51N 16.02 E
Genzano di Roma 14 Fi 41.42N 11.41 E
Geographe Bay 57 Ch 33.35S 115.15 E
Geographe Channel 59 Cd 24.40S 113.20 E
Geographical Society Øer 41 Jd 72.40N 22.20W
Geokčaj 16 Oi 40.40N 47.42 E
Geok-Tepe 19 Fh 38.10N 57.58 E
Geomagnetic Pole (1975) (EN) 66 Hf 78.40S 109.33 E
Georga, Zemlja- 21 Ga 80.30N 49.00 E
George 38 Md 58.30N 66.00W
George 37 Cf 33.58S 22.24 E
George, Lake- [Austl.] 59 Jg 35.05S 149.25 E
George, Lake- [Fl.-U.S.] 44 Gk 29.17N 81.36W
George, Lake- [Ug.] 36 Fc 0.00 30.12 E
George, Lake- [U.S.] 44 Kd 43.35N 73.35W
George Gill Range 59 Gd 24.15S 131.35 E
Georges Bank (EN) 43 Nc 41.15N 67.30W
George Sound 62 Bf 44.50S 167.20 E
George Town 58 Fi 41.06S 146.50 E
Georgetown 45 Hk 30.38N 97.41W
George Town 22 Mi 5.25N 100.20 E
Georgetown [Austl.] 58 Ff 18.18S 143.33 E
Georgetown [Bah.] 49 Jb 23.30N 75.46W
Georgetown [Cay.Is.] 47 He 19.18N 81.23W
Georgetown [De.-U.S.] 44 Jf 38.42N 75.23W
Georgetown [Gam.] 31 Fg 13.32N 14.46W
Georgetown [Guy.] 53 Ke 6.48N 58.10W
Georgetown [Ky.-U.S.] 44 Ef 38.13N 84.33W
Georgetown [Oh.-U.S.] 44 Ff 38.52N 83.54W
Georgetown [S.C.-U.S.] 43 Le 33.23N 79.18W
Georgetown [St.Hel.] 31 Fi 7.56S 14.25W
Georgetown [St.Vin.] 50 Ff 13.16N 61.08W
George V Coast 66 Je 68.30S 147.30 E
George VI Sound 66 Qf 71.00S 68.00W
George West 45 Gl 28.20N 98.07W
Georgia [2] 43 Ke 32.50N 83.15W
Georgia (EN) 5 Kg 42.00N 44.00 E
Georgia, Strait of - 42 Fg 49.00N 123.20W
Georgia del Sur, Islas-/ South Georgia 66 Ad 54.15S 36.45W
Georgian Bay 38 Ke 45.15N 80.50W
Georgian SSR (EN)= Gruzinskaja SSR [2] 19 Eg 42.00N 44.00 E
Georgijevka [Kaz.-U.S.S.R.] 19 Hg 43.02N 74.43 E
Georgijevka [Kaz.-U.S.S.R.] 19 If 49.19N 81.35 E
Georgijevsk 16 Mg 44.09N 43.28 E
Georgina River 57 Eg 23.30S 139.47 E
Georgsmarienhütte 10 Ed 52.16N 8.02 E
Gera 10 Ie 51.08N 10.56 E
Gera 10 If 50.52N 12.05 E
Gera [2] 10 Hf 50.45N 11.55 E
Geraardsbergen/Grammont 12 Fd 50.46N 3.52 E
Gerais, Chapadão dos- 55 Jc 17.40S 45.35W
Geral, Serra- [Braz.] 55 Gi 29.10S 50.15W
Geral, Serra- [Braz.] 52 Kh 26.30S 50.30W
Geral, Serra- [Braz.] 55 Gf 23.54S 50.46W
Geral da Serra, Coxilha- 55 Ej 30.20S 55.15W
Geral de Goiás, Serra- 52 Lg 13.00S 46.15W
Geraldine 62 Df 44.05S 171.15 E
Geral do Paraná, Serra- 55 Ib 14.45S 47.30W
Geraldton [Austl.] 58 Cg 28.46S 114.36 E
Geraldton [Ont.-Can.] 42 Ig 49.44N 86.57W
Gérardmer 11 Mf 48.04N 6.53 E
Geräsh 24 Pi 27.40N 54.06 E
Gerbiči, Gora- 20 Fc 66.39N 105.02 E
Gerca 15 Ja 48.10N 26.17 E
Gercüş 24 Id 37.34N 41.23 E
Gerecse 10 Oi 47.41N 18.29 E
Gerede 24 Eb 40.52N 32.39 E
Gerede 24 Eb 40.48N 32.12 E
Gerês, Serra do- 13 Ec 41.48N 8.00W
Gereshk 23 Jc 31.48N 64.34 E
Gérgal 13 Jg 37.07N 2.33W
Gering 45 Ef 41.50N 103.40W
Gerlachovský štít 10 Qg 49.12N 20.09 E
Gerlogubi 35 Hd 6.56N 45.03 E
Gerlos 14 Gc 47.14N 12.02 E
Gerlovo 15 Kf 43.03N 27.35 E
German Democratic Republic (EN)=Deutsche Demokratische Republik [1] 6 He 52.00N 12.30 E
Germania 55 Al 34.34S 62.03W
Germania Land 41 Kc 76.50N 20.00W
Germany, Federal Republic of- (EN)=Bundesrepublik Deutschland [1] 6 Ge 51.00N 9.00 E
Germencik 15 Kl 37.51N 27.37 E
Germersheim 12 Ke 49.13N 8.22 E
Germī 23 Hc 33.32N 54.58 E
Germi 24 Mc 39.01N 48.03 E
Germiston 37 De 26.15S 28.05 E
Gernsbach 12 Kf 48.46N 8.19 E
Gernsheim 12 Ke 49.45N 8.29 E
Gero 28 Ng 35.48N 137.14 E
Gerolstein 12 Id 50.13N 6.40 E
Gerona [3] 13 Ob 42.10N 2.40 E
Gerona/Girona 13 Oc 41.59N 2.49 E
Gerpinnes 12 Gd 50.20N 4.31 E
Gers 11 Gj 44.09N 0.39 E
Gers [3] 11 Gk 43.40N 0.30 E
Gersprenz 12 Le 49.59N 9.04 E
Gêrzê 27 De 32.20N 84.04 E
Gerze 24 Fb 41.48N 35.12 E
Gescher 12 Jc 51.57N 7.00 E
Geseke 12 Kc 51.39N 8.31 E
Geser 26 Jg 3.53S 130.54 E
Gesunda 8 Fd 60.54N 14.32 E
Gesunden 8 Fa 63.10N 15.55 E
Geta 7 Ef 60.23N 19.50 E
Getafe 13 Id 40.18N 3.43W
Gete 11 Ld 50.55N 5.08 E
Getinge 7 Ch 56.49N 12.44 E
Gettysburg 45 Gd 45.01N 99.57W
Gettysburg Seamount (EN) 32 Eb 36.32N 11.37W
Getúlio Vargas 55 Fh 27.50S 52.16W
Getz Ice Shelf 66 Nf 74.15S 125.00W
Geul 12 Hd 50.40N 5.43 E
Gévaudan 11 Jj 44.27N 3.30 E
Gevelsberg 12 Jc 51.19N 7.20 E
Gevgelija 15 Fh 41.08N 22.31 E
Gévora 13 Ff 38.53N 6.57W
Gevsjön 8 Ea 63.25N 12.40 E
Gewane 35 Gc 10.10N 40.39 E
Gex 11 Mh 46.20N 6.04 E
Gexianzhuang → Qinghe 28 Cf 37.03N 115.39 E
Geyersberg 10 Fg 49.50N 9.30 E
Geyik Daği 24 Ed 36.54N 32.10 E
Geyikli 15 Jj 39.48N 26.12 E
Geyser, Banc du- 37 Hb 12.25S 46.25 E
Geysir 5 Dc 64.19N 20.18W
Geyve 24 Db 40.30N 30.18 E
Ghabāri, Darb al- 24 Cj 25.10N 29.50 E
Ghadāmis 31 He 30.08N 9.30 E
Ghadduwah 33 Bd 26.26N 14.18 E
Ghaghara 21 Kg 24.52N 84.55 E
Ghaghe 63a Db 7.23S 158.12 E
Ghallah, Wādī al- 30 Jg 10.25N 27.32 E
Ghamrah, Wādī al- 24 Hj 25.47N 38.45 E
Ghana [1] 31 Gh 8.00N 2.00W
Ghanzi 31 Jk 21.42S 21.38 E
Ghanzi [3] 37 Cd 22.00S 23.00 E
Ghār ad Dimā' 14 Cn 36.27N 8.26 E
Gharaqābād 24 Me 35.06N 49.50 E
Gharbī, Al Hajar al- 24 Qj 24.10N 56.15 E
Gharbīyah, Aş Şaḩrā' al-= Western Desert (EN) 30 Jf 27.30N 28.00 E
Ghardaïa 31 He 32.29N 3.40 E
Ghārib, Jabal- 33 Fd 28.07N 32.54 E
Gharrāf, Shaţţ al- 24 Kf 32.30N 45.48 E
Gharsah, Shaţţ al- 32 Ic 34.06N 7.50 E
Gharyān 33 Bc 32.10N 13.01 E
Gharyān [3] 33 Bc 30.35N 12.00 E
Ghāt 31 If 24.58N 10.11 E
Ghatere 63a Db 7.58S 159.01 E
Ghaţţī 24 Gg 31.16N 37.31 E
Ghazāl, Baḩr al- 35 Ed 9.31N 30.25 E
Ghazal, Bahr el- 30 Ig 13.01N 15.28 E
Ghazal, Bahr el- 35 Bc 14.00N 16.30 E
Ghazaouet 32 Gb 35.06N 1.51W
Ghazipur 25 Gc 25.35N 83.34 E
Ghaznī 22 If 33.33N 68.26 E
Ghaznī [3] 23 Kc 33.00N 68.00 E
Ghent (EN)=Gand/Gent 11 Jc 51.03N 3.43 E
Ghent (EN)=Gent/Gand 11 Jc 51.03N 3.43 E
Gheorghe Gheorghiu-Dej 15 Jc 46.12N 26.46 E
Gheorghieni 15 Ic 46.43N 25.37 E
Gheorghiu-Dej 19 De 51.00N 39.31 E
Gherla 15 Gb 47.02N 23.55 E
Ghidigeni 15 Kc 46.03N 27.30 E
Ghidole (EN)=Gidole 35 Fd 5.37N 37.29 E
Ghilarza 14 Cj 40.07N 8.50 E
Ghimeş, Pasul- 15 Jc 46.33N 26.07 E
Ghisonaccia 11a Ba 42.00N 9.24 E
Ghizunabeana Islands 63a Db 7.33S 158.45 E
Ghowr [3] 23 Jc 34.00N 65.00 E
Ghriss 13 Mi 35.15N 0.10 E
Ghubbat al Qamar 21 Hh 16.00N 52.30 E
Ghudāf, Wādī al- 24 Jf 32.56N 43.30 E
Ghurāb, Jabal al- 24 Hf 34.00N 38.42 E
Ghurayrah 33 Hf 18.37N 42.41 E
Ghūriān 23 Jc 34.21N 61.30 E
Ghurrah, Jabal al- 14 Cn 36.36N 8.23 E
Ghuzayyil, Sabkhat- 33 Dd 29.50N 19.45 E
Giaginskaja 16 Lg 44.47N 40.05 E
Giala, Jabal- 24 Ei 27.20N 32.57 E
Gialo Oasis (EN)=Jālū, Wāḩāt- 30 Jf 29.00N 21.20 E
Gialoúsa 24 Fe 35.35N 34.15 E
Gia Nghia 25 Lf 11.59N 107.42 E
Giannutri 14 Fh 42.15N 11.05 E
Giant's Causeway/Clochán an Aifir 9 Gf 55.15N 6.35W
Giarre 14 Jm 37.43N 15.11 E
Gibara 49 Ic 21.07N 76.08W
Gibbon Point 51b Bb 18.14N 63.00W
Gibb River 59 Fc 16.25S 126.25 E
Gibbs Islands 66 Re 61.30S 55.31W
Gibellina 14 Gm 37.47N 12.58 E
Gibeon [3] 37 Bd 25.00S 18.30 E
Gibeon 37 Be 25.09S 17.43 E
Gibostad 7 Db 69.21N 18.00 E
Gibraleón 13 Fg 37.23N 6.58W
Gibraltar 6 Fh 36.11N 5.22W
Gibraltar [5] 6 Fh 36.11N 5.22W
Gibraltar, Estrecho de-= Gibraltar, Strait of- (EN) 5 Fh 35.57N 5.36W
Gibraltar, Strait of- (EN)= Djebel Ţāriq, El Bōghāz- 5 Fh 35.57N 5.36W
Gibraltar, Strait of- (EN)= Gibraltar, Estrecho de- 5 Fh 35.57N 5.36W
Gibson Desert 57 Dg 24.30S 126.00 E
Gidami 35 Ed 8.58N 34.40 E
Giddings 45 Hk 30.11N 96.56W
Gidigič 15 Lb 47.04N 28.38 E
Gidole=Ghidole (EN) 35 Fd 5.37N 37.29 E
Gien 11 Ig 47.42N 2.38 E
Giens, Presqu'île de- 11 Mk 43.02N 6.08 E
Gier 11 Ki 45.35N 4.46 E
Gießen 10 Ef 50.35N 8.39 E
Gieten 12 Ia 53.01N 6.48 E
Giethoorn 12 Ib 52.43N 6.07 E
Gifford 42 Jb 70.21N 83.05W
Gifford Seamount (EN) 52 Hi 39.00S 82.00W
Gifhorn 10 Gd 52.29N 10.33 E
Gift Lake 42 Fe 55.49N 115.57W
Gifu 22 Pf 35.25N 136.45 E
Gifu Ken [2] 28 Ng 35.50N 137.00 E
Gigant 16 Lf 46.29N 41.20 E
Giganta, Cerro- 47 Bc 26.07N 111.36W
Giganta, Sierra de la- 47 Bc 26.18N 111.39W
Gigante 54 Cc 2.24N 75.34W
Gigen 15 Hf 43.42N 24.29 E
Gigha 9 Hf 55.41N 5.44W
Giglio 14 Eh 42.20N 10.55 E
Gijón 6 Fg 43.32N 5.40W
Gikongoro 36 Ec 2.30S 29.35 E
Gila Bend 46 Ij 32.57N 112.43W
Gila Bend Mountains 46 Ij 33.10N 113.10W
Gilān [3] 23 Gb 37.00N 49.50 E
Gīlān-e-Gharb 24 Ke 34.08N 45.55 E
Gila River 43 Ee 32.43N 114.33W
Gilbert, Mount- 46 Ca 50.51N 124.20W
Gilbert Islands 57 Ie 0.01S 174.00 E
Gilbert River 59 Ic 16.35S 141.15 E
Gilbert Seamount (EN) 40 If 52.50N 150.10W
Gilbués 54 Ie 9.50S 45.21W
Gilé 37 Fc 16.09S 38.19 E
Giles Meteorological Station 59 Fe 25.02S 128.18 E
Gilford Island 46 Ba 50.45N 126.25W
Gilgandra 59 Jf 31.42S 148.39 E
Gilgău 15 Gb 47.17N 23.43 E
Gilgil 36 Gc 0.30S 36.19 E
Gilgit 25 Ea 35.44N 74.38 E
Gilgit 22 Jf 35.55N 74.18 E
Gilijuj 20 Hf 54.17N 127.05 E
Gillam 42 Ie 56.21N 94.43W
Gilleleje 8 Eh 56.07N 12.19 E
Gillen, Lake- 59 Ee 26.10S 124.40 E
Gillenfeld 12 Id 50.07N 6.54 E
Gillette 43 Fc 44.18N 105.30W
Gillian, Lake - 42 Jc 69.30N 75.30W
Gillingham 9 Nj 51.24N 0.33 E
Gilo 35 Ed 8.10N 33.15 E
Gilort 15 Ge 44.36N 23.27 E
Gilroy 46 Eh 37.00N 121.34W
Giluwe, Mount- 60 Ci 6.04S 143.53 E
Gilvān 24 Md 36.47N 49.08 E
Gimån 8 Gb 62.28N 16.20 E
Gimbi 35 Fd 9.10N 35.51 E
Gimie, Mount- 50 Ff 13.52N 61.01W
Gimli 42 Hf 50.39N 97.00W
Gimo 8 Hd 60.11N 18.11 E
Gimolskoje, Ozero- 7 He 63.00N 32.15 E
Gimone 11 Hk 44.00N 1.06 E
Ginda 35 Fb 15.27N 39.06 E
Ginetu 63a Ac 9.30S 152.43 E

Index Symbols

[1] Independent Nation
[2] State, Region
[3] District, County
[4] Municipality
[5] Colony, Dependency
Continent
Physical Region
Historical or Cultural Region
Mount, Mountain
Volcano
Hill
Mountains, Mountain Range
Hills, Escarpment
Plateau, Upland
Pass, Gap
Plain, Lowland
Delta
Salt Flat
Valley, Canyon
Crater, Cave
Karst Features
Depression
Polder
Desert, Dunes
Forest, Woods
Heath, Steppe
Oasis
Cape, Point
Coast, Beach
Cliff
Peninsula
Isthmus
Sandbank
Island
Atoll
Rock, Reef
Islands, Archipelago
Rocks, Reefs
Coral Reef
Well, Spring
Geyser
River, Stream
Waterfall Rapids
River Mouth, Estuary
Lake
Salt Lake
Intermittent Lake
Reservoir
Swamp, Pond
Canal
Glacier
Ice Shelf, Pack Ice
Ocean
Sea
Gulf, Bay
Strait, Fjord
Lagoon
Bank
Seamount
Tablemount
Ridge
Shelf
Basin
Escarpment, Sea Scarp
Fracture
Trench, Abyss
National Park, Reserve
Point of Interest
Recreation Site
Cave, Cavern
Historic Site
Ruins
Wall, Walls
Church, Abbey
Temple
Scientific Station
Airport
Port
Lighthouse
Mine
Tunnel
Dam, Bridge

Gin Gin 59 Kd 25.00S 151.58 E
Gingin 59 Df 31.21S 115.42 E
Gingoog 26 Ie 8.50N 125.07 E
Ginir 35 Gd 7.08N 40.43 E
Ginosa 14 Kj 40.35N 16.45 E
Ginowan 29b Ab 26.17N 127.45 E
Ginzo de Limia 13 Eb 42.03N 7.43W
Giofra Oasis (EN)=Jufrah, Wāḥāt al- 30 If 29.10N 16.00 E
Gioia, Golfo di- 14 Jl 38.30N 15.45 E
Gioia del Colle 14 Kj 40.48N 16.55 E
Gioia Tauro 14 Jl 38.25N 15.54 E
Gion 35 Fd 8.24N 37.55 E
Gióna Óros 15 Fk 38.35N 22.15 E
Giovi, Passo dei- 14 Cf 44.33N 8.57 E
Giraltovce 10 Rg 49.07N 21.31 E
Girardot 54 Dc 4.18N 74.49W
Girdle Ness 9 Kd 57.08N 2.02W
Giresun 23 Ea 40.55N 38.24 E
Giresun Dağları 24 Hb 40.40N 38.10 E
Giri 36 Cb 0.28N 17.59 E
Giridih 25 Hd 24.11N 86.18 E
Giriftu 36 Gb 2.00N 39.45 E
Girne/Kyrenia 24 Ee 35.20N 33.19 E
Girón 54 Cd 3.10S 79.09W
Girona/Gerona 13 Oc 41.59N 2.49 E
Gironde 11 Fj 44.55N 0.30W
Gironde 5 Ff 45.35N 1.03W
Gironella 13 Nb 42.02N 1.53 E
Girou 11 Hk 43.46N 1.23 E
Girvan 9 If 55.15N 4.51W
Girvas 7 He 62.31N 33.44 E
Gisborne 58 Ih 38.39S 178.01 E
Gisenyi 36 Ec 1.42S 29.15 E
Gislaved 8 Eg 57.18N 13.32 E
Gisors 11 He 49.17N 1.47 E
Gissar 18 Ge 38.31N 68.36 E
Gissarski Hrebet 18 Ge 39.00N 68.40 E
Gistad 8 Ff 58.27N 15.55 E
Gistel 12 Ec 51.10N 2.57 E
Gistral 13 Ea 43.28N 7.35W
Gitarama 36 Ec 2.05S 29.16 E
Gitega 36 Ec 3.26S 29.56 E
Gitu 24 Me 35.20N 48.05 E
Giudicarie, Valli- 14 Ed 46.00N 10.40 E
Giulianova 14 Hh 42.45N 13.57 E
Giumalău, Vîrful- 15 Ib 47.26N 25.29 E
Giurgeni 15 Ke 44.35N 27.48 E
Giurgiu 15 If 43.53N 25.58 E
Give 8 Ci 55.51N 9.15 E
Givors 11 Ki 45.35N 4.46 E
Givry-en-Argonne 12 Gf 48.57N 4.53 E
Givry Island 64d Bb 7.07N 151.53 E
Giwa 34 Gc 11.18N 7.27 E
Giza (EN)=Al Jīzah 31 Ke 30.01N 31.13 E
Gižduvan 19 Gg 40.06N 64.40 E
Gižiga 20 Ld 62.03N 160.30 E
Gižiginskaja Guba 20 Kd 61.10N 158.30 E
Gizo 63a Cc 8.07S 156.50 E
Gizo 60 Fi 8.06S 156.51 E
Giżycko 10 Rb 54.03N 21.47 E
Gjalicës, Mali i- 15 Dg 42.01N 20.28 E
Gjamyš, Gora- 16 Oi 40.20N 46.25 E
Gjende 8 Cc 61.30N 8.35 E
Gjerstad 8 Cf 58.52N 9.00 E
Gjevilvatn 8 Cb 62.40N 9.25 E
Gjirokastra 15 Di 40.05N 20.10 E
Gjoa Haven 39 Jc 68.38N 95.57W
Gjøvik 6 Hc 60.48N 10.42 E
Gjuhës, Kep i- 15 Ci 40.25N 19.18 E
Glace Bay 42 Lg 46.12N 59.57W
Glacier Bay 40 Le 58.40N 136.00W
Glacier Peak 43 Cb 48.07N 121.07W
Glacier Strait 42 Ja 76.15N 79.00W
Gladbeck 12 Ic 51.34N 6.59 E
Gladenbach 12 Kd 50.46N 8.34 E
Gladewater 45 Ij 32.33N 94.56W
Gladstone [Austl.] 58 Gg 23.51S 151.16 E
Gladstone [Man.-Can.] 45 Ga 50.15N 98.50W
Gladstone [Mi.-U.S.] 44 Dc 45.51N 87.03W
Gladstone [Mo.-U.S.] 45 Ig 39.13N 94.34W
Glafsfjorden 8 Ee 59.35N 12.35 E
Glåma 5 Hd 59.12N 10.57 E
Gláma 7a Ab 65.48N 23.00W
Glamis Castle 9 Ke 56.37N 3.00W
Glamoč 23 Ff 44.03N 16.51 E
Glan 7 Dg 58.35N 15.55 E
Glan [Aus.] 14 Id 46.36N 14.25 E
Glan [F.R.G.] 10 Dg 49.47N 7.43 E
Glan-Münchweiler 12 Je 49.28N 7.26 E
Glarner Alpen 14 Cd 46.55N 9.00 E
Glärnisch 14 Cd 47.00N 9.00 E
Glarus 14 Dd 46.55N 9.05 E
Glarus 14 Dc 47.03N 9.04 E
Glasgow [Ky.-U.S.] 44 Eg 37.00N 85.55W
Glasgow [Mt.-U.S.] 43 Fb 48.12N 106.38W
Glasgow [Scot.-U.K.] 6 Fd 55.53N 4.15W
Glashütte 10 Jf 50.51N 13.47 E
Glass 9 Id 57.25N 4.30W
Glassboro 44 Jf 39.42N 75.07W
Glass Mountains 45 Ek 30.25N 103.15W
Glastonbury 9 Kj 51.09N 2.43W
Glauchau 10 If 50.49N 12.32 E
Glava 8 Ee 59.33N 12.34 E
Glazov 6 Ld 58.09N 52.40 E
Gleann Dá Loch/Glendalough 9 Gh 53.00N 6.20W
Gledićske Planine 15 Df 43.49N 20.55 E
Gleinalpe 14 Jc 47.10N 15.05 E
Gleisdorf 14 Jc 47.06N 15.43 E
Glen 12 Bb 52.50N 0.07W
Glénan, Iles de- 11 Cg 47.43N 4.00W
Glen Arbor 44 Ec 44.53N 85.58W
Glenavy 62 Df 44.55S 171.06 E
Glen Canyon 46 Jh 37.05N 111.41W
Glencoe [Mn.-U.S.] 45 Id 44.46N 94.09W
Glencoe [S.Afr.] 37 Ee 28.12S 30.07 E
Glendale [Az.-U.S.] 43 Ee 33.32N 112.11W
Glendale [Ca.-U.S.] 43 De 34.10N 118.17W
Glendalough/Gleann Dá Loch 9 Gh 53.00N 6.20W
Glendive 43 Gb 47.06N 104.43W
Glendo Reservoir 46 Me 42.31N 104.58W
Glenhope 61 Dh 41.39S 172.39 E
Glen Innes 58 Gg 29.44S 151.44 E
Glennallen 40 Jd 62.07N 145.33W
Glenner 14 Dd 46.46N 9.12 E
Glenns Ferry 46 He 42.57N 115.18W
Glenorchy 62 Cf 44.52S 168.24 E
Glenrock 46 Me 42.52N 105.52W
Glen Rose 45 Hj 32.14N 97.45W
Glenrothes 9 Je 56.12N 3.05W
Glens Falls 44 Kd 43.17N 73.41W
Glenville 44 Gf 38.57N 80.51W
Glenwood [Ia.-U.S.] 45 If 41.03N 95.45W
Glenwood [Mn.-U.S.] 45 Id 45.39N 95.23W
Glenwood Springs 43 Fd 39.32N 107.19W
Glibokaja 15 Ja 48.05N 26.00 E
Glina 14 Ke 45.20N 16.06 E
Glinjany 10 Ug 49.46N 24.33 E
Glittertind 5 Gc 61.39N 8.33 E
Gliwice 10 Of 50.17N 18.40 E
Globe 43 Ee 33.24N 110.47W
Globino 16 He 49.24N 33.18 E
Głogów 10 Me 51.40N 16.05 E
Glomfjord 7 Cc 66.49N 13.58 E
Glommersträsk 7 Ed 65.16N 19.38 E
Glonn 10 Hh 48.11N 11.45 E
Glorieuses, Iles- 30 Lj 11.30S 47.20 E
Glottof, Mount- 40 Ie 57.30N 153.30W
Gloucester 9 Kj 51.55N 2.15W
Gloucester [Eng.-U.K.] 9 Kj 51.53N 2.14W
Gloucester [Ma.-U.S.] 44 Ld 42.41N 70.39W
Gloucester, Cape- 60 Di 5.27S 148.25 E
Gloucestershire 9 Lj 51.50N 1.55W
Glover Island 51p Bb 11.59N 61.47W
Glover's Reef 49 De 16.49N 87.48W
Gloversville 44 Jd 43.03N 74.21W
Głowno 10 Pe 51.58N 19.44 E
Głubczyce 10 Nf 50.13N 17.49 E
Glubokoje [Bye.-U.S.S.R.] 19 Cd 55.08N 27.41 E
Glubokoje [Kaz.-U.S.S.R.] 19 Ie 50.06N 82.19 E
Glubokoje, Ozero- 8 Md 60.30N 29.25 E
Głuchołazy 10 Nf 50.20N 17.22 E
Glücksburg 10 Fb 54.50N 9.33 E
Glückstadt 10 Fc 53.47N 9.25 E
Gluhov 19 De 51.43N 33.57 E
Gluša 16 Fc 53.06N 28.52 E
Glyngøre 8 Ch 56.46N 8.52 E
Gmünd [Aus.] 14 Hd 46.54N 13.32 E
Gmünd [Aus.] 14 Ib 48.46N 14.59 E
Gmunden 14 Hc 47.55N 13.48 E
Gnarp 7 De 62.03N 17.16 E
Gnesta 7 Dg 59.03N 17.18 E
Gniben 8 Dh 56.01N 11.18 E
Gniew 10 Oc 53.51N 18.49 E
Gniewkowo 10 Od 52.54N 18.25 E
Gniezno 10 Nd 52.31N 17.37 E
Gnjilane 15 Eg 42.28N 21.29 E
Gnosjö 7 Ch 57.22N 13.44 E
Gnowangerup 59 Df 33.56S 117.50 E
Goa, Damān and Diu 25 Ee 15.35N 74.00 E
Goageb 37 Be 26.44S 17.15 E
Goālpāra 25 Ic 26.10N 90.37 E
Goat 63b Dd 18.42S 169.17 E
Goat Island 51d Ba 17.44N 61.51W
Goat Point 51d Ba 17.44N 61.51W
Goba 31 Kh 7.01N 39.59 E
Gobabis 31 Ik 22.30S 18.58 E
Gobabis 37 Bd 22.00S 19.00 E
Göbel 15 Lj 40.00N 28.09 E
Gober 34 Gc 13.48N 6.51 E
Gobernador Gregores 56 Fg 48.46S 70.15W
Gobernador Ingeniero Valentín Virasoro 56 Ic 28.03S 56.02W
Gobernador Mansilla 55 Ck 32.33S 59.22W
Gobi, Pustynja-=Gobi Desert (EN) 21 Me 43.00N 106.00 E
Gobi Altai (EN)=Gobijski Altaj 21 Me 44.00N 102.00 E
Gobi Desert (EN)=Gobi, Pustynja- 21 Me 43.00N 106.00 E
Gobijski Altaj=Gobi Altai (EN) 21 Me 44.00N 102.00 E
Gobō 28 Mh 33.53N 135.10 E
Göçbeyli 15 Kj 39.13N 27.25 E
Goceano 14 Dj 40.30N 9.15 E
Goceano, Catena del- 14 Cj 40.30N 9.00 E
Goce Delčev 15 Gh 41.33N 23.42 E
Goch 10 Ce 51.40N 6.10 E
Gochas 37 Bd 24.55S 18.55 E
Goczałkowickie, Jezioro- 10 Og 49.53N 18.50 E
Göd 10 Pi 47.42N 19.08 E
Godafoss 7a Cb 65.41N 17.33W
Godalming 12 Bc 51.11N 0.36W
Godär 24 Qh 29.45N 57.30 E
Godār-e Shah 24 Me 34.45N 48.10 E
Godāvari 21 Kh 17.00N 81.45 E
Godbout, Rivière- 44 Na 49.21N 67.42W
Gode 35 Gd 5.55N 43.40 E
Godeč 15 Gf 43.01N 23.03 E
Godelbukta Breidvika 66 Df 70.15S 24.15 E
Goderich 44 Gd 43.45N 81.43W
Goderville 12 Ce 49.39N 0.22 E
Godhavn/Qeqertarssuaq 67 Nc 69.20N 53.35W
Godhra 25 Ed 22.45N 73.38 E
Godinlabe 35 Hd 5.54N 46.40 E
Gödöllő 10 Pi 47.36N 19.22 E
Godoy Cruz 56 Gd 32.55S 68.50W
Gods Lake 42 If 54.40N 94.09W
Gods Lake 42 If 54.40N 94.20W
Gods Mercy, Bay of - 42 Id 63.30N 86.10W
Gods River 42 Ie 56.22N 92.52W
Godthåb/Nûk 67 Nc 64.15N 51.40W
Godthåbfjord 41 Gf 64.20N 51.30W
Godwin Austen (EN)=K2 21 Jf 35.53N 76.30 E
Godwin Austen (EN)=Qogir Feng 21 Jf 35.53N 76.30 E
Goedereede 12 Fc 51.49N 3.58 E
Goéland, Lac au- 42 Jg 49.45N 76.50W
Goélands, Lac aux- 42 Le 55.30N 64.30W
Goële 12 Ee 49.10N 2.40 E
Goelette Island 37b Bc 10.13S 51.08 E
Goeree 11 Jc 51.50N 3.55 E
Goes 11 Jc 51.30N 3.54 E
Gogama 42 Jg 47.40N 81.43W
Gō-Gawa 29 Cd 35.01N 132.13 E
Gogebic Range 44 Cb 46.45N 89.25W
Gogland, Ostrov- 7 Gf 60.05N 27.00 E
Gog Magog Hills 12 Cb 52.09N 0.11 E
Gogounou 34 Fc 10.50N 2.50 E
Gogrial 35 Dd 8.32N 28.07 E
Gogu, Vîrful- 15 Fd 45.12N 22.30 E
Gogui 34 Db 15.39N 9.21W
Goğu Karadeniz Dağları 24 Ib 40.40N 40.00 E
Gohelle 12 Ed 50.28N 2.45 E
Goiandira 54 Ig 18.08S 48.06W
Goianésia 54 Ig 15.19S 49.04W
Goiânia 53 Lg 16.40S 49.16W
Goianinha 54 Ke 6.16S 35.12W
Goiás 54 If 12.00S 48.00W
Goiás 54 Hg 15.56S 50.08W
Goiatuba 54 Ig 18.01S 49.22W
Goikul 64a Bc 7.22N 134.36 E
Göinge 8 Eh 56.20N 13.50 E
Goio-Erê 56 Jb 24.12S 53.01W
Goioxim 55 Gg 25.14S 52.01W
Goirle 12 Hc 51.34N 5.05 E
Góis 13 Dd 40.09N 8.07W
Goito 14 Ee 45.15N 10.40 E
Gojam 35 Fc 10.33N 37.35 E
Gojō 29 Dd 34.21N 135.42 E
Gojōme 29 Gb 39.56N 140.07 E
Gojra 25 Eb 31.09N 72.41 E
Gojthski, Pereval- 16 Kg 44.15N 39.18 E
Gokase-Gawa 29 Be 32.35N 131.42 E
Gokasho-Wan 29 Ed 34.20N 136.40 E
Gökbel Dağı 15 Kl 37.28N 28.00 E
Gökçay 24 Ed 36.36N 33.23 E
Gökçeada 24 Ac 40.10N 25.50 E
Gökçeören 15 Lk 38.35N 28.32 E
Gökçeyazi 15 Kj 39.38N 27.39 E
Gökdere 24 Ed 36.39N 33.35 E
Gökırmak 24 Fb 41.24N 35.08 E
Göksu [Tur.] 24 Fd 36.20N 34.05 E
Göksu [Tur.] 24 Fd 37.37N 35.35 E
Göksu [Tur.] 15 Mi 40.23N 29.58 E
Göksun 24 Gc 38.03N 36.30 E
Gök Tepe 15 Mm 36.53N 29.17 E
Göktepe 15 Ll 37.16N 28.36 E
Gokwe 37 Dc 18.13S 28.55 E
Gol 7 Bf 60.42N 8.57 E
Golāghāt 25 Ic 26.31N 93.58 E
Golaja Pristan 16 Hf 46.29N 32.31 E
Gołańcz 10 Nd 52.57N 17.18 E
Golconda [Il.-U.S.] 45 Lh 37.22N 88.29W
Golconda [Nv.-U.S.] 46 Gf 40.57N 117.30W
Gölcük 24 Cb 40.44N 29.44 E
Golčův Jeníkov 10 Lg 49.49N 15.30 E
Gołdap 10 Sb 54.19N 22.19 E
Gold Beach 46 Ce 42.25N 124.25W
Gold Coast 58 Gg 27.58S 153.25 E
Gold Coast 30 Gh 5.20N 0.45W
Golden [B.C.-Can.] 42 Ff 51.18N 116.58W
Golden [Co.-U.S.] 45 Dg 39.46N 105.13W
Golden Bay 62 Ed 40.50S 172.50 E
Goldendale 46 Ed 45.49N 120.50W
Goldene Aue 10 Ge 51.25N 11.00 E
Golden Gate 46 Dh 37.49N 122.29W
Golden Hinde 42 Eg 49.39N 125.45W
Golden Meadow 45 Kl 29.23N 90.16W
Golden Vale/Machaire na Mumhan 9 Fi 52.30N 8.00W
Goldfield 46 Gh 37.42N 117.14W
Gold River 46 Bb 49.41N 126.08W
Goldsboro 43 Ld 35.23N 77.59W
Goldsworthy 59 Dd 20.20S 119.30 E
Göle 24 Jb 40.48N 42.36 E
Golegã 13 De 39.24N 8.29W
Goleniów 10 Kc 53.36N 14.50 E
Golešnica 15 Eh 41.42N 21.33 E
Goleta, Cerro- 48 Ih 18.38N 100.04W
Golfito 47 Hg 8.38N 83.11W
Golfo Aranci 14 Dj 41.00N 9.37 E
Gölgeli Dağları 15 Ml 37.15N 29.06 E
Gölhisar 15 Ml 37.08N 29.30 E
Goliad 45 Hl 28.40N 97.23W
Golija [Yugo.] 15 Df 43.19N 20.18 E
Golija [Yugo.] 15 Bf 43.02N 18.47 E
Goljak 15 Eg 42.44N 21.31 E
Goljama Kamčija 15 Kf 43.03N 27.29 E
Goljama Sjutkja 15 Hh 41.54N 24.01 E
Goljamo Konare 15 Hg 42.16N 24.33 E
Goljam Perelik 15 Hh 41.36N 24.34 E
Goljam Persenk 15 Hh 41.49N 24.33 E
Gölköy 24 Gb 40.15N 37.26 E
Gölkük 15 Kj 39.19N 27.59 E
Göllheim 12 Ke 49.35N 8.03 E
Gölmarmara 15 Kk 38.42N 27.56 E
Golmud He 27 Gd 36.54N 95.11 E
Golo 11a Ba 42.31N 9.32 E
Goloby 10 Ve 51.06N 25.06 E
Gologory 10 Ug 49.35N 24.30 E
Gololcha 35 Gd 8.12N 40.05 E
Golovin 40 Gd 64.33N 163.02W
Golovnin Seamount (EN) 20 Kg 46.50N 157.00 E
Golpāyegān 23 Hc 33.27N 50.18 E
Gölpazarı 24 Db 40.17N 30.19 E
Golšanka 10 Kb 54.00N 26.16 E
Golspie 9 Jd 57.58N 3.58W
Gol Tappeh 24 Kd 36.35N 45.45 E
Golubac 15 Ee 44.39N 21.38 E
Golub-Dobrzyń 10 Pc 53.08N 19.02 E
Golungo Alto 36 Bd 9.08S 14.47 E
Golyšmanovo 19 Gd 56.23N 68.23 E
Goma 31 Ji 1.37S 29.12 E
Gómara 13 Jc 41.37N 2.13W
Gombe 31 Ig 10.17N 11.10 E
Gombi 34 Hc 10.10N 12.44 E
Gomel 6 Je 52.25N 31.00 E
Gomelskaja Oblast 19 Ce 52.20N 29.40 E
Gomera 30 Ff 28.06N 17.08W
Gómez Farías 48 Ie 24.57N 101.02W
Gómez Palacio 47 Dc 25.34N 103.30W
Gomo Co 27 Ee 33.45N 85.35 E
Goms 14 Cd 46.25N 8.10 E
Gonābād 23 Ic 34.20N 58.42 E
Gonaïves 47 Je 19.27N 72.43W
Gonam 20 Ie 57.18N 131.20 E
Gonâve, Golfe de la- 47 Je 19.00N 73.30W
Gonâve, Ile de la- 47 Je 18.51N 73.03W
Gonbad-e Qābūs 23 Ib 37.15N 55.09 E
Gonda 25 Gc 27.08N 81.56 E
Gonder 35 Fc 12.00N 38.00 E
Gonder 31 Kg 12.38N 37.27 E
Gondia 25 Gd 21.27N 80.12 E
Gondo 30 Gg 14.20N 3.10W
Gondomar 13 Dc 41.09N 8.32W
Gondwana 21 Kg 23.00N 81.00 E
Gönen 24 Bb 40.06N 27.39 E
Gönen 24 Bb 40.06N 27.36 E
Gonfreville-l'Orcher 12 Ce 49.30N 0.14 E
Gong'an (Doushi) 27 Je 30.05N 112.12 E
Gongbo'gyamda 27 Ff 29.59N 93.25 E
Gonggar 27 Ff 29.17N 90.50 E
Gongga Shan 21 Mg 29.34N 101.53 E
Gonghe 27 Hd 36.21N 100.47 E
Gongliu/Tokkuztara 27 Dc 43.30N 82.15 E
Gongola 30 Ih 9.30N 12.04 E
Gongola 34 Hd 8.40N 11.20 E
Gongpoquan 27 Gc 41.50N 97.00 E
Gongshan 27 Gf 27.39N 98.35 E
Gongxian 27 Kf 26.05N 119.32 E
Gongxian (Xiaoyi) 28 Bg 34.46N 112.57 E
Gongzhuling→Huaide 27 Lc 43.30N 124.52 E
Goñi 55 Dk 33.31S 56.24W
Goniądz 10 Sc 53.30N 22.45 E
Gonīshān 24 Pd 37.04N 54.06 E
Gonjo 27 Ge 30.52N 98.20 E
Gonohe 29 Ga 40.31N 141.19 E
Go-no-ura 29 Ae 33.45N 129.41 E
Gönuk 24 Ic 39.00N 40.41 E
Gonzales 45 Hl 29.30N 97.27W
Gonzáles, Riacho- 55 Df 22.48S 57.54W
González 48 Jf 22.50N 98.27W
Goodenough, Cape- 66 Ie 66.16S 126.10 E
Goodenough Bay 59 Ja 9.55S 150.00 E
Goodenough Island 60 Ei 9.22S 150.16 E
Good Hope, Cape of-/Groeie Hoop, Kaap die- 30 Il 34.21S 18.28 E
Goodhouse 37 Be 28.57S 18.13 E
Gooding 46 He 42.56N 114.43W
Goodland 43 Gd 39.21N 101.43W
Goodnews Bay 40 Ge 59.07N 161.35W
Goodsir, Mount- 46 Ga 51.12N 116.20W
Good Spirit Lake 46 Na 51.34N 102.40W
Goodwin Sands 12 Dc 51.15N 1.35 E
Goodyear 46 Ij 33.26N 112.21W
Goole 9 Mh 53.42N 0.52W
Goomalling 59 Df 31.19S 116.49 E
Goondiwindi 58 Gg 28.32S 150.19 E
Goonyella 59 Jd 21.43S 147.58 E
Goor 12 Ib 52.14N 6.37 E
Goose Bay 39 Md 53.19N 60.24W
Goose Lake 43 Cc 41.57N 120.25W
Goose River 45 Hc 47.28N 96.52W
Gopło, Jezioro- 10 Od 52.35N 18.20 E
Göppingen 10 Fh 48.42N 9.40 E
Góra 10 Me 51.40N 16.33 E
Gora 15 Di 40.40N 20.30 E
Góra Kalwaria 10 Re 51.59N 21.12 E
Gorakhpur 22 Kg 26.45N 83.22 E
Goransko 15 Bf 43.07N 18.50 E
Gorata 15 Ih 41.45N 25.55 E
Goražde 14 Mg 43.40N 18.59 E
Gorda 46 Ei 35.55N 121.27W
Gorda, Cayo 49 Ff 15.55N 82.15W
Gorda, Punta- [Ca.-U.S.] 46 Cf 40.16N 124.20W
Gorda, Punta- [Cuba] 49 Fb 22.24N 82.10W
Gorda, Punta- [Nic.] 49 Ff 14.21N 83.12W
Gördes 15 Lk 38.54N 28.18 E
Gördes 15 Kj 38.46N 27.58 E
Gordil 35 Cd 9.44N 21.35 E
Gordior 24 Ec 39.37N 32.00 E
Gordon [Nb.-U.S.] 45 Ee 42.48N 102.12W
Gordon [Wi.-U.S.] 45 Kc 46.15N 91.47W
Gordon, Lake- 59 Jh 43.05S 146.05 E
Gordon Horne Peak 46 Fa 51.46N 118.50W
Gordonvale 59 Jc 17.05S 145.47 E
Goré 35 Bd 7.55N 16.38 E
Gore [Eth.] 35 Fd 8.09N 35.34 E
Gore [N.Z.] 62 Cg 46.06S 168.56 E
Görele 24 Hb 41.02N 39.00 E
Görenez Dağı 15 Lk 39.00N 28.01 E
Gorenjsko 14 Id 46.20N 14.10 E
Gorey/Guaire 9 Gi 52.40N 6.18W
Gorgān 24 Pd 36.59N 54.05 E
Gorgān 24 Jf 33.21N 43.40 E
Gorgān, Khalīj-e- 24 Od 36.40N 53.50 E
Gorgany 10 Jh 48.30N 24.15 E
Gorgin 24 Ld 36.15N 47.55 E
Gorgol 32 Ef 15.45N 13.00W
Gorgol el Abiod 32 Ef 16.14N 12.58W
Gorgona 14 Dg 43.25N 9.55 E
Gorgona, Isla- 54 Cc 2.59N 78.12W
Gorgora 35 Fc 12.14N 37.17 E
Gorham 44 Lc 44.23N 71.11W
Gori 19 Eg 42.00N 44.02 E
Gorinchem 11 Kc 51.50N 5.00 E
Goring 12 Ac 51.31N 1.08W
Goris 16 Oj 39.31N 46.22 E
Gorizia 14 He 45.57N 13.38 E
Gorj 15 Gd 45.00N 23.20 E
Gorjačegorsk 20 De 55.24N 88.55 E
Gorjači Kljuc 16 Kg 44.36N 39.07 E
Gorjanci 14 Je 45.45N 15.20 E
Gorki [Bye.-U.S.S.R.] 16 Gb 54.17N 31.00 E
Gorki [R.S.F.S.R.] 6 Kd 57.38N 45.05 E
Gorki [R.S.F.S.R.] 20 Bc 65.05N 65.15 E
Gorko-Solenoje, Ozero- 16 Oe 49.20N 46.05 E
Gorkovskaja Oblast 19 Ed 56.15N 44.45 E
Gorkovskoje Vodohranilišče =Gorky Reservoir (EN) 5 Kd 57.00N 43.10 E
Gorkum 10 Hf 50.10N 11.08 E
Gorky Reservoir (EN)= Gorkovskoje Vodohr. 5 Kd 57.00N 43.10 E
Gørlev 8 Di 55.32N 11.14 E
Gorlice 10 Rg 49.40N 21.10 E
Görlitz 10 Ke 51.10N 15.00 E
Gorlovka 6 Jf 48.18N 38.03 E
Gornalunga 14 Jm 37.24N 15.03 E
Gorna Orjahovica 15 If 43.07N 25.41 E
Gornjak [R.S.F.S.R.] 20 Df 51.00N 81.29 E
Gornjak [Ukr.-U.S.S.R.] 10 Uf 50.16N 24.13 E
Gornji Milanovac 15 De 44.02N 20.27 E
Gornji Vakuf 23 Fg 43.56N 17.36 E
Gorno-Altajsk 22 Kd 51.58N 85.58 E
Gorno-Altajskaja Avtonomnaja Oblast 20 Df 51.00N 87.00 E
Gorno-Badahšanskaja Avtonomnaja Oblast 19 Hh 38.15N 73.00 E
Gorno-Čujski 20 Ge 57.40N 111.40 E
Gornozavodsk [R.S.F.S.R.] 20 Jg 46.30N 141.55 E
Gornozavodsk [R.S.F.S.R.] 17 Ig 58.25N 58.20 E
Gorny [R.S.F.S.R.] 20 Ih 44.50N 133.56 E
Gorny [R.S.F.S.R.] 16 Pd 51.45N 48.34 E
Gorny [R.S.F.S.R.] 20 If 50.48N 136.26 E
Gornyje Ključi 28 Lb 45.15N 133.30 E
Gorochan 35 Fd 9.26N 37.05 E
Gorodec [R.S.F.S.R.] 19 Ed 56.40N 43.30 E
Gorodec [R.S.F.S.R.] 8 Mf 58.30N 29.55 E
Gorodenka 16 De 48.42N 25.32 E
Gorodišče [Bye.-U.S.S.R.] 10 Vc 53.16N 26.03 E
Gorodišče [R.S.F.S.R.] 16 Nc 53.16N 45.42 E
Gorodišče [Ukr.-U.S.S.R.] 16 Ge 49.17N 31.27 E
Gorodnica 16 Ed 50.49N 27.22 E
Gorodnja 16 Gd 51.55N 31.31 E
Gorodok [Bye.-U.S.S.R.] 19 Cd 55.26N 29.59 E
Gorodok [Ukr.-U.S.S.R.] 16 Ee 49.10N 26.31 E
Gorodok [Ukr.-U.S.S.R.] 16 Ce 49.47N 23.39 E
Gorodovikovsk 19 Ef 46.05N 41.59 E
Gorohov 10 Uf 50.28N 24.47 E
Gorohovec 7 Kh 56.12N 42.42 E
Goroka 58 Fe 6.02S 145.22 E
Gorom-Gorom 34 Ec 14.26N 0.14W
Gorong, Kepulauan- 26 Jg 4.05S 131.20 E
Gorongosa, Serra da- 37 Ec 18.24S 34.06 E
Gorontalo 22 Oi 0.33N 123.03 E
Goroual 34 Fc 14.42N 0.53 E
Górowo Iławeckie 10 Qb 54.17N 20.30 E
Gorron 11 Ff 48.25N 0.49W
Goršečnoje 16 Kd 51.33N 38.09 E
Gorski Kotar 14 Ie 45.26N 14.40 E
Gorssel 12 Ib 52.12N 6.13 E
Gort 9 Eh 53.04N 8.50W
Goru, Vîrful- 15 Jd 45.48N 26.25 E
Görükle 15 Li 40.14N 28.50 E
Goryn 19 Ce 52.09N 27.17 E
Gorzów 10 Ld 54.25N 15.15 E
Gorzów Wielkopolski 10 Ld 52.44N 15.15 E
Goschen Strait 59 Kb 10.09S 150.56 E
Gosen 28 Of 37.44N 139.11 E
Gosford 59 Kf 33.26S 151.21 E
Goshen 44 Ee 41.35N 85.50W
Goshogawara 28 Pd 40.48N 140.27 E
Gosier 51e Bb 16.12N 61.30W
Goslar 10 Ge 51.54N 10.26 E
Gospić 14 Jf 44.33N 15.23 E
Gosport 9 Lk 50.48N 1.08W
Gossen 8 Bb 62.50N 6.55 E
Gossi 34 Eb 15.47N 1.15W
Gossinga 35 Dd 8.39N 25.59 E
Gostivar 15 Dh 41.48N 20.54 E
Gostyń 10 Me 51.53N 17.00 E
Gostynin 10 Pd 52.26N 19.29 E
Gota älv 5 Hd 57.42N 11.52 E
Göta Kanal 5 Hd 58.50N 13.58 E
Götaland 5 Hd 57.30N 14.30 E
Götaland 7 Dg 57.30N 14.30 E
Göteborg 6 Hd 57.43N 11.58 E
Göteborg och Bohus 7 Cg 58.30N 11.30 E
Gotel Mountains 30 Ih 7.00N 11.40 E
Gotemba 29 Fd 35.18N 138.56 E
Götene 7 Cg 58.32N 13.29 E
Gotha 10 Gf 50.57N 10.43 E
Gothenburg 45 Ff 40.56N 100.09W
Gothèye 34 Fc 13.52N 1.34 E
Gotland 7 Eh 57.30N 18.30 E
Gotland 5 Hd 57.30N 18.30 E
Gotō-Nada 29 Ae 32.45N 129.30 E
Gotō-Rettō 27 Me 32.50N 129.00 E
Gotowasi 26 If 0.38N 128.26 E
Gotska Sandön 7 Eg 58.25N 19.15 E
Gōtsu 28 Lg 35.00N 132.14 E
Göttingen 10 Fe 51.32N 9.56 E
Gottwaldov 10 Ng 49.13N 17.39 E
Goubangzi 28 Fd 41.23N 121.48 E
Gouda 11 Kc 52.01N 4.43 E
Goudiri 34 Cc 14.11N 12.43W
Gouet 11 Df 48.32N 2.45W
Gough Island 30 Gm 40.20S 10.00W
Gough Lake 46 Ia 52.02N 112.28W
Gouin, Réservoir- 42 Kg 48.35N 74.50W
Goulbin Kaba 34 Gc 13.42N 6.19 E
Goulburn 58 Fh 34.45S 149.43 E

Index Symbols

[1] Independent Nation
[2] State, Region
[3] District, County
[4] Municipality
[5] Colony, Dependency
Continent
Physical Region
Historical or Cultural Region
Mount, Mountain
Volcano
Hill
Mountains, Mountain Range
Hills, Escarpment
Plateau, Upland
Pass, Gap
Plain, Lowland
Delta
Salt Flat
Valley, Canyon
Crater, Cave
Karst Features
Depression
Polder
Desert, Dunes
Forest, Woods
Heath, Steppe
Oasis
Cape, Point
Coast, Beach
Cliff
Peninsula
Isthmus
Sandbank
Island
Atoll
Rock, Reef
Islands, Archipelago
Rocks, Reefs
Coral Reef
Well, Spring
Geyser
River, Stream
Waterfall Rapids
River Mouth, Estuary
Lake
Salt Lake
Intermittent Lake
Reservoir
Swamp, Pond
Canal
Glacier
Ice Shelf, Pack Ice
Ocean
Sea
Gulf, Bay
Strait, Fjord
Lagoon
Bank
Seamount
Tablemount
Ridge
Shelf
Basin
Escarpment, Sea Scarp
Fracture
Trench, Abyss
National Park, Reserve
Point of Interest
Recreation Site
Cave, Cavern
Historic Site
Ruins
Wall, Walls
Church, Abbey
Temple
Scientific Station
Airport
Port
Lighthouse
Mine
Tunnel
Dam, Bridge

Index Symbols

[1] Independent Nation	Historical or Cultural Region
[2] State, Region	Mount, Mountain
[3] District, County	Volcano
[4] Municipality	Hill
[5] Colony, Dependency	Mountains, Mountain Range
Continent	Hills, Escarpment
Physical Region	Plateau, Upland

Pass, Gap	Depression
Plain, Lowland	Polder
Delta	Desert, Dunes
Salt Flat	Forest, Woods
Valley, Canyon	Heath, Steppe
Crater, Cave	Oasis
Karst Features	Cape, Point

Coast, Beach	Rock, Reef
Cliff	Islands, Archipelago
Peninsula	Rocks, Reefs
Isthmus	Coral Reef
Sandbank	Well, Spring
Island	Geyser
Atoll	River, Stream

Waterfall Rapids	Canal
River Mouth, Estuary	Glacier
Lake	Ice Shelf, Pack Ice
Salt Lake	Ocean
Intermittent Lake	Gulf, Bay
Sea	Strait, Fjord
Swamp, Pond	Basin

Lagoon	Escarpment, Sea Scarp
Bank	Fracture
Seamount	Trench, Abyss
Tableland	National Park, Reserve
Ridge	Point of Interest
Shelf	Recreation Site
Cave, Cavern	Scientific Station
	Airport

Historic Site	Port
Ruins	Lighthouse
Wall, Walls	Mine
Church, Abbey	Tunnel
Temple	Dam, Bridge

Groenlo 12 Ib 52.04N 6.39 E
Groesbeek 12 Hc 51.47N 5.56 E
Grofa, Gora- 15 Ha 48.34N 24.03 E
Groix 11 Cg 47.38N 3.28W
Groix, Ile de- 11 Cg 47.38N 3.28W
Grójec 10 Qe 51.52N 20.52 E
Gröll Seamount (EN) 54 Lf 14.00S 32.00W
Gromnik 10 Nf 50.42N 17.07 E
Gronau (Westfalen) 10 Dd 52.12N 7.02 E
Grong 7 Cd 64.30N 12.27 E
Groningen [3] 12 Ia 53.13N 6.33 E
Groningen [Neth.] 6 Ge 53.13N 6.33 E
Groningen [Sur.] 54 Gb 5.48N 55.28W
Groninger-wad 12 Ia 53.27N 6.25 E
Groningerwad 12 Ia 53.25N 6.30 E
Grønland/Kalaallit Nunaat=Greenland (EN) 38 Pb 70.00N 40.00W
Grønland/Kalaallit Nunaat=Greenland (EN) [5] 67 Nd 70.00N 40.00W
Grønlandshavet=Greenland Sea (EN) 67 Ld 77.00N 1.00W
Grønnedal 41 Hf 61.20N 47.45W
Grönskara 8 Fg 57.05N 15.44 E
Groot 30 Jl 33.45S 24.58 E
Groot Baai 51b Ab 18.01N 63.04W
Groote Eylandt 57 Ef 14.00S 136.40 E
Grootfontein 31 Ij 19.32S 18.05 E
Grootfontein [3] 37 Bc 19.00S 19.00 E
Groot-Karasberge=Great Karasberge (EN) 30 Ik 27.20S 18.45 E
Groot Karoo=Great Karroo (EN) 30 Jl 33.00S 22.00 E
Grootlaagte 37 Cd 20.55S 21.27 E
Groot Namaland/Great Namaland 37 Be 26.00S 17.00 E
Grootvloer 37 Ce 30.00S 20.40 E
Gropeni 15 Kd 45.05N 27.54 E
Gros Caps, Pointe des- 51e Bb 16.28N 61.25W
Gros Islet Bay 51k Ba 14.05N 60.58W
Gros Islets 51k Ba 14.05N 60.58W
Gros-Morne 51h Ab 14.43N 61.01W
Gros-Morne 42 Lg 49.00N 57.22W
Grosne 11 Kh 46.42N 4.56 E
Gros Piton 51k Ab 13.49N 61.04W
Große Aa 12 Jb 52.25N 7.23 E
Große Aue 12 Kb 52.30N 8.38 E
Großefehn 12 Ja 53.24N 7.33 E
Große Laaber 10 Ih 48.50N 12.30 E
Großenhain 10 Je 51.17N 13.33 E
Großenkneten 12 Kb 52.57N 8.16 E
Grosse Pointe 51e Bb 16.01N 61.17W
Großer Arber 10 Jg 49.07N 13.07 E
Großer Gleichberg 10 Gf 50.23N 10.35 E
Großer Inselsberg 10 Gf 50.52N 10.28 E
Grosseto 14 Fh 42.46N 11.08 E
Grosseto, Formiche di- 14 Eh 42.40N 10.55 E
Groß-Gerau 10 Eg 49.55N 8.29 E
Großglockner 5 Hf 47.04N 12.42 E
Großräschen 10 Je 51.35N 14.00 E
Groß-Umstadt 12 Ke 49.52N 8.56 E
Großvenediger 14 Gc 47.06N 12.21 E
Grostenquin 12 If 48.59N 6.44 E
Gros Ventre Range 46 Je 43.30N 110.15W
Groswater Bay 38 Nd 54.20N 57.30W
Grøtavær 7 Db 68.58N 16.16 E
Grote Nete 12 Gc 51.07N 4.34 E
Grotli 7 Be 62.01N 7.40 E
Grottaglie 14 Lj 40.32N 17.26 E
Grottammare 14 Hh 42.59N 13.52 E
Groumania 34 Ed 7.55N 4.00W
Groundhog River 44 Ga 49.43N 81.58W
Grouse Creek Mountains 46 If 41.55N 113.50W
Grove Mountains 66 Ff 72.59S 74.53 E
Groves 45 Jl 29.57N 93.55W
Grovfjord 7 Db 68.41N 17.09 E
Grow, Idaarderadeel- 12 Ha 53.06N 5.50 E
Grozny 6 Kg 43.20N 45.42 E
Grubišno Polje 14 Le 45.42N 17.10 E
Grudovo 15 Kg 42.21N 27.10 E
Grudziądz 10 Oc 53.29N 18.45 E
Grumento Nova 14 Jj 40.17N 15.53 E
Grumo Appula 14 Ki 41.01N 16.42 E
Grums 8 Ee 59.21N 13.06 E
Grünau 37 Be 27.47S 18.23 E
Grünberg 12 Kd 50.36N 8.57 E
Gründau 12 Ld 50.14N 9.05 E
Grundy 44 Fg 37.17N 82.06W
Gruñidera 48 Ie 24.15N 101.58W
Grünstadt 12 Ke 49.34N 8.10 E
Grunwald 10 Qc 53.30N 20.05 E
Gruppo di Brenta 14 Ed 46.10N 10.55 E
Gruyère 14 Bd 46.40N 7.10 E
Gruža 15 Df 43.54N 20.47 E
Gruzinskaja Sovetskaja Socialističeskaja Respublika [2] 19 Eg 42.00N 44.00 E
Gruzinskaja SSR/Sakartvelos Sabčata Socialisturi Respublica [2] 19 Eg 42.00N 44.00 E
Gruzinskaja SSR=Georgian SSR (EN) [2] 19 Eg 42.00N 44.00 E
Grybów 10 Qg 49.38N 20.56 E
Grycksbo 8 Fd 60.41N 15.28 E
Gryfice 10 Lc 53.56N 15.12 E
Gryfino 10 Kc 53.15N 14.30 E
Grythyttan 8 Fe 59.42N 14.32 E
Grytviken 66 Ad 54.17S 36.31W
Gstaad 14 Bd 46.28N 7.17 E
Guacanayabo, Golfo de- 47 Id 20.28N 77.30W
Guacara 50 Cg 10.14N 67.53W
Guaçu 55 Ef 22.11S 54.31W
Guadaioz 13 Hg 37.50N 4.51W
Guadaira 13 Fg 37.20N 6.01W
Guadalajara [3] 13 Jd 40.50N 2.30W
Guadalajara [Mex.] 39 Ig 20.40N 103.20W
Guadalajara [Sp.] 13 Id 40.38N 3.10W
Guadalaviar 13 Kd 40.21N 1.08W
Guadalbullón 13 Ig 37.59N 3.47W
Guadalcanal 13 Gf 38.06N 5.49W
Guadalcanal Island 57 He 9.32S 160.12 E
Guadalén 13 If 38.05N 3.32W
Guadalentín o Sangonera 13 Kg 37.59N 1.04W
Guadalete 13 Fh 36.35N 6.13W
Guadalfeo 13 Ih 36.43N 3.35W
Guadalimar 13 Ig 37.59N 3.44W
Guadalmena 13 Jf 38.20N 2.55W
Guadalmez 13 Gf 38.46N 5.04W
Guadalope 13 Lc 41.15N 0.03W
Guadalquivir 5 Fh 36.47N 6.22W
Guadalupe [Mex.] 47 Dc 25.41N 100.15W
Guadalupe [Mex.] 48 Hf 22.45N 102.31W
Guadalupe [Mex.] 48 Id 26.12N 101.23W
Guadalupe [Sp.] 13 Ge 39.27N 5.19W
Guadalupe, Isla de- 38 Hg 29.00N 118.16W
Guadalupe, Sierra de- 13 Ge 39.25N 5.25W
Guadalupe Bravos 48 Fb 31.23N 106.07W
Guadalupe Mountains 45 Dj 32.20N 105.00W
Guadalupe Peak 43 Ge 31.50N 104.52W
Guadalupe River 45 Hl 28.30N 96.53W
Guadalupe Victoria, Presa- 48 Gf 23.50N 104.55W
Guadalupe y Calvo 48 Fd 26.06N 106.58W
Guadarrama 13 He 39.53N 4.10W
Guadarrama, Puerto de- 13 Hd 40.43N 4.10W
Guadarrama, Sierra de- 13 Id 40.55N 4.00W
Guadazaón 13 Ke 39.42N 1.36W
Guadeloupe 38 Mh 16.15N 61.35W
Guadeloupe [5] 39 Mh 16.15N 61.35W
Guadeloupe, Canal de la-=Guadeloupe Passage (EN) 47 Le 16.40N 61.50W
Guadeloupe Passage 50 Fd 16.40N 61.50W
Guadeloupe Passage (EN)=Guadeloupe, Canal de la- 47 Le 16.40N 61.50W
Guadiana 5 Fh 37.14N 7.22W
Guadiana, Canal del- 13 Ie 39.20N 3.20W
Guadiana, Ojos del- 13 Ie 39.08N 3.31W
Guadiana Menor 13 Ig 37.56N 3.15W
Guadiaro 13 Gh 36.17N 5.17W
Guadiela 13 Jd 40.22N 2.49W
Guadix 13 Ig 37.18N 3.08W
Guafo, Boca del- 56 Ff 43.40S 74.15W
Guafo, Isla- 56 Ff 43.36S 74.43W
Guaiba 56 Jd 30.06S 51.19W
Guaiba, Rio- 55 Gj 30.15S 51.12W
Guaimaca 49 Df 14.52N 86.51W
Guaimorato, Laguna de- 49 Ef 15.58N 85.55W
Guainía [2] 54 Ec 2.30N 69.00W
Guainía, Rio- 52 Je 2.01N 67.07W
Guaiquinima, Cerro- 54 Fb 5.49N 63.40W
Guaira [3] 55 Dg 25.45S 56.30W
Guaira [Braz.] 56 Jb 24.04S 54.15W
Guaira [Braz.] 55 He 20.19S 48.18W
Guaira Falls (EN) = Sete Quedas, Saltos das- 56 Jb 24.02S 54.16W
Guairas 55 Ja 12.39S 44.16W
Guaire/Gorey 9 Gi 52.40N 6.18W
Guaitecas, Islas- 56 Ff 43.57S 73.50W
Guajaba, Cayo- 49 Ic 21.50N 77.30W
Guajará Mirim 53 Jg 10.48S 65.22W
Guajira, Peninsula de la- 52 Id 12.00N 71.30W
Guajolotes, Sierra del- 48 Ge 26.00N 105.15W
Guakolak, Tanjung- 26 Eh 6.50S 105.14 E
Gualaco 49 Df 15.06N 86.07W
Gualán 49 Cf 15.08N 89.22W
Gualdo Tadino 14 Gg 43.14N 12.47 E
Gualeguay 55 Ck 33.09S 59.20W
Gualeguay, Rio- 55 Ck 33.19S 59.39W
Gualeguaychu 56 Id 33.01S 58.31W
Gualeguaychú, Rio- 55 Ck 33.05S 58.25W
Gualicho, Salina del- 56 Gf 40.24S 65.15W
Guam 58 Fc 13.28N 144.47 E
Guam 57 Fc 13.28N 144.47 E
Guamini 56 He 37.02S 62.25W
Guampi, Sierra de- 54 Eb 6.00N 65.35W
Guamuchil 47 Cc 25.22N 108.22W
Gua Musang 26 Df 4.53N 101.58 E
Gu'an 28 De 39.24N 116.10 E
Guanabacoa 49 Fb 23.07N 82.18W
Guanabara, Baía de- 55 Kf 22.50S 43.10W
Guanacaste [3] 49 Eh 10.30N 85.15W
Guanacaste, Cordillera de- 49 Eh 10.45N 85.05W
Guanacevi 48 Ge 25.56N 105.57W
Guanahacabibes, Golfo de- 49 Eb 22.08N 84.35W
Guanahacabibes, Peninsula de- 49 Ec 21.57N 84.35W
Guana Island 51a Db 18.29N 64.34W
Guanaja 49 Ee 16.27N 85.54W
Guanaja, Isla de- 49 Ee 16.30N 85.55W
Guanajay 49 Fb 22.55N 82.42W
Guanajibo 51a Ab 18.10N 67.09W
Guanajibo, Punta- 51a Ab 18.12N 67.10W
Guanajuato 47 Dd 21.01N 101.15W
Guanajuato [2] 47 Dd 21.00N 101.00W
Guanambi 54 Jf 14.13S 42.47W
Guanare 54 Eb 9.03N 69.45W
Guanare, Rio- 54 Ch 8.13N 67.46W
Guanare Viejo, Rio- 49 Mi 8.19N 68.10W
Guanarito 50 Bh 8.42N 69.12W
Guandacol 56 Gc 29.31S 68.32W
Guandi Shan 27 Jd 38.09N 111.27 E
Guane 47 Hd 22.12N 84.05W
Guangde 27 Ke 30.51N 119.26 E
Guangdong Sheng (Kuang-tung Sheng)=Kwangtung (EN) [2] 27 Jg 23.00N 113.00 E
Guangfeng 28 Ej 28.27N 118.12 E
Guanghua 27 Je 32.18N 111.45 E
Guangji (Wuxue) 27 Kf 29.58N 115.32 E
Guangling 28 Ce 39.46N 114.16 E
Guangmao Shan 27 Hf 26.48N 100.56 E
Guangming Ding 28 Ei 30.09N 118.11 E
Guangnan 27 Ig 24.02N 105.04 E
Guangrao 28 Ef 37.03N 118.25 E
Guangshan 28 Ci 32.02N 114.53 E
Guangshui 28 Ci 31.37N 114.01 E
Guangxi Zhuangzu Zizhiqu (Kuang-hsi-chuang-tsu Tzu-chih-ch'ü)=Kwangsi Chuang (EN) [2] 27 Ig 24.00N 109.00 E
Guangyuan 22 Mf 32.27N 105.55 E
Guangzhou=Canton (EN) 22 Ng 23.07N 113.18 E
Guan He 28 Ch 32.18N 115.44 E
Guánica 51a Bc 17.59N 66.56W
Guanipa, Rio- 50 Eh 9.56N 62.26W
Guannan (Xin'anzhen) 28 Eg 34.04N 119.21 E
Guantánamo [3] 49 Jc 20.10N 75.00W
Guantanamo 39 Lg 20.08N 75.12W
Guantánamo, Bahía de- 49 Jd 20.00N 75.10W
Guantánamo Bay 47 Id 20.00N 75.10W
Guantanamo Bay Naval Station 49 Jd 20.00N 75.08W
Guantao (Nanguantao) 28 Cf 36.33N 115.18 E
Guanting Shuiku 28 Cd 40.13N 115.36 E
Guanxian 22 Mf 31.00N 103.38 E
Guanyun (Dayishan) 28 Eg 34.18N 119.14 E
Guapé 55 Je 20.47S 45.55W
Guapi 54 Cc 2.35N 77.55W
Guápiles 49 Fh 10.13N 83.46W
Guapó 55 Hc 16.51S 49.33W
Guaporé 55 Gi 29.10S 51.54W
Guaporé 56 Jc 28.51S 51.54W
Guaporé, Rio- 52 Jg 11.55S 65.04W
Guaqui 54 Eg 16.35S 68.51W
Guará 55 Gg 25.23S 51.17W
Guara, Sierra de- 13 Lb 42.17N 0.10W
Guarabira 54 Ke 6.51S 35.29W
Guaranda 54 Cd 1.35S 78.59W
Guaraniacu 56 Jc 25.06S 52.52W
Guarani de Goiás 55 Ia 13.57S 46.28W
Guarapiche, Rio- 50 Eh 9.57N 62.52W
Guarapuava 56 Jc 25.23S 51.27W
Guaraqueçaba 55 Hg 25.17S 48.21W
Guararapes 55 Ge 21.15S 50.38W
Guaratinguetá 55 Jf 22.49S 45.13W
Guaratuba 55 Hg 25.54S 48.34W
Guarayos, Rio- 55 Bb 14.38S 62.11W
Guarda 13 Ed 40.32N 7.16W
Guarda [2] 13 Ed 40.40N 7.10W
Guardafui, Cape-(EN)='Asayr 30 Mg 11.49N 51.15 E
Guardal 13 Jg 37.36N 2.45W
Guarda-Mor 55 Ic 17.47S 47.06W
Guardiagrele 14 Ih 42.11N 14.13 E
Guardian Seamount (EN) 38 Ki 9.32N 87.40W
Guardo 13 Hb 42.47N 4.50W
Guardunha, Serra da- 13 Ed 40.05N 7.31W
Guarei, Rio- 55 Ff 22.40S 53.34W
Guareña 13 Gc 41.29N 5.23W
Guarenas 50 Cg 10.28N 66.37W
Guaribas, Rio- 55 Jc 16.22S 45.03W
Guaribe, Rio- 50 Dh 9.53N 65.11W
Guárico [2] 54 Eb 8.40N 66.35W
Guárico, Embalse del- 50 Ch 9.00N 67.20W
Guarico, Rio- 54 Eb 7.55N 67.23W
Guariquito, Rio- 50 Ci 7.40N 66.18W
Guarita, Rio- 55 Fh 27.11S 53.44W
Guaritico, Caño- 50 Bi 7.52N 68.53W
Guaritire, Rio- 55 Ba 13.43S 60.38W
Guarujá 55 If 24.00S 46.16W
Guarulhos 56 Kb 23.28S 46.32W
Guasave 47 Cc 25.34N 108.27W
Guasdualito 54 Db 7.15N 70.44W
Guasipati 54 Fb 7.28N 61.54W
Guasopa 63a Ac 9.14S 152.55 E
Guastalla 14 Ef 44.55N 10.39 E
Guatemala 39 Jh 14.38N 90.31W
Guatemala [3] 49 Bf 14.40N 90.30W
Guatemala [1] 39 Jh 14.38N 90.31W
Guatemala Basin (EN) 3 Mh 11.00N 95.00W
Guateque [Col.] 54 Db 5.05N 73.30W
Guateque [Col.] 54 Db 5.00N 73.28W
Guatimozin 55 Ak 33.27S 62.27W
Guatisimiña 54 Fc 4.33N 63.57W
Guatraché 56 He 37.40S 63.32W
Guaviare, Rio- 52 Je 4.03N 67.44W
Guaviravi 55 Di 29.22S 56.50W
Guaxupé 55 Ie 21.18S 46.42W
Guayabal [Cuba] 49 Ic 20.42N 77.36W
Guayabal [Ven.] 50 Ci 8.00N 67.24W
Guayabero, Rio- 52 Je 4.03N 67.44W
Guayalejo, Rio- 48 Kf 22.13N 97.52W
Guayama 49 Ne 17.59N 66.07W
Guayana, Macizo de la- = Guiana Highlands (EN) 52 Ke 5.00N 60.00W
Guayana Basin (EN) 3 Ci 10.00N 52.00W
Guayaneco, Archipiélago- 56 Eg 47.45S 75.10W
Guayanés, Punta- 51a Cb 18.04N 65.48W
Guayanilla 51a Bb 18.02N 66.47W
Guayanilla, Bahía de- 51a Bc 17.58N 66.45W
Guayape, Rio- 49 Df 14.26N 86.02W
Guayaquil 53 If 2.10S 79.50W
Guayaquil, Golfo de- 52 Hf 3.00S 80.30W
Guaycurú, Rio- 55 Ch 27.19S 58.45W
Guaymas 39 Hg 27.56N 110.54W
Guayquiraró, Rio- 55 Cj 30.10S 58.34W
Guba [Eth.] 35 Fc 11.15N 35.20 E
Guba [Zaire] 36 Ee 10.38S 26.25 E
Guba Dolgaja 19 Fa 70.19N 58.45 E
Gubaha 19 Fd 58.52N 57.36 E
Guban 30 Lg 10.15N 44.26 E
Gubbio 14 Gg 43.21N 12.35 E
Gubdor 17 Hf 60.15N 56.35 E
Guber 10 Rb 54.13N 21.02 E
Gubin 10 Ke 51.56N 14.45 E
Gubio 34 Hc 12.30N 12.47 E
Gubkin 19 De 51.17N 37.33 E
Gúdar, Sierra de- 13 Ld 40.27N 0.42W
Gudara 19 Hh 38.23N 72.42 E
Gudauta 16 Lh 43.07N 40.37 E
Gudbrandsdalen 7 Bf 61.30N 10.00 E
Gudenå 8 Dh 56.29N 10.13 E
Gudermes 19 Eg 43.22N 46.08 E
Gudivāda 25 Ge 16.27N 80.59 E
Gudiyāttam 25 Ff 12.57N 78.52 E
Gudou Shan 27 Jg 22.12N 112.57 E
Güdül 24 Eb 40.13N 32.15 E
Güdür 25 Ff 14.08N 79.51 E
Gudvangen 8 Bd 60.52N 6.50 E
Guebwiller 11 Ng 47.55N 7.12 E
Guéckédou 34 Cd 8.33N 10.09W
Guelma [3] 32 Ib 36.15N 7.30 E
Guelma 32 Ib 36.28N 7.26 E
Guelph 42 Jh 43.33N 80.15W
Guelta Zemmur 32 Ed 25.08N 12.22W
Guemar 32 Ic 33.29N 6.48 E
Guéméné-Penfao 11 Eg 47.38N 1.50W
Guénange 12 Ie 49.18N 6.11 E
Guéné 34 Fc 11.44N 3.13 E
Guer 11 Dg 47.54N 2.07W
Guéra [3] 35 Bc 11.30N 18.30 E
Güera 32 De 20.52N 17.03W
Guéra, Massif de- 30 Ig 11.55N 18.12 E
Guérande 11 Dg 47.20N 2.26W
Guerara 32 Hc 32.48N 4.30 E
Guercif 32 Gc 34.14N 3.22W
Guerdjoumane, Djebel- 13 Oh 36.25N 2.51 E
Güere, Rio- 50 Dh 9.50N 65.08W
Guéréda 35 Cc 14.31N 22.05 E
Guéret 11 Hh 46.10N 1.52 E
Guérin-Kouka 34 Fd 9.41N 0.37 E
Guernica y Luno 13 Ja 43.19N 2.41W
Guernsey 9 Kl 49.27N 2.35W
Guerrero [2] 47 De 17.40N 100.00W
Guerrero 48 Ic 28.20N 100.26W
Guessou-Sud 34 Fc 10.03N 2.38 E
Guest Peninsula 66 Mf 76.18S 148.00W
Guge 35 Fd 6.12N 37.30 E
Gügerd, Kūh-e- 24 Oe 34.50N 53.00 E
Guglionesi 14 Ii 41.55N 14.55 E
Guguan Island 57 Fc 17.19N 145.51 E
Guia 55 Db 15.22S 56.14W
Guia Lopes da Laguna 55 De 21.26S 56.07W
Guiana Highlands (EN) = Guayana, Macizo de la- 52 Ke 5.00N 60.00W
Guiana Island 51d Bb 17.06N 61.44W
Guichi (Chizhou) 27 Ke 30.38N 117.30 E
Guichón 55 Dk 32.21S 57.12W
Guide 27 Hd 36.00N 101.30 E
Guider 34 Hd 9.56N 13.57 E
Guidimaka [3] 32 Ef 15.30N 12.00W
Guidimouni 34 Gc 13.42N 9.30 E
Guiding 27 If 26.33N 107.16 E
Guidong 27 Jf 26.11N 113.58 E
Guiers 11 Li 45.37N 5.37 E
Guiglo 34 Dd 6.33N 7.29W
Guiglo [3] 34 Dd 6.30N 7.40W
Guijá 37 Ed 24.29S 33.00 E
Güija, Lago de- 49 Cf 14.13N 89.34W
Gui Jiang 21 Ng 23.28N 111.18 E
Guijk en Sint Agatha 12 Hc 51.44N 5.52 E
Guijuelo 13 Gd 40.33N 5.40W
Guil 11 Mj 44.40N 6.36 E
Guildford 9 Mj 51.14N 0.35W
Guiler Gol 28 Ga 46.03N 122.06 E
Guilin 22 Ng 25.21N 110.15 E
Guillaume Delisle, Lac- 42 Je 56.25N 76.00W
Guillestre 11 Mj 44.40N 6.39 E
Guilvinec 11 Bg 47.47N 4.17W
Guimarães [Braz.] 54 Jd 2.08S 44.36W
Guimarães [Port.] 13 Dc 41.27N 8.18W
Guimaras 26 Hd 10.35N 122.37 E
Guinchos Cay 49 Hb 22.45N 78.06W
Guinea (EN)=Guinée [1] 31 Fg 11.00N 10.00W
Guinea, Gulf of- 30 Hh 2.00N 2.30 E
Guinea, Gulf of- (EN)=Guinée, Golfe de- 30 Hh 2.00N 2.30 E
Guinea Basin (EN) 3 Di 0.00 5.00W
Guinea-Bissau (EN)=Guiné-Bissau [1] 31 Fg 12.00N 15.00W
Guinea Ecuatorial=Equatorial Guinea (EN) [1] 31 Hh 2.00N 9.00 E
Guinea Rise (EN) 3 Dj 4.00S 0.00
Guiné-Bissau=Guinea-Bissau (EN) [1] 31 Fg 12.00N 15.00W
Guinée=Guinea (EN) [1] 31 Fg 11.00N 10.00W
Guinée, Golfe de-=Guinea, Gulf of- (EN) 30 Hh 2.00N 2.30 E
Guinée Forestière [3] 34 Dd 8.40N 9.50W
Guinée Maritime [3] 34 Cc 10.00N 14.00W
Guînes 12 Dd 50.52N 1.52 E
Güines 47 Hd 22.50N 82.02W
Guingamp 11 Cf 48.33N 3.09W
Guinguinéo 34 Bc 14.16N 15.57W
Guiones, Punta- 49 Eh 9.54N 85.41W
Guiping 27 Ig 23.23N 110.00 E
Guipúzcoa [3] 13 Ja 43.10N 2.10W
Guir, Hamada du- 30 Ge 31.00N 3.20W
Güira de Melena 49 Fb 22.48N 82.30W
Guiratinga 54 Hg 16.21S 53.45W
Güiria 54 Fa 10.34N 62.18W
Guiscard 12 Fe 49.39N 3.03 E
Guise 11 Je 49.54N 3.38 E
Guitiriz 13 Ea 43.11N 7.54W
Guiuan 26 Id 11.02N 125.43 E
Guixi 27 Kf 28.18N 117.15 E
Guixian 27 Ig 23.10N 109.35 E
Guiyang 22 Mg 26.38N 106.43 E
Guizhou Sheng (Kuei-chou Sheng)=Kweichow (EN) [2] 27 If 27.00N 107.00 E
Gujan-Mestras 11 Ej 44.38N 1.04W
Gujarāt [3] 25 Ed 22.51N 71.30 E
Gujarāt 21 Jg 22.51N 71.30 E
Gujranwala 22 Jf 32.09N 74.11 E
Gujrāt 25 Eb 32.34N 74.05 E
Gukovo 16 Ke 48.04N 39.58 E
Gulang 27 Hd 37.30N 102.54 E
Gulbarga 22 Jh 17.20N 76.50 E
Gulbene 7 Gh 57.12N 26.49 E
Gulča 19 Hg 40.19N 73.33 E
Gulf 55 Ad 19.08S 62.01W
Gulf Breeze 44 Dj 30.22N 87.07W
Gulf Coastal Plain 38 Jf 31.00N 92.00W
Gulfport 43 Je 30.22N 89.06W
Gulian 27 La 52.58N 122.09 E
Gulin 27 If 28.02N 105.47 E
Gulistan 19 Gg 40.30N 68.45 E
Guliya Shan 27 Lb 49.48N 122.25 E
Gulja 20 Hf 54.43N 121.03 E
Gulja/Yining 27 Dc 43.54N 81.21 E
Guljajpole 16 Jf 47.37N 36.18 E
Gulkana 40 Jd 62.16N 145.23W
Gulkeviči 16 Lg 45.19N 40.44 E
Gull Bay 45 Lb 49.47N 89.02W
Gulleråsen 8 Fc 61.04N 15.11 E
Gullfoss 7a Bb 64.20N 20.08W
Gullkronafjärd 8 Jd 60.05N 22.15 E
Gull Lake 42 Gf 50.08N 108.27W
Gullringen 8 Fg 57.48N 15.42 E
Gull River 45 Lb 49.50N 89.04W
Gullspång 8 Ff 58.59N 14.06 E
Güllü 15 Mk 38.16N 29.07 E
Güllük 24 Bd 37.14N 27.36 E
Gülpinar 15 Jj 39.32N 26.07 E
Gülşehir 24 Fc 38.45N 34.38 E
Gulstav 8 Dj 54.43N 10.41 E
Gulu 31 Kh 2.47N 32.18 E
Guma /Pishan 27 Cd 37.38N 78.19 E
Gumbiri, Jabal- 35 Ee 4.18N 30.57 E
Gumel 34 Gc 12.38N 9.23 E
Gummersbach 10 De 51.02N 7.33 E
Gummi 34 Gc 12.09N 5.07 E
Gümüşçey 15 Ki 40.17N 27.17 E
Gümüşhacıköy 24 Fb 40.53N 35.14 E
Gümüşhane 23 Ea 40.27N 39.29 E
Gümüşsu 15 Nk 38.14N 30.01 E
Guna 35 Fc 11.44N 38.15 E
Guna 25 Fd 24.19N 77.19 E
Gundagai 59 Jg 35.04S 148.07 E
Gundji 36 Db 2.05N 21.27 E
Gündoğdu 15 Ki 40.15N 27.07 E
Gündoğmuş 24 Ed 36.48N 32.01 E
Güney 15 Mk 38.09N 29.05 E
Güneydoğu Toroslar 21 Gf 38.30N 41.00 E
Gungu 36 Cd 5.44S 19.19 E
Gunma Ken [2] 28 Of 36.20N 139.05 E
Gunnar 42 Ge 59.23N 108.53W
Gunnbjørns Fjeld 67 Mc 68.55N 29.20W
Gunnedah 59 Kf 30.59S 150.15 E
Gunnison 43 Fd 38.33N 106.56W
Gunt 18 Hf 37.30N 71.03 E
Guntakal 25 Fe 15.10N 77.23 E
Guntersville 44 Dh 34.21N 86.18W
Guntersville Lake 44 Dh 34.45N 86.03W
Guntūr 22 Kh 16.18N 80.27 E
Gunungapi, Pulau- 26 Ih 6.38S 126.40 E
Gunungsitoli 26 Cf 1.17N 97.37 E
Günz 10 Gh 48.27N 10.16 E
Günzburg 10 Gh 48.27N 10.16 E
Gunzenhausen 10 Gg 49.06N 10.45 E
Guo He 28 Dh 32.58N 117.13 E
Guojiadian 28 Hc 43.20N 124.37 E
Guoyang 28 Dh 33.31N 116.12 E
Guozhen 28 Bj 29.24N 113.09 E
Gurahonţ 15 Fc 46.16N 22.21 E
Gura Humorului 15 Ib 47.33N 25.54 E
Gurban Obo 27 Jc 43.06N 112.28 E
Gurbantünggüt Shamo 27 Eb 45.30N 87.30 E
Gurdžaani 16 Ni 41.43N 45.48 E
Güre 15 Mk 38.39N 29.10 E
Gurgei, Jabal- 35 Cc 13.50N 24.19 E
Gurghiului, Munţii- 15 Ic 46.41N 25.12 E
Gurgueia, Rio- 52 Lf 6.50S 43.24W
Guri — Raúl Leoni, Represa- 54 Fb 7.30N 63.00W
Gurjev 6 Lf 47.07N 51.56 E
Gurjevsk 20 Df 54.20N 86.00 E
Gurjevskaja Oblast [3] 19 Ff 47.30N 52.00 E
Gurk 14 Id 46.36N 14.31 E
Gurk 14 Id 46.52N 14.18 E
Gurktaler Alpen 14 Hd 46.55N 14.00 E
Guro 37 Ec 17.26S 33.20 E
Gürpınar 24 Jc 38.18N 43.25 E
Gurskoje 20 If 50.20N 138.05 E
Gurskøy 7 Ae 62.15N 5.40 E
Gürsu 15 Mi 40.13N 29.12 E
Guruè 37 Fc 15.28S 36.59 E
Gurumeti 36 Fc 2.05S 33.57 E
Gürün 24 Gc 38.43N 37.17 E
Gurupá 54 Hd 1.25S 51.39W
Gurupi 53 Lg 11.43S 49.04W
Gurupi, Rio- 52 Lf 1.13S 46.06W
Gurupi, Serra do- 54 Id 5.00S 47.30W
Guru Sikhar 25 Ed 24.39N 72.46 E
Gus 7 Ji 55.00N 41.12 E
Gusau 31 Hg 12.10N 6.40 E
Gusev 16 Ce 54.37N 22.12 E
Gushan 28 Ge 39.54N 123.36 E
Gushi 27 Ke 32.02N 115.39 E
Gushikawa 29b Ab 26.21N 127.52 E
Gūshk 24 Ph 28.13N 55.52 E
Gus-Hrustalny 7 Ji 55.38N 40.40 E
Gusinaja, Guba- 20 Kb 72.00N 150.00 E
Gusinaja Zemlja, Poluostrov- 19 Fa 71.50N 52.00 E
Gusinje 15 Cg 42.34N 19.50 E
Gusinoozersk 20 Ff 51.17N 106.30 E
Guspini 14 Ck 39.32N 8.37 E
Güssing 14 Kc 47.04N 16.20 E
Gustav Holm, Kap- 41 Ie 66.45N 34.00W
Gustavia 51b Bc 17.54N 62.52W

Index Symbols

[1] Independent Nation
[2] State, Region
[3] District, County
[4] Municipality
[5] Colony, Dependency
Continent
Physical Region
Historical or Cultural Region
Mount, Mountain
Volcano
Hill
Mountains, Mountain Range
Hills, Escarpment
Plateau, Upland
Pass, Gap
Plain, Lowland
Delta
Salt Flat
Valley, Canyon
Crater, Cave
Karst Features
Depression
Polder
Desert, Dunes
Forest, Woods
Heath, Steppe
Oasis
Cape, Point
Coast, Beach
Cliff
Peninsula
Isthmus
Sandbank
Island
Atoll
Rock, Reef
Islands, Archipelago
Rocks, Reefs
Coral Reef
Well, Spring
Geyser
River, Stream
Waterfall Rapids
River Mouth, Estuary
Lake
Salt Lake
Intermittent Lake
Reservoir
Swamp, Pond
Canal
Glacier
Ice Shelf, Pack Ice
Ocean
Sea
Gulf, Bay
Strait, Fjord
Lagoon
Bank
Seamount
Tablemount
Ridge
Shelf
Basin
Escarpment, Sea Scarp
Fracture
Trench, Abyss
National Park, Reserve
Point of Interest
Recreation Site
Cave, Cavern
Historic Site
Ruins
Wall, Walls
Church, Abbey
Temple
Scientific Station
Airport
Port
Lighthouse
Mine
Tunnel
Dam, Bridge

Gustavs/Kustavi	8	Id	60.30N	21.25 E
Gustavs/Kustavi	8	Id	60.33N	21.21 E
Gustavsfors	8	Ee	59.12N	12.06 E
Gustavus	40	Le	58.25N	135.44W
Güstrow	10	Ic	53.48N	12.10 E
Gusum	8	Gf	58.16N	16.29 E
Gütersloh	10	Ee	51.54N	8.23 E
Guthrie [Ok.-U.S.]	45	Hi	35.53N	97.25W
Guthrie [Tx.-U.S.]	45	Fj	33.37N	100.19W
Gutian	27	Kf	26.40N	118.42 E
Gutiérrez Zamora	48	Kg	20.27N	97.05W
Gutii, Vîrful-	15	Gb	47.42N	23.52 E
Guting → Yutai	28	Dg	35.00N	116.40 E
Gutland	11	Me	49.40N	6.10 E
Gutu	37	Ec	19.39S	31.10 E
Guyana [1]	53	Ke	5.00N	59.00W
Guyane Française = French Guiana (EN) [5]	53	Ke	4.00N	53.00W
Guyang	27	Jc	41.02N	110.04 E
Guyenne	11	Gj	44.35N	1.00 E
Guymon	43	Gd	36.41N	101.29W
Guyonneau, Anse-	51e	Ab	16.14N	61.47W
Guyuan	27	Id	36.01N	106.17 E
Guyuan (Pingdingbu)	28	Cd	41.40N	115.41 E
Guzar	18	Fe	38.37N	66.18 E
Güzelyurt/Mórphou	24	Ee	35.12N	32.59 E
Gūzhān	24	Le	34.20N	46.57 E
Guzhen	28	Dh	33.20N	117.19 E
Guzhou → Rongjiang	27	If	25.58N	108.30 E
Guzmán, Laguna de-	48	Fb	31.20N	107.30W
Gvardejsk	7	Ei	54.40N	21.03 E
Gvardejskoje	16	Hg	45.06N	33.59 E
Gvary	8	Ce	59.23N	9.09 E
Gwa	25	Ie	17.36N	94.35 E
Gwadabawa	34	Gc	13.22N	5.14 E
Gwādar	22	Ig	25.07N	62.19 E
Gwai	30	Jj	17.59S	26.52 E
Gwai	37	Dc	19.17S	27.39 E
Gwalior	22	Jg	26.13N	78.10 E
Gwanda	37	Dd	20.56S	29.00 E
Gwane	36	Eb	4.43N	25.50 E
Gwda	10	Mc	53.04N	16.44 E
Gweebarra Bay/Béal an Bheara	9	Eg	54.52N	8.20W
Gwelo	31	Jj	19.27S	29.49 E
Gwent [3]	9	Kj	51.45N	2.55W
Gweta	37	Dd	20.13S	25.14 E
Gwydir River	59	Je	29.27S	149.48 E
Gwynedd [3]	9	Ji	52.50N	3.50W
Gyaca	27	Ff	29.09N	92.38 E
Gya'gya → Saga	27	Ef	29.22N	85.15 E
Gyai Qu	27	Fe	31.30N	94.40 E
Gyaisi/Jiulong	27	Hf	28.58N	101.33 E
Gya La	27	Gf	29.05N	98.41 E
Gyala Shankou	27	Gf	29.05N	98.41 E
Gyangzê	27	Ef	29.00N	89.38 E
Gyaring Co	27	Ee	31.10N	88.15 E
Gyaring Hu	27	Ge	34.55N	98.00 E
Gyda	20	Cb	70.52N	78.30 E
Gydanskaja Guba	20	Cb	71.20N	76.30 E
Gydanski Poluostrov = Gyda Peninsula (EN)	21	Jb	70.50N	79.00 E
Gyda Peninsula (EN) = Gydanski Poluostrov	21	Jb	70.50N	79.00 E
Gyigang → Zayü	27	Gf	28.43N	97.25 E
Gyirong (Zongga)	27	Ef	28.57N	85.12 E
Gyldenløves Fjord	41	Hf	64.10N	40.30W
Gyldenløves Høj	8	Di	55.33N	11.52 E
Gympie	58	Gg	26.11S	152.40 E
Gyoma	10	Qj	46.56N	20.50 E
Gyöngyös	10	Pi	47.47N	19.56 E
Győr	6	Hf	47.41N	17.38 E
Győr [2]	10	Ni	47.40N	17.39 E
Győr-Sopron [2]	10	Ni	47.40N	17.15 E
Gypsumville	42	Hf	51.45N	98.35W
Gysinge	8	Gd	60.17N	16.53 E
Gyttorp	8	Fe	59.31N	14.58 E
Gyula	10	Rj	46.39N	21.17 E

H

Haacht	12	Gd	50.59N	4.38 E
Häädemeeste/Hjademeste	8	Uf	58.00N	24.28 E
Ha'afeva	65b	Ba	19.57S	174.43W
Haafusia	64h	Bb	13.18S	176.09W
Haag, Mount-	66	Qf	77.40S	79.00W
Haaksbergen	12	Ib	52.09N	6.45 E
Haamstede, Westerschouwen-	12	Fc	51.42N	3.45 E
Haanja Kõrgustik	8	Lg	57.30N	27.30 E
Ha'ano	65b	Ba	19.40S	174.17W
Ha'apai Group	57	Jf	19.47S	174.27W
Haapajärvi	7	Fe	63.45N	25.20 E
Haapamäki	8	Kb	62.15N	24.28 E
Haapasaari	8	Ld	60.15N	27.10 E
Haapaselkä [Fin.]	8	Mc	61.35N	28.15 E
Haapaselkä [Fin.]	8	Mb	62.10N	28.10 E
Haapiti	65e	Fc	17.34S	149.52W
Haapsalu	19	Cd	58.57N	23.32 E
Ha'arava	24	Fg	30.58N	32.24 E
Haardt	10	Dg	49.15N	8.00 E
Haardtkopf	12	Je	49.51N	7.04 E
Haaren, Wünnenberg-	12	Kc	51.34N	8.44 E
Haarlem	11	Kb	52.23N	4.38 E
Haarlemmermeer	12	Gb	52.20N	4.41 E
Haarlerberg	12	Ib	52.20N	6.25 E
Haarstrang	12	Kc	51.30N	8.20 E
Haast	58	Hi	43.52S	169.01 E
Haast Pass	62	Cf	44.06S	169.21 E
Habahe/Kaba	27	Eb	47.53N	86.12 E
Habarovsk	22	Pe	48.27N	135.06 E
Habarovski Kraj [3]	20	If	53.00N	137.00 E
Ḩabarūt	23	Hf	17.22N	52.42 E
Ḩabashīyah, Jabal-	35	Ib	16.45N	50.05 E
Habaswein	36	Gb	1.01N	39.29 E
Habay [Alta.-Can.]	42	Fe	58.52N	118.45W
Habay [Bel.]	12	He	49.45N	5.38 E
Habay [Som.]	35	Ge	1.08N	43.46 E
Ḩabbān	35	Hc	14.21N	47.05 E
Ḩabbānīyah, Hawr al-	24	Jf	33.17N	43.29 E
Habibas, Iles-	13	Ki	35.44N	1.08W
Habichtswald	10	Fe	51.20N	9.25 E
Habo	8	Fg	57.55N	14.04 E
Haboro	27	Pc	44.22N	141.42 E
Ḩabshān	24	Ok	23.50N	53.37 E
Hache	10	Ec	53.05N	8.50 E
Hachenburg	12	Jd	50.39N	7.50 E
Hachijō	29	Fe	35.15N	139.45 E
Hachijō-Fuji	29	Fe	33.08N	139.46 E
Hachijō-Jima	27	Oe	33.05N	139.50 E
Hachiman	29	Ed	35.46N	136.57 E
Hachimori	29	Fa	40.22N	140.00 E
Hachinohe	22	Qe	40.30N	141.29 E
Hachiōji	29	Fd	35.39N	139.18 E
Hachiro-Gata	29	Fa	40.00N	140.00 E
Hacibey De	24	Kd	36.58N	44.18 E
Hackar Dağı	24	Ib	40.50N	41.10 E
Hackås	7	De	62.55N	14.31 E
Håckren	8	Ea	63.10N	13.35 E
Hačmas	19	Eg	41.25N	48.52 E
Hadagang	28	Kb	45.24N	131.12 E
Hadamar	12	Kd	50.27N	8.03 E
Ḩaḑan, Ḩarrat-	33	He	21.30N	41.23 E
Hadano	29	Fd	35.22N	139.14 E
Ḩadāribah, Ra's al-	35	Fa	22.04N	36.54 E
Hadd, Ra's al-	21	Hg	22.32N	59.59 E
Haddad	30	Ig	14.40N	18.46 E
Ḩadded	35	Hc	10.10N	48.28 E
Haddington	9	Kf	55.58N	2.47W
Haddummati Atoll	25a	Bb	1.45N	73.30 E
Hadejia	34	Hc	12.27N	10.03 E
Hadejia	34	Hc	12.50N	10.51 E
Hadeland	8	Dd	60.25N	10.35 E
Hadeln	10	Ec	53.45N	8.45 E
Hadera	24	Ff	32.26N	34.55 E
Haderslev	7	Bi	55.15N	9.30 E
Hadībah	23	Hg	12.39N	54.02 E
Hadım	24	Ed	36.59N	32.28 E
Hadimköy	24	Cb	41.09N	28.37 E
Hadīyah	23	Ed	25.34N	38.41 E
Hadjer el Hamis	35	Ac	12.51N	14.50 E
Hadjout	13	Oh	36.31N	2.25 E
Hadleigh	12	Cb	52.03N	0.56 E
Hadley Bay	42	Gb	72.30N	108.30W
Ha Dong	25	Ld	20.58N	105.46 E
Ḩaḑramawt	21	Gh	15.00N	50.00 E
Hadrian's Wall	9	Kg	54.59N	2.26W
Hadsten	8	Dh	56.20N	10.03 E
Hadsund	8	Dh	56.43N	10.07 E
Hadytajaha	17	Nc	66.57N	69.12 E
Hadyženk	16	Kg	44.25N	39.31 E
Hadzibeiski Liman	15	Nc	46.40N	30.30 E
Haedo, Cuchilla de-	55	Dj	31.40S	56.18W
Haeju	28	He	38.02N	125.42 E
Haena	60	Oc	22.13N	159.34W
Ḩafar al 'Atk	24	Lj	25.56N	46.47 E
Ḩafar al Bāţin	23	Gd	28.27N	46.00 E
Haffner Bjerg	41	Fc	76.30N	63.00W
Ḩaffūz	14	Do	35.38N	9.40 E
Hafik	24	Gc	39.52N	37.24 E
Ḩafīrat al 'Aydā	23	Ed	26.26N	39.12 E
Ḩafit	24	Pk	23.59N	55.49 E
Ḩafit, Jabal-	24	Pj	24.03N	55.46 E
Hafnarfjördur	7a	Bb	64.04N	21.57W
Haft Gel	24	Mg	31.27N	49.27 E
Hāfūn	35	Ic	10.10N	51.05 E
Hāfūn, Rās- = Hafun, Ras- (EN)	30	Mg	10.27N	51.24 E
Hafun, Ras- (EN) = Hāfūn, Rās-	30	Mg	10.27N	51.24 E
Hāfūn Bay North	35	Ic	10.37N	51.15 E
Hāfūn Bay South	35	Ic	10.15N	51.05 E
Hagadera	36	Hb	0.02N	40.17 E
Hagby	8	Gh	56.33N	16.10 E
Hageland	12	Gd	50.55N	4.45 E
Hagemeister	40	Ge	58.40N	161.00W
Hagen	10	De	51.21N	7.28 E
Hagenow	10	Hc	53.26N	11.12 E
Hagere Hiywet	35	Fd	8.58N	37.53 E
Hagerman	46	He	42.49N	114.54W
Hagerstown	43	Ld	39.39N	77.43W
Hagetmau	11	Fk	43.40N	0.35W
Hagfors	7	Cf	60.02N	13.42 E
Häggenås	8	Fa	63.24N	14.55 E
Hagi	28	Kg	34.24N	131.25 E
Ha Giang	25	Kd	22.50N	104.59 E
Hágios Theódóros	24	Fe	35.20N	34.01 E
Hagman, Puntan-	64b	Ba	15.09N	145.48 E
Hagondange	11	Me	49.15N	6.10 E
Hags Head/Ceanna Cailllighe	9	Di	52.57N	9.28W
Hague, Cap de la-	5	Ff	49.43N	1.57W
Haguenau	11	Nf	48.49N	7.47 E
Hagunia	32	Ed	27.26N	12.24W
Hahajima-Rettō	60	Cb	26.37N	142.10 E
Hahns Peak	45	Cf	40.56N	107.01W
Hahót	10	Mj	46.38N	16.56 E
Hai'an	28	Fh	32.33N	120.26 E
Haicheng	27	Lc	40.51N	122.43 E
Haidenaab	10	Ig	49.35N	12.08 E
Hai Duong	25	Ld	20.56N	106.19 E
Haifa (EN) = Hefa	22	Ff	32.50N	35.00 E
Haifeng	27	Kg	22.58N	115.21 E
Haiger	12	Kd	50.45N	8.13 E
Hai He	28	De	38.57N	117.43 E
Haikakan Sovetakan Socialistakan Respublika/Armjanskaja SSR [2]	19	Eg	40.00N	45.00 E
Haikang (Leizhou)	27	Jg	20.56N	110.06 E
Haikou	22	Ng	20.05N	110.20 E
Ḩā'il	22	Gg	27.33N	41.42 E
Hailang He	28	Jb	44.33N	129.33 E
Hailar	22	Ne	49.14N	119.42 E
Hailar He	21	Ne	49.30N	117.50 E
Hailin	27	Mc	44.35N	129.22 E
Hailong (Meihekou)	27	Mc	42.32N	125.37 E
Hailsham	12	Cd	50.52N	0.16 E
Hailun	27	Mb	47.29N	126.55 E
Hailuoto/Karlö	5	Ib	65.02N	24.42 E
Haima Tan	27	Kd	10.52N	116.53 E
Haimen [China]	28	Fi	31.53N	121.10 E
Haimen [China]	28	Fj	28.40N	121.27 E
Haina	12	Kc	51.03N	8.56 E
Hainan Dao	21	Mh	19.00N	109.00 E
Hainaut	11	Jd	50.20N	3.50 E
Hainaut [3]	12	Fd	50.30N	4.00 E
Hainburg an der Donau	14	Kb	48.09N	16.56 E
Haines	39	Fd	59.14N	135.27W
Haines Junction	42	Dd	60.45N	137.30W
Hainich	10	Ge	51.05N	10.27 E
Hainleite	10	Ge	51.20N	10.48 E
Hai Phong	22	Mg	20.52N	106.41 E
Haïti = Haiti (EN) [1]	39	Lh	19.00N	72.25W
Haiti (EN) = Haïti [1]	39	Lh	19.00N	72.25W
Haixing (Suji)	28	De	38.10N	117.29 E
Haixin Shan	27	Hd	37.00N	100.03 E
Haiyan (Sanjiaocheng)	27	Hd	36.58N	100.50 E
Haiyan (Wuyuanzhen)	28	Fi	30.31N	120.56 E
Haiyang (Dongoun)	28	Ff	36.46N	121.09 E
Haiyang Dao	28	Ge	39.03N	123.12 E
Haiyou → Sanmen	27	Lf	29.08N	121.22 E
Haiyuan	27	Id	36.35N	105.40 E
Haizhou	28	Eg	34.34N	119.08 E
Haizhou Wan	21	Nf	35.00N	119.30 E
Ḩajar Banga	35	Cc	11.30N	23.00 E
Hajdarken	19	Hh	39.55N	71.24 E
Hajdú-Bihar [2]	10	Ri	47.25N	21.30 E
Hajdúböszörmény	10	Ri	47.40N	21.31 E
Hajdúhadház	10	Ri	47.41N	21.40 E
Hajdúnánás	10	Ri	47.51N	21.26 E
Hajdúság	10	Ri	47.35N	21.30 E
Hajdúszoboszló	10	Ri	47.27N	21.24 E
Hajihi-Zaki	29	Fb	38.19N	138.31 E
Ḩājjīābād [Iran]	24	Ph	28.19N	55.55 E
Ḩājjīābād [Iran]	24	Ph	28.21N	54.27 E
Ḩājjīabād-e Māsīleh	24	Ne	34.49N	51.13 E
Hajnówka	10	Td	52.45N	23.36 E
Hajós	10	Pj	46.24N	19.07 E
Hajpudyrskaja Guba	17	Ib	68.40N	59.30 E
Haka	25	Id	22.39N	93.37 E
Hakase-Yama	29	Fc	37.22N	139.43 E
Hakasskaja Avtonomnaja Oblast [3]	20	Df	53.30N	90.00 E
Hakata-Wan	29	Be	33.40N	130.20 E
Hakefjord	8	Dg	57.41N	11.44 E
Hakkâri	23	Fb	37.34N	43.45 E
Hakken-Zan	29	Dd	34.10N	135.54 E
Hakkōda San	29	Ga	40.40N	140.53 E
Hako-Dake	29a	Ca	44.40N	142.25 E
Hakodate	22	Qe	41.45N	140.43 E
Hakone-Yama	29	Fd	35.13N	139.00 E
Hakui	28	Nf	36.53N	136.47 E
Hakupu	64k	Bb	19.06S	169.50W
Haku-San	29	Ec	36.09N	136.45 E
Hal/Halle	11	Kd	50.44N	4.14 E
Halab	24	Md	36.17N	48.03 E
Ḩalab = Aleppo (EN)	22	Ff	36.12N	37.10 E
Ḩalabjah	24	Ke	35.10N	45.59 E
Halač	19	Gh	39.04N	64.53 E
Halachó	48	Ng	20.29N	90.05W
Halahei	28	Ga	46.11N	122.46 E
Ḩalā'ib	31	Kf	22.13N	36.38 E
Halalii Lake	65a	Ab	21.52N	160.11W
Halangingie Point	64k	Bb	19.03S	169.58W
Håladeven	8	Ff	58.05N	14.45 E
Halawa	65a	Eb	21.10N	156.44W
Halawa, Cape-	65a	Eb	21.10N	156.43W
Ḩalbā	24	Ge	34.33N	36.05 E
Halberstadt	10	He	51.54N	11.03 E
Halcon, Mount-	26	Hd	13.16N	121.00 E
Haldean-Sogotyn-Daba	27	Gb	49.05N	97.55 E
Halden	7	Cg	59.09N	11.23 E
Haldensleben	10	Hd	52.18N	11.25 E
Haldia	25	Hd	22.08N	88.05 E
Haldwani	25	Fc	29.13N	79.31 E
Hale, Mount-	59	De	26.00S	117.10 E
Haleakala Crater	65a	Ec	20.43N	156.12W
Haleiwa	65a	Cb	21.36N	158.06W
Halemaumau	65a	Fd	19.24N	155.17W
Hale River	59	Hd	24.56S	135.53 E
Halesworth	12	Db	52.21N	1.30 E
Haleyville	44	Dh	34.14N	87.37W
Ḩalfā al Gadida	31	Kg	15.19N	35.34 E
Half Assini	34	Ed	5.03N	2.53W
Halfeti	24	Gd	37.15N	37.52 E
Halfway	42	Fe	56.13N	121.26W
Halh-Gol	27	Kb	48.01N	118.10 E
Haliburton	44	Hc	45.03N	78.33W
Halifax	39	Me	44.39N	63.36W
Halifax, Mount-	59	Jc	19.05S	146.20 E
Halifax Bay	59	Jc	18.50S	146.30 E
Hālīl	23	Id	27.28N	58.44 E
Halīleh, Ra's-e-	24	Nh	28.46N	50.56 E
Halilovo	16	Ud	51.27N	58.10 E
Ḩalin	35	Hd	9.08N	48.47 E
Haliut → Urad Zhonghou Lianheqi	27	Ic	41.34N	108.32 E
Haljala	8	Le	59.22N	26.09 E
Haljasavej	20	Cd	63.20N	78.30 E
Hall	40	Ed	60.40N	173.05W
Halladale	9	Jc	58.30N	3.50W
Hallam Peak	46	Fa	52.11N	118.46W
Halland	8	Eh	57.00N	12.45 E
Halland [2]	7	Ch	56.45N	13.00 E
Hallandsås	8	Eh	56.23N	13.00 E
Halla-san	28	Ih	33.22N	126.32 E
Ḩallat 'Ammār	24	Gh	29.08N	36.02 E
Hall Beach	42	Jc	68.10N	81.56W
Halle	10	He	51.30N	12.00 E
Halle [2]	10	He	51.30N	11.50 E
Halle/Hal	11	Kd	50.44N	4.14 E
Halle (Westfalen)	12	Kb	52.05N	8.22 E
Halleberg	8	Ef	58.23N	12.25 E
Hällefors	8	Fe	59.47N	14.30 E
Hälleforsnäs	8	Ge	59.10N	16.30 E
Halleim	14	Hc	47.41N	13.06 E
Hällekis	8	Ef	58.38N	13.25 E
Hallen	7	De	63.11N	14.05 E
Hallenberg	12	Kc	51.07N	8.38 E
Hallencourt	12	De	49.59N	1.53 E
Halle-Neustadt	10	He	51.31N	11.53 E
Hallertau	10	Hh	48.35N	11.50 E
Hällestad	8	Ff	58.44N	15.34 E
Hallettsville	45	Hl	29.27N	96.57W
Halley Bay	66	Af	75.31S	26.38W
Halli	8	Kc	61.52N	24.50 E
Hallie-Jackson Bank (EN)	63c	Ba	9.45S	166.10 E
Halligen	10	Eb	54.35N	8.35 E
Hallingdal	7	Bf	60.40N	9.15 E
Hallingdalselva	8	Cd	60.23N	9.35 E
Hallingskarvet	5	Gc	60.37N	7.45 E
Hall Islands	57	Gd	8.37N	152.00 E
Halliste Jõgi	8	Kf	58.23N	24.25 E
Hall Lake	42	Jc	68.40N	82.20W
Hall Land	41	Fb	81.12N	61.10W
Hallock	45	Hb	48.47N	96.57W
Hall Peninsula	38	Mc	63.30N	66.00W
Hallsberg	7	Dg	59.04N	15.07 E
Halls Creek	58	Df	18.13S	127.40 E
Hallstahammar	7	Dg	59.37N	16.13 E
Hallstatt	14	Hb	47.33N	13.39 E
Hallstavik	7	Ef	60.03N	18.36 E
Halluin	12	Fd	50.47N	3.08 E
Halmahera	57	Dd	1.00N	128.00 E
Halmahera, Laut- = Halmahera Sea (EN)	57	De	1.00S	129.00 E
Halmahera Sea (EN) = Halmahera, Laut-	57	De	1.00S	129.00 E
Halmer-Ju	19	Gb	67.58N	64.40 E
Halmeu	15	Gb	47.58N	23.01 E
Halmstad	6	Hd	56.39N	12.50 E
Haloze	14	Jd	46.20N	15.50 E
Ḩalq al Wādī	32	Jb	36.49N	10.18 E
Hals	7	Cg	57.00N	10.19 E
Hälsingland	8	Gc	61.30N	17.00 E
Halsön	8	Ib	62.50N	21.10 E
Halstead	12	Cc	51.57N	0.38 E
Halsteren	12	Gc	51.32N	4.16 E
Haltang He	27	Fd	39.00N	94.40 E
Halten Bank (EN)	7	Bd	64.45N	8.45 E
Haltern	12	Jc	51.44N	7.11 E
Haltiatunturi	7	Eb	69.18N	21.16 E
Haltom City	45	Hj	32.48N	97.16W
Halturin	19	Ed	58.35N	48.55 E
Hālūl	24	Oj	25.40N	52.25 E
Halver	12	Jc	51.12N	7.29 E
Ham	11	Je	49.45N	3.04 E
Ham, Roches de-	12	Ae	49.02N	1.02W
Hamada	29	Cd	34.53N	132.03 E
Hamadān	22	Gf	34.48N	48.30 E
Hamadān [3]	23	Gb	35.00N	48.40 E
Hamadia	13	Ni	35.28N	1.52 E
Hamaguir	32	Gc	30.54N	3.02W
Hamāh	23	Eb	35.08N	36.45 E
Hamakita	29	Ed	34.49N	137.45 E
Hamamasu	29a	Bb	43.36N	141.21 E
Hamamatsu	27	Oe	34.42N	137.44 E
Hamanaka	29a	Db	43.05N	145.05 E
Hamanaka-Wan	29a	Db	43.07N	145.10 E
Hamana-Ko	29	Ed	34.45N	137.34 E
Hamanen, Oued el-	32	Hd	25.52N	1.26 E
Hamaoka	29	Fd	34.39N	138.07 E
Hamar	6	Hc	60.48N	11.06 E
Hamar-Daran, Hrebet-	20	Ff	51.10N	105.00 E
Hamasaka	29	Dd	35.38N	134.27 E
Ḩamāţah, Jabal-	33	Ge	24.12N	35.00 E
Hamatonbetsu	28	Qb	45.07N	142.23 E
Hambantota	25	Gg	6.10N	81.07 E
Hambre, Cayos del-	49	Fb	22.15N	82.47W
Hamburg [2]	10	Fc	53.35N	10.00 E
Hamburg [F.R.G.]	6	Ge	53.33N	10.00 E
Hamburg [S.Afr.]	37	Df	33.18S	27.28 E
Hamburg-Altona	10	Fc	53.33N	9.57 E
Hamburg-Harburg	10	Fc	53.28N	10.00 E
Hamburgsund	8	Df	58.33N	11.16 E
Ḩamḑah	33	Hf	19.02N	43.36 E
Ḩamḑh, Wādī al-	21	Fg	25.58N	36.42 E
Häme [2]	7	Ff	61.30N	24.30 E
Häme	8	Kc	61.30N	25.30 E
Hämeenkangas	8	Jc	61.45N	22.40 E
Hämeenlinna/Tavastehus	7	Ff	61.00N	24.27 E
Hämeenselkä	8	Kb	62.30N	25.00 E
Hamelin Pool	59	Ce	26.15S	114.05 E
Hameln	10	Fd	52.06N	9.21 E
Hamero Hadad	35	Gd	7.28N	42.13 E
Hamersley Range	59	Dd	21.55S	116.45 E
Hamgyŏng-Namdo [2]	28	Id	40.00N	127.30 E
Hamgyŏng-Pukto [2]	28	Jd	41.45N	129.50 E
Hamgyŏng-Sanmaek	28	Jd	41.00N	128.45 E
Hamhŭng	22	Of	39.54N	127.32 E
Hami/Kumul	22	Le	42.48N	93.27 E
Ḩamīdīyeh	24	Mg	31.29N	48.26 E
Hamilton [Austl.]	59	Ig	37.45S	142.02 E
Hamilton [Ber.]	39	Mf	32.17N	64.46W
Hamilton [Mt.-U.S.]	43	Eb	46.15N	114.09W
Hamilton [N.Z.]	58	Ih	37.47S	175.17 E
Hamilton [Oh.-U.S.]	43	Kd	39.23N	84.33W
Hamilton [Ont.-Can.]	39	Le	43.15N	79.51W
Hamilton [Scot.-U.K.]	9	If	55.47N	4.03W
Hamilton [Tx.-U.S.]	45	Gk	31.42N	98.07W
Hamilton, Lake-	45	Ji	34.30N	93.05W
Hamilton, Mount-	46	Hg	39.14N	115.32W
Hamilton River	59	Hd	23.30S	139.47 E
Ḩamīn, Wādī al-	33	Dc	30.28N	22.00 E
Hamina/Fredrikshamn	7	Gf	60.34N	27.12 E
Hamm	10	De	51.41N	7.48 E
Ḩammām al 'Alīl	24	Jd	36.10N	43.16 E
Ḩammām al Anf	32	Jb	36.44N	10.20 E
Ḩammāmāt	32	Jb	36.24N	10.37 E
Ḩammāmāt, Khalīj-	32	Jb	36.05N	10.40 E
Hammam Bou Hadjar	13	Li	35.23N	0.58W
Hammami	30	Ff	23.03N	11.30W
Hammam Righa	13	Oh	36.23N	2.24 E
Ḩammār, Hawr al-	23	Gc	30.50N	47.10 E
Hammarstrand	8	Ga	63.06N	16.21 E
Hamme	12	Gc	51.06N	4.08 E
Hammelburg	10	Ff	50.07N	9.54 E
Hammerdal	7	De	63.36N	15.21 E
Hammeren	8	Fi	55.18N	14.47 E
Hammerfest	6	Ia	70.40N	23.45 E
Hamminkeln	12	Ic	51.44N	6.35 E
Hamminkeln-Dingden	12	Ic	51.46N	6.37 E
Hammond [In.-U.S.]	44	De	41.36N	87.30W
Hammond [La.-U.S.]	43	Ie	30.30N	90.28W
Hammonton	44	Jf	39.38N	74.48W
Hamont, Hamont-Achel-	12	Hc	51.15N	5.33 E
Hamont-Achel	12	Hc	51.15N	5.33 E
Hamont-Achel-Hamont	12	Hc	51.15N	5.33 E
Hamoyet, Jabal-	30	Kg	17.33N	38.02 E
Hampden	62	Df	45.20S	170.49 E
Hampshire [3]	9	Lk	51.00N	1.10W
Hampshire Downs	9	Lj	51.15N	1.15W
Hampton [Ia.-U.S.]	45	Je	42.45N	93.12W
Hampton [Va.-U.S.]	44	Ig	37.02N	76.23W
Hampton Butte	46	Ee	43.46N	120.17W
Hamp'yong	28	Ig	35.04N	126.31 E
Ḩamrā'	35	Dc	10.54N	29.54 E
Hamra [R.S.F.S.R.]	20	Gd	60.17N	114.10 E
Hamra [Swe.]	8	Fc	61.39N	15.00 E
Ḩamrā', Al Ḩamādah al-	30	If	29.30N	12.00 E
Hamra, Saguia el-	30	Ff	27.24N	13.43W
Hamrān	24	Kd	36.22N	45.44 E
Ḩamrat ash Shaykh	35	Dc	14.35N	27.58 E
Ḩamrīn, Jabal-	24	Ke	34.30N	44.30 E
Hāmūn-e Hirmand, Daryācheh-ye-	23	Jc	31.30N	61.20 E
Han	34	Ec	10.41N	2.27W
Hana	60	Oc	20.45N	155.59W
Hanahan	44	Hi	32.55N	80.00W
Hanaizum	29	Gb	38.51N	141.12 E
Ḩanak	23	Ed	25.33N	36.56 E
Hanalei	65a	Ba	22.13N	159.30W
Hanamaki	28	Pe	39.23N	141.07 E
Hanang	30	Ki	4.26S	35.24 E
Hanaoka	29	Ga	40.21N	140.34 E
Hanapepe	65a	Bb	21.55N	159.35W
Hanau	10	Ef	50.08N	8.55 E
Han-Bogdo	27	Ic	43.12N	107.10 E
Hanceville	42	Ff	51.55N	123.02W
Hancheng	27	Jd	35.30N	110.25 E
Hanchuan	28	Bi	30.39N	113.46 E
Hancock	44	Cb	47.07N	88.35W
Handa	29	Ed	34.53N	136.56 E
Handan	22	Nf	36.35N	114.28 E
Handen	8	He	59.10N	18.08 E
Handeni	36	Gd	5.26S	38.01 E
Handlová	10	Oh	48.44N	18.46 E
Handöl	8	Ea	63.16N	12.26 E
Handyga	22	Pc	62.40N	135.36 E
Ha̱negev = Negev Desert (EN)	24	Fg	30.30N	34.55 E
Hanford	46	Fh	36.20N	119.39W
Hangaj, Hrebet- (Changajn Nuruu) = Khangai Mountains (EN)	21	Le	47.30N	100.00 E
Han-gang	27	Md	37.45N	126.11 E
Hanga Roa	65d	Ab	27.09S	109.26W
Hang'bu He	28	Di	31.33N	117.05 E
Hanggin Houqi (Xamba)	27	Ic	40.59N	107.07 E
Hanggin Qi (Xin Zhen)	27	Id	39.54N	108.55 E
Hangö/Hanko	7	Fg	59.50N	22.57 E
Hangöudde/Hankoniemi	8	Je	59.50N	23.10 E
Hangu	28	De	39.16N	117.50 E
Hangzhou	22	Of	30.18N	120.11 E
Hangzhou Wan	28	Fi	30.25N	121.00 E
Ḩanīsh	33	Hg	13.45N	42.45 E
Ḩanīsh al Kabīr, Jazīrat al-	33	Hg	13.43N	42.45 E
Hanja, Vozvyšennost-	8	Lg	57.30N	27.30 E
Ḩanjūrah, Ra's-	24	Pj	24.44N	54.39 E
Hanka, Ozero- = Khanka Lake (EN)	21	Pe	45.00N	132.24 E
Hankasalmi	8	Lb	62.23N	26.26 E
Hankensbüttel	10	Gd	52.44N	10.36 E
Hanko/Hangö	7	Fg	59.50N	22.57 E
Hankoniemi/Hangöudde	8	Je	59.50N	23.10 E
Hankou, Wuhan-	28	Ci	30.35N	114.16 E
Hanksville	46	Jg	38.25N	110.10W
Hanlar	16	Oi	40.34N	46.20 E
Hanmej, Gora-	17	Lc	67.08N	66.00 E
Hanmer Springs	62	Ee	42.31S	172.50 E
Hann, Mount-	59	Fc	15.50S	125.50 E
Hanna [Alta.-Can.]	42	Gf	51.38N	111.54W
Hanna [Wy.-U.S.]	46	Lf	41.52N	106.34W
Hannah Bay	42	Jf	51.15N	79.50W
Hannibal	43	Id	39.42N	91.22W
Hanningfield Reservoir	12	Cc	51.37N	0.28 E
Hannō	29	Fd	35.53N	139.17 E
Hannover	6	Ge	52.22N	9.43 E
Hann River	59	Fc	17.10S	126.10 E
Hannuit/Hannut	12	Hd	50.40N	5.05 E
Hannut/Hannuit	12	Hd	50.40N	5.05 E
Hano	8	Fi	56.00N	14.50 E
Hanöbukten	8	Fi	55.45N	14.30 E
Ha Noi	22	Mg	21.02N	105.51 E
Hanover [N.H.-U.S.]	44	Kd	43.42N	72.17W
Hanover [Ont.-Can.]	44	Gc	44.09N	81.02W
Hanover [Pa.-U.S.]	44	If	39.47N	76.59W
Hanover [S.Afr.]	37	Cf	31.04S	24.29 E
Hanover, Isla-	56	Fh	51.00S	74.40W
Hanpan, Cape-	59	Ka	5.01S	154.37 E
Han Pijesak	14	Mf	44.05N	18.57 E

Index Symbols

- [1] Independent Nation
- [2] State, Region
- [3] District, County
- [4] Municipality
- [5] Colony, Dependency
- Continent
- Physical Region
- Historical or Cultural Region
- Mount, Mountain
- Volcano
- Hill
- Mountains, Mountain Range
- Hills, Escarpment
- Plateau, Upland
- Pass, Gap
- Plain, Lowland
- Delta
- Salt Flat
- Valley, Canyon
- Crater, Cave
- Karst Features
- Depression
- Polder
- Desert, Dunes
- Forest, Woods
- Heath, Steppe
- Oasis
- Cape, Point
- Coast, Beach
- Cliff
- Peninsula
- Isthmus
- Sandbank
- Island
- Atoll
- Rock, Reef
- Islands, Archipelago
- Rocks, Reefs
- Coral Reef
- Well, Spring
- Geyser
- River, Stream
- Waterfall Rapids
- River Mouth, Estuary
- Lake
- Salt Lake
- Intermittent Lake
- Reservoir
- Swamp, Pond
- Canal
- Glacier
- Ice Shelf, Pack Ice
- Ocean
- Sea
- Gulf, Bay
- Strait, Fjord
- Lagoon
- Bank
- Seamount
- Tablemount
- Ridge
- Shelf
- Basin
- Escarpment, Sea Scarp
- Fracture
- Trench, Abyss
- National Park, Reserve
- Point of Interest
- Recreation Site
- Cave, Cavern
- Historic Site
- Ruins
- Wall, Walls
- Church, Abbey
- Temple
- Scientific Station
- Airport
- Port
- Lighthouse
- Mine
- Tunnel
- Dam, Bridge

Hansen Mountains 66 Ee 68.16S 58.47E
Hanshan 28 Ei 31.43N 118.07E
Hanshou 28 Aj 28.55N 111.58E
Han Shui 21 Nf 30.34N 114.17E
Hanstholm 8 Cg 57.07N 8.38E
Han Sum 28 Eb 44.33N 119.58E
Han-sur-Lesse, Rochefort- 12 Hd 50.08N 5.11E
Han-sur-Nied 12 If 48.59N 6.26E
Hantajskoje, Ozero- 20 Ec 68.25N 91.00E
Hantau 19 Hg 44.13N 73.48E
Hantengri Feng 27 Dc 42.03N 80.11E
Hants 9 Lj 51.10N 1.10W
Hanty-Mansijsk 22 Ic 61.00N 69.06E
Hanty-Mansijski Nacionalny Okrug [3] 19 Hc 62.00N 72.30E
Hantzsch 42 Kc 67.32N 72.26W
Hanušovice 10 Mf 50.05N 16.55E
Hanwang 27 He 31.25N 104.13E
Hanyang 28 Ci 30.34N 114.01E
Hanyang, Wuhan- 28 Ci 30.33N 114.16E
Hanyū 29 Fc 36.11N 139.32E
Hanyuan (Fulin) 27 Hf 29.25N 102.12E
Hanzhong [China] 22 Mf 32.59N 107.11E
Hanzhong [China] 27 Ie 33.07N 107.00E
Hanzhuang 28 Dg 34.38N 117.23E
Hao Atoll 57 Mf 18.15S 140.54W
Haouach 30 Ig 16.30N 19.55E
Haoud el Hamra 32 Ic 31.58N 5.59E
Hao Xi 28 Ej 28.28N 119.56E
Haoxue 28 Bi 30.02N 112.25E
Haparanda 7 Fd 65.50N 24.10E
Hapčeranga 20 Gg 49.42N 112.20E
Hapsu 28 Jd 41.13N 128.51E
Ḩaql 24 Fh 29.18N 34.57E
Ḩaql al Barqan 24 Lh 28.55N 47.57E
Ḩaql al Manāqish 24 Lh 29.02N 47.32E
Ḩaql as Şābirīyah 24 Lh 29.48N 47.50E
Hara, Zaliv-/Hara Laht 8 Ke 59.35N 25.30E
Hara-Ajrag 27 Ib 45.50N 109.20E
Harabali 19 Ef 47.25N 47.16E
Ḩaraḑ 23 Ge 24.14N 49.11E
Haraiki Atoll 57 Mf 17.28S 143.27W
Hara Laht/Hara, Zaliv- 8 Ke 59.35N 25.30E
Haramachi 28 Pf 37.38N 140.58E
Haram Dāgh 23 Gb 37.35N 46.43E
Harami, Pereval- 16 Oh 42.48N 46.12E
Harand 24 Of 32.34N 52.26E
Harani'ia Point 63a Ed 10.21S 161.16E
Hara Nur 27 Fb 48.05N 93.12E
Ḩarardēre 35 He 4.32N 47.53E
Harare 31 Kj 17.50S 31.10E
Harat 35 Fb 16.05N 39.28E
Hara-Tas, Krjaž- 20 Fb 72.00N 107.00E
Haratini 64n Bc 10.28S 160.58W
Ḩarat Zuwayyah 31 Jf 24.14N 21.59E
Hara-Us-Nur 27 Fb 48.00N 92.10E
Haraz 35 Bc 13.57N 19.26E
Ḩarāz 24 Od 36.40N 52.43E
Harāzah, Jabal- 35 Eb 15.03N 30.27E
Haraze 35 Cd 9.55N 20.48E
Harbel 34 Cd 6.16N 10.21W
Harbin 22 Oe 45.45N 126.37E
Harbor Beach 44 Fd 43.51N 82.39W
Harbour Breton 42 Lg 47.29N 55.50W
Harbour Grace 42 Mg 47.41N 53.15W
Harburg, Hamburg- 10 Fc 53.28N 10.00E
Harcourt 44 Ob 46.30N 65.15W
Harcuvar Mountains 46 Ii 34.00N 113.30W
Harcyzsk 16 Kf 47.59N 38.11E
Hardanger 8 Bd 60.20N 6.30E
Hardangerfjorden 5 Gc 60.10N 6.00E
Hardangerjøkulen 8 Bd 60.35N 7.25E
Hardangervidda 7 Bf 60.20N 7.30E
Hardelot Plage, Neufchâtel Hardelot- 12 Dd 50.38N 1.35E
Hardenberg 12 Ib 52.34N 6.37E
Harderwijk 11 Lb 52.21N 5.36E
Hardin 43 Fb 45.44N 107.37W
Harding 37 Df 30.34S 29.58E
Hardinsburg 44 Dg 37.47N 86.28W
Härdler 12 Kc 51.06N 8.14E
Hardoi 25 Gc 27.25N 80.07E
Hardy, Peninsula- 56 Gi 55.25S 68.30W
Hareid 8 Bb 62.22N 6.02E
Hareidlandet 7 Ae 62.20N 5.55E
Hare Indian 42 Ec 66.18N 128.38W
Harelbeke 12 Fd 50.51N 3.18E
Haren 12 Ia 53.11N 6.38E
Haren (Ems) 12 Jb 52.47N 7.14E
Harer 31 Lh 9.18N 42.08E
Harerge [3] 35 Gd 9.00N 41.30E
Harēri Mālinwarfā 35 He 4.34N 47.21E
Harewa 35 Gd 9.54N 41.58E
Harfleur 12 Ce 49.30N 0.12E
Harg 8 Hd 60.11N 18.24E
Hargeysa 31 Lh 9.30N 44.03E
Harghita [2] 15 Ic 46.25N 25.45E
Harghita, Munţii- 15 Ic 46.31N 25.33E
Harghita, Vîrful- 15 Ic 46.27N 25.35E
Hargla 8 Lg 57.31N 26.25E
Harhorin 27 Hb 47.13N 102.50E
Har Hu 38.15N 97.40E
Ḩarīb 23 Gg 14.56N 45.30E
Haricha, Hamâda el- 34 Ea 22.36N 3.31W
Harihari 62 De 43.09S 170.34E
Hari Kurk 8 Je 59.00N 22.50E
Harim 24 Gd 36.12N 36.31E
Ḩarīm, Jabal al- 24 Qj 25.58N 56.14E
Harima-Nada 29 Dd 34.30N 134.35E
Haringey, London- 12 Bc 51.36N 0.06W
Harīrūd 21 If 37.24N 60.38E
Härjångsfjället 8 Ea 63.01N 12.35E
Harjavalta 7 Ff 61.19N 22.08E
Härjedalen 8 Eb 62.20N 13.05E
Härjehågna 8 Ec 61.44N 12.08E
Hårkan 8 Fa 63.20N 14.55E
Harkov 6 Je 50.00N 36.15E
Harkovskaja Oblast [3] 19 Df 49.40N 36.30E
Harlan [Ia.-U.S.] 45 If 41.39N 95.19W
Harlan [Ky.-U.S.] 44 Fg 36.51N 83.19W
Harlan County Lake 45 Gf 40.04N 99.16W
Harlech Castle 9 Ii 52.52N 4.07W
Harlem 46 Kb 48.32N 108.47W
Harleston 12 Db 52.24N 1.18E
Harlingen [Neth.] 11 La 53.10N 5.24E
Harlingen [Tx.-U.S.] 43 Hf 26.11N 97.42W
Harlovka 7 Ib 68.47N 37.20E
Harlovka 7 Ib 68.47N 37.15E
Harlow 9 Nj 51.47N 0.08E
Harlowton 46 Kc 46.26N 109.50W
Harlu 7 Hf 61.51N 30.54E
Hărman 15 Id 45.43N 25.41E
Harmancık 24 Cc 39.41N 29.10E
Harmånger 7 Df 61.56N 17.13E
Harmanli 15 Ih 41.56N 25.54E
Harmil 35 Gb 16.30N 40.12E
Harmony 45 Ke 43.33N 91.59W
Harnai 25 Ee 17.48N 73.06E
Harney Basin 38 Ge 43.15N 120.40W
Harney Lake 43 Dc 43.14N 119.07W
Harney Peak 43 Gc 44.00N 103.30W
Härnön 8 Gb 62.35N 18.00E
Härnösand 6 Hc 62.38N 17.56E
Haro 13 Jb 42.35N 2.51W
Harovsk 19 Ed 59.59N 40.11E
Harøya 8 Bb 62.45N 6.25E
Harøyfjorden 8 Bb 62.45N 6.35E
Harpenden 12 Bc 51.48N 0.21W
Harper [Ks.-U.S.] 45 Gh 37.17N 98.01W
Harper [Lbr.] 31 Gh 4.22N 7.43W
Harper, Mount- 40 Kd 64.14N 143.50W
Harper Pass 62 De 42.44S 171.53E
Harplinge 8 Eh 56.45N 12.43E
Harqin Qi (Jinshan) 28 Ed 41.57N 118.40E
Harqin Zuoyi Monggolzu Zizhixian 28 Ed 41.05N 119.40E
Ḩarrah 23 Hg 14.57N 50.19E
Ḩarrat al 'Uwayrid 23 Ed 27.00N 37.30E
Harricana 42 Jf 51.10N 79.47W
Harricana, Rivière- 44 Ha 51.10N 79.45W
Harrington-Harbour 42 Lf 50.26N 59.30W
Harris 9 Gd 57.53N 6.55W
Harris 51c Bc 16.28N 62.10W
Harris, Lake- 44 Gk 28.46N 81.49W
Harris, Sound of- 9 Fd 57.45N 7.08W
Harrisburg 39 Le 40.16N 76.52W
Harrismith 37 De 28.18S 29.03E
Harrison [Ar.-U.S.] 45 Jh 36.14N 93.07W
Harrison [Mi.-U.S.] 44 Ec 44.01N 84.48W
Harrison [Nb.-U.S.] 45 Ee 42.41N 103.53W
Harrison, Cape- 42 Lf 54.56N 57.55W
Harrison Bay 40 Ib 70.30N 151.30W
Harrisonburg 44 Hf 38.27N 78.54W
Harrison Lake 46 Eb 49.31N 121.59W
Harrison Point 51q Ab 13.18N 59.38W
Harrisonville 45 Ig 38.39N 94.21W
Harrisville [Mi.-U.S.] 44 Fc 44.39N 83.17W
Harrisville [W.V.-U.S.] 44 Gf 39.13N 81.04W
Harrodsburg 44 Eg 37.46N 84.51W
Harrogate 9 Lh 54.00N 1.33W
Harrow, London- 12 Bc 51.36N 0.20W
Harry S. Truman Reservoir 45 Jg 38.00N 93.45W
Har Sai Shan 27 Gd 35.26N 97.41E
Harsewinkel 12 Kc 51.58N 8.14E
Harshō 35 Hc 11.17N 47.30E
Harsim 24 Lf 33.48N 46.50E
Harsin 24 Le 34.16N 47.35E
Harstad 7 Db 68.47N 16.30E
Harsvik 7 Cd 64.03N 10.02E
Hart 44 Dd 43.42N 86.22W
Hart 42 Dc 65.51N 136.22W
Hartao 28 Gc 42.30N 122.08E
Hartbees 30 Jk 28.45S 20.33E
Hartberg 14 Jc 47.17N 15.58E
Hårteigen 8 Bd 60.12N 7.04E
Hartford [Ct.-U.S.] 39 Le 41.46N 72.41W
Hartford [Ky.-U.S.] 44 Dg 37.27N 86.55W
Hartford City 44 Ee 40.29N 85.23W
Hartington 45 He 42.37N 97.16W
Hartland 44 Nb 46.18N 67.32W
Hartland Point 9 Ij 51.02N 4.31W
Hartlepool 9 Lg 54.42N 1.11W
Hartley 37 Ec 18.07S 30.08E
Hartmannberge 37 Ac 17.30S 12.23E
Hartola 7 Gf 61.35N 26.01E
Harts 28.24S 24.18E
Hartselle 44 Dh 34.27N 86.56W
Harts Range 59 Gd 23.05S 134.55E
Hartsville 44 Gh 34.23N 80.04W
Hartwell 44 Fh 34.21N 82.56W
Hartwell Lake 44 Fh 34.30N 82.55W
Harun, Bukit- 26 Gf 4.06N 115.46E
Haruno 29 Ce 33.30N 133.30E
Harves Bank (EN) 51c Ac 16.52N 62.35W
Harvey [Austl.] 59 Df 33.05S 115.54E
Harvey [N.D.-U.S.] 43 Hb 47.47N 99.56W
Harvey Bay 59 Kd 25.00S 153.00E
Harwich 9 Oj 51.57N 1.17E
Haryana [3] 25 Fc 29.30N 76.30E
Harz 5 He 51.45N 10.30E
Hasaki 29 Gd 35.44N 140.48E
Hasama 29 Gb 38.42N 141.13E
Hasan 19 Ih 42.26N 130.39E
Ḩasanābād [Iran] 24 Ph 28.47N 54.19E
Ḩasanābād [Iran] 24 Nd 36.28N 50.17E
Hasan Daği 23 Db 38.08N 34.12E
Ḩasan Langī 24 Qi 27.22N 56.52E
Hasavjurt 16 Oh 43.16N 46.35E
Hāsbayyā 24 Ff 33.43N 35.52E
Hasdo 25 Hd 21.44N 82.44E
Hase 10 Dd 52.41N 7.18E
Hasekijata 15 Kg 42.08N 27.30E
Hasenkamp 55 Cj 31.31S 59.51W
Hashimoto 29 Dd 34.19N 135.37E
Hashtpar 24 Md 37.48N 48.55E
Hasi Hausert 32 Ee 22.35N 14.18W
Haskell 43 He 33.10N 99.44W
Haskerland 12 Hb 52.58N 5.47E
Haskerland-Joure 12 Hb 52.58N 5.47E
Haskovo 15 Ih 41.56N 25.33E
Haskovo [2] 15 Ih 41.50N 25.55E
Hasle 8 Fi 55.11N 14.43E
Haslemere 9 Mj 51.06N 0.43W
Haslev 8 Di 55.20N 11.58E
Hăşmaşu Mare, Vîrful- 15 Ic 46.30N 25.50E
Haspengouws Plateau/Hesbaye 11 Ld 50.35N 5.10E
Haspres 12 Fd 50.15N 3.25E
Hassa 24 Gd 36.50N 36.29E
Hassan 25 Ff 13.00N 76.05E
Hassberge 10 Gf 50.12N 10.29E
Hassela 7 De 62.07N 16.42E
Hassel Sound 42 Ha 78.30N 99.00W
Hasselt 11 Ld 50.56N 5.20E
Hassi Bel Guebbour 32 Id 28.30N 6.41E
Hassi el Ghella 13 Ki 35.27N 1.03W
Hassi-Mamèche 13 Mi 35.51N 0.04E
Hassi Messaoud 31 He 31.43N 6.03E
Hassi R'mel 32 Hc 32.55N 3.16E
Hassi Serouenout 32 Ie 24.00N 7.50E
Hässleholm 7 Ch 56.09N 13.46E
Hässlö 8 Fh 56.05N 15.25E
Haßloch 12 Ke 49.23N 8.16E
Hastière 12 Gd 50.13N 4.50E
Hastière-par-delà 12 Gd 50.13N 4.50E
Hastière-par-delà, Hastière- 12 Gd 50.13N 4.50E
Hastings [Bar.] 51q Ab 13.04N 59.35W
Hastings [Eng.-U.K.] 9 Nk 50.51N 0.36E
Hastings [Mi.-U.S.] 44 Ed 42.39N 85.17W
Hastings [Mn.-U.S.] 45 Jd 44.44N 92.51W
Hastings [Nb.-U.S.] 43 Hc 40.35N 98.23W
Hastings [N.Z.] 61 Eg 39.38S 176.50E
Hästveda 8 Eh 56.16N 13.56E
Hašuri 16 Mi 41.59N 43.33E
Hasvik 7 Fa 70.29N 22.09E
Ḩasy al Qaţţār 33 Ec 30.14N 27.11E
Ḩasy Hague 33 Bd 26.17N 10.31E
Hat'ae-Do 28 Hg 34.23N 125.17E
Hatanga 22 Mb 71.58N 102.30E
Hatanga 21 Mb 72.55N 106.00E
Hatch 45 Cj 32.40N 107.09W
Hatches Creek 59 Hd 20.56S 135.12E
Haţeg 15 Fd 45.37N 22.57E
Hatgal 27 Ha 50.26N 100.09E
Ḩaţībah, Ra's- 23 Ee 21.59N 38.55E
Ha Tien 25 Kf 10.23N 104.29E
Ha Tinh 25 Le 18.20N 105.54E
Hato Mayor 49 Md 18.46N 69.15W
Ḩattá, Jabal- 24 Qj 24.45N 56.04E
Hattem 12 Ib 52.28N 6.06E
Hatten 12 Ka 53.03N 8.23E
Hatteras, Cape- 38 Lf 35.13N 75.32W
Hatteras Inlet 44 Jh 35.00N 75.40W
Hatteras Island 43 Ld 35.25N 75.30W
Hattfjelldal 7 Cd 65.36N 14.00E
Hattiesburg 43 Je 31.19N 89.16W
Hattingen 12 Jc 51.24N 7.10E
Hatu Iti, Ile- 61 Ma 8.42S 140.43W
Hatutaa, Ile- 57 Me 7.30S 140.38W
Hatvan 10 Pi 47.40N 19.41E
Hat Yai 25 Kg 7.01N 100.27E
Hatyrka 20 Md 62.03N 175.05E
Hau Bon 25 Lf 13.24N 108.27E
Haubourdin 12 Ed 50.36N 2.59E
Hauge 7 Bg 58.21N 6.17E
Haugesund 6 Gd 59.25N 5.18E
Hauho 8 Kc 61.10N 24.33E
Hauhungaroa Range 62 Fc 38.40S 175.35E
Haukeligrend 7 Bg 59.51N 7.11E
Haukipudas 7 Fd 65.15N 25.28E
Haukivesi 5 Ic 62.05N 28.30E
Haukivuori 8 Lb 62.01N 27.13E
Hauraha 63a Ed 10.49S 161.57E
Hauraki Gulf 61 Eg 36.35S 175.00E
Hauroko, Lake- 62 Bf 45.55S 167.20E
Hausa 32 Ed 27.06N 11.01W
Hausruck 14 Hb 48.07N 13.35E
Haut, Isle au- 44 Mc 44.03N 68.38W
Haut Atlas=High Atlas (EN) 30 Ge 32.00N 6.00W
Haute-Champagne 11 Kf 49.18N 4.15E
Haute-Corse [3] 11a Aa 42.30N 9.00E
Haute-Garonne [3] 11 Hk 43.25N 1.30E
Haute-Guinée [3] 34 Dc 11.30N 10.00W
Haute-Kotto [3] 35 Cd 7.00N 23.00E
Haute-Loire [3] 11 Ji 45.05N 4.00E
Haute-Marne [3] 11 Lf 48.05N 5.10E
Hauterive 44 Ma 49.11N 68.16W
Hautes-Alpes [3] 11 Mj 44.40N 6.30E
Haute-Sangha [3] 35 Be 4.30N 16.00E
Haute-Saône [3] 11 Mg 47.40N 6.10E
Haute-Saône, Plateau de- 11 Lg 47.50N 6.00E
Haute-Savoie [3] 11 Mi 46.00N 6.20E
Hautes Fagnes/Hoge Venen 10 Bf 50.30N 6.00E
Hautes-Pyrénées [3] 11 Gk 43.00N 0.10E
Haute-Vienne [3] 11 Hi 45.50N 1.10E
Haute-Volta=Upper Volta (EN) [1] 31 Gg 13.00N 2.00W
Haut-Mbomou [3] 35 Dd 6.00N 26.00E
Hautmont 11 Jd 50.15N 3.56E
Haut-Ogooué [3] 36 Bc 2.00S 14.00E
Haut Rhin [3] 11 Ng 48.00N 7.20E
Hauts-Bassins [3] 34 Ec 12.30N 4.30W
Hauts-de-Seine [3] 11 If 48.50N 2.11E
Hauts-Plateaux 30 He 34.00N 0.01E
Haut-Zaïre [2] 36 Eb 2.30N 25.30E
Hauula 65a 21.36N 157.54W
Hauz-Han 18 Cf 37.16N 61.15E
Hauz-Hanskoje Vodohr. 18 Cf 37.10N 61.20E
Havana 45 Kf 40.18N 90.04W
Havana (EN)=La Habana 39 Kg 23.08N 82.22W
Havant 9 Mk 50.51N 0.59W
Havast 18 Gd 40.16N 68.51E
Havasu, Lake- 46 Hi 34.30N 114.20W
Havel 10 Hd 52.53N 11.58E
Havelange 12 Hd 50.23N 5.14E
Havelange-Méan 12 Hd 50.22N 5.20E
Havelberg 10 Id 52.49N 12.05E
Havelland 10 Id 52.25N 12.45E
Havelländisches Luch 10 Id 52.40N 12.40E
Havelock [N.C.-U.S.] 44 Ih 34.53N 76.54W
Havelock [N.Z.] 62 Ed 41.17S 173.46E
Havelock North 62 Gc 39.40S 176.53E
Havelte 12 Ib 52.46N 6.16E
Haverfordwest 9 Ij 51.49N 4.58W
Haverhill [Eng.-U.K.] 9 Ni 52.05N 0.26E
Haverhill [Ma.-U.S.] 44 Ld 42.47N 71.05W
Havering, London- 12 Cc 51.36N 0.11E
Havířov 10 Og 49.48N 18.27E
Havlíčkův Brod 10 Lg 49.36N 15.34E
Havøysund 7 Fa 71.03N 24.40E
Havran 24 Bc 39.33N 27.06E
Havre 39 Ie 48.33N 109.41W
Havre-Saint-Pierre 39 Md 50.15N 63.36W
Havsa 15 Jh 41.33N 26.49E
Havza 24 Fb 41.05N 35.45E
Hawaii [2] 58 Kb 24.00N 167.00W
Hawaiian Islands 57 Kb 24.00N 167.00W
Hawaiian Ridge (EN) 3 Kg 24.00N 165.00W
Hawaii Island 57 Lc 19.30N 155.30W
Ḩawallī 23 Gd 29.19N 48.02E
Ḩawār 24 Nj 25.40N 50.45E
Hawarden 62 Ee 42.56S 172.39E
Ḩawashīyah, Wādī- 24 Eh 28.31N 32.58E
Hawaymī, Sha'īb al- 24 Kg 30.58N 44.15E
Hawd 30 Lh 7.40N 47.43E
Ḩawḑ Al Waqf 24 Ei 26.03N 32.22E
Hawea, Lake- 62 Cf 44.30S 169.20E
Hawera 61 Dg 39.35S 174.17E
Hawi 58 Lb 20.14N 155.50W
Hawick 9 Kf 55.25N 2.47W
Ḩawīzah, Hawr al- 24 Lg 31.35N 47.38E
Hawkdun Range 62 Cf 44.50S 170.00E
Hawke Bay 61 Eg 39.25S 177.20E
Hawke Harbour 42 Lf 53.01N 55.50W
Hawker 59 Hf 31.53S 138.25E
Hawkes, Mount- 66 Rg 83.55S 56.05W
Hawke's Bay [2] 62 Gc 39.30S 176.40E
Hawkesbury 44 Jc 45.36N 74.37W
Hawkhurst 12 Cc 51.02N 0.30E
Hawkinsville 44 Fi 32.17N 83.28W
Hawksbill 44 Hf 38.33N 78.23W
Hawk Springs 46 Mf 41.48N 104.09W
Ḩawmat as Sūq 32 Jc 33.53N 10.51E
Hawng Tuk 25 Jd 20.28N 99.56E
Ḩawrā' 35 Hb 15.43N 48.18E
Hawrān, Wādī al- 23 Fc 33.58N 42.34E
Ḩawsh 'Īsá 24 Dg 30.55N 30.17E
Hawthorne 43 Dd 38.32N 118.38W
Hawthorne, Mount- 66 Pf 72.10S 98.39W
Haxtun 45 Ef 40.39N 102.38W
Hay 58 Fh 34.30S 144.51E
Hay 38 Hc 60.51N 115.44W
Hayachine-San 29 Gb 39.34N 141.29E
Hayakita 29a Bb 42.45N 141.48E
Hayange 11 Me 49.20N 6.03E
Hayasui-no-Seto 28 Kh 33.20N 132.00E
Hayato 29 Bf 31.45N 130.43E
Haybān 35 Ec 11.13N 30.31E
Haybān, Jabal- 35 Ec 11.15N 30.31E
Hayden 46 Jj 33.00N 110.47W
Hayes [Man.-Can.] 42 Ie 57.00N 92.15W
Hayes [N.W.T.-Can.] 42 Hc 67.20N 95.02W
Hayes, Mount- 40 Jd 63.37N 146.43W
Hayes Halvø=Hayes Peninsula (EN) 67 Od 77.40N 64.30W
Hayes Peninsula (EN)= Hayes Halvø 67 Od 77.40N 64.30W
Ḩayl 24 Qj 24.33N 56.06E
Hayl, Wādī al- 24 He 34.47N 39.18E
Hayling Island 12 Bd 50.48N 0.58W
Haymana 24 Ec 39.27N 32.30E
Haymana Platosu 24 Ec 39.25N 32.45E
Haynin 23 Gf 15.50N 48.18E
Hayrabolu 24 Bb 41.12N 27.06E
Ḩayrān 33 Hf 16.02N 42.49E
Hay River 59 Hd 25.00S 138.00E
Hay River 39 Hc 60.51N 115.40W
Hayrūt 35 Ib 15.59N 52.09E
Hays 43 Hd 38.53N 99.20W
Hay Springs 45 Ee 42.41N 102.41W
Haystack Peak 46 Ig 39.50N 113.55W
Hayward [Ca.-U.S.] 46 Dh 37.40N 122.05W
Hayward [Wi.-U.S.] 45 Kc 46.01N 91.29W
Haywards Heath 12 Bc 51.00N 0.06W
Hazar, Wādī- 35 Hb 17.50N 49.07E
Hazarasp 18 Cd 41.19N 61.08E
Hazard 44 Fg 37.15N 83.12W
Hazar Gölü 24 Hc 38.30N 39.25E
Hazāribāgh 25 Hd 23.59N 85.21E
Hazebrouck 11 Id 50.43N 2.32E
Hazelton 42 Ee 55.15N 127.40W
Hazen 45 Fc 47.18N 101.38W
Hazen Strait 42 Ga 77.15N 110.00W
Ḩaẕeva 24 Fg 30.48N 35.15E
Hazlehurst [Ga.-U.S.] 44 Fj 31.52N 82.36W
Hazlehurst [Ms.-U.S.] 45 Kk 31.52N 90.24W
Hazleton 44 Je 40.58N 76.00W
Hazlett, Lake- 59 Fd 21.30S 128.50E
Hazrah, Ra's al- 24 Nj 24.22N 51.36E
Hazro 24 Ic 38.15N 40.47E
Heacham 12 Cb 52.55N 0.29E
Headley 12 Bc 51.07N 0.49W
Healdsburg 46 Dg 38.37N 122.52W
Heanor 12 Aa 53.00N 1.18W
Heard Island 30 On 53.00S 73.35E
Hearne 45 Hk 30.53N 96.36W
Hearst 42 Jg 49.41N 83.40W
Heart River 45 Fc 46.47N 100.51W
Heathrow Airport London 12 Bc 51.28N 0.30W
Hebbronville 45 Gm 27.18N 98.41W
Hebei Sheng (Ho-pei Sheng) =Hopeh (EN) [2] 27 Kd 39.00N 116.00E
Heber City 46 Jf 40.30N 111.25W
Hebi 27 Jd 35.53N 114.09E
Hebian 27 Jd 38.35N 113.06E
Hebiji 28 Cf 36.00N 114.08E
Hebrides 5 Fd 57.00N 6.30W
Hebrides, Sea of the- 9 Ge 57.00N 7.00W
Hebron [N.D.-U.S.] 45 Ec 46.54N 102.03W
Hebron [Newf.-Can.] 42 Le 58.15N 62.35W
Heby 8 Ge 59.56N 16.53E
Hecate Strait 42 Ef 53.20N 131.00W
Hecelchakán 48 Ng 20.10N 90.08W
Hechi (Jinchengjiang) 27 Ig 24.44N 108.02E
Hechingen 10 Eh 48.21N 8.59E
Hechuan 27 Ie 30.07N 106.15E
Hecla 45 Gd 45.43N 98.09W
Hecla and Griper Bay 42 Ga 76.00N 111.30W
Hecla Island 45 Ha 51.08N 96.45W
Heddalsvatnet 8 Ce 59.30N 9.15E
Hede 7 Ce 62.25N 13.30E
Hede → Sheyang 28 Fh 33.47N 120.15E
Hedemarken 8 Dd 60.50N 11.20E
Hedemora 7 Df 60.17N 15.59E
Hedensted 8 Ci 55.46N 9.42E
Hedesunda 7 Df 60.25N 17.00E
Hedesunda fjärdarna 8 Gd 60.20N 17.00E
Hedmark [2] 7 Cf 61.30N 11.45E
Hedo-Misaki 29b Bb 26.52N 128.16E
Heemskerk 12 Gb 52.30N 4.42E
Heemstede 12 Gb 52.21N 4.37E
Heerenveen 11 Lb 52.57N 5.55E
Heerhugowaard 12 Gb 52.40N 4.50E
Heerlen 11 Ld 50.54N 5.59E
Hefa=Haifa (EN) 22 Ff 32.50N 35.00E
Hefei 22 Nf 31.47N 117.15E
Hefeng 27 Jf 29.49N 110.01E
Hegang 22 Pe 47.20N 130.12E
Hegau 10 Ei 47.50N 8.45E
Hegura Jima 27 Od 37.50N 136.55E
Heide 10 Fb 54.12N 9.06E
Heidelberg 10 Fg 49.25N 8.42E
Heidenheim an der Brenz 10 Gh 48.41N 10.09E
Heidenreichstein 14 Jb 48.52N 15.07E
Hei-Gawa 29 Gb 39.38N 141.58E
Heigun-Tō 29 Ce 33.47N 132.15E
Hei He 27 Hd 38.15N 100.15E
Heihe → Aihui 22 Od 50.13N 127.26E
Heilbron 37 De 27.21S 27.58E
Heilbronn 10 Fg 49.08N 9.13E
Heiligenblut 14 Gd 47.02N 12.50E
Heiligenhafen 10 Gb 54.22N 10.59E
Heiligenhaus 12 Ic 51.19N 6.58E
Heiligenstadt 10 Ge 51.23N 10.08E
Heilinzi 28 Ib 44.33N 126.41E
Heilong Jiang 21 Qd 52.56N 141.10E
Heilongjiang Sheng (Hei-lung-chiang Sheng)= Heilungkiang (EN) [2] 27 Mb 48.00N 128.00E
Heiloo 12 Gb 52.36N 4.43E
Hei-lung-chiang Sheng → Heilongjiang Sheng=Heilungkiang (EN) [2] 27 Mb 48.00N 128.00E
Heilungkiang (EN)= Heilongjiang Sheng (Hei-lung-chiang Sheng) [2] 27 Mb 48.00N 128.00E
Heilungkiang (EN)=Hei-lung-chiang Sheng → Heilongjiang Sheng [2] 27 Mb 48.00N 128.00E
Heimaey 7a c 63.26N 20.17W
Heimbach 12 Id 50.38N 6.29E
Heimdal 7 Ce 63.21N 10.22E
Heimsheim 12 Kf 48.48N 8.51E
Heinävesi 7 Ge 62.26N 28.36E
Heinola 7 Gf 61.13N 26.02E
Heinsberg 12 Ic 51.04N 6.05E
Heishan 28 Gd 41.42N 122.07E
Heishan Xia 27 Hd 37.18N 104.39E
Heishui [China] 28 Ec 42.06N 119.22E
Heishui [China] 27 He 32.03N 103.05E
Heist, Knokke- 12 Fc 51.21N 3.15E
Heist-op-den-Berg 12 Gc 51.05N 4.43E
Hei-Zaki 29 Hb 39.39N 142.00E
Hejgijaha 17 Pd 65.27N 72.50E
Hejian 28 De 38.27N 116.05E
Hejing 27 Ec 42.18N 86.18E
Hejjaha 17 Kb 68.18N 62.32E
Hekimhan 24 Gc 38.49N 37.56E
Hekinan 29 Ed 34.52N 136.58E
Hekla 5 Ec 64.00N 19.40W
Hekou 28 Ci 31.20N 114.25E
Hekou → Yanshan 28 Dj 28.18N 117.41E
Hel 10 Ob 54.37N 18.48E
Helagsfjället 7 Ce 62.55N 12.27E
Helan 27 Id 38.35N 106.16E
Helan Shan 27 Id 39.00N 106.00E
Helden's Point 51c Ab 17.24N 62.50W
Helena [Ar.-U.S.] 43 Ie 34.32N 90.35W
Helena [Guy.] 54 Gb 6.41N 57.55W
Helena [Mt.-U.S.] 39 He 46.36N 112.01W
Helen Glacier 66 Ge 66.40S 93.55E
Helen Reef 57 Ed 2.53N 131.47E
Helensburgh 9 Ie 56.01N 4.44W
Helensville 62 Fb 36.40S 174.27E
Helgaå 8 Fi 55.53N 14.08E
Helgasjön 8 Fh 56.55N 14.45E
Helgeland 7 Cd 66.15N 13.05E
Helgoland 10 Db 54.12N 7.53E

Index Symbols

[1] Independent Nation
[2] State, Region
[3] District, County
[4] Municipality
[5] Colony, Dependency
Continent
Physical Region

Historical or Cultural Region
Mount, Mountain
Volcano
Hill
Mountains, Mountain Range
Hills, Escarpment
Plateau, Upland

Pass, Gap
Plain, Lowland
Delta
Salt Flat
Valley, Canyon
Crater, Cave
Karst Features

Depression
Polder
Desert, Dunes
Forest, Woods
Heath, Steppe
Oasis
Cape, Point

Coast, Beach
Cliff
Peninsula
Isthmus
Sandbank
Island
Atoll

Rock, Reef
Islands, Archipelago
Rocks, Reefs
Coral Reef
Well, Spring
Geyser
River, Stream

Waterfall Rapids
River Mouth, Estuary
Lake
Salt Lake
Intermittent Lake
Reservoir
Swamp, Pond

Canal
Glacier
Ice Shelf, Pack Ice
Ocean
Sea
Gulf, Bay
Strait, Fjord

Lagoon
Bank
Seamount
Tablemount
Ridge
Shelf
Basin

Escarpment, Sea Scarp
Fracture
Trench, Abyss
National Park, Reserve
Point of Interest
Recreation Site
Cave, Cavern

Historic Site
Ruins
Wall, Walls
Church, Abbey
Temple
Scientific Station
Airport

Port
Lighthouse
Mine
Tunnel
Dam, Bridge

Helgoländer Bucht	10	Eb	54.10N	8.04 E
Helikón Óros	15	Fk	38.20N	22.50 E
Helixi	28	Ei	30.39N	119.01 E
Heljulja	8	Nc	61.37N	30.38 E
Hella	7a	Bc	63.50N	20.24W
Hellberge	10	Hd	52.34N	11.17 E
Hělleh	24	Nh	29.10N	50.40 E
Hellendoorn	11	Mb	52.24N	6.26 E
Hellendoorn-Nijverdal	12	Ib	52.22N	6.27 E
Hellenic Trough (EN)	5	Ii	35.00N	24.00 E
Hellental	12	Id	50.29N	6.26 E
Hellesylt	7	Be	62.05N	6.54 E
Hellín	13	Kf	38.31N	1.41W
Hells Canyon	43	Db	45.20N	116.45W
Hellweg	12	Kc	51.40N	8.00 E
Helmand	21	If	31.12N	61.34 E
Helmand [3]	23	Jc	31.00N	64.00 E
Helme	10	He	51.20N	11.20 E
Helmeringhausen	37	Be	25.54S	16.57 E
Helmond	11	Lc	51.29N	5.40 E
Helmsdale	9	Jc	58.10N	3.40W
Helmsdale	9	Jc	58.07N	3.40W
Helmstedt	10	Gd	52.14N	11.00 E
Helong	27	Mc	42.32N	129.00 E
Helpe Majeure	12	Fd	50.11N	3.47 E
Helpringham	12	Bb	52.56N	0.18W
Helpter Berge	10	Jc	53.30N	13.36 E
Helsingborg	6	Hd	56.03N	12.42 E
Helsinge	8	Eh	56.01N	12.12 E
Helsingfors/Helsinki	6	Ic	60.10N	24.58 E
Helsingør	7	Ch	56.02N	12.37 E
Helsinki/Helsingfors	6	Ic	60.10N	24.58 E
Helska, Mierzeja-	10	Ob	54.45N	18.39 E
Helston	9	Hk	50.05N	5.16W
Helvecia	55	Bj	31.06S	60.05W
Helwān (EN)=Ḩulwān	33	Fd	29.51N	31.20 E
Ḩemār	24	Qg	31.42N	57.31 E
Hemčik	20	Ef	51.40N	92.10 E
Hemel Hempstead	9	Mj	51.46N	0.28W
Hemer	12	Jc	51.23N	7.46 E
Hemnesberget	7	Cc	66.14N	13.38 E
Hemsby	12	Db	52.41N	1.42 E
Hemse	8	Hg	57.14N	18.22 E
Hemsedal	8	Cd	60.50N	8.40 E
Hemsö	7	Ee	62.45N	18.05 E
Hen	8	Dd	60.13N	10.14 E
Henan	27	He	34.33N	101.55 E
Hen and Chickens Islands	62	Fa	35.55S	174.45 E
Henan Sheng (Ho-nan Sheng)=Honan (EN) [2]	27	Je	34.00N	114.00 E
Henares	13	Id	40.24N	3.30W
Henashi-Zaki	29	Fa	40.37N	139.51 E
Henbury	59	Gd	24.35S	133.15 E
Hendaye	11	Ek	43.22N	1.47W
Hendek	24	Db	40.48N	30.45 E
Henderson [Arg.]	55	Bm	36.18S	61.43W
Henderson [Ky.-U.S.]	44	Dg	37.50N	87.35W
Henderson [N.C.-U.S.]	44	Hg	36.20N	78.25W
Henderson [Nv.-U.S.]	43	Dd	36.02N	115.01W
Henderson [Tx.-U.S.]	45	Ij	32.09N	94.48W
Henderson Island	57	Og	24.22S	128.19W
Henderson Seamount (EN)	43	Df	25.34N	119.33W
Hendersonville [N.C.-U.S.]	44	Fh	35.19N	82.28W
Hendersonville [Tn.-U.S.]	44	Dg	36.18N	86.37W
Hendījān	24	Mg	30.14N	49.43 E
Hendorābī, Jazīreh-ye-	24	Oi	26.40N	53.37 E
Hendrik Verwderddam	30	Km	46.36S	37.55 E
Hengām, Jazīreh-ye-	24	Pi	26.39N	55.53 E
Hengduan Shan	21	Lg	27.30N	99.00 E
Hengelo [Neth.]	11	Mb	52.15N	6.45 E
Hengelo [Neth.]	12	Ib	52.03N	6.20 E
Heng Shan [China]	27	Jd	39.42N	113.45 E
Hengshan [China]	27	Jf	27.16N	112.51 E
Heng Shan [China]	27	Jf	27.18N	112.41 E
Hengshan [China]	27	Id	37.51N	109.20 E
Hengshan [China]	28	Kb	45.24N	131.01 E
Hengshui	27	Kd	37.39N	115.46 E
Hengxian	27	Ig	22.46N	109.15 E
Hengyang	22	Ng	26.56N	112.35 E
Henik Lakes	42	Hd	61.05N	97.20W
Hénin-Liétard	11	Id	50.25N	2.56 E
Henley-on-Thames	12	Bc	51.32N	0.54W
Hennan	8	Fb	62.05N	15.45 E
Hennan	7	De	62.02N	15.54 E
Hennebont	11	Cg	47.48N	3.17W
Hennef (Sieg)	12	Jd	50.47N	7.17 E
Hennigsdorf bei Berlin	10	Jd	52.38N	13.12 E
Henrietta Maria, Cape -	42	Je	55.09N	82.19W
Henrietty, Ostrov-	20	Ka	77.00N	157.00 E
Henry, Mount-	46	Hb	48.53N	115.31W
Henry Bay	66	Ie	66.40S	120.40 E
Henryetta	45	Ii	35.27N	95.59W
Henry Kater Peninsula	42	Kk	69.15N	67.30W
Henry Mountains	46	Jh	37.55N	110.50W
Henrys Fork River	46	Je	43.45N	111.56W
Henslow, Cape-	63a	Ec	9.56S	160.38 E
Hentej	21	Me	48.50N	109.00 E
Hentiesbaai	37	Ad	22.08S	14.18 E
Henzada	22	Lh	17.38N	95.28 E
Heping → Yanhe	27	If	28.31N	108.28 E
Heppenheim (Bergstraße)	12	Ke	49.38N	8.39 E
Heppner	46	Fd	45.21N	119.33W
Hepu (Lianzhou)	27	Ig	21.40N	109.12 E
Hequ	27	Jd	39.22N	111.15 E
Herakol Dağı	24	Id	37.45N	42.35 E
Heralds Cays	59	Jc	16.55S	149.10 E
Herāt [3]	23	Jc	34.30N	62.00 E
Herāt	22	If	34.20N	62.12 E
Hérault [3]	11	Jk	43.40N	3.30 E
Hérault	11	Jk	43.17N	3.26 E
Herbert [N.Z.]	62	Df	45.13S	170.46 E
Herbert [Sask.-Can.]	46	La	50.26N	107.12W
Herberton	59	Jc	17.23S	145.23 E
Herbert River	59	Jc	18.32S	146.17 E
Herborn	10	Ef	50.41N	8.19 E
Herby	10	Of	50.45N	18.40 E
Hercegnovi	15	Bg	42.27N	18.32 E
Hercegovina	14	Lg	43.00N	17.50 E
Hercegovina	5	Hg	43.00N	17.50 E
Herdubreid	7a	Cb	65.11N	16.21W
Heredia [3]	49	Fh	10.30N	84.00W
Heredia	47	Hf	10.00N	84.07W
Hereford	9	Ki	52.15N	2.50W
Hereford [Eng.-U.K.]	9	Ki	52.04N	2.43W
Hereford [Tx.-U.S.]	43	Ge	34.49N	102.24W
Hereford and Worcester [3]	9	Ki	52.10N	2.35W
Hereheretue Atoll	57	Mf	19.54S	144.58W
Hereke	15	Mi	40.48N	29.39 E
Herekino	62	Ea	35.16S	173.13 E
Herent	12	Gd	50.54N	4.40 E
Herentals	12	Gc	51.11N	4.50 E
Herfølge	8	Ei	55.25N	12.10 E
Herford	10	Ed	52.08N	8.41 E
Héricourt	11	Mg	47.35N	6.45 E
Herington	45	Hg	38.40N	96.57W
Heriot	61	Ci	45.51S	169.16 E
Herīs	24	Lc	38.14N	47.07 E
Herisau	14	Dc	47.24N	9.16 E
Herk	12	Hd	50.58N	5.07 E
Herk-de-Stad	12	Hd	50.56N	5.10 E
Herkimer	44	Jd	43.02N	74.59W
Herlen He	27	Kb	48.48N	117.00 E
Hermagor	14	Hd	46.37N	13.22 E
Hermanas	48	Id	27.14N	101.14W
Herma Ness	9	Ma	60.50N	0.54W
Hermano Peak	45	Bh	37.17N	108.48W
Hermansverk	8	Bc	61.11N	6.51 E
Hermanus	37	Bf	34.25S	19.16 E
Hermeskeil	12	Ie	49.39N	6.57 E
Hermiston	46	Fd	45.51N	119.17W
Hermitage	62	De	43.44S	170.05 E
Hermit Islands	57	Fe	1.32S	145.05 E
Hermosa de Santa Rosa, Sierra-	48	Id	28.00N	101.45W
Hermosillo	39	Hg	29.04N	110.58W
Hermoso Campo	55	Bh	27.36S	61.21W
Hérnad	10	Qh	48.00N	20.58 E
Hernandarias	56	Jc	25.22S	54.45W
Hernández [Arg.]	55	Bk	32.21S	60.02W
Hernández [Mex.]	48	Hf	23.02N	102.02W
Hernani	13	Ka	43.16N	1.58W
Herne	10	De	51.33N	7.13 E
Herne Bay	9	Oj	51.23N	1.08 E
Herning	6	Gd	56.08N	8.59 E
Heroica Alvarado	48	Lh	18.46N	95.46W
Heroica Tlapacoyan	48	Kh	19.58N	97.13W
Heroica Zitácuaro	48	Ih	19.24N	100.22W
Herouville-Saint-Clair	12	Be	49.12N	0.19W
Herowābād	24	Md	37.37N	48.32 E
Herradura	55	Ch	26.29S	58.18W
Herre	8	Ce	59.06N	9.34 E
Herrera	55	Ck	32.26S	58.38W
Herrera [3]	49	Gj	7.54N	80.38W
Herrera del Duque	13	Ge	39.10N	5.03W
Herrera de Pisuerga	13	Hb	42.36N	4.20W
Herrero, Punta-	48	Ph	19.10N	87.30W
Herrljunga	8	Ef	58.05N	13.02 E
Hers	11	Hk	43.47N	1.20 E
Herschel	42	Dc	69.35N	139.05W
Herselt	12	Gc	51.03N	4.53 E
Herserange	12	He	49.31N	5.47 E
Hershey	44	Ie	40.17N	76.39W
Hersilia	55	Bj	30.00S	61.51W
Herson	6	Jf	46.38N	32.35 E
Hersonesskí, Mys-	16	Hg	44.33N	33.25 E
Hersonskaja Oblast [3]	19	Df	46.40N	33.30 E
Herstal	11	Ld	50.40N	5.38 E
Herten	12	Jc	51.36N	7.08 E
Hertford	9	Mj	51.50N	0.05W
Hertford	9	Mj	51.48N	0.05W
Hertfordshire [3]	9	Mj	51.45N	0.20W
Hertugen Af Orleans Land	41	Jc	78.15N	21.12W
Hervás	13	Gd	40.16N	5.51W
Herve	12	Hd	50.38N	5.48 E
Herve, Plateau van-/Herveland	12	Hd	50.40N	5.50 E
Herveland/Herve, Plateau van-	12	Hd	50.40N	5.50 E
Hervey Bay	59	Ke	25.15S	152.50 E
Herzberg	10	Je	51.41N	13.14 E
Herzberg am Harz	10	Ge	51.39N	10.20 E
Herzebrock	12	Kc	51.53N	8.15 E
Herzele	12	Fd	50.53N	3.53 E
Herzliyya	24	Ff	32.10N	34.51 E
Herzogenrath	12	Id	50.52N	6.06 E
Herzog-Ernst-Bucht (Vahsel Bay)	66	Af	77.48S	34.39W
Hesāmābād	24	Me	35.52N	48.25 E
Hesbaye/Haspengouws Plateau	11	Ld	50.35N	5.10 E
Hesdin	11	Id	50.22N	2.02 E
Hesel	12	Ja	53.18N	7.36 E
Heshī	24	Md	37.30N	48.15 E
Heshun	27	Jd	37.18N	113.32 E
Hesse (EN)=Hessen [2]	10	Ff	50.30N	9.15 E
Hesselberg	10	Gg	49.05N	10.35 E
Hesselø	8	Dh	56.10N	11.45 E
Hessen	12	Ke	49.47N	8.08 E
Hessen=Hesse (EN) [2]	10	Ff	50.30N	9.15 E
Hess Tablemount (EN)	57	Jc	17.50N	174.15W
Heta	21	Mb	71.54N	102.00 E
Heta	20	Eb	71.35N	99.45 E
Hettange-Grande	12	Ie	49.24N	6.09 E
Hettinger	45	Ec	46.00N	102.39W
Heuberg	10	Eh	48.06N	8.55 E
Heuchin	12	Ed	50.28N	2.16 E
Heuru	63a	Ed	10.12S	161.25 E
Hève, Cap de la-	11	Fe	49.31N	0.04W
Heves	10	Qi	47.36N	20.17 E
Heves [2]	10	Qi	47.50N	20.15 E
Hexham	9	Kg	54.58N	2.06W
Hexi	27	Hf	27.44N	102.09 E
Hexian	28	Ei	31.43N	118.22 E
Hexian (Babu)	27	Jg	24.28N	111.34 E
Hexigten Qi (Jingfeng)	27	Kc	43.15N	117.31 E
Heydarābād	24	Kd	37.06N	45.27 E
Heysham	9	Kg	54.02N	2.54W
Heyuan	27	Jg	23.41N	114.43 E
Heywood	59	Ig	38.08S	141.38 E
Heze (Caozhou)	27	Kd	35.14N	115.28 E
Hezuo	27	Hd	35.02N	102.57 E
Hialeah	44	Gm	25.49N	80.17W
Hiawatha	45	Ig	39.51N	95.32W
Hibara-Ko	29	Gc	37.42N	140.03 E
Hibbing	43	Ib	47.25N	92.56W
Hibernia Reef	59	Eb	12.00S	123.25 E
Hibiki-Nada	29	Bd	34.15N	130.40 E
Hibiny	7	Hc	67.40N	33.35 E
Hiburi-Jima	29	Ce	33.10N	132.18 E
Hickman	44	Cg	36.34N	89.11W
Hickory	44	Gh	35.44N	81.21W
Hick's Cay	49	Ce	17.39N	88.08W
Hida-Gawa	29	Ed	35.25N	137.03 E
Hidaka [Jap.]	28	Qc	42.53N	142.28 E
Hidaka [Jap.]	29	Dd	35.28N	134.47 E
Hidaka-Gawa	29	De	33.53N	135.08 E
Hidaka Sanmyaku	28	Qc	42.25N	142.50 E
Hidalgo [2]	47	Ed	20.30N	99.00W
Hidalgo [Mex.]	47	Ed	24.15N	99.26W
Hidalgo [Mex.]	48	Jd	27.47N	99.52W
Hidalgo del Parral	39	Ig	26.56N	105.40W
Hida-Sanchi	29	Ec	36.20N	137.00 E
Hida-Sanmyaku	28	Nf	36.10N	137.30 E
Hiddensee	10	Jb	54.33N	13.07 E
Hidra	8	Bf	58.15N	6.35 E
Hidrolândia	55	Hc	16.58S	49.16W
Hidrolina	55	Hb	14.37S	49.25W
Hieflau	14	Ic	47.36N	14.44 E
Hiei-Zan	29	Dd	35.05N	135.50 E
Hienghène	61	Cd	20.35S	164.56 E
Hierro	30	Ff	27.45N	18.00W
Higashi	29b	b	26.38N	128.08 E
Higashihiroshima	29	Cd	34.25N	132.43 E
Higashi-izu	29	Fd	34.48N	139.02 E
Higashi-matsuyama	29	Fc	36.02N	139.22 E
Higashimuroran	29a	Bb	42.21N	141.02 E
Higashine	28	Pe	38.26N	140.24 E
Higashiōsaka	29	Dd	34.40N	135.37 E
Higashi Rishiri	29a	Ba	45.16N	141.15 E
Higashi-Shina-Kai=East China Sea (EN)	21	Og	29.00N	125.00 E
Higgins	45	Fh	36.07N	100.02W
Higham Ferrers	12	Bb	52.18N	0.35W
High Atlas (EN)=Haut Atlas	30	Ge	32.00N	6.00W
Highland [3]	9	Id	57.30N	5.00W
Highland Park	45	Me	42.11N	87.48W
High Level	42	Fe	58.30N	117.05W
Highmore	45	Gd	44.31N	99.27W
High Plains	38	If	38.30N	103.00W
High Point	43	Ld	35.58N	79.59W
High Prairie	42	Fe	55.27N	116.30W
High River	42	Gf	50.35N	113.52W
Highrock Lake	42	He	55.49N	100.23W
High Springs	44	Fk	29.50N	82.36W
High Tatra (EN)=Vysoké Tatry	10	Pg	49.10N	20.00 E
High Willhays	9	Jk	50.41N	3.59W
Highwood Mountains	46	Jc	47.25N	110.30W
High Wycombe	9	Mj	51.38N	0.46W
Higuera de Zaragoza	48	Ee	25.59N	109.16W
Higüero, Punta-	49	Nd	18.22N	67.16W
Higuerote	50	Cg	10.29N	66.06W
Higüey	49	Md	18.37N	68.43W
Hiidenvesi	8	Kd	60.20N	24.10 E
Hii-Gawa	29	Cd	35.26N	132.52 E
Hiiraan [3]	35	He	4.00N	45.30 E
Hiitola	7	Gf	61.16N	29.42 E
Hiiumaa/Hiuma	5	Id	58.50N	22.40 E
Hijar	13	Lc	41.10N	0.27W
Ḩijāz	23	Ee	24.30N	38.30 E
Hijāz, Jabal al-	33	Hf	19.45N	41.55 E
Hiji	29	Be	33.22N	131.32 E
Hiji-Gawa	29	Ce	33.36N	132.29 E
Hikami	29	Dd	35.11N	135.02 E
Hikari	28	Kh	33.58N	131.56 E
Hiketa	29	Dd	34.13N	134.24 E
Hikiä	8	Kd	60.45N	24.55 E
Hiki-Gawa	29	De	33.35N	135.26 E
Ḩikmah, Ra's al-	24	Bg	31.17N	27.44 E
Hikone	28	Ng	35.15N	136.15 E
Hiko-San	29	Be	33.29N	130.56 E
Hikueru Atoll	61	Mc	17.36S	142.37W
Hikurangi	62	Hb	37.55S	178.04 E
Hikurangi	62	Fa	35.36S	174.17 E
Hila	26	Ih	7.35S	127.24 E
Hilāl, Ra's al-	33	Dc	32.55N	22.11 E
Hiland	46	Le	43.08N	107.18W
Hilchenbach	12	Kc	51.00N	8.06 E
Hildburghausen	10	Gf	50.25N	10.45 E
Hilden	12	Ic	51.10N	6.56 E
Hildesheim	10	Fd	52.09N	9.58 E
Hillaby, Mount-	50	Gf	13.12N	59.35W
Hillared	8	Eg	57.38N	13.09 E
Hillary Coast	6	Kf	79.00S	161.00 E
Hill Bank	49	Ce	17.35N	88.42W
Hill City	45	Gg	39.22N	99.51W
Hillcrest Center	46	Fi	35.23N	118.57W
Hille	12	Kb	52.20N	8.45 E
Hillegom	12	Gb	52.18N	4.35 E
Hillekrog	8	Dj	54.36N	11.30 E
Hillerød	8	Ei	55.56N	12.19 E
Hillerstorp	8	Eg	57.19N	13.52 E
Hillesheim	12	Id	50.19N	6.41 E
Hillingdon, London-	12	Bc	51.31N	0.27W
Hillsboro [Il.-U.S.]	45	Lg	39.09N	89.29W
Hillsboro [N.D.-U.S.]	45	Hc	47.26N	97.03W
Hillsboro [Oh.-U.S.]	44	Ff	39.12N	83.37W
Hillsboro [Or.-U.S.]	46	Dd	45.31N	122.59W
Hillsboro [Tx.-U.S.]	45	Hj	32.01N	97.08W
Hillsborough	51p	Cb	12.29N	61.26W
Hillsdale	44	Ee	41.55N	84.38W
Hillsville	44	Gg	36.46N	80.44W
Hillswich	9	La	60.28N	1.30W
Hilo	58	Lc	19.44N	155.05W
Hilo Bay	65a	Fd	19.44N	155.05W
Hilok	21	Md	51.19N	106.59 E
Hilok	20	Gf	51.22N	110.30 E
Hilton Head Island	44	Gi	32.12N	80.45W
Hiltrup, Münster-	12	Jc	51.54N	7.38 E
Hilvan	24	Hd	37.30N	38.58 E
Hilvarenbeek	12	Hc	51.29N	5.08 E
Hilversum	11	Lb	52.14N	5.10 E
Himāchal Prādesh [3]	25	Fb	31.00N	78.00 E
Himalaya=Himalayas (EN)	21	Kg	29.00N	83.00 E
Himalayas (EN)=Himalaya	21	Kg	29.00N	83.00 E
Himara	15	Ci	40.07N	19.44 E
Himeji	27	Ne	34.49N	134.42 E
Hime-Jima	29	Be	33.43N	131.40 E
Hime-Kawa	29	Ec	37.02N	137.50 E
Hime-Shima	29	Ae	32.49N	128.41 E
Hime-Zaki	29	Fb	38.05N	138.34 E
Himi	28	Nf	36.51N	136.59 E
Himki	7	Ii	55.56N	37.28 E
Himmelbjerget	8	Ch	56.06N	9.42 E
Himmerfjärden	8	Ge	59.00N	17.43 E
Himmerland	8	Ch	56.50N	9.45 E
Himo	36	Gc	3.23S	37.33 E
Ḩimş=Homs (E)	22	Ff	34.44N	36.43 E
Hims, Bahrat-	24	Ge	34.39N	36.34 E
Hinai	29	Ga	40.13N	140.35 E
Hinca Renancó	56	Hd	34.50S	64.23W
Hinche	49	Kd	19.09N	72.01W
Hinchinbrook	40	Jd	60.22N	146.30W
Hinchinbrook Island	59	Jc	18.25S	146.15 E
Hinckley	12	Ab	52.32N	1.22W
Hindås	8	Eg	57.42N	12.27 E
Hindhead	12	Bc	51.06N	0.44W
Ḩindi, Badwēynta-=Indian Ocean (EN)	3	Gl	21.00S	82.00 E
Hindmarsh, Lake-	59	Ig	36.05S	141.55 E
Hinds	62	Df	44.00S	171.34 E
Hindsholm	8	Di	55.33N	10.40 E
Hindukush	21	Jf	35.00N	71.00 E
Hindustan	21	Jg	25.00N	79.00 E
Hinesville	44	Gj	31.51N	81.36W
Hinganghāt	25	Fd	20.34N	78.50 E
Hınıs	24	Ic	39.22N	41.44 E
Hınıs	24	Jc	39.18N	42.12 E
Hinlopenstretet	41	Oc	79.15N	21.00 E
Hinnøya	5	Hb	68.30N	16.00 E
Hino-Gawa	29	Cd	35.27N	133.22 E
Hinojosa del Duque	13	Gf	38.30N	5.09W
Hinokage	29	Be	32.39N	131.24 E
Hi-no-Misaki	29	Cd	35.26N	132.38 E
Hino-Misaki	29	De	33.53N	135.04 E
Hinterrhein	14	Dd	46.49N	9.25 E
Hinton	42	Ff	53.25N	117.34W
Hi-Numa	29	Gc	36.16N	140.30 E
Hınzır Burun	24	Fb	36.22N	35.45 E
Hiou	63b	Ca	13.08S	166.33 E
Hipólito	48	Ie	25.41N	101.26W
Hippolytushoef, Wieringen-	12	Gb	52.54N	4.59 E
Hippone	14	Bn	36.52N	7.44 E
Hirado	28	Jh	33.22N	129.33 E
Hirado-Shima	28	Jh	33.19N	129.32 E
Hiraka	29	Gb	39.16N	140.29 E
Hirakata	29	Dd	34.48N	135.38 E
Hīrākud	25	Gd	21.15N	84.15 E
Hiraman	36	Gc	1.07S	39.55 E
Hiranai	29a	Bc	40.54N	140.57 E
Hirara	27	Mg	24.48N	125.17 E
Hira-Shima	29	Ae	33.01N	129.15 E
Hirata	29	Cd	35.26N	132.49 E
Hiratsuka	29	Fd	35.19N	139.19 E
Hirfanlı barajı Gölü	24	Ec	39.10N	33.32 E
Hirgis	27	Fb	49.32N	93.48 E
Hirgis-Nur	21	Le	49.12N	93.24 E
Hirhafok	32	Ie	23.29N	5.45 E
Hîrlău	15	Jb	47.26N	26.54 E
Hiromi	29	Ce	33.15N	132.38 E
Hiroo	27	Pc	42.17N	143.19 E
Hirosaki	27	Pc	40.35N	140.28 E
Hiroshima	22	Pf	34.24N	132.27 E
Hiroshima Ken [2]	28	Lg	34.35N	132.50 E
Hiroshima-Wan	29	Cd	34.10N	132.20 E
Hirschhorn (Neckar)	12	Ke	49.27N	8.54 E
Hirson	11	Ke	49.55N	4.05 E
Hîrşova	15	Ke	44.41N	27.56 E
Hîrtibaciu	15	Hd	45.44N	24.14 E
Hirtshals	7	Bh	57.35N	9.58 E
Hirvensalmi	8	Lc	61.38N	26.48 E
Ḩis	35	Hc	10.50N	46.54 E
Hisai	29	Ed	34.40N	136.28 E
Hisaka-Shima	29	Ae	32.48N	128.52 E
Hisar	15	Jg	42.35N	27.00 E
Hisar	25	Fc	29.10N	75.43 E
Hisarcik	15	Mj	39.15N	29.15 E
Hisarja	15	Hg	42.30N	24.42 E
Ḩismā	24	Fh	28.30N	35.50 E
Ḩişn al 'Abr	33	If	16.08N	47.14 E
Ḩişn aş Şaḩābī	33	Dc	30.01N	20.48 E
Hispaniola (EN)=La Española	38	Lh	19.00N	71.00W
Histon	12	Cb	52.15N	0.06 E
Histria	15	Le	44.30N	28.45 E
Hīt	24	Jf	33.38N	42.49 E
Hita	28	Kh	33.19N	130.56 E
Hitachi	28	Pf	36.36N	140.39 E
Hitachi-ōta	29	Gc	36.32N	140.31 E
Hitchin	12	Bc	51.57N	0.16W
Hitiaa	65e	Fc	17.36S	149.18W
Hitotsuse-Gawa	29	Be	32.03N	131.31 E
Hitoyoshi	28	Kh	32.15N	130.45 E
Hitra	5	Gc	63.30N	8.45 E
Hiuchi-ga-Take	29	Fc	36.57N	139.17 E
Hiuchi-Nada	29	Cd	34.05N	133.15 E
Hiuma/Hiiumaa	5	Id	58.50N	22.40 E
Hiv	16	Oi	41.46N	47.57 E
Hiva	19	Gg	41.25N	60.23 E
Hiva Oa, Ile-	57	Ne	9.45S	139.00W
Hiw	24	Ei	26.01N	32.16 E
Hjademeste/Häädemeeste	8	Uf	58.00N	24.28 E
Hjallerup	8	Dg	57.10N	10.09 E
Hjälmare kanal	8	Fe	59.25N	15.55 E
Hjälmaren	5	Hd	59.15N	15.45 E
Hjelm	8	Dh	56.10N	10.50 E
Hjelmelandsvågen	7	Bg	59.15N	6.10 E
Hjelmsøya	7	Fa	71.05N	24.43 E
Hjerkinn	8	Cb	62.13N	9.32 E
Hjo	7	Dg	58.18N	14.17 E
Hjørring	7	Bh	57.28N	9.59 E
Hlatikulu	37	Ee	26.58S	31.19 E
Hlavní město Praha [3]	10	Kf	50.05N	14.25 E
Hlavní město SSR Bratislava [3]	10	Nh	48.10N	17.10 E
Hlinsko	10	Lg	49.46N	15.54 E
Hlohovec	10	Nh	48.25N	17.48 E
Hluhluwe	37	Ee	28.02S	32.17 E
Hmelnickaja Oblast [3]	19	Cf	49.30N	27.00 E
Hmelnicki	19	Cf	49.24N	26.57 E
Hmelnik	16	Ee	49.33N	27.59 E
Hnilec	10	Rh	48.53N	21.01 E
Ho	34	Fd	6.36N	0.28 E
Hoa Binh	25	Ld	20.50N	105.20 E
Hoai Nhon	25	Lf	14.26N	109.01 E
Hoanib	37	Ac	19.23S	13.06 E
Hoare Bay	42	Lc	65.30N	63.10W
Hoback Peak	46	Je	43.10N	110.33W
Hobart [Austl.]	58	Fi	42.53S	147.19 E
Hobart [Ok.-U.S.]	45	Gi	35.01N	99.06W
Hobbs	43	Ge	32.42N	103.08W
Hobbs Coast	66	Nf	74.50S	131.00W
Hobda	16	Sd	50.55N	54.38 E
Hoboken, Antwerpen-	12	Gc	51.10N	4.21 E
Hoboksar	27	Eb	46.47N	85.43 E
Hobq Shamo	27	Ic	40.30N	108.00 E
Hobro	7	Bh	56.38N	9.48 E
Hoburgen	7	Eh	56.55N	18.07 E
Hobyā	31	Lh	5.20N	48.38 E
Hocalar	15	Mk	38.37N	29.57 E
Hochalmspitze	14	Hc	47.01N	13.19 E
Hochfeiler/Gran Pilastro	14	Fd	46.58N	11.44 E
Hochgolling	14	Hc	47.16N	13.45 E
Ho Chi Minh (Saigon)	22	Mh	10.45N	106.40 E
Hochschwab	14	Jc	47.36N	15.05 E
Höchstadt an der Aisch	10	Gg	49.42N	10.44 E
Hochstetters Forland	41	Kc	75.45N	20.00W
Höchst im Odenwald	12	Ke	49.48N	9.00 E
Hochtor	14	Gc	47.05N	12.48 E
Hockenheim	12	Ke	49.19N	8.33 E
Hodaka-Dake	29	Ec	36.17N	137.39 E
Hodda	35	Ic	11.30N	50.45 E
Hoddesdon	12	Cc	51.45N	0.00
Hodgenville	44	Eg	37.34N	85.44W
Hodh	30	Gg	16.10N	8.40W
Hodh ech Chargui [3]	32	Ff	17.00N	7.15W
Hodh el Gharbi [3]	32	Ff	16.30N	10.00W
Hódmezővásárhely	10	Qj	46.25N	20.20 E
Hodna, Chott el-	32	Hb	35.25N	4.45 E
Hodna, Monts du-	32	Hb	35.50N	4.50 E
Hodna, Plaine du-	13	Qi	35.35N	4.35 E
Hodonín	10	Nh	48.52N	17.08 E
Hodorov	16	De	49.25N	24.18 E
Hodžambas	18	Ee	38.06N	65.01 E
Hodža-Pirjah, Gora-	18	Fe	38.47N	67.35 E
Hodžejli	19	Fg	42.23N	59.20 E
Hœdic, Ile de-	11	Dg	47.20N	2.52W
Hoegaarden	12	Gd	50.47N	4.53 E
Hoei/Huy	11	Ld	50.31N	5.14 E
Hoë Karoo	30	Jl	30.00S	21.30 E
Hoek van Holland	11	Kc	51.59N	4.09 E
Hoeselt	12	Hd	50.51N	5.29 E
Hof	10	Hf	50.19N	11.55 E
Höfdakaupstadur	7a	Bb	65.50N	20.19W
Hofgeismar	10	Fe	51.29N	9.24 E
Hofheim	12	Kd	50.05N	8.27 E
Hofmeyr	37	Df	31.39S	25.50 E
Höfn	7a	Cb	64.15N	15.13W
Hofsjökull	5	Ec	64.49N	18.48W
Hōfu	28	Kg	34.03N	131.34 E
Höganäs	8	Eh	56.12N	12.33 E
Hogarth, Mount-	59	Hd	21.48S	136.58 E
Hogback Mountain	46	Id	44.54N	112.07W
Hog Cliffs	51d	Ba	17.38N	61.44W
Hoge Venen/Hautes Fagnes	10	Bf	50.30N	6.00 E
Högfors/Karkkila	7	Ff	60.32N	24.11 E
Hog Island	51p	Bb	12.00N	61.44W
Hogne, Somme-Leuze-	12	Hd	50.15N	5.17 E
Hog Point	51d	Ba	17.43N	61.48W
Högsby	7	Dh	57.10N	16.02 E
Høgste Breakulen	8	Bc	61.41N	7.02 E
Høgstegia	8	Db	62.23N	10.08 E
Hogsty Reef	49	Kc	21.41N	73.49W
Hŏhang-nyŏng	28	Jd	41.48N	128.20 E
Hohe Acht	10	Cf	50.23N	7.00 E
Hohe Eifel	12	Id	50.16N	6.50 E
Hohenau	55	Eh	27.05S	55.45W
Hohenems	14	Dc	47.22N	9.41 E
Hohenloher Ebene	10	Fg	49.20N	9.40 E
Hohes Venn	10	Bf	50.30N	6.00 E
Hohe Tauern	14	Gc	47.10N	12.30 E
Hohhot	22	Ne	40.51N	111.38 E
Hōhoku	29	Bd	34.17N	130.57 E
Höhr-Grenzhausen	12	Jd	50.26N	7.40 E
Höhtiäinen	8	Mb	62.50N	29.40 E
Hoh Xil Hu	27	Fd	35.35N	91.06 E
Hoh Xil Shan	21	Lf	35.20N	91.00 E
Hoi An	25	Le	15.52N	108.19 E

Index Symbols

- [1] Independent Nation
- [2] State, Region
- [3] District, County
- [4] Municipality
- Colony, Dependency
- Continent
- Physical Region
- Historical or Cultural Region
- Mount, Mountain
- Volcano
- Hill
- Mountains, Mountain Range
- Hills, Escarpment
- Plateau, Upland
- Pass, Gap
- Plain, Lowland
- Delta
- Salt Flat
- Valley, Canyon
- Crater, Cave
- Karst Features
- Depression
- Polder
- Desert, Dunes
- Forest, Woods
- Heath, Steppe
- Oasis
- Cape, Point
- Coast, Beach
- Cliff
- Peninsula
- Isthmus
- Sandbank
- Island
- Atoll
- Rock, Reef
- Islands, Archipelago
- Rocks, Reefs
- Coral Reef
- Well, Spring
- Geyser
- River, Stream
- Waterfall Rapids
- River Mouth, Estuary
- Lake
- Salt Lake
- Intermittent Lake
- Reservoir
- Swamp, Pond
- Canal
- Glacier
- Ice Shelf, Pack Ice
- Ocean
- Sea
- Gulf, Bay
- Strait, Fjord
- Lagoon
- Bank
- Seamount
- Tablemount
- Ridge
- Shelf
- Basin
- Escarpment, Sea Scarp
- Fracture
- Trench, Abyss
- National Park, Reserve
- Point of Interest
- Recreation Site
- Cave, Cavern
- Historic Site
- Ruins
- Wall, Walls
- Church, Abbey
- Temple
- Scientific Station
- Airport
- Port
- Lighthouse
- Mine
- Tunnel
- Dam, Bridge

International Map Index

Hude (Oldenburg)	12	Ka	53.07N 8.28 E
Huder	27	Lb	49.59N 121.30 E
Hudiksvall	6	Hc	61.44N 17.07 E
Hudson	38	Le	40.42N 74.02W
Hudson [Fl.-U.S.]	44	Fk	28.22N 82.42W
Hudson [N.Y.-U.S.]	44	Kd	42.15N 73.47W
Hudson, Lake-	45	Ih	36.20N 95.05W
Hudson Bay	42	Hf	52.52N 102.23W
Hudson Bay	38	Kd	60.00N 86.00W
Hudson Canyon (EN)	44	Kf	39.27N 72.12W
Hudson Hope	42	Fe	56.02N 121.55W
Hudson Land	41	Jd	73.45N 22.30W
Hudson Mountains	66	Pf	74.32S 99.20W
Hudson Strait	38	Lc	62.30N 72.00W
Hudžirt	27	Hb	47.05N 102.45 E
Hue	22	Mh	16.28N 107.36 E
Huebra	13	Fc	41.02N 6.48W
Huehuecúicui, Punta-	56	Ff	41.47S 74.02W
Hueco Mountains	45	Dj	32.05N 105.55W
Huedin	15	Gc	46.52N 23.03 E
Huehuetenango	49	Bf	15.40N 91.35W
Huehuetenango	47	Fe	15.20N 91.28W
Huejutla de Reyes	48	Jg	21.08N 98.25W
Huelgoat	11	Cf	48.22N 3.45W
Huelma	13	Ig	37.39N 3.27W
Huelva	13	Fg	37.40N 7.00W
Huelva	6	Fh	37.16N 6.57W
Huelva, Ribera de-	13	Gg	37.27N 6.00W
Huércal Overa	13	Kg	37.23N 1.57W
Huerfano Mountain	45	Bh	36.30N 108.10W
Huertas, Cabo de-	13	Lf	38.21N 0.24W
Huerva	13	Lc	41.39N 0.52W
Huesca	13	Lb	42.08N 0.25W
Huesca	13	Lb	42.10N 0.10W
Huéscar	13	Jg	37.49N 2.32W
Hueso, Sierra del-	48	Gb	30.15N 105.20W
Huesos, Arroyo de los-	55	Cm	36.30S 59.09W
Huetamo de Núñez	48	Ih	18.35N 100.53W
Huete	13	Jd	40.08N 2.41W
Hufrat an Naḩās	35	Cd	9.45N 24.19 E
Huftarøy	8	Ad	60.05N 5.15 E
Hugh Butler Lake	45	Ff	40.22N 100.42W
Hughenden	58	Fg	20.51S 144.12 E
Hughes	40	Ic	66.03N 154.16W
Hughes Range	46	Hb	49.55N 115.28W
Hugo	45	Ii	34.01N 95.31W
Huguan	28	Bf	36.05N 113.12 E
Huhur He	28	Fc	43.55N 120.47 E
Huiʼan	27	Kf	25.07N 118.47 E
Huiarau Range	62	Gc	38.35S 177.10 E
Huib-Hochplato	37	Be	27.10S 16.50 E
Huichang	27	Kf	25.33N 115.45 E
Huicheng → Shexian	28	Ej	29.53N 118.27 E
Huicholes, Sierra de los-	48	Gf	22.00N 104.00W
Huichʼon	27	Mc	40.10N 126.17 E
Huifa He	28	Ic	43.06N 126.53 E
Hui He [China]	27	Kb	48.51N 119.12 E
Hui He [China]	28	Be	39.21N 112.37 E
Huiji He	28	Ch	33.53N 115.37 E
Huila	54	Cc	2.30N 75.45W
Huila	36	Ce	15.00S 15.00 E
Huila, Nevado del-	52	Ie	3.00N 76.00W
Huilai	27	Kg	23.05N 116.18 E
Huili	27	Hf	26.37N 102.19 E
Huimanguillo	48	Mi	17.51N 93.23W
Huimin	27	Kd	37.29N 117.30 E
Huinan (Chaoyang)	28	Ic	42.41N 126.03 E
Huisne	11	Gg	47.59N 0.11 E
Huissen	12	Hc	51.56N 5.55 E
Huiten Nur	27	Fd	35.30N 91.55 E
Huittinen	8	Jc	61.11N 22.42 E
Huivuilay, Isla de-	48	Dd	27.03N 110.01W
Huixian [China]	28	Bg	35.27N 113.47 E
Huixian [China]	27	Ie	33.46N 106.06 E
Huixtla	47	Fe	15.09N 92.28W
Huize	27	Hf	26.28N 103.18 E
Huizen	12	Hb	52.18N 5.16 E
Huizhou	27	Jg	23.02N 114.28 E
Hukou	28	Dj	29.44N 116.14 E
Hu Kou	28	Bg	36.09N 110.20 E
Hüksan-Chedo	27	Me	34.30N 125.20 E
Hukuntsi	37	Cd	23.59S 21.44 E
Hulan	27	Mb	46.03N 126.36 E
Hulan He	27	Mb	45.54N 126.42 E
Hulayfaʼ	23	Fd	26.00N 40.47 E
Hulett	46	Md	44.41N 104.36W
Hulga	17	Ad	64.15N 60.58 E
Hulin	27	Nb	45.52N 132.58 E
Hulin He	28	Hb	45.19N 124.06 E
Hull	42	Jg	45.26N 75.43W
Hull → Kingston-upon-Hull	6	Fe	53.45N 0.20W
Hull → Orona Atoll	57	Je	4.29S 172.10W
Hull Bay	66	Nf	74.55S 137.40W
Hull Glacier	66	Nf	75.05S 137.15W
Hull Mountain	46	Dg	39.31N 122.59W
Hüls, Krefeld-	12	Ic	51.22N 6.31 E
Hultsfred	7	Dh	57.29N 15.50 E
Huludao	27	Lc	40.44N 120.59 E
Hulun Nur	21	Ne	49.00N 117.30 E
Ḩulwān=Helwān (EN)	33	Fd	29.51N 31.20 E
Hulwāt, Qūr al-	24	Hh	28.49N 38.50 E
Huma [China]	27	Ma	51.44N 126.36 E
Huma [Ton.]	65b	Bc	21.19S 174.56W
Humacao	49	Od	18.09N 65.50W
Huma He	27	Ma	51.42N 126.42 E
Humaitá [Braz.]	53	Jf	7.31S 63.02W
Humaitá [Par.]	56	Ic	27.03S 58.33W
Humansdorp	37	Cf	34.02S 24.46 E
Humbe	36	Bf	16.42S 14.54 E
Humber	5	Fe	53.40N 0.10W
Humberside	9	Mh	53.55N 0.30W
Humbolat River	61	Cd	21.53S 166.25 E
Humboldt [Ia.-U.S.]	45	Ie	42.43N 94.13W
Humboldt [Nb.-U.S.]	17	If	40.10N 95.57W
Humboldt [Sask.-Can.]	42	Gf	52.12N 105.07W
Humboldt [Tn.-U.S.]	44	Ch	35.49N 88.55W
Humboldt Gletscher	41	Fc	79.40N 63.45W
Humboldt Range	46	Ff	40.15N 118.10W
Hume, Lake-	59	Jg	36.05S 147.05 E
Humenné	10	Rh	48.56N 21.55 E
Hummelfjell	8	Db	62.27N 11.17 E
Hümmling, Der-	10	Dd	52.52N 7.31 E
Humphreys Peak	38	Hf	35.20N 111.40W
Humppila	7	Ff	60.56N 23.22 E
Humuya, Rio-	49	Df	15.13N 87.57W
Hün	31	If	29.07N 15.56 E
Húnaflói	5	Db	65.50N 20.50W
Hunan Sheng (Hu-nan Sheng)	27	Jf	28.00N 112.00 E
Hu-nan Sheng → Hunan	27	Jf	28.00N 112.00 E
Hunchun	28	Kc	42.52N 130.21 E
Hundested	8	Di	55.58N 11.52 E
Hunedoara	15	Fd	45.45N 22.52 E
Hünfeld	10	Ff	50.40N 9.46 E
Hünfelden	12	Kd	50.19N 8.11 E
Hunga Haʼapai	65b	Ab	20.33S 175.24W
Hungary (EN) = Magyarország	6	Hf	47.00N 20.00 E
Hunga Tonga	65b	Ab	20.32S 175.23W
Hungen	12	Kd	50.28N 8.54 E
Hüngnam	27	Md	39.50N 127.38 E
Hungry Horse Reservoir	46	Ib	48.22N 113.30W
Hun He [China]	28	Be	39.47N 113.15 E
Hun He [China]	28	Gd	40.41N 122.12 E
Hunhedoara	15	Fd	45.45N 22.54 E
Hunish, Rubha-	9	Gd	57.43N 6.20W
Hunjiang	28	Hd	40.52N 125.42 E
Hunne	27	Mc	41.55N 126.27 E
Hunneberg	8	Ef	58.20N 12.27 E
Hunnebostrand	8	Df	58.27N 11.18 E
Hunsrück	10	Cg	49.50N 6.40 E
Hunstanton	9	Ni	52.57N 0.30 E
Hunte	10	Ed	52.30N 8.19 E
Hunter, Ile-	57	Ig	22.24S 172.03 E
Hunter Island	59	Ih	40.30S 144.45 E
Hunter Ridge (EN)	57	Ig	21.30S 174.30 E
Hunter River	59	Kf	32.30S 151.42 E
Hunterville	62	Fc	39.56S 175.34 E
Huntingdon	9	Mi	52.30N 0.10W
Huntingdon [Eng.-U.K.]	9	Mi	52.20N 0.12W
Huntingdon [Que.-Can.]	44	He	40.31N 78.02W
Huntingdon [In.-U.S.]	44	Jc	45.05N 74.08W
Huntington [In.-U.S.]	44	Ee	40.53N 85.30W
Huntington [W.V.-U.S.]	43	Kd	38.24N 82.26W
Huntly [N.Z.]	62	Fb	37.33S 175.10 E
Huntly [Scot.-U.K.]	9	Kd	57.27N 2.47W
Huntsville [Al.-U.S.]	39	Kf	34.44N 86.35W
Huntsville [Ont.-Can.]	42	Jg	45.20N 79.13W
Huntsville [Tx.-U.S.]	43	He	30.43N 95.33W
Hunucmá	48	Og	21.01N 89.52W
Hünxe	12	Ic	51.39N 6.47 E
Huocheng (Shuiding)	27	Dc	44.03N 80.49 E
Huojia	28	Bg	35.16N 113.39 E
Huolongmen	27	Mb	49.49N 125.49 E
Huolu	28	Ce	38.05N 114.18 E
Huon, Ile-	57	If	18.01S 162.57 E
Huon Gulf	59	Ja	7.10S 147.25 E
Huon Peninsula	60	Di	6.25S 147.30 E
Huonville	59	Jh	43.01S 147.02 E
Huoqin	28	Dh	32.21N 116.17 E
Huoshan	27	Ke	31.19N 116.20 E
Huo Shan [China]	27	Jd	37.00N 111.52 E
Huo Shan [China]	27	Ke	31.06N 116.12 E
Huoxian	27	Jd	36.39N 111.47 E
Hupeh → Baltit	11	Ma	53.13N 6.40 E
Hupei → Hubei Sheng (Hu-pei Sheng)	27	Je	31.00N 112.00 E
Hu-pei Sheng → Hubei Sheng = Hopeh (EN)	27	Je	31.00N 112.00 E
Hür	24	Qg	30.50N 57.07 E
Hurama → Hongyuan	27	He	32.45N 102.38 E
Huränd	24	Lc	38.40N 47.20 E
Hurd, Cape-	44	Gc	45.13N 81.44W
Hurdalssjøen	8	Dd	60.20N 11.05 E
Hurd Deep = La Grande Trench (EN)	9	Kl	49.40N 3.00W
Hurdiyo	35	Ic	10.32N 51.08 E
Huron	11	If	48.30N 2.10 E
Huron, Lake-	45	Lb	48.50N 89.29W
Huron Mountains	44	Db	46.45N 87.45W
Hurricane	46	Ih	37.11N 113.17W
Hurricane Cliffs	46	Ih	37.00N 113.05W
Hurrungane	8	Bc	61.27N 7.51 E
Hursley	12	Ac	51.01N 1.24W
Hurst	45	Hj	32.49N 97.09W
Hurstpierpoint	12	Bd	50.55N 0.10W
Hürth	10	Cf	50.52N 6.52 E
Hurum	8	De	59.35N 10.35 E
Hurum	24	Hh	28.49N 38.50 E
Hurunui	62	Ee	42.54S 173.18 E
Hurup	8	Ch	56.45N 8.25 E
Húsavík	5	Lc	66.41N 28.04 E
Hushan → Cixi	7a	Ca	66.03N 17.54 E
Huskvarna	28	Fi	30.10N 121.14 E
Huslia	8	Fg	57.48N 14.16 E
Husnes	40	Hc	66.45N 156.25W
Husnesfjorden	8	Ae	59.52N 5.46 E
Hussigny-Godbrange	12	He	49.29N 5.52 E
Hust	16	Ce	48.10N 23.27 E
Hustadvika	8	Ba	63.00N 7.05 E
Hustad	10	Fb	54.28N 9.03 E
Husum [F.R.G.]	7	Bh	54.20N 19.10 E
Husum [Swe.]	27	Hb	49.23N 102.43 E
Hutag	43	Hd	38.05N 97.56W
Hutchinson [Ks.-U.S.]			

Index Symbols

1 Independent Nation	Pass, Gap
2 State, Region	Plain, Lowland
3 District, County	Delta
4 Municipality	Salt Flat
5 Colony, Dependency	Forest, Woods
6 Continent	Heath, Steppe
7 Physical Region	Oasis
	Cape, Point
Historical or Cultural Region	Depression
Mount, Mountain	Polder
Volcano	Desert, Dunes
Hill	Sandbank
Mountains, Mountain Range	Island
Hills, Escarpment	
Plateau, Upland	Karst Features
	Cliff
	Peninsula
	Isthmus
	Crater, Cave
Coast, Beach	Rock, Reef
Islands, Archipelago	
Rocks, Reefs	
Coral Reef	
Well, Spring	
Geyser	
River, Stream	
Waterfall Rapids	Canal
River Mouth, Estuary	Glacier
Lake	Ice Shelf, Pack Ice
Salt Lake	Ocean
Intermittent Lake	Sea
Reservoir	Gulf, Bay
Swamp, Pond	Strait, Fjord
Lagoon	Historic Site
Bank	Ruins
Seamount	Wall, Walls
Tablemount	Church, Abbey
Ridge	Temple
Shelf	Scientific Station
Basin	Airport
Escarpment, Sea Scarp	Port
Fracture	Lighthouse
Trench, Abyss	Mine
National Park, Reserve	Tunnel
Point of Interest	Dam, Bridge
Recreation Site	
Cave, Cavern	

Ilbengja	20	Hd	62.55N	124.10 E
Ile-à-la-Crosse	42	Ge	55.27N	107.53W
Ilebo	31	Ji	4.44S	20.33 E
Ile de France	11	Ie	49.00N	2.20 E
Ile de France	41	Kc	77.45N	27.45W
Ile de France, Côte de l'-	11	Jf	48.55N	3.50 E
Ilek	19	Fe	51.32N	53.27 E
Ilek	5	Le	51.30N	53.20 E
Ileksa	7	Ie	62.30N	36.57 E
Ilerh	32	He	21.40N	2.22 E
Ileša	7	Le	62.37N	46.35 E
Ilesha [Nig.]	34	Fd	8.55N	3.25 E
Ilesha [Nig.]	34	Fd	7.37N	4.44 E
Ilet	7	Li	55.57N	48.14 E
Ilfov [2]	15	Je	44.30N	26.20 E
Ilfracombe	9	Ij	51.13N	4.08W
Ilgaz	24	Eb	40.56N	33.38 E
Ilgaz Dağları	24	Eb	41.00N	33.35 E
Ilgın	24	Dc	38.17N	31.55 E
Ilha Grande	54	Ed	0.27S	65.02W
Ilha Grande, Baía da-	55	Jf	23.09S	44.30W
Ilhas Desertas	32	Dc	32.30N	16.30W
Ilhavo	13	Dd	40.36N	8.40W
Ilhéus	53	Mg	14.49S	39.02W
Ili	21	Je	45.24N	74.08 E
Ilia	15	Fd	45.56N	22.39 E
Iliamna	40	Ie	59.45N	154.54W
Iliamna Lake	40	He	59.30N	155.00W
İliç	24	Hc	39.28N	38.34 E
Ilič	18	Gd	40.55N	68.29 E
Ilica	15	Kj	39.52N	27.46 E
Iličevsk [Abz.-U.S.S.R.]	16	Nj	39.33N	44.59 E
Iličevsk [Ukr.-U.S.S.R.]	19	Df	46.18N	30.37 E
Ilidža	14	Mg	43.50N	18.19 E
Iligan	22	Oi	8.14N	124.14 E
Iligan Bay	26	He	8.25N	124.05 E
Ilim	20	Fe	56.50N	103.25 E
Ilimskoje Vodohranilišče	20	Fe	57.20N	102.30 E
Ilinski [R.S.F.S.R.]	7	Hf	61.02N	32.42 E
Ilinski [R.S.F.S.R.]	20	Jg	47.59N	142.21 E
Ilinski [R.S.F.S.R.]	17	Gg	58.35N	55.41 E
Ilion	44	Jd	43.01N	75.04W
Ilio Point	65a	Db	21.13N	157.16W
Ilir	20	Fe	55.13N	100.45 E
Ilirska Bistrica	14	Ie	45.34N	14.16 E
Iljaly	18	Bd	41.53N	59.40 E
Ilkal	25	Fe	15.58N	76.08 E
Ilkeston	12	Ab	52.58N	1.18W
Ill	11	Nf	48.40N	7.53 E
Illampu, Nevado del-	54	Eg	15.50S	68.34W
Illana Bay	26	He	7.25N	123.45 E
Illapel	56	Fd	31.38S	71.10W
Illbillee, Mount-	59	Ge	27.02S	132.30 E
Ille	11	Ef	48.08N	1.40W
Ille-et-Vilaine [3]	11	Ef	48.10N	1.30W
Illéla	34	Gc	14.28N	5.15 E
Iller	10	Fh	48.23N	9.58 E
Illescas	13	Id	40.07N	3.50W
Ille-sur-Têt	11	Il	42.40N	2.37 E
Illi, Ba-	35	Bc	10.44N	16.21 E
Illimani, Nevado del-	52	Jg	16.39S	67.48W
Illingen	12	Je	49.22N	7.03 E
Illinois	38	Jf	38.58N	90.27W
Illinois [2]	43	Jd	40.00N	89.00W
Illinois Peak	46	Hc	47.02N	115.04W
Illizi	31	Hf	26.29N	8.28 E
Ilm	10	He	51.07N	11.40 E
Ilmajoki	8	Jb	62.44N	22.34 E
Ilmen, Ozero-	5	Jd	58.20N	31.20 E
Ilmenau	10	Gf	50.41N	10.54 E
Ilmenau	10	Gc	53.23N	10.10 E
Il Montello	14	Ge	45.49N	12.07 E
Ilo	54	Dg	17.38S	71.20W
Iloilo	22	Oh	10.42N	122.34 E
Ilok	14	Ne	45.13N	19.23 E
Ilomantsi	7	He	62.40N	30.55 E
Ilorin	31	Hh	8.30N	4.33 E
Iloron, Cerro-	48	Gg	20.57N	104.22W
Ilova	14	Ke	45.25N	16.45 E
Ilovik	14	If	44.27N	14.33 E
Ilovlja	16	Ne	49.18N	44.01 E
Ilovlja	16	Me	49.14N	43.54 E
Ilpyrski	20	Le	59.52N	164.12 E
Ilski	16	Kg	44.51N	38.32 E
Iltin	20	Nc	67.52N	178.48W
Ilubabor [3]	35	Ed	7.50N	35.00 E
Ilūkste/Ilukste	8	Li	55.58N	26.26 E
Ilukste/Ilūkste	8	Li	55.58N	26.26 E
Ilulissat/Jakobshavn	67	Nc	69.20N	50.50W
Ilwaki	26	Ih	7.56S	126.26 E
Ilyč	17	He	62.32N	56.40 E
Ilz	10	Jh	48.35N	13.30 E
Iłżanka	10	Re	51.14N	21.47 E
Imabari	28	Lg	34.03N	133.00 E
Imagane	28	Pc	42.26N	140.01 E
Imaichi	28	Of	36.43N	139.41 E
Imán, Sierra del-	55	Eh	27.42S	55.28W
Imanburluk	17	Mj	53.40N	67.15 E
Imandra, Ozero-	5	Jb	67.30N	33.00 E
Imano-Yama	29	Ce	32.51N	132.49 E
Imari	28	Jh	33.16N	129.53 E
Imaruí	55	Hi	28.21S	48.49W
Imataca, Serranía de-	50	Fi	7.45N	61.00W
Imatra	7	Gf	61.10N	28.46 E
Imazu	29	Ed	35.24N	136.01 E
Imbabah, Al Qāhirah-	33	Fc	30.05N	31.13 E
Imba-Numa	29	Gd	35.45N	140.14 E
Imbert	49	Ld	19.45N	70.50W
Imbituba	56	Kc	28.14S	48.40W
Imeni 26 Bakinskih Komissarov [Abz.-U.S.S.R.]	19	Eh	39.19N	49.12 E
Imeni 26 Bakinskih Komissarov [Tur.-U.S.S.R.]	19	Fh	39.21N	54.12 E
İmeni Gastello	20	Jd	61.35N	147.59 E
İmeni Karla Liebknechta	16	Id	51.38N	35.29 E
İmeni Mariny Raskovoj	20	Jd	62.05N	146.30 E
İmeni Poliny Osipenko	20	If	52.23N	136.25 E
Imi	31	Lh	6.28N	42.11 E
Imilili	32	De	22.50N	15.54W
Imi n'Tanout	32	Fc	31.03N	8.08W
Imišli	19	Eh	39.53N	48.03 E
Imjin-gang	28	If	37.47N	126.40 E
Imlay	46	Ff	40.42N	118.07W
Immenstadt im Allgäu	10	Gi	47.34N	10.13 E
Imo [2]	34	Gd	5.30N	7.20 E
Imola	14	Ff	44.21N	11.42 E
Imotski	14	Lg	43.27N	17.13 E
Imperatriz	53	Lf	5.32S	47.29W
Imperia	14	Cg	43.53N	8.03 E
Imperial	45	Ff	40.31N	101.39W
Imperial de Aragón, Canal-	13	Kb	42.02N	1.33W
Imperial Valley	46	Hj	32.50N	115.30W
Impfondo	31	Ih	1.37N	18.04 E
Imphāl	22	Lg	24.49N	93.57 E
Imphy	11	Jh	46.56N	3.15 E
Impilanti	7	Hf	61.41N	31.12 E
Imrali Adasi	15	Li	40.32N	28.32 E
Imst	14	Ec	47.14N	10.44 E
Imtan	24	Gf	32.24N	36.49 E
Imuris	48	Db	30.47N	110.52W
Im-Zouren	13	Ii	35.04N	3.50W
Ina	28	Ng	35.50N	137.57 E
Ina	10	Kc	53.32N	14.38 E
I-n-Abanrherit	34	Gb	17.58N	6.05 E
Inabu	29	Ed	35.13N	137.30 E
Inaccessible Islands	66	Re	60.34S	46.44W
Inacessible Island	30	Fi	37.17S	12.45W
I-n-Afaleleh	32	Ie	23.34N	9.12 E
I Naftan, Puntan-	64b	Ba	15.05N	145.45 E
Ina-Gawa	29	Fc	37.23N	139.18 E
I-n-Amenas	31	Hf	28.03N	9.33 E
Inami	29	De	33.48N	135.12 E
Inanba-Jima	29	Fe	33.39N	139.18 E
Inangahua Junction	62	Dd	41.52S	171.56 E
Inanwatan	26	Jg	2.08S	132.10 E
Iñapari	54	Ef	10.57S	69.35W
Inarajan	64c	Bb	13.16N	144.45 E
I-n-Arhâta	34	Ea	21.09N	0.18W
Inari	6	Ib	68.54N	27.01 E
Inari, Lake- (EN)= Inarijärvi	5	Ib	69.00N	28.00 E
Inarijärvi=Inari, Lake- (EN)	5	Ib	69.00N	28.00 E
Inawashiro	29	Gc	37.34N	140.05 E
Inawashiro-Ko	28	Pf	37.30N	140.03 E
I-n Azaoua	34	Ga	20.47N	7.31 E
I-n-Azaoua	34	Ga	20.54N	7.28 E
Inazawa	29	Ed	35.15N	136.47 E
Inca	13	Oe	39.43N	2.54 E
Inca de Oro	56	Gc	26.45S	69.54W
Incaguasi	56	Fc	29.13S	71.03W
Ince Burun	15	Ki	40.28N	27.16 E
İnce Burun	23	Da	42.07N	34.56 E
İncekum Burun	24	Ed	36.13N	33.58 E
Inceler	15	Ml	37.42N	29.35 E
I-n-Chaouâg	34	Fb	16.23N	0.10 E
Inchcape (Bell Rock)	9	Ke	56.26N	2.24W
Inchiri [3]	32	Df	20.00N	15.00W
Inch'ŏn	22	Of	37.28N	126.38 E
Incirliova	15	Kl	37.50N	27.43 E
Incudine	11a	Bb	41.51N	9.12 E
Indaiá, Rio-	55	Jd	18.27S	45.22W
Indaia Grande, Ribeirão-	55	Fd	19.31S	52.29W
Indaiatuba	55	If	23.05S	47.14W
Indal	8	Gb	62.34N	17.06 E
Indalsälven	7	De	62.31N	17.27 E
Inda Selase	35	Fc	14.06N	38.17 E
Indawgyi	25	Jc	25.08N	96.20 E
Indefatigable Banks	9	Ph	53.35N	2.20 E
Independence [Ca.-U.S.]	46	Fh	36.48N	118.12W
Independence [Ia.-U.S.]	45	Ke	42.28N	91.54W
Independence [Ks.-U.S.]	43	Hd	37.13N	95.42W
Independence [Mo.-U.S.]	45	Ig	39.05N	94.04W
Independence [Va.-U.S.]	44	Gg	36.38N	81.11W
Independence Fjord	67	Me	82.00N	30.25W
Independence Mountains	46	Gf	41.15N	116.05W
Independência [Braz.]	54	Je	5.23S	40.19W
Independência [Braz.]	55	Fa	13.34S	53.57W
Independenta	15	Kd	45.29N	27.45 E
Inder → Jalaid Qi	27	Lb	46.41N	122.52 E
Inder, Ozero-	16	Qe	48.25N	51.55 E
Inderborski	6	Lf	48.32N	51.47 E
India (EN)	21	Jh	20.00N	77.00 E
India (EN)=Bhārat Juktarashtra [1]	22	Jh	20.00N	77.00 E
India Muerta, Arroyo de la-	55	Fk	33.40S	54.04W
Indiana [2]	43	Jc	40.00N	86.15W
Indiana	44	He	40.39N	79.11W
Indianapolis	39	Kf	39.46N	86.09W
Indian Church	49	Ce	17.45N	88.40W
Indian Creek Point	51d	Bb	17.00N	61.43W
Indian Harbour	42	Lf	54.27N	57.13W
Indian Head	42	Hf	50.32N	103.40W
Indian Ocean	3	Gl	21.00S	82.00 E
Indian Ocean (EN)=Ḩindi, Badwēynta-	3	Gl	21.00S	82.00 E
Indian Ocean (EN)=Indico, Oceano-	3	Gl	21.00S	82.00 E
Indian Ocean (EN)=Indien, Océan-	3	Gl	21.00S	82.00 E
Indian Ocean (EN)=Indiese Oseaan-	3	Gl	21.00S	82.00 E
Indian Ocean (EN)= Indonesia, Samudera-	3	Gl	21.00S	82.00 E
Indianola	45	Kj	33.27N	90.39W
Indianópolis	55	Id	19.02S	47.55W
Indian Peak	46	Ig	38.16N	113.53W
Indian Rock	46	Ec	46.01N	120.49W
Indian Springs	43	Dd	36.34N	115.40W
Indiantown	44	Gl	27.01N	80.28W
Indian Town Point	51d	Bb	17.06N	61.40W
Indiapora	55	Gd	19.57S	50.17W
Indias Occidentales=West Indies (EN)	47	Je	19.00N	70.00W
Indico, Oceano-=Indian Ocean (EN)	3	Gl	21.00S	82.00 E
Indien, Océan-=Indian Ocean (EN)	3	Gl	21.00S	82.00 E
Indiese, Oseaan-=Indian Ocean (EN)	3	Gl	21.00S	82.00 E
Indiga	19	Eb	67.41N	49.00 E
Indigirka	21	Qb	70.48N	148.54 E
Indigskaja Guba	17	Dc	67.45N	48.20 E
Inđija	15	Dd	45.03N	20.05 E
Indio	43	De	33.43N	116.13W
Indio, Río-	49	Fh	10.57N	83.44W
Indio Rico	55	Bn	38.19S	60.53W
Indispensable Reefs	57	Hf	12.40S	160.25 E
Indispensable Strait	63a	Ec	9.00S	160.30 E
Indochina (EN)	21	Mh	16.00N	107.00 E
Indonesia [1]	22	Nj	5.00S	120.00 E
Indonesia, Samudera-= Indian Ocean (EN)	3	Gl	21.00S	82.00 E
Indore	22	Jg	22.43N	75.50 E
Indra	8	Li	55.53N	27.40 E
Indragiri	26	Dg	0.22S	103.26 E
Indramayu	26	Eh	6.20S	108.19 E
Indrāvati	25	Ge	18.44N	80.16 E
Indre	11	Gg	47.14N	0.11 E
Indre [3]	11	Hh	46.50N	1.40 E
Indre Arna	8	Ad	60.26N	5.30 E
Indre-et-Loire [3]	11	Gg	47.15N	0.45 E
Indus	21	Ig	24.20N	67.47 E
İnebolu	23	Da	41.58N	33.46 E
Inece	15	Kh	41.41N	27.04 E
Inecik	15	Ki	40.56N	27.16 E
İnegöl	23	Ca	40.05N	29.31 E
Inés Indart	55	Bl	34.24S	60.33W
Ineu	15	Ec	46.26N	21.51 E
Ineu, Vîrful-	15	Hb	47.32N	24.53 E
Inezgane	32	Fc	30.21N	9.32W
I-n-Ezzane	32	Je	23.29N	11.15 E
Inferior, Laguna-	48	Li	16.15N	94.45W
Infiernillo, Presa del-	47	De	18.35N	101.45W
Infiesto	13	Ga	43.21N	5.22W
Infreschi, Punta degli-	14	Jk	39.59N	15.25 E
Ingá	54	Ke	7.17S	35.36W
Inga	36	Bd	5.39S	13.39 E
Ingå/Inkoo	7	Ff	60.03N	24.01 E
Ingabu	25	Je	17.49N	95.16 E
Ingaí, Rio-	55	Je	21.10S	44.52W
I-n Gall	34	Gb	16.47N	6.56 E
Ingarö	8	He	59.15N	18.30 E
Ingavi	55	Bb	15.02S	60.29W
Ingelheim am Rhein	12	Ke	49.59N	8.02 E
Ingelmunster	12	Fd	50.55N	3.15 E
Ingelstad	8	Fh	56.45N	14.55 E
Ingende	36	Cc	0.15S	18.57 E
Ingeniero Guillermo N. Juarez	56	Hb	23.54S	61.51W
Ingeniero Jacobacci	56	Gf	41.18S	69.35W
Ingeniero Luiggi	56	He	35.25S	64.29W
Ingenio Santa Ana	56	Gc	27.28S	65.41W
Ingermanland (EN)	5	Id	59.00N	30.00 E
Ingham	58	Ff	18.39S	146.10 E
Ingička	18	Ee	39.47N	65.58 E
Inglefield Bredning	41	Fc	77.40N	65.00W
Inglefield Land	41	Fc	78.44N	68.20W
Inglewood [Austl.]	59	Ke	28.25S	151.05 E
Inglewood [Ca.-U.S.]	46	Fj	33.58N	118.21W
Inglewood [N.Z.]	62	Fc	39.09S	174.12 E
Ingolf Fjord	41	Kb	80.35N	17.35W
Ingólfshödi	7a	Cc	63.48N	16.39W
Ingolstadt	10	Hh	48.46N	11.26 E
Ingrid Christensen Kyst	66	Fe	69.30S	76.00 E
I-n-Guezzâm	31	Hg	19.32N	5.42 E
Ingul	16	Gf	47.02N	31.59 E
Ingulec	16	Hf	46.41N	32.48 E
Ingulec	19	Df	47.43N	33.10 E
Inguri	16	Lh	42.24N	41.32 E
Inhaca, Ilha da-	30	Kk	26.02S	32.58 E
Inhambane	31	Kk	23.52S	35.23 E
Inhambane [3]	37	Ed	23.00S	34.30 E
Inhambane, Baía de-	37	Fd	23.50S	35.20 E
Inhaminga	37	Fc	18.25S	35.01 E
Inhanduí-Guaçu, Rio-	55	Fe	21.37S	52.59W
Inhanduízinho, Rio-	55	Fe	21.34S	53.36W
Inharrime	37	Fd	24.28S	35.01 E
Inhassoro	37	Fd	21.32S	35.12 E
Inhaúma	55	Ja	13.01S	44.39W
I-n-Hihaou	32	He	23.00N	2.00 E
Inhobi, Rio-	55	Ef	23.45S	54.40W
Inhumas	54	Ig	16.22S	49.30W
Iniö	8	Id	60.25N	21.25 E
Inírida, Río-	52	Je	3.55N	67.52W
Inis/Ennis	9	Ei	52.50N	8.59W
Inis Airc/Inishark	9	Ch	53.37N	10.16W
Inis Bó Finne/Inishbofin	9	Ch	53.38N	10.12W
Inis Ceithleann/Enniskillen	9	Fg	54.21N	7.38W
Inis Córthaidh/Enniscorthy	9	Gi	52.30N	6.34W
Inis Diomáin/Ennistymon	9	Di	52.57N	9.13W
Inis Eoghain/Inishowen Peninsula	9	Ff	55.15N	7.20W
Inishark/Inis Airc	9	Ch	53.37N	10.16W
Inishbofin/Inis Bó Finne	9	Ch	53.38N	10.12W
Inisheer/Inis Oírr	9	Dh	53.03N	9.31W
Inishkea	9	Cg	54.08N	10.11W
Inishmaan/Inis Meáin	9	Dh	53.05N	9.35W
Inishmore/Árainn	9	Dh	53.07N	9.45W
Inishmurray/Inis Muirígh	9	Eg	54.26N	8.40W
Inishowen Peninsula/Inis Eoghain	9	Ff	55.15N	7.20W
Inishtranull	9	Ff	55.27N	7.14W
Inishturk/Inis Toirc	9	Ch	53.43N	10.05W
Inis Meáin/Inishmaan	9	Dh	53.05N	9.35W
Inis Muirígh/Inishmurray	9	Eg	54.26N	8.40W
Inis Oírr/Inisheer	9	Dh	53.03N	9.31W
Inis Toirc/Inishturk	9	Ch	53.43N	10.05W
Inja	20	Je	59.22N	144.50 E
Inja [R.S.F.S.R.]	20	Je	59.30N	144.48 E
Inja [R.S.F.S.R.]	20	Df	50.27N	86.42 E
Injeŭp	28	Je	38.04N	128.10 E
Injibara	35	Fc	10.55N	36.58 E
Injune	59	Je	25.51S	148.34 E
I-n-Kak	34	Fb	16.20N	0.17 E
Inkisi	36	Bc	4.46S	14.52 E
Inkoo/Ingå	7	Ff	60.03N	24.01 E
Inland Kaikoura Range	62	Ee	42.00S	173.35 E
Inland Sea (EN)= Setonaikai	21	Pf	34.10N	133.00 E
Inn	5	Hf	48.35N	13.28 E
Innamincka	59	Ie	27.45S	140.44 E
Inner Hebrides	9	Ge	57.00N	6.45W
Inner Mongolia (EN)=Nei Monggol Zizhiqu (Nei-meng-ku Tzu-chih-ch'ü) [2]	27	Jc	44.00N	112.00 E
Inner Silver Pit	9	Nh	53.30N	0.40 E
Inner Sound	9	Hd	57.30N	5.55W
Innerste	10	Fd	52.15N	9.50 E
Innisfail [Alta.-Can.]	46	Ia	52.02N	113.57W
Innisfail [Austl.]	59	Jc	17.32S	146.02 E
Innokentjevka	20	Ig	49.42N	136.55 E
Innokentjevski	20	Jg	48.38N	140.12 E
Innoko	40	Hd	62.14N	159.45W
Innsbruck	6	Hf	47.16N	11.24 E
Innuksuac	42	Je	58.27N	78.08W
Innviertel	14	Hb	48.15N	13.15 E
Innvikfjorden	8	Bc	61.50N	6.35 E
Inny/An Eithne	9	Fh	53.35N	7.50W
Ino	29	Ce	33.33N	133.26 E
Inobonto	26	Hf	0.52N	123.57 E
Inongo	31	Ii	1.57S	18.16 E
Inoni	36	Cc	3.04S	15.39 E
Inönü	15	Nj	39.48N	30.09 E
I-n-Ouagar	34	Gb	16.12N	6.54 E
Inoucdjauac	39	Ld	58.30N	78.15W
I-n-Ouzzal	32	He	21.34N	1.59 E
Inowrocław	10	Od	52.48N	18.15 E
I-n-Salah	31	Hf	27.13N	2.28 E
Insar	7	Ki	54.42N	45.18 E
Insar	7	Kj	53.52N	44.23 E
Inscription, Cape-	57	Cg	25.30S	112.59 E
Insjön	8	Fd	60.41N	15.05 E
Ińsko	10	Lc	53.27N	15.33 E
Instruč	8	Ij	54.39N	21.48 E
Insurăţei	15	Ke	44.55N	27.36 E
Inta	6	Mb	66.05N	60.08 E
I-n-Tabezas	34	Fb	17.54N	1.50 E
I-n-Tallak	34	Fb	16.19N	3.15 E
Intepe	15	Ji	40.00N	26.20 E
Interlaken	14	Bd	46.41N	7.52 E
International Falls	43	Ib	48.36N	93.25W
Interview	25	If	12.55N	92.43 E
Inthanon, Doi-	25	Je	18.35N	98.29 E
Intibucá [3]	49	Cf	14.20N	88.15W
Intiyaco	56	Hc	28.39S	60.05W
Intorsura Buzaului	15	Jd	45.41N	26.02 E
Intracoastal Waterway	45	Im	28.45N	95.40W
Inubō-Zaki	29	Gd	35.42N	140.52 E
Inutil, Bahia-	56	Fh	52.45S	71.24W
Inuvik	39	Fc	68.25N	133.30W
Inuyama	29	Ed	35.23N	136.56 E
Inva	17	Gg	58.59N	55.40 E
Inveraray	9	He	56.13N	5.05W
Invercargill	58	Hi	46.25S	168.21 E
Inverell	59	Ke	29.47S	151.07 E
Inverness	6	Fd	57.27N	4.15W
Inverurie	9	Kd	57.17N	2.23W
Investigator Group	57	Eh	33.45S	134.30 E
Investigator Strait	59	Hg	35.25S	137.10 E
Inyangani	30	Kj	18.18S	32.51 E
Inyangani	37	Ec	18.13S	32.46 E
Inyati	37	Dc	19.40S	28.51 E
Inyazura	37	Ec	18.43S	32.10 E
Inyo Mountains	46	Gh	36.50N	117.45W
Inza	19	Ee	53.53N	46.28 E
Inzá	54	Cc	2.33N	76.04W
Inžavino	16	Mc	52.19N	42.31 E
Inzer	17	Hi	54.30N	56.28 E
Inzer	17	Hi	54.14N	57.34 E
Inzia	36	Cc	3.45S	17.57 E
Iō/Kazan-Rettō=Volcano Islands (EN)	21	Qg	25.00N	141.00 E
Ioánnina	6	Ih	39.40N	20.50 E
Ioanninon, Límni-	15	Dj	39.40N	20.53 E
Iokanga	7	Jb	68.03N	39.40 E
Iola	45	Ih	37.55N	95.24W
Iolotan	19	Gh	37.18N	62.21 E
Iona	9	Ge	56.19N	6.25W
Iona	36	Bf	16.52S	12.34 E
Ionava/Jonava	7	Fi	55.05N	24.17 E
Ion Corvin	15	Ke	44.07N	27.48 E
Ione	46	Eg	38.21N	120.56W
Ionia	44	Ed	42.59N	85.04W
Ionian Basin (EN)	5	Hh	36.00N	20.00 E
Ionian Islands (EN)=Iónioi Nísoi	5	Ih	38.30N	20.30 E
Ionian Sea (EN)=Ionio, Mar-	5	Hh	39.00N	19.00 E
Ionian Sea (EN)=Iónion Pélagos	5	Hh	39.00N	19.00 E
Ionio, Mar-=Ionian Sea (EN)	5	Hh	39.00N	19.00 E
Iónioi Nísoi [2]	15	Dk	38.40N	20.10 E
Iónioi Nísoi=Ionian Islands (EN)	5	Ih	38.30N	20.30 E
Iónion Pélagos=Ionian Sea (EN)	5	Hh	39.00N	19.00 E
Ioniškelis/Joniškélis	8	Ki	56.00N	24.14 E
Ioniškis/Joniškis	7	Fh	56.16N	23.37 E
Iony, Ostrov-	20	Je	56.15N	143.20 E
Iori	16	Oi	41.03N	46.27 E
Ios	15	Im	36.44N	25.18 E
Ios	15	Im	36.42N	25.20 E
Iō-Shima	28	Ki	31.51N	130.13 E
Iowa [2]	43	Ic	42.15N	93.15W
Iowa City	43	Ic	41.40N	91.32W
Iowa Falls	45	Je	42.31N	93.16W
Iowa Park	45	Gj	33.57N	98.40W
Iowa River	45	Kf	41.10N	91.02W
Iō-Yama	29a	Da	44.10N	145.10 E
Ipa	16	Fc	52.07N	29.12 E
Ipameri	54	Ig	17.43S	48.09W
Ipatovo	19	Ef	45.43N	42.53 E
Ipaumirim	54	Ke	6.47S	38.43W
Ipel'	10	Oi	47.49N	18.52 E
Ipiales	54	Cc	0.50N	77.37W
Ipiaú	54	Kf	14.08S	39.44W
Ipiranga	55	Gg	25.01S	50.35W
Ipiros [2]	15	Dj	39.30N	20.40 E
Ipiros=Epirus (EN)	15	Dj	39.30N	20.40 E
Ipiros=Epirus (EN)	5	Ih	39.30N	20.40 E
Ipixuma, Rio-	54	Fe	5.50S	63.00W
Ipixuna	54	De	7.34S	72.36W
Ipoh	22	Mi	4.35N	101.05 E
Ipoly	10	Oi	47.49N	18.52 E
Iporã	55	Ff	23.59S	53.37W
Iporá	54	Hg	16.28S	51.07W
Ippy	35	Cd	6.15N	21.12 E
Ipsala	24	Bb	40.55N	26.23 E
Ipsízonos Óros	15	Gi	40.28N	23.34 E
Ipswich [Austl.]	58	Gg	27.36S	152.46 E
Ipswich [Eng.-U.K.]	6	Ge	52.04N	1.10 E
Ipswich [S.D.-U.S.]	45	Gd	45.27N	99.02W
Ipu	54	Jd	4.20S	40.42W
Iput	16	Gc	52.26N	31.05 E
Iquique	53	Ih	20.13S	70.10W
Iquitos	53	If	3.50S	73.15W
Iraan	45	Fk	30.54N	101.54W
Ira Banda	35	Cd	5.57N	22.06 E
Irabu-Jima	27	Mg	24.50N	125.10 E
Iracoubo	54	Hb	5.29N	53.13W
Iraël	17	Gd	64.27N	55.08 E
Irago-Suidō	29	Ed	34.35N	136.55 E
Irago-Zaki	29	Ed	34.35N	137.01 E
Iráklia	15	Gh	41.10N	23.16 E
Iráklia	15	Im	36.50N	25.26 E
Iráklion	6	Ih	35.20N	25.08 E
Irān=Iran (EN) [1]	22	Hf	32.00N	53.00 E
Iran (EN)=Irān [1]	22	Hf	32.00N	53.00 E
Iran, Pegunungan-=Iran Mountains (EN)	21	Ni	2.05N	114.55 E
Iran, Plateau of- (EN)	21	Hf	32.00N	56.00 E
Irani, Serra do-	55	Fh	27.00S	52.12W
Iran Mountains (EN)=Iran, Pegunungan-	21	Ni	2.05N	114.55 E
Irānshahr	22	Ig	27.13N	60.41 E
Irapa	50	Eg	10.34N	62.35W
Irapuá, Arroio-	55	Fj	30.15S	53.10W
Irapuato	39	Ig	20.41N	101.28W
Iraq (EN)=Al 'Irāq [1]	22	Gf	33.00N	44.00 E
'Irāq al 'Arabi	24	Kg	31.50N	45.50 E
Irati	13	Kb	42.35N	1.16W
Irati	56	Jc	25.27S	50.39W
Irazú, Volcán-	38	Ki	9.59N	83.51W
Irbeni Väin	8	Ig	57.48N	22.05 E
Irbid	23	Ec	32.33N	35.51 E
Irbiktepe	15	Jh	41.00N	26.30 E
Irbit	17	Kh	57.42N	63.07 E
Irbit	19	Gd	57.41N	63.03 E
Irebu	36	Cc	0.37S	17.45 E
Irecê	54	Jf	11.18S	41.52W
Iregua	13	Jb	42.27N	2.24W
Ireland	5	Fe	53.00N	8.00W
Ireland/Éire [1]	6	Fe	53.00N	8.00W
Ireland Trough (EN)	5	Ed	55.00N	12.40W
Iren	17	Hh	57.27N	56.59 E
Ireng River	54	Gc	3.33N	59.51W
Irês Corações	54	Ih	21.42S	45.16W
Iretama	55	Fg	24.27S	52.02W
Irgiz	19	Gf	48.13N	62.08 E
Irgiz	19	Gf	48.36N	61.16 E
Irharrhar [Alg.]	30	Hf	28.00N	6.15 E
Irharrhar [Alg.]	32	Ie	21.01N	6.01 E
Irherm	32	Fc	30.04N	8.26W
Iri	28	Ig	35.56N	126.57 E
Iriba	31	Jg	15.07N	22.15 E
Irîgui	30	Gg	16.43N	5.30W
Iriklinski	16	Ud	51.39N	58.38 E
Iriklinskoje Vodohranilišče	16	Ud	51.45N	58.45 E
Iringa [3]	36	Gd	8.00S	35.30 E
Iringa	31	Ki	7.46S	35.42 E
Irinja, Gora-	20	Fe	58.20N	104.30 E
Iriomote Jima	27	Lg	24.20N	123.50 E
Iriona	49	Ef	15.57N	85.11W
Iriri, Rio-	52	Kf	3.52S	52.37W
Irish Sea	5	Fe	53.30N	5.20W
Irish Sea (EN)=Muir Eireann	5	Fe	53.30N	5.20W
Irituia	54	Id	1.46S	47.26W
Irkeštam	18	Ie	39.38N	73.55 E
Irkutsk	22	Md	52.16N	104.20 E
Irkutskaja Oblast [3]	20	Fe	56.00N	104.00 E
Irlir, Gora-	18	Dc	42.40N	63.30 E
Irminio	14	In	36.46N	14.36 E
Irnijärvi	7	Gd	65.36N	29.05 E
Iro, Lac-	35	Bc	10.06N	19.25 E
Iroise	11	Bf	48.15N	4.55W
Iron Gate (EN) = Portile de Fier	5	Ig	44.41N	22.31 E
Iron Knob	59	Hf	32.44S	137.08 E
Iron Mountain	43	Jb	45.49N	88.04W
Iron Mountains	9	Fg	54.15N	7.50W
Iron River [Mi.-U.S.]	43	Jb	46.05N	88.39W
Iron River [Wi.-U.S.]	45	Kc	46.34N	91.24W
Ironside Mountain	46	Fd	44.15N	118.08W
Ironton [Mo.-U.S.]	45	Kh	37.36N	90.38W
Ironton [Oh.-U.S.]	44	Ff	38.32N	82.40W
Ironwood	43	Ib	46.27N	90.10W
Iroquois Falls	42	Jg	48.46N	80.41W
Irō-Zaki	28	Og	34.35N	138.55 E

Index Symbols

[1] Independent Nation
[2] State, Region
[3] District, County
[4] Municipality
[5] Colony, Dependency
Continent
Physical Region
Historical or Cultural Region
Mount, Mountain
Volcano
Hill
Mountains, Mountain Range
Hills, Escarpment
Plateau, Upland
Pass, Gap
Plain, Lowland
Delta
Salt Flat
Valley, Canyon
Crater, Cave
Karst Features
Depression
Polder
Desert, Dunes
Forest, Woods
Heath, Steppe
Oasis
Cape, Point
Coast, Beach
Cliff
Peninsula
Isthmus
Sandbank
Island
Atoll
Rock, Reef
Islands, Archipelago
Rocks, Reefs
Coral Reef
Well, Spring
Geyser
River, Stream
Waterfall Rapids
River Mouth, Estuary
Lake
Salt Lake
Intermittent Lake
Reservoir
Swamp, Pond
Canal
Glacier
Ice Shelf, Pack Ice
Ocean
Sea
Gulf, Bay
Strait, Fjord
Lagoon
Bank
Seamount
Tablemount
Ridge
Shelf
Basin
Escarpment, Sea Scarp
Fracture
Trench, Abyss
National Park, Reserve
Point of Interest
Recreation Site
Cave, Cavern
Historic Site
Ruins
Wall, Walls
Church, Abbey
Temple
Scientific Station
Airport
Port
Lighthouse
Mine
Tunnel
Dam, Bridge

Irpen	19	De	50.31N	30.16 E
Irpinia	14	Ij	40.55N	15.00 E
Irrawaddy [3]	25	Ie	17.00N	95.00 E
Irrawaddy	21	Lh	15.50N	95.06 E
Irrawaddy, Mouths of the- (EN)	21	Lh	16.30N	95.00 E
Irrel	12	Ie	49.51N	6.28 E
Irsâva	10	Th	48.15N	23.05 E
Irsina	14	Kj	40.45N	16.14 E
Irtek	16	Rd	51.29N	52.42 E
Irthlingborough	12	Bb	52.19N	0.36W
Irtyš	21	Ic	61.04N	68.52 E
Irtyšsk	19	He	53.21N	75.27 E
Irumu	36	Eb	1.27N	29.52 E
Irún	13	Ka	43.21N	1.47W
Irurzun	13	Kb	42.55N	1.50W
Irves Šaurums	8	Ig	57.48N	22.05 E
Irvine	9	If	55.37N	4.40W
Irving	45	Hj	32.49N	96.56W
Is, Jabal-	35	Fa	21.49N	35.39 E
Isa, Ra's-	33	Hf	15.11N	42.39 E
Isabel	45	Fd	45.24N	101.26W
Isabel, Bahia-	54a	Ab	0.38S	91.25W
Isabela	51a	Ab	18.31N	67.07W
Isabela → Basilan City	26	He	6.42N	121.58 E
Isabela, Cabo-	49	Ld	19.56N	71.01W
Isabela, Isla- [Ec.]	52	Gf	0.30S	91.06W
Isabela, Isla- [Mex.]	48	Gg	21.51N	105.55W
Isabella, Cordillera-	47	Gf	13.30N	85.30W
Isabel Segunda	49	Od	18.09N	65.27W
Isabey	15	Ml	38.00N	29.24 E
Isaccea	15	Ld	45.16N	28.28 E
Isachsen	39	Ib	78.50N	103.30W
Isafjörour	6	Db	66.03N	23.09W
Isahaya	28	Jh	32.50N	130.03 E
Isakov, Seamount (EN)	57	Ga	31.35N	151.07 E
Isaku/Iisaku	8	Le	59.14N	27.41 E
Isana, Rio-	54	Ec	0.26N	67.19W
Isandja	36	Dc	2.59S	22.00 E
Isanga	36	Dc	1.26S	22.18 E
Isangi	36	Db	0.46N	24.15 E
Isanlu Makutu	34	Gd	8.16N	5.48 E
Isaouane-n-Irrarraren	32	Id	27.15N	8.00 E
Isaouane-n-Tifernine	32	Id	27.00N	7.30 E
Isar	10	Ih	48.49N	12.58 E
Isarco/Eisack	14	Fd	46.27N	11.18 E
Isarco, Valle-/Eisacktal	14	Fd	46.45N	11.35 E
Isbergues	12	Ed	50.37N	2.27 E
Iscayachi	54	Eh	21.31S	65.03W
Ischgl	14	Ec	47.01N	10.17 E
Ischia	14	Hj	40.45N	13.55 E
Ischia	14	Hj	40.44N	13.57 E
Ise	27	Oe	34.29N	136.42 E
Isefjord	8	Di	55.50N	11.50 E
Išejevka	7	Li	54.28N	48.17 E
Isen	10	Ih	48.20N	12.45 E
Isenach	12	Ke	49.38N	8.28 E
Isen-Zaki	29b	Bb	27.39N	128.55 E
Iseo, Lago d'-	14	Ee	45.45N	10.05 E
Iseran, Col de l'-	11	Ni	45.25N	7.02 E
Isère	11	Kj	44.59N	4.51 E
Isère [3]	11	Li	45.10N	5.50 E
Iserit, Gora-	17	If	61.08N	59.10 E
Iserlohn	10	De	51.22N	7.42 E
Isernia	14	Ii	41.36N	14.14 E
Isesaki	29	Fc	36.19N	139.12 E
Iset	21	Id	56.36N	66.24 E
Isetskoje	17	Lh	56.29N	65.21 E
Ise-Wan	28	Ng	34.40N	136.42 E
Iseyin	34	Fd	7.58N	3.36 E
Isfahan (EN)=Eşfahān	22	Hf	32.40N	51.38 E
Isfana	18	Ge	39.51N	69.32 E
Isfara	18	Hd	40.07N	70.38 E
Isfendiyar Dağları	23	Da	41.45N	34.10 E
Isfjorden	41	Nc	78.15N	15.00 E
Isha Baydabo	31	Lh	3.04N	43.48 E
Ishasha River	36	Ec	0.50S	29.40 E
Ishavet=Arctic Ocean (EN)	67	Be	85.00N	170.00 E
Isherton	54	Gc	2.19N	59.22W
Ishigaki	27	Lg	24.20N	124.09 E
Ishikari	29a	Bb	43.13N	141.18 E
Ishikari-Dake	29a	Cb	43.33N	143.00 E
Ishikari-Gawa	29a	Bb	43.15N	141.20 E
Ishikari-Heiya	29a	Bb	43.00N	141.40 E
Ishikari-Wan	27	Pc	43.25N	141.00 E
Ishikawa [Jap.]	27	Mf	26.27N	127.50 E
Ishikawa [Jap.]	29	Gc	37.09N	140.27 E
Ishikawa Ken [2]	28	Nf	36.35N	136.40 E
Ishim Steppe (EN)= Išimskaja Step	21	Id	55.00N	67.30 E
Ishinomaki	27	Pd	38.25N	141.18 E
Ishinomaki-Wan	29	Gb	38.20N	141.15 E
Ishioka	28	Pf	36.11N	140.16 E
Ishitate-San	29	De	33.44N	134.03 E
Ishizuchi-Yama	29	Ce	33.45N	133.05 E
Ishodnaja, Gora-	20	Nd	64.50N	173.26W
Ishpeming	44	Db	46.30N	87.40W
Isidro Alves	55	Ee	20.09S	55.12W
Isigny-sur-Mer	11	Ee	49.19N	1.06W
Isii	29	Dd	34.04N	134.26 E
Işıklar Dağı	24	Bb	40.50N	27.05 E
Işıkli	15	Mk	38.19N	29.51 E
Isikli Göl	15	Mk	38.14N	29.55 E
Isili	14	Dk	39.44N	9.06 E
Isilkul	19	He	54.55N	71.16 E
Išim	22	Id	56.09N	69.27 E
Išim	21	Jd	57.45N	71.12 E
Išimbaj	19	Fe	53.28N	56.02 E
Išimskaja Step=Ishim Steppe (EN)	21	Id	55.00N	67.30 E
Isinga	20	Gf	52.55N	112.00 E
Isiolo	36	Gb	0.21N	37.35 E
Isiro	31	Jh	2.48N	27.41 E
Isisford	59	Id	24.16S	144.26 E
Isjangulovo	17	Hj	52.12N	56.36 E
Iskandar	18	Gd	41.35N	69.43 E
Iskăr	15	Hf	43.44N	24.27 E
Iskăr, Jazovir-	15	Gg	42.25N	23.35 E
Iškašim	19	Hh	36.44N	71.39 E
İskenderun=Alexandretta (EN)	22	Ff	36.37N	36.07 E
İskenderun Körfezi= Alexandretta, Gulf of- (EN)	23	Eb	36.30N	35.40 E
İskilip	24	Fb	40.45N	34.29 E
Iski-Naukat	18	Id	40.14N	72.41 E
Iskininski	18	Rf	47.13N	52.36 E
Iskitim	20	Df	54.38N	83.18 E
Iskushuban	35	Ic	10.13N	50.14 E
Iskut	42	Ee	56.45N	131.48W
Isla-Cristina	13	Eg	37.12N	7.19W
Íslâhiye	24	Gd	37.26N	36.41 E
Islāmābād	22	Jf	33.42N	73.10 E
Islāmābād → Anantnāg	25	Fb	33.44N	75.09 E
Isla Mujeres	48	Pg	21.12N	86.43W
Island=Iceland (EN) [1]	6	Eb	65.00N	18.00W
Island=Iceland (EN)	5	Eb	65.00N	18.00W
Island Harbour	51b	Ab	18.16N	63.02W
Island Lagoon	59	Hf	31.30S	136.40 E
Island Lake	42	If	53.45N	94.30W
Island Lake	42	If	53.58N	94.46W
Island Pond	44	Lc	44.50N	71.53W
Islands, Bay of - [Can.]	42	Lg	49.10N	58.15W
Islands, Bay of- [N.Z.]	62	Fa	35.10S	174.10 E
Islao, Massif de l'-	30	Lk	22.30S	45.20 E
Islas de la Bahia [3]	49	De	16.20N	86.30W
Islay	5	Fd	55.46N	6.10W
Islaz	15	Hf	43.44N	24.45 E
Isle	11	Fj	44.55N	0.15W
Isle of Man [5]	9	Ig	54.15N	4.30W
Isle of Wight [3]	9	Lk	50.40N	1.15W
Isleta	45	Ci	34.55N	106.42W
Isle-Verte	44	Ma	48.01N	69.22W
Ismael Cortinas	55	Dk	33.56S	57.08W
Ismailia (EN)=Al Ismā'īlīyah	33	Fc	30.35N	32.16 E
Ismailly	16	Pi	40.47N	48.13 E
Ismantorps Borg	8	Gh	56.45N	16.40 E
Isnā	31	Kf	25.18N	32.33 E
Isny im Allgäu	10	Gi	47.42N	10.02 E
Isojärvi	8	Ic	61.45N	21.45 E
Isojoki	7	Ee	62.07N	21.58 E
Isojoki/Storå	7	Ee	62.07N	21.58 E
Isoka	36	Fe	10.08S	32.38 E
Isola del Liri	14	Hi	41.41N	13.34 E
Isola di Capo Rizzuto	14	Ll	38.58N	17.05 E
Isonzo	14	He	45.43N	13.33 E
Isonzo (EN)=Soča	14	He	45.43N	13.33 E
Isosyöte	7	Gd	65.37N	27.35 E
Isparta	23	Db	37.46N	30.33 E
Isperih	15	Jf	43.43N	26.50 E
Ispica	14	In	36.47N	14.55 E
Ispir	24	Ib	40.29N	41.00 E
Ispiriz Dağı	24	Jc	38.03N	43.55 E
Israel (EN)=Yisra'el [1]	22	Ff	31.30N	35.00 E
Isratu	35	Fb	16.20N	39.55 E
Issa	8	Mh	56.55N	28.50 E
Issano	54	Gb	5.49N	59.25W
Issaran, Ra's-	24	Eh	28.50N	32.56 E
Issel	10	Cd	52.00N	6.10 E
Isser	13	Ph	36.51N	3.40 E
Issia [3]	34	Dd	6.30N	6.35W
Issia	34	Dd	6.29N	6.35W
Issoire	11	Ji	45.33N	3.15 E
Issoudun	11	Hh	46.57N	2.00 E
Issyk	18	Kc	43.20N	77.28 E
Issyk-Kul, Ozero-	21	Je	42.25N	77.15 E
Issyk-Kulskaja Oblast [3]	19	Hg	42.10N	78.00 E
Ist	14	If	44.17N	14.47 E
İstanbul	22	Ee	41.01N	28.58 E
İstanbul-Bakırköy	15	Li	40.59N	28.52 E
İstanbul-Beyoğlu	15	Lh	41.02N	28.59 E
İstanbul Boğazi=Bosporus (EN)	5	Ig	41.00N	29.00 E
İstanbul-Kadıköy	15	Mi	40.59N	29.01 E
Isteren	8	Db	62.00N	11.50 E
Istgāh-e Eqbālīyeh	24	Ne	35.50N	50.45 E
Isthilart	55	Dj	31.11S	57.58W
Istiaia	15	Gk	38.57N	23.09 E
Istisu	16	Nj	39.57N	46.00 E
Istmina	54	Cb	5.09N	76.42W
Isto, Mount-	38	Ec	69.12N	143.48W
Istok	15	Dg	42.47N	20.29 E
Istokpoga, Lake-	44	Gl	27.22N	81.17W
Istra = Istria (EN)	5	Hf	45.00N	14.00 E
Istres	11	Kk	43.31N	4.59 E
Istria	15	Le	44.34N	28.43 E
Istria (EN) = Istra	5	Hf	45.00N	14.00 E
Isulan	26	He	7.02N	124.29 E
Itabaiana	54	Kf	10.41S	37.26W
Itabaianinha	54	Kf	11.16S	37.47W
Itaberá	55	Hf	23.51S	49.09W
Itaberaba	54	Jf	12.32S	40.18W
Itaberaí	55	Ig	16.02S	49.48W
Itabira	54	Jg	19.37S	43.13W
Itabirito	55	Ke	20.15S	43.48W
Itabuna	53	Mg	14.48S	39.16W
Itacaiúna, Rio-	54	Ie	5.21S	49.08W
Itacarambi	55	Jb	15.01S	44.03W
Itacoatiara	53	Kf	3.08S	58.25W
Itacolomi, Pico do-	55	Ke	20.26S	43.29W
Itacuai, Rio-	54	Dd	4.20S	70.12W
Itacumbi	55	Ei	28.44S	55.08W
Itacurubí del Rosario	55	Dg	24.29S	56.41W
Itaguari, Rio-	55	Jb	14.11S	44.40W
Itaguaru	55	Hb	15.44S	49.37W
Itaguí	54	Cb	6.12N	75.40W
Itaimbèzinho	55	Gi	28.38S	50.34W
Itaituba	53	Kf	4.17S	55.59W
Itajai	53	Lh	26.53S	48.39W
Itajai Açu, Rio-	55	Hh	26.54S	48.41W
Itajubá	54	Ih	22.26S	45.27W
Itajuípe	54	Kf	14.41S	39.22W
Itaka	20	Gf	53.54N	118.42 E
Italia = Italy (EN) [1]	6	Hg	42.50N	12.50 E
Itálica	13	Fg	37.25N	6.05W
Italy (EN) = Italia [1]	6	Hg	42.50N	12.50 E
Itambacuri	54	Jg	18.01S	41.42W
Itambé, Pico de-	52	Lg	18.23S	43.21W
Itämeri=Baltic, Sea (EN)	5	Hd	57.00N	19.00 E
Itampolo	37	Gd	24.41S	43.57 E
Itanagar	25	Ic	26.57N	93.15 E
Itanará, Rio-	55	Eg	24.00S	55.53W
Itanhaém	56	Kb	24.11S	46.47W
Itano	29	Dd	34.09N	134.28 E
Itapaci	55	Hb	14.57S	49.34W
Itapagé	54	Kd	3.41S	39.34W
Itapajipe	55	Hd	19.54S	49.22W
Itaparanã, Rio-	54	Fe	5.47S	63.03W
Itapebi	54	Kg	15.56S	39.32W
Itapecerica	55	Je	20.28S	45.07W
Itapecuru-Mirim	54	Jd	3.24S	44.20W
Itapemirim	54	Jh	21.01S	40.50W
Itaperina, Pointe-	30	Lk	24.59S	47.06 E
Itaperuna	54	Jh	21.12S	41.54W
Itapetinga	54	Jg	15.15S	40.15W
Itapetininga	56	Kb	23.36S	48.03W
Itapetininga, Rio-	55	Hf	23.35S	48.27W
Itapeva	55	Hf	23.58S	48.52W
Itapeva, Lagoa-	55	Hi	29.30S	49.55W
Itapicuru, Rio- [Braz.]	54	Kf	11.47S	37.32W
Itapicuru, Rio- [Braz.]	52	Lf	2.52S	44.12W
Itapipoca	54	Kd	3.31S	39.33W
Itapiranga [Braz.]	54	Gd	2.45S	58.01W
Itapiranga [Braz.]	55	Fh	27.08S	53.43W
Itapirapuã, Pico-	55	Hg	24.17S	49.12W
Itápolis	55	He	21.35S	48.46W
Itaporã	55	Ef	22.01S	54.54W
Itaporanga [Braz.]	55	Hf	23.42S	49.29W
Itaporanga [Braz.]	54	Ke	7.18S	38.10W
Itapúa [3]	55	Eh	26.50S	55.50W
Itapuã	55	Gj	30.16S	51.01W
Itapuranga	55	Ig	15.35S	49.59W
Itaqui	56	Ic	29.08S	56.33W
Itaquyry	55	Eg	24.56S	55.13W
Itararé	55	Hg	24.07S	49.20W
Itararé, Rio-	55	Hf	23.10S	49.42W
Itārsi	25	Fd	22.37N	77.45 E
Itarumã	55	Gd	18.42S	51.25W
Itati	55	Ch	27.16S	58.15W
Itatinga	55	Hf	23.07S	48.36W
Itatski	20	De	56.07N	89.20 E
Itaum	55	Ef	22.00S	55.20W
Itaúna	54	Jh	20.04S	44.34W
Itaya-Tōge	29	Gc	37.50N	140.13 E
Itbāy	30	Kf	22.00N	35.30 E
Itbayat	26	Hb	20.46N	121.50 E
Itchen	12	Ad	50.57N	1.22W
Ite	54	Dg	17.50S	70.58W
Itéa	15	Fk	38.26N	22.25 E
Ithaca	43	Lc	42.26N	76.30W
Ithaca (EN)=Itháki	15	Dk	38.24N	20.40 E
Itháki	15	Dk	38.22N	20.43 E
Itháki = Ithaca (EN)	15	Dk	38.24N	20.40 E
Ith Hils	10	Fd	52.05N	9.35 E
Ithnayn, Harrat-	24	Ii	26.40N	40.10 E
Itigi	36	Fd	5.42S	34.29 E
Itimbiri	30	Jh	2.02N	22.44 E
Itiopya=Ethiopia (EN) [1]	31	Kh	9.00N	39.00 E
Itiquira	54	Hg	17.05S	54.56W
Itiquira, Rio-	52	Kg	17.18S	56.44W
Itirapina	55	If	22.15S	47.49W
Itiúba	54	Kf	10.43S	39.51W
Itivdleq	41	Ge	66.38N	53.51W
Itō	28	Og	34.58N	139.05 E
Itoigawa	28	Nf	37.02N	137.51 E
Itoko	36	Dc	1.00S	21.45 E
Itoman	29b	Ab	26.07N	127.40 E
Iton	11	Hf	49.09N	1.12 E
Itremo, Massif de l'-	37	Hd	20.45S	46.30 E
Itsā	24	Dh	29.15N	30.48 E
Itsukaichi	29	Cd	34.22N	132.22 E
Itsuki	29	Be	32.24N	130.50 E
Ittiri	14	Cj	40.36N	8.34 E
Itu [Braz.]	55	If	23.16S	47.19W
Itu [Nig.]	34	Gd	5.12N	7.59 E
Itu, Rio-	55	Ei	29.25S	55.51W
Itui, Rio-	54	Dd	4.38S	70.19W
Ituiutaba	54	Ig	18.58S	49.28W
Itula	36	Ec	3.29S	27.52 E
Itumbiara	54	Ig	18.25S	49.13W
Itumkale	16	Nh	42.43N	45.35 E
Ituna	46	Na	51.10N	103.30W
Itungi Port	36	Fd	9.35S	33.56 E
Itupiranga	54	Ie	5.09S	49.20W
Iturama	55	Gd	19.44S	50.11W
Iturbide	48	Oh	19.40N	89.37W
Ituri	30	Jh	1.40N	27.01 E
Iturregui	55	Bm	36.50S	61.08W
Iturup, Ostrov-	21	Qe	44.54N	147.30 E
Iturup, Ostrov-/Etorofu Tō	21	Qe	44.54N	147.30 E
Itutinga	55	Je	21.18S	44.40W
Ituverava	56	Kb	20.20S	47.47W
Ituxi, Rio-	52	Jf	7.18S	64.51W
Ituzaingó	55	Dh	27.36S	56.41W
Itz	10	Gg	49.58N	10.52 E
Itzehoe	10	Fc	53.55N	9.31 E
Ivacevići	16	Dc	52.43N	25.21 E
Ivai	55	Gg	25.01S	50.52W
Ivai, Rio- [Braz.]	55	Fi	29.08S	53.16W
Ivai, Rio- [Braz.]	52	Kh	23.18S	53.42W
Ivaiporã	55	Gg	24.15S	51.45W
Ivajlovgrad	15	Jh	41.32N	26.08 E
Ivakoany, Massif de l'-	37	Hd	23.50S	46.25 E
Ivalojoki	7	Gc	68.43N	27.36 E
Ivančice	10	Mg	49.06N	16.22 E
Ivangorod	7	Gg	59.23N	28.20 E
Ivangrad	15	Cg	42.51N	19.52 E
Ivanhoe	58	Fh	32.54S	144.18 E
Ivanić-Grad	14	Ke	45.42N	16.24 E
Ivaniči	10	Uf	50.38N	24.24 E
Ivanjica	15	Df	43.35N	20.14 E
Ivanjska	14	Lf	44.55N	17.04 E
Ivankov	16	Fd	50.57N	29.58 E
Ivano-Frankovo	10	Tg	49.52N	23.46 E
Ivano-Frankovsk	6	If	48.55N	24.43 E
Ivano-Frankovskaja Oblast [3]	19	Cf	48.40N	24.40 E
Ivanovka [R.S.F.S.R.]	20	Hf	50.18N	127.59 E
Ivanovka [Ukr.-U.S.S.R.]	16	Gf	46.57N	30.28 E
Ivanovo [Bye.-U.S.S.R.]	16	Dc	52.10N	25.32 E
Ivanovo [R.S.F.S.R.]	6	Kd	57.00N	40.59 E
Ivanovskaja Oblast [3]	19	Ed	57.00N	41.50 E
Ivanovskoje	8	Me	59.12N	28.59 E
Ivanšćica	14	Kd	46.11N	16.10 E
Ivdel	19	Gc	60.42N	60.28 E
Ivenec	8	Lk	53.55N	26.49 E
Ivigtut	41	Hf	61.15N	48.00W
Ivindo	30	Ii	0.09S	12.09 E
Ivinheima	55	Ff	22.10S	53.37W
Ivinheima, Rio-	54	Hh	23.14S	53.42W
Ivinski razliv	7	If	61.10N	35.00 E
Iviza (EN)=Eivissa/Ibiza	5	Gh	39.00N	1.25 E
Iviza (EN)=Ibiza/Eivissa	5	Gh	39.00N	1.25 E
Ivje	10	Vc	53.55N	25.51 E
Ivohibe	37	Hd	22.29S	46.52 E
Ivoire, Côte d'-=Ivory Coast (EN)	30	Gh	5.00N	5.00W
Ivolândia	55	Gc	16.34S	50.51W
Ivory Coast (EN)=Côte d'Ivoire [1]	31	Gh	8.00N	5.00W
Ivory Coast (EN)=Ivoire, Côte d'-	30	Gh	5.00N	5.00W
Ivösjön	8	Fh	56.05N	14.25 E
Ivrea	14	Be	45.28N	7.52 E
Ivrindi	15	Kj	39.34N	27.29 E
Ivry-la-Bataille	12	Df	48.53N	1.28 E
Ivry-sur-Seine	12	Ef	48.49N	2.23 E
Ivujivik	39	Lc	62.25N	77.54W
Iwai-Shima	29	Be	33.47N	131.58 E
Iwaizumi	28	Pe	39.50N	141.48 E
Iwaki	22	Qf	36.55N	140.48 E
Iwaki-Gawa	29	Ga	41.01N	140.22 E
Iwaki-Hisanohama	29	Gc	37.09N	140.59 E
Iwaki-Jōban	29	Gc	37.02N	140.50 E
Iwaki-Kawamae	29	Gc	37.12N	140.45 E
Iwaki-Miwa	29	Gc	37.09N	140.42 E
Iwaki-Nakoso	29	Gc	36.56N	140.48 E
Iwaki-Onahama	29	Gc	36.57N	140.53 E
Iwaki-San	29	Ga	40.40N	140.20 E
Iwaki-Taira	29	Gc	37.05N	140.50 E
Iwaki-Uchigō	29	Gc	37.04N	140.50 E
Iwaki-Yoshima	29	Gc	37.05N	140.50 E
Iwaki-Yotsukura	29	Gc	37.07N	140.58 E
Iwakuni	27	Ne	34.09N	132.11 E
Iwami	29	Dd	35.35N	134.20 E
Iwami-Kōgen	29	Cd	35.00N	132.30 E
Iwamizawa	27	Pc	43.12N	141.46 E
Iwanai	28	Pc	42.58N	140.30 E
Iwanuma	29	Gb	38.07N	140.52 E
Iwase	29	Gc	36.21N	140.06 E
Iwasuge-Yama	29	Fc	36.44N	138.32 E
Iwata	29	Ed	34.42N	137.48 E
Iwate	28	Pe	39.30N	141.30 E
Iwate Ken [2]	28	Pe	39.30N	141.15 E
Iwate San	28	Pe	39.49N	141.26 E
Iwo	34	Fd	7.38N	4.11 E
Iwŏn	27	Mc	40.19N	128.37 E
Iwuy	12	Fd	50.14N	3.19 E
Ixiamas	54	Ef	13.45S	68.09W
Ixmiquilpan	48	Jg	20.29N	99.14W
Ixopo	37	Ef	30.08S	30.00 E
Ixtapa, Punta-	48	Ii	17.39N	101.40W
Ixtepec	47	Ee	16.34N	95.06W
Ixtlahuacán del Rio	48	Hg	20.52N	103.15W
Ixtlán del Rio	47	Dd	21.02N	104.22W
Iyah	35	Hd	9.00N	49.38 E
Iyo	28	Lh	33.46N	132.42 E
Iyo-mishima	29	Ce	33.58N	133.33 E
Iyo-Nada	29	Ce	33.40N	132.15 E
Iž	7	Mh	56.00N	52.41 E
Iž	14	Jf	44.03N	15.06 E
Izabal [3]	49	Cf	15.30N	89.00W
Izabal, Lago de-	47	Ge	15.30N	89.10W
Izad Khvāst	24	Og	31.31N	52.07 E
Izamal	47	Gd	20.56N	89.01W
Izamal	48	Og	20.56N	89.01W
Izapa	47	Ff	14.55N	92.10W
'Izbat al Jājah	24	Dj	24.48N	30.35 E
'Izbat Dush	24	Dj	24.34N	30.42 E
Izberbaš	19	Eg	42.33N	47.52 E
Izbiceni	15	Hf	43.50N	24.39 E
Izborsk	8	Mg	57.39N	28.01 E
Izegem	12	Fd	50.55N	3.12 E
Izeh	24	Mg	31.50N	49.50 E
Izena-Shima	29b	Ab	26.56N	127.56 E
Iževsk	6	Ld	56.51N	53.14 E
Izjaslav	16	Ed	50.09N	26.51 E
Izjum	19	Df	49.12N	37.17 E
Izki	23	Ie	22.57N	57.49 E
Izma	5	Lb	65.19N	52.54 E
Izma	17	Fd	65.02N	53.55 E
Izmail	6	If	45.21N	28.50 E
İzmir=Smyrna (EN)	22	Ef	38.25N	27.09 E
Izmir, Gulf of- (EN)=İzmir Körfezi	24	Bc	38.30N	26.50 E
İzmir-Bornova	24	Bc	38.27N	27.14 E
İzmir Körfezi=Izmir, Gulf of- (EN)	24	Bc	38.30N	26.50 E
İzmit	22	Ee	40.46N	29.55 E
İzmit Körfezi	24	Cb	40.45N	29.35 E
İzmor	24	Ab	40.11N	25.55 E
Iznajar, Embalse de-	13	Hg	37.15N	4.30W
Iznalloz	13	Ig	37.23N	3.31W
İznik	24	Cb	40.26N	29.43 E
İznik Gölü	23	Ca	40.26N	29.30 E
Izobilny	16	Lg	45.19N	41.42 E
Izola	14	He	45.32N	13.40 E
Izōrskaja Vozvyšennost	8	Me	59.35N	29.30 E
Izozog, Bañados del-	54	Fg	18.50S	62.10W
Izra'	24	Gf	32.51N	36.15 E
Izsák	10	Pj	46.48N	19.22 E
Iztočni Rodopi	15	Ih	41.44N	25.31 E
Izúcar de Matamoros	48	Jh	18.36N	98.28W
Izu-Hantō	28	Og	34.55N	138.55 E
Izuhara	28	Jg	34.12N	129.17 E
Izu Islands (EN)=Izu-shotō	21	Pf	32.00N	140.00 E
Izumi [Jap.]	28	Kh	32.05N	130.22 E
Izumi [Jap.]	29	Dd	34.29N	135.26 E
Izumi [Jap.]	29	Gb	38.19N	140.51 E
Izumi-sano	29	Dd	34.24N	135.18 E
Izumo	28	Lg	35.22N	132.46 E
Izu-Shotō=Izu Islands (EN)	21	Pf	32.00N	140.00 E
Izvesti CIK, Ostrova-= Izvestiya Tsik Islands (EN)	20	Da	75.55N	82.30 E
Izvestiya Tsik Islands (EN)= Izvesti CIK, Ostrova-	20	Da	75.55N	82.30 E

J

Jaala	8	Lc	61.03N	26.29 E
Jaama/Jama	8	Lf	58.59N	27.45 E
Jääsjärvi	8	Lc	61.35N	26.05 E
Jaba	24	Qe	35.55N	56.35 E
Jabal, Bahr al-=Mountain Nile (EN)	30	Kh	9.30N	30.30 E
Jabal Abū Rujmayn	24	Ge	34.50N	37.56 E
Jabal al Awliyā'	35	Eb	15.14N	32.30 E
Jabal az Zannah	24	Oj	24.11N	52.38 E
Jabalón	13	Hf	38.53N	4.05W
Jabalpur	22	Jg	23.10N	79.57 E
Jabal Şabāyā	33	Hf	18.35N	41.03 E
Jabālyah	24	Fg	31.32N	34.29 E
Jabal Zuqar, Jazīrat-	33	Hg	14.00N	42.45 E
Jabbārah	33	Hf	19.27N	40.03 E
Jabbeke	12	Fc	51.11N	3.05 E
Jabjabah, Wādī-	35	Ea	22.37N	33.17 E
Jablah	24	Fe	35.21N	35.55 E
Jablanac	14	If	44.43N	14.53 E
Jablanica	15	Dh	41.15N	20.30 E
Jablanica [Bul.]	15	Hf	43.01N	24.06 E
Jablanica [Yugo.]	14	Lg	43.39N	17.45 E
Jabločny	20	Jg	47.09N	142.03 E
Jablonec nad Nisou	10	Lf	50.44N	15.10 E
Jablonicki, Pereval-	5	If	48.18N	24.28 E
Jablonovo	20	Gf	51.51N	112.50 E
Jablonovy Hrebet= Yablonovy Range (EN)	21	Nd	53.30N	115.00 E
Jablunkovský průsmyk	10	Og	49.31N	18.45 E
Jaboatão	54	Ke	8.07S	35.01W
Jaboti	55	De	20.48S	56.23W
Jabrīn	24	Ni	27.51N	51.26 E
Jabuka	14	Jg	43.05N	15.28 E
Jabung, Tanjung-	26	Dg	1.01S	104.22 E
Jabuticabal	56	Kb	21.16S	48.19W
Jabuticatubas	55	Kd	19.30S	43.45W
Jaca	13	Lb	42.34N	0.33W
Jacaltenango	49	Bf	15.40N	91.44W
Jacaré, Rio-	55	Je	21.03S	45.16W
Jacarei	55	Jf	23.19S	45.58W
Jacarezinho	56	Kb	23.09S	49.59W
Jáchal, Rio-	52	Ji	30.44S	68.08W
Jaciara [Braz.]	55	Ib	14.12S	46.41W
Jaciara [Braz.]	55	Eb	15.59S	54.57W
Jackman	44	Lc	45.38N	70.16W
Jack Mountain	46	Eb	48.47N	120.57W
Jackpot	46	Hf	41.59N	114.09W
Jacksboro	45	Gj	33.13N	98.10W
Jacks Mountain	44	Ie	40.45N	77.30W
Jackson [Al.-U.S.]	44	Dj	31.31N	87.53W
Jackson [Bar.]	51q	Ab	13.10N	59.43W
Jackson [Ky.-U.S.]	44	Fg	37.33N	83.23W
Jackson [Mi.-U.S.]	43	Kc	42.15N	84.24W
Jackson [Mn.-U.S.]	45	Ie	43.37N	94.59W
Jackson [Mo.-U.S.]	45	Lh	37.23N	89.40W
Jackson [Ms.-U.S.]	39	Jf	32.18N	90.12W
Jackson [Oh.-U.S.]	44	Ff	39.03N	82.40W
Jackson [Tn.-U.S.]	43	Jd	35.37N	88.49W
Jackson [Wy.-U.S.]	46	Je	43.29N	110.38W
Jackson, Cape-	62	Fd	40.59S	174.19 E
Jackson, Mount- [Ant.]	66	Qf	71.23S	63.22W
Jackson, Mount- [Austl.]	59	Df	30.15S	119.16 E
Jackson Bay	62	Ce	43.55S	168.40 E
Jackson Head	62	Ce	43.58S	168.37 E
Jackson Lake	46	Je	43.55N	110.40W
Jacksonville [Ar.-U.S.]	45	Ji	34.52N	92.07W
Jacksonville [Fl.-U.S.]	39	Kf	30.20N	81.40W
Jacksonville [Il.-U.S.]	45	Kg	39.44N	90.14W
Jacksonville [N.C.-U.S.]	43	Le	34.45N	77.26W
Jacksonville [Tx.-U.S.]	43	He	31.58N	95.17W
Jacksonville Beach	43	Ke	30.18N	81.24W
Jacmel	47	Je	18.14N	72.32W
Jacobābād	25	Dc	28.17N	68.26 E
Jacobina	54	Jf	11.11S	40.31W
Jacob Lake	46	Ih	36.45N	112.13W
Jacobs	45	La	50.15N	89.46W
Jacona de Plancarte	48	Hh	19.57N	102.16W
Jacques-Cartier, Détroit de -	42	Lg	50.00N	63.30W
Jacques-Cartier, Mont -	42	Kg	48.58N	65.57W
Jacuba, Rio-	55	Fd	18.25S	52.28W
Jacuí, Rio-	52	Ki	30.02S	51.15W
Jacuí-Mirim, Rio-	55	Fi	28.51S	53.07W
Jacundá	54	Id	4.33S	49.28W
Jacundá, Rio-	54	Hd	1.57S	50.26W
Jacupiranga	56	Kb	24.42S	48.00W
Jada	34	Hd	8.46N	12.09 E
Jadal	34	Fb	18.37N	5.00 E

Index Symbols

[1] Independent Nation
[2] State, Region
[3] District, County
[4] Municipality
[5] Colony, Dependency
Continent
Physical Region

Historical or Cultural Region
Mount, Mountain
Volcano
Hill
Mountains, Mountain Range
Hills, Escarpment
Plateau, Upland

Pass, Gap
Plain, Lowland
Delta
Salt Flat
Valley, Canyon
Crater, Cave
Karst Features

Depression
Polder
Desert, Dunes
Forest, Woods
Heath, Steppe
Oasis
Cape, Point

Coast, Beach
Cliff
Peninsula
Isthmus
Sandbank
Island
Atoll

Rock, Reef
Islands, Archipelago
Rocks, Reefs
Coral Reef
Well, Spring
Geyser
River, Stream

Waterfall Rapids
River Mouth, Estuary
Lake
Salt Lake
Intermittent Lake
Reservoir
Swamp, Pond

Canal
Glacier
Ice Shelf, Pack Ice
Ocean
Sea
Gulf, Bay
Strait, Fjord

Lagoon
Bank
Seamount
Tablemount
Ridge
Shelf
Basin

Escarpment, Sea Scarp
Fracture
Trench, Abyss
National Park, Reserve
Point of Interest
Recreation Site
Cave, Cavern

Historic Site
Ruins
Wall, Walls
Church, Abbey
Temple
Scientific Station
Airport

Port
Lighthouse
Mine
Tunnel
Dam, Bridge

Name	Page	Grid	Lat.	Long.
Jiaoxian	27	Kd	36.20N	120.00 E
Jiaozhou-Wan	28	Ff	36.10N	120.15 E
Jiaozuo	22	Nf	35.15N	113.18 E
Jiashan	28	Fi	30.51N	120.54 E
Jiashan (Mingguang)	28	Dh	32.47N	118.00 E
Jiashi/Payzawat	27	Cd	39.29N	76.39 E
Jiawang	28	Dg	34.27N	117.26 E
Jiaxian	28	Bh	33.58N	113.13 E
Jiaxing	27	Le	30.44N	120.46 E
Jiayin (Chaoyang)	27	Nb	48.52N	130.21 E
Jiayu	27	Jf	30.00N	113.57 E
Jiayuguan	27	Gd	39.49N	98.18 E
Jibalei	35	Ic	10.07N	50.47 E
Jibão, Serra do-	55	Jb	14.48S	45.15W
Jibiya	34	Gc	13.06N	7.14 E
Jibou	15	Gb	47.16N	23.15 E
Jicarón, Isla-	49	Gj	7.16N	81.47W
Jičín	10	Lf	50.26N	15.22 E
Jiddah	22	Fg	21.29N	39.12 E
Jiddat al Ḩarāsīs	23	Ie	20.05N	56.00 E
Jiehu → Yinan	28	Eg	35.33N	118.27 E
Jieshou	28	Ch	33.17N	115.22 E
Jiesjjavrre	7	Fb	69.40N	24.12 E
Jiexiu	27	Jd	37.00N	112.00 E
Jieyang	27	Kg	23.32N	116.25 E
Jieznas/Eznas	8	Kj	54.34N	24.17 E
Jifn, Wādī al-	24	Jj	25.48N	42.15 E
Jiftūn, Jazā'ir-	24	Ei	27.13N	33.56 E
Jīgley	35	He	4.25N	45.22 E
Jiguaní	49	Ic	20.22N	76.26W
Jigüey, Bahía de-	49	Hb	22.08N	78.05W
Jigzhi	27	He	33.28N	101.29 E
Jihlava	10	Mh	48.55N	16.37 E
Jihlava	10	Lg	49.24N	15.34 E
Jihlavské vrchy	10	Lg	49.15N	15.20 E
Jihočeský kraj [3]	10	Kg	49.05N	14.30 E
Jihomoravský kraj [3]	10	Mg	49.10N	16.40 E
Jijel	32	Ib	36.48N	5.46 E
Jijel [3]	32	Ib	36.45N	5.45 E
Jijia	15	Lc	46.54N	28.05 E
Jijiga	35	Gd	9.21N	42.48 E
Jijona	13	Lf	38.32N	0.30W
Jikharrah	33	Dd	29.17N	21.38 E
Jilava	15	Je	44.20N	26.05 E
Jilf al Kabīr, Haḑabat al-	33	Ee	23.30N	26.00 E
Jilib	31	Lh	0.29N	42.47 E
Jilin	27	Mc	43.51N	126.33 E
Jilin Sheng (Chi-lin Sheng) =Kirin (EN) [2]	27	Mc	43.00N	126.00 E
Jiliu He	27	La	52.02N	120.41 E
Jiloca	13	Kc	41.21N	1.39W
Jima=Jimma (EN)	31	Kh	7.39N	36.49 E
Jimāl, Wādī-	24	Fj	24.40N	35.06 E
Jimaní	49	Ld	18.28N	71.51W
Jimbe	36	De	11.05S	24.00 E
Jimbolia	15	Dd	45.48N	20.43 E
Jimena	13	Ig	37.50N	3.28W
Jimena de la Frontera	13	Gh	36.26N	5.27W
Jiménez	47	Dc	27.08N	104.55W
Jiménez del Teul	48	Gf	23.10N	104.05W
Jimma (EN)=Jima	31	Kh	7.39N	36.49 E
Jimo	28	Ff	36.24N	120.27 E
Jimsar	27	Ec	43.59N	89.04 E
Jimulco	48	He	25.20N	103.10W
Jināh	24	Dj	25.20N	30.31 E
Jinan=Tsinan (EN)	22	Nf	36.35N	117.00 E
Jincheng [China]	27	Jd	35.32N	112.53 E
Jincheng [China]	28	Fd	41.12N	121.25 E
Jinchuan /Quqên	27	He	31.02N	102.02 E
Jind	25	Fc	29.19N	76.19 E
Jindřichův Hradec	10	Kg	49.09N	15.00 E
Jinfo Shan	27	If	29.01N	107.14 E
Jing/Jinghe	27	Dc	44.39N	82.50 E
Jing'an	28	Cj	28.51N	115.21 E
Jingbian (Zhangjiapan)	27	Id	37.32N	108.45 E
Jingde	28	Ei	30.18N	118.30 E
Jingdezhen	22	Ng	29.18N	117.18 E
Jingfeng → Hexigten Qi	27	Kc	43.15N	117.31 E
Jinggang Shan	27	Jf	26.42N	114.07 E
Jinggu	27	Hg	23.28N	100.39 E
Jinghai	28	De	38.57N	116.56 E
Jinghe/Jing	27	Dc	44.39N	82.50 E
Jinghong (Yunjinghong)	27	Hg	21.59N	100.48 E
Jinghong Dao	27	Je	9.45N	114.28 E
Jingjiang	28	Fh	32.01N	120.15 E
Jingle	28	Ae	38.22N	111.56 E
Jingmen	27	Je	31.00N	112.11 E
Jingning	27	Id	35.30N	105.45 E
Jingping → Pinglu	28	Be	39.32N	112.14 E
Jingpo Hu	28	Jc	43.50N	128.53 E
Jingshan	28	Bi	31.04N	113.08 E
Jingtai	27	Hd	37.10N	104.08 E
Jingxian [China]	27	If	26.40N	109.37 E
Jingxian [China]	27	Ke	30.41N	118.29 E
Jingxing (Weishui)	28	Ce	38.03N	114.09 E
Jingyu	28	Ic	42.25N	126.48 E
Jingyuan	27	Hd	36.35N	104.40 E
Jingzhi	28	Ef	36.18N	119.22 E
Jingzhou → Jiangling	27	Je	30.21N	112.10 E
Jinhu (Licheng)	28	Eh	33.01N	119.01 E
Jinhua	27	Kf	29.09N	119.38 E
Jining [China]	22	Nf	37.26N	116.36 E
Jining [China]	22	Ne	41.02N	113.07 E
Jinja	31	Kh	0.26N	33.13 E
Jin Jiang	28	Cj	28.23N	115.48 E
Jinkou	28	Ci	30.20N	114.07 E
Jinotega [3]	49	Eg	14.00N	85.25W
Jinotega	47	Gf	13.06N	86.00W
Jinotepe	47	Gf	11.51N	86.12W
Jinping	27	Hg	22.45N	103.15 E
Jinsha	27	If	27.18N	106.16 E
Jinsha → Nantong	28	Fh	32.06N	120.52 E
Jinshan	28	Fi	30.54N	121.09 E
Jinshan → Harqin Qi	28	Ed	41.57N	118.40 E
Jinshi	28	Aj	29.03N	111.52 E
Jinta	27	Gc	40.00N	99.00 E
Jintan	28	Ei	31.45N	119.34 E
Jinxi	27	Lc	40.46N	120.50 E
Jinxian [China]	27	Ld	39.06N	121.44 E
Jinxian [China]	28	Dj	28.21N	116.16 E
Jinxiang	28	Dg	35.04N	116.19 E
Jinyang	27	Hf	27.39N	103.12 E
Jinyun	28	Fj	28.39N	120.05 E
Jinzhai (Meishan)	28	Ci	31.40N	115.52 E
Jinzhou	22	Oe	41.09N	121.08 E
Jinzū-Gawa	29	Ec	36.45N	137.13 E
Jiparaná, Rio-	52	Jf	8.03S	62.52W
Jipijapa	54	Bd	1.22S	80.34W
Jiquilisco	49	Cg	13.19N	88.35W
Jiquilisco, Bahía de-	49	Cg	13.10N	88.28W
Jirjā	33	Fd	26.20N	31.53 E
Jishou	27	If	28.18N	109.43 E
Jishu	28	Ib	44.16N	126.50 E
Jisr ash Shughur	24	Ge	35.48N	36.19 E
Jiu	15	Gd	43.47N	23.48 E
Jiucai Ling	27	Jf	25.33N	111.18 E
Jiucheng → Wucheng	28	Df	37.12N	116.04 E
Jiujiang	22	Ng	29.39N	116.00 E
Jiuling Shan	27	Jf	28.55N	114.50 E
Jiulong/Gyaisi	27	Hf	28.58N	101.33 E
Jiuquan (Suzhou)	22	Lf	39.46N	98.34 E
Jiurongcheng	28	Gf	37.22N	122.33 E
Jiutai	27	Mc	44.10N	125.50 E
Jīwani, Rās-	25	Cc	25.01N	61.44 E
Jixi [China]	28	Ei	30.04N	118.36 E
Jixi [China]	22	Pe	45.15N	130.55 E
Jixian [China]	28	Cg	35.23N	114.04 E
Jixian [China]	28	Cf	37.34N	115.34 E
Jixian [China]	28	Dd	40.03N	117.24 E
Jiyang	28	Df	36.59N	117.11 E
Jiyuan	28	Bg	35.06N	112.35 E
Jiyun He	28	De	39.05N	117.45 E
Jiz, Wādī al-	35	Ib	16.12N	52.14 E
Jīzān	22	Gh	16.54N	42.32 E
Jize	28	Cf	36.54N	114.52 E
Jizera	10	Kf	50.10N	14.43 E
Jizerské Hory	10	Lf	50.50N	15.13 E
Jizl, Wādī al-	24	Hj	25.39N	38.25 E
Jizō-Zaki	28	Lg	35.33N	133.18 E
Jmbe	36	De	10.20S	16.40 E
Jnchengjiang → Hechi	27	Ig	24.44N	108.02 E
Joaçaba	55	Gh	27.10S	51.30W
Joal-Fadiout	34	Bc	14.10N	16.51W
João Câmara	54	Ke	5.32S	35.48W
João Monlevade	55	Kd	19.50S	43.08W
João Pessoa	53	Mf	7.07S	34.52W
João Pinheiro	54	Ig	17.45S	46.10W
Joaquín V. González	56	Hb	25.00S	64.11W
Jobado	49	Ic	20.54N	77.17W
Jódar	13	Ig	37.50N	3.21W
Jodhpur	22	Jg	26.17N	73.02 E
Jodoigne/Geldenaken	12	Gd	50.43N	4.52 E
Joensuu	6	Ic	62.36N	29.46 E
Joerg Plateau	66	Qf	75.00S	69.30W
Joes Hill	64g	Bb	1.48N	157.19W
Jōetsu	27	Od	37.06N	138.15 E
Joeuf	12	Ie	49.14N	6.01 E
Jôf di Montasio	14	Hd	46.26N	13.26 E
Joffre, Mount-	46	Ha	50.32N	115.13W
Jogbani	25	Hc	26.25N	87.15 E
Jõgeva/Jygeva	7	Gg	58.46N	26.26 E
Joghatāy	24	Qd	36.36N	57.01 E
Joghatāy, Kūh-e-	24	Qd	36.30N	57.00 E
Jōhana	29	Ec	36.31N	136.54 E
Johannesburg	31	Jk	26.15S	28.00 E
Jōhen	29	Ce	32.57N	132.35 E
John Day	46	Fd	44.25N	118.57W
John Day River	43	Cb	45.44N	120.39W
John H. Kerr Reservoir	44	Hg	36.31N	78.18W
John Martin Reservoir	45	Eg	38.05N	103.02W
John o' Groat's	9	Jc	58.38N	3.05W
Johnson	45	Fh	37.34N	101.45W
Johnson, Pico de-	48	Cc	29.13N	112.07W
Johnson City [Tn.-U.S.]	43	Kd	36.19N	82.21W
Johnson City [Tx.-U.S.]	45	Gk	30.17N	98.25W
Johnsons Crossing	42	Ed	60.29N	133.17W
Johnsons Point	51d	Bb	17.02N	61.53W
Johnstone, Lake-	59	Ef	32.20S	120.40 E
Johnstone Strait	46	Ca	50.25N	126.00W
Johnston Island	57	Kc	17.00N	168.30W
Johnston Island [5]	58	Kc	17.00N	168.30W
Johnstown [N.Y.-U.S.]	44	Jd	43.01N	74.22W
Johnstown [Pa.-U.S.]	43	Lc	40.20N	78.56W
Johor Baharu	22	Mi	1.28N	103.45 E
Joia	55	Ei	28.39S	54.08W
Joigny	11	Jg	47.59N	3.24 E
Joinvile	53	Lh	26.18S	48.50W
Joinville	11	Lf	48.27N	5.08 E
Joinville Island	66	Re	63.15S	55.45W
Jokau	35	Ed	8.24N	33.49 E
Jokela	8	Kd	60.33N	24.59 E
Jokelbugten	41	Kc	78.25N	19.00W
Jokioinen	8	Jd	60.49N	23.28 E
Jokkmokk	7	Ec	66.36N	19.51 E
Jøkuleggi	8	Cc	61.03N	8.12 E
Jolfā	24	Kc	38.57N	45.38 E
Joliet	43	Jc	41.32N	88.05W
Joliette	42	Kg	46.01N	73.26W
Jolo	26	He	6.00N	121.00 E
Jolo Group	21	Oi	6.00N	121.09 E
Jølstravatnet	8	Bc	61.30N	6.15 E
Jomala	8	Hd	60.09N	19.58 E
Jombang	26	Fh	7.33S	112.14 E
Jomda	27	Ge	31.37N	98.20 E
Jönåker	8	Gf	58.44N	16.40 E
Jonava/Ionava	7	Fi	55.05N	24.17 E
Jonê	27	He	34.35N	103.32 E
Jones Bank	9	Fl	49.50N	8.00W
Jonesboro [Ar.-U.S.]	43	Id	35.50N	90.42W
Jonesboro [La.-U.S.]	45	Jj	32.15N	92.43W
Jones Mountains	66	Pf	73.32S	94.00W
Jones Sound	38	Kb	76.00N	85.00W
Jonesville	44	Fg	36.41N	83.06W
Jonglei [3]	35	Ed	7.20N	32.00 E
Jonglei	35	Ed	6.50N	31.18 E
Jonglei, Tur'ah-=Jonglei Canal (EN)	35	Ed	9.22N	31.30 E
Jonglei Canal (EN)=Jonglei, Tur'ah-	35	Ed	9.22N	31.30 E
Joniškélis/Ioniškelis	8	Ki	56.00N	24.14 E
Joniškis/Ioniškis	7	Fh	56.16N	23.37 E
Jönköping	6	Hd	57.47N	14.11 E
Jönköping [2]	7	Dh	57.30N	14.30 E
Jonquière	42	Kg	48.25N	71.15W
Jonuta	48	Mh	18.05N	92.08W
Jonzac	11	Fi	45.27N	0.26W
Joplin	39	Jf	37.06N	94.31W
Jordan	43	Fb	47.19N	106.55W
Jordan	23	Ec	31.46N	35.33 E
Jordan (EN)=Al Urdun [1]	22	Ff	31.00N	36.00 E
Jordan Valley	46	Ge	42.58N	117.03W
Jordão, Rio-	55	Fg	25.46S	52.07W
Jorhāt	22	Lg	26.45N	94.13 E
Jörn	7	Ed	65.04N	20.02 E
Joroinen	7	Ge	62.11N	27.50 E
Jørpelànd	7	Bg	59.01N	6.03 E
Jos	31	Hh	9.55N	8.54 E
José A. Guisasola	55	Bn	38.40S	61.05W
José Battle y Ordóñez	55	Ek	33.28S	55.07W
José Bonifácio	55	He	21.03S	49.41W
José de San Martín	56	Ff	44.02S	70.29W
Joselandia	55	Dc	16.32S	56.12W
José Otávio	55	Ej	31.17S	54.07W
José Pedro Varela	55	Ek	33.27S	54.32W
Joseph, Lake-	44	Hc	45.14N	79.45W
Joseph Bonaparte Gulf	57	Df	14.55S	128.15 E
Josephine Seamount (EN)	5	Eh	36.52N	14.20W
Joseph Lake	42	Kf	52.48N	65.17W
Joshimath	25	Fb	30.34N	79.34 E
Joškar-Ola	6	Kd	56.40N	47.55 E
Jos Plateau	30	Hh	10.00N	9.30 E
Josselin	11	Dg	47.57N	2.33W
Jostedalen	8	Bc	61.35N	7.20 E
Jostedalsbreen	7	Bf	61.40N	7.00 E
Jostefonn	8	Bc	61.26N	6.33 E
Jost Van Dyke	51a	Db	18.28N	64.45W
Jotunheimen	5	Gc	61.40N	8.20 E
Joubertberge	37	Ac	18.45S	13.55 E
Joué-lès-Tours	11	Gg	47.21N	0.40 E
Jouquara, Rio-	55	Db	15.06S	57.06W
Joure, Haskerland-	12	Hb	52.58N	5.47 E
Joutsa	7	Gf	61.44N	26.07 E
Joutseno	7	Gf	61.06N	28.30 E
Jovan, Deli-	15	Fe	44.15N	22.13 E
Jovellanos	49	Gb	22.48N	81.12W
Joviânia	55	Hc	17.49S	49.30W
Jowhar	31	Lh	2.46N	45.32 E
Jow Kār	24	Me	34.26N	48.42 E
Jowzjān [3]	23	Kb	36.30N	66.00 E
Joya, Laguna de la-	48	Mj	15.55N	93.40W
Jreïda	32	Df	18.19N	16.03W
Jrian Jaya [3]	26	Kg	3.55S	138.00 E
Juan Aldama	47	Dd	24.19N	103.21W
Juana Ramírez, Isla-	48	Kg	21.50N	97.40W
Juan Blanquier	55	Cl	35.46S	59.18W
Juancheng	28	Cg	35.33N	115.30 E
Juan de Fuca, Strait of-	38	Ge	48.20N	124.00W
Juan de Nova, Ile-	30	Lj	17.03S	42.45 E
Juan E. Barra	55	Bm	37.48S	60.29W
Juan Fernández, Archipielago-=Juan Fernández, Islands (EN)	52	Ii	33.00S	80.00W
Juan Fernandez Islands (EN)=Juan Fernández, Archipielago-	52	Ii	33.00S	80.00W
Juan G. Bazán	55	Bg	24.33S	60.50W
Juangriego	50	Eg	11.05N	63.57W
Juanjuy	54	Ce	7.11S	76.45W
Juan L. Lacaze	55	Dl	34.26S	57.27W
Juárez [Arg.]	56	Ie	37.40S	59.48W
Juárez [Mex.]	48	Id	27.37N	100.44W
Juárez, Sierra de-	48	Bb	32.00N	115.50W
Juarzohn	34	Dd	5.20N	8.58W
Juàzeirinho	54	Ke	7.04S	36.35W
Juàzeiro	53	Lf	9.25S	40.30W
Juàzeiro do Norte	53	Mf	7.12S	39.20W
Jūbā	31	Kh	4.51N	31.37 E
Juba (EN)=Ganāne, Webi-	30	Lh	0.15S	42.38 E
Juba, Rio-	55	Db	14.59S	57.44W
Jūbāl, Maḑīq-	24	Ei	27.40N	33.55 E
Jubaland (EN)	30	Lh	1.00N	42.00 E
Jubayl [Eg.]	24	Eh	28.12N	33.38 E
Jubayl [Leb.]	24	Fe	34.07N	35.39 E
Jubayt [Sud.]	35	Fb	18.57N	36.50 E
Jubayt [Sud.]	35	Fa	20.59N	36.18 E
Jubbada Dhexe [3]	35	Ge	1.15N	42.30 E
Jubbada Hoose [3]	35	Gf	0.30S	42.00 E
Jubbah	24	Ih	28.02N	40.56 E
Jubilee Lake	59	Fe	29.10S	126.40 E
Juby, Cap-	30	Ff	27.57N	12.55W
Júcar/Xúquer	5	Fh	39.09N	0.14W
Juçara	55	Gb	15.53S	50.51W
Jucaro	49	Hc	21.37N	78.51W
Jüchen	12	Ic	51.06N	6.30 E
Juchipila	48	Hg	21.25N	103.07W
Juchipila, Río-	48	Hg	21.03N	103.25W
Juchitán de Zaragoza	39	Jh	16.26N	95.01W
Jučjugej	20	Jd	63.20N	142.15 E
Judas, Punta-	49	Ei	9.31N	84.32W
Judayyidat 'Ar'ar	23	Fc	31.22N	41.26 E
Judenburg	14	Ic	47.10N	14.40 E
Juding Shan	27	He	31.30N	104.00 E
Judith Mountains	46	Kc	47.12N	109.15W
Judith River	46	Kc	47.44N	109.38W
Judoma	20	Ie	59.08N	135.03 E
Judomski Hrebet	20	Jd	61.05N	141.30 E
Juegang → Rudong	28	Fh	32.19N	121.11 E
Juelsminde	8	Di	55.43N	10.01 E
Jufrah, Wāḩāt al-=Giofra Oasis (EÑ)	30	If	29.10N	16.00 E
Jug	5	Kc	60.45N	46.20 E
Jug	17	Hh	57.43N	56.12 E
Jugo-Osetinskaja Avtonomnaja Oblast [3]	19	Eg	42.20N	44.05 E
Jugorski Poluostrov	17	Kb	69.30N	62.30 E
Jugorski Šar, Proliv-	19	Gb	69.45N	60.35 E
Jugoslavija = Yugoslavia (EN) [1]	6	Hg	44.00N	19.00 E
Jugo-Tala	20	Kc	66.03N	151.05 E
Jugydjan	17	Gf	61.42N	54.58 E
Juhaym	24	Kh	29.36N	45.24 E
Juhnov	16	Ib	54.43N	35.12 E
Juhor	15	Ef	43.50N	21.15 E
Juhoslovenská nížina	10	Ph	48.10N	19.40 E
Juhua Dao	28	Fd	40.32N	120.48 E
Juigalpa	49	Eg	12.05N	85.24W
Juina, Rio-	55	Ca	12.36S	58.57W
Juine	11	If	48.32N	2.23 E
Juininha, Rio-	55	Ca	12.55S	59.13W
Juist	10	Cc	53.40N	7.00 E
Juiz de Fora	53	Lh	21.45S	43.20W
Jujuy [2]	56	Gb	23.00S	66.00W
Jukagirskoje Ploskogorje	20	Kc	66.00N	155.30 E
Jukonda	17	Mg	59.38N	67.20 E
Juksejevo	17	Gg	59.52N	54.16 E
Jula	7	Ke	63.48N	44.44 E
Juldybajevo	17	Hj	52.20N	57.52 E
Julesburg	45	Ef	40.59N	102.16W
Juli	54	Eg	16.13S	69.27W
Juliaca	54	Dg	15.30S	70.08W
Julia Creek	59	Id	20.39S	141.45 E
Julian Alps (EN)=Julijske Alpe	14	Hd	46.20N	13.45 E
Juliana Top	54	Gc	3.41N	56.32W
Julianehåb/Qaqortoq	67	Nc	60.50N	46.10W
Jülich	10	Cf	50.56N	6.22 E
Jülicher Borde	12	Id	50.50N	6.30 E
Julijske Alpe=Julian Alps (EN)	14	Hd	46.20N	13.45 E
Julimes	48	Gc	28.25N	105.27W
Júlio de Castilhos	55	Fi	29.14S	53.41W
Jullundur	22	Jf	31.19N	75.34 E
Julong/New Kowloon	22	Ng	22.20N	114.09 E
Julu	28	Cf	37.13N	115.02 E
Juma	7	Hd	65.05N	33.13 E
Juma He	28	De	39.31N	116.08 E
Jumet, Charleroi-	11	Kd	50.27N	4.26 E
Jumièges	12	Ce	49.26N	0.49 E
Jumilla	13	Kf	38.29N	1.17W
Jümme	12	Ja	53.13N	7.31 E
Junāgadh	25	Ed	21.31N	70.28 E
Junan (Shizilu)	28	Eg	35.10N	118.50 E
Junaynah, Ra's al-	24	Eh	29.01N	33.58 E
Juncal	48	De	24.50N	111.47W
Juncos	51a	Cb	18.13N	65.55W
Junction [Tx.-U.S.]	45	Gk	30.29N	99.46W
Junction [Ut.-U.S.]	46	Ig	38.14N	112.13W
Junction City	43	Hd	39.02N	96.50W
Jundiaí	56	Kb	23.11S	46.52W
Jundiaí do Sul	55	Gf	23.27S	50.17W
Jundūbah	32	Ib	36.30N	8.45 E
Jundūbah [3]	32	Ib	36.28N	8.41 E
Juneau	39	Fd	57.20N	134.27W
Junee	59	Jf	34.52S	147.35 E
Jungar Qi (Shagedu)	27	Jd	39.37N	110.58 E
Jungfrau	14	Bd	46.32N	7.58 E
Junggar Pendi=Dzungarian Basin	21	Ke	45.00N	88.00 E
Junín [2]	54	Df	11.30S	75.00W
Junín [Arg.]	53	Ji	34.35S	60.57W
Junín [Peru]	54	Cf	11.10S	76.00W
Junín, Lago de-	54	Cf	11.02S	76.05W
Junín de los Andes	56	Fe	39.56S	71.05W
Juniville	12	Ge	49.24N	4.23 E
Jūniyah	24	Ff	33.59N	35.38 E
Junjaha	17	Jc	66.25N	62.00 E
Junlian	27	Hf	28.12N	104.34 E
Junsele	7	De	63.41N	16.54 E
Juntura	46	Fe	43.45N	118.05W
Junxian (Danjiang)	27	Je	32.31N	111.32 E
Juodupė	8	Kh	56.03N	25.44 E
Juojärvi	8	Mb	62.45N	28.35 E
Juoksengi	7	Fc	66.34N	23.51 E
Jupiá, Reprêsa de-	56	Jb	20.47S	51.39W
Juquiá	55	Ig	24.19S	47.38W
Juquiá, Rio-	55	Ig	24.22S	47.49W
Juquiá, Serra do-	55	Gg	25.10S	52.00W
Jur	20	Ie	59.48N	137.29 E
Jur	30	Jh	8.39N	29.18 E
Jura [2]	14	Ac	47.25N	6.15 E
Jura	5	Gf	46.45N	6.30 E
Jura [3]	11	Lh	46.50N	5.50 E
Jura	9	Hf	56.00N	5.50W
Jura/Jūra	7	Fi	55.03N	22.10 E
Jūra/Jura	7	Fi	55.03N	22.10 E
Jura, Sound of-	9	Hf	55.55N	5.22W
Juradó	54	Cb	7.07N	77.46W
Juratiški	8	Kj	54.02N	26.00 E
Juraybī'āt	24	Lh	29.50N	46.03 E
Juraybȳ'āt	24	Kh	29.08N	45.30 E
Jurbarkas	7	Fi	55.08N	22.47 E
Jurdī, Wādī-	24	Ei	26.33N	32.44 E
Jurga	20	De	55.42N	84.55 E
Jurgamyš	17	Li	55.25N	64.28 E
Juribej	17	Nb	68.55N	69.05 E
Jurien Bay	59	Cf	30.15S	115.00 E
Jurigue, Rio-	55	Ec	16.29S	54.37W
Jurilovca	15	Le	44.46N	28.52 E
Jurja	7	Lg	59.03N	49.20 E
Jurjaha	17	Gc	66.42N	56.00 E
Jurjevec	7	Kh	57.22N	43.06 E
Jurjev-Polski	7	Jh	56.31N	39.44 E
Jurjuzan	17	Hi	55.43N	56.57 E
Jurjuzan	17	Ii	54.52N	58.28 E
Jurla	17	Gg	59.20N	54.16 E
Jurmala/Jūrmala	19	Cd	56.59N	23.38 E
Jūrmala/Jurmala	19	Cd	56.59N	23.38 E
Jurmo	8	Ie	59.50N	21.35 E
Jurong	28	Ei	31.56N	119.10 E
Juruá	54	Ed	3.27S	66.03W
Juruá, Rio-	52	Jf	2.37S	65.44W
Juruena, Rio-	52	Kf	7.20S	58.03W
Jurumirim, Reprêsa de-	56	Kb	23.20S	49.00W
Juruti	54	Gd	2.09S	56.04W
Jurva	8	Ib	62.41N	21.59 E
Jusan-Kō	29a	Bc	41.00N	140.20 E
Jusayrah	24	Nj	25.53N	50.36 E
Jusheng	27	Mb	48.44N	126.37 E
Ju Shui	28	Ci	31.09N	114.52 E
Juškozero	19	Dc	64.45N	32.08 E
Jussarö	8	Je	59.50N	23.35 E
Justo Daract	5€	Gd	33.52S	65.11W
Jusva	17	Gg	58.59N	54.57 E
Jutaí	54	Ee	5.11S	68.54W
Jutaí, Rio-	52	Jf	2.43S	66.57W
Jüterbg	10	Je	51.59N	13.05 E
Juti	55	Ef	22.52S	54.37W
Jutiapa [3]	49	Bf	14.10N	89.50W
Jutiapa [Guat.]	47	Gf	14.17N	89.54W
Jutiapa [Hond.]	49	Df	15.46N	86.34W
Juticalpa	47	Gf	14.42N	86.15W
Jutland (EN)=Jylland	5	Gd	56.00N	9.15 E
Juuka	7	Ge	63.14N	29.15 E
Juva	7	Gf	61.54N	27.51 E
Juventud, Isla de la-=Pines, Isle of- (EN)	38	Kg	21.40N	82.50W
Juxian	27	Kd	35.33N	118.45 E
Jūybār	24	Od	36.38N	52.53 E
Juye	28	Dg	35.23N	116.05 E
Jūyom	24	Oh	28.10N	54.02 E
Juža	7	Kh	56.36N	42.01 E
Južnaja Keltma	17	Gf	60.30N	55.40 E
Južna Morava	15	Ef	43.41N	21.24 E
Južni Rodopi	15	Ih	41.15N	25.30 E
Južnoje	20	Jg	46.13N	143.27 E
Južno-Jenisejski	20	Ee	58.48N	94.45 E
Južno-Kurilsk	20	Jh	44.05N	145.52 E
Južno-Sahalinsk	22	Qe	46.58N	142.42 E
Južno-Uralsk	19	Ge	54.26N	61.15 E
Južny, Mys-	20	Ke	57.42N	156.55 E
Južny Bug	5	Jf	46.59N	31.58 E
Južny Ural=Southern Urals (EN)	5	Le	54.00N	58.30 E
Jygeva/Jõgeva	7	Gg	58.46N	26.26 E
Jylland=Jutland (EN)	5	Gd	56.00N	9.15 E
Jylland Bank	8	Bh	56.55N	7.20 E
Jyske Ås	8	Dg	57.15N	10.14 E
Jyväskylä	6	Ic	62.14N	25.44 E

K

Name	Page	Grid	Lat.	Long.
K2=Godwin Austen (EN)	21	Jf	35.53N	76.30 E
Ka	34	Fc	11.39N	4.11 E
Kaabong	36	Fb	3.31N	34.09 E
Kaahka	19	Fh	37.21N	59.38 E
Kaala	65a	Cb	21.31N	158.09W
Kaala-Gomén	63b	Be	20.40S	164.24 E
Kaalualu Bay	65a	Fe	18.58N	155.37W
Kaamanen	7	Gb	69.06N	27.12 E
Kaap Kruis	37	Ad	21.46S	13.58 E
Kaap Plateau (EN)=Kaapplato	30	Jk	27.30S	23.45 E
Kaapplato=Kaap Plateau (EN)	30	Jk	27.30S	23.45 E
Kaapprovinsie/Cape Province [2]	37	Cf	32.00S	22.00 E
Kaapstad / Cape Town	31	Il	33.55S	18.22 E
Kaarst	12	Ic	51.15N	6.37 E
Kaarta	34	Cc	14.35N	10.00W
Kaba/Habahe	27	Eb	47.53N	86.12 E
Kabaena, Pulau-	26	Hh	5.15S	121.55 E
Kabah	48	Og	20.07N	89.29W
Kabala	34	Cd	9.35N	11.33W
Kabale	36	Ec	1.15S	29.59 E
Kabalega Falls	36	Fb	2.17N	31.41 E
Kabalo	31	Ji	6.03S	26.55 E
Kabaman	63a	Aa	4.38S	152.42 E
Kabambare	36	Ec	4.16S	27.07 E
Kabamet	36	Gb	0.30N	35.45 E
Kabanjahe	26	Cf	3.06N	98.30 E
Kabardino-Balkarskaja ASSR [3]	19	Eg	43.30N	43.30 E
Kabare	36	Ec	2.29S	28.48 E
Kabasalan	26	He	7.48N	122.45 E
Kaba-Shima [Jap.]	29	Ae	32.45N	129.00 E
Kaba-Shima [Jap.]	29	Ae	32.34N	129.47 E
Kabba	34	Gd	7.50N	6.04 E
Kåbdalis	7	Ec	66.09N	20.00 E
Kaberamaido	36	Fb	1.45N	33.10 E
Kabetogama Lake	45	Jb	48.28N	92.59W
Kabhegy	10	Ni	47.03N	17.39 E
Kabinakagami Lake	44	Ea	48.58N	84.25W
Kabinda	31	Ji	6.08S	24.29 E
Kabīr, Wādī al-	14	Dn	36.23N	9.52 E
Kabīr Kūh	24	Lf	33.25N	46.45 E
Kabkābīyah	35	Cc	13.39N	24.05 E
Kableškovo	15	Kg	42.39N	27.34 E
Kabna	35	Eb	19.10N	32.41 E
Kabo	35	Bd	7.35N	18.38 E
Kabompo	36	De	13.36S	24.12 E
Kabompo	30	Jj	14.11S	23.11 E
Kabondo Dianda	36	Ed	8.53S	25.40 E
Kabongo	36	Ed	7.19S	25.35 E
Kabou	34	Fd	9.27N	0.49 E
Kabūdiyāh, Ra's-	32	Jb	35.14N	11.10 E
Kabūd Rāhang	24	Me	35.12N	48.44 E
Kābul	22	If	34.31N	69.12 E
Kābul [3]	23	Kc	34.30N	69.00 E
Kābul	21	Jf	33.55N	72.14 E
Kabunda	36	Ee	12.13S	29.23 E

Index Symbols

[1] Independent Nation
[2] State, Region
[3] District, County
[4] Municipality
[5] Colony, Dependency
Continent
Physical Region
Historical or Cultural Region
Mount, Mountain
Volcano
Hill
Mountains, Mountain Range
Hills, Escarpment
Plateau, Upland
Pass, Gap
Plain, Lowland
Delta
Salt Flat
Valley, Canyon
Crater, Cave
Karst Features
Depression
Polder
Desert, Dunes
Forest, Woods
Heath, Steppe
Oasis
Cape, Point
Coast, Beach
Cliff
Peninsula
Isthmus
Sandbank
Island
Atoll
Rock, Reef
Islands, Archipelago
Rocks, Reefs
Coral Reef
Well, Spring
Geyser
River, Stream
Waterfall Rapids
River Mouth, Estuary
Lake
Salt Lake
Intermittent Lake
Reservoir
Swamp, Pond
Canal
Glacier
Ice Shelf, Pack Ice
Ocean
Sea
Gulf, Bay
Strait, Fjord
Lagoon
Bank
Seamount
Tablemount
Ridge
Shelf
Basin
Escarpment, Sea Scarp
Fracture
Trench, Abyss
National Park, Reserve
Point of Interest
Recreation Site
Cave, Cavern
Historic Site
Ruins
Wall, Walls
Church, Abbey
Temple
Scientific Station
Airport
Port
Lighthouse
Mine
Tunnel
Dam, Bridge

Kabunga 36 Ec 1.42S 28.08 E
Kaburuang, Pulau- 26 If 3.48N 126.48 E
Kabushi-ga-Take 29 Fd 35.54N 138.44 E
Kabwe 31 Jj 14.27S 28.27 E
Kabylie 32 Ib 36.15N 5.25 E
Kača 16 Hg 44.44N 33.32 E
Kačanik 15 Eg 42.14N 21.15 E
Kačanovo 8 Lg 57.24N 27.53 E
Kačergine 8 Jj 54.53N 23.49 E
Kachia 34 Gd 9.52N 7.57 E
Kachikau 37 Cc 18.09S 24.29 E
Kachin [2] 25 Jc 26.00N 97.30 E
Kačiry 19 He 53.04N 76.07 E
Kačkanar 19 Fd 58.42N 59.35 E
Kačug 20 Ff 54.00N 105.52 E
Kaczawa 10 Me 51.18N 16.27 E
Kadada 16 Oc 53.09N 46.01 E
Kadaň 10 Jf 50.23N 13.16 E
Kadan Kyun 25 Jf 12.30N 98.22 E
Kadeï 30 Ih 3.31N 16.03 E
Kadijevka 19 Df 48.32N 38.40 E
Kadiköy 24 Bb 40.51N 26.50 E
Kadıköy, İstanbul 15 Mi 40.59N 29.01 E
Kadina 59 Hf 33.58S 137.43 E
Kadınhanı 24 Ec 38.15N 32.14 E
Kadiolo 34 Dc 10.34N 5.45W
Kadiri 25 Ff 14.07N 78.10 E
Kadirli 23 Eb 37.23N 36.05 E
Kadja 35 Cc 12.02N 22.28 E
Kadmat Island 25 Ef 11.14N 72.47 E
Kadnikov 7 Jg 59.30N 40.24 E
Kadoka 45 Fe 43.50N 101.31W
Kaduj 7 Ig 59.14N 37.09 E
Kaduna [2] 34 Gc 11.00N 7.30 E
Kaduna 30 Hh 8.45N 5.48 E
Kaduna 31 Hg 10.31N 7.26 E
Kāduqlī 31 Jg 11.01N 29.43 E
Kadykčan 20 Jd 63.05N 146.58 E
Kadžaran 16 Oj 39.11N 46.10 E
Kadžerom 17 Gd 64.41N 55.54 E
Kadži-Saj 18 Kc 42.08N 77.10 E
Kaech'ŏn 28 He 39.42N 125.53 E
Kaédi 31 Fg 16.08N 13.31W
Kaélé 34 Hc 10.07N 14.27 E
Kaena Point 65a Cb 21.35N 158.17W
Kaeo 62 Ea 35.06S 173.47 E
Kaesŏng 22 Of 37.58N 126.33 E
Kaesŏng Si [2] 28 Ie 38.05N 126.30 E
Kāf 24 Gg 31.24N 37.29 E
Kafakumba 36 Dd 9.41S 23.44 E
Kafan 19 Eh 39.12N 46.28 E
Kafanchan 34 Gd 9.35N 8.18 E
Kaffrine 34 Bc 14.06N 15.33W
Kafia Kingi 35 Cd 9.16N 24.25 E
Kafiréos, Dhiékplous- 15 Hl 38.00N 24.40 E
Kafirévs, Ákra- 15 Hk 38.10N 24.35 E
Kafr ad Dawwār 24 Dg 31.08N 30.07 E
Kafr ash Shaykh 33 Fc 31.07N 30.56 E
Kafta 35 Fc 13.54N 37.11 E
Kafu 36 Fb 1.39N 32.05 E
Kafue 30 Ef 15.56S 28.55 E
Kafue 31 Jj 15.47S 28.11 E
Kafue Dam 36 Ef 15.45S 28.28 E
Kafue Flats 36 Ef 15.40S 26.25 E
Kafufu 36 Fd 7.12S 31.31 E
Kaga 28 Nf 36.18N 136.18 E
Kaga Bandoro 35 Bd 7.02N 19.13 E
Kagalaska 40a Cb 51.47N 176.23W
Kagalnik 16 Kf 47.04N 39.18 E
Kagami 29 Be 32.34N 130.40 E
Kagan 19 Gh 39.43N 64.32 E
Kagarlyk 16 Ge 49.53N 30.56 E
Kagawa Ken [2] 28 Mg 34.15N 134.15 E
Kagera 30 Ki 0.57S 31.47 E
Kağızman 24 Jb 40.09N 43.07 E
Kagoshima 22 Pf 31.36N 130.33 E
Kagoshima Bay (EN)= Kagoshima-Wan 28 Ki 31.27N 130.40 E
Kagoshima Ken [2] 28 Ki 31.45N 130.40 E
Kagoshima-Taniyama 29 Bf 31.31N 130.31 E
Kagoshima-Wan= Kagoshima Bay (EN) 28 Ki 31.27N 130.40 E
Kagul 15 Ld 45.32N 28.27 E
Kagul 19 Cf 45.53N 28.14 E
Kahal Tabelbala 32 Gd 28.45N 2.15W
Kahama 36 Fc 3.50S 32.36 E
Kahemba 31 Ii 7.17S 19.00 E
Kahi 16 Oi 41.23N 46.59 E
Kahiu Point 65a Eb 21.13N 156.58W
Kahler Asten 10 Ee 51.11N 8.29 E
Kahnūj 24 Qi 27.58N 57.47 E
Kahoku 29 Gb 38.30N 141.20 E
Kahoku-Gata 29 Ec 36.40N 136.40 E
Kahoolawe Island 57 Lb 20.33N 156.35W
Kahouanne, Ilet à- 51e Ab 16.22N 61.47W
Kahovka 19 Df 46.47N 33.32 E
Kahovskoje Vodohranilišče =Kakhovka Reservoir (EN) 5 Jf 47.25N 34.10 E
Kahramanmaraş 23 Eb 37.36N 36.55 E
Kahrūyeh 24 Ng 31.43N 51.48 E
Kâhta 24 Hd 37.46N 38.36 E
Kahuku 65a Db 21.41N 157.57W
Kahuku Point 65a Db 21.43N 157.59W
Kahului 65a Ec 20.53N 156.27W
Kahului Bay 65a Ec 20.55N 156.30W
Kahurangi Point 62 Ed 40.46S 172.13 E
Kai, Kepulauan- 57 Ee 5.35S 132.45 E
Kaiama 34 Fd 9.36N 3.57 E
Kaiapoi 62 Ee 43.23S 172.39 E
Kaibab Plateau 46 Ih 36.30N 112.15W
Kai Besar 26 Jh 5.35S 133.00 E
Kaidu He/Karaxabar He 27 Ec 41.55N 86.38 E
Kaieteur Falls 54 Gc 5.10N 59.28W
Kaifeng 22 Nf 34.45N 114.25 E
Kaihua 28 Ej 29.10N 118.24 E
Kai Kecil 26 Jh 5.45S 132.40 E
Kaikohe 62 Ea 35.24S 173.48 E
Kaikoura 61 Dh 42.25S 173.41 E
Kaili 27 If 26.35N 107.59 E
Kailu 27 Lc 43.37N 121.19 E
Kailua [Hi.-U.S.] 65a Fd 19.39N 155.59W
Kailua [Hi.-U.S.] 65a Db 21.23N 157.44W
Kaimana 26 Jg 3.39S 133.45 E
Kaimanawa Mountains 62 Fc 39.15S 176.00 E
Kaimon-Dake 29 Bf 31.10N 130.32 E
Kain, Tournai- 12 Fd 50.38N 3.22 E
Kainach 14 Jd 46.54N 15.31 E
Kainan [Jap.] 29 Dd 34.09N 135.12 E
Kainan [Jap.] 29 De 33.36N 134.22 E
Kainantu 60 Di 6.15S 145.53 E
Kainji Dam 34 Fd 9.55N 4.40 E
Kainji Reservoir 34 Fc 10.30N 4.35 E
Kaipara Harbour 62 Fb 36.25S 174.15 E
Kaiparowits Plateau 46 Jh 37.20N 111.15W
Kaiser Franz Josephs Fjord 41 Jd 73.30N 24.00W
Kaisersesch 12 Jd 50.14N 7.09 E
Kaiserslautern 10 Dg 49.27N 7.45 E
Kaiserstuhl 10 Dh 48.06N 7.40 E
Kaishantun 27 Mc 42.43N 129.37 E
Kaišiadorys/Kajšjadoris 7 Fi 54.53N 24.31 E
Kaita 29 Cd 34.20N 132.32 E
Kaitaia 62 Ea 35.07S 173.14 E
Kaitangata 62 Cg 46.17S 169.51 E
Kaithal 25 Fc 29.48N 76.23 E
Kaitong → Tongyu 27 Lc 44.47N 123.05 E
Kaituma River 50 Gh 8.11N 59.41W
Kaiwaka 61 Dg 36.10S 174.26 E
Kaiwi Channel 60 Oc 21.13N 157.30W
Kaixian 27 Ie 31.10N 108.25 E
Kaiyuan [China] 27 Lc 42.33N 124.04 E
Kaiyuan [China] 27 Hg 23.47N 103.15 E
Kaiyuh Mountains 40 Hd 64.00N 158.00W
Kaja 30 Jg 12.02N 22.28 E
Kajaani 6 Ic 64.14N 27.41 E
Kajaapu 26 Dh 5.26S 102.24 E
Kajabbi 58 Fg 20.02S 140.02 E
Kajak 20 Fb 71.30N 103.15 E
Kajang 26 Df 2.59N 101.47 E
Kajdak, Sor- 16 Rg 44.40N 53.30 E
Kajerkan 20 Dc 69.25N 87.30 E
Kajiado 36 Gc 1.51S 36.47 E
Kajiki 29 Bf 31.44N 130.40 E
Kajmakčalan 15 Ei 40.58N 21.48 E
Kajnar 15 Lb 47.50N 28.06 E
Kajo Kaji 35 Ee 3.53N 31.40 E
Kajrakkumskoje Vodohranilišče 18 Hd 40.20N 70.05 E
Kajrakty 19 Hf 48.31N 73.14 E
Kajšjadoris/Kaišiadorys 7 Fi 54.53N 24.31 E
Kajuru 34 Gc 10.19N 7.41 E
Kaka 35 Fd 7.28N 39.06 E
Kākā 35 Ec 10.36N 32.11 E
Kakagi Lake 45 Jb 49.13N 93.52W
Kakamas 37 Ce 28.45S 20.33 E
Kakamega 36 Fb 0.17N 34.45 E
Kakamigahara 29 Ed 35.25N 136.50 E
Kakanj 14 Mf 44.08N 18.05 E
Kaka Point 65a Ec 20.32N 156.33W
Kakata 34 Cd 6.32N 10.21W
Kake 29 Cd 34.36N 132.19 E
Kakegawa 29 Ed 34.46N 138.00 E
Kakenge 36 Dc 4.51S 21.55 E
Kakeroma-Jima 29b Ba 28.08N 129.15 E
Kakhovka Reservoir (EN)= Kahovskoje Vodohranilišče 5 Jf 47.25N 34.10 E
Kākī 24 Nh 28.19N 51.34 E
Kākināda 22 Kh 16.56N 82.13 E
Kakisa Lake 42 Fd 60.55N 117.40W
Kakizaki 29 Fc 37.16N 138.22 E
Kaklkan 24 Cd 36.15N 29.24 E
Kakogawa 29 Dd 34.46N 134.51 E
Kakpin 34 Ed 8.39N 3.48W
Kaktovik 40 Kb 70.08N 143.37W
Kakuda 29 Gc 37.58N 140.47 E
Kakuma 36 Fb 3.43N 34.52 E
Kakunodate 28 Pe 39.40N 140.32 E
Kakva 17 Jg 59.37N 60.50 E
Kakya 36 Gc 1.36S 39.02 E
Kalaa 13 Mi 35.35N 0.20 E
Kalaa Khasba 14 Co 35.38N 8.36 E
Kalaallit Nunaat/Grønland= Greenland (EN) [5] 39 Pb 70.00N 40.00W
Kalaallit Nunaat/Grønland= Greenland (EN) 38 Pb 70.00N 40.00W
Kalabahi 26 Hh 8.13S 124.31 E
Kalabáka 15 Ej 39.42N 21.38 E
Kalabera 64b Ba 15.14N 145.48 E
Kalabo 36 De 14.58S 22.41 E
Kalâbsha 33 Fe 23.33N 32.50 E
Kalač 19 Ee 50.23N 41.01 E
Kalačinsk 19 Hd 55.03N 74.34 E
Kalač-na-Donu 19 Ef 48.43N 43.32 E
Kaladan 25 Id 20.09N 92.57 E
Ka Lae 60 Od 18.55N 155.41W
Kalahari Desert 30 Jk 23.00S 22.00 E
Kalaheo 65a Bb 21.56N 159.32W
Kalai-Mor 19 Gh 35.37N 62.31 E
Kalaj Humo 18 He 38.25N 70.47 E
Kalajoki 7 Fd 64.15N 23.57 E
Kalakan 20 Ge 55.10N 116.45 E
Kalaldi 34 Hd 6.30N 14.04 E
Kalāleh 24 Pd 37.25N 55.40 E
Kalámai 6 Ih 37.02N 22.07 E
Kalamákion 15 Gl 37.55N 23.43 E
Kalamazoo 43 Jc 42.17N 85.32W
Kalambo Falls 36 Fd 8.36S 31.14 E
Kalamitski Zaliv 16 Hg 45.00N 33.25 E
Kálamos 15 Dk 38.37N 20.55 E
Kalamunda, Perth- 59 Df 31.57S 116.03 E
Kalan 23 Eb 39.07N 39.32 E
Kalandula 31 Ii 9.06S 15.58 E
Kalanshiyū, Sarīr- 30 Jf 27.00N 21.30 E
Kalao, Pulau- 26 Hh 7.18S 120.58 E
Kalaotoa, Pulau- 26 Hh 7.22S 121.47 E
Kalapana 65a Gd 19.21N 154.59W
Kalaraš 16 Ff 47.16N 28.16 E
Kälarne 8 Gb 62.59N 16.05 E
Kalarski Hrebet 20 Ge 56.30N 118.50 E
Kalasin [Indon.] 26 Ff 0.12N 114.16 E
Kalasin [Thai.] 25 Ke 16.29N 103.31 E
Kalāt 25 Dc 29.02N 66.35 E
Kalāteh 24 Pd 36.29N 54.10 E
Kalau 65b Bc 21.28S 174.57W
Kalaupapa 65a Eb 21.12N 156.59W
Kalaus 16 Ng 45.43N 44.07 E
Kalavárdha 15 Km 36.20N 27.57 E
Kálavrita 15 Fk 38.02N 22.07 E
Kalbā' 24 Qj 25.03N 56.21 E
Kalbīyah, Sabkhat al- 14 Eo 35.51N 10.17 E
Kaldbakur 7a Ab 65.49N 23.39W
Kaldygajty 16 Re 49.20N 52.38 E
Kale [Tur.] 24 Cd 37.26N 28.51 E
Kale [Tur.] 24 Cd 36.14N 29.59 E
Kalecik 24 Eb 40.06N 33.25 E
Kalehe 36 Ec 2.06S 28.55 E
Kalemie 31 Ji 5.56S 29.12 E
Kāl-e Shur 23 Jb 35.05N 60.59 E
Kalevala 19 Db 65.12N 31.10 E
Kalewa 25 Id 23.12N 94.18 E
Kaleybar 24 Lc 38.47N 47.02 E
Kalgoorlie 58 Dh 30.45S 121.28 E
Kaliakoúdha 15 Ek 38.48N 21.46 E
Kaliakra, Nos- 15 Lf 43.18N 28.30 E
Kalibo 26 Hd 11.43N 122.22 E
Kalí Límni 15 Kn 35.35N 27.08 E
Kalima 31 Ji 2.34S 26.37 E
Kalimantan/Borneo 21 Ni 1.00N 114.00 E
Kalimantan Barat [3] 26 Ff 0.01N 110.30 E
Kalimantan Selatan [3] 26 Gg 2.30S 115.30 E
Kalimantan Tengah [3] 26 Fg 2.00S 113.30 E
Kalimantan Timur [3] 26 Gf 1.30N 116.30 E
Kálimnos 15 Jm 36.57N 26.59 E
Kálimnos 15 Jl 37.00N 27.00 E
Kalinin [R.S.F.S.R.] 6 Jd 56.52N 35.55 E
Kalinin [Tur.-U.S.S.R.] 19 Fg 42.07N 59.40 E
Kalininabad 18 Gf 37.53N 68.57 E
Kaliningrad [R.S.F.S.R.] 6 Ie 54.43N 20.30 E
Kaliningrad [R.S.F.S.R.] 7 Ii 55.55N 37.57 E
Kaliningradskaja Oblast [3] 19 Ce 54.45N 21.20 E
Kalinino [Arm.-U.S.S.R.] 16 Ni 41.08N 44.14 E
Kalinino [R.S.F.S.R.] 16 Kg 45.05N 38.59 E
Kalininsk [Mold.-U.S.S.R.] 15 Ka 48.07N 27.16 E
Kalininsk [R.S.F.S.R.] 16 Nd 51.30N 44.30 E
Kalininskaja Oblast [3] 19 Dd 57.20N 34.40 E
Kalinkoviči 19 Ce 52.07N 29.23 E
Kalino 17 Hg 58.15N 57.35 E
Kalinovik 14 Mg 43.31N 18.26 E
Kalinovka 16 Fe 49.29N 28.32 E
Kaliro 36 Fb 0.54N 33.30 E
Kalispell 39 He 48.12N 114.19W
Kalisz [2] 10 Of 51.45N 18.05 E
Kalisz 10 Oe 51.46N 18.06 E
Kalisz Pomorski 10 Lc 53.19N 15.54 E
Kalitva 16 Le 48.10N 40.46 E
Kaliua 36 Fd 5.04S 31.48 E
Kalix 7 Fd 65.51N 23.08 E
Kalixälven 7 Fd 65.47N 23.13 E
Kalja 17 Jf 60.20N 60.01 E
Kaljazin 19 Dd 57.15N 37.55 E
Kalkandere 24 Ib 40.55N 40.28 E
Kalkar 12 Ic 51.44N 6.18 E
Kalkaska 44 Ec 44.44N 85.11W
Kalkfeld 37 Bd 20.53S 16.11 E
Kalkfontein 37 Cd 22.07S 20.54 E
Kalkim 15 Kj 39.48N 27.13 E
Kalkrand 37 Bd 24.03S 17.33 E
Kall 7 Ce 63.28N 13.15 E
Kållands Halvö 8 Ef 58.35N 13.05 E
Kållandsö 8 Ef 58.40N 13.10 E
Kallaste 7 Gg 58.41N 27.08 E
Kallavesi 5 Ic 62.50N 27.45 E
Kalletal 12 Kb 52.08N 8.57 E
Kallhäll 8 Ge 59.27N 17.48 E
Kallídhromon Óros 15 Fk 38.44N 22.34 E
Kallinge 7 Dh 56.14N 15.17 E
Kallonís, Kolpos- 15 Jj 39.07N 26.08 E
Kallsjön 7 Ce 63.35N 13.00 E
Kalmar 6 Hd 56.40N 16.22 E
Kalmar [2] 7 Dh 57.20N 16.00 E
Kalmarsund 7 Dh 56.40N 16.25 E
Kalmit 12 Ke 49.19N 8.05 E
Kalmius 16 Jf 47.03N 37.34 E
Kalmthout 12 Gc 51.23N 4.28 E
Kalmyckaja ASSR [3] 19 Ef 46.30N 45.30 E
Kalmykovo 16 Qe 49.05N 51.47 E
Kalnciems 8 Jh 56.48N 23.34 E
Kalnik 14 Kd 46.10N 16.30 E
Kalocsa 10 Oj 46.32N 19.00 E
Kalofer 15 Hg 42.37N 24.59 E
Kalohi Channel 65a Ec 21.00N 156.56W
Kaloko 36 Ed 6.47S 25.47 E
Kalole 36 Ec 3.42S 27.22 E
Kaloli Point 65a Gd 19.37N 154.57W
Kalomo 36 Ef 17.02S 26.30 E
Kalpa 25 Fb 31.37N 78.10 E
Kalpákion 15 Dj 39.53N 20.35 E
Kalpeni Island 25 Ef 10.05N 73.38 E
Kalpin 27 Cc 40.31N 79.03 E
Kalsūbai 21 Jh 19.36N 73.43 E
Kaltern/Caldaro 14 Fd 46.25N 11.14 E
Kaltungo 34 Hd 9.49N 11.19 E
Kaluga 6 Je 54.31N 36.16 E
Kalulushi 36 Ee 12.50S 28.05 E
Kalumburu Mission 59 Fb 14.18S 126.39 E
Kalundborg 7 Ci 55.41N 11.06 E
Kaluš 19 Cf 49.03N 24.23 E
Kałuszyn 10 Rd 52.13N 21.49 E
Kalužskaja Oblast [3] 19 De 54.20N 35.30 E
Kalvåg 8 Ac 61.46N 4.53 E
Kalvarija 7 Fi 54.27N 23.14 E
Kalya 36 Fd 6.28S 30.03 E
Kalyān 25 Ee 19.15N 73.09 E
Kám 10 Mi 47.06N 16.53 E
Kama 36 Ec 3.32S 27.07 E
Kama [R.S.F.S.R.] 17 Nf 60.27N 69.00 E
Kama [U.S.S.R.] 5 Ld 55.45N 52.00 E
Kamae 29 Be 32.48N 131.56 E
Kamaï 35 Ba 21.12N 17.30 E
Kamaing 25 Jc 25.31N 96.44 E
Kamaishi 28 Pe 39.16N 141.53 E
Kamakou 65a Eb 21.07N 156.52W
Kamakura 29 Fd 35.19N 139.32 E
Kamālia 25 Eb 30.44N 72.39 E
Kamalo 65a Eb 21.03N 156.53W
Kaman 24 Ec 39.25N 33.45 E
Kamand, Āb-e- 24 Mf 33.28N 49.04 E
Kamanjab 37 Ac 19.35S 14.51 E
Kamanyola 36 Ec 2.46S 29.00 E
Kamaran 23 Ff 15.12N 42.35 E
Kamarang 54 Fb 5.53N 60.35W
Kama Reservoir (EN)= Kamskoje Vodohranilišče 5 Ld 58.50N 56.15 E
Kamaši 19 Gh 38.48N 66.29 E
Kamativi 37 Dc 18.19S 27.03 E
Kambalda 59 Ef 31.10S 121.37 E
Kambalnaja Sopka, Vulkan- 20 Kf 51.17N 156.57 E
Kambara 29 Fd 35.07N 138.36 E
Kambara 63d Cc 18.57S 178.57W
Kambarka 7 Nh 56.18N 54.14 E
Kambia 34 Cd 9.07N 12.55W
Kambja 8 Lf 58.11N 26.43 E
Kambove 36 Ee 10.52S 26.35 E
Kamčatka 20 Le 56.10N 162.30 E
Kamčatka, Poluostrov-= Kamchatka Peninsula (EN) 21 Rd 56.00N 160.00 E
Kamčatskaja Oblast [3] 20 Kf 54.50N 159.00 E
Kamčatski Zaliv 20 Le 55.30N 163.00 E
Kamchatka Peninsula (EN) =Kamčatka, Poluostrov- 21 Rd 56.00N 160.00 E
Kamčija 15 Kf 43.02N 27.53 E
Kamčijska Plato 15 Kg 42.56N 27.32 E
Kameda [Jap.] 29 Fc 37.52N 139.06 E
Kameda [Jap.] 29a Bc 41.49N 140.46 E
Kameda-Hantō 29a Bc 41.45N 141.00 E
Kámeiros 15 Km 36.18N 27.56 E
Kamelik 16 Pc 52.06N 49.30 E
Kamen 12 Jc 51.36N 7.40 E
Kaménai 15 Im 36.25N 25.25 E
Kamende 36 Dd 6.28S 24.33 E
Kamenec 10 Td 52.23N 23.49 E
Kamenec-Podolski 19 Cf 48.39N 26.33 E
Kamenijak, Rt- 14 Hf 44.46N 13.56 E
Kamenka [Kaz.-U.S.S.R.] 16 Qd 51.07N 50.20 E
Kamenka [Mold.-U.S.S.R.] 16 Fe 48.03N 28.45 E
Kamenka [R.S.F.S.R.] 16 Kd 50.43N 39.25 E
Kamenka [R.S.F.S.R.] 19 Ee 53.13N 44.03 E
Kamenka [R.S.F.S.R.] 7 Kd 65.54N 44.04 E
Kamenka [R.S.F.S.R.] 28 Nb 44.28N 136.01 E
Kamenka [Ukr.-U.S.S.R.] 19 Df 49.03N 32.06 E
Kamenka-Bugskaja 10 Uf 50.01N 24.25 E
Kamenka-Dneprovskaja 16 If 47.29N 34.29 E
Kamen-Kaširski 16 Dd 51.36N 24.59 E
Kamen-na-Obi 20 Df 53.47N 81.20 E
Kamennogorsk 7 Gf 60.59N 29.12 E
Kamennoje, Ozero- 7 Hd 64.30N 30.15 E
Kamennomostski 16 Lg 44.17N 40.12 E
Kamen-Rybolov 28 Kb 44.45N 132.04 E
Kamenskoje 20 Ld 62.30N 166.12 E
Kamensk-Šahtinski 16 Le 48.18N 40.16 E
Kamensk-Uralski 22 Id 56.28N 61.54 E
Kamenz/Kamjenc 10 Ke 51.16N 14.06 E
Kameoka 29 Dd 35.00N 135.35 E
Kameškovo 7 Jh 56.22N 41.01 E
Kamet 25 Fd 30.55N 79.35 E
Kameyama 29 Ed 34.51N 136.27 E
Kami-Agata 29 Ad 34.38N 129.25 E
Kamiah 46 Gc 46.14N 116.02W
Kamicharo 29a Cb 43.11N 143.52 E
Kamienna 10 Re 51.06N 21.47 E
Kamienna Góra 10 Mf 50.47N 16.01 E
Kamień Pomorski 10 Kc 53.58N 14.46 E
Kamiénsk 10 Pe 51.12N 19.30 E
Kamieskroon 37 Bf 30.09S 17.56 E
Kami-furano 29a Cb 43.29N 142.27 E
Kamiiso 28 Pd 41.49N 140.39 E
Kamiita 29 Dd 34.08N 134.24 E
Kamiji 36 Dd 6.39S 23.17 E
Kamikawa 29a Cb 43.50N 142.47 E
Kami-Koshiki-Jima 29 Af 31.50N 129.55 E
Kamina 31 Ji 8.44S 24.59 E
Kaminak Lake 42 Id 62.13N 95.00W
Kaminokuni 29a Bc 41.48N 140.05 E
Kamino-Shima 29 Ad 34.30N 129.25 E
Kaminoyama 28 Pe 38.09N 140.17 E
Kaminuriak Lake 42 Hd 63.00N 95.45W
Kamioka 28 Nf 36.16N 137.18 E
Kami-shihoro 29a Cb 43.13N 143.16 E
Kamisunagawa 29a Bb 43.28N 141.58 E
Kamitsushima 29 Ad 34.39N 129.28 E
Kamituga 36 Ec 3.04S 28.11 E
Kamiyama 29 De 33.58N 134.21 E
Kami-yūbetsu 29a Ca 44.11N 143.34 E
Kamjenc/Kamenz 10 Ke 51.16N 14.06 E
Kamloops 39 Gd 50.40N 120.20W
Kamloops Plateau 46 Ea 50.10N 120.35W
Kamnik 14 Id 46.14N 14.37 E
Kamo [Arm.-U.S.S.R.] 16 Ni 40.22N 45.05 E
Kamo [Jap.] 29 Fc 37.39N 139.03 E
Kamo [N.Z.] 62 Fa 35.41S 174.17 E
Kamōda-Misaki 29 De 33.50N 134.45 E
Kamogawa 29 Gd 35.06N 140.05 E
Kamp 14 Jb 48.23N 15.48 E
Kampala 31 Kh 0.19N 32.35 E
Kampar 26 Df 4.18N 101.09 E
Kampar 26 Mi 0.32N 103.08 E
Kampen 11 Lb 52.33N 5.54 E
Kampene 36 Ec 3.36S 26.40 E
Kamphaeng Phet 25 Je 16.26N 99.33 E
Kamp-Lintford 12 Ic 51.30N 6.32 E
Kamp'o 28 Jg 35.48N 129.30 E
Kâmpóng Cham 22 Mh 12.00N 105.27 E
Kâmpóng Chhnâng 25 Kf 12.15N 104.40 E
Kâmpóng Saôm 22 Mh 10.38N 103.30 E
Kâmpóng Saôm, Chhâk- 25 Kf 10.50N 103.32 E
Kâmpóng Thum 25 Kf 12.42N 104.54 E
Kâmpôt 25 Kf 10.37N 104.11 E
Kampti 34 Ec 10.08N 3.27W
Kampuchea (Cambodia) [1] 22 Mh 13.00N 105.00 E
Kamrau, Teluk- 26 Jg 3.32S 133.37 E
Kamsack 42 Hf 51.34N 101.54W
Kamsar 34 Cc 10.40N 14.36W
Kamskoje Ustje 7 Li 55.14N 49.16 E
Kamskoje Vodohranilišče= Kama Reservoir (EN) 5 Ld 58.50N 56.15 E
Kam Summa 35 Ge 0.21N 42.44 E
Kamuenai 29a Bb 43.08N 140.26 E
Kamui-Dake 29a Cb 42.25N 142.52 E
Kamui-Misaki 27 Pc 43.20N 140.20 E
Kámuk, Cerro- 49 Fi 9.17N 83.04W
Kamvoúnia Óri 15 Ei 40.00N 21.52 E
Kāmyārān 24 Le 34.47N 46.56 E
Kamyšin 6 Ke 50.06N 45.24 E
Kamyšlov 19 Gd 56.52N 62.43 E
Kamyšovaja Buhta 16 Hg 44.31N 33.33 E
Kamysty-Ajat 17 Jj 53.01N 61.35 E
Kamyzjak 19 Ef 46.06N 48.05 E
Kan 24 Ne 35.45N 51.16 E
Kan 20 Ee 56.31N 93.47 E
Kana 37 Dc 18.32S 27.24 E
Kanaaupscow 42 Jf 54.01N 76.32W
Kanaaupscow 42 Jf 53.40N 77.08W
Kanab 43 Ed 37.03N 112.32W
Kanab Creek 46 Ih 36.24N 112.38W
Kanaga 40a Cb 51.45N 177.10W
Kanagawa Ken [2] 28 Og 35.30N 139.10 E
Kanaliasem 26 Dg 1.44S 103.35 E
Kanami-Zaki 29b Bb 27.53N 128.58 E
Kananga 31 Ji 5.54S 22.25 E
Kanariktok 42 Le 55.03N 60.10W
Kanaš 7 Li 55.31N 47.31 E
Kanathea 63d Cb 17.16S 179.09W
Kanaya 29 Fd 34.48N 138.07 E
Kanayama 29 Ed 35.39N 137.09 E
Kanazawa 22 Pf 36.34N 136.39 E
Kanbalu 25 Jd 23.12N 95.31 E
Kanbe 25 Je 16.42N 96.01 E
Kanchanaburi 25 Jf 14.02N 99.33 E
Kānchenjunga 21 Kg 27.42N 88.08 E
Kānchipuram 25 Ff 12.50N 79.43 E
Kandalakša 6 Jb 67.09N 32.21 E
Kandalaksha, Gulf of- (EN) =Kandalakšski Zaliv 5 Jb 66.35N 32.45 E
Kandalakšski Zaliv= Kandalaksha, Gulf of- (EN) 5 Jb 66.35N 32.45 E
Kandangan 26 Gg 2.47S 115.16 E
Kándanos 15 Gn 35.20N 23.44 E
Kandava 7 Fh 57.03N 22.46 E
Kandavu Island 57 If 19.00S 178.13 E
Kandavu Passage 63d Ac 18.45S 178.00 E
Kandel 12 Ke 49.05N 8.12 E
Kandel 10 Eh 48.04N 8.01 E
Kandhelioúsa 15 Jm 36.30N 26.58 E
Kandi 31 Hg 11.08N 2.56 E
Kandıra 24 Db 41.04N 30.09 E
Kandla 25 Ed 23.02N 70.14 E
Kando-Gawa 29 Cd 35.22N 132.40 E
Kandovān, Gardaneh-ye- 24 Nd 36.09N 51.18 E
Kandrian 60 Di 6.13S 149.33 E
Kandry 17 Gi 54.34N 54.10 E
Kandy 22 Ki 7.18N 80.38 E
Kane 44 He 41.40N 78.48W
Kane Bassin 67 Od 79.35N 67.00W
Kaneh 24 Pi 27.04N 54.18 E
Kanem [3] 35 Bc 15.00N 16.00 E
Kanem 30 Ig 14.45N 15.30 E
Kaneohe 60 Oc 21.25N 157.48W
Kaneohe Bay 65a Db 21.28N 157.48W
Kánestron, Ákra- 15 Gj 39.56N 23.45 E
Kanev 16 Ge 49.42N 31.29 E
Kanevskaja 19 Df 46.06N 38.58 E
Kaneyama 29 Fc 37.27N 139.30 E
Kang 37 Cd 23.44S 22.50 E
Kangaba 34 Dc 11.56N 8.25W
Kangal 24 Gc 39.15N 37.24 E
Kangalassy 20 Hd 62.17N 129.58 E
Kangâmiut 41 Ge 65.39N 53.55W
Kangān [Iran] 24 Oi 27.50N 52.03 E
Kangān [Iran] 24 Qj 25.48N 57.28 E
Kangar 26 De 6.26N 100.12 E
Kangaré 34 Dc 11.37N 8.08W
Kangaroo Island 57 Eh 35.50S 137.05 E
Kangasala 8 Kc 61.28N 24.05 E
Kangasniemi 7 Gf 61.59N 26.38 E
Kangâtsiaq 41 Ge 68.20N 53.18W
Kangāvar 24 Le 34.30N 47.58 E
Kangbao 28 Cd 41.51N 114.37 E
Kangding/Dardo 27 He 30.01N 101.58 E
Kangean, Kepulauan-= Kangean Islands (EN) 26 Gh 6.55S 115.30 E
Kangean, Pulau- 26 Gh 6.54S 115.20 E
Kangean Islands (EN)= Kangean, Kepulauan- 26 Gh 6.55S 115.30 E
Kangeeak Point 42 Lc 68.01N 64.45W
Kangen 30 Kh 6.47N 33.09 E
Kangerdlugssuaq 41 Ie 68.20N 31.40W
Kangetet 36 Gb 1.58N 36.06 E

Index Symbols

[1] Independent Nation
[2] State, Region
[3] District, County
[4] Municipality
[5] Colony, Dependency
Continent
Physical Region
Historical or Cultural Region
Mount, Mountain
Volcano
Hill
Mountains, Mountain Range
Hills, Escarpment
Plateau, Upland
Pass, Gap
Plain, Lowland
Delta
Salt Flat
Valley, Canyon
Crater, Cave
Karst Features
Depression
Polder
Desert, Dunes
Forest, Woods
Heath, Steppe
Oasis
Cape, Point
Coast, Beach
Cliff
Peninsula
Isthmus
Sandbank
Island
Atoll
Rock, Reef
Islands, Archipelago
Rocks, Reefs
Coral Reef
Well, Spring
Geyser
River, Stream
Waterfall Rapids
River Mouth, Estuary
Lake
Salt Lake
Intermittent Lake
Reservoir
Swamp, Pond
Canal
Glacier
Ice Shelf, Pack Ice
Ocean
Sea
Gulf, Bay
Strait, Fjord
Lagoon
Bank
Seamount
Tablemount
Ridge
Shelf
Basin
Escarpment, Sea Scarp
Fracture
Trench, Abyss
National Park, Reserve
Point of Interest
Recreation Site
Cave, Cavern
Historic Site
Ruins
Wall, Walls
Church, Abbey
Temple
Scientific Station
Airport
Port
Lighthouse
Mine
Tunnel
Dam, Bridge

Kanggup'o 28 Id 41.07N 127.31 E
Kanggye 27 Mc 40.58N 126.36 E
Kangi 35 Dd 8.10N 27.39 E
Kangjin 28 Ig 34.38N 126.46 E
Kangmar 27 Ef 28.32N 89.43 E
Kangnŭng 27 Md 37.44N 128.54 E
Kango 36 Bb 0.09N 10.08 E
Kangondu 36 Gc 1.06S 37.42 E
Kangping 28 Gc 42.45N 123.20 E
Kangrinboqê Feng 27 De 31.04N 81.30 E
Kangto 25 Ic 27.52N 92.30 E
Kangwŏn-Do [N.Kor.] [2] 28 Ie 38.45N 127.35 E
Kangwŏn-Do [S.Kor.] [2] 28 Jf 37.45N 128.15 E
Kani 34 Dd 8.29N 6.36W
Kaniama 36 Dd 7.31S 24.11 E
Kanibadam 18 Hd 40.17N 70.25 E
Kaniet Islands 57 Fe 0.53S 145.30 E
Kanija 15 Lc 46.16N 28.13 E
Kanimeh 18 Ed 40.18N 65.09 E
Kanina 15 Ci 40.26N 19.31 E
Kanin Kamen 17 Bb 68.15N 45.15 E
Kanin Nos 19 Eb 68.39N 43.14 E
Kanin Nos, Mys- 5 Kb 68.39N 43.16 E
Kanin Peninsula (EN)= Kanin Poluostrov 5 Kb 68.00N 45.00 E
Kanin Poluostrov=Kanin Peninsula (EN) 5 Kb 68.00N 45.00 E
Kanioumé 34 Eb 15.46N 3.09W
Kanita 29a Bc 41.02N 140.38 E
Kanjiža 15 Dc 46.04N 20.03 E
Kankaanpää 7 Ff 61.48N 22.25 E
Kankakee 43 Jc 41.07N 87.52W
Kankakee River 45 Lf 41.23N 88.16W
Kankalabé 34 Cc 11.00N 12.00W
Kankan 31 Gg 10.23N 9.18W
Kanker 25 Gd 20.17N 81.29 E
Kankesanturai 25 Gg 9.49N 80.02 E
Kankossa 32 Ef 15.55N 11.31W
Kankunski 20 He 57.39N 126.25 E
Kanla 10 Hf 50.48N 11.35 E
Kanmav Kyun 25 Jf 11.40N 98.28 E
Kanmon-Kaikyō 29 Bd 33.56N 130.57 E
Kanmuri-Yama 29 Cd 34.28N 132.05 E
Kannapolis 43 Kd 35.30N 80.37W
Kannone-Jima 28 Jj 28.51N 128.58 E
Kannonkoski 8 Kb 62.58N 25.15 E
Kannus 7 Fe 63.54N 23.54 E
Kano [2] 34 Gc 12.00N 9.00 E
Kano 31 Hg 12.00N 8.31 E
Kanona 36 Fe 13.04S 30.38 E
Kan'onji 28 Lg 34.07N 133.39 E
Kanoya 28 Ki 31.23N 130.51 E
Kanozero, Ozero- 7 Ic 67.00N 34.05 E
Kānpur 22 Kg 26.28N 80.21 E
Kansas 38 Jf 39.07N 94.36W
Kansas [2] 43 Hd 38.45N 98.15W
Kansas City [Ks.-U.S.] 39 Jf 39.07N 94.39W
Kansas City [Mo.-U.S.] 39 Jf 39.05N 94.35W
Kanshi 27 Kg 24.57N 116.52 E
Kansk 22 Ld 56.13N 95.41 E
Kansŏng 28 Je 38.22N 128.28 E
Kansu (EN)=Gansu Sheng (Kan-su Sheng) [2] 27 Hd 38.00N 102.00 E
Kansu (EN)=Kan-su Sheng→Gansu Sheng [2] 27 Hd 38.00N 102.00 E
Kan-su Sheng→Gansu Sheng=Kansu (EN) [2] 27 Hd 38.00N 102.00 E
Kansyat 26 Kg 2.15S 138.51 E
Kant 18 Jc 42.52N 74.50 E
Kantang 25 Jg 7.23N 99.32 E
Kantchari 34 Fc 12.29N 1.31 E
Kanté 34 Fd 9.57N 1.03 E
Kantemirovka 19 Df 49.45N 39.53 E
Kantō-Heiya 29 Fc 36.00N 139.30 E
Kanton Atoll 57 Je 2.50S 171.41W
Kantō-Sanchi 29 Fc 36.00N 138.45 E
Kantubek 18 Bb 45.06N 59.16 E
Kanturk/Ceann Toirc 9 Ei 52.10N 8.55W
Kanuma 29 Fc 36.34N 139.45 E
Kanye 31 Jk 24.58S 25.21 E
Kanyu 37 Cd 20.04S 24.36 E
Kanzenze 36 Ee 10.31S 25.12 E
Kao 65b Aa 19.40S 175.01W
Kaohsiung 22 Og 22.38N 120.17 E
Kaôk Nhêk 25 Lf 13.05N 107.04 E
Kaoko Otavi 37 Ac 18.15S 13.37 E
Kaokoveld [3] 37 Ac 18.00S 13.00 E
Kaokoveld 30 Ij 19.30S 13.30 E
Kaolack 31 Fg 14.09N 16.04W
Kao Neua, Col de- 25 Le 18.23N 105.10 E
Kaouadja 35 Cd 8.00N 23.14 E
Kaouar 34 Hb 19.05N 12.52 E
Kapaa 65a Ba 22.05N 159.19W
Kapanga 31 Ji 8.21S 22.35 E
Kapar 24 Ld 36.32N 47.30 E
Kapčagaj 19 Hg 43.52N 77.03 E
Kapčagajskoje Vodohranilišče 19 Hg 43.45N 78.00 E
Kapchorwa 36 Fb 1.24N 34.27 E
Kap Dan 41 Ie 65.32N 37.30W
Kapelle 12 Fc 51.39N 3.57 E
Kapellskär 8 He 59.43N 19.04 E
Kapena 36 Ee 10.47S 28.20 E
Kapenguria 36 Gb 1.14N 35.07 E
Kapfenberg 14 Jc 47.26N 15.18 E
Kapidaği Yarimadası 15 Ki 40.28N 27.50 E
Kapingamarangi Atoll 57 Gd 1.04N 154.46 E
Kapingamarangi Rise (EN) 57 Gd 1.00N 157.00 E
Kapiri Mposhi 36 Ee 13.58S 28.41 E
Kāpīsā [3] 23 Kc 34.45N 69.30 E
Kapit 26 Ff 2.01N 112.56 E
Kapiti Island 62 Fd 40.50S 174.55 E
Kapka, Massif du- 35 Cb 15.07N 21.45 E
Kapoeta 31 Kh 4.47N 33.35 E
Kapona 36 Ed 7.11S 29.09 E
Kapos 10 Oj 46.44N 18.29 E
Kaposvár 10 Nj 46.22N 17.48 E
Kapp 8 Dd 60.42N 10.52 E
Kappeln 10 Fb 54.40N 9.56 E
Kapša 7 Hg 59.52N 33.45 E
Kapsan 28 Jd 41.05N 128.18 E
Kapsukas 7 Fi 54.33N 23.23 E
Kapuas [Indon.] 26 Mj 0.25S 109.40 E
Kapuas [Indon.] 26 Fg 3.01S 114.20 E
Kapuas Hulu, Pegunungan-=Kapuas Mountains (EN) 26 Ff 1.25N 113.15 E
Kapuas Mountains (EN)= Kapuas Hulu, Pegunungan 26 Ff 1.25N 113.15 E
Kapugargin 15 Lm 36.40N 28.50 E
Kapušany 10 Rg 49.03N 21.21 E
Kapuskasing 39 Ke 49.25N 82.26W
Kapustin Jar 16 Ne 48.35N 45.45 E
Kapustoje 7 Ic 67.17N 34.12 E
Kaputdžuh, Gora- 16 Oj 39.12N 46.01 E
Kapuvár 10 Ni 47.36N 17.02 E
Kara 17 Lb 69.10N 64.45 E
Kara 34 Fd 9.33N 1.12 E
Kara [3] 34 Fd 9.35N 1.05 E
Kara Ada [Tur.] 15 Km 36.58N 27.28 E
Kara Ada [Tur.] 15 Jk 38.25N 26.20 E
Kara-Balta 19 Hg 42.49N 73.57 E
Karabas 19 Hf 49.30N 73.00 E
Karabaš 17 Ji 55.29N 60.13 E
Karabekaul 19 Gh 38.28N 64.10 E
Karabiga 15 Ki 40.24N 27.18 E
Karabil, Vozvyšennost- 18 Df 36.20N 63.30 E
Kara-Bogaz-Gol 19 Fg 41.01N 52.59 E
Kara-Bogaz-Gol, proliv- 16 Ri 41.04N 52.59 E
Kara-Bogaz-Gol, Zaliv- 5 Lg 41.00N 53.15 E
Karabuk 23 Da 41.12N 32.37 E
Karabulak [Kaz.-U.S.S.R.] 18 Lb 44.54N 78.29 E
Karabulak [Kaz.-U.S.S.R.] 19 Gg 42.31N 69.47 E
Kara Burun 15 Km 36.32N 27.58 E
Karaburun [Tur.] 24 Cb 41.21N 28.40 E
Karaburun [Tur.] 24 Bc 38.37N 26.31 E
Karabutak 19 Gf 49.57N 60.08 E
Karacabey 24 Cb 40.13N 28.21 E
Karaca Dağ 24 Hd 37.40N 39.50 E
Karačajevo-Čerkessakaja Avtonomnaja Oblast [3] 19 Eg 43.45N 41.45 E
Karačajevsk 16 Lh 43.44N 41.58 E
Karacaköy 24 Cb 41.22N 28.30 E
Karacaoğlan 15 Kh 41.32N 27.04 E
Karacasu 24 Cd 37.43N 28.37 E
Karačev 19 De 53.04N 34.59 E
Karāchi 22 Ig 24.52N 67.03 E
Kara Dağ [Tur.] 24 Jd 37.40N 43.42 E
Kara Dağ [Tur.] 24 Ed 37.23N 33.10 E
Karadah 16 Oh 42.29N 46.54 E
Karadeniz=Black Sea (EN) 5 Jg 43.00N 35.00 E
Kara Dong 27 Dd 38.26N 81.50 E
Karagajly 19 Hf 49.20N 75.48 E
Karaganda 22 Je 49.50N 73.10 E
Karagandinskaja Oblast [3] 19 Hf 50.00N 74.00 E
Karaginski, Ostrov- 21 Sd 58.48N 164.05 E
Karaginski Zaliv 21 Sd 58.50N 164.00 E
Kara Gölü 15 Mm 36.42N 29.50 E
Karagoš, Gora- 20 Df 51.44N 89.24 E
Karahalli 15 Mk 38.20N 29.32 E
Karaidelski 17 Hi 55.49N 57.05 E
Kara-Irtyš 21 Ke 47.52N 84.16 E
Karaisali 24 Fd 37.16N 35.03 E
Karaj 24 Ne 35.48N 50.59 E
Karaj 24 Ne 35.07N 51.35 E
Karak, Gora- 19 Gg 44.59N 63.05 E
Kara-Kala 19 Fh 38.28N 56.18 E
Karakalpak ASSR (EN)= Karakalpakskaja ASSR [3] 19 Fg 43.30N 59.00 E
Karakalpakskaja ASSR= Karakalpak ASSR (EN) [3] 19 Fg 43.30N 59.00 E
Karakax/Moyu 27 Cd 37.17N 79.42 E
Karakax He 27 Dd 38.06N 80.24 E
Karakeçi 24 Hd 37.26N 39.26 E
Karakelong, Pulau- 26 If 4.15N 126.48 E
Karakoçan 24 Ic 38.02N 40.07 E
Karakoin, Ozero- 18 Ga 46.10N 68.40 E
Karakojsu 16 Oh 42.30N 47.05 E
Karakolka 18 Kd 41.29N 77.24 E
Karakoram 21 Jf 34.00N 78.00 E
Karakoram Pass 21 Jf 35.30N 77.50 E
Karakore 35 Gc 10.25N 40.01 E
Karakoro 34 Cc 14.43N 12.03 E
Karakorum Shan 27 Cd 36.00N 76.00 E
Karakorum Shankou 27 Cd 35.30N 77.50 E
Karaköse 23 Fb 39.44N 43.03 E
Karaköy 24 Ic 39.04N 41.42 E
Kara-Kul 18 Id 41.34N 72.47 E
Karakul, Ozero- 19 Hh 39.05N 73.25 E
Karakumski kanal imeni V.I. Lenina 19 Gh 37.42N 64.20 E
Karakumy 21 Hf 39.00N 60.00 E
Karakuwisa 37 Bc 18.56S 19.40 E
Karam 20 Fe 55.09N 107.37 E
Karama 26 Gg 2.18S 119.06 E
Karaman 23 Db 37.11N 33.14 E
Karamanli 15 Ml 37.22N 29.49 E
Karamay 22 Ke 45.30N 84.55 E
Karamea 61 Dh 41.15S 172.06 E
Karamea Bight 62 Dd 41.25S 171.50 E
Karamet-Nijaz 19 Gh 37.43N 64.31 E
Karamiran He 27 Dd 37.50N 84.35 E
Karamiran Shankou 27 Ed 36.15N 87.05 E
Karamiševo 8 Mg 57.44N 28.50 E
Karamoja [3] 36 Fb 2.45N 34.15 E
Karamürsel 15 Mi 40.42N 29.36 E
Kara-myk 19 Hh 39.30N 71.51 E
Karamyš 16 Nd 51.18N 45.00 E
Karān 24 Mi 27.43N 49.49 E
Karaova 15 Kl 37.05N 27.40 E
Karapınar 24 Ed 37.43N 33.33 E
Kara-Saki 29 Ad 34.40N 129.29 E
Kara-Sal 16 Mf 47.18N 43.36 E
Karasay 27 Dd 36.48N 83.48 E
Karasburg 31 Ik 28.00S 18.43 E
Kara Sea (EN)=Karskoje More 67 Hd 76.00N 80.00 E
Karašica 14 Me 45.36N 18.36 E
Karasjok 7 Fb 69.27N 25.30 E
Kara Strait (EN)=Karskije Vorota, Proliv- 21 Hb 70.30N 58.00 E
Karasu 24 Db 41.04N 30.47 E
Karasu [Tur.] 21 Ff 38.52N 38.48 E
Karasu [Tur.] 24 Ic 38.49N 41.28 E
Karasu [Tur.] 24 Jc 38.32N 43.10 E
Karasu Dağları 24 Ic 39.30N 40.45 E
Karasuk 20 Cf 53.44N 78.08 E
Karasuk 20 Cf 53.35N 77.30 E
Karasuyama 29 Gc 36.39N 140.08 E
Karatá, Laguna- 49 Fg 13.56N 83.30W
Karatal 19 Hf 46.26N 77.10 E
Karataş [Tur.] 24 Fd 36.36N 35.21 E
Karataş [Tur.] 15 Lk 38.34N 28.17 E
Karataş Burun 24 Fb 36.35N 35.22 E
Karatau 19 Hg 43.10N 70.29 E
Karatau, Hrebet- 21 Ie 43.40N 69.00 E
Karatj 7 Ec 66.43N 18.33 E
Karatobe 16 Re 49.42N 53.33 E
Karaton 19 Ff 46.25N 53.34 E
Karatsu 28 Jh 33.26N 130.00 E
Karatsu-Wan 29 Be 33.30N 130.00 E
Kara-Turgaj 21 Ie 48.01N 62.45 E
Karaul [Kaz.-U.S.S.R.] 19 Hf 49.00N 79.20 E
Karaul [R.S.F.S.R.] 20 Db 70.10N 83.08 E
Karaulbazar 18 Ee 39.29N 64.47 E
Karaulkala 18 Bc 42.18N 58.41 E
Karáva 15 Ej 39.19N 21.36 E
Karavanke 14 Id 46.25N 14.25 E
Karavastase, Gjiri i- 15 Ci 40.55N 19.30 E
Karavastase, Laguna e- 15 Ci 40.55N 19.30 E
Karávi 15 Gm 36.45N 23.35 E
Karavonísia 15 Jn 35.59N 26.26 E
Karawa 36 Db 3.20N 20.18 E
Karaxabar He/Kaidu He 27 Ec 41.55N 86.38 E
Karažal 19 Hf 47.59N 70.53 E
Karbalā' 22 Gf 32.36N 44.02 E
Karbalā [3] 24 Jf 32.30N 43.45 E
Kårbole 7 Df 61.59N 15.19 E
Karcag 10 Qi 47.19N 20.56 E
Kardhámaina 15 Km 36.47N 27.09 E
Kardhámila 15 Jk 38.31N 26.06 E
Kardhiotissa 15 Im 36.38N 25.01 E
Kardhítsa 15 Ej 39.22N 21.55 E
Kärdla/Kjardla 7 Fg 59.01N 22.42 E
Kărdžali 15 Ih 41.39N 25.22 E
Kărdžali [2] 15 Ih 41.30N 25.30 E
Kareha, Jbel- 13 Gi 35.15N 5.30W
Karelia (EN) 5 Jc 64.00N 32.00 E
Karelskaja ASSR [3] 19 Dc 63.30N 33.30 E
Karema 36 Fd 6.49S 30.26 E
Karen [2] 25 Je 17.30N 97.45 E
Karen 25 If 12.51N 92.53 E
Karesuando 7 Fb 68.27N 22.29 E
Karêt 30 Gf 24.00N 7.30W
Kärevere/Kjarevere 8 Lf 58.23N 26.30 E
Kargala 16 Sd 51.59N 55.10 E
Kargapazarı Dağı 24 Ib 40.07N 41.35 E
Kargapolje 17 Li 55.57N 64.27 E
Kargasok 20 De 59.07N 81.01 E
Kargat 20 De 55.10N 80.17 E
Kargı 24 Fb 41.08N 34.30 E
Kargil 25 Fb 34.34N 76.06 E
Kargilik/Yecheng 22 Jf 37.54N 77.26 E
Kargopol 19 Dc 61.32N 38.58 E
Karhula 7 Gf 60.31N 26.57 E
Kari 34 Hc 11.14N 10.34 E
Kariaí 6 Ig 40.15N 24.15 E
Kariba 31 Jj 16.30S 28.45 E
Kariba, Lake- 30 Jj 17.00S 28.00 E
Kariba-Dake 29a Ab 42.37N 139.56 E
Kariba Dam 37 Dc 16.30S 28.50 E
Karibib 31 Ik 21.58S 15.51 E
Karibib [3] 37 Bd 22.00S 16.00 E
Kariet-Arkmane 13 Ji 35.06N 2.45W
Karigasniemi 7 Fb 69.24N 25.50 E
Karijärvi 8 Jc 61.35N 22.30 E
Karikachi Tōge 29a Cb 43.10N 142.40 E
Kārikāl 25 Ff 10.55N 79.50 E
Karikari, Cape- 62 Ea 34.47S 173.24 E
Karima (EN)=Kuraymah 31 Kg 18.33N 31.51 E
Karimama 34 Fc 12.04N 3.11 E
Karimata, Kepulauan-= Karimata Islands (EN) 26 Eg 1.25S 109.05 E
Karimata, Pulau- 26 Eg 1.36S 108.55 E
Karimata, Selat-=Karimata Strait (EN) 21 Mj 2.05S 108.40 E
Karimata Islands (EN)= Karimata, Kepulauan- 26 Eg 1.25S 109.05 E
Karimata Strait (EN)= Karimata, Selat- 21 Mj 2.05S 108.40 E
Karīmganj 25 Id 24.42N 92.33 E
Karīmnagar 25 Fe 18.26N 79.09 E
Karimunjawa, Kepulauan-= Karimunjawa Islands (EN) 26 Fh 5.50S 110.25 E
Karimunjawa Islands (EN)= Karimunjawa, Kepulauan- 26 Fh 5.50S 110.25 E
Karin [Som.] 35 Hc 10.59N 49.13 E
Karin [Som.] 35 Hc 10.51N 45.45 E
Karis/Karjaa 7 Ff 60.05N 23.40 E
Karisimbi 30 Ji 1.30S 29.27 E
Káristos 15 Hk 38.01N 24.25 E
Karjaa/Karis 7 Ff 60.05N 23.40 E
Karkār 35 Hd 9.57N 49.20 E
Karkaralinsk 19 Hf 49.23N 75.31 E
Karkar Island 57 Fe 4.40S 146.00 E
Karkas, Kūh-e 24 Nf 33.27N 51.48 E
Karkheh 23 Gc 31.31N 47.55 E
Karkinitski zaliv 5 Jf 45.55N 33.00 E
Karkkila/Högfors 7 Ff 60.32N 24.11 E
Karkku 8 Jc 61.25N 23.01 E
Kärkölä 8 Kd 60.55N 25.15 E
Kärla/Kjarla 8 Jf 58.16N 22.05 E
Karlholm 8 Gd 60.31N 17.37 E
Karlik Shan 21 Le 43.00N 94.30 E
Karlino 10 Lb 54.03N 15.51 E
Karliova 24 Ic 39.18N 41.01 E
Karl Marx, Pik- 19 Hh 37.08N 72.29 E
Karl-Marx-Stadt 6 He 50.50N 12.55 E
Karl-Marx-Stadt [2] 10 If 50.45N 12.50 E
Karlö/Hailuoto 5 Ib 65.02N 24.42 E
Karlobag 14 Jf 44.32N 15.05 E
Karlovac 14 Je 45.29N 15.33 E
Karlovka 16 Ie 49.28N 35.08 E
Karlovo 15 Hg 42.38N 24.48 E
Karlovy Vary 10 If 50.14N 12.52 E
Karlsbad 12 Kf 48.55N 8.35 E
Karlsborg 7 Df 58.32N 14.31 E
Karlshamn 7 Dh 56.10N 14.51 E
Karlskoga 7 Dg 59.20N 14.31 E
Karlskrona 6 Hd 56.10N 15.35 E
Karlsöarna 8 Gg 57.15N 18.00 E
Karlsruhe 10 Eg 49.01N 8.24 E
Karlstad [Mn.-U.S.] 45 Hb 48.35N 96.31W
Karlstad [Swe.] 6 Hd 59.22N 13.30 E
Karluk 40 Ie 57.34N 154.28W
Karmah=Kerma (EN) 35 Eb 19.38N 30.25 E
Karmana 18 Ed 40.09N 65.15 E
Karmøy 7 Ag 59.15N 5.15 E
Karnāli 25 Gc 28.45N 81.16 E
Karnataka (Mysore) [3] 25 Ff 13.30N 76.00 E
Karnobat 15 Jg 42.39N 26.59 E
Kärnten = Carinthia (EN) [2] 14 Hd 46.45N 14.00 E
Kärnten = Carinthia (EN) 14 Hd 46.45N 14.00 E
Karoi 37 Dc 16.50S 29.40 E
Karonga 31 Ki 9.56S 33.56 E
Karora 35 Fb 17.39N 38.22 E
Káros 15 Im 36.53N 25.39 E
Kárpathos 15 Kn 35.30N 27.14 E
Kárpathos=Karpathos (EN) 5 Ih 35.40N 27.10 E
Karpathos (EN)= Kárpathos 5 Ih 35.40N 27.10 E
Karpáthou, Stenón- 15 Kn 35.50N 27.30 E
Karpenision 15 Ek 38.55N 21.47 E
Karpinsk 17 Jg 59.45N 60.01 E
Karpuzlu 15 Kl 37.33N 27.50 E
Kars 23 Fa 40.37N 43.05 E
Karsakpaj 19 Gf 47.48N 66.45 E
Kärsämäki 7 Fe 64.00N 25.46 E
Karsava/Kārsava 7 Gh 56.47N 27.42 E
Kārsava/Karsava 7 Gh 56.47N 27.42 E
Karši 22 If 38.53N 65.48 E
Karşiyaka 15 Ki 40.26N 28.00 E
Karsiyaka 15 Kk 38.27N 27.07 E
Karskije Vorota, Proliv-= Kara Strait (EN) 21 Hb 70.30N 58.00 E
Karskoje More=Kara Sea (EN) 67 Hd 76.00N 80.00 E
Kars Platosu 24 Jb 40.40N 43.07 E
Karst (EN)=Kras 5 Hf 45.48N 14.00 E
Kårsta 8 He 59.39N 18.14 E
Karstula 7 Fe 62.52N 24.47 E
Kartal 24 Cb 40.53N 29.10 E
Kartaly 19 Ge 53.03N 60.40 E
Kartaly-Ajat 17 Jj 53.01N 61.50 E
Karttula 8 Lb 62.53N 26.58 E
Kartuzy 10 Ob 54.20N 18.12 E
Karumai 29 Ga 40.20N 141.28 E
Karumba 59 Ic 17.29S 140.50 E
Karūn 21 Gf 30.25N 48.12 E
Karungi 7 Fc 66.03N 23.57 E
Karungu 36 Fc 0.51S 34.09 E
Karunki 7 Fc 66.02N 24.01 E
Karūr 25 Ff 10.57N 78.05 E
Karvia 7 Fe 62.08N 22.34 E
Karviná 10 Og 49.51N 18.32 E
Kārwār 25 Ef 14.48N 74.08 E
Karwendel Gebirge 14 Fc 47.28N 11.20 E
Karymskoje 20 Gf 51.37N 114.21 E
Kas 35 Cc 12.34N 24.14 E
Kaş 24 Cd 36.12N 29.38 E
Kasaba [Tur.] 15 Mm 36.18N 29.44 E
Kasaba [Zam.] 36 Ee 10.44S 29.43 E
Kasado-Shima 29 Be 33.57N 131.50 E
Kasah 16 Mi 40.03N 43.52 E
Kasai 29 Dd 34.56N 134.49 E
Kasai 30 Ii 3.02S 16.57 E
Kasai Occidental [2] 36 Dc 5.00S 21.30 E
Kasai Oriental [2] 36 Dc 3.00S 23.00 E
Kasaji 36 De 10.22S 23.27 E
Kasaku 36 Ec 1.55S 25.50 E
Kasama [Jap.] 29 Gc 36.22N 140.16 E
Kasama [Zam.] 31 Kj 10.13S 31.12 E
Kasan 18 Ee 39.01N 65.35 E
Kasane 31 Jj 17.48S 25.09 E
Kasanga 36 Fd 8.28S 31.09 E
Kasangulu 36 Bc 4.36S 15.10 E
Kasansaj 18 Hd 41.10N 71.32 E
Kasaoka 29 Cd 34.30N 133.29 E
Kāsaragod 25 Ef 12.30N 75.00 E
Kasari 29b Ba 28.27N 129.41 E
Kašary 16 Le 49.02N 41.03 E
Kasatori-Yama 29 Ce 33.33N 132.55 E
Kasba Lake 42 Hd 60.20N 102.10W
Kasba Tatla 32 Fc 32.36N 6.16W
Kaseda 28 Ki 31.25N 130.19 E
Kasempa 36 Ee 13.27S 25.50 E
Kasenga 31 Jj 10.22S 28.37 E
Kasenye 36 Fb 1.24N 30.26 E
Kasese [Ug.] 36 Fb 0.10N 30.05 E
Kasese [Zaire] 36 Ec 1.38S 27.07 E
Kashaf 23 Jb 35.58N 61.07 E
Kāshān 22 Hf 33.59N 51.29 E
Kashi 22 Jf 39.29N 75.58 E
Kashihara 29 Dd 34.31N 135.47 E
Kashima [Jap.] 29 Cd 35.31N 132.59 E
Kashima [Jap.] 29 Gd 35.58N 140.38 E
Kashima [Jap.] 29 Be 33.07N 130.07 E
Kashima-Nada 29 Gc 36.30N 140.45 E
Kashiobwe 36 Ed 9.39S 28.37 E
Kashiwazaki 28 Of 37.25N 138.30 E
Kashkū'īyeh 24 Qh 28.58N 56.37 E
Kāshmar 23 Ib 35.12N 58.27 E
Kashmir 21 Jf 34.00N 76.00 E
Kashmor 25 Dc 28.26N 69.35 E
Kasimov 19 Ee 54.59N 41.28 E
Kašin 19 Dd 57.23N 37.37 E
Kasindi 36 Eb 0.02N 29.43 E
Kaširа 7 Ji 54.52N 38.11 E
Kasiruta, Pulau- 26 Ig 0.25S 127.12 E
Kasisty 20 Fb 73.40N 109.45 E
Kaškadarinskaja Oblast [3] 19 Gh 38.50N 66.10 E
Kaškadarja 18 Ee 39.35N 64.38 E
Kaskaskia River 45 Lh 37.59N 89.56W
Kaskelen 19 Hg 43.09N 76.37 E
Kaskinen/Kaskö 7 Ee 62.23N 21.13 E
Kaskö/Kaskinen 7 Ee 62.23N 21.13 E
Kasli 17 Ji 55.53N 60.48 E
Kaslo 46 Gb 49.55N 116.55W
Kasongo 31 Ji 4.27S 26.40 E
Kasongo-Lunda 36 Cd 6.28S 16.49 E
Kásos 15 Jn 35.25N 26.55 E
Kásou, Stenón- 15 Jn 35.25N 26.35 E
Kaspi 16 Ni 41.58N 44.25 E
Kaspičan 15 Kf 43.18N 27.11 E
Kaspijsk 19 Eg 42.57N 47.35 E
Kaspijski 19 Ef 45.25N 47.22 E
Kaspijskoje More=Caspian Sea (EN) 5 Lg 42.00N 50.30 E
Kasplja 16 Gb 55.24N 30.43 E
Kasr, Ra's- 35 Fb 18.04N 38.33 E
Kassaar/Kassar 8 Jf 58.47N 22.40 E
Kassalā 31 Kg 15.28N 36.24 E
Kassalā [3] 35 Fc 14.40N 35.30 E
Kassándra 15 Gi 40.00N 23.30 E
Kassandra, Gulf of- (EN) = Kassándras, Kólpos- 15 Gi 40.05N 23.30 E
Kassándras, Ákra- 15 Gj 39.57N 23.21 E
Kassándras, Kólpos- = Kassandra, Gulf of- (EN) 15 Gi 40.05N 23.30 E
Kassar/Kassaar 8 Jf 58.47N 22.40 E
Kassel 10 Fe 51.19N 9.30 E
Kassinga 36 Cf 15.06S 16.06 E
Kassiópi 15 Cj 39.47N 19.55 E
Kastamonu 23 Da 41.22N 33.47 E
Kastanéai 15 Jh 41.39N 26.28 E
Kastellaun 12 Jd 50.04N 7.27 E
Kastéllion [Grc.] 15 In 35.12N 25.20 E
Kastéllion [Grc.] 15 Gn 35.30N 23.39 E
Kastéllos, Ákra- 15 Kn 35.23N 27.09 E
Kasterlee 12 Gc 51.15N 4.57 E
Kastlösa 8 Gh 56.28N 16.25 E
Kastoría 15 Ei 40.31N 21.16 E
Kastorías, Límni- 15 Ei 40.31N 21.18 E
Kastornoje 16 Kd 51.51N 38.07 E
Kastós 15 Dk 38.35N 20.55 E
Kasuga 29 Be 33.32N 130.27 E
Kasugai 29 Ed 35.14N 136.58 E
Kasulu 36 Fc 4.34S 30.06 E
Kasumbalesa 36 Ee 12.13S 27.48 E
Kasumi 29 Dd 35.38N 134.38 E
Kasumi-ga-Ura 28 Pf 36.00N 140.25 E
Kasumkent 16 Pi 41.42N 48.10 E
Kasungan 26 Fg 1.58S 113.24 E
Kasungu 36 Fe 13.02S 33.29 E
Kasupe 36 Gf 15.10S 35.18 E
Kasūr 25 Eb 31.07N 74.27 E
Kaszuby 10 Ob 54.10N 18.15 E
Kataba 31 Jj 16.05S 25.10 E
Katahdin, Mount- 43 Nb 45.55N 68.55W
Katajsk 17 Kh 56.18N 62.35 E
Katako-Kombe 36 Dc 3.24S 24.25 E
Katanga 36 Ed 10.00S 25.30 E
Katanga 20 Fd 60.10N 102.10 E
Katangli 20 Jf 51.43N 143.16 E
Katanning 59 Df 33.42S 117.33 E
Katav-Ivanovsk 17 Ii 54.47N 58.15 E
Katchall 25 Ig 7.57N 93.22 E
Katchi 32 Ef 17.00N 13.55W
Katende, Chutes de- 36 Dd 6.30S 22.10 E
Kateríni 15 Fi 40.16N 22.30 E
Katesh 36 Gc 4.31S 35.23 E
Katete 36 Fe 14.06S 32.05 E
Katha 25 Jd 24.11N 96.21 E
Katherine 58 Ef 14.28S 132.16 E
Katherine River 59 Gb 14.39S 131.42 E
Kāthiāwār 21 Jg 21.58N 70.30 E
Kathmandu 22 Kg 27.43N 85.19 E
Kathua 36 Gc 1.17S 39.03 E
Kati 34 Dc 12.43N 8.05W
Katihār 25 Hc 25.32N 87.35 E
Katiki, Volcán- 65d Bb 27.06S 109.16W
Katima Mulilo 36 Df 17.28S 24.14 E
Katiola 34 Dd 8.08N 5.06W
Katiola [3] 34 Dd 8.13N 5.02W
Katiu Atoll 61 Mc 16.26S 144.22W
Katla 7a Bc 63.36N 18.58W
Katlabuh, Ozero- 15 Ld 45.25N 29.00 E
Katlanovo 15 Eh 41.54N 21.41 E
Katmai, Mount- 40 Ie 58.17N 154.56W
Káto Akhaía 15 Ek 38.09N 21.33 E
Katofio 36 Ee 11.02S 28.01 E
Katompi 36 Ed 6.11S 26.20 E
Katonga 36 Fb 0.10N 30.40 E
Katon-Karagaj 19 If 49.11N 85.37 E
Káto Ólimbos 15 Fj 39.55N 22.28 E
Katoomba 59 Kf 33.42S 150.18 E
Katopasa, Gunung- 26 Hg 1.14S 121.25 E

Index Symbols

[1] Independent Nation
[2] State, Region
[3] District, County
[4] Municipality
[5] Colony, Dependency
Continent
Physical Region
Historical or Cultural Region
Mount, Mountain
Volcano
Hill
Mountains, Mountain Range
Hills, Escarpment
Plateau, Upland
Pass, Gap
Plain, Lowland
Delta
Salt Flat
Valley, Canyon
Crater, Cave
Karst Features
Depression
Polder
Desert, Dunes
Forest, Woods
Heath, Steppe
Oasis
Cape, Point
Coast, Beach
Cliff
Peninsula
Isthmus
Sandbank
Island
Atoll
Rock, Reef
Islands, Archipelago
Rocks, Reefs
Coral Reef
Well, Spring
Geyser
River, Stream
Waterfall Rapids
River Mouth, Estuary
Lake
Salt Lake
Intermittent Lake
Reservoir
Swamp, Pond
Canal
Glacier
Ice Shelf, Pack Ice
Ocean
Sea
Gulf, Bay
Strait, Fjord
Lagoon
Bank
Seamount
Tablemount
Ridge
Shelf
Basin
Escarpment, Sea Scarp
Fracture
Trench, Abyss
National Park, Reserve
Point of Interest
Recreation Site
Cave, Cavern
Historic Site
Ruins
Wall, Walls
Church, Abbey
Temple
Scientific Station
Airport
Port
Lighthouse
Mine
Tunnel
Dam, Bridge

Katowice [2] 10 Of 50.15N 19.00 E
Katowice 6 He 50.16N 19.00 E
Katrancık Dağı 24 Dd 37.27N 30.25 E
Kātrīnā, Jabal- 30 Kf 28.31N 33.57 E
Katrineholm 7 Dg 59.00N 16.12 E
Katsina 31 Hg 13.00N 7.36 E
Katsina Ala 34 Gd 7.48N 8.52 E
Katsumoto 28 Jh 33.51N 129.42 E
Katsuta 28 Pf 36.24N 140.32 E
Katsuura 28 Pg 35.08N 140.18 E
Katsuyama [Jap.] 28 Nf 36.03N 136.30 E
Katsuyama [Jap.] 29 Cd 35.06N 133.41 E
Kattakurgan 19 Gh 39.55N 66.15 E
Kattavia 15 Kn 35.57N 27.46 E
Kattegat 5 Hd 57.00N 11.00 E
Katthammarsvik 8 Hg 57.26N 18.50 E
Katulo, Lagh- 36 Hb 2.08N 40.56 E
Katumbi 36 Fe 10.49S 33.32 E
Katun 21 Kd 52.25N 85.05 E
Katwijk aan Zee 11 Kb 52.13N 4.24 E
Katwijk aan Zee, Katwijk- 12 Gb 52.12N 4.25 E
Katwijk-Katwijk aan Zee 12 Gb 52.12N 4.25 E
Katzenelnbogen 12 Jd 50.17N 7.57 E
Kau 26 If 1.11N 127.54 E
Kauai Channel 60 Oc 21.45N 158.50W
Kauai Island 57 Lb 22.03N 159.30W
Kaub 12 Jd 50.05N 7.46 E
Kauehi Atoll 61 Lc 15.51S 145.09W
Kaufbeuren 10 Gi 47.53N 10.37 E
Kauhajoki 7 Fe 62.26N 22.11 E
Kauhava 7 Fe 63.06N 23.05 E
Kauiki Head 60 Oc 20.46N 155.59W
Kaukauna 45 Ld 44.17N 88.17W
Kaukauveld 30 Jk 20.00S 21.50 E
Kaukonen 7 Fc 67.29N 24.54 E
Kaukura Atoll 57 Mf 15.45S 146.42W
Kaula Island 57 Kb 21.40N 160.32W
Kaulakahi Channel 65a Ba 22.02N 159.53W
Kaumalapau 65a Ec 20.47N 156.59W
Kaunakakai 60 Oc 21.05N 157.02W
Kaunas 6 Ie 54.54N 23.54 E
Kaunasskoje Vodohranilišče /Kauno Marios 8 Kj 54.50N 24.15 E
Kauniainen/Grankulla 8 Kd 60.13N 24.45 E
Kauno Marios/Kaunasskoje Vodohranilišče 8 Kj 54.50N 24.15 E
Kaunos 15 Lm 36.50N 28.35 E
Kaupanger 7 Bf 61.11N 7.14 E
Kau Paulatmada, Gunung- 26 Ig 3.15S 126.09 E
Kaura Namoda 34 Gc 12.36N 6.35 E
Kauriāla Ghāt 25 Gc 28.27N 80.59 E
Kaušany 16 Ff 46.39N 29.25 E
Kaustinen 7 Fe 63.32N 23.42 E
Kautokeino 7 Fb 68.59N 23.08 E
Kavacik 15 Lj 39.40N 28.30 E
Kavadarci 15 Fh 41.26N 22.01 E
Kavaja 15 Ch 41.11N 19.33 E
Kavak [Tur.] 15 Ji 40.36N 26.54 E
Kavak [Tur.] 24 Gb 41.05N 36.03 E
Kavaklidere 15 Ll 37.26N 28.22 E
Kavála 6 Ig 40.56N 24.25 E
Kavála, Kólpos- 15 Hi 40.52N 24.25 E
Kavalerovo 20 Ih 44.19N 135.05 E
Kavali 25 Ff 14.55N 79.59 E
Kavār 24 Oh 29.11N 52.44 E
Kavaratti 22 Jh 10.33N 72.38 E
Kavaratti Island 25 Ef 10.33N 72.38 E
Kavarna 15 Lf 43.25N 28.20 E
Kavarskas/Kovarskas 8 Ki 55.24N 25.03 E
Kavendou, Mont- 30 Fg 10.41N 12.12W
Kavieng 60 Eh 2.34S 150.48 E
Kavīr, Dasht-e- 21 Hf 34.40N 54.30 E
Kavkaz 16 Jg 45.21N 36.12 E
Kavkaz, Bolšoj-=Caucasus (EN) 5 Kg 42.30N 45.00 E
Kävlinge 8 Ei 55.48N 13.06 E
Kävlingeån 8 Ei 55.47N 13.06 E
Kawa 35 Eb 19.10N 30.39 E
Kawabe 29 Gb 39.39N 140.15 E
Kawachi-nagano 29 Dd 34.27N 135.34 E
Kawagoe 29 Fd 35.55N 139.28 E
Kawaguchi 29 Fd 35.48N 139.42 E
Kawaihae Bay 65a Fc 20.02N 155.51W
Kawaihoa Point 65a Ab 21.47N 160.12W
Kawakawa 62 Fa 35.23S 174.04 E
Kawalusu, Pulau- 26 If 4.15N 125.19 E
Kawamata 29 Gc 37.40N 140.36 E
Kawambwa 36 Ed 9.47S 29.05 E
Kawaminami 29 Be 32.12N 131.32 E
Kawamoto 29 Cd 34.59N 132.29 E
Kawanishi 29 Gc 37.59N 140.03 E
Kawanoe 29 Cd 34.01N 133.34 E
Kawartha Lakes 44 Hc 44.32N 78.30W
Kawasaki [Jap.] 29 Gb 38.10N 140.38 E
Kawasaki [Jap.] 28 Og 35.32N 139.43 E
Kawashiri-Misaki 29 Bd 34.26N 130.58 E
Kawauchi 29a Bc 41.12N 141.00 E
Kawau Island 62 Fb 36.25S 174.50 E
Kawaura 29 Be 32.21N 130.05 E
Kawerau 62 Gc 38.05S 176.42 E
Kawhia 62 Fc 38.04S 174.49 E
Kawich Range 46 Gh 37.40N 116.30W
Kawio, Kepulauan- 26 If 4.30N 125.30 E
Kawkareik 25 Je 16.33N 98.14 E
Kawm Umbū 33 Fe 24.28N 32.57 E
Kawthaung 25 Jg 9.59N 98.33 E
Kaxgar He 21 Jf 39.46N 78.15 E
Kax He 27 Dc 43.37N 81.48 E
Kaya 34 Ec 13.05N 1.05W
Kayah [2] 25 Je 19.15N 97.30 E
Kayak 40 Ke 59.52N 144.30W
Kayali Daği 15 Jj 39.58N 26.38 E
Kayan 21 Ni 2.55N 117.35 E
Kayanga 34 Bc 11.58N 15.00W
Kayangel Islands 57 Ed 8.04N 134.43 E
Kayangel Passage 64a Ba 8.01N 134.42 E
Kaycee 46 Le 43.43N 106.38W
Kayenta 46 Jh 36.44N 110.17W
Kayes [3] 34 Cc 14.00N 11.00W
Kayes 31 Fg 14.26N 11.27W
Kayoa, Pulau- 26 Ig 0.05S 127.25 E
Kayseri 22 Ff 38.43N 35.30 E
Kayuagung 26 Dg 3.24S 104.50 E
Kayu Ara, Pulau- 26 Ef 1.31N 106.26 E
Kazačje 20 Ib 70.40N 136.13 E
Kazah 16 Ni 41.05N 45.22 E
Kazahskaja Sovetskaja Socialističeskaja Respublika [2] 19 Gf 48.00N 68.00 E
Kazahskaja SSR/Kazak Sovettik Socialistik Respublikasy [2] 19 Gf 48.00N 68.00 E
Kazahskaja SSR=Kazakh SSR (EN) [2] 19 Gf 48.00N 68.00 E
Kazahski Melkosopočnik= Kazakh Hills (EN) 21 Je 49.00N 73.00 E
Kazahskij Zaliv 16 Rh 42.40N 52.25 E
Kazakh Hills (EN)= Kazahski Melkosopočnik 21 Je 49.00N 73.00 E
Kazakh SSR (EN)= Kazahskaja SSR [2] 19 Gf 48.00N 68.00 E
Kazakhstan (EN) 21 Hd 51.11N 52.52 E
Kazaklija 15 Lc 46.05N 28.38 E
Kazak Sovettik Socialistik Respublikasy [2] 19 Gf 48.00N 68.00 E
Kazalak 15 Ke 44.03N 27.24 E
Kazalinsk 19 Gf 45.46N 62.07 E
Kazan 6 Kd 55.45N 49.08 E
Kazan 38 Jc 64.02N 95.30W
Kazandžik 19 Fh 39.17N 55.34 E
Kazanka 7 Li 55.48N 49.05 E
Kazanka 16 Hf 47.50N 32.49 E
Kazanlăk 15 Ig 42.37N 25.24 E
Kazan-Rettō/Iō=Volcano Islands (EN) 21 Qg 25.00N 141.00 E
Kazanskoje 19 Gd 55.38N 69.14 E
Kazarman 19 Hg 41.20N 74.02 E
Kazatin 19 Cf 49.43N 28.50 E
Kazbek, Gora- 5 Kg 42.42N 44.31 E
Kaz Daği 23 Cb 39.42N 26.50 E
Kaz Daği 15 Mk 38.35N 29.15 E
Kāzerūn 22 Hg 29.37N 51.38 E
Kažim 17 Ef 60.20N 51.32 E
Kazi-Magomed 16 Pi 40.02N 48.56 E
Kazimierza Wielka 10 Qf 50.16N 20.30 E
Kāzımkarabekir 24 Ed 37.14N 32.59 E
Kazincbarcika 10 Qh 48.15N 20.38 E
Kazinga Channel 36 Ec 0.13S 29.53 E
Kazlu-Rūda/Kazlu-Ruda 8 Jj 54.42N 23.32 E
Kazlu-Ruda/Kazlų-Rūda 8 Jj 54.42N 23.32 E
Kazo 29 Fc 36.08N 139.36 E
Kaztalovka 16 Pe 49.46N 48.44 E
Kazumba 36 Dd 6.25S 22.02 E
Kazuno 28 Pd 40.14N 140.48 E
Kazym 19 Gc 63.54N 65.50 E
Kazyr 20 Ef 53.50N 92.53 E
Kcynia 10 Nd 53.00N 17.30 E
Kdyně 10 Jg 49.24N 13.02 E
Ké 35 Bb 18.32N 17.55 E
Kéa 15 Hl 37.37N 24.20 E
Kéa 15 Hl 37.39N 24.20 E
Keaau 65a Fd 19.37N 155.03W
Keahole Point 65a Ed 19.44N 156.04W
Kealaikahiki Channel 65a Ec 20.37N 156.50W
Kealaikahiki Point 65a Ec 20.32N 156.42W
Kealakekua Bay 65a Fd 19.28N 155.56W
Keams Canyon 46 Ji 35.49N 110.12W
Keanae 65a Ec 20.52N 156.09W
Keanapapa Point 65a Dc 20.54N 157.04W
Kearney 43 Hc 40.42N 99.05W
Kearns 46 Jf 40.39N 111.59W
Kéas, Stenón- 15 Hl 37.40N 24.12 E
Keats Bank (EN) 57 Id 5.23N 173.28 E
Keb 8 Mg 57.44N 28.38 E
Keban Gölü 23 Eb 38.53N 39.00 E
Kébémer 34 Bb 15.22N 16.27W
Kebir, Oued el- 14 Bn 36.51N 7.57 E
Kebnekaise 5 Hb 67.53N 18.33 E
Kebri Dehar 31 Lh 6.45N 44.17 E
Kebumen 26 Eh 7.40S 109.39 E
Kecel 10 Pj 46.32N 19.16 E
Kechika 42 Ee 59.38N 127.09W
Kecskemét 10 Pj 46.54N 19.42 E
Kėdainiai/Kedajnjaj 7 Fi 55.18N 23.59 E
Kedajnjaj/Kėdainiai 7 Fi 55.18N 23.59 E
Kedgwick 44 Nb 47.39N 67.21W
Kediri 22 Nj 7.49S 112.01 E
Kédougou 34 Cc 12.33N 12.11W
Kedva 17 Fd 64.14N 53.30 E
Kędzierzyn-Koźle 10 Of 50.20N 18.10 E
Keele 42 Fd 64.24N 124.47W
Keele Peak 38 Fc 63.26N 130.19W
Keeling Islands→Cocos Islands 21 Lk 12.10S 96.55 E
Keeling Islands→Cocos Islands [5] 22 Lk 12.10S 96.55 E
Keelung 22 Og 25.08N 121.44 E
Keene 44 Kd 42.55N 72.17W
Keer-Weer, Cape- 59 Ib 13.58S 141.30 E
Keetmanshoop 31 Ik 26.36S 18.08 E
Keetmanshoop [3] 37 Be 26.30S 18.30 E
Keewatin 42 Ig 49.46N 94.34W
Keewatin, District of- [3] 42 Hd 64.00N 96.00W
Kefa [3] 35 Fd 7.00N 36.00 E
Kefallinía=Cephalonia (EN) 5 Ih 38.15N 20.35 E
Kefamenanu 26 Hh 9.27S 124.29 E
Kefar Sava 24 Ff 32.10N 34.54 E
Keffi 34 Gd 8.51N 7.52 E
Keflavík 7a Ab 64.01N 22.34W
Kegen 19 Hg 42.58N 79.12 E
Kegums 8 Kh 56.41N 24.44 E
Kehdingen 10 Fc 53.45N 9.20 E
Kehl 10 Dh 48.35N 7.49 E
Kehra 7 Fg 59.19N 25.18 E
Keighley 9 Lh 53.52N 1.54W
Keila/Kejla 7 Fg 59.19N 24.27 E
Keila Jõgi/Kejla 8 Ke 59.25N 24.15 E
Keimoes 37 Ce 28.41S 21.00 E
Keipel Bank (EN) 59 Le 25.15S 159.30E
Keïta 34 Gc 14.46N 5.46 E
Kéïta, Bahr- 35 Bd 9.14N 18.21 E
Keitele 5 Ic 62.55N 26.00 E
Keith [Austl.] 59 Ig 36.06S 140.21 E
Keith [Scot.-U.K.] 9 Kd 57.32N 2.57W
Keith Arm 42 Fc 65.20N 122.00W
Keiyasi 63d Ab 17.53S 177.45 E
Kejla/Keila 7 Fg 59.19N 24.27 E
Kejla/Keila Jõgi 8 Ke 59.25N 24.15 E
Kejvy 7 Ic 67.30N 37.45 E
Kekaha 65a Bb 21.58N 159.43W
Kekerengu 62 Ee 42.00S 174.00 E
Kékes 10 Qi 47.52N 20.01 E
Keklau 64a Bb 7.35N 134.39 E
Kelafo 35 Gd 5.37N 44.13 E
Kelakam 34 Hc 13.35N 11.44 E
Kela Met 35 Fb 15.50N 38.23 E
Kelan 27 Jd 38.44N 111.34 E
Kelang 22 Mi 3.02N 101.27 E
Kelasa, Selat-=Gaspar Strait (EN) 26 Eg 2.40S 107.15 E
Kelberg 12 Id 50.18N 6.55 E
Kelcyra 15 Di 40.19N 20.11 E
Kelefesia 65b Bb 20.30S 174.44W
Kelekçi 15 Ml 37.14N 29.28 E
Kelem 35 Fe 4.49N 35.59 E
Keles 15 Mj 39.55N 29.14 E
Keles 18 Gd 41.02N 68.37 E
Kelheim 10 Hh 48.55N 11.52 E
Kelifely, Causse du- 37 Hc 17.15S 45.30 E
Kelifski Uzboj 18 Ef 37.45N 64.40 E
Keli Hāji Ibrāhīm 24 Kd 36.42N 45.00 E
Kelkheim 12 Kd 50.08N 8.27 E
Kelkit 23 Ea 36.32N 40.46 E
Kelkit 24 Hb 40.08N 39.27 E
Kellé 36 Bc 0.06S 14.33 E
Kellerberrin 59 Df 31.38S 117.43 E
Kellerwald 10 Fe 51.03N 9.10 E
Kellett, Cape- 42 Eb 72.57N 125.27W
Kellett Strait 42 Fa 75.50N 117.40W
Kellog 20 Dd 62.27N 86.35 E
Kellogg 43 Db 47.32N 116.07W
Kelloselkä 7 Gc 66.56N 29.00 E
Kells/Ceanannas Mór 9 Gh 53.44N 6.53W
Kelmė/Kelme 7 Fi 55.39N 22.58 E
Kelme/Kelmė 7 Fi 55.39N 22.58 E
Kelmency 15 Ja 48.27N 26.47 E
Kelmis/La Calamine 12 Hd 50.43N 6.00 E
Kélo 35 Bd 9.15N 15.48 E
Kelowna 39 He 49.53N 119.29W
Kelsey 42 He 56.00N 97.00W
Kelsey Bay 42 Ef 50.24N 125.57W
Kelso 46 Dc 46.09N 122.54W
Kelso Bank 59 Ld 24.10S 159.10 E
Kelso Bank (EN) 59 Ld 24.10S 159.30 E
Kel Tepe [Tur.] 24 Eb 41.05N 32.27 E
Kel Tepe [Tur.] 15 Ni 40.39N 30.06 E
Keltie, Mount- 66 Jf 79.15S 159.00 E
Keluang 26 Df 2.02N 103.19 E
Kelvin Seamount (EN) 43 Od 38.50N 64.00W
Kelyeḥēd 35 Hd 8.44N 49.10 E
Kem 19 Dc 64.57N 34.31 E
Kema 7 If 60.19N 37.15 E
Ké Macina 34 Dc 13.57N 5.23W
Kemah 24 Hc 39.36N 39.02 E
Kemaliye 24 Hc 39.16N 38.29 E
Kemalpaşa 24 Cc 40.00N 28.20 E
Kemalpaşa 15 Kk 38.25N 27.26 E
Kembé 35 Ce 4.36N 21.54 E
Kemer [Tur.] 15 Mm 36.28N 29.21 E
Kemer [Tur.] 24 Dd 36.36N 30.34 E
Kemer Baraji 15 Ll 37.30N 28.35 E
Kemeri/Ķemeri 8 Jh 56.56N 23.25 E
Ķemeri/Kemeri 8 Jh 56.56N 23.25 E
Kemerovo 22 Kd 55.20N 86.05 E
Kemerovskaja Oblast [3] 20 De 55.00N 87.00 E
Kemi 6 Ib 65.44N 24.34 E
Kemijärvi 7 Gc 66.40N 27.25 E
Kemijärvi=Kenni, Lake- (EN) 7 Gc 66.36N 27.24 E
Kemijoki 5 Ib 65.47N 24.30 E
Kemiö 8 Jd 60.10N 22.40 E
Kemiö/Kimito 8 Jd 60.10N 22.40 E
Kemlja 7 Ki 54.43N 45.15 E
Kemmerer 46 Jf 41.48N 110.32W
Kémo-Gribingui [3] 35 Bd 6.00N 19.00 E
Kemp, Lake- 45 Gj 33.45N 99.13W
Kempaž 17 Jd 64.03N 61.02 E
Kempele 7 Fd 64.55N 25.30 E
Kempen 12 Ic 51.22N 6.25 E
Kempen/Campine 11 Lc 51.10N 5.20 E
Kempendjaj 20 Gd 62.02N 118.42 E
Kempenich 12 Jd 50.25N 7.08 E
Kemp Land 66 Ee 67.10S 58.00 E
Kemps Bay 49 Ia 24.02N 77.33W
Kempsey 59 Kf 31.05S 152.50 E
Kempston 12 Bb 52.06N 0.29W
Kempt, Lac- 42 Kg 47.25N 74.15W
Kempten 10 Gi 47.43N 10.19 E
Ken 25 Hc 25.46N 80.31 E
Ken, Loch- 9 If 55.02N 4.02W
Kena 7 Je 62.06N 39.05 E
Kenadsa 32 Gc 31.34N 2.26W
Kenai 39 Dc 60.33N 151.15W
Kenai Mountains 40 Ie 60.00N 150.00W
Kenai Peninsula 38 Ed 60.10N 150.00W
Kendal 9 Kg 54.20N 2.45W
Kendall 44 Gm 25.41N 80.19W
Kendall, Cape- 42 Id 63.36N 87.13W
Kendallville 44 Ee 41.27N 85.16W
Kendari 22 Oj 3.57S 122.35 E
Kendawangan 26 Fg 2.32S 110.12 E
Kenema 31 Fh 7.52N 11.12W
Kenge 31 Ii 4.52S 16.59 E
Kengere 36 Ee 11.10S 25.28 E
Keng Tung 25 Jd 21.17N 99.36 E
Kenhardt 37 Ce 29.19S 21.12 E
Kéniéba 34 Cc 12.50N 11.14W
Keningau 26 Ge 5.20N 116.10 E
Kenitra 31 Ge 34.16N 6.36W
Kenitra [3] 32 Fc 34.00N 6.00W
Kenli (Xishuanghe) 28 Ef 37.35N 118.30 E
Kenmare 43 Gb 48.40N 102.05W
Kenmare/Neidín 9 Dj 51.53N 9.35W
Kenmare River/An Ribhéar 9 Dj 51.50N 9.50W
Kennebunk 44 Ld 43.23N 70.33W
Kennedy Peak 25 Id 23.19N 93.46 E
Kennedy Range 59 Cd 24.30S 115.00 E
Kenner 45 Ki 29.59N 90.15W
Kennet 9 Mj 51.28N 0.57W
Kennett 45 Kh 36.14N 90.03W
Kennewick 46 Fc 46.12N 119.07W
Kenni, Lake- (EN)= Kemijärvi 7 Gc 66.36N 27.24 E
Kennington 12 Cc 51.09N 0.53 E
Kenn Reef 57 Gg 21.10S 155.50 E
Kénogami 44 La 48.26N 71.14W
Kénogami, Lac- 44 La 48.21N 71.28W
Kenogami River 42 Jf 51.06N 84.29W
Keno Hill 42 Dd 63.54N 135.18W
Kenora 39 Je 49.47N 94.29W
Kenosha 43 Jc 42.35N 87.49W
Kent 9 Nj 51.10N 0.55 E
Kent [3] 9 Nj 51.20N 0.55 E
Kent [S.L.] 34 Cd 8.10N 13.10W
Kent [Wa.-U.S.] 46 Dc 47.23N 122.14W
Kent, Vale of- 9 Nj 51.10N 0.30 E
Kentau 19 Gg 43.32N 68.33 E
Kent Group 59 Jg 39.30S 147.20 E
Kenton 44 Fe 40.38N 83.38W
Kent Peninsula 42 Gc 68.30N 107.00W
Kentucky [2] 43 Jd 37.30N 85.15W
Kentucky Lake 43 Jd 36.25N 88.05W
Kentucky River 44 Ef 38.41N 85.11W
Kenya [1] 31 Kh 1.00N 38.00 E
Kenya, Mount-/Kirinyaga 30 Ki 0.10S 37.20 E
Keokea 65a Ec 20.42N 156.21W
Keokuk 43 Ic 40.24N 91.24W
Keonjhargarh 25 Hd 21.38N 85.35 E
Keowee, Lake- 44 Fh 34.55N 82.50W
Kepe 7 Hd 65.09N 32.08 E
Kepi 26 Kh 6.32S 139.19 E
Kępno 10 Ne 51.17N 17.59 E
Kepsut 24 Cc 39.41N 28.09 E
Kerala [3] 25 Ff 11.00N 76.30 E
Kerama-Rettō 29b Ab 26.10N 127.15 E
Kerang 59 Ig 35.44S 143.55 E
Keratéa 15 Gl 37.48N 23.59 E
Kerava/Kervo 8 Kd 60.24N 25.07 E
Kerč 6 Jf 45.22N 36.27 E
Kerčenski Poluostrov 16 Ig 45.15N 36.00 E
Kerčenski Proliv 5 Jf 45.22N 36.38 E
Kerdhilion Óros 15 Gi 40.47N 23.39 E
Kerema 60 Di 7.58S 145.46 E
Keren 35 Fb 15.47N 38.27 E
Keret, Ozero- 7 Hd 65.50N 32.50 E
Kerewan 34 Bc 13.29N 16.06W
Kerguélen 30 Nm 49.20S 69.30 E
Kerguélen, Iles- 30 Nm 49.15S 69.10 E
Kerguelen Plateau (EN) 3 Go 55.00S 75.00 E
Kericho 36 Gc 0.22S 35.17 E
Keri Kera 35 Ec 12.21N 32.46 E
Kerimäki 8 Mc 61.55N 29.17 E
Kerinci, Gunung- 21 Mj 1.42S 101.16 E
Kerio 30 Kh 2.59N 36.07 E
Kerion 15 Dl 37.40N 20.49 E
Keriya/Yutian 22 Kf 36.52N 81.42 E
Keriya He 27 Dd 38.30N 82.10 E
Keriya Shankou 27 Dd 35.12N 81.44 E
Kerka 10 Mj 46.28N 16.36 E
Kerken 12 Ic 51.27N 6.26 E
Kerkennah Islands (EN)= Qarqannah, Juzur- 30 Ie 34.44N 11.12 E
Kerketevs Óros 15 Jl 37.44N 26.38 E
Kerki 19 Gh 37.50N 65.13 E
Kerkini Óros 15 Fh 41.21N 22.50 E
Kérkira 15 Cj 39.36N 19.55 E
Kérkira=Corfu (EN) 5 Hh 39.40N 19.45 E
Kerkiras, Stenón- = Corfu, Strait of- (EN) 15 Dj 39.35N 20.05 E
Kerkrade 12 Id 50.52N 6.04 E
Kerma (EN)=Karmah 35 Eb 19.38N 30.25 E
Kermadec Islands 57 Jh 30.00S 178.30W
Kermadec Ridge (EN) 57 Jh 30.30S 178.30W
Kermadec Trench (EN) 3 Km 30.00S 177.00W
Kermajarvi 8 Mb 62.30N 28.40 E
Kermān [3] 23 Ic 30.50N 57.50 E
Kermān 22 Hf 30.17N 57.05 E
Kermānshāh 22 Gf 34.19N 47.04 E
Kermānshāhān [3] 23 Gc 34.15N 47.20 E
Kermānshāhān 24 Pg 31.17N 54.55 E
Kerme Körfezi 15 Kl 37.02N 28.00 E
Kermit 45 Ek 31.51N 103.06W
Kern River 46 Fi 35.13N 119.17W
Kérouané 34 Dd 9.16N 9.01W
Kerpen 12 Id 50.52N 6.41 E
Kerrobert 42 Gf 51.55N 109.08W
Kerrville 43 He 30.03N 99.08W
Kerry/Ciarraí [2] 9 Di 52.10N 9.30W
Kerry, Mountains of- 9 Dj 51.55N 9.50W
Kertamulya 26 Eg 0.23N 109.09 E
Kerteh 26 Df 4.31N 103.27 E
Kerteminde 8 Di 55.27N 10.40 E
Kerulen (Cherlen) 21 Ne 48.48N 117.00 E
Kervo/Kerava 8 Kd 60.24N 25.07 E
Kerzaz 32 Gd 29.27N 1.25W
Keržeenec 7 Kh 56.04N 45.01 E
Kesagami Lake 42 Jf 50.23N 80.10W
Kesälahti 8 Mc 61.54N 29.50 E
Keşan 23 Ca 40.51N 26.37 E
Keşap 24 Hb 40.55N 38.31 E
Kesen'numa 28 Pe 38.54N 141.35 E
Kesen'numa-Wan 29 Gb 38.50N 141.35 E
Keshan 27 Mb 48.04N 125.51 E
Keskastel 12 Jf 48.58N 7.02 E
Keskin 24 Ec 39.41N 33.37 E
Keski-Suomi [2] 7 Fe 62.30N 25.30 E
Kestenga 7 Hd 65.53N 31.45 E
Keswick 9 Jg 54.37N 3.08W
Keszthely 10 Nj 46.46N 17.15 E
Ket 21 Kd 58.55N 81.32 E
Kéta 34 Fd 5.55N 0.59 E
Keta, Ozero- 20 Dc 68.45N 90.00 E
Ketanda 20 Jd 60.38N 141.30 E
Ketapang 22 Mj 1.52S 109.59 E
Ketchikan 39 Fd 55.21N 131.35W
Ketchum 43 Ec 43.41N 114.22W
Ketchum Mountain 45 Fk 31.15N 101.00W
Kete Krachi 34 Ed 7.46N 0.03W
Ketelmeer 12 Hb 52.35N 5.45 E
Ketli, Jbel- 13 Gi 35.22N 5.17W
Ketmen, Hrebet- 18 Lc 43.20N 80.00 E
Kétou 34 Fd 7.22N 2.36 E
Kętrzyn 10 Rb 54.06N 21.23 E
Kettering [Eng.-U.K.] 9 Mi 52.24N 0.44W
Kettering [Oh.-U.S.] 44 Ef 39.41N 84.10W
Kettle River 46 Fb 48.42N 118.07W
Kettle River Range 46 Fb 48.30N 118.40W
Keuka Lake 44 Id 42.27N 77.10W
Keur Massène 32 Df 16.33N 16.14W
Keuruu 7 Fe 62.16N 24.42 E
Keuruunselkä 8 Kb 62.10N 24.40 E
Kevelaer 12 Ic 51.35N 6.15 E
Kew 49 Kc 21.54N 72.02W
Kewanee 43 Jc 41.14N 89.56W
Keweenaw Bay 44 Cb 46.56N 88.23W
Keweenaw Peninsula 43 Jb 47.12N 88.25W
Key, Lough-/Loch Cé 9 Eg 54.00N 8.15W
Keya Paha River 45 Ge 42.54N 99.00W
Keyhole Reservoir 46 Md 44.21N 104.51W
Key Largo 44 Gm 25.04N 80.28W
Keypel Bank (EN) 59 Le 25.15S 159.30 E
Keystone Lake 45 Hh 36.15N 96.25W
Key West 39 Kg 24.33N 81.48W
Kez 7 Mh 57.56N 53.43 E
Kezi 37 Dd 20.55S 28.29 E
Kežma 20 Fe 59.02N 101.09 E
Kežmarok 10 Qg 49.08N 20.25 E
Kgalagadi [3] 37 Ce 25.00S 22.00 E
Kgatleng [3] 37 Dd 24.28S 26.05 E
Kghoti 37 Cd 24.55S 21.59 E
Khabr, Kūh-e- 23 Id 28.50N 56.26 E
Khābūr, Nahr al- 24 Ie 35.08N 40.26 E
Khadari, Wādī al- 35 Dc 10.29N 27.00 E
Khādim, Shūshat al- 24 Bh 28.35N 27.43 E
Khadki (Kirkee) 25 Ee 18.34N 73.52 E
Khadra 13 Mh 36.15N 0.35 E
Khafs Banbān 24 Lj 25.31N 46.27 E
Khairónia 15 Fk 38.30N 22.51 E
Khairpur 25 Dc 27.32N 68.46 E
Khāīz, Kūh-e- 24 Ng 30.27N 50.55 E
Khakhea 37 Cd 24.42S 23.30 E
Khalatse 25 Fb 34.20N 76.49 E
Khalīj-e Fārs=Persian Gulf (EN) 21 Hg 27.00N 51.00 E
Khálki 15 Km 36.13N 27.37 E
Khálki 15 Km 36.14N 27.36 E
Khalkidhiki=Chalcidice (EN) 5 Ig 40.25N 23.25 E
Khalkís 15 Gk 38.28N 23.36 E
Khaluf 23 Ie 20.29N 57.59 E
Khambhāt 25 Ed 22.18N 72.37 E
Khambhāt, Gulf of- 21 Jg 21.00N 72.30 E
Khāmgaon 25 Fd 20.41N 76.34 E
Khamili 15 Jn 35.52N 26.14 E
Khamir 23 Ff 15.59N 43.57 E
Khāmis, Ash Shallāl al-= Fifth Cataract (EN) 30 Kg 18.23N 33.47 E
Khamīs Mushayţ 27 Ff 18.18N 42.44 E
Khammam 25 Ge 17.15N 80.09 E
Khamseh 24 Md 36.40N 48.50 E
Khan 37 Ad 22.42S 14.54 E
Khān 24 Qj 24.13N 56.20 E
Khānābād 23 Kb 36.41N 69.07 E
Khān al Baghdādī 24 Jf 33.51N 42.33 E
Khān al Hammād 24 Kf 32.19N 44.17 E
Khānaqīn 23 Gc 34.21N 45.22 E
Khān az Zabīb 24 Gg 31.28N 36.06 E
Khandwa 25 Fd 21.50N 76.20 E
Khāneh Sorkh, Gardaneh-ye- 24 Qh 29.49N 56.06 E
Khānewāl 25 Eb 30.18N 71.56 E
Khangai Mountains (EN)= Changajn Nuruu→Hangaj, Hrebet- 21 Le 47.30N 100.00 E
Khangai Mountains (EN)= Hangaj, Hrebet- (Changajn Nuruu) 21 Le 47.30N 100.00 E
Khanh Hung 25 Lg 9.36N 105.58 E
Khánia 6 Ih 35.31N 24.02 E
Khanion, Kólpos- 15 Gn 35.35N 23.50 E
Khanka, Lake- (EN)=Hanka, Ozero- 21 Pe 45.00N 132.24 E
Khanka Lake (EN)=Xingkai Hu 21 Pe 45.00N 132.24 E
Khānpur 25 Ec 28.39N 70.39 E
Khān Shaykhūn 24 Ge 35.26N 36.38 E
Khān Takhtī 24 Kc 38.09N 44.55 E
Khān Yūnus 24 Fg 31.21N 34.19 E
Khānzīr, Rās- 35 Hc 10.50N 45.50 E

Index Symbols

[1] Independent Nation
[2] State, Region
[3] District, County
[4] Municipality
[5] Colony, Dependency
Continent
Physical Region
Historical or Cultural Region
Mount, Mountain
Volcano
Hill
Mountains, Mountain Range
Hills, Escarpment
Plateau, Upland
Pass, Gap
Plain, Lowland
Delta
Salt Flat
Valley, Canyon
Crater, Cave
Karst Features
Depression
Polder
Desert, Dunes
Forest, Woods
Heath, Steppe
Oasis
Cape, Point
Coast, Beach
Cliff
Peninsula
Isthmus
Sandbank
Island
Atoll
Rock, Reef
Islands, Archipelago
Rocks, Reefs
Coral Reef
Well, Spring
Geyser
River, Stream
Waterfall Rapids
River Mouth, Estuary
Lake
Salt Lake
Intermittent Lake
Reservoir
Swamp, Pond
Canal
Glacier
Ice Shelf, Pack Ice
Ocean
Sea
Gulf, Bay
Strait, Fjord
Lagoon
Bank
Seamount
Tablemount
Ridge
Shelf
Basin
Escarpment, Sea Scarp
Fracture
Trench, Abyss
National Park, Reserve
Point of Interest
Recreation Site
Cave, Cavern
Historic Site
Ruins
Wall, Walls
Church, Abbey
Temple
Scientific Station
Airport
Port
Lighthouse
Mine
Tunnel
Dam, Bridge

Khao Laem 25 Kf 14.19N 101.11 E
Khao Miang 25 Ke 17.42N 101.01 E
Khao Mokochu 25 Je 15.56N 99.06 E
Khao Saming 25 Kf 12.16N 102.26 E
Khar 24 Me 35.53N 48.55 E
Kharagpur 22 Kg 22.20N 87.20 E
Khárakas 15 In 35.01N 25.07 E
Khārān 24 Qh 28.55N 57.09 E
Kharānaq 24 Pf 32.20N 54.39 E
Kharānaq, Kūh-e- 24 Pf 32.10N 54.39 E
Kharga Oasis (EN)= Khārijah, Waḩāt al- 30 Kf 25.20N 30.35 E
Khārijah, Wāḩāt al-= Kharga Oasis (EN) 30 Kf 25.20N 30.35 E
Kharīţ, Wādī al- 24 Ej 24.26N 33.03 E
Kharīţah, Shiqqat al- 33 If 17.10N 47.50 E
Khārk 24 Nh 29.15N 50.20 E
Khārk, Jazīreh-ye- 23 Hd 29.15N 50.20 E
Khār Khū 24 Og 31.39N 53.46 E
Kharmān, Kūh-e- 23 Hd 29.13N 53.35 E
Kharshah, Qārat al- 24 Bg 30.35N 27.25 E
Khartoum (EN)=Al Kharţūm [3] 35 Eb 15.50N 33.00 E
Khartoum (EN)=Al Kharţūm 31 Kg 15.36N 32.32 E
Khartoum North (EN)=Al Kharţūm Baḩrī 31 Kg 15.38N 32.33 E
Khāsh 23 Jc 31.31N 62.52 E
Khāsh 23 Jc 31.11N 62.05 E
Khashm al Qirbah 35 Fc 14.58N 35.55 E
Khāsi Jaintia 21 Lg 25.35N 91.38 E
Khatikhon, Yam-= Mediterranean Sea (EN) 5 Hh 35.00N 20.00 E
Khaţţ 33 Dd 28.40N 22.40 E
Khātūn, Kūh-e- 24 Og 30.25N 53.38 E
Khawr al Fakkān 24 Qk 25.21N 56.22 E
Khawr āl Juḩaysh 35 Ia 20.36N 50.59 E
Khawr al Mufattaḩ 24 Mh 28.40N 48.25 E
Khawr Umm Qasr 24 Lg 30.02N 47.56 E
Khay' 23 Ff 18.45N 41.24 E
Khaybar 23 Ed 25.42N 39.31 E
Khaybar, Ḩarrat- 24 Hj 25.30N 39.45 E
Khazzī, Qārat- 30 Jf 21.26N 24.30 E
Khemis 13 Qh 36.10N 4.04 E
Khemis Anjra 13 Gi 35.41N 5.32W
Khémis Beni Arouss 13 Gi 35.19N 5.38W
Khemis Miliana 32 Hb 36.16N 2.13 E
Khemissat 32 Fc 33.49N 6.04W
Khemisset [3] 32 Fc 33.49N 6.00W
Khemmarat 25 Ke 16.03N 105.11 E
Khenchela 32 Ib 35.26N 7.08 E
Khenifra 32 Fc 32.56N 5.40W
Khenifra [3] 32 Fc 33.00N 5.08W
Kherāmeh 24 Oh 29.32N 53.21 E
Khersan 24 Ng 31.33N 50.22 E
Khersónisos Akrotíri 15 Hn 35.35N 24.10 E
Kheyrābād [Iran] 24 Mg 31.49N 48.23 E
Kheyrābād [Iran] 24 Ph 29.26N 55.19 E
Khionótripa 15 Hh 41.18N 24.05 E
Khíos 15 Jk 38.22N 26.08 E
Khíos=Chios (EN) 5 Ih 38.22N 26.00 E
Khirbat Isrīyah 24 Ge 35.21N 37.46 E
Khirr, Nahr al- 24 Kf 33.17N 44.21 E
Khlomón Óros 15 Fk 38.36N 23.00 E
Khlong Yai 25 Kf 11.46N 102.53 E
Khokhropār 25 Ec 25.42N 70.12 E
Khok Kloi 25 Jg 8.17N 98.19 E
Khok Samrong 25 Ke 15.03N 100.44 E
Kholm 23 Kb 36.42N 67.41 E
Khomām 24 Md 37.22N 49.40 E
Khomas Highland (EN)= Khomas Hochland 30 Ik 22.40S 16.20 E
Khomas Hochland=Khomas Highland (EN) 30 Ik 22.40S 16.20 E
Khomeyn 24 Nf 33.38N 50.04 E
Khonj 24 Oi 27.52N 53.27 E
Khon Kaen 25 Ke 16.26N 102.50 E
Khonsār 24 Nf 33.21N 50.19 E
Khóra 15 El 37.03N 21.43 E
Khor Anghar 35 Gc 12.27N 43.18 E
Khorāsān 21 Hf 34.00N 56.00 E
Khorāsān [3] 23 Ic 35.00N 58.00 E
Khorāsānī, Godār-e 24 Qg 30.44N 57.03 E
Khóra Sfakíon 15 Hn 35.12N 24.09 E
Khormūj, Kūh-e- 23 Hd 28.43N 51.22 E
Khorof Harar 36 Hb 2.14N 40.44 E
Khorramābād 23 Gc 33.30N 48.20 E
Khorramshahr 23 Gc 30.25N 48.11 E
Khorsābād 24 Jd 36.38N 43.17 E
Khoshyeylāq 24 Pd 36.53N 55.15 E
Khosrowābād 24 Mg 30.00N 48.25 E
Khosrowshah 24 Ld 37.57N 46.03 E
Khouribga [3] 32 Fc 32.56N 6.36W
Khouribga 32 Fc 32.53N 6.54W
Khowst 23 Kc 33.22N 69.57 E
Khrisí 15 Io 34.52N 25.42 E
Khrisoúpolis 15 Hi 40.59N 24.42 E
Khristianá 15 Im 36.14N 25.13 E
Khu Dağı 24 Jc 38.35N 43.40 E
Khuff [Lib.] 33 Cd 28.17N 18.20 E
Khuff [Sau.Ar.] 23 Ed 25.20N 37.20 E
Khulna 22 Kg 22.48N 89.33 E
Khūrān 24 Pi 26.50N 55.40 E
Khurayş 23 Gd 25.05N 48.02 E
Khurayt 35 Dc 13.57N 26.02 E
Khurīyā Murīyā, Jazā'ir-= Kuria Muria Islands (EN) 21 Hh 17.30N 56.00 E
Khurr, Wādī al- 24 Jg 30.52N 42.10 E
Khursanīyah 24 Mi 27.18N 49.16 E
Khūshābar 24 Md 37.59N 48.54 E
Khutse 37 Cd 23.20S 24.34 E
Khuwayy 35 Dc 13.05N 29.14 E
Khuzdār 25 Dc 27.48N 66.37 E
Khūzestān [3] 23 Gc 32.00N 48.30 E
Khūzestān 21 Gf 30.33N 50.00 E
Khvojeh Lāk, Kūh-e- 24 Le 35.43N 46.29 E
Khvor 24 Pf 33.47N 55.03 E
Khvorāsgān 24 Nf 32.39N 51.45 E
Khvormūj 24 Nh 28.39N 51.23 E
Khvoshkūh 24 Qi 27.37N 56.41 E
Khvoy 24 Kc 38.33N 44.58 E
Khyber Pass 25 Eb 34.05N 71.10 E
Kia 63a Db 7.32S 158.26 E
Kia 63d Bb 16.14S 179.05 E
Kiamba 26 He 5.59N 124.37 E
Kiambi 36 Ed 7.20S 28.01 E
Kiamichi River 45 Ij 33.57N 95.14W
Kiangarow, Mount- 59 Ke 26.49S 151.33 E
Kiangsi (EN)=Chiang-hsi Sheng→Jangxi Sheng [2] 27 Kf 28.00N 116.00 E
Kiangsi (EN)=Jangxi Sheng (Chiang-hsi Sheng) [2] 27 Kf 28.00N 116.00 E
Kiangsu (EN)=Chiang-su Sheng→Jiangsu Sheng [2] 27 Ke 33.00N 120.00 E
Kiangsu (EN)=Jiangsu Sheng (Chiang-su Sheng) [2] 27 Ke 33.00N 120.00 E
Kiantajärvi 7 Gd 65.03N 29.07 E
Kiáton 15 Fk 38.01N 22.45 E
Kibali 36 Eb 3.37N 28.34 E
Kibangou 36 Bc 3.27S 12.21 E
Kibartaj/Kybartai 8 Jj 54.38N 22.44 E
Kibasira Swamp 36 Gd 8.20S 36.18 E
Kibau 36 Gd 8.35S 35.17 E
Kibaya 36 Gd 5.18S 36.34 E
Kibbish 35 Fe 4.40N 35.53 E
Kiberg 7 Ha 70.17N 31.00 E
Kibikogen 29 Cd 34.45N 133.15 E
Kiboko 36 Gc 2.15S 37.42 E
Kibombo 36 Ec 3.54S 25.55 E
Kibondo 36 Fc 3.35S 30.42 E
Kibre Mengist 35 Fd 5.58N 39.00 E
Kıbrıs/Kypros=Cyprus (EN) [1] 22 Ff 35.00N 33.00 E
Kıbrıs/Kypros=Cyprus (EN) 21 Ff 35.00N 33.00 E
Kibungo 36 Fc 2.10S 30.32 E
Kibuye 36 Ec 2.03S 29.21 E
Kibwezi 36 Gc 2.25S 37.58 E
Kičevo 15 Dh 41.31N 20.58 E
Kichi Kichi 35 Bb 17.36N 17.19 E
Kicking Horse Pass 42 Ff 51.50N 116.30W
Kidal 31 Hg 18.26N 1.24 E
Kidapawan 26 Ie 7.01N 125.03 E
Kidatu 36 Gd 7.42S 36.57 E
Kidira 34 Cc 14.28N 12.13W
Kidnappers, Cape- 62 Gc 39.38S 177.06 E
Kiekie 65a Ab 21.53N 160.13W
Kiel 6 He 54.20N 10.08 E
Kiel Canal (EN)=Nord-Ostsee Kanal 5 Ge 53.53N 9.08 E
Kielce 6 Ie 50.52N 20.37 E
Kielce [2] 10 Qf 50.50N 20.35 E
Kieler Bucht 10 Gb 54.35N 10.35 E
Kienge 36 Ee 10.33S 27.33 E
Kierspe 12 Jc 51.08N 7.35 E
Kieta 58 Ge 6.15S 155.37 E
Kietrz 10 Of 50.05N 18.01 E
Kiev (EN)=Kijev 6 Je 50.26N 30.31 E
Kiev Reservoir (EN)= Kijevskoje Vodohranilišče 5 Je 51.00N 30.25 E
Kiffa 31 Fg 16.36N 11.23W
Kifisiá 15 Gk 38.04N 23.49 E
Kifisós 15 Gk 38.26N 23.15 E
Kifrī 24 Ke 34.42N 44.58 E
Kigač 16 Pf 46.28N 49.08 E
Kigali 31 Ki 1.57S 30.04 E
Kiğı 24 Ic 39.19N 40.21 E
Kigille 35 Ed 8.40N 34.02 E
Kigoma 31 Ji 4.52S 29.38 E
Kigoma [3] 36 Fc 4.50S 30.05 E
Kigosi 36 Fc 4.40S 31.27 E
Kihelkonna 8 If 58.20N 21.54 E
Kihniö 8 Jb 62.12N 23.11 E
Kihnu 7 Fg 58.10N 24.00 E
Kiholo 65a Fd 19.51N 155.55W
Kiholo Bay 65a Fd 19.52N 155.56W
Kihti/Skiftet 8 Id 60.15N 21.05 E
Kii-Hantō 27 Oe 34.00N 135.45 E
Kiikka 8 Jc 61.20N 22.46 E
Kiil 16 Se 49.27N 54.50 E
Kiiminki 7 Fd 65.08N 25.44 E
Kii-Sanchi 29 Dd 34.15N 135.50 E
Kii-Suido 28 Mh 34.00N 134.55 E
Kija 20 De 56.52N 86.40 E
Kijev=Kiev (EN) 6 Je 50.26N 30.31 E
Kijevka 19 He 50.16N 71.34 E
Kijevskaja Oblast [3] 19 De 50.20N 30.45 E
Kijevskoje Vodohranilišče= Kiev Reservoir (EN) 5 Je 51.00N 30.25 E
Kijma 19 Ge 51.35N 67.34 E
Kikai-Jima 27 Mf 28.15N 130.00 E
Kikerino 8 Me 59.23N 29.38 E
Kikinda 15 Dd 45.50N 20.29 E
Kikládhes = Cyclades (EN) 5 Ih 37.00N 25.10 E
Kikonai 28 Pd 41.40N 140.26 E
Kikori 58 Fe 7.25S 144.13 E
Kikori River 57 Fe 7.23S 144.16 E
Kikuchi 29 Be 32.59N 130.49 E
Kikuma 29 Cd 34.03N 132.51 E
Kikvidze 16 Md 50.44N 43.03 E
Kikwit 31 Ii 5.02S 18.49 E
Kil [Nor.] 8 Cf 58.52N 9.19 E
Kil [Swe.] 7 Cg 59.30N 13.19 E
Kilafors 7 Df 61.15N 16.33 E
Kilambé, Cerro- 49 Eg 13.34N 85.42W
Kilauea 65a Ba 22.13N 159.25W
Kilauea Crater 65a Fd 19.24N 155.17W
Kilauea Point 65a Ba 22.14N 159.24W
Kilbrannan Sound 9 Hf 55.40N 5.25W
Kilbuck Mountains 40 Hd 60.30N 159.45W
Kilchu 27 Mc 40.58N 129.20 E
Kilcoy 59 Ke 26.57S 152.33 E
Kildare/Cill Dara [2] 9 Gh 53.15N 6.45W
Kildare/Cill Dara 9 Gh 53.10N 6.55W
Kildin, Ostrov- 7 Ib 69.20N 34.10 E
Kilembe 36 Cd 5.42S 19.55 E
Kilgore 45 Ij 32.23N 94.53W
Kilgoris 36 Fc 1.00S 34.53 E
Kiliao He 21 Oe 43.24N 123.42 E
Kiliç 15 Mi 40.40N 29.23 E
Kilifi 36 Gc 3.38S 39.51 E
Kili Island 57 Hd 5.39N 169.04 E
Kilija 19 Cf 45.27N 29.14 E
Kilijskoje girlo 15 Md 45.13N 29.43 E
Kilimanjaro [3] 36 Gc 4.00S 37.40 E
Kilimanjaro, Mount- 30 Ki 3.04S 37.22 E
Kilimli 24 Db 41.29N 31.50 E
Kilinailau Islands 60 Fh 4.45S 155.20 E
Kilindoni 31 Ki 7.55S 39.39 E
Kilingi-Nõmme/Kilingi-Nymme 7 Fg 58.08N 24.59 E
Kilingi-Nymme/Kilingi-Nõmme 7 Fg 58.08N 24.59 E
Kilis 23 Eb 36.44N 37.05 E
Kilitbahir 24 Bb 40.12N 26.20 E
Kilkee/Cill Chaoi 9 Di 52.41N 9.38W
Kilkenny/Cill Chainnigh 9 Fi 52.39N 7.15W
Kilkenny/Cill Chainnigh [2] 9 Fi 52.40N 7.20W
Kilkieran Bay 9 Dh 53.15N 9.45W
Kilkís 15 Fi 41.00N 22.52 E
Killala Bay/Cuan Chill Ala 9 Dg 54.15N 9.10W
Killarney/Cill Airne 9 Di 52.03N 9.30W
Killary Harbour/An Caoláire Rua 9 Dh 53.38N 9.55W
Killdeer 45 Ec 47.22N 102.45W
Killeen 43 He 31.08N 97.44W
Killinck 42 Ld 60.25N 64.40W
Killíni 15 El 37.56N 21.09 E
Killíni Óros 15 Fl 37.55N 22.26 E
Kilmallock/Cill Mocheallóg 9 Ei 52.25N 8.35W
Kilmarnock 9 If 55.37N 4.30W
Kilmez 7 Mh 56.58N 50.29 E
Kilmez 7 Mh 57.03N 51.24 E
Kilmore 59 Ig 37.18S 144.57 E
Kilombero 36 Gd 8.31S 37.22 E
Kilosa 31 Ki 6.50S 36.59 E
Kilpisjärvi 7 Eb 69.03N 20.48 E
Kilp-Javr 7 Hb 69.07N 32.28 E
Kilrush/Cill Rois 9 Di 52.39N 9.29W
Kilsbergen 8 Fe 59.20N 14.45 E
Kiltān Island 25 Ef 11.29N 73.00 E
Kilwa 36 Ed 9.17S 28.20 E
Kilwa Kisiwani 31 Ki 8.58S 39.30 E
Kilwa Kivinje 36 Gd 8.45S 39.24 E
Kilwa Masoko 36 Gd 8.56S 39.31 E
Kilyos → Kumköy 15 Mh 41.15N 29.02 E
Kim 45 Eh 37.15N 103.21W
Kimamba 36 Gd 6.47S 37.08 E
Kimba 59 Hf 33.09S 136.25 E
Kimball [Nb.-U.S.] 45 Ef 41.14N 103.40W
Kimball [S.D.-U.S.] 45 Ge 43.45N 98.57W
Kimball, Mount- 40 Kd 63.14N 144.39W
Kimbe 59 Ka 5.31S 150.12 E
Kimbe Bay 60 Ei 5.30S 150.30 E
Kimberley 57 Df 16.00S 126.00 E
Kimberley [B.C.-Can.] 42 Fg 49.41N 115.59W
Kimberley [S.Afr.] 31 Jk 28.43S 24.46 E
Kimberley Plateau 59 Fc 17.00S 127.00 E
Kimch'aek (Sŏngjin) 27 Mc 40.41N 129.12 E
Kimch'ŏn 27 Md 36.07N 128.07 E
Kimhandu 30 Ki 7.05S 37.35 E
Kími 15 Hk 38.38N 24.06 E
Kimito 8 Jd 60.10N 22.40 E
Kimito/Kemiö 8 Jd 60.10N 22.40 E
Kimje 28 Ig 35.48N 126.53 E
Kimobetsu 29a Bb 42.47N 140.56 E
Kímolos 15 Hm 36.48N 24.34 E
Kimongo 36 Bc 4.29S 12.58 E
Kimovsk 19 De 54.01N 38.36 E
Kimpu-San 29 Fd 35.52N 138.37 E
Kimry 19 Dd 56.52N 37.24 E
Kimvula 36 Cd 5.44S 15.58 E
Kinabalu, Gunong- 21 Ni 6.05N 116.33 E
Kinabatangan 26 Ge 5.42N 118.23 E
Kinango 36 Gc 4.08S 39.19 E
Kínaros 15 Jm 36.59N 26.17 E
Kincardine 42 Jh 44.11N 81.38W
Kind 8 Eg 57.35N 13.25 E
Kinda 36 Ed 9.18S 25.04 E
Kinda 8 Ff 58.05N 15.40 E
Kindamba 36 Bc 3.44S 14.31 E
Kinder 45 Jk 30.29N 92.51W
Kinder Scout 9 Lh 53.23N 1.52W
Kindersley 42 Gf 51.27N 109.10W
Kindi 34 Ec 12.26N 2.01W
Kindia 31 Fg 10.04N 12.51W
Kindu 31 Ji 2.57S 25.56 E
Kinel 7 Mj 53.14N 50.40 E
Kinesi 36 Fc 1.28S 33.52 E
Kinešma 19 Ed 57.28N 42.16 E
King 63a Aa 4.24S 152.43 E
King, Cayos- 49 Fg 12.45N 83.20W
Kingaroy 59 Ke 26.33S 151.50 E
King Christian 42 Ha 77.45N 102.00W
King Christian IX Land (EN) = Kong Christian IX Land 67 Mc 68.00N 36.30W
King Christian X Land (EN) = Kong Christian X Land 67 Md 72.20N 32.30W
King City 43 Cd 36.13N 121.08W
King Edward River 59 Fb 14.14S 126.35 E
Kingfisher 45 Hi 35.52N 97.56W
King Frederik VI Coast (EN) =Kong Frederik VI Kyst 67 Nc 63.00N 43.30W
King Frederik VIII Land (EN) = Kong Frederik VIII Land 67 Md 78.30N 28.00W
King George Island 66 Re 62.00S 58.15W
King George Islands 42 Je 57.15N 78.30W
King George Sound 59 Dg 35.10S 118.10 E
Kingisepp 7 Gg 59.23N 28.37 E
Kingisepp/Kingissepp 19 Cd 58.17N 22.29 E
King Island 57 Fh 39.50S 144.00 E
Kingissepp/Kingisepp 19 Cd 58.17N 22.29 E
King Lear Peak 46 Ff 41.12N 118.34W
King Leopold Ranges 59 Fc 17.30S 125.45 E
Kingman [Az.-U.S.] 43 Ed 35.12N 114.04W
Kingman [Ks.-U.S.] 45 Gh 37.39N 98.07W
Kingman Reef 57 Kd 6.19N 162.28W
Kingombe [Zaire] 36 Ec 2.35S 26.37 E
Kingombe [Zaire] 36 Ec 3.52S 26.35 E
Kingoome Inlet 46 Ba 50.49N 126.13W
Kingoonya 58 Eh 30.54S 135.18 E
King Peninsula 66 Of 73.12S 101.00W
Kingsclere 12 Ac 51.19N 1.15W
Kingscote 59 Hg 35.40S 137.38 E
King's Lynn 9 Ni 52.45N 0.24 E
King Sound 57 Df 17.00S 123.30 E
Kings Peak [Ca.-U.S.] 46 Cf 40.10N 124.08W
Kings Peak [U.S.] 38 He 40.46N 110.22W
Kingsport 43 Kd 36.32N 82.33W
Kings River 46 Fh 36.03N 119.49W
Kingston [Jam.] 39 Lh 18.00N 76.50W
Kingston [Nor.I.] 58 Hg 29.04S 167.58 E
Kingston [N.Y.-U.S.] 43 Mc 41.55N 74.00W
Kingston [N.Z.] 61 Ci 45.20S 168.43 E
Kingston [Ont.-Can.] 39 Le 44.14N 76.30W
Kingston Peak 46 Hi 35.42N 115.52W
Kingston South East 58 Eh 36.50S 139.51 E
Kingston-upon-Hull (Hull) 6 Fe 53.45N 0.20W
Kingston-upon-Thames, London- 9 Mj 51.28N 0.19W
Kingstown 39 Mh 13.09N 61.14W
Kingsville 43 Hf 27.31N 97.52W
Kings Worthy 12 Ac 51.05N 1.18W
Kingussie 9 Id 57.05N 4.04W
King William 38 Jc 69.00N 97.30W
King William's Town 31 Jl 32.51S 27.22 E
Kiniama 36 Ee 11.26S 28.19 E
Kınık 24 Bc 39.05N 27.23 E
Kinkala 36 Bc 4.22S 14.46 E
Kinlochleven 9 Ie 56.43N 4.58W
Kinna 8 Eg 57.30N 12.41 E
Kinnairds Head 9 Ld 57.42N 2.00W
Kinnared 8 Eg 57.02N 13.06 E
Kinnekulle 8 Ef 58.35N 13.23 E
Kinneret, Yam- 24 Ff 32.48N 35.35 E
Kino-Kawa 29 Dd 34.13N 135.08 E
Kinomoto 29 Ed 35.31N 136.13 E
Kinoosao 42 He 57.06N 102.01W
Kinós Kefalaí 15 Fj 39.25N 22.34 E
Kinross 9 Je 56.13N 3.27W
Kinsale/cionn tSáile 9 Ej 51.42N 8.32W
Kinsale, Old Head of-/An Seancheann 9 Ej 51.36N 8.32W
Kinsangire 36 Gd 7.26S 38.35 E
Kinsarvik 7 Bf 60.23N 6.43 E
Kinshasa [2] 36 Cc 4.00S 16.00 E
Kinshasa (Leopoldville) 31 Ii 4.18S 15.18 E
Kinsley 45 Gh 37.55N 99.25W
Kinston 43 Ld 35.16N 77.35W
Kintampo 34 Ed 8.03N 1.43W
Kintap 26 Gg 3.51S 115.13 E
Kintyre 9 Hf 55.32N 5.35W
Kintyre, Mull of- 9 Hf 55.17N 5.55W
Kin-Wan 29b Ab 26.25N 127.54 E
Kinyan 34 Dc 11.51N 6.01W
Kinyeti 30 Kh 3.57N 32.54 E
Kinzig [Eur.] 10 Dh 48.37N 7.49 E
Kinzig [F.R.G.] 10 Ef 50.08N 8.54 E
Kioa 63d Bb 16.39S 179.55 E
Kipaka 36 Ec 4.09S 26.30 E
Kiparissia 15 El 37.15N 21.40 E
Kiparissia, Gulf of- (EN) = Kiparissiakós Kólpos 15 El 37.30N 21.25 E
Kiparissiakós Kólpos = Kiparissia, Gulf of- (EN) 15 El 37.30N 21.25 E
Kipawa, Lac- 42 Jg 46.55N 79.00W
Kipembawe 36 Fd 7.39S 33.24 E
Kipengere Range 30 Ki 9.10S 34.15 E
Kiperčeny 15 Lb 47.32N 28.40 E
Kipili 36 Fd 7.26S 30.36 E
Kipini 36 Hc 2.32S 40.31 E
Kipling 45 Ea 50.10N 102.38W
Kippure 9 Gh 53.11N 6.20W
Kiprarenukk, Mys-/Undva Neem 8 If 58.25N 21.45 E
Kipushi 36 Ee 11.46S 27.14 E
Kirakira 58 Hf 10.27S 161.56 E
Kiraz 24 Cc 39.21N 27.25 E
Kirazlı 24 Bb 40.01N 26.40 E
Kirbla 8 Jf 58.42N 23.49 E
Kircasalih 15 Jh 41.23N 26.48 E
Kirchberg (Hunsrüch) 12 Je 49.57N 7.24 E
Kirchhain 12 Kd 50.49N 8.58 E
Kirchheimbolanden 12 Ke 49.40N 8.01 E
Kirchheim unter Teck 10 Fh 48.39N 9.27 E
Kirchhundem 12 Kc 51.06N 8.06 E
Kirchhundem-Rahrbach 12 Jc 51.02N 7.59 E
Kirchlengern 12 Kb 52.12N 8.38 E
Kirdimi 35 Bb 18.11N 18.38 E
Kireç 15 Lj 39.33N 28.22 E
Kirenga 21 Md 57.47N 107.59 E
Kirensk 22 Md 57.46N 108.08 E
Kirghiz SSR (EN)= Kirgizskaja SSR [2] 19 Hg 41.30N 75.00 E
Kirghiz Steppe (EN) 5 Lf 49.30N 50.30 E
Kirgizskaja Sovetskaja Socialističeskaja Respublika [2] 19 Hg 41.30N 75.00 E
Kirgizskaja SSR/Kyrgyz Sovetik Socialistik Respublikasy [2] 19 Hg 41.30N 75.00 E
Kirgizskaja SSR=Kirghiz SSR (EN) [2] 19 Hg 41.30N 75.00 E
Kirgizski Hrebet 19 Hg 42.30N 74.00 E
Kiri 36 Cc 1.27S 19.00 E
Kiribati [1] 58 Je 0.01S 174.00 E
Kirikhan 24 Gd 36.32N 36.19 E
Kırıkkale 23 Db 39.50N 33.31 E
Kirillov 7 Jg 59.54N 38.27 E
Kirillovskoje 8 Md 60.28N 29.28 E
Kirin (EN)=Chi-lin Sheng→Jilin Sheng [2] 27 Mc 43.00N 126.00 E
Kirin (EN)=Jilin Sheng (Chi-lin Sheng) [2] 27 Mc 43.00N 126.00 E
Kirinyaga/Kenya, Mount- 30 Ki 0.10S 37.20 E
Kirishima-Yama 29 Bf 31.56N 130.52 E
Kiriši 19 Dd 59.27N 32.02 E
Kiritimati Atoll (Christmas) 57 Ld 1.52N 157.20W
Kirja 7 Li 55.05N 46.52 E
Kirkağaç 24 Bc 39.06N 27.40 E
Kirkby Lonsdale 9 Kg 54.13N 2.36W
Kirkcaldy 9 Je 56.07N 3.10W
Kirkcudbright 9 Ig 54.50N 4.03W
Kirkee→Khadki 25 Ee 18.34N 73.52 E
Kirkenær 7 Cf 60.28N 12.03 E
Kirkenes 6 Jb 69.43N 30.03 E
Kirkjubæjarklaustur 7a Bc 63.47N 18.04W
Kirkkonummi/Kyrkslätt 8 Kd 60.07N 24.26 E
Kirkland 46 Dc 47.41N 122.12W
Kirkland Lake 39 Ke 48.09N 80.02W
Kırklareli 23 Ca 41.44N 27.12 E
Kirkpatrick, Mont- 66 Kg 84.20S 166.19 E
Kırkpınar Dağı 24 Fd 37.14N 34.15 E
Kirksville 43 Ic 40.12N 92.35W
Kirkūk 22 Gf 35.28N 44.23 E
Kirkwall 9 Kc 58.59N 2.58W
Kirkwood [Mo.-U.S.] 45 Kg 38.35N 90.24W
Kirkwood [S.Afr.] 37 Df 33.22S 25.15 E
Kırlangıç Burun 24 Dd 36.13N 30.25 E
Kirn 10 Dg 49.47N 7.27 E
Kirobasi 24 Ed 36.43N 33.52 E
Kirov [R.S.F.S.R.] 19 De 54.03N 34.21 E
Kirov [R.S.F.S.R.] 6 Kd 58.33N 49.42 E
Kirova, Zaliv- 16 Pj 39.05N 49.05 E
Kirovabad 6 Kg 40.40N 46.22 E
Kirovakan 19 Eg 40.48N 44.28 E
Kirovgrad 17 Jh 57.26N 60.04 E
Kirovo 18 Hd 40.28N 70.34 E
Kirovo-Čepeck 19 Fd 58.35N 50.03 E
Kirovograd 6 Jf 48.30N 32.18 E
Kirovogradskaja Oblast [3] 19 Df 48.20N 31.50 E
Kirovsk [R.S.F.S.R.] 19 Db 67.37N 33.37 E
Kirovsk [R.S.F.S.R.] 7 Hg 59.53N 31.01 E
Kirovsk [Tur.-U.S.S.R.] 18 Cf 37.43N 60.24 E
Kirovskaja Oblast [3] 19 Ed 58.30N 50.00 E
Kirovski [Kaz.-U.S.S.R.] 19 Hg 44.53N 78.12 E
Kirovski [R.S.F.S.R.] 20 Ig 45.05N 133.27 E
Kirovski [R.S.F.S.R.] 16 Pg 45.48N 48.08 E
Kirovski [R.S.F.S.R.] 20 Kf 54.25N 155.37 E
Kirovski [R.S.F.S.R.] 20 Hf 54.26N 127.00 E
Kirovskoje 18 Hc 42.39N 71.35 E
Kirpilski Liman 16 Kg 45.50N 38.05 E
Kirriemuir 9 Je 56.41N 3.01W
Kirs 19 Fd 59.21N 52.18 E
Kirsanov 16 Mc 52.41N 42.45 E
Kırsşehir 23 Db 39.09N 34.10 E
Kīrthar Range 21 Ig 27.00N 67.20 E
Kirton 12 Bb 52.55N 0.03W
Kiruna 6 Ib 67.51N 20.13 E
Kirundu 36 Ec 0.44S 25.32 E
Kiryū 29 Fc 36.25N 139.20 E
Kiržač 7 Jh 56.11N 38.53 E
Kisa 7 Dh 57.59N 15.37 E
Kisabi 36 Ed 8.03S 29.11 E
Kisač 15 Cd 45.21N 19.44 E
Kisakata 29 Fb 39.14N 139.54 E
Kisaki 36 Gd 7.28S 37.36 E
Kisalföld 10 Mi 47.30N 17.00 E
Kisangani 31 Jh 0.25N 25.12 E
Kisarazu 29 Fd 35.23N 139.55 E
Kisbér 10 Oi 47.30N 18.02 E
Kiselevsk 20 Df 54.03N 86.49 E
Kiserawe 36 Gd 6.54S 39.05 E
Kishangarh 25 Ec 26.34N 74.52 E
Kishb, Harraţ al- 33 He 22.47N 41.30 E
Kishi 34 Fd 9.05N 3.51 E
Kishiwada 28 Mg 34.28N 135.22 E
Kisii 36 Fc 0.41S 34.46 E
Kisiju 36 Gd 7.24S 39.20 E
Kišinev 6 If 46.59N 28.52 E
Kısır Dağı 24 Jb 40.58N 43.04 E
Kiska 40a Bb 52.00N 177.30 E
Kiska Volcano 40a Bb 52.07N 177.36 E
Kisko 8 Jd 60.14N 23.29 E
Kiskörei Víztároló 10 Qi 47.44N 20.40 E
Kiskórös 10 Pj 46.37N 19.18 E
Kiskunfélegyháza 10 Pj 46.33N 19.51 E
Kiskunhalas 10 Pj 46.26N 19.30 E
Kiskunmajsa 10 Pj 46.29N 19.45 E
Kiskunság 10 Pj 46.35N 19.15 E
Kislovodsk 19 Eg 43.54N 42.42 E
Kismanyo 31 Li 0.22S 42.32 E
Kisofukushima 29 Ed 35.51N 137.41 E
Kiso-Gawa 28 Ng 35.05N 136.45 E
Kisoro 36 Ec 1.17S 29.41 E
Kiso-Sanmyaku 29 Ed 35.45N 137.45 E
Kisria, Daiet el- 13 Oi 35.44N 2.47 E
Kissámou, Kólpos- 15 Gn 35.35N 23.40 E
Kissidougou 34 Cd 9.11N 10.06W
Kissimmee 44 Gk 28.18N 81.24W
Kissimmee, Lake- 44 Gl 27.55N 81.16W
Kissū, Jabal- 35 Da 21.35N 25.09 E
Kistelek 10 Pj 46.28N 19.59 E
Kisterenye 10 Ph 48.01N 19.50 E

Index Symbols

[1] Independent Nation
[2] State, Region
[3] District, County
[4] Municipality
[5] Colony, Dependency
Continent
Physical Region
Historical or Cultural Region
Mount, Mountain
Volcano
Hill
Mountains, Mountain Range
Hills, Escarpment
Plateau, Upland
Pass, Gap
Plain, Lowland
Delta
Salt Flat
Valley, Canyon
Crater, Cave
Karst Features
Depression
Polder
Desert, Dunes
Forest, Woods
Heath, Steppe
Oasis
Cape, Point
Coast, Beach
Cliff
Peninsula
Isthmus
Sandbank
Island
Atoll
Rock, Reef
Islands, Archipelago
Rocks, Reefs
Coral Reef
Well, Spring
Geyser
River, Stream
Waterfall Rapids
River Mouth, Estuary
Lake
Salt Lake
Intermittent Lake
Reservoir
Swamp, Pond
Canal
Glacier
Ice Shelf, Pack Ice
Ocean
Sea
Gulf, Bay
Strait, Fjord
Lagoon
Bank
Seamount
Tablemount
Ridge
Shelf
Basin
Escarpment, Sea Scarp
Fracture
Trench, Abyss
National Park, Reserve
Point of Interest
Recreation Site
Cave, Cavern
Historic Site
Ruins
Wall, Walls
Church, Abbey
Temple
Scientific Station
Airport
Port
Lighthouse
Mine
Tunnel
Dam, Bridge

Kisújszállás 10 Qi 47.13N 20.46 E
Kisuki 29 Cd 35.17N 132.54 E
Kisumu 31 Kf 0.06S 34.45 E
Kisvárda 10 Sh 48.13N 22.05 E
Kita 31 Gg 13.03N 9.30W
Kitab 19 Gh 39.08N 66.54 E
Kita-Daitō-Jima 27 Nf 25.55N 131.20 E
Kitaibaraki 28 Pf 36.48N 140.45 E
Kita-lō-Jima 60 Cb 25.26N 141.17 E
Kitaj, Ozero- 15 Md 45.35N 29.15 E
Kitakami 27 Pd 39.30N 141.10 E
Kitakami-Gawa 29 Gb 38.25N 141.19 E
Kitakami-Sanchi 29 Gb 39.30N 141.30 E
Kitakata 28 Of 37.39N 139.52 E
Kitakyūshū 22 Pf 33.53N 130.50 E
Kitale 31 Kh 1.01N 35.00 E
Kitamaiaioi 29a Cb 43.33N 143.57 E
Kitami 27 Pc 43.48N 143.54 E
Kitami-Fuji 29a Cb 43.42N 143.14 E
Kitami-Sanchi 28 Qb 44.30N 142.30 E
Kitami Tōge 29a Cb 43.55N 142.55 E
Kitan-Kaikyō 29 Dd 34.15N 135.00 E
Kita-Taiheyō=Pacific Ocean (EN) 60 Ch 22.00N 167.00 E
Kita-Ura 29 Gc 36.00N 140.34 E
Kit Carson 45 Eg 38.46N 102.48W
Kitchener 42 Jh 43.27N 80.29W
Kitee 7 He 62.06N 30.09 E
Kitessa 35 Dd 5.22N 25.22 E
Kitgum 36 Fb 3.19N 32.53 E
Kithira=Cythera (EN) 15 Fm 36.09N 23.00 E
Kithira=Kythera (EN) 5 Ih 36.15N 23.00 E
Kithira Channel (EN)=Kithiron Dhiékplous 15 Fm 36.00N 23.00 E
Kithíron, Dhiékplous-=Kithira Channel (EN) 15 Fm 36.00N 23.00 E
Kithnos 15 Hl 37.25N 24.26 E
Kithnos 15 Hl 37.23N 24.25 E
Kithnou, Stenón- 15 Hl 37.25N 24.30 E
Kitimat 39 Gd 54.05N 128.38W
Kitimat Ranges 42 Ef 53.58N 128.39W
Kitoushi-Yama 29a Cb 43.27N 143.25 E
Kitriani 15 Hm 36.54N 24.44 E
Kitridge Point 51q Bb 13.09N 59.25W
Kitros 15 Fi 40.22N 22.35 E
Kitsuki 29 Be 33.25N 131.37 E
Kittanning 44 He 40.49N 79.31W
Kittery 44 Ld 43.05N 70.45W
Kittilä 7 Fc 67.40N 24.54 E
Kitui 31 Ki 1.22S 38.01 E
Kitunda 36 Fd 6.48S 33.13 E
Kitutu 36 Ec 3.17S 28.05 E
Kitwe-Nkana 31 Jj 12.49S 28.13 E
Kitzbühel 14 Gc 47.27N 12.23 E
Kitzbüheler Alpen 14 Gc 47.20N 12.20 E
Kitzingen 10 Gg 49.44N 10.10 E
Kiunga [Kenya] 36 Hc 1.45S 41.29 E
Kiunga [Pap.N.Gui.] 60 Ci 6.07S 141.18 E
Kiuruvesi 7 Ge 63.39N 26.37 E
Kivalina 40 Gc 67.59N 164.33W
Kivercy 16 Dd 50.50N 25.31 E
Kivijärvi [Fin.] 8 Ld 60.55N 27.40 E
Kivijärvi [Fin.] 7 Fe 63.10N 25.09 E
Kivik 7 Di 55.41N 14.15 E
Kiviõli/Kiviyli 7 Gg 59.23N 26.59 E
Kiviyli/Kiviõli 7 Gg 59.23N 26.59 E
Kivu [2] 36 Ec 2.30S 27.30 E
Kivu, Lac-=Kivu, Lake- (EN) 30 Ii 2.00S 29.10 E
Kivu, Lake- (EN)=Kivu, Lac- 30 Ii 2.00S 29.10 E
Kiwai Island 60 Ci 8.30S 143.25 E
Kıyāmaki Dāgh 24 Kc 38.47N 45.51 E
Kıyıköy 24 Cb 41.25N 28.01 E
Kiyosato 29a Db 43.51N 144.35 E
Kizel 19 Fd 59.03N 57.40 E
Kizema 7 Kf 61.09N 44.46 E
Kizilcabölük 15 Ml 37.37N 29.01 E
Kızılca Dağı 24 Cd 36.55N 29.52 E
Kızılcahaman 24 Eb 40.28N 32.39 E
Kızıl Dağ 24 Ed 36.25N 32.42 E
Kizilhisar 15 Ml 37.33N 29.18 E
Kızılırmak 21 Fe 41.45N 35.59 E
Kızılırmak 24 Eb 40.22N 33.59 E
Kiziljurt 16 Oh 43.13N 46.55 E
Kizilskoje 17 Ij 52.44N 58.54 E
Kızıltepe 24 Id 37.12N 40.36 E
Kizimen, Vulkan- 20 Le 55.03N 160.27 E
Kizinga 20 Ff 51.51N 109.55 E
Kizir 20 Ef 54.10N 93.30 E
Kizljar 19 Eg 43.50N 46.42 E
Kizljarski Zaliv 16 Og 44.35N 46.55 E
Kizukuri 29a Bc 40.48N 140.22 E
Kizyl-Arvat 19 Fh 39.01N 56.20 E
Kizyl-Atrek 19 Fh 37.38N 54.47 E
Kizyl-Su 19 Fh 39.46N 53.01 E
Kjahta 20 Ff 50.26N 106.25 E
Kjalvaz 16 Pj 38.38N 48.20 E
Kjardla/Kärdla 7 Fg 59.01N 22.42 E
Kjarevere/Kärevere 8 Lf 58.23N 26.30 E
Kjarla/Kärla 8 Jf 58.16N 22.05 E
Kjellerup 8 Ch 56.17N 9.26 E
Kjøllefjord 7 Ga 70.56N 27.27 E
Kjölur 7a Bb 64.50N 19.25W
Kjøpsvik 7 Db 68.06N 16.21 E
Kjubjume 20 Jd 63.28N 140.30 E
Kjurdamir 19 Eg 40.20N 48.07 E
Kjusjur 20 Hb 70.35N 127.45 E
Kjustendil 15 Fg 42.17N 22.41 E
Kjustendil [2] 15 Fg 42.17N 22.41 E
Kiyosumi-Yama 29 Gd 35.10N 140.09 E
Klabat, Gunung- 26 If 1.28N 125.02 E
Kladanj 23 Gf 44.14N 18.42 E
Kladno 10 Kf 50.09N 14.07 E
Kladovo 15 Fe 44.37N 22.37 E
Klagenfurt 6 Hf 46.38N 14.18 E
Klaipėda/Klajpeda 6 Id 55.43N 21.07 E
Klajpeda/Klaipėda 6 Id 55.43N 21.07 E
Klamath 46 Cf 41.32N 124.02W
Klamath Falls 39 Ge 42.13N 121.46W
Klamath Mountains 43 Cc 41.40N 123.20W
Klamath River 46 Cf 41.33N 124.04W
Klamono 26 Jg 1.08S 131.30 E
Klarälven 5 Hd 59.23N 13.32 E
Klaten 26 Fh 7.42S 110.35 E
Klatovy 10 Jg 49.24N 13.19 E
Klavreström 8 Fg 57.08N 15.08 E
Klawer 37 Bf 31.44S 18.36 E
Klazienaveen, Emmen- 12 Jb 52.44N 7.01 E
Kleck 16 Ec 53.03N 26.40 E
Kłecko 10 Nd 52.38N 17.26 E
Kleinblittersdorf 12 Je 49.09N 7.02 E
Kleine Nete 12 Gc 51.08N 4.34 E
Kleine Sluis, Anna Paulowna- 12 Gb 52.52N 4.52 E
Klein-Karoo=Little Karroo (EN) 37 Cf 33.42S 21.20 E
Kleinsee 37 Be 29.40S 17.05 E
Klekovača 14 Kf 44.26N 16.31 E
Kléla 34 Dc 11.40N 5.40W
Kleppe 8 Af 58.46N 5.40 E
Klerksdorp 37 De 26.58S 26.39 E
Kletnja 19 De 53.27N 33.17 E
Kletski 16 Me 49.19N 43.04 E
Kleve 10 Ce 51.47N 6.09 E
Klibreck, Ben- 9 Ic 58.19N 4.30W
Klička 20 Gf 50.24N 118.01 E
Klimoviči 19 De 53.37N 32.01 E
Klimovo 16 Hc 52.23N 32.16 E
Klin 19 Dd 56.20N 36.42 E
Klina 15 Dg 42.37N 20.35 E
Klincy 19 De 52.46N 32.17 E
Klingbach 12 Ke 49.11N 8.24 E
Klingenthal 10 If 50.22N 12.28 E
Klinovec 10 If 50.24N 12.58 E
Klintehamn 7 Eh 57.24N 18.12 E
Klippan 8 Eh 56.08N 13.06 E
Kliplaat 37 Cf 33.02S 24.21 E
Kliškovcy 15 Ja 48.23N 26.13 E
Klisura 15 Hg 42.42N 24.27 E
Klitmøller 8 Cg 57.02N 8.31 E
Kljazma 5 Kd 56.10N 42.58 E
Ključevskaja Sopka, Vulkan- 21 Sd 56.04N 160.38 E
Kljuci 20 Le 56.14N 160.58 E
Kłobuck 10 Of 50.55N 18.57 E
Kłodawa 10 Od 52.16N 18.55 E
Kłodzka, Kotlina- 10 Mf 50.30N 16.35 E
Kłodzko 10 Mf 50.28N 16.40 E
Kløfta 8 Dd 60.04N 11.09 E
Kloga/Klooga 8 Ke 59.24N 24.10 E
Klomnice 10 Pf 50.56N 19.21 E
Klondike Plateau 42 Dd 63.10N 139.55W
Klondike River 42 Dd 64.03N 139.26W
Klooga/Kloga 8 Ke 59.24N 24.10 E
Kloosteezande, Hontenisse- 12 Gc 51.23N 4.00 E
Klosi 15 Dh 41.29N 20.06 E
Klosterneuburg 14 Kb 48.18N 16.19 E
Klosters/Claustra 14 Dd 46.52N 9.52 E
Kloten 14 Cc 47.27N 8.35 E
Klotz, Lac- 42 Kd 60.40N 73.00W
Kluane Lake 42 Dd 61.15N 138.40W
Kluczbork 10 Of 50.59N 18.13 E
Knaben 8 Bf 58.39N 7.04 E
Knäred 8 Eh 56.32N 13.19 E
Kneža 15 Hf 43.30N 24.05 E
Knife River 45 Fc 47.20N 101.23W
Knin 14 Kf 44.02N 16.12 E
Knislinge 8 Fh 56.11N 14.05 E
Knittelfeld 14 Ic 47.13N 14.49 E
Knivsta 8 Ge 59.43N 17.48 E
Knjaževac 15 Ff 43.34N 22.15 E
Knobly Mountain 44 Hf 39.15N 79.05W
Knockmealdown Mountains/Cnoc Mhaoldonn 9 Fi 52.15N 8.00W
Knokke-Heist [Bel.] 12 Fc 51.21N 3.15 E
Knokke-Heist [Bel.] 11 Jc 51.21N 3.17 E
Knokke-Westkapelle 12 Fc 51.19N 3.18 E
Knolls grund 8 Gg 57.30N 17.30 E
Knøsen 8 Dg 57.12N 10.18 E
Knosós=Cnossus (EN) 15 In 35.18N 25.10 E
Knox, Cape- 42 Ef 54.11N 133.05W
Knox Coast 66 He 66.30S 105.00 E
Knoxville [Ia.-U.S.] 45 Jf 41.19N 93.06W
Knoxville [Tn.-U.S.] 39 Kf 35.58N 83.56W
Knud Rasmussen Land 67 Nd 80.00N 55.00W
Knüllgebirge 10 Ff 50.50N 9.30 E
Knutsholstind 8 Cc 61.26N 8.34 E
Knysna 31 Jl 34.02S 23.02 E
Ko, Kut 25 Kf 11.40N 102.35 E
Koartac 42 Kd 60.50N 69.30W
Koba 26 Eg 2.29S 106.24 E
Koba, Pulau- 26 Jh 6.25S 134.28 E
Kobar Sink 35 Gc 14.00N 40.30 E
Kobayashi 28 Ki 31.59N 130.59 E
Kobdo 22 Le 48.01N 91.38 E
Kobdo (Chovd) 27 Fb 48.06N 92.11 E
Kōbe 22 Pf 34.41N 135.10 E
Kobeljaki 16 Ie 49.08N 34.12 E
København [2] 8 Ei 55.40N 12.10 E
København=Copenhagen (EN) 6 Hi 55.40N 12.35 E
Kobenni 32 Ff 15.55N 9.05W
Kobern-Gondorf 12 Jd 50.19N 7.28 E
Kobjaj 20 Hd 63.30N 126.26 E
Koblenz 10 Df 50.21N 7.36 E
Kobo 35 Fc 12.09N 39.39 E
Koboldo 20 If 52.58N 132.42 E
Kobra 7 Mg 59.19N 50.54 E
Kobrin 19 Ce 52.13N 24.23 E
Kobrinskoje 8 Ne 59.22N 30.14 E
Kobroor, Pulau- 26 Jh 6.12S 134.32 E
Kobuk 38 Cc 66.45N 161.00W
Kobuleti 16 Li 41.47N 41.45 E
Koca 24 Eb 41.41N 32.15 E
Kocabaş 24 Bb 40.22N 27.19 E
Koca Çay 15 Lj 38.43N 28.30 E
Koca Çay [Tur.] 24 Bb 40.08N 27.57 E
Koca Çay [Tur.] 24 Cd 36.17N 29.16 E
Koca Çay/Orhaneli 15 Lj 39.56N 28.32 E
Kočani 15 Fh 41.55N 22.25 E
Kocasu 15 Mj 39.42N 29.31 E
Kočečum 20 Fd 64.17N 100.10 E
Kočetovka 16 Lc 53.01N 40.31 E
Kočevje 14 Ie 45.39N 14.51 E
Kočevski rog 14 Ie 45.41N 15.00 E
Koch 42 Jc 69.35N 78.20W
Köch'ang 28 Ig 35.41N 127.55 E
Ko Chang 25 Kf 12.00N 102.23 E
Kōchi 27 Ne 33.33N 133.33 E
Kōchi Ken [2] 28 Lh 33.20N 133.30 E
Kochisar Ovası 24 Ec 38.50N 33.30 E
Kock 10 Se 51.39N 22.27 E
Kočkorka 18 Jc 42.11N 75.45 E
Kočmar 15 Kf 43.41N 27.28 E
Kočubej 19 Eg 44.23N 46.31 E
Kočubejevskoje 16 Lg 44.41N 41.50 E
Kodiak 39 Dd 57.48N 152.23W
Kodiak 38 Dd 57.30N 153.30W
Kodino 7 Je 63.44N 39.40 E
Kodok 35 Ed 9.53N 32.07 E
Kodomari 29a Bc 41.08N 140.18 E
Kodori 16 Lh 42.49N 41.10 E
Kodry 15 Lb 47.15N 28.15 E
Kodyma 16 Ge 48.01N 30.48 E
Kodža Balkan 15 Jg 42.50N 27.00 E
Koekenaap 37 Bf 31.29S 18.19 E
Koes 37 Be 25.59S 19.08 E
Kofa Mountains 46 Ij 33.20N 114.00W
Kofarli 15 Kl 37.45N 27.42 E
Kofaz 24 Bb 41.58N 27.12 E
Koffiefontein 37 Ce 29.30S 25.00 E
Kofiau, Pulau- 26 Ig 1.11S 129.50 E
Köflach 14 Jc 47.04N 15.05 E
Koforidua 31 Gh 6.05N 0.15W
Kōfu [Jap.] 29 Cd 35.18N 133.29 E
Kōfu [Jap.] 27 Od 35.39N 138.35 E
Koga 29 Fc 36.12N 139.42 E
Kogaluc 42 Je 59.38N 77.30W
Kōge 29 Dd 35.24N 134.15 E
Køge 7 Ci 55.27N 12.11 E
Køge Bugt 8 Ei 55.30N 12.20 E
Kogel 17 He 62.38N 57.07 E
Kogilnik 15 Md 45.51N 29.38 E
Kogilnik (Kunduk) 15 Md 45.51N 29.38 E
Kogon 34 Cc 11.09N 14.42W
Kogota 29 Gb 38.32N 141.01 E
Kohala Mountains 65a Fc 20.05N 155.43W
Kohāt 25 Eb 33.35N 71.26 E
Kohila 8 Ke 59.11N 24.40 E
Kohima 25 Ic 25.40N 94.07 E
Koh-i-Mārān 25 Dc 29.05N 66.50 E
Kohinggo 63a Cc 8.13S 157.10 E
Kohma 7 Jh 56.57N 41.07 E
Kohtla-Jarve/Kohtla-Järve 19 Cd 59.25N 27.14 E
Kohtla-Järve/Kohtla-Jarve 19 Cd 59.25N 27.14 E
Kohu Dağı 15 Mm 36.30N 29.50 E
Kohunlich 48 Oh 18.30N 88.55W
Koide 29 Fc 37.14N 138.57 E
Koigi/Kojgi 8 Kf 58.49N 25.40 E
Koin 17 Ee 63.10N 51.15 E
Koindu 34 Cd 8.28N 10.20W
Koitere 7 He 62.58N 30.45 E
Kojā 23 Jd 25.34N 61.13 E
Kojandytau 18 Lb 44.20N 78.45 E
Kojda 7 Kc 66.23N 42.31 E
Koje-Do 28 Jg 34.52N 128.37 E
Kojetín 10 Ng 49.21N 17.20 E
Kojgi/Koigi 8 Kf 58.49N 25.40 E
Ko-Jima [Jap.] 29 Fe 33.07N 139.40 E
Ko-Jima [Jap.] 28 Od 41.22N 139.47 E
Kojō 27 Md 38.57N 127.52 E
Kojonup 59 Df 33.50S 117.09 E
Kojtaš 18 Fd 40.14N 67.22 E
Kojtezek, Pereval- 18 If 37.29N 72.45 E
Kojur 24 Nd 36.23N 51.43 E
Kojva 17 Ig 58.15N 58.14 E
Kokab 35 Cc 10.03N 22.04 E
Kokai-Gawa 29 Gd 35.52N 140.08 E
Kokand 22 Je 40.33N 70.57 E
Kōkar 7 Eg 59.55N 20.55 E
Kökarsfjärden 8 Ie 59.55N 20.45 E
Kokas 26 Jg 2.42S 132.26 E
Kokava nad Rimavicou 10 Ph 48.34N 19.50 E
Kokawa 29 Dd 34.17N 135.26 E
Kokčetav 22 Id 53.17N 69.25 E
Kokčetavskaja Oblast [3] 19 Ge 53.30N 70.00 E
Kokemäenjoki 8 Ic 61.33N 21.42 E
Kokemäki/Kumo 7 Ff 61.15N 22.21 E
Kok-Jangak 19 Hg 40.59N 73.15 E
Kokkina 24 Ee 35.10N 32.36 E
Kokkola/Gamlakarleby 6 Ic 63.50N 23.07 E
Koko [Eth.] 35 Fc 10.20N 36.04 E
Koko [Nig.] 34 Fc 11.26N 4.30 E
Kokomo 43 Jc 40.29N 86.08W
Kokonau 26 Kg 4.43S 136.26 E
Kokong 37 Cd 24.27S 23.03 E
Koko Nor (EN)=Qinghai Hu 21 Mf 37.00N 100.20 E
Kokpekty 19 If 48.45N 82.24 E
Kokšaal-Tau, Hrebet- 19 Hg 41.00N 78.00 E
Kokšenga 7 Kf 61.27N 42.38 E
Koksijde 12 Ec 51.06N 2.39 E
Koksoak 42 Ke 58.31N 68.11W
Kokstad 31 Jl 30.32S 29.29 E
Koktal 18 Lb 44.05N 79.44 E
Koktokay/Fuyun 22 Ke 47.13N 89.39 E
Kokubu 28 Ki 31.44N 130.46 E
Kola 19 Db 68.53N 33.01 E
Kola, Pulau- 26 Jh 5.30S 134.35 E
Kolahun 34 Cd 8.17N 10.05W
Kolaka 26 Hg 4.03S 121.36 E
Kolamadulu Atoll 25a Bb 2.25N 73.10 E
Kola Peninsula (EN)=Kolski Poluostrov 5 Jb 67.30N 37.00 E
Kolār Gold Fields 25 Ff 12.55N 78.17 E
Kolari 7 Fc 67.20N 23.48 E
Kólarovo 10 Ni 47.55N 18.00 E
Kolašin 15 Cg 42.49N 19.32 E
Kolbäck 8 Ge 59.34N 16.15 E
Kolbäcksån 8 Ge 59.32N 16.16 E
Kolbio 36 Hc 1.09S 41.12 E
Kolbuszowa 10 Rf 50.15N 21.47 E
Kolby 8 Di 55.48N 10.33 E
Kolčugino 7 Jh 56.16N 39.23 E
Kolda 34 Cc 12.53N 14.57W
Kolding 6 Gd 55.31N 9.29 E
Kole [Zaire] 36 Dc 3.31S 22.27 E
Kole [Zaire] 36 Eb 2.07N 25.26 E
Koléa 13 Oh 36.38N 2.46 E
Kolendo 20 Jf 53.43N 142.57 E
Kolente 34 Cd 8.55N 13.08W
Kolesnoje 15 Mc 46.04N 29.45 E
Kolga 8 Ke 59.28N 25.29 E
Kolga, Zaliv-/Kolga Laht 8 Ke 59.30N 25.15 E
Kolga Laht/Kolga, Zaliv- 8 Ke 59.30N 25.15 E
Kolgompja, Mys- 8 Me 59.44N 28.35 E
Kolgujev, Ostrov- 5 Kb 69.05N 49.15 E
Kolhāpur 22 Jh 16.42N 74.13 E
Kolhozabad 18 Gf 37.35N 68.39 E
Kolhozbentskoje, Vodohranilišče- 18 Df 37.10N 62.30 E
Koli 7 Ge 63.06N 29.53 E
Kolimbiné 34 Cc 14.45N 11.00 E
Kolín 10 Lf 50.02N 15.13 E
Kolito 35 Fd 7.25N 38.07 E
Koljučinskaja Guba 20 Nc 66.50N 174.30W
Kolka 8 Jg 57.44N 22.27 E
Kolkasrags 7 Fh 57.46N 22.37 E
Kolki 16 Dd 51.07N 25.42 E
Kollinai 15 Fl 37.17N 22.22 E
Kollumúli 7a Cb 65.47N 14.21W
Kolmården 8 Gf 58.41N 16.35 E
Köln=Cologne (EN) 6 Ge 50.56N 6.57 E
Köln-Lövenich 12 Id 50.57N 6.50 E
Kolno 10 Rc 53.25N 21.56 E
Köln-Porz 10 Df 50.53N 7.03 E
Koło 10 Od 52.12N 18.38 E
Koloa 65a Bb 21.54N 159.28W
Kołobrzeg 10 Lb 54.12N 15.33 E
Kolodnja 16 Hb 54.49N 32.11 E
Kologriv 7 Kg 58.51N 44.17 E
Kolokani 34 Dc 13.34N 8.03W
Koloko 34 Dc 11.05N 5.19W
Kolokolkova Guba 17 Fb 68.30N 52.30 E
Kololo 35 Gd 7.27N 41.59 E
Kolombangara Island 60 Fi 8.00S 157.05 E
Kolomna 6 Jd 55.05N 38.49 E
Kolomyja 19 Cf 48.32N 25.01 E
Kolondiéba 34 Dc 11.06N 6.53W
Kolonga 65b Ac 21.08S 175.04W
Kolonodale 26 Hg 2.00S 121.19 E
Kolosovka 19 Hd 56.28N 73.36 E
Kolossa 34 Dc 13.52N 7.35W
Kolovai 65b Ac 21.06S 175.20W
Kolozero, Ozero- 7 Hb 68.15N 33.15 E
Kolp 7 Ig 59.20N 36.50 E
Kolpaševo 22 Kd 58.20N 82.50 E
Kolpino 7 Hg 59.45N 30.33 E
Kolpny 16 Jc 52.16N 37.00 E
Kolski Poluostrov=Kola Peninsula (EN) 5 Jb 67.30N 37.00 E
Koltubanovski 16 Rc 52.57N 52.02 E
Kolubara 15 De 44.40N 20.15 E
Koluszki 10 Pe 51.44N 19.49 E
Koluton 19 Ge 51.42N 69.25 E
Kolva [R.S.F.S.R.] 19 Fb 65.55N 57.20 E
Kolva [R.S.F.S.R.] 17 Hf 60.22N 56.33 E
Kolvickoje, Ozero- 7 Hc 67.05N 33.30 E
Kolvrå 8 Ch 56.18N 9.08 E
Kolwezi 31 Jj 10.43S 25.28 E
Kolyma 21 Sc 69.30N 161.00 E
Kolyma Plain (EN)=Kolymskaja Nizmennost 21 Rc 68.30N 154.00 E
Kolyma Range (EN)=Kolymskoje Nagorje 21 Rc 62.30N 155.00 E
Kolymskaja Nizmennost=Kolyma Plain (EN) 21 Rc 68.30N 154.00 E
Kolymskoje Nagorje=Kolyma Range (EN) 21 Rc 62.30N 155.00 E
Kolyšlej 16 Nc 52.40N 44.31 E
Kolžat 19 Ig 43.29N 80.37 E
Kom 15 Gf 43.10N 23.03 E
Kom 36 Gb 1.05N 38.02 E
Komádi 10 Rj 47.00N 21.30 E
Komadugu Gana 34 Hc 13.05N 12.24 E
Komadugu Yobe 30 Ig 13.42N 13.24 E
Komagane 29 Ed 35.43N 137.54 E
Koma-ga-Take [Jap.] 29 Fd 35.45N 138.13 E
Koma-ga-Take [Jap.] 29 Gb 39.47N 140.50 E
Koma-ga-Take [Jap.] 29a Bb 42.04N 140.40 E
Komandorskie Islands (EN)=Komandorskije Ostrova 21 Sd 55.00N 167.00 E
Komandorskije Ostrova=Komandorski Islands (EN) 21 Sd 55.00N 167.00 E
Komandorskiye Basin (EN) 20 Le 57.00N 168.00 E
Komarin 16 Gd 51.27N 30.32 E
Komarno 10 Tg 49.34N 23.43 E
Komárno 10 Oi 47.46N 18.09 E
Komárom [2] 10 Oi 47.40N 18.15 E
Komárom 10 Oi 47.44N 18.07 E
Komatipoort 37 Ee 25.25S 31.55 E
Komatsu 27 Od 36.24N 136.37 E
Komatsujima 29 Dd 34.01N 134.35 E
Komba, Pulau- 26 Hh 7.47S 123.35 E
Kombissiri 34 Ec 12.04N 1.20W
Kombolcha 35 Fc 11.05N 39.45 E
Komebail Lagoon 64a Ac 7.24N 134.27 E
Komen/Comines 12 Ed 50.46N 2.59 E
Komi ASSR [3] 19 Fc 64.00N 55.00 E
Komi-Permjacki Nacionalny Okrug [3] 19 Fd 60.00N 54.30 E
Komló 10 Oj 46.12N 18.16 E
Kommunarsk 16 Ke 48.27N 38.52 E
Kommunary 8 Nd 60.55N 30.10 E
Kommunizma, Pik-=Communism Peak (EN) 21 Jf 38.57N 72.08 E
Komodo, Pulau- 26 Gh 8.36S 119.30 E
Komoé 30 Gh 5.12N 3.44W
Komoé [3] 34 Ec 10.25N 4.20W
Komono 36 Bc 3.15S 13.14 E
Komoran, Pulau- 26 Kh 8.18S 138.45 E
Komoro 29 Fc 36.19N 138.24 E
Komotini 15 Ih 41.07N 25.24 E
Komovi 15 Cg 42.41N 19.39 E
Kompasberg 30 Jl 31.46S 24.32 E
Komrat 16 Ff 46.17N 28.38 E
Komsa 20 Dd 61.40N 89.25 E
Komsomolec 19 Ge 53.45N 62.02 E
Komsomolec, Ostrov- 21 La 80.30N 95.00 E
Komsomolec, Zaliv- 16 Rg 45.30N 52.45 E
Komsomolsk [R.S.F.S.R.] 7 Jh 57.02N 40.22 E
Komsomolsk [R.S.F.S.R.] 20 De 57.25N 86.02 E
Komsomolsk [Tur.-U.S.S.R.] 19 Gh 39.02N 63.36 E
Komsomolski [Kaz.-U.S.S.R.] 19 Ff 47.20N 53.44 E
Komsomolski [R.S.F.S.R.] 16 Og 45.22N 46.01 E
Komsomolski [R.S.F.S.R.] 7 Ki 54.27N 45.45 E
Komsomolski [R.S.F.S.R.] 19 Gb 67.35N 63.47 E
Komsomolski [R.S.F.S.R.] 17 Kf 61.20N 63.15 E
Komsomolski [R.S.F.S.R.] 20 Mc 69.12N 172.55 E
Komsomolsk-na-Amure 22 Pd 50.36N 137.02 E
Komsomolsk-na-Ustjurte 19 Fg 44.07N 58.17 E
Komsomolskoje [Ukr.-U.S.S.R.] 16 Je 49.36N 36.33 E
Komsomolskoje [Ukr.-U.S.S.R.] 16 Kf 47.37N 38.05 E
Komsomolskoj Pravdy, Ostrova- 20 Fa 77.15N 107.30 E
Kōmun-Do 28 Ig 34.02N 127.19 E
Kömür Burun 15 Jk 38.39N 26.25 E
Komusan 27 Mc 42.07N 129.42 E
Kona 34 Ec 14.57N 3.53W
Kona Coast 65a Fd 19.35N 155.56W
Konakovo 19 Dd 56.42N 36.46 E
Konar 23 Lc 34.25N 70.32 E
Konārak 25 Hh 19.54N 86.07 E
Konarha [3] 23 Lb 35.15N 71.00 E
Konda 19 Gc 60.40N 69.46 E
Kondagaon 25 Ge 19.36N 81.40 E
Kondinin 59 Df 32.30S 118.16 E
Kondinskoje 17 Mg 59.40N 67.25 E
Kondoa 31 Ki 4.54S 35.47 E
Kondopoga 6 Jc 62.13N 34.17 E
Kondratjevo 8 Md 60.36N 28.02 E
Kondrovo 19 De 54.49N 35.55 E
Kondurča 7 Mj 53.31N 50.24 E
Koné 61 Bd 21.04S 164.52 E
Konečnaja 19 He 50.45N 78.27 E
Konevic, Ostrov- 8 Nd 60.50N 30.45 E
Kong 34 Ed 9.09N 4.37W
Kông 25 Lf 13.32N 105.58 E
Kông, Kaôh- 25 Kf 11.20N 103.00 E
Konga/Koonga 8 Jf 58.34N 24.00 E
Kongauru 64a Ac 7.04N 134.17 E
Kong Christian IX Land=King Christian IX Land (EN) 67 Mc 68.00N 36.30W
Kong Christian X Land=King Christian X Land (EN) 67 Md 72.20N 32.30W
Kongeå 8 Ci 55.23N 8.39 E
Kong Frederik VIII Land=King Frederik VIII Land (EN) 67 Md 78.30N 28.00W
Kong Frederik VI Kyst=King Frederik VI Coast (EN) 67 Nc 63.00N 43.30W
Konginkangas 8 Kb 62.46N 25.48 E
Kongju 28 If 36.27N 127.08 E
Kong Karls Land 41 Oc 78.50N 28.00 E
Kong Kong 35 Ed 7.26N 33.14 E
Kongolo 31 Ji 5.23S 27.00 E
Kongor 35 Ed 7.10N 31.21 E
Kong Oscars Fjord 67 Md 72.20N 23.00W
Kongoussi 34 Ec 13.19N 1.32W
Kongsberg 7 Bg 59.39N 9.39 E
Kongsøya 41 Oc 78.55N 28.40 E
Kongsvinger 7 Cf 60.12N 12.00 E
Kongur Shan 21 Jf 38.40N 75.21 E
Kongwa 36 Gd 6.12S 36.25 E
Kong Wilhelms Land 41 Jc 75.48N 23.15W
Koniecpol 10 Pf 50.48N 19.41 E
Königslutter am Elm 10 Gd 52.15N 10.49 E
Königswinter 12 Jd 50.41N 7.11 E
Königs Wusterhausen 10 Jd 52.17N 13.37 E
Konin 10 Od 52.13N 18.16 E
Konin [2] 10 Od 52.15N 18.15 E
Konispoli 15 Dj 39.39N 20.10 E
Kónitsa 15 Di 40.03N 20.45 E
Konj 14 Kg 43.43N 16.55 E
Konjed Jān 24 Nf 33.30N 50.27 E
Konjic 14 Lg 43.39N 17.58 E
Konjuh 14 Mf 44.18N 18.33 E
Konkan 25 Ee 18.05N 73.25 E
Konkiep 37 Be 28.00S 17.23 E
Konko 36 Ed 10.12S 27.27 E
Konkouré 34 Cd 9.58N 13.42W
Konnevesi 8 Lb 62.40N 26.35 E
Konnevesi 8 Lb 62.37N 26.19 E
Konnivesi 8 Lc 61.10N 26.10 E
Konoša 6 Kc 60.58N 40.15 E

Index Symbols

- [1] Independent Nation
- [2] State, Region
- [3] District, County
- [4] Municipality
- [5] Colony, Dependency
- Continent
- Physical Region
- Historical or Cultural Region
- Mount, Mountain
- Volcano
- Hill
- Mountains, Mountain Range
- Hills, Escarpment
- Plateau, Upland
- Pass, Gap
- Plain, Lowland
- Delta
- Salt Flat
- Valley, Canyon
- Crater, Cave
- Karst Features
- Depression
- Polder
- Desert, Dunes
- Forest, Woods
- Heath, Steppe
- Oasis
- Cape, Point
- Coast, Beach
- Cliff
- Peninsula
- Isthmus
- Sandbank
- Island
- Atoll
- Rock, Reef
- Islands, Archipelago
- Rocks, Reefs
- Coral Reef
- Well, Spring
- Geyser
- River, Stream
- Waterfall Rapids
- River Mouth, Estuary
- Lake
- Salt Lake
- Intermittent Lake
- Reservoir
- Swamp, Pond
- Canal
- Glacier
- Ice Shelf, Pack Ice
- Ocean
- Sea
- Gulf, Bay
- Strait, Fjord
- Lagoon
- Bank
- Seamount
- Tablemount
- Ridge
- Shelf
- Basin
- Escarpment, Sea Scarp
- Fracture
- Trench, Abyss
- National Park, Reserve
- Point of Interest
- Recreation Site
- Cave, Cavern
- Historic Site
- Ruins
- Wall, Walls
- Church, Abbey
- Temple
- Scientific Station
- Airport
- Port
- Lighthouse
- Mine
- Tunnel
- Dam, Bridge

Kōnosu 29 Fc 36.04N 139.30 E
Konotop 6 Je 51.14N 33.12 E
Konqi He 21 Ke 41.48N 86.47 E
Konrei 64a Bb 7.43N 134.37 E
Konsei-Tōge 29 Fc 36.52N 139.22 E
Konsen-Daichi 29a Db 43.20N 144.50 E
Końskie 10 Qe 51.12N 20.26 E
Konstantinovka 16 Je 48.29N 37.43 E
Konstantinovsk 16 Lf 47.35N 41.05 E
Konstanz 10 Fi 47.40N 9.11 E
Kontagora 31 Hg 10.24N 5.29 E
Kontcha 34 Hd 7.58N 12.14 E
Kontich 12 Gc 51.08N 4.27 E
Kontiolahti 7 Ge 62.46N 29.51 E
Kontiomäki 7 Gd 64.21N 28.09 E
Kontum 25 Lf 14.21N 108.00 E
Kontum, Plateau de- 25 Lf 13.55N 108.05 E
Konusin, Mys- 7 Kc 67.10N 43.50 E
Konya 22 Ff 37.52N 32.31 E
Konya Ovası 24 Ed 37.30N 33.20 E
Konz 12 Ie 49.42N 6.35 E
Konza 36 Gc 1.45S 37.07 E
Konžakovski Kamen, Gora- 5 Ld 59.38N 59.08 E
Koocanusa, Lake- 46 Hb 48.45N 115.15W
Kook, Punta- 65d Ab 27.08S 109.26W
Koolau Range 65a Db 21.21N 157.47W
Koonga/Konga 8 Jf 58.34N 24.00 E
Koorda 59 Df 30.50S 117.29 E
Koosa 8 Lf 58.33N 27.07 E
Kootenay Lake 46 Gb 49.35N 116.50W
Kootenay River 38 He 49.15N 117.39W
Kopa 18 Jc 43.31N 75.48 E
Kopaonik 15 Df 43.15N 20.50 E
Kópasker 7a Ca 66.18N 16.27W
Kópavogur 7a Bb 64.06N 21.55W
Kopejsk 19 Gd 55.08N 61.39 E
Koper 14 He 45.33N 13.44 E
Kopervik 7 Ag 59.17N 5.18 E
Kopetdag, Hrebet- 21 Hf 37.45N 58.15 E
Kop Geçidi 24 Ib 40.01N 40.28 E
Ko Phangan 25 Jg 9.45N 100.00 E
Köping 7 Dg 59.31N 16.00 E
Köpingsvik 8 Gh 56.53N 16.43 E
Kopjevo 20 Df 54.59N 89.55 E
Kopliku 15 Cg 42.13N 19.26 E
Köpmanholmen 7 Ee 63.10N 18.34 E
Koporje 8 Me 59.40N 29.08 E
Koporski Zaliv 8 Me 59.45N 28.45 E
Koppal 25 Fe 15.21N 76.09 E
Koppang 7 Cf 61.34N 11.04 E
Koppány 10 Oj 46.35N 18.26 E
Kopparberg 8 Fe 59.52N 14.59 E
Kopparberg [2] 7 Df 61.00N 14.30 E
Kopparstenarna 8 Hf 58.32N 19.20 E
Koppom 8 Ee 59.43N 12.09 E
Koprivnica 14 Kd 46.10N 16.50 E
Kopru 24 Dd 36.49N 31.10 E
Köprüören 15 Mj 39.30N 29.47 E
Korab 5 Ig 41.44N 20.32 E
Korablino 7 Jj 53.57N 40.00 E
Korahe 35 Gd 6.36N 44.16 E
Korak 64a Bc 7.21N 134.34 E
Koralpe 14 Id 46.45N 15.00 E
Koramlik 27 Ed 37.32N 85.42 E
Korana 14 Je 45.30N 15.35 E
Korangi 25 Dd 24.47N 67.08 E
Koraput 25 Ge 18.49N 82.43 E
Korba 25 Gd 22.21N 82.41 E
Korbach 10 Ee 51.17N 8.52 E
Körby 8 Ei 55.51N 13.59 E
Korça 15 Di 40.37N 20.46 E
Korčula 14 Kh 42.57N 16.55 E
Korčula 14 Lh 42.58N 17.08 E
Korčulanski Kanal 14 Kg 43.03N 16.40 E
Kordān 24 Ne 35.56N 50.50 E
Kordel 12 Ie 49.50N 6.38 E
Kordestān [3] 23 Gb 35.30N 47.00 E
Kord Küy 23 Hb 36.48N 54.07 E
Kordun 14 Je 45.10N 15.35 E
Korea Bay (EN)=Sŏjosŏn-man 21 Of 39.15N 125.00 E
Korean Peninsula (EN) 21 Of 35.30N 125.30 E
Korea Strait (EN)=Taehan-Haehyŏp 21 Of 34.40N 129.00 E
Korea Strait (EN)=Tsushima-Kaikyō 21 Of 34.40N 129.00 E
Korec 16 Ed 50.37N 27.10 E
Korem 35 Fc 12.30N 39.32 E
Korenovsk 19 Df 45.28N 39.28 E
Korf 20 Ld 60.18N 166.01 E
Korfovski 20 Ig 48.11N 135.04 E
Korgen 7 Cc 66.05N 13.50 E
Kõrgesaare/Kyrgesare 8 Je 59.00N 22.25 E
Korhogo 31 Gh 9.27N 5.38W
Korhogo [3] 34 Dd 9.35N 5.55W
Koribundu 34 Cd 7.43N 11.42W
Korienzé 34 Eb 15.24N 3.47W
Korinthiakós Kólpos=Corinth, Gulf of- (EN) 5 Ih 38.12N 22.30 E
Kórinthos 15 Fl 37.55N 22.53 E
Kórinthos = Corinth (EN) 15 Fl 37.55N 22.53 E
Korinthou, Dhiórix- = Corinth Canal (EN) 15 Fl 37.57N 22.58 E
Koriolei 31 Lh 1.48N 44.30 E
Kőrishegy 10 Ni 47.12N 17.49 E
Koritnik 15 Dg 42.05N 20.34 E
Kōriyama 27 Pd 37.24N 140.23 E
Korjakskaja Sopka, Vulkan- 21 Rd 53.20N 158.47 E
Korjakski Nacionalny okrug [3] 20 Le 60.00N 163.00 E
Korjakskoje Nagorje=Koryak Range (EN) 21 Tc 62.30N 172.00 E
Korjažma 19 Ec 61.18N 47.07 E
Korjukovka 16 Hd 51.47N 32.17 E
Korkino 17 Ji 54.54N 61.25 E
Korkodon 20 Kd 64.43N 154.05 E
Korkuteli 24 Dd 37.04N 30.13 E
Korla 22 Ke 41.44N 86.09 E
Kormakiti Burun 24 Ee 35.24N 32.56 E
Körmend 10 Mi 47.01N 16.36 E
Kormy, Gora- 20 Fd 62.15N 106.08 E
Kornati 14 Jg 43.49N 15.20 E
Kornejevka 17 Ni 54.01N 68.27 E
Kornešty 15 Kb 47.23N 28.00 E
Korneuburg 14 Kb 48.21N 16.20 E
Kórnik 10 Nd 52.17N 17.04 E
Kornsjø 7 Cg 58.57N 11.39 E
Koro 34 Ec 14.05N 3.04W
Koroba 59 Ia 5.40S 142.45 E
Koroča 16 Jd 50.50N 37.13 E
Köroğlu Dağları 23 Da 40.40N 32.35 E
Köroğlu Tepe 24 Db 40.31N 31.53 E
Korogwe 36 Gd 5.09S 38.29 E
Koro Island 57 If 17.32S 179.42 E
Koroit 59 Ig 38.17S 142.22 E
Korolevo 10 Th 48.08N 23.07 E
Korolevu 63d Ac 18.12S 177.53 E
Korom, Bahr 35 Bc 10.35N 19.45 E
Koromiri 64p Cc 21.15S 159.43W
Koronadal 26 He 6.12N 125.01 E
Korónia, Límni- 15 Gi 40.40N 23.10 E
Koronowo 10 Nc 53.19N 17.57 E
Koronowski e, Jezioro- 10 Nc 53.22N 17.55 E
Koror 57 Ed 7.20N 134.30 E
Koror 58 Ed 7.20N 134.29 E
Körös 10 Qj 46.43N 20.12 E
Koro Sea 61 Ec 18.00S 180.00
Korosten 6 Ie 50.57N 28.39 E
Korostyšev 16 Fd 50.18N 29.05 E
Korotaiha 17 Jb 68.55N 60.55 E
Koro Toro 31 Ig 16.05N 18.30 E
Korovin Volcano 40a Db 52.22N 174.10W
Korpijärvi 8 Lc 61.15N 27.10 E
Korpilahti 7 Fe 62.01N 25.33 E
Korpo/Korppoo 8 Id 60.10N 21.35 E
Korppoo/Korpo 8 Id 60.10N 21.35 E
Korsakov 20 Jg 46.37N 142.51 E
Korshäs 7 Ee 62.47N 21.12 E
Korsholm/Mustasaari 8 Ia 63.05N 21.43 E
Korso 8 Kd 60.21N 25.06 E
Korsør 7 Ci 55.20N 11.09 E
Korsun-Ševčenkovski 16 Ge 49.26N 31.18 E
Korsze 10 Rb 54.10N 21.09 E
Kortemark 12 Fc 51.02N 3.02 E
Kortrijk/Courtrai 11 Jd 50.50N 3.16 E
Korucu 15 Kj 39.28N 27.22 E
Koru Dağ 15 Ji 40.42N 26.45 E
Koryak Range (EN)=Korjakskoje Nagorje 21 Tc 62.30N 172.00 E
Korzybie 10 Mb 54.18N 16.50 E
Kos 15 Km 36.53N 27.18 E
Kos 15 Km 36.50N 27.10 E
Kosa 17 Gg 59.56N 55.01 E
Kosa 17 Gf 60.11N 55.10 E
Kosai 29 Ed 34.43N 137.30 E
Kosaja Gora 16 Jb 54.09N 37.31 E
Kosaka 29 Ga 40.20N 140.44 E
Kō-Saki 29 Ad 34.05N 129.13 E
Ko Samui 25 Jg 9.30N 99.58 E
Kosan-ŭp 27 Md 38.51N 127.25 E
Koscagyl 16 Rf 46.52N 53.47 E
Kościan 10 Md 52.06N 16.38 E
Kościerzyna 10 Nb 54.08N 18.00 E
Kosciusko 45 Lj 32.58N 89.35W
Kosciusko, Mount- 57 Fg 36.27S 148.16 E
Kose/Koze 8 Ke 59.11N 25.05 E
Köse Dağ 24 Gb 40.06N 37.58 E
Kosha 35 Ea 20.49N 30.32 E
Koshigaya 29 Fd 35.55N 139.45 E
Koshiji 29 Fc 37.24N 138.45 E
Koshiki-Kaikyō 29 Bf 31.45N 130.05 E
Koshiki Rettō 27 Me 31.45N 129.45 E
Koshimizu 29a Db 43.51N 144.25 E
Kōshoku 28 Of 36.38N 138.06 E
Kōshyū Seamount (EN) 29 Df 31.35N 135.50 E
Košice 6 If 48.43N 21.15 E
Kosjerić 15 Cf 44.00N 19.55 E
Kosju 17 Ic 66.18N 59.53 E
Kosju 17 Id 65.38N 58.59 E
Köşk 15 Ll 37.51N 28.03 E
Koski 8 Jd 60.39N 23.09 E
Koskolovo 8 Me 59.34N 28.30 E
Koslan 19 Ec 63.29N 48.52 E
Kosma 17 Dd 65.43N 49.50 E
Kosmaj 15 De 44.28N 20.33 E
Kosŏng 27 Md 38.40N 128.19 E
Kosov 15 Ia 48.15N 25.08 E
Kosovo 15 Eg 42.40N 21.05 E
Kosovo [3] 15 Dg 42.35N 21.00 E
Kosovska Mitrovica 15 Dg 42.53N 20.52 E
Kosrae (Kusaie) 57 Hd 5.19N 162.59 E
Kossol Passage 64a Bb 7.52N 134.36 E
Kossol Reef 64a Bb 7.57N 134.41 E
Kossou, Barrage de- 34 Dd 7.01N 5.29W
Kossovo 16 Dc 52.47N 25.10 E
Kostajnica 14 Ke 45.13N 16.33 E
Kostenec 15 Gg 42.16N 23.49 E
Koster 37 De 25.57S 26.42 E
Kosteröarna 8 Df 58.55N 11.05 E
Kostjukoviči 16 Hc 53.23N 32.06 E
Kostjukovka 16 Gc 52.32N 30.58 E
Kostolac 15 Ee 44.44N 21.12 E
Kostopol 16 Ed 50.53N 26.29 E
Kostriževka 15 Ia 48.31N 25.45 E
Kostroma 6 Kd 57.47N 40.59 E
Kostromskaja Oblast [3] 19 Ed 58.30N 44.00 E
Kostrzyń 10 Nd 52.25N 17.14 E
Kostrzyn 10 Kd 52.37N 14.39 E
Kosva 17 Hg 58.50N 56.45 E
Koszalin 10 Mb 54.12N 16.09 E
Koszalin [2] 10 Mb 54.10N 16.10 E
Kőszeg 10 Mi 47.23N 16.33 E
Kota 22 Jg 25.16N 75.55 E
Kotaagung 26 Dh 5.30S 104.38 E
Kota Baharu 22 Mi 6.08N 102.15 E
Kotabaru 26 Gg 3.14S 116.13 E
Kotabumi 22 Mj 4.50S 104.54 E
Kotadabok 26 Dg 0.30S 104.33 E
Kota Kinabalu 22 Ni 5.59N 116.04 E
Kotamobagu 26 Hf 0.46N 124.19 E
Ko Tao 25 Jf 10.05N 99.52 E
Kotari 14 Jf 44.05N 15.30 E
Ko Tarutau 25 Jg 6.35N 99.40 E
Kota Tinggi 26 Df 1.44N 103.54 E
Kotel 15 Jg 42.53N 26.27 E
Kotelnič 19 Ed 58.20N 48.20 E
Kotelnikovo 16 Mf 47.38N 43.09 E
Kotelny, Ostrov- 21 Pb 75.45N 138.44 E
Kotelva 16 Id 50.03N 34.45 E
Köthen 10 He 51.45N 11.58 E
Kotido 36 Fb 3.00N 34.09 E
Kotjužany 29 Gb 47.50N 28.27 E
Kotka 7 Gf 60.28N 26.55 E
Kot Kapūra 25 Eb 30.35N 74.54 E
Kotlas 6 Kc 61.16N 46.35 E
Kotlenik 15 Df 43.51N 20.42 E
Kotlenski prohod 15 Jg 42.53N 26.27 E
Kotlik 40 Gd 63.02N 163.33W
Kotlin, Ostrov- 8 Md 60.00N 29.45 E
Kotly 8 Me 59.30N 28.48 E
Kotobi 34 Ed 6.42N 4.08W
Kotohira 29 Cd 34.11N 133.48 E
Koton Karifi 34 Gd 8.06N 6.48 E
Kotor 15 Bg 42.25N 18.46 E
Kotorosl 7 Jh 57.38N 39.57 E
Kotorska, Boka- 15 Bg 42.25N 18.40 E
Kotor Varoš 14 Lf 44.37N 17.22 E
Kotouba 34 Ed 8.41N 3.12W
Kotovo 19 Ee 50.18N 44.48 E
Kotovsk [Mold.-U.S.S.R.] 16 Ff 46.49N 28.33 E
Kotovsk [R.S.F.S.R.] 19 Ee 52.35N 41.32 E
Kotovsk [Ukr.-U.S.S.R.] 19 Cf 47.43N 29.33 E
Kotra 10 Uc 53.32N 24.17 E
Kotri 25 Dc 25.22N 68.18 E
Kötschach 14 Gd 46.40N 13.00 E
Kottayam 25 Fg 9.35N 76.31 E
Kotte 25 Gg 6.54N 80.02 E
Kotto 30 Jh 4.14N 22.02 E
Kotton 35 Id 9.37N 50.32 E
Kotu 65b Ba 19.57S 174.48W
Kotu Group 57 Jg 20.00S 174.45W
Kotuj 21 Mb 71.55N 102.05 E
Kotujkan 20 Fb 70.40N 103.25 E
Koturdepe 16 Rj 39.26N 53.40 E
Kotzebue 39 Cc 66.53N 162.39W
Kotzebue Sound 38 Cc 66.20N 163.00W
Kouandé 34 Fc 10.20N 1.42 E
Kouango 35 Be 4.58N 19.59 E
Kouba Modounga 35 Bb 15.40N 18.15 E
Koudougou 31 Gg 11.44N 4.31W
Kouéré 34 Ec 10.27N 3.59W
Koufália 15 Fi 40.47N 22.35 E
Koufonísion [Grc.] 15 Jo 34.56N 26.10 E
Koufonísion [Grc.] 15 Im 36.55N 25.35 E
Koufonísiou, Stenón- 15 Jo 35.00N 26.10 E
Kouilou [3] 36 Bc 4.00S 12.00 E
Kouilou 30 Ii 4.28S 11.41 E
Koukdjuak 42 Kc 66.47N 73.10W
Kouki 35 Bd 7.10N 17.18 E
Koukourou 35 Cd 7.12N 20.02 E
Koulamoutou 36 Bc 1.08S 12.29 E
Koulikoro 34 Dc 12.51N 7.34W
Koulountou 34 Cc 13.15N 13.37W
Koumac 58 Hg 20.30S 164.12 E
Koumac, Grand Récif de- 63b Be 20.32S 164.04 E
Koumbi-Saleh 32 Ff 15.47N 7.58W
Koumi 29 Fc 36.05N 138.28 E
Koumpentoum 34 Cc 13.59N 14.34W
Koumra 35 Bd 8.55N 17.33 E
Koundara 31 Fg 12.29N 13.18W
Koundian 34 Cc 13.08N 10.42W
Kounoúpoi 15 Jm 36.32N 26.27 E
Kounradski 19 Hf 46.57N 75.01 E
Kounta 34 Eb 17.30N 0.40W
Koupéla 34 Ec 12.11N 0.21W
Kouqian → Yongji 28 Ic 43.40N 126.30 E
Kourou 54 Hb 5.09N 52.39W
Kouroussa 34 Dc 10.39N 9.53W
Koury 34 Ec 12.10N 4.48W
Koussané 34 Cc 14.52N 11.15W
Kousséri 34 Ic 12.05N 15.02 E
Koussi, Emi- 30 Ig 19.55N 18.30 E
Koutiala 31 Gg 12.23N 5.27W
Koutoumo 63b Cf 22.40S 167.32 E
Koutous 34 Hc 14.30N 10.00 E
Kouvola 7 Gf 60.52N 26.42 E
Kouyou 36 Cc 0.45S 16.38 E
Kova 20 Fe 58.20N 100.20 E
Kovač 15 Cf 43.31N 19.07 E
Kovačica 15 Dd 45.06N 20.38 E
Koval 10 Pd 52.31N 19.10 E
Kovalevka 15 Nc 46.42N 30.31 E
Kovarskas/Kavarskas 8 Ki 55.24N 25.03 E
Kovdor 19 Db 67.33N 30.25 E
Kovdozero, Ozero- 7 Hc 66.47N 32.00 E
Kovel 19 Ce 51.13N 24.43 E
Kovenskaja 17 Mf 61.24N 67.39 E
Kovin 15 De 44.45N 20.59 E
Kovinskaja Grjada 20 Fe 57.15N 101.00 E
Kovrov 19 Ed 56.24N 41.20 E
Kovylkino 7 Ki 54.02N 43.58 E
Kowŏn 27 Md 39.26N 127.15 E
Kowtal-e Do Rāh 23 Lb 36.07N 71.15 E
Kowt-e 'Ashrow 23 Kc 34.27N 68.48 E
Kōyama 29 Bf 31.19N 130.57 E
Köyceğiz 24 Cd 36.55N 28.43 E
Köyceğiz Gölü 15 Lm 36.55N 28.40 E
Koyoshi-Gawa 29 Gb 39.24N 140.01 E
Koyuk 40 Gd 64.56N 161.08W
Koyukuk 38 Dc 64.56N 157.30W
Kozaklı 24 Fc 39.13N 34.49 E
Kozan 24 Fd 37.27N 35.49 E
Kozáni 15 Ei 40.18N 21.47 E
Kozara 14 Ke 45.00N 16.55 E
Kozawa 29a Bb 42.58N 140.40 E
Koze/Kose 8 Ke 59.11N 25.05 E
Kozelsk 19 De 54.01N 35.46 E
Koževnikovo 20 De 56.18N 84.00 E
Kozhikode → Calicut 22 Jh 11.19N 75.46 E
Kozienice 10 Re 51.35N 21.33 E
Kožim 17 Id 65.43N 59.31 E
Kožim 17 Id 65.45N 59.15 E
Kozima 14 He 45.37N 13.56 E
Kozjak 15 Eh 41.06N 21.54 E
Kozloduj 15 Gf 43.47N 23.44 E
Kozlovka 7 Li 55.52N 48.13 E
Kozlovščina 10 Vc 53.14N 25.20 E
Kozlu 24 Db 41.25N 31.46 E
Kozluk 24 Ic 38.11N 41.29 E
Koźmin 10 Ne 51.50N 17.28 E
Kozmodemjansk 7 Lh 56.20N 46.36 E
Kožozero, Ozero- 7 Je 63.05N 38.05 E
Kożuchów 10 Le 51.45N 15.35 E
Kožuf 15 Fh 41.09N 22.10 E
Kōzu-Shima 27 Oe 34.15N 139.10 E
Kožva 17 Hd 65.07N 56.57 E
Kožva 17 Hd 65.10N 57.00 E
Kozyrevsk 20 Ke 56.59N 159.59 E
Kpalimé 34 Fd 6.54N 0.38 E
Kpandu 34 Fd 7.00N 0.18 E
Kpessi 34 Fd 8.04N 1.16 E
Kra, Isthmus of- (EN)=Kra, Khokhok- 21 Lh 10.20N 99.00 E
Kra, Khokhok-=Kra, Isthmus of- (EN) 21 Lh 10.20N 99.00 E
Kraba 15 Ch 41.12N 19.59 E
Krabbfjärden 8 Gf 58.45N 17.40 E
Krabi 25 Jg 8.05N 98.53 E
Krabit, Mali i- 15 Cg 42.07N 19.59 E
Kra Buri 25 Jf 10.24N 98.47 E
Krâchéh 22 Mh 12.29N 106.01 E
Kragerø 7 Bg 58.52N 9.25 E
Kragujevac 15 De 44.01N 20.55 E
Kraichbach 12 Ke 49.22N 8.31 E
Kraichgau 12 Eg 49.10N 8.50 E
Kraichtal 12 Ke 49.07N 8.46 E
Krajina 14 Kf 44.45N 16.35 E
Krajina 15 Fe 44.10N 22.30 E
Krajište 15 Fg 42.35N 22.25 E
Krajnovka 16 Oh 43.57N 47.24 E
Kråka 8 Ca 63.28N 9.00 E
Krakatau, Gunung- 21 Mj 6.07S 105.24 E
Krak des Chevaliers 24 Ge 34.46N 36.19 E
Krakovec 10 Tg 49.56N 23.13 E
Kraków [2] 10 Pf 50.05N 20.00 E
Kraków 6 He 50.03N 19.58 E
Kraków-Nowa Huta 10 Qf 50.04N 20.05 E
Krakowsko-Częstochowska, Wyżyna- 10 Pf 50.50N 19.15 E
Kralendijk 50 Bf 12.10N 68.16W
Kraljevica 14 Ie 45.16N 14.34 E
Kraljevo 15 Df 43.44N 20.43 E
Kralupy nad Vltavou 10 Kf 50.14N 14.19 E
Kramatorsk 16 Je 48.43N 37.32 E
Kramfors 7 De 62.56N 17.47 E
Krammer 12 Gc 51.38N 4.15 E
Kranenburg 12 Ic 51.47N 6.01 E
Kranidhion 15 Gl 37.23N 23.09 E
Kranj 14 Id 46.14N 14.22 E
Krapina 14 Jd 46.10N 15.53 E
Krapkowice 10 Nf 50.29N 17.56 E
Kras=Karst (EN) 5 Hf 45.48N 14.00 E
Krasavino 19 Ec 60.59N 46.28 E
Krasiczyn 10 Sg 49.48N 22.39 E
Krasilov 16 Ee 49.37N 26.59 E
Kraskino 28 Kc 42.44N 130.48 E
Kraslava/Krāslava 7 Gi 55.54N 27.10 E
Krāslava/Kraslava 7 Gi 55.54N 27.10 E
Krasnaja Poljana 16 Lh 43.40N 40.12 E
Kraśnik 10 Sf 50.56N 22.13 E
Kraśnik Fabryczny, Kraśnik- 10 Sf 50.58N 22.12 E
Kraśnik-Kraśnik Fabryczny 10 Sf 50.58N 22.12 E
Krasnoarmejsk [Kaz.-U.S.S.R.] 19 Ge 53.57N 69.43 E
Krasnoarmejsk [R.S.F.S.R.] 19 Ee 51.02N 45.42 E
Krasnoarmejsk [Ukr.-U.S.S.R.] 16 Je 48.11N 37.12 E
Krasnoarmejski 20 Mc 69.37N 172.02 E
Krasnodar 6 Jf 45.02N 39.00 E
Krasnodarski Kraj [3] 19 Df 45.20N 39.30 E
Krasnodon 16 Ke 48.17N 39.44 E
Krasnogorodskoje 8 Mh 56.47N 28.18 E
Krasnogorsk [R.S.F.S.R.] 20 Jg 48.26N 142.10 E
Krasnogorsk [R.S.F.S.R.] 7 Ii 55.51N 37.20 E
Krasnogorski 17 Ji 54.36N 61.15 E
Krasnograd 19 Df 49.22N 35.27 E
Krasnogvardejsk 18 Fe 39.45N 67.16 E
Krasnogvardejskoje 16 Lg 45.49N 41.31 E
Krasnoholmski 19 Gh 56.02N 55.05 E
Krasnoilsk 15 Ia 48.02N 25.48 E
Krasnojarsk 22 Ld 56.01N 92.50 E
Krasnojarski 17 Ij 51.58N 59.57 E
Krasnojarski Kraj [3] 20 Ee 57.30N 95.00 E
Krasnojarskoje Vodohranilišče 20 Ee 55.05N 91.30 E
Krasnoje 10 Ug 49.49N 24.39 E
Krasnoje Selo 7 Hg 59.43N 30.03 E
Krasnoje Znamja 18 Df 36.50N 62.29 E
Krasnokamensk 20 Gf 50.00N 118.05 E
Krasnokamsk 19 Fd 58.04N 55.45 E
Krasnokutsk 19 He 52.59N 75.59 E
Krasnolesje 8 Jj 54.23N 22.25 E
Krasnolesny 16 Kd 51.52N 39.35 E
Krasnooktjabrski [Kirg.-U.S.S.R.] 18 Jc 42.45N 74.20 E
Krasnooktjabrski [R.S.F.S.R.] 7 Lh 56.43N 47.37 E
Krasnooskolskoje Vodohranilišče 16 Je 49.25N 37.35 E
Krasnoostrovski 8 Md 60.12N 28.39 E
Krasnoperekopsk 19 Df 45.57N 33.47 E
Krasnorečenski 28 Mb 44.38N 135.15 E
Krasnoščelje 7 Ic 67.23N 37.02 E
Krasnoselki 10 Uc 53.14N 24.30 E
Krasnoselkup 20 Dc 65.41N 82.28 E
Krasnoslobodsk [R.S.F.S.R.] 16 Ne 48.40N 44.31 E
Krasnoslobodsk [R.S.F.S.R.] 7 Ki 54.27N 43.47 E
Krasnoturinsk 19 Gd 59.46N 60.18 E
Krasnoufimsk 19 Fd 56.37N 57.46 E
Krasnouralsk 19 Gd 58.24N 60.03 E
Krasnousolski 19 Fe 53.54N 56.29 E
Krasnovišersk 19 Fc 60.23N 57.03 E
Krasnovodsk 22 He 40.00N 53.00 E
Krasnovodskaja Oblast [3] 19 Fh 39.50N 55.00 E
Krasnovodski Poluostrov 16 Rc 40.30N 53.15 E
Krasnovodski Zaliv 16 Rj 39.50N 53.15 E
Krasnozatonski 19 Fc 61.41N 51.01 E
Krasnozavodsk 7 Jh 56.29N 38.13 E
Krasnoznamensk [Kaz.-U.S.S.R.] 19 Ge 51.03N 69.30 E
Krasnoznamensk [R.S.F.S.R.] 8 Jj 54.52N 22.27 E
Krasny Čikoj 20 Ff 50.25N 108.45 E
Krasny Holm 7 Ig 58.04N 37.09 E
Krasny Jar [R.S.F.S.R.] 20 De 57.07N 84.40 E
Krasny Jar [R.S.F.S.R.] 19 Hd 55.14N 72.56 E
Krasnyje Barrikady 16 Of 46.13N 47.50 E
Krasnyje Okny 15 Mb 47.34N 29.23 E
Krasny Kut 19 Ee 50.58N 46.58 E
Krasny Liman 16 Je 48.59N 37.47 E
Krasny Luč 16 Ke 48.09N 38.57 E
Krasny Oktjabr 19 Gd 55.37N 64.48 E
Krasny Profintern 7 Jh 57.47N 40.29 E
Krasnystaw 10 Tf 50.59N 23.10 E
Krasny Sulin 16 Lf 47.53N 40.09 E
Kratovo 15 Fg 42.05N 22.12 E
Kraulshavn 41 Gd 74.10N 57.00W
Krâvanh, Chuŏr Phnum- 21 Mh 12.00N 103.15 E
Krawang 26 Eh 6.19S 107.17 E
Krefeld 10 Ce 51.20N 6.34 E
Krefeld-Hüls 12 Ic 51.22N 6.31 E
Kremastá, Límni- 15 Ek 38.50N 21.30 E
Kremenchug Reservoir (EN) =Kremenčugskoje Vodohranilišče 5 Jf 49.20N 32.30 E
Kremenčug 6 Jf 49.04N 33.25 E
Kremenčugskoje Vodohranilišče=Kremenchug Reservoir (EN) 5 Jf 49.20N 32.30 E
Kremenec 16 Dd 50.06N 25.43 E
Kremennaja 16 Ke 49.03N 38.14 E
Kremmling 45 Cf 40.03N 106.24W
Krems 14 Jb 48.25N 15.36 E
Krems an der Donau 14 Jb 48.25N 15.36 E
Kremsmünster 14 Ib 48.03N 14.08 E
Krenitzin Islands 40a Eb 54.08N 166.00W
Kresta, Zaliv- 20 Nc 65.30N 179.00W
Krestcy 7 Hg 58.15N 32.31 E
Krestovy, Pereval- 16 Nh 42.32N 44.30 E
Kretek 26 Fh 7.59S 110.19 E
Kretinga 7 Ei 55.55N 21.17 E
Kreuzau 12 Id 50.45N 6.29 E
Kreuzberg 10 Ff 50.22N 9.58 E
Kreuzlingen 14 Dc 47.39N 9.10 E
Kreuztal 10 Df 50.58N 7.59 E
Kria Vrisi 15 Fi 40.41N 22.18 E
Kribi 31 Hh 2.57N 9.55 E
Kričev 19 De 53.43N 31.43 E
Kričim 15 Hg 42.08N 24.31 E
Krim 14 Ie 45.56N 14.28 E
Krimml 14 Gc 47.13N 12.11 E
Krimpen aan den IJssel 12 Gc 51.55N 4.35 E
Kriós, Ákra- 5 Ih 35.14N 23.35 E
Krishna 21 Kh 15.57N 80.59 E
Krishnanagar 25 Hd 23.24N 88.30 E
Kristdala 8 Gg 57.24N 16.11 E
Kristiansand 6 Gd 58.10N 8.00 E
Kristianstad 7 Dh 56.02N 14.08 E
Kristianstad [2] 7 Ch 56.15N 14.00 E
Kristiansund 6 Gc 63.07N 7.45 E
Kristiinankaupunki/Kristinestad 7 Ee 62.17N 21.23 E
Kristineberg 7 Ed 65.04N 18.35 E
Kristinehamn 7 Dg 59.20N 14.07 E
Kristinestad/Kristiinankaupunki 7 Ee 62.17N 21.23 E
Kriti = Crete (EN) 5 Ih 35.15N 24.45 E
Kriti = Crete (EN) [2] 15 Hn 35.35N 25.00 E
Kritikón Pélagos = Crete, Sea of- (EN) 15 Hn 36.00N 25.00 E
Krivaja 14 Mf 44.27N 18.10 E
Kriva Palanka 15 Fg 42.12N 22.21 E
Krivići 8 Lj 54.44N 27.20 E
Krivodol 15 Gf 43.23N 23.29 E
Krivoje Ozero 16 Gf 47.57N 30.21 E
Krivoj Rog 6 Jf 47.54N 33.21 E
Križevci 14 Kd 46.02N 16.32 E
Krk 14 Ie 45.05N 14.35 E
Krk 14 Ie 45.02N 14.35 E
Krka [Yugo.] 14 Jg 43.43N 15.51 E
Krka [Yugo.] 14 Je 45.53N 15.36 E
Krkonoše 10 Lf 50.46N 15.35 E
Krn 14 Hd 46.16N 13.40 E
Krndija 14 Le 45.27N 17.55 E
Krnjača, Beograd- 15 De 44.52N 20.28 E
Krnov 10 Nf 50.05N 17.41 E
Krobia 10 Me 51.47N 16.58 E
Krøderen 8 Cd 60.15N 9.40 E
Krokeai 15 Fm 36.53N 22.33 E
Krokek 8 Gf 58.40N 16.24 E
Kroken 7 Dd 65.22N 14.16 E

Index Symbols

[1] Independent Nation
[2] State, Region
[3] District, County
[4] Municipality
[5] Colony, Dependency
Continent
Physical Region
Historical or Cultural Region
Mount, Mountain
Volcano
Hill
Mountains, Mountain Range
Hills, Escarpment
Plateau, Upland
Pass, Gap
Plain, Lowland
Delta
Salt Flat
Valley, Canyon
Crater, Cave
Karst Features
Depression
Polder
Desert, Dunes
Forest, Woods
Heath, Steppe
Oasis
Cape, Point
Coast, Beach
Cliff
Peninsula
Isthmus
Sandbank
Island
Atoll
Rock, Reef
Islands, Archipelago
Rocks, Reefs
Coral Reef
Well, Spring
Geyser
River, Stream
Waterfall Rapids
River Mouth, Estuary
Lake
Salt Lake
Intermittent Lake
Reservoir
Swamp, Pond
Canal
Glacier
Ice Shelf, Pack Ice
Ocean
Sea
Gulf, Bay
Strait, Fjord
Lagoon
Bank
Seamount
Tablemount
Ridge
Shelf
Basin
Escarpment, Sea Scarp
Fracture
Trench, Abyss
National Park, Reserve
Point of Interest
Recreation Site
Cave, Cavern
Historic Site
Ruins
Wall, Walls
Church, Abbey
Temple
Scientific Station
Airport
Port
Lighthouse
Mine
Tunnel
Dam, Bridge

Kwangsi Chuang (EN)= Guangxi Zhuangzu Zizhiqu (Kuang-hsi-chuang-tsu Tzu-chih-ch'ü) [2] 27 Ig 24.00N 109.00 E
Kwangsi Chuang (EN)= Kuang-hsi-chuang-tsu Tzu-chih-ch'ü→Guangxi Zhuangzu Zizhiqu [2] 27 Ig 24.00N 109.00 E
Kwangtung (EN)= Guangdong Sheng (Kuang-tung Sheng) [2] 27 Jg 23.00N 113.00 E
Kwangtung (EN)=Kuang-tun Sheng→Guangdong Sheng [2] 27 Jg 23.00N 113.00 E
Kwanmo-bong 28 Jd 41.42N 129.13 E
Kwara [2] 34 Fd 8.30N 5.00 E
Kweichow (EN)=Guizhou Sheng (Kuei-chou Sheng) [2] 27 If 27.00N 107.00 E
Kweichow (EN)=Kuei-chou Sheng→Guizhou Sheng [2] 27 If 27.00N 107.00 E
Kweneng [3] 37 Cd 24.00S 24.00 E
Kwenge 30 Ii 4.50S 18.44 E
Kwethluk 40 Gd 60.49N 161.27W
Kwidzyn 10 Oc 53.45N 18.56 E
Kwigillingok 40 Ge 59.51N 163.08W
Kwilu 30 Ii 3.22S 17.22 E
Kwisa 10 Le 51.35N 15.25 E
Kwoka, Gunung- 26 Jg 0.31S 132.27 E
Kyabé 31 Ih 9.27N 18.57 E
Kyabram 59 Jg 36.19S 145.03 E
Kyaikkami 25 Je 16.04N 97.34 E
Kyaikto 25 Je 17.18N 97.01 E
Kyaka 36 Fc 1.16S 31.25 E
Kyancutta 58 Eh 33.08S 135.34 E
Kyan-Zaki 29b Ab 26.05N 127.40 E
Kyaukpyu 25 Id 20.51N 92.58 E
Kyaukse 25 Jd 21.36N 96.08 E
Kybartai/Kibartaj 8 Jj 54.38N 22.44 E
Kyeintali 25 Ie 18.00N 94.29 E
Kyelang 25 Fb 32.35N 77.02 E
Kyffhauser 10 He 51.25N 11.10 E
Kyjov 10 Ng 49.01N 17.08 E
Kyle, Lake- 37 Ed 20.12S 31.00 E
Kyle of Lochalsh 9 Hd 57.17N 5.43W
Kyll 10 Cg 49.48N 6.42 E
Kyllburg 12 Id 50.02N 6.35 E
Kyma 7 Ld 64.48N 47.31 E
Kymi [2] 7 Gf 61.00N 28.00 E
Kymijoki 8 Ld 60.30N 26.52 E
Kyn 17 Ih 57.52N 58.32 E
Kynnefjäll 8 Df 58.42N 11.41 E
Kynsivesi 8 Lb 62.25N 26.10 E
Kyoga, Lake- 30 Kh 1.30N 33.00 E
Kyōga-Dake 29 Be 33.00N 130.05 E
Kyōga-Misaki 28 Mg 35.45N 135.11 E
Kyonan 29 Fd 35.07N 139.49 E
Kyŏnggi-Do [2] 28 If 37.30N 127.15 E
Kyŏnggi-man 28 Hf 37.25N 126.00 E
Kyŏngju 27 Md 35.50N 129.13 E
Kyŏngsang-Namdo [2] 28 Jg 35.15N 128.30 E
Kyŏngsang-Pukto [2] 28 Jf 36.20N 128.40 E
Kyŏngsŏng 28 Jd 41.40N 129.40 E
Kyōto 22 Pf 35.00N 135.45 E
Kyōto Fu [2] 28 Mg 35.25N 135.15 E
Kypros/Kıbrıs=Cyprus (EN) [1] 22 Ff 35.00N 33.00 E
Kypros/Kıbrıs=Cyprus (EN) 21 Ff 35.00N 33.00 E
Kyra 20 Gg 49.36N 111.58 E
Kyren 20 Ff 51.41N 102.10 E
Kyrenia/Girne 24 Ee 35.20N 33.19 E
Kyrgesare/Kõrgesaare 8 Je 59.00N 22.25 E
Kyrgyz Sovetik Socialistik Respublikasy/Kirgizskaja SSR [2] 19 Hg 41.30N 75.00 E
Kyritz 10 Id 52.57N 12.24 E
Kyrkheden 8 Ed 60.10N 13.29 E
Kyrksæterora 7 Be 63.17N 9.06 E
Kyrkslätt/Kirkkonummi 8 Kd 60.07N 24.26 E
Kyrö 8 Jd 60.42N 22.45 E
Kyrönjoki 8 Ia 63.14N 21.45 E
Kyrösjärvi 8 Jc 61.45N 23.10 E
Kyröskoski 8 Jc 61.40N 23.11 E
Kyštym 19 Gd 55.42N 60.34 E
Kysucké Nové Mesto 10 Og 49.18N 18.48 E
Kythera (EN)=Kithira 5 Ih 36.15N 23.00 E
Kythraia 24 Ee 35.15N 33.29 E
Kyuquot Sound 46 Bb 49.55N 127.25W
Kyūshū 21 Pf 32.50N 131.00 E
Kyushu-Palau Ridge (EN) 3 Ih 20.00N 136.00 E
Kyushū-Sanchi 29 Be 32.40N 131.10 E
Kyyjärvi 7 Fe 63.02N 24.34 E
Kyyvesi 8 Lc 61.55N 27.05 E
Kyzikos 24 Bb 40.28N 27.47 E
Kyzyl 22 Ld 51.42N 94.27 E
Kyzylart, Pereval- 19 Hh 39.22N 73.20 E
Kyzyl-Kija 19 Hg 40.14N 72.12 E
Kyzylkum 21 Ie 42.00N 64.00 E
Kyzylrabot 19 Hh 37.28N 74.45 E
Kyzylsu [U.S.S.R.] 18 Gf 37.22N 69.22 E
Kyzylsu [U.S.S.R.] 18 He 39.17N 71.25 E
Kyzylžar 19 Gf 48.17N 69.49 E
Kzyl-Orda 22 Ie 44.48N 65.28 E
Kzyl-Ordinskaja Oblast [3] 19 Gf 45.00N 65.00 E
Kzyltu 19 He 53.41N 72.15 E

L

Laa an der Thaya 14 Kb 48.43N 16.23 E
Laakdal 12 Gc 51.05N 4.59 E
La Alberca 13 Fd 40.29N 6.06W
La Alcarria 13 Jd 40.31N 2.45W
La Almunia de Doña Godina 13 Kc 41.29N 1.22W
La Ametlla de Mar 13 Md 40.54N 0.48 E
La Ardilla, Cerro- 48 Hf 22.15N 102.40W
La Armuña 13 Gc 41.05N 5.35W
Laasphe 12 Kd 50.56N 8.24 E
La Asunción 54 Fa 11.02N 63.53W
Laau Point 65a Db 21.06N 157.16W
Laayoune 13 Ni 35.42N 2.00 E
Lab 15 Eg 43.31N 21.01 E
Laba 16 Kg 45.10N 39.40 E
La Babia 48 Hc 28.34N 102.04W
Laba Daği 15 Kl 37.22N 27.33 E
Labaddey 35 Ge 0.32N 42.45 E
Labadie Bank 9 Ek 50.30N 8.15W
La Banda 56 Hc 27.44S 64.15W
La Bañeza 13 Gb 42.18N 5.54W
La Barca 48 Hg 20.17N 102.34W
Labardén 55 Cm 36.57S 58.06W
La Barge 46 Je 42.16N 110.12W
La Barra, Punta- 49 Lh 11.30N 70.10W
La-Barre-en-Ouche 12 Cf 48.57N 0.40 E
La Baule-Escoublac 11 Dg 47.17N 2.24W
Labbezanga 34 Fc 14.59N 0.43 E
Labé 31 Fg 11.19N 12.17W
Labe=Elbe (EN) 5 Ge 53.50N 9.00 E
La Belle 44 Gl 26.46N 81.26W
Labelle 44 Jb 46.17N 74.45W
La Berzosa 13 Fd 40.35N 6.40W
Labin 14 Ie 45.05N 14.08 E
Labinsk 19 Eg 44.35N 40.44 E
Labis 26 Df 2.23N 103.02 E
La Bisbal/La Bisbal d'Empordà 13 Pc 41.57N 3.03 E
La Bisbal d'Empordà/La Bisbal 13 Pc 41.57N 3.03 E
La Blanca, Laguna- 55 Bj 30.14S 60.38W
Laboe 10 Gb 54.24N 10.13 E
Laborec 10 Rh 48.31N 21.54 E
Laborie 51k Bb 13.45N 61.00W
Labota 26 Hg 2.52S 122.10 E
Labouheyre 11 Fj 44.13N 0.55W
Laboulaye 56 Hd 34.07S 63.24W
Labra, Peña- 13 Ha 43.03N 4.26W
Labrador 38 Md 55.00N 70.00W
Labrador, Coast of- 38 Me 56.00N 60.35W
Labrador Basin (EN) 3 Dd 53.00N 48.00W
Labrador City 39 Md 52.57N 66.54W
Labrador Sea 38 Nd 57.00N 53.00W
Labrang→Xiahe 27 Hd 35.18N 102.30 E
Lábrea 53 Jf 7.16S 64.46W
Labrieville 44 Ma 49.19N 69.34W
Labrit 11 Fj 44.06N 0.33W
Labuan, Pulau- 26 Ge 5.19N 115.13 E
Labudalin→Ergun Youqi 27 La 50.16N 120.09 E
Labuha 26 Ig 0.37S 127.29 E
Labuhan 26 Eh 6.22S 105.50 E
Labuhanbajo 26 Gh 8.29S 119.54 E
Labuhanbilik 26 Df 2.31N 100.10 E
Labuk, Teluk- 26 Ge 6.10N 117.50 E
La Bureba 13 Ib 42.36N 3.24W
Labutta 25 Ie 16.09N 94.46 E
Labytnangi 22 Ic 66.39N 66.21 E
Lac [3] 35 Ac 13.30N 14.20 E
Lača, Ozero- 7 Jf 61.20N 38.50 E
La Cadena 48 Ge 25.53N 104.12W
La Calamine/Kelmis 12 Hd 50.43N 6.00 E
La Calandria 55 Cj 30.48S 58.39W
Lac Allard 42 Lf 50.30N 63.30W
La Campiña 13 Hg 37.45N 4.45W
Lacanau 11 Ej 44.59N 1.05W
Lacanau, Étang de- 11 Ej 44.58N 1.07W
Lacanau-Océan 11 Ei 45.00N 1.12W
Lacantún, Rio- 48 Ni 16.36N 90.39W
La-Capelle 11 Je 49.58N 3.55 E
Laćarak 15 Ce 45.00N 19.34 E
La Carlota [Arg.] 56 Hd 33.26S 63.18W
La Carlota [Phil.] 26 Hd 10.25N 122.55 E
La Carlota [Sp.] 13 Hg 37.40N 4.56W
La Carolina 13 If 38.15N 3.37W
Lacaune 11 Ik 43.43N 2.42 E
Lacaune, Monts de- 11 Ik 43.40N 2.36 E
Laccadive Islands 21 Jh 11.00N 72.00 E
Lac du Bonnet 45 Ha 50.35N 96.05W
La Ceiba [Hond.] 39 Kh 15.47N 86.50W
La Ceiba [Ven.] 49 Li 9.28N 71.04W
Lacepede Bay 59 Hg 36.45S 139.45 E
Lacepede Islands 59 Ec 16.50S 122.10 E
La Cerdaña/La Cerdanya 13 Nb 42.24N 1.40 E
La Cerdanya/La Cerdaña 13 Nb 42.24N 1.40 E
Lacey 46 Dc 47.07N 122.49W
Lac Giao 25 Lf 12.40N 108.03 E
La Chaise-Dieu 11 Ji 45.19N 3.42 E
La Charité-sur-Loire 11 Jg 47.11N 3.01 E
La Châtre 11 Hh 46.35N 1.59 E
La Chaux-de-Fonds 14 Ac 47.06N 6.50 E
Lachay, Punta- 54 Cf 11.18S 77.39W
La China, Sierra- 55 Bm 36.47S 60.34W
Lachine 44 Kc 45.26N 73.40W
Lachlan River 57 Fh 34.21S 143.57 E
La Chorrera [Col.] 54 Dd 0.45S 73.00W
La Chorrera [Pan.] 47 Ig 8.53N 79.47W
Laçi 15 Ch 41.38N 19.43 E
Laçin 16 Oj 39.39N 46.33 E
La Ciotat 11 Lk 43.10N 5.36 E
Łąck 10 Pd 52.28N 19.40 E
Lackawanna 44 Hd 42.49N 78.49W
Lac La Biche 42 Gf 54.46N 111.58W
Lac la Martre 42 Fd 63.21N 117.00W
Lac Mégantic 42 Kg 45.35N 70.53W
La Colina 55 Bm 37.20S 61.32W
La Coloma 49 Fb 22.15N 83.34W
La Colorada 48 Dc 28.41N 110.25W
Lacombe 42 Gf 52.28N 113.44W
Lacon 45 Lf 41.02N 89.24W
La Concepción [Pan.] 49 Fi 8.31N 82.37W
La Concepción [Ven.] 49 Lh 10.48N 71.46W
La Concha 48 Gg 21.46N 105.29W
Laconi 14 Dk 39.51N 9.03 E
Laconia 43 Mc 43.32N 71.29W
Laconia, Gulf of- (EN) = Lakonikós Kólpos 15 Fm 36.35N 22.40 E
La Coronilla 55 Fk 33.44S 53.31W
La Coruña 6 Fg 43.22N 8.23W
La Coruña [3] 13 Da 43.10N 8.25W
La Côte-Saint-André 11 Li 45.23N 5.15 E
La Couronne 11 Gi 45.37N 0.06 E
La Courtine-le-Trucq 11 Ii 45.42N 2.16 E
Lacq 11 Fk 43.25N 0.38W
Lacroix-sur-Meuse 12 Hf 48.58N 5.31 E
La Crosse [Ks.-U.S.] 45 Gg 38.32N 99.18W
La Crosse [Wi.-U.S.] 39 Je 43.49N 91.15W
La Cruz [Arg.] 56 Ic 29.10S 56.38W
La Cruz [C.R.] 49 Eh 11.04N 85.39W
La Cruz [Mex.] 47 Cd 23.55N 106.54W
La Cruz [Ur.] 56 Id 33.56S 56.15W
La Cruz de Rio Grande 49 Eg 13.06N 84.10W
La Cruz de Taratara 49 Mh 11.03N 69.44W
La Cuesta 48 Hc 28.45N 102.25W
La Cumbre 56 Hd 30.58S 64.30W
Lac Yora 35 Cb 19.08N 20.35 E
Ladário 55 Dd 19.01S 57.35W
Ladbergen 12 Jb 52.08N 7.45 E
Lądek-Zdrój 10 Mf 50.21N 16.50 E
Ladenburg 12 Ke 49.28N 8.37 E
La Désirade 50 Fd 16.19N 61.03W
La Digue Island 37b Ca 4.21S 55.50 E
Lādik 24 Fb 40.36N 36.45 E
Ladismith 37 Cf 33.30S 21.16 E
Ladispoli 14 Gi 41.56N 12.05 E
Lado, Jabal- 35 Ed 5.06N 31.35 E
Ladoga, Lake- (EN)= Ladožkoje Ozero 5 Jc 61.00N 31.00 E
Ladong 27 Ig 24.49N 109.34 E
La Dorada 54 Db 5.22N 74.42W
Ladožkoje Ozero=Ladoga, Lake (EN) 5 Jc 61.00N 31.00 E
Ladrones, Islas- 49 Fj 7.52N 82.26W
Laduškin 8 Ij 54.35N 20.10 E
Ladva-Vetka 7 If 61.20N 34.29 E
Lady Ann Strait 42 Ja 75.45N 80.00W
Ladybrand 37 De 29.19S 27.25 E
Lady Evelyn Lake 44 Gb 47.20N 80.10W
Lady Newnes Ice Shelf 66 Kf 73.40S 167.30 E
Ladysmith [B.C.-Can.] 46 Db 48.58N 123.49W
Ladysmith [S.Afr.] 31 Jk 28.34S 29.45 E
Ladysmith [Wi.-U.S.] 43 Ib 45.28N 91.07W
Ladyžin 16 Fe 48.40N 29.13 E
Lae 58 Fe 6.43S 147.01 E
Lae Atoll 57 Hd 8.56N 166.14 E
La Eduvigis 55 Ch 26.50S 59.05W
Laem, Khao- 25 Kf 14.19N 101.11 E
Laer [F.R.G.] 12 Kb 52.06N 8.05 E
Laer [F.R.G.] 12 Jb 52.04N 7.21 E
Lærdalsøyri 7 Bf 61.06N 7.29 E
La Escala/L'Escala 13 Pb 42.07N 3.08 E
La Esmeralda 54 Ec 3.10N 65.33W
Læsø 7 Bh 57.15N 10.00 E
Læsø Rende 8 Dg 57.15N 10.45 E
La Española=Hispaniola (EN) 38 Lh 19.00N 71.00W
La Esperanza [Bol.] 54 Ff 14.34S 62.10W
La Esperanza [Hond.] 49 Cf 14.20N 88.10W
La Estrada 13 Db 42.41N 8.29W
Lafayette [Al.-U.S.] 44 Ei 32.54N 85.24W
Lafayette [In.-U.S.] 43 Jc 40.25N 86.53W
Lafayette [La.-U.S.] 39 Jf 30.14N 92.01W
La Fère 12 Fe 49.40N 3.22 E
La Ferrière-sur-Risle 12 Cf 48.59N 0.48 E
La Ferté-Bernard 11 Gf 48.11N 0.40 E
La Ferté-Frênel 12 Cf 48.50N 0.30 E
La Ferté-Macé 11 Ff 48.36N 0.22W
La Ferté-Milon 12 Fe 49.10N 3.07 E
La Ferté-Saint-Aubin 11 Hg 47.43N 1.56 E
La Ferté-sous-Jouarre 11 Jf 48.57N 3.08 E
Laffān, Ra's- 24 Nj 25.54N 51.35 E
Lafia 34 Gd 8.29N 8.31 E
Lafiagi 34 Gd 8.52N 5.15 E
La Flèche 11 Fg 47.42N 0.05W
Lafnitz 14 Kc 46.57N 16.16 E
La Foa 63b Be 21.43S 165.49 E
La Follette 44 Eg 36.23N 84.07W
La Fria 49 Ki 8.13N 72.15W
Laft 24 Pi 26.54N 55.46 E
La Fuente de San Esteban 13 Fd 40.48N 6.15W
Laga, Monti della- 14 Hh 42.45N 13.35 E
La Galite (EN)=Jāliṭah 30 He 37.32N 8.56 E
La Gallareta 55 Bi 29.34S 60.23W
Lagamar 55 Id 18.13S 46.48W
Lagan 8 Eh 56.33N 12.56 E
Lagan 8 Eh 56.55N 13.59 E
Lagan/Abhainn an Lagáin 9 Hg 54.37N 5.53W
Lagarina, Val- 14 Fe 45.50N 11.10 E
La Garita Mountains 45 Ch 38.00N 106.40W
Lagarto 54 Kf 10.54S 37.41W
Lagash 24 Lg 31.27N 46.13 E
Lagawe 26 Hc 16.49N 121.06 E
Lage 12 Kc 51.59N 8.48 E
Lågen 7 Cf 61.08N 10.25 E
Lagh Bogal 36 Gb 0.42N 40.55 E
Laghmān [3] 23 Lb 35.00N 70.15 E
Laghouat 31 He 33.48N 2.53 E
Laghouat [3] 32 Hc 33.30N 3.15 E
La Gloria 49 Ki 8.38N 73.48W
Lagny 11 If 48.52N 2.43 E
Lagoa 13 Dg 37.08N 8.27W
Lagôa 55 Eb 14.08S 55.20W
Lagoa da Prata 55 Je 20.01S 45.33W
Lagoa Vermelha 56 Jc 28.13S 51.32W
Lagodehi 16 Oi 41.50N 46.14 E
La Gomera 49 Bf 14.05N 91.03W
Lagonegro 14 Jj 40.07N 15.46 E
Lagonoy Gulf 26 Hd 13.35N 123.45 E
Lagoon 64n Ab 10.23S 161.05W
Lagos 13 Dg 37.06N 8.40W
Lagos 31 Hh 6.27N 3.23 E
Lágos 15 Ih 41.01N 25.07 E
Lagos [2] 34 Fd 6.30N 3.30 E
Lagos, Baia de- 13 Dg 37.06N 8.39W
Lagosa 36 Ed 5.57S 29.53 E
Lagos de Moreno 47 Dd 21.21N 101.55W
La Grand-Combe 11 Kj 44.13N 4.02 E
La Grande 43 Db 45.20N 118.05W
La Grande Fosse 9 Kl 49.40N 3.00W
La Grande-Motte 11 Kk 43.34N 4.07 E
La Grande Rivière 38 Ld 53.50N 79.00W
La Grande Trench (EN)= Hurd Deep 9 Kl 49.40N 3.00W
La Grange 44 Ef 38.24N 85.23W
Lagrange 44 Ee 41.39N 85.25W
La Grange [Ga.-U.S.] 43 Je 33.02N 85.02W
La Grange [Tx.-U.S.] 45 Hl 29.54N 96.52W
La Gran Sabana 54 Fb 5.30N 61.30W
La Grita 54 Db 8.08N 71.59W
Lagskär 8 He 59.50N 20.00 E
La Guaira 53 Jd 10.36N 66.56W
La Guajira [2] 54 Da 11.30N 72.30W
Lagua Lichan, Puntan- 64b Ba 15.16N 145.50 E
Laguardia 13 Jb 42.33N 2.35W
La Guardia [Sp.] 13 Dc 41.54N 8.53W
La Guardia [Sp.] 13 Ie 39.47N 3.29W
La Guasima 48 Kg 21.06N 97.49W
La Guerche-sur-l'Aubois 11 Ih 46.57N 2.57 E
Laguiole 11 Ij 44.41N 2.51 E
Laguna 56 Kc 28.29S 48.47W
Laguna Alsina 55 Am 36.49S 62.13W
Laguna Beach 46 Gj 33.33N 117.51W
Laguna Blanca 55 Cg 25.08S 58.15W
Laguna de Bay 26 Hd 14.23N 121.15 E
Laguna Limpia 55 Ch 26.29S 59.41W
Laguna Mountains 46 Gj 32.55N 116.25W
Laguna Paiva 56 Hd 31.19S 60.39W
Laguna Superior 47 Fe 16.20N 94.25W
Laguna Veneta 14 Ge 45.25N 12.20 E
Laguna Yema 55 Bg 24.15S 61.15W
Lagunillas [Bol.] 54 Fg 19.38S 63.43W
Lagunillas [Mex.] 48 Ii 17.50N 101.44W
Lagunillas [Ven.] 49 Lh 10.08N 71.16W
Lagunillas [Ven.] 49 Li 8.31N 71.24W
Laha 27 Lb 48.13N 124.36 E
La Habana [3] 49 Fb 22.45N 82.10W
La Habana=Havana (EN) 39 Kg 23.08N 82.22W
Lahad Datu 26 Ge 5.02N 118.19 E
Laham 34 Fc 14.54N 4.25 E
Lahat 26 Dg 3.48S 103.32 E
Lahdenpohja 7 Hf 61.33N 30.13 E
Lahewa 26 Cf 1.24N 97.11 E
Lahij 23 Fg 13.04N 44.53 E
Lāhījān 23 Hb 37.12N 50.01 E
Lahn 10 Df 50.18N 7.37 E
Lahnstein 12 Jd 50.20N 7.29 E
Laholm 7 Ch 56.31N 13.02 E
Laholmsbukten 8 Eh 56.35N 12.50 E
Lahore 22 Jf 31.35N 74.18 E
Lahr 10 Dh 48.20N 7.52 E
Lahti 6 Ic 60.58N 25.40 E
Laï 31 Ih 9.24N 16.18 E
Laiagam 60 Ci 5.31S 143.39 E
Lai'an 28 Eh 32.28N 118.26 E
Lai Chau 25 Kd 22.02N 103.10 E
Laich o'Moray 9 Jd 57.40N 3.30W
Laie 65a Db 21.39N 157.56W
Laifeng 27 If 29.31N 109.23 E
Laighean/Leinster 9 Gh 53.00N 7.00W
L'Aigle 11 Gf 48.45N 0.38 E
Laignes 11 Kg 47.50N 4.22 E
Laihia 7 Fe 62.58N 22.01 E
Lainioälven 7 Fc 67.22N 22.39 E
Lairg 9 Ic 58.01N 4.25W
Lairi 35 Bc 10.49N 17.06 E
Lairi, Batha de- 35 Bc 12.28N 16.45 E
Lais 26 Dg 3.32S 102.03 E
La Isabela 49 Gb 22.57N 80.01W
Laisamis 36 Gb 1.36N 37.48 E
Laiševo 7 Li 55.26N 49.32 E
Laishui 28 Ce 39.23N 115.42 E
Laisvall 7 Dc 66.08N 17.10 E
Laitila 7 Ef 60.53N 21.41 E
Laiwu 28 Df 36.12N 117.40 E
Laiwui 26 Ig 1.22S 127.40 E
Laixi (Shuiji) 28 Ff 36.52N 120.31 E
Laiyang 27 Ld 36.59N 120.39 E
Laiyuan 27 Jd 39.19N 114.43 E
Laizhou Wan 28 Ef 37.30N 119.30 E
Laja 56 Fe 37.16S 72.42W
Laja 17 Hc 66.20N 56.16 E
La Jara 13 He 39.40N 4.55W
Lajeado 55 Gi 29.27S 51.58W
Lajeado, Serra do- 55 Hd 19.08S 49.56W
Lājerd 24 Oe 35.24N 53.04 E
Lajes [Braz.] 54 Ke 5.41S 36.14W
Lajes [Braz.] 53 Kh 27.48S 50.19W
Lajes do Pico 32 Bb 38.23N 28.16W
Lajosmizse 10 Pi 47.01N 19.33 E
La Junta [Co.-U.S.] 43 Gd 37.59N 103.33W
La Junta [Mex.] 48 Fc 28.28N 107.20W
Lak Bor 36 Hb 1.18N 40.40 E
Lake Cargelligo 59 Jf 33.18S 146.23 E
Lake Charles 39 Jf 30.12N 93.12W
Lake City 43 Ke 30.12N 82.38W
Lake District 9 Jg 54.30N 3.10W
Lake Fork Creek 46 Jf 40.13N 110.07W
Lake Geneva 45 Le 42.36N 88.26W
Lake George 44 Kd 43.25N 73.45W
Lake Grace 59 Df 33.06S 118.28 E
Lake Harbour 42 Kd 62.51N 69.53W
Lake Havasu City 46 Hi 34.27N 114.22W
Lake Itasca 45 Ic 46.51N 95.13W
Lake Jackson 45 Il 29.02N 95.27W
Lake King 59 Df 33.05S 119.40 E
Lakeland 43 Kf 28.03N 81.57W
Lake Louise 46 Ga 51.26N 116.11W
Lakemba 63d Cc 18.13S 178.47W
Lakemba Passage 63d Cb 17.53S 178.32W
Lake Mills 45 Je 43.25N 93.32W
Lake Minchumina 40 Ia 63.53N 152.19W
Lake Murray 60 Ci 6.54S 141.28 E
Lake Oswego 46 Dd 45.26N 122.39W
Lake Placid 44 Kc 44.18N 73.59W
Lake Providence 45 Kj 32.48N 91.11W
Lake Pukaki 62 Df 44.11S 170.08 E
Lake Range 46 Ff 40.15N 119.25W
Lake River 42 Jf 54.28N 82.30W
Lakes Entrance 59 Jg 37.53S 147.59 E
Lakeside 46 If 41.13N 112.57W
Lake Tekapo 62 Df 44.00S 170.29 E
Lakeview 43 Cc 42.11N 120.21W
Lakeville 45 Jd 44.39N 93.14W
Lake Wales 44 Gl 27.55N 81.35W
Lakewood [Co.-U.S.] 45 Dg 39.44N 105.06W
Lakewood [Oh.-U.S.] 44 Ge 41.29N 81.50W
Lake Worth 44 Gl 26.37N 80.03W
Lakhdar, Chergui Kef- 13 Pi 35.57N 3.16 E
Lakhdaria 13 Ph 36.34N 3.35 E
Lāki 15 Hh 41.50N 24.50 E
Lakin 45 Fh 37.58N 101.15W
Lakinsk 7 Jh 56.04N 39.58 E
Lákmos Óros 15 Ej 39.40N 21.07 E
Lakon, Ile- 57 Hf 14.17S 167.30 E
Lakonikós Kólpos = Laconia, Gulf of- (EN) 15 Fm 36.35N 22.40 E
Lakota [3] 34 Dd 5.53N 5.42W
Lakota [I.C.] 34 Dd 5.51N 5.41W
Lakota [N.D.-U.S.] 45 Gb 48.02N 98.21W
Laksefjorden 7 Ga 70.58N 27.00 E
Lakselv 7 Fa 70.03N 25.01 E
Lakshadweep [3] 25 Ef 11.00N 72.00 E
La Laguna 55 Bb 14.30S 61.06W
Lalanna 37 Hd 23.28S 45.05 E
Lalapaşa 15 Jh 41.50N 26.44 E
Lāleh Zār, Kūh-e- 23 Hg 29.24N 56.46 E
La Leonesa 55 Ch 27.03S 58.43W
Lāli 24 Mf 32.21N 49.06 E
Lalibela 35 Fc 12.00N 39.04 E
La Libertad [2] 54 Ce 8.00S 78.30W
La Libertad [ElSal.] 47 Gf 13.29N 89.16W
La Libertad [Guat.] 49 Be 16.47N 90.07W
La Libertad [Guat.] 49 Bf 15.30N 91.50W
La Libertad [Hond.] 49 Df 14.43N 87.36W
La Ligua 56 Fd 32.27S 71.14W
Lalín 13 Db 42.39N 8.07W
La Linea 13 Gh 36.10N 5.19W
Lalin He 28 Hb 45.28N 125.43 E
Lalitpur 25 Fd 24.41N 78.25 E
Lalla Khedidja 13 Qh 36.27N 4.14 E
Lālmanir Hāt 25 Hc 25.54N 89.27 E
La Loche 42 Ge 56.29N 109.27W
La Loupe 11 Hf 48.28N 1.01 E
La Louvière 11 Kd 50.29N 4.11 E
L'Alpe-d'Huez 11 Mi 45.06N 6.04 E
La Lucila 55 Bj 30.25S 61.01W
Lalzit, Gjiri i- 15 Ch 41.31N 19.29 E
La Machine 11 Jh 46.53N 3.28 E
La Maddalena 14 Di 41.13N 9.24 E
La Maiella 5 Hg 42.05N 14.07 E
La Maladeta/Malditos, Montes- 13 Mb 42.40N 0.50 E
La Malbaie 42 Kg 47.39N 70.10W
La Mancha 5 Fh 39.05N 3.00W
La Manche 5 Fe 50.20N 1.00W
Lamap 61 Cc 16.26S 167.43 E
Lamar 43 Gd 38.05N 102.37W
La Maragateria 13 Fb 42.25N 6.10W
La Marina 13 Lf 38.35N 0.05W
La Marmora 14 Dk 39.59N 9.20 E
La Marque 45 Il 29.22N 94.58W
Lamas 54 Ce 6.25S 76.35W
Lamastre 11 Kj 44.59N 4.35 E
Lamawan 28 Ad 40.05N 111.25 E
Lambach 14 Hb 48.05N 13.53 E
Lamballe 11 Df 48.28N 2.31W
Lambar, Rio- 55 Jd 19.30S 45.00W
Lambaréné 31 Ii 0.42S 10.13 E
Lambari 55 Je 21.58S 45.21W
Lambasa 61 Ec 16.26S 179.24 E
Lambay/Reachrainn 9 Gh 53.29N 6.01W
Lambayeque [2] 54 Ce 6.20S 80.00W
Lambayeque 54 Ce 6.42S 79.55W
Lambert Glacier 66 Ff 71.00S 70.00 E
Lambert Land 41 Jc 79.10N 21.00W
Lamberts Bay 31 Il 32.05S 18.17 E
Lambro 14 De 45.08N 9.32 E
Lambsheim 12 Ke 49.31N 8.17 E
Lambton, Cape- 42 Fb 71.04N 123.08W
Lamé 35 Ad 9.15N 14.32 E
Lame Deer 46 Ld 45.37N 106.40W
Lamego 13 Ec 41.06N 7.49W
Lamentin 51e Ab 16.16N 61.38W
La Mesa 46 Gj 32.46N 117.01W
Lamesa 43 Ge 32.44N 101.57W
La Meta 14 Hj 41.41N 13.56 E
Lamezia Terme 14 Kl 38.59N 16.17 E
Lamia 15 Fk 38.54N 22.26 E
Lamina 55 De 20.34S 56.14W
Lamlam, Mount- 64c Bb 13.20N 144.40 E
Lammermuir Hills 9 Kf 55.52N 2.40W
Lammhult 8 Fg 57.10N 14.35 E
Lammi 7 Ff 61.05N 25.01 E
Lamoil 64d Ba 7.39N 151.41 E
Lamon Bay 21 Oh 14.25N 122.00 E
Lamone 14 Gf 44.29N 12.08 E
Lamoni 45 Jf 40.37N 93.56W
Lamont 44 Fj 30.21N 83.50W
La Montaña 52 If 10.00S 72.50W
La Moraña 13 Hd 40.45N 4.55W
La Mosquitia 49 Ef 15.00N 84.20W
La Mothe-Achard 11 Eh 46.37N 1.40W
Lamotrek Atoll 57 Fd 7.30N 146.20 E

Index Symbols

[1] Independent Nation
[2] State, Region
[3] District, County
[4] Municipality
[5] Colony, Dependency
Continent
Physical Region
Historical or Cultural Region
Mount, Mountain
Volcano
Hill
Mountains, Mountain Range
Hills, Escarpment
Plateau, Upland
Pass, Gap
Plain, Lowland
Delta
Salt Flat
Valley, Canyon
Crater, Cave
Karst Features
Depression
Polder
Desert, Dunes
Forest, Woods
Heath, Steppe
Oasis
Cape, Point
Coast, Beach
Cliff
Peninsula
Isthmus
Sandbank
Island
Atoll
Rock, Reef
Islands, Archipelago
Rocks, Reefs
Coral Reef
Well, Spring
Geyser
River, Stream
Waterfall Rapids
River Mouth, Estuary
Lake
Salt Lake
Intermittent Lake
Reservoir
Swamp, Pond
Canal
Glacier
Ice Shelf, Pack Ice
Ocean
Sea
Gulf, Bay
Strait, Fjord
Lagoon
Bank
Seamount
Tablemount
Ridge
Shelf
Basin
Escarpment, Sea Scarp
Fracture
Trench, Abyss
National Park, Reserve
Point of Interest
Recreation Site
Cave, Cavern
Historic Site
Ruins
Wall, Walls
Church, Abbey
Temple
Scientific Station
Airport
Port
Lighthouse
Mine
Tunnel
Dam, Bridge

Lamotte-Beuvron 11 Ig 47.36N 2.01 E
La Moure 45 Gc 46.21N 98.18W
Lampang 25 Je 18.16N 99.34 E
Lampasas 45 Gk 31.03N 98.12W
Lampazos de Naranjo 48 Id 27.01N 100.31W
Lampedusa 14 Go 35.30N 12.35 E
Lampertheim 10 Eg 49.36N 8.28 E
Lampeter 9 Ii 52.07N 4.05W
Lamphun 25 Je 18.35N 99.00 E
Lampione 14 Go 35.35N 12.20 E
Lampung [3] 26 Dg 5.00S 105.00 E
Lamu 31 Li 2.16S 40.54 E
Lamud 54 Ce 6.09S 77.55W
La Mure 11 Lj 44.54N 5.47 E
Lan 16 Ec 52.09N 27.18 E
Lana 14 Fd 46.37N 11.09 E
Lana, Rio de la- 48 Li 17.49N 95.09W
Lanai City 65a Ec 20.50N 156.55W
Lanaihale 65a Ec 20.49N 156.52W
Lanai Island 57 Lb 20.50N 156.55W
Lanaken 12 Hd 50.53N 5.39 E
Lanark 9 Jf 55.41N 3.48W
Lanbi Kyun 25 Jf 10.50N 98.15 E
Lancang (Menglangba) 27 Gg 22.37N 99.57 E
Lancang Jiang=Mekong (EN) 21 Mh 10.15N 105.55 E
Lancashire [3] 9 Kh 53.55N 2.40W
Lancashire Plain 9 Kh 53.40N 2.45W
Lancaster 9 Kh 53.45N 2.50W
Lancaster [Ca.-U.S.] 43 De 34.42N 118.08W
Lancaster [Eng.-U.K.] 9 Kg 54.03N 2.48W
Lancaster [Mo.-U.S.] 45 Jf 40.31N 92.32W
Lancaster [N.H.-U.S.] 44 Lc 44.29N 71.34W
Lancaster [Oh.-U.S.] 44 Ff 39.43N 82.37W
Lancaster [Ont.-Can.] 44 Jc 45.12N 74.30W
Lancaster [Pa.-U.S.] 43 Lc 40.01N 76.19W
Lancaster [S.C.-U.S.] 44 Gh 34.43N 80.47W
Lancaster Sound 38 Kb 74.13N 84.00W
Lançeiro 55 Fe 20.59S 53.43W
Lancelin 59 Df 31.01S 115.19 E
Lanciano 14 Ih 42.14N 14.23 E
Lančin 15 Ha 48.31N 24.49 E
Lancun 28 Ff 36.25N 120.11 E
Łańcut 10 Sf 50.05N 22.13 E
Land 8 Cd 60.45N 10.00 E
Lândana 36 Bd 5.15S 12.10 E
Landau an der Isar 10 Ih 48.41N 12.41 E
Landau in der Pfalz 10 Eg 49.12N 8.07 E
Land Bay 66 Mf 75.25S 141.45W
Landeck 14 Ec 47.08N 10.34 E
Landen 12 Hd 50.45N 5.05 E
Lander 43 Fc 42.50N 108.44W
Landerneau 11 Bf 48.27N 4.15W
Lander River 59 Gd 20.25S 132.00 E
Landeryd 8 Eg 57.05N 13.16 E
Landes 11 Fj 44.15N 1.00W
Landes [3] 11 Fj 44.00N 0.50W
Landesbergen 12 Lb 52.34N 9.08 E
Landeta 55 Ak 32.01S 62.04W
Landete 13 Ke 39.54N 1.22W
Landfallis 25 If 13.40N 93.02 E
Land Glacier 66 Mf 75.40S 141.45W
Landi Kotal 25 Eb 34.06N 71.09 E
Landless Corner 36 Ee 14.53S 28.04 E
Landrecies 12 Fd 50.08N 3.42 E
Landsberg am Lech 10 Gh 48.03N 10.52 E
Landsbro 8 Fg 57.22N 14.54 E
Land's End 5 Fe 50.03N 5.44W
Lands End 42 Fa 76.25N 122.45W
Landshut 10 Ih 48.32N 12.09 E
Landskrona 8 Ei 55.52N 12.50 E
Landsort 8 Gf 58.45N 17.50 E
Landsortsdjupet 8 Hf 58.40N 18.30 E
Landstuhl 12 Je 49.25N 7.34 E
Landusky 46 Kc 47.54N 108.37W
La Neuve-Lyre 12 Cf 48.54N 0.45 E
Lanfeng → Lankao 28 Cg 34.49N 114.48 E
Lang 46 Mb 49.56N 104.23W
La'nga Co 27 De 30.41N 81.17 E
Langadhás 15 Gi 40.45N 23.04 E
Langádhia 15 Fl 37.39N 22.03 E
Långan 7 De 63.19N 14.44 E
Langano, Lake- 35 Fd 7.36N 38.43 E
Langao 27 Ie 32.20N 108.53 E
Langara 26 Hg 4.02S 123.00 E
Langarfoss 7a Cb 65.35N 14.15W
Langasian 26 Ie 8.16N 125.39 E
Langdon 45 Gb 48.46N 98.22W
Langeac 11 Ji 45.06N 3.29 E
Langeais 11 Gg 47.20N 0.24 E
Langeb 35 Fb 17.46N 36.41 E
Langebaan 37 Bf 33.06S 18.02 E
Langeberg 37 Cf 33.56S 20.45 E
Langedijk 12 Gb 52.42N 4.48 E
Langeland 7 Ci 55.00N 10.50 E
Langelands Bælt 8 Dj 54.50N 10.55 E
Längelmävesi 8 Kc 61.30N 24.20 E
Langen 12 Ke 49.59N 8.40 E
Langenberg 12 Kc 51.17N 8.34 E
Langenburg 45 Fa 50.50N 101.43W
Langenfeld (Rheinland) 12 Ic 51.06N 6.57 E
Langenhagen 10 Fd 52.27N 9.45 E
Langenselbold 12 Ld 50.11N 9.02 E
Langenthal 14 Bc 47.13N 7.49 E
Langeoog 10 Dc 53.46N 7.32 E
Langeri 20 Jf 50.08N 143.20 E
Langesund 8 Ce 59.00N 9.45 E
Langesundsfjorden 8 Cf 59.00N 9.48 E
Langevåg 8 Bb 62.27N 6.12 E
Langfang → Anci 27 Kd 39.29N 116.40 E
Långfjället 8 Eb 62.10N 12.20 E
Langfjorden 8 Bb 62.45N 7.30 E
Langhe 14 Bf 44.30N 8.00 E
Langholm 9 Kf 55.09N 3.00W
Langjökull 5 Ec 64.39N 20.00W
Langkawi, Pulau- 26 Ce 6.22N 99.48 E
Langkon 26 Ge 6.32N 116.42 E
Langlade 44 Ja 48.12N 75.57W
Langnau im Emmental 14 Bd 46.56N 7.46 E
Langogne 11 Jj 44.43N 3.51 E
Langon 11 Fj 44.33N 0.15W
Langorūd 24 Md 37.11N 50.10 E
Langøya 7 Db 68.44N 14.50 E
Langreo 13 Ga 43.18N 5.41W
Langres 11 Lg 47.52N 5.20 E
Langres, Plateau de- 5 Gf 47.41N 5.03 E
Langrune-sur-Mer 12 Be 49.19N 0.22W
Langsa 22 Li 4.28N 97.58 E
Långsele 8 Ga 63.11N 17.04 E
Långshyttan 8 Gd 60.27N 16.01 E
Lang Son 25 Ld 21.50N 106.44 E
Lang Suan 25 Jg 9.55N 99.07 E
Languedoc 5 Gg 44.00N 4.00 E
Languedoc 11 Jj 44.00N 4.00 E
Langueyú, Arroyo- 55 Cm 36.39S 58.27W
Langwedel 12 Lb 52.58N 9.13 E
Langxi 28 Ei 31.08N 119.11 E
Langzhong 27 Ie 31.40N 106.04 E
Lan Hsu 27 Lg 22.00N 121.30 E
Laniel 44 Hb 47.06N 79.15W
Lanin, Volcán- 52 Ii 39.38S 71.30W
Lankao 27 Cd 35.12N 79.50 E
Lankao (Lanfeng) 27 Kg 21.00N 116.00 E
Lankao (Lanfeng) 28 Cg 34.49N 114.48 E
Länkipohja 8 Kc 61.44N 24.48 E
Lannemezan 11 Gk 43.08N 0.23 E
Lannemezan, Plateau de- 11 Gk 43.09N 0.27 E
Lannion 11 Cf 48.44N 3.28W
Lannion, Baie de- 11 Cf 48.43N 3.34W
La Noria 56 Gb 20.23S 69.53W
Lansdowne House 42 If 52.13N 87.53W
L'Anse 44 Cb 46.45N 88.27W
Lansing [Ia.-U.S.] 45 Ke 43.22N 91.13W
Lansing [Mi.-U.S.] 39 Ke 42.43N 84.34W
Lansjärv 7 Fc 66.39N 22.12 E
Łańskie, Jezioro- 10 Qc 53.33N 20.30 E
Lantar 20 Ie 56.05N 137.35 E
Lanta Yai, Ko- 25 Jg 7.35N 99.03 E
Lanteri 55 Ci 28.50S 59.39W
Lanterne 11 Mg 47.44N 6.03 E
Lanús 55 Cl 34.43S 58.24W
Lanusei 14 Dk 39.53N 9.32 E
Lanvaux, Landes de- 11 Dg 47.47N 2.36W
Lanxi [China] 28 Ej 29.13N 119.28 E
Lanxi [China] 28 Ha 46.15N 126.16 E
Lanxian (Dongcun) 28 Ae 38.17N 111.38 E
Lanyi He 28 Ae 38.40N 110.53 E
Lanzarote 30 Ff 29.00N 13.40W
Lanzhou 22 Mf 36.03N 103.41 E
Lanzo Torinese 14 Be 45.16N 7.28 E
Lao 14 Jk 39.47N 15.48 E
Laoag 22 Oh 18.12N 120.36 E
Laoang 26 Id 12.34N 125.00 E
Lao Cai 22 Mg 22.30N 103.57 E
Laocheng 28 Hc 42.37N 124.04 E
Laoha He 27 Lc 43.24N 120.39 E
Lao He 28 Cj 29.02N 115.47 E
Laohuanghe Kou 28 Ef 37.39N 119.02 E
Laois [2] 9 Fi 53.00N 7.30W
Laojunmiao → Yumen 22 Lf 39.50N 97.44 E
Laojun Shan 27 Je 33.45N 111.38 E
Lao Ling 28 Id 41.24N 126.10 E
Laon 11 Je 49.34N 3.37 E
Laona 45 Ld 45.34N 88.40W
Laonnois 12 Fe 49.35N 3.40 E
La Orchila, Isla- 54 Ea 11.48N 66.10W
La Oroya 53 Ig 11.32S 75.57W
Laos [1] 22 Mh 18.00N 105.00 E
Laoshan (Licun) 28 Ff 36.10N 120.25 E
Laotougou 28 Jc 42.54N 129.09 E
Laou 13 Gi 35.26N 5.05W
Laoye Ling 28 Kb 44.50N 130.10 E
Lapa 56 Kc 25.45S 49.42W
Lapai 34 Gd 9.03N 6.43 E
Lapalisse 11 Jh 46.15N 3.38 E
La Palma 30 Ff 28.40N 17.52W
La Palma [ElSal.] 49 Cf 14.19N 89.11W
La Palma [Pan.] 47 Ig 8.25N 78.09W
La Palma del Condado 13 Fg 37.23N 6.33W
La Paloma 55 El 34.40S 54.10W
La Pampa [2] 56 Ge 37.00S 66.00W
La Panne/De Panne 12 Ec 51.06N 2.35 E
La Paragua 54 Fb 6.50N 63.20W
La Partida, Isla- 48 De 24.30N 110.25W
La Paz [3] 49 Df 14.15N 87.50W
La Paz [2] 54 Eg 15.00S 68.00W
La Paz [Arg.] 56 Id 30.45S 59.39W
La Paz [Arg.] 56 Gd 33.28S 67.33W
La Paz [Bol.] 53 Jg 16.30S 68.09W
La Paz [Col.] 49 Kh 10.23N 73.10W
La Paz [Hond.] 47 Gf 14.16N 87.40W
La Paz [Mex.] 39 Hg 24.10N 110.18W
La Paz [Ur.] 55 Dl 34.46S 56.13W
La Paz [Ven.] 49 Lh 10.41N 72.00W
La Paz, Bahía de- 47 Bd 24.09N 110.25W
La Paz, Llano de- 48 De 24.00N 110.30W
La Paz Centro 49 Dg 12.20N 86.41W
La Pedrera 54 Ed 1.18S 69.40W
Lapeer 44 Fd 43.03N 83.19W
La Pelada 55 Bj 30.52S 60.59W
La Pérouse, Bahía- 65d Bb 27.04S 109.18W
La Perouse Strait (EN)=Laperuza, Proliv- 21 Qe 45.30N 142.00 E
La Perouse Strait (EN)=Sōya-Kaikyō 21 Qe 45.30N 142.00 E
Laperuza, Proliv-=La Perouse Strait (EN) 21 Qe 45.30N 142.00 E
La Pesca 47 Ed 23.47N 97.47W
Lápethos 24 Ee 35.20N 33.10 E
La Petite Pierre 12 Jf 48.52N 7.19 E
La Picasa, Laguna- 55 Al 34.20S 62.14W
La Piedad Cavadas 48 Hg 20.21N 102.00W
La Pine 46 Ee 43.40N 121.30W
Lapinjärvi/Lappträsk 8 Ld 60.36N 26.09 E
Lapinlahti 7 Ge 63.22N 27.30 E
La Plaine 51g Bb 15.20N 61.15W
La Plana 13 Ld 40.00N 0.05W
Lapland (EN)=Lappi 5 Ib 66.50N 22.00 E
Lapland (EN)=Lappland 5 Ib 66.50N 22.00 E
La Plant 45 Fd 45.10N 100.38W
La Plata 53 Ki 34.55S 57.57W
La Pobla de Lillet 13 Nb 42.15N 1.59 E
La Pobla de Segur/Pobla de Segur 13 Mb 42.15N 0.58 E
La Pocatièr 44 Lb 47.21N 70.02W
La Porte 44 De 41.36N 86.43W
Lapovo 15 Ee 44.11N 21.06 E
Lappajärvi 7 Fe 63.08N 23.40 E
Lappeenranta/Villmanstrand 6 Ic 61.04N 28.11 E
Lappfjärd/Lapväärtti 8 Ib 62.15N 21.32 E
Lappi [2] 7 Gc 67.40N 26.30 E
Lappi 8 Ic 61.06N 21.50 E
Lappi=Lapland (EN) 5 Ib 66.50N 22.00 E
Lappland=Lapland (EN) 5 Ib 66.50N 22.00 E
Lappo/Lapua 7 Fe 62.57N 23.00 E
Lappträsk/Lapinjärvi 8 Ld 60.36N 26.09 E
Lapri 20 He 55.45N 124.59 E
Laprida 56 He 37.33S 60.49W
Lâpseki 24 Bb 40.20N 26.41 E
Laptev Sea (EN)=Laptevyh, More- 67 Fd 76.00N 126.00 E
Laptevyh, More-=Laptev Sea (EN) 67 Fd 76.00N 126.00 E
Lapua/Lappo 7 Fe 62.57N 23.00 E
La Puebla 13 Pe 39.46N 3.01 E
La Puebla de Cazalla 13 Gg 37.14N 5.19W
Lapuna 55 Ba 13.19S 60.28W
La Puntilla 52 Hf 2.11S 81.01W
La Purísima 48 Cd 26.10N 112.04W
Lăpuş 15 Hb 47.30N 24.01 E
Lăpuş 15 Gb 47.39N 23.24 E
La Push 46 Cc 47.55N 124.38W
Lapväärtti/Lappfjärd 8 Ib 62.15N 21.32 E
Łapy 10 Sd 53.00N 22.53 E
Laqīyat al Arba'in 35 Da 20.03N 28.02 E
La Quemada 48 Hf 22.27N 102.45W
La Quiaca 56 Gb 22.06S 65.37W
L'Aquila 6 Hg 42.22N 13.22 E
Lar 23 Hd 27.41N 54.17 E
Lara [2] 54 Ea 10.10N 69.50W
Larache 32 Fb 35.12N 6.09W
Laragne-Montéglin 11 Lj 44.19N 5.49 E
Lārak 23 Id 26.52N 56.22 E
La Rambla 13 Hg 37.36N 4.44W
Laramie 39 Ie 41.19N 105.35W
Laramie Mountains 43 Fc 42.00N 105.40W
Laramie Peak 46 Me 42.17N 105.27W
Laramie River 46 Me 42.12N 104.32W
Laranjal, Rio- 55 Ff 23.12S 53.45W
Laranjeiras do Sul 56 Jc 25.25S 52.25W
Larantuka 26 Hh 8.21S 122.59 E
Larat 26 Jh 7.09S 131.45 E
Larat, Pulau- 26 Jh 7.10S 131.50 E
La Raya 49 Ji 8.20N 74.34W
L'Arba 13 Ph 36.34N 3.09 E
L'Arbaa-Naït-Irathen 13 Qh 36.38N 4.12 E
L'Arbresle 11 Ki 45.50N 4.37 E
Lärbro 7 Eh 57.47N 18.47 E
Larche, Col de- 11 Mj 44.25N 6.53 E
Larde 37 Fc 16.28S 39.43 E
Larderello 14 Eg 43.14N 10.53 E
La Réale 11 Fj 44.35N 0.02W
Laredo [Sp.] 13 Ia 43.24N 3.25W
Laredo [Tx.-U.S.] 39 Jg 27.31N 99.30W
Laren 12 Hb 52.16N 5.16 E
Lārestān 21 Hg 27.00N 55.30 E
Larestan 24 Pi 27.00N 55.30 E
Large Island 51p Cb 12.24N 61.30W
Largentière 11 Kj 44.32N 4.18 E
L'Argentière-la-Bessée 11 Mj 44.47N 6.33 E
Largo, Cayo- 49 Gc 21.38N 81.28W
Largs 9 If 55.48N 4.52W
La Ribagorça/Ribagorza 13 Mb 42.15N 0.30 E
La Ribera 13 Kb 42.30N 2.00W
Larimore 45 Hc 47.54N 97.38W
Larino 14 Ii 41.48N 14.54 E
La Rioja [2] 56 Gc 30.00S 67.30W
La Rioja 13 Jb 42.20N 2.20W
La Rioja 53 Jh 29.25S 66.50W
Lárisa 6 Ih 39.38N 22.25 E
La Rivière-Thibouville, Nassandres- 12 Ce 49.07N 0.44 E
Lārkāna 25 Dc 27.33N 68.13 E
Larmor-Plage 11 Cg 47.42N 3.23W
Larnaka/Lárnax 23 Dc 34.55N 33.38 E
Lárnax/Larnaka 23 Dc 34.55N 33.38 E
Larne/Latharna 9 Hg 54.51N 5.49W
Larned 45 Gg 38.11N 99.06W
La Robla 13 Gb 42.48N 5.37W
La Roche 63b De 21.28S 168.02 E
La Roche-en-Ardenne 11 Ld 50.11N 5.35 E
La Rochefoucauld 11 Gi 45.44N 0.23 E
La Roche-Guyon 12 De 49.05N 1.38 E
La Rochelle 6 Ff 46.10N 1.09W
La Roche-sur-Yon 11 Eh 46.40N 1.26W
La Roda 13 Je 39.13N 2.09W
La Romana 47 Ke 18.25N 68.58W
La Ronge 42 Ge 55.06N 105.17W
La Ronge, Lac- 38 Id 55.05N 104.59W
Larose 45 Kl 29.35N 90.23W
La Rosita 48 Ic 28.24N 101.43W
Larouco 13 Ec 41.56N 7.40W
Larreynaga 49 Dg 12.40N 86.34W
Larrey Point 59 Dc 20.00S 119.10 E
Larrimah 58 Ef 15.35S 133.12 E
Larsa 24 Kg 31.16N 45.49 E
Lars Christensen Kyst 66 Fe 69.30S 68.00 E
Larsen, Mount- 66 Kf 74.51S 162.12 E
Larsen Ice Shelf 66 Qe 68.30S 62.30W
Lartijas Padomju Socialistiska Respublika/Latvijskaja SSR [2] 19 Cd 57.00N 25.00 E
La Rumorosa 48 Aa 32.34N 116.06W
Laruns 11 Fk 43.00N 0.25W
Larvik 7 Bg 59.04N 10.00 E
La Sabana [Arg.] 55 Ch 27.52S 59.57W
La Sabana [Col.] 54 Ec 2.20N 68.32W
Las Adjuntas, Presa de- 48 Jf 23.55N 98.45W
La Sagra 13 Id 40.05N 4.00W
La Sagra 13 Jg 37.57N 2.34W
La Salle 45 Lf 41.20N 89.06W
La Salle, Pic- 47 Je 18.22N 71.59W
La Sal Mountains 46 Kg 38.30N 109.10W
Las Alpujarras 13 Ih 36.50N 3.25W
La Sanabria 13 Fb 42.08N 6.30W
Las Animas 45 Eg 38.04N 103.13W
Lās 'ānōd 35 Hd 8.26N 47.24 E
La Sarre 42 Jg 48.48N 79.12W
Las Aves, Islas- 54 Ea 11.58N 67.33W
Las Avispas 55 Bi 29.53S 61.18W
Las Bardenas 13 Kb 42.10N 1.25W
Las Bonitas 50 Di 7.52N 65.40W
Las Breñas 56 Hc 27.05S 61.05W
Las Cabezas de San Juan 13 Gh 36.59N 5.56W
Lascahobas 49 Ld 18.50N 71.56W
Lascano 55 Ek 33.40S 54.12W
Las Casitas, Cerro- 47 Cd 23.31N 109.53W
Lascaux, Grotte de- 11 Hi 45.03N 1.11 E
Las Cejas 56 Hc 26.53S 64.44W
Las Chilcas, Arroyo- 55 Cm 37.16S 58.26W
Las Choapas 47 Fe 17.55N 94.05W
Las Cinco Villas 13 Kb 42.05N 1.07W
Las Cruces 43 Fe 32.23N 106.29W
Läsdäred 35 Hc 10.10N 46.01 E
Lās Dawa'o 35 Hc 10.22N 49.03 E
La Segarra 13 Nc 41.30N 1.10 E
La Selva 13 Oc 41.40N 2.50 E
La Serena 13 Gf 38.45N 5.30W
La Serena 53 Ih 29.54S 71.16W
La Seu d'Urgell/Seo de Urgel 13 Nb 42.21N 1.28 E
La-Seyne-sur-Mer 11 Lk 43.06N 5.53 E
Las Flores 56 Ie 36.03S 59.07W
Lāsh-e Joveyn 23 Jc 31.43N 61.37 E
Las Heras 56 Gd 32.51S 68.49W
Lashkar Gāh 22 If 31.35N 64.21 E
Las Hurdes 13 Fd 40.20N 6.20W
La Sila 5 Hh 39.15N 16.30 E
Łasin 10 Pc 53.32N 19.05 E
Łask 10 Pe 51.36N 19.07 E
Las Lajas 56 Fe 38.31S 70.22W
Las Lomitas 56 Hb 24.42S 60.36W
Las Margaritas 48 Ni 16.19N 91.59W
Las Mariñas 13 Da 43.20N 8.15W
Las Marismas 13 Fg 37.00N 6.15W
Las Mercedes 54 Eb 9.07N 66.24W
Las Mestenas 48 Gc 28.13N 104.35W
Las Minas, Cerro- 47 Gf 14.33N 88.39W
Las Minas, Sierra de- 47 Ge 15.05N 90.00W
Las Mixtecas, Sierra del- 48 Ki 17.45N 97.15W
La Sola, Isla- 54 Fa 11.20N 63.34W
La Solana 13 If 38.56N 3.14W
Lasolo 26 Hg 3.29S 122.04 E
La Sorcière 51k Bb 13.59N 60.56W
La Souterraine 11 Hh 46.14N 1.29 E
Las Palmas [3] 32 Ed 28.20N 14.20W
Las Palmas de Gran Canaria 31 Ff 28.06N 15.24W
Las Petas 55 Cc 16.23S 59.11W
La Spezia 6 Gg 44.07N 9.50 E
Las Piedras 56 Id 34.45S 56.13W
Las Plumas 53 Jj 43.40S 67.15W
Lās Qoray 35 Hc 11.15N 48.22 E
Las Rosas 55 Bk 32.28S 61.34W
Lassen Peak 43 Cc 40.29N 121.31W
Lassigny 12 Ee 49.35N 2.51 E
Laßnitz 14 Jd 46.46N 15.32 E
Lasso 64b Ba 15.02N 145.38 E
Las Tablas 49 Gj 7.46N 80.17W
Last Mountain Lake 42 Gf 51.10N 105.15W
Las Toscas 55 Ci 28.21S 59.17W
Lastoursville 36 Bc 0.49S 12.42 E
Lastovo 14 Kh 42.46N 16.55 E
Lastovo 14 Kh 42.45N 16.50 E
Lastovski kanal 14 Kh 42.50N 16.59 E
Las Tres Virgenes, Volcán- 47 Bc 27.27N 112.34W
Las Tunas [3] 49 Ic 21.00N 77.00W
Las Tunas, Punta- 51a Bb 18.30N 66.37W
Las Varillas 56 Hd 31.52S 62.43W
Las Vegas [N.M.-U.S.] 43 Fd 35.36N 105.13W
Las Vegas [Nv.-U.S.] 39 Hf 36.11N 115.08W
Las Villuercas 13 Ge 39.33N 5.27W
Łaszczów 10 Tf 50.32N 23.40 E
Lata 65c Db 14.14S 169.29W
Latacunga 54 Cd 0.55S 78.37W
La Tagua 54 Dd 0.03S 74.40W
Latakia (EN)=Al Lādhiqīyah 22 Ff 35.31N 35.07 E
Latarc, Causse du- 11 Jk 43.57N 3.11 E
Late Island 61 Gc 18.48S 174.39W
Laterza 14 Kj 40.37N 16.48 E
La Teste 11 Ej 44.38N 1.09W
Latgale 8 Lh 56.45N 27.30 E
Latgales Augstiene/Latgalskaja Vozvyšennost 8 Lh 56.10N 27.30 E
Latgalskaja Vozvyšennost/Latgales Augstiene 8 Lh 56.10N 27.30 E
Latharna/Larne 9 Hg 54.51N 5.49W
Lathen 12 Jb 52.52N 7.19 E
La Tigra 55 Bh 27.06S 60.34W
Latina 14 Gi 41.28N 12.52 E
Latisana 14 Ge 45.47N 13.00 E
Latium (EN) = Lazio [2] 14 Gh 42.02N 12.23 E
La Toja 13 Db 42.27N 8.50W
La Toma 56 Gd 33.03S 65.37W
La Tontouta 63b Ce 22.00S 166.15 E
Latorica 10 Rh 48.28N 21.50 E
La Tortuga, Isla- 54 Ea 10.56N 65.20W
La-Tour-du-Pin 11 Li 45.34N 5.27 E
La Trimouille 11 Hh 46.28N 1.03 E
La Trinidad 49 Dg 12.58N 86.14W
La Trinidad de Orichuna 50 Bi 7.07N 69.45W
La Trinité 50 Fe 14.44N 60.58W
Latronico 14 Kj 40.05N 16.01 E
Lattari, Monti- 14 Ij 40.40N 14.30 E
La Tuque 42 Kg 47.27N 72.47W
Lātūr 25 Fe 18.24N 76.35 E
Latvian SSR (EN)=Latvijas PSR [2] 19 Cd 57.00N 25.00 E
Latvijas PSR=Latvian SSR (EN) [2] 19 Cd 57.00N 25.00 E
Latvijskaja Sovetskaja Socialističeskaja Respublika [2] 19 Cd 57.00N 25.00 E
Latvijskaja SSR/Latvijas Padomju Socialistiska Respublika [2] 19 Cd 57.00N 25.00 E
Lau 30 Kh 6.56N 30.16 E
Laubach 12 Kd 50.33N 8.59 E
Lauchert 10 Fh 48.05N 9.15 E
Lauchhammer 10 Je 51.30N 13.48 E
Lauenburg 10 Gc 53.22N 10.34 E
Lauf an der Pegnitz 10 Hg 49.31N 11.17 E
Laughlan Islands 63a Ac 9.15S 153.40 E
Laughlin Peak 45 Dh 36.38N 104.12W
Lau Group 57 Jf 18.20S 178.30W
Lauhanvuori 8 Jb 62.10N 22.10 E
Laujar de Andarax 13 Jh 36.59N 2.51W
Laukaa 7 Fe 62.25N 25.57 E
Laukuva 8 Ji 55.35N 22.08 E
Laulau, Bahia- 64b Ba 15.08N 145.46 E
Launceston [Austl.] 58 Fi 41.26S 147.08 E
Launceston [Eng.-U.K.] 9 Ik 50.38N 4.21W
La Unión [Bol.] 55 Bb 15.18S 61.05W
La Unión [Chile] 56 Ff 40.17S 73.05W
La Unión [Col.] 54 Cc 1.37N 77.08W
La Unión [ElSal.] 47 Gf 13.20N 87.51W
La Unión [Mex.] 48 Ii 17.58N 101.49W
La Unión [Peru] 54 Ce 9.46S 76.48W
La Unión [Sp.] 13 Lg 37.37N 0.52W
La Unión [Ven.] 49 Ni 8.13N 67.46W
Laura 59 Ic 15.34S 144.28 E
La Urbana 50 Ci 7.08N 66.56W
Laurel [Ms.-U.S.] 43 Je 31.42N 89.08W
Laurel [Mt.-U.S.] 43 Fb 45.40N 108.46W
Laureles 55 Ej 31.23S 55.52W
Laurel Hill 44 He 40.02N 79.17W
Laurel Mountain 44 Hf 39.20N 79.50W
Laurens 44 Fh 34.30N 82.01W
Laurentian Plateau (EN)=Laurentien, Plateau- 38 Md 50.00N 70.00W
Laurentian Scarp 44 Ic 45.50N 76.15W
Laurentide Scarp 44 Kb 46.38N 73.00W
Laurentien, Plateau-=Laurentian Plateau (EN) 38 Md 50.00N 70.00W
Lauria 14 Jj 40.02N 15.50 E
Lau Ridge (EN) 3 Kl 25.00S 179.00 E
Laurie River 42 He 56.00N 100.58W
Laurinburg 44 Hh 34.47N 79.27W
Laurium 44 Cb 47.14N 88.26W
Lauro Muller 55 Hi 28.24S 49.23W
Lausanne 6 Gf 46.30N 6.40 E
Lausitzer Gebirge 10 Kf 50.48N 14.40 E
Lausitzer Neiße 10 Kd 52.04N 14.46 E
Laut, Pulau- 26 Ef 4.43N 107.59 E
Laut, Pulau- 21 Nj 3.40S 116.10 E
Lautaret, Col du- 11 Mi 45.02N 6.24 E
Lautaro 56 Fe 38.31S 72.27W
Lautém 26 Ih 8.22S 126.54 E
Lauter 10 Eg 48.58N 8.11 E
Lauterbach 10 Ff 50.38N 9.24 E
Lauterbourg 12 Kf 48.59N 8.11 E
Lauterecken 12 Je 49.39N 7.36 E
Lauthala 63d Cb 16.45S 179.41W
Laut Kecil, Kepulauan- 26 Gg 4.50S 115.45 E
Lautoka 61 Ec 17.37S 177.27 E
Lauvergne Island 64d Cb 7.00N 152.00 E
Lauwersmeer 12 Ia 53.25N 6.15 E
Lauzerte 11 Hj 44.15N 1.08 E
Lauzon 44 Lb 46.50N 71.10W
Lauzoue 11 Gj 44.03N 0.15 E
Lava 10 Rb 54.37N 21.14 E
Lava, Nosy- [Mad.] 37 Hb 12.49S 48.41 E
Lava, Nosy- [Mad.] 37 Hb 14.33S 47.36 E
Lavaca River 45 Hl 28.50N 96.36W
Lava Flow 45 Bi 34.45N 108.20W
Laval 11 Ff 48.01N 0.46W
Lavalle 55 Ci 29.01S 59.11W
Lavalleja [2] 55 El 34.00S 55.00W
Lāvān, Jazīreh-ye- 23 Hd 26.48N 53.00 E
Lavanggu 63a Ed 11.37S 160.15 E
Lavant 14 Id 46.38N 14.56 E
Lavapié, Punta- 52 Ii 37.09S 73.35W
Lāvar Meydān 24 Pg 30.20N 54.30 E
Lavassaare 8 Kf 58.29N 24.16 E
Lavaur 11 Hk 43.42N 1.49 E
La Vecilla 13 Gb 42.51N 5.24W
La Vega 47 Je 19.13N 70.31W
La Vela de Coro 49 Mh 11.27N 69.34W
Lavelanet 11 Hl 42.56N 1.51 E
Lavello 14 Ji 41.03N 15.48 E
La Venta 47 Fe 18.08N 94.03W
Laventie 12 Ed 50.38N 2.46 E
La Ventura 48 Ie 24.37N 100.54W
La Vera 13 Gd 40.05N 5.30W
L'Averdy, Cape- 63a Ba 5.33S 155.04 E
Laverton 59 Ee 28.38S 122.25 E
Lavia 7 Ff 61.36N 22.36 E
La Victoria 54 Ea 10.14N 67.20W
La Vila Jojosa/Villajoyosa 13 Lf 38.30N 0.14W
La Villita, Presa- 48 Hh 18.05N 102.05W
La Viña 54 Ce 6.54S 79.28W

Index Symbols

[1] Independent Nation
[2] State, Region
[3] District, County
[4] Municipality
[5] Colony, Dependency
Continent
Physical Region
Historical or Cultural Region
Mount, Mountain
Volcano
Hill
Mountains, Mountain Range
Hills, Escarpment
Plateau, Upland
Pass, Gap
Plain, Lowland
Delta
Salt Flat
Valley, Canyon
Crater, Cave
Karst Features
Depression
Polder
Desert, Dunes
Forest, Woods
Heath, Steppe
Oasis
Cape, Point
Coast, Beach
Cliff
Peninsula
Isthmus
Sandbank
Island
Atoll
Rock, Reef
Islands, Archipelago
Rocks, Reefs
Coral Reef
Well, Spring
Geyser
River, Stream
Waterfall Rapids
River Mouth, Estuary
Lake
Salt Lake
Intermittent Lake
Reservoir
Swamp, Pond
Canal
Glacier
Ice Shelf, Pack Ice
Ocean
Sea
Gulf, Bay
Strait, Fjord
Lagoon
Bank
Seamount
Tablemount
Ridge
Shelf
Basin
Escarpment, Sea Scarp
Fracture
Trench, Abyss
National Park, Reserve
Point of Interest
Recreation Site
Cave, Cavern
Historic Site
Ruins
Wall, Walls
Church, Abbey
Temple
Scientific Station
Airport
Port
Lighthouse
Mine
Tunnel
Dam, Bridge

La Vôge 11 Mf 48.05N 6.05 E
Lavoisier Island 66 Qe 66.12S 66.44W
Lavougba 35 Cd 5.37N 23.19 E
La Voulte-sur-Rhône 11 Kj 44.48N 4.47 E
Lavouras 55 Db 14.59S 56.47W
Lavras 54 Jh 21.14S 45.00W
Lavras do Sul 55 Fj 30.49S 53.55W
Lavrentija 20 Nc 65.33N 171.02W
Lávrion 15 Hl 37.43N 24.03 E
Lavumisa 37 Ee 27.15S 31.55 E
Lawas 26 Gf 4.51N 115.24 E
Lawdar 23 Gg 13.53N 45.52 E
Lawe 12 Ed 50.38N 2.42 E
Lawers, Ben- 9 Ie 56.33N 4.15W
Lawit, Gunong- 26 Ff 1.23N 112.55 E
Lawqah 24 Jh 29.49N 42.45 E
Lawra 34 Ec 10.39N 2.52W
Lawrence [Ks.-U.S.] 43 Hd 38.58N 95.14W
Lawrence [Ma.-U.S.] 43 Mc 42.42N 71.09W
Lawrence [N.Z.] 62 Cf 45.55S 169.42 E
Lawrenceburg [Ky.-U.S.] 44 Ef 38.02N 84.54W
Lawrenceburg [Tn.-U.S.] 44 Dh 35.15N 87.20W
Lawson, Mount- 59 Ja 7.44S 146.37 E
Lawton 39 Jf 34.37N 98.25W
Lawu, Gunung- 21 Nj 7.38S 111.11 E
Lawz, Jabal al- 24 Fh 28.41N 35.18 E
Laxå 7 Dg 58.59N 14.37 E
Lay 11 Eh 46.18N 1.17W
Laylá 23 Ge 22.17N 46.45 E
Layon 11 Fg 47.20N 0.45W
Layou 51g Bb 15.23N 61.26W
Layou 51n Ba 13.12N 61.17W
Laysan Island 57 Jb 25.50N 171.50W
Layton 46 Jf 41.04N 111.58W
La Zarca 48 Ge 25.50N 104.44W
Lazarev 20 Jf 52.13N 141.35 E
Lazarevac 15 De 44.23N 20.16 E
Lázaro Cárdenas, Presa- 48 Ge 25.35N 105.05W
Lazdijai/Lazdijaj 7 Fi 54.13N 23.33 E
Lazdijaj/Lazdijai 7 Fi 54.13N 23.33 E
Lāzeh 24 Oi 26.48N 53.22 E
Lazio = Latium (EN) [2] 14 Gh 42.02N 12.23 E
Lazo 28 Mc 43.25N 134.01 E
Lazovsk 16 Ff 47.38N 28.12 E
Łazy 10 Pf 50.27N 19.26 E
Lea 9 Nj 51.30N 0.01 E
Lead 43 Gc 44.21N 103.46W
Leader 46 Ka 50.53N 109.31W
Lead Hill 45 Jh 37.06N 92.38W
Leadville 43 Fd 39.15N 106.20W
Leaf River 45 Lk 31.00N 88.45W
League City 45 Il 29.31N 95.05W
Leamington 44 Fd 42.03N 82.36W
Leandro N. Alem 55 Bl 34.30S 61.24W
Leane, Lough-/Loch Léin 9 Di 52.05N 9.35W
Le'an Jiang 28 Dj 28.58N 116.41 E
Learmonth 59 Cd 22.13S 114.04 E
Leavenworth [Ks.-U.S.] 45 Ig 39.19N 94.55W
Leavenworth [Wa.-U.S.] 46 Ec 47.36N 120.40W
Łeba 10 Nb 54.47N 17.33 E
Łeba 10 Nb 54.43N 17.25 E
Lebach 12 Ie 49.24N 6.55 E
Lébamba 36 Bc 2.12S 11.30 E
Lebanon [In.-U.S.] 44 De 40.03N 86.28W
Lebanon [Ky.-U.S.] 44 Eg 37.34N 85.15W
Lebanon [Mo.-U.S.] 45 Jh 37.41N 92.40W
Lebanon [N.H.-U.S.] 44 Kd 43.38N 72.15W
Lebanon [Or.-U.S.] 46 Dd 44.32N 122.54W
Lebanon [Pa.-U.S.] 44 Ie 40.21N 76.25W
Lebanon [Tn.-U.S.] 44 Dg 36.12N 86.18W
Lebanon (EN)=Lubnān [1] 22 Ff 33.50N 35.50 E
Lebanon Mountains (EN)= Lubnān, Jabal- 23 Ec 34.00N 36.30 E
Lebap 18 Cd 41.02N 61.54 E
Le Bec-Hellouin 12 Ce 49.14N 0.43 E
Lebedin 19 De 50.36N 34.30 E
Lebediny 20 He 58.25N 125.58 E
Lebedjan 19 De 53.02N 39.07 E
Le Bény-Bocage 12 Bf 48.56N 0.50W
Lebjažje [Kaz.-U.S.S.R.] 19 He 51.28N 77.46 E
Lebjažje [R.S.F.S.R.] 17 Mi 55.16N 66.29 E
Le Blanc 11 Hh 46.38N 1.04 E
Lebo 36 Db 4.29N 23.57 E
Lebomboberge 30 Kk 26.15S 32.00 E
Lebombo Mountains 30 Kk 26.15S 32.00 E
Lębork 10 Nb 54.33N 17.44 E
Le Bourget 12 Ef 48.56N 2.25 E
Lebrija 13 Fh 36.55N 6.04W
Łebsko, Jezioro- 10 Nb 54.44N 17.24 E
Lebu 56 Fe 37.37S 73.39W
Le Carbet 51h Ab 14.43N 61.11W
Le Cateau 12 Fd 50.06N 3.33 E
Le Catelet 12 Fd 50.01N 3.15 E
Lecce 6 Hg 40.23N 18.11 E
Lecco 14 De 45.51N 9.23 E
Lech 10 Gh 48.44N 10.56 E
Lech 14 Ec 47.12N 10.09 E
Le Champ du Feu 11 Nf 48.24N 7.15 E
Lechang 27 Jf 25.15N 113.25 E
Le Château-d'Oléron 11 Ei 45.54N 1.12W
Le Chesne 11 Ke 49.31N 4.46 E
Le Cheylard 11 Kj 44.54N 4.25 E
Lechfeld 10 Gh 48.10N 10.50 E
Lechiguiri, Cerro- 48 Li 16.43N 95.30W
Lechtaler Alpen 14 Ec 47.15N 10.30 E
Léconi 36 Bc 1.11S 13.16 E
Léconi 36 Bc 1.35S 14.14 E
Le Cornate 14 Eg 43.10N 10.58 E
Le Coudray-Saint-Germer 12 De 49.25N 1.50 E
Le Creusot 11 Kh 46.48N 4.26 E
Le Croisic 11 Dg 47.18N 2.30W
Le Crotoy 12 Dd 50.13N 1.37 E
Łęczna 10 Se 51.19N 22.52 E
Łęczyca 10 Pd 52.04N 19.13 E
Led 7 Ke 62.20N 43.00 E
Lede 12 Fd 50.57N 3.59 E
Ledesma 13 Gc 41.05N 6.00W
Le Diamant 51h Ac 14.29N 61.02W
Ledjanaja, Gora- [R.S.F.S.R.] 21 Tc 61.45N 171.15 E
Ledjanaja, Gora- [R.S.F.S.R.] 21 Qe 49.28N 142.45 E
Lednik Entuziastov 66 Cf 70.30S 16.00 E
Lednik Mušketova 66 Cf 72.00S 14.00 E
Ledo, Cabo- 36 Bd 9.41S 13.12 E
Ledolom Tajmyrski 66 Ge 66.00S 83.00 E
Le Donjon 11 Jh 46.21N 3.48 E
Le Dorat 11 Hh 46.13N 1.05 E
Lędyczek 10 Mc 53.33N 16.58 E
Lee/An Laoi 9 Ej 51.55N 8.30W
Leech Lake 43 Ib 47.09N 94.23W
Leeds [Al.-U.S.] 44 Di 33.33N 86.33W
Leeds [Eng.-U.K.] 6 Fe 53.50N 1.35W
Leeds [N.D.-U.S.] 45 Gb 48.17N 99.27W
Leek 12 Ia 53.10N 6.24 E
Leer 10 Dc 53.14N 7.26 E
Leer (Ostfriesland) 10 Dc 53.14N 7.26 E
Leerdam 12 Hc 51.53N 5.06 E
Lées 11 Fk 43.38N 0.14W
Leesburg 43 Kf 29.49N 81.53W
Leeste, Weyhe- 12 Kb 52.59N 8.50 E
Leesville 45 Jk 31.08N 93.16W
Leeuwarden 11 La 53.12N 5.46 E
Leeuwarderadeel 12 Ha 53.16N 5.46 E
Leeuwarderadeel-Stiens 12 Ha 53.16N 5.46 E
Leeuwin, Cape- 59 Cf 34.25S 115.00 E
Leeward Islands 47 Le 17.00N 63.00W
Leeward Islands (EN)=Sous le Vent, Iles- 57 Lf 16.38S 151.30W
Léfini 36 Cc 2.57S 16.10 E
Lefka 15 Jh 41.52N 26.16 E
Lefke/Levka 24 Ee 35.07N 32.51 E
Lefkosa/Levkōsia=Nicosia (EN) 22 Ff 35.10N 33.22 E
Le François 51h Bb 14.37N 60.54W
Lefroy, Lake- 59 Ef 31.15S 121.40 E
Łęg 10 Rf 50.38N 21.49 E
Leganés 13 Id 40.19N 3.45W
Legazpi 22 Oh 13.09N 123.44 E
Legden 12 Jb 52.02N 7.06 E
Legges Tor 59 Jh 41.32S 147.40 E
Leggett 46 Dg 39.52N 123.43W
Leghorn (EN)=Livorno 6 Hg 43.33N 10.19 E
Legionowo 10 Qd 52.25N 20.56 E
Léglise 12 He 49.48N 5.32 E
Legnago 14 Fe 45.11N 11.18 E
Legnano 14 Ce 45.36N 8.54 E
Legnica [2] 10 Me 51.15N 16.10 E
Legnica 10 Me 51.13N 16.09 E
Le Grand-Quevilly 12 De 49.25N 1.02 E
Le Grand Veymont 11 Lj 44.52N 5.32 E
Le Grau-du-Roi 11 Kk 43.32N 4.08 E
Léguer 11 Cf 48.44N 3.32W
Leh 25 Fb 34.10N 77.35 E
Le Havre 6 Gf 49.30N 0.08 E
Lehi 46 Jf 40.24N 111.51W
Lehmann 55 Bj 31.08S 61.27W
Le Hohneck 11 Nf 48.02N 7.01 E
Le Houlme 12 De 49.31N 1.02 E
Lehrte 10 Fd 52.23N 9.58 E
Lehtimäki 8 Jb 62.47N 23.55 E
Lehua Island 65a Aa 22.01N 160.06W
Lehututu 37 Cd 23.53S 21.49 E
Leibnitz 14 Jd 46.46N 15.32 E
Leibo 27 Hf 28.13N 103.34 E
Leicester 6 Fe 52.38N 1.05W
Leicester 9 Mi 52.40N 1.00W
Leicestershire [3] 9 Mi 52.38N 1.00W
Leichhardt Range 59 Jd 20.40S 147.05 E
Leichhardt River 59 Hc 17.35S 139.48 E
Leiden 11 Kc 52.09N 4.30 E
Leidschendam 12 Gb 52.05N 4.26 E
Leie 11 Jc 51.03N 3.43 E
Leifear/Lifford 9 Fg 54.50N 7.29W
Leigh Creek 58 Eh 30.28S 138.25 E
Leighton Buzzard 12 Bc 51.55N 0.39W
Leigong Shan 27 If 26.23N 108.15 E
Leikanger 7 Ae 62.07N 5.20 E
Léim an Mhadaidh/Limavady 9 Gf 55.03N 6.57W
Leimen 12 Ke 49.21N 8.41 E
Leimus 49 Ef 14.44N 84.07W
Leine 10 Fd 52.40N 9.40 E
Leinster/Laighean 9 Gh 53.00N 7.00W
Leipzig 6 He 51.18N 12.20 E
Leipzig [2] 10 Ie 51.20N 12.20 E
Leira 8 Cd 60.58N 9.18 E
Leiria [2] 13 De 39.40N 8.50W
Leiria 13 De 39.45N 8.48W
Leirvik 7 Ag 59.47N 5.30 E
Leisi/Lejsi 8 Jf 58.33N 22.30 E
Leisler, Mount- 59 Fd 23.30S 129.20 E
Leiston 12 Db 52.12N 1.34 E
Leitariegos, Puerto de- 13 Fa 43.00N 6.25W
Leitha 14 Lc 47.52N 17.18 E
Leithagebirge 14 Kc 47.58N 16.40 E
Leitir Ceanainn/Letterkenny 9 Fg 54.57N 7.44W
Leitrim/Liatroim [2] 9 Eg 54.20N 8.20W
Leiva, Cerro- 54 Dc 2.54N 74.48W
Leiyang 27 Jf 26.30N 112.57 E
Leizhou → Haikang 27 Jg 20.56N 110.06 E
Leizhou Bandao 21 Ng 20.40N 110.05 E
Lejasciems 8 Lg 57.08N 26.36 E
Lejsi/Leisi 8 Jf 58.33N 22.30 E
Lek 11 Lc 52.00N 6.00 E
Leka 7 Cd 65.05N 11.37 E
Lékana 36 Cc 2.19S 14.36 E
Leketi, Monts de la- 30 Ii 2.34S 14.17 E
Lekhainá 15 El 37.56N 21.16 E
Lekhal 13 Ph 36.20N 3.51 E
Lekitobi 26 Hg 1.58S 124.33 E
Lekki Lagoon 34 Fd 6.30N 4.07 E
Leknes 7 Cb 68.10N 13.42 E
Łęknica 10 Ke 51.32N 14.48 E
Lékoumou [3] 36 Bc 3.00S 13.50 E
Leksand 7 Df 60.44N 15.01 E
Leksozero, Ozero- 7 He 63.45N 31.00 E
Leksula 26 Ig 3.46S 126.31 E
Leksvik 7 Ce 63.40N 10.37 E
Le Lamentin 50 Fe 14.37N 61.01W
Leland 45 Kj 33.24N 90.54W
Lelång 8 Ee 59.10N 12.10 E
Le Lavandou 11 Mk 43.08N 6.22 E
Lelčicy 16 Fd 51.49N 28.21 E
Leleiwi Point 65a Gd 19.44N 155.00W
Lelepa 63b Dc 17.36S 168.13 E
Leleque 56 Ff 42.23S 71.03W
Leli 63a Ec 8.45S 161.02 E
Leli → Tianlin 27 Ig 24.22N 106.11 E
Lelija 14 Mg 43.26N 18.29 E
Leling 28 Df 37.44N 117.13 E
Léliogat 63b Ce 21.18S 167.35 E
Lelle 7 Fg 58.53N 25.00 E
Le Locle 14 Ac 47.05N 6.45 E
Le Lorrain 51h Ab 14.50N 61.04W
Lelystad 11 Lb 52.31N 5.27 E
Le Madonie 14 Hm 37.50N 14.00 E
Le Maire, Estrecho de- 56 Hh 54.50S 65.00W
Léman, Lac-=Geneva, Lake- (EN) 5 Gf 46.25N 6.30 E
Leman Bank 9 Oh 53.10N 1.58 E
Lemankoa 63a Ba 5.03S 154.34 E
Le Mans 6 Gf 48.00N 0.12 E
Le Marin 51h Bc 14.28N 60.52W
Le Mars 45 He 42.47N 96.10W
Le Mas-d'Azil 11 Hk 43.05N 1.22 E
Lembach 12 Je 49.00N 7.48 E
Lembeck 12 Ic 51.44N 6.59 E
Lemberg 12 Je 49.00N 7.23 E
Lembolovskaja Vozvyšennost 8 Md 60.50N 30.15 E
Lembruch 12 Kb 52.32N 8.21 E
Leme 55 If 22.12S 47.24W
Lemelerberg 12 Ib 52.29N 6.23 E
Lemesós/Limassol 23 Dc 34.40N 33.02 E
Lemgo 10 Ed 52.02N 8.54 E
Lemhi Range 46 Id 44.30N 113.25W
Lemieux Islands 42 Ld 64.00N 64.20W
Lemju 17 He 63.50N 56.57 E
Lemland 8 Id 60.05N 20.10 E
Lemmer, Lemsterland- 12 Hb 52.51N 5.42 E
Lemmon 43 Gb 45.56N 102.10W
Lemmon, Mount- 46 Jj 32.26N 110.47W
Lemnos (EN)=Límnos 5 Ih 39.55N 25.15 E
Le-Molay-Littry 12 Be 49.15N 0.53W
Le-Mont-Saint-Michel 11 Ef 48.38N 1.30W
Le Morne Rouge 51h Ab 14.46N 61.08W
Lemotol Bay 64d Bb 7.21N 151.35 E
Le Moyne, Lac - 42 Ke 57.00N 68.00W
Lempa, Río- 47 Gf 13.14N 88.49W
Lempäälä 8 Jc 61.19N 23.45 E
Lempira [3] 49 Cf 14.20N 88.40W
L'Empordà/Ampurdán 13 Ob 42.12N 2.45 E
Lemro 25 Id 20.25N 93.20 E
Lemsid 32 Ed 26.33N 13.51W
Lemsterland 12 Hb 52.51N 5.42 E
Lemsterland-Lemmer 12 Hb 52.51N 5.42 E
Le Murge 5 Hg 40.50N 16.40 E
Le Muy 11 Mk 43.28N 6.33 E
Lemvig 8 Ch 56.32N 8.18 E
Lemya 17 Jc 66.30N 62.00 E
Lena 21 Ob 72.25N 126.40 E
Lena, Mount- 46 Kf 40.50N 109.27W
Lénakel 63b Dd 19.32S 169.16 E
Lena Mountains (EN) = Prilenskoje Plato 21 Oc 60.45N 125.00 E
Lena Tablemount (EN) 30 Ln 53.00S 45.00 E
Lençóis Paulista 55 Hf 22.36S 48.47W
Lendava 14 Kd 46.34N 16.27 E
Lendery 7 He 63.26N 31.12 E
Lendinara 14 Fe 45.05N 11.36 E
Le Neubourg 12 Ce 49.09N 0.55 E
Lenger 19 Gg 42.10N 69.55 E
Lengerich 10 Dd 52.11N 7.52 E
Lengoué 36 Cb 0.49N 15.47 E
Lengshuijiang 27 Jf 27.41N 111.28 E
Lengua de Vaca, Punta- 56 Fd 30.14S 71.38W
Lengulu 36 Eb 3.15N 26.30 E
Lenhovda 7 Dh 57.00N 15.17 E
Lenina, Pik-=Lenin Peak (EN) 21 Jf 39.19N 73.01 E
Leninabad 22 Ie 40.17N 69.37 E
Leninabadskaja Oblast [3] 19 Gh 40.00N 69.10 E
Leninakan 6 Kg 40.47N 43.50 E
Lenin Canal (EN)=Volgo-Donskoj sudohodny kanal imeni V. I. Lenina 5 Kf 48.40N 43.37 E
Leningrad 6 Jc 59.55N 30.15 E
Leningradskaja 66 Je 69.30S 159.23 E
Leningradskaja 16 Kf 46.17N 39.25 E
Leningradskaja Oblast [3] 19 Dd 60.00N 31.40 E
Leningradski [R.S.F.S.R.] 20 Mc 69.17N 178.10 E
Leningradski [Tad.-U.S.S.R.] 19 Hh 38.09N 70.01 E
Lenino 16 Ig 45.17N 35.44 E
Leninogorsk [Kaz.-U.S.S.R.] 22 Kd 50.27N 83.32 E
Leninogorsk [R.S.F.S.R.] 19 Fe 54.38N 52.30 E
Lenin Peak (EN)=Lenina, Pik- 21 Jf 39.19N 73.01 E
Leninsk [R.S.F.S.R.] 16 Ne 48.42N 45.11 E
Leninsk [Tur.-U.S.S.R.] 18 Bc 42.04N 59.24 E
Leninsk [Uzb.-U.S.S.R.] 18 Id 40.40N 72.20 E
Leninski [Kaz.-U.S.S.R.] 19 He 52.13N 76.50 E
Leninski [Mold.-U.S.S.R.] 15 Lb 47.50N 28.16 E
Leninski [R.S.F.S.R.] 20 He 58.32N 125.58 E
Leninsk-Kuznecki 22 Kd 54.38N 86.10 E
Leninskoje [Kaz.-U.S.S.R.] 19 Ge 54.05N 65.23 E
Leninskoje [R.S.F.S.R.] 7 Lg 58.21N 47.07 E
Leninskoje [R.S.F.S.R.] 20 Ig 47.59N 132.38 E
Leninváros 10 Ri 47.56N 21.05 E
Lenkoran 6 Kh 38.44N 48.50 E
Lenne 10 De 51.25N 7.30 E
Lenne 12 Jc 51.15N 7.50 E
Lennestadt 12 Kc 51.08N 8.01 E
Lennestadt-Grevenbrück 12 Kc 51.08N 8.01 E
Lennox Hills 9 Ie 56.05N 4.10W
Leno-Angarskoje Plato 20 Fe 55.00N 104.30 E
Lenoir 44 Gh 35.55N 81.32W
Le Nouvion-en-Thiérache 12 Fd 50.01N 3.47 E
Lens 11 Id 50.26N 2.50 E
Lensk 22 Nc 61.00N 114.50 E
Lenti 10 Mi 46.37N 16.33 E
Lentiira 7 Gd 64.21N 29.50 E
Lentini 14 Jm 37.17N 15.01 E
Lentua 7 Gd 64.14N 29.36 E
Lentvaris 8 Kj 54.38N 25.13 E
Léo 34 Ec 11.06N 2.06W
Leoben 14 Jc 47.23N 15.06 E
Léogâne 49 Kd 18.31N 72.38W
Leok 26 Hf 1.11N 121.26 E
Leola 45 Gd 45.43N 98.56W
Leominster 9 Ki 52.14N 2.45W
León 13 Gc 42.00N 6.00W
Léon 11 Ek 43.53N 1.18W
León [Mex.] 39 Ig 21.10N 101.42W
León [Nic.] [3] 49 Dg 12.35N 86.35W
León [Nic.] 39 Kh 12.26N 86.54W
León [Sp.] 6 Fg 42.36N 5.34W
León [Sp.] [3] 13 Gb 42.40N 6.00W
León, Montes de- 13 Fb 42.30N 6.20W
León, Puerto del- 13 Hh 36.50N 4.21W
Leonardville 37 Bd 23.29S 18.49 E
Leonberg 12 Kf 48.48N 9.01 E
Leone, Monte- 14 Cd 46.15N 8.10 E
Leones 55 Ak 32.39S 62.18W
Leonessa 14 Gh 42.34N 12.58 E
Leonforte 14 Im 37.38N 14.23 E
Leōnídhion 15 Fl 37.10N 22.52 E
Leonora 58 Dg 28.53S 121.20 E
Leon River 45 Hk 30.59N 97.24W
Leopold and Astrid Coast 66 Ge 67.10S 84.10 E
Leopoldina 54 Jh 21.32S 42.38W
Leopold McClintock, Cape - 42 Fa 77.38N 116.20W
Leopoldo de Bulhões 55 Hc 16.37S 48.46W
Leopoldsburg 12 Hc 51.07N 5.15 E
Leopoldville → Kinshasa 31 Ii 4.18S 15.18 E
Leovo 16 Ff 46.29N 28.15 E
Lepa 65c Bb 14.01S 171.28W
Le Palais 11 Cg 47.21N 3.09W
Lepar, Pulau- 26 Eg 2.57S 106.50 E
Le Parcq 12 Ed 50.23N 2.06 E
Lepaterique 49 Df 14.02N 87.27W
Lepe 13 Eg 37.15N 7.12W
Lepel 19 Ce 54.53N 28.46 E
Lepenica 15 Ee 44.10N 21.08 E
Le Petit Caux 12 De 49.55N 1.20 E
Le Petit-Couronne 12 De 49.23N 1.01 E
Le Petit-Quevilly 12 De 49.26N 1.02 E
Lephepe 37 Dd 23.22S 25.52 E
Leping 27 Kf 28.59N 117.07 E
Lepini, Monti- 14 Gi 41.35N 13.00 E
Le Plessis-Belleville 12 Ee 49.06N 2.46 E
Le Pont-de-Claix 11 Li 45.07N 5.42 E
Le Portel 12 Dd 50.42N 1.34 E
Leppävesi 8 Kb 62.15N 25.55 E
Leppävirta 8 Lb 62.29N 27.47 E
Le Prêcheur 51h Ab 14.48N 61.14W
Lepsøya 8 Bb 62.35N 6.10 E
Lepsy 18 La 46.18N 78.20 E
Lepsy 19 Hf 46.12N 78.55 E
Leptis Magna 33 Bc 32.38N 14.18 E
Le Puy 11 Ji 45.02N 3.53 E
Leqemt (EN)=Nekemt 31 Kh 9.05N 36.33 E
Le Quesnoy 12 Fd 50.15N 3.38 E
Lercara Friddi 14 Hm 37.45N 13.36 E
Lerchenfeld Glacier 66 Af 77.50S 34.50W
Lere 34 Gc 10.23N 8.35 E
Léré 35 Ad 9.39N 14.13 E
Lérida 54 Dc 0.06N 70.43W
Lérida [3] 13 Nc 42.00N 1.10 E
Lérida/Lleida 13 Mc 41.37N 0.37 E
Lérins, Iles de- 11 Nk 43.31N 7.03 E
Lerma 13 Ib 42.02N 3.45W
Lerma, Río- 48 Hg 20.13N 102.46W
Lermontov 16 Mg 44.06N 42.45 E
Le Robert 51h Bb 14.41N 60.57W
Léros 15 Jl 37.08N 26.50 E
Lerum 7 Ch 57.46N 12.16 E
Lerwick 9 La 60.09N 1.09W
Léry 12 De 49.17N 1.13 E
Les Abrets 11 Li 45.32N 5.35 E
Le Saint-Esprit 51h Bb 14.34N 60.57W
Les Alberes/Albères, Montes- 11 In 42.28N 2.56 E
Les Allobroges 63b Dc 16.47S 168.09 E
Les Andelys 11 He 49.15N 1.25 E
Les Anses-d'Arlets 51h Ac 14.29N 61.05W
Les-Baux-de-Provence 11 Kk 43.45N 4.48 E
Les Borges Blanques/Borjas Blancas 13 Mc 41.31N 0.52 E
Lesbos (EN)=Lésvos 5 Ih 39.10N 26.32 E
L'Escala/La Escala 13 Pb 42.07N 3.08 E
Les Cayes 47 Je 18.12N 73.45W
Les Coëvrons 11 Ff 48.12N 0.10W
Le Serre 14 Kl 38.30N 16.30 E
Les Escoumins 44 Ma 48.25N 69.29W
Les Eyzies-de-Tayac 11 Hj 44.56N 1.01 E
Les Falaises 12 Ce 49.44N 0.21 E
Leshan 27 Hf 29.34N 103.45 E
Les Herbiers 11 Eh 46.52N 1.01W
Lesina, Lago di- 14 Ji 41.55N 15.25 E
Lesja 8 Cb 62.07N 8.52 E
Lesjöfors 7 Dg 59.59N 14.11 E
Leskino 20 Cb 72.25N 79.40 E
Lesko 10 Sg 49.29N 22.21 E
Leskov 66 Ad 56.40S 28.10W
Leskovac 15 Eg 42.59N 21.57 E
Leskoviku 15 Di 40.09N 20.35 E
Les Mangles 51e Ab 16.23N 61.27W
Les Mauges 11 Fg 47.10N 1.00W
Les Minquiers 9 Km 48.58N 2.08W
Les Monédières 11 Hi 45.30N 1.52 E
Les Mureaux 12 Df 49.00N 1.55 E
Lesnaja 10 Vd 52.55N 25.52 E
Lesnaja 16 Cc 52.11N 23.30 E
Lesneven 11 Bf 48.34N 4.19W
Lešnica 15 Ce 44.39N 19.19 E
Lesnoj [R.S.F.S.R.] 19 Gd 57.01N 67.50 E
Lesnoj [R.S.F.S.R.] 19 Fd 59.49N 52.10 E
Lesnoj, Ostrov- 8 Md 60.02N 28.20 E
Lesný 10 If 50.02N 12.37 E
Lesogorski 8 Mc 61.01N 28.51 E
Lesosibirsk 22 Ld 58.15N 92.30 E
Lesotho [1] 31 Jk 29.30S 28.30 E
Lesozavodsk 20 Ig 45.26N 133.25 E
Lesozavodski 7 Hc 66.45N 32.50 E
Lesparre-Médoc 11 Fi 45.18N 0.56W
L'Espérance Rock 57 Jh 31.26S 178.54W
Les Ponts-de-Cé 11 Fg 47.25N 0.31W
Les Posets 13 Mb 42.39N 0.25 E
Les Sables-d'Olonne 11 Eh 46.30N 1.47W
Lessay 11 Ee 49.13N 1.32W
Lesse 11 Kd 50.14N 4.54 E
Lessebo 7 Dh 56.45N 15.16 E
Lessen/Lessines 12 Fd 50.43N 3.50 E
Les Sept Iles 11 Cf 48.53N 3.28W
Lesser Antilles (EN)= Antillas Menores 38 Mh 15.00N 61.00W
Lesser Caucasus (EN)= Maly Kavkaz 5 Kg 41.00N 44.35 E
Lesser Khingan Range (EN)= Xiao Hinggan Ling 21 Oe 48.45N 127.00 E
Lesser Slave Lake 38 Hd 55.25N 115.30W
Lesser Sunda Islands (EN) 21 Oj 9.13S 121.12 E
Lessines/Lessen 12 Fd 50.43N 3.50 E
Lessini 14 Fe 45.41N 11.13 E
Les Tantes 51p Bb 12.19N 61.33W
Les Thilliers-en-Vexin 12 De 49.14N 1.36 E
Les Triagoz 11 Cf 48.53N 3.40W
Les Trois-Ilets 51h Ab 14.33N 61.03W
Lešukonskoje 7 Kd 64.52N 45.40 E
Lésvos=Lesbos (EN) 5 Ih 39.10N 26.32 E
Leszno [2] 10 Me 51.50N 16.35 E
Leszno 10 Me 51.51N 16.35 E
Letälven 8 Fe 59.05N 14.20 E
Le Tanargue 11 Kj 44.37N 4.09 E
Letchworth 12 Bc 51.58N 0.13W
Letea, Ostrovul- 15 Md 45.20N 29.20 E
Le Teil 11 Kj 44.33N 4.41 E
Letenye 10 Mj 46.26N 16.44 E
Lethbridge 39 He 49.42N 110.50W
Lethem 53 Ke 3.20N 59.50W
Le Thillot 11 Mg 47.53N 6.46 E
Leti, Kepulauan-=Leti Islands (EN) 26 Ih 8.13S 127.50 E
Letiahau 30 Jk 21.04S 24.25 E
Leticia 53 Jf 4.09S 69.57W
Leti Islands (EN)=Leti, Kepulauan- 26 Ih 8.13S 127.50 E
Leting 28 Ee 39.25N 118.55 E
Letka 7 Mg 58.59N 50.14 E
Letlhakane 37 Dd 21.25S 25.36 E
Letnerečenski 7 Id 64.19N 34.25 E
Letni Bereg 7 Jd 64.50N 38.20 E
Letohrad 10 Mf 50.03N 16.31 E
Le Touquet-Paris-Plage 11 Hd 50.31N 1.35 E
Letovice 10 Mg 49.33N 16.36 E
Letpadan 25 Je 17.47N 95.45 E
Le Translay 12 De 49.58N 1.41 E
Le Tréport 11 Hd 50.04N 1.22 E
Letsôk-aw Kyun 25 Jf 11.37N 98.15 E
Letterkenny/Leitir = Ceanainn 9 Fg 54.57N 7.44W
Leu 15 Ge 44.11N 24.00 E
Leuca 14 Mk 39.48N 18.21 E
Leucas (EN) = Levkás 15 Dk 38.43N 20.38 E
Leucate 11 Jl 42.55N 3.02 E
Leucate, Étang de- 11 Il 42.51N 3.00 E
Leuk 14 Bd 46.20N 7.38 E
Leukónoikon 24 Ee 35.15N 33.42 E
Leulumoega 65c Ba 13.49S 171.55W
Leuna 10 Ie 51.19N 12.01 E
Leušeny 15 Lc 46.51N 28.11 E
Leuser, Gunung- 21 Li 3.45N 97.11 E
Leutkirch im Allgäu 10 Gi 47.50N 10.02 E
Leuven/Louvain 11 Kd 50.53N 4.42 E
Leuze-en-Hainaut 12 Fd 50.36N 3.36 E
Levádhia 15 Fk 38.26N 22.53 E
Levaja Hetta 20 Cc 65.15N 73.20 E
Levanger 7 Ce 63.45N 11.18 E
Levante, Riviera di- 14 Df 44.15N 9.30 E
Levanzo 14 Gm 38.00N 12.20 E
Levaši 16 Oh 42.27N 47.20 E
Le Vauclin 51h Bb 14.33N 60.51W
Levelland 45 Ej 33.35N 102.23W
Lévêque, Cape- 59 Ec 16.25S 122.55 E
Le Verdon-sur-Mer 11 Ei 45.33N 1.04W
Leverkusen 10 Ce 51.01N 6.59 E
Leverkusen-Opladen 10 De 51.04N 7.01 E
Lévèzou 11 Ij 44.09N 2.53 E
Levice 10 Oh 48.13N 18.37 E
Levico Terme 14 Fd 46.01N 11.18 E
Le Vigan 11 Jk 43.59N 3.36 E
Levin 61 Eh 40.37S 175.17 E
Lévis 42 Kg 46.48N 71.10W
Levisa Fork 44 Ff 38.06N 82.37W
Levítha 15 Jm 37.00N 26.28 E
Levittown 44 Je 40.09N 74.50W
Levka/Lefke 24 Ee 35.07N 32.51 E
Levká Óri 15 Gn 35.20N 24.00 E
Levkás 15 Dk 38.50N 20.42 E
Levkás = Leucas (EN) 15 Dk 38.43N 20.38 E

Index Symbols

[1] Independent Nation
[2] State, Region
[3] District, County
[4] Municipality
[5] Colony, Dependency
Continent
Physical Region
Historical or Cultural Region
Mount, Mountain
Volcano
Hill
Mountains, Mountain Range
Hills, Escarpment
Plateau, Upland
Pass, Gap
Plain, Lowland
Delta
Salt Flat
Valley, Canyon
Crater, Cave
Karst Features
Depression
Polder
Desert, Dunes
Forest, Woods
Heath, Steppe
Oasis
Cape, Point
Coast, Beach
Cliff
Peninsula
Isthmus
Sandbank
Island
Atoll
Rock, Reef
Islands, Archipelago
Rocks, Reefs
Coral Reef
Well, Spring
Geyser
River, Stream
Waterfall Rapids
River Mouth, Estuary
Lake
Salt Lake
Intermittent Lake
Reservoir
Swamp, Pond
Canal
Glacier
Ice Shelf, Pack Ice
Ocean
Sea
Gulf, Bay
Strait, Fjord
Lagoon
Bank
Seamount
Tablemount
Ridge
Shelf
Basin
Escarpment, Sea Scarp
Fracture
Trench, Abyss
National Park, Reserve
Point of Interest
Recreation Site
Cave, Cavern
Historic Site
Ruins
Wall, Walls
Church, Abbey
Temple
Scientific Station
Airport
Port
Lighthouse
Mine
Tunnel
Dam, Bridge

Levkōsia/Lefkosa=Nicosia (EN) 22 Ff 35.10N 33.22 E
Levoča 10 Qg 49.02N 20.35 E
Levroux 11 Hh 46.59N 1.37 E
Levski 15 If 43.22N 25.08 E
Lev Tolstoj 16 Kc 53.12N 39.28 E
Levuka 63d Bb 17.41S 178.50 E
Levuo/Lévuo 8 Kh 56.02N 24.28 E
Lévuo/Levuo 8 Kh 56.02N 24.28 E
Lewes [De.-U.S.] 44 Jf 38.47N 75.08W
Lewes [Eng.-U.K.] 9 Nk 50.52N 0.01 E
Lewin Brzeski 10 Nf 50.46N 17.37 E
Lewis, Butt of- 9 Gc 58.31N 6.15W
Lewis, Isle of- 5 Fd 58.10N 6.40W
Lewis and Clark Lake 45 He 42.50N 97.45W
Lewisburg 44 Gg 37.49N 80.28W
Lewis Pass 62 Ee 42.24S 172.24 E
Lewis Range 38 He 48.30N 113.15W
Lewis River 46 Dd 45.51N 122.48W
Lewis Smith Lake 44 Dh 34.00N 87.07W
Lewiston [Id.-U.S.] 39 He 46.25N 117.01W
Lewiston [Me.-U.S.] 43 Mc 44.06N 70.13W
Lewistown [Mt.-U.S.] 43 Fb 47.04N 109.26W
Lewistown [Pa.-U.S.] 44 Ie 40.37N 77.36W
Lewisville 45 Jj 33.22N 93.35W
Lexington [Ky.-U.S.] 39 Kf 38.03N 84.30W
Lexington [Nb.-U.S.] 43 Hc 40.47N 99.45W
Lexington [N.C.-U.S.] 44 Gh 35.49N 80.15W
Lexington [Ok.-U.S.] 45 Hi 35.01N 97.20W
Lexington [Va.-U.S.] 44 Hg 37.47N 79.27W
Leygues, Iles- 30 Nm 48.45S 69.30 E
Leyre 11 Ej 44.39N 1.01W
Leysdown-on-Sea 12 Cc 51.23N 0.55 E
Leyte 21 Oh 10.50N 124.50 E
Lez 11 Kj 44.13N 4.43 E
Ležajsk 10 Sf 50.16N 22.24 E
Lézard, Pointe à- 51e Ab 16.08N 61.47W
Lézarde, Rivière- 51h Ab 14.36N 61.01W
Lezha 15 Ch 41.47N 19.39 E
Lézignan-Corbières 11 Ik 43.12N 2.46 E
Lgov 19 De 51.41N 35.17 E
Lhari 27 Fe 30.48N 93.25 E
Lhasa 22 Lg 29.42N 91.07 E
Lhazê 27 Ef 29.13N 87.44 E
Lhazhong 27 Ee 31.28N 86.36 E
Lhokseumawe 26 Ce 5.10N 97.08 E
Lhoksukon 26 Ce 5.03N 97.19 E
L'Hôpital 12 Ie 49.10N 6.44 E
Lhorong 27 Ge 30.45N 95.48 E
L'Hospitalet de l'Infant/Hospitalet del Infante 13 Md 40.59N 0.56 E
Lhozhag 27 Ff 28.18N 90.51 E
Lhünzhub (Poindo) 27 Fe 30.17N 91.20 E
Liádhi 15 Jm 36.55N 26.10 E
Liákoura 15 Fk 38.32N 22.37 E
Liamone 11a Aa 42.04N 8.43 E
Liancheng 27 Kf 25.48N 116.48 E
Liancourt 12 Ee 49.20N 2.28 E
Liane 12 Dd 50.43N 1.36 E
Liangcheng 28 Bd 40.32N 112.28 E
Liangpran, Gunung- 26 Ff 1.04N 114.23 E
Liangshan (Houji) 28 Dg 35.48N 116.07 E
Liangzhou→Wuwei 22 Mf 37.58N 102.48 E
Liangzi Hu 27 Je 30.15N 114.32 E
Lianjiang 27 Jg 21.42N 110.14 E
Lianshui 28 Eh 33.47N 119.16 E
Lianxian 27 Jg 24.48N 112.26 E
Lianyin 27 La 53.26N 123.50 E
Lianyungang 27 Ke 34.38N 119.27 E
Lianyungang (Xinpu) 28 Nf 34.34N 119.15 E
Lianzhou → Hepu 27 Ig 21.40N 109.12 E
Lianzhushan 28 Kb 45.28N 131.45 E
Liaocheng 27 Kd 36.27N 115.58 E
Liaodong Bandao=Liaotung Peninsula (EN) 21 Of 40.00N 122.20 E
Liaodong Wan=Liaotung, Gulf of- (EN) 27 Lc 40.00N 121.30 E
Liao He 21 Oe 40.39N 122.12 E
Liaoning Sheng (Liao-ning Sheng) [2] 27 Lc 41.00N 123.00 E
Liao-ning Sheng→Liaoning Sheng [2] 27 Lc 41.00N 123.00 E
Liaotung, Gulf of- (EN)=Liaodong Wan 27 Lc 40.00N 121.30 E
Liaotung Peninsula (EN)=Liaodong Bandao 21 Of 40.00N 122.20 E
Liaoyang 27 Lc 41.16N 123.10 E
Liaoyuan 22 Oe 42.55N 125.09 E
Liaozhong 28 Gd 41.30N 122.42 E
Liard 38 Gc 61.52N 121.18W
Liard River 42 Ee 59.15N 126.09W
Liat, Pulau- 26 Eg 2.53S 107.05 E
Liatorp 8 Fh 56.40N 14.16 E
Liatroim/Leitrim [2] 9 Eg 54.20N 8.20W
Liban 30 Lh 5.05N 40.05 E
Libano 55 Bm 37.32S 61.18W
Libby 46 Hb 48.23N 115.33W
Libenge 31 Ih 3.39N 18.38 E
Libengé 36 Cb 3.39N 18.38 E
Liberal 43 Gd 37.02N 100.55W
Liberec 10 Lf 50.46N 15.03 E
Liberia 47 Gf 10.38N 85.27W
Liberia [1] 31 Fh 6.00N 10.00W
Libertad [Ur.] 55 Dl 34.38S 56.39W
Libertad [Ven.] 49 Li 8.08N 71.28W
Libertad [Ven.] 54 Eb 8.20N 69.37W
Libertade, Rio- 54 He 9.35S 52.17W
Libertador General Bernardo O'Higgins [2] 56 Fd 33.35S 70.45W
Libertador Gen. San Martin 56 Hb 23.48S 64.48W
Libertador General San Martin, Cumbre del- 52 Jh 24.55S 66.40W
Liberty [Mo.-U.S.] 45 Ig 39.15N 94.25W
Liberty [Tx.-U.S.] 45 Ik 30.03N 94.47W
Libīyā=Libya (EN) [1] 31 If 27.00N 17.00 E
Libīyah, Aş Şaḩrā' al-=Libyan Desert (EN) 30 Jf 24.00N 25.00 E
Libo 27 If 25.28N 107.52 E
Libobo, Tanjung- 26 Ig 0.54S 128.28 E
Liboi 36 Hb 0.24N 40.57 E
Libourne 11 Fj 44.55N 0.14W
Libramont-Chevigny 12 He 49.55N 5.23 E
Librazhdi 15 Dh 41.11N 20.19 E
Libreville 31 Hh 0.23N 9.27 E
Libro Point 26 Gd 11.26N 119.29 E
Libya (EN)=Libīyā [1] 31 If 27.00N 17.00 E
Libyan Desert (EN)= Libīyah, Aş Şaḩrā' al- 30 Jf 24.00N 25.00 E
Licantén 56 Fe 34.59S 72.00W
Licata 14 Hm 37.06N 13.56 E
Lice 24 Ic 38.28N 40.39 E
Licenciado Matienzo 55 Cm 37.55S 58.54W
Lich 12 Kd 50.31N 8.50 E
Licheng → Jinhu 28 Eh 33.01N 119.01 E
Lichfield 9 Li 52.42N 1.48W
Lichinga 31 Kj 13.20S 35.20 E
Lichtenau 12 Kc 51.37N 8.54 E
Lichtenburg 37 De 26.08S 26.08 E
Lichtenfels 10 Hf 50.09N 11.04 E
Lichtenvoorde 12 Ic 51.59N 6.34 E
Licking River 44 Ef 39.06N 84.30W
Licosa, Punta- 14 Ij 40.15N 14.54 E
Licuare 37 Fc 17.54S 36.49 E
Licun → Laoshan 28 Ff 36.10N 120.25 E
Licungo 37 Fc 17.40S 37.22 E
Lida 19 Ce 53.56N 25.18 E
Lidan 8 Ef 58.31N 13.09 E
Liddel 9 Kf 55.04N 2.57W
Liddon Gulf 42 Gb 75.00N 113.30W
Liden 7 De 62.42N 16.48 E
Lidhorikion 15 Fk 38.32N 22.12 E
Lidhult 8 Eh 56.50N 13.26 E
Lidingö 7 Eg 59.22N 18.08 E
Lidköping 7 Cg 58.30N 13.10 E
Lido 34 Fc 12.54N 3.44 E
Lido, Venezia- 14 Ge 45.25N 12.22 E
Lido di Ostia 14 Gi 41.44N 12.16 E
Lidzbark 10 Pc 53.17N 19.49 E
Lidzbark Warmiński 10 Qb 54.09N 20.35 E
Lié 11 Df 48.00N 2.40W
Liebenau 12 Lb 52.36N 9.06 E
Liebig, Mount- 59 Gd 23.15S 131.20 E
Liechtenstein [1] 6 Gf 47.10N 9.30 E
Liège [3] 12 Hd 50.30N 5.40 E
Liège/Luik 6 Ge 50.38N 5.34 E
Lieksa 7 He 63.19N 30.01 E
Lielupe 7 Fh 57.03N 23.56 E
Lielvarde/Lielvärde 8 Kh 56.40N 24.49 E
Lielvärde/Lielvarde 8 Kh 56.40N 24.49 E
Lienen 12 Jb 52.09N 7.59 E
Lienz 14 Gd 46.50N 12.47 E
Liepaja/Liepāja 6 Id 56.35N 21.01 E
Liepāja/Liepaja 6 Id 56.35N 21.01 E
Liepajas, Ozero-/Liepājas Ezers 8 Ih 56.35N 20.35 E
Liepājas ezers/Liepaja, Ozero- 8 Ih 56.35N 20.35 E
Liepna 8 Lg 57.16N 27.35 E
Liepupe 8 Kg 57.22N 24.22 E
Lier/Lierre 11 Kc 51.08N 4.34 E
Lierbyen 8 De 59.47N 10.14 E
Lierneux 12 Hd 50.17N 5.48 E
Lierre/Lier 11 Kc 51.08N 4.34 E
Liesborn, Wadersloh- 12 Kc 51.43N 8.16 E
Lieser 10 Dg 49.55N 7.01 E
Liesing 14 Jc 47.20N 15.02 E
Liestal 14 Bc 47.29N 7.44 E
Liești 15 Kd 45.37N 27.31 E
Lieto 8 Jd 60.30N 22.27 E
Lietuvos Tarybu Socialistine Respublika/Litovskaja SSR [2] 19 Cd 56.00N 24.00 E
Lietuvos TSR=Lithuanian SSR (EN) [2] 19 Cd 56.00N 24.00 E
Lietvesi 8 Lc 61.30N 28.00 E
Lieurey 12 Ce 49.14N 0.29 E
Lieuvin 11 Ge 49.10N 0.30 E
Lievestuoreenjärvi 8 Lb 62.20N 26.10 E
Liévin 11 Id 50.25N 2.46 E
Lievre, Rivière du- 44 Jc 45.35N 75.25W
Liezen 14 Ic 47.34N 14.14 E
Lifford/Leifear 9 Fg 54.50N 7.29W
Li Fiord 42 Ia 80.17N 94.35W
Lifjell 8 Ce 59.30N 8.52 E
Lifou, Ile- 57 Hg 20.53S 167.13 E
Lifuka 65b Ba 19.48S 174.21W
Ligatne/Līgatne 8 Kg 57.07N 25.00 E
Līgatne/Ligatne 8 Kg 57.07N 25.00 E
Lighthouse Reef 49 De 17.20N 87.32W
Lignano Sabbiadoro 14 He 45.52N 13.09 E
Lignières 11 Ih 46.45N 2.10 E
Lignon 11 Ki 45.44N 4.08 E
Ligny-en-Barrois 11 Lf 48.41N 5.20 E
Ligonha 37 Fc 16.51S 39.09 E
Ligure, Mar-=Ligurian Sea (EN) 5 Gg 43.30N 9.00 E
Liguria [2] 14 Cf 44.30N 8.50 E
Ligurian Sea (EN)=Ligure, Mar- 5 Gg 43.30N 9.00 E
Lihir Group 57 Ge 3.05S 152.40 E
Lihme 8 Ch 56.36N 8.44 E
Lihoslavl 7 Ih 57.09N 35.29 E
Lihou Reefs and Cays 57 Gf 17.25S 151.40 E
Lihue 60 Oc 21.59N 159.22W
Lihula 7 Fg 58.44N 23.49 E
Liinahamari 7 Hb 69.40N 31.22 E
Lijiang (Dayan) 22 Mg 26.56N 100.15 E
Lijin 28 Ef 37.29N 118.15 E
Lika 14 Jf 44.46N 15.10 E
Lika 14 Jf 44.30N 15.30 E
Likasi 31 Jj 10.59S 26.43 E
Likati 36 Db 2.53N 24.03 E
Likati 36 Db 3.21N 23.53 E
Likėnai/Likenaj 8 Kh 56.11N 24.42 E
Likenaj/Likėnai 8 Kh 56.11N 24.42 E
Likenäs 8 Ed 60.37N 13.02 E
Likhapani 25 Jc 27.19N 95.54 E
Likiep Atoll 57 Hc 9.53N 169.09 E
Likolo 36 Cc 0.43S 19.40 E
Likoma Island 36 Fe 12.04S 34.44 E
Likoto 36 Dc 1.10S 24.45 E
Likouala [3] 36 Cb 2.00N 17.30 E
Likouala 36 Cc 1.13S 16.48 E
Likouala aux Herbes 36 Cc 0.50S 17.11 E
Liku 64k Bb 19.02S 169.47W
L'Ile Rousse 11a Aa 42.38N 8.56 E
Lilibeo, Capo-→Boeo, Capo- 14 Gm 37.34N 12.41 E
Lilienfeld 14 Jb 48.01N 15.38 E
Lilienthal 12 Ka 53.08N 8.55 E
Lilla Edet 7 Cg 58.08N 12.08 E
Lille [Bel.] 12 Gc 51.14N 4.50 E
Lille [Fr.] 6 Ge 50.38N 3.04 E
Lille Bælt=Little Belt (EN) 5 Gd 55.20N 9.45 E
Lillebonne 11 Ge 49.31N 0.33 E
Lille Fiskebanke 8 Bh 56.56N 6.20 E
Lillehammer 7 Cf 61.08N 10.30 E
Lille Hellefiske Bank (EN) 41 Ge 65.05N 54.00W
Lillers 11 Id 50.34N 2.29 E
Lillesand 7 Bg 58.15N 8.24 E
Lillestrøm 8 De 59.57N 11.05 E
Lillhärdal 7 Df 61.51N 14.04 E
Lillie Glacier 66 Kf 70.45S 163.55 E
Lillo 13 Ie 39.43N 3.18W
Lillooet 42 Ff 50.42N 121.56W
Lillooet Range 46 Eb 50.00N 121.45W
Lillooet River 42 Fg 49.45N 122.10W
Lilongwe 31 Kj 13.59S 33.47 E
Liloy 26 He 8.08N 122.40 E
Lim [Afr.] 35 Bd 7.54N 15.46 E
Lim [Yugo.] 14 Ng 43.45N 19.13 E
Lima 13 Dc 41.41N 8.50W
Lima [2] 54 Cf 12.00S 76.35W
Lima [Mt.-U.S.] 46 Id 44.38N 112.36W
Lima [Oh.-U.S.] 43 Kc 40.43N 84.06W
Lima [Par.] 55 Df 23.54S 56.20W
Lima [Peru] 53 Ig 12.03S 77.03W
Lima [Swe.] 8 Ed 60.56N 13.21 E
Lima, Pulau-Pulau- 26 Gg 3.03S 107.24 E
Limagne 11 Jh 46.00N 3.20 E
Limah 24 Qj 25.56N 56.25 E
Liman [R.S.F.S.R.] 16 Og 45.45N 47.14 E
Liman [Ukr.-U.S.S.R.] 15 Md 45.42N 29.46 E
Limanskoje 15 Mc 46.38N 29.54 E
Limari, Rio- 56 Fd 30.44S 71.43W
Limassol/Lemesós 23 Dc 34.40N 33.02 E
Limavady/Léim an Mhadaidh 9 Gf 55.03N 6.57W
Limay 12 Df 48.59N 1.44 E
Limay, Rio- 52 Ji 38.59S 68.00W
Limbara 14 Dj 40.51N 9.10 E
Limbaži 7 Fh 57.31N 24.47 E
Limbé 49 Kd 19.42N 72.24W
Limbe, Blantyre- 36 Gf 15.49S 35.03 E
Limbot 63b Cb 14.12S 167.34 E
Limboto 26 Hf 0.37N 122.57 E
Limbourg 12 Hd 50.37N 5.56 E
Limbourg/Limburg 11 Lc 51.05N 5.40 E
Limburg [Bel.] [3] 12 Hc 51.00N 5.30 E
Limburg [Neth.] [3] 12 Hc 51.14N 5.50 E
Limburg/Limbourg 11 Lc 51.05N 5.40 E
Limburg an der Lahn 10 Ef 50.23N 8.03 E
Limedsforsen 8 Ed 60.54N 13.23 E
Limeira 56 Kb 22.34S 47.24W
Limerick/Luimneach [2] 9 Ei 52.30N 9.00W
Limerick/Luimneach 6 Fe 52.40N 8.38W
Limestone, Hadabat- 33 Fe 24.50N 32.00 E
Limfjorden 5 Gd 56.55N 9.10 E
Limia 13 Dc 41.41N 8.50W
Limingen 7 Cd 64.47N 13.36 E
Liminka 7 Fd 64.49N 25.29 E
Limmat 14 Cc 47.30N 8.15 E
Limmen Bight 59 Hb 14.45S 135.40 E
Limmen Bight River 59 Hc 15.15S 135.30 E
Limni 15 Gk 38.46N 23.19 E
Limnos=Lemnos (EN) 5 Ih 39.55N 25.15 E
Limoeiro 54 Ke 7.52S 35.27W
Limoges 6 Gf 45.51N 1.15 E
Limogne, Causse de- 11 Hj 44.20N 1.55 E
Limon 43 Gd 39.16N 103.41W
Limón [3] 49 Fi 10.00N 83.15W
Limón [C.R.] 39 Kh 10.00N 83.02W
Limón [Hond.] 49 Ef 15.52N 85.33W
Limone Piemonte 14 Bf 44.12N 7.34 E
Limousin 11 Hi 45.30N 1.50 E
Limousin, Plateau du- 11 Hi 45.50N 1.10 E
Limoux 11 Ik 43.04N 2.14 E
Limpopo 30 Jk 25.12S 33.32 E
Limu Ling 27 Ie 19.02N 109.43 E
Limuru 36 Gc 1.06S 36.39 E
Līnah 24 Jh 28.42N 43.48 E
Lin'an 27 Ke 30.14N 119.39 E
Linapacan 26 Gd 11.27N 119.49 E
Linares [Chile] 53 Ii 35.51S 71.36W
Linares [Mex.] 47 Ed 24.52N 99.34W
Linares [Sp.] 13 If 38.05N 3.38W
Linares Viejo 55 Bf 23.09S 61.46W
Linaro, Capo- 14 Fh 42.02N 11.50 E
Lincang 22 Mg 23.48N 100.04 E
Lincheng 28 Cf 37.26N 114.34 E
Lincheng→Xuecheng 28 Dg 34.48N 117.14 E
Lincoln 9 Mh 53.20N 0.30W
Lincoln [Arg.] 56 Hd 34.52S 61.32W
Lincoln [Eng.-U.K.] 9 Mh 53.14N 0.33W
Lincoln [Il.-U.S.] 45 Lf 40.09N 89.22W
Lincoln [Nb.-U.S.] 39 Je 40.48N 96.42W
Lincoln [N.Z.] 62 Ee 43.38S 172.29 E
Lincoln, Mount- 45 Cg 39.21N 106.07W
Lincoln City 46 Cd 44.59N 124.01W
Lincoln Sea 67 Ne 83.00N 56.00W
Lincolnshire [3] 9 Mh 53.00N 0.10W
Lindashalvøya 8 Ad 60.40N 5.15 E
Lindau 10 Fi 47.33N 9.41 E
Linde [Neth.] 12 Hb 52.49N 5.52 E
Linde [R.S.F.S.R.] 20 Hd 64.59N 124.36 E
Linden [Guy.] 54 Gb 6.00N 58.18W
Linden [Tn.-U.S.] 44 Dh 35.37N 87.50W
Lindenows Fjord 41 Hf 60.25N 43.00W
Linderödsåsen 8 Ei 55.53N 13.56 E
Lindesberg 7 Dg 59.35N 15.15 E
Lindesnes 5 Gd 58.00N 7.02 E
Lindhorst 12 Lb 52.22N 9.17 E
Lindhos 15 Lm 36.06N 28.04 E
Lindi [3] 36 Gd 9.30S 38.20 E
Lindi 31 Ki 10.00S 39.43 E
Lindi 30 Jh 0.33N 25.05 E
Lindis Pass 62 Cf 44.35S 169.39 E
Lindlar 12 Jc 51.01N 7.23 E
Lindome 8 Eg 57.34N 12.05 E
Lindong→Bairin Zuoqi 27 Kc 43.59N 119.22 E
Lindsay [Ca.-U.S.] 46 Fh 36.12N 119.05W
Lindsay [Ont.-Can.] 44 Hc 44.21N 78.44W
Lindsdal 8 Gh 56.44N 16.18 E
Line Islands 57 Le 0.01S 157.00W
Linfen 27 Jd 36.03N 111.32 E
Lingayen 22 Oh 16.01N 120.14 E
Lingayen Gulf 26 Hc 16.15N 120.14 E
Lingbi 28 Dh 33.33N 117.33 E
Lingbo 7 Df 61.03N 16.41 E
Lingchuan 28 Bg 35.46N 113.16 E
Lingen (Ems) 10 Dd 52.31N 7.19 E
Lingfield 12 Bc 51.10N 0.01W
Lingga, Kepulauan-=Lingga Archipelago (EN) 21 Mj 0.02S 104.35 E
Lingga, Pulau- 26 Dg 0.12S 104.35 E
Lingga Archipelago (EN)= Lingga, Kepulauan- 21 Mj 0.02S 104.35 E
Linghed 8 Fd 60.47N 15.51 E
Lingling 27 Jf 26.24N 111.41 E
Lingomo 36 Db 0.38N 21.59 E
Lingqiu 28 Ce 39.26N 114.14 E
Lingshan 27 Ig 22.30N 109.17 E
Lingshan Dao 28 Fg 35.45N 120.10 E
Lingshi 28 Af 36.50N 111.46 E
Lingshou 28 Ce 38.18N 114.22 E
Linguère 31 Fg 15.24N 15.07W
Lingwu 27 Id 38.05N 106.20 E
Lingxian 28 Df 37.20N 116.35 E
Lingyuan 28 Ed 41.15N 119.23 E
Linh, Ngoc- 21 Mh 15.04N 107.59 E
Linhai 27 La 51.36N 124.22 E
Linhai (Taizhou) 27 Lf 28.52N 121.08 E
Linhares 54 Jg 19.25S 40.04W
Linhe 27 Ic 40.49N 107.28 E
Linhuaiguan 28 Dh 32.54N 117.39 E
Linjiang 28 Id 41.49N 126.55 E
Linköping 6 Hd 58.25N 15.37 E
Linkou 27 Nb 45.18N 130.18 E
Linkuva 8 Jh 56.02N 23.58 E
Linlü Shan 28 Bf 36.02N 113.42 E
Linn, Mount- 46 Df 40.03N 122.48W
Linneryd 8 Fh 56.40N 15.07 E
Linnhe, Loch- 9 He 56.37N 5.25W
Linnich 12 Id 50.59N 6.16 E
Linosa 14 Go 35.50N 12.50 E
Linovo 10 Ud 52.28N 24.35 E
Linqing 27 Kd 36.48N 115.49 E
Linqu 28 Ef 36.31N 118.32 E
Linquan 28 Ch 33.04N 115.16 E
Linru 28 Bg 34.10N 112.51 E
Lins 56 Kb 21.40S 49.45W
Linsell 8 Eb 62.09N 13.53 E
Linshu (Xiazhuang) 28 Eg 34.56N 118.38 E
Linslade 12 Bc 51.55N 0.40W
Linta 37 Ge 25.02S 44.05 E
Lintao 27 Hd 35.20N 104.00 E
Linthal 14 Cd 46.55N 9.00 E
Linton [Eng.-U.K.] 12 Cb 52.06N 0.16 E
Linton [N.D.-U.S.] 45 Fc 46.16N 100.14W
Linxi [China] 22 Ne 43.36N 118.02 E
Linxi [China] 28 Ee 39.42N 118.26 E
Linxia 22 Mf 35.28N 102.59 E
Linxian 27 Jd 37.57N 111.00 E
Linxiang 28 Bj 29.29N 113.28 E
Linyi [China] 28 Df 37.11N 116.51 E
Linyi [China]' 27 Kd 35.09N 118.15 E
Linz 6 Hf 48.18N 14.18 E
Linze (Shahezhen) 27 Hd 39.10N 100.21 E
Lion, Golfe du-=Lion, Gulf of- (EN) 5 Gg 43.00N 4.00 E
Lion, Gulf of- (EN)=Lion, Golfe du- 5 Gg 43.00N 4.00 E
Lions Den 37 Ec 17.16S 30.02 E
Lion-sur-Mer 12 Be 49.18N 0.19W
Lioppa 26 Ih 7.40S 126.00 E
Lios Mór/Lismore 9 Fi 52.08N 7.55W
Lios na gCearrbhach/Lisburn 9 Gg 54.31N 6.03W
Lios Tuathail/Listowel 9 Di 52.27N 9.29W
Liouesso 36 Cb 1.02N 15.43 E
Lipa 26 Hd 13.57N 121.10 E
Lipany 10 Qg 49.10N 20.58 E
Lipari 14 Il 38.30N 14.55 E
Lipari 14 Il 38.28N 14.57 E
Lipari Islands (EN)=Eolie o Lipari, Isole- 5 Hh 38.35N 14.55 E
Lipeck 6 Je 52.37N 39.35 E
Lipeckaja Oblast [3] 19 De 52.45N 39.10 E
Lipenská přehradní nádrž 10 Kh 48.45N 14.05 E
Liperi 7 Ge 62.32N 29.22 E
Lipez, Cordillera de- 54 Eh 22.00S 66.45W
Liphook 12 Bc 51.04N 0.48W
Lipkani 15 Ja 48.13N 26.48 E
Lipljan 15 Eg 42.32N 21.08 E
Lipno 10 Pd 52.51N 19.10 E
Lipova 15 Ec 46.05N 21.42 E
Lipovcy 20 Ih 44.15N 131.45 E
Lippborg, Lippetal- 12 Kc 51.40N 8.02 E
Lippe 10 Ce 51.39N 6.38 E
Lipper Bergland 12 Kb 52.05N 8.57 E
Lippetal 12 Kc 51.40N 8.13 E
Lippetal-Eickelborn 12 Kc 51.39N 8.13 E
Lippetal-Lippborg 12 Kc 51.40N 8.02 E
Lippischer Wald 12 Kc 51.56N 8.45 E
Lippstadt 10 Ee 51.40N 8.21 E
Lipsko 10 Re 51.09N 21.39 E
Lipsoí 15 Jl 37.20N 26.45 E
Liptako 30 Hg 14.15N 0.02 E
Liptovský Mikuláš 10 Pg 49.05N 19.38 E
Lira 36 Fb 2.15N 32.54 E
Liranga 36 Cc 0.40S 17.36 E
Liri 14 Hi 41.25N 13.52 E
Liria 13 Le 39.38N 0.36W
Lis 13 De 39.53N 8.58W
Lisa 15 Cf 43.08N 19.42 E
Lisac 15 Eg 42.45N 21.56 E
Lisakovsk 19 Ge 52.33N 62.28 E
Lisala 31 Jh 2.09N 21.31 E
Lisboa [2] 13 Ce 39.00N 9.08W
Lisboa=Lisbon (EN) 6 Fh 38.43N 9.08W
Lisbon 45 Hc 46.27N 97.41W
Lisbon (EN)=Lisboa 6 Fh 38.43N 9.08W
Lisbon Canyon (EN) 13 Cf 38.20N 9.20W
Lisburn/Lios na gCearrbhach 9 Gg 54.31N 6.03W
Lisburne, Cape- 40 Fc 68.52N 166.14W
Liscannor Bay/Bá Thuath Reanna 9 Di 52.55N 9.25W
Lisec 10 Uh 48.48N 24.45 E
Li Shan 28 Ag 35.25N 111.58 E
Lishi 27 Jd 37.29N 111.08 E
Lishu 28 Hc 43.19N 124.20 E
Lishui 27 Kf 28.30N 119.55 E
Lisianski Island 57 Jb 26.02N 174.00W
Lisičansk 19 Df 48.53N 38.28 E
Lisieux 11 Ge 49.09N 0.14 E
Liska 15 Dh 41.19N 20.58 E
L'Isle-Adam 12 Ee 49.07N 2.14 E
L'Isle-Jourdain 11 Hk 43.37N 1.05 E
L'Isle sur-la-Sorgue 11 Lk 43.55N 5.03 E
Lismore 58 Gg 28.48S 153.17 E
Lismore/Lios Mór 9 Fi 52.08N 7.55W
Liss 24 Hg 31.14N 38.31 E
Liss 12 Bc 51.02N 0.54W
List 10 Ea 55.01N 8.26 E
Lista 8 Bf 58.10N 6.40 E
Listafjorden 8 Bf 58.10N 6.35 E
Lister, Mount- 66 Kf 78.04S 162.41 E
Lištica 14 Lg 43.23N 17.39 E
Listowel/Lios Tuathail 9 Di 52.27N 9.29W
Listowel 44 Gd 43.44N 80.57W
Liswarta 10 Pe 51.06N 19.01 E
Lit 8 Fa 63.19N 14.49 E
Litang [China] 27 Ig 23.12N 109.05 E
Litang [China] 27 He 30.02N 100.18 E
Litani Rivier 54 Hc 3.18N 54.06W
Litchfield 45 Id 45.08N 94.31W
Lithgow 58 Gh 33.29S 150.09 E
Lithinon, Ákra- 15 Ho 34.55N 24.44 E
Lithuania (EN) 5 Id 56.00N 24.00 E
Lithuanian SSR (EN)= Lietuvos TSR [2] 19 Cd 56.00N 24.00 E
Litókhoron 15 Fi 40.06N 22.30 E
Litoměřice 10 Kf 50.32N 14.08 E
Litovel 10 Ng 49.43N 17.05 E
Litovko 20 Ig 49.17N 135.10 E
Litovskaja Sovetskaja Socialističeskaja Respublika [2] 19 Cd 56.00N 24.00 E
Litovskaja SSR/Lietuvos Tarybu Socialistine Respublika [2] 19 Cd 56.00N 24.00 E
Little Abaco Island 47 Ic 26.53N 77.43W
Little Abitibi River 44 Ha 49.29N 79.32W
Little Aden 23 Fg 12.45N 44.52 E
Little America 46 Kf 41.32N 109.47W
Little Andaman 21 Lh 10.45N 92.30 E
Little Bahama Bank (EN) 47 Ic 26.30N 78.00W
Little Barrier Island 62 Fb 36.10S 175.05 E
Little Beaver Creek 45 Ec 46.17N 103.56W
Little Belt (EN)=Lille Bælt 5 Gd 55.20N 9.45 E
Little Belt Mountains 46 Jc 46.45N 110.35W
Little Blue River 45 Hg 39.41N 96.40W
Little Bow River 46 Ib 49.53N 112.29W
Little Carpathians (EN) = Malé Karpaty 10 Nh 48.30N 17.20 E
Little Cayman 47 He 19.41N 80.03W
Little Colorado River 38 He 36.11N 111.48W
Little Current 42 Jg 45.58N 81.56W
Little Current 42 Jf 50.57N 84.36W
Little Dry Creek 46 Lc 47.21N 106.22W
Little Exuma Island 49 Jb 23.27N 75.37W
Little Falls 43 Ib 45.59N 94.21W
Littlefield 45 Ej 33.55N 102.20W
Little Fort 46 Ea 51.25N 120.12W
Little Grand Rapids 42 Hf 52.02N 95.25W
Little Halibut Bank 9 Lc 58.20N 1.15W
Littlehampton 12 Bd 50.48N 0.32W
Little Inagua Island 47 Jd 21.30N 73.00W
Little Karroo (EN)=Klein-Karoo 37 Cf 33.42S 21.20 E
Little Missouri 38 Ie 47.30N 102.25W
Little Namaland (EN)= Namakwaland 37 Be 29.00S 17.00 E
Little Nicobar 25 Ig 7.20N 93.40 E
Little Ouse 9 Ni 52.30N 0.22 E
Littleport 12 Cb 52.27N 0.18 E
Little Powder River 46 Md 45.28N 105.20W
Little Quill Lake 46 Ma 51.55N 104.05W
Little River 62 Ee 43.46S 172.47 E
Little Rock 39 Jf 34.44N 92.15W
Little Rocky Mountains 46 Kb 48.00N 108.45W

Index Symbols

[1] Independent Nation
[2] State, Region
[3] District, County
[4] Municipality
[5] Colony, Dependency
Continent
Physical Region
Historical or Cultural Region
Mount, Mountain
Volcano
Hill
Mountains, Mountain Range
Hills, Escarpment
Plateau, Upland
Pass, Gap
Plain, Lowland
Delta
Salt Flat
Valley, Canyon
Crater, Cave
Karst Features
Depression
Polder
Desert, Dunes
Forest, Woods
Heath, Steppe
Oasis
Cape, Point
Coast, Beach
Cliff
Peninsula
Isthmus
Sandbank
Island
Atoll
Rock, Reef
Islands, Archipelago
Rocks, Reefs
Coral Reef
Well, Spring
Geyser
River, Stream
Waterfall Rapids
River Mouth, Estuary
Lake
Salt Lake
Intermittent Lake
Reservoir
Swamp, Pond
Canal
Glacier
Ice Shelf, Pack Ice
Ocean
Sea
Gulf, Bay
Strait, Fjord
Lagoon
Bank
Seamount
Tablemount
Ridge
Shelf
Basin
Escarpment, Sea Scarp
Fracture
Trench, Abyss
National Park, Reserve
Point of Interest
Recreation Site
Cave, Cavern
Historic Site
Ruins
Wall, Walls
Church, Abbey
Temple
Scientific Station
Airport
Port
Lighthouse
Mine
Tunnel
Dam, Bridge

International Map Index

Name	Page	Grid	Lat	Long
Little Scarcies	34	Cd	8.51N	13.09W
Little Sioux River	45	Hf	41.49N	96.04W
Little Sitkin	40a	Cb	51.55N	178.30 E
Little Smoky	42	Fe	55.39N	117.37W
Little Snake River	45	Bf	40.27N	108.26W
Littleton [Co.-U.S.]	45	Dg	39.37N	105.01W
Littleton [N.H.-U.S.]	44	Lc	44.18N	71.46W
Little White River [Ont.-Can.]	44	Fb	46.15N	83.00W
Little White River [S.D.-U.S.]	45	Fe	43.44N	100.40W
Littoral [3]	34	He	4.30N	10.00 E
Litvinov	10	Jf	50.36N	13.36 E
Liuba	27	Ie	33.39N	106.53 E
Liuhe	27	Mc	42.16N	125.45 E
Liu He [China]	28	Gd	41.48N	122.43 E
Liu He [China]	28	Ic	42.46N	126.13 E
Liuheng Dao	28	Gj	29.43N	122.08 E
Liujia Xia	27	Hd	35.50N	103.00 E
Liukang Tenggaja, Kepulauan-	26	Gh	6.45S	118.50 E
Liupai → Tian'e	27	If	25.05N	107.12 E
Liupan Shan	27	Id	35.40N	106.15 E
Liuqu He	28	Fd	40.10N	120.15 E
Liuwa Plain	36	De	14.27S	22.25 E
Liuyang	28	Bj	28.09N	113.38 E
Liuzhangzhen → Yuanqu	27	Jd	35.19N	111.44 E
Liuzhou	22	Mg	24.22N	109.20 E
Līvāni/Līvany	5	Gh	56.22N	26.12 E
Livanjsko Polje	14	Kg	43.51N	16.50 E
Līvany/Līvāni	7	Gh	56.22N	26.12 E
Livarot	12	Ce	49.01N	0.09 E
Livengood	40	Jc	65.32N	148.33W
Livenza	14	Ge	45.35N	12.51 E
Livenzi	15	Ge	44.14N	23.47 E
Live Oak	44	Fj	30.18N	82.59W
Livermore	45	Dk	30.37N	104.08W
Livermore, Mount-	45	Dk	30.37N	104.08W
Liverpool [Eng.-U.K.]	6	Fe	53.25N	2.55W
Liverpool [N.S.-Can.]	42	Lh	44.02N	64.43W
Liverpool, Cape -	42	Jb	73.38N	78.05W
Liverpool Bay [Can.]	42	Ec	70.00N	129.00W
Liverpool Bay [Eng.-U.K.]	9	Jh	53.30N	3.16W
Liverpool Range	59	Kf	31.40S	150.30 E
Liverpool River	59	Gb	12.00S	134.00 E
Livigno	14	Ed	46.32N	10.04 E
Livingston [Guat.]	49	Cf	15.50N	88.45W
Livingston [Mt.-U.S.]	43	Eb	45.40N	110.34W
Livingston [Newf.-Can.]	42	Kf	53.40N	66.10W
Livingston [Tn.-U.S.]	44	Eg	36.23N	85.19W
Livingston [Tx.-U.S.]	45	Ik	30.43N	94.56W
Livingston, Lake-	45	Ik	30.45N	95.10W
Livingstone, Chutes de-= Livingstone Falls (EN)	30	Ii	4.50S	14.30 E
Livingstone Falls (EN) = Livingstone, Chutes de-	30	Ii	4.50S	14.30 E
Livingstone Memorial	36	Fe	12.19S	30.18 E
Livingstone Mountains	36	Fd	9.45S	34.20 E
Livingstonia	36	Fe	10.36S	34.07 E
Livingston Island	66	Qe	62.36S	60.30W
Livno	14	Lg	43.50N	17.01 E
Livny	19	De	52.28N	37.37 E
Livonia	44	Fd	42.25N	83.23W
Livonia (EN)=Livonija	5	Id	58.50N	27.30 E
Livonija=Livonia (EN)	5	Id	58.50N	27.30 E
Livorno=Leghorn (EN)	8	Hg	43.33N	10.19 E
Livradois, Monts du-	11	Ji	45.30N	3.33 E
Livramento do Brumado	54	Jf	13.39S	41.50W
Livron-sur-Drôme	11	Kj	44.46N	4.51 E
Liwale	36	Gd	9.46S	37.56 E
Liwiec	10	Rd	52.35N	21.33 E
Liwonde	36	Gf	15.01S	35.13 E
Lixi	17	Hf	26.21N	102.03 E
Lixian [China]	27	Ie	34.11N	105.02 E
Lixian [China]	27	Jf	29.40N	111.45 E
Lixin	28	Ce	38.29N	115.34 E
Lixoúrion	15	Dk	38.12N	20.26 E
Liyang	28	Ei	31.26N	119.29 E
Lizard	9	Hl	49.57N	5.13W
Lizard Point	5	Ff	49.56N	5.13W
Lizhu	28	Fj	29.58N	120.26 E
Lizy sur Ourcq	12	Fe	49.01N	3.02 E
Ljady	8	Mf	58.35N	28.55 E
Ljahoviči	16	Ec	53.04N	26.15 E
Ljahovskije Ostrova= Lyakhov Islands (EN)	21	Qb	73.30N	141.00 E
Ljalja	5	Jj	59.10N	61.30 E
Ljamin	17	Of	61.18N	71.45 E
Ljangar	18	Ed	40.23N	65.59 E
Ljangasovo	7	Lg	58.33N	49.29 E
Ljapin	17	Ke	63.38N	61.58 E
Ljaskelja	8	Nc	61.39N	31.03 E
Ljaskovec	15	If	43.06N	25.43 E
Ljig	15	De	44.14N	20.15 E
Ljuban [Bye.-U.S.S.R.]	16	Ec	52.48N	27.59 E
Ljuban [R.S.F.S.R.]	7	Hg	59.22N	31.13 E
Ljubar	16	Ee	49.55N	27.44 E
Ljubaščevka	15	Nb	47.50N	30.07 E
Ljubelj	14	Id	46.26N	14.16 E
Ljubercy	19	De	55.40N	37.55 E
Ljubešov	10	Ve	51.45N	25.37 E
Ljubim	7	Jg	58.22N	40.41 E
Ljubimec	15	Jh	41.50N	26.05 E
Ljubinje	14	Mh	42.57N	18.06 E
Ljubljana	15	Cf	43.20N	19.07 E
Ljuboml	8	Hf	46.02N	14.30 E
Ljubotin	16	Cd	51.15N	23.59 E
Ljubovija	16	Le	49.59N	35.55 E
Ljubuški	15	Lg	44.12N	17.33 E
Ljubytino	19	De	53.51N	34.28 E
Ljugarn	8	Ei	57.19N	18.42 E
Ljungan	5	Hc	62.19N	17.23 E
Ljungaverk	8	Gb	62.29N	16.03 E
Ljungby	7	Ch	56.50N	13.56 E
Ljungbyholm	8	Gh	56.38N	16.10 E
Ljungdalen	7	Ce	62.51N	12.47 E
Ljungsbro	8	Ff	58.31N	15.30 E
Ljungskile	8	Df	58.14N	11.55 E
Ljusdal	7	Df	61.50N	16.05 E
Ljusnan	5	Hc	61.12N	17.08 E
Ljusne	7	Df	61.13N	17.08 E
Ljusterö	8	He	59.30N	18.35 E
Ljuta	8	Mf	58.33N	28.45 E
Llandilo	9	Jj	51.53N	3.59W
Llandovery	9	Jj	51.59N	3.48W
Llandrindod Wells	9	Ji	52.15N	3.23W
Llandudno	9	Jh	53.19N	3.49W
Llanelli	9	Ij	51.42N	4.10W
Llanes	13	Ha	43.25N	4.45W
Llangefni	9	Ih	53.16N	4.18W
Llangollen	9	Ji	52.58N	3.10W
Llano	45	Gk	30.45N	98.41W
Llano Estacado	38	If	33.30N	102.40W
Llano River	45	Gk	30.35N	98.25W
Llanos	52	Je	5.00N	70.00W
Llanos de Sonora	47	Bc	28.20N	111.00W
Llanquihue, Lago-	56	Ff	41.08S	72.48W
Llata	54	Ce	9.25S	76.47W
Lleida/Lérida	13	Mc	41.37N	0.37 E
Llerena	13	Ff	38.14N	6.01W
Lleyn	9	Ii	52.54N	4.30W
Llica	54	Eg	19.52S	68.16W
Llivia	13	Nb	42.28N	1.59 E
Llobregat	13	Oc	41.19N	2.09 E
Lloret de Mar	13	Oc	41.42N	2.51 E
Llorona, Punta-	49	Fi	8.37N	83.44W
Llorri/Orri, Pic d'-	13	Nb	42.23N	1.12 E
Lloydminster	42	Gf	53.17N	110.00W
Lluchmayor	13	Oe	39.29N	2.54 E
Llullaillaco, Volcán-	52	Jh	24.43S	68.33W
Lo	63b	Ca	13.21S	166.38 E
Loa	46	Jg	38.24N	111.38W
Loa, Rio-	56	Fb	21.26S	70.04W
Loanatit, Pointe-	63b	Dd	19.21S	169.14 E
Loango	30	Ji	4.17S	20.02 E
Loano	36	Bc	4.39S	11.48 E
Loban	7	Mh	56.59N	51.12 E
Lobatse	31	Jk	25.13S	25.41 E
Lobau/Lubji	10	Ke	51.06N	14.40 E
Lobaye	30	Ih	3.41N	18.35 E
Lobenstein	10	Hf	50.27N	11.39 E
Loberia	56	Ie	38.09S	58.47W
Lobito	10	Lc	53.39N	15.36 E
Lobos	31	Ij	12.22S	13.34 E
Lobos, Cabo-	34	Dd	6.02N	6.47W
Lobos, Cay-	56	Ie	35.11S	59.06W
Lobos, Cayo-	32	Ed	28.45N	13.49W
Lobos, Isla-	48	Cc	29.55N	112.45W
Lobos, Islas de-	49	Ib	22.24N	77.32W
Lobos de Afuera, Islas-	48	Ph	18.22N	87.24W
Lobos de Tierra, Isla-	48	Dd	27.20N	110.36W
Lobva	54	Be	6.57S	80.42W
Łobżonka	54	Be	6.27S	80.52W
Locana	19	Gd	59.12N	60.30 E
Locarno	10	Nc	53.07N	17.18 E
Loch Aillionn/Allen, Lough-	14	Cd	46.10N	8.48 E
Loch Arabhach/Arrow, Lough-	9	Eg	54.08N	8.08W
Lochboisdale	9	Eg	54.05N	8.20W
Loch Cairlinn/Carlingford Lough	9	Fd	57.09N	7.19W
Loch Ce/Key, Lough-	9	Gg	54.05N	6.14W
Loch Coirib/Corrib, Lough	9	Fg	54.00N	8.15W
Loch Con/Conn, Lough-	9	Dh	53.05N	9.10W
Loch Cuan/Strangford Lough	9	Dg	54.04N	9.20W
Loch Deirgeirt/Derg, Lough-	9	Hg	54.26N	5.36W
Lochearnhead	9	Ei	53.00N	8.20W
Loch Éirne Iochtair/Lower Lough Erne	9	Ie	56.23N	4.18W
Loch Éirne Uachtair/Upper Lough Erne	9	Fg	54.30N	7.50W
Lochem	9	Fg	54.20N	7.30W
Loches	12	Ib	52.10N	6.25 E
Loch Feabhail/Foyle, Lough-	11	Gg	47.08N	1.00 E
Loch Garman/Wexford	9	Ff	55.05N	7.10W
Loch Garman/Wexford [2]	9	Fe	52.20N	6.27W
Lochgilphead	9	Gi	52.20N	6.40W
Loch Hinnin/Ennell, Lough-	9	He	56.03N	5.26W
Lochinver	9	Fh	53.28N	7.24W
Loch Lao/Belfast Lough	9	Hc	58.09N	5.15W
Loch Léin/Leane, Lough-	9	Hg	54.40N	5.50W
Loch Leven	9	Di	52.05N	9.30W
Loch Long	9	Je	56.13N	3.10W
Lochmaddy	9	Ie	56.04N	4.50W
Loch Measca/Mask, Lough-	9	Fd	57.36N	7.10W
Lochnagar	9	Dh	53.35N	9.20W
Loch nEathach/Neagh, Lough-	9	Je	56.55N	3.10W
Loch Ness	9	Gg	54.38N	6.24W
Łochów	9	Id	57.15N	4.30W
Loch Pholl an Phúca/Poulaphuca Reservoir	10	Rd	52.32N	21.48 E
Loch Ri/Ree, Lough-	9	Gd	53.10N	6.30W
Lochsa River	9	Fh	53.35N	8.00W
Loch Sileann/Sheelin, Lough-	46	Hc	46.08N	115.36W
Loch Suili/Swilly, Lough-	9	Fh	53.48N	7.20W
Loch Uí Ghadra/Gara, Lough-	9	Ff	55.10N	7.38W
	9	Eh	53.55N	8.30W
Lochy	9	He	56.49N	5.06W
Lochy, Loch-	9	Ie	56.55N	4.55W
Lockerbie	9	Jf	55.07N	3.22W
Lockhart	45	Hl	29.53N	97.41W
Lock Haven	44	Ie	41.09N	77.28W
Löcknitz	10	Hc	53.07N	11.16 E
Lockport	44	Hd	43.11N	78.39W
Locminé	11	Dg	47.53N	2.50W
Locri	14	Kl	38.14N	16.16 E
Lod	24	Fj	31.58N	34.54 E
Lodalskåpa	7	Bf	61.47N	7.12 E
Loddon	12	Sb	52.31N	1.29 E
Loddon River	59	Ig	36.41S	143.55 E
Lodejnoje Pole	19	Dc	60.44N	33.33 E
Lodève	11	Jk	43.43N	3.19 E
Lodi [Ca.-U.S.]	46	Eg	38.08N	121.16W
Lodi [It.]	14	De	45.19N	9.30 E
Lødingen	7	Db	68.25N	16.00 E
Lodja	31	Ji	3.29S	23.26 E
Lodosa	13	Jb	42.25N	2.05W
Lödöse	8	Ef	58.02N	12.08 E
Lodwar	31	Kh	3.07N	35.36 E
Łódź	6	He	51.46N	19.30 E
Łódź [2]	10	Pe	51.45N	19.30 E
Loei	25	Ke	17.32N	101.34 E
Loeriesfontein	37	Bf	30.56S	19.26 E
Lofanga	65b	Ba	19.50S	174.33W
Loffa	30	Fh	6.36N	11.05W
Loffa [3]	34	Hd	7.45N	10.00W
Lofoten	3	Ga	68.30N	15.00 E
Lofoten Basin (EN)	5	Ga	70.00N	4.00 E
Lofsdalen	8	Eb	62.07N	13.16 E
Loftahammar	8	Gg	57.52N	16.40 E
Loga	34	Fc	13.37N	3.14 E
Logan [N.M.-U.S.]	45	Ei	35.22N	103.25W
Logan [Ut.-U.S.]	44	Fj	39.32N	82.24W
Logan [W.V.-U.S.]	43	Ec	41.44N	111.50W
Logan, Mount- [Can.]	44	Fj	37.52N	81.58W
Logan, Mount- [Wa.-U.S.]	38	Ec	60.34N	140.24W
Logan Martin Lake	44	Di	33.40N	86.15W
Logansport	44	De	40.45N	86.21W
Loge	30	Ii	7.49S	13.06 E
Logojsk	30	Ig	12.06N	15.02 E
Logone	34	Ic	11.37N	15.06 E
Logone Birni	35	Bd	8.40N	16.00 E
Logone Occidental [3]	30	Ih	9.07N	16.26 E
Logone Occidental	35	Bd	8.20N	16.30 E
Logone Oriental [3]	35	Bd	9.07N	16.26 E
Logone Oriental	13	Jb	42.15N	2.30W
Logroño	55	Bi	29.30S	61.42W
Logroño [Arg.]	13	Jb	42.28N	2.27W
Logroño [Sp.]	13	Ge	39.20N	5.29W
Logrosán	7	Bh	56.58N	9.15 E
Løgstør	14	Cj	40.35N	8.40 E
Loguduro	8	Ci	55.03N	8.57 E
Løgumkloster	7a	Cb	65.15N	14.30W
Løgurinn	12	Ge	49.50N	1.24 E
Lohja/Lojo	7	Ff	60.15N	24.05 E
Lohjanjärvi	8	Jd	60.15N	23.55 E
Lohjanselkä/Lojo åsen	8	Kd	60.15N	24.10 E
Löhme	12	Kb	51.41N	8.42 E
Lohne	10	Ed	52.11N	8.41 E
Lohne	12	Kb	52.40N	8.14 E
Lohra	12	Kd	50.44N	8.38 E
Lohr am Main	11	Lf	49.59N	9.35 E
Lohusuu/Lokusu	16	Lf	58.53N	27.01 E
Lohvica	16	Md	50.22N	33.15 E
Loi, Phou-	25	Kd	20.16N	103.12 E
Loi-Kaw	25	Je	19.41N	97.13 E
Loile	36	Dc	0.52S	20.12 E
Loimaa	7	Ff	60.51N	23.03 E
Loimijoki	8	Jc	61.13N	22.38 E
Loing	11	If	48.23N	2.48 E
Loir	11	Fg	47.33N	0.32W
Loir, Vaux du-	11	Gg	47.45N	0.25 E
Loire [3]	11	Ji	45.30N	4.00 E
Loire	5	Ff	47.16N	2.11W
Loire, Canal latéral à la-	11	Jh	46.29N	3.59 E
Loire, Val de-	11	Hg	47.40N	1.35 E
Loire-Atlantique [3]	11	Eg	47.15N	1.50W
Loiret [3]	11	Ig	47.55N	2.20 E
Loir-et-Cher [3]	11	Hg	47.30N	1.30 E
Loison	12	Ge	49.30N	5.17 E
Loja [Ec.]	53	If	4.00S	79.13W
Loja [Sp.]	13	Hg	37.10N	4.09W
Lojo/Lohja	7	Ff	60.15N	24.05 E
Lojo åsen/Lohjanselkä	8	Kd	60.15N	24.10 E
Loka	35	Ef	4.16N	31.01 E
Lokači	10	Uf	50.43N	24.44 E
Lokalahti	8	Id	60.41N	21.28 E
Lokandu	36	Ec	2.31S	25.47 E
Lokantekojärvi	7	Gc	68.56N	27.47 E
Lokbatan	16	Pi	40.21N	49.42 E
Løken	8	Cg	59.48N	11.29 E
Lokeren	11	Jc	51.06N	4.00 E
Lokichar	36	Fb	2.23S	35.39 E
Lokichokio	36	Fb	4.12N	34.21 E
Lokitaung	36	Gb	4.15N	35.45 E
Løkken [Den.]	7	Bg	57.22N	9.43 E
Løkken [Nor.]	7	Be	63.05N	9.36 E
Loko	34	Gd	8.00N	7.50 E
Lokoja	34	Gd	7.48N	6.44 E
Lokoja	34	Ie	2.41N	15.19 E
Lokolama	36	Cc	1.43S	18.23 E
Lokolo	36	Cc	1.43S	19.35 E
Lokomo	35	Bf	2.34N	15.36 E
Lokoro	30	Ii	2.00S	18.07 E
Lokossa	34	Fd	6.38N	1.43 E
Lokoti	16	Ic	52.33N	34.31 E
Loks Land	42	Md	62.27N	64.30W
Lokuru	63a	Cc	8.35S	157.20 E
Lokusu/Lohusuu	16	Lf	58.53N	27.01 E
Lokwa Kangole	36	Gb	3.32N	35.54 E
Lol	30	Jh	9.13N	28.59 E
Lola	34	Dd	7.48N	8.32W
Lolimi	35	Ee	4.35N	33.59 E
Loliondo	36	Gc	2.03S	35.37 E
Lolland	5	He	54.45N	11.30 E
Lollar	12	Kd	50.38N	8.42 E
Lolo	36	Db	2.13N	23.00 E
Lolo	36	Bc	0.40S	12.52 E
Lolo Pass	46	Hc	46.40N	114.33W
Lolodorf	34	He	3.14N	10.44 E
Loloma	26	Gf	3.30N	116.31 E
Lom	15	Gf	43.49N	23.14 E
Lom [Afr.]	34	Hd	5.20N	13.24 E
Lom [Bul.]	15	Gf	43.50N	23.15 E
Loma Bonita	48	Lh	18.07N	95.53W
Lomaloma	63d	Cb	17.17S	178.59W
Lomami	30	Dh	0.46N	24.16 E
Loma Mountains	30	Fh	9.10N	11.07W
Lomas de Vallejos	55	Bh	27.44S	57.56W
Loma Verde	55	Cl	35.16S	58.24W
Lomba	36	Df	15.36S	21.32 E
Lombarda, Serra-	54	Hc	2.50N	51.50W
Lombarde, Prealpi-	14	De	46.00N	9.30 E
Lombardia = Lombardy (EN) [2]	65b	Ba	19.50S	174.33W
Lombardy (EN) = Lombardia [2]	14	De	45.40N	9.30 E
Lomblen, Pulau-	21	Oj	8.25S	123.30 E
Lombok, Pulau-	21	Nj	8.45S	116.30 E
Lombok, Selat-	26	Gh	8.30S	115.50 E
Lomé	31	Hh	6.08N	1.13 E
Lomela	34	Fc	13.37N	3.14 E
Lomela	30	Ji	0.14S	20.42 E
Lomellina	14	Ce	45.15N	8.45 E
Lomémeti	63b	Dd	19.30S	169.27 E
Lomié	34	He	3.10N	13.37 E
Lomgxi	15	Cf	44.32N	23.14 E
Łomża	8	Ej	55.41N	13.05 E
Lomma	12	Nd	50.08N	5.10 E
Lomme	11	Lc	51.14N	5.18 E
Lommel	10	Ug	49.02N	24.47 E
Lomnica	9	Ie	56.08N	4.38W
Lomond, Loch-	12	Cd	59.55N	29.40 E
Lomonosov	19	Ge	52.50N	66.28 E
Lomonosovki	30	Ig	12.06N	15.02 E
Lomonosov Ridge (EN)	67	De	88.00N	140.00 E
Lomont	11	Mg	47.21N	6.36 E
Lompobatang, Gunung-	26	Gh	5.20S	119.55 E
Lompoc	43	Ce	34.38N	120.27W
Lomsegga	7	Bf	61.49N	8.22 E
Łomża	13	Jb	42.15N	2.30W
Łomża [2]	10	Sc	53.11N	22.05 E
Lønahorg	8	Bd	60.42N	6.25 E
Loncoche	56	Fe	39.22S	72.38W
Londa	25	Le	15.28N	74.31 E
Londerzeel	12	Gc	51.01N	4.18 E
Londiani	36	Gc	0.10S	35.36 E
Londinières	12	De	49.50N	1.24 E
London [Eng.-U.K.]	6	Fe	51.30N	0.10W
London [Kir.]	64g	Bb	1.58N	157.29W
London [Ky.-U.S.]	44	Eg	37.08N	84.05W
London [Ont.-Can.]	39	Ke	42.59N	81.14W
London-Barnet	12	Bc	51.39N	0.12W
London-Bexley	12	Cc	51.26N	0.09 E
London-Bromley	12	Cc	51.25N	0.01 E
London-Croydon	12	Bc	51.23N	0.07W
Londonderry/Doire	6	Fd	55.00N	7.19W
Londonderry, Cape-	59	Fb	13.45S	126.55 E
London-Ealing	12	Bc	51.30N	0.19W
London-Enfield	12	Bc	51.40N	0.04W
London-Greenwich	9	Mj	51.28N	0.00
London-Haringey	12	Bc	51.36N	0.06W
London-Harrow	12	Bc	51.36N	0.20W
London-Havering	12	Cc	51.36N	0.11 E
London-Hillingdon	12	Bc	51.31N	0.27W
London-Kingston-upon-Thames	9	Mj	51.28N	0.19W
London-Redbridge	12	Cc	51.35N	0.08 E
London-Sutton	12	Bc	51.21N	0.12W
London-Wandsworth	12	Bc	51.27N	0.12W
London-Westminster	12	Bc	51.30N	0.07W
Londra	53	Kh	23.18S	51.09W
Londrina	46	Nb	49.07N	103.00W
Lone Pine	14	He	49.30N	5.17 E
Longa	36	Ce	14.41S	18.29 E
Longá [Ang.]	36	Cf	16.25S	19.04 E
Longá [Ang.]	36	Be	10.15S	13.30 E
Longa, Proliv= De Long Strait (EN)	21	Tb	70.20N	178.00 E
Longá, Rio-	54	Jd	3.09S	41.56W
Long Akah	26	Ff	3.16N	114.47 E
Longarone	14	Gd	46.16N	12.18 E
Longbangun	26	Gg	0.06N	114.45 E
Long Bay [Bar.]	51q	Bb	13.04N	59.29W
Long Bay [S.C.-U.S.]	7	Gc	68.56N	27.47 E
Long Beach [Ca.-U.S.]	39	Hf	33.46N	118.11W
Long Beach [N.Y.-U.S.]	44	Ke	40.35N	73.40W
Long Beach [Wa.-U.S.]	46	Ec	46.21N	124.03W
Long Branch	44	Ke	40.17N	73.59W
Long Buckby	36	Bb	2.23S	35.39 E
Long Cay	36	Ab	4.12N	34.21 E
Longchuan	36	Gb	5.45S	35.45 E
Long Creek	27	Kg	24.10N	115.17 E
Long Eaton	46	Nb	49.07N	103.00W
Longfang	28	Ha	46.31N	125.02 E
Longford/An Longfort [2]	9	Fh	53.44N	7.40W
Longford/An Longfort	9	Fh	53.44N	7.47W
Long Forties	5	Fd	57.00N	0.30 E
Longhua	28	Dd	41.18N	117.44 E
Longhui	28	Dd	41.18N	117.44 E
Long Island [Atg.]	51d	Bb	17.08N	61.45W
Long Island [Bah.]	42	Ld	23.10N	75.10W
Long Island [Can.]	42	Jf	54.50N	79.20W
Long Island [Can.]	44	Nc	44.20N	66.15W
Long Island [Pap.N.Gui.]	57	Fe	5.36S	148.00 E
Long Island [U.S.]	38	Le	40.50N	73.00W
Long Island Sound	44	Ke	41.05N	72.58W
Longjiang	27	Lb	47.20N	123.09 E
Longjuzhai → Danfeng	27	Je	33.44N	110.22 E
Longkou	5	He	54.45N	11.30 E
Longlac	42	Ig	49.50N	86.32W
Long Lake [N.D.-U.S.]	45	Fc	46.43N	100.07W
Long Lake [Ont.-Can.]	45	Mb	49.32N	86.45W
Longmalinau	26	Gf	3.30N	116.31 E
Long Men	27	Je	34.40N	110.30 E
Longmont	45	Df	40.10N	105.06W
Longnan	27	Jg	24.54N	114.48 E
Longobucco	14	Kk	39.27N	16.37 E
Longoz	15	Kf	43.02N	27.41 E
Longping → Luodian	27	If	25.26N	106.47 E
Long Point	44	Gd	42.34N	80.15W
Long Point Bay	44	Gd	42.40N	80.14W
Longpujungan	26	Gf	2.34N	115.40 E
Longquan	27	Kf	28.06N	119.05 E
Long Range Mountains	42	Lg	48.00N	58.30W
Longreach	58	Fg	23.26S	144.15 E
Long Sand	12	Dc	51.37N	1.10 E
Longs Peak	38	Ie	40.15N	105.37W
Long Sutton	12	Cb	52.47N	0.08 E
Longtan	28	Eh	32.10N	119.03 E
Longtown	9	Kf	55.01N	2.58W
Longué	12	Ee	49.52N	2.21 E
Longueau	12	Ee	49.52N	2.21 E
Longueville-sur-Scie	12	De	49.48N	1.06 E
Longuyon	11	Le	49.26N	5.36 E
Long Valley	46	Ji	34.37N	111.16W
Longview [Tx.-U.S.]	43	Ie	32.30N	94.44W
Longview [Wa.-U.S.]	43	Cb	46.08N	122.57W
Longwu	27	Hg	24.07N	102.18 E
Longwy	11	Le	49.31N	5.46 E
Longxi	27	Hd	35.00N	104.38 E
Longxian → Wengyuan	27	Jg	24.21N	114.13 E
Longxi Shan	27	Kf	26.35N	117.17 E
Long Xuyen	25	Lf	10.23N	105.25 E
Longyan	27	Kf	25.06N	117.01 E
Longyao	28	Cf	37.21N	114.46 E
Longyearbyen	67	Kd	78.13N	15.38 E
Longyou	28	Ej	29.11N	119.10 E
Longzhou	27	Ig	22.23N	106.49 E
Lonigo	14	Fe	45.23N	11.23 E
Löningen	10	Dd	52.44N	7.46 E
Lonja	14	Ke	45.24N	16.41 E
Lonjsko Polje	14	Ke	45.24N	16.42 E
Lönsboda	8	Fh	56.24N	14.19 E
Lons-le-Saunier	11	Lh	46.40N	5.33 E
Lontra, Ribeirão-	55	Fe	21.28S	53.37W
Lookout, Cape- [N.C.-U.S.]	43	Le	34.35N	76.32W
Lookout, Cape- [Or.-U.S.]	46	Dd	45.20N	124.00W
Lookout Mountain	44	Dh	34.40N	85.20W
Lookout Pass	43	Db	47.27N	115.42W
Loolmalasin	36	Gc	3.03S	35.49 E
Loop Head/Ceann Léime	9	Di	52.34N	9.56W
Loosdrechtse Plassen	12	Hb	52.10N	5.08 E
Lop	27	Dd	37.01N	80.16 E
Lopatina, Gora-	21	Qd	50.52N	143.10 E
Lopatino	16	Nc	52.37N	45.47 E
Lopatka, Mys-	21	Rd	50.52N	156.40 E
Lop Buri	25	Kf	14.48N	100.37 E
Lopča	55	Fe	55.44N	122.45 E
Lopévi	63b	Cb	16.30S	168.21 E
Lopez, Cap-= Lopez, Cape- (EN)	30	Hi	0.37S	8.43 E
Lopez, Cape-(EN)= Lopez, Cap-	30	Hi	0.37S	8.43 E
Lop Nur	21	Le	40.30N	90.30 E
Lopnur/Yuli	27	Ec	41.22N	86.09 E
Lopori	30	Ih	1.14N	19.49 E
Loppersum	12	Ic	53.19N	6.45 E
Lopphavet	7	Ea	70.25N	22.00 E
Lopud	8	Kd	60.43N	24.27 E
Łopuszno	10	Qf	50.57N	20.15 E
Lora del Rio	13	Gg	37.39N	5.32W
Lorain	43	Kc	41.28N	82.11W
Loran, Boca-	51h	Bb	9.00N	60.45W
Lorca	13	Kg	37.40N	1.42W
Lorch	12	Jd	50.03N	7.49 E
Lord Howe Island	57	Gh	31.35S	159.05 E
Lord Howe Rise (EN)	3	Jm	32.00S	162.00 E
Lord Mayor Bay	42	Ic	69.45N	92.00W
Lordsburg	45	Bj	32.21N	108.43W
Loreley	12	Jd	50.08N	7.43 E
Lorena	55	Jf	22.44S	45.08W
Lorengau	60	Dh	2.01S	147.17 E
Lorestān [3]	23	Gc	33.30N	48.40 E
Loreto	54	Dd	5.00S	75.00W
Loreto [Arg.]	54	Db	27.46S	57.17W
Loreto [Bol.]	54	Fg	15.13S	64.40W
Loreto [Braz.]	54	Ie	7.05S	45.09W
Loreto [It.]	14	Hg	43.26N	13.36 E
Loreto [Mex.]	47	Bc	22.16N	101.58W
Loreto [Par.]	55	Bf	26.01N	111.21W
Loreto Aprutino	14	Hh	42.26N	13.59 E
Lorica	54	Cb	9.14N	75.49W
Lorient	6	Ef	47.45N	3.22W
Lőrinci	10	Pi	47.44N	19.41 E
Lorn, Firth of-	9	He	56.20N	5.40W
Lorne	59	Ig	38.33S	143.59 E
Lörrach	11	Mh	47.37N	7.40 E
Lorrain, Plateau-	51h	Aa	14.50N	61.03W
Lorraine, Rivière du-	11	Lf	49.00N	6.30 E
Lorraine [3]	28	Dj	29.37N	116.12 E
Lorraine, Plaine-	11	Lf	48.10N	5.50 E
Lorsch	12	Je	49.39N	8.34 E
Los	12	Ke	60.15N	15.10 E
Los, Îles de- (EN)	34	Cd	9.30N	13.48W

Index Symbols

- [1] Independent Nation
- [2] State, Region
- [3] District, County
- [4] Municipality
- [5] Colony, Dependency
- Continent
- Physical Region
- Historical or Cultural Region
- Mount, Mountain
- Volcano
- Hill
- Mountains, Mountain Range
- Hills, Escarpment
- Plateau, Upland
- Pass, Gap
- Plain, Lowland
- Delta
- Salt Flat
- Valley, Canyon
- Crater, Cave
- Karst Features
- Depression
- Polder
- Desert, Dunes
- Forest, Woods
- Heath, Steppe
- Oasis
- Cape, Point
- Coast, Beach
- Cliff
- Peninsula
- Isthmus
- Sandbank
- Island
- Atoll
- Rock, Reef
- Islands, Archipelago
- Rocks, Reefs
- Coral Reef
- Well, Spring
- Geyser
- River, Stream
- Waterfall Rapids
- River Mouth, Estuary
- Lake
- Salt Lake
- Intermittent Lake
- Sea
- Swamp, Pond
- Canal
- Glacier
- Ice Shelf, Pack Ice
- Ocean
- Ridge
- Shelf
- Strait, Fjord
- Lagoon
- Bank
- Seamount
- Tablemount
- National Park, Reserve
- Point of Interest
- Basin
- Escarpment, Sea Scarp
- Fracture
- Trench, Abyss
- Recreation Site
- Cave, Cavern
- Historic Site
- Ruins
- Wall, Walls
- Church, Abbey
- Temple
- Scientific Station
- Airport
- Port
- Lighthouse
- Mine
- Tunnel
- Dam, Bridge

Index Symbols

[1] Independent Nation	⊟ Historical or Cultural Region	⊟ Pass, Gap
[2] State, Region	⊟ Mount, Mountain	⊟ Plain, Lowland
[3] District, County	⊟ Volcano	⊟ Delta
[4] Municipality	⊟ Hill	⊟ Salt Flat
[5] Colony, Dependency	⊟ Mountains, Mountain Range	⊟ Valley, Canyon
■ Continent	⊟ Hills, Escarpment	⊟ Crater, Cave
[6] Physical Region	⊟ Plateau, Upland	⊟ Karst Features

⊟ Depression	⊟ Coast, Beach	⊟ Rock, Reef
⊟ Polder	⊟ Cliff	⊟ Islands, Archipelago
⊟ Desert, Dunes	⊟ Peninsula	⊟ Rocks, Reefs
⊟ Forest, Woods	⊟ Isthmus	⊟ Coral Reef
⊟ Heath, Steppe	⊟ Sandbank	⊟ Well, Spring
⊟ Oasis	⊟ Island	⊟ Geyser
⊟ Cape, Point	⊟ Atoll	⊟ River, Stream

⊟ Waterfall Rapids	⊟ Canal	⊟ Lagoon
⊟ River Mouth, Estuary	⊟ Glacier	⊟ Bank
⊟ Lake	⊟ Ice Shelf, Pack Ice	⊟ Seamount
⊟ Salt Lake	⊟ Ocean	⊟ Tablemount
⊟ Intermittent Lake	⊟ Sea	⊟ Ridge
⊟ Reservoir	⊟ Gulf, Bay	⊟ Shelf
⊟ Swamp, Pond	⊟ Strait, Fjord	⊟ Basin

⊟ Escarpment, Sea Scarp	⊟ Historic Site	⊟ Port
⊟ Fracture	⊟ Ruins	⊟ Lighthouse
⊟ Trench, Abyss	⊟ Wall, Walls	⊟ Mine
⊟ National Park, Reserve	⊟ Church, Abbey	⊟ Tunnel
⊟ Point of Interest	⊟ Temple	⊟ Dam, Bridge
⊟ Recreation Site	⊟ Scientific Station	
⊟ Cave, Cavern	⊟ Airport	

Name	Page	Grid	Lat.	Long.
Luy de France	11	Fk	43.38N	0.47W
Luyi	28	Ch	33.51N	115.28 E
Luz	55	Jd	19.48S	45.41W
Luz, Costa de la-	13	Fh	36.40N	6.20W
Luza	19	Ec	60.39N	47.15 E
Luza	5	Kc	60.40N	46.25 E
Luzarches	12	Ee	49.07N	2.25 E
Luzern [2]	14	Cc	47.05N	8.10 E
Luzern = Lucerne (EN)	14	Cc	47.05N	8.20 E
Luzhai	27	Ig	24.31N	109.46 E
Luzhangjie → Lushui	27	Gf	26.00N	98.50 E
Luzhou	22	Mg	28.55N	105.20 E
Luziânia	54	Ig	16.15S	47.56W
Luzická Nisa	10	Kd	52.04N	14.46 E
Luzilândia	54	Jd	3.28S	42.22W
Lužnice	10	Kg	49.16N	14.25 E
Luzon	21	Oh	16.00N	121.00 E
Luzon Sea	26	Gd	12.30N	119.00 E
Luzon Strait (EN)	21	Og	21.00N	122.00 E
Luz-Saint-Sauveur	11	Gl	42.52N	0.01 E
Lužskaja Guba	8	Me	59.35N	28.25 E
Lužskaja Vozvyšennost	8	Mf	58.15N	28.45 E
Luzy	11	Jh	46.47N	3.58 E
Łużyca	10	Oe	51.33N	18.15 E
Lvov	6	If	49.50N	24.00 E
Lvovskaja Oblast [3]	19	Cf	49.45N	24.00 E
Lwowa	60	Hj	10.44S	165.45 E
Lwówek	10	Md	52.28N	16.10 E
Lwówek Śląski	10	Le	51.07N	15.35 E
Lyakhov Islands (EN)= Ljahovskije Ostrova	21	Qb	73.30N	141.00 E
Lyall, Mount-	62	Bf	45.17S	167.33 E
Lyallpur	22	Jf	31.25N	73.05 E
Lychsele	7	Ed	64.36N	18.40 E
Lycia	15	Mm	36.30N	29.30 E
Lyckeby	8	Fh	56.12N	15.39 E
Lyckebyån	8	Fh	56.11N	15.40 E
Lyčkovo	7	Hh	57.57N	32.24 E
Lydd	9	Nk	50.57N	0.55 E
Lydd Airport	12	Cd	50.58N	0.56 E
Lydenburg	37	Ee	25.10S	30.29 E
Lydia	15	Lk	38.35N	28.30 E
Lygna	8	Bf	58.10N	7.02 E
Lygnern	8	Eg	57.29N	12.20 E
Lyme Bay	9	Kk	50.38N	3.00W
Lyminge	12	Dc	51.07N	1.05 E
Lymington	9	Lk	50.46N	1.33W
Łyna	10	Rb	54.37N	21.14 E
Lynchburg	43	Ld	37.24N	79.09W
Lynd	58	Ff	18.56S	144.30 E
Lynden	46	Db	48.57N	122.27W
Lyndon River	59	Cd	23.29S	114.06 E
Lyngdal	7	Bg	58.08N	7.05 E
Lyngen	7	Eb	69.58N	20.30 E
Lyngør	8	Cf	58.38N	9.10 E
Lyngseidet	7	Eb	69.35N	20.13 E
Lynn	44	Ld	42.28N	70.57W
Lynnaj, Gora-	20	Ld	62.55N	163.58 E
Lynn Canal	40	Le	58.50N	135.15W
Lynn Deeps	12	Cb	52.58N	0.20 E
Lynn Lake	39	Id	56.51N	101.03W
Lyntupy	8	Li	55.02N	26.27 E
Lynx Lake	42	Gd	62.25N	106.20W
Lyon	6	Gf	45.45N	4.51 E
Lyon Inlet	42	Jc	66.20N	83.40W
Lyonnais, Monts du-	11	Ki	45.40N	4.30 E
Lyon River	59	De	25.00S	115.20 E
Lyons [Ga.-U.S.]	44	Fi	32.12N	82.19W
Lyons [Ks.-U.S.]	45	Gg	38.21N	98.12W
Lyons, Forêt de-	12	De	49.25N	1.30 E
Lyons-la-Forêt	12	De	49.24N	1.28 E
Lyra Reef	60	Eh	1.50S	153.35 E
Lys	11	Jc	51.03N	3.43 E
Łysa Góra	10	Nd	52.07N	17.33 E
Lysaja, Gora-	8	Lj	54.12N	27.40 E
Lysá nad Labem	10	Kf	50.12N	14.50 E
Lysefjorden	8	Be	59.00N	6.14 E
Lysekil	7	Cf	58.16N	11.26 E
Lyskovo	19	Ed	56.03N	45.03 E
Lyss	14	Bc	47.04N	7.37 E
Lysva	19	Fd	58.07N	57.47 E
Lytham Saint Anne's	9	Jh	53.45N	3.01W
Lyttelton	62	Ee	43.36S	172.43 E
Lytton	46	Ea	50.14N	121.34W
Lyža	17	Hd	65.42N	56.40 E

M

Name	Page	Grid	Lat.	Long.
Ma, Oued el-	32	Fe	24.03N	9.10W
Ma, Song	25	Le	19.45N	105.55 E
Maâdis, Djebel-	13	Qi	35.52N	4.44 E
Maalaea Bay	65a	Ec	20.47N	156.29W
Ma'āmīr	24	Mg	30.04N	48.20 E
Ma'ān	23	Ec	30.12N	35.44 E
Ma'ānīyah	24	Jg	30.44N	43.00 E
Maanselkä	5	Ib	68.07N	28.29 E
Maanselka	7	Ge	63.54N	28.30 E
Ma'anshan	27	Ke	31.38N	118.30 E
Maardu	8	Ke	59.28N	24.56 E
Maarianhamina/Mariehamn	7	Ef	60.06N	19.57 E
Ma 'arrat an Nu 'mān	24	Ge	35.38N	36.40 E
Maarssen	12	Hb	52.08N	5.03 E
Maas=Meuse (EN)	5	Ge	51.49N	5.01 E
Maaseik	11	Lc	51.06N	5.48 E
Maaseik-Neeroeteren	12	Hc	51.05N	5.42 E
Maasin	26	Hd	10.08N	124.50 E
Maasmechelen/Mechelen	12	Hd	50.57N	5.40 E
Maassluis	12	Gc	51.55N	4.17 E
Maastricht	11	Ld	50.52N	5.43 E
Maasupa	63a	Ec	9.18S	161.15 E
Ma'āzah, Al Haḑabat al-	33	Fd	27.44N	31.44 E
Mabalane	37	Ed	23.38S	32.31 E
Mabaruma	50	Gh	8.12N	59.47W
Mabechi-Gawa	29	Ga	40.31N	141.31 E
Mabella	45	Lb	48.37N	89.58W
Mabel Lake	46	Fa	50.35N	118.44W
Mablethorpe	9	Nh	53.21N	0.15 E
Mabote	37	Ed	22.03S	34.08 E
Ma'būs Yūsuf	31	Jf	25.45N	21.00 E
Maçaão	13	Ee	39.33N	8.00W
McAdam	42	Kg	45.36N	67.20W
Macajaí, Rio-	54	Fc	2.25N	60.50W
McAllen	43	Hf	26.12N	98.15W
Macaloge	37	Fb	12.25S	35.25 E
Mac Alpine Lake	42	Hc	66.40N	102.50W
Macambará	55	Di	29.08S	56.03W
Macamic	44	Ha	48.48N	79.01W
Macamic, Lac-	44	Ha	48.46N	79.00W
Macao (EN)=Aomen/Macau [5]	22	Ng	22.10N	113.33 E
Macao (EN)=Aomen/Macau	27	Jg	22.12N	113.33 E
Macao (EN)=Macau/Aomen [5]	22	Ng	22.10N	113.33 E
Macao (EN)=Macau/Aomen	27	Jg	22.12N	113.33 E
Macapá	53	Ke	0.02N	51.03W
Macará	54	Cd	4.21S	79.56W
Macaracas	49	Gj	7.44N	80.33W
Macareo, Caño-	54	Fb	9.47N	61.36W
McArthur	44	Ff	39.14N	82.29W
Mc Arthur River	59	Hc	15.54S	136.40 E
Maçãs	13	Fc	41.29N	6.39W
Macas	54	Cd	2.18S	78.06W
Macatete, Sierra de-	48	Dd	28.00N	110.05W
Macau	53	Mf	5.07S	36.38W
Macau/Aomen=Macao (EN)	27	Jg	22.12N	113.33 E
Macau/Aomen=Macao (EN) [5]	22	Ng	22.10N	113.33 E
Macaúbas	54	Jf	13.02S	42.42W
Macauley Island	57	Ih	30.13S	178.33W
Macaya, Pic de-	47	Je	18.23N	74.02W
McBeth Fiord	42	Kc	69.43N	69.20W
McCamey	45'	Ek	31.08N	102.13W
McCammon	46	Ie	42.39N	112.12W
Mc Carthy	40	Kd	61.26N	142.55W
McClellanville	44	Hi	33.06N	79.28W
MacClenny	44	Fj	30.18N	82.07W
Macclesfield	9	Kh	53.16N	2.07W
Macclesfield Bank (EN)	26	Fc	15.50N	114.20 E
McClintock	42	Ie	57.48N	94.12W
McClintock, Mount-	66	Jg	80.13S	157.26 E
Mc Clintock Channel	38	Ib	71.00N	101.00W
McCluer Gulf (EN)=Berau, Teluk-	26	Jg	2.30S	132.30 E
Mc Clure Strait	38	Hb	74.30N	116.00W
McClusky	45	Fc	47.29N	100.27W
McComb	43	Ie	31.14N	90.27W
McConaughy, Lake-	45	Ff	41.18N	101.46W
McConnelsville	44	Gf	39.39N	81.51W
McCook	43	Gc	40.12N	100.38W
McCormick	44	Fi	33.55N	82.19W
McDame	42	Ee	59.13N	129.14W
McDermitt	46	Gf	41.59N	117.36W
Macdhui, Ben-	9	Jd	57.04N	3.40W
Macdonald, Lake-	59	Fd	23.30S	129.00 E
Mc Donald Islands	30	On	52.59S	72.50 E
McDonald Peak [Ca.-U.S.]	46	Ef	40.58N	120.26W
McDonald Peak [Mt.-U.S.]	46	Ic	47.29N	113.46W
Macdonald Range	46	Hb	49.12N	114.46W
Macdonnell Ranges	57	Eg	23.45S	132.20 E
McDouglas Sound	42	Hd	75.15N	97.30W
Macduff	9	Kd	57.40N	2.29W
Macedo de Cavaleiros	13	Fc	41.32N	6.58W
Macedonia (EN)= Makedhonía	5	Ig	41.00N	23.00 E
Macedonia (EN)= Makedhonía	15	Fh	41.00N	23.00 E
Macedonia (EN) = Makedonija [2]	15	Eh	41.50N	22.00 E
Macedonia (EN)= Makedonija	5	Ig	41.00N	23.00 E
Macedonia (EN)= Makedonija	15	Fh	41.00N	23.00 E
Maceió	53	Mf	9.40S	35.43W
Macenta	34	Dd	8.33N	9.28W
Macerata	14	Hg	43.18N	13.27 E
McGehee	45	Kj	33.38N	91.24W
McGill	46	Hg	39.23N	114.47W
Macgillycuddy's Reeks/Na Cruacha Dubha	9	Di	52.00N	9.50W
McGrath	40	Hd	62.58N	155.38W
MacGregor	45	Gb	49.57N	98.49W
McGregor	45	Jc	46.36N	93.19W
McGregor Lake	46	Ia	50.31N	112.53W
Mc Gregor Range	59	Ie	26.40S	142.45 E
McGuire, Mount-	46	Hd	45.10N	114.36W
Machachi	54	Cd	0.30S	78.34W
Machado	55	Je	21.41S	45.56W
Machagai	56	Hc	26.56S	60.03W
Machaila	37	Ed	22.15S	32.58 E
Machaire na Mumhan/ Golden Vale	9	Fi	52.30N	8.00W
Machaire Rátha/Maghera	9	Gg	54.51N	6.40W
Machakos	36	Gc	1.31S	37.16 E
Machala	54	Cd	3.16S	79.58W
Machaneng	37	Dd	23.12S	27.30 E
Machareti	54	Fh	20.49S	63.24W
Machar Marshes	35	Ed	9.20N	33.10 E
Machattie, Lake-	59	Hd	24.50S	139.48 E
Machault	12	Ge	49.21N	4.30 E
Macheke	37	Ec	18.05S	31.51 E
Macheng	27	Je	31.10N	115.00 E
Machias	44	Nc	44.43N	67.28W
Machida	29	Fd	35.32N	139.27 E
Machilipatnam (Bandar)	25	Ge	16.10N	81.08 E
Machiques	54	Da	10.04N	72.34W
Machona, Laguna-	48	Mh	18.20N	93.40W
Machów	10	Rf	50.34N	21.40 E
Machupicchu	53	Ig	13.07S	72.34W
Macia	37	Ef	25.02S	33.06 E
Mc Ilwraith Range	59	Ib	13.45S	143.20 E
Măcin	15	Ld	45.15N	28.09 E
Macina	30	Gg	14.30N	5.00W
McIntosh	45	Fd	45.55N	101.21W
Macintyre River	59	Je	29.25S	148.45 E
Maçka	24	Hb	40.50N	39.38 E
Mackay [Austl.]	58	Fg	21.09S	149.11 E
Mackay [Id.-U.S.]	46	Ie	43.55N	113.37W
Mackay, Lake-	57	Dg	22.30S	129.00 E
McKay Lake	45	Mb	49.35N	86.22W
McKean Atoll	57	Je	3.36S	174.08W
McKeand	42	Kd	63.00N	65.05W
McKeesport	44	He	40.21N	79.52W
Mackenzie	38	Fc	69.15N	134.08W
McKenzie	44	Cg	36.08N	88.31W
Mackenzie, District of- [3]	42	Gd	65.00N	115.00W
Mackenzie Bay [Ant.]	66	Fe	68.20S	71.15 E
Mackenzie Bay [Can.]	38	Fc	69.00N	136.30W
McKenzie Island	42	If	51.05N	93.48W
Mackenzie King	38	Hb	77.45N	111.00W
Mackenzie Mountains	38	Gc	64.00N	130.00W
McKenzie River	46	Dd	44.07N	123.06W
Mackenzie River	59	Jd	24.00S	149.55 E
McKerrow, Lake-	62	Cf	44.30S	168.05 E
Mackinac, Straits of-	43	Kb	45.49N	82.45W
Mackinaw City	44	Ec	45.47N	84.44W
McKinley, Mount-	38	Dc	63.30N	151.00W
McKinley Park	40	Jd	63.44N	148.54W
McKinney	45	Hj	33.12N	96.37W
Mackinnon Road	36	Gc	3.44S	39.03 E
McLaughlin	45	Fd	45.49N	100.49W
McLean	45	Fi	35.14N	100.36W
McLeans Town	44	Il	26.39N	77.59W
Maclean Strait	42	Ha	77.30N	103.10W
Maclear	37	Df	31.02S	28.23 E
Macleay River	59	Kf	30.52S	153.01 E
Mc Leod, Lake-	57	Cg	24.10S	113.35 E
McLeod Bay	42	Gd	62.53N	110.15W
McLeod Lake	42	Ff	54.59N	123.02W
McLoughlin, Mount-	46	De	42.27N	122.19W
McLure	46	Ea	51.03N	120.14W
Macmillan	42	Dd	62.52N	135.55W
McMillan, Lake-	45	Dj	32.40N	104.20W
McMillan Pass	42	Ed	63.00N	130.00W
McMinnville [Or.-U.S.]	46	Dd	45.13N	123.12W
McMinnville [Tn.-U.S.]	44	Eh	35.41N	85.46W
McMurdo	66	Kf	77.51S	166.37 E
McNaughton Lake	42	Ff	52.40N	117.50W
Macomb	45	Kf	40.27N	90.40W
Macomer	14	Cj	40.16N	8.47 E
Macomia	37	Gb	12.15S	40.08 E
Mâcon	11	Kh	46.18N	4.50 E
Macon [Ga.-U.S.]	39	Kf	32.50N	83.38W
Macon [Mo.-U.S.]	45	Jg	39.44N	92.28W
Macon [Ms.-U.S.]	45	Lj	33.07N	88.34W
Macondo	36	De	12.36S	23.43 E
Mâconnais, Monts du-	11	Kh	46.18N	4.45 E
Macoris, Cabo-	49	Ld	19.47N	70.28W
Macouba	51h	Ab	14.52N	61.09W
McPherson	43	Hd	38.22N	97.40W
Mc Pherson Range	59	Ke	28.20S	153.00 E
Macquarie	66	Jd	54.30S	158.30 E
Macquarie Harbour	59	Jh	42.20S	145.25 E
Macquarie Ridge (EN)	3	Jo	57.00S	159.00 E
Macquarie River	57	Fh	30.07S	147.24 E
Mac Robertson Land	66	Fe	70.00S	65.00 E
Macroom/Maigh Chromtha	9	Ej	51.54N	8.57W
Macugnaga	14	Be	45.58N	7.58 E
Macujer	54	Dc	0.24N	73.07W
Macuro	50	Fg	10.39N	61.56W
Macusani	54	Df	14.05S	70.26W
Macuspana	48	Mi	17.48N	92.36W
Mačva	15	Ce	44.49N	19.30 E
McVicar Arm	42	Fc	65.10N	120.30W
Ma'dabā	24	Fg	31.43N	35.48 E
Madagali	34	Hc	10.53N	13.38 E
Madagascar	30	Lj	20.00S	47.00 E
Madagascar (EN)= Madagasikara [1]	31	Lj	19.00S	46.00 E
Madagascar Basin (EN)	3	Fl	27.00S	53.00 E
Madagascar Plateau (EN)	3	Fm	30.00S	45.00 E
Madagasikara=Madagascar (EN) [1]	31	Lj	19.00S	46.00 E
Madā'in Şāliḩ	24	Gi	26.48N	37.53 E
Madalai	64a	Ac	7.20N	134.28 E
Madama	34	Ha	21.58N	13.39 E
Madan	15	Hh	41.30N	24.57 E
Madang	58	Fe	5.13S	145.48 E
Madanīyīn	31	Ie	33.21N	10.30 E
Madanīyīn [3]	32	Jc	33.00N	10.45 E
Madaoua	34	Gc	14.05N	5.58 E
Madara	15	Kf	43.17N	27.06 E
Madara-Shima	29	Ae	33.35N	129.45 E
Madaroumfa	34	Gc	13.18N	7.09 E
Madau	63a	Ac	9.00S	152.26 E
Madawaska Highlands	44	Hc	45.20N	78.15W
Maddalena	14	Di	41.15N	9.25 E
Maddalena, Colle della-	11	Mj	44.25N	6.53 E
Maddaloni	14	Ii	41.02N	14.23 E
Made, Made en Drimmelen-	12	Gc	51.41N	4.48 E
Made en Drimmelen	12	Gc	51.41N	4.48 E
Made en Drimmelen-Made	12	Gc	51.41N	4.48 E
Madeir	35	Dd	7.50N	29.12 E
Madeira [5]	31	Fe	32.40N	16.45W
Madeira	30	Fe	32.44N	17.00W
Madeira, Arquipélago da-= Madeira Islands (EN)	30	Fe	32.40N	16.45W
Madeira, Rio-	52	Kf	3.22S	58.45W
Madeira Islands (EN)= Madeira, Arquipélago da-	30	Fe	32.40N	16.45W
Madeleine, Ile de la -	42	Lg	47.26N	61.44W
Madeleine, Monts de la-	11	Jh	46.03N	3.50 E
Maden	24	Hc	38.23N	39.40 E
Madenassa Veld	30	Jj	19.00N	25.30 E
Madera [Ca.-U.S.]	46	Eh	36.57N	120.03W
Madera [Mex.]	47	Cc	29.12N	108.07W
Mader-Chih	13	Ri	35.26N	5.07 E
Madero, Puerto del-	13	Jc	41.48N	2.05W
Madesimo	14	Dd	46.26N	9.21 E
Madgaon	25	Ee	15.22N	73.49 E
Madhya Pradesh [3]	25	Fd	22.00N	79.00 E
Madimba	36	Cc	4.58S	15.08 E
Madina do Boé	34	Cc	11.45N	14.13W
Madinani	34	Dd	9.37N	6.57W
Madīnat al Abyār	33	Dc	32.11N	20.36 E
Madīnat ash Sha'b	22	Gh	12.50N	44.56 E
Madingo-Kayes	36	Bc	4.10S	12.18 E
Madingou	36	Bc	4.09S	13.34 E
Madirovalo	37	Hc	16.29S	46.30 E
Madison [Fl.-U.S.]	44	Fj	30.28N	83.25W
Madison [In.-U.S.]	44	Ef	38.44N	85.23W
Madison [Mn.-U.S.]	45	Hd	45.01N	96.11W
Madison [S.D.-U.S.]	45	He	44.00N	97.07W
Madison [Wi.-U.S.]	39	Ke	43.05N	89.22W
Madison [W.V.-U.S.]	44	Gf	38.03N	81.50W
Madison Range	46	Jd	45.15N	111.20W
Madison River	46	Jd	45.56N	111.30W
Madisonville	43	Jd	37.20N	87.30W
Madiun	26	Fh	7.37S	111.31 E
Mado Gashi	36	Gb	0.44N	39.10 E
Madoi (Huangheyan)	22	Lf	35.00N	98.56 E
Madon	11	Mf	48.36N	6.06 E
Madona	7	Gh	56.53N	26.20 E
Madra Dağı	15	Kj	39.23N	27.12 E
Madrakah, Ra's al-	23	If	18.59N	57.45 E
Madranbaba Dağı	15	Ll	37.38N	28.12 E
Madras [India]	22	Kh	13.05N	80.17 E
Madras [Or.-U.S.]	46	Ed	44.38N	121.08W
Madre, Laguna- [Mex.]	47	Ed	25.00N	97.40W
Madre, Laguna- [Tx.-U.S.]	43	Hf	27.00N	97.35W
Madre, Sierra-	38	Jh	15.20N	92.20W
Madre de Dios [2]	54	Df	12.00S	70.15W
Madre de Dios	54	Df	12.36S	69.59W
Madre de Dios, Isla-	52	Ik	50.15S	75.05W
Madre de Dios, Río-	52	Jg	10.59S	66.08W
Madre del Sur, Sierra-= Southern Sierra Madre (EN)	38	Jj	17.00N	100.00W
Madre Occidental, Sierra-= Western Sierra Madre (EN)	38	Ig	25.00N	105.00W
Madre Oriental, Sierra-= Eastern Sierra Madre (EN)	38	Jg	22.00N	99.30W
Madrid [3]	13	Id	40.30N	3.40W
Madrid	6	Fg	40.24N	3.41W
Madrid-Aravaca	13	Id	40.27N	3.47W
Madridejos	13	Ie	39.28N	3.32W
Madrid-El Pardo	13	Id	40.32N	3.46W
Madrid-Vallecas	13	Id	40.23N	3.37W
Madrid-Villaverde	13	Id	40.21N	3.42W
Madrigal de las Altas Torres	13	Hc	41.05N	5.00W
Mad River	46	Cf	40.57N	124.07W
Madriz [3]	49	Dg	13.30N	86.30W
Madrona, Sierra-	13	Hf	38.25N	4.10W
Madula	36	Eb	0.28N	25.23 E
Madura, Palau-	21	Nj	7.00S	113.20 E
Madurai	22	Ji	9.56N	78.07 E
Madvār, Kūh-e-	23	Hc	30.36N	54.52 E
Madwīn	33	Cd	28.42N	17.31 E
Madyan	21	Fg	27.40N	35.35 E
Madžalis	16	Oh	42.08N	47.50 E
Maebara	29	Be	33.34N	130.13 E
Maebashi	27	Od	36.23N	139.04 E
Mae Hong Son	25	Je	19.16N	97.56 E
Mæl	8	Ce	59.56N	8.48 E
Mae Nam Khong=Mekong (EN)	21	Mh	10.15N	105.55 E
Maesawa	29	Gb	39.03N	141.07 E
Mae Sot	25	Je	16.40N	98.35 E
Maestra, Sierra-	38	Lh	20.00N	76.45W
Maevatanana	37	Hc	16.56S	46.49 E
Maéwo, Ile-	57	Hf	15.10S	168.10 E
Mafeteng	37	De	29.45S	27.18 E
Mafia Channel	36	Gd	7.50S	39.35 E
Mafia Island	30	Ki	7.50S	39.50 E
Mafikeng	31	Jk	25.53S	25.39 E
Mafra [Braz.]	56	Kc	26.07S	49.49W
Mafra [Port.]	13	Cf	38.56N	9.20W
Magadan	22	Rd	59.34N	150.48 E
Magadanskaja Oblast [3]	20	Kd	62.30N	154.00 E
Magadi	36	Gc	1.54S	36.17 E
Magallanes, Estrecho de- = Magellan, Strait of- (EN)	52	Ik	54.00S	71.00W
Magallanes y Antártica Chilena [2]	56	Fh	51.30S	73.30W
Magangué	54	Db	9.14N	74.46W
Maganik	15	Cg	42.44N	19.16 E
Maganoy	26	He	6.51N	124.31 E
Magaria	34	Gc	12.59N	8.50 E
Magazine Mountain	45	Ji	35.10N	93.38W
Magdagači	20	Hf	53.29N	125.55 E
Magdala	55	Bm	36.06S	61.42W
Magdalena [2]	54	Db	10.00N	74.15W
Magdalena [Arg.]	55	Dl	35.04S	57.32W
Magdalena [Bol.]	54	Ff	13.20S	64.08W
Magdalena [Mex.]	47	Bb	30.38N	110.57W
Magdalena [N.M.-U.S.]	45	Ci	34.07N	107.14W
Magdalena, Bahía-	48	Ce	24.35N	112.00W
Magdalena, Isla-	47	Bd	24.55N	112.15W
Magdalena, Llano de la-	47	Bd	24.30N	111.40W
Magdalena, Río- [Col.]	52	Id	11.06N	74.51W
Magdalena, Río- [Mex.]	48	Cb	30.48N	112.32W
Magda Plateau	42	Jb	72.18N	82.55W
Magdeburg	6	He	52.10N	11.40 E
Magdeburg [2]	10	Hd	52.15N	11.35 E
Magdeburger Börde	10	Hd	52.00N	11.30 E
Magdelaine Cays	57	Gf	16.35S	150.15 E
Magee	45	Lk	31.52N	89.44W
Magee, Island-/Oileán Mhic Aodha	9	Hg	54.50N	5.50W
Magelang	26	Fh	7.28S	110.13 E
Magellan, Strait of- (EN) = Magallanes, Estrecho de-	52	Ik	54.00S	71.00W
Magellan Seamounts (EN)	57	Gc	17.30N	152.00 E
Magenta	14	Ce	45.28N	8.53 E
Magerøya	7	Fa	71.03N	25.45 E
Magetan	26	Fh	7.39S	111.20 E
Maggiorasca	14	Df	44.33N	9.29 E
Maggiore, Lago-	14	Ce	45.55N	8.40 E
Maghāghah	33	Fd	28.39N	30.50 E
Maghama	32	Ef	15.31N	12.50W
Maghera/Machaire Rátha	9	Gg	54.51N	6.40W
Maghnia	32	Gc	34.51N	1.44W
Magic Reservoir	46	He	43.20N	114.18W
Mágina, Sierra-	13	Ig	37.45N	3.30W
Magistralny	20	Fe	56.03N	107.35 E
Maglaj	14	Mf	44.33N	18.06 E
Măglenik	15	Ih	41.20N	25.45 E
Maglie	14	Mj	40.07N	18.18 E
Măgliž	15	Ig	42.36N	25.33 E
Magnetawan River	44	Gc	45.46N	80.37W
Magnetic Island	59	Jc	19.10S	146.50 E
Magnitka	17	Ii	55.21N	59.43 E
Magnitnaja, Gora-	17	Ij	53.10N	59.10 E
Magnitogorsk	6	Le	53.27N	59.04 E
Magnolia	45	Jj	33.16N	93.14W
Magnor	7	Cg	59.57N	12.12 E
Magny-en-Vexin	11	He	49.09N	1.47 E
Mago	20	Jf	53.18N	140.20 E
Mágoé	37	Ec	15.48S	31.43 E
Magoebaskloof	37	Ed	23.51S	30.02 E
Magog	44	Kc	45.16N	72.09W
Magosa=Famagusta (EN)	23	Dc	35.07N	33.57 E
Magra [Alg.]	13	Qi	35.29N	4.58 E
Magra [It.]	14	Df	44.03N	9.58 E
Magtá Lahjar	32	Ef	17.50N	13.20W
Maguarinho, Cabo-	54	Id	0.20S	48.20W
Magude	37	Ee	25.02S	32.40 E
Magumeri	34	Hc	12.07N	12.49 E
Magura, Gora-	10	Th	48.50N	23.44 E
Magwe [3]	25	Jd	20.00N	95.00 E
Magwe	22	Lg	20.09N	94.55 E
Magyarország=Hungary (EN) [1]	6	Hf	47.00N	20.00 E
Mahābād	23	Gb	36.45N	45.53 E
Mahabalipuram	25	Gf	12.37N	80.12 E
Mahabe	37	Hc	17.05S	45.20 E
Mahabo	37	Gd	20.21S	44.39 E
Mahačkala	6	Kg	42.58N	47.30 E
Mahadday Wēyne	35	He	3.00N	45.32 E
Mahādeo Range	25	Ee	17.50N	74.15 E
Mahafaly, Plateau-	37	Gd	24.30S	44.00 E
Mahagi	36	Fb	2.18N	30.59 E
Mahajamba	37	Hc	15.33S	47.08 E
Mahājan	25	Ec	28.47N	73.50 E
Mahajanga	31	Lj	15.17S	46.43 E
Mahajanga [3]	37	Hc	16.30S	47.00 E
Mahajilo	37	Hc	19.42S	45.22 E
Mahakam	21	Nj	0.35S	117.17 E
Mahalapye	37	Dd	23.07S	26.46 E
Mahalevona	37	Hc	15.26S	49.55 E
Mahallāt	24	Nf	33.55N	50.27 E
Mahamid	35	Cb	15.09N	20.25 E
Māhān	24	Qg	30.05N	57.19 E
Mahānadi	21	Kg	20.19N	86.45 E
Mahanoro	37	Hc	19.53S	48.49 E
Maharadze	19	Eg	41.53N	42.01 E
Mahārāshtra [3]	25	Ee	18.00N	75.00 E
Mahārlū, Daryācheh-ye-	24	Oh	29.25N	52.50 E
Maḩās	35	He	4.24N	46.07 E
Maha Sarakham	25	Ke	16.12N	103.16 E
Mahavavy	30	Lj	15.57S	45.54 E
Mahbés	32	Dd	27.10N	9.50W
Maḩḑah	24	Pj	24.24N	55.59 E
Mahdia	54	Gb	5.16N	59.09W
Mahe	25	Ff	11.42N	75.32 E
Mahébourg	37a	Bb	20.24S	57.42 E
Mahé Island	30	Mi	4.40S	55.28 E
Mahendra Giri	25	Ge	18.58N	84.21 E
Mahenge	31	Ki	8.41S	36.43 E
Maheno	62	Df	45.10S	170.50 E
Mahi	25	Ed	22.16N	72.58 E
Mahia Peninsula	61	Eg	39.10S	177.55 E
Mahmudābād	24	Lc	39.25N	47.15 E
Mahmūdābād	24	Od	36.38N	52.15 E
Mahmūd-e 'Erāqī	23	Kb	35.01N	69.20 E
Mahmudiye	24	Dc	39.30N	31.00 E
Mahmutşevketpaşa	15	Mh	41.09N	29.11 E
Māhneshān	24	Ld	36.45N	47.38 E
Mahnevo	17	Jg	58.27N	61.42 E
Mahnomen	45	Ic	47.19N	95.59W
Mahón/Mao	13	Qe	39.53N	4.15 E
Mahoré/Mayotte	30	Lj	12.50S	45.10 E
Mahrāt, Jabal-	35	Ib	17.00N	52.00 E
Mahsana	25	Ed	23.36N	72.24 E
Mahuan Dao	27	Kd	10.50N	115.47 E
Mahua Point	63a	Fd	10.28S	162.05 E
Maiana Atoll	57	Id	0.55N	173.00 E
Maïao, Ile- (Tubai-Manu)	57	Lf	17.34S	150.35W
Maicao	54	Da	11.23N	72.15W
Maicasagi, Lac-	44	Ia	49.52N	76.48W
Maîche	11	Mg	47.15N	6.48 E
Maicuru, Rio-	54	Hd	2.10S	54.17W
Maidenhead	12	Bc	51.31N	0.42W
Maidstone	9	Nj	51.17N	0.32 E
Maiduguri	31	Ig	11.51N	13.09 E
Maigh Chromtha/Macroom	9	Ej	51.54N	8.57W
Maigudo	35	Fd	7.26N	37.10 E
Maihara	29	Ed	35.20N	136.18 E
Maikala Range	25	Gd	22.30N	81.30 E
Maiko	36	Eb	0.14N	25.33 E
Maikona	36	Gb	2.56N	37.38 E
Maikoor, Pulau-	26	Jh	6.15S	134.15 E
Main	10	Ef	50.00N	8.18 E
Maínalon Óros	15	Fl	37.40N	22.15 E

Index Symbols

[1] Independent Nation
[2] State, Region
[3] District, County
[4] Municipality
[5] Colony, Dependency
Continent
Physical Region
Historical or Cultural Region
Mount, Mountain
Volcano
Hill
Mountains, Mountain Range
Hills, Escarpment
Plateau, Upland
Pass, Gap
Plain, Lowland
Delta
Salt Flat
Valley, Canyon
Crater, Cave
Karst Features
Depression
Polder
Desert, Dunes
Forest, Woods
Heath, Steppe
Oasis
Cape, Point
Coast, Beach
Cliff
Peninsula
Isthmus
Sandbank
Island
Atoll
Rock, Reef
Islands, Archipelago
Rocks, Reefs
Coral Reef
Well, Spring
Geyser
River, Stream
Waterfall Rapids
River Mouth, Estuary
Lake
Salt Lake
Intermittent Lake
Reservoir
Swamp, Pond
Canal
Glacier
Ice Shelf, Pack Ice
Ocean
Sea
Gulf, Bay
Strait, Fjord
Lagoon
Bank
Seamount
Tablemount
Ridge
Shelf
Basin
Escarpment, Sea Scarp
Fracture
Trench, Abyss
National Park, Reserve
Point of Interest
Recreation Site
Cave, Cavern
Historic Site
Ruins
Wall, Walls
Church, Abbey
Temple
Scientific Station
Airport
Port
Lighthouse
Mine
Tunnel
Dam, Bridge

Main Barrier Range 59 If 31.25 S 141.25 E
Mainburg 10 Hh 48.39N 11.47 E
Main Camp 64g Ba 2.01N 157.25W
Main Channel 44 Gc 45.22N 81.50W
Mai-Ndombe, Lac- 30 Ii 2.10 S 18.15 E
Main-Donau-Kanal 10 Gg 49.55N 10.50 E
Maindong → Coqên 27 Ee 31.15N 85.13 E
Maine 11 Ff 48.15N 0.10W
Maine [2] 43 Nb 45.15N 69.15W
Maine [Fr.] 11 Fg 47.25N 0.37W
Maine [Fr.] 11 Eg 47.09N 1.27W
Maine, Gulf of- 38 Me 43.00N 68.00W
Maine-et-Loire [3] 11 Fg 47.30N 0.20W
Maïné-Soroa 34 Hc 13.18N 12.02 E
Mainistir Fhear Maí/Fermoy 9 Ei 52.08N 8.16W
Mainistir na Búille/Boyle 9 Eh 53.58N 8.18W
Mainistir na Corann/Midleton 9 Ej 51.55N 8.10W
Mainistir na Féile/Abbeyfeale 9 Di 52.24N 9.18W
Mainit, Lake- 26 Ie 9.26N 125.32 E
Mainland [Scot.-U.K.] 5 Fc 60.20N 1.22W
Mainland [Scot.-U.K.] 5 Fd 59.00N 3.10W
Maintal 12 Kd 50.08N 8.51 E
Maintenon 11 Hf 48.35N 1.35 E
Maintirano 31 Lj 18.03 S 44.03 E
Mainz 10 Eg 50.00N 8.15 E
Maio 32 Cf 23.10N 15.10W
Maio 30 Eg 15.15N 23.10W
Maipo, Volcán- 52 Ji 34.10 S 69.50W
Maipú 56 Ie 36.52 S 57.52W
Maiquetia 54 Ea 10.36N 66.57W
Maira 14 Bf 44.49N 7.38 E
Mairi 54 Jf 11.43 S 40.08W
Mairipotaba 55 Hc 17.21 S 49.31W
Maisān [3] 24 Lg 32.00N 47.00 E
Maisí, Punta- 47 Jd 20.15N 74.09W
Maišiagala/Maišjagala 8 Kj 54.51N 25.14 E
Maišjagala/Maišiagala 8 Kj 54.51N 25.14 E
Maïter 13 Qi 35.23N 4.17 E
Maitland [Austl.] 59 Hf 34.22 S 137.40 E
Maitland [Austl.] 58 Gh 32.44 S 151.33 E
Maíz, Isla Grande del- 49 Fg 12.10N 83.03W
Maíz, Isla Pequeña del- 49 Fg 12.18N 82.59W
Maíz, Islas del- 47 Hf 12.15N 83.00W
Maizhokunggar 27 Ff 29.50N 91.40 E
Maizières-lès-Metz 12 Ie 49.13N 6.09 E
Maizuru 28 Mg 35.27N 135.20 E
Maizuru-Nishimaizuru 29 Dd 35.28N 135.19 E
Maizuru-Wan 29 Dd 35.30N 135.20 E
Maja 21 Pd 60.17N 134.41 E
Majagual 49 Ji 8.35N 74.37W
Majakovski 16 Mh 42.02N 42.47 E
Majangat 27 Fb 48.20N 91.58 E
Majardah, Wādī- 14 Em 37.07N 10.13 E
Majāz al Bāb 14 Dn 36.39N 9.37 E
Majdanpek 15 Ee 44.25N 21.56 E
Majene 22 Nj 3.33 S 118.57 E
Majērtēn = Mijirtein (EN) 30 Lh 9.00N 50.00 E
Majevica 14 Mf 44.40N 18.40 E
Maji 35 Fd 6.10N 35.35 E
Majia He 27 Kd 38.09N 117.53 E
Majja 20 Id 61.38N 130.25 E
Majkain 19 He 51.27N 75.52 E
Majkamys 18 Ka 46.34N 77.37 E
Majkop 6 Kg 44.35N 40.07 E
Majli-Saj 18 Id 41.15N 72.30 E
Majma'ah 24 Kj 25.54N 45.20 E
Majmak 19 Hg 42.40N 71.14 E
Majmakan 20 Ie 57.30N 135.23 E
Majmeča 20 Fb 71.20N 104.15 E
Majn 20 Mc 65.03N 172.10 E
Majna [R.S.F.S.R.] 20 Ef 53.00N 91.28 E
Majna [R.S.F.S.R.] 7 Li 54.09N 47.37 E
Major, Puig- 13 Oe 39.48N 2.48 E
Major, Puig-/Mayor, Puig- 13 Oe 39.48N 2.48 E
Majorca (EN) = Mallorca 5 Gh 39.30N 3.00 E
Majrur 35 Db 16.40N 26.53 E
Majski [R.S.F.S.R.] 16 Nh 43.36N 44.03 E
Majski [R.S.F.S.R.] 20 Hf 52.18N 129.38 E
Maju, Pulau 26 If 1.20N 126.25 E
Majuro Atoll 57 Id 7.09N 171.12 E
Makabana 31 Ii 3.28 S 12.36 E
Makaha 65a Cb 21.29N 158.13W
Makahuena Point 65a Bb 21.52N 159.27W
Makalamabedi 37 Cd 20.20 S 23.53 E
Makale 26 Gg 3.06 S 119.51 E
Makallé 56 Ic 27.13 S 59.17W
Makalondi 34 Fc 12.50N 1.41 E
Makamby, Nosy- 37 Hc 15.42 S 45.54 E
Makanči 19 If 46.51N 81.57 E
Makanza 36 Cb 1.36N 19.07 E
Makapala 65a Fc 20.13N 155.45W
Makapu Point 64k Ba 18.59 S 169.55W
Makapuu Head 65a Db 21.18N 157.39W
Makara, Prohod- 15 Ih 41.16N 25.26 E
Mákares 15 Il 37.05N 25.42 E
Makarfi 34 Gc 11.23N 7.53 E
Makari 34 Hc 12.35N 14.28 E
Makari Mountains 36 Ed 6.05 S 29.50 E
Makarjev 7 Kh 57.57N 43.49 E
Makarov 20 Jg 48.39N 142.51 E
Makarov Basin (EN) 67 Ce 87.00N 170.00 E
Makarov Seamount (EN) 57 Gb 29.30N 153.30 E
Makarska 14 Lg 43.18N 17.02 E
Makā Rūd 24 Nd 36.21N 51.16 E
Makasar → Ujung Pandang 22 Nj 5.07 S 119.24 E
Makasar, Selat- = Makassar Strait (EN) 21 Nj 2.00 S 117.30 E
Makassar Strait (EN) = Makasar, Selat- 21 Nj 2.00 S 117.30 E
Makat 6 Lf 47.40N 53.28 E
Makatea, Ile- 57 Mf 15.50 S 148.15W
Makaw 25 Jc 26.27N 96.42 E
Makawao 65a Ec 20.51N 156.19W
Makay, Massif du- 37 Hd 21.15 S 45.15 E
Makedhonía [2] 15 Fi 40.40N 22.30 E
Makedhonía = Macedonia (EN) 15 Fh 41.00N 23.00 E
Makedhonía = Macedonia (EN) 5 Ig 41.00N 23.00 E
Makedonija = Macedonia (EN) 5 Ig 41.00N 23.00 E
Makedonija = Macedonia (EN) [2] 15 Eh 41.50N 22.00 E
Makedonija = Macedonia (EN) 15 Fh 41.00N 23.00 E
Makejevka 16 Jf 48.00N 37.58 E
Makelulu, Mount- 64a Bb 7.34N 134.35 E
Makemo Atoll 57 Mf 16.35 S 143.40W
Makeni 31 Fh 8.53N 12.03W
Makgadikgadi Pans 30 Jk 20.50 S 25.30 E
Makhfar al Buşayyah 24 Lg 30.08N 46.07 E
Makhfar al Hammām 24 He 35.51N 38.45 E
Makhmūr 24 Je 35.46N 43.35 E
Makhyah, Wādī- 23 Gf 17.40N 49.01 E
Maki 29 Fc 37.45N 138.52 E
Makian, Pulau- 26 If 0.20N 127.25 E
Makikihi 62 Df 44.38 S 171.09 E
Makinsk 19 He 52.40N 70.26 E
Makkah = Mecca (EN) 22 Fg 21.27N 39.49 E
Makkovik 42 Le 55.05N 59.11W
Maknassy 32 Ic 34.37N 9.36 E
Makó 10 Qj 46.13N 20.29 E
Makokou 31 Ih 0.34N 12.52 E
Makongai 63d Bb 17.27 S 178.58 E
Makongolosi 36 Fd 8.24 S 33.09 E
Makorako 62 Gc 39.09 S 176.03 E
Makoua 31 Ih 0.01N 15.39 E
Makoura 63b Dc 17.08 S 168.26 E
Makov 10 Og 49.22N 18.29 E
Maków Mazowiecki 10 Rd 52.52N 21.06 E
Makrá 15 Im 36.16N 25.53 E
Makrān 21 Hg 26.00N 60.00 E
Makrónisos 15 Hl 37.42N 24.07 E
Maksatiha 7 Ih 57.48N 35.55 E
Makteïr 30 Ff 21.50N 11.40W
Makthar 14 Do 35.50N 9.13 E
Makthar 32 Ib 35.51N 9.12 E
Makū 23 Hd 27.52N 52.26 E
Mākū 24 Kc 39.17N 44.31 E
Makubetsu 29a Cb 42.54N 143.19 E
Makumbato 36 Fd 8.51 S 34.50 E
Makumbi 36 Dd 5.51 S 20.41 E
Makunduchi 36 Gd 6.25 S 39.33 E
Makung 27 Kg 23.35N 119.35 E
Makurazaki 28 Ki 31.16N 139.19 E
Makurdi 31 Hh 7.44N 8.32 E
Makushin Volcano 40a Eb 53.53N 166.50W
Makušino 19 Gd 55.13N 67.13 E
Makuyuni 36 Gc 3.33 S 36.06 E
Malå 7 Ed 65.11N 18.44 E
Mala/Mallow 9 Ei 52.08N 8.39W
Mala, Punta- 47 Ig 7.28N 80.00W
Malabang 26 He 7.38N 124.03 E
Malabar Coast 21 Jh 10.00N 76.15 E
Malabo 31 Hh 3.45N 8.47 E
Malabrigo 55 Ci 29.20 S 59.58W
Malacca, Strait of- (EN) = Melaka, Selat- 21 Mi 2.30N 101.20 E
Malacky 10 Nh 48.27N 17.01 E
Malad City 46 Ie 42.12N 112.15W
Malá Fatra 10 Og 49.08N 18.50 E
Málaga [3] 13 Hh 36.48N 4.45W
Málaga [Col.] 54 Db 6.42N 72.44W
Málaga [Sp.] 6 Fh 36.43N 4.25W
Malagarasi 30 Ji 5.12 S 29.47 E
Malagón 13 Ie 39.10N 3.51W
Malaimbandi 37 Hd 20.20 S 45.36 E
Malaita Island 57 He 9.00 S 161.00 E
Malaja Kuonamka 20 Gb 70.50N 113.20 E
Malaja Ob 20 Bc 66.08N 65.50 E
Malaja Sosva 19 Gc 63.10N 64.22 E
Malaja Višera 19 Dd 58.52N 32.14 E
Malaja Viska 16 Ge 48.39N 31.38 E
Malakāl 31 Kh 9.31N 31.39 E
Malakal Harbor 64a Ac 7.20N 134.26 E
Malakal Pass 64a Ac 7.17N 134.28 E
Mala Kapela 14 Jf 44.55N 15.28 E
Malakobi 63a Db 7.19 S 158.07 E
Mallamalla Range 25 Fe 16.17N 79.29 E
Malang 22 Nj 7.59 S 112.37 E
Malange [3] 36 Cd 9.30 S 16.30 E
Malange 31 Ii 9.33 S 16.22 E
Malangen 7 Eb 69.30N 18.20 E
Malanville 34 Fc 11.52N 3.23 E
Malao 63b Cb 15.10 S 166.51 E
Mała Panew 10 Nf 50.44N 17.52 E
Mälaren 5 Hd 59.30N 17.15 E
Malargüe 56 Ge 35.28 S 69.35W
Malartic, Lac- 44 Ha 48.15N 78.05W
Malaspina Glacier 40 Ke 59.50N 140.30W
Malatya 22 Ff 38.21N 38.19 E
Malāvi 24 Lf 33.10N 47.50 E
Malawi [1] 31 Kj 13.30 S 34.00 E
Malawi, Lake- 30 Kj 12.00 S 34.30 E
Malaya 26 Df 4.00N 102.00 E
Malaybalay 26 Ie 8.09N 125.05 E
Malāyer 24 Me 34.16N 48.12 E
Malāyer 23 Gc 34.17N 48.50 E
Malay Peninsula (EN) 21 Mi 6.00N 102.00 E
Malaysia [1] 22 Mi 4.00N 102.00 E
Malaysia, Semenanjung- [2] 26 Df 4.00N 102.00 E
Malazgirt 24 Jc 39.09N 42.31 E
Malberg 12 Id 50.03N 6.35 E
Mālbor 24 Og 30.45N 52.05 E
Malbork 10 Pb 54.02N 19.01 E
Malbrán 56 Hc 29.21 S 62.27W
Malchin 10 Ic 53.44N 12.47 E
Maldegem 12 Fc 51.13N 3.27 E
Malden 45 Lh 36.34N 89.57W
Malden Island 57 Le 4.03 S 154.59W
Malditos, Montes-/La Maladeta 13 Mb 42.40N 0.50 E
Maldive Islands 21 Ji 3.15N 73.00 E
Mal di Ventre 14 Ck 40.00N 8.20 E
Maldives [1] 22 Ji 3.15N 73.00 E
Maldon 9 Nj 51.45N 0.40 E
Maldonado [2] 55 El 34.40 S 54.55W
Maldonado 56 Jd 34.54 S 54.57W
Maldonado, Punta- 48 Ji 16.20N 98.35W
Male 22 Ji 4.10N 73.30 E
Malé 14 Ed 46.21N 10.55 E
Mâle, Lac du- 44 Ja 48.30N 75.30W
Malea, Cape- (EN) = Maléas, Ákra- 15 Gm 36.26N 23.12 E
Maléas, Ákra- = Malea, Cape- (EN) 15 Gm 36.26N 23.12 E
Male Atoll 21 Ji 4.29N 73.30 E
Malebo, Pool- 30 Ii 4.17 S 15.20 E
Mālegaon 25 Ed 20.33N 74.32 E
Maléha 34 Dc 11.48N 9.43W
Malek 35 Ed 6.04N 31.36 E
Malé Karpaty = Little Carpathians (EN) 10 Nh 48.30N 17.20 E
Malek Kandī 24 Ld 37.09N 46.06 E
Malékoula, Ile 57 Hf 16.15 S 167.30 E
Malema 37 Fb 14.57 S 37.25 E
Malemba Nkulu 36 Ed 8.02 S 26.48 E
Malenga 7 Ie 63.50N 36.25 E
Măleruş 15 Id 45.54N 25.32 E
Malesherbes 11 If 48.18N 2.25 E
Malgobek 16 Nh 43.32N 44.34 E
Malgomaj 7 Dd 64.47N 16.12 E
Malhada 55 Kb 14.21 S 43.47W
Malhanski Hrebet 20 Ff 50.30N 109.00 E
Malhão da Estrêla 13 Ed 40.19N 7.37W
Malha Wells 35 Db 15.08N 26.12 E
Malheur Lake 43 Dc 43.20N 118.45W
Malheur River 46 Gd 44.03N 116.59W
Mali [1] 31 Gg 17.00N 4.00W
Mali 34 Cc 12.05N 12.18W
Mali 25 Jc 25.42N 97.30 E
Mali 63d Bb 16.20 S 179.21 E
Mália 15 In 35.17N 25.28 E
Maliakós Kólpos 15 Fk 38.52N 22.38 E
Malik, Wādī al- 30 Kg 18.02N 30.58 E
Mali kanal 15 Cd 45.42N 19.19 E
Malik Sīah, Kūh-i- 23 Jd 29.51N 60.52 E
Målilla 8 Fg 57.23N 15.48 E
Mali Lošinj 14 If 44.32N 14.28 E
Malimba, Monts- 36 Ed 7.32 S 29.30 E
Malin 16 Fd 50.46N 29.14 E
Malinalco 48 Jh 18.57N 99.30W
Malinaltepec 48 Ji 17.03N 98.40W
Malindi 31 Li 3.13 S 40.07 E
Malines/Mechelen 11 Kc 51.02N 4.29 E
Malin Head/Cionn Mhálanna 5 Fd 55.23N 7.24W
Malino, Bukit- 26 Hf 0.45N 120.47 E
Malinovoje Ozero 20 Cf 51.40N 79.55 E
Malinyi 36 Gd 8.56 S 36.08 E
Malipo 27 Hg 23.07N 104.42 E
Maliqi 15 Di 40.43N 20.41 E
Malita 26 Ie 6.25N 125.36 E
Maljen 15 De 44.07N 20.03 E
Maljovica 15 Gg 42.11N 23.22 E
Malka 16 Nh 43.44N 44.15 E
Malkara 24 Bb 40.53N 26.54 E
Malki Lom 15 Jf 43.39N 26.04 E
Malko Tărnovo 15 Kh 41.59N 27.32 E
Mallacoota 59 Jg 37.30 S 149.50 E
Mallaig 9 Hd 57.00N 5.50W
Mallāq, Wādī- 14 Cn 36.32N 8.51 E
Mallawī 33 Fd 27.44N 30.50 E
Mallery Lake 42 Hd 64.00N 98.00W
Malles Venosta / Mals 14 Ed 46.41N 10.32 E
Mallet 55 Gg 25.55 S 50.50W
Mallorca = Majorca (EN) 5 Gh 39.30N 3.00 E
Mallow/Mala 9 Ei 52.08N 8.39W
Malm 7 Cd 64.04N 11.13 E
Malmbäck 8 Fg 57.35N 14.28 E
Malmberget 7 Ec 67.10N 20.40 E
Malmédy 11 Md 50.26N 6.02 E
Malmesbury 37 Bf 33.28 S 18.44 E
Malmö 6 Hd 55.36N 13.00 E
Malmöhus [2] 7 Ci 55.45N 13.30 E
Malmön 8 Df 58.21N 11.20 E
Malmslätt 8 Ff 58.25N 15.30 E
Malmyž 19 Fd 56.31N 50.41 E
Malo 63b Cb 15.41 S 167.10 E
Maloarhangelsk 16 Jc 52.26N 36.29 E
Maloelap 57 Id 8.45N 171.03 E
Maloggia/Malojapaß 14 Dd 46.24N 9.41 E
Malojapaß/Maloggia 14 Dd 46.24N 9.41 E
Malojaroslavec 16 Jb 55.02N 36.28 E
Maloje Polesje 10 Jf 50.10N 24.30 E
Malolo 63d Ab 17.45 S 177.10 E
Malolos 26 Hd 14.51N 120.49 E
Malombe, Lake- 36 Ge 14.38 S 35.12 E
Malone 44 Jc 44.52N 74.19W
Malonga 36 De 10.24 S 23.10 E
Małopolska 10 Pf 50.45N 20.00 E
Malorita 16 Dd 51.48N 24.05 E
Malošujka 7 Ie 63.47N 37.22 E
Måløy 7 Af 61.56N 5.07 E
Malozemelskaja Tundra 17 Ec 68.00N 52.00 E
Malpaso 48 Mi 17.20N 93.30W
Malpelo, Isla de- 52 He 3.59N 81.35W
Malprabha 25 Fe 16.12N 76.03 E
Mals / Malles Venosta 14 Ed 46.41N 10.32 E
Malsch 12 Kf 48.53N 8.20 E
Malše 10 Kh 48.59N 14.29 E
Malta 5 Hh 35.54N 14.31 E
Malta [1] 6 Hh 35.50N 14.30 E
Malta [Lat.-U.S.S.R.] 8 Lh 56.18N 27.15 E
Malta [Mt.-U.S.] 43 Fb 48.21N 107.52W
Malta, Canale di- [Eur.] = Malta Channel (EN) 14 In 36.30N 14.30 E
Malta Channel (EN) = Malta, Canale di- [Eur.] 14 In 36.30N 14.30 E
Maltahöhe [3] 37 Bd 25.00 S 16.30 E
Maltahöhe 31 Ik 24.50 S 17.00 E
Maltepe 15 Mi 40.55N 29.08 E
Malton 9 Mg 54.08N 0.48W
Maluku [3] 26 Ig 4.00 S 128.00 E
Maluku, Kepulauan- = Moluccas (EN) 57 De 2.00 S 128.00 E
Maluku, Laut- = Molucca Sea (EN) 21 Oj 0.05 S 125.00 E
Malumfashi 34 Gc 11.48N 7.37 E
Malunda 26 Gg 3.00 S 118.50 E
Malung 7 Cf 60.40N 13.44 E
Malungsfors 8 Ed 60.44N 13.33 E
Malūţ 35 Ec 10.26N 32.12 E
Maluu 63a Ec 8.21 S 160.38 E
Malvern [Ar.-U.S.] 45 Ji 34.22N 92.49W
Malvern [Eng.-U.K.] 9 Ki 52.07N 2.19W
Malvinas 55 Ci 29.37 S 58.59W
Malvinas, Islas-/Falkland Islands [5] 53 Kk 51.45 S 59.00W
Malvinas, Islas-/Falkland Islands 52 Kk 51.45 S 59.00W
Maly, Ostrov- 8 Ld 60.02N 27.58 E
Malya 36 Fc 2.59 S 33.31 E
Maly Anjuj 20 Lc 68.35N 161.03 E
Maly Čeremšan 7 Mi 54.20N 50.01 E
Malý Dunaj 10 Nh 48.08N 17.09 E
Malygina, Proliv- 20 Cb 73.00N 70.30 E
Maly Jenisej 20 Ef 51.40N 94.26 E
Maly Kavkaz = Lesser Caucasus (EN) 5 Kg 41.00N 44.35 E
Maly Ljahovski, Ostrov- 20 Jb 74.07N 140.36 E
Maly Tajmyr, Ostrov- 20 Fa 78.08N 107.08 E
Maly Uzen 5 Kf 48.50N 49.38 E
Mama 20 Ge 58.20N 112.54 E
Mamadyš 7 Mi 55.45N 51.24 E
Mamagota 63a Bb 6.46 S 155.24 E
Mamaia 15 Le 44.17N 28.37 E
Mamakan 20 Ge 57.48N 114.05 E
Mamantel 48 Nh 18.33N 91.05W
Mamanutha Group 63d Ab 17.34 S 177.04 E
Mamaqān 24 Kd 37.51N 45.59 E
Mambaj 55 Ib 14.28 S 46.07W
Mambajao 26 He 9.15N 124.43 E
Mambasa 36 Eb 1.21N 29.03 E
Mambéré 35 Be 3.31N 16.03 E
Mambili 36 Cb 0.07N 16.08 E
Mamborê 55 Fg 24.18 S 52.32W
Mambova 36 Ef 17.44 S 25.11 E
Mambrui 36 Hc 3.07 S 40.09 E
Mamburao 26 Hd 13.14N 120.35 E
Mamedkala 16 Ph 42.12N 48.06 E
Mamer 12 Ie 49.38N 6.02 E
Mamers 11 Gf 48.21N 0.23 E
Mamfe 34 Gd 5.46N 9.17 E
Mamiá, Lago- 54 Fd 4.15 S 63.05W
Mamisonski, Pereval- 16 Mh 42.43N 43.45 E
Mamljutka 19 Ge 54.57N 68.35 E
Mammoth Cave 44 Dg 37.10N 86.08W
Mammoth Hot Springs 46 Jd 44.59N 110.43W
Mamoré, Río- 52 Jg 10.23 S 65.53W
Mamou 31 Fg 10.23N 12.05W
Mampikony 37 Hc 16.05 S 47.37 E
Mampodre, Picos de- 13 Ga 43.02N 5.12W
Mampong 34 Ed 7.04N 1.24W
Mamry, Jezioro- 10 Rb 54.08N 21.42 E
Mamuju 26 Gg 2.41 S 118.54 E
Mamuno 37 Cd 22.17 S 20.02 E
Ma'mūrah, Ra's al- 14 En 36.27N 10.49 E
Mamurokawa 29 Gb 38.54N 140.15 E
Mamutzu 37 Hb 12.47 S 45.14 E
Man 31 Gh 7.24N 7.33W
Man [3] 34 Dd 7.13N 7.41W
Man, Calf of- 9 Ig 54.03N 4.48W
Man, Isle of- 5 Fe 54.15N 4.30W
Mana 60 Oc 22.02N 159.46W
Mana 20 Ee 55.57N 92.28 E
Manacapuru 54 Fd 3.18 S 60.37W
Manacor 13 Pe 39.34N 3.12 E
Manado 22 Oi 1.29N 124.51 E
Managua 39 Kh 12.09N 86.17W
Managua [3] 49 Dg 12.05N 86.20W
Managua, Lago de- 47 Gf 12.20N 86.20W
Manakara 31 Lk 22.07 S 48.00 E
Manama (EN) = Al Manāmah 22 Hg 26.13N 50.35 E
Manambolo 37 Gc 19.19 S 44.17 E
Manam Island 57 Fe 4.05 S 145.03 E
Manamo, Caño- 54 Fb 9.55N 62.16W
Mananara 37 Hc 16.10 S 49.45 E
Mananara 37 Hd 23.21 S 47.42 E
Mananjary 31 Lk 21.14 S 48.17 E
Manankoro 34 Dc 10.28N 7.25W
Manantenina 37 Hd 24.17 S 47.18 E
Manaoba 63a Ec 8.19 S 160.47 E
Manapire, Río- 50 Ci 7.42N 66.07W
Manapouri 58 Hi 45.34 S 167.36 E
Manapouri, Lake- 62 Bf 45.30 S 167.30 E
Manār, Jabal- 33 Hg 14.10N 44.17 E
Manas 22 Ke 44.18N 86.13 E
Manas, Gora- 18 Hc 42.18N 71.06 E
Manas He 27 Eb 45.38N 85.12 E
Manas Hu 27 Eb 45.45N 85.55 E
Manasija, Manastir- 15 Ee 44.06N 21.28 E
Manatí 49 Ic 21.19N 76.56W
Manati 49 Nd 18.26N 66.29W
Manatuto 26 Ih 8.30 S 126.01 E
Manaure 49 Kh 11.46N 72.28W
Manaus 53 Jf 3.08 S 60.01W
Manavgat 24 Dd 36.47N 31.26 E
Manbij 24 Gd 36.31N 37.57 E
Manbūbnagar 25 Fe 16.44N 77.59 E
Mancelona 44 Ec 44.54N 85.04W
Mancha Real 13 Ig 37.47N 3.37W
Manche [3] 11 Ee 49.00N 1.10W
Mancheng 28 Ce 38.57N 115.19 E
Manchester [Ct.-U.S.] 44 Ke 41.47N 72.31W
Manchester [Eng.-U.K.] 6 Fe 53.30N 2.15W
Manchester [Ia.-U.S.] 45 Ke 42.29N 91.27W
Manchester [Ky.-U.S.] 44 Fg 37.09N 83.46W
Manchester [N.H.-U.S.] 43 Mc 42.59N 71.28W
Manchester [Tn.-U.S.] 44 Dh 35.29N 86.05W
Manchok 34 Gd 9.40N 8.31 E
Manchuria (EN) 22 Oe 47.00N 125.00 E
Manciano 14 Fh 42.35N 11.31 E
Mand 23 Hd 28.11N 51.17 E
Manda [Chad] 35 Bd 9.11N 18.13 E
Manda [Tan.] 36 Fe 10.28 S 34.35 E
Manda, Jabal- 35 Cd 8.39N 24.27 E
Mandabe 37 Gd 21.02 S 44.56 E
Mandaguari 56 Jb 23.32 S 51.42W
Manda Island 36 Hc 2.17 S 40.57 E
Mandal 7 Bg 58.02N 7.27 E
Mandalay [3] 25 Jd 21.00N 96.00 E
Mandalay 22 Lg 22.00N 96.05 E
Mandal-Gobi 27 Ib 45.45N 106.12 E
Mandalī 24 Kf 33.45N 45.32 E
Mandalselva 8 Bf 58.02N 7.28 E
Mandalt → Sonid Zuoqi 27 Kc 43.50N 116.45 E
Mandalya körfezi 24 Bd 37.12N 27.20 E
Mandan 43 Gb 46.50N 100.54W
Mandaon 26 Hd 12.13N 123.17 E
Mandara, Monts- = Mandara Mountains (EN) 34 Hc 10.45N 13.40 E
Mandara Mountains (EN) = Mandara, Monts- 34 Hc 10.45N 13.40 E
Mandas 14 Dk 39.38N 9.07 E
Mandasor 25 Fd 24.04N 75.04 E
Mandera 31 Lh 3.56N 41.52 E
Manderscheid 12 Id 50.06N 6.49 E
Mandeville 49 Id 18.02N 77.30W
Mandi 25 Fb 31.43N 76.55 E
Mandiana 34 Dc 10.38N 8.41W
Mandimba 37 Fb 14.21 S 35.39 E
Mandingues, Monts- 34 Cc 13.00N 11.00W
Mandioli, Pulau- 26 Ig 0.44 S 127.14 E
Mandioré, Laguna- 55 Dd 18.08 S 57.33W
Mandirituba 55 Hg 25.46 S 49.19W
Mandji 36 Bc 1.42 S 10.24 E
Mandla 25 Gd 22.36N 80.23 E
Mandø 8 Ci 55.15N 8.35 E
Mandoúdhion 15 Gk 38.48N 23.29 E
Mandrákion 15 Km 36.36N 27.08 E
Mandritsara 37 Hc 15.49 S 48.48 E
Mandurah 59 Df 32.32 S 115.43 E
Manduria 14 Lj 40.24N 17.38 E
Māndvi 25 Dd 22.50N 69.22 E
Mandya 25 Ff 12.33N 76.54 E
Måne 8 Ce 59.56N 8.48 E
Măneciu Ungureni 15 Id 45.19N 25.59 E
Manendragarh 25 Gd 23.10N 82.35 E
Maneromango 36 Gd 7.16 S 38.46 E
Manevići 16 Dd 51.19N 25.33 E
Manfalūţ 33 Fd 27.19N 30.58 E
Manfredonia 14 Ji 41.38N 15.55 E
Manfredonia, Golfo di- 14 Ki 41.35N 16.05 E
Manga [Afr.] 30 Ig 15.00N 14.00 E
Manga [Braz.] 54 Jf 14.46 S 43.56W
Mangabeiras, Chapada das- 52 Lg 10.00 S 46.30W
Mangai 36 Cc 4.03 S 19.35 E
Mangaia Island 57 Lg 21.55 S 157.55W
Mangakino 62 Fc 38.22 S 175.46 E
Mangalia 15 Lf 43.48N 28.35 E
Mangalmé 35 Bc 12.21N 19.37 E
Mangalore 22 Jh 12.52N 74.53 E
Mangareva, Ile- 57 Ng 23.07 S 134.57W
Mangfall 10 Ii 47.51N 12.08 E
Manggar 26 Eg 2.53 S 108.16 E
Manggautu 63a Dd 11.30 S 159.59 E
Mangin Yoma 25 Jd 24.20N 95.42 E
Mangistau 16 Qg 44.03N 51.57 E
Mangit 19 Gg 42.07N 60.01 E
Mangkalihat, Tanjung- 26 Gf 1.02N 118.59 E
Manglares, Cabo- 54 Cc 1.36N 79.02W
Mangnai 27 Fd 37.48N 91.55 E
Mangniu He 28 Ib 45.10N 126.58 E
Mango [Fiji] 63d Cb 17.27 S 179.09W
Mango [Ton.] 65b Bb 20.20 S 174.43W
Mangoche 36 Ge 14.28 S 35.16 E
Mangoky [Mad.] 37 Hd 23.27 S 45.13 E
Mangoky [Mad.] 30 Lk 21.29 S 43.41 E
Mangole, Pulau- 26 Ig 1.53 S 125.50 E
Mangonui 62 Ea 34.59 S 173.32 E
Mangrove Cay 49 Ia 24.51N 76.14W
Mangrullo, Cuchilla- 55 Fk 32.27 S 53.50W
Mangshi → Luxi 27 Gg 24.29N 98.40 E
Mangualde 13 Ed 40.36N 7.46W
Mangueira, Lagoa- 56 Jd 33.06 S 52.48W
Mangueni, Plateau de- 30 If 22.35N 12.40 E
Mangui 27 La 52.03N 122.09 E
Mangula 37 Ec 16.52 S 30.08 E
Mangum 45 Gi 34.53N 99.30W
Manguredjipa 36 Eb 0.21N 28.44 E
Mangyšlak 19 Fg 43.40N 51.15 E
Mangyšlak, Plato- 19 Fg 43.25N 53.00 E
Mangyšlakskaja Oblast [3] 19 Fg 44.00N 53.30 E
Mangyšlakski Zaliv 16 Qg 44.45N 51.00 E
Manhattan 43 Hd 39.11N 96.35W
Manhica 37 Ee 25.24 S 32.48 E
Mani 36 Ed 6.27 S 25.20 E
Maní 54 Dc 4.49N 72.17W
Mānī', Wādī al- 24 Ie 34.16N 41.02 E
Mania 37 Hc 19.42 S 45.22 E
Maniago 14 Gd 46.10N 12.43 E
Manica [3] 37 Ec 19.00 S 33.20 E
Manica 37 Ec 18.56 S 32.53 E
Manicaland [3] 37 Ec 19.00 S 32.30 E
Manicoré 53 Jf 5.49 S 61.17W

Index Symbols

[1] Independent Nation
[2] State, Region
[3] District, County
[4] Municipality
[5] Colony, Dependency
Continent
Physical Region
Historical or Cultural Region
Mount, Mountain
Volcano
Hill
Mountains, Mountain Range
Hills, Escarpment
Plateau, Upland
Pass, Gap
Plain, Lowland
Delta
Salt Flat
Valley, Canyon
Crater, Cave
Karst Features
Depression
Polder
Desert, Dunes
Forest, Woods
Heath, Steppe
Oasis
Cape, Point
Coast, Beach
Cliff
Peninsula
Isthmus
Sandbank
Island
Atoll
Rock, Reef
Islands, Archipelago
Rocks, Reefs
Coral Reef
Well, Spring
Geyser
River, Stream
Waterfall Rapids
River Mouth, Estuary
Lake
Salt Lake
Intermittent Lake
Reservoir
Swamp, Pond
Canal
Glacier
Ice Shelf, Pack Ice
Ocean
Sea
Gulf, Bay
Strait, Fjord
Lagoon
Bank
Seamount
Tablemount
Ridge
Shelf
Basin
Escarpment, Sea Scarp
Fracture
Trench, Abyss
National Park, Reserve
Point of Interest
Recreation Site
Cave, Cavern
Historic Site
Ruins
Wall, Walls
Church, Abbey
Temple
Scientific Station
Airport
Port
Lighthouse
Mine
Tunnel
Dam, Bridge

Manicoré, Rio- � 54 Fe 5.51 S 61.19 W
Manicouagan � 42 Kg 49.10 N 68.15 W
Manicouagan 42 Kf 51.00 N 68.20 W
Manicouagan, Réservoir- 38 Md 51.30 N 68.19 W
Manigotagan 45 Ha 51.06 N 96.18 W
Manihi Atoll 57 Mf 14.24 S 145.56 W
Manihiki Anchorage 64n Ab 10.23 S 161.03 W
Manihiki Atoll 57 Kf 10.24 S 161.01 W
Manika, Plateau de la- 36 Ed 10.00 S 26.00 E
Manila [Phil.] 22 Oh 14.35 N 121.00 E
Manila [Ut.-U.S.] 46 Kf 40.59 N 109.43 W
Manila Bay 21 Oh 14.30 N 120.45 E
Manilaid/Manilajd 8 Kf 58.08 N 24.03 E
Manilajd/Manilaid 8 Kf 58.08 N 24.03 E
Manily 20 Ld 62.30 N 165.20 E
Maningrida Settlement 59 Gb 12.05 S 134.10 E
Maniouro, Pointe- 63b Dc 17.41 S 168.35 E
Manipa, Selat- 26 Ig 3.20 S 127.23 E
Manipur [3] 25 Id 25.00 N 94.00 E
Manipur 25 Id 22.52 N 94.05 E
Manisa 23 Cb 38.36 N 27.26 E
Manisa Daği 15 Kk 38.33 N 27.28 E
Manises 13 Le 39.29 N 0.27 W
Manissau a-Missu, Rio- 54 Hf 10.58 S 53.20 W
Manistee 44 Dc 44.15 N 86.18 W
Manistee River 44 Dc 44.15 N 86.21 W
Manistique 43 Jb 45.57 N 86.15 W
Manitique Lake 44 Eb 46.15 N 85.45 W
Manitoba [3] 42 Hf 55.00 N 97.00 W
Manitoba, Lake- 38 Jd 51.00 N 98.45 W
Manitou Islands 44 Ec 45.10 N 86.00 W
Manitou Lake 44 Gc 45.48 N 82.00 W
Manitoulin Island 42 Jg 45.45 N 82.30 W
Manitou Springs 45 Dg 38.52 N 104.55 W
Manitouwadge 45 Nb 49.08 N 85.47 W
Manitowoc 43 Jc 44.06 N 87.40 W
Manitsoq/Sukkertoppen 41 Ge 65.25 N 53.00 W
Maniwaki 42 Jg 46.23 N 75.58 W
Manizales 53 Ie 5.05 N 75.32 W
Manja 17 Jd 64.23 N 60.50 E
Manja 37 Gd 21.23 S 44.20 E
Manjača 14 Lf 44.35 N 17.05 E
Manjacaze 37 Ed 24.42 S 33.33 E
Manjakandriana 37 Hc 18.55 S 47.47 E
Manji 29a Bb 43.09 N 141.59 E
Manjimup 59 Df 34.14 S 116.09 E
Mänjra 25 Fe 18.49 N 77.52 E
Män Kät 25 Jd 22.05 N 98.01 E
Mankato [Ks.-U.S.] 45 Gg 39.47 N 98.12 W
Mankato [Mn.-U.S.] 43 Ic 44.10 N 94.01 W
Mankono 34 Dd 8.04 N 6.12 W
Mankono [3] 34 Dd 7.58 N 6.02 W
Mankoya 31 Jj 14.50 S 25.00 E
Manley Hot Springs 40 Ic 65.00 N 150.37 W
Manlleu 13 Ob 42.00 N 2.17 E
Manmad 25 Ed 20.15 N 74.27 E
Manmanoc, Mount- 26 Hc 17.40 N 121.06 E
Manna 26 Dh 4.27 S 102.55 E
Mannahill 59 Hf 32.26 S 139.59 E
Mannar 25 Fg 8.59 N 79.54 E
Mannar, Gulf of- 21 Ji 8.30 N 79.00 E
Mannheim 6 Gf 49.29 N 8.28 E
Manning [Alta.-Can.] 42 Fe 56.55 N 117.33 W
Manning [S.C.-U.S.] 44 Gi 33.42 N 80.12 W
Manning, Cape- 64g Ba 2.02 N 157.26 W
Manning Strait 63a Db 7.24 S 158.04 E
Manningtree 12 Dc 51.57 N 1.04 E
Mann Ranges 59 Fe 26.00 S 129.30 E
Mann River 59 Gb 12.20 S 134.07 E
Mannu, Capo- 14 Cj 40.02 N 8.22 E
Mannu, Rio- [It.] 14 Cj 40.50 N 8.23 E
Mannu, Rio- [It.] 14 Dj 40.41 N 8.59 E
Mano 34 Cd 6.56 N 11.31 W
Mano [Jap.] 29 Fc 37.58 N 138.20 E
Mano [S.L.] 34 Cd 7.55 N 12.00 W
Manoa 54 Ee 9.40 S 65.27 W
Man of War, Cayos- 49 Fg 13.02 N 83.22 W
Manokwari 26 Je 0.52 S 134.05 E
Manombo 37 Gd 23.58 S 43.28 E
Manompana 37 Hc 16.41 S 49.45 E
Manonga 36 Fc 4.08 S 34.12 E
Manono 31 Ji 7.18 S 27.25 E
Manono 65c Aa 13.50 S 172.05 W
Manosque 11 Lk 43.50 N 5.47 E
Manouane, Lac- 42 Kf 50.40 N 70.45 W
Mano-Wan 38 Ie 37.30 N 138.15 E
Manp'ojin 28 Id 41.09 N 126.17 E
Manra Atoll (Sydney) 57 Je 4.27 S 171.15 W
Manresa 13 Nc 41.44 N 1.50 E
Mansa 31 Jj 11.12 S 28.53 E
Mansa Konko 34 Bc 13.28 N 15.33 W
Mansel 38 Lc 62.00 N 79.50 W
Mansfield [Austl.] 59 Jg 37.03 S 146.05 E
Mansfield [Eng.-U.K.] 9 Lh 53.09 N 1.11 W
Mansfield [La.-U.S.] 45 Jj 32.02 N 93.43 W
Mansfield [Oh.-U.S.] 43 Kc 40.46 N 82.31 W
Mansfield [Pa.-U.S.] 44 Ie 41.47 N 77.05 W
Mansfield, Mount- 44 Kc 44.33 N 72.49 W
Mansle 11 Gi 45.52 N 0.11 E
Manso, Rio- 55 Db 14.42 S 56.14 W
Manso, Rio- ou Mortes, Rio
das- 52 Kg 11.45 S 50.44 W
Mansôa 34 Bc 12.04 N 15.19 W
Mansourah 13 Qh 36.04 N 4.28 E
Mansourah, Djebel- 13 Qh 36.02 N 4.28 E
Manta 54 Bd 0.57 S 80.42 W
Manta, Bahía de- 54 Bd 0.50 S 80.40 W
Mantalingajan, Mount- 26 Ge 8.48 N 117.40 E
Manteca 46 Cg 37.48 N 121.13 W
Mantecal [Ven.] 50 Di 6.52 N 65.38 W
Mantecal [Ven.] 50 Bi 7.33 N 69.09 W
Manteigas 13 Ed 40.24 N 7.32 W
Manteo 44 Jh 35.55 N 75.40 W
Mantes-la-Jolie 11 Hf 48.59 N 1.43 E
Manti 46 Jg 39.16 N 111.38 W
Mantiqueira, Serra da- 52 Lh 22.00 S 44.45 W
Manto 49 Df 14.55 N 86.23 W

Manton 44 Ec 44.24 N 85.24 W
Mantova 14 Ee 45.09 N 10.48 E
Mäntsälä 8 Kd 60.38 N 25.20 E
Mänttä 7 Fe 62.02 N 24.38 E
Mantua 49 Eb 22.17 N 84.17 W
Manturovo 19 Ed 58.22 N 44.44 E
Mäntyharju 7 Gf 61.25 N 26.53 E
Mäntyluoto 8 Ic 61.35 N 21.29 E
Manu 54 Df 12.15 S 70.50 W
Manuae Atoll 57 Lf 19.21 S 158.56 W
Manua Islands 57 Kf 14.13 S 169.35 W
Manuangi Atoll 57 Lf 19.12 S 141.16 W
Manúbah 14 En 36.48 N 10.06 E
Manuel 48 Jf 22.44 N 98.19 W
Manuel Alves, Rio- 54 If 11.19 S 48.28 W
Manuel Bonavides 48 Hc 29.05 N 103.55 W
Manuel Derqui 55 Ch 27.50 S 58.48 W
Manuel J. Cobo 55 Dl 35.49 S 57.54 W
Manuel Ocampo 55 Bk 33.46 S 60.39 W
Manuga Reefs 63a Ad 11.00 S 153.21 E
Manui, Pulau- 26 Hg 3.35 S 123.08 E
Manujän 24 Qi 27.24 N 57.32 E
Manukau 24 Hf 33.10 N 38.50 E
Manulu Lagoon 58 Ih 36.56 S 174.56 E
Manulu Lagoon 64g Bb 1.56 N 157.20 W
Manus Island 57 Fe 2.05 S 147.00 E
Many 45 Jk 31.34 N 93.29 W
Manyara, Lake- 36 Gc 3.35 S 35.50 E
Manyas 24 Bb 40.02 N 27.58 E
Manyč 5 Kf 47.15 N 40.00 E
Manyč-Gudilo, Ozero- 5 Kf 46.25 N 42.35 E
Manyoni 36 Fd 5.45 S 34.50 E
Manzala, Puerto del- 15 Ie 42.30 N 6.10 W
Manzanares 13 Ie 39.00 N 3.22 W
Manzaneda, Cabeza de- 13 Eb 42.20 N 7.15 W
Manzanilla 13 Fg 37.23 N 6.25 W
Manzanillo [Cuba] 39 Lg 20.21 N 77.07 W
Manzanillo [Mex.] 39 Ih 19.03 N 104.20 W
Manzanillo, Bahía de- [Dom.Rep.] 49 Ld 19.45 N 71.46 W
Manzanillo, Bahía de- [Mex.] 48 Gh 19.04 N 104.25 W
Manzanillo, Punta- 49 Hi 9.38 N 79.32 W
Manzano Mountains 45 Ci 34.45 N 106.20 W
Manzhouli 22 Ne 49.33 N 117.28 E
Manzil Bû Ruqaybah 24 Eg 31.15 N 32.00 E
Manzilah, Bubayrat al- 32 Ib 37.10 N 9.48 E
Manzil bü Zalafah 14 En 36.41 N 10.35 E
Manzil Tamin 14 En 36.47 N 10.59 E
Manzini 37 Ee 26.29 S 31.22 E
Mao 63b Dc 17.29 S 168.29 E
Mao [Chad] 31 Ig 14.07 N 15.19 E
Mao [Dom.Rep.] 49 Ld 19.34 N 71.05 W
Mao/Mahón 13 Qe 39.53 N 4.15 E
Maoke, Pegunungan- 57 Ee 4.00 S 138.00 E
Maomao Shan 27 Hd 37.12 N 103.10 E
Maoming 22 Nj 21.41 N 110.52 E
Maoniu Shan 27 He 32.50 N 104.12 E
Maotou Shan 27 Hg 24.31 N 100.38 E
Maouri, Dallol- 34 Fc 12.05 N 3.32 E
Mapai 37 Ed 22.51 S 31.58 E
Mapanda 36 Gd 9.32 S 34.16 E
Mapati 37 Hb 14.43 N 13.00 E
Mapi 64g Ba 2.02 N 157.26 W
Mapi 26 Jf 0.50 N 134.20 E
Mapimí, Bolsón de- 38 Ig 27.30 N 103.15 W
Mapinhane 37 Ed 22.15 S 35.07 E
Mapire 50 Di 7.45 N 64.42 W
Mapiri 54 Eg 15.15 S 68.10 W
Maple Creek 42 Gg 49.55 N 109.27 W
Maprik 60 Ch 3.38 S 143.03 E
Mapuera, Rio- 54 Ge 1.05 S 57.02 W
Maputo 37 Ee 26.00 S 32.30 E
Maputo (Lourenço Marques) 31 Kk 25.58 S 32.34 E
Maputo, Baía de- 30 Kk 26.05 S 33.00 E
Maqên (Dawu) 27 He 34.29 N 100.01 E
Maqran, Wâdî al- 33 Ie 20.55 N 47.12 E
Maqu 27 He 34.05 N 101.45 E

Kanbab 27 Df 29.36 N 84.09 E
Maquela do Zombo 31 Ii 6.03 S 15.08 E
Maquinchao 56 Gf 41.15 S 68.44 W
Maquoketa 45 Ke 42.04 N 90.40 W
Mar, Serra do- 52 Lh 25.00 S 48.00 W
Mara 36 Fc 1.31 S 33.56 E
Mara [3] 36 Fc 2.30 S 34.00 E
Maraã 54 Ed 1.50 S 65.22 W
Marab 35 Fc 14.54 N 37.55 E
Marabá 54 Ie 5.21 S 49.07 W
Marabahan 26 Fg 3.00 S 114.45 E
Marabá Paulista 55 Gf 22.06 S 51.56 W
Maraca, Ilha de- 54 Ha 2.05 N 50.25 W
Maracaibo 53 Id 10.40 N 71.37 W
Maracaibo, Lago de- = 52 Ie 9.50 N 71.30 W
Maracaibo, Lake- (EN) = 52 Ie 9.50 N 71.30 W
Maracaibo, Lago de- 52 Ie 9.50 N 71.30 W
Maracaju 54 Gh 21.38 S 55.09 W
Maracaju, Serra de- [Braz.] 52 Kh 21.00 S 55.00 W
Maracaju, Serra de- [S.Amer.] 55 Ef 23.57 S 55.01 W
Maracanã 54 Id 0.46 S 47.27 W
Maracás 54 Jf 13.26 S 40.27 W
Maracay 50 Ci 10.15 N 67.36 W
Marädah 34 Ih 29.14 N 19.13 E
Maradi 31 Hg 13.29 N 7.06 E
Marägheh 24 Nf 37.23 N 46.40 E
Maraho 54 Jf 13.45 S 42.50 W
Marahuaca, Cerro- 50 Ek 3.34 N 65.27 W
Marajó, Baía de- 54 Id 1.00 S 48.30 W
Marajó, Ilha de- 52 Lf 1.00 S 49.30 W
Marakei Atoll 57 Id 1.58 N 173.25 E
Maralal 36 Gb 1.06 N 36.42 E

Maralinga 59 Gf 30.13 S 131.35 E
Maralwexi/Bachu 27 Cc 39.46 N 78.15 E
Maramag 26 He 7.46 N 125.00 E
Maramasike Island 60 Gi 9.30 S 161.25 E
Maramba 31 Jj 17.51 S 25.52 E
Marampa 34 Cd 8.41 N 12.28 W
Maramureş [2] 15 Gb 47.40 N 24.00 E
Maranchón 13 Jc 41.03 N 2.12 W
Marand 23 Gb 38.26 N 45.46 E
Marandellas 37 Ec 18.10 S 31.36 E
Marang 26 De 5.12 N 103.13 E
Maranhão [2] 54 Ie 5.00 S 45.00 W
Maranhão, Rio- 54 If 14.34 S 49.02 W
Marano, Laguna di- 14 He 45.44 N 13.10 E
Maranoa River 59 Je 27.50 S 148.37 E
Marañón, Rio- 52 Jf 4.30 S 73.35 W
Marans 11 Fh 46.18 N 1.00 W
Marão 37 Ed 24.18 S 34.07 E
Marão, Serra do- 13 Ec 41.15 N 7.55 W
Maraoué 34 Dd 6.54 N 5.31 W
Marapanim 54 Id 0.42 S 47.42 W
Marapi, Gunung- 26 Dg 0.23 S 100.28 E
Marargiu, Capo- 14 Cj 40.20 N 8.23 E
Marari, Serra do- 55 Ha 13.58 S 49.09 W
Mara Rosa 54 If 14.00 N 147.30 E
Mârâseşti 15 Kd 45.53 N 27.14 E
Maratea 14 Jk 39.59 N 15.43 E
Marathón 36 Gc 3.35 S 35.50 E
Marathon 15 Gk 38.09 N 23.58 E
Marathon 45 Dk 30.12 N 103.15 W
Maratua, Pulau- 26 Gf 2.15 N 118.36 E
Marau 55 Fi 28.27 S 52.12 W
Maravari 63a Dc 9.17 S 156.44 E
Marävêh Tappeh 24 Pd 37.55 N 55.57 E
Maravilha 55 Fh 26.47 S 53.09 W
Maravilhas Creek 45 El 29.34 N 102.47 W
Maravovo 63a Dc 9.17 S 159.38 E
Maräwah 33 Dc 32.29 N 21.25 E
Marawi 26 He 8.13 N 124.15 E
Marawiy 35 Eb 18.29 N 31.49 E
Marayes 56 Gd 31.29 S 67.20 W
Marbella 13 Hh 36.31 N 4.53 W
Marble Bar 59 Dd 21.11 S 119.44 E
Marble Canyon 46 Jh 36.30 N 111.50 W
Marble Falls 45 Gk 30.34 N 98.17 W
Marble Hall 37 Dd 24.57 S 29.13 E
Marburg an der Lahn 10 Ef 50.49 N 8.46 E
Marca, Ponta da- 30 Ij 16.31 S 11.42 E
Marcal 31 Ni 47.38 N 17.32 E
Marcala 49 Df 14.07 N 88.00 W
Marçal Daǧlari 15 Kf 37.09 N 28.00 E
Marcali 10 Nj 46.35 N 17.25 E
March 10 Mh 48.10 N 16.59 E
March 9 Ni 52.33 N 0.06 E
Marche 11 Hh 46.10 N 1.30 E
Marche = Marches (EN) [2] 11 Hh 43.30 N 13.15 E
Marche, Plateau de la- 11 Hh 46.16 N 1.30 E
Marche-en-Famenne 11 Ld 50.14 N 5.20 E
Marchena 13 Gg 37.20 N 5.24 W
Marchena, Isla- 54a Aa 0.20 N 90.30 W
Marches (EN) = Marche [2] 11 Hh 43.30 N 13.15 E
Marchesato 14 Kk 39.05 N 17.00 E
Marchfeld 10 Kb 48.15 N 16.50 E
Mar Chiquita, Laguna- 55 Dm 37.37 S 57.24 W
Mar Chiquita, Laguna- 52 Ji 30.42 S 62.36 W
Marciana Marina 14 Eh 42.48 N 10.12 E
Marcigny 11 Kh 46.16 N 4.02 E
Marcilly-sur-Eure 17 Df 48.49 N 1.21 E
Marcinelle, Charleroi- 54 Eg 15.15 S 68.10 W
Marck 12 Dd 50.57 N 1.57 E
Marcoing 12 Fd 50.07 N 3.11 E
Marcos Juárez 56 Hd 32.42 S 62.06 W
Marcus Baker, Mount- 40 Jd 61.26 N 147.45 W
Marcus Island (EN) = Minami-Tori-Shima 57 Gb 26.32 N 142.09 E
Marcy, Mount- 43 Mc 44.07 N 73.56 W
Mardakert 10 Oi 40.12 N 46.52 E
Mardakjan 16 Qi 40.29 N 50.12 E
Mardän 25 Eb 34.09 N 71.52 E
Mardarovka 15 Mb 47.30 N 29.40 E
Mar del Plata 53 Ki 38.01 S 57.35 W
Marden 12 Cc 51.10 N 0.30 E
Mardin 23 Fb 37.18 N 40.44 E
Mardin Daǧlari 24 Id 37.20 N 41.00 E
Maré, Ile- 57 Hg 21.30 S 168.00 E
Mare, Muntele- 15 Gc 46.29 N 23.14 E
Marechal Cândido Rondon 54 Gh 24.34 S 54.04 W
Maree, Loch- 9 Hd 57.40 N 5.30 W
Mareeba 59 Jc 17.00 S 145.26 E
Märeǧ 35 He 3.47 N 47.18 E
Maremma 14 Fh 42.30 N 11.30 E
Marennes 11 Ei 45.49 N 1.07 W
Marettimo 14 Gm 37.56 N 12.05 E
Marfa 45 Dk 30.18 N 104.01 W
Marfil, Laguna- 55 Jd 30.15 S 30.15 E
Margai Caka 27 Ee 35.10 N 86.55 E
Marganec 19 Df 47.38 N 34.40 E
Margaret River 59 Df 33.57 S 115.04 E
Margarida 55 De 21.41 S 56.44 W
Margarita, Isla de- 53 Ie 11.00 N 64.00 W
Margariton 53 Jf 39.21 N 20.26 E
Margate [Eng.-U.K.] 9 Oj 51.24 N 1.24 E
Margate [S.Afr.] 37 De 30.53 S 30.15 E
Margerie, Monts de la- 11 Jj 44.50 N 3.25 E
Marghera, Venezia- 14 Ge 45.28 N 12.44 E
Margherita di Savoia 14 Ki 41.23 N 16.09 E
Marghine, Catena del- 14 Cj 40.20 N 8.50 E
Marghita 15 Fb 47.20 N 22.20 E
Marghûb, Küh-e- 24 Of 33.06 N 57.30 E
Margilan 19 Fd 40.28 N 71.46 E
Margina 15 Fd 45.51 N 22.16 E
Marguerite Bay 66 Qe 68.30 S 68.30 W
Margut 12 Gc 49.35 N 5.16 E
Marha 20 Gb 1.06 N 36.42 E

Marha 21 Nc 63.20 N 118.50 E
Mari 16 He 34.39 N 40.53 E
Mari 24 Ee 34.44 N 33.18 E
Maria Atoll [W.F.] 60 Gi 9.30 S 161.25 E
Maria Atoll [W.F.] 57 Lg 21.48 S 154.41 W
Maria Cleofas, Isla- 48 Fg 21.16 N 106.14 W
Maria Elena 56 Gb 22.21 S 69.40 W
Mariager 8 Ch 56.39 N 10.00 E
Mariager Fjord 8 Dh 56.40 N 10.20 E
Maria Grande, Arroyo- 55 Ci 29.21 S 58.45 W
Maria Ignacia 55 Cm 37.24 S 59.30 W
Maria Island [Austl.] 59 Jh 42.40 S 148.05 E
Maria Island [Austl.] 59 Hb 14.55 S 135.40 E
Maria Island [St.Luc.] 51k Bb 13.44 N 60.56 W
Mariakani 36 Gc 3.52 S 39.28 E
Maria Laach 12 Jd 50.25 N 7.15 E
Maria Madre, Isla- 48 Fg 21.35 N 106.33 W
Maria Magdalena, Isla- 48 Fg 21.25 N 106.25 W
Mariana Islands 57 Hc 16.00 N 145.30 E
Marianao 34 Dd 6.54 N 5.31 W
Mariana Trench (EN) 3 Ih 14.00 N 147.30 E
Marianna [Ar.-U.S.] 45 Ki 34.46 N 90.46 W
Marianna [Fl.-U.S.] 44 Kj 30.47 N 85.14 W
Marianne I. Loza 55 Ci 29.22 S 58.12 W
Mariánské Lázně 10 Ig 49.58 N 12.43 E
Marias, Islas- 38 Ig 21.25 N 106.28 W
Marias Pass 46 Ib 48.19 N 113.21 W
Marias River 43 Eb 47.56 N 110.30 W
Maria Theresa Reef 57 Lh 36.58 S 151.23 W
Mariato, Punta- 47 Hg 7.13 N 80.53 W
Maria van Diemen, Cape- 62 Ea 34.29 S 172.39 E
Mariazell 14 Jc 47.46 N 15.19 E
Ma'rib 23 Gf 15.30 N 45.21 E
Maribo 8 Dj 54.46 N 11.31 E
Maribor 14 Jd 46.33 N 15.39 E
Marica 5 Ig 40.52 N 26.12 E
Marica 15 Ij 42.05 N 25.40 E
Maricao 51a Bb 18.10 N 66.58 W
Maricopa 46 Ij 33.04 N 112.03 W
Maricourt 42 Kd 61.36 N 71.57 W
Marid 35 Dd 6.05 N 29.24 E
Maridi 13 Hh 36.31 N 4.53 W
Marié, Rio- 54 Ed 0.25 S 66.26 W
Marie Byrd Land (EN) 66 Nf 80.00 S 120.00 W
Mariec 7 Lh 56.31 N 49.51 E
Marie Galante 47 Le 15.56 N 61.16 W
Marie-Galante, Canal de- 51e Bc 15.55 N 61.25 W
Mariehamn/Maarianhamina 7 Ef 60.06 N 19.57 E
Marie Louise Island 37b Bb 6.11 S 53.09 E
Mariembourg, Couvin- 12 Gd 50.04 N 4.31 E
Marienburg 12 Jd 50.04 N 7.08 E
Marienmünster 12 Lc 51.50 N 9.13 E
Marienstatt 12 Jd 50.40 N 7.49 E
Mariental 31 Jk 24.36 S 17.59 E
Marietta [Ga.-U.S.] 43 Ke 33.57 N 84.33 W
Marietta [Oh.-U.S.] 44 Gf 39.26 N 81.27 W
Mariga 34 Gd 9.36 N 5.57 E
Marignac 11 Gl 42.55 N 0.39 E
Marignane 11 Lk 43.25 N 5.13 E
Marigot [Dom.] 50 Ec 15.32 N 61.18 W
Marigot [Guad.] 51e Bb 18.04 N 63.06 W
Marigot [Haiti] 49 Kd 18.14 N 72.19 W
Marigot [Mart.] 51h Ab 14.49 N 61.02 W
Marigot [St.Luc.] 51k Ab 13.58 N 61.02 W
Mariinsk 20 Be 56.13 N 87.45 E
Mariinski Posad 7 Lh 56.08 N 47.48 E
Mariinskoje 21 Oe 51.43 N 140.19 E
Marijovo 15 Eh 41.04 N 21.45 E
Marijskaja ASSR [3] 19 Ed 56.40 N 48.00 E
Marília 56 Jb 22.13 S 50.01 W
Mariluz 55 Fg 24.02 S 53.13 W
Marimba 36 Gd 8.22 S 17.02 E
Marimbondo, Cachoeira do- 55 He 20.18 S 49.10 W
Marin 13 Db 42.23 N 8.42 W
Marin, Cul-de-Sac du- 51h Bc 14.27 N 60.53 W
Marina di Catanzaro 14 Kl 38.49 N 16.36 E
Marina di Gioiosa Ionica 14 Kl 38.18 N 16.20 E
Marina di Pisa 14 Ef 43.40 N 10.16 E
Marina di Ravenna 14 Gf 44.29 N 12.17 E
Marina Grande 19 Ce 53.31 N 28.12 E
Marinduque 26 He 13.24 N 121.58 E
Marineland 44 De 29.43 N 81.12 W
Marines 12 De 49.09 N 1.59 E
Marinette 43 Jb 45.06 N 87.38 W
Maringá 56 Jb 23.25 S 51.55 W
Marinha Grande 13 De 39.45 N 8.56 W
Marino [It.] 14 Gi 41.46 N 12.39 E
Marino [San.] 63b Bb 14.59 S 168.03 E
Marins, Pico dos- 55 Jf 22.27 S 45.10 W
Marion [Al.-U.S.] 44 Di 32.38 N 87.19 W
Marion [Ia.-U.S.] 45 Ke 42.02 N 91.36 W
Marion [Il.-U.S.] 45 Lh 37.44 N 88.56 W
Marion [Oh.-U.S.] 44 Fe 40.35 N 83.08 W
Marion [S.C.-U.S.] 44 Hh 34.11 N 79.23 W
Marion, Lake- 44 Gi 33.30 N 80.25 W
Marion Reefs 57 Gf 19.10 S 152.20 E
Maripa 50 Di 7.26 N 65.09 W
Mariposa 46 Dg 37.29 N 119.58 W
Mariquita, Cerro- 50 Ei 9.51 N 64.55 W
Marisa 26 He 0.28 N 121.56 E
Mariscal Estigarribia 54 Gg 22.02 S 60.38 W
Maritime [3] 34 Ee 7.00 N 1.20 E
Maritsa, Caño- 50 Pi 9.43 N 61.02 W
Mariusa, Isla- 50 Fh 9.45 N 61.02 W
Mariván 24 Le 35.31 N 46.10 E
Märjamaa/Marjamaa 8 Kf 58.54 N 24.21 E
Märjamaa/Marjamaa 8 Kf 58.54 N 24.21 E
Marjanovka [R.S.F.S.R.] 19 He 54.58 N 72.38 E

Marjanovka [Ukr.-U.S.S.R.] 10 Uf 50.23 N 24.55 E
Mark 12 Gc 51.39 N 4.39 E
Mark [F.R.G.] 12 Jc 51.13 N 7.36 E
Mark [Swe.] 8 Eg 53.75 N 12.35 E
Marka 31 Lh 1.43 N 44.46 E
Markako, Ozero- 19 Hf 48.45 N 85.50 E
Markala 34 Dc 13.39 N 6.05 W
Markam (Gartog) 27 Gf 29.32 N 98.33 E
Markaryd 7 Hc 56.26 N 13.36 E
Marken 12 Hb 52.27 N 5.05 E
Markerwaard 12 Hb 52.31 N 5.15 E
Market Deeping 12 Bb 52.40 N 0.18 W
Market Harborough 9 Mi 52.29 N 0.55 W
Markham, Mount- 66 Kg 82.51 S 161.21 E
Markham Bay 42 Kd 63.30 N 71.40 W
Markham River 59 Ja 6.35 S 146.25 E
Marki 10 Rd 52.20 N 21.07 E
Märkische Schweiz 10 Jc 52.35 N 14.00 E
Markit 27 Cd 38.53 N 77.35 E
Markounda 35 Hd 7.37 N 16.59 E
Markovac 15 Ee 44.14 N 21.06 E
Markovka 16 Ke 49.31 N 39.32 E
Markovo 22 Tc 64.40 N 170.25 E
Markoye 34 Fc 14.39 N 0.02 E
Marksburg 12 Jd 50.16 N 7.40 E
Marksville 45 Jk 31.08 N 92.04 W
Marktoberdorf 10 Gi 47.47 N 10.37 E
Marktredwitz 10 If 50.00 N 12.05 E
Markulešty 15 Lb 47.51 N 28.07 E
Marl 10 Dd 51.39 N 7.05 E
Marlagne 12 Gd 50.25 N 4.40 E
Marlborough [2] 62 Ed 41.50 S 173.40 E
Marlborough [Austl.] 59 Jd 22.49 S 149.53 E
Marlborough [Guy.] 50 Gi 7.29 N 58.38 W
Marle 11 Je 49.44 N 3.46 E
Marlin 45 Hk 31.18 N 96.53 W
Marlinton 44 Gf 38.14 N 80.06 W
Marlow [Eng.-U.K.] 12 Bc 51.34 N 0.46 W
Marlow [Ok.-U.S.] 45 Hi 34.39 N 97.57 W
Marmande 11 Gj 44.30 N 0.10 E
Marmara 24 Bb 40.35 N 27.33 E
Marmara, Sea of- (EN) = Marmara Denizi 5 Ig 40.40 N 28.15 E
Marmara Adasi 24 Bb 40.38 N 27.37 E
Marmara Denizi = Marmara, Sea of- (EN) 5 Ig 40.40 N 28.15 E
Marmara Ereğlisi 15 Kf 40.58 N 27.57 E
Marmara Gölü 15 Lk 38.37 N 28.02 E
Marmarica (EN) = Barqah al Bahriyah 37b Bb 30 Je 31.40 N 24.30 E
Marmaris 23 Cb 36.51 N 28.16 E
Marmelos, Rio- 54 Fe 6.08 S 61.47 W
Marmion Lake 45 Kb 48.54 N 91.30 W
Marmolada 12 Jd 50.44 N 7.49 E
Marmora 44 Ic 44.29 N 77.41 W
Marmore, Cascata delle- 14 Gh 42.35 N 12.45 E
Marne 10 Cc 53.57 N 9.00 E
Marne 9 Gf 48.49 N 2.24 E
Marne à la Saône, Canal de la- 11 Kf 48.55 N 4.10 E
Marne au Rhin, Canal de la- 11 Kf 48.44 N 4.36 E
Mârnes 7 Dc 67.09 N 14.06 E
Marneuli 16 Ni 41.29 N 44.45 E
Maro 35 Bd 8.25 N 18.46 E
Maroa 54 Dd 2.43 N 67.33 W
Maroantsetra 31 Lj 15.27 S 49.44 E
Marokau Atoll 61 Mc 18.02 S 142.17 W
Marolambo 37 Hb 14.11 S 48.06 E
Maromme 11 Hf 48.58 E
Maromokotro 37 Hb 14.01 S 48.58 E
Maroni, Fleuve- 52 Ke 5.45 N 53.58 W
Marónia 11 Hi 45.56 N 25.31 E
Maroochydore 59 Ke 26.39 S 153.06 E
Maro Reef 57 Jb 25.25 N 170.35 W
Maros 26 Gg 5.00 S 119.34 E
Maroua 31 Ig 10.36 N 14.20 E
Marovoay 37 Hc 16.06 S 46.37 E
Marovoay 37 Hb 16.06 S 46.37 E
Marowijne River 54 Hc 5.45 N 53.58 W
Marquard 37 Dd 28.54 S 27.28 E
Mar Qu 37 Dd 27.28 E
Marquesas Islands (EN) = Marquises, Iles- 43 Jb 46.33 N 87.24 W
Marquette 43 Jb 46.33 N 87.24 W
Marquion 51p Bb 12.06 N 61.37 W
Marquis [Gren.] 51p Bb 12.06 N 61.37 W
Marquis [St.Luc.] 51k Ba 14.02 N 60.55 W
Marquis, Cape- 51k Ba 14.03 N 60.54 W
Marquise 12 Dd 50.49 N 1.42 E
Marquesas Islands (EN) = Iles Marquises 57 Ne 9.00 S 139.30 W
Marracuene 37 Ee 25.44 S 32.41 E
Marradi 14 Ff 44.04 N 11.37 E
Marrah, Jabal- 30 Jg 13.04 N 24.21 E
Marrak 33 Hf 16.26 N 41.54 E
Marrakech 13 Qh 31.38 N 8.00 W
Marrakech 33 Ec 32.00 N 8.00 W
Marrawah 59 Ih 40.55 S 144.41 E
Marree 58 Eg 29.39 S 138.04 E
Marreh, Küh-e- 24 Oh 29.15 N 52.20 E
Marrah 33 Fd 25.05 N 34.54 E
Marresalskije Koški,
Ostrova- 17 Mb 69.44 N 66.59 E
Marrti 7 Gc 67.28 N 28.22 E
Marrupa 37 Fb 13.12 S 37.30 E
Marsá al 'Alam 33 Fd 25.05 N 34.54 E
Marsá al Burayqah 33 Cc 30.25 N 19.35 E

Index Symbols

Symbol	Meaning
[1]	Independent Nation
[2]	State, Region
[3]	District, County
[4]	Municipality
[5]	Colony, Dependency
■	Continent
▨	Physical Region
▣	Historical or Cultural Region
▲	Mount, Mountain
▲	Volcano
▲	Hill
▲	Mountains, Mountain Range
▲	Hills, Escarpment
▱	Plateau, Upland
⌣	Pass, Gap
▬	Plain, Lowland
▭	Delta
▭	Salt Flat
⋁	Valley, Canyon
●	Crater, Cave
▦	Karst Features
▭	Depression
▭	Polder
▭	Desert, Dunes
▭	Forest, Woods
▭	Heath, Steppe
▭	Oasis
▭	Cape, Point
▭	Coast, Beach
▭	Cliff
▭	Peninsula
▭	Isthmus
▭	Sandbank
▭	Island
⊙	Atoll
▨	Rock, Reef
▨	Islands, Archipelago
▨	Rocks, Reefs
▨	Coral Reef
▨	Waterfall Rapids
▨	River Mouth, Estuary
▨	Lake
▨	Salt Lake
▨	Intermittent Lake
▨	Sea
▨	Gulf, Bay
▨	Strait, Fjord
▨	Well, Spring
▨	Geyser
▨	Reservoir
▨	Swamp, Pond
▨	River, Stream
▨	Canal
▨	Glacier
▨	Ice Shelf, Pack Ice
▨	Ocean
▨	Sea
▨	Shelf
▨	Basin
▨	Lagoon
▨	Bank
▨	Seamount
▨	Tablemount
▨	Ridge
▨	Escarpment, Sea Scarp
▨	Fracture
▨	Trench, Abyss
▨	National Park, Reserve
▨	Point of Interest
▨	Recreation Site
▨	Cave, Cavern
▨	Historic Site
▨	Ruins
▨	Church, Abbey
▨	Temple
▨	Scientific Station
▨	Airport
▨	Port
▨	Lighthouse
▨	Mine
▨	Wall, Walls
▨	Tunnel
▨	Dam, Bridge

Marsá al Uwayjah 33 Cc 30.55N 17.52 E
Marsa Ben Mehidi 13 Ji 35.05N 2.11W
Marsabit 31 Kh 2.20N 37.59 E
Marsala 14 Gm 37.48N 12.26 E
Marsá Sha'b 35 Fa 22.52N 35.47 E
Marsá Umm Ghayj 24 Fj 25.38N 34.30 E
Marsberg 10 Ee 51.27N 8.51 E
Marsciano 14 Gh 42.54N 12.20 E
Marsdiep 12 Gb 52.58N 4.45 E
Marseille=Marseilles (EN) 6 Gg 43.18N 5.24 E
Marseille-en-Beauvaisis 11 He 49.35N 1.57 E
Marseilles (EN)=Marseille 6 Gg 43.18N 5.24 E
Marshall [Ak.-U.S.] 40 Gd 61.52N 162.04W
Marshall [Ar.-U.S.] 45 Ji 35.55N 92.38W
Marshall [Il.-U.S.] 45 Mg 39.23N 87.42W
Marshall [Lbr.] 34 Cd 6.09N 10.23W
Marshall [Mn.-U.S.] 43 Hc 44.27N 95.47W
Marshall [Mo.-U.S.] 45 Jg 39.07N 93.12W
Marshall [Tx.-U.S.] 43 Ie 32.33N 94.23W
Marshall Islands 58 Hd 9.00N 168.00 E
Marshall Islands 57 Hd 9.00N 168.00 E
Marshall River 59 Hd 22.59 S 136.59 E
Marshalltown 43 Ic 42.03N 92.54W
Marshfield 45 Kd 44.40N 90.10W
Marsh Harbour 47 Ic 26.33N 77.03W
Mārshinān, Kūh-e- 24 Of 32.53N 52.24 E
Marsh Island 45 Kl 29.35N 91.53W
Marsica 14 Hi 41.55N 13.35 E
Marsico Nuovo 14 Jj 40.25N 15.44 E
Marsjaty 17 Jf 60.05N 60.29 E
Marsland 45 Ee 42.29N 103.16W
Mars-la-Tour 12 He 49.06N 5.54 E
Marson 12 Gf 48.55N 4.32 E
Märsta 8 Ge 59.37N 17.51 E
Marstal 8 Dj 54.51N 10.31 E
Marstrand 8 Dg 57.53N 11.35 E
Marta 14 Fh 42.14N 11.42 E
Martaban 25 Je 16.32N 97.37 E
Martaban, Gulf of- (EN) 21 Lh 16.30N 97.00 E
Martap 34 Hd 6.54N 13.03 E
Martapura [Indon.] 26 Dg 4.19 S 104.22 E
Martapura [Indon.] 26 Fg 3.25 S 114.51 E
Martelange/Martelingen 12 He 49.50N 5.44 E
Martelingen/Martelange 12 He 49.50N 5.44 E
Martés, Sierra de- 13 Le 39.20N 0.57W
Martha's Vineyard 43 Mc 41.25N 70.40W
Martigny 14 Bd 46.06N 7.05 E
Martigues 11 Lk 43.24N 5.03 E
Martil 13 Gi 35.37N 5.17W
Martim Vaz, Ilhas- 52 Nh 20.30 S 28.51W
Martin 13 Lc 41.18N 0.19W
Martin [Czech.] 10 Og 49.04N 18.55 E
Martin [S.D.-U.S.] 43 Gc 43.10N 101.44W
Martin [Tn.-U.S.] 44 Cg 36.21N 88.51W
Martina Franca 14 Lj 40.42N 17.20 E
Martinez de Hoz 55 Bl 35.19 S 61.37W
Martinez de la Torre 48 Kg 20.04N 97.03W
Martin Garcia, Isla- 55 Cl 34.11 S 58.15W
Martin Hills 66 Pg 82.04 S 88.01W
Martinho Campos 55 Jd 19.20 S 45.13W
Martinique 38 Mh 14.40N 61.00W
Martinique 39 Mh 14.40N 61.00W
Martinique, Canal de la-=Martinique Passage (EN) 47 Le 15.10N 61.20W
Martinique Passage 50 Fe 15.10N 61.20W
Martinique Passage (EN)=Martinique, Canal de la- 47 Le 15.10N 61.20W
Martin Lake 44 Ei 32.50N 85.55W
Martin Peninsula 66 Of 74.25 S 114.10W
Martinsburg 44 If 39.28N 77.59W
Martins Ferry 44 Ge 40.07N 80.45W
Martinsville [In.-U.S.] 44 Df 39.26N 86.25W
Martinsville [Va.-U.S.] 43 Ld 36.43N 79.53W
Marton 62 Fd 40.05 S 175.23 E
Martos 13 Ig 37.43N 3.58W
Martre, Lac la- 42 Fd 63.20N 118.00W
Martuk 19 Fe 50.47N 56.31 E
Martuni 16 Ni 40.06N 45.18 E
Maru 34 Gc 12.21N 6.24 E
Marud 25 Ee 18.19N 72.58 E
Marudi 26 Ff 4.11N 114.19 E
Marudu, Teluk- 26 Ge 6.45N 116.55 E
Marugame 29 Cd 34.18N 133.47 E
Maruko 29 Fc 36.19N 138.15 E
Mārūn 24 Mg 31.02N 49.36 E
Marungu, Monts- 30 Ji 7.42 S 30.00 E
Maruoka 29 Ec 36.09N 136.16 E
Maruseppu 29a Ca 44.01N 143.19 E
Marutea Atoll [W.F.] 57 Ng 21.30 S 135.34W
Marutea Atoll [W.F.] 57 Mf 17.00 S 143.10W
Maruyama-Gawa 29 Dd 35.40N 134.50 E
Marvão 13 Ee 39.24N 7.23W
Marvast 24 Pg 30.30N 54.15 E
Marvast, Kavīr-e- 24 Pg 30.20N 54.25 E
Mårvatn 8 Cd 60.10N 8.15 E
Marv-Dasht 23 Hd 29.50N 52.40 E
Marvejols 11 Jj 44.33N 3.17 E
Marvine, Mount- 46 Jg 38.40N 111.39W
Marx 16 Od 51.42N 46.46 E
Mary 22 If 37.36N 61.50 E
Maryborough [Austl.] 58 Gg 25.32 S 152.42 E
Maryborough [Austl.] 59 Ig 37.03 S 143.45 E
Marydale 37 Ce 29.23 S 22.05 E
Maryjskaja Oblast 19 Gh 37.15N 62.30 E
Maryland 43 Ld 39.00N 76.45W
Maryland 34 De 4.45N 8.00W
Maryport 9 Jg 54.43N 3.30W
Mary River 59 Gb 12.53 S 131.38 E
Marysville [Ca.-U.S.] 46 Eg 39.09N 121.35W
Marysville [Ks.-U.S.] 45 Hg 39.51N 96.39W
Marysville [N.B.-Can.] 44 Nc 45.59N 66.35W
Marysville [Oh.-U.S.] 44 Fe 40.13N 83.22W
Marysville [Wa.-U.S.] 46 Db 48.03N 122.11W
Maryville [Mo.-U.S.] 43 Ic 40.21N 94.52W
Maryville [Tn.-U.S.] 44 Fh 35.46N 83.58W
Marzūq 31 If 25.55N 13.55 E
Marzūq, Ḩamādat- 33 Bd 26.00N 12.30 E
Marzuq, Şaḩrā'- 30 If 24.30N 13.00 E
Masachapa 49 Dh 11.47N 86.31W
Masāhīm, Kūh-e- 24 Pg 30.21N 55.20 E
Masai Steppe 30 Ki 4.45 S 37.00 E
Masaka 36 Fc 0.20 S 31.44 E
Masākin 32 Jb 35.44N 10.35 E
Masalembo, Kepulauan- 26 Fh 5.30 S 114.26 E
Masally 19 Eh 39.01N 48.40 E
Masalog, Puntan- 64b Ba 15.01N 145.41 E
Masan 27 Md 35.11N 128.24 E
Masasi 31 Kj 10.43 S 38.48 E
Masaya 49 Dh 12.00N 86.10W
Masaya 47 Gf 11.58N 86.06W
Masbate 21 Oh 12.15N 123.30 E
Masbate 26 Hd 12.10N 123.35 E
Mascara 32 Hb 35.24N 0.08 E
Mascara 32 Hb 35.30N 0.15 E
Mascareignes, Iles-/Mascarene Islands 30 Mk 21.00 S 57.00 E
Mascarene Basin (EN) 3 Fk 15.00 S 56.00 E
Mascarene Islands/Mascareignes, Iles- 30 Mk 21.00 S 57.00 E
Mascarene Plateau (EN) 3 Gk 10.00 S 60.00 E
Mascota 48 Gg 20.32N 104.49W
Masela, Pulau- 26 Ih 8.09 S 129.50 E
Maseru 31 Jk 29.28 S 27.29 E
Maşfūţ 24 Qk 24.48N 56.06 E
Mashaba 37 Ed 20.02 S 30.29 E
Mashābih 24 Gj 25.37N 36.32 E
Mashan 28 Kb 45.12N 130.32 E
Mashhad 22 Hf 36.18N 59.36 E
Mashike 28 Pc 43.51N 141.31 E
Mashiki 29 Be 32.47N 130.50 E
Mashīz 24 Qh 29.56N 56.37 E
Mashkel 21 Ig 28.02N 63.25 E
Mashonaland North 37 Ec 17.00 S 31.00 E
Mashonaland South 37 Ec 18.00 S 31.00 E
Mashra' ar Raqq 35 Dd 8.25N 29.16 E
Mashū-Ko 29a Db 43.35N 144.30 E
Masiaca 48 Ed 26.45N 109.18W
Masīlah, Wādī al- 21 Hh 15.10N 51.08 E
Masi-Manimba 36 Cc 4.46 S 17.55 E
Masindi 36 Fb 1.42N 31.43 E
Maşīrah, Jazīrat- 21 Hg 20.29N 58.33 E
Maşīrah, Khalīj- 21 Hg 20.15N 57.40 E
Masisi 36 Ec 1.24 S 28.49 E
Masjed-Soleymān 23 Gc 31.58N 49.18 E
Mask, Lough-/Loch Measca 9 Dh 53.35N 9.20W
Maskanah 24 Hd 36.01N 38.05 E
Maskelynes, Iles- 63b Cc 16.32 S 167.49 E
Maslovare 14 Lf 44.34N 17.33 E
Masoala, Cap- 30 Mj 15.59 S 50.13 E
Masoala, Presqu'île de- 37 Ic 15.40 S 50.12 E
Mason 45 Gk 30.45N 99.14W
Mason Bay 62 Bg 46.55 S 167.45 E
Mason City 39 Je 43.09N 93.12W
Masovia (EN)=Mazowsze 5 Ie 52.40N 20.20 E
Masparro, Río- 49 Mi 8.04N 69.26W
Masqaţ=Muscat (EN) 22 Hg 23.29N 58.33 E
Massa 14 Ef 44.01N 10.09 E
Massachusetts 43 Mc 42.15N 71.50W
Massachusetts Bay 44 Ld 42.20N 70.50W
Massaciuccoli, Lago di- 14 Eg 43.50N 10.20 E
Massafra 14 Lj 40.35N 17.07 E
Massaguet 35 Bc 12.28N 15.26 E
Massakori 35 Bc 13.00N 15.44 E
Massa Marittima 14 Eg 43.03N 10.53 E
Massangano 36 Bd 9.37 S 14.17 E
Massangena 37 Ed 21.32 S 32.57 E
Massapê 54 Jd 3.31 S 40.19W
Massawa (EN)=Mitsiwa 31 Kg 15.37N 39.39 E
Massena 43 Mc 44.56N 74.57W
Massénya 35 Bc 11.24N 16.10 E
Masset 42 Ef 54.02N 132.09W
Masseube 11 Gk 43.26N 0.35 E
Massey Sound 42 Ia 78.00N 94.00W
Massiac 11 Ji 45.15N 3.13 E
Massiaru 8 Kg 57.52N 24.27 E
Massillon 44 Ge 40.48N 81.32W
Massinga 37 Fd 23.20 S 35.22 E
Masson Island 66 Ge 66.08 S 96.34 E
Massuma 36 De 14.05 S 22.00 E
Mastābah 33 Ge 20.49N 39.26 E
Maštaga 16 Pi 40.32N 49.59 E
Masterton 61 Eh 40.57 S 175.39 E
Mastūrah 33 Ge 23.06N 38.50 E
Masuda 27 Ne 34.40N 131.51 E
Māsūleh 24 Md 37.10N 48.59 E
Masurai, Gunung- 26 Dg 2.30 S 101.51 E
Masuria (EN) 5 Ie 53.50N 21.30 E
Masurian Lakes (EN) 5 Ie 53.45N 21.45 E
Maşyāf 24 Ge 35.03N 36.21 E
Maszewo 10 Lc 53.29N 15.02 E
Mataabé, Cap- 63b Cb 15.38 S 166.46 E
Matabeleland North 37 Dc 19.00 S 27.30 E
Matabeleland South 37 Dd 21.00 S 29.30 E
Matachel 13 Ff 38.50N 6.17W
Matachewan 42 Jg 47.56N 80.39W
Matacu 55 Bc 17.21 S 61.28W
Matadi 31 Ii 5.49 S 13.27 E
Matador 45 Fi 34.01N 100.49W
Matagalpa 49 Eg 13.00N 85.30W
Matagalpa 39 Kh 12.53N 85.57W
Matagami 42 Jg 49.45N 77.35W
Matagami, Lac- 44 Ia 49.54N 77.32W
Mata Gassīle 35 Ge 2.30N 42.16 E
Matagorda Bay 45 Hl 28.35N 96.20W
Matagorda Island 43 Hf 28.15N 96.30W
Matagorda Peninsula 45 Hl 28.32N 96.07W
Mataiea 65e Fc 17.46 S 149.25W
Mataiva Atoll 57 Mf 14.53 S 148.40W
Mataj 19 Hf 45.51N 78.43 E
Matak, Pulau- 26 Ef 3.18N 106.16 E
Matakana Island 62 Gb 37.35 S 176.05 E
Matala 36 Ce 14.43 S 15.02 E
Matalaa, Pointe- 64h Bc 13.20 S 176.08W
Matale 25 Gg 7.28N 80.37 E
Mataliele 37 Df 30.24 S 28.43 E
Matam 34 Cb 15.40N 13.15W
Matamey 34 Gc 13.26N 8.28 E
Matamoros [Mex.] 47 Dc 25.32N 103.15W
Matamoros [Mex.] 39 Jg 25.53N 97.30W
Matana, Danau- 26 Hg 2.28 S 121.20 E
Ma'ţan as Sarra 33 De 21.41N 21.52 E
Matancita 48 De 25.09N 111.59W
Matane 42 Kg 48.51N 67.32W
Matankari 34 Fc 13.46N 4.01 E
Matanza 55 Cl 34.33 S 58.35W
Matanzas 39 Kg 23.03N 81.35W
Matanzas 49 Gb 22.40N 81.10W
Matão 55 He 21.35 S 48.22W
Matapalo, Cabo- 49 Fi 8.23N 83.19W
Matapan, Cape- (EN)=Tainaron, Ákra- 5 Ih 36.23N 22.29 E
Matape, Río- 48 Dc 28.17N 110.41W
Mata Point 64k Bb 19.07 S 169.50W
Matara 35 Fc 14.35N 39.28 E
Matara 25 Gg 5.56N 80.33 E
Mataram 22 Nj 8.35 S 116.07 E
Mataranka 59 Gb 14.56 S 133.07 E
Mataró 13 Oc 41.32N 2.27 E
Matarraña/Matarranya 13 Mc 41.14N 0.22 E
Matarranya/Matarraña 13 Mc 41.14N 0.22 E
Mataso 63b Dc 17.15 S 168.25 E
Matatula, Cape- 65c Cb 14.15 S 170.34W
Mataura 62 Cg 46.34 S 168.44 E
Mataura 62 Cg 46.12 S 168.52 E
Mata-Utu 58 Jf 13.17 S 176.08W
Mata-Utu, Baie de- 64h Bb 13.19 S 176.07W
Matavai 61 Gb 13.28 S 172.35W
Matavera 64p Cb 21.13 S 159.44W
Mataverj 65d Ab 27.10 S 109.27W
Matawai 62 Gc 38.21 S 177.32 E
Matawin, Réservoir- 44 Kb 46.45N 73.50W
Matawin, Rivière- 44 Kb 46.55N 72.55W
Maţāy 24 Dh 28.25N 30.46 E
Maţbakhayn 33 Hf 17.29N 41.48 E
Matca 15 Kd 45.51N 27.32 E
Matemo, Ilha- 37 Gb 12.13 S 40.36 E
Matera 14 Kj 40.40N 16.36 E
Matese 14 Ii 41.25N 14.20 E
Mátészalka 10 Si 47.57N 22.20 E
Matfors 7 De 62.21N 17.02 E
Matha 11 Fi 45.52N 0.19W
Mathematicians Seamounts (EN) 47 Be 15.30N 111.00W
Matheson 44 Ga 48.32N 80.28W
Mathis 45 Hl 28.06N 97.50W
Mathrákion 15 Cj 39.46N 19.31 E
Mathura 25 Fc 27.30N 77.41 E
Mati 15 Ch 41.39N 19.34 E
Mati 26 Ie 6.57N 126.13 E
Matias Cardoso 55 Kb 14.52 S 43.56W
Matías Romero 47 Ee 16.53N 95.02W
Maticora, Río- 49 Lh 11.01N 71.09W
Matina 49 Fh 10.05N 83.17W
Matinha 54 Id 3.06 S 45.02W
Māţir 32 Ib 37.03N 9.40 E
Matiyure, Río- 50 Ci 7.36N 67.39W
Matkaselkja 8 Nc 61.57N 30.33 E
Mātmāţah 32 Ic 33.33N 9.58 E
Matnog 26 Hd 12.35N 124.05 E
Mato, Cerro- 50 Di 7.15N 65.14W
Mato, Río- 50 Di 7.09N 65.07W
Matočkin Šar, Proliv- 19 Fa 73.30N 54.55 E
Mato Grosso 54 Gf 14.00 S 56.00W
Mato Grosso [Braz.] 55 Dd 18.18 S 57.20W
Mato Grosso [Braz.] 53 Kg 15.00 S 59.57W
Mato Grosso, Planalto do-=Mato Grosso, Plateau of- (EN) 52 Kg 15.30 S 56.00W
Mato Grosso, Plateau of- (EN)=Mato Grosso, Planalto do- 52 Kg 15.30 S 56.00W
Mato Grosso do Sul 54 Hg 20.00 S 55.00W
Matos Costa 55 Gh 26.27 S 51.09W
Matosinhos 13 Dc 41.11N 8.42W
Matou 28 Cj 29.50N 115.32 E
Matov→Qiuxian 28 Cf 36.47N 114.30 E
Mátra 5 Hf 47.53N 19.57 E
Maţrah 23 Ie 23.29N 58.31 E
Matrei in Osttirol 14 Gc 47.00N 12.32 E
Maţrūḩ 31 Je 31.21N 27.14 E
Matsiatra 37 Hd 21.25 S 45.33 E
Matsudo 28 Og 35.48N 139.55 E
Matsue 27 Nd 35.28N 133.04 E
Matsukawa [Jap.] 29 Gc 37.40N 140.28 E
Matsukawa [Jap.] 29 Ed 35.36N 137.53 E
Matsu Liehtao 27 Kf 26.05N 119.56 E
Matsumae 29a Bc 41.26N 140.07 E
Matsumae-Hantō 29a Bc 41.40N 140.15 E
Matsumoto 27 Od 36.14N 137.58 E
Matsuo 29 Gb 39.58N 141.02 E
Matsu-Ōminato 29a Bc 41.16N 141.09 E
Matsusaka 28 Ng 34.34N 136.32 E
Matsushima 29 Gb 38.22N 141.04 E
Matsutō 29 Ec 36.31N 136.33 E
Matsuura 29 Ae 33.22N 129.42 E
Matsuyama 22 Pf 33.50N 132.45 E
Matsuzaki 29 Fd 34.44N 138.45 E
Mattagami Lake 44 Gb 47.57N 81.35W
Mattagami River 42 Jf 50.43N 81.30W
Mattawa 42 Jg 46.19N 78.42W
Matterhorn [Eur.] 14 Be 45.58N 7.39 E
Matterhorn [Nv.-U.S.] 46 Hf 41.49N 115.23W
Matthew, Ile- 57 Ig 22.20 S 171.20 E
Matthews Ridge 54 Fb 7.30N 60.10W
Matthew Town 47 Jd 20.57N 73.40W
Maţţī, Sabhat- 35 Ia 23.30N 52.00 E
Mattighofen 14 Hb 48.06N 13.09 E
Mattoon 45 Lg 39.29N 88.22W
Matua, Ostrov- 20 Kg 48.00N 153.10 E
Matucana 54 Cf 11.51 S 76.24W
Matuku Island 61 Ec 19.10 S 179.46 E
Matundu 36 Db 4.21N 23.40 E
Matundu 36 Gd 8.50 S 39.30 E
Maturin 53 Je 9.45N 63.11W
Matvejev Kurgan 16 Kf 47.34N 38.55 E
Maúa 37 Fb 13.52 S 37.09 E
Maubeuge 11 Jd 50.17N 3.58 E
Ma-ubin 25 Je 16.44N 95.39 E
Maudheimvidda 66 Bf 74.00 S 8.00W
Maud Seamount (EN) 66 Ce 65.00 S 2.35 E
Maués 54 Gd 3.24 S 57.42W
Maués, Rio- 54 Gd 3.22 S 57.44W
Mau Escarpment 36 Gc 0.40 S 36.02 E
Maug Islands 57 Fb 20.01N 145.13 E
Maui Island 57 Lb 20.45N 156.20W
Mauke Island 57 Lg 20.09 S 157.23W
Mau Kyun 25 Jf 12.45N 98.20 E
Mauldre 12 Df 48.59N 1.49 E
Maule 56 Fe 35.45 S 72.15W
Mauléon 11 Fh 46.55N 0.45W
Mauléon-Licharre 11 Fk 43.14N 0.53W
Maullin 56 Ff 41.38 S 73.37W
Maumee 44 Fe 41.34N 83.39W
Maumere 26 Hh 8.37 S 122.14 E
Maun 31 Jj 19.58 S 23.26 E
Maun 14 If 44.26N 14.55 E
Mauna Kea 57 Lc 19.50N 155.28W
Maunaloa 65a Db 21.08N 157.13W
Mauna Loa 65a Fd 19.28N 155.36W
Maunath 25 Gc 25.40N 82.38 E
Maunawili 65a Db 21.21N 157.47W
Maunga Roa 64p Bb 21.13 S 159.48W
Maungdaw 25 Id 20.49N 92.22 E
Mauncir, Lac - 42 Fc 67.30N 125.00W
Maupihaa Atoll (Mopelia, Atoll-) 57 Lf 16.50 S 153.55W
Maupin 46 Ed 45.11N 121.05W
Maupiti, Ile- 57 Lf 16.27 S 152.15W
Maurepas, Lake- 45 Kk 30.15N 90.30W
Maures 11 Mk 43.16N 6.23 E
Mauriac 11 Ii 45.13N 2.20 E
Maurice, Lake- 59 Ge 29.30 S 131.00 E
Maurienne 11 Mi 45.13N 6.30 E
Mauritania (EN)=Mūrītāniyā 31 Fg 20.00N 12.00W
Mauriti 54 Ke 7.23 S 38.46W
Mauritius 30 Mk 20.17 S 57.33 E
Mauritius 31 Mj 18.00 S 57.40 E
Mauron 11 Df 48.05N 2.18W
Maurs 11 Ij 44.43N 2.12 E
Mauston 45 Ke 43.48N 90.05W
Mauthausen 14 Ib 48.14N 14.31 E
Mauzé-sur-le-Mignon 11 Fh 46.12N 0.40W
Mavinga 36 Df 15.47 S 20.24 E
Mavita 37 Ec 19.32 S 33.09 E
Mavrovoúni [Grc.] 15 Fj 39.37N 22.47 E
Mavrovoúni [Grc.] 15 Gh 41.07N 23.08 E
Mawchi 25 Je 18.49N 97.09 E
Mawei 27 Kf 26.02N 119.30 E
Mawlaik 25 Id 23.38N 94.25 E
Mawqaq 24 Ii 27.25N 41.08 E
Mawr, Wādī- 23 Ff 15.41N 42.42 E
Mawson 66 Fe 67.36 S 62.53 E
Mawson Coast 66 Fe 67.40 S 63.30 E
Mawson Escarpment 66 Ff 73.05 S 68.10 E
Maxcanú 47 Fd 20.35N 90.01W
Maxixe 37 Fd 23.51 S 35.21 E
Maxwell Bay 42 Ib 74.32N 89.00W
May, Isle of- 9 Ke 56.10N 2.30W
Maya, Pulau- 26 Eg 1.10 S 109.35 E
Mayaguana Island 47 Jd 22.23N 72.57W
Mayaguana Passage 49 Kb 22.32N 73.15W
Mayagüez 47 Ke 18.12N 67.09W
Mayahi 34 Gc 13.58N 7.40 E
Mayama 36 Bc 3.51 S 14.54 E
Mayāmey 24 Pd 36.24N 55.42 E
Maya Mountains 47 Ge 16.40N 88.50W
Mayapan 47 Gd 20.38N 89.27W
Mayarí 49 Jc 20.40N 75.41W
Maybell 45 Bf 40.31N 108.05W
Maychew 35 Fc 12.46N 39.34 E
Mayḑ 35 Hc 10.57N 47.06 E
Maydān 24 Ke 34.55N 45.37 E
Maydena 59 Jh 42.55 S 146.30 E
Maydī 23 Ff 16.18N 42.48 E
Mayen 10 Df 50.20N 7.13 E
Mayenne 11 Ff 48.18N 0.37W
Mayenne 11 Fg 47.30N 0.32W
Mayenne 11 Ff 48.05N 0.40W
Mayfa'ah 35 Hc 14.16N 47.35 E
Mayfield 44 Cg 36.44N 88.38W
May Glacier 66 Ie 67.00 S 130.00 E
Mayi He 28 Jb 45.52N 128.46 E
Maymyo 25 Jd 22.02N 96.28 E
Maynas 54 Dd 3.00 S 75.00W
Mayo 39 Fc 63.35N 135.54W
Mayo/Muigheo 9 Dh 53.50N 9.30W
Mayo, Mountains of- 9 Dg 54.05N 9.30W
Mayo, Río- 48 Ed 26.45N 109.47W
Mayo Darlé 34 Hd 6.30N 11.55 E
Mayo-Kébbi 35 Ad 9.18N 13.33 E
Mayo-Kébbi 35 Bd 10.00N 15.30 E
Mayoko 36 Bc 2.18 S 12.49 E
Mayon, Mount- 21 Oh 13.15N 123.41 E
Mayor, Puig- 13 Oe 39.48N 2.48 E
Mayor, Puig-/Major, Puig- 13 Oe 39.48N 2.48 E
Mayor Island 62 Gb 37.15 S 176.15 E
Mayor Pablo Lagerenza 56 Ha 19.58 S 60.45W
Mayotte 31 Lj 12.50 S 45.10 E
Mayotte/Mahoré 30 Lj 12.50 S 45.10 E
May Pen 47 Ie 17.58N 77.14W
Mayraira Point 26 Hc 18.39N 120.51 E
Mayran, Laguna de- 48 He 25.45N 102.45W
Mayreau Island 51n Bb 12.39N 61.23W
May-sur-Orne 12 Be 49.06N 0.22W
Maysville 44 Ff 38.39N 83.46W
Mayumba [Gabon] 31 Ii 3.25 S 10.39 E
Mayumba [Zaire] 36 Ed 7.16 S 27.03 E
Mayum La 27 De 30.35N 82.27 E
Mayville 44 Hd 42.15N 79.32W
Mayyit, Al Baḩr al-=Dead Sea (EN) 21 Ff 31.30N 35.30 E
Mazabuka 36 Ef 15.51 S 27.46 E
Mazagão 54 Hd 0.07 S 51.17W
Mazamet 11 Ik 43.30N 2.24 E
Māzandarān 23 Hb 36.00N 54.00 E
Māzandarān, Daryā-ye-=Caspian Sea (EN) 5 Lg 42.00N 50.30 E
Mazar 27 Cd 36.27N 77.03 E
Mazara del Vallo 14 Gm 37.39N 12.35 E
Mazār-e Sharīf 22 If 36.42N 67.06 E
Mazarrón, Golfo de- 13 Kg 37.30N 1.18W
Mazartag 27 Dd 38.29N 80.50 E
Mazaruni River 54 Gb 6.25N 58.38W
Mazatenango 47 Ff 14.32N 91.30W
Mazatlán 39 Ig 23.13N 106.25W
Mažeikiai/Mažejkjaj 7 Fh 56.20N 22.22 E
Mažejkjaj/Mažeikiai 7 Fh 56.20N 22.22 E
Mazḩafah, Jabal- 24 Fh 28.48N 34.57 E
Maẓhūr, 'Irq al- 24 Ji 27.25N 43.55 E
Mazinga 51c Ab 17.29N 62.58W
Mazirbe 8 Jg 57.40N 22.10 E
Mazoe 37 Ec 17.30 S 30.58 E
Mazoe 30 Kj 16.32 S 33.25 E
Mazomeno 36 Ec 4.55 S 27.13 E
Mazong Shan 27 Gc 41.33N 97.10 E
Mazowsze 10 Qd 52.40N 20.20 E
Mazowsze=Masovia (EN) 5 Ie 52.40N 20.20 E
Mazsalaca 8 Kg 57.45N 24.59 E
Mazunga 37 Dd 21.44 S 29.52 E
Mazurskie, Pojezierze- 10 Qc 53.40N 21.00 E
Mazzarino 14 Im 37.18N 14.13 E
Mba 63d Ab 17.32 S 177.42 E
Mbabane 31 Kk 26.18 S 31.07 E
Mbabo, Tchabal- 34 Hd 7.16N 12.09 E
Mbacké 34 Bc 14.48N 15.55W
Mbaéré 35 Be 3.47N 17.31 E
Mbaïki 31 Ih 3.53N 18.00 E
Mbakaou 34 Hd 6.19N 12.49 E
Mbakaou, Barrage de- 34 Hd 6.25N 13.00 E
Mbala 31 Ki 8.50 S 31.22 E
Mbalam 34 He 2.13N 13.49 E
Mbale 31 Kh 1.05N 34.10 E
Mbali 35 Be 4.27N 18.20 E
Mbalmayo 34 He 3.31N 11.30 E
Mbam 30 Ih 4.24N 11.17 E
Mbamba Bay 36 Fe 11.17 S 34.46 E
Mbandaka 31 Ih 0.04N 18.16 E
Mbanga 34 Ge 4.30N 9.34 E
Mbanika 63a Dc 9.05 S 159.12 E
Mbanza Congo 36 Bd 6.16 S 14.15 E
Mbanza-Ngungu 31 Ii 5.35 S 14.47 E
Mbarangandu 36 Gd 8.57 S 37.24 E
Mbarara 36 Fc 0.36 S 30.38 E
Mbari 35 Ce 4.34N 22.43 E
Mbatiki 63d Bb 17.46 S 179.08 E
Mbava 63a Cb 7.49 S 156.37 E
Mbé 34 Hd 7.51N 13.36 E
Mbengga 63d Bc 18.23 S 178.08 E
Mbengwi 34 Hd 6.01N 10.00 E
Mbéré 35 Bd 9.07N 16.26 E
Mbeya 31 Ki 8.54 S 33.27 E
Mbeya 36 Fd 8.00 S 33.30 E
Mbi 35 Be 4.28N 18.07 E
Mbigou 36 Bc 1.53 S 11.56 E
Mbinda 31 Ii 2.07 S 12.52 E
Mbinga 36 Ge 10.56 S 35.01 E
Mbingué 34 Dc 10.00N 5.54W
Mbini 34 Ge 1.34N 9.37 E
Mbini 34 He 1.30N 10.00 E
Mbini 30 Ih 1.30N 10.30 E
Mboki 35 Dd 5.19N 25.58 E
Mbokonimbeti 63a Ec 8.57 S 160.05 E
Mbomo 36 Bb 0.24N 14.44 E
Mbomou=Bomu (EN) 35 Cd 5.30N 23.30 E
Mbomou=Bomu (EN) 30 Jh 4.08N 22.26 E
Mborokua 63a Dc 9.02 S 158.44 E
Mbour 34 Bc 14.24N 16.58W
Mbout 32 Ef 16.01N 12.35W
Mbozi 36 Fd 9.02 S 32.56 E
Mbrés 35 Bd 6.40N 19.48 E
M'Bridge 36 Bd 7.14 S 12.52 E
Mbua 63d Bb 16.48 S 178.37 E
Mbuji-Mayi 31 Ji 6.09 S 23.33 E
Mbulo 63a Dc 8.46 S 158.21 E
Mbulu 36 Gc 3.51 S 35.32 E
Mburucuyá 55 Ci 28.03 S 58.14W
Mbutha 63d Bb 16.39 S 179.51 E
Mbuyuni 36 Gd 7.23 S 36.32 E
Mbwemburu 36 Gd 9.29 S 39.39 E
Mcalester 43 He 34.56N 95.46W
Mcensk 19 De 53.17N 36.32 E
M'Chedallah 13 Qh 36.22N 4.16 E
Mcherrah 32 Gd 27.00N 4.30W
Mchinga 36 Gd 9.44 S 39.42 E
Mchinji 36 Fe 13.48 S 32.54 E
Mdandu 36 Fd 9.09 S 34.42 E
M'Daourouch 14 Bn 36.05N 7.49 E
Mdennah 32 Gd 25.00N 4.50W
Mdiq 13 Gi 35.41N 5.19W
Mead 44 Fa 49.29N 83.50W
Mead, Lake- 43 Ed 36.05N 114.25W
Meade 40 Hb 70.50N 156.25W
Meade 45 Fh 37.17N 100.20W
Meade Peak 46 Je 42.30N 111.15W
Meadow Lake 42 Gf 54.07N 108.20W
Meadville 44 Ge 41.38N 80.10W
Me-akan-Dake 29a Cb 43.23N 143.59 E
Mealhada 13 Dd 40.22N 8.27W

Index Symbols

1 Independent Nation
2 State, Region
3 District, County
4 Municipality
5 Colony, Dependency
Continent
Physical Region
Historical or Cultural Region
Mount, Mountain
Volcano
Hill
Mountains, Mountain Range
Hills, Escarpment
Plateau, Upland
Pass, Gap
Plain, Lowland
Delta
Salt Flat
Valley, Canyon
Crater, Cave
Karst Features
Depression
Polder
Desert, Dunes
Forest, Woods
Heath, Steppe
Oasis
Cape, Point
Coast, Beach
Cliff
Peninsula
Isthmus
Sandbank
Island
Atoll
Rock, Reef
Islands, Archipelago
Rocks, Reefs
Coral Reef
Well, Spring
Geyser
River, Stream
Waterfall Rapids
River Mouth, Estuary
Lake
Salt Lake
Intermittent Lake
Reservoir
Swamp, Pond
Canal
Glacier
Ice Shelf, Pack Ice
Ocean
Sea
Gulf, Bay
Strait, Fjord
Lagoon
Bank
Seamount
Tablemount
Ridge
Shelf
Basin
Escarpment, Sea Scarp
Fracture
Trench, Abyss
National Park, Reserve
Point of Interest
Recreation Site
Cave, Cavern
Historic Site
Ruins
Wall, Walls
Church, Abbey
Temple
Scientific Station
Airport
Port
Lighthouse
Mine
Tunnel
Dam, Bridge

Mealy Mountains 42 Lf 53.20N 59.30W
Meama 65b Ba 19.45S 174.34W
Méan, Havelange- 12 Hd 50.22N 5.20 E
Meander Reef 26 Ge 8.09N 119.14 E
Meander River 42 Fe 59.02N 117.42W
Meanguera, Isla- 49 Dg 13.12N 87.43W
Mearim, Rio- 52 Lf 3.04S 44.35W
Meath/An Mhí [2] 9 Gh 53.35N 6.40W
Meaux 11 If 48.57N 2.52 E
Mecca (EN)=Makkah 22 Fg 21.27N 39.49 E
Mechara 35 Gd 8.34N 40.28 E
Mechelen/Maasmechelen 12 Hd 50.57N 5.40 E
Mechelen/Malines 11 Kc 51.02N 4.29 E
Mecheraa-Asfa 13 Ni 35.24N 1.03 E
Mecheria 32 Gc 33.33N 0.17W
Mechernich 12 Id 50.36N 6.39 E
Mechongué 55 Cn 38.09S 58.13W
Mecidiye 15 Ji 40.38N 26.32 E
Mecitözü 24 Fb 40.31N 35.19 E
Mecklenburgischer Höhenrücken 10 Ic 53.40N 12.10 E
Mecklenburg 10 Hc 53.30N 12.00 E
Mecklenburger Bucht 10 Hb 54.20N 11.40 E
Mecklenburger Schweiz 10 Ic 53.45N 12.35 E
Mecoacán, Laguna- 48 Mh 18.20N 93.10W
Meconta 37 Fb 14.59S 39.50 E
Mecsek 10 Oj 46.10N 18.18 E
Mecubúri 37 Gb 14.10S 40.31 E
Mecúfi 37 Gb 13.17S 40.33 E
Mecula 37 Fb 12.05S 37.39 E
Médala 32 Ff 15.30N 5.37W
Medan 22 Li 3.35N 98.40 E
Médanos [Arg.] 56 He 38.50S 62.41W
Médanos [Arg.] 55 Ck 33.24S 59.05W
Medanosa, Punta- 56 Gg 48.06S 65.55W
Mede 14 Ce 45.06N 8.44 E
Médéa 32 Hb 36.16N 2.45 E
Médéa [3] 32 Hb 36.20N 3.25 E
Medebach 12 Kc 51.12N 8.43 E
Medellín 26 Hd 11.08N 123.58 E
Medellín 53 Ie 6.15N 75.35W
Medelpad 8 Gb 62.35N 16.15 E
Medemblik 12 Hb 52.46N 5.06 E
Medenica 10 Tg 49.21N 23.45 E
Mederdra 32 Df 16.54N 15.40W
Medetziz 24 Fd 37.25N 34.40 E
Medford [Or.-U.S.] 39 Ge 42.19N 122.52W
Medford [Wi.-U.S.] 45 Kd 45.09N 90.20W
Medgidia 15 Le 44.15N 28.17 E
Medi 35 Ed 5.06N 30.44 E
Media Luna, Arrecife de la- 49 Ff 15.13N 82.36W
Medianeira 55 Eg 25.17S 54.05W
Mediaş 15 Hc 46.10N 24.21 E
Medical Lake 46 Gc 47.34N 117.41W
Medicine Bow 46 Lf 41.54N 106.12W
Medicine Bow Mountains 46 Lf 41.10N 106.25W
Medicine Butte 46 Jf 41.29N 110.48W
Medicine Hat 39 Hd 50.03N 110.40W
Medicine Lake 46 Mb 48.28N 104.24W
Medicine Lodge 45 Gh 37.17N 98.35W
Međimurje 14 Kd 46.25N 16.30 E
Medina (EN)=Al Madīnah [Sau.Ar.] 22 Fg 24.28N 39.36 E
Medina Az-Zahra 13 Hg 37.52N 4.50W
Medinaceli 13 Jc 41.10N 2.26W
Medina del Campo 13 Hc 41.18N 4.55W
Medina de Rioseco 13 Gc 41.53N 5.02W
Medina-Sidonia 13 Gh 36.27N 5.55W
Medininkai/Medininkaj 8 Kj 54.32N 25.46 E
Medininkaj/Medininkai 8 Kj 54.32N 25.46 E
Medio, Arroyo del- 55 Bk 33.16S 60.15W
Mediterranean Sea (EN)= Akdeniz 5 Hh 35.00N 20.00 E
Mediterranean Sea (EN)= Khatikhon, Yam- 5 Hh 35.00N 20.00 E
Mediterranean Sea (EN)= Méditerranée, Mer- 5 Hh 35.00N 20.00 E
Mediterranean Sea (EN)= Mediterraneo, Mar- 5 Hh 35.00N 20.00 E
Mediterranean Sea (EN)= Mediterráneo, Mar- 5 Hh 35.00N 20.00 E
Mediterranean Sea (EN)= Mesoyéios Thálassa 5 Hh 35.00N 20.00 E
Mediterranean Sea (EN)= Mutawassiţ, Al Baḩr al- 5 Hh 35.00N 20.00 E
Méditerranée, Mer-= Mediterranean Sea (EN) 5 Hh 35.00N 20.00 E
Mediterráneo, Mar-= Mediterranean Sea (EN) 5 Hh 35.00N 20.00 E
Mediterraneo, Mar-= Mediterranean Sea (EN) 5 Hh 35.00N 20.00 E
Medje 36 Eb 2.25N 27.18 E
Medjerda, Monts de la- 32 Ib 36.35N 8.15 E
Mednogorsk 19 Fe 51.26N 57.40 E
Mednyj, Ostrov- 20 Lf 54.40N 167.50 E
Médoc 11 Fi 45.00N 1.00W
Mêdog 27 Gf 29.18N 95.27 E
Médouneu 36 Bb 1.01N 10.48 E
Medveđa 15 Eg 42.51N 21.36 E
Medvedica [R.S.F.S.R.] 5 Kf 49.35N 42.41 E
Medvedica [R.S.F.S.R.] 7 Ih 57.05N 37.31 E
Medvednica 14 Je 45.55N 15.58 E
Medvedok 7 Mh 57.24N 50.06 E
Medvenka 16 Jd 51.27N 36.08 E
Medveži, Ostrova-=Bear Islands (EN) 21 Sb 70.52N 161.26 E
Medvežjegorsk 19 Dc 62.56N 34.29 E
Medway 12 Cc 51.23N 0.31 E
Medzilaborce 10 Rg 49.16N 21.55 E
Meekatharra 58 Cg 26.36S 118.29 E
Meeker 45 Cf 40.02N 107.55W
Meerane 10 If 50.51N 12.28 E
Meerbusch 12 Ic 51.16N 6.40 E
Meerut 25 Fc 28.59N 77.42 E
Meeteetse 46 Kd 44.09N 108.52W
Mefarlane, Lake- 59 Hf 32.00S 136.40 E
Mega [Eth.] 31 Kh 4.03N 38.20 E
Mega [Indon.] 26 Jg 0.41S 131.53 E
Mega, Pulau- 26 Dg 4.00S 101.02 E
Megalo 35 Gd 6.52N 40.47 E
Megálon Khorion 15 Km 36.27N 27.21 E
Megalópolis 15 Fl 37.24N 22.08 E
Megálo Sofráno 15 Jm 36.04N 26.25 E
Meganisión 15 Dk 38.38N 20.43 E
Meganom, Mys- 16 Ig 44.48N 35.05 E
Mégara 15 Gk 38.00N 23.21 E
Megève 11 Mi 45.52N 6.37 E
Meghalaya [3] 25 Ic 26.00N 91.00 E
Megid 33 Dd 28.35N 22.10 E
Megion 19 Hc 61.00N 76.15 E
Megiscane, Lac- 44 Ia 48.30N 76.04W
Megri 16 Oj 38.55N 46.15 E
Mehadia 15 Fe 44.54N 22.22 E
Mehaigne 12 Hd 50.32N 5.13 E
Meharry, Mount- 59 Dd 23.00S 118.35 E
Mehdia 13 Ni 35.25N 1.45 E
Mehdīshahr 24 Oe 35.44N 53.22 E
Mehedinţi [2] 15 Fe 44.30N 23.00 E
Mehetia, Ile- 61 Lc 17.52S 148.03W
Mehrabān 24 Lc 38.05N 47.08 E
Mehrān 24 Pi 26.52N 55.24 E
Mehrān 24 Lf 33.07N 46.10 E
Mehrenga 7 Je 63.17N 41.20 E
Mehrīz 24 Pg 31.35N 54.28 E
Mehtar Lām 23 Lc 34.39N 70.10 E
Mehun-sur-Yèvre 11 Ig 47.09N 2.13 E
Meia Meia 36 Gd 5.49S 35.48 E
Meia Ponte, Rio- 54 Ig 18.32S 49.36W
Meiganga 34 Hd 6.31N 14.18 E
Meighen 42 Ha 79.55N 99.00W
Meihekou→Hailong 27 Mc 42.32N 125.37 E
Meiktila 25 Jd 20.52N 95.52 E
Meilü→Wuchuan 27 Jg 21.28N 110.44 E
Meinerzhagen 12 Jc 51.07N 7.39 E
Meiningen 10 Gf 50.33N 10.25 E
Meio, Rio do- 55 Ja 13.20S 44.34W
Meisenheim 12 Je 49.43N 7.40 E
Meishan [China] 27 He 30.05N 103.48 E
Meishan [China] 28 Ei 31.06N 119.43 E
Meishan → Jinzhai 28 Ci 31.40N 115.52 E
Meißen 10 Je 51.09N 13.29 E
Meißner 10 Fe 51.12N 9.50 E
Meitan (Yiquan) 27 If 27.48N 107.32 E
Meixian 27 Kg 24.21N 116.07 E
Meiyukou 28 Bd 40.01N 113.08 E
Méjean, Causse- 11 Jj 44.16N 3.22 E
Mejillones 56 Fb 23.06S 70.27W
Mékambo 36 Bb 1.01N 13.56 E
Mekdela 35 Fc 11.28N 39.20 E
Mekele=Meqele (EN) 31 Kg 13.30N 39.28 E
Mékhé 34 Bb 15.07N 16.38W
Mekherrhane, Sebkha- 30 Hf 26.22N 1.20 E
Meknès [3] 32 Fc 33.00N 5.30W
Meknès 31 Ge 33.54N 5.32W
Mekong (EN)=Lancang Jiang 21 Mh 10.15N 105.55 E
Mekong (EN)=Mae Nam Khong 21 Mh 10.15N 105.55 E
Mekong (EN)=Mékôngk 21 Mh 10.15N 105.55 E
Mekong (EN)=Mènam Khong 21 Mh 10.15N 105.55 E
Mekong Delta (EN) 21 Mi 10.20N 106.40 E
Mekongga, Gunung- 26 Hg 3.35S 121.15 E
Mékôngk=Mekong (EN) 21 Mh 10.15N 105.55 E
Mekoryuk 40 Fd 60.23N 166.12W
Mékrou 34 Fc 12.24N 2.49 E
Mel, Ilha do- 55 Hg 25.31S 48.20W
Melaab 13 Ni 35.43N 1.20 E
Mēlādēn 35 Hc 10.25N 49.52 E
Melaka 22 Mi 2.12N 102.15 E
Melaka, Selat-=Malacca, Strait of- (EN) 21 Mi 2.30N 101.20 E
Melamo, Cabo- 30 Lj 14.24S 40.49 E
Melanesia 57 Hf 13.00S 164.00 E
Melanesian Basin (EN) 3 Jj 0.05S 160.35 E
Melawi 26 Ff 0.05N 111.29 E
Melbourne [Ar.-U.S.] 45 Kh 36.04N 91.54W
Melbourne [Austl.] 58 Fh 37.49S 144.58 E
Melbourne [Eng.-U.K.] 12 Ab 52.49N 1.26W
Melbourne [Fl.-U.S.] 43 Kf 28.05N 80.37W
Melbourne-Dandenong 59 Jg 37.59S 145.12 E
Melchor Múzquiz 47 Dc 27.53N 101.31W
Melchor Ocampo 48 Hi 17.59N 102.11W
Meldorf 10 Fb 54.05N 9.05 E
Mele, Capo- 14 Cg 43.57N 8.10 E
Melekeiok 64a Bc 7.29N 134.38 E
Melela 37 Fc 17.04S 38.36 E
Melenci 15 Dd 45.31N 20.19 E
Melenki 7 Ed 55.23N 41.42 E
Meleto Dağı 24 Ic 38.35N 41.32 E
Meleuz 19 Fe 52.58N 55.59 E
Mélèzes, Rivière aux- 42 Ke 57.00N 69.00W
Melfa 14 Hi 41.30N 13.35 E
Melfi [Chad] 35 Bc 11.04N 17.56 E
Melfi [It.] 14 Jj 41.00N 15.39 E
Melfort 42 Hf 52.52N 104.36W
Melgaço 54 Hd 1.47S 50.44W
Melibocus 12 Eg 49.42N 8.40 E
Melilla 31 Ge 35.19N 2.58W
Melincué, Laguna- 55 Bk 33.42S 61.28W
Melipilla 56 Fd 33.42S 71.13W
Melita 45 Fb 49.16N 101.00W
Meliti 15 Ei 40.50N 21.35 E
Melito di Porto Salvo 14 Jm 37.55N 15.47 E
Melito di Porto Salvo, Punta di- 14 Jm 37.57N 15.45 E
Melitopol 6 Jf 46.50N 35.22 E
Melk 14 Jb 48.13N 15.19 E
Mella 14 Ee 45.13N 10.13 E
Mellakou 13 Ni 35.15N 1.14 E
Mellanfryken 8 Ee 59.40N 13.15 E
Melle [Fr.] 11 Fh 46.13N 0.08W
Melle [F.R.G.] 12 Kb 52.12N 8.21 E
Mellen 45 Kc 46.20N 90.40W
Mellerud 7 Cg 58.42N 12.28 E
Mellish Reef 59 Lc 17.25S 155.50 E
Mellish Seamount (EN) 57 Ia 34.00N 178.15 E
Mellit 35 Dc 14.08N 25.33 E
Mělník 10 Kf 50.21N 14.30 E
Melnik 15 Gh 41.31N 23.24 E
Melo 53 Ki 32.22S 54.11W
Melo, Rio- 55 De 21.25S 57.55W
Melrhir, Chott- 30 He 34.20N 6.20 E
Melrose 46 Id 45.38N 112.40W
Melsetter 37 Ec 19.48S 32.50 E
Melsungen 10 Fe 51.08N 9.33 E
Meltaus 7 Fc 66.54N 25.22 E
Melton Constable 12 Db 52.51N 1.02 E
Melton Mowbray 9 Mi 52.46N 0.53W
Meluco 37 Fb 12.33S 39.37 E
Meluli 37 Fc 16.28S 39.44 E
Melun 11 If 48.32N 2.40 E
Melville 38 Ib 75.15N 110.00W
Melville 46 Na 50.55N 102.48W
Melville, Cape- 59 Ib 14.10S 144.30 E
Melville, Lake- 42 Lf 53.42N 59.30W
Melville Bay 59 Hb 12.05S 136.45 E
Melville Bay (EN)=Melville Bugt 67 Od 75.35N 62.30W
Melville Bugt=Melville Bay (EN) 67 Od 75.35N 62.30W
Melville Hills 42 Fc 69.20N 123.00W
Melville Island 57 Ef 11.40S 131.00 E
Melville Peninsula 38 Kc 68.00N 84.00W
Melville Sound 42 Gc 68.05N 107.30W
Melvin, Lough- 9 Eg 54.25N 8.10W
Mélykút 10 Pj 46.13N 19.23 E
Memaliaj 15 Ci 40.20N 19.58 E
Memambetsu 29a Db 43.55N 144.11 E
Memba, Baia de- 37 Gb 14.11S 40.35 E
Memberamo 26 Kg 1.28S 137.52 E
Memboro 26 Gh 9.22S 119.32 E
Mēmele 8 Kh 56.24N 24.10 E
Memmert 10 Cc 53.39N 6.53 E
Memmingen 10 Gi 47.59N 10.10 E
Mempawan 26 Ef 0.22N 108.58 E
Memphis 33 Fd 29.52N 31.15 E
Memphis [Mo.-U.S.] 45 Jf 40.28N 92.10W
Memphis [Tn.-U.S.] 39 Jf 35.08N 90.03W
Memphis [Tx.-U.S.] 45 Fi 34.44N 100.32W
Memrut Dağı 24 Jc 38.40N 42.12 E
Memuro 28 Qc 42.55N 143.03 E
Memuro-Dake 29a Cb 42.52N 142.45 E
Mena 35 Gd 5.30N 41.06 E
Mena [Ar.-U.S.] 45 Ii 34.35N 94.15W
Mena [Ukr.-U.S.S.R.] 19 De 51.33N 32.14 E
Menabe 30 Lk 20.00S 44.40 E
Menai Strait 9 Ih 53.12N 4.12W
Ménaka 31 Hg 15.55N 2.26 E
Mènam Khong=Mekong (EN) 21 Mh 10.15N 105.55 E
Menangalaku 26 Gh 9.36S 119.01 E
Menard 45 Gk 30.55N 99.47W
Menawashei 35 Dc 12.40N 25.01 E
Menčul, Gora- 10 Th 48.16N 23.49 E
Mendala, Puncak- 26 Lg 4.44S 140.20 E
Mendanau, Pulau- 26 Eg 2.51S 107.26 E
Mendanha 55 Kd 18.06S 43.30W
Mende 11 Jj 44.31N 3.30 E
Mendebo 30 Kh 6.50N 39.40 E
Mendelejevsk 7 Mi 55.57N 52.22 E
Menden (Sauerland) 10 De 51.26N 7.48 E
Mendes 13 Mi 35.39N 0.52 E
Méndez 48 Je 25.07N 98.34W
Mendi [Eth.] 35 Fd 9.48N 35.05 E
Mendi [Pap.N.Gui.] 60 Ci 6.10S 143.40 E
Mendig 12 Jd 50.22N 7.16 E
Mendip Hills 9 Kj 51.15N 2.40W
Mendocino 46 Dg 39.19N 123.48W
Mendocino, Cape- 38 Ge 40.25N 124.25W
Mendocino Fracture Zone (EN) 3 Lf 40.00N 145.00W
Mendota [Ca.-U.S.] 46 Eh 36.45N 120.23W
Mendota [Il.-U.S.] 45 Lf 41.33N 89.07W
Mendoza 53 Ji 32.54S 68.50W
Mendoza [2] 56 Gd 34.30S 68.30W
Mené, Landes du- 11 Df 48.15N 2.32W
Mene de Mauroa 49 Lh 10.43N 71.01W
Mene Grande 54 Db 9.49S 70.56W
Menemen 24 Bc 38.36N 27.04 E
Menen/Menin 11 Jd 50.48N 3.07 E
Meneng Point 64e Bb 0.33S 166.57 E
Meneses 55 Dj 30.53S 56.30W
Ménez Hom 11 Bf 48.13N 4.16W
Menfi 14 Gm 37.36N 12.58 E
Mengcheng 27 Ke 33.11N 116.30 E
Mengdingjie 27 Gg 23.31N 99.07 E
Menggala 26 Eg 4.28S 105.17 E
Mengibar 13 Ig 37.58N 3.48W
Mengjin 28 Bg 34.50N 112.26 E
Mengla 27 Hg 21.30N 101.35 E
Menglangba→Lancang 27 Gg 22.37N 99.57 E
Menglian 27 Gg 22.20N 99.27 E
Mengoun Huizu Zizhixian 28 De 38.04N 117.06 E
Mengyin 28 Dg 35.42N 117.56 E
Mengzi 22 Mg 23.23N 103.34 E
Menihek Lakes 42 Kf 54.00N 66.30W
Menin/Menen 11 Jd 50.48N 3.07 E
Menindee 59 If 32.24S 142.26 E
Menindee Lake 59 If 32.00S 142.23 E
Meningie 59 Hg 35.42S 139.20 E
Menjapa, Gunung- 26 Gf 1.05N 116.05 E
Menno 45 He 43.14N 97.34W
Menoikion Óros 15 Gh 41.11N 23.48 E
Menominee 44 Dc 45.07N 87.39W
Menongue 31 Ij 14.40S 17.39 E
Menor, Mar- 13 Lg 37.43N 0.48W
Menorca=Minorca (EN) 5 Gg 40.00N 4.00 E
Menor do Araguaia, Braço- ou Javaes 54 He 9.50S 50.12W
Mentana 14 Gh 42.02N 12.38 E
Mentasta Lake 40 Kd 62.55N 143.45W
Mentawai, Kepulauan-= Mentawai Islands (EN) 21 Lj 2.00S 99.30 E
Mentawai, Selat- 21 Lj 2.00S 99.30 E
Mentawai Islands (EN)= Mentawai, Kepulauan- 21 Lj 2.00S 99.30 E
Menton 11 Nk 43.47N 7.30 E
Mentougou 28 De 39.56N 116.02 E
Menyuan 27 Hd 37.30N 101.35 E
Menzelinsk 7 Mi 55.45N 53.09 E
Menzies 59 Ee 29.41S 121.02 E
Menzies, Mount- 66 Ff 73.30S 61.50 E
Meon 12 Ad 50.49N 1.15W
Meoqui 47 Cc 28.17N 105.29W
Meponda 37 Eb 13.25S 34.52 E
Meppel 11 Mb 52.42N 6.11 E
Meppen 10 Dd 52.41N 7.19 E
Meqele(EN)=Mekele 31 Kg 13.30N 39.28 E
Mê Qu 27 He 33.58N 102.10 E
Mequinenza, Pantà de-/ Mequinenza, Embalse de- 13 Lc 41.15N 0.02W
Mequinenza, Embalse de-/ Mequinenza, Pantà de- 13 Lc 41.15N 0.02W
Mera 14 Dd 46.11N 9.25 E
Merabello, Gulf of- (EN) = Merabéllou, Kólpos- 15 In 35.14N 25.47 E
Merabéllou, Kólpos- = Merabello, Gulf of- (EN) 15 In 35.14N 25.47 E
Merak 26 Eh 5.56S 106.00 E
Meråker 7 Ce 63.26N 11.45 E
Méralab 63b Db 14.27S 168.03 E
Meramangye, Lake- 59 Ge 28.25S 132.15 E
Meran / Merano 14 Fd 46.40N 11.09 E
Merano / Meran 14 Fd 46.40N 11.09 E
Meratus, Pegunungan- 26 Gg 2.45S 115.40 E
Merauke 58 Fe 8.28S 140.20 E
Mercadal 13 Qe 39.59N 4.05 E
Mercato Saraceno 14 Gg 43.57N 12.12 E
Merced 43 Cd 37.18N 120.29W
Mercedario, Cerro- 52 Ii 31.59S 70.14W
Mercedes [Arg.] 56 Id 34.39S 59.27W
Mercedes [Arg.] 56 Ic 29.12S 58.05W
Mercedes [Arg.] 53 Ji 33.40S 65.30W
Mercedes [Ur.] 53 Ki 33.16S 58.01W
Merchants Bay 42 Lc 67.10N 62.50W
Merchtem 12 Gd 50.58N 4.14 E
Mercury Islands 62 Fb 36.35S 175.50 E
Mercy, Cape- 42 Ld 64.56N 63.40W
Mercy Bay 42 Fb 74.15N 118.10W
Meredith, Cape- 56 Hh 52.15S 60.38W
Meredith, Lake- 45 Fi 35.36N 101.42W
Meredoua 32 Hd 25.20N 2.05 E
Merefa 19 Df 49.51N 36.00 E
Merelbeke 12 Fd 51.00N 3.45 E
Merenga 20 Kd 61.43N 156.05 E
Mergui 22 Lh 12.26N 98.36 E
Mergui Archipelago 21 Lh 12.00N 98.00 E
Méri 34 Hc 10.47N 14.06 E
Meriç 15 Jh 41.11N 26.25 E
Meriç 24 Bb 40.52N 26.12 E
Mérida [2] 54 Db 8.30N 71.10W
Mérida [Mex.] 39 Kg 20.58N 89.37W
Mérida [Sp.] 13 Ff 38.55N 6.20W
Mérida [Ven.] 53 Ie 8.36N 71.08W
Merida, Cordillera de- 52 Ie 8.40N 71.00W
Meridian 39 Kf 32.22N 88.42W
Mérig 63b Cb 14.19S 167.48 E
Mérignac 11 Fj 44.50N 0.38W
Merikarvia 7 Ef 61.51N 21.30 E
Merín, Laguna- 56 Jd 32.45S 52.50W
Meringur 59 If 34.24S 141.29 E
Merir Island 57 Ed 4.19N 132.19 E
Merizo 64c Bb 13.16N 144.40 E
Merke 18 Ic 42.52N 73.12 E
Merkem, Houthulst- 12 Ed 50.57N 2.51 E
Merkine/Merkinė 8 Kj 54.07N 24.20 E
Merkinė/Merkine 8 Kj 54.07N 24.20 E
Merkis/Merkys 7 Fi 54.10N 24.11 E
Merksem, Antwerpen- 12 Gc 51.15N 4.27 E
Merksplas 12 Gc 51.22N 4.52 E
Merkys/Merkis 7 Fi 54.10N 24.11 E
Meroe 35 Eb 16.56N 33.59 E
Meroe 35 Eb 16.05N 33.55 E
Merouane, Chott- 32 Ic 34.00N 6.02 E
Merredin 59 Df 31.29S 118.16 E
Merrick 9 If 55.08N 4.29W
Merrill 43 Jb 45.11N 89.41W
Merriman 45 Fe 42.55N 101.42W
Merritt 42 Ff 50.07N 120.47W
Merritt Island 43 Kf 28.21N 80.42W
Merritt Reservoir 45 Fe 42.35N 100.55W
Mersa Fatma 35 Gc 14.53N 40.19 E
Mersa Teklay 35 Fb 17.25N 38.45 E
Mersea Island 12 Cc 51.47N 0.57 E
Merseburg 10 He 51.22N 12.00 E
Mers el Kebir 13 Li 35.44N 0.43W
Mersey 9 Kh 53.25N 3.00W
Merseyside [3] 9 Kh 53.30N 3.00W
Mersin 23 Db 36.48N 34.38 E
Mersing 26 Df 2.26N 103.50 E
Mers-les-Bains 12 Dd 50.04N 1.23 E
Mērsrags/Mersrags 8 Jg 57.19N 23.01 E
Mersrags/Mērsrags 8 Jg 57.19N 23.01 E
Merta 25 Ec 26.39N 74.02 E
Merta Road 25 Ec 26.43N 73.55 E
Mertert 12 Ie 49.42N 6.29 E
Merthyr Tydfil 9 Jj 51.46N 3.23W
Merti 36 Gb 1.04N 38.40 E
Mértola 13 Eg 37.38N 7.40W
Mertule Maryam 35 Fc 10.50N 38.15 E
Mertvy Kultuk, Sor- 16 Rg 45.30N 53.40 E
Mertz Glacier 66 Je 67.40S 144.45 E
Meru 36 Gb 0.03N 37.39 E
Méru 11 Ie 49.14N 2.08 E
Meru, Mount- 36 Gc 3.14S 36.45 E
Merure 55 Fb 15.33S 53.05W
Merville 12 Ed 50.38N 2.38 E
Merzifon 23 Ea 40.53N 35.29 E
Merzig 10 Cg 49.27N 6.38 E
Meša 7 Li 55.34N 49.24 E
Mesa [Az.-U.S.] 39 Hf 33.25N 111.50W
Mesa [Co.-U.S.] 45 Bg 39.14N 108.08W
Mesabi Range 45 Jc 47.30N 92.50W
Mesagne 14 Lj 40.34N 17.48 E
Mescalero 45 Dj 33.09N 105.46W
Meščera=Moscow Basin 5 Kd 55.00N 40.30 E
Meschede 10 Ee 51.21N 8.17 E
Mescit Dağı 24 Ib 40.22N 41.11 E
Meščovsk 16 Ib 54.19N 35.18 E
Mesegon 64d Bb 7.09N 151.55 E
Mesfinto 35 Fc 13.28N 37.23 E
Me-Shima 28 Jh 32.01N 128.25 E
Meshkinshahr 24 Lc 38.24N 47.40 E
Mesima 14 Jl 38.30N 15.55 E
Mesjagutovo 17 Ii 55.35N 58.20 E
Meskiana 14 Bo 35.38N 7.40 E
Meskiana, Oued- 14 Bo 35.48N 7.53 E
Meslo 35 Fd 6.22N 39.50 E
Mesnil-Val, Criel-sur-Mer- 12 Dd 50.03N 1.20 E
Mesola 14 Gf 44.55N 12.14 E
Mesolóngion 15 Ek 38.22N 21.26 E
Mesopotamia 52 Kh 30.00S 58.00W
Mesopotamia (EN) 23 Fc 34.00N 44.00 E
Mesoyéios Thálassa= Mediterranean Sea (EN) 5 Hh 35.00N 20.00 E
Mesquite [Nv.-U.S.] 46 Hh 36.48N 114.04W
Mesquite [Tx.-U.S.] 45 Hj 32.46N 96.36W
Mesra 13 Mi 35.50N 0.10 E
Messaad 32 Hc 34.10N 3.30 E
Messalo 30 Lj 11.40S 40.46 E
Messará, Órmos- 15 Ho 35.00N 24.40 E
Messina [It.] 6 Hh 38.11N 15.34 E
Messina [S.Afr.] 31 Kk 22.23S 30.00 E
Messina, Strait of- (EN) = Messina, Stretto di- 5 Hh 38.15N 15.35 E
Messina, Stretto di- = Messina, Strait of- (EN) 5 Hh 38.15N 15.35 E
Messini 15 El 37.15N 21.50 E
Messini 15 Fl 37.03N 22.01 E
Messiniakós Kólpos 15 Fm 36.45N 22.10 E
Messojaha 20 Cc 67.52N 77.27 E
Mesta 15 Hi 40.51N 24.44 E
Mestecăniş, Pasul- 15 Ib 47.28N 25.20 E
Mesters Vig 41 Jd 72.15N 24.20W
Mestia 16 Mh 43.03N 42.43 E
Mestre, Espigão- 54 If 12.30S 46.00W
Mestre, Venezia- 14 Ge 45.29N 12.14 E
Mesuji 26 Eg 4.08S 105.52 E
Meta [2] 54 Dc 3.30N 73.00W
Meta, Río- 50 Je 6.12N 67.28W
Meta Incognita Peninsula 38 Mc 62.40N 68.00W
Metairie 45 Kl 29.59N 90.09W
Metaliferi, Munţii- 15 Fc 46.10N 22.50 E
Metallifere, Colline- 14 Eg 43.10N 10.55 E
Metán 56 Hc 25.29S 64.57W
Metangula 37 Eb 12.43S 34.49 E
Metaponto 14 Kj 40.20N 16.50 E
Metauro 14 Hg 43.50N 13.03 E
Metautu 65c Ba 13.57S 171.54W
Meteghan 44 Nc 44.11N 66.10W
Metelen 12 Jb 52.09N 7.12 E
Metéora 15 Ej 39.43N 21.40 E
Meteor Seamount (EN) 30 Hm 48.00S 8.30 E
Meteor Trench (EN) 3 Do 55.00S 27.00 E
Méthana 15 Gl 37.35N 23.23 E
Methánon, Khersónisos- 15 Gl 37.36N 23.22 E
Methven 62 De 43.38S 171.38 E
Methwold 12 Cb 52.31N 0.33 E
Metković 14 Lg 43.03N 17.39 E
Metlakatla 40 Me 55.08N 131.35W
Metlika 14 Je 45.39N 15.19 E
Metlili Chaamba 32 Hc 32.16N 3.38 E
Metmárfag 32 Ed 26.26N 13.26W
Metohija 15 Dg 42.40N 20.27 E
Metro 26 Eh 5.05S 105.20 E
Metropolis 45 Lh 37.09N 88.44W
Métsovon 15 Ej 39.46N 21.11 E
Métsovon, Zigós- = Métsovon Pass (EN) 15 Ej 39.47N 21.15 E
Métsovon Pass (EN) = Métsovon, Zigós- 15 Ej 39.47N 21.15 E
Mettet 12 Gd 50.19N 4.40 E
Mettingen 12 Jb 52.19N 7.47 E
Mettlach 12 Ie 49.30N 6.36 E
Mettmann 12 Ic 51.15N 6.58 E
Metu 31 Kh 8.20N 35.38 E
Metuje 10 Lf 50.20N 15.55 E
Metz 6 Gf 49.08N 6.10 E
Metzervisse 12 Ie 49.19N 6.17 E
Meu 11 Ef 48.02N 1.47W
Meulaboh 26 Cf 4.09N 96.08 E
Meulan 12 De 49.01N 1.54 E
Meulebeke 12 Fd 50.57N 3.17 E
Meureudu 26 Ce 5.16N 96.16 E
Meurthe 11 Mf 48.47N 6.09 E
Meurthe-et-Moselle [3] 11 Mf 48.35N 6.10 E
Meuse [3] 11 Lf 49.00N 5.30 E
Meuse 5 Ge 51.49N 5.01 E
Meuse (EN)=Maas 5 Ge 51.49N 5.01 E
Meuse, Côtes de- 11 Le 49.10N 5.30 E
Meuzenti 35 Bb 18.14N 17.06 E
Mexia 45 Hk 31.41N 96.29W
Mexiana, Ilha 54 Ic 0.00 49.35W
Mexicali 39 Hf 32.40N 115.29W
Mexicana, Altiplanicie-= Mexico, Plateau of- (EN) 38 Ig 25.30N 104.00W
Mexican Hat 46 Kh 37.09N 109.52W
Mexicanos, Laguna de los- 48 Fc 28.09N 106.57W
Mexico 45 Kg 39.10N 91.53W
México [1] 39 Ig 23.00N 102.00W

Index Symbols

[1] Independent Nation
[2] State, Region
[3] District, County
[4] Municipality
[5] Colony, Dependency
Continent
Physical Region
Historical or Cultural Region
Mount, Mountain
Volcano
Hill
Mountains, Mountain Range
Hills, Escarpment
Plateau, Upland
Pass, Gap
Plain, Lowland
Delta
Salt Flat
Valley, Canyon
Crater, Cave
Karst Features
Depression
Polder
Desert, Dunes
Forest, Woods
Heath, Steppe
Oasis
Cape, Point
Coast, Beach
Cliff
Peninsula
Isthmus
Sandbank
Island
Atoll
Rock, Reef
Islands, Archipelago
Rocks, Reefs
Coral Reef
Well, Spring
Geyser
River, Stream
Waterfall Rapids
River Mouth, Estuary
Lake
Salt Lake
Intermittent Lake
Reservoir
Swamp, Pond
Canal
Glacier
Ice Shelf, Pack Ice
Ocean
Sea
Gulf, Bay
Strait, Fjord
Lagoon
Bank
Seamount
Tablemount
Ridge
Shelf
Basin
Escarpment, Sea Scarp
Fracture
Trench, Abyss
National Park, Reserve
Point of Interest
Recreation Site
Cave, Cavern
Historic Site
Ruins
Wall, Walls
Church, Abbey
Temple
Scientific Station
Airport
Port
Lighthouse
Mine
Tunnel
Dam, Bridge

Index Symbols

[1] Independent Nation	[=] Historical or Cultural Region	Pass, Gap	Depression	Coast, Beach	Rock, Reef	Waterfall Rapids	Canal	Lagoon	Escarpment, Sea Scarp	Historic Site	Port
[2] State, Region	Mount, Mountain	Plain, Lowland	Polder	Cliff	Islands, Archipelago	River Mouth, Estuary	Glacier	Bank	Fracture	Ruins	Lighthouse
[3] District, County	Volcano	Delta	Desert, Dunes	Peninsula	Rocks, Reefs	Lake	Ice Shelf, Pack Ice	Seamount	Trench, Abyss	Wall, Walls	Mine
[4] Municipality	Hill	Salt Flat	Forest, Woods	Isthmus	Coral Reef	Salt Lake	Ocean	Tablemount	National Park, Reserve	Church, Abbey	Tunnel
[5] Colony, Dependency	Mountains, Mountain Range	Valley, Canyon	Heath, Steppe	Sandbank	Well, Spring	Intermittent Lake	Sea	Ridge	Point of Interest	Temple	Dam, Bridge
Continent	Hills, Escarpment	Crater, Cave	Oasis	Island	Geyser	Reservoir	Gulf, Bay	Shelf	Recreation Site	Scientific Station	
Physical Region	Plateau, Upland	Karst Features	Cape, Point	Atoll	River, Stream	Swamp, Pond	Strait, Fjord	Basin	Cave, Cavern	Airport	

Name	Page	Grid	Lat.	Long.
Mitsamiouli	37	Gb	11.23S	43.18 E
Mitsinjo	37	Hc	16.00S	45.52 E
Mitsio, Nosy-	37	Hb	12.54S	48.36 E
Mitsiwa=Massawa (EN)	31	Kg	15.37N	39.39 E
Mitsiwa Channel	35	Fb	15.30N	40.00 E
Mitsuishi	29a	Cb	42.15N	142.33 E
Mitsukaido	29	Fc	36.01N	139.59 E
Mitsuke	29	Fc	37.32N	138.56 E
Mitsushima	29	Ad	34.16N	129.20 E
Mittelfranken	10	Gg	49.20N	10.40 E
Mittelland	14	Bd	46.50N	7.05 E
Mittellandkanal	5	He	52.16N	11.41 E
Mittelmark	10	Jd	52.20N	13.20 E
Mittenwald	10	Hi	47.27N	11.15 E
Mittersheim	12	If	48.52N	6.56 E
Mittersill	14	Gc	47.16N	12.29 E
Mittweida	10	If	50.59N	12.59 E
Mitú	53	Ie	1.08N	70.03W
Mitumba, Monts-=Mitumba Range (EN)	30	Ji	6.00S	29.00 E
Mitumba Range (EN)= Mitumba, Monts-	30	Ji	6.00S	29.00 E
Mituva	8	Jj	55.00N	22.45 E
Mitwaba	36	Ed	8.38S	27.20 E
Mitzic	36	Bb	0.47N	11.34 E
Miura	29	Fd	35.08N	139.37 E
Miura-Hantō	29	Fd	35.15N	139.40 E
Mixco Viejo	49	Bf	14.52N	90.40W
Mixian	28	Bg	34.31N	113.22 E
Mixteco, Río-	48	Jh	18.11N	98.30W
Miya-Gawa	29	Ed	34.32N	136.42 E
Miyagi Ken [2]	28	Pe	38.30N	140.50 E
Miyagusuku-Jima	29b	Ab	26.22N	127.59 E
Miyāh, Wādī al- [Eg.]	24	Ej	25.00N	33.23 E
Miyāh, Wādī al- [Sau. Ar.]	24	Gi	26.06N	36.31 E
Miyāh, Wādī al- [Syr.]	24	He	34.44N	39.57 E
Miyake-Jima	27	Oe	34.05N	139.30 E
Miyako	27	Pd	39.38N	141.57 E
Miyako-Jima	27	Mg	24.45N	125.20 E
Miyakonojō	28	Ki	31.44N	131.04 E
Miyako-Rettō	27	Lg	24.25N	125.00 E
Miyako-Wan	29	Hb	39.40N	142.00 E
Miyama	29	Dd	35.17N	135.34 E
Miyanojō	29	Bf	31.54N	130.27 E
Miyanoura-Dake	28	Ki	30.20N	130.29 E
Miyata	29	Be	33.45N	130.45 E
Miyazaki	27	Ne	31.54N	131.26 E
Miyazaki Ken [2]	28	Kh	32.05N	131.20 E
Miyazu	28	Mg	35.32N	135.11 E
Miyazuka-Yama	29	Fd	34.24N	139.16 E
Miyazu-Wan	29	Dd	35.35N	135.13 E
Miyoshi	28	Lg	34.48N	132.51 E
Miyun	27	Kc	40.22N	116.53 E
Miyun Shuiku	28	Dd	40.31N	116.58 E
Mizan Teferi	35	Fd	6.53N	35.28 E
Mizdah	33	Bc	31.26N	12.59 E
Mizen Head/Carn Ui Néid	5	Fe	51.27N	9.49W
Mizil	15	Je	45.01N	26.27 E
Mizorām [3]	25	Id	23.00N	93.00 E
Mizque	54	Eg	17.56S	65.19W
Mizuho	29	Cd	34.50N	132.29 E
Mizuho	66	Ef	70.43S	40.20 E
Mizunami	29	Ed	35.22N	137.15 E
Mizusawa	28	Pe	39.08N	141.08 E
Mjadel	8	Lj	54.54N	27.03 E
Mjakiševo	8	Mh	56.30N	28.54 E
Mjakit	20	Kd	61.23N	152.10 E
Mjällom	8	Ha	62.59N	18.26 E
Mjaundža	20	Jd	63.02N	147.13 E
Mjölby	7	Dg	58.19N	15.08 E
Mjøndalen	8	De	59.45N	10.01 E
Mjorn	8	Eg	57.54N	12.25 E
Mjøsa	5	Hc	60.40N	11.00 E
Mkoani	36	Gd	5.22S	39.39 E
Mkokotoni	36	Gd	5.52S	39.15 E
Mkushi Bona	36	Ee	13.37S	29.23 E
Mkushi River	36	Fe	13.33S	29.40 E
Mkuze	37	Ee	27.10S	32.00 E
Mladá Boleslav	10	Kf	50.21N	14.54 E
Mladenovac	15	De	44.26N	20.42 E
Mlava	15	Ee	44.45N	21.14 E
Mława	10	Qc	53.06N	20.23 E
Mljet	14	Lh	42.45N	17.30 E
Mljetski kanal	14	Lh	42.48N	17.35 E
Mmadinare	37	Dd	21.53S	27.45 E
Mnichovo Hradiště	10	Kf	50.32N	14.59 E
Mnogoveršinny	20	If	53.55N	139.50 E
Moa	49	Jc	20.40N	74.56W
Moa	34	Cd	6.59N	11.36W
Moa, Pulau-	26	Ih	8.10S	127.56 E
Moab	43	Fd	38.35N	109.33W
Moabi	36	Bc	2.24S	10.59 E
Moala	63d	Bc	18.36S	179.53 E
Moamba	37	Ee	25.36S	32.15 E
Moanda [Gabon]	36	Bc	1.34S	13.11 E
Moanda [Zaire]	36	Bd	5.56S	12.21 E
Moatize	37	Ec	16.10S	33.46 E
Moba	31	Ji	7.03S	29.47 E
Mobara	29	Gd	35.25N	140.17 E
Mobārakeh	24	Nf	32.20N	51.30 E
Mobaye	31	Jh	4.19N	21.11 E
Mobayi-Mbongo	36	Db	4.18N	21.11 E
Mobeka	36	Cb	1.53N	19.46 E
Moberly	43	Id	39.25N	92.26W
Mobile	39	Kf	30.42N	88.05W
Mobile Bay	43	Je	30.25N	88.00W
Mobridge	43	Gb	45.32N	100.26W
Mobuto Sese Seko, Lac-= Albert, Lake- (EN)	30	Kh	1.40N	31.00 E
Moca	49	Ld	19.24N	70.31W
Moçambique= Mozambique (EN) [1]	31	Kj	18.15S	35.00 E
Moçambique= Mozambique (EN)	31	Lk	15.03S	40.45 E
Moçambique, Canal de-= Mozambique Channel (EN)	30	Lk	20.00S	43.00 E
Moçâmedes [3]	36	Bf	15.20S	12.30 E
Moçâmedes	31	Ij	15.12S	12.10 E
Mocapra, Río-	50	Ci	7.56N	66.46W
Mocha, Isla-	56	Fe	38.22S	73.56W
Moc Hoa	25	Lf	10.46N	105.56 E
Mochudi	37	Dd	24.23S	26.08 E
Mocimboa da Praia	31	Lj	11.20S	40.21 E
Möckeln	8	Fh	56.40N	14.10 E
Mockfjärd	8	Fd	60.30N	14.58 E
Môco, Serra-	30	Ij	12.28S	15.10 E
Mocoa	54	Cc	1.09N	76.38W
Mococa	55	Ie	21.28S	47.01W
Mocoví	55	Ci	28.24S	59.42W
Moctezuma [Mex.]	47	Cc	29.48N	109.42W
Moctezuma [Mex.]	48	If	22.45N	101.05W
Moctezuma [Mex.]	48	Fb	30.12N	106.26W
Moctezuma, Rio [Mex.]	48	Ec	29.09N	109.40W
Moctezuma, Río- [Mex.]	48	Jg	21.59N	98.34W
Mocuba	31	Kj	16.51S	36.56 E
Mocubúri	37	Fb	14.39S	38.54 E
Močurica	15	Jg	42.31N	26.32 E
Modane	11	Mi	45.12N	6.40 E
Modderrivier	37	Ce	29.02S	24.37 E
Modena [It.]	14	Ef	44.40N	10.55 E
Modena [Ut.-U.S.]	46	Ih	37.49N	113.55W
Moder	11	Of	48.49N	8.06 E
Modesto	43	Cd	37.39N	120.59W
Modica	14	In	36.52N	14.46 E
Modjamboli	36	Db	2.28N	22.06 E
Modjigo	34	Hb	17.09N	13.12 E
Mödling	14	Kb	48.05N	16.28 E
Modriča	14	Mf	44.58N	18.18 E
Modum	8	Ce	59.55N	10.00 E
Moe	59	Jg	38.10S	146.15 E
Moelv	7	Cf	60.56N	10.42 E
Moen	64d	Bb	7.26N	151.52 E
Moengo	54	Hb	5.37N	54.24W
Moen-jo-Daro	25	Dc	27.19N	68.07 E
Moenkopi Wash	46	Ji	35.54N	111.26W
Moerbeke	12	Fc	51.10N	3.56 E
Moers	10	Ce	51.27N	6.39 E
Moeskroen/Mouscron	11	Jd	50.44N	3.13 E
Moffat	9	Jf	55.20N	3.27W
Moga	36	Ec	2.21S	26.49 E
Mogadishu (EN)= Muqdisho	31	Lh	2.03N	45.22 E
Mogadouro	13	Fc	41.20N	6.43W
Mogadouro, Serra do-	13	Fc	41.19N	6.40W
Mogāl	24	Nd	36.35N	50.35 E
Mogalakwena	37	Dd	22.27S	28.55 E
Mogami	29	Gb	38.45N	140.30 E
Mogami-Gawa	28	Oe	38.54N	139.50 E
Mogami Trench (EN)	29	Fb	39.00N	139.00 E
Mogaung	25	Jc	25.18N	96.56 E
Mogho	35	Ge	4.49N	40.19 E
Mogielnica	10	Qe	51.42N	20.43 E
Mogilev	6	Je	53.56N	30.18 E
Mogilev-Podolski	16	Ee	48.27N	27.48 E
Mogilevskaja Oblast [3]	19	De	53.45N	30.30 E
Mogilno	10	Nd	52.40N	17.58 E
Mogincual	37	Gc	15.34S	40.24 E
Mogoča	22	Nd	53.44N	119.44 E
Mogočin	20	De	57.43N	83.40 E
Mogogh	35	Ed	8.26N	31.19 E
Mogojto	20	Gf	54.25N	110.27 E
Mogojtuj	20	Gf	51.15N	114.58 E
Mogok	25	Jd	22.55N	96.30 E
Mogollon Rim	43	Ee	34.20N	111.00W
Mogotes, Punta-	55	Dn	38.06S	57.33W
Mogotón, Pico-	49	Dg	13.45N	86.23W
Mogreïn	31	Ff	25.13N	11.34W
Mogroum	35	Bc	11.06N	15.25 E
Moguer	13	Fg	37.16N	6.50W
Mogzon	20	Gf	51.42N	111.59 E
Mohács	10	Ok	45.59N	18.42 E
Mohaka	62	Gc	39.07S	177.12 E
Mohaka	62	Gc	39.07S	177.12 E
Mohales Hoek	37	Df	30.15S	27.25 E
Mohall	45	Fb	48.46N	101.31W
Moḩammadābād	24	Pg	31.47N	54.27 E
Mohammadia	13	Mi	35.35N	0.04 E
Mohammedia	32	Fc	33.42N	7.24W
Mohanganj	25	Id	24.54N	90.59 E
Mohang-ni	28	If	36.46N	126.08 E
Mohave, Lake-	43	Ed	35.25N	114.38W
Mohawk Mountains	46	Ij	32.25N	113.25W
Mohe	22	Od	53.27N	122.18 E
Moheda	8	Fh	57.00N	14.34 E
Moheli/Mwali	30	Lj	12.15S	43.45 E
Moher, Cliffs of-/Aillte an Mhothair	9	Di	52.58N	9.27W
Mohican, Cape-	40	Fd	60.12N	167.28W
Mohinora	38	Ig	26.06N	107.04W
Möhnesee	12	Kc	51.29N	8.05 E
Mohns Ridge (EN)	5	Ga	73.00N	5.00 E
Moholm	8	Ff	58.37N	14.02 E
Mohon, Charleville-Mézierès-	12	Ge	49.46N	4.43 E
Mohon Peak	46	Ii	34.57N	113.15W
Mohoro	36	Gd	8.08S	39.10 E
Mohotani, Ile-	61	Na	9.59S	138.49W
Mohovaja	20	Kf	53.01N	158.38 E
Moi	8	Bf	58.28N	6.32 E
Moikovac	15	Cg	42.58N	19.35 E
Moimenta da Beira	13	Ed	40.59N	7.37W
Moindou	63b	Be	21.42S	165.41 E
Moineşti	15	Jc	46.28N	26.29 E
Moírai	15	Hn	35.03N	24.52 E
Mo i Rana	6	Hb	66.18N	14.08 E
Mõisaküla/Myjzakjula	7	Fg	58.07N	25.10 E
Moisés Ville	55	Bj	30.43S	61.29W
Moisie	42	Kf	50.13N	66.06W
Moisie	42	Kf	50.11N	66.06W
Moissac	11	Hj	44.06N	1.05 E
Moïssala	35	Bd	8.21N	17.46 E
Moitaco	50	Dh	8.01N	61.21W
Möja	8	He	59.25N	18.55 E
Mojácar	13	Kg	37.08N	1.51W
Mojada, Sierra-	48	Hd	27.15N	103.45W
Mojana, Caño-	49	Ji	9.02N	74.46W
Mojave	43	Dd	35.03N	118.10W
Mojave Desert	38	Hf	35.00N	117.00W
Mojiguaçu, Rio-	55	He	20.53S	48.10W
Moji Mirim	55	If	22.26S	46.57W
Mojjero	20	Fc	68.44N	103.30 E
Mojo	35	Fd	8.36N	39.09 E
Mojo	35	Gd	8.00N	41.50 E
Mojos, Llanos de-	52	Jg	15.00S	65.00W
Moju, Rio-	54	Id	1.40S	48.25W
Mojynty	19	Hf	47.10N	73.18 E
Mokambo	36	Ee	12.25S	28.21 E
Mokapu Peninsula	65a	Db	21.26N	157.45W
Mokau	62	Fc	38.42S	174.35 E
Mokau	61	Dg	38.41S	174.37 E
Mokhotlong	37	De	29.17S	29.05 E
Mokil Atoll	57	Gd	6.40N	159.47 E
Moklakan	20	Gf	54.48N	118.56 E
Möklinta	8	Gd	60.05N	16.32 E
Mokochu, Khao-	25	Je	15.56N	99.06 E
Mokohinau Islands	62	Fa	35.55S	175.05 E
Mokolo	34	Hc	10.45N	13.48 E
Mokp'o	22	Of	34.47N	126.23 E
Mokra Gora	15	Dg	42.50N	20.25 E
Mokrany	10	Ue	51.48N	24.23 E
Mokrin	15	Dd	45.56N	20.25 E
Mokša	5	Ke	54.44N	41.53 E
Mokwa	34	Gd	9.17N	5.03 E
Mol	11	Lc	51.11N	5.07 E
Mola di Bari	14	Li	41.04N	17.05 E
Molango	48	Jg	20.47N	98.43W
Moláoi	15	Fm	36.48N	22.51 E
Molara	14	Dj	40.50N	9.45 E
Molas, Punta-	48	Pg	20.35N	86.44W
Molat	14	If	44.13N	14.50 E
Molatón	13	Kf	38.59N	1.24W
Moldau (EN)=Vltava	5	He	50.21N	14.30 E
Moldava nad Bodvou	10	Qh	48.37N	21.00 E
Moldavia (EN) = Moldova	15	Jc	46.30N	27.00 E
Moldavia (EN)=Moldova	5	If	46.30N	27.00 E
Moldavian SSR (EN)= Moldavskaja SSR [2]	19	Cf	47.00N	29.00 E
Moldavskaja Sovetskaja Socialističeskaja Respublika [2]	19	Cf	47.00N	29.00 E
Moldavskaja SSR/ Respublika Sovetike Sočialiste Moldovenjaske [2]	19	Cf	47.00N	29.00 E
Moldavskaja SSR= Moldavian SSR (EN) [2]	19	Cf	47.00N	29.00 E
Molde	6	Gc	62.44N	7.11 E
Moldefjorden	8	Bb	62.45N	7.05 E
Moldotau, Hrebet-	18	Jd	40.00N	74.50 E
Moldova	15	Jc	46.54N	26.58 E
Moldova = Moldavia (EN)	15	Jc	46.30N	27.00 E
Moldova = Moldavia (EN)	5	If	46.30N	27.00 E
Moldova Nouă	15	Ee	44.44N	21.41 E
Moldoveanu, Vîrful-	5	If	45.36N	24.44 E
Moldoviţa	15	Ib	47.41N	25.32 E
Mole	12	Bc	51.24N	0.20W
Moléne, Ile de-	11	Bf	48.24N	4.58W
Molens van Kinderdijk	12	Gc	51.52N	4.40 E
Molepolole	31	Jk	24.25S	25.30 E
Môle Saint-Nicolas	49	Kd	19.47N	73.22W
Moletai/Moletaj	8	Ki	55.13N	25.36 E
Moletaj/Moletai	8	Ki	55.13N	25.36 E
Molfetta	14	Ki	41.12N	16.36 E
Molihong Shan	28	Hc	42.11N	124.43 E
Molina, Parameras de-	13	Jd	40.55N	2.01W
Molina de Aragón	13	Kd	40.51N	1.53W
Molina de Segura	13	Kf	38.03N	1.12W
Moline	45	Kf	41.30N	90.31W
Moliniere Point	51p	Bb	12.05N	61.45W
Molise [2]	14	Ii	41.40N	14.30 E
Molkābād	24	Oe	34.32N	52.35 E
Molkom	8	Ee	59.36N	13.43 E
Möll	14	Hd	46.50N	13.26 E
Moll	55	Cl	35.04S	59.39W
Mollafeneri	15	Mi	40.54N	29.30 E
Mölle	8	Eh	56.17N	12.29 E
Mollendo	53	Ig	17.02S	72.01W
Molliens-Dreuil	12	Ee	49.52N	2.01 E
Mölln	10	Gc	53.38N	10.41 E
Mollösund	8	Df	58.04N	11.28 E
Mölndal	7	Ch	57.39N	12.01 E
Mölnlycke	8	Ef	57.39N	12.09 E
Moločansk	16	If	47.10N	35.36 E
Moločny, Liman-	16	If	46.30N	35.20 E
Molócuè	37	Fc	17.03S	38.52 E
Molodečno	19	Ce	54.19N	26.53 E
Molodežnaja	66	Ee	67.40S	45.51 E
Molodi	8	Mf	58.00N	28.52 E
Molodogvardejskoje	19	He	54.07N	70.50 E
Mologa	5	Jd	58.50N	37.11 E
Molokai Island	57	Lb	21.08N	157.00W
Moloma	7	Lg	58.20N	48.28 E
Molong	59	Jf	33.06S	148.52 E
Molopo	30	Jk	28.31S	20.13 E
Moloundou	34	Ie	2.02N	15.13 E
Molteno	37	Df	31.24S	26.22 E
Molu, Pulau-	26	Jh	6.45S	131.33 E
Moluccas (EN)=Maluku, Kepulauan-	57	De	2.00S	128.00 E
Molucca Sea (EN)=Maluku, Laut-	21	Oj	0.05S	125.00 E
Molygino	20	Ee	58.11N	94.45 E
Moma	20	Jc	66.20N	143.06 E
Moma	37	Fc	16.44S	39.14 E
Mombaça	54	Ke	5.45S	39.28W
Mombasa	31	Ki	4.03S	39.40 E
Mombo	36	Gc	4.53S	38.17 E
Momboyo	36	Cc	0.16S	19.00 E
Mombuca, Serra da-	55	Fd	18.15S	52.26W
Momčilgrad	15	Ih	41.32N	25.25 E
Mömling	12	Le	49.50N	9.09 E
Momotombo, Volcán-	49	Dg	12.26N	86.33W
Mompono	36	Db	0.04N	21.48 E
Mompós	54	Db	9.14N	74.27W
Momski Hrebet	20	Jc	66.00N	145.00 E
Mon [2]	25	Je	17.22N	97.20 E
Møn	7	Ci	55.00N	12.20 E
Mona, Canal de la-=Mona Passage (EN)	38	Mh	18.30N	67.45W
Mona, Isla-	47	Ke	18.05N	67.54W
Mona, Punta-	49	Fi	9.38N	82.37W
Monach Islands	9	Fd	57.32N	7.40W
Monaco [1]	6	Gg	43.42N	7.23 E
Monadhliath Mountains	9	Id	57.15N	4.10W
Monagas [2]	54	Fb	9.20N	63.00W
Monaghan/Muineachán [2]	9	Gg	54.10N	7.00W
Monaghan/Muineachán	9	Gg	54.15N	6.58W
Monahans	45	Ek	31.36N	102.54W
Mona Passage (EN)=Mona, Canal de la-	38	Mh	18.30N	67.45W
Monapo	37	Gb	14.55S	40.18 E
Monarch Mountain	42	Ef	51.54N	125.54W
Monashee Mountains	42	Ff	51.00N	118.43W
Monastyrščina	16	Gb	54.19N	31.48 E
Monatélé	34	He	4.16N	11.12 E
Monbetsu [Jap.]	28	Qc	42.28N	142.07 E
Monbetsu [Jap.]	27	Pc	44.21N	143.22 E
Monbetsu-Shokotsu	29a	Ca	44.23N	143.16 E
Moncalieri	14	Be	45.00N	7.41 E
Moncalvo	14	Ce	45.03N	8.16 E
Monção [Braz.]	54	Id	3.30S	45.15W
Monção [Port.]	13	Db	42.05N	8.29W
Moncayo	13	Kc	41.46N	1.50W
Moncayo, Sierra del-	13	Kc	41.45N	1.50W
Mončegorsk	19	Db	67.56N	32.58 E
Mönchengladbach	10	Ce	51.12N	6.26 E
Mönchengladbach-Rheydt	12	Ic	51.10N	6.27 E
Mönchengladbach-Wickrath	12	Ic	51.08N	6.25 E
Mönchgut	10	Jb	54.20N	13.40 E
Monchique	13	Dg	37.19N	8.33W
Monchique, Serra de-	13	Dg	37.19N	8.36W
Monclova	39	Ig	26.54N	101.25W
Moncton	39	Me	46.06N	64.07W
Mondai	55	Fh	27.05S	53.25W
Mondego	13	Dd	40.09N	8.52W
Mondego, Cabo-	13	Dd	40.11N	8.55W
Mondeville	12	Be	49.10N	0.19W
Mondjoko	36	Dc	1.41S	21.12 E
Mondo	35	Bc	13.43N	15.32 E
Mondoñedo	13	Ea	43.26N	7.22W
Mondorf-les-Bains/Bad Mondorf	12	Ie	49.30N	6.17 E
Mondoubleau	11	Gg	47.59N	0.54 E
Mondoví	14	Bf	44.23N	7.49 E
Mondragone	14	Hi	41.07N	13.53 E
Mondy	20	Ff	51.40N	100.59 E
Monemvasía	15	Gm	36.41N	23.03 E
Monessen	44	He	40.09N	79.53W
Monett	45	Jh	36.55N	93.55W
Monfalcone	14	He	45.49N	13.32 E
Monferrato	14	Cf	44.55N	8.05 E
Monforte	13	Ee	39.03N	7.26W
Monforte de Lemos	13	Eb	42.31N	7.30W
Monga	36	Db	4.12N	22.49 E
Mongala	36	Cb	1.53N	19.46 E
Mongalla	35	Ed	5.12N	31.46 E
Mongbwalu	36	Fb	1.57N	30.02 E
Mong Cai	25	Ld	21.32N	107.58 E
Monger, Lake-	59	De	29.15S	117.05 E
Mongga	63a	Cb	7.57S	156.59 E
Monggolküre/Zhaosu	27	Dc	43.10N	81.07 E
Monghyr	25	Hc	25.23N	86.28 E
Monginevro, Colle del-	11	Mj	44.56N	6.44 E
Mongo	31	Ig	12.11N	18.42 E
Mongo	34	Cd	9.34N	12.11W
Mongol Altajn Nuruu→Mongolski Altaj= Mongolian Altai (EN)	21	Le	46.30N	93.00 E
Mongol Ard-Uls=Mongolia (EN) [1]	22	Me	47.00N	104.00 E
Mongolia (EN)=Mongol Ard-Uls [1]	22	Me	47.00N	104.00 E
Mongolian Altai (EN)= Mongol Altajn Nuruu→Mongolski Altaj	21	Le	46.30N	93.00 E
Mongolian Altai (EN)= Mongolski Altaj (Mongol Altajn Nuruu)	21	Le	46.30N	93.00 E
Mongolski Altaj (Mongol Altajn Nuruu)=Mongolian Altai (EN)	21	Le	46.30N	93.00 E
Mongonu	34	Hc	12.41N	13.36 E
Mongororo	35	Cc	12.01N	22.28 E
Mongoumba	35	Be	3.38N	18.36 E
Möng Pan	25	Jd	20.19N	98.22 E
Mongrove, Punta-	48	Hi	17.56N	102.11W
Mongu	31	Jj	15.17S	23.08 E
Monguel	32	Ef	16.25N	13.08W
Möng Yai	25	Jd	22.25N	98.02 E
Monheim	12	Ic	51.05N	6.53 E
Mönichkirchen	14	Kc	47.30N	16.02 E
Mon Idée, Auvillers-lès-Forges-	12	Ge	49.52N	4.21 E
Monigotes	55	Bj	30.30S	61.39W
Moní Hosiou Louká	15	Fk	38.24N	22.49 E
Monistrol-sur-Loire	11	Ki	45.17N	4.10 E
Monito, Isla-	51a	Ab	18.09N	67.56W
Monitor Peak	46	Gg	38.50N	116.32W
Monitor Range	46	Gg	38.45N	116.40W
Monjolos	55	Jd	18.18S	44.05W
Monkayo	26	Ie	7.50N	126.00 E
Monkey Bay	36	Fe	14.05S	34.55 E
Monkey Point	49	Fg	11.36N	83.39W
Monkey River	49	Ce	16.22N	88.29W
Mońki	10	Sc	53.24N	22.49 E
Monkoto	36	Dc	1.38S	20.39 E
Monmouth [Il.-U.S.]	45	Kf	40.55N	90.39W
Monmouth	9	Kj	51.45N	3.00W
Monmouth [Or.-U.S.]	46	Dd	44.51N	123.14W
Monmouth [Wales-U.K.]	9	Kj	51.50N	2.43W
Monmouth Mountain	46	Da	51.00N	123.47W
Mönne	10	De	51.28N	7.30 E
Monnikendam	12	Hb	52.27N	5.02 E
Monnow	9	Kj	51.48N	2.42W
Mono	63a	Bb	7.20S	155.35 E
Mono [3]	34	Fd	6.45N	1.50 E
Monobe-Gawa	29	Ce	33.32N	133.42 E
Mono Lake	43	Dd	38.00N	119.00W
Monólithos	15	Km	36.07N	27.45 E
Monopoli	14	Lj	40.57N	17.18 E
Monor	10	Pi	47.21N	19.27 E
Monou	35	Cb	16.24N	22.11 E
Monóvar	13	Lf	38.26N	0.50W
Monowai, Lake-	62	Bf	45.55S	167.25 E
Monreal	12	Jd	50.18N	7.10 E
Monreal del Campo	13	Kd	40.47N	1.21W
Monreale	14	Hl	38.05N	13.17 E
Monroe [Ga.-U.S.]	44	Fi	33.47N	83.43W
Monroe [La.-U.S.]	39	Jf	32.33N	92.07W
Monroe [Mi.-U.S.]	44	Fe	41.55N	83.24W
Monroe [N.C.-U.S.]	44	Gh	34.59N	80.33W
Monroe [Or.-U.S.]	46	Dd	44.19N	123.18W
Monroe [Wi.-U.S.]	45	Le	42.36N	89.38W
Monroe, Lake-	44	Df	39.05N	86.25W
Monroe City	45	Kg	39.39N	91.44W
Monroeville	44	Dj	31.31N	87.20W
Monrovia	31	Fh	6.19N	10.48W
Mons/Bergen	11	Jd	50.27N	3.56 E
Monsanto	13	Ed	40.02N	7.07W
Monschau	10	Cf	50.33N	6.15 E
Monselice	14	Fe	45.14N	11.45 E
Monserrate, Isla-	48	De	25.41N	111.05W
Monsheim	12	Ke	49.38N	8.12 E
Møns Klint	8	Ej	54.58N	12.33 E
Mönsterås	7	Dh	57.02N	16.26 E
Montabaur	10	Df	50.26N	7.50 E
Montagna Grande	14	Gm	37.56N	12.44 E
Montagne	11	Jh	46.10N	3.40 E
Montagu	66	Ad	58.25S	26.20W
Montague	40	Je	60.00N	147.30W
Montague, Isla-	48	Bb	31.45N	114.48W
Montaigu	11	Eh	46.59N	1.19W
Montalbán	13	Ld	40.50N	0.48W
Montalbano Ionico	14	Kj	40.17N	16.34 E
Montalcino	14	Fg	43.03N	11.29 E
Montalegre	13	Ec	41.49N	7.48W
Montalto di Castro	14	Fh	42.21N	11.37 E
Montalto Uffugo	14	Kk	39.24N	16.09 E
Montalvânia	55	Jb	14.28S	44.32W
Montana [2]	43	Eb	47.00N	110.00W
Montana	14	Bd	46.18N	7.30 E
Montánchez	13	Fe	39.13N	6.09W
Montánchez, Sierra de-	13	Ge	39.15N	5.55W
Montargis	11	Ig	48.00N	2.45 E
Montataire	12	Ee	49.16N	2.26 E
Montauban [Fr.]	11	Hj	44.01N	1.21 E
Montauban [Fr.]	11	Df	48.12N	2.03W
Montauk Point	44	Le	41.04N	71.52W
Montbard	11	Kg	47.37N	4.20 E
Montbéliard	11	Mg	47.31N	6.48 E
Montblanc	13	Nc	41.22N	1.10 E
Mont Blanc	5	Gf	45.50N	6.52 E
Montbrison	11	Ki	45.36N	4.03 E
Montceau-les-Mines	11	Kh	46.40N	4.22 E
Mont Cenis, Col du-	5	Gf	45.15N	6.54 E
Montchanin	11	Kh	46.45N	4.27 E
Mont Darwin	37	Ec	16.46S	31.35 E
Mont-de-Marsan	11	Fk	43.53N	0.30W
Montdidier	11	Ie	49.39N	2.34 E
Mont Dore	11	Ii	45.34N	2.49 E
Mont-Dore	63b	Cf	22.17S	166.35 E
Monte, Laguna del-	55	Am	37.00S	62.28W
Monteagudo	54	Fg	19.49S	63.59W
Monte Alban	39	Jh	17.02N	96.45W
Monte Alegre	54	Hd	2.01S	54.04W
Monte Alegre, Rio-	55	Gc	17.16S	50.41W
Monte Alegre de Goiás	55	Ia	13.14S	47.10W
Montealegre del Castillo	13	Kf	38.47N	1.19W
Monte Alegre de Minas	55	Hd	18.52S	48.52W
Monte Azul	54	Jg	15.09S	42.53W
Montebello	44	Jc	45.39N	74.56W
Monte Bello Islands	59	Dd	20.25S	115.30 E
Monte Carlo	11	Nk	43.44N	7.25 E
Montecarlo	55	Eh	26.34S	54.47W
Monte Carmelo	55	Id	18.43S	47.29W
Monte Caseros	56	Id	30.15S	57.39W
Montecatini Terme	14	Eg	43.23N	10.45 E
Montecchio Maggiore	14	Fe	45.30N	11.24 E
Monte Comán	56	Gd	34.36S	67.54W
Montecristi	49	Ld	19.52N	71.39W
Montecristo	14	Eh	42.20N	10.20 E
Monte Cristo	55	Bb	14.43S	61.14W
Monte Ermoso	55	Bn	38.55S	61.33W
Monte Escobedo	48	Hf	22.18N	103.35W
Montefalco	14	Gh	42.52N	12.39 E
Montefeltro	14	Gg	43.55N	12.15 E
Montefiascone	14	Gh	42.32N	12.02 E
Montefrío	13	Hg	37.19N	4.01W
Montego Bay	39	Lh	18.30N	77.55W
Monteiro	54	Ke	7.53S	37.07W
Montelíbano	49	Ji	8.02N	75.29W
Montélimar	11	Kj	44.34N	4.45 E
Monte Lindo, Arroyo-	55	Cg	25.28S	59.25W
Monte Lindo, Río-	56	Ib	23.56S	57.12W
Monte Lindo Chico, Riacho-	55	Dg	25.53S	57.53W

Index Symbols

[1] Independent Nation
[2] State, Region
[3] District, County
[4] Municipality
[5] Colony, Dependency
Continent
Physical Region
Historical or Cultural Region
Mount, Mountain
Volcano
Hill
Mountains, Mountain Range
Hills, Escarpment
Plateau, Upland
Pass, Gap
Plain, Lowland
Delta
Salt Flat
Valley, Canyon
Crater, Cave
Karst Features
Depression
Polder
Desert, Dunes
Forest, Woods
Heath, Steppe
Oasis
Cape, Point
Coast, Beach
Cliff
Peninsula
Isthmus
Sandbank
Island
Atoll
Rock, Reef
Islands, Archipelago
Rocks, Reefs
Coral Reef
Well, Spring
Geyser
River, Stream
Waterfall Rapids
River Mouth, Estuary
Lake
Salt Lake
Intermittent Lake
Reservoir
Swamp, Pond
Canal
Glacier
Ice Shelf, Pack Ice
Ocean
Sea
Gulf, Bay
Strait, Fjord
Lagoon
Bank
Seamount
Tablemount
Ridge
Shelf
Basin
Escarpment, Sea Scarp
Fracture
Trench, Abyss
National Park, Reserve
Point of Interest
Recreation Site
Cave, Cavern
Historic Site
Ruins
Wall, Walls
Church, Abbey
Temple
Scientific Station
Airport
Port
Lighthouse
Mine
Tunnel
Dam, Bridge

Monte Lindo Grande, Riacho- 55 Cg 25.45 S 58.06W
Montello [Nv.-U.S.] 46 Hf 41.16N 114.12W
Montello [Wi.-U.S.] 45 Le 43.48N 89.20W
Montemorelos 47 Ec 25.12N 99.49W
Montemor-o-Novo 13 Df 38.39N 8.13W
Montemor-o-Velho 13 Dd 40.10N 8.41W
Montemuro, Serra de- 13 Dc 40.58N 8.01W
Montenegro 56 Jc 29.42 S 51.28W
Montenegro (EN) = Crna Gora [2] 15 Cg 42.30N 19.18 E
Montenegro (EN)=Crna Gora 15 Cg 42.30N 19.18 E
Monte Plata 49 Md 18.48N 69.47W
Montepuez 37 Gb 12.32 S 40.27 E
Montepuez 37 Fb 13.07 S 39.00 E
Montepulciano 14 Fg 43.05N 11.47 E
Monte Quemado 56 Hc 25.48 S 62.52W
Monte Real 13 De 39.51N 8.52W
Montereale, Passo di- 14 Hh 42.31N 13.13 E
Montereau-Faut-Yonne 11 If 48.23N 2.57 E
Monterey 43 Cd 36.37N 121.55W
Monterey Bay 43 Cd 36.45N 121.55W
Montería 53 Ie 8.46N 75.53W
Montero 54 Fg 17.20 S 63.15W
Monteros 56 Gc 27.10 S 65.30W
Monterotondo 14 Gh 42.03N 12.37 E
Monterrey 39 Ig 25.40N 100.19W
Montesano 46 Dc 46.59N 123.36W
Monte San Savino 14 Fg 43.20N 11.43 E
Monte Sant'Angelo 14 Ji 41.42N 15.57 E
Monte Santu, Capo di- 14 Dj 45.05N 9.44 E
Montes Claros 53 Lg 16.43 S 43.52W
Montes Claros de Goiás 55 Gb 15.54 S 51.13W
Montesilvano 14 Ih 42.31N 14.09 E
Montevarchi 14 Fg 43.31N 11.34 E
Montevideo [2] 55 Dl 34.50 S 56.10W
Montevideo [Mn.-U.S.] 45 Id 44.57N 95.43W
Montevideo [Ur.] 53 Ki 34.53 S 56.11W
Monte Vista 45 Ch 37.35N 106.09W
Montfaucon 12 He 49.17N 5.08 E
Montfort-l'Amaury 12 Df 48.47N 1.49 E
Montfort-sur-Risle 12 Ce 49.18N 0.40 E
Montgenèvre, Col de- 11 Mj 44.56N 6.44 E
Montgomery 39 Kf 32.23N 86.18W
Montgomery Pass 46 Fh 38.00N 118.20W
Montguyon 11 Fi 45.13N 0.11W
Monthermé 12 Ge 49.53N 4.44 E
Monthey 14 Ad 46.15N 6.56 E
Monthois 12 Ge 49.19N 4.43 E
Monticello [Ar.-U.S.] 45 Kj 33.38N 91.47W
Monticello [Fl.-U.S.] 44 Fj 30.33N 83.52W
Monticello [Ia.-U.S.] 45 Ke 42.15N 91.12W
Monticello [In.-U.S.] 44 De 40.45N 86.46W
Monticello [Ky.-U.S.] 44 Eg 36.50N 84.51W
Monticello [N.Y.-U.S.] 44 Je 41.39N 74.41W
Monticello [Ut.-U.S.] 43 Fd 37.52N 109.21W
Montiel 13 Jf 38.42N 2.52W
Montiel, Campo de- 13 Jf 38.46N 2.44W
Montiel, Cuchilla de- 55 Cj 31.05 S 59.10W
Montignac 11 Hi 45.04N 1.10 E
Montigny-le-Roi 11 Lf 48.00N 5.30 E
Montigny-les-Metz 11 Me 49.06N 6.09 E
Montigny-le-Tilleul 12 Gd 50.23N 4.22 E
Montijo [Pan.] 49 Gj 7.59N 81.03W
Montijo [Port.] 13 Df 38.42N 8.58W
Montijo [Sp.] 13 Ff 38.55N 6.37W
Montijo, Golfo de- 49 Gj 7.40N 81.07W
Montilla 13 Hg 37.35N 4.38W
Montividiu 55 Gc 17.24 S 51.14W
Montivilliers 11 Ge 49.33N 0.12 E
Mont Joli 42 Kg 48.35N 68.11W
Mont-Laurier 42 Jg 46.33N 75.30W
Mont Louis 44 Oa 49.15N 65.43W
Mont-Louis 11 Il 42.31N 2.07 E
Montluçon 11 Ih 46.20N 2.36 E
Montmagny 42 Kg 46.59N 70.33W
Montmarault 11 Ih 46.19N 2.57 E
Montmédy 11 Le 49.31N 5.22 E
Montmirail 11 Jf 48.52N 3.32 E
Montmorency 12 Ef 49.00N 2.20 E
Montmorillon 11 Gh 46.26N 0.52 E
Montmort-Lucy 12 Ff 48.55N 3.49 E
Monto 59 Kd 24.52 S 151.07 E
Montoire-sur-le-Loir 11 Gg 47.45N 0.52 E
Montone 14 Gf 44.24N 12.14 E
Montoro 13 Hf 38.01N 4.23W
Montpelier [Id.-U.S.] 43 Ec 42.19N 111.18W
Montpelier [Vt.-U.S.] 39 Le 44.16N 72.35W
Montpellier 6 Gg 43.36N 3.53 E
Montpon-Ménestérol 11 Gi 45.01N 0.10 E
Montréal 39 Le 45.31N 73.34W
Montreal Lake 42 Gf 54.20N 105.40W
Montreal River 44 Hb 47.08N 79.27W
Montréjeau 11 Gk 43.05N 0.35 E
Montreuil [Fr.] 11 Hd 50.28N 1.46 E
Montreuil [Fr.] 12 Ef 48.52N 2.26 E
Montreuil-l'Argillé 12 Cf 48.56N 0.29 E
Montreux 14 Ad 46.26N 6.55 E
Montrose [Co.-U.S.] 43 Fd 38.29N 107.53W
Montrose [Scot.-U.K.] 9 Ke 56.43N 2.29W
Monts, Pointe des- 44 Na 49.19N 67.23W
Mont-Saint-Aignan 12 De 49.28N 1.05 E
Mont-Saint-Michel, Baie du- 11 Ef 48.40N 1.40W
Montsalvy 11 Ij 44.42N 2.30 E
Montsant, Serra del-/Montsant, Sierra de- 13 Mc 41.17N 0.50 E
Montsant, Sierra de-/Montsant, Serra del- 13 Mc 41.17N 0.50 E
Montsec, Serra del-/Montsech, Sierra del- 13 Mb 42.02N 0.50 E
Montsech, Sierra del-/Montsec, Serra del- 13 Mb 42.02N 0.50 E
Montseny/Pallars, Montsent de- 13 Nb 42.29N 1.02 E
Montseny, Sierra de- 13 Oc 41.48N 2.24 E
Montserrado [3] 34 Cd 6.35N 10.35W
Montserrat [5] 39 Mh 16.45N 62.12W
Montserrat, Monasterio de- 13 Nc 41.35N 1.49 E
Montserrat, Monasterio de-/Montserrat, Monèstir de- 13 Nc 41.35N 1.49 E
Montserrat, Monèstir de- 13 Nc 41.35N 1.49 E
Montserrat, Monèstir de-/Montserrat, Monasterio de- 13 Nc 41.35N 1.49 E
Montuosa, Isla- 49 Fj 7.28N 82.14W
Montville 12 De 49.33N 1.07 E
Monument Peak 46 He 42.07N 114.14W
Monument Valley 46 Jh 36.50N 110.20W
Monveda 36 Db 2.57N 21.27 E
Monviso 5 Gg 44.40N 7.07 E
Monywa 25 Jd 22.07N 95.08 E
Monza 14 De 45.35N 9.16 E
Monze 36 Ef 16.16 S 27.29 E
Monzen 29 Ec 37.17N 136.46 E
Monzón 13 Mc 41.55N 0.12 E
Mo'oka 29 Fc 36.27N 139.59 E
Moonbeam 44 Fa 49.25N 82.11W
Moonie 59 Ke 27.40 S 150.19 E
Moonie River 59 Je 29.19 S 148.43 E
Moonta 59 Hf 34.04 S 137.35 E
Moora 58 Ch 30.39 S 116.00 E
Moorcroft 46 Md 44.16N 104.57W
Moore 45 Hi 35.20N 97.29W
Moore, Lake- 57 Cg 29.50 S 117.35 E
Moorea, Ile- 57 Mf 17.32 S 149.50W
Moore's Island 44 Il 26.18N 77.33W
Moorhead 43 Hb 46.53N 96.45W
Moormerland 12 Ja 53.18N 7.26 E
Moormerland-Neermoor 12 Ja 53.18N 7.26 E
Moorreesburg 37 Bf 33.09 S 18.40 E
Moosburg an der Isar 10 Hh 48.28N 11.56 E
Moose 38 Kd 50.48N 81.18W
Moosehead Lake 43 Nb 45.40N 69.40W
Moose Jaw 39 Id 50.23N 105.32W
Moose Jaw River 46 Ma 50.34N 105.17W
Moose Lake 45 Jc 46.25N 92.45W
Mooselookmeguntic Lake 44 Lc 44.53N 70.48W
Moose Mountain 45 Eb 49.45N 102.37W
Moose Mountain Creek 45 Eb 49.12N 102.10W
Moosomin 42 Hf 50.09N 101.40W
Moosonee 39 Kd 51.17N 80.39W
Mopeia 37 Fc 17.59 S 35.43 E
Mopelia, Atoll- → Maupihaa Atoll 57 Lf 16.50 S 153.55W
Mopti 31 Gg 14.30N 4.12W
Mopti [3] 34 Ec 14.40N 4.15W
Moqokorei 35 He 4.04N 46.08 E
Moquegua [2] 54 Dg 16.50 S 70.55W
Moquegua 54 Dg 17.12 S 70.56W
Mór 10 Oi 47.23N 18.12 E
Mor, Glen- 9 Id 57.10N 4.40W
Mora [Cam.] 34 Hc 11.03N 14.09 E
Mora [Port.] 13 Df 38.56N 8.10W
Mora [Sp.] 13 Ie 39.41N 3.46W
Mora [Swe.] 7 Df 61.00N 14.33 E
Morača 15 Cg 42.16N 19.09 E
Morača, Manastir- 15 Cg 42.46N 19.24 E
Morādābād 22 Jg 28.50N 78.47 E
Morada Nova de Minas 55 Jd 18.25 S 45.22W
Móra d'Ebre/Mora de Ebro 13 Mc 41.05N 0.38 E
Mora de Ebro/Móra d'Ebre 13 Mc 41.05N 0.38 E
Mora de Rubielos 13 Ld 40.15N 0.45W
Morafenobe 37 Gc 17.49 S 44.55 E
Morąg 10 Pc 53.56N 19.56 E
Mórahalom 10 Pj 46.13N 19.53 E
Moraleda, Canal- 56 Ff 44.30 S 73.30W
Moraleja 13 Fd 40.04N 6.39W
Morales [Col.] 49 Ki 8.17N 73.52W
Morales [Guat.] 49 Cf 15.29N 88.49W
Morales, Laguna- 48 Kf 23.35N 97.45W
Moramanga 37 Hc 18.57 S 48.11 E
Moran 46 Je 43.50N 110.28W
Morane Atoll 57 Ng 23.10 S 137.07W
Morangas, Ribeirão- 55 Fd 19.39 S 52.19W
Morant Bay 49 Ie 17.53N 76.25W
Morant Cays 47 Ie 17.24N 75.59W
Morant Point 49 Ie 17.55N 76.10W
Morar, Loch- 9 He 56.58N 5.45W
Morarano 37 Hc 17.46 S 48.10 E
Mora River 45 Di 35.44N 104.23W
Moraska, Góra- 10 Md 52.30N 16.52 E
Morat/Murten 14 Bd 46.56N 7.08 E
Morata, Puerto de- 13 Kc 41.29N 1.31W
Moratalla 13 Kf 38.12N 1.53W
Moratuwa 25 Fg 6.46N 79.53 E
Morava 5 Hf 48.10N 16.59 E
Morava=Moravia (EN) 5 Hf 49.30N 17.00 E
Morava=Moravia (EN) 10 Mg 49.30N 17.00 E
Moravia (EN)=Morava 5 Hf 49.30N 17.00 E
Moravia (EN)=Morava 10 Mg 49.30N 17.00 E
Moravian Gate (EN)=Moravská Brána 5 Hf 49.33N 17.42 E
Moravian Upland (EN)=Českomoravská Vrchovina 5 Hf 49.20N 15.30 E
Moravica 15 Df 43.51N 20.05 E
Moravská Brána=Moravian Gate(EN) 5 Hf 49.33N 17.42 E
Moravské Budějovice 10 Lg 49.03N 15.49 E
Morawa 59 De 29.13 S 116.00 E
Morawhanna 54 Gb 8.16N 59.45W
Moray Firth 5 Fd 57.50N 3.30W
Morbach 12 Je 49.49N 7.07 E
Morbihan [3] 11 Dg 47.55N 2.50W
Morbihan 11 Dg 47.35N 2.48W
Morbylånga 7 Dh 56.31N 16.23 E
Morcenx 11 Fj 44.02N 0.55W
Mordāb 24 Md 37.26N 49.25 E
Mordaga 27 La 51.14N 120.43 E
Morden 42 Hg 49.11N 98.05W
Mordovo 16 Lc 52.05N 40.46 E
Mordovskaja ASSR [3] 19 Ee 54.20N 44.30 E
Möre 8 Fh 56.25N 15.55 E
More, Ben- 9 Ie 56.23N 4.31W
Morea 37 Bd 22.41 S 15.54 E
More Assynt, Ben- 9 Ic 58.07N 4.51W
Moreau River 43 Gb 45.18N 100.43W
Morecambe 9 Kg 54.04N 2.53W
Morecambe Bay 9 Kg 54.07N 3.00W
Moree 58 Fg 29.28 S 149.51 E
Morehead [Ky.-U.S.] 44 Ff 38.11N 83.25W
Morehead [Pap.N.Gui.] 60 Ci 8.50 S 141.57 E
Morehead City 39 Lf 34.43N 76.43W
Moreiz, Gora- 19 Gb 69.30N 62.05 E
Moreju 17 Ib 68.20N 59.45 E
Morelia 39 Ih 19.42N 101.07W
Morella 13 Ld 40.37N 0.06W
Morelos 48 Ic 28.25N 100.53W
Morelos [2] 47 Ee 18.45N 99.00W
Morena, Sierra- 5 Fh 38.00N 5.00W
Moreni 15 Ie 44.59N 25.39 E
Møre og Romsdal [2] 7 Be 62.40N 7.50 E
Moresby 42 Ef 52.45N 131.50W
Moreton Bay 59 Ke 27.20 S 153.15 E
Moreton Island 59 Ke 27.10 S 153.25 E
Moret-sur-Loing 11 If 48.22N 2.49 E
Moreuil 11 Ie 49.46N 2.29 E
Morez 11 Mh 46.31N 6.02 E
Morezu 15 Hd 45.09N 24.01 E
Mörfelden 12 Ke 49.59N 8.34 E
Morgan City 45 Kl 29.42N 91.12W
Morganfield 44 Dg 37.41N 87.55W
Morganton 44 Gh 35.45N 81.41W
Morgantown [Ky.-U.S.] 44 Dg 37.14N 86.41W
Morgantown [W.V.-U.S.] 44 Hf 39.38N 79.57W
Morges 14 Ad 46.31N 6.30 E
Morghāb 23 Jb 38.18N 61.12 E
Morhange 11 Mf 48.55N 6.38 E
Mori [China] 27 Fc 43.49N 90.11 E
Mori [Jap.] 28 Pc 42.06N 140.35 E
Moriarty 45 Ci 34.59N 106.03W
Morichal Largo, Río- 50 Eh 9.27N 62.25W
Moriguchi 29 Dd 34.44N 135.34 E
Morin Dawa (Nirji) 27 Lb 48.30N 124.28 E
Morioka 22 Qf 39.42N 141.09 E
Moriyoshi 29 Ga 40.07N 140.22 E
Moriyoshi-Yama 29 Gb 39.59N 140.33 E
Morjärv 7 Fc 66.04N 22.43 E
Morki 7 Lh 56.28N 49.00 E
Morko 8 Gf 59.00N 17.40 E
Morkoka 20 Gc 65.03N 115.40 E
Mørkøv 8 Di 55.40N 11.32 E
Morlaix 11 Cf 48.35N 3.50W
Morlanwelz 12 Gd 50.27N 4.14 E
Mörlunda 8 Fg 57.19N 15.51 E
Mormanno 14 Jk 39.53N 15.59 E
Morne-à-l'Eau 50 Fd 16.21N 61.31W
Morne Diablotin 47 Le 15.30N 61.24W
Mornington, Isla- 56 Eg 49.45 S 75.23W
Mornington Island 59 Hc 16.35 S 139.24 E
Moro 46 Ed 45.29N 120.44W
Morobe 58 Fe 7.45 S 147.37 E
Morocco (EN)=Al Maghrib [1] 31 Ge 32.00N 5.50W
Morogoro 31 Ki 6.49 S 37.40 E
Morogoro [3] 36 Gd 8.20 S 37.00 E
Moro Gulf 26 He 6.51N 123.00 E
Moroleón 48 Ig 20.08N 101.12W
Morombe 31 Lk 21.44 S 43.23 E
Morón [Arg.] 55 Cl 34.39 S 58.37W
Morón [Cuba] 47 Id 22.06N 78.38W
Morón [Ven.] 54 Ea 10.29N 68.11W
Morona, Río- 54 Cd 4.45 S 77.04W
Morondava 31 Lk 20.15 S 44.17 E
Morón de la Frontera 13 Gg 37.08N 5.27W
Morones, Sierra- 48 Hg 21.55N 103.05W
Moroni 31 Lj 11.41 S 43.16 E
Moron Us He 21 Lf 34.42N 94.50 E
Morotai, Pulau- 57 Dd 2.20N 128.25 E
Moroto 31 Kh 2.32N 34.39 E
Morovița 15 Ed 45.16N 21.16 E
Morozov 15 Ig 42.30N 25.10 E
Morozovsk 19 Ef 48.20N 41.50 E
Morpeth 9 Lf 55.10N 1.41W
Morphou/Güzelyurt 24 Ee 35.12N 32.59 E
Morrilton 45 Ji 35.09N 92.45W
Morrinhos 54 Ig 17.44 S 49.07W
Morrinsville 62 Fb 37.39 S 175.32 E
Morris [Il.-U.S.] 45 Lf 41.22N 88.26W
Morris [Man.-Can.] 42 Hg 49.21N 97.22W
Morris [Mn.-U.S.] 45 Id 45.35N 95.55W
Morris, Mount- 59 Ge 26.09 S 131.04 E
Morrisburg 44 Jc 44.54N 75.11W
Morris Jesup, Kap- 67 Me 83.45N 35.50W
Morrison Dennis Cays 49 Ff 14.28N 82.53W
Morristown 44 Fg 36.13N 83.18W
Morrito 49 Eh 11.37N 85.05W
Morro, Punta del- 48 Kh 19.51N 96.27W
Morro Bay 43 Cd 35.22N 120.51W
Morro do Chapéu 54 Jf 11.33 S 41.09W
Morrosquillo, Golfo de- 49 Ji 9.35N 75.40W
Morro Vermelho, Serra do- 55 Jc 17.45 S 45.20W
Mörrum 8 Fh 56.11N 14.45 E
Morrumbala 37 Fc 17.20 S 35.35 E
Morrumbene 37 Fd 23.39 S 35.20 E
Mörrumsån 8 Fh 56.09N 14.44 E
Mors 8 Ch 56.50N 8.45 E
Moršansk 19 Ee 53.26N 41.49 E
Morsbach 12 Jd 50.52N 7.45 E
Morsberg 12 Ke 49.43N 8.54 E
Mörsil 7 Ce 63.19N 13.38 E
Mörskom/Myrskylä 8 Kd 60.40N 25.51 E
Morsott 14 Co 35.40N 8.01 E
Mortagne 11 Mf 48.33N 6.27 E
Mortagne-au-Perche 11 Gf 48.31N 0.33 E
Mortagne-sur-Sèvre 11 Fg 47.00N 0.57W
Mortain 11 Ff 48.39N 0.56W
Mortara 14 Ce 45.15N 8.44 E
Mortcha 30 Jg 16.00N 21.10 E
Morteau 11 Mg 47.04N 6.37 E
Morteaux-Couliboeuf 12 Bf 48.56N 0.04W
Morteros 56 Hd 30.42 S 62.00W
Mortes, Rio das- 55 Je 21.09 S 44.53W
Mortesoro 35 Ec 10.12N 34.09 E
Mortlock Islands 57 Gd 5.27N 153.40 E
Morton 46 Dc 46.33N 122.17W
Mortsel 12 Gc 51.10N 4.28 E
Morumbi 55 Ef 23.46 S 54.06W
Morvan 11 Jg 47.05N 4.00 E
Morven 59 Je 26.25 S 147.07 E
Morvern 9 He 56.35N 5.50W
Morvi 25 Ed 22.49N 70.50 E
Morwell 58 Fh 38.14 S 146.24 E
Morzine 11 Mh 46.11N 6.43 E
Moržovec, Ostrov- 7 Kc 66.45N 42.35 E
Moša 7 Je 62.25N 39.48 E
Mosbach 10 Fg 49.21N 9.09 E
Mosby 8 Bf 58.14N 7.54 E
Moščny, Ostrov- 7 Gg 60.00N 27.50 E
Mosconi 55 Bl 35.44 S 60.34W
Moscos Islands 25 Jf 14.00N 97.45 E
Moscow [Id.-U.S.] 43 Db 46.44N 116.59W
Moscow (EN)=Moskva 5 Jd 55.08N 38.50 E
Moscow (EN)=Moskva [R.S.F.S.R.] 6 Jd 55.45N 37.35 E
Moscow Basin (EN)=Meščera 5 Kd 55.00N 40.30 E
Moscow Canal (EN)=Moskvy, kanal imeni- 5 Jd 56.43N 37.08 E
Moscow Upland (EN)=Moskovskaja Vozvyšennost 5 Jd 56.30N 37.30 E
Mosel=Moselle (EN) 5 Ge 50.22N 7.36 E
Moselberge 12 Ie 49.57N 6.56 E
Moselle [3] 11 Me 49.00N 6.30 E
Moselle 5 Ge 50.22N 7.36 E
Moselle (EN)=Mosel 5 Ge 50.22N 7.36 E
Moses Lake 43 Db 47.08N 119.17W
Mosgiel 61 Di 45.53 S 170.22 E
Moshi 31 Ki 3.21 S 37.20 E
Mosina 10 Md 52.16N 16.51 E
Mosjøen 7 Cd 65.50N 13.12 E
Moskalvo 20 Jf 53.39N 142.37 E
Moskenesøy 7 Cc 67.59N 13.00 E
Moskovskaja Oblast [3] 19 Dd 55.45N 37.45 E
Moskovskaja Vozvyšennost =Moscow Upland (EN) 5 Jd 56.30N 37.30 E
Moskovski 18 Gf 37.40N 69.39 E
Moskva [R.S.F.S.R.] = Moscow (EN) 6 Jd 55.45N 37.35 E
Moskva [Tur.-U.S.S.R.] 18 Ee 38.27N 64.24 E
Moskva=Moscow (EN) 5 Jd 55.08N 38.50 E
Moskva, Pik- 18 He 38.55N 71.52 E
Moskvy, kanal imeni-=Moscow Canal (EN) 5 Jd 56.43N 37.08 E
Moslavačka Gora 14 Ke 45.38N 16.42 E
Moso 63b Dc 17.32 S 168.15 E
Mosomane 37 Dd 24.01 S 26.19 E
Mosoni-Duna 10 Ni 47.44N 17.47 E
Mosonmagyaróvár 10 Ni 47.52N 17.17 E
Mosor 14 Kg 43.30N 16.40 E
Mosquero 45 Ei 35.47N 103.58W
Mosquito, Baie - 42 Jd 60.40N 78.00W
Mosquito Coast (EN)=Mosquitos, Costa de- 38 Kh 13.00N 83.45W
Mosquito, Riacho- 55 Cf 22.12 S 57.57W
Mosquitos, Costa de-=Mosquito Coast (EN) 38 Kh 13.00N 83.45W
Mosquitos, Golfo de los- 38 Ki 9.00N 81.20W
Moss 6 Hd 59.26N 10.42 E
Mossaka 36 Cc 1.13 S 16.48 E
Mossâmedes 55 Gc 16.07 S 50.11W
Mossbank 46 Mb 49.55N 105.59W
Mossburn 61 Ci 45.41 S 168.15 E
Mosselbaai 31 Jl 34.11 S 22.08 E
Mossendjo 36 Bc 2.57 S 12.44 E
Mossman 58 Ff 16.28 S 145.22 E
Mossø 8 Ch 56.05N 9.50 E
Mossoró 53 Mf 5.11 S 37.20W
Moss Point 45 Lk 30.25N 88.29W
Mossuril 37 Gb 14.58 S 40.40 E
Most 10 Jf 50.32N 13.39 E
Mostaganem [3] 32 Hb 35.40N 0.30 E
Mostaganem 31 He 35.56N 0.05 E
Mostar 14 Lg 43.21N 17.49 E
Mostardas 55 Gj 31.06 S 50.57W
Møsting, Kap- 41 Hf 63.45N 41.00W
Mostiska 16 Ce 49.48N 23.09 E
Mostiştea 15 Je 44.15N 26.54 E
Most na Soci 14 Hd 46.09N 13.45 E
Mostovskoj 16 Lg 44.22N 40.48 E
Mosty 19 Ce 53.27N 24.33 E
Mosul (EN)=Al Mawşil 22 Gf 36.20N 43.08 E
Møsvatn 7 Bg 59.50N 8.05 E
Mota 63b Ca 13.40 S 167.42 E
Mota 35 Fc 11.05N 37.53 E
Motaba 36 Cb 2.03N 18.03 E
Motacusito 55 Bc 17.35 S 61.31W
Mota del Marques 13 Gc 41.38N 5.10W
Motagua 38 Kh 15.44N 88.14W
Motajica 14 Le 45.04N 17.40 E
Motala 7 Dg 58.33N 15.03 E
Motala ström 8 Gf 58.38N 16.10 E
Motatán 49 Li 9.24N 70.36W
Motatán, Río- 49 Li 9.32N 71.02W
Motegi 29 Gc 36.32N 140.10 E
Motehuala 47 Dd 23.39N 100.39W
Mothe 63d Cc 18.40 S 178.30W
Motherwell 9 Jf 55.48N 4.00W
Motihāri 25 Gc 26.39N 84.55 E
Motilla del Palancar 13 Ke 39.34N 1.53W
Motiti Island 62 Gb 37.40 S 176.25 E
Motlav 63b Ca 13.40 S 167.40 E
Motobu 29b Ab 26.40N 127.55 E
Motol 10 Vd 52.17N 25.40 E
Motovski Zaliv 7 Hb 69.30N 32.30 E
Motoyoshi 29 Gb 38.48N 141.31 E
Motozintla de Mendoza 48 Mj 15.22N 92.14W
Motril 13 Ih 36.45N 3.31W
Motru 15 Ge 44.33N 23.27 E
Motru 15 Fe 44.48N 23.00 E
Motsuta-Misaki 29a Ab 42.36N 139.49 E
Mott 45 Ec 46.22N 102.20W
Motteville 12 Ce 49.38N 0.51 E
Motu 62 Gb 37.51 S 177.35 E
Motueka 62 Ed 41.07 S 173.01 E
Motuhora Island 62 Gb 37.50 S 177.00 E
Motu-Iti 65d Ac 27.11 S 109.27W
Motu-Iti → Tupai Atoll 61 Kc 16.17 S 151.50W
Motul 47 Gd 21.06N 89.17W
Motu-Nui 65d Ac 27.12 S 109.28W
Motu One Atoll 57 Lf 15.48 S 154.33W
Motupae 64n Ac 10.27 S 161.02W
Motupena Point 63a Bb 6.32 S 155.09 E
Moturiki 63d Bb 17.46 S 178.45 E
Motutapu 64p Cb 21.14 S 159.43W
Motu Tautara 65d Ab 27.05 S 109.26W
Motutunga Atoll 57 Mf 17.06 S 144.22W
Moubray Bay 66 Kf 72.11 S 170.15 E
Mouchard 11 Lh 46.58N 5.48 E
Mouchoir Bank (EN) 47 Jd 20.57N 70.42W
Mouchoir Passage 49 Lc 21.10N 71.00W
Moudjéria 32 Ef 17.52N 12.20W
Mouila 31 Ii 1.52 S 11.01 E
Mouka 35 Cd 7.16N 21.52 E
Moul 34 Hb 15.03N 13.18 E
Mould Bay 39 Hb 76.15N 119.30W
Moule 50 Fd 16.20N 61.21W
Moule à Chique, Cap- 51k Bb 13.43N 60.57W
Moulins 11 Jh 46.34N 3.20 E
Moulmein 22 Le 16.30N 97.38 E
Moulouya 30 Ge 35.06N 2.20W
Moult 12 Be 49.07N 0.10W
Moultrie 44 Fj 31.11N 83.47W
Moultrie, Lake- 44 Gi 33.20N 80.05W
Mouly, Pointe de- 63b Ce 20.43 S 166.23 E
Moúnda, Ákra- 15 Dk 38.03N 20.47 E
Moundou 31 Ih 8.34N 16.05 E
Moundsville 44 Gf 39.54N 80.44W
Mo'unga'one 65b Ba 19.38 S 174.29W
Moungoudou 36 Bc 2.40 S 12.41 E
Mountainair 45 Ci 34.31N 106.15W
Mountain Grove 45 Jh 37.08N 92.16W
Mountain Home [Ar.-U.S.] 45 Jh 36.21N 92.23W
Mountain Home [Id.-U.S.] 43 Dc 43.08N 115.41W
Mountain Nile (EN)=Jabal, Baḩr al- 30 Kh 9.30N 30.30 E
Mountain Village 40 Gd 62.05N 163.44W
Mount Airy 44 Gg 36.31N 80.37W
Mount Barker 59 Df 34.38 S 117.40 E
Mount Carmel 45 Mf 38.25N 87.46W
Mount Desert Island 44 Mc 44.20N 68.20W
Mount Douglas 58 Fg 21.30 S 146.50 E
Mount Eba 59 Hf 30.12 S 135.40 E
Mount Forest 44 Gd 43.59N 80.44W
Mount Frere 37 Df 31.00 S 28.58 E
Mount Gambier 58 Fh 37.50 S 140.46 E
Mount Hagen 60 Ci 5.52 S 144.13 E
Mount Hope 59 Hf 34.07 S 135.23 E
Mount Isa 58 Eg 20.44 S 139.30 E
Mountlake Terrace 46 Dc 47.47N 122.18W
Mount Lavinia 25 Fg 6.50N 79.52 E
Mount Lebanon 44 Ge 40.23N 80.03W
Mount Lofty Ranges 59 Hg 35.15 S 138.50 E
Mount Magnet 58 Cg 28.04 S 117.49 E
Mount Maunganui 61 Eg 37.38 S 176.12 E
Mount Morgan 59 Kd 23.39 S 150.23 E
Mountnorris Bay 59 Gb 11.20 S 132.45 E
Mount Peck 46 Ha 50.10N 115.02W
Mount Pleasant [Ia.-U.S.] 45 Kf 40.58N 91.33W
Mount Pleasant [Mi.-U.S.] 44 Ed 43.35N 84.47W
Mount Pleasant [S.C.-U.S.] 44 Hi 32.47N 79.52W
Mount Pleasant [Tx.-U.S.] 45 Ij 33.09N 94.58W
Mount Pleasant [Ut.-U.S.] 46 Jg 39.33N 111.27W
Mount's Bay 9 Hk 50.03N 5.25W
Mount Somers 62 De 43.42 S 171.25 E
Mount Sterling [Il.-U.S.] 45 Kg 39.59N 90.45W
Mount Sterling [Ky.-U.S.] .44 Ff 38.04N 83.56W
Mount Vancouver 42 Dd 60.20N 139.41W
Mount Vernon [Al.-U.S.] 44 Cj 31.05N 88.01W
Mount Vernon [Austl.] 59 Dd 24.13 S 118.14 E
Mount Vernon [Il.-U.S.] 43 Jd 38.19N 88.55W
Mount Vernon [In.-U.S.] 44 Dg 37.56N 87.54W
Mount Vernon [Ky.-U.S.] 44 Eg 37.21N 84.20W
Mount Vernon [Oh.-U.S.] 44 Fe 40.23N 82.30W
Mount Vernon [Wa.-U.S.] 43 Cb 48.25N 122.20W
Moura [Austl.] 59 Jd 24.35 S 150.00 E
Moura [Port.] 13 Ef 38.08N 7.27W
Mourão 13 Ef 38.23N 7.21W
Mourdi 35 Cb 17.50N 22.25 E
Mourdi, Dépression du-=Mourdi Depression (EN) 30 Jg 18.10N 23.00 E
Mourdiah 34 Dc 14.26N 7.31W
Mourdi Depression (EN)=Mourdi, Dépression du- 30 Jg 18.10N 23.00 E
Mourmelon-le-Grand 12 Ge 49.08N 4.22 E
Mourne Mountains/Beanna Boirche 9 Gg 54.10N 6.04W
Mouscron/Moeskroen 11 Jd 50.44N 3.13 E
Moussoro 31 Ig 13.39N 16.29 E
Moustiers-Sainte-Marie 11 Mk 43.51N 6.13 E
Moutier/Münster 14 Bc 47.16N 7.22 E
Moutiers 11 Mi 45.29N 6.32 E
Moutong 26 Hf 0.28N 121.13 E
Mouy 12 Ee 49.19N 2.19 E
Mouydir 30 Hf 25.00N 4.10 E
Mouyondzi 36 Bc 3.58 S 13.57 E
Mouzaia 13 Oh 36.28N 2.41 E
Mouzon 12 He 49.36N 5.05 E
Movas 48 Ec 28.10N 109.25W

Index Symbols

[1] Independent Nation
[2] State, Region
[3] District, County
[4] Municipality
[5] Colony, Dependency
Continent
Physical Region
Historical or Cultural Region
Mount, Mountain
Volcano
Hill
Mountains, Mountain Range
Hills, Escarpment
Plateau, Upland
Pass, Gap
Plain, Lowland
Delta
Salt Flat
Valley, Canyon
Crater, Cave
Karst Features
Depression
Polder
Desert, Dunes
Forest, Woods
Heath, Steppe
Oasis
Cape, Point
Coast, Beach
Cliff
Peninsula
Isthmus
Sandbank
Island
Atoll
Rock, Reef
Islands, Archipelago
Rocks, Reefs
Coral Reef
Well, Spring
Geyser
River, Stream
Waterfall Rapids
River Mouth, Estuary
Lake
Salt Lake
Intermittent Lake
Reservoir
Swamp, Pond
Canal
Glacier
Ice Shelf, Pack Ice
Ocean
Sea
Gulf, Bay
Strait, Fjord
Lagoon
Bank
Seamount
Tablemount
Ridge
Shelf
Basin
Escarpment, Sea Scarp
Fracture
Trench, Abyss
National Park, Reserve
Point of Interest
Recreation Site
Cave, Cavern
Historic Site
Ruins
Wall, Walls
Church, Abbey
Temple
Scientific Station
Airport
Port
Lighthouse
Mine
Tunnel
Dam, Bridge

Moxico [3] 36 De 12.00S 20.00 E
Moxico 36 De 11.51S 20.01 E
Moy/An Mhuaidh 9 Dg 54.12N 9.08W
Moyahua 48 Hg 21.16N 103.10W
Moyale [Eth.] 31 Kh 3.32N 39.04 E
Moyale [Kenya] 36 Gb 3.32N 39.03 E
Moyamba 34 Cd 8.10N 12.26W
Moÿ-de-l'Aisne 12 Fe 49.45N 3.22 E
Moyen Atlas=Middle Atlas (EN) 30 Ge 33.30N 4.30W
Moyen-Chari [3] 35 Bd 9.00N 18.00 E
Moyenne Guinée [3] 34 Cc 11.15N 12.30W
Moyenneville 12 Dd 50.04N 1.45 E
Moyen-Ogooué [3] 36 Bc 0.30S 10.30 E
Moyeuvre-Grande 12 Ie 49.15N 6.02 E
Moyo 36 Fb 3.40N 31.43 E
Moyo, Pulau- 26 Gh 8.15S 117.34 E
Moyobamba 53 If 6.02S 76.58W
Moyowosi 36 Fc 4.50S 31.24 E
Moyto 35 Bc 12.35N 16.33 E
Moyu/Karakax 27 Cd 37.17N 79.42 E
Možajsk 7 Ii 55.32N 36.02 E
Mozambique (EN)=Moçambique [1] 31 Kj 18.15S 35.00 E
Mozambique (EN)=Moçambique 31 Lk 15.03S 40.45 E
Mozambique, Canal de-=Mozambique Channel (EN) 30 Lk 20.00S 43.00 E
Mozambique Channel (EN)=Moçambique, Canal de- 30 Lk 20.00S 43.00 E
Mozambique Channel (EN)=Mozambique, Canal de- 30 Lk 20.00S 43.00 E
Mozambique Plateau (EN) 30 Kl 32.00S 35.00 E
Mozdok 19 Eg 43.44N 44.38 E
Možga 19 Fd 56.28N 52.13 E
Mozuli 8 Mh 56.32N 28.14 E
Mozyr 19 Ce 52.02N 29.16 E
Mpala 36 Ed 6.45S 29.31 E
Mpanda 31 Ki 6.22S 31.02 E
Mpigi 36 Fb 0.15N 32.20 E
Mpika 31 Kj 11.50S 31.27 E
Mpoko 35 Be 4.19N 18.33 E
Mporokoso 36 Fd 9.23S 30.08 E
Mpouia 36 Cc 2.37S 16.13 E
Mpui 36 Fd 8.21S 31.50 E
Mpulungu 36 Fd 8.46S 31.07 E
Mpwapwa 36 Gd 6.21S 36.29 E
Mrągowo 10 Rc 53.52N 21.19 E
Mrakovo 17 Hj 52.43N 56.38 E
Mrewa 37 Ec 17.39S 31.47 E
Mrkonjić Grad 14 Lf 44.25N 17.06 E
Mrocza 10 Nc 53.14N 17.36 E
Mroga 10 Pd 52.09N 19.42 E
Msangesi 36 Ge 11.40S 36.45 E
Msid, Djebel- 14 Cn 36.25N 8.04 E
Msif 13 Qi 35.23N 4.45 E
M'Sila 13 Qi 35.31N 4.30 E
M'Sila [3] 32 Hb 35.00N 4.30 E
M'Sila 32 Hb 35.42N 4.33 E
Mšinskaja 8 Nf 58.55N 30.03 E
Msta 5 Jd 58.25N 31.20 E
Mstislavl 16 Gc 53.59N 31.45 E
Mszana Dolna 10 Qg 49.42N 20.05 E
Mtakuja 36 Fd 7.22S 30.37 E
Mtama 36 Ge 10.18S 39.22 E
Mtelo 36 Gb 1.39N 35.23 E
Mtera Reservoir 36 Gd 7.01S 35.55 E
Mtito Andei 36 Gc 2.41S 38.10 E
Mtoko 37 Ec 17.24S 32.13 E
Mtubatuba 37 Ee 28.30S 32.08 E
Mtwara [3] 36 Ge 10.40S 39.00 E
Mtwara 31 Lj 10.16S 40.11 E
Mu, Cerro- 49 Ki 9.29N 73.07W
Mua 64h Ac 13.21S 176.10W
Mu'a 65b Ac 21.11S 175.07W
Mua, Baie de- 64h Bc 13.23S 176.09W
Muaná 54 Id 1.32S 49.13W
Muang Huon 25 Kd 20.09N 101.27 E
Muang Khammouan 25 Ke 17.24N 104.48 E
Muang Không 25 Lf 14.07N 105.51 E
Muang Khôngxédôn 25 Le 15.34N 105.49 E
Muang Khoua 25 Kd 21.05N 102.31 E
Muang Pak Lay 25 Ke 18.12N 101.25 E
Muang Pakxan 25 Ke 18.22N 103.39 E
Muang Pakxong 25 Le 15.11N 106.14 E
Muang Sing 25 Kd 21.11N 101.09 E
Muang Tahoi 25 Le 16.10N 106.38 E
Muang Thai=Thailand (EN) [1] 22 Lh 15.00N 100.00 E
Muang Vangviang 25 Ke 18.56N 102.27 E
Muang Xaignabouri 25 Ke 19.15N 101.45 E
Muang Xay 25 Kd 20.42N 101.59 E
Muang Xépôn 25 Le 16.41N 106.14 E
Muanzanza 36 Dd 6.32S 20.51 E
Muar 26 Df 2.02N 102.34 E
Muaraaman 26 Dg 3.07S 102.12 E
Muarabungo 26 Dg 1.28S 102.07 E
Muaraenim 26 Dg 3.39S 103.48 E
Muaralasan 26 Gf 1.48N 117.12 E
Muarapajang 26 Gg 1.32S 115.48 E
Muarasiberut 26 Cg 1.36S 99.11 E
Muarasiram 26 Gg 0.46S 116.11 E
Muaratebo 26 Dg 1.30S 102.26 E
Muaratewe 26 Fg 0.57S 114.53 E
Muarawahau 26 Gf 1.02N 116.52 E
Mubarek 18 Ee 39.16N 65.07 E
Mubende 36 Fb 0.35N 31.23 E
Mubi 31 Ig 10.16N 13.16 E
Much 12 Jd 50.55N 7.24 E
Muchinga Escarpment 36 Fe 13.40S 30.00 E
Muchinga Mountains 30 Kj 12.00S 31.45 E
Muck 9 Ge 56.50N 6.14W
Mücke 12 Ld 50.37N 9.02 E
Mucojo 37 Gb 12.04S 40.28 E
Muconda 36 De 10.34S 21.20 E
Mucua 37 Ec 18.09S 34.58 E
Mucubela 37 Fc 16.54S 37.49 E
Mucuchíes 49 Li 8.45N 70.55W
Mucumbura 37 Ec 16.10S 31.42 E
Mucur 24 Fc 39.04N 34.23 E
Mucusso 36 Df 18.00S 21.25 E
Mudan Jang 21 Oe 46.18N 129.31 E
Mudanjiang 22 Oe 44.35N 129.34 E
Mudanya 24 Cb 40.22N 28.52 E
Muddy Gap 46 Le 42.22N 107.27W
Mudgee 59 Jf 32.36S 149.35 E
Mud Lake 46 Ie 43.53N 112.24W
Mud Lake 46 Gh 37.55N 117.05W
Mudon 25 Je 16.15N 97.44 E
Mudug [3] 35 Hd 6.30N 48.00 E
Mudug 35 Hd 6.20N 47.00 E
Mudurnu 24 Db 40.28N 31.13 E
Muecate 37 Fb 14.53S 39.38 E
Mueda 37 Fb 11.39S 39.33 E
Muerto, Cayo- 49 Ff 14.34N 82.44W
Muerto, Mar- 48 Li 16.10N 94.10W
Mufulira 31 Jj 12.33S 28.14 E
Mufu Shan 27 Jf 29.15N 114.20 E
Mufu Shan 27 Jf 29.00N 113.50 E
Mugello 14 Fg 43.55N 11.25 E
Múggia 14 He 45.36N 13.46 E
Mughshin, Wādī- 35 Ib 19.44N 55.00 E
Mugi 29 De 33.40N 134.25 E
Mu Gia, Deo- 25 Le 17.40N 105.47 E
Mugila, Monts- 36 Ed 6.49S 29.08 E
Muğla 23 Cb 37.12N 28.22 E
Mugodžary 21 He 49.00N 58.40 E
Mugur an Na'ām 24 Ig 31.56N 40.30 E
Muhaiwir 24 If 33.28N 40.59 E
Muḩammad, Ra's- 33 Fd 27.42N 34.13 E
Muḩammad Oawl 35 Fa 20.54N 37.05 E
Muhen 20 Ig 48.10N 136.08 E
Muheza 36 Gd 5.10S 38.47 E
Muhīt, Al Baḩr al-=Atlantic Ocean (EN) 3 Di 2.00N 25.00W
Mühlacker 10 Eh 48.57N 8.50 E
Mühldorf am Inn 10 Ih 48.15N 12.32 E
Mühlhausen in Thüringen 10 Ge 51.13N 10.27 E
Mühlig-Hofmann Gebirge 66 Cf 72.00S 5.20 E
Mühlviertel 14 Ib 48.30N 14.10 E
Muhoršibir 20 Ff 51.01N 107.50 E
Muhos 7 Gd 64.50N 26.01 E
Muhu 7 Fg 58.35N 23.15 E
Muhu 8 Jf 58.37N 23.05 E
Muhu, Proliv-/Muhu Väin 8 Jf 58.45N 23.15 E
Muhulu 36 Ec 1.03S 27.17 E
Muhu Väin/Muhu, Proliv- 8 Jf 58.45N 23.15 E
Muhuwesi 36 Ge 11.16S 37.58 E
Muiderslot 12 Hb 52.20N 5.06 E
Muigheo/Mayo [2] 9 Dh 53.50N 9.30W
Muikamachi 28 Of 37.04N 138.53 E
Muineachán/Monaghan [2] 9 Gg 54.10N 7.00W
Muineachán/Monaghan 9 Gg 54.15N 6.58W
Muine Bheag 9 Gi 52.42N 6.57W
Muir Bhreatan=Saint George's Channel (EN) 5 Fe 52.00N 6.00W
Muir Eireann=Irish Sea (EN) 5 Fe 53.30N 5.20W
Muiron Islands 59 Cd 21.35S 114.20 E
Muir Seamount (EN) 38 Mf 33.41N 63.32W
Muite 37 Fb 14.02S 39.02 E
Mujeres, Isla- 48 Pg 21.13N 86.43W
Mujezerski 7 He 63.57N 32.01 E
Muji 27 Cd 37.27N 78.33 E
Mujnak 19 Fg 43.44N 59.02 E
Mujnakski Zaliv 18 Bc 43.50N 58.40 E
Mujunkum, Peski- 21 Je 44.00N 70.30 E
Mukačevo 19 Cf 48.26N 22.45 E
Mukah 26 Ff 2.54N 112.06 E
Mukawa 29a Bb 42.35N 141.55 E
Mu-Kawa 29a Bb 42.33N 141.53 E
Mukawwar 35 Fa 20.48N 37.13 E
Mukdahan 25 Ke 16.31N 104.42 E
Mukden → Shenyang 22 Oe 41.48N 123.24 E
Mukeru 64a Bc 7.25N 134.30 E
Mukho 28 Jf 37.33N 129.07 E
Mukinbudin 59 Df 30.54S 118.13 E
Mukojima-Rettō 60 Cb 27.37N 142.10 E
Mukomuko 26 Dg 2.35S 101.07 E
Muksu 18 He 39.17N 71.25 E
Mula 25 Dc 27.57N 67.36 E
Mula 13 Kf 38.03N 1.30W
Mulainagiri 25 Ff 13.24N 75.43 E
Mulaku Atoll 25a Bb 2.57N 73.34 E
Mulaly 19 Hf 45.27N 78.20 E
Mulan 27 Mb 46.00N 128.02 E
Mulanje 30 Kj 16.03S 35.31 E
Mulanje 36 Gf 16.02S 35.30 E
Mulatre, Point- 51g Bb 15.17N 61.15W
Mulatupo Sasardí 49 Ii 8.57N 77.45W
Mulchatna 40 Hd 59.39N 157.08W
Mulchén 56 Fe 37.34S 72.14W
Mulda 17 Kc 67.28N 63.34 E
Mulde 10 Ie 51.48N 12.10 E
Mulebreen 66 Ee 67.28S 59.21 E
Mulegé 47 Bc 26.53N 112.01W
Mulegé, Sierra de- 47 Bc 37.30N 112.40W
Mulenda 36 Dc 4.18S 24.58 E
Muleshoe 45 Ei 34.13N 102.43W
Mulgrave Island 59 Ib 10.05S 142.10 E
Mulhacén 5 Fh 37.03N 3.19W
Mülheim an der Ruhr 12 Ic 51.26N 6.53 E
Mülheim-Kärlich 12 Jd 50.23N 7.30 E
Mulhouse 6 Gf 47.45N 7.20 E
Muli (Bowa) 27 Hf 27.55N 101.13 E
Mulifanua 65c Aa 13.50S 172.02W
Muling 28 Kb 44.34N 130.12 E
Muling (Bamiantong) 28 Kb 44.55N 130.32 E
Muling Guan 28 Ef 36.10N 118.46 E
Muling He 28 Lb 45.53N 133.30 E
Mull, Island of- 5 Fd 56.27N 6.00W
Mull, Sound of- 9 He 56.35N 5.50W
Mullen 45 Fe 42.03N 101.01W
Mullens 44 Gg 37.35N 81.25W
Muller, Pegunungan- 26 Ff 0.40N 113.50 E
Mullet Peninsula/An Muirthead 9 Cg 54.15N 10.04W
Mullett Lake 44 Ec 45.30N 84.30W
Mullewa 59 De 28.33S 115.31 E
Müllheim 10 Di 47.48N 7.38 E
Mullingar/An Muileann gCearr 9 Fh 53.32N 7.20W
Mullsjö 8 Eg 57.55N 13.53 E
Mulobezi 36 Ef 16.47S 25.10 E
Mulock Glacier 66 Jf 79.03S 159.10 E
Mulongo 36 Ed 7.50S 26.57 E
Multān 22 Jf 30.11N 71.29 E
Multé 48 Ni 17.41N 91.24W
Multia 8 Kb 62.25N 24.47 E
Multien 12 Ee 49.05N 2.55 E
Mulu, Gunong- 26 Ff 4.03N 114.56 E
Mulvane 45 Hh 37.29N 97.14W
Mulymja 17 Lf 60.12N 64.32 E
Mumbué 36 Ce 13.53S 17.19 E
Mumbwa 36 Ee 14.59S 27.04 E
Mumhan/Munster 9 Ei 52.30N 9.00W
Mumra 16 Og 45.43N 47.41 E
Mun 21 Mh 15.19N 105.30 E
Muna 48 Og 20.29N 89.43W
Muna 21 Oc 67.52N 123.10 E
Muna, Pulau- 26 Hg 5.00S 122.30 E
Munābāo 25 Ec 25.45N 70.17 E
Munamägi/Munamjagi 8 Lg 57.38N 27.10 E
Munamjagi/Munamägi 8 Lg 57.38N 27.10 E
Munaybarah, Sharm- 24 Gi 26.04N 36.38 E
Muncar 26 Fh 8.29S 114.21 E
Münchberg 10 Hf 50.12N 11.47 E
München=Munich (EN) 6 Hf 48.09N 11.35 E
Münchhausen 12 Kd 50.57N 8.43 E
Muncho Lake 42 Ee 58.56N 125.46W
Munch'ŏn 28 Ie 39.14N 127.22 E
Muncie 43 Jc 40.11N 85.23W
Munda 63a Cc 8.19S 157.15 E
Mundaring, Perth- 59 Df 31.54S 116.10 E
Munday 45 Gj 33.27N 99.38W
Mundemba 34 Ge 4.59N 8.40 E
Münden 10 Fe 51.25N 9.41 E
Mundesley 12 Db 52.52N 1.25 E
Mundford 12 Cb 52.30N 0.39 E
Mundiwindi 58 Dg 23.52S 120.09 E
Mundo 13 Kf 38.19N 1.40W
Mundo Novo 54 Jf 11.52S 40.28W
Munellës, Mali i- 15 Dh 41.58N 20.06 E
Munera 13 Je 39.02N 2.28W
Mungana 59 Ic 17.07S 144.24 E
Mungbere 31 Jh 2.38N 28.30 E
Mungindi 59 Je 28.58S 148.59 E
Munhango 36 Ce 12.10S 18.34 E
Munh-Hajrhan-Ula 21 Le 46.40N 91.30 E
Munich (EN)=München 6 Hf 48.09N 11.35 E
Muniesa 13 Lc 41.02N 0.48W
Munīfah 23 Gd 27.38N 49.00 E
Munising 44 Db 46.25N 86.40W
Munkedal 7 Cg 58.29N 11.41 E
Munkfors 7 Cg 59.50N 13.32 E
Munku Sardik, Gora- 21 Md 51.45N 100.20 E
Muñoz Gamero, Peninsula- 56 Fh 52.30S 73.10W
Munsan 28 If 37.55N 126.22 E
Münsingen 10 Fh 48.25N 9.30 E
Munster 11 Nf 48.03N 7.08 E
Münster [F.R.G.] 12 Ke 49.55N 8.52 E
Münster [F.R.G.] 10 De 51.58N 7.38 E
Münster/Moutier 14 Bc 47.16N 7.22 E
Munster/Mumhan 9 Ei 52.30N 9.00W
Münster-Hiltrup 12 Jc 51.54N 7.38 E
Münsterland [F.R.G.] 12 Kb 52.45N 8.10 E
Münsterland [F.R.G.] 10 De 52.00N 7.30 E
Münstermaifeld 12 Jd 50.15N 7.22 E
Muntenia 15 Ie 44.00N 26.00 E
Munteni Buzău 15 Je 44.38N 26.59 E
Muntok 26 Eg 2.04S 105.11 E
Munzur Dağları 24 Hc 39.30N 39.10 E
Muojärvi 7 Gd 65.56N 28.36 E
Muong Sen 25 Ke 19.24N 104.08 E
Muonio 6 Ib 67.57N 23.42 E
Muonioälven Muonionijoki 5 Ib 67.11N 23.34 E
Muping 28 Ff 37.23N 121.36 E
Muqaddam 35 Eb 18.04N 31.30 E
Muqayshiţ 24 Oj 24.10N 53.45 E
Muqdisho=Mogadishu (EN) 31 Lh 2 03N 45.22 E
Mur 5 Hf 46.18N 16.55 E
Mura 5 Hf 46.18N 16.55 E
Muradiye [Tur.] 15 Kk 38.39N 27.24 E
Muradiye [Tur.] 24 Jc 39.00N 43.43 E
Murafa 16 Fe 48.13N 28.14 E
Murakami 28 Oe 38.14N 139.29 E
Murallón, Cerro- 52 Ij 49.48S 73.25W
Muráň 10 Qh 48.45N 20.02 E
Mur'aňyo 35 Ic 11.41N 50.27 E
Muraši 19 Ed 59.24N 48.59 E
Murat 21 Ff 38.52N 38.48 E
Murat 11 Ii 45.07N 2.52 E
Murat Dağı 23 Cb 38.55N 29.43 E
Muratlı [Tur.] 24 Ib 41.29N 41.41 E
Muratlı [Tur.] 15 Kh 41.10N 27.30 E
Murau 14 Ic 47.06N 14.10 E
Muravera 14 Dk 39.25N 9.34 E
Murayama 29 Gb 38.29N 140.23 E
Mürchen Khvort 24 Nf 33.06N 51.30 E
Murchison 62 Ed 41.48S 172.20 E
Murchison, Mount- [Austl.] 59 De 26.46S 116.25 E
Murchison, Mount- [N.Z.] 62 De 43.01S 171.17 E
Murchison River 57 Cg 27.50S 114.00 E
Murcia 6 Fh 37.59N 1.07W
Murcia [3] 13 Kg 38.00N 1.30W
Murcia 13 Kf 38.30N 1.45W
Mur-de-Barrez 11 Ij 44.51N 2.39 E
Murdo 45 Fe 43.53N 100.43W
Mürefte 15 Ki 40.40N 27.14 E
Muren 22 Me 49.38N 100.10 E
Mureş 5 If 46.15N 20.12 E
Mureş [2] 15 Hc 46.30N 24.40 E
Muret 11 Hk 43.28N 1.21 E
Murfreesboro 43 Jd 35.51N 86.23W
Murg 10 Eh 48.55N 8.10 E
Murgab 21 If 38.18N 61.12 E
Murgab [Tad.-U.S.S.R.] 19 Hh 38.10N 73.59 E
Murgab [Tur.-U.S.S.R.] 18 Df 37.32N 62.01 E
Murgaš 15 Gg 42.50N 23.40 E
Murgeni 15 Lc 46.12N 28.01 E
Murgon 59 Ke 26.15S 151.57 E
Muri 64p Cc 21.15S 159.43W
Muriaé 54 Jh 21.08S 42.22W
Murici 54 Ke 9.19S 35.56W
Muriege 36 Dd 9.53S 21.13 E
Murihiti 64n Ab 10.23S 161.02W
Murilo Atoll 57 Gd 8.40N 152.11 E
Mūrītāniyā=Mauritania (EN) [1] 31 Fg 20.00N 12.00W
Müritz 10 Ic 53.25N 12.43 E
Murkong Selek 25 Jc 27.44N 95.18 E
Murmansk 6 Jb 68.58N 33.05 E
Murmanskaja Oblast [3] 19 Db 68.00N 35.30 E
Murmaši 19 Db 68.49N 32.49 E
Murnau 10 Hi 47.41N 11.12 E
Muro 13 Pe 39.44N 3.03 E
Muro, Capo di- 11a Ab 41.44N 8.40 E
Muro Lucano 14 Jj 40.45N 15.29 E
Murom 6 Kd 55.34N 42.02 E
Muromcevo 19 Hd 56.23N 75.14 E
Muroran 22 Qe 42.18N 140.59 E
Muros 13 Cb 42.47N 9.02W
Muros y Noya, Ría de- 13 Db 42.45N 9.00W
Muroto 27 Ne 33.18N 134.09 E
Muroto Zaki 28 Mh 33.16N 134.10 E
Murowana Goślina 10 Nd 52.35N 17.01 E
Murphy [Id.-U.S.] 46 Ge 43.13N 116.33W
Murphy [N.C.-U.S.] 44 Eh 35.05N 84.01W
Murphysboro 45 Lh 37.46N 89.20W
Murrah al Kubrá, Al Buḩayrah al- 24 Eg 30.20N 32.23 E
Murray [Ky.-U.S.] 44 Cg 36.37N 88.19W
Murray [Ut.-U.S.] 46 Jf 40.40N 111.53W
Murray, Lake- [Pap.N.Gui.] 60 Ci 7.00S 141.30 E
Murray, Lake- [S.C.-U.S.] 44 Gh 34.04N 81.23W
Murray Bridge 59 Hg 35.07S 139.17 E
Murray Fracture zone (EN) 3 Lf 34.00N 135.00W
Murray Islands 59 Ia 9.55S 144.05 E
Murray Ridge (EN) 3 Gg 21.00N 61.50 E
Murray River 57 Eh 35.22S 139.22 E
Murraysburg 37 Cf 31.58S 23.47 E
Murro di Porco, Capo- 14 Jm 37.00N 15.20 E
Murrumbidgee River 57 Fh 34.43S 143.12 E
Murrupula 37 Fc 15.27S 38.47 E
Murska Sobota 14 Kd 46.40N 16.10 E
Murten/Morat 14 Bd 46.56N 7.08 E
Murter 14 Jg 43.47N 15.37 E
Murtle Lake 46 Fa 52.08N 119.38W
Murud, Gunong- 26 Gf 3.52N 115.30 E
Murupara 62 Gc 38.27S 176.42 E
Mururoa Atoll 57 Ng 21.52S 138.55W
Murwāra 25 Gd 23.51N 80.24 E
Murwillumbah 59 Ke 28.19S 153.24 E
Mürz 14 Jc 47.24N 15.17 E
Mürzzuschlag 14 Jc 47.36N 15.41 E
Muş 23 Fb 38.44N 41.30 E
Muša/Mūša 7 Fh 56.24N 24.12 E
Mūša/Muša 7 Fh 56.24N 24.12 E
Mūsa, Jabal-=Sinai, Mount- (EN) 24 Eh 28.32N 33.59 E
Musa Ali 35 Gc 12.30N 42.27 E
Musāfī 24 Qk 25.18N 56.10 E
Musā'id 33 Ed 31.36N 25.03 E
Musala 5 Ig 42.11N 23.34 E
Musallam 24 Lg 31.53N 46.56 E
Musan 27 Mc 42.14N 129.13 E
Musandam Peninsula 24 Qi 26.18N 56.24 E
Musay'īd 24 Nj 25.00N 51.33 E
Musaymir 33 Hg 13.27N 44.37 E
Muscat (EN)=Masqaţ 22 Hg 23.29N 58.33 E
Muscat and Oman (EN) → Oman (EN) [1] 22 Hg 21.00N 57.00 E
Muscatine 45 Kf 41.25N 91.03W
Musgrave 58 Ff 14.47S 143.30 E
Musgrave Ranges 57 Eg 26.10S 131.50 E
Mūshā 24 Di 27.07N 31.14 E
Mus-Haja, Gora- 21 Qc 62.35N 140.50 E
Mushāsh al 'Ashawī 24 Mj 24.12N 48.50 E
Mushāsh Ramlān 24 Mj 24.25N 49.15 E
Mushayrib, Ra's- 24 Nj 24.18N 51.44 E
Mushie 36 Cc 3.01S 16.54 E
Mūsi 25 Ge 15.20N 80.06 E
Musi 21 Mj 2.20S 104.56 E
Mūsiān 24 Lf 32.28N 47.26 E
Musicians Seamounts (EN) 57 Kb 29.00N 162.00W
Muskegon 43 Jc 43.14N 86.16W
Muskegon Heights 44 Dd 43.12N 86.12W
Muskegon River 44 Dd 43.14N 86.20W
Muskö 8 He 59.00N 18.05 E
Muskogee 43 Hd 35.45N 95.22W
Muskoka, Lake- 44 Hc 45.00N 79.25W
Musoma 31 Ki 1.30S 33.48 E
Musone 14 Hg 43.28N 13.38 E
Mussaţţaḩah, Al Jazīrah al- 14 Em 37.11N 10.20 E
Mussau Island 60 Dh 1.25S 149.38 E
Musselkanaal, Stadskanaal- 12 Jb 52.56N 7.02 E
Musselshell River 43 Fb 47.21N 107.58W
Mussende 36 Ce 10.31S 16.02 E
Mussidan 11 Gi 45.02N 0.22 E
Mussòmeli 14 Hm 37.35N 13.45 E
Must 27 Fb 46.40N 92.40 E
Muşţafá, Ra's- 14 Fn 36.50N 11.07 E
Mustafakemalpaşa 24 Cb 40.02N 28.24 E
Mustahil 35 Gd 5.15N 44.44 E
Mustāng 25 Gc 29.11N 83.58 E
Mustang Draw 45 Fj 32.00N 101.40W
Mustang Island 45 Hm 28.00N 96.55W
Mustasaari/Korsholm 8 Ia 63.05N 21.43 E
Musters, Lago- 56 Gg 45.27S 69.13W
Mustique Island 50 Ff 12.39N 61.15W
Mustjala 8 Jf 58.25N 22.04 E
Mustla 7 Fg 58.14N 25.52 E
Mustvee 7 Gg 58.52N 26.59 E
Musu-dan 28 Jd 40.50N 129.43 E
Muswellbrook 59 Kf 32.16S 150.53 E
Muszyna 10 Qg 49.21N 20.54 E
Mut 24 Ed 36.39N 33.27 E
Mūţ 33 Ed 25.29N 28.59 E
Mūtaf, Ra's al- 23 Hd 27.41N 51.27 E
Mutalau 64k Ba 18.56S 169.50W
Mutarara 31 Kj 17.27S 35.04 E
Mutatá 54 Cb 7.16N 76.32W
Mutawassiţ, Al Baḩr al-=Mediterranean Sea (EN) 5 Hh 35.00N 20.00 E
Mutha 36 Gc 1.48S 38.26 E
Muting 26 Lh 7.23S 140.20 E
Mutis, Gunung- 26 Hh 9.34S 124.14 E
Mutoraj 20 Fd 61.20N 100.20 E
Mutsamudu 31 Lj 12.09S 44.25 E
Mutshatsha 36 De 10.39S 24.27 E
Mutsu 27 Pc 41.05N 140.55 E
Mutsu-Wan 28 Pd 41.10N 140.55 E
Muttaburra 59 Id 22.36S 144.33 E
Mutterstadt 12 Ke 49.27N 8.21 E
Mutton/Oiléan Coarach 9 Di 52.49N 9.31W
Mutton Bird Islands 62 Bg 47.15S 167.25 E
Mutuali 37 Fb 14.53S 37.00 E
Mutún 55 Dd 19.10S 57.54W
Mutunópolis 55 Ha 13.40S 49.15W
Mutusjärvi 7 Gb 69.31N 26.57 E
Muurame 8 Kb 62.08N 25.40 E
Mu Us Shamo=Ordos Desert (EN) 21 Mf 38.45N 109.10 E
Muxima 36 Bd 9.32S 13.57 E
Muyinga 36 Fc 2.51S 30.20 E
Muy Muy 49 Eg 12.46N 85.38W
Muzaffarābād 25 Eb 34.22N 73.28 E
Muzaffargarh 25 Eb 30.04N 71.12 E
Muzaffarnagar 25 Fc 29.28N 77.41 E
Muzaffarpur 25 Hc 26.07N 85.24 E
Muzambinho 55 Ie 21.22S 46.32W
Muzat He 27 Dc 41.15N 83.27 E
Muži 20 Bc 65.27N 64.40 E
Muzillac 11 Dg 47.33N 2.29W
Mužlja 15 Dd 45.21N 20.25 E
Muztag [China] 21 Kf 35.55N 80.20 E
Muztag [China] 21 Kf 36.25N 87.25 E
Muztagata 27 Cd 38.17N 75.07 E
Mvolo 35 Dd 6.03N 29.56 E
Mvomero 36 Gd 6.20S 37.25 E
Mvoung 36 Bb 0.04N 12.18 E
Mwadingusha 36 Ee 10.45S 27.15 E
Mwali/Mohéli 30 Lj 12.15S 43.45 E
Mwanza [3] 36 Fc 2.30S 32.30 E
Mwanza [Mwi.] 36 Ff 15.37S 34.31 E
Mwanza [Tan.] 31 Ki 2.31S 32.54 E
Mwanza [Zaire] 36 Ed 7.54S 26.45 E
Mwatate 36 Gc 3.30S 38.23 E
Mweelrea 9 Dh 53.38N 9.50W
Mweka 31 Ji 4.51S 21.34 E
Mwene Ditu 31 Ji 7.03S 23.27 E
Mwenga 36 Ec 3.02S 28.26 E
Mweru, Lake- 30 Ji 9.00S 28.45 E
Mweru Wantipa, Lake- 36 Ed 8.42S 29.46 E
Mwimbi 36 Fd 8.39S 31.40 E
Mwinilunga 36 De 11.44S 24.26 E
Mya 30 He 31.40N 5.15 E
Myaing 25 Id 21.37N 94.51 E
Myanaung 25 Je 18.17N 95.19 E
Myanma-Nainggan-Daw → Burma [1] 22 Lg 22.00N 98.00 E
Myaungmya 25 Ie 16.36N 94.56 E
Mycenae (EN) = Mikínai 15 Fl 37.43N 22.45 E
Myebon 25 Id 20.03N 93.22 E
Myingyan 22 Lg 21.28N 95.23 E
Myinmoletkat Taung 25 Jf 13.28N 98.48 E
Myitta 25 Jf 14.10N 98.31 E
Myjava 10 Mh 48.33N 16.58 E
Myjzakjula/Mõisaküla 7 Fg 58.07N 25.10 E
Mykulkin, Mys- 17 Cc 67.48N 46.40 E
Mylius Erichsens Land 41 Jb 81.40N 24.00W
Myltkyinā 22 Lg 25.23N 97.24 E
Mymensingh 25 Id 24.45N 90.24 E
Mynämäki 7 Ef 60.40N 22.00 E
Mynaral 19 Hf 45.22N 73.39 E
Myōkō-Zan 29 Fc 36.52N 138.06 E
Mýrdalsjökull 7a Bc 63.40N 19.06W
Myre 7 Db 68.51N 15.05 E
Myrskylä/Mörskom 8 Kd 60.40N 25.51 E
Myrtle Beach 43 Le 33.42N 78.54W
Myrtle Point 46 Ce 43.04N 124.08W
Mysen 7 Cg 59.33N 11.20 E
Mysia 15 Kj 39.30N 28.00 E
Myśla 10 Kd 52.40N 14.29 E
Myślenice 10 Pg 49.51N 19.56 E
Myślibórz 10 Kd 52.55N 14.52 E
Mysore 22 Jh 12.18N 76.39 E
Mysore → Karnataka [3] 25 Ff 13.30N 76.00 E
Mys Saryč 16 Hg 44.23N 33.45 E
Myszków 10 Pf 50.36N 19.20 E
Myszyniec 10 Rc 53.24N 21.21 E
My Tho 22 Mh 10.21N 106.21 E
Mytišči 7 Ii 55.56N 37.46 E
Mývatn 7a Cb 65.36N 17.00W

Index Symbols

[1] Independent Nation
[2] State, Region
[3] District, County
[4] Municipality
[5] Colony, Dependency
Continent
Physical Region
Historical or Cultural Region
Mount, Mountain
Volcano
Hill
Mountains, Mountain Range
Hills, Escarpment
Plateau, Upland
Pass, Gap
Plain, Lowland
Delta
Salt Flat
Valley, Canyon
Crater, Cave
Karst Features
Depression
Polder
Desert, Dunes
Forest, Woods
Heath, Steppe
Oasis
Cape, Point
Coast, Beach
Cliff
Peninsula
Isthmus
Sandbank
Island
Atoll
Rock, Reef
Islands, Archipelago
Rocks, Reefs
Coral Reef
Well, Spring
Geyser
River, Stream
Waterfall Rapids
River Mouth, Estuary
Lake
Salt Lake
Intermittent Lake
Reservoir
Swamp, Pond
Canal
Glacier
Ice Shelf, Pack Ice
Ocean
Sea
Gulf, Bay
Strait, Fjord
Lagoon
Bank
Seamount
Tablemount
Ridge
Shelf
Basin
Escarpment, Sea Scarp
Fracture
Trench, Abyss
National Park, Reserve
Point of Interest
Recreation Site
Cave, Cavern
Historic Site
Ruins
Wall, Walls
Church, Abbey
Temple
Scientific Station
Airport
Port
Lighthouse
Mine
Tunnel
Dam, Bridge

Myzeqeja 15 Ci 41.01N 19.36 E
M'Zab 32 Hc 32.35N 3.20 E
Mže 10 Jg 49.46N 13.24 E
Mziha 36 Gd 5.54S 37.47 E
Mzimba 36 Fe 11.54S 33.36 E
Mzuzu 31 Kj 11.27S 33.55 E

N

Naab 10 Ig 49.01N 12.02 E
Naaldwijk 12 Gc 51.59N 4.12 E
Naalehu 65a Fd 19.04N 155.35W
Naantali/Nådendal 7 Ff 60.27N 22.02 E
Naarden 12 Hb 52.18N 5.10 E
Naas/An Nás 9 Gh 53.13N 6.39W
Nababid 35 Gd 9.38N 43.29 E
Nabão 13 De 39.31N 8.21W
Nabari 29 Ed 34.37N 136.05 E
Naberera 36 Gc 4.12S 36.56 E
Naberežnyje Čelny 6 Ld 55.42N 52.19 E
Nābha 25 Fb 30.22N 76.09 E
Nabileque, Rio- 55 De 20.55S 57.49W
Nabire 58 Ee 3.22S 135.29 E
Nabī Shu'ayb, Jabal an- 21 Gh 15.17N 43.59 E
Nabq 24 Fh 28.04N 34.25 E
Nābul 31 Ie 36.27N 10.44 E
Nābul [3] 32 Jb 36.45N 10.45 E
Nābulus 24 Ff 32.13N 35.16 E
Nabusanke 36 Fb 0.01N 32.03 E
Nacala 37 Gb 14.33S 40.40 E
Nacala-a-Velha 31 Lj 14.33S 40.36 E
Nacaome 49 Dg 13.31N 87.30W
Nacaroa 37 Fb 14.23S 39.55 E
Nacereddine 13 Ph 36.08N 3.26 E
Nachikatsuura 29 De 33.39N 135.55 E
Nachingwea 36 Ge 10.23S 38.46 E
Nachi-San 29 De 33.42N 135.51 E
Náchod 10 Mf 50.26N 16.10 E
Nachuge 25 If 10.35N 92.28 E
Nachvak Fiord 42 Le 59.03N 63.45W
Nacka 7 Ee 59.18N 18.10 E
Ná Clocha Liatha/Greystones 9 Gh 53.09N 6.04W
Nacogdoches 45 Ik 31.36N 94.39W
Na Comaraigh/Comeragh Mountains 9 Fi 52.13N 7.35W
Nacori, Sierra- 48 Ec 29.50N 108.50W
Nacozari, Río- 48 Ec 29.48N 109.42W
Nacozari de García 47 Cb 30.24N 109.39W
Na Cruacha/Blue Stack 9 Eg 54.45N 8.06W
Na Cruacha Dubha/Macgillycuddy's Reeks 9 Di 52.00N 9.50W
Nacunday, Río- 55 Eh 26.03S 54.45W
Nada → Danxian 27 Ih 19.38N 109.32 E
Nådendal/Naantali 7 Ff 60.27N 22.02 E
Nadiād 25 Ed 22.42N 72.52 E
Nădlac 15 Dc 46.10N 20.45 E
Nador [3] 32 Gb 35.00N 3.00W
Nador 32 Gb 35.11N 2.56W
Nádusa 15 Fi 40.38N 22.04 E
Nadvoicy 19 Dc 63.52N 34.20 E
Nadvornaja 16 De 48.38N 24.34 E
Nadym 22 Jc 65.35N 72.42 E
Naeba-San 29 Fc 36.51N 138.41 E
Nærbø 8 Af 58.40N 5.39 E
Næstved 7 Ci 55.14N 11.46 E
Nafada 34 Hc 11.06N 11.20 E
Näfels 14 Dc 47.06N 9.04 E
Naftah 14 Dn 36.57N 9.04 E
Naftan Rock 64b Bb 14.50N 145.32 E
Naft-e-Safīd 24 Mg 31.40N 49.17 E
Naft-e-Shāh 24 Kf 33.59N 45.30 E
Naft Khāneh 24 Ke 34.02N 45.28 E
Nafūsah, Jabal- 30 Ie 31.50N 12.00 E
Nāg 25 Dc 27.24N 65.08 E
Naga 22 Oh 13.28N 123.39 E
Nâga, Kreb en- 32 Fe 24.00N 6.00W
Nagagami Lake 44 Ea 49.28N 85.02W
Nagagami River 45 Na 50.25N 84.20W
Nagahama [Jap.] 29 Ed 35.23N 136.16 E
Nagahama [Jap.] 29 Ce 33.36N 132.29 E
Nagai 29 Gb 38.06N 140.02 E
Nagai 40 Ge 55.11N 159.55W
Na Gaibhlte/Galty Mountains 9 Ei 52.23N 8.11W
Nāgāland [3] 25 Ic 26.30N 94.00 E
Nagano 22 Pf 36.39N 138.11 E
Nagano Ken [2] 28 Nf 36.10N 138.00 E
Nagano-Matsushiro 29 Fc 36.34N 138.10 E
Nagano-Shinonoi 29 Fc 36.35N 138.06 E
Nagaoka 27 Od 37.27N 138.51 E
Nāgappattinam 25 Ff 10.46N 79.50 E
Nagara-Gawa 29 Ed 35.02N 136.43 E
Nagarote 49 Dg 12.16N 86.34W
Nagarzê 27 Ff 28.59N 90.28 E
Nagasaki 22 Of 32.47N 129.56 E
Nagasaki-Hantō 29 Ae 32.40N 129.45 E
Nagasaki Ken [2] 28 Jh 33.00N 129.50 E
Naga-Shima 29 Ce 33.50N 132.05 E
Nagashima 29 Ed 34.12N 136.19 E
Nagashima 29 Be 32.10N 130.10 E
Naga-Shima-Kaikyō 29 Be 32.15N 130.10 E
Nagato 28 Kg 34.21N 131.10 E
Nagayo 29 Ae 32.50N 129.52 E
Nāgda 25 Fd 23.27N 75.25 E
Nāgercoil 25 Fg 8.10N 77.26 E
Naghora Point 60 Gj 10.50S 162.24 E
Nagichot 35 Ee 4.16N 33.34 E
Nagi-San 29 Dd 35.10N 134.10 E
Nagiso 29 Ed 35.36N 137.36 E
Nago 27 Mf 26.35N 128.01 E
Nagold 10 Eh 48.52N 8.42 E
Nagorno-Karabahskaja Avtonomnaja Oblast [3] 19 Eh 39.55N 46.45 E
Nagorny [R.S.F.S.R.] 20 He 55.45N 124.58 E
Nagorny [R.S.F.S.R.] 20 Md 63.10N 179.05 E
Nagorsk 7 Mg 59.21N 50.48 E
Nago-Wan 29b Ab 26.35N 127.55 E
Nagoya 22 Pf 35.10N 136.55 E
Nāgpur 22 Jg 21.09N 79.06 E
Nagqu 22 Lf 31.30N 92.00 E
Nag's Head 51c Ab 17.13N 62.38W
Nagua 49 Md 19.23N 69.50W
Naguabo 51a Cb 18.13N 65.44W
Nagyatád 10 Nj 46.13N 17.22 E
Nagybajom 10 Mj 46.23N 16.31 E
Nagyecsed 10 Si 47.52N 22.24 E
Nagyhalász 10 Rh 48.08N 21.46 E
Nagykálló 10 Ri 47.53N 21.51 E
Nagykanizsa 10 Mj 46.27N 16.59 E
Nagykáta 10 Pi 47.25N 19.45 E
Nagykőrös 10 Pi 47.02N 19.47 E
Nagykunság 10 Qj 46.55N 20.15 E
Nagy-Milic 10 Rh 48.35N 21.28 E
Naha 22 Og 26.13N 127.40 E
Nahanni Butte 42 Fd 61.04N 123.24W
Nahari 29 De 33.25N 134.01 E
Naharyya 24 Ff 33.00N 35.05 E
Nahāvand 23 Gc 34.12N 48.22 E
Nahe 10 Dg 49.58N 7.57 E
Nahičevan 6 Kh 39.13N 45.27 E
Nahičevanskaja ASSR [3] 19 Eh 39.15N 45.35 E
Na'hīmābād 24 Qg 30.51N 56.31 E
Nahodka 22 Pe 42.48N 132.52 E
Nahr al 'Āsī=Orontes (EN) 23 Eb 36.02N 35.58 E
Nahr Quassel 13 Oi 35.45N 2.46 E
Nahuala, Laguna- 48 Ji 16.50N 99.40W
Nahuel Huapi, Lago- 56 Ff 40.58S 71.30W
Nahunta 44 Gj 31.12N 81.59W
Naie 29a Bb 43.24N 141.52 E
Naiguatá, Pico- 54 Ea 10.33N 66.46W
Naila 10 Hf 50.19N 11.42 E
Naiman Qi (Daqin Tal) 27 Lc 42.49N 120.38 E
Nain 39 Md 57.00N 61.40W
Nā'in 24 Of 32.52N 53.05 E
Na'īnābād 24 Pd 36.14N 54.39 E
Nairai 63d Bb 17.49S 179.24 E
Nairn 9 Jd 57.35N 3.53W
Nairobi 31 Ki 1.17S 36.49 E
Nairobi [3] 36 Gc 1.17S 36.50 E
Naissaar/Najssar 8 Ke 59.35N 24.25 E
Naitamba 63d Cb 17.01S 179.17W
Naizishan 28 Ic 43.41N 127.27 E
Najafābād 23 Hc 32.37N 51.21 E
Najd 23 Fe 25.00N 44.30 E
Najd 21 Gg 25.00N 44.30 E
Nájera 13 Jb 42.25N 2.44W
Najerilla 13 Jb 42.31N 2.42W
Naj' Ḩammādī 33 Fd 26.03N 32.15 E
Najibābād 25 Fc 29.58N 78.10 E
Najin 27 Nc 42.15N 130.18 E
Najō 29 Ec 35.47N 136.12 E
Najrān 33 Hf 17.30N 44.10 E
Najrān 33 Hf 17.30N 44.10 E
Najssar/Naissaar 8 Ke 59.35N 24.25 E
Najstenjarvi 7 He 62.18N 32.42 E
Naju 28 Ig 35.02N 126.43 E
Najzataš, Pereval- 18 If 37.52N 73.46 E
Nakadōri-Jima 28 Jh 32.58N 129.05 E
Nakagawa 29a Ca 44.47N 142.05 E
Naka-Gawa [Jap.] 29 Gc 36.20N 140.36 E
Naka-Gawa [Jap.] 29 De 33.56N 134.42 E
Nakagusuku-Wan 29b Ab 26.15N 127.50 E
Nakahechi 29 De 33.47N 135.29 E
Naka-lō-Jima 60 Cc 24.47N 141.20 E
Naka-Jima 29 Ce 33.58N 132.37 E
Nakajō 28 Oe 38.03N 139.24 E
Naka-Koshiki-Jima 29 Af 31.48N 129.50 E
Nakalele Point 65a Eb 21.02N 156.35W
Nakama 29 Be 33.50N 130.43 E
Nakaminato 29 Gc 36.22N 140.36 E
Nakamura 28 Lh 32.59N 132.56 E
Nakanai Mountains 59 Ka 5.35S 151.10 E
Nakano 29 Fc 36.45N 138.22 E
Naka-no-Dake 29 Fc 37.04N 139.06 E
Nakanojō 29 Fc 36.35N 138.51 E
Naka-no-Shima 28 Lf 36.05N 133.04 E
Naka-no- Shima 27 Mf 29.50N 129.50 E
Nakasato 29a Bc 40.58N 140.26 E
Naka-satsunai 29a Cb 42.42N 143.08 E
Nakashibetsu 28 Rc 43.36N 145.00 E
Nakasongola 36 Fb 1.19N 32.28 E
Nakatonbetsu 29a Ca 44.58N 142.17 E
Nakatsu 28 Kh 33.34N 131.13 E
Nakatsugawa 28 Ng 35.29N 137.30 E
Nakfa 35 Fb 16.40N 38.30 E
Nakhon Pathom 25 Kf 13.49N 100.06 E
Nakhon Phanom 25 Mh 17.22N 104.46 E
Nakhon Ratchasima 22 Mh 14.57N 102.09 E
Nakhon Sawan 22 Mh 15.42N 100.06 E
Nakhon Si Thammarat 22 Li 8.26N 99.58 E
Nakijin 29b Ab 26.42N 127.59 E
Nakina 39 Kd 50.10N 86.42W
Nakkila 8 Ic 61.22N 22.00 E
Nakło nad Notecia 10 Nc 53.08N 17.35 E
Naknek 40 He 58.44N 157.02W
Nakonde 36 Fd 9.19S 32.46 E
Nakskov 7 Ci 54.50N 11.09 E
Näkten 8 Fb 62.50N 14.40 E
Naktong-gang 28 Jg 35.07N 128.57 E
Nakuru 31 Ki 0.20S 35.56 E
Nakusp 46 Ga 50.15N 117.48W
Nāl 25 Dc 26.02N 65.29 E
Nalajch → Nalajha 27 Ib 47.45N 107.16 E
Nalajha (Nalajch) 27 Ib 47.45N 107.16 E
Nalčik 6 Kg 43.29N 43.37 E
Nallıhan 24 Db 40.11N 31.21 E
Nalón 13 Fa 43.32N 6.04W
Nālūt 31 Ie 31.52N 10.59 E
Nalwasha 36 Gc 0.43S 36.26 E
Na Machairi/Brandon Head 9 Ci 52.16N 10.15W
Namacurra 37 Fc 17.29S 37.01 E
Namai Bay 64a Bb 7.32N 134.39 E
Namak, Daryācheh-ye-=Namak Lake (EN) 21 Hf 34.45N 51.36 E
Namak Lake (EN)=Namak, Daryācheh-ye- 21 Hf 34.45N 51.36 E
Namakan Lake 45 Jb 48.27N 92.35W
Namak-e Mīghān, Kavīr-e- 24 Me 34.13N 49.49 E
Namakia 37 Hc 15.56S 45.48 E
Namakwaland=Little Namamland (EN) 37 Be 29.00S 17.00 E
Namanga 36 Gc 2.33S 36.47 E
Namangan 22 Je 41.00N 71.40 E
Namanganskaja Oblast [3] 19 Hg 41.00N 71.20 E
Namanyere 36 Fd 7.31S 31.03 E
Namapa 37 Fb 13.43S 39.50 E
Namaqua Seamount (EN) 37 Af 31.30S 11.20 E
Namarrói 37 Fc 15.57S 36.51 E
Namasagali 36 Fb 1.01N 32.57 E
Namasale 36 Fb 1.30N 32.37 E
Namatanai 60 Eh 3.40S 152.27 E
Namathu 63d Bb 17.21S 179.26 E
Nambavatu 63d Bb 16.36S 178.55 E
Namber 26 Jg 1.04S 134.49 E
Nambour 59 Ke 26.38S 152.58 E
Nambouwalu 61 Ec 16.59S 178.42 E
Nam Can 25 Kg 8.46N 104.59 E
Namche Bazar 25 Hc 27.49N 86.43 E
Nam Co 21 Lf 30.45N 90.35 E
Namčy 20 Hd 62.35N 129.40 E
Namdalen 7 Cd 64.38N 12.35 E
Nam Dinh 22 Mg 20.25N 106.10 E
Nämdö 8 He 59.10N 18.40 E
Nam Du, Quan Dao- 25 Kg 9.42N 104.22 E
Namêche, Andenne- 12 Hd 50.28N 5.00 E
Namelakl Passage 64a Bc 7.24N 134.38 E
Namen/Namur 11 Kd 50.28N 4.52 E
Namerikawa 29 Ec 36.45N 137.20 E
Náměšt nad Oslavou 10 Mg 49.12N 16.09 E
Nametil 37 Fc 15.43S 39.21 E
Namib Desert/Namibwoestyn 30 Ik 23.00S 15.00 E
Namibia (South West Africa) [1] 31 Ik 22.00S 17.00 E
Namibwoestyn/Namib Desert 30 Ik 23.00S 15.00 E
Namie 28 Pf 37.29N 140.59 E
Namīn 24 Mc 38.25N 48.30 E
Namioka 29 Ga 40.42N 140.35 E
Namiquipa 48 Fc 29.15N 107.40W
Namiranga 37 Gb 10.33S 40.30 E
Namjagbarwa Feng 21 Lg 29.38N 95.04 E
Namja La 27 Df 29.58N 82.34 E
Namkham 25 Jd 23.50N 97.41 E
Namlea 26 Ig 3.18S 127.06 E
Namling 27 Ef 29.44N 89.05 E
Namnoi, Khao- 25 Jf 10.36N 98.38 E
Namoi River 59 Je 30.00S 148.07 E
Namoluk Island 57 Gd 5.55N 153.08 E
Namonuito Atoll 57 Gd 8.46N 150.02 E
Namorik Atoll 57 Hd 5.36N 168.07 E
Namous 32 Gc 30.28N 0.14W
Nampa 43 Dc 43.34N 116.34W
Nampala 34 Db 15.17N 5.33W
Nam Phan=Cochin China (EN) 21 Mg 11.00N 107.00 E
Nam Phong 25 Ke 16.45N 102.52 E
Nampi 28 De 38.02N 116.42 E
Namp'o 27 Md 38.44N 125.25 E
Nampula [3] 37 Fb 15.00S 39.30 E
Nampula 31 Kj 15.07S 39.15 E
Namsê Shankou 27 Df 29.58N 82.34 E
Namsos 6 Hc 64.30N 11.30 E
Namtu 25 Jd 23.05N 97.24 E
Namu 46 Ba 51.49N 127.52W
Namu Atoll 57 Hd 8.00N 168.10 E
Namuka-I-Lau 63d Cc 18.51S 178.38W
Namúli, Serra- 30 Kj 15.21S 37.00 E
Namuno 37 Fb 13.37S 38.48 E
Namur [3] 12 Gd 50.20N 4.50 E
Namur/Namen 11 Kd 50.28N 4.52 E
Namur-Saint Servais 12 Gd 50.28N 4.50 E
Namuruputh 36 Gb 4.34N 35.57 E
Namur-Wépion 12 Gd 50.25N 4.52 E
Namutoni 37 Bc 18.30S 17.55 E
Namwala 36 Ef 15.45S 26.26 E
Namwŏn 28 Ig 35.24N 127.23 E
Namysłów 10 Ne 51.05N 17.42 E
Nan 21 Mh 15.42N 100.09 E
Nan 25 Ke 18.48N 100.46 E
Nana 35 Bd 5.00N 15.50 E
Nana Barya 35 Bd 7.59N 17.43 E
Nanae 29a Bc 41.53N 140.41 E
Nanaimo 42 Fg 49.10N 123.56W
Nanakuli 65a Cb 21.23N 158.08W
Nana-Mambéré [3] 35 Bd 6.00N 16.00 E
Nanango 59 Ke 26.40S 152.00 E
Nanao 27 Od 37.03N 136.58 E
Nanao-Wan 29 Ec 37.10N 137.00 E
Nanatsu-Shima 29 Ec 37.35N 136.50 E
Nancha 27 Mb 47.08N 129.09 E
Nanchang 22 Ng 28.40N 115.58 E
Nancheng 27 Kf 27.32N 116.36 E
Nanchong 22 Mf 30.47N 106.03 E
Nancowry 25 Ig 7.59N 93.32 E
Nancy 6 Gf 48.41N 6.12 E
Nanda Devi 21 Jf 30.23N 79.59 E
Nandaime 49 Dh 11.46N 86.03W
Nandan [China] 27 Ig 24.59N 107.31 E
Nandan [Jap.] 28 Mg 34.15N 134.43 E
Nandaran → Qingyuan 28 Ce 38.46N 115.29 E
Nander 22 Jh 19.09N 77.20 E
Nandewar Range 59 Kf 30.40S 151.10 E
Nandi 61 Ec 17.48S 177.25 E
Nandu Jiang 27 Jg 20.04N 110.22 E
Nanduri 63d Bb 16.27S 179.09 E
Nandyāl 25 Fe 15.29N 78.29 E
Nanfen 28 Gd 41.06N 123.45 E
Nanfeng 27 Kf 27.15N 116.30 E
Nanga-Eboko 34 He 4.41N 12.22 E
Nanga Parbat 21 Jf 35.15N 74.36 E
Nangapinoh 26 Fg 0.20S 111.44 E
Nangarhār [3] 23 Lc 34.15N 70.30 E
Nangatayap 26 Fg 1.32S 110.34 E
Nangis 11 If 48.33N 3.00 E
Nangnim-san 28 Id 40.21N 126.55 E
Nangnim-Sanmaek 28 Id 40.30N 127.00 E
Nangong 27 Kd 37.22N 115.23 E
Nangqên 27 Ge 32.15N 96.13 E
Nanguan 28 Af 36.42N 111.41 E
Nanguantao → Guantao 28 Cf 36.33N 115.18 E
Nangweshi 36 Df 16.26S 23.20 E
Nan Hai=South China Sea (EN) 21 Ni 10.00N 113.00 E
Nanhaoqian → Shangyi 28 Bd 41.06N 113.58 E
Nanhe 28 Cf 36.58N 114.41 E
Nanhua 27 Hf 25.16N 101.18 E
Nanhui 28 Fi 31.03N 121.46 E
Nan Hulsan Hu 27 Gd 36.45N 95.45 E
Nanjian 27 Hf 25.05N 100.32 E
Nanjiang 27 Ie 32.22N 106.45 E
Nanjing=Nanking (EN) 22 Nf 31.59N 118.51 E
Nankai Trough (EN) 27 Ne 32.00N 135.00 E
Nanking (EN)=Nanjing 22 Nf 31.59N 118.51 E
Nankoku 28 Lh 33.39N 133.44 E
Nanle 28 Cf 36.06N 115.12 E
Nanling 28 Ei 30.55N 118.19 E
Nan Ling 21 Ng 25.00N 112.00 E
Nanlou Shan 28 Ic 43.24N 126.40 E
Nanma → Yiyuan 28 Ef 36.11N 118.10 E
Nanning 22 Mg 22.50N 108.18 E
Nannup 59 Df 33.59S 115.45 E
Nanortalik 41 Hf 60.32N 45.45W
Nanpan Jiang 27 Ig 24.56N 106.12 E
Nānpāra 25 Gc 27.52N 81.30 E
Nanping [China] 22 Ng 26.42N 118.09 E
Nanping [China] 27 He 33.15N 104.13 E
Nanpu 28 Ee 39.16N 118.12 E
Nanqiao → Fengxian 28 Fi 30.55N 121.27 E
Nansei-Shotō=Ryukyu Islands (EN) 21 Og 26.30N 128.00 E
Nansen Cordillera (EN) 67 Ge 87.00N 90.00 E
Nansen Land 41 Hb 83.20N 46.00W
Nanshan Islands (EN)=Nansha Qundao 21 Ni 9.40N 113.30 E
Nansha Qundao=Nanshan Islands (EN) 21 Ni 9.40N 113.30 E
Nansio 36 Fc 2.08S 33.03 E
Nant 11 Jj 44.01N 3.18 E
Nantais, Lac - 42 Kd 61.00N 73.50W
Nanterre 11 If 48.54N 2.12 E
Nantes 6 Ff 47.13N 1.33W
Nantes à Brest, Can. de- 11 Bf 48.12N 4.06W
Nanteuil-le-Haudouin 12 Ee 49.08N 2.48 E
Nanticoke 44 Je 41.13N 76.00W
Nantō 29 Ed 34.17N 136.29 E
Nantong 27 Le 32.00N 120.52 E
Nantong (Jinsha) 28 Fh 32.06N 120.52 E
Nantou 27 Lg 23.54N 120.51 E
Nantua 11 Lh 46.09N 5.37 E
Nantucket 44 Le 41.17N 70.06W
Nantucket Island 43 Mc 41.16N 70.03W
Nantucket Sound 44 Le 41.30N 70.15W
Nanuku Passage 63d Cb 16.45S 179.15W
Nanuku Reef 63d Cb 16.40S 179.26W
Nanumanga Island 57 Ie 6.18S 176.20 E
Nanumea Atoll 57 Ie 5.43S 176.00 E
Nanuque 54 Jg 17.50S 40.21W
Nanusa, Pulau-Pulau- 26 If 4.42N 127.06 E
Nanwan Shuiku 28 Bh 32.02N 113.57 E
Nanwei Dao 27 Je 8.42N 111.40 E
Nanweng He 27 Ma 51.10N 125.59 E
Nanxian 28 Bj 29.22N 112.25 E
Nanxiang 28 Fi 31.18N 121.17 E
Nanxiong 27 Jf 25.13N 114.18 E
Nanxun 28 Fi 30.53N 120.26 E
Nanyandang Shan 27 Lf 27.37N 120.06 E
Nanyang 22 Nf 32.56N 112.32 E
Nanyang Hu 28 Dg 35.15N 116.39 E
Nanyō 28 Pe 38.03N 140.10 E
Nanyuki 31 Kh 0.01N 37.04 E
Nanzhang 27 Je 31.45N 111.53 E
Nanzhao 27 Je 33.28N 112.29 E
Nao, Cabo de la- 5 Gh 38.44N 0.14 E
Naococane, Lac- 42 Kf 52.50N 70.40W
Naoero/Nauru [1] 58 He 0.31S 166.56 E
Naoetsu 29 Fc 37.11N 138.14 E
Não-me-Toque 55 Fi 28.28S 52.49W
Naours, Souterrains de- 12 Ed 50.05N 2.17 E
Napa 46 Dg 38.18N 122.17W
Napanee 44 Ic 44.15N 76.57W
Napassoq 41 Ge 65.45N 52.38W
Napata 35 Eb 18.29N 31.51 E
Na-Peng 25 Lg 23.10N 98.26 E
Napf 14 Bc 47.01N 7.57 E
Napier 58 Ih 39.30S 176.54 E
Napier, Mount- 59 Fc 17.32S 129.10 E
Napier Mountains 66 Ee 66.30S 53.40 E
Naples [Fl.-U.S.] 43 Kf 26.08N 81.48W
Naples [Id.-U.S.] 46 Gb 48.34N 116.24W
Naples (EN) = Napoli 6 Hg 40.50N 14.15 E
Naples, Gulf of- (EN) = Napoli, Golfo di- 14 Ij 40.45N 14.10 E
Napo 27 Ig 23.25N 105.49 E
Napo, Río- 52 If 3.20S 72.40W
Napoleon 45 Gc 46.30N 99.46W
Napoli = Naples (EN) 6 Hg 40.50N 14.15 E
Napoli, Golfo di- = Naples, Gulf of- (EN) 14 Ij 40.45N 14.10 E
Napostá 55 An 38.26S 62.15W
Napuka, Ile- 57 Mf 14.12S 141.15W
Naqa 35 Eb 16.16N 33.17 E
Naqadeh 23 Gb 36.57N 45.23 E
Naqsh-e-Rostam 24 Og 30.01N 52.50 E
Nar 9 Ni 52.45N 0.24 E
Nāra 25 Dc 24.07N 69.07 E
Nara [Jap.] 27 Oe 34.41N 135.50 E
Nara [Mali] 34 Db 15.11N 7.15W
Naračenskibani 15 Hh 41.54N 24.45 E
Naracoorte 59 Ig 36.58S 140.44 E
Nara-Ken [2] 28 Mg 34.20N 135.55 E
Naranjo 48 Ee 25.48N 108.31W
Naranjos [Bol.] 55 Cd 18.38S 59.09W
Naranjos [Mex.] 48 Kg 21.21N 97.41W
Narao 29 Ae 32.52N 129.04 E
Narathiwat 25 Kg 6.25N 101.48 E
Nārāyanganj 25 Id 23.37N 90.30 E
Narbonne 11 Ik 43.11N 3.00 E
Narca, Ponta da- 36 Bd 6.07S 12.16 E
Narcea 13 Fa 43.28N 6.06W
Narcondam 25 If 13.15N 94.30 E
Nardó 14 Mj 40.11N 18.02 E
Naré 55 Bj 30.58S 60.28W
Nares Land 41 Hb 82.25N 47.30W
Nares Strait 38 Lb 78.50N 73.00W
Narew 10 Td 52.55N 23.29 E
Narew 10 Qd 52.26N 20.42 E
Narian, Pointe- 63b Be 20.05S 164.00 E
Narin Gol 27 Fd 36.54N 92.51 E
Nariño [2] 54 Cc 1.30N 78.00W
Narita 29 Gd 35.47N 140.18 E
Narjan-Mar 6 Lb 67.39N 53.00 E
Närke 8 Ff 59.05N 15.05 E
Narlı 24 Gd 37.27N 37.09 E
Narmada 21 Jg 21.38N 72.36 E
Narman 24 Ib 40.21N 41.52 E
Nārnaul 25 Fc 28.03N 76.06 E
Narni 14 Gh 42.31N 12.31 E
Naroč 8 Lj 54.27N 26.45 E
Naroč 8 Lj 54.57N 26.49 E
Naroč, Ozero- 16 Eb 54.50N 26.45 E
Naroda 17 Jd 64.15N 61.00 E
Narodnaja, Gora- 5 Mb 65.04N 60.09 E
Naro-Fominsk 19 Dd 55.24N 36.43 E
Narok 36 Gc 1.05S 35.52 E
Narovlja 16 Fd 51.48N 29.31 E
Närpes/Närpio 8 Ib 62.28N 21.20 E
Närpio/Närpes 8 Ib 62.28N 21.20 E
Narrabri 59 Jf 30.19S 149.47 E
Narrandera 59 Jf 34.45S 146.33 E
Narrogin 59 Df 32.56S 117.10 E
Narromine 59 Jf 32.14S 148.15 E
Narrows, The- 51c Ab 17.12N 62.38W
Narryer, Mount- 59 De 26.30S 116.25 E
Narsimhapur 25 Fd 22.57N 79.12 E
Narssalik 41 Hf 61.42N 49.11W
Narssaq [Grld.] 41 Hf 61.00N 46.00W
Narssaq [Grld.] 41 Gf 64.00N 51.33W
Narssarssuaq 41 Hf 61.10N 45.15W
Narthákion 15 Fj 39.14N 22.22 E
Nartkala 16 Mh 43.32N 43.47 E
Narubis 37 Be 26.55S 18.35 E
Narugo 29 Gb 38.44N 140.43 E
Năruja 15 Jd 45.50N 26.47 E
Naru-Shima 29 Ae 32.50N 128.56 E
Naruto 28 Mg 34.11N 134.37 E
Naruto-Kaikyō 29 Dd 34.15N 134.40 E
Narva 7 Gg 59.29N 28.02 E
Narva 6 Id 59.23N 28.11 E
Narva Jõesuu/Narva-Jyesuu 8 Me 59.21N 28.04 E
Narva-Jyesuu/Narva Jõesuu 8 Me 59.21N 28.04 E
Narva laht 7 Gg 59.30N 27.40 E
Narvik 6 Hb 68.26N 17.25 E
Narvski Zaliv 7 Gg 59.30N 27.40 E
Narvskoje Vodohranilišče 8 Me 59.10N 28.30 E
Narym 20 De 58.58N 81.40 E
Naryn 21 Je 40.54N 71.45 E
Naryn 22 Je 41.26N 75.59 E
Naryncol 19 Ig 42.43N 80.08 E
Narynskaja Oblast [3] 19 Hg 41.20N 75.40 E
Nås 7 Df 60.27N 14.29 E
Na Sailtí/Saltee Islands 9 Gi 52.07N 6.36W
Näsåker 7 De 63.23N 16.54 E
Nasarawa 34 Gd 8.32N 7.43 E
Năsăud 15 Hb 47.17N 24.24 E
Nasawa 63b Db 15.12S 168.06 E
Na Sceirí/Skerries 9 Gh 53.35N 6.07W
Nash Point 9 Jj 51.24N 3.27W
Nashtārud 24 Nd 36.45N 51.02 E
Nashua 44 Ld 42.44N 71.28W
Nashville [Ar.-U.S.] 45 Jj 33.57N 93.51W
Nashville [Ga.-U.S.] 44 Fj 31.12N 83.15W
Nashville [Il.-U.S.] 45 Lg 38.21N 89.23W
Nashville [In.-U.S.] 44 Df 39.12N 86.15W
Nashville [Tn.-U.S.] 39 Kf 36.09N 86.48W
Nashville Seamount (EN) 38 Nf 35.00N 57.20W
Našice 14 Me 45.30N 18.06 E
Nasielsk 10 Qd 52.36N 20.48 E
Näsijärvi 5 Ic 61.35N 23.40 E
Nāsik 22 Jg 20.05N 73.48 E
Nāşir 35 Ed 8.36N 33.04 E
Naskaupi 42 Lf 53.47N 60.51W
Nasorolevu 63d Bb 16.38S 179.24 E
Naşr [Eg.] 24 Dg 30.36N 30.23 E
Naşr [Lib.] 33 Dd 28.59N 21.13 E
Naşrābād 24 Of 32.09N 52.08 E
Nass 42 Ee 55.00N 129.50W
Nassandres 12 Ce 49.07N 0.44 E
Nassandres-La Rivière Thibouville 12 Ce 49.07N 0.44 E
Nassau [Bah.] 39 Lg 25.05N 77.21W
Nassau [F.R.G.] 12 Jd 50.19N 7.48 E
Nassau, Bahia- 56 Gi 55.25S 67.40W
Nassau Island 57 Kf 11.33S 165.25W
Nassau River 59 Ic 15.58S 141.30 E
Nasser, Birkat-=Nasser, Lake-(EN) 30 Kf 22.40N 32.00 E

Index Symbols

[1] Independent Nation
[2] State, Region
[3] District, County
[4] Municipality
[5] Colony, Dependency
Continent
Physical Region
Historical or Cultural Region
Mount, Mountain
Volcano
Hill
Mountains, Mountain Range
Hills, Escarpment
Plateau, Upland
Pass, Gap
Plain, Lowland
Delta
Salt Flat
Valley, Canyon
Crater, Cave
Karst Features
Depression
Polder
Desert, Dunes
Forest, Woods
Heath, Steppe
Oasis
Cape, Point
Coast, Beach
Cliff
Peninsula
Isthmus
Sandbank
Island
Atoll
Rock, Reef
Islands, Archipelago
Rocks, Reefs
Coral Reef
Well, Spring
Geyser
River, Stream
Waterfall Rapids
River Mouth, Estuary
Lake
Salt Lake
Intermittent Lake
Reservoir
Swamp, Pond
Canal
Glacier
Ice Shelf, Pack Ice
Ocean
Sea
Gulf, Bay
Strait, Fjord
Lagoon
Bank
Seamount
Tablemount
Ridge
Shelf
Basin
Escarpment, Sea Scarp
Fracture
Trench, Abyss
National Park, Reserve
Point of Interest
Recreation Site
Cave, Cavern
Historic Site
Ruins
Wall, Walls
Church, Abbey
Temple
Scientific Station
Airport
Port
Lighthouse
Mine
Tunnel
Dam, Bridge

Nasser, Lake-(EN)=Nasser, Birkat- ≈	30	Kf	22.40N	32.00 E
Nassian	34	Ed	9.24N	4.29W
Nässjö	7	Dh	57.39N	14.41 E
Nassogne	12	Hd	50.08N	5.21 E
Na Staighrí Dubha/ Blackstairs Mountains ⛰	9	Gi	52.33N	6.49W
Nastapoka Islands ⊞	42	Je	56.50N	76.50W
Nastätten	12	Jd	50.12N	7.52 E
Nastola	8	Kd	60.57N	25.56 E
Nasu	29	Gc	37.02N	140.06 E
Nasu-Dake ▲	29	Fc	37.07N	139.58 E
Näsviken	8	Gc	61.45N	16.52 E
Natá	49	Gi	8.20N	80.31W
Nata ∿	30	Jk	20.14S	26.10 E
Nata	37	Dd	20.13S	26.11 E
Natal [2]	37	Ee	29.00S	30.00 E
Natal [B.C.-Can.]	46	Hb	49.44N	114.50W
Natal [Braz.]	53	Mf	5.47S	35.13W
Natal [Indon.]	26	Cf	0.33N	99.07 E
Natal Basin (EN) ⌣	3	Fm	30.00S	40.00 E
Natanz	24	Nf	33.31N	51.54 E
Natashquan ∿	42	Lf	50.09N	61.37W
Natashquan	42	Lf	50.11N	61.49W
Natchez	43	Ie	31.34N	91.23W
Natchitoches	43	Ie	31.46N	93.05W
Natewa Bay ◧	63d	Bb	16.35S	179.40 E
Nathorsts Land ⊠	41	Jd	72.20N	27.00W
Nathula ◆	63d	Ab	16.53S	177.25 E
Natitingou	31	Hg	10.19N	1.22 E
Natityāy, Jabal- ▲	33	Fe	23.01N	34.22 E
Natividad, Isla- ◆	48	Bd	27.55N	115.10W
Natividade	54	If	11.43S	47.47W
Natori	28	Pe	38.11N	140.58 E
Natron, Lake- ≈	30	Ki	2.25S	36.00 E
Naṭrūn, Wādī an- ⌴	24	Dg	30.25N	30.13 E
Natsudomari-Zaki ►	29a	Bc	41.00N	140.53 E
Nåttarö ◆	8	Hf	58.50N	18.10 E
Nättraby	8	Fh	56.12N	15.31 E
Natuna Besar, Pulau- ◆	26	Ef	4.00N	108.15 E
Natuna Islands (EN)= Bunguran, Kepulauan- ⊞	21	Mi	2.45N	109.00 E
Naturaliste, Cape- ►	57	Ch	33.32S	115.01 E
Naturaliste Channel ▬	59	Ce	25.25S	113.00 E
Naturita	45	Bg	38.14N	108.34W
Naturno / Naturns	14	Ed	46.39N	11.00 E
Naturns / Naturno	14	Ed	46.39N	11.00 E
Nau	18	Gd	40.09N	69.22 E
Nau, Cap de la-/Nao, Cabo de la- ►	5	Gh	38.44N	0.14 E
Naucelle	11	Ij	44.12N	2.21 E
Nauėji-Akmjane/Naujoji-Akmenė	7	Fh	56.21N	22.50 E
Naugo/Nauvo ◆	8	Id	60.10N	21.50 E
Nauhcampatépetl → Cofre de Perote, Cerro- ▲	48	Kh	19.29N	97.08W
Nauja Bay ◧	42	Kc	68.58N	75.00W
Naujamestis/Naujamiestis	8	Ki	55.41N	24.09 E
Naujamiestis/Naujamestis	8	Ki	55.41N	24.09 E
Naujoji-Akmenė/Nauėji-Akmjane	7	Fh	56.21N	22.50 E
Naukluft ⛰	37	Bd	24.10S	16.10 E
Naumburg [F.R.G.]	12	Lc	51.15N	9.10 E
Naumburg [G.D.R.]	10	He	51.09N	11.49 E
Nā'ūr	24	Fg	31.53N	35.50 E
Nauru ◆	57	He	0.31S	166.56 E
Nauru/Naoero [1]	58	He	0.31S	166.56 E
Nauški	20	Ff	50.28N	106.07 E
Nausori	61	Ec	18.02S	178.32 E
Nauta	54	Dd	4.32S	73.33W
Nautanwa	25	Gc	27.26N	83.25 E
Nautla	48	Kg	20.13N	96.47W
Nauvo/Naugo ◆	8	Id	60.10N	21.50 E
Nava	48	Ic	28.25N	100.45W
Navacerrada, Puerto de- ⌓	13	Id	40.47N	4.00W
Nava del Rey	13	Gc	41.20N	5.05W
Navahermosa	13	He	39.38N	4.28W
Navajo Mountain ▲	46	Jh	37.02N	110.52W
Navajo Reservoir ⊟	45	Ch	36.55N	107.30W
Navalmoral de la Mata	13	Ge	39.54N	5.32W
Navan/An Uaimh	9	Gh	53.39N	6.41W
Navarin, Mys- ►	21	Tc	62.16N	179.10 E
Navarino, Isla- ◆	52	Jk	55.05S	67.40W
Navarra [3]	13	Kb	42.45N	1.40W
Navarra=Navarre (EN) ⊡	13	Kb	43.00N	1.30W
Navarre (EN)=Navarra ⊡	13	Kb	43.00N	1.30W
Navarro	55	Cl	35.01S	59.16W
Navarro Mills Lake ≈	45	Hk	31.56N	96.45W
Navašino	7	Ki	55.33N	42.12 E
Navasota	45	Hk	30.23N	96.05W
Navasota River ∿	45	Hk	30.20N	96.09W
Navassa ◆	47	Ie	18.24N	75.01W
Navaste Jõgi/Navesti ∿	8	Kf	58.56N	24.58 E
Nävekvarn	8	Gf	58.38N	16.49 E
Naver ∿	9	Ic	58.30N	4.15W
Navesti/Navaste Jõgi ∿	8	Kf	58.56N	24.58 E
Navia	13	Fa	43.32N	6.43W
Navia ∿	13	Fa	43.33N	6.44W
Navidad, Bahía de- ◧	48	Gh	19.10N	104.45W
Navidad Bank (EN) ⋯	49	Mc	20.00N	68.50W
Naviti ◆	63d	Ab	17.07S	177.15 E
Navlja ∿	16	Ic	52.42N	34.03 E
Navlja	19	De	52.50N	34.31 E
Năvodari	15	Le	44.19N	28.36 E
Navoi	19	Gg	40.10N	65.15 E
Navoja	47	Cc	27.06N	109.26W
Navolato	48	Fe	24.47N	107.42W
Navoloki	7	Jh	57.28N	41.59 E
Návpaktos	15	Ek	38.24N	21.50 E
Návplion	15	Fl	37.34N	22.48 E
Navrongo	34	Ec	10.54N	1.06W
Navsāri	25	Ed	20.55N	72.55 E
Navtílos ◆	15	Gn	35.57N	23.13 E
Navua	63d	Bc	18.13S	178.10 E
Navy Board Inlet ▬	42	Jb	73.30N	81.00W
Nawa	24	Gf	32.53N	36.03 E
Nawābshāh	25	Dc	26.15N	68.25 E
Nawāṣif, Ḩarrat- ◭	33	He	21.20N	42.10 E
Ņaws, Ra's- ►	23	If	17.18N	55.16 E
Náxos	15	Il	37.06N	25.23 E
Naxos ⁙	14	Jm	37.49N	15.15 E
Náxos=Naxos (EN) ◆	5	Ih	37.02N	25.35 E
Naxos (EN)=Náxos ◆	5	Ih	37.02N	25.35 E
Nayarit [2]	47	Cd	22.00N	105.00W
Nayarit, Sierra- ⛰	47	Dd	22.00N	103.50W
Nayau ◆	63d	Cb	17.58S	179.03W
Nāy Band [Iran]	24	Oi	27.23N	52.38 E
Nāy Band [Iran]	24	Qf	32.20N	57.34 E
Nāy Band, Ra's-e- ►	24	Oi	27.23N	52.34 E
Nayoro	27	Pc	44.21N	142.28 E
Nazaré [Braz.]	54	Kf	13.02S	39.00W
Nazaré [Port.]	13	Ce	39.36N	9.04W
Nazareth (EN)=Nazerat	24	Ff	32.42N	35.18 E
Nazarovo	20	Ee	56.01N	90.36 E
Nazas	48	Ge	25.14N	104.08W
Nazas, Río- ∿	38	Ig	25.35N	105.00W
Nazca	53	Ig	14.50S	74.55W
Nazca Ridge (EN) ⋀	3	Nl	22.00S	82.00W
Naze	27	Mf	28.23N	129.30 E
Nazerat=Nazareth (EN)	24	Ff	32.42N	35.18 E
Nazilli	23	Cb	37.55N	28.21 E
Nazimiye	24	Hc	39.11N	39.50 E
Nazimovo	20	Ee	59.30N	90.58 E
Nazino	20	Cd	60.15N	78.58 E
Nazlū ∿	24	Kd	37.42N	45.16 E
Nazran	16	Nh	43.15N	44.46 E
Nazret	35	Fd	8.34N	39.18 E
Nazw'a	23	Ie	22.54N	57.31 E
Nazym ∿	17	Nf	61.12N	68.57 E
Nazyvajevsk	19	Hd	55.34N	71.21 E
Nbâk	32	Ef	17.15N	14.59W
Nchanga	36	Ee	12.31S	27.52 E
Ncheu	36	Fe	14.49S	34.38 E
Ndala	36	Fc	4.46S	33.16 E
Ndalatando	36	Bd	9.18S	14.54 E
Ndali	34	Fd	9.51N	2.43 E
Ndélé	31	Jh	8.24N	20.39 E
Ndélélé	34	He	4.02N	14.56 E
Ndendé	36	Bc	2.23S	11.23 E
Ndindi	36	Bc	3.46S	11.09 E
N'djamena (Fort-Lamy)	31	Ig	12.07N	15.03 E
Ndola	31	Jj	12.58S	28.38 E
Ndouana, Pointe- ►	63b	Dc	16.35S	168.09 E
Ndrhamcha, Sebkha de- ≊	32	Df	18.45N	15.48W
Nduindui	60	Fi	9.48S	159.58 E
Ndui Ndui	63b	Cb	15.24S	167.46 E
Né ∿	11	Fi	45.40N	0.23W
Nea	63c	Ab	10.51S	165.47 E
Nea ∿	7	Ce	63.13N	11.02 E
Néa Alikarnassós	15	In	35.20N	25.09 E
Néa Artáki	15	Gk	38.31N	23.38 E
Neagari	29	Ec	36.26N	136.26 E
Neagh, Lough-/Loch nEathach ≈	5	Fe	54.38N	6.24W
Neagră, Marea-=Black Sea (EN) ≣	5	Jg	43.00N	35.00 E
Neah Bay	46	Cb	48.22N	124.37W
Néa Ionía	15	Fj	39.23N	22.56 E
Neajlov ∿	15	Je	44.11N	26.12 E
Neale, Lake- ≈	59	Fd	24.20S	130.00 E
Neamț [2]	15	Jb	47.00N	26.20 E
Neápolis [Grc.]	15	In	35.15N	25.37 E
Neápolis [Grc.]	15	Ei	40.19N	21.23 E
Neápolis [Grc.]	15	Gm	36.31N	23.04 E
Near Islands ⊞	38	Bd	52.40N	173.30W
Neath ∿	9	Jj	51.37N	3.50W
Neath	9	Jj	51.40N	3.48W
Néa Zíkhni	15	Gh	41.02N	23.50 E
Néba ◆	63b	Ae	20.09S	163.55 E
Nebaj	49	Bf	15.24N	91.08W
Nebbou	34	Ec	11.18N	1.53W
Nebit-Dag	22	Hf	39.30N	54.22 E
Neblina, Pico da- ▲	52	Je	1.08N	66.10W
Nebo	59	Jd	21.40S	148.39 E
Nebo, Mount- ▲	46	Jg	39.49N	111.46W
Nebolči	7	Hg	59.08N	33.21 E
Nebraska [2]	43	Gc	41.30N	100.00W
Nebraska City	43	Hc	40.41N	95.52W
Nebrodi (Caronie) ⛰	14	Im	37.55N	14.35 E
Necedah	45	Kd	44.02N	90.03W
Nechako ∿	42	Ff	53.55N	122.44W
Nechako Reservoir ⊟	42	Ef	53.00N	126.10W
Nechar, Djebel- ▲	13	Qi	35.52N	4.59 E
Neches River ∿	45	Jl	29.55N	93.52W
Nechí	49	Ji	8.07N	74.46W
Nechí, Río- ∿	49	Ji	8.08N	74.46W
Neckako Plateau ◭	42	Ff	53.25N	124.40W
Neckar ∿	10	Eg	49.31N	8.26 E
Neckarsulm	10	Fg	49.11N	9.14 E
Necker Island ◆	57	Kb	23.35N	164.42W
Necochea	53	Ki	38.34S	58.45W
Necy	12	Bf	48.50N	0.07W
Nedeley	35	Bb	15.34N	18.10 E
Nederland	45	Jl	29.58N	93.59W
Nederland=Netherlands (EN) [1]	6	Ge	52.15N	5.30 E
Nederlandse Antillen [5]	50	Ec	18.06N	63.10W
Nederlandse Antillen = Netherlands Antilles (EN) [5]	53	Jd	12.15N	69.00W
Neder-Rijn = Lower Rhine (EN) ∿	11	Mc	51.59N	6.20 E
Nêdong	22	Lg	29.14N	91.46 E
Nedstrand	8	Ae	59.21N	5.51 E
Nedstrandefjorden ▬	8	Ae	59.20N	5.50 E
Neede	12	Ib	52.08N	6.37 E
Needham Market	12	Db	52.09N	1.02 E
Needham's Point ►	51q	Ab	13.05N	59.36W
Needles	43	Ee	34.51N	114.37W
Neembucú [3]	55	Dh	27.00S	58.00W
Neenah	45	Ld	44.11N	88.28W
Neepawa	45	Ga	50.13N	99.29W
Neermoor, Moormerland-	12	Ja	53.18N	7.26 E
Neeroeteren, Maaseik-	12	Hc	51.05N	5.42 E
Neerpelt	12	Hc	51.13N	5.25 E
Nefasit	35	Fb	15.18N	39.04 E
Nefedova	19	Hd	58.48N	72.34 E
Né Finn/Nephin ▲	9	Dg	54.01N	9.22W
Neftah	32	Ic	33.52N	7.53 E
Neftečala	16	Pj	39.19N	49.13 E
Neftegorsk [R.S.F.S.R.]	16	Kg	44.22N	39.42 E
Neftegorsk [R.S.F.S.R.]	20	Jf	53.00N	143.00 E
Neftegorsk [R.S.F.S.R.]	19	Fe	52.45N	51.13 E
Neftejugansk	19	Hc	61.05N	72.45 E
Neftekamsk	19	Fd	56.06N	54.17 E
Neftekumsk	19	Eg	44.43N	44.59 E
Neftjanyje Kamin	16	Qi	40.15N	50.49 E
Negage	36	Cd	7.46S	15.18 E
Negara	26	Fh	8.22S	114.37 E
Negele=Neghelle (EN)	31	Kh	5.20N	39.37 E
Negev Desert (EN)= Ħanegev ◢	24	Fg	30.30N	34.55 E
Neghelle (EN)=Negele	31	Kh	5.20N	39.37 E
Negla, Arroyo- ∿	55	Df	22.52S	56.41W
Negola	36	Be	14.10S	14.30 E
Negomano	37	Fb	11.26S	38.33 E
Negombo	25	Fg	7.13N	79.50 E
Negonego Atoll ⊙	57	Mf	18.47S	141.48W
Negotin	15	Fe	44.13N	22.32 E
Negotino	15	Fh	41.29N	22.06 E
Negra, Cordillera- ⛰	54	Ce	9.25S	77.40W
Negra, Coxilha- ⛰	55	Ej	31.02S	55.45W
Negra, Peña- ▲	13	Fb	42.11N	6.30W
Negra, Ponta- ►	55	Jf	23.21S	44.36W
Negra, Punta- ►	52	Hf	6.06S	81.10W
Negra, Serra- ⛰	55	Fc	16.30S	52.10W
Negra o de los Difuntos, Laguna- ►	55	Fl	34.03S	53.40W
Negreira	13	Db	42.54N	8.44W
Negreni	15	He	44.34N	24.36 E
Negrești	15	Gb	47.52N	23.26 E
Negrine	32	Ic	34.29N	7.31 E
Negrinho, Rio- ∿	55	Ed	19.20S	55.05W
Negro, Cabo- ►	13	Gi	35.41N	5.17W
Negro, Río- [Arg.] ∿	55	Ch	27.27S	58.54W
Negro, Río- [Arg.] ∿	52	Jj	41.02S	62.47W
Negro, Río- [Bol.] ∿	54	Ff	14.11S	63.07W
Negro, Rio- [Braz.] ∿	54	Gg	19.13S	57.17W
Negro, Rio- [Braz.] ∿	56	Jc	26.01S	50.30W
Negro, Río- [Par.] ∿	56	Ib	24.23S	57.11W
Negro, Rio- [S.Amer.] ∿	52	Kf	3.08S	59.55W
Negro, Río- [S.Amer.] ∿	55	Ce	20.11S	58.10W
Negro, Río- [Ur.] ∿	52	Ki	33.24S	58.22W
Negros ◆	21	Oi	10.00N	123.00 E
Negru, Rîu- ∿	15	Id	45.45N	25.46 E
Negru Vodă	15	Lf	43.49N	28.12 E
Nehajevski	16	Ld	50.27N	41.46 E
Nehalem River ∿	46	Dd	45.40N	123.56W
Nehāvand	24	Me	35.56N	49.31 E
Nehe	27	Lb	48.28N	124.53 E
Nehoiu	15	Jd	45.26N	26.17 E
Néhoué, Baie de-	63b	Be	20.21S	164.09 E
Neiba	49	Ld	18.28N	71.25W
Neiba, Bahía de- ◧	49	Ld	18.15N	71.02W
Neidín/Kenmare	9	Dj	51.53N	9.35W
Neige, Crêt de la- ▲	11	Lh	46.16N	5.56 E
Neiges, Piton des- ▲	30	Mk	21.05S	55.29 E
Neijiang	22	Mg	29.38N	104.58 E
Neilton	46	Dc	47.25N	123.52W
Nei-meng-ku Tzu-chih-ch'ü → Nei Monggol Zizhiqu [2]	27	Jc	44.00N	112.00 E
Nei Monggol Gaoyuan ◭	21	Ne	42.00N	111.00 E
Nei Monggol Zizhiqu (Nei-meng-ku Tzu-chih-ch'ü)=Inner Mongolia (EN) [2]	27	Jc	44.00N	112.00 E
Neiqiu	28	Cf	37.17N	114.30 E
Neiva	53	Ie	2.56N	75.18W
Neja	19	Ed	58.19N	43.52 E
Nejanilini Lake ≈	42	He	59.30N	97.50W
Nejdek	10	If	50.19N	12.44 E
Nejo	35	Fd	9.30N	35.32 E
Nejva ∿	17	Kh	57.54N	62.18 E
Nekemt=Leqemt (EN)	31	Kh	9.05N	36.33 E
Neksø	8	Fi	55.04N	15.09 E
Nelemnoje	20	Kc	65.23N	151.08 E
Nelgese ∿	20	Ic	66.40N	136.30 E
Nelichu ▲	35	Ed	6.08N	34.25 E
Nelidovo	19	Dd	56.13N	32.50 E
Neligh	45	Ge	42.08N	98.02W
Neljaty	20	Ge	56.29N	115.50 E
Nelkan	20	Jd	64.15N	143.03 E
Nellore	22	Jh	12.56N	79.08 E
Nelma	20	Ig	47.40N	139.08 E
Nelson [2]	62	Ed	41.45S	172.30 E
Nelson ∿	38	Jd	57.04N	92.30W
Nelson [B.C.-Can.]	42	Fg	49.29N	117.17W
Nelson [N.Z.]	58	Ii	41.16S	173.15 E
Nelson, Cape- [Austl.] ►	57	Fh	38.26S	141.33 E
Nelson, Cape- [Pap.N.Gui.] ►	59	Ja	9.00S	149.15 E
Nelson Island ◆	40	Gd	60.35N	164.45W
Nelson's Dockyard ⌂	51d	Bb	17.00N	61.46W
Nelspruit	31	Kk	25.30S	30.58 E
Néma	31	Gg	16.36N	7.15W
Néma, Dahr- ▲	32	Ff	16.14N	7.30W
Neman ∿	5	Id	55.18N	21.23 E
Neman	7	Fi	55.03N	22.01 E
Nembrala	26	Hi	10.53S	122.50 E
Nemda ∿	7	Kh	57.31N	43.15 E
Neméa	15	Fl	37.49N	22.39 E
Neméa ⁙	15	Fl	37.49N	22.40 E
Nëmërçkes, Mali i- ▲	15	Di	40.08N	20.24 E
Nemenčinė	8	Kj	54.50N	25.39 E
Nëmërçkes, Mali i- ▲	15	Di	40.08N	20.24 E
Nemira, Vîrful- ▲	15	Jc	46.15N	26.19 E
Nemirov [Ukr.-U.S.S.R.]	10	Tf	50.08N	23.28 E
Nemirov [Ukr.-U.S.S.R.]	16	Fe	48.59N	28.50 E
Némiscau	42	Jf	51.30N	77.00W
Nemjuga ∿	7	Kd	65.29N	43.40 E
Nemours	11	If	48.16N	2.42 E
Nemunas ∿	5	Id	55.18N	21.23 E
Nemunėlis ∿	8	Kh	56.24N	24.10 E
Nemuro	27	Qc	43.20N	145.35 E
Nemuro-Hantō ⊏	29a	Db	43.20N	145.35 E
Nemuro-Kaikyō=Nemuro Strait (EN) ▬	20	Jh	43.50N	145.30 E
Nemuro Strait (EN)= Kunaširski Proliv ▬	20	Jh	43.50N	145.30 E
Nemuro Strait (EN)= Nemuro-Kaikyō ▬	20	Jh	43.50N	145.30 E
Nemuro-Wan ◧	29a	Db	43.25N	145.25 E
Nenagh/An tAonach	9	Ei	52.52N	8.12W
Nenana ∿	40	Jd	64.30N	149.00W
Nenana	40	Jd	64.34N	149.07W
Nendo Island ◆	57	Hf	10.40S	165.54 E
Nene ∿	9	Ni	52.48N	0.13 E
Nenecki Nacionalny Okrug [3]	19	Fb	67.30N	54.00 E
Nenjiang	22	Oe	49.10N	125.12 E
Nen Jiang ∿	21	Oe	45.26N	124.39 E
Neo	29	Ed	35.38N	136.37 E
Neodesha	45	Ih	37.25N	95.41W
Néon Karlovásion	15	Jl	37.47N	26.42 E
Neosho	45	Ih	36.52N	94.22W
Neosho River ∿	45	Ih	35.48N	95.18W
Néouvielle, Massif de- ⛰	11	Gl	42.51N	0.07 E
Nepal [1]	22	Kg	28.00N	84.00 E
Nepalganj	25	Gc	28.03N	81.37 E
Nephi	43	Ed	39.43N	111.50W
Nephin/Né Finn ▲	9	Dg	54.01N	9.22W
Nepisiguit River ∿	44	Ob	47.37N	65.38W
Nepoko ∿	30	Jh	1.40N	27.01 E
Nepomuk	10	Jg	49.29N	13.34 E
Ner ∿	10	Od	52.10N	18.40 E
Nera [It.] ∿	14	Gh	42.26N	12.24 E
Nera [Rom.] ∿	15	Ee	44.49N	21.22 E
Nérac	11	Gj	44.08N	0.21 E
Neratovice	10	Kf	50.16N	14.31 E
Nerău	15	Dd	45.58N	20.34 E
Nerča ∿	20	Gf	51.54N	116.30 E
Nerčinsk	20	Gf	51.58N	116.35 E
Nerčinski Zavod	20	Gf	51.17N	119.30 E
Nerehta	19	Ed	57.28N	40.34 E
Nereju	15	Jd	45.42N	26.43 E
Nereta	8	Kh	56.12N	25.24 E
Neretva ∿	14	Lg	43.02N	17.27 E
Neretvanski kanal ▬	14	Lg	43.03N	17.11 E
Nerica ∿	17	Fd	65.20N	52.45 E
Neringa	7	Ei	55.24N	21.05 E
Neringa ≡	7	Ei	55.18N	21.00 E
Neringa-Joudkrante/ Neringa-Juodkrantė	8	Ii	55.35N	21.01 E
Neringa-Juodkrantė/ Neringa-Juodkrante	8	Ii	55.35N	21.01 E
Neringa-Nida	8	Ii	55.18N	20.53 E
Neringa-Preila/Neringa-Prejla	8	Ii	55.20N	20.59 E
Neringa-Prejla/Neringa-Preila	8	Ii	55.20N	20.59 E
Neriquinha	36	Df	15.45S	21.33 E
Neris/Njaris ∿	8	Kj	54.55N	25.45 E
Nerja	13	Ih	36.44N	3.52W
Nerjungri	20	He	56.40N	124.47 E
Nerl [R.S.F.S.R.] ∿	7	Jh	56.11N	40.34 E
Nerl [R.S.F.S.R.] ∿	7	Ih	57.07N	37.39 E
Nerpio	13	Jf	38.09N	2.18W
Nerussa ∿	16	Hc	52.33N	33.47 E
Nerva	13	Fg	37.42N	6.32W
Nervi, Genova-	14	Df	44.23N	9.02 E
Nervión ∿	13	Ja	43.14N	2.53W
Nes	8	Cd	60.34N	9.59 E
Nes, Ameland-	12	Ha	53.26N	5.48 E
Nesbyen	7	Bf	60.34N	9.06 E
Nesebăr	15	Kg	42.39N	27.44 E
Nesjøen ≈	8	Db	63.00N	12.00 E
Neskaupstaður	7a	Db	65.09N	13.42W
Nesle	12	Ee	49.46N	2.45 E
Nesna	7	Cc	66.12N	13.02 E
Ness City	45	Gg	38.27N	99.54W
Nesterov [R.S.F.S.R.]	7	Fi	54.42N	22.34 E
Nesterov [Ukr.-U.S.S.R.]	16	Cd	50.03N	24.00 E
Néstos ∿	15	Hi	40.51N	24.44 E
Nesttun	8	Ad	60.19N	5.20 E
Nesviž	16	Ec	53.13N	26.39 E
Netanya	24	Ff	32.20N	34.51 E
Netcong	44	Je	40.54N	74.43W
Nete ∿	11	Kc	51.10N	4.15 E
Nethe ∿	12	Lc	51.44N	9.23 E
Netherdale	59	Jd	21.08S	148.32 E
Netherlands (EN)= Nederland [1]	6	Ge	52.15N	5.30 E
Netherlands Antilles (EN) = Nederlandse Antillen [5]	53	Jd	12.15N	69.00W
Neto ∿	14	Lk	39.12N	17.09 E
Netphen	12	Kd	50.55N	8.06 E
Nettebach ∿	12	Jd	50.26N	7.28 E
Nettersheim	12	Id	50.30N	6.38 E
Nettetal	12	Ic	51.18N	6.12 E
Nettiling Lake ≈	38	Lc	66.30N	70.40W
Nettuno	14	Gi	41.27N	12.39 E
Netzahualcóyotl, Presa- ⊟	48	Mi	17.00N	93.30W
Neubourg, Campagne du- ⊠	11	Ge	49.08N	1.00 E
Neubrandenburg	10	Jc	53.34N	13.16 E
Neubrandenburg [2]	10	Jc	53.35N	13.15 E
Neuburg an der Donau	10	Hh	48.44N	11.11 E
Neuchâtel [2]	14	Ac	47.05N	6.50 E
Neuchâtel/Neuenburg	14	Ad	46.59N	6.56 E
Neuchâtel, Lac de- / Neuenburger See ≈	14	Ad	46.55N	6.55 E
Neuenbürg	12	Kf	48.50N	8.35 E
Neuenburg/Neuchâtel	14	Ad	46.59N	6.56 E
Neuenburger See/ Neuchâtel, Lac de- ≈	14	Ad	46.55N	6.55 E
Neuenhaus	12	Ib	52.30N	6.58 E
Neuenkirchen	12	Jb	52.15N	7.22 E
Neuerburg	12	Id	50.01N	6.18 E
Neufchâteau [Bel.]	11	Le	49.51N	5.26 E
Neufchâteau [Fr.]	11	Lf	48.21N	5.42 E
Neufchâtel-en-Bray	11	He	49.44N	1.27 E
Neufchâtel-Hardelot	12	Dd	50.37N	1.38 E
Neufchâtel Hardelot-Hardelot Plage	12	Dd	50.38N	1.35 E
Neufchâtel-sur-Aisne	12	Ge	49.26N	4.02 E
Neuffossé, Canal de- ═	12	Ed	50.45N	2.15 E
Neuhaus am Rennweg	10	Hf	50.31N	11.09 E
Neuilly-en-Thelle	12	Ee	49.13N	2.17 E
Neuilly-Saint-Front	12	Fe	49.10N	3.16 E
Neu-Isenburg	12	Kd	50.03N	8.42 E
Neukirchen-Vluyn	12	Ic	51.27N	6.35 E
Neum	14	Lh	42.55N	17.38 E
Neumagen Dhron	12	Ie	49.51N	6.54 E
Neumarkter Sattel ⌓	14	Id	47.06N	14.22 E
Neumarkt in der Oberpfalz	10	Hg	49.17N	11.28 E
Neumünster	10	Fb	54.04N	9.59 E
Neunkirchen [Aus.]	14	Kc	47.43N	16.05 E
Neunkirchen [F.R.G.]	10	Dg	49.21N	7.11 E
Neunkirchen [F.R.G.]	12	Jd	50.51N	7.20 E
Neunkirchen [F.R.G.]	12	Kd	50.48N	8.00 E
Neuquén	53	Ji	39.00S	68.05W
Neuquén [2]	56	Ge	39.00S	70.00W
Neuquén, Río- ∿	52	Ji	38.59S	68.00W
Neurupping	10	Id	52.56N	12.48 E
Neuse River ∿	44	Ih	35.06N	76.30W
Neusiedl am See	14	Kc	47.56N	16.50 E
Neusiedler See (Fertö) ≈	10	Mi	47.50N	16.45 E
Neuß	10	Ce	51.12N	6.42 E
Neustadt (Hessen)	12	Ld	50.51N	9.07 E
Neustadt am Rübenberge	10	Fd	52.30N	9.28 E
Neustadt an der Aisch	10	Gg	49.35N	10.36 E
Neustadt an der Orla	10	Hf	50.44N	11.45 E
Neustadt an der Weinstraße	10	Eg	49.21N	8.09 E
Neustadt bei Couburg	10	Hf	50.19N	11.07 E
Neustadt in Holstein	10	Gb	54.06N	10.49 E
Neustrelitz	10	Jc	53.22N	13.05 E
Neu-Ulm	10	Gh	48.24N	10.01 E
Neuville-les-Dieppe	12	De	49.55N	1.06 E
Neuville-sur-Saône	11	Ki	45.52N	4.51 E
Neuwerk ◆	10	Ec	53.55N	8.30 E
Neuwied	10	Df	50.26N	7.28 E
Neva ∿	5	Jd	59.55N	30.15 E
Nevada [2]	43	Dd	39.00N	117.00W
Nevada [Ia.-U.S.]	45	Je	42.01N	93.27W
Nevada [Mo.-U.S.]	43	Id	37.51N	94.22W
Nevada, Sierra- [Sp.] ⛰	5	Fh	37.05N	3.10W
Nevada, Sierra- [U.S.] ⛰	38	Hf	38.00N	119.15W
Nevada del Cocuy, Sierra- ⛰	52	Ie	6.10N	72.15W
Nevada de Santa Marta, Sierra- ⛰	52	Id	10.50N	73.40W
Nevado, Cerro- ▲	52	Ie	3.59N	74.04W
Nevado de Ampato ▲	52	Ig	15.50S	71.52W
Neve, Serra da- ⛰	30	Ij	13.52S	13.26 E
Nevel	19	Cd	56.02N	29.55 E
Nevele	12	Fc	51.02N	3.33 E
Nevelsk	20	Jg	46.37N	141.57 E
Neverkino	16	Oc	52.47N	46.48 E
Nevers	11	Jg	46.59N	3.10 E
Nevesinje	14	Mg	43.16N	18.07 E
Nevinnomyssk	19	Eg	44.38N	41.58 E
Nevis ◆	47	Le	17.10N	62.34W
Nevis, Ben- ▲	5	Fd	56.48N	5.01W
Nevis Peak ▲	51c	Ab	17.10N	62.34W
Nevjansk	19	Gd	57.32N	60.13 E
Nevşehir	23	Db	38.38N	34.43 E
Nevskoje	28	Lb	45.42N	133.40 E
Newala	36	Ge	10.56S	39.18 E
New Albany [In.-U.S.]	43	Jd	38.18N	85.49W
New Albany [Ms.-U.S.]	45	Li	34.29N	89.00W
New Alresford	12	Ac	51.05N	1.10W
New Amsterdam	53	Ke	6.17N	57.36W
Newark [De.-U.S.]	44	Jf	39.41N	75.45W
Newark [N.J.-U.S.]	43	Mc	40.44N	74.11W
Newark [N.Y.-U.S.]	44	Id	43.03N	77.06W
Newark [Oh.-U.S.]	43	Kc	40.03N	82.25W
Newark-on-Trent	9	Mh	53.05N	0.49W
New Bedford	43	Mc	41.38N	70.56W
New Bern	43	Ld	35.07N	77.03W
Newberry [Mi.-U.S.]	44	Eb	46.21N	85.30W
Newberry [S.C.-U.S.]	44	Gh	34.17N	81.37W
New Braunfels	43	Hf	29.42N	98.08W
New Britain	44	Ke	41.40N	72.47W
New Britain Island ◆	57	Ge	5.40S	151.00 E
New Britain Trench (EN) ∇	60	Ei	6.00S	153.00 E
New Brunswick	44	Je	40.29N	74.27W
New Brunswick [3]	42	Kg	46.30N	66.45W
New Buckenham	12	Db	52.28N	1.05 E
New Buffalo	44	De	41.47N	86.45W
Newburgh	43	Mc	41.30N	74.00W
Newbury	9	Lj	51.25N	1.20W
New Caledonia (EN) = Nouvelle-Calédonie [5]	58	Hg	21.30S	165.30 E
New Caledonia (EN)= Nouvelle-Calédonie ◆	57	Hg	21.30S	165.30 E
New Caledonia Basin (EN) ⌣	3	Jm	30.00S	165.00 E
New Carlisle	44	Oa	48.01N	65.20W
New Castile (EN)=Castilla la Nueva ⊡	13	Id	40.00N	3.45W
New Castle [In.-U.S.]	44	Ef	39.55N	85.22W
New Castle [Pa.-U.S.]	43	Kc	41.00N	80.22W
Newcastle [Austl.]	58	Gh	32.56S	151.46 E
Newcastle [N.B.-Can.]	42	Kg	47.00N	65.34W
Newcastle [N.Ire.-U.K.]	9	Hg	54.12N	5.54W
Newcastle [S.Afr.]	37	De	27.49S	29.55 E
Newcastle [St.C.N.]	51c	Ab	17.13N	62.34W
Newcastle/An Caisleán Nua	9	Hg	54.12N	5.54W
Newcastle Creek ∿	59	Gc	17.20S	133.23 E
Newcastle-under-Lyme	9	Kh	53.00N	2.14W

Index Symbols

- [1] Independent Nation
- [2] State, Region
- [3] District, County
- [4] Municipality
- [5] Colony, Dependency
- ■ Continent
- ⊠ Physical Region
- ⊡ Historical or Cultural Region
- ▲ Mount, Mountain
- ⏶ Volcano
- ◠ Hill
- ⛰ Mountains, Mountain Range
- ⌒ Hills, Escarpment
- ◭ Plateau, Upland
- ⌓ Pass, Gap
- ▁ Plain, Lowland
- ◣ Delta
- ▭ Salt Flat
- ∨ Valley, Canyon
- ◯ Crater, Cave
- ⁂ Karst Features
- ⌴ Depression
- ▤ Polder
- ◢ Desert, Dunes
- ♣ Forest, Woods
- ⁕ Heath, Steppe
- ✻ Oasis
- ► Cape, Point
- ≡ Coast, Beach
- ⌈ Cliff
- ⊏ Peninsula
- ⋈ Isthmus
- ≋ Sandbank
- ◆ Island
- ⊙ Atoll
- ⁜ Rock, Reef
- ⊞ Islands, Archipelago
- ✲ Rocks, Reefs
- ❋ Coral Reef
- ⊚ Well, Spring
- ⇡ Geyser
- ∿ River, Stream
- ⫽ Waterfall Rapids
- ⋎ River Mouth, Estuary
- ≈ Lake
- ≊ Salt Lake
- ≃ Intermittent Lake
- ⊟ Reservoir
- ⵈ Swamp, Pond
- ═ Canal
- ❄ Glacier
- ❅ Ice Shelf, Pack Ice
- ▦ Ocean
- ≣ Sea
- ◧ Gulf, Bay
- ▬ Strait, Fjord
- ◎ Lagoon
- ⋯ Bank
- ⏅ Seamount
- ⊓ Tablemount
- ⋀ Ridge
- ⊐ Shelf
- ⌣ Basin
- ⌐ Escarpment, Sea Scarp
- ⚡ Fracture
- ∇ Trench, Abyss
- ✿ National Park, Reserve
- ✦ Point of Interest
- ⚑ Recreation Site
- ◖ Cave, Cavern
- ⌂ Historic Site
- ⁙ Ruins
- ▥ Wall, Walls
- ✝ Church, Abbey
- ⛩ Temple
- ⚗ Scientific Station
- ✈ Airport
- ⚓ Port
- ☼ Lighthouse
- ⚒ Mine
- ⋂ Tunnel
- ⌇ Dam, Bridge

Newcastle-upon-Tyne 6 Fd 54.59N 1.35W
Newcastle Waters 58 Ef 17.24S 133.24 E
Newcastle West/An Caisleán Nua 9 Di 52.27N 9.03W
New Delhi 22 Jg 28.36N 77.12 E
New Denver 46 Ga 50.00N 117.22W
Newell 45 Ed 44.43N 103.25W
Newell, Lake- 46 Ja 50.25N 111.56W
New England 38 Le 44.00N 71.20W
New England Range 57 Gh 30.00S 151.50 E
New England Seamounts (EN) 38 Mf 38.00N 61.00W
Newenham, Cape- 40 Ge 58.37N 162.12W
New Forest 9 Lk 50.55N 1.35W
Newfoundland [3] 42 Lf 52.00N 56.00W
Newfoundland, Island of- 38 Ne 48.30N 56.00W
Newfoundland Basin (EN) 3 De 45.00N 40.00W
New Galloway 9 If 55.05N 4.10W
New Georgia 57 Ge 8.30S 157.20 E
New Georgia Island 60 Fi 8.15S 157.30 E
New Georgia Sound (The Slot) 60 Fi 8.00S 158.10 E
New Glasgow 42 Lg 45.35N 62.39W
New Guinea/Pulau Irian 57 Fe 5.00S 140.00 E
New Guinea Trench (EN) 60 Bg 0.05N 135.50 E
New Hampshire [2] 43 Mc 43.35N 71.40W
New Hampton 45 Je 43.03N 92.19W
New Hanover Island 57 Ge 2.30S 150.15 E
New Harmony 44 Df 38.08N 87.56W
New Haven 39 Le 41.18N 72.56W
Newhaven 9 Nk 50.47N 0.03 E
New Hebrides/Nouvelles Hébrides 57 Hf 16.01S 167.01 E
New Hebrides Trench (EN) 3 Jl 20.00S 168.00 E
New Iberia 43 If 30.00N 91.49W
New Ireland Island 57 Ge 3.20S 152.00 E
New Jersey [2] 43 Mc 40.15N 74.30W
New Kowloon/Julong 22 Ng 22.20N 114.09 E
New Liskeard 42 Jg 47.30N 79.40W
New London 43 Mc 41.21N 72.07W
New Madrid 45 Lh 36.36N 89.32W
Newman 59 Dd 23.15S 119.35 E
Newmarket [Eng.-U.K.] 9 Ni 52.15N 0.25 E
Newmarket [Ont.-Can.] 44 Hc 44.03N 79.28W
New Martinsville 44 Gf 39.39N 80.52W
New Meadows 46 Gd 44.58N 116.32W
New Mexico [2] 43 Fe 34.30N 106.00W
Newnan 44 Ei 33.23N 84.48W
New Norfolk 59 Jh 42.47S 147.03 E
New Orleans 39 Jg 29.58N 90.07W
New Philadelphia 44 Ge 40.30N 81.27W
New Pine Creek 46 Ee 42.01N 120.18W
New-Plymouth 58 Ih 39.04S 174.04 E
Newport [Ar.-U.S.] 45 Ki 35.37N 91.17W
Newport [Eng.-U.K.] 12 Cc 51.59N 0.15 E
Newport [Eng.-U.K.] 9 Lk 50.42N 1.18W
Newport [Fl.-U.S.] 44 Ej 30.14N 84.12W
Newport [Or.-U.S.] 43 Cc 44.38N 124.03W
Newport [R.I.-U.S.] 44 Le 41.30N 71.19W
Newport [Tn.-U.S.] 44 Fh 35.58N 83.11W
Newport [Vt.-U.S.] 44 Kc 44.56N 72.13W
Newport [Wales-U.K.] 9 Kj 51.35N 3.00W
Newport [Wa.-U.S.] 46 Gb 48.11N 117.03W
Newport Beach 43 De 33.37N 117.54W
Newport News 39 Lf 37.04N 76.28W
Newport Pagnell 12 Bb 52.05N 0.43W
New Providence Island 47 Ic 25.02N 77.24W
Newquay 9 Hk 50.25N 5.05W
New Quebec Crater (EN) = Nouveau-Québec, Cratère du- 42 Kd 61.30N 73.55W
New Richmond [Oh.-U.S.] 44 Ef 38.57N 84.16W
New Richmond [Que.-Can.] 44 Oa 48.10N 65.52W
New River [Blz.] 49 Cd 18.22N 88.24W
New River [Guy.] 54 Gc 3.23N 57.36W
New River [U.S.] 44 Ff 38.50N 82.06W
New Rockford 45 Gc 47.41N 99.15W
New Romney 12 Cd 50.59N 0.56 E
New Ross/Ros Mhic Thriúin 9 Gi 52.24N 6.56W
Newry/an t-Iúr 9 Gg 54.11N 6.20W
New Salem 45 Fc 46.51N 101.25W
New Sandy Bay 51n Ba 13.20N 61.08W
New Schwabenland (EN) 66 Cf 72.30S 1.00 E
New Siberia (EN) = Novaja Sibir, Ostrov- 21 Qb 75.00N 149.00 E
New Siberian Islands (EN) = Novosibirskije Ostrova 21 Qb 75.00N 142.00 E
New Smyrna Beach 44 Gk 29.02N 80.56W
New South Wales 59 Jf 33.00S 146.00 E
Newton [Ia.-U.S.] 45 Jf 41.42N 93.03W
Newton [Il.-U.S.] 45 Lg 38.59N 88.10W
Newton [Ks.-U.S.] 43 Hd 38.03N 97.21W
Newton [Ma.-U.S.] 44 Ld 42.21N 71.13W
Newton [Ms.-U.S.] 45 Lj 32.19N 89.10W
Newton [N.J.-U.S.] 44 Je 41.03N 74.45W
Newton Abbot 9 Jk 50.32N 3.36W
Newton Stewart 9 Ig 54.57N 4.29W
Newtontoppen 67 Kd 72.02N 17.30 E
New Town 45 Ec 47.59N 102.30W
Newtown 9 Ji 52.32N 3.19W
Newtownabbey/Baile na Mainistreach 9 Hg 54.42N 5.54W
Newtownards/Baile Nua na hArda 9 Hg 54.36N 5.41W
New Ulm 43 Ic 44.19N 94.28W
New Westminster 42 Fg 49.12N 122.55W
New York 39 Le 40.43N 74.01W
New York [2] 43 Lc 43.00N 75.00W
New York State Barge Canal 44 Hd 43.05N 78.43W
New Zealand [1] 58 Ii 41.00S 174.00 E
New Zealand 57 Ii 41.00S 174.00 E
Nexpa, Rio- 48 Hh 18.05N 102.46W
Neyagawa 29 Dd 34.46N 135.36 E
Neyrīz 24 Ph 29.12N 54.19 E
Neyshābūr 23 Ib 36.12N 58.50 E
Nežárka 10 Kg 49.11N 14.43 E
Nežin 19 De 51.02N 31.57 E
Ngabé 36 Cc 3.12S 16.11 E
Ngahere 62 De 42.24S 171.26 E
Ngajangel 64a Ba 8.05N 134.43 E
Ngala 34 Hc 12.20N 14.11 E
Ngaliema, Chutes-=Stanley Falls (EN) 30 Jh 0.30N 25.30 E
Ngamegei Passage 64a Bb 7.44N 134.34 E
Ngami, Lake- 37 Cd 20.37S 22.40 E
Ngamiland [3] 37 Cc 19.09S 22.47 E
Ngamring 27 Ef 29.14N 87.12 E
Ngangala 35 Ee 4.42N 31.55 E
Ngangerabeli Plain 36 Hc 1.30S 40.15 E
Ngangla Ringco 27 De 31.40N 83.00 E
Nganglong Kangri 27 De 32.45N 81.12 E
Nganglong Kangri 21 Kf 32.00N 83.00 E
Ngangzê Co 27 Ee 31.00N 86.55 E
Ngao 25 Je 18.45N 99.59 E
Ngaoundéré 31 Ih 7.19N 13.35 E
Ngapara 62 Df 44.57S 170.45 E
Ngara 36 Fc 2.28S 30.39 E
Ngardmau 64a Bb 7.37N 134.35 E
Ngardmau Bay 64a Bb 7.39N 134.35 E
Ngardololok 64a Ac 7.00N 134.16 E
Ngaregur 64a Bb 7.45N 134.38 E
Ngarekeukl 64a Ac 7.00N 134.14 E
Ngariungs 64a Ba 8.03N 134.43 E
Ngaruangl 64a Ba 8.10N 134.39 E
Ngaruangl Passage 64a Ba 8.07N 134.40 E
Ngaruawahia 62 Fb 37.40S 175.09 E
Ngaruroro 62 Gc 39.34S 176.55 E
Ngatangiia 64p Cb 21.14S 159.43W
Ngatangiia Harbour 64p Cb 21.14S 159.43W
Ngateguil, Point- 64a Bc 7.26N 134.37 E
Ngatik Atoll 57 Gd 5.51N 157.16 E
Ngatpang 64a Bc 7.28N 134.32 E
Ngau Island 63d Bc 18.02S 179.18 E
Ngauruhoe 62 Fc 39.09S 175.38 E
Ngawa/Aba 27 He 32.55N 101.45 E
Ngayu 36 Eb 1.35N 27.13 E
Ngemelis Islands 64a Ac 7.07N 134.15 E
Ngeregong 64a Ac 7.07N 134.22 E
Ngergoi 64a Ac 7.05N 134.17 E
Ngesebus 64a Ac 7.03N 134.16 E
Nggamea 63d Cb 16.46S 179.46W
Nggatokae 63a Dc 8.46S 158.11 E
Nggela Pile 63a Ec 9.08S 160.20 E
Nggela Sule 63a Ec 9.03S 160.12 E
Nggelelevu 63d Cb 16.05S 179.09W
Ngidinga 36 Cd 5.37S 15.17 E
Ngiro, Ewaso- 36 Gb 0.28N 39.55 E
Ngiva 31 Ij 17.03S 15.47 E
Ngo 36 Cc 2.29S 15.45 E
Ngoangoa 35 Dd 5.58N 25.10 E
Ngobasangel 64a Ac 7.16N 134.20 E
Ngoko 36 Cb 1.40N 16.03 E
Ngola Shankou 27 Gd 35.30N 99.36 E
Ngoma 36 Ef 15.58S 25.56 E
Ngoring Hu 27 Gd 35.00N 97.30 E
Ngorongoro Crater 30 Ki 3.10S 35.35 E
Ngoui 34 Cb 16.09N 13.55W
Ngouna 63b Dc 17.26S 168.21 E
Ngounié [3] 36 Bc 2.00S 11.00 E
Ngounié 36 Bc 0.37S 10.18 E
Ngoura 35 Bc 12.52N 16.27 E
Ngouri 35 Bc 13.38N 15.22 E
Ngourti 34 Hb 15.19N 13.12 E
Ngousouboot, Pointe- 63b Ca 13.58S 167.27 E
Ngudu 36 Fc 2.58S 33.20 E
Nguigmi 31 Ig 14.15N 13.07 E
Ngulu Atoll 57 Ed 8.18N 137.29 E
Nguni 36 Gc 0.50S 38.20 E
Ngunza 31 Ij 11.12S 13.51 E
Nguru 31 Ig 12.53N 10.28 E
Nhachengue 37 Fd 22.51S 35.11 E
Nhamundá 54 Gd 2.14S 56.43W
Nhamundá, Rio- 54 Gd 2.12S 56.41W
Nhandeara 55 Ge 20.40S 50.02W
Nhandutiba 55 Jb 14.37S 44.12W
Nharea 36 Ce 11.28S 16.53 E
Nha Trang 22 Mh 12.15N 109.11 E
Nhecolândia 55 Dd 19.16S 57.04W
Nhia 36 Be 10.15S 14.12 E
Nhulunbuy 58 Ef 12.00S 35.58 E
Niafounké 35 Eb 15.56N 4.00W
Niagara Escarpment 44 Gc 44.30N 80.35W
Niagara Falls 38 Le 43.05N 79.04W
Niagara Falls [N.Y.-U.S.] 43 Lc 43.06N 79.02W
Niagara Falls [Ont.-Can.] 42 Jh 43.06N 79.04W
Niagara River 44 Hd 43.15N 79.04W
Niagassola 34 Dc 12.19N 9.07W
Niah 26 Ff 3.52N 113.44 E
Niakaramandougou 34 Dd 8.40N 5.17W
Niamey 31 Hg 13.31N 2.07 E
Niamey [2] 34 Fc 14.00N 2.00 E
Niandan 34 Dc 10.35N 9.45W
Niangara 31 Jh 3.42N 27.52 E
Niangay, Lac- 34 Eb 15.50N 3.00W
Niangoloko 34 Ec 10.17N 4.55W
Nia-Nia 36 Eb 1.24N 27.36 E
Nianzishan 27 Lb 47.31N 122.50 E
Niao Dao 27 Gd 37.20N 99.50 E
Niaoshu Shan 27 He 34.54N 104.04 E
Niari [3] 36 Bc 4.30S 13.00 E
Niari 36 Bc 3.56S 12.12 E
Nias, Pulau- 21 Li 1.05N 97.35 E
Niassa [3] 37 Fb 13.00S 36.00 E
Niassa, Lago-=Nyasa, Lake- (EN) 30 Kj 12.00S 34.30 E
Niau, Ile- 57 Mf 16.09S 146.21W
Nibāk 24 Nj 24.24N 50.50 E
Nibe 8 Ch 56.59N 9.38 E
Nica 7 Lh 57.29N 64.33 E
Nica/Nīca 8 Ih 56.25N 20.56 E
Nica/Nīca 8 Ih 56.25N 20.56 E
Nicanor Olivera 55 Cn 38.17S 59.12W
Nicaragua [1] 39 Kh 13.00N 85.00W
Nicaragua, Lago de-=Nicaragua, Lake- (EN) 38 Kh 11.35N 85.25W
Nicaragua, Lake- (EN)=Nicaragua, Lago de- 38 Kh 11.35N 85.25W
Nicastro 14 Kl 38.59N 16.19 E
Nice 6 Gg 43.42N 7.15 E
Niceville 44 Dj 30.31N 86.29W
Nichicum, Lac- 42 Kf 53.08N 70.55W
Nichinan [Jap.] 29 Cd 35.10N 133.16 E
Nichinan [Jap.] 28 Ki 31.36N 131.23 E
Nicholas Channel 49 Gb 23.25N 80.05W
Nicholas Channel (EN)=Nicolás, Canal- 47 Hd 23.25N 80.05W
Nicholasville 44 Eg 37.53N 84.34W
Nicholls Town 49 Ia 25.08N 78.00W
Nicholson Range 59 De 27.15S 116.45 E
Nicholson River 57 Ef 17.31S 139.36 E
Nickerson Ice Shelf 66 Mf 75.45S 145.00W
Nickol Bay 59 Dd 20.40S 116.50 E
Nicobar Islands 21 Li 8.00N 93.30 E
Nicocli 49 Ii 8.26N 76.48W
Nicolajevka 15 Nb 47.33N 30.41 E
Nicola River 46 Ea 50.25N 121.18W
Nicolás, Canal-=Nicholas Channel (EN) 47 Hd 23.25N 80.05W
Nicolet 44 Kb 46.14N 72.37W
Nicopolis (EN) = Nikópolis 15 Dj 39.00N 20.45 E
Nicosia 14 Im 37.45N 14.24 E
Nicosia (EN)=Lefkosa/Levkôsia 22 Ff 35.10N 33.22 E
Nicosia (EN)=Levkôsia/Lefkosa 22 Ff 35.10N 33.22 E
Nicotera 14 Jl 38.33N 15.56 E
Nicoya 47 Gf 10.09N 85.27W
Nicoya, Golfo de- 47 Hg 9.47N 84.48W
Nicoya, Peninsula de-=Nicoya Peninsula (EN) 38 Ki 10.00N 85.25W
Nicoya Peninsula (EN)=Nicoya, Peninsula de- 38 Ki 10.00N 85.25W
Nicuadala 37 Fc 17.37S 36.50 E
Niculiţel 15 Ld 45.11N 28.29 E
Nida 10 Qf 50.18N 20.52 E
Nidda 12 Ld 50.25N 9.00 E
Nidda 10 Ef 50.06N 8.34 E
Nidder 12 Kd 50.12N 8.47 E
Nideggen 12 Id 50.42N 6.29 E
Nidelva [Nor.] 8 Cf 58.24N 8.48 E
Nidelva [Nor.] 8 Da 63.26N 10.25 E
Nido, Sierra del- 48 Fc 29.30N 106.45W
Nidže 15 Ei 41.00N 21.50 E
Nidzica 10 Qf 50.12N 20.40 E
Nidzica 10 Qc 53.22N 20.26 E
Nidzkie, Jezioro- 10 Rc 53.37N 21.30 E
Niebüll 10 Eb 54.48N 8.50 E
Nied 12 Ie 49.23N 6.40 E
Nieddu 14 Dj 40.44N 9.34 E
Niederbayern 10 Ih 48.35N 12.30 E
Niederbronn-les-Bains 11 Nf 48.58N 7.38 E
Niedere Tauern 14 Hc 47.20N 14.00 E
Niederlausitz 10 Ke 51.40N 14.15 E
Nieder-Olm 12 Ke 49.54N 8.13 E
Niederösterreich = Lower Austria (EN) [2] 14 Jb 48.30N 15.45 E
Niedersachsen=Lower Saxony (EN) [2] 10 Fd 52.00N 10.00 E
Niederwald 10 Df 50.10N 8.00 E
Niederzier 12 Id 50.53N 6.28 E
Niefang 34 He 1.50N 10.14 E
Niegocin, Jezioro- 10 Rb 54.00N 21.50 E
Niel 12 Gc 51.07N 4.20 E
Nielfa, Puerto de- 13 Hf 38.32N 4.23W
Niéllé 34 Dc 10.12N 5.38W
Niellim 35 Bd 9.42N 17.49 E
Niemba 36 Ed 5.57S 28.26 E
Niemba 36 Ed 5.57S 28.26 E
Niemodlin 10 Nf 50.39N 17.37 E
Niéna 34 Dc 11.25N 6.20W
Nienburg (Weser) 10 Fd 52.38N 9.13 E
Niepołomice 10 Qf 50.03N 20.13 E
Niermalak, Pointe- 63b Cb 14.21S 167.24 E
Niers 12 Be 51.43N 5.57 E
Nierstein 12 Ke 49.53N 8.20 E
Niesky/Niska 10 Ke 51.18N 14.49 E
Nieszawa 10 Od 52.50N 18.55 E
Nieuport/Nieuwpoort 11 Ic 51.08N 2.45 E
Nieuw Amsterdam 54 Gb 5.53N 55.05W
Nieuwe-Pekela 12 Ia 53.04N 6.59 E
Nieuweschans 12 Ja 53.11N 7.15 E
Nieuw Milligen, Apeldoorn- 12 Hb 52.14N 5.45 E
Nieuw Nickerie 53 Ke 5.57N 56.59W
Nieuwolda 12 Ia 53.14N 6.59 E
Nieuwoudtville 37 Bf 31.22S 19.06 E
Nieuwpoort/Nieuport 11 Ic 51.08N 2.45 E
Nieuw Weerdinge, Emmen- 12 Jb 52.52N 7.01 E
Nieves 48 He 24.00N 103.01W
Nièvre [3] 11 Jg 47.05N 3.30 E
Nièvre 11 Jh 46.59N 3.10 E
Nigata 28 Lg 34.13N 132.29 E
Niğde 23 Db 37.59N 34.42 E
Nigenān 24 Qe 34.13N 57.19 E
Niger [1] 31 Hg 16.00N 8.00 E
Niger 30 Hh 5.33N 6.33 E
Niger [2] 34 Gd 9.40N 6.00 E
Niger Basin (EN) 30 Gg 15.00N 2.00 E
Niger Delta 30 Hh 4.50N 6.00 E
Nigeria [1] 31 Hh 10.00N 8.00 E
Night Hawk Lake 44 Ga 48.28N 81.00W
Nightingale Island 30 Fi 37.24S 12.28W
Nigrita 15 Gi 40.54N 23.30 E
Nihiru Atoll 57 Mf 16.42S 142.50W
Nihoa Island 57 Kb 23.06N 161.58W
Nihonmatsu 28 Pf 37.35N 140.26 E
Nihuil, Embalse del- 56 Ge 35.05S 68.45W
Niigata 22 Pf 37.55N 139.03 E
Niigata Ken [2] 28 Of 37.30N 138.50 E
Niihama 28 Lh 33.58N 133.16 E
Niihau Island 57 Kb 21.55N 160.10W
Nii-Jima 27 Oe 34.20N 139.15 E
Niikappu-Gawa 29a Cb 42.22N 142.16 E
Niimi 28 Lg 34.59N 133.28 E
Niisato 29 Gb 39.36N 141.49 E
Niitsu 28 Of 37.48N 139.07 E
Nijar 13 Jh 36.58N 2.12W
Nijkerk 12 Hb 52.14N 5.29 E
Nijlen 12 Gc 51.10N 4.39 E
Nijmegen 11 Lc 51.50N 5.50 E
Nijvel/Nivelles 11 Kd 50.36N 4.20 E
Nijverdal, Hellendoorn- 12 Ib 52.22N 6.27 E
Nikel 19 Db 69.24N 30.13 E
Niki 15 Ei 40.55N 21.25 E
Nikitin Seamount (EN) 21 Kj 3.00S 83.00 E
Nikki 34 Fd 9.56N 3.12 E
Nikkō 29 Fc 36.44N 139.35 E
Nikolajev [Ukr.-U.S.S.R.] 16 Ce 49.32N 23.58 E
Nikolajev [Ukr.-U.S.S.R.] 6 Jf 46.58N 32.00 E
Nikolajevka 18 Kc 43.37N 77.01 E
Nikolajevo 8 Mf 58.14N 29.32 E
Nikolajevsk 19 Ee 50.02N 45.31 E
Nikolajevskaja Oblast [3] 19 Df 47.20N 32.00 E
Nikolajevski 20 Hf 54.50N 129.25 E
Nikolajevsk-na-Amure 22 Qd 53.08N 140.44 E
Nikolsk [R.S.F.S.R.] 19 Ee 53.42N 46.03 E
Nikolsk [R.S.F.S.R.] 19 Ed 59.33N 45.31 E
Nikolski [Ak.-U.S.] 40a Eb 53.15N 168.22W
Nikolski [Kaz.-U.S.S.R.] 19 Gf 47.55N 67.33 E
Nikonga 36 Fc 4.40S 31.28 E
Nikopol [Bul.] 15 Hf 43.42N 24.54 E
Nikopol [Ukr.-U.S.S.R.] 19 Df 47.35N 34.25 E
Nikópolis = Nicopolis (EN) 15 Dj 39.00N 20.45 E
Nikpey 24 Md 36.50N 48.10 E
Niksar 24 Gb 40.36N 36.58 E
Nikšić 15 Bg 42.46N 18.58 E
Nikumaroro Atoll (Gardner) 57 Je 4.40S 174.32W
Nikunau Island 57 Ie 1.23S 176.26 E
Nil, Kūh-e- 24 Ng 30.52N 50.49 E
Nil, Nahr an-=Nile (EN) 30 Ke 30.10N 31.06 E
Nila, Pulau- 26 Ih 6.44S 129.31 E
Nilakka 7 Ge 63.07N 26.33 E
Niland 46 Hj 33.14N 115.31W
Nilandu Atoll 25a Bb 3.00N 72.55 E
Nile [3] 36 Fb 3.00N 31.30 E
Nile (EN)=Nil, Nahr an- 30 Ke 30.10N 31.06 E
Nile Delta (EN) 30 Ke 31.20N 31.00 E
Nileh, Kūh-e- 24 Nf 32.59N 50.32 E
Niles 44 De 41.50N 86.15W
Nilka 27 Dc 43.47N 82.20 E
Nil Kowtal 23 Kc 34.48N 67.22 E
Nilsiä 7 Ge 63.12N 28.05 E
Nilüfer 15 Li 40.18N 28.27 E
Nimba [3] 34 Dd 6.45N 8.45W
Nimba, Monts-=Nimba Mountains (EN) 30 Gh 7.35N 8.28W
Nimba Mountains (EN)=Nimba, Monts- 30 Gh 7.35N 8.28W
Nîmes 6 Gg 43.50N 4.21 E
Nimjad 32 Df 17.25N 15.41W
Nimmitabel 59 Jg 36.31S 149.16 E
Nimpkish River 46 Ba 50.32N 126.59W
Nimrode Glacier 66 Kg 82.27S 161.00 E
Nimrud 24 Jd 36.06N 43.20 E
Nimrūz [3] 23 Jc 30.30N 62.00 E
Nims 12 Ie 49.51N 6.28 E
Nimule 31 Kh 3.36N 32.03 E
Nimūn, Punta- 48 Ng 20.46N 90.25W
Nin 14 Jf 44.14N 15.11 E
Nina 37 Bd 22.57S 18.14 E
Nīnawā [3] 24 Je 35.45N 42.45 E
Nīnawā=Nineveh (EN) 23 Fb 36.22N 43.09 E
Nine Degree Channel 21 Ji 9.00N 73.00 E
Ninetyeast Ridge (EN) 3 Gj 10.00S 90.00 E
Ninety Mile Beach [Austl.] 59 Jg 38.15S 147.25 E
Ninety Mile Beach [N.Z.] 62 Ea 34.45S 173.00 E
Nineveh (EN)=Nīnawā 23 Fb 36.22N 43.09 E
Ning'an 27 Mc 44.22N 129.23 E
Ningbo 22 Og 29.55N 121.28 E
Ningcheng (Tianyi) 27 Kc 41.34N 119.25 E
Ningde 27 Kf 26.44N 119.29 E
Ningdu 27 Kf 26.31N 115.59 E
Ningguo 28 Ei 30.39N 119.00 E
Ninghai 28 Fj 29.19N 121.26 E
Ning-hsia-hui-tsu Tzu-chih-ch'ü→Ningxia Huizu Zizhiqu=Ningsia Hui (EN) [2] 27 Id 37.00N 106.00 E
Ningjin [China] 28 Df 37.39N 116.48 E
Ningjin [China] 28 Cf 37.37N 114.55 E
Ningjing Shan 27 Ge 31.45N 97.15 E
Ninglang 27 Hf 27.17N 100.52 E
Ningling 28 Cg 34.27N 115.18 E
Ningnan 27 Hf 27.05N 102.44 E
Ningqiang 27 Ie 32.48N 106.15 E
Ningsia Hui (EN)=Ning-hsia-hui-tsu Tzu-chih-ch'ü→Ningxia Huizu Zizhiqu [2] 27 Id 37.00N 106.00 E
Ningsia Hui (EN)=Ningxia Huizu Zizhiqu (Ning-hsia-hui-tsu Tzu-chih-ch'ü) [2] 27 Id 37.00N 106.00 E
Ningwu 27 Jd 38.59N 112.14 E
Ningxia Huizu Zizhiqu (Ning-hsia-hui-tsu Tzu-chih-ch'ü)=Ningsia Hui (EN) [2] 27 Id 37.00N 106.00 E
Ningxian 27 Id 35.27N 107.50 E
Ningxiang 28 Bj 28.16N 112.33 E
Ningyang 28 Dg 35.45N 116.48 E
Ningyō-Tōge 29 Cd 35.19N 133.56 E
Ninh Binh 25 Ld 20.15N 105.59 E
Ninh Hoa 25 Lf 12.29N 109.08 E
Ninigo Group 57 Fe 1.15S 144.15 E
Niniva 65b Ba 19.46S 174.38W
Ninnis Glacier 66 Je 68.12S 147.12 E
Ninohe 27 Pc 40.16N 141.18 E
Ninove 12 Fd 50.50N 4.00 E
Nioaque 54 Gh 21.08S 55.48W
Niobrara 38 Je 42.45N 98.00W
Niobrara 45 He 42.25N 98.00W
Nioghalvfjerdsfjorden 41 Kc 79.30N 18.45W
Nioki 36 Cc 2.43S 17.41 E
Niono 34 Dc 14.15N 6.00W
Nioro du Rip 34 Bc 13.45N 15.48W
Nioro du Sahel 31 Gg 15.14N 9.37W
Niort 11 Fh 46.19N 0.28W
Nipawin 42 Hf 53.22N 104.00W
Nipe, Bahia de- 49 Jc 20.47N 75.42W
Nipesotsu-Yama 29a Cb 43.27N 143.02 E
Nipigon 39 Ke 49.01N 88.16W
Nipigon, Lake- 38 Ke 49.50N 88.30W
Nipigon Bay 45 Mb 48.53N 87.50W
Nipissing, Lake- 38 Le 46.17N 80.00W
Nippon=Japan (EN) [1] 22 Pf 38.00N 137.00 E
Nippon-Kai=Japan, Sea of- (EN) 21 Pf 40.00N 134.00 E
Nippur 24 Kf 32.10N 45.10 E
Niquelândia 54 If 14.27S 48.27W
Niquero 49 Ic 20.03N 77.35W
Niquitao, Teta de- 49 Li 9.07N 70.30W
Niquivil 56 Gd 30.25S 68.42W
Nīr 24 Lc 38.02N 47.59 E
Nirasaki 29 Fd 35.43N 138.27 E
Nirji → Morin Dawa 27 Lb 48.30N 124.28 E
Nirmal 25 Fe 19.06N 78.21 E
Niš 6 Ig 43.19N 21.54 E
Nisa 13 Ee 39.31N 7.39W
Nişāb 23 Gg 14.24N 46.38 E
Nisāh, Sha'īb- 24 Lj 24.11N 47.11 E
Nišava 15 Ef 43.22N 21.46 E
Niscemi 14 Im 37.09N 14.23 E
Nishibetsu-Gawa 29a Db 43.23N 145.17 E
Nishikawa 29 Gb 38.26N 140.08 E
Nishiki 29 Bd 34.16N 131.57 E
Nishinomiya 29 Dd 34.43N 135.20 E
Nishino'omote 27 Ne 30.44N 131.00 E
Nishino-Shima 60 Cb 27.30N 140.53 E
Nishi-No-Shima 28 Lf 36.06N 133.00 E
Nishiokoppe 29a Ca 44.20N 142.57 E
Nishi-Sonogi-Hantō 29 Ae 32.55N 129.45 E
Nishiwaki 29 Dd 34.59N 134.58 E
Nisiros 15 Km 36.35N 27.10 E
Niska/Niesky 10 Ke 51.18N 14.49 E
Niška Banja 15 Ff 43.18N 22.01 E
Nisko 10 Sf 50.31N 22.09 E
Nismes, Viroinval- 12 Gd 50.05N 4.33 E
Nisoi Aiyaiou [2] 15 Il 37.40N 25.40 E
Nisporeny 16 Ff 47.06N 28.10 E
Nissan 8 Eh 56.40N 12.51 E
Nissan 63a Ba 4.30S 154.14 E
Nisser 8 Ce 59.10N 8.30 E
Nissum Bredning 8 Ch 56.40N 8.20 E
Nissum Fjord 8 Ch 56.20N 8.15 E
Nita 29 Cd 35.12N 133.00 E
Nitchequon 42 Kf 53.15N 70.44W
Niterói 53 Lh 22.53S 43.07W
Nith 9 Jf 55.00N 3.35W
Nitra 10 Oi 47.46N 18.10 E
Nitra 10 Oh 48.19N 18.05 E
Niuafo'ou Island 57 Jf 15.35S 175.38W
Niuatoputapu Island 57 Jf 15.57S 173.45W
Niue [5] 58 Kf 19.02S 169.55W
Niue Island 57 Kf 19.02S 169.55W
Niu'erhe 27 La 51.30N 121.40 E
Niufu 29a Ca 44.35N 142.35 E
Niulakita Island 57 If 10.45S 179.30 E
Niutaca, Corrente- 55 De 20.42S 57.37W
Niutao Island 57 Ie 6.06S 177.16 E
Niutg, Gunung- 26 Ef 1.00N 109.55 E
Niutoushan 27 Ke 31.00N 119.35 E
Niuzhuang 28 Gd 40.57N 122.30 E
Nivala 7 Fe 63.58N 25.01 E
Nive 11 Ek 43.30N 1.29W
Nivelles/Nijvel 11 Kd 50.36N 4.20 E
Nivernais 11 Jg 47.00N 3.30 E
Nivernais, Canal du- 11 Jg 47.40N 3.40 E
Nivernais, Côtes du- 11 Jg 47.10N 3.30 E
Nivillers 12 Ee 49.28N 2.10 E
Nixon 45 Hl 29.16N 97.46W
Niya/Minfeng 27 Dd 37.04N 82.46 E
Niyābād 24 Le 35.12N 46.20 E
Niyodo-Gawa 29 Ce 33.28N 133.29 E
Nīza 24 Ph 28.25N 55.55 E
Nizāmābād 25 Fe 18.40N 78.07 E
Nižankoviči 10 Sg 49.40N 22.48 E
Nizip 23 Eb 37.01N 37.46 E
Nízke Tatry = Low Tatra (EN) 10 Ph 48.54N 19.40 E
Nízký-Jeseník 10 Ng 49.50N 17.30 E
Nižná 10 Pg 49.19N 19.32 E
Nižneangarsk 22 Md 55.47N 109.33 E
Nižnegorski 16 Ig 45.27N 34.44 E
Nižnejansk 20 Ib 71.24N 136.00 E
Nižnekamsk 19 Fd 55.38N 51.49 E
Nižnekolymsk 20 Lc 68.38N 160.56 E
Nižnetroicki 17 Fi 54.20N 53.41 E
Nižneudinsk 20 Ef 54.54N 99.03 E
Nižnevartovsk 22 Jc 61.00N 77.00 E
Nižni Baskunčak 19 Ef 48.13N 46.50 E
Nižni Bestjah 20 Hd 61.48N 129.55 E
Nižni Casučej 20 Gf 50.27N 115.08 E
Nižnije Serogozy 16 If 46.49N 34.24 E
Nižni Kuranah 20 He 58.40N 125.48 E
Nižni Lomov 19 Ee 53.32N 43.41 E
Nižni Odes 17 Ge 63.40N 54.52 E

Index Symbols

- [1] Independent Nation
- [2] State, Region
- [3] District, County
- [4] Municipality
- [5] Colony, Dependency
- Continent
- Physical Region
- Historical or Cultural Region
- Mount, Mountain
- Volcano
- Hill
- Mountains, Mountain Range
- Hills, Escarpment
- Plateau, Upland
- Pass, Gap
- Plain, Lowland
- Delta
- Salt Flat
- Valley, Canyon
- Crater, Cave
- Karst Features
- Depression
- Polder
- Desert, Dunes
- Forest, Woods
- Heath, Steppe
- Oasis
- Cape, Point
- Coast, Beach
- Cliff
- Peninsula
- Isthmus
- Sandbank
- Island
- Atoll
- Rock, Reef
- Islands, Archipelago
- Rocks, Reefs
- Coral Reef
- Well, Spring
- Geyser
- River, Stream
- Waterfall Rapids
- River Mouth, Estuary
- Lake
- Salt Lake
- Intermittent Lake
- Reservoir
- Swamp, Pond
- Canal
- Glacier
- Ice Shelf, Pack Ice
- Ocean
- Sea
- Gulf, Bay
- Strait, Fjord
- Lagoon
- Bank
- Seamount
- Tablemount
- Ridge
- Shelf
- Basin
- Escarpment, Sea Scarp
- Fracture
- Trench, Abyss
- National Park, Reserve
- Point of Interest
- Recreation Site
- Cave, Cavern
- Historic Site
- Ruins
- Wall, Walls
- Church, Abbey
- Temple
- Scientific Station
- Airport
- Port
- Lighthouse
- Mine
- Tunnel
- Dam, Bridge

Name	Page	Grid	Lat.	Long.
Nižni Oseredok, Ostrov- ◈	16	Pg	45.45N	48.35 E
Nižni Tagil	6	Ld	57.55N	59.57 E
Nižni Trajanov Val = Lower Trajan's Wall (EN) ▥	15	Ld	45.45N	28.30 E
Nižnjaja Omra	17	Ge	62.46N	55.46 E
Nižnjaja Peša	19	Eb	66.43N	47.36 E
Nižnjaja Pojma	20	Ee	56.08N	97.18 E
Nižnjaja Salda	17	Jg	58.05N	60.48 E
Nižnjaja Tavda	19	Gd	57.40N	66.12 E
Nižnjaja Tojma ≈	7	Ke	62.22N	44.15 E
Nižnjaja Tunguska = Lower Tunguska (EN) ≈	21	Kc	65.48N	88.04 E
Nižnjaja Tura	17	Ig	58.37N	59.49 E
Nižnjaja Zolotica	7	Jd	65.41N	40.13 E
Nižny Pjandž	18	Gf	37.14N	68.35 E
Nizza Monferrato	14	Cf	44.46N	8.21 E
Njajs ≈	17	Je	62.25N	60.47 E
Njamunas ≈	5	Id	55.18N	21.23 E
Njandoma	19	Ec	61.43N	40.12 E
Njaris/Neris ≈	8	Kj	54.55N	25.45 E
Njazepetrovsk	17	Ih	56.03N	59.38 E
Njazidja/Grande Comore ◈	30	Lj	11.35 S	43.20 E
Njegoš ⛰	15	Bg	42.53N	18.45 E
Njinjo	36	Gd	8.48 S	38.54 E
Njombe ≈	30	Ki	6.56 S	35.06 E
Njombe	31	Ki	9.20 S	34.46 E
Njudung ⊠	8	Fg	57.25N	14.50 E
Njuja	20	Gd	60.32N	116.25 E
Njuk, Ozero- ◒	7	Hd	64.25N	31.45 E
Njuksenica	7	Kf	60.28N	44.15 E
Njukža ≈	20	He	56.30N	121.40 E
Njunes ▲	7	Eb	68.45N	19.30 E
Njurba	22	Nc	63.17N	118.20 E
Njurundabommen	7	De	62.16N	17.22 E
Njutånger	8	Gc	61.37N	17.03 E
Njuvčim	17	Ef	61.22N	50.42 E
Nkai	37	Dc	19.00 S	28.54 E
Nkambe	34	Hd	6.38N	10.40 E
Nkawkaw	34	Ed	6.33N	0.46W
Nkayi	31	Ii	4.05 S	13.18 E
Nkhata Bay	36	Fe	11.36 S	34.18 E
Nkongsamba	31	Hh	4.57N	9.56 E
Nkota Kota	31	Kj	12.55 S	34.18 E
Nkululu ≈	36	Fd	6.26 S	32.49 E
Nkusi ≈	36	Fb	1.07N	30.40 E
Nkwalini	37	Ee	28.45 S	31.30 E
'Nmai ≈	25	Jc	25.42N	97.30 E
Nmaki ≈	24	Pg	31.16N	55.29 E
Nnewi	34	Gd	6.01N	6.55 E
Nō	29	Ec	37.05N	137.59 E
Noailles	12	Ee	49.20N	2.12 E
Noākhāli	25	Id	22.49N	91.06 E
Noatak	40	Gc	67.34N	162.59W
Nobel	44	Gc	45.25N	80.06W
Nobeoka	27	Ne	32.35N	131.40 E
Noblesville	44	Ee	40.03N	86.00W
Noboribetsu	28	Pc	42.25N	141.11 E
Noce ≈	14	Fd	46.09N	11.04 E
Nocra ◈	35	Fc	15.40N	39.55 E
Nodaway River ≈	45	Ig	39.54N	94.58W
Noēn	27	Hc	43.15N	102.20 E
Noeuf, Ile des- ◈	37b	Bb	6.14 S	53.03 E
Noeux-les-Mines	12	Ed	50.29N	2.40 E
Nogajskaja Step ⋎	16	Ng	44.15N	46.00 E
Nogales [Az.-U.S.]	43	Ee	31.21N	110.55W
Nogales [Mex.]	39	Hf	31.20N	110.56W
Nogaro	11	Fk	43.46N	0.02W
Nogat ≈	10	Pb	54.11N	19.15 E
Nōgata	29	Be	33.44N	130.44 E
Nogent-le-Rotrou	11	Gf	48.19N	0.50 E
Nogent-sur-Marne	12	Ef	48.50N	2.29 E
Nogent-sur-Oise	12	Ee	49.16N	2.28 E
Nogent-sur-Seine	11	Jf	48.29N	3.30 E
Noginsk [R.S.F.S.R.]	20	Ed	64.25N	91.10 E
Noginsk [R.S.F.S.R.]	19	Dd	55.54N	38.28 E
Nogliki	20	Jf	51.45N	143.15 E
Nōgo-Hakusan ▲	29	Ed	35.46N	136.31 E
Nogoyá	56	Id	32.24 S	59.48W
Nogoya, Arroyo- ≈	55	Ck	32.55 S	59.59W
Nógrád [2]	10	Ph	48.00N	19.35 E
Nogueira, Serra da- ⛰	13	Fc	41.42N	6.52W
Noguera Pallaresa ≈	13	Mb	42.15N	0.54 E
Noguera Ribagorçana/Noguera Ribagorzana ≈	13	Mc	41.40N	0.43 E
Noguera Ribagorzana/Noguera Ribagorçana ≈	13	Mc	41.40N	0.43 E
Noh, Laguna- ◒	48	Nh	18.40N	90.20W
Nohain ≈	11	Ig	47.24N	2.55 E
Noheji	28	Pd	40.52N	141.08 E
Nohfelden	12	Je	49.35N	7.09 E
Noidore, Rio- ≈	55	Fb	14.50 S	52.34W
Noir, Causse- ⌓	11	Jj	44.09N	3.15 E
Noire, Montagne- ▲	11	Ik	43.28N	2.18 E
Noires, Montagnes- ⛰	11	Cf	48.09N	3.40W
Noirétable	11	Ji	45.49N	3.46 E
Noirmoutier, Ile de- ◈	11	Dh	46.58N	2.12W
Noirmoutier-en-l'Ile	11	Dg	47.00N	2.15W
Nojima-Zaki ▶	29	Fd	34.54N	139.50 E
Nojiri-Ko ◒	29	Fc	36.49N	138.13 E
Noka	63c	Bb	10.40 S	166.03 E
Nokaneng	37	Cc	19.40 S	22.12 E
Nokia	7	Ff	61.28N	23.30 E
Nok Kundi	25	Cc	28.48N	62.46 E
Nokomis	46	Ma	51.30N	105.00W
Nokou	35	Ac	14.35N	14.47 E
Nokra	35	Fb	15.42N	39.56 E
Nol	8	Eg	57.55N	12.03 E
Nola [C.A.R.]	35	Be	3.32N	16.04 E
Nola [It.]	14	Ij	40.55N	14.33 E
Nolin Lake ◒	44	Dg	37.20N	86.10W
Nolinsk	19	Ed	57.33N	50.00 E
Nomad	58	Fe	6.21 S	142.12 E
Noma Omuramba ≈	37	Cc	19.10 S	22.16 E
Noma-Zaki ▶	29	Bf	31.25N	130.06 E
Nombre de Dios	48	Gf	23.51N	104.14W
Nome	39	Cc	64.30N	165.24W
Nomeny	12	If	48.54N	6.14 E
Nomo-Saki ▶	29	Ae	32.35N	129.45 E
Nomozaki	29	Ae	32.35N	129.45 E
Nomuka ◈	65b	Bb	20.15 S	174.48W
Nomuka Group ⧉	57	Jg	20.20 S	174.45W
Nomuka Iki ◈	65b	Bb	20.17 S	174.49W
Nomwin Atoll ⊙	57	Gd	8.32N	151.47 E
Nonacho Lake ◒	42	Gd	62.40N	109.30W
Nonancourt	12	Df	48.46N	1.12 E
Nonette ≈	12	Ee	49.12N	2.24 E
Nong'an	27	Mc	44.24N	125.08 E
Nong Han	25	Ke	17.21N	103.06 E
Nong Khai	22	Mh	17.52N	102.45 E
Nongoma	37	Ee	27.53 S	31.38 E
Nonoava	48	Fd	27.28N	106.44W
Nonouti Atoll ⊙	57	Ie	0.40 S	174.21 E
Nonsan	28	If	36.12N	127.05 E
Nonsuch Bay ◖	51d	Bb	17.03N	61.42W
Nontron	11	Gi	45.32N	0.40 E
Noord-Beveland ◈	12	Fc	51.35N	3.45 E
Noord-Brabant [3]	12	Gc	51.30N	5.00 E
Noord-Holland [3]	12	Gb	52.40N	4.50 E
Noordhollandskanaal ≡	11	Kb	52.55N	4.50 E
Noordoewer	37	Be	28.45 S	17.37 E
Noordoostpolder ⊠	11	Lb	52.42N	5.45 E
Noordoostpolder	12	Hb	52.42N	5.44 E
Noordoostpolder-Emmeloord	12	Hb	52.42N	5.44 E
Noordwijk aan Zee	11	Kb	52.14N	4.26 E
Noordwijk aan Zee, Noordwijk-	12	Gb	52.14N	4.26 E
Noordwijk-Noordwijk aan Zee	12	Gb	52.14N	4.26 E
Noordzee = North Sea (EN) ≋	5	Gd	55.20N	3.00 E
Noordzeekanaal ≡	11	Kb	52.30N	4.35 E
Noormarkku/Norrmark	8	Ic	61.35N	21.52 E
Noorvik	40	Gc	66.50N	161.12W
Nootka Island ◈	46	Bb	49.32N	126.42W
Nootka Sound ◖	46	Bb	49.33N	126.38W
Nóqui	36	Bd	5.50 S	13.27 E
Nora [It.]	14	Dk	39.00N	9.02 E
Nora [Swe.]	7	Dg	59.31N	15.02 E
Noranda	42	Jg	48.15N	79.01W
Noraskog ⊠	8	Fe	59.40N	14.50 E
Norberg	8	Fd	60.04N	15.56 E
Norcia	14	Hh	42.48N	13.05 E
Nord	41	Kb	81.45N	17.30W
Nord [Cam.] [3]	34	Hd	9.00N	13.50 E
Nord [Fr.] [3]	11	Jd	50.20N	3.40 E
Nord [U.V.] [3]	34	Ec	13.40N	2.50W
Nord, Canal du- ≡	11	Id	49.57N	2.55 E
Nord, Mer du- = North Sea (EN) ≋	5	Gd	55.20N	3.00 E
Nordausques	12	Ed	50.49N	2.05 E
Nordaustlandet ◈	67	Jd	79.48N	22.24 E
Nordborg	8	Ci	55.03N	9.45 E
Nordby	8	Ci	55.27N	8.25 E
Norddeutsches Tiefland = North German Plain (EN) ⊠	5	He	53.00N	11.00 E
Norden	10	Dc	53.36N	7.12 E
Nordenham	10	Ec	53.39N	8.29 E
Nordenskjölda, Ostrova- = Nordenskjöld, Archipelago (EN) ⧉	20	Ea	76.50N	96.00 E
Nordenskjöld Archipelago (EN) = Nordenskjölda, Ostrova- ⧉	20	Ea	76.50N	96.00 E
Norderney ◈	10	Dc	53.42N	7.10 E
Norderstedt	10	Fc	53.41N	9.58 E
Nordfjord ⊠	8	Bc	61.50N	6.15 E
Nordfjord ═	7	Af	61.55N	5.10 E
Nordfjordeid	7	Af	61.54N	6.00 E
Nordfold	7	Dc	67.46N	15.12 E
Nordfriesische Inseln = North Frisian Islands (EN) ⧉	10	Ea	54.50N	8.30 E
Nordfriesland ⊠	10	Eb	54.40N	8.55 E
Nordgau ⊠	10	Hg	49.15N	11.50 E
Nordgrønland = North Greenland (EN) [2]	41	Gc	79.30N	50.00W
Nordhausen	10	Ge	51.31N	10.48 E
Nordhordland ⊠	8	Ad	60.50N	5.50 E
Nordhorn	10	Dd	52.26N	7.05 E
Nord-Jylland [2]	8	Cg	57.15N	10.00 E
Nordkapp [Nor.] = North Cape (EN) ▶	5	Ia	71.11N	25.48 E
Nordkapp [Sval.] ▶	41	Nb	80.31N	20.00 E
Nordkinn ◨	5	Ia	71.08N	27.39 E
Nordkinnhalvøya ◨	7	Ga	70.55N	27.45 E
Nord-Kvaløy ◈	7	Ea	70.10N	19.11 E
Nordland [3]	7	Cc	67.06N	13.20 E
Nördlingen	10	Gh	48.51N	10.30 E
Nordloher Tief ≈	12	Ja	53.10N	7.45 E
Nordmark	8	Fe	59.50N	14.06 E
Nordmøre ⊠	8	Ca	63.00N	8.30 E
Nordostrundingen ▶	67	Le	81.30N	11.00W
Nord-Ostsee Kanal = Kiel Canal (EN) ≡	5	Ge	53.53N	9.08 E
Nord-Ouest [3]	34	Hd	6.30N	10.30 E
Nordøyane ⧉	8	Bb	62.40N	6.15 E
Nordreisa	7	Eb	69.46N	21.03 E
Nordre Rønner ◈	8	Dg	57.22N	10.56 E
Nordrhein-Westfalen = North Rhine-Westphalia (EN) [2]	10	De	51.30N	7.30 E
Nordsee = North Sea (EN) ≋	5	Gd	55.20N	3.00 E
Nordsjøen = North Sea (EN) ≋	5	Gd	55.20N	3.00 E
Nordskjobotn	7	Eb	69.13N	19.34 E
Nordsøen = North Sea (EN) ≋	5	Gd	55.20N	3.00 E
Nord Strand ◈	10	Eb	54.30N	8.55 E
Nordtiroler Kalkalpen ⛰	10	Hi	47.30N	11.30 E
Nord-Trøndelag [2]	7	Cd	64.25N	12.00 E
Nordwestfjord ═	41	Jd	71.30N	26.30W
Nore/An Fheoir ≈	9	Gi	52.25N	6.58W
Norefjell ▲	8	Cd	60.16N	9.29 E
Norefjorden ◒	8	Cd	60.10N	9.00 E
Norfolk ⊟	9	Oi	52.40N	1.05 E
Norfolk [3]	9	Mi	52.45N	0.40W
Norfolk [Nb.-U.S.]	43	Hc	42.02N	97.25W
Norfolk [Va.-U.S.]	39	Lf	38.40N	76.14W
Norfolk Island [5]	58	Hg	29.05 S	167.59 E
Norfolk Island ◈	57	Hg	29.05 S	167.59 E
Norfolk Ridge (EN) ⋀	57	Hg	29.00 S	168.00 E
Norfork Lake ◒	45	Jh	36.25N	92.10W
Norg	12	Ia	53.04N	6.32 E
Norge = Norway (EN) [1]	6	Gc	62.00N	10.00 E
Norheimsund	7	Bf	60.22N	6.08 E
Norikura-Dake ▲	29	Ec	36.06N	137.33 E
Norilsk	22	Kc	69.20N	88.06 E
Normal	45	Lf	40.31N	88.59W
Norman	43	Hd	35.15N	97.26W
Norman, Lake- ◒	44	Gh	35.35N	81.00W
Normanby Island ◈	60	Ej	10.00 S	151.00 E
Normanby River ≈	59	Ib	14.25 S	144.08 E
Normand, Bocage- ♣	11	Ef	49.00N	1.10W
Normandie = Normandy (EN) ⊟	11	Gf	49.00N	0.10 E
Normandie = Normandy (EN) ⊠	5	Gf	49.00N	0.10 E
Normandie, Collines de- = Normandy Hills (EN) ∩	5	Ff	48.50N	0.40W
Normandin	44	Ka	48.52N	72.30W
Normandy (EN) = Normandie ⊟	11	Gf	49.00N	0.10 E
Normandy (EN) = Normandie ⊠	5	Gf	49.00N	0.10 E
Normandy Hills (EN) = Normandie, Collines de- ∩	5	Ff	48.50N	0.40W
Norman Island ◈	51a	Db	18.20N	64.37W
Norman River ≈	59	Ic	17.28 S	140.39 E
Normanton	58	Ff	17.40 S	141.05 E
Norman Wells	39	Gc	65.17N	126.51W
Norquinco	56	Ff	41.51 S	70.54W
Norra Dellen ◒	8	Gc	61.55N	16.40 E
Norrahammar	8	Fg	57.42N	14.06 E
Norrala	8	Gc	61.22N	16.59 E
Norra Midsjöbanken ▤	8	Gh	56.10N	17.30 E
Norra Ny	7	Cf	60.24N	13.15 E
Norra Storfjället ▲	7	Dd	65.53N	15.14 E
Norrbotten [2]	7	Ec	67.26N	19.35 E
Nørre Åby	8	Ci	55.27N	9.54 E
Nørre Alslev	8	Dj	54.54N	11.54 E
Nørre-Nebel	8	Ci	55.47N	8.18 E
Norrent-Fontes	12	Ed	50.35N	2.24 E
Nørresundby	7	Bh	57.04N	9.55 E
Norrhult	7	Dh	57.08N	15.10 E
Norris Lake ◒	44	Fg	36.20N	83.55W
Norristown	44	Je	40.07N	75.20W
Norrköping	6	Hd	58.36N	16.11 E
Norrland ⊠	5	Hc	64.27N	17.20 E
Norrland ⊟	7	Dd	65.00N	18.00 E
Norrmark/Noormarkku	8	Ic	61.35N	21.52 E
Norrsundet	8	Gd	60.56N	17.08 E
Norrtälje	7	Eg	59.46N	18.42 E
Norseman	58	Dh	32.12 S	121.46 E
Norsewood	62	Gd	40.04 S	176.13 E
Norsjö	7	Ed	64.55N	19.29 E
Norsjø ◒	8	Ce	59.20N	9.20 E
Norsk	20	Hf	52.20N	129.59 E
Norske Havet = Norwegian, Sea (EN) ≋	5	Gc	70.00N	2.00 E
Norske Øer ⧉	41	Kc	79.00N	18.00W
Norsoup	63b	Cc	16.04 S	167.23 E
Norte, Baia- ◖	55	Hh	27.30 S	48.35W
Norte, Cabo- [Braz.] ▶	54	Ic	1.40N	50.00W
Norte, Cabo- [Pas.] ▶	65d	Ab	27.03 S	109.24W
Norte, Canal do- ═	54	Hc	0.30N	50.30W
Norte, Punta- ▶	56	Hf	42.04 S	63.45W
Norte, Serra do- ⛰	54	Gf	11.00 S	59.00W
Norte del Cabo San Antonio, Punta- ▶	56	Ie	36.17 S	56.47W
Norte de Santander [2]	54	Db	8.00N	73.00W
Nortelândia	54	Gf	14.25 S	56.48W
North, Cape - ▶	42	Lg	47.02N	60.25W
North Adams	44	Kd	42.42N	73.02W
Northallerton	9	Lg	54.20N	1.26W
Northam [Austl.]	58	Ch	31.39 S	116.40 E
Northam [S.Afr.]	37	Dd	24.58 S	27.11 E
North America ■	38	Jf	40.00N	95.00W
North American Basin (EN) ◡	3	Cf	30.00N	60.00W
Northampton ⊟	9	Mi	52.30N	1.00W
Northampton [Austl.]	59	Ce	28.21 S	114.37 E
Northampton [Eng.-U.K.]	9	Mi	52.14N	0.54W
Northampton [Ma.-U.S.]	44	Kd	42.19N	72.38W
Northampton Seamounts (EN) ⩚	57	Jb	25.20N	172.04W
Northamptonshire [3]	9	Mi	52.25N	0.55W
North Andaman ◈	25	If	13.15N	92.55 E
North Arm ◖	42	Gd	62.00N	114.30W
North Astrolabe Reef ❋	63d	Bc	18.39 S	178.32 E
North Augusta	44	Gi	33.30N	81.58W
North Aulatsivik ◈	42	Le	59.45N	64.04W
North Australian Basin ◡	3	Hk	14.30 S	116.30 E
North Battleford	39	Id	52.47N	108.17W
North Bay	39	Le	46.19N	79.28W
North Belcher Islands ⧉	42	Je	56.45N	79.45W
North Berwick	9	Ke	56.04N	2.44W
North Buganda [3]	36	Fb	0.50N	32.10 E
North Caicos ◈	49	Lc	21.56N	71.59W
North Canadian River ≈	43	Hd	35.17N	95.31W
North Cape ▶	57	Ih	34.25 S	173.03 E
North Cape (EN) = Nordkapp [Nor.] ▶	5	Ia	71.11N	25.48 E
North Caribou Lake ◒	42	If	52.48N	90.45W
North Carolina [2]	43	Ld	35.30N	80.00W
North Channel ═	42	Jg	46.02N	82.50W
North Channel/Sruth na Maoile ═	5	Fd	55.10N	5.40W
Northchapel	12	Bc	51.03N	0.38W
North Charleston	44	Hi	32.53N	80.00W
North Chicago	45	Me	42.20N	87.51W
North Cove	46	Cc	46.47N	124.06W
North Dakota [2]	43	Gb	47.30N	100.15W
North Downs ∩	9	Nj	51.20N	0.10 E
North East	44	Hd	42.13N	79.51W
North-East [3]	37	Dd	21.00 S	27.30 E
Northeast Cape	40	Fd	63.18N	168.42W
North-Eastern [3]	36	Hb	1.00N	40.15 E
Northeast Islands ⧉	64d	Ba	7.36N	151.57 E
Northeast Pacific Basin (EN) ◡	3	Lg	20.00N	140.00W
Northeast Pass ═	64d	Ba	7.30N	151.59 E
North East Point ▶	64g	Bb	1.57N	157.16W
Northeast Point [Bah.] ▶	49	Kc	21.18N	72.54W
Northeast Point [Bah.] ▶	49	Kb	22.43N	73.50W
Northeast Providence Channel ═	47	Ic	25.40N	77.09W
Northeim	10	Fe	51.42N	10.00 E
North Entrance ═	64a	Bb	7.59N	134.37 E
Northern [Ghana] [3]	34	Ed	9.30N	1.00W
Northern [Mwi.] [3]	36	Fe	11.00 S	34.00 E
Northern [S.L.] [3]	34	Cd	9.15N	11.45W
Northern [Ug.] [3]	36	Fb	2.45N	32.45 E
Northern [Zam.] [3]	36	Fe	11.00 S	31.00 E
Northern Cay ◈	49	De	17.27N	87.28W
Northern Cook Islands ⧉	57	Kf	10.00 S	161.00W
Northern Dvina (EN) = Severnaja Dvina ≈	5	Kc	64.32N	40.30 E
Northern Guinea ⊠	30	Gh	8.30N	1.00W
Northern Indian Lake ◒	42	He	57.20N	97.17W
Northern Ireland [2]	9	Gg	54.40N	6.45W
Northern Mariana Islands [5]	58	Fc	16.00N	145.30 E
Northern Sporades (EN) = Vórioi Sporádhes, Nísoi- ⧉	5	Ih	39.15N	23.55 E
Northern Territory	59	Gc	20.00 S	134.00 E
Northern Urals (EN) = Severny Ural ⛰	5	Lc	62.00N	59.00 E
Northern Uvals (EN) = Severnyje Uvaly ∩	5	Kd	59.30N	49.00 E
North Esk ≈	9	Ke	56.45N	2.30W
Northfield	45	Jd	44.27N	93.09W
North Fiji Basin (EN) ◡	3	Jk	16.00 S	174.00 E
North Foreland ▶	9	Oj	51.23N	1.27 E
North Fork Grand River ≈	45	Ed	45.47N	102.16W
North Fork John Day River ≈	46	Fd	44.45N	119.38W
North Fork Moreau River ≈	45	Ed	45.09N	102.50W
North Fork Pass ⌣	42	Dd	64.00N	138.00W
North Fork Powder River ≈	46	Le	43.40N	106.30W
North Fork Red ≈	45	Gi	34.25N	99.14W
North Fort Myers	44	Gl	26.40N	81.54W
North Frisian Islands (EN) = Nordfriesische Inseln ⧉	10	Ea	54.50N	8.30 E
North German Plain (EN) = Norddeutsches Tiefland ⊠	5	He	53.00N	11.00 E
North Greenland (EN) = Nordgrønland [2]	41	Gc	79.30N	50.00W
North Highlands	46	Eg	38.40N	121.23W
North Horr	36	Gb	3.19N	37.04 E
North Island [N.Z.] ◈	57	Ih	39.00 S	176.00 E
North Island [Sey.] ◈	37b	Bc	10.07 S	51.11 E
North Kent ◈	42	Ia	76.40N	90.15W
North Korea (EN) = Chosŏn M.I.K. [1]	22	Oe	40.00N	127.30 E
North Lakhimpur	25	Ic	27.14N	94.07 E
Northland [2]	62	Ea	35.30 S	173.40 E
North Las Vegas	46	Hh	36.12N	115.07W
North Lincoln Land ⊠	42	Ja	76.15N	80.00W
North Little Rock	43	Ie	34.46N	92.14W
North Loup River ≈	45	Gf	41.17N	98.23W
North Magnetic Pole (1980)	67	Qd	77.03N	101.08W
North Malosmadulu Atoll ⊙	25a	Ba	5.35N	72.55 E
North Mamm Peak ▲	45	Cg	39.23N	107.52W
North Mayreau Channel	51n	Bb	12.41N	61.20W
North Miami	44	Gm	25.56N	80.09W
North Minch ═	5	Fd	58.05N	5.55W
North Palisade ▲	46	Fh	37.10N	118.38W
North Pass [F.S.M.] ═	64d	Ba	7.41N	151.48 E
North Pass [U.S.] ═	45	Ll	29.10N	89.15W
North Platte	43	Gc	41.08N	100.46W
North Platte ≈	38	Ie	41.15N	100.45W
North Point ▶	64n	Ab	10.22 S	161.02W
North Point [Bar.] ▶	51q	Ab	13.20N	59.36W
North Pole	67	Ge	90.00N	0.00
Northport	44	Di	33.14N	87.35W
North Powder	46	Gd	45.03N	117.55W
North Raccoon River ≈	45	Jf	41.35N	93.31W
North Reef ❋	63a	Ee	12.13 S	160.04 E
North Rhine-Westphalia (EN) = Nordrhein-Westfalen [2]	10	De	51.30N	7.30 E
North Rim	46	Ih	36.12N	112.03W
North River	42	Ie	58.53N	94.42W
North Rona ◈	9	Hb	59.10N	5.40W
North Ronaldsay ◈	9	Kb	59.25N	2.30W
North Saskatchewan ≈	38	Id	53.15N	105.06W
North Sea ≋	5	Gd	55.20N	3.00 E
North Sea (EN) = Noordzee ≋	5	Gd	55.20N	3.00 E
North Sea (EN) = Nord, Mer du- ≋	5	Gd	55.20N	3.00 E
North Sea (EN) = Nordsee ≋	5	Gd	55.20N	3.00 E
North Sea (EN) = Nordsjøen ≋	5	Gd	55.20N	3.00 E
North Sea (EN) = Nordsøen ≋	5	Gd	55.20N	3.00 E
North Sentinel ◈	25	If	11.33N	92.15 E
North Shoshone Peak ▲	46	Gg	39.10N	117.29W
North Siberian Plain (EN) = Severo-Sibirskaja Niz. ▭	21	Mb	72.00N	104.00 E
North Sound ═	51d	Bb	17.07N	61.45W
North Sound ◖	49	Gd	19.25N	81.26W
North Stradbroke Island ◈	59	Ke	27.35 S	153.30 E
North Taranaki Bight ◖	62	Fc	38.50 S	174.25 E
North Thompson ≈	42	Ff	50.41N	120.11W
North Tokelau Trough (EN) ⌵	3	Kj	3.00 S	165.00W
North Tonawanda	44	Hd	43.02N	78.54W
North Trap ◈	62	Bg	47.20 S	167.55 E
North Tyne ≈	9	Kg	54.59N	2.08W
North Uist ◈	9	Fd	57.37N	7.22W
Northumberland [3]	9	Kf	55.15N	2.10W
Northumberland ⊟	9	Kf	55.15N	2.05W
Northumberland Islands ⧉	57	Gg	21.40 S	150.00 E
Northumberland Strait ═	42	Lg	46.00N	63.30W
North Umpqua River ≈	46	De	43.16N	123.27W
North Vancouver	46	Db	49.19N	123.04W
North Walsham	12	Db	52.49N	1.23 E
Northway	40	Kd	62.59N	141.43W
North West Bluff ✱	51c	Bc	16.49N	62.12W
North West Cape ▶	57	Cg	21.45 S	114.10 E
North-Western [3]	36	Ee	13.00 S	25.00 E
Northwest Frontier [3]	25	Eb	33.00N	70.30 E
North West Highlands ∩	5	Fd	57.30N	5.00W
Northwest Pacific Basin (EN) ◡	3	Je	40.00N	155.00 E
North West Point ▶	64g	Ab	2.02N	157.30W
Northwest Providence Channel ≡	44	Hl	26.10N	78.20W
Northwest Reef ✱	64a	Bb	7.59N	134.33 E
North West River	42	Lf	53.32N	60.09W
Northwest Territories [3]	42	Hc	66.00N	102.00W
Northwich	9	Kh	53.16N	2.32W
North York Moors	9	Mg	54.25N	0.50W
North Yorkshire [3]	9	Lg	54.15N	1.40W
Norton [Ks.-U.S.]	43	Gd	39.50N	100.01W
Norton [Va.-U.S.]	44	Fg	36.56N	82.37W
Norton [Zimb.]	37	Ec	17.53 S	30.41 E
Norton Bay ◖	40	Gd	64.45N	161.15W
Norton Sound ═	38	Cc	64.45N	161.15W
Norvegia, Kapp- ▶	66	Bf	71.25 S	12.18W
Norwalk [Ct.-U.S.]	44	Ke	41.07N	73.27W
Norwalk [Oh.-U.S.]	44	Fe	41.14N	82.37W
Norway	44	Dc	45.47N	87.55W
Norway (EN) = Norge [1]	6	Gc	62.00N	10.00 E
Norway Bay ◖	42	Hb	71.00N	104.35W
Norway House	42	Hf	53.58N	97.50W
Norwegian Basin (EN) ◡	3	Dc	68.00N	2.00W
Norwegian Bay ◖	42	Ij	77.45N	90.30W
Norwegian Sea (EN) = Norske Havet ≋	5	Gc	70.00N	2.00 E
Norwegian Trench (EN) ⌵	5	Gd	59.00N	4.30 E
Norwich [Ct.-U.S.]	44	Ke	41.32N	72.05W
Norwich [Eng.-U.K.]	6	Ge	52.38N	1.18 E
Norwich [N.Y.-U.S.]	44	Jd	42.33N	75.33W
Norwich Airport ✈	12	Db	52.40N	1.18 E
Norwood	44	Ef	39.10N	84.28W
Nosappu-Misaki ▶	29a	Db	43.23N	145.47 E
Noshappu-Misaki ▶	29a	Ba	45.27N	141.39 E
Noshiro	27	Pc	40.12N	140.02 E
Nosovaja	19	Fb	68.15N	54.31 E
Nosovka	19	De	50.54N	31.37 E
Nosratābād	23	Id	29.54N	59.59 E
Nossa Senhora das Candeias	54	Kf	12.40 S	38.33W
Nossa Senhora do Livramento	55	Db	15.48 S	56.22W
Noss Head ▶	9	Jc	58.30N	3.05W
Nossob ≈	30	Jk	26.55 S	20.40 E
Nossop ≈	37	Ce	26.55 S	20.40 E
Nosy-Be ◈	30	Lj	13.20 S	48.15 E
Nosy-Be	31	Lj	13.22 S	48.16 E
Nosy-Varika	37	Hd	20.35 S	48.30 E
Nota ≈	7	Hb	68.07N	30.10 E
Notch Peak ▲	46	Ig	39.08N	113.24W
Noteć ≈	10	Ld	52.44N	15.26 E
Notecka, Puszcza- ♣	10	Ld	52.45N	16.00 E
Note Kemopla ▶	63c	b	10.55 S	165.51 E
Notengo, Laguna de- ◎	48	Ji	16.15N	98.10W
Notía Píndhos ⛰	15	Ej	39.30N	21.20 E
Nótioi Sporádhes = Dodecanese (EN) ⧉	5	Ih	36.00N	27.00 E
Nótios Evvoïkós Kólpos ◖	15	Gk	38.20N	23.50 E
Nötö ◈	8	Ie	60.00N	21.45 E
Noto [It.]	14	Jn	36.53N	15.04 E
Noto [Jap.]	28	Nf	37.18N	137.09 E
Noto, Golfo di- ◖	14	Jn	36.50N	15.10 E
Notodden	7	Bg	59.34N	9.17 E
Noto-Hantō ◨	27	Od	37.20N	137.00 E
Noto-Jima ◈	29	Ec	37.07N	137.00 E
Notoro-Ko ◒	29a	Da	44.05N	144.10 E
Notoro-Misaki ▶	29a	Da	44.07N	144.15 E
Notranjsko ⊠	14	Ie	45.46N	14.26 E
Notre-Dame, Monts- ⛰	38	Me	48.00N	69.00W
Notre Dame Bay ◖	42	Mg	49.50N	55.00W
Notre-Dame-de-Courson	12	Cf	48.59N	0.16 E
Notre-Dame-de-Gravenchon	12	Ce	49.29N	0.35 E
Notre Dame-du-Lac	44	Mb	47.38N	68.49W
Notre-Dame-du-Nord	44	Hb	47.36N	79.29W
Notsé	34	Fd	6.59N	1.12 E
Notsuke-Zaki ▶	29a	Db	43.34N	145.19 E
Nottawasaga Bay ◖	44	Gc	44.40N	80.30W
Nottaway ≈	38	Ld	51.25N	79.50W
Notterøy ◈	8	De	59.15N	10.25 E
Nottingham	6	Fe	52.58N	1.10W
Nottingham ◈	42	Jd	63.20N	78.00W
Nottingham ⊟	9	Mh	53.05N	1.00W
Nottinghamshire [3]	9	Mh	53.10N	0.55W
Nottoway River ≈	44	Ig	36.33N	76.55W
Nottuln	12	Jc	51.56N	7.21 E
Notukeu Creek ≈	46	Lb	49.55N	106.30W
Nouâdhibou	31	Ff	20.54N	17.01W
Nouâdhibou, Dahklet- ◖	32	De	21.00N	16.50W
Nouâdhibou, Râs- = Blanc Cape- (EN) ▶	30	Ff	20.46N	17.03W
Nouakchott	31	Fg	18.07N	15.59W
Nouakchott, District de- [3]	32	Df	18.06N	15.57W
Nouamrhar	32	Df	19.22N	16.31W
Nouméa	58	Hg	22.16 S	166.26 E
Nouna	34	Ec	12.44N	3.52W
Noupoort	37	Cf	31.10 S	24.57 E

Index Symbols

[1] Independent Nation
[2] State, Region
[3] District, County
[4] Municipality
[5] Colony, Dependency
■ Continent
⊠ Physical Region

⊟ Historical or Cultural Region
▲ Mount, Mountain
▲ Volcano
∩ Hill
⛰ Mountains, Mountain Range
∩ Hills, Escarpment
⌓ Plateau, Upland

⌣ Pass, Gap
▭ Plain, Lowland
≈ Delta
▭ Salt Flat
∨ Valley, Canyon
◠ Crater, Cave
⁂ Karst Features

⌄ Depression
▦ Polder
∵ Desert, Dunes
♣ Forest, Woods
⋎ Heath, Steppe
⊕ Oasis
▶ Cape, Point

⌒ Coast, Beach
◖ Cliff
◨ Peninsula
⋈ Isthmus
▱ Sandbank
◈ Island
⊙ Atoll

✱ Rock, Reef
⧉ Islands, Archipelago
✱ Rocks, Reefs
❋ Coral Reef
◎ Well, Spring
◎ Geyser
≈ River, Stream

≈ Waterfall Rapids
◒ River Mouth, Estuary
◒ Lake
◒ Salt Lake
◒ Intermittent Lake
◒ Reservoir
∴ Swamp, Pond

≡ Canal
❄ Glacier
❄ Ice Shelf, Pack Ice
≋ Ocean
≋ Sea
◖ Gulf, Bay
═ Strait, Fjord

◎ Lagoon
▤ Bank
⩚ Seamount
⩚ Tablemount
⋀ Ridge
▱ Shelf
◡ Basin

⌇ Escarpment, Sea Scarp
⌇ Fracture
⌵ Trench, Abyss
⚘ National Park, Reserve
✦ Point of Interest
✦ Recreation Site
◠ Cave, Cavern

▲ Historic Site
∴ Ruins
▥ Wall, Walls
✝ Church, Abbey
✝ Temple
✦ Scientific Station
✈ Airport

⚓ Port
✱ Lighthouse
⚒ Mine
◠ Tunnel
═ Dam, Bridge

Nouveau-Comptoir	42	Jf	52.35N	78.40W
Nouveau-Québec, Cratère du- = New Quebec Crater (EN) ◡	42	Kd	61.30N	73.55W
Nouvelle-Calédonie = New Caledonia (EN) ⑤	58	Hg	21.30S	165.30 E
Nouvelle-Calédonie=New Caledonia (EN) ◆	57	Hg	21.30S	165.30 E
Nouvelle-France, Cap de - ►	42	Kd	62.33N	73.35W
Nouvelles Hébrides/New Hebrides ❖	57	Hf	16.01S	167.01 E
Nouvion	12	Dd	50.12N	1.47 E
Nouzonville	11	Ke	49.49N	4.45 E
Novabad	18	He	39.01N	70.09 E
Nová Baňa	10	Oh	48.26N	18.39 E
Nová Bystřice	10	Lg	49.02N	15.06 E
Nova Cruz	54	Ke	6.28S	35.26W
Nova Esperança	55	Ff	23.08S	52.13W
Nova Friburgo	54	Jh	22.16S	42.32W
Nova Gaia	36	Ce	10.05S	17.32 E
Nova Gorica	14	He	45.57N	13.39 E
Nova Gradiška	14	Le	45.16N	17.23 E
Nova Granada	55	He	20.29S	49.19W
Nova Iguaçu	53	Lh	22.45S	43.27W
Novaja Igirma	20	Fe	57.10N	103.55 E
Novaja-Ivanovka	15	Md	45.59N	29.04 E
Novaja Kahovka	16	Hf	46.43N	33.23 E
Novaja Kazanka	16	Pe	48.58N	49.37 E
Novaja Ladoga	7	Hf	60.05N	32.16 E
Novaja Ljálja	19	Gd	59.03N	60.36 E
Novaja Odessa	16	Gf	47.18N	31.47 E
Novaja Sibir, Ostrov-=New Siberia (EN) ◆	21	Qb	75.00N	149.00 E
Novaja Vodolaga	16	Ie	49.45N	35.52 E
Novaja Zemlja=Novaya Zemlya (EN) ❖	21	Hb	74.00N	57.00 E
Nova Lamego	34	Cc	12.17N	14.13W
Nova Lima	54	Jh	19.59S	43.51W
Nova Londrina	55	Ff	22.45S	53.00W
Nova Mambone	37	Fd	20.58S	35.00 E
Nova Olinda do Norte	54	Gd	3.45S	59.03W
Nová Paka	10	Lf	50.29N	15.31 E
Nova Prata	55	Gi	28.47S	51.36W
Novara	14	Ce	45.28N	8.38 E
Nova Roma	55	Ia	13.51S	46.57W
Nova Russas	54	Jd	4.42S	40.34W
Nova Scotia ③	42	Lh	45.00N	63.00W
Nova Scotia ◧	38	Me	45.00N	63.00W
Nova Sintra	32	Cf	14.54N	24.40W
Nova Sofala	37	Ed	20.10S	34.44 E
Novato	46	Dg	38.06N	122.34W
Nova Varoš	15	Cf	43.28N	19.49 E
Nova Venécia	54	Jg	18.43S	40.24W
Novaya Zemlya (EN)= Novaja Zemlja ❖	21	Hb	74.00N	57.00 E
Nova Zagora	15	Jg	42.29N	26.01 E
Novelda	13	Lf	38.23N	0.46W
Novellara	14	Ef	44.51N	10.44 E
Nové Mesto nad Váhom	10	Nh	48.46N	17.50 E
Nové Zámky	10	Oi	47.59N	18.11 E
Novgorod	6	Jd	58.31N	31.17 E
Novgorodka	8	Mg	57.00N	28.37 E
Novgorod-Severski	19	De	52.01N	33.16 E
Novgorodskaja Oblast ③	19	Dd	58.20N	32.40 E
Novi Bečej	15	Dd	45.36N	20.08 E
Novigrad [Yugo.]	14	He	45.19N	13.34 E
Novigrad [Yugo.]	14	Jf	44.11N	15.33 E
Novi Kričim	15	Hg	42.03N	24.28 E
Novi Ligure	14	Cf	44.46N	8.47 E
Novillero	48	Gf	22.21N	105.39W
Novion-Porcien	12	Ge	49.36N	4.25 E
Novi Pazar [Bul.]	15	Kf	43.21N	27.12 E
Novi Pazar [Yugo.]	15	Df	43.08N	20.31 E
Novi Sad	6	Hf	45.15N	19.50 E
Novi Travnik	14	Lf	44.10N	17.39 E
Novi Vinodolski	14	Ie	45.08N	14.47 E
Novoaleksandrovsk	16	Lg	45.24N	41.14 E
Novoaleksejevka [Kaz.-U.S.S.R.]	16	Sd	50.08N	55.42 E
Novoaleksejevka [Ukr.-U.S.S.R.]	16	If	46.16N	34.39 E
Novoaltajsk	20	Df	53.24N	83.58 E
Novoanninski	19	Ee	50.31N	42.45 E
Novoarhangelsk	16	Ge	48.39N	30.50 E
Novo Aripuanã	54	Fe	5.08S	60.22W
Novoazovsk	16	Kf	47.05N	38.05 E
Novobirjusinski	20	Ee	56.58N	97.55 E
Novobogdanovka	16	If	47.05N	35.18 E
Novočeboksarsk	7	Lh	56.08N	47.29 E
Novočeremšansk	7	Mi	54.23N	50.10 E
Novočerkassk	19	Ef	47.25N	40.03 E
Novodevičje	7	Lj	53.35N	48.51 E
Novograd-Volynski	19	Ce	50.36N	27.36 E
Novogrudok	16	Dc	53.37N	25.50 E
Nôvo Hamburgo	56	Jc	29.41S	51.08W
Novohopërsk	16	Ld	51.06N	41.37 E
Novo Horizonte	55	He	21.28S	49.13W
Novoizborsk	8	Mg	57.43N	28.05 E
Novojenisejsk	20	Ee	58.19N	92.27 E
Novojerudinski	20	Ee	59.47N	93.30 E
Novokačalinsk	20	Ig	45.05N	131.59 E
Novokazalinsk	22	Ie	45.50N	62.10 E
Novokubansk	16	Lg	45.06N	41.01 E
Novokujbyševsk	19	Ee	53.08N	49.58 E
Novokuzneck	22	Kd	53.45N	87.06 E
Novolazarevskaja ⊗	66	Cf	70.46S	11.50 E
Novolukoml	7	Gi	54.38N	29.07 E
Novo Mesto	14	Je	45.48N	15.10 E
Novomičurinsk	7	Ji	54.02N	39.48 E
Novomihajlovka	20	Ih	44.17N	133.50 E
Novo Miloševo	15	Dd	45.43N	20.18 E
Novomirgorod	16	Ge	48.45N	31.39 E
Novomoskovsk [R.S.F.S.R.]	6	Je	54.05N	38.13 E
Novomoskovsk [Ukr.-U.S.S.R.]	19	Df	48.37N	35.16 E
Novonikolajevski	16	Md	50.55N	42.24 E
Novoorsk	19	Fe	51.24N	58.59 E
Novopokrovskaja	16	Lg	45.56N	40.42 E
Novopolock	19	Cd	55.31N	28.40 E
Novorossijsk	6	Jg	44.45N	37.45 E
Novorybnaja	20	Fb	72.50N	105.45 E
Novoržev	19	Cd	57.02N	29.20 E
Novo-Šahtinsk	19	Df	47.47N	39.54 E
Novoselica	15	Ja	48.13N	26.17 E
Novoselje	8	Mf	58.05N	29.00 E
Novoselki	10	Ud	52.04N	24.25 E
Novoselovo	20	Ef	54.55N	91.00 E
Novosergijevka	19	Fe	52.03N	53.39 E
Novosibirsk	22	Kd	55.02N	82.55 E
Novosibirskaja Oblast ③	20	Ce	55.30N	80.00 E
Novosibirskije Ostrova= New Siberian Islands (EN) ❖	21	Qb	75.00N	142.00 E
Novosibirskoje Vodohranilišče ◙	20	Df	54.40N	82.35 E
Novosil	16	Jc	52.59N	37.01 E
Novosineglazovski	17	Ji	55.05N	61.25 E
Novosokolniki	19	Dd	56.19N	30.12 E
Novospasskoje	7	Lj	53.09N	47.44 E
Novotroick	19	Fe	51.12N	58.35 E
Novotroickoje	19	Hg	43.39N	73.45 E
Novoukrainka	16	Ge	48.19N	31.32 E
Novouljanovsk	7	Li	54.10N	48.23 E
Novouzensk	19	Ee	50.29N	48.08 E
Novovjatsk	7	Lg	58.31N	49.43 E
Novovolynsk	19	Ce	50.46N	24.09 E
Novovoronežski	16	Kd	51.17N	39.16 E
Novozybkov	19	De	52.32N	32.00 E
Novska	14	Ke	45.20N	16.59 E
Novy Bug	16	Hf	47.43N	32.29 E
Nový Bydžov	10	Lf	50.15N	15.29 E
Novy Jaričev	10	Ug	49.50N	24.21 E
Novyje Aneny	15	Mc	46.53N	29.13 E
Novyje Burasy	16	Oc	52.06N	46.06 E
Nový Jičín	10	Og	49.36N	18.01 E
Novy Oskol	19	De	50.43N	37.54 E
Novy Pogost	8	Li	55.30N	27.32 E
Novy Port	22	Jc	67.40N	72.52 E
Novy Tap	17	Mh	56.55N	67.15 E
Novy Terek ∿	16	Oh	43.37N	47.25 E
Novy Uzen	19	Fg	43.19N	52.55 E
Novy Vasjugan	20	Ce	58.34N	76.29 E
Novy Zaj	7	Mi	55.17N	52.02 E
Nowa Dęba	10	Rf	50.26N	21.46 E
Nowa Huta, Kraków-	10	Qf	50.04N	20.05 E
Nowa Ruda	10	Mf	50.35N	16.31 E
Nowa Sarzyna	10	Sf	50.23N	22.22 E
Nowa Sól	10	Le	51.48N	15.44 E
Now Bandegān	24	Oh	28.52N	53.53 E
Nowbarān	24	Me	35.08N	49.42 E
Nowdesheh	24	Le	35.11N	46.15 E
Nowe	10	Oc	53.40N	18.43 E
Nowe Miasto Lubawskie	10	Pc	53.27N	19.35 E
Nowe Miasto-nad-Pilicą	10	Qe	51.38N	20.35 E
Nowe Warpno	10	Kc	53.44N	14.20 E
Nowfel low Shātow	24	Ne	34.27N	50.55 E
Nowgong	25	Ic	26.21N	92.40 E
Nowogard	10	Lc	53.40N	15.08 E
Nowogród	10	Rc	53.15N	21.53 E
Nowood River ∿	46	Ld	44.17N	107.58W
Nowra	59	Kf	34.53S	150.36 E
Nowshahr	24	Nd	36.39N	51.31 E
Nowy Dwór Gdański	10	Pb	54.13N	19.06 E
Nowy Dwór Mazowiecki	10	Qd	52.26N	20.43 E
Nowy Korczyn	10	Qf	50.20N	20.50 E
Nowy Sącz ②	10	Qg	49.40N	20.40 E
Nowy Sącz	10	Qg	49.38N	20.42 E
Nowy Targ	10	Qg	49.29N	20.02 E
Nowy Tomyśl	10	Md	52.20N	16.07 E
Noya	13	Db	42.47N	8.53W
Noya/Anoia ∿	13	Nc	41.28N	1.56 E
Noyant	11	Gg	47.31N	0.08 E
Noyon	11	Ie	49.35N	3.00 E
Nozaki-Jima ◆	29	Ae	33.11N	129.08 E
Nozay	11	Eg	47.34N	1.38W
Nsanje	36	Gf	16.55S	35.16 E
Nsawan	34	Ed	5.48N	0.21W
Nschodnia ∿	10	Rf	50.30N	21.18 E
Nsefu	36	Fe	13.03S	32.07 E
Nsukka	34	Gd	6.52N	7.23 E
Ntadembele	36	Cc	2.11S	17.08 E
Ntchisi	36	Fe	13.22S	34.00 E
Ntem ∿	30	Hh	2.10N	9.57 E
Ntoum	36	Ab	0.22N	9.47 E
Ntui	34	He	4.27N	11.38 E
Ntusi	36	Fb	0.03N	31.13 E
Nuageuses, Iles- ❖	30	Nm	48.40S	68.58 E
Nuanetsi	37	Ed	21.22S	30.45 E
Nuanetsi ∿	30	Kk	22.40S	31.49 E
Nūbah, Jibāl an- ⛰	30	Kg	12.00N	30.45 E
Nubian Desert (EN)= Nūbiyah, Aş Şaḩrā' an- ⁘	30	Kf	20.30N	33.00 E
Nūbiyah, Aş Şaḩrā' an-= Nubian Desert (EN) ⁘	30	Kf	20.30N	33.00 E
Nudha ◆	63a	Ec	9.32S	160.48 E
Nueces Plain ▁	43	Hf	28.30N	99.15W
Nueces River ∿	43	Hf	27.50N	97.30W
Nueltin Lake ◍	38	Jc	60.50N	99.30W
Nü'er He ∿	28	Fd	41.06N	121.09 E
Nueva Asunción ③	55	Be	21.00S	60.20W
Nueva Ciudad Guerrero	48	Jd	26.35N	99.15W
Nueva Esparta ②	54	Fa	11.00N	64.00W
Nueva Germania	55	Df	23.54S	56.34W
Nueva Gerona	47	Hd	21.53N	82.48W
Nueva Imperial	56	Fe	38.44S	72.57W
Nueva Italia de Ruiz	48	Hh	19.01N	102.06W
Nueva Ocotepeque	49	Cf	14.24N	89.13W
Nueva Palmira	55	Ck	33.53S	58.25W
Nueva Rosita	39	Ig	27.57N	101.13W
Nueva San Salvador	47	Gf	13.41N	89.17W
Nueva Segovia ③	49	Dg	13.40N	86.10W
Nueve de Julio	56	He	35.27S	60.52W
Nuevitas	47	Id	21.33N	77.16W
Nuevitas, Bahía de- ⊂	49	Ic	21.30N	77.12W
Nuevo, Cayo- ✣	48	Mg	21.51N	92.05W
Nuevo, Golfo- ⊂	52	Jj	42.42S	64.36W
Nuevo Berlín	55	Ck	32.59S	58.03W
Nuevo Casas Grandes	39	If	30.25N	107.55W
Nuevo Laredo	39	Jg	27.30N	99.31W
Nuevo León ②	47	Ec	25.40N	100.00W
Nuevo Mundo, Cerro- ▲	54	Eh	21.55S	66.53W
Nuevo Rocafuerte	54	Cd	0.56S	75.25W
Nugaal ③	35	Hd	8.30N	48.00 E
Nugālēd, Dēh- ∿	30	Lh	7.58N	49.51 E
Nugālēd, Dōho- ∨	35	Hd	8.35N	48.35 E
Nûgâtsiaq	41	Gd	71.39N	53.45W
Nugget Point ►	62	Cg	46.27S	169.49 E
Nûgssuaq ◧	41	Gd	70.30N	51.30W
Nuguria Islands ❖	57	Ge	3.20S	154.45 E
Nuguš ∿	17	Gj	53.05N	56.00 E
Nuhaka	62	Gc	39.02S	177.45 E
Nui Atoll ⊙	57	Ie	7.15S	177.10 E
Nuijama	8	Md	60.58N	28.32 E
Nuiqsut	40	Ib	70.20N	151.00W
Nu Jang ∿	21	Lh	16.31N	97.37 E
Nûk/Godthåb	67	Nc	64.15N	51.40W
Nukapu ◆	63c	Ab	10.07S	165.59 E
Nukey Bluff ▲	59	Hf	32.35S	135.40 E
Nukhayb	23	Fc	32.02N	42.15 E
Nukhaylak	31	Jg	19.08N	26.20 E
Nukiki	63a	Cb	6.45S	156.29 E
Nukuaéta ◆	64h	Ac	13.22S	176.11W
Nuku'alofa	58	Jg	21.08S	175.12W
Nukufetau Atoll ⊙	57	Ie	8.00S	178.22 E
Nukufotu ◆	64h	Bb	13.11S	176.10W
Nukuhifala ◆	64h	Bb	13.17S	176.05W
Nukuhione ◆	64h	Bb	13.16S	176.06W
Nuku Hiva, Ile- ◆	57	Me	8.54S	140.06W
Nukulaelae Atoll ⊙	57	Ie	9.23S	179.52 E
Nukuloa ◆	64h	Bb	13.11S	176.09W
Nukumanu Islands ❖	57	Ge	4.30S	159.30 E
Nukumbasanga ◆	63d	Cb	16.18S	179.15W
Nukunonu Atoll ⊙	57	Je	9.10S	171.53W
Nukuoro Atoll ⊙	57	Gd	3.51N	154.58 E
Nukus	22	He	42.50N	59.29 E
Nukutapu ◆	64h	Bb	13.13S	176.08W
Nukuteatea ◆	64h	Bb	13.12S	176.08W
Nulato	40	Hd	64.43N	158.06W
Nules	13	Le	39.51N	0.09W
Nullagine	58	Dg	21.53S	120.06 E
Nullagine River ∿	59	Ed	20.43S	120.33 E
Nullarbor	59	Gf	31.26S	130.55 E
Nullarbor Plain ▁	57	Dh	31.00S	129.00 E
Nulu'erhu Shan ⛰	27	Kc	41.40N	119.50 E
Numakawa	29a	Ba	45.15N	141.51 E
Numan	34	Hd	9.28N	12.02 E
Numancia [Phil.]	26	Ie	9.52N	125.58 E
Numancia [Sp.]	13	Jc	41.47N	2.30W
Numanohata	29a	Bb	42.40N	141.41 E
Numata [Jap.]	29a	Bb	43.49N	141.55 E
Numata [Jap.]	28	Of	36.38N	139.03 E
Numatinna ∿	35	Dd	7.14N	27.37 E
Numazu	28	Og	35.06N	138.52 E
Nümbrecht	12	Jd	50.54N	7.33 E
Numedal ⊠	7	Bf	60.05N	9.05 E
Numena	36	Ee	11.46S	26.31 E
Número Cinco, Canal- ═	55	Cm	37.14S	58.06W
Número Doce, Canal- ═	55	Cm	36.30S	59.08W
Número Dos, Canal- ═	55	Cm	36.51S	58.03W
Número Nueve, Canal- ═	55	Cm	36.08S	58.36W
Número Once, Canal- ═	55	Bm	36.28S	60.01W
Número Quince, Canal- ═	55	Dl	35.55S	57.45W
Número Uno, Canal- ═	55	Cm	36.40S	58.35W
Numfoor, Pulau- ◆	26	Jg	1.03S	134.54 E
Nuneaton	9	Li	52.32N	1.28W
Nungarin	59	Df	31.11S	118.06 E
Nungnain Sum	27	Kb	45.45N	118.56 E
Nungo	37	Fb	13.25S	37.46 E
Nunivak ◆	38	Cd	60.00N	166.30W
Nunkirchen, Wadern-	12	Ie	49.32N	6.53 E
Nunn	45	Df	40.45N	104.46W
Nunspeet	12	Hb	52.22N	5.46 E
Nunukan Timur, Pulau- ◆	26	Gf	4.05N	117.40 E
Nuomin He ∿	27	Lb	48.21N	124.32 E
Nuorgam	7	Ga	70.05N	27.51 E
Nuoro	6	Gg	40.19N	9.20 E
Nupani ◆	63c	Ab	10.04S	165.40 E
Nūq	24	Pg	30.55N	55.35 E
Nuqayr	24	Mi	27.48N	48.21 E
Nuqrah	24	Ij	25.34N	41.24 E
Nuqruş, Jabal- ▲	33	Fe	24.49N	34.36 E
Nuquí	54	Cb	5.43N	77.16W
Nūr ∿	24	Od	36.15N	52.20 E
Nūr	24	Pg	31.25N	54.20 E
Nura	19	Gf	48.57N	62.20 E
Nura ∿	21	Id	50.30N	69.59 E
Nūrābād	24	Ng	30.48N	51.27 E
Nuraghe Santu Antine	14	Cj	40.29N	8.45 E
Nurata	19	Gg	40.34N	65.35 E
Nur Dağları ⛰	24	Gd	36.45N	36.20 E
Nure ∿	14	De	45.03N	9.49 E
Nurek	19	Gh	38.25N	69.20 E
Nurhak Dağı ▲	23	Eb	38.04N	37.29 E
Nūrī ⁂	35	Eb	18.30N	32.02 E
Nurki	20	Ie	56.42N	138.28 E
Nurlat	19	Fe	54.28N	50.48 E
Nurlati	7	Li	55.38N	48.17 E
Nurmes	7	Ge	63.33N	29.07 E
Nurmijärvi	8	Kd	60.28N	24.48 E
Nurmo	8	Jb	62.50N	22.54 E
Nürnberg	6	Hf	49.27N	11.05 E
Nurra ⊠	14	Cj	40.45N	8.15 E
Nurri, Mount- ▲	59	Jf	31.42S	146.02 E
Nurugas	37	Bc	19.11S	18.54 E
Nurzec ∿	10	Sd	52.33N	22.28 E
Nusa Tenggara Barat ③	26	Gh	8.50S	117.30 E
Nusa Tenggara Timur ③	26	Hh	9.30S	122.00 E
Nusaybin	24	Id	37.03N	41.13 E
Nushagak ∿	40	He	58.57N	158.29W
Nushan ⛰	27	Gf	25.00N	99.00 E
Nu-Shima ◆	29	Dd	34.10N	134.50 E
Nutak	42	Le	57.31N	62.00W
Nuttal	25	Dc	28.45N	68.08 E
Nuutele ◆	65c	Bb	14.02S	171.22W
Nuwākot	25	Gc	28.08N	83.53 E
Nuwara	25	Gg	6.58N	80.46 E
Nuwaybi 'al Muzayyinah	33	Fd	28.58N	34.39 E
Nyabing	59	Df	33.32S	118.09 E
Nyagquka/Yajiang	27	He	30.07N	100.58 E
Nyagrong/Xinlong	27	He	30.57N	100.12 E
Nyahanga	36	Fc	2.23S	33.33 E
Nyahua ∿	36	Fc	4.58S	33.34 E
Nyainqêntanglha Feng ▲	27	Fe	30.12N	90.33 E
Nyainqêntanglha Shan ⛰	21	Kf	30.10N	90.00 E
Nyakanazi	36	Fc	3.00S	31.15 E
Nyala	31	Jg	12.03N	24.53 E
Nyalam	27	Ef	28.15N	85.55 E
Ny-Ålesund	41	Nc	78.56N	11.57 E
Nyalikungu	36	Fc	3.11S	33.47 E
Nyamandhlovu	37	Dc	19.51S	28.16 E
Nyamapanda	37	Ec	16.55S	32.52 E
Nyamlell	35	Dd	9.07N	26.58 E
Nyamtumbo	36	Ge	10.30S	36.06 E
Nyanding ∿	35	Ed	8.40N	32.41 E
Nyanga ∿	30	Ii	2.58S	10.15 E
Nyanga ③	36	Bc	3.00S	11.00 E
Nyanza ③	36	Fc	0.30S	34.30 E
Nyanza-Lac	36	Ec	4.21S	29.36 E
Nyasa, Lake- (EN)=Niassa, Lago- ◍	30	Kj	12.00S	34.30 E
Nyaunglebin	25	Je	17.57N	96.44 E
Nyborg	7	Ci	55.19N	10.48 E
Nybro	7	Dh	56.45N	15.54 E
Nyda ∿	17	Pc	66.40N	72.50 E
Nyda	20	Cc	66.36N	72.54 E
Nyeboe Land ⊠	41	Gb	81.45N	56.40W
Nyêmo	27	Ff	29.30N	90.07 E
Nyeri	36	Gc	0.25S	36.57 E
Nyerol	35	Ed	8.41N	32.02 E
Ny Friesland ◧	41	Nc	79.30N	17.00 E
Nyhammar	8	Fd	60.17N	14.58 E
Nyhem	8	Fb	62.54N	15.40 E
Nyika ⊠	30	Ki	2.37S	38.44 E
Nyika Plateau ▰	30	Kj	10.40S	33.50 E
Nyikog Qu ∿	27	He	30.24N	100.40 E
Nyimba	36	Fe	14.33S	30.48 E
Nyingchi	27	Ff	29.38N	94.23 E
Nyírbátor	10	Si	47.50N	22.08 E
Nyíregyháza	10	Ri	47.57N	21.43 E
Nyiri Desert ⁘	36	Gc	2.20S	37.20 E
Nyiro, Mount- ▲	36	Gb	2.08N	36.51 E
Nyírség ⊠	10	Ri	47.50N	21.55 E
Nykøbing [Den.]	7	Ci	54.46N	11.53 E
Nykøbing [Den.]	7	Ci	55.55N	11.41 E
Nykøbing [Den.]	8	Ch	56.48N	8.52 E
Nyköping	7	Dg	58.45N	17.00 E
Nyköpingsån ∿	8	Gf	58.45N	17.01 E
Nykroppa	8	Fe	59.38N	14.18 E
Nyland	8	Ga	63.00N	17.46 E
Nylstroom	37	Dd	24.42S	28.20 E
Nymburk	10	Lf	50.11N	15.03 E
Nymphe Bank (EN) ≡	9	Fj	51.30N	7.05W
Nynäshamn	7	Dg	58.54N	17.57 E
Nyngan	58	Fh	31.34S	147.11 E
Nyon	14	Ad	46.23N	6.15 E
Nyong ∿	30	Hh	3.17N	9.54 E
Nyonga	36	Fd	6.43S	32.04 E
Nyons	11	Lj	44.22N	5.08 E
Nýřany	10	Jg	49.43N	13.13 E
Nyrob	17	Hf	60.42N	56.45 E
Nyš	20	Jf	51.30N	142.49 E
Nysa	10	Nf	50.29N	17.20 E
Nysa Kłodzka ∿	10	Nf	50.49N	17.50 E
Nysa Łuzycka ∿	10	Kd	52.04N	14.46 E
Nyslott/Savonlinna	7	Gf	61.52N	28.53 E
Nyssa	46	Ge	43.53N	117.00W
Nystad/Uusikaupunki	7	Ef	60.48N	21.25 E
Nysted	8	Dj	54.40N	11.45 E
Nytva	19	Fd	57.56N	55.20 E
Nyūdō-Zaki ►	28	Od	40.00N	139.35 E
Nyunzu	36	Ed	5.57S	28.01 E
Nyūzen	29	Ec	36.56N	137.30 E
Nzambi	36	Bc	3.58S	11.16 E
Nzara	35	De	4.40N	28.14 E
Nzega	36	Fc	4.13S	33.11 E
Nzérékoré	31	Gh	7.45N	8.49W
Nzeto	36	Bd	7.05S	12.50 E
Nzi ∿	30	Gh	5.57N	4.50W
Nzilo, Barrage de- ⩇	36	Ee	10.35S	25.30 E
Nzo ∿	34	Dd	6.16N	7.03W
Nzoro ∿	36	Eb	3.18N	29.26 E
Nzwali/Anjouan ◆	30	Lj	12.15S	44.25 E

O

Oa, Mull of- ►	9	Gf	55.35N	6.20W
Oahe, Lake- ◍	38	Ie	45.30N	100.25W
Oahu Island ◆	57	Lb	21.30N	158.00W
O-akan-Dake ▲	29a	Db	43.27N	144.10 E
Oakdale [Ca.-U.S.]	46	Eh	37.46N	120.51W
Oakdale [La.-U.S.]	45	Jk	30.49N	92.40W
Oakham	9	Mi	52.40N	0.44W
Oak Harbor	46	Db	48.18N	122.39W
Oak Lake ◍	45	Fb	49.40N	100.45W
Oakland [Ca.-U.S.]	39	Gf	37.47N	122.13W
Oakland [Md.-U.S.]	44	Hf	39.25N	79.24W
Oakley [Id.-U.S.]	46	Ie	42.15N	113.53W
Oakley [Ks.-U.S.]	43	Gd	39.08N	100.51W
Oak Park	45	Mf	41.53N	87.48W
Oak Ridge	43	Kd	36.01N	84.16W
Oakridge	46	De	43.45N	122.28W
Oakville	44	Hd	43.27N	79.41W
Oamaru	61	Di	45.05S	170.59 E
Oancea	15	Ld	45.55N	28.06 E
Oani-Gawa ∿	29	Ga	40.12N	140.16 E
Ōarai	29	Gc	36.18N	140.33 E
Oaro	62	Ee	42.31S	173.30 E
Oasis	46	Hf	41.01N	114.37W
Oasis ▣	32	Hd	26.00N	5.00 E
Oates Coast ⌇	66	Jf	70.00S	160.00 E
Oaxaca ②	47	Ee	17.00N	96.30W
Oaxaca, Sierra Madre de- ⛰	48	Ki	17.30N	96.30W
Oaxaca de Juárez	39	Jh	17.03N	96.43W
Ob ∿	21	Ic	66.45N	69.30 E
Oba	42	Jg	48.55N	84.17W
Obala	34	He	4.10N	11.32 E
Obama [Jap.]	28	Mg	35.30N	135.45 E
Obama [Jap.]	29	Be	32.43N	130.13 E
Obama-Wan ⊂	29	Dd	35.30N	135.40 E
Oban [N.Z.]	61	Ci	46.52S	168.10 E
Oban [Scot.-U.K.]	9	He	56.25N	5.29W
Obanazawa	28	Pe	38.36N	140.24 E
Obando	53	Je	4.07N	67.45W
Oban Hills ⌒	34	Gd	5.30N	8.35 E
Obeliai/Obeljaj	8	Ki	55.58N	25.59 E
Obeljaj/Obeliai	8	Ki	55.58N	25.59 E
Oberá	56	Ic	27.29S	55.08W
Oberbayern ⊠	10	Hi	47.50N	11.50 E
Oberderdingen	12	Ke	49.04N	8.48 E
Oberfranken ⊠	10	Hf	50.10N	11.30 E
Oberhausen	10	Ce	51.28N	6.51 E
Oberkirchen, Schmallenberg-	12	Kc	51.09N	8.18 E
Oberland [Switz.] ⊠	14	Bd	46.35N	7.30 E
Oberland [Switz.] ⊠	14	Dd	46.45N	9.05 E
Oberlausitz ⊠	10	Ke	51.15N	14.30 E
Oberlin	45	Fg	39.49N	100.32W
Obermoschel	12	Je	49.44N	7.46 E
Obernkirchen	12	Lb	52.16N	9.08 E
Oberösterreich=Upper Austria (EN) ②	14	Hb	48.15N	14.00 E
Oberpfalz ⊠	10	Ig	49.30N	12.10 E
Oberpfälzer Wald= Bohemian Forest (EN) ⛰	10	Ig	49.50N	12.30 E
Oberpullendorf	14	Kc	47.30N	16.31 E
Ober-Ramstadt	12	Ke	49.50N	8.45 E
Oberstdorf	10	Gi	47.24N	10.16 E
Oberursel (Taunus)	12	Kd	50.12N	8.35 E
Obervellach	14	Hd	46.56N	13.12 E
Oberwesel	12	Jd	50.06N	7.44 E
Ob Gulf (EN)=Obskaja Guba ⊂	21	Jc	69.00N	73.00 E
Obi, Kepulauan- ❖	26	Ig	1.30S	127.45 E
Obi, Pulau- ◆	57	De	1.30S	127.45 E
Obi, Selat- ⫘	26	Ig	0.52S	127.33 E
Óbidos [Braz.]	53	Kf	1.55S	55.31W
Óbidos [Port.]	13	Ce	39.22N	9.09W
Obihiro	27	Pc	42.55N	143.12 E
Obilić	15	Eg	42.41N	21.05 E
Obira	29a	Ba	44.01N	141.38 E
Obispos	49	Li	8.36N	70.05W
Obispo Trejo	56	Hd	30.46S	63.25W
Obitočnaja Kosa ▂	16	Jf	46.35N	36.15 E
Oblučje	20	Ig	48.59N	131.05 E
Obninsk	19	Dd	55.05N	36.37 E
Obo	31	Jh	5.24N	26.30 E
Obock	35	Gc	11.57N	43.17 E
Obojan	19	De	51.13N	36.16 E
Obokote	36	Ec	0.52S	26.19 E
Obol ∿	7	Gi	55.24N	29.01 E
Oborniki	10	Md	52.39N	16.51 E
Obouya	36	Cc	0.56S	15.43 E
Obozerski	19	Ec	63.28N	40.20 E
Obra ∿	10	Ld	52.36N	15.28 E
Obrenovac	15	De	44.39N	20.12 E
Obrovac	14	Jf	44.12N	15.41 E
Obrovo	10	Vd	52.27N	25.43 E
Obruchev Rise (EN) ⋀	20	Lf	52.30N	166.00 E
Obruk Platosu ▰	24	Ec	38.02N	33.30 E
Obšči Syrt ⌒	5	Le	51.50N	51.00 E
Obskaja Guba=Ob Gulf (EN) ⊂	21	Jc	69.00N	73.00 E
Ob' Tablemount (EN) ⊓	30	Ln	52.30S	42.00 E
Ōbu	29	Ed	35.01N	136.58 E
Obuasi	34	Ed	6.12N	1.40W
Obudu	34	Gd	6.40N	9.10 E
Obuhov	16	Gd	50.07N	30.37 E
Obva ∿	17	Gg	58.35N	55.25 E
Obzor	15	Kg	42.49N	27.53 E
Oca ∿	13	Ib	42.46N	3.26W
Oca, Montes de- ⛰	13	Ib	42.20N	3.15W
Očakov	19	Df	46.38N	31.33 E
Ocala	43	Kf	29.11N	82.07W
Očamcira	16	Lh	42.46N	41.27 E
Ocampo [Mex.]	48	Hd	27.20N	102.21W
Ocampo [Mex.]	48	Ec	28.11N	108.23W
Ocaña [Col.]	54	Db	8.15N	73.20W
Ocaña [Sp.]	13	Ie	39.56N	3.31W
Occhito, Lago di- ◍	14	Ii	41.35N	14.55 E
Ocean Bight ⊂	49	Kc	21.15N	73.15W
Ocean City [Md.-U.S.]	43	Ld	38.20N	75.05W
Ocean City [N.J.-U.S.]	44	Jf	39.16N	74.35W
Ocean Falls	42	Ef	52.21N	127.40W
Oceania ■	57	Ie	5.00S	175.00E
Ocean Point ►	44	Il	26.16N	77.03W
Oceanside	43	De	33.12N	117.23W
Ocean Springs	45	Lk	30.25N	88.50W
Ocejón, Pico- ▲	13	Ic	41.07N	3.15W
Očenyrd, Gora- ▲	17	Mb	68.05N	66.20 E
Očer	19	Fd	57.53N	54.45 E
Ochagavia	13	Kb	42.55N	1.05W
Ochiai	29	Cd	35.02N	133.45 E
Ochi-Gata ◒	29	Ec	36.55N	136.48 E
Ochiishi-Misaki ►	29a	Db	43.10N	145.28 E
Ochil Hills ⌒	9	Je	56.23N	3.35W
Och'onjang	28	Jd	40.55N	128.50 E
Ocho Rios	49	Id	18.25N	77.07W
Ochsenfurt	10	Gg	49.39N	10.05 E
Ochtrup	12	Jb	52.13N	7.11 E
Ockelbo	7	Dd	60.53N	16.43 E
Öckerö	8	Dg	57.43N	11.39 E
Ocmulgee River ∿	44	Fj	31.58N	82.32W
Ocna Mureş	15	Gc	46.23N	23.51 E

Index Symbols

① Independent Nation
② State, Region
③ District, County
④ Municipality
⑤ Colony, Dependency
■ Continent
⊠ Physical Region
▣ Historical or Cultural Region
▲ Mount, Mountain
🌋 Volcano
◠ Hill
⛰ Mountains, Mountain Range
⌒ Hills, Escarpment
▰ Plateau, Upland
⋎ Pass, Gap
▁ Plain, Lowland
◣ Delta
▦ Salt Flat
∨ Valley, Canyon
◡ Crater, Cave
✪ Karst Features
⌣ Depression
▬ Polder
⁘ Desert, Dunes
♣ Forest, Woods
❦ Heath, Steppe
✿ Oasis
► Cape, Point
⌇ Coast, Beach
⌈ Cliff
◧ Peninsula
⧖ Isthmus
▂ Sandbank
◆ Island
⊙ Atoll
✣ Rock, Reef
❖ Islands, Archipelago
✤ Rocks, Reefs
✺ Coral Reef
◉ Well, Spring
⛲ Geyser
∿ River, Stream
↯ Waterfall Rapids
⥤ River Mouth, Estuary
◍ Lake
◌ Salt Lake
◔ Intermittent Lake
◙ Reservoir
≈ Swamp, Pond
═ Canal
❄ Glacier
❅ Ice Shelf, Pack Ice
▒ Ocean
▓ Sea
⊂ Gulf, Bay
⫘ Strait, Fjord
◒ Lagoon
≡ Bank
⩙ Seamount
⊓ Tablemount
⋀ Ridge
⊐ Shelf
⊔ Basin
⌐ Escarpment, Sea Scarp
⚡ Fracture
⊽ Trench, Abyss
⛨ National Park, Reserve
✱ Point of Interest
☼ Recreation Site
⌓ Cave, Cavern
⚑ Historic Site
⁂ Ruins
▥ Wall, Walls
✝ Church, Abbey
⛩ Temple
⊗ Scientific Station
✈ Airport
⚓ Port
⛯ Lighthouse
⚒ Mine
∩ Tunnel
⩇ Dam, Bridge

Ocna Sibiului 15 Hc 45.53N 24.03 E
Ocoa, Bahía de- 49 Ld 18.22N 70.39W
Oconee River 44 Fj 31.58N 82.32W
Oconto 45 Md 44.55N 87.52W
Ocosingo 48 Mi 17.04N 92.15W
Ocotal 49 Dg 13.38N 86.29W
Ocotepeque [3] 49 Cf 14.30N 89.00W
Ocotlán 47 Dd 20.21N 102.46W
Ocotlán de Morelos 48 Ki 16.48N 96.43W
Ocracoke Inlet 44 Ih 35.10N 76.05W
Ocracoke Island 44 Jh 35.09N 75.53W
Ocreza 13 Ee 39.32N 7.50W
Octeville-sur-Mer 12 Ce 49.33N 0.07 E
October Revolution Island (EN)=Oktjabrskoj Revoljuci, Ostrov- 21 Lb 79.30N 97.00 E
Ocú 49 Gj 7.57N 80.47W
Ocumare del Tuy 50 Cg 10.07N 66.46W
Oda [Ghana] 34 Ed 5.55N 0.59W
Oda [Jap.] 29 Ce 33.34N 132.48 E
Ōda 28 Lg 35.11N 132.30 E
Oda, Jabal- 35 Fa 20.21N 36.39 E
Ódáðahraun 7a Cb 65.09N 17.00W
Ōdai 29 Ed 34.24N 136.24 E
Odaigahara-San 29 Ed 34.11N 136.06 E
Odalen 8 Dd 60.15N 11.40 E
Ōdate 28 Pd 40.16N 140.34 E
Odawara 28 Og 35.15N 139.10 E
Odda 7 Bf 60.04N 6.33 E
Odder 8 Di 55.58N 10.10 E
Odeleite 13 Eg 37.21N 7.27W
Odemira 13 Dg 37.36N 8.38W
Ödemiş 24 Bc 38.13N 27.59 E
Odendaalsrus 37 De 27.48S 26.45 E
Odense 6 Hd 55.24N 10.23 E
Odenthal 12 Jc 51.02N 7.07 E
Odenwald 10 Eg 49.40N 9.00 E
Oder [Eur.] 5 He 53.40N 14.33 E
Oder [F.R.G.] 10 Ge 51.40N 10.02 E
Oderbruch 10 Kd 52.40N 14.15 E
Oderské vrchy 10 Ng 49.40N 17.45 E
Oderzo 14 Ge 45.47N 12.29 E
Ödeshög 7 Dg 58.14N 14.39 E
Odessa [Tx.-U.S.] 39 If 31.51N 102.22W
Odessa [Ukr.-U.S.S.R.] 6 Jf 46.28N 30.44 E
Odessa [Wa.-U.S.] 46 Fc 47.20N 118.41W
Odesskaja Oblast [3] 19 Df 46.45N 30.30 E
Odet 11 Bg 47.52N 4.06W
Odiel 13 Fg 37.10N 6.54W
Odienné 31 Gh 9.30N 7.34W
Odienné [3] 34 Dd 9.45N 7.45W
Odivelas 13 Df 38.12N 8.18W
Ödmården 8 Gc 61.05N 16.40 E
Odobeşti 15 Kd 45.46N 27.03 E
Ödöngk 25 Kf 11.48N 104.45 E
Odoorn 12 Ib 52.51N 6.50 E
Odorheiu Secuiesc 15 Ic 46.18N 25.18 E
Ōdose-Zaki 29a Bc 40.46N 140.03 E
Odra 5 He 53.40N 14.33 E
Ōdwēyne 35 Hd 9.23N 45.04 E
Odžaci 15 Cd 45.31N 19.16 E
Odžak 14 Me 45.01N 18.18 E
Odzi 37 Ec 19.47S 32.24 E
Oeiras 13 Eg 37.38N 7.40W
Oeiras [Braz.] 54 Je 7.01S 42.08W
Oeiras [Port.] 13 Cf 38.41N 9.19W
Oelde 12 Kc 51.49N 8.09 E
Oelerbeek 12 Ib 52.21N 6.38 E
Oelrichs 45 Ee 43.15N 103.10W
Oelsnitz 10 If 50.25N 12.10 E
Oelwein 45 Ke 42.41N 91.55W
Oeno Island 57 Ng 23.56S 130.44W
Oer-Erkenschwick 12 Jc 51.38N 7.15 E
Oeste, Punta- 51a Ab 18.05N 67.57W
Oeventrop, Arnsberg- 12 Kc 51.24N 8.08 E
Ōe-Yama 29 Dd 35.27N 135.06 E
Of 24 Ib 40.57N 40.16 E
O'Fallon Creek 46 Mc 46.50N 105.09W
Ofanto 14 Ki 41.21N 16.13 E
Ofaqim 24 Fg 31.17N 34.37 E
Offa 34 Fd 8.09N 4.43 E
Offaly/Uíbh Fhailí [2] 9 Fh 53.20N 7.30W
Offenbach am Main 10 Ef 50.06N 8.46 E
Offenbach-Hundheim 12 Je 49.37N 7.33 E
Offenburg 10 Dh 48.29N 7.56 E
Offida 14 Hh 42.56N 13.41 E
Offoué 36 Bc 0.04S 11.44 E
Offranville 12 De 49.52N 1.03 E
Ofidhoúsa 15 Jm 36.33N 26.09 E
Ofolanga 65b Ba 19.36S 174.27W
Ofu 65c Db 14.11S 169.42W
Ōfunato 28 Pe 39.04N 141.43 E
Oga 28 Oe 40.43N 141.18 E
Ogachi 29 Gb 39.05N 140.28 E
Ogaden 30 Lh 7.30N 45.00 E
Oga-Hantō 28 Oe 39.55N 139.50 E
Ōgaki 28 Ng 35.21N 136.37 E
Ogallala 43 Gc 41.08N 101.43W
Ogasawara-Shotō=Bonin Islands (EN) 21 Qg 27.00N 142.10 E
Ogawara-Ko 29a Bc 40.45N 141.20 E
Ogbomosho 31 Hh 8.08N 4.16 E
Ogden 39 He 41.14N 111.58W
Ogdensburg 44 Jc 44.42N 75.31W
Ogeechee River 44 Gj 31.51N 81.06W
Oghāsh 24 Lc 39.10N 46.55 E
Ogi 29 Fc 37.50N 138.16 E
Ogilvie Mountains 42 Dc 65.00N 140.00W
Ogi-no-Sen 29 Dd 35.26N 134.26 E
Oginski Kanal 16 Dc 52.20N 25.55 E
Oglanly 16 Sj 39.50N 54.33 E
Oglethorpe 44 Ei 31.28N 84.04W
Ogliastra 14 Dk 39.55N 9.35 E
Oglio 14 Ee 45.02N 10.39 E
Ognon 11 Lg 47.20N 5.29 E
Ogo 35 Hd 9.48N 45.35 E
Ogoamas, Bulu- 26 Hf 0.40N 120.12 E
Ogodža 20 If 52.48N 132.40 E
Ogoja 34 Gd 6.40N 8.48 E
Ogoki 42 If 51.38N 85.56W
Ogoki 42 If 51.38N 85.55W
Ogoki Reservoir 42 If 51.35N 86.00W
Ogonëk 20 Ie 59.40N 138.01 E
Ogooué 30 Hi 0.49S 9.00 E
Ogooué-Ivindo [3] 36 Bb 0.30N 13.00 E
Ogooué-Lolo [3] 36 Bc 1.00S 13.00 E
Ogooué-Maritime [3] 36 Ac 2.00S 9.30 E
Ogōri [Jap.] 29 Bd 34.06N 131.25 E
Ogōri [Jap.] 29 Be 33.24N 130.34 E
Ogosta 15 Gf 43.45N 23.51 E
Ogražden 15 Fh 41.30N 22.55 E
Ogre 8 Kh 56.42N 24.33 E
Ogre 7 Fh 56.50N 24.39 E
Ogulin 14 Je 45.16N 15.14 E
Ogun [2] 34 Fd 7.00N 3.40 E
Oguni [Jap.] 29 Fb 38.04N 139.45 E
Oguni [Jap.] 29 Be 33.07N 131.04 E
Ogurčinski, Ostrov- 16 Rj 38.55N 53.05 E
Oğuzeli 24 Gd 37.00N 37.30 E
Oha 22 Qd 53.34N 142.56 E
Ohai 62 Bf 45.56S 167.57 E
Ohakune 62 Fc 39.25S 175.25 E
Ohanet 32 Id 28.40N 8.50 E
Ohansk 17 Gh 57.42N 55.25 E
Ōhara 29 Gd 35.15N 140.23 E
Ōhasama 29 Gb 39.28N 141.17 E
Ohata 20 Je 59.20N 143.05 E
Ōhata 28 Pd 41.24N 141.10 E
Ohau, Lake- 62 Cf 44.15S 169.50 E
Ohey 12 Hd 50.26N 5.08 E
O'Higgins, Cabo- 65d Bb 27.05S 109.15W
Ohio 38 Kf 36.59N 89.08W
Ohio [2] 43 Kc 40.15N 82.45W
Ohm 10 Ef 50.51N 8.48 E
Ohmberge 10 Ge 51.30N 10.28 E
'Ohonua 65b Bc 21.20S 174.57W
Ohopoho 31 Ij 18.03S 13.45 E
Ohotsk 22 Qd 59.23N 143.18 E
Ohotskoje More=Okhotsk, Sea of- (EN) 21 Qd 53.00N 150.00 E
Ohre 10 Hd 52.18N 11.47 E
Ohře 10 Kf 50.32N 14.08 E
Ohrid 15 Dh 41.07N 20.48 E
Ohrid, Lake- (EN) = Ohridsko Jezero 5 Ig 41.00N 20.45 E
Ohrid, Lake- (EN) = Ohrit, Liqen i- 5 Ig 41.00N 20.45 E
Ohridsko Jezero=Ohrid, Lake- (EN) 5 Ig 41.00N 20.45 E
Öhringen 10 Fg 49.12N 9.30 E
Ohrit, Liqen i- = Ohrid, Lake- (EN) 5 Ig 41.00N 20.45 E
Ohura 62 Fc 38.51S 174.59 E
Oiapoque 54 Hc 3.50N 51.50W
Oich 9 Id 57.10N 4.45W
Oi-Gawa 29 Fd 34.46N 138.17 E
Oil City 44 He 41.26N 79.44W
Oildale 46 Fi 35.25N 119.01W
Oileán Baoi/Dursey 9 Cj 51.36N 10.12W
Oileán Ciarraí/Castleisland 9 Di 52.14N 9.27W
Oileán Coarach/Mutton 9 Di 52.49N 9.31W
Oileán Mhic Aodha/Magee, Island- 9 Hg 54.50N 5.50W
Oinoúsai 15 Jk 38.32N 26.13 E
Oinoúsai, Nisoi- 15 Jk 38.31N 26.14 E
Oirschot 12 Hc 51.30N 5.18 E
Oisans 11 Mi 45.02N 6.02 E
Oise [3] 11 Ie 49.30N 2.30 E
Oise 11 Ie 49.00N 2.04 E
Oise à l'Aisne, Canal de l'- 11 Je 49.36N 3.11 E
Oisemont 12 De 49.57N 1.46 E
Oissel 12 De 49.20N 1.06 E
Oisterwijk 12 Hc 51.35N 5.11 E
Oistins 51q Ab 13.04N 59.32W
Oistins Bay 51q Ab 13.03N 59.33W
Ōita 27 Ne 33.14N 131.36 E
Ōita Ken [2] 28 Kh 33.15N 131.20 E
Oiti Óros 15 Fk 38.49N 22.17 E
Oituz, Pasul- 15 Jc 46.03N 26.23 E
Oiwake 29a Bb 42.52N 141.48 E
Ojat 7 Hf 60.31N 33.05 E
Öje 8 Ed 60.49N 13.51 E
Ojestos de Jalisco 48 Ig 21.50N 101.35W
Ojika-Jima 29 Ae 33.13N 129.03 E
O-Jima 29 Be 34.00N 130.45 E
Ojinaga 47 Dc 29.34N 104.25W
Ojiya 28 Of 37.18N 138.48 E
Ojmjakon 20 Jd 63.28N 142.49 E
Ojocaliente 48 Hf 22.34N 102.15W
Ojo Caliente 48 Fb 30.25N 106.33W
Ojos del Salado, Nevado- 52 Jh 27.06S 68.32W
Ojos Negros 13 Kd 40.44N 1.30W
Ojtal 19 Hg 42.54N 73.21 E
Oka [R.S.F.S.R.] 21 Md 55.00N 102.03 E
Oka [U.S.S.R.] 5 Kd 56.20N 43.59 E
Okaba 26 Kh 8.06S 139.42 E
Okahandja [3] 37 Bd 21.30S 17.30 E
Okahandja 31 Ik 21.59S 16.58 E
Okahukura 62 Fc 38.47S 175.14 E
Okaihau 62 Ea 35.19S 173.46 E
Okak Islands 42 Le 57.28N 61.48W
Okanagan Lake 42 Fg 49.55N 119.30W
Okano 36 Bb 0.05S 10.57 E
Okanogan River 43 Db 48.06N 119.43W
Okapa 59 Ja 6.31S 145.32 E
Okāra 25 Eb 30.49N 73.27 E
Okarem 19 Fh 38.07N 54.05 E
Okato 62 Ec 39.12S 173.53 E
Okaukuejo 37 Bc 19.10S 15.54 E
Okavango 30 Jj 18.53N 22.24 E
Okavango [3] 37 Cc 18.00S 21.00 E
Okavango Swamp 30 Jj 19.30S 23.00 E
Ōkawa 29 Be 33.12N 130.23 E
Okaya 28 Of 36.03N 138.03 E
Okayama 22 Pf 34.39N 133.55 E
Okayama Ken [2] 28 Lg 34.50N 133.45 E
Okazaki 28 Ng 34.57N 137.10 E
Okeechobee 44 Gl 27.15N 80.50W
Okeechobee, Lake- 38 Kg 26.55N 80.45W
Okefenokee Swamp 44 Fj 30.42N 82.20W
Okehampton 9 Jk 50.44N 4.00W
Okene 34 Gd 7.33N 6.14 E
Oker 10 Gd 52.30N 10.22 E
Oketo 29a Cb 43.41N 143.32 E
Okha 25 Dd 22.27N 69.04 E
Ókhi Óros 15 Hk 38.04N 24.28 E
Okhotsk, Sea of- (EN)= Hok-Kai 21 Qd 53.00N 150.00 E
Okhotsk, Sea of- (EN)= Ohotskoje More 21 Qd 53.00N 150.00 E
Okhthonía, Ákra- 15 Hk 38.32N 24.14 E
Oki-Daitō-Jima 27 Ng 24.30N 131.00 E
Okiep 37 Be 29.39S 17.53 E
Okinawa 29b Ab 26.20N 127.47 E
Okinawa Islands (EN)= Okinawa-Shotō 21 Og 26.40N 128.00 E
Okinawa-Jima 27 Mf 26.40N 128.20 E
Okinawa Ken [2] 29b Ab 26.31N 127.59 E
Okinawa-Shotō=Okinawa Islands (EN) 21 Og 26.40N 128.00 E
Okinoerabu-Jima 27 Mf 27.20N 128.35 E
Okino-Shima [Jap.] 29 Ce 32.44N 132.33 E
Okino-Shima [Jap.] 29 Bd 34.15N 130.08 E
Okino-Tori-Shima 21 Pg 20.25N 136.00 E
Oki Ridge (EN) 28 Mf 37.00N 135.00 E
Oki-Shotō 27 Nd 36.00N 132.50 E
Okitipupa 34 Fd 6.30N 4.48 E
Oki Trench (EN) 29 Dc 37.00N 135.30 E
Oklahoma [2] 43 Hd 35.30N 98.00W
Oklahoma City 39 Jf 35.28N 97.32W
Okmulgee 45 Ii 35.37N 95.58W
Oknica 15 Ka 48.22N 27.24 E
Oko 35 Fa 22.20N 35.56 E
Okoko 36 Fb 2.06N 33.53 E
Okolo 36 Fb 2.40N 31.09 E
Okolona 44 Ef 38.08N 85.41W
Okondja 36 Bc 0.41S 13.47 E
Okonek 10 Mc 53.33N 16.50 E
Okoppe 28 Qb 44.28N 143.08 E
Okotoks 46 Ia 50.44N 113.59W
Okoyo 36 Cc 1.28S 15.04 E
Okrzeika 10 Re 51.40N 21.30 E
Øksfjord 7 Fa 70.14N 22.22 E
Oksino 17 Fc 67.33N 52.10 E
Okstindane 5 Hb 66.02N 14.10 E
Oktemberjan 16 Ni 40.09N 44.03 E
Oktjabrsk [Kaz.-U.S.S.R.] 6 Lf 48.40N 57.11 E
Oktjabrsk [R.S.F.S.R.] 7 Lj 53.13N 48.40 E
Oktjabrski [Bye.-U.S.S.R.] 16 Fc 52.38N 28.54 E
Oktjabrski [Kaz.-U.S.S.R.] 17 Kj 52.37N 62.43 E
Oktjabrski [R.S.F.S.R.] 20 Ee 56.05N 99.25 E
Oktjabrski [R.S.F.S.R.] 19 Fe 54.31N 53.28 E
Oktjabrski [R.S.F.S.R.] 17 Hh 56.31N 57.12 E
Oktjabrski [R.S.F.S.R.] 7 Kf 61.05N 43.08 E
Oktjabrski [R.S.F.S.R.] 20 Hf 53.00N 128.42 E
Oktjabrski [R.S.F.S.R.] 20 Kf 52.38N 156.15 E
Oktjabrski [R.S.F.S.R.] 16 Mf 47.56N 43.38 E
Oktjabrskoje 19 Gc 62.28N 66.01 E
Oktjabrskoj Revoljuci, Ostrov-=October Revolution Island (EN) 21 Lb 79.30N 97.00 E
Oku 29b Bb 26.50N 128.17 E
Ōkuchi 28 Kh 32.04N 130.37 E
Okulovka 7 Hg 58.24N 33.18 E
Okushiri 28 Oc 42.09N 139.29 E
Okushiri-Kaikyō 29a Ab 42.15N 139.40 E
Okushiri-Tō 27 Oc 42.10N 139.25 E
Okuta 34 Fd 9.13N 3.11 E
Oku Tango-Hantō 29 Dd 35.40N 135.10 E
Okwa 30 Jk 22.26S 22.58 E
Ola 20 Ke 59.37N 151.20 E
Ólafsfjörđur 7a Ba 66.04N 18.39W
Ólafsvík 7a Ab 64.53N 23.43W
Ola Grande, Punta- 51a Bc 17.55N 66.08W
Olaine/Olajne 7 Fh 56.49N 23.59 E
Olajne/Olaine 7 Fh 56.49N 23.59 E
Olancha 46 Gh 36.17N 117.59W
Olanchito 49 Df 15.30N 86.35W
Olancho [3] 49 Ef 14.45N 86.00W
Öland 5 Hd 56.45N 16.40 E
Ölands norra udde 8 Gg 57.22N 17.05 E
Ölands södra grund 8 Gh 55.40N 17.25 E
Ölands södra udde 8 Gh 56.11N 16.24 E
Olanga 7 Hc 66.08N 30.38 E
Olathe 45 Ig 38.53N 94.49W
Olavarría 53 Ji 36.53S 60.20W
Oława 10 Nf 50.57N 17.17 E
Oława 10 Nf 50.57N 17.17 E
Olbernhau 10 Jf 50.40N 13.20 E
Olbia 6 Gg 40.55N 9.31 E
Olbia, Golfo di- 14 Dj 40.55N 9.40 E
Old Bahama Channel 49 Ib 22.30N 78.05W
Old Bahama Channel (EN)= Bahamas, Canal Viejo de- 49 Ib 22.30N 78.05W
Old Castile (EN)=Castilla la Vieja 13 Ic 41.30N 4.00W
Old Crow 39 Fc 67.35N 139.50W
Oldeani 36 Gc 3.21S 35.33 E
Oldebroek 12 Hb 52.26N 5.53 E
Oldenburg 10 Ec 53.10N 8.12 E
Oldenburg in Holstein 10 Gb 54.18N 10.53 E
Oldenzaal 11 Mb 52.19N 6.56 E
Old Faithful Geyser 46 Jd 44.30N 110.45W
Old Fletton 12 Bb 52.34N 0.15W
Oldham 9 Kh 53.33N 2.07W
Old Hickory Lake 44 Dg 36.18N 86.30W
Oldman River 46 Jb 49.56N 111.42W
Old Marsh Bed 59 Gd 20.55S 130.30 E
Old Mkuski 36 Ee 14.22S 29.22 E
Old Road 51d Bb 17.01N 61.50W
Old Road Town 51c Ab 17.19N 62.48W
Olds 42 Gf 51.47N 114.06W
Old Town 44 Mc 44.56N 68.39W
Old Wives Lake 46 Ma 50.06N 106.00W
Olean 44 Hd 42.05N 78.26W
Olecko 10 Sb 54.03N 22.30 E
Oleiros 13 Ee 39.55N 7.55W
Olëkma 21 Oc 60.22N 120.42 E
Olëkminsk 22 Oc 60.30N 120.15 E
Olëkminski Stanovik 20 Gf 54.00N 119.00 E
Ølen 7 Ag 59.36N 5.48 E
Olenegorsk 19 Db 68.10N 33.13 E
Olenëk 21 Nb 73.00N 119.55 E
Olenëkski Zaliv 20 Hb 73.10N 121.00 E
Olenica 7 Ic 66.29N 35.19 E
Olenj, Ostrov- 20 Cb 72.25N 77.45 E
Olenty 16 Re 49.45N 52.10 E
Oléron, Île d'- 5 Ff 45.56N 1.18W
Olesko 10 Ug 49.53N 24.58 E
Oleśnica 10 Ne 51.13N 17.23 E
Olesno 10 Of 50.53N 18.25 E
Olevsk 16 Ed 51.13N 27.41 E
Olga 20 Ih 43.46N 135.21 E
Olga, Mount- 59 Ge 25.19S 130.46 E
Olgastretet 41 Oc 78.30N 24.00 E
Ølgod 8 Ci 55.49N 8.37 E
Olhão 13 Eg 37.02N 7.50W
Olhovatka 16 Kd 50.17N 39.17 E
Oli 34 Fd 9.40N 4.29 E
Oliana 13 Nb 42.04N 1.19 E
Olib 14 If 44.23N 14.47 E
Oliena 14 Dj 40.16N 9.24 E
Olifants [Afr.] 30 Kk 24.03S 32.40 E
Olifants [Nam.] 37 Be 25.30S 19.30 E
Olifantshoek 37 Ce 27.57S 22.42 E
Olimarao Atoll 57 Fd 7.42N 145.53 E
Olimbía 15 El 37.39N 21.38 E
Ólimbos 15 Kn 35.44N 27.13 E
Ólimbos, Óros-=Olympus, Mount- (EN) 5 Ig 40.05N 22.21 E
Ólimbos Óros 15 Jj 39.05N 26.20 E
Olimpia 55 Hf 20.44S 48.54W
Olinda 54 Le 8.01S 34.51W
Olite 13 Kb 42.29N 1.39W
Oliva [Arg.] 56 Hd 32.03S 63.34W
Oliva [Sp.] 13 Lf 38.55N 0.07W
Oliva, Monasterio de la- 13 Kb 42.20N 1.25W
Oliva de la Frontera 13 Ff 38.16N 6.55W
Oliveira 55 Je 20.41S 44.49W
Oliveira dos Brejinhos 54 Jf 12.19S 42.54W
Olivença 37 Fb 11.46S 35.13 E
Olivenza 13 Ef 38.41N 7.06W
Oliver 46 Fb 49.11N 119.33W
Olivet 11 Hg 47.52N 1.54 E
Olivia 45 Id 44.46N 94.59W
Olja 16 Og 45.47N 47.35 E
Olji Moron He 28 Fb 44.16N 121.42 E
Oljutorski, Mys- 21 Td 59.55N 170.25 E
Oljutorski Zaliv 20 Ld 60.00N 168.00 E
Olkusz 10 Pf 50.17N 19.35 E
Ollan 64d Bb 7.14N 151.38 E
Ollerton 12 Aa 53.13N 1.01W
Olmedo 13 Hc 41.17N 4.41W
Olmos 54 Ce 5.59S 79.46W
Olney [Eng.-U.K.] 12 Bb 52.09N 0.42W
Olney [Il.-U.S.] 45 Lg 38.44N 88.05W
Olney [Tx.-U.S.] 45 Gj 33.22N 98.45W
Oloči 20 Gf 51.20N 119.53 E
Olofström 7 Dh 56.16N 14.30 E
Oloitokitok 36 Gc 2.56S 37.30 E
Oloj 20 Kc 66.20N 159.29 E
Olojski Hrebet 20 Lc 65.50N 162.30 E
Olombo 36 Cc 1.18S 15.53 E
Ólomburi 63a Ec 8.59S 161.09 E
Olomouc 6 Hf 49.36N 17.16 E
Olona 14 De 45.06N 9.21 E
Olonec 19 Dc 61.01N 32.58 E
Olonešty 15 Mc 46.29N 29.52 E
Olongapo 22 Oh 14.50N 120.16 E
Oloron, Gave d'- 11 Ek 43.33N 1.05W
Oloron-Sainte-Marie 11 Fk 43.12N 0.36W
Olosega 65c Db 14.11S 169.39W
Olot 13 Ob 42.11N 2.29 E
Olovjannaja 20 Gf 50.56N 115.35 E
Olovo 14 Mf 44.07N 18.35 E
Olpe 10 De 51.02N 7.51 E
Olpoy 63b Cb 14.52S 166.33 E
Olroyd River 59 Ib 14.10S 141.50 E
Olsberg 12 Kc 51.21N 8.30 E
Olshammar 8 Ff 58.45N 14.48 E
Olst 12 Ib 52.20N 6.08 E
Olsztyn 6 Ie 53.48N 20.29 E
Olsztyn [2] 10 Qc 53.50N 20.30 E
Olsztynek 10 Qc 53.36N 20.17 E
Olt [2] 15 He 44.25N 24.30 E
Olt 5 If 43.43N 24.51 E
Oltedal 8 Bf 58.50N 6.02 E
Olten 14 Bc 47.22N 7.55 E
Olteni 15 Ie 44.11N 25.17 E
Oltenia 15 Ge 44.30N 23.30 E
Olteniţa 15 Je 44.05N 26.38 E
Olteţ 15 He 44.14N 24.27 E
Oltu 24 Ib 40.33N 41.59 E
Oluanpi 27 Lg 21.54N 120.51 E
Olutanga 26 He 7.22N 122.52 E
Olvera 13 Gh 36.56N 5.16W
Olym 16 Kc 52.27N 38.05 E
Olympia 39 Ge 47.03N 122.53W
Olympic Mountains 46 Dc 47.50N 123.45W
Olympus, Mount- 38 Ge 47.48N 123.43W
Olympus, Mount- (EN)= Ólimbos, Óros- 5 Ig 40.05N 22.21 E
Om 20 Cf 54.59N 73.22 E
Ōma 29a Bc 41.30N 140.55 E
Oma 17 Cc 66.45N 46.20 E
Ōmachi 28 Nf 36.30N 137.52 E
Omae-Zaki 29 Fd 34.36N 138.14 E
Ōmagari 28 Pe 39.27N 140.29 E
Omagh/An Ómaigh 9 Fg 54.36N 7.18W
Omaha 39 Je 41.16N 95.57W
Omak 46 Fb 48.24N 119.31W
Omakau 62 Cf 45.06S 169.36 E
Omak Lake 46 Fb 48.16N 119.23W
Oman (EN)='Umān [1] 22 Hg 21.00N 57.00 E
Oman, Gulf of- (EN)= 'Umān, Khalīj- 21 Hg 25.00N 58.00 E
Omarama 61 Ch 44.29S 169.58 E
Omar Gambon 35 He 3.10N 45.47 E
Omaru-Gawa 29 Be 32.07N 131.34 E
Omaruru 37 Bd 21.28S 15.56 E
Omaruru [3] 37 Bd 21.30S 15.00 E
Omatako 37 Bd 21.07S 16.43 E
Omatako, Omuramba- 30 Jj 17.57S 20.25 E
Omate 54 Dg 16.41S 70.59W
Ōma-Zaki 29a Bc 41.32N 140.55 E
Ombai, Selat- 26 Hh 8.30S 125.00 E
Ombella-Mpoko [3] 35 Bd 5.00N 18.00 E
Omberg 8 Ff 58.20N 14.39 E
Ombo 8 Ae 59.15N 6.00 E
Omboué 36 Ac 1.34S 9.15 E
Ombrone 14 Fh 42.39N 11.01 E
Ombu 27 Ee 31.18N 86.33 E
Omčak 20 Jd 61.38N 147.55 E
Omdurman (EN)=Umm Durmān 31 Kg 15.38N 32.30 E
Ōme 29 Fd 35.47N 139.15 E
Omegna 14 Ce 45.53N 8.24 E
Omeo 59 Jg 37.06S 147.36 E
Ömerköy 15 Lj 39.50N 28.04 E
Ometepe, Isla de- 47 Gf 11.30N 85.35W
Ometepec 47 Ee 16.41N 98.25W
Omhajer 35 Fc 14.19N 36.40 E
Ōmihachiman 29 Ed 35.08N 136.05 E
Omihi 62 Ee 43.01S 172.51 E
Omineca 42 Fe 56.05N 124.05W
Omineca Mountains 42 Ee 56.35N 125.55W
Omiš 14 Kg 43.27N 16.42 E
Ōmi-Shima [Jap.] 29 Bd 34.25N 131.15 E
Ōmi-Shima [Jap.] 29 Cd 34.15N 133.00 E
Omitara 37 Bd 22.18S 18.01 E
Ōmiya 27 Od 35.54N 139.38 E
Ommanney Bay 42 Hb 73.00N 101.00W
Omme Å 8 Ci 55.55N 8.25 E
Ommen 12 Ib 52.31N 6.25 E
Omo 30 Kh 4.32N 36.04 E
Omø 8 Di 55.10N 11.10 E
Omoa, Bahía de- 49 Cf 15.50N 88.10W
Omodeo, Lago- 14 Cj 40.10N 8.55 E
Omoloj 20 Ib 71.08N 132.01 E
Omolon 21 Rc 68.42N 158.36 E
Omolon 20 Lc 65.12N 160.27 E
Omono-Gawa 29 Gb 39.44N 140.04 E
Omont 12 Ge 49.36N 4.44 E
Omoto-Gawa 29 Gb 39.51N 141.58 E
Omsk 22 Jd 55.00N 73.24 E
Omskaja Oblast [3] 19 Hd 56.00N 72.30 E
Omsukčan 20 Kd 62.27N 155.50 E
Omsukčanski Hrebet 20 Kd 63.00N 155.10 E
Ōmu 28 Qb 44.34N 142.58 E
Omu, Vîrful- 15 Id 45.26N 25.25 E
Omulew 10 Rc 53.05N 21.32 E
Ōmura 28 Jh 32.54N 129.57 E
Ōmura-Wan 29 Ae 33.00N 129.50 E
Omurtag 15 Jf 43.06N 26.25 E
Ōmuta 28 Kh 33.02N 130.27 E
Omutinski 19 Gd 56.31N 67.45 E
Omutninsk 19 Fd 58.43N 52.12 E
Oña 13 Ib 42.44N 3.24W
Onagawa 29 Gb 38.26N 141.27 E
Onakayale 37 Bc 17.30S 15.01 E
Onaman Lake 45 Ma 50.00N 87.29W
Onamia 45 Jc 46.04N 93.40W
Onamue 64d Bb 7.21N 151.31 E
Onaping Lake 44 Gb 46.57N 81.30W
Onatchiway, Lac- 44 La 49.03N 71.03W
Onawa 45 He 42.02N 96.06W
Onch'ŏn 28 He 38.49N 125.13 E
Oncócua 36 Bf 16.40S 13.24 E
Onda 13 Le 39.58N 0.15W
Ondangua 31 Ij 17.55S 16.00 E
Ondárroa 13 Ja 43.19N 2.25W
Ondava 10 Rh 48.27N 21.48 E
Ondo [2] 34 Gd 7.00N 5.00 E
Ondo [Jap.] 29 Cd 34.12N 132.32 E
Ondo [Nig.] 34 Fd 7.06N 4.50 E
Ondor Sum 28 Bc 42.30N 113.00 E
Ondozero, Ozero- 7 He 63.40N 33.15 E
One and Half Degree Channel 21 Ji 1.30N 73.10 E
Oneata 63d Cc 18.27S 178.29W
Oneata Passage 63d Cc 18.32S 178.28W
Onega 6 Jc 63.57N 38.05 E
Onega 5 Jc 63.58N 37.55 E
Onega, Lake- (EN)= Onežskoje Ozero 5 Jc 61.30N 35.45 E
Onega Peninsula (EN)= Onežski Poluostrov 5 Jc 64.35N 38.00 E
One Hundred Mile House 42 Ff 51.38N 121.16W
Oneida 44 Jd 43.04N 75.40W
Oneida Lake 44 Jd 43.13N 76.00W
O'Neil 43 Hc 42.27N 98.39W
Ōnejime 29 Bf 31.14N 130.47 E
Onekotan, Ostrov- 21 Re 49.25N 154.45 E
Oneonta [Al.-U.S.] 44 Di 33.57N 86.29W
Oneonta [N.Y.-U.S.] 44 Jd 42.28N 75.04W
Oneroa 64p Cb 21.15S 159.43W
Onežskaja Guba 5 Jc 64.20N 36.30 E
Onežski Poluostrov=Onega Peninsula (EN) 5 Jc 64.35N 38.00 E
Onežskoje Ozero=Onega, Lake- (EN) 5 Jc 61.30N 35.45 E
Ongea Levu 63d Cc 19.08S 178.24W

Index Symbols

[1] Independent Nation
[2] State, Region
[3] District, County
[4] Municipality
[5] Colony, Dependency
Continent
Physical Region
Historical or Cultural Region
Mount, Mountain
Volcano
Hill
Mountains, Mountain Range
Hills, Escarpment
Plateau, Upland
Pass, Gap
Plain, Lowland
Delta
Salt Flat
Valley, Canyon
Crater, Cave
Karst Features
Depression
Polder
Desert, Dunes
Forest, Woods
Heath, Steppe
Oasis
Cape, Point
Coast, Beach
Cliff
Peninsula
Isthmus
Sandbank
Island
Atoll
Rock, Reef
Islands, Archipelago
Rocks, Reefs
Coral Reef
Well, Spring
Geyser
River, Stream
Waterfall Rapids
River Mouth, Estuary
Lake
Salt Lake
Intermittent Lake
Reservoir
Swamp, Pond
Canal
Glacier
Ice Shelf, Pack Ice
Ocean
Sea
Gulf, Bay
Strait, Fjord
Lagoon
Bank
Seamount
Tablemount
Ridge
Shelf
Basin
Escarpment, Sea Scarp
Fracture
Trench, Abyss
National Park, Reserve
Point of Interest
Recreation Site
Cave, Cavern
Historic Site
Ruins
Wall, Walls
Church, Abbey
Temple
Scientific Station
Airport
Port
Lighthouse
Mine
Tunnel
Dam, Bridge

Ongijn-Gol 27 Hc 44.30N 103.40 E
Ongjin 27 Md 37.56N 125.22 E
Ongniud Qi (Wudan) 27 Kc 42.58N 119.01 E
Ongole 25 Ge 15.30N 80.03 E
Ongon 27 Jb 45.49N 113.08 E
Onhaye 12 Gd 50.15N 4.50 E
Oni 16 Mh 42.35N 43.27 E
Onigajō-Yama 29 Ce 33.07N 132.41 E
Onilany 30 Lk 23.34S 43.45 E
Onishibetsu 29a Ca 45.21N 142.06 E
Onitsha 31 Hh 6.10N 6.47 E
Ono 29 Dd 34.51N 134.57 E
Ono 63d Bc 18.54S 178.29 E
Ōno [Jap.] 28 Ng 35.59N 136.29 E
Ōno [Jap.] 29 Cd 34.18N 132.17 E
Onoda 29 Be 33.59N 131.11 E
Ōno-Gawa 29 Be 33.15N 131.43 E
Ōnohara-Jima 29 Fd 34.02N 139.23 E
Onohoj 20 Ff 51.55N 108.01 E
Ono-i-Lau Islands 57 Jg 20.39S 178.42W
Onojō 29 Be 33.34N 130.29 E
Onomichi 28 Lg 34.25N 133.12 E
Onon 21 Nd 51.42N 115.50 E
Onoto 50 Dh 9.36N 65.12W
Onotoa Atoll 57 Ie 1.52S 175.34 E
Ons, Isla de- 13 Db 42.23N 8.56W
Onsala 7 Ch 57.25N 12.01 E
Onseepkans 37 Be 28.45S 19.17 E
Onslow 58 Cg 21.39S 115.06 E
Onslow Bay 43 Le 34.20N 77.20W
On-Take 29 Bf 31.35N 130.39 E
Ontake-San 29 Ed 35.53N 137.29 E
Ontario [3] 42 If 50.00N 86.00W
Ontario [Ca.-U.S.] 46 Gi 34.04N 117.39W
Ontario [Or.-U.S.] 43 Dc 44.02N 116.58W
Ontario, Lake- 38 Le 43.40N 78.00W
Ontario Peninsula 38 Ke 43.50N 81.00W
Onteniente/Ontinyent 13 Lf 38.49N 0.37W
Ontinyent/Onteniente 13 Lf 38.49N 0.37W
Ontojärvi 7 Gd 64.08N 29.09 E
Ontonagon 44 Cb 46.52N 89.19W
Ontong Java Atoll 57 Ge 5.20S 159.30 E
Ō-Numa 29a Bc 41.59N 140.41 E
Oodnadatta 58 Eg 27.33S 135.28 E
Ooidonk 12 Fc 51.01N 3.35 E
Ookala 65a Fc 20.01N 155.17W
Ooldea 58 Eh 30.27S 131.50 E
Oologah Lake 45 Ih 36.39N 95.36W
Ooltgensplaat, Oostflakkee- 12 Gc 51.41N 4.21 E
Oostburg 12 Fc 51.20N 3.30 E
Oostelijk Flevoland 12 Hb 52.30N 5.40 E
Oostende/Ostende 11 Ic 51.14N 2.55 E
Oosterhout 11 Kc 51.38N 4.51 E
Oosterschelde=East Schelde (EN) 11 Jc 51.30N 4.00 E
Oosterwolde, Ooststellingwerf- 12 Ha 53.00N 6.18 E
Oosterzele 12 Fd 50.57N 3.48 E
Oostflakkee 12 Gc 51.41N 4.21 E
Oostflakkee-Ooltgensplaat 12 Gc 51.41N 4.21 E
Oostkamp 12 Fc 51.09N 3.14 E
Oost-Souburg, Vlissingen- 12 Fc 51.28N 3.36 E
Ooststellingwerf 12 Ib 53.00N 6.18 E
Ooststellingwerf-Oosterwolde 12 Ha 53.00N 6.18 E
Oost Vieland, Vieland- 12 Ha 53.17N 5.06 E
Oost-Vlaanderen [3] 12 Fc 51.00N 3.40 E
Ootmarsum 12 Ib 52.25N 6.54 E
Opala 36 Dc 0.37S 24.21 E
Opalenica 10 Md 52.19N 16.23 E
Opanake 25 Gg 6.36N 80.37 E
Opari 35 Ee 3.56N 32.03 E
Oparino 7 Lg 59.53N 48.25 E
Opasatika 44 Fa 49.31N 82.58W
Opasatika Lake 44 Fa 49.06N 83.08W
Opasatika River 44 Fa 50.15N 82.25W
Opatija 14 Ie 45.20N 14.19 E
Opatów 10 Rf 50.49N 21.26 E
Opatówka 10 Rf 50.42N 21.50 E
Opava 10 Ng 49.57N 17.54 E
Opava 10 Og 49.51N 18.17 E
Opelika 43 Je 32.39N 85.23W
Opelousas 45 Jk 30.32N 92.05W
Opémisca, Lac- 44 Ja 49.58N 74.57W
Opheim 46 Lb 48.51N 106.24W
Ophir 40 Hd 63.10N 156.31W
Ophthalmia Range 59 Dd 23.15S 119.30 E
Opienge 36 Eb 0.12N 27.30 E
Opihikao 65a Gd 19.26N 154.53W
Opinaca 42 Jf 52.14N 78.02W
Opiscotéo, Lac- 42 Kf 53.09N 68.10W
Opladen, Leverkusen- 10 De 51.04N 7.01 E
Opobo 34 Ge 4.34N 7.27 E
Opočka 19 Cd 56.42N 28.41 E
Opoczno 10 Qe 51.23N 20.17 E
Opole [2] 10 Nf 50.40N 17.55 E
Opole 10 Nf 50.41N 17.55 E
Opole Lubelskie 10 Re 51.09N 21.58 E
Oporny 19 Ff 46.13N 54.29 E
Opotiki 62 Gc 38.01S 177.17 E
Opp 44 Dj 31.17N 86.22W
Oppa-Wan 29 Gb 38.35N 141.30 E
Oppdal 7 Be 62.36N 9.40 E
Oppenheim 10 Eg 49.51N 8.21 E
Oppland [2] 7 Bf 61.10N 9.40 E
Opportunity 46 Gc 47.39N 117.15W
Opsa 8 Li 55.31N 26.54 E
Opsterland 12 Ia 53.03N 6.04 E
Opsterland-Beetsterzwaag 12 Ia 53.03N 6.04 E
Opua 61 Dg 35.18S 174.07 E
Opunake 62 Ec 39.27S 173.51 E
Oputo 48 Eb 30.03N 109.20W
Oquossoc 44 Lc 45.04N 70.44W
Or 16 Ud 51.12N 58.33 E
Ōra 33 Cd 28.20N 19.35 E
Oradea 6 If 47.04N 21.56 E
Orahovac 15 Dg 42.24N 20.40 E
Orahovica 14 Le 45.32N 17.53 E
Orai 25 Fc 25.59N 79.28 E
Oraibi Wash 46 Ji 35.26N 110.49W
Oran 31 Ge 35.42N 0.38W
Oran [3] 32 Gb 36.00N 0.35W
Orange [Austl.] 58 Fh 33.17S 149.06 E
Orange [Fr.] 11 Kj 44.08N 4.48 E
Orange [Tx.-U.S.] 43 Ie 30.01N 93.44W
Orange [Va.-U.S.] 44 Hf 38.14N 78.07W
Orange/Oranje 30 Ik 28.38N 16.27 E
Orange, Cabo- 52 Ke 4.24N 51.33W
Orangeburg 43 Ke 33.30N 80.52W
Orange Free State/Oranje Vrystaat [2] 37 De 29.00S 26.00 E
Orange Lake 44 Fk 29.25N 82.13W
Orange Park 44 Gj 30.10N 81.42W
Orangeville 44 Gd 43.55N 80.06W
Orange Walk 47 Ge 18.06N 88.33W
Orango 30 Fg 11.05N 16.08W
Oranienburg 10 Jd 52.45N 13.14 E
Oranje/Orange 30 Ik 28.38N 16.27 E
Oranje Gebergte 54 Hc 3.00N 55.00W
Oranjemund 37 Be 28.38S 16.24 E
Oranjestad 54 Da 12.33N 70.06W
Oranje Vrystaat/Orange Free State [2] 37 De 29.00S 26.00 E
Oranžerei 16 Og 45.50N 47.36 E
Orapa 37 Dd 21.16S 25.22 E
Orăştie 15 Gd 45.50N 23.12 E
Orava 10 Pg 49.08N 19.10 E
Oravița 15 Ed 45.02N 21.42 E
Orayská Priehradní Nádrž 10 Pg 49.20N 19.35 E
Orb 11 Jk 43.15N 3.18 E
Orba 14 Cf 44.53N 8.37 E
Orba Co 27 De 34.33N 81.06 E
Ørbæk 8 Di 55.16N 10.41 E
Orbec 12 Ce 49.01N 0.25 E
Orbetello 14 Fh 42.27N 11.13 E
Orbetello, Laguna di- 14 Fh 42.25N 11.15 E
Orbigo 13 Gc 41.58N 5.40W
Orbiquet 12 Ce 49.09N 0.14 E
Orbost 59 Jg 37.42S 148.27 E
Örbyhus 8 Gd 60.14N 17.42 E
Orcadas 66 Re 60.40S 44.30W
Orcas Island 46 Db 48.39N 122.55W
Orchies 12 Fd 50.28N 3.14 E
Orchon → Orhon 21 Md 50.21N 106.05 E
Orcia 14 Fh 42.58N 11.21 E
Orco 14 Be 45.10N 7.52 E
Ord, Mount- 59 Fc 17.20S 125.35 E
Órdenes 13 Da 43.04N 8.24W
Ordos Desert (EN)=Mu Us Shamo 21 Mf 38.45N 109.10 E
Ord River 57 Df 15.30S 128.21 E
Ordu 23 Ea 41.00N 37.53 E
Ordubad 16 Oj 38.55N 46.01 E
Ordynskoje 20 Df 54.22N 81.58 E
Ordžonikidze [Ukr.-U.R.S.S.] 16 If 47.40N 34.04 E
Ordžonikidze [Kaz.-U.S.S.R.] 17 Jj 52.25N 61.45 E
Ordžonikidze [R.S.F.S.R.] 6 Kg 43.03N 44.40 E
Ordžonikidzeabad 19 Gh 38.34N 69.02 E
Ore älv 8 Fc 61.08N 14.35 E
Orebić 14 Lh 42.58N 17.11 E
Örebro 6 Hd 59.17N 15.13 E
Örebro [2] 7 Dg 59.30N 15.00 E
Oredež 8 Nf 58.50N 30.13 E
Oregon 44 Fe 41.38N 83.28W
Oregon [2] 43 Cc 44.00N 121.00W
Oregon City 43 Cb 45.21N 122.36W
Oregon Inlet 44 Jh 35.50N 75.35W
Öregrund 8 Hd 60.20N 18.26 E
Orehov 16 If 47.34N 35.47 E
Orehovo-Zujevo 6 Jd 55.49N 38.59 E
Orel 6 Je 52.59N 36.05 E
Orel 16 Ie 48.31N 34.55 E
Orel, Gora- 20 Jf 53.55N 140.01 E
Orellana [Peru] 54 Ce 6.54S 75.04W
Orellana [Peru] 54 Cd 4.40S 78.10W
Orem 43 Ec 40.19N 111.42W
Ore Mountains (EN)= Erzgebirge 5 He 50.30N 13.15 E
Ore Mountains (EN)= Krušné Hory 5 He 50.30N 13.15 E
Ören 24 Bd 37.18N 29.17 E
Orenbel 24 Hb 40.00N 39.10 E
Orenburg 6 Le 51.54N 55.06 E
Orenburgskaja Oblast [3] 19 Fe 52.00N 55.00 E
Örencik 24 Cc 39.16N 29.34 E
Orense [3] 13 Eb 42.10N 7.30W
Orense [Arg.] 56 Ie 38.40S 59.47W
Orense [Sp.] 13 Eb 42.20N 7.51W
Oreón, Dhíavlos- 15 Fk 38.54N 22.55 E
Orepuki 62 Bg 46.17S 167.44 E
Orestiás 15 Jh 41.30N 26.31 E
Øresund 5 Hd 55.50N 12.40 E
Oreti 62 Cg 46.28S 168.17 E
Orewa 62 Fb 36.35S 174.42 E
Orford 12 Db 52.05N 1.32 E
Orford Ness 9 Oi 52.05N 1.34 E
Orgañá/Organyà 13 Nb 42.13N 1.20 E
Organ Needle 45 Cj 32.21N 106.33W
Organyà/Orgañá 13 Nb 42.13N 1.20 E
Orgaz 13 Ie 39.39N 3.54W
Orgejev 19 Cf 47.23N 28.50 E
Orgelet 11 Lh 46.31N 5.37 E
Orgon Tal 28 Bc 43.20N 112.40 E
Orgosolo 14 Dj 40.12N 9.21 E
Orgūn 23 Kc 32.57N 69.11 E
Orhaneli 15 Lj 39.54N 29.00 E
Orhaneli/Koca Çay 15 Lj 39.56N 28.32 E
Orhangazi 15 Mi 40.30N 29.18 E
Orhomenós 15 Fk 38.35N 22.54 E
Orhon (Orchon) 21 Md 50.21N 106.05 E
Orhy, Pico de- 13 La 42.59N 1.00W
Oria 13 Ja 43.17N 2.08W
Orichuna, Río- 50 Bi 7.30N 68.13W
Orick 46 Cf 41.17N 124.04W
Oriental 48 Kh 19.22N 97.37W
Oriental, Cordillera- 49 Md 18.55N 69.15W
Oriente 56 He 38.44S 60.37W
Orihuela 13 Lf 38.05N 0.57W
Oriku 15 Ci 40.17N 19.25 E
Óri Lekánis 15 Hh 41.08N 24.33 E
Orillia 42 Jh 44.37N 79.25W
Orimattila 7 Ff 60.48N 25.45 E
Orinoco, Río- 52 Je 8.37N 62.15W
Oripää 8 Jd 60.51N 22.41 E
Orissa [3] 25 Gd 21.00N 84.00 E
Orissaare/Orissare 7 Fg 58.34N 23.05 E
Orissare/Orissaare 7 Fg 58.34N 23.05 E
Oristano 14 Ck 39.54N 8.36 E
Oristano, Golfo di- 14 Ck 39.50N 8.30 E
Orituco, Río- 50 Ch 8.45N 67.27W
Orivesi 5 Ic 62.15N 29.25 E
Orivesi 7 Ff 61.41N 24.21 E
Oriximiná 54 Gd 1.45S 55.52W
Orizaba 39 Jh 18.51N 97.06W
Orizaba, Pico de- (Citlaltépetl, Volcán-) 38 Jh 19.01N 97.16W
Orizona 55 Hc 17.03S 48.18W
Orjahovo 15 Gf 43.44N 23.58 E
Ørje 8 De 59.29N 11.39 E
Orjen 15 Bg 42.34N 18.33 E
Orjiva 13 Ih 36.54N 3.25W
Orkanger 7 Be 63.19N 9.52 E
Orkdalen 8 Ca 63.15N 9.50 E
Örkelljunga 8 Eh 56.17N 13.17 E
Orkla 8 Ca 63.18N 9.50 E
Orkney 37 De 27.00S 26.39 E
Orkney [3] 9 Kb 59.00N 3.00W
Orkney Islands 5 Fd 59.00N 3.00W
Orlândia 55 Ie 20.43S 47.53W
Orlando 39 Kg 28.32N 81.23W
Orlando, Capo d'- 14 Il 38.10N 14.45 E
Orlanka 10 Td 52.52N 23.12 E
Orléanais 11 Hf 48.40N 1.20 E
Orléans 6 Gf 47.55N 1.54 E
Orlice 10 Lf 50.12N 15.49 E
Orlické Hory 10 Mf 50.10N 16.30 E
Orlik 20 Ef 52.30N 99.55 E
Orlovskaja Oblast [3] 19 De 52.45N 36.30 E
Orlovski 16 Mf 46.52N 42.06 E
Orlovski, mys- 7 Jc 67.16N 41.18 E
Orly 11 If 48.45N 2.24 E
Ormāra 25 Cc 25.12N 64.38 E
Ormes 12 Ce 49.03N 0.59 E
Ormoc 26 Hd 11.00N 124.37 E
Ormond 62 Gc 38.33S 177.55 E
Ormond Beach 44 Gk 29.17N 81.02W
Ornain 11 Kf 48.46N 4.47 E
Ornans 11 Mg 47.06N 6.09 E
Ornäs 8 Fd 60.31N 15.32 E
Orne [3] 11 Gf 48.40N 0.05 E
Orne [Fr.] 11 Ie 49.17N 6.11 E
Orne [Fr.] 11 Be 49.19N 0.14W
Orne Seamount (EN) 61 Je 27.30S 157.30W
Orneta 10 Qb 54.08N 20.08 E
Ornö 7 Eg 59.05N 18.25 E
Ornsköldsvik 7 Ee 63.18N 18.43 E
Oro 28 Id 40.01N 127.27 E
Oro, Río de- 55 Ch 27.04S 58.34W
Oro, Río del- 48 Ge 25.35N 105.03W
Orocué 54 Dc 4.48N 71.20W
Orodara 34 Ec 10.59N 4.55W
Orofino 46 Gc 46.29N 116.15W
Orogrande 45 Cj 32.23N 106.08W
Orohena, Mont- 65e Fc 17.31S 149.28W
Oroluk Atoll 57 Gd 7.32N 155.18 E
Orom 36 Fb 3.20N 33.40 E
Oromocto 42 Kg 45.51N 66.29W
Oron 34 Ge 4.50N 8.14 E
Orona Atoll (Hull) 57 Je 4.29S 172.10W
Orongo 65d Ac 27.10S 109.26W
Oronsay 9 Ge 56.01N 6.14W
Orontes (EN)=Nahr al 'Āsī 23 Eb 36.02N 35.58 E
Oropesa [Sp.] 13 Ge 39.55N 5.10W
Oropesa [Sp.] 13 Ld 40.06N 0.09W
Oroqen Zizhiqi (Alihe) 27 La 50.35N 123.42 E
Oroquieta 26 He 8.29N 123.48 E
Orós 54 Ke 6.15S 38.55W
Orós, Açude- 54 Ke 6.15S 39.05W
Orosei 14 Dj 40.23N 9.42 E
Orosei, Golfo di- 14 Dj 40.15N 9.45 E
Orosháza 10 Qj 46.34N 20.40 E
Oro-Shima 29 Be 33.52N 130.02 E
Oroszlány 10 Oi 47.29N 18.19 E
Orote Peninsula 64c Bb 13.26N 144.38 E
Orote Point 64c Bb 13.27N 144.37 E
Orotukan 20 Kd 62.17N 151.50 E
Oroville [Ca.-U.S.] 46 Eg 39.31N 121.33W
Oroville [Wa.-U.S.] 46 Fb 48.56N 119.26W
Orp-Jauche 12 Gd 50.40N 4.57 E
Orqohan 27 Lb 49.36N 121.23 E
Orr 45 Jb 48.03N 92.50W
Orrefors 8 Fh 56.50N 15.45 E
Orri, Pic d'-/Llorri 13 Nb 42.23N 1.12 E
Orša 6 Je 54.30N 30.24 E
Orsa 7 Df 61.07N 14.37 E
Orsasjön 8 Fc 61.05N 14.35 E
Orsay 12 Ef 48.42N 2.11 E
Orsjön 8 Gc 61.35N 16.20 E
Orsk 6 Le 51.12N 58.34 E
Orşova 15 Fe 44.42N 22.25 E
Ørsta 7 Be 62.12N 6.09 E
Örsundsbro 8 Ge 59.44N 17.18 E
Orta, Lago d'- 14 Ce 45.50N 8.25 E
Ortaca 24 Cd 36.49N 28.47 E
Ortakent 15 Kl 37.02N 27.21 E
Ortaklar 15 Kl 37.53N 27.30 E
Orta Nova 14 Ji 41.19N 15.42 E
Orte 14 Gh 42.27N 12.23 E
Ortegal, Cabo- 13 Ea 43.45N 7.53W
Ortenberg 12 Ld 50.21N 9.03 E
Orthez 11 Fk 43.29N 0.46W
Orthon, Río- 54 Ef 10.50S 66.04W
Ortigueira [Braz.] 56 Jb 24.12S 50.55W
Ortigueira [Sp.] 13 Fa 43.34N 6.44W
Ortisei / Sankt Ulrich 14 Fd 46.34N 11.40 E
Ortiz [Mex.] 48 Dc 28.15N 110.43W
Ortiz [Ven.] 50 Ch 9.37N 67.17W
Ortlergruppe/Ortles 14 Ed 46.30N 10.40 E
Ortles/Ortlergruppe 14 Ed 46.30N 10.40 E
Ortolo 11a Ab 41.30N 8.55 E
Ortona 14 Ih 42.21N 14.24 E
Ortonville 45 Hd 45.19N 96.27W
Orto-Tokoj 18 Kc 42.20N 76.02 E
Örtze 10 Fd 52.40N 9.57 E
Orukuizu 64a Ac 7.10N 134.17 E
Orūmīyeh 22 Gf 37.33N 45.04 E
Orūmīyeh, Daryācheh-ye-= Urmia, Lake- (EN) 21 Gf 37.40N 45.30 E
Oruro [2] 54 Eg 18.40S 67.30W
Oruro 53 Jg 17.59S 67.09W
Orust 8 Df 58.10N 11.38 E
Orūzgān [3] 23 Kc 33.15N 66.00 E
Orūzgān 23 Kc 32.56N 66.38 E
Orval, Abbaye d'- 12 He 49.38N 5.22 E
Orvault 11 Eg 47.16N 1.37W
Orvieto 14 Gh 42.43N 12.07 E
Orville Escarpment 66 Qf 75.45S 65.30W
Órvilos, Óros- 15 Gh 41.23N 23.36 E
Orwell 12 Dc 51.58N 1.18 E
Orxois 12 Fe 49.08N 3.12 E
Orz 10 Rd 52.50N 21.30 E
Orzinuovi 14 De 45.24N 9.55 E
Orzyc 10 Rd 52.47N 21.13 E
Orzysz 10 Rc 53.49N 21.56 E
Oš 19 Hg 40.32N 72.50 E
Os 7 Ce 62.30N 11.12 E
Osa 19 Fd 57.17N 55.26 E
Oša 8 Lh 56.21N 26.29 E
Osa 10 Oc 53.33N 18.45 E
Osa, Península de- 47 Hg 8.35N 83.33W
Osage 45 Je 43.17N 92.49W
Osage River 43 Id 38.35N 91.57W
Osaka 29 Ed 35.57N 137.14 E
Ōsaka 22 Pf 34.40N 135.30 E
Osaka Bay (EN)=Ōsaka-Wan 28 Mg 34.36N 135.27 E
Ōsaka-Fu [2] 28 Mg 34.45N 135.35 E
Osakarovka 19 He 50.32N 72.39 E
Ōsaka-Wan=Osaka Bay (EN) 28 Mg 34.36N 135.27 E
Osăm 15 Hf 43.42N 24.51 E
Osan 28 If 37.09N 127.04 E
Osasco 55 If 23.32S 46.46W
Osat 14 Nf 44.02N 19.20 E
Osawatomie 45 Ig 38.31N 94.57W
Osborne 45 Gg 39.26N 98.42W
Osburger Hochwald 12 Ie 49.40N 6.50 E
Osby 7 Ch 56.22N 13.59 E
Osceola [Ar.-U.S.] 45 Li 35.42N 89.58W
Osceola [Ia.-U.S.] 43 Ic 41.02N 93.46W
Osceola [Mo.-U.S.] 45 Jh 38.03N 93.42W
Oschatz 10 Je 51.18N 13.07 E
Oschersleben 10 Hd 52.02N 11.15 E
Oschiri 14 Dj 40.43N 9.06 E
Osen 7 Cd 64.18N 10.31 E
Osered 16 Ld 50.01N 40.48 E
Osetr 16 Kb 55.00N 38.45 E
Ōse-Zaki 28 Jh 32.38N 128.42 E
Oshamanbe 28 Pc 42.30N 140.22 E
Oshawa 42 Jh 43.54N 78.51W
Oshekehia Lake 37 Bc 18.08S 15.45 E
Oshika 29 Gb 38.17N 141.31 E
Oshika-Hantō 28 Pe 38.22N 141.27 E
Oshikango 37 Bc 17.22S 15.55 E
Oshima 29 Ce 33.55N 132.11 E
Ō-Shima [Jap.] 29 De 33.28N 135.50 E
Ō-Shima [Jap.] 29 Ae 33.30N 129.33 E
Ō-Shima [Jap.] 29 Ae 32.34N 128.54 E
Ō-Shima [Jap.] 29 Be 33.54N 130.27 E
Ō-Shima [Jap.] 27 Oe 34.45N 139.30 E
Ōshima [Jap.] 29 Fd 34.44N 139.20 E
Ō-Shima [Jap.] 29 Bf 31.32N 131.25 E
Ō-Shima [Jap.] 29 De 33.38N 134.30 E
Ō-Shima [Jap.] 29 Cd 34.10N 133.05 E
Ōshima [Jap.] 29 Ae 33.04N 129.36 E
Ō-Shima [Jap.] 28 Od 41.30N 139.15 E
Ō-Shima [Jap.] 28 Jh 32.04N 128.26 E
Oshima-Hantō 28 Pd 41.40N 140.30 E
Ōshima-Kaikyō 29b Ba 28.10N 129.15 E
Oshkosh [Nb.-U.S.] 45 Ef 41.24N 102.21W
Oshkosh [Wi.-U.S.] 43 Jc 44.01N 88.33W
Oshnaviyeh 24 Kd 37.02N 45.06 E
Oshogbo 31 Hh 7.46N 4.34 E
Oshtorān Kūh 23 Gc 33.20N 49.16 E
Oshtorīnān 24 Me 34.01N 48.38 E
Oshwe 36 Cc 3.24S 19.30 E
Osich'ŏn-ni 28 Jd 41.25N 128.16 E
Osijek 6 Hf 45.33N 18.42 E
Osilo 14 Cj 40.45N 8.40 E
Osimo 14 Hg 43.28N 13.29 E
Osinki 7 Lj 52.52N 49.31 E
Osinniki 20 Df 53.37N 87.31 E
Osipaonica 15 Ee 44.33N 21.04 E
Osipoviči 16 Fc 53.19N 28.40 E
Osječenica 14 Kf 44.29N 16.17 E
Oskaloosa 45 Jf 41.18N 92.39W
Oskarshamn 7 Dh 57.16N 16.26 E
Oskarström 8 Eh 56.48N 12.58 E
Oskélanéo 44 Ja 48.08N 75.05W
Oskino 20 Fd 60.48N 107.58 E
Öskjuvatn 7a Cb 65.02N 16.45W
Oskol 16 Je 49.06N 37.25 E
Oskū 24 Ld 37.55N 46.06 E
Oslava 10 Mg 49.05N 16.22 E
Ösling 11 Le 49.55N 6.00 E
Osljanka, Gora- 17 Ig 59.10N 58.33 E
Oslo [2] 7 Cg 59.55N 10.45 E
Oslo 6 Hd 59.55N 10.45 E
Oslofjorden 5 Hd 59.20N 10.35 E
Osmānābād 25 Fe 18.10N 76.03 E
Osmancık 24 Fb 40.59N 34.49 E
Osmaneli 15 Ni 40.22N 30.01 E
Osmaniye 23 Eb 37.05N 36.14 E
Osmino 8 Mf 58.54N 29.15 E
Ošmjanskaja Vozvyšennost 8 Kj 54.30N 26.00 E
Ošmjany 16 Db 54.27N 25.57 E
Ösmo 8 Gf 58.59N 17.54 E
Osmussaar/Osmussar 8 Je 59.20N 23.15 E
Osmussar/Osmussaar 8 Je 59.20N 23.15 E
Osnabrück 6 Ge 52.16N 8.03 E
Osning 12 Kb 52.10N 8.05 E
Oso, Sierra del- 48 Gd 26.00N 105.25W
Osobłoga 10 Nf 50.27N 17.58 E
Osogovske Planine 15 Fg 42.10N 22.30 E
Osor 14 If 44.42N 14.24 E
Osório 56 Jc 29.54S 50.16W
Osorno 53 Ij 40.34S 73.09W
Osoyoos 42 Fg 49.02N 119.28W
Osøyra 7 Af 60.11N 5.28 E
Ospino 50 Bh 9.18N 69.27W
Osprey Reef 57 Ff 13.55S 146.40 E
Oss 11 Lc 51.46N 5.31 E
Ossa, Mount- 57 Fi 41.54S 146.01 E
Óssa, Óros- 15 Fj 39.49N 22.40 E
Ossabaw Island 44 Gj 31.47N 81.06W
Ossa de Montiel 13 Jf 38.58N 2.45W
Osse 11 Gj 44.07N 0.17 E
Ossining 44 Ke 41.10N 73.52W
Ossjøen 8 Dc 61.15N 11.55 E
Oŝskaja Oblast [3] 19 Hg 40.45N 73.20 E
Ossora 20 Le 59.15N 163.02 E
Östanvik 8 Fc 61.10N 15.13 E
Ostaškov 19 Dd 57.09N 33.07 E
Ostbevern 12 Jb 52.03N 7.51 E
Oste 10 Fc 53.33N 9.10 E
Ostende/Oostende 11 Ic 51.14N 2.55 E
Oster 16 Gd 50.55N 30.57 E
Oster [Ukr.-U.S.S.R.] 16 Gd 50.53N 30.55 E
Oster [U.S.S.R.] 16 Gc 53.47N 31.45 E
Osterburg in der Altmark 10 Hd 52.47N 11.44 E
Österbybruk 8 Gd 60.12N 17.54 E
Österdalälven 7 Df 60.33N 15.08 E
Østerdalen 7 Cf 62.00N 10.40 E
Osterfjorden 8 Ad 60.30N 5.20 E
Österforse 8 Ga 63.09N 17.01 E
Östergarnsholm 8 Hg 57.25N 19.00 E
Östergötland 8 Ff 58.25N 15.35 E
Östergötland [2] 7 Dg 58.25N 15.45 E
Osterholz Scharmbeck 10 Ec 53.14N 8.48 E
Österlen 8 Fi 55.30N 14.10 E
Ostermark/Teuva 7 Ee 62.29N 21.44 E
Osterode am Harz 10 Ge 51.44N 10.11 E
Osterøya 7 Af 60.35N 5.35 E
Österreich = Austria (EN) [1] 6 Hf 47.30N 14.00 E
Östersjön=Baltic Sea (EN) 5 Hd 57.00N 19.00 E
Østersøen=Baltic Sea (EN) 5 Hd 57.00N 19.00 E
Östersund 6 Hc 63.11N 14.39 E
Osterwick, Rosendahl- 12 Jb 52.01N 7.12 E
Østfold [2] 7 Cg 59.20N 11.30 E
Ostfriesische Inseln=East Frisian Islands (EN) 10 Dc 53.45N 7.25 E
Ostfriesland=East Friesland (EN) 10 Dc 53.20N 7.40 E
Østgrønland=East Greenland (EN) [2] 41 Id 72.00N 35.00W
Östhammar 7 Ed 60.16N 18.22 E
Osthofen 12 Ke 49.42N 8.20 E
Östmark 8 Ed 60.17N 12.45 E
Ostrach 10 Fh 48.05N 9.25 E
Östra Silen 8 Ee 59.15N 12.20 E
Ostrava 6 Hf 49.50N 18.17 E
Ostrhauderfehn 12 Ja 53.08N 7.37 E
Ostróda 10 Pc 53.43N 19.59 E
Ostrog 16 Ed 50.19N 26.32 E
Ostrogožsk 19 De 50.52N 39.05 E
Ostrołęka [2] 10 Rc 53.05N 21.35 E
Ostrołęka 10 Rc 53.06N 21.34 E
Ostrošicki Gorodok 8 Lj 54.03N 27.46 E
Ostrov [Bye.-U.S.S.R.] 10 Vd 52.48N 26.01 E
Ostrov [Czech.] 10 If 50.18N 12.57 E
Ostrov [Rom.] 15 Ke 44.07N 27.22 E
Ostrov [R.S.F.S.R.] 19 Cd 57.23N 28.22 E
Ostrov [R.S.F.S.R.] 8 Mf 58.28N 28.44 E
Ostrovec 8 Lj 54.38N 26.06 E
Ostrovicës, Mali i- 15 Di 40.34N 20.27 E
Ostrovskoje 7 Kh 57.50N 42.13 E
Ostrov Zmeiny 16 Gg 45.15N 30.12 E
Ostrowiec Świętokrzyski 10 Rf 50.57N 21.23 E
Ostrów Lubelski 10 Se 51.30N 22.52 E
Ostrów Mazowiecka 10 Rd 52.49N 21.54 E
Ostrów Wielkopolski 10 Ne 51.39N 17.49 E
Ostryna 10 Uc 53.41N 24.37 E
Ostrzeszów 10 Ne 51.25N 17.57 E
Ostsee=Baltic Sea (EN) 5 Hd 57.00N 19.00 E
Oststeirisches Hügelland 14 Jd 47.00N 15.45 E
Osttirol 14 Gd 46.55N 12.30 E
Ostuni 14 Lj 40.44N 17.35 E
Osumi 15 Ci 40.48N 19.52 E
Ōsumi 29 Bf 31.36N 130.59 E
Ōsumi-Hantō 29 Bf 31.15N 130.50 E
Osumi Islands (EN)=Ōsumi-Shotō 21 Pf 30.35N 130.59 E
Ōsumi-Shotō=Osumi Islands (EN) 21 Pf 30.35N 130.59 E
Osuna 13 Gg 37.14N 5.07W
Osveja 8 Mi 55.59N 28.10 E
Osvejskoje, Ozero- 8 Mh 56.00N 28.15 E
Oswego 43 Lc 43.27N 76.31W
Oswestry 9 Ji 52.52N 3.04W

Index Symbols

[1] Independent Nation
[2] State, Region
[3] District, County
[4] Municipality
[5] Colony, Dependency
Continent
Physical Region
Historical or Cultural Region
Mount, Mountain
Volcano
Hill
Mountains, Mountain Range
Hills, Escarpment
Plateau, Upland
Pass, Gap
Plain, Lowland
Delta
Salt Flat
Valley, Canyon
Crater, Cave
Karst Features
Depression
Polder
Desert, Dunes
Forest, Woods
Heath, Steppe
Oasis
Cape, Point
Coast, Beach
Cliff
Peninsula
Isthmus
Sandbank
Island
Atoll
Rock, Reef
Islands, Archipelago
Rocks, Reefs
Coral Reef
Well, Spring
Geyser
River, Stream
Waterfall Rapids
River Mouth, Estuary
Lake
Salt Lake
Intermittent Lake
Reservoir
Swamp, Pond
Canal
Glacier
Ice Shelf, Pack Ice
Ocean
Sea
Gulf, Bay
Strait, Fjord
Lagoon
Bank
Seamount
Tablemount
Ridge
Shelf
Basin
Escarpment, Sea Scarp
Fracture
Trench, Abyss
National Park, Reserve
Point of Interest
Recreation Site
Cave, Cavern
Historic Site
Ruins
Wall, Walls
Church, Abbey
Temple
Scientific Station
Airport
Port
Lighthouse
Mine
Tunnel
Dam, Bridge

Oświęcim	10	Pf	50.03N	19.12 E
Osyka	45	Kk	31.00N	90.28W
Ōta	29	Fc	36.18N	139.22 E
Ota	29	Ec	35.56N	136.03 E
Otago [2]	62	Cf	45.00S	169.10 E
Otago Peninsula	62	Df	45.50S	170.45 E
Ōtake	28	Lg	34.12N	132.13 E
Otakeho	62	Fc	39.33S	174.03 E
Otaki	62	Fd	40.45S	175.08 E
Ōtakime-Yama	29	Gc	37.22N	140.42 E
Otanoshike	29a	Db	43.01N	144.16 E
Otar	19	Hg	43.31N	75.12 E
Otaru	27	Pc	43.13N	141.00 E
Otautau	62	Bg	46.09S	168.00 E
Otava	10	Kg	49.26N	14.12 E
Otava	8	Lc	61.39N	27.04 E
Otavi	37	Bc	19.39S	17.20 E
Ōtawara	28	Pf	36.52N	140.02 E
Otelu Roşu	15	Fd	45.32N	22.22 E
Otematata	62	Df	44.37S	170.11 E
Otepää/Otepja	7	Gg	58.03N	26.30 E
Otepää, Vozvyšennost-/ Otepää Kõrgustik	8	Lf	58.00N	26.40 E
Otepää Kõrgustik/Otepää, Vozvyšennost-	8	Lf	58.00N	26.40 E
Otepja/Otepää	7	Gg	58.03N	26.30 E
Oteros	47	Cc	26.55N	108.30W
Othain	12	He	49.31N	5.23 E
Othello	46	Fc	46.50N	119.10W
Othonoi	15	Cj	39.50N	19.25 E
Óthris Óros	15	Fj	39.02N	22.37 E
Oti	30	Hh	7.48N	0.08 E
Otira	62	De	42.51S	171.33 E
Otish, Monts-	38	Md	52.45N	69.15W
Otjikondo	37	Bc	19.50S	15.23 E
Otjimbingwe	37	Bd	22.21S	16.08 E
Otjiwarongo	31	Ik	20.29S	16.36 E
Otjiwarongo [3]	37	Bd	20.30S	17.30 E
Otjosondjou, Omuramba-	30	Ij	19.55S	20.00 E
Otjosondu	37	Bd	21.12S	17.58 E
Otmuchowskie, Jezioro-	10	Nf	50.27N	17.15 E
Otnes	7	Cf	61.46N	11.12 E
Otobe	29a	Bc	41.57N	140.08 E
Otočac	14	Jf	44.52N	15.14 E
Otofuke	29a	Cb	42.59N	143.10 E
Otofuke-Gawa	29a	Cb	42.56N	143.12 E
Otog Qi (Ulan)	27	Id	39.07N	108.00 E
Otoineppu	29a	Ca	44.43N	142.16 E
Otok	14	Me	45.09N	18.53 E
Otopeni	15	Je	44.33N	26.04 E
Otorohanga	62	Fc	38.11S	175.12 E
Otorten, Gora-	17	If	61.50N	59.13 E
Ōtoyo	29	Ce	33.46N	133.40 E
Otra	5	Gd	58.09N	8.00 E
Otradnaja	16	Lg	44.23N	41.31 E
Otradnoje, Ozero-	8	Nd	60.50N	30.25 E
Otradny	7	Mj	53.23N	51.24 E
Otranto	14	Mj	40.09N	18.30 E
Otranto, Canale d'-= Otranto, Strait of- (EN)	5	Hg	40.00N	19.00 E
Otranto, Capo d'-	14	Mj	40.06N	18.31 E
Otranto, Strait of- (EN)= Otranto, Canale d'-	5	Hg	40.00N	19.00 E
Otranto, Strait of- (EN)= Otrantos, Kanali i-	15	Bi	40.00N	19.00 E
Otranto, Terra d'-	14	Mj	40.20N	18.15 E
Otrantos, Kanali i-=Otranto, Strait of- (EN)	15	Bi	40.00N	19.00 E
Ötscher	14	Jc	47.51N	15.12 E
Ōtsu	28	Mg	35.00N	135.52 E
Ōtsuchi	28	Pe	39.21N	141.54 E
Ōtsuki [Jap.]	29	Fd	35.36N	138.54 E
Ōtsuki [Jap.]	29	Ce	32.50N	132.41 E
Otta	8	Cc	61.46N	9.31 E
Otta	7	Bf	61.46N	9.32 E
Otta	64d	Bb	7.09N	151.54 E
Ottadalen	8	Bc	61.55N	8.00 E
Ottana	14	Dj	40.15N	9.05 E
Otta Pass	64d	Bb	7.09N	151.53 E
Ottawa [Il.-U.S.]	45	Lf	41.21N	88.51W
Ottawa [Ks.-U.S.]	43	Hd	38.37N	95.16W
Ottawa [Oh.-U.S.]	44	Ee	41.02N	84.03W
Ottawa [Ont.-Can.]	39	Le	45.25N	75.42W
Ottawa Islands	38	Kd	59.30N	80.10W
Ottawa River	38	Le	45.20N	73.58W
Ottemby	7	Dh	56.16N	16.24 E
Otterberg	12	Je	49.30N	7.46 E
Otter Creek	44	Fk	29.19N	82.48W
Otterndorf	10	Ec	53.48N	8.54 E
Otteroy	8	Bb	62.40N	6.50 E
Otter Rapids	44	Ga	50.15N	81.45W
Otterup	8	Di	55.31N	10.24 E
Ottumwa	43	Ic	41.01N	92.25W
Ottweiler	12	Je	49.23N	7.10 E
Otukpa	34	Gd	7.05N	7.40 E
Otumpa	55	Ah	27.19S	62.13W
Otuquis, Bañados de-	54	Gg	19.20S	58.30W
Otuquis, Río-	55	Cd	19.41S	58.20W
Oturkpo	34	Gd	7.13N	8.09 E
Otu Tolu Group	65b	Bb	20.21S	174.32W
Otuzco	54	Ce	7.54S	78.35W
Otway, Cape-	59	Ig	38.52S	143.31 E
Otwock	10	Rd	52.07N	21.16 E
Otynja	10	Uh	48.40N	24.57 E
Ötz	14	Ec	47.12N	10.54 E
Ötztaler Ache	14	Ec	47.14N	10.50 E
Ötztaler Alpen	10	Gi	46.45N	10.55 E
Ou	25	Kd	20.04N	102.13 E
'O'ua	65b	Bb	20.02S	174.41W
Oua	63b	Ce	21.14S	167.05 E
Ouachita, Lake-	45	Ji	34.40N	93.25W
Ouachita Mountains	38	Jf	34.40N	94.25W
Ouachita River	43	Ie	31.38N	91.49W
Ouadane	31	Ff	20.57N	11.35W
Ouaddaï [3]	35	Cc	13.00N	21.00 E
Ouaddaï	30	Jg	13.00N	21.00 E
Ouagadougou	31	Gg	12.22N	1.31W
Ouahigouya	31	Gg	13.35N	2.25W
Ouaka [3]	35	Cd	6.00N	21.00 E
Ouaka	30	Ih	4.59N	19.56 E
Oualata	32	Ff	17.18N	7.00W
Oualata, Dahr-	32	Ff	17.48N	7.24W
Oualidia	32	Fc	32.44N	9.02W
Ouallam	34	Fc	14.19N	2.05 E
Ouallene	32	He	24.35N	1.17 E
Ouanda-Djallé	35	Cd	8.54N	22.48 E
Ouandjia	35	Cd	8.35N	23.12 E
Ouandjia	35	Cd	9.35N	21.43 E
Ouango	35	Ce	4.19N	22.33 E
Ouangolodougou	34	Dd	9.58N	5.09W
Ouanne	11	Ig	47.57N	2.47 E
Ouarane	30	Ff	21.00N	10.00W
Ouargaye	34	Fc	11.32N	0.01 E
Ouargla	31	He	31.57N	5.20 E
Ouargla [3]	32	Id	30.00N	6.30 E
Ouarkziz, Jbel-	30	Gf	28.00N	8.20W
Ouarra	30	Jh	5.05N	24.26 E
Ouarsenis, Djebel-	13	Ni	35.53N	1.38 E
Ouarsenis, Massif de l'-	32	Hb	35.50N	2.05 E
Ouarzazate [3]	32	Fc	31.00N	6.30W
Ouarzazate	32	Fc	30.55N	6.55W
Oubangui	30	Ii	0.30S	17.42 E
Ouborré, Pointe-	63b	Dd	18.47S	169.16 E
Ouche, Pays d'-	11	Gf	48.55N	0.45 E
Ōuchi	29	Gb	39.27N	140.06 E
Oud Beijerland	12	Gc	51.50N	4.26 E
Oude IJssel	12	Ic	52.00N	6.10 E
Oudenaarde/Audenarde	11	Jd	50.51N	3.36 E
Oudenbosch	12	Gc	51.35N	4.34 E
Oude Rijn	11	Kb	52.05N	4.20 E
Oudon	11	Fg	47.37N	0.42W
Oudtshoorn	31	Jl	33.35S	22.14 E
Oued Ben Tili	32	Fd	25.48N	9.32W
Oued el Abtal	13	Mi	35.27N	0.41 E
Oued Fodda	13	Nh	36.11N	1.32 E
Oued Lili	13	Ni	35.31N	1.16 E
Oued Rhiou	32	Hb	35.58N	0.55 E
Oued-Taria	13	Mi	35.07N	0.05 E
Oued Tlelat	13	Li	35.33N	0.27W
Oued Zem	31	Ge	32.52N	6.34W
Ouégoa	63b	Be	20.21S	164.26 E
Ouéllé	34	Ed	7.18N	4.01W
Ouémé	30	Hh	6.29N	2.32 E
Ouémé [3]	34	Fd	7.00N	2.35 E
Ouen	63b	Cf	22.26S	166.48 E
Ouenza	32	Ib	35.57N	8.07 E
Ouenza, Djebel-	14	Co	35.57N	8.05 E
Ouessa	34	Ec	11.03N	2.47W
Ouessant, Ile d'-	11	Af	48.28N	5.05W
Ouesso	31	Ih	1.37N	16.04 E
Ouest [3]	34	Hd	5.20N	10.30 E
Ouest, Baie de l'-	64h	Ab	13.15S	176.13W
Ouezzane	32	Fc	34.48N	5.36W
Oughter, Lough-	9	Fg	54.00N	7.29W
Ouham [3]	35	Bd	7.00N	18.00 E
Ouham	30	Ih	9.18N	18.14 E
Ouham-Pendé [3]	35	Bd	7.00N	16.00 E
Ouidah	34	Fd	6.22N	2.05 E
Ouistreham	11	Fe	49.17N	0.15W
Ouistreham-Riva Bella	12	Be	49.17N	0.16W
Oujda [3]	32	Gc	33.00N	2.00W
Oujda	31	Ge	34.40N	1.54W
Oujeft	32	Ee	20.02N	13.03W
Oulainen	7	Fd	64.16N	24.57 E
Oulchy-le-Château	12	Fe	49.12N	3.21 E
Ouled Djellal	32	Ic	34.25N	5.04 E
Ouled Naïl, Monts des-	32	Hc	34.40N	3.25 E
Oulou, Bahr-	35	Cd	9.48N	21.32 E
Oulu [2]	7	Gd	65.00N	27.00 E
Oulu/Uleåborg	6	Ib	65.01N	25.30 E
Oulu, Lake- (EN)= Oulujärvi	5	Ic	64.20N	27.15 E
Oulujärvi=Oulu, Lake- (EN)	5	Ic	64.20N	27.15 E
Oulujoki	5	Ib	65.01N	25.25 E
Oum Chalouba	31	Jg	15.48N	20.46 E
Oumé [3]	34	Dd	6.25N	5.30W
Oumé	34	Dd	6.23N	5.25W
Oum el Bouaghi [3]	32	Ib	35.30N	7.10 E
Oum el Bouaghi	32	Ib	35.53N	7.07 E
Oum er Rbia	30	Ge	33.19N	8.20W
Oum Hadjer	35	Bc	13.18N	19.41 E
Oumm ed Droûs Guebli, Sebkhet-	32	Ee	24.03N	11.45W
Oumm ed Droûs Telli, Sebkhet-	32	Ee	24.20N	11.30W
Ounasjoki	5	Ib	66.30N	25.45 E
Oundle	12	Bb	52.29N	0.28W
Ounianga	35	Cb	19.10N	20.30 E
Ounianga Kébir	31	Jg	19.04N	20.29 E
Ountivou	34	Fd	7.21N	1.34 E
Ouolosséboougou	34	Dc	12.00N	7.55W
Oupeye	12	Hd	50.42N	5.39 E
Oupu	27	Ma	52.45N	126.00 E
Our	12	Ie	49.53N	6.18 E
Ouray	45	Cg	38.01N	107.40W
Ouray, Mount-	45	Cg	38.25N	106.14W
Ource	11	Kf	48.06N	4.23 E
Ourcq	11	Je	49.01N	3.01 E
Ourcq, Canal de l'-	11	If	48.51N	2.22 E
Ourém	54	Id	1.33S	47.06W
Ouricuri	54	Je	7.35S	40.05W
Ourinhos	53	Lh	22.59S	49.52W
Ouro, Rio do-	55	Ha	13.20S	48.59W
Ouro Fino	55	If	22.17S	46.22W
Ouro Prêto	54	Jh	20.23S	43.30W
Ourthe [Bel.]	11	Ld	50.38N	5.35 E
Ourville-en-Caux	12	Ce	49.44N	0.36 E
Ous	19	Gc	60.55N	61.31 E
Ōu-Sanmyaku	28	Pe	39.00N	141.00 E
Ouse [Eng.-U.K.]	9	Nk	50.47N	0.03 E
Ouse [Eng.-U.K.]	9	Mh	53.42N	0.41W
Oust	11	Dg	47.35N	2.06W
Outagouna	34	Fb	15.11N	0.43 E
Outaouais, Rivière-	38	Le	45.20N	73.58W
Outardes, Rivière aux-	42	Kg	49.05N	68.23W
Outat Oulad El Hajj	32	Gc	33.21N	3.42W
Outer Dowsing	9	Oh	53.25N	1.05 E
Outer Hebrides	9	Fd	57.50N	7.32W
Outer Santa Barbara Passage	46	Fj	33.10N	118.30W
Outer Silver Pit	9	Og	54.05N	2.00 E
Outjo	31	Ik	20.08S	16.08 E
Outjo [3]	37	Ac	19.30S	14.30 E
Outlook	46	La	51.30N	107.03W
Outokumpu	7	Ge	62.44N	29.01 E
Outram Mountain	46	Eb	49.19N	121.05W
Outreau	12	Dd	50.42N	1.35 E
Out Skerries	9	Ma	60.30N	0.50W
Outwell	12	Cb	52.37N	0.14 E
Ouvéa, Ile-	57	Hg	20.35S	166.35 E
Ouvèze	11	Kk	43.59N	4.51 E
Ouxian	28	Ej	28.58N	118.53 E
Ouyen	59	Ig	35.04S	142.20 E
Ouyou Bézédinga	34	Hb	16.32N	13.15 E
Ouzera	13	Oh	36.15N	2.51 E
Ovacık [Tur.]	24	Ed	36.11N	33.40 E
Ovacık [Tur.]	24	Hc	39.22N	39.13 E
Ovada	14	Cf	44.38N	8.38 E
Ova Gölü	15	Mm	36.16N	29.22 E
Ovakent	15	Lk	38.06N	28.02 E
Ovalau Island	63d	Bb	17.40S	178.48 E
Ovalle	53	Ii	30.36S	71.12W
Oval Peak	46	Eb	48.15N	120.25W
Ovamboland	37	Bc	18.30S	16.00 E
Ovamboland [3]	37	Bc	18.00S	16.00 E
Ovan	36	Bb	0.30N	12.10 E
Ovanåker	7	Df	61.21N	15.54 E
Ovar	13	Dd	40.52N	8.38W
Ovau	63a	Cb	6.48S	156.02 E
Ovejas	49	Ji	9.32N	75.14W
Overath	12	Jd	50.57N	7.18 E
Øverbygd	7	Eb	69.01N	19.18 E
Overflakke	11	Kc	51.45N	4.10 E
Overhalla	7	Cd	64.30N	12.00 E
Overije	12	Gd	50.46N	4.32 E
Overijssel [3]	12	Ib	52.25N	6.30 E
Överkalix	7	Fc	66.19N	22.50 E
Overland Park	45	Ig	38.59N	94.40W
Övermark/Ylimarkku	8	Ib	62.37N	21.28 E
Overpelt	12	Hc	51.12N	5.25 E
Overri	34	Gd	5.29N	7.02 E
Overton	46	Hh	36.33N	114.27W
Övertorneå	7	Fc	66.23N	23.40 E
Överum	8	Gg	57.59N	16.19 E
Ovidiu	15	Le	44.16N	28.34 E
Oviedo [3]	13	Ga	43.20N	6.00W
Oviedo [Dom.Rep.]	49	Le	17.47N	71.22W
Oviedo [Sp.]	6	Fg	43.22N	5.50W
Oviši	8	Ig	57.34N	21.35 E
Ovo, Capo dell'-	14	Lj	40.18N	17.30 E
Øvre Årdal	7	Bf	61.19N	7.48 E
Övre Fryken	8	Ed	60.00N	13.05 E
Övre Soppero	7	Eb	68.05N	21.41 E
Ovruč	19	Ce	51.19N	28.50 E
Ovsjanka	20	Hf	53.32N	126.58 E
Owaka	62	Cg	46.27S	169.40 E
Owando	31	Ii	0.29S	15.55 E
Ōwani	28	Pd	40.31N	140.35 E
Owase	28	Ng	34.04N	136.12 E
Owatonna	43	Ic	44.05N	93.14W
Owego	44	Id	42.06N	76.16W
Owen, Mount-	62	Ed	41.33S	172.32 E
Owendo	36	Ab	0.17N	9.30 E
Owen Falls Dam	36	Fb	0.24N	33.11 E
Owensboro	43	Jd	37.46N	87.07W
Owens Lake	46	Gh	36.25N	117.56W
Owen Sound	42	Jh	44.34N	80.56W
Owens River	46	Gh	36.31N	117.57W
Owen Stanley Range	57	Fe	9.20S	148.00 E
Owl Creek Mountains	46	Ke	43.30N	108.35W
Ownay, Kowlal-e-	23	Kc	34.27N	68.22 E
Owo	34	Gd	7.11N	5.35 E
Owosso	44	Ed	43.00N	84.10W
Owyhee	46	Gf	41.57N	116.06W
Owyhee, Lake-	46	Ge	43.28N	117.20W
Owyhee Mountains	46	Ge	43.00N	116.45W
Owyhee River [U.S.]	46	Ge	43.40N	117.16W
Owyhee River [U.S.]	43	Dc	43.46N	117.02W
Oxberg	8	Fc	61.07N	14.10 E
Oxbow	45	Eb	49.14N	102.11W
Oxelösund	7	Dg	58.40N	17.06 E
Oxford	9	Lj	51.50N	1.30W
Oxford [Eng.-U.K.]	6	Fe	51.46N	1.15W
Oxford [Ms.-U.S.]	45	Li	34.22N	89.32W
Oxford [N.C.-U.S.]	44	Hg	36.19N	78.35W
Oxford [N.Z.]	62	Ee	43.17S	172.11 E
Oxford Lake	42	Hf	54.50N	95.35W
Oxfordshire [3]	9	Lj	51.50N	1.20W
Oxia	15	Ek	38.18N	21.06 E
Oxkutzcab	48	Og	20.18N	89.25W
Oxnard	43	De	34.12N	119.11W
Ox or Slieve Gamph Mountains/Sliabh Gamh	9	Eg	54.10N	8.50W
Oxted	12	Bc	51.14N	0.01W
Oyabe	29	Ec	36.40N	136.52 E
Oyahue	53	Jh	21.08S	68.45W
O-Yama	29	Fd	34.04N	139.31 E
Oyama	28	Of	36.21N	139.50 E
Ōyama	29	Ec	36.35N	137.18 E
Ōyano	29	Be	32.35N	130.27 E
Oyapock, Fleuve-	52	Ke	4.08N	51.40W
Oyem	31	Ih	1.37N	11.35 E
Oyen	46	Ja	51.22N	110.28W
Øyeren	8	De	59.50N	11.14 E
Oykel	9	Id	57.50N	4.25W
Oyo [2]	34	Fd	8.00N	3.50 E
Oyo [Nig.]	34	Fd	7.51N	3.56 E
Oyo [Sud.]	35	Fa	21.55N	36.06 E
Oyodo-Gawa	29	Bf	31.55N	131.28 E
Oyonnax	11	Lh	46.15N	5.40 E
Oyster Bay	59	Jh	42.10S	148.10 E
Øystese	8	Bd	60.23N	6.13 E
Özalp	24	Jc	38.39N	43.59 E
Ozamiz	26	He	8.08N	123.50 E
Ozark	44	Ej	31.28N	85.38W
Ozark Plateau	38	Jf	37.00N	93.00W
Ozark Reservoir	45	Ii	35.25N	94.05W
Ozarks, Lake of the-	43	Id	37.39N	92.50W
Ózd	10	Qh	48.13N	20.18 E
Ozeblin	14	Jf	44.35N	15.53 E
Ozernoj, Zaliv-	20	Le	57.00N	163.20 E
Ozernovski	20	Kf	51.21N	156.32 E
Ozerny	16	Vd	51.08N	60.55 E
Ozersk	8	Ij	54.24N	21.59 E
Ozery [Bye.-U.S.S.R.]	10	Uc	53.38N	24.18 E
Ozery [R.S.F.S.R.]	7	Ji	54.54N	38.32 E
Ožezdy	19	Gf	48.03N	67.09 E
Ozieri	14	Cj	40.35N	9.00 E
Ozinki	19	Ee	51.12N	49.47 E
Ožogina	20	Kc	66.12N	151.05 E
Ozona	43	Ge	30.43N	101.12W
Ozorków	10	Pe	51.58N	19.19 E
Ozouri	36	Ac	0.55S	8.55 E
Ozren [Yugo.]	14	Mf	44.37N	18.15 E
Ozren [Yugo.]	14	Mg	43.59N	18.30 E
Ozren [Yugo.]	15	Ef	43.36N	21.54 E
Ōzu [Jap.]	29	Be	32.52N	130.52 E
Ōzu [Jap.]	28	Lh	33.30N	132.23 E

P

Pääjärvi	8	Kb	62.50N	24.45 E
Paama	63b	Dc	16.28S	168.13 E
Pa-an	25	Je	16.53N	97.38 E
Paar	10	Hh	48.45N	11.35 E
Paarl	31	Il	33.45S	18.56 E
Paauilo	65a	Fc	20.03N	155.22W
Paavola	7	Fd	64.36N	25.12 E
Pabbay	9	Fd	57.47N	7.20W
Pabellón, Ensenada del-	48	Fe	24.27N	107.36W
Pabianice	10	Pe	51.40N	19.22 E
Pābna	25	Hd	24.00N	89.15 E
Pabradė/Pabrade	7	Fi	54.59N	25.50 E
Pabrade/Pabradė	7	Fi	54.59N	25.50 E
Pacaás Novos, Serra dos-	54	Ff	10.50S	64.00W
Pacajá, Rio-	54	Hd	1.56S	50.55W
Pacajus	54	Kd	4.10S	38.28W
Pacaraima, Serra-	52	Je	4.30N	60.40W
Pacasmayo	54	Ce	7.24S	79.34W
Paceco	14	Gm	37.59N	12.33 E
Pachala	35	Ed	7.10N	34.06 E
Pacheco	48	Eb	30.06N	108.21W
Pachino	14	Jn	36.43N	15.05 E
Pachitea, Río-	54	De	8.46S	74.32W
Pachuca de Soto	47	Ed	20.07N	98.44W
Pacific-Antarctic Ridge (EN)	3	Kp	62.00S	157.00W
Pacific City	46	Dd	45.12N	123.57W
Pacific Grove	46	Eh	36.38N	121.56W
Pacific Islands, Trust Territory of the-	58	Gc	10.00N	155.00 E
Pacífico, Océano-=Pacific Ocean (EN)	3	Ki	5.00N	155.00W
Pacific Ocean	3	Ki	5.00N	155.00W
Pacific Ocean (EN)=Kita-Taiheiyō	60	Ch	22.00N	167.00 E
Pacific Ocean (EN)= Pacífico, Océano-	3	Ki	5.00N	155.00W
Pacific Ocean (EN)= Pacifique, Océan-	3	Ki	5.00N	155.00W
Pacific Ocean (EN)= Taiheiyō	3	Ki	5.00N	155.00W
Pacific Ocean (EN)=Tihi Okean	3	Ki	5.00N	155.00W
Pacific Ranges	42	Ef	50.55N	125.10W
Pacifique, Océan-=Pacific Ocean (EN)	3	Ki	5.00N	155.00W
Packsattel	14	Id	46.58N	14.58 E
Pacuí, Rio-	55	Jc	16.46S	45.01W
Pacuneiro, Rio-	55	Fa	13.02S	53.25W
Pacy-sur-Eure	12	De	49.01N	1.23 E
Paczków	10	Mf	50.27N	17.00 E
Padana, Pianura-=Po Valley (EN)	5	Gf	45.20N	10.00 E
Padang	22	Mj	0.57S	100.21 E
Padangsidempuan	26	Cf	1.22N	99.16 E
Padangtikar, Pulau-	26	Eg	0.50S	109.30 E
Padany	7	He	63.19N	33.25 E
Padasjoki	8	Kc	61.21N	25.17 E
Padauiri, Rio-	54	Fd	0.15S	64.05W
Paddle Prairie	42	Fe	58.02N	117.50W
Paderborn	10	Ee	51.43N	8.46 E
Paderborn-Elsen	12	Kc	51.44N	8.41 E
Paderborn-Schloß Neuhaus	12	Kc	51.44N	8.42 E
Padeş, Vîrful-	15	Fd	45.40N	22.20 E
Padilla	54	Fg	19.19S	64.20W
Padina	15	Ke	44.50N	27.07 E
Padornelo, Portillo del-	13	Fb	42.03N	6.50W
Padova = Padua (EN)	14	Fe	45.25N	11.53 E
Padre, Morro do-	55	Ic	16.48S	47.35W
Padre Bernardo	55	Hb	15.21S	48.30W
Padre Island	43	Hf	27.00N	97.15W
Padrón	13	Db	42.44N	8.40W
Padua (EN) = Padova	14	Fe	45.25N	11.53 E
Paducah [Ky.-U.S.]	39	Kf	37.05N	88.36W
Paducah [Tx.-U.S.]	45	Fi	34.01N	100.18W
Padula	14	Jj	40.20N	15.39 E
Paea	65e	Fc	17.41S	149.35W
Paegam-san	28	Id	40.35N	126.15 E
Paengnyong-Do	27	Ld	38.00N	124.40 E
Paeroa	61	Eg	37.23S	175.41 E
Paestum	14	Jj	40.25N	15.01 E
Paeu	63c	Bb	11.22S	166.50 E
Pafuri	37	Ed	22.26S	31.20 E
Pag	14	Jf	44.27N	15.03 E
Pag	14	If	44.30N	15.00 E
Pagadian	26	He	7.49N	123.25 E
Pagai, Kepulauan-=Pagi Islands (EN)	21	Lj	2.45S	100.00 E
Pagai Selatan	26	Dg	3.00S	100.20 E
Pagai Utara	26	Cg	2.42S	100.07 E
Pagan Island	57	Fc	18.07N	145.46 E
Pagasitikós Kólpos	15	Fj	39.15N	23.00 E
Pagatan	26	Gg	3.36S	115.56 E
Pagat Point	64c	Bb	13.30N	144.53 E
Page	46	Jh	36.57N	111.27W
Pagėgiai	8	Ii	55.09N	21.54 E
Paget, Mount-	66	Ad	54.26S	36.33W
Pagi Islands (EN)=Pagai, Kepulauan-	21	Lj	2.45S	100.00 E
Paglia	14	Gh	42.42N	12.11 E
Pago Bay	64c	Bb	13.25N	144.48 E
Pagoda Point	21	Lh	15.57N	94.15 E
Pāgodār	24	Qh	28.10N	57.22 E
Pago Pago	58	Jf	14.16S	170.42W
Pago Pago Harbor	65c	Cb	14.17S	170.40W
Pago Redondo	55	Ci	29.35S	59.13W
Pagosa Springs	45	Ch	37.16N	107.01W
Pagoua Bay	51g	Ba	15.32N	61.17W
Pagwa River	45	Na	50.01N	85.10W
Pahači	20	Ld	60.30N	169.00 E
Pahala	65a	Fd	19.12N	155.29W
Pàhara, Laguna-	49	Ff	14.18N	83.15W
Pahiatua	62	Fd	40.27S	175.50 E
Pahkāing Bum	21	Lg	26.00N	95.30 E
Pahoa	65a	Gd	19.30N	154.57W
Pahokee	44	Gl	26.49N	80.40W
Pahtakor	18	Fd	40.16N	67.55 E
Pahute Mesa	46	Gh	37.20N	116.40W
Païa	63b	Dc	16.35S	168.12 E
Paide/Pajde	7	Fg	58.57N	25.35 E
Paignton	9	Jk	50.28N	3.30W
Päijänne	5	Ic	61.35N	23.30 E
Páïkon Óros	15	Fi	40.56N	22.21 E
Paila	48	He	25.39N	102.07W
Pailîn	25	Kf	12.51N	102.36 E
Pailitas	49	Ki	8.58N	73.38W
Pailolo Channel	65a	Eb	21.05N	156.42W
Paimio/Pemar	8	Jd	60.27N	22.42 E
Paimionjoki	8	Jd	60.25N	22.40 E
Paimpol	11	Cf	48.46N	3.03W
Painan	26	Dg	1.21S	100.34 E
Paine, Mount-	66	Mg	86.46S	147.32W
Painel	55	Gh	27.55S	50.06W
Painesville	44	Ge	41.43N	81.15W
Painted Desert	43	Ed	36.00N	111.20W
Paintsville	44	Fg	37.49N	82.48W
País do Vinho	13	Ec	41.15N	7.55W
Paisley	9	If	55.50N	4.26W
Paita	54	Be	5.06S	81.07W
Païta	63b	Cf	22.08S	166.22 E
Paiva	13	Dc	41.04N	8.16W
Paj	7	If	61.43N	34.28 E
Pajala	7	Fc	67.12N	23.22 E
Pajares, Puerto de-	13	Ga	43.00N	5.46W
Pajaros, Punta-	48	Ph	19.36N	87.25W
Pajaros Point	51a	Db	18.31N	64.18W
Pajatén	54	Ce	7.29S	77.22W
Pajde/Paide	7	Fg	58.57N	25.35 E
Pajęczno	10	Oe	51.09N	19.00 E
Pajer, Gora-	19	Gb	66.40N	64.20 E
Paj-Hoj	5	Mb	69.00N	62.30 E
Pajule	36	Fb	2.58N	32.56 E
Pakanbaru	22	Mi	0.32N	101.27 E
Pakaraima Mountains	54	Fb	4.05N	61.30W
Pakch'on	28	He	39.44N	125.35 E
Pakhiá	15	Im	36.16N	25.50 E
Pakhna	24	Ee	34.46N	32.48 E
Pákhnes	15	Gn	35.18N	23.58 E
Paki	34	Gc	11.30N	8.09 E
Pakima	36	Dc	3.21S	24.06 E
Pakin Atoll	57	Gd	7.04N	157.48 E
Pakistan [1]	22	Ig	30.00N	70.00 E
Pakleni Otoci	14	Kg	43.10N	16.23 E
Pakokku	25	Jd	21.17N	95.06 E
Pakowki Lake	46	Jb	49.22N	110.57W
Pak Phanang	25	Kg	8.21N	100.12 E
Pakrac	14	Le	45.26N	17.12 E
Pakruois/Pakruojis	7	Fi	55.57N	23.50 E
Pakruojis/Pakruois	7	Fi	55.57N	23.50 E
Paks	10	Oj	46.38N	18.52 E
Paktīā [3]	23	Kc	33.30N	69.30 E
Pakwach	36	Fb	2.28N	31.30 E
Pakxé	22	Mh	15.07N	105.47 E
Pakxèng	25	Kd	20.10N	102.40 E
Pala	35	Ad	9.22N	14.54 E
Palacca Point	49	Kc	21.15N	73.26W
Palacios [Arg.]	55	Bj	30.43S	61.37W
Palacios [Tx.-U.S.]	45	Hl	28.42N	96.13W
Palafrugell	13	Pc	41.55N	3.10 E
Palagruža	14	Kh	42.24N	16.15 E
Palaiokastrítsa	15	Cj	39.40N	19.41 E
Palaiokhóra	15	Gn	35.14N	23.41 E
Palaiseau	12	Ef	48.43N	2.15 E
Palamás	15	Fj	39.28N	22.05 E
Palamós	13	Pc	41.51N	3.08 E
Palamuse/Palamuze	8	Lf	58.39N	26.35 E
Palamut	15	Kk	38.59N	27.41 E
Palamuze/Palamuse	8	Lf	58.39N	26.35 E
Palana	22	Rd	59.07N	159.58 E
Palancia	13	Le	39.40N	0.12W
Palanga	19	Cd	55.57N	21.05 E
Palangkaraya	26	Fg	2.16S	113.56 E
Pālanpur	25	Ed	24.10N	72.26 E

Index Symbols

[1] Independent Nation
[2] State, Region
[3] District, County
[4] Municipality
[5] Colony, Dependency
Continent
Physical Region
Historical or Cultural Region
Mount, Mountain
Volcano
Hill
Mountains, Mountain Range
Hills, Escarpment
Plateau, Upland
Pass, Gap
Plain, Lowland
Delta
Salt Flat
Valley, Canyon
Crater, Cave
Karst Features
Depression
Polder
Desert, Dunes
Forest, Woods
Heath, Steppe
Oasis
Cape, Point
Coast, Beach
Cliff
Peninsula
Isthmus
Sandbank
Island
Atoll
Rock, Reef
Islands, Archipelago
Rocks, Reefs
Coral Reef
Well, Spring
Geyser
River, Stream
Waterfall Rapids
River Mouth, Estuary
Lake
Salt Lake
Intermittent Lake
Reservoir
Swamp, Pond
Canal
Glacier
Ice Shelf, Pack Ice
Ocean
Sea
Gulf, Bay
Strait, Fjord
Lagoon
Bank
Seamount
Tablemount
Ridge
Shelf
Basin
Escarpment, Sea Scarp
Fracture
Trench, Abyss
National Park, Reserve
Point of Interest
Recreation Site
Cave, Cavern
Historic Site
Ruins
Wall, Walls
Church, Abbey
Temple
Scientific Station
Airport
Port
Lighthouse
Mine
Tunnel
Dam, Bridge

Palaoa Point 65a Ec 20.44N 156.58W
Palapye 31 Jk 22.33S 27.08 E
Palasa 26 Hf 0.29N 120.24 E
Palatka [Fl.-U.S.] 43 Kf 29.39N 81.38W
Palatka [R.S.F.S.R.] 20 Kd 60.05N 151.00 E
Palau 14 Di 41.11N 9.23 E
Palau [5] 58 Ed 7.30N 134.30 E
Palau Islands 57 Ed 7.30N 134.30 E
Palauli 65c Aa 13.44S 172.16W
Palauli Bay 65c Aa 13.47S 172.14W
Palau Trench (EN) 60 Af 6.30N 134.30 E
Palavas-les-Flots 11 Jk 43.32N 3.56 E
Palaw 25 Jf 12.58N 98.39 E
Palawan 21 Ni 9.30N 118.30 E
Palawan Passage 26 Gd 10.00N 118.00 E
Palayan 26 Hc 15.33N 121.06 E
Pälayankottai 25 Fg 8.43N 77.44 E
Palazzo, Punta- 11a Aa 42.22N 8.33 E
Palazzolo Acreide 14 Im 37.04N 14.54 E
Palazzolo sull'Oglio 14 De 45.36N 9.53 E
Paldiski 19 Cd 59.20N 24.06 E
Pale di San Martino 14 Fd 46.14N 11.53 E
Paleleh 26 Hf 1.04N 121.57 E
Palembang 22 Mj 2.55S 104.45 E
Palena 14 Ii 41.59N 14.08 E
Palencia [3] 13 Hb 42.25N 4.30W
Palencia 13 Hb 42.01N 4.32W
Palen Lake 46 Hj 33.46N 115.12W
Palenque 39 Jh 17.30N 92.00W
Palenque [Mex.] 48 Ni 17.31N 91.58W
Palenque [Pan.] 49 Hi 9.13N 79.41W
Palenque, Punta- 49 Ld 18.14N 70.09W
Palermo 6 Hh 38.07N 13.22 E
Palermo, Golfo di- 14 Hl 38.10N 13.25 E
Palestine 43 He 31.46N 95.38W
Palestine (EN) 23 Dc 32.15N 34.47 E
Palestrina 14 Gi 41.50N 12.53 E
Pälghät 25 Ff 10.47N 76.39 E
Palgrave Point 37 Ad 20.28S 13.16 E
Palhoça 55 Hh 27.38S 48.40W
Päli 25 Ec 25.46N 73.20 E
Palinuro 14 Jj 40.02N 15.17 E
Palinuro, Capo- 14 Jj 40.02N 15.16 E
Palisades Reservoir 46 Je 43.04N 111.26W
Paliseul 12 He 49.54N 5.08 E
Palivere 8 Jf 59.00N 23.45 E
Palizada 48 Mh 18.15N 92.05W
Paljakka 7 Gd 64.45N 28.07 E
Paljavaam 20 Mc 68.50N 170.50 E
Paljenik 5 Hg 44.15N 17.36 E
Pälkäne 8 Kc 61.20N 24.16 E
Palkino 8 Mg 57.29N 28.10 E
Palk Strait 21 Ji 10.00N 79.45 E
Palla Bianca/Weißkugel 14 Ed 46.48N 10.44 E
Pallars 13 Mb 42.25N 0.55 E
Pallars, Montsent de-/
Montseny 13 Nb 42.29N 1.02 E
Pallasovka 19 Ee 50.03N 46.55 E
Pallastunturi 7 Fb 68.06N 24.02 E
Palliser, Cape- 61 Eh 41.37S 175.16 E
Palliser, Iles- 57 Mf 15.30S 146.30W
Palma [Moz.] 37 Gb 10.46S 40.28 E
Palma [Sp.] 6 Gh 39.34N 2.39 E
Palma, Badia de-/Palma,
Bahia de- 13 Oe 39.27N 2.35 E
Palma, Bahia de-/Palma,
Badia de- 13 Oe 39.27N 2.35 E
Palma, Rio- 54 If 12.33S 47.52W
Palma, Sierra de la- 48 Id 26.00N 101.35W
Palma del Rio 13 Gg 37.42N 5.17W
Palma di Montechiaro 14 Hm 37.11N 13.46 E
Palmar, Laguna del- 55 Bi 29.35S 60.42W
Palmar, Rio- 49 Lh 10.11N 71.52W
Palmar, Salto- 55 Cg 24.18S 59.18W
Palmares 54 Ke 8.41S 35.36W
Palmares do Sul 55 Gj 30.16S 50.31W
Palmarito 54 Db 7.37N 70.10W
Palmarola 14 Gj 40.55N 12.50 E
Palmar Sur 47 Hg 8.58N 83.29W
Palmas 56 Jc 26.30S 52.00W
Palmas, Cape- 30 Gh 4.22N 7.44W
Palmas, Golfo di- 14 Cl 39.00N 8.30 E
Palmas Bellas 49 Gi 9.14N 80.05W
Palma Soriano 47 Id 20.13N 76.00W
Palm Bay 44 Gk 28.01N 80.35W
Palm Beach 43 Kf 26.42N 80.02W
Palmdale 46 Fi 34.35N 118.07W
Palmeira 55 Gg 25.25S 50.00W
Palmeira das Missões 56 Jc 27.55S 53.17W
Palmeira dos Indios 54 Ke 9.25S 36.37W
Palmeirais 54 Je 5.58S 43.04W
Palmeiras, Rio- 55 Gb 15.25S 51.10W
Palmeiras de Goiás 55 Hc 16.47S 49.53W
Palmeirinhas, Ponta das- 30 Ii 9.05S 13.00 E
Palmela 13 Df 38.34N 8.54W
Palmer 40 Jd 61.36N 149.07W
Palmer Archipelago 66 Qe 64.10S 62.00W
Palmer Land (EN) 66 Qf 71.30S 65.00W
Palmer Station 66 Qe 64.46S 64.05W
Palmerston 57 Df 45.29S 170.43 E
Palmerston Atoll 57 Kf 18.04S 163.10W
Palmerston North 58 Ii 40.28S 175.17 E
Palmetto Point 51d Ba 17.35N 61.52W
Palmi 14 Jl 38.21N 15.51 E
Palmira [Col.] 53 Ie 3.32N 76.16W
Palmira [Cuba] 49 Gb 22.14N 80.23W
Palm Islands 59 Jc 18.40S 146.30 E
Palmital 55 Fg 24.39S 52.16W
Palmitas 55 Dk 33.27S 57.48W
Palmito 55 Cd 18.53S 58.22W
Palmitos 55 Fh 27.05S 53.08W
Palm Springs 43 De 33.50N 116.33W
Palmyra 23 Ec 34.33N 38.17 E
Palmyra Atoll 57 Kd 5.52N 162.06W
Palo Alto 43 Cd 37.27N 122.09W
Paloh 26 Ef 1.43N 109.18 E
Paloich 35 Ec 10.28N 32.32 E
Palomani, Nevado- 52 Jg 14.38S 69.14W
Palomar Mountain 43 De 33.22N 116.50W
Palomera, Sierra- 13 Kd 40.40N 1.12W
Palopo 22 Oj 3.00S 120.12 E
Palos, Cabo de- 5 Fh 37.38N 0.41W
Palo Santo 55 Cg 25.34S 59.21W
Palotina 55 Fg 24.17S 53.50W
Palouse River 46 Fc 46.35N 118.13W
Palpa 54 Cf 14.32S 75.11W
Palsa 8 Lg 57.23N 26.24 E
Pålsboda 8 Fe 59.04N 15.20 E
Paltamo 7 Gd 64.25N 27.50 E
Palu [Indon.] 22 Nj 0.53S 119.53 E
Palu [Tur.] 24 Hc 38.42N 39.57 E
Palu, Pulau- 26 Hh 8.20S 121.43 E
Pam 63b Be 20.15S 164.17 E
Pama 34 Fc 11.15N 0.42 E
Påmark/Pomarkku 8 Ic 61.42N 22.00 E
Pambarra 37 Fd 21.56S 35.06 E
Pambeguwa 34 Gc 10.40N 8.17 E
Pamekasan 26 Fh 7.10S 113.28 E
Pamiers 11 Hk 43.07N 1.36 E
Pamir 21 Jf 38.00N 73.00 E
Pamir 19 Hh 37.01N 72.41 E
Pâmiut/Frederikshåb 41 Hf 62.00N 49.45W
Pamlico Sound 43 Ld 35.20N 75.55W
Pampa 43 Gd 35.32N 100.58W
Pampa del Indio 55 Ch 26.02S 59.55W
Pampa del Infierno 55 Bh 26.31S 61.10W
Pampa de los Guanacos 56 Hc 26.14S 61.51W
Pampas 54 Df 12.24S 74.54W
Pampas 52 Ji 35.00S 63.00W
Pampeiro 55 Ej 30.38S 55.16W
Pamplona [Col.] 54 Db 7.23N 72.38W
Pamplona [Sp.] 6 Fg 42.49N 1.38W
Pamukkale 15 Ml 37.47N 29.04 E
Pamukova 15 Ni 40.31N 30.09 E
Pamunkey River 44 Ig 37.32N 76.48W
Pan, Tierra del- 13 Gc 41.50N 6.00W
Pana 36 Bc 1.41S 12.39 E
Panagjurište 15 Hg 42.30N 24.11 E
Panaitan, Pulau- 26 Eh 6.36S 105.12 E
Panaitolikón Óros 15 Ek 38.43N 21.39 E
Panaji (Panjim) 22 Jh 15.29N 73.50 E
Panakhaïkón Óros 15 Ek 38.12N 21.54 E
Panamá [1] 39 Li 9.00N 80.00W
Panamá = Panama (EN) [3] 49 Hi 9.00N 79.00W
Panamá=Panama City (EN) 39 Li 8.58N 79.31W
Panama (EN) = Panamá [3] 49 Hi 9.00N 79.00W
Panamá, Bahia de- 49 Hi 8.50N 79.15W
Panamá, Canal de-=
Panama Canal (EN) 47 Ig 9.20N 79.55W
Panamá, Golfo de-=
Panama, Gulf of- (EN) 38 Li 8.00N 79.10W
Panama, Gulf of- (EN)=
Panamá, Golfo de- 38 Li 8.00N 79.10W
Panama, Isthmus of- (EN)=
Panamá, Istmo de- 38 Li 9.20N 79.30W
Panamá, Istmo de-=
Panama, Isthmus of- (EN) 38 Li 9.20N 79.30W
Panama Canal (EN)=
Panamá, Canal de- 47 Ig 9.20N 79.55W
Panama City [La.-U.S.] 39 Kf 30.10N 85.41W
Panama City (EN)=Panamá 39 Li 8.58N 79.31W
Panamá La Vieja 49 Hi 9.00N 79.29W
Panambi 55 Fi 28.18S 53.30W
Panamint Range 46 Gh 36.30N 117.20W
Panao 54 Ce 9.49S 76.00W
Panarea 14 Jl 38.40N 15.05 E
Panaro 14 Ff 44.55N 11.25 E
Pana Tinai 63a Ad 11.14S 153.10 E
Pana-Wina 63a Ad 11.11S 153.01 E
Panay 21 Oh 11.15N 122.30 E
Pancake Range 46 Hg 39.00N 115.45W
Pančevo 15 De 44.52N 20.39 E
Pančićev vrh 15 Df 43.15N 20.45 E
Panciu 15 Kd 45.54N 27.05 E
Pancros 63b Db 15.58S 168.12 E
Panda 37 Ed 24.03S 34.43 E
Panda ma Tenga 37 Dc 18.32S 25.38 E
Pandan 26 Hd 11.43N 122.06 E
Pan de Azúcar 55 El 34.48S 55.14W
Pandeiros, Ribeirão- 55 Jb 15.42S 44.36W
Pandelis/Pandėlys 8 Kh 56.01N 25.21 E
Pandėlys/Pandelis 8 Kh 56.01N 25.21 E
Pandharpur 25 Fe 17.40N 75.20 E
Pándheon 15 Fi 40.05N 22.20 E
Pāndhurna 25 Fd 21.36N 78.31 E
Pandivere Kõrgustik/
Pandivere Vozvyšennost 8 Le 59.00N 26.15 E
Pandivere Vozvyšennost/
Pandivere Kõrgustik 8 Le 59.00N 26.15 E
Pando 56 Id 34.43S 55.57W
Pando [2] 54 Ef 11.20S 67.40W
Pandokrátor 15 Cj 39.45N 19.52 E
Pandora 49 Fi 9.45N 82.57W
Pandrup 8 Cg 57.14N 9.41 E
Pandu 36 Cb 4.59N 19.16 E
Panevežys/Panevėžys 19 Cd 55.44N 24.22 E
Panevėžys/Panevežys 19 Cd 55.44N 24.22 E
Panfilov 19 Ig 44.08N 80.01 E
Panga 36 Eb 1.51N 26.25 E
Pangai 65b Ba 19.48S 174.21W
Pangaion Óros 15 Hi 40.50N 24.05 E
Panganes, Canal de- 30 Lk 22.48S 47.50 E
Pangani 36 Gd 5.26S 38.58 E
Pangani or Ruvu 36 Gc 5.26S 38.58 E
Pange 12 Ie 49.05N 6.22 E
Panggoe 58 Ge 7.01S 157.05 E
Pangi 36 Ec 3.11S 26.38 E
Pangkajene 26 Gg 4.50S 119.32 E
Pangkalanberandan 26 Cf 4.01N 98.17 E
Pangkalanbuun 26 Fg 2.41S 111.37 E
Pangkalaseang, Tanjung- 26 Hg 0.42S 123.26 E
Pangkalpinang 26 Eg 2.08S 106.08 E
Pangnirtung 39 Mc 66.08N 65.44W
Pang-Pang 63b Dc 17.41S 168.32 E
Panguitch 43 Ed 37.49N 112.26W
Panguma 34 Cd 8.24N 11.13W
Pangutaran Group 26 He 6.15N 120.30 E
Panhandle 45 Fi 35.21N 101.23W
Pania Mutombo 36 Dd 5.11S 23.51 E
Paniau 65a Ab 21.57N 160.05W
Panié, Mont- 61 Bd 20.36S 164.46 E
Pānīpat 25 Fc 29.23N 76.58 E
Paniza, Puerto de- 13 Kc 41.15N 1.20W
Panjang 26 Eh 5.29S 105.18 E
Panjang, Pulau- 26 Ef 2.44N 108.55 E
Panjgūr 25 Cc 26.58N 64.06 E
Panjim → Panaji 22 Jh 15.29N 73.50 E
Panjwīn 24 Ke 35.36N 45.58 E
Pankow, Berlin- 10 Jd 52.34N 13.24 E
Pankshin 34 Gd 9.20N 9.27 E
P'anmunjŏm 28 If 37.57N 126.40 E
Panopah 26 Fg 1.56S 111.11 E
Panorama 56 Jb 21.21S 51.51W
Panshan 28 Gd 41.12N 122.03 E
Panshi 27 Mc 42.56N 126.02 E
Pant 12 Cc 51.53N 0.39 E
Pantanal 52 Kg 18.00S 56.00W
Pantar, Pulau- 26 Hh 8.25S 124.07 E
Pantego 44 Ih 35.34N 76.36W
Pantelleria 14 Fn 36.50N 11.57 E
Pantelleria 5 Hh 36.45N 12.00 E
Pantelleria, Canale di- 14 Fn 36.40N 11.45 E
Pante Makassar 26 Hh 9.12S 124.23 E
Pantoja 54 Cd 0.58S 75.10W
Pánuco 48 Jf 22.03N 98.10W
Pánuco 38 Jg 22.16N 97.47W
Panxian 27 Hf 25.45N 104.39 E
Panyam 34 Gd 9.25N 9.13 E
Panzi 36 Cd 7.13S 17.58 E
Panzós 49 Cf 15.24N 89.40W
Pao, Rio- [Ven.] 50 Bh 8.33N 68.01W
Pao, Rio- [Ven.] 50 Dh 8.06N 64.17W
Paola [It.] 14 Kk 39.21N 16.03 E
Paola [Ks.-U.S.] 45 Ig 38.35N 94.53W
Paoli 44 Df 38.33N 86.28W
Paopao 65eFc 17.30S 149.49W
Paoua 35 Bd 7.15N 16.26 E
Pápa 10 Ni 47.20N 17.28 E
Papa 65a Fd 19.13N 155.52W
Papaaloa 65a Fd 19.59N 155.13W
Papagaios 55 Jd 19.32S 44.45W
Papagayo, Golfo del- 47 Gf 10.45N 85.45W
Papaikou 65a Fd 19.47N 155.06W
Papakura 62 Fb 37.03S 174.57 E
Papaloapan, Rio- 48 Lh 18.42N 95.38W
Papanduva 55 Gh 26.25S 50.09W
Papangpanjang 26 Dg 0.27S 100.25 E
Papantla de Olarte 47 Ed 20.27N 97.19W
Papar 26 Ge 5.44N 115.56 E
Paparoa Range 62 De 42.05S 171.35 E
Papa Stour 9 La 60.30N 1.40W
Papa Westray 9 Kb 59.22N 2.54W
Papeete 58 Mf 17.32S 149.34W
Papenburg 10 Dc 53.04N 7.24 E
Papenburg-Aschendorf
(Ems) 12 Ja 53.04N 7.22 E
Papenoo 65eFc 17.30S 149.25W
Papes Ezers/Papes
Ozero 8 Ih 56.15N 20.55 E
Papes Ozero/Papes
Ezers 8 Ih 56.15N 20.55 E
Papetoai 65eFc 17.30S 149.52W
Papey 7a Cb 64.36N 14.11W
Paphos/Baf 24 Ee 34.50N 32.35 E
Papija 15 Kg 42.07N 27.51 E
Papikion Óros 15 Ih 41.15N 25.18 E
Papilé/Papile 8 Jh 56.09N 22.45 E
Papile/Papilé 8 Jh 56.09N 22.45 E
Papillion 45 Hf 41.09N 96.03W
Papua, Gulf of- 57 Fe 8.32S 145.00 E
Papua New Guinea [1] 58 Fe 6.00S 150.00 E
Papua Passage 64p Bc 21.15S 159.47W
Papuk 14 Le 45.31N 17.39 E
Papun 25 Je 18.04N 97.27 E
Para 7 Ji 54.23N 40.53 E
Pará [2] 54 Hd 4.00S 53.00W
Pará, Rio- 55 Jd 19.13S 45.07W
Para, Rio- 52 Lf 1.30S 48.55W
Parabel 20 De 58.40N 81.30 E
Parabel 20 De 58.43N 81.31 E
Paraburdoo 59 Dd 23.15S 117.45 E
Paracas 54 Cf 13.49S 76.16W
Paracatu 54 Ig 17.13S 46.52W
Paracatu, Rio- [Braz.] 55 Ic 17.30S 46.32W
Paracatu, Rio- [Braz.] 55 Jc 16.30S 45.04W
Paracel Islands (EN)=Xisha
Qundao 21 Nh 16.30N 112.15 E
Pārachinār 25 Eb 33.54N 70.06 E
Paraćin 15 Ef 43.52N 21.25 E
Paracuru 54 Kd 3.24S 39.04W
Parada Km 329 55 Ek 32.30S 55.25W
Paradip 25 Hd 20.19N 86.42 E
Paradise [Ca.-U.S.] 46 Eg 39.46N 121.37W
Paradise [Mi.-U.S.] 44 Eb 46.38N 85.03W
Paragould 45 Kh 36.03N 90.29W
Paragua, Rio- 54 Fb 6.55N 62.55W
Paraguá, Rio- 54 Ff 13.34S 61.53W
Paraguaçu, Rio- 52 Mg 12.45S 38.54W
Paraguaçu Paulista 55 Gf 22.25S 50.34W
Paraguai, Rio- 52 Kh 27.18S 58.38W
Paraguaipoa 49 Lh 11.21N 71.57W
Paraguaná, Peninsula de-
52 Jd 11.55N 70.00W
Paraguari [3] 55 Dg 26.00S 57.10W
Paraguari 56 Ic 25.38S 57.09W
Paraguay [1] 53 Kh 23.00S 58.00W
Paraguay, Rio- 52 Kh 27.18S 58.38W
Paraiba [2] 54 Ke 7.10S 36.30W
Paraiba do Sul, Rio- 52 Lh 21.37S 41.03W
Paraibuna, Represa do- 55 Jf 23.25S 45.35W
Paraibuna, Rio- 55 Jf 23.22S 45.40W
Parainen/Pargas 7 Ff 60.18N 22.18 E
Paraiso [Braz.] 55 Fd 19.03S 52.59W
Paraiso [Mex.] 48 Mh 18.24N 93.14W
Paraiso, Rio- 55 Bb 15.08S 61.52W
Parakou 31 Hh 9.21N 2.37 E
Param 64d Bb 7.22N 151.48 E
Paramaribo 53 Ke 5.50N 55.10W
Paramera, Sierra de la- 13 Hd 40.30N 4.46W
Paramithiá 15 Dj 39.28N 20.31 E
Paramušir, Ostrov- 21 Rd 50.25N 155.50 E
Paraná 53 Ji 31.45S 60.30W
Paraná [2] 56 Jb 24.00S 51.00W
Paraná, Pico- 55 Hg 25.14S 48.48W
Paraná, Rio- 52 Ki 33.43S 59.15W
Paranã, Rio- 52 Lg 12.30S 48.14W
Paraná de las Palmas, Rio- 55 Cl 34.18S 58.33W
Paranaguá 53 Lh 25.31S 48.30W
Paraná-Guazú, Rio- 55 Ck 34.00S 58.25W
Paranaíba 54 Hg 19.40S 51.11W
Paranaíba, Rio- 52 Kh 20.07S 51.05W
Paranaiguara 55 Gd 18.53S 50.28W
Paranapanema, Rio- 52 Kh 22.40S 53.09W
Paranapiacaba, Serra do- 52 Lh 24.20S 49.00W
Paranapuã-Guaçu, Ponta
do- 55 Ig 24.24S 47.00W
Paranavai 56 Jb 23.04S 52.28W
Parandak 24 Ne 35.21N 50.42 E
Paranéstion 15 Hh 41.16N 24.30 E
Paranhos 55 Ef 23.55S 55.25W
Paraoa Atoll 57 Mf 19.09S 140.43W
Paraopeba 55 Jd 19.18S 44.25W
Paraopeba, Rio- 55 Jd 18.50S 45.11W
Parapara 63b Ca 13.32S 167.20 E
Paraparaumu 62 Fd 40.55S 175.00 E
Paraspóri 15 Kn 35.54N 27.14 E
Parati 55 Jf 23.13S 44.43W
Paratodos, Serra- 55 Jb 14.40S 44.50W
Paratunka 20 Kf 52.52N 158.12 E
Pārāu, Kūh-e- 24 Le 34.37N 47.05 E
Paraúna 55 Gc 17.02S 50.26W
Paravae 64n Bc 10.27S 160.58W
Paray-le-Monial 11 Kh 46.27N 4.07 E
Parbati 25 Fc 25.51N 76.36 E
Parbhani 25 Fe 19.16N 76.47 E
Parchim 10 Hc 53.26N 11.51 E
Parczew 10 Se 51.39N 22.54 E
Pardo 55 Cm 36.15S 59.22W
Pardo, Rio- [Braz.] 55 Fi 29.59S 52.23W
Pardo, Rio- [Braz.] 54 Hh 21.46S 52.09W
Pardo, Rio- [Braz.] 55 He 20.10S 48.38W
Pardo, Rio- [Braz.] 55 Hf 22.55S 49.58W
Pardo, Rio- [Braz.] 55 Jb 15.48S 44.48W
Pardo, Rio- [Braz.] 54 Kg 15.39S 38.57W
Pardubice 10 Lf 50.02N 15.45 E
Parea 65eEb 16.49S 150.58W
Parecis, Chapada dos- 52 Kg 13.00S 60.00W
Parecis, Rio- 55 Da 12.56S 56.43W
Paredes de Nava 13 Hb 42.09N 4.41W
Parelhas 54 Ke 6.41S 36.39W
Paren 20 Ld 62.28N 163.05 E
Parent 42 Kg 47.55N 74.37W
Parentis-en-Born 11 Ej 44.21N 1.04W
Pareora 62 Df 44.29S 171.13 E
Parepare 22 Nj 4.01S 119.38 E
Párga 15 Dj 39.17N 20.24 E
Pargas/Parainen 7 Ff 60.18N 22.18 E
Pargolovo 8 Nd 60.03N 30.30 E
Parham 51d Bb 17.05N 61.46W
Parhar 19 Gh 37.31N 69.23 E
Pari, Rio- 55 Db 15.36S 56.08W
Paria, Golfo de-/Paria, Gulf
of- 54 Fa 10.20N 62.00W
Paria, Gulf of-/Paria, Golfo
de- 54 Fa 10.20N 62.00W
Paria, Peninsula de- 50 Eg 10.40N 62.30W
Pariaguán 54 Fb 8.51N 64.43W
Pariaman 26 Dg 0.38S 100.08 E
Paria River 46 Jh 36.52N 111.36W
Paricutín, Volcán- 48 Hh 19.28N 102.15W
Parida, Isla- 49 Fi 8.07N 82.20W
Pari das Pedras 55 Ja 12.45S 44.47W
Parigi 26 Hg 0.48S 120.10 E
Parika 54 Gb 6.52N 58.25W
Parikkala 7 Gf 61.33N 29.30 E
Parima, Serra- 52 Je 3.00N 64.20W
Parinacota 56 Ga 18.12S 69.16W
Pariñas, Punta- 52 Hf 4.40S 81.20W
Paringul Mare, Vîrful- 15 Gd 45.20N 23.30 E
Parintins 53 Kf 2.36S 56.44W
Paris [Fr.] 6 Gf 48.52N 2.20 E
Paris [Il.-U.S.] 45 Mg 39.36N 87.42W
Paris [Kir.] 64g Ab 1.56N 157.31W
Paris [Ky.-U.S.] 44 Ef 38.13N 84.14W
Paris [Tn.-U.S.] 44 Cg 36.19N 88.20W
Paris [Tx.-U.S.] 43 He 33.40N 95.33W
Paris Basin (EN)=Parisien,
Bassin- 5 Gf 49.00N 2.00 E
Parisien, Bassin-=Paris
Basin (EN) 5 Gf 49.00N 2.00 E
Parita 49 Gi 8.00N 80.31W
Parita, Bahia de- 49 Gi 8.08N 80.24W
Parit Buntar 26 De 5.07N 100.30 E
Parkano 7 Fe 62.01N 23.01 E
Parkent 18 Gd 41.18N 69.40 E
Parker 46 Hi 34.09N 114.17W
Parker, Mount- 59 Fc 17.10S 128.20 E
Parkersburg 43 Kd 39.17N 81.33W
Parker Seamount (EN) 40 If 52.35N 151.15W
Parkes 58 Fh 33.08S 148.11 E
Park Falls 45 Kd 45.56N 90.32W
Parkland 46 Dc 47.09N 122.26W
Park Range 43 Fc 40.00N 106.30W
Park Rapids 45 Ic 46.55N 95.04W
Park River 45 Hb 48.24N 97.45W
Park Valley 46 If 41.50N 113.21W
Parma 14 Ef 44.56N 10.26 E
Parma [It.] 6 Hg 44.48N 10.20 E
Parma [Oh.-U.S.] 44 Ge 41.24N 81.44W
Parnaguá 54 Jf 10.13S 44.38W
Parnaíba 53 Lf 2.54S 41.47W
Parnaíba, Rio- 52 Lf 3.00S 41.50W
Parnamirim [Braz.] 54 Ke 8.05S 39.34W
Parnamirim [Braz.] 54 Ke 5.55S 35.15W
Parnarama 54 Je 5.41S 43.06W
Parnassós Óros=Parnassus
(EN) 5 Ih 38.30N 22.37 E
Parnassus 62 Ee 42.43S 173.17 E
Parnassus (EN)=Parnassós
Óros 5 Ih 38.30N 22.37 E
Párnis Óros 15 Gk 38.10N 23.40 E
Párnon Óros 15 Fl 37.12N 22.38 E
Pärnu/Pjarnu 6 Id 58.24N 24.32 E
Pärnu-Jaagupi/Pjarnu-
Jagupi 8 Kf 58.36N 24.25 E
Pärnu Jõgi/Pjarnu 7 Fg 58.23N 24.34 E
Pärnu Laht/Pjarnu, Zaliv-
7 Fg 58.15N 24.25 E
Parola 8 Kc 61.03N 24.22 E
Paroo River 57 Fh 31.28S 143.32 E
Paropamisus/Salseleh-ye
Safid Kūh 21 If 34.30N 63.30 E
Páros 15 Il 37.05N 25.09 E
Páros 15 Il 37.06N 25.12 E
Parowan 46 Ih 37.51N 112.57W
Parpaillon 11 Mj 44.35N 6.40 E
Parque Industrial 55 Jd 19.57S 44.01W
Parral 56 Fe 36.09S 71.50W
Parral, Rio- 48 Gd 27.35N 105.25W
Parras, Sierra de- 48 He 25.25N 102.00W
Parras de la Fuente 47 Dc 25.25N 102.11W
Parravicini 55 Dm 36.27S 57.46W
Parrett 9 Jj 51.13N 3.01W
Parrita 49 Ei 9.30N 84.19W
Parry, Cape - 42 Fb 70.12N 124.35W
Parry, Kap- [Grld.] 41 Jd 72.28N 22.00W
Parry, Kap- [Grld.] 41 Ec 77.00N 71.00W
Parry Bay 42 Jc 68.00N 82.00W
Parry Islands 38 Ib 76.00N 110.00W
Parry Peninsula 42 Fc 69.45N 124.35W
Parry Sound 42 Jg 45.21N 80.02W
Parsęta 10 Lb 54.12N 15.33 E
Parsons [Ks.-U.S.] 43 Hd 37.20N 95.16W
Parsons [W.V.-U.S.] 44 Hf 39.06N 79.43W
Parsons Range 59 Hb 13.30S 135.15 E
Partanna 14 Gm 37.43N 12.53 E
Parthenay 11 Fh 46.39N 0.15W
Partille 8 Eg 57.44N 12.07 E
Partinico 14 Hl 38.03N 13.07 E
Partizansk 20 Ih 43.13N 133.05 E
Partizánske 10 Oh 48.38N 18.23 E
Partizanskoje 20 Ee 55.30N 94.30 E
Paru, Rio- 52 Kf 1.33S 52.38W
Paru de Este, Rio- 54 Hc 1.10N 54.40W
Paru de Oeste, Rio- 54 Hc 1.30S 56.00W
Paruru 63a Ec 9.51S 160.49 E
Parvān [3] 23 Kb 35.15N 69.30 E
Pârvomaj 15 Ig 42.06N 25.13 E
Parys 37 De 27.04S 27.16 E
Paša 7 Hf 60.28N 32.55 E
Pasadena [Ca.-U.S.] 39 Hf 34.09N 118.09W
Pasadena [Tx.-U.S.] 45 Il 29.42N 95.13W
Paşaeli Yarimadası 15 Lh 41.20N 28.25 E
Paşalimani Adası 15 Ki 40.28N 27.37 E
Pasangkaju 26 Gg 1.10S 119.20 E
Pāsārgād 24 Og 30.17N 52.55 E
Pasarwajo 26 Hh 5.29S 122.50 E
Pascagoula 43 Je 30.23N 88.31W
Paşcani 15 Jb 47.15N 26.44 E
Pasco 43 Db 46.14N 119.06W
Pasco [2] 54 Cf 10.30S 75.15W
Pascoal 55 Ba 13.38S 61.06W
Pascoal, Monte- 54 Kg 16.54S 39.24W
Pascua, Isla de-/Rapa Nui=
Easter Island (EN) 57 Qg 27.07S 109.22W
Pas-de-Calais [3] 11 Id 50.30N 2.20 E
Pas-en-Artois 12 Ed 50.09N 2.30 E
Pasewalk 10 Jc 53.31N 13.59 E
Pasinler 24 Ib 40.00N 41.41 E
Pašino 20 De 55.11N 83.02 E
Pasión, Rio de la- 49 Be 16.28N 90.33W
Pasir Mas 26 De 6.02N 102.08 E
Pasirpengarayan 26 Df 0.51N 100.16 E
Pasir Puteh 26 De 5.50N 102.24 E
Påskallavik 8 Gg 57.10N 16.27 E
Paškovski 16 Kg 45.01N 39.05 E
Pasłęk 10 Pb 54.05N 19.39 E
Pasłęka 10 Pb 54.25N 19.50 E
Pašman 14 Jg 43.57N 15.21 E
Pasni 22 Ig 25.16N 63.28 E
Paso de Indios 56 Gf 43.52S 69.06W
Paso del Cerro 55 Ej 31.31S 55.46W
Paso de los Libres 56 Ic 29.43S 57.05W
Paso de los Toros 56 Id 32.49S 56.31W
Paso Tranqueras 55 Ej 31.12S 55.45W
Passamaquoddy Bay 44 Nc 45.06N 66.59W
Passa Três, Serra- 55 Hb 14.40S 49.30W
Passau 10 Jh 48.35N 13.29 E
Passero, Capo- 14 Jn 36.40N 15.10 E
Passo Fundo 53 Kh 28.15S 52.24W
Passo Fundo, Rio- 55 Fh 27.16S 52.42W
Passos 54 Ig 20.43S 46.37W
Pastaza, Rio- 52 If 4.50S 76.25W
Pasteur 56 He 35.08S 62.14W
Pasto 53 Ie 1.13N 77.17W
Pastora Peak 46 Kh 36.47N 109.10W
Pastoria, Laguna de- 48 Ki 16.00N 97.40W
Pastos Bons 54 Je 6.36S 44.05W
Pastrana 13 Jd 40.25N 2.55W
Paštrik 15 Dg 42.14N 20.32 E
Pasubio 14 Fe 45.47N 11.10 E
Pasvalis/Pasvalys 7 Fh 56.02N 24.28 E
Pasvalys/Pasvalis 7 Fh 56.02N 24.28 E
Pásztó 10 Pi 47.55N 19.42 E

Index Symbols

- [1] Independent Nation
- [2] State, Region
- [3] District, County
- [5] Municipality
- [5] Colony, Dependency
- Continent
- Physical Region
- Historical or Cultural Region
- Mount, Mountain
- Volcano
- Hill
- Mountains, Mountain Range
- Hills, Escarpment
- Plateau, Upland
- Pass, Gap
- Plain, Lowland
- Delta
- Salt Flat
- Valley, Canyon
- Crater, Cave
- Karst Features
- Depression
- Polder
- Desert, Dunes
- Forest, Woods
- Heath, Steppe
- Oasis
- Cape, Point
- Coast, Beach
- Cliff
- Peninsula
- Isthmus
- Sandbank
- Island
- Atoll
- Rock, Reef
- Islands, Archipelago
- Rocks, Reefs
- Coral Reef
- Well, Spring
- Geyser
- River, Stream
- Waterfall Rapids
- River Mouth, Estuary
- Lake
- Salt Lake
- Intermittent Lake
- Reservoir
- Swamp, Pond
- Canal
- Glacier
- Ice Shelf, Pack Ice
- Ocean
- Sea
- Gulf, Bay
- Strait, Fjord
- Lagoon
- Bank
- Seamount
- Tablemount
- Ridge
- Shelf
- Basin
- Escarpment, Sea Scarp
- Fracture
- Trench, Abyss
- National Park, Reserve
- Point of Interest
- Recreation Site
- Cave, Cavern
- Historic Site
- Ruins
- Wall, Walls
- Church, Abbey
- Temple
- Scientific Station
- Airport
- Port
- Lighthouse
- Mine
- Tunnel
- Dam, Bridge

Patagonia	52	Jj	44.00S	68.00W
Patagonica, Cordillera-	52	Ij	46.00S	71.30W
Patan	25	Hc	27.40N	85.20 E
Pātan	25	Ed	23.50N	72.07 E
Patani	26	If	0.18N	128.48 E
Pata Peninsula	64d	Bb	7.23N	151.35 E
Patchogue	44	Ke	40.46N	73.01W
Pate	36	Hc	2.08S	41.00 E
Patea	62	Fc	39.46S	174.29 E
Patea	62	Fc	39.46S	174.30 E
Pategi	34	Gd	8.44N	5.45 E
Patensie	37	Cf	33.46S	24.49 E
Paternò	14	Jm	37.34N	15.54 E
Paterson	43	Mc	40.55N	74.10W
Paterson Inlet	62	Bg	46.55S	168.00 E
Paterson Range	59	Ed	21.45S	122.05 E
Pathānkot	25	Fb	32.17N	75.39 E
Pathfinder Reservoir	46	Le	42.30N	106.50W
Pathfinder Seamount (EN)	40	Kf	50.55N	143.15W
Pathiu	25	Jf	10.41N	99.20 E
Patía, Río-	54	Cc	2.13N	78.40W
Patiāla	25	Fb	30.19N	76.24 E
Patiño, Estero-	55	Cg	24.05S	59.55W
Patio	65e	Db	16.35S	151.29W
Pati Point	64c	Ba	13.36N	144.57 E
Pătîrlagele	15	Jd	45.19N	26.21 E
Pativilca	54	Cf	10.42S	77.47W
Pátmos	15	Jl	37.19N	26.34 E
Pátmos	15	Jl	37.20N	26.33 E
Patna	22	Kg	25.36N	85.07 E
Patnos	24	Jc	39.14N	42.52 E
Pato Branco	56	Jc	26.13S	52.40W
Patom Plateau (EN)= Patomskoje Nagorje	20	Ge	59.00N	115.30 E
Patomskoje Nagorje=Patom Plateau (EN)	20	Ge	59.00N	115.30 E
Patos	53	Mf	7.01S	37.16W
Patos, Isla de-	50	Fg	10.38N	61.52W
Patos, Lagoa dos-	52	Ki	31.06S	51.15W
Patos, Laguna de los-	55	Aj	30.25S	62.15W
Patos, Ribeirão dos-	55	Gd	18.58S	50.30W
Patos, Rio dos- [Braz.]	55	Da	13.33S	56.29W
Patos, Rio dos- [Braz.]	55	Hb	14.59S	48.46W
Patos de Minas	53	Lg	18.35S	46.32W
Patosi	15	Ci	40.38N	19.39 E
Patquía	56	Gd	30.03S	66.53W
Pátrai	6	Ih	38.15N	21.44 E
Patrai, Gulf of- (EN) = Patraïkós Kólpos	15	Ek	38.15N	21.30 E
Patraïkós Kólpos = Patrai, Gulf of- (EN)	15	Ek	38.15N	21.30 E
Patricio Lynch, Isla-	56	Eg	48.36S	75.26W
Patricios	55	Bl	35.27S	60.42W
Patrocínio	54	Ig	18.57S	46.59W
Patta Island	30	Li	2.07S	41.03 E
Pattani	25	Kg	6.51N	101.16 E
Patteson, Passage-	63b	Db	15.26S	168.09 E
Patti	14	Il	38.08N	14.58 E
Patti, Golfo di-	14	Jl	38.10N	15.05 E
Patton Seamount (EN)	38	Dd	54.40N	150.30W
Pattullo, Mount -	42	Ee	56.14N	129.39W
Patu	54	Ke	6.06S	37.38W
Patuākhāli	25	Id	22.16N	90.18 E
Patuca, Punta-	49	Ef	15.51N	84.18W
Patuca, Río-	47	He	15.50N	84.18W
Pătulele	15	Fe	44.21N	22.47 E
Patutahi	62	Gc	38.37S	177.53 E
Patuxent Range	66	Qg	84.43S	64.30W
Pátzcuaro	48	Ih	19.31N	101.36W
Pau	11	Fk	43.18N	0.22W
Pau, Gave de-	11	Ek	43.33N	1.12W
Paucartambo	54	Df	13.18S	71.40W
Paucerne, Río-	55	Ba	13.34S	61.14W
Pau dos Ferros	54	Ke	6.07S	38.10W
Pauillac	11	Fi	45.12N	0.45W
Pauini	54	Ee	7.40S	66.58W
Pauini, Rio-	54	Ee	7.47S	67.15W
Pauksa Taung	25	Ie	19.55N	94.18 E
Paulatuk	39	Gc	69.23N	124.00W
Paulaya, Río-	49	Ef	15.51N	85.06W
Paulding Bay	66	Ie	66.35S	123.00 E
Paulina Peak	46	Ee	43.41N	121.15W
Păuliş	15	Ec	46.07N	21.35 E
Paulistana	54	Je	8.09S	41.09W
Paulo Afonso	53	Mf	9.21S	38.14W
Paulo Afonso, Cachoeira de-	52	Mf	9.24S	38.12W
Pauls Valley	45	Hi	34.44N	97.13W
Paungde	25	Je	18.29N	95.30 E
Pavant Range	46	Ig	39.00N	112.15W
Pāveh	24	Le	35.03N	46.22 E
Pavia	14	De	45.10N	9.10 E
Pavilly	12	Ce	49.34N	0.58 E
Pāvilosta/Pavilosta	7	Eh	56.55N	21.13 E
Pavilosta/Pāvilosta	7	Eh	56.55N	21.13 E
Pavlikeni	15	If	43.14N	25.18 E
Pavlodar	22	Jd	52.18N	76.57 E
Pavlodarskaja Oblast [3]	19	He	52.00N	76.30 E
Pavlof Islands	40	Ge	55.15N	161.20W
Pavlof Volcano	40	Ge	55.24N	161.55W
Pavlograd	16	Ie	48.32N	35.53 E
Pavlovka	17	Hi	55.25N	56.33 E
Pavlovo	19	Ed	55.58N	43.04 E
Pavlov Seamount (EN)	20	Lf	50.40N	162.00 E
Pavlovsk	16	Ld	50.27N	40.08 E
Pavlovskaja	19	Df	46.06N	39.48 E
Pavullo nel Frignano	14	Ef	44.20N	10.50 E
Pavuvu	63a	Dc	9.04S	159.08 E
Pawa	63a	Ed	10.15S	161.44 E
Pawhuska	45	Hh	36.40N	96.20W
Pawnee	45	Hh	36.20N	96.48W
Pawnee River	45	Gg	38.10N	99.06W
Pawtucket	44	Le	41.53N	71.23W
Paximádhia, Nisidhes-	15	Ho	35.00N	24.35 E
Paxoí	15	Dj	39.12N	20.10 E
Paxson	40	Jd	63.02N	145.30W
Payakumbuk	26	Dg	0.14S	100.38 E
Payas, Cerro-	49	Ef	15.50N	85.00W
Payerne	14	Ad	46.49N	6.58 E
Payette	46	Gd	44.05N	116.57W
Payette	43	Dc	44.05N	116.56W
Payne, Baie-	42	Ke	59.55N	69.35W
Payne, Lac -	42	Ke	59.30N	74.00W
Paysandú [2]	55	Dk	32.00S	57.15W
Paysandú	53	Ki	32.19S	58.05W
Pays de Léon	11	Bf	48.28N	4.30W
Pays d'Othe	11	Jf	48.06N	3.37 E
Payson [Az.-U.S.]	46	Ji	34.14N	111.20W
Payson [Ut.-U.S.]	46	Jf	40.03N	111.44W
Payzawat/Jiashi	27	Cd	39.29N	76.39 E
Pāzanān	24	Mg	30.35N	49.59 E
Pazar	24	Ib	41.11N	40.53 E
Pazarbası Burun	24	Db	41.13N	30.17 E
Pazarcık	24	Gd	37.31N	37.19 E
Pazardžik	15	Hg	42.12N	24.20 E
Pazardžik [2]	15	Hg	42.12N	24.20 E
Pazarköy	15	Kj	39.51N	27.24 E
Pazaryeri	24	Cc	40.00N	29.54 E
Pazin	14	He	45.14N	13.56 E
Pčinja	15	Eh	41.49N	21.40 E
Pea	65b	Ac	21.11S	175.14W
Peabirú	55	Ff	23.54S	52.20W
Peace Point	42	Ge	59.12N	112.33W
Peace River	39	Hd	56.14N	117.17W
Peace River [Can.]	38	Hd	56.14N	117.17W
Peace River [Fl.-U.S.]	44	Fl	26.55N	82.05W
Peachland	46	Fb	49.46N	119.44W
Peach Springs	46	Ii	35.32N	113.25W
Peacock Hills	42	Gc	66.05N	110.00W
Peak District	9	Lh	53.17N	1.45W
Peake Creek	59	He	28.05S	136.07 E
Peaked Mountain	44	Mb	46.34N	68.49W
Peale, Mount-	43	Fd	38.26N	109.14W
Pearl	45	Lb	48.42N	88.44W
Pearland	45	Il	29.34N	95.17W
Pearl and Hermes Reef	57	Jb	27.55N	175.45W
Pearl City	65a	Db	21.23N	157.58W
Pearl Harbor	65a	Cb	21.20N	158.00W
Pearl River	43	Je	30.11N	89.32W
Pearsall	45	Gl	28.53N	99.06W
Pearsoll Peak	46	De	42.18N	123.50W
Peary Channel	42	Ha	79.25N	101.00W
Peary Land	67	Me	82.40N	30.00W
Pease River	45	Gi	34.12N	99.07W
Pebane	37	Fc	17.14S	38.10 E
Pebas	54	Dd	3.20S	71.49W
Peć	15	Dg	42.39N	20.18 E
Peca	14	Id	46.29N	14.48 E
Peças, Ilha das-	55	Hg	25.26S	48.19W
Pecatonica River	45	Le	42.29N	89.03W
Pečenežskoje Vodohranilišče	16	Jd	50.05N	36.50 E
Pečenga	6	Jb	69.33N	31.07 E
Pečenga	7	Hb	69.39N	31.27 E
Pechea	15	Kd	45.38N	27.48 E
Pechora (EN)=Pečora	5	Lb	68.13N	54.10 E
Pechora (EN)=Pečora	6	Lb	65.10N	57.11 E
Pechora Bay (EN)= Pečorskaja Guba	19	Fb	68.40N	54.45 E
Pechora Sea (EN)= Pečorskoje More	19	Fb	69.45N	54.30 E
Pecica	15	Ec	46.10N	21.04 E
Peçin	15	Kl	37.19N	27.45 E
Peckelsheim, Willebadessen-	12	Lc	51.36N	9.08 E
Pečora=Pechora (EN)	6	Lb	65.10N	57.11 E
Pečora=Pechora (EN)	5	Lb	68.13N	54.10 E
Pecora, Capo-	14	Ck	39.27N	8.23 E
Pečorskaja Guba=Pechora Bay (EN)	19	Fb	68.40N	54.45 E
Pečorskoje More=Pechora Sea (EN)	19	Fb	69.45N	54.30 E
Pečory	7	Gh	57.49N	27.38 E
Pecos	43	Ge	31.25N	103.30W
Pecos	38	Ig	29.42N	101.22W
Pecos Plain	43	Ge	33.20N	104.30W
Pécs	6	Hf	46.05N	18.14 E
Pécs [2]	10	Oj	46.06N	18.15 E
Pedasí	49	Gj	7.32N	80.02W
Pedder, Lake-	59	Jh	43.00S	146.15 E
Peddie	37	Df	33.14S	27.07 E
Pededze	8	Lh	56.53N	27.01 E
Pedernales [Dom.Rep.]	49	Ld	18.02N	71.45W
Pedernales [Ven.]	50	Eh	9.58N	62.16W
Pedernales, Salar de-	56	Gc	26.15S	69.10W
Pedja Jõgi	8	Lf	58.20N	26.10 E
Pêdo Shankou	27	Df	29.12N	83.26 E
Pedra Azul	54	Jg	16.01S	41.16W
Pedra Branca	54	Ke	5.27S	39.43W
Pedra do Sino	55	Kf	22.27S	43.03W
Pedra Lume	32	Cf	16.46N	22.54W
Pedras, Rio das-	55	Ia	13.30S	47.09W
Pedras Altas, Coxilha-	55	Fj	31.45S	53.35W
Pedregal	54	Da	11.01N	70.08W
Pedreiras	54	Jd	4.34S	44.39W
Pedriceña	48	He	25.06N	103.47W
Pedrizas, Puerto de las-	13	Hh	36.55N	4.30W
Pedro Afonso	54	Ie	8.59S	48.11W
Pedro Bank (EN)	49	He	17.00N	78.30W
Pedro Betancourt	49	Gb	22.44N	81.17W
Pedro Cays	47	Ie	17.00N	77.50W
Pedro de Valdivia	56	Gb	22.37S	69.38W
Pedro Gomes	55	Ed	18.04S	54.32W
Pedro Gonzáles, Isla-	49	Hi	8.24N	79.06W
Pedro II	54	Jd	4.25S	41.28W
Pedro II, Ilha-	54	Ec	1.10N	66.44W
Pedro Juan Caballero	56	Ib	22.34S	55.37W
Pedro Leopoldo	55	Jd	19.38S	44.03W
Pedro Luro	56	He	39.29S	62.41W
Pedro Lustoza	55	Gg	25.49S	51.51W
Pedro Montoya	48	Jg	21.38N	99.49W
Pedro Osorio	56	Jd	31.51S	52.45W
Pedro R. Fernández	55	Ci	28.45S	58.39W
Pedro Severo	55	Ec	17.40S	54.02W
Pedroso, Sierra del-	13	Gf	38.35N	5.35W
Peebles	9	Jf	55.39N	3.12W
Pee Dee River	38	Lf	33.21N	79.16W
Peekskill	44	Ke	41.18N	73.56W
Peel	38	Fc	67.37N	134.40W
Peel	11	Lc	51.25N	5.50 E
Peel	9	Ig	54.13N	4.40W
Peel Sound	42	Hb	73.00N	96.00W
Peene	10	Jb	54.09N	13.46 E
Peer	12	Hc	51.08N	5.28 E
Peera Peera Poolanna Lake	59	He	26.30S	138.00 E
Peetz	45	Ef	40.58N	103.07W
Pegasus, Port-	62	Bg	47.10S	167.40 E
Pegasus Bay	61	Dh	43.20S	172.50 E
Pegnitz	10	Gg	49.29N	11.00 E
Pegnitz	10	Hg	49.45N	11.33 E
Pego	13	Lf	38.51N	0.07W
Pegtymel	20	Mc	69.47N	174.00 E
Pegu	22	Lh	17.30N	96.30 E
Pegu [3]	25	Je	17.52N	95.40 E
Pegu Yoma	21	Lh	19.00N	95.50 E
Pegwell Bay	12	Dc	51.18N	1.23 E
Pehčevo	15	Fh	41.46N	22.54 E
Pehlivanköy	15	Jh	41.21N	26.55 E
Pehuajó	56	He	35.48S	61.53W
Pei-ching Shih → Beijing Shi [4]	27	Kc	40.15N	116.30 E
Peine	10	Gd	52.19N	10.14 E
Peipsi järv=Peipus, Lake- (EN)	5	Id	58.45N	27.30 E
Peipus, Lake- (EN)= Čudskoje Ozero	5	Id	58.45N	27.30 E
Peipus, Lake- (EN)=Peipsi järv	5	Id	58.45N	27.30 E
Peixe	54	If	12.03S	48.32W
Peixe, Lagoa do-	55	Gj	31.18S	51.00W
Peixe, Rio do- [Braz.]	55	Ge	21.31S	51.58W
Peixe, Rio do- [Braz.]	55	Gb	14.06S	50.51W
Peixe, Rio do- [Braz.]	55	Hc	17.37S	48.29W
Peixe, Rio do- [Braz.]	55	Fc	16.32S	52.38W
Peixe, Rio do- [Braz.]	55	Gh	27.27S	51.54W
Peixe de Couro, Rio-	55	Ec	17.21S	55.29W
Peixes, Rio dos-	55	Hb	15.10S	49.30W
Peixian (Yunhe)	28	Dg	34.44N	116.56 E
Peixoto, Represa de-	54	Ih	20.30S	46.30W
Pejantan, Pulau-	26	Ef	0.07N	107.14 E
Pëjde/Pöide	8	Jf	58.30N	22.50 E
Pek	15	Ee	44.46N	21.33 E
Pekalongan	26	Eh	6.53S	109.40 E
Pekan	26	Df	3.30N	103.25 E
Pekin	43	Jc	40.35N	89.40W
Peking (EN)=Beijing	22	Nf	39.55N	116.23 E
Pekulnei, Hrebet-	20	Mc	66.30N	176.00 E
Pelabuhanratu	26	Eh	6.59S	106.33 E
Pelagie, Isole-	5	Hh	35.40N	12.40 E
Pelagonija	15	Eh	41.05N	21.30 E
Pélagos	15	Hj	39.20N	24.05 E
Pelaihari	26	Fg	3.48S	114.45 E
Pelat, Mont-	11	Mj	44.16N	6.42 E
Pelawanbesar	26	Gf	1.10N	117.54 E
Pélé	63b	Dc	17.30S	168.24 E
Peleaga, Vîrful-	15	Fd	45.22N	22.53 E
Peleduj	20	Ge	59.40N	112.38 E
Pelée, Montagne-	47	Le	14.48N	61.10W
Pelee, Point-	44	Fe	41.54N	82.30W
Pelee Island	44	Fe	41.46N	82.39W
Peleliu Island	57	Ed	7.01N	134.15 E
Peleng, Pulau-	26	Hg	1.20S	123.10 E
Pelhřimov	10	Lg	49.26N	15.13 E
Pelican Lake	45	Gb	49.20N	99.35W
Pelicanpunt	37	Ad	22.54S	14.26 E
Peligre, Lac de-	49	Ld	18.52N	71.56W
Pelinaion Óros	15	Ik	38.32N	26.00 E
Pelješac	14	Lh	42.55N	17.25 E
Pelkosenniemi	7	Gc	67.07N	27.30 E
Pella	45	Jf	41.25N	92.55W
Pélla	15	Fi	40.46N	22.34 E
Pellegrini	56	He	36.16S	63.09W
Pellice	14	Bf	44.50N	7.38 E
Pellinge/Pellinki	8	Kd	60.15N	25.50 E
Pellinki/Pellinge	8	Kd	60.15N	25.50 E
Pello	7	Fc	66.47N	24.01 E
Pellworm	10	Eb	54.30N	8.40 E
Pelly	38	Fc	62.47N	137.19W
Pelly Bay	42	Ic	68.50N	90.10W
Pelly Bay	39	Kc	68.52N	89.55W
Pelly Crossing	42	Dd	62.50N	136.35W
Pelly Mountains	42	Ed	61.30N	132.00W
Peloncillo Mountains	46	Kj	32.15N	109.10W
Pelón de Nado, Cerro-	48	Jg	20.05N	99.55W
Peloponnesus (EN)= Pelopónnisos	5	Ih	37.40N	22.00 E
Peloponnesus (EN) = Pelopónnisos	15	El	37.40N	22.00 E
Pelopónnisos [2]	15	El	37.40N	22.00 E
Pelopónnisos = Peloponnesus (EN)	15	El	37.40N	22.00 E
Pelopónnisos= Peloponnesus (EN)	5	Ih	37.40N	22.00 E
Peloritani	14	Jl	38.05N	15.20 E
Peloro, Capo- o Faro, Punta del-	14	Jl	38.16N	15.39 E
Pelotas	53	Ki	31.46S	52.20W
Pelotas, Rio-	56	Jc	27.28S	51.55W
Pelplin	10	Oc	53.56N	18.42 E
Pelvoux, Massif du-	5	Gg	44.55N	6.20 E
Pelym	19	Gd	59.40N	63.05 E
Pelymski Tuman, Ozero-	17	Kf	60.05N	63.05 E
Pemalang	26	Eh	6.54S	109.22 E
Pemar/Paimio	8	Jd	60.27N	22.42 E
Pematangsiantar	22	Li	2.57N	99.03 E
Pemba [3]	36	Hd	5.02S	40.00 E
Pemba [Moz.]	31	Lj	12.57S	40.30 E
Pemba [Zam.]	36	Ef	16.31S	27.22 E
Pemba Channel	36	Gd	5.10S	39.20 E
Pemba Island	30	Ki	5.10S	39.48 E
Pemberton [Austl.]	59	Df	34.28S	116.01 E
Pemberton [B.C.-Can.]	46	Da	50.20N	122.48W
Pembina	42	Gf	54.45N	114.17W
Pembina	43	Hb	48.58N	97.15W
Pembina River	43	Hb	48.56N	97.15W
Pembroke [Ont.-Can.]	42	Jg	45.49N	77.07W
Pembroke [Wales-U.K.]	9	Ij	51.41N	4.55W
Pembuang	26	Fg	3.24S	112.33 E
Peña, Sierra de la-	13	Lb	42.31N	0.38W
Penafiel	13	Dc	41.12N	8.17W
Peñafiel	13	Hc	41.36N	4.07W
Peñagolosa/Penyagolosa	13	Ld	40.13N	0.21W
Peña Gorda, Cerro-	48	Gg	20.40N	104.55W
Peñalara	13	Id	40.51N	3.57W
Penalva	54	Id	3.18S	45.10W
Penamacor	13	Ed	40.10N	7.10W
Peña Nevada, Cerro-	38	Jg	23.46N	99.52W
Penápolis	55	Ge	21.24S	50.04W
Peñaranda de Bracamonte	13	Gd	40.54N	5.12W
Peñarroya	13	Ld	40.28N	0.43W
Peñarroya-Pueblonuevo	13	Gf	38.18N	5.16W
Peñas, Cabo de-	5	Fg	43.39N	5.51W
Penas, Golfo de-	52	Ij	47.22S	74.50W
Peñas, Punta-	54	Fa	10.44N	61.51W
Peñasco, Rio-	45	Dj	32.45N	104.19W
Pendé	35	Ad	9.07N	16.26 E
Pendembu [S.L.]	34	Cd	9.06N	12.12W
Pendembu [S.L.]	34	Cd	8.06N	10.42W
Pendik	15	Mi	40.53N	29.13 E
Pendjari	34	Fc	10.54N	0.51 E
Pendle Hill	9	Kh	53.52N	2.17W
Pendleton	39	He	45.40N	118.47W
Pendolo	26	Hg	2.05S	120.42 E
Pend Oreille Lake	43	Db	48.10N	116.11W
Pend Oreille River	43	Db	49.04N	117.37W
Pendžikent	19	Gh	39.29N	67.38 E
Peneda	13	Dc	41.58N	8.15W
Penedo	54	Kf	10.17S	36.36W
Penetanguishene	44	Hc	44.47N	79.55W
Penganga	25	Fe	19.53N	79.09 E
Pengcheng	27	Jd	36.25N	114.08 E
Penge	36	Dd	5.31S	24.37 E
Pengho Jiao	27	Jc	16.03N	112.35 E
Penghu Liehtao= Pescadores (EN)	27	Kg	23.30N	119.30 E
Penglai (Dengzhou)	27	Ld	37.44N	120.45 E
Pengshui	27	If	29.17N	108.13 E
Pengze	27	Kf	29.52N	116.34 E
Penha	55	Hh	26.46S	48.39W
Penhalonga	37	Ec	18.54S	32.40 E
Penibético, Sistema-	13	Ig	37.00N	3.30W
Peniche	13	Ce	39.21N	9.23W
Penicuik	9	Jf	55.50N	3.14W
Penida, Nusa-	26	Gh	8.44S	115.32 E
Península Ibérica=Iberian Peninsula (EN)	5	Fg	40.00N	4.00W
Peñíscola	13	Md	40.21N	0.25 E
Penisola Salentina= Salentine Peninsula (EN)	5	Hg	40.30N	18.00 E
Penitente, Serra do-	54	Ie	8.45S	46.20W
Pénjamo	48	Ig	20.26N	101.44W
Penju, Kepulauan-	26	Ih	5.22S	127.46 E
Penmarch, Pointe de-	11	Bg	47.48N	4.22W
Penne	14	Hh	42.27N	13.55 E
Penne, Punta-	14	Lj	40.41N	17.56 E
Pennell Coast	66	Kf	71.00S	167.00 E
Penner	21	Kh	14.35N	80.10 E
Penn Hills	44	He	40.28N	79.53W
Pennines	5	Fe	54.10N	2.05W
Pennsylvania [2]	43	Lc	40.45N	77.30W
Penn Yan	44	Id	42.41N	77.03W
Penny Ice Cap	42	Kc	67.00N	65.10W
Penny Strait	42	Ha	76.35N	97.10W
Peno	7	Hh	56.57N	32.45 E
Penobscot Bay	44	Mc	44.15N	68.52W
Penobscot River	43	Nc	44.30N	68.50W
Penola	59	Ig	37.23S	140.50 E
Peñón del Rosario, Cerro-	48	Jh	19.40N	98.12W
Penong	58	Eh	31.55S	133.01 E
Penonomé	47	Hg	8.31N	80.22W
Pénot, Mont-	63b	Cc	16.20S	167.31 E
Penrhyn Atoll	57	Le	9.00S	158.00W
Penrith	9	Kg	54.40N	2.44W
Penrith, Sydney-	59	Kf	33.45S	150.42 E
Pensacola	39	Kf	30.25N	87.13W
Pensacola Mountains	66	Rg	83.45S	55.00W
Pensacola Seamount (EN)	57	Lc	18.17N	157.20W
Pensamiento	55	Bb	14.44S	61.35W
Pensiangan	26	Gf	4.33N	116.19 E
Pentecôte, Ile-	57	Hf	15.45S	168.10 E
Penticton	42	Fg	49.30N	119.35W
Pentland	59	Jd	20.32S	145.24 E
Pentland Firth	9	Jc	58.44N	3.13W
Pentland Hills	9	Jf	55.48N	3.23W
Penwith	9	Hk	50.13N	5.40W
Penyagolosa/Peñagolosa	13	Ld	40.13N	0.21W
Penza	6	Ke	53.13N	45.00 E
Penzance	6	Ff	50.07N	5.33W
Penzenskaja Oblast [3]	19	Ee	53.15N	44.40 E
Penzhina Bay (EN)= Penžinskaja Guba	20	Ld	61.00N	163.00 E
Penžina	21	Sc	62.28N	165.18 E
Penžinskaja Guba= Penzhina Bay (EN)	20	Ld	61.00N	163.00 E
Penžinski Hrebet	20	Ld	62.15N	166.35 E
Peoples Creek	46	Kb	48.24N	108.19W
Peoria	39	Ke	40.42N	89.36W
Peoúia	24	Ee	34.53N	32.23 E
Pepa	36	Ed	7.42S	29.47 E
Pepel	34	Cd	8.35N	13.03W
Peperiguaçu, Rio-	55	Fh	27.10S	53.50W
Peqini	15	Ch	41.03N	19.45 E
Pequena, Lagoa-	55	Fj	31.36S	52.04W
Pequiri, Rio-	54	Gg	17.23S	55.38W
Perabumulih	26	Dg	3.27S	104.15 E
Perälä	8	Ib	62.28N	21.36 E
Perales, Puerto de-	13	Fd	40.15N	6.41W
Pérama	15	Hn	35.22N	24.42 E
Peräseinäjoki	8	Jb	62.34N	23.04 E
Perche, Col de la-	11	Il	42.30N	2.06 E
Perche, Collines du-	11	Gf	48.25N	0.40 E
Percival Lakes	59	Ed	21.25S	125.00 E
Percy Islands	59	Kd	21.40S	150.15 E
Perdasdefogu	14	Dk	39.41N	9.26 E
Perdida, Sierra-	48	Hd	27.30N	103.30W
Perdido, Monte-	5	Gg	42.40N	0.05 E
Perdido, Rio-	55	Df	22.10S	57.33W
Perdizes	55	Id	19.21S	47.17W
Perečin	10	Sh	48.44N	22.29 E
Pereginskoje	16	De	48.49N	24.12 E
Pereira	54	Cc	4.48N	75.42W
Pereira Barreto	56	Jb	20.38S	51.07W
Perejaslav-Hmelnicki	16	Gd	50.04N	31.27 E
Perejil, Isla de-	13	Ig	35.55N	5.26W
Pereljub	16	Qd	51.52N	50.20 E
Peremennyj, Cape-	66	He	66.08S	105.30 E
Peremyšliany	10	Ug	49.38N	24.35 E
Perenjori	59	De	29.26S	116.17 E
Pereščepino	16	Ie	48.59N	35.22 E
Pereslavl-Zalesski	7	Jh	56.45N	38.55 E
Peretu	15	Ie	44.03N	25.05 E
Peretyčiha	20	Ig	47.10N	138.35 E
Perevolocki	16	Sd	51.51N	54.15 E
Pergamino	56	Hd	33.53S	60.35W
Pergamon	15	Kj	39.08N	27.13 E
Perge	24	Dd	37.00N	30.10 E
Pergine Valsugana	14	Fd	46.04N	11.14 E
Pergola	14	Gg	43.34N	12.50 E
Perham	45	Ic	46.36N	95.34W
Perho	7	Fe	63.13N	24.25 E
Periam	15	Dc	46.03N	20.52 E
Péribonca, Rivière-	42	Kg	48.44N	72.06W
Perico	56	Hb	24.23S	65.00W
Pericos	48	Fe	25.03N	107.42W
Périgord	11	Gi	45.00N	0.30 E
Perigoso, Canal-	54	Ic	0.05N	49.40W
Périgueux	11	Gi	45.11N	0.43 E
Perijá, Sierra de-	52	Ie	10.00N	73.00W
Peristerá	15	Gj	39.12N	23.59 E
Perito Moreno	53	Ij	46.36S	70.56W
Perkam, Tanjung-=Urville, Cape d'- (EN)	26	Kg	1.28S	137.54 E
Perković	14	Kg	43.41N	16.06 E
Perlas, Archipiélago de las-	47	Ig	8.25N	79.00W
Perlas, Cayos de-	49	Fg	12.28N	83.28W
Perlas, Laguna de-	49	Fg	12.30N	83.40W
Perlas, Punta de-	49	Fg	12.23N	83.30W
Perleberg	10	Hc	53.04N	11.52 E
Perlez	15	Dd	45.12N	20.23 E
Perm	6	Ld	58.00N	56.15 E
Përmeti	15	Di	40.14N	20.21 E
Permskaja Oblast [3]	19	Fd	59.00N	57.00 E
Pernambuco [2]	54	Ke	8.30S	37.30W
Pernik	15	Gg	42.36N	23.02 E
Pernik [2]	15	Fg	42.35N	22.50 E
Perniö/Bjärna	7	Ff	60.12N	23.08 E
Péronne	11	Ie	49.56N	2.56 E
Perote	48	Kh	19.34N	97.14W
Perpignan	6	Gg	42.41N	2.53 E
Perro, Laguna del-	45	Di	34.40N	105.57W
Perros-Guirec	11	Cf	48.49N	3.27W
Perry [Fl.-U.S.]	44	Fj	30.07N	83.35W
Perry [Ga.-U.S.]	44	Fi	32.27N	83.44W
Perry [Ia.-U.S.]	45	If	41.50N	94.06W
Perry [Ok.-U.S.]	45	Hh	36.17N	97.17W
Perry Lake	45	Ig	39.20N	95.30W
Perryton	45	Fh	36.24N	100.48W
Perryville	40	He	55.54N	159.10W
Persan	12	Ee	49.09N	2.16 E
Perşani, Munţii-	15	Id	45.40N	25.15 E
Persberg	8	Fe	59.45N	14.15 E
Persembe	24	Gb	41.04N	37.46 E
Persepolis	24	Oh	29.57N	52.52 E
Perseverancia	54	Ff	14.44S	62.48W
Persian Gulf (EN)=Al-Khalīj al-'Arabi	21	Hg	27.00N	51.00 E
Persian Gulf (EN)=Khalīj-e Fārs	21	Hg	27.00N	51.00 E
Perstorp	8	Eh	56.08N	13.23 E
Pertek	24	Hc	38.50N	39.22 E
Perth [Austl.]	58	Ch	31.56S	115.50 E
Perth [Ont.-Can.]	44	Ic	44.54N	76.15W
Perth [Scot.-U.K.]	9	Je	56.24N	3.28W
Perth Amboy	44	Je	40.32N	74.17W
Perth-Andover	44	Nb	46.44N	67.42W
Perth-Armadale	59	Df	32.09S	116.00 E
Perth-Fremantle	59	Df	32.03S	115.45 E
Perth-Kalamunda	59	Df	31.57S	116.03 E
Perth-Mundaring	59	Df	31.54S	116.10 E
Perthus, Col de-/Portús, Coll del-	13	Ob	42.28N	2.51 E
Perthus, Col du-	13	Ob	42.28N	2.51 E
Pertuis	11	Lk	43.41N	5.30 E
Pertusato, Capo-	11a	Bb	41.21N	9.11 E
Perú [1]	53	Ig	10.00S	76.00W
Peru [Il.-U.S.]	45	Lf	41.20N	89.08W
Peru [In.-U.S.]	44	De	40.45N	86.04W
Perú, Altiplano del-	54	Df	15.00S	72.00W
Peruaçu, Rio-	55	Jb	15.11S	44.07W
Peru Basin (EN)	3	Mk	17.00S	90.00W
Peru-Chile Trench (EN)	3	Nl	20.00S	73.00W
Perugia	6	Hg	43.08N	12.22 E
Perugorría	55	Ci	29.20S	58.37W
Peruíbe	55	Ig	24.19S	47.00W
Perušić	14	Jf	44.39N	15.22 E
Péruwelz	12	Fd	50.31N	3.35 E

Index Symbols

- [1] Independent Nation
- [2] State, Region
- [3] District, County
- [4] Municipality
- [5] Colony, Dependency
- Continent
- Physical Region
- Historical or Cultural Region
- Mount, Mountain
- Volcano
- Hill
- Mountains, Mountain Range
- Hills, Escarpment
- Plateau, Upland
- Pass, Gap
- Plain, Lowland
- Delta
- Salt Flat
- Valley, Canyon
- Crater, Cave
- Karst Features
- Depression
- Polder
- Desert, Dunes
- Forest, Woods
- Heath, Steppe
- Oasis
- Cape, Point
- Coast, Beach
- Cliff
- Peninsula
- Isthmus
- Sandbank
- Island
- Atoll
- Rock, Reef
- Islands, Archipelago
- Rocks, Reefs
- Coral Reef
- Well, Spring
- Geyser
- River, Stream
- Waterfall Rapids
- River Mouth, Estuary
- Lake
- Salt Lake
- Intermittent Lake
- Reservoir
- Swamp, Pond
- Canal
- Glacier
- Ice Shelf, Pack Ice
- Ocean
- Sea
- Gulf, Bay
- Strait, Fjord
- Lagoon
- Bank
- Seamount
- Tablemount
- Ridge
- Shelf
- Basin
- Escarpment, Sea Scarp
- Fracture
- Trench, Abyss
- National Park, Reserve
- Point of Interest
- Recreation Site
- Cave, Cavern
- Historic Site
- Ruins
- Wall, Walls
- Church, Abbey
- Temple
- Scientific Station
- Airport
- Port
- Lighthouse
- Mine
- Tunnel
- Dam, Bridge

Index Symbols

[1] Independent Nation	Historical or Cultural Region	Pass, Gap
[2] State, Region	Mount, Mountain	Plain, Lowland
[3] District, County	Volcano	Delta
[4] Municipality	Hill	Salt Flat
[5] Colony, Dependency	Mountains, Mountain Range	Valley, Canyon
Continent	Hills, Escarpment	Crater, Cave
Physical Region	Plateau, Upland	Karst Features

Depression	Coast, Beach	Rock, Reef
Polder	Cliff	Islands, Archipelago
Desert, Dunes	Peninsula	Rocks, Reefs
Forest, Woods	Isthmus	Coral Reef
Heath, Steppe	Sandbank	Well, Spring
Oasis	Island	Geyser
Cape, Point	Atoll	River, Stream

Waterfall Rapids	Canal	Lagoon
River Mouth, Estuary	Glacier	Bank
Lake	Ice Shelf, Pack Ice	Seamount
Salt Lake	Ocean	Tablemount
Intermittent Lake	Sea	Ridge
Reservoir	Gulf, Bay	Shelf
Swamp, Pond	Strait, Fjord	Basin

Escarpment, Sea Scarp	Historic Site	Port
Fracture	Ruins	Lighthouse
Trench, Abyss	Wall, Walls	Mine
National Park, Reserve	Church, Abbey	Tunnel
Point of Interest	Temple	Dam, Bridge
Recreation Site	Scientific Station	
Cave, Cavern	Airport	

Pisano 14 Eg 43.46N 10.33 E
Pisar 64d Cb 7.19N 152.01 E
Pisciotta 14 Jj 40.06N 15.14 E
Pisco 53 Ig 13.42S 76.13W
Pişcolt 15 Fb 47.35N 22.18 E
Pisek 10 Kg 49.19N 14.10 E
Pishan/Guma 27 Cd 37.38N 78.19 E
Pīsh Qal'eh 24 Qd 37.35N 57.05 E
Pīshvā 24 Ne 35.18N 51.44 E
Piso Firme 55 Ba 13.41S 61.52W
Pissa 7 Ei 54.39N 21.50 E
Pisshiri-Dake 29a Ba 44.20N 141.55 E
Pista 7 Hd 65.28N 30.45 E
Pisticci 14 Kj 40.23N 16.33 E
Pistoia 14 Eg 43.55N 10.54 E
Pisuerga 13 Hc 41.33N 4.52W
Pisz 10 Rc 53.38N 21.49 E
Pita 34 Cc 11.05N 12.24W
Pitalito 54 Cc 1.53N 76.02W
Pitanga 56 Jb 24.46S 51.44W
Pitanga, Serra da- 55 Gg 24.52S 51.48W
Pitangui 55 Jd 19.40S 44.54W
Pitcairn [5] 58 Og 24.00S 129.00W
Pitcairn Island 57 Ng 25.04S 130.05W
Piteå 7 Ed 65.20N 21.30 E
Piteälven 5 Ib 65.14N 21.32 E
Piteşti 6 Ig 44.51N 24.52 E
Pithiviers 11 If 48.10N 2.15 E
Pithorāgarh 25 Gc 29.35N 80.13 E
Piti 36 Fd 7.00S 32.44 E
Piti 64c Bb 13.28N 144.41 E
Pitiquito 48 Dc 30.42N 112.02W
Pitkjaranta 19 Dc 61.35N 31.31 E
Pitkkala 8 Jc 61.28N 23.34 E
Pitljar 20 Bc 65.52N 65.55 E
Pitlochry 9 Je 56.43N 3.45W
Pitomača 14 Le 45.57N 17.14 E
Piton, Pointe du- 51e Ba 16.30N 61.27W
Pit River 43 Cc 40.45N 122.22W
Pitrufquén 56 Fe 38.59S 72.39W
Pitt 42 Ef 53.40N 129.50W
Pitt Island 57 Ji 44.20S 176.10W
Pittsburg 43 Id 37.25N 94.42W
Pittsburgh 39 Le 40.26N 80.00W
Pittsfield [Il.-U.S.] 45 Kg 39.36N 90.48W
Pittsfield [Ma.-U.S.] 44 Kd 42.27N 73.15W
Pittsfield [Me.-U.S.] 44 Mc 44.47N 69.23W
Pitt Strait 62 Jf 44.10S 176.20W
Pitu 26 If 1.41N 128.01 E
Piúí 55 Je 20.28S 45.58W
Piura 53 Hf 5.12S 80.38W
Piura [2] 54 Be 5.00S 80.20W
Piuthān 25 Gc 28.06N 82.52 E
Piva 15 Bf 43.21N 18.51 E
Pivan 20 If 50.27N 137.05 E
Pivijay 49 Jh 10.28N 74.38W
Pižma [R.S.F.S.R.] 7 Lh 57.36N 48.58 E
Pižma [R.S.F.S.R.] 17 Fd 65.24N 52.05 E
Pizzo 14 Kl 38.44N 16.40 E
Pjakupur 20 Cd 65.00N 77.48 E
Pjalica 7 Jc 66.12N 39.32 E
Pjalma 19 Dc 62.27N 35.53 E
Pjana 7 Ki 55.37N 45.58 E
Pjandž 19 Gh 37.15N 69.07 E
Pjandž 21 If 37.06N 68.20 E
Pjaozero, Ozero- 5 Jb 66.05N 30.55 E
Pjarnu/Pärnu 6 Id 58.24N 24.32 E
Pjarnu/Pärnu Jõgi 7 Fg 58.23N 24.34 E
Pjarnu, Zaliv-/Pärnu Laht 7 Fg 58.15N 24.25 E
Pjarnu-Jagupi/Pärnu-Jaagupi 8 Kf 58.36N 24.25 E
Pjasina 21 Kb 73.47N 87.01 E
Pjasino, Ozero- 20 Dc 69.45N 87.30 E
Pjasinski Zaliv 20 Db 74.00N 85.00 E
Pjatigorsk 6 Kg 44.03N 43.04 E
Pjatihatki 16 He 48.27N 33.40 E
Pjórsá 5 Dc 63.45N 20.50W
Pjussi/Püssi 8 Le 59.17N 26.57 E
Pkulagalid 64a Bb 7.36N 134.33 E
Pkulagasemieg 64a Ac 7.08N 134.23 E
Pkurengel 64a Ac 7.27N 134.28 E
Plá 55 Bl 35.07S 60.13W
Placentia 42 Mg 47.14N 53.58W
Placentia Bay 38 Ne 47.15N 54.30W
Placer 26 Hd 11.52N 123.55 E
Placerville 46 Eg 38.43N 120.48W
Placetas 47 Id 22.19N 79.40W
Plácido Rosas 55 Fk 32.45S 53.44W
Plačkovci 15 Ig 42.49N 25.28 E
Plačkovica 15 Fh 41.46N 22.32 E
Plainfield 44 Je 40.37N 74.25W
Plains [Mt.-U.S.] 46 Hc 47.27N 114.53W
Plains [Tx.-U.S.] 45 Ej 33.11N 102.50W
Plainview [Nb.-U.S.] 45 He 42.21N 97.47W
Plainview [Tx.-U.S.] 43 Ge 34.11N 101.43W
Plainville 45 Gg 39.14N 99.18W
Pláka, Ákra- 15 Ii 40.02N 25.25 E
Plake 15 Eh 41.14N 21.02 E
Plampang 26 Gh 8.48S 117.48 E
Planá 10 Ig 49.52N 12.44 E
Plana Cays 49 Kb 22.37N 73.33W
Plana o Nueva Tabarca, Isla- 13 Lf 38.10N 0.28W
Planco, Peñón- 48 Ge 24.35N 104.15W
Plane, Ile- 13 Li 35.46N 0.54W
Planeta Rica 54 Cb 8.25N 75.35W
Planet Depth (EN) 3 Hi 10.20S 110.30 E
Planézes 11 Ij 45.00N 2.50 E
Plankinton 45 Ge 43.43N 98.29W
Plantation 44 Gl 26.05N 80.14W
Plantaurel 11 Hk 43.04N 1.30 E
Plant City 44 Fk 28.01N 82.08W
Plasencia 13 Fd 40.02N 6.05W
Plast 19 Ge 54.22N 60.55 E
Plaster Rock 44 Nb 46.54N 67.24W
Plastun 20 Ih 44.48N 136.17 E
Plasy 10 Jg 49.56N 13.24 E
Plata, Rio de la- [P.R.] 51a Bb 18.30N 66.14W
Plata, Rio de la- [S.Amer.] 52 Ki 35.00S 57.00W
Plataiai 15 Gk 38.13N 23.16 E
Platani 14 Hm 37.24N 13.16 E
Plateau [2] 34 Gd 8.50N 9.00 E
Plateau [3] 36 Cc 2.10S 15.00 E
Plateau, Khorat- 21 Mh 15.30N 102.50 E
Plateaux [3] 34 Fd 7.30N 1.10 E
Platen, Kapp- 41 Ob 80.31N 22.48 E
Plati 15 Fi 40.39N 22.32 E
Plato 54 Db 9.47N 74.47W
Platte 45 Ge 43.23N 98.51W
Platte 38 Je 43.23N 98.51W
Platte Island 30 Mi 5.52S 55.23 E
Platte River 45 Ig 39.16N 94.50W
Platteville 45 Ke 42.44N 90.29W
Plattsburgh 43 Mc 44.42N 73.29W
Plattsmouth 45 If 41.01N 95.53W
Plau 10 Ic 53.27N 12.16 E
Plauen 10 If 50.30N 12.08 E
Plauer See 10 Ic 53.30N 12.20 E
Plav 15 Cg 42.36N 19.57 E
Plavecký Mikuláš 10 Nh 48.30N 17.18 E
Pļaviņas/Pljavinjas 7 Fh 56.38N 25.46 E
Plavsk 16 Jc 53.43N 37.18 E
Playa Azul 47 De 17.59N 102.24W
Playa Noriega, Laguna- 48 Dc 29.10N 111.50W
Playa Vicente 48 Li 17.50N 95.49W
Playón Chico 49 Hi 9.18N 78.14W
Pleasanton [Ks.-U.S.] 45 Ig 38.11N 94.43W
Pleasanton [Tx.-U.S.] 45 Gl 28.58N 98.29W
Pleasant Point 62 Df 44.16S 171.08 E
Pleasant Valley 45 Fi 35.15N 101.48W
Plechý 10 Jh 48.49N 13.53 E
Pleiku 25 Lf 13.59N 108.00 E
Pleiße 10 Ie 51.20N 12.22 E
Plekinge 8 Fh 56.20N 15.05 E
Pleniţa 15 Ge 44.13N 23.11 E
Plenty, Bay of- 57 Ih 37.45S 177.10 E
Plentywood 43 Gb 48.47N 104.34W
Plešcenicy 16 Eb 54.29N 27.55 E
Pleseck 19 Ec 62.44N 40.18 E
Plešivec 10 Qh 48.33N 20.25 E
Pleşu, Vîrful- 15 Fc 46.32N 22.11 E
Pleszew 10 Ne 51.54N 17.48 E
Plétipi, Lac- 42 Kf 51.42N 70.08W
Plettenberg 12 Jc 51.13N 7.53 E
Plettenbergbaai 37 Cf 34.03S 23.22 E
Pleven [2] 15 Hf 43.25N 24.37 E
Pleven 6 Ig 43.25N 24.37 E
Plibo 34 De 4.35N 7.40W
Pliska 15 Kf 43.22N 27.07 E
Pliszka 10 Kd 52.15N 14.40 E
Plitvice 14 Jf 44.54N 15.36 E
Pljavinjas/Pļaviņas 7 Fh 56.38N 25.46 E
Plješevica 14 Jf 44.45N 15.45 E
Pljevlja 15 Cf 43.21N 19.21 E
Pljusa 7 Gg 58.25N 29.20 E
Pljusa 7 Gg 59.13N 28.11 E
Ploča, Rt- 14 Jg 43.30N 15.58 E
Plôce 14 Lg 43.04N 17.26 E
Płock [2] 10 Pd 52.35N 19.45 E
Płock 10 Pd 52.33N 19.43 E
Ploërmel 11 Dg 47.56N 2.24W
Ploieşti 6 Ig 44.57N 26.01 E
Plomárion 15 Jk 38.59N 26.22 E
Plomb du Cantal 11 Ii 45.03N 2.46 E
Plön 10 Gb 54.10N 10.26 E
Płonia 10 Kc 53.25N 14.36 E
Płonka 10 Qd 52.37N 20.30 E
Płońsk 10 Qd 52.38N 20.23 E
Plopana 15 Kc 46.41N 27.13 E
Płoty 10 Lc 53.50N 15.16 E
Plouguerneau 11 Bf 48.36N 4.30W
Plovdiv [2] 15 Hg 42.09N 24.45 E
Plovdiv 6 Ig 42.09N 24.45 E
Plummer 46 Gc 47.20N 116.53W
Plumridge Lakes 59 Fe 29.30S 125.25 E
Plumtree 37 Dd 20.31S 27.48 E
Plungė/Plunge 7 Ei 55.56N 21.48 E
Plunge/Plungė 7 Ei 55.56N 21.48 E
Plymouth [Eng.-U.K.] 6 Fe 50.23N 4.10W
Plymouth [In.-U.S.] 44 De 41.21N 86.19W
Plymouth [Ma.-U.S.] 44 Le 41.58N 70.41W
Plymouth [Mont.] 47 Le 16.42N 62.13W
Plymouth Sound 9 Ik 50.25N 4.05W
Plzeň=Pilsen (EN) 6 Hf 49.45N 13.24 E
Plzeňská pahorkatina 10 Jg 49.50N 13.15 E
Pniewy 10 Md 52.31N 16.15 E
Pô 34 Ec 11.10N 1.09W
Po 5 Hg 44.57N 12.05 E
Po, Colline del- 14 Be 45.05N 7.50 E
Po, Foci del-=Po, Mouths of the- (EN) 14 Gf 44.52N 12.30 E
Po, Mouths of the- (EN)=Po, Foci del- 14 Gf 44.52N 12.30 E
Poarta de Fier a Transilvaniei, Pasul- 15 Fd 45.25N 22.40 E
Poarta Orientală, Pasul- 15 Fd 45.08N 22.20 E
Poás, Volcán- 49 Eh 10.11N 84.13W
Pobé 34 Fd 6.58N 2.41 E
Pobeda, Gora- 21 Qc 65.12N 146.12 E
Pobeda Ice Island 66 Ge 64.30S 97.00 E
Pobedy, Pik- 21 Ke 42.02N 80.05 E
Pobla de Segur/La Pobla de Segur 13 Mb 42.15N 0.58 E
Poblet, Monasterio de-/Poblet, Monèstir de- 13 Nc 41.20N 1.05 E
Poblet, Monèstir de-/Poblet, Monasterio de- 13 Nc 41.20N 1.05 E
Pobrežije 15 Jf 43.56N 26.21 E
Pocahontas 35 Ig 36.16N 90.58W
Pocatello 39 He 42.52N 112.27W
Počep 16 Hc 52.57N 33.28 E
Pocerina 15 Ce 44.38N 19.35 E
Počinok 19 De 54.23N 32.29 E
Počitelj 14 Lg 43.08N 17.44 E
Pocito, Sierra del- 13 He 39.20N 4.05W
Pocito Casas 48 Dc 28.32N 111.06W
Pocklington Reef 60 Fj 11.00S 155.00 E
Poções 54 Jf 14.31S 40.21W
Poço Fundo, Cachoeira- 55 Jc 16.10S 45.51W
Poconé 54 Gg 16.15S 56.37W
Pocono Mountains 44 Je 41.10N 75.20W
Poços de Caldas 54 Ih 21.48S 46.34W
Pocri 49 Gj 7.40N 80.07W
Podborovje [R.S.F.S.R.] 8 Mg 57.51N 28.46 E
Podborovje [R.S.F.S.R.] 7 Ig 59.32N 35.01 E
Podbrezová 10 Ph 48.49N 19.31 E
Podčerje 17 He 63.55N 57.30 E
Poděbrady 10 Lf 50.09N 15.07 E
Podgajcy 10 Vg 49.12N 25.12 E
Podgorina 15 Ce 44.15N 19.56 E
Po di Volano 14 Gf 44.49N 12.15 E
Podjuga 7 Jf 61.07N 40.54 E
Podkamennaja Tunguska=Stony Tunguska (EN) 21 Lc 61.36N 90.18 E
Podlasie 10 Sd 52.30N 23.00 E
Podlaska, Nizina- 10 Sc 53.00N 22.45 E
Podlužje 15 Ce 44.45N 19.55 E
Podolia (EN)=Podolskaja Vozvyšennost 5 If 49.00N 28.00 E
Podolsk 19 Dd 55.27N 37.33 E
Podolskaja Vozvyšennost=Podolia (EN) 5 If 49.00N 28.00 E
Podor 34 Cb 16.40N 14.57W
Podporožje 19 Dc 60.54N 34.09 E
Podravina 14 Le 45.40N 17.40 E
Podravska Slatina 14 Le 45.42N 17.42 E
Podrima 15 Dg 42.24N 20.33 E
Podromanija 14 Mg 43.54N 18.46 E
Podsvilje 8 Mi 55.09N 28.01 E
Podujevo 15 Eg 42.55N 21.12 E
Podunajská nížina 10 Nh 48.00N 17.40 E
Podvološino 20 Fe 58.15N 108.25 E
Poel 10 Hb 54.00N 11.26 E
Poeniţa, Vîrful- 15 Gc 46.15N 23.20 E
Pofadder 37 Be 29.10S 19.22 E
Pogăniş 15 Ed 45.41N 21.21 E
Pogar 16 Hc 52.33N 33.16 E
Poggibonsi 14 Fg 43.28N 11.09 E
Pöggstall 14 Jb 48.19N 15.11 E
Pogibi 20 Jf 52.15N 141.45 E
Pogny 12 Gf 48.52N 4.29 E
Pogoanele 15 Je 44.55N 27.00 E
Pogórze Karpackie 10 Qg 49.52N 21.00 E
Pogradeci 15 Di 40.54N 20.39 E
Pograničny 20 Ih 44.26N 131.20 E
Pogrebišče 16 Fe 49.29N 29.14 E
Poguba Xoréu, Rio- 55 Ec 16.29S 54.58W
P'ohang 27 Md 36.02N 129.22 E
Pohja/Pojo 8 Jd 60.06N 23.31 E
Pohjankangas 8 Jc 62.00N 22.30 E
Pohjanlahti=Bothnia, Gulf of- (EN) 5 Hc 63.00N 20.00 E
Pohjanmaa 8 Jb 63.00N 22.30 E
Pohjois-Karjala [2] 7 Ge 63.00N 30.00 E
Pohlheim 12 Kd 50.32N 8.42 E
Pohorje 14 Jd 46.32N 15.28 E
Po Hu 28 Di 30.15N 116.32 E
Pohue Bay 65a Fd 19.01N 155.48W
Pohvistnevo 19 Fe 53.40N 52.08 E
Poiana Mare 15 Gf 43.55N 23.04 E
Poiana Ruscă, Munţii 15 Fd 45.41N 22.30 E
Pöide/Pējde 8 Jf 58.30N 22.50 E
Poie 36 Dc 2.55S 23.10 E
Poindimié 61 Cd 20.56S 165.20 E
Poindo → Lhünzhub 27 Fe 30.17N 91.20 E
Poinsett, Cape- 66 He 65.42S 113.18 E
Poinsett, Lake- 45 Hd 44.34N 97.05W
Point Arena 46 Dg 38.55N 123.41W
Point au Fer Island 45 Kl 29.15N 91.15W
Pointe-à-Pitre 47 Le 16.14N 61.32W
Pointe Duble 51e Bb 16.20N 61.00W
Pointe-Noire 51e Ab 16.14N 61.47W
Pointe Noire 31 Ii 4.48S 11.51 E
Point Hope 40 Fc 68.21N 166.41W
Point Lake 42 Gc 65.15N 113.00W
Point Lay 40 Gc 69.45N 163.03W
Point Pleasant [N.J.-U.S.] 44 Je 40.06N 74.02W
Point Pleasant [W.V.-U.S.] 44 Ff 38.53N 82.07W
Poisson-Blanc, Lac- 44 Jc 46.00N 75.44W
Poissonnier Point 59 Dc 20.00S 119.10 E
Poissy 11 If 48.56N 2.03 E
Poitevin, Marais- 11 Eh 46.22N 1.06W
Poitiers 6 Gf 46.35N 0.20 E
Poitou 11 Fh 46.40N 0.30W
Poitou, Plaines et Seuil du- 11 Gh 46.26N 0.17 E
Poivre Islands 37b Bb 5.46S 53.19 E
Poix-de-Picardie 11 He 49.47N 1.59 E
Poix-Terron 12 Ge 49.39N 4.39 E
Pojarkovo 20 Hg 49.42N 128.50 E
Pojkovski 19 Hc 60.59N 72.00 E
Pojo/Pohja 8 Jd 60.06N 23.31 E
Pojuba, Rio- 55 Ec 16.30S 54.59W
Pokaran 25 Ec 26.55N 71.55 E
Pokhara 25 Gc 28.14N 83.59 E
Poko 36 Eb 3.09N 26.53 E
Pokoinu 64p Bb 21.12S 159.49W
Pokój 10 Nf 50.56N 17.50 E
Pokrovka 18 Lc 42.19N 78.01 E
Pokrovsk 20 Hd 61.29N 129.10 E
Pokrovskoje [R.S.F.S.R.] 16 Jc 52.38N 36.51 E
Pokrovskoje [Ukr.-U.S.S.R.] 16 Jf 47.59N 36.13 E
Pokšenga 7 Kd 64.01N 44.15 E
Pokutje 15 Ia 48.20N 25.05 E
Pola 7 Hg 58.05N 31.40 E
Polabí 10 Lf 50.10N 15.10 E
Polacca 46 Ji 35.50N 110.23W
Pola de Laviana 13 Ga 43.15N 5.34W
Pola de Lena 13 Ga 43.10N 5.49W
Pola de Siero 13 Ga 43.23N 5.40W
Polanco 55 Ek 33.54S 55.09W
Poland 64g Ab 1.52N 157.33W
Poland (EN)=Polska [1] 6 He 52.00N 19.00 E
Polanów 10 Mb 54.08N 16.39 E
Polar Plateau 66 Cg 90.00S 0.00
Polar Urals (EN)=Poljarny Ural 5 Mb 66.55N 64.30 E
Polatlı 23 Db 39.36N 32.09 E
Polch 12 Jd 50.18N 7.19 E
Połczyn Zdrój 10 Mc 53.46N 16.06 E
Pol-e Khomrī 23 Kb 35.56N 68.43 E
Pole of Inaccessibility (EN) 66 Eg 82.06S 54.58 E
Pol-e-Safīd 24 Od 36.06N 53.01 E
Polesella 14 Ff 44.58N 11.45 E
Polesie Lubelskie 10 Te 51.30N 23.20 E
Polesine 14 Fe 45.00N 11.45 E
Polesje=Polesye (EN) 5 Ie 52.00N 27.00 E
Polessk 8 Ij 54.51N 21.02 E
Polesskoje 16 Fd 51.16N 29.27 E
Polesye (EN)=Polesje 5 Ie 52.00N 27.00 E
Polevskoj 19 Gd 56.28N 60.11 E
Polewali 26 Gg 3.25S 119.20 E
Poležan 15 Gh 41.43N 23.30 E
Polgár 10 Ri 47.52N 21.07 E
Pölgyo 28 Ig 34.51N 127.21 E
Poli 34 Hd 8.29N 13.15 E
Políaigos 15 Hm 36.46N 24.38 E
Poliçani 15 Di 40.08N 20.21 E
Policastro, Golfo di- 14 Jk 40.00N 15.35 E
Police 10 Kc 53.33N 14.35 E
Policoro 14 Kj 40.13N 16.41 E
Poligny 11 Lh 46.50N 5.43 E
Poligus 20 Ed 61.58N 94.40 E
Polikastron 15 Fh 41.00N 22.34 E
Polikhnitos 15 Jj 39.05N 26.11 E
Polillo Islands 21 Oh 14.50N 122.05 E
Pólis 24 Ee 35.02N 32.25 E
Polist 7 Hg 58.07N 31.32 E
Polistena 14 Kl 38.24N 16.04 E
Políyiros 15 Gi 40.23N 23.27 E
Poljarny [R.S.F.S.R.] 19 Db 69.13N 33.28 E
Poljarny [R.S.F.S.R.] 20 Mc 69.01N 178.45 E
Poljarny Ural=Polar Urals (EN) 5 Mb 66.55N 64.30 E
Polkowice 10 Me 51.32N 16.06 E
Pöllau 14 Jc 47.18N 15.50 E
Polle 64d Bb 7.20N 151.15 E
Pollença/Pollensa 13 Pe 39.53N 3.01 E
Pollensa/Pollença 13 Pe 39.53N 3.01 E
Pollino 5 Hh 39.55N 16.10 E
Polochic, Rio- 49 Cf 15.28N 89.22W
Polock 19 Cd 55.29N 28.52 E
Polog 15 Dh 42.00N 21.00 E
Pologi 19 Df 47.28N 36.15 E
Polonina 10 Jh 48.30N 23.30 E
Polonnaruwa 25 Gg 7.56N 81.00 E
Polonnoje 16 Ed 50.06N 27.29 E
Polousny Krjaž 20 Jc 69.30N 144.00 E
Polska=Poland (EN) [1] 6 He 52.00N 19.00 E
Polski Gradec 15 Jg 42.11N 26.06 E
Polski Trămbeš 15 If 43.22N 25.38 E
Polson 46 Hc 47.41N 114.09W
Poltár 10 Ph 48.27N 19.48 E
Poltava 6 Jf 49.35N 34.34 E
Poltavka 19 He 54.22N 71.45 E
Poltavskaja Oblast [3] 19 Df 49.45N 33.50 E
Põltsamaa/Pyltsamaa 8 Lf 58.23N 26.08 E
Põltsamaa/Pyltsamaa 7 Fg 58.39N 25.59 E
Poluj 20 Bc 66.30N 66.31 E
Polunočnoje 19 Gc 60.52N 60.25 E
Polür 24 Oe 32.52N 52.03 E
Põlva/Pylva 7 Gg 58.04N 27.06 E
Polvijärvi 7 Ge 62.51N 29.22 E
Polynesia 57 Le 4.00S 156.00W
Polynésie Française=French Polynesia (EN) [5] 58 Mf 16.00S 145.00W
Pom, Laguna de- 48 Mh 18.35N 92.15W
Pomarance 14 Eg 43.18N 10.52 E
Pomarkku/Påmark 8 Ic 61.42N 22.00 E
Pombal [Braz.] 54 Ke 6.46S 37.47W
Pombal [Port.] 13 De 39.55N 8.38W
Pombo, Rio- 55 Fe 20.53S 52.23W
Pomerania (EN)=Pommern 5 He 54.00N 16.00 E
Pomerania (EN)=Pommern 10 Lc 54.00N 16.00 E
Pomeranian Bay (EN)=Pommersche Bucht 10 Kb 54.20N 14.20 E
Pomeranian Bay (EN)=Pomorska, Zatoka- 10 Kb 54.20N 14.20 E
Pomeroy 44 Ff 39.03N 82.03W
Pomio 58 Ge 5.32S 151.30 E
Pomme de Terre Reservoir 45 Jh 37.51N 93.19W
Pommern=Pomerania (EN) 10 Lc 54.00N 16.00 E
Pommern=Pomerania (EN) 5 He 54.00N 16.00 E
Pommersche Bucht=Pomeranian Bay (EN) 10 Kb 54.20N 14.20 E
Pommersfelden 10 Gg 49.46N 10.49 E
Pomona 46 Gi 34.04N 117.45W
Pomona Lake 45 Ig 38.40N 95.35W
Pomorije 15 Kg 42.33N 27.39 E
Pomorska, Zatoka-=Pomeranian Bay (EN) 10 Kb 54.20N 14.20 E
Pomorski Bereg 7 Id 64.00N 36.15 E
Pomorskie, Pojezierze- 10 Mc 53.30N 16.30 E
Pomorski Proliv 19 Eb 68.40N 50.00 E
Pomošnaja 16 Ge 48.14N 31.29 E
Pompano Beach 44 Gl 26.15N 80.07W
Pompei 14 Ij 40.45N 14.30 E
Pompeu 55 Jd 19.12S 44.59W
Ponape 58 Gd 6.52N 158.15 E
Ponape Island 57 Gd 6.55N 158.15 E
Ponca City 43 Hd 36.42N 97.05W
Ponce 39 Mh 18.01N 66.37W
Poncheville, Lac- 44 Ia 50.12N 76.55W
Pondcreek 45 Hh 36.40N 97.48W
Pondicherry 25 Ff 11.56N 79.53 E
Pondicherry [3] 25 Ff 11.55N 79.45 E
Pond Inlet 39 Lb 72.41N 78.00W
Pond Inlet 42 Jb 72.48N 77.00W
Ponea 64n Ac 10.28S 161.01W
Ponente, Riviera di- 14 Cf 44.10N 8.20 E
Ponérihouen 63b Be 21.05S 165.24 E
Pones 64d Bb 7.12N 151.59 E
Ponferrada 13 Fb 42.33N 6.35W
Pongaroa 62 Gd 40.33S 176.11 E
Pongo 30 Jh 8.42N 27.40 E
Pongola 37 Ee 26.52S 32.20 E
Pong Qu 27 Ef 26.49N 87.09 E
Poniatowa 10 Se 51.11N 22.05 E
Ponoj 6 Kb 67.05N 41.07 E
Ponoj 5 Kb 66.59N 41.10 E
Ponomarevka 16 Sc 53.09N 54.12 E
Ponorogo 26 Fh 7.52S 111.27 E
Pons 11 Fi 45.35N 0.33W
Pons/Ponts 13 Nc 41.55N 1.12 E
Ponsul 13 Ee 39.40N 7.31W
Pont-à-Celles 12 Gd 50.30N 4.21 E
Ponta Delgada 31 Ee 37.44N 25.40W
Ponta Delgada [3] 32 Bb 37.48N 25.30W
Ponta Grossa 53 Kh 25.05S 50.09W
Pont-à-Mousson 11 Mf 48.54N 6.04 E
Ponta Porã 53 Kh 22.32S 55.43W
Pontarlier 11 Mh 46.54N 6.22 E
Pontassieve 14 Fg 43.46N 11.26 E
Pont-Audemer 11 Ge 49.21N 0.31 E
Pontaut 55 Bm 37.44S 61.20W
Pontávert 12 Fe 49.25N 3.49 E
Pontchartrain, Lake- 43 Ie 30.10N 90.10W
Pontchâteau 11 Dg 47.26N 2.05W
Pont-de-l'Arche 12 De 49.18N 1.10 E
Pont de Suert 13 Mb 42.24N 0.45 E
Pont-de-Vaux 11 Kh 46.26N 4.56 E
Ponte Alta 55 Gh 27.29S 50.23W
Ponte Alta, Serra da- 55 Id 19.42S 47.40W
Ponte Branca 55 Fc 16.27S 52.40W
Pontecorvo 14 Hi 41.27N 13.40 E
Ponte de Lima 13 Dc 41.46N 8.35W
Ponte de Pedra 55 Ec 17.06S 54.23W
Ponte de Pedrā 55 Da 13.35S 57.21W
Pontedera 14 Eg 43.40N 10.38 E
Ponte de Sor 13 De 39.15N 8.01W
Ponte Firme, Chapada da- 55 Id 18.05S 46.25W
Ponteix 46 Lb 49.49N 107.30W
Ponte Nova 54 Jh 20.24S 42.54W
Pontés e Lacerda 55 Cb 15.11S 59.21W
Pontevedra [3] 13 Db 42.30N 8.30W
Pontevedra 13 Db 42.26N 8.38W
Pontevedra, Ria de- 13 Db 42.22N 8.45W
Ponte Vermelha 55 Ed 19.29S 54.25W
Pont-Farcy 12 Af 48.56N 1.02W
Pontfaverger-Moronvilliers 12 Ge 49.18N 4.19 E
Ponthieu 11 Hd 50.10N 1.55 E
Pontiac [Il.-U.S.] 45 Lf 40.53N 88.38W
Pontiac [Mi.-U.S.] 44 Fd 42.37N 83.18W
Pontianak 22 Mj 0.02S 109.20 E
Pontian Kechil 26 Df 1.29N 103.23 E
Pontine Islands (EN)=Ponziane, Isole- 14 Gj 40.55N 13.00 E
Pontivy 11 Df 48.04N 2.59W
Pontivy, Pays de- 11 Dg 48.00N 3.00W
Pont-l'Abbé 11 Bg 47.52N 4.13W
Pont-l'Evêque 12 Ce 49.18N 0.11 E
Pontoise 11 Ie 49.03N 2.06 E
Pontorson 11 Ef 48.33N 1.31W
Pontremoli 14 Df 44.22N 9.53 E
Pontresina 14 Dd 46.28N 9.53 E
Ponts/Pons 13 Nc 41.55N 1.12 E
Pont-Sainte-Maxence 12 Ee 49.18N 2.36 E
Pont-Saint-Esprit 11 Kj 44.15N 4.39 E
Pontypool 9 Jj 51.43N 3.02W
Ponza 14 Gj 40.54N 12.58 E
Ponza 14 Gj 40.55N 12.55 E
Ponziane, Isole-=Pontine Islands (EN) 14 Gj 40.55N 13.00 E
Pool [3] 36 Bc 3.30S 15.00 E
Poole 9 Lk 50.43N 1.59W
Poona→Pune 22 Jh 18.32N 73.52 E
Poopó 54 Eg 18.23S 66.59W
Poopó, Lago de-=Poopó, Lake- (EN) 52 Jg 18.45S 67.07W
Poopó, Lake- (EN)=Poopó, Lago de- 52 Jg 18.45S 67.07W
Poor Knights Islands 62 Fa 35.30S 174.45 E
Pōōsaspea Neem/Pyzaspea 8 Je 59.15N 23.25 E
Popakai 54 Gc 3.22N 55.25W
Popayán 53 Ie 2.27N 76.36W
Poperinge 12 Id 50.51N 2.43 E
Poperinge-Watou 12 Ed 50.51N 2.37 E
Popigaj 20 Gb 71.55N 110.47 E
Popigaj 20 Fb 72.55N 106.00 E
Poplar 46 Mb 48.07N 105.12W
Poplar 42 Hf 53.00N 97.18W
Poplar Bluff 43 Id 36.45N 90.24W
Poplar River 46 Mb 48.05N 105.11W
Popocatépetl, Volcán- 38 Jh 19.02N 98.38W
Popokabaka 36 Cd 5.42S 16.35 E
Popoli 14 Hh 42.10N 13.50 E
Popomanaseu, Mount- 63a Ec 9.42S 160.03 E
Popondetta 60 Di 8.46S 148.14 E
Popovo 15 Jf 43.21N 26.14 E
Poppberg 10 Hg 49.20N 11.45 E
Poppel, Ravels- 12 Hc 51.27N 5.02 E
Poprad 10 Qg 49.38N 20.42 E
Poprad 6 If 49.03N 20.19 E
Poptún 49 Ce 16.21N 89.26W
Por 10 Tf 50.48N 23.01 E
Porangahau 62 Gd 40.18S 176.38 E

Index Symbols

[1] Independent Nation
[2] State, Region
[3] District, County
[4] Municipality
[5] Colony, Dependency
Continent
Physical Region
Historical or Cultural Region
Mount, Mountain
Volcano
Hill
Mountains, Mountain Range
Hills, Escarpment
Plateau, Upland
Pass, Gap
Plain, Lowland
Delta
Salt Flat
Valley, Canyon
Crater, Cave
Karst Features
Depression
Polder
Desert, Dunes
Forest, Woods
Heath, Steppe
Oasis
Cape, Point
Coast, Beach
Cliff
Peninsula
Isthmus
Sandbank
Island
Atoll
Rock, Reef
Islands, Archipelago
Rocks, Reefs
Coral Reef
Well, Spring
Geyser
River, Stream
Waterfall Rapids
River Mouth, Estuary
Lake
Salt Lake
Intermittent Lake
Reservoir
Swamp, Pond
Canal
Glacier
Ice Shelf, Pack Ice
Ocean
Sea
Gulf, Bay
Strait, Fjord
Lagoon
Bank
Seamount
Tablemount
Ridge
Shelf
Basin
Escarpment, Sea Scarp
Fracture
Trench, Abyss
National Park, Reserve
Point of Interest
Recreation Site
Cave, Cavern
Historic Site
Ruins
Wall, Walls
Church, Abbey
Temple
Scientific Station
Airport
Port
Lighthouse
Mine
Tunnel
Dam, Bridge

Porangatu	55	Ha	13.26 S	49.10 W
Porbandar	25	Dd	21.38 N	69.36 E
Porcien	12	Ge	49.40 N	4.20 E
Porcos, Rio dos-	55	Ja	12.42 S	45.07 W
Porcuna	13	Hg	37.52 N	4.11 W
Porcupine	38	Ec	66.35 N	145.15 W
Porcupine	44	Ga	48.32 N	81.10 W
Porcupine Bank (EN)	5	Ee	53.20 N	13.30 W
Porcupine Hills	46	Ha	50.05 N	114.10 W
Porcupine Plain	42	Dc	67.30 N	137.30 W
Pordenone	14	Ge	45.57 N	12.39 E
Poreč	14	He	45.13 N	13.37 E
Poreč	15	Fe	44.20 N	22.05 E
Porecatú	55	Gf	22.43 S	51.24 W
Porećje	8	Kk	53.53 N	24.08 E
Poreckoje	7	Li	55.13 N	46.19 E
Porhov	19	Cd	57.45 N	29.32 E
Pori/Björneborg	6	Ic	61.29 N	21.47 E
Porion	15	Gn	35.58 N	23.16 E
Porirua	61	Dh	41.08 S	174.50 E
Pórisvatn	7a	Bb	64.20 N	18.55 W
Porjus	7	Ec	66.57 N	19.49 E
Porkkala	8	Ke	59.55 N	24.25 E
Porlamar	54	Fa	10.57 N	63.51 W
Porma	13	Gb	42.29 N	5.28 W
Pornic	11	Dg	47.07 N	2.06 W
Poronajsk	22	Qe	49.14 N	143.04 E
Poronin	10	Qg	49.20 N	20.04 E
Póros	15	Gl	37.30 N	23.31 E
Póros	15	Gl	37.30 N	23.27 E
Poroshiri-Dake	28	Qc	42.42 N	142.35 E
Porosozero	7	He	62.44 N	32.42 E
Porozovo	10	Ud	52.54 N	24.27 E
Porpoise Bay	66	Ie	66.30 S	128.30 E
Porquis Junction	44	Ga	48.43 N	80.52 W
Porrentruy	14	Bc	47.25 N	7.10 E
Porreras	13	Oe	39.31 N	3.00 E
Porretta, Passo della-	14	Ef	44.02 N	10.56 E
Porretta Terme	14	Ef	44.09 N	10.59 E
Porsangen	5	Ia	70.50 N	26.00 E
Porsangerhalvøya	7	Fa	70.50 N	25.00 E
Porsgrunn	7	Bg	59.09 N	9.40 E
Pórshöfn	7a	Ca	66.10 N	15.20 W
Porsuk	24	Dc	39.42 N	31.59 E
Portachuelo	54	Fg	17.21 S	63.24 W
Portadown/Port an Dúnáin	9	Gg	54.26 N	6.27 W
Portage	45	Le	43.33 N	89.28 W
Portage la Prairie	42	Hg	49.57 N	98.18 W
Port Alberni	42	Fg	49.14 N	124.48 W
Portalegre	13	Ee	39.17 N	7.26 W
Portalegre [2]	13	Ee	39.15 N	7.35 W
Portales	43	Ge	34.11 N	103.20 W
Port-Alfred	42	Kg	48.20 N	70.53 W
Port Alfred	37	Df	33.36 S	26.55 E
Port Alice	42	Ef	50.23 N	127.27 W
Port Allegany	44	He	41.48 N	78.18 W
Port an Dúnáin/Portadown	9	Gg	54.26 N	6.27 W
Port Angeles	43	Cb	48.07 N	123.27 W
Port Antonio	47	Ie	18.11 N	76.28 W
Port Arthur [Austl.]	59	Jh	43.09 S	147.51 E
Port Arthur [Tx.-U.S.]	39	Jg	29.55 N	93.55 W
Port Arthur (EN)=Lüshun	27	Ld	38.50 N	121.13 E
Port Augusta	58	Eh	32.30 S	137.46 E
Port-Au-Prince	39	Lh	18.32 N	72.20 W
Port-au-Prince, Baie de-	49	Kd	18.40 N	72.30 W
Port Austin	44	Fc	44.03 N	83.01 W
Port aux Français	31	Om	49.25 S	70.10 E
Porta Westfalica	12	Kb	52.15 N	8.56 E
Port-Bergé-Vao Vao	37	Hc	15.33 S	47.38 E
Port Blair	22	Lh	11.36 N	92.45 E
Port-Bou/Portbou	13	Pb	42.25 N	3.10 E
Portbou/Port-Bou	13	Pb	42.25 N	3.10 E
Port Burwell [Newf.-Can.]	39	Mc	60.25 N	64.49 W
Port Burwell [Ont.-Can.]	44	Gd	42.39 N	80.49 W
Port-Cartier	42	Kf	50.01 N	66.53 W
Port Chalmers	62	Df	45.49 S	170.37 E
Port Charlotte	43	Kf	26.59 N	82.06 W
Port Clinton	44	Fe	41.30 N	82.58 W
Port Coquitlam	46	Db	49.16 N	122.46 W
Port-de-Bouc	11	Kk	43.24 N	4.59 E
Port-de-Paix	49	Kd	19.57 N	72.50 W
Port Dickson	26	Df	2.31 N	101.48 E
Port Edward	37	Ef	31.03 S	30.13 E
Portel [Braz.]	54	Hd	1.57 S	50.49 W
Portel [Port.]	13	Ef	38.18 N	7.42 W
Port Elgin	44	Gc	44.26 N	81.24 W
Port Elizabeth [S.Afr.]	31	Jl	33.58 S	25.40 E
Port Elizabeth [St.Vin.]	51n	Ba	13.00 N	61.16 W
Port Ellen	9	Gf	55.39 N	6.12 W
Port-en-Bessin-Huppain	11	Fe	49.21 N	0.45 W
Port Erin	9	Ig	54.05 N	4.43 W
Porter Point	51n	Ba	13.23 N	61.11 W
Porterville [Ca.-U.S.]	43	Dd	36.04 N	119.01 W
Porterville [S.Afr.]	37	Bf	33.00 S	19.00 E
Portete, Bahia de-	49	Lg	12.13 N	71.55 W
Port Fairy	59	Ig	38.23 S	142.14 E
Port Fitzroy	62	Fb	36.10 S	175.21 E
Port-Gentil	31	Hi	0.43 S	8.47 E
Port Gibson	45	Kk	31.58 N	90.58 W
Port Harcourt	31	Hh	4.46 N	7.01 E
Port Hardy	42	Ef	50.43 N	127.29 W
Port Hawkesbury	42	Lg	45.37 N	61.21 W
Porthcawl	9	Jj	51.29 N	3.43 W
Port Hedland	58	Cg	20.19 S	118.34 E
Port Heiden	40	He	56.55 N	158.41 W
Port Hope Simpson	42	Lf	52.30 N	56.17 W
Port Huron	43	Kc	42.58 N	82.27 W
Portile de Fier = Iron Gate (EN)	5	Ig	44.41 N	22.31 E
Port-Ilič	16	Pj	38.53 N	48.51 E
Portimão	13	Dg	37.08 N	8.32 W
Port Isabel	45	Hm	26.04 N	97.13 W
Portița	15	Le	44.41 N	29.00 E
Port Láirge/Waterford [2]	9	Fi	52.10 N	7.40 W
Port Láirge/Waterford	6	Fe	52.15 N	7.06 W
Portland [Austl.]	59	Ig	38.21 S	141.36 E
Portland [Eng.-U.K.]	9	Kk	50.33 N	2.27 W
Portland [In.-U.S.]	44	Ee	40.26 N	84.59 W
Portland [Me.-U.S.]	39	Le	43.39 N	70.17 W
Portland [N.D.-U.S.]	45	Hc	47.30 N	97.22 W
Portland [N.Z.]	62	Fa	35.48 S	174.20 E
Portland [Or.-U.S.]	39	Ge	45.33 N	122.36 W
Portland [Tx.-U.S.]	45	Hm	27.53 N	97.20 W
Portland, Bill of-	9	Kk	50.31 N	2.28 W
Portland, Promontoire -	42	Je	58.41 N	78.33 W
Portland Bight	49	Ie	17.57 N	77.08 W
Portland Island	62	Gc	39.20 S	177.50 E
Portland Point	49	Ie	17.42 N	77.11 W
Port-la-Nouvelle	11	Jk	43.01 N	3.03 E
Portlaoise/Port Laoise	9	Fh	53.02 N	7.17 W
Port Laoise/Portlaoise	9	Fh	53.02 N	7.17 W
Port Lavaca	43	Hf	28.37 N	96.38 W
Port Lincoln	58	Eh	34.44 S	135.52 E
Port Loko	34	Cd	8.46 N	12.47 W
Port Louis	50	Fd	16.25 N	61.32 W
Port-Louis	31	Mk	20.10 S	57.30 E
Port Macquarie	59	Kf	31.26 S	152.44 E
Portmadoc	9	Ii	52.55 N	4.08 W
Port Maria	49	Id	18.22 N	76.54 W
Port-Menier	42	Lg	49.49 N	64.20 W
Port Moller	40	Ge	55.59 N	160.34 W
Port Moody	46	Db	49.17 N	122.51 W
Port Moresby	58	Fe	9.30 S	147.07 E
Port Nelson	42	Ie	57.04 N	92.30 W
Portneuf, Rivière-	44	Ma	48.37 N	69.05 W
Port Nolloth	31	Ik	29.17 S	16.51 E
Port Nouveau-Québec	39	Md	58.35 N	65.59 W
Porto [2]	13	Dc	41.15 N	8.20 W
Porto [Fr.]	11a	Aa	42.16 N	8.42 E
Porto [Port.]	6	Fg	41.09 N	8.37 W
Porto, Golfe de-	11a	Aa	42.16 N	8.37 E
Pôrto Acre	54	Ee	9.34 S	67.31 W
Porto Alegre [Braz.]	53	Ki	30.04 S	51.11 W
Porto Alegre [SaoT.P.]	34	Ge	0.02 N	6.32 E
Porto Alexandre	31	Ij	15.48 S	11.52 E
Porto Amboim	31	Ij	10.44 S	13.45 E
Porto Azzurro	14	Eh	42.46 N	10.24 E
Portobelo	49	Hi	9.33 N	79.39 W
Pôrto Cedro	55	Ed	18.17 S	55.02 W
Porto Cervo	14	Di	41.08 N	9.35 E
Porto Curupai	55	Ff	22.50 S	53.53 W
Porto de Moz	53	Kf	1.45 S	52.14 W
Porto Empedocle	14	Hm	37.17 N	13.32 E
Porto Esperança [Braz.]	55	Dd	19.37 S	57.27 W
Porto Esperança [Braz.]	55	Db	14.02 S	56.06 W
Porto Esperança [Braz.]	55	Dc	17.47 S	57.07 W
Porto Esperidião	55	Cb	15.51 S	58.28 W
Porto Estrêla	55	Db	15.20 S	57.14 W
Portoferraio	14	Eh	42.49 N	10.19 E
Port of Ness	9	Gc	58.30 N	6.15 W
Pôrto Franco	54	Ie	6.20 S	47.24 W
Port of Spain	53	Jd	10.39 N	61.31 W
Porto Fundação	55	Ea	13.39 S	55.18 W
Portogruaro	14	Ge	45.47 N	12.50 E
Porto Lucena	55	Eh	27.51 S	55.01 W
Pörtom/Pirttikyla	8	Ib	62.42 N	21.37 E
Portomaggiore	14	Ff	44.42 N	11.48 E
Porto Mendes	55	Eg	24.30 S	54.20 W
Porto Moniz	32	Dc	32.51 N	17.10 W
Porto Moroco	55	Ea	13.24 S	55.35 W
Porto Morrinho	55	Dc	16.38 S	57.49 W
Porto Murtinho	53	Kh	21.42 S	57.52 W
Porto Novo [Ben.]	31	Hh	6.29 N	2.37 E
Porto Novo [C.V.]	32	Bf	17.07 N	25.04 W
Port Orford	46	Ce	42.45 N	124.30 W
Porto San Giorgio	14	Hg	43.11 N	13.48 E
Pôrto Santana	54	Hd	0.03 S	51.11 W
Porto Sant'Elpidio	14	Hg	43.15 N	13.45 E
Porto Santo	30	Fe	33.04 N	16.20 W
Porto Santo Stefano	14	Fh	42.26 N	11.07 E
Portoscuso	14	Ck	39.12 N	8.23 E
Pôrto Seguro	54	Kg	16.26 S	39.05 W
Porto Tolle	14	Gf	44.56 N	12.22 E
Porto Torres	14	Cj	40.50 N	8.24 E
Porto União	55	Gh	26.15 S	51.05 W
Pôrto Válter	54	De	8.15 S	72.45 W
Porto Vecchio	11a	Bb	41.35 N	9.17 E
Porto Velho	53	Jf	8.46 S	63.54 W
Portoviejo	53	Hf	1.03 S	80.27 W
Porto Xavier	55	Eh	27.54 S	55.08 W
Port Phillip Bay	59	Ig	38.05 S	144.50 E
Port Pirie	58	Eh	33.11 S	138.01 E
Portree	9	Gd	57.24 N	6.12 W
Port Renfrew	46	Cb	48.33 N	124.25 W
Port Rois/Portrush	9	Gf	55.12 N	6.40 W
Port Royal	44	If	38.10 N	77.12 W
Portrush/Port Rois	9	Gf	55.12 N	6.40 W
Port Said (EN)=Būr Sa'īd	31	Ke	31.16 N	32.18 E
Port Saint Joe	43	Jf	29.49 N	85.18 W
Port Saint Johns	37	Df	31.38 S	29.33 E
Port-Saint-Louis-du-Rhône	11	Kk	43.23 N	4.48 E
Port-Salut	49	Kd	18.05 N	73.55 W
Port Saunders	42	Lf	50.39 N	57.18 W
Port Shepstone	31	Kl	30.46 S	30.22 E
Portsmouth [Dom.]	50	Fe	15.35 N	61.28 W
Portsmouth [Eng.-U.K.]	9	Lk	50.48 N	1.05 W
Portsmouth [N.H.-U.S.]	43	Mc	43.03 N	70.47 W
Portsmouth [Oh.-U.S.]	43	Kd	38.45 N	82.59 W
Portsmouth [Va.-U.S.]	43	Ld	36.50 N	76.26 W
Portsmouth City Airport	12	Ad	50.46 N	1.04 W
Port Sudan (EN)=Būr Sūdān	31	Kg	19.37 N	37.14 E
Port Sulphur	45	Ll	29.29 N	89.42 W
Port Talbot	9	Jj	51.36 N	3.47 W
Porttipahdantekojärvi	7	Gb	68.06 N	26.33 E
Port Townsend	46	Db	48.07 N	122.46 W
Portugal [1]	6	Fh	39.30 N	8.00 W
Portugalete	13	Ia	43.19 N	3.01 W
Portuguesa [2]	54	Eb	9.10 N	69.15 W
Portuguesa, Río-	54	Eb	7.57 N	67.32 W
Portuguesa, Sierra de-	50	Bh	9.35 N	69.45 W
Portuguese Guinea (EN) → Guinea Bissau (EN) [1]	31	Fg	12.00 N	15.00 W
Portús, Coll del-/Perthus, Col de-	13	Ob	42.28 N	2.51 E
Port-Vendres	11	Jl	42.31 N	3.07 E
Port-Vila	58	Hf	17.44 S	168.19 E
Port Wakefield	59	Hf	34.11 S	138.09 E
Port Washington	45	Me	43.23 N	87.53 W
Porvenir [Bol.]	54	Ef	11.15 S	68.41 W
Porvenir [Bol.]	55	Ba	13.59 S	61.39 W
Porvenir [Chile]	56	Fh	53.18 S	70.22 W
Porvenir [Ur.]	55	Dk	32.23 S	57.59 W
Porvoo/Borgå	7	Ff	60.24 N	25.40 E
Porvoonjoki	8	Kd	60.23 N	25.40 E
Porz, Köln-	10	Df	50.53 N	7.03 E
Posada, Fiume di-	14	Dj	40.39 N	9.45 E
Posadas [Arg.]	53	Kh	27.25 S	55.50 W
Posadas [Sp.]	13	Gg	37.48 N	5.06 W
Posavina	15	De	44.33 N	20.04 E
Poschiavo	14	Ed	46.20 N	10.04 E
Pošehonje-Volodarsk	7	Jg	58.30 N	39.08 E
Posht-e Bādām	24	Pf	33.02 N	55.23 E
Posio	7	Gc	66.06 N	28.09 E
Posjet	28	Kc	42.39 N	130.48 E
Poskam/Zepu	27	Cd	38.12 N	77.18 E
Poso	22	Oj	1.23 S	120.44 E
Poso, Danau-	26	Hg	1.52 S	120.35 E
Posof	24	Jb	41.31 N	42.42 E
Posŏng	28	Ig	34.46 N	127.05 E
Pospeliha	20	Df	52.02 N	81.56 E
Posse	54	If	14.05 S	46.22 W
Possession, Ile de la-	30	Mm	46.14 S	49.55 E
Possession Island	37	Be	27.01 S	15.30 E
Pößneck	10	Hf	50.42 N	11.36 E
Post	45	Fj	33.12 N	101.23 W
Posta de San Martin	55	Bk	33.09 S	60.31 W
Postavy	19	Cd	55.07 N	26.50 E
Poste-de-la-Baleine	42	Je	55.20 N	76.50 W
Poste Maurice Cortier/Bidon V	32	He	22.18 N	1.05 E
Poste Weygand	32	He	24.29 N	0.40 E
Postmasburg	37	Ce	28.18 S	23.05 E
Postojna	14	Ie	45.47 N	14.14 E
Posto Simões Lopes	55	Eb	14.14 S	54.41 W
Postville [Ia.-U.S.]	45	Ke	43.05 N	91.34 W
Postville [Newf.-Can.]	42	Lf	54.55 N	59.58 W
Potchefstroom	37	De	26.46 S	27.01 E
Poteau	45	Ii	35.03 N	94.37 W
Potenza	14	Hg	43.25 N	13.40 E
Potenza	14	Jj	40.38 N	15.48 E
Poteriteri, Lake-	62	Bg	46.05 S	167.05 E
Potes	13	Ha	43.09 N	4.37 W
Potgietersrus	37	Dd	24.15 S	28.55 E
Potholes Reservoir	46	Fc	47.01 N	119.19 W
Poti	6	Kg	42.08 N	41.39 E
Poti, Rio-	54	Je	5.02 S	42.50 W
Potigny	12	Bf	48.58 N	0.14 W
Potiskum	31	Ig	11.43 N	11.04 E
Potnarhvin	63b	Dd	18.45 S	169.12 E
Potomac	38	Lf	38.00 N	76.18 W
Potosí [2]	54	Eh	20.40 S	67.00 W
Potosí [Bol.]	53	Jg	19.35 S	65.45 W
Potosí [Mex.]	47	Dd	24.51 N	100.19 W
Potosí, Bahía-	48	Ii	17.35 N	101.30 W
Potosí, Cerro-	48	Ie	24.52 N	100.13 W
Pototan	26	Hd	10.55 N	122.40 E
Potrerillos	56	Gc	26.26 S	69.29 W
Potrero, Rio-	55	Bc	17.32 S	61.35 W
Potsdam [2]	10	Id	52.30 N	13.00 E
Potsdam [G.D.R.]	10	Jd	52.24 N	13.04 E
Potsdam [N.Y.-U.S.]	44	Jc	44.40 N	75.01 W
Pott	63b	Ad	19.35 S	163.36 E
Potters Bar	12	Bc	51.41 N	0.10 W
Pottstown	44	Je	40.15 N	75.38 W
Pottsville	44	Ie	40.42 N	76.13 W
Pouancé	11	Eg	47.45 N	1.10 W
Pouébo	63b	Be	20.24 S	164.34 E
Pouembout	63b	Be	21.08 S	164.54 E
Poughkeepsie	44	Ke	41.43 N	73.56 W
Poulaphuca Reservoir/Loch Pholl an Phúca	9	Gh	53.10 N	6.30 W
Poum	63b	Be	20.14 S	164.01 E
Pourtalé	55	Bm	37.02 S	60.36 W
Pouso Alegre	54	Ih	22.13 S	45.56 W
Pouss	34	Ic	10.51 N	15.03 E
Poutasi	65c	Bb	14.01 S	171.41 W
Poŭthĭsăt	25	Kf	12.32 N	103.55 E
Poutrincourt, Lac-	44	Ja	49.13 N	74.04 W
Po Valley (EN)=Padana, Pianura-	5	Gf	45.20 N	10.00 E
Považská Bystrica	10	Og	49.07 N	18.28 E
Považský Inovec	10	Nh	48.35 N	18.00 E
Povenec	7	Ie	62.51 N	34.45 E
Poverty Bay	62	Gc	38.45 S	178.00 E
Povlen	15	Ce	44.09 N	19.44 E
Póvoa de Varzim	13	Dc	41.23 N	8.46 W
Povorino	16	Md	51.12 N	42.17 E
Povungnituk	42	Jd	60.03 N	77.16 W
Povungnituk	39	Lc	60.02 N	77.10 W
Powassan	44	Hb	46.05 N	79.22 W
Powder River [U.S.]	43	Fb	46.44 N	105.26 W
Powder River [Or.-U.S.]	46	Gd	44.45 N	117.03 W
Powell	46	Kd	44.45 N	108.46 W
Powell, Lake- [U.S.]	43	Ed	37.25 N	110.45 W
Powell Lake [Can.]	46	Ca	50.11 N	124.24 W
Powell River	42	Fg	49.52 N	124.33 W
Powers	44	Dc	45.39 N	87.32 W
Powers Lake	45	Eb	48.34 N	102.39 W
Powidzkie, Jezioro-	10	Nc	52.24 N	17.57 E
Powys [3]	9	Ji	52.25 N	3.20 W
Poxoréu	54	Hg	15.50 S	54.23 W
Poxoréu, Rio- [Braz.]	55	Ec	16.32 S	54.46 W
Poxoréu, Rio- [Braz.]	55	Ec	16.08 S	54.14 W
Poya	63b	Be	21.21 S	165.09 E
Poyang Hu	21	Ng	29.00 N	116.25 E
Poza de la Sal	13	Ib	42.40 N	3.30 W
Pozanti	24	Fd	37.25 N	34.52 E
Požarevac	15	Ee	44.37 N	21.12 E
Poza Rica de Hidalgo	39	Jg	20.33 N	97.27 W
Požarskoje	28	Ma	46.16 N	134.04 E
Požega	15	Df	43.51 N	20.02 E
Poznań [2]	10	Pd	52.25 N	19.55 E
Poznań	6	He	52.25 N	16.55 E
Pozoblanco	13	Hf	38.22 N	4.51 W
Pozo Borrado	55	Bi	28.56 S	61.41 W
Pozo Colorado	55	Cf	23.22 S	58.55 W
Pozo del Mortero	55	Bg	24.24 S	61.02 W
Pozo del Tigre	55	Bc	17.34 S	61.59 W
Pozo Dulce	55	Ai	29.04 S	62.02 W
Pozos, Punta-	56	Gg	47.57 S	65.47 W
Pozuelos	54	Fa	10.11 N	64.39 W
Pozzallo	14	In	36.43 N	14.51 E
Pozzuoli	14	Ij	40.49 N	14.07 E
Pra [Ghana]	34	Ed	6.27 N	1.47 W
Pra [R.S.F.S.R.]	7	Ji	54.45 N	41.01 E
Prabuty	10	Pc	53.46 N	19.10 E
Prachatice	10	Jg	49.01 N	14.00 E
Prachin Buri	25	Kf	14.02 N	101.22 E
Prachuap Khiri Khan	25	Jf	11.48 N	99.47 E
Praděd	10	Nf	50.06 N	17.14 E
Prades	11	Il	42.37 N	2.26 E
Prado	54	Kg	17.21 S	39.13 W
Præstø	8	Ei	55.07 N	12.03 E
Prague (EN)=Praha	6	He	50.05 N	14.26 E
Praha=Prague (EN)	6	He	50.05 N	14.26 E
Prahova [2]	15	Id	45.10 N	26.00 E
Praia	31	Eg	14.55 N	23.31 W
Praia a Mare	14	Jk	39.54 N	15.47 E
Praia da Rocha	13	Dg	37.07 N	8.32 W
Praia Rica	55	Eb	14.51 S	55.33 W
Praid	15	Ic	46.33 N	25.08 E
Prainha	54	Hd	1.48 S	53.29 W
Prairie Dog Town Fork	45	Gi	34.26 N	99.21 W
Prairie du Chien	45	Ke	43.03 N	91.09 W
Prangli	8	Ke	59.38 N	24.50 E
Prānhita	25	Fe	18.49 N	79.55 E
Prapat	26	Cf	2.40 N	98.56 E
Prasat	25	Kf	14.38 N	103.24 E
Praslin	51k	Bb	13.53 N	60.54 W
Praslin, Port-	51k	Bb	13.53 N	60.54 W
Praslin Island	37b	Ca	4.19 S	55.44 E
Prasonisìon	15	Kn	35.52 N	27.46 E
Prat, Isla-	56	Fg	48.15 S	75.00 W
Prata	54	Ig	19.18 S	48.55 W
Prata, Rio da-	55	Hd	18.49 S	49.54 W
Pratapgarh	25	Ed	24.02 N	74.47 E
Prat de Llobregat/El Prat de Llobregat	13	Oc	41.20 N	2.06 E
Prato	14	Fg	43.53 N	11.06 E
Pratomagno	14	Fg	43.40 N	11.40 E
Pratt	43	Hd	37.39 N	98.44 W
Prättigau	14	Dd	46.55 N	9.40 E
Pratt Seamount (EN)	40	Ke	56.10 N	142.30 W
Prattville	44	Di	32.28 N	86.29 W
Pratudinho, Rio-	55	Ja	13.58 S	45.10 W
Pravda	18	Cf	36.50 N	60.33 E
Pravda Coast	66	Ge	67.00 S	94.00 E
Pravdinsk [R.S.F.S.R.]	8	Ij	54.28 N	21.00 E
Pravdinsk [R.S.F.S.R.]	7	Kh	56.33 N	43.33 E
Pravia	13	Fa	43.29 N	6.07 W
Praxedis G. Guerrero	48	Gb	31.22 N	106.00 W
Praya	26	Gh	8.42 S	116.17 E
Prealpi Venete	14	Fd	46.25 N	11.50 E
Predazzo	14	Fd	46.19 N	11.36 E
Predeal	15	Id	45.30 N	25.34 E
Predeal, Pasul-	15	Id	45.28 N	25.36 E
Predel	14	Hd	46.25 N	13.35 E
Predivinsk	20	Ee	57.04 N	93.37 E
Predporožny	20	Jd	65.00 N	143.20 E
Pré-en-Pail	11	Ff	48.27 N	0.12 W
Preetz	10	Gb	54.14 N	10.17 E
Pregolia	7	Ei	54.42 N	20.24 E
Pregradnaja	16	Lh	43.58 N	41.12 E
Preiļi/Prejli	7	Gh	56.19 N	26.48 E
Preissac, Lac-	44	Ha	48.25 N	78.28 W
Prejli/Preiļi	7	Gh	56.19 N	26.48 E
Prekmurje	14	Kd	46.45 N	16.15 E
Prekornica	15	Cg	42.40 N	19.12 E
Prekule/Priekulé	8	Ii	55.36 N	21.12 E
Přelouč	10	Lf	50.02 N	15.33 E
Premià de Mar/Premiá de Mar	13	Oc	41.29 N	2.22 E
Premiá de Mar/Premià de Mar	13	Oc	41.29 N	2.22 E
Premnitz	10	Id	52.32 N	12.20 E
Premuda	14	If	44.21 N	14.37 E
Prenaj/Prienai	7	Fi	54.39 N	23.59 E
Prenj	14	Lg	43.32 N	17.52 E
Prenjasi	15	Dh	41.04 N	20.32 E
Prentice	45	Kd	45.33 N	90.17 W
Prentiss	45	Lk	31.36 N	89.52 W
Prenzlau	10	Jc	53.19 N	13.52 E
Preobraženije	20	Ih	42.58 N	133.55 E
Preobraženka	20	Fd	60.04 N	107.58 E
Preparis Island	25	If	14.52 N	93.41 E
Preparis North Channel	25	Ie	15.27 N	94.05 E
Preparis South Channel	25	If	14.45 N	94.05 E
Přerov	10	Ng	49.27 N	17.27 E
Prescelly, Mynydd-	9	Ij	51.58 N	4.42 W
Prescott [Ar.-U.S.]	45	Jj	33.48 N	93.23 W
Prescott [Az.-U.S.]	43	Ee	34.33 N	112.28 W
Preševo	15	Eg	42.19 N	21.39 E
Presho	45	Fe	43.53 N	100.04 W
Presicce	14	Mk	39.54 N	18.16 E
Presidencia Roque Sáenz Peña	53	Jh	26.50 S	60.30 W
Presidente Epitácio	56	Jb	21.46 S	52.06 W
Presidente Frei	66	Re	62.12 S	58.55 W
Presidente Hayes [3]	55	Cf	24.00 S	59.00 W
Presidente Juscelino	55	Jd	18.39 S	44.05 W
Presidente Murtinho	55	Fb	15.39 S	53.54 W
Presidente Olegário	55	Id	18.25 S	46.25 W
Presidente Prudente	56	Jb	22.07 S	51.22 W
Presidente Venceslau	55	Ge	21.52 S	51.50 W
President Thiers Seamount (EN)	57	Lg	24.39 S	145.51 W
Presidio	43	Gf	29.33 N	104.23 W
Presidio, Río del-	48	Ff	23.06 N	106.17 W
Preslav	15	Jf	43.10 N	26.49 E
Presnovka	17	Mi	54.40 N	67.09 E
Prešov	10	Rh	49.00 N	21.14 E
Prespa	15	Hh	41.43 N	24.53 E
Prespa, Lake- (EN)= Prespansko jezero	5	Ig	40.55 N	21.00 E
Prespansko jezero=Prespa, Lake- (EN)	5	Ig	40.55 N	21.00 E
Presque Isle	43	Nb	46.41 N	68.01 W
Prestea	34	Ed	5.26 N	2.09 W
Přeštice	10	Jg	49.35 N	13.21 E
Preston [Eng.-U.K.]	9	Kh	53.46 N	2.42 W
Preston [Id.-U.S.]	43	Ec	42.06 N	111.53 W
Preston [Ont.-Can.]	44	Gd	43.23 N	80.21 W
Prestonsburg	44	Fg	37.40 N	82.46 W
Preststranda	8	Ce	59.06 N	9.04 E
Prestwick	9	If	55.30 N	4.37 W
Prêto, Rio- [Braz.]	54	Jf	11.21 S	43.52 W
Prêto, Rio- [Braz.]	55	Gd	18.44 S	50.23 W
Prêto, Rio- [Braz.]	55	Ic	17.00 S	46.12 W
Prêto, Rio- [Braz.]	55	Ha	13.37 S	48.06 W
Preto do Igapó Açu, Rio-	54	Gd	4.26 S	59.48 W
Pretoria	31	Jk	25.45 S	28.10 E
Pretty Rock Butte	45	Fc	46.10 N	101.42 W
Preußisch-Oldendorf	12	Kb	52.18 N	8.30 E
Préveza	15	Dk	38.57 N	20.45 E
Prey	12	Df	48.58 N	1.13 E
Prey Vêng	25	Lf	11.29 N	105.19 E
Priangarskoje Plato	20	Ee	57.30 N	97.00 E
Priargunsk	20	Gf	50.27 N	119.00 E
Pribelski	17	Hi	54.24 N	56.29 E
Pribilof Islands	38	Cd	57.00 N	170.00 W
Priboj	15	Cf	43.35 N	19.32 E
Příbram	10	Kg	49.42 N	14.01 E
Price [Que.-Can.]	44	Ma	48.39 N	68.12 W
Price [Ut.-U.S.]	46	Jg	39.36 N	110.48 W
Price River	46	Jg	39.10 N	110.06 W
Prichard	44	Cj	30.44 N	88.05 W
Prickly Pear Cays	51b	Ab	18.16 N	63.11 W
Prickly Point	51p	Bc	11.59 N	61.45 W
Pridneprovskaja Vozvyšennost=Dnepr Upland (EN)	5	Jf	49.00 N	32.00 E
Priego	13	Jd	40.27 N	2.18 W
Priego de Córdoba	13	Hg	37.26 N	4.11 W
Priei, Măgura-	15	Fc	46.58 N	22.50 E
Priekule	7	Eh	56.29 N	21.37 E
Priekulė/Prekule	8	Ii	55.36 N	21.12 E
Prienai/Prenaj	7	Fi	54.39 N	23.59 E
Priene	24	Bd	37.40 N	27.13 E
Prieska	31	Jk	29.40 S	22.42 E
Priest Lake	46	Gb	48.34 N	116.52 W
Prieta, Peña-	13	Ha	43.01 N	4.44 W
Prieta, Sierra-	48	Cb	31.15 N	112.55 W
Prievidza	10	Oh	48.46 N	18.39 E
Prignitz	10	Hc	53.00 N	12.00 E
Prijedor	14	Kf	44.59 N	16.42 E
Prijepolje	15	Cf	43.24 N	19.39 E
Prijutovo	19	Fe	53.58 N	53.58 E
Prikaspijskaja Nizmennost= Caspian Depression (EN)	5	Lf	48.00 N	52.00 E
Prilenskoje Plato = Lena Mountains (EN)	21	Oc	60.45 N	125.00 E
Prilep	15	Eh	41.21 N	21.34 E
Priluki	19	De	50.36 N	32.24 E
Primavera	66	Qe	64.09 S	60.57 W
Primeira Cruz	54	Jd	2.30 S	43.26 W
Primorje	8	Hj	54.56 N	20.00 E
Primorsk [R.S.F.S.R.]	7	Gf	60.22 N	28.36 E
Primorsk [Ukr.-U.S.S.R.]	16	Jf	46.43 N	36.22 E
Primorski Hrebet	20	Ff	52.30 N	106.00 E
Primorski Kraj [3]	20	Ig	45.30 N	135.30 E
Primorsko	15	Kg	42.16 N	27.46 E
Primorsko-Ahtarsk	19	Df	46.03 N	38.11 E
Primorskoje [R.S.F.S.R.]	8	Ld	60.32 N	27.56 E
Primorskoje [Ukr.-U.S.S.R.]	15	Nd	45.59 N	30.15 E
Primošten	14	Jg	43.36 N	15.55 E
Primrose Lake	42	Gf	54.55 N	109.45 W
Prims	10	Cg	49.20 N	6.44 E
Prince Albert	39	Id	53.12 N	104.46 W
Prince Albert Mountains	66	Jf	76.00 S	161.30 E
Prince Albert Peninsula	42	Fb	72.30 N	116.00 W
Prince Albert Road	37	Cf	33.13 S	22.02 E
Prince Albert Sound	42	Gb	70.25 N	115.00 W
Prince Alfred, Cape -	42	Fb	74.05 N	124.29 W
Prince Charles	38	Lc	67.50 N	76.00 W
Prince Charles Mountains	66	Ff	72.00 S	67.00 E
Prince-de-Galles, Cap -	42	Kd	61.36 N	71.30 W
Prince Edward	30	Km	46.33 S	37.57 E
Prince Edward Island [3]	42	Lg	46.30 N	63.00 W
Prince Edward Island	38	Me	46.30 N	63.00 W
Prince Edward Islands	30	Km	46.35 S	37.56 E
Prince George	39	Gd	53.55 N	122.49 W
Prince Gustaf Adolf Sea	38	Ib	78.30 N	107.00 W
Prince of Wales [Ak.-U.S.]	40	Me	55.47 N	132.50 W
Prince of Wales [Can.]	38	Jb	72.40 N	99.00 W
Prince of Wales, Cape-	38	Cc	65.40 N	168.05 W
Prince of Wales Island	59	Ib	10.40 S	142.10 E
Prince of Wales Mountains	42	Ja	77.45 N	78.00 W
Prince of Wales Strait	42	Fb	72.45 N	118.00 W
Prince Patrick	38	Hb	76.45 N	119.30 W
Prince Regent Inlet	42	Ib	72.45 N	90.30 W
Prince Rupert	39	Fd	54.19 N	130.19 W
Prince Rupert Bay	51g	Ba	15.34 N	61.29 W
Prince Rupert Bluff	51g	Ba	15.35 N	61.29 W
Princes Risborough	12	Bc	51.43 N	0.49 W
Princess Anne	44	Jf	38.12 N	75.41 W
Princess Charlotte Bay	59	Ib	14.25 S	144.00 E
Princess Elizabeth Land	66	Ff	70.00 S	80.00 E

Index Symbols

[1] Independent Nation
[2] State, Region
[3] District, County
[4] Municipality
[5] Colony, Dependency
Continent
Physical Region
Historical or Cultural Region
Mount, Mountain
Volcano
Hill
Mountains, Mountain Range
Hills, Escarpment
Plateau, Upland
Pass, Gap
Plain, Lowland
Delta
Salt Flat
Valley, Canyon
Crater, Cave
Karst Features
Depression
Polder
Desert, Dunes
Forest, Woods
Heath, Steppe
Oasis
Cape, Point
Coast, Beach
Cliff
Peninsula
Isthmus
Sandbank
Island
Atoll
Rock, Reef
Islands, Archipelago
Rocks, Reefs
Coral Reef
Well, Spring
Geyser
River, Stream
Waterfall Rapids
River Mouth, Estuary
Lake
Salt Lake
Intermittent Lake
Reservoir
Swamp, Pond
Canal
Glacier
Ice Shelf, Pack Ice
Ocean
Sea
Gulf, Bay
Strait, Fjord
Lagoon
Bank
Seamount
Tablemount
Ridge
Shelf
Basin
Escarpment, Sea Scarp
Fracture
Trench, Abyss
National Park, Reserve
Point of Interest
Recreation Site
Cave, Cavern
Historic Site
Ruins
Wall, Walls
Church, Abbey
Temple
Scientific Station
Airport
Port
Lighthouse
Mine
Tunnel
Dam, Bridge

Index Symbols

[1] Independent Nation	[2] State, Region	[3] District, County
[4] Municipality	[5] Colony, Dependency	■ Continent
[X] Physical Region		

- Historical or Cultural Region
- Mount, Mountain
- Volcano
- Hill
- Mountains, Mountain Range
- Hills, Escarpment
- Plateau, Upland
- Pass, Gap
- Plain, Lowland
- Delta
- Salt Flat
- Valley, Canyon
- Crater, Cave
- Karst Features
- Depression
- Polder
- Cliff
- Peninsula
- Forest, Woods
- Isthmus
- Oasis
- Cape, Point
- Coast, Beach
- Islands, Archipelago
- Rocks, Reefs
- Coral Reef
- Sandbank
- Island
- Atoll
- Rock, Reef
- Waterfall Rapids
- River Mouth, Estuary
- Lake
- Salt Lake
- Intermittent Lake
- Sea
- Gulf, Bay
- Strait, Fjord
- Canal
- Glacier
- Ice Shelf, Pack Ice
- Well, Spring
- Geyser
- Reservoir
- Swamp, Pond
- Lagoon
- Bank
- Seamount
- Tablemount
- Ridge
- Shelf
- Basin
- Escarpment, Sea Scarp
- Fracture
- Trench, Abyss
- National Park, Reserve
- Point of Interest
- Recreation Site
- Cave, Cavern
- Historic Site
- Ruins
- Wall, Walls
- Church, Abbey
- Temple
- Scientific Station
- Airport
- Port
- Lighthouse
- Mine
- Tunnel
- Dam, Bridge

Index Symbols

[1]	Independent Nation
[2]	State, Region
[3]	District, County
[4]	Municipality
[5]	Colony, Dependency
■	Continent
⌧	Physical Region
⌧	Historical or Cultural Region
▲	Mount, Mountain
▲	Volcano
▲	Hill
⌧	Mountains, Mountain Range
⌧	Hills, Escarpment
⌧	Plateau, Upland
⌧	Pass, Gap
⌧	Plain, Lowland
⌧	Delta
⌧	Salt Flat
⌧	Valley, Canyon
⌧	Crater, Cave
⌧	Karst Features
⌧	Depression
⌧	Polder
⌧	Desert, Dunes
⌧	Forest, Steppe
⌧	Heath, Steppe
⌧	Oasis
⌧	Cape, Point
⌧	Coast, Beach
⌧	Cliff
⌧	Peninsula
⌧	Isthmus
⌧	Sandbank
⌧	Island
⌧	Atoll
⌧	Rock, Reef
⌧	Islands, Archipelago
⌧	Rocks, Reefs
⌧	Coral Reef
⌧	Well, Spring
⌧	Geyser
⌧	River, Stream
⌧	Waterfall Rapids
⌧	River Mouth, Estuary
⌧	Lake
⌧	Salt Lake
⌧	Intermittent Lake
⌧	Reservoir
⌧	Swamp, Pond
⌧	Canal
⌧	Glacier
⌧	Ice Shelf, Pack Ice
⌧	Ocean
⌧	Sea
⌧	Gulf, Bay
⌧	Strait, Fjord
⌧	Lagoon
⌧	Bank
⌧	Seamount
⌧	Tableland
⌧	Ridge
⌧	Shelf
⌧	Basin
⌧	Escarpment, Sea Scarp
⌧	Fracture
⌧	Trench, Abyss
⌧	National Park, Reserve
⌧	Point of Interest
⌧	Recreation Site
⌧	Cave, Cavern
⌧	Historic Site
⌧	Ruins
⌧	Wall, Walls
⌧	Church, Abbey
⌧	Temple
⌧	Scientific Station
⌧	Airport
⌧	Port
⌧	Lighthouse
⌧	Mine
⌧	Tunnel
⌧	Dam, Bridge

Name	Page	Grid	Lat.	Long.
Rājshāhi	25	Hd	24.22N	88.36 E
Rakahanga Atoll	57	Kl	10.02S	161.05W
Rakaia	62	Ee	43.54S	172.13 E
Rakaia	62	Ee	43.45S	172.01 E
Rakan, Ra's-	24	Ni	26.10N	51.13 E
Rakata, Pulau-	26	Eh	6.10S	105.26 E
Raka Zangbo	27	Ef	29.24N	87.58 E
Rakhawt, Wādī-	35	Ib	18.16N	51.50 E
Rakht-e Shāh	24	Mf	33.17N	49.23 E
Rakitnoje	28	Mb	45.36N	134.17 E
Rakitovo	15	Hh	41.59N	24.05 E
Rakkestad	8	De	59.26N	11.21 E
Rakoniewice	10	Md	52.10N	16.16 E
Rakops	37	Cd	21.01S	24.20 E
Rakovnicka panev	10	Jf	50.10N	13.30 E
Rakovník	10	Jf	50.06N	13.43 E
Rakovski	15	Hg	42.18N	24.58 E
Raków	10	Rf	50.42N	21.03 E
Rakušečny, Mys-	16	Qh	42.52N	51.55 E
Råkvåg	7	Ce	63.46N	10.05 E
Rakvere	7	Gg	59.22N	26.22 E
Raleigh [N.C.-U.S.]	39	Lf	35.47N	78.39W
Raleigh [Ont.-Can.]	45	Kb	49.31N	91.56W
Raleigh Bay	44	Ih	35.00N	76.20W
Ralik Chain	57	Hd	8.00N	167.00 E
Rama	47	Hf	12.09N	84.15W
Rama, Río-	49	Eg	12.08N	84.13W
Ramādah	32	Jc	32.19N	10.24 E
Ramaḏīn, Wādī-	24	Ej	24.57N	32.34 E
Ramales de la Victoria	13	Ia	43.15N	3.27W
Ramalho, Serra do-	55	Ja	13.45S	44.00W
Ramapo Bank (EN)	57	Fb	27.15N	145.10 E
Ramatlabama	37	De	25.37S	25.30 E
Ramberg	10	He	51.45N	11.05 E
Rambervillers	11	Mf	48.21N	6.38 E
Rambi	63d	Cb	16.30S	179.59W
Rambouillet	11	Hf	48.39N	1.50 E
Rambutyo Island	57	Fe	2.18S	147.48 E
Rāmhormoz	24	Mg	31.16N	49.36 E
Ramigala/Ramygala	8	Ki	55.28N	24.23 E
Ramis	35	Gd	8.02N	41.36 E
Ramla	24	Fg	31.55N	34.52 E
Ramlīyah, 'Aqabat ar-	24	Di	26.01N	30.42 E
Ramlu	35	Gc	13.20N	41.45 E
Ramm, Jabal-	24	Fh	29.35N	35.24 E
Rammāk, Ghurd ar-	24	Ch	29.40N	29.20 E
Rāmnagar	25	Fc	29.24N	79.07 E
Ramnäs	8	Ge	59.46N	16.12 E
Ramón Santamarina	55	Cn	38.26S	59.20W
Ramos	63a	Ec	8.16S	160.11 E
Ramos, Río-	48	Ge	25.35N	105.03W
Ramotswa	37	Dd	24.52S	25.50 E
Rāmpur	25	Fc	28.49N	79.02 E
Ramree	25	Ie	19.06N	93.48 E
Rams	24	Qj	25.53N	56.02 E
Rāmsar	24	Nd	36.53N	50.41 E
Ramsele	7	De	63.33N	16.29 E
Ramsey [Eng.-U.K.]	12	Bb	52.27N	0.07W
Ramsey [Ont.-Can.]	44	Fb	47.29N	82.24W
Ramsey [U.K.]	9	Ig	54.20N	4.21W
Ramsey Lake	42	Jg	47.20N	83.00W
Ramsgate	9	Oj	51.20N	1.25 E
Rāmshīr	24	Mg	30.50N	49.30 E
Ramsjö	7	De	62.11N	15.39 E
Ramstein-Miesenbach	12	Je	49.27N	7.32 E
Ramsund	7	Db	68.29N	16.32 E
Ramu	60	Di	4.02S	144.41 E
Ramu	36	Hb	3.56N	41.13 E
Ramvik	7	De	62.49N	17.51 E
Ramville, Ilet-	51h	Bb	14.42N	60.53W
Ramygala/Ramigala	8	Ki	55.28N	24.23 E
Rana	7	Dc	66.20N	14.08 E
Rañadoiro, Sierra del-	13	Fa	43.20N	6.45W
Ranai	26	Ef	3.55N	108.23 E
Ranakah, Potjo-	26	Hh	8.38S	120.31 E
Rana Kao, Volcán-	65d	Ac	27.11S	109.27W
Rana Roi, Volcán-	65d	Ab	27.05S	109.23W
Rana Roraka, Volcán-	65d	Bb	27.07S	109.18W
Ranau	26	Ge	5.58N	116.41 E
Ranča	14	Lf	44.24N	17.22 E
Rancagua	53	Ii	34.10S	70.45W
Rance	11	Ef	48.31N	1.59W
Rance, Sivry-Rance-	12	Gd	50.09N	4.16 E
Rancharia	55	Gf	22.15S	50.55W
Ranchería, Río-	49	Kh	11.34N	72.54W
Rānchī	22	Kg	23.21N	85.20 E
Ranchos	55	Cl	35.32S	58.22W
Ranco, Lago-	56	Ff	40.14S	72.24W
Randa	35	Gc	11.51N	42.40 E
Randaberg	8	Ae	59.00N	5.36 E
Randazzo	14	Im	37.53N	14.57 E
Randers	7	Ch	56.28N	10.03 E
Randers Fjord	8	Dh	56.35N	10.20 E
Randijaure	7	Ec	66.42N	19.18 E
Randow	10	Kc	53.41N	14.04 E
Randsfjorden	7	Cf	60.25N	10.25 E
Ranérou	34	Cb	15.18N	13.58W
Ranfurly	62	Df	45.08S	170.06 E
Rangasa, Tanjung-	26	Gg	3.33S	118.56 E
Ranger	45	Gj	32.28N	98.41W
Rangiora	62	Ee	43.18S	172.36 E
Rangiroa Atoll	57	Mf	15.10S	147.35W
Rangitaiki	62	Gb	37.55S	176.53 E
Rangitata	62	Df	44.10S	171.30 E
Rangitikei	62	Fd	40.17S	175.13 E
Rangkasbitung	26	Eh	6.21S	106.15 E
Rangoon	22	Lh	16.47N	96.10 E
Rangoon [3]	25	Je	16.40N	95.20 E
Rangpur	25	Hc	25.44N	89.16 E
Rāniyah	24	Kd	36.15N	44.53 E
Rankin Inlet	39	Jc	62.45N	92.10W
Rankoshi	29a	Bb	42.47N	140.31 E
Rannoch, Loch-	9	Ie	56.41N	4.20W
Ranobe	37	Gc	17.10S	44.08 E
Ranon	63b	Dc	16.09S	168.07 E
Ranong	25	Jg	9.59N	98.40 E
Ranongga Island	60	Fi	8.05S	156.34 E
Ranova	16	Lb	54.07N	40.14 E
Ransaren	7	Dd	65.14N	14.59 E
Rantabe	37	Hc	15.42S	49.39 E
Rantasalmi	8	Mb	62.04N	28.18 E
Rantaupanjang	26	Fg	1.23S	112.04 E
Rantauprapat	26	Cf	2.06N	99.50 E
Rantekombola, Bulu-	21	Oj	3.21S	120.01 E
Rantoul	45	Lf	40.19N	88.09W
Ranua	7	Gd	65.55N	26.32 E
Ranyah, Wādī-	33	He	21.18N	43.20 E
Raohe	27	Nb	46.48N	133.58 E
Raon-l'Étape	11	Mf	48.24N	6.51 E
Raoui, Erg er-	32	Gd	29.15N	2.45W
Raoul Island	57	Jg	29.15S	177.52W
Raoyang	28	Ce	38.14N	115.44 E
Raoyang He	28	Gd	41.13N	122.12 E
Rapa, Ile-	57	Mg	27.36S	144.20W
Rapallo	14	Df	44.21N	9.14 E
Rapang	26	Gg	3.50S	119.48 E
Rapa Nui/Pascua, Isla de-=Easter Island (EN)	57	Qg	27.07S	109.22W
Raper, Cape -	42	Kc	69.41N	67.24W
Rapid City	39	Ie	44.05N	103.14W
Rapid Creek	45	Ee	43.54N	102.37W
Rapid River	44	Dc	45.58N	86.59W
Räpina/Rjapina	8	Lf	58.03N	27.35 E
Rapla	7	Fg	59.02N	24.47 E
Rappahannock River	44	Ig	37.34N	76.18W
Rápulo, Río-	52	Jg	13.43S	65.32W
Rāqūbah	31	If	28.58N	19.02 E
Raraka Atoll	57	Mf	16.10S	144.54W
Raroia Atoll	57	Mf	16.05S	142.26W
Rarotonga Island	57	Lg	21.14S	159.46W
Rasa, Punta-	52	Jj	40.51S	62.19W
Ra's Abū Daraj	24	Eh	29.23N	32.33 E
Ra's Abū Rudays	24	Eh	28.53N	33.11 E
Ra's Abū Shajarah	35	Fa	21.04N	37.14 E
Ra's Ajdīr	33	Bc	33.09N	11.34 E
Ra's al 'Ayn	24	Id	36.51N	40.04 E
Ra's al-Barr	24	Dg	31.31N	31.50 E
Ra's al Ḥikmah	24	Bg	31.08N	27.50 E
Ra's al Jabal	14	Em	37.13N	10.08 E
Ra's al Khafjī	24	Mh	28.25N	48.30 E
Ra's al Khaymah	23	Id	25.47N	55.57 E
Ra's al Mish'āb	24	Mh	28.12N	48.37 E
Ra's al Unūf	33	Cc	30.31N	18.34 E
Ra's an Naqb	24	Fh	30.00N	35.29 E
Ra's as Sidr	24	Eh	29.36N	32.40 E
Ra's at Tannūrah	24	Ni	26.42N	50.10 E
Ras Beddouza	30	Ge	32.22N	9.18W
Ras Dashan	30	Kg	13.19N	38.20 E
Raseiniai/Rasejnjaj	7	Fi	55.23N	23.07 E
Rasejnjaj/Raseiniai	7	Fi	55.23N	23.07 E
Râs el Mâ	34	Eb	16.37N	4.27W
Ras-el-Ma	13	Ji	35.08N	2.29W
Ras el Oued	13	Ri	35.57N	5.02 E
Ra's Ghārib	33	Fd	28.21N	33.06 E
Rashād	35	Ec	11.51N	31.04 E
Rāshayyā	24	Ff	33.30N	35.51 E
Rashīd=Rosetta (EN)	33	Fc	31.24N	30.25 E
Rashīd, Maṣabb-	24	Dg	31.30N	30.20 E
Rasht	22	Gf	37.16N	49.36 E
Rāsiga 'Alūla	35	Ic	11.59N	50.50 E
Rās Jumbo	35	Gf	1.37S	41.31 E
Raška	15	Df	43.18N	20.38 E
Ra's Madhar, Jabal-	24	Gj	25.46N	37.32 E
Ra's Matārimah	24	Eh	29.27N	32.43 E
Rasmussen Basin	42	Hc	67.56N	95.15W
Rason Lake	59	Ee	28.45S	124.20 E
Rasskazovo	19	Ee	52.39N	41.57 E
Rasšua, Ostrov-	20	Kg	47.40N	153.00 E
Rassvet	20	Ee	57.00N	91.32 E
Ras-Tarf, Cap-	13	Ii	35.17N	3.41W
Rastatt	10	Eh	48.51N	8.12 E
Rastede	12	Ka	53.15N	8.12 E
Rastigaissa	7	Ga	70.03N	26.18 E
Råstojaure	7	Eb	68.45N	20.30 E
Ra's Ţurunbī	24	Fj	25.40N	34.35 E
Rasūl	24	Pi	27.10N	55.30 E
Ra's Zayt	33	Fd	27.56N	33.31 E
Rat	40a	Bb	51.55N	178.20 E
Ratak Chain	57	Id	9.00N	171.00 E
Ratangarh	25	Ec	28.05N	74.36 E
Rätansbyn	7	De	62.29N	14.32 E
Rat Buri	25	Jf	13.32N	99.49 E
Rathbun Lake	45	Jf	40.54N	93.05W
Ráth Droma/Rathdrum	9	Gi	52.56N	6.13W
Rathdrum/Ráth Droma	9	Gi	52.56N	6.13W
Rathenow	10	Id	52.36N	12.20 E
Rathlin Island/Reachlainn	9	Gf	55.18N	6.13W
Ráth Luirc/An Ráth	9	Ei	52.21N	8.41W
Rathor, Pik-	18	If	37.55N	72.14 E
Rätikon	14	Dc	47.03N	9.40 E
Ratingen	12	Ic	51.18N	6.51 E
Rätische Alpen=Rhaetian Alps (EN)	14	Dd	46.30N	10.00 E
Rat Islands	38	Ad	52.00N	178.00 E
Ratlām	25	Fd	23.19N	75.04 E
Ratmanova, Ostrov-	20	Lc	35.45N	169.00W
Ratnāgiri	25	Ee	16.59N	73.18 E
Ratnapura	25	Gg	6.41N	80.24 E
Ratno	16	Dd	51.42N	24.31 E
Raton	43	Gd	36.54N	104.24W
Ratqh, Wādī ar-	24	Ie	34.25N	40.55 E
Rätta	20	Dd	63.35N	84.05 E
Rattlesnake Hills	46	Le	42.45N	107.10W
Rattray Head	9	Ld	57.38N	1.46W
Rättvik	7	Df	60.53N	15.06 E
Ratz, Mount-	38	Fd	57.23N	132.19W
Ratzeburg	10	Gc	53.42N	10.46 E
Raub	26	Df	3.48N	101.52 E
Rauch	56	Ie	36.46S	59.06W
Raucourt-et-Flaba	12	Ge	49.36N	4.57 E
Raudeberg	8	Ab	61.59N	5.09 E
Rauer Islands	66	Fe	68.51S	77.50 E
Raufarhöfn	7a	Ca	66.27N	15.57W
Raufjellet	8	Dc	61.15N	11.00 E
Raufoss	7	Cf	60.43N	10.37 E
Raukotaha	64n	Ac	10.28S	161.01W
Raukumara Range	62	Gc	38.00S	178.00 E
Rauland	8	Be	59.44N	8.00 E
Raúl Leoni, Represa- (Guri)	54	Fb	7.30N	63.00W
Rauma	7	Be	62.33N	7.43 E
Rauma/Raumo	7	Ef	61.08N	21.30 E
Raumo/Rauma	7	Ef	61.08N	21.30 E
Rauna	8	Kg	57.14N	25.39 E
Raunds	12	Bb	52.20N	0.32W
Raurimu	62	Fc	39.07S	175.24 E
Raurkela	22	Kg	22.13N	84.53 E
Rausu	28	Rb	44.01N	145.12 E
Rausu-Dake	29a	Da	44.06N	145.07 E
Rautalampi	8	Lb	62.38N	26.50 E
Ravahere Atoll	57	Mf	18.14S	142.09W
Ravan	14	Mf	44.15N	18.16 E
Ravanica, Manastir-	15	Ef	43.58N	21.30 E
Ravānsar	24	Le	34.43N	46.40 E
Ravanusa	14	Hm	37.16N	13.58 E
Rāvar	24	Qg	31.12N	56.53 E
Rava-Russkaja	16	Cd	50.13N	23.37 E
Ravels	12	Gc	51.22N	4.59 E
Ravelsbach	14	Jb	48.30N	15.50 E
Ravels-Poppel	12	Hc	51.27N	5.02 E
Ravenna [It.]	14	Gf	44.25N	12.12 E
Ravenna [Nb.-U.S.]	45	Gf	41.02N	98.55W
Ravensburg	10	Fi	47.47N	9.37 E
Ravenshoe	58	Ff	17.37S	145.29 E
Ravensthorpe	59	Ef	33.35S	120.02 E
Ravi	21	Jf	30.35N	71.49 E
Ravnina	19	Gh	37.57N	62.42 E
Rawaki Atoll (Phoenix)	57	Je	3.43S	170.43W
Rāwalpindi	22	Jf	33.35N	73.03 E
Rawa Mazowiecka	10	Qe	51.46N	20.16 E
Rawāndūz	24	Kd	36.37N	44.31 E
Rawdah	24	Ie	35.15N	41.05 E
Rawene	62	Ea	35.24S	173.30 E
Rawicz	10	Me	51.37N	16.52 E
Rawka	10	Qd	52.07N	20.08 E
Rawlinna	58	Dh	31.01S	125.20 E
Rawlins	43	Fc	41.47N	107.14W
Rawlinson Range	59	Fd	24.50S	128.00 E
Rawson [Arg.]	55	Bl	34.36S	60.04W
Rawson [Arg.]	53	Jj	43.18S	65.06W
Rawura, Ras-	36	He	10.20S	40.30 E
Raxaul	25	Gc	26.59N	84.51 E
Ray, Cape -	42	Lg	47.37N	59.19W
Raya, Bukit-	21	Nj	1.32S	111.05 E
Rayadrug	25	Ff	14.42N	76.52 E
Rayāt	24	Kd	36.40N	44.58 E
Rayleigh	12	Cc	51.35N	0.37 E
Raymond [Alta.-Can.]	46	Ib	49.27N	112.39W
Raymond [Wa.-U.S.]	46	Dc	46.41N	123.44W
Raymondville	43	Hf	26.29N	97.47W
Rayne	45	Jk	30.14N	92.16W
Rayón [Mex.]	48	Jg	21.51N	99.40W
Rayón [Mex.]	48	Dc	29.43N	110.35W
Rayones	48	Ie	25.01N	100.05W
Rayong	25	Kf	12.40N	101.17 E
Raysūt	23	Hf	16.54N	54.02 E
Raytown	45	Ig	39.00N	94.28W
Raz, Pointe du-	11	Bf	48.02N	4.44W
Razan	24	Me	35.23N	49.02 E
Razdan	16	Ni	40.28N	44.43 E
Razdelnaja	16	Gf	46.50N	30.05 E
Razdolinsk	20	Ee	58.25N	94.44 E
Razdolnaja	28	Kc	43.20N	131.49 E
Razdolnoje [R.S.F.S.R.]	28	Kc	43.33N	131.55 E
Razdolnoje [Ukr.-U.S.S.R.]	16	Hg	45.47N	33.30 E
Razgrad	15	Jf	43.32N	26.31 E
Razgrad [2]	15	Jf	43.32N	26.31 E
Razī	24	Mc	38.32N	48.08 E
Raziku/Raasiku	8	Ke	59.22N	25.11 E
Razlog	15	Gh	41.53N	23.28 E
Razo	32	Cf	16.37N	24.36W
Ré, Ile de-	5	Ff	46.12N	1.25W
Reachlainn	9	Gf	55.18N	6.13W
Reachlainn/Rathlin Island	9	Gf	55.18N	6.13W
Reachrainn/Lambay	9	Gh	53.29N	6.01W
Read	42	Gc	69.12N	114.30W
Reading [Eng.-U.K.]	9	Mj	51.28N	0.59W
Reading [Pa.-U.S.]	43	Lc	40.20N	75.55W
Real, Cordillera- [Bol.]	54	Eg	16.30S	68.30W
Real, Cordillera- [Ec.]	52	If	3.00S	78.00W
Real Audiencia	55	Cm	36.11S	58.35W
Real del Castillo	48	Aa	31.58N	116.19W
Realicó	56	He	35.02S	64.15W
Réalmont	11	Ik	43.47N	2.12 E
Reao Atoll	57	Nf	18.31S	136.23W
Reatini, Monti-	14	Gh	42.35N	12.50 E
Rebais	12	Ff	48.51N	3.14 E
Rebecca, Lake-	59	Ee	29.55S	122.10 E
Rebiana Oasis (EN)=Rabyānah, Wāḥāt al-	33	De	24.14N	21.59 E
Rebollera	13	Hf	38.25N	4.02W
Reboly	7	He	63.52N	30.47 E
Rebord Manamblen	37	Hd	24.05S	46.30 E
Rebun	28	Pb	45.23N	141.02 E
Rebun-Dake	29a	Ba	45.22N	141.01 E
Rebun-Suidō	29a	Ba	45.15N	141.05 E
Rebun-Tō	27	Pb	45.23N	141.10 E
Recalde	55	Bm	36.39S	61.05W
Recanati	14	Hg	43.24N	13.32 E
Recaş	15	Ed	45.48N	21.30 E
Recherche, Archipelago of the-	57	Dh	34.06S	122.45 E
Rečica	19	De	52.22N	30.25 E
Recife	53	Mf	8.03S	34.54W
Recife, Cape-	30	Jl	34.02S	25.45 E
Recke	12	Jb	52.23N	7.43 E
Recklinghausen	10	De	51.37N	7.12 E
Recknitz	10	Ib	54.14N	12.28 E
Recoaro Terme	14	Fe	45.42N	11.13 E
Reconquista	56	Ic	29.09S	59.39W
Recovery Glacier	66	Ag	81.10S	28.00W
Recreo	56	Gc	29.16S	65.04W
Recz	10	Lc	53.16N	15.33 E
Reda	10	Ob	54.38N	18.30 E
Redange	12	He	49.46N	5.54 E
Red Bank	44	Eh	35.07N	85.17W
Red Bay	42	Lf	51.44N	56.25W
Red Bluff	43	Cc	40.11N	122.15W
Red Bluff Reservoir	45	Ek	31.57N	103.56W
Redbridge, London-	12	Cc	51.35N	0.08 E
Red Butte	46	Ii	35.55N	112.03W
Redcar	9	Lg	54.37N	1.04W
Red Cliff	51c	Ab	17.05N	62.32W
Redcliff	37	Dc	19.02S	29.50 E
Redcliffe, Mount-	59	Ee	28.25S	121.32 E
Red Cloud	45	Gf	40.05N	98.32W
Red Deer	39	Hd	52.16N	113.48W
Red Deer [Can.]	42	Hf	52.55N	101.27W
Red Deer [Can.]	38	Id	50.56N	109.54W
Redding	39	Ge	40.35N	122.24W
Redditch	9	Li	52.19N	1.56W
Rede	9	Kf	55.08N	2.13W
Redenção	54	Kd	4.13S	38.43W
Redfield	43	Hc	44.53N	98.31W
Red Hill	65a	Ec	20.43N	156.15W
Red Hills	45	Gh	37.25N	99.25W
Redkino	7	Ih	56.40N	36.19 E
Red Lake	42	If	51.05N	93.55W
Red Lake	42	If	51.03N	93.49W
Red Lake River	45	Hc	47.55N	97.01W
Red Lakes	43	Ib	48.05N	94.45W
Redlands	46	Gi	34.03N	117.11W
Red Lodge	46	Kd	45.11N	109.15W
Redmond	43	Cc	44.17N	121.11W
Red Mountain [Ca.-U.S.]	46	Df	41.35N	123.06W
Red Mountain [Mt.-U.S.]	46	Ic	47.07N	112.44W
Red Oak	45	If	41.01N	95.14W
Redon	11	Dg	47.39N	2.05W
Redonda	50	Ed	16.55N	62.19W
Redondela	13	Db	42.17N	8.36W
Redondo	13	Ef	38.39N	7.33W
Redondo Beach	46	Fj	33.51N	118.23W
Redoubt Volcano	38	Dc	60.29N	152.45W
Red River [N.Amer.]	38	Jd	50.24N	96.48W
Red River [U.S.]	38	Jf	31.00N	91.40W
Red River (EN)=Hông, Sông-	21	Mg	20.17N	106.34 E
Red River (EN)=Yuan Jiang [Asia]	21	Mg	20.17N	106.34 E
Red Rock, Lake-	45	Jf	41.30N	93.20W
Red Rock River	46	Id	44.59N	112.52W
Redruth	9	Hk	50.13N	5.14W
Red Sea (EN)=Aḥmar, Al Baḥr al-	30	Kf	25.00N	38.00 E
Redstone	42	Fd	64.17N	124.33W
Redstone	46	Da	52.08N	123.42W
Red Volta (EN)=Volta Rouge	30	Gh	10.34N	0.30W
Redwater Creek	46	Mb	48.03N	105.13W
Red Wing	43	Ic	44.34N	92.31W
Redwood City	46	Dh	37.29N	122.13W
Redwood Falls	45	Id	44.32N	95.07W
Ree, Lough-/Loch Rí	9	Fh	53.35N	8.00W
Reed City	44	Ed	43.53N	85.31W
Reedley	46	Fh	36.24N	119.37W
Reeds Peak	45	Cj	33.09N	107.51W
Reedsport	43	Cc	43.42N	124.06W
Reedy Glacier	66	Ng	85.30S	134.00W
Reef Islands	57	Hf	10.15S	166.10 E
Reefton	62	De	42.07S	171.52 E
Reepham	12	Db	52.45N	1.07 E
Rees	12	Ic	51.46N	6.24 E
Reese River	46	Gf	40.39N	116.54W
Refahiye	24	Hc	39.54N	38.46 E
Reforma, Río-	48	Ed	26.56N	108.12W
Reftele	8	Eg	57.11N	13.35 E
Reftinski	17	Jh	57.10N	61.43 E
Refugio	45	Hl	28.18N	97.17W
Refugio, Punta-	48	Cc	29.30N	113.30W
Rega	10	Lb	54.10N	15.18 E
Regar	19	Gh	38.34N	68.13 E
Regen	10	Jh	48.58N	13.08 E
Regen	10	Ig	49.01N	12.06 E
Regensburg	6	Hf	49.01N	12.06 E
Reggane	31	Hf	26.42N	0.10 E
Regge	12	Ib	52.26N	6.29 E
Reggio di Calabria	6	Hh	38.06N	15.39 E
Reggio nell'Emilia	14	Ef	44.43N	10.36 E
Reghin	15	Hc	46.46N	24.42 E
Regina [Fr.Gui.]	54	Hc	4.19N	52.08W
Regina [Sask.-Can.]	39	Id	50.25N	104.39W
Registan (EN)=Rīgestān	21	If	31.00N	65.00 E
Registro	55	Ig	24.30S	47.50W
Registro do Araguaia	55	Gb	15.44S	51.50W
Regnitz	10	Gg	49.54N	10.49 E
Regocijo	48	Gf	23.35N	105.11W
Reguengos de Monsaraz	13	Ef	38.25N	7.32W
Rehburg-Loccum	12	Lb	52.28N	9.14 E
Rehoboth [3]	37	Bd	23.50S	17.00 E
Rehoboth	37	Bd	23.18S	17.03 E
Reḥovot	24	Fg	31.54N	34.49 E
Reichelsheim (Odenwald)	12	Ke	49.43N	8.51 E
Reichenbach	10	If	50.37N	12.18 E
Reichshoffen	12	Jf	48.56N	7.40 E
Reichshoft	12	Jd	50.55N	7.39 E
Reichshoft-Denklingen	12	Jd	50.55N	7.39 E
Reidsville	44	Hg	36.21N	79.40W
Reigate	9	Mj	51.14N	0.13W
Reims	6	Gf	49.15N	4.02 E
Rein=Rhine (EN)	5	Ge	51.52N	6.02 E
Reina Adelaida, Archipiélago-	52	Ik	52.10S	74.25W
Reindeer	42	He	55.34N	103.10W
Reindeer Bank (EN)	51p	Ac	11.50N	62.05W
Reindeer Lake	38	Id	57.15N	102.40W
Reineskarvet	8	Cd	60.47N	8.13 E
Reinga, Cape-	62	Ea	34.25S	172.41 E
Reinhardswald	10	Fe	51.30N	9.30 E
Reinheim	12	Je	49.08N	7.11 E
Reinosa	13	Ha	43.00N	4.08W
Reisa	7	Eb	69.48N	21.00 E
Reitoru Atoll	57	Mf	17.52S	143.05W
Reitz	37	De	27.53S	28.31 E
Rejmyra	8	Ff	58.50N	15.55 E
Rejowiec Fabryczny	10	Te	51.08N	23.13 E
Reka Devnja	15	Kf	43.13N	27.36 E
Rekarne	8	Ge	59.20N	16.25 E
Reken	12	Jc	51.48N	7.03 E
Reliance	39	Ic	62.42N	109.08W
Relizane	32	Hb	35.45N	0.33 E
Remagen	12	Jd	50.34N	7.14 E
Remarkable, Mount-	59	Hf	32.48S	138.10 E
Rembang	26	Fh	6.42S	111.20 E
Remedios	49	Gi	8.14N	81.51W
Remedios, Punta-	49	Cg	13.31N	89.49W
Remedios, Río-	49	Mh	11.01N	69.15W
Remich	12	Ie	49.32N	6.22 E
Rémire	54	Hc	4.53N	52.17W
Remiremont	11	Mf	48.01N	6.35 E
Remire Reef	37b	Bb	5.05S	53.22 E
Remontnoje	16	Mf	46.33N	43.40 E
Remoulins	11	Kk	43.56N	4.34 E
Remscheid	10	De	51.11N	7.12 E
Rena	7	Cf	61.08N	11.22 E
Rena	8	Dc	61.08N	11.23 E
Renaix/Ronse	11	Jd	50.45N	3.36 E
Renana, Fossa-	5	Gf	48.40N	7.50 E
Renard Islands	63a	Ad	10.50S	153.00 E
Renaud Island	66	Qe	65.40S	66.00W
Rende	14	Kk	39.20N	16.11 E
Rendezvous Bay	51b	Ab	18.10N	63.07W
Rend Lake	45	Lg	38.05N	88.58W
Rendova Island	60	Fi	8.32S	157.20 E
Rendsburg	10	Fb	54.18N	9.40 E
Renfrew	42	Jg	45.28N	76.41W
Rengat	26	Dg	0.24S	102.33 E
Rengo	56	Fd	34.25S	70.52W
Reni	16	Fg	45.29N	28.18 E
Renko	8	Kd	60.54N	24.17 E
Renkum	12	Hc	51.58N	5.45 E
Renland	41	Jd	71.15N	27.20W
Renmark	58	Fh	34.11S	140.45 E
Rennell, Islas-	56	Fh	52.00S	74.00W
Rennell Island	57	Hf	11.40S	160.10 E
Rennes	6	Ff	48.05N	1.41W
Rennes, Bassin de-	11	Ef	48.05N	1.40W
Rennesøy	8	Ae	59.05N	5.40 E
Rennick Glacier	66	Kf	70.30S	161.45 E
Rennie Lake	42	Gd	61.10N	105.30W
Reno	39	Hf	39.31N	119.48W
Reno	14	Gf	44.38N	12.16 E
Renqiu	28	De	38.42N	116.06 E
Rensselaer [In.-U.S.]	44	De	40.57N	87.09W
Rensselaer [N.Y.-U.S.]	44	Kd	42.37N	73.44W
Renterría	13	Ka	43.19N	1.54W
Renton	46	Dc	47.30N	122.11W
Renwez	12	Ge	49.50N	4.36 E
Renxian	28	Cf	37.07N	114.41 E
Reo	26	Hh	8.19S	120.30 E
Repartimento, Serra do-	55	Jc	17.40S	44.50W
Répce	10	Ni	47.41N	17.02 E
Repino	8	Md	60.10N	29.58 E
Repong, Pulau-	26	Ef	2.22N	105.53 E
Reposaari/Räfsö	8	Ic	61.37N	21.27 E
Republic	46	Fb	48.39N	118.44W
Republican	38	Jf	39.03N	96.48W
Repulse Bay	39	Kc	66.32N	86.15W
Repulse Bay [Austl.]	59	Jd	20.35S	148.45 E
Repulse Bay [Can.]	42	Ic	66.20N	86.00W
Repvåg	7	Fa	70.45N	25.41 E
Requena [Peru]	54	Dd	5.00S	73.50W
Requena [Sp.]	13	Ke	39.29N	1.06W
Requin Bay	51p	Bb	12.02N	61.38W
Réquista	11	Ij	44.02N	2.32 E
Reşadiye Yarimadası	15	Km	36.40N	27.45 E
Reschenpass/Resia, Passo di-	14	Ed	46.50N	10.30 E
Resen	15	Eh	41.05N	21.01 E
Reserva	55	Gg	24.38S	50.52W
Reserve	45	Bj	33.43N	108.45W
Rešetilovka	16	Ie	49.33N	34.05 E
Reshui	27	Hd	37.38N	100.30 E
Resia, Passo di-/Reschenpass	14	Ed	46.50N	10.30 E
Resistencia	53	Kh	27.30S	58.59W
Reşiţa	15	Ed	45.18N	21.55 E
Resko	10	Lc	53.47N	15.25 E
Reso/Raisio	7	Ff	60.29N	22.11 E
Resolute	39	Jb	74.41N	94.54W
Resolution	38	Mc	61.30N	65.00W
Resolution Island	42	Ld	61.35N	64.39W
Resolution Island	62	Bf	45.40S	166.35 E
Respublikai Soveth Socialisti Todžikiston/Tadžikskaja SSR [2]	19	Hh	39.00N	71.00 E
Respublika Sovetike Sočialiste Moldovenjaske/Moldavskaja SSR [2]	19	Cf	47.00N	29.00 E
Ressa	16	Ib	54.45N	35.10 E
Ressons-sur-Matz	12	Ee	49.33N	2.45 E
Restigouche River	44	Na	48.04N	66.20W
Restinga de Sefton, Isla-	52	Hi	37.00S	83.50W
Restinga Sêca	55	Fi	29.49S	53.23W
Reszel	10	Rb	54.04N	21.09 E
Retalhuleu [3]	49	Bf	14.20N	91.50W
Retalhuleu	47	Ff	14.32N	91.41W
Retavas/Rietavas	8	Ii	55.43N	21.49 E
Retezatului, Munţii-	15	Fd	45.25N	23.00 E
Rethel	11	Ke	49.31N	4.22 E
Rethem (Aller)	12	Lb	52.47N	9.23 E
Réthinnon	15	Hn	35.22N	24.28 E
Retie	12	Hc	51.17N	5.05 E

Index Symbols

- [1] Independent Nation
- [2] State, Region
- [3] District, County
- Municipality
- Colony, Dependency
- Continent
- Physical Region
- Historical or Cultural Region
- Mount, Mountain
- Volcano
- Hill
- Mountains, Mountain Range
- Hills, Escarpment
- Plateau, Upland
- Pass, Gap
- Plain, Lowland
- Delta
- Salt Flat
- Valley, Canyon
- Crater, Cave
- Karst Features
- Depression
- Polder
- Desert, Dunes
- Forest, Woods
- Heath, Steppe
- Oasis
- Cape, Point
- Coast, Beach
- Cliff
- Peninsula
- Isthmus
- Sandbank
- Island
- Atoll
- Rock, Reef
- Islands, Archipelago
- Rocks, Reefs
- Coral Reef
- Well, Spring
- Geyser
- River, Stream
- Waterfall Rapids
- River Mouth, Estuary
- Lake
- Salt Lake
- Intermittent Lake
- Reservoir
- Swamp, Pond
- Canal
- Glacier
- Ice Shelf, Pack Ice
- Ocean
- Sea
- Gulf, Bay
- Strait, Fjord
- Lagoon
- Bank
- Seamount
- Tablemount
- Ridge
- Shelf
- Basin
- Escarpment, Sea Scarp
- Fracture
- Trench, Abyss
- National Park, Reserve
- Point of Interest
- Recreation Site
- Cave, Cavern
- Historic Site
- Ruins
- Wall, Walls
- Church, Abbey
- Temple
- Scientific Station
- Airport
- Port
- Lighthouse
- Mine
- Tunnel
- Dam, Bridge

Index Symbols

[1] Independent Nation	⊞ Historical or Cultural Region	◸ Pass, Gap
[2] State, Region	▲ Mount, Mountain	◺ Plain, Lowland
[3] District, County	▲ Volcano	◿ Delta
[4] Municipality	▲ Hill	◹ Salt Flat
[5] Colony, Dependency	⩙ Mountains, Mountain Range	◿ Valley, Canyon
[6] Continent	⩙ Hills, Escarpment	◹ Crater, Cave
◨ Physical Region	⬒ Plateau, Upland	◹ Karst Features

▢ Depression	▨ Coast, Beach	▨ Rock, Reef
▢ Polder	◺ Cliff	▨ Islands, Archipelago
◸ Desert, Dunes	◹ Peninsula	▨ Rocks, Reefs
▣ Forest, Woods	◺ Isthmus	▨ Coral Reef
▨ Heath, Steppe	◹ Sandbank	▨ Well, Spring
◹ Oasis	◹ Island	▨ Geyser
◹ Cape, Point	◹ Atoll	▨ River, Stream

▨ Waterfall Rapids	▭ Canal	▨ Lagoon
▨ River Mouth, Estuary	▭ Glacier	▭ Bank
▭ Lake	▭ Ice Shelf, Pack Ice	▨ Seamount
▭ Salt Lake	▭ Ocean	▭ Trench, Abyss
▭ Intermittent Lake	▭ Sea	▭ Tablemount
▭ Reservoir	▭ Ridge	▭ Shelf
▭ Swamp, Pond	◠ Gulf, Bay	▭ Basin

▨ Escarpment, Sea Scarp	▨ Historic Site
▨ Fracture	▨ Ruins
▨ Trench, Abyss	▨ Wall, Walls
▨ National Park, Reserve	▨ Church, Abbey
▨ Point of Interest	▨ Temple
▨ Recreation Site	▨ Scientific Station
▨ Cave, Cavern	▨ Airport

⚓ Port
◈ Lighthouse
⚒ Mine
) Tunnel
▭ Dam, Bridge

Index Symbols

- [1] Independent Nation
- [2] State, Region
- [3] District, County
- [4] Municipality
- [5] Colony, Dependency
- Continent
- Physical Region
- Historical or Cultural Region
- Mount, Mountain
- Volcano
- Hill
- Mountains, Mountain Range
- Hills, Escarpment
- Plateau, Upland
- Pass, Gap
- Plain, Lowland
- Delta
- Salt Flat
- Valley, Canyon
- Crater, Cave
- Karst Features
- Depression
- Polder
- Desert, Dunes
- Forest, Woods
- Heath, Steppe
- Oasis
- Cape, Point
- Coast, Beach
- Cliff
- Peninsula
- Isthmus
- Sandbank
- Island
- Atoll
- Rock, Reef
- Islands, Archipelago
- Rocks, Reefs
- Coral Reef
- Well, Spring
- Geyser
- River, Stream
- Waterfall Rapids
- River Mouth, Estuary
- Lake
- Salt Lake
- Intermittent Lake
- Sea
- Gulf, Bay
- Strait, Fjord
- Swamp, Pond
- Canal
- Glacier
- Ice Shelf, Pack Ice
- Ocean
- Reservoir
- Shelf
- Basin
- Lagoon
- Bank
- Seamount
- Tablemount
- Ridge
- Cave, Cavern
- Escarpment, Sea Scarp
- Fracture
- Trench, Abyss
- National Park, Reserve
- Point of Interest
- Recreation Site
- Scientific Station
- Airport
- Historic Site
- Ruins
- Wall, Walls
- Church, Abbey
- Temple
- Scientific Station
- Port
- Lighthouse
- Mine
- Tunnel
- Dam, Bridge

Index Symbols

[1] Independent Nation	▣ Historical or Cultural Region	◫ Pass, Gap
[2] State, Region	▲ Mount, Mountain	◫ Plain, Lowland
[3] District, County	▲ Volcano	◫ Delta
[4] Municipality	● Hill	◫ Salt Flat
[5] Colony, Dependency	▲ Mountains, Mountain Range	◫ Valley, Canyon
■ Continent	Hills, Escarpment	◫ Crater, Cave
◫ Physical Region	Plateau, Upland	◫ Karst Features

◫ Depression	◫ Coast, Beach	◫ Rock, Reef	◫ Waterfall Rapids
◫ Polder	◫ Cliff	◫ Islands, Archipelago	◫ River Mouth, Estuary
◫ Desert, Dunes	◫ Peninsula	◫ Rocks, Reefs	◫ Lake
◫ Forest, Woods	◫ Isthmus	◫ Coral Reef	◫ Salt Lake
◫ Heath, Steppe	◫ Sandbank	◫ Well, Spring	◫ Intermittent Lake
◫ Oasis	◫ Island	◫ Geyser	◫ Reservoir
◫ Cape, Point	◫ Atoll	◫ River, Stream	◫ Swamp, Pond

◫ Canal	◫ Lagoon	◫ Escarpment, Sea Scarp	◫ Historic Site	◫ Port
◫ Glacier	◫ Bank	◫ Fracture	◫ Ruins	◫ Lighthouse
◫ Ice Shelf, Pack Ice	◫ Seamount	◫ Trench, Abyss	◫ Wall, Walls	◫ Mine
◫ Ocean	◫ Tablemount	◫ National Park, Reserve	◫ Church, Abbey	◫ Tunnel
◫ Sea	◫ Ridge	◫ Point of Interest	◫ Temple	◫ Dam, Bridge
◫ Gulf, Bay	◫ Shelf	◫ Recreation Site	◫ Scientific Station	
◫ Strait, Fjord	◫ Basin	◫ Cave, Cavern	◫ Airport	

Index Symbols

[1] Independent Nation	⊡ Historical or Cultural Region	⊟ Pass, Gap
[2] State, Region	▲ Mount, Mountain	⬚ Plain, Lowland
[3] District, County	▲ Volcano	◿ Delta
[4] Municipality	◬ Hill	⬚ Salt Flat
[5] Colony, Dependency	▲ Mountains, Mountain Range	⬚ Valley, Canyon
■ Continent	◿ Hills, Escarpment	⬚ Crater, Cave
⊠ Physical Region	⬟ Plateau, Upland	⬚ Karst Features

⬚ Depression	⬚ Coast, Beach	⬚ Rock, Reef
⬚ Polder	⬚ Cliff	⬚ Islands, Archipelago
⬚ Desert, Dunes	⬚ Peninsula	⬚ Rocks, Reefs
⬚ Forest, Woods	⬚ Isthmus	⬚ Coral Reef
⬚ Heath, Steppe	⬚ Sandbank	⬚ Well, Spring
⬚ Oasis	⬚ Island	⬚ Geyser
⬚ Cape, Point	⬚ Atoll	⬚ River, Stream

⬚ Waterfall Rapids	⬚ Canal	⬚ Lagoon
⬚ River Mouth, Estuary	⬚ Glacier	⬚ Bank
⬚ Lake	⬚ Ice Shelf, Pack Ice	⬚ Seamount
⬚ Salt Lake	⬚ Ocean	⬚ Tablemount
⬚ Intermittent Lake	⬚ Ridge	⬚ Trench, Abyss
⬚ Sea	⬚ Shelf	⬚ National Park, Reserve
⬚ Gulf, Bay	⬚ Basin	⬚ Recreation Site
⬚ Strait, Fjord		⬚ Cave, Cavern

⬚ Escarpment, Sea Scarp	⬚ Historic Site	⬚ Port
⬚ Fracture	⬚ Ruins	⬚ Lighthouse
⬚ Wall, Walls	⬚ Point of Interest	⬚ Mine
⬚ Church, Abbey		⬚ Tunnel
⬚ Temple		⬚ Dam, Bridge
⬚ Scientific Station		
⬚ Airport		

Index Symbols

[1] Independent Nation	Historical or Cultural Region	Pass, Gap	Depression	Coast, Beach	Rock, Reef	Waterfall Rapids	Canal	Lagoon	Escarpment, Sea Scarp	Historic Site	Port
[2] State, Region	Mount, Mountain	Plain, Lowland	Polder	Cliff	Islands, Archipelago	River Mouth, Estuary	Glacier	Bank	Fracture	Ruins	Lighthouse
[3] District, County	Volcano	Delta	Desert, Dunes	Peninsula	Rocks, Reefs	Ice Shelf, Pack Ice	Seamount	Trench, Abyss	Wall, Walls	Mine
[4] Municipality	Hill	Salt Flat	Forest, Woods	Isthmus	Coral Reef	Lake	Ocean	Tablemount	National Park, Reserve	Church, Abbey	Tunnel
[5] Colony, Dependency	Mountains, Mountain Range	Valley, Canyon	Heath, Steppe	Sandbank	Well, Spring	Salt Lake	Sea	Ridge	Point of Interest	Temple	Dam, Bridge
Continent	Hills, Escarpment	Crater, Cave	Oasis	Island	Geyser	Intermittent Lake	Gulf, Bay	Shelf	Recreation Site	Scientific Station	
Physical Region	Plateau, Upland	Karst Features	Cape, Point	Atoll	River, Stream	Reservoir	Strait, Fjord	Basin	Cave, Cavern	Airport	

Index Symbols

[1] Independent Nation	▭ Historical or Cultural Region	⌣ Pass, Gap	▭ Depression	▨ Coast, Beach	▨ Rock, Reef	▨ Waterfall Rapids	▭ Canal	▨ Lagoon	▨ Escarpment, Sea Scarp	▨ Historic Site	▨ Port
[2] State, Region	▲ Mount, Mountain	▨ Plain, Lowland	▨ Polder	▨ Cliff	▨ Islands, Archipelago	▨ River Mouth, Estuary	▨ Glacier	▨ Bank	▨ Fracture	▨ Ruins	▨ Lighthouse
[3] District, County	▲ Volcano	▨ Delta	▨ Desert, Dunes	▨ Peninsula	▨ Rocks, Reefs	▨ Ice Shelf, Pack Ice	▨ Seamount	▨ Trench, Abyss	▨ Wall, Walls	▨ Mine	
[4] Municipality	▨ Hill	▨ Salt Flat	▨ Forest, Woods	▨ Isthmus	▨ Coral Reef	▨ Lake	▨ Tablemount	▨ National Park, Reserve	▨ Church, Abbey	▨ Tunnel	
[5] Colony, Dependency	▨ Mountains, Mountain Range	▨ Valley, Canyon	▨ Heath, Steppe	▨ Sandbank	▨ Well, Spring	▨ Salt Lake	▨ Shelf	▨ Point of Interest	▨ Temple	▨ Dam, Bridge	
◇ Continent	▨ Hills, Escarpment	▨ Crater, Cave	▨ Oasis	▨ Island	▨ Geyser	▨ Intermittent Lake	▨ Ridge	▨ Recreation Site	▨ Scientific Station		
▨ Physical Region	▨ Plateau, Upland	▨ Karst Features	▨ Cape, Point	▨ Atoll	▨ River, Stream	▨ Swamp, Pond	▨ Strait, Fjord	▨ Basin	▨ Cave, Cavern	▨ Airport	

São Mateus, Rio- ☐	55	la	13.48 S	46.54 W
São Miguel ⊡	30	Ee	37.47 N	25.30 W
São Miguel, Rio- ☐	55	Ic	16.03 S	46.07 W
São Miguel do Araguaia	55	Ga	13.19 S	50.13 W
São Miguel d'Oeste	55	Fh	26.45 S	53.34 W
Saona, Isla- ⊡	49	Md	18.09 N	68.40 W
Saône ☐	5	Gf	45.44 N	4.50 E
Saône-et-Loire ③	11	Kh	46.40 N	4.30 E
Saonek	26	Jg	0.28 S	130.47 E
São Nicolau ☐	30	Eg	16.35 N	24.15 W
São Nicolau [Ang.]	36	Be	14.15 S	12.24 E
São Nicolau [Braz.]	55	Ei	28.11 S	55.16 W
São Patricio, Rio- ☐	55	Hb	15.02 S	49.15 W
São Paulo	53	Lh	23.32 S	46.37 W
São Paulo ②	56	Kb	22.00 S	49.00 W
São Paulo de Olivença	54	Ed	3.27 S	68.48 W
São Pedro, Ribeirão ☐	55	Ic	16.54 S	46.32 W
São Pedro do Sul [Braz.]	55	Ei	29.37 S	54.10 W
São Pedro do Sul [Port.]	13	Dd	40.45 N	8.04 W
São Pedro e São Paulo,				
Penedos de- ⊠	52	Ne	0.56 N	29.22 W
São Raimundo Nonato	54	Je	9.01 S	42.42 W
São Romão [Braz.]	55	Ed	18.33 S	54.27 W
São Romão [Braz.]	54	Ig	16.22 S	45.04 W
São Roque	55	De	21.43 S	57.46 W
São Roque, Cabo de- ⊠	52	Mf	5.29 S	35.16 W
São Roque, Serra de- ☑	55	Ib	14.40 S	46.50 W
São Sebastião	55	Ei	23.48 S	45.25 W
São Sebastião, Ilha de- ⊡	52	Lh	23.50 S	45.18 W
São Sebastião, Ponta- ➤	30	Kk	22.05 S	35.24 E
São Sebastião				
da Boa Vista	54	Id	1.42 S	49.31 W
São Sebastião				
do Paraíso	54	Ih	20.55 S	47.00 W
São Sepé	55	Fj	30.10 S	53.34 W
São Simão	54	Hg	18.56 S	50.30 W
São Tiago ⊡	30	Eg	15.05 N	23.40 W
São Tomé ⊠	30	Hh	0.12 N	6.39 E
São Tomé	31	Hh	0.20 N	6.44 E
São Tomé, Cabo de- ➤	54	Jh	22.00 S	40.59 W
Sao Tome and Principe (EN)				
= São Tomé e Principe ①	31	Hh	1.00 N	7.00 E
São Tomé e Principe = Sao				
Tome and Principe (EN) ①	31	Hh	1.00 N	7.00 E
Saoura ⊠	32	Gd	27.50 N	2.50 W
Saoura ☐	30	Gf	28.48 N	0.50 W
São Vicente ⊠	30	Eg	16.50 N	25.00 W
São Vicente [Braz.]	55	Ia	13.38 S	46.31 W
São Vicente [Braz.]	56	Kb	23.58 S	46.23 W
São Vicente, Cabo de- ➤	5	Fh	37.01 N	9.00 W
São Xavier, Serra de- ☑	55	Ei	29.15 S	54.15 W
Sápai	15	Ih	41.02 N	25.42 E
Sapanca	15	Ni	40.41 N	30.16 E
Sapanca Gölü ☐	15	Ni	40.43 N	30.15 E
Sape [Braz.]	54	Ke	7.06 S	35.13 W
Sape [Indon.]	26	Gh	8.34 S	118.59 E
Sape, Selat- ☑	26	Gh	8.39 S	119.18 E
Sapele	34	Gd	5.55 N	5.42 E
Sapelo Island ⊡	44	Gj	31.28 N	81.15 W
Şaphane	15	Mj	39.01 N	29.14 E
Şaphane Dağı ☑	15	Mj	39.03 N	29.16 E
Sapiéntza ⊡	15	Em	36.45 N	21.42 E
Šapkina ☐	17	Fc	66.44 N	52.25 E
Sapo, Serranía del- ☑	49	Hi	7.50 N	78.17 W
Sapóne	34	Ec	12.03 N	1.36 W
Sapopema	55	Gf	23.55 S	50.35 W
Saposoa	54	Ce	6.56 S	76.48 W
Sapphire Mountains ☑	46	Ic	46.20 N	113.45 W
Sapporo	22	Qe	43.03 N	141.21 E
Sapri	14	Jj	40.04 N	15.38 E
Sapucaí, Rio- ☐	55	He	20.08 S	48.27 W
Sapulpa	43	Hd	36.00 N	96.06 W
Sapulut	26	Gf	4.42 N	116.29 E
Sâqiyat Sidi Yûsuf	14	Cn	36.13 N	8.21 E
Saqqez	23	Gb	36.14 N	46.16 E
Saráb	23	Gb	37.56 N	47.32 E
Saraburi	25	Kf	14.30 N	100.55 E
Saraf Doungous	35	Bc	12.33 N	19.42 E
Sarafjagán	24	Ne	34.28 N	50.28 E
Saragmatha = Everest,				
Mount- (EN)	21	Kg	27.59 N	86.56 E
Saragossa (EN) = Zaragoza				
[Sp.]	6	Fg	41.38 N	0.53 W
Sarai	7	Jj	53.44 N	41.03 E
Sarajevo	14	Mg	43.50 N	18.25 E
Saraji Mine	59	Jd	22.30 S	148.20 E
Sarakhs	23	Jb	36.32 N	61.11 E
Sarakiná ☐	15	Hk	38.40 N	24.37 E
Šarakol	17	Kj	52.03 N	62.47 E
Saraktaš	19	Fe	51.47 N	56.18 E
Saraland	44	Cj	30.49 N	88.02 W
Saramati ☑	25	Jc	25.44 N	95.02 E
Saran	19	Hf	49.46 N	72.52 E
Saran, Gunung- ☑	26	Fg	0.25 S	111.18 E
Saranac Lake	44	Jc	44.20 N	74.08 W
Saranci	15	Gg	42.43 N	23.46 E
Saranda	15	Cj	39.52 N	20.00 E
Sarandi	55	Fh	27.56 S	52.55 W
Sarandi del Yi	55	Ek	33.21 S	55.38 W
Sarandi Grande	55	Dk	33.44 S	56.20 W
Šaranga	7	Lh	57.12 N	46.34 E
Sarangani Bay ☑	26	le	5.57 N	125.11 E
Sarangani Islands ⊡	26	le	5.25 N	125.26 E
Saranley	35	Ge	2.23 N	42.16 E
Saransk	6	Ke	54.11 N	45.11 E
Sarapul	6	Ld	56.28 N	53.48 E
Sarapulskoje	20	Ig	48.50 N	135.58 E
Sarare	49	Mi	9.47 N	69.10 W
Sararé, Rio- ☐	55	De	14.51 S	59.40 W
Sarasota	43	Kf	27.20 N	82.34 W
Sarata	15	Ne	46.01 N	29.41 E
Sărățel	15	Kb	47.03 N	27.25 E
Saratoga	11	Lf	41.27 N	106.48 W
Saratoga Springs	43	Mc	43.04 N	73.47 W
Saratok	26	Ff	1.24 N	111.31 E
Saratov	6	Ke	51.34 N	46.02 E
Saratov Reservoir (EN) =				
Saratovskoje				
Vodohranilišče ☐	5	Ke	52.50 N	47.50 E
Saratovskaja Oblast ③	19	Ee	51.30 N	47.00 E
Saratovskoje Vodohranilišče				
= Saratov Reservoir (EN)				
☐	5	Ke	52.50 N	47.50 E
Saravan	25	Le	15.43 N	106.25 E
Sarawak ②	26	Ff	2.30 N	113.30 E
Saray	24	Bb	41.26 N	27.55 E
Saraya	34	Cc	12.50 N	11.45 W
Saräyä	24	Fe	35.47 N	35.58 E
Sarayköy	24	Cd	37.55 N	28.56 E
Sarbāz	23	Jd	26.39 N	61.15 E
Sârbogárd	10	Oj	46.53 N	18.38 E
Sarca ☐	14	Ee	45.52 N	10.52 E
Sarcelle, Passe de la- ☑	63b	Cf	22.28 S	167.13 E
Sarcelles	12	Ef	49.00 N	2.23 E
Sarcidano ☑	14	Dk	39.40 N	9.15 E
Sardara	14	Ck	39.37 N	8.49 E
Sar Dasht [Iran]	24	Mf	32.32 N	48.52 E
Sar Dasht [Iran]	24	Kd	36.09 N	45.28 E
Sardegna ②	14	Cj	40.00 N	9.00 E
Sardegna = Sardinia (EN)				
⊡	5	Gh	40.00 N	9.00 E
Sardegna, Mar di- ☑	14	Bk	40.00 N	8.00 E
Sardes ☑	15	Lk	38.29 N	28.03 E
Sardinal	49	Eh	10.31 N	85.39 W
Sardinata	54	Db	8.07 N	72.48 W
Sardinia (EN) =				
Sardegna ⊡	5	Gh	40.00 N	9.00 E
Sardis Lake ☐	45	Li	34.27 N	89.43 W
Sarektjåkkå ☑	7	Dc	67.25 N	17.46 E
Sarema/Saaremaa ⊡	5	Id	58.25 N	22.30 E
Sar-e Pol	23	Kb	36.14 N	65.55 E
Sar Eskand Khan	24	Ld	37.29 N	47.04 E
Sar-e Yazd	24	Pg	31.36 N	54.35 E
Sargasso Sea ☑	38	Mg	29.00 N	65.00 W
Sargodha	25	Eb	32.05 N	72.40 E
Šargun	18	Fe	38.31 N	67.59 E
Sarh	31	Ih	9.09 N	18.23 E
Sarhe ☐	11	Fg	47.30 N	0.32 W
Sarhro, Jebel- ☑	32	Fc	31.00 N	6.00 W
Sári [Iran]	22	Hf	36.34 N	53.04 E
Sári [Iraq]	24	Jd	34.42 N	42.44 E
Sariá ⊡	15	Kn	35.50 N	27.15 E
Saríçakaya	24	Db	40.02 N	30.31 E
Sarigan Island ⊡	57	Fc	16.42 N	145.47 E
Sarigöl	24	Cc	38.14 N	28.43 E
Sarikamiş	24	Jb	40.15 N	42.35 E
Sarikaya	24	Fc	39.48 N	35.24 E
Sarikei	26	Ff	2.07 N	111.31 E
Sariköy	15	Ki	40.12 N	27.36 E
Sarina	59	Jd	21.26 S	149.13 E
Sarine ☐	14	Bd	46.59 N	7.16 E
Sariñena	13	Lc	41.48 N	0.10 W
Sarioğlan	24	Fc	39.05 N	35.59 E
Sarir	33	Dd	27.30 N	22.30 E
Sariwŏn	27	Md	38.30 N	125.45 E
Sariyer	24	Cb	41.10 N	29.03 E
Sarj, Jabal as- ☑	14	Do	35.56 N	9.32 E
Šarja	6	Kd	58.24 N	45.30 E
Sark ⊡	9	Kl	49.26 N	2.21 W
Sarkad	10	Rj	46.45 N	21.23 E
Sarkand	19	Hf	45.25 N	79.54 E
Šarkikaraağaç	24	Dc	38.04 N	31.23 E
Sarkişla	24	Gc	39.21 N	36.26 E
Šarkovščina	8	Li	55.22 N	27.32 E
Sarköy	24	Bb	40.37 N	27.06 E
Sarlat-la-Canéda	11	Hj	44.53 N	1.13 E
Šarlyk	16	Sc	52.54 N	54.42 E
Sarmi	58	Ee	1.51 S	138.44 E
Sarmiento	53	Jj	45.35 S	69.05 W
Sarmizegetuza	15	Fd	45.31 N	22.47 E
Sárna	8	Ec	61.41 N	13.08 E
Sarnen	14	Cd	46.54 N	8.15 E
Sarny	19	Ce	51.21 N	26.36 E
Saroako	26	Hg	2.31 S	121.22 E
Sarolangun	26	Dg	2.18 S	102.42 E
Saroma-Ko ☐	29a	Ca	44.02 N	143.45 E
Šaromy	20	Kf	54.23 N	158.14 E
Saronic Gulf (EN) =				
Saronikós Kólpos ☑	15	Gl	37.45 N	23.30 E
Saronikós Kólpos = Saronic				
Gulf (EN) ☑	15	Gl	37.45 N	23.30 E
Saronno	14	De	45.38 N	9.02 E
Saros, Gulf of- (EN) =				
Saros Körfezi ☑	24	Bb	40.30 N	26.20 E
Saros Körfezi = Saros, Gulf				
of- (EN) ☑	24	Bb	40.30 N	26.20 E
Sárospatak	10	Rh	48.19 N	21.35 E
Sar Passage ☑	64a	Ac	7.12 N	134.23 E
Sarpinskije Ozera ☐	16	Nf	47.45 N	45.00 E
Sar Planina ☑	15	Dg	42.05 N	21.05 E
Sarpsborg	8	De	59.17 N	11.07 E
Sarqaq	41	Gd	70.00 N	51.39 W
Sarrabus ☑	14	Dk	39.20 N	9.30 E
Sarralbe	11	Ne	49.00 N	7.01 E
Sarrat, Wâdī - ☐	14	Co	35.59 N	8.23 E
Sarre ☐	9	Og	49.42 N	6.34 E
Sarrebourg	11	Ne	48.44 N	7.03 E
Sarreguemines	11	Ne	49.06 N	7.03 E
Sarre-Union	11	Ne	48.56 N	7.03 E
Sarria	13	Eb	42.47 N	7.24 W
Sarstún, Rio- ☐	49	Cf	15.54 N	88.54 W
Sartène	11a	Ab	41.37 N	8.59 E
Sartu → Anda	28	Ha	46.35 N	125.00 E
Saru-Gawa ☐	29a	Cb	42.30 N	142.00 E
Saruhanli	24	Bc	38.44 N	27.34 E
Sarukaishi-Gawa ☐	29	Gb	39.25 N	141.08 E

Sárüq	24	Me	34.25 N	49.30 E
Saruyama-Misaki ➤	29	Ec	37.18 N	136.43 E
Sárvár	14	Mi	47.15 N	16.56 E
Sarvestán	24	Oh	29.16 N	53.13 E
Sárviz ☐	10	Oj	46.22 N	18.48 E
Saryagač	18	Hc	41.28 N	69.11 E
Sarybarak	18	Hc	43.24 N	71.29 E
Sary-Bulak	18	Jd	41.54 N	75.47 E
Saryč, Mys- ➤	5	Jg	44.23 N	33.45 E
Saryg-Sep	20	Ef	51.30 N	95.40 E
Sary-Išikotrau ☑	18	Kb	45.15 N	76.25 E
Sarykamys	19	Hf	46.00 N	53.41 E
Sarykamyškoje, Ozero- ☐	19	Fg	41.58 N	57.58 E
Sarykolski Hrebet ☑	18	Je	38.30 N	74.15 E
Šaryn-Gol	27	lb	49.20 N	106.30 E
Saryozek	19	Hf	46.05 N	73.38 E
Sarysu ☐	19	Gf	45.12 N	66.45 E
Sary-Taš	19	Hh	39.44 N	73.16 E
Saryžaz	18	Lc	42.54 N	79.31 E
Sarzana	14	Df	44.07 N	9.58 E
Sasabe	48	Db	31.27 N	111.31 W
Sasabeneh	35	Gd	8.00 N	43.44 E
Sasa-ga-Mine ☑	29	Cd	33.49 N	133.17 E
Sasago-Tōge ☑	29	Fd	35.37 N	138.45 E
Sasamungga	63a	Cb	7.02 S	156.47 E
Sasarám	25	Gc	24.57 N	84.02 E
Sasari, Mount- ☑	63a	Dc	8.11 S	159.33 E
Sascut	15	Kc	46.11 N	27.04 E
Sásd	10	Oj	46.15 N	18.07 E
Sasebo	27	Me	33.12 N	129.44 E
Saseginaga, Lac- ☐	44	Hb	47.05 N	78.34 W
Saskatchewan ③	42	Gf	54.00 N	106.00 W
Saskatchewan ☐	38	Jd	53.12 N	99.16 W
Saskatoon	39	Id	52.07 N	106.38 W
Saskylah	20	Gb	72.00 N	114.00 E
Saslaya, Cerro- ☑	49	Eg	13.45 N	85.03 W
Sasovo	14	Se	54.22 N	41.54 E
Sassafras Mountain ☑	44	Fh	35.03 N	82.48 W
Sassandra ☐	30	Ga	4.58 N	6.05 W
Sassandra ③	34	Dd	5.20 N	6.10 W
Sassandra	31	Gh	4.57 N	6.05 W
Sassari	6	Gg	40.43 N	8.34 E
Sassenberg	12	Kc	51.59 N	8.03 E
Sassenheim	12	Gb	52.14 N	4.33 E
Sassetot-le-Mauconduit	12	Ce	49.48 N	0.32 E
Saßnitz	10	Jb	54.31 N	13.39 E
Sasso Marconi	14	Ff	44.24 N	11.15 E
Sassuolo	14	Ff	44.33 N	10.47 E
Sastobe	18	Hc	42.34 N	70.03 E
Sastre	55	Dj	31.45 S	61.50 W
Sasyk, Ozero- (Kunduk) ☐	16	Kg	45.45 N	29.40 E
Sasykkol, Ozero- ☐	19	If	46.40 N	81.00 E
Sata	29	Bf	31.04 N	130.42 E
Sata, Cape- (EN) = Sata				
Misaki ➤	21	Pf	30.59 N	130.37 E
Satakunta ☑	8	Jc	61.30 N	23.00 E
Sata-Misaki = Sata, Cape-				
(EN) ➤	21	Pf	30.59 N	130.37 E
Satan, Pointe de- ➤	63b	Dd	19.00 S	169.17 E
Sátara	25	Ee	17.41 N	73.59 E
Sataua	65c	Aa	13.28 S	172.40 W
Satawal Island ⊡	57	Fd	7.21 N	147.02 E
Satawan Atoll ☑	57	Gd	5.25 N	153.35 E
Satellite Bay ☑	42	Fa	77.25 N	117.15 W
Sáter	7	Ec	60.30 N	18.45 E
Satihaure ☐	7	Ec	67.30 N	18.45 E
Satipo	54	Df	11.16 S	74.37 W
Satit ☐	35	Fc	14.20 N	35.50 E
Satka	19	Fd	55.03 N	59.01 E
Šatki	7	Ki	55.11 N	44.08 E
Sätmäla Range ☑	25	Fe	19.30 N	78.45 E
Satna	25	Gd	24.35 N	80.50 E
Šator ☑	14	Kf	44.09 N	16.37 E
Sátoraljaújhely	10	Rh	48.24 N	21.40 E
Sátpura Range ☑	21	Jg	21.25 N	76.10 E
Satsuma-Hantō ➤	29	Bf	31.25 N	130.25 E
Satsunai-Gawa ☐	29a	Cb	42.55 N	143.15 E
Satsunan-Shotō ☐	27	Mf	29.00 N	130.00 E
Sattahip	25	Kf	12.39 N	100.54 E
Satulung	15	Gb	47.34 N	23.26 E
Satu Mare	15	Fb	47.48 N	22.53 E
Satu Mare ②	15	Fb	47.48 N	22.56 E
Satun	25	Kg	6.39 N	100.03 E
Saturniná ou Papagaio, Rio-				
☐	55	Ca	13.55 S	58.18 W
Saualpe ☑	14	Id	46.50 N	14.40 E
Sauce	56	Ja	30.00 S	58.46 W
Sauce Corto, Arroyo- ☐	55	Bm	36.55 S	61.48 W
Sauceda Mountains ☑	48	Cb	32.30 N	112.30 W
Sauce Grande, Rio- ☐	55	Bn	38.59 S	61.07 W
Saucillo	47	Cc	28.01 N	105.17 W
Sauda	8	Be	59.39 N	6.20 E
Saudade, Serra da- [Braz.]				
☑	55	Jd	19.20 S	45.50 W
Saudade, Serra da- [Braz.]				
☑	55	Fc	16.20 S	53.53 W
Saudárkrókur	7a	Bb	65.45 N	19.39 W
Saudi Arabia (EN) = Al				
'Arabiyah As-Su'ūdiyah ①	22	Gg	25.00 N	45.00 E
Sauer [Eur.] ☐	10	Cg	49.44 N	6.31 E
Sauer [Fr.] ☐	12	Kf	48.55 N	8.10 E
Sauerland ☑	10	De	51.10 N	8.00 E
Saüèruiná, Rio- ☐	55	Cb	12.05 S	58.40 W
Sauga Jõgi ☐	8	Kf	58.19 N	24.25 E
Saugatuck	44	Dd	42.40 N	86.12 W
Saugues	11	Jj	44.58 N	3.33 E
Sauk Centre	43	Id	45.44 N	94.57 W
Sauk Rapids	45	Id	45.34 N	94.09 W
Saül	54	Hc	3.37 N	53.12 W
Saulder	18	Gb	42.43 N	68.24 E
Sauldre ☐	11	Hg	47.16 N	1.30 E
Saulieu	11	Kg	47.16 N	4.14 E
Saulkrasti/Saulkrasty ☐	7	Fh	57.17 N	24.29 E
Saulkrasty/Saulkrasti	7	Fh	57.17 N	24.29 E
Saulnois ☑	12	If	48.52 N	6.30 E

Sault	11	Lj	44.05 N	5.25 E
Sault Sainte Marie [Mi.-U.S.]	43	Kb	46.30 N	84.21 W
Sault Sainte Marie				
[Ont.-Can.]	39	Ke	46.31 N	84.20 W
Saumarez Reefs ⊡	57	Gg	21.50 S	153.40 E
Saumâtre, Étang- ☐	49	Kd	18.35 N	72.00 W
Saumur	11	Fg	47.16 N	0.05 W
Saunders ⊡	66	Ad	57.47 S	26.27 W
Saunders Coast ☑	66	Mf	77.45 S	150.00 W
Saurimo	31	Ji	9.38 S	20.24 E
Sauro ☐	14	Kj	40.18 N	16.21 E
Sautar	36	Ce	11.09 S	18.25 E
Sauteurs	51p	Bb	12.14 N	61.38 W
Sauvagnon	11	Fj	44.22 N	3.17 E
Sauvo/Sagu	8	Jd	60.21 N	22.42 E
Sauwald ☑	14	Hb	48.28 N	13.40 E
Sava ☐	5	Ig	44.50 N	20.28 E
Savage River	59	Jh	41.33 S	145.09 E
Savai'i Island ⊡	57	Jf	13.35 S	172.25 W
Savalou	34	Fd	7.56 N	1.58 E
Savanes ③	34	Fc	10.30 N	0.30 E
Savan Island ⊡	51n	Bb	12.48 N	61.12 W
Savannah	45	Ke	42.05 N	90.08 W
Savannah [Ga.-U.S.]	39	Kf	32.04 N	81.05 W
Savannah [Tn.-U.S.]	44	Ch	35.14 N	88.14 W
Savannah Beach	44	Gi	32.01 N	80.51 W
Savannakhét	22	Mh	16.33 N	104.45 E
Savanne-la-Mar	49	le	18.13 N	78.08 W
Savanne	45	Kb	48.59 N	90.12 W
Savannes Bay ☑	51k	Bb	13.45 N	60.56 W
Savant Lake	42	If	50.15 N	90.42 W
Savant Lake ☐	45	Ka	50.30 N	90.20 W
Savaştepe	24	Bc	39.22 N	27.40 E
Savdiri	35	Dc	14.25 N	29.05 E
Save ☐	31	Hh	8.02 N	2.29 E
Save [Afr.] ☐	30	Kk	21.00 S	35.02 E
Save [Fr.] ☐	11	Hk	43.47 N	1.17 E
Saveân ☐	8	Dg	57.43 N	11.59 E
Säveh	23	Hb	35.01 N	50.20 E
Säveni	15	Jb	47.57 N	26.52 E
Saverdun	11	Hk	43.14 N	1.35 E
Saverne	11	Nf	48.44 N	7.22 E
Savigliano	14	Bf	44.38 N	7.40 E
Savigsivik	41	Fc	76.00 N	64.45 W
Savinje ☐	14	Jc	46.51 N	26.28 E
Savinjske Alpe ☑	14	Id	46.20 N	14.30 E
Savinski	19	Ec	62.57 N	40.13 E
Savio ☐	14	Gf	44.19 N	12.20 E
Sävirşin	16	Ki	46.00 N	22.14 E
Savitaipale	7	Gf	61.12 N	27.42 E
Savnik	15	Cg	42.57 N	19.06 E
Savo ☑	63a	Dc	9.08 S	159.48 E
Savo ☐	8	Lb	62.30 N	27.30 E
Savoie ③	11	Mi	45.30 N	6.25 E
Savoie = Savoy (EN) ☑	11	Mi	45.24 N	6.30 E
Savona	14	Cf	44.17 N	8.30 E
Savonlinna/Nyslott	7	Gf	61.52 N	28.53 E
Savonranta	8	Lb	62.11 N	29.12 E
Savonselkä ☑	8	Lb	62.05 N	27.20 E
Savoonga	40	Ed	63.42 N	170.27 W
Savoy (EN) = Savoie ☑	11	Mi	45.24 N	6.30 E
Savsat	24	Jb	41.15 N	42.20 E
Savsjö	7	Dh	57.25 N	14.40 E
Savudrija, Rt- ➤	14	Hd	45.30 N	13.31 E
Savukoski	7	Gc	67.17 N	28.10 E
Savur	24	Jd	37.33 N	40.53 E
Savusavu	61	Ec	17.34 S	178.15 E
Savusavu Bay ☑	63d	Bb	16.45 S	179.15 E
Savu Sea (EN) = Sawu,				
Laut- ☑	21	Oj	9.40 S	122.00 E
Savuto ☐	14	Kk	39.20 N	16.06 E
Sawahlunto	26	Dg	0.40 S	100.47 E
Sawai Mädhopur	25	Fc	25.59 N	76.22 E
Sawäkin	31	Kg	19.07 N	37.20 E
Sawäkin, Jazā'ir-=Suakin				
Archipelago (EN) ⊡	30	Kg	19.07 N	37.20 E
Sawankhalok	25	Je	17.19 N	99.54 E
Sawara	29	Gd	35.53 N	140.49 E
Sawasaki-Hana ➤	28	Of	37.47 N	138.12 E
Sawatch Range ☑	45	Cg	39.10 N	106.25 W
Sawbä > Sobat (EN) ☐	30	Kh	9.45 N	31.45 E
Sawbridgeworth	12	Cc	51.49 N	0.09 E
Sawdā', Jabal as- ☑	33	Cd	28.40 N	15.30 E
Sawfajjin ☐	33	Cd	31.54 N	15.07 E
Sawhāj=Sohag (EN)	31	Kf	26.30 N	31.42 E
Sawkanah	33	Cd	29.04 N	15.47 E
Sawla	34	Ec	9.17 N	2.25 W
Sawqirah	23	If	18.10 N	56.30 E
Şawqirah, Ghubbat- ☑	23	If	18.35 N	56.45 E
Sawtooth Mountains ☑	46	Hc	44.00 N	115.00 W
Sawu, Kepulauan- ☐	26	Hi	10.30 S	121.50 E
Sawu, Laut-=Savu Sea				
(EN) ☑	21	Oj	9.40 S	122.00 E
Sawu, Pulau- ⊡	23	Ok	10.30 S	121.54 E
Şawwän, Ard as- ☑	24	Gg	31.00 N	37.00 E
Sax	13	Lf	38.32 N	0.49 W
Saxby River ☐	59	le	18.25 S	140.53 E
Saxmundham	12	Db	52.13 N	1.30 E
Saxony (EN) = Sachsen ☑	10	Jd	51.00 N	13.30 E
Say	34	Fc	13.07 N	2.21 E
Sayabec	44	Na	48.36 N	67.37 W
Saya de Malha Bank (EN)				
☑	30	Nj	10.00 S	61.00 E
Sayago ☑	13	Fc	41.20 N	6.10 W
Sayan	54	Cf	11.08 S	77.12 W
Sayang, Pulau- ⊡	26	Hf	0.18 N	129.54 E
Sayaxché	49	Be	16.31 N	90.10 W
Saydá	23	Ec	33.33 N	35.22 E
Saybüt	22	Hh	15.12 N	51.14 E
Saylorville Lake ☐	45	Jf	41.48 N	93.46 W
Säynätsalo	8	Kb	62.08 N	25.46 E
Sayö	29	Dd	35.01 N	134.22 E
Sayram Hu ☐	27	Dc	44.35 N	81.10 E

Sayula	48	Hh	19.52 N	103.37 W
Saywün	35	Hb	15.56 N	48.47 E
Sazanit, Ishull i- ⊡	15	Ci	40.30 N	19.16 E
Sázava ☐	10	Kg	49.53 N	14.24 E
Sázava	10	Kg	49.52 N	14.54 E
Sbaa	32	Gd	28.13 N	0.10 W
Sbisseb ☐	13	Pi	35.42 N	3.51 E
Scaër	11	Cf	48.02 N	3.42 W
Scafell Pike ☑	9	Jg	54.27 N	3.12 W
Scalea	14	Jk	39.49 N	15.47 E
Scalone, Passo dello- ☑	14	Jk	39.38 N	15.57 E
Scammon, Laguna- ☑	48	Bd	27.45 N	114.15 W
Scammon Bay	40	Fd	61.53 N	165.38 W
Scandinavia (EN) ☑	5	Hb	65.00 N	16.00 E
Scanno	14	Hi	41.54 N	13.53 E
Scansano	14	Fh	42.41 N	11.20 E
Scapa Flow ☑	9	Jc	58.54 N	3.05 W
Scapegoat Mountain ☑	46	Ic	47.19 N	112.50 W
Ščapino	20	Ke	55.15 N	159.25 E
Ščara ☐	16	Dc	53.27 N	24.44 E
Scaramia, Capo- ➤	14	In	36.47 N	14.29 E
Scarba ⊡	9	He	56.11 N	5.42 W
Scarborough [Eng.-U.K.]	9	Mg	54.17 N	0.24 W
Scarborough [Trin.]	54	Fa	11.11 N	60.44 W
Ščastje	11	Jd	50.30 N	3.27 E
Ščastje	16	Ke	48.44 N	39.14 E
Sceaux	12	Ef	48.47 N	2.17 E
Ščekino	16	Jb	54.01 N	37.29 E
Ščekurja ☐	17	Ad	61.56 N	60.52 E
Ščeljajur	19	Fb	65.21 N	53.25 E
Ščerbakty	19	Ie	52.29 N	78.14 E
Ščerbinovka	16	Kc	50.35 N	10.57 E
Schaalsee ☐	12	Gd	53.35 N	10.57 E
Schaarbeek/Schaerbeek	12	Gd	50.51 N	4.23 E
Schaerbeek/Schaarbeek	12	Gd	50.51 N	4.23 E
Schaffhausen ②	14	Cc	47.45 N	8.40 E
Schaffhausen	14	Cc	47.40 N	8.40 E
Schagen	12	Gb	52.48 N	4.48 E
Schärding	14	Hb	48.27 N	13.26 E
Scharmützelsee ☐	10	Kd	52.15 N	14.03 E
Scharnhörn ⊡	10	Cc	53.57 N	8.25 E
Scheeßel	12	La	53.10 N	9.29 E
Schefferville	39	Md	54.47 N	64.49 W
Scheibbs	14	Jb	48.00 N	15.10 E
Schela	15	Gd	45.10 N	23.18 E
Schelde ☐	11	Kc	51.22 N	4.15 E
Schelde (EN) = Escaut ☐	11	Kc	51.22 N	4.15 E
Schell Creek Range ☑	43	Ed	39.10 N	114.40 W
Schenectady	43	Mc	42.48 N	73.57 W
Scheno	35	Fd	9.35 N	39.25 E
Scherfede, Warburg-	12	Lc	51.32 N	9.02 E
Scherpenheuvel-Zichem	12	Gd	50.59 N	4.59 E
Scheveningen, 's-				
Gravenhage-	11	Kb	52.06 N	4.18 E
Schiedam	11	Kc	51.55 N	4.24 E
Schiermonnikoog ⊡	11	Ma	53.28 N	6.15 E
Schifferstadt	12	Ke	49.23 N	8.22 E
Schiffgraben ☐	10	Hd	52.02 N	11.10 E
Schifflange	12	Je	49.30 N	6.01 E
Schijndel	12	Hc	51.37 N	5.28 E
Schiltigheim	11	Nf	48.36 N	7.45 E
Schio	14	Fe	45.43 N	11.21 E
Schipbeek ☐	12	Ib	52.15 N	6.14 E
Schladming	14	Hc	47.23 N	13.41 E
Schlei ☑	10	Fb	54.35 N	9.50 E
Schleiden	10	Cf	50.32 N	6.28 E
Schleiz	10	Hf	50.35 N	11.49 E
Schleswig	5	Gc	54.31 N	9.33 E
Schleswig Holstein ②	10	Gb	54.00 N	10.30 E
Schlitz	10	Ff	50.40 N	9.34 E
Schloß Holte-Stukenbrock	12	Kc	51.55 N	8.36 E
Schloß Neuhaus, Paderborn-	12	Ke	49.23 N	8.42 E
Schluchsee ☐	10	Ei	47.49 N	8.10 E
Schlüchtern	10	Ff	50.21 N	9.31 E
Schmallenberg	12	Lc	51.09 N	8.18 E
Schmallenberg-Bödefeld-				
Freiheit	12	Kc	51.15 N	8.24 E
Schmallenberg-Oberkirchen	12	Kc	51.09 N	8.18 E
Schmelz	12	Ie	49.26 N	6.51 E
Schmida	14	Kb	48.20 N	16.14 E
Schneeberg	10	If	50.36 N	12.38 E
Schneeberg [Aus.] ☑	14	Ic	47.46 N	15.52 E
Schneeberg [F.R.G.] ☑	10	Hf	50.00 N	11.51 E
Schneifel ☑	10	Cf	50.16 N	6.23 E
Schoberpaß ☑	14	Ic	47.27 N	14.40 E
Schoberspitze ☑	14	Hc	47.05 N	13.05 E
Schœlcher	51h	Ab	14.37 N	61.06 W
Schönecken	10	Cf	50.01 N	11.45 E
Schongau	10	Gi	47.49 N	10.54 E
Schöningen	10	Hd	52.08 N	10.57 E
Schoondijke	12	Fc	51.21 N	3.33 E
Schoonebeek	12	Ib	52.40 N	6.53 E
Schoonhoven	12	Gc	51.55 N	4.51 E
Schorfheide ☑	10	Jd	52.55 N	13.35 E
Schoten	12	Ld	50.30 N	9.08 E
Schotten	12	Fe	50.30 N	9.08 E
Schouten Islands ⊡	57	Fe	3.30 S	144.30 E
Schouwen ⊡	11	Jc	51.43 N	3.50 E
Schramberg	10	Eh	48.14 N	8.23 E
Schreiber	42	Jf	48.48 N	87.15 W
Schriesheim	12	Ke	49.29 N	8.40 E
Schrobenhausen	10	Hh	48.33 N	11.16 E
Schruns	14	Dc	47.04 N	9.55 E
Schuls / Scuol	14	Ec	46.48 N	10.18 E
Schultz Lake ☐	42	Hd	64.45 N	97.30 W
Schussen ☐	10	Fi	47.37 N	9.32 E
Schüttorf	12	Jb	52.19 N	7.14 E
Schwabach	10	Gg	49.20 N	11.02 E
Schwaben=Swabia (EN) ☑	10	Gh	48.20 N	10.30 E
Schwäbisch-Bayerisches				
Alpenvorland=Swabian-				
Bavarian Plateau (EN) ☑	10	Hi	48.10 N	10.30 E
Schwäbische Alb=Swabian				
Jura (EN) ☑	5	Gf	48.25 N	9.30 E

Index Symbols

① Independent Nation	▣ Historical or Cultural Region	⊟ Pass, Gap	⊟ Depression	▤ Coast, Beach	⊞ Rock, Reef	⊟ Waterfall Rapids	⊟ Canal	⊟ Lagoon	⊞ Escarpment, Sea Scarp	⊞ Historic Site	⊠ Port
② State, Region	▲ Mount, Mountain	⊟ Plain, Lowland	⊟ Polder	⊟ Cliff	⊞ Islands, Archipelago	⊟ River Mouth, Estuary	⊟ Bank	⊞ Glacier	⊞ Fracture	⊞ Ruins	⊠ Lighthouse
③ District, County	▲ Volcano	⊟ Delta	⊟ Desert, Dunes	▤ Peninsula	⊞ Rocks, Reefs	⊟ Lake	⊞ Ice Shelf, Pack Ice	⊞ Seamount	⊞ Trench, Abyss	⊞ Wall, Walls	⊠ Mine
④ Municipality	▲ Hill	⊟ Salt Flat	⊟ Forest, Woods	⊟ Isthmus	⊞ Coral Reef	⊟ Salt Lake	⊞ Ocean	⊞ Tableland	⊞ National Park, Reserve	⊞ Church, Abbey	⊠ Tunnel
⑤ Colony, Dependency	▲ Mountains, Mountain Range	⊟ Valley, Canyon	⊟ Heath, Steppe	⊟ Sandbank	⊞ Well, Spring	⊟ Intermittent Lake	⊞ Sea	⊞ Ridge	⊞ Point of Interest	⊞ Temple	⊠ Dam, Bridge
⊟ Continent	▲ Hills, Escarpment	⊟ Crater, Cave	⊟ Oasis	⊟ Island	⊞ Geyser	⊟ Reservoir	⊞ Gulf, Bay	⊞ Shelf	⊞ Recreation Site	⊞ Scientific Station	
⊠ Physical Region	▲ Plateau, Upland	⊟ Karst Features	⊟ Cape, Point	⊟ Atoll	⊟ River, Stream	⊟ Swamp, Pond	⊞ Strait, Fjord	⊞ Basin	⊞ Cave, Cavern	⊞ Airport	

Schwäbisch Gmünd 10 Fh 48.48N 9.47 E
Schwäbisch Hall 10 Fg 49.06N 9.44 E
Schwalbach (Saar) 12 Ie 49.18N 6.49 E
Schwalm 12 Lc 51.07N 9.24 E
Schwalm 10 Ff 50.45N 9.25 E
Schwalmstadt 10 Ff 50.55N 9.12 E
Schwalmtal 12 Ic 51.15N 6.15 E
Schwandorf 10 Ig 49.20N 12.07 E
Schwaner, Pegunungan- 26 Fg 0.40S 112.40 E
Schwanewede 12 Ka 53.14N 8.36 E
Schwarzach 10 Ig 49.30N 12.10 E
Schwarzbach 12 Je 49.17N 7.40 E
Schwarze Elster 10 Ie 51.49N 12.51 E
Schwarzer Mann 12 Id 50.15N 6.22 E
Schwarzrand 37 Be 26.00S 17.10 E
Schwarzwald=Black Forest (EN) 5 Gf 48.00N 8.15 E
Schwarzwalder Hochwald 12 Ie 49.39N 6.55 E
Schwatka Mountains 40 Hc 67.25N 157.00W
Schwaz 14 Fc 47.20N 11.42 E
Schwechat 14 Kb 48.08N 16.28 E
Schwechat 14 Kb 48.08N 16.28 E
Schwedt 10 Kc 53.04N 14.18 E
Schweich 12 Ie 49.49N 6.45 E
Schweinfurt 10 Gf 50.03N 10.14 E
Schweiz / Suisse / Svizra / Svizzera = Switzerland (EN) [1] 6 Gf 46.00N 8.30 E
Schweizer-Reneke 37 De 27.11S 25.18 E
Schwelm 12 Jc 51.17N 7.17 E
Schwerin [2] 10 Hc 53.35N 11.25 E
Schwerin 10 Hc 53.38N 11.23 E
Schweriner See 10 Hc 53.45N 11.28 E
Schwerte 12 Jc 51.27N 7.34 E
Schwetzingen 12 Ke 49.23N 8.34 E
Schwielochsee 10 Kd 52.03N 14.12 E
Schwyz [2] 14 Cc 47.10N 8.50 E
Schwyz 14 Cc 47.03N 8.40 E
Sciacca 14 Hm 37.31N 13.03 E
Scicli 14 In 36.47N 14.42 E
Ščigry 19 De 51.53N 36.55 E
Scilly, Isles of- 5 Ff 49.57N 6.15W
Scioto River 44 Ff 38.44N 83.01W
Ščirec 10 Tg 49.34N 23.54 E
Scobey 46 Mb 48.47N 105.25W
Scordia 14 Im 37.18N 14.51 E
Scoresby Land 41 Jd 71.45N 26.30W
Scoresbysund 67 Md 70.35N 21.40W
Scoresby Sund 67 Md 70.20N 23.30W
Scorff 11 Cg 47.46N 3.21W
Ščors 19 De 51.48N 31.59 E
Scotia Ridge (EN) 3 Co 57.00S 45.00W
Scotia Sea (EN) 52 Mk 57.00S 40.00W
Scotland [2] 9 Ie 56.30N 4.30W
Scotland 5 Fd 56.30N 4.30W
Scotlandville 45 Kk 30.31N 91.11W
Scotstown 44 Lc 45.31N 71.17W
Scott 42 Gf 52.27N 108.23W
Scott, Cape- [Austl.] 59 Fb 13.30S 129.50 E
Scott, Cape - [B.C.-Can.] 42 Ef 50.47N 128.25W
Scott, Mount- 46 De 42.56N 122.01W
Scott Base 66 Kf 77.51S 166.46 E
Scottburgh 37 Ef 30.19S 30.40 E
Scott Channel 46 Aa 50.45N 128.30W
Scott City 45 Fg 38.29N 100.54W
Scott Coast 66 Kf 76.30S 162.30 E
Scott Glacier [Ant.] 66 He 66.15S 100.05 E
Scott Glacier [Ant.] 66 Mg 85.45S 153.00W
Scott Inlet 42 Kb 71.05N 71.05W
Scott Island 66 Le 67.24S 179.55W
Scott Islands 46 Aa 50.48N 128.40W
Scott Peak 46 Id 44.21N 112.50W
Scott Reef 59 Eb 14.00S 121.50 E
Scottsbluff 39 Ie 41.52N 103.40W
Scottsboro 44 Dh 34.40N 86.01W
Scottsburg 44 Ef 38.41N 85.46W
Scottsdale [Austl.] 59 Jh 41.10S 147.31 E
Scottsdale [Az.-U.S.] 43 Ee 33.30N 111.56W
Scotts Head 51g Bb 15.13N 61.23W
Scottsville 44 Dg 36.45N 86.11W
Scottville 44 Dd 43.59N 86.17W
Scranton 39 Le 41.24N 75.40W
Scrivia 14 Ce 45.03N 8.54 E
Scrub Cays 49 Ia 24.07N 76.55W
Scrub Island 51b Bb 18.17N 62.57W
Ščučin 16 Dc 53.39N 24.48 E
Ščučinsk 19 He 53.00N 70.11 E
Ščučja 17 Nc 66.45N 68.20 E
Ščučje 19 Gd 55.15N 62.43 E
Scugog, Lake- 44 Hc 44.10N 78.51W
Ščugor 17 Hd 64.12N 57.32 E
Scunthorpe 9 Mh 53.36N 0.38W
Scuol / Schuls 14 Ed 46.48N 10.17 E
Scutari, Lake- (EN)= Shkodrës, Liqen i- 5 Hg 42.10N 19.20 E
Scutari, Lake- (EN)= Skadarsko Jezero 5 Hg 42.10N 19.20 E
Seaford 9 Nk 50.46N 0.06 E
Seahorse Point 42 Jd 63.47N 80.10W
Sea Islands 43 Ke 31.20N 81.20W
Seal 42 Ie 59.04N 94.47W
Seal Island 44 Nd 43.30N 66.01W
Sealpunt 30 Jl 34.06S 23.24 E
Searcy 45 Ki 35.15N 91.44W
Searles Lake 46 Gi 35.43N 117.20W
Seaside [Ca.-U.S.] 46 Eh 36.37N 121.50W
Seaside [Or.-U.S.] 46 Dc 46.01N 123.55W
Seattle 39 Ge 47.36N 122.20W
Seaward Kaikoura Range 62 Ee 42.15S 173.35 E
Seba 26 Hi 10.29S 121.50 E
Sébaco 49 Dg 12.51N 86.06W
Sebago Lake 44 Ld 43.50N 70.35W
Sebaiera 22 Ee 24.51N 13.02W
Sebaou 13 Ph 36.55N 3.51 E
Sebastian, Cape- 46 Ce 42.19N 124.26W
Sebastián Vizcaíno, Bahía- 38 Hg 28.00N 114.30W
Sebastopol 46 Dg 38.24N 122.49W
Sebatik, Pulau- 26 Gf 4.10N 117.45 E
Sebba 34 Fc 13.26N 0.32 E
Sebderat 35 Fb 15.27N 36.39 E
Sébé 36 Bc 1.02S 13.06 E
Šebekino 19 De 50.27N 37.00 E
Sébékoro 34 Dc 12.49N 8.50W
Seberi 55 Fh 27.29S 53.24W
Sebeş 15 Gd 45.58N 23.34 E
Sebeş 15 Gd 46.00N 23.34 E
Sebes-Körös 15 Dc 46.55N 20.59 E
Sebeşului, Munţii- 15 Gd 45.38N 23.27 E
Sebewaing 44 Fd 43.44N 83.27W
Sebež 19 Cd 56.19N 28.31 E
Sebha Oasis (EN)=Sabhā, Wāḩāt 30 If 27.00N 14.25 E
Şebınkarahisar 24 Hb 40.18N 38.26 E
Sebiş 15 Fc 46.22N 22.07 E
Sebou 30 Ge 34.16N 6.41W
Sebring 44 Gl 27.30N 81.26W
Sebugal 13 Ed 40.21N 7.05W
Sebuku, Pulau- 26 Gg 3.30S 116.22 E
Šebunino 20 Jg 46.24N 141.56 E
Secas, Islas- 49 Gi 7.58N 82.02W
Secchia 14 Ee 45.04N 11.00 E
Sechura 54 Be 5.33S 80.51W
Sechura, Bahía de- 54 Be 5.40S 81.00W
Sechura, Desierto de- 54 Be 6.00S 80.30W
Seckau 14 Ic 47.16N 14.47 E
Seclin 12 Fd 50.33N 3.02 E
Secondigny 11 Fh 46.37N 0.25W
Secos, Ilhéus- 32 Cf 14.58N 24.40W
Secretary Island 62 Bf 45.15S 166.55 E
Sécure, Río- 54 Fg 15.10S 64.52W
Seda 8 Kg 57.38N 25.12 E
Sêda 13 Df 38.56N 8.03W
Seda [Lat.-U.S.S.R.] 8 Kg 57.32N 25.43 E
Seda [Lith.-U.S.S.R.] 8 Jh 56.10N 22.00 E
Sedalia 43 Id 38.42N 93.14W
Sedan 11 Ke 49.42N 4.57 E
Sedanka 40a Eb 53.50N 166.10W
Sedano 13 Ib 42.43N 3.45W
Sedbergh 9 Kg 54.20N 2.31W
Seddenga 35 Ea 20.33N 30.18 E
Seddon 62 Fd 41.40S 174.04 E
Seddon, Kap- 41 Gc 75.20N 58.45W
Seddonville 62 Dd 41.33S 171.59 E
Seddülbahir 15 Ji 40.03N 26.10 E
Sedelnikovo 19 Hd 56.57N 75.18 E
Séderon 11 Lj 44.12N 5.32 E
Sédhiou 34 Bc 12.44N 15.33W
Sedini 14 Ci 40.51N 8.49 E
Šedok 16 Lg 44.13N 40.52 E
Sedom 24 Fg 31.04N 35.24 E
Sedona 46 Ji 34.52N 111.46W
Sedrada 14 Bn 36.08N 7.32 E
Šédro 14 Kg 43.05N 16.42 E
Sedro Woolley 46 Db 48.30N 122.14W
Šeduva 7 Fi 55.48N 23.45 E
Sée 11 Ef 48.39N 1.26W
Seeheim [F.R.G.] 12 Ke 49.46N 8.40 E
Seeheim [Nam.] 37 Be 26.50S 17.45 E
Seeis 37 Bd 22.29S 17.39 E
Seeland 14 Bc 47.05N 7.05 E
Seeling, Mount- 66 Og 82.28S 103.00W
Seelow 10 Kd 52.31N 14.23 E
Sées 11 Gf 48.36N 0.10 E
Seesen 10 Ge 51.54N 10.11 E
Seewarte Seamounts (EN) 30 Ee 33.00N 28.30W
Şefaatli 24 Fc 39.31N 34.46 E
Sefadu 34 Cd 8.39N 10.59W
Seferihisar 24 Bc 38.11N 26.51 E
Séféto 34 Dc 14.08N 9.51W
Sefīd Dasht 24 Nf 32.09N 51.10 E
Sefrou 32 Gc 33.50N 4.50W
Sefuri-San 29 Be 33.26N 130.22 E
Segaf, Kepulauan- 26 Jg 2.10S 130.28 E
Ségalas 11 Ij 44.09N 2.30 E
Segamat 26 Df 2.30N 102.49 E
Segangane 13 Ii 35.10N 3.01W
Şegarcea 15 Ge 44.06N 23.45 E
Šegarka 20 De 57.16N 84.02 E
Segbana 34 Fc 10.56N 3.42 E
Segeg 35 Gd 7.40N 42.50 E
Segesta 14 Gm 37.55N 12.50 E
Segeža 6 Jc 63.44N 34.19 E
Seghe 63a Cc 8.25S 157.51 E
Seglinge 8 Id 60.15N 20.40 E
Segmon 8 Ee 59.17N 13.01 E
Segorbe 13 Le 39.51N 0.29W
Ségou [3] 34 Dc 14.00N 6.20W
Ségou 31 Gg 13.27N 6.15W
Segovia 13 Hd 40.57N 4.07W
Segovia [3] 13 Ic 41.10N 4.00W
Segozero, Ozero- 5 Jc 63.18N 33.45 E
Segré 11 Fg 47.41N 0.52W
Segre 13 Mc 41.40N 0.43 E
Seguam 40a Db 52.17N 172.30W
Séguédine 34 Ha 20.12N 12.59 E
Séguéla 34 Dd 7.57N 6.40W
Séguéla [3] 34 Dd 8.05N 6.32W
Seguin 43 Hf 29.34N 97.58W
Segula 40a Bb 52.01N 178.07 E
Segura 13 Lf 38.06N 0.38W
Segura, Sierra de- 13 Jf 38.00N 2.45W
Segura de la Sierra 13 Jf 38.18N 2.39W
Sehithwa 37 Cd 20.27S 22.42 E
Seia 13 Ed 40.25N 7.42W
Seibal 49 Be 16.27N 90.05W
Seiche 11 Eg 48.00N 1.46W
Seiland 7 Fa 70.25N 23.15 E
Seiling 45 Gh 36.09N 98.56W
Seille [Fr.] 11 Me 49.07N 6.11 E
Seille [Fr.] 11 Kh 46.31N 4.56 E
Sein, Ile de- 11 Bf 48.02N 4.51W
Seinäjoki 7 Fe 62.47N 22.50 E
Seine 5 Gf 49.26N 0.26 E
Seine, Baie de la-=Seine, Bay of the- (EN) 5 Ff 49.30N 0.30W
Seine, Bay of the- (EN)= Seine, Baie de la- 5 Ff 49.30N 0.30W
Seine, Val de- 11 Jf 48.30N 3.20 E
Seine-et-Marne [3] 11 If 48.30N 3.00 E
Seine-Maritime [3] 11 Ge 49.45N 1.00 E
Seine-Saint-Denis [3] 11 If 48.55N 2.30 E
Seine Seamount (EN) 5 Ei 33.45N 14.25W
Seini 15 Gb 47.45N 23.17 E
Seistan (EN)=Sīstān 21 If 30.30N 62.00 E
Seixal 13 Cf 38.38N 9.06W
Sējaha 20 Cb 70.10N 72.30 E
Sejerø 8 Di 55.55N 11.10 E
Sejerø Bugt 8 Di 55.50N 11.15 E
Sejm 5 Je 51.27N 32.34 E
Sejmčan 20 Kd 62.52N 152.27 E
Sejny 10 Tb 54.07N 23.20 E
Sekakes 37 Df 30.04S 28.21 E
Sekenke 36 Fc 4.16S 34.10 E
Šeki 19 Eg 41.10N 47.11 E
Seki [Jap.] 29 Ed 35.28N 136.54 E
Seki [Tur.] 24 Cd 36.44N 29.33 E
Sekincau, Gunung- 26 Dh 5.05S 104.18 E
Seki-Zaki 29b Be 33.16N 131.54 E
Sekoma 37 Cd 24.36S 23.58 E
Sekondi-Takoradi 31 Gh 4.53N 1.45W
Sekota 35 Fc 12.37N 39.03 E
Šeksna 19 Dd 59.13N 38.32 E
Šelagski, Mys- 20 Mb 70.10N 170.45 E
Selah 46 Ec 46.39N 120.32W
Selajar, Pulau- 26 Hh 6.05S 120.30 E
Selajar, Selat- 26 Hh 5.42S 120.28 E
Selaön 8 Ge 59.25N 17.10 E
Selaru, Pulau- 26 Jh 8.09S 131.00 E
Selatan, Cape- (EN)= Selatan, Tanjung- 21 Nj 4.10S 113.48 E
Selatan, Tanjung-=Selatan, Cape- (EN) 21 Nj 4.10S 113.48 E
Selawik 40 Gc 66.37N 160.03W
Selawik Lake 40 Hc 66.30N 160.40W
Selb 10 If 50.10N 12.08 E
Selbjørn 8 Ae 60.00N 5.10 E
Selbjørnsfjorden 8 Ae 59.55N 5.10 E
Selbu 8 Da 63.13N 11.02 E
Selbukta 66 Bf 71.40S 12.25W
Selbusjøen 8 Da 63.15N 10.55 E
Selby [Eng.-U.K.] 9 Lh 53.48N 1.04W
Selby [S.D.-U.S.] 45 Fd 45.31N 100.02W
Selco 16 Ic 53.23N 34.05 E
Selçuk 24 Bd 37.56N 27.22 E
Seldovia 40 Ie 59.27N 151.43W
Sele 14 Ij 40.29N 14.56 E
Sele, Piana del- 14 Ij 40.30N 14.55 E
Selebi-Pikwe 31 Jk 22.13S 27.58 E
Selečka Planina 15 Eh 41.05N 21.35 E
Šelehov 20 Ff 52.10N 104.01 E
Selemdža 21 Od 51.49N 128.53 E
Selencia 24 Kf 33.04N 44.33 E
Selendi 15 Lk 38.40N 28.41 E
Selendi 15 Lk 38.45N 28.53 E
Selenduma 20 Ff 50.55N 106.10 E
Selenga (Selenge) 21 Md 52.16N 106.16 E
Selenge [Mong.] 27 Hb 49.25N 103.59 E
Selenge [Zaire] 36 Cc 1.58S 18.11 E
Selenge→Selenga 21 Md 52.16N 106.16 E
Selenginsk 20 Ff 51.59N 106.57 E
Selenica 15 Ci 40.32N 19.38 E
Selennjah 20 Jc 67.55N 145.00 E
Sélestat 11 Nf 48.16N 7.27 E
Selety 19 He 53.06N 73.00 E
Seletyteniz, Ozero- 19 He 53.15N 73.15 E
Selevac 15 De 44.30N 20.53 E
Seleznevo 8 Md 60.44N 28.37 E
Selfoss 7a Bc 63.56N 21.00W
Seli 34 Cd 8.33N 12.48W
Sélibabi 32 Ef 15.10N 12.11W
Seliger, Ozero- 19 Dd 57.20N 33.05 E
Seligman 46 Ii 35.20N 112.53W
Šelihova, Zaliv-=Shelikhov Gulf (EN) 21 Rc 60.00N 158.00 E
Selimağa 15 Lj 39.35N 28.33 E
Selimiye 24 Bd 37.24N 27.40 E
Selingenstadt 12 Kd 50.03N 8.59 E
Selinunte 14 Gm 37.35N 12.48 E
Selizarovo 7 Hh 56.51N 33.29 E
Seljatin 15 Ib 47.52N 25.14 E
Selje 8 Ab 62.03N 5.22 E
Seljord 7 Bg 59.29N 8.37 E
Selkirk [Man.-Can.] 45 Ha 50.09N 96.52W
Selkirk [Scot.-U.K.] 9 Kf 55.33N 2.50W
Selkirk Mountains 42 Ff 50.00N 117.00W
Sella 13 Ga 43.28N 5.04W
Sellasia 15 Fl 37.10N 22.25 E
Selle 12 Fd 50.19N 3.23 E
Selles-sur-Cher 11 Hg 47.16N 1.33 E
Sells 46 Jk 31.55N 111.53W
Selm 12 Jc 51.42N 7.28 E
Selma [Al.-U.S.] 43 Je 32.25N 87.01W
Selma [Ca.-U.S.] 46 Fh 36.34N 119.37W
Selmer 44 Ch 35.11N 88.36W
Selmęt Wielki, Jezioro- 10 Sc 53.50N 22.30 E
Šelon 7 Hg 58.14N 30.50 E
Selong 26 Gh 8.39S 116.32 E
Selsey 12 Bd 50.44N 0.47W
Selsey Bill 9 Mk 50.43N 0.48W
Seltz 12 Kf 48.53N 8.06 E
Selu, Pulau- 26 Jh 7.32S 130.54 E
Selukwe 37 Dc 19.40S 30.00 E
Sélune 11 Ef 48.39N 1.26W
Selva 55 Ai 29.46S 62.03W
Selvagens, Ilhas- 30 Fe 30.05N 15.55W
Selvånå 24 Kd 37.25N 44.51 E
Selvas 52 Jf 5.00S 68.00W
Selway River 46 Hc 46.08N 115.36W
Selwyn, Détroit de- 63b Dc 16.04S 168.11 E
Selwyn Lake 42 He 60.00N 104.30W
Selwyn Mountains 38 Fc 63.10N 130.20W
Selwyn Range 57 Fg 21.35S 140.35 E
Selz 12 Ke 49.59N 8.02 E
Šemaha 16 Pi 40.39N 48.38 E
Semani 15 Ci 40.54N 19.26 E
Semara 31 Ff 26.44N 11.41W
Semarang 22 Nj 6.58S 110.25 E
Sematan 26 Ef 1.48N 109.46 E
Semau, Pulau- 26 Hi 10.13S 123.22 E
Sembakung 26 Gf 3.47N 117.30 E
Sembé 36 Bb 1.39N 14.36 E
Semberija 14 Nf 44.45N 19.10 E
Sembuan 26 Gg 0.19S 115.30 E
Semenicului, Munţii- 15 Fd 45.05N 22.05 E
Semenov 7 Kh 56.49N 44.29 E
Semenovka 16 Hc 52.11N 32.40 E
Semeru, Gunung- 21 Nj 7.58S 113.35 E
Semichi Islands 40a Db 52.42N 174.00 E
Semidi Islands 40 He 56.07N 156.44W
Semiluki 19 De 51.43N 39.02 E
Semily 10 Lf 50.36N 15.20 E
Seminoe Reservoir 46 Le 42.00N 106.50W
Seminole [Ok.-U.S.] 45 Hi 35.14N 96.14W
Seminole [Tx.-U.S.] 45 Ej 32.43N 102.39W
Seminole, Lake- 43 Ke 30.46N 84.50W
Semipalatinsk 22 Kd 50.28N 80.13 E
Semipalatinskaja Oblast [3] 19 If 48.30N 80.10 E
Semirara Islands 26 Hd 11.57N 121.27 E
Semīrom 24 Ng 31.22N 51.47 E
Semisopochnoi 40a Cb 52.00N 179.35 E
Semitau 26 Ff 0.33N 111.58 E
Semiun, Pulau- 26 Ef 4.31N 107.44 E
Semizbugy 19 He 50.12N 74.48 E
Semliki 30 Kh 1.14N 30.28 E
Semmering 14 Jc 47.38N 15.49 E
Semnām [3] 23 Hb 35.00N 53.30 E
Semnān 22 Hf 35.33N 53.24 E
Semnon 11 Eg 47.54N 1.45W
Semois 11 Ke 49.53N 4.45 E
Šemonaiha 19 Ie 50.39N 81.54 E
Semporna 26 Gf 4.28N 118.36 E
Semuda 26 Fg 2.51S 112.58 E
Semur-en-Auxois 11 Kg 47.29N 4.20 E
Sên 25 Kf 12.32N 104.28 E
Senador Mourão 55 Kc 17.51S 43.22W
Senador Pompeu 54 Ke 5.35S 39.22W
Senaja 26 Ge 6.45N 117.03 E
Sena Madureira 54 Ee 9.04S 68.40W
Senanga 36 Df 16.07S 23.16 E
Senarpont 12 De 49.53N 1.43 E
Senatobia 45 Li 34.39N 89.58W
Sendai [Jap.] 28 Ki 31.49N 130.18 E
Sendai [Jap.] 22 Qf 38.15N 140.53 E
Sendai-Gawa [Jap.] 29 Bf 31.51N 130.12 E
Sendai-Gawa [Jap.] 29 Dd 35.34N 134.11 E
Sendai-Wan 28 Pe 38.10N 141.15 E
Senden 12 Jc 51.51N 7.30 E
Sendenhorst 12 Jc 51.50N 7.50 E
Senderg 24 Qi 26.52N 57.37 E
Seneca 45 Hg 39.50N 96.04W
Seneca Lake 44 Id 42.40N 76.57W
Sénégal=Senegal (EN) 30 Fg 15.48N 16.32W
Sénégal=Senegal (EN) [1] 31 Fg 14.00N 14.00W
Senegal (EN)=Sénégal [1] 31 Fg 14.00N 14.00W
Senegal (EN)=Sénégal 30 Fg 15.48N 16.32W
Sénégal Oriental [3] 34 Cc 13.30N 13.00W
Senekal 37 De 28.30S 27.32 E
Senetosa, Punta di- 11a Ab 41.33N 8.47 E
Seney 44 Eb 46.21N 85.56W
Senftenberg/Zły Komorow 10 Ke 51.31N 14.01 E
Sengata 22 Ni 0.28N 117.33 E
Sengilej 7 Lj 53.58N 48.46 E
Senguerr, Río- 56 Gg 45.32S 68.54W
Sengwa 37 Dc 17.05S 28.03 E
Senhor do Bonfim 53 Lg 10.27S 40.11W
Senica 10 Nh 48.41N 17.23 E
Senigallia 14 Hg 43.43N 13.13 E
Senirkent 24 Dc 38.07N 30.33 E
Senj 14 If 45.00N 14.54 E
Senja 5 Hb 69.20N 17.30 E
Senjsko Bilo 14 Jf 44.55N 15.03 E
Senkaku-Shotō 27 Lf 25.45N 124.00 E
Şenkaya 24 Jb 40.35N 42.21 E
Senkevičevka 10 Vf 50.29N 25.05 E
Šenkursk 19 Ec 62.08N 42.53 E
Senlin Shan 28 Kc 43.12N 130.38 E
Senlis 11 Ie 49.12N 2.35 E
Senmonorom 25 Lf 12.27N 107.12 E
Senn, Dahr Ou- 32 Ef 17.55N 11.00W
Sennestadt, Bielefeld- 12 Kc 51.57N 8.35 E
Senneterre 42 Jg 48.24N 77.14W
Senno 7 Gi 54.47N 29.41 E
Sennoj 16 Oc 52.07N 46.59 E
Senorbì 14 Dk 39.32N 9.08 E
Senqu 37 Be 28.38S 16.27 E
Sens 11 Jf 48.12N 3.17 E
Sensée 12 Fd 50.16N 3.06 E
Sensuntepeque 49 Cg 13.52N 88.38W
Senta 15 Dd 45.56N 20.05 E
Sentinel Peak 42 Ff 54.58N 122.00W
Sentinel Range 66 Pf 78.10S 85.30W
Senyavin Islands 57 Gd 6.55N 158.00 E
Şenyurt 24 Id 37.06N 40.40 E
Senzaki-Wan 29 Bd 34.25N 131.20 E
Senžarka 17 Mi 54.45N 67.50 E
Seo de Urgel/La Seu d'Urgell 13 Nb 42.21N 1.28 E
Seoni 25 Fd 22.05N 79.32 E
Seoul (EN)=Sŏul 22 Of 37.34N 127.00 E
Séoune 11 Gj 44.10N 0.41 E
Sepanjang, Pulau- 26 Gh 7.10S 115.50 E
Separation Point 62 Ed 40.47S 173.00 E
Sepetovka 19 Ce 50.12N 27.04 E
Sepik River 57 Fe 3.51S 144.34 E
Sępólno Krajeńskie 10 Nc 53.28N 17.32 E
Sępopol 10 Qb 54.15N 21.00 E
Sępopolska, Nizina- 10 Rb 54.15N 21.10 E
Septemvri 15 Hg 42.13N 24.06 E
Septentrional, Cordillera- 49 Ld 19.35N 70.45W
Septeuil 12 Df 48.54N 1.41 E
Sept-Iles 39 Md 50.12N 66.23W
Sepúlveda 13 Ic 41.18N 3.45W
Sequeros 13 Fd 40.31N 6.01W
Sequillo 13 Gc 41.45N 5.30W
Sera 29 Cd 34.36N 133.01 E
Sera, Pulau- 26 Jh 7.40S 131.05 E
Šerabad 19 Gh 37.43N 66.59 E
Šerabad 18 Ff 37.22N 67.03 E
Serafettın Dağları 24 Ic 39.05N 41.10 E
Serafimovič 16 Me 49.36N 42.47 E
Serahs 19 Gh 36.30N 61.13 E
Seraidi 14 Bn 36.55N 7.40 E
Seraing 11 Ld 50.36N 5.31 E
Seram 57 De 3.00S 129.00 E
Seram, Laut-=Ceram Sea (EN) 57 De 2.30S 128.00 E
Serang 26 Eh 6.07S 106.09 E
Serasan, Pulau- 26 Ef 2.30N 109.03 E
Serasan, Selat- 26 Ef 2.20S 109.00 E
Serbia (EN) = Srbija [2] 15 Df 44.00N 21.00 E
Serbia (EN) = Srbija 5 Ig 43.00N 21.00 E
Serbia (EN)=Srbija 15 Df 44.00N 21.00 E
Şercaia 15 Id 45.50N 25.08 E
Serchio 14 Eg 43.47N 10.16 E
Serdo 35 Gc 11.58N 41.18 E
Serdoba 16 Nc 52.34N 44.01 E
Serdobsk 19 Ee 52.29N 44.16 E
Sereba 35 Gc 13.12N 40.32 E
Serebrjansk 19 If 49.43N 83.20 E
Serebrjanski 7 Ib 68.52N 35.32 E
Sered' 10 Nh 48.17N 17.45 E
Seredka 8 Mf 58.10N 28.25 E
Şereflikoçhisar 24 Ec 38.56N 33.33 E
Serein 11 Jg 47.55N 3.31 E
Seremban 26 Df 2.43N 101.56 E
Serengeti Plain 36 Fc 2.50S 35.00 E
Serenje 36 Fe 13.14S 30.14 E
Šereševo 10 Ud 52.31N 24.19 E
Seret 16 De 48.38N 25.52 E
Serfopoúla 15 Hl 37.15N 24.36 E
Sergač 19 Ed 55.33N 45.28 E
Sergeievka 28 Lc 43.23N 133.22 E
Sergeja Kirova, Ostrova- 20 Da 77.10N 90.00 E
Sergejevka [Kaz.-U.S.S.R.] 19 Ge 53.51N 67.28 E
Sergejevka [R.S.F.S.R.] 28 Kb 44.20N 131.40 E
Sergino 22 Ic 62.30N 65.40 E
Sergipe [2] 54 Kf 10.30S 37.10W
Sergokala 16 Oh 42.30N 47.40 E
Sergozero, Ozero- 7 Ic 66.45N 36.50 E
Seria 26 Ff 4.37N 114.19 E
Serian 26 Ff 1.10N 110.34 E
Seriana, Val- 14 De 45.50N 9.50 E
Seribu, Kepulauan- 26 Fh 5.36S 106.33 E
Sérifontaine 12 De 49.21N 1.46 E
Sérifos 15 Hl 37.09N 24.30 E
Sérifos 15 Hl 37.10N 24.30 E
Serifou, Stenón- 15 Hl 37.15N 24.30 E
Serik 24 Dd 36.55N 31.06 E
Seringapatam Reef 59 Eb 13.40S 122.05 E
Serio 14 De 45.16N 9.45 E
Šerlovaja Gora 20 Gf 50.34N 116.18 E
Sermata, Kepulauan- 26 Ih 8.10S 128.40 E
Sermilik 41 Ie 66.00N 38.45W
Sernovodsk 7 Mj 53.54N 51.09 E
Sernur 7 Lh 56.57N 49.11 E
Sernyje Vody 7 Mj 53.53N 50.59 E
Sero 24 Kd 37.33N 44.40 E
Serock 10 Rd 52.31N 21.03 E
Serodino 55 Bk 32.37S 60.57W
Serov 22 Id 59.29N 60.31 E
Serowe 31 Jk 22.23S 26.43 E
Serpa 13 Eg 37.56N 7.36W
Serpent, Vallée du- 34 Dc 14.50N 8.00W
Serpentine Lakes 59 Fe 28.30S 129.10 E
Serpent's Mouth/Serpiente, Boca de la- 54 Fa 10.10N 61.58W
Serpiente, Boca de la-/ Serpent's Mouth 54 Fa 10.10N 61.58W
Serpis 13 Lf 38.59N 0.09W
Serpnevoje 15 Lc 46.23N 28.59 E
Serpuhov 6 Je 54.55N 37.25 E
Serra, Aparados da- 55 Hi 28.45S 49.45W
Serra Bonita 55 Ib 15.13S 46.49W
Serra das Araras 55 Jb 15.30S 45.21W
Serra do Navio 53 Ke 0.59N 52.03W
Serra do Salitre 55 Id 19.06S 46.41W
Serra Dourada 55 Ka 12.50S 43.56W
Sérrai 15 Gh 41.05N 23.33 E
Serralada Litoral Catalana/ Cadena Costero Catalana= Catalan Coastal Range (EN) 5 Gg 41.35N 1.40 E
Serralada Pirinenca= Pyrenees (EN) 5 Gg 42.40N 1.00 E
Serrana Bank 47 Hf 14.23N 80.12W
Serranilla Bank 47 Ie 15.50N 79.50W
Serranópolis 55 Fd 18.16S 52.00W
Serra San Bruno 14 Kl 38.35N 16.20 E
Serrat, Cap- 32 Ib 37.14N 9.13 E
Serra Talhada 54 Ke 7.59S 38.18W
Serre 11 Je 49.41N 3.23 E
Serre, Massif de la- 11 Lg 47.10N 5.35 E
Serre-Ponçon, Réservoir de- 11 Mj 44.27N 6.16 E
Serres 11 Lj 44.26N 5.43 E
Serrezuela 56 Gd 30.38S 65.23W
Serrinha 54 Kf 11.39S 39.00W
Serriola, Bocca- 14 Gg 43.31N 12.21 E
Serro 55 Kd 18.37S 43.23W
Serrota 13 Gd 40.30N 5.04W
Serrote, Rio- 55 Ee 21.27S 54.40W

Index Symbols

[1] Independent Nation
[2] State, Region
[3] District, County
[4] Municipality
[5] Colony, Dependency
Continent
Physical Region
Historical or Cultural Region
Mount, Mountain
Volcano
Hill
Mountains, Mountain Range
Hills, Escarpment
Plateau, Upland
Pass, Gap
Plain, Lowland
Delta
Salt Flat
Valley, Canyon
Crater, Cave
Karst Features
Depression
Polder
Desert, Dunes
Forest, Woods
Heath, Steppe
Oasis
Cape, Point
Coast, Beach
Cliff
Peninsula
Isthmus
Sandbank
Island
Atoll
Rock, Reef
Islands, Archipelago
Rocks, Reefs
Coral Reef
Well, Spring
Geyser
River, Stream
Waterfall Rapids
River Mouth, Estuary
Lake
Salt Lake
Intermittent Lake
Reservoir
Swamp, Pond
Canal
Glacier
Ice Shelf, Pack Ice
Ocean
Sea
Gulf, Bay
Strait, Fjord
Lagoon
Bank
Seamount
Tablemount
Ridge
Shelf
Basin
Escarpment, Sea Scarp
Fracture
Trench, Abyss
National Park, Reserve
Point of Interest
Recreation Site
Cave, Cavern
Historic Site
Ruins
Wall, Walls
Church, Abbey
Temple
Scientific Station
Airport
Port
Lighthouse
Mine
Tunnel
Dam, Bridge

Sersou, Plateau du- 13 Ni 35.30N 2.00 E
Sertã 13 De 39.48N 8.06W
Sertão 52 Lg 10.00S 41.00W
Sertãozinho 55 Ie 21.08S 47.59W
Sêrtar 27 He 32.20N 100.20 E
Serti 34 Hd 7.30N 11.22 E
Serua, Pulau- 26 Jh 6.18S 130.01 E
Serui 26 Kg 1.53S 136.14 E
Serule 37 Dd 21.55S 27.19 E
Sérvia 15 Ei 40.11N 22.00 E
Sêrxü 27 Ge 32.56N 98.02 E
Seryitsi 15 Ii 40.00N 25.10 E
Seryševo 20 Hf 51.02N 128.25 E
Sesayap 26 Gf 3.36N 117.15 E
Sese 36 Eb 2.11N 25.47 E
Seseganaga Lake 45 Ka 50.10N 90.15W
Sese Islands 36 Fc 0.20S 32.20 E
Sesfontein 37 Ac 19.07S 13.39 E
Sesheke 36 Df 17.29S 24.18 E
Sesia 14 Ce 45.05N 8.37 E
Sesibi 35 Ea 20.05N 30.31 E
Sesimbra 13 Cf 38.26N 9.06W
Šešma 7 Mi 55.20N 51.12 E
Sesnut 8 Be 59.42N 7.21 E
Sessa Aurunca 14 Hi 41.14N 13.56 E
Ses Salines, Cap de-/Salinas, Cabo de- 13 Pe 39.16N 3.03 E
Sestao 13 Ja 43.18N 3.00W
Sesto Fiorentino 14 Fg 43.50N 11.12 E
Sesto San Giovanni 14 De 45.32N 9.14 E
Sestriere 14 Af 44.57N 6.53 E
Sestri Levante 14 Df 44.16N 9.24 E
Sestroreck 7 Gf 60.06N 29.59 E
Šešupė 7 Fi 55.00N 22.10 E
Šešuvis 8 Ji 55.12N 22.31 E
Sesvenna, Piz- 14 Ed 46.42N 10.25 E
Sesvete 14 Ke 45.50N 16.07 E
Šeta/Šėta 8 Ki 55.14N 24.18 E
Šėta/Šeta 8 Ki 55.14N 24.18 E
Setaka 29 Be 33.09N 130.28 E
Setana 28 Oc 42.26N 139.51 E
Sète 11 Jk 43.24N 3.41 E
Sete de Setembro, Rio- 55 Fa 12.56S 52.51W
Sete Lagoas 54 Jg 19.27S 44.14W
Setenil 13 Gh 36.51N 5.11W
Sete Quedas, Saltos das-=Guaira Falls (EN) 56 Jb 24.02S 54.16W
Setermoen 7 Eb 68.52N 18.28 E
Setesdal 7 Bg 59.05N 7.35 E
Setesdalsheiane 8 Be 59.30N 7.10 E
Seti 25 Gc 28.58N 81.06 E
Sétif [3] 32 Ib 36.05N 5.00 E
Sétif 31 He 36.12N 5.24 E
Seto 29 Ed 35.13N 137.05 E
Setonaikai=Inland Sea (EN) 21 Pf 34.10N 133.00 E
Setouchi 29b Ba 28.08N 129.20 E
Šetpe 19 Fg 44.06N 52.02 E
Settat 32 Fc 33.00N 7.37W
Settat [3] 32 Fc 33.00N 7.30W
Setté Cama 36 Ac 2.32S 9.45 E
Sette-Daban, Hrebet- 20 Id 62.00N 138.00 E
Settle 9 Kg 54.04N 2.16W
Setúbal [2] 13 Df 38.20N 8.30W
Setúbal 6 Fh 38.32N 8.54W
Setúbal, Baía de- 13 Df 38.27N 8.53W
Setúbal o de Guadalupe, Laguna- 55 Bj 31.33S 60.35W
Seudre 11 Ei 45.48N 1.09W
Seugne 11 Fi 45.42N 0.32W
Seui 14 Dk 39.50N 9.19 E
Seuil-d'Argonne 12 Hf 48.58N 5.03 E
Seul, Lac- 38 Jd 50.20N 92.30W
Seulles 12 Be 49.20N 0.27W
Seurre 11 Lg 47.00N 5.09 E
Sevan 19 Eg 40.32N 44.57 E
Sevan, Lake- (EN)=Sevan, Ozero- 5 Kg 40.20N 45.20 E
Sevan, Ozero-=Sevan, Lake- (EN) 5 Kg 40.20N 45.20 E
Sévaré 34 Ec 14.32N 4.06W
Sevastopol 6 Jg 44.36N 33.32 E
Ševčenko 22 He 43.35N 51.05 E
Ševčenko, Zaliv- 16 Ca 46.30N 60.15 E
Sevenoaks 9 Nj 51.16N 0.12 E
Sever 13 Ee 39.40N 7.32W
Sévérac-le-Château 11 Jj 44.19N 3.04 E
Severn 9 Kj 51.20N 3.10W
Severn [Can.] 38 Kd 56.02N 87.36W
Severn [U.K.] 9 Kj 51.35N 2.40W
Severnaja Dvina=Northern Dvina (EN) 5 Kc 64.32N 40.30 E
Severnaja Keltma 17 Ff 61.30N 54.00 E
Severnaja Pseašho, Gora- 16 Lh 43.47N 40.30 E
Severnaja Sosva 19 Gc 64.10N 65.28 E
Severnaja Zemlja=Severnaya Zemlya (EN) 21 Lb 79.30N 98.00 E
Severnaya Zemlya (EN)=Severnaja Zemlja 21 Lb 79.30N 98.00 E
Severn Lake 42 If 53.52N 90.58W
Severnoje [R.S.F.S.R.] 16 Rb 54.05N 52.32 E
Severnoje [R.S.F.S.R.] 20 Ce 56.21N 78.23 E
Severny 19 Gb 67.38N 64.06 E
Severnyje Uvaly=Northern Uvals (EN) 5 Kd 59.30N 49.00 E
Severny Kommunar 17 Gg 58.23N 54.02 E
Severny Ledovity Okean=Arctic Ocean (EN) 67 Be 85.00N 170.00 E
Severny Ural=Northern Urals (EN) 5 Lc 62.00N 59.00 E
Severobajkalsk 20 Fe 55.40N 109.25 E
Severočeský kraj [3] 10 Kf 50.35N 14.15 E
Severodoneck 16 Ke 48.57N 38.31 E
Severodvinsk 6 Jc 64.34N 39.50 E
Severo-Jenisejski 20 Ed 60.28N 93.01 E
Severo-Kazahstanskaja Oblast [3] 19 Ge 54.30N 68.00 E
Severo-Krymski Kanal 16 Ig 45.30N 34.35 E
Severo-Kurilsk 22 Rd 50.40N 156.08 E
Severomoravský kraj [3] 10 Ng 49.45N 17.50 E
Severomorsk 19 Db 69.04N 33.24 E
Severo-Osetinskaja ASSR [3] 19 Eg 43.00N 44.10 E
Severo-Sibirskaja Nizmennost=North Siberian Plain (EN) 21 Mb 72.00N 104.00 E
Severouralsk 19 Gc 60.09N 60.01 E
Sevier 46 Ig 38.35N 112.14W
Sevier Bridge Reservoir 46 Jg 39.21N 111.57W
Sevier Desert 46 Ig 39.25N 112.50W
Sevier Lake 43 Ed 38.55N 113.09W
Sevier River 43 Ed 39.04N 113.06W
Sevilla [3] 13 Gg 37.30N 5.30W
Sevilla [Col.] 54 Cc 4.16N 75.53W
Sevilla [Sp.]=Seville (EN) 6 Fh 37.23N 5.59W
Sevilla, Isla- 49 Fi 8.14N 82.24W
Seville (EN)=Sevilla [Sp.] 6 Fh 37.23N 5.59W
Sevlijevo 15 If 43.01N 25.06 E
Sèvre Nantaise 11 Eg 47.12N 1.33W
Sèvre Niortaise 11 Eh 46.18N 1.08W
Sevron 11 Lh 46.32N 5.16 E
Sevsk 16 Ic 52.08N 34.30 E
Sewa 34 Cd 7.18N 12.08W
Seward [Ak.-U.S.] 39 Ec 60.06N 149.26W
Seward [Nb.-U.S.] 45 Hf 40.55N 97.06W
Seward Peninsula 38 Cc 65.00N 164.00W
Sewell 56 Fd 34.05S 70.21W
Seyāhkal 24 Md 37.09N 49.52 E
Seybaplaya 48 Nh 19.39N 90.40W
Seybaplaya, Punta- 48 Nh 19.45N 90.42W
Seybouse, Oued- 14 Bn 36.53N 7.46 E
Seychelles [1] 31 Mi 8.00S 55.00 E
Seychelles Islands 30 Mi 4.35S 55.40 E
Seydān 24 Og 30.01N 53.01 E
Seydişehir 24 Dd 37.25N 31.51 E
Seyðisfjörður 6 Eb 65.16N 14.00W
Seyfe Gölü 24 Fc 39.13N 34.23 E
Seyf Tāleh 24 Le 35.57N 46.19 E
Seyhan 23 Db 36.43N 34.53 E
Seyitgazi 24 Dc 39.27N 30.43 E
Seyitömer 15 Mj 39.34N 29.52 E
Seyla' 35 Gc 11.21N 43.30 E
Seymour [Austl.] 59 Jg 37.02S 145.08 E
Seymour [In.-U.S.] 44 Ef 38.58N 85.53W
Seymour [Mo.-U.S.] 45 Jh 37.09N 92.46W
Seymour [S.Afr.] 37 Df 32.33S 26.46 E
Seymour [Tx.-U.S.] 43 He 33.35N 99.16W
Sezana 14 He 45.42N 13.52 E
Sézanne 11 Jf 48.43N 3.43 E
Sfaktiria 15 Em 36.56N 21.40 E
Sfax (EN)=Şafāqis [3] 32 Jc 34.30N 10.30 E
Sfax (EN)=Şafāqis 31 Ie 34.44N 10.46 E
Sferracavallo, Capo- 14 Dk 39.43N 9.40 E
Sfintu Gheorghe [Rom.] 15 Me 44.53N 29.26 E
Sfintu Gheorghe [Rom.] 15 Id 45.52N 25.47 E
Sfintu Gheorghe, Braţul- 15 Me 44.53N 29.36 E
Sfintu Gheorghe, Ostrovul- 15 Md 45.07N 29.22 E
Sfizef 13 Li 35.14N 0.15W
's-Gravenhage/Den Haag=The Hague (EN) 6 Ge 52.06N 4.18 E
's-Gravenhage-Scheveningen 11 Kb 52.06N 4.18 E
Shaan-hsi Sheng→Shaanxi Sheng=Shensi (EN) [2] 27 Id 36.00N 109.00 E
Shaanxi Sheng (Shaan-hsi Sheng)=Shensi (EN) [2] 27 Id 36.00N 109.00 E
Shaba [2] 36 Ed 8.30S 25.00 E
Sha'bah, Wādī ash- 24 Ij 25.59N 41.55 E
Shabani 37 Ed 20.19S 30.04 E
Shabeellaha Dhexe [3] 35 He 3.00N 46.00 E
Shabellaha Hoose [3] 35 Ge 2.00N 44.40 E
Shabēlle, Webi-=Shebeli Webi (EN) 30 Lh 0.12S 42.45 E
Shabestar 24 Kc 38.11N 45.42 E
Shabunda 36 Ec 2.42S 27.20 E
Shache/Yarkant 27 Cd 38.24N 77.15 E
Shacheng → Huailai 27 Kc 40.29N 115.30 E
Shackleton Coast 66 Kg 82.00S 162.00 E
Shackleton Glacier 66 Lg 84.35S 176.15W
Shackleton Ice Shelf 66 He 66.00S 101.00 E
Shackleton Range 66 Ag 80.40S 26.00W
Shaddādī 24 Id 36.02N 40.45 E
Shādegān 24 Mg 30.40N 48.38 E
Shadwān, Jazīrat- 33 Fd 27.30N 33.55 E
Shaftesbury 9 Kk 51.01N 2.12W
Shagedu→Jungar Qi 27 Jd 39.37N 110.58 E
Shāghir Bazar 24 Id 36.52N 40.53 E
Shag Rocks 66 Rd 54.26S 36.33W
Shāh 'Abbās 24 Oe 34.44N 52.10 E
Shah Alam 26 Df 3.05N 101.29 E
Shahdol 25 Gd 23.13N 81.18 E
Sha He [China] 28 Ch 33.39N 114.38 E
Sha He [China] 28 Cf 37.09N 114.46 E
Shahezhen → Linze 27 Hd 39.10N 100.21 E
Shah Jahān, Kūh-e- 24 Qd 37.02N 57.54 E
Shahjahānpur 25 Fc 27.53N 79.55 E
Shah Kūh 23 Hb 36.35N 54.31 E
Shahmīrzād 24 Oe 35.47N 53.20 E
Shāhpūr 24 Nh 32.50N 51.45 E
Shāhpūr 24 Nh 29.39N 51.03 E
Shahrak 24 Nd 36.14N 50.40 E
Shahr-e-Bābak 24 Pg 30.10N 55.09 E
Shahr-e Khafr 24 Oh 28.56N 53.14 E
Shahr Kord 23 Hc 32.19N 50.50 E
Shāhrūd 24 Md 37.17N 48.43 E
Shahu, Kūh-e- 24 Le 34.45N 46.30 E
Shāh Zeyd 24 Od 36.13N 52.22 E
Shā'ib al Banāt, Jabal- 30 Kf 26.59N 33.29 E
Sha'īt, Wādī- 24 Ej 24.33N 33.01 E
Shakaga-Dake 29 Be 33.11N 130.53 E
Shakawe 31 Ji 18.23S 21.51 E
Shak Bay (Denham) 59 Ce 25.55S 113.32 E
Shaker Heights 44 Ge 41.29N 81.36W
Shaki 34 Fd 8.40N 3.23 E
Shakotan-Dake 29a Bb 43.16N 140.26 E
Shakotan-Hantō 29a Bb 43.15N 140.35 E
Shakotan-Misaki 29a Bb 43.23N 140.28 E
Shaktoolik 40 Gd 64.20N 161.09W
Shāl 24 Me 35.54N 49.46 E
Shala, Lake- 35 Fd 7.29N 38.32 E
Shalamzār 24 Nf 32.02N 50.49 E
Shalānbōd 35 Ge 1.40N 44.42 E
Shaler Mountains 42 Gb 71.45N 111.00W
Shaliuhe → Gangca 27 Hd 37.30N 100.14 E
Shaluli Shan 21 Lf 30.45N 99.45 E
Shām, Bādiyat ash-=Syrian Desert (EN) 21 Ff 32.00N 40.00 E
Shām, Jabal ash- 21 Hg 23.10N 57.20 E
Shamattawa 42 Ie 55.52N 92.05W
Shambe 35 Ed 7.07N 30.46 E
Shambu 35 Fd 9.33N 37.07 E
Shamīl 24 Qi 27.30N 56.53 E
Shāmīyah 21 Ff 34.00N 39.59 E
Shammar, Jabal- 21 Gg 27.20N 41.45 E
Shamo, Lake- 35 Fd 5.50N 37.40 E
Shamokin 44 Ie 40.47N 76.34W
Shamrock 45 Fi 35.13N 100.15W
Shams 24 Pg 31.04N 55.02 E
Shamsī 35 Db 19.03N 29.54 E
Shamwa 37 Ec 17.18S 31.34 E
Shan [2] 25 Jd 22.00N 98.00 E
Shandī 31 Kg 16.42N 33.26 E
Shandian He 28 Dc 42.20N 116.20 E
Shandong Bandao=Shantung Peninsula (EN) 21 Of 37.00N 121.00 E
Shandong Sheng (Shan-tung Sheng)=Shantung (EN) [2] 27 Kd 36.00N 119.00 E
Shandūr Pass 25 Ea 36.04N 72.31 E
Shangani 37 Dc 19.42S 29.22 E
Shangani 37 Dc 18.30S 27.11 E
Shangbahe 28 Ci 30.39N 115.06 E
Shangcai 28 Ch 33.16N 114.15 E
Shangcheng 28 Ci 31.49N 115.24 E
Shangdu 28 Bc 41.33N 113.32 E
Shanggao 28 Cj 28.15N 114.55 E
Shanghai 22 Of 31.14N 121.28 E
Shanghai Shi (Shang-hai Shih) [4] 27 Le 31.14N 121.28 E
Shang-hai Shih→Shanghai Shi [4] 27 Le 31.14N 121.28 E
Shanghang 27 Kf 25.04N 116.21 E
Shanghe 28 Df 37.19N 117.09 E
Shanghekou 27 Lc 40.26N 124.51 E
Shangpaihe → Feixi 28 Di 31.42N 117.09 E
Shangqiu (Zhuji) 27 Ke 34.24N 115.37 E
Shangrao 27 Kf 28.29N 117.59 E
Shan Guan 27 Kf 27.28N 117.05 E
Shangxian 27 Ie 33.55N 109.57 E
Shangyi (Nanhaoqian) 28 Bd 41.06N 113.58 E
Shangyu (Baiguan) 28 Fi 30.01N 120.53 E
Shangzhi 27 Mb 45.13N 127.55 E
Shanhaiguan 28 Ed 40.01N 119.45 E
Shanhetun 28 Ib 44.43N 127.14 E
Shan-hsi Sheng→Shanxi Sheng=Shansi (EN) [2] 27 Jd 37.00N 112.00 E
Shanklin 12 Ad 50.37N 1.11W
Shanmatang Ding 27 Jg 24.45N 111.50 E
Shannon 41 Kc 75.20N 18.10W
Shannon 62 Fd 40.33S 175.25 E
Shannon/Aerfort na Sionainne 9 Ei 52.42N 8.57W
Shannon/An tSionainn 5 Fe 52.36N 9.41W
Shannon, Mount- 59 Ie 29.58S 141.30 E
Shannon, Mouth of the- 9 Di 52.30N 9.53W
Shanshan (Piqan) 27 Fc 42.52N 90.10 E
Shansi (EN)=Shan-hsi Sheng→Shanxi Sheng [2] 27 Jd 37.00N 112.00 E
Shansi (EN)=Shanxi Sheng (Shan-hsi Sheng) [2] 27 Jd 37.00N 112.00 E
Shansonggang 28 Ic 42.30N 126.13 E
Shanṭah, Ra's- 24 Qi 26.22N 56.26 E
Shantar Islands (EN)=Šantarskije Ostrova 21 Pd 55.00N 137.36 E
Shantou 22 Ng 23.26N 116.42 E
Shantung (EN)=Shandong Sheng (Shan-tung Sheng) [2] 27 Kd 36.00N 119.00 E
Shantung (EN)=Shan-tung Sheng→Shandong Sheng [2] 27 Kd 36.00N 119.00 E
Shantung Peninsula (EN)=Shandong Bandao 21 Of 37.00N 121.00 E
Shan-tung Sheng→Shandong Sheng=Shantung (EN) [2] 27 Kd 36.00N 119.00 E
Shanxian 28 Dg 34.47N 116.05 E
Shanxi Sheng (Shan-hsi Sheng)=Shansi (EN) [2] 27 Jd 37.00N 112.00 E
Shanyin (Daiyue) 28 Be 39.30N 112.48 E
Shanyincheng 28 Be 39.27N 112.56 E
Shaoguan 22 Ng 24.57N 113.34 E
Shaoshan 27 Jf 27.55N 112.32 E
Shaowu 27 Kf 27.21N 117.29 E
Shaoxing 22 Og 30.00N 120.30 E
Shaoyang 22 Ng 27.13N 111.31 E
Shapinsay 9 Kb 59.03N 2.51W
Shaqlāwah 24 Kd 36.23N 44.18 E
Shaqq al Ju'ayfir 35 Db 15.16N 26.00 E
Shaqrā' 23 Gg 13.21N 45.42 E
Shaqū 24 Qi 27.14N 56.32 E
Sharāf 24 Jg 30.37N 43.45 E
Sharafah 35 Dc 12.04N 27.07 E
Sharafkhāneh 24 Kc 38.11N 45.29 E
Sharāh, Jibāl ash- 24 Fg 30.10N 35.30 E
Sharā 'Iwah 24 Oj 25.02N 52.14 E
Shareh 24 Kd 37.38N 44.50 E
Shari 27 Pc 43.55N 144.40 E
Sharī, Buḥayrat- 24 Ke 34.23N 44.07 E
Shari-Dake 29a Db 43.46N 144.43 E
Sharifābād [Iran] 24 Nd 36.12N 50.08 E
Sharifābād [Iran] 24 Ne 35.25N 51.47 E
Shark Bay 57 Cg 25.30S 113.30 E
Sharm ash Shaykh 33 Fd 27.50N 34.16 E
Sharon 44 Ge 41.16N 80.30W
Sharon Springs 45 Fg 38.54N 101.45W
Sharp 9 Fc 58.05N 7.05W
Sharqīyah, Aş Şaḥrā' ash-=Arabian Desert (EN) 30 Kf 28.00N 32.00 E
Sharshar, Jabal- 24 Dk 23.52N 30.20 E
Shary 23 Fd 27.15N 43.27 E
Shashe 37 Dd 21.24S 27.27 E
Shashemene 35 Fd 7.13N 38.36 E
Shashi 22 Nf 30.22N 112.11 E
Shashi 30 Jk 22.12S 29.21 E
Shasta, Mount- 38 Ge 41.20N 122.20W
Shasta Lake 43 Cc 40.50N 122.25W
Shāţī', Wādī ash- 33 Bd 27.10N 13.25 E
Shattuck 45 Gh 36.16N 99.53W
Shaunavon 42 Gg 49.40N 108.25W
Shawan 27 Ec 44.21N 85.37 E
Shawano 45 Ld 44.47N 88.36W
Shawinigan 42 Kg 46.33N 72.45W
Shawnee 43 Hd 35.20N 96.55W
Shawneetown 45 Lh 37.42N 88.08W
Shaw River 59 Dd 20.20S 119.17 E
Shāwshāw, Jabal- 24 Ci 26.03N 28.56 E
Shayang 28 Bi 30.42N 112.34 E
Shaybārā 24 Gj 25.25N 36.51 E
Shaykh Aḥmad 24 Lf 32.53N 46.26 E
Shaykh Fāris 24 Lf 32.05N 47.36 E
Shaykh Sa'd 24 Lf 32.34N 46.17 E
Shaykh 'Uthmān 23 Fg 12.52N 44.59 E
Shebar, Kowtal-e- 23 Kc 34.54N 68.14 E
Shebele, Wabe-=Shebeli Webi (EN) 30 Lh 0.12S 42.45 E
Shebeli Webi (EN)=Shabēlle, Webi- 30 Lh 0.12S 42.45 E
Shebeli Webi (EN)=Shebele, Wabe- 30 Lh 0.12S 42.45 E
Sheberghān 22 If 36.41N 65.45 E
Sheboygan 45 Me 43.46N 87.44W
Shebshi Mountains 30 Ih 8.30N 11.45 E
Shedin Peak 42 Ee 55.50N 127.00W
Sheelin, Lough-/Loch Síleann 9 Fh 53.48N 7.20W
Sheenjek 40 Kc 66.45N 144.33W
Sheep Haven/Cuan na gCaorach 9 Ff 55.10N 7.52W
Sheep Mountain 46 Hj 32.32N 114.14W
Sheep Range 46 Hh 36.45N 115.05W
s'Heerenberg, Bergh- 12 Ic 51.53N 6.16 E
Sheerness 9 Nj 51.27N 0.45 E
Sheffield [Al.-U.S.] 44 Dh 34.46N 87.40W
Sheffield [Eng.-U.K.] 6 Fe 53.23N 1.30W
Sheffield [Tx.-U.S.] 45 Fk 30.43N 101.50W
Shefford 12 Bb 52.02N 0.20W
Shek Hasan 35 Fc 12.04N 35.53 E
Shek Husen 35 Gd 7.45N 40.42 E
Shelburne [N.S.-Can.] 42 Kh 43.46N 65.19W
Shelburne [Ont.-Can.] 44 Gc 44.04N 80.12W
Shelby [Mt.-U.S.] 43 Eb 48.30N 111.51W
Shelby [N.C.-U.S.] 44 Gh 35.17N 81.32W
Shelbyville [Il.-U.S.] 45 Lg 39.24N 88.48W
Shelbyville [In.-U.S.] 44 Ef 39.31N 85.47W
Shelbyville [Tn.-U.S.] 44 Dh 35.29N 86.27W
Shelbyville, Lake- 45 Lg 39.30N 88.40W
Sheldon 45 Ie 43.11N 95.51W
Sheldon Point 40 Gd 63.32N 164.52W
Shelikhov Gulf (EN)=Šelihova, Zaliv- 21 Rc 60.00N 158.00 E
Shelikof Strait 40 Ie 57.30N 155.00W
Shell 46 Ld 44.33N 107.44W
Shellbrook 42 Gf 53.13N 106.24W
Shellharbour 58 Gh 34.35S 150.52 E
Shelter Point 62 Cg 47.06S 168.13 E
Shelton 46 Dc 47.13N 123.06W
Shenandoah 45 If 40.46N 95.22W
Shenandoah Mountain 44 Hf 38.58N 79.00W
Shenandoah Valley 44 Hf 38.45N 78.45W
Shenchi 28 Be 39.05N 112.11 E
Shendam 34 Gd 8.53N 9.32 E
Shending Shan 27 Nb 46.34N 133.27 E
Shenge 34 Cd 7.55N 12.57W
Shëngjini 15 Ch 41.49N 19.35 E
Shengsi (Caiyuanzhen) 28 Gi 30.42N 122.29 E
Shengsi Liedao 27 Le 30.45N 122.40 E
Shengxian 27 Lf 29.35N 120.45 E
Shengze 28 Fi 30.55N 120.39 E
Shenjiamen → Putuo 28 Gj 29.57N 122.18 E
Shenmu 27 Jd 38.52N 110.35 E
Shenqiu (Huaidian) 27 Ke 33.27N 115.05 E
Shensi (EN)=Shaan-hsi Sheng→Shaanxi Sheng [2] 27 Id 36.00N 109.00 E
Shensi (EN)=Shaanxi Sheng (Shaan-hsi Sheng) [2] 27 Id 36.00N 109.00 E
Shenton, Mount- 59 Ee 28.00S 123.22 E
Shenxian 28 Ce 38.01N 115.33 E
Shenyang (Mukden) 22 Oe 41.48N 123.24 E
Shenze 28 Ce 38.11N 115.11 E
Shepherd, Iles-=Shepherd Islands (EN) 63b Dc 16.55S 168.35 E
Shepherd Islands (EN)=Shepherd, Iles- 63b Dc 16.55S 168.35 E
Shepparton 58 Fh 36.23S 145.25 E
Sheppey 9 Nj 51.24N 0.50 E
Shepshed 12 Ab 52.45N 1.17W
Sheqi 28 Bh 33.04N 112.56 E
Sherard, Cape- 42 Jb 74.36N 80.10W
Sherard Osborn Fjord 41 Gb 82.10N 51.30W
Sherborne 9 Kk 50.57N 2.31W
Sherbro Island 30 Fh 7.33N 12.40W
Sherbrooke 39 Le 45.24N 71.54W
Sherda 35 Ba 20.08N 16.45 E
Shere Hill 34 Gd 9.57N 9.03 E
Sheridan [Mt.-U.S.] 46 Id 45.27N 112.12W
Sheridan [Wy.-U.S.] 39 Ie 44.48N 106.58W
Sheridan Lake 45 Eg 38.30N 102.15W
Sheringham 9 Oi 52.57N 1.12 E
Sherman 43 He 33.38N 96.36W
Sherman Station 44 Mc 45.54N 68.26W
Sherridon 42 He 55.07N 101.05W
's-Hertogenbosch/Den Bosch 11 Lc 51.41N 5.19 E
Sherwood Forest 9 Lh 53.10N 1.10W
She Shui 28 Ci 30.52N 114.22 E
Shetland [3] 9 La 60.30N 1.30W
Shetland Islands (Zetland) 5 Fc 60.30N 1.30W
Shewa [3] 35 Fd 9.20N 38.55 E
Shewa Gimira 35 Fd 7.00N 35.50 E
Shexian 28 Bf 36.33N 113.40 E
Shexian (Huicheng) 28 Ej 29.53N 118.27 E
Sheyang (Hede) 28 Fh 33.47N 120.15 E
Sheyenne River 43 Hb 47.05N 96.50W
Shiant Islands 9 Gd 57.54N 6.30W
Shibām 35 Hb 15.56N 48.38 E
Shibamīnah, Wādī- 23 Ie 22.12N 55.30 E
Shibata [Jap.] 28 Of 37.57N 139.20 E
Shibata [Jap.] 29 Gb 38.05N 140.50 E
Shibayama-Gata 29 Ec 36.21N 136.23 E
Shibazhan 27 Ma 42.28N 125.20 E
Shibecha 28 Rc 43.17N 144.36 E
Shibetsu [Jap.] 28 Rc 43.40N 145.08 E
Shibetsu [Jap.] 27 Pc 44.10N 142.23 E
Shibetsu-Gawa 29a Db 43.40N 145.06 E
Shibin al Kawm 33 Fc 30.33N 31.01 E
Shibiutan 29a Ca 44.47N 142.35 E
Shibi-Zan 29 Bf 31.59N 130.22 E
Shib Kūh 23 Hd 27.20N 52.40 E
Shibukawa 28 Of 36.29N 139.00 E
Shibushi 29 Bf 31.28N 131.07 E
Shibushi-Wan 28 Ki 31.25N 131.12 E
Shichinohe 29 Ga 40.41N 141.10 E
Shichiyo Islands 64d Bb 7.23N 151.40 E
Shidao 27 Ld 36.51N 122.18 E
Shido 29 Dd 34.19N 134.10 E
Shidongsi → Gaolan 27 Hd 36.23N 103.55 E
Shiel, Loch- 9 He 56.50N 5.50W
Shiga Ken [2] 28 Ng 35.10N 136.10 E
Shigu 27 Gf 26.54N 99.44 E
Shi He 28 Ch 32.32N 115.52 E
Shihezi 27 Ec 44.18N 86.02 E
Shiiba 29 Be 32.28N 131.09 E
Shijaku 15 Ch 41.20N 19.34 E
Shijiazhuang 22 Nf 38.00N 114.30 E
Shijiusuo 28 Eg 35.24N 119.32 E
Shika 29 Ec 37.01N 136.46 E
Shikabe 29a Bb 42.02N 140.47 E
Shikārpur 25 Dc 27.57N 68.38 E
Shiki Islands 64d Bb 7.24N 151.53 E
Shikine-Jima 29 Fd 34.19N 139.13 E
Shikoku 21 Pf 33.30N 133.30 E
Shikoku Basin (EN) 27 Oe 30.00N 135.30 E
Shikoku-Sanchi 29 Ce 33.45N 133.35 E
Shikotsu-Ko 28 Pc 42.48N 141.20 E
Shilabo 35 Gd 6.05N 44.45 E
Shiliu → Changjiang 27 Ih 19.20N 109.03 E
Shilla 25 Fb 32.24N 78.12 E
Shillong 22 Lg 25.34N 91.53 E
Shimabara 28 Kh 32.47N 130.22 E
Shimabara-Hantō 29 Be 32.45N 130.15 E
Shimabara-Wan 29 Be 32.50N 130.30 E
Shimada 29 Fd 34.49N 138.09 E
Shima-Hantō 29 Ed 34.25N 136.45 E
Shimane-Hantō 29 Cd 35.30N 133.00 E
Shimane Ken [2] 28 Lg 35.00N 132.20 E
Shimanto-Gawa 29 Ce 32.56N 133.00 E
Shimaura-Tō 29 Bd 34.50N 131.50 E
Shimian 27 Hf 29.10N 102.26 E
Shimizu [Jap.] 29a Cb 43.01N 142.51 E
Shimizu [Jap.] 28 Og 35.01N 138.29 E
Shimizu-Tōge 29 Fc 36.53N 138.55 E
Shimoda 28 Og 34.40N 138.57 E
Shimodate 29 Fc 36.19N 139.58 E
Shimoga 22 Jh 13.55N 75.34 E
Shimo-Jima 29 Be 32.25N 130.05 E
Shimokawa 29a Ca 44.18N 142.38 E
Shimokita-Hantō 29a Bc 41.15N 141.05 E
Shimo-Koshiki-Jima 29 Af 31.40N 129.40 E
Shimo la Tewa 36 Gc 3.57S 39.44 E
Shimoni 36 Gc 4.39S 39.23 E
Shimonoseki 27 Ne 33.57N 130.57 E
Shimono-Shima 27 Ad 34.15N 129.15 E
Shimotsu 29 Dd 34.07N 135.08 E
Shimotsuma 29 Fc 36.11N 139.58 E
Shin, Loch- 9 Ic 58.07N 4.32W
Shinano 29 Fc 36.47N 138.10 E
Shinano-Gawa 29 Fc 37.57N 139.04 E
Shināş 24 Qj 24.43N 56.27 E
Shindand 23 Jc 33.18N 62.08 E
Shinga 36 Dc 3.16S 24.38 E
Shingbwiyang 25 Jc 26.41N 96.13 E
Shingū 27 Oe 33.44N 135.59 E
Shingwidzi 37 Ed 23.01S 30.43 E
Shinji 29 Cd 35.24N 132.54 E
Shinji-Ko 28 Lg 35.27N 133.02 E
Shinjō 27 Pd 38.46N 140.18 E
Shinkafe 34 Gc 13.05N 6.31 E
Shinminato 29 Ec 36.47N 137.04 E
Shinnanyō 29 Bd 34.05N 131.45 E
Shinshiro 29 Ed 34.53N 137.30 E
Shintoku 28 Qc 43.12N 142.55 E
Shintotsugawa 29a Bb 43.32N 141.40 E
Shinyanga 31 Ki 3.40S 33.26 E
Shinyanga [3] 36 Fc 3.30S 33.00 E
Shiogama 29 Gb 38.19N 141.01 E
Shiojiri 28 Nf 36.06N 137.58 E
Shiokubi-Misaki 29a Bc 41.43N 140.57 E
Shio-no-Misaki 27 Oe 33.25N 135.45 E
Shipai → Huaining 28 Di 30.25N 116.39 E

Index Symbols

[1] Independent Nation
[2] State, Region
[3] District, County
[4] Municipality
[5] Colony, Dependency
Continent
Physical Region
Historical or Cultural Region
Mount, Mountain
Volcano
Hill
Mountains, Mountain Range
Hills, Escarpment
Plateau, Upland
Pass, Gap
Plain, Lowland
Delta
Salt Flat
Valley, Canyon
Crater, Cave
Karst Features
Depression
Polder
Desert, Dunes
Forest, Woods
Heath, Steppe
Oasis
Cape, Point
Coast, Beach
Cliff
Peninsula
Isthmus
Sandbank
Island
Atoll
Rock, Reef
Islands, Archipelago
Rocks, Reefs
Coral Reef
Well, Spring
Geyser
River, Stream
Waterfall Rapids
River Mouth, Estuary
Lake
Salt Lake
Intermittent Lake
Reservoir
Swamp, Pond
Canal
Glacier
Ice Shelf, Pack Ice
Ocean
Sea
Gulf, Bay
Strait, Fjord
Lagoon
Bank
Seamount
Tablemount
Ridge
Shelf
Basin
Escarpment, Sea Scarp
Fracture
Trench, Abyss
National Park, Reserve
Point of Interest
Recreation Site
Cave, Cavern
Historic Site
Ruins
Wall, Walls
Church, Abbey
Temple
Scientific Station
Airport
Port
Lighthouse
Mine
Tunnel
Dam, Bridge

Shiping 27 Hg 23.44N 102.28 E
Shipki La 27 Ce 31.49N 78.45 E
Shippegan 42 Lg 47.45N 64.42W
Shiprock 45 Bh 36.47N 108.41W
Shipshaw, Rivière- 44 La 48.30N 71.15W
Shipu 28 Fj 29.17N 121.57 E
Shipugi Shankou 27 Ce 31.49N 78.45 E
Shiquan 27 Ie 33.05N 108.15 E
Shiquanhe 22 Jf 32.24N 79.52 E
Shiquan He 27 Ce 32.28N 79.44 E
Shiragami Dake 29 Ga 40.30N 140.01 E
Shiragami-Misaki 28 Pd 41.25N 140.12 E
Shirahama 29 De 33.40N 135.20 E
Shirakawa [Jap.] 29 Ed 35.36N 137.12 E
Shirakawa [Jap.] 29 Ec 36.17N 136.53 E
Shirakawa [Jap.] 28 Pf 37.07N 140.13 E
Shirane-San [Jap.] 27 Od 36.48N 139.22 E
Shirane-San [Jap.] 29 Fd 35.40N 138.13 E
Shirane-San [Jap.] 29 Fc 36.38N 138.32 E
Shiranuka 28 Rc 42.57N 144.05 E
Shiraoi 28 Pc 42.31N 141.16 E
Shirase Coast 66 Mf 78.30S 156.00W
Shirataka 29 Gb 38.11N 140.06 E
Shirataki 29a Cb 43.53N 143.09 E
Shīrāz 22 Hg 29.36N 52.32 E
Shirbīn 24 Dg 31.11N 31.32 E
Shire 30 Kj 17.42S 35.19 E
Shiren 28 Id 41.54N 126.34 E
Shiretoko-Dake 29a Da 44.15N 145.14 E
Shiretoko-Hantō 29a Da 44.00N 145.00 E
Shiretoko-Misaki 27 Qc 44.21N 145.20 E
Shīrgāh 24 Od 36.17N 52.54 E
Shiribetsu-Gawa 29a Bb 42.52N 140.21 E
Shiriha-Misaki 29a Db 42.56N 144.45 E
Shirikishinai 29a Bc 41.48N 141.05 E
Shīrīn 24 Qi 27.10N 56.41 E
Shīrīn sū 24 Me 35.29N 48.27 E
Shiriya-Zaki 27 Pc 41.26N 141.28 E
Shīr Kūh 21 Hf 31.37N 54.04 E
Shirley Mountains 46 Le 42.15N 106.30W
Shiroishi 28 Pe 38.00N 140.37 E
Shirone 29 Fc 37.46N 139.00 E
Shirotori 29 Ed 35.53N 136.52 E
Shirouma-Dake 29 Ec 36.45N 137.46 E
Shirshov Ridge (EN) 20 Me 57.30N 171.00 E
Shīrvān 24 Lf 33.33N 46.49 E
Shirwan Mazīn 24 Kd 37.03N 44.10 E
Shishaldin Volcano 38 Cd 54.45N 163.57W
Shishi-Jima 29 Be 32.17N 130.15 E
Shishmaref 40 Fc 66.14N 166.09W
Shishou 27 Jf 29.42N 112.23 E
Shitai (Qili) 28 Di 30.12N 117.28 E
Shitara 29 Ed 35.05N 137.34 E
Shitou Shan 27 Ma 51.02N 125.12 E
Shivwits Plateau 46 Ih 36.10N 113.40W
Shiwa 28 Pe 39.33N 141.35 E
Shiwan Dashan 27 Ig 21.45N 107.35 E
Shiwa Ngandu 36 Fe 11.12S 31.43 E
Shiwpuri 25 Fc 25.26N 77.39 E
Shixian 28 Jc 43.05N 129.46 E
Shiyan 27 Je 32.34N 110.48 E
Shiyang He 27 Hd 39.00N 103.25 E
Shizilu → Junan 28 Eg 35.10N 118.50 E
Shizugawa 29 Gb 38.40N 141.28 E
Shizui 28 Ic 43.03N 126.09 E
Shizuishan (Dawukou) 27 Id 39.03N 106.24 E
Shizukuishi 29 Gb 39.42N 140.59 E
Shizunai 28 Qc 42.20N 142.22 E
Shizunai-Gawa 29a Cb 42.20N 142.22 E
Shizuoka 22 Pf 34.58N 138.23 E
Shizuoka Ken [2] 28 Og 35.00N 138.25 E
Shkodra 6 Hg 42.05N 19.30 E
Shkodrës, Liqen i-=Scutari, Lake- (EN) 5 Hg 42.10N 19.20 E
Shkumbini 15 Ch 41.01N 19.26 E
Shoal Lake 45 Fa 50.26N 100.34W
Shoal Lake 45 Ib 49.32N 95.00W
Shoal Lakes 45 Ha 50.20N 97.40W
Shōbara 28 Lg 34.51N 133.01 E
Shodo-Shima 29 Dd 34.30N 134.15 E
Shō-Gawa 29 Ec 36.47N 137.04 E
Shokanbetsu-Dake 29a Bb 43.43N 141.31 E
Shokotsu-Gawa 29a Ca 44.23N 143.17 E
Sholāpur 22 Jh 17.41N 75.55 E
Shoqān 24 Qd 37.20N 56.58 E
Shoranūr 25 Ff 10.46N 76.17 E
Shoreham-by-Sea 9 Mk 50.49N 0.16W
Shortland Islands 60 Fi 6.55S 155.53 E
Shosambetsu 29a Ba 44.32N 141.46 E
Shoshone 46 He 42.56N 114.24W
Shoshone Mountains 43 Dd 39.15N 117.25W
Shoshone Peak 46 Gh 36.56N 116.16W
Shoshone River 46 Kd 44.52N 108.11W
Shoshong 37 Dd 23.02S 26.31 E
Shoshoni 46 Ke 43.14N 108.07W
Shotor Khūn 23 Jc 34.20N 64.55 E
Shouchang 28 Ej 29.23N 119.12 E
Shouguang 28 Ef 36.53N 118.44 E
Shouxian (Shouyang) 28 Dh 32.35N 116.47 E
Shouyang → Shouxian 28 Dh 32.35N 116.47 E
Shōwa 29 Gb 39.51N 140.03 E
Show Low 46 Ji 34.15N 110.02W
Shqiperia=Albania (EN) [1] 6 Hg 41.00N 20.00 E
Shreveport 39 Jf 32.30N 93.45W
Shrewsbury 9 Ki 52.43N 2.45W
Shuangcheng 27 Mb 45.21N 126.17 E
Shuangjiang 27 Gg 23.27N 99.50 E
Shuangjiang → Tongdao 27 If 26.14N 109.45 E
Shuangliao 27 Lc 43.30N 123.30 E
Shuangyang 27 Mc 43.31N 125.28 E
Shuangyashan 22 Pe 46.37N 131.10 E
Shucheng 28 Di 31.28N 116.57 E
Shufu 27 Cd 39.27N 75.52 E
Shuguri Falls 36 Gd 8.31S 37.23 E
Shu He 28 Eg 34.07N 118.30 E
Shuicheng 27 Hf 26.34N 104.52 E
Shuiding → Huocheng 27 Dc 44.03N 80.49 E
Shuiji → Laixi 28 Ff 36.52N 120.31 E
Shuijiahu → Changfeng 28 Dh 32.29N 117.10 E
Shuikou → Jianghua 27 Jg 24.58N 111.56 E
Shuiye 28 Cf 36.08N 114.06 E
Shuizhai → Xiangcheng 28 Ch 33.27N 114.53 E
Shūl 24 Ng 30.10N 51.38 E
Shulan 27 Mc 44.26N 126.55 E
Shule 27 Cd 39.25N 76.06 E
Shule He 21 Le 40.20N 92.50 E
Shulu (Xinji) 28 Cf 37.56N 115.14 E
Shumagin Islands 40 He 55.07N 159.45W
Shumarinai-Ko 29a Ca 44.20N 142.13 E
Shunayn, Sabkhat- 33 Dc 30.10N 21.00 E
Shungnak 40 Hc 66.53N 157.02W
Shunyi 28 Dd 40.09N 116.38 E
Shuolong 27 Ig 22.51N 106.55 E
Shuoxian 27 Jd 39.18N 112.25 E
Shūr [Iran] 24 Pi 26.59N 55.47 E
Shūr [Iran] 24 Oh 28.12N 52.09 E
Shūr [Iran] 24 Ne 35.09N 51.30 E
Shūr [Iran] 24 Oh 28.33N 53.12 E
Shūr Āb 24 Pg 31.45N 55.15 E
Shurāb 23 Ic 33.07N 55.18 E
Shūsf 23 Jc 31.48N 60.01 E
Shūsh 24 Mf 32.12N 48.17 E
Shushica 15 Ci 40.34N 19.34 E
Shūshtar 23 Gc 32.03N 48.51 E
Shuswap Lake 46 Fa 50.57N 119.15W
Shūt 24 Oe 34.44N 52.53 E
Shuwak 35 Fc 14.23N 35.52 E
Shuyang 27 Ke 34.01N 118.52 E
Shuzenji 29 Fd 34.58N 138.55 E
Shwebo 25 Jd 22.34N 95.42 E
Shwell 25 Jd 23.56N 96.17 E
Shyok 25 Fa 35.13N 75.53 E
Sia 26 Jh 6.49S 134.19 E
Siagne 11 Mk 43.32N 6.57 E
Siāh Band 23 Kc 33.25N 65.21 E
Sīah-Chashmeh 24 Kc 39.04N 44.23 E
Sīāh-Kūh 24 Oe 34.38N 52.16 E
Siak 26 Df 1.13N 102.09 E
Sialkot [Pak.] 25 Ea 35.15N 73.17 E
Sialkot [Pak.] 22 Jf 32.30N 74.31 E
Sianów 10 Mb 54.15N 16.16 E
Siantan, Pulau- 26 Ef 3.10N 106.15 E
Siargao 26 Ie 9.53N 126.02 E
Šiaškotan, Ostrov- 21 Re 48.49N 154.06 E
Siátista 15 Ei 40.16N 21.33 E
Siau, Pulau- 26 If 2.42N 125.24 E
Šiauliai/Šjauljaj 6 Id 55.53N 23.19 E
Siavonga 36 Ef 16.32S 28.43 E
Siazan 19 Eg 41.04N 49.06 E
Sibā'ī, Jabal as- 33 Fd 25.43N 34.09 E
Sibaj 19 Fe 52.42N 58.39 E
Sibari 14 Kk 39.45N 16.27 E
Sibasa 37 Ed 22.56S 30.29 E
Šibenik 14 Jg 43.44N 15.53 E
Siberimanua 26 Cg 2.09S 99.34 E
Siberut, Pulau- 21 Lj 1.20S 98.55 E
Siberut, Selat- 26 Cg 0.42S 98.35 E
Sibi 25 Dc 29.33N 67.53 E
Sibigo 26 Cf 2.51N 95.55 E
Sibillini, Monti- 14 Hh 42.55N 13.15 E
Sibircatajaha 17 Lb 69.05N 64.43 E
Sibircevo 20 Ih 44.16N 132.20 E
Sibirjakova, Ostrov- 20 Cb 72.50N 79.00 E
Sibiti 36 Bc 3.41S 13.21 E
Sibiu [2] 15 Hd 45.46N 24.12 E
Sibiu 6 If 45.48N 24.09 E
Sibolga 22 Li 1.45N 98.48 E
Sibsāgar 25 Ic 26.59N 94.38 E
Sibu 22 Ni 2.18N 111.49 E
Sibuguey Bay 26 He 7.30N 122.40 E
Sibut 31 Ih 5.44N 19.05 E
Sibutu Islands 26 Gf 4.45N 119.20 E
Sibutu Passage 26 Gf 4.56N 119.36 E
Sibuyan 26 Hd 12.25N 122.34 E
Sibuyan Sea 26 Hd 12.50N 122.40 E
Siby 34 Dc 12.22N 8.22W
Sibyllenstein 10 Ke 51.12N 14.05 E
Sicani, Monti- 14 Hm 37.40N 13.15 E
Sicasica 54 Eg 17.22S 67.45W
Si Chon 25 Jg 9.00N 99.56 E
Sichuan Pendi 21 Mf 30.01N 105.00 E
Sichuan Sheng (Ssu-ch'uan Sheng)=Szechwan (EN) [2] 27 He 30.00N 103.00 E
Sicilia [2] 14 Im 37.45N 14.15 E
Sicilia = Sicily (EN) 5 Hh 37.30N 14.00 E
Sicilia, Canale di-=Sicily, Strait of- (EN) 5 Hh 37.20N 11.20 E
Sicilia, Mar di- 14 Gn 36.30N 13.00 E
Sicily (EN) = Sicilia 5 Hh 37.30N 14.00 E
Sicily, Strait of- (EN)= Sicilia, Canale di- 5 Hh 37.20N 11.20 E
Sicily, Strait of- (EN)= Tūnis, Canal de- 5 Hh 37.20N 11.20 E
Sico Tinto, Río- 49 Ef 15.58N 84.58W
Sicuani 53 Ig 14.15S 71.15W
Šid 15 Cd 45.08N 19.14 E
Sidamo [3] 35 Fd 5.48N 38.50 E
Siddipet 25 Fe 18.06N 78.51 E
Side 24 Dd 36.46N 31.22 E
Sidéradougou 34 Ec 10.40N 4.15W
Siderno 14 Kl 38.16N 16.18 E
Siders/Sierre 14 Bd 46.17N 7.32 E
Šiderty 19 He 52.32N 74.50 E
Šiderty 19 He 51.40N 74.50 E
Sídheros, Ákra- 15 Jn 35.19N 26.19 E
Sidhirókastron 15 Gh 41.14N 23.23 E
Sīdī 'Abd ar Raḩmān 24 Cg 30.58N 28.44 E
Sidi Aïch 13 Qh 36.37N 4.41 E
Sidi-Akacha 13 Nh 36.28N 1.18 E
Sidi Ali 13 Mh 36.06N 0.25 E
Sīdī'Alī al Makkī, Ra's- 14 Em 37.11N 10.17 E
Sīdī Barrānī 33 Ec 31.36N 25.55 E
Sidi Bel Abbes [3] 32 Gc 34.45N 0.35W
Sidi Bel Abbes 32 Gb 35.12N 0.38W
Sidi Bennour 32 Fc 32.39N 8.26W
Sidi di Daoud 13 Ph 36.51N 3.52 E
Sidi Ifni 31 Ff 29.33N 10.10W
Sidi Kacem 32 Fc 34.13N 5.42W
Sidikalang 26 Cf 2.45N 98.19 E
Sidi Lakhdar 13 Mh 36.10N 0.27 E
Sīdī Zayd, Jabal- 14 En 36.29N 10.20 E
Sidlaw Hills 9 Ke 56.30N 3.00W
Sidmouth 9 Jk 50.41N 3.15W
Sidney [B.C.-Can.] 42 Fg 48.39N 123.24W
Sidney [Mt.-U.S.] 43 Gb 47.43N 104.09W
Sidney [Nb.-U.S.] 43 Gc 41.09N 102.59W
Sidney [Oh.-U.S.] 44 Ee 40.16N 84.10W
Sidney Lanier, Lake- 44 Fh 34.15N 83.57W
Sidobre 11 Ik 43.40N 2.30 E
Sidorovsk 20 Dc 66.35N 82.30 E
Sidra 10 Tc 53.33N 23.30 E
Sidra, Gulf of-(EN)=Surt, Khalīj- 30 Ie 31.30N 18.00 E
Sidrolândia 55 Ee 20.55S 54.58W
Siedlce [2] 10 Sd 52.10N 22.15 E
Siedlce 10 Sd 52.11N 22.16 E
Siedlecka, Wysoczyzna- 10 Sd 52.10N 22.15 E
Sieg [F.R.G.] 10 Df 50.45N 7.05 E
Sieg [F.R.G.] 12 Kd 50.55N 8.01 E
Siegburg 10 Df 50.48N 7.12 E
Siegen 10 Ef 50.52N 8.02 E
Siemiatycze 10 Sd 52.26N 22.53 E
Siĕmréab 25 Kf 13.22N 103.51 E
Siena 14 Fg 43.19N 11.21 E
Sieniawa 10 Sf 50.11N 22.36 E
Sienne 11 Ee 49.00N 1.34W
Sieradz 10 Oe 51.36N 18.45 E
Sieradz [2] 10 Oe 51.35N 18.45 E
Sieradzka, Niecka- 10 Oe 51.35N 18.50 E
Sierck-les-Bains 12 Ie 49.26N 6.21 E
Sierpc 10 Pd 52.52N 19.41 E
Sierra Blanca 45 Dk 31.11N 105.21W
Sierra Blanca Peak 43 Fe 33.23N 105.48W
Sierra Colorada 56 Gf 40.35S 67.48W
Sierra Leone [1] 31 Fh 8.30N 11.30W
Sierra Leone Basin (EN) 3 Di 5.00N 17.00W
Sierra Leone Rise (EN) 3 Di 5.30N 21.00W
Sierra Madre 21 Oh 16.20N 122.00 E
Sierra Mojada 47 Dc 27.17N 103.42W
Sierre/Siders 14 Bd 46.17N 7.32 E
Siete Palmas 55 Cg 25.13S 58.20W
Siete Puntas, Río- 55 Df 23.34S 57.20W
Şieu 15 Hb 47.11N 24.13 E
Sifié 34 Dd 7.59N 6.55W
Sífnos 15 Hm 37.00N 24.40 E
Sig 32 Gb 35.32N 0.11W
Siğacik Körfezi 15 Jk 38.12N 26.45 E
Sigean 11 Ik 43.02N 2.59 E
Sighetu Marmaţiei 15 Gb 47.56N 23.53 E
Sighişoara 15 Hc 46.13N 24.48 E
Sigli 26 Ce 5.23N 95.57 E
Siglufjördur 7a Ba 66.09N 18.55W
Sigmaringen 10 Fh 48.05N 9.13 E
Signal Peak 46 Hj 33.22N 114.03W
Signy Island 66 Re 60.43S 45.38W
Signy-l'Abbaye 12 Ge 49.42N 4.25 E
Signy-le-Petit 12 Ge 49.54N 4.17 E
Sigtuna 7 Dg 59.37N 17.43 E
Siguanea, Ensenada de la- 49 Fc 21.38N 83.05W
Siguatepeque 49 Df 14.32N 87.49W
Sigüenza 13 Jc 41.04N 2.38W
Siguiri 31 Gg 11.25N 9.10W
Sigulda 7 Fh 57.09N 24.53 E
Si He 28 Dg 35.11N 116.42 E
Sihong 28 Eh 33.28N 118.13 E
Sihote-Alin 21 Pe 48.00N 138.00 E
Sihou → Changdao 28 Ff 37.56N 120.42 E
Sihuas 54 Ce 8.34S 77.37W
Siikainen 8 Ic 61.52N 21.50 E
Siilinjärvi 7 Ge 63.02N 27.40 E
Siirt 23 Fb 37.56N 41.57 E
Sijunjung 26 Dg 0.42S 100.58 E
Sikaiana 63a Fc 8.22S 162.45 E
Sikakap 26 Dg 2.46S 100.13 E
Sikanni Chief 42 Fe 58.17N 121.46W
Sīkar 25 Fc 27.37N 75.09 E
Sikasso 31 Gg 11.20N 5.40W
Sikasso [3] 34 Dc 10.55N 7.00W
Sikéa [Grc.] 15 Fm 36.46N 22.56 E
Sikéa [Grc.] 15 Gi 40.03N 23.58 E
Sikeston 43 Jd 36.53N 89.35W
Síkinos 15 Im 36.50N 25.05 E
Sikkim [3] 25 Hc 27.50N 88.30 E
Siklós 10 Ok 45.51N 18.18 E
Sikonge 36 Fd 5.38S 32.46 E
Šikotan, Ostrov/Tō, Shikotan- 20 Jh 43.47N 146.45 E
Siktjah 20 Hc 69.55N 125.10 E
Sil 13 Eb 42.27N 7.43W
Sila Grande 14 Kk 39.20N 16.30 E
Sila Greca 14 Kk 39.30N 16.30 E
Šilale/Šilalė 7 Fi 55.29N 22.12 E
Šilalė/Šilale 7 Fi 55.29N 22.12 E
Silao 48 Ig 20.56N 101.26W
Silaogou 28 Be 39.59N 113.03 E
Sila Piccola 14 Kk 39.05N 16.35 E
Silba 14 If 44.23N 14.42 E
Silchar 25 Id 24.49N 92.48 E
Šilda 16 Ud 51.47N 59.50 E
Sildagapet 8 Ab 62.05N 5.10 E
Sile 14 Ge 45.28N 12.35 E
Şile 24 Cb 41.05N 29.35 E
Šilega 19 Ec 64.03N 44.02 E
Silesia (EN)=Śląsk 10 Me 51.00N 16.45 E
Silesia (EN)=Śląsk 5 He 51.00N 16.45 E
Silet 32 He 22.39N 4.35 E
Silhouette Island 37b Ca 4.29S 55.14 E
Silifke 23 Db 36.22N 33.56 E
Siligir 20 Gc 68.27N 114.50 E
Silīguri 22 Kg 26.42N 88.26 E
Siling Co 21 Kf 31.50N 89.00 E
Siling Jiao 27 Ke 8.20N 115.27 E
Silisili, Mauga- 65c Aa 13.35S 172.27W
Silistra [2] 15 Kf 44.07N 27.16 E
Silistra 15 Ke 44.07N 27.16 E
Silivri 24 Cb 41.04N 28.15 E
Siljan 7 Df 60.50N 14.45 E
Šilka 20 Gf 51.51N 116.02 E
Šilka 21 Od 53.22N 121.32 E
Silkeborg 7 Bh 56.10N 9.34 E
Sillamäe/Sillamjae 7 Gg 59.24N 27.43 E
Sillamjae/Sillamäe 7 Gg 59.24N 27.43 E
Sillaro 14 Ff 44.34N 11.51 E
Silleiro, Cabo- 13 Db 42.07N 8.54W
Sillé-le-Guillaume 11 Ff 48.12N 0.08W
Sillian 14 Gd 46.45N 12.25 E
Sillil 35 Gc 11.00N 43.26 E
Siloam Springs 45 Ih 36.11N 94.32W
Siloana Plains 36 Df 17.15S 23.10 E
Šilovo 19 Ee 54.24N 40.52 E
Silsbee 45 Ik 30.21N 94.11W
Siltou 35 Bb 16.52N 15.43 E
Šilutė/Šilute 19 Cd 55.21N 21.30 E
Šilute/Šilutė 19 Cd 55.21N 21.30 E
Silvan 24 Ic 38.08N 41.01 E
Silvassa 25 Ed 20.20N 73.05 E
Silver Bank (EN) 49 Mc 20.30N 69.45W
Silver Bay 43 Ib 47.17N 91.16W
Silver City 43 Fe 32.46N 108.17W
Silverdalen 8 Fg 57.32N 15.44 E
Silver Lake 46 Ee 43.06N 120.53W
Silver Spring 44 If 39.02N 77.03W
Silver Springs 46 Fg 39.25N 119.13W
Silverthrone Mountain 46 Ba 51.31N 126.06W
Silverton [Co.-U.S.] 45 Ch 37.49N 107.40W
Silverton [Tx.-U.S.] 45 Fi 34.28N 101.19W
Silves [Braz.] 54 Gd 2.54S 58.27W
Silves [Port.] 13 Dg 37.11N 8.26W
Silvi 14 Ih 42.34N 14.06 E
Silvia 54 Cc 2.37N 76.24W
Silviers River 46 Fe 43.22N 118.48W
Silvretta 14 Ed 46.50N 10.15 E
Silyānah [3] 32 Ib 36.00N 9.30 E
Silyānah 32 Ib 36.05N 9.22 E
Silyānah, Wādī- 14 Dn 36.33N 9.25 E
Sim 17 Hi 54.59N 57.41 E
Sim 17 Hi 54.32N 56.30 E
Sim, Cap- 32 Fc 31.23N 9.51W
Simanggang 26 Ff 1.15N 111.26 E
Šimanovsk 20 Hf 52.01N 127.36 E
Simao 27 Hg 22.40N 101.02 E
Simard, Lac- 44 Hb 47.38N 78.40W
Sīmareh 24 Mf 32.08N 48.03 E
Simav 23 Ca 40.23N 28.31 E
Simav 24 Cc 39.05N 28.59 E
Simav Dağ 15 Lj 39.04N 28.54 E
Simav Gölü 15 Lj 39.09N 28.55 E
Simayama-Jima 29 Ae 32.40N 128.38 E
Simba 36 Db 0.36N 22.55 E
Simbo 36 Fc 4.53S 29.44 E
Simbo 63a Cc 8.18S 156.34 E
Simbruini, Monti- 14 Hj 41.55N 13.15 E
Simcoe 44 Gd 42.50N 80.18W
Simcoe, Lake - 42 Jh 44.27N 79.20W
Simen 35 Fc 13.25N 38.00 E
Simenti 34 Cc 13.00N 13.25W
Simeria 15 Gd 45.51N 23.01 E
Simeto 14 Jm 37.24N 15.06 E
Simeulue, Pulau- 21 Li 2.35N 96.05 E
Simferopol 6 Jf 44.57N 34.06 E
Simhah, Jabal- 23 Hf 17.20N 54.50 E
Simi 15 Km 36.36N 27.50 E
Simi 15 Km 36.35N 27.50 E
Simití 49 Kj 7.58N 73.58W
Simitli 15 Gh 41.53N 23.06 E
Simla 22 Jf 31.06N 77.10 E
Şimleu Silvaniei 15 Fb 47.14N 22.48 E
Simmental 14 Bd 46.35N 7.25 E
Simmerath 12 Id 50.36N 6.18 E
Simmerbach 12 Je 49.48N 7.31 E
Simmern 10 Dg 49.59N 7.31 E
Simmertal 12 Je 49.48N 7.33 E
Simnas 8 Jj 54.20N 23.45 E
Simo 7 Fd 65.39N 24.55 E
Simojärvi 7 Gc 66.06N 27.03 E
Simojoki 7 Fd 65.37N 25.03 E
Simojovel de Allende 48 Mi 17.12N 92.38W
Simonstown 37 Bf 34.14S 18.26 E
Simpele 7 Gf 61.26N 29.22 E
Simpelejärvi 8 Mc 61.30N 29.25 E
Simplon 14 Bd 46.15N 8.00 E
Simpson Desert 57 Eg 25.00S 137.00 E
Simpson Hill 59 Fe 26.30S 126.30 E
Simpson Peninsula 42 Ic 68.45N 89.10W
Simrishamn 7 Di 55.33N 14.20 E
Simsonbaai 51b Ab 18.02N 63.08W
Simušir, Ostrov- 21 Re 46.58N 152.02 E
Sina 25 Fe 17.22N 75.54 E
Sīnā'=Sinai Peninsula (EN) 30 Kf 29.30N 34.00 E
Sinabang 26 Cf 2.29N 96.23 E
Sinaḑaqo 35 Hd 5.22N 46.22 E
Sinai, Mount- (EN)=Mūsa, Jabal- 24 Eh 28.32N 33.59 E
Sinaia 15 Id 45.21N 25.33 E
Sinai Peninsula (EN)= Sīnā' 30 Kf 29.30N 34.00 E
Sinajana 64c Bb 13.28N 144.45W
Sinaloa [2] 47 Cc 25.00N 107.30W
Sinaloa, Llanos de- 47 Cc 25.00N 107.30W
Sinaloa, Río- 48 Ee 25.18N 108.30W
Sinaloa de Leyva 48 Ee 25.50N 108.14W
Sinalunga 14 Fg 43.12N 11.44 E
Sinamaica 54 Da 11.05N 71.51W
Sinan 27 If 27.56N 108.11 E
Sinara 17 Kh 56.17N 62.23 E
Sīnāwin 33 Bc 31.02N 10.36 E
Sinazongwe 36 Ef 17.15S 27.28 E
Şincai 15 Hc 46.39N 24.23 E
Sincanli 24 Dc 38.45N 30.15 E
Sincé 49 Ji 9.14N 75.06W
Sincelejo 53 Ie 9.18N 75.24W
Sinch'am 28 Jc 42.07N 129.25 E
Sinch'ang 28 Jd 40.07N 128.28 E
Sinch'on 28 He 38.28N 125.27 E
Sinclair, Lake- 44 Fi 33.11N 83.16W
Sind [3] 25 Cc 25.30N 69.00 E
Sind 21 Ig 25.30N 69.00 E
Sindal 8 Dg 57.28N 10.13 E
Sindangbarang 26 Eh 7.27S 107.08 E
Sindara 36 Bc 1.02S 10.40 E
Sindelfingen-Böblingen 10 Fh 48.41N 9.01 E
Sindfeld 12 Kc 51.32N 8.48 E
Sindi 7 Fg 58.24N 24.42 E
Sındırgı 24 Cc 39.14N 28.10 E
Sindirgi Geçidi 15 Lj 39.10N 28.04 E
Sîndominic 15 Ic 46.35N 25.47 E
Sindri 25 Hd 23.42N 86.29 E
Sinegorje 20 Kd 62.03N 150.25 E
Sinegorski 16 Le 48.00N 40.53 E
Šine-Ider 27 Gb 48.56N 99.33 E
Sinekli 15 Lh 41.14N 28.12 E
Sinelnikovo 16 Ie 48.18N 35.31 E
Sines 13 Dg 37.57N 8.52W
Sines, Cabo de- 13 Dg 37.57N 8.53W
Sine-Saloum [3] 34 Bc 14.00N 15.50W
Singako 35 Bd 9.50N 19.29 E
Singapore / Singapura 22 Mi 1.17N 103.51 E
Singapore Strait (EN)= Singapura, Selat- 26 Df 1.15N 104.00 E
Singapura / Singapore 22 Mi 1.17N 103.51 E
Singapura, Selat-= Singapore Strait (EN) 26 Df 1.15N 104.00 E
Singaraja 26 Gh 8.07S 115.06 E
Singatoka 63d Ac 18.08S 177.30 E
Sing Buri 25 Kf 14.53N 100.25 E
Singen 10 Ei 47.46N 8.50 E
Sîngeroz Băi 15 Hb 47.22N 24.41 E
Singida [3] 36 Fd 5.30S 34.30 E
Singida 31 Ki 4.49S 34.45 E
Singitic Gulf (EN) = Singitikós Kólpos 15 Gi 40.10N 23.55 E
Singitikós Kólpos = Singitic Gulf (EN) 15 Gi 40.10N 23.55 E
Singkaling Hkamti 25 Jc 26.00N 95.42 E
Singkang 26 Hg 4.08S 120.01 E
Singkawang 26 Ef 0.54N 109.00 E
Singkep, Pulau- 26 Dg 0.30S 104.25 E
Singkil 26 Cf 2.17N 97.49 E
Singleton [Austl.] 59 Kf 32.34S 151.10 E
Singleton [Eng.-U.K.] 12 Bd 50.55N 0.44W
Singleton, Mount- 59 De 29.28S 117.18 E
Singö 8 Hd 60.10N 18.45 E
Siniscola 14 Dj 40.34N 9.41 E
Sini vrăh 15 Ih 41.51N 25.01 E
Sinj 14 Kg 43.42N 16.38 E
Sinjah 35 Ec 13.09N 33.56 E
Sinjai 26 Hh 5.07S 120.15 E
Sinjaja 8 Mg 57.05N 28.33 E
Sinjajevina 15 Cf 43.00N 19.18 E
Sinjār 24 Id 36.19N 41.52 E
Sinjār, Jabal- 24 Id 36.23N 41.52 E
Sinjuža 16 Ge 48.03N 30.50 E
Sinkiang (EN)= Hsin-chiang-wei-wu-erh Tzu-chih-ch'ü → Xinjiang Uygur Zizhiqu [2] 27 Ec 42.00N 86.00 E
Sinkiang (EN)= Xinjiang Uygur Zizhiqu (Hsin-chiang-wei-wu-erh Tzu-chih-ch'ü) [2] 27 Ec 42.00N 86.00 E
Sin-le-Noble 12 Fd 50.22N 3.07 E
Sinmi-Do 28 He 39.33N 124.53 E
Sinn 12 Kd 50.39N 8.20 E
Sinn al Kadhdhāb 33 Fe 23.30N 32.05 E
Sinnamary 54 Hb 5.23N 53.00W
Sinni 14 Kj 40.08N 16.41 E
Sînnicolau Mare 15 Dc 46.05N 20.38 E
Sinnūris 24 Dh 29.25N 30.52 E
Sinnyŏng 28 Jf 36.02N 128.47 E
Sinoe [3] 34 Dd 5.20N 8.40W
Sinoe, Lacul- 15 Le 44.38N 28.53 E
Sinoia 31 Kj 17.22S 30.12 E
Sinop 23 Ea 41.59N 35.09 E
Sinop Burun 24 Fa 42.02N 35.12 E
Sinp'o 28 Jd 40.02N 128.12 E
Sinsang 28 Ie 39.39N 127.25 E
Sinsheim 10 Eg 49.15N 8.53 E
Sint-Amandsberg, Gent- 12 Fc 51.04N 3.45 E
Sîntana 15 Ec 46.21N 21.30 E
Sint-Andries, Brugge- 12 Fc 51.12N 3.10 E
Sintang 26 Ff 0.04N 111.30 E
Sint Eustatius 47 Le 17.30N 62.59W
Sint-Gillis-Waas 12 Gc 51.13N 4.08 E
Sint Kruis 50 Bf 12.18N 69.08W
Sint Laureins 12 Fc 51.15N 3.31 E
Sint Maarten 50 Ec 18.04N 63.04W
Sint Nicolaas 50 Bf 12.26N 69.55W
Sint Niklaas/Saint-Nicolas 11 Kc 51.10N 4.08 E
Sint-Oedenrode 12 Hc 51.34N 5.28 E
Sinton 45 Hl 28.02N 97.33W
Sint-Pieters-Leeuw 12 Gd 50.47N 4.14 E
Sintra 13 Cf 38.48N 9.23W
Sint-Truiden/Saint-Trond 11 Ld 50.49N 5.12 E
Sintu 35 Fd 8.12N 36.56 E
Sinú, Río- 49 Ji 9.24N 75.49W
Sinŭiju 22 Oe 40.06N 124.24 E
Sinujīf 35 Hd 8.30N 48.59 E
Sinzig 12 Jd 50.33N 7.15 E
Sió 10 Oj 46.23N 18.40 E
Siocon 26 He 7.42N 122.08 E
Siófok 10 Oj 46.54N 18.03 E
Sioma 36 Df 16.40S 23.35 E

Index Symbols

- [1] Independent Nation
- [2] State, Region
- [3] District, County
- Municipality
- Colony, Dependency
- Continent
- Physical Region
- Historical or Cultural Region
- Mount, Mountain
- Volcano
- Hill
- Mountains, Mountain Range
- Hills, Escarpment
- Plateau, Upland
- Pass, Gap
- Plain, Lowland
- Delta
- Salt Flat
- Valley, Canyon
- Crater, Cave
- Karst Features
- Depression
- Polder
- Desert, Dunes
- Forest, Woods
- Heath, Steppe
- Oasis
- Cape, Point
- Coast, Beach
- Cliff
- Peninsula
- Isthmus
- Sandbank
- Island
- Atoll
- Rock, Reef
- Islands, Archipelago
- Rocks, Reefs
- Coral Reef
- Well, Spring
- Geyser
- River, Stream
- Waterfall Rapids
- River Mouth, Estuary
- Lake
- Salt Lake
- Intermittent Lake
- Reservoir
- Swamp, Pond
- Canal
- Glacier
- Ice Shelf, Pack Ice
- Ocean
- Sea
- Gulf, Bay
- Strait, Fjord
- Lagoon
- Bank
- Seamount
- Tablemount
- Ridge
- Shelf
- Basin
- Escarpment, Sea Scarp
- Fracture
- Trench, Abyss
- National Park, Reserve
- Point of Interest
- Recreation Site
- Cave, Cavern
- Historic Site
- Ruins
- Wall, Walls
- Church, Abbey
- Temple
- Scientific Station
- Airport
- Port
- Lighthouse
- Mine
- Tunnel
- Dam, Bridge

Name	Page	Grid	Lat.	Long.
Sion/Sitten	14	Bd	46.15N	7.20 E
Siorapaluk	41	Ec	77.39N	71.00W
Sioule	11	Jh	46.22N	3.19 E
Sioux City	39	Je	42.30N	96.23W
Sioux Falls	39	Je	43.32N	96.44W
Sioux Lookout	42	If	50.06N	91.55W
Sipalay	26	He	9.45N	122.24 E
Šipan	14	Lh	42.43N	17.54 E
Siparia	50	Fg	10.08N	61.30W
Šipčenski prohod	15	Ig	42.46N	25.19 E
Siping	22	Oe	43.11N	124.24 E
Sipiwesk	42	He	55.27N	97.24W
Sipiwesk Lake	42	He	55.05N	97.35W
Siple, Mount-	66	Nf	73.15 S	126.06W
Siple Coast	66	Mg	82.00 S	153.00W
Siple Island	66	Nf	73.39 S	125.00W
Siple Station	66	Pf	75.55 S	83.55W
Sipolilo	37	Ec	16.39 S	30.42 E
Sipora, Pulau-	26	Cg	2.12 S	99.40 E
Sippola	8	Ld	60.44N	27.00 E
Siqueira Campos	55	Hf	23.42 S	49.50W
Siquia, Río-	49	Eg	12.09N	84.13W
Siquijor	26	He	9.13N	123.31 E
Siquisique	54	Ea	10.34N	69.42W
Šira	20	Ef	54.29N	90.02 E
Sira	8	Be	58.17N	6.24 E
Sira	7	Bg	58.25N	6.38 E
Şir Abū Nu'Ayr	24	Pj	25.13N	54.13 E
Si Racha	25	Kf	13.10N	100.57 E
Siracusa=Syracuse (EN)	6	Hh	37.04N	15.18 E
Sir Alexander, Mount -	42	Ff	53.56N	120.23W
Sirasso	34	Dd	9.16N	6.06W
Şirāţ, Jabal-	33	Hf	17.00N	43.50 E
Sirba	34	Fc	13.46N	1.40 E
Şir Banī Yās	24	Oj	24.19N	52.37 E
Sirdalen	8	Bf	58.50N	6.40 E
Sirdalsvatn	8	Bf	58.35N	6.40 E
Sire [Eth.]	35	Fd	8.58N	37.00 E
Sire [Eth.]	35	Fd	8.16N	39.30 E
Sir Edward Pellew Group	59	Hc	15.40 S	136.50 E
Siret	5	If	45.24N	28.01 E
Siret	15	Jb	47.57N	26.04 E
Sirevåg	7	Ag	58.30N	5.47 E
Sīrīk	23	Id	26.29N	57.09 E
Sirik, Tanjong-	26	Ff	2.46N	111.19 E
Sirina	15	Jm	36.21N	26.41 E
Sirino	14	Jj	40.07N	15.50 E
Sirius Seamount (EN)	40	Gf	52.00N	160.50W
Širjajevo	16	Gf	47.24N	30.13 E
Sir James Mac Brian, Mount-	42	Ed	62.08N	127.40W
Sirjān, Kavīr-e-	24	Ph	29.30N	55.30 E
Sirmione	14	Ee	45.29N	10.36 E
Şırnak	24	Jd	37.32N	42.28 E
Širokaja Pad	20	Jf	50.15N	142.11 E
Široki	20	Jd	63.04N	148.01 E
Širokoje	16	Hf	47.38N	33.14 E
Sironcha	25	Fe	18.50N	79.58 E
Siros	15	Hl	37.26N	24.55 E
Sirpsindiği	15	Jh	41.50N	26.29 E
Sirr, Nafūd as-	24	Kj	25.15N	44.45 E
Sirrayn	33	Hf	19.38N	40.36 E
Sirretta Peak	46	Fi	35.59N	118.20W
Sīrrī, Jazīreh-ye-	24	Pj	25.55N	54.32 E
Sirsa	25	Fc	29.32N	75.01 E
Sir Sandford, Mount-	46	Ga	51.40N	117.52W
Sirte Desert (EN)=As Sidrah	30	Ie	30.30N	17.30 E
Sir Thomas, Mount-	59	Fe	27.11 S	129.46 E
Širvintos	7	Fi	55.03N	25.01 E
Sir Wilfrid Laurier, Mount -	42	Ff	52.48N	119.45W
Sisak	14	Ke	45.29N	16.22 E
Si Sa Ket	25	Ke	15.07N	104.19 E
Sisakht	24	Ng	30.47N	51.33 E
Sisal	48	Ng	21.10N	90.02W
Sisante	13	Je	39.25N	2.13W
Sisargas, Islas-	13	Da	43.22N	8.50W
Šišćhid-Gol	27	Ga	51.30N	97.10 E
Sishen	37	Ce	27.55 S	22.59 E
Sishui	28	Dg	35.40N	117.17 E
Sisian	16	Oj	39.31N	46.03 E
Sisili	34	Ec	10.16N	1.15W
Sisimiut/Holsteinsborg	67	Nc	67.05N	53.45W
Siskiyou Mountains	46	Df	41.55N	123.15W
Sisöphŏn	25	Kf	13.35N	102.59 E
Sissano	60	Ch	3.00 S	142.03 E
Sisseton	45	Hd	45.40N	97.03W
Sissonne	12	Fe	49.34N	3.54 E
Sīstān=Seistan (EN)	21	If	30.30N	62.00 E
Sistema Central	5	Fg	40.30N	5.00W
Sistema Ibérico=Iberian Mountains (EN)	5	Fg	41.30N	2.30W
Sistemas Béticos	5	Fh	37.35N	3.30W
Sisteron	11	Lj	44.12N	5.56 E
Sisters	46	Ed	44.17N	121.33W
Sistranda	7	Be	63.43N	8.50 E
Sitāpur	25	Gc	27.34N	80.41 E
Sitasjaure	7	Dc	68.00N	17.25 E
Siteki	37	Ee	26.27 S	31.57 E
Sitges	13	Nc	41.14N	1.49 E
Sithonia	15	Gi	40.05N	23.55 E
Sitia	15	Jn	35.12N	26.07 E
Sitio d'Abadia	55	Ib	14.48 S	46.16W
Sitio Nuevo	49	Jh	10.46N	74.43W
Sitka	39	Fd	57.03N	135.14W
Sitkalidak	40	Ie	57.10N	153.10W
Sitna	15	Kb	47.30N	27.10 E
Sitnica	15	Dg	42.53N	20.52 E
Sitona	35	Fc	14.23N	37.22 E
Sitrah [Bhr.]	24	Ni	26.10N	50.40 E
Sitrah [Eg.]	24	Bh	28.42N	26.54 E
Sittang	25	Je	17.10N	96.58 E
Sittard	11	Ld	51.00N	5.53 E
Sittee Point	49	Ce	16.48N	88.15W
Sitten/Sion	14	Bd	46.15N	7.20 E
Sittingbourne	12	Cc	51.20N	0.45 E
Sittwe (Akyab)	22	Lg	20.09N	92.54 E
Siuna	49	Eg	13.44N	84.46W
Siuslaw River	46	Cd	44.01N	124.08W
Siva	7	Mh	56.49N	53.55 E
Sivac	15	Cd	45.42N	19.23 E
Sivaki	20	Hf	52.38N	126.45 E
Sivas	22	Ff	39.50N	37.03 E
Sivaš, Ozero-	16	Ig	45.50N	34.40 E
Sivasli	15	Mk	38.30N	29.42 E
Šiveluč, Vulkan-	20	Le	56.33N	161.25 E
Sivera, Ozero-/Sivera Ezers	8	Li	55.58N	27.25 E
Sivera Ezers/Sivera, Ozero-	8	Li	55.58N	27.25 E
Siverek	23	Eb	37.45N	39.19 E
Siverski	7	Hg	59.22N	30.02 E
Sivomaskinski	17	Kc	66.40N	62.31 E
Sivrice	24	Hc	38.27N	39.19 E
Sivrihisar	24	Dc	39.27N	31.34 E
Sivry-Rance	12	Gd	50.10N	4.16 E
Sivry Rance-Rance	12	Gd	50.09N	4.16 E
Sivry-sur-Meuse	12	He	49.19N	5.16 E
Siwah	31	Jf	29.12N	25.31 E
Siwah, Wāḩāt-=Siwa Oasis (EN)	30	Jf	29.10N	25.40 E
Siwalik Range	21	Jg	29.00N	80.00 E
Siwān	25	Gc	26.13N	84.22 E
Siwa Oasis (EN)=Sīwah, Wāḩāt-	30	Jf	29.10N	25.40 E
Sixaola, Río-	49	Fi	9.35N	82.34W
Six Cross Road	51q	Bb	13.07N	59.28W
Six-Fours-la-Plage	11	Lk	43.06N	5.51 E
Sixian	28	Dh	33.29N	117.53 E
Six Men's Bay	51q	Ab	13.16N	59.38W
Sixth Cataract (EN)=Sablūkah, Ash Shallāl as-	30	Kg	16.20N	32.42 E
Siyah-Chaman	24	Ld	37.35N	47.10 E
Siyang (Zhongxing)	28	Eh	33.43N	118.40 E
Siziwang Qi (Ulan Hua)	28	Ad	41.31N	111.41 E
Sjaelland=Zealand (EN)	5	Hd	55.30N	11.45 E
Sjamozero, Ozero-	7	Hf	61.55N	33.15 E
Sjare/Sääre	8	Ig	57.57N	21.53 E
Sjas	7	Hf	60.10N	32.31 E
Sjasstroj	7	Hf	60.09N	32.36 E
Sjašupe	7	Fi	55.00N	22.10 E
Šjauljaj/Šiauliai	6	Id	55.53N	23.19 E
Sjenica	15	Cf	43.16N	20.00 E
Sjnjaja	20	Hd	61.00N	126.57 E
Sjoa	8	Cc	61.41N	9.33 E
Sjöbo	8	Ei	55.38N	13.42 E
Sjøholt	7	Be	62.29N	6.50 E
Sjujutlijka	15	Ig	42.17N	25.55 E
Sjun	17	Gi	55.43N	54.17 E
Sjuøyane	41	Ob	80.43N	20.45 E
Skadarsko Jezero=Scutari, Lake- (EN)	5	Hg	42.10N	19.20 E
Skadovsk	19	Df	46.07N	32.56 E
Skælskør	8	Di	55.15N	11.19 E
Skærbæk	8	Ci	55.09N	8.46 E
Skagatá	7a	Ba	66.07N	20.06W
Skagen	7	Ch	57.44N	10.36 E
Skagern	8	Ff	59.00N	14.15 E
Skagerrak	5	Gd	57.45N	9.00 E
Skaget	8	Cc	61.17N	9.12 E
Skagit River	46	Db	48.20N	122.25W
Skagway	39	Fd	59.28N	135.19W
Skaidi	7	Fa	70.26N	24.30 E
Skaland	7	Db	69.27N	17.18 E
Skälderviken	8	Eh	56.20N	12.40 E
Skålevik	8	Bf	58.04N	8.00 E
Skalisty Golec, Gora- [R.S.F.S.R.]	20	Ge	56.20N	119.10 E
Skalisty Golec, Gora- [R.S.F.S.R.]	20	Ie	55.55N	130.35 E
Skanderborg	7	Bh	56.02N	9.56 E
Skåne	5	Hd	56.00N	13.30 E
Skånevik	8	Ae	59.44N	5.59 E
Skänninge	8	Ff	58.24N	15.05 E
Skanör	8	Ei	55.25N	12.52 E
Skántzoura	15	Hj	39.05N	24.07 E
Skara	7	Cg	58.22N	13.25 E
Skaraborg [2]	7	Cg	58.20N	13.30 E
Skarblacka	8	Ff	58.34N	15.54 E
Skārdu	25	Fa	35.18N	75.37 E
Skärhamn	8	Dg	57.59N	11.33 E
Skarnes	8	Dd	60.15N	11.41 E
Skarsstind	8	Cb	62.03N	8.35 E
Skarsvåg	7	Fa	71.06N	25.56 E
Skarszewy	10	Ob	54.05N	18.27 E
Skarvdalsegga	8	Cb	62.09N	8.03 E
Skaryszew	10	Re	51.19N	21.15 E
Skarżysko-Kamienna	10	Qe	51.08N	20.53 E
Skasøy	8	Ca	63.20N	8.35 E
Skät	15	Gf	43.44N	23.51 E
Skattkärr	8	Ee	59.25N	13.41 E
Skattungbyn	8	Fc	61.12N	14.52 E
Skaudvile/Skaudvilė	7	Fi	55.27N	22.33 E
Skaudvilė/Skaudvile	7	Fi	55.27N	22.33 E
Skaulen	8	Be	59.38N	6.35 E
Skawa	10	Pf	50.02N	19.26 E
Skawina	10	Pg	49.59N	19.49 E
Skee	8	Df	58.56N	11.19 E
Skeena	38	Fd	54.09N	130.02W
Skeena Mountains	42	Ee	56.45N	128.40W
Skegness	9	Nh	53.10N	0.21 E
Skeidarársandur	7a	Cc	63.54N	17.14W
Skeldon	54	Gb	5.53N	57.08W
Skeleton Coast	37	Ac	17.50 S	12.45 E
Skellefteå	6	Ic	64.46N	20.57 E
Skellefteälven	5	Ic	64.42N	21.06 E
Skelleftehamn	7	Ed	64.41N	21.14 E
Skënderbeut, Mali i-	15	Ch	41.35N	19.50 E
Skene	8	Eg	57.29N	12.38 E
Skerki Bank (EN)	32	Jb	37.45N	10.50 E
Skerries/Na Sceiri	9	Gh	53.35N	6.07W
Skerryvore	9	Fe	56.20N	7.05W
Skhiza	15	Em	36.44N	21.46 E
Skhoinoúsa	15	Im	36.50N	25.30 E
Ski	7	Cg	59.43N	10.50 E
Skiathos	15	Gj	39.10N	23.28 E
Skiathos	15	Gj	39.10N	23.29 E
Skibbereen/An Sciobairin	9	Dj	51.33N	9.15W
Skibotn	7	Eb	69.24N	20.16 E
Skidel	16	Dc	53.38N	24.17 E
Skien	6	Gd	59.12N	9.36 E
Skierniewice	10	Qe	51.58N	20.08 E
Skierniewice [2]	10	Qe	52.00N	20.10 E
Skiftet/Kihti	8	Id	60.15N	21.05 E
Skikda	31	He	36.52N	6.54 E
Skikda [3]	32	Ib	36.45N	6.50 E
Skillet Fork	45	Lg	38.08N	88.07W
Skillingaryd	8	Fg	57.26N	14.05 E
Skinári, Ákra-	15	Dl	37.56N	20.42 E
Skinnskatteberg	8	Fe	59.50N	15.41 E
Skipton	9	Kh	53.58N	2.01W
Skiptvet	8	De	59.28N	11.11 E
Skiropoúla	15	Hk	38.50N	24.21 E
Skiros	15	Hk	38.54N	24.34 E
Skiros	15	Hk	38.53N	24.32 E
Skive	7	Bh	56.34N	9.02 E
Skive Å	8	Ch	56.34N	9.04 E
Skjærhalden	8	De	59.02N	11.02 E
Skjåk	8	Cc	61.52N	8.22 E
Skjálfandafljót	7a	Cb	65.59N	17.38W
Skjeberg	8	De	59.14N	11.12 E
Skjern	7	Bi	55.57N	8.30 E
Skjern Å	7	Bi	55.55N	8.24 E
Skjervøy	7	Ea	70.02N	20.59 E
Skjoldungen	41	Hf	63.20N	41.20W
Sklad	20	Hb	71.52N	123.35 E
Šklov	16	Gb	54.14N	30.18 E
Skobeleva, Pik-	18	Ie	39.51N	72.47 E
Skærfjorden	41	Kc	77.30N	19.10W
Škofja Loka	14	Id	46.10N	14.18 E
Skog	8	Gc	61.10N	16.55 E
Skógafoss	7a	Bc	63.32N	19.31W
Skoghall	8	Ee	59.19N	13.26 E
Skogshorn	8	Cd	60.53N	8.42 E
Skokie	45	Me	42.02N	87.46W
Skole	10	Th	48.58N	23.32 E
Skópelos	15	Gj	39.07N	23.44 E
Skópelos	15	Gj	39.10N	23.40 E
Skopi	15	Jn	35.11N	26.02 E
Skopin	7	Jj	53.52N	39.37 E
Skopje	6	Ig	42.00N	21.29 E
Skórcz	10	Oc	53.48N	18.32 E
Skorovatn	7	Cd	64.39N	13.07 E
Skorpa	8	Ac	61.35N	4.50 E
Skørping	8	Ch	56.50N	9.53 E
Skorpiós	15	Dk	38.42N	20.45 E
Škotovo	28	Lc	43.20N	132.21 E
Skotselv	8	Ce	59.51N	9.53 E
Skoura	32	Fc	31.04N	6.43W
Skövde	7	Cg	58.24N	13.50 E
Skovorodino	22	Od	53.59N	123.55 E
Skowhegan	44	Mc	44.46N	69.43W
Skradin	14	Jg	43.49N	15.56 E
Skreia	8	Dd	60.34N	11.04 E
Skreia	8	Dd	60.39N	10.56 E
Skrekken	8	Bd	60.13N	7.49 E
Skridulaupen	8	Bc	61.55N	7.35 E
Skrimkolla	8	Cb	62.23N	9.04 E
Skriveri/Skriveri	8	Kh	56.37N	25.10 E
Skriveri/Skriveri	8	Kh	56.37N	25.10 E
Skrunda	7	Eh	56.41N	22.00 E
Skrwa	10	Pd	52.33N	19.32 E
Skudenesfjorden	8	Ae	59.05N	5.20 E
Skudeneshavn	7	Ag	59.09N	5.17 E
Skuodas	7	Eh	56.17N	21.31 E
Skurup	8	Ei	55.28N	13.30 E
Skutskär	8	Gd	60.38N	17.25 E
Skvira	16	Fe	49.44N	29.42 E
Skwierzyna	10	Ld	52.35N	15.30 E
Skye, Island of-	5	Fd	57.15N	6.10W
Slagelse	7	Ci	55.24N	11.22 E
Slagnäs	7	Ed	65.36N	18.10 E
Slamet, Gunung-	21	Mj	7.14 S	109.12 E
Slaná	10	Ri	47.56N	21.08 E
Slancy	19	Cd	59.08N	28.02 E
Slaney/An tSláine	9	Gi	52.21N	6.30W
Slănic	15	Id	45.15N	25.56 E
Slănic Moldova	15	Jc	46.12N	26.26 E
Slannik	15	Jf	43.06N	26.13 E
Slano	14	Lh	42.47N	17.54 E
Slaný	10	Kf	50.14N	14.06 E
Ślązk=Silesia (EN)	10	Me	51.00N	16.45 E
Ślązk=Silesia (EN)	5	He	51.00N	16.45 E
Śląska, Wyżyna-	10	Of	50.28N	18.40 E
Slate Islands	45	Mb	48.34N	86.45W
Slatina	15	He	44.26N	24.22 E
Slatina	10	Ph	48.32N	19.10 E
Slaton	45	Fj	33.26N	101.39W
Slave Coast	30	Hh	6.00N	3.30 E
Slave Lake	42	Ge	55.17N	114.46W
Slave River	42	Hc	61.18N	113.39W
Slavgorod [Bye.-U.S.S.R.]	16	Gc	53.27N	31.01 E
Slavgorod [R.S.F.S.R.]	20	Cf	53.03N	78.48 E
Slavičin	10	Ng	49.06N	17.53 E
Slavjanka	20	Ih	42.55N	131.20 E
Slavjanka	15	Gh	41.23N	23.36 E
Slavjansk	6	Jf	48.52N	37.37 E
Slavjansk-na-Kubani	19	Df	45.15N	38.08 E
Slavkoje	10	Th	48.45N	23.31 E
Slavkoviči	8	Mg	57.37N	29.10 E
Slavonija (EN) = Slavonija	5	Hf	45.00N	18.00 E
Slavonia (EN)=Slavonija	14	Le	45.00N	18.00 E
Slavonija=Slavonia (EN)	14	Le	45.00N	18.00 E
Slavonija = Slavonia (EN)	5	Hf	45.00N	18.00 E
Slavonska Požega	14	Le	45.20N	17.41 E
Slavonski Brod	14	Me	45.09N	18.02 E
Slavsk	8	Ii	55.01N	21.37 E
Slavuta	19	Ce	50.18N	26.52 E
Sława	10	Me	51.53N	16.04 E
Sławatycze	10	Te	51.43N	23.30 E
Sławno	10	Mb	54.22N	16.40 E
Slayton	45	Id	44.01N	95.45W
Sleaford	9	Mh	53.00N	0.24W
Slea Head/Ceann Sléibhe	9	Ci	52.06N	10.27W
Sleat, Sound of-	9	Hd	57.10N	5.50W
Sleen	12	Ib	52.47N	6.49 E
Sleeper Islands	42	Je	57.25N	79.50W
Sléibhte Chill Mhantáin/Wicklow Mountains	9	Gh	53.02N	6.24W
Sleidinge, Evergem-	12	Fc	51.08N	3.41 E
Slesin	10	Od	52.23N	18.19 E
Slessor Glacier	66	Af	79.50 S	28.30W
Slessor Peak	66	Qe	66.31 S	64.58W
Slettefjell	8	Cc	61.13N	8.44 E
Sletterhage	8	Dh	56.06N	10.31 E
Ślęża	10	Me	51.10N	16.58 E
Ślęża	10	Mf	50.52N	16.45 E
Sliabh Bearnach/Slieve Bernagh	9	Ei	52.50N	8.35W
Sliabh Bladhma/Slieve Bloom	9	Fh	53.10N	7.35W
Sliabh Eachtai/Slieve Aughty	9	Eh	53.10N	8.30W
Sliabh Gamh/Ox or Slieve Gamph Mountains	9	Eg	54.10N	8.50W
Sliabh Mis/Slieve Mish	9	Di	52.10N	9.50W
Sliabh Speirin/Sperrin Mountains	9	Fg	54.50N	7.05W
Slidell	45	Lk	30.17N	89.47W
Slide Mountain	44	Jd	42.00N	74.23W
Slidre	8	Cc	61.10N	9.00 E
Sliedrecht	12	Gc	51.50N	4.46 E
Slieve Aughty/Sliabh Eachtai	9	Eh	53.10N	8.30W
Slieve Bernagh/Sliabh Bearnach	9	Ei	52.50N	8.35W
Slieve Bloom/Sliabh Bladhma	9	Fh	53.10N	7.35W
Slievefelim Mountains	9	Ei	52.45N	8.15W
Slieve Mish/Sliabh Mis	9	Di	52.10N	9.50W
Sligeach/Sligo [2]	9	Eg	54.10N	8.40W
Sligeach/Sligo	6	Fe	54.17N	8.28W
Sligo/Sligeach [2]	9	Eg	54.10N	8.40W
Sligo/Sligeach	6	Fe	54.17N	8.28W
Sligo Bay/Cuan Shligigh	9	Eg	54.20N	8.40W
Slinge	12	Ib	52.08N	6.31 E
Slingebeek	12	Ic	51.59N	6.18 E
Slite	8	Hg	57.43N	18.48 E
Sliven	15	Jg	42.40N	26.19 E
Sliven [2]	15	Jg	42.40N	26.19 E
Slivnica	15	Gg	42.51N	23.02 E
Sljudjanka	20	Ff	51.38N	103.40 E
Slobodka	15	Mb	47.54N	29.12 E
Slobodskoj	19	Fd	58.47N	50.12 E
Slobodzeja	16	Ff	46.43N	29.43 E
Slobozia [Rom.]	15	Ke	44.34N	27.22 E
Slobozia [Rom.]	15	Ie	44.30N	25.11 E
Slochteren	12	Ia	53.12N	6.50 E
Slocum Mountain	46	Gi	35.18N	117.13W
Slonim	19	Ce	53.05N	25.18 E
Sloten	12	Hb	52.54N	5.40 E
Slotermeer	12	Hb	52.55N	5.40 E
Slough	9	Mj	51.31N	0.36W
Slovakia (EN)=Slovensko	10	Ph	48.45N	19.30 E
Slovakia (EN)=Slovensko	5	Hf	48.45N	19.30 E
Slovečna	16	Fd	51.41N	29.42 E
Slovenia (EN) = Slovenija	5	Hf	46.00N	15.00 E
Slovenia (EN) = Slovenija	14	Id	46.00N	15.00 E
Slovenia (EN) = Slovenija [2]	14	Id	46.00N	15.00 E
Slovenija=Slovenia (EN) [2]	14	Id	46.00N	15.00 E
Slovenija = Slovenia (EN)	14	Id	46.00N	15.00 E
Slovenija = Slovenia (EN)	5	Hf	46.00N	15.00 E
Slovenska Bistrica	14	Jd	46.24N	15.34 E
Slovenske Gorice	14	Jd	46.35N	15.55 E
Slovenské rudohorie	10	Ph	48.45N	20.00 E
Slovensko [2]	10	Ph	48.45N	19.30 E
Slovensko=Slovakia (EN)	5	Hf	48.45N	19.30 E
Slovensko=Slovakia (EN)	10	Ph	48.45N	19.30 E
Slovenský kras	10	Qh	48.35N	20.40 E
Słubice	10	Kd	52.20N	14.35 E
Sluč [Bye.-U.S.S.R.]	16	Ec	52.08N	27.32 E
Sluč [Ukr.-U.S.S.R.]	16	Ed	51.37N	26.38 E
Sluck	19	Ce	53.02N	27.31 E
Slunj	14	Je	45.07N	15.35 E
Słupca	10	Nd	52.19N	17.52 E
Słupia	10	Mb	54.35N	16.50 E
Słupsk	10	Nb	54.28N	17.01 E
Słupsk [2]	10	Mb	54.30N	17.00 E
Slyne Head/Ceann Gólaim	9	Ch	53.24N	10.13W
Småland	7	Dh	57.20N	15.05 E
Smålandsfarvandet	8	Di	55.06N	11.20 E
Smålandsstenar	8	Eg	57.10N	13.24 E
Smalininkai/Smalininkaj	8	Ji	55.01N	22.32 E
Smalininkaj/Smalininkai	8	Ji	55.01N	22.32 E
Smallingerland-Drachten	11	Ma	53.06N	6.05 E
Smallwood Reservoir	38	Md	54.00N	64.30W
Smederevo	15	De	44.39N	20.56 E
Smederevska Palanka	15	De	44.22N	20.58 E
Smedjebacken	7	Df	60.08N	15.25 E
Smela	19	Df	49.13N	31.53 E
Smidovič	20	Ig	48.36N	133.50 E
Šmidta, Mys-	20	Nc	68.45N	178.40W
Šmidta, Ostrov-	21	La	81.08N	90.48 E
Šmidta, Poluostrov-	20	Jf	54.15N	142.40 E
Śmigiel	10	Md	52.01N	16.32 E
Smilde	12	Ib	52.56N	6.28 E
Smiltene	7	Fh	57.28N	25.56 E
Smirnovo	17	Ni	54.31N	69.28 E
Smirnyh	20	Jg	49.45N	142.53 E
Smith	55	Bl	35.30 S	61.36W
Smith Arm	42	Fc	66.15N	124.00W
Smith Bay [Ak.-U.S.]	40	Ib	70.51N	154.25W
Smith Bay [Can.]	42	Ja	77.15N	79.00W
Smith Center	45	Gg	39.47N	98.47W
Smithers	42	Ef	54.47N	127.10W
Smithfield [S.Afr.]	37	Df	30.09 S	26.30 E
Smithfield [Ut.-U.S.]	46	Jf	41.50N	111.50W
Smith Knoll	9	Pi	52.50N	2.10 E
Smith Mountain Lake	44	Hg	37.10N	79.40W
Smith Peak	46	Gb	48.50N	116.39W
Smith River	46	Jc	47.25N	111.29W
Smiths Falls	42	Jh	44.54N	76.01W
Smith Sound	46	Ba	51.18N	127.48W
Smithton	58	Fi	40.51 S	145.07 E
Smjadovo	15	Kf	43.04N	27.01 E
Smjörfjoll	7a	Cb	65.35N	14.46W
Smögen	8	Df	58.21N	11.13 E
Smoke Creek Desert	46	Ff	40.30N	119.40W
Smokey Dome	46	He	43.29N	114.56W
Smoky Bay	59	Gf	32.20 S	133.45 E
Smoky Cape	59	Kf	30.56 S	153.05 E
Smoky Falls	42	Jf	50.03N	82.10W
Smoky Hill	38	Jf	39.03N	96.48W
Smoky Hills	45	Gg	39.15N	99.00W
Smoky River	42	Fe	56.11N	117.19W
Smøla	7	Be	63.25N	8.00 E
Smolensk	6	Je	54.47N	32.03 E
Smolenskaja Oblast [3]	19	De	55.00N	33.00 E
Smolenskaja Vozvyšennost =Smolensk Upland (EN)	5	Je	54.40N	33.00 E
Smolensk Upland (EN)= Smolenskaja Vozvyšennost	5	Je	54.40N	33.00 E
Smolevići	16	Fb	54.03N	28.02 E
Smolianica	10	Ud	52.40N	24.40 E
Smólikas Óros	5	Ig	40.06N	20.55 E
Smoljan	15	Hh	41.35N	24.41 E
Smoljan [2]	15	Hh	41.40N	24.40 E
Smooth Rock Falls	44	Ga	49.20N	81.39W
Smorgon	19	Ce	54.31N	26.23 E
Smørstabbren	8	Cc	61.32N	8.06 E
Smrdeš	15	Fh	41.33N	22.28 E
Smygehamn	8	Ei	55.21N	13.22 E
Smygehuk	8	Ei	55.21N	13.23 E
Smyley, Cape-	66	Qf	72.00 S	78.50W
Smyrna	44	Ei	33.53N	84.31W
Smyrna (EN)=İzmir	22	Ef	38.25N	27.09 E
Smyšljajevka	7	Mj	53.17N	50.24 E
Smythe, Mount-	38	Gd	57.50N	124.59W
Snacke Point	51b	Bb	18.17N	62.58W
Snæfell	7a	Cb	64.48N	15.34W
Snaefell	9	Ig	54.16N	4.27W
Snæfellsjökull	7a	Ab	64.49N	23.46W
Snag	42	Dd	62.23N	140.22W
Snake Bay Settlement	59	Gb	11.25 S	130.40 E
Snake Range	46	Hg	39.00N	114.15W
Snake River [Can.]	42	Ec	65.57N	134.13W
Snake River [U.S.]	38	He	46.12N	119.02W
Snake River Plain	43	Ec	42.45N	114.30W
Snare	42	Fd	63.15N	116.08W
Snares Islands	61	Ci	48.00 S	166.35 E
Snarumselva	8	Cc	59.57N	9.58 E
Snåsa	7	Cd	64.15N	12.22 E
Sneek	11	La	53.02N	5.40 E
Snekermeer	11	La	52.59N	5.40 E
Snežnaja, Gora-	20	Lc	65.18N	165.30 E
Snežnik	14	Ie	45.26N	14.36 E
Snežnogorsk	20	Dc	68.15N	87.35 E
Šneżnoje	16	Kf	47.59N	38.50 E
Śniardwy, Jezioro-	10	Rc	53.46N	21.44 E
Śnieżka	5	He	50.45N	15.43 E
Śnieżnik	10	Mf	50.12N	16.50 E
Snigirevka	16	Hf	47.04N	32.45 E
Snillfjord	8	Ca	63.24N	9.30 E
Snina	10	Sh	48.59N	22.08 E
Snizort, Loch-	9	Gd	57.30N	6.25W
Snjatyn	16	De	48.29N	25.34 E
Snøhetta	5	Gc	62.20N	9.17 E
Snohomish	46	Dc	47.55N	122.06W
Snønuten	8	Be	59.31N	6.54 E
Snøonipa	8	Bc	61.42N	6.41 E
Snota	8	Cb	62.51N	9.06 E
Snov	16	Gd	51.32N	31.33 E
Snowbird Lake	42	Hd	60.40N	102.50W
Snowdon	5	Fe	53.04N	4.05W
Snowdonia	9	Jh	53.05N	3.55W
Snowdrift	42	Gd	62.23N	110.47W
Snowflake	46	Ji	34.30N	110.05W
Snow Hill	44	Jf	38.11N	75.24W
Snow Lake	42	Hf	54.53N	100.02W
Snow Mountain	43	Cd	39.23N	122.46W
Snowshoe Peak	46	Hb	48.13N	115.41W
Snowville	46	If	41.58N	112.43W
Snowy Mountain [B.C.-Can.]	46	Fb	49.02N	119.57W
Snowy Mountain [N.Y.-U.S.]	44	Jd	43.42N	74.23W
Snowy Mountains	59	Jg	36.30 S	148.20 E
Snowy River	59	Jg	37.48 S	148.32 E
Snudy, Ozero-	8	Li	55.40N	27.15 E
Snug Corner	49	Kb	22.32N	73.53W
Snuōl	25	Lf	12.04N	106.26 E
Snyder	43	Ge	32.44N	100.55W
Soalala	37	Hc	16.07 S	45.21 E
Soalara	37	Gd	23.35 S	43.44 E
Soanierana-Ivongo	37	Hc	16.54 S	49.34 E
Soar	12	Ab	52.52N	1.17W
Şoarş	15	Hd	45.56N	24.55 E
Soavinandriana	37	Hc	19.10 S	46.43 E
Sob [R.S.F.S.R.]	17	Mc	66.20N	66.02 E

Index Symbols

[1] Independent Nation	Historical or Cultural Region	Pass, Gap	Depression	Coast, Beach	Rock, Reef	Waterfall Rapids	Canal	Lagoon	Escarpment, Sea Scarp	Historic Site	Port
[2] State, Region	Mount, Mountain	Plain, Lowland	Polder	Cliff	Islands, Archipelago	River Mouth, Estuary	Glacier	Bank	Fracture	Ruins	Lighthouse
[3] District, County	Volcano	Delta	Desert, Dunes	Peninsula	Rocks, Reefs	Lake	Ice Shelf, Pack Ice	Seamount	Trench, Abyss	Wall, Walls	Mine
[4] Municipality	Hill	Salt Flat	Forest, Woods	Isthmus	Coral Reef	Salt Lake	Ocean	Tablemount	National Park, Reserve	Church, Abbey	Tunnel
[5] Colony, Dependency	Mountains, Mountain Range	Valley, Canyon	Heath, Steppe	Sandbank	Well, Spring	Intermittent Lake	Sea	Ridge	Point of Interest	Temple	Dam, Bridge
Continent	Hills, Escarpment	Crater, Cave	Oasis	Island	Geyser	Reservoir	Gulf, Bay	Shelf	Recreation Site	Scientific Station	
Physical Region	Plateau, Upland	Karst Features	Cape, Point	Atoll	River, Stream	Swamp, Pond	Strait, Fjord	Basin	Cave, Cavern	Airport	

Index Symbols

[1] Independent Nation
[2] State, Region
[3] District, County
[4] Municipality
[5] Colony, Dependency
Continent
Physical Region
Historical or Cultural Region
Mount, Mountain
Volcano
Hill
Mountains, Mountain Range
Hills, Escarpment
Plateau, Upland
Pass, Gap
Plain, Lowland
Delta
Salt Flat
Valley, Canyon
Crater, Cave
Karst Features
Depression
Polder
Desert, Dunes
Forest, Woods
Heath, Steppe
Oasis
Cape, Point
Coast, Beach
Cliff
Peninsula
Isthmus
Sandbank
Island
Atoll
Rock, Reef
Islands, Archipelago
Rocks, Reef
Coral Reef
Well, Spring
Geyser
River, Stream
Waterfall Rapids
River Mouth, Estuary
Lake
Salt Lake
Intermittent Lake
Sea
Gulf, Bay
Strait, Fjord
Canal
Glacier
Ice Shelf, Pack Ice
Ocean
Reservoir
Swamp, Pond
Lagoon
Bank
Seamount
Tablemount
Ridge
Shelf
Basin
Escarpment, Sea Scarp
Fracture
Trench, Abyss
National Park, Reserve
Point of Interest
Recreation Site
Cave, Cavern
Historic Site
Ruins
Wall, Walls
Church, Abbey
Temple
Scientific Station
Airport
Port
Lighthouse
Mine
Tunnel
Dam, Bridge

South Korea (EN)=Taehan-Min'guk 22 Of 38.00N 127.30 E
South Lake Tahoe 46 Eg 38.57N 120.01W
Southland 62 Bf 45.45S 168.00 E
South Loup River 45 Gf 41.04N 98.40W
South Lueti 36 Df 16.14S 23.12 E
South Magnetic Pole (1980) 66 Ie 65.08S 139.03 E
South Malosmadulu Atoll 25a Ba 5.10N 72.58 E
South Mountain 46 Ge 42.44N 116.54W
South Nahanni 42 Fd 61.03N 123.22W
South Negril Point 47 Ie 18.16N 78.22W
South Orkney Islands 66 Re 60.35S 45.30W
South Pass 38 Ie 42.22N 108.55W
South Pass [F.S.M.] 64d Bb 7.14N 151.48 E
South Pass [U.S.] 45 Ll 28.55N 89.20W
South Platte 38 Ie 41.07N 100.42W
South Point 51q Ab 13.02N 59.31W
South Pole 66 Bg 90.00S 0.00
South Porcupine 44 Ga 48.28N 81.13W
Southport [Eng.-U.K.] 9 Jh 53.39N 3.01W
Southport [N.C.-U.S.] 44 Hi 33.55N 78.01W
South Reef 63a Ee 13.00S 160.32 E
South Ronaldsay 9 Kc 58.46N 2.50W
South Rukuru 36 Fe 10.44S 34.14 E
South Saint Paul 45 Jd 44.52N 93.02W
South Sandwich Islands 66 Ad 56.00S 26.30W
South Sandwich Trench (EN) 3 Do 56.30S 25.00W
South Saskatchewan River 38 Id 53.15N 105.05W
South Shetland Islands 66 Re 62.00S 58.00W
South Shields 9 Lg 55.00N 1.25W
South Sioux City 45 He 42.28N 96.24W
South Sister 46 Ed 44.12N 121.45W
South Taranaki Bight 62 Fc 39.40S 174.15 E
South Trap 62 Bg 47.30S 167.55 E
South Tyne 9 Kg 54.59N 2.08W
South Uist 9 Fd 57.15N 7.24W
South Umpqua River 46 De 43.20N 123.25W
•Southwell 12 Ba 53.04N 0.57W
South Wellesley Islands 59 Hc 17.05S 139.25 E
South West Africa→Namibia 31 Ik 22.00S 17.00 E
Southwest Cape 57 Hi 47.17S 167.27 E
South West Cape 59 Jh 43.34S 146.02 E
Southwest Cape 51a Dc 17.42N 64.53W
Southwest Indian Ridge (EN) 3 Fm 32.00S 55.00 E
Southwest Miramichi River 44 Ob 46.50N 65.45W
Southwest Pacific Basin (EN) 3 Km 40.00S 150.00W
Southwest Pass 45 Ll 29.00N 89.20W
Southwest Point 49 Jb 22.10N 74.10W
South West Point 64g Ab 1.52N 157.33W
South West Point 51p Cb 12.27N 61.30W
Southwold 9 Oi 52.20N 1.40 E
South Yorkshire 9 Lh 53.30N 1.25W
Soutpansberg 37 Dd 22.58S 29.50 E
Soverato 14 Kl 38.41N 16.33 E
Sovetabad 18 Gd 40.14N 69.42 E
Sovetsk [R.S.F.S.R.] 19 Ed 57.36N 48.58 E
Sovetsk [R.S.F.S.R.] 19 Cd 55.05N 21.52 E
Sovetskaja Gavan 22 Qe 48.58N 140.18 E
Sovetski [R.S.F.S.R.] 7 Lh 56.47N 48.30 E
Sovetski [R.S.F.S.R.] 8 Md 60.29N 28.40 E
Sovetski [R.S.F.S.R.] 19 Gc 61.20N 63.29 E
Sovetskoje 19 Ef 47.17N 44.30 E
Soviet Union (EN)→Union of Soviet Socialist Republics (EN) 22 Jd 60.00N 80.00 E
Şowghān 24 Qh 28.20N 56.54 E
Sowie, Góry- 10 Mf 50.38N 16.30 E
Sōya 29a Ba 45.28N 141.53 E
Sōya-Kaikyō=La Perouse Strait (EN) 21 Qe 45.30N 142.00 E
Sōya-Misaki 27 Pb 45.31N 141.56 E
Soyatita 48 Fe 25.45N 107.22W
Soyo 36 Bd 6.05S 12.20 E
Sož 5 Je 51.57N 30.48 E
Sozopol 15 Kg 42.25N 27.42 E
Spa 11 Ld 50.29N 5.52 E
Spain (EN)=España 6 Fg 40.00N 4.00W
Špakovskoje 16 Lg 45.06N 42.00 E
Spalding 9 Mi 52.47N 0.10W
Spanish Fork 46 Jf 40.07N 111.39W
Spanish Peak 46 Fd 44.24N 119.46W
Spanish Point 51d Ba 17.33N 61.44W
Spanish Sahara (EN)→Western Sahara (EN) 31 Ff 24.30N 13.00W
Spanish Town [B.V.I.] 51a Db 18.27N 64.26W
Spanish Town [Jam.] 47 Ie 17.59N 76.57W
Sparbu 7 Ce 63.55N 11.28 E
Spargi, Isola- 14 Di 41.15N 9.20 E
Sparks 43 Dd 39.32N 119.45W
Sparreholm 8 Ge 59.04N 16.49 E
Sparta [Il.-U.S.] 45 Lg 38.07N 89.42W
Sparta [N.C.-U.S.] 44 Gg 36.30N 81.07W
Sparta [Tn.-U.S.] 44 Eh 35.56N 85.29W
Sparta [Wi.-U.S.] 45 Ke 43.57N 90.47W
Sparta (EN)=Spárti 15 Fl 37.05N 22.26 E
Spartanburg 43 Ke 34.57N 81.55W
Spartel, Cap- 30 Ge 35.48N 5.56W
Spárti=Sparta (EN) 15 Fl 37.05N 22.26 E
Spartivento, Capo- [It.] 14 Cl 38.53N 8.50 E
Spartivento, Capo- [It.] 5 Hh 37.55N 16.04 E
Spas-Demensk 16 Ib 54.24N 34.01 E
Spas-Klepiki 7 Ji 55.10N 40.13 E
Spassk-Rjazanski 7 Ji 54.27N 40.22 E
Spátha, Ákra-=Spatha, Cape- (EN) 15 Gn 35.42N 23.44 E
Spatha, Cape- (EN)=Spátha, Ákra- 15 Gn 35.42N 23.44 E
Spearfish 43 Gc 44.30N 103.52W
Spearman 45 Fh 36.12N 101.12W
Speedway 44 Df 39.47N 86.15W
Speicher 12 Ie 49.56N 6.38 E
Speightstown 50 Gf 13.15N 59.39W
Speke Gulf 36 Fc 2.20S 33.15 E
Spello 14 Gh 42.59N 12.40 E
Spenard 40 Jd 61.11N 149.55W
Spence Bay 39 Jc 69.32N 93.31W
Spencer [Ia.-U.S.] 43 Hc 43.09N 95.09W
Spencer [In.-U.S.] 44 Df 39.17N 86.46W
Spencer [Nb.-U.S.] 45 Ge 42.53N 98.42W
Spencer [W.V.-U.S.] 44 Gf 38.48N 81.22W
Spencer, Cape- 59 Hg 35.18S 136.53 E
Spencer Gulf 57 Eh 34.00S 137.00 E
Spenge 12 Kb 52.08N 8.29 E
Spenser Mountains 62 Ee 42.10S 172.35 E
Sperillen 8 Dd 60.30N 10.05 E
Sperkhiós 15 Fk 38.52N 22.34 E
Sperlonga 14 Hi 41.15N 13.26 E
Sperone, Capo- 14 Cl 38.55N 8.25 E
Sperrin Mountains/Sliabh Speirín 9 Fg 54.50N 7.05W
Spessart 10 Fg 49.55N 9.30 E
Spétsai 15 Gl 37.16N 23.09 E
Spétsai 15 Gl 37.16N 23.08 E
Spey 9 Jd 57.40N 3.06W
Spey Bay 9 Jd 57.40N 3.05W
Speyer 10 Eg 49.19N 8.26 E
Speyer-bach 12 Ke 49.19N 8.27 E
Speyside 50 Fg 11.18N 60.32W
Spezzano Albanese 14 Kk 39.40N 16.19 E
Spicer Islands 42 Jc 68.10N 79.00W
Spiekeroog 10 Dc 53.46N 7.42 E
Spiez 14 Bd 46.41N 7.42 E
Spijkenisse 12 Gc 51.51N 4.21 E
Spilimbergo 14 Gd 46.07N 12.54 E
Spilion 15 Hn 35.13N 24.32 E
Spilsby 12 Ca 53.11N 0.06 E
Spina 14 Gf 44.42N 12.08 E
Spinazzola 14 Kj 40.58N 16.05 E
Spincourt 12 He 49.20N 5.40 E
Spirit River 42 Fe 55.47N 118.50W
Spirovo 7 Ih 57.27N 35.01 E
Spiš 10 Qg 49.05N 20.30 E
Spišská Nová Ves 10 Qh 48.57N 20.34 E
Spitak 16 Ni 40.49N 44.14 E
Spitsbergen 67 Kd 78.00N 19.00 E
Spitsbergen 67 Kd 78.45N 16.00 E
Spittal an der Drau 14 Hd 46.48N 13.30 E
Spitzbergen Bank (EN) 41 Oc 76.00N 23.00 E
Spjelkavik 7 Be 62.28N 6.23 E
Split 6 Hg 43.31N 16.26 E
Split Lake 42 He 56.10N 96.10W
Spluga, Passo dello- 14 Dd 46.29N 9.20 E
Splügenpaß 14 Dd 46.29N 9.20 E
Spōgi/Špogi 8 Lh 56.02N 26.52 E
Špogi/Spōgi 8 Lh 56.02N 26.52 E
Spokane 39 He 47.40N 117.23W
Spokane, Mount- 46 Gc 47.55N 117.07W
Spokane River 46 Fc 47.44N 118.20W
Špola 19 Df 49.01N 31.24 E
Spoleto 14 Gh 42.44N 12.44 E
Spooner 45 Kd 45.50N 91.53W
Spoon River 45 Kf 40.18N 90.04W
Sporovo 10 Vd 52.25N 25.27 E
Spotsylvania 44 If 38.12N 77.35W
Sprague 46 Gc 47.18N 117.59W
Sprague River 46 Ee 42.34N 121.51W
Spray 46 Fd 44.50N 119.48W
Spreča 14 Mf 44.44N 18.06 E
Spree 10 Jd 52.32N 13.13 E
Spreewald 10 Je 51.55N 14.00 E
Spremberg/Grodk 10 Ke 51.33N 14.22 E
Sprengisandur 7a Bb 64.40N 18.07W
Springbok 31 Ik 29.43S 17.15 E
Spring Creek 45 Fd 45.45N 100.18W
Springdale 45 Ih 36.11N 94.08W
Springe 10 Fd 52.13N 9.33 E
Springer 45 Dh 36.22N 104.36W
Springer, Mount- 44 Ja 49.48N 74.51W
Springerville 46 Ki 34.08N 109.17W
Springfield [Co.-U.S.] 45 Eh 37.24N 102.37W
Springfield [Il.-U.S.] 39 Kf 39.47N 89.40W
Springfield [Ma.-U.S.] 43 Mc 42.07N 72.36W
Springfield [Mn.-U.S.] 45 Id 44.14N 94.59W
Springfield [Mo.-U.S.] 39 Jf 37.14N 93.17W
Springfield [N.Z.] 62 De 43.20S 171.56 E
Springfield [Oh.-U.S.] 43 Kd 39.55N 83.48W
Springfield [Or.-U.S.] 43 Cc 44.03N 123.01W
Springfield [S.D.-U.S.] 45 He 42.49N 97.54W
Springfield [Tn.-U.S.] 44 Dg 36.31N 86.52W
Springfontein 37 Df 30.19S 25.36 E
Spring Garden 54 Gb 6.59N 58.31W
Spring Hall 51q Ab 13.19N 59.36W
Springhill [La.-U.S.] 45 Jj 33.00N 93.28W
Springhill [N.S.-Can.] 42 Lg 45.39N 64.03W
Spring Mountains 46 Hh 36.10N 115.40W
Springs 37 De 26.13S 28.25 E
Springsure 59 Jd 24.07S 148.05 E
Spring Valley 46 Hg 39.10N 114.30W
Spring Valley 45 Je 43.41N 92.23W
Springville 46 Jf 40.10N 111.37W
Spruce Knob 38 Lf 38.42N 79.32W
Spruce Mountain [Az.-U.S.] 46 Ii 34.28N 112.24W
Spruce Mountain [Nv.-U.S.] 46 Hf 40.33N 114.49W
Spulico, Capo- 14 Kk 39.58N 16.38 E
Spurn Head 9 Nh 53.34N 0.07 E
Squamish 42 Fg 49.42N 123.09W
Squillace 14 Kl 38.47N 16.31 E
Squillace, Golfo di- 14 Kl 38.45N 16.50 E
Squinzano 14 Mj 40.26N 18.02 E
Srbica 15 Dg 42.45N 20.47 E
Srbija=Serbia (EN) 15 Df 44.00N 21.00 E
Srbija=Serbia (EN) 15 Df 44.00N 21.00 E
Srbija=Serbia (EN) 5 Ig 43.00N 21.00 E
Srbobran 15 Cd 45.33N 19.48 E
Srê Âmběl 25 Kf 11.07N 103.46 E
Sredinny Hrebet 21 Rd 56.00N 158.00 E
Sredna Gora 15 Hg 42.30N 25.00 E
Srednekolymsk 20 Kc 67.27N 153.41 E
Srednerusskaja Vozvyšennost=Central Russian Uplands (EN) 5 Je 52.00N 38.00 E
Srednesatyginski Tuman, Ozero- 17 Lg 59.45N 65.25 E
Srednesibirskoje Ploskogorje=Central Siberian Uplands (EN) 21 Mc 65.00N 105.00 E
Sredni Kujto, Ozero- 7 Hd 65.05N 31.30 E
Sredni Ural=Central Urals (EN) 5 Ld 58.00N 59.00 E
Sredni Urgal 20 If 51.13N 132.58 E
Sredni Verecki, Pereval- 16 Ce 48.49N 23.07 E
Srednjaja Ahtuba 16 Ne 48.43N 44.52 E
Srednjaja Olëkma 20 He 55.26N 120.40 E
Śrem 10 Nd 52.08N 17.01 E
Sremska Mitrovica 15 Ce 44.58N 19.37 E
Sremski Karlovci 15 Cd 45.12N 19.56 E
Sretensk 22 Nd 52.15N 117.43 E
Sri Gangānagar 25 Ec 29.55N 73.53 E
Srijem 15 Cd 45.00N 19.40 E
Srīkākulam 25 Ge 18.18N 83.54 E
Sri Lanka (Ceylon) 22 Ki 7.40N 80.50 E
Srīnagar 22 Jf 34.05N 74.49 E
Srivardhan 25 Ee 18.02N 73.01 E
Środa Śląska 10 Me 51.10N 16.36 E
Środa Wielkopolska 10 Nd 52.14N 17.17 E
Srpska Crnja 15 Dd 45.43N 20.42 E
Sruth na Maoile/North Channel 5 Fd 55.10N 5.40W
SSSR=Union of Soviet Socialist Republics (USSR) (EN) 22 Jd 60.00N 80.00 E
SSSR→Sojuz Sovetskih Socialističeskih Respublik 22 Jd 60.00N 80.00 E
Ssu-ch'uan Sheng→Sichuan Sheng=Szechwan (EN) 27 He 30.00N 103.00 E
Staaten River 59 Ic 16.24S 141.17 E
Stabroek 12 Gc 51.20N 4.22 E
Stack Skerry 9 Ib 59.02N 4.30W
Stade 10 Fc 53.36N 9.29 E
Staden 12 Fd 50.59N 3.01 E
Stadhavet 8 Ab 62.15N 5.05 E
Stådjan 8 Ec 61.58N 12.52 E
Stadlandet 8 Ab 62.05N 5.20 E
Stadskanaal 11 Ma 53.00N 6.55 E
Stadskanaal-Musselkanaal 12 Jb 52.56N 7.02 E
Stadthagen 12 Lb 52.19N 9.12 E
Stadtkyll 12 Id 50.21N 6.32 E
Stadtlohn 12 Ic 51.59N 6.56 E
Stadtoldendorf 10 Fe 51.54N 9.39 E
Staffa 9 Ge 56.25N 6.10W
Staffanstorp 8 Ei 55.38N 13.13 E
Staffelsee 10 Hi 47.42N 11.10 E
Staffora 14 De 45.04N 9.01 E
Stafford 9 Li 52.50N 2.00W
Stafford 9 Ki 52.48N 2.07W
Staffordshire 9 Li 52.55N 2.00W
Staicele/Stajcele 8 Kg 57.44N 24.39 E
Stainach 14 Ic 47.32N 14.06 E
Staines 12 Bc 51.26N 0.31W
Stajcele/Staicele 8 Kg 57.44N 24.39 E
Stakčin 10 Sg 49.00N 22.13 E
Stalać 15 Ef 43.40N 21.25 E
Stalham 12 Db 52.46N 1.31 E
Stalingrad→Volgograd 6 Kf 48.44N 44.25 E
Ställdalen 8 Fe 59.56N 14.56 E
Stalowa Wola 10 Sf 50.35N 22.02 E
Starnberger See 10 Ii 47.55N 12.20 E
Stamford [Ct.-U.S.] 44 Ke 41.03N 73.32W
Stamford [Eng.-U.K.] 9 Mi 52.39N 0.29W
Stamford [Tx.-U.S.] 45 Gj 32.57N 99.48W
Stamford, Lake- 45 Gj 33.05N 99.35W
Stampriet 37 Bd 24.20S 18.28 E
Stamsund 7 Cb 68.08N 13.51 E
Stanberry 45 If 40.13N 94.35W
Stancija Jakkabag 18 Fe 38.59N 66.42 E
Stancija-Karakul 19 Gh 39.30N 63.50 E
Standerton 37 De 26.58S 29.07 E
Standish 44 Fd 44.00N 83.57W
Stanford 46 Jc 47.09N 110.13W
Stånga 8 Hg 57.17N 18.28 E
Stångån 8 Ff 58.27N 15.37 E
Stange 8 Dd 60.43N 11.11 E
Stanger 37 Ee 29.27S 31.14 E
Stanke Dimitrov 15 Gg 42.16N 23.07 E
Stanley [Austl.] 59 Jh 40.46S 145.18 E
Stanley [Falk. Is.] 53 Kk 51.42S 57.51W
Stanley [N.D.-U.S.] 45 Eb 48.19N 102.23W
Stanley Falls (EN)=Ngaliema, Chutes- 30 Jh 0.30N 25.30 E
Stann Creek 49 Ce 16.50N 88.30W
Stanovoje Nagorje=Stanovoy Upland (EN) 21 Nd 56.00N 114.00 E
Stanovoj Hrebet=Stanovoy Range (EN) 21 Od 56.20N 126.00 E
Stanovoy Upland (EN)=Stanovoje Nagorje 21 Nd 56.00N 114.00 E
Stans 14 Cd 46.58N 8.22 E
Stansted Airport 12 Cc 51.54N 0.13 E
Stansted Mountfitchet 12 Cc 51.54N 0.12 E
Stanthorpe 59 Ke 28.39S 151.57 E
Stanton Banks 9 Fe 56.15N 7.50W
Staphorst 12 Ib 52.38N 6.14 E
Staples 45 Ic 46.21N 94.48W
Stapleton 45 Ff 41.29N 100.31W
Stąporków 10 Qe 51.09N 20.34 E
Starachowice 10 Re 51.03N 21.04 E
Staraja Majna 7 Li 54.36N 48.59 E
Staraja Russa 19 Dd 57.59N 31.23 E
Staraja-Vyževka 10 Ue 51.27N 24.34 E
Stará Ľubovňa 10 Qg 49.18N 20.42 E
Stara Moravica 15 Cd 45.52N 19.28 E
Stara Pazova 15 De 44.59N 20.10 E
Stara Planina=Balkan Mountains (EN) 5 Ig 43.15N 25.00 E
Stara Zagora 15 Ig 42.25N 25.38 E
Stara Zagora 6 Ig 42.25N 25.38 E
Starbuck Island 57 Le 5.37S 155.53W
Staretina 14 Kf 44.02N 16.43 E
Stargard Szczeciński 10 Lc 53.20N 15.02 E
Stari Begejski kanal 15 Dd 45.29N 20.25 E
Starica 7 Ih 56.30N 34.56 E
Starigrad 14 Kg 43.11N 16.36 E
Stari Vlah 15 Df 43.23N 20.10 E
Starke 44 Fk 29.57N 82.07W
Starkville 45 Lj 33.28N 88.48W
Starnberg 10 Hh 48.00N 11.21 E
Starobelsk 19 Df 49.15N 38.58 E
Starodub 19 De 52.35N 32.46 E
Starogard Gdański 10 Oc 53.59N 18.33 E
Starokonstantinov 16 Ee 49.43N 27.13 E
Starominskaja 19 Df 46.31N 39.06 E
Staroščerbinovskaja 16 Kf 46.37N 38.42 E
Starosubhangulovo 17 Hj 53.06N 57.20 E
Starotimoškino 7 Lj 53.43N 47.32 E
Start Point 9 Jk 50.13N 3.38W
Staryje Dorogi 16 Fc 53.02N 28.17 E
Stary Krym 16 Ig 45.02N 35.05 E
Stary Oskol 19 De 51.18N 37.51 E
Stary Sambor 16 Ce 49.29N 23.01 E
Stary Terek 16 Og 44.01N 47.24 E
Staßfurt 10 He 51.52N 11.35 E
Staszów 10 Rf 50.34N 21.10 E
State College 44 Ie 40.48N 77.52W
Staten Island (EN)=Estados, Isla de los- 52 Jk 54.47S 64.15W
Statesboro 44 Gi 32.27N 81.47W
Statesville 44 Gh 35.47N 80.53W
Stathelle 8 Ce 59.03N 9.41 E
Stathmós Krioneríou 15 Ek 38.20N 21.35 E
Statland 7 Cd 64.30N 11.08 E
Staunton 43 Ld 38.10N 79.05W
Stavanger 6 Gd 58.58N 5.45 E
Stavelot 12 Hd 50.23N 5.56 E
Staveren 11 Lb 52.53N 5.22 E
Stavern 8 Df 59.00N 10.02 E
Stavnoje 10 Sh 48.59N 22.45 E
Stavropol 6 Kf 45.02N 41.59 E
Stavropolskaja Vozvyšennost 16 Mg 45.10N 43.00 E
Stavropolski Kraj 19 Eg 45.00N 43.15 E
Stavrós [Grc.] 15 Fj 39.19N 22.14 E
Stavrós [Grc.] 15 Gi 40.40N 23.42 E
Stavroúpolis 15 Hh 41.12N 24.42 E
Stawell 59 Ig 37.04S 142.46 E
Stawiski 10 Sc 53.23N 22.09 E
Stawiszyn 10 Oe 51.55N 18.07 E
Stayton 46 Dd 44.48N 122.48W
Steamboat Springs 43 Fc 40.29N 106.50W
Stebnik 10 Tg 49.14N 23.34 E
Stedingen 12 Ka 53.10N 8.30 E
Steele 45 Gc 46.51N 99.55W
Steelpoort 37 Ed 24.48S 30.12 E
Steenbergen 12 Gc 51.35N 4.19 E
Steen River 42 Fe 59.38N 117.06W
Steensby Inlet 42 Jb 70.10N 78.25W
Steenstrups Gletscher 41 Gc 75.15N 57.30W
Steenvoorde 12 Ed 50.48N 2.35 E
Steenwijk 11 Mb 52.47N 6.08 E
Ştefăneşti 15 Kb 47.48N 27.12 E
Stefanie, Lake- (EN)=Chew Bahir 30 Kh 4.38N 36.50 E
Stefansson 42 Gb 73.30N 105.30W
Ştefleşti, Vîrful- 15 Gd 45.32N 23.48 E
Stege 8 Ej 54.59N 12.18 E
Steiermark=Styria (EN) 14 Ic 47.15N 15.00 E
Steiermark=Styria (EN) 14 Ic 47.15N 15.00 E
Steigerwald 10 Gg 49.40N 10.20 E
Steilrandberge 37 Ac 17.53S 13.20 E
Steinach 14 Fc 47.05N 11.28 E
Steinbach 42 Hg 49.32N 96.41W
Steinen, Rio- 54 Hf 12.05S 53.46W
Steinfeld (Oldenburg) 12 Kb 52.36N 8.13 E
Steinfort/Steinfurt 12 He 49.40N 5.55 E
Steinfurt 10 Dd 52.09N 7.20 E
Steinfurt/Steinfort 12 He 49.40N 5.55 E
Steinfurt-Borghorst 12 Jb 52.08N 7.25 E
Steinhagen 12 Kb 52.01N 8.24 E
Steinhausen 37 Bd 21.49S 18.20 E
Steinheim 12 Lc 51.51N 9.06 E
Steinhuder Meer 10 Fd 52.28N 9.19 E
Steinkjer 7 Cd 64.01N 11.30 E
Steinkopf 37 Be 29.18S 17.43 E
Steinshamn 8 Bb 62.47N 6.29 E
Steinsøy 7 Ac 61.00N 4.30 E
Steirisch-Niederösterreichische Kalkalpen 14 Jc 47.45N 15.30 E
Stekene 12 Gc 51.12N 4.02 E
Stekolny 20 Ke 60.00N 150.50 E
Stella 37 Ce 26.33S 24.53 E
Stellenbosch 37 Bf 33.58S 18.50 E
Stello 11a Ba 42.47N 9.25 E
Stelvio, Passo dello-/Stilfser Joch 14 Ed 46.32N 10.27 E
Stemwede 12 Kb 52.26N 8.26 E
Stenay 11 Le 49.29N 5.11 E
Stendal 10 Hd 52.36N 11.51 E
Stende 8 Jg 57.10N 22.28 E
Stende 8 Jg 57.40N 21.57 E
Stenhouse Bay 59 Hg 35.17S 136.56 E
Stenstorp 8 Ef 58.16N 13.43 E
Stenungsund 7 Cg 58.05N 11.49 E
Stepanakert 6 Kh 39.49N 46.44 E
Stepanavan 16 Ni 40.59N 44.20 E
Stephens, Cape- 62 Ed 40.42S 173.57 E
Stephens, Mount- 66 Rg 83.23S 51.27W
Stephens Passage 40 Me 57.50N 133.50W
Stephenville [Newf.-Can.] 42 Lg 48.33N 58.35W
Stephenville [Tx.-U.S.] 45 Gj 32.13N 98.12W
Steps Point 65c Cb 14.22S 170.45W
Sterea Ellás kai Évvoia 15 Hk 38.20N 24.30 E
Sterkstroom 37 Df 31.32S 26.32 E
Sterlibaševo 17 Gj 53.28N 55.15 E
Sterling [Co.-U.S.] 43 Gc 40.37N 103.13W
Sterling [Il.-U.S.] 45 Lf 41.48N 89.42W
Sterling City 45 Fk 31.50N 100.59W
Sterlitamak 6 Le 53.37N 55.58 E
Šternberk 10 Ng 49.44N 17.19 E
Sterzing/Vipiteno 14 Fd 46.54N 11.26 E
Stettin (EN)=Szczecin 6 He 53.24N 14.32 E
Stettiner Haff 10 Kc 53.46N 14.14 E
Stettler 42 Gf 52.19N 112.43W
Steubenville 43 Kc 40.22N 80.39W
Stevenage 9 Mj 51.54N 0.11W
Stevenson Entrance 40 Ie 57.45N 152.20W
Stevens Point 43 Jc 44.31N 89.34W
Stewart 42 Dd 63.18N 139.24W
Stewart 42 Ee 55.56N 129.59W
Stewart Crossing 42 Dd 63.19N 136.33W
Stewart Island 57 Hi 47.00S 167.50 E
Stewart Islands 57 He 8.20S 162.40 E
Steyerberg 12 Lb 52.34N 9.02 E
Steyning 12 Bd 50.53N 0.20W
Steynsburg 37 Df 31.15S 25.49 E
Steyr 14 Ib 48.02N 14.25 E
Steyr 14 Ib 48.03N 14.25 E
Štiavnické vrchy 10 Oh 48.15N 18.50 E
Stidia 13 Li 35.50N 0.05W
Stiene 8 Kg 57.19N 24.28 E
Stiens, Leeuwarderadeel- 12 Ha 53.16N 5.46 E
Stigliano 14 Kj 40.24N 16.14 E
St. Ignace 43 Kb 45.52N 84.43W
Stigtomta 8 Gf 58.48N 16.47 E
Stikine 38 Fd 56.40N 132.30W
Stikine Ranges 42 Ee 57.35N 131.00W
Stilfser Joch/Stelvio, Passo dello- 14 Ed 46.32N 10.27 E
Stilfontein 37 De 26.50S 26.50 E
Stilis 15 Fk 38.55N 22.37 E
Stillwater [Mn.-U.S.] 45 Jd 45.04N 92.49W
Stillwater [Ok.-U.S.] 43 Hd 36.07N 97.04W
Stillwater Range 46 Fg 39.50N 118.15W
Stilo 14 Kl 38.29N 16.28 E
Stilo, Punta- 14 Kl 38.27N 16.35 E
Štimlje 15 Eg 42.26N 21.03 E
Stînişoarei, Munţii- 15 Ib 47.20N 26.00 E
Stinnett 45 Fi 35.50N 101.27W
Štip 15 Fh 41.44N 22.12 E
Stirling 9 Je 56.07N 3.57W
Stirling Range 59 Df 34.25S 117.50 E
Stjernøya 7 Fa 70.18N 22.45 E
Stjørdalshalsen 7 Ce 63.28N 10.44 E
Stobi 15 Eh 41.33N 21.59 E
Stobrawa 10 Nf 50.50N 17.32 E
Stocka 8 Gc 61.54N 17.20 E
Stockach 10 Fi 47.51N 9.01 E
Stockbridge 12 Ac 51.06N 1.29W
Stockerau 14 Kb 48.23N 16.13 E
Stockholm 7 Dg 59.20N 18.00 E
Stockholm 6 Hd 59.20N 18.03 E
Stockport 9 Kh 53.25N 2.10W
Stocks Seamount (EN) 52 Mg 12.15S 32.00W
Stockton [Ca.-U.S.] 39 Gf 37.57N 121.17W
Stockton [Mo.-U.S.] 45 Jh 37.42N 93.48W
Stockton Lake 45 Jh 37.40N 93.45W
Stockton-on-Tees 9 Lg 54.34N 1.19W
Stockton Plateau 45 Ge 30.30N 102.30W
Stoczek Łukowski 10 Re 51.58N 21.58 E
Stöde 7 De 62.25N 16.35 E
Stoêng Trêng 25 Lf 13.31N 105.58 E
Stoer, Point of- 9 Hc 58.20N 5.25W
Stogovo 15 Dh 41.29N 20.39 E
Stohod 10 Ve 51.52N 25.44 E
Stoholm 8 Ch 56.29N 9.10 E
Stoj, Gora- 16 Ce 48.39N 23.15 E
Stojba 22 Pd 52.49N 131.43 E
Stoke-on-Trent 9 Kh 53.00N 2.10W
Stokksnes 7a Cb 64.14N 14.58W
Stokmarknes 7 Db 68.34N 14.55 E
Stol 15 Fe 44.11N 22.09 E
Stolac 14 Lg 43.05N 17.58 E
Stolbcy 16 Ec 53.31N 26.43 E
Stolberg 10 Cf 50.46N 6.14 E
Stolbovoj, Ostrov- 20 Ib 74.05N 136.00 E
Stolin 16 Ed 51.57N 26.52 E
Stolzenau 12 Lb 52.31N 9.04 E
Ston 14 Lh 42.50N 17.42 E
Stone 9 Ki 52.54N 2.10W
Stonehaven 9 Ke 56.58N 2.13W
Stonehenge 9 Lj 51.11N 1.49W
Stonehenge 59 Id 24.22S 143.17 E
Stoner 45 Bh 37.37N 108.18W
Stonewall 45 Ha 50.09N 97.21W
Stony 40 Hd 61.45N 156.35W
Stony Rapids 42 Ge 59.16N 105.50W
Stony River 40 Hd 61.47N 156.41W
Stony Stratford 12 Bb 52.03N 0.51W
Stony Tunguska (EN)=Podkamennaja Tunguska 21 Lc 61.36N 90.18 E
Stör 10 Fc 53.50N 9.25 E
Storå 8 Ch 56.19N 8.19 E
Storå 8 Fe 59.43N 15.08 E
Storå/Isojoki 7 Ee 62.07N 21.58 E
Stora Gla 8 Ee 59.30N 12.30 E
Stora Le 8 De 59.05N 11.55 E
Stora Lulevatten 7 Ec 67.08N 19.20 E
Storavan 7 Ed 65.42N 18.12 E
Storby 8 Hd 60.13N 19.34 E
Stord 7 Ag 59.55N 5.25 E
Storöa 7 Ee 62.07N 21.58 E
Stordal 8 Bb 62.23N 7.01 E

Index Symbols

Independent Nation · State, Region · District, County · Municipality · Colony, Dependency · Continent · Physical Region · Historical or Cultural Region · Mount, Mountain · Volcano · Hill · Mountains, Mountain Range · Hills, Escarpment · Plateau, Upland · Pass, Gap · Plain, Lowland · Delta · Salt Flat · Valley, Canyon · Crater, Cave · Karst Features · Depression · Polder · Desert, Dunes · Forest, Woods · Heath, Steppe · Oasis · Cape, Point · Coast, Beach · Cliff · Peninsula · Isthmus · Sandbank · Island · Atoll · Rock, Reef · Islands, Archipelago · Rocks, Reefs · Coral Reef · Well, Spring · Geyser · River, Stream · Waterfall Rapids · River Mouth, Estuary · Lake · Salt Lake · Intermittent Lake · Reservoir · Swamp, Pond · Canal · Glacier · Ice Shelf, Pack Ice · Ocean · Sea · Gulf, Bay · Strait, Fjord · Lagoon · Bank · Seamount · Tablemount · Ridge · Shelf · Basin · Escarpment, Sea Scarp · Fracture · Trench, Abyss · National Park, Reserve · Point of Interest · Recreation Site · Cave, Cavern · Historic Site · Ruins · Wall, Walls · Church, Abbey · Temple · Scientific Station · Airport · Port · Lighthouse · Mine · Tunnel · Dam, Bridge

Index Symbols

① Independent Nation · ② State, Region · ③ District, County · ④ Municipality · ⑤ Colony, Dependency · ■ Continent · Physical Region · Historical or Cultural Region · Mount, Mountain · Volcano · Hill · Mountains, Mountain Range · Hills, Escarpment · Plateau, Upland · Pass, Gap · Plain, Lowland · Delta · Salt Flat · Valley, Canyon · Crater, Cave · Karst Features · Depression · Polder · Desert, Dunes · Forest, Woods · Heath, Steppe · Oasis · Cape, Point · Coast, Beach · Cliff · Peninsula · Isthmus · Sandbank · Island · Atoll · Rock, Reef · Islands, Archipelago · Rocks, Reefs · Coral Reef · Well, Spring · Geyser · River, Stream · Waterfall Rapids · River Mouth, Estuary · Lake · Salt Lake · Intermittent Lake · Reservoir · Ocean · Sea · Gulf, Bay · Strait, Fjord · Swamp, Pond · Canal · Glacier · Ice Shelf, Pack Ice · Bank · Seamount · Tablemount · Ridge · Shelf · Basin · Lagoon · Escarpment, Sea Scarp · Fracture · Trench, Abyss · National Park, Reserve · Point of Interest · Recreation Site · Cave, Cavern · Historic Site · Ruins · Wall, Walls · Church, Abbey · Temple · Scientific Station · Port · Lighthouse · Mine · Tunnel · Dam, Bridge · Airport

Surahammar	8	Ge	59.43N	16.13 E
Sūrak	23	Id	25.43N	58.48 E
Surakarta	22	Nj	7.35 S	110.50 E
Şūrān	24	Ge	35.17N	36.45 E
Šurany	10	Oh	48.06N	18.11 E
Surar	35	Gd	7.29N	40.54 E
Surat	22	Jg	21.10N	72.50 E
Surat Thani	22	Li	9.06N	99.20 E
Surаž [Bye.-U.S.S.R.]	7	Hi	55.26N	30.43 E
Suraž [R.S.F.S.R.]	19	De	53.02N	32.29 E
Surčin	15	De	44.47N	20.17 E
Sur del Cabo San Antonio, Punta- ►	56	Ie	36.52 S	56.40W
Surduc	15	Gb	47.15N	23.21 E
Sûre ≈	10	Cg	49.44N	6.31 E
Surendranagar	25	Ed	22.42N	71.41 E
Surgères	11	Fh	46.06N	0.45W
Surgut	22	Jc	61.14N	73.20 E
Surgutiha	20	Dd	63.47N	87.20 E
Surhandarinskaja Oblast ③	19	Gh	38.00N	67.30 E
Surhandarja ≈	18	Ff	37.14N	67.20 E
Surhob ≈	19	Hh	38.54N	70.04 E
Surigao	26	Ie	9.45N	125.30 E
Surin	25	Kf	14.53N	103.30 E
Suriname ①	53	Ke	4.00N	56.00W
Suripá, Río- ≈	49	Mj	7.47N	69.53W
Sūrīyah=Syria (EN) ①	22	Ff	35.00N	38.00 E
Sūrmaq	24	Og	31.03N	52.48 E
Surmelin ≈	12	Fe	49.04N	3.31 E
Sürmene	24	Ib	40.55N	40.07 E
Surna ≈	8	Cb	62.59N	8.40 E
Surnadalsøra	8	Cb	62.59N	8.39 E
Surovikino	19	Ef	48.36N	42.54 E
Surovo	20	Fe	55.39N	105.36 E
Sur-Pakri/Suur-Pakri ◆	8	Je	59.50N	23.45 E
Surprise, Ile- ◆	63b	Ad	18.32 S	163.02 E
Surprise, Lac- ◍	44	Ja	49.20N	74.57W
Surrey ③	9	Mj	51.25N	0.30W
Surrey ▣	9	Mj	51.20N	0.05W
Sursee	14	Cc	47.10N	8.07 E
Sursk	16	Nc	53.04N	45.42 E
Surskoje	7	Li	54.31N	46.44 E
Surt	31	Ie	31.13N	16.35 E
Surt, Khalīj-=Sidra, Gulf of-(EN) ◧	30	Ie	31.30N	18.00 E
Surte	8	Eg	57.49N	12.01 E
Surtsey ◆	7a	Bc	63.20N	20.38W
Sürüç	24	Hd	36.58N	38.24 E
Surud Ad ▲	30	Lg	10.42N	47.09 E
Suruga-Wan ◧	28	Og	34.55N	138.35 E
Surulangun	26	Dg	2.37 S	102.45 E
Survey Pass ⌣	40	Ic	67.52N	154.10W
Sur-Vjajn/Suur Väin ≡	8	Jf	58.30N	23.20 E
Surwold	12	Jb	52.57N	7.31 E
Suså ≈	8	Di	55.11N	11.46 E
Šuša	16	Oj	39.43N	46.44 E
Susa [It.]	14	Be	45.08N	7.03 E
Susa [Jap.]	29	Bd	34.37N	131.36 E
Susa, Val di- ∨	14	Be	45.10N	7.10 E
Sušac ◆	14	Kh	42.46N	16.30 E
Sūsah [Lib.]	33	Dc	32.54N	21.58 E
Sūsah [Tun.] =Sousse (EN)	31	Ie	35.49N	10.38 E
Sūsah=Sousse (EN) ③	32	Jb	35.45N	10.30 E
Susak	14	If	44.31N	14.18 E
Susaki	27	Ne	33.22N	133.17 E
Susami	29	De	33.33N	135.29 E
Susamyr	18	Ic	42.09N	73.59 E
Susanville	43	Cc	40.25N	120.39W
Suşehri	24	Hb	40.11N	38.06 E
Suseja ≈	8	Kh	56.23N	25.00 E
Šušenskoje	20	Ef	53.19N	92.01 E
Sušice	10	Jg	49.14N	13.30 E
Susitna ≈	40	Id	61.16N	150.30W
Suslonger	7	Lh	56.18N	48.12 E
Susoh	26	Cf	3.43N	96.50 E
Susong	26	Di	30.10N	116.06 E
Suspiro	55	Ej	30.38 S	54.22W
Suspiro del Moro, Puerto del- ⌣	13	Ig	37.08N	3.40W
Susquehanna River ≈	43	Ld	39.33N	76.05W
Susques	56	Gb	23.25 S	66.29W
Sussex ▣	9	Mk	50.55N	0.30W
Sussex	44	Oc	45.43N	65.31W
Sussex, Vale of- ∨	9	Mk	51.00N	0.15W
Susubona	63a	Dc	8.19 S	159.27 E
Susuman	22	Qc	62.47N	148.10 E
Susurluk	24	Cc	39.54N	28.10 E
Susuzmüsellim	15	Kh	41.06N	27.03 E
Šušvė ≈	8	Ji	55.08N	23.53 E
Susz	10	Pc	53.44N	19.20 E
Suţeşti	15	Kd	45.13N	27.26 E
Sutherland	37	Cf	32.24 S	20.40 E
Sutherland Falls ⤓	62	Bf	44.48 S	167.44 E
Sutherlin	46	De	43.25N	123.19W
Sutla ≈	14	Je	45.51N	15.41 E
Sutlej ≈	21	Jg	29.23N	71.02 E
Sutton	44	Gf	38.41N	80.43W
Sutton, London-	12	Bc	51.21N	0.12W
Sutton Bridge	12	Cb	52.46N	0.11 E
Sutton in Ashfield	12	Aa	53.07N	1.16W
Sutton Scotney	12	Ac	51.09N	1.20W
Suttor River ≈	59	Jd	21.25 S	147.45 E
Suttsu	28	Pc	42.48N	140.14 E
Sütüler	24	Dd	37.30N	30.59 E
Sutwik ◆	40	He	56.34N	157.05W
Su'uholo	63a	Ec	9.46 S	161.58 E
Suunduk ≈	16	Ud	51.46N	58.46 E
Suure-Jaani	7	Fg	58.31N	25.29 E
Suur-Pakri/Sur-Pakri ◆	8	Je	59.50N	23.45 E
Suur Väin/Sur-Vjajn ≡	8	Jf	58.30N	23.20 E
Suva	58	If	18.08 S	178.25 E
Suvadiva Atoll ⊙	21	Ji	0.30N	73.13 E
Suva Gora ⛰	15	Eh	41.51N	21.03 E
Suva Planina ⛰	15	Ff	43.08N	22.13 E
Suvasvesi ◍	7	Ge	62.40N	28.10 E
Suvorov	16	Jb	54.08N	36.32 E
Suvorovo [Mold.-U.S.S.R.]	15	Mc	46.33N	29.35 E
Suvorovo [Ukr.-U.S.S.R.]	15	Ld	45.35N	29.00 E
Suvorovskaja	16	Mg	44.10N	42.38 E
Suwa	28	Of	36.02N	138.08 E
Suwa-Ko ◍	29	Fc	36.03N	138.05 E
Suwałki	10	Sb	54.07N	22.56 E
Suwałki ②	10	Sb	54.05N	22.55 E
Suwalskie, Pojezierze- ⧗	10	Sb	54.15N	23.00 E
Suwannee River ≈	44	Fk	29.18N	83.09W
Suwanose-Jima ◆	27	Mf	29.40N	129.45 E
Suwarrow Atoll ⊙	57	Kf	13.15 S	163.05W
Suwayqīyah, Hawr as- ◍	24	Lf	32.40N	46.03 E
Suways, Khalīj as-=Suez, Gulf of-(EN) ◧	30	Kf	28.10N	33.27 E
Suways, Qanāt as-=Suez Canal (EN) ═	30	Ke	29.55N	32.33 E
Suwŏn	27	Md	37.16N	127.01 E
Suxian	27	Ke	33.36N	116.58 E
Suzaka	29	Fc	36.39N	138.18 E
Suzdal	7	Jh	56.28N	40.27 E
Suzhou	22	Of	31.16N	120.37 E
Suzhou/Jiuquan	22	Lf	39.46N	98.34 E
Suzi He ≈	28	Hd	41.56N	124.20 E
Suzu	27	Od	37.25N	137.17 E
Suzuka	29	Ed	34.51N	136.35 E
Suzuka-Sanmyaku ⛰	29	Ed	35.10N	136.20 E
Suzu-Misaki ►	28	Nf	37.28N	137.20 E
Suzun	20	Df	53.47N	82.19 E
Suzzara	14	Ef	45.00N	10.45 E
Særholthalvøya ⊳	7	Ga	70.30N	26.05 E
Svågan ≈	8	Gc	61.54N	16.33 E
Svalbard ⑤	67	Kd	78.00N	20.00 E
Svaljava	16	Ce	48.32N	22.59 E
Svalöv	8	Ei	55.55N	13.06 E
Svaneholm	8	Ee	59.11N	12.33 E
Svaneke	7	Di	55.08N	15.09 E
Svängsta	8	Fh	56.16N	14.46 E
Svanøy ◆	8	Ac	61.30N	5.05 E
Svapa ≈	16	Id	51.44N	34.59 E
Svappavaara	7	Ec	67.39N	21.04 E
Svärdsjö	8	Fd	60.45N	15.55 E
Svartå	8	Fe	59.08N	14.31 E
Svartälven ≈	8	Fe	59.20N	14.35 E
Svartån [Swe.] ≈	8	Fe	59.17N	15.15 E
Svartån [Swe.] ≈	8	Ff	58.28N	15.33 E
Svartån [Swe.] ≈	8	Ge	59.37N	16.33 E
Svartenhuk Halvø= Svartenhuk Peninsula (EN) ⊳	41	Gd	71.30N	55.20W
Svartenhuk Peninsula (EN) =Svartenhuk, Halvø ⊳	41	Gd	71.30N	55.20W
Svartisen ❄	7	Cc	66.38N	13.58 E
Svatoj Nos, Mys- ►	20	Jb	72.45N	140.45 E
Svatovo	19	Df	49.24N	38.13 E
Svay Riĕng	25	Lf	11.05N	105.48 E
Sveabreen ❄	66	Cf	72.08 S	1.53 E
Sveagruva	41	Nc	78.39N	16.25 E
Svealand ▣	7	Dd	60.30N	15.30 E
Svealand ⧗	5	Hc	60.30N	15.30 E
Svedala	8	Ei	55.30N	13.14 E
Sveg	7	De	62.02N	14.21 E
Švėkšna	8	Ii	55.32N	21.30 E
Svelgen	7	Af	61.45N	5.18 E
Svelvik	8	De	59.37N	10.24 E
Švenčėneljaj/Švenčioneliai	7	Gi	55.09N	26.02 E
Švenčėnis/Švenčionys	7	Gi	55.07N	26.12 E
Švenčioneliai/Švenčėneljaj	7	Gi	55.09N	26.02 E
Švenčionys/Švenčėnis	7	Gi	55.07N	26.12 E
Svendborg	7	Ci	55.03N	10.37 E
Svendsen Peninsula ⊳	42	Ja	77.50N	84.00W
Svenljunga	7	Ch	57.30N	13.07 E
Svenska högarna ✲	8	He	59.35N	19.35 E
Svenskøya ◆	41	Oc	78.43N	26.30 E
Svenstavik	7	De	62.46N	14.27 E
Šventoj/Šventoji	8	Ih	56.04N	20.59 E
Šventoji ≈	7	Fi	55.05N	24.24 E
Šventoji/Šventoj	8	Ih	56.04N	20.59 E
Sverdlovsk	22	Id	56.51N	60.36 E
Sverdlovskaja Oblast ③	19	Gd	59.00N	62.00 E
Sverdrup, Ostrov- ◆	20	Cb	74.30N	79.35 E
Sverdrup Channel ≡	42	Ha	80.00N	96.30W
Sverdrup Islands ◆	38	Jb	79.00N	98.00W
Sverige=Sweden (EN) ①	6	Hc	62.00N	15.00 E
Svetac ◆	14	Jg	43.02N	15.45 E
Svēte/Svete ≈	8	Jh	56.40N	23.38 E
Svete/Svēte ≈	8	Jh	56.40N	23.38 E
Sveti Naum ⌂	15	Di	40.55N	20.45 E
Sveti Nikola, Prohod- ⌣	15	Ff	43.27N	22.36 E
Sveti Nikole	15	Eh	41.52N	21.57 E
Sveti Stefan	15	Bg	42.16N	18.54 E
Svetlaja	20	Ig	46.31N	138.18 E
Svetli	20	Ge	58.34N	116.00 E
Svetlogorsk [Bye.-U.S.S.R.]	19	Ce	52.38N	29.42 E
Svetlogorsk [R.S.F.S.R.]	8	Ij	54.55N	20.08 E
Svetlograd	19	Ef	45.19N	42.40 E
Svetlovodsk	16	He	49.02N	33.15 E
Svetly [R.S.F.S.R.]	19	Ge	50.51N	60.53 E
Svetly [R.S.F.S.R.]	7	Ei	54.41N	20.08 E
Svetly Jar	16	Ne	48.29N	44.46 E
Svetogorsk	7	Gf	61.07N	28.58 E
Svetozarevo	15	Ef	43.59N	21.15 E
Sviča ≈	10	Ug	49.04N	24.06 E
Svid ≈	7	Jf	61.13N	38.45 E
Svidník	10	Rg	49.18N	21.35 E
Svidník ▲	10	Kg	49.23N	14.58 E
Svijaga ≈	19	Ed	55.39N	48.28 E
Svilaja ⛰	14	Kg	43.50N	16.26 E
Svilengrad	15	Jh	41.46N	26.12 E
Svincovy Rudnik	18	Ff	37.52N	66.28 E
Svinecea Mare, Vîrful- ▲	15	Fe	44.48N	22.09 E
Svir ≈	5	Jc	60.30N	32.48 E
Svir	8	Lj	54.50N	26.34 E
Svirica	7	Hf	60.30N	32.54 E
Svirsk	20	Ff	53.04N	103.18 E
Svisloč ≈	16	Fc	53.27N	28.59 E
Svisloč	16	Dc	53.03N	24.07 E
Svištov	15	If	43.37N	25.20 E
Svit	10	Qg	49.03N	20.12 E
Svitava ≈	10	Mg	49.11N	16.38 E
Svitavy	10	Mg	49.46N	16.27 E
Svizra / Svizzera / Schweiz / Suisse = Switzerland (EN) ①	6	Gf	46.00N	8.30 E
Svizzera / Schweiz / Suisse / Svizra = Switzerland (EN) ①	6	Gf	46.00N	8.30 E
Svjatoj Nos, Mys- ►	5	Jb	68.10N	39.43 E
Svobodny	22	Od	51.24N	128.07 E
Svoge	15	Gg	42.58N	23.21 E
Svolvær	7	Db	68.14N	14.34 E
Svratka ≈	10	Mh	48.52N	16.38 E
Svrljig	15	Ff	43.25N	22.08 E
Svulrya	8	Ed	60.25N	12.24 E
Svytaya Anna Trough (EN) ⊻	67	He	80.00N	70.00 E
Swabia (EN)=Schwaben ⧗	10	Gh	48.20N	10.30 E
Swabian-Bavarian Plateau (EN)=Schwäbisch-Bayerisches Alpenvorland ▬	5	Hf	48.15N	10.30 E
Swabian Jura (EN)= Schwäbische Alb ⛰	5	Gf	48.25N	9.30 E
Swaffham	12	Cb	52.39N	0.41 E
Swain Reefs ✺	57	Gg	21.40 S	152.15 E
Swains Atoll ⊙	57	Jf	11.03 S	171.05W
Swainsboro	44	Fi	32.36N	82.20W
Swakop ≈	37	Ad	22.41 S	14.31 E
Swakopmund ③	37	Ad	22.30 S	15.00 E
Swakopmund	31	Ik	22.41 S	14.34 E
Swale ≈	9	Lg	54.06N	1.20W
Swalmen	12	Ic	51.14N	6.02 E
Swanage	9	Lk	50.37N	1.58W
Swan Hill	59	Ig	35.21 S	143.34 E
Swan Range ⛰	46	Ic	47.50N	113.40W
Swan River	42	Hf	52.06N	101.16W
Swansboro	44	Ih	34.36N	77.07W
Swansea [Austl.]	59	Jh	42.08 S	148.04 E
Swansea [Wales-U.K.]	6	Fe	51.38N	3.57W
Swansea Bay ◧	9	Jj	51.35N	3.52W
Swans Island ◆	44	Mc	44.10N	68.25W
Swanson Lake ◍	45	Ff	40.09N	101.06W
Swan Valley	46	Je	43.28N	111.20W
Swartberge ⛰	30	Jl	33.23 S	21.48 E
Swarzędz	10	Nd	52.26N	17.05 E
Swastika	44	Ga	48.07N	80.12W
Swaziland ①	31	Kk	26.30 S	31.10 E
Sweden (EN)=Sverige ①	6	Hc	62.00N	15.00 E
Swedru	34	Ed	5.32N	0.42W
Sweet Grass Hills ⋒	46	Jb	48.55N	111.30W
Sweet Home	46	Dd	44.24N	122.44W
Sweetwater	43	Ge	32.28N	100.25W
Sweetwater River ≈	43	Fc	42.31N	107.02W
Swellendam	37	Cf	34.02 S	20.26 E
Świder ≈	10	Rd	52.08N	21.12 E
Świdnica	10	Mf	50.51N	16.29 E
Świdnik	10	Se	51.14N	22.41 E
Świdwin	10	Lc	53.47N	15.47 E
Świebodzin	10	Ld	52.15N	15.32 E
Świecie	10	Oc	53.25N	18.28 E
Świętej Anny, Góra- ▲	10	Of	50.28N	18.13 E
Świętokrzyskie, Góry- ▲	10	Qf	50.55N	21.00 E
Swift Current	42	Gf	50.17N	107.50W
Swift Current Creek ≈	46	La	50.40N	107.44W
Swift River	42	Ed	60.05N	131.11W
Swilly, Lough-/Loch Suili ◧	9	Ff	55.10N	7.38W
Swinburne, Cape - ►	42	Hb	71.14N	98.33W
Swindon	9	Lj	51.34N	1.47W
Swinford/Béal Átha na Muice	9	Eh	53.57N	8.57W
Świnoujście	10	Kc	53.53N	14.14 E
Swischenahner Meer ◍	12	Ka	53.12N	8.01 E
Swisttal	12	Id	50.44N	6.54 E
Switzerland (EN) = Schweiz / Suisse / Svizra / Svizzera ①	6	Gf	46.00N	8.30 E
Switzerland (EN) = Suisse / Svizra / Svizzera / Schweiz ①	6	Gf	46.00N	8.30 E
Switzerland (EN) = Svizra / Svizzera / Schweiz / Suisse ①	6	Gf	46.00N	8.30 E
Switzerland (EN) = Svizzera / Schweiz / Suisse / Svizra ①	6	Gf	46.00N	8.30 E
Syčevka	16	Ib	55.51N	34.15 E
Syców	10	Ne	51.19N	17.43 E
Sydfalster-Gedser	7	Ci	54.35N	11.57 E
Sydkap Ice Cap ❄	42	Ja	76.30N	85.00W
Sydney [Austl.]	58	Gh	33.52 S	151.13 E
Sydney [N.S.-Can.]	39	Me	46.09N	60.11W
Sydney → Manra Atoll ⊙	57	Je	4.27 S	171.15W
Sydney-Campbelltown	59	Kf	34.04 S	150.49 E
Sydney Lake ◍	45	Ia	50.40N	94.24W
Sydney Mines	42	Lg	46.14N	60.12W
Sydney-Penrith	59	Kf	33.45 S	150.42 E
Syktyvkar	6	Lc	61.40N	50.46 E
Sylacauga	44	Di	33.10N	86.15W
Sylane ▲	7	Ce	63.02N	12.13 E
Sylarna ▲	7	Ce	63.02N	12.13 E
Sylhet	25	Id	24.54N	91.52 E
Sylling	8	De	59.54N	10.17 E
Sylt ◆	10	Eb	54.55N	8.20 E
Sylva ≈	17	Hh	57.40N	56.57 E
Sylvania	44	Gi	32.45N	81.38W
Sylvania Tablemount (EN) ⊼	60	Ge	11.58N	165.00 E
Sylvan Pass ⌣	43	Ec	44.28N	110.08W
Sylvester	44	Fj	31.32N	83.49W
Sylvester, Lake- ◍	59	Hc	18.50 S	135.50 E
Sym ≈	20	Ed	60.15N	90.02 E
Syndassko	20	Fb	73.14N	108.05 E
Synja ≈	17	Ld	65.12N	64.45 E
Synnfjell ▲	8	Cc	61.05N	9.45 E
Syowa ⚛	66	De	69.00 S	39.35 E
Syracuse [Ks.-U.S.]	45	Fh	37.59N	101.45W
Syracuse [N.Y.-U.S.]	39	Le	43.03N	76.09W
Syracuse (EN)=Siracusa	6	Hh	37.04N	15.18 E
Syrdarinskaja Oblast ③	19	Gg	40.30N	68.40 E
Syrdarja	19	Gg	40.52N	68.38 E
Syrdarja=Syr Darya (EN) ≈	21	Ie	46.03N	61.00 E
Syr Darya (EN)= Syrdarja ≈	21	Ie	46.03N	61.00 E
Syria (EN) ⧗	21	Ff	35.00N	38.00 E
Syria (EN)=Sūrīyah ①	22	Ff	35.00N	38.00 E
Syriam	25	Je	16.46N	96.15 E
Syrian Desert- (EN)=Shām, Bādiyat ash- ∴	21	Ff	32.00N	40.00 E
Syrkovoje, Ozero- ◍	17	Lf	60.40N	65.00 E
Syrski	16	Kc	52.36N	39.28 E
Sysert	17	Jh	56.31N	60.49 E
Sysmä	7	Ff	61.30N	25.41 E
Sysola ≈	19	Fc	61.42N	50.58 E
Sysslebäck	8	Ed	60.44N	12.52 E
Sysulp, Gora- ▲	15	Ha	48.29N	24.17 E
Syverma, Plato- ▬	21	Lc	67.00N	99.00 E
Syzran	6	Ke	53.09N	48.27 E
Szabolcs-Szatmár ②	10	Sh	48.00N	22.10 E
Szamocin	10	Nc	53.02N	17.08 E
Szamos ≈	15	Fa	48.07N	22.20 E
Szamotuły	10	Md	52.37N	16.35 E
Szarvas	10	Qj	46.52N	20.33 E
Szczawnica Krościenko	10	Qg	49.26N	20.30 E
Szczebrzeszyn	10	Sf	50.42N	22.59 E
Szczecin ②	10	Kc	52.35N	14.30 E
Szczecin=Stettin (EN)	6	He	53.24N	14.32 E
Szczecinek	10	Mc	53.43N	16.42 E
Szczeciński, Zalew- ◧	10	Kc	53.46N	14.14 E
Szczekociny	10	Pf	50.38N	19.50 E
Szczerców	10	Pe	51.18N	19.09 E
Szczucin	10	Rf	50.18N	21.04 E
Szczuczyn	10	Sc	53.34N	22.18 E
Szczytno	10	Qc	53.34N	21.00 E
Szechwan (EN)=Sichuan Sheng (Ssu-ch'uan Sheng) ②	27	He	30.00N	103.00 E
Szechwan (EN)=Ssu-ch'uan Sheng → Sichuan Sheng ②	27	He	30.00N	103.00 E
Szécsény	10	Ph	48.05N	19.31 E
Szeged	6	If	46.15N	20.10 E
Szeged ②	10	Qj	46.16N	20.08 E
Szeghalom	10	Ri	47.02N	21.10 E
Székesfehérvár	6	Hf	47.12N	18.25 E
Szekszárd	10	Oj	46.21N	18.43 E
Szendrő	10	Qh	48.24N	20.44 E
Szentendre	10	Pi	47.40N	19.05 E
Szentes	10	Qj	46.39N	20.16 E
Szentgotthárd	10	Mj	46.57N	16.17 E
Szerencs	10	Rh	48.10N	21.12 E
Szeskie Wzgórza ▲	10	Sb	54.14N	22.22 E
Szigetvár	10	Nj	46.03N	17.48 E
Szkwa ≈	10	Rc	53.10N	21.45 E
Szlichtyngowa	10	Me	51.43N	16.15 E
Szob	10	Oi	47.49N	18.52 E
Szolnok	10	Qi	47.11N	20.12 E
Szolnok ②	10	Qi	47.15N	20.30 E
Szombathely	10	Mi	47.14N	16.37 E
Szprotawa	10	Le	51.34N	15.33 E
Szreniawa ≈	10	Qf	50.10N	20.35 E
Sztum	10	Pc	53.56N	19.01 E
Szubin	10	Nc	53.00N	17.44 E
Szydłów	10	Rf	50.35N	21.01 E
Szydłowiec	10	Qe	51.14N	20.51 E

T

Taakoka ◆	64p	Cc	21.15 S	159.43W
Taalintendas/Dalsbruk	8	Jd	60.02N	22.31 E
Taavetti	8	Ld	60.55N	27.34 E
Tab	10	Oj	46.44N	18.02 E
Tabacal	56	Hb	23.16 S	64.15W
Ţābah	24	Ji	27.02N	42.08 E
Tabaqah	24	He	35.52N	38.34 E
Tabar Islands ⁂	57	Ge	2.50 S	152.00 E
Ţabarqah	32	Ib	36.57N	8.45 E
Ţabas	24	Qf	33.36N	56.54 E
Tabasará, Serranía de- ⛰	49	Gi	8.33N	81.40W
Tabasco ②	47	Fe	18.00N	92.40W
Tabasco y Campeche, Llanos de- ▭	47	Fe	18.15N	91.00W
Tabašino	7	Lh	56.59N	47.43 E
Tābask, Kūh-e- ▲	24	Nh	29.52N	51.49 E
Tabay	55	Ci	28.18 S	58.17W
Tabelbala	32	Gd	29.24N	3.15W
Taber	42	Gg	49.47N	112.08W
Taberg	8	Fg	57.41N	14.05 E
Taberg ▲	8	Fg	57.41N	14.05 E
Tabernacle	51c	Ab	17.23N	62.46W
Tabernas	13	Jg	37.03N	2.23W
Tabernes de Valldigna	13	Le	39.04N	0.16W
Tabiteuea Atoll ⊙	57	Ie	1.20 S	174.50 E
Tabla	34	Fc	13.46N	3.01 E
Tablas ◆	26	Hd	12.24N	122.02 E
Tablas Strait ≡	26	Hd	12.40N	121.48 E
Tablat	13	Ph	36.25N	3.19 E
Tablazo, Bahía del- ◧	49	Lh	10.52N	71.35W
Table Cape ►	62	Gc	39.06 S	178.00 E
Table Rock Lake ◍	45	Jh	36.35N	93.30W
Tabocas	55	Jb	14.39 S	45.28W
Taboco, Rio- ≈	55	Ed	19.53 S	55.58W
Tabola ≈	16	Pg	45.53N	48.20 E
Tábor	10	Kg	49.25N	14.41 E
Tabora	31	Ki	5.01 S	32.48 E
Tabora ③	36	Fd	5.20 S	32.30 E
Tabory	17	Lg	58.31N	64.33 E
Tabou	31	Gh	4.25N	7.21W
Tabrīz	22	Gf	38.05N	46.18 E
Tábua	13	Dd	40.21N	8.02W
Tabuaeran Atoll (Fanning) ⊙	57	Ld	3.52N	159.20W
Tabūk	22	Fg	28.23N	36.35 E
Tabuk	26	Hc	17.24N	121.25 E
Ţaburbah	14	Dn	36.50N	9.50 E
Tabursuq	14	Dn	36.28N	9.15 E
Tabursuq, Monts de- ⛰	14	Dn	36.25N	9.05 E
Tabusintac	44	Ob	47.24N	65.02W
Tabwemasana ▲	63b	Cb	15.22 S	166.45 E
Täby	7	Eg	59.30N	18.03 E
Tacámbaro de Codallos	48	Ih	19.14N	101.28W
Tacarcuna, Cerro- ▲	49	Ij	8.05N	77.17W
Tacarigua, Laguna de- ◎	50	Dg	10.15N	65.50W
Tacheng/Qoqek	22	Ke	46.45N	82.57 E
Tachibana-Wan ◧	29	Be	32.45N	130.05 E
Tachichilte, Isla de- ◆	48	Ee	24.59N	108.04W
Tachikawa [Jap.]	29	Fd	35.42N	139.23 E
Tachikawa [Jap.]	29	Fb	38.48N	139.58 E
Táchira ②	54	Db	7.50N	72.05W
Tachiumet	33	Bd	26.19N	10.03 E
Tachov	10	Ig	49.48N	12.40 E
Tachungnya	64b	Bb	14.58N	145.36 E
Tacinski	16	Le	48.13N	41.17 E
Tacir	15	Mi	40.32N	29.44 E
Tacloban	22	Oh	11.15N	125.00 E
Tacna	53	Ig	18.01 S	70.15W
Tacna ②	54	Dg	17.40 S	70.20W
Tacoma	39	Ge	47.15N	122.27W
Tacotalpa, Río- ≈	48	Mi	17.50N	92.52W
Tacuaral	55	Cd	18.59 S	58.07W
Tacuarembó ②	55	Ek	32.10 S	55.30W
Tacuarembó, Río- ≈	55	Ek	32.25 S	55.29W
Tacuarí, Río- ≈	55	Fk	32.46 S	53.18W
Tacuati	55	Df	23.27 S	56.35W
Tadami	29	Fc	37.21N	139.17 E
Tadami-Gawa ≈	29	Fc	37.38N	139.45 E
Tadarimana, Rio- ≈	55	Ec	16.29 S	54.31W
Tademaït, Plateau du- ▬	30	Hf	28.30N	2.15 E
Tadine	63b	Ce	21.33 S	167.53 E
Tadjeraout ≈	32	He	21.17N	1.20 E
Tadjetaret ≈	32	Ie	22.00N	7.30 E
Tadjourah	35	Gc	11.45N	42.54 E
Tadjourah, Golfe de- ◧	35	Gc	11.45N	43.00 E
Tadoule Lake ◍	42	He	58.35N	98.20W
Tadoussac	44	Ma	48.09N	69.43W
Tadzhik SSR (EN)= Tadžikskaja SSR ②	19	Hh	39.00N	71.00 E
Tadžikskaja Sovetskaja Socialističeskaja Respublika ②	19	Hh	39.00N	71.00 E
Tadžikskaja SSR/ Respublikai Soveth Socialisti Todžikiston ②	19	Hh	39.00N	71.00 E
Tadžikskaja SSR=Tadzhik SSR (EN) ②	19	Hh	39.00N	71.00 E
T'aebaek-Sanmaek ⛰	21	Of	37.40N	128.50 E
Taechon	28	If	36.21N	126.36 E
T'aech'on	28	He	39.55N	125.30 E
Taedong-gang ≈	28	He	38.42N	125.15 E
Taegu	22	Of	35.52N	128.36 E
Taeha-dong	28	Kf	37.31N	130.48 E
Taehan-Haehyŏp=Korea Strait (EN) ≡	21	Of	34.40N	129.00 E
Taehan-Min' guk=South Korea (EN) ①	22	Of	38.00N	127.30 E
Taehuksan-Do ◆	28	Hg	34.40N	125.25 E
Taejŏn	22	Of	36.20N	127.26 E
Tafahi Island ◆	57	Jf	15.52 S	173.55W
Tafalla	13	Kb	42.31N	1.40W
Tafassasset ≈	30	If	21.56N	10.12 E
Tafassasset, Ténéré du- ⧗	34	Ha	21.20N	11.00 E
Taff ≈	9	Jj	51.27N	3.09W
Tafilalt ☘	32	Gc	31.18N	4.18W
Tafiré	34	Dd	9.04N	5.10W
Tafí Viejo	56	Gc	26.44 S	65.16W
Taflan	24	Gb	41.25N	36.09 E
Tafna ≈	13	Ki	35.18N	1.28W
Tafraout	32	Fd	29.43N	9.00W
Tafresh	24	Ne	34.41N	50.01 E
Taft	24	Pg	31.45N	54.14 E
Taftān, Kuh-e- ▲	21	Ig	28.36N	61.06 E
Taftanāz	24	Ge	35.59N	36.47 E
Taga	65c	Aa	13.46 S	172.28W
Taga Dzong	25	Hc	27.04N	89.53 E
Tagajō	29	Gb	38.18N	140.58 E
Tagama ⧗	30	Hg	15.50N	8.12 E
Taganrog	6	Jf	47.12N	38.56 E
Taganrogski Zaliv ◧	16	Kf	46.50N	38.25 E
Tagant ③	32	Ef	18.30N	10.30W
Tagant ⛰	30	Fg	17.31N	12.07W
Tagarev, Gora- ▲	18	Ae	38.19N	57.18 E
Tagawa	29	Be	33.39N	130.48 E
Tagbilaran	26	He	9.39N	123.51 E
Tageru, Jabal- ▲	35	Db	16.25N	27.10 E
Taggia	14	Bg	43.52N	7.51 E
Taghit	32	Gc	30.55N	2.02W
Tagil ≈	17	Kg	58.33N	62.30 E
Tagish Lake ◍	42	Ed	60.00N	134.00W
Tagliamento ≈	14	He	45.38N	13.06 E
Taglio di Po	14	Ge	45.00N	12.12 E
Tagomago, Isla de- ◆	13	Ne	39.02N	1.39 E
Tagounit	32	Fd	29.58N	5.35W
Tagpochau, Ogso- ▲	64b	Ba	15.11N	145.45 E
Tāgrīfat	33	Cd	29.12N	17.21 E
Taguatinga	54	If	12.25 S	46.26W
Taguersimet	32	De	24.09N	15.07W
Tagula	63a	Ad	11.20 S	153.00 E
Tagula Island ◆	57	Gf	11.30 S	153.30 E
Tagum	26	Ie	7.21N	125.50 E
Tagus (EN)=Tajo ≈	5	Fh	38.40N	9.24W
Tagus (EN)=Tejo ≈	5	Fh	38.40N	9.24W
Tah	32	Ed	27.37N	12.50W
Tahaa, Ile- ◆	61	Kc	16.38 S	151.30W
Tahakopa	62	Cg	46.31 S	169.23 E
Tahan, Gunong- ▲	21	Mi	4.39N	102.14 E
Tahanea Atoll ⊙	57	Mf	16.52 S	144.45W

Index Symbols

① Independent Nation
② State, Region
③ District, County
④ Municipality
⑤ Colony, Dependency
■ Continent
⧗ Physical Region
▣ Historical or Cultural Region
▲ Mount, Mountain
△ Volcano
∩ Hill
⛰ Mountains, Mountain Range
⋒ Hills, Escarpment
▬ Plateau, Upland
⌣ Pass, Gap
▭ Plain, Lowland
Δ Delta
▤ Salt Flat
∨ Valley, Canyon
◡ Crater, Cave
⌬ Karst Features
∪ Depression
⊔ Polder
∴ Desert, Dunes
♣ Forest, Woods
⋀ Heath, Steppe
☘ Oasis
► Cape, Point
⌇ Coast, Beach
▌ Cliff
⊳ Peninsula
⋈ Isthmus
▂ Sandbank
◆ Island
⊙ Atoll
✱ Rock, Reef
⁂ Islands, Archipelago
✲ Rocks, Reefs
✺ Coral Reef
◉ Well, Spring
⛲ Geyser
≈ River, Stream
⤓ Waterfall Rapids
⋔ River Mouth, Estuary
◍ Lake
◌ Salt Lake
◯ Intermittent Lake
◑ Reservoir
ψ Swamp, Pond
═ Canal
❄ Glacier
❅ Ice Shelf, Pack Ice
≋ Ocean
∿ Sea
◧ Gulf, Bay
≡ Strait, Fjord
◎ Lagoon
▦ Bank
⋏ Seamount
⊼ Tablemount
⌃ Ridge
▱ Shelf
⊍ Basin
⌐ Escarpment, Sea Scarp
↯ Fracture
⊻ Trench, Abyss
♠ National Park, Reserve
★ Point of Interest
☀ Recreation Site
⌓ Cave, Cavern
⌂ Historic Site
⁖ Ruins
▥ Wall, Walls
✝ Church, Abbey
⛩ Temple
⚛ Scientific Station
✈ Airport
⚓ Port
☼ Lighthouse
⚒ Mine
⊓ Tunnel
⫽ Dam, Bridge

Tenterfield 59 Ke 29.03S 152.01 E
Tenuku 25 Ge 81.40N 16.45 E
Tenuze/Teenuse Jõgi 7 Jf 58.44N 23.58 E
Ten-Zan 29 Be 33.20N 130.08 E
Teocaltiche 48 Hg 21.26N 102.35W
Teodelina 55 Bl 34.11S 61.32W
Teodoro Sampaio 55 Ff 22.31S 52.10W
Teófilo Otoni 53 Lg 17.51S 41.30W
Teotepec, Cerro- 38 Ih 16.50N 100.50W
Teotihuacan 47 Ee 19.44N 98.50W
Teotilán del Camino 48 Kh 18.08N 97.05W
Tepa [Indon.] 26 Ih 7.52S 129.31 E
Tepa [W.F.] 64h Bb 13.19S 176.09W
Te Pae Roa Ngake o Tuko 64n Bb 10.23S 161.00W
Tepako, Pointe- 64h Bb 13.16S 176.08W
Tepalcatepec, Río- 48 Ih 18.35N 101.59W
Tepa Point 64k Bb 19.07S 169.56W
Tepatitlán de Morelos 48 Hg 20.49N 102.44W
Tepehuanes 47 Cc 25.21N 105.44W
Tepehuanes, Río- 48 Ge 25.11N 105.26W
Tepehuanes, Sierra de- 47 Cc 25.00N 105.40W
Tepelena 15 Di 40.18N 20.01 E
Tepi 35 Fd 7.03N 35.30 E
Tepic 39 Ig 21.30N 104.54W
Teplá 10 Ig 49.59N 12.52 E
Teplá 10 If 50.14N 12.52 E
Teplice 10 Jf 50.39N 13.50 E
Tepoca, Bahía de- 48 Cb 30.15N 112.50W
Tepopa, Cabo- 48 Cc 29.20N 112.25W
Te Puka 64n Ac 10.26S 161.02W
Te Puke 62 Gb 37.47S 176.20 E
Tequepa, Bahía de- 48 Ii 17.17N 101.05W
Tequila 48 Hg 20.54N 103.47W
Tequisquiapan 48 Jg 20.31N 99.52W
Ter 13 Pb 42.01N 3.12 E
Téra 31 Hg 14.01N 0.45 E
Tera [Port.] 13 Df 38.56N 8.03W
Tera [Sp.] 13 Gc 41.54N 5.44W
Teradomari 29 Fc 37.38N 138.45 E
Terai 21 Kg 26.30N 85.15 E
Teraina Island (Washington) 57 Kd 4.43N 160.24W
Terakeka 35 Ed 5.26N 31.45 E
Teramo 14 Hh 42.39N 13.42 E
Terampa 26 Ef 3.14N 106.14 E
Ter Apel, Vlagtwedde- 12 Jb 52.52N 7.06 E
Terborg, Wisch- 12 Ic 51.55N 6.22 E
Tercan 24 Ic 39.47N 40.24 E
Terceira 30 Ee 38.43N 27.13W
Tercero, Río- 56 Hd 32.55S 62.19W
Terebovlja 16 De 49.18N 25.42 E
Terehovka 28 Kc 43.38N 131.55 E
Terek 16 Nh 43.29N 44.08 E
Terek 5 Kg 43.44N 47.30 E
Térékolé 34 Cb 15.07N 10.53W
Terek-Saj 18 Hd 41.29N 71.13 E
Terenos 55 Ee 20.26S 54.50W
Teresa Cristina 55 Gg 24.48S 51.07W
Teresina 53 Lf 5.05S 42.49W
Teresinha 54 Hc 0.58N 52.02W
Tereška 16 Od 51.50N 46.45 E
Terespol 10 Td 52.05N 23.36 E
Teressa 25 Ig 8.15N 93.10 E
Teresva 16 Cf 47.59N 23.15 E
Terevaka, Cerro- 65d Ab 27.05S 109.23W
Tergnier 11 Je 49.39N 3.18 E
Terhazza 34 Ea 23.36N 4.56W
Teriberka 7 Ib 69.10N 35.10 E
Teriberka 7 Ib 69.09N 35.08 E
Terlingua Creek 45 El 29.10N 103.36W
Termas de Río Hondo 56 Hc 27.29S 64.52W
Terme 24 Gb 41.12N 36.59 E
Termez 22 If 37.14N 67.16 E
Termini Imerese 14 Hm 37.59N 13.42 E
Termini Imerese, Golfo di- 14 Hl 38.00N 13.45 E
Terminillo 14 Hh 42.28N 13.01 E
Términos, Laguna de- 47 Fe 18.37N 91.33W
Termit, Massif de- 34 Hb 16.15N 11.17 E
Termit-Kaoboul 34 Hb 15.43N 11.37 E
Termoli 14 Ii 42.00N 15.00 E
Termonde/Dendermonde 12 Gc 51.02N 4.07 E
Ternaard, Westdongeradeel- 12 Ha 53.23N 5.58 E
Ternate 25 If 0.48N 127.24 E
Ternej 20 Ig 45.05N 136.35 E
Terneuzen 11 Jc 51.20N 3.50 E
Terni 14 Gh 42.34N 12.37 E
Ternitz 14 Kc 47.43N 16.02 E
Ternois 12 Ed 50.25N 2.19 E
Ternopol 6 If 49.34N 25.38 E
Ternopolskaja Oblast [3] 19 Cf 49.20N 25.35 E
Terpenija, Mys- 20 Jg 48.38N 144.40 E
Terpenija, Zaliv- 21 Qe 49.00N 143.30 E
Terrace 42 Ef 54.31N 128.35W
Terrace Bay 45 Mb 48.47N 87.09W
Terracina 14 Hi 41.17N 13.15 E
Terra de Basto 13 Ec 41.25N 8.00W
Terra Firma 37 Ce 25.36S 23.24 E
Terråk 7 Cd 65.05N 12.25 E
Terralba 14 Ck 39.43N 8.39 E
Terra Rica 55 Ff 22.43S 52.38W
Terrebonne Bay 45 Kl 29.09N 90.35W
Terre-de-Bas 51e Ac 15.51N 61.39W
Terre-de-Haut 51e Ac 15.58N 61.35W
Terre Froides 11 Li 45.30N 5.30 E
Terre Haute 43 Jd 39.28N 87.24W
Terrell 45 Hj 32.44N 96.17W
Terre Plaine 11 Jg 47.25N 4.00 E
Terril 13 Gh 37.00N 5.11W
Territoire de Belfort [3] 11 Mg 47.45N 7.00 E
Terruca 13 Fc 41.45N 6.25W
Terry 46 Mc 46.47N 105.19W
Tersa 16 Nd 50.46N 44.42 E
Terschelling 12 Ha 53.21N 5.13 E
Terschelling 11 La 53.24N 5.20 E
Terschelling-West-Terschelling 12 Ha 53.21N 5.13 E
Tersef 35 Bc 12.55N 16.49 E
Terskej-Alatau, Hrebet- 19 Hg 42.10N 78.45 E
Terski Bereg 7 Jc 66.10N 39.30 E
Tersko-Kumski Kanal 16 Ng 44.47N 44.37 E
Terter 16 Oi 40.27N 47.16 E
Teruel 13 Kd 40.21N 1.06W
Teruel [3] 13 Ld 40.40N 0.40W
Tervakoski 8 Kd 60.48N 24.37 E
Tervel 15 Kf 43.45N 27.24 E
Tervo 8 Lb 62.57N 26.45 E
Tervola 7 Fc 66.05N 24.48 E
Tes 27 Fa 50.27N 93.30 E
Teša 7 Ki 55.38N 42.10 E
Tesalia 54 Cc 2.29N 75.44W
Tesaret 32 Hd 25.40N 2.43 E
Tesdrero, Cerro- 48 Hf 22.47N 103.04W
Teseney 35 Fb 15.07N 36.40 E
Teshekpuk Lake 40 Ib 70.35N 153.30W
Teshikaga 28 Rc 43.29N 144.28 E
Teshio 28 Pb 44.53N 141.44 E
Teshio-Dake 28 Qc 43.58N 142.50 E
Teshio-Gawa 28 Pb 44.53N 141.44 E
Teshio-Sanchi 29a Ba 44.20N 142.00 E
Tesijn → Tesijn Gol 21 Ld 50.28N 93.04 E
Tesijn Gol (Tesijn) 21 Ld 50.28N 93.04 E
Teslić 14 Lf 44.37N 17.52 E
Teslin 42 Ed 61.34N 134.50W
Teslin 42 Ed 60.09N 132.45W
Teslin Lake 42 Ed 60.00N 132.30W
Teslui 15 He 44.09N 24.29 E
Tesocoma 48 Ed 27.41N 109.16W
Tesouras, Rio- 55 Gb 14.36S 50.51W
Tesouro 55 Fc 16.04S 53.34W
Tessala, Monts du- 13 Li 35.15N 0.45W
Tessalit 31 Hf 20.14N 0.59 E
Tessaoua 34 Gc 13.45N 7.59 E
Tessenderlo 12 Hc 51.04N 5.05 E
Test 9 Lk 50.55N 1.29W
Test, Tizi n'- 32 Fc 30.50N 8.20W
Testa, Capo- 14 Di 41.14N 9.08 E
Têt 11 Jl 42.44N 3.02 E
Tetari, Cerro- 49 Ki 9.59N 72.55W
Tetas, Punta- 56 Fc 23.31S 70.38W
Tete 31 Kj 16.10S 33.36 E
Tete [3] 37 Ec 15.30S 33.00 E
Te Teko 62 Gc 38.02S 176.48 E
Tetepare Island 63a Cc 8.45S 157.35 E
Téterchen 12 Ie 49.14N 6.34 E
Tetere 63a Ec 9.25S 160.15 E
Teterev 16 Gd 51.01N 30.08 E
Teterow 10 Ic 53.47N 12.34 E
Teteven 15 Hg 42.55N 24.16 E
Tetiaroa Atoll 57 Mf 17.05S 149.32W
Tetijev 16 Fe 49.23N 29.41 E
Tetjuši 7 Li 54.57N 48.49 E
Teton Peak 46 Ic 47.55N 112.48W
Teton Range 46 Je 43.50N 110.55W
Teton River 46 Jc 47.56N 110.31W
Tétouan 31 Ge 35.34N 5.22W
Tétouan [3] 32 Fb 35.35N 5.30W
Tetovo 15 Dg 42.01N 20.59 E
Tetri-Ckaro 16 Ni 41.33N 44.27 E
Teuco, Río- 55 Bg 25.38S 60.12W
Teufelskopf 12 Ie 49.36N 6.49 E
Teulada 14 Cl 38.58N 8.46 E
Teulada, Capo- 5 Gh 38.52N 8.38 E
Téul de Gonzales Ortega 48 Hg 21.28N 103.29W
Teun, Pulau- 26 Ih 6.59S 129.08 E
Teupasenti 49 Df 14.13N 86.42W
Teuquito, Río- 55 Bg 24.22S 61.09W
Teuri-Tō 29a Ba 44.25N 141.20 E
Teutoburger Wald 10 Ee 52.10N 8.15 E
Teuva/Ostermark 7 Ee 62.29N 21.44 E
Teuz 15 Ec 46.39N 21.33 E
Tevai 63c Bb 11.37S 166.55 E
Tevaïtoa 65e Db 16.46S 151.28W
Tevere = Tiber (EN) 5 Hg 41.44N 12.14 E
Teverya 24 Ff 32.47N 35.32 E
Teviot 9 Kf 55.36N 2.26W
Tevli 10 Ud 52.19N 24.23 E
Tevriz 19 Hd 57.34N 72.24 E
Tevšruleh 27 Hb 47.25N 101.55 E
Te Waewae Bay 62 Bg 46.15S 167.30 E
Tewkesbury 9 Kj 51.59N 2.09W
Têwo (Dêngkagoin) 27 He 34.03N 103.21 E
Texada Island 46 Cb 49.40N 124.24W
Texarkana [Ar.-U.S.] 43 Ie 33.26N 94.02W
Texarkana [Tx.-U.S.] 39 Jf 33.26N 94.03W
Texas 59 Ke 28.51S 151.11 E
Texas [2] 43 He 31.30N 99.00W
Texas City 43 If 29.23N 94.54W
Texcoco 48 Jh 19.31N 98.53W
Texel 12 Ga 53.03N 4.47 E
Texel 11 Ka 53.05N 4.45 E
Texel-De Koog 12 Ga 53.07N 4.46 E
Texel-Den Burg 12 Ga 53.03N 4.47 E
Texoma, Lake- 43 He 33.55N 96.37W
Teyéa = Tegea (EN) 15 Fl 37.27N 22.25 E
Teza 7 Jh 56.32N 41.57 E
Teze-Jel 19 Gh 37.55N 60.22 E
Teziutlán 47 Ee 19.49N 97.21W
Tezpur 25 Ic 26.38N 92.48 E
Tha-anne 42 Id 60.31N 94.37W
Thabana Ntlenyana 30 Jk 29.30S 29.15 E
Thabazimbi 37 Dd 24.41S 27.21 E
Thai, Ao- = Thailand, Gulf of- (EN) 21 Mh 10.00N 102.00 E
Thai Binh 25 Ld 20.27N 106.20 E
Thailand (EN) = Muang Thai [1] 22 Mh 15.00N 100.00 E
Thailand, Gulf of- (EN) = Thai, Ao- 21 Mh 10.00N 102.00 E
Thai Nguyen 25 Ld 21.36N 105.50 E
Thal 25 Eb 31.30N 71.40 E
Thālith, Ash Shallāl ath- = Third Cataract (EN) 30 Kg 19.49N 30.19 E
Thamad Bū Ḩashīshah 33 Cd 25.50N 18.05 E
Thamarīd 35 Ib 17.39N 54.02 E
Thame 12 Bc 51.45N 0.59W
Thames 61 Eg 37.08S 175.33 E
Thames 5 Ge 51.28N 0.43 E
Thames River 44 Fd 42.19N 82.28W
Thamūd 23 Gf 17.15N 49.54 E
Thāna 22 Jh 19.12N 72.58 E
Thandaung 25 Je 19.04N 96.41 E
Thanh Hoa 22 Mh 19.48N 105.46 E
Thanjāvūr 25 Ff 10.48N 79.09 E
Thann 11 Ng 47.49N 7.05 E
Thaon-les-Vosges 11 Mf 48.15N 6.25 E
Thap Sakae 25 Jf 11.14N 99.31 E
Thar/Great Indian Desert 21 Ig 27.00N 70.00 E
Thargomindah 59 Ie 28.00S 143.49 E
Tharrawaddy 25 Je 17.39N 95.48 E
Tharros 14 Ck 39.54N 8.28 E
Tharthār, Baḩr ath- 23 Fc 33.59N 43.12 E
Tharthār, Wādī ath- 23 Fc 33.59N 43.12 E
Thasi Gang Dzong 25 Ic 27.19N 91.34 E
Thásos 5 Ig 40.49N 24.42 E
Thásos 15 Hi 40.47N 24.43 E
Thásou, Dhíavlos- 15 Hi 40.49N 24.42 E
Thathlīth, Wādī- 33 He 20.25N 44.55 E
Thau, Bassin de- 11 Jk 43.23N 3.36 E
Thaxted 12 Cc 51.57N 0.22 E
Thaya 10 Mh 48.37N 16.56 E
Thayetchaung 25 Jf 13.52N 98.16 E
Thayetmyo 25 Je 19.19N 95.11 E
Thaywthadangyi Kyun 25 Jf 12.20N 98.00 E
The Alberga River 59 He 27.06S 135.33 E
The Aldermen Islands 62 Gb 37.00S 176.05 E
Thebai = Thebes (EN) 33 Fd 25.43N 32.35 E
Thebes (EN) = Thebai 33 Fd 25.43N 32.35 E
Thebes (EN) = Thívai 15 Gk 38.19N 23.19 E
The Black Sugarloaf 59 Kf 31.20S 151.33 E
The Borders 9 Kf 55.35N 2.50W
The Bottom 50 Ed 17.38N 63.15W
The Broads 9 Oi 52.40N 1.30 E
The Cheviot 9 Kf 55.28N 2.09W
The Cheviot Hills 9 Kf 55.30N 2.10W
The Crane 51q Bb 13.06N 59.26W
The Dalles 43 Cb 45.36N 121.10W
Thedford 43 Gc 41.59N 100.35W
The Entrance 59 Kf 33.21S 151.30 E
The Everglades 43 Kf 26.00N 81.00W
The Fens 9 Mi 5.24N 0.02W
The Gap 46 Jh 36.25N 111.30W
The Granites 59 Gd 20.35S 130.21 E
The Hague (EN) = Den Haag /'s-Gravenhage 6 Ge 52.06N 4.18 E
The Hague (EN) = 's-Gravenhage/Den Haag 6 Ge 52.06N 4.18 E
The Knob 44 He 41.14N 78.22W
The Little Minch 9 Gd 57.35N 6.55W
Thelle 12 De 49.23N 1.51 E
Thelon 38 Jc 64.16N 96.05W
The Macumba River 57 Eg 27.45S 136.50 E
The Merse 9 Kf 55.50N 2.10W
The Naze 12 Dc 51.42N 1.47 E
The Neales River 59 He 28.08S 136.47 E
The Needles 9 Lk 50.39N 1.34W
Theniet el Had 13 Oi 35.32N 2.01 E
Theodore 59 Kd 24.57S 150.05 E
Theológos 15 Hi 40.40N 24.42 E
The Pas 39 Id 53.50N 101.15W
The Pillories 51n Bb 12.54N 61.12W
Thérain 11 Ie 49.15N 2.27 E
Thermaïkós Kólpos = Salonika, Gulf of- (EN) 5 Ig 40.20N 22.45 E
Thermopilai = Thermopylae (EN) 15 Fk 38.48N 22.32 E
Thermopolis 43 Fc 43.39N 108.13W
Thermopylae (EN) = Thermopílai 15 Fk 38.48N 22.32 E
Thérouanne 12 Ed 50.38N 2.15 E
The Round Mountain 59 Kf 30.27S 152.16 E
The Sandlings 9 Oi 52.10N 1.30 E
Thesiger Bay 42 Fb 71.30N 124.00W
The Slot → New Georgia Sound 60 Fi 8.00S 158.10 E
The Solent Spithead 9 Lk 50.46N 1.20W
Thessalia [2] 15 Fj 39.30N 22.10 E
Thessalia = Thessaly (EN) 5 Ih 39.30N 22.10 E
Thessalía = Thessaly (EN) 15 Fj 39.30N 22.10 E
Thessalon 44 Fb 46.15N 83.34W
Thessaloniki = Salonika (EN) 6 Ig 40.38N 22.56 E
Thessaly (EN) = Thessalía 15 Fj 39.30N 22.10 E
Thessaly (EN) = Thessalia 5 Ih 39.30N 22.10 E
The Stevenson River 59 He 27.06S 135.33 E
Thet 12 Cb 52.24N 0.45 E
Thetford 9 Ni 52.25N 0.45 E
Thetford Mines 44 Lb 46.05N 71.18W
The Twins 62 Ed 41.14S 172.40 E
Theux 12 Hd 50.33N 5.49 E
The Valley 47 Le 18.03N 63.04W
The Warburton River 59 He 27.55S 137.28 E
The Wash 5 Ge 52.55N 0.15 E
The Weald 9 Nj 51.05N 0.05 E
The Witties 49 Ff 14.10N 82.45W
The Wolds 9 Mh 53.20N 0.10W
Thiaucourt-Regniéville 12 Hf 48.57N 5.52 E
Thiberville 12 Ce 49.08N 0.27 E
Thibodaux 45 Kl 29.48N 90.49W
Thief River Falls 43 Hb 48.07N 96.10W
Thiel Mountains 66 Pg 85.15S 91.00W
Thiene 14 Fe 45.42N 11.29 E
Thiérache, Collines de la- 11 Je 49.48N 3.55 E
Thiers 11 Ji 45.51N 3.34 E
Thiès 31 Fg 14.48N 16.56W
Thiès [3] 34 Bc 14.45N 16.50W
Thiesi 14 Cj 40.31N 8.43 E
Thika 36 Gc 1.03S 37.05 E
Thikombia 61 Fc 15.44S 179.55W
Thimerais 11 Hf 48.40N 1.20 E
Thimphu 22 Kg 27.28N 89.39 E
Thio 61 Cd 21.37S 166.14 E
Thionville 11 Me 49.22N 6.10 E
Thiou 34 Ec 13.48N 2.40W
Thíra 15 Im 36.25N 25.26 E
Thíra = Thira (EN) 15 Im 36.24N 25.26 E
Thira (EN) = Thíra 15 Im 36.24N 25.26 E
Thirasia 15 Im 36.25N 25.20 E
Third Cataract (EN) = Thālith, Ash Shallāl ath- 30 Kg 19.49N 30.19 E
Thirsk 9 Lg 54.14N 1.20W
Thisted 7 Bh 56.57N 8.42 E
Thithia 63d Cb 17.45S 179.18W
Thiu Khao Phetchabun 25 Ke 16.20N 100.55 E
Thívai = Thebes (EN) 15 Gk 38.19N 23.19 E
Thiviers 11 Gi 45.25N 0.55 E
Thlewiaza 42 Id 60.28N 94.42W
Thoa 42 Gd 60.31N 109.45W
Tho Chu, Dao- 25 Kg 9.00N 103.50 E
Thoen 25 Je 17.41N 99.14 E
Tholen 12 Gc 51.32N 4.13 E
Tholen 11 Kc 51.35N 4.05 E
Tholey 12 Je 49.29N 7.04 E
Thomasset, Rocher- 57 Nf 10.21S 138.25W
Thomaston 44 Ei 32.54N 84.20W
Thomasville [Al.-U.S.] 44 Dj 32.18N 87.47W
Thomasville [Ga.-U.S.] 43 Ke 30.50N 83.59W
Thomasville [N.C.-U.S.] 44 Gh 35.53N 80.05W
Thompson 42 He 55.45N 97.45W
Thompson Falls 46 Hc 47.36N 115.21W
Thompson River 45 Jg 39.45N 93.36W
Thompson Sound 62 Bf 45.10S 167.00 E
Thomsen 42 Fb 73.40N 119.30W
Thomson 44 Fi 33.28N 82.30W
Thomson River 59 Ie 25.11S 142.53 E
Thomson's Falls 36 Gb 0.02N 36.22 E
Thon 12 Fe 49.53N 3.55 E
Thon Buri 22 Mh 13.43N 100.24 E
Thong Pha Phum 25 Jf 14.44N 98.38 E
Thongwa 25 Je 16.46N 96.32 E
Thonon-les-Bains 11 Mh 46.22N 6.29 E
Thoreau 45 Bi 35.24N 108.13W
Thornaby-on-Tees 9 Lg 54.34N 1.18W
Thornbury 61 Ci 46.17S 168.06 E
Thorney 12 Bb 52.37N 0.06W
Thornhill 9 Jf 55.18N 3.40W
Thorshavn 6 Fc 62.01N 6.46W
Thouars 11 Fh 46.58N 0.13W
Thouet 11 Fg 47.17N 0.06W
Thrace (EN) = Thráki 15 Jh 41.20N 26.45 E
Thrace (EN) = Thráki 5 Ig 41.20N 26.45 E
Thrace (EN) = Trakya 15 Jh 41.20N 26.45 E
Thrace (EN) = Trakya 5 Ig 41.20N 26.45 E
Thráki [2] 15 Ih 41.10N 25.30 E
Thráki = Thrace (EN) 5 Ig 41.20N 26.45 E
Thráki = Thrace (EN) 15 Jh 41.20N 26.45 E
Thrakikón Pélagos 15 Hi 40.30N 25.00 E
Thrapston 12 Bb 52.24N 0.32W
Three Forks 43 Eb 45.54N 111.33W
Three Kings Islands 57 Ih 34.10S 172.10 E
Three Kings Trough (EN) 3 Jm 32.00S 170.30 E
Three Points, Cape- 30 Gh 4.45N 2.06W
Three Rivers 44 Ee 41.57N 85.38W
Three Sisters Islands 63a Ed 10.10S 161.57 E
Throckmorton 45 Gj 33.11N 99.11W
Throssel, Lake- 59 Ee 27.25S 124.15 E
Thua 36 Gc 1.17S 40.00 E
Thuin 11 Kd 50.20N 4.17 E
Thule 66 Ad 59.27S 27.19W
Thule/Qânâq 67 Od 77.35N 69.40W
Thule, Mount - 42 Jb 73.00N 78.27W
Thun 14 Bd 46.45N 7.40 E
Thunder Bay 39 Ke 48.23N 89.15W
Thunder Bay [Mi.-U.S.] 44 Fc 45.04N 83.25W
Thunder Bay [Ont.-Can.] 45 Lb 48.24N 89.00W
Thunder Butte 45 Fd 45.19N 101.53W
Thuner See 14 Bd 46.40N 7.45 E
Thung Song 25 Jg 8.11N 99.41 E
Thur 14 Cc 47.36N 8.35 E
Thurgau [2] 14 Dc 47.40N 9.10 E
Thüringen 10 Gf 50.40N 11.00 E
Thüringer Wald = Thuringian Forest (EN) 5 He 50.30N 11.00 E
Thuringian Forest (EN) = Thüringer Wald 5 He 50.30N 11.00 E
Thurles/Durlas 9 Fi 52.41N 7.49W
Thurrock 9 Nj 51.28N 0.20 E
Thursday Island 59 Ib 10.35S 142.13 E
Thurso 6 Fd 58.35N 3.32W
Thurso 9 Jc 58.35N 3.30W
Thurston Island 66 Pf 72.06S 99.00W
Thury-Harcourt 12 Bf 48.59N 0.29W
Thusis/Tusaun 14 Dd 46.42N 9.26 E
Thuwayrāt, Nafūd ath- 24 Kj 26.00N 44.50 E
Thuy Phong 25 Lf 11.14N 108.43 E
Thwaites Iceberg Tongue 66 Of 74.00S 108.30W
Thy 8 Ch 57.00N 8.30 E
Thyborøn 8 Ch 56.42N 8.13 E
Tianbaoshan 28 Jc 42.57N 128.57 E
Tianchang 27 Ke 32.37N 119.00 E
Tiandong (Pingma) 27 Ig 23.40N 107.09 E
Tian'e (Liupai) 27 If 25.05N 107.12 E
Tianguá 54 Jd 3.44S 40.59W
Tianjin = Tientsin (EN) 22 Nf 39.08N 117.12 E
Tianjin Shi (T'ien-chin Shih) [4] 27 Kd 39.08N 117.12 E
Tianjun (Xinyuan) 22 Lf 37.18N 99.15 E
Tianlin (Leli) 27 Ig 24.22N 106.11 E
Tian Ling 28 Kb 44.24N 130.10 E
Tianmen 27 Je 30.40N 113.10 E
Tianmu Shan 28 Ei 30.31N 119.36 E
Tianmu Xi 28 Ej 29.59N 119.24 E
Tianqiaoling 27 Mc 43.35N 129.35 E
Tian Shan 21 Ke 42.00N 80.01 E
Tianshan → Ar Horqin Qi 27 Lc 43.55N 120.05 E
Tianshifu 27 Lc 41.15N 124.20 E
Tianshui 22 Mf 34.35N 105.43 E
Tiantal 28 Fj 29.08N 121.00 E
Tianwangsi 28 Ei 31.45N 119.12 E
Tianyi → Ningcheng 27 Kc 41.34N 119.25 E
Tianzhen 28 Cd 40.24N 114.05 E
Tianzhen → Gaoqing 28 Df 37.10N 117.50 E
Tianzhuangtai 28 Gd 40.49N 122.06 E
Tiaraju 55 Ej 30.15S 54.23W
Tiarei 65e Fc 17.32S 149.20W
Tiaret [3] 32 Hc 34.50N 1.30 E
Tiaret 31 He 35.20N 1.14 E
Tiaret, Monts de- 13 Ni 35.26N 1.15 E
Tiassalé 34 Ed 5.54N 4.50W
Tiavea 65c Ba 13.57S 171.24W
Ţīb, Ra's Aţ- = Bon, Cape- (EN) 30 Ie 37.05N 11.03 E
Tibaji 55 Gg 24.30S 50.24W
Tibaji, Rio- 55 Gf 22.47S 51.01W
Tibasti, Sarīr- 30 If 24.00N 17.00 E
Tibati 31 Ih 6.28N 12.38 E
Tiber (EN) = Tevere 5 Hg 41.44N 12.14 E
Tiberina, Val- 14 Gg 43.30N 12.10 E
Tibesti 30 If 21.30N 17.30 E
Tibet (EN) = Xizang Zizhiqu (Hsi-tsang Tzu-chih-ch'ü) [2] 27 Ee 32.00N 90.00 E
Tibet, Plateau of- (EN) = Qing Zang Gaoyuan 21 Kf 32.30N 87.00 E
Tibidabo 13 Oc 41.25N 2.07 E
Tibni 24 He 35.35N 30.49 E
Tibro 8 Ff 58.26N 14.10 E
Tibú 49 Ki 8.40N 72.42W
Tibugà, Golfo de- 54 Cb 5.45N 77.20W
Tiburón, Capo- 49 Ii 8.42N 77.21W
Tiburon, Isla- 47 Bc 29.00N 112.25W
Ticao 26 Hd 12.31N 123.42 E
Tice 44 Gl 26.41N 81.49W
Tichá Orlice 10 Mf 50.09N 16.05 E
Tîchît 31 Gg 18.26N 9.31W
Tîchît, Dahr- 32 Ff 18.30N 9.25W
Tichka, Tizı n'- 32 Fc 31.17N 7.21W
Tichla 32 Ee 21.36N 14.58W
Ticino [2] 14 Cd 46.20N 9.00 E
Ticino 14 De 45.09N 9.14 E
Ticul 47 Gd 20.24N 89.32W
Tidaholm 7 Cg 58.11N 13.57 E
Tidan 8 Ef 58.42N 13.48 E
Tiddim 25 Id 23.22N 93.40 E
Tidikelt, Plaine du- 30 Hf 27.00N 1.30 E
Tidirhine 32 Gc 34.51N 4.31W
Tidjikja 31 Fg 18.32N 11.27W
Tidore 26 If 0.40N 127.26 E
Tidra, Ile- 30 Fg 19.44N 16.24W
Tiebissou 34 Dd 7.10N 5.13W
Tiechang 28 Id 41.40N 126.12 E
Tiel 11 Lc 51.54N 5.25 E
Tieli 27 Mb 47.04N 128.02 E
Tieling 28 Gc 42.18N 123.51 E
Tielt 11 Jc 51.00N 3.20 E
Tienba 34 Dd 8.30N 7.10W
T'ien-chin Shih → Tianjin Shi [4] 27 Kd 39.08N 117.12 E
Tienen/Tirlemont 12 Gd 50.48N 4.57 E
Tiengemeten 12 Gc 51.45N 5.20 E
Tientsin (EN) = Tianjin 22 Nf 39.08N 117.12 E
Tieroko, Tarso- 35 Ba 20.45N 17.52 E
Tierp 7 Df 60.20N 17.30 E
Tierra Amarilla [Chile] 56 Fc 27.29S 70.17W
Tierra Amarilla [N.M.-U.S.] 45 Ch 36.42N 106.33W
Tierra Blanca 47 Ee 18.27N 96.21W
Tierra Colorada 48 Ji 17.10N 99.35W
Tierra del Fuego [2] 56 Gh 54.00S 67.00W
Tierra del Fuego (EN) = Tierra del Fuego, Isla Grande de- 52 Jk 54.00S 69.00W
Tierra del Fuego, Isla Grande de- = Tierra del Fuego (EN) 52 Jk 54.00S 69.00W
Tierralta 54 Cb 8.10N 76.04W
Tiétar 13 Fe 39.50N 6.01W
Tietê, Rio- 52 Kh 20.40S 51.35W
Tietjerksteradeel 12 Ia 53.12N 6.00 E
Tietjerksteradeel-Bergum 12 Hb 52.17N 5.58 E
Tifariti 32 Ed 26.09N 10.33W
Tiffany Mountain 46 Fb 48.40N 119.56W
Tiffin 44 Fe 41.07N 83.11W
Tifton 43 Ke 31.27N 83.31W
Tiga 63b Ce 21.08S 167.49 E
Tigalda 40a Fb 54.05N 165.05W
Tigăneşti 15 If 43.54N 25.22 E
Tighennif 13 Mi 35.25N 0.15 E
Tigil 20 Ke 57.57N 158.20 E
Tigil 20 Ke 57.48N 158.40 E
Tignère 34 Hd 7.22N 12.39 E
Tigray [3] 35 Fc 14.00N 39.00 E
Tigre 48 Hh 19.53N 102.59W
Tigre, Cerro del- 48 Jf 23.03N 99.16W
Tigre, Río- [S.Amer.] 52 If 4.30S 74.10W
Tigre, Río- [Ven.] 50 Eh 9.20N 62.30W
Tigris (EN) = Dicle 21 Gf 31.00N 47.25 E
Tigris (EN) = Dijlah 21 Gf 31.00N 47.25 E
Tigrovy Hvost, Mys- 18 Bc 43.57N 58.45 E
Tiguent 32 Df 17.15N 16.00W
Tiguentourine 32 Id 27.43N 9.33 E
Tigui 35 Bb 18.38N 18.47 E
Tigzirt 13 Qh 36.54N 4.07 E
Tīh, Jabal at- 33 Fd 29.35N 34.00 E
Tīh, Şaḩrā' at- = At Tīh Desert (EN) 33 Fc 30.05N 34.00 E
Tihāmat 23 Ff 18.30N 41.30 E
Tihāmat Ash Shām 33 Hf 19.15N 41.10 E

Index Symbols

[1] Independent Nation
[2] State, Region
[3] District, County
[4] Municipality
[5] Colony, Dependency
Continent
Physical Region
Historical or Cultural Region
Mount, Mountain
Volcano
Hill
Mountains, Mountain Range
Hills, Escarpment
Plateau, Upland
Pass, Gap
Plain, Lowland
Delta
Salt Flat
Valley, Canyon
Crater, Cave
Karst Features
Depression
Polder
Desert, Dunes
Forest, Woods
Heath, Steppe
Oasis
Cape, Point
Coast, Beach
Cliff
Peninsula
Isthmus
Sandbank
Island
Atoll
Rock, Reef
Islands, Archipelago
Rocks, Reefs
Coral Reef
Well, Spring
Geyser
River, Stream
Waterfall Rapids
River Mouth, Estuary
Lake
Salt Lake
Intermittent Lake
Reservoir
Swamp, Pond
Canal
Glacier
Ice Shelf, Pack Ice
Ocean
Sea
Gulf, Bay
Strait, Fjord
Lagoon
Bank
Seamount
Tablemount
Ridge
Shelf
Basin
Escarpment, Sea Scarp
Fracture
Trench, Abyss
National Park, Reserve
Point of Interest
Recreation Site
Cave, Cavern
Historic Site
Ruins
Wall, Walls
Church, Abbey
Temple
Scientific Station
Airport
Port
Lighthouse
Mine
Tunnel
Dam, Bridge

Index Symbols

[1] Independent Nation	Historical or Cultural Region	Pass, Gap
[2] State, Region	Mount, Mountain	Plain, Lowland
[3] District, County	Volcano	Delta
[4] Municipality	Hill	Salt Flat
[5] Colony, Dependency	Mountains, Mountain Range	Valley, Canyon
[] Continent	Hills, Escarpment	Crater, Cave
[] Physical Region	Plateau, Upland	Karst Features

Depression	Coast, Beach	Rock, Reef
Polder	Cliff	Islands, Archipelago
Desert, Dunes	Peninsula	Rocks, Reefs
Forest, Woods	Isthmus	Coral Reef
Heath, Steppe	Sandbank	Well, Spring
Oasis	Island	Geyser
Cape, Point	Atoll	River, Stream

Waterfall Rapids	Canal	Lagoon
River Mouth, Estuary	Bank	Escarpment, Sea Scarp
Lake	Glacier	Seamount
Salt Lake	Ice Shelf, Pack Ice	Tablemount
Ocean	Sea	Trench, Abyss
Intermittent Lake	Ridge	National Park, Reserve
Reservoir	Gulf, Bay	Point of Interest
Swamp, Pond	Shelf	Recreation Site
	Strait, Fjord	Cave, Cavern
	Basin	

Historic Site	Port
Ruins	Lighthouse
Church, Abbey	Wall, Walls
Temple	Mine
Scientific Station	Tunnel
Airport	Dam, Bridge

Tongaat	37	Ee	29.37S	31.03 E
Tonga Islands	57	Jf	20.00S	175.00W
Tonga Ridge (EN)	57	Jg	21.00S	175.00W
Tongariki	63b	Dc	17.01S	168.37 E
Tongatapu Group	57	Jg	21.10S	175.10W
Tongatapu Island	61	Fd	21.10S	175.10W
Tonga Trench (EN)	3	Kl	20.00S	173.00W
Tongbai	28	Bh	32.21N	113.24 E
Tongbai Shan	27	Je	32.20N	113.14 E
Tongcheng [China]	28	Bj	29.15N	113.49 E
Tongcheng [China]	28	Di	31.04N	116.56 E
Tongcheng → Dong'e	28	Df	36.19N	116.14 E
Tongchuan	27	Id	35.10N	109.03 E
Tongdao (Shuangjiang)	27	If	26.14N	109.45 E
Tongde	27	Hd	35.29N	100.32 E
Tongeren/Tongres	11	Ld	50.47N	5.28 E
Tonggu	28	Cj	28.33N	114.21 E
Tongguzbasti	27	Dd	38.23N	82.00 E
Tonggu Zhang	27	Kg	24.12N	116.22 E
Tong-Hae = Japan, Sea of- (EN)	21	Pf	40.00N	134.00 E
Tonghai	22	Mg	24.15N	102.45 E
Tonghe	27	Mb	46.01N	128.42 E
Tonghua	22	Oe	41.43N	125.55 E
Tongjiang	27	Nb	47.39N	132.30 E
Tongjosŏn-man	21	Of	39.30N	128.00 E
Tongliao	22	Oe	43.37N	122.15 E
Tongling	27	Ke	30.49N	117.47 E
Tonglu	28	Ej	29.48N	119.39 E
Tongmun'gŏ-ri	27	Mc	40.58N	127.08 E
Tongoa	63b	Dc	16.54S	168.33 E
Tongoy	56	Fd	30.15S	71.30W
Tongren [China]	27	If	27.45N	109.09 E
Tongren [China]	27	Hd	35.40N	102.07 E
Tongres/Tongeren	11	Ld	50.47N	5.28 E
Tongsa Dzong	25	Ic	27.31N	90.30 E
Tongshan	28	Cj	29.36N	114.30 E
Tongta	25	Jd	21.20N	99.16 E
Tongtian He/Zhi Qu	21	Lf	33.26N	96.36 E
Tongue	9	Ic	58.28N	4.25W
Tongue of the Ocean	49	Ia	24.12N	77.10W
Tongue River	43	Fb	46.24N	105.52W
Tongxian	27	Kd	39.52N	116.38 E
Tongxin	27	Id	36.59N	105.50 E
Tongxu	28	Cg	34.29N	114.27 E
Tongyu (Kaitong)	27	Lc	44.47N	123.05 E
Tongyu Yunhe	28	Eg	34.46N	119.51 E
Tongzi	27	If	28.09N	106.50 E
Tonichi	48	Ec	28.35N	109.34W
Tönisvorst	12	Ic	51.19N	6.28 E
Tonj	35	Dd	7.17N	28.45 E
Tonj	30	Jh	7.31N	29.25 E
Tonk	25	Fc	26.10N	75.47 E
Tonkin (EN) = Bac-Phan	21	Mg	22.00N	105.00 E
Tonkin, Gulf of- (EN) = Beibu Wan	21	Mh	20.00N	108.00 E
Tonkin, Gulf of- (EN) = Vinh Bac Phan	21	Mh	20.00N	108.00 E
Tônlé Sab, Bœng- = Tonle Sap (EN)	21	Mh	13.00N	104.00 E
Tonle Sap (EN) = Tônlé Sab, Bœng-	21	Mh	13.00N	104.00 E
Tonnay-Charente	11	Fi	45.57N	0.54W
Tonneins	11	Gj	44.23N	0.19 E
Tönning	10	Eb	54.19N	8.57 E
Tōno	28	Pe	39.19N	141.32 E
Tonopah	43	Dd	38.04N	117.14W
Tonoshō	29	Dd	34.29N	134.11 E
Tonosí	49	Gj	7.24N	80.27W
Tønsberg	7	Cg	59.17N	10.25 E
Tonstad	7	Bg	58.40N	6.43 E
Tonumeia	65b	Bb	20.28S	174.46W
Tonya	24	Hb	40.53N	39.16 E
Tooele	43	Ec	40.32N	112.18W
Toora-Hem	20	Ef	52.28N	96.22 E
Tootsi	8	Kf	58.34N	24.43 E
Toovoomba	58	Gg	27.33S	151.57 E
Topalu	15	Le	44.33N	28.03 E
Topa Taung	25	Jd	21.08N	95.12 E
Topeka	39	Jf	39.03N	95.41W
Topki	20	De	55.18N	85.40 E
Topko, Gora-	20	Ie	57.00N	137.23 E
Topl'a	10	Rh	48.45N	21.45 E
Topleţ	15	Fe	44.48N	22.24 E
Toplica	15	Ef	43.13N	21.51 E
Topliţa	15	Ic	46.55N	25.20 E
Topola	15	De	44.16N	20.42 E
Topol'čany	10	Oh	48.34N	18.10 E
Topolnica	15	Hg	42.11N	24.18 E
Topolobampo	47	Cc	25.36N	109.03W
Topolobampo, Bahía de-	48	Ee	25.30N	109.05W
Topolog	15	Hd	44.56N	24.16 E
Topolovgrad	15	Jg	42.05N	26.20 E
Topozero, Ozero-	5	Jb	65.40N	32.00 E
Toppenish	46	Ec	46.23N	120.19W
Toprakkale	24	Gd	37.06N	36.07 E
Top Springs	59	Gc	16.38S	131.50 E
Toquepala	54	Eg	17.38S	69.56W
Tor	35	Ed	7.51N	33.36 E
Tora	64d	Ba	7.39N	151.53 E
Toraigh/Tory Island	9	Ef	55.16N	8.13W
Tora Island Pass	64d	Ba	7.39N	151.53 E
Toråker	8	Gd	60.31N	16.29 E
Torbalı	24	Bc	38.10N	27.21 E
Torbat-e Heydarīyeh	22	Hf	35.16N	59.13 E
Torbat-e Jam	23	Jb	35.14N	60.36 E
Torbay	9	Jk	50.28N	3.30W
Torbert, Mount-	40	Id	61.25N	152.24W
Torch Lake	44	Ec	45.00N	85.19W
Torčin	10	Vf	50.44N	25.05 E
Tordesillas	13	Hc	41.30N	5.00W
Tordino	14	Hh	42.44N	13.59 E
Töre	7	Fd	65.54N	22.39 E
Töreboda	7	Dg	58.43N	14.08 E
Torekov	8	Eh	56.26N	12.37 E
Torenberg	11	Lb	52.15N	5.55 E
Torez	16	Kf	47.59N	38.41 E
Torgau	10	Ie	51.34N	13.00 E
Torgelow	10	Kc	53.38N	14.01 E
Torgun	16	Od	50.10N	46.20 E
Torhamn	8	Fh	56.05N	15.50 E
Torhout	11	Jc	51.04N	3.06 E
Toribulu	26	Hg	0.19S	120.01 E
Torigni-sur-Vire	12	Be	49.05N	0.59W
Torii-Tōge	29	Ed	35.59N	137.49 E
Tori-Jima	29b	Ab	26.35N	126.50 E
Torino = Turin (EN)	6	Gf	45.03N	7.40 E
Toriparu	55	Fc	16.20S	53.55W
Tori-Shima [Jap.]	27	Pe	30.25N	140.15 E
Tori-Shima [Jap.]	29b	Bb	27.52N	128.14 E
Torit	35	Ee	4.24N	32.34 E
Torixoreu	54	Hg	16.15S	52.26W
Torkoviči	7	Hg	58.53N	30.20 E
Törmänen	7	Gb	68.36N	27.29 E
Tormes	13	Fc	41.18N	6.29W
Tornado Mountain	46	Hb	49.58N	114.39W
Tornavacas, Puerto de-	13	Gd	40.16N	5.37W
Torneå/Tornio	7	Fd	65.51N	24.08 E
Torneälven	5	Ib	65.48N	24.08 E
Torneträsk	7	Eb	68.22N	19.06 E
Torngat Mountains	38	Md	59.00N	64.00W
Tornio/Torneå	7	Fd	65.51N	24.08 E
Tornionjoki	5	Ib	65.48N	24.08 E
Tornquist	55	An	38.06S	62.14W
Toro	13	Gc	41.31N	5.24W
Toro	8	Gf	58.50N	17.50 E
Toro, Cerro del-	52	Jh	29.08S	69.48W
Toro, Isla del-	48	Kg	21.35N	97.32W
Toro, Monte-	13	Qe	39.59N	4.07 E
Toroiaga, Vîrful-	15	Hb	47.44N	24.43 E
Torokina	63a	Bb	6.14S	155.03 E
Tōro-Ko	29a	Db	43.08N	144.30 E
Törökszentmiklós	10	Qi	47.11N	20.25 E
Torola, Río-	49	Cg	13.52N	88.30W
Toronto	39	Le	43.39N	79.23W
Toropec	19	Dd	56.31N	31.39 E
Tororo	36	Fb	0.41N	34.11 E
Toros Dağları = Taurus Mountains (EN)	21	Ff	37.00N	33.00 E
Torquato Severo	55	Ej	31.02S	54.11W
Torquay	9	Jk	50.29N	3.29W
Torrá, Cerro-	52	Ie	4.38N	76.15W
Torrance	46	Fj	33.50N	118.19W
Torre Annunziata	14	Ij	40.45N	14.27 E
Torreblanca	13	Md	40.13N	0.12 E
Torrecilla	13	Hh	36.41N	5.00W
Torrecilla en Cameros	13	Jb	42.16N	2.37W
Torre del Greco	14	Ij	40.47N	14.22 E
Torre del Mar	13	Hh	36.44N	4.06W
Torredembarra	13	Nc	41.09N	1.24 E
Torre de Moncorvo	13	Ec	41.10N	7.03W
Torre de' Passeri	14	Hh	42.14N	13.56 E
Torredonjimeno	13	Ig	37.46N	3.57W
Torrejón de Ardoz	13	Id	40.27N	3.29W
Torrelaguna	13	Id	40.50N	3.32W
Torrelavega	13	Ha	43.21N	4.03W
Torre Miró, Puerto de-	13	Ld	40.42N	0.05W
Torremolinos	13	Hh	36.37N	4.30W
Torrens, Lake-	57	Eh	31.00S	137.50 E
Torrens Creek	59	Jd	20.46S	145.02 E
Torrent de l'Horta/Torrente	13	Le	39.26N	0.28W
Torrente/Torrent de l'Horta	13	Le	39.26N	0.28W
Torrenueva	13	If	38.38N	3.22W
Torreón	39	Ig	25.33N	103.26W
Torre-Pacheco	13	Lg	37.44N	0.57W
Torre Pellice	14	Bf	44.49N	7.13 E
Torres	64d	Ab	7.19N	151.27 E
Tôrres	56	Kc	29.21S	49.44W
Torrès, Iles- = Torres Islands (EN)	57	Hf	13.15S	166.37 E
Torres Islands (EN) = Torrès, Iles-	57	Hf	13.15S	166.37 E
Torres Novas	13	De	39.29N	8.32W
Torres Strait	57	Ff	10.25S	142.10 E
Torres Vedras	13	Ce	39.06N	9.16W
Torrevieja	13	Lg	37.59N	0.41W
Torridon, Loch-	9	Hd	57.35N	5.50W
Torriglia	14	Df	44.31N	9.10 E
Torrijos	13	He	39.59N	4.17W
Torrington [Ct.-U.S.]	44	Ke	41.48N	73.08W
Torrington [Wy.-U.S.]	43	Gc	42.04N	104.11W
Torroella de Montgrí	13	Pb	42.02N	3.08 E
Torröjen	7	Cf	63.55N	12.56 E
Torrox	13	Ih	36.46N	3.58W
Torsås	7	Dh	56.24N	16.00 E
Torsby	7	Cf	60.08N	13.00 E
Torshälla	8	Ge	59.25N	16.28 E
Torsken	7	Db	69.20N	17.06 E
Torsö	7	Cg	58.50N	13.50 E
Torto	14	Hm	37.58N	13.46 E
Tortola	47	Le	18.27N	64.36W
Tortoli	14	Dk	39.55N	9.39 E
Tortona	14	Cf	44.54N	8.52 E
Tortorici	14	Il	38.02N	14.49 E
Tortosa	13	Md	40.48N	0.31 E
Tortosa, Cabo de-/Tortosa, Cap de-	13	Md	40.43N	0.55 E
Tortosa, Cap de-/Tortosa, Cabo de-	13	Md	40.43N	0.55 E
Tortue, Ile de la-	47	Jd	20.04N	72.49W
Tortuga, Isla-	48	Dd	27.26N	111.55W
Tortum	24	Ib	40.19N	41.35 E
Torud	24	Pe	35.26N	55.07 E
Torugart, Pereval-	21	Je	40.32N	75.24 E
Torul	24	Hb	40.35N	39.18 E
Toruń [2]	10	Oc	53.00N	18.35 E
Toruń	10	Oc	53.02N	18.35 E
Torunos	49	Li	8.30N	70.04W
Toruńska, Kotlina-	10	Oc	53.00N	18.30 E
Torup	7	Ch	56.58N	13.05 E
Tõrva/Tyrva	7	Fg	58.01N	25.59 E
Tory Island/Toraigh	9	Ef	55.16N	8.13W
Torysa	10	Rh	48.39N	21.21 E
Toržok	19	Dd	57.03N	35.01 E
Tosa	28	Lh	33.29N	133.25 E
Tosas, Puerto de-/Toses, Port de-	13	Ob	42.20N	2.01 E
Tosashimizu	28	Lh	32.46N	132.57 E
Tosa-Wan	28	Lh	33.25N	133.35 E
Tosa-yamada	29	Ce	33.36N	133.40 E
Toscana = Tuscany (EN) [2]	14	Eg	43.25N	11.00 E
Toses, Port de-/Tosas, Puerto de-	13	Ob	42.20N	2.01 E
Toshibetsu-Gawa [Jap.]	29a	Cb	42.54N	143.25 E
Toshibetsu-Gawa [Jap.]	29a	Ab	42.25N	139.48 E
Tōshi-Jima	29	Ed	34.31N	136.52 E
To-Shima	29	Fd	34.31N	139.17 E
Tosno	7	Hg	59.34N	30.50 E
Toson-Cengel	27	Gb	48.47N	98.15 E
Toson Hu	27	Gd	37.08N	96.52 E
Töss	14	Cc	47.33N	8.33 E
Tossa de Mar	13	Oc	41.43N	2.56 E
Tostado	56	Hc	29.14S	61.46W
Tõstamaa/Tystama	8	Jf	58.17N	23.52 E
Tosu	29	Be	33.22N	130.30 E
Tosya	24	Fb	41.01N	34.02 E
Totak	8	Be	59.40N	7.55 E
Totana	13	Kg	37.46N	1.30W
Toten	8	Dd	60.40N	10.50 E
Toteng	37	Cd	20.23S	22.59 E
Tôtes	11	He	49.41N	1.03 E
Totes Gebirge	14	Hc	47.42N	13.55 E
Tōtias	35	Ge	3.57N	43.58 E
Totland	12	Ad	50.40N	1.32W
Totma	19	Ed	60.00N	42.45 E
Totness	54	Gb	5.53N	56.19W
Toto	36	Bd	7.10S	14.25 E
Totonicapán [3]	49	Bf	15.00N	91.20W
Totonicapán	47	Ff	14.55N	91.22W
Totora	54	Eg	17.42S	65.09W
Totoras	55	Bk	32.35S	61.11W
Totota	34	Dd	6.49N	9.56W
Totoya	63d	Cc	18.57S	179.50W
Totten Glacier	66	He	66.45S	116.10 E
Totton	12	Ad	50.55N	1.29W
Tottori	27	Nd	35.30N	134.14 E
Tottori Ken [2]	28	Lg	35.25N	133.50 E
Tou, Motu-	64p	Bb	21.11S	159.48W
Touâjil	32	Ee	21.45N	12.35W
Touat	30	Gf	27.40N	0.01W
Touba [3]	34	Dd	8.15N	7.45W
Touba	34	Dd	8.17N	7.41W
Toubkal, Jebel-	30	Ge	31.03N	7.55W
Touch	11	Hk	43.38N	1.24 E
Toucy	11	Jg	47.44N	3.18 E
Tougan	34	Ec	13.04N	3.04W
Touggourt	31	He	33.06N	6.04 E
Tougué	34	Cc	11.27N	11.41W
Touho	63b	Be	20.47S	165.14 E
Touil	32	Hb	35.33N	2.36 E
Toûîl	13	Oi	35.33N	2.36 E
Toukoto	34	Dc	13.28N	9.52W
Toul	11	Lf	48.41N	5.54 E
Toulépleu	34	Dd	6.35N	8.25W
Toulon	6	Gg	43.07N	5.56 E
Toulouse	6	Gg	43.36N	1.26 E
Toulumne River	46	Eh	37.36N	121.10W
Toumodi	34	Dd	6.33N	5.01W
Tounassine, Hamada-	32	Fd	28.36N	5.10W
Toungo	34	Hd	8.07N	12.03 E
Toungoo	22	Lh	18.56N	96.26 E
Touques	11	Ge	49.22N	0.06 E
Toura	35	Bc	10.30N	15.19 E
Touraine	11	Hg	47.12N	1.30 E
Touraine, Val de-	11	Hg	47.20N	1.30 E
Tourcoing	11	Jd	50.43N	3.09 E
Touriñan, Cabo de-	13	Ca	43.03N	9.18W
Tourine	32	Ee	22.00N	12.15W
Tournai/Doornik	11	Jd	50.36N	3.23 E
Tournai-Kain	12	Fd	50.38N	3.22 E
Tournon	11	Ki	45.04N	4.50 E
Tournus	11	Kh	46.34N	4.54 E
Touros	54	Ke	5.12S	35.28W
Tours	6	Gf	47.23N	0.41 E
Tourteron	12	Ge	49.32N	4.39 E
Toury	11	Hf	48.12N	1.56 E
Touside, Pic-	35	Ba	21.02N	16.25 E
Toussoro	35	Cd	9.02N	23.55 E
Toutouba	63b	Cb	15.34S	167.16 E
Touwsrivier	37	Cf	33.20S	20.00 E
Toužim	10	If	50.04N	12.59 E
Tovar	49	Li	8.20N	71.46W
Tovarkovski	16	Kc	53.43N	38.13 E
Tovdalselva	8	Cf	58.12N	8.06 E
Tove	12	Bb	52.04N	0.50W
Tōwa	29	Gb	39.23N	141.15 E
Towada	28	Pd	40.35N	141.13 E
Towada-Kō	29	Ga	40.28N	140.55 E
Towanda	44	Ie	41.46N	76.27W
Tower	45	Jc	47.48N	92.17W
Towner	45	Fb	48.21N	100.25W
Townsend	46	Jc	46.19N	111.31W
Townshend, Cape-	59	Kd	22.15S	150.30 E
Townsville	58	Ff	19.16S	146.48 E
Towot	35	Ed	6.12N	34.25 E
Towson	44	If	39.24N	76.36W
Towuti, Danau-	26	Hg	2.45S	121.32 E
Toxkan He	27	Dc	41.08N	80.11 E
Tōya	29a	Bb	42.39N	140.48 E
Toyah Creek	45	Ek	31.18N	103.27W
Tōya-Ko	28	Pc	42.33N	140.50 E
Toyama	22	Pf	36.41N	137.13 E
Toyama Ken [2]	28	Nf	30.40N	137.10 E
Toyama Trench (EN)	29	Ec	38.00N	138.00 E
Toyama-Wan	28	Nf	37.00N	137.15 E
Tōyō	28	Mh	33.22N	134.18 E
Toyohashi	27	Oe	34.46N	137.23 E
Toyokoro	29a	Cb	42.48N	143.28 E
Toyonaka	29	Dd	34.47N	135.28 E
Toyo'oka	27	Od	35.33N	137.54 E
Toyosaka	29	Fc	37.55N	139.12 E
Toyota	28	Ng	35.05N	137.09 E
Toyotama	29	Ad	34.27N	129.19 E
Toyotomi	29a	Ba	45.08N	141.47 E
Toyoura	29	Bd	34.10N	130.55 E
Trabancos	13	Gc	41.27N	5.11W
Traben Trabach	12	Je	49.57N	7.07 E
Trabzon	22	Fe	40.59N	39.43 E
Traer	45	Je	42.12N	92.28W
Trafalgar, Cabo-	13	Fh	36.11N	6.02W
Tragacete	13	Kd	40.21N	1.51W
Traiguén	56	Fe	38.15S	72.41W
Trail	39	He	49.06N	117.43W
Traill	41	Jd	72.45N	24.00W
Traíras, Rio-	55	Hb	14.07S	48.31W
Trairi	54	Kd	3.17S	39.15W
Traisen	14	Jb	48.22N	15.46 E
Trakai/Trakaj	7	Fi	54.38N	24.57 E
Trakaj/Trakai	7	Fi	54.38N	24.57 E
Trakt	17	Ee	62.44N	51.11 E
Trakya = Thrace (EN)	15	Jh	41.20N	26.45 E
Trakya = Thrace (EN)	5	Ig	41.20N	26.45 E
Tralee/Trá Lí	9	Di	52.16N	9.42W
Tralee Bay/Bá Thrá Lí	9	Di	52.15N	9.59W
Trá Lí/Tralee	9	Di	52.16N	9.42W
Trá Mhór/Tramore	9	Fi	52.10N	7.10W
Tramore/Trá Mhór	9	Fi	52.10N	7.10W
Tramping Lake	46	Ka	52.10N	108.48W
Trăn	15	Fg	42.50N	22.39 E
Tranås	7	Dg	58.03N	14.59 E
Trancoso	13	Ed	40.47N	7.21W
Tranebjerg	8	Di	55.50N	10.36 E
Tranemo	8	Eg	57.29N	13.21 E
Trang	22	Li	7.33N	99.36 E
Trani	14	Ki	41.17N	16.25 E
Transantarctic Mountains (EN)	66	Lg	85.00S	175.00W
Transcaucasia (EN)	5	Kg	41.00N	45.00 E
Transilvania = Transylvania (EN)	15	Hc	46.30N	25.00 E
Transilvania = Transylvania (EN)	5	If	46.30N	25.00 E
Transkei	30	Jl	31.30S	29.00 E
Transkei	37	Df	32.45S	28.30 E
Transtrand	8	Ec	61.05N	13.19 E
Transtrandsfjällen	8	Ec	61.15N	12.58 E
Transvaal [2]	37	Dd	25.00S	30.00 E
Transylvania (EN) = Transilvania	15	Hc	46.30N	25.00 E
Transylvania (EN) = Transilvania	5	If	46.30N	25.00 E
Transylvanian Alps (EN) = Carpații Meridionali	5	If	45.30N	24.15 E
Trants Bay	51c	Bc	16.46N	62.09W
Trapani	6	Hh	38.01N	12.29 E
Trapper Peak	46	Hd	45.54N	114.18W
Trappes	12	Ef	48.47N	2.01 E
Traralgon	59	Jg	38.12S	146.32 E
Trarza [3]	32	Ef	18.00N	15.00W
Trarza	30	Fg	17.20N	14.40W
Traşcăului, Munții-	15	Gc	46.23N	23.33 E
Trasimeno, Lago-	14	Gg	43.10N	12.05 E
Träslövsläge	8	Eg	57.04N	12.16 E
Trás os Montes e Alto Douro	13	Ec	41.30N	7.15W
Trat	25	Kf	12.13N	102.16 E
Traun	14	Ib	48.13N	14.14 E
Traun	14	Ib	48.16N	14.22 E
Traunsee	14	Hc	47.52N	13.48 E
Traunstein	10	Ii	47.53N	12.39 E
Trave	10	Gc	53.54N	10.50 E
Travemünde, Lübeck-	10	Gc	53.57N	10.52 E
Travers, Mount-	61	Dh	42.01S	172.44 E
Traverse, Lake-	45	Hd	45.43N	96.40W
Traverse City	43	Jc	44.46N	85.37W
Traverse Islands	66	Ad	56.36S	27.43W
Travers Reservoir	46	Ia	50.14N	112.51W
Travesia	49	Df	15.20N	87.53W
Travis, Lake-	45	Hk	30.27N	98.00W
Travnik	23	Ff	44.14N	17.40 E
Travo	11a	Bb	41.54N	9.24 E
Trbovlje	14	Jd	46.10N	15.03 E
Treasurers	63c	Ba	9.53S	167.09 E
Treasury Islands	63a	Bb	7.22S	155.37 E
Trebbia	14	De	45.04N	9.41 E
Třebíč	10	Lg	49.13N	15.53 E
Trebinje	14	Mh	42.43N	18.21 E
Trebisacce	14	Kk	39.52N	16.32 E
Trebišnjica	14	Lg	43.01N	17.47 E
Trebišov	10	Rh	48.40N	21.43 E
Treblinka	10	Sd	52.40N	22.03 E
Trebnje	14	Je	45.54N	15.01 E
Třeboň	10	Kg	49.01N	14.48 E
Třeboňska pánev	10	Kg	49.00N	14.50 E
Trégorrois	11	Cf	48.45N	3.15W
Tregrosse Islets	57	Gf	17.40S	150.45 E
Tréguier	11	Cf	48.47N	3.14W
Treherne	45	Gb	49.38N	98.41W
Treignac	11	Hi	45.32N	1.48 E
Treinta y Tres [2]	55	Ek	33.00S	54.15W
Treinta y Tres	56	Jd	33.14S	54.23W
Treis-Karden	12	Jd	50.11N	7.17 E
Trélazé	11	Fg	47.27N	0.28W
Trelew	56	Gf	43.15S	65.18W
Trelleborg	6	Hd	55.22N	13.10 E
Trélon	12	Gd	50.04N	4.06 E
Tremadoc Bay	9	Ii	52.40N	4.10W
Tremblant, Mount-	38	Le	46.15N	74.34W
Tremiti, Isole- = Tremiti Islands (EN)	5	Hg	42.10N	15.30 E
Tremiti Islands (EN) = Tremiti, Isole-	5	Hg	42.10N	15.30 E
Tremonton	46	If	41.43N	112.10W
Tremp	13	Mb	42.10N	0.54 E
Třemšín	10	Jg	49.33N	13.48 E
Trenche, Rivière-	44	Kb	47.35N	72.58W
Trenčín	10	Oh	48.54N	18.04 E
Trenque Lauguen	56	He	35.58S	62.42W
Trent	9	Mh	53.42N	0.41W
Trent, Vale of-	9	Li	52.45N	1.50W
Trentino-Alto Adige / Südtirol [2]	14	Fd	46.30N	11.20 E
Trento	14	Fd	46.04N	11.08 E
Trenton [Mo.-U.S.]	45	Jf	40.05N	93.37W
Trenton [N.J.-U.S.]	39	Le	40.13N	74.45W
Trenton [Ont.-Can.]	44	Ic	44.06N	77.35W
Tréon	12	Df	48.41N	1.20 E
Trepassey	42	Mg	46.44N	53.22W
Tres Arboles [Ur.]	56	Id	32.24S	56.43W
Tres Arroyos	53	Ji	38.22S	60.15W
Tres Bocas	55	Ck	32.44S	59.45W
Tres Carações	54	Ih	21.42S	45.16W
Tres Cruces, Cerro-	48	Mj	15.28N	92.24W
Três de Maio	55	Eh	27.47S	54.14W
Tres Esquinas	54	Cc	0.43N	75.15W
Tres Isletas	55	Bh	26.21S	60.26W
Treska	15	Eh	41.59N	21.19 E
Treskavica	14	Mg	43.35N	18.24 E
Três Lagoas	53	Kh	20.48S	51.43W
Três Marias, Represa-	54	Ig	18.15S	45.15W
Tres Montes, Peninsula-	56	Eg	46.50S	75.30W
Três Passos	56	Jc	27.27S	53.56W
Tres Picos, Cerro- [Arg.]	52	Ji	38.09S	61.57W
Tres Picos, Cerro- [Mex.]	48	Li	16.36N	94.13W
Três Pontas	55	Je	21.22S	45.31W
Tres Puntas, Cabo- [Arg.]	52	Jj	47.06S	65.53W
Tres Puntas, Cabo- [Guat.]	49	Cf	15.58N	88.37W
Três Ranchos	55	Id	18.22S	47.47W
Três Rios	55	Kf	22.07S	43.12W
Třešť	10	Lg	49.18N	15.28 E
Tres Valles	48	Kh	18.15N	96.08W
Tres Zapotes	47	Ee	18.28N	95.24W
Tretten	7	Cf	61.19N	10.19 E
Treuer Range	59	Gd	22.15S	130.50 E
Treungen	8	Ce	59.02N	8.33 E
Trêve, Lac la-	44	Ja	49.58N	75.31W
Trevi	14	Gh	42.52N	12.45 E
Trévières	12	Be	49.19N	0.54W
Treviglio	14	De	45.31N	9.35 E
Trevinca, Peña-	13	Fb	42.15N	6.46W
Treviño	13	Jb	42.44N	2.45W
Treviso	14	Ge	45.40N	12.15 E
Trevose Head	9	Hk	50.33N	5.01W
Trgovište	15	Fg	42.21N	22.06 E
Triánda	15	Lm	36.24N	28.10 E
Triangle	37	Ed	21.02S	31.28 E
Triángulos, Arrecifes-	48	Mg	20.57N	92.16W
Trianísia	15	Jm	36.18N	26.45 E
Tribeč	10	Oh	48.27N	18.15 E
Tribune	45	Fg	38.28N	101.45W
Tricarico	14	Kj	40.37N	16.09 E
Tricase	14	Mk	39.56N	18.22 E
Trichūr	25	Ff	10.31N	76.13 E
Tri City	46	De	43.02N	123.15W
Trie-Château	12	De	49.17N	1.50 E
Triel-sur-Seine	12	Ef	48.59N	2.01 E
Trier	10	Cg	49.45N	6.38 E
Trier-Ehrang	12	Ie	49.49N	6.41 E
Trier-Pfalzel	12	Ie	49.46N	6.41 E
Trieste	6	Hf	45.40N	13.46 E
Trieste, Golfo di-	14	He	45.40N	13.30 E
Trieux	11	Cf	48.50N	3.03W
Trifels	12	Je	49.11N	7.59 E
Triglav	5	Hf	46.23N	13.50 E
Trigno	14	Ih	42.04N	14.48 E
Trikala	15	Ej	39.33N	21.46 E
Trikhonis, Límni-	15	Ek	38.34N	21.30 E
Trikomo/Trikomon	24	Ee	35.17N	33.52 E
Trikomon/Trikomo	24	Ee	35.17N	33.52 E
Trikora, Puncak-	26	Kg	4.15S	138.45 E
Trilport	12	Ef	48.57N	2.57 E
Trim/Baile Átha Troim	9	Gh	53.34N	6.47W
Trincheras	48	Gc	28.55N	104.18W
Trincomalee	22	Ki	8.34N	81.14 E
Trindade	54	Ig	16.40S	49.30W
Trindade, Ilha da-	52	Nh	20.31S	29.19W
Třinec	10	Og	49.41N	18.42 E
Tring	12	Bc	51.47N	0.39W
Tringía	15	Ej	39.38N	21.25 E
Trinidad	52	Jd	10.30N	61.15W
Trinidad [Bol.]	53	Jg	14.47S	64.47W
Trinidad [Ca.-U.S.]	46	Cf	41.07N	124.07W
Trinidad [Co.-U.S.]	39	If	37.10N	104.31W
Trinidad [Cuba]	47	Id	21.48N	79.59W
Trinidad [Mex.]	48	Ec	28.25N	109.06W
Trinidad [Ur.]	56	Id	33.32S	56.54W
Trinidad, Golfo-	56	Eg	49.55S	75.25W
Trinidad, Isla-	55	Bn	39.08S	61.58W
Trinidad, Laguna-	55	Be	20.21S	61.35W
Trinidad and Tobago [1]	53	Jd	11.00N	61.00W
Trinidade Spur (EN)	3	Cl	21.00S	35.00W
Trinitapoli	14	Ki	41.21N	16.05 E
Trinity	45	Ik	30.57N	95.22W
Trinity	38	Jg	29.47N	94.42W
Trinity Bay [Austl.]	59	Jc	16.25S	145.35 E
Trinity Bay [Can.]	42	Mg	48.15N	53.10W
Trinity Islands	40	Ie	56.33N	154.25W
Trinity Range	46	Ff	40.20N	118.45W
Trinity River	46	Df	41.11N	123.42W
Trinkitat	35	Fb	18.41N	37.43 E
Trino	14	Ce	45.12N	8.18 E
Trionto	14	Kk	39.37N	16.45 E
Trionto, Capo-	14	Kk	39.37N	16.45 E
Triora	14	Bf	43.59N	7.46 E
Tripoli (EN) = Ţarābulus [3]	33	Bc	32.40N	13.15 E
Tripoli (EN) = Ţarābulus [Leb.]	23	Ec	34.26N	35.51 E
Tripoli (EN) = Ţarābulus [Lib.]	31	Ie	32.54N	13.11 E
Trípolis	15	Fl	37.31N	22.22 E
Tripolitania (EN) = Tarabulus	30	Ie	31.00N	14.00 E
Tripolitania (EN) = Ţarābulus	33	Bc	30.00N	15.00 E

Index Symbols

[1] Independent Nation
[2] State, Region
[3] District, County
[4] Municipality
[5] Colony, Dependency
Continent
Physical Region
Historical or Cultural Region
Mount, Mountain
Volcano
Hill
Mountains, Mountain Range
Hills, Escarpment
Plateau, Upland
Pass, Gap
Plain, Lowland
Delta
Salt Flat
Valley, Canyon
Crater, Cave
Karst Features
Depression
Polder
Desert, Dunes
Forest, Woods
Heath, Steppe
Oasis
Cape, Point
Coast, Beach
Cliff
Peninsula
Isthmus
Sandbank
Island
Atoll
Rock, Reef
Islands, Archipelago
Rocks, Reefs
Coral Reef
Well, Spring
Geyser
River, Stream
Waterfall Rapids
River Mouth, Estuary
Lake
Salt Lake
Intermittent Lake
Reservoir
Swamp, Pond
Canal
Glacier
Ice Shelf, Pack Ice
Ocean
Sea
Gulf, Bay
Strait, Fjord
Lagoon
Bank
Seamount
Tablemount
Ridge
Shelf
Basin
Escarpment, Sea Scarp
Fracture
Trench, Abyss
National Park, Reserve
Point of Interest
Recreation Site
Cave, Cavern
Historic Site
Ruins
Wall, Walls
Church, Abbey
Temple
Scientific Station
Airport
Port
Lighthouse
Mine
Tunnel
Dam, Bridge

Tripura [3] 25 Id 24.00N 92.00 E
Trisanna 14 Ec 47.07N 10.30 E
Tristan da Cunha 30 Fi 37.05S 12.17W
Tristan da Cunha Group 30 Fi 37.15S 12.30W
Triste, Golfo- 50 Bg 10.40N 68.10W
Triunfo 55 Ee 20.46S 55.47W
Trivandrum 22 Ji 8.29N 76.55 E
Trivento 14 Ii 41.47N 14.33 E
Trjavna 15 Ig 42.52N 25.30 E
Trnava 10 Nh 48.22N 17.35 E
Troarn 12 Be 49.11N 0.11W
Trobriand Islands 57 Ge 8.30S 151.05 E
Trödje 8 Gd 60.49N 17.12 E
Trofors 7 Cd 65.34N 13.25 E
Trögd 8 Ge 59.30N 17.15 E
Trogir 14 Kg 43.32N 16.15 E
Troglav [Yugo.] 14 Kg 43.58N 16.36 E
Troglav [Yugo.] 14 Mg 43.02N 18.33 E
Trøgstad 8 De 59.38N 11.18 E
Troia 14 Ji 41.22N 15.18 E
Troick [R.S.F.S.R.] 22 Id 54.06N 61.35 E
Troick [R.S.F.S.R.] 20 Ee 57.23N 94.55 E
Troickoje [R.S.F.S.R.] 20 Df 52.58N 84.45 E
Troickoje [R.S.F.S.R.] 20 Ig 49.30N 136.32 E
Troickoje [Ukr.-U.S.S.R.] 15 Nb 47.38N 30.12 E
Troicko Pečorsk 19 Fc 62.44N 56.06 E
Troina 14 Im 37.47N 14.36 E
Troisdorf 12 Jd 50.49N 7.10 E
Trois Fourches, Cap des- 32 Gb 35.26N 2.58W
Trois-Pistoles 44 Ma 48.07N 69.10W
Trois Pitons, Morne- 51g Bb 15.22N 61.20W
Trois-Ponts 12 Hd 50.22N 5.52 E
Trois-Rivières [Guad.] 51e Ac 15.59N 61.39W
Trois-Rivières [Que.-Can.] 39 Le 46.21N 72.33W
Troissereux 12 Ee 49.29N 2.03 E
Troisvierges/Ulflingen 12 Hd 50.07N 6.00 E
Trojah 15 Hg 42.53N 24.43 E
Trojanovka 10 Ve 51.21N 25.25 E
Trojanski Manastir 15 Hg 42.53N 24.48 E
Trojanski prohod 15 Hg 42.48N 24.40 E
Trojebratski 19 Ge 54.25N 66.03 E
Trollhättan 7 Cg 58.16N 12.18 E
Trollheimen 7 Be 62.50N 9.05 E
Trollhetta 8 Cb 62.51N 9.19 E
Trolltindane 8 Bd 62.29N 7.43 E
Tromba 55 Ha 13.28S 48.45W
Trombetas, Rio- 52 Kf 1.55S 55.35W
Tromelin 30 Mj 15.52S 54.25 E
Tromøya 8 Cf 58.30N 8.50 E
Troms [3] 7 Eb 69.07N 19.15 E
Tromsø 6 Hb 69.40N 19.00 E
Tron 8 Db 62.10N 10.43 E
Tronador, Monte- 52 Ij 41.10S 71.54W
Trondheim 6 Hc 63.25N 10.25 E
Trondheimsfjorden 5 Hc 63.40N 10.50 E
Tronto 14 Hh 42.54N 13.55 E
Tropea 14 Jl 38.41N 15.54 E
Tropeiros, Serra dos- 55 Jb 14.43S 44.33W
Tropoja 15 Dg 42.24N 20.10 E
Trosa 7 Dg 58.54N 17.33 E
Troškūnai/Troškunaj 8 Ki 55.32N 24.59 E
Troškunaj/Troškūnai 8 Ki 55.32N 24.59 E
Trostberg 10 Ih 48.02N 12.33 E
Trostjanec 16 Id 50.29N 34.59 E
Trotuş 15 Kc 46.03N 27.14 E
Trou Gras Point 51k Bb 13.52N 60.53W
Troumasse 51k Bb 13.49N 60.54W
Trout Lake [Mi.-U.S.] 44 Eb 46.12N 85.01W
Trout Lake [N.W.T.-Can.] 42 Fd 60.35N 121.10W
Trout Lake [Ont.-Can.] 42 If 51.12N 93.19W
Trout Lake [Ont.-Can.] 42 If 53.54N 89.56W
Trout Peak 46 Kd 44.36N 109.32W
Trout River 42 Lg 49.29N 58.08W
Trouville-sur-Mer 11 Ge 49.22N 0.05 E
Trowbridge 9 Kj 51.20N 2.13W
Troy [Al.-U.S.] 43 Je 31.48N 85.58W
Troy [Mo.-U.S.] 45 Kg 38.59N 90.59W
Troy [Mt.-U.S.] 46 Hb 48.28N 115.53W
Tröy [N.Y.-U.S.] 43 Mc 42.43N 73.40W
Troy [Oh.-U.S.] 44 Ee 40.02N 84.12W
Troy (EN)=Truva 24 Bc 39.57N 26.15 E
Troyes 6 Gf 48.18N 4.05 E
Troy Peak 43 Dd 38.19N 115.30W
Trstenik 15 Df 43.37N 21.00 E
Trubčevsk 19 De 52.36N 33.46 E
Truc Giang 25 Lf 10.14N 106.23 E
Truchas Peak 45 Di 35.58N 105.39W
Trucial Coast (EN) 21 Hg 24.00N 53.00 E
Trucial States (EN)→United Arab Emirates (EN) [1] 22 Hg 24.00N 54.00 E
Truckee 46 Eg 39.20N 120.11W
Trudfront 16 Og 45.56N 47.41 E
Trudovoje 20 Ih 43.18N 132.05 E
Trufanova 7 Kd 64.29N 44.05 E
Trujillo [2] 54 Db 9.25N 70.30W
Trujillo [Hond.] 47 Ge 15.55N 86.00W
Trujillo [Peru] 53 If 8.10S 79.02W
Trujillo [Sp.] 13 Ge 39.28N 5.53W
Trujillo [Ven.] 54 Db 9.22N 70.26W
Trujillo, Rio- 48 Hf 23.39N 103.08W
Truk Islands 57 Gd 7.25N 151.47 E
Trumann 45 Ki 35.41N 90.31W
Trumbull, Mount- 43 Ed 36.25N 113.10W
Trun 12 Gf 48.51N 0.02 E
Trung Phan=Annam (EN) 21 Me 15.00N 108.00 E
Truro [Eng.-U.K.] 9 Hk 50.16N 5.03W
Truro [N.S.-Can.] 39 Me 45.22N 63.16W
Truskavec 16 Ce 49.17N 23.34 E
Truth or Consequences (Hot Springs) 43 Fe 33.08N 107.15W
Trutnov 10 Lf 50.34N 15.54 E
Truva=Troy (EN) 24 Bc 39.57N 26.15 E
Truyère 11 Ij 44.38N 2.34 E
Trysil 8 Ec 61.25N 12.25 E
Trysil 7 Cf 61.18N 12.16 E
Trysilelva 5 Hd 59.23N 13.32 E
Trysilfjellet 8 Ec 61.18N 12.11 E
Trzcianka 10 Mc 53.03N 16.28 E
Trzcińsko Zdrój 10 Kd 52.58N 14.35 E
Trzebiatów 10 Lb 54.04N 15.14 E
Trzebież 10 Kc 53.42N 14.31 E
Trzebinia-Siersza 10 Pf 50.11N 19.25 E
Trzebnica 10 Ne 51.19N 17.03 E
Trzebnicki, Wał- 10 Me 51.30N 16.20 E
Trzebnickie, Wzgórza- 10 Me 51.15N 17.00 E
Trzemeszno 10 Nd 52.35N 17.50 E
Tsaidam Basin (EN)= Qaidam Pendi 27 Fd 37.00N 95.00 E
Tsamandá, Óri- 15 Dj 39.48N 20.21 E
Tsarap 25 Fb 33.31N 76.56 E
Tsaratanana 37 Hc 16.46S 47.38 E
Tsaratanana (EN)= Tsaratanana, Massif du- 30 Lj 14.00S 49.00 E
Tsaratanana, Massif du-= Tsaratanana (EN) 30 Lj 14.00S 49.00 E
Tsau 37 Cd 20.10S 22.27 E
Tsavo 36 Gc 2.59S 38.28 E
Tses 37 Be 25.58S 18.08 E
Tsévié 34 Fd 6.25N 1.13 E
Tshabong 31 Jk 26.02S 22.06 E
Tshane 31 Jk 24.01S 21.43 E
Tshangalele, Lac- 36 Ee 10.55S 27.03 E
Tshela 31 Ii 4.59S 12.56 E
Tshesebe 37 Dd 20.43S 27.37 E
Tshibala 36 Dd 6.56S 21.28 E
Tshibamba 36 Dd 9.06S 22.34 E
Tshikapa 31 Ji 6.25S 20.48 E
Tshilenge 36 Dd 6.15S 23.46 E
Tshimbalanga 36 Dd 9.43S 23.06 E
Tshimbulu 36 Dd 6.29S 22.51 E
Tshinsenda 36 Ee 12.16S 27.55 E
Tshofa 36 Ed 5.14S 25.15 E
Tshopo 36 Eb 0.33N 25.07 E
Tshuapa 30 Ji 0.14S 20.42 E
Tshwaane 37 Cd 22.38S 22.05 E
Tsiafajavona 37 Hc 19.21S 47.15 E
Tsihombe 37 He 25.17S 45.30 E
Tsimlyansk Reservoir (EN)= Cimljanskoje Vodohranilišče 5 Kf 48.00N 43.00 E
Tsinan (EN)=Jinan 22 Nf 36.35N 117.00 E
Tsinghai (EN)=Ch'ing-hai Sheng→Qinghai Sheng [2] 27 Gd 36.00N 96.00 E
Tsinghai (EN)=Qinghai Sheng (Ch'ing-hai Sheng) [2] 27 Gd 36.00N 96.00 E
Tsingtao (EN)=Qingdao 22 Of 36.05N 120.21 E
Tsiribihina 37 Gc 19.42S 44.31 E
Tsiroanomandidy 37 Hc 18.50S 46.00 E
Tsis 64d Bb 7.18N 151.50 E
Tsjokkarassa 7 Fb 69.59N 24.32 E
Tsodilo Hill 37 Cc 18.50S 21.45 E
Tsu 27 Oe 34.43N 136.31 E
Tsubame 29 Fc 37.39N 138.56 E
Tsubata 28 Nf 36.40N 136.44 E
Tsubetsu 29a Db 43.43N 144.01 E
Tsuchiura 28 Pf 36.05N 140.12 E
Tsugaru-Hantō 29a Bc 41.00N 140.30 E
Tsugaru-Kaikyō=Tsugaru Strait (EN) 21 Qe 41.40N 140.55 E
Tsugaru Strait (EN)= Tsugaru-Kaikyō 21 Qe 41.40N 140.55 E
Tsuken-Jima 29b Ab 26.15N 127.57 E
Tsukidate 29 Gb 38.44N 141.01 E
Tsukigata 29a Bb 43.20N 141.39 E
Tsukuba-San 29 Gc 36.13N 140.06 E
Tsukumi 29 Be 33.04N 131.52 E
Tsukura-Se 29 Af 31.18N 129.47 E
Tsukushi-Sanchi 29 Be 33.25N 130.30 E
Tsumeb 31 Ij 19.13S 17.42 E
Tsumeb [3] 37 Bc 19.00S 17.30 E
Tsumkwe 37 Cc 19.32S 20.30 E
Tsuna 29 Dd 34.26N 134.54 E
Tsuno-Shima 29 Bd 34.22N 130.52 E
Tsuru 29 Fd 35.35N 138.50 E
Tsuruga 27 Od 35.39N 136.04 E
Tsuruga-Wan 29 Ed 35.45N 136.05 E
Tsurugi 29 Ec 36.26N 136.37 E
Tsurugi-San 29 De 33.51N 134.03 E
Tsurui 29a Db 43.14N 144.21 E
Tsurumi-Dake 29 Be 33.18N 131.27 E
Tsurumi-Saki 29 Ce 32.56N 132.05 E
Tsuruoka 28 Oe 38.44N 139.50 E
Tsuruta 29 Ga 40.44N 140.26 E
Tsushima 21 Of 34.30N 129.20 E
Tsushima [Jap.] 29 Ce 33.07N 132.30 E
Tsushima [Jap.] 29 Ed 35.10N 136.43 E
Tsushima-Kaikyō=Korea Strait (EN) 21 Of 34.40N 129.00 E
Tsuwano 29 Bd 34.28N 131.46 E
Tsuyama 28 Lg 35.03N 134.00 E
Tua 13 Ec 41.13N 7.26W
Tuai 62 Gc 38.49S 177.08 E
Tuaim/Tuam 9 Eh 53.31N 8.50W
Tuakau 62 Fb 37.15S 174.57 E
Tual 26 Jh 5.40S 132.45 E
Tuam/Tuaim 9 Eh 53.31N 8.50W
Tuamotu, Iles-=Tuamotu Archipelago (EN) 57 Mf 19.00S 142.00W
Tuamotu Archipelago (EN) =Tuamotu, Iles- 57 Mf 19.00S 142.00W
Tuamotu Ridge (EN) 3 Ll 20.00S 145.00W
Tuapa 64k Ba 18.57S 169.54W
Tuapse 6 Jg 44.07N 39.05 E
Tuaran 26 Ge 6.11N 116.14 E
Tuasivi 65c Aa 13.40S 172.07W
Tuasivi, Cape- 65c Aa 13.40S 172.07W
Tuatapere 61 Ci 46.08S 167.41 E
Tuba 20 Ef 54.00N 91.40 E
Tuba City 46 Jh 36.08N 111.14W
Tubai, Ile- 57 Mg 23.18S 149.30W
Tubai-Manu→Maiao, Ile- 57 Lf 17.34S 150.35W
Tubal, Wādī at- 24 Jf 32.19N 42.13 E
Tuban 26 Fh 6.54S 112.03 E
Tubarão 56 Kc 28.30S 49.01W
Ṭubayq, Jabal at- 24 Gh 29.32N 37.30 E
Tubbataha Reefs 26 Ge 8.51N 119.56 E
Tubeke/Tubize 12 Gd 50.41N 4.12 E
Tübingen 10 Fh 48.32N 9.03 E
Tubize/Tubeke 12 Gd 50.41N 4.12 E
Ṭubruq=Tobruk (EN) 31 Je 32.05N 23.59 E
Tubuaï, Iles-/Australes, Iles-=Tubuai Islands (EN) 57 Lg 23.00S 150.00W
Tubuai Islands (EN)= Australes, Iles-/Tubuaï, Iles- 57 Lg 23.00S 150.00W
Tubuai Islands (EN)= Tubuaï, Iles-/Australes, Iles- 57 Lg 23.00S 150.00W
Tubutama 48 Db 30.53N 111.29W
Tucacas 54 Ea 10.48N 68.19W
Tucacas, Punta- 49 Mh 10.52N 68.13W
Tucavaca 55 Cd 18.36S 58.55W
Tucavaca, Rio- 55 Cd 18.37S 58.59W
Tuchola 10 Nc 53.35N 17.50 E
Tucholska, Równina- 10 Oc 53.40N 18.30 E
Tuchów 10 Rg 49.54N 21.03 E
Tucker Glacier 66 Kf 72.35S 169.20 E
Tucson 39 Hf 32.13N 110.58W
Tucuarembó 56 Id 31.44S 55.59W
Tucumán [2] 56 Gc 27.00S 65.30W
Tucumcari 43 Gd 35.10N 103.44W
Tucunuí 54 Id 3.42S 49.27W
Tucupido 54 Eb 9.17N 65.47W
Tucupita 54 Fb 9.04N 62.03W
Tudela 13 Kb 42.05N 1.36W
Tudia, Sierra de- 13 Ff 38.05N 6.20W
Tudmur 23 Ec 34.33N 38.17 E
Tudora 15 Jb 47.31N 26.38 E
Tuela 13 Ec 41.30N 7.12W
Tuensang 25 Ic 26.17N 94.40 E
Tuerto 13 Gb 42.18N 5.53W
Tufanbeyli 24 Gc 38.18N 36.11 E
Tufi 58 Fe 9.08S 149.20 E
Tugela 30 Kk 29.14S 31.30 E
Tug Fork 44 Ff 38.25N 82.35W
Tuguegarao 26 Hc 17.37N 121.44 E
Tugulym 17 Lh 57.04N 64.39 E
Tugur 20 If 53.51N 136.52 E
Tuhai He 28 Ee 38.05N 118.13 E
Tujiabu→Yongxiu 27 Kf 29.05N 115.49 E
Tujmazy 19 Fe 54.36N 53.42 E
Tukan 17 Hj 53.50N 57.31 E
Tukangbesi, Kepulauan-= Tukangbesi Islands (EN) 26 Hh 5.40S 123.50 E
Tukangbesi Islands (EN)= Tukangbesi, Kepulauan- 26 Hh 5.40S 123.50 E
Tukayel 35 Hd 8.05N 45.20 E
Tukayyid 24 Kh 29.47N 45.36 E
Tukituki 62 Gc 39.36S 176.56 E
Tuko Village 64n Ab 10.22S 161.02W
Tūkrah 33 Dc 32.32N 20.34 E
Tuktoyaktuk 39 Fc 69.27N 133.02W
Tukums 7 Fh 56.59N 23.10 E
Tukuringra, Hrebet- 20 Hf 54.30N 126.00 E
Tukuyu 36 Fd 9.15S 33.39 E
Tula 47 Ed 20.06N 99.19W
Tula 36 Gc 0.50S 39.51 E
Tula [Mex.] 48 Jf 23.00N 99.43W
Tula [R.S.F.S.R.] 6 Je 54.12N 37.37 E
Tula de Allende 48 Jg 20.03N 99.21W
Tula Mountains 66 Ee 66.54S 51.06 E
Tulancingo 47 Ed 20.05N 98.22W
Tulare 46 Fh 36.13N 119.21W
Tulare Lake Bed 46 Fh 36.03N 119.49W
Tularosa 45 Cj 33.04N 106.01W
Tularosa Valley 45 Cj 32.45N 106.10W
Tulcán 54 Cc 0.48N 77.43W
Tulcea [2] 15 Md 45.12N 29.10 E
Tulcea 15 Ld 45.10N 28.48 E
Tulčin 16 Fe 48.39N 28.52 E
Tulelake 46 Ef 41.57N 121.29W
Tulemalu Lake 42 Hd 62.55N 99.25W
Tulgheş 15 Ic 46.57N 25.46 E
Tuli 37 Dd 21.55S 29.12 E
Tuli 37 Dd 21.48S 29.04 E
Tulia 45 Fi 34.32N 101.46W
Tulihe 27 La 50.30N 121.51 E
Tullahoma 44 Dh 35.22N 86.11W
Tullamore/An Tulach Mhór 9 Fh 53.16N 7.30W
Tulle 11 Hi 45.16N 1.46 E
Tulln 14 Kb 48.22N 16.03 E
Tulln 14 Kb 48.20N 16.03 E
Tullner Becken 14 Jb 48.25N 15.55 E
Tullow/An Tulach 9 Gi 52.48N 6.44W
Tullus 35 Cc 11.03N 24.33 E
Tully 59 Jc 17.56S 145.56 E
Ṭulmaythah 33 Dc 32.43N 20.57 E
Tuloma 5 Jb 68.52N 32.49 E
Tulos, Ozero- 7 He 63.35N 30.35 E
Tulsa 39 Jf 36.09N 95.58W
Tulskaja Oblast [3] 19 De 54.00N 37.30 E
Tuluá 54 Cc 4.05N 76.12W
Tuluksak 40 Gd 61.06N 160.58W
Tulum 47 Gd 20.15N 87.27W
Tulum 48 Pg 20.13N 87.28W
Tulun 22 Md 54.35N 100.33 E
Tulungagung 26 Fh 8.04S 111.54 E
Tuma 7 Ji 55.10N 40.36 E
Tuma, Rio- 49 Eg 13.03N 84.44W
Tumaco 53 Ie 1.49N 78.46W
Tumaco, Rada de- 54 Cc 1.50N 78.40W
Tumacuarí, Pico- 54 Fc 1.15N 64.40W
Tuman-gang 28 Kc 42.18N 130.41 E
Tumba 8 Ge 59.12N 17.49 E
Tumbarumba 59 Jg 35.47S 148.01 E
Tumbes [2] 54 Bd 3.50S 80.30W
Tumbes 53 Hf 4.05S 80.35W
Tumča 7 Hc 66.35N 31.45 E
Tumd Youqi 27 Jc 40.33N 110.32 E
Tumd Zuoqi 27 Jc 40.43N 111.06 E
Tumen 22 Oe 42.58N 129.49 E
Tumen Jiang 28 Kc 42.18N 130.41 E
Tumeremo 54 Fb 7.18N 61.30W
Tumkur 25 Ff 13.21N 77.05 E
Tummel 9 Je 56.43N 3.44W
Tummo 33 Be 23.00N 14.10 E
Tumon Bay 64c Ba 13.31N 144.48 E
Tumpat 26 De 6.12N 102.10 E
Tumu 34 Ec 10.52N 1.59W
Tumucumaque, Serra- 52 Ke 2.20N 55.00W
Tumwater 46 Dc 47.01N 122.54W
Tuna, Punta- 51a Cc 18.00N 65.52W
Tunapuna 50 Fg 10.38N 61.23W
Tunas 55 Hg 24.58S 49.06W
Tunas, Sierra de las- 48 Fc 29.40N 107.15W
Tunas Chicas, Laguna- 55 Am 36.01S 62.20W
Tunaydah 24 Cj 25.31N 29.21 E
Tunçbilek 15 Mj 39.37N 29.29 E
Tunduma 36 Fd 9.18S 32.46 E
Tunduru 36 Ge 11.07S 37.21 E
Tundža 15 Jh 41.40N 26.34 E
Tunga 34 Gd 8.07N 9.12 E
Tungabhadra 25 Fe 15.57N 78.15 E
Tungaru 35 Ec 10.14N 30.42 E
Tungnaá 7a Bb 64.10N 19.34W
Tungokočen 20 Gf 53.33N 115.34 E
Tungsten 42 Ed 62.05N 127.42W
Tungua 65b Bb 20.01S 174.46W
Tuni 25 Ge 17.21N 82.33 E
Tūnis=Tunis (EN) [3] 32 Jb 36.30N 10.00 E
Tūnis=Tunis (EN) 31 Ie 36.48N 10.11 E
Tūnis=Tunisia (EN) [1] 31 He 34.00N 9.00 E
Tunis (EN)=Tūnis 31 Ie 36.48N 10.11 E
Tunis (EN)=Tūnis [3] 32 Jb 36.30N 10.00 E
Tūnis, Canal de-=Sicily, Strait of- (EN) 5 Hh 37.20N 11.20 E
Tūnis, Khalīj- 32 Jb 37.00N 10.30 E
Tunisia (EN)=Tūnis [1] 31 He 34.00N 9.00 E
Tunja 53 Ie 5.31N 73.22W
Tunkhannock 44 Je 41.32N 75.57W
Tunliu 28 Bf 36.18N 112.53 E
Tunnhovdfjorden 8 Cd 60.25N 8.55 E
Tunø 8 Di 55.55N 10.25 E
Tunumuk 42 Ec 69.00N 134.57W
Tununak 40 Fd 60.35N 165.16W
Tunungayualok 42 Le 56.05N 61.05W
Tunxi 27 Kf 29.45N 118.15 E
Tuo He 28 Dh 33.16N 117.45 E
Tuo Jang 27 If 28.55N 105.26 E
Tuostah 20 Ic 67.50N 135.40 E
Tuotuo He 27 Fe 34.03N 92.46 E
Tuotuohe/Tanggulashanqu 22 Lf 34.15N 92.29 E
Tupã 56 Jb 21.56S 50.30W
Tupaciguara 55 Hd 18.35S 48.42W
Tupai Atoll (Motu-Iti) 61 Kc 16.17S 151.50W
Tupanciretã 56 Jc 29.05S 53.51W
Tupelo 43 Je 34.16N 88.43W
Tupik 20 Gf 54.28N 119.57 E
Tupinambarana, Ilha- 54 Gd 3.00S 58.00W
Tupiraçaba 55 Hb 14.29S 48.34W
Tupper Lake 44 Jc 44.13N 74.29W
Tupungato, Cerro- 56 Gd 33.22S 69.47W
Tuquan 27 Lb 45.22N 121.33 E
Túquerres 54 Cc 1.06N 77.37W
Tur 15 Fa 48.04N 22.33 E
Tura 19 Gd 57.12N 66.56 E
Tura [India] 25 Ic 25.31N 90.13 E
Tura [R.S.F.S.R.] 22 Mc 64.17N 100.15 E
Turabah [Sau.Ar.] 23 Fe 21.13N 41.39 E
Turabah [Sau.Ar.] 23 Fd 28.13N 42.59 E
Turagua, Serranías- 50 Di 7.20N 64.35W
Turakina 62 Fd 40.02S 175.13 E
Turan 24 Qe 35.40N 56.50 E
Turan 20 Ef 52.08N 93.55 E
Turana, Hrebet- 20 If 51.30N 132.00 E
Turangi 62 Fc 38.59S 175.48 E
Turano 14 Gh 42.26N 12.47 E
Turanskaja Nizmennost 21 Ie 44.30N 63.00 E
Turawa 10 Of 50.45N 18.05 E
Turawskie, Jezioro- 10 Of 50.43N 18.10 E
Turbaco 49 Jh 10.19N 75.25W
Turbat 25 Cc 25.59N 63.04 E
Turbo 53 Ie 8.06N 76.43W
Turcoaia 15 Ld 45.07N 28.11 E
Turda 15 Gc 46.34N 23.47 E
Türeh 24 Me 34.02N 49.17 E
Tureia Atoll 57 Ng 20.50S 138.32W
Turek 10 Od 52.02N 18.30 E
Turenki 8 Kd 60.55N 24.38 E
Turfan Depression (EN)= Turpan Pendi 21 Ke 42.30N 89.30 E
Turgai Gates (EN)= Turgajskaja Ložbina 21 Id 51.00N 64.30 E
Turgai Upland (EN)= Turgajskoje Plato 21 Id 51.00N 64.00 E
Turgaj [Kaz.-U.S.S.R.] 19 Gf 49.38N 63.28 E
Turgaj [U.S.S.R.] 21 Ie 48.01N 62.45 E
Turgajskaja Ložbina=Turgai Gates (EN) 21 Id 51.00N 64.30 E
Turgajskaja Oblast [3] 19 Ge 50.30N 66.00 E
Turgajskoje Plato=Turgai Upland (EN) 21 Id 51.00N 64.00 E
Turgeon, Rivière- 44 Ha 50.00N 78.55W
Turgutlu 24 Bc 38.30N 27.50 E
Turhal 24 Gb 40.24N 36.06 E
Türi/Tjuri 7 Fg 58.50N 25.27 E
Turia 13 Le 39.27N 0.19W
Turiaçu, Baía de- 54 Id 1.30S 45.15W
Turiec 10 Og 49.06N 18.52 E
Turijsk 10 Ue 51.10N 24.37 E
Turimiquire, Cerro- 54 Fa 10.03N 64.00W
Turin (EN) = Torino 6 Gf 45.03N 7.40 E
Turinsk 19 Gd 58.03N 63.42 E
Turja 16 Dd 51.48N 24.52 E
Turka [R.S.F.S.R.] 20 Ff 52.57N 108.13 E
Turka [Ukr.-U.S.S.R.] 10 Tg 49.07N 23.01 E
Turkana 36 Gb 4.00N 35.30 E
Turkana, Lake-/Rudolf, Lake- 30 Kh 3.30N 36.00 E
Türkeli 24 Fb 41.57N 34.21 E
Turkestanski Hrebet 19 Gh 39.35N 69.00 E
Turkestan 22 Ie 43.18N 68.15 E
Türkeve 10 Qi 47.06N 20.45 E
Turkey (EN)=Türkiye [1] 22 Fg 39.00N 35.00 E
Turkey Creek 59 Fc 17.02S 128.12 E
Turki 16 Mc 52.01N 43.16 E
Türkiye=Turkey (EN) [1] 22 Fg 39.00N 35.00 E
Turkmenistan Sovet Socialistik Respublikasy/Turkmenskaja SSR [2] 19 Fh 40.00N 60.00 E
Turkmen-Kala 18 Df 37.26N 62.19 E
Turkmenskaja Sovetskaja Socialističeskaja Respublika [2] 19 Fh 40.00N 60.00 E
Turkmenskaja SSR/Turkmenistan Sovet Socialistik Respublikasy [2] 19 Fh 40.00N 60.00 E
Turkmenskaja SSR= Turkmen SSR (EN) [2] 19 Fh 40.00N 60.00 E
Turkmenski Zaliv 16 Ff 39.00N 53.30 E
Turkmen SSR (EN)= Turkmenskaja SSR [2] 19 Fh 40.00N 60.00 E
Türkoğlu 24 Gd 37.31N 36.49 E
Turks and Caicos Islands [5] 39 Ff 21.45N 71.35W
Turks Island Passage 49 Lc 21.25N 71.19W
Turks Islands 47 Jd 21.24N 71.07W
Turku/Åbo 6 Ic 60.27N 22.17 E
Turku-Pori [2] 7 Ff 61.00N 22.30 E
Turkwel 36 Gb 3.06N 36.06 E
Turlock 46 Eh 37.30N 120.51W
Turmantas 8 Li 55.42N 26.34 E
Turnagain, Cape- 62 Gd 40.30S 176.37 E
Turneffe Islands 47 Ge 17.22N 87.51W
Turnhout 11 Kc 51.19N 4.57 E
Turnov 10 Lf 50.35N 15.09 E
Turnu Roşu, Pasul- 15 Hd 45.33N 24.16 E
Turnu Măgurele 15 Hf 43.45N 24.52 E
Turočak 20 Df 52.16N 87.05 E
Turó de L'Home 13 Oc 41.45N 2.25 E
Turopolje 14 Ke 45.38N 16.07 E
Turpan 22 Ke 42.56N 89.10 E
Turpan Pendi=Turfan Depression 21 Ke 42.30N 89.30 E
Turquino, Pico- 47 Ie 19.59N 76.51W
Turrialba 49 Fi 9.54N 83.41W
Tursuntski Tuman, Ozero- 17 Kf 60.35N 63.55 E
Turtas 17 Ng 58.57N 69.10 E
Turtas 17 Ng 59.06N 68.50 E
Turtkul 19 Gg 41.35N 61.00 E
Turtle Mountain 45 Fb 49.05N 100.15W
Turugart Shankou 21 Je 40.32N 75.24 E
Turuhan 20 Dc 65.56N 87.42 E
Turuhansk 20 Dc 65.49N 87.59 E
Turvânia 55 Gc 16.39S 50.09W
Turvo 55 Hi 28.56S 49.41W
Turvo, Rio- [Braz.] 55 Hd 19.56S 49.55W
Turvo, Rio- [Braz.] 55 Gc 17.46S 50.12W
Tusaun/Thusis 14 Dd 46.42N 9.26 E
Tuscaloosa 43 Je 33.13N 87.33W
Tuscan Archipelago (EN)= Arcipelago Toscano 5 Hg 42.45N 10.20 E
Tuscania 14 Fh 42.25N 11.52 E
Tuscany (EN) = Toscana [2] 14 Eg 43.25N 11.00 E
Tuscarora Mountain 44 Ie 40.10N 77.45W
Tuscarora Mountains 46 Gf 41.00N 116.20W
Tuščibas, Zaliv- 18 Ba 46.10N 59.45 E
Tuscola 45 Lg 39.48N 88.17W
Tusenøyane 41 Oc 77.05N 22.00 E
Tuskar 16 Jd 51.40N 36.15 E
Tuskegee 44 Ei 32.26N 85.42W
Tuşnad Băi 15 Ic 46.09N 25.51 E
Tustna 8 Ca 63.10N 8.05 E
Tuszymka 10 Rf 50.09N 21.30 E
Tuszyn 10 Pe 51.37N 19.34 E
Tutajev 19 Dd 57.52N 39.32 E
Tutak 24 Jc 39.32N 42.46 E
Tuticorin 25 Fg 8.47N 78.08 E
Tutira 62 Gc 39.12S 176.53 E
Tutóia 54 Jd 2.45S 42.16W
Tutoko Peak 62 Bf 44.36S 167.58 E
Tutončana 20 Ed 64.05N 93.50 E
Tutova 15 Kc 46.06N 27.32 E
Tutrakan 15 Je 44.03N 26.37 E
Tuttle Creek Lake 45 Hg 39.22N 96.40W
Tuttlingen 10 Ei 47.59N 8.49 E
Tutuala 26 Ih 8.24S 127.15 E
Tutuila Island 57 Jf 14.18S 170.42W
Tutupaca, Volcán- 54 Dg 17.01S 70.22W
Tuupovaara 8 Nb 62.29N 30.36 E
Tuusniemi 7 Ge 62.49N 28.30 E
Tuvalu (Ellice Islands) [1] 58 Ie 8.00S 178.00 E
Tuvalu Islands 57 Ie 8.00S 178.00 E
Tuvana-i-Ra Island 61 Fd 21.00S 178.43W
Tuvana-i-Tholo Island 57 Ig 21.02S 178.49W
Tuvinskaja ASSR [3] 20 Ef 51.30N 94.00 E
Tuvutha 63d Cb 17.40S 178.48W
Tuwayq, Jabal- 21 Gg 25.30N 46.20 E
Tuxer Alpen 14 Fc 47.10N 11.45 E
Tuxford 12 Ba 53.13N 0.53W
Tuxpan 48 Hh 19.33N 103.24W
Tuxpán 47 Cd 21.57N 105.18W
Tuxpan, Arrecife- 48 Kg 21.02N 97.13W
Tuxpan, Rio- 48 Kg 20.53N 97.18W
Tuxpán de Rodriguez Cano 47 Ed 20.57N 97.24W
Tuxtla Gutiérrez 39 Jh 16.45N 93.07W
Túy 13 Db 42.03N 8.38W
Tuy, Rio- 50 Dg 10.24N 65.59W
Tuy An 25 Lf 13.17N 109.16 E

Index Symbols

[1] Independent Nation
[2] State, Region
[3] District, County
[4] Municipality
[5] Colony, Dependency
Continent
Physical Region

Historical or Cultural Region
Mount, Mountain
Volcano
Hill
Mountains, Mountain Range
Hills, Escarpment
Plateau, Upland

Pass, Gap
Plain, Lowland
Delta
Salt Flat
Valley, Canyon
Crater, Cave
Karst Features

Depression
Polder
Desert, Dunes
Forest, Woods
Heath, Steppe
Oasis
Cape, Point

Coast, Beach
Cliff
Peninsula
Isthmus
Sandbank
Island
Atoll

Rock, Reef
Islands, Archipelago
Rocks, Reefs
Coral Reef
Well, Spring
Geyser
River, Stream

Waterfall Rapids
River Mouth, Estuary
Lake
Salt Lake
Intermittent Lake
Reservoir
Swamp, Pond

Canal
Glacier
Ice Shelf, Pack Ice
Ocean
Sea
Gulf, Bay
Strait, Fjord

Lagoon
Bank
Seamount
Tablemount
Ridge
Shelf
Basin

Escarpment, Sea Scarp
Fracture
Trench, Abyss
National Park, Reserve
Point of Interest
Recreation Site
Cave, Cavern

Historic Site
Ruins
Wall, Walls
Church, Abbey
Temple
Scientific Station
Airport

Port
Lighthouse
Mine
Tunnel
Dam, Bridge

Tuy Hoa 25 Lf 13.05N 109.18 E
Tüyserkān 24 Me 34.33N 48.27 E
Tuz, Lake- (EN)=Tuz Gölü 21 Ff 38.45N 33.25 E
Tuz Gölü=Tuz, Lake- (EN) 21 Ff 38.45N 33.25 E
Tuzkan, Ozero- 18 Fd 40.35N 67.30 E
Tūz Khurmātū 23 Fc 34.53N 44.38 E
Tuzla 14 Mf 44.33N 18.41 E
Tuzlov 16 Lf 47.23N 40.08 E
Tuzluca 24 Jb 40.03N 43.39 E
Tuzly 15 Nd 45.56N 30.05 E
Tvååker 8 Eg 57.03N 12.24 E
Tvårdica 15 Ig 42.42N 25.54 E
Tvedestrand 7 Bg 58.37N 8.55 E
Tverca 7 Ih 56.52N 35.59 E
Tweed 9 Lf 55.46N 2.00W
Tweedsmuir Hills 9 Jf 55.30N 3.22W
Tweerivier 37 Be 25.35S 19.37 E
Twello, Voorst- 12 Ib 52.14N 6.07 E
Twente 11 Mb 52.17N 6.40 E
Twentekanaal 12 Ib 52.13N 6.53 E
Twilight Cove 59 Ff 32.20S 126.00 E
Twin Buttes Reservoir 45 Fk 31.20N 100.35W
Twin Falls 39 He 42.34N 114.28W
Twin Islands 42 Jf 53.50N 80.00W
Twin Peaks 46 Hd 44.35N 114.29W
Twisp 46 Eb 48.22N 120.07W
Twiste 12 Lc 51.29N 9.09 E
Twistringen 10 Ed 52.48N 8.39 E
Two Butte Creek 45 Eg 38.02N 102.08W
Two Harbors 45 Kc 47.01N 91.40W
Two Rivers 45 Md 44.09N 87.34W
Two Thumb Range 62 De 43.45S 170.40 E
Tychy 10 Of 50.09N 18.59 E
Tyczyn 10 Sg 49.58N 22.02 E
Tydal 7 Ce 63.04N 11.34 E
Tygda 20 Hf 53.07N 126.20 E
Tyin 8 Cc 61.15N 8.15 E
Tyin 8 Cc 61.14N 8.14 E
Tyler 43 He 32.21N 95.18W
Tylertown 45 Kk 31.07N 90.09W
Tylösand 8 Eh 56.39N 12.44 E
Tylöskog 8 Ff 58.40N 15.10 E
Tym 20 De 59.30N 80.07 E
Tymovskoje 20 Jf 50.50N 142.41 E
Tympákion 15 Hn 35.06N 24.45 E
Tynda 22 Od 53.07N 126.20 E
Tyne 9 Lf 55.01N 1.26W
Tyne and Wear [3] 9 Lg 55.00N 1.35W
Tynemouth 9 Lf 55.01N 1.24W
Týn nad Vltavou 10 Kg 49.14N 14.26 E
Tynset 7 Ce 62.17N 10.47 E
Tyra, Cayos- 49 Fg 12.50N 83.20W
Tyrifjorden 8 De 60.05N 10.10 E
Tyringe 8 Eh 56.10N 13.35 E
Tyrma 20 If 50.01N 132.10 E
Tyrnyauz 16 Mh 43.23N 42.56 E
Tyrol (EN)=Tirol [2] 14 Fc 47.10N 11.25 E
Tyrol (EN)=Tirol/Tirolo 14 Fd 47.00N 11.20 E
Tyrol (EN)=Tirolo/Tirol 14 Fd 47.00N 11.20 E
Tyrone 44 He 40.41N 78.15W
Tyrrell, Lake- 59 Ig 35.20S 142.50 E
Tyrrel Lake 42 Gd 63.05N 105.30W
Tyrrhenian Basin (EN) 5 Hh 40.00N 13.00 E
Tyrrhenian Sea (EN)=Tirreno, Mar- 5 Hh 40.00N 12.00 E
Tyrva/Tõrva 7 Fg 58.01N 25.59 E
Tyrvää 8 Jc 61.21N 22.53 E
Tysmenica 10 Uh 48.49N 24.56 E
Tyśmienica 10 Se 51.33N 22.30 E
Tysnesøy 7 Af 60.00N 5.35 E
Tysse 8 Ad 60.22N 5.45 E
Tyssedal 8 Bd 60.07N 6.34 E
Tystama/Tõstamaa 8 Jf 58.17N 23.52 E
Tystberga 8 Gf 58.52N 17.15 E
Tyszowce 10 Tf 50.36N 23.41 E
Tytuvėnai/Tituvenaj 8 Ji 55.33N 23.09 E
Tywyn 9 Ii 52.35N 4.05W
Tzanconeja, Rio- 48 Ni 16.51N 91.47W
Tzaneen 37 Ed 23.50S 30.09 E
Tzintzuntzan 48 Ih 19.38N 101.34W
Tzucacab 48 Og 20.04N 89.05W

U

Uaboe 64e Ab 0.31S 166.54 E
Uacurizal, Ilha do- 55 Dc 16.25S 56.05W
Ua Huka, Ile- 57 Ne 8.54S 139.33W
Uanukuhahaki 65b Ba 19.58S 174.29W
Ua Pou, Ile- 57 Me 9.23S 140.03W
Uaroo 59 Dd 23.00S 115.10 E
Uatumã, Rio- 52 Kf 2.26S 57.37W
Uaupés 53 Jf 0.08S 67.05W
Uaupés, Rio- 52 Je 0.02N 67.16W
Uaxactún 47 Ge 17.25N 89.29W
Ub 15 De 44.27N 20.05 E
Ubá 54 Jh 21.07S 42.56W
Übach-Palenberg [F.R.G.] 10 Cf 50.56N 6.05 E
Ubagan 19 Ge 54.23N 64.40 E
Ubaila 24 If 33.06N 40.15 E
Ubaitaba 54 Kf 14.18S 39.20W
Ubajay 55 Cj 31.47S 58.18W
Ubangi 30 Ii 0.30S 17.42 E
Ubatuba 55 Jf 23.26S 45.04W
Ubay 26 Hd 10.03N 124.28 E
Ubaye 11 Mj 44.28N 6.18 E
Ubayyiḍ, Wādī al- 23 Fc 32.34N 43.48 E
Ube 28 Kh 33.56N 131.15 E
Ubeda 13 If 38.01N 3.22W
Ubekendt Ejland 41 Gd 71.10N 53.45W
Uberaba 53 Lg 19.45S 47.55W
Uberaba, Lagoa- 55 Dc 17.30S 57.45W
Uberlândia 53 Lg 18.56S 48.18W
Überlingen 10 Fi 47.46N 9.10 E
Ubiaja 34 Gd 6.39N 6.23 E
Ubiña, Peña- 13 Ga 43.01N 5.57W
Ubiratã 55 Fg 24.32S 52.56W
Ubon Ratchathani 22 Mh 15.15N 104.54 E
Ubort 16 Fc 52.06N 28.30 E
Ubrique 13 Gh 36.41N 5.27W
Ubsu-Nur (Uvs nuur) 21 Ld 50.20N 92.45 E
Ubundu 31 Ji 0.21S 25.29 E
Učaly 19 Fe 54.20N 59.31 E
Učami 20 Ed 63.50N 96.39 E
Ucaral 19 If 46.08N 80.52 E
Ucayali, Rio- 52 If 4.30S 73.30W
Uccle/Ukkel 12 Gd 50.48N 4.19 E
Üçdoruk Tepe 24 Ib 40.45N 41.05 E
Ucero 13 Ic 41.31N 3.04W
Uchiko 29 Ce 33.34N 132.38 E
Uchi Lake 45 Ja 51.05N 92.35W
Uchinomi 29 Dd 34.30N 134.19 E
Uchinoura 29 Bf 31.16N 131.05 E
Uchiura-Wan 28 Pc 42.18N 140.35 E
Uchte 12 Ed 52.30N 8.55 E
Učka 14 Ie 45.17N 14.12 E
Uckange 12 Ie 49.18N 6.09 E
Uckermark 10 Jc 53.10N 13.35 E
Uckfield 12 Cd 50.58N 0.06 E
Učkuduk 19 Gg 42.10N 63.30 E
Učkurgan 18 Id 41.01N 72.04 E
Ucrainskaja Sovetskaja Socialističeskaja Respublika [2] 19 Df 49.00N 32.00 E
Ucross 46 Ld 44.33N 106.31W
Ucua 36 Bd 8.40S 14.12 E
Učur 20 Pd 58.48N 130.35 E
Uda [R.S.F.S.R.] 21 Pd 54.42N 135.14 E
Uda [R.S.F.S.R.] 20 Ff 51.45N 107.25 E
Uda [R.S.F.S.R.] 20 Ee 56.05N 99.34 E
Udačny 20 Gc 66.25N 112.20 E
Udaipur 22 Jg 24.35N 73.41 E
Udaj 16 Hd 50.05N 33.07 E
Udaquiola 55 Cm 36.34S 58.31W
Udbina 14 Jf 44.32N 15.46 E
Uddevalla 7 Cg 58.21N 11.55 E
Uddjaure 5 Hb 65.58N 17.50 E
Uden 12 Hc 51.40N 5.37 E
Udgir 25 Fe 18.23N 77.07 E
Udhampur 25 Fb 32.56N 75.08 E
Udimski 7 Kf 61.09N 45.52 E
Udine 14 Hd 46.03N 13.14 E
Udipi 25 Ef 13.21N 74.45 E
Udmurtskaja ASSR [3] 19 Fd 57.20N 52.50 E
Udoha 8 Mg 57.58N 29.50 E
Udomlja 7 Ih 57.56N 35.02 E
Udone-Jima 29 Fd 34.28N 139.17 E
Udon Thani 25 Ke 17.25N 102.48 E
Udot 64d Bb 7.23N 151.43 E
Udskaja Guba 21 Pd 55.00N 136.00 E
Udskoje 20 If 54.36N 134.30 E
Udy 16 Je 49.47N 36.35 E
Udžary 16 Oi 40.31N 47.40 E
Udzungwa Range 36 Gd 8.05S 35.50 E
Uebonti 26 Hg 0.55S 121.38 E
Uecker 10 Kc 53.45N 14.04 E
Ueckermünde 10 Kc 53.44N 14.03 E
Ueda 27 Od 36.24N 138.16 E
Uele 30 Jh 4.09N 22.26 E
Uelen 20 Oc 66.13N 169.48W
Uelzen 10 Gd 52.58N 10.34 E
Ueno 29 Ed 34.46N 136.06 E
Uere 30 Jh 3.42N 25.24 E
Ufa 5 Le 54.40N 56.00 E
Ufa 6 Le 54.44N 55.56 E
Uftjuga 7 Lf 61.28N 46.12 E
Ugab 30 Ik 21.12S 13.38 E
Ugale/Ugāle 8 Ig 57.19N 21.52 E
Ugāle/Ugale 8 Ig 57.19N 21.52 E
Ugalla 36 Fd 5.08S 30.42 E
Uganda [1] 31 Kh 1.00N 32.00 E
Ugărčin 15 Hf 43.06N 24.25 E
Ugashik 40 He 57.32N 157.25W
Ughelli 34 Gd 5.30N 5.59 E
Ugijar 13 Ih 36.57N 3.03W
Uglegorsk 20 Jg 49.05N 142.06 E
Uglekamensk 20 Ih 43.18N 133.08 E
Ugleuralski 17 Hg 58.59N 57.38 E
Uglič 19 Dd 57.33N 38.23 E
Ugljan 14 Jf 44.05N 15.10 E
Uglovoje 28 Lc 43.20N 132.06 E
Ugnev 10 Tf 50.20N 23.45 E
Ugo 29 Gb 39.13N 140.23 E
Ugolnyje Kopi 20 Md 64.42N 177.50 E
Ugoma 36 Ec 4.55S 26.50 E
Ugra 19 De 54.30N 36.07 E
Ugtal-Cajdam 27 Ib 48.25N 105.30 E
Uh 10 Rh 48.33N 22.00 E
Uherské Hradiště 10 Ng 49.04N 17.27 E
Uhlava 10 Jg 49.45N 13.23 E
Uhlenhorst 37 Bd 23.45S 17.55 E
Uhta 6 Lc 63.33N 53.40 E
Uibh Fhaili/Offaly [2] 9 Fh 53.20N 7.30W
Uig 9 Gd 57.30N 6.20W
Uige 31 Ii 7.35S 15.04 E
Uige [3] 36 Cd 7.00S 15.30 E
'Uiha 65b Ba 19.54S 174.25W
Uijec 64d Bb 7.10N 151.57 E
Ŭijŏngbu 28 If 37.44N 127.02 E
Uiju 28 Hd 40.12N 124.32 E
Uil 19 Ff 48.36N 52.30 E
Uil 19 Ff 49.04N 54.42 E
Uilpata, Gora- 16 Mh 42.47N 43.44 E
Uinta Mountains 43 Ec 40.45N 110.05W
Uinta River 46 Kf 40.14N 109.51W
Uis 37 Ad 21.08S 14.49 E
Ŭisŏng 28 Jf 36.21N 128.42 E
Uitenhage 31 Jl 33.40S 25.28 E
Uithoorn 12 Gb 52.14N 4.52 E
Uithuizen 12 Ia 53.25N 6.42 E
Uithuizerwad 12 Ia 53.30N 6.40 E
Ujae Atoll 57 Hd 9.05N 165.40 E
Ujān 24 Og 30.45N 52.05 E
Ujandina 20 Jc 68.23N 145.50 E
Ujar 20 Ee 55.48N 94.20 E
Ujarrás 49 Fi 9.50N 83.40W
Ujedinenija, Ostrov- 20 Da 77.30N 82.30 E
Ujelang Atoll 57 Hd 9.49N 160.55 E
Újfehértó 10 Ri 47.48N 21.41 E
Uji 29 Dd 34.53N 135.47 E
Uji 19 Ge 54.20N 63.58 E
Uji-Guntō 28 Ji 31.10N 129.28 E
Ujije 29 Fc 36.41N 139.57 E
Ujiji 31 Ji 4.55S 29.41 E
Ujjain 22 Jg 23.11N 75.46 E
Ujunglamuru 26 Gg 4.40S 119.58 E
Ujung Pandang (Makasar) 22 Nj 5.07S 119.24 E
Uk 20 Ee 55.04N 98.52 E
Ukata 34 Gc 10.50N 5.50 E
Ukeng, Bukit- 26 Gf 1.45N 115.08 E
Ukerewe Island 36 Fc 2.03S 33.00 E
Uke-Shima 29b Ba 28.02N 129.15 E
Ukhayḍir 24 Jf 32.26N 43.36 E
Ukiah [Ca.-U.S.] 43 Cd 39.09N 123.13W
Ukiah [Or.-U.S.] 46 Fd 45.08N 118.56W
Uki Ni Masi 63a Ed 10.15S 161.44 E
Ukkel/Uccle 12 Gd 50.48N 4.19 E
Ukmerge/Ukmergė 7 Fi 55.14N 24.47 E
Ukmergė/Ukmerge 7 Fi 55.14N 24.47 E
Ukraine (EN) 5 Jf 49.00N 32.00 E
Ukrainian SSR (EN)=Ukrainskaja SSR [2] 19 Df 49.00N 32.00 E
Ukrainskaja SSR/Ukrainska Radyanska Socialistična Respublika [2] 19 Df 49.00N 32.00 E
Ukrainskaja SSR=Ukrainian SSR (EN) [2] 19 Df 49.00N 32.00 E
Ukrainska Radyanska Socialistična Respublika/Ukrainskaja SSR [2] 19 Df 49.00N 32.00 E
Ukrina 14 Le 45.05N 17.56 E
Uku-Jima 29 Ae 33.16N 129.07 E
Ula 24 Cd 37.05N 28.26 E
Ulah Lake 45 Hh 36.58N 96.10W
Ulaidh/Ulster 9 Gg 54.30N 7.00W
Ulalu 64d Bb 7.25N 151.40 E
Ulan (Xiligou) 27 Gd 36.55N 98.16 E
Ulan→Otog Qi 27 Id 39.07N 108.00 E
Ulanbaatar→Ulan-Bator 22 Me 47.55N 106.53 E
Ulan-Badrah 28 Ac 43.58N 110.37 E
Ulan-Bator (Ulaanbaatar) 22 Me 47.55N 106.53 E
Ulanbel 19 Hg 44.49N 71.10 E
Ulan-Burgasy, Hrebet- 20 Ff 52.30N 108.30 E
Ulangom 22 Le 49.58N 92.02 E
Ulanhad/Chifeng 27 Kc 42.16N 118.57 E
Ulan Hol 19 Ef 45.27N 46.46 E
Ulan Hot/Horqin Youyi Qianqi 22 Oe 46.04N 122.00 E
Ulan Hua → Siziwang Qi 28 Ad 41.31N 111.41 E
Ulan-Hus 27 Eb 49.02N 89.23 E
Ulanów 10 Sf 50.30N 22.16 E
Ulansuhai Nur 27 Ic 40.56N 108.49 E
Ulan-Tajga 27 Ga 50.45N 98.30 E
Ulan-Ude 22 Md 51.50N 107.37 E
Ulan Ul Hu 27 Fe 34.45N 90.25 E
Ulas 24 Gc 39.27N 37.03 E
Ulawa Island 60 Gi 9.46S 161.57 E
Ulbeja 20 Je 59.20N 144.25 E
Ulchin 28 Jf 36.59N 129.24 E
Ulcinj 15 Ch 41.56N 19.13 E
Uleåborg/Oulu 6 Ib 65.01N 25.30 E
Ulefoss 7 Bg 59.17N 9.16 E
Ulegej 22 Ke 48.56N 89.57 E
Ulety 20 Gf 51.22N 112.30 E
Uleza 15 Ch 41.40N 19.53 E
Ulfborg 8 Ch 56.16N 8.20 E
Ulflingen/Troisvierges 12 Hd 50.07N 6.00 E
Ulft, Gendringen- 12 Ic 51.54N 6.24 E
Ulgain Gol 27 Kb 45.31N 117.50 E
Ulhāsnagar 25 Ee 19.10N 73.07 E
Uliastai→Dong Ujimqin Qi 27 Kc 45.31N 116.58 E
Uliga 58 Id 7.09N 171.13 E
Ulindi 30 Ji 1.40S 25.52 E
Ulithi Atoll 57 Ed 9.58N 139.40 E
Ulja 20 Je 58.48N 141.40 E
Uljanovka [R.S.F.S.R.] 8 Ne 59.37N 30.55 E
Uljanovka [Ukr.-U.S.S.R.] 16 Ge 48.20N 30.13 E
Uljanovsk 6 Ke 54.20N 48.24 E
Uljanovskaja Oblast [3] 19 Ee 54.00N 48.00 E
Uljanovski 19 He 50.05N 73.45 E
Uljasutaj 22 Le 47.45N 96.49 E
Ulkan 20 Fe 55.55N 107.55 E
Ulla 13 Db 42.39N 8.44W
Ullapool 9 Hd 57.54N 5.10W
Ullared 7 Ch 57.08N 12.43 E
Ulldecona 13 Md 40.36N 0.27 E
Ullsfjorden 7 Eb 69.58N 20.00 E
Ullswater 9 Kg 54.34N 2.54W
Ullŭng-Do 28 Kf 37.29N 130.52 E
Ullvettern 8 Fe 59.25N 14.15 E
Ulm 10 Fh 48.25N 10.00 E
Ulmen 12 Id 50.13N 6.59 E
Ulmeni 15 Jd 45.04N 26.39 E
Ulmu 15 Je 44.16N 26.55 E
Ulongwé 37 Eb 14.43S 34.21 E
Ulricehamn 7 Ch 57.47N 13.25 E
Ulrichstein 12 Ld 50.35N 9.12 E
Ulrum 12 Ia 53.22N 6.20 E
Ulrum-Zoutkamp 12 Ia 53.20N 6.18 E
Ulsan 27 Md 35.33N 129.19 E
Ulsteinvik 7 Ae 62.20N 5.53 E
Ulster 10 Ff 50.51N 9.59 E
Ulster/Ulaidh 9 Gg 54.30N 7.00W
Ulster Canal 9 Gg 54.27N 6.40W
Ulu 35 Ec 10.43N 33.29 E
Ulu/Uulu 8 Kf 58.13N 24.29 E
Ulúa, Rio- 47 Ge 15.56N 87.43W
Ulubat Gölü 24 Cb 40.10N 28.35 E
Ulubey 24 Cc 38.09N 29.33 E
Uludağ 23 Ca 40.04N 29.13 E
Uludere 24 Jd 37.27N 42.51 E
Uluggat/Wuqia 27 Cd 39.40N 75.07 E
Ulukışla 24 Fd 37.33N 34.30 E
Ulungur He 21 Ke 46.58N 87.28 E
Ulungur Hu 27 Eb 47.20N 87.10 E
Ulus 24 Eb 41.35N 32.39 E
Ulus Dağ 15 Lj 39.18N 28.24 E
Ulva 9 Ge 56.28N 6.12W
Ulverston 9 Jg 54.12N 3.06W
Ulverstone 59 Jh 41.09S 146.10 E
Ulvik 8 Bd 60.34N 6.54 E
Ulvön 8 Ha 63.05N 18.40 E
Ulysses 45 Fh 37.35N 101.22W
Ulytau 19 Gf 48.35N 67.05 E
Ulytau, Gora- 19 Gf 48.45N 67.00 E
Uly-Žilanšik 19 Gf 48.51N 63.47 E
Uma 27 La 52.36N 120.38 E
Umag 14 He 45.25N 13.32 E
Umala 54 Eg 17.24S 67.58W
Umán 48 Og 20.53N 89.45W
Uman 64d Bb 7.18N 151.53 E
Uman 19 Df 48.47N 30.09 E
'Umān 21 Hg 22.10N 58.00 E
'Umān=Oman (EN) [1] 22 Hg 21.00N 57.00 E
'Umān, Khalīj-=Oman, Gulf of- (EN) 21 Hg 25.00N 58.00 E
Umanak 41 Gd 70.36N 52.15W
Ümánarssuaq/Farvel, Kap- 67 Nb 59.50N 43.50W
Umatac 64c Bb 13.18N 144.40 E
Umba 19 Db 66.41N 34.17 E
Umbelasha 35 Cd 9.51N 24.50 E
Umbertide 14 Gg 43.18N 12.20 E
Umberto de Campos 54 Jd 2.37S 43.27W
Umboi Island 57 Fe 5.36S 148.00 E
Umbozero, Ozero- 7 Ic 67.45N 34.20 E
Umbria [2] 14 Gh 43.00N 12.30 E
Ume 37 Dc 17.15S 28.20 E
Umeå 6 Ic 63.50N 20.15 E
Umeälven 5 Ic 63.47N 20.16 E
Umm al Arānib 33 Bd 26.08N 14.45 E
Umm al Hayf, Wādī- 23 Hf 18.37N 53.59 E
Umm al Jamaājim 24 Ki 26.59N 45.19 E
Umm al Qaywayn 23 Id 25.35N 55.34 E
Ummanz 10 Jb 54.30N 13.10 E
Umm ar Rizam 33 Dc 32.32N 23.00 E
Umm as Samīm 23 Ie 21.30N 56.45 E
Umm Bāb 24 Nj 25.12N 50.48 E
Umm Bel 35 Dc 13.32N 28.04 E
Umm Buru 35 Cb 15.01N 23.36 E
Umm Dhibbān 35 Dc 14.14N 29.37 E
Umm Durmān=Omdurman (EN) 31 Kg 15.38N 32.30 E
Umm Inderaba 35 Eb 15.12N 31.54 E
Umm Kaddādah 35 Dc 13.36N 26.42 E
Umm Lajj 23 Ed 25.04N 37.13 E
Umm Naqqāt, Jabal- 24 Fj 25.30N 34.14 E
Umm Qam'ul 24 Pj 24.47N 54.42 E
Umm Ruwābah 31 Kg 12.54N 31.13 E
Umm Sayyālah 35 Ec 14.25N 31.00 E
Umm Urūmah 24 Gj 25.46N 36.33 E
Umnak 38 Cd 58.25N 168.10W
Umne-Gobi 27 Fb 49.06N 91.43 E
Umpqua River 46 Ce 43.42N 124.03W
Umpulu 36 Ce 12.42S 17.40 E
Umsini, Gunung- 26 Jg 1.35S 133.30 E
Umtali 31 Kj 18.58S 32.40 E
Umtata 31 Jl 31.35S 28.47 E
Umuarama 56 Jb 23.45S 53.20W
Umurbey 15 Ji 40.14N 26.36 E
Umvukwes 37 Ec 17.01S 30.52 E
Umvuma 37 Ec 19.19S 30.35 E
Umzingwani 37 Dd 22.12S 29.56 E
Una 14 Ke 45.16N 16.55 E
Unabetsu-Dake 29a Db 43.52N 144.51 E
Unac 14 Kf 44.29N 16.08 E
Unai 54 Ig 16.23S 46.53W
Unalakleet 40 Gd 63.53N 160.47W
Unalaska 38 Cd 53.45N 166.45W
Unare, Rio- 50 Dg 10.06N 65.12W
Unauna, Pulau- 26 Hg 0.10S 121.35 E
'Unayzah [Jor.] 24 Fg 30.29N 35.48 E
'Unayzah [Sau. Ar.] 22 Gg 26.06N 43.56 E
Uncia 54 Eg 18.27S 66.37W
Uncompahgre Peak 43 Fd 38.04N 107.28W
Uncompahgre Plateau 45 Bg 38.30N 108.25W
Unden 8 Ff 58.45N 14.25 E
Underberg 37 De 29.50S 29.22 E
Under-Han 22 Ne 47.19N 110.39 E
Undjuljung 20 Hc 66.20N 124.40 E
Undu Point 63d Cb 16.08S 179.57W
Undva Neem/Kiprarenukk, Mys- 8 If 58.25N 21.45 E
Uneča 16 Hc 52.50N 32.44 E
'Ung, Jabal al- 14 Dn 36.45N 9.35 E
Unga 40 Ge 55.15N 160.45W
Ungava, Péninsule d'-=Ungava Peninsula (EN) 38 Lc 60.00N 74.00W
Ungava Bay 38 Md 59.30N 67.30W
Ungava Peninsula (EN)=Ungava, Péninsule d'- 38 Lc 60.00N 74.00W
Ungeny 16 Ef 47.13N 27.50 E
Unggi 28 Kc 42.21N 130.23 E
Ungureni 15 Jb 47.53N 26.47 E
Ungwatiri 35 Fb 16.55N 36.05 E
União 54 Jd 4.35S 42.52W
União da Vitória 56 Jc 26.13S 51.05W
União dos Palmares 54 Ke 9.10S 36.02W
Uničov 10 Ng 49.49N 17.07 E
Uniejów 10 Oe 51.58N 18.49 E
Unije 14 If 44.38N 14.15 E
Unimak 38 Cd 54.50N 164.00W
Unimak Pass 40 Gf 54.35N 164.43W
Unini, Rio- 54 Fd 1.41S 61.30W
Union [Mo.-U.S.] 45 Kg 38.27N 91.00W
Union [S.C.-U.S.] 44 Gh 34.42N 81.37W
Union City 44 Cg 36.26N 89.03W
Uniondale 37 Cf 33.40S 23.08 E
Unión de Reyes 49 Gb 22.48N 81.32W
Unión de Tula 48 Gh 19.58N 104.16W
Union Island 50 Ff 12.36N 61.26W
Union Islands/Tokelau 57 Je 9.00S 171.45W
Union of Soviet Socialist Republics (USSR) (EN)=SSSR [1] 22 Jd 60.00N 80.00 E
Union Seamount (EN) 42 Eg 49.35N 132.45W
Union Springs 44 Ei 32.09N 85.49W
Uniontown 44 Hf 39.54N 79.44W
Unionville 45 Jf 40.29N 93.01W
United Arab Emirates (EN)=Al Imārāt al 'Arabīyah al Muttaḥidah [1] 22 Hg 24.00N 54.00 E
United Arab Republic (EN) → Egypt (EN) [1] 31 Jf 27.00N 30.00 E
United Kingdom [1] 6 Fe 54.00N 2.00W
United Kingdom of Great Britain and Northern Ireland [1] 6 Fe 54.00N 2.00W
United States [1] 39 Jf 38.00N 97.00W
United States of America [1] 39 Jf 38.00N 97.00W
Unity [Or.-U.S.] 46 Fd 44.29N 118.13W
Unity [Sask.-Can.] 42 Gf 52.27N 109.10W
Universales, Montes- 13 Kd 40.18N 1.33W
University City 45 Kg 38.39N 90.19W
Unna 10 De 51.32N 7.41 E
Unnāb, Wādī al- 24 Gg 30.11N 36.39 E
Unnukka 8 Lb 62.25N 27.55 E
Unst 5 Fc 60.45N 0.55W
Unstrut 10 He 51.10N 11.48 E
Unterfranken 10 Fg 50.00N 10.00 E
Unterwalden-Nidwalden [2] 14 Cd 46.55N 8.30 E
Unterwalden-Obwalden [2] 14 Cd 46.50N 8.20 E
Unuli Horog 27 Fd 35.12N 91.58 E
Ünye 23 Ea 41.08N 37.17 E
Unža 5 Kd 57.20N 43.08 E
Unzen-Dake 29 Be 32.45N 130.17 E
Uoleva 65b Ba 19.51S 174.24W
Uozu 28 Nf 36.48N 137.24 E
Upa 10 Lf 50.22N 15.54 E
Upata 54 Fb 8.01N 62.24W
Upemba, Lac- 36 Ed 8.36S 26.26 E
Upernavik 41 Gd 72.20N 56.00W
Upin 26 Ig 2.56S 129.11 E
Upington 31 Jk 28.25S 21.15 E
Upland 12 Kc 51.18N 8.42 E
Upolu Island 57 Jf 13.55S 171.45W
Upolu Point 60 Oc 20.16N 155.52W
Upper [3] 34 Ec 10.30N 1.30W
Upper Arlington 44 Fe 40.01N 83.03W
Upper Arrow Lake 46 Ga 50.30N 117.55W
Upper Austria (EN)=Oberösterreich [2] 14 Hb 48.15N 14.00 E
Upper Hutt 62 Fd 41.07S 175.04 E
Upper Klamath Lake 43 Cc 42.23N 122.00W
Upper Lake 46 Ef 41.44N 120.08W
Upper Lough Erne/Loch Éirne Uachtair 9 Fg 54.20N 7.30W
Upper Red Lake 45 Ib 48.10N 94.40W
Upper Sandusky 44 Fe 40.48N 83.17W
Upper Sheik 35 Hd 9.57N 45.09 E
Upper Thames Valley 9 Lj 51.40N 1.40W
Upper Trajan's Wall (EN)=Verhni Traijanov Val 15 Lc 46.40N 29.00 E
Upper Volta (EN)=Haute-Volta [1] 31 Gg 13.00N 2.00W
Uppingham 12 Bb 52.35N 0.43W
Uppland 8 Gd 60.00N 17.50 E
Upplands Väsby 8 Ge 59.31N 17.54 E
Uppsala [2] 7 Df 60.00N 17.45 E
Uppsala 6 Hd 59.52N 17.38 E
Upsala 45 Kb 49.02N 90.29W
Upshi 25 Fb 33.50N 77.49 E
Upton 46 Md 44.06N 104.38W
Uqbān 33 Hf 15.30N 42.23 E
'Uqlat aș Șuqūr 24 Jj 25.53N 42.15 E
Uqturpan/Wushi 27 Cc 41.10N 79.16 E
Ur 23 Gc 30.58N 46.06 E
Urabá, Golfo de- 54 Cb 8.25N 77.00W
Uracoa 50 Eh 9.00N 62.21W
Uracoa, Rio- 50 Eh 9.08N 62.20W
Uradarja 18 Fe 38.51N 66.02 E
Urad Qianqi 27 Ic 40.49N 108.37 E
Urad Zhonghou Lianheqi (Haliut) 27 Ic 41.34N 108.32 E
Uraga-Suido 29 Fd 35.15N 139.45 E
Ura-Guba 7 Hb 69.18N 32.48 E
Urahoro 29a Cb 42.48N 143.38 E
Urahoro-Gawa 29a Cb 42.44N 143.40 E
Uraj 19 Gc 60.08N 64.40 E
Urakawa 28 Qc 42.09N 142.47 E
Ural 5 Lf 47.00N 51.48 E
Ural Mountains (EN)=Uralskije Gory 5 Ld 57.00N 60.00 E
Uralsk 6 Le 51.14N 51.22 E
Uralskaja Oblast [3] 19 Ff 49.45N 51.00 E
Uralskije Gory=Ural Mountains (EN) 5 Ld 57.00N 60.00 E
Urambo 36 Fd 5.04S 32.03 E
Uranium City 39 Id 59.34N 108.36W
Uraricoera 54 Fc 3.27N 60.59W
Uraricoera, Rio- 52 Je 3.02N 60.30W
Ura-Tjube 19 Gh 39.53N 69.01 E
Urawa 28 Og 35.51N 139.39 E
'Uray'irah 24 Mj 25.57N 48.53 E
Urayq, Nafūd al- 24 Jj 25.17N 42.25 E
Urbana [Il.-U.S.] 45 Lf 40.07N 88.12W
Urbana [Oh.-U.S.] 44 Fe 40.06N 83.45W
Urbandale 45 Jf 41.38N 93.48W
Urbania 14 Gg 43.40N 12.31 E

Index Symbols

[1] Independent Nation
[2] State, Region
[3] District, County
[4] Municipality
[5] Colony, Dependency
Continent
Physical Region
Historical or Cultural Region
Mount, Mountain
Volcano
Hill
Mountains, Mountain Range
Hills, Escarpment
Plateau, Upland
Pass, Gap
Plain, Lowland
Delta
Salt Flat
Valley, Canyon
Crater, Cave
Karst Features
Depression
Polder
Desert, Dunes
Forest, Woods
Heath, Steppe
Oasis
Cape, Point
Coast, Beach
Cliff
Peninsula
Isthmus
Sandbank
Island
Atoll
Rock, Reef
Islands, Archipelago
Rocks, Reefs
Coral Reef
Well, Spring
Geyser
River, Stream
Waterfall Rapids
River Mouth, Estuary
Lake
Salt Lake
Intermittent Lake
Reservoir
Swamp, Pond
Canal
Glacier
Ice Shelf, Pack Ice
Ocean
Sea
Gulf, Bay
Strait, Fjord
Lagoon
Bank
Seamount
Tablemount
Ridge
Shelf
Basin
Escarpment, Sea Scarp
Fracture
Trench, Abyss
National Park, Reserve
Point of Interest
Recreation Site
Cave, Cavern
Historic Site
Ruins
Wall, Walls
Church, Abbey
Temple
Scientific Station
Airport
Port
Lighthouse
Mine
Tunnel
Dam, Bridge

Index Symbols

[1] Independent Nation
[2] State, Region
[3] District, County
[4] Municipality
[5] Colony, Dependency
Continent
Physical Region

Historical or Cultural Region
Mount, Mountain
Volcano
Hill
Mountains, Mountain Range
Hills, Escarpment
Plateau, Upland

Pass, Gap
Plain, Lowland
Delta
Salt Flat
Valley, Canyon
Crater, Cave
Karst Features

Depression
Polder
Desert, Dunes
Forest, Woods
Heath, Steppe
Oasis
Cape, Point

Coast, Beach
Cliff
Peninsula
Isthmus
Sandbank
Island
Atoll

Rock, Reef
Islands, Archipelago
Rocks, Reefs
Coral Reef
Well, Spring
Geyser
River, Stream

Waterfall Rapids
River Mouth, Estuary
Lake
Salt Lake
Intermittent Lake
Sea
Swamp, Pond

Canal
Glacier
Ice Shelf, Pack Ice
Ocean
Gulf, Bay
Strait, Fjord

Lagoon
Bank
Seamount
Tablemount
Ridge
Shelf
Basin

Escarpment, Sea Scarp
Fracture
Trench, Abyss
National Park, Reserve
Point of Interest
Recreation Site
Cave, Cavern

Historic Site
Ruins
Wall, Walls
Church, Abbey
Temple
Scientific Station
Airport

Port
Lighthouse
Mine
Tunnel
Dam, Bridge

Index Symbols

International Map Index

Vittangi 7 Ec 67.41N 21.39 E
Vitteaux 11 Kg 47.24N 4.32 E
Vittel 11 Lf 48.12N 5.57 E
Vittinge 8 Ge 59.54N 17.04 E
Vittoria 14 In 36.57N 14.32 E
Vittorio Veneto 14 Ge 45.59N 12.18 E
Vityaz Depth (EN) 3 Je 44.00N 151.00 E
Vityaz i Depth (EN) 3 Ih 11.20N 141.30 E
Vityaz II Depth (EN) 3 Kl 23.27S 175.00W
Vityaz III Depth (EN) 3 Km 32.00S 178.00W
Vityaz Seamount (EN) 57 Jc 13.30N 173.15W
Vityaz Trench (EN) 3 Jj 10.00S 170.00 E
Vivarais, Monts du- 11 Ki 44.55N 4.15 E
Vivarais, Plateau du- 11 Kj 44.50N 4.45 E
Viver 13 Le 39.55N 0.36W
Vivero 13 Ea 43.40N 7.35W
Viverone, Lago di- 13 Ea 45.25N 8.05 E
Vivi 20 Ed 63.52N 97.50 E
Vivian 45 Jj 32.53N 93.59W
Viviers 11 Kj 44.29N 4.41 E
Vivo 37 Dd 23.03S 29.17 E
Vivoratá 55 Dm 37.40S 57.39W
Vivorillo, Cayos- 49 Ff 15.50N 83.18W
Viwa 63d Ab 17.08S 176.56 E
Vizcaíno, Desierto de- 47 Bc 27.40N 114.40W
Vizcaíno, Sierra- 48 Bd 27.20N 114.00W
Vizcaya 13 Ja 43.15N 2.55W
Vizcaya, Golfo de- 5 Fg 44.00N 4.00W
Vize 15 Kh 41.34N 27.45 E
Vize, Ostrov 21 Jb 79.30N 77.00 E
Vizianagaram 25 Ge 18.07N 83.25 E
Vizille 11 Li 45.05N 5.46 E
Vizinga 19 Fc 61.05N 50.10 E
Viziru 15 Kd 45.00N 27.42 E
Vižnica 16 De 48.14N 25.12 E
Vizzini 14 In 37.10N 14.45 E
Vjaike-Maarja/Väike-Maarja 8 Le 59.04N 26.12 E
Vjajke-Pakri/Väike-Pakri 8 Je 59.50N 23.50 E
Vjajke-Vjajn/Väik Vain 8 Ne 59.00N 23.10 E
Vjalje, Ozero- 8 Ne 59.00N 30.20 E
Vjalozero, Ozero- 7 Ic 66.50N 35.10 E
Vjandra/Vändra 7 Fg 58.40N 25.01 E
Vjartsilja 7 He 62.10N 30.48 E
Vjatka 5 Ld 55.36N 51.30 E
Vjatskije Poljany 19 Fd 56.14N 51.04 E
Vjatski Uval 7 Lg 58.00N 49.45 E
Vjazemski 20 Ig 47.31N 134.45 E
Vjazma 6 Jd 55.13N 34.18 E
Vjazniki 7 Kh 56.15N 42.12 E
Vjeio, Rio- 49 Dg 12.17N 86.54W
Vjosa 15 Ci 40.37N 19.20 E
Vlaamse Banken 12 Ec 51.15N 2.30 E
Vlaanderen/Flandres=Flanders (EN) 5 Ge 51.00N 3.20 E
Vlaanderen/Flandres=Flanders (EN) 11 Jc 51.00N 3.20 E
Vlaardingen 11 Kc 51.54N 4.21 E
Vlădeasa, Vîrful- 15 Fc 46.45N 22.48 E
Vlădeni 15 Kb 47.25N 27.20 E
Vladičin Han 15 Fg 42.43N 22.04 E
Vladimir 6 Kd 56.10N 40.25 E
Vladimirskaja Oblast [3] 19 Ed 56.00N 40.40 E
Vladimirski Tupik 15 Hb 55.42N 33.18 E
Vladimir-Volynski 19 Ce 50.51N 24.22 E
Vladivostok 22 Pe 43.10N 131.56 E
Vlad Tepeş 15 Ke 44.21N 27.05 E
Vlagtwedde 12 Ja 53.02N 7.08 E
Vlagtwedde-Ter Apel 12 Jb 52.52N 7.06 E
Vlahina 15 Fi 41.54N 22.52 E
Vlăhița 15 Ic 46.21N 25.31 E
Vlamse Vlakte=Flanders Plain (EN) 11 Id 50.40N 2.50 E
Vlasenica 14 Mf 44.11N 18.57 E
Vlašic [Yugo.] 14 Lf 44.19N 17.40 E
Vlašim 10 Kg 49.42N 14.54 E
Vlasotince 15 Fg 42.58N 22.08 E
Vlasovo 20 Ib 70.40N 134.35 E
Vlieland 11 Ka 53.15N 5.00 E
Vlieland 12 Ha 53.17N 5.06 E
Vlieland-Oost Vlieland 12 Ha 53.17N 5.06 E
Vliestroom 12 Ha 53.17N 5.06 E
Vlissingen 11 Jc 51.26N 3.35 E
Vlissingen-Oost-Souburg 12 Fc 51.28N 3.36 E
Vloesberg/Flobecq 12 Gd 50.44N 3.44 E
Vlora 6 Hg 40.27N 19.30 E
Vlorës, Gjiri i- 15 Ci 40.25N 19.25 E
Vlotho 12 Kb 52.10N 8.51 E
Vltava=Moldau (EN) 5 He 50.21N 14.30 E
Vöcklabruck 14 Jg 43.46N 15.47 E
Vodla 7 If 61.49N 36.00 E
Vodlozero, Ozero- 7 Ie 62.20N 37.00 E
Vodňany 10 Kg 49.09N 14.11 E
Vodnjan 14 Hf 44.57N 13.51 E
Vodny 17 Fe 63.32N 53.20 E
Voerde (Niederrhein) 12 Ce 51.35N 6.41 E
Voeren/Fouron 12 Hd 50.45N 5.48 E
Vogel Peak 34 Hd 8.24N 11.47 E
Vogelsberg 10 Ff 50.30N 9.15 E
Voghera 14 Ee 44.59N 9.01 E
Vogtland 10 If 50.30N 12.05 E
Voh 63b Be 20.58S 164.42 E
Võhandu Jõgi/Vyhandu 8 Lf 58.03N 27.40 E
Vohémar 37 Ib 13.22S 50.00 E
Vohipeno 37 Hd 22.20S 47.52 E
Vöhl 12 Kc 51.12N 8.56 E
Vohma 7 Ld 58.45N 46.36 E
Vohma 19 Ed 58.58N 46.45 E
Voi 31 Ki 3.23S 38.34 E
Voikoski 7 Ke 61.16N 26.44 E
Võion Õros 31 Gh 8.25N 9.45W
Voire 11 Kf 48.27N 4.25 E
Voiron 11 Li 45.22N 5.35 E
Voitsberg 14 Jc 47.02N 15.09 E
Voiviis, Limni- 15 Fj 39.32N 22.45 E
Vojens 8 Ci 55.15N 9.19 E

Vojkar 17 Ld 65.38N 64.40 E
Vojmsjön 7 Dd 65.00N 16.24 E
Vojnić 14 Je 45.19N 15.42 E
Vojnilov 10 Ug 49.04N 24.33 E
Vojvodina [3] 15 Cd 45.00N 20.00 E
Voj-Vož 19 Fc 62.56N 54.59 E
Voknavolok 7 Hd 64.57N 30.31 E
Vokré, Hoséré- 30 Ih 8.21N 13.15 E
Volary 10 Jh 48.55N 13.54 E
Volcán 49 Fi 8.46N 82.38W
Volcanica, Cordillera- 38 Ih 18.00N 101.00W
Volcano 65a Fd 19.26N 155.20W
Volcano Islands (EN)=Iõ/Kazan-Rettõ 21 Qg 25.00N 141.00 E
Volcano Islands (EN)=Kazan-Rettõ/Iõ 21 Qg 25.00N 141.00 E
Volcán Rana Roi 65d Ab 27.05S 109.23W
Volčansk [R.S.F.S.R.] 17 Jg 59.59N 60.04 E
Volčansk [Ukr.-U.S.S.R.] 16 Jd 50.16N 37.01 E
Volčiha 20 Df 52.02N 80.23 E
Volda 7 Be 62.09N 6.06 E
Voldafjorden 8 Ab 62.10N 6.00 E
Volga 5 Kf 45.55N 47.52 E
Volga 7 Jh 57.57N 38.25 E
Volga-Baltic Canal (EN)=Volgo-Baltijski vodny put imeni V. I. Lenina 5 Jd 59.58N 37.10 E
Volga Delta (EN) 5 Kf 46.30N 47.00 E
Volga Hills (EN)=Privolžskaja Vozvyšennost 5 Ke 52.00N 46.00 E
Volgo-Baltijski vodny put imeni V.I. Lenina=Volga-Baltic Canal (EN) 5 Jd 59.58N 37.10 E
Volgodonsk 19 Ef 47.33N 42.08 E
Volgo-Donsko sudohodny kanal imeni V. I. Lenina=Lenin Canal (EN) 5 Kf 48.40N 43.37 E
Volgograd (Stalingrad) 6 Kf 48.44N 44.25 E
Volgograd Reservoir (EN)=Volgogradskoje Vodohranilišče 5 Kf 49.20N 45.00 E
Volgogradskaja Oblast [3] 19 Ef 49.30N 44.30 E
Volgogradskoje Vodohranilišče=Volgograd Reservoir (EN) 5 Kf 49.20N 45.00 E
Volhov 5 Jc 60.08N 32.20 E
Volhov 9 Jd 59.55N 32.20 E
Volhynia 5 Ie 51.00N 25.00 E
Volissós 15 Ik 38.29N 25.55 E
Volja 7 Jf 61.21N 61.16 E
Volka 10 Vd 52.43N 25.43 E
Völkermarkt 14 Id 46.39N 14.38 E
Völklingen 10 Cg 49.15N 6.51 E
Volkmarsen 12 Lc 51.24N 9.07 E
Volkovysk 16 Dc 53.10N 24.31 E
Volkovysskaja Vozvyšennost 10 Kc 53.10N 24.30 E
Volksrust 37 De 27.24S 29.53 E
Vollenhove 12 Hb 52.40N 5.57 E
Vollsjö 8 Ei 55.42N 13.46 E
Volme 12 Jc 51.24N 7.27 E
Volmunster 12 Je 49.07N 7.21 E
Volna, Gora- 20 Kd 63.30N 154.57 E
Volnjansk 16 If 47.54N 35.29 E
Volnovaha 16 Jf 47.37N 37.36 E
Voločajevka 2-ja 20 Jg 48.36N 134.36 E
Voločisk 16 Ee 49.31N 26.13 E
Volodarsk 7 Kh 56.14N 43.13 E
Volodarski 16 Pf 46.26N 48.31 E
Volodarskoje 19 Ge 53.18N 68.08 E
Vologda 5 Jb 59.12N 39.55 E
Vologodskaja Oblast [3] 19 Ed 60.00N 41.00 E
Volokolamsk 7 Id 56.03N 35.58 E
Volokonovka 16 Jd 50.29N 37.52 E
Vólos 6 Ih 39.22N 22.57 E
Vološka 7 Jf 61.42N 39.15 E
Vološka 7 Jf 61.21N 40.03 E
Volosovo 7 Gg 58.29N 29.31 E
Volovec 10 Ug 48.42N 23.17 E
Volovo 16 Kc 53.35N 38.01 E
Voložin 16 Eb 54.06N 26.32 E
Volquart Boons Kyst 41 Jd 70.20N 24.20W
Volsini, Monti- 14 Hd 42.40N 11.55 E
Volsk 19 Ee 52.02N 47.23 E
Volta 30 Hh 5.46N 0.41 E
Volta 34 Fd 7.00N 0.30 E
Volta Blanche=White Volta (EN) 30 Gh 8.38N 0.59W
Volta Lake 30 Hh 7.30N 0.15 E
Volta Noire=Black Volta (EN) 30 Gh 8.38N 1.30W
Volta Noire=Black Volta (EN) 34 Ec 12.30N 4.00W
Volta Redonda 53 Lh 22.32S 44.07W
Volta Rouge=Red Volta (EN) 30 Gh 10.34N 0.30W
Volterra 14 Eg 42.43N 10.51 E
Voltoya 13 Hc 41.13N 4.31W
Voltri, Genova- 14 Cf 44.26N 8.45 E
Volturino 14 Jj 40.25N 15.48 E
Volturno 14 Hi 41.01N 13.55 E
Volubilis 32 Fc 34.04N 5.33W
Vólvi, Limni- 15 Gi 40.41N 23.33 E
Volynska Grjada 10 Ue 51.10N 25.00 E
Volynskaja Oblast [3] 19 Ce 51.10N 25.00 E
Volynskaja Vozvyšennost 10 Ue 50.00N 25.00 E
Volžsk 19 Ed 55.55N 48.19 E
Volžski [R.S.F.S.R.] 6 Kf 48.48N 44.44 E
Volžski [R.S.F.S.R.] 7 Mj 53.26N 50.08 E
Voma 63d Bc 18.00S 178.08 E
Vonavona 63a Cc 8.12S 157.05 E
Vondrozo 37 Hd 22.47S 47.20 E
Von Frank Mountain 40 Id 63.33N 154.20W
Vónitsa 15 Dk 38.55N 20.53 E
Vonne 11 Gh 46.25N 0.15 E

Võnnu/Vynnu 8 Lf 58.15N 27.10 E
Voorne 12 Gc 51.52N 4.05 E
Voorschoten 12 Gb 52.08N 4.28 E
Voorst 12 Ib 52.10N 6.09 E
Voorst-Twello 12 Ib 52.14N 6.07 E
Vop 16 Hb 54.56N 32.44 E
Vopnafjördur 7a Cb 65.45N 14.50W
Vora 15 Ch 41.23N 19.40 E
Võra/Võyri 8 Ja 63.09N 22.15 E
Vorarlberg [2] 14 Dc 47.15N 9.50 E
Vóras Óros 15 Ei 41.00N 21.50 E
Vorau 14 Jc 47.24N 15.53 E
Vorden 12 Ib 52.06N 6.20 E
Vorderrhein 14 Dd 46.49N 9.26 E
Vordingborg 7 Ci 55.01N 11.55 E
Voreifel 12 Jd 50.10N 7.00 E
Vorga Šor 17 Kc 67.35N 63.40 E
Voria Pindhos 15 Dj 40.20N 20.55 E
Vórioi Sporádhes, Nisoi-=Northern Sporades (EN) 15 Ih 39.15N 23.55 E
Vórios Evvoïkós Kólpos=Évvoia, Gulf of- (EN) 15 Gk 38.45N 23.10 E
Vorkuta 6 Mb 67.27N 63.58 E
Vorma 7 Cf 60.09N 11.27 E
Vorma 8 Je 59.02N 23.05 E
Vormsi 7 Fg 59.00N 23.15 E
Vorniceni 15 Jf 47.59N 26.40 E
Vorogovo 20 Dd 60.58N 89.28 E
Vorona 16 Md 51.22N 42.03 E
Voroncovo [R.S.F.S.R.] 20 Ib 71.40N 83.40 E
Voroncovo [R.S.F.S.R.] 8 Mg 57.15N 28.49 E
Voronež 6 Je 51.40N 39.10 E
Voronežskaja Oblast [3] 19 Df 49.00N 39.10 E
Voronin Trough (EN) 67 Ge 80.00N 85.00 E
Voronja 7 Ib 69.09N 35.47 E
Voronovo 6 Kj 54.09N 25.19 E
Voropajevo 8 Li 55.07N 27.19 E
Vorošilovgrad 6 Jf 48.34N 39.20 E
Vorošilovgradskaja Oblast [3] 19 Df 49.00N 39.10 E
Vorotan 16 Oj 39.15N 46.43 E
Vorotynec 7 Kh 56.02N 45.52 E
Voróžba 16 Id 51.10N 34.11 E
Vorskla 16 Je 48.52N 34.05 E
Vorsma 7 Ki 55.58N 43.17 E
Võrts Järv/Vyrtsjarv, Ozero- 7 Gg 58.15N 26.05 E
Võru/Vyru 8 Lf 57.52N 27.05 E
Voruh 18 He 39.52N 70.35 E
Vosges 5 Gf 48.30N 7.10 E
Vosges [3] 11 Mf 48.10N 6.20 E
Voskresensk 7 Ji 55.22N 38.42 E
Voskresenskoje 7 Kh 56.51N 45.27 E
Voss 8 Bd 60.40N 6.30 E
Vossa 8 Ad 60.39N 5.42 E
Vossevangen 8 Bd 60.39N 6.26 E
Vostočno-Kazahstanskaja Oblast [3] 19 If 49.00N 84.00 E
Vostočno-Kounradski 19 Hf 46.58N 75.07 E
Vostočno Sibirskoje More=East Siberian Sea (EN) 67 Cd 74.00N 166.00 E
Vostočny [R.S.F.S.R.] 20 Jg 48.19N 142.40 E
Vostočny [R.S.F.S.R.] 17 Jg 58.48N 61.52 E
Vostočny, Hrebet- 20 Lf 55.00N 160.30 E
Vostočny Sajan=Eastern Sayans (EN) 21 Ld 53.00N 97.00 E
Vostok 66 Hf 78.28S 106.48 E
Vostok Island 57 Lf 10.06S 152.23W
Vostrecovo 20 Jg 45.56N 134.59 E
Vošu/Vyzu 6 Ke 59.30N 25.50 E
Votkinsk 19 Fd 57.05N 53.59 E
Votkinskoje Vodohranilišče=Votkinsk Reservoir (EN) 5 Ld 57.30N 55.10 E
Votkinsk Reservoir (EN)=Votkinskoje Vodohranilišče 5 Ld 57.30N 55.10 E
Votuporanga 55 He 20.24S 49.59W
Vouga 36 Ce 12.14S 16.48 E
Vouga 13 Dd 40.41N 8.40W
Vouillé 15 Hc 46.38N 0.10 E
Voulgára 15 Ej 39.06N 21.54 E
Vouliagméni 15 Gl 37.49N 23.47 E
Voúrinos Óros 15 Ei 40.11N 21.40 E
Voúxa, Ákra- 15 Gn 35.38N 23.36 E
Vouziers 11 Ke 49.24N 4.42 E
Voves 11 He 48.16N 1.38 E
Vovodo 35 Cd 5.40N 24.21 E
Voxna 8 Fg 61.17N 15.34 E
Voxnan 8 Gg 61.17N 16.26 E
Voyeykov Ice Shelf 66 Ie 66.20S 124.38 E
Võyri/Võrå 8 Ja 63.09N 22.15 E
Vože, Ozero- 18 Bb 60.35N 39.05 E
Vožega 7 Jf 60.33N 39.13 E
Voznesenje 7 If 61.01N 35.27 E
Voznesensk 19 Df 47.35N 31.20 E
Vozroždenija, Ostrov- 18 Bb 45.05N 59.15 E
Vraca [2] 15 Gh 43.12N 23.33 E
Vraca 15 Dh 41.54N 20.45 E
Vracov 14 Lf 48.59N 17.01 E
Vradijevka 16 Gf 47.51N 30.34 E
Vrakhiónas 15 Dl 37.48N 20.45 E
Vran 14 Lg 43.39N 17.27 E
Vrancea [2] 15 Jc 45.50N 26.42 E
Vranica 14 Lg 43.57N 17.44 E
Vranje 15 Fh 43.33N 21.54 E
Vranov nad Topľou 10 Rh 48.54N 21.41 E
Vráška čuka, Prohod- 15 Fh 43.50N 22.23 E
Vratnica 15 Eh 42.18N 21.07 E
Vratnik, prohod- 15 Jh 42.49N 26.10 E
Vrbas 15 Cd 45.34N 19.39 E
Vrbno pod Pradědem 10 Nf 50.08N 17.23 E
Vrbovsko 14 Jf 45.22N 15.05 E

Vrchlabí 10 Lf 50.38N 15.37 E
Vrede 37 De 27.30S 29.06 E
Vreden 12 Ib 52.02N 6.50 E
Vredenburg 37 Bf 32.54S 17.59 E
Vredendal 37 Bf 31.41S 18.35 E
Vresse, Vresse-sur-Semois- 12 Ge 49.52N 4.56 E
Vresse-sur-Semois 12 Ge 49.52N 4.56 E
Vresse-sur-Semois-Vresse 12 Ge 49.52N 4.56 E
Vretstorp 8 Fe 59.02N 14.52 E
Vrhnika 14 Id 45.58N 14.18 E
Vries 12 Ia 53.05N 6.36 E
Vriezenveen 12 Ib 52.26N 6.36 E
Vrigstad 8 Fg 57.21N 14.28 E
Vron 12 Dd 50.19N 1.45 E
Vršac 15 Ed 45.07N 21.18 E
Vryburg 31 Jk 26.55S 24.45 E
Vryheid 37 Ee 27.52S 30.38 E
Vsetin 10 Ng 49.21N 18.00 E
Vsevidof, Mount- 40a Eb 53.07N 168.43W
Vsevoložsk 7 Hf 60.04N 30.41 E
Vstrečny 20 Lc 68.00N 165.58 E
Vtačnik 10 Pg 48.42N 18.37 E
Vuanggava 63d Cc 18.52S 178.54W
Vučitrn 15 Dg 42.49N 20.58 E
Vučjak 15 Fh 41.28N 22.20 E
Vuka 14 Me 45.21N 19.00 E
Vukovar 14 Me 45.21N 19.00 E
Vuktyl 19 Fc 63.50N 57.25 E
Vulavu 63d Dc 8.31S 159.48 E
Vulcan 15 Gd 45.23N 23.16 E
Vulcan, Vîrful- 15 Fc 46.14N 22.58 E
Vulcano 14 Il 38.25N 15.00 E
Vulkanešty 16 Fg 45.38N 28.27 E
Vulture 14 Jj 40.57N 15.38 E
Vung Tau 25 Lf 10.21N 107.04 E
Vunindawa 63d Bb 17.49S 178.19 E
Vunisea Station 61 Je 19.03S 178.09 E
Vuohijärvi 8 Lc 61.10N 26.40 E
Vuoksa 8 Nd 60.35N 30.42 E
Vuoksa, Ozero- [R.S.F.S.R.] 8 Mc 61.00N 30.00 E
Vuoksa, Ozero- [R.S.F.S.R.] 8 Md 60.38N 29.55 E
Vuollerim 7 Ec 66.25N 20.36 E
Vuosjärvi 8 Ka 63.00N 25.00 E
Vuotso 7 Gb 68.06N 27.08 E
Vuranimala 63a Ec 9.05S 160.51 E
Vyborg 6 Ic 60.42N 28.45 E
Vyčegda 5 Kc 61.18N 46.36 E
Vyčegodski 17 Lf 61.17N 46.48 E
Vychodočeský kraj [3] 10 Lf 50.10N 16.00 E
Východoslovenská nížina 10 Rh 48.35N 21.50 E
Východoslovenský kraj [3] 10 Rg 49.00N 21.15 E
Vyg 5 Jc 63.17N 35.17 E
Vygoda [Ukr.-U.S.S.R.] 15 Nc 46.38N 30.24 E
Vygoda [Ukr.-U.S.S.R.] 10 Uh 48.52N 24.01 E
Vygozero, Ozero- 5 Jc 63.35N 34.45 E
Vyhandu/Võhandu Jõgi 5 Jc 58.03N 27.40 E
Vyja 7 Le 62.57N 46.42 E
Vyksa 19 Ed 55.20N 42.12 E
Vym 19 Fc 62.13N 50.23 E
Vynnu/Võnnu 8 Lf 58.15N 27.10 E
Vyrica 19 Dd 59.24N 30.19 E
Vyrnwy 9 Ki 52.45N 2.50W
Vyrtsjarv, Ozero-/Võrts Järv 7 Gg 58.15N 26.05 E
Vyru/Võru 19 Cd 57.52N 27.05 E
Vyša 16 Mb 54.03N 42.06 E
Vyšgorod 16 Gd 50.38N 30.29 E
Vyšgorodok 8 Mg 56.55N 28.05 E
Vyškov 10 Mg 49.17N 17.00 E
Vyškov, pereval 15 Jb 48.38N 23.45 E
Vyšni Voloček 7 Th 57.37N 34.32 E
Vysock 7 Gf 60.36N 28.36 E
Vysoké Tatry=High Tatra (EN) 10 Pg 49.10N 20.00 E
Vysokogorny 20 Lf 50.07N 139.10 E
Vysokogorsk 28 Mb 44.23N 135.23 E
Vysokoje 5 Ib 52.22N 23.26 E
Vysokovsk 7 Ih 56.21N 36.29 E
Vyšši Brod 10 Kh 48.37N 14.18 E
Vytebet 16 Ic 53.53N 35.38 E
Vytegra 19 Dc 61.01N 36.28 E
Vyvenka 20 Ld 60.10N 165.20 E
Vyzu/Vošu 6 Ke 59.30N 25.50 E
Vzmorje 20 Jg 47.45N 142.30 E

W

Wa 34 Ec 10.03N 2.29W
Waal 11 Kc 51.55N 4.30 E
Waalre 12 Hc 51.23N 5.27 E
Waalwijk 12 Hc 51.41N 5.04 E
Waar, Meos- 26 Ja 2.05S 134.23 E
Waardgronden 11a Ha 53.12N 5.05 E
Waarschoot 12 Fc 51.09N 3.36 E
Wabana 42 Mg 47.38N 52.57W
Wabao, Cap- 63b Ce 21.36S 167.51 E
Wabasca 42 Fe 56.00N 113.53W
Wabasca 42 Fe 58.22N 115.20W
Wabash 38 Kf 37.46N 88.02W
Wabash 12 Ee 40.48N 85.49W
Wabash River 45 Lh 37.46N 88.02W
Wabowden 42 Hd 54.55N 98.38W
Wabu Hu 27 Kf 32.25N 116.55 E
Wabush 42 Ld 52.55N 66.52W
Wachile 35 Hc 4.34N 39.03 E
Wachusett Seamount (EN) 57 Lh 32.00S 151.20W
Waco 39 Jf 31.55N 97.08W
Waconda Lake 45 Gg 39.30N 98.30W
Wad Bandah 35 Dc 13.06N 27.57 E
Wadayama 29 Dd 35.20N 134.51 E

Waddän 33 Cd 29.10N 16.08 E
Waddän, Jabal- 33 Cd 29.20N 16.20 E
Waddeneilanden=West Frisian Islands (EN) 11 Ka 53.30N 5.00 E
Waddenzee 11 Ka 53.30N 5.30 E
Waddington, Mount- 38 Gd 51.23N 125.15W
Wadena 45 Ic 46.26N 95.08W
Wadern 12 Ie 49.32N 6.53 E
Wadern-Nunkirchen 12 Ie 49.32N 6.53 E
Wadersloh 12 Kc 51.44N 8.15 E
Wadersloh-Liesborn 12 Kc 51.43N 8.16 E
Wadesboro 44 Gh 34.58N 80.04W
Wadhams 46 Ba 51.30N 127.31W
Wädi Bishah 23 Fe 21.24N 43.26 E
Wädi Fajr 23 Ec 30.17N 38.18 E
Wädi Ḥalfa' 31 Kf 21.56N 31.20 E
Wädi Jimäl, Jaziírat- 23 Fj 24.40N 35.10 E
Wädi Müsá 24 Fg 30.19N 35.29 E
Wädi Shiban 35 Ib 18.10N 52.57 E
Wad Madaní 14 Kg 14.24N 33.32 E
Wad Nimr 35 Lc 14.32N 32.08 E
Wadowice 10 Pg 49.53N 19.30 E
Wadsworth 46 Fg 39.38N 119.17W
Wafangdian → Fuxian 27 Ld 39.38N 121.59 E
Wafrah 23 Gd 28.25N 47.56 E
Waga-Gawa 29 Gb 39.18N 141.07 E
Wagenfeld 12 Kb 52.33N 8.35 E
Wagenfeld-Ströhen 12 Kb 52.32N 8.39 E
Wageningen 12 Hc 51.57N 5.41 E
Wager, Qar- 35 Hc 10.01N 45.30 E
Wager Bay 38 Kc 65.26N 88.40W
Wagga Wagga 58 Fh 35.07S 147.22 E
Waghäusel 9 Fh 49.15N 8.30 E
Wagin 58 Ch 33.18S 117.21 E
Waginger See 10 Ii 47.58N 12.50 E
Wagon Mound 45 Dh 36.01N 104.42W
Wagontire Mountain 46 Fe 43.21N 119.53W
Wagrien 10 Gb 54.15N 10.45 E
Wagrowiec 10 Nd 52.49N 17.11 E
Wah 25 Eb 33.48N 72.42 E
Waha 31 If 28.10N 19.57 E
Wahai 26 Ig 2.48S 129.30 E
Wahiawa 60 Oc 21.30N 158.02W
Wahoo 45 Hf 41.13N 96.37W
Wahpeton 43 Hb 46.16N 96.36W
Waialeale, Mount- 65a Ba 22.04N 159.30W
Waialua 65a Cb 21.35N 158.08W
Waianae 65a Cb 21.27N 158.12W
Waiau 62 Ee 42.47S 173.22 E
Waiau 61 Dh 42.39S 173.03 E
Waiblingen 10 Hh 48.50N 9.18 E
Waibstadt 12 Ke 49.18N 8.56 E
Waidhofen an der Thaya 14 Jb 48.49N 15.17 E
Waidhofen an der Ybbs 14 Ic 47.58N 14.46 E
Waigame 26 Ig 1.50S 129.49 E
Waigeo, Pulau- 57 Ee 0.14S 130.45 E
Waihi 62 Fb 37.24S 175.50 E
Waihou 62 Fb 37.10S 175.33 E
Waikabubak 26 Jh 9.38S 119.25 E
Waikare, Lake- 62 Fb 37.25S 175.10 E
Waikaremoana, Lake- 61 Eg 38.45S 177.05 E
Waikato 62 Fb 37.23S 174.43 E
Waikawa 62 Cg 46.38S 169.08 E
Waikouaiti 62 Df 45.36S 170.41 E
Wailangilala 63d Eb 16.45S 179.06W
Wailua 65a Ba 22.03N 159.20W
Wailuku 60 Oc 20.53N 156.30W
Waimamaku 62 Ea 35.34S 173.29 E
Waimanalo Beach 65a Db 21.20N 157.42W
Waimangaroa 62 Bd 41.43S 171.46 E
Waimate 62 Df 44.45S 171.03 E
Waimea 65a Fc 20.02N 155.40W
Wainfleet All Saints 12 Ca 53.06N 0.15 E
Waingamba 26 Jh 19.36N 79.48 E
Waingapu 26 Jh 9.39S 120.16 E
Waini Point 50 Gb 8.24N 59.49W
Waini River 50 Gb 8.24N 59.51W
Wainwright [Ak.-U.S.] 40 Gb 70.38N 160.01W
Wainwright [Alta.-Can.] 42 Gf 52.49N 110.52W
Waiouru 62 Fc 39.29S 175.40 E
Waipahu 65a Cb 21.23N 158.01W
Waipara 62 Df 43.03S 172.45 E
Waipawa 62 Gc 39.56S 176.35 E
Waipiro 62 Hc 38.02S 178.20 E
Waipu 62 Fa 35.59S 174.26 E
Waipukurau 62 Gc 39.59S 176.33 E
Wairakei 62 Fc 38.37S 176.05 E
Wairarapa, Lake- 62 Fd 41.15S 175.15 E
Wairau 62 Fd 41.31S 174.03 E
Wairoa 61 Eg 39.03S 177.26 E
Wairoa 62 Ea 36.05S 173.59 E
Waitaki 62 Cf 44.56S 171.09 E
Waitangi 61 Di 43.56S 176.34W
Waitara 62 Fc 39.00S 174.14 E
Waitati 62 Df 45.45S 170.34 E
Waitemata 62 Fb 36.50S 174.40 E
Waitotara 62 Fc 39.48S 174.44 E
Waiwerang 26 Hh 8.23S 123.09 E
Waiyevo 61 Fc 16.48S 179.59 E
Wäjid 35 Ge 3.50N 43.14 E
Wajima 28 Nf 37.24N 136.54 E
Wajir 31 Ih 1.42N 40.04 E
Waka [Eth.] 35 Hc 7.09N 37.19 E
Waka [Zaïre] 36 Db 1.01N 20.13 E
Wakamatsu-Shima 29 Ae 32.54N 129.00 E
Wakasa-Wan 28 Mf 35.45N 135.40 E
Wakatipu, Lake- 62 Cf 45.05S 168.35 E
Wakaya 63d Bb 17.37S 179.00 E
Wakayama 28 Mf 34.13N 135.11 E
Wakayama Ken [2] 28 Mh 33.55N 135.20 E
Wa Keeney 45 Gg 39.01N 99.53W
Wakefield [Eng.-U.K.] 9 Lh 53.42N 1.29W
Wakefield [N.Z.] 62 Ed 41.24S 173.03 E

Index Symbols

[1] Independent Nation
[2] State, Region
[3] District, County
[4] Municipality
[5] Colony, Dependency
Continent
Physical Region

Historical or Cultural Region
Mount, Mountain
Volcano
Hill
Mountains, Mountain Range
Hills, Escarpment
Plateau, Upland

Pass, Gap
Plain, Lowland
Delta
Salt Flat
Valley, Canyon
Crater, Cave
Karst Features

Depression
Polder
Cliff
Desert, Dunes
Forest, Woods
Heath, Steppe
Oasis
Cape, Point

Coast, Beach
Islands, Archipelago
Rocks, Reefs
Coral Reef
Well, Spring
Geyser
Island
Atoll

Rock, Reef
Waterfall Rapids
River Mouth, Estuary
Lake
Salt Lake
Intermittent Lake
Reservoir
Swamp, Pond
River, Stream

Canal
Glacier
Ice Shelf, Pack Ice
Ocean
Sea
Gulf, Bay
Strait, Fjord

Lagoon
Bank
Seamount
Tablemount
Ridge
Shelf
Basin

Escarpment, Sea Scarp
Fracture
Trench, Abyss
National Park, Reserve
Point of Interest
Recreation Site
Cave, Cavern

Historic Site
Ruins
Wall, Walls
Church, Abbey
Temple
Scientific Station
Airport

Port
Lighthouse
Mine
Tunnel
Dam, Bridge

Wake Island [5]	58	Jd	19.18N	166.36W
Wake Island	57	Hc	19.18N	166.36 E
Wakkanai	22	Qe	45.25N	141.40 E
Wakunai	63a	Ba	5.52S	155.13 E
Wakuya	29	Gb	38.33N	141.05 E
Wala	36	Fd	5.46S	32.04 E
Walachia (EN) = Valahia	5	Ig	44.00N	25.00 E
Walachia (EN) = Valahia	15	He	44.00N	25.00 E
Wałbrzych [2]	10	Mf	50.45N	16.15 E
Wałbrzych	6	He	50.46N	16.17 E
Walchensee	10	Hi	47.35N	11.20 E
Walcheren	11	Jc	51.33N	3.35 E
Walcott, Lake-	46	Ie	42.40N	113.23W
Walcourt	12	Gd	50.15N	4.25 E
Walcourt-Fraire	12	Gd	50.16N	4.30 E
Wałcz	10	Mc	53.17N	16.28 E
Waldböckelheim	12	Je	49.49N	7.43 E
Waldbröl	10	Df	50.53N	7.37 E
Waldeck	12	Kc	51.17N	8.50 E
Waldeck	12	Lc	51.12N	9.05 E
Waldems	12	Kd	50.15N	8.18 E
Walden	45	Cf	40.44N	106.17W
Waldfischbach-Burgalben	12	Je	49.17N	7.40 E
Waldkirchen	10	Jh	48.44N	13.36 E
Waldkraiburg	10	Ih	48.12N	12.25 E
Wald-Michelbach	12	Ke	49.34N	8.49 E
Waldnaab	10	Ig	49.35N	12.07 E
Waldorf	44	If	38.37N	76.54W
Waldrach	12	Ie	49.45N	6.45 E
Waldron	45	Ii	34.54N	94.05W
Waldshut	10	Ei	47.37N	8.13 E
Waldviertel	14	Jb	48.30N	15.30 E
Waleabahi, Pulau-	26	Hg	0.15S	122.20 E
Wales	40	Fc	65.36N	168.05W
Wales	42	Ic	67.50N	86.40W
Wales	5	Fe	52.30N	3.30W
Wales [2]	9	Ji	52.30N	3.30W
Walewale	34	Ec	10.21N	0.48W
Walferdange	12	Ie	49.39N	6.08 E
Walgett	58	Fh	30.01S	148.07 E
Walgreen Coast	66	Of	75.15S	105.00W
Walhalla	45	Hb	48.55N	97.55W
Walikale	36	Ec	1.25S	28.03 E
Walker	45	Jc	47.06N	94.35W
Walker Lake	43	Dd	38.40N	118.43W
Walkerston	59	Jd	21.10S	149.10 E
Wall	45	Ed	44.01N	102.14W
Wallace	46	Hc	47.28N	115.56W
Wallaceburg	44	Fd	42.36N	82.23W
Wallangarra	59	Ke	28.56S	151.56 E
Wallaroo	59	Hf	33.56S	137.38 E
Wallary Island	59	Ic	15.05S	141.50 E
Wallasey	9	Jh	53.26N	3.03W
Walla Walla	43	Db	46.08N	118.20W
Walldorf	12	Ke	49.20N	8.39 E
Wallenhorst	12	Kb	52.21N	8.01 E
Wallibu	51n	Ba	13.19N	61.15W
Wallingford	12	Ac	51.36N	1.08W
Wallis, Iles-=Wallis Islands (EN)	57	Jf	13.18S	176.10W
Wallis and Futuna (EN)= Wallis-et-Futuna, Iles- [5]	58	Jf	14.00S	177.00W
Walliser Alpen/Alpes Valaisannes	14	Bd	46.10N	7.30 E
Wallis-et-Futuna, Iles-= Wallis and Futuna (EN) [5]	58	Jf	14.00S	177.00W
Wallis Islands (EN)=Wallis, Iles-	57	Jf	13.18S	176.10W
Wallowa	46	Gd	45.34N	117.32W
Wallowa Mountains	46	Gd	45.10N	117.30W
Walmer	12	Dc	51.12N	1.24 E
Walney, Isle of-	9	Jg	54.07N	3.15W
Walnut Ridge	43	Id	36.04N	90.57W
Walpole, Ile-	57	Hg	22.37S	168.57 E
Walrus Islands	40	Ge	58.45N	160.20W
Walsall	9	Li	52.35N	1.58W
Walsenburg	43	Gd	37.37N	104.47W
Walsrode	10	Fd	52.52N	9.35 E
Walterboro	44	Gi	32.54N	80.39W
Walter F. George Lake	44	Ej	31.49N	85.08W
Walter Lake	43	Dd	38.44N	118.43W
Walters	45	Gi	34.22N	98.19W
Waltershausen	10	Gf	50.54N	10.34 E
Waltham	44	Ic	45.58N	76.57W
Walton-on-the-Naze	12	Dc	51.51N	1.17 E
Waltrop	12	Jc	51.38N	7.24 E
Walvisbaai/Walvis Bay [3]	37	Ad	23.00S	14.30 E
Walvisbaai=Walvis Bay (EN)	31	Ik	22.59S	14.31 E
Walvisbaai=Walvis Bay (EN) [5]	31	Ik	22.59S	14.31 E
Walvisbaai=Walvis Bay (EN)	30	Ik	22.57S	14.30 E
Walvis Bay/Walvisbaai [3]	37	Ad	23.00S	14.30 E
Walvis Bay (EN)= Walvisbaai	30	Ik	22.57S	14.30 E
Walvis Bay (EN)= Walvisbaai [3]	31	Ik	22.59S	14.31 E
Walvis Bay (EN)= Walvisbaai	31	Ik	22.59S	14.31 E
Walvis Ridge (EN)	3	El	28.00S	3.00 E
Wamba	30	Ii	3.56S	17.12 E
Wamba [Kenya]	36	Gb	0.59N	37.19 E
Wamba [Nig.]	34	Gd	8.56N	8.36 E
Wamba [Zaire]	36	Eb	2.09N	28.00 E
Wamena	26	Kg	4.00S	138.57 E
Wami	30	Ki	6.08S	38.49 E
Wampusirpi	49	Ef	15.15N	84.37W
Wamsutter	46	Lf	41.40N	107.58W
Wan	26	Kh	8.23S	137.56 E
Wana	25	Db	32.17N	69.35 E
Wanaka	58	Hi	44.42S	169.08 E
Wanaka, Lake-	62	Cf	44.30S	169.10 E
Wan'an	27	Jf	26.32N	114.48 E
Wanapiri	26	Kg	4.33S	135.59 E
Wanapitei Lake	44	Gb	46.45N	80.45W
Wandel Hav=Wandel Sea (EN)	41	Gb	83.00N	15.00W
Wandel Sea (EN)=Wandel Hav	41	Gb	83.00N	15.00W
Wandsworth, London-	12	Bc	51.27N	0.12W
Wanganui	62	Fc	39.58S	175.00 E
Wanganui	61	Eg	39.56S	175.02 E
Wangaratta	59	Jg	36.22S	146.20 E
Wangcun [China]	28	Df	36.41N	117.42 E
Wangcun [China]	27	Jd	39.58N	112.53 E
Wangda/Zogang	27	Gf	29.37N	97.58 E
Wangdu	28	Ce	38.43N	115.09 E
Wangen in Allgäu	10	Fi	47.41N	9.50 E
Wangerooge	10	Dc	53.46N	7.55 E
Wanggameti, Gunung-	26	Hi	10.07S	120.14 E
Wanggezhuang → Jiaonan	28	Eg	35.53N	119.58 E
Wangiwangi, Pulau-	26	Hh	5.20S	123.35 E
Wangjiang	28	Di	30.08N	116.41 E
Wangkui	27	Mb	46.50N	126.29 E
Wangpan Yang	21	Of	30.33N	121.26 E
Wangping	27	Mc	43.18N	129.46 E
Wangying → Huaiyin	28	Eh	33.35N	119.02 E
Wani, Laguna-	49	Ff	14.50N	83.25W
Wanie-Rukula	36	Eb	0.14N	25.34 E
Wanitsuka-Yama	29	Bf	31.45N	131.17 E
Wankie	31	Jj	18.21S	26.30 E
Wanlewēyn	35	Ge	2.35N	44.55 E
Wan Namton	25	Jd	22.03N	99.33 E
Wannian (Chenying)	28	Dj	28.42N	117.04 E
Wanning	27	Jh	18.59N	110.24 E
Wanquan	28	Cd	40.52N	114.44 E
Wansbeck	9	Lf	55.10N	1.34W
Wan Shui	28	Di	30.30N	117.01 E
Wanxian	22	Mf	30.48N	108.21 E
Wanyuan	27	Ie	32.03N	108.04 E
Wanzai	28	Cj	28.06N	114.27 E
Wanzhi → Wuhu	28	Ei	31.21N	118.23 E
Wapato	46	Ec	46.27N	120.25W
Wapiti	46	Kd	44.28N	109.28W
Wapiti	42	Fe	55.08N	118.19W
Wapsipinicon River	45	Kf	41.44N	90.20W
Waqooyi Galbeed [3]	35	Gc	10.00N	44.00 E
Warangal	22	Jh	18.18N	79.35 E
Waratah Bay	59	Jg	38.50S	146.05 E
Warburg	10	Fe	51.30N	9.10 E
Warburger Borde	12	Lc	51.35N	9.12 E
Warburg-Scherfede	12	Lc	51.32N	9.02 E
Warburton Bay	42	Gd	63.50N	111.30W
Warburton Mission	59	Fe	26.10S	126.35 E
Warburton Range	59	Fe	26.10S	126.40 E
Ward	62	Fd	41.50S	174.08 E
Warden	37	De	27.56S	29.00 E
Wardenburg	12	Ka	53.04N	8.12 E
Wardha	25	Fd	20.45N	78.37 E
Ward Hunt Strait	59	Ja	9.25S	149.55 E
Ware [B.C.-Can.]	42	Ee	57.27N	125.38W
Ware [Eng.-U.K.]	12	Bc	51.49N	0.01W
Waregem	12	Fd	50.53N	3.25 E
Waremme/Borgworm	11	Ld	50.42N	5.15 E
Waren [G.D.R.]	10	Ic	53.31N	12.41 E
Waren [Indon.]	58	Ee	2.16S	136.20 E
Warendorf	10	De	51.57N	7.59 E
Warin Chamrap	25	Ke	15.14N	104.52 E
Warka	10	Re	51.47N	21.10 E
Warkworth	62	Fb	36.24S	174.40 E
Warmbad [3]	37	Be	28.00S	18.30 E
Warmbad [Nam.]	37	Be	28.29S	18.41 E
Warmbad [S.Afr.]	37	Dd	24.53S	28.17 E
Warming Land	41	Gb	81.50N	52.45W
Warmington	12	Ab	52.08N	1.24W
Warminster	9	Kj	51.13N	2.12W
Warm Springs [Nv.-U.S.]	46	Gg	38.13N	116.20W
Warm Springs [Or.-U.S.]	46	Ed	44.46N	121.16W
Warnemünde, Rostock-	10	Ib	54.10N	12.05 E
Warner, Mount-	46	Da	51.03N	123.12W
Warner Mountains	43	Cc	41.40N	120.20W
Warner Peak	46	Fe	42.27N	119.44W
Warner Robins	43	Ke	32.37N	83.36W
Warner Valley	46	Fe	42.30N	119.55W
Warnes	54	Fg	17.30S	63.10W
Warnow	10	Ib	54.06N	12.09 E
Waroona	59	Df	32.50S	115.55 E
Warragul	59	Jg	38.10S	145.56 E
Warrego Range	59	Je	25.00S	145.45 E
Warrego River	57	Fh	30.24S	145.21 E
Warren [Ar.-U.S.]	45	Jj	33.38N	92.05W
Warren [Mi.-U.S.]	44	Fd	42.28N	83.01W
Warren [Mn.-U.S.]	45	Hb	48.12N	96.46W
Warren [Oh.-U.S.]	43	Kc	41.15N	80.49W
Warren [Pa.-U.S.]	44	He	41.52N	79.09W
Warrenpoint/An Pointe	9	Gg	54.06N	6.15W
Warrensburg	45	Jg	38.46N	93.44W
Warrenton	37	Ce	28.09S	24.47 E
Warri	34	Gd	5.31N	5.45 E
Warrington [Eng.-U.K.]	9	Kh	53.24N	2.37W
Warrington [Fl.-U.S.]	44	Dj	30.23N	87.16W
Warrior Reefs	59	Ia	9.35S	143.10 E
Warrnambool	58	Fh	38.23S	142.29 E
Warroad	43	Hb	48.54N	95.19W
Warrumbungle Range	59	Jf	31.30S	149.40 E
Warsaw [In.-U.S.]	44	Ee	41.14N	85.51W
Warsaw [Mo.-U.S.]	45	Jg	38.15N	93.23W
Warsaw [N.Y.-U.S.]	44	Hd	42.45N	78.07W
Warsaw (EN)=Warszawa	6	Ie	52.15N	21.00 E
Warshīkh	35	He	2.18N	45.48 E
Warstein	12	Kc	51.27N	8.22 E
Warstein-Belecke	12	Kc	51.29N	8.20 E
Warszawa [2]	10	Qd	52.15N	21.00 E
Warszawa=Warsaw (EN)	6	Ie	52.15N	21.00 E
Warta	5	He	52.35N	14.39 E
Waru	26	Jg	3.24S	130.40 E
Warwich	59	Ke	28.13S	152.02 E
Warwick	9	Li	52.25N	1.30W
Warwick [Eng.-U.K.]	9	Li	52.17N	1.34W
Warwick [R.I.-U.S.]	44	Le	41.42N	71.23W
Warwickshire [3]	9	Li	52.10N	1.35W
Wasagu	34	Gc	11.22N	5.48 E
Wasatch Range	38	He	41.15N	111.30W
Wascana Creek	46	Ma	50.40N	104.55W
Wasco	46	Fi	35.36N	119.20W
Waseca	45	Jd	44.05N	93.30W
Washburn	45	Fc	47.17N	101.02W
Washess Bay	64g	Ab	1.49N	157.31W
Wāshim	25	Fd	20.10N	76.58 E
Washington [2]	43	Cb	47.30N	120.30W
Washington [D.C.-U.S.]	39	Lf	38.54N	77.01W
Washington [Eng.-U.K.]	9	Lg	54.54N	1.31W
Washington [Ga.-U.S.]	44	Fi	33.44N	82.44W
Washington [Ia.-U.S.]	45	Kf	41.18N	91.42W
Washington [In.-U.S.]	44	Df	38.40N	87.10W
Washington [N.C.-U.S.]	44	Ih	35.33N	77.03W
Washington [Pa.-U.S.]	44	Ge	40.11N	80.16W
Washington → Teraina Island	57	Kd	4.43N	160.24W
Washington, Mount-	38	Le	44.15N	71.15W
Washington Court House	44	Ff	39.32N	83.29W
Washington Island	45	Md	45.23N	86.55W
Washington Land	41	Fb	80.15N	65.00W
Washita River	45	Hi	34.12N	96.50W
Washtucna	46	Fc	46.45N	118.19W
Wasile	26	If	1.04N	127.59 E
Wasilków	10	Tc	53.12N	23.12 E
Wasior	26	Jg	2.43S	134.30 E
Wāsiṭ [3]	24	Lf	32.35N	46.00 E
Wāsiṭ	24	Lf	32.11N	46.18 E
Wąsosz	10	Me	51.34N	16.42 E
Waspán	47	Hf	14.44N	83.58W
Wassamu	29a	Ca	44.02N	142.24 E
Wassenaar	12	Gb	52.09N	4.24 E
Wassenberg	12	Ic	51.06N	6.09 E
Wasserburg am Inn	10	Ih	48.04N	12.14 E
Wasserkuppe	10	Ff	50.30N	9.56 E
Wassigny	12	Fd	50.01N	3.36 E
Wassuk Range	46	Fg	38.40N	118.50W
Wassy	11	Kf	48.30N	4.57 E
Waswanipi, Lac-	44	Ia	49.32N	76.29W
Watampone	22	Oj	4.32S	120.20 E
Watansoppeng	26	Gg	4.21S	119.53 E
Watari	29	Gb	38.02N	140.51 E
Waterbeach	12	Cb	52.16N	0.12 E
Waterberg	37	Bd	20.25S	17.15 E
Waterbury	43	Mc	41.33N	73.02W
Water Cays	49	Ib	23.40N	77.45W
Wateree Pond	44	Gh	34.25N	80.50W
Waterford/Port Láirge	6	Fe	52.15N	7.06W
Waterford/Port Láirge [2]	9	Fi	52.10N	7.40W
Waterford Harbour/Cuan Phort Láirge	9	Gi	52.10N	6.57W
Wateringues	11	Ic	51.00N	2.30 E
Waterloo [Bel.]	11	Kd	50.43N	4.24 E
Waterloo [Ia.-U.S.]	43	Ic	42.30N	92.20W
Waterloo [Il.-U.S.]	45	Kg	38.20N	90.09W
Waterlooville	12	Ad	50.52N	1.01W
Watersmeet	44	Cb	46.18N	89.11W
Watertown [N.Y.-U.S.]	43	Lc	43.57N	75.56W
Watertown [S.D.-U.S.]	43	Hc	44.54N	97.07W
Watertown [Wi.-U.S.]	45	Le	43.12N	88.43W
Waterville	43	Nc	44.33N	69.38W
Watford	9	Mj	51.40N	0.25W
Watford City	45	Ec	47.48N	103.17W
Wa'th	35	Ed	8.10N	32.07 E
Watheroo	59	Df	30.17S	116.04 E
Watīr, Wādī-	24	Fh	29.01N	34.40 E
Watkins Glen	44	Id	42.23N	76.53W
Watling → San Salvador	47	Jd	24.02N	74.28W
Watlington	12	Ac	51.38N	1.00W
Watonga	45	Gi	35.51N	98.25W
Watou, Poperinge-	12	Ed	50.51N	2.37 E
Watrous	42	Gf	51.40N	105.28W
Watsa	31	Jh	3.03N	29.32 E
Watseka	45	Mf	40.47N	87.44W
Watsi [C.R.]	49	Fi	9.37N	82.52W
Watsi [Zaire]	36	Dc	0.19S	21.04 E
Watsi Kengo	36	Dc	0.48S	20.33 E
Watson Lake	39	Gc	60.07N	128.48W
Watsonville	46	Eh	36.55N	121.45W
Watt, Morne-	51g	Bb	15.19N	61.19W
Watton	12	Cb	52.34N	0.50 E
Watts Bar Lake	44	Eh	35.48N	84.39W
Wattwil	14	Dc	47.18N	9.05 E
Watubela, Kepulauan-	26	Jg	4.35S	131.40 E
Wau	59	Ja	7.20S	146.45 E
Waubay Lake	45	Hd	45.25N	97.25W
Wauchope	59	Kf	31.27S	152.44 E
Wauchula	44	Gl	27.33N	81.49W
Waucoba Mountain	46	Fh	37.00N	118.01W
Waukara, Gunung-	26	Gg	1.15S	119.42 E
Waukarlycarly, Lake-	59	Ed	21.25S	121.50 E
Waukegan	43	Jc	42.22N	87.50W
Waukesha	45	Le	43.01N	88.14W
Waupaca	45	Ld	44.21N	89.05W
Wausau	43	Jc	44.59N	89.39W
Wauseon	44	Ee	41.33N	84.09W
Wauwatosa	45	Me	43.03N	88.00W
Wave Hill	59	Gc	17.29S	130.57 E
Waveney	9	Oi	52.28N	1.45 E
Waver/Wavre	11	Kd	50.43N	4.37 E
Waverly [Ia.-U.S.]	45	Je	42.44N	92.29W
Waverly [Oh.-U.S.]	44	Ff	39.07N	82.59W
Waverly [Tn.-U.S.]	44	Dg	36.05N	87.48W
Waves	44	Jh	35.37N	75.29W
Wavre/Waver	11	Kd	50.43N	4.37 E
Wāw	31	Jh	7.42N	28.00 E
Wawa [Nig.]	34	Fd	9.55N	4.27 E
Wawa [Ont.-Can.]	42	Jg	47.59N	84.47W
Wawa, Rio-	49	Fg	13.53N	83.28W
Wāw al Kabīr	31	If	25.20N	16.43 E
Wāw an Nāmūs	33	Ce	24.55N	19.45 E
Wāw Nahr	35	Dd	7.03N	27.13 E
Wawo	26	Hg	3.41S	121.02 E
Wawotobi	26	Hg	3.51S	122.06 E
Waxahachie	45	Hj	32.24N	96.51W
Waxweiler	12	Id	50.06N	6.22 E
Waxxari	27	Ed	38.37N	87.22 E
Way, Lake-	59	Ee	26.50S	120.20 E
Waya	63d	Ab	17.18S	177.08 E
Wayabula	26	If	2.17N	128.12 E
Wayan	46	Je	43.00N	111.22W
Waycross	43	Ke	31.13N	82.21W
Wayne [Nb.-U.S.]	45	He	42.14N	97.01W
Wayne [W.V.-U.S.]	44	Ff	38.14N	82.27W
Waynesboro [Ga.-U.S.]	44	Fi	33.06N	82.01W
Waynesboro [Ms.-U.S.]	45	Lk	31.40N	88.39W
Waynesboro [Pa.-U.S.]	44	If	39.45N	77.36W
Waynesboro [Va.-U.S.]	44	Hf	38.04N	78.54W
Waynesville [Mo.-U.S.]	45	Jh	37.50N	92.12W
Waynesville [N.C.-U.S.]	44	Fh	35.29N	83.00W
Waynoka	45	Gh	36.35N	98.53W
Waziers	12	Fd	50.23N	3.07 E
Wda	10	Oc	53.25N	18.29 E
Wdzydze, Jezioro-	10	Nc	54.00N	17.50 E
Wé	61	Cd	20.55S	167.16 E
We, Pulau-	26	Ce	5.51N	95.18 E
Wear	9	Lg	54.55N	1.22W
Weatherford [Ok.-U.S.]	45	Gi	35.32N	98.42W
Weatherford [Tx.-U.S.]	43	He	32.46N	97.48W
Weaverville	46	Df	40.44N	122.56W
Weber	62	Gd	40.24S	176.20 E
Webster	45	Hd	45.20N	97.31W
Webster City	45	Je	42.28N	93.49W
Webster Springs	44	Gf	38.29N	80.25W
Weda	26	If	0.21N	127.52 E
Weda, Teluk-	26	If	0.20N	128.00 E
Weddell Island	56	Hh	51.50S	61.00W
Weddel Sea (EN)	66	Rf	72.00S	45.00W
Wedel	10	Fc	53.35N	9.41 E
Wedgeport	44	Od	43.44N	65.59W
Wedza	37	Ec	18.35S	31.35 E
Weed	46	Df	41.25N	122.27W
Weener	10	Dc	53.10N	7.21 E
Weerdinge, Emmen-	12	Ib	52.49N	6.57 E
Weert	11	Lc	51.15N	5.43 E
Weesp	12	Hb	52.18N	5.02 E
Wegberg	12	Ic	51.09N	6.16 E
Węgliniec	10	Le	51.17N	15.13 E
Węgorzewo	10	Rb	54.14N	21.44 E
Węgrów	10	Sd	52.25N	22.01 E
Wehni	35	Fc	12.40N	36.42 E
Weichang (Zhuizishan)	28	Kc	41.55N	117.45 E
Weida	10	If	50.46N	12.04 E
Weiden in der Oberpfalz	10	Ig	49.41N	12.10 E
Weifang	22	Nf	36.43N	119.06 E
Weihai	27	Ld	37.27N	122.02 E
Weihe	28	Jb	44.55N	128.23 E
Wei He	21	Nf	34.36N	110.10 E
Weilburg	10	Ef	50.29N	8.15 E
Weilerbach	12	Je	49.29N	7.38 E
Weilerswist	12	Id	50.46N	6.50 E
Weilheim in Oberbayern	10	Hi	47.50N	11.09 E
Weilmünster	12	Kd	50.26N	8.21 E
Weimar [F.R.G.]	12	Kd	50.46N	8.43 E
Weimar [G.D.R.]	10	Hf	50.59N	11.19 E
Weinan	27	Ie	34.30N	109.34 E
Weingarten	10	Fi	47.48N	9.38 E
Weinheim	10	Eg	49.33N	8.40 E
Weining	27	Hf	26.46N	104.18 E
Weinsberger Wald	14	Ib	48.25N	15.00 E
Weinstraße	12	Ke	49.20N	8.05 E
Weinviertel	14	Kb	48.35N	16.30 E
Weipa	58	Ff	12.41S	141.52 E
Weirton	44	Ge	40.24N	80.37W
Weiser	46	Gd	44.15N	116.58W
Weiser River	46	Gd	44.15N	116.59W
Weishan Hu	27	Ke	34.35N	117.15 E
Weishi	28	Cg	34.25N	114.10 E
Weishui → Jingxing	28	Ce	38.03N	114.09 E
Weiße Elster	10	He	51.26N	11.57 E
Weißenberg	12	Je	49.15N	7.49 E
Weißenburg in Bayern	10	Gg	49.02N	10.59 E
Weißenfels	10	He	51.12N	11.58 E
Weißer Main	10	Hf	50.05N	11.24 E
Weißerstein	12	Id	50.24N	6.22 E
Weißkugel/Palla Bianca	14	Ed	46.48N	10.44 E
Weiss Lake	44	Eh	34.15N	85.35W
Weißwasser/Běła Woda	10	Ke	51.31N	14.38 E
Weitra	14	Ib	48.42N	14.53 E
Weixi	27	Gf	27.13N	99.19 E
Weixian	28	Cf	36.59N	115.15 E
Weixin (Zhaxi)	27	If	27.46N	105.04 E
Weiz	14	Jc	47.13N	15.37 E
Wejherowo	10	Ob	54.37N	18.15 E
Welbourn Hill	58	Eg	27.21S	134.06 E
Welch	44	Gg	37.26N	81.36W
Weldiya	35	Fc	11.48N	39.35 E
Weld Range	59	De	26.55S	117.25 E
Welega [3]	35	Fd	8.38N	35.40 E
Welel	35	Ed	8.56N	34.52 E
Weligama	25	Gg	5.58N	80.25 E
Welkenraedt	12	Hd	50.39N	5.58 E
Welker Seamount (EN)	40	Ke	55.07N	140.20W
Welkite	35	Fd	8.17N	37.49 E
Welkom	31	Jk	27.59S	26.45 E
Welland	42	Jh	42.59N	79.15W
Welland	9	Ni	52.53N	0.02 E
Welland Canal	44	Hd	43.14N	79.13W
Wellesley Islands	57	Ef	16.45S	139.30 E
Wellin	12	Hd	50.05N	5.07 E
Wellingborough	9	Mi	52.19N	0.42W
Wellington [2]	62	Fd	40.10S	175.30 E
Wellington [Austl.]	59	Jf	32.33S	148.57 E
Wellington [Eng.-U.K.]	9	Jk	50.59N	3.14W
Wellington [Ks.-U.S.]	45	Hh	37.16N	97.24W
Wellington [Nv.-U.S.]	46	Fg	38.45N	119.22W
Wellington [N.Z.]	58	Ii	41.17S	174.46 E
Wellington, Isla-	52	Ij	49.20S	74.40W
Wellington, Lake-	59	Jg	38.10S	147.15 E
Wellington Channel	42	Ia	75.10N	93.00W
Wells [Eng.-U.K.]	9	Kj	51.13N	2.39W
Wells [Nv.-U.S.]	43	Dc	41.07N	115.01W
Wells, Lake-	59	Ee	26.45S	123.15 E
Wells, Mount-	59	Fc	17.26S	127.14 E
Wellsboro	44	Ie	41.45N	77.18W
Wellsford	62	Fb	36.18S	174.31 E
Wells-next-the-Sea	9	Ni	52.58N	0.51 E
Wellton	46	Hj	32.40N	114.08W
Welmel	35	Gd	5.35N	40.55 E
Wełna	10	Md	52.36N	16.50 E
Welo [3]	35	Fc	12.00N	40.00 E
Wels	14	Ib	48.10N	14.02 E
Welshpool	9	Ji	52.40N	3.09W
Welver	12	Jc	51.37N	7.58 E
Welwitschia	37	Ad	20.21S	14.57 E
Welwyn Garden City	9	Mj	51.48N	0.13W
Wema	36	Dc	0.26S	21.38 E
Wemding	10	Gh	48.52N	10.43 E
Wen'an	28	De	38.52N	116.30 E
Wenatchee	43	Cb	47.25N	120.19W
Wenatchee Mountains	46	Ec	47.20N	120.45W
Wenchang	27	Jh	19.43N	110.44 E
Wenchi	34	Ed	7.44N	2.06W
Wenchit	35	Fc	10.03N	38.35 E
Wenden	12	Jd	50.58N	7.52 E
Wendeng	27	Ld	37.10N	122.01 E
Wendland	10	Gc	53.10N	11.00 E
Wendo	35	Fd	6.37N	38.25 E
Wengyuan (Longxian)	27	Jg	24.21N	114.13 E
Wen He	28	Ef	37.06N	119.29 E
Wenling	27	Lf	28.23N	121.22 E
Wenquan	27	Fe	33.15N	91.55 E
Wenquan/Arixang	27	Dc	44.59N	81.04 E
Wenshan	27	Hg	23.22N	104.23 E
Wenshui	28	Bf	37.26N	112.01 E
Wensu	27	Dc	41.15N	80.14 E
Wensum	12	Db	52.37N	1.22 E
Wentworth	59	If	34.07S	141.55 E
Wenxian	27	He	32.52N	104.40 E
Wenzhou	22	Og	27.57N	120.38 E
Wenzhu	27	Jf	27.00N	114.00 E
Wepener	37	De	29.46S	27.00 E
Wépion, Namur-	12	Gd	50.25N	4.52 E
Werda	37	Ce	25.16S	23.17 E
Werder	31	Lh	7.00N	45.21 E
Werder	10	Jc	53.40N	13.25 E
Werdohl	12	Jc	51.16N	7.46 E
Were Ilu	35	Fc	10.38N	39.23 E
Werkendam	12	Gc	51.49N	4.55 E
Werl	12	Jc	51.33N	7.55 E
Werlte	12	Jb	52.51N	7.41 E
Wermelskirchen	12	Jc	51.09N	7.13 E
Werne	12	Jc	51.40N	7.38 E
Wernigerode	10	Ge	51.50N	10.47 E
Werra	5	Ge	51.26N	9.39 E
Werribee	59	Ig	37.54S	144.40 E
Werris Creek	59	Kf	31.21S	150.39 E
Werse	12	Jb	52.02N	7.41 E
Wertach	10	Gh	48.24N	10.53 E
Wertheim	10	Fg	49.45N	9.31 E
Wesel	10	Ce	51.40N	6.37 E
Weser	5	Ge	53.32N	8.34 E
Weserbergland	10	Fe	51.55N	9.30 E
Wesergebirge	10	Fd	52.15N	9.10 E
Weslaco	45	Gm	26.09N	98.01W
Wesley	51g	Ba	15.34N	61.19W
Wesleyville	42	Mg	49.09N	53.34W
Wessel, Cape-	59	Hb	11.00S	136.45 E
Wesseling	12	Id	50.50N	6.59 E
Wessel Islands	57	Ef	12.00S	136.45 E
Wessington Springs	45	Gd	44.05N	98.34W
West Allis	45	Me	43.01N	88.00W
West Baines River	59	Gc	15.26S	130.08 E
West Bay	45	Ll	29.00N	89.30W
West Bend	45	Le	43.25N	88.11W
West Bengal [3]	25	Hd	24.00N	88.00 E
West Berlin (EN)=Berlin (West)	6	He	52.31N	13.24 E
West Branch	44	Ec	44.17N	84.14W
West Bridgford	12	Ab	52.55N	1.07W
West Bromwich	9	Li	52.31N	1.59W
Westbrook	44	Ld	43.41N	70.21W
West Burra	9	La	60.05N	1.10W
West Caicos	49	Kc	21.47N	72.17W
West Cape	57	Hi	45.55S	166.26 E
West Caroline Basin (EN)	3	Ii	4.00N	138.00 E
West Carpathians (EN)= Západné Karpaty	10	Og	49.30N	19.00 E
West Des Moines	45	Jf	41.35N	93.43W
Westdongeradeel	12	Ha	53.23N	5.58 E
Westdongeradeel-Holwerd	12	Ha	53.22N	5.54 E
Westdongeradeel-Ternaard	12	Ha	53.23N	5.58 E
Westeinderplassen	12	Gb	52.15N	4.30 E
West Elk Mountains	45	Cg	38.40N	107.15W
West End	44	Hl	26.41N	78.58W
Westende, Middelkerke-	12	Ec	51.10N	2.46 E
West End Village	51b	Ab	18.11N	63.09W
West Entrance	64a	Bb	7.57N	134.30 E
Westerbork	12	Ib	52.51N	6.36 E
Westerburg	12	Jd	50.34N	7.59 E
Westerland	10	Eb	54.54N	8.18 E
Westerlo	12	Gc	51.05N	4.55 E
Western [Ghana] [3]	34	Ed	5.30N	2.30W
Western [Kenya] [3]	36	Fb	0.30N	34.35 E
Western [S.L.] [3]	34	Cd	8.20N	13.00W
Western [Ug.] [3]	36	Fb	1.00N	31.00 E
Western [Zam.] [3]	36	Df	15.00S	24.00 E
Western Australia [2]	59	Ed	25.00S	122.00 E
Western Desert (EN)= Gharbīyah, Aṣ Ṣaḥrā' Al-	30	Jf	27.30N	28.00 E
Western Dvina (EN)= Zapadnaja Dvina	5	Id	57.04N	24.03 E
Western Entrance	63a	Bb	6.55S	155.40 E
Western Ghats/Sahyadri	21	Jh	14.00N	75.00 E
Western Isles [3]	9	Fd	57.40N	7.10W
Western Port	59	Jg	38.25S	145.10 E
Western River	42	Gc	66.22N	107.15W
Western Sahara (EN) [5]	31	Ff	24.30N	13.00W

Index Symbols

[1] Independent Nation; [2] State, Region; [3] District, County; [4] Municipality; [5] Colony, Dependency; Continent; Physical Region

Historical or Cultural Region; Mount, Mountain; Volcano; Hill; Mountains, Mountain Range; Hills, Escarpment; Plateau, Upland

Pass, Gap; Plain, Lowland; Delta; Salt Flat; Valley, Canyon; Crater, Cave; Karst Features

Depression; Polder; Desert, Dunes; Forest, Woods; Heath, Steppe; Oasis; Cape, Point

Coast, Beach; Cliff; Peninsula; Isthmus; Sandbank; Island; Atoll

Rock, Reef; Islands, Archipelago; Rocks, Reefs; Coral Reef; Well, Spring; Geyser; River, Stream

Waterfall Rapids; River Mouth, Estuary; Lake; Salt Lake; Intermittent Lake; Reservoir; Swamp, Pond

Canal; Glacier; Ice Shelf, Pack Ice; Ocean; Sea; Gulf, Bay; Strait, Fjord

Lagoon; Bank; Seamount; Tablemount; Ridge; Shelf; Basin

Escarpment, Sea Scarp; Fracture; Trench, Abyss; National Park, Reserve; Point of Interest; Recreation Site; Cave, Cavern

Historic Site; Ruins; Wall, Walls; Church, Abbey; Temple; Scientific Station; Airport

Port; Lighthouse; Mine; Tunnel; Dam, Bridge

Index Symbols

[1]	Independent Nation
[2]	State, Region
[3]	District, County
[4]	Municipality
[5]	Colony, Dependency
■	Continent
⊠	Physical Region
=	Historical or Cultural Region
▲	Mount, Mountain
▲	Volcano
▲	Hill
▲	Mountains, Mountain Range
▲	Hills, Escarpment
⊡	Plateau, Upland
⊡	Pass, Gap
⊡	Plain, Lowland
⊡	Polder
⊠	Delta
⊠	Salt Flat
⊡	Valley, Canyon
⊡	Crater, Cave
⊠	Karst Features
⊡	Depression
⊠	Desert, Dunes
⊡	Forest, Woods
⊡	Heath, Steppe
⊡	Oasis
⊠	Cape, Point
⊡	Coast, Beach
⊡	Cliff
⊡	Peninsula
⊡	Isthmus
⊡	Sandbank
⊟	Island
⊡	Atoll
⊠	Rock, Reef
⊡	Islands, Archipelago
⊡	Rocks, Reefs
⊡	Coral Reef
⊡	Well, Spring
⊡	Geyser
⊠	River, Stream
⊠	Waterfall Rapids
⊠	River Mouth, Estuary
⊡	Lake
⊡	Salt Lake
⊡	Intermittent Lake
⊡	Reservoir
⊡	Swamp, Pond
⊡	Canal
⊡	Glacier
⊡	Bank
⊡	Ice Shelf, Pack Ice
⊡	Ocean
⊡	Sea
⊡	Gulf, Bay
⊡	Strait, Fjord
⊡	Lagoon
⊡	Seamount
⊡	Tablemount
⊡	Ridge
⊡	Shelf
⊡	Basin
⊡	Escarpment, Sea Scarp
⊡	Fracture
⊡	Trench, Abyss
⊡	National Park, Reserve
⊡	Point of Interest
⊡	Recreation Site
⊡	Cave, Cavern
⊡	Historic Site
⊡	Ruins
⊡	Wall, Walls
⊡	Church, Abbey
⊡	Temple
⊡	Scientific Station
⊡	Airport
⊡	Port
⊡	Lighthouse
⊡	Mine
⊡	Tunnel
⊡	Dam, Bridge

Index Symbols

[1] Independent Nation
[2] State, Region
[3] District, County
[4] Municipality
[5] Colony, Dependency
[6] Continent
[7] Physical Region

Historical or Cultural Region
Mount, Mountain
Volcano
Hill
Mountains, Mountain Range
Hills, Escarpment
Plateau, Upland

Pass, Gap
Plain, Lowland
Delta
Salt Flat
Valley, Canyon
Crater, Cave
Karst Features

Depression
Polder
Desert, Dunes
Forest, Woods
Heath, Steppe
Oasis
Cape, Point

Coast, Beach
Cliff
Peninsula
Isthmus
Sandbank
Island
Atoll

Rock, Reef
Islands, Archipelago
Rocks, Reefs
Coral Reef
Well, Spring
Geyser
River, Stream

Waterfall Rapids
River Mouth, Estuary
Lake
Salt Lake
Intermittent Lake
Reservoir
Swamp, Pond

Canal
Glacier
Ice Shelf, Pack Ice
Ocean
Sea
Gulf, Bay
Strait, Fjord

Lagoon
Bank
Seamount
Tablemount
Ridge
Shelf
Basin

Escarpment, Sea Scarp
Fracture
Trench, Abyss
National Park, Reserve
Point of Interest
Recreation Site
Cave, Cavern

Historic Site
Ruins
Wall, Walls
Church, Abbey
Temple
Scientific Station
Airport

Port
Lighthouse
Mine
Tunnel
Dam, Bridge

Index Symbols

[1] Independent Nation	⌧ Historical or Cultural Region	⊿ Pass, Gap	⌧ Depression	⌧ Coast, Beach
[2] State, Region	⌧ Mount, Mountain	⌧ Plain, Lowland	⌧ Polder	⌧ Cliff
[3] District, County	▲ Volcano	⌧ Delta	⌧ Desert, Dunes	⌧ Peninsula
[4] Municipality	⌧ Hill	⌧ Salt Flat	⌧ Forest, Woods	⌧ Isthmus
[5] Colony, Dependency	⌧ Mountains, Mountain Range	⌧ Valley, Canyon	⌧ Heath, Steppe	⌧ Sandbank
⌧ Continent	⌧ Hills, Escarpment	⌧ Crater, Cave	⌧ Oasis	⌧ Island
⌧ Physical Region	⌧ Plateau, Upland	⌧ Karst Features	⌧ Cape, Point	⌧ Atoll

⌧ Rock, Reef	⌧ Waterfall Rapids	⌧ Canal	⌧ Lagoon
⌧ Islands, Archipelago	⌧ River Mouth, Estuary	⌧ Glacier	⌧ Bank
⌧ Rocks, Reefs	⌧ Lake	⌧ Ice Shelf, Pack Ice	⌧ Seamount
⌧ Coral Reef	⌧ Salt Lake	⌧ Ocean	⌧ Tablemount
⌧ Well, Spring	⌧ Intermittent Lake	⌧ Sea	⌧ Ridge
⌧ Geyser	⌧ Reservoir	⌧ Gulf, Bay	⌧ Shelf
⌧ River, Stream	⌧ Swamp, Pond	⌧ Strait, Fjord	⌧ Basin

⌧ Escarpment, Sea Scarp	⌧ Historic Site
⌧ Fracture	⌧ Ruins
⌧ Trench, Abyss	⌧ Wall, Walls
⌧ National Park, Reserve	⌧ Church, Abbey
⌧ Point of Interest	⌧ Temple
⌧ Recreation Site	⌧ Scientific Station
⌧ Cave, Cavern	⌧ Airport

⌧ Port	
⌧ Lighthouse	
⌧ Mine	
⌧ Tunnel	
⌧ Dam, Bridge	

Yuzawa [Jap.] 29 Fc 36.56N 138.47 E
Yuzhou→Chongqing=
Chungking (EN) 22 Mg 29.34N 106.27 E
Yvel 11 Dg 47.59N 2.23W
Yvelines [3] 11 Hf 48.50N 1.50 E
Yverdon 14 Ad 46.46N 6.40 E
Yvetot 11 Ge 49.37N 0.46 E
Yvette 12 Ef 48.40N 2.20 E
Yxlan 8 He 59.40N 18.50 E
Yxningen 8 Gf 58.15N 16.20 E

Z

Zaajatskaja 17 Jj 52.53N 61.35 E
Zaalajski Hrebet 18 Ie 39.25N 72.50 E
Zaanstad 11 Kb 52.26N 4.49 E
Žabaj 17 Nj 51.42N 68.22 E
Zabajkalsk 20 Gg 49.40N 117.21 E
Zabarjad 33 Ge 23.37N 36.12 E
Zāb-e Kūchek 24 Ke 36.00N 45.15 E
Zabīb, Ra's az- 14 Em 37.16N 10.04 E
Zabid 23 Fg 14.12N 43.18 E
Zabīd, Wādī- 23 Fg 14.07N 43.06 E
Žabinka 16 Dc 52.13N 24.01 E
Ząbkowice Śląskie 10 Mf 50.36N 16.53 E
Žabljak 15 Cf 43.09N 19.08 E
Zabłudów 10 Tc 53.01N 23.20 E
Zabok 14 Jd 46.02N 15.55 E
Zābol [3] 23 Kc 32.00N 67.15 E
Zabolotje [Bye.-U.S.S.R.] 8 Kk 53.56N 24.46 E
Zabolotje [Ukr.-U.S.S.R.] 10 Ue 51.37N 24.26 E
Zabolotov 15 Ia 48.25N 25.23 E
Zabré 34 Ec 11.10N 0.38W
Zábřeh 10 Mg 49.53N 16.52 E
Zabrze 10 Of 50.18N 18.46 E
Zacapa [3] 49 Cf 15.00N 89.30W
Zacapa 47 Gf 14.58N 89.32W
Zacapu 48 Ih 19.50N 101.43W
Zacatecas 39 Ig 22.47N 102.35W
Zacatecas [2] 47 Dd 23.00N 103.00W
Zacatecoluca 49 Cg 13.30N 88.52W
Zacatepec 48 Jh 18.39N 99.12W
Zacatlán 48 Kh 19.56N 97.58W
Zaccar, Djebel- 13 Oh 36.20N 2.13 E
Zacoalco de Torres 48 Hg 20.14N 103.35W
Zacualtipán 48 Jg 20.39N 98.36W
Zaculeu 49 Bf 15.21N 91.29W
Zadar 6 Hg 44.07N 15.15 E
Zadarski Kanal 14 Jf 44.10N 15.10 E
Zadetkyi Kyun 25 Jg 9.58N 98.13 E
Zadi 36 Bc 4.46S 14.52 E
Zadoi 27 Fe 33.10N 94.58 E
Zadonsk 16 Kc 52.23N 38.58 E
Za'farānah 33 Fd 29.07N 32.33 E
Zafferano, Capo- 14 Hl 38.07N 13.32 E
Ẓafir 23 He 23.07N 53.46 E
Zafra 13 Ff 38.25N 6.25W
Żagań 10 Le 51.37N 15.19 E
Zagare/Žagarė 8 Jh 56.19N 23.14 E
Žagarė/Zagare 8 Jh 56.19N 23.14 E
Zāgheh 24 Mf 33.30N 48.42 E
Zāgh Marz 24 Od 36.47N 53.17 E
Zaghrah, Wādī- 24 Fh 28.40N 34.20 E
Zaghwān 32 Jb 36.24N 10.09 E
Zaghwān [3] 32 Jb 36.25N 10.10 E
Zaghwān, Jabal- 14 En 36.21N 10.07 E
Zagora 31 Ge 30.19N 5.50W
Zagora 14 Kg 43.40N 16.15 E
Zagória 15 Dj 39.45N 20.50 E
Zagorje 14 Jd 46.05N 16.00 E
Zagorodje 10 Vd 52.15N 25.30 E
Zagórów 10 Nd 52.11N 17.55 E
Zagorsk 6 Jd 56.18N 38.08 E
Zagórz, Sanok- 10 Sg 49.31N 22.17 E
Zagreb 6 Hf 45.48N 16.00 E
Zāgros, Kūhhā-ye-=Zagros
Mountains (EN) 21 Gf 33.40N 47.00 E
Zagros Mountains (EN)=
Zāgros, Kūhhā-ye- 21 Gf 33.40N 47.00 E
Žagubica 15 Ee 44.12N 21.48 E
Za'gya Zangbo 27 Ee 31.55N 88.58 E
Zagyva 10 Qi 47.10N 20.12 E
Zāhedān 22 Ig 29.30N 60.52 E
Zahlah 24 Ff 33.51N 35.53 E
Zahmet 19 Gh 37.48N 62.29 E
Ẓahrān 33 Hf 17.40N 43.30 E
Zahrez Chergui 13 Pi 35.14N 3.32 E
Zailijski Alatau, Hrebet- 18 Kc 43.00N 77.00 E
Žailma 19 Ge 51.32N 61.40 E
Zaire 30 Ii 6.04S 12.24 E
Zaire 30 Ii 6.04S 12.24 E
Zaire [3] 36 Bd 6.30S 13.30 E
Zaire (Congo, Dem. Rep. of
the-) [1] 31 Ji 1.00S 25.00 E
Zaisan, Lake- (EN)=Zajsan,
Ozero- 21 Ke 48.10N 83.50 E
Zaj 7 Mi 55.36N 51.40 E
Zaječar 15 Ff 43.54N 22.17 E
Zajsan 22 Ke 47.30N 84.55 E
Zajsan, Ozero-=Zaisan,
Lake- (EN) 21 Ke 48.10N 83.50 E
Zak 30 Jk 29.39S 21.11 E
Zaka 37 Ed 20.20S 31.29 E
Zakamensk 20 Ff 50.23N 103.20 E
Zakarpatskaja Oblast [3] 19 Cf 48.20N 23.20 E
Zakataly 19 Eg 41.38N 46.37 E
Zakhāro 15 El 37.29N 21.39 E
Zākhū 23 Fb 37.08N 42.41 E
Zákinthos 15 Dl 37.47N 20.54 E
Zákinthos=Zante (EN) 5 Ih 37.47N 20.47 E
Zakinthou Dhiavlos- 15 Dl 37.50N 21.00 E
Zakopane 10 Pg 49.19N 19.57 E
Zakouma 35 Bc 10.54N 19.49 E
Žaksy 19 Ge 51.53N 67.20 E
Zala [2] 10 Mj 46.40N 16.50 E

Zala 10 Nj 46.43N 17.16 E
Zālābiyah 24 He 35.39N 39.51 E
Zalaegerszeg 10 Mj 46.50N 16.51 E
Zalāf 24 Gf 32.55N 37.20 E
Zalalövő 10 Mj 46.51N 16.36 E
Zalamea de la Serena 13 Gf 38.39N 5.39W
Zalamea la Real 13 Fg 37.41N 6.39W
Zalantum→Butha Qi 27 Lb 48.02N 122.42 E
Zalari 20 Ff 53.36N 102.32 E
Zalaszentgrót 10 Nj 46.57N 17.05 E
Zalău 15 Gb 47.12N 23.03 E
Zaleščiki 16 De 48.39N 25.44 E
Ẓalim 23 Fe 22.43N 42.10 E
Zalingei 35 Cc 12.54N 23.29 E
Zalṭan 33 Cd 28.55N 19.50 E
Zaltbommel 12 Hc 51.49N 5.17 E
Žaltidjal 15 Ih 41.30N 25.05 E
Žaltyr 19 Ge 51.35N 69.58 E
Žaltyr, Ozero- 16 Qf 47.25N 51.05 E
Zamakh 23 Gf 16.28N 47.35 E
Zamami-Shima 29b Ab 26.15N 127.18 E
Zamarkh 33 If 16.30N 47.18 E
Zambeze=Zambezi (EN)
30 Kj 18.50N 36.17 E
Zambezi (EN)=Zambeze 30 Kj 18.50N 36.17 E
Zambézia [3] 37 Fc 17.00S 37.00 E
Zambezi Escarpment 37 Ec 16.15S 30.10 E
Zambia [1] 31 Jj 15.00S 30.00 E
Zamboanga 22 Oi 6.54N 122.04 E
Zamboanga Peninsula 26 He 7.32N 122.16 E
Zambrah, Jazīrat- 32 Jb 37.08N 10.48 E
Zambrano 49 Ji 9.45N 74.49W
Zambrów 10 Sd 53.00N 22.15 E
Zambué 37 Ec 15.07S 30.49 E
Zamfara 34 Fc 12.02N 4.03 E
Zamkova, Gora- 10 Vc 53.34N 25.53 E
Zamkowa, Góra- 10 Qb 54.25N 20.25 E
Zammar 24 Jd 36.47N 42.40 E
Zamora [3] 13 Gc 41.45N 6.00W
Zamora [Ec.] 54 Cd 4.04S 78.52W
Zamora [Sp.] 13 Gc 41.30N 5.45W
Zamora, Rio- 54 Cd 2.59S 78.15W
Zamora de Hidalgo 47 De 19.59N 102.16W
Zamość [2] 10 Tf 50.44N 23.15 E
Zamość 10 Tf 50.44N 23.15 E
Zampa-Misaki 29b Ab 26.26N 127.43 E
Zamtang (Gamda) 27 He 32.23N 101.05 E
Zamuro, Punta- 49 Mh 11.26N 68.50W
Zamzam 33 Cc 31.24N 15.17 E
Žanaozen 36 Bc 2.51S 13.50 E
Žanatas 19 Gg 43.36N 69.43 E
Zancara 13 Ie 39.18N 3.18W
Zanda (Toling) 27 Ce 31.28N 79.50 E
Zandvoort 11 Kb 52.22N 4.32 E
Zanesville 43 Kd 39.55N 82.02W
Zangelan 16 Oj 39.05N 46.38 E
Zanhuang 28 Cf 37.38N 114.26 E
Zanjān [3] 23 Gb 36.35N 48.15 E
Zanjān 23 Gb 36.40N 48.29 E
Zanjānrūd 24 Ld 37.08N 47.47 E
Zannone 14 Hj 40.55N 13.05 E
Zante (EN)=Zákinthos 5 Ih 37.47N 20.47 E
Zanthus 59 Ef 31.02S 123.34 E
Zanzibar 31 Ki 6.10S 39.11 E
Zanzibar [3] 36 Gd 6.00S 39.50 E
Zanzibar [2] 36 Gd 6.10S 39.20 E
Zanzibar Channel 36 Gd 6.00S 39.00 E
Zanzibar Island 30 Ki 6.10S 39.20 E
Zaolin 27 Jd 39.09N 113.03 E
Zaō-San 29 Gb 38.08N 140.28 E
Zaouatallaz 32 Ie 24.52N 8.26 E
Zaousfana 32 Gc 30.30N 2.18W
Zaoyang 27 Je 32.08N 112.45 E
Zaozerny 20 Ee 55.57N 94.42 E
Zaozhuang 27 Ke 34.58N 117.34 E
Zapacos Norte, Rio- 55 Ac 17.03S 62.23W
Zapacos Sur, Rio- 55 Ac 17.03S 62.23W
Zapadnaja Dvina 7 Hh 56.17N 32.03 E
Zapadnaja Dvina=Western
Dvina (EN) 5 Id 57.04N 24.03 E
Západna Morava 15 Ef 43.41N 21.24 E
Západné Karpaty=West
Carpathians (EN) 10 Og 49.30N 19.00 E
Zapadni Rodopi 15 Hh 41.45N 24.05 E
Zapadno-Karelskaja
Vozvyšennost 7 He 63.40N 31.40 E
Zapadno Sibirskaja Ravnina
=West Siberian Plain (EN)
21 Jc 60.00N 75.00 E
Zapadny Sajan=Western
Sayans (EN) 21 Ld 53.00N 94.00 E
Západočeský kraj [3] 10 Ig 49.45N 13.00 E
Západoslovenský kraj [3] 10 Nh 48.20N 18.00 E
Zapala 53 Ii 38.55S 70.05W
Zapardiel 13 Gc 41.29N 5.02W
Zapata 45 Gm 26.52N 99.19W
Zapata, Peninsula de- 49 Gb 22.20N 81.35W
Zapatera, Isla- 49 Eh 11.45N 85.50W
Zapatosa,
Cienaga de- 49 Ki 9.05N 73.50W
Zapljusje 8 Mf 58.24N 29.56 E
Zapoljarny 19 Db 69.26N 30.48 E
Zapopan 48 Hg 20.43N 103.24W
Zaporožje 6 Jf 47.50N 35.10 E
Zaporožskaja Oblast [3] 19 Df 47.15N 35.50 E
Zapotitlán, Punta- 48 Lh 18.33N 94.49W
Zapovednik Beloveżskaja
Pušča 10 Kd 52.45N 24.15 E
Za Qu 27 Ge 32.00N 96.55 E
Zara 24 Gc 39.55N 37.48 E
Zarāf, Baḥr az- 35 Ed 9.25N 31.10 E
Zarafšan 19 Gg 41.39N 64.10 E
Zaragoza [3] 13 Lc 41.35N 1.00W
Zaragoza [Col.] 54 Db 7.30N 74.52W
Zaragoza [Mex.] 47 Jf 23.58N 99.46W
Zaragoza [Mex.] 48 Ic 28.29N 100.55W
Zaragoza [Mex.] 48 If 22.02N 100.44W

Zaragoza [Sp.] =Saragossa
(EN) 6 Fg 41.38N 0.53W
Zarajsk 7 Ji 54.47N 38.53 E
Zarand [Iran] 24 Qg 30.48N 56.53 E
Zarand [Iran] 24 Me 35.08N 49.00 E
Zarand-e-Kohneh 24 Ne 35.17N 50.30 E
Zărandului, Munții- 15 Fc 46.10N 22.15 E
Zaranj 22 If 31.06N 61.53 E
Zarasai/Zarasaj 7 Gi 55.43N 26.19 E
Zarasaj/Zarasai 7 Gi 55.43N 26.19 E
Zárate 53 Ki 34.05S 59.02W
Zarauz 13 Ja 43.17N 2.10W
Zaraza 54 Eb 9.21N 65.19W
Žarcovski 7 Hi 55.53N 32.16 E
Zard Kūh 21 Hf 32.22N 50.04 E
Zardob 16 Oi 40.14N 47.42 E
Zarečensk 7 Hc 66.40N 31.23 E
Zarghaṭ 24 Ii 26.32N 40.29 E
Zarghun 25 Db 30.31N 68.50 E
Zarghūn Shahr 23 Kc 32.51N 68.25 E
Zaria 31 Hg 11.04N 7.42 E
Žarkamys 19 Ff 47.59N 56.29 E
Žarma 19 If 48.48N 80.55 E
Zărnești 15 Id 45.33N 25.18 E
Zarqān 24 Oh 29.46N 52.43 E
Zarrīneh 24 Kd 37.05N 45.40 E
Zarrīnshahr 24 Nf 32.30N 51.25 E
Zaruma 54 Cd 3.42S 79.38W
Zarumilla 54 Bd 3.30S 80.16W
Żary 10 Le 51.38N 15.09 E
Žaryk 19 Hf 48.52N 72.54 E
Zarzaïtine 32 Id 28.05N 9.45 E
Zasa 8 Lh 56.15N 26.01 E
Zāskar 25 Fb 34.10N 77.20 E
Žaškov 16 Ge 49.15N 30.09 E
Zaslavl 8 Lj 54.00N 27.22 E
Zaslavskoje
Vodohranilišče 8 Lj 54.00N 27.30 E
Zastavna 15 Ia 48.25N 25.49 E
Zastron 37 Df 30.18S 27.07 E
Žatec 10 Jf 50.20N 13.33 E
Zatišje 15 Mb 47.47N 29.48 E
Zatobolsk 17 Kj 53.12N 63.43 E
Zatoka 15 Nc 46.07N 30.25 E
Zauche 10 Id 52.15N 12.35 E
Žavadovskogo Island 66 Ge 66.30S 86.00 E
Zavāreh 24 Of 33.30N 52.29 E
Zaventem 12 Gd 50.53N 4.28 E
Zavety Iljiča 20 Jg 49.02N 140.19 E
Zavidovići 14 Mf 44.27N 18.09 E
Zavitinsk 20 Hg 50.01N 129.26 E
Zavodoukovsk 19 Gd 56.33N 66.32 E
Zavodovski 66 Ad 56.20S 27.35W
Zavolžje 7 Kh 56.38N 43.21 E
Zavolžsk 7 Kh 57.32N 42.10 E
Zawidów 10 Le 51.01N 15.02 E
Zawiercie 10 Pf 50.30N 19.25 E
Zawīlah 33 Cd 26.10N 15.07 E
Zāwiyat al Mukhaylā 33 Dc 32.10N 22.17 E
Zāwiyat Masūs 33 Dc 31.35N 21.01 E
Zāwiyat Qirzah 33 Bc 31.00N 14.20 E
Zāwiyat Shammās 24 Bg 31.31N 26.24 E
Zawr, Ra's az- 24 Mi 27.26N 49.19 E
Zaya 14 Kb 48.31N 16.55 E
Zāyandeh 24 Of 32.20N 52.50 E
Zaydūn, Wādī- 24 Ej 25.53N 33.04 E
Zayü (Gyigang) 27 Gf 28.43N 97.25 E
Zaza, Rio- 49 Hc 21.37N 79.32W
Zazir 32 If 19.50N 5.13 E
Zbaraž 16 De 49.42N 25.47 E
Zbąszyń 10 Ld 52.16N 15.55 E
Zborov 10 Vg 49.37N 25.09 E
Ždanichý les 10 Mg 49.05N 16.50 E
Ždanov 6 Jf 47.06N 37.33 E
Ždanovsk 16 Oj 39.45N 47.33 E
Žďárské vrchy 10 Mg 49.35N 16.03 E
Ždiar 10 Qg 49.16N 20.15 E
Zdolbunov 16 Ed 50.33N 26.15 E
Zduńska Wola 10 Oe 51.36N 18.57 E
Zealand (EN)=Sjælland 5 Hd 55.30N 11.45 E
Zebediela 37 Dd 24.19S 29.16 E
Zebēs, Mali i- 15 Dh 41.55N 20.14 E
Zebil 15 Le 44.57N 28.46 E
Zeča 14 If 44.46N 14.19 E
Zeddine 13 Nh 36.12N 1.50 E
Zedelgem 12 Fc 51.09N 3.08 E
Zeehan 58 Fi 41.53S 145.20 E
Zeeland 11 Jc 51.27N 3.45 E
Zeeland [3] 12 Fc 51.27N 3.45 E
Zeerust 37 De 25.33S 26.06 E
Zefat 24 Ff 32.58N 35.30 E
Zegrzyńskie, Jezioro- 10 Rd 52.30N 21.05 E
Zehdenick 10 Jd 52.59N 13.20 E
Zeil, Mount- 59 Gd 23.25S 132.25 E
Žeimelis/Zeimjalis 8 Jh 56.14N 23.58 E
Žeimena/Žeimena 7 Fi 54.54N 23.53 E
Zeimjalis/Žeimelis 8 Jh 56.14N 23.58 E
Zeist 11 Lb 52.05N 5.15 E
Zeitz 10 Ie 51.03N 12.09 E
Zeja 21 Od 50.13N 127.35 E
Zeja 22 Od 53.45N 127.15 E
Žejmena/Žeimena 7 Fi 54.54N 23.53 E
Zejskoje Vodohranilišče 20 Hf 54.40N 127.30 E
Zékog 27 Hd 35.00N 101.35 E
Želanija, Mys- 21 Ib 76.57N 68.35 E
Zelaya [3] 49 Eg 13.00N 84.00W
Želča 8 Lf 58.18N 27.50 E
Zele 12 Gc 51.04N 4.02 E
Żelechów 10 Re 51.49N 21.54 E
Zelee, Cape- 63a Ec 9.44S 161.34 E
Zelenaja Rošča 8 Md 60.08N 29.14 E
Zelenčukskaja 16 Lh 43.51N 41.34 E
Zelengora 14 Mg 43.22N 18.35 E
Zelenoborsk 19 Gc 61.29N 63.59 E
Zelenoborski 19 Db 66.50N 32.18 E
Zelenodolsk 19 Ed 55.53N 48.31 E
Zelenogorsk 19 Cc 60.12N 29.42 E

Zelenograd 7 Ih 56.01N 37.12 E
Zelenogradsk 8 Ij 54.57N 20.27 E
Zelenokumsk 19 Eg 44.23N 43.53 E
Zeletin 15 Kc 46.03N 27.23 E
Železné hory 10 Lg 49.50N 15.45 E
Zeleznik 15 De 44.43N 20.23 E
Železnodorožny [R.S.F.S.R.] 20 Fe 57.55N 102.50 E
Železnodorožny [R.S.F.S.R.] 7 Ei 54.23N 21.19 E
Železnodorožny [R.S.F.S.R.] 19 Fc 62.37N 50.55 E
Železnogorsk 19 De 52.21N 35.23 E
Železnogorsk-Tlimski 20 Fe 56.40N 104.05 E
Železnovodsk 16 Mg 44.08N 43.00 E
Zelfana 32 Hc 32.24N 4.14 E
Želiezovce 10 Oh 48.03N 18.40 E
Želivka 10 Lg 49.43N 15.06 E
Željin 15 Df 43.29N 20.48 E
Zell am See 14 Gc 47.19N 12.47 E
Zell am Ziller 14 Fc 47.14N 11.53 E
Zelów 10 Pe 51.28N 19.13 E
Želtau Ajtau 18 Ib 44.30N 74.00 E
Želtyje Vody 16 He 48.23N 33.31 E
Želudok 10 Vc 53.33N 25.07 E
Želva 8 Ki 55.13N 25.13 E
Zelva 10 Uc 53.04N 24.54 E
Zelzate 11 Jc 51.12N 3.49 E
Žemaičių Aukštuma/
Žemajtskaja
Vozvyšennost 8 Ji 55.45N 22.30 E
Žemaiciy-Naumiestis/
Žemajčju-Naumiestis 8 Ii 55.21N 21.37 E
Žemaitija 8 Ji 55.55N 22.30 E
Žemajčju-Naumiestis/
Žemaiciy-Naumiestis 8 Ii 55.21N 21.37 E
Zemajtskaja Vozvyšennost/
Žemaičių Aukštuma 8 Ji 55.45N 22.30 E
Zembin 8 Mj 54.24N 28.19 E
Zembretta, Ile- 14 Em 37.07N 10.53 E
Zemetčino 16 Mc 53.31N 42.38 E
Zemgale 8 Kh 56.30N 25.00 E
Zémio 35 Dd 5.19N 25.08 E
Zemmora 13 Mi 35.43N 0.45 E
Zemmour 30 Ff 25.30N 12.00W
Zemplinska Sirava, údolná
nádrž- 10 Sh 48.50N 22.02 E
Zempoala 47 Ee 19.27N 96.23W
Zempoaltepec 38 Jh 17.00N 96.50W
Zemra, Djebel- 13 Pi 35.14N 3.54 E
Zemst 12 Gd 50.59N 4.28 E
Zemun, Beograd- 15 De 44.53N 20.25 E
Zengfeng Shan 28 Jc 42.25N 128.44 E
Zenica 23 Ff 44.13N 17.55 E
Zenkov 16 Id 50.13N 34.22 E
Zenne 12 Gc 51.04N 4.26 E
Zenobia Peak 45 Bf 40.40N 108.48W
Zentsūji 29 Cd 34.14N 133.47 E
Zenzach 13 Pi 35.21N 3.22 E
Zenza do Itombe 36 Bd 9.16S 14.13 E
Žepče 14 Mf 44.26N 18.03 E
Zepu/Poskam 27 Cd 38.12N 77.18 E
Zéralda 13 Oh 36.43N 2.50 E
Zeravšan 21 If 39.22N 63.45 E
Zeravšan 18 Ge 39.10N 68.40 E
Zeravšanski Hrebet 19 Gh 39.15N 68.30 E
Zerbst 10 Ie 51.58N 12.05 E
Žerdevka 19 Ee 51.53N 41.28 E
Zerind 15 Ec 46.37N 21.31 E
Zermatt 14 Bd 46.02N 7.44 E
Zernez 14 Ed 46.42N 10.07 E
Zernograd 19 Ef 46.48N 40.19 E
Zeroua 13 Ph 36.22N 3.21 E
Žešart 17 De 62.05N 49.31 E
Zestafoni 16 Mh 42.07N 43.02 E
Zeta 15 Cg 42.28N 19.16 E
Zetland→Shetland
Islands 5 Fc 60.30N 1.30W
Žetybaj 19 Fg 43.34N 52.04 E
Žetykol Ozero- 16 Vd 51.05N 60.55 E
Zeune Islands 63a Bb 6.18S 155.50 E
Zeven 10 Fc 53.18N 9.17 E
Zevenaar 12 Ic 51.55N 6.05 E
Zevenbergen 12 Gc 51.38N 4.36 E
Zeydābād 24 Ph 29.37N 55.33 E
Zeydār 24 Pd 36.20N 55.53 E
Zeytinbaği 15 Li 40.23N 28.47 E
Zeytindağ 15 Kk 38.58N 27.04 E
Zêzere 13 De 39.28N 8.20W
Žežmarjaj/Žiežmariai 8 Kj 54.47N 24.36 E
Zghartā 24 Fe 34.24N 35.54 E
Zgierz 10 Pe 51.52N 19.25 E
Zgorzelec 10 Le 51.12N 15.01 E
Zhabdun→Zhongba 22 Kg 29.41N 84.10 E
Zhag'yab 27 Ge 30.40N 97.40 E
Zhangbei 27 Jc 41.13N 114.43 E
Zhangde→Anyang 22 Nf 36.01N 114.25 E
Zhangdian→Zibo 27 Kd 36.48N 118.04 E
Zhangguangcai 28 Jb 45.00N 129.00 E
Zhang He 28 Cf 36.27N 114.42 E
Zhangjiakou 22 Ne 40.49N 114.57 E
Zhangjiapan → Jingbian 27 Id 37.32N 108.45 E
Zhangling 27 La 52.39N 123.31 E
Zhanglou 28 Dh 32.40N 116.47 E
Zhangping 28 Cf 25.25N 117.27 E
Zhangqiu (Mingshui) 28 Df 36.44N 117.33 E
Zhangshuzhen → Qingjiang 27 Kf 28.02N 115.31 E
Zhangwei Xinhe 28 Dg 38.13N 117.48 E
Zhangwu 27 Lc 42.23N 122.33 E
Zhangye 22 Mf 38.57N 100.28 E
Zhangzhou 22 Ng 24.38N 117.39 E
Zhangzi 27 Jd 36.04N 112.53 E
Zhan He 27 Mb 49.21N 128.07 E
Zhanhua (Fuguo) 28 Ef 37.42N 118.08 E
Zhanjiang 22 Ng 21.13N 110.23 E
Zhanyi 27 Hf 25.40N 103.46 E
Zhao'an 27 Kg 23.49N 117.10 E
Zhaodong 27 Mb 46.04N 125.56 E
Zhaoge→Qixian 28 Cg 35.35N 114.12 E
Zhaojue 27 Hf 28.02N 102.50 E

Zhaoqing 27 Jg 23.04N 112.28 E
Zhaosu/Mongolküre 27 Dc 43.10N 81.07 E
Zhaosutai He 28 Gc 42.42N 123.35 E
Zhaotong 22 Mg 27.20N 103.46 E
Zhaoxian 28 Cf 37.46N 114.46 E
Zhaoyang Hu 28 Dg 35.00N 116.48 E
Zhaoyuan [China] 28 Ff 37.22N 120.23 E
Zhaoyuan [China] 28 Hb 45.30N 125.06 E
Zhaozhou 28 Hb 45.42N 125.15 E
Zhari Namco 27 Ee 31.05N 85.35 E
Zhaxi→Weixin 27 If 27.46N 105.04 E
Zhaxi Co 27 Ee 32.12N 85.10 E
Zhecheng 28 Cg 34.05N 115.17 E
Zheduo Shankou 27 He 30.06N 101.48 E
Zhejiang Sheng (Che-Chiang
Sheng) [2] 27 Kf 29.00N 120.00 E
Zhen'an 27 Ie 33.27N 109.10 E
Zhenba 27 Ie 32.37N 107.50 E
Zhenghe 27 Kf 27.20N 118.58 E
Zhenghe Qunjiao 26 Fd 10.20N 114.20 E
Zhenglan Qi (Dund Hot) 28 Cc 42.14N 115.59 E
Zhengxiangbai Qi (Qagan
Nur) 27 Jc 42.16N 114.59 E
Zhengyang 28 Ci 32.36N 114.23 E
Zhengzhou 22 Nf 34.42N 113.41 E
Zhenhai 28 Fj 29.57N 121.43 E
Zhenjiang 27 Ke 32.03N 119.26 E
Zhenkang (Fengweiba) 27 Gg 23.54N 99.00 E
Zhenlai 27 Lb 45.50N 123.14 E
Zhenning 27 If 26.05N 105.46 E
Zhenping 28 Bh 33.02N 112.14 E
Zhenxiong 27 Hf 27.28N 104.52 E
Zhenyuan 27 Hg 23.52N 100.53 E
Zhenyuan (Wuyang) 27 If 27.05N 108.26 E
Zhicheng 27 Je 30.17N 111.29 E
Zhidan (Bao'an) 27 Id 36.48N 108.46 E
Zhidoi 27 Ge 34.46N 95.46 E
Zhijiang 27 If 27.32N 109.42 E
Zhi Qu/Tongtian He 21 Lf 33.26N 96.36 E
Zhiziluo→Bijiang 27 Gf 26.39N 99.00 E
Zhob 25 Db 32.04N 69.50 E
Zhongba (Zhabdun) 22 Kg 29.41N 84.10 E
Zhongba → Jiangyou 27 He 31.48N 104.39 E
Zhongdian 27 Gf 27.42N 99.41 E
Zhönggyü 21 Mg 35.00N 105.00 E
Zhonghua Renmin
Gongheguo=China (EN)
[1] 22 Mf 35.00N 105.00 E
Zhongjian Dao 26 Fc 15.52N 111.13 E
Zhongmou 28 Cg 34.45N 114.01 E
Zhongning 27 Id 37.28N 105.41 E
Zhongshan 27 Jg 22.31N 113.23 E
Zhongwei 22 Mf 37.30N 105.09 E
Zhongxian 27 Ie 30.20N 108.02 E
Zhongxiang 27 Je 31.10N 112.38 E
Zhongxing→Siyang 28 Eh 33.43N 118.40 E
Zhongyaozhan 27 Ma 50.46N 125.53 E
Zhongye Qundao 26 Fd 11.20N 114.30 E
Zhoukoudianzhen 28 Ce 39.41N 115.55 E
Zhoukouzhen 27 Je 33.32N 114.40 E
Zhoushan Dao 28 Gi 30.00N 122.00 E
Zhoushan Qundao 21 Of 30.00N 122.00 E
Zhuanghe 27 Ld 39.42N 122.58 E
Zhucheng 27 Kd 35.58N 119.28 E
Zhu Dao 28 Fe 39.05N 121.10 E
Zhuggu 27 He 33.46N 104.18 E
Zhuhe 28 Bj 29.44N 113.07 E
Zhuizishan → Weichang 27 Kc 41.55N 117.39 E
Zhuji 28 Fj 29.43N 120.13 E
Zhuji→Shangqiu 27 Ke 34.24N 115.37 E
Zhujiang Kou 27 Jg 22.20N 113.45 E
Zhumadian 27 Je 32.54N 114.03 E
Zhuolu 28 Cd 40.23N 115.13 E
Zhuoxian 27 Kd 39.26N 116.00 E
Zhuozhang He 28 Bf 36.36N 113.10 E
Zhuozi 28 Bd 40.52N 112.33 E
Zhuozi Shan 27 Id 39.36N 107.00 E
Zhushan 27 Je 32.16N 110.12 E
Zhuzhou 22 Ng 27.52N 113.12 E
Ziama Mansouria 32 Ib 36.40N 5.29 E
Ziar nad Hronom 10 Oh 48.36N 18.52 E
Ẓibā' 23 Ed 27.21N 35.40 E
Zibo (Zhangdian) 27 Kd 36.48N 118.04 E
Zicavo 11a Bb 41.54N 9.08 E
Židačov 10 Ug 49.17N 24.12 E
Zielona Góra 10 Le 51.56N 15.31 E
Zielona Góra [2] 10 Le 51.55N 15.30 E
Zierikzee 11 Jc 51.38N 3.55 E
Žiežmariai/Žežmarjaj 8 Kj 54.47N 24.36 E
Ziftá 24 Dg 30.43N 31.15 E
Žigalovo 20 Ff 54.48N 105.08 E
Zigana Geçidi 24 Hb 40.38N 39.25 E
Žigansk 20 Hc 66.45N 123.30 E
Zigey 35 Bc 14.43N 15.47 E
Zighan, Wāḥāt- 33 Dd 25.35N 22.06 E
Zigong 22 Mg 29.24N 104.48 E
Zigui 27 Je 31.01N 110.42 E
Ziguinchor 31 Fg 12.35N 16.16W
Žigulevsk 19 Ee 53.27N 49.29 E
Zihuatanejo 47 De 17.38N 101.33W
Zijing Shan 27 Jd 37.12N 112.50 E
Zijpenberg 12 Hb 52.04N 6.00 E
Zilālet 34 Gb 18.28N 7.48 E
Zile 23 Ea 40.18N 35.54 E
Žilina 6 Hf 49.14N 18.45 E
Žilino 8 Ij 54.55N 21.48 E
Zillah 31 If 28.33N 17.35 E
Ziller 14 Fc 47.24N 11.50 E
Zillertaler Alpen 10 Hi 47.00N 11.55 E
Žiloj 16 Qi 40.19N 50.33 E
Zilupe 7 Gh 56.25N 28.07 E
Zima 22 Md 53.55N 102.04 E
Zimapán 48 Jg 20.45N 99.21W
Zimatlán de Alvarez 48 Ki 16.52N 96.47W
Zimba 36 Ef 17.02S 26.30 E
Zimbabwe 37 Ed 20.16S 30.55 E
Zimbabwe (Rhodesia) [1] 31 Jj 20.00S 30.00 E

Index Symbols

[1] Independent Nation
[2] State, Region
[3] District, County
[4] Municipality
[5] Colony, Dependency
Continent
Physical Region
Historical or Cultural Region
Mount, Mountain
Volcano
Hill
Mountains, Mountain Range
Hills, Escarpment
Plateau, Upland
Pass, Gap
Plain, Lowland
Delta
Salt Flat
Valley, Canyon
Crater, Cave
Karst Features
Depression
Polder
Desert, Dunes
Forest, Woods
Heath, Steppe
Oasis
Cape, Point
Coast, Beach
Cliff
Peninsula
Isthmus
Sandbank
Island
Atoll
Rock, Reef
Islands, Archipelago
Rocks, Reefs
Coral Reef
Well, Spring
Geyser
River, Stream
Waterfall Rapids
River Mouth, Estuary
Lake
Salt Lake
Intermittent Lake
Reservoir
Swamp, Pond
Canal
Glacier
Ice Shelf, Pack Ice
Ocean
Sea
Gulf, Bay
Strait, Fjord
Lagoon
Bank
Seamount
Tablemount
Ridge
Shelf
Basin
Escarpment, Sea Scarp
Fracture
Trench, Abyss
National Park, Reserve
Point of Interest
Recreation Site
Cave, Cavern
Historic Site
Ruins
Wall, Walls
Church, Abbey
Temple
Scientific Station
Airport
Port
Lighthouse
Mine
Tunnel
Dam, Bridge

Name	Map	Grid	Lat	Long
Zimbor	15	Gc	47.00N	23.16 E
Zimi	34	Cd	7.19N	11.18W
Zimni Bereg	7	Jd	66.00N	40.45 E
Zimnicea	15	If	43.40N	25.22 E
Zimovniki	16	Mf	47.08N	42.29 E
Zina	34	Hc	11.16N	14.58 E
Zincirli	24	Gd	37.00N	36.41 E
Zinder	31	Hg	13.48N	8.59 E
Zinder [2]	34	Hb	15.00N	10.00 E
Zinga	35	Be	3.43N	18.35 E
Zingst	10	Ib	54.25N	12.50 E
Zinjibăr	33	Ig	13.08N	45.23 E
Zinnik/Soignies	11	Kd	50.35N	4.04 E
Zinsel du Nord	12	Jf	48.49N	7.44 E
Zion [Il.-U.S.]	45	Me	42.27N	87.50W
Zion [St.C.N.]	51c	Ab	17.09N	62.32W
Zipaquirá	54	Db	5.02N	74.01W
Zirc	10	Ni	47.16N	17.52 E
Žirje	14	Jg	43.39N	15.40 E
Zirkel, Mount-	45	Cf	40.52N	106.36W
Žirnovsk	19	Ee	51.01N	44.48 E
Ziro	25	Ic	27.32N	93.32 E
Zi Shui	27	Jf	28.41N	112.43 E
Žitava	10	Oi	47.53N	18.11 E
Žitkoviči	16	Fc	52.16N	28.02 E
Zitkovo	7	Gf	60.42N	29.23 E
Žitomir	6	Ie	50.16N	28.40 E
Žitomirskaja Oblast [3]	19	Ce	50.40N	28.30 E
Zittau	10	Kf	50.54N	14.50 E
Zitterwald	12	Id	50.27N	6.25 E
Zitundo	37	Ee	26.44S	32.49 E
Živinice	14	Mf	44.27N	18.39 E
Ziwa Magharibi [3]	36	Fc	2.00S	31.30 E
Ziway, Lake-	35	Fd	8.00N	38.48 E
Ziya He	28	De	38.39N	117.33 E
Ziyang	27	Ie	32.34N	108.37 E
Žiz	32	Gc	30.29N	4.26W
Žizdra	16	Ic	53.45N	34.43 E
Žizdra	16	Jb	54.14N	36.12 E
Zlatar	15	Cf	43.23N	19.51 E
Zlaté Moravce	10	Oh	48.23N	18.24 E
Zlatibor	15	Cf	43.40N	19.43 E
Zlatica	15	Hg	42.43N	24.08 E
Zlatica	15	Dd	45.49N	20.10 E
Zlatijata	15	Gf	43.40N	23.36 E
Zlatiški prohod	15	Hg	42.45N	24.05 E
Zlatna	15	Gc	46.07N	23.13 E
Zlatograd	15	Ih	41.23N	25.06 E
Zlatoust	6	Ld	55.10N	59.40 E
Zlatoustovsk	20	If	52.59N	133.41 E
Zletovo	15	Fh	41.59N	22.15 E
Žlobin	33	Bc	32.28N	14.34 E
Zlobin	19	De	52.59N	30.03 E
Złocieniec	10	Mc	53.33N	16.01 E
Złoczew	10	Oe	51.25N	18.36 E
Zlot	15	Ee	44.01N	21.59 E
Złotoryja	10	Le	51.08N	15.55 E
Złotów	10	Nc	53.22N	17.02 E
Zły Komorow/Senftenberg	10	Ke	51.31N	14.01 E
Zlynka	16	Gc	52.27N	31.44 E
Zmeinogorsk	20	Df	51.10N	82.13 E
Žmerinka	19	Cf	49.02N	28.05 E
Żmigród	10	Me	51.29N	16.55 E
Zmijev	16	Je	49.41N	36.20 E
Zmijevka	16	Jc	52.40N	36.24 E
Zna	7	Ih	57.33N	34.25 E
Znamenka [R.S.F.S.R.]	16	Lc	52.24N	41.28 E
Znamenka [Ukr.-U.S.S.R.]	16	He	48.41N	32.40 E
Znamensk	8	Ij	54.39N	21.15 E
Znamenskoje	19	Hd	57.08N	73.55 E
Žnin	10	Nd	52.52N	17.43 E
Znojmo	10	Mh	48.51N	16.03 E
Zobia	36	Eb	2.53N	26.02 E
Zóbuè	37	Ec	15.36S	34.26 E
Žodino	16	Fb	54.07N	28.19 E
Žodiški	8	Lj	54.40N	26.33 E
Zoetermeer	12	Gb	52.04N	4.30 E
Zogang/Wangda	27	Gf	29.37N	97.58 E
Žohova, Ostrov-	20	Ka	76.10N	153.05 E
Zohreh	24	Mg	30.04N	49.34 E
Zolgě	27	He	33.38N	103.00 E
Zoločev [Ukr.-U.S.S.R.]	16	Id	50.18N	35.59 E
Zoločev [Ukr.-U.S.S.R.]	19	Cf	49.49N	24.58 E
Zolotaja Gora	20	Hf	54.21N	126.41 E
Zolotoje	16	Ke	48.40N	38.30 E
Zolotonoša	16	He	49.40N	32.02 E
Zolotuhino	16	Jc	52.07N	36.25 E
Žolymbet	19	He	51.45N	71.44 E
Zomba	31	Kj	15.23S	35.20 E
Zongga → Gyirong	27	Ef	28.57N	85.12 E
Zongo	36	Cb	4.21N	18.36 E
Zonguldak	23	Da	41.27N	31.49 E
Zongyang	28	Di	30.42N	117.12 E
Zonkwa	34	Gd	9.47N	8.17 E
Zonnebeke	12	Ed	50.52N	2.59 E
Zontehuitz, Cerro-	48	Mi	16.50N	92.38W
Zonúz	24	Kc	38.35N	45.50 E
Zonza	11a	Bb	41.44N	9.10 E
Zorita	13	Ge	39.17N	5.42W
Zorkassa, Gora-	18	Qa	38.01N	68.10 E
Zorleni	15	Kc	46.16N	27.43 E
Zorritos	54	Bd	3.40S	80.40W
Zorzor	34	Dd	7.47N	9.26W
Zottegem	12	Fd	50.52N	3.48 E
Zou	34	Fd	8.00N	2.15 E
Zouar	31	If	20.27N	16.32 E
Zouïrât	31	Ff	22.46N	12.27W
Zoutkamp, Ulrum-	12	Ia	53.20N	6.18 E
Zouxian	28	Dg	35.24N	116.59 E
Zôvten	15	Nb	47.14N	30.14 E
Žovtnevoje	16	Hf	46.52N	32.02 E
Zpouping	28	Df	36.53N	117.44 E
Zrenjanin	15	Dd	45.23N	20.23 E
Zrinska Gora	14	Ke	45.10N	16.15 E
Zrmanja	14	Jf	44.12N	15.35 E
Zruč nad Sázavou	10	Lg	49.45N	15.07 E
Zschopau	10	Je	51.08N	13.03 E
Žuantobe	19	Gg	44.47N	68.52 E
Zuata, Rio-	50	Di	7.52N	65.22W
Zubayr, Jazā'ir az-	33	Hf	15.05N	42.08 E
Zubcov	7	Ih	56.10N	34.31 E
Zubova Poljana	7	Ki	54.05N	42.50 E
Zudañez	54	Fg	19.06S	64.44W
Zuénoula	34	Dd	7.26N	6.03W
Zuénoula [3]	34	Dd	7.22N	6.12W
Zuera	13	Lc	41.52N	0.47W
Zufäf	33	Hf	16.43N	41.46 E
Zufallspitze/Cevedale	14	Ed	46.27N	10.37 E
Žufär	21	Hh	17.30N	54.00 E
Zug [Switz.]	14	Cc	47.10N	8.40 E
Zug [2]	14	Cc	47.10N	8.30 E
Zug [W.Sah.]	32	Ee	21.36N	14.09W
Zugdidi	19	Eg	42.29N	41.48 E
Zugersee	14	Cc	47.10N	8.30 E
Zugspitze	10	Gi	47.25N	10.59 E
Zuid Beveland	12	Fc	51.25N	3.45 E
Zuidelijke Flevoland	12	Hb	52.25N	5.20 E
Zuid-Holland [3]	12	Gc	52.00N	4.30 E
Zuid-Ijsselmeerpolders [3]	12	Hb	52.20N	5.20 E
Zuidlaren	12	Ia	53.06N	6.42 E
Zuid-Willemsvaart	12	Hd	50.50N	5.41 E
Zuidwolde	12	Ib	52.40N	6.25 E
Zújar	13	Ge	39.01N	5.47W
Zújar, Embalse del-	13	Gf	38.50N	5.20W
Zujevka	19	Fd	58.26N	51.12 E
Žukovka	19	De	53.33N	33.47 E
Žukovski	7	Ji	55.37N	38.12 E
Zula	35	Fb	15.14N	39.40 E
Zulia [2]	54	Db	10.00N	72.10W
Zulia, Rio-	49	Ki	9.04N	72.18W
Zülpich	12	Id	50.42N	6.39 E
Zumbo	37	Ec	15.36S	30.25 E
Zundert	12	Gc	51.29N	4.40 E
Zungeru	34	Gd	9.48N	6.09 E
Zunhua	28	Dd	40.12N	117.58 E
Zuni	45	Bi	35.04N	108.51W
Zuni River	46	Ki	34.39N	109.40W
Zunyi	22	Mg	27.40N	106.56 E
Zuoquan	28	Bf	37.05N	113.22 E
Zuoyun	28	Be	39.58N	112.40 E
Županja	14	Me	45.04N	18.42 E
Zuqâq	33	Hf	18.04N	40.48 E
Zurak	34	Hd	9.14N	10.34 E
Zürich [2]	14	Cc	47.30N	8.30 E
Zürich	6	Gf	47.20N	8.35 E
Zurich, Lake- (EN) = Zürichsee	14	Cc	47.15N	8.45 E
Zürichsee = Zurich, Lake- (EN)	14	Cc	47.15N	8.45 E
Zurmi	34	Gc	12.47N	6.47 E
Žuromin	10	Pc	53.04N	19.55 E
Zuru	34	Gc	11.26N	5.14 E
Zuša	16	Jc	53.27N	36.25 E
Zusam	10	Gh	48.42N	10.45 E
Zutiua, Rio-	54	Id	3.43S	45.30W
Zutphen	11	Mb	52.08N	6.12 E
Zuwärah	33	Bc	32.56N	12.06 E
Zvenigorodka	16	Ge	49.04N	30.59 E
Zverinogolovskoje	17	Li	54.28N	64.50 E
Zvezdny	20	Fe	56.40N	106.30 E
Zvičina	10	Lf	50.25N	15.41 E
Žvirca	10	Uf	50.24N	24.16 E
Zvolen	10	Ph	48.35N	19.08 E
Zvornik	14	Nf	44.23N	19.07 E
Zwardoń	10	Og	49.30N	18.59 E
Zwarte Bank=Black Bank (EN)	12	Fa	53.15N	3.55 E
Zweibrücken	10	Dg	49.15N	7.22 E
Zweisimmen	14	Bd	46.34N	7.25 E
Zwesten	12	Lc	51.03N	9.11 E
Zwettl in Niederösterreich	10	If	50.44N	12.30 E
Zwickau	14	Jb	48.37N	15.10 E
Zwickauer Mulde	10	Ie	51.10N	12.48 E
Zwierzyniec	10	Sf	50.37N	22.58 E
Zwiesel	10	Jg	49.01N	13.14 E
Zwijndrecht	12	Gc	51.50N	4.41 E
Zwischenahn	10	Dc	53.11N	8.00 E
Zwoleń	10	Re	51.22N	21.35 E
Zwolle	11	Mb	52.30N	6.05 E
Žychlin	10	Pd	52.15N	19.38 E
Żyrardów	10	Qd	52.04N	20.25 E
Zyrjanka	20	Kc	65.45N	105.51 E
Zyrjanovsk	19	If	49.45N	84.16 E
Żywiec	10	Pg	49.41N	19.12 E

Index Symbols

[1] Independent Nation	Desert, Dunes	Lake
[2] State, Region	Forest, Woods	Salt Lake
[3] District, County	Heath, Steppe	Intermittent Lake
[4] Municipality	Oasis	Reservoir
[5] Colony, Dependency	Cape, Point	Swamp, Pond
Continent	Coast, Beach	Canal
Physical Region	Cliff	Glacier
Historical or Cultural Region	Peninsula	Ice Shelf, Pack Ice
Mount, Mountain	Isthmus	Ocean
Volcano	Sandbank	Sea
Hill	Island	Gulf, Bay
Mountains, Mountain Range	Atoll	Strait, Fjord
Hills, Escarpment	Rock, Reef	Lagoon
Plateau, Upland	Islands, Archipelago	Bank
Pass, Gap	Rocks, Reefs	Seamount
Plain, Lowland	Coral Reef	Tablemount
Delta	Well, Spring	Ridge
Salt Flat	Geyser	Shelf
Valley, Canyon	River, Stream	Basin
Crater, Cave	Waterfall Rapids	Escarpment, Sea Scarp
Karst Features	River Mouth, Estuary	Fracture
Depression		Trench, Abyss
Polder		National Park, Reserve

Historic Site	Port
Ruins	Lighthouse
Wall, Walls	Mine
Church, Abbey	Tunnel
Temple	Dam, Bridge
Scientific Station	
Airport	
Point of Interest	
Recreation Site	
Cave, Cavern